Proceedings of

SMC 2013

10th Sound and Music Computing Conference

July 30 - August 2, 2013
KTH Royal Institute of Technology
Stockholm, Sweden

Edited by Roberto Bresin

Bibliographic information published by the Deutsche Nationalbibliothek

The Deutsche Nationalbibliothek lists this publication in the Deutsche Nationalbibliografie; detailed bibliographic data are available in the Internet at http://dnb.d-nb.de .

Cover by Kjetil Falkenberg Hansen
The website of this book is http://smcnetwork.org/resources/smc2013

ISBN 978-3-8325-3472-1

Logos Verlag Berlin GmbH
Comeniushof, Gubener Str. 47,
10243 Berlin
Tel.: +49 (0)30 42 85 10 90
Fax: +49 (0)30 42 85 10 92
INTERNET: http://www.logos-verlag.de

Contents

Sonic interaction design 461

Sound processing 523

Technical program committee

Anna Rita Addessi, University of Bologna, Italy
Anders Askenfelt, KTH, Sweden
Federico Avanzini, University of Padova, Italy
Roberto Bresin, KTH, Sweden
Murray Campbell, University of Edinburgh, UK
Sofia Dahl, Aalborg University in Copenhagen, Denmark
Matthias Demoucron, Ghent University, Belgium
Gianpaolo Evangelista, Linköping University, Sweden
Emilia Gomez, UPF, Barcelona, Spain
Benoit Fabre, UPMC, France
Anders Friberg, KTH, Sweden
Leonardo Fuks, Rio de Janeiro Federal University, Brasil
Bruno L Giordano, University of Glasgow, UK
Werner Goebl, University of Music and Performing Arts Vienna, Austria
Kjetil Hansen, KTH, Sweden
Alexander Refsum Jensenius, University of Oslo, Norway
Malte Kob, Hochschule für Musik Detmold, Germany
Petri Laukka, Stockholm University, Sweden
Erwin Schoonderwaldt, Hanover University of Music, Drama and Media, Germany
Stefania Serafin, Aalborg University in Copenhagen, Denmark
Patrick Susini, IRCAM, France
Sten Ternström, KTH, Sweden
Vesa Välimäki, Aalto University, Finland

Reviewers

Adhitya, Sara
Ahlbäck, Sven
Alexandre, Enrique
Allison, Jesse
Almeida, André
Anders, Torsten
Andrade Esquef, Paulo Antonio
Antonacci, Fabio
Antunes, Jose
Arar, Raphael
Ashley, Richard
Atienza, Ricardo
Aucouturier, Jean-Julien
Auvray, Roman
Avanzini, Federico
Baldan, Stefano
Bank, Balázs
Barrass, Stephen
Barthet, Mathieu
Bello, Juan P.
Benetos, Emmanouil
Beskow, Jonas
Bevilacqua, Frederic
Bilbao, Stefan
Birkett, Stephen
Bishop, Laura
Bissinger, George
Blauert, Jens
Bonada, Jordi
Bosch, Juan J.
Bosi, Mathieu
Boutillon, Xavier
Boyer, Eric
Bozkurt, Baris
Buen, Anders
Buick, James
Burger, Birgitta
Burgoyne, J. A.
Cambouropoulos, Emilios
Canazza, Sergio
Caramiaux, Baptiste
Carlsson, Peter
Causse, René
Chaigne, Antoine
Chandra, Arjun
Chatron, Jacques
Chen, Alex
Chick, John
Chon, Song Hui
Château, Noël
Comajuncosas, Josep M
Curtin, Joseph
Cuthbert, Michael Scott
Daffern, Helena
Dalmont, Jean-Pierre
Dannenberg, Roger
Daudet, Laurent
Davies, Matthew
de Francisco, Martha
de Götzen, Amalia
De La Cuadra, Patricio
De Poli, Giovanni
De Quay, Yago
Debut, Vincent
Delle Monache, Stefano
Demoucron, Matthias
Depalle, Philippe
Ege, Kerem
Elblaus, Ludvig
Erkut, Cumhur
Essl, Georg
Eveno, Pauline
Farrùs, Mireia
Fernstrom, Mikael
Flossmann, Sebastian
Fontana, Federico
Freour, Vincent
Friberg, Anders
Fritz, Claudia
Germain, Francois
Geronazzo, Michele
Gilbert, Joel
Gingras, Bruno
Giordano, Nicholas
Godøy, Rolf Inge
Gough, Colin
Gouyon, Fabien
Grani, Francesco
Grassi, Massimo
Grosshauser, Tobias
Grothe, Timo
Guastavino, Catherine
Gómez, Daniel
Hacihabiboglu, Huseyin
Hattwick, Ian
Hellmer, Kahl
Herrera, Perfecto
Himberg, Tommi
Hirschberg, Avraham
Hofmann, Alex
Houix, Olivier
Howard, David
Hunt, Andy
Härmä, Aki
Jackowski, Dariusz
Janer, Jordi
Jansson, Erik
Jensen, Kristoffer
Johnson, Rose
Katz, Brian
Kausel, Wilfried
Kemp, Jonathan
Kereliuk, Corey
Kergomard, Jean
Kirke, Alexis
Klapuri, Anssi
Kleimola, Jari
Klien, Volkmar
Koehly, Rodolphe
Kojs, Juraj
Kretz, Johannes
Kronland-Martinet, Richard
Lartillot, Olivier
Lavandier, Mathieu
Le Carrou, Jean-Loic
Lee, Edward Jangwon
Lehtonen, Heidi-Maria
Lembke, Sven-Amin
Lindborg, Permagnus
Lindström, Erik
Lopez Arteaga, Ines
Lorenz-Kierakiewitz, Klaus-Hendrik
MacRitchie, Jennifer
Maculewicz, Justyna
Madison, Guy
Malloch, Joseph

Mamou-Mani, Adrien
Mansour, Hossein
Marchand, Sylvain
Mauch, Matthias
Mauro, Davide Andrea
McAdams, Steve
McLennan, John
Meunier, Sabine
Misdariis, Nicolas
Moelants, Dirk
Moore, Thomas
Mores, Robert
Morreale, Fabio
Myers, Arnold
Naveda, Luiz
Nederveen, Kees
Newton, Michael
Nicol, Rozenn
Nieto, Oriol
Noisternig, Markus
Nymoen, Kristian
O'Modhrain, Sile
Overholt, Daniel
Pabon, Peter
Papadopoulos, Helene
Papetti, Stefano
Parker, Julian
Parncutt, Richard
Parseihian, Gaëtan
Pauletto, Sandra
Pearce, Marcus
Penttinen, Henri
Percival, Graham
Peters, Nils
Petiot, Jean-Francois
Pätynen, Jukka
Rabenstein, Rudolf
Raphael, Christopher
Rasamimanana, Nicolas
Richardson, Bernard
Rigaud, Francois
Roads, Curtis
Rocchesso, Davide
Rodà, Antonio
Roebel, Axel
Rämö, Jussi
Saari, Pasi
Saitis, Charalampos
Savioja, Lauri
Scavone, Gary
Scherrer, Bertrand
Schmidt, Erik
Schön, Daniele
Schwarz, Diemo
Senturk, Sertan
Serrà, Joan
Sharp, David
Sinclair, Stephen
Skogstad, Ståle A.
Smith, Julius
Smyth, Tamara
Sordo, Mohamed
Spagnol, Simone
Sprechmann, Pablo
Sujbert, László
Sundberg, Johan
Taillard, Pierre André
Temperley, David
Thoret, Etienne
Timmers, Renee
Toiviainen, Petri
Torin, Alberto
Torresen, Jim
Touzé, Cyril
Trail, Shawn
Trento, Stefano
Turchet, Luca
Tørresen, Jim
Umbert, Marti
Upham, Finn
Van Nort, Doug
van Vugt, Floris
Van Walstijn, Maarten
Vempala, Naresh
Vergara, Sossio
Vergez, Christophe
Volpe, Gualtiero
Wanderley, Marcelo
Weinreich, Gabriel
Widholm, Gregor
Wingstedt, Johnny
Winters, Michael
Wolfe, Joe
Woodhouse, Jim
Woolley, Alan
Yeo, Woon Seung
Zambon, Stefano
Zeiner-Henriksen, Hans
Özbek, Erdal

Preface

Welcome to the fourth Stockholm Music Acoustics Conference (SMAC 2013), July 30 – August 3, 2013. This time SMAC is run in parallel with the Sound and Music Computing Conference (SMC 2013). SMAC 2013 continues the series of music acoustics conferences in Stockholm, started 30 years ago. Following the tradition of SMAC 83, SMAC 93, and SMAC 03, SMAC 2013 covers the traditional fields of music acoustics, including musical instruments, singing voice, perception, and physical modeling. The fields of music perception and performance are this time covered by SMC 2013, as well as the rapidly growing research in sonic interaction design, sound processing and music information retrieval

A good reason for keeping the broad perspective from earlier SMACs is to offer the possibility of at least a partial overview of the many fascinating research areas which address the wonderful combination of performing arts, physics, creativity, and life experience called music. In order to give this perspective SMAC 2013 and SMC 2013 feature a number of invited presentations (the exact number being 13), in which outstanding researchers, old and young, will present overviews of their areas up to and including the research frontier.

SMAC 03 was run in two parallel sections. In the 2013 edition, one of the two sessions is the SMC conference. SMC is rapidly establishing as one of the most important conference series in the field of sound and music computing. This year SMC celebrates the 10th edition. SMC 2013 is jointly hosted by the Sound and Music Computing Research Group at the Royal Institute of Technology (KTH) and the Department of Composition, Conducting and Music Theory at the Royal College of Music (KMH) in Stockholm. KTH is responsible for the scientific part and KMH will host the music performances.

The theme for SMAC and SMC this year is "*Sound Science, Sound Experience.*" During the past five decades, the domain of music acoustics has widened from studies of the acoustics of musical instruments and voice, including basic elements of musical perception and performance, to investigations of how humans experience and interact with sounds and music. Increasingly, the knowledge is put into industrial, societal and psychological perspectives. The age-old dream of bridging science and art has found new and bountiful ground in the field of Sound and Music Computing.

Besides all scientific sessions SMAC and SMC 2013 will include many memorable events, including three concerts organized by KMH, Rencon Performance Rendering Contest, an electroacoustic pub, a Swedish summer night banquet in the archipelago of Stockholm, and above all, numerous occasions to meet friends and colleagues, old and new.

WE WELCOME YOU ALL TO SMAC 2013 & SMC 2013 !

Sten Ternström, Roberto Bresin, Anders Friberg, Anders Askenfelt

Keynotes

EXPLOITING DOMAIN KNOWLEDGE IN MUSIC INFORMATION RESEARCH

Xavier Serra
Music Technology Group
Universitat Pompeu Fabra, Barcelona
xavier.serra@upf.edu

ABSTRACT

Music Information Research (MIR) is a discipline that aims to understand and model music from an information processing perspective, but the successful approaches used in MIR are going beyond the traditional data processing methodologies. Most of the great advancements have been the result of combining engineering disciplines such as audio signal processing and machine learning with non-engineering disciplines such as music perception and music theory. One of the challenges in MIR is to automatically describe music audio signals, thus to develop methodologies to extract musically useful information from audio recordings. In this paper we claim that if we want to advance in this direction we should maximize the use of musical knowledge in all the steps of our research tasks. To support this claim we overview some of the work being carried out in CompMusic, a project that aims to analyze and automatically describe the music of several non-western music traditions.

1. INTRODUCTION

The field of MIR has greatly grown in the past two decades and the number of disciplines involved has expanded. The MIR research community is evolving and changing accordingly, specially due to the incorporation of researchers coming from fields such as Speech Processing, Text Retrieval or Computer Vision. These changes might have been influential in the fact that most of the current research is centered in data processing methodologies, thus with a bottom-up perspective. Most of the approaches used are not specific to musical problems and there is a recent agreement in the community on the need to explore new methodological approaches that can complement the currently used data processing ones.

The recently published MIR roadmap [1] identifies current research challenges while reviewing the relevant state of the art. It lists challenges related to the gathering and organization of machine-readable musical data, to the development of data representations, and to the methodologies for processing and understanding that data, taking into account domain knowledge and bringing expertise from relevant scientific and engineering disciplines. The Roadmap also looks into a user perspective, thus promoting the need to understand the user roles within the music communication chain and to develop technologies for the interaction of these users with music data. Finally, the roadmap emphasizes the fact that music is a communication phenomenon that involves people and communities immersed in specific social and cultural contexts, thus it claims that MIR should aim at developing methodologies for processing musical data that capture these contexts.

There is a widespread consensus in the MIR community on the need to emphasize knowledge-driven methodologies. Collaboration should be promoted with disciplines such as Musicology, Psychology, and Sociology. But the key question is: how can we use the knowledge generated from these disciplines as part of the methodologies being used in MIR?

Most MIR projects are carried out following a common set of steps. After defining the problem, the data to be analyzed is gathered, a methodology is developed to process the data, experiments are run in which the methods are applied to the data, and finally the results are evaluated. The main point that we want to emphasize in this paper is the need to use musical knowledge, domain knowledge, in every one of these steps. The problem, the data, the method and the evaluation steps, all have to be musically meaningful and musically relevant. Many published articles have not given enough consideration to the musical issues and as a result the obtained results lack the impact intended by the authors.

The most direct way of adding domain knowledge in a research project is by incorporating domain experts in the research team. This is fundamental. But even then, how can we represent and express specific musical concepts in the data and methodologies used in an MIR project? Given that many music traditions have developed and use formalizations/representations in the education and transmission of their music, a good starting point are the formalisms developed by the music scholars of those traditions. These formalisms can then be incorporated into the MIR-specific computational methodologies.

Next we present some issues related to musical knowledge representation and then we go over how we address these issues in the CompMusic project.

2. MUSICAL KNOWLEDGE REPRESENTATION

Knowledge engineering is a discipline that involves integrating knowledge into computer systems in order to solve complex problems normally requiring a high level of human expertise. In the currently favored modeling view of the field, the knowledge engineer attempts to model the knowledge and problem solving techniques of the domain expert. [1] A major concern in knowledge engineering is the construction of domain specific ontologies, which are structural frameworks for organizing information and that are used as a form of knowledge representations [2].

Music is a complex phenomenon that can be approached and studied from a multitude of perspectives. Even the definition of music vary according to culture and social context. [2] From a knowledge engineering perspective the only way to agree on a set of musical formalisms and concepts is to narrow down the domain to a level in which we can find a sufficient scholarly consensus, without reaching a domain size so small that is of no use. A practical approximation is to constrain the domain to a particular music culture and to a particular application. For example, the Music Ontology project [3] is developing and maintaining several ontologies of music production concepts and it is basically centered on western commercial music. In the CompMusic project we have decided to focus on five music cultures and we are working towards the particular application of music discovery of audio content.

An ontology specifies concepts, attributes, relations, constraints, and instances in a domain. For creating music ontologies the most useful types of information sources are the encyclopaedias and dictionaries, ideally written by music scholars specialists on the chosen domain. From these sources we can gather all the relevant concepts used in a specific domain area, but it is not easy to gather the relations between concepts. Musicological books and articles are very useful but they are often not precise enough for extracting clearly formalized concepts and relationships. At the same time it is not easy to find clear agreement between different information sources, thus there is always the need to involve domain experts and to account for the fact that there are no single and long-lived formalizations. No matter what information source we start from, even written by the most academically reputed scholar, it will be impossible to come up with complete and persistent ontologies. Thus, we should develop systems that can handle multiple versions of an ontology and that can support dynamic ontologies.

There has been little work in the development of domain specific ontologies for music and efforts are needed to create them. The existing and most related initiatives are the repositories of structured information that are being created as collaborative on-line projects. Two of the larger and most important projects of relevance to music are Musicbrainz [4] and DBpedia. [5]

MusicBrainz is an open music encyclopedia that collects music metadata and makes it available to the public. It aims to form a trusty central database to identify music CDs. In MusicBrainz anyone can add the metadata of CDs such as the names of tracks, the label of the release and the artists featured in the album. Yet, MusicBrainz is more ambitious than just being a database of metadata of CDs, it also allows to add detailed information about the music, such as personal details of artists, composer/lyricist information, or the specific date of a performance. Even more, the MusicBrainz database can maintain relationships between the data entities.

The DBpedia project is a community effort to extract structured information from Wikipedia and to make this information available on the Web. Through DBpedia we can ask sophisticated queries against Wikipedia, and we can link different data sets on the Web to Wikipedia data. DBpedia is at the core of the W3C Linking Opendata community effort [6] and MusicBrainz is the main music project within that community. All the information generated by these projects is available as open data sets using the RDF specification. These RDF links enable to navigate between data items in various data sources using a search language like SPARQL. [7]

In the context of MIR we are interested in describing and organizing the musical concepts and entities observed in audio recordings, scores, and writings on music. We generally get data/information both from existing data repositories and from the processing of the data. The automatic, or semiautomatic, structuring and integration of all this information is one of the main research efforts in MIR.

3. THE CASE OF COMPMUSIC

In the CompMusic project we work on the automatic description of music by emphasizing the use of domain knowledge of particular music traditions. We are focusing on five music cultures: Turkish-makam (Turkey), Arab-Andalusian (Maghreb), Beijing Opera (China), Carnatic (South-India) and Hindustani (North-India). There are many great traditions that we could have also chosen, but we had to limit ourselves and we were looking for traditions that: (1) had musical personalities contrasting with the popular western music of the last few decades, (2) had alive performance practices and strong social and cultural relevance, (3) had musicological and cultural studies available about them, and (4) it was feasible to collect sufficient and coherent machine-readable music data. At the same time we wanted to have a diverse set of music repertoires to study a variety of new and diverse MIR problems. The target application of CompMusic is to develop a system to browse through audio music collections of the chosen cultures, a system with which to discover characteristics of the music and relationships between different musical concepts. For a list of articles resulting from this research we refer to the project's website. [8]

[1] http://en.wikipedia.org/wiki/Knowledge_engineering

[2] http://en.wikipedia.org/wiki/Music

[3] http://musicontology.com/

[4] http://musicbrainz.org

[5] http://dbpedia.org

[6] http://www.w3.org/wiki/SweoIG/TaskForces/CommunityProjects/LinkingOpenData

[7] http://en.wikipedia.org/wiki/SPARQL

[8] http://compmusic.upf.edu

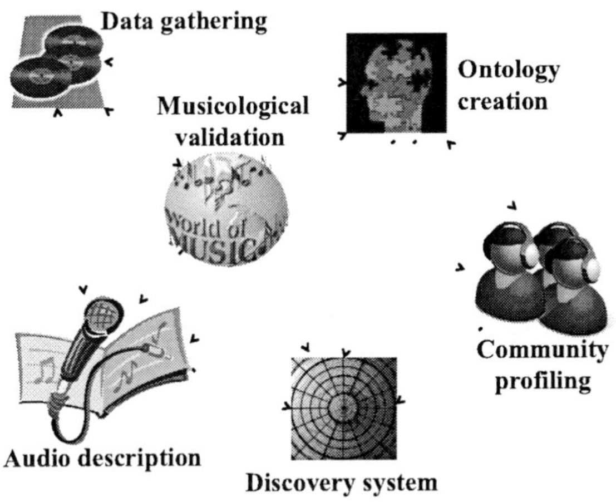

Figure 1. Diagram of the tasks being carried out in CompMusic for every musical culture.

Figure 1 shows a diagram of the specific research tasks that are being carried out for all the music traditions. However, in order to emphasize our point, here we overview CompMusic by going through the basic and most common tasks in MIR projects.

3.1 Problem definition

Defining relevant problems is the single most important step in any research project. For the case of CompMusic we wanted to work on problems that could take advantage of the musical specificities of each tradition and that could result in technologies for musically meaningful explorations of audio music collections. This is a large project and thus we were able to be ambitious in the problem formulations.

In the five music traditions chosen, melody and rhythm are, arguably, the two most important musical facets. At the same time each tradition has a different way to understand both melody and rhythm. These complementary facts offer the possibility to focus on just these two musical facets while being able to explore a large variety of problems and methodologies.

In the project we have involved music experts and researchers coming from all the cultures we are studying. With their input we have defined specific problems to work on. Impossible to detail here all the identified issues; so let's just mention the basic concepts that are framing most of our automatic music description tasks. In the indian traditions *rāga* and *tāla* are the driving melodic and rhythmic concepts and in Turkish-makam music the corresponding melodic and rhythmic frameworks are the *makam* and *usul*. In Arab-Andalusian music the *nawba* is a fundamental structuring concept that defines the melodic and rhythmic characteristics and in Beijing Opera the *shengqiang* and the *banshi* are the basic concepts underlying melody and meter. We could go very deep into each of these concepts but for the purpose of MIR, given that we are just starting in this direction, basic musicological studies have been sufficient for defining the musical issues of relevance for our project, at least for now.

3.2 Data collections

Properly collecting and organizing the data is a crucial and demanding task. The basic types of machine readable data used CompMusic are: audio recordings, editorial metadata, scores, and social data. In the research done so far we have focused on the audio recordings and the accompanying metadata.

Experts advised us in the selection of the CDs for each repertoire, with the goal to gather in the course of the project at least 500 hours of curated audio per collection. For the selection of the CDs it was important to choose recordings by recognized and representative artists, with reliable editorial information. As a result of musical and research considerations each collection has special characteristics. For example the Carnatic collection is basically composed of live recordings of concerts and the Beijing Opera collection is composed of CDs in which a single artists sings a compilation of arias.

To store the editorial metadata of the CDs we use MusicBrainz. However MusicBrainz was designed to support western popular music and it lacks the support for some of our culture specific concepts. Given the community-based development of MusicBrainz, we are involved in the addition of the culture specific concepts that we need and in contributing to make sure that it can properly support our music repertoires. For example, MusicBrainz now supports most of the instruments used in our music traditions and we are in the way to add support for concepts such as *rāga* and *tāla*.

The musical cultures studied have developed as oral traditions but they also use music notations, scores, and these are useful to study and describe some musical characteristics. However few scores are available in machine readable form and so far we have been able to gather a well curated collection of scores for Turkish-makam music.[9] It has been easier to obtain the lyrics, also very relevant, of the vocal pieces that we are gathering, which represent a large percentage of all our music.

Social data is a valuable source of information to work on issues like community profiling. The challenge is to identify on-line communities with discussion forums dedicated to particular music traditions and available to be crawled and studied computationally. So far we have identified and studied an on-line community for Carnatic music.[10]

3.3 Data processing

The most common data processing methodologies used in MIR come from the fields of signal processing and machine learning; being both extensively used in CompMusic.

With signal processing methods we extract features from audio recordings, in our case features that describe melodic and rhythmic characteristics of the music. We focus on audio features that are perceptually relevant and on top of which we can apply music considerations. Features that we extract include: prominent pitch, intonation profiles [3],

[9] SymbTr (`http://compmusic.upf.edu/node/140`)
[10] `http://www.rasikas.org/forum/index.php`

loudness, note onset location, and brightness. These are meaningful features that can be used to study and to describe musical concepts and at the same time they are basic features from which to extract higher level descriptors. To compute these features we use Essentia, [11] an audio analysis library developed by our research group.

With machine learning methods we obtain higher level descriptors and identify musically meaningful categories. For example we have computed the tonic pitch for the case of indian music [4] and performed structural segmentations of many pieces. A fundamental problem of the machine learning methods is that they behave like black boxes, solving a given task without helping much in the understanding of the solution. For our purposes we try to minimize this problem by using well selected and musically meaningful features as input and by emphasizing supervised approaches in which the training set has been labelled by music experts. Also we choose machine learning methods, like decision trees, that generate explicit rules that might be easier to understand, specially if the number of input features is small.

One of the key research problems in CompMusic is the identification and characterization of melodic and rhythmic patterns. For this task we need to develop meaningful similarity measures so we can compare patterns from the extracted audio features and organize them into categories. Important here is to use melody and rhythm representations that make sense for the given culture and that can be invariant to non-relevant music transformations, such as transposition and tempo change. So far we have applied some supervised approaches using dynamic time warping methods [5].

The most common bottleneck in statistical and machine learning methods are the training sets. In CompMusic we have put a lot of effort in having data collections for training that are carefully labelled by experts. We are working towards having complete ontologies that can capture all the relevant attributes and relationships of the data and metadata of each collection, thus resulting in well structured training sets that can be used in a variety of problems.

3.4 Evaluation

The evaluation has become a fundamental part of any MIR project and there is much concern on developing proper evaluations at the system level [6]. To evaluate an MIR system we have to characterize the usage experience of the users who will employ it, thus we need to have a system with a clear application and identified target users.

For the case of CompMusic we are developing technologies with which to discover musically relevant relationships within specific audio music collections and our target users are the music lovers of the particular music tradition that the collection belongs to. To carry proper evaluations we are developing a web-based software application, Dunya, [12] that lets users interact with an audio music collection using the technologies developed in the project. The application displays the content of various culture specific entities and their relationships. Users can listen to the recordings and navigate through the collection by exploring information that is related to the currently viewed entity, either through links that reflect ontological relationships or by using culturally relevant similarity measures.

We are evaluating specific technologies using ground truth data and we will evaluate the overall Dunya system with user tests. Not many evaluations have yet been done but we will make sure that the user evaluation results are used for improving the technologies being developed.

4. CONCLUSIONS

Music Information Research is a field very much tied to the domain that it studies, Music. Any music information processing task reaches a glass ceiling quite early on unless domain knowledge is added into the research methodology. In this article we have argued in favour of this point by using as example the problem of automatically describing audio recording of specific music cultures for the purpose of discovering relationship between the entities that can be identified in them. The project CompMusic started two years ago and has three more years to go, but with the obtained results we have already shown the usefulness of exploiting domain knowledge.

Acknowledgments

The CompMusic project is funded by the European Research Council under the European Union's Seventh Framework Programme (FP7/2007-2013) / ERC grant agreement 267583.

5. REFERENCES

[1] X. Serra, M. Magas, E. Benetos, M. Chudy, S. Dixon, A. Flexer, E. Gómez, F. Gouyon, P. Herrera, S. Jordà, O. Paytuvi, G. Peeters, J. Schlüter, H. Vinet, and G. Widmer, *Roadmap for Music Information ReSearch*, G. Peeters, Ed., 2013. [Online]. Available: http://mires.eecs.qmul.ac.uk/wiki/index.php/Roadmap

[2] R. Brachman and H. Levesque, *Knowledge Representation and Reasoning*. Morgan Kaufmann, 2004.

[3] G. K. Koduri, J. Serrà, and X. Serra, "Characterization of intonation in carnatic music by parametrizing pitch histograms," *Proc. ISMIR*, pp. 199–204, 2012.

[4] J. Salamon, S. Gulati, and X. Serra, "A multipitch approach to tonic identification in indian classical music," *Proc. ISMIR*, pp. 499–504, 2012.

[5] J. C. Ross, T. Vinutha, and P. Rao, "Detecting melodic motifs from audio for hindustani classical music," *Proc. ISMIR*, pp. 193–198, 2012.

[6] J. Urbano, M. Schedl, and X. Serra, "Evaluation in music information retrieval," *Journal of Intelligent Information Systems*, In Press.

[11] http://essentia.upf.edu

[12] http://dunya.compmusic.upf.edu

MUSIC AS THE GOAL OF TRAINING AND MEANS OF REHABILITATION: EVIDENCE FROM BRAIN SCIENCE

Mari Tervaniemi
Cognitive Brain Research Unit
Institute of Behavioural Sciences,
University of Helsinki
Finnish Centre of Excellence in Interdisciplinary Music Research, University of Jyväskylä, Finland
mari.tervaniemi@helsinki.fi

ABSTRACT

During the past three decades, our knowledge about brain functions and its structures underlying music perception, performance, and emotions has accumulated relatively quickly. Cortical and subcortical brain areas involved in these musical functions have been identified using various techniques and paradigms.

In the present talk, I will introduce recent findings revealing enhanced brain mechanisms during long-term musical training, as well as by informal music activities at home. Furthermore, I will present examples of how casual music activities, such as music listening and singing, can be used in neurological rehabilitation to promote health and wellbeing in patients and their family members.

In sum, these findings promote the use of music in formal and informal settings across the whole life span in healthy participants, as well as with individuals with special needs.

1. INTRODUCTION

During the past 30 years, pioneering knowledge about the neural basis of musical activities has been acquired in several complementary empirical and methodological frameworks. The earliest endeavors aimed at determining the brain functions involved in music-sound perception and cognition in healthy adult participants. Thereafter a developmental approach was also adopted. In parallel, investigations on musical expertise were started.

Currently, these lines of research are still active, but they are appended by systematic studies on music emotions and preferences as a newly established field of neuroaesthetics. Importantly, findings in all these fields of neurosciences of music are systematically used in applied settings in education and rehabilitation.

In the following, the basic brain functions and structures of music processing will be described (Section 2), and followed by key findings in music development (Section 3) and music rehabilitation (Section 4). The paper will end with general conclusions.

2. MUSIC IN THE BRAIN

All sounds are perceived via neural transfer from the inner ear and subcortical nuclei to the auditory cortices in the temporal lobes in both left and right hemispheres. In the case of music, this sound-specific activation of primary auditory areas in the upper part of the Sylvian fissure is necessary, but not sufficient for an elaborated musical perception to form, and emotions to emerge. It needs to be supplemented by further neural activation in the brain areas governing cross-modal (e.g., audio-visual and audio-motor) processes, focused attention, and regulation of emotions and alertness [1]. Since these functions are determined by highly distributed neural networks which occupy many brain areas, it is safe to say that for intentional and emotional music listening we need most parts of our brain. In the case of music performance this is even more apparent – then the cerebellum and sensory as well as motor cortices also need to be active and in sync.

3. DEVELOPMENT OF MUSIC SKILLS

3.1 Studies on adults

Knowing now which parts of the brain are activated by music listening and performance, we can ask what are the brain areas that can be shaped by musical expertise.

Initial findings in this area emphasized neuroplasticity as observed in the primary sensory areas in the cortex - particularly in the auditory [2] and in the somatosensory [3] areas. These brain responses were stronger in musicians than in laymen and, importantly, stronger in those musicians who started their training early (before the age of seven) than in those who started later.

More recently, these findings were replicated using several brain research methods on both brain function and brain structure [4]. Additionally, they were augmented by results indicating that musicians are not "a homogenous group of experts in sound and motorics". Instead, they display different structural brain indices and neural auditory responses as a function of their background in training, for instance, with regard to the primary instrument and music genre they are most attached with [5, 6].

These studies on adult musicians were considered as an interesting window to the outcome of neuroplasticity in the music domain. Yet, they unfortunately left unanswered whether there was a neurocognitive readiness already present in the brains of those "musicians-to-be" prior to their training. In other words, could it be that the musicians in general, and the early starters in particular, had some skills which motivated their parents to pursue musical training' For instance, they display sensitivity to music in general, accurate discrimination and error detection in pitch and rhythm, preference to sing or play any instrument, or even a non-instrument like a table or a box.

3.2 Studies on children

When studying children and their development during music training, we are able to complete initial investigations to the onset of the music training. By these means, we can determine the "kick-off" level of their neural and behavioral functions, and can compare that to "control" children who have hobbies with a comparable frequency and intensity as the musically oriented children, but without the involvement of sound-related actions. These recordings are conducted first before the training onset, and second, after the commencement of the training (e.g., after 6 or 12 months).

In the first studies in this field, however, this opportunity was not used. Yet, these pioneering findings strongly indicated that already after a relatively brief 1-year training program, music had enhanced timbre-specific brain responses to the child's own instrument [7] implying training-induced modulation of the auditory brain activity. Due to these strong findings, follow-up studies were started. In these studies, the participating children were either randomly allocated into music activities or other (e.g., painting, theater) activities [8]; or, they were recruited from children who were randomly allocated into different music programs [9].

These studies point strongly towards the following conclusions: First, music training facilitates the auditory (perceptual, cognitive) and motor functions which are crucial to music perception and performance, namely, auditory, motor, and neural transfer between the left and right hemispheres [9]. Second, even informal, familial music activities at home, such as singing, dancing/moving with the music, listening to music, etc.; can modulate brain indices reflecting attentional functions [10].

4. MUSIC REHABILITATION

If music activities can boost a healthy, normally developing brain as the previous subsection documented, would it also be feasible to assume that music can "repair" brain functions after brain damage? This has been the assumption and justification for various kinds of music therapy and music rehabilitation for some time. However, only recently has this assumption received systematic scientific support. One of these successful initiatives with neurological patients will be introduced below. Further evidence to support the use of music in clinical settings, particularly in patients with memory disorders, will be given in the talk.

4.1 Music listening in neurological rehabilitation

A stroke, a sudden disorder in the blood circulation in the brain, can cause various perceptual, motor, and/or cognitive impairments. Thanks to the neuroplasticity of the brain, those impairments can be rehabilitated and sometimes even fully recovered; however, symptoms often remain and may even lead them to retire.

Since any neurological rehabilitation is most effective right after the damage, it was our intention to look for a treatment which is readily available after hospitalization. Music listening was the most obvious choice - readily available and cheap to implement. We recruited 60 patients who had had an acute stroke and randomly assigned them to three groups: 1) music listening (experimental group), 2) audio-book listening (control group with non-musical auditory stimulation), 3) standard care (control group). Their recovery was followed by a multitude of testing in listening [11], neuropsychological functions [12], and brain activity, [13] as well as interviews [14].

It turned out that the patients who were guided to listen to their favorite music for about one hour a day for two months had the fastest recovery as indicated in the cognitive tests for attention and memory. Additionally, the patients guided to listen to music or audio books had less confusion and depression, so, in other words, their emotional recovery was advanced compared to patients who belonged to the control group (with standard care but no further rehabilitation on top of that).

5. GENERAL CONCLUSIONS

During past two-three decades, our knowledge about the brain functions underlying music activities has accumulated relatively quickly. Currently, we are at the stage of finding and evaluating ways to improve brain functions by using music, e.g., with children and with neurological patients. We can predict that music has a great potential to facilitate emotional and cognitive functions on various groups of participants with special needs in learning and rehabilitation.

6. REFERENCES

[1] Levitin, D.J. & Tirovolas, A.K. (2009). Current advances in the cognitive neuroscience of music *Annals of the New York Academy of Science,*. **1156**, 211–231.

[2] Pantev, C., Oostenveld, R., Engelien, A., Ross, B., Roberts, L. and Hoke, M. (1998). Increased auditory cortical representation in musicians. *Nature*, **392**, 811–814.

[3] Elbert, T., Pantev, C., Wienbruch, C., Rockstroh, B. and Taub, E. (1995). Increased cortical representation of the fingers of the left hand in string players. *Science*, **270**, 305–307.

[4] Münte, T.F., Altenmüller, E. and Jäncke, L. (2002). The musician's brain as a model of neuroplasticity. *Nature Rev Neurosci*, **3**, 473–478.

[5] Tervaniemi, M. (2009). Musicians – same or different? *Annals of the New York Academy of Sciences*, **1169**, 151–156.

[6] Vuust, P., Brattico, E., Seppänen, M., Näätänen, R, Tervaniemi, M. (2012). The sound of music: Differentiating musicians using a fast, musical multi-feature mismatch negativity paradigm. *Neuropsychologia*, **50**, 1432–1443.

[7] Shahin, A.J., Roberts, L.E., Chau, W., Trainor, L.J., Miller L.M. (2008). Music training leads to the development of timbre-specific gamma band activity. NeuroImage, **41**, 13–22.

[8] Moreno, S. Bialystok, E., Barac, R., Schellenberg, E.G., Cepeda, N.J., Chau, T. (2011). Short-term music trainin enhances verbal intelligence and executive function. *Psychological Science*, **22**, 1425–1433.

[9] Hyde, K.L., Lerch, J., Norton, A., Forgeard, M., Winner, E., Evans, A.C., Schlaug, G. (2009). Musical training shapes structural brain development. *Journal of Neuroscience*, **29**, 19–25.

[10] Putkinen, V., Tervaniemi, M., Huotilainen, M. (2013). Informal musical activities are linked to auditory discrimination and attention in 2-3-year-old children: an event-related potential study. *European Journal of Neuroscience*, **37**, 654–661

[11] Särkämö, T., Tervaniemi, M., Soinila, S., Autti, T., Silvennoinen, H.M., Laine, M., Hietanen, M. (2009). Cognitive deficits associated with acquired amusia after stroke: a neuropsychological follow-up study. *Neuropsychologia*, **47**, 2642–2651.

[12] Särkämö T., Tervaniemi M., Laitinen S., Forsblom A., Soinila S., Mikkonen M., Autti T., Silvennoinen H.M., Erkkilä, J., Laine M., Peretz I., Hietanen M. (2008). Music listening enhances cognitive recovery and mood after middle cerebral artery stroke. *Brain*, **131**, 866–876.

[13] Särkämö T., Pihko., E., Laitinen S., Forsblom A., Soinila S., Mikkonen M., Autti T., Silvennoinen H.M., Erkkilä, J., Laine M., Peretz I., Hietanen M., Tervaniemi, M. (2010). Music and speech listening enhance the recovery of early sensory processing after stroke. *Journal of Cognitive Neuroscience*, **22**, 2716–2127.

[14] Forsblom, A., Laitinen, S., Särkämö, T., Tervaniemi, M. (2009). Therapeutic role of music listening in stroke rehabilitation. *Annals of the New York Academy of Sciences*, **1169**, 426–430.

Perception

MEASURING THE INTERACTION BETWEEN BASSOON AND HORN PLAYERS IN ACHIEVING TIMBRE BLEND

Sven-Amin Lembke **Scott Levine** **Martha de Francisco** **Stephen McAdams**
Centre for Interdisciplinary Research in Music Media and Technology, Schulich School of Music, McGill University
sven-amin.lembke@mail.mcgill.ca

ABSTRACT

Our study investigates the interactive relationship between bassoon and horn players in achieving timbre blend during musical performance. The interaction is studied in a behavioral experiment, measuring the timbral adjustments performers employ. Several timbre descriptors serve as acoustic measures, quantifying global and formant-based spectral-envelope properties. Furthermore, musicians' self-assessment of their performances is measured through behavioral ratings. The performances are investigated across four factors, i.e., room acoustics, communication directivity, musical voicing, and leading vs. accompanying roles. Findings from ANOVAs suggest that differences in role assignments and communication directivity between performers lead to timbral adjustments. These effects are more pronounced for horn than for bassoon and performer interdependencies appear to be most important for unison voicing.

1. INTRODUCTION

In orchestration practice, composers rely on their experience and intuition to obtain instrument combinations that lead to blended timbres, i.e., combinations exhibiting higher degrees of perceptual fusion. Previous research on timbre blending has emphasized explanations of the degree of blend through correlations with acoustic instrument properties. However, the contribution of musical performance factors to the actual realization of timbre blend remains largely unexplored. Past investigations of timbre blending between orchestral instruments have instead primarily employed stimuli that were created by a mix of solo-instrument recordings [1, 2], with their findings not fully extending to more realistic scenarios. In musical practice, blend is always performed by two or more musicians in an interactive relationship that allows for timbral adjustments between performers. Our investigation focuses on this interactive relationship between two performers attempting to blend together.

A previous investigation of performer interaction focused on synchrony between two pianists [3]. Experimental factors such as performer role or acoustical feedback were investigated, showing asymmetric dependency of players acting as *followers* on the *leading* pianists. Furthermore, under impaired acoustical feedback, performers increasingly relied on visual cues to maintain synchrony, which argues for investigations of performance-related factors involving auditory properties alone to exclude the possibility of visual communication between performers. With regard to common examples from the orchestral repertoire, musicians performing in a blended pairing may involve either doubled performances in (pitch) unison or paired phrases in non-unison. In both scenarios, one of the performers would usually assume the leading role, with that role commonly also being associated with the top voice in non-unison cases. It therefore may be hypothesized that followers would adjust their timbres to the leading performer and not vice versa. Moreover, a general validity of this unilateral dependency should not result in the leader performing differently, if they were to receive no auditory feedback from the follower, as might occur in unfavorable studio or live-performance situations.

Performer interaction in achieving timbre blend is investigated in a behavioral experiment for an instrument combination that finds widespread use in the orchestral repertoire, namely, the combination of bassoon and (French) horn. Orchestration treatises discuss these two instruments as forming a common blended pairing [4–7], with these observations reflected in findings of high degrees of blend in perceptual investigations [1, 2]. The horn is often considered an unofficial member of the woodwind section, bearing a timbral versatility that succeeds in blending with woodwinds, brasses, and even strings. Given the relevance to orchestration practice, the investigation of musical performance situates musicians in approximation to the ecologically valid setting of a concert hall, realized through controlled and reproducible virtual performance environments. The measurement of musical performance is conducted in both behavioral and acoustic domains.

2. METHODS

2.1 Experimental design

The behavioral experiment addresses a series of research questions. The principal aim investigates what instrument-specific adjustments are employed in achieving timbre blend and how these interact in a performance scenario with two musicians. These interactions are furthermore studied as a function of musical and acoustical factors. The experiment is based on a mixed-model design, with the two instruments implemented as a between-participants factor. All remaining factors employ a repeated-measures design, to rule out the possibility that individual differences for instruments and playing technique or style are confounded with the investigated effects for musical and acoustical factors.

2.1.1 Musical factors

Two within-participant, independent variables involve the performer role and the influence of different musical voice contexts. The former considers one instrumentalist taking on the role of *leader*, whereas the other performer acts as *follower*, i.e., takes on an accompanying role. According to the 'voice' factor, musicians either perform a melodic phrase in *unison* or a musically related, two-voice phrase in *non-unison*. The musical excerpts are taken from Mendelssohn-Bartholdy's *A Midsummer Night's Dream*, Op. 61, No. 7 (measures 1-16). In this orchestral excerpt, the chosen instrument combination is featured prominently, with a horn solo being accompanied by two bassoons. All phrases were transposed by a fifth down to A major from the original key of E major, to reduce the impact of player fatigue through repeated performances in high instrument registers. The solo melody functions as the unison excerpt, denoted A; the two accompanying voices serve as the top and bottom voices in the non-unison condition, denoted B and C, respectively, with B being assigned to the leader.

2.1.2 Acoustical factors

Another pair of within-participant variables considers effects for communication directivity between performers and the room-acoustical properties of performance venues. The 'communication' factor assesses the influence of whether both performers are able to hear each other or only the follower hears the leader, denoted *two-way* or *one-way*, respectively. For the 'room' factor, the influence of room acoustics is assessed for two different performance spaces: musicians are simulated as performing in either a large, multipurpose performance space (Music Multimedia Room) or in a mid-sized recital hall (Tanna Schulich Hall). [1]

2.1.3 Procedure

Two participants were tested in a single experimental session, being instructed to perform together to achieve the highest possible degree of blend. Each musician underwent three repetitions of 16 different experimental conditions (four factors by two treatment levels, 2^4), leading to a total of 48 experimental trials. The total duration of the experiment was around two hours, including a break scheduled after half of the trials. To avoid disorientation of musicians through strongly varying performer-role and voice assignments, the musical factors were blocked. Participants assumed the role of either leader or follower throughout the first or second half of the experiment. Furthermore, shorter eight-trial blocks grouped conditions based on voice assignment (e.g., four unison trials, another four non-unison), with the repetitions occurring after each block. For instance, a given participant would begin as leader for 24 trials, performing the first repetition of four unison trials, then proceed to four non-unison trials, followed by the second repetition of the same four unison trials, etc. The four possible block-ordering schemes were counterbalanced across all participants and instruments. The acoustical-factor combinations were encapsulated inside sub-blocks of four trials and randomized in order. Three practice trials were conducted under the guidance of the two experimenters, presenting the experimental conditions encountered at the beginning of individual block-ordering schemes.

2.1.4 Participants

Sixteen musicians participated in the experiment and were primarily recruited from the Schulich School of Music at McGill University and the music faculty of the Université de Montréal. The bassoonists, three female and five male, had a median age of 21 years (range 18-31). The hornists, six female and two male, had a median age of 20 years (range 17-44). Across both instruments, 10 participants considered themselves as professional musicians, and overall, the musicians reported to play or practice their respective instruments for the median duration of 21 hours per week. All musicians were remunerated with 35 CAD for their participation.

2.1.5 Performance measures

The musical performances were evaluated with the help of a set of behavioral and acoustic measures, which focus on capturing features related to timbre blending. Behavioral measures comprise two ratings that participants provided after each experimental trial. The first rating assessed how well musicians thought they performed individually given their assigned role, on a continuous scale with the verbal anchors *very badly* and *very well*. The second measure acquired ratings on the perceived degree of achieved timbre blend with the other performer, on a continuous scale with the verbal anchors *low blend* and *high blend*. The acoustic measures consist of a number of spectral-envelope descriptors, which are discussed in Section 2.3.

2.2 Technical realization

The experiment was conducted in two research laboratories at the Centre for Interdisciplinary Research in Music Media and Technology (CIRMMT) at McGill University. Separate laboratory spaces were called for in order to create individual acoustical environments for each participant, ensuring the capture of separate source signals as well as preventing visual cues between performers. Each performance laboratory was treated to be relatively non-reverberant, with a $RT_{60} < 0.5$ s. Performers received instructions to prepare for performances of assigned roles and excerpts and also provided their behavioral ratings through dedicated computer interfaces. Furthermore, the performances were synchronized by attending to a video monitor transmitting a silent conductor cue track.

Each musician's performance was captured through an omnidirectional high-voltage microphone, which were matched across laboratories. Both microphone signals were routed to a control room, where preamplification gain was digitally matched across both performance spaces. The analog

[1] Both venues are located at the Schulich School of Music, McGill University. More details under http://www.mcgill.ca/music/about-us/facilities. (Last accessed on March 20, 2013.)

signals were converted to 96 kHz / 24-bit PCM digital data, recorded at full resolution for later acoustical analysis and at the same time fed into separate convolution engines, processing the source signals with different sets of binaural impulse responses (IRs). Individualized binaural signals, based on the acoustical factors, were then fed to headphones for each performer. Headphone amplifier volume was held constant, as were the circumaural closed-ear headphones. The convolution introduced a system latency of 805 samples, resulting in delayed arrival of the room feedback by about 8.4 ms, affecting both performers equally and thus not assumed to influence their interaction. The IRs had been previously collected in the concert halls discussed in Section 2.1.2, with RT_{60} for the smaller and larger halls being 1.3 and 2.1 s, respectively. IRs were measured with a binaural head-and-torso system, positioning the excitation source and receiver appropriately for a typical orchestral setup: horns on the conductor's left front side and bassoons on the conductor's right front.

2.3 Acoustic descriptors

For the instruments bassoon and horn, the existence of largely pitch-invariant, local spectral maxima has been reported [8–10], which are also termed *formants* by analogy with the human voice. Furthermore, frequency alignment of formants between instruments has been argued to contribute to the perception of blend [2], with certain aspects of this hypothesis having been replicated in further perceptual investigations [11], confirming the significant contribution of the most prominent formants. On the other hand, global spectral-envelope descriptors, such as the spectral centroid, have also been reported to correlate with the perception of blend [1].

Time-variant spectral envelopes are obtained through *True Envelope* (TE) estimation [12]. The TE algorithm applies iterative cepstral smoothing on STFT-magnitude spectra, with the computed estimates using a constant cepstral order oriented at fundamental frequencies $f_0 \leq 300$ Hz. A formant-analysis algorithm, based on the detection of local spectral maxima and plateaus, i.e., regions of spectral-envelope slopes approximating zero, identifies and classifies up to three formants within a dynamic range of 50 dB. The frequencies of formant maximums (e.g., F_1) serve as descriptors. In addition, the most prominent formant F_1, also termed *main* formant, involves pairs of descriptor frequencies delimiting upper or lower bounds at which the magnitude has decreased by 3 dB or 6 dB (e.g., upper $F_{3dB}^{\rightarrow}$ and lower $F_{3dB}^{\leftarrow}$ bounds relative to F_1). These formant descriptors are illustrated for a spectral-envelope estimate of a single participant's performance in Fig. 1, based on median magnitudes over time. In addition, relative magnitude differences between spectral-envelope regions are considered: for example, $\Delta L_{1vsRest}$ quantifies the level difference between F_1 and the averaged magnitude for frequencies $f > F_{6dB}^{\rightarrow}$. The spectral-envelope estimates furthermore serve as the basis for the computation of the spectral centroid S_c (amplitude-weighted frequency average) and slope S_s (linear regression of the spectrum) [13]. These serve as global, formant-independent descriptors of general spectral trends in the frequency and magnitude dimensions, respectively.

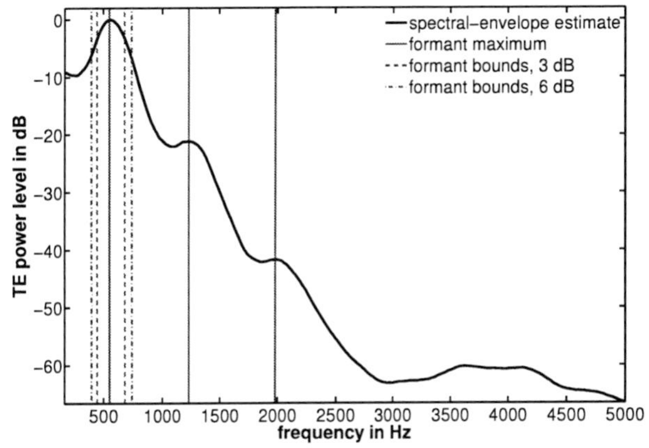

Figure 1. Time-averaged spectral-envelope estimate and its formant description for a single bassoon performance of the unison excerpt.

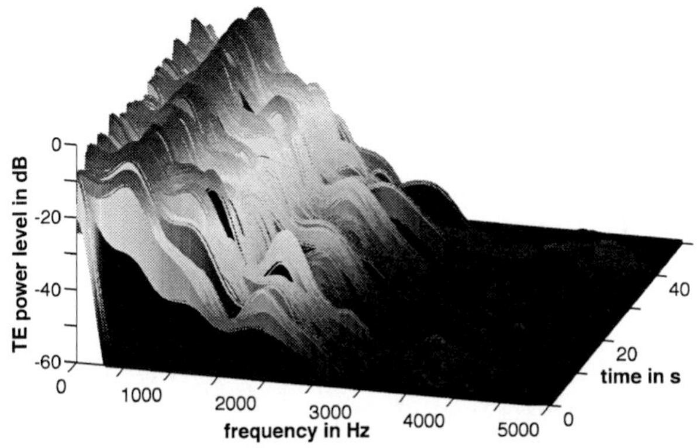

Figure 2. Temporal evolution of *True Envelopes* for the same performance as in Fig. 1.

From qualitative evaluations of spectro-temporal representations for both instruments conducted prior to running the experiment, the chosen spectral-envelope description could be confirmed as capturing relevant features associated with timbral modifications. The main formants F_1 for both instruments are located around 500 Hz and, as illustrated in Fig. 2 for the bassoon, they remain relatively stable across pitch and dynamic range. It also became apparent that the players' control over instrumental timbre is constrained, more so for bassoon than for horn. The main formants of horns are broader, less defined, and more variable in location, which affords horn players greater timbral control. For both instruments, the strongest variability is achieved for changes in dynamic markings, which in the chosen excerpt are limited to a single, notated change (e.g., *crescendo-descrescendo*) in measures 13-14.

3. RESULTS AND DISCUSSION

The strongest trends for effects between instruments and the remaining factors should already become apparent from inferential statistics computed on the behavioral and time-averaged acoustic measures. Moreover, it will not be possible to address more complex effects found across the

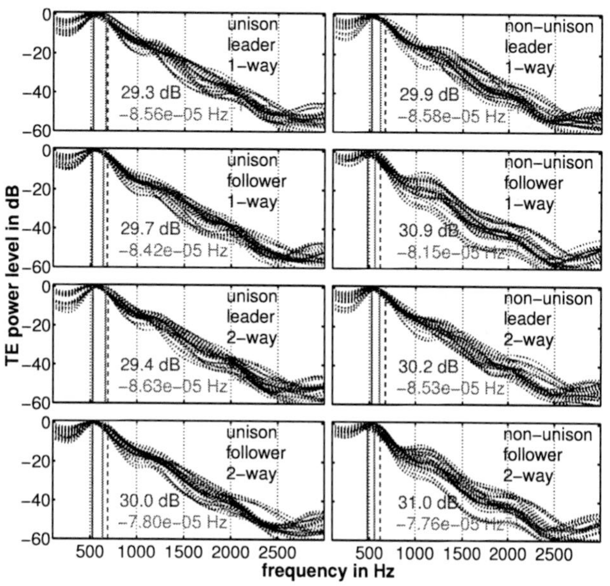

Figure 3. Bassoonists' spectral envelopes and median acoustic-descriptor values per factor combination 'voice'×'role'×'communication'. Formant description in red: F_1 (solid line), $F_{3dB}^{\rightarrow}$ (dashed line), and $\Delta L_{1vsRest}$ (numerical value). Global descriptors in green: S_c (line) and S_s (numerical value).

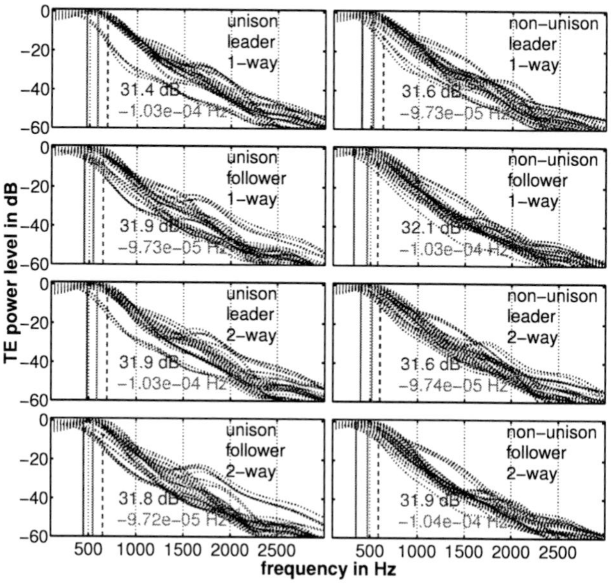

Figure 4. Hornists' spectral envelopes and median acoustic-descriptor values per factor combination 'voice'×'role'×'communication'. See caption of Fig. 3 for legend.

time course of performances within the scope of this paper. Given that amongst the acquired data some performances were qualitatively better than others, the entire dataset with three repetitions per condition is reduced by retaining only the two performances per participant that yield the highest self-assessed performance ratings. [2] Separate performances are considered as independent cases, i.e., corresponding to a total number of 16 cases (eight performers × two repetitions) per instrument. Mixed-model ANOVAs involving the between-participants factor 'instrument' and the within-participants factors 'role', 'voice', 'room', and 'communication' were computed, assuming a significance level of $\alpha = .05$. Both behavioral measures as well as the acoustic measures F_1, $F_{3dB}^{\rightarrow}$, $\Delta L_{1vsRest}$, S_c, and S_s were considered as dependent variables in separate analyses. [3] We will focus on a discussion of the main and two-way interaction effects, as higher-order interactions are generally difficult to draw conclusions from.

The time-averaged spectral envelopes of performances and their trends across the acoustic descriptors are visualized for bassoon and horn in Figs. 3 and 4, respectively. For the sake of clarity, the data set has been collapsed over the two levels of the 'room' factor, as this factor does not lead to any statistically significant effects. The figures display complete sets of time-averaged spectral envelopes across 32 performances (16 cases × two rooms) across the eight remaining factor combinations. Furthermore, the corresponding median values for the acoustic descriptors are depicted as well; formant-related descriptors (red) and global descriptors (green). It should be noted that differences in medians computed across participants do not directly correspond to how within-participant variables are evaluated in repeated-measures ANOVAs, with the latter having greater statistical power in detecting effects.

3.1 Main effects

The main effects for 'instrument' are obtained for all acoustic variables, but for none of the behavioral measures. This suggests that the differences are based on systematic deviations between the spectral envelopes of the instruments alone, without bassoonists or hornists judging the assessment of their performances differently. As anticipated and illustrated in Figs. 3 and 4, the spectral-envelope profiles for both instruments bear some resemblance in shape, while notable differences do exist. The strongest differences are found for the descriptors S_c $[F(1,30) = 36.8,\ p < .001,\ \eta_p^2 = .551]$ and F_1 $[F(1,30) = 21.4,\ p < .001,\ \eta_p^2 = .416]$. While on average the bassoons' main formants are located slightly above 500 Hz, the horns' F_1s lie slightly below that frequency, with an analogous frequency difference for S_c. At the same time, the location of both instruments' $F_{3dB}^{\rightarrow}$ is more similar, reflected in a less pronounced difference $[F(1,30) = 7.0,\ p = .013,\ \eta_p^2 = .190]$. Differences for the descriptors of relative magnitude differences yield comparable statistical effect sizes (η_p^2).

With regard to within-participant factors, the strongest effects are found for 'voice'. The global descriptor S_c $[F(1,30) = 165.7,\ p < .001,\ \eta_p^2 = .847]$ and the formant descriptors F_1 and $F_{3dB}^{\rightarrow}$ $[F(1,30) \approx 86.0,\ p < .001,\ \eta_p^2 \approx .740]$

[2] Due to unforeseen technical issues during two experimental sessions, data for a total of five trials were rendered unusable. However, these only concern conditions for which two remaining repetitions were still available, and these were used for the statistical analyses.

[3] Shapiro-Wilk tests on case-based residuals per factor combination yield slight deviations from normality. Across all seven dependent variables and 16 factor combinations, violations are obtained for 23% of tests at $\alpha = .05$, reducing to 6% at $\alpha = .01$. Given the limited number of violations and the known robustness of ANOVAs run on equal sample sizes per factor combination, the statistics are still assumed to be valid.

		bassoon			horn		
vc.	f_0	F_1	$F_{\overrightarrow{3dB}}$	S_c	F_1	$F_{\overrightarrow{3dB}}$	S_c
A	100	100	100	100	100	100	100
B	84	96	97	92	80	89	87
C	63	98	97	91	78	88	86

Table 1. Comparison of frequencies between voice excerpts A, B, and C relative to A (in %), reporting median descriptor values across all non-'voice' factor combinations. The variable fundamental frequency f_0 corresponds to the lowest pitch in each excerpt.

exhibit strong effects, suggesting the presence of systematic differences between unison and non-unison excerpts. As is apparent in the figures, the descriptor frequencies shift downward in the lower-pitched non-unison conditions. Table 1 quantifies these frequency shifts across all performed musical excerpts and compares them to the corresponding shifts in pitch register. Variations in pitch are quantified through f_0 for the lowest pitch occurring in each voice excerpt (i.e., A, B, and C). Although the shifts in descriptor values follow the same trend as for pitch, their deviations remain more constrained compared to the maximum pitch change of 37%. For the bassoon, the formant descriptors are relatively stable and only shift downwards by about 3%, whereas S_c decreases by about 9% for both non-unison excerpts. The horn deviations are most strongly pronounced for F_1, with a downward shift of 21%, whereas the remaining descriptors deviate by about 13%. Across both instruments, $F_{\overrightarrow{3dB}}$ exhibits the weakest dependency on pitch. Overall, these differences appear to stem more from pitch covariation inherent to instrument acoustics than intentional spectral adjustments evoked by the performers.

In addition, the 'voice' factor yields the only main effects with behavioral measures. For the blend ratings, a moderate effect is obtained [$F(1,30) = 13.3$, $p = .001$, $\eta_p^2 = .308$], which is based on the fact that unison performances lead to higher blend. The weak main effect for musicians' judgments of their performance [$F(1,30) = 6.0$, $p = .020$, $\eta_p^2 = .168$] is more complex in nature, as it involves several interaction effects and therefore will be discussed further in Section 3.2.

The 'role' factor yields main effects across all acoustic measures. The strongest effects are again obtained for S_c [$F(1,30) = 95.5$, $p < .001$, $\eta_p^2 = .761$] and $F_{\overrightarrow{3dB}}$ [$F(1,30) = 31.4$, $p < .001$, $\eta_p^2 = .512$], which yield lower frequencies in the follower condition. This trend is clearly observable in Figs. 3 and 4, especially in the unison conditions that do not exhibit the confounding covariation with pitch discussed above. For the unison conditions in Fig. 3, the relationship between $F_{\overrightarrow{3dB}}$ and S_c is characterized by the latter decreasing relative to the former. Given the stable main formant in this example, the downward shift in centroid implies a reduction of spectral magnitudes located above $F_{\overrightarrow{3dB}}$. Relating these observations to the interaction between performers as a function of their role assignments, followers adjust their spectral envelopes towards being slightly 'darker' in timbre than those of the leaders, without affecting the main formant as much. Along these lines, a single, weak main effect for the factor 'communication' with $F_{\overrightarrow{3dB}}$ [$F(1,30) = 4.5$, $p = .041$, $\eta_p^2 = .131$] provides another interesting insight. This effect suggests that in the one-way-communication scenario, both musicians perform more 'timidly' by exhibiting lower $F_{\overrightarrow{3dB}}$. In this scenario the leader is unable to hear the follower, which implies that leaders tend to adjust their sounds toward 'darker' timbres, in order to ensure the achievement of blend under the communication impairment.

3.2 Interaction effects

There are several cases of the between-participants factor 'instrument' interacting with the within-participant factors 'role' or 'voice', which are mainly related to effects being more pronounced for the horn, likely due its greater timbral versatility. For example, the horn exhibits more drastic differences along all acoustic measures as a function of performer role as well as being more prone to pitch covariation across different voice excerpts. A similar case concerns the descriptor S_c and an interaction effect 'role' × 'voice', which is explained by the augmented pitch separation for non-unison voices inducing increased S_c differences between performer roles. In the interest of brevity, no detailed report of the statistics will be made.

As mentioned above, the behavioral measure of individual performance judgments and the 'voice' factor yield complex dependencies based on two-way interactions with 'role' [$F(1,30) = 6.6$, $p = .015$, $\eta_p^2 = .181$] and 'communication' [$F(1,30) = 9.5$, $p = .004$, $\eta_p^2 = .241$]. Assuming that the larger effect size conveys the more dominant influence, only in unison performances do musicians rate their performances higher for unimpaired, two-way communication, whereas the ratings for non-unison performances appear to be unaffected by communication directivity. The second interaction involves musicians rating themselves as having performed their role better as followers than as leaders in unison conditions, with the inverse relationship holding for non-unison performances. In addition, the modulating three-way interaction with the additional factor 'instrument' [$F(1,30) = 4.9$, $p = .035$, $\eta_p^2 = .139$] motivates a reinterpretation with respect to non-unison performances. It suggests that hornists acting as followers rate their performances worse than as leaders, with the contrary applying to bassoonists. This could be related to the playability of the bottom non-unison voice, set in the low pitch register, having been reported as being harder for horns than for bassoons. Overall, these interdependencies suggest that for unison performances, communication impairment has a stronger effect on performers and that followers perform their roles more satisfactorily than leaders.

4. CONCLUSIONS

Both acoustic and behavioral measures succeed in revealing effects of performer interaction within the context of achieving timbre blend. The strongest implication for interaction is found across performer roles. Performers acting as followers adjust their timbres to be 'darker' (i.e., exhibiting lower spectral centroids) compared to their performances as leaders. In the leader role, musicians indicate being less satisfied with their performances, implying that this role bears a larger responsibility for the joint performance (e.g., regarding phrasing, intonation, timing). Hence, leaders may be more critical of their own performance or the resulting blend outcome. In the absence of acoustical feedback from the followers, this increased responsibility may have also encouraged leaders to orient their playing towards avoiding 'brighter' timbres.

Effects found between instruments and between voicings covary with systematic differences in instrument acoustics and pitch range. As a result, the assessment of their actual influence on performer interaction is difficult. This translates to analogous difficulties regarding certain acoustic measures being more sensitive to one instrument or the presence of pitch differences. However, the acoustical analyses based on both pitch-invariant formant traits (e.g., F_1, $F_{\overrightarrow{3dB}}$) and global spectral traits (e.g., S_c) aid in evaluating the different contributions. Across both instruments, $F_{\overrightarrow{3dB}}$ appears least affected by instrument and pitch covariation, and it also leads to the only effect obtained for communication directivity. These observations agree with findings suggesting that $F_{\overrightarrow{3dB}}$ serves as a perceptually salient feature in correlating blend ratings with spectral-envelope traits [10]. Furthermore, the behavioral measures convey that performer interactions appear to be more critical in unison than in non-unison contexts, as the perceived degree of blend is also higher in the first case.

The reported findings will have to be considered preliminary until further analyses are conducted on time-variant datasets. These analyses are expected to provide more insight into effects related to performer interactions that are left concealed in the time-averaged representations as well as allowing two other important influences on timbre blend to be addressed, i.e., intonation and synchrony. While musicians may have succeeded in compensating for effects between room-acoustical environments over the entire duration of performances, the 'room' factor may still become relevant on a finer timescale.

In conclusion, results from this experiment will be valuable to both performance and orchestration practice. For musicians, rules to improve timbre blending between performers could be deduced from effects obtained across musical and acoustical factors. With regard to orchestration, its practitioners will benefit from knowing to what extent performers can affect blend and, conversely, what instrument-specific acoustic properties remain unaffected. These constraints would only emphasize the crucial importance of selecting suitable instrument combinations.

Acknowledgments

The authors would like to thank Harold Kilianski, Yves Méthot, and Julien Boissinot at CIRMMT for their technical assistance. This research was funded in part by a CIRMMT Student Award to Scott Levine and Sven-Amin Lembke as well as a grant from the Canadian Natural Sciences and Engineering Research Council and a Canada Research Chair to Stephen McAdams.

5. REFERENCES

[1] G. J. Sandell, "Roles for spectral centroid and other factors in determining "blended" instrument pairings in orchestration," *Music Perception*, vol. 13, pp. 209–246, 1995.

[2] C. Reuter, *Die auditive Diskrimination von Orchesterinstrumenten - Verschmelzung und Heraushörbarkeit von Instrumentalklangfarben im Ensemblespiel.* Frankfurt am Main: P. Lang, 1996.

[3] W. Goebl and C. Palmer, "Synchronization of timing and motion among performing musicians," *Music Perception*, vol. 26, no. 5, pp. 427–438, 2009.

[4] N. Rimsky-Korsakov, *Principles of orchestration*, M. Steinberg, Ed. New York: Dover Publications, 1964.

[5] C. Koechlin, *Traité de l'orchestration : en quatre volumes.* Paris: M. Eschig, 1954.

[6] G. J. Sandell, "Concurrent timbres in orchestration: a perceptual study of factors determining blend," PhD thesis, Northwestern University, 1991.

[7] C. Reuter, *Klangfarbe und Instrumentation: Geschichte—Ursachen—Wirkung.* Frankfurt am Main: P. Lang, 2002.

[8] K. E. Schumann, "Physik der Klangfarben," Professorial dissertation, Universität Berlin, 1929.

[9] D. Luce and J. Clark, "Physical correlates of brass-instrument tones," *Journal of the Acoustical Society of America*, vol. 42, no. 6, pp. 1232–1243, 1967.

[10] S.-A. Lembke and S. McAdams, "Spectral-envelope characteristics and perceptual timbre blending," In preparation.

[11] ——, "Timbre blending of wind instruments : acoustics and perception," in *Proc. 5th International Conference of Students of Systematic Musicology / SysMus12*, Montreal, Canada, 2012, pp. 1–5.

[12] F. Villavicencio, A. Röbel, and X. Rodet, "Improving LPC spectral envelope extraction of voiced speech by True-Envelope estimation," in *Proc. IEEE International Conference on Acoustics, Speech, and Signal Processing*, 2006, pp. I–869–I–872.

[13] G. Peeters, B. L. Giordano, P. Susini, N. Misdariis, and S. McAdams, "The Timbre Toolbox: extracting audio descriptors from musical signals," *Journal of the Acoustical Society of America*, vol. 130, no. 5, pp. 2902–2916, 2011.

A social network integrated game experiment to relate tapping to speed perception and explore rhythm reproduction

Guillaume Bellec
ENSTA Paristech
bellec@ensta.fr

Anders Elowsson, Anders Friberg
Royal Institute of Technology,
Speech, Music and Hearing
{afriberg,elov}@kth.se

Daniel Wolff, Tillman Weyde
City University London,
Department of Computer Science
{daniel.wolff.1,t.e.weyde}@city.ac.uk

ABSTRACT

During recent years, games with a purpose (GWAPs) have become increasingly popular for studying human behaviour [1–4]. However, no standardised method for web-based game experiments has been proposed so far. We present here our approach comprising an extended version of the CaSimIR social game framework [5] for data collection, mini-games for tempo and rhythm tapping, and an initial analysis of the data collected so far. The game presented here is part of the Spot The Odd Song Out game, which is freely available for use on Facebook and on the Web [1].

We present the GWAP method in some detail and a preliminary analysis of data collected. We relate the tapping data to perceptual ratings obtained in previous work. The results suggest that the tapped tempo data collected in a GWAP can be used to predict perceived speed. I toned down the above statement as I understand from the results section that our data are not as good as When averaging the rhythmic performances of a group of 10 players in the second experiment, the tapping frequency shows a pattern that corresponds to the time signature of the music played. Our experience shows that more effort in design and during runtime is required than in a traditional experiment. Our experiment is still running and available on line.

1. INTRODUCTION

Collecting perceptual data from listening experiments is a tedious task and the resulting data sets are typically small (tens or hundreds of entries). On the other hand, in music information retrieval (MIR), the size of music collections has exceeded 10 million songs (20m in the Spotify Library [2], 12m in iTunes store in 2010 [3]). To also gather perceptual data on music on a larger scale, the concept of games with a purpose (GWAPs), as defined in 2006 by von Ahn [6], has been applied in some recent MIR projects [1–3,5]. In comparison to traditional experiments, the number of participants in a GWAP can be very large at low cost (TagATune reached 14442 unique players [1]). However, the design and evaluation of GWAPs requires more effort than traditional experiments, as there is less control over the experimental conditions and no human interaction with the subject during the experiment.

Social networks have reached world wide popularity in a relatively short time. Facebook was founded in 2004, and had one billion monthly active users in December 2012. Integrating a GWAP into social networks is thus an opportunity to reach potentially large numbers of players and to gather contextual information.

This paper presents the tempo and rhythm sections of the *Spot The Odd Song Out* Facebook game. This paper is complementary to ongoing work [7] examining 'speed' as a perceptual intermediate used to model higher level semantic attributes such as sadness vs. happiness.

In this work we address the following questions:

- Can we use a GWAP for collecting tapped tempo data, and if so how?
- Is the distribution of tempi of each musical example a good predictor of speed?
- If we let users tap rhythms freely along to music, can we find relevant patterns in the data?

The remainder of this paper is organised as follows: Section 2 describes the software architecture and the design of the two mini-games used in this study. Section 3 presents the collected results. Section 4 discusses the data analysis and reflects on the method. Section 5 summarises the results and discusses future work.

2. METHOD

In this section, we describe the application architecture as well as the design for the tempo tapping and rhythm tapping experiments with GWAPs.

2.1 Application architecture

The GWAP presented here is built with the CaSimIR API and game framework. CaSimIR as well as the method and the user interface to collect similarity data have been introduced in [5].

[1] http://apps.facebook.com/spottheoddsongout/ and http://mi.soi.city.ac.uk/camir/game/
[2] https://www.spotify.com/se/about-us/press/information/
[3] http://www.apple.com/pr/library/2010/02/25iTunes-Store-Tops-10-Billion-Songs-Sold.html

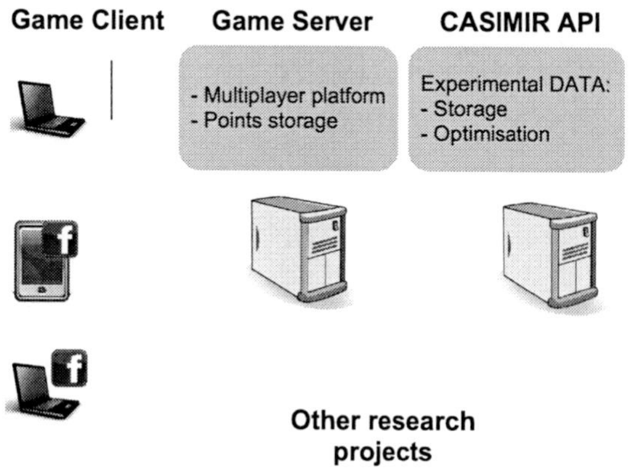

Figure 1. The application is organised in three layers: the client, the CaSimIR game server and the CaSimIR API. The API deals with the collection, organisation and selection of experimental data. The game server is separated from the game client to make the multi-player game accessible across different devices and operating systems.

The CaSimIR framework supports the development of social games with a purpose, providing a multi-player platform, high scores, social network integration and compatibility over a large range of browsers and devices. The CaSimIR API is a machine-to-machine interface between the game and the database systems, providing storage and controlled selection of experimental data.

From the developer's point of view, the client interface structures the game as a sequence of mini-games, which are part of the modular architecture. In the latest release of the Spot The Odd Song Out game, we provide three mini games studying different aspects of music: music similarity, tempo and rhythm.

2.1.1 The CaSimIR API: the data collecting system

The CaSimIR API provides an interface between the game and the database. Its two main purposes are firstly to gather and relate the data from different instances and different applications into a central database. Secondly the API also manages the selection of stimuli in order to achieve intended data properties, e.g. a certain number of subject responses per stimulus, or connectedness of graphs in the result coverage.

The API controls the number of responses for each song and returns a song according to the intended data set properties. In the "tap tempo" mini-game, for example, the API checks whether 70% of the songs have been annotated at least 7 times. Once this condition is achieved, new songs will be added to a subset and presented to future users.

Each time a player joins the game, they are authenticated in the API according to a unique key related to their IP or Facebook profile. Similarly, songs are uniquely referenced from the MagnaTagATune [1] and the Million Song Dataset [8] dataset. Thus data can be related by song and user across different games, supporting the comparison and aggregation of results from different studies.

2.1.2 The CaSimIR game framework

In comparison to traditional experiments or to web surveys a GWAP has additional requirements. A game design needs more software functionality to provide an engaging experience. Especially the cooperative aspect of a multi-player increases enjoyability and involvement of the subjects, but it poses further challenges: e.g. players with variable latencies, different Java Script interpretation across browsers and the need for AI-players to avoid empty matches. CaSimIR aims to provide a modular multi-player game environment that many projects can easily adapt to their needs, without having to re-implement basic functionalities such as data management, player synchronisation or social sharing.

Most existing GWAPs simulate a multi-player experience or restrict interaction to a high score table. In contrast, Spot The Odd Song Out features almost real-time interaction, a display menu, high scores and Facebook integration in addition to the mini-games for data collection. All mini-games feature basic gaming functionality such as a navigation menu, volume control and the display of the status of collaborating players.

To encourage players to return, options to customise the game experience are provided: Players may use points earned before to buy a new avatar or a genre in the music similarity mini-game. We also provide high scores tables, modern graphics, and social advertisement on Facebook to attract players.

2.1.3 Client-side JavaScript and implementation issues

The game client runs on mobile devices and computers in a web browser supporting HTML5. We use LimeJS [4] game-framework and the Google Closure Library [5] to achieve compatibility over many devices and browsers. By providing a tested multi-platform framework, CaSimIR makes it easier for researchers to develop GWAPs.

2.2 Game experience and user interface

The user plays sequence of mini-games and against three other players. Each mini-game corresponds to one experiment, the current succession being "odd-one-out", "tap tempo", "odd-one-out", "tap rhythm", "odd-one-out", "tap tempo". The "odd-one-out" mini-game is described in [5]. During each mini-game, the player is asked to perform a task within 60 seconds. Once all players have completed the task, or on time-out, the results are compared and points are awarded.

We aimed to make the games easily understandable with short explanation. In the design stage we found that implicit information from images, titles and overall layout has a stronger influence on the user than lengthy instructions. Thus the tasks are described in few short sentences in the first appearance of each mini-game and descriptive images and animations are provided. In the first run of a mini-game, the interface provides additional information.

[4] `http://www.limejs.com/`
[5] `https://developers.google.com/closure/library/`

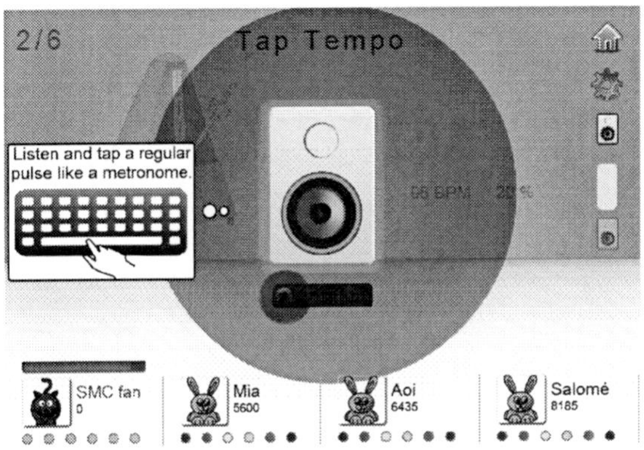

Figure 2. Screenshot of the "tap tempo" mini-game.

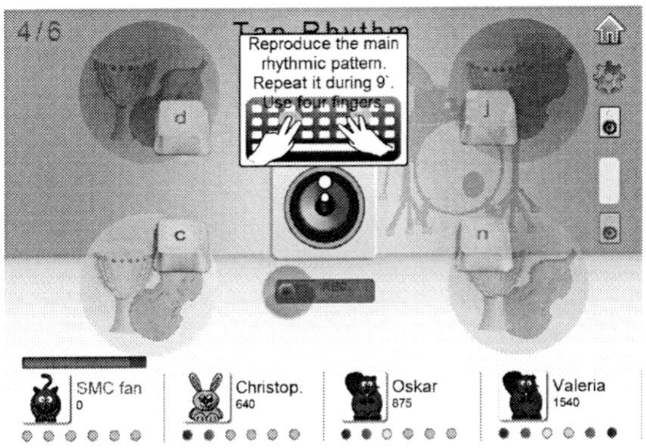

Figure 3. Screenshot of the "tap rhythm" mini-game.

The data of these runs is still recorded but can be identified in evaluations.

We use rules and rewards to encourage "well-behaved" responses, and avoid cheating or random behaviour. It is also important not to bias the experiment by rewarding very particular inputs. We use two approaches for awarding points: basing rewards on a parameter that is independent of the studied parameter (all the tempo octaves correspond to a correct answer) and rewarding agreements of players.

The dataset for the experiments described here contains audio for 100 ring tones synthesised from MIDI and songs from the Million Song Dataset [8] and is used for both the "tap tempo" and the "tap rhythm" mini-games.

2.2.1 *The "tap tempo" mini-game*

The "tap tempo" mini-game is designed to study how players tap a tempo. As the mini-game appears, an instruction explains the task. It shows an animated icon of a finger hitting the space bar of a keyboard and a note: "Listen and tap a regular pulse like a metronome." A large icon of a metronome in shown the background. The user listens to the audio clip while clicking on the mouse or hitting any key of the keyboard to reproduce the perceived pulse. Depending on the speed of the tapping, the timings of 8 to 16 taps performed by the player are recorded in ms. At each tap a red flash provides visual feedback. The player has to wait for the other players to finish the task before being shown the results and the rewards. The tempo and the relative precision error accumulated during tapping are displayed in the evaluation.

For the evaluation we only use the intervals between the taps, because the tap positions in relation to the music are subject to latencies that we can not control. The four players are ranked and get 0, 5, 10 or 20 points, based on the ranking score R_{tempo}, where lower values are better. R_{tempo} is the weighted sum of the irregularity indicator ind_{reg} and the imprecision indicator ind_{pre}

$$R_{tempo} = c_1 ind_{reg} + c_2 ind_{pres} \quad (1)$$

We manually determined $c_1 = 0.1$ and $c_2 = 0.1$ so that the reward is low for users with incoherent balance between regularity and precision.

Let vector t contain the times of the different taps, T the median time difference of successive taps. We define the irregularity indicator

$$ind_{reg} = \sum_{i}^{n} \frac{t_i - t_{i-1}}{T}. \quad (2)$$

The imprecision indicator needs to be minimal for octaves of the tempo, thus we use

$$m = \max\left(\frac{T}{T_{ref}}, \frac{T_{ref}}{T}\right) \quad (3)$$

$$ind_{pre} = m - round(m) \quad (4)$$

where T_{ref} the reciprocal of the tempo. ind_{pre} will also be minimal for integer multiples greater than 2, 3 authorise a ternary subdivision of the bar and higher values did not appear in our data.

In the results screen following each mini-game, the tempi given by all the players are shown coloured from green to red depending on the imprecision indicator. The relative error in percent is displayed in the same way according to the irregularity indicator. The earned points (0 - 20) are also displayed.

2.2.2 *The "tap rhythm" mini-game*

The "tap rhythm" game is designed to encourage complex rhythmic performances. The screen shows four circles of different colours and a drum kit is shown in the background. On each of the circles we display the letter D,C,J or N and a picture of a djembe and a double bass. By hitting the keys for the letters users can tap different rhythms or instruments which together form a rhythmic pattern. An instruction bubble explains: "Reproduce the main rhythmic pattern. Repeat it during 9 sec. Use four fingers." When the user hits one of the four keys, the corresponding circle blinks as a visual feedback. After pressing play and taping for the first time, the user's taps are recorded during nine seconds. When the rating is displayed an instruction bubble explained that it is based on complexity and precision of the tapping sequence. The users are ranked according to their performances and get from 0 to 20 points. In the rating computation and the presented preliminary analysis, the recorded taps of the four keys are merged to a single tap sequence.

We define the precision indicator on the same way as in the "tap tempo" mini-game, but the inverse of the frequency maximising the squared spectrum of the tap sequence is used instead of the median time difference of successive taps.

The complexity indicator ranges from 0 to 36 and is defined as growing each time one of the three highest peaks of the squared spectrum goes below one of the threshold values 0.025,0.02,0.016 and 0.013. We manually determined these threshold values so that:

- a random performance will obtain the three peaks under the thresholds values,
- an isochronous sequence will have the second and third peaks lower than the thresholds,
- poly-rhythms - repeating a one bar pattern containing multiple intervals - are promoted by giving three peaks over the thresholds.

The players are ranked according to the value:

$$R_{rhythm} = \frac{1}{1 + d_1 ind_{comp}} + \frac{1}{1 + d_2 ind_{pres}} \quad (5)$$

The constants $d_1 = 0.05$ and $d_2 = 0.2$ are determined manually like the threshold values.

These rating functions are not optimised estimators of tempo, rhythmic accuracy or complexity, but we feel that they are meaningful enough to support enjoyable game play and encourage participants to enter meaningful data.

3. PRELIMINARY RESULTS

The presented results are based on data collected during an internal testing period of two weeks and one week following the official release on Facebook and the web. The database contains 904 tempo estimations and 396 rhythm estimations. These were provided by 114 Facebook users and 50 further unique users of the web version. For the majority of these users, attributes including age, gender, country and further demographic data have been collected. A measurement of the accuracy of the recording of the taps led to an error below 30 ms in most cases and 100 ms in one particular case.

3.1 Testers' feedback

During the internal testing we provided computers and iPad devices to the players, observed how they understood the tasks and asked them for feedback following each match. Testers found the game was enjoyable but the mini-games would deserve more explanations to be understood from the beginning. Many testers were unsure what to do in the "tap rhythm" mini-game. Many non-musician players expressed that they felt the "tap rhythm" and sometimes the "tap tempo" games were too difficult. However, testers with a musical background appreciated this part of the game.

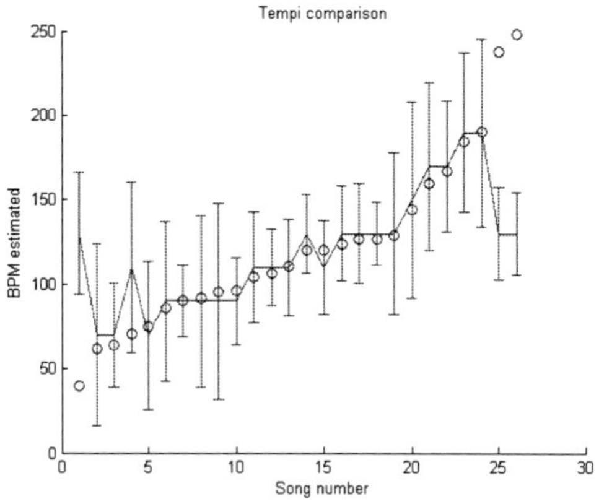

Figure 4. Comparison of tapped tempo (red line) vs ground truth (blue dots). The red curve follows the dominant tempo estimated from tapping. Red bars indicate the standard deviation of the user data. The computed/expert ground truth tempo and the tapped tempo agree in most of the cases. Extreme tempi tend to be tapped as multiples or divisions in a range of about 70 to 180 BPM.

3.2 Precision of tempo estimations

In order to filter out tap sequences given by players who did not actually try to perform the intended task, we used a set of "relevance thresholds". With the following thresholds for the "tap tempo" we obtain 46% of relevant tap sequences:

- the average tempo is between 30 and 300 BPM
- the relative standard deviation of time intervals is below 25%
- the maximum of relative deviation is under 35%

Players without musical background were sometimes adapting their taps with strong rhythmic changes or paused tapping. Most of those values are filtered out.

We compared the tapped tempo to a computed ground truth tempo: The tempo extraction is based on a percussive onset detection in the audio files [9] and agrees with the expert tempo for every song of the ringtones dataset, which was mainly used in the "tap tempo" mini-game. For the songs from the Million Song Dataset, we used tempo estimations provided by The Echo Nest.

3.3 Tempo and perceived speed

By *speed* we mean subjective ratings of "how fast" a piece of music is on a scale from "not at all" (0) to "very much" (see [10] for more detail). The relation between speed perception and tempo is not straightforward. E.g. the perceived tempo for a certain music example is not necessarily the same for all listeners. There are usually different metric levels present at the same time in a piece, and the one that is chosen as the most salient tempo can vary among listeners. This can be referred to as the tempo octave issue studied in [11–13]. For our study, we use three different tempo estimates:

Method	R-Square
Centroid	0.59
Tapped	0.51
Expert	0.61

Table 1. Linear regression of the correlation between speed and the listed variables.

- expert tempo - estimated by a music expert,
- tapped tempo - the most frequently tapped tempo within the players,
- computed tempo - is determined by an algorithm [9].

Madison et al. [10] relate expert tempo to speed ratings, concluding that speed can be modelled as a sigmoid function of an expert tempo. Elowsson et al. [9] find that a computed tempo and a combination of custom features for onset and computed tempo could predict up to 90% of estimations.

Levy [11] used a web based application to collect the speed labelled as fast, intermediate or slow while asking the user to tap the tempo. The purpose was to correct possible tempo octave errors in a computed tempo. Determining speed from the tempo distribution with this dataset is not straightforward, because only three categories of speed are used and a bias may be introduced by the subject being asked to tap and evaluate speed at the same time.

3.4 Tempo distribution

For each song we computed the centroid of the tempo distribution given by the tapped estimations. Madison et al. [10] relate expert tempo values to speed estimations with a sigmoid curve. We computed a linear regression to compare the correlation between perceived speed collected in a separate experiment described here [7] and the centroid of the tapped distribution, the tapped tempo, and the tempo ground truth. The results are summarised in a table 1 and figure 5.

3.5 Rhythmic pattern identification

The data acquired from the second experiment are analysed as an onset list. Based on this list we compute a main rhythmic pattern description: To each onset we associate a Gaussian function with a standard deviation of 50ms. We define the bar period as four beats in the ground truth tempo. Inspired by the Beat Spectrum published by Jonathan Foote et al. [14], for each offset we sum the corresponding positions of the tap signal over the bar periods starting. This results in a pattern representing the accumulated tap incidence over the time of one bar. We sum over all performances to obtain an estimation of the main tapped pattern of the song. This pattern is compared to a pattern extracted using a computed onset list over the audio file. In this experiment the offset is hard to define, as for recorded taps, the time when audio playback starts could

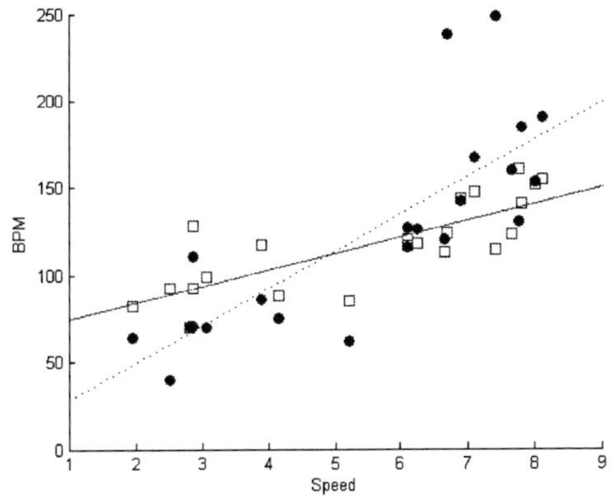

Figure 5. Regression for tapped tempo centroids (squares) and ground truth (filled circles). Regression of centroids is plotted as red line (75 - 200BPM), and regression of tempo ground truth is plotted as black dotted line. The X-axis represent the speed and the Y-axis represent the tempo.

not be accurately recorded. We recreated the offset by assuming that the player taps on the first beat more than at any other time in the bar.

4. DISCUSSION

4.1 General assumption on tempo estimations

In nearly all cases (figure 4), the tapped tempo data reproduced the ground truth tempo given by computer and experts, with tempo octave disagreements occurring only for extreme tempi. When a tempo octave can be ambiguous, indicated by more than one valid tapped tempo centroid, non-musician players disagreeing with the ground truth tend to prefer tempi close to 120 BPM.

4.2 Tempo distribution

The centroids of the tempo distribution and the expert tempi in figure 5 show similar performances as indicators of the speed ratings. Madison et al. [10] indeed describe a high correlation between speed and expert tempo. We have not yet collected sufficient data to allow for a more wide-ranging comparison. The above correlations of tempo centroid and expert tempo are still encouraging to infer perceptual speed from tempo centroids. The tapped tempo itself proved an inferior predictor of perceptual speed.

For musically trained subjects, tempo-related tasks appear relatively easy. On the other hand, non-musician subjects had often great difficulty in reproducing the tempo. MacDougall et al. [15] state that 120 BPM correspond to a "resonant frequency" of the human body. Madison et al. suggest the tendency of performing a tempo in a middle range tempo between 90 and 150 BPM. A non-musician may have trouble to produce a pulse out of this natural range from a motor point of view. On the other hand, a music expert will be able to pick a tempo multiple more representative of his perception of speed in the musical piece. This would explain both the disagreement of the crowd and

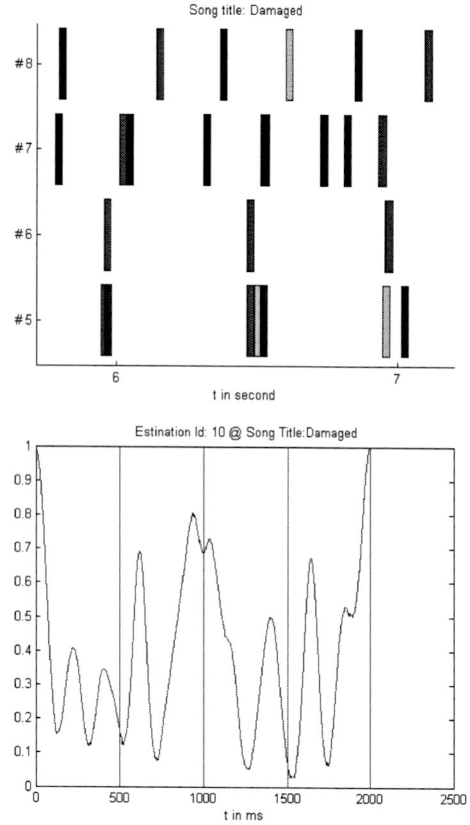

Figure 6. (top) Rows depict onset times from "tap rhythm" performances for 4 users, with colours identifying different fingers. (bottom) Accumulated tap incidence pattern for a single performance, red vertical lines locate predicted beat positions.

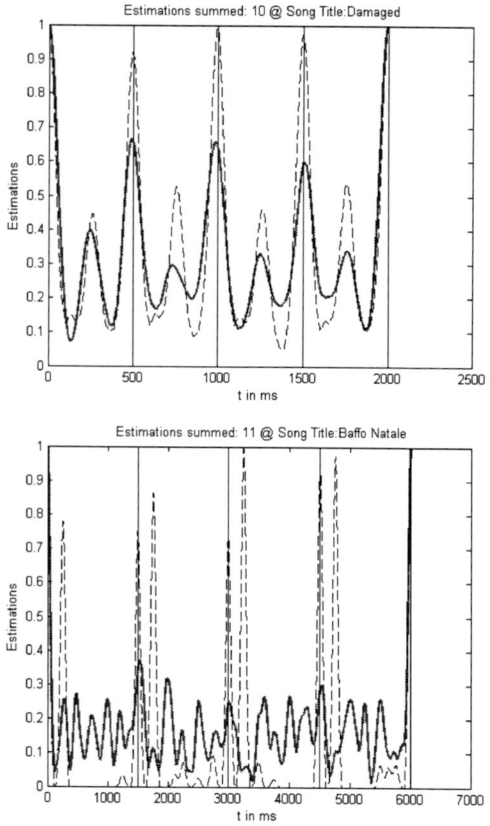

Figure 7. Averaged tap incidence pattern over several performances for 2 songs (top) Song "Damaged", time signature 4/4, averaged over 10 data entries. (bottom) Song "Baffo Natale", time signature 12/8, averaged over 11 data entries. The beat patterns are plotted as continuous graphs (-). For comparison, the dashed curves (–) represent beat patterns automatically extracted from audio.

the expert in extreme ranges as well as the higher correlation for the expert tempo compared to the most frequently tapped tempo.

4.3 Tapping free rhythms with four fingers

Many different behaviours can be identified in the collected data (Figure 6). The task was designed to give interpretive freedom to the player, in contrast to the very strict "tap tempo" mini-games. Unfortunately, many players perceived it as hard to understand and perform. This may be due to the interpretative freedom and multi-limb and finger coordination as well as rhythmic skills required by the task. The main aim of this second task was to identify which metric positions would be emphasised by players. This could have led to more complex or irregular patterns such as syncopation, swing or groove, useful for extending the regular notion of tempo.

During analysis we found that, by summing the main pattern tapped by ten players or more, (see Figure 7) we converge to a hierarchical description of the time division in the bar. In most of the cases, this hierarchical description corresponds to the actual time signature a music expert would assign to the music piece: a hierarchical sequence of regular subdivisions of the bar is indicated by the most represented onsets. With a standard $4/4$ (four quarters) audio stimulus, a clear majority tapped beat corresponds to the first beat of the period. However, there is a bias here, as we do not know the absolute time of each tap. To overcome this problem we shift each performance's maximum of accumulated tap incidence to the beginning of the pattern. The lower peaks represent the three other beats of the bar. Eights are tapped as well, but no lower subdivisions of the bar are represented.

Figure 7 compares players' patterns to the patterns extracted from the audio clip. In most of the cases, the tapped pattern corresponds very closely to the onset identified in the song. Yet in a song containing twelve subdivisions per bar, players agree on the song signature even if the automatically extracted onsets barely finds this in the music.

In this preliminary study, we have considered the tapping with the four fingers as having an equivalent role. This representation led to an interesting result but did not represent rhythmic irregularity of some songs as expected. The dataset could be further explored, e.g. by comparing players using 1,2,3 and 4 fingers or identifying reproduced pattern in a particular bar of the song.

5. CONCLUSIONS AND FUTURE WORK

In this paper we have described the CaSimIR API, a modular GWAP framework, and evaluated its applicability to research in tempo, rhythm and speed using two experiments: "tap tempo" and "tap rhythm". The CaSimIR framework allowed for the recording of taps in reasonable accuracy. The programming of automated answer scripts via bots should be discouragingly complex. This is due to integrity testing of submitted user data and the general complexity of the interaction with the game-style user interface.

5.1 Results of the tapping experiments

For "tap tempo", we were able to collect a large dataset of new tempo estimations, and found the collected data strongly reproduced ground truth data, encouraging the use of GWAP's to collect more tempo information about music, which could be used for inferring perceptual speed.

The "tap rhythm" mini-game also allowed for the collection of rhythmic patterns. Although we encountered some usability problems, rhythmic patterns were extracted and used for analysis by combining data from several users. When asking a group of people to perform a rhythm freely with four fingers, the data was relatively noisy. However, the averaged pattern still converged to a regular hierarchical subdivision of the bar similar to a traditional time signature.

After a preliminary data collection period of a few of weeks, we raise questions to be explored in future studies: In order to further investigate the relation of speed perception and collected tempo data, we need precise numerical results and more data. The exploration of the "tap rhythm" dataset encourages further research into characterising rhythm singularities or particularities in motion related to the reproduction of rhythms. Results of these experiments might also relate to other perceptual features such as rhythmic complexity or clarity.

5.2 Lessons learned in using a GWAP

The CaSimIR framework addresses many challenges related to the GWAP approach: It provides a multi-player platform, survey example selection, and manages data storage allowing for combination of different data collection ventures.

The game has reached enough players to observe interesting details using this experiment. Although the mass effect of a GWAP based experiment is appealing, it is not granted: Many players did not return to the game, and it proved hard to maintain a constant amount of players participating. Other GWAPs such as HerdIt [2,3] have reached a threshold of 500 players, TagATune even reached an audience of almost 15,000 players. Reaching such a success is a hard task and requires appealing game as well as a long term effort including regular additions and advertising. The number of players needed for particular studies may not justify the complexity of the application compared to a study with large promotion [11].

As earlier games focussed on collecting textual annotations, we show that recent technology allows for collecting tempo data on a large scale of users. The tightly timed game interaction promotes high attention of users, but means of controlling the users' context such as noise, type of speakers and sound levels could not be applied. Although we found the visual feedback helpful, we did not measure the influence on the performer. Despite the preliminary nature of our data collection and the moderate timing precision, our data still allowed to validate and identify human perception specificities, which is appropriate for a preliminary study. Communication and interaction between users is important and should be improved, as collaborative playing might be a key to attract more players.

6. REFERENCES

[1] E. Law and L. von Ahn, "Input-agreement: a new mechanism for collecting data using human computation games," in *Proc. of the SIGCHI Conference on Human Factors in Computing Systems*, 2009.

[2] D. Turnbull, R. Liu, L.Barrington, and G.Lanckriet, "A game-based approach for collecting semantic annotations of music," in *Austrian Computer Society*, 2007.

[3] L. Barrington, D. Turnbull, D. O'Malley, and G. Lanckriet, "User-centered design of a social game to tag music," in *Proc. of the ACM SIGKDD Workshop on Human Computation*, 2007.

[4] M. L. Mandel and D. P. Ellis, "A web-based game for collecting music metadata," *Journal of New Music Research*, 2008.

[5] D. Wolff, G. Bellec, and T. Weyde, "A music similarity game prototype using the CASimIR API," in *Online Proc. of ISMIR Late Breaking Sessions*, 2012.

[6] L. von Ahn, "Game with a purpose," *Computer*, 2006.

[7] A. Elowsson, A. Friberg, and G. Madison, "Tempo estimation of popular music," in *Submitted*, 2013.

[8] T.Bertin-Mahieux, D. Ellis, B.Whitman, and P. Lamere, "The million song dataset," in *Proc. of the 12th International Society for Music Information Retrieval Conference*, 2011.

[9] A.Elowsson and A.Friberg, "Modelling perception of speed in music audio," in *Forthcoming for Proc. of SMC*, 2013.

[10] G. Madison and J. Paulin, "Ratings of speed in real music as a function of both original and manipulated beat tempo," *Acoustical Society of America*, 2009.

[11] M. Levy, "Improving perceptual tempo estimation with crowd-sourced annotations," in *Proc. of ISMIR*, 2010.

[12] M. McKinney and D. Moelants, "Deviations from the resonance theory of tempo induction," in *Proc of Interdisciplinary Musicology*, R. Parncutt, A. Kessler, and F. Zimmer, Eds., 2004.

[13] J. Hockman and I. Fujinaga, "Fast vs slow: Learning tempo octaves from user data," in *Proc. of ISMIR*, 2010.

[14] J. Foote, "The beat spectrum: a new approach to rhythm analysis," in *In Proc. IEEE Int. Conf. on Multimedia and Expo*, 2001.

[15] H. G. MacDougall and S. T. Moore, "Marching to the beat of the same drummer: the spontaneous tempo of human locomotion," *Human Movement Science*, 2005.

Methods for Real Time Harmonic Excitation of Acoustic Signals

Sean Enderby
Department of Digital Media Technology
Birmingham City University
Birmingham, UK
sean.enderby@mail.bcu.ac.uk

Zlatko Baracskai
Department of Digital Media Technology
Birmingham City University
Birmingham, UK
zlatko.baracskai@bcu.ac.uk

Cham Athwal
Department of Digital Media Technology
Birmingham City University
Birmingham, UK
cham.athwal@bcu.ac.uk

ABSTRACT

In this paper three methods for the introduction of new harmonic content to an acoustic signal are assessed. Each method extracts the amplitude envelope of the fundamental frequency in a signal and applies it to a newly generated harmonic. In one method this is achieved in the frequency domain through use of the short time Fourier transform. The other two methods process audio in the time domain using either instantaneous amplitude and phase measurements or single side band automodulation.

The results from a set of preliminary listening tests are discussed and compared against objective measurements based on psychoacoustic models. It is suggested that frequency domain processing is too inaccurate where low latency is required and a time domain approach is preferential. The two time domain approaches show similar levels of accuracy, however it is considered that extracting the amplitude envelope of harmonics other than the fundamental could increase accuracy. It is noted that the instantaneous amplitude and phase method provides more flexibility in order to achieve this.

1. INTRODUCTION

Harmonic excitation involves the introduction of new harmonic content to an audio signal. This can be used to increase the perceived quality of a piece of audio. They can also be used to restore old recordings where the recording medium may have deteriorated or was not able to capture high frequency signals. [1].

Pitched sounds arise from resonant systems that produce a harmonic spectrum with complex evolution and envelope. In sound synthesis the detailed harmonic spectrum can be produced by synthesising the harmonics separately or by using higher order nonlinearities to process the fundamental. Chebyshev polynomials allow synthesising any proportion of harmonics by applying a transfer function to a full amplitude sine wave [2]. In the context of real-time processing this technique is ideal for its zero latency, however it is not suitable for exciting harmonics of acoustic sounds as the non-unit amplitude produces a varying mixture of the desired and the lower order harmonics as shown in Figure 1.

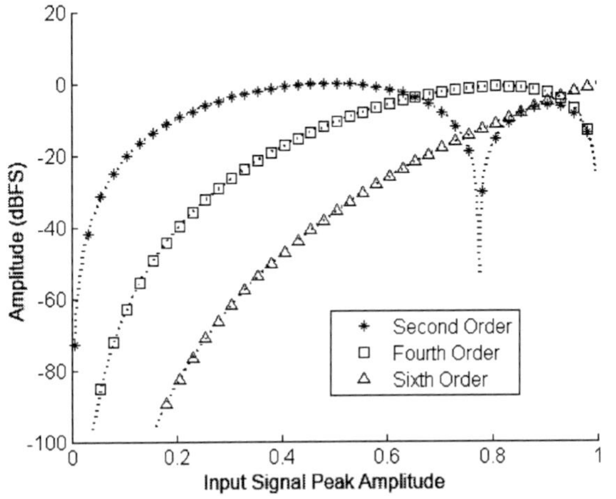

Figure 1: The levels of unwanted harmonics introduced when using Chebyshev polynomials to synthesise the 6th order harmonic of sine waves with various peak amplitudes.

A simple method to introduce new harmonic content to a signal is through the application of a static nonlinear system. The value of each input sample is mapped, using some nonlinear function, to a new output value. Examples of these types of systems are given in [3]. For a sinusoidal input each of these systems will introduce a characteristic set of harmonics. The order and amplitude of these harmonics is defined by the nonlinear function used to process the signal.

The downside of these methods is that more than one harmonic is introduced to the signal. This is not desirable in situations where only a specific harmonic is required. This paper deals with methods by which single harmonics can be introduced to a signal with as little extraneous frequency content as possible.

Three such methods are be described in Section 2. The methods are then assessed on their latency and their ability to introduce specific harmonics into a pitched signal. The later is done through use of perceptual listening tests, as described in Section 3, and a perceptual distortion metric. The results of these test are then compared in order to determine which harmonic excitation method is most suitable for real time applications.

2. METHODS

The process by which individual harmonics will be introduced to a signal can be broken down into four stages.

- Calculate the fundamental frequency of the input signal.
- Extract the amplitude envelope of the fundamental in the input signal.
- Synthesise a new signal with the frequency of the desired harmonic and the amplitude envelope of the fundamental.
- Scale the synthesised harmonic and mix it back into the original input signal.

Three different methods for the synthesis of new harmonics are assessed in this paper. Each has been named according to the mathematical transforms on which they are based. The methods are based on:

- The Short Time Fourier Transform (STFT).
- Instantaneous amplitude and phase measurements (IAP).
- Single side band automodulation (SSB).

2.1 Short Time Fourier Transform

The STFT can be used to analyse the frequency content of sequential time frames of the input signal. This frame based processing introduces an inherent delay into the system. The challenge with generating harmonics using the STFT is to keep the frame length short enough to keep latency from being perceptible whilst still maintaining enough frequency resolution to accurately synthesise the new harmonic [4].

The acceptable levels of latency in live music situations are discussed in [5]. It is suggested that the acceptable level varies from 1.4ms to 42ms depending on the instrument and monitoring system. The frame length used needs to be kept short enough such that the latency of the entire system does not exceed these limits.

The phase vocoder technique can be used to scale the frequency of the fundamental to the desired harmonic. This is achieved by zeroing the bins for frequencies greater than the fundamental in the DFT data for each frame. The new frequency domain data can then be pitch shifted via a phase vocoder to the frequency of the desired harmonic. It was found that when using short frame lengths pitch shifting of several octaves is not achievable due to the poor frequency resolution. This means that higher order harmonics could not be generated.

A simpler method is to calculate the amplitude of the fundamental frequency in each time frame. These values can then be linearly interpolated in order to approximate the amplitude envelope of the fundamental. This amplitude can then be applied during the synthesis of a harmonic with the desired frequency. This allows for a better accuracy for short STFT frame lengths but it does rely on knowing the frequency of the fundamental precicely. The samples used in the listening tests discussed in Section 3 were created using this method.

2.2 Instantaneous Amplitude and Phase

In this technique the fundamental of the input signal is isolated using a low pass filter. The amplitude envelope of the fundamental can then be found using measurements of instantaneous amplitude.

The principles of instantaneous amplitude and phase are discussed in [6]. To take these measurements the filtered signal must be converted to its analytic form. In a true analytic signal the real part will be the original input signal and the imaginary part its Hilbert transform. Calculating a true analytic signal is not possible without introducing delay to the system. The more delay introduced the more accurate the analytic signal will be.

A low latency alternative is to use a pair of all pass filters whose phase responses differ by $\frac{\pi}{2}$ radians across a large proportion of the audible bandwidth. An example of such a pair of filters is given in [7]. Simple calculations can be applied to the output of these filters to produce two new signals. One is a signal which represents the amplitude envelope of the fundamental ($a[t]$) and the other represents the phase of the fundamental ($\phi[t]$). Due to the filters used the phase measurements will not represent the phase of the fundamental in the the original signal. The change in phase measurement with time however, will be consistent with the frequency of the fundamental.

Once the measurements of amplitude and phase have been taken, the new harmonic can be synthesised as done in [8]. Equation 1 shows the calculation for synthesising the nth harmonic ($h[t]$).

$$h[t] = a[t] \cos(n\phi[t]) \tag{1}$$

The accuracy of this method is largely dependant on the order of the low pass filter used to isolate the fundamental. The higher the order of the filter the better the isolation of the fundamental. This leads to less extraneous frequencies being introduced in the synthesis of the new harmonic.

2.3 Single Side Band Automodulation

With this technique, as with the IAP technique, the fundamental is isolated using a low pass filter and then further filtering is applied in order to create an analytic signal. This analytic signal can then be raised to a power in order to scale its pitch to that of the desired harmonic. The underlying principle is that of de Moirve's formula (Equation 2) and single side band modulation.

$$(\cos(x) + i\sin(x))^n = \cos(nx) + i\sin(nx) \tag{2}$$

When signals are multiplied together (or multiplied by them selves in this case) an upper and lower sideband are created. These sidebands are comprised of various intermodulation frequencies which are the sums and differences of the frequencies in the input signals. If the two signals are converted to their analytic representations first only a single sideband will be created. This is the concept of single side band modulation as discussed in [9]. For the generation of harmonics the analytic signal of the fundamental is multiplied with itself rather than a modulator wave. This gives rise to the idea of single side band automodulation.

Where $z[t]$ represents the analytic signal for the fundamental the nth harmonic can be calculated using equation 3.

$$h[t] = \mathrm{Re}(z[t]^n) \tag{3}$$

As with the IAP technique the accuracy of this process relies on the fundamental being well isolated. The better isolated the fundamental the less unwanted intermodulation frequencies will be present in the synthesised harmonic.

An advantage of this technique is that the amplitude envelope of the fundamental does not have to be measured, as such it requires the least computation of the discussed methods. This is beneficial for real time processing but it does cause inaccuracies in the amplitude envelope of the generated harmonic. If the nth harmonic were generated, its amplitude envelope would be the amplitude envelope of the fundamental raised to the power n.

3. LISTENING TESTS

A preliminary series of subjective listening tests were undertaken in order to assess the accuracy of each of the described methods. The assessment criteria for the listening tests were based on the following statement. "If some harmonic content is removed from an audio signal and then reintroduced through harmonic excitation. The newly produced signal should sound the same as the original signal". This is similar to the method by which the quality of perceptual coding algorithms is assessed. This allows a listening test methodology similar to MUSHRA [10] to be used effectively.

To create the stimuli for the listening test four different audio samples were each processed in nine different ways. The four unprocessed samples were:

- A bowed cello sample.
- A clarinet sample.
- A synthesised harmonic sound.
- A piano sample.

Each of the samples were of the instrument playing a single sustained note. The synthesised sample has very little energy at frequencies that are not its harmonics. This should make it easier to excite harmonics in as the fundamental can be isolated more easily. Owing to the acoustic nature of the other samples they have more energy at these non harmonic frequencies.

In order to reduce the number of variables each of the unprocessed samples was analysed prior to the creation of the test stimuli. The fundamental frequency of each sample was measured along with the amplitudes of the third through ninth harmonics. This information was then used in the reconstruction of the signal. This allowed for any inaccuracies which may be involved with real time calculation of the fundamental frequency or amplitudes of harmonics to be mitigated. Allowing the accuracy of the harmonic generation algorithms to be assessed more thoroughly.

For each sample the third through ninth harmonics were filtered out as shown by the spectrograms in Figure 2. This was in order to cause significant degradation in the quality of the sample such that the difference is plainly audible to the majority of listeners. The second harmonic was left in the signal in order to pose a challenge to the IAP and SSB techniques. As mentioned previously the accuracy of these methods is dependant on how well the fundamental is isolated. Retaining the second harmonic allows for the effects of filter order on the accuracy of the technique to be assessed.

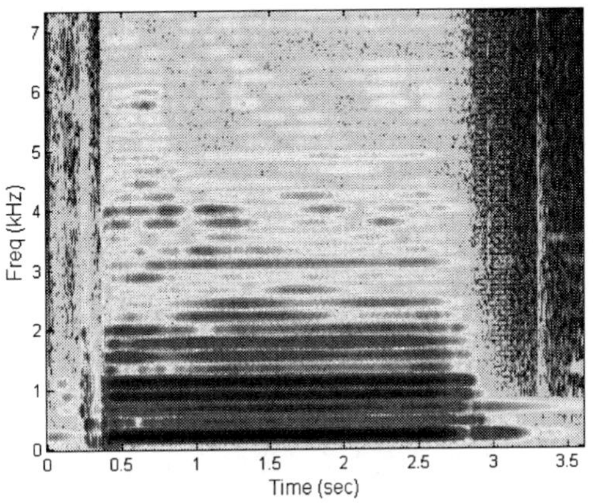

(a) Original Signal

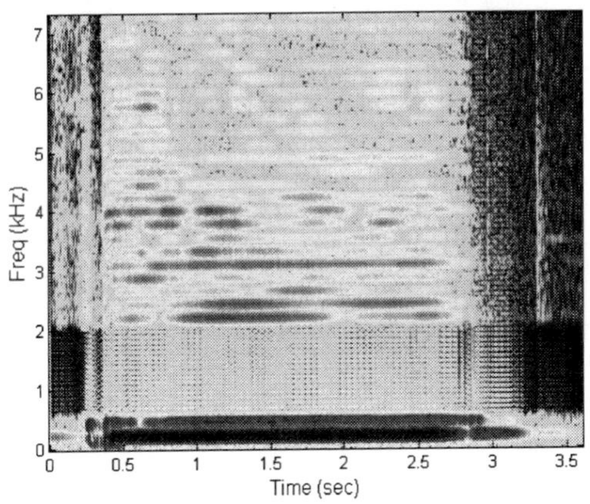

(b) Signal with Harmonics Removed

Figure 2: Spectrograms showing the frequency content of the cello sample before and after the harmonics were removed.

The filtered signal was then processed using the techniques discussed in Section 2. Each technique was used to create three stimuli, each with different parameters. For the STFT method, frame lengths of 50, 100 and 500 samples were used. For the IAP and SSB stimuli FIR filters with kernel lengths of 50, 100 and 500 samples were used to isolate the fundamental.

In line with the ITU recommendations [10] test subjects were presented with all the processed versions of a particular sample at once along with a reference sample (the unprocessed sample). Subjects could listen to the samples in any order and as many times as they required. Subjects

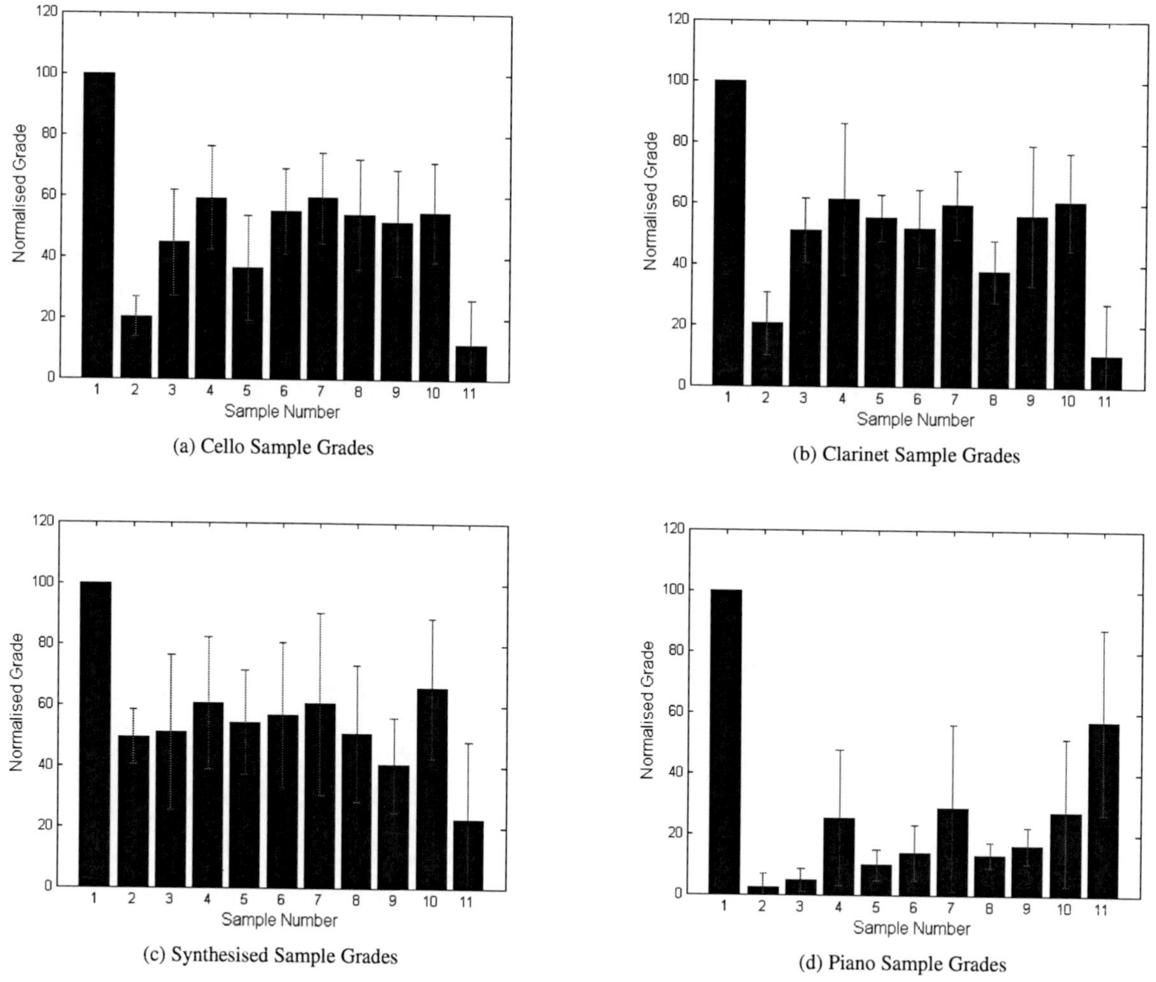

Figure 3: Mean grades and confidence intervals for each of the stimuli.

were asked to rate how well each processed samples recreated the reference sample on a scale from 0 to 100. The scale is shown in Figure 4.

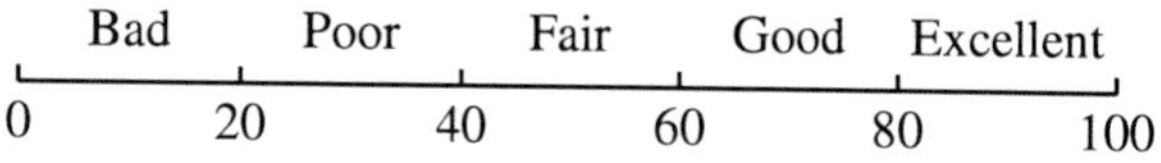

Figure 4: Listening Test Grading Scale

Among the samples to be graded are a hidden reference and anchor. The hidden reference is the same as the reference sample so should be given a score of 100. The anchor is the sample with the third through ninth harmonics removed. As no attempt was made to reintroduce the harmonics, this stimuli should be graded worse that the stimuli which have undergone harmonic excitation.

4. RESULTS

4.1 Listening Test Results

Preliminary testing has been undertaken with six test subjects. While this not a sufficient amount to provide confident assessments for each of the processing algorithms, it was sufficient to find basic patterns in the accuracy achieved by using a different method or changing the parameters of the method.

The grades given by each test subject were normalised to the range of 0 to 100. The mean grade given for each stimulus was then calculated. As suggested in the ITU recommendations [10] a 95% confidence interval was also calculated for each stimulus.

Figure 3 shows the results obtained from this preliminary testing. Each separate graph relates to a particular reference sample. The sample numbers relate to different processing algorithms as follows:

1. The hidden reference sample.
2. STFT reconstructed sample with a frame length of 50 samples.
3. STFT reconstructed sample with a frame length of 100 samples.
4. STFT reconstructed sample with a frame length of 500 samples.
5. SSB reconstructed sample using a filter kernel length of 50 samples.

6. SSB reconstructed sample using a filter kernel length of 100 samples.

7. SSB reconstructed sample using a filter kernel length of 500 samples.

8. IAP reconstructed sample using a filter kernel length of 50 samples.

9. IAP reconstructed sample using a filter kernel length of 100 samples.

10. IAP reconstructed sample using a filter kernel length of 500 samples.

11. The hidden anchor sample.

The error bars on each bar in the graphs show the 95% confidence interval for that stimulus.

It is immediately apparent that the confidence intervals are fairly large. For most of the stimuli this can be attributed to only having a small cohort of test subjects.

Across the three acoustically recorded samples (Cello, Clarinet and Piano) there is an increase in the perceived accuracy of the algorithms as the frame or filter kernel length is increased as seen in Figures 3a, b and d. The lowest grades in each of these are given to the STFT processing with the shortest window length. The IAP and SSB techniques show greater accuracy while introducing less latency. For the electronically synthesised sample however the different processing algorithms are all given similar grades but with a wider variance in grades between different test subjects.

This could be attributed to the synthetic nature of the sample. There is very little energy in the sample at frequencies that are not harmonics. This makes it easy to isolate the fundamental and generate accurate new harmonics. Because of this even the processed samples which used short filter of frame lengths will be accurate. As all the processed samples sound fairly similar it is then difficult for the test subject to determine where on the scale they should be placed.

In the acoustic signals there is much more energy in frequencies which are not harmonics. This makes it more difficult to generate accurate harmonics so the differences between stimuli with different frame or filter lengths are more perceptible. As the subject is given a larger range of accuracies to assess it is easier for them to place them on the scale in a consistent manner.

The piano sample used is of special interest as its fun-

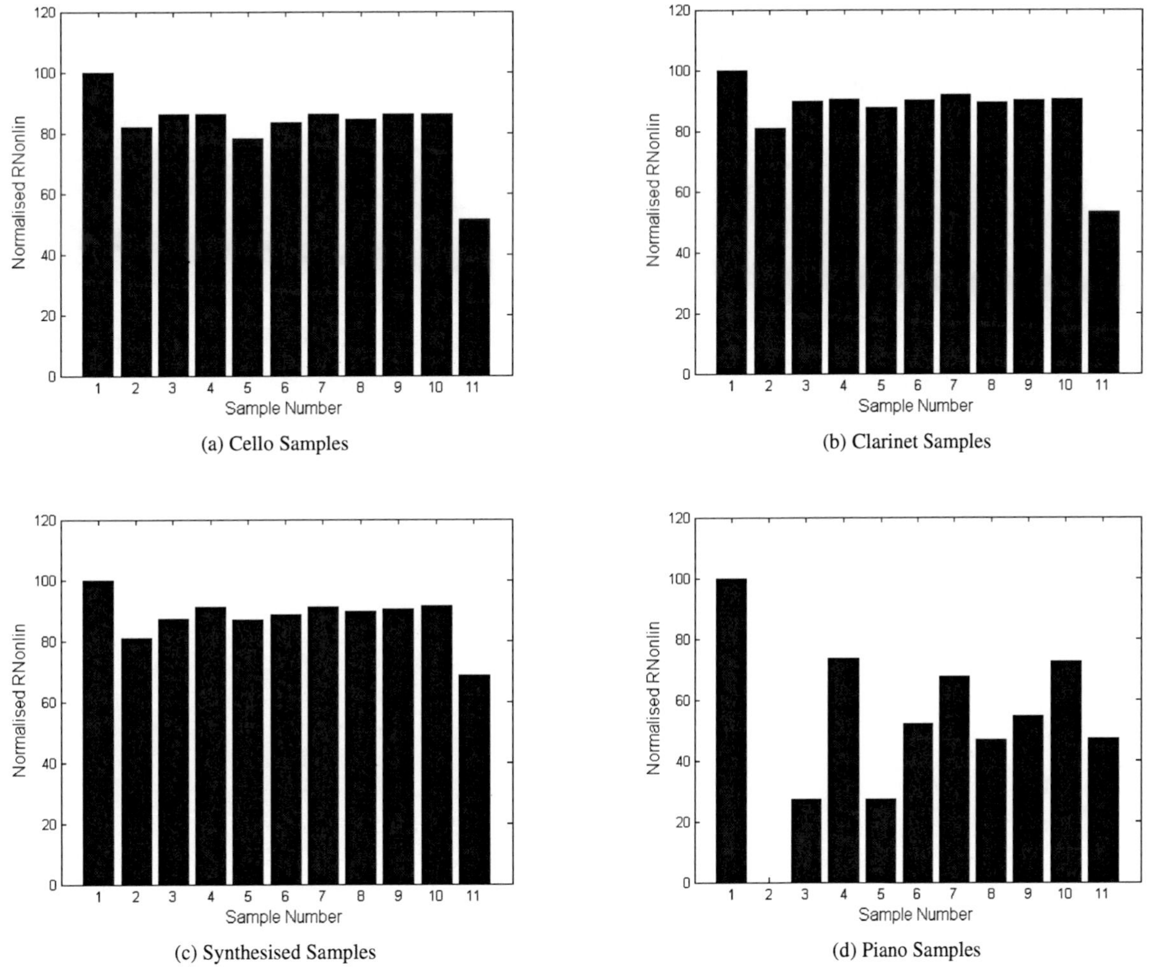

(a) Cello Samples

(b) Clarinet Samples

(c) Synthesised Samples

(d) Piano Samples

Figure 5: R_{nonlin} measurements for each of the listening test stimuli.

damental frequency is heavily damped. This led to the second harmonic in the signal being the most prominent. As the processing used relies on the amplitude envelope of the fundamental to generate new harmonics this lead to accuracy problems. Figure 3d shows that the reconstruction of the piano sample was not successful. The anchor signal has been graded higher than all of the reconstructed samples. The harmonic excitation has served to make the filtered signal sound less like the original rather than more.

4.2 R_{nonlin} Results

The R_{nonlin} metric was developed for predicting the perceived quality of nonlinearly distorted signals. The process by which it is measured is described in [11]. The metric uses psychoacoustic models and correlation measurements to determine how similar a distorted signal sounds to the undistorted signal. This is very similar to the assessment criteria of the subjective listening tests.

The R_{nonlin} value for each of the listening test stimuli were calculated and are shown in Figure 5. As the R_{nonlin} metric returns a value between 0 and 1 the results have again been normalised to the range of 0 to 100. These values are used to support the results obtained from the listening tests as the cohort of test subjects was not large enough to provide conclusive results.

The results in Figure 5 support some of the correlations noticed in Figure 3. It is shown that increasing the frame or filter kernel length will produce a signal which is objectively more similar to the reference sample. It has also shown that for samples with a prominent fundamental (Figures 5a, b and c) the reconstructed samples are more similar to the original than the anchor sample is.

Figure 5d again highlights the inaccuracies of the discussed methods when the input signal has a severely damped fundamental. Some of the reconstructed samples are less similar to the original than the anchor signal. This was also apparent from the results shown in Figure 3d. Section 5 will suggest methods by which this problem may be overcome.

5. FURTHER ISSUES

5.1 Fundamental Amplitude Envelope

Scaling the amplitude envelope of the fundamental and applying it to the generated harmonic has caused some problems with accuracy. Most obviously in the reconstruction of the Piano sample, where the fundamental was damped and hence its amplitude envelope did not reflect those of the higher order harmonics.

More subtle issues also arose in the reconstructed Cello samples. Figure 6 shows spectrograms of the Cello sample before and after reconstruction using the IAP method.

The decay portion of each of these samples are substantially different from one another. In the original signal (Figure 6a) the first and third harmonics decay in amplitude over a longer period than any of the other harmonics. As the reconstructed harmonics all use the amplitude envelope of the fundamental they also have this extended delay

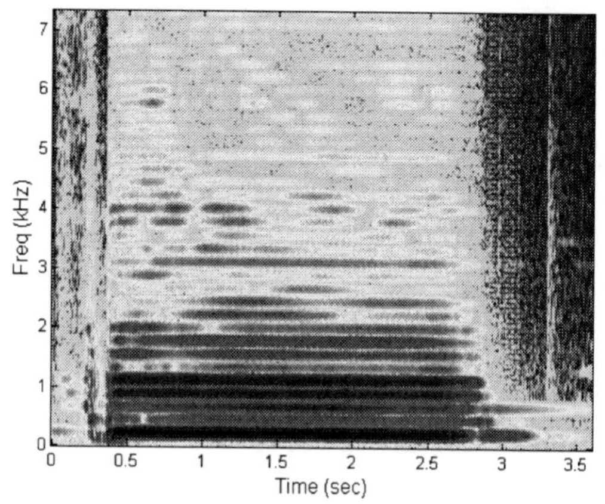

(a) Original Signal

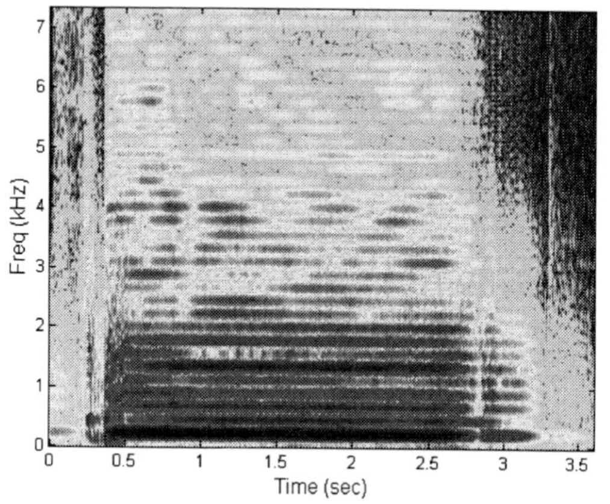

(b) IAP Reconstruction (50 Sample Filter kernel)

Figure 6: Spectrograms showing the frequency content of the cello sample before and after reconstruction with the IAP method.

time, as shown in Figure 6b. This results in an audible difference in the two samples during the decay phase.

A proposed method to increase accuracy in these cases is to use the amplitude envelope of harmonics closer to the one being generated rather than that of the fundamental. It may also prove more accurate to use the amplitude envelope of a harmonic with the same parity as the one being generated. Note in Figure 6a that the first and third harmonic have an extended decay but not the second.

This is only achievable using the STFT and IAP methods. While the SSB method is fast to compute it does not measure the amplitude envelope of the harmonic used as the input. It merely pitch shifts it by an integer multiple. This means that unless the fundamental is used as the input not every harmonic can be generated.

In the samples made for the experiment discussed in Section 3, a large amount of the harmonics were removed prior to harmonic excitation. This meant there was little choice of harmonics to extract an amplitude envelope from. In a more ideal situation the amplitude envelope could be taken from the nearest harmonic with the same parity as the one being generated. Thus an improvement that could be made to the samples created for the experiment would be to use the amplitude envelope of the second harmonic to generate the even order harmonics. Evidently further experimentation is needed to examine what effect this would have on accuracy.

5.2 Post Filtering

Another issue apparent in the samples is the extra high order harmonics that are generated using the SSB and IAP techniques. Any extraneous frequencies in the isolated fundamental will cause these higher order harmonics to be generated along with the desired one. A simple way to overcome this is to apply a band pass filter at the frequency of the desired harmonic after it has been generated. This post filtering process reduces the amount of extraneous high order harmonics in the output signal as evidenced in Figure 7. The extended decay seen at the higher frequencies in Figure 7a are seen to be reduced by the application of post filtering (Figure 7b).

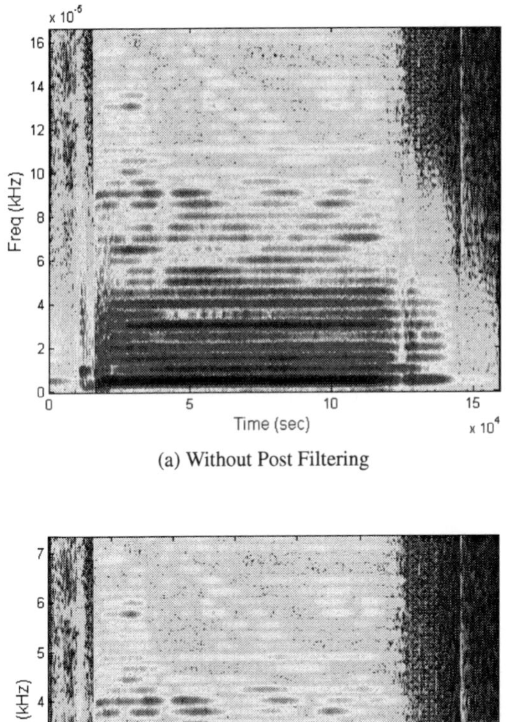

(a) Without Post Filtering

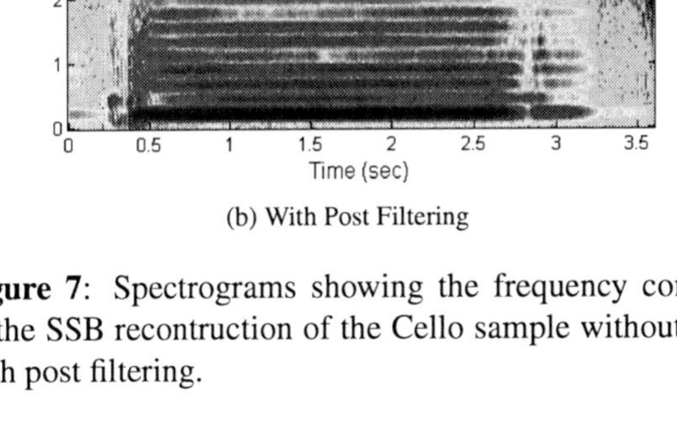

(b) With Post Filtering

Figure 7: Spectrograms showing the frequency content of the SSB recontruction of the Cello sample without and with post filtering.

6. CONCLUSION

It has been shown that resynthesising harmonics using the amplitude envelope of the fundamental gives varying degrees of accuracy depending on the input signal. It is suggested that to increase this accuracy the amplitude envelopes of harmonics closer to those being synthesised could be used. Further experimentation is needed in order to determine the effect this will have on accuracy.

It is also suggested that in order to introduce new harmonics to an audio signal with as little latency as possible, time domain approaches (IAP and SSB) are preferential to a frequency domain approach (STFT). From the preliminary listening tests conducted it is not possible to conclude which of the two time domain approaches is superior.

Were latency the prime concern the SSB method would be appropriate as it requires the least computation. If it can be shown that using the amplitude envelope of harmonics other than the fundamental to synthesise new harmonics would improve accuracy, the more flexible IAP technique would be more appropriate.

7. REFERENCES

[1] J. Chalupper, "Aural exciter and loudness maximizer: What's psychoacoustic about -psychoacoustic processors?-," in *Audio Engineering Society Convention 109*, Sep 2000.

[2] C. Dodge and T. A. Jerse, *Computer Music: Synthesis, Composition and Performance*, 2nd ed. Schirmer: Thomson Learning, 1997.

[3] D. T. Yeh, "Digital implementations of musical distortion circuits by analysis and simulation," Ph.D. dissertation, Stanford University, 2009.

[4] A. De Götzen, N. Bernardini, and D. Arfib, "Traditional (?) implementations of a phase-vocoder: The tricks of the trade," in *DAFx-00*, Dec 2000.

[5] M. Lester and J. Boley, "The effects of latency on live sound monitoring," in *Audio Engineering Society Convention 123*, Oct 2007.

[6] B. Picinbono, "On instantaneous amplitude and phase of signals," *Signal Processing, IEEE Transactions on*, vol. 45, no. 3, pp. 552–560, 1997.

[7] O. Niemitalo. (2003, Jul) Hilbert transform.

[8] M. Puckette, "Patch for guitar," in *Pure Data Convention, Montreal*, Aug 2007.

[9] M. Corinthios, *Signals, Systems, Transforms, and Digital Signal Processing with MATLAB*. Taylor & Francis Group, 2009.

[10] Recommendation ITU-R BS.1534-1, "Methods for the subjective assessment of intermediate quality level of coding systems," 2001.

[11] C. Tan, B. C. J. Moore, N. Zacharov, and M. Ville-Veikko, "Predicting the perceived quality of nonlinearly distorted music and speech signals," *J. Audio Eng. Soc*, vol. 52, no. 7/8, pp. 699–711, 2004.

SENSITIVITY TO LOUDSPEAKER PERMUTATIONS DURING AN EIGHT-CHANNEL ARRAY REPRODUCTION OF PIANO NOTES

Federico Fontana, Yuri De Pra
University of Udine
Department of Mathematics and Computer Science
federico.fontana@uniud.it
yuridepra@libero.it

Alberto Amendola
University of Parma
Department of Industrial Engineering
ame2@libero.it

ABSTRACT

An experiment has been conducted, in which ten pianists with different skill rated the sound realism and scene accuracy of a sequence of piano notes reproduced by a linear loudspeaker array, whose channel positions were changed during the test so to define different spatial patterns for the same sequence. Only exaggerated channel permutations produced significant downgrade of both qualities, furthermore without introducing appreciable changes of the apparent listening position. These results suggest that an accurate multi-channel reproduction of the frontal waves may not be crucial for determining the perceived quality of a digital piano.

1. INTRODUCTION

The quality of a digital piano depends on every design aspect of the electronic instrument, and involves current makers in a complex process that typically requires several iterations along the development cycle. Even if optimal source sounds are at hand, such as the output from a modern physically-based model or an accurate recording of the pressure field taken in the proximity of the real instrument, nevertheless the recipes that are needed to correctly display these sounds to the pianist remain a matter of experience and craft. Particularly in the case of piano sound reproduction, the rendering systems that have been proposed to fill the distance between the source and the listening point represent a manifold family spanning the history of digital pianos, ranging from standardized loudspeaker configurations [1] up to more recent arrangements aiming in particular at increasing sense of depth [2].

Performers declare to be especially sensitive to changes in the sound coming from their instrument. On the other hand, the role and importance played by the auditory cues when a piano is perceived to sound different is not obvious. In a pioneering paper, Mary Cochran claimed the insensitivity of pianists to piano tone quality [3]. Galembo and Askenfelt showed that a group of expert pianists lost much of their recognition ability when listening to three different pianos, even if they had been able to identify them easily and accurately during a previous performing task [4]. Recent literature marks the difference existing between playing as opposed to listening to a piano: such two activities would in fact lead the pianist to develop different impressions about the quality of the instrument [5, 6].

The proposed research considers a collection of accurate multi-channel recorded piano notes, that were presented to a group of pianists via a calibrated array of eight small loudspeakers. Distortions were introduced during the listening test by exchanging the output channels, and subjective impressions about the realism of the sound and the auditory scene were gathered along with the apparent listening position. Our analysis suggests that only the largest permutations, in a sense that will be defined later, cause significant corruption of both qualities furthermore without clear implications on the auditory scene description.

2. EXPERIMENT

The experiment was intended to pilot a broader research aiming at clarifying whether pianists, while listening to reproduced piano sounds in the inside of a normal room, are able to discriminate differences in the spatial-temporal envelope of the *partial* components forming each note: if proved to exist, this ability may concur to characterize the *apparent source width* [7] of the instrument, and hence be exploited to create auditory sense of depth and "spaciousness" similar to those pianists declare to experience when they play a real (especially grand) piano.

The evolution in space and time of such envelopes mainly depends on the radiation properties of the soundboard [8]. A linear array of small loudspeakers reproduces at least some patterns of radiation at a central listening point in front of the array, within a reasonably wide frequency range. For this reason, this system represents a solution for achieving sufficiently accurate reproductions of a piano soundfield in the performer's listening area, at reasonable cost.

Before experimenting on the perception of differences in the reproduced partial components, we decided to first test whether a group of pianists was able to discriminate major distortions in the soundfield: did the subjects judge the distorted soundfields to be less consistent and/or to sound worse, then it could make sense to increase the precision of the reproduction and to focus the investigation on specific perceptual effects, and the cues at their origin. Rather, our experiment suggests that the pianists' ability to discrimi-

Figure 1. Recording session: microphone setup.

nate a reproduced piano soundfield distortion in terms of perceived realism is lower than expected.

2.1 Stimuli

Six *mezzo forte* piano notes (C4, E4, C2, A4 major, D4, C5) were selected from a huge collection, result of a recording session made in July 2012 at the Viscount International SpA semi-anechoic room based in Mondaino (RN) - Italy, using a Seiler model 1849 piano that was tuned and prepared for the occasion, and then played by a professional pianist and sound designer consulting for the company. Such notes were collated together one after the other, hence forming a slow scale lasting about thirty seconds.

Fig. 1 illustrates the recording setup consisting of a linear array of 30 Bruel&Kjær model 4188 omnidirectional microphones, calibrated and made available by Angelo Farina's acoustics research group at the University of Parma, along with an M-Audio multi-channel sound interface. The array was positioned in such a way to capture the soundfield in front of the cover, which was left open.

The reproduction was realized avoiding any signal processing, by just reporting eight equally-spaced recorded channels onto a single-pressure chamber linear array made with 2.5" Ciare loudspeaker units, prepared by the same research group. The array was driven by four t.amp model S75 stereo power amplifiers. Before feeding such amplifiers, the frequency range below 60 Hz was cut in each channel by an 48 dB/octave linear phase digital filter, to prevent injection of energy in the low frequency in the respective loudspeaker; in parallel, the sound in the low frequency range was isolated using a complementary filter, accepting a downmix of the eight channels and then sending its output to a Mitsubishi 8" active woofer standing below the array. Note that the fundamental components of all notes forming the scale have a frequency above 60 Hz, hence none of them was mixed down into the woofer. Finally, the 8+1 output channels were played by Adobe Audition running on a desktop PC, which drove an M-audio Delta 1010 audio card.

Fig. 2 shows the alignment between the microphone and the loudspeaker array, with the piano keyboard taken as reference: the eight loudspeakers, hence, reproduced the

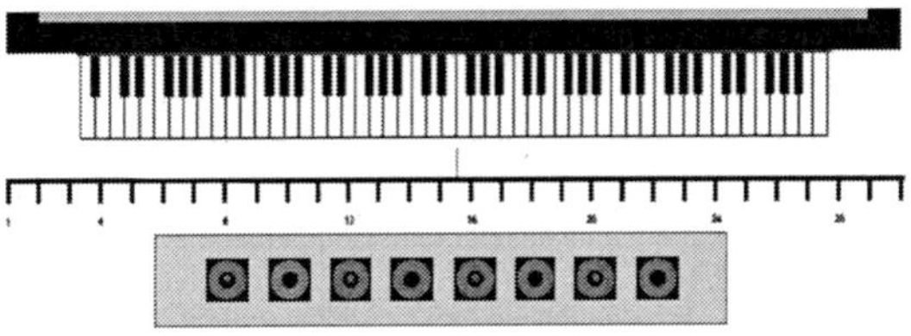

Figure 2. Microphone/loudspeaker alignment.

recorded channels no. 8, 10, 12, 14, 16, 18, 20 and 22, respectively. From here on we will associate such recorded channels respectively to the loudspeakers 1, 2, 3, 4, 5, 6, 7, 8, numbered left to right.

Ten reproduction patterns were prepared using the eight channels: two of them were formed respectively by quadruplicating two, and duplicating four recorded channels over the loudspeakers; the third one was left untouched; the remaining seven were obtained by permutations of the inputs. All patterns are listed in Table 1 below.

Pattern no.	Configuration	Label
1	11118888	Magnified stereophony
2	11336688	Magnified quadraphony
3	12345678	Original
4	21436587	Swapped adjacent ones
5	34127856	Swapped adjacent pairs
6	56781234	Swapped quadruples
7	73258146	Random no. 1
8	78345612	Swapped edge pairs
9	87654321	Reverse panning
10	51843276	Random no. 2

Table 1. Output patterns.

2.2 Subjects

Three professional pianists, four piano practitioners, and three amateur sound engineers having regular contact with the instrument were involved in the test, for a total of seven male and three female (age 13-49, avg 33.2 years old). All reported normal hearing ability and understood the Italian language. On a scale ranging 1 to 7 they declared sufficient (2) to excellent (7) knowledge of the instrument (avg 4.7).

2.3 Setup and method

The experiment was set up in a silent, dry room (approximately $3 \times 3 \times 2.75$ meters) having walls partially covered with damping foam. In addition to the active array, four loudspeakers were located each at one corner of the room, furthermore two additional eight-channel arrays were put in front of the listener: the presence of such idle systems added uncertainty in the listeners about the sources that were going to be used during the experiment.

Subjects had to sit on a chair at the center of the room, approximately one meter far from the loudspeaker array. While sitting, every subject was given a tabletop computer on which (s)he could respectively rate the *realism of the*

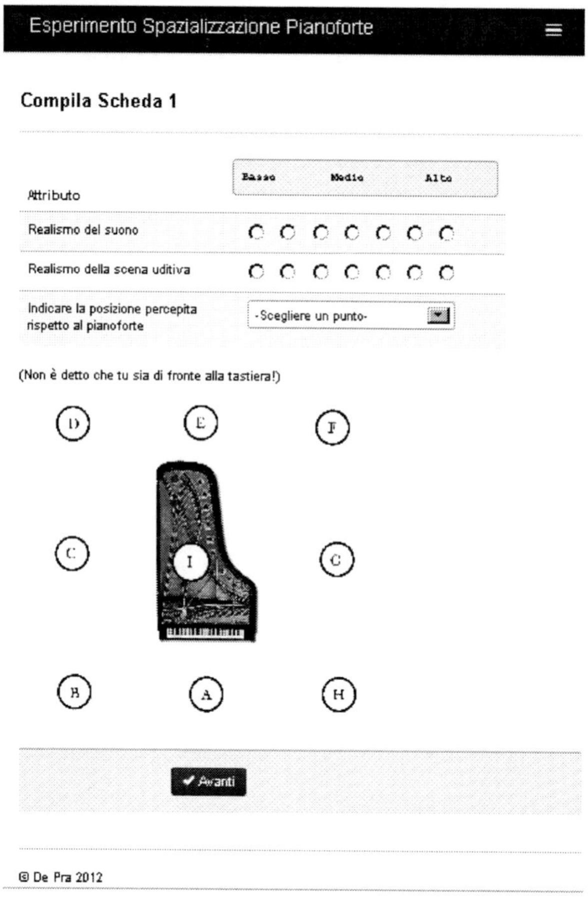

Figure 3. Graphical user interface used for the tests.

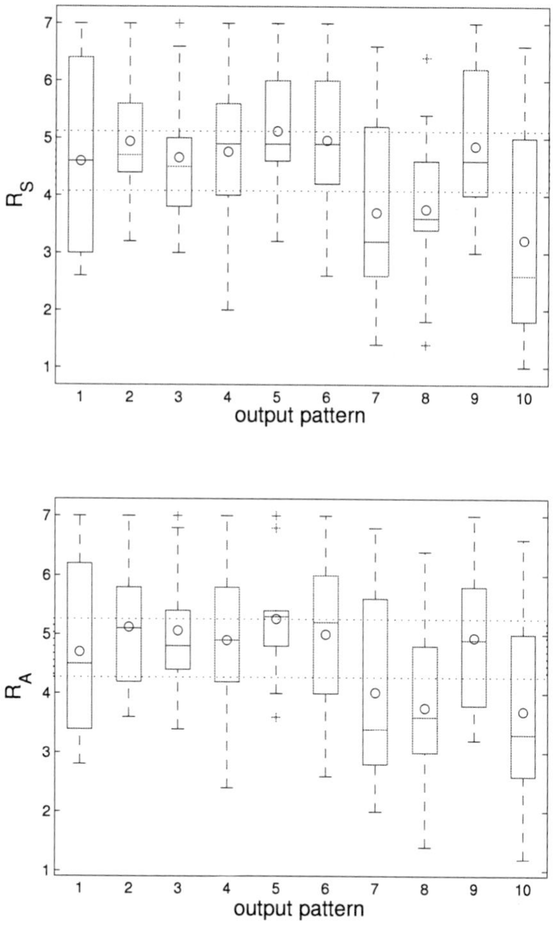

Figure 4. Boxplots showing median, 25th and 75th percentiles with their extreme datapoints, average values ('o') and outliers ('+') for each output pattern rated R_S (above) and R_A (below), respectively. On either boxplot, the rectangle in dashed line gathers average values within the respective HSD range, edged by the largest average.

sound R_S and the *realism of the auditory scene* R_A on a scale ranging 1 (poor) to 7 (excellent), as well as choose his or her own *relative position* R_P in the virtual scene among nine possible listening points, labeled A to I in alphabetical order (see Fig. 3). Before the test, the subject was given verbal instructions about the scale (s)he was going to listen to, as well as about the use of the graphical interface.

The test consisted of listening to a balanced random distribution of the patterns, each repeated five times for a total of fifty trials. During each trial, every subject listened to the musical scale and then rated R_S, R_A and R_P by selecting the corresponding value in the graphical interface; finally, (s)he submitted her or his selections by pushing a software button. After each submission a new trial was started: this procedure allowed in particular for rating a scale and go to the next one by submitting before the end of the current sound, or conversely to pause at the end of a trial by delaying the respective submission. In this way subjects could optimize the flow of the test, which took approximately 40 minutes to be completed.

3. RESULTS

Fig. 4 (above) plots, for each pattern in the respective box, the median of the corresponding rate R_S, the 25th and 75th percentiles with their extreme datapoints, the average values and the outliers. The same boxes are displayed for each pattern rated R_A, below in the figure. Both plots have been obtained using the `boxplot` function of Matlab.

An informal inspection suggests the existence of a significant decay in both sound and scene realism when the patterns 7,8 and 10 are displayed. In fact, significant differences in the average subjective rates exist among patterns, concerning in general the perceived realism of both sounds (repeated-measures anova: $F(9,81) = 8.2056$, $p = 1.44e\text{-}8$) and auditory scenes (repeated-measures anova: $F(9,81) = 6.9137$, $p = 2.50e\text{-}7$). However, only relatively few pairs are actually responsible for such differences: concerning sound realism, a Tukey's HSD value amounting to 1.048 has been computed; concerning the realism of the scene, we obtained a Tukey's HSD value amounting to 1.031. Essentially these results confirm the eye inspection of Fig. 4, in which we have added a rectangle in dashed line in either boxplot, grouping averages within the respective HSD including the largest value: even if such rectangles do not strictly split the respective averages in two categories based on the significance of their paired differences — compare for instance patterns 1 and 7 in both boxplots — nevertheless they give a useful picture about the significance of most paired comparisons.

The apparent listening positions exhibit a broad spectrum of selections, that are summarized in Fig. 5. Also on the light of the significance observed regarding the realism of the auditory scene, no statistical analysis of such apparent positions has been attempted: their dependence on the output pattern is instead left to the reader's qualitative inspection of the same figure, and will be informally discussed in the next section.

Some subjects showed large deviations around their average ratings, at least for some patterns. Concerning sound realism, the largest std values across subjects respectively amounted to 1.79, 2.35, 1.0, 1.48, 1.79, 2.83, 1.95, 1.58, 0.89, 0.54; within subjects, the same values amounted to 2.05, 2.30, 2.30, 1.64, 1.67, 1.94, 1.73, 2.83, 2.34, 1.73. Similar ranges were found for the realism of the scene. During the final debriefing, all subjects expressed positive surprise for the unexpected quality of the multi-channel sound reproduction, and consequent satisfaction for their participation in the experiment.

4. DISCUSSION

The first consideration concerns the perceived realism of the sounds. Perhaps surprisingly, listeners did not judge the realism as significantly lower but for few patterns. A deeper look to Fig. 4 suggests that the random distributions of the output channels were judged to form kind of "worst category" in terms of sound realism. Pattern 8 suffers from a lower average rating as well: this evidence may depend on the higher degree of distortion coming from swapping the edge pairs of the multi-channel output.

This consideration is reinforced by the results on the perceived realism of the auditory scene, in which patterns 7, 8 and 10 again show significant differences against the other stimuli. Together, both results suggest that listeners may correlate the realism of the sounds with the realism of the auditory scene, and, perhaps, downgrade both of them once a distortion threshold is reached.

To quantify this idea in simple terms, we have computed a figure of penalty P_i for each pattern $i = 1, \ldots, 10$. The penalty value is obtained by summing up nine "scores of neighborhood", one for each pair of subsequent loudspeakers in the array, based on the following rule: a loudspeaker pair scores zero if both speakers reproduce the same channel n; otherwise the same pair scores $k - 1$, in which k is the distance between the reproduced channel numbers (e.g., the pair scores $k - 1$ if its speakers respectively reproduce the channels n and $n + k$, or $n + k$ and n). In particular, it follows that a score of neighborhood equals zero if the corresponding loudspeaker pair reproduces the same channel as well as two adjacent channels irrespectively of their orientation along the array. Based on this rule we can compute a penalty for each pattern, and obtain the list appearing in Table 2, which is in fairly good correspondence with the judgments on realism.

As a second consideration, let us instead consider the perceived similarities among patterns. How can it be that pianists declare to be so sensitive to the piano sound quality and the related auditory scene during playing, and conversely our group on average failed in discriminating the realism of most multi-channel presentations once the order of such channels was changed in the array? [1] An inspection channel-by-channel (see Fig. 6) of the temporal envelopes of the fundamental, first and second partial component of the note C4 used for the stimuli, computed by processing every channel of the array with a bank of heterodyne filters each fitted on a partial component by means of a dynamic programming search algorithm [9,10], shows the existence of local relative differences among the envelope amplitudes amounting to 20 dB and more. Switching such components among channels should translate in appreciable changes of the resulting soundfield.

i	1	2	3	4	5	6	7	8	9	10
P_i	6	4	0	6	5	6	16	8	0	15

Table 2. Pattern penalties.

At least two arguments can be attempted to support this relative insensitivity of our group to loudspeaker permutations in the array. i) A professional pianist who is asked to evaluate a novel instrument definitely prefers to play instead of simply listening to it: only if engaged in an interactive task does the performer feel him or herself sufficiently confident as an evaluator. It is possible that most variations in the soundfield that were presented during the experiment cannot be perceived by pianists, as far as they are engaged in a passive listening task. ii) We speculate that our subjects had specific listening practice with their own piano, conversely they were not used to judge sounds coming from an unknown instrument. Both arguments do not contradict rigorous studies, investigating on the perceived acoustics of a piano made through listening as opposed to performance tests, especially concerning judgments on its tone and touch quality [5,6].

The conclusions about the relative insensitivity of pianists to loudspeaker permutations may be further supported by the wide scope of apparent listening points (see Fig. 5) subjects selected during the test. The breadth of this scope is almost certainly also a result of the known tendency of subjects to make, during a test, multiple choices from a palette of possible answers when the stimuli actually do not bring significant information for that choice. Mainly due to this suspicion, the blocks in Fig. 5 hardly establish any significance. However, some considerations are worth being done: i) pattern 1 seems to establish a polarization around the "I" position, that is, the center of the instrument. This fact does not contradict the stereophonic nature of the corresponding stimulus, and the existence of phase cancellations among identical components reproduced by multiple speakers, hence the possible net loss of spatial cues otherwise present in the other stimuli; ii) the random patterns, i.e. 7 and 10, seem to evoke relative positioning of the piano off the frontal plane. This fact fits with the decreased

[1] This evidence does not imply that pianists did not detect *relative* differences among patterns. However measurable using a different experimental procedure, at present their discovery would have provided few insight for reproduction system design purposes.

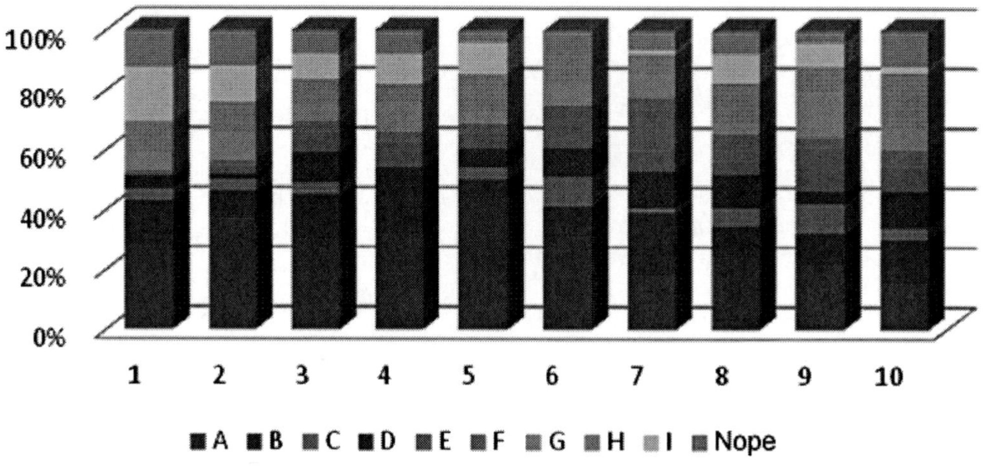

Figure 5. Apparent listening positions as functions of the output pattern.

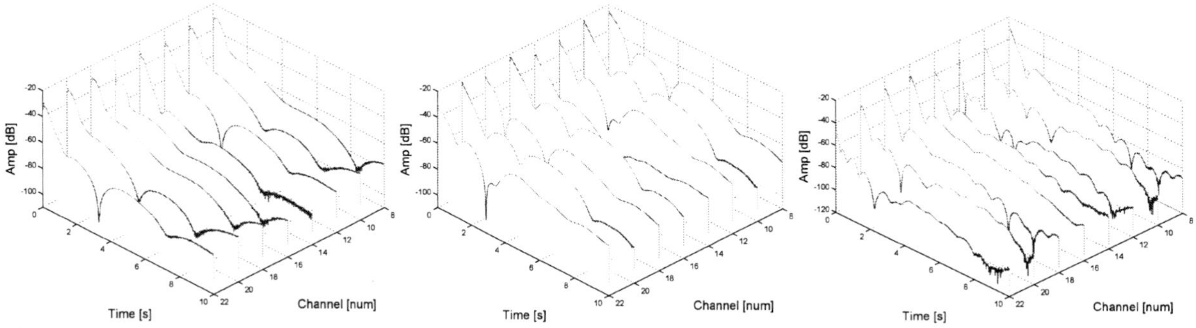

Figure 6. Temporal envelopes, channel-by-channel, of the fundamental (left plot), 1st partial (center plot), and 2nd partial (right plot) component of the note C4 used for the stimuli.

perceived realism of the auditory scene; finally, iii) reversing the output positions in the array (pattern 9) apparently does not translate in a significant impression of listening to the piano from its back (i.e., from positions "D", "E" or "F"): this point is further commented in the next paragraph.

The perceived realism obtained by reversing the array points to a discussion about the ability of pianists to perceive the direction of arrival of a piano note. Traditional studies in the field have investigated the question limitedly to the stereophonic or binaural reproduction of piano sounds, furthermore considering the instrument as a concentrated sound source [12–14]. Even if stereophonic panning has been used in digital pianos to lateralize the notes based on the key/hammer position, and the interactive rendering of piano sounds through headphones is nowadays object of more advanced studies [11], nevertheless in a real piano only the initial noise of the key and hammer mechanics before the strike, responsible for the creation of the so-called *touch precursor* [15], may provide sufficient lateralization cues to a listener sitting in front of the keyboard: the following mechanical energy in fact is distributed across the bridge, soundboard and keybed while radiating from the instrument. The observation of a 10 ms temporal window containing the signal attacks for the note C4, see Fig. 7, suggests that the relative delays and amplitude differences among channels are not large enough to elicit lateralization cues. On the other hand, should such cues be present in the sound then their reversal along the array would have created confusion in listeners who, conversely, in their answers neither downgraded the realism of the corresponding auditory scene nor polarized the apparent listening point toward the back of the instrument.

Similarly to the explanation given for motivating the stability of the perceived realism in presence of loudspeaker permutations in the array, independently of the existence of a precedence effect we conjecture that the localization of a note during playing is locked to the corresponding key position by the somatosensory cues of hand proprioception. Holding this locking effect, then the same position can be robustly recalled during listening: this previously learnt process may suppress the auditory localization of the same note via lateralization cues, in particular resolving any potential incongruence between the proprioceptive and auditory information. All this said, a rigorous discussion of the apparent listening points emerging from the tests appears to have limited consistency here, and should rather be reinforced through future experimentation.

5. CONCLUSIONS

The results of this research may support decisions of digital piano makers, who are often challenged by the idea

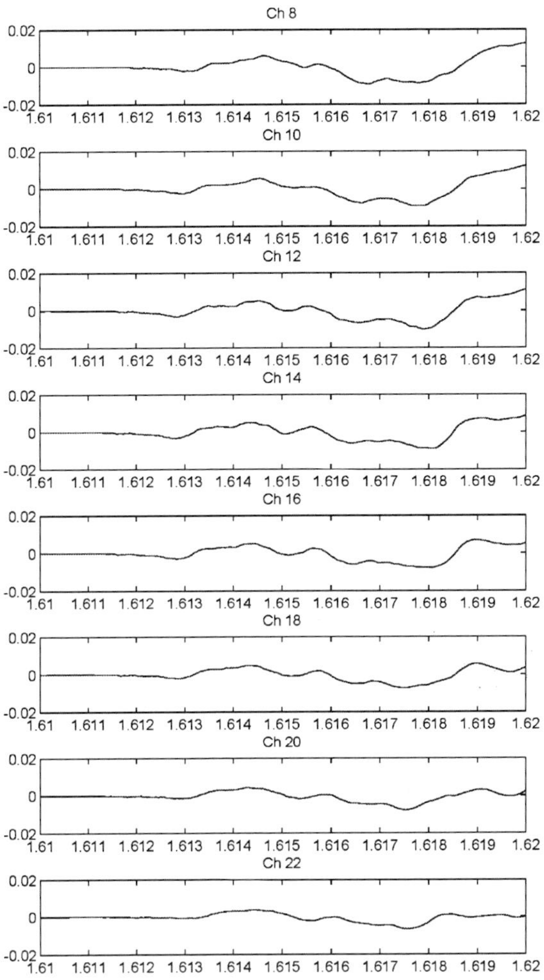

Figure 7. Temporal windows (10 ms) containing the attack of C4 on each channel.

of increasing the number of frontal output channels as a mean for improving the sound of their products. Holding some methodological immaturity as with many pilot studies, in the limit of its findings this paper suggests that such an option, and the consequent increase in hardware costs, must be pondered carefully. Besides this qualitative conclusion, the experiment leaves questions open concerning its repeatability over broader pitch and dynamic ranges, and across different subjective impressions. The scalability of the results to different array sizes and technologies should be dealt with as well. More in general, the exact nature of the auditory cues linking the objective to the perceived accuracy of a multi-channel piano reproduction is still largely unexplored.

Acknowledgments

The authors acknowledge the support of Viscount International SpA during the recording session. The calibrated microphones and recording equipment were courtesy of Angelo Farina and his research team. Stefano Zambon has permitted use of his software for computing the partial component envelopes appearing in Fig. 6. Submission of this paper was granted by the project PiaNo - *Piano from Nothing*, funded by Intel Corporation, Santa Clara, CA 95052.

6. REFERENCES

[1] R. D. Lawson, "Loudspeaker system for electronic piano," US Patent 5 789 693, Aug., 1998.

[2] S. Koseki, R. Mantani, N. Sugiyama, and T. Tamaki, "Method for making electronic tones close to acoustic tones, recording system and tone generating system," EU Patent EP1 357 538A3, Apr., 2003.

[3] M. Cochran, "Insensitiveness to tone quality," *The Australasian Journal of Psychology and Philosophy*, vol. 9, no. 2, pp. 131–133, 1931.

[4] A. Galembo and A. Askenfelt, "Quality assessment of musical instruments - Effects of multimodality," in *5th Triennial Conference of the European Society for the Cognitive Sciences of Music (ESCOM5)*, Hannover, Germany, Sep. 8-13 2003.

[5] A. Askenfelt, A. Galembo, and L. L. Cuddy, "On the acoustics and psychology of piano touch and tone," *The Journal of the Acoustical Society of America*, vol. 103, no. 5, p. 2873, 1998.

[6] W. Goebl, R. Bresin, and A. Galembo, "Once again: The perception of piano touch and tone. Can touch audibly change piano sound independently of intensity?" in *Proceedings of the International Symposium on Musical Acoustics (ISMA2004)*, Nara, Japan, Mar. 31 – Apr. 4 2004, pp. 332–335.

[7] D. Griesinger, "The psychoacoustics of apparent source width, spaciousness and envelopment in performance spaces," *Acustica*, vol. 83, pp. 721–731, 1997.

[8] N. H. Fletcher and T. D. Rossing, *The Physics of Musical Instruments*. New York: Springer-Verlag, 1991.

[9] M. Karjalainen, P. Esquef, P. Antsalo, A. Mäkivirta, and V. Välimäki, "Frequency-zooming arma modeling of resonant and reverberant systems," *J. Audio Engineering Society*, vol. 50, no. 12, pp. 1012–1029, 2002.

[10] F. Rigaud, B. David, and L. Daudet, "A parametric model of piano tuning," in *Proc. 14th International Conference On Digital Audio Effects*, Paris, France, Sep. 19-23 2011, pp. 393–399.

[11] S. Kim, A. Ramesh, M. Ikeda, and W. L. Martens, "Enhancing headphone reproduction of an electronic piano: Control of dynamic interaural level differences coupled with a players active head movement," in *Proc. 20th International Congress on Acoustics (ICA 2010)*, Sydney, Australia, Aug. 23-27 2010.

[12] H. Wallach, E. B. Newman, and M. R. Rosenzweig, "The precedence effect in sound localization," *The American journal of psychology*, vol. 62, no. 3, pp. 315–336, 1949.

[13] C. Tsakostas and J. Blauert, "Some new experiments on the precedence effect," *FORTSCHRITTE DER AKUSTIK*, vol. 27, pp. 486–487, 2001.

[14] B. Supper, T. Brookes, and F. Rumsey, "A lateral angle tool for spatial auditory analysis," in *Proc. Audio Engineering Society Convention 116*, no. 6068, Berlin, Germany, May 8-11 2004.

[15] A. Askenfelt, "Observations on the transient components of the piano tone," *STL-QPSR*, vol. 34, no. 4, pp. 15–22, 1993, web available at http://www.speech.kth.se/qpsr.

REINFORCEMENT LEARNING MODELS FOR ACQUIRING EMOTIONAL MUSICAL MODES

Tsubasa Tanaka
Tokyo University of the Arts
s1311923@fa.geidai.ac.jp

Hidefumi Ohmura
Japan Science Technology Agency, ERATO,
Okanoya Emotional Information Project
and RIKEN Brain Science Institute
ohmura@brain.riken.jp

Kiyoshi Furukawa
Tokyo University of the Arts
kf@zkm.de

ABSTRACT

Music is deeply related to emotions. The relationships between musical modes and emotions are especially strong. This has been recognized since the age of ancient Greece. However, finding a mode that represents a specific emotion well by psychological experiments is not easy because there are so many modes mathematically. To deal with this problem, we propose a method to generate modes that represent emotions with an engineering approach that uses reinforcement learning rather than a psychological approach. Since this method gradually adapts a mode to a target emotion, we can expect to obtain a desirable mode without enumerating all the possible modes one by one. However, this method needs a human evaluator who trains the mode. In consideration of reducing the burden on the evaluator, we have designed four function approximation models of the action-value function. As a result of a pilot experiment, the best model could acquire modes that represent "high" representational power of happiness, sadness and tenderness and "a little high" representational power of fear. Additionally, we propose a musicological concept "interval scale" that is derived from the second model and show a possibility of applying it to compose music.

1. INTRODUCTION

There are strong relationships between musical modes and emotions. If we think of bright major mode and dark minor mode, then this is obvious. These relationships have been recognized since the age of ancient Greece. In Plato's *The Republic* [1], Socrates argues, from an educational viewpoint, that "sad" Lydian mode and "loose" Ionian mode should not be used and that only Dorian and Phrygian modes, which represent "courage" and "moderation" respectively, should be used. [1] Aristotle argues in *Politics* [2] that "aggressive" modes and "enthusiastic" modes can be used in some cases, though Dorian is the most suitable mode for educational purpose because it is the most "calm" and "masculine" mode.

[1] Greek modes mentioned here are different from church modes, though the names are identical.

In recent decades, empirical research of finding correspondence between modes and emotions has been conducted. Kastner et al. [3] performed an experiment about major and minor modes that used illustrations of facial expressions as emotion labels for children. All of the 38 subjects between the age of three and 12 could perceive positive emotion from major mode and negative emotion from minor mode. Hill et al. [4] conducted an experiment in which the subjects listen to Bach's melodies that consist of Ionian or Phrygian modes and judge which of the modes correspond to "salvation" or "condemnation." The results shows that Ionian mode corresponds to salvation and Phrygian mode corresponds to condemnation. Ramos et al. [5] mapped seven church modes to the two-dimensional plane of valence and arousal and analyzed the differences of emotions represented by respective church modes. Thompson et al. [6] also found that atonality and chromatic harmony are related to "anger." In India, there are many types of mode called "raga," and it is said that Indian musicians can generate various moods by selecting ragas [7]. [2]

A significant difficulty in studying the correspondence between modes and emotions is that there are a very large number of modes mathematically, though we can only investigate a small number of modes practically. Calculated simply, the number of modes (as pitch class sets) in n-tone tuning is 2^n (4096 in 12-tone). Individual investigation is needed for each tuning. Because of this difficulty, most research only treats major and minor modes. Even the research that treats seven church modes like [5] would be approved as highly motivated work. Moreover, if we try to deal with not only mere pitch class sets, but also modes that include tendencies of melodic behavior, the number of modes increases further.

To avoid this difficulty, we propose a new method based on an engineering approach that uses reinforcement learning [9] rather than a psychological approach. In the approach, a mode gradually changes to adapt to a target emotion by feedback given by a human evaluator. It is expected that this method will enable us to obtain desirable modes that represent target emotions well without investigating a very large number of fixed modes. Another possible advantage of this method is that it may be adaptable to individual, cultural, and educational differences.

[2] Raga is not just a scale. It contains melodic behavior and is regarded as a kind of mode [8]. We use the term mode as a pitch class set that contains tendencies of melodic behavior.

There are some previous studies about application of reinforcement learning in music. They include the research [10] in which a musical agent adapts its parameters to the degree of musical tension desired by a human evaluator. The research [11] that intends to imitate polyphonic musical styles by reinforcement learning from musical scores is also included in such studies. As far as we know, our research is the first attempt to adapt modes to emotions using reinforcement learning.

The outline of this paper is as follows: Section 2 explains the basic methods of reinforcement learning. Section 3 presents our method of learning modes using reinforcement learning, and four function approximation models are introduced. Section 4 reports the results of pilot experiment that evaluates and compares the performances of the four models. Section 5 provides additional remark and proposes a musicological concept "interval scale" that is derived from the second model. Section 6 summarizes this paper.

2. REINFORCEMENT LEARNING

2.1 Basic Framework

Reinforcement learning is an unsupervised machine learning techniques in which an *agent* in an *environment* learns optimal actions through trial and error. The environment repeats state transitions within the state space S at each time step t. The agent observes the *state* $s \in S$ of the environment and takes an *action* $a \in A(s)$, where $A(s)$ is the set of actions available in the state s. Partly as a consequence of its action, the agent receives a *reward* r from the environment. The aim of the agent is to maximize the *return* R_t defined as:

$$R_t = \sum_{k=0}^{\infty} \gamma^k r_{t+k+1}, \tag{1}$$

where γ is a parameter, $0 \leq \gamma \leq 1$, called the *discount rate*.As γ approaches to 1, the agent takes future rewards into account more strongly.

Using the received reward r as a clue, the agent estimates the value of s, which is denoted by $V(s)$, and the value of the action a at s, which is denoted by $Q(s,a)$. $V(s)$ is called the *state-value function*, and $Q(s,a)$ is called the *action-value function*. $V(s)$ and $Q(s,a)$ are defined as:

$$V(s) = E\{R_t | s_t = s\}, \tag{2}$$

$$Q(s,a) = E\{R_t | s_t = s, a_t = a\}. \tag{3}$$

In many cases, the environment satisfies the Markov property and is called a *Markov Decision Process* (MDP), and the state and action spaces are finite. In MDP, s moves to the next state s' by transition probability $P^a_{ss'}$ when the agent takes an action a. And then, environment gives the agent the reward r whose expected value is $R^a_{ss'}$. Thus, MDP is characterized by $P^a_{ss'}$ and $R^a_{ss'}$.

On the other hand, the agent has a preference in selecting its actions. The agent in a state s takes an action a by probability $\pi(s,a)$. This π is called the *policy*. The value of $\pi(s,a)$ is determined by referring to $V(s)$ or $Q(s,a)$, in many cases, and the values of $V(s)$, $Q(s,a)$ and $\pi(s,a)$ are improved as time passes.

If $P^a_{ss'}$ and $R^a_{ss'}$ are known and $\gamma < 1$, $V(s)$ and $Q(s,a)$ can be obtained by solving a simultaneous equation called *Bellman equation* without trial and error. In many cases, however, the environment is unknown, and the agent learns through trial and error under $\pi(s,a)$.

2.2 Bootstrapping and Episode

There are many types of reinforcement learning method in unknown environments. The difference between the methods that update value functions step by step and the methods that update value functions after an *episode* ends is especially important for this study, where an episode means a finite series of states experienced under $\pi(s,a)$. This subsection explains the difference.

The general expressions of improvement of the value functions are the following update rules that make $V(s)$ and $Q(s,a)$ closer to the target R_t:

$$V(s_t) \leftarrow V(s_t) + \alpha[R_t - V(s_t)], \tag{4}$$

$$Q(s_t,a_t) \leftarrow Q(s_t,a_t) + \alpha[R_t - Q(s_t,a_t)], \tag{5}$$

where α is called a step-size parameter that determine the degree of learning in one step. In general, calculating R_t according to equation 1 in a naive manner would require infinite time and is therefore impossible. To make it possible to learn $V(s)$ in real time, the next equation

$$\begin{aligned} V(s) &= E\{R_t | s_t = s\} \\ &= E\{\sum_{k=0}^{\infty} \gamma^k r_{t+k+1} | s_t = s\} \\ &= E\{r_{t+1} + \gamma \sum_{k=0}^{\infty} \gamma^k r_{t+k+2} | s_t = s\} \\ &= E\{r_{t+1} + \gamma V(s_{t+1}) | s_t = s\} \end{aligned} \tag{6}$$

is used to approximate R_t. For example, *TD(0)*, which is a method that updates $V(s)$ step by step, estimates R_t indirectly from the immidiate reward r_{t+1} and $V(s_{t+1})$ by the following update rule:

$$V(s_t) \leftarrow V(s_t) + \alpha[r_{t+1} + \gamma V(s_{t+1}) - V(s_t)]. \tag{7}$$

This type of method that estimate the state values indirectly using the estimated values of other states is called *bootstrapping* method. Similar methods can be taken for $Q(s,a)$, too.

On the other hand, there are some cases where the exact calculation is possible. If the series $\{s_t\}_{t=1}^{\infty}$ is divided into the episodes that end in a finite time, R_t can be determined after reaching the ends of the episodes. In such cases, we can directly update $V(s)$ and $Q(s,a)$ that correspond to the states and actions appearing in the episode using the actual R_t by the update rules (4) and (5). This method is called *Montes Carlo method*.

Bootstrapping methods include *TD-learning*, *Q-learning* and *Sarsa* and the methods whose unit is an episode include Monte Carlo method and *profit sharing*. In this study, we adopt Monte Carlo method.

2.3 Function Approximation, Gradient Descent

To train $Q(s,a)$ about all the pairs of (s,a), long time and large data are required. Therefore, *generalization* of experience is important. Generalization makes it possible to estimate $Q(s,a)$ of which (s,a) has not been experienced yet to an extent. It is accomplished when $Q(s,a)$ is approximated by a function of a parameter vector $\vec{\theta} = (\theta_0, \theta_1, \cdots, \theta_{n-1})^T$ whose number of the elements n is smaller than the number of combinations of s and a.

A *linear approximation* is one of the simplest in such *function approximations*. It approximates $Q(s,a)$ using a *feature vector* $\vec{\phi}(s,a) = (\phi_0(s,a), \phi_1(s,a), \cdots \phi_{n-1}(s,a))^T$ that corresponds to $\vec{\theta}$, and $Q(s,a)$ is expressed as:

$$Q(s,a) = \vec{\theta}^T \cdot \vec{\phi} = \sum_{i=0}^{n-1} \theta_i \cdot \phi_i(s,a). \tag{8}$$

When $Q(s,a)$ is generalized by $\vec{\theta}$, *gradient descent* is often used to update $\vec{\theta}$. It moves the parameters to the direction that decreases the objective function most steeply to minimize it. In this study, the objective function is the square error of the difference between R_t and $Q(s,a)$. The gradient of the square error is calculated as:

$$\nabla_{\vec{\theta}}[R_t - Q(s,a)]^2 = -2[R_t - Q(s,a)]\nabla_{\vec{\theta}}Q(s,a). \tag{9}$$

From this equation, the update rule is expressed as:

$$\vec{\theta} \leftarrow \vec{\theta} + \alpha[R_t - Q(s,a)]\nabla_{\vec{\theta}}Q(s,a). \tag{10}$$

In the case of the linear approximation (8), the gradient can be easily calcurated as:

$$\begin{aligned}\nabla_{\vec{\theta}}Q(s,a) &= \left(\frac{\partial Q(s,a)}{\partial \theta_0}, \cdots, \frac{\partial Q(s,a)}{\partial \theta_{n-1}}\right)^T \\ &= (\phi_0(s,a), \phi_1(s,a), \cdots \phi_{n-1}(s,a))^T \\ &= \vec{\phi}(s,a),\end{aligned} \tag{11}$$

then the update rule is expressed as:

$$\vec{\theta} \leftarrow \vec{\theta} + \alpha[R_t - Q(s,a)] \cdot \vec{\phi}(s,a). \tag{12}$$

3. PROPOSED METHOD

3.1 Target

The aim of this study is to obtain a "mode that represents the target emotion E." We define this concept as follows:

Definition 1. [3] Let us consider tone series (ordered list) $e = (s_1, s_2, \cdots, s_T)$ that is generated from a first order Markov chain M on the state space S, where S is the pitch classes of n equal temperament $\mathbb{Z}_n = \{0, 1, 2, \cdots, n-1\}$. When e is generated repeatedly from M and a human evaluator evaluates that e represents the target emotion E well on average, we call M a "mode that represents the emotion E," and denote M by M_E.This definition makes possible to include the tendencies of melodic movements and distinguish a "mode" from a "scale" that is represented by a mere probability distribution of the pitch classes.

[3] For the sake of simplicity, we treat only the equal temperaments (especially that of 12 tone in the experiment).

3.2 Monte Carlo Method

As was mentioned in subsection 2.2, we apply Monte Carlo method to obtain M_E. This subsection explains how to apply it.

The action $a \in A(s)$ ($\forall s \in S$, $A(s) = \mathbb{Z}_n$) is defined as the melodic interval from the current pitch class s to the next pitch class s'. s' is determined uniquely by s and a ($P^a_{ss'} = 1$), and it equals $(s + a) \bmod n$. Tone series $e = (s_1, s_2, \cdots, s_T)$ is used as the episode. This e is stochastically generated by $\pi(s,a)$ that is defined later. After each episode finishes, the human evaluator decides the reward r_T. Because the evaluation is for all of the states and actions in e, γ is set as 1. Based on this r_T, $V(s)$ and $Q(s,a)$ whose s and a appear in the episode are updated by the rules (4) and (5).

r_T is an integer between -3 and 3 that corresponds to the degree of how much representational power of the emotion E the tone series e has. The meanings of these values are: 3 (very high), 2 (high), 1 (a little high), 0 (neither high nor low), -1 (a little low), -2 (low), -3 (very low). Under such rewards, the state-value function $V(s)$ reflects the necessity of s to express the emotion E and $Q(s,a)$ reflects the necessity of the melodic movement a from s to s'.

Here, let us consider the meaning of the policy π. $\pi(s,a)$ is equal to $Pr(s'|s)$, the transition probability from s to s'. Therefore, π derives a Markov chain. After the convergence of learning an emotion E and the achievement of a high average score, the Markov chain derived from π becomes M_E, a mode that represents the emotion E.

3.3 Policy

In this study, $\pi(s,a)$ that is used to generate the episodes is defined as follows:

$$\pi(s,a) = \begin{cases} \dfrac{Q(s,a)}{\sum\limits_{u(\in A(s))\ s.t.\ 0<Q(s,u)} Q(s,u)} & if\ \ 0 < Q(s,a) \\ 0 & otherwise. \end{cases} \tag{13}$$

By this definition, the transition with the positive action-value $Q(s,a)$ will appear according to the probability proportional to $Q(s,a)$, and transition with the negative action value will not appear at all. This policy is expected to eliminate the transitions that are not necessary to represent the target emotion. However, once $Q(s,a)$ becomes under 0, a stops appearing at s. Therefore, it is necessary to prevent the failure to appreciate $Q(s,a)$ by ill fortune. To prevent it, the initial values of $Q(s,a)$ are set as optimistic values (3.0, for example).Optimistic initial values are also known to encourage broad exploration of the state space and action space [9].

3.4 Function Approximation Models

The domain of $Q(s,a)$ is the direct product of the state space and the action space, and $Q(s,a)$ has n^2 values to learn in this case. Learning all these values is inefficient. In this section, therefore, we build four function approximation models. The performances of these models are compared to each other in the next section.

In these function approximations, a parameter vector $\vec{\theta}$ that is common to four models is introduced under the assumption that the melodic interval a has its own worthiness not depending on the pitch class s. This $\vec{\theta}$ consists of $2n$ parameters. The parameters from θ_0 to θ_{n-1} are used to represent the worthinesses of the pitch classes from 0 to $n-1$ respectively and the parameters from θ_n to θ_{2n-1} are used to represent the worthinesses of the melodic intervals from 0 to $n-1$ respectively.

3.4.1 Model 1: Pitch Class Model

This first model approximates $Q(s, a)$ by disregarding the melodic interval a. Only the parameter for the pitch class s', which is the state reached after the transition, is taken into account. In the linear approximation (8), the feature vector of this model is expressed as follows:

$$\phi_i(s,a) = \phi_i(s') = \begin{cases} 1 & if\ i = s' \\ 0 & otherwise. \end{cases} \tag{14}$$

The action-value function of this model is expressed as:

$$Q_1(s,a) = \sum_{i=0}^{2n-1} \theta_i \cdot \phi_i(s,a) = \theta_{s'}. \tag{15}$$

In this model, the Markov chain derived from π doesn't depend on the current state s, and it is degenerated to the probability distribution $Pr(s')$.

3.4.2 Model 2: Melodic Intervel Model

In contrast with the first model, the second model approximates $Q(s, a)$ by disregarding s'. Only the parameter for the melodic interval a is taken into account. In the linear approximation (8), the feature vector of this model is expressed as follows:

$$\phi_i(s,a) = \phi_i(a) = \begin{cases} 1 & if\ i = n + a \\ 0 & otherwise. \end{cases} \tag{16}$$

The action-value function of this model is expressed as:

$$Q_2(s,a) = \sum_{i=0}^{2n-1} \theta_i \cdot \phi_i(s,a) = \theta_{n+a} \tag{17}$$

In this model, the Markov chain derived from π doesn't depend on s or s', and it is degenerated to the probability distribution $Pr(a)$.

3.4.3 Model 3: Additive Model

The third model approximates $Q(s, a)$ by the sum of the parameters for s' and a. In the linear approximation (8), the feature vector of this model is expressed as follows:

$$\phi_i(s,a) = \begin{cases} 1 & if\ i = s'\ or\ i = n + a \\ 0 & otherwise. \end{cases} \tag{18}$$

The action-value function of this model is expressed as:

$$Q_3(s,a) = \sum_{i=0}^{2n-1} \theta_i \cdot \phi_i(s,a) = \theta_{s'} + \theta_{n+a} \tag{19}$$

3.4.4 Model 4: Multiplicative Sigmoid Model

The fourth model is designed to have a synergetic effect of the parameters for s' and a. The action-value function is approximated by the parameters for both s' and a transformed by the *sigmoid function*:

$$\sigma(\theta) = \frac{1}{(1 + e^{-\theta})}. \tag{20}$$

The sigmoid function has a pair of horizontal asymptotes. It approaches to 0 as $\theta \to -\infty$ and approaches to 1 as $\theta \to \infty$, respectively. Using these properties, the range of $\sigma(\theta)$ can be controled. The action-value function of this model is expressed as:

$$Q_4(s,a) = 6\sigma(\theta_{s'})\sigma(\theta_{n+a}) - 3. \tag{21}$$

Here, we determined the values of the coefficient and the intercept so that $Q_4(s, a)$ is bounded as $-3 < Q_4(s, a) < 3$. Because the derivative of the sigmoid function is expressed as:

$$\frac{d\sigma(\theta)}{d\theta} = \sigma(\theta)(1 - \sigma(\theta)), \tag{22}$$

the gradient of $Q_4(s, a)$ can be calculated using the following partial derivative:

$$\frac{\partial Q_4(s,a)}{\partial \theta_i} = \begin{cases} 6\sigma(\theta_{s'})(1-\sigma(\theta_{s'}))\sigma(\theta_{n+a}) & (i = s') \\ 6\sigma(\theta_{n+a})(1-\sigma(\theta_{n+a}))\sigma(\theta_{s'}) & (i = n+a) \\ 0 & (otherwise). \end{cases} \tag{23}$$

4. PILOT EXPERIMENT

In order to examine whether learning musical mode is possible with the proposed method and compare the parformances of four models, the first author (he is studying music at the university) carried out a pilot evaluation experiment as an evaluator. n was set as 12. $V(s)$ is also learned by the update rule (4) to see dominant pitch classes.

4.1 Experimental Conditions

As the target emotions, happiness, sadness, fear, and tenderness were selected by referring to the circumplex model adopted by Juslin et al. (Fig. 1 [12]). In this model, many categories of emotions are arranged on a two dimensional plane of valence and arousal. The four emotions are the representatives of the respective quadrants of the two dimensional plane.

The tone series e used as the episode was set up as follows: T was set up as a small number, 5, because there is a fear that learning does not progress speedily if the length of a tone series T is too long. Tonic was set as C (MIDI number 60) and the note at the beginning of the episode was fixed as the tonic. This is because there is a fear that the learning does not progress due to a confusion of keys.

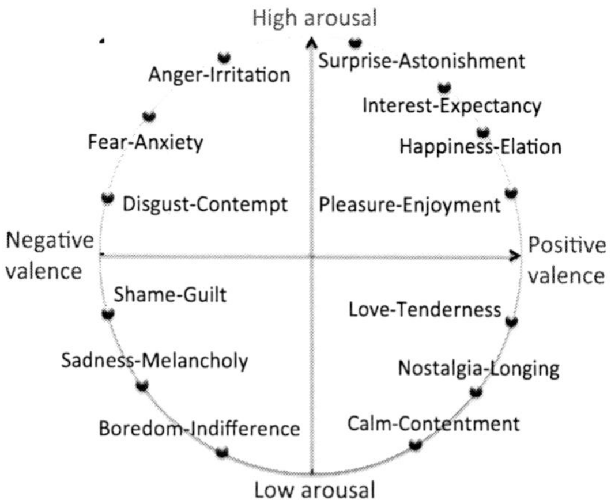

Figure 1. Circumplex model of emotion categories.

In order to evaluate the episodes accurately, each episode was repeated until the evaluator was able to become confident of the evaluation. When the evaluator felt that the learning reached a deadlock, the learning was ended. We adopted this deadlock as the definition of the convergence. twelve pitch classes were represented by the MIDI numbers from 60 to 71. The step-size parameter α was set as 0.1. The durations of the notes were fixed as 300ms, and the timbre of the piano (MIDI) was used.

4.2 Results

4.2.1 Reward Transition

The learning processes about the respective emotions by the four models are shown in Fig. 2. The mean rewards of the latest 10 episodes are shown by the lines. We can observe that there are tendencies of convergence toward higher mean rewards than 0 by around the 150th episode. This shows the success of the proposed method to a certain degree. However, the melodic interval model receives smaller rewards (between 0 and 1, in many cases) than other models. This probably indicates that pitch classes have more important roles in representing the emotions than melodic intervals.

The pitch class model and the multiplicative sigmoid model show comparatively good performances in every emotion. They received "high" mean rewards around 2 except for "fear," and they received "a little high" mean rewards around 1 in "fear." The multiplicative sigmoid model dominates the pitch class model in "tenderness." However, the pitch class model converges earlier than the multiplicative sigmoid model. This might be because the former model uses fewer parameters (the parameters for the states s are virtually not used.).

4.2.2 Acquired Modes

The parameters of $\vec{\theta}$ after training are shown in Fig. 3. From this figure, it is observed that the multiplicative sigmoid model (blue) shares the features of ups and downs of the black pitch class model (from θ_0 to θ_{11}) and the features of the red melodic interval model (from θ_{12} to θ_{23}).

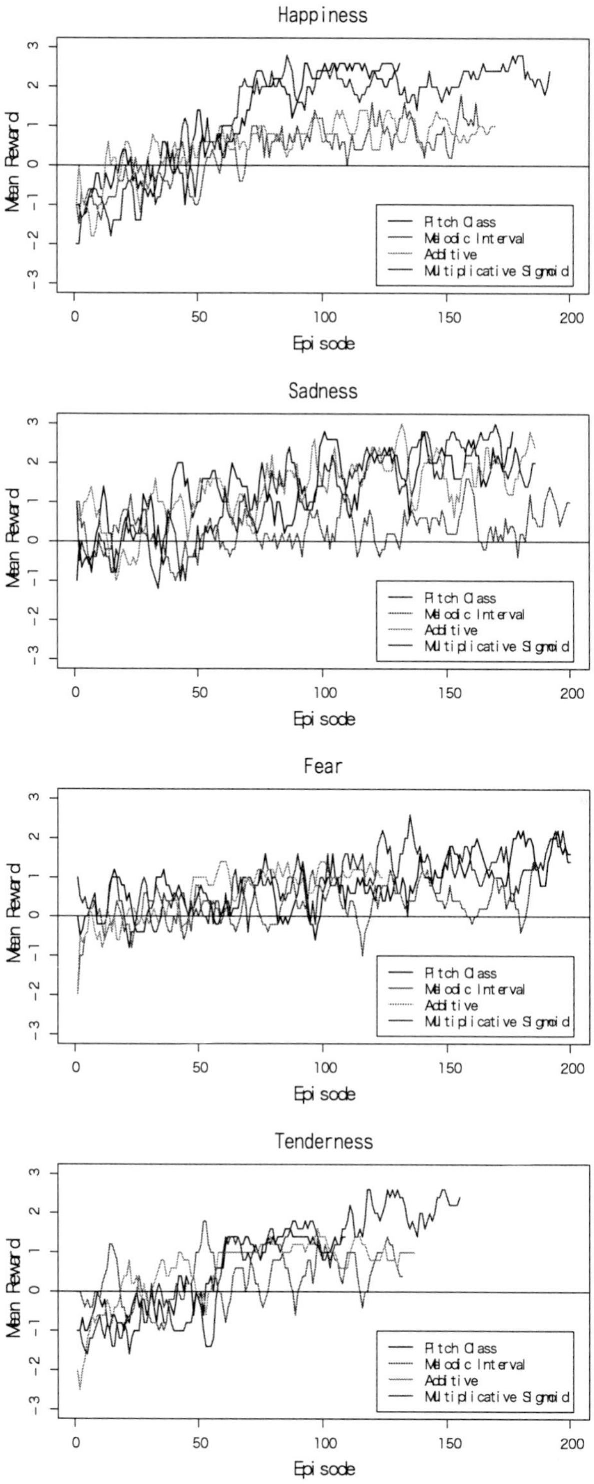

Figure 2. Mean rewards.

While each element of the gradients takes 0 or 1 in other models than the multiplicative sigmoid model, the multiplicative sigmoid model has interdependences between the states and the actions in its gradient. This interdependence may be the reason of the dominance of the multiplicative sigmoid model. However, the shapes of ups and downs from θ_0 to θ_{11} are more clear than those of θ_{12} to θ_{23}. This may also suggest that pitch classes are more important in representing emotions than melodic intervals.

Fig. 4 shows the value function $V(s)$. The set of s whose

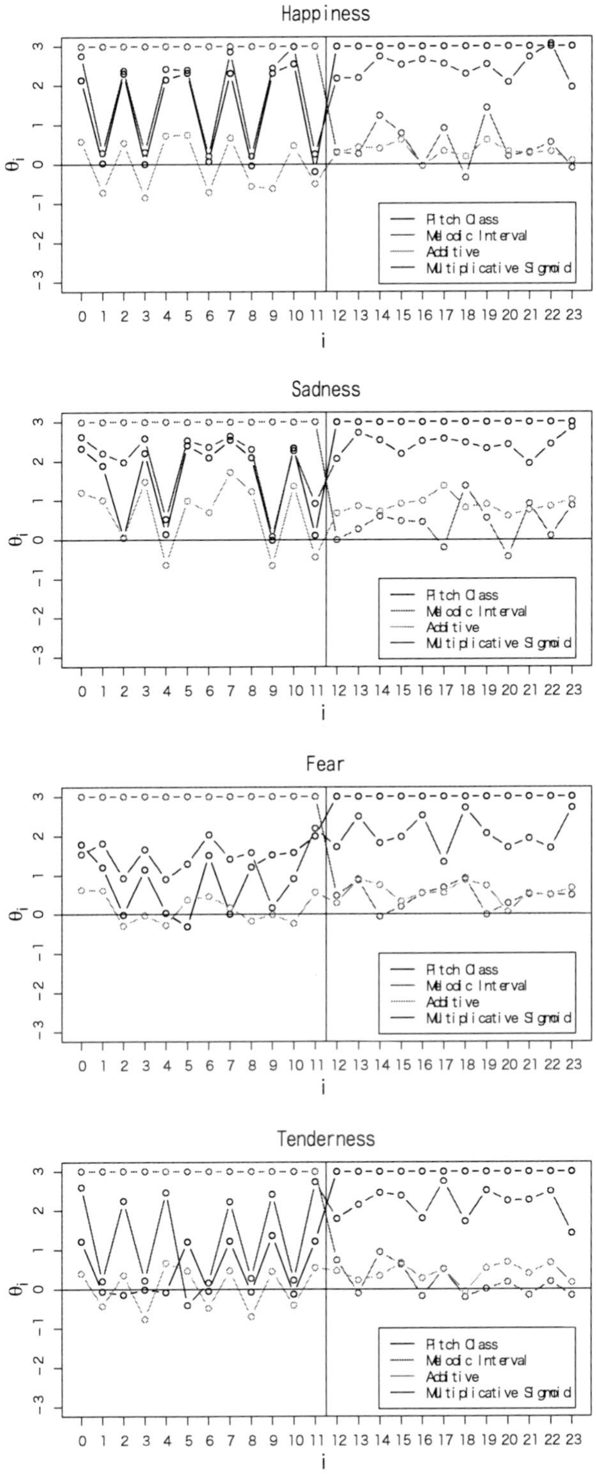

Figure 3. $\vec{\theta}$ after training.

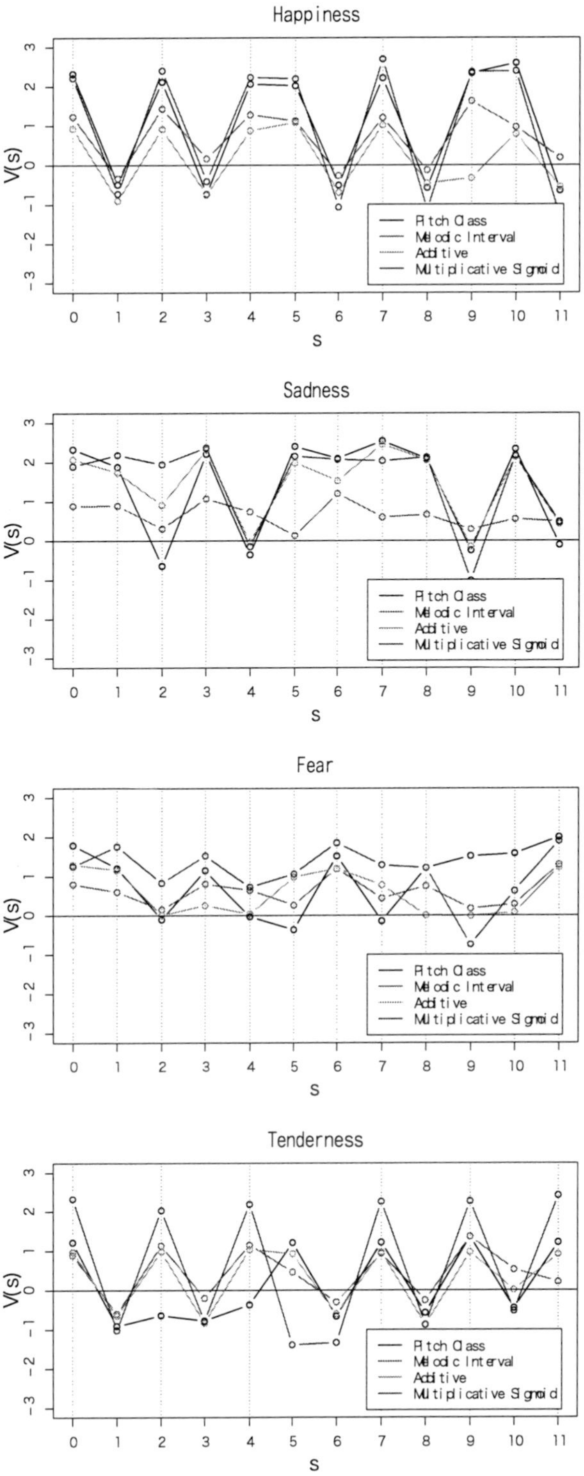

Figure 4. V(s) after training.

$V(s)$ is clearly larger than 0 means the aspect of the mode as a "scale," which consists of only pitch classes. These are represented by the vertical dotted lines (these lines refer to the multiplicative sigmoid model, which has the best performance). We can observe that the mode of happiness is identical to Mixolydian mode (on C). The mode of sadness is a Locrian mode to which the pitch D and G are added. The mode of fear can be interpreted as a mode of sadness to which E and B are added. The mode of tenderness is identical to a subset of Ionian mode (major mode).

In the research [5], music samples of the combinations of three tempi and seven church modes are mapped to the two-dimensional plane of valence and arousal. Although it is not easy to interpret the results of the research because of the difference of tempo, the results can be interpreted, at least, that Mixolydian mode and Ionian mode have high arousal, and the Locrian mode has low arousal. This is consistent with the results of our experiment that the mode of happiness, which is considered to have high arousal, was Mixolydian mode and the mode of sadness, which is con-

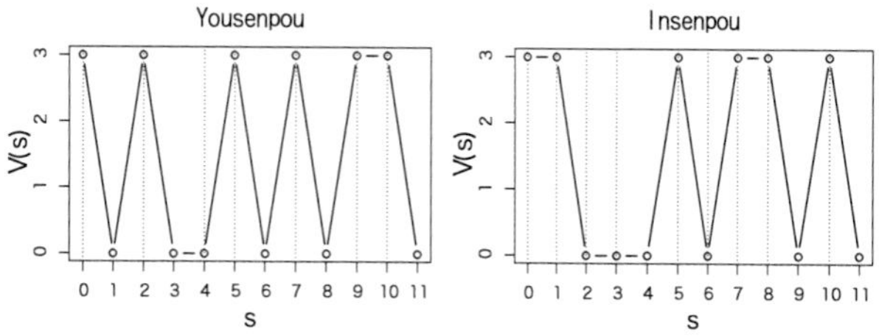

Figure 5. Japanese traditional modes (ascending and descending forms are merged) [8]. Yosenpou (bright mode) is embedded in the mode of happiness and insenpou (dark mode) is embedded in the mode of sadness. The pitch class sets of the modes of happiness and sadness are represented by the vertical dotted lines.

sidered to have low arousal, was similar to Locrian mode. However, our result that the mode of tenderness was similar to Ionian mode appears to be inconsistent with the result of the research. Considering that the mode of tenderness was a subset of Ionian mode and not the exact Ionian mode, a hypothesis that not using all of the pitch classes of Ionian mode was effective to lower the arousal and to represent tenderness can be suggested. Also from the modes acquired by our experiment, we can make hypotheses that the number of pitch classes is correlated with the height of the arousal and that the number of pitch classes is inversely correlated with the height of the valence. Further investigation of such relations between the constitutions of pitch classes and the types of emotions is an future subject.

Interestingly, a pair of traditional Japanese modes, "yousenpou" and "insenpou," are embedded in the modes of happiness and sadness, respectively. "Yousenpou" means "bright mode" and "insenpou" means "dark mode" in Japanese. These modes are shown in Fig. 5. These results may suggest that the fact that the evaluator was Japanese affected the results and that there is a consistency between the culture and the results of the training due to the adaptive method. It will be also valuable to investigate personal, cultural, and educational differences by a larger scale experiment in the future.

5. ADDITIONAL REMARK

Although the experiment in the previous section indicates that the second melodic interval model is inferior to the other models, it works to some extent. Moreover, it is musicologically very important. In this section, we present the concept "interval scale" derived from the second model and show that the concept can be an alternative basis of music composition (especially in atonal music).

The concept "scale" usually just means a constitution of pitch classes, and the constitution of melodic intervals is of second importance in many cases. However, we define "interval scale" as a concept that reversed it. That is to say, "interval scale" just means a set of melodic intervals, and the constitution of pitch classes is not restricted. "Interval scale" is exactly the object to which we tried to obtain by using the second model. To distinguish "interval scale" with usual scale, we call an usual scale a "pitch scale."

Figure 6. The opening of Ligeti's Étude No. 2.

It is obvious that a musical piece based on a pitch scale exists. However, is there a musical piece based on some interval scales? Ligeti's piano piece "Étude No. 2: Cordes à vide" may be an good example. The title means "open string." As is guessed from it, ascending and descending perfect fifths (intervals of 5 and 7) are used all over the piece. Fig. 6 shows the opening of this piece.

The collection of all the melodic intervals between adjacent eighth notes in Fig. 6 is $\{5, 6, 7, 8\}$. The number of the elements of this set is small, and there is a feature that the elements are consecutive numbers. The interval 6 and 8 are adjacent to 5 and 7 respectively, and 6 and 8 make it possible to transpose the motions of perfect fifths mildly and play a role of preventing fixation of the melodies.

On the other hand, the pitch scale of this part of the piece includes all the pitch classes, and it is, therefore, chromatic scale. When a piece is based on an interval scale, it is not accidental that a pitch scale becomes the chromatic scale. That is because the interval 7, for example, can generate all the pitch classes passing through the circle of fifths. Conversely, even if a piece of music is atonal music, it is conceivable that an characteristic interval scale is implicitly used in the piece. The Ligeti's piece shows that interval scale can be used as a basis of composing atonal music.

To characterize interval scale from the standpoint of emotion, we define the following pair of concepts that are related to the first and the second models.

Definition 2. After the reinforcement learning of the emotion E by the first model has converged on a mean reward larger than 0, we call $\{s \in \mathbb{Z}_n | \theta_s > \epsilon\}$ "a pitch scale that represents the emotion E," where ϵ is an adequate threshold.

Definition 3. After the reinforcement learning of the emotion E by the second model has converged on a mean reward larger than 0, we call $\{a \in \mathbb{Z}_n | \theta_{a+n} > \epsilon\}$ "an interval scale that represents the emotion E," where ϵ is an adequate threshold.

By these definitions and the results of the experiment, Mixolydian mode, for example, is a pitch scale that represents happiness and the interval set $\{2, 3, 5, 7, 10\}$ is an interval scale that represents happiness. Although finding an existing music piece based on specific interval scales will be difficult, the proposed method may be useful to select appropriate interval scales for emotional expressions in composing music from now on. What is important is that interval scales may be useful to express emotions even in atonal music.

In reinforcement learning, by the way, the state-value function $V(s)$, which disregards the action a, and the action-value function $Q(s,a)$, which depends on both s and a, are used. However, why is the following action-value function $W(a)$, which disregards s, not used?:

$$W(a) = E\{R_t | a_t = a\}. \quad (24)$$

This is probably because, in most of the problems of reinforcement learning, reaching the goal states is treated as the purpose and the actions are regarded as interchangeable with other alternative actions. This bias that gives priority to the states rather than the actions may have something to do with the fact that interval scale has not been focused on in music. However, when the actions themselves are also important like in music, the value function like $W(a)$ may become important. θ_{n+a} in the proposed method corresponds to such values of a independent of s.

6. CONCLUSION

We proposed a method to obtain modes that represent target emotions based on reinforcement learning, and four function approximation models were proposed and compared to each other. As a consequence of the pilot experiment of learning four categories of emotions, the multiplicative sigmoid model, which was the best model in the four models, could generate the modes that have high representational power of happiness, sadness and tenderness and the mode that has a little high representational power of fear. From comparison of the models, it was suggested that pitch classes are more important for representing the emotions than melodic intervals. The mode of happiness was identical to Mixolydian mode and it consists of 7 pitch classes. Japanese yousenpou was embedded in it. The mode of sadness was a Locrian mode to which the pitch D and G are added and it consists of 9 pitch classes. Japanese insenpou was also embedded in it. The mode of fear was a mode of 11 pitch classes without the pitch class 9. The mode of tenderness was a subset of Ionian mode and it consists of 6 pitch classes. From these, we hypothesized that the number of pitch classes is correlated with the height of the arousal and inversely correlated with the height of the valence. However, further experiments are needed to confirm these hypotheses. Additionally, we presented the concept "interval scale," which was derived from the second function approximation model, and the possibility of applying it to compose atonal music was suggested.

The following issues are included in the future subjects:

- Further investigation of the proposed method in more categories of emotions.
- Application of the proposed method to other tunings such as microtonal tunings and non-octave tunings.
- Investigation of personal, cultural, educational influences.
- Expansion of the proposed method to other musical elements such as timbre, register, tempo, rhythm, and chord.
- Mathematical and musicological investigations about the property of interval scales and application of the concept to compose music.

Acknowledgments: This work was supported by Grant-in-Aid for JSPS Fellows Grant Number 12J11238.

7. REFERENCES

[1] Plato: *The Republic*. N. Fujisawa (Translation): *Kokka Vol.1*, pp.209-213, Iwanami Shoten (2005).

[2] Aristotelis: *The Politics*. M. Yamamoto (Translation): *Seijigaku*, pp.368-381, Iwanami Shoten (1997).

[3] M. P. Kastner and R. G. Crowder: Perception of the major/minor distinction: IV. Emotional connotations in young children. Music Perception, 8, 189-202 (1990).

[4] D. S. Hill, S. B. Kamenetsky, and S. E. Trehub: Relations among text, mode, and medium: Historical and empirical perspective, Music Perception, 14, 3-21 (1996).

[5] D. Ramos, J. L. O. Bueno and E. Bigand: Manipulating Greek musical modes and tempo affects perceive perceived musical emotion in musicians and non-musicians, BRAZILIAN JOURNAL OF MEDICAL AND BIOLOGICAL RESEARCH, Vol.44(2), pp.165-172 (2011).

[6] W. F. Thompson and B. Robitaille: Can composers express emotions through music?, Empirical Studies of the Arts, Vol.10:1, pp.79-89 (1992).

[7] A. P. Merriam: The anthropology of music. Chicago: Northwestern University Press (1964).

[8] S. Sadie et al. (Eds.): *The New GROVE Dictionary of Music and Musicians*, Macmillan Publishers Limited, London (1980).

[9] R. S. Sutton and A. G. Barto: *Reinforcement Learning: An Introduction* , The MIT Press, (1998).

[10] S. Le Groux, and Paul F. M. J. Verschure: Towards Adaptive Music Generation by Reinforcement Learning of Musical Tension, Proc. *SMC*, pp.160-165 (2010).

[11] M. V. Butz, O. Sigaud, G. Pezzulo and G. Baldassarre (Eds.): *Anticipatory Behavior in Adaptive Learning Systems*: A. Cont, S. Dubnov, and G. Assayag: Anticipatory Model of Musical Style Imitation using Collaborative and Competitive Reinforcement Learning, pp.285-306, Springer (2007).

[12] P. N. Juslin and J. A. Sloboda (Eds.): *Handbook of Music and Emotion - Theory, Research, Applications*, Oxford University Press (2010).

[13] G. Ligeti: *Études pour piano premier livre*, pp.14-19, SCHOTT (1986).

About the Impact of Audio Quality on Overall Listening Experience

Michael Schoeffler
International Audio Laboratories Erlangen
michael.schoeffler@audiolabs-erlangen.de

Jürgen Herre
International Audio Laboratories Erlangen
juergen.herre@audiolabs-erlangen.de

ABSTRACT

When listening to music, rating the overall listening experience takes many different aspects into account, e. g. the provided audio quality, the listener's mood, the song that is played back etc. Music that is distributed over the Internet is usually encoded into a compressed audio format. Compressed audio formats are evaluated by expert listeners who rate these audio formats according to the perceived audio quality. Much effort is put into researching techniques for encoding music by having better audio quality at lower bit rates. Nevertheless, the beneficial effect that the audio quality has on the overall listening experience is not fully known.

This paper presents the results of an experiment that was carried out to examine the influence that a song and audio quality have on the overall listening experience. The 27 participants rated their personal overall listening experience of music items which were played back in different levels of audio quality.

Since listeners have different preferences when rating overall listening experience, the participants were divided into two groups of listeners according to their responses: song likers and audio quality likers. For both types of listeners, the effect of the audio quality on the rating of overall listening experience is shown.

1. INTRODUCTION

When we listen to music, it is probably not only the music itself which makes us like it or not. For a rating of the overall listening experience, we probably put emotional aspects into account which e. g. could be an individual experience we made in our life that we are connecting to the song [1]. The influence of such emotional aspects and their impact on the overall listening experience differs from person to person and research is far away from fully understanding the effects of emotions in music [2]. Besides emotion-related aspects, the provided audio quality probably influences the overall listening experience as well. This influence of audio quality becomes apparent when we listen to broadcast radio, and the reception is getting so poor that we turn off the radio or switch to another channel.

In the context of digital distribution, music is provided in uncompressed or compressed formats. Since the upcoming of MP3, compressed formats have become more popular and are nowadays used by most of the Internet music providers. In the last decades, a lot of research effort has been put into improving the audio quality of compressed music. For the evaluation of compressed formats, MUSHRA [3] or BS.1116-1 [4] are often used where the rating is done by so-called expert listeners trained to focus on audio quality related differences between a given reference and the compressed audio signal while suppressing emotional influences. Since the audio quality rated according to MUSHRA or BS.1116-1 does not fully correlate with overall listening experience, the question arises: What is the impact of higher audio quality on the overall listening experience?

2. RELATED WORK

In 2005, James L. Barbour published a study for answering the question whether normal listeners are able to identify any significant differences between multichannel audio codecs [5]. He came to the conclusion that normal consumers listening to commercial releases on good quality audio equipment at home are able to perceive differences between some uncompressed and compressed digital audio delivery formats, depending of the style of music, the production values of the surround mix and the data rate.

In 2005, Francis Rumsey *et al.* presented the results of two experiments with the purpose to find out what relationships between experienced listener ratings of multichannel audio quality and naïve listener preferences exist [6]. They stated that there is a relatively large similarity between the basic audio quality scores acquired from the experienced listeners and preference scores elicited from the naïve listeners.

Blauert and Jekosch structured the broad field of sound quality evaluation into a four-layer model [7]. They defined Aural-communication Quality as the most abstract layer containing the so-called product-sound quality which is the quality from an user's point of view.

In this paper the term overall listening experience covers all aspects which are taken into account by listeners when rating music. Therefore, the term overall listening experience as it is used in this paper is related to Quality of Experience (QoE). An overview about Quality of Experience models is given by Laghari and Connelly [8].

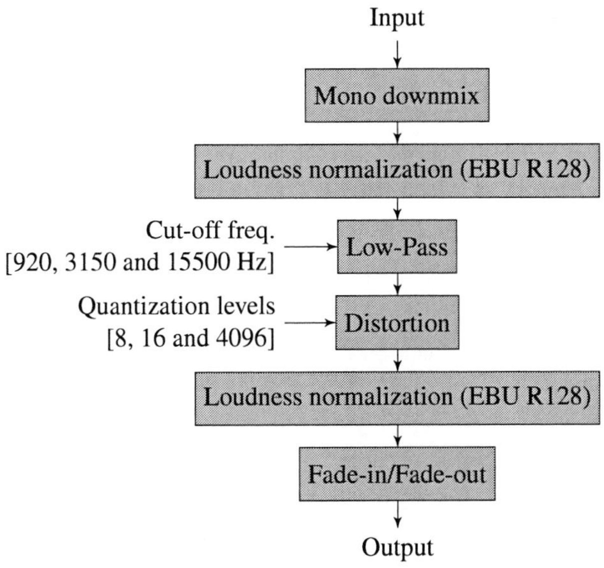

Figure 1. Block diagram of the stimuli manipulation.

3. EXPERIMENT

3.1 Stimuli

Six music excerpts having nine different audio quality levels served as stimuli. The audio quality levels were obtained by limiting the bandwidth and distorting the music excerpt in the frequency domain. The cut-off frequencies used for limiting the bandwidth were 920 Hz, 3150 Hz and 15500 Hz. Distortion was introduced by quantizing the magnitudes of the spectral coefficients in 8, 16 and 4096 quantization levels. The purpose of the different audio quality levels was to add artifacts which are common when encoding music into compressed audio formats. An overview of the processing applied to the stimuli is depicted in Figure 1.

The challenge in the music excerpt selection was to find excerpts that have an emotional influence on the participants, while each audio quality level should result in approximately the same perceived audio quality for all music excerpts.

For having a strong emotional influence on the participant, the song and its level of awareness of the music excerpt were decided to be important. Therefore 79 music excerpts of ten seconds duration were chosen from a large database such that a recognizable part of the song (e. g. refrain) was selected. Moreover, the song had to be ranked in known record charts which was expected to represent the level of awareness. In the second selection step, the spectral flatness and spectral centroid of the 79 music excerpts were computed.

The spectral flatness was used as a simple feature for roughly representing the perceived effect of distortion in the frequency domain:

$$spectral\ flatness = \frac{\sqrt[N]{\prod_{n=0}^{N-1} X(n)}}{\frac{\sum_{n=0}^{N-1} X(n)}{N}}, \quad (1)$$

where $X(n)$ is the magnitude of bin number n and N is the total number of bins.

Song	Interpret	Flatness	Centroid[Hz]
Feel	Robbie Williams	0.289	3736
Hold on me	Marlon Roudette	0.299	3636
Love Today	Mika	0.308	3887
Paid my Dues	Anastacia	0.317	3556
Summertime	Kenny Chesney	0.306	3658
Respect Yourself	Joe Cocker	0.343	3595

Table 1. Selected music excerpts and their spectral flatness and spectral centroid.

The spectral centroid was used as a representing feature for limiting the bandwidth:

$$spectral\ centroid = \frac{\sum_{n=0}^{N-1} f(n)\, X(n)}{\sum_{n=0}^{N-1} X(n)}, \quad (2)$$

where $X(n)$ is the magnitude of bin number n, $f(n)$ is the center frequency of bin number n and N is the total number of bins.

A cluster of 20 music excerpts represented by their spectral flatness and spectral centroid was computed, where the sum of the Euclidean distances between all nodes was minimal. In a final step, the selected 20 music excerpts were manually reduced to 6 excerpts according to their expected emotional influence on the overall listening experience. Table 1 shows the final selection of music excerpts including their spectral flatness and spectral centroid.

The selected music excerpts were down-mixed from stereo to mono and their loudness was normalized according to EBU R128 recommendation [9].

The low-pass filter for limiting the bandwidth was realized by two biquad filters in series. The cut-off frequencies (920 Hz, 3150 Hz and 15500 Hz) for limiting the bandwidth correspond to the cut-off frequencies of the 8th, 16th and 24th critical band of the Bark scale [10].

To introduce distortion, the magnitudes of spectral coefficients obtained from short-time Fourier Transform (STFT) were quantized. The boundaries for the quantization intervals were calculated as follows:

$$Q_{\text{Bound}}(i) = 1.0 - \sqrt{\frac{\log(N-i)}{\log N}}, \quad (3)$$

where i is the boundary index and N the number of total boundaries. The corresponding quantization value for each interval is calculated as follows:

$$Q_{\text{Value}}(i) = \begin{cases} 0 & \text{if } i = 0 \\ \frac{Q_{\text{Bound}}(i)+Q_{\text{Bound}}(i+1)}{2} & \text{if } i > 0 \end{cases}, \quad (4)$$

where i is the interval index. Input values are mapped to quantization values according to

$$Q(x) = Q_{\text{Value}}(i), \quad (5)$$

when $Q_{\text{Bound}}(i) \leq Q(x)$ and $Q_{\text{Bound}}(i+1) > Q(x)$. The details of the distortion processing including frequency domain transformation are depicted as a block diagram in Figure 2. For the STFT, a square-root Hann window with

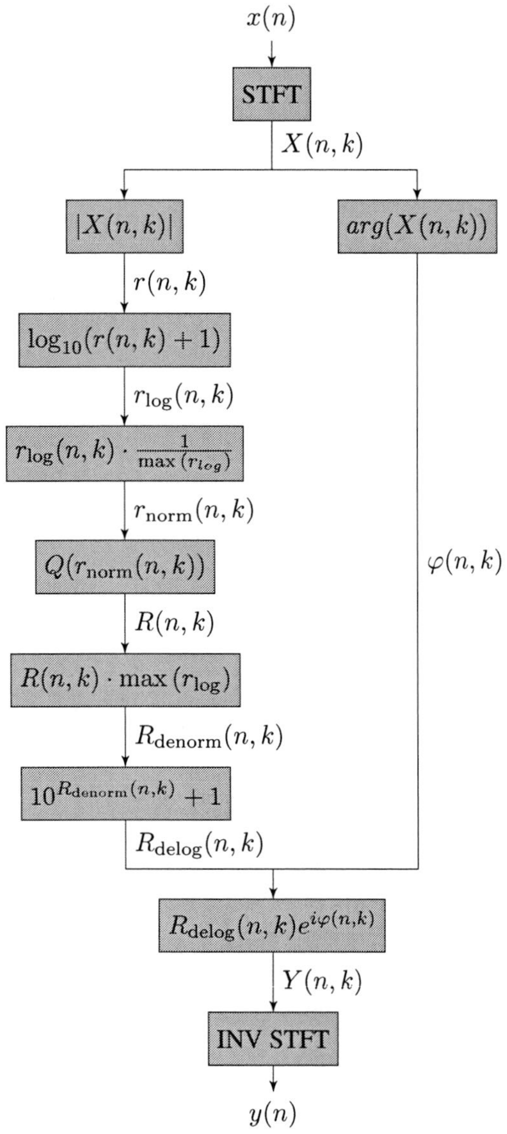

Figure 2. Block diagram of quantization.

a size of 512 samples and an overlap size of 256 samples was used. Before quantization, the values were normalized from 0 to 1 by using the maximum value as target value 1.

After processing the distortion, the loudness was again normalized using the EBU R128 recommendation. The last processing step consisted of adding a 500 ms fade-in and fade-out effect to the music excerpts.

3.2 Participants

The experiment was attended by 27 participants including researchers, students and related persons of the International Audio Laboratories Erlangen. 12 participants had a professional background in audio and 18 participants were familiar with listening tests. 25 participants were between 20 and 29 years old and 2 were between 30 and 39 years old. Since especially the participants with a professional background in audio are in touch with audio quality in their everyday work, it was assumed that these participants are more sensitive to audio quality than randomly selected participants with not such background. Detailed information about the participants are described in Table 2.

Total	Age group	professionals	listening test
27	25 [20-29]	15 [no]	9 [no]
			6 [yes]
		10 [yes]	10 [yes]
	2 [30-39]	2 [yes]	2 [yes]

Table 2. Information about the participants.

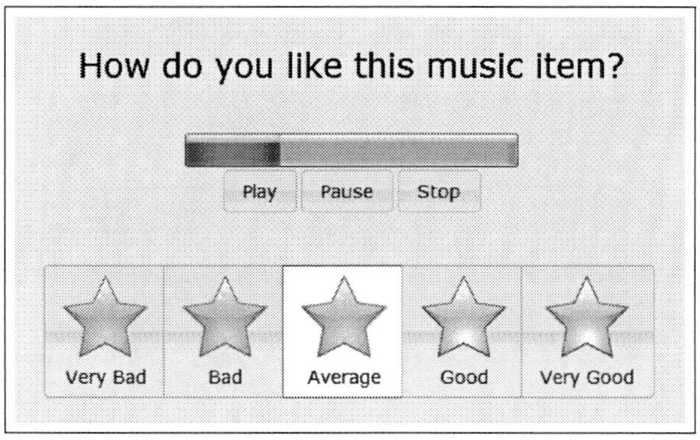

Figure 3. Experiment User Interface.

3.3 Method

The participants were instructed to rate the music excerpts in how much they like it by using a five-star scale. They were told that the music excerpts differ in song and quality. In the instruction, it was also emphasized that it is asked for the listener's personal rating and they should put everything into account what they would do in a real world scenario. This additional instruction note was added since pilot tests showed that some listeners tend to rate only the audio quality no matter what instructions say. The reason for this is that very often the listening experiments conducted at our institute focus on audio quality.

After reading the instructions the participants did a training. This training phase was added to familiarize the participants with the rating scale, range of audio quality levels and songs. During the training phase the participants listened to all six music excerpts, each in lowest quality (bandwidth = 920 Hz and distortion = 8 quantization levels) and highest quality (bandwidth = 15500 Hz and distortion = 4096 quantization levels), making 24 items in total. Pilot tests showed that adding this training phase leads to more reliable responses but as a consequence listeners tend to become more audio quality aware. For the training, the same experiment question and scale were used as for the actual listening test which started right after the training.

Then, the participants listened to 54 items (6 music excerpts · 3 bandwidth levels · 3 distortion levels). The experiment question was formulated as follows: "How do you like this music item?". Participants were allowed to play back an item as often as they wanted. The participants rated the items by using a five-star Likert scale. The stars were labeled with "Very Bad", "Bad", "Average", "Good" and "Very Good". The user interface is shown in Figure 3.

At last, the participants were asked how much was their

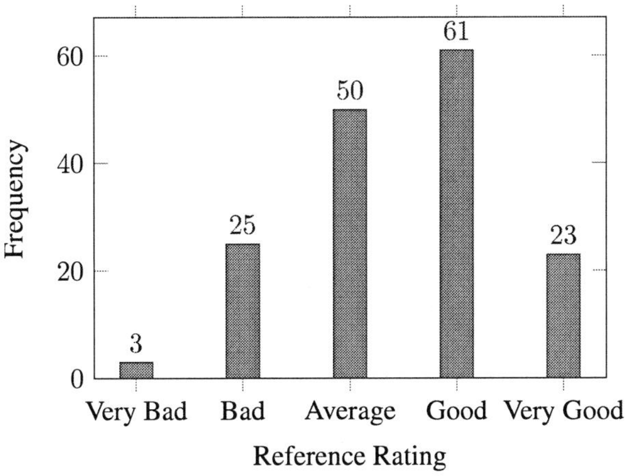

Figure 4. Distribution of all 162 *Reference Ratings* (6 items · 27 participants).

Variable	Kendall's Tau	p-Value
Bandwidth	0.552	0
Distortion	0.142	2.908e-10
Reference Rating	0.269	0

Table 3. Correlation between *Overall Listening Experience* and *Bandwidth, Distortion* and *Reference Rating.*

overall listening experience rating influenced by the audio quality and the song. The responses were given by a Likert scale with the values "Strongly Agree", "Agree", "Neutral", "Disagree" and "Strongly Disagree".

The experiment was done using open electrostatic Stax SR-507 headphones with SRM-600 driver unit. The system was calibrated to 75 dBA SPL for a 1000 Hz sine. Completing the listening test took each participant about 15 minutes. As mentioned before, the music excerpts were normalized according to EBU R128 which recommends to normalize at -23 dB.

4. RESULTS

The main hypothesis is formulated as whether bandwidth and distortion correlates with rating of overall listening experience. *Overall Listening Experience* is the dependent variable and *Bandwidth* (representing cut-off frequency) and *Distortion* (representing quantization levels) are the independent variables. Another variable, *Reference Rating*, is calculated from *Overall Listening Experience* for the statistical analysis. *Reference Rating* is the response of *Overall Listening Experience* that was given when *Bandwidth* is 15500 Hz and *Distortion* has 4096 quantization levels. Distribution of reference ratings are depicted as histogram in Figure 4.

Table 3 shows the results of correlations with *Overall Listening Experience* by using Kendall's Tau (0 = no correlation, 1 = perfect correlation) which is a ranked correlation coefficient. The correlation and all following calculations are calculated without the data which was used for *Reference Rating*, since this data is used as independent variable and e. g. including would lead to higher correlation values.

Correlation with bandwidth is very strong ($= 0.552$) which

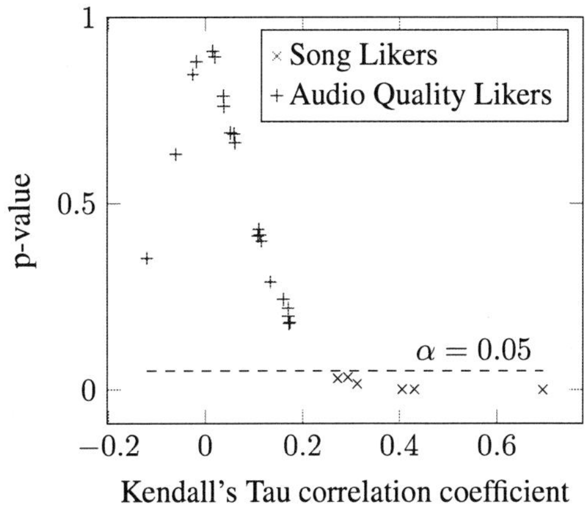

Figure 5. Kendall's Tau correlation between *Overall Listening Experience* and *Reference Rating* and its p-value for each participant. All participants having a correlation coefficient greater than 0.25 are marked as song likers.

is expected since very low levels of bandwidth were used. The very weak correlation between *Overall Listening Experience* and *Distortion* ($= 0.142$) is a bit surprising, as the first two levels of distortion were very low, too. *Reference Rating* which probably contains some information about participant's emotional value for a music excerpt has a medium correlation ($= 0.269$).

An individual calculation of Kendall's Tau Correlation between *Overall Listening Experience* and *Reference Rating* for each participant points out that participants have different preferences in rating overall listening experience. Figure 5 shows Kendall's Tau correlation between *Overall Listening Experience* and *Reference Rating* to their p-values for each participant. The results show that a group of participants had at least a medium correlation to *Reference Rating* (≥ 0.25) while their p-values are below a significance level of $\alpha = 0.05$. These participants are considered to be more influenced by the song that is played back than the other participants who have weaker correlations.

For further analysis all participants who have a Kendall's Tau coefficient greater than 0.25 are assigned to the song likers group. The remaining participants are assigned to audio quality likers. To avoid confusion, participants who are in the song likers group could also have a strong correlation between their rating and an audio quality variable. In addition, the spread of correlation coefficients shows that the correlation with the song is rather a continuum. The main reason for defining only two groups is that a more detailed distinction would require a larger amount of participants to avoid under-representation.

When correlation values are calculated separately for song likers and audio quality likers, the emotional influence becomes more obvious. For the song likers, *Reference Rating* correlates nearly the same as *Bandwidth* to *Overall Listening Rating*. Due to the high p-value, no reliable statement can be made for *Distortion*. Correlation values for audio quality likers and song likers are shown in Table 4 and 5.

In Figure 6, the ratio between *Overall Listening Experi-*

Variable	Kendall's Tau	p-Value
Bandwidth	0.530	0
Distortion	0.018	0.516
Reference Rating	0.192	6.961e-13

Table 4. Correlation between *Overall Listening Experience* and *Bandwidth, Distortion* and *Reference Rating* of audio quality likers.

Variable	Kendall's Tau	p-Value
Bandwidth	0.430	0
Distortion	0.002	0.972
Reference Rating	0.405	8.882e-16

Table 5. Correlation between *Overall Listening Experience* and *Bandwidth, Distortion* and *Reference Rating* of song likers listeners.

ence and *Reference Rating* for each *Bandwidth* is shown. A ratio value of 1 would mean that *Overall Listening Experience* for the particular *Bandwidth* level is the same as for *Bandwidth* = 15500 Hz and a ratio of 1.5 would mean the rating was 50% higher. One can see that audio quality likers have lower values than song likers. This means that audio quality likers are more critical in their rating when audio quality is decreased. Besides that, the ratio values of audio quality likers decrease more for each bandwidth limitation level than for song likers.

A cumulative link model of *Overall Listening Experience* was calculated (Table 6). As the previous analysis indicated, *Bandwidth* had more influence on *Overall Listening Experience* than *Distortion*. Furthermore, song likers gave slightly higher ratings.

At the end of the experiment the participants were asked how much their rating was influenced by song and audio quality. It was expected that song likers do much more strongly agree that their rating was influenced by the song compared to audio quality likers. As Figure 7 shows such a trend could not be confirmed. Figure 8 shows that for both types of listeners audio quality is important for their rating.

5. DISCUSSION

The presented results indicate that all ratings were strongly correlated with bandwidth. Interesting is the fact that the mean of *Overall Listening Experience* to *Reference Rating* ratio for song likers had a value of 0.75 ($0.\overline{6}7$ for audio quality likers) for *Bandwidth* of 3150 Hz. Such a bandwidth degradation is considered as a strong impairment and a much lower ratio was expected. Some participants who rated lower bandwidths the same or higher than reference bandwidth stated that lower bandwidths reminds them of festivals or concerts resulting in a positive effect on their rating.

We assume that especially the song likers would rate lower bandwidths in a real world scenario much higher than in this experiment. Many participants reported that they got annoyed by listening to the same songs repeatedly which made them focus on audio quality. Since this reaction was

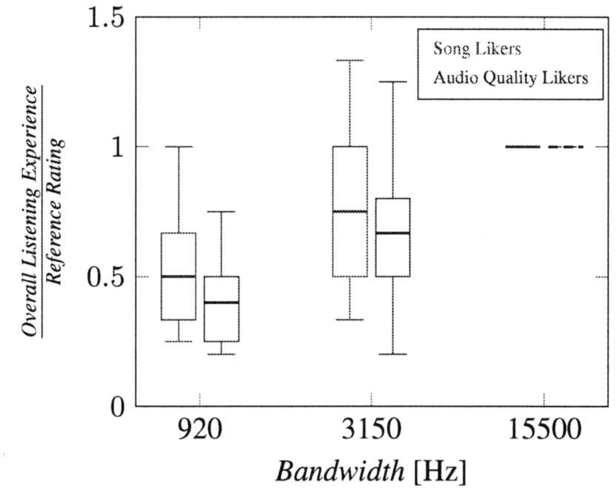

Figure 6. *Overall Listening Rating* to *Reference Rating* ratio for all three bandwidths. Only samples with *Distortion* of 4096 levels are included.

Coefficient	Estimate	Std. Error	z-value	p-value
Bandwidth = 3150	2.0788	0.1433	14.505	<2e-16
Bandwidth = 15500	3.9807	0.1840	21.632	<2e-16
Distortion = 16	0.7560	0.1294	5.842	5.17e-09
Distortion = 4096	1.0305	0.1554	6.632	3.32e-11
Reference Rating = 2	3.4240	1.0729	3.191	0.00142
Reference Rating = 3	4.8280	1.0697	4.513	6.38e-06
Reference Rating = 4	5.7951	1.0712	5.410	6.31e-08
Reference Rating = 5	5.7654	1.0797	5.340	9.32e-08
Liker Type = song	0.2750	0.1386	1.984	0.04728
Threshold coefficients:				
	Estimate	Std. Error	z-value	
very bad|bad	6.685	1.082	6.178	
bad|average	8.596	1.093	7.867	
average|good	10.550	1.103	9.563	
good|very good	12.953	1.128	11.480	
Residual Deviance: 2704.485				
AIC: 2730.485				

Table 6. Cumulative Link Model of *Overall Listening Experience*.

expected, we integrated the very long training phase where participants listened to each song twice (best quality and worst quality). Therefore, we assumed that at the beginning of the actual experiment the participants were more influenced by audio quality than they would be without the training phase. This was also reported by several song likers that their sensitivity to audio quality increased due to the training phase. Since in a real world scenario, listeners have no reference what the music they are listening to sounds in best quality, their ratings would not be as critical as in this experiment.

Some participants reported about the distortion that it felt like being masked by the bandwidth limitation which is also seen in the statistical analysis results where distortion correlates very weakly with *Overall Listening Experience*. It should not be concluded from the results that bandwidth is more important than distortion for *Overall Listening Experience* since only three levels of each variable were examined. Moreover, music can be distorted in frequency domain in various ways, other algorithms for distortion might lead to other results. It was also reported that it is harder to remember the best quality reference of distortion than it is for bandwidth. It can be assumed that for non-expert

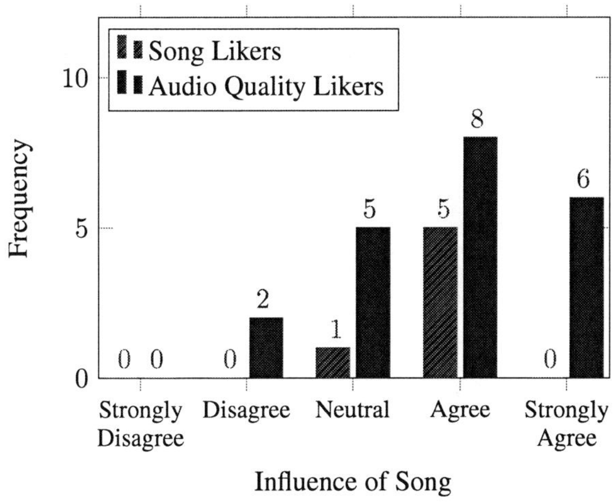

Figure 7. Distribution of participants' responses of how much their rating was influenced by the song.

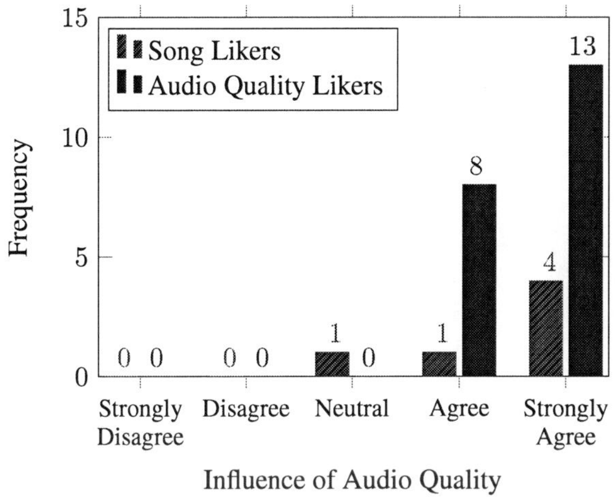

Figure 8. Distribution of participants' responses of how much their rating was influenced by audio quality.

listeners building a short-time reference for bandwidth is easier than for frequency domain distortion.

In our statistical analysis, *Reference Rating* was used as some sort of dependent variable like *Bandwidth* and *Distortion*. This means when the selection of music excerpts matches a participant's taste of music, *Reference Rating* has higher values in average than if the selection would not match his taste of music. This results in an unequally distributed data of *Overall Listening Experience* for *Reference Rating*. To overcome, one would need to ask each participant before the test for five songs which would be rated from one to five stars and use them as stimuli. But then each participant would listen to different songs where limiting the bandwidth or distortion would result in different perceived audio quality artifacts. That is why we carefully selected six music excerpts from a large database where differences of the perceived artifacts were within reasonable limits.

6. CONCLUSIONS

The results of the experiment show that rating music in overall listening experience is strongly influenced by bandwidth when the listeners is presented a reference of the music in maximum available bandwidth. In this experiment, the participants were familiarized with the minimum and maximum available bandwidth by a training phase.

The participants were divided into two types of listeners by using the correlation between reference rating and overall listening experience: audio quality likers and song likers. Audio quality likers have stronger correlation with bandwidth and their rating was more critical than song likers' rating.

Further research will look into the effect of bandwidth limitation on overall listening experience in more detail.

7. REFERENCES

[1] P. N. Juslin and D. Västfjäll, "Emotional responses to music: the need to consider underlying mechanisms." *Behavioral and brain sciences*, vol. 31, no. 5, pp. 559–621, Oct. 2008.

[2] K. R. Scherer and M. R. Zentner, "Emotional Effects of Music : Production Rules," in *Music and Emotion: Theory and Research*. London, England: Oxford University Press, 2001, ch. 16, pp. 361–392.

[3] International Telecommunications Union, "ITU-R BS . 1534-1 (Method for the subjective assessment of intermediate quality level of coding systems)," 2003.

[4] International Telecommunications Union, "ITU-R BS.1116-1 (Methods for the subjective assessment of small impairments in audio systems including multichannel sound systems)," 1997.

[5] J. L. Barbour, "Subjective Consumer Evaluation of Multi-Channel Audio Codecs," in *Audio Engineering Society Convention 119*, New York, 2005.

[6] F. Rumsey, S. Zielinski, R. Kassier, and S. Bech, "Relationships between experienced listener ratings of multichannel audio quality and naïve listener preferences," *The Journal of the Acoustical Society of America*, vol. 117, no. 6, pp. 3832–3840, 2005.

[7] J. Blauert and U. Jekosch, "A Layer Model of Sound Quality," *Journal of the Audio Engineering Society*, vol. 60, no. 1/2, pp. 4–12, 2012.

[8] K. u. R. Laghari and K. Connelly, "Toward total quality of experience: A QoE model in a communication ecosystem," *IEEE Communications Magazine*, vol. 50, no. 4, pp. 58–65, 2012.

[9] EBU, "Loudness normalisation and permitted maximum level of audio signals (EBU Recommendation R 128)," Geneva, pp. 1–5, 2011.

[10] E. Zwicker, "Subdivision of the Audible Frequency Range into Critical Bands (Frequenzgruppen)," *J. Acoust. Soc. Am.*, vol. 33, no. 2, pp. 248–248, 1961.

EFFECT OF TIMBRE ON MELODY RECOGNITION IN THREE-VOICE COUNTERPOINT MUSIC

Song Hui Chon, Kevin Schwartzbach, Bennett Smith, Stephen McAdams
CIRMMT (Centre for Interdisciplinary Research in Music Media and Technology)
Schulich School of Music
McGill University
songhui.chon@mail.mcgill.ca

ABSTRACT

Timbre saliency refers to the attention-capturing quality of timbre. Can we make one musical line stand out of multiple concurrent lines using a highly salient timbre on it? This is the question we ask in this paper using a melody recognition task in counterpoint music.

Three-voice stimuli were generated using instrument timbres that were chosen following specific conditions of timbre saliency and timbre dissimilarity. A listening experiment was carried out with 36 musicians without absolute pitch. No effect of gender was found in the recognition data. Although a strong difference was observed for the middle voice from mono-timbre to multi-timbre conditions, timbre saliency and timbre dissimilarity conditions did not appear to have systematic effects on the average recognition rate as we hypothesized. This could be due to the variability in the excerpts used for certain conditions, or more fundamentally, because the context effect of each voice position might have been much bigger than the effects of timbre conditions we were trying to measure. A further discussion is presented on possible context effects.

1. INTRODUCTION

1.1 Timbre Saliency

Timbre saliency is a new concept we proposed regarding the attention-capturing quality of timbre [1]. It was measured using tapping to perceptually isochronous ABAB sequences, the pitch (C4), loudness and effective duration of which were all equalized. The duration of each stimulus was controlled by imposing a raised cosine decay envelope at a point corresponding to the effective duration of 200 ms on a recorded sample from the Vienna Symphonic Library [2]. All sounds were selected from those playing mezzoforte in the most basic manner (such as bowing on the cello rather than plucking). The hypothesis was that the more salient a timbre is, the more attention it will draw from the participants, and hence be tapped to more often. Figure 1 shows the one-dimensional saliency scale obtained from CLASCAL [3]. Although the saliency scale is one-dimensional, it is presented in two dimensions because of the seven instruments closely positioned around 0.

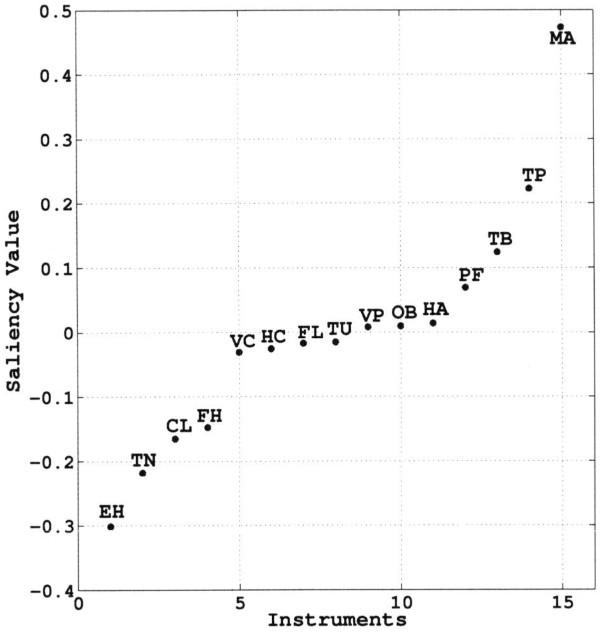

Figure 1. One-dimensional timbre saliency space of 15 timbres: Clarinet (CL), English Horn (EH), French Horn (FH), Flute (FL), Harp (HA), Harpsichord (HC), Marimba (MA), Oboe (OB), Piano (PF), Trombone (TN), Trumpet (TP), Tuba (TU), Tubular Bells (TB), Violoncello (VC), and Vibraphone (VP).

As saliency refers to the character of an object that makes it stand out from its surroundings, we next studied the effect of saliency on the perceived blending of concurrent unison dyads [4]. 105 composite sounds were created using pairs of non-identical timbres that were used in the tapping experiment [1]. Rating data from 60 people showed that, as we hypothesized, a highly salient timbre would not blend well with others, although the degree of correlation was mild at most. Attack time and spectral centroid were most efficient in describing the blend ratings, which are the two acoustic features that were reported in previous studies of the blend perception [5, 6], verifying that a sound will tend to blend better when it has more low-frequency energy and when it starts slowly.

After studying the effect of timbre saliency on the simplest musical situation of unison concurrent dyads, the next step is an investigation in a more musically realistic scenario. For example, it has been known that the entries of inner voices are more difficult to detect than those of outer voices in polyphonic music [7]. Therefore, can we enhance the detection of an inner voice by applying a salient instrument timbre to it?

To answer this question, we decided to employ a melody recognition task. Iverson, and Bey & McAdams found that having two highly dissimilar timbres helped the recognition of the target melodies that were interleaved with distractors [8,9]. Using concurrent melodies, Huron observed that in general musicians were capable of correctly identifying the number of voices, although the performance degraded as the number of voices increased, especially beyond three [7]. Gregory found that concurrent melodies that had simultaneous note onsets in the same pitch range in a related key tended to be easier to perceive if they were distinguished by timbre differences [10]. Although this result suggests that listeners can attend to more than one musical line at a time, it might need to be interpreted with caution because the voices in musical excerpts in the study were not controlled carefully and some excerpts might have been too well-known (such as the one from Mozart's *Don Giovanni*).

As we aimed to expand the study of the effect of timbre saliency in a more musically realistic setting, the method of melody recognition in counterpoint music was deemed to be appropriate. There are two or more musical lines with virtually equal musical importance. Since the authors, who knew the melodies in the excerpts by heart, could not listen to all voices in an excerpt at once, it is practically impossible for listeners to attend to every note of every voice. Therefore they would tend to focus on whatever voice catches their attention. Hence, if we can control the timbre saliency of the voices in music, listeners' tendency to attend to a specific voice must reflect the voice's saliency. But since it is difficult for us to figure out which voice each listener is hearing out at a given moment, we decided to use a comparison task based on melody recognition. If, for example, a listener happened to focus more on the high voice melody and was tested with a high-voice comparison melody, he or she would be more likely to answer correctly than someone who happened to focus on the low voice. Therefore performance in this task should covary with voice prominence.

Since this is a very complex experiment, we had to run two experiments for preparation. One was to study the dissimilarity of the timbres that were used in our saliency experiment (Section 1.2). The other was a melody comparison experiment to make sure that the changes on a voice were easy enough to hear out in isolation (Section 3). The design of musical stimuli, which took place before the melody comparison experiment, is explained in detail in Section 2. Section 4 discusses the main experiment, then finally a general discussion and conclusions are presented in Section 5.

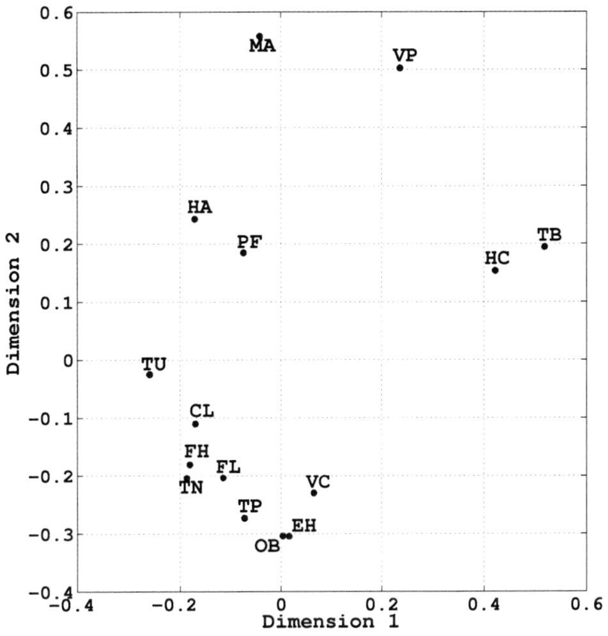

Figure 2. Two-dimensional timbre dissimilarity space. See Fig. 1 caption for abbreviations.

1.2 Timbre Dissimilarity

A classic timbre dissimilarity experiment was carried out using the same set of 15 isolated instrument sounds used in the timbre saliency experiment [1]. Twenty participants, balanced in gender and musicianship were recruited, with ages from 19 to 39 with a median age of 26.5 years.

Repeated-measures ANOVAs on dissimilarity ratings showed no effect of gender or musicianship. The dissimilarity judgments were formed into 20 individual lower triangular matrices, then analyzed by CLASCAL [3] to obtain the dissimilarity space. The best solution turned out to have two dimensions with specificities and five latent classes of participants (Figure 2).

Note that the percussive instruments are all located above the $y = 0$ line. This suggests that the second dimension may be related to attack time. Correlations were computed between each of the two dimensions and the acoustic features computed by the Timbre Toolbox [11]. The first dimension shows a high correlation with spectral centroid in the ERB-FFT spectrum, $r(13) = .845, p < .0001$, and the second dimension a moderate correlation with attack time, $r(13) = -.692, p = .004$. This is in agreement with previous studies in timbre dissimilarity showing that attack time and spectral centroid are two of the most important acoustic features [12–17].

This two-dimensional timbre dissimilarity space in Figure 2 will provide a basis for the selection of stimuli for Experiments 1 and 2. This is necessary because it is not feasible to study all 15 timbres' effect on melody recognition, and therefore we need to select timbres that best represent the experimental conditions. This timbre dissimilarity space will also be essential in data analysis as the dissimilarity distance is one of the main parameters for Experiment 2.

Figure 3. An example excerpt and corresponding comparison melodies

2. MUSICAL STIMULUS DESIGN

A number of excerpts and their comparison melodies are needed to avoid any unexpected training effect from participants. We selected nine excerpts from J.S. Bach's *Trio Sonatas for Organ*, BWV 525 – 530, because the music was already clearly written for three-voices (right hand, left hand and pedal) and relatively unknown in comparison with other three-voice pieces (such as the *Sinfonias*).

We looked for the parts with all three voices clearly in action with about equal note onset density. Any excerpts with voice crossings were avoided. We also did some editing of the excerpts such as transposing the melodies to a new key (often to accommodate the playing ranges of selected instruments), changing the pitch of a note (often by an octave) to avoid voice crossing, or breaking a longer note into two shorter notes to maintain the note onset density.

For each voice in each excerpt, a comparison melody was composed by changing the pitches of two notes, which resulted in a different pitch contour, following the approach in auditory streaming studies using interleaved melodies [9]. An example is shown in Figure 3. The first two measures show the three-voice excerpt by Bach and the last two measures the corresponding comparison melodies. In the actual experiment all three voices in an excerpt will play together, whereas the three comparison melodies will never be heard together.

The excerpts were first encoded in Finale [18], the MIDI timings of which were exported to Logic [19]. The stimuli were created using the recorded samples in the Vienna Symphonic Library [2] based on the MIDI timing information. The specific timbre combinations used for stimulus generation are presented in the next section.

2.1 Timbre Combinations

A subset of instruments was chosen that would best represent the timbre saliency and timbre dissimilarity conditions from the two spaces in Figures 1 and 2, respectively. We decided to focus on a subset of timbre combinations in which two timbres are similar and the other one is different (i.e., two are close to each other and the third one is far from these two in timbre *dissimilarity* space), and one is a highly salient timbre and two others are of lower saliency. Three timbre dissimilarity conditions combined with three timbre saliency conditions resulted in nine conditions (Table 1).

D1, D2 and D3 represent the three *dissimilarity* conditions according to the assignments of three timbres to three voices. Among the three timbres, T1, T2 and T3, *T3* is always the "far" timbre and is highlighted in blue italics. Similarly, S1, S2 and S3 represent the three *saliency* conditions. The "High" saliency timbre of the three timbres is highlighted in a bold red font. For example, the D1S1 column in Table 1 shows that in this condition high and middle voices have timbres that are of low saliency and close in dissimilarity space. This factorial combination of saliency and dissimilarity allows us to test their separate contributions to melody recognition, as well as their potential interaction.

Even though there are nine conditions, it turns out that only four sets of timbre assignments are required – {D1S1, D2S2, D3S3}, {D1S2}, {D1S3, D2S3, D3S2}, and {D2S1, D3S1}, as specified with four types of fonts in Table 2. These combinations were chosen considering not only the relative positions in timbre dissimilarity and timbre saliency spaces, but also the instrument ranges, because some instruments cannot play higher notes in the top voice and others cannot play the lower notes in the bottom voice.

In addition, we need to test the same-timbre version of all stimuli, to determine baseline performance in the absence of timbre differences. We decided to use the piano (PF) for this, not only because it has a sufficient range for all excerpts, but because its timbre is quite homogeneous over the middle range, which is used primarily in the current study.

In searching for the right timbre combinations for the conditions specified in Table 2, we had to make some compromises by using some instruments with medium saliency. More specifically, Harpsichord (HC) was used in place of some lower saliency instruments. This was the best we could do with the two given spaces (Figures 1 and 2), especially because nine out of fifteen timbres were located together in the lower left corner of the timbre dissimilarity space (Fig. 2).

3. EXPERIMENT 1: MELODY DISCRIMINATION

The goal of this experiment was to verify that the changes in pairs of melodies were easy enough to detect in isolation

Table 1. Timbre conditions for three-voice excerpts

	D1S1	D1S2	D1S3	D2S1	D2S2	D2S3	D3S1	D3S2	D3S3
High	T1L	T1L	T1**H**	T2L	T2L	T2**H**	*T3*L	*T3*L	*T3***H**
Middle	T2L	T2**H**	T2L	*T3*L	*T3***H**	*T3*L	T1L	T1**H**	T1L
Low	*T3***H**	*T3*L	*T3*L	T1**H**	T1L	T1L	T2**H**	T2L	T2L

Table 2. Timbre assignments for three-voice excerpts

	D1S1	D1S2	**D1S3**	*D2S1*	D2S2	**D2S3**	*D3S1*	**D3S2**	D3S3
High	T1L	T1L	**T1H**	*T2L*	T2L	**T2H**	*T3L*	**T3L**	T3H
Middle	T2L	T2H	**T2L**	*T3L*	T3H	**T3L**	*T1L*	**T1H**	T1L
Low	T3H	T3L	**T3L**	*T1H*	T1L	**T1L**	*T2H*	**T2L**	T2L
T1	CL	EH	**TP**	*MA*	TN	**TN**	*VP*	**TP**	CL
T2	TN	TP	**TN**	*VP*	CL	**TP**	*MA*	**TN**	TN
T3	MA	HC	**HC**	*CL*	MA	**HC**	*CL*	**HC**	MA

at least 75% of the time, because if participants cannot hear changes in corresponding melodies in isolation, they will not be able to hear out changes on one voice in a mixture with other voice(s). The stimuli were 108 ordered pairs of "original" and "comparison" multi-timbre melodies from all three voices in nine excerpts: original-original, original-comparison, comparison-original, and comparison-comparison. These were presented to the participants in a random order without an option to repeat. Participants were required to indicate whether a given pair of melodies was identical or not on the graphic user interface, which then automatically proceeded to the next trial.

Twenty musicians (10 males) without absolute pitch were recruited, aged from 18 to 37 with a median of 24 years. There was quite a large variability in the participants' average performances, ranging from 69% to 92% correct, with a median of 84%. All melody pairs showed correct discrimination above 75% with the exception of one pair at 72.5%. As the 75% threshold was somewhat arbitrary and 72.5% is not too far from 75%, we decided to proceed to the main experiment using the current modified melodies without any further adjustments.

4. EXPERIMENT 2: MELODY RECOGNITION IN THREE-VOICE COUNTERPOINT MUSIC

4.1 Methods

This experiment studied the role of timbre dissimilarity and saliency in melody recognition in counterpoint music. Stimuli were the three-voice Bach excerpts, as well as the individual monophonic melodies. For each trial, a multi-voice excerpt would play first, followed by a monophonic melody. The monophonic melody could be the original or comparison melody corresponding to one of the voices in the preceding excerpt. Participants were required to indicate whether the monophonic melody was the same as or different from a voice in the excerpt by pressing on the appropriate button on the graphic user interface. There was no option to listen to the stimuli again to prevent participants from strategically learning all voices by attending to one voice each time over repeats. Once an answer was submitted, the next trial would start automatically, playing a new multi-voice excerpt.

Thirty-six musicians without absolute pitch took part in the experiment. Their ages ranged from 18 to 37, with a median of 24 years. There were equal numbers of males and females. Nineteen of them identified themselves as "professional" musicians and the rest as "amateurs". In terms of their listening habits, 15 claimed to be "harmony-listeners" and 21 to be "melody-listeners." Although we have not come across any literature on the effect of this listening habit on the listeners perception of voices in counterpoint music, we thought the melody-listeners might focus on one prominent voice whereas the harmony-listeners would focus on emergent properties of all voices.

4.2 Results

4.2.1 Average Performance Per Condition

The main goal of this experiment was to examine the melody recognition performance in terms of timbre conditions based on timbre saliency and timbre dissimilarity. For this purpose, we computed the average recognition rate over all melodies used per voice per condition and compared those average values (Figure 4). The horizontal axis shows the saliency conditions and each line represents the dissimilarity conditions.

Considering only the mean values (blue dots, black stars and red triangles), we see they loosely follow a v-shape, although sometimes flipped upside down or almost flattened. The three v-shaped lines in the middle voice appear to maintain the same direction, which suggests that the timbre saliency condition may play an important role in the recognition of the middle voices. The fact that the lines keep a similar shape in the middle voice graph but not in other two voices implies a possible main effect of voice position or an interaction between timbre saliency and voice position.

A three-way repeated measures ANOVA was performed on the average recognition rate per condition as the dependent variable. The voice position (high, middle or low), dissimilarity and saliency conditions in Table 1 were within-subjects factors. The only significant effects were interactions between voice position and saliency, $F(4, 140) =$

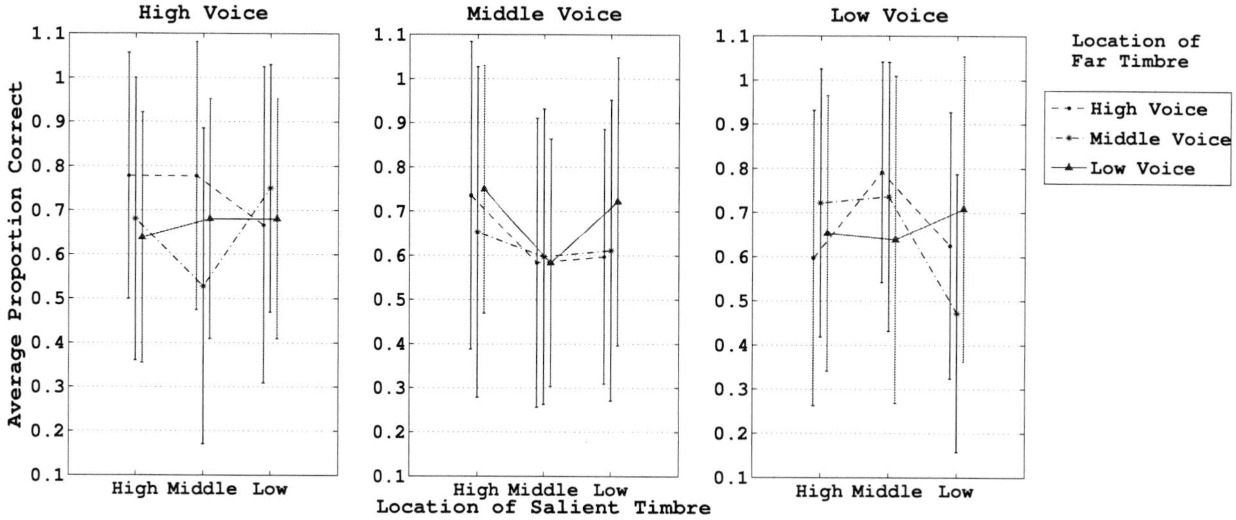

Figure 4. Results for three-voice excerpts. The error bars show ± one standard deviation.

$3.86, p = .005$, and between voice type, saliency, and dissimilarity, $F(8, 280) = 3.14, p = .002$. None of the other effects was significant.

The significant voice position × saliency interaction means that our hypothesis that the effect of saliency condition differs across voices was correct. This may imply that the innate 'voice prominence' from this musical structure may have a bigger impact on melody recognition than the controlled timbre conditions. The significant three-way interaction of voice position, dissimilarity and saliency indicates that the two-way interaction effect between dissimilarity and saliency differs depending on the voice type. This is in agreement with the fact that in Figure 4, the dissimilarity × saliency interaction (i.e., the angles of v-shape lines) seems to be higher for high and low voices, but negligible for the middle voice.

Two-way ANOVAs were performed to study the effect of timbre dissimilarity and timbre saliency for each voice type. On the high voice, the interaction effect was significant, $F(4, 140) = 3.12, p = .017$, but not the main effects of timbre dissimilarity, $F(2, 70) = 2.28, p = .11$, or of timbre saliency, $F(2, 70) = 0.91, p = .41$. In the high-voice graph of Figure 4, the locations of the nine points, corresponding to average performance across participants in nine timbral conditions, are quite different according to timbre conditions, although their vertical or horizontal (per line) averages do not show significant differences (hence non-significant main effects).

On the middle voice, the main effect of timbre saliency turned out to be significant, $F(2, 70) = 4.69, p = .012$, but not timbre dissimilarity, $F(2, 70) = 1.04, p = .36$, nor their interaction $F(4, 140) = 0.71, p = .59$. The three lines in the middle voice graphs of Figure 4 have similar shapes (hence no significant interaction effect) and locations (hence no significant main effect of dissimilarity). The nine points representing the nine conditions have very different vertical means (therefore a significant main effect of saliency), but not so different horizontal means (hence a non-significant main effect of dissimilarity). What is strange is that the performance on the middle voice was at its worst when the salient timbre was on the middle voice. This can be observed in all three dissimilarity conditions, probably suggesting that the effect of a salient timbre was minimal on the middle voice. It is also hard to understand why the recognition performance on the middle voice (black dash-dotted line connecting stars) was the worst when the far timbre was assigned to the middle voice. In summary, this graph seems to suggest the absence of our hypothesized effects of dissimilarity or saliency on the middle voice.

A two-way ANOVA on the low voice showed two significant effects: the main effect of timbre saliency, $F(2, 70) = 3.66, p = .031$, and its interaction with timbre dissimilarity, $F(4, 140) = 4.56, p = .002$. The main effect of timbre dissimilarity was not significant, $F(2, 70) = 0.28, p = .75$. The v-shapes face different directions, reflecting the significant interaction effect. Although the per-dissimilarity condition (i.e., per-line) averages are all located in a similar area (hence no main effect of dissimilarity), the vertical means are at different locations, confirming the significant main effect of saliency. However, it is strange to see that the vertical mean was at its lowest when the salient timbre was on the low voice. Having the salient timbre on the low voice was expected to help the recognition performance, but apparently it did not. A close look reveals that the performance was not too bad when the salient timbre was on the low voice and the far timbre was on the high or low voice. But somehow having a far timbre on the middle voice hindered the recognition of the low voice melody so much that the performance actually fell below 50%. This might result from the saliency differences inherent in the stimuli: somehow the low voice melodies were not salient at all and participants' attention was drawn to the salient high-voice melodies in the given condition.

Overall, it is quite disappointing to see that recognition was not highest (with an exception of the high voice) when a voice had both the salient and the far timbre, which had been hypothesized to have the maximum effect on the recognition task. For example, the high voice graph on the left of Figure 4 reaches the maximum performance at the left blue dot, when the salient and far timbre happened to be on the high voice, but this is not the case in the other two

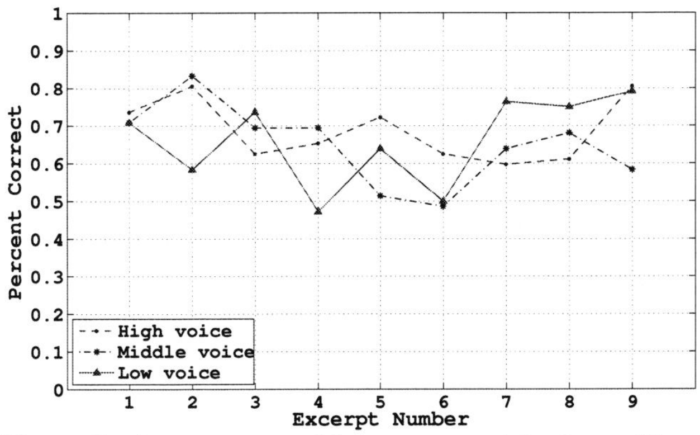

Figure 5. Average recognition per excerpt in the multi-timbre conditions

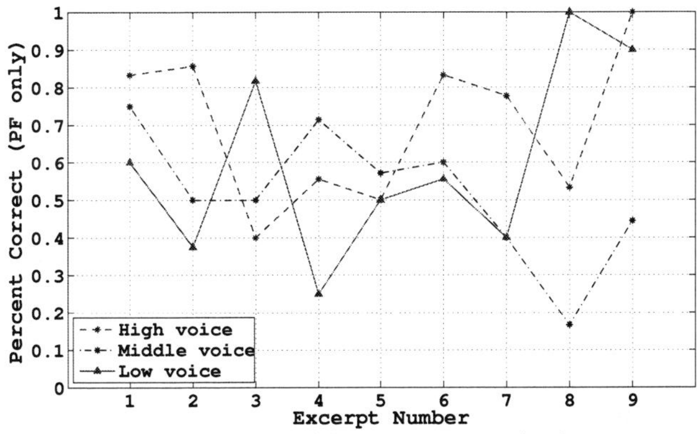

Figure 6. Average recognition per excerpt in the mono-timbre condition

graphs. The black star in the middle of the dash-dotted line of the middle voice graph, which was hypothesized to be the highest point, is located much lower than the actual highest point (a red triangle). In fact, it is puzzling to see the low performance on the middle voice when it was played with the salient timbre. We began to wonder if the middle voice melodies used for this condition happened to be too difficult. To study this, we decided to analyze the average recognition performance for each stimulus, which is presented in the next section.

4.2.2 *Average Performance Per Excerpt*

The average recognition rates of the nine excerpts across all participants are shown in Figures 5 and 6. There is quite a bit of variability across the excerpts used. This might be due to the fact that some excerpts are more difficult to remember than others. At first glance, the multi-timbre average curves look a bit different from the mono-timbre ones, but paired-sample t tests show that these seeming differences are mostly non-significant. One marginally significant difference was found on the middle voice, $t(8) = 1.89, p = .096$, where the average recognition rate of the middle voice in multi-timbre condition was 0.65 ($STD = 0.11$), whereas that in the mono-timbre condition was 0.52 ($STD = 0.18$). This may suggest that having a distinctive timbre on the middle voice, which is usually the most difficult to listen to in the given musical structure, helps its recognition slightly.

Since the average performance per excerpt varied quite a bit, we came to wonder if this is related to how easily the changes in corresponding voices could be heard out in Experiment 1. Hence, the average recognition rate per excerpt was analyzed in terms of the average percent correct values from Experiment 1. Spearman's rank correlation showed that no correlation was significant. This lack of correlation could reflect the fact that the current experimental task is too complex to be successfully predicted by the control experiment result.

4.3 Discussion

In this experiment, we studied the effects of timbre saliency and timbre dissimilarity on the melody recognition in counterpoint music with nine three-voice excerpts in nine timbre conditions. Considering previous work in auditory streaming that has shown that greater timbre dissimilarity leads to better recognition of interleaved melodies [8, 9], as well as our measurement of timbre saliency [1], we hypothesized that a highly dissimilar or a highly salient timbre would enhance a voice's prominence in a multi-voice texture. We were also confident of our choice of counterpoint music excerpts, where each voice had about equal musical importance.

However, the results from 36 musicians did not confirm our hypothesis. Analysis of per-condition performance of middle and low voices showed a significant effect of saliency, although not in the direction we expected: the average performance was poorer when the salient timbre was located on the target voice. This is completely against our hypothesis, and essentially nullifies the conjecture of the timbre saliency's effect on melody recognition in multipart music.

In searching for an answer to this unexpected pattern, we looked at the average recognition performance for each of the excerpts used. It turned out that there was a large difference in per-excerpt performance, which could have come from various degrees of memorability that affected the recognition performance. This variance in per-excerpt performance could also have contributed to differences in per-condition performance.

As there were no significant differences in average recognition of each excerpt-voice according to the timbre conditions (multi-timbre vs. mono-timbre), with an exception only for the middle voice, the lack of effect of timbre saliency may actually indicate a greater 'voice prominence' in the given musical structure than whatever timbral effects we expected. After all, we had not studied the intrinsic saliency of each voice in the three-voice counterpoint structure. This could be a case of the experimental context affecting the measurement of saliency differences of the objects in the experiment.

However, the fact that the average recognition of the middle voice was marginally higher in the multi-timbre condition in comparison with the mono-timbre condition does speak for the case of timbral effects. The middle voice, which is the most difficult to listen to in three-voice music, became easier to recognize with the use of a timbre different from those on the other voices. Unfortunately, this effect seems too weak to be reflected and measured properly in the current experimental setup.

The large variance in recognition performance also makes us hesitate in drawing firm conclusions based on the analysis. In the per-condition performance, all the means and the respective confidence intervals overlapped without exception. Hence, the analyses based on mean values lose their effectiveness when we consider the large variance.

It was disappointing not to see the expected effects of timbre saliency and timbre dissimilarity. What we saw instead was another incidence of a context effect, which was possibly a lot stronger than our planned timbral effects in this experiment. To clarify unanswered questions, another experiment using the untested portion of the current stimuli seems to be in order, which will provide data that can complement this experiment so that we can apprehend the big picture.

5. SUMMARY & GENERAL DISCUSSION

To examine the effect of timbre saliency and timbre dissimilarity in a more realistic music listening setting, a melody recognition experiment was carried out as a natural extension of the previous study of the perception of blend in concurrent unison dyads [4]. As a mild negative relationship between timbre saliency and the perceived blend was observed in the concurrent unison dyads, we hypothesized that a highly salient timbre would show little blend with other voices in the musical texture and therefore be heard out more easily. Also considering the effect of timbre dissimilarity, we expected to confirm previous findings in the auditory streaming literature [8,9] that a highly dissimilar timbre on a voice would help detect changes in that voice more easily in the presence of other voices in multipart music.

The high voice did not show any main effects of timbre saliency and timbre dissimilarity conditions; it is already the most prominent voice in the chosen musical structure. This 'voice prominence' was probably a lot more salient than any possible additional benefits from timbre saliency and dissimilarity conditions. There was a significant interaction effect observed though, suggesting that the effect of timbre dissimilarity varied with timbre saliency (and vice versa). Middle and low voices showed a significant effect of timbre saliency condition, but this effect did not go in the same direction as our hypothesis. In fact, the average recognition performance was lowest when the salient timbre was located on the target voice. This was completely unexpected, and we are still puzzled by it.

So we decided to look into the per-excerpt average performance, hoping that it would shed light that could explain the aforementioned observations on middle and high voices. When each excerpt's average recognition performance in multi-timbre condition was contrasted with that in mono-timbre condition, the only marginally significant difference was observed on the middle voice. The recognition performance was much higher on average (by 13%) in the multi-timbre condition. This suggests that the middle voice, which has the least 'voice prominence' in the chosen musical structure, benefited from having a different timbre from the other voices, which agrees with previous literature on timbral effects on auditory streaming.

However, the fact that this additional benefit did not make any significant differences in average performances per timbre condition led us to think about the context effects again. As we hypothesized, there exists an intrinsic saliency for each object and an extrinsic saliency for each context in which the object's saliency is measured. Considering this, the limit in our experiment might have been that we did not consider the inherent prominence of each voice position in the musical form that was selected for the experiment. Even the strong recognition improvement on the middle voice in the condition with multiple timbres may not have covaried systematically with the hypothesized timbre conditions, which could be why there is lack of effect of the timbre conditions.

Reflecting on the complexity of Experiment 2, we wonder if we should have started with a simpler experiment. Perhaps it would help to carry out a new experiment with simplified conditions to verify the effect of timbre saliency and timbre dissimilarity, where the stimuli have only two conditions – a "high" condition with a highly salient and dissimilar (i.e., far in dissimilarity space) timbre and a "low" condition with a not-so-salient and similar timbre. This should be able to clearly contrast the performance in each condition to examine the effect of timbre saliency and timbre dissimilarity. We can also conduct Experiment 2 again with the set of stimuli that were not tested currently. Because each three-voice excerpt in a particular timbre combination was tested with only one voice, we can make use of the untested voices and run the same analysis on the combined data.

Another idea is to conduct an experiment utilizing top-down attention instead of the current melody recognition paradigm, which depends on bottom-up attention and short-term memory. Imagine that a short cue, an isolated note at a certain pitch and timbre, is played right before a polyphonic excerpt is played. What happens to the recognition rate? Do listeners tend to get drawn more towards the voice close to the pitch of the cue? Or to the voice that has the same timbre? This may bring us to an interesting interaction of top-down and bottom-up attention together.

Also, more fundamentally, the relationship between timbre saliency and timbre dissimilarity needs to be examined. In the design of experiments in this paper, we proceeded from assumptions that timbre saliency and timbre dissimilarity would be at least somewhat related to each other and that there would not be any negative interaction between them. Do our assumptions still hold? What is the difference between saliency and dissimilarity? Can one explain the other? After studying their relationship, we might have a new insight to bring to understanding the current results.

One thing that we learned from carrying out this complex experiment is that counterpoint music is such a sophisticated art that it could not be sufficiently analyzed with our model. Saliency is a function of context, and our measure of timbre saliency might not have been effective in the context of melody recognition in counterpoint music, especially when each voice position's prominence is unknown. As this was our first attempt to explain the perception of multipart music in terms of timbre saliency, any findings are important. However disappointing or puzzling the findings were, these will lead to a new journey with more questions to answer, which will eventually help us understand what catches our attention in music, which was the starting point of timbre saliency.

Acknowledgments

This work was funded by grants from the Canadian Natural Sciences and Engineering Research Council (NSERC) and the Canada Research Chairs (CRC) program to Stephen McAdams and by the Centre for Interdisciplinary Research in Music Media and Technology (CIRMMT) to Song Hui Chon. A special thanks to the members of the Music Perception and Cognition Lab for discussions in the design of the experiment.

6. REFERENCES

[1] S. H. Chon and S. McAdams, "Investigation of timbre saliency, the attention-capturing quality of timbre," *Proceedings of the Acoustics 2012 Hong Kong (Invited Paper)*, 2012.

[2] (2011) Vienna symphonic library. Vienna Symphonic Library GmbH. [Online]. Available: http://vsl.co.at

[3] S. Winsberg and G. De Soete, "A latent-class approach to fitting the weighted euclidean model, clascal," *Psychometrika*, vol. 58, pp. 315–330, 1993.

[4] S. H. Chon and S. McAdams, "Exploring blending as a function of timbre saliency," *Proceedings of the 12th International Conference of Music Perception and Cognition*, 2012.

[5] G. J. Sandell, "Roles for spectral centroid and other factors in determining "blended" instrument pairings in orchestration," *Music Perception*, vol. 13, pp. 209–246, 1995.

[6] D. Tardieu and S. McAdams, "Perception of dyads of impulsive and sustained sounds," *Music Perception*, vol. 30, no. 2, pp. 117–128, 2012.

[7] D. Huron, "Voice denumerability in polyphonic music of homogeneous timbres," *Music Perception*, vol. 6, no. 4, pp. 361–382, 1989.

[8] P. Iverson, "Auditory stream segregation by musical timbre: Effects of static and dynamic acoustic attributes," *Journal of Experimental Psychology*, vol. 21, no. 4, pp. 751–763, 1995.

[9] C. Bey and S. McAdams, "Postrecognition of interleaved melodies as an indirect measure of auditory stream formation," *Journal of Experimental Psychology: Human Perception and Performance*, vol. 29, no. 2, pp. 267–279, 2003.

[10] A. H. Gregory, "Listening to polyphonic music," *Psychology of Music*, vol. 18, pp. 163–170, 1990.

[11] G. Peeters, P. Susini, N. Misdariis, B. L. Giordano, and S. McAdams, "The timbre toolbox: Extracting audio descriptors from musical signals," *Journal of the Acoustical Society of America*, vol. 130, no. 5, pp. 2902–2916, 2011.

[12] J. M. Grey, "Multidimensional perceptual scaling of musical timbres," *Journal of the Acoustical Society of America*, vol. 61, pp. 1270–1277, 1977.

[13] J. M. Grey and J. W. Gordon, "Perceptual effects of spectral modifications on musical timbres," *Journal of the Acoustical Society of America*, vol. 63, pp. 1493–1500, 1978.

[14] C. L. Krumhansl, "Why is musical timbre so hard to understand?" in *Structure and Perception of Electroacoustic Sound and Music*, S. Nielzen and O. Olsson, Eds. Amsterdam: Excerpta Medica, 1989, pp. 44–53.

[15] S. McAdams, S. Winsberg, S. Donnadieu, G. De Soete, and J. Krimphoff, "Perceptual scaling of synthesized musical timbres: Common dimensions, specificities, and latent subject classes," *Psychol Res*, vol. 58, pp. 177–192, 1995.

[16] S. Lakatos, "A common perceptual space for harmonic and percussive timbres," *Perception & Psychophysics*, vol. 62, no. 7, pp. 1426–1439, 2000.

[17] A. Caclin, S. McAdams, B. K. Smith, and S. Winsberg, "Acoustic correlates of timbre space dimensions: A confirmatory study using synthetic tones," *Journal of the Acoustical Society of America*, vol. 118, no. 1, pp. 471–482, 2005.

[18] (2012) Finale. MakeMusic, Inc. Eden Prairie, MN.

[19] (2012) Logic. Apple Computer. Cupertino, CA.

THE IMPORTANCE OF AMPLITUDE ENVELOPE: SURVEYING THE TEMPORAL STRUCTURE OF SOUNDS IN PERCEPTUAL RESEARCH

Jessica Gillard
McMaster Institute for Music and the Mind
gillarj@mcmaster.ca

Michael Schutz
McMaster Institute for Music and the Mind
schutz@mcmaster.ca

ABSTRACT

Our lab's research has repeatedly documented significant differences in the outcomes of perception experiments using *flat* (i.e. sustained) vs. *percussive* (i.e. decaying) tones [1, 2]. Some of these findings contrast with well-established theories and models, and we suspect this discrepancy stems from a traditional focus on *flat* tones in psychophysical research on auditory perception. To explore this issue, we surveyed 94 articles published in *Attention, Perception & Psychophysics,* classifying the temporal structure (i.e. amplitude envelope) of each sound using five categories: *flat* (i.e. sustained with abruptly ending offsets), *percussive* (i.e. naturally decaying offsets), *click train* (i.e. a series of rapid sound-bursts), *other*, and *not specified* (i.e. insufficient specification with respect to temporal structure). The use of *flat* tones (31%) clearly outnumbered *percussive* (4.5%). This under-utilization of *percussive* sounds is intriguing, given their ecological prevalence outside the lab [3,4]. Interestingly, 55% of the tones encountered fell within the *not specified* category. This is not indicative of general neglect, as these articles frequently specified other details such as spectral envelope, headphone model, and model of computer/synthesizer. This suggests that temporal structure's full importance has not traditionally been recognized, and that it represents a rich area for future research and exploration.

1. INTRODUCTION

Research in the field of audition has a long history of using artificial (i.e. sustained or '*flat*') tones to assess perceptual and cognitive ability. While these *flat* tones lend themselves well for the kinds of rigorously controlled stimuli desirable in an experimental or clinical setting, they offer little resemblance to the types of sounds heard outside the laboratory or audiologist's office [5].

1.1 Stimuli used in auditory perception research

In broad strokes, this issue has been addressed in the literature previously by William Gaver [3, 4], who argued that auditory perception research largely focuses on specific *attributes* of sounds, such as pitch, loudness or timbre. This contrasts with our listening outside the laboratory, which is generally focused more on the *events* producing sounds. Gaver referred to this event-based perception as 'everyday listening' – conveying its pervasive nature in real world settings. For instance, when listening to two hands colliding, one might remark that it 'sounds like hands clapping', not that 'it sounds like a spectrally dense burst of noise with a sharp onset' [6]. Such scenarios can also be observed in laboratory settings – in free identification tasks, participants often describe sounds based on the events creating them rather than their attributes (unless the source is ambiguous) [7].

Such event-based perception can be derived in part from a sound's temporal structure or amplitude envelope. Impact sounds such as handclaps, footsteps and door slams are pervasive in our environment and carry detailed information regarding the materials and force used, particularly in their offset. While this information is easily derived from ecologically valid impact sounds, this is not the case for the abruptly ending *flat* tones commonly used in auditory perception research. In fact, previous studies in our lab have repeatedly shown striking differences in outcomes when using sounds with abruptly-ending *flat* vs. more naturalistic, gradually decaying '*percussive*' tones in a variety of tasks [1, 2]. Examples of *flat* and *percussive* tones used in those experiments can been seen in Figure 1.

1.2 Temporal structure and sensory integration

Our interest in this issue began with a seemingly unrelated debate among percussionist in which some argue that stroke length can influence perceived note duration, with longer gestures making 'long' notes and shorter gestures making 'short' notes. To test this hypothesis empirically we asked participants to rate the durations of tones paired with videos of a professional marimbist making either long or short striking gestures, while ignoring the visual information [1].

When paired with *flat* tones, the visual information (i.e. gestures) did not influence perceived tone durations.

However, when paired with *percussive* tones, long gestures made the tones sound 'longer' and short gestures made the tones sound 'shorter'. Curiously, the use of sounds with naturally decaying offset leads to *qualitatively different outcomes* on a seemingly unrelated sensory integration task.

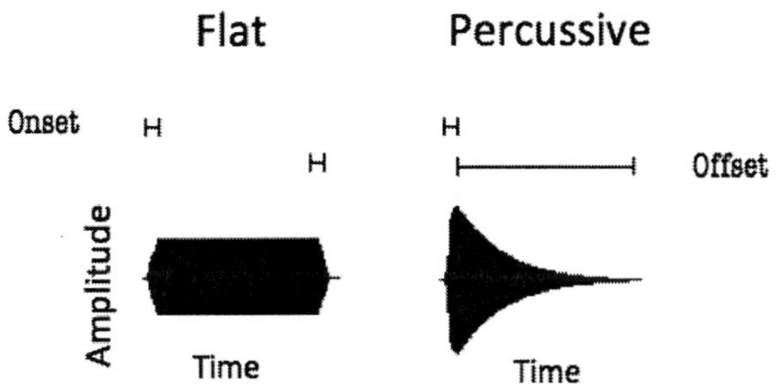

Figure 1. Examples of *flat* (left) and *percussive* (right) tones used in previous experiments [1, 2]. *Flat* tones are characterized by a quick onset, indefinite sustain period and abrupt offset. *Percussive* tones are characterized by a quick onset, followed by an immediate exponentially decaying offset.

This finding is surprising, as it conflicts with the widely held notion that visual information does not affect auditory judgments of duration [8] (although vision is known to affect other aspects, such as localization [9]). This finding has been replicated using point-light displays [10] and a single dot using simplified motion paths [11], suggesting that this discrepancy cannot be fully explained by the use of visual information depicting a marimbist rather than a more traditional visual stimulus. This observation led to our interest in exploring the degree to which this discrepancy can be explained by differences in the perception of sounds with natural vs. artificial envelopes. In other words: is this previously unobserved visual influence on auditory judgments of event duration driven by categorical differences in the perception of ecologically common naturally-decaying sounds vs. the artificial abruptly-ending sounds?

It is worth mentioning that previous studies have used tones with 'ramped' (i.e. increasing in intensity over time) and 'damped' (i.e. decreasing in intensity over time) amplitude envelopes to investigate the perception of streaming vs. bouncing of converging visual stimuli [12]. Overall, damped tones produced the perception of bouncing visual stimuli whereas ramped tones produced the perception of bouncing and streaming equally. This finding is not surprising, as impact events do not typically produce sounds with ramped temporal structures and therefore should not integrate with the visual stimuli. Likewise, if we attempted to replicate this experiment using *flat* and percussive tones, we would expect fewer 'bounce' responses for *flat* tones as *flat* temporal structures are not indicative of an impact event.

1.3 Duration judgment strategies

Intriguingly, differences in the outcomes of perceptual tasks involving *flat* and *percussive* tones are not limited to sensory integration. Other members of our team have found evidence for the use of different strategies when estimating the duration of *flat* vs. *percussive* tones [2]. With *flat* tones participants are able to use what we call a 'marker strategy', marking the onset and offset of a tone to derive the duration. Consistent with the pacemaker-accumulator model [13], participants may be neurally tracking the accumulation of time-markers between the onset and offset of *flat* tones. Such approaches are ill-suited to frequently encountered *percussive* tones, where we suspect participants might use what we refer to as a 'prediction strategy' in which an estimation of the moment of tone completion can be derived by the rate of offset decay.

When we presented these two types of tones uniformly blocked, we found no difference in the precision of duration judgments, suggesting that participants could easily adopt one strategy over the other. However, when we mixed *flat* and *percussive* tones within a block, participants performed significantly worse on duration estimations of *percussive* tones. In other words, when participants are unable to predict what tone type will be presented in the next trial, they cannot select the optimal strategy. Instead, participants presumably resorted to the 'marker strategy' – a viable but less optimal tactic for estimating the duration of decaying *percussive* tones.

These findings of perceptual differences in both audiovisual integration and tone duration estimation tasks raises the question of whether we process sounds with *percussive* temporal structures in a categorically different way than the *flat* tones commonly used in a research setting. Together, this work (along with other differences observed between *percussive* and *flat* tones in an associative memory task [14]) motivated us to explore the temporal structure of sounds used in auditory perception research. As part of a large-scale effort by several members of our research team, here we surveyed the sounds in one prominent journal, in order to determine the relative prevalence of *flat* vs. *percussive* tones.

2. METHOD

We chose to use *Attention, Perception, & Psychophysics* (formerly *Perception & Psychophysics*) as the basis for our survey, with the intention of selecting roughly one hundred articles focused on human perception of non-speech sounds. Searching *PsycInfo* using the terms '*Perception & Psychophysics*' (Publication), 'Auditory' (Identifier/Key Word) and NOT 'Speech', 'Language', 'Phonetic' and 'Dialect' (Identifiers/Key Words) yielded 422 articles. From this pool we composed our sample by selecting the first two articles from each year of the publication (1966-2012), for a total of 94 articles.

Article	Experiment Num	Sound categories	Functional category	Point weighting	Envelope category
Radeau & Bertelson, 1978 [16]	1	1	stimulus	1.0	percussive
Shinn-Cunnigham, 2000 [17]	1	1	target	1.0	click train
Five experiments, each using	2		target	1.0	click train
a single type of sound	3		target	1.0	click train
	4		target	1.0	click train
	5		target	1.0	click train
Boltz, Mashburn, Jones & Johnson, 1985 [18]	1	2	stimulus	0.5	flat
Two experiments, each using	1		warning tone	0.5	not specified
two types of sounds	2	2	stimulus	0.5	flat
	2		warning tone	0.5	not specified
Stilp, Alexander, Keifte & Kluender, 2010 [19]	1	3	target A	0.33	other
Two experiments, each using	1		target B	0.33	other
three types of sounds	1		precursor	0.33	not specified
	2	3	target A	0.33	other
	2		target B	0.33	other
	2		precursor	0.33	not specified

Table 1. Each experiment received a single point, which we distributed equally amongst the functional categories of the sounds used.

We modeled our approach of sound categorization after an earlier survey of articles in the journal *Music Perception* conducted by the MAPLE Lab [15]. As in that study, we classified only the auditory components and coded all experiments (n=212) in the 94 articles individually. We allocated one point to each experiment, subdividing based on the number of sound categories employed. For example, we allocated a point weighting of 1 to experiments using a single sound. If an experiment contained two sounds (i.e. a target and a probe), we allocated each sound category a point weighting of 0.5. If these categories contained multiple sounds, we split the category's weighting equally. Examples of point weight distributions are illustrated in Table 1 [16:19].

2.1 Categories of primary classification

We classified each sound into one of five categories: (1) *flat*, (2) *percussive*, (3) *click train*, (4) *other*, and (5) *not specified*. We classified sounds as *flat* if the description included a period of sustain with rise/fall times. For example, Watson and Clopton had a "550-Hz sinusoid, 150msec in duration…gated with a rise-decay time of 25msec" [20] (suggesting a sustain period of 100msec). Other examples of *flat* descriptions included more ambiguous descriptions such as 'fade-ins and fade-outs to avoid clicks' [21], which imply rise/fall times of an unspecified duration.

We classified sounds as *percussive* if they consisted of a sharp onset followed by a period of exponential decay. Although rarely explicitly described this way, *percussive* temporal structures are implied by the sound produced by certain instruments and/or materials. Therefore, we included studies using traditional percussive sounds such as cowbell [22], chimes [23], bells [23], and bongos [16], as well as impact sounds such as footsteps [24], hand claps [23] and objects dropped on a surface [25] in the *percussive* category. Additionally, we classified piano tones [22] as *percussive* given that they are produced by impact events (i.e. a hammer striking a string).

We classified sounds as *click trains* if they consisted of a series of repeated stimuli over a short duration. In most cases, these stimuli were explicitly described as 'click trains' or 'pulses in a train'. One study described its sounds as "a series of free-field acoustic clicks" [26], which we also included in this category.

The *other* category encompassed sounds with specified envelopes other than those described previously. This included natural sounds such as recordings of complex environmental sounds [23], and tones produced by brass and wind instruments [19, 23], as well as artificial sounds such as amplitude modulated tones [27] and 'pyramid' tones (i.e. with linear rise/fall times but no sustain period) [28, 29].

We treated our final classification of *not specified* as a 'category of last resort', used only when the information regarding temporal structure was insufficient to classify stimuli into one of the previous four categories. For cases in which stimuli were *not specified* in their description but available online, we simply downloaded the stimuli and classified them accordingly. In the current survey, one paper failing to specify the temporal structure included a link to a webpage containing the stimuli. Therefore we determined the envelope shape by analyzing these files [23].

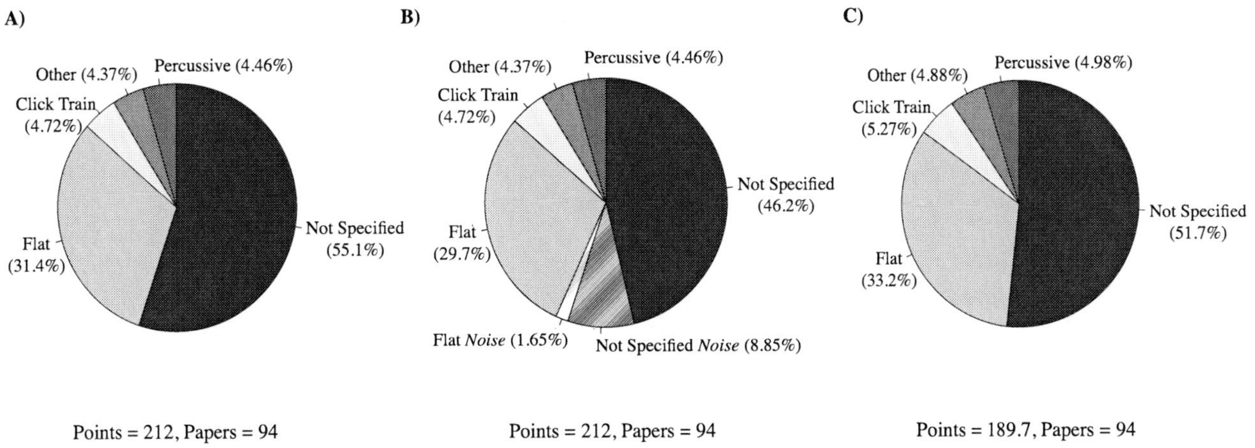

Figure 2. Distribution of the temporal structures of sounds used in *Attention, Perception & Psychophysics*, 1966-2012. Depicts the distribution of envelope types when (A) masking or background noise is included, (B) separated and (C) removed (note the smaller number of "points" included in panel c). Ultimately, decisions regarding the classification of noise do not meaningfully alter the results of this survey.

Amplitude modulated tones presented an interesting classification challenge. At slow rates (i.e. 3Hz) modulators can effectively change the amplitude envelope from *flat* to a sinusoid-like shape. However, at faster rates (i.e. periods sufficiently shorter than the tone's duration) the modulators are too fast to play a significant role on amplitude envelope. Only one paper in our sample used a slow modulation rate (3Hz [27]); the rest exceeded 20Hz. Therefore we placed the 3Hz amplitude modulated tones in *other* category, and classified the remaining amplitude modulated tones (with modulators ranging from 80Hz to 200Hz) according to the previously stated criteria.

2.2 Secondary classifications

In addition to our main focus on temporal structure, we classified other important stimulus characteristics such as the spectral structure, duration, and intensity. Additionally, we noted descriptions of technical equipment information such as headphone model and the model of sound generators so as to gauge methodological diligence. We used the following criteria for this supplemental information:

2.2.1 Spectral information

Spectral information included descriptions such as pure/sine tones, complex tones, white noise, amplitude modulated tones, etc. If an instrument produced a sound, we simply used the instrument name as gross aspects of their spectral structure are already well known. We used the category *not specified (spectral information)* when the spectral structure was not given.

2.2.2 Duration

Duration simply tracked the temporal length of the sound. In the case of *click trains*, we recorded durations in two ways: the duration of individual clicks (if given) and the duration of the train. We denoted descriptions of sounds that did not include duration information as *not specified (duration)*.

2.2.3 Intensity

We recoded the intensities of sounds in decibels, or if described as being presented at a 'comfortable listening level'. If insufficient information was provided regarding sound pressure level, we recorded these sounds as *not specified (intensity)*.

2.2.4 Equipment

As with the spectral information, duration and intensity, we recorded the make and model of equipment (i.e. headphones, speakers, tone generators and computers) given in experimental descriptions. If no information was provided, we recorded these as *not specified (equipment)*.

3. RESULTS

3.1 Fairly accounting for masking noise

We came across several instances where experiments made use of a target or signal in addition to masking or background noise. In these experiments we often found that the target or signal would be specified in terms of its temporal structure, but the masking or background noise would not. Mindful of the possibility of artificially inflating our *not specified* category, we plotted the survey data in three ways: including the masking/background noise (Figure 2A), specifying the proportions of background/masking noise separately (Figure 2B) and, removing it from the sample entirely (Figure 2C). As seen in Figure 2, these considerations did not significantly change the outcome of the survey. Therefore, all reported results are based on the full survey, counting all data points including background and masking noise.

3.2 Outcomes of classifications

As seen in Figure 2A, the majority of sounds (55.1%) used in *Attention, Perception & Psychophysics* fell within the *not specified* category in terms of their temporal structure. This finding echoes the results of an earlier survey classifying the types of sounds used in the journal *Music Perception*, in which *not specified* also formed the largest category [15]. As in that survey, we speculate that many of the *not specified* tones actually have *flat* temporal structures. If so, then tones with artificial abruptly ending offsets comprise 93% of the experiments surveyed (i.e. *not specified, flat, click trains* as well as amplitude modulated and pyramid tones classified in the *other* category), with less than 7% of experiments making use of sounds with more naturalistic offsets (with *percussive* sounds making up almost two thirds – 4.46%).

This disproportionate focus on tones with abruptly ending artificial envelopes rather than sounds with envelopes more indicative of those encountered in everyday perceiving raises intriguing questions about the generalizability of this research to real world listening.

3.3 Specifications for the *not specified* tones

It is worthwhile to note that the lack of specification of temporal structure is not an indication of a lack of attention to detail on the part of the authors. In fact, within the *not specified* category 61.9% of studies specified another important acoustic parameter known to affect perception – spectral structure. Intriguingly, 66.5% of studies in the *not specified* category denoted the exact model of speaker (i.e. "Sony SRS-A91", "Harman/Kardon HK-195", "Acoustic Profile PSL 0.5") or headphones (i.e. "Sennheiser HD465", "Sony MDR CD250", "AKG-K270", "Beyer DT-49"), used for the experiment and 52% specified the precise model of tone generator (i.e. "Grason-Stadler 455C noise generator", "Hewlett-Packard 200 ABR oscillator", "Wavetek Model 116 oscillator") used to produce the stimuli.

These comparatively high proportions of specification with respect to spectral structure and technical equipment indicate that authors and reviewers frequently felt compelled to include in-depth technical information. Therefore the lack of specification of regarding temporal structure does not indicate negligence to detail, but rather demonstrates that temporal structure has not been previously recognized as playing a meaningful role in the outcome of perceptual experiments—or at least a role less significant than that of the specific model of headphone used to deliver sounds, or the specific tone generator used to synthesize a pure tone.

4. DISCUSSION

Previous work conducted by our research team has repeatedly shown that a sound's temporal structure has the ability to qualitatively change the outcome of perceptual experiments. In an audiovisual integration task, long and short striking gestures did not influence tone duration estimations when paired with *flat* tones. However, when paired with *percussive* tones, short gestures made the tones sound 'shorter' and long gestures made tones sound 'longer' [1]. Similarly, it appears that participants adopt different strategies to estimate the duration of *flat* vs. *percussive* tones [2]. When tones are uniformly blocked, participants adopt a 'marker strategy' – marking the beginning and end – to estimate the duration of *flat* tones and a 'predictor strategy' – deriving an estimation based on the rate of decay – for *percussive* tones.

Beyond perceptual experiments, we have also found differences in performance on a more cognitive task involving associative memory of tone sequences [14]. In this experiment we asked participants to associate ten everyday objects with ten short 4-note melodies that were either *percussive* or *flat*. The results indicate that participants not only learned the associations faster, but could recall significantly more object-associations when hearing *percussive* tone sequences.

These findings suggest that we process sound with naturally decaying offsets in a qualitatively different way than the abruptly ending *flat* tones. While impact sounds exhibiting naturally decaying temporal structures are pervasive in our everyday listening [3], these types of sounds have not historically been used in auditory perception research. Instead, *flat* sounds with artificial sustain periods and abrupt offsets appear to dominate psychophysical research on auditory perception. This survey helps to test our intuitions regarding a long-standing bias towards sounds with artificial envelopes by establishing a set of data capable of commenting on this issue of broad relevance to the auditory perception community.

As anticipated, the proportion of *flat* tones (31.4%) significantly outnumbered the proportion of *percussive* tones (4.46%) in the current survey. This finding differs from our previous survey of the journal *Music Perception*, in which the proportions of *percussive* and *flat* tones were almost equivalent (i.e. 26.9% for *percussive* and 27.6% for *flat*) [15]. This difference may be due to a larger focus on listening to natural (i.e. acoustic) sounds in the case of *Music Perception*, compared to a more psychophysical approach in the case of *Attention, Perception & Psychophysics*. Despite these differences, we did find that *not specified* formed the largest proportion of sounds within each journal. In the current survey, *not specified* in fact encompassed the majority of the sample – 55.1%. This is appreciably more than the 35% encountered in *Music Perception*. Therefore these findings extend our previous results, demonstrating that the general lack of amplitude envelope specification is not limited to a single journal. The degree to which this is a widespread issue within the field of auditory perception remains an open question—albeit one we are currently exploring by surveying other journals.

It is also worthwhile to mention that the exploration of the temporal structure of sounds is not a new idea. In fact, over the last few decades a small group of researchers have been conducting experiments that focus specifically on the perceptual differences produced by varying temporal structures. For instance, these researchers are finding that 'ramped' sounds (i.e. increasing in intensity over time) are consistently perceived as longer than 'damped' sounds (i.e. decreasing in intensity over time) of equal duration, when presented alone [30, 31] or accompanied by a visual stimulus [12, 32]. This suggests that the importance of amplitude envelope in auditory perception research is starting to be recognized and has great potential to flourish.

4.1 Further thoughts on the *not specified* tones

Due to the ease with which *flat* tones can be created and the control afforded, we suspect that many of the *not specified* sounds in the current survey are actually *flat* in nature. Working on this assumption and noting that *click trains* exhibit abruptly ending offsets, we suspect that 93% of sounds surveyed used abruptly ending envelopes (i.e. *flat*, *not specified*, *click trains* as well as amplitude modulated and pyramid tones within the *other* category) that may afford different processing strategies and lead to different experimental outcomes than would be obtained using sounds with more natural envelopes. In contrast, *percussive* sounds with naturally decaying envelopes are used in just 4.46% of experiments surveyed, despite their ubiquity in everyday listening [3].

Although we suspect the *not specified* sounds are in fact *flat,* it would be irresponsible to draw any strong conclusions based on this assumption. As this information was not explicitly provided, researchers attempting to replicate the reported results would not be able to recreate the described stimuli. This lack of specification with regards to temporal structure does not however suggest an inattention to methodological detail. Within the *not specified* category, there is evidence authors went to great lengths to rigorously specify important methodological details. For example, a large proportion (66.5%) of studies in the *not specified* category included the exact model of speakers or headphones used to deliver the stimuli – details that could arguably not significantly influence the overall outcome of the experiment.

Additionally, the spectral structure of the sound as well as other equipment details, such as the model of tone generator and computer, were commonly included in the descriptions of *not specified* stimuli. This attention to detail with respect to other aspects of the methodological and technical details suggests that temporal structure has simply not been recognized as a parameter that could inherently influence results.

4.2 Implications for auditory research and future directions

As a result of our lab's findings in audiovisual integration [1] and tone duration estimation [2] tasks using *flat* and *percussive* tones, we have reason to believe that temporal structure can be an influential parameter in auditory perception research. Given the sophistication of modern sound synthesis tools, we now have the ability to generate sounds with more realistic envelopes while still tightly controlling other parameters. Consequently, researchers are well equipped to assess our perceptual system with sounds paralleling those encountered in the real world. To help others interested in exploring these issues, we are now sharing the software we have developed to generate *flat* and *percussive* tones (Figure 1), which is freely available at www.maplelab.net/software. In the future, we plan to expand our survey to other important auditory perception journals such as the *Journal of the Acoustical Society or America* and *Hearing Research.* Ultimately, we believe temporal structure is a parameter with great potential for fruitful future research, and hope that our survey can help inspire interest in this under-studied aspect of auditory perception.

Acknowledgments

We would like to acknowledge financial assistance for this research through grants to Dr. Michael Schutz from the Natural Sciences and Engineering Research Council of Canada (NSERC RGPIN/386603-2010), Ontario Early Researcher Award (ER 10-07-195) the Canadian Foundation for Innovation (CFI-LOF 30101), and the McMaster University Arts Research Board (ARB) program.

5. REFERENCES

[1] M. Schutz, "Crossmodal integration: The search for unity" Doctoral thesis, University of Virginia, 2009.

[2] M. Schutz, G. Vallet, and D. Shore, "Exploring the role of amplitude envelope in duration estimation: Evidence for two strategies" Presented at Auditory, Perception, Cognition, and Action Meeting, Minneapolis, 2012, pp.7.

[3] W. Gaver, "What in the world do we hear? An ecological approach to auditory event perception" in Ecological Psychology, 1993, pp. 1-29.

[4] W. Gaver, "How do we hear in the world? Explorations in ecological acoustics" in Ecological Psychology, 1993, pp. 285-313.

[5] Acoustical Society of America, American National Standard Specification for Audiometers. American National Standards Institute, 2010.

[6] N. Vanderveer, "Ecological acoustics: Human perception of environmental sounds", Doctoral Dissertation, Georgia Institute of Technology, 1979.

[7] W. Gaver, "Everyday listening and auditory icons" Doctoral Dissertation, University of California, San Diego, 1988.

[8] S. Guttman, L. Gilroy and R. Blake, "Hearing what the eyes see: Auditory encoding of visual temporal sequences" in Psychological Science, 2005, pp. 228-235.

[9] C. Jackson, "Visual Factors in auditory localization" in Quarterly Journal of Experiment Psychology, 1953, pp. 37-41.

[10] M. Schutz and M. Kubovy, "Deconstructing a musical illusion: Point-light representations capture

salient properties of impact motions" in Canadian Acoustics, 2009, pp. 23-28.

[11] J. Armontrout, M. Schutz and M. Kubovy, "Visual determinants of a cross-modal illusion" in Attention, Perception & Psychophysics, 2009, pp. 1618-1627.

[12] M. Grassi and C. Casco, "Audiovisual bounce-inducing effect: Attention alone does not explain why the discs are bouncing" in Journal of Experimental Psychology: Human Perception and Performance, 2009, pp. 235-243.

[13] C. Buhusi and W. Meck, "What makes us tick? Functional and neural mechanisms of interval timing" in Nature Reviews Neuroscience, 2005, pp. 755-765.

[14] M. Schutz, J. Stefanucci, S. Baum and A. Roth "Name that percussive tune: Associative memory and amplitude envelope", Under Review.

[15] M. Schutz and J. Vaisberg, "Surveying the temporal structure of sounds used in Music Perception" in Music Perception, In Press.

[16] M. Radeau and P. Bertelson, "Cognitive factors and adaptation to auditory-visual discordance" in Perception & Psychophysics, 1978, pp. 341-343.

[17] B. Shinn-Cunningham, "Adapting to remapped auditory localization cues: A decision-theory model" in Perception & Psychophysics, 2000, pp. 33-47.

[18] M. Boltz, E. Mashburn, M. Jones and W. Johnson, "Serial-pattern structure and temporal-order recognition" in Perception & Psychophysics, 1985, pp. 209-217.

[19] C. Stilp, J. Alexander, M. Kiefte and K. Kluender, "Auditory color constancy: Calibration to reliable spectral properties across nonspeech context and targets" in Attention, Perception & Psychophysics, 2010, pp. 470-480.

[20] C. Watson and B. Clopton, "Motivated changes of auditory sensitivity in a simple detection task" in Perception & Psychophysics, 1969, pp. 281-287.

[21] P. Bertelson, J. Vroomen, B de Gelder and J. Driver, "The ventriloquist effect does not depend on the direction of deliberate visual attention" in Perception & Psychophysics, 2000, pp. 321-332.

[22] P. Pfordresher and C Plamer, "Effect of hearing the past, present, or future during music performance" in Perception & Psychophysics, 2006, pp. 362-376.

[23] M. Gregg and A. Samuel, "The importance of semantics in auditory representations" in Attention, Perception & Psychophysics, 2009, pp. 607-619.

[24] R. Pastore, J. Flint, J. Gaston and M. Solomon, "Auditory event perception: The source-perception loop for posture in human gait" in Perception & Psychophysics, 2008, pp. 13-29.

[25] M. Grassi, "Do we hear size or sound? Balls dropped on plates" in Perception & Psychophysics, 2005, pp. 274-284.

[26] W. Uttal and P. Smith, "Contralateral and heteromodal interaction effects in somatosensation: Do they exist?" in Perception & Psychophysics, 1967, pp. 363-368.

[27] L. Riecke, A van Opstal and E Formisano, " The auditory continuity illusion: A parametric investigation and filter model" in Perception & Psychophysics, 2008, pp. 1-12.

[28] B. Wright and M. Fitzgerald, "The time course of attention in a simple auditory detection task" in Perception & Psychophysics, 2004, pp. 508-516.

[29] E. Hasuo, Y. Nakajima, S, Osawa and H. Fujishima, "Effect of temporal shapes of sound markers on the perception of interonset intervals" in Attention, Perception & Psychophysics, 2012, pp. 430-445.

[30] R. Schlauch, D. Ries and J. Di Giovanni, "Duration Discrimination and subjective duration for ramped and damped sounds" in Journal of the Acoustical Society of America, 2001, pp. 2880-2887.

[31] M. Grassi and C. Darwin, "The subjective duration of ramped and damped sounds" in Perception & Psychophysics, 2006, pp. 1382-1392.

[32] J. Neuhoff, "Perceptual bias for rising tones" in Nature, 1998, pp. 123-124.

Modeling of Melodic Rhythm Based on Entropy toward Creating Expectation and Emotion

Hidefumi Ohmura
JST, ERATO, Okanoya Emotional Information Project, Japan, and Riken, Saitama, Japan
ohmura@brain.riken.jp

Takuro Shibayama
Tokyo Denki University, Saitama, Japan
takuro@mail.dendai.ac.jp

Satoshi Shibuya
Tokyo Denki University, Saitama, Japan
shibuya@rd.dendai.ac.jp

Tatsuji Takahashi
Tokyo Denki University, Saitama, Japan
tatsuji@mail.dendai.ac.jp

Kazuo Okanoya
JST, ERATO, Okanoya Emotional Information Project, Japan, Riken, saitama, Japan, and The University of Tokyo, Tokyo, Japan
kazuookanoya@gmail.com

Kiyoshi Furukawa
Tokyo University of the Arts, Tokyo, Japan
furukawa@zkm.de

ABSTRACT

The act of listening to music can be regarded as a sequence of expectations about the nature of the next segment in the musical piece. While listening to music, the listener infers how the next section of a musical piece would sound based on whether or not the previous inferences were confirmed. However, if the listener's expectations continue to be satisfied, the listener will gradually want a change in the music. Therefore, the pleasant betrayal of the listener's expectations is important to evoke emotion in music. The increase and decrease of local complexities in the music structure are deeply involved in the betrayal of expectation. Nevertheless, no quantitative research has been conducted in this area of study. We already validated that entropy in sets of note pitches are closely related to the listeners' feeling of complexity. Therefore, in this paper, we propose a model that is able to generate a melodic rhythm based on entropy in sets of note values, and then we validate the suitability of the model in terms of complexities of rhythm through a psychological experiment.

1. INTRODUCTION

Meyer pointed out that the deviations of expectations arouse emotions when listening to music [1], based on Dewey's theory that conflict causes emotions [2]. Narmour defined the relation between expectation and deviation/realization as the IR (implication-realization) theory [3]. Huron also proposed the ITPRA Theory of Expectation [4]. These research studies indicate that the deviation/realization of expectations could have an influence on musically induced emotions. In these theories, the generation and deviation/realization of expectation are defined as rules based on intuitive feelings; therefore, the theories are difficult to implement directly on computers.

Therefore, we propose a model to calculate the deviation/realization of expectation to be able to generate music automatically within a perspective. Deviation from the expectation of the listener when listening to music is brought by the partial or complete disregard of rules that were accepted in advance. This indicates an increase of entropy from the viewpoint of informatics theory because of its augmented uncertainties. These uncertainties have a commonality with the complexity in the optimal-complexity model [5], which illustrates the relation between complexity and pleasure. This commonality suggests the existence of a relation between uncertainty and emotion. Therefore, uncertainty could be calculated, based on the order of the musical sequence generated using entropy. The important characteristic of this research is the viewpoint that controlling entropy in melodies elicits emotions.

Generally, melodies can be described as sets of pitches and values of musical notes. Timbre is also one of the elements that indicate the characteristics of melodies; however, we used a melody-generation system that considers only the pitches of musical notes. In this paper, the model about the uncertainty of rhythm was the basis for the generation of rhythm in our melodies, while we focused our attention to the duration of musical notes that form the melody. Then we developed the system of melody generation and verified the appropriateness of this model by experiment.

2. MUSICAL CONSTRUCTION AND COMPLEXITY

2.1 Musical Construction for Musical Expectation

Based on Meyer's theory that emotion arises when the music deviates from the listener's expectations, Narmour proposed the IR theory, which treats the listener's expectation as an "implication." Two sequential notes have a specific relation, which creates an expectation or "implication" of the next note. The third musical note brings the "realization" for the "implication." If the listener incorrectly guessed the third musical note, then the music evokes emotion. We attempted to generate melodies by developing a system that produces the various pitch transition possibilities of two sequential notes with symmetry biases, which is a human illogical reasoning process brought on by human intuition [6]. As a result, this system, which is the core of this research, was able to generate melodies that can offer the listener musical coordination or musical unpredictability. Through these analyses of melodies, we find that the feelings of *unity* and *unpredictability* are closely related to entropy in expressing musical complexities, a similar close relationship could exist between melodic rhythm and entropy.

2.2 Entropy

The theories for musical deviation/realization of expectations are not appropriate for computer system implementations, because they are based on intuition and are not quantitative but qualitative. We propose a computation model of complexity to create musical deviation/realization of expectations so that we can develop an automatic system to create music that can evoke musical emotion. To substantiate the model of musical complexity, we use information theory [1], which provides the quantity of information to be delivered. Music elicits a listener's emotion with temporal structures of musical notes. By modeling the structures based on information theory, we can create music that can evoke emotions.

In information theory, when event i occurs, the amounts of information are defined as

$$I = -\log p_i \quad (1)$$

where p_i is the probability of event i. When n events occur with the probabilities $p_1, p_2, \cdots p_n$, the expected values are calculated as

$$H = -\sum_{i=1}^{n} p_i \log p_i \quad (2)$$

The value H represents the amount of information to be delivered, i.e., the degree of uncertainty and complexity.

3. PROPOSED MODEL

3.1 Creation of Melodic Rhythm

Melody is characterized by many factors, such as note value (duration of a note), pitch (frequency), and timbre (tone color). We developed a system that automatically creates complex melodies using the relationships among the pitches of notes. The entropy of the transitions between pitches creates the human cognition of complexity.

In this paper, we propose a model of complexity by adjusting the note value. The minimum rhythmic pattern is pulse-framed by a repeated arbitrary time interval, which is called a metrical structure. A pulse becomes a complex

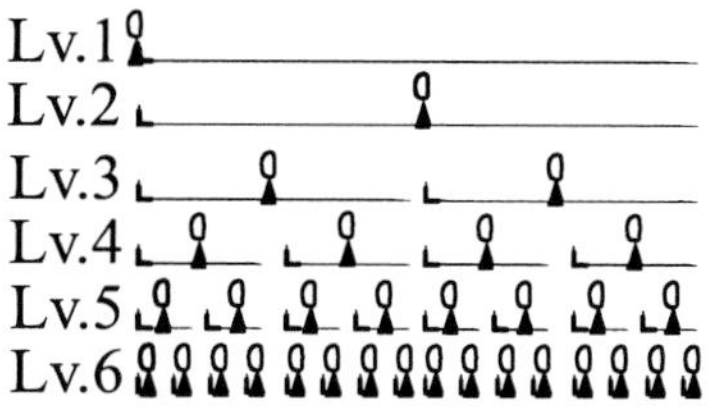

Figure 1. How to divide metrical structure

rhythm by extending or shortening the note value. To create rhythm, notes are positioned on a metrical structure, and their positions divide the metrical structures. Repeated divisions by a prime number can create various positions in a metrical structure. The typical number of division used in music is two or three. Five or higher divisions are infrequently used, probably because humans have difficulty perceiving such rhythms. For example, a quintuplet note or five beats are understood to be 2 + 3, and a septuplet note or seven beats are understood to be 2 + 2 + 3. Moreover, a rhythm with a mixed number of divisions is more difficult to perceive [8]. They suggest divisions by two or three to create melodic rhythm patterns. In this study, we only consider a division by two for the sake of simplicity.

Figure 1 shows the division of a metrical structure and the note positions at each level. Lv.1 includes a position created, but not a division. Lv.2 includes a position created in a division by one. Similarly, the levels Lv.3, Lv.4, Lv.5, and Lv.6 include positions created in divisions by two, three, four, and five, respectively. At four-quarter time, a whole note is set at a position as in Lv.1, and thirty-second notes are set at positions as in Lv.6. Although divisions greater than Lv.6 exist, they are not necessarily elements of a melodic rhythm, because sixty-four and shorter notes may not be perceived by the listener. Therefore, we use positions of notes from Lv.1 to Lv.6 only. In this research, a metrical structure consists of 32 positions, and the melodic rhythm is created by selecting these 32 positions.

3.2 Creation of Entropy

Entropy is calculated from the probabilities of selecting a position out of 32 positions. From Lv.1 to Lv.6, each position has a weight. A lower position has a greater weight than higher positions. The reason is that listeners may have difficulty perceiving notes at a higher position, because dividing a position creates new positions in the next higher level.

$$f(x) = \frac{1}{\sqrt{2\pi\sigma^2}} \exp\left(-\frac{(x-\mu)^2}{2\sigma^2}\right) \quad (3)$$

Table 1. weights and probability ($\sigma = 10$)

	Lv. 1	Lv. 2	Lv. 3	Lv. 4	Lv. 5	Lv. 6
x	0	12	24	36	48	60
w	9978	4855	560	16	1	1
p	0.647	0.315	0.036	0.001	0.000	0.000

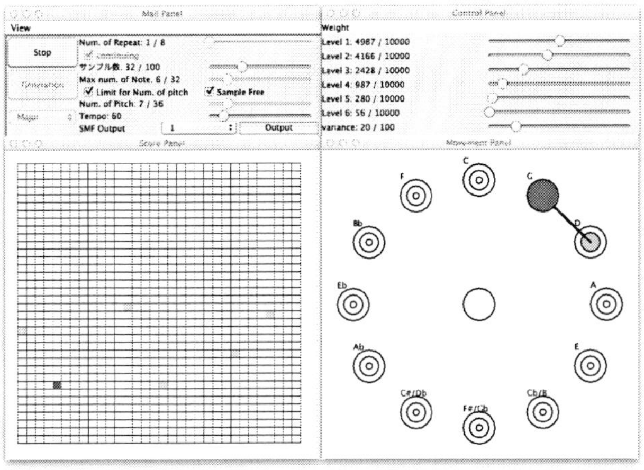

Figure 2. The application system with the model

This equation describes the normal distribution with the mean μ and variance σ^2. The division at each level is substituted for x in the equation. μ is 0. By controlling σ, we can obtain values such as the weights of each position. We calculate the magnitude of the weights as

$$w = f(x) \times 2.5 \times 10^5 \qquad (4)$$

For example, when $\sigma = 10$ and each x is set as indicated in Table 1, we obtain the weight w and the probability p as shown in Table 1 using (3) and (4). By entering these probabilities in (2), we get entropy $H = 1.115$. Melodic rhythms are created by probabilities, and our experimental melodies are introduced in 4.3.

3.3 Implementation of Model

We implemented the model in a system written in Java. The system can be downloaded from "http://emotion.brain.riken.jp/music/app/CMM.jar." It has an interface consisting of four panels, as shown in Figure 2.

The Main Panel, which is located at the top-left corner, has a melody generation button, a play melody button, a selector of identical metrical iteration counts, a check box for automatic continuous creation of metrical structures, a selector of the sample size, a selector of the limitation in the number of notes in a metrical structure, a selector of the number of pitches, a selector of the tempo, and the SMF output button.

The Control Panel, which is located at the top-right corner, has selectors of weights for each level and a selector of the variance σ. Although each selector of weight is independent, all weights are decided by selecting the variance.

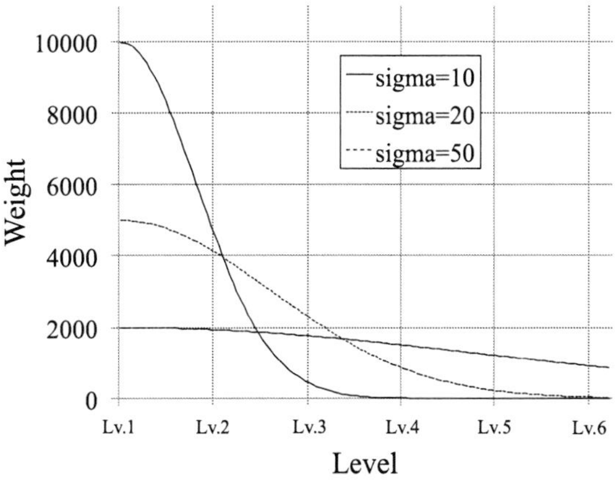

Figure 3. Three Gaussian curves for melodies

Table 2. Experimental parameter

σ	p						H
	Lv.1	Lv.2	Lv.3	Lv.4	Lv.5	Lv.6	
10	0.647	0.315	0.036	0.001	0.000	0.000	1.115
20	0.389	0.323	0.188	0.076	0.022	0.004	1.947
50	0.210	0.204	0.188	0.163	0.133	0.102	2.544

The Score Panel, which is located at the bottom-left corner, shows a melody being created as a 32×32 sequencer whose x-axis indicates time and whose y-axis indicates the pitch.

The Movement Panel, which is located at the bottom-right corner, shows the movement of pitch as a red ball in circle of fifths. A big circle means higher pitch, and a small circle means lower pitch.

The Device Selection Panel, which is hidden, allows the selection of MIDI devices.

4. EXPERIMENT

4.1 Experimental Purpose and Participants

The purpose of the experiment is to confirm that the listener can distinguish differences between melodies based on different entropies.

Out of 25 participants, five did not understand the purpose of the experiment: two participants assigned the same points to all melodies, and three participants compared the melodies with popular music. Therefore, we analyzed the data of only 20 participants (men: 11, women: 9; mean age: 31.57, SD: 9.11).

4.2 Experimental System

The experiment was conducted on a Webpage written in PHP and JavaScript. Each participant accessed the site with arbitrary computers. After listening to the melodies with players on the experimental Webpage, they ap-

Figure 4. Sample of melodies

praised the melodies by assigning appraisal labels. They were instructed to listen in a quiet environment or with an earphone or a headphone and to adjust the volume to a comfortable level.

4.3 Experimental Melody

We created melodies under three conditions ($\sigma = 10, 20, 50$), whose settings in a Gaussian curve are shown in Figure 3. Table 2 shows the probabilities and entropies of those three conditions. Melodies created from these three conditions were called Melody 1, Melody 2, and Melody 3. All melodies lasted for one minute and consisted of eight bars. Each bar in each melody had six notes. We generated at least 75 melodies, so that each participant listened to three unique melodies. Figure 4 shows a sample of the melodies at each level. The melodies were played for the participants in a random order to avoid order effects.

4.4 Appraisal Label

Participants were provided the following appraisal labels to identify their sensory perception of the melodies. The words in parentheses are abbreviations, which we used as appellative appraisal labels. Participants appraised the melodies on a five-point scale, where 1 is the lowest appraisal meaning they feel nothing, and 5 is the highest appraisal meaning they feel something strongly.

- You feel the rhythm. (*Rhythm*)
- You feel a musical unity. (*Unity*)
- You feel a complexity. (*Complexity*)
- You feel amusement. (*Amusement*)
- You feel positive emotion. (*Positive*)
- You feel negative emotion. (*Negative*)
- You like it. (*Like*)

The orders of the appraised labels were randomized for each participant to avoid order effects.

Table 3. Means and result of ANOVA *$p<0.05$, **$p<0.01$

Melody		1 ($H = 1.115$)	2 ($H = 1.947$)	3 ($H = 2.544$)
Rhythm	Mean (SD)	3.4 (0.995)	3.15 (1.137)	2.25 (1.020)
	ANOVA	$F(2,57) = 6.609, p = 0.003^{**}$		
Unity	Mean (SD)	2.85 (0.988)	2.55 (0.999)	2.05 (0.945)
	ANOVA	$F(2,57) = 3.420, p = 0.040^{*}$		
Complexity	Mean (SD)	2.85 (1.127)	2.65 (1.182)	3.55 (1.050)
	ANOVA	$F(2,57) = 3.262, p = 0.046^{*}$		
Amusement	Mean (SD)	2.8 (1.005)	2.75 (0.786)	2.85 (1.226)
	ANOVA	$F(2,57) = 0.479, p = 0.953$		
Positive	Mean (SD)	2.45 (1.146)	2.45 (0.887)	2.55 (1.356)
	ANOVA	$F(2,57) = 0.508, p = 0.951$		
Negative	Mean (SD)	2.2 (1.005)	2.1 (1.071)	2.45 (1.099)
	ANOVA	$F(2,57) = 0.579, p = 0.564$		
Like	Mean (SD)	2.2 (0.952)	2.6 (1.273)	2.4 (1.429)
	ANOVA	$F(2,57) = 0.525, p = 0.594$		

4.5 Experimental Procedure

The experiment was conducted using the following procedure:

1. Accessing the experimental Webpage with arbitrary computers.
2. Reading the experimental manual, and answering questions such as age and gender.
3. Listening to melodies, and appraising them.
4. Completing the appraisal of the melodies and sending the appraisal data.

4.6 Experimental Result

We analyzed the appraisal data for each appraisal label using ANOVA. Table 3 shows the results.

Rhythm, *Unity*, and *Complexity* showed significant differences among the melodies; therefore, we analyzed them using multiple comparisons (Bonferroni). In *Rhythm*, the mean score of Melody 3 is higher than that of Melody 1 (p = 0.003), and the mean score of Melody 3 is higher than that of Melody 2 (p = 0.180). In *Unity*, the mean score of Melody 3 is lower than that of Melody 1 (p = 0.037). In *Complexity*, the differences are not significant, but the mean score of Melody 3 is lower than that of Melody 1 (p = 0. 055).

Amusement, *Positive*, *Negative*, and *Like* have no significant differences.

5. DISCUSSION

5.1 Experimental Purpose and Participants

Adjusting entropy leads to variations of appraisal about *Rhythm*, *Unity*, and *Complexity*. Therefore, the model of melodic rhythm is validated by our results. The differences between Melody 1 and Melody 2 are significant, but that between Melody 1 and Melody 3 and that between Melody 2 and Melody 3 do not tend to be significant. The reason may be that the listener could not sense small differences in entropies but could recognize big differences. A threshold of feeling could exist, and we will examine that possibility as a future task.

The differences in the appraisal of *Complexity* are significant. One reason might be that the experimental melodies were only based on values, and the pitches of notes were random; therefore, other properties of the melody might have created the feeling of *Complexity*. It is also possible that value and pitch are not independent, but interactive.

Amusement, *Positive*, *Negative*, and *Like* are not affected by adjusting the entropy, possibly because emotion and liking are elicited by deviation/realization of expectation. In this paper, we proposed the model of rhythmic complexity, which could provide elements of deviation/realization. As a next step, we will implement these models.

6. CONCLUSIONS

We are developing a system that automatically creates melody based on deviation/realization of musical expectations. In this paper, we proposed the model of melodic rhythm based on entropy, and we verified that the model can provide musical complexity, which is one of the musical elements that elicit emotions.

7. REFERENCES

[1] L. B. Meyer, "Emotion and meaning in music," University of Chicago Press, 1956.

[2] J. Dewey, "The theory of emotion: I: Emotional attitude," Psychological Review, Vol.1, No. 6, pp. 553–569, 1894.

[3] E. Narmour, "The analysis and cognition of basic melodic structures," University of Chicago Press, 1990.

[4] D. Huron, "Sweet anticipation: Music and the psychology of expectation," MIT Press, 2006.

[5] D. E. Berlyne, "Aesthetics and psychobiology," Appleton Century Crofts, 1971.

[6] H. Ohmura, T. Shibayama, T. Takahashi, T. Shibuya, K. Furukawa, and K. Okanoya, "Melody Generation System Based on Generalization by Human Causal Intuition," Proceeding of SICE Annual Conference 2012, pp. 2005–2010, 2012.

[7] C. E. Shannon, "The mathematical theory of communication," The University of Illinois Press 1949.

[8] P. Essens, "Hierarchical organization of temporal patterns," Perception & Psychophysics, Vol. 40, pp. 69–73, 1986.

Design of an Interactive Earphone Simulator and Results from a Perceptual Experiment

PerMagnus Lindborg
Nanyang Technology University
permagnus@ntu.edu.sg

Miracle Lim Jia Yi
Nanyang Technological University
miraclejoseph.lim@gmail.com

ABSTRACT

The article outlines a psychoacoustically founded method to describe the acoustic performance of earphones in two dimensions, *Spectral Shape* and *Stereo Image Coherence.* In a test set of 14 typical earphones, these dimensions explained 66.2% of total variability in 11 acoustic features based on Bark band energy distribution. We designed an interactive *Earphone Simulator* software that allows smooth interpolation between measured earphones, and employed it in a controlled experiment (N=30). Results showed that the preferred 'virtual earphone' sound was different between two test conditions, silence and commuter noise, both in terms of gain level and spectral shape. We discuss possible development of the simulator design for use in perceptual research as well as in commercial applications.

1. INTRODUCTION

One of the most common situations for music consumption today might very well be that of listening over earphones while on a suburban train or bus during rush hours. The acoustic performance of commercially available earphones is highly variable, and it is not clear to what extent objective audio quality measures predict people's preference in a given listening context. Portable audiovisual entertainment devices are increasingly popular and sales figures of earphones have increased exponentially within the past decade. According to *Cellular-news*, combined headphone and earphone sales in Southeast Asia went up by 7% during the first half of 2010 alone, and even more so in Singapore [1]. The growing demand is one indicator of the direction in which technology is changing lifestyle and habits in the early 21st century.

This is the background for a project to investigate the perceived quality of earphones. A questionnaire survey of listening habits of commuters on public transport in Singapore was conducted (N=94). Among other things, it revealed that people use earphones in a wide price range: from 'free' (e.g. included with player or phone) to several hundred dollars worth. Results showed a positive relationship between cost and perceived quality. However, we suspected a less direct relationship with objective audio quality, itself a multidimensional measure that would have to be calculated from acoustic features.

Fourteen earphones were selected, with characteristics typical of those observed in the survey findings, and their acoustic performance was measured in studio. A controlled experiment with volunteers was designed to determine perceptual ratings of sound quality, as well as visual aesthetics, physical comfort, and perceived sound quality in conditions of 'lab silence' and ambient noise. To achieve a high degree of ecologic validity, we used in the noise condition actual soundscape recordings from a commuter train, reproduced at the SPL that was registered on-site.

1. AIMS FOR THE SIMULATION

To be able to make predictions of earphone sound quality ratings, we developed an interactive earphone simulator to be part of the experiment. The design was made in order to minimise bias and to let the person doing the ratings quickly find the preferred 'virtual earphone' sound in a given condition, i.e. in a noisy environment or in lab silence.

It has been shown that perceptual ratings of subjective features are correlated with loudness level. In a real-life situation, such as listening to music while commuting, the user adjusts for optimal loudness considering factors such as the kind of sound (e.g. music style), the internal emotional state and cognitive attitude, while taking into account the level of noise in the prevailing sonic environment. As a consequence, in an experimental setting, the user must be allowed to adjust the playback gain for optimal experience when shifting between different earphones. The trivial observation about actual usage also implies that SPL on its own is not a meaningful feature for earphone acoustic performance. Therefore, we hypothesised that frequency magnitude response and stereo image would be sufficient to describe earphone sound quality.

For the research project as a whole, several other acoustic features were considered, i.e. noise isolation, harmonic distorsion, and impedance matching, as well as non-acoustic features such as physical comfort, visual aesthetic, and price. The results are reported in [4]. How multimodal perceptual features relate to objective acoustic features is discussed in [9] and goes beyond the scope of the present text.

In what follows, we first describe how the acoustic measurements were made. Then, the design of an interactive *Earphone Simulator* and an implementation using the acoustic measurements. Finally, we report results from a controlled pilot experiment (N=30).

2. ACOUSTIC MEASUREMENTS

Table 1 lists the selection of 14 commercially available earphones, representative of those typically used by commuters on buses and trains in Singapore. Purchase prices were in a range from zero ('free') to around 400 USD. Four use buds placed in the outer ear, and ten use in-ear buds of different shape and material, such as foam, smooth silicon, and 'tree' shaped silicon.

1. Procedure

Measurements were made in accordance with best practices as in [6]. Impulse-response recordings were conducted in an acoustically isolated sound booth. A time-smoothed impulse or 'swept sine wave' (logarithmic, 30 seconds) was generated. The frequency range 12...22050 Hz was chosen in order to cover the defined range of Bark bands. Recall that the lower limit of band 1 is 50 Hz, and the higher limit of band 24 is 15500 Hz. The chirp was played back via a sound card (*Echo AudioFire4*) through one earphone at a time, with earbuds fitted in left and right pinnae of a manikin head (*Neumann KU100*). Left and right responses were captured by built-in reference microphones. A total of 33 stereo recordings were made of the 14 earphones, with left-right swapping of earphone buds in the manikin pinnae to minimise any bias introduced by frequency response mismatch between the microphones. Custom software developed in *Max* (*Cycling'74*) was then used to calculate each channel's energy content in 24 Bark bands [2], [3]. Plots of the earphone responses in units of Bark band are shown in Figure 1.

2. Results

Numerous features of the profiles were investigated before a parsimonious set of features could be settled upon. Seven measures of frequency magnitude response were calculated on the response averaged across left and right channels. Note that the relation between levels in broad Bark band regions and the total SPL is a measure of spectral shape. Means were calculated on amplitude, i.e. linear pressure equivalent, while slope was calculated on levels expressed on a decibel scale [5].

- *BB_pki* = index for the Bark band with highest level;
- *SPL_low* = mean of Bark bands 1...8 minus total SPL;
- *SPL_mid* = mean of bands 9...16 minus total SPL;
- *SPL_high* = mean of bands 17...24 minus total SPL;
- *R_low* = regression slope (Pearson's *r*) of bands 1...8;
- *R_mid* = slope of bands 9...16; and
- *R_high* = slope of bands 17...24.

Four measures of left/right channel matching were calculated on the separate response of left and right channel. Note that the correlation *r* between responses was considered but not included in the final selection.

- *ChD_rms* = root mean square of channel differences;
- *ChD_low* = RMS of differences in bands 1...8;
- *ChD_mid* = RMS of differences in bands 9...16; and
- *ChD_high* = RMS of differences in bands 17...24.

Numeric values for these measures are listed in Table 1.

3. Analysis

The interrelationships of the features were investigated with a Principal Component Analysis approach. The first two components together explain 66.2% of the variability in the data. The original solution was rotated so as produce two derived dimensions whose meaning could easily be interpreted. The first axis, explaining 43.0%, describes *Spectral Shape*: low values correspond to earphones with 'boomy' sound, and high values to those with 'brighter' character. The second axis, explaining 23.2%, describes *Stereo Image Coherence*: low values mean that left and right channels have differing Bark band profiles, and high values that responses are closely matching. Each earphone thus occupies a position in a plane with orthogonal axes. Figure 2 shows a biplot of the rotated PCA.

3. AN EARPHONE SIMULATOR

A software simulation was designed to enable participants in the ensuing perceptual experiment to interactively select their preferred 'virtual earphone' sound.

1. Interpolation space

Each of the 14 measured earphones is represented by an {x, y} position, or node, in the plane with axes corresponding to *Spatial Shape* and *Stereo Image Coherence*, i.e. the two rotated PC dimensions. The Bark band left/right profiles of an intermediate point in this plane can be estimated as a linear interpolation of values from two or more fixed positions weighted by the inverse of their Euclidian distance to that point. The design was implemented in a Max patcher, using *FTM* [7] to store 51 values for each earphone, i.e. name, PC-derived position, and measured frequency response levels in 24 Bark bands per channel. The size of the region within which an earphone measurement contributes to an interpolation must be decided. Because the 14 measurements are not equally distributed in the plane we have defined, the size of the region around some nodes must be extended so as to achieve smooth interpolations and minimise non-covered space. A solution was found heuristically where each region is a circle with radius adjusted so as to cover the two closest neighbours and exactly touch the third. The interpolation space is visualised in Figure 3.

Table 1. Values of the selected acoustic measures of 14 earphones.

	BB_pki	SPL_low	SPL_mid	SPL_high	R_low	R_mid	R_high	ChD_rms	ChD_low	ChD_mid	ChD_high	PC1	PC2
A	15	-24.56	-5.88	-7.27	0.86	0.94	-0.84	1.66	0.99	2.50	1.03	1.86	1.54
B	15	-16.13	-5.79	-9.62	0.95	0.72	-0.92	5.37	6.83	3.54	5.22	0.89	-0.51
C	4	-8.41	-10.31	-10.04	0.64	-0.95	-0.93	2.58	2.84	1.65	3.04	-1.66	0.54
D	16	-9.51	-7.66	-11.99	0.41	0.37	-0.94	3.35	2.60	2.17	4.71	-0.59	0.61
E	12	-20.06	-4.04	-11.29	1.00	-0.07	-0.70	1.44	2.11	0.86	1.03	1.30	1.13
F	19	-9.42	-9.49	-9.72	0.71	-0.93	-0.64	3.70	4.86	3.66	2.01	0.33	-1.09
G	16	-19.36	-6.59	-7.45	0.99	0.95	-0.93	3.75	5.62	2.18	2.42	1.50	0.59
H	22	-22.71	-9.95	-4.31	0.97	0.99	-0.60	4.15	5.16	4.91	1.03	2.67	-0.33
I	1	-4.52	-12.41	-15.61	-0.99	0.72	-0.97	1.27	0.84	0.69	1.92	-4.03	1.85
J1	14	-8.90	-7.44	-13.29	0.64	0.82	-0.92	1.33	0.91	0.63	2.02	-0.51	1.69
J2	14	-9.86	-6.78	-13.14	0.98	0.47	-0.92	7.78	12.71	1.43	4.24	0.10	-2.48
J3	14	-23.32	-4.86	-8.86	0.96	0.88	-0.91	1.74	1.64	0.83	2.40	1.56	1.66
J4	17	-10.00	-6.95	-12.59	0.81	0.83	-0.97	4.03	6.55	0.67	2.31	0.14	0.10
K	3	-5.87	-9.53	-16.07	-0.72	-0.12	-0.73	13.23	10.20	13.31	15.61	-3.55	-5.28

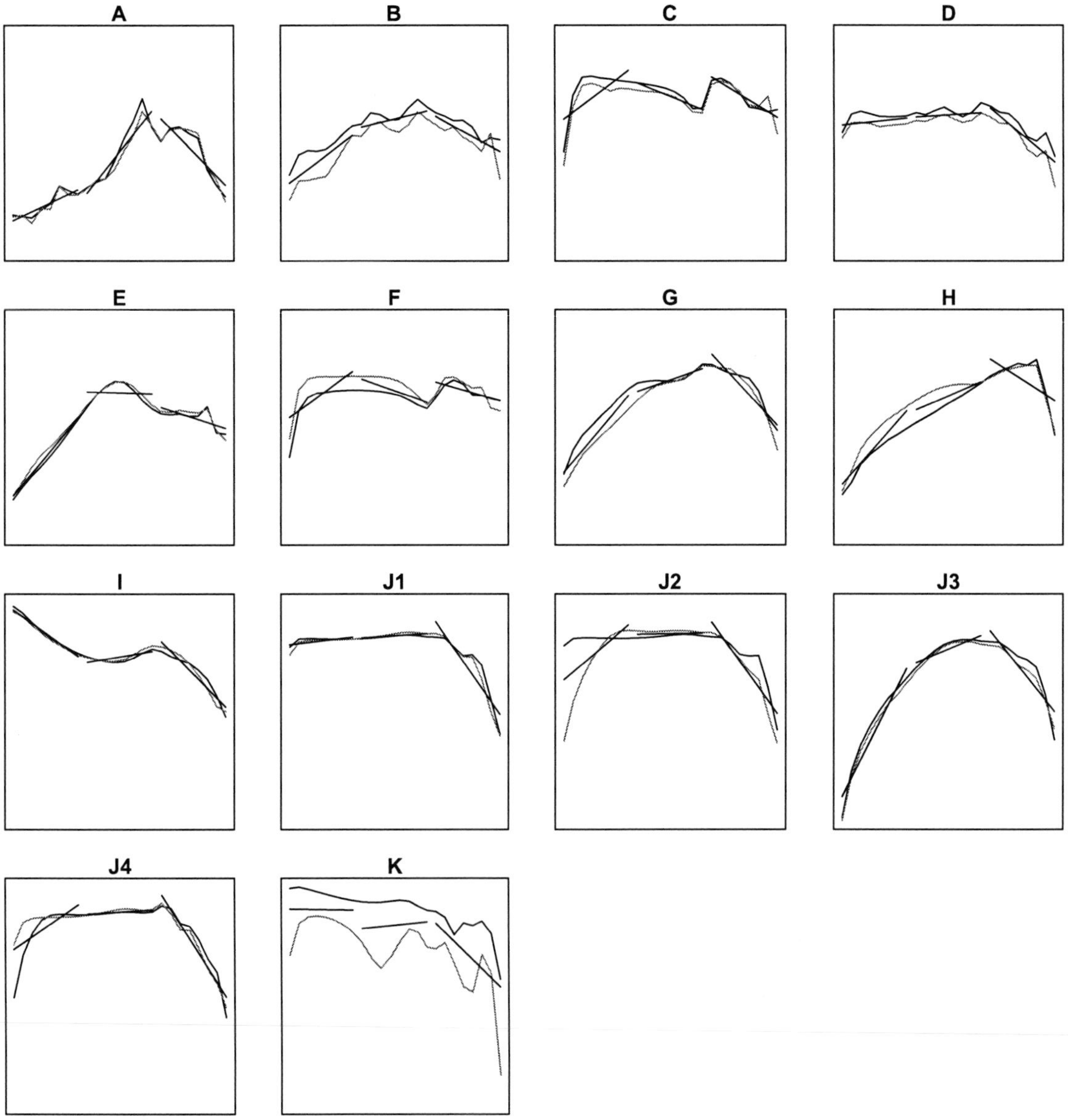

Figure 1. Averaged frequency responses of 14 earphones in 24 Bark bands for left (blue) and right (red) channels. Linear regression lines ('slopes', black) are indicated for channel average ('mono mix') in low, mid, and treble Bark band ranges.

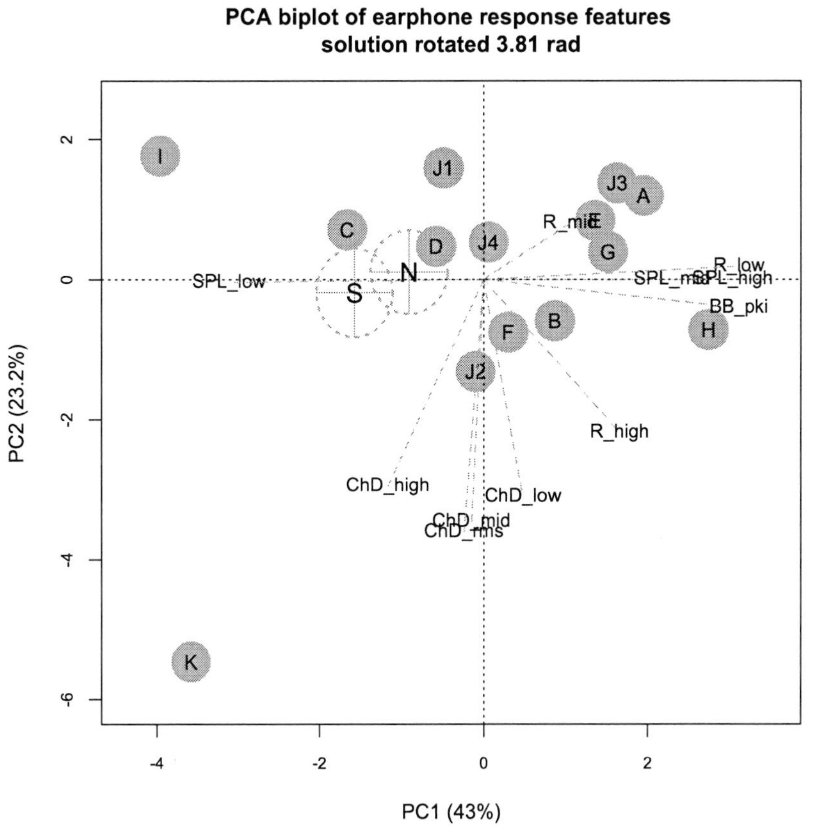

Figure 2. PCA biplot of 14 earphones where 11 acoustic measurements are projected onto a plane with axes *Spectral Shape* and *Stereo Image Coherence.* 'S' and 'N' refer to the preferred virtual earphone sound in *Silent* and *Noise* conditions (mean position across 30 participants, surrounded by 95% confidence ellipses).

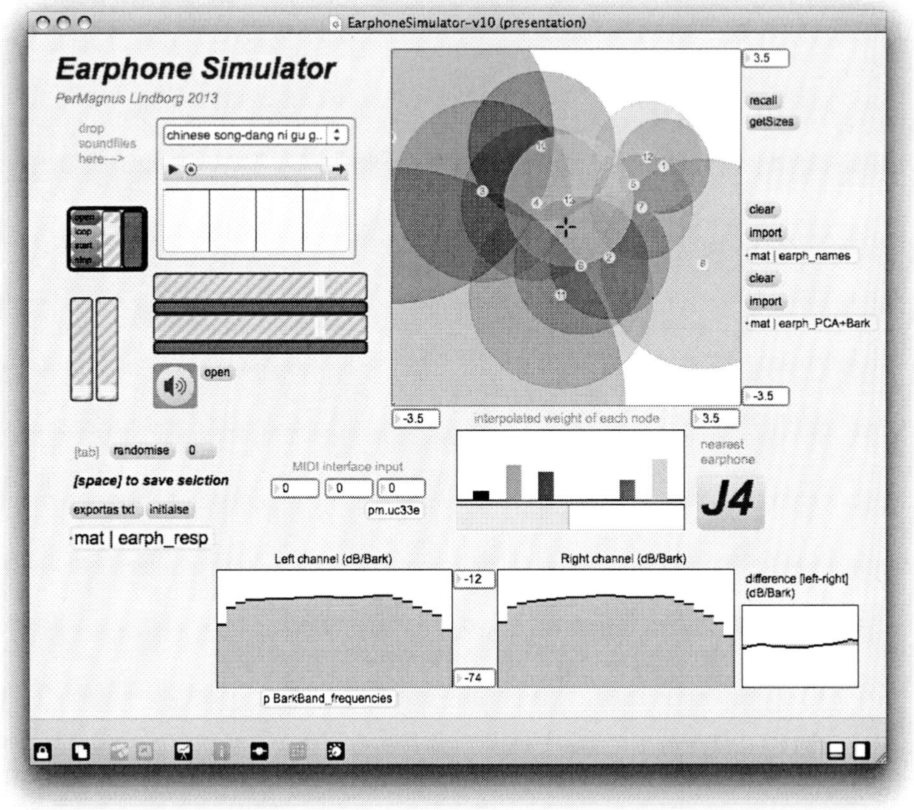

Figure 3. User interface for the Earphone Simulation. The square with the colourful circles corresponds exactly to the 2-dimensional plane yielded by the PCA. It is a visualisation of the space used for interpolation of Bark band profiles.

2. Slider interface

The patcher receives interactive input from three sliders of a USB MIDI interface (*Evolution UC33e*). One slider allows the adjustment of gain level, for reasons discussed above. The two other sliders are mapped to the PCA-derived dimensions, in a particular way. When using a physical input device to represent some perceptual dimension, there might be tacit assumptions such as "increased pitch goes upwards" or "increasing loudness goes rightwards", and so forth. Such 'cliché' mappings can introduce response bias. To reduce this bias, the design randomises slider mappings (input slider -> x or y axis) as well as whether sliders and axes are mapped straight, or mirrored. This gives eight different arrangements. Since the mapping is not communicated to the person doing the rating, she must inform herself through attentive listening while moving the sliders of the interface. For each rating stimulus, e.g. a sound excerpt or a new condition, the mapping is randomised. Further, in order to insure against 'lazy clicking' bias, the software verifies that a certain amount, i.e. at least 10 out of 14 nodes have been 'heard' (have been part of an interpolation), before a preference rating is accepted and saved to disk.

3. Filterbank

The interpolated 2x24 values, determining the Bark band profiles of the channels of a 'virtual earphone', are sent to a filter bank, implemented as a set of parallel 3rd-order Butterworth bandpass filters with centre frequency and bandwidth as in [2], [3]. The user can thus smoothly move between different kinds of earphone filtering, and eventually select what s/he consideres the optimal sound. In the experiment, reference earphones with a very flat frequency response were used (*Etymotic ER-2*). Compared to the commercial earphones that are simulated, these earphones can be considered transparent. According to the manufacturer, their passive isolation with 'shallow insertion'. Finally, the Bark profiles for the preferred sound are saved to disk, together with the amount of gain adjustment for playback level. The *Earphone Simulator* interface is shown in Figure 3.

4. EXPERIMENT

The software was employed in a controlled experiment, as part of a pilot research project to investigate several aspects of earphones [4].

1. Procedure

30 volunteers completed the experiment, one at a time, taking approximately 10 minutes of the test session. Participants received a movie voucher as a token of appreciation. The participant was fitted with the set of reference earphones (*ER-2)* and presented with the interface (*UC33e)*. As stimuli, songs were selected randomly from a collection that had been normalised in terms of RMS. The participant was informed that two sliders control "the sound" (but not in what way) and that one slider controls "the volume". There were two conditions, presented in random order. The 'Lab Silence' condition (ie. the sound studio) was measured at Leq(A, 60s)=39.8 dB, Leq(C)=65.4 dB. The 'Commuter Noise' condition, where a recording from the interior of a Singaporean MRT train during rush hour was played back at the level registered at the original site, was in studio measured at Leq(A)=75.7 dB, Leq(C)=82.6 dB. Hence the difference in ambient noise level between conditions was substantial. The participant's task was to move the three interface sliders so as to select the "best sound" for the given condition. They repeated the task 6 times or more for each condition, and were free to change songs at any time. As described above, the mapping of slider movement to PCA dimension changed randomly between 8 different configurations every time a new song was selected. This obliged the participant to listen out carefully for how the sliders affected the sound output. To sum up, three parameters determining the preferred virtual earphone were collected. They are here referred to as *Spectral Shape*, *Stereo Image Coherence*, and *Level.* The first two are identical to the {x, y} position in the 2-dimensional rotated PCA plane, described above.

In the first round (N_1=13) a procedure problem caused gain levels to be incorrectly saved. Serendipitously, screenshots had been taken of the GUI for all participants preferred setting in either condition, and in several cases for both conditions. From the latter, correct gain adjustments could be read directly, and for the remaining, reasonable estimates could be inferred with a conservative *ad hoc* method. As a result, *Level* values were similar to those in round two (very carefully registered), but because of the conservative estimate made, they showed a less pronounced difference between conditions.

2. Results

Means (on linear pressure equivalent where appropriate) were calculated for each participant and condition. A repeated-measures MANOVA with *Spectral Shape*, *Stereo Image Coherence*, and *Level* as dependent variables, and *Condition* as independent variable, yielded the results in Table 2.

Table 2. Main results from repeated-measures MANOVA of Condition onto 3 parameters of the preferred virtual earphone. Cohen's *d* uses the pooled standard deviation method.

variable	F(1, 29)	p	*d*	ω^2
Spectral Shape	7.32	0.0113 *	0.531	0.196
St. Img. Coherence	0.580	0.452	0.179	0.019
Level	11.7	0.0019 **	0.667	0.280

As expected, *Level* was clearly different between conditions. It was on average 4.2 dB higher during the noise condition, with 95% confidence interval {3.2…7.8} dB. The effect size was two-thirds of a standard deviation, and *Condition* explained 28% of the variance in *Level.* Interestingly, there was a significant difference in *Spectral Shape* between conditions. During the noise condition, participants preferred an earphone sound with larger ratio between higher Bark bands energy to lower Bark bands energy, i.e. *SPL_high* divided by *SPL_low;* see Section 2.2, and Figure 4. Given that the commuter train sonic environments (e.g. the recording used in the noise condition) contains a lot of low-frequency energy, music would be heard more clearly through an earphone with a high-frequency spectral bias. The effect size was slightly more than half a standard deviation, and *Condition* explained nearly 20% of the variance in *Spectral Shape*. For *Stereo Image Coherence* the difference between conditions was not significant.

In Figure 2 the positions of the optimal (preferred) virtual earphone sound can be seen, in both conditions ('S'=*Lab Silence*, 'N'=*Commuter Noise)*. Note that neither corresponds exactly with the sound profile of any of the 14 measured earphones.

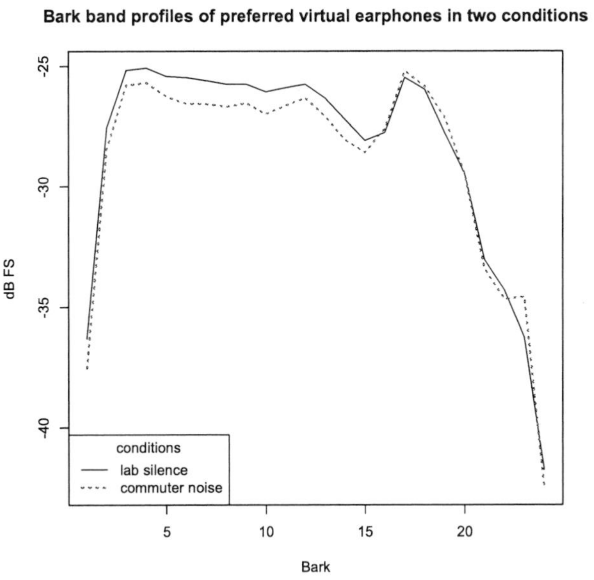

Figure 4. Bark band profiles of preferred virtual earphones (mean across participants). Blue line is in the 'lab silence' condition, and dashed red line is in the 'commuter noise' condition.

3. CONCLUSION

We have described a psychoacoustically founded method to analyse acoustic measurements of earphones and the design of a prototype *Earphone Simulator* software. A pilot experiment employing the Simulator showed that, in addition to (gain) *Level, Spectral Shape* was a useful dimension along which listeners differentiated their preferred sound under two ambient noise conditions.

One reviewer of this article brought to our attention recent work [8] by Rämö and Välimäki on software simulation of headphones in quiet and noisy situations. The authors measured the frequency response and isolation capabilities of different headphones. This is a highly interesting work that merits further study, in particular in regards to the reference headphone calibration method and the inclusion of noise isolation in the simulation software. We believe that the Earphone Simulator described in this article has features that are not described in their work, in particular the possibility to create a 'virtual earphone sound' by smooth linear interpolation between measured, real-life earphones and using a physical interface. One interesting avenue of future work could be to integrate the methods in [8] with those we have presented here.

We believe that interactive simulations enable certain kinds of perceptual investigation and that they extendable. Further development could aim to integrate all parts of the method here described in a single software, i.e. impulse-response measurements, PCA, interactive interpolation, and perceptual ratings. Such a software would be adaptable to various research design scenarios involving perceptual ratings of earphones, headphones, or loudspeakers of any type. It would also potentially be valuable in a commercial situation where a user needs to make an optimal selection within a set of loudspeaker options, depending on personal preferences of sound quality as well as other factors.

4. ACKNOWLEDGMENTS

The 1st author is the supervisor of the 2nd author's undergraduate Final Year Project. The work here reported mainly concerns the contribution of the 1st author and represents only a part of the research work undertaken for the FYP. We thank the anonymous SMAC-SMC reviewers for their valuable comments.

5. REFERENCES

[1] Cellular-news. (2011) "Increased Demand for More Sophisticated Headphones, Earphones, and Headsets". http://www.cellular-news.com/story/51102.php (April 2013)

[2] Zwicker, E. and Fastl, H. (1990, -9). *Psychoacoustics Facts and Models*. Springer-Verlag, Munich Germany (2nd edition).

[3] Loy, G. (2007). "Psychophysical Basis of Sound". Chapter 6 in *Musimathics. The Mathematical Foundations of Music*. Vol. 1 & 2. MIT Press, England.

[4] Lim, M. J. Y. & Lindborg, PM. (2013). "How much does Quality Matter? Listening over earphones on Buses and Trains". *Proc. ICME3*. Jyväskylä, Finland.

[5] British Standards Institution (2007). *Acoustics - Definitions of Basic Quantities and Terms*. BSi ISO/TR 25417:2007.

[6] British Standards Institution (2009). *Acoustics - Measurements of room acoustic parameters*. BSi ISO 3382-1:2009.

[7] FTM & Co. http://ftm.ircam.fr/ (April 2013).

[8] Rämö, J. & Välimäki, V. (2012). "Signal Processing Framework for Virtual Headphone Listening Tests in a Noisy Environment". *132nd AES Convention*.

[9] Lindborg, PerMagnus (2013, submitted). "Perception of soundscapes correlates with acoustic features and is moderated by personality traits."

How Predictable Do We Like Our Music? Eliciting Aesthetic Preferences With The Melody Triangle Mobile App

Henrik Ekeus[1], Samer A. Abdallah[2], Peter W. McOwan[1], Mark D. Plumbley[1]
[1]Centre for Digital Music, Queen Mary University of London
[2]Department of Computer Science, University College London
{hekeus,peter.mcowan,mark.plumbley}@eecs.qmul.ac.uk
s.abdallah@ucl.ac.uk

ABSTRACT

The Melody Triangle is a smartphone application for Android that lets users easily create musical patterns and textures. The user creates melodies by specifying positions within a triangle, and these positions correspond to the information theoretic properties of generated musical sequences. A model of human expectation and surprise in the perception of music, *information dynamics*, is used to 'map out' a musical generative system's parameter space, in this case Markov chains. This enables a user to explore the possibilities afforded by Markov chains, not by directly selecting their parameters, but by specifying the subjective *predictability* of the output sequence. As users of the app find melodies and patterns they like, they are encouraged to press a 'like' button, where their setting are uploaded to our servers for analysis. Collecting the 'liked' settings of many users worldwide will allow us to elicit trends and commonalities in aesthetic preferences across users of the app, and to investigate how these might relate to the information-dynamic model of human expectation and surprise. We outline some of the relevant ideas from information dynamics and how the Melody Triangle is defined in terms of these. We then describe the Melody Triangle mobile application, how it is being used to collect research data and how the collected data will be evaluated.

1. INTRODUCTION

The use of generative stochastic processes in music composition has been widespread for decades—for instance Iannis Xenakis applied probabilistic mathematical models to the creation of musical materials [1]. However it can sometimes be difficult for a composer to find desirable parameters and navigate the possibilities of a generative algorithm intuitively.

The Melody Triangle is an interface for the discovery of melodic content where the parameter space of a stochastic generative musical process, the Markov chain, is 'mapped out' according to the *predictability* of the output. The Melody Triangle was developed in the context of *information dynamics* [2]; an information theoretic approach to modelling human expectation and surprise in the perception of music. Users of the Melody Triangle do not select the parameters to generative processes directly, rather they provide input in the form of a position within a triangle, and this maps to the information theoretic properties of an output melody. For instance one corner of the triangle returns completely random melodies, while an other area yields entirely predictable and periodic patterns, the entirety of the triangle covering a spectrum of predictability of the output melodies.

In section 2 we review the concepts and ideas behind information dynamics, and outline the information measures that lead to the development of the Melody Triangle, which have been described in greater detail in our previous work [2]. In section 3 we describe how these information measures are used to construct the Melody Triangle, and how the triangular interface is used to retrieve patterns of symbols that are then mapped to notes or percussive sounds. The Melody Triangle has in previous work been implemented as an interactive installation and as a desktop application, these implementations are described and evaluated in [3]. In section 4 we describe the Melody Triangle mobile app for Android, which is the main contribution of this paper. We outline its features, how it allows users to share their settings with each other, and how it is currently being used to collect data for research. We then describe how the collected data will be interpreted to identify trends and commonalities in aesthetic preferences across users of the app, and to determine if parallels between these preferences and the information dynamics models can be made.

2. INFORMATION DYNAMICS

The relationship between Shannon's [4] information theory and music and art in general has been the subject of some interest since the 1950s [5–9]. The general thesis is that perceptible qualities and subjective states like uncertainty, surprise, complexity, tension, and interestingness are closely related to information-theoretic quantities like entropy, relative entropy, and mutual information.

Music is an inherently dynamic process. An essential aspect of this is that music is experienced as a phenomenon that unfolds in time, rather than being apprehended as a static object presented in its entirety. Meyer [8] and Narmour [10] argued that the experience depends on how we change and revise our conceptions *as events happen*, on how expectation and prediction interact with occurrence, and that, to a large degree, the way to understand the effect of music is to focus on this 'kinetics' of expectation and surprise.

Prediction and expectation are essentially probabilistic concepts and can be treated mathematically using probability theory. We suppose that when we listen to music, expectations are created on the basis of our familiarity with various styles of music and our ability to detect and learn statistical regularities in the music as they emerge. There is experimental evidence that human listeners are able to internalise statistical knowledge about musical structure [11], and also that statistical models can form an effective basis for computational analysis of music [12–14].

Information dynamics considers several different kinds of predictability in musical patterns, how these might be quantified using the tools of information theory, and how they shape or affect the listening experience. Our working hypothesis is that listeners maintain a dynamically evolving probabilistic belief state that enables them to make predictions about how a piece of music will continue.

They do this using both the immediate context of the piece as well as using previous musical experience, such as a familiarity with musical styles and conventions. As the music unfolds, listeners continually revise this belief state, which includes predictive distributions over possible future events. These changes in probabilistic beliefs can be associated with quantities of information; these are the focus of information dynamics.

In this next section we briefly describe the information measures that we use to define the Melody Triangle, however a more complete overview of information dynamics and some of its applications can be found in [2] and [15].

2.1 Sequential Information Measures

Consider a sequence of symbols from the viewpoint of an observer at a certain time, and split the sequence into a single symbol in the *present* (X_t), an infinite *past* ($\overleftarrow{X}_t$) and the infinite *future* ($\overrightarrow{X}_t$). The symbols arrive at a constant, uniform rate.

The *entropy rate* of a random process is a well-known, basic measure of its randomness or unpredictablity. The entropy rate is the entropy, H, of the *present* given the *past*:

$$h_\mu = H(X_t|\overleftarrow{X}_t). \qquad (1)$$

that is, it represents our average uncertainty about the present symbol *given* that we have observed everything before it. Processes with zero entropy rate can be predicted perfectly given enough of the preceding context.

The *multi-information rate* ρ_μ [16] is the mutual information, I, between the 'past' and the 'present':

$$\rho_\mu = I(\overleftarrow{X}_t; X_t) = H(X_t) - H(X_t|\overleftarrow{X}_t). \qquad (2)$$

Multi-information rate can be thought of as measures of *redundancy*, quantifying the extent to which the same information is to be found in all parts of the sequence. It is a measure of how much the predictability of the process depends on knowing the preceding context. It is the difference between the entropy of a single element of the sequence in isolation (imagine choosing a note from a musical score at random with your eyes closed and then trying to guess the note) and its entropy after taking into account the preceding context: If the previous symbols reduce our uncertainty about the present symbol a great deal, then the redundancy is high. For example, if we know that a sequence consists of a repeating cycle such as ... b, c, d, a, b, c, d, a ..., but we do not know which was the first symbol, then the redundancy is high, as $H(X_t)$ is high (because we have no idea about the present symbol in isolation), but $H(X_t|\overleftarrow{X}_t)$ is zero, because knowing the previous symbol immediately tells us what the present symbol is.

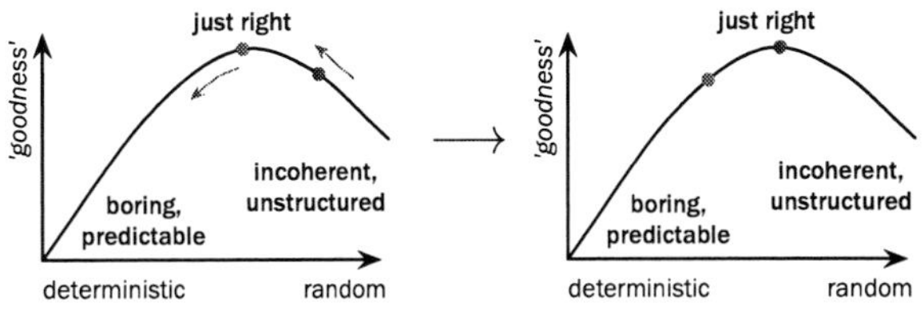

Figure 1: The Wundt curve relating randomness/complexity with perceived value. Repeated exposure sometimes results in a move to the left along the curve [17].

The *predictive information rate* (PIR) [2] brings in our uncertainty about the future. It is a measure of how much each symbol reduces our uncertainty about the future as it is observed, *given* that we have observed the past:

$$b_\mu = I(X_t; \overrightarrow{X}_t|\overleftarrow{X}_t) = H(\overrightarrow{X}_t|\overleftarrow{X}_t) - H(\overrightarrow{X}_t|X_t, \overleftarrow{X}_t). \quad (3)$$

It is a measure of the mutual information between the 'present' and the 'future' given the 'past'. In other words, it is a measure of the *new* information in each symbol.

The behaviour of the predictive information rate make it interesting from a compositional point of view. The definition of the PIR is such that it is low both for extremely regular processes, such as constant or periodic sequences, *and* low for extremely random processes, where each symbol is chosen independently of the others, in a kind of 'white noise'. In the former case, the pattern, once established, is completely predictable and therefore there is no *new* information in subsequent observations. In the latter case, the randomness and independence of all elements of the sequence means that, though potentially surprising, each observation carries no information about the ones to come. Processes with high PIR maintain a certain kind of balance between predictability and unpredictability in such a way that the observer must continually pay attention to each new observation as it occurs in order to make the best possible predictions about the evolution of the sequence. This balance between predictability and unpredictability is reminiscent of the inverted 'U' shape of the Wundt curve (see Fig. 1), which summarises the observations of Wundt [18] that stimuli are most pleasing at intermediate levels of novelty or disorder, where there is a balance between 'order' and 'chaos'.

A similar shape is visible in the upper envelope of the plot in Fig. 3a, which is a 3-D scatter plot of the information measures for hundreds of first-order, eight state Markov

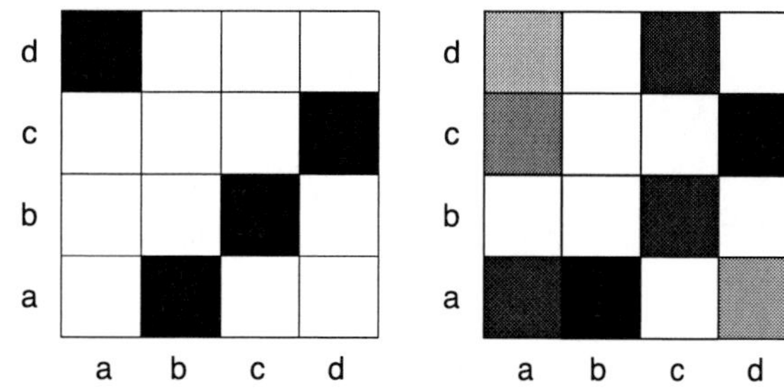

Figure 2: Two transition matrixes representing Markov chains. The shade of grey represents the probabilities of transition from one symbol to the next (white=0, black=1). The current symbol is along the bottom, and the next symbol is along the left. The left hand matrix has no uncertainty; it represents a periodic pattern (a,d,c,b,a,d,c,b,a,d,c,b,a. . .). The right hand matrix contains unpredictability but nonetheless is not completely without perceivable structure (we know for instance that any 'b' will always be followed by an 'a' and preceded by a 'c'), it is of a higher entropy rate.

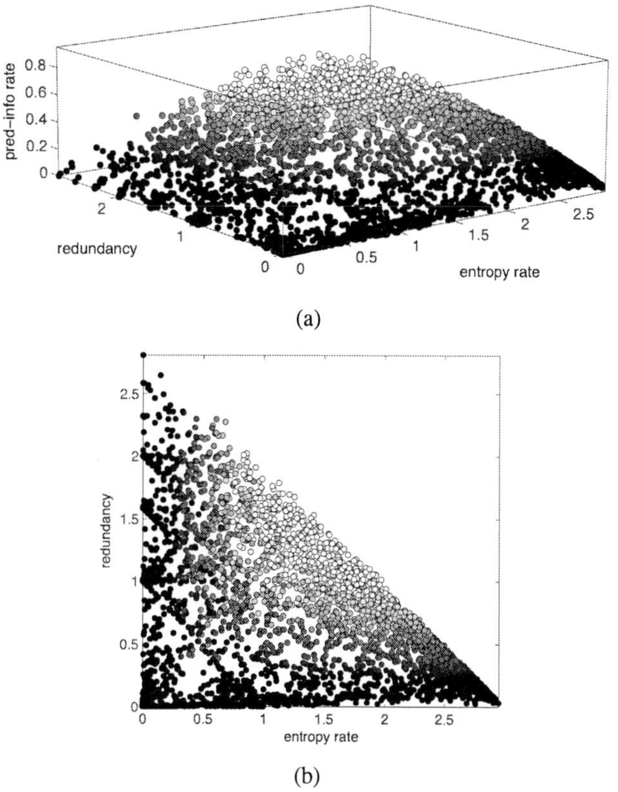

Figure 3: The population of hundreds of randomly generated 8-state transition matrices in the 3D space of entropy rate (h_μ), redundancy (ρ_μ) and predictive information rate (b_μ), all in bits. As can be seen in (a) the distribution as a whole makes a curved sheet, with the highest PIR values found at intermediate entropy and redundancy. Although not visible in this plot, it is largely hollow in the middle. As can be seen in (b), the same plot with the PIR dimension projected out forms a right angled triangle, this is the triangle which corresponds to the interface of the Melody Triangle.

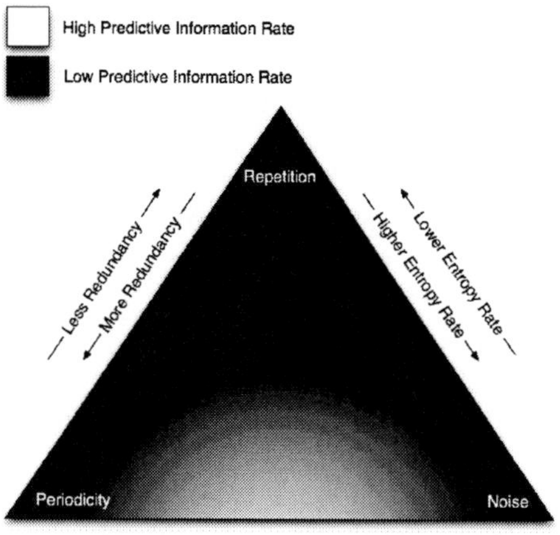

Figure 4: The Melody Triangle

chain transition matrices.The coordinates of the 'information space' are entropy rate (h_μ), redundancy (ρ_μ), and predictive information rate (b_μ). The matrices are generated by a hierarchical Dirichlet sampling method [19] to increase the probability of generating very sparse transition matrices, and get a good spread that reaches the edges and corners of the space. The points along the 'redundancy' axis correspond to periodic Markov chains. Those along the 'entropy' axis produce uncorrelated sequences with no temporal structure. Processes with high PIR are to be found at intermediate levels of entropy and redundancy.

These observations led us to construct the 'Melody Triangle'.

3. THE MELODY TRIANGLE

The Melody Triangle is an interface that is designed around this natural distribution of Markov chain transition matrices in the information space of entropy rate (h_μ), redundancy (ρ_μ) and predictive information rate (b_μ), as illustrated in Fig. 3a.

The distribution of transition matrices in this space forms a relatively thin curved sheet. Thus, it is a reasonable simplification to project out the third dimension (the PIR) and present an interface that is just two dimensional, resulting in a right-angled triangle, as can be seen in Fig. 3b.

The right-angled triangle is rotated and stretched to form an equilateral triangle with the 'redundancy'/'entropy rate' vertex at the top, the 'redundancy' axis down the left-hand side, and the 'entropy rate' axis down the right, as shown in Fig. 4. This is our 'Melody Triangle' and forms the interface by which the system is controlled.

3.1 Usage

The user selects a point within the triangle, this is mapped into the information space and the nearest transition matrix is used to generate a sequence of values which are then sonified either as pitched notes or percussive sounds.

Though the interface is 2D, the third dimension (predictive information rate) is implicitly present, as transition matrices retrieved from along the centre line of the triangle will tend to have higher PIR. As shown in Fig. 4, the corners correspond to three different extremes of predictability and unpredictability, which could be loosely characterised as 'periodicity', 'noise' and 'repetition'. Melodies from the 'noise' corner (high h_μ, low ρ_μ and low b_μ) have no discernible pattern; those along the 'periodicity' to 'repetition' edge are all cyclic patterns that get shorter as we approach the 'repetition' corner, until each is just one repeating note. Those along the opposite edge consist of independent random notes from non-uniform distributions. Areas between the left and right edges will tend to have higher predictive information rate (b_μ), and we hypothesise that, under the appropriate conditions, these will be perceived as more 'interesting' or 'melodic.' These melodies have some level of unpredictability, but are not completely random. Or, conversely, are predictable, but not entirely so.

Given coordinates corresponding to a point in the triangle, we select from a pre-built library of random processes, choosing one whose entropy rate and redundancy match the desired values. The implementations discussed in this paper use first order Markov chains as the content generator, since it is easy to compute the theoretically exact values of entropy rate, redundancy and predictive information rate given the transition matrix of the Markov chain. However, in principle, any generative system could be used to create the library of sequences, given an appropriate probabilistic listener model supporting the estimation of entropy rate and redundancy.

The Markov chain based implementation generates streams of symbols in the abstract; the alphabet of symbols is then mapped to a set of distinct sounds, such as pitched notes in a scale or a set of percussive sounds. By layering these streams, intricate musical textures can be created. The number of states in the generated Markov chains corresponds to the number of audio samples used, however the output of the Melody Triangle could even be mapped to non sonic outputs such as visible shapes, colours, or movements.

The information measures that define the Melody Triangle assume a constant rate of symbols, and thus the output sequences proceed at a constant, uniform rate. Although the placing of events in time and rhythm has a strong effect on expectations, surprise and satisfaction in music, the system does not, as yet, address this temporal dimension. Additionally the system does not address the culturally defined expectations of melodic structure that result from our exposure to tonal music; all symbols are considered equal, regardless of what note in a scale they are mapped to.

4. THE MOBILE APP

The Melody Triangle has been implemented as an interactive multi-user installation, as a desktop composition tool, and most recently as a mobile app for the Android platform. It was launched on 28th March 2013, and is free to download from the Google Play app store. [1] A description of the interactive installation and the desktop versions of the Melody Triangle, as well as some user trials can be read in [3].

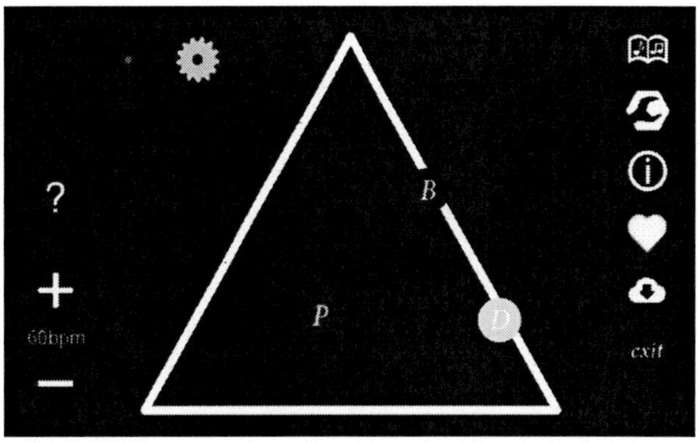

Figure 5: Screenshot of the Melody Triangle mobile app for Android. The letters on the tokens correspond to the instrument they are currently assigned to. P=piano, B=bass, D=drums.

To support the crowdsourcing of data, the app needs to provide enough musical variety to engage users. A simple implementation (with for instance, one single concurrent melody, at one single rate and timbre), would make data analysis easier and more straight forward, however the limit musical appeal would make it difficult to collect data from the public. In the next sections we outline the features of the app, describe how the data is collected, and how it will be analysed.

4.1 Features

As seen in Fig. 5, the app provides three tokens that can be dragged in to the triangle using the touch screen. It is with these tokens that the user selects the points in the triangle that will generate sequences, and thus three sequences can be played simultaneously. Each token can be assigned to one of three instruments: piano, bass, drums. The user can change what instrument is assigned to each token by pressing on the token's holder position on the top left. In addition to changing the instrument, the user can also change the register of the instrument; the piano has three octaves, the bass has two. Additionally the user can select the number of notes per beat, as well as specifying whether this token's notes should be delayed to come on the off-beat, allowing for syncopation between the sequences generated by the tokens.

There are also some global controls; the master beats-per-minute can be changed with the '+/-' buttons on the left, and there is an additional settings menu were the user can choose between the diatonic scale, harmonic scale or the pentatonic scale.

The mobile app is pre-populated with two sets of over 8000 matrixes that densely cover the triangular interface. For the diatonic and harmonic scale (and for the drums samples) the transition matrixes contain 8 states, and for the pentatonic scale 6 states. Whenever a transition matrix is selected by placing a token in the triangle, the symbol-to-note mapping is shuffled. This allows the same transition matrix to correspond to multiple melodies. One state for each of the matrixes is mapped to a rest, allowing for some

[1] The download link and some sample audio can be found at http://melodytriangle.eecs.qmul.ac.uk/

rhythmic variety and to increase the musicality of the output. When a user taps one of the tokens in the triangle it re-shuffles the symbol-to-note mapping while keeping the same transition matrix.

The current transition matrices, settings of each token and the global settings constitute the 'state' of the system. A user can save their favourites states locally as presets or share them with the world by pressing the 'like' button.

4.2 Collecting Data - 'Likes' and the Melody Triangle 'Radio'

Onscreen notifications encourage users of the app to press the 'like' button (the heart icon on the right of the screen) whenever they enjoy what they are hearing. When they do so, the current state of the system is stored and assigned a unique 6 character hash code, referred to as a 'song id'. The users are given the option to enter a username, or may choose to remain anonymous. This state is encoded into a small file and uploaded to our servers at Queen Mary, University of London. Geographical information is also stored.

It is possible for users of the app to share settings with each other. By pressing the cloud icon on the right of the screen, the user can type in any song id. When they do so the app downloads the state file from the server and loads the state on to the user's phone. Additionally the app can go into 'radio mode', where the users can quickly and easily audition other users' uploaded states. Upon entering radio mode, the app downloads a randomly selected uploaded state. An additional button appears on the interface, a 'skip' button, which whenever it is pressed the app downloads another randomly selected state. Again the users are encouraged (via on screen notifications) to whenever they enjoy one of the downloaded states, to press the 'like' button. This allows us over time to build a kind of crowdsourced ranking of the uploaded states, as more popular states get more likes. Users can modify downloaded states and then 'like' those, hence states can evolve from other states, and so any uploaded state keeps a history of previous states so that we may track their evolution.

To further encourage uploads and participations, there is a 'Hall of Fame' (see Fig. 6) available at the project website. It shows a list of the users who have contributed the most by uploading many states, as well as chart of most popular songs when 'liked' in radio mode.

In previous work [3] we attempted to carry out a lab study to find links between the information theoretic measures of the Melody Triangle and aesthetic preferences, however it quickly became clear that lab conditions were not practical to get significant amounts of data. The Melody Triangle mobile phone app provides an alternative means of collecting data, while engaging crowds with a unique citizen science project.

4.3 Interpreting Crowdsourced Data

By collecting many liked settings from users all over the world, it may be possible to identify trends and commonalities across these settings. A submitted setting contains all the information relating to the current state of the app, this forms a feature vector that includes the information measures of the currently playing Markov chains, the current note-to-symbol mappings, instrument/register choices, scale, notes per beat for every token and master BPM. Given a submitted state we can extract a number of additional features that are not explicitly stored in the data representing the state of the system, but that are implicitly available by observing the output. This includes the frequencies of notes and melodic intervals for each melody, and by looking across concurrent melodies, inter-melody intervals allowing us to extract harmonic information.

TOP UPLOADERS

Username	Number of Uploads
Anonymous users	96
BLUE	15
MRSPACEMAN	12
FFFFRED	9
HDC	7
EX	7
CONKI	4

TOP SONGS

Chart Position	SongID	Composer	Recent Likes
1	T31FFJV	EX	7
2	MW9PCSG	EX	6
3	TOEM3G8	*Anonymous user*	5
3	TMREXLE	*Anonymous user*	5
3	M7GEMIO	*Anonymous user*	5
3	TWQNOXT	*Anonymous user*	5

Figure 6: The Melody Triangle 'Hall of Fame' as of 9th of June 2013. The top list shows the most prolific users who have shared the most settings by pressing the 'like' button. The lower list shows the top ranked songs based on the number of 'likes' a state has received by other users while in 'Radio Mode'. The hall of fame can be found at http://melodytriangle.eecs.qmul.ac.uk/

We can look for clusters in the feature space to answer a variety of questions. For instance we can identify what the most common intervals are, both within a melody, and across concurrent melodies, and whether these correspond to the more consonant intervals. We can look for the average information values of the Markov chains, and see how these vary based on the number of concurrent tokens, the rate at which notes are output, or register for instance. We can see if the states that receive the greatest like-to-download ratio in 'Radio mode' have similar information properties to each other.

We are in the active state of research [2] and a full analysis is yet to be carried out. However it is already clear from data collected so far that the more 'predictable' half of the triangle (the half with lower entropy rate and higher redundancy) is preferred to the 'unpredictable' half of the triangle. Additionally it has been observed that the visual layout of the interface has an influence on the parameter choices; a number of states contain tokens lined up in rows or columns. Approximately 20% of states submitted so far contain only the drum sounds, and these may lend themselves to a more straight-forward information theo-

[2] As of June 9th 2013, there have been 173 submitted settings. The collected data is being made available to researchers at the project website: http://melodytriangle.eecs.qmul.ac.uk/data.

retic analysis as these are not subject to cultural melodic expectations.

Clusterings in the state-space of the data may provide us with the means to link the information dynamic models and its measures to aesthetic preferences. Additionally if we get enough entries, the geographical information may allow us to determine if there are any cultural differences between users based on countries or continents.

5. CONCLUSION

We presented the Melody Triangle; an interface for the discovery of melodic content where the input — positions within a triangle — corresponds to the predictability of the output melodies. The Melody Triangle is contextualised in *information dynamics*; an information theoretic approach to modelling human expectation and surprise. We outlined the relevant ideas behind information dynamics and described three key information theoretic measures; entropy rate, redundancy and a measure of *predictive information rate*, which describes the gain in information made by current observations about the future, but which are not already known from past observations. We described how the natural distribution of randomly generated Markov chains in terms of these measures lead us to design the Melody Triangle.

We described the Melody Triangle mobile app, a free app for Android, and outlined how it collects data for research by uploading the 'liked' settings of users to our servers. We describe the app's 'radio mode' that enables users to quickly audition other uploaded states provide feedback to form a crowd-sourced rankings table of most popular settings. Finally we outline how the collected data will be used to look for trends and commonalities in the uploaded settings, and to help identify any relationship between the information-dynamic model of human expectation and aesthetic preference.

Acknowledgments

This work is supported by an EPSRC Doctoral Training Centre EP/G03723X/1 (HE), GR/S82213/01 and EP/E045235/1(SA), an EPSRC Leadership Fellowship, EP/G007144/1 (MDP) and EPSRC IDyOM2 EP/H013059/1. The Melody Triangle mobile app was developed with QApps and supported by impactQM, funded by the EPSRC.

6. REFERENCES

[1] I. Xenakis, *Formalized Music: Thought and Mathematics in Composition.* Stuyvesant, NY: Pendragon Press, 1992.

[2] S. Abdallah and M. Plumbley, "Information dynamics: patterns of expectation and surprise in the perception of music," *Connection Science*, vol. 21, no. 2, pp. 89–117, 2009.

[3] H. Ekeus, S. Abdallah, and M. Plumbley, "The Melody Triangle: Exploring Pattern and Predictability in Music," in *Proc. Musical Metacreation (MUME), 1st International Workshop on*, Palo Alto, USA, October 2012, pp. 35–42.

[4] C. E. Shannon, "A mathematical theory of communication," *The Bell System Technical Journal*, vol. 27, pp. 379–423,623–656, 1948.

[5] J. E. Youngblood, "Style as information," *Journal of Music Theory*, vol. 2, pp. 24–35, 1958.

[6] E. Coons and D. Kraehenbuehl, "Information as a measure of structure in music," *Journal of Music Theory*, vol. 2, no. 2, pp. 127–161, 1958.

[7] A. Moles, *Information Theory and Esthetic Perception.* University of Illinois Press, 1966.

[8] L. B. Meyer, *Music, the Arts and Ideas: Patterns and Predictions in Twentieth-Century Culture.* University of Chicago Press, 1967.

[9] J. E. Cohen, "Information theory and music," *Behavioral Science*, vol. 7, no. 2, pp. 137–163, 1962.

[10] E. Narmour, *Beyond Schenkerism.* University of Chicago Press, 1977.

[11] J. R. Saffran, E. K. Johnson, R. N. Aslin, and E. L. Newport, "Statistical learning of tone sequences by human infants and adults," *Cognition*, vol. 70, no. 1, pp. 27–52, 1999.

[12] D. Conklin and I. H. Witten, "Multiple viewpoint systems for music prediction," *Journal of New Music Research*, vol. 24, no. 1, pp. 51–73, 1995.

[13] D. Ponsford, G. A. Wiggins, and C. S. Mellish, "Statistical learning of harmonic movement," *Journal of New Music Research*, vol. 28, no. 2, pp. 150–177, 1999.

[14] M. T. Pearce, "The construction and evaluation of statistical models of melodic structure in music perception and composition," Ph.D. dissertation, Department of Computing, City University, London, 2005.

[15] S. A. Abdallah, H. Ekeus, P. Foster, A. Robertson, and M. D. Plumbley, "Cognitive music modelling: An information dynamics approach," in *Proc. Cognitive Information Processing (CIP), 3rd International Workshop on*, Parador de Baiona, Spain, May 2012.

[16] S. Dubnov, "Generalization of spectral flatness measure for non-gaussian linear processes," *Signal Processing Letters, IEEE*, vol. 11, no. 8, pp. 698–701, 2004.

[17] D. E. Berlyne, *Aesthetics and Psychobiology.* New York: Appleton Century Crofts, 1971.

[18] W. Wundt, *Outlines of Psychology.* Lepzig: Englemann, 1897.

[19] Y. W. Teh, "A hierarchical Bayesian language model based on Pitman-Yor processes," in *Proc. of the 21st International Conf. on Computational Linguistics and 44th Annual Meeting of the ACL*, Sydney, Australia, June 2006, pp. 985–992.

A MULTIPITCH ESTIMATION ALGORITHM BASED ON FUNDAMENTAL FREQUENCIES AND PRIME HARMONICS

Arturo Camacho
School of Computer Science and Informatics
University of Costa Rica
arturo.camacho@ecci.ucr.ac.cr

Iosef Kaver-Oreamuno
Research Center for Info. & Comm. Techs.
University of Costa Rica
iosefkaver@gmail.com

ABSTRACT

An algorithm named Prime-multiF0 for the estimation of multiple pitches in a signal is proposed. Unlike other algorithms that consider all harmonics of every pitch candidate, our algorithm considers only on the fundamental frequency and prime harmonics. This approach is shown to work extremely well with chords made of intervals no smaller than a minor third. A test suite was created using synthetic signals of sawtooth, square, and triangle waves; major, minor, diminished and augmented triads in fundamental and first and second inversion, and spanning a bass range of three octaves. Experimental results show that our algorithm was able to detect the correct notes (after rounding to the closest semitone) for all the sawtooth and square waves in the test set, and for 99.3% of the triangle waves, failing only on very high pitch notes.

1. INTRODUCTION

The first attempts to solve the problem of estimating pitch in monophonic signals can be traced back to the 1960s, according to a review of early algorithms in [1]. More recent and successful approaches to solve the problem are presented in [2] and [3]. These algorithms can be applied to solve problems in speech coding [4], speech therapy [5], and music information retrieval [6], but they fail to solve complex music problems like transcription, which require estimating the pitch of concurrent signals [7].

In solving the multipitch problem, [8] and [9] are among the most successful algorithms. They both use an auditory model to split the signal in bands (notably two in [8]), apply half-wave rectification to generate extra harmonics, compute a generalized summary autocorrelation function (SACF), and process this SACF to obtain pitches from its peaks. In [8] the process consists in enhancing the SACF by setting negative values to zero and subtracting from the SACF stretched copies of itself to eliminate spurious peaks (notably the root of the chord). In [9] the most salient peak of the SACF is used to estimate the pitch of one of the signals. Then, an attempt is made to remove the recognized signal from the spectrum, and the SACF is recomputed on

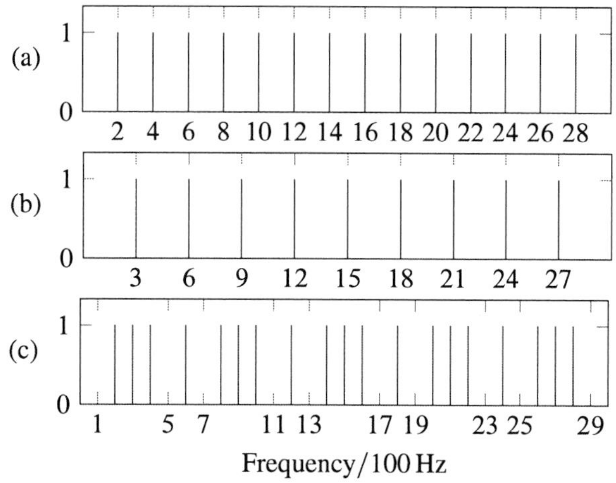

Figure 1: Spectral components of (a) a signal with fundamental frequency 200 Hz, (b) a signal with fundamental frequency 300 Hz, and (c) a signal combining both 200 Hz and 300 Hz signals. In the latter case, the numbers along the horizontal axis are the frequencies for which there are no harmonics in the spectrum, which would correspond to missing harmonics of a signal whose fundamental frequency is 100 Hz (the maximum common divisor of 200 Hz and 300 Hz).

the modified spectrum to recognize another pitch. The process is repeated for the other sound sources.

The approaches in [8] and [9] use a generalized autocorrelation function consisting in the inverse Fourier transform of the magnitude of the signal's modified spectrum (with extra harmonics), raised to a certain power. A closer look reveals that this function computes a score for each pitch candidate based on the number and magnitude of the peaks found at harmonics of the candidate in the modified spectrum. To illustrate the rationale behind this idea, Fig. 1(a) and (b) shows the spectral components of two harmonic signals with fundamental frequencies 200 Hz and 300 Hz, and Fig. 1(c) shows the components of the combined signal. The signals are assumed to be limited to a maximum frequency of 3 kHz (they are sampled at 6 kHz), which means that the 200 Hz tone has 15 harmonics and the 300 Hz tone has 10 harmonics. Based on the scoring schema stated above, their respective scores would be 15 and 10. However, since 100 Hz is the root of the chord (i.e., all harmonics are multiples of 100), that frequency would receive a score of 20, corresponding to the total number of harmonics in (c). The score for the (combined) 100 Hz signal would then be higher than the score for the individual tones, which would cause autocorrelation to fail at estimating the correct fundamental frequency of these types of combined signals.

In order to overcome this shortcoming of autocorrelation, a different approach could be used that gives credit to a pitch candidate based solely on those peaks located at its fundamental frequency and prime harmonics. Using this approach, the 200 Hz candidate would receive a score of 7 (for the components at 2, 4, 6, 10, 14, 22, and 26 in Fig. 1-a), the 300 Hz candidate would receive a score of 5 (for the components at 3, 6, 9, 15, and 21 in Fig. 1-b), and the 100 Hz candidate would receive score of 2 (for the components at 2 and 3 in Fig. 1-c), leaving 200 Hz and 300 Hz as the indisputable winners. It can be shown that, under this approach, no candidate can receive credit for more than one harmonic of any tone with a fundamental frequency larger than that one of the candidate, and that will be the approach used in this work.

The theoretical advantage of identifying tones based on their prime harmonics was identified by Klapuri [10]. However, he abandoned this approach on posterior works (e.g., [9]). Prime harmonics were are successfully used in [3] for the single pitch estimation problem. Surprisingly, some novel features proposed in that work, like the measurement of frequency using the Equivalent Rectangular Bandwidth scale (ERB) [11], the weighting of the harmonics as the inverse of their frequency, and the normalization of the kernel, did not work well here and had to be removed. Except for that, the algorithm proposed here is identical to that one in [3], with the only novelty being its application to the multipitch problem, plus the incorporation of an *enhancement* to the pitch candidates' scores proposed in [8].

The rest of the paper is organized as follows. Section 2 describes the proposed method, Section 3 presents and discusses the results, and Section 4 outlines our conclusions.

2. METHOD

The proposed method, named Prime-multiF0, works as follows. It divides the signal in windows, computes the spectrum in each window, and applies an integral transform to the spectrum to obtain a score for each pitch candidate. Then, negatives scores are set to zero and a subharmonic subtraction step is performed to enhance the scores. Finally, a peak-selection method is applied to detect the different pitches. The details of the method are described next.

To compute the score of a pitch candidate f, the authors of [3] recommend to use of a Hann window of size $8/f$. The use of this window type and size makes the width of the spectral lobes match the width of the positive part of of the kernel of the transform. This means that the spectrum of the signal at time t should be computed as:

$$X(t,f') = \int_{-\infty}^{\infty} w\left(8/f, t'-t\right) x\left(t'\right) e^{-2\pi i f' t'} dt', \quad (1)$$

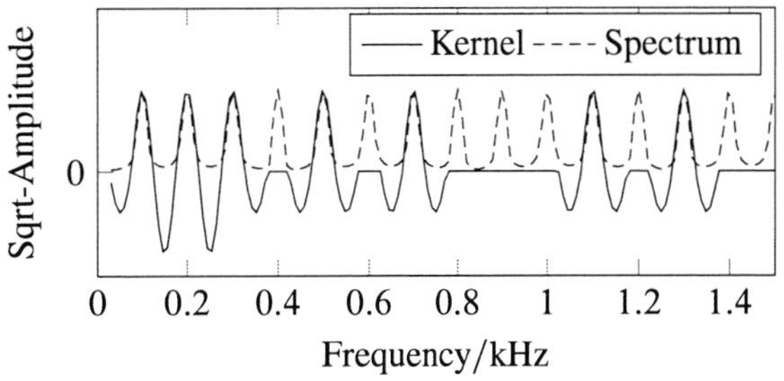

Figure 2: Spectrum of a signal with fundamental frequency 100 Hz and kernel that allows to recognize its pitch.

where

$$w(T,t) = \begin{cases} \frac{1}{2}\left(1+\cos\left(\pi(t'-t)/T\right)\right), & \text{if } |t| < T/2 \\ 0, & \text{otherwise.} \end{cases} \quad (2)$$

Then, the score of a candidate f at time t should be computed as the integral transform

$$S(t,f) = \int_{0}^{\infty} K\left(f,f'\right) |X(t,f)|^{1/2} \, df' \quad (3)$$

with kernel

$$K(f,f') = K_1(f,f') + \sum_{j \in \mathbb{P}} K_j(f,f'), \quad (4)$$

where

$$K_j(f,f') = \begin{cases} \cos(2\pi f'/f), & \text{if } |f'/f - j| < \frac{1}{4} \\ \frac{1}{2}\cos(2\pi f'/f), & \text{if } \frac{1}{4} < |f'/f - j| < \frac{3}{4} \\ 0, & \text{otherwise,} \end{cases} \quad (5)$$

and $\mathbb{P}$ is the set of prime numbers. Each component of the kernel has the purpose to give credit to the candidate if there is energy at its j-th harmonic. [1] This is illustrated in Fig. 2, which shows the spectrum of a signal with fundamental frequency 100 Hz and the kernel with same frequency.

Unfortunately, it is computationally expensive to compute a different Fourier transform for each pitch candidate. Hence, we adopt a schema to reduce the number of transforms computed, at the price of a decreased match between the width of the spectral lobes and the width of the components of the kernel. Under this scheme, transforms are computed using only window sizes that are powers of two (in number of samples), and the score of each candidate is produced as a linear combination of the scores obtained for that candidate using the two closest power-of-two window sizes. More precisely, the scores are computed as follows:

$$S(t,f) = (1-\lambda)\, S_0(t,f) + \lambda S_1(t,f) \quad (6)$$

where $S_0(t,f)$ and $S_1(t,f)$ are computed as in (3), but using the two closest power-of-two window sizes N_0 =

[1] The use of the square-root amplitude of the spectrum in (3) approximates the growth of loudness with amplitude [12], and the use of a cosine in (5) allows for inharmonicity in the signals. Both are explained in more detail in [3].

2^L and $N_1 = 2^{L+1}$ (in samples), respectively; and λ is obtained from N^*, the optimal window size (in samples) for a candidate f, with $N^* = 2^{L+\lambda} = [8f_s/f]$, where $L \in \mathbb{N}, 0 \le \lambda < 1$, and f_s is the sampling rate of the signal).

Finally, the scores computed in (6) are enhanced by applying a variation of the approach proposed in [8]. The original enhancement consists in setting to zero all negative scores and subtracting from each score the scores of multiples of the candidate. This has the purpose of reducing the scores of the inevitable peaks at common divisors of the pitches (e.g., the root of the chord). The proposed variation uses only scalings by a prime factor:

$$S'(t,f) = S^+(t,f) - \sum_{k \in \mathbb{P}} S^+(t,kf), \qquad (7)$$

where

$$S^+(t,f) = \max\{0, S(t,f)\} \qquad (8)$$

is a clipped version of $S(t,f)$ to nonnegative values.

Ideally, one would wish to use (7) itself to determine the pitch of the notes being played at time t, but $S'(t,f)$ is a little bit unstable over short periods of time. Therefore, it is recommended to integrate it over some period of time in order to obtain a more reliable estimate of the notes' pitch. In our experiments we obtained good results integrating over 0.3 s.

The algorithm implementation we used was written in the MATLAB programming language. The integrals in (1) and (3) were approximated by sums using as step sizes $\Delta t' = 1/f_s$ and $\Delta f' = f_s/N$, where f_s is the sampling frequency of the signal and N is the window size (in samples).

3. RESULTS

In order to test the algorithm, we used chords consisting of major, minor, diminished and augmented triads. All triads were played in root position, first inversion and second inversion, except for augmented chords, for which inversions are indistinguishable from other augmented chord in root position. This made for a total of ten chord profiles. The bass was let run from C_3 (about 130.8 Hz) to B_5 (about 987.8 Hz) for a total of 36 different basses and 360 chords. The chords were generated using synthetic signals sampled at a rate of 48 kHz and with a duration of 0.3 s. The signals consisted of sawtooth, square, and triangle waves. These types of signals were chosen because of their popularity in the literature and their interesting spectral characteristics:

Sawtooth waves The amplitude of their harmonics decays inversely proportional to frequency.

Square waves Have only even harmonics. Their amplitude decays inversely proportional to frequency.

Triangle waves Have only even harmonics. Their amplitude decays inversely proportional to the square of frequency.

Each chord was built using only signals of the same type and each type was used to build each of the chords. This made for a total of 1440 chords. Since every chord has three notes, the total number of notes was 4320.

Table 1: Error rates for the evaluated algorithms on sawtooth, square, and triangle waves.

	Error rate	
Signal type	Prime-multiF0	Klapuri
Sawtooth waves	0.00%	0.00%
Square waves	0.00%	0.74%
Triangle waves	0.74%	0.28%

The performance of the algorithm was compared to that one in [9]. The pitch search range used to test the algorithms was from 30 to 5 kHz (based on psychoacoustic experiments [13–15]) and the resolution was a quarter of a semitone. For the proposed algorithm, the candidate with the highest score was matched to the closest note of the chord, the candidate with the second highest score was matched to the next available closest note (as long as the distance to the previously detected note exceeds 2.5 semitones), and the third best candidate was matched to the last note of the chord (as long as the distance to the previously detected notes exceeds 2.5 semitones). [2] Since the notes of the chords and the pitch candidates shared the same tuning (A_4 = 440 Hz) and the resolution used for the candidates was one quarter of a semitone, all errors were a multiple of that quantity. For Klapuri's algorithm, we matched each note outputted by the algorithm to the closest note of the chord. A note was considered to be in error if its distance to the assigned note exceeded half a semitone.

Table 1 shows the error rates classified by signal type. The proposed algorithm (Prime-multiF0) produced no errors for sawtooth and square waves, and an error rate of 0.74% for triangle waves. On the other hand, the algorithm proposed by Klapuri produced no errors for sawtooth waveforms, but error rates of 0.74% and 0.28% for square and triangle waves, respectively.

Errors tend to occur only at the very high and low ends of the chosen pitch range for the signals. This is illustrated in Fig. 3, which shows the cumulative error rate as a function of bass. Errors from Prime-multiF0 occur only with basses above E_5 (660 Hz), and errors from Klapuri's algorithm occur in a similar range for square waves, and with basses below G_3 (196 Hz) for triangle waves. This means that both algorithms produce good results for the most common pitch range for chords (i.e., the *middle* octave: between C_4 and B_4).

For illustrative purposes, we show in Figs. 4–6 the average scores produced by Prime-multiF0 for each type of chord as a function of the distance to the bass in semitones. [3]

[2] Candidates located at less than 2.5 semitones of previously recognized pitches are not considered because we empirically found that the algorithm, in its current state, does not work well for intervals smaller than a minor third (three semitones).

[3] The scores were normalized to the maximum score in each chord before taking averages. This was done to avoid a bias toward chords with overall higher scores, and to reduce the variance in Fig. 4. Averages were taken over different signal types (i.e., sawtooth, square, and triangle waves.)

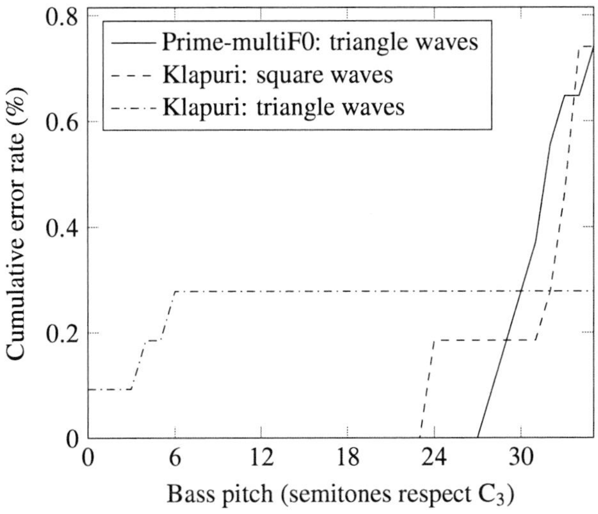

Figure 3: Cumulative error rates as a function of distance of the bass respect C_3. Most errors occur at the low or high ends of the bass range used in the experiment.

4. CONCLUSION

A new estimation algorithm for multipitch signals was proposed. This algorithm, named Prime-multiF0, was successful in detecting the pitch of chords played with synthetic signals consisting of sawtooth, square and triangle waves, for a wide range of pitch. Its performance was slightly better than a well known algorithm in the literature. However, both algorithms performed exceedingly well, and more tests with natural signals need to be performed to obtain more realistic results.

5. REFERENCES

[1] W. Hess, *Pitch Determination of Speech Signals*. Springer, 1983.

[2] A. de Cheveigné and H. Kawahara, "YIN, a fundamental frequency estimator for speech and music," *J. Acoust. Soc. Am.*, vol. 111, no. 4, pp. 1917–1930, 2002.

[3] A. Camacho and J. G. Harris, "A sawtooth waveform inspired pitch estimator for speech and music," *J. Acoust. Soc. Am.*, vol. 124, pp. 1638–1652, 2008.

[4] A. S. Spanias, "Speech coding: a tutorial review," *Proceedings of the IEEE*, vol. 82, no. 10, pp. 1541 –1582, 1994.

[5] J. Hillenbrand and R. A. Houde, "Acoustic correlates of breathy vocal quality: Dysphonic voices and continuous speech," *Journal of Speech, Language and Hearing Research*, vol. 39, no. 2, p. 311, 1996.

[6] R. B. Dannenberg, W. P. Birmingham, G. P. Tzanetakis, C. P. Meek, N. P. Hu, and B. P. Pardo, "The musart testbed for query-by-humming evaluation," *Comput. Music J.*, vol. 28, pp. 34–48, June 2004.

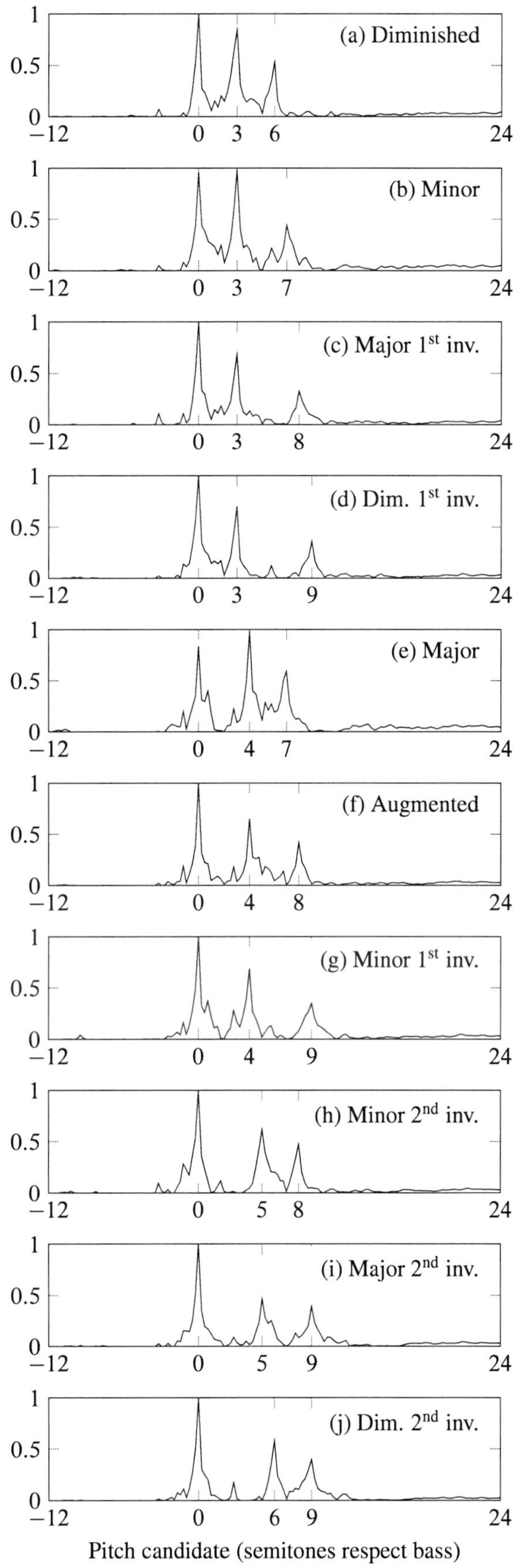

Figure 4: Average scores produced by the Prime-multiF0 algorithm for chords produced using *sawtooth* waveforms.

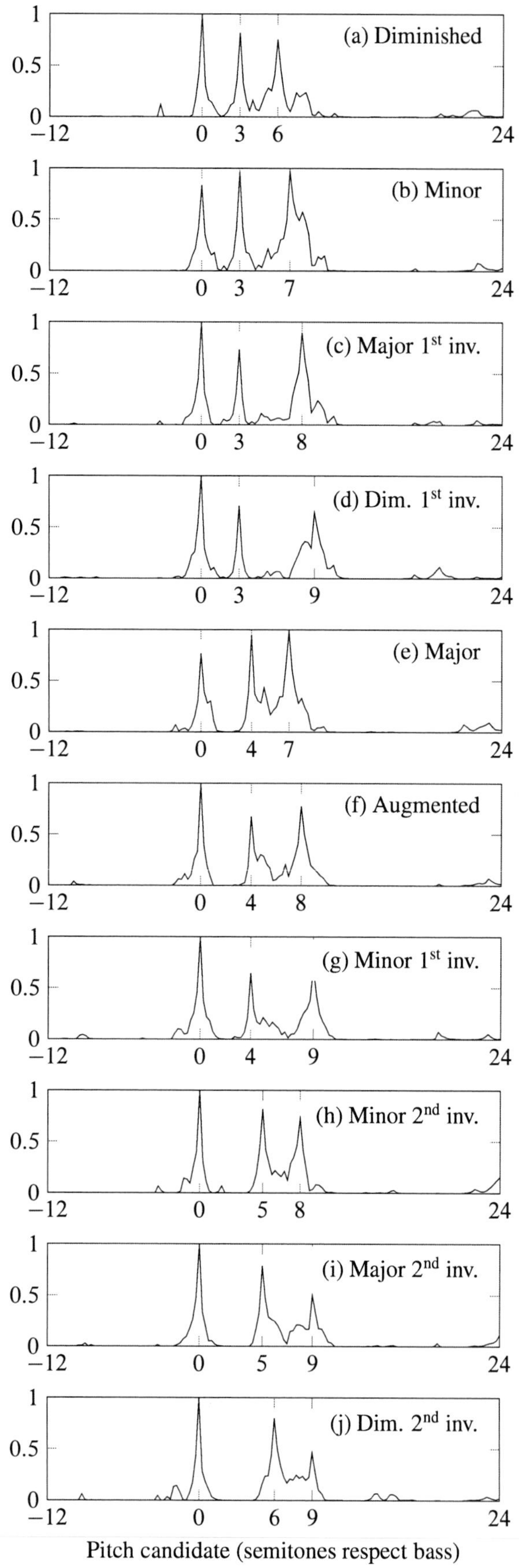

Figure 5: Average scores produced by the Prime-multiF0 algorithm for chords produced using *square* waveforms.

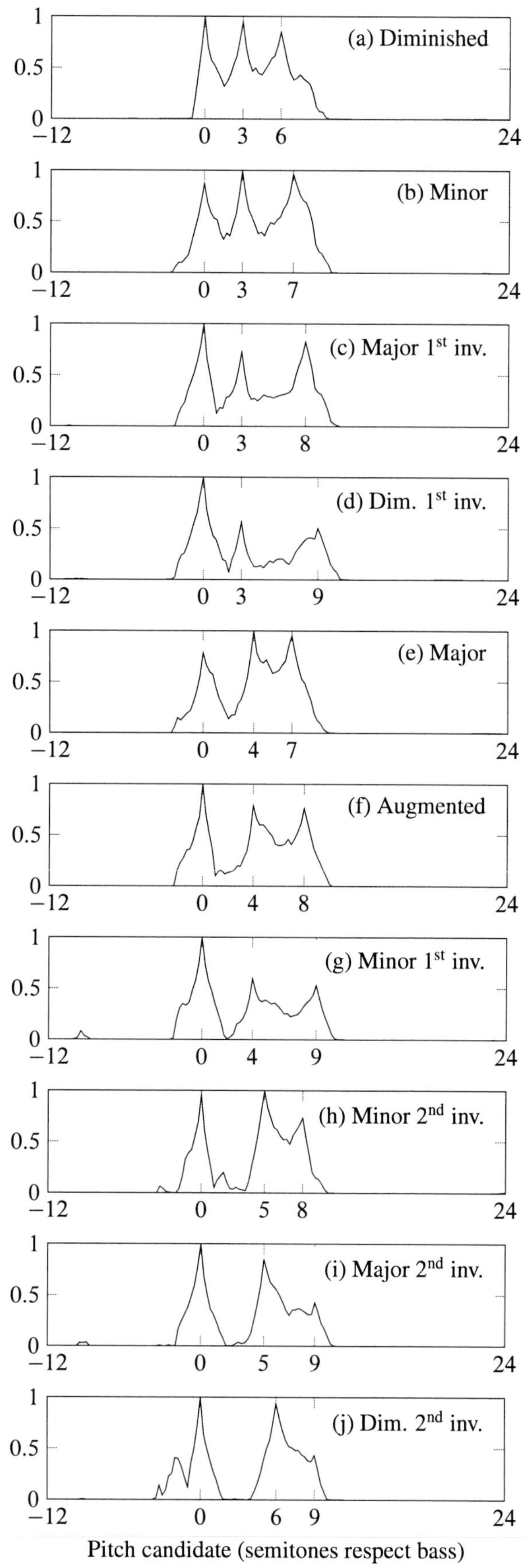

Figure 6: Average scores produced by the Prime-multiF0 algorithm for chords produced using *triangle* waveforms.

[7] A. P. Klapuri, "Automatic music transcription as we know it today," *Journal of New Music Research*, vol. 33, no. 3, pp. 269–282, 2004.

[8] T. Tolonen and M. Karjalainen, "A computationally efficient multipitch analysis model," *Speech and Audio Processing, IEEE Transactions on*, vol. 8, no. 6, pp. 708 –716, nov 2000.

[9] A. Klapuri, "Multipitch analysis of polyphonic music and speech signals using an auditory model," *IEEE Trans. Audio, Speech, Lang. Process.*, vol. 16, pp. 255–266, 2008.

[10] A. Klapuri, "Number theoretical means of resolving a mixture of several harmonic sounds," in *Proceedings of the European Signal Processing Conference*, 1998.

[11] B. R. Glasberg and B. C. J. Moore, "Derivation of auditory filter shapes from notched-noise data," *Hearing Research*, vol. 47, no. 1-2, pp. 103–138, 1990.

[12] H. Takeshima, Y. Suzuki, K. Ozawa, M. Kumagai, and T. Sone, "Comparison of loudness functions suitable for drawing equal-loudness level contours," *Acoust. Sci. Tech*, vol. 24, no. 2, pp. 61–68, 2003.

[13] C. Semal and L. Demany, "The upper limit of 'musical' pitch," *Music Perception: An Interdisciplinary Journal*, vol. 8, no. 2, pp. 165–176, 1990.

[14] K. Krumbholz, R. D. Patterson, and D. Pressnitzer, "The lower limit of pitch as determined by rate discrimination," *J. Acoust. Soc. Am.*, vol. 108, no. 3, pp. 1170–1180, 2000.

[15] D. Pressnitzer, R. D. Patterson, and K. Krumbholz, "The lower limit of melodic pitch," *J. Acoust. Soc. Am.*, vol. 109, no. 5, pp. 2074–2084, 2001.

Human-machine interaction

CHILD/MACHINE INTERACTION IN REFLEXIVE ENVIRONMENT. THE MIROR PLATFORM

Anna Rita Addessi

University of Bologna, Italy
annarita.addessi@unibo.it

ABSTRACT

This paper introduces the MIROR Platform, an innovative adaptive device for music and dance education, proposed in the framework of the EU-ICT project MIROR-Musical Interaction Relying On Reflexion. In concluding the MIROR project, 3 software applications (MIROR-Impro, MIROR-Compo and MIROR-Body Gesture) and the draft version of the User's and Teacher's Guides have been accomplished. In this paper, the technological and pedagogical principles of the MIROR platform, notably the "reflexive interaction" paradigm, the 3 applications and related experiments will be introduced. Finally, the draft of the full architecture of the platform is presented.

1. THE MIROR PLATFORM

The MIROR Platform is an innovative adaptive device for early childhood music and dance education, proposed in the framework of the EU-ICT MIROR-Music Interaction Relying On Reflexion.[1] It acts as an advanced cognitive tutor, designed to promote abilities in the field of music improvisation, composition and creative movement. The MIROR platform is designed to implement "reflexive interactive musical systems" (IRMS in short) [1], within technology-enhanced learning. On the basis of the interesting results observed with children and the first prototype of IRMS, the Continuator [2], in the context of the MIROR Project, we proposed, indeed, to extend the IRMS with the analysis and synthesis of multisensory expressive gesture [3], to increase its impact on the musical pedagogy of young children. In so doing, the MIROR Platform was conceived as an educational device composed by several software applications exploiting the reflexive interaction paradigm not only in music improvisation but also in the field of body and creative movement. The platform is not designed, however, to teach a specific instrument and instrumental skills, though it can also be used with this aim. It has been conceived rather as a "device" to stimulate and enhance musical creativity of children.

2. TARGET GROUP SCENARIOS

The MIROR Platform is developed in the area of music and motor education of children aged from 2 to 10 years. Indeed, one of the challenges set by the MIROR proposal was that of building tools of technology enhanced learning addressing very young children, not only with regard to formal music education contexts, but also to foster children's music and motor creativity in informal contexts, and in the school. The targets are a number of settings and contexts: from nursery, kindergartens and the primary school, to music schools, dance schools, children centres, children hospitals, and social inclusion contexts such as centres for immigrants and social centres. Furthermore, the platform is also conceived for therapeutic and rehabilitation settings and scenarios. Teachers' training classes are another target group: both general programmes of teacher training, and classes aimed at the formation of music and dance teachers. Indeed, the platform can be used to foster the music and motor creativity of teachers, as well as a tool to learn how to use the reflexive interaction paradigm as a new way to teach music and dance.

3. CHILD/MACHINE INTERACTION IN REFLEXIVE ENVIRONMENT

The basic hypothesis of the MIROR Project is that "reflexive interaction" enhances music learning and musical creativity in young children. According to Pachet [1, 4], the reflexive interaction paradigm is based on the idea of letting users manipulate virtual copies of themselves, through specifically designed machine-learning software referred to as interactive reflexive musical systems. The idea was to develop a machine that gives users the perception of interacting with something similar to themselves. In this case, the machine does not exactly mimic the user's proposal, but her/his own musical style, or, in other words, her/his own musical identity.

The subsequent experiments with adults, e.g., see [1], and especially with children, e.g. see [2], immediately demonstrated the potential of these reflexive systems for the development of creative musical experiences. Despite the apparent simplicity of the mechanism, IRMS generate

1 The MIROR Project is coordinated by the University of Bologna. The Consortium is composed by Bologna, SONY France-Paris, University of Genoa, University of Gothenburg, National and Kapodistrian University of Athens, University of Exeter and Compedia Ltd, Israel. For more information on the project, see the official website: www.mirorproject.eu.

very complex reactions, where the children are expected to form differentiated judgements about "self" and "others". In literature, these forms of awareness are considered crucial for the building of the child's identity. IRMS, by means of its mirror effect, help towards the construction of a "musical self". One innovative feature of the IRMS is the creation of a natural, organic dialogue with the child. This dialogue is based on the mechanism of repetition and variation, which is, in fact, at the heart of reflexive interaction: the system's repetition of the input given by the child allows the child to perceive the response of the system as a sort of sound image of him/herself. Moreover, this is the moment when the child shows an absolute attraction towards this other that appears similar to him/herself. The interesting thing is that it is not a mere repetition/imitation/echo, but rather a repetition that is always constantly varied. It is precisely the co-presence of something that is repeated along with something different that seems to make the reflexive interaction a sort of device of attraction first, and then of stimulation of interest to become involved in the interaction.

Starting from the observation of children interacting with the interactive reflexive musical systems, several theories have been considered to explain human behaviours in action during the interaction with a reflexive system. From a systematic perspective, the theoretical framework of the reflexive interaction paradigm could include references ranging from the myth of Echo (Ovid), to the more recent semiological paradigmatic analysis [5, 6], and the theory of similarity perception in listening to music [7]. The capacity to replicate the behaviour of others is to a certain extent grounded on the non-conscious mechanisms of the mirror neuron system (MNS), a network of neurons, which becomes active during the execution and observation of actions [8]. The studies presented so far highlight the complexity of the processes set in place during an interaction between child and reflexive machines: *imitation*, *imitation recognition*, *self-imitation*, *repetition/variation* represent processes that develop in the first months of life and which structure the Self of the child and her/his interaction with the surrounding environment [9, 10, 11]. Anzieu [12], calls this kind of infant experience "musical wrapping" of the Self, in which the Self is described like the first embryo of the personality felt as a unit, an individuality, and which expresses one of the more archaic shapes of repetition: the *echo*. Another important aspect that we can draw from this literature is the importance of reflexive interaction as a *dynamic process*: the experience of repetition/variation is carried out within affective and emotional conditions, the *amodal* experience that Stern [13] calls "affective contours", which are the outcome of the child's interaction experiences. The mechanism of repetition/variation can also be explained by recent studies in neuroscience, which underline the neural and cognitive mechanisms that allow one to transform and manipulate existing representations. Zatorre [14], suggests that the dorsal pathway of auditory processing performs equivalent operations on musical inputs. The results allow new hypotheses about how novel musical ideas may emerge from pre-existing musical images.

4. REFLEXIVE INTERACTION MEETS BODY GESTURE ANALYSIS

An important extension of IRMS into the MIROR Platform is the pedagogical exploitation of the possibility of communicating with the machine through body "gestures". These issues are addressed by introducing the *expressive gesture analysis* [3], implemented in the MIROR-Body Gesture prototype. The term "gesture" is an expression of the mediation between mind and physical environment, and it is distinguished from action, movement and motion because it refers to both of them in relationship with the meaningful level of human behaviours. The research in the field of embodied music cognition [15, 16], highlighted the fundamental role of the body in relation to human musical activities. The concept of "resonance" by Leman [16] has much in common with reflexive interaction and helps to better understand the relationship between reflexive interaction and perception of the body.

5. REFLEXIVE INTERACTION REQUIREMENTS

A number of characteristics emerged as being the most interesting to retain and generalise for developing IRMS in the field of technology-enhanced learning.

5.1 Technical Requirements

According to Pachet [1, 4], the following technical requirements of IRMS can be listed:

Reflexive interactive systems are a particular "class of interactive systems in which users can interact with virtual copies of themselves, or at least with agents that have a mimetic capacity and can evolve in an organic fashion." [1, p. 360]. Their focus is not on solving a given, well-defined problem, such as querying a database, but rather on helping users express hidden ideas.

"Similarity or Mirroring effect: The IRMS produce musical sounds like what the user is (...) able to produce. This similarity must be easily recognisable by the user, who experiences the sensation of interacting with a copy of her/himself." [1, p. 360]

*"Agnosticism***:** The system's ability to reproduce the user's personality is learned automatically and agnostically, i.e. without human intervention." In the case of the Continuator, for instance, "no pre-programmed musical information is given to the system".[1, p. 360]

"Scaffolding of complexity. Incremental learning ensures that the IRMS keeps evolving and consequently that the user will interact with it for a long time. Each interaction with the system contributes to changing its future behaviour. Incremental learning is a way to endow the system with an organic feel, typical of open, natural systems, as opposed to pre-programmed, closed-world systems. This scaffolding of complexity implies in turn a

number of technical constraints, such as the ability for the IRMS to store/retrieve models incrementally." [1, p. 360]

Build virtual images of users: Designing systems that effectively build virtual images of users in several disciplines. These images are built with the help of real time machine-learning components, which build models of the users that are continuously updated.

Feedback by designing an image of the user: unlike feedback systems, reflexive interactions do not consist of feeding back the output of a system to its input. They consist of influencing the actions of the user by providing her/him with a carefully designed image of her/himself.

Learn the behaviour of the user: RI software are essentially intelligent mirrors that learn the "behaviour" of the users.

Technically, this image is most of the time imperfect, for many reasons, including the intrinsic limitations of machine-learning systems. However, it is precisely this imperfection that produces the desired creation of side effects.

Side effect: target objects (e.g. a melody, a drawing, a taxonomy, etc.) are not produced *directly* by man-machine interactions, but as *side effects* of these mirroring interactions.

Collaborative production of object: Mirroring interactions can then take place in which the system continuously learns from the user, *to collaboratively produce an object.*

The *basic playing mode* of the IRMS is a particular kind of turn-taking between the user and the system governed by three principles: 1. Automatic detection of phrase endings. 2. The duration of the phrase generated by the IRMS should be set to be the same as the duration of the last input phrase. 3. Priority is given to the user.[4]

5.2. User Requirements

An empirical list of children user requirements concerning the reflexive paradigm has been derived from the results of the experiments with children [2, 17].

5.2.1 Modes of interaction

Repetition/variation (mirroring, reflexion): This is the "core" of reflexive interaction. The particular ability of the system to imitate the style of whoever is playing generates dialogues based on repetition and variation. Or rather, we observed that a real dialogue between the child and the system actually begins as soon as the child recognises something from her/his own proposal in the system's reply, and tries to answer by repeating and varying what s/he has just heard

Turn-taking: The children learn the implicit rule of turn-taking. They stop and listen to the system's reply, respecting the "turn-taking" with the system. Turn-taking lets you hear and be heard, it is a rule of interaction that is applied intuitively.

Regular timing of turns: The duration of the phrase generated by the system was set to be the same as the duration of the last input phrase. Bullowa [18], sustained that in order to share meaning with the adult, rhythms must also be shared and that this sharing is at the basis of communication.

Temporal contingency: the MIROR-Impro detects phrase endings by using a (dynamic) temporal threshold (typically about 400 milliseconds). Research on infant/mother interaction supports these "requirements": in the presence of maternal stimulations that are *non-contingent* (i.e. the mother does not respect the timing of the interaction), lacking in emotional sharing, or are excessive and intrusive, the behaviour of the child is characterised by passiveness or disorganisation.

Role-taking: this is the moment when one of the two interlocutors takes the partner into account and as a consequence regulates his/her own behaviour according to that of the other. Children are, for example, able to adapt their language when speaking to children younger than them.

Co-regulation of the communication: during the dialogue, the child and the system adapt to each other and co-regulate the contents and the timing of the interaction [19].

5.2.2 User Experience

To interact and manipulate a virtual copy of themselves. The children are allowed to manipulate virtual copies of themselves, and to reflect about their own musical style.

Imitation, self-imitation, imitation recognition: the children should be involved in several processes of imitation, self-imitation and imitation recognition and be able to control them for communicative purposes.

The life cycle of interaction: it deals with the temporal dynamic of the interaction, which is an important factor for the children's musical experience. We noticed several moments in child/Continuator interaction, characterised by different emotional and cognitive states: Surprise, Excitement, Concentration and analytical attention, moments of Engagement and Readjustment, Relaunching, Exploration, Invention, Attunement.

Flow state [20]: it should be possible to observe higher level of flow experience in children interacting with the IRMS.

The invention of rules: The children learned the rules of the system: it replies by playing alone, it replies when you stop playing (turn-taking), it repeats what you play, it repeats with variations (or 'errors'), it's capable of establishing a dialogue made up of repetition/variation, it does not always respect the rules, you can teach the system, and the rules of the system can be taught to others.

Joint attention: Of particular interest are the relationships established between two children playing together, and between them and the system: playing, listening, exploring together, watching the partner's reactions, playing separately, alternating, or conflicting. A typical situation encountered was the phenomenon of 'joint attention': more precisely, one of the children would force the other to stop playing in order to listen to the situation.

The system develops and enhances *self-regulated and self-initiated activities, self-efficacy, autonomy, and intrinsic motivation.*

Music-maker in style: The system stimulated and reinforced conducts of an exploratory type, but it also prompted inventive conducts. Both in the exploration and in the improvisations themselves, we can see very personalised styles in the children's approach to producing sounds, in their handling of the instrument and other equipment, and their working out plans of action to satisfy their own goals. The IRMS might be able to reinforce these individual styles, and allow their development and evolution.

6. PEDAGOGICAL CONCEPTS

According to the requirements above introduced, it is possible to describe several pedagogical concepts of the reflexive interaction paradigm and of the MIROR Platform. However, one of the results of the research conducted in the framework of the MIROR Project is that even if some pedagogical theories can be used to define the "reflexive" pedagogy, actually the reflexive interaction paradigm cannot be fully described by any of the pedagogical categories already existing. Instead, this paradigm proposes a novel and innovative pedagogical perspective dealing with the child / machine interaction. The IRMS could represent a new and original application of technology-enhanced learning.

6.1. The pedagogical framework

Priority to children's and Learner-centred learning: the centre of the attention in the reflexive interaction process is not the end product, but the subject engaged in the interaction. Reflexive interaction naturally produces a learner-centred approach.

Adaptive: The system adapts itself constantly and in an organic way to the musical style of the user, that is to say to everyone's style. It reinforces the children's musical style (both musical and learning style)

The 'teaching method' is based on turn-taking and regular timing of turns, on the strategies of mirroring, modelling and scaffolding [21, 22], and on starting up 'affect attunement' [16], intrinsic motivation, collaborative playing and joint attention.

Not to be programmed with fixed musical objectives, as for examples software for ear training, chord recognition etc. *Side effect*: the musical products and the learning objects should be the result of the interaction, as a side effect.

The system possesses the properties of transparency, involving "a shift from the representation of music to the music itself" [23], the children only interact by playing, without other graphic or mechanical interfaces (e.g. mouse, buttons, switches etc.), *and reflection,* in the sense that it is the system itself that helps the user to understand the mechanism of interaction; the rules are learnt during the interaction.

The factor of distance: the children are able to interrupt the game when they want, thus preserving the factor of "distance" between child and machine, vital from aesthetic and pedagogical points of view [24].

The attractiveness. The IRMS avoid the monotony of mere repetition, by introducing variation continuously, the "error", as an "imperfect machine". The only interface is the keyboard. The findings show that the attractiveness of IRMS is based on the conceptual and technical features of the software rather than external or nicely designed interfaces.

Collaborative playing in classroom setting: the double role of an IRMS, as virtual partner and tutor, enhances music creativity in children based on exploration and socialisation: sharing the discoveries and the newly invented games with partner and teacher. Furthermore, classroom activities with the IRMS enhance the self-regulation of the group of children in the use of the equipment and in managing the turns to play.

Music improvisation: the improvisations revealed rhythmic and melodic patterns, synchronisation on the same pulse, forms of song and accompaniment, individual improvisation styles, brief formal constructions based on imitation, repetition, alternation and contrast. With IRMS children learn to improvise by interacting with a computer, which is necessary if their teacher cannot, or does not want to improvise.

Creativity in child/machine interaction: the reflexive interaction paradigm proposed for music learning and cognition, and its connected theories (such as flow theory) could be applied not only to music education but also as a novel paradigm to the studying of general cognitive and creative processes. "Reflexive" learning is not learning by imitation. On the contrary, during RI the learning mechanism is activated by the experience "to be imitated".

IRMS also exploit the Vygotskian concept of zone of proximal development (ZPD). However, the difference with the Vygotskian concept of ZPD is that the IRMS are not *more* capable than children: they are agnostic systems and adapt themselves in an intuitive way to the child's musical knowledge during the interaction. In this way, IRMS establish an interaction between pairs, where the mirroring reflection creates a balance between challenges and skills, a basis to create Flow experiences [20] and creative processes. This characteristic will enable the MIROR Platform to enhance self-regulation, self-initiated activities, and the learner-centred approach. IRMS support children in mixing old musical skills with new ones, in an original and autotelic way, according to the "cognitive fiction" perspective [25], where the innovative technology enables the subject to see and listen in a more original way, bringing out previous childhood experiences.

Finally, the MIROR project owes to the Laban Movement Analysis (LMA), elaborated by the Hungarian dance artist and theorist Rudolf Laban (1879-1958). LMA has been widely used in the field of dance education and was applied also to music and movement education. This analytical approach is the basis of the *expressive gesture analysis* implemented by the MIROR-Body Gesture application.

6.2 Reflexive Listening

The listening behaviour of children interacting with the Continuator and MIROR Impro was particularly rich and varied: concentrated, analytical, but also symbolic. A particularly interesting aspect is the quality of the children's listening to their own productions while they played, heightened by the interactive element that encourages them to listen carefully so as to compare their own pieces with the reply and new proposal of the system, and to identify repetitions and differences. As already reiterated many times, in the world of teaching, listening to one's own musical productions while playing is one of the main objectives of music education [e.g. 26]. Different types of listening stimulated by the reflexive interaction can be distinguished:

Attentive and analytical listening: children listen carefully to the system's answers, they seem to be seeking to understand the rules that govern them;

Embodied listening: while listening to the system the children dance and move their body freely, interpreting the sounds they hear;

Tutoring: In sessions in pairs, the child who already knows the system usually guides her/his partner;

Empathic listening: children follow the musical evolution of the system "affectionately" and treat it like a living thing;

Joint listening: in games in pairs or in groups, listening becomes socialised; the children share the experience through looks, words, gestures;

Ecstatic listening: sometimes listening achieves moments of genuine ecstasy, of pure aesthetic pleasure, followed by expressions of joy: "It's beautiful!";

Autotelic listening: in many cases, however, the listening becomes particularly intense, concentrated, deeply intimate, regardless of everything else;

Listening by immersion or multi-modal listening: some children were seen to participate with their whole body, bringing into play every single electronic component available;

Symbolic listening: children dramatise a story or a character that mimics the response of the system, or invent a story while the system's replies serve as a soundtrack;

Listening to their productions: the children are encouraged to listen carefully and compare their productions with the response of the system, to identify repetitions and differences;

Listening "pseudo-distracted": Interaction through moments of great effort and times when the interaction seems loose, but not interrupted;

Virtual Listening: one of the most interesting acts observed was staring at an invisible point in space, a trait that characterises the conduct of enjoyment developed through the increasing use of means of reproduction, from the walk-man to the IPod;

Intertextual listening: finally, the IRMS could be placed in an aesthetics of the fragment and of intertext, being itself by definition a machine that produces intertexts. Dialoguing with it generates a kind of intertextual listening in children during which they are asked to interactively build and reconstruct the fragments of their own musical discourse, relaunched by the system, using those of the system's answer and the friend's. And it is this variation which attracts the child and motivates her/him to produce a new answer, to develop a musical idea: ultimately, to produce musical "meaning".

6.3. The MIROR Platform as a "device" for music and dance creativity

In the pedagogical field, the "device" has been defined as the concrete mediation that the teacher should individuate in reference to the specific situation, in order to allow children focusing their attention on the sound and the movements, and on their characteristics [26]. From this perspective, the MIROR platform can be defined as a "device" to enhance musical and dance creativity and invention in children. That is a tool to enhance children's creative conducts, both in music improvisation, composition and dance education.

6.3.1 The Practices

Several practices can be implemented with the 3 components of the MIROR Platform. We can distinguish 3 kinds of practices:

Practice 1: the children use the software applications of MIROR Platform. This is properly the setting of MIROR applications, that is the child/machine reflexive interaction. In this kind of practice, the reflexive interaction develops between child/ren and system.

Practice 2: the children and the teacher use the MIROR Platform together. In this practice the teacher acts as mediator between the child/ren and the applications.

Practice 3: the teachers use the MIROR Platform. In this kind of practice, the reflexive interaction is established between teacher and system. Indeed, the MIROR platform can also be used for teachers' music and dance education (Figure 1).

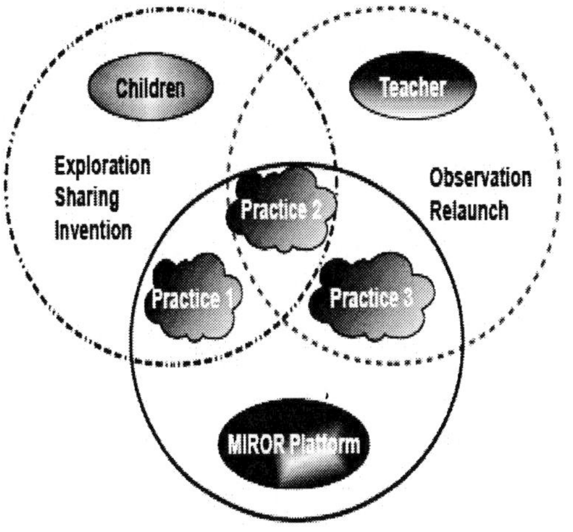

Figure 1: Creative Practices with Children/Teacher/MIROR platform.

7. THE SOFTWARE APPLICATIONS: MIROR-IMPRO, MIROR-COMPO, MIROR-BODY GESTURE

The MIROR project aimed to develop 3 software applications of the MIROR platform: MIROR-Impro, MIROR-Compo and MIROR-Body Gesture. They have been designed and developed by the engineers of Sony team [27] and of the University of Genoa [28, 29], in cooperation with the other partners: experts in psychology and pedagogy of music, which are the Universities of Bologna, Athens, Exeter and Gothenburg, and an expert in children educational software, which is Compedia Ltd.

7.1 MIROR-Impro

MIROR Impro software is linked to a normal midi-linked keyboard. When the children play something, making up a music phrase of their own and then pause, the software creates and immediately plays a "reflexive" reply that is based on the child's input. What is very new and interesting about this software is that the children can improvise with the computer as a kind of partner, discovering what elements in the replies stay the same or what changes. The educational aim of this software is both to support children in learning to improvise and to encourage their aural awareness through play in which they can control the levels of challenge by their own input. The reflexive interaction, with its mechanism of repetition/variation, triggers a dialogue between the two partners during which the improvisation process develops.

7.2 MIROR-Compo

MIROR-Compo allows children the composition of music: it acts as a sort of "musical scaffolding" that allows the children the combination of several musical phrases on the basis of their own style and musical taste. In this MIROR Platform application, the reflexive interaction paradigm is employed so that the software produces musical phrases similar to the opening sentences produced by the child. The educational aim of this software is to support children in creating music, storytelling, and engaging in collaborative compositions in a classroom context as well as in the family.

7.3 MIROR-Body Gesture

MIROR-Body Gesture was conceived so as to pick up the children's movements and convert them into "reflexive" sound, i.e. sound with the same characteristics of the related movement (heavy/light, fast/slow, and so on). In this way, the children can dance and create music via movement, and control their own improvisations and compositions. The educational aim of this software is to support children in discovering musicality through embodiment, i.e., by means of their own body, its movement, and its dynamic nature. MIROR-Body Gesture is composed by 2 components: BeSound and The Potter.

8. EXPERIMENTS WITH CHILDREN AND MIROR APPLICATIONS

A vast number of psychological and pedagogical experiments are being carried out in the framework of the MIROR project in order to implement the 3 applications - Impro, Compo and Body Gesture - and test them with children and teachers.

8.1 Psychological experiments

The Protocol no 1, "Music making with MIROR-Improvisation", showed interesting results concerning the analysis of the flow experience of children interacting with the Miror-Impro [17]. In the field of human/machine interaction, Leman, Lesaffre, Nijs, and Deweppe [30] and Leman [21], indicate the theory of flow as one of the areas of expertise which should be explored to study human/machine interaction. The experimental results with children and MIROR-Impro showed that the *Flow emotional state* increases not only when children play with the system, but also when they play using the set-up Same, that is the more "reflexive" set-up used in the experiment, as the system's output melody is musically much closer to the user's input melody. These results would support, in terms of quantitative data, a wide range of qualitative observations related to the mechanism of mirroring, repetition/variation, imitation, turn-taking, co-regulation, which characterise reflexive interaction, showing that they are able to create flow experience, well-being and creativity process.

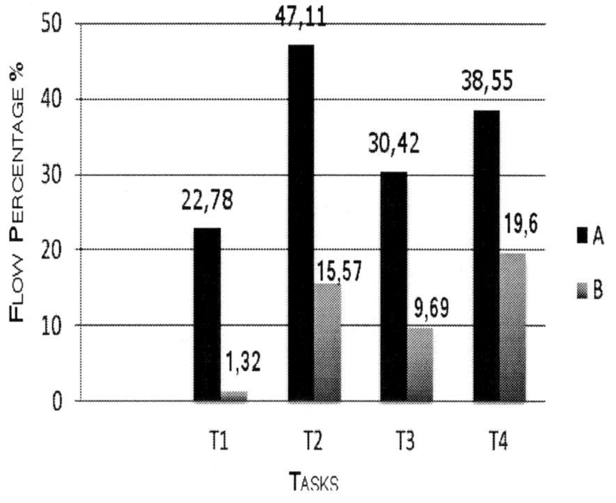

FIGURE 2. Percentage of the presence of flow with the set up A (same) and set up B (very different) in each task (set up A*set up B: t = 8.151; df = 3; p =.004). T1=the child plays the keyboard; T2=the child plays the keyboard with MIROR-Impro; T3= the child plays the keyboard with a friend; T4= the child plays the keyboard with the MIROR-Impro with a friend.

The results of the protocol no 1 also raised some problematic aspects related to the reflexive qualities of the Impro's replies that should be improved. Alexakis et al. [31] introduced a computer assisted music analysis, in order to assess the progress of children's creativity skills when using the MIROR-Impro. The results would suggest a potential progress of several variables, which might be indicative of creativity advancement. Other exploratory studies showed further scenarios in schooling contexts [e.g. 32, 33], nursery schools included [34], and suggested several recommendations for the implementation of the applications, according to the "spiral model" of collaboration adopted by the MIROR Consortium [e.g. 35].

8.2 Pedagogical experiments

In the second phase of the project, an extensive package of pedagogical experiments are being carried out by the partners and members of the Advisory and Liaison Board, in several European countries, in order to validate the MIROR applications in different scenarios, therapeutic and rehabilitative settings included. The Protocol no 2, "Teaching to improvise" has been carried out in order to verify if the reflexive interaction is necessary and sufficient to enhance children's ability to improvise. Focus groups with university students have been organised to explore the pedagogical conceptions developed in the context of reflexive interaction. The data analyses are being carried out. See the official website of the MIROR Project for further information and update.

8.3 The User's and Teacher's Guides

The User's and Teacher's guides are pedagogical practices and guides for teachers and children, to be used with MIROR applications. The deliverable 6.2 is the first draft of the Guides, composed with the contributions of the partners expert in music and dance education: UNIBO, NKUA, UGOT and UNEXE.

8.4 Theoretical contributions

On one hand, the experimental results have allowed supporting a series of theoretical hypotheses presented in the theoretical framework. On the other hand, they also raised a number of issues regarding some problematic aspects of the reflexive interaction paradigm, thus prompting further investigations in the field of embodied music cognition, pedagogical and multicultural contexts.

9. FUTURE STEPS AND CHALLENGES

In concluding the MIROR project, 3 software applications (MIROR-Impro, MIROR-Compo and MIROR-Body Gesture) and the draft version of the User's and Teacher's Guides have been accomplished.

The future challenge is to realise the MIROR platform by designing and implementing the learning/teaching environment and related architecture and technology tools (platform interface, tutorials, forum, data base, learning objects, etc.). The concept of the MIROR platform architecture includes the following parts:

The MIROR Platform interface: The interface will introduce the links to each application and to the other tools of the Platform.

Software applications with related interfaces, manuals and tutorials: MIROR Impro, MIROR-Compo and MIROR-Body Gesture. New software applications could be added in the future, based on the reflexive interaction paradigm.

The User's and Teacher's Guides: The User's and Teacher's guides are pedagogical practices and guides for teachers and children, to be used with MIROR Platform.

Practices for: educational settings (nursery, kindergarten, primary school), music schools, schools of dance, at home, therapeutic settings, teacher training, etc.

Children_Log: to upload interesting children compositions, improvisations and choreographies.

Work in progress: to upload interesting practices, experiments and videos, documenting the research work in progress.

Forums: for teachers, for researchers, for children, for parents, for the MIROR community.

Feedbacks: to upload feedback for software implementation, usability, user experience.

Publications: to upload or suggest interesting publications.

News and Events: dissemination of the project results.

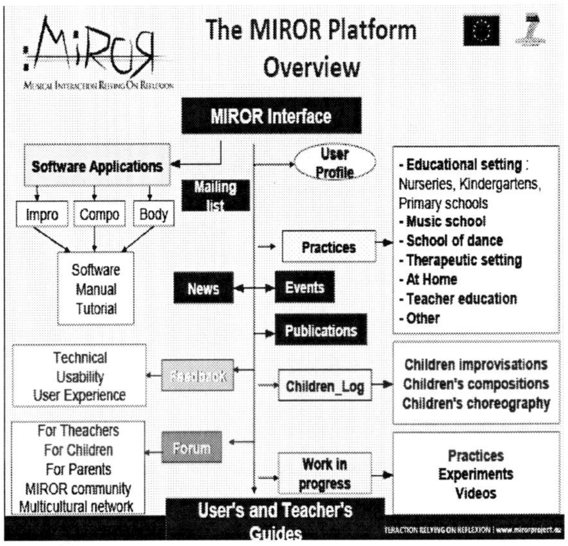

Figure 3: The overview of the MIROR Platform architecture showing the most important parts as described in the section above.

Acknowledgments

This study was partially supported by the EU-ICT Project MIROR-Musical Interaction Relying On Reflexion.

REFERENCES

[1] F. Pachet, "Enhancing individual creativity with interactive musical reflexive systems", in I. Deliège & G. Wiggins (Eds), *Musical Creativity*, Psychology Press, pp. 358-375, 2006.

[2] A.R. Addessi and F. Pachet, "Experiments with a musical machine. Musical style replication in 3/5 year old children", *British J. of Music Education*, vol. 22, no. 1, pp. 21–46, 2005.

[3] A. Camurri, C. Canepa, S. Ghisio, and G. Volpe, "Automatic classication of expressive hand gestures on tangible acoustic interfaces according to Laban's theory of Effort", in *Gesture in Human-Computer Interaction and Simulation,* Springer Verlag, pp. 151–162, 2009.

[4] F. Pachet, Music interaction with style. *J. of New Music Research*, vol. 32, no. 3, pp. 333–341, 2003.

[5] N. Ruwet, "Méthodes d'analyse en musicologie". *Revue belge de Musicologie*, 20, pp. 65–90, 1966.

[6] N, Meeùs, "Le rapports associatifs comme déterminants du style". *Analyse Musicale*, no. 32, pp. 9–13, 1996.

[7] I. Deliège (Ed.), "Music Similarity", *Musicae Scientiae,* Special Issue, 2003.

[8] G. Rizzolatti, L. Fadiga, L. Fogassi, and V. Gallese, "From mirror neurons to imitation: Facts and speculations", in A, Meltzoff and W. Prinz (Eds.), *The Imitative Mind. Development, Evolution, and Brain Bases*, CUP, pp. 247–266, 2002.

[9] J. Nadel, and G. Butterworth (Eds.), *Imitation in Infancy,* Cambridge University Press, 1999.

[10] M. Papousěk, "Le comportament parental intuitif", in I. Deliège nd J. Sloboda (Eds.), *Naissance et dévelopement du sens musical,* Presses Universitaires de France, pp. 101-130, 1995.

[11] M. Imberty, *La musique creause le temps. De Wagner à Boulez: musique, psychologie, psychoanalyse,* L'Harmattan, 2005.

[12] D. Anzieu, *Les enveloppes psychiques*, Dunod, 1996.

[13] D. Stern, *The First Relationship,* Harvard University Press, 1977.

[14] R.J. Zatorre, "Beyond auditory cortex: working with musical thoughts", in *Annals of the New York Academy of Sciences*, no. 1252, pp. 222–228, 2012.

[15] M. Leman, *Embodied Music Cognition and Mediation Technology*, MIT Press, 2007.

[16] R.G. Godøy and M. Leman (Eds.), *Musical Gestures. Sound, Movement, and Meaning.* Routledge, 2010.

[17] A.R. Addessi, L. Ferrari, and F. Carugati, "Observing and measuring the Flow experience in children", in *Proc. ICMPC and Conf. of ESCOM*, Thessaloniki, pp. 20-30, 2012.

[18] M. Bullowa, "Introduction. Prelinguistic communication: A field for scientific research", in M. Bullowa (Ed.), *Before speech: The Beginning of Human Communication,* CUP, pp. 1–62 , 1979.

[19] A. Fogel, "Oltre gli individui: un approccio storico-relazionale alla teoria e alla ricerca sulla comunicazione", in M.L. Genta (Ed.), *Il rapporto madre-bambino,* Carocci, pp. 123–161, 2000.

[20] M. Csikzsentmihalyi, *Flow: The Psychology of Optimal Experience.* Harper & Row, 1990.

[21] J. Bruner, *Child's Talk: Learning to Use Language,* Norton, 1983.

[22] L. Vygotsky, *Thought and language,* MIT Press. 1962.

[23] G. Folkestad, D. Hargreaves and B. Lindström, "Compositional strategies in computer-based music-making" *British Journal of Music Education*, vol. 15, no. 1, pp. 83–97, 1998.

[24] P. Bertolini and M. Dallari, "A proposito di giudizio estetico", in *Il giudizio estetico nell'eposca dei mass media,* Libreria Musicale Italiana, pp. 23-34, 2003.

[25] L. Guerra, *Educazione e tecnologie*, Junior, 2002.

[26] F. Delalande, *Le condotte musicali.* CLUEB, 1993.

[27] F. Pachet, P. Roy and G. Barbieri, "Finite-Length Markov processes with constraints", *Proc. of Int. Joint Conf. Artificial Intelligence,* Barcelona, 2011.

[28] G. Volpe, G. Varni, A.R. Addessi and B. Mazzarino, "BeSound: Embodied reflexion for music education in childhood", in *Proc. Int. Conf. Interaction Design and Children*, Bremen, 2012.

[29] G. Varni, G. Volpe, R. Sagoleo, M. Mancini and G. Lepri, "Interactive reflexive and embodied exploration of sound qualities with BeSound", in *Proc. Int. Conf. Interaction Design and Children*, New York, 2013.

[30] M. Leman, M. Lesaffre, L. Nijs and A. Deweppe, "User-oriented studies in embodied music cognition research", *Musicae Scientiae*, Special Issue, pp. 203–224, 2010.

[31] A. Alexakis, A. Khatchatourov, A. Triantafyllaki and C. Anagnostopoulou, "Measuring musical creativity advancement", in *Proc. Conf. Stockholm Music Acoustic & Conf. Sound and Music Computing*, Stockholm, 2013.

[32] A. Triantafyllaki, C. Anagnostopoulou and A. Alexakis, "An exploratory study of young children's technology-enabling improvisation", in *Proc. ICMPC and Conf. of ESCOM*, Thessaloniki, pp. 1009-1015, 2012.

[33] C. Wallerstedt, P. Lagerlof, "Exploring turn-taking in children's interaction with a new music technology", *HeKupu*, vol. 2, no 5, pp. 20-31, 2011.

[34] L. Ferrari and A.R. Addessi,"Early exploration of digital sound", in *Proc. Conf. European Network of Music Educators and Researchers of Young Children*, The Hague, 2013.

[35] A.R. Addessi, R. Cardoso, M. Maffioli, F. Regazzi, G. Volpe, G. Varni and B. Mazarino, "Designing the MIROR-Body Gesture framework for music and dance creativity", in *Proc. Int. Symposium of Musical Cognition,* Belém, 2013.

3D GESTURAL INTERACTION WITH HARMONIC PITCH SPACE

Thomas W. Hedges
Queen Mary University of London
London, UK
twh30@eecs.qmul.ac.uk

Andrew P. McPherson
Queen Mary University of London
London, UK
andrewm@eecs.qmul.ac.uk

ABSTRACT

This paper presents an interface allowing users to intuitively interact with harmonic pitch space through gestures in physical space. Although harmonic pitch spaces are a well-defined concept within the circles of academic musicology, they often fail to engage with non-musicians or musicians outside academia. A three-dimensional *tonnetz* founded on root progression theories is conceived and a graphical representation rendered for visual feedback. Users navigate the tonnetz with two-handed gestures captured in three-dimensional space with a purpose built video colour-tracking system. Root transitions and pivot tone triads are used to navigate the tonnetz and trigger audio feedback generated with MIDI.

Keywords: Harmonic pitch space, Interactive, Gesture, Tonnetz, Root progression theory.

1. INTRODUCTION

In musicology, the construction of harmonic pitch spaces as cognitive models for music perception has been a fruitful area of research for the past four or so decades [1]. In particular, various tonnetz models have become a useful spatial metaphor for tonal, harmonic and pitch relations [1, 2, 8, 12, 13]. However, for musicians outside of musicological circles and non-musicians such constructs may seem unintuitive or abstract.

We present a new interface for three-dimensional, two-handed gestural interaction with a tonnetz model. Since the interface relies on simple gestures, it does not necessitate musical instrument skills or music theoretical knowledge but aims to allow users to intuitively explore the underlying principles of tonal harmony. As such, the interface has strong didactic properties and will be of interest to music educators and students, as well as a wider variety of performers, composers and even non-musicians.

1.1. Related Works and Interfaces

The current paper aims to build on the work of several related studies and interfaces. Simon Holland's *Harmony Space* [6, 7] allows users to navigate a two dimensional tonnetz (Figure 1) with whole body gestures, working within the context of music education. The interactive system exists in two versions: [6] manually tracks users movements around a tonnetz projected onto a floor space and [7] captures footfalls and arm gestures with pressure sensors and accelerometers. *Harmony Space's* tonnetz, derived from a cyclic group theoretic model [8] for musical pitch, can be summarised as a two dimensional grid ordering pitches by major thirds along the horizontal axis and minor thirds along the vertical. Two further important intervallic pitch structures can be derived from the two diagonals, corresponding to fifth and semitone relations respectively. Pitch-nodes within a diatonic scale are visually marked. For example, in Figure 1 the seven diatonic tones of D major are underlined; Harmony Space uses black and white backgrounds to identify diatonic tones. [6, 7] are fundamentally didactic interfaces, placing strong emphasis on the understanding of music and harmony implicitly with the aid of gestures, a fundamental concept of the current paper.

	Maj. 3rd >				
Min. 3th V	D	F#	B♭	D	F#
	B	E♭	G	B	E♭
	A♭	C	E	A♭	C
	F	A	C#	F	A
	D	F#	B♭	D	F#

Figure 1. A section of *Harmony Space's* tonnetz, ordered by major and minor thirds.

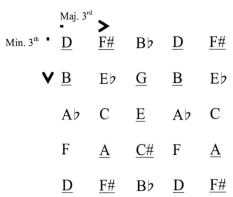

Similar matrix-based interfaces have been used to augment performance and improvisation on musical instruments [9]. Adeney's *HarmonyGrid* consists of four grids controlling musical parameters (volume, rhythm, timbre and harmony) with a four-by-four matrix covering a floor area of approximately two meters squared. Performers' motions are tracked with an overhead webcam, triggering and controlling audio in real time. The system is optimised for musical performance, and therefore the chord layout does not reflect any music theoretical constructs.

A larger scale interactive interface for music education is presented in [10], tracking user location by GPS. A neo-Riemannian tonnetz governs physical distances between pitch-nodes with level of musical consonance. The planar tonnetz is mapped onto a physical space where pitch-nodes are placed approximately 80m apart and triggered when users entered an 'influence' radius for each node. Overlapping 'influence' radiuses allow users to trigger more than one node at a time, generating various dyads and major or minor triads. The large-scale nature of the interface creates a novel interactive system for music students. However, it is limited to the GPS resolution: an accuracy of 1-3 meters and a measurement every second. Given its scale, this is not necessarily problematic but it negates the possibility of using the interface in 'real time' since the rate of harmonic change would be slower than almost all styles and genres of music.

Chew's [11] MuSA.RT Opus 2 interactive system for tonal and harmonic visualisation differs from the above approaches in two significant ways. Firstly, tonal and harmonic space is navigated purely through performance as opposed to user gestures. Input from a MIDI stream is parsed with a tonal induction algorithm which controls the movement of long term and short term 'centres of effect', and 'closest triad' on the visualisation. Secondly, the tonal and harmonic space is represented with a sophisticated nested spiral array model in contrast to the matrix-based tonnetz models described above. The resulting interface allows performers and audiences to visualise in detail the tonal landscape of a piece of music as it evolves.

1.2. Relation to Previous Work

With the above approaches in mind, we present an interface for users to intuitively navigate a tonnetz model without the need for specific prior skills or knowledge. It is important for such interfaces to be founded on musicologically convincing harmonic pitch models as they give structure in the audio feedback to the user. Since Chew's Spiral Array model [11] is intended to visualise performances, it does not seem a good candidate for a gestural interface. The complex nature of the spiral structure is unlikely to be easy to navigate intuitively with simple gestures. [9] presents intuitive and simple interactions (in conjunction with performance) but does not seek to engage with music theoretical concepts. [6] notes the didactic importance of whole-body gestures, but reports the physical limitation they can entail on harmonic transitions around a physical tonnetz. Therefore, we propose an interface with a richer set of gestures to navigate a harmonic pitch space, thus reducing any physical limitations and giving users flexible and intuitive interaction.

2. THE TONNETZ

2.1. Musicological Perspectives

A brief overview of harmonic and pitch spaces is useful at this point. Both map chords or notes into a multidimensional space such that objects close together in the space are closely related musically. However, whereas pitch space maps individual notes into a space [2], harmonic space maps whole chords, typically represented by a root pitch [6]. Often useful systems are an amalgamation of the two, with the objects in the space representing individual pitches that can be grouped into chords [12].

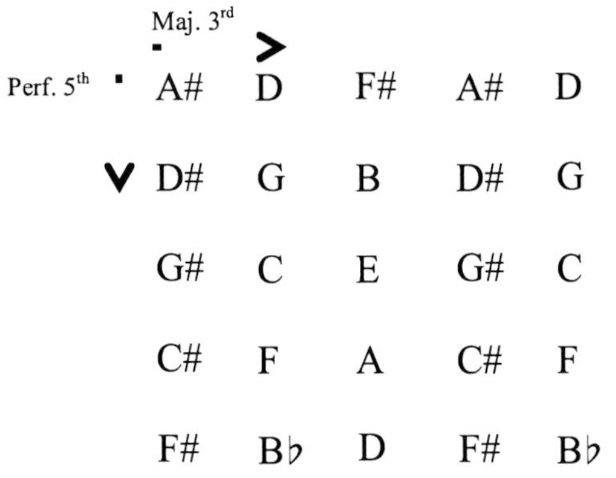

Figure 2. A section of Longuet-Higgins' infinite tonnetz ordered by major thirds and perfect fifths.

The dimensionality and complexity of harmonic spaces can vary considerably. Simple spaces map chords onto an infinite *x-y* plane [2] (Figure 2), referred to as a tonnetz or tone grid, ordered by fifths or thirds. A more complex tonnetz is at the core of Neo-Riemannian theory and consists of tessellated equilateral triangles with triads formed from the pitches at points of each triangle. Here, chord progressions are described by a combination of just three core transformation functions [12]. The dimensionality of a tonnetz can be increased to form 5-dimensional toroidal spaces, accounting for octave equivalence [13]. Similarly, octave equivalence is often described with spiral structures, as exhibited by [11].

Since the proposed interface aims to be intuitive and easy to navigate with gestures, a complex, high-dimensional harmonic space is rejected in favour of a simpler construct. It is important that a user can easily relate between the harmonic and physical spaces, so a three-dimensional matrix-based construct is presented in Section 2.3 as the musicological basis for the interface.

2.2. Root Progression Theories

A simple three-dimensional harmonic space demands a compact music theoretical grounding, as a complex model for harmony would map poorly onto a low dimensional harmonic space. Root progression theories [3, 4, 5] are extremely compact and often powerful models for tonal harmony, collapsing harmonies to a single note (root) [3] to explain harmonic progression. A permissible set of root transitions by consonant intervals (major thirds and sixths, minor thirds and sixths, and perfect fourths and fifths) is defined [3] and subsequently categorised into symmetrically opposed groups: dominant and subdominant [4, 5], to explain tonal harmony. Compared to functional approaches to harmony this generates a far more compact set of six (paired) permissible harmonic transitions. This small set lend themselves to simple tonnetz architectures since the three pairs of transitions can be represented on three axes. As such, the proposed interface orders its three axes by major thirds, minor thirds, and perfect fifths. Each axis can be interpreted as representing dominant root progressions in one direction (e.g. a descending fifth) and subdominant progressions in the other (e.g. an ascending fifth) [c.f 4].

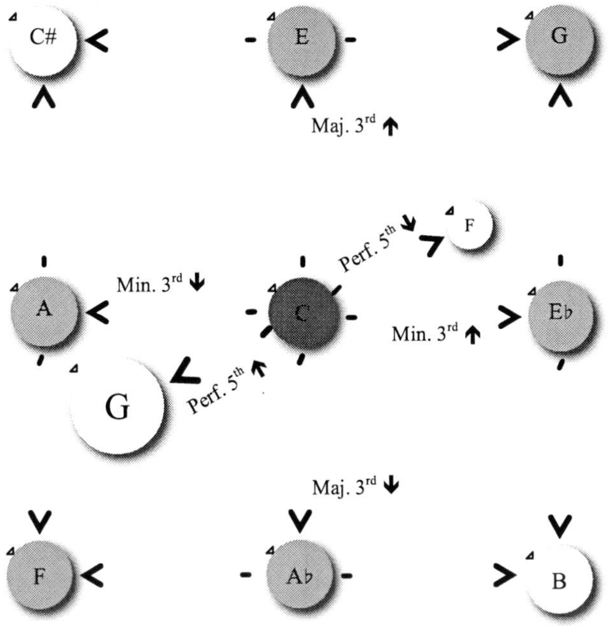

Figure 3. The 3D Tonnetz with the six labelled root progression vectors and pivot and triad notes in red and blue respectively.

2.3. The 3D Tonnetz

The 3D Tonnetz forming the musical model for the interface is based on an amalgamation of two common two-dimensional tonnetze. Longuet-Higgins' tonnetz [2] (Figure 2) consists of a matrix of major thirds and perfect fifths, whilst *Harmony Space's* tonnetz [6] (Figure 1) comprises of major and minor thirds. Bearing intervallic invertibility in mind, these intervals form the set of permissible consonant root transitions outlined in Section 2.2 [4]. Figure 3 maps this set of six root transitions as vectors to form the 3D Tonnetz for this interface. Note that the *x-y* plane forms *Harmony Space's* tonnetz [6], and the *y-z* plane Longuet-Higgins' tonnetz [2].

The 3D Tonnetz poses some interesting structural properties, lending it specifically to a musicologically grounded gestural interface. A single node can be selected as a pivot note (red) from which six permissible transitions to other nodes along the *x*, *y* or *z*-axes of the tonnetz can be made in accordance with [4]. From the pivot node, two triad nodes (blue) on the *x-y* plane can be selected from adjacent nodes to form six major or minor triads, expanding harmonic options available to users for creative purposes.

For example, from the pivot note C (highlighted in red in Figure 3), E and G can be selected as triad notes (in blue) to form a C major triad, E♭ and G for C minor, and E♭ and A♭ for an A♭ major triad. In theory, diminished and augmented triads, as well as other non-diatonic sets of three pitches, could be selected from adjacent nodes, but for simplicity and usability, the proposed interface is restricted to major and minor triads. For visual clarity, selecting blue triad nodes adjacent on the *z*-axis is also prohibited.

2.4. Musicological Visual Analysis

Harmonic pitch spaces are useful tools for visualising the harmonic landscape of a piece of music. The root progression architecture of the 3D Tonnetz lends itself in particular to visual musicological analyses for the Classical (strongly favouring cycle of fifths progressions) and Romantic eras (with a wider variety of harmonic progressions). Two brief demonstrations are given below, mapping the root progressions of a few phrases onto the harmonic space defined in Section 2.3.

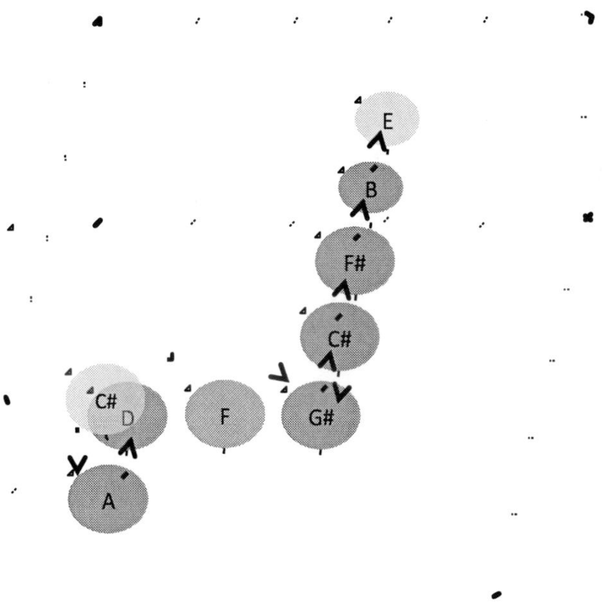

Figure 4. A visualisation of Beethoven's Piano Sonata, Op. 27 No. 2, bars 1-9.

2.4.1. Beethoven's Piano Sonata Op. 27 No. 2

The opening two phrases of Beethoven's 'Moonlight Sonata' are a relatively straightforward example of how a tonal piece of music maps onto the 3D Tonnetz (Figure 4). Although the initial root progression is a descending third (C# - A or i^7 – VI), the majority of progressions operate along the fifths axis. The undulation between C# (i) and G# (V) in bars 5-7 gives way to a cycle of fifths towards a perfect cadence in E major, represented by a series of forward steps along the *z*-axis in the space. The progression from D (II♭) to G# (V) is conceived as a leap of two minor thirds along the *y*-axis, skipping F.

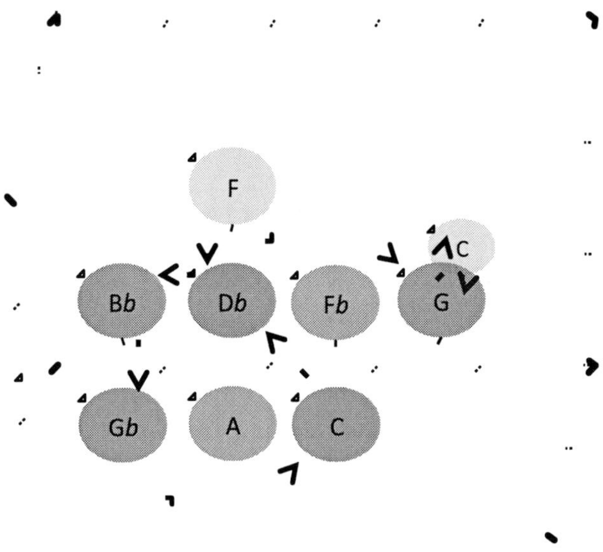

Figure 5. A visualisation of Brahms' Clarinet Sonata, Op. 120 No. 1, bars 5-12.

2.4.2. Brahms Clarinet Sonata Op. 120 No. 1

By contrast, the first subject of Brahms' Clarinet Sonata in F minor is strongly characterised by its movement around the *x-y* plane (Figure 5). The initial Brahmsian chain of falling thirds (F – D♭ – B♭ - G♭) manifests itself in a down - left - down motion in the harmonic space. The more adventurous romantic harmony requires a series of leaps from G♭ (II♭) to C (V) to D♭ (VI) and finally to G (V of v). Although more complex than Figure 4 in terms of spatial movement, the movements along the *z*-axis at the end give a clear visual indicator of the cadential closure of the phrase.

3. THE INTERFACE

The interactive interface comprises of three distinct components. A graphical representation gives users visual feedback of their position in the 3D Tonnetz (as described in Section 2.3), a colour-tracking system captures two-handed gestures from users, and a simple system gives audio feedback over MIDI.

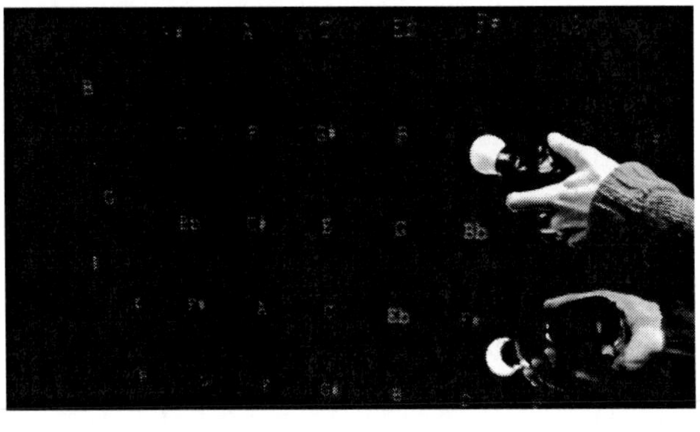

Figure 6. The red and blue controllers in front of a projection of the 3D Tonnetz.

The interface setup is comprised of the graphical representation of the 3D Tonnetz (Figure 7) projected onto a black sheet, with the user holding two LED-lit Ping-Pong balls mounted on controllers each with on/off button switches (Figure 6). To aid users, a small graphic of the locations of both balls can be shown in the lower right of the display or on a separate screen (Figure 8).

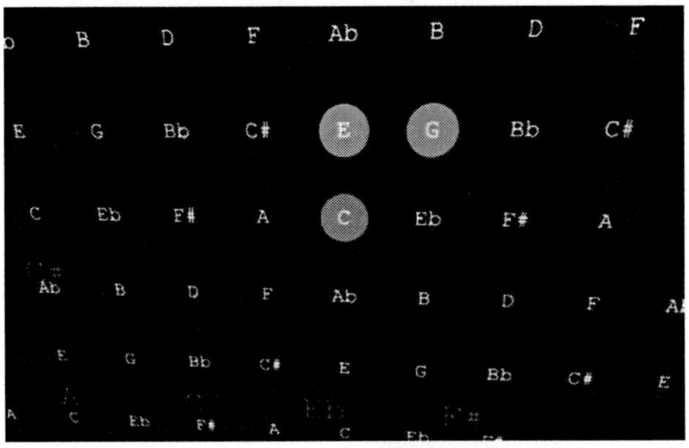

Figure 7. The graphical representation for the three-dimensional tonnetz rendered in Processing.

3.1. Visualisation of the 3D Tonnetz

The graphical representation of the harmonic pitch space was written in Processing[1] with OPENGL rendering (Figure 7). Nodes built with object-oriented programming represent pitches, displaying the corresponding note names. Users are presented with *Harmony Space's* tonnetz [6] on the *x-y* plane of the matrix, with Longuet-Higgins' tonnetz [2] going 'into' the screen on the *y-z* axis. Note names update with respect to the pivot pitch, maintaining intervallic relations for adjacent pitches. However, non-adjacent pitches are written enharmonically with the fewest possible number of accidentals. Nodes selected as the pivot and triad nodes are lit red and blue respectively, with the corresponding *x-y* plane highlighted. To give users the impression of moving though a physical space, the camera viewpoint tracks pivot note transitions with smooth glides.

3.2. Gestural Recognition

A gesture tracking system for the interactive interface is required to recognise two-armed gestures in three-dimensional space in real time and update the graphical representation. In selecting a tracking system, further preference was given to systems that were low-cost, preferably to be run from a laptop with an in-built webcam. Three methods were trialled for the interface: Oliver's [14] MANO controller, a detailed hand gesture recognition system; *blobscanner*[2], a hand-tracking library written in the Processing environment; and a purpose built colour-tracking system written in the Max/Jitter[3] programming environment to track LED-lit hand-held controllers. The MANO controller is able to pick up detailed hand gestures without time lag, but requires a restrictive back-lit, black background setup, which ties the user to a small area, in a similar manner to a touch-screen controller.

[1] `http://processing.org/`
[2] `https://code.google.com/p/blobscanner/`
[3] `http://cycling74.com/products/max/video-jitter/`

Blobscanner is less restrictive in setup, but time lag makes it impractical for true real-time interactions with musical spaces. The purpose built Max/Jitter colour tracking system was chosen for the interactive system since it is unrestrictive in setup, fast and accurate, as well as being low-cost since it does not require specialised motion tracking equipment. Furthermore, button switches on the LED controllers provide additional functionality over hand gesture recognition systems as they can instantly be turned on or off.

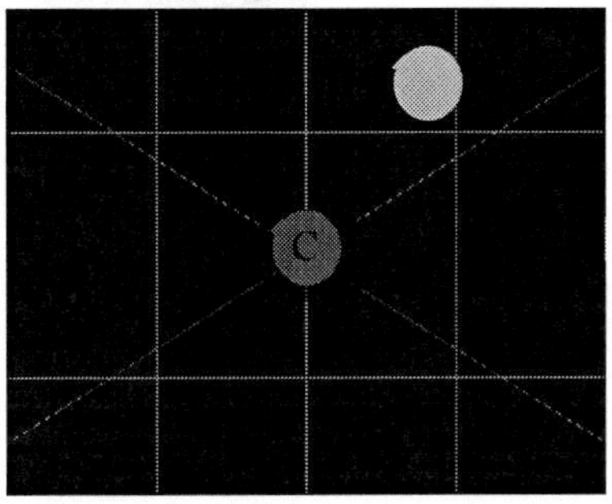

Figure 8. The 'clock face' triad selection interface.

The system tracks red and blue LED-lit Ping-Pong balls mounted on non-reflective controllers, held in each of the users hands. Video is captured with a webcam set to a low exposure time to maximize the difference in brightness between the LED light and the background. For *up down*, *left* and *right* gestures, x and y co-ordinates are obtained by finding the centre point of a bounding box of all the coloured pixels defined within a specified RGB range. For example, the red bounding box selected pixels with red values of 0.5 – 1, blue: 0 – 0.2 and green: 0 – 0.2. For *forward* gestures, the width of the bounding box is chosen to represent the size of the ball, and so movement through the z-axis. An alternative solution is to take the area of the box to map onto the z-axis. However, since the area has an inverse-quadratic relationship with distance from the camera, and the width only an inversionally proportional relationship, width maps better for the interface.

To map gestures to navigate the red node (as described in Section 2.3) around the tonnetz, *up, down, left, right* and *forward* messages are triggered after the red ball passes a threshold, which incorporates hysteresis to avoid spurious repeat triggers. Messages are only triggered once, until the red ball passes back through the threshold. *Back* messages are triggered when the red ball is turned off.

Gestures with the blue ball control the two blue nodes (described in Section 2.3) to select triads on the x-y plane. The angle between the blue ball and the centre of the screen is calculated, creating a 'clock face' interface with regions representing different triads (Figure 8). A region is selected when the blue ball moves into the region, or is turned on in that region. A 'play' message is triggered whenever the blue ball is turned on or when it has changed region.

As such, the functions of navigation (the red ball) and triad selection (the blue ball) are separated between the controllers. When triggered, all messages are sent over Open Sound Control (OSC) to the graphical representation running on Processing.

3.3. Audio Feedback

Audio output for the interface is governed by OSC messages sent from Processing to Max/MSP, which triggers various MIDI messages to an internal MIDI synthesizer application. Simply outputting the three notes of the triad selected in the tonnetz gives little control over inversion and creates weak voice leadings with parallel fifths whenever consecutive root position chords are played. To counteract this undesirable effect the triad is first converted to root position and transposed to several octaves simultaneously, generating a total of 19 MIDI notes. The large quantity of notes (somewhat counter intuitively) reduces the impact of parallel movement since the notes all have the same timbre and, therefore, cannot be easily streamed into distinct channels.

4. PRELIMINARY USER TEST

A simple preliminary user test was conducted to judge the quality of the interface as an interactive tool. In particular, the test aimed to identify any weaknesses in the gesture recognition system for future development and provide an indicator of how intuitive the interface was as a whole. Four participants were selected who had not used the interface before, with musical experience ranging from 0 to 8 years.

The test comprised of four stages. Firstly, the user was taught each of the six gestures for the red and blue controllers separately, making twelve gestures in total. For each gesture the number of attempts before a successful trigger was noted. In the second stage, four navigation tasks test how well the red pivot note can be moved around the 3D Tonnetz. The user was asked to move the red pivot note to a position up to two steps away, with any combination of *up, down, left, right, forward* and *back* gestures. Again, the number of attempts before successfully completing each task was recorded. In the third stage, the user was asked to follow three typical harmonic sequences represented as vector maps, for example, a descending cycle of fifths, or a falling third rising forth sequence. Finally, the user was given the opportunity to freely explore the interface.

4.1. Results

In general, the gesture recognition was successful for the novice participants: 79% of gestures triggering correctly on the first attempt and 98% by the second attempt for the initial instructional stage, which consisted of the user learning each gesture for each controller in turn (twelve in total). Of the four navigation tasks, one requiring a step forwards on the z-axis (a descending fifth) followed by a move in the x-y plane proved most difficult, with users requiring between 2 and 6 attempts. During harmonic sequence navigation tasks, forward steps (descending fifths) also proved problematic with users making nearly twice as many errors in harmonic progressions with descending fifths compared to progressions that did not.

During the exploration stage, users exhibited a variety of gestural styles. The participant who had struggled most with the navigational tasks strongly preferred the blue 'clock face' controller, keeping the red relatively static. Two participants combined arm gestures with leg movement, either bending at the knees or lunging forwards with one leg to trigger the forward step.

4.2. Discussion

Although the interface appeared to be relatively intuitive with a high success rate in the instructional stage, the test identified the *forward* gesture as difficult to operate. Since this gesture corresponds to a descending fifth, a crucial progression in tonal music, a quick solution might be to use the 'red light off' gesture to descend a fifth and the forward gesture to ascend a fifth. However, a more permanent solution would be to improve the colour tracking along the z-axis, either by counting red or blue pixels to determine the size or adding a separate camera to the side of the user and simply track location.

5. CONCLUSIONS

The main contribution of this work is to provide the basic framework for an interface allowing users to navigate harmonic pitch space with gestures in three-dimensional space. The 3D Tonnetz based on [2, 6] and [3, 4, 5] was proposed as a model of harmony for the interface. A system to track two-handed gestures in real time was devised and simple audio feedback generated over MIDI.

A preliminary user study showed that some aspects of gesture recognition worked well but others, particularly z-axis motion (descending fifths), could be improved.

The strong didactic properties of the installation [c.f. 6] can be utilised by music students and teachers in conjunction with music theory, analysis and composition studies.

Furthermore, since the 3D Tonnetz is grounded firmly on root progression theories [3, 4, 5], the interface can be usefully applied to the field of music analysis. Empirical studies [5, 15] have shown that root progressions differ fundamentally between pre-tonal and tonal music. As such, the interface could provide an interesting visual tool to map these two genres of music for comparison.

Finally, with development to the audio system, the interface could be used in musical performances, both allowing performers to use gestures rather than instruments and for audiences to visualise musical performances.

6. REFERENCES

[1] I. Cross, "Pitch Schemata", in *Perception and Cognition of Music*. I. Deliège, and J. Sloboda, (Eds.), Psychology Press, 1997, pp.357-390

[2] C. H. Longuet-Higgins, "The Perception of Music," in *Proceedings of the Royal Society: Series B*, 1979, pp.307-322.

[3] J.-P. Rameau, *Treatise on Harmony*. P. Gossett (trans.), Dover Publications, 1971.

[4] N. Meeus, "Toward a Post-Schoenbergian Grammar of Tonal and Pre-Tonal Harmonic Progressions," in *Music Theory Online*, 2000.

[5] D. Tymoczko, "Function Theories: A Statistical Approach," *Musurgia*, 2003, pp.35-64.

[6] S. Holland et. al., "Running up Blueberry Hill: Prototyping Whole Body Interaction in Harmony Space," in *Proc. of the Third Int. Conf. on Tangible Embedded Interaction*, Cambridge, 2009, pp.93-98.

[7] S. Holland et. al., "Whole Body Interaction in Abstract Domains" in *Whole Body Interaction*. D. England (Ed.), Springer Verlag, 2011, pp.19-34.

[8] G. J. Balzano, "The Group-theoretic Description of 12-fold and Microtonal Pitch Systems," in *Computer Music J.*, 1980, pp.66-84.

[9] R. Adeney and A. R. Brown, "Performing with Grid Music Systems," in *Improvise: The Australasian Computer Music Conf.*, Brisbane, 2009, pp.102-109.

[10] R. Behringer and J. Elliot, "Linking Physical Space with the Riemann Tonnetz for Exploration of Western Tonality," in *Music Education*. J. Hermida and M. Ferrero (Eds.), Nova Science Publishers, 2009, pp.131-143.

[11] E. Chew and A. R. J. François, "Interactive Multi-scale Visualizations of Tonal Evolution in MuSA.RT Opus 2," in *Special Issue on Music Visualization and Education, ACM Computers in Entertainment*, N. Lee (Eds.), 2005, pp.1-16.

[12] R. Cohn, "Neo-Riemannian Operations, Parsimonious Trichords, and their *Tonnetz* Representations", in *J. Music Theory*, 1997, pp.1-66

[13] R. N. Shepard, "Structural Representations of Musical Pitch," in *The Psychology of Music*. D. Deutsch (Ed.), Academic Press, 1982, pp.334-390.

[14] J. Oliver, "The MANO Controller: A Video Based Hand Tracking System," in *Proc. Int. Computer Music Conf.*, New York, 2010.

[15] T. Hedges and M. Rohrmeier. "Exploring Rameau and Beyond: a Corpus Study of Root Progression Theories," in *Proc. Mathematics and Computation in Music*, 2011, pp.334-337.

AUDIO-TACTILE FEEDBACK IN MUSICAL GESTURE PRIMITIVES: FINGER PRESSING

Hanna Järveläinen, Stefano Papetti, Sébastien Schiesser
ICST, Zurich University of the Arts
name.surname@zhdk.ch

Tobias Grosshauser
Wearable Computing lab, ETH Zurich
tobias.grosshauser@ife.ee.ethz.ch

ABSTRACT

We present a study on the effect of auditory and vibrotactile cues in a finger-pressing task. During a training phase subjects learned three target forces, and had to reproduce them during an experiment, under different feedback conditions. Results show that audio-tactile augmentation allowed subjects to achieve memorized target forces with improved accuracy. A tabletop device capable of recording normal force and displaying vibrotactile feedback was implemented to run several experiments. This study is first in a series of planned investigations on the role of audio-haptic feedback and perception in relation to musical gestures primitives.

1. INTRODUCTION

The synergy of tactile, auditory and kinesthetic cues generally plays a central role while performing on acoustic and electro-acoustic musical instruments. Indeed, several studies [1–3] support the idea that tactile and kinesthetic feedback inform sophisticated control strategies which enable experienced musicians to achieve top performance levels (e.g. precise timing, accurate intonation), and support expressivity and self-monitoring.

Conversely, while modern digital musical interfaces (DMIs) can track to different extent input gestures, they provide haptic feedback only as by-product of their built-in mechanics, if any. This missing physical link between DMIs and performers prevents the latter to enter the engagement and embodiment normally established in tactual interactions with traditional instruments, and alters the action-perception loop [4]. In this perspective, the addition of advanced audio-haptic to future DMIs is expected to offer enhanced playability, performance and expressivity. Currently, however, the development of actuated musical interfaces is often grounded on practice and intuition, leading to the production of one-of-a-kind devices [5], while only rarely a systematic approach is taken into account [6], or general guidelines are produced [7–9].

To overcome this, we suggest that a scientifically founded, multidisciplinary approach is necessary, which should involve experts from fields such as human-machine interaction, musical practice, applied psychology and engineering. The present work belongs to a series of ongoing investigations aimed at collecting novel qualitative and quantitative results on the role of audio-haptic feedback and perception in interactions with musical instruments and digital musical interfaces. By following a systematic bottom-up approach – starting with focus on gesture primitives observed in instrumental practice (such as pressing, plucking, sliding, etc.) that will be then combined in more articulated ones – we aim at isolating cross-modal and multisensory phenomena, and at identifying gestures and tasks where the auditory and tactile channels appear crucial to musical performance. The long-term goal is to establish well-grounded guidelines for the implementation of actuated musical interfaces.

In this paper a study is presented, which investigates the effect of audio-tactile cues on reaching target finger-pressing forces that have been previously learned in a training phase. Despite considering simplified input gestures and feedback stimuli, our experiment was designed to imitate real-world playing conditions, where musicians would learn the response of an instrument, and would then perform on it by relying on memorized standards (e.g. from kinesthetic memory).

The present work is the continuation of a preliminary study [10] which is here expanded by re-analyzing the experimental data with more fitting and robust statistical methods, and taking into consideration different groups of subjects according to their musical skills. Moreover, an original discussion of the new results has been added, and the general coverage of the experiment extended.

Similar studies on the effect of haptic feedback on finger-force control are e.g. [11, 12], however these do not take into consideration auditory feedback, nor they rely on memorized force targets.

Other studies which make use of actuated interfaces to investigate the effects of auditory and vibrotactile feedback in tasks related to musical performance are e.g. [13–16].

2. EXPERIMENT

The experiment considered the gesture of pressing with the finger on a flat, rigid surface.

Our hypothesis was that auditory and tactile feedback provided interactively by such surface would support subjects in reaching target pressing-force levels.

Figure 1. The touch box interface used in the experiment for recording normal finger forces and providing vibrotactile feedback.

2.1 Apparatus and signal flow

The experiment made use of a tabletop interface developed for this purpose, and housed in a small 3D-printed plastic box (see Figure 1). The touch box interface offers a top panel embedding an Interlink 406 force sensing resistor (FSR) which records normal force. The analog force signal provided by the FSR is fed into an Arduino UNO board which uniformly samples it at 1920 Hz with 10 bit resolution [17]. The Arduino is connected via USB to a host laptop running Pure Data, where the digital data are recorded and used to control a sound synthesis algorithm (see 2.2). The audio signal generated by the synthesis algorithm is output through a RME Fireface 800 audio interface, and used to provide both auditory and vibrotactile feedback: the former is sent to a pair of Sennheiser HD 202 headphones, while the latter is sent to a battery-powered audio amplifier feeding a HiWave HIAX13C02-8/RH audio exciter which is attached to the touch box's top panel.

The box construction was optimized so that the embedded exciter produces vibrations on the touch panel with minimum sound emission. This allows to segregate the auditory and vibrotactile feedback separately.

Additionally, the experimental setup offered an 'OK' button allowing the subjects to mark their currently applied force (see 2.3).

The round-trip latency of a comparable system, which used a similar software/hardware setup for force data acquisition and audio-tactile feedback generation, was measured under 20 ms [17].

2.2 Stimuli and conditions

A simple sine wave was chosen as audio-tactile feedback signal, whose amplitude varied proportionally to the pressing-force applied on the touch panel, thus implementing a metaphor that is commonly found in musical practice, and especially on DMIs. The maximum intensity of the vibrotactile stimulus – corresponding to the maximum force manageable by the FSR – was empirically set to the high-

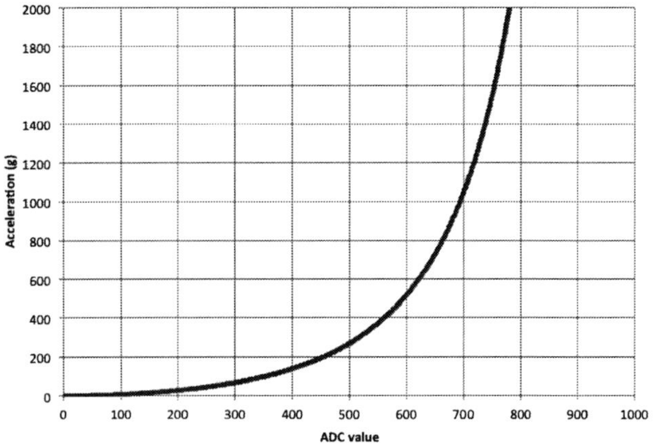

Figure 2. Characteristic showing input acceleration (g-force) vs. sampled force values (10 bit ADC)

est level that could be produced by the amplifier-exciter combination without perceivable distortion. Similarly, the frequency of the sine wave was empirically chosen in order to maximize the produced vibrotactile sensation [2] at any output level, and consequently set to 200 Hz.

Four *feedback conditions* were considered in the experiment: neutral condition (N), without active feedback; auditory feedback only (A), provided through headphones; auditory and vibrotactile feedback (AV); vibrotactile feedback only (V). In the latter condition, in order to cancel any residual sound emission produced by the interface, a masking noise signal was sent through the headphones.

The experiment was run under three *target conditions* (standards), each corresponding to a different pressing-force level. The targets were chosen empirically according to low, medium and high pressing-forces, within the data range of the interface (values within 0-1023, corresponding to 10-bit resolution): the low target was set to 400, the medium one to 650 and the high target to 850.

By combining the "acceleration-to-voltage" characteristic of the Interlink 406 FSR, and the "voltage-to-ADC values" characteristic of the Arduino UNO board, we extracted the curve shown in Figure 2. This allows one to approximately figure out the acceleration (g-force) values corresponding to the sampled force values output by the Arduino's ADC. Since the curve was obtained from general characteristics provided by the products' data sheet rather than from actual measurements on our interface, it has to be considered as a qualitative reference only.

2.3 Design and procedure

Fourteen subjects (average age 33 years old) participated in the experiment: five of them were pianists, five other musicians and four non-musicians. The musicians were either professionals or in professional training, while the non-musicians had no more than a couple of years of experience with any musical instrument. All subjects reported normal hearing and sense of touch.

The task was to reach a given standard among low, medium or high target forces, under one of the four feedback conditions (N, A, V and AV), thus leading to 12 possible combinations of target forces and feedback conditions. The test followed a 2-factor within subjects design, where each subject was tested under each combination of conditions. All combinations were repeated 10 times for each subject, resulting in 120 trials that were presented in randomized order.

The subjects sat at a desk, on which the touch box interface and the 'OK' button had been arranged, and were instructed to lean their forearm (dominant hand) on a arm rest and to press one finger on the interface's top panel. Also, they were asked to choose and use the same finger throughout the experiment, and not to touch the box with other fingers.

To begin with, the subjects entered a short *training phase* (lasting 2-4 minutes) in which they had to learn the target pressing-forces, and could freely practice to reproduce them. This was done by providing an additional audio signal through the headphones: three different beeping tones – each corresponding to one target – signaled when the applied force was within an acceptable range (± 50 units) around a target. During this phase, the AV and N feedback conditions were alternated (1-2 minutes each), and when the former condition was on, the subjects were instructed to pay attention to the intensity of the vibrotactile and auditory feedback. During the experimental session, after each block of 30 trials, the subjects were allowed to shortly retrain to refresh their memory.

During the actual trials the beeping tones signaling the targets were removed, and the subjects had to adjust their pressing-force "from memory", until they believed they had reached the asked target. At that point they had to press the 'OK' button with their free hand, while maintaining the pressing-force on the touch panel.

The experiment was conducted in a sound-proof chamber and each experimental session lasted approximately one hour, including breaks and training.

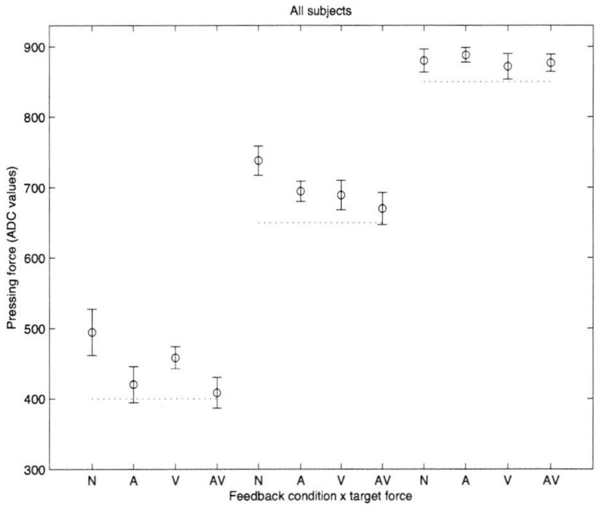

Figure 3. Mean results over all the subjects (errorbars: 95% CI, considering variability due to condition manipulation only, according to [18]). Target forces given by dashed lines: low = 400, medium = 650, high = 850).

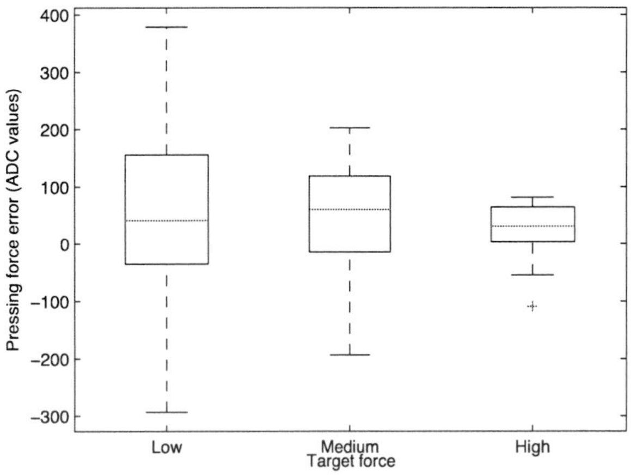

Figure 4. Box-plot of results for each target force (median and 25th / 75th percentiles describing between-subjects variability), collapsed over feedback conditions.

3. RESULTS

To prevent the possible effect (reported by some of the subjects) of having to press with both hands at the same time, the dependent variable – i.e. pressing-force on the touch panel – was measured as the average over a 10 ms time window, starting 100 ms before the subject pressed the 'OK' button.

The measurements, amounting to 1344 different recordings, included 9 missing data points which were ignored in the analyses.

The data considered for the analysis of each subject was given by the mean over the last 8 repetitions of each combination of conditions, thus regarding the first 2 repetitions as practice. These data are shown in Figure 3, which demonstrates a common trend for both low and medium targets: with audio-tactile feedback (condition AV) the mean results are nearest to the target, while they clearly overshoot with no feedback (condition N); results for the audio-only (A) and vibrotactile-only (V) conditions are somewhere between these extremes.

A large difference in variance over the target force levels was observed both within each subject's 8 repeated measurements and between subjects, shown in Figure 4. This violates the assumption of variance homogeneity for ANOVA. Therefore the data were analyzed using the *aligned rank transform*, a nonparametric method for factorial within-subjects analyses using ANOVA procedures, generalized for n factors in [19].

The analysis shows a significant main effect for the feedback factor ($F_{(3,143)} = 16$, $p < 0.0001$), when the force data were normalized by subtracting the corresponding target force from each condition (i.e. respectively 400, 650 and 850 for the low, medium and high conditions). No significant effect was observed for the target force level ($F_{(2,143)} = 0.7$, $p = 0.52$), but the interaction "feedback $\times$ target level" was significant with $F_{(6,143)} = 6.0$, $p < 0.0001$.

The interaction plots in Figure 5 show that for the low target force, mean errors are much smaller in presence of auditory or audio-tactile feedback (A, AV) than with no

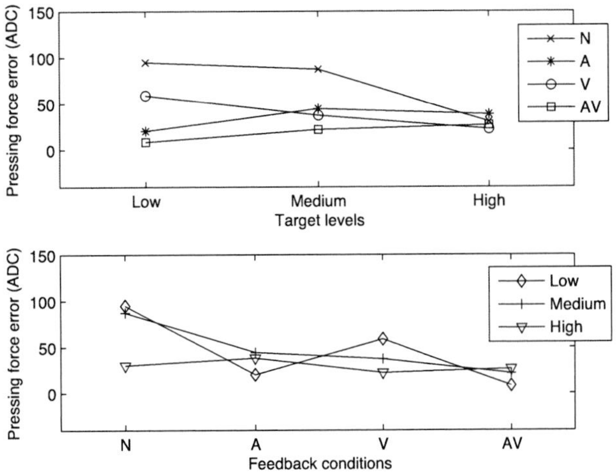

Figure 5. Interaction plots. Top panel: mean errors at the three target forces, presented for each feedback condition. Bottom panel: mean errors at the four feedback conditions, presented for each target force level.

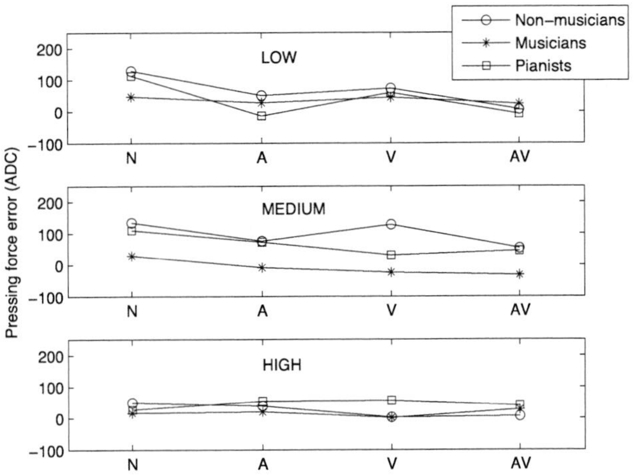

Figure 6. Mean errors for non-musicians, pianists and other musicians, for low (top panel), medium (middle panel), and high (bottom panel) target forces.

feedback (N). For the high target force, however, the results are almost equivalent at all feedback conditions.

Pairwise comparisons between the feedback conditions, collapsed over the target force levels, were performed by the *Wilcoxon signed-rank test* with *Bonferroni correction*, for significance level cutoff $\alpha = 0.05/5 = 0.01$. These results show significantly different medians between the N–AV pair ($p < 0.0001$), N–A ($p < 0.0001$), N–V ($p < 0.0001$) and V–AV ($p < 0.0001$), but not for A–V ($p = 0.22$) and hardly for A–AV ($p = 0.007$).

Finally, differences between groups of subjects according to their musical skills were investigated, which are presented in Figure 6. General observations are that pianists benefited most from auditory feedback at the low target force level, while for other factor combinations they performed only slightly better than non-musicians. An exception is the vibrotactile condition at medium target level, where non-musicians performed clearly worse than either of the musician groups. Other musicians performed evenly well at all factor combinations, and at medium target level even clearly better than the other two groups.

4. DISCUSSION

From the results described above for the employed setup, it can be generally concluded that audio-tactile feedback, and to a lesser degree auditory feedback alone, made it generally easier to reach a given target pressing-force, compared to the condition when no active feedback was present. Notably the results also show that the addition of the vibrotactile component to the auditory feedback generally improved the performance. The vibrotactile feedback alone looks instead less effective than the audio-tactile one.

The lower variance at the high target force further suggests that the task was easier with higher pressing force and more difficult at lower pressing forces. Thus one may accept the hypothesis that auditory, and especially audio-tactile feedback facilitate reaching force targets in conditions where the task is difficult.

The performance of pianists – generally similar to that of non-musicians and under par compared to other musicians – may be explained considering that the task of pressing continuously on the touch box interface was clearly distant from that of hitting the keys on the piano. Moreover, in their instrumental practice, pianists are not in direct contact with the source of sound and vibration, which are instead mediated through the keys and hammer mechanics. This may result in less developed tactile sensitivity compared to e.g. players of stringed instruments, who perform by direct contact with the strings. In this regard, different studies [1, 20] showed that vibrations on stringed instruments are clearly perceivable by the player during performance, while vibrations on the piano are generally hardly felt at the fingers. It must be considered however that, due to difficulties in recruiting subjects, our sample size is small and it does not allow reliable statistical inference. As an example, a *Kruskal-Wallis test* on the "N–low target" combination was faintly non-significant ($\chi^2 = 4.86$, $p = 0.09$), giving no evidence for true differences in medians between the independent groups. Therefore it remains a future task to test more thoroughly performance differences among classes of musicians and non-musicians.

4.1 Issues

The experiment proved somewhat problematic at the high target force, where the results have a much lower variance than at the other two targets. The same is true for intra-subject variability: for all subjects the varying range of the 10 repetitions of each high-target conditions combination was typically much smaller than for the low or medium targets. One explanation lies in the nonlinear sensitivity curve of the touch box interface, shown in Figure 2), hence to equal small changes in the pressing-force correspond ADC values variations that are larger in the low range than in the high one. In this regard we plan to linearize the system, e.g. according to what suggested in [21]. Another explanation is that subjects found it easier to be accurate when applying a hard rather than a soft pressing-force.

Fatigue was neither noticed in the recorded data, nor reported by the subjects. Practice effects during the course of the 10 repetitions of each combination of conditions were not observed, except during the first two repetitions for some subjects. However, future test designs should address the possible learning and kinesthetic memory effects, e.g. by varying the standard randomly within a narrow force range and presenting it before each trial.

Concerning the auditory feedback, according to the standardized equal loudness curves (ISO226:2003), the perceived loudness (phons) of a 200 Hz sine tone increases somewhat faster than the sound pressure level (dB) in the over 70 dB range than in the softer range, suggesting that a difference of 1 dB causes a greater difference in perceived loudness. However, in this occasion no loudness recordings could be performed, since at the time of writing we do not have instrumentation suitable for measurements on headphones.

Finally, it is known that sensitivity to vibrations depends on stimulus location, stimulus frequency and contact area [2]. In this regard, it is worth noticing that while most subjects performed the experiment placing their finger-pad on the touch panel, a few of them used their fingertip.

4.2 Other remarks

While visual feedback was not prevented explicitly, some subjects chose to perform the experiment with their eyes closed to better focus on the auditory and tactile sensations.

Related research involving memory in action-perception tasks is reported by Morris *et al.* [22], who found that haptic feedback enhanced force skill learning in sensorimotor tasks. Their study concerned visual and haptic force feedback and focused on the effect of three training modalities (visual only, haptic only, or both), while in the test phase the subjects relied only on force recall. In the present study, training was given to all subjects first without feedback and then with audio-tactile feedback, thus the effect of training on recall could not be measured. However it is expected that, in a normal musical scenario, the player learns the behavior of the instrument in presence of both auditory and haptic feedback.

An aspect requiring further measurements is that of the relative importance of kinestethic and tactile feedback. In the present study, tactile feedback was in fact always present even in the neutral condition N through sensations of the fingertip, augmented by a vibrotactile signal in the V and AV feedback conditions. Thus it was not possible to completely separate the tactile and kinesthetic channels, as was done in a study by Srinivasan and Chen [23], who repeated force tracking experiments in normal conditions and with locally anesthetized finger tips. They found that while absence of tactile feedback resulted in somewhat higher force tracking errors, absence of augmented visual feedback increased the error with target force magnitude, indicating that without augmented visual feedback the force tracking task was more difficult with high target forces. This contradicts with our findings for high target forces, which indicate the smallest errors regardless of feedback condition. Future experiments will be designed taking this aspect into account, while pressing forces will be measured in terms of Newtons instead of ADC values.

Also, we planned to perform vibration measurements on our interface for the different experimental conditions, and compare these data with known psychophysiological results [24].

Our choice of audio-tactile stimuli (sine wave) was motivated by the desire of keeping the setup as simple and controllable as possible. In future implementation we plan to consider the use of physically-based sound models that react in a dynamic way to the user's gestures. Nevertheless this could introduce interference at a cognitive and perceptual level that might be difficult to isolate in an experimental setting.

5. CONCLUSION

A pilot experiment has been described, which investigated the role of auditory and vibrotactile feedback in a finger-pressing task. At each trial, subjects had to aim at one of three memorized target pressing-forces, under different feedback conditions (no active feedback, audio only, vibrotactile only and audio-tactile). Our analysis show that the audio-tactile augmentation allowed subjects to reach a given target force with the best accuracy.

The present work is first in a series of planned experiments that will systematically measure performance for various musically relevant gesture primitives, in relation to auditory and haptic cues. In this way, we aim at providing useful guidelines for the implementation of future actuated digital musical instruments, that will enable improved performance control (e.g. precise timing, accurate intonation, articulation), expressivity and playability.

Acknowledgments

The authors wish to thank Martin Fröhlich for building the touch box interface, and Marco Civolani for providing the Arduino firmware for data acquisition.

6. REFERENCES

[1] A. Askenfelt and E. V. Jansson, "On vibration sensation and finger touch in stringed instrument playing," *Music Perception: An Interdisciplinary Journal*, vol. 9, no. 3, pp. pp. 311–349, 1992.

[2] R. T. Verrillo, "Vibration sensation in humans," *Music Perception*, vol. 9, no. 3, pp. 281–302, 1992.

[3] J. Rovan and V. Hayward, "Typology of tactile sounds and their synthesis in gesture-driven computer music performance," in *In Trends in Gestural Control of Music*, M. Wanderley and M. Battier, Eds. IRCAM, 2000, pp. 297–320.

[4] J. Lagarde and J. A. S. Kelso, "Binding of movement, sound and touch: multimodal coordination dynamics," *Experimental Brain Research*, vol. 173, pp. 673–688, 2006.

[5] D. Overholt, E. Berdahl, and R. Hamilton, "Advancements in actuated musical instruments," *Organised Sound*, vol. 16, no. 02, pp. 154–165, Jun 2011.

[6] S. O'Modhrain and C. Chafe, "Incorporating Haptic Feedback into Interfaces for Music Applications," in *Proc. of ISORA, World Automation Conference*, 2000.

[7] S. O'Modhrain, "A framework for the evaluation of digital musical instruments," *Computer Music J.*, vol. 35, no. 1, pp. 28–42, Mar. 2011. [Online]. Available: http://dx.doi.org/10.1162/COMJ_a_00038

[8] M. T. Marshall and M. M. Wanderley, "Examining the effects of embedded vibrotactile feedback on the feel of a digital musical instrument," in *Proc. Conf. on New Interfaces for Musical Expression*, ser. NIME, Jun. 2011.

[9] D. M. Birnbaum and M. M. Wanderley, "A systematic approach to musical vibrotactile feedback," in *Proc. Int. Computer Music Conf. (ICMC)*, 2007.

[10] S. Papetti, H. Järveläinen, S. Schiesser, and T. Grosshauser, "Effects of audio-tactile feedback on force accuracy in a finger pressing task," in *Proc. Int. Workshop on Haptic and Audio Interaction Design (HAID)*, 2013.

[11] L. Jiang, M. R. Cutkosky, J. Ruutiainen, and R. Raisamo, "Improving finger force control with vibrational haptic feedback for multiple sclerosis," in *Proc. of the IASTED Int. Conf. on Telehealth/Assistive Technologies*, ser. Telehealth/AT '08. Anaheim, CA, USA: ACTA Press, 2008, pp. 110–115.

[12] T. Ahmaniemi, "Effect of dynamic vibrotactile feedback on the control of isometric finger force," *IEEE Trans. on Haptics*, 2012.

[13] F. Fontana, S. Papetti, M. Civolani, V. del Bello, and B. Bank, "An exploration on the influence of vibrotactile cues during digital piano playing," in *Proc. Int. Conf. on Sound and Music Computing (SMC)*, Padua, Italy, 2011.

[14] B. Giordano, F. Avanzini, M. Wanderley, and S. McAdams, "Multisensory integration in percussion performance," in *10ème Congrès Francais d'Acoustique*, Lyon, France, 2010.

[15] S. Dahl and R. Bresin, "Is the player more influenced by the auditory than the tactile feedback from the instrument?" in *Proc. Conf. on Digital Audio Effects (DAFX)*, Limerick, Ireland, 2001, pp. 194–197.

[16] D. Birnbaum, "The touch flute: Exploring roles of vibrotactile feedback in musical performance," McGill University, Tech report, 2003.

[17] M. Civolani, F. Fontana, and S. Papetti, "Efficient acquisition of force data in interactive shoe designs," in *Haptic and Audio Interaction Design (HAID)*. Copenhagen, Denmark: Springer, 2010.

[18] D. Cousineau, "Confidence intervals in within-subject designs: A simpler solution to Loftus and Masson's method," *Tutorials in Quantitative Methods for Psychology*, vol. 1, no. 1, pp. 42–45, 2005.

[19] J. O. Wobbrock, L. Findlater, D. Gergle, and J. J. Higgins, "The aligned rank transform for nonparametric factorial analyses using only anova procedures," in *Proc. of the SIGCHI Conf. on Human Factors in Computing Systems*, ser. CHI '11. New York, NY, USA: ACM, 2011, pp. 143–146.

[20] C. Chafe, "Tactile audio feedback," in *Proc. Int. Computer Music Conf. (ICMC)*, 1993.

[21] C. Stewart, M. Rohs, S. Kratz, and G. Essl, "Characteristics of pressure-based input for mobile devices," in *Proc. of the SIGCHI Conf. on Human Factors in Computing Systems*, ser. CHI '10. New York, NY, USA: ACM, 2010, pp. 801–810. [Online]. Available: http://doi.acm.org/10.1145/1753326.1753444

[22] D. Morris, H. Tan, F. Barbagli, T. Chang, and K. Salisbury, "Haptic Feedback Enhances Force Skill Learning," in *Second Joint EuroHaptics Conf. and Symposium on Haptic Interfaces for Virtual Environment and Teleoperator Systems (WHC'07)*, 2007.

[23] M. A. Srinivasan and J. Chen, "Human performance in controlling normal forces of contact with rigid objects," in *Advances in Robotics, Mechatronics, and Haptic Interfaces (ASME)*, 1993.

[24] R. T. Verrillo, "Psychophysics of vibrotactile stimulation," *The Journal of the Acoustical Society of America*, vol. 77, no. 1, pp. 225–232, 1985.

VocaRefiner: An Interactive Singing Recording System with Integration of Multiple Singing Recordings

Tomoyasu Nakano **Masataka Goto**
National Institute of Advanced Industrial Science and Technology (AIST), Japan
{t.nakano, m.goto}[at]aist.go.jp

ABSTRACT

This paper presents a singing recording system, *VocaRefiner*, that enables a singer to make a better singing recording by integrating multiple recordings of a song he or she has sung repeatedly. It features a function called *clickable lyrics*, with which the singer can click a word in the displayed lyrics to start recording from that word. Clickable lyrics facilitate efficient multiple recordings because the singer can easily and quickly repeat recordings of a phrase until satisfied. Each of the recordings is automatically aligned to the music-synchronized lyrics for comparison by using a *phonetic alignment* technique. Our system also features a function, called *three-element decomposition*, that analyzes each recording to decompose it into three essential elements: F_0, power, and spectral envelope. This enables the singer to select good elements from different recordings and use them to synthesize a better recording by taking full advantage of the singer's ability. Pitch correction and time stretching are also supported so that singers can overcome limitations in their singing skills. VocaRefiner was implemented by combining existing signal processing methods with new estimation methods for achieving high-accuracy robust F_0 and group delay, which we propose to improve the synthesized quality.

1. INTRODUCTION

When singers perform live in front of an audience they only have one chance. If they forget the lyrics or sing out of time with the accompaniment then these mistakes cannot be corrected, though singing out-of-tune could be fixed by using real-time pitch correction (e.g., Auto-tune or [1]). However, when vocals are recorded in a studio setting, the situation is quite different. Many attempts, or "takes", at singing the entire song, or sections within it, can be recorded. Indeed, if time and cost are not an issue, this process can continue until either the singer or someone else (*e.g.*, a producer or recording engineer) is completely satisfied with the performance. The vocal track which eventually appears on the final recording is often reconstituted from different sections of various takes and, to a greater and greater degree, subjected to automatic pitch correction

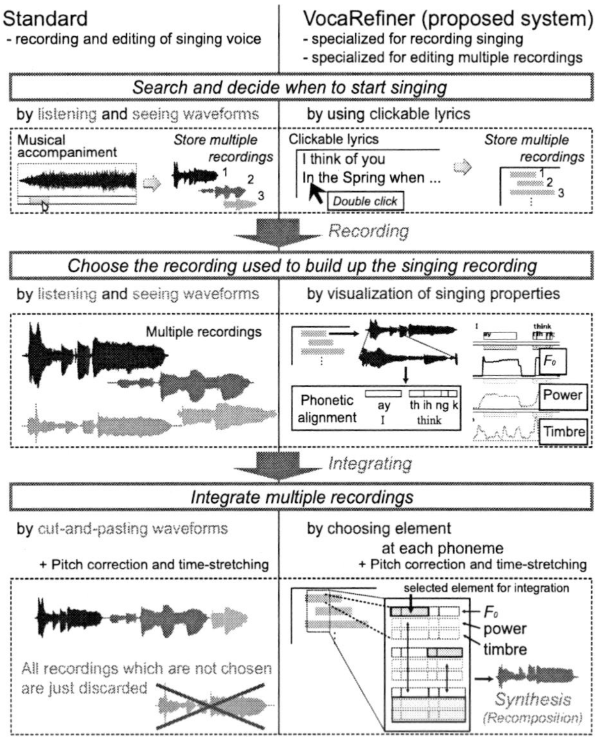

Figure 1. A comparison of VocaRefiner with the standard recording and editing procedure.

(*e.g.*, Auto-tune) to "fix" any notes which are sung out of tune. What is left over at the end of this process is simply discarded as it is of no further use. This "standard" process of recording singing voice is summarized in the left side of Figure 1.

Although this procedure for recording and editing vocals is widespread, it has some drawbacks. First, it is extremely time-consuming to manually listen through multiple takes and subjectively determine the "best" parts to be saved for the final version. Second, the manipulation of multi-track waveforms through "cut-and-paste" and the use of pitch correction software requires specialist technical knowledge which may be too complex for the amateur singer recording music in their home.

To address these shortcomings, we have developed an interactive singing recording system called *VocaRefiner*, which lets a singer make multiple recordings interactively and edit them while visualizing analysis of the recordings. VocaRefiner has three functions (shown in the right side of Figure 1) which are specialized for recording, editing and processing singing recordings.

1. *Interactive recording with clickable lyrics*: This allows a singer to immediately navigate to the part of the song he or she wants to sing without the need to visually inspect the audio waveform.
2. *Visualization of singing analysis*: This enables the singer to see an analysis of the recorded singing which captures three essential elements of singing voice: F_0 (pitch), power (loudness), and spectral envelope (voice timbre).
3. *Integration by recomposition and manipulation*: This allows the singer to select elements among multiple recordings at the phoneme level and recombine them to synthesize an integrated result. In addition to the direct recombination of phonemes, VocaRefiner also has pitch-correction and time-stretching functionality to give the user even more control over their performance.

The use of these three functions draws out the latent potential of existing singing recordings to the greatest degree possible, and enables the amateur singer to use advanced technologies in a manner which is both intuitive to use and enhances creative possibilities of music creation through singing.

The remainder of this paper is structured as follows. In Section 2 we present an overview of the main motivation, the target users for VocaRefiner, and the originality of this study. In Section 3 we describe VocaRefiner's functionality and usage. The signal processing back-end which drives VocaRefiner is described in Section 4 along with results on the performance of the F_0 detection method. In Section 5 we discuss the role and potential impact of VocaRefiner in the wider context of singing, and finally, in Section 6 we summarize the key outcomes from the paper.

We provide a website with video demonstrations of VocaRefiner at http://staff.aist.go.jp/t.nakano/VocaRefiner/.

2. VOCAREFINER: AN INTERACTIVE SINGING-RECORDING SYSTEM

This section describes the goal of our system and shortcomings of standard approaches. To achieve the goal and to overcome the shortcomings, we then propose our original solutions of VocaRefiner.

2.1 Goal of VocaRefiner

The aim of this study is to enable amateur singers recording music in their home to create high-quality singing recordings efficiently and effectively. Many amateur singers have recently started making personal recordings of songs and have uploaded them to video and audio sharing services on the web. For example, over 600,000 music video clips including singing recordings by amateur singers have been uploaded to the most popular Japanese video-sharing service *Nico Nico Douga* (http://www.nicovideo.jp). There are many listeners who enjoy such amateur singing which is illustrated by the fact that, as of April 2013 on Nico Nico Douga, over 4250 video clips by amateur singers received over one hundred thousand page views, over 190 video clips had more than one million page views, and the top five video clips had more than five million page views.

In Japanese culture, it is common for the singers not to show their faces in video clips. In this way, their recordings can be appreciated purely on the quality of the singing. In fact, amateur singers have become very well-known just by their voices and released commercially-available compact discs from recording companies. This is a kind of the new culture for music creation and appreciation driven by massive influx of user-generated content (UGC) on web services like Nico Nico Douga.

This creates a need and demand for making personal singing recordings at home. Most amateur singers record their singing voice at home without help from other people (*e.g.*, studio engineers). To fully produce the recordings, they must complete the entire process shown in the left side of Figure 1 by themselves. To create high-quality singing recordings, singers typically use traditional recording software or a digital audio workstation on a personal computer to recording multiple takes of their singing, again and again until they are satisfied. They then cut-and-paste multi-track waveforms and sometimes use pitch correction software (*e.g.*, Auto-tune). This traditional approach is inefficient and time-consuming, and requires specialist technical knowledge which may be a barrier for some would-be singers. We therefore study a novel recording system specialized for personal singing recording. Our eventual goal with this work is to facilitate and encourage even greater numbers of singers to create vocal recordings with better control and to actively participate in UGC music culture.

2.2 Originality of VocaRefiner

In this paper we present an alternative to the standard approach of recording singing voice by providing a novel interactive singing recording system *VocaRefiner*. It has an original efficient and effective interface based on visualizing analysis of singing voice and driven by signal processing technologies. We propose a novel use of the lyrics to specify when to start the singing recording and also propose an interactive visualization and integration of multiple recordings.

Although lyrics have already been clickable on some music players [2], they only allowed users to change the playback position for listening. VocaRefiner presents a novel use of lyrics alignment for recording purposes.

Multiple recordings were also not fully utilized for integration into the final high-quality recording, with most recordings being simply discarded if they are not explicitly selected. For example, recordings with good lyrics but incorrect pitch and recordings with correct-pitch singing but a mistake in the lyrics generally cannot be used in the final recording. However, VocaRefiner can make full use of bad recordings that would otherwise be discarded in the standard approach.

Although there has not been much research into the assistance of singing recording, some studies exist for visu-

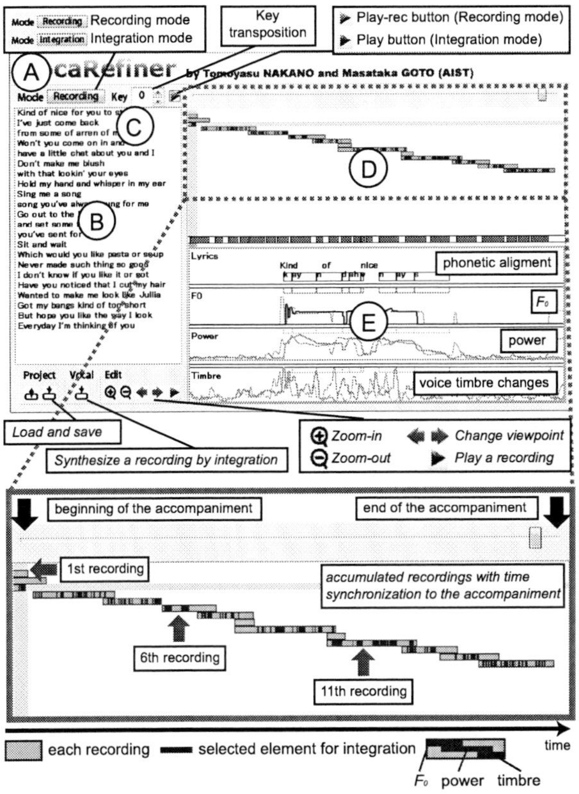

Figure 2. An example VocaRefiner screen. The recordings are displayed as rectangles.

alizing analysis of singing voices to improve singing skills [3, 4]. Singing analysis has also been used for other purposes, such as time-stretching based on phase vocoder [5], voice-conversion [6], and voice-morphing [7]. However, we believe that no other research currently exists which deals with both the analysis and integration of multiple singing recordings as in VocaRefiner.

3. INTERFACE OF VOCAREFINER

The VocaRefiner system, shown in Figure 2, is built around components which encapsulate the following three functions:

1. Interactive recording by clickable lyrics
2. Visualization by automatic singing analysis
3. Integration by recomposition and manipulation

These functions can be used within the two main modes of VocaRefiner, "recording mode" and "integration mode", which are selected using button Ⓐ in Figure 2.

In recording mode the user first selects the target lyrics of the song they wish to sing (which can currently be in English or Japanese, marked Ⓑ) and loads the musical accompaniment.

To facilitate the alignment of lyrics with music and clickable lyric functionality, the representation of the lyrics must be richer than a simple text file containing the words of the song. It must also contain timing information - where each word has an associated onset time and the lyrics must also include the pronunciation of each word. It is possible to estimate this information automatically, however this process can produce some errors which require manual correction. Given the normal text file of lyrics, we therefore automatically convert it into the VocaRefiner format and then manually correct errors if any.

The accompaniment can include a synthesized guide melody or vocal (e.g. prepared by a singing synthesis system) to make it easier for the user to sing along with the lyrics. In the case where the user is recording a cover version of an original song they can include the original vocal of the song for this purpose.

If the user is unable to sing the song in original key, they can make use of a transposition function (marked Ⓒ), to shift the accompaniment to a more comfortable range.

3.1 Interactive Recording with Clickable Lyrics

The clickable lyrics function, which is built around the time-synchronization of lyrics to audio (described in Section 4.1), enables a singer who makes a mistake in the pitch or lyrics to start singing that part again immediately. Such seamless re-recording can offer a new avenue for recording singing, in particular for the amateur singer recording at home. One case where this could be particularly useful is when attempting to sing the first note of a song, where it can be hard to hit the right note straight away. Using clickable lyrics, the singer can repeat the phrase they will to sing recording each version until they are happy they have it right. By recording vocals in this way, a singer could also easily try different styles of singing the same phrase (storing each one aligned to the accompaniment), which could help them to experiment more in their singing style.

Because the lyrics and music are synchronized in time, when the singer clicks the lyrics, the accompaniment is played back on headphones (to prevent recording the accompaniment as well as the vocal) from the specified time and the voice sung by the user is recorded in time with the accompaniment. In addition, if the singer only wants to sing a particular section of the song, this section can be selected using the mouse.

The recording process can also be started by clicking the "play-rec" button indicated by the red triangle (close to Ⓒ) or by using the mouse to drag the slider located to the right of the button.

With this type of functionality, the clickable lyrics component can facilitate the efficient recording of multiple takes, where a singer can repeat an individual phrase over and over until they are satisfied. In this way, our work extends existing work into lyrics and audio synchronization [2], which has, up until now, only been applied to playback systems which cannot record and align singing input.

3.2 Visualization by Automatic Singing Analysis

Two types of visualization are implemented in VocaRefiner. The first of which addresses the timing information of multiple recordings. Each separate recording is indicated by a rectangle displayed at Ⓓ, as shown on Figure 2, whose length indicates its duration. The rectangles of multiple recordings, which appear stacked on top of one

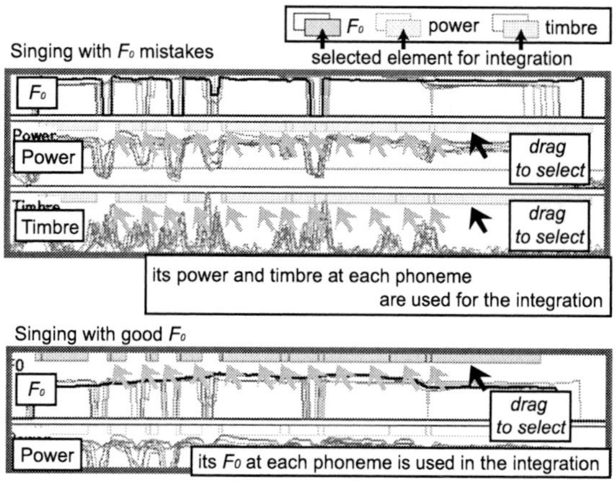

Figure 3. Selecting voice elements to integrate.

another, can be used to see which parts of a song were sung many times, and can be useful for singers to find challenging parts requiring additional practice.

The second visualization shows the results of analyzing the singing recordings. This analysis takes place immediately after the each recording has taken place. First, the recording is automatically aligned to the lyrics via the pronunciation and timing using a *phonetic alignment* technique. VocaRefiner estimates and then displays *three elements* of each recording: F_0, power, and spectral envelope using techniques described in Section 4.2. These elements are used later for the recomposition of recordings from multiple takes.

An example of the analysis is shown at the point marked Ⓔ in Figure 2. The location of the rectangles in Figure 2 shows the onset and offset time of each phoneme. The blue line, the light green line, and the darker green line indicate trajectories of selected part used for integration of F_0, power, and voice timbre changes, respectively. The superimposed gray lines (which correspond to other recordings) are parts not selected for integration.

Such superimposed views are useful for seeing differences between the recordings without the need for repeated playback. In particular this can highlight recordings where the wrong note has been sung (without the need to listen back to the recording), and also show the singer the points where the timbre of their voice has changed.

3.3 Integration by Recomposition and Manipulation

The integration can be achieved by two main methods: "recomposition" and "manipulation" along with an additional technique for error repair. Their operation with VocaRefiner are described in the following subsections, and the technology behind them in Section 4.3.

3.3.1 Recomposition

The recomposition process involves direct interaction from the user where the elements they wish to use at each phoneme are selected with the mouse. These selected elements are used for synthesizing the recording.

In the situation where multiple recordings have been made for a particular section, VocaRefiner assumes that

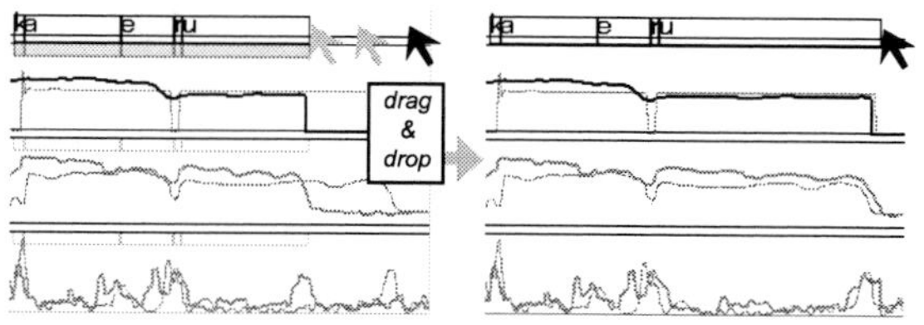

Figure 4. Time-stretching a phoneme. The length of the final phoneme /u/ is extended, and its F_0, power, and voice timbre are also stretched accordingly.

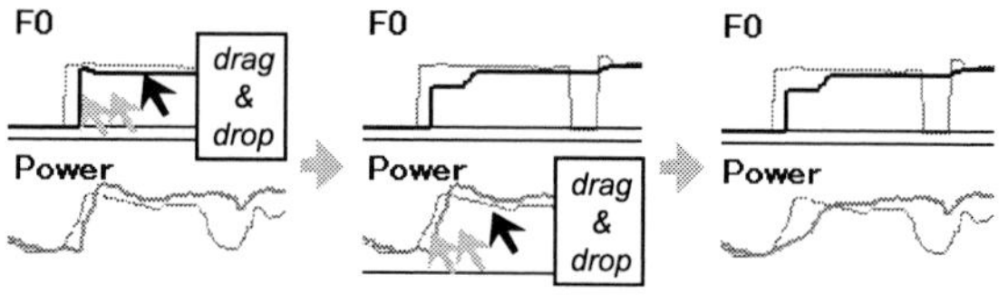

Figure 5. F_0 and power can be adjusted using the mouse.

the most recently recorded take will be of good quality, and therefore selects this by default.

3.3.2 Manipulation

Two modes of manipulation are available to the user, one which modifies the phoneme timing and the other which modifies the singing style. The modification of phoneme timing changes the phoneme onset and duration (via time-stretching), and the manipulation of singing style is achieved through changes to the F_0 and power.

A common situation requiring timing manipulation occurs when a phoneme is too short and needs to be lengthened. Figure 4 shows that when the length of the final phoneme /u/ is extended, the F_0, power, and spectral envelope of the phoneme are also stretched accordingly. Onset times can also be adjusted without the need for time-stretching.

Figure 5 shows that F_0 and power can be independently adjusted using the mouse. In addition to these local changes, the overall key of the recording can be also changed (Fig. 6) by global transposition.

3.3.3 Error Repair

Because occasional errors are unavoidable when recomposition and manipulation are based on the results of automatic analysis, it is important to recognize this possibility and provide the singer the means for correcting mistakes. The most critical errors that could require correction relate to the F_0 estimation and phonetic alignment. Such errors can be easily fixed through a simple interaction, as shown in Figure 7.

When an octave error occurs in F_0 estimation it can be repaired by dragging the mouse to specify the correct time-frequency range. In fact, octave errors can be eliminated by specifying the desired time-frequency range after recording. The more recordings of the same phrase there are, the easier it is to determine the correct time-frequency range, because the singer can make a judgement from many F_0 trajectories, where most have been correctly analysed.

Phonetic alignment errors are repaired by dragging the mouse to change the estimated phonetic boundaries. Fig-

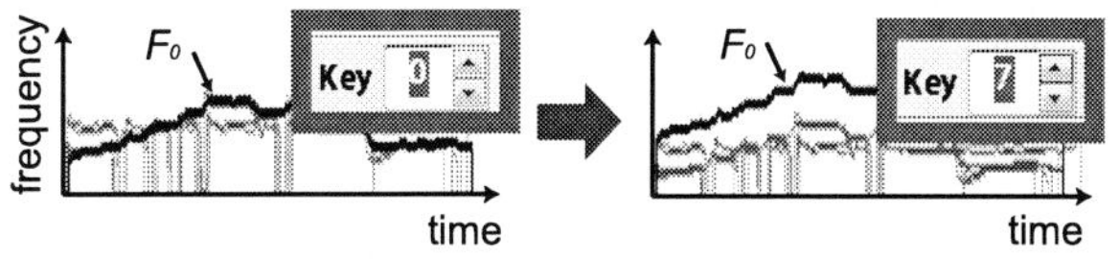

Figure 6. Example of a shift to a higher key.

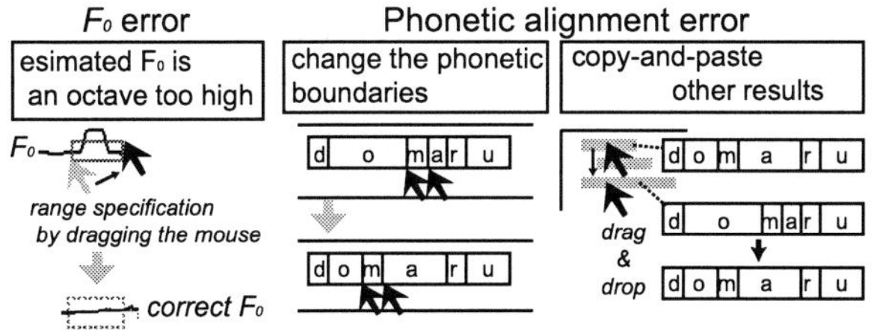

Figure 7. Error repair. An F_0 error is repaired by dragging the mouse to specify the correct time-frequency range (the red rectangle), and then a new F_0 trajectory is estimated from this range.

ure 7 shows the correction of the wrong duration of a phoneme /o/. Moreover, estimation results from other recordings can be used to correct errors by a simple copy-and-paste process. This function can be used to correct the situation where the alignment of a recording has many errors, for example, when a singer chose to hum the melody instead of sing the lyrics.

4. SIGNAL PROCESSING FOR THE IMPLEMENTATION

The functionality of VocaRefiner is built around advanced signal processing techniques for the estimation of F_0, power, spectral envelope and group delay in singing voice. While we make use of some standard techniques for this analysis, *e.g.*, F_0 [8,9], spectral envelope [8], and group delay [10], and build upon our own previous work in this area [11,12] we also present novel contributions for F_0 and group delay estimation to meet the need for very high accuracy frequency and phase estimation in VocaRefiner. In evaluating the new F_0 detection method for singing voice (in Section 4.4), we demonstrate that our method exceeds the current state of the art.

Throughout this paper, singing samples are monaural solo vocal recordings digitised at 16 bit / 44.1 kHz. The discrete analysis time step (1 *frame-time*) is 1 ms. Time t in this paper is the time measured in frame-time units. All spectral envelopes and group delay are represented by 4097 frequency bins (8192 FFT length).

4.1 Signal Processing For Interactive Recording

Methods for estimating pronunciation and timing information and for transposing the key of the accompaniment are required for interactive recording. Phoneme-level pronunciation of English lyrics is determined using the CMU pronouncing dictionary[1], and the pronunciation of Japanese lyrics is estimated by using a Japanese language morphological analyzer MeCab[2].

Timing information is estimated by first having the singer sing the target song once. The system then synchronizes the phoneme-level pronunciation of the lyrics with the recordings. This synchronization is called *phonetic alignment* and is estimated through Viterbi alignment with a monophone hidden Markov model (HMM). Two HMMs were trained with English and Japanese songs, respectively. The English songs came from the RWC Music Database (Popular Music [13], Music Genre [14], and Royalty-Free Music [13]) and the Japanese songs are in the RWC Music Database (Popular Music [13]).

When a singer wishes to transpose the key of the accompaniment in VocaRefiner, we use a well-known phase vocoder technique [5], which operates offline.

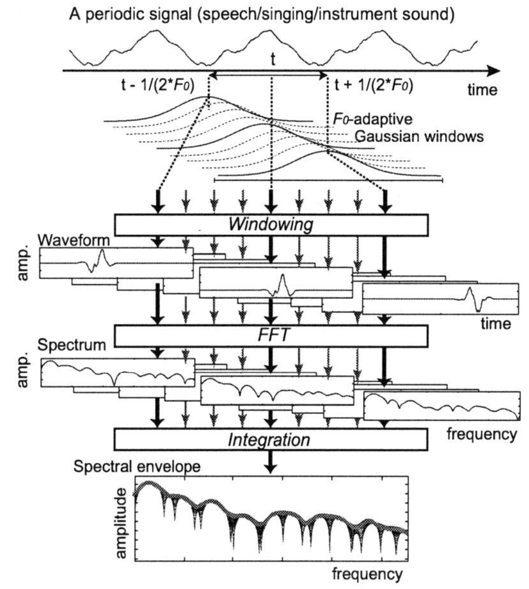

Figure 8. Overview of F_0-adaptive multi-frame integration analysis.

4.2 Signal Processing For Visualizing

A phonetic alignment method and three-element decomposition method are required for implementing this function. The phonetic alignment method is the same as that described above.

The system estimates the fundamental frequency (F_0), power, and spectral envelope of each recording.

$F_0(t)$ values are estimated using the method of Goto *et al.* [11]. $F_0(t)$ are linear-scale frequency values (Hz) estimated by applying a Hanning window whose length is 1024 samples (about 64 ms) and resampling at 16 kHz.

Spectral envelopes are estimated using F_0-adaptive multi-frame integration analysis [12]. This method can estimate spectral envelopes with appropriate shape and high temporal resolution. Figure 8 shows an overview of the analysis. First, F_0-adaptive Gaussian windows are used for spectrum analysis (F_0*-adaptive* analysis). Then neighborhood frames are integrated to estimate the target spectral envelope (*multi-frame integration* analysis).

[1] http://www.speech.cs.cmu.edu/cgi-bin/cmudict

[2] http://mecab.sourceforge.net/

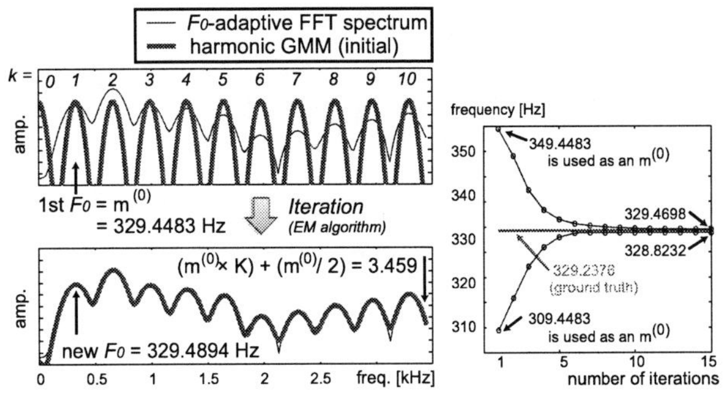

Figure 9. Iterative F_0 results estimated by the harmonic GMM.

The power is calculated from the spectral envelope by summation of the frequency axis at each time frame.

4.3 Signal Processing For Integration

For high-quality resynthesis, the three elements should be estimated accurately and with high temporal resolution. For this purpose we propose a new F_0 re-estimation technique, called *F_0-adaptive F_0 estimation method.* It is highly accurate and has the requisite high temporal resolution. To generate the phase spectrum used in resynthesis we also propose a new method for estimating group delay [10].

4.3.1 F_0-adaptive F_0 estimation method

Using the technique in [11] we perform an initial estimate of the F_0 which we call the *1st F_0* and use this as input to the F_0-adaptive F_0 estimation method. The basic idea behind our new method is that high temporal resolution can be obtained by shortening the analysis window length for F_0 estimation as much as possible. Moreover we exploit the knowledge that harmonic components at lower frequencies of the amplitude spectrum of FFT can be used to estimate F_0 accurately, as they contain relatively reliable information whereas aperiodic components often dominant at higher frequencies.

To obtain high accuracy and high temporal resolution, we propose a harmonic GMM (Gaussian mixture model). We fit the GMM to the FFT spectrum estimated by an *F_0 adaptive analysis* that uses F_0-adaptive Gaussian windows and uses the 1st F_0 used as an initial value. Hereafter, the 1st F_0 is described as $m^{(0)}$.

We designed an F_0-adaptation window by using a Gaussian function. Let $w(\tau)$ be a Gaussian window function of time τ defined as follows, where $\sigma(t)$ is the standard deviation of the Gaussian distribution and $F_0(t)$ is the fundamental frequency for analysis time t.

$$w(\tau) = \exp(-\frac{\tau^2}{2\sigma(t)^2}) \quad (1)$$

$$\sigma(t) = \frac{\alpha}{F_0(t)} \times \frac{1}{3} \quad (2)$$

To set the value of α, we follow the approach for high-accuracy spectral envelope estimation in [15] and assign α=2.5.

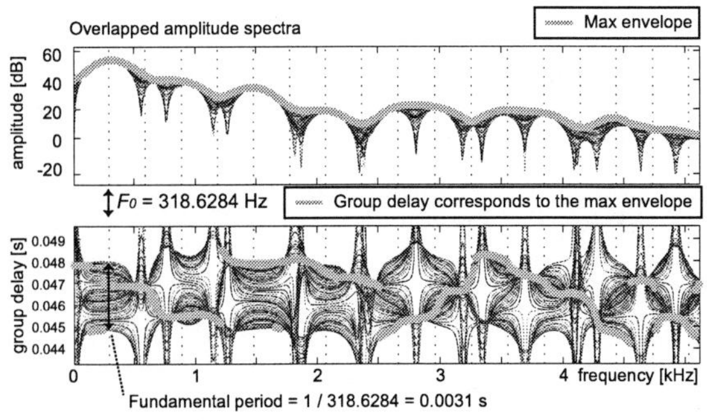

Figure 10. Overlapped STFT results showing the maximum envelope (top) and corresponding group delays (bottom).

A harmonic GMM $G(f;m,\omega_k,\sigma_k)$ for frequency f is designed as follows:

$$G(f;m,\omega_k,\sigma_k) = \sum_{k=0}^{K} \frac{\omega_k}{\sqrt{2\pi\sigma_k^2}} \exp(-\frac{(f-(m\times k))^2}{2\sigma_k^2}) \quad (3)$$

where K is the number of harmonics, for which K=10 was found to provide a high quality output. The Gaussian function parameters m, ω_k, and σ_k can be estimated using the well-known expectation and maximization (EM) algorithm, which is fitted to the F_0-adaptive FFT spectrum in the frequency range $[0,(K\times m^{(0)})+m^{(0)}/2]$. In the iteration process of the EM algorithm, σ_k can be replaced with a range constraint, $[\epsilon, m]$, where $\epsilon = 2.2204\times 10^{-16}$. The estimated m is used as the new estimated $F_0(t)$.

4.3.2 Normalized Group Delay Estimation Method Based on F_0-Adaptive Multi-Frame Integration Analysis

To enable the estimation of the phase spectrum for resynthesis, we propose a robust group delay estimation method. Although the previous method [12] relied upon pitch marks to estimate the group delay, the proposed method is more robust because it does not require them. The basic idea of this estimation is to use an F_0-adaptive multi-frame integration analysis based on the spectral envelope estimation approach in [12]. To estimate group delay, the F_0-adaptive analysis and a multi-frame integration analysis are conducted. In the integration, maximum envelopes are selected and their corresponding group delays are used as the target group delays. The group delay at each time can be estimated by using the method described in [10]. Figure 10 shows an example of extracting the maximum envelopes and corresponding group delays.

The estimated group delay has discontinuities along the frequency axis caused by the fundamental period. The group delay $\hat{g}(f,t)$ is therefore normalized with the range $(-\pi,\pi]$ and will be given by sin and cos functions as follows:

$$g(f,t) = \frac{\bmod\ (\hat{g}(f,t)-\hat{g}(\beta\times F_0(t),t), 1/F_0(t))}{F_0(t)} \quad (4)$$

$$g_\pi(f,t) = (g(f,t)\times 2\pi)-\pi \quad (5)$$

$$g_x(f,t) = \cos(g_\pi(f,t)) \quad (6)$$

$$g_y(f,t) = \sin(g_\pi(f,t)) \quad (7)$$

Here $\bmod\ (x,y)$ is a residual. The $\hat{g}(f,t)-\hat{g}(\beta\times F_0(t),t)$ component is used to eliminate an offset

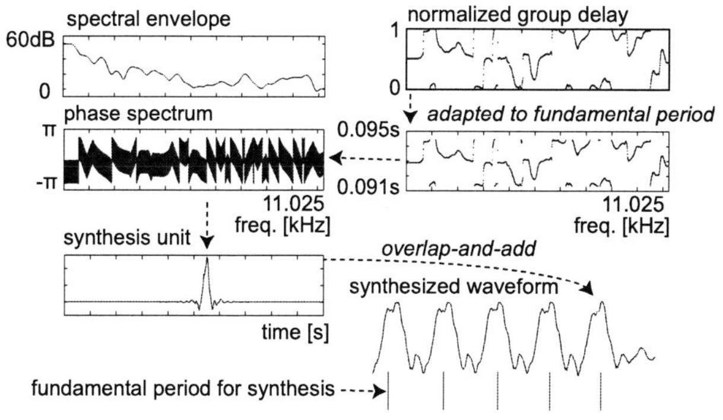

Figure 11. Singing synthesis by F_0-synchronous overlap-and-add method from spectral envelope and group delay.

of the analysis time, and β is set to 1.5 (an intermediate frequency between the first and second harmonics) as setting β=1.0 (the fundamental frequency) allowed undesirable fluctuations to remain.

There are also discontinuities along time axis. These are smoothed along both the time and frequency directions using a 2-dimensional FIR low-pass filter. Since the estimated group delay of frequency bins under F_0 is known to be unreliable, we finally smooth the group delay of bins under F_0 so that it can take the same value of the group delay at F_0.

4.3.3 Singing Synthesis Using Normalized Group Delay

The singing-synthesis method used to make the final recording needs to reflect integrating and editing results. Our implementation of singing synthesis from spectral envelopes and group delays is based on the well-known F_0-synchronous overlap-and-add method (Fig. 11).

The normalized group delays $g_x(f,t)$ and $g_y(f,t)$ are adapted to the synthesized fundamental period $1/F_0(t)_{syn}$ as follows:

$$g(f,t) = \frac{1}{F_0(t)_{syn}} \times \frac{(g_\pi(f,t)+\pi)}{2\pi} \quad (8)$$

$$g_\pi(f,t) = \begin{cases} \tan^{-1}\left(\frac{g_y(f,t)}{g_x(f,t)}\right) & (g_x(f,t) > 0) \\ \tan^{-1}\left(\frac{g_y(f,t)}{g_x(f,t)}\right) + \pi & (g_x(f,t) < 0) \\ (3\times\pi)/2 & (g_y(f,t) < 0, g_x(f,t) = 0) \\ \pi/2 & (g_y(f,t) > 0, g_x(f,t) = 0) \end{cases} \quad (9)$$

Then the phase spectrum used to generate the synthesized unit is computed from the adapted group delay. The phase spectrum can be obtained by integration of the group delay, as in [10].

4.4 Experiments and Results

To evaluate the effectiveness of the iterative F_0 estimation method we examine its use when applied as a secondary processing stage on three well-known existing F_0 methods: Goto [11][3], SWIPE [9], and STRAIGHT [8]. In each case we provide our iterative F_0 estimation method with the initial output from these systems and derive a new F_0 result. The frequency range is used as $[100, 700]$ Hz for all the methods.

[3] The 1st author reimplemented Goto's method for speech signals.

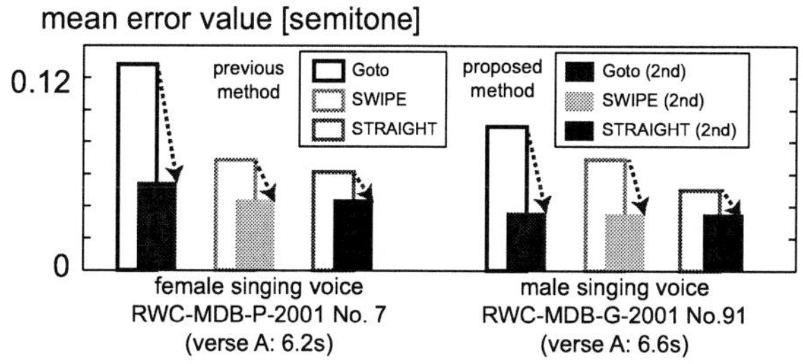

Figure 12. Estimation accuracies (mean error value) of the proposed re-estimation method (described as "2nd") compared with those of Goto [11], SWIPE [9], and STRAIGHT [8].

Estimation accuracy is determined by finding the mean error value, ϵ_f, defined by

$$\epsilon_f = \frac{1}{T_f}\sum_t |f_g(t) - f_n(t)| \quad (10)$$

$$f_n(t) = 12 \times \log_2 \frac{F_0(t)}{440} + 69 \quad (11)$$

where T_f is the number of voiced frames, and $f_g(t)$ is the ground truth value. The $f_n(t)$ and $f_g(t)$ are log-scale frequency values relative to the MIDI note number.

To compare the performance of the algorithms, we use synthesized and resynthesized natural sound examples in the RWC Music Database (Popular Music [13] and Music Genre [14]). To prepare the ground truth, $f_g(t)$, we used singing voices resynthesized from natural singing examples using the STRAIGHT algorithm [8].

Results in Figure 12 show that the F_0 estimation across each of the methods is highly accurate, with very low, ϵ_f, both for male and female signing voice. Furthermore we can see that, for each of the three algorithms, the inclusion of our iterative estimation method improves performance. In this way, our iterative method could be applied to any F_0 estimation algorithm as an additional processing step to increase accuracy.

Regarding the estimation of spectral envelope and group delay, it is not feasible to perform a similar objective analysis. Therefore in Figure 13 we present a comparison between the estimated spectral envelope and group delay from a singing recording and a synthesized singing voice. By inspection it is clear that both the spectral envelope and group delay between the two signals are highly similar, which indicates the robustness of our method.

5. DISCUSSION

There are two ways to make high-quality singing content currently and in the future. One way is for singers to improve their voices by training with a professional teacher or using singing-training software. This can be considered the "traditional" way. The alternative is to improve one's singing "expression" skill by editing and integrating, *i.e.*, through practice and training with software tools. This paper presented a system for expanding the possibilities via this new emerging second way. We recognise that these two ways can be used for different purposes and have different qualities of pleasantness. We also believe that, in

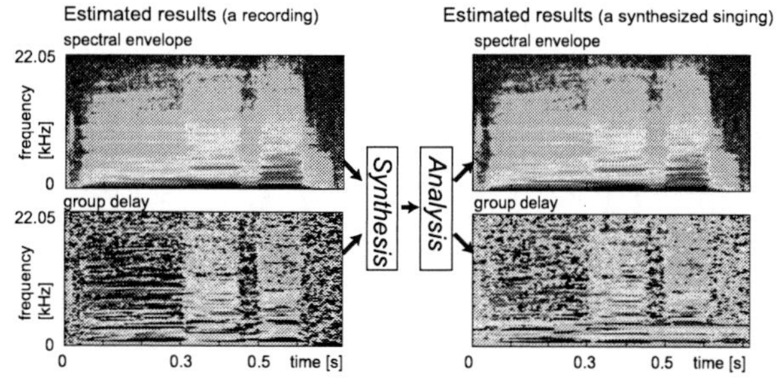

Figure 13. Examples of estimated spectral envelope and group delay and of analysis results for a synthesized singing voice.

the future, they could become equally important. A high-quality singing recording produced in the traditional way can create an emotional response in the listeners who appreciate the "physical control" of the singer. On the other hand, a high-quality singing recording improved using a tool like VocaRefiner can reach listeners in a different way, where they can appreciate the level of expression within a kind of "singing representation" created through skilled technical manipulation. In both cases, there is a shared common purpose of vocal expression and reaching listeners on a personal and emotional level.

The standard function of recording vocals has only focused on the acquisition of the vocal signal using microphones, pre-amps and digital audio workstations, etc. However, in this paper we explore a new paradigm for recording, where the process can become interactive. By allowing a singer to record their voice with a lyrics-based recording system opens new possibilities for interactive sound recording which could change how music is recorded in the future, *e.g.*, when applied to recording other instruments such as drums, guitars, and piano.

6. CONCLUSIONS

In this paper we present an interactive singing recording system called VocaRefiner to help amateur singers make high quality vocal recordings at home. VocaRefiner comes with a suite of powerful tools driven by advanced signal processing techniques for voice analysis (including robust F_0 and group delay estimation), which allow for easy recording, editing and manipulation of recordings. In addition, VocaRefiner has the unique ability to integrate the "best parts" from different takes, even down to the phoneme level. By selecting between takes and correcting errors in pitch and timing, an amateur singer can create recordings which capture the full potential of their voice, or even go beyond it. Furthermore, the ability to visually inspect objective information about their singing (*e.g.*, pitch, loudness and timbre) could help singers better understand their voices and encourage them to experiment more in their singing style. Hence VocaRefiner can also act as an educational tool.

In future work we intend to further improve the synthesis quality and to implement other music understanding functions including beat tracking and structure visualization [16], towards a more complete interactive recording environment.

Acknowledgments

We would like to thank Matthew Davies (CREST/AIST) for proofreading. This research utilized the RWC Music Database "RWC-MDB-P-2001" (Popular Music), "RWC-MDB-G-2001" (Music Genre), and "RWC-MDB-R-2001" (Royalty-Free Music). This research was supported in part by OngaCrest, CREST, JST.

7. REFERENCES

[1] K. Nakano, M. Morise, and T. Nishiura, "Vocal manipulation based on pitch transcription and its application to interactive entertainment for karaoke," in *LNCS: Haptic and Audio Interaction Design*, vol. 6851, 2011, pp. 52–60.

[2] H. Fujihara, M. Goto, J. Ogata, and H. G. Okuno, "Lyricsynchronizer: Automatic synchronization system between musical audio signals and lyrics," in *IEEE Journal of Selected Topics in Signal Processing*, 2011, pp. 311–316.

[3] D. Hoppe, M. Sadakata, and P. Desain, "Development of real-time visual feedback assistance in singing training: a review," *Journal of computer assisted learning*, vol. 22, pp. 308–316, 2006.

[4] T. Nakano, M. Goto, and Y. Hiraga, "MiruSinger: A singing skill visualization interface using real-time feedback and music cd recordings as referential data," in *Proc. ISMW 2007*, 2008, pp. 75–76.

[5] U. Zölzer and X. Amatriain, *DAFX - Digital Audio Effects*. Wiley, 2002.

[6] T. Toda, A. Black, and K. Tokuda, "Voice conversion based on maximum likelihood estimation of spectral parameter trajectory," *IEEE Trans. ASLP*, vol. 15, no. 8, pp. 2222–2235, 2007.

[7] H. Kawahara, R. Nisimura, T. Irino, M. Morise, T. Takahashi, and H. Banno, "Temporally variable multi-aspect auditory morphing enabling extrapolation without objective and perceptual breakdown," in *Proc. ICASSP 2009*, 2009, pp. 3905–3908.

[8] H. Kawahara, I. Masuda-Katsuse, and A. de Cheveigne, "Restructuring speech representations using a pitch adaptive time-frequency smoothing and an instantaneous frequency based on F0 extraction: Possible role of a repetitive structure in sounds," *Speech Communication*, vol. 27, pp. 187–207, 1999.

[9] A. Camacho, *SWIPE: A Sawtooth Waveform Inspired Pitch Estimator for Speech And Music*. Ph.D. Thesis, University of Florida, 2007.

[10] H. Banno, L. Jinlin, S. Nakamura, K. Shikano, and H. Kawahara, "Efficient representation of short-time phase based on group delay," in *Proc. ICASSP1998*, 1998, pp. 861–864.

[11] M. Goto, K. Itou, and S. Hayamizu, "A real-time filled pause detection system for spontaneous speech recognition," in *Proc. Eurospeech '99*, 1999, pp. 227–230.

[12] T. Nakano and M. Goto, "A spectral envelope estimation method based on F0-adaptive multi-frame integration analysis," in *Proc. SAPA-SCALE Conference 2012*, 2012, pp. 11–16.

[13] M. Goto, H. Hashiguchi, T. Nishimura, and R. Oka, "RWC music database: Popular, classical, and jazz music databases," in *Proc. ISMIR 2002*, 2002, pp. 287–288.

[14] ——, "RWC music database: Music genre database and musical instrument sound database," in *Proc. ISMIR 2003*, 2003, pp. 229–230.

[15] H. Kawahara and M. Morise, "Technical foundations of TANDEM-STRAIGHT, a speech analysis, modification and synthesis framework," *Sadhana: Academy Proceedings in Engineering Sciences*, vol. 36, no. 5, pp. 713–727, 2011.

[16] M. Goto, K. Yoshii, H. Fujihara, M. Mauch, and T. Nakano, "Songle: A web service for active music listening improved by user contributions," in *Proc. ISMIR 2011*, 2011, pp. 311–316.

Multi-scale design of interactive music systems : the libTuiles experiment

David Janin, Florent Berthaut, Myriam Desainte-Catherine
LaBRI, Université de Bordeaux, CNRS UMR 5800
351, cours de la libération
F-33405 Talence, FRANCE
{janin|berthaut|myriam}@labri.fr

ABSTRACT

The design and implementation of an *interactive music system* is a difficult task. It necessitates the description of complex interplays between two design layers at least : the real time synchronous layer for audio processing, and the symbolic event based layer for interaction handling. Tiled programming is a recent proposal that aims at combining with a single metaphor: tiled signals, the distinct programmatic features that are used in these two layers. The libTuiles experiment presented in this paper is a first experimental implementation of such a new design principle.

1. INTRODUCTION

1.1 Background

Nowadays, many specialized languages can be used for the design and implementation of musical systems. Be them textual like *Supercollider/Chuck* [1] or *Faust* [2], or visual like *Max/Msp* or *PureData* [3], these languages mostly inherit from the synchronous programming language paradigms that allow for powerful descriptions of signal processing mechanisms.

However, programming interactive musical systems remains a delicate task. In particular, maintaining the time/rhythmic coherence of musical systems govern by the unpredictable arrival of asynchronous events is a difficult task. This can be partly explained by the heterogeneous time scales or layers at which such systems need to be described. Audio processing necessitates low level real time synchronous programming mechanisms while interaction handling necessitates high level event based system design tools.

Such a difficulty, partially adressed by the GALS design style [4], remains a challenging issue. Despite considerable effort, there is still a lack of high level metaphors or paradigms allowing for a hierarchical, multi-scale and modular description of dynamic time structuring mechanisms.

Among other proposals, the *i-score* sequencer [5] integrates an explicit specification mechanism that allows for the high level description of the relative positioning of musical objects, hence their potential *overlapping*. Together with explicit input control points and dynamic mechanisms for solving position constraints, the *i-score* sequencer thus already offers an abstract description of dynamic time structuration. However, by lack of additional control flow structures such as conditionals and loops, its applicability remains limited.

Independently, in the lines of the structuralist approach developed for musical linguistic [6], recent studies [7] emphasize the fact that, for computer assisted music systems, a key issue lays in the precise modeling of *behaviors overlaps* that recurrently occur in such (multi-agent) musical systems. Further studies, more oriented towards abstract and untimed models, provide evidences that an entire and well-developed mathematical field, *inverse semigroup theory* [8], is suitable for developing an associated language theory of *overlapping structures* [9–11].

1.2 Outline

The work presented here aims at combining the high-level time specification mechanisms offered by the *i-score* approach with the modeling power provided by languages of overlapping structures, and with the efficient signal processing provided by the synchronous languages.

Implementing an advanced synchronization algebra of audio or musical patterns [12], the *libTuiles*, first appears as a fairly versatile multi-scale and hierarchical mixing tool. In the long run, the *libTuiles* also aims at becoming the first *execution engine* for the T-calculus [13] : the programming language theoretic counterpart of the experiment presented here.

The *libTuiles* can be connected to the real time synchronous audio thread provided by the *JACK* audio server. An additional granular synthesis module for producing audio signals that can be stretched makes it even more easy to use with tiled sound files. It is also linked with other existing tools such as the *Faust* [2] synchronous programming language.

Last but not least, a graphical interface, the *LiveTuiles*, inspired by live looping interfaces such as *Drile* [14], allows for *live performance* experiments of the underlying metaphors and concepts.

2. MODELING OF MUSICAL PROCESSES

Modeling musical system behaviors, be them *on time* when systems are running, or *offtime* when systems are being designed, one faces the long standing and complex question of musical objects representation. Many proposals, often incomparable, are available. The *libTuiles* presented in this paper is based on a rather formal model : *tiled signals*, that have been formalized as an attempt to clarify the situation.

2.1 The structure space of musical objects

There already exist many formalisms applicable to the modeling of music. Each of them provides answers for specific application perspectives, usage constraints and thus approximates the musical objects that are described. An immediate difficulty is therefore to understand *what* the characteristics of these models are and *which* one of their features we truly need for designing interactive music systems.

For instance, in a *western music score*, notes and rhythms are pictured in such a way that, in particular, the fast reading of melodic and rhythmic lines by musicians is made easier. In particular, bars and metric structures indicate on every system how musicians should synchronize their plays.

When modeling music for designing a music system, the visual aspect of music score is probably of a fairly low interest. However, there already appear two dimensions of some abstract modeling space where the various models of music lay. The first one, the *time axis* (T), is depicted by the sequence of notes, the succession of bars, and so on. The second one, the *parallel axis* (P), appears in the many music systems that are to be played in parallel by musicians.

Analyzing further music scores such as, for instance, popular melody annotated with chords as in jazz music scores, a third dimension appears, the *abstraction dimension* (A). Indeed, music is often described at various level of abstractions such as melodic lines, chords progressions, stylistic annotations, and so on.

Though often implicit, a fourth dimension also appears when modeling interactive (or improvised) music. It is the *interaction (or alternative) axis* (I) that allows, for instance, the descriptions of how musicians (say in a jazz band) can adapt their plays to the real time performance of a given soloist according to some stylistic rules.

In other words, music models adapted to the design of interactive music systems lay in an at least four dimensional space that is depicted in Figure 1.

Of course, such a four dimensional modeling space for musical objects is highly debatable. Even more, there may be some description of music that mix so much these dimensions that it no longer make sense to distinguish them. Still, positioning a given musical model in such a space may help clarifying our understanding of its features. Then, a complex musical object can be abstracted as some partial function

$$M : (A) \times (I) \times (T) \times (P) \rightarrow V$$

from that structure space to some set of values V.

For instance, the structure of standard *piano roll* that are displayed on computer screens typically lay in the two dimensional space formed by the time axis (T) and the parallelism axis (P). Another typical example is the *musical transcription and analysis* of a recorded performance. As all possible interactions have been resolved during the performance, it lays in the three dimensional space formed by time (T), parallelism (P) and abstraction (A).

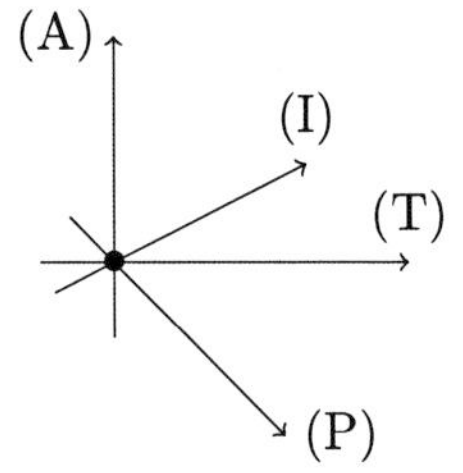

Figure 1. The 4D structure space of music

Interactive pieces of music just like *reactive systems* can be modeled by *branching structures* (or input/ output discrete automata) that describe, in every state, the potential behaviors of those systems that depend and evolve with the external events that are received. Such branching structures typically lay in the two dimensional space formed by the (abstract) time axis (T) and the interaction axis (I).

Another important feature of this structure space is that the *nature* of scales changes with abstraction.

This is especially clear in the time axis (T). At the lowest level, we have a *synchronous real-time, signal based, layer*, almost continuous. The time scale is just a sequence of regular time clicks, e.g. one click per 1/44000s with standard quantization. Above, at the interaction level, the time scale is more irregular. For instance, at the interaction level, the time scale models the arrival date of events, and its precision hardly goes below 1/100s. This is the *asynchronous real-time, event based, layer.*

On the opposite side, at the most abstract level, the time scale is a sequence of totally ordered musical events, e.g. the alegro, adagio, scherzo and sonata movements of a symphony. In between, times scales can be defined as partially ordered sets of events (causally ordered), or sets of partially overlapping intervals (melodic lines), or even mixture of these two models... These are various *symbolic time, event-based, layers.*

One can observe that such an abstraction dependent heterogeneous nature of scales also appear in the other axis. Interaction events, modeling for instance musicians' gestures, can vary from discrete events, e.g. a click on a pedal, from almost continuous finite signals, e.g. pitch pend modulation.

Designing tools for the conception of computerized music systems therefore requires to handle the combined modeling of all these heterogeneous scales.

2.2 The synchronization algebra

In every music system, be it for mixing signals, or more generally for arbitrary multi-channel signal processing, one of the most fundamental operation consists in positioning in time, one relative to the other, the signals to be processed. This feature is depicted in Figure 2. Such an operation, that lays in the two

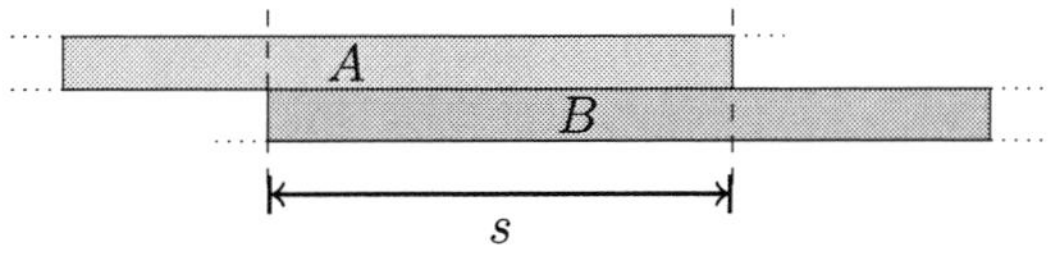

Figure 2. External synchronization

dimensional space of time (T) and parallelism (P), is often performed by means of an *external synchronization* mechanism where the relative positioning of the signals depends on the result of their combined analysis, for example relying on onset detections.

Commonly used by sound engineers in music studios, such an approach however lacks compositionality. Some audio or musical analysis may need to be performed again and again each time a new signal (or musical object) has to be positioned with respect to the previous ones. In order to avoid such a useless repeated analysis, audio processing applications are thus equipped with various and somehow adhoc notions of *time stamps* or *sync. marks* that annotate the tracks onto which these signals are positioned. It occurs that such technical tricks can be formalized with great benefits via the notion of *tiled signals*. Indeed, *tiled signals* appear when one wants to *internalize* such synchronization marks.

Simply said, a tiled signal is a signal equipped with two additional bars that delimit what are called the *synchronization window* of the tiled signal. By contrast, the position in time of the entire signal is called the *realization window*. More formally, for every signal A, the relative positioning of the synchronization window with respect to the realization window can be modeled by specifying two values : the left offset l_A and the right offset r_A, as depicted in Figure 3. With s_A the duration of the synchronization window, the resulting duration of the realization window is given by $l_A + s_A + r_A$. The resulting triple (l_A, s_A, r_A) is called the *synchronization profile* of the tiled signal A. With this model, synchronizing two tiled signals only amounts to positioning the second bar of the first

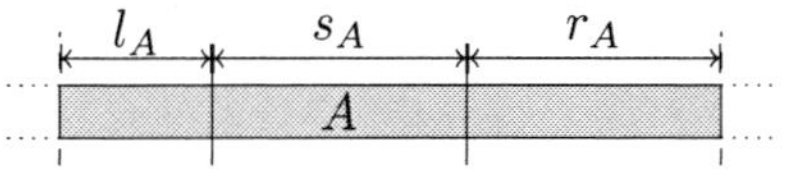

Figure 3. Synchronization vs realization windows

tiled signal right at the same time as the first bar of the second timed signal. This is depicted in Figure 4. The resulting synchronized product of two tiled sig-

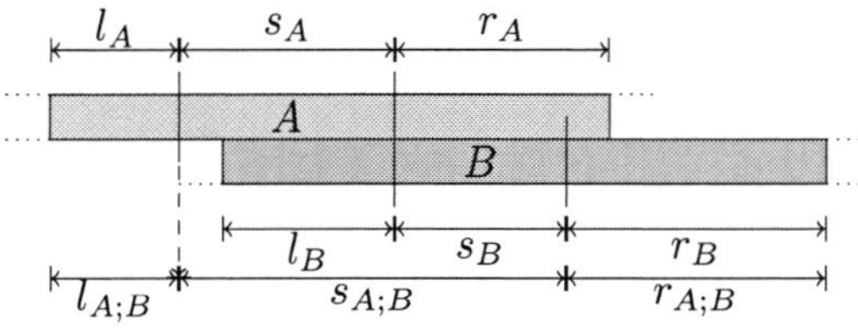

Figure 4. Internal synchronization

nals A and B is denoted $SEQ(A, B)$ or simply $A; B$. An immediate observation is that the synchronization product $A; B$ of two tiled signals A and B is indeed compositional since, as depicted in Figure 4, the newly built signal is again a tiled signal.

It occurs that the synchronization product $A; B$ defined above over tiled signals is an associative operation over tiled signals. The resulting algebraic structure is thus a semigroup. Aiming at defining interactive signal handling, with signals that are dynamically received, processed or synthesized, this is a much welcome property.

From a programing paradigm point of view, the synchronized product $A; B$ of two tiled signals A and B can be understood in two ways:

- at an abstract event-based layer : $A; B$ means that *"event" A is followed by "event" B*,
- at the concrete synchronous layer: $A; B$ means that *"signal" A is synchronized with "signal" B* with possible overlaps.

In other words, depending on the chosen time scale, every tiled signal can be seen both as an *asynchronous event* (on the logical time scale) or as a *synchronous signal* (on the synchronous realtime scale). In other words, the tiled signal approach is *multi-scale*.

The resulting algebra is described further in [12]. It is shown, in particular, that additional left and right Resync operators can be derived from the structure of tiled signals. They are depicted in Figure 5. Together

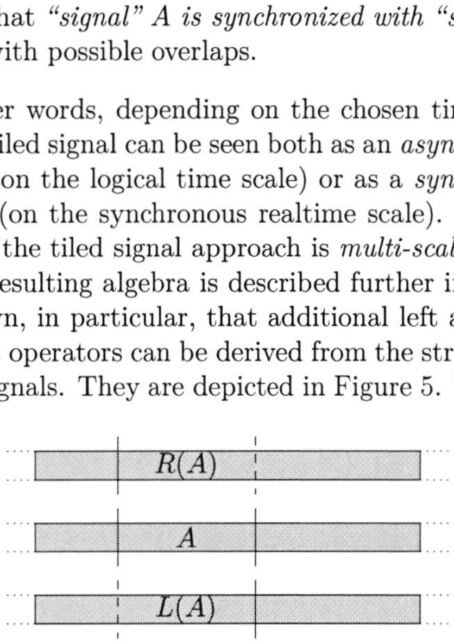

Figure 5. Right and left *Resync* operators

with the sequential product, these resets operators considerably increase the expressive power of tiled signal expressions.

Indeed, one can define $Fork(A, B) = R(A); B$ with a synchronization of A and B at the beginning of their synchronization windows. This situation is depicted in Figure 6. One can also define $Join(A, B) = A; L(B)$

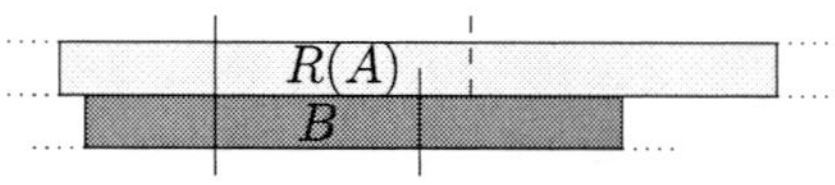

Figure 6. The derived operator *Fork*

with a synchronization of A and B at the end of their synchronization windows. This situation is depicted in Figure 7. In other words, handling multi-channel sig-

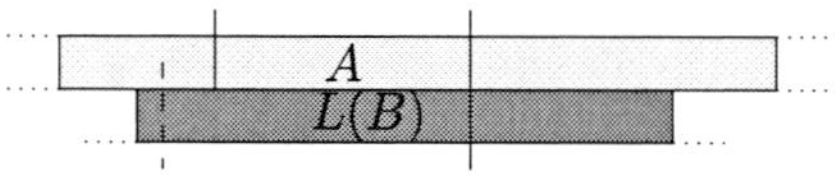

Figure 7. The derived operator *Join*

nals that can seen both at the synchronous scale and at the event-based scale, our proposal thus provides descriptions of musical object in the three dimensional space $(T) \times (P) \times (A)$. The way the interaction dimension (I) is handled and experimented is the purpose of the remaining sections.

Remark. In the T-calculus presented in [13], the synchronization algebra is extended further with additional typed operators that can be applied to synchronized products of tiles. Rather subtle signal processing operators can then be derived.

3. IMPLEMENTING THE ALGEBRA

In this section, we describe the software components of the *libTuiles* library. In particular, we present the *libTuiles* API, the synchronous sound engine that is controlled by the asynchronous execution of the tuiles, and an object-oriented architecture dedicated to messaging between musical threads.

3.1 LibTuiles: building and playing trees of tiles

LibTuiles is a C++ software library that allows for the creation and the execution of trees of synchronized tiles. In these trees, each tile is given an unsigned integer as unique identifier. The following methods of the class TuilesManager are used to build and play the tiles.

addLeaf(const float& d, unsigned int& id) creates a new leaf tile with an initial length set to d and assigns its identifier to the id variable.

addLoop(const unsigned int& idChild, unsigned int& loopID) creates a new tile by applying the *Loop* operator to the tile with the idChild identifier and assign the new identifier to the loopID variable.

addSeq(const unsigned int& idChild1, const unsigned int& idChild2, unsigned int& opID), **addFork(...)** and **addJoin(...)** create a tile by applying respectively the *Seq*, *Fork* and *Join* operators to the tiles with the identifiers idChild1 and idChild2. The id of the resulting tile is assigned to the variable opID.

setTuileLength(const unsigned int& id, const float& l) applies the *Stretch* operator with value l to the tile identified by id.

setTuileLeftOffset(const unsigned int& id, const float& lo) applies the *Resync* operator in order to set the left offset of the synchronization window of the tile with the id identifier.

setTuileRightOffset(const unsigned int& id, const float& ro) applies the *Resync* operator in order to set the right offset of the synchronization window of the tile with the id identifier.

setBpm(const float& bpm) sets the tempo at which the tree is played.

setRoot(const unsigned int& id) sets the tile with identifier id as root of the tree.

play() et stop() respectively starts and stops playing the tree.

removeTuile(const unsigned int& id) removes the tile with identifier id from the tree.

clear() removes all the tiles from the tree.

Internally, the manipulation and execution of the tree are done in a separate thread, in order to avoid slowing down when computations are done in the main application thread, for example using a graphical interface. The inter-threads communication mechanism is described in section 3.3.

When playing the tree, the temporal progression is computed in the root tile and spreads down the tree. Each operator computes the progression of its children based on the parameters of their synchronization and realization intervals. The play position in each tile is computed at any time t. Therefore, it is possible to know the absolute position of each tile within the tree. Because the temporal progression is computed for each node of the tree relatively to its parent node, it is also possible to dynamically modify the tree while playing it.

Activation and deactivation commands are sent from the playing thread respectively when tiles enter and leave their realization intervals. Lengths commands are also sent when *Stretch* operators are applied or when the main tempo is modified. Absolute position commands are also sent whenever the tree is modified. Therefore, a synchronous audio synthesis/processing engine, such as the one described in section 3.2, receives all the commands required to temporally manage the processes associated to tiles.

Tiles properties can be accessed by calling the method **getTuileProps(const unsigned int& id)** which returns a structure associated to the tile with the identified id. This structure contains the various properties of the associated tile such as the length of the realization interval, the left and right offsets of the synchronization interval and the absolute position in the tree. This mechanisms allows for example for the update of tiles representations in a graphical user interface, as these properties may be impacted by manipulations of other tiles of the tree.

3.2 A synchronous engine for temporal structuring of musical processes

LibTuiles is connected to a synchronous synthesis/processing engine based on the JACK sound server. This engine receives tiles activation/deactivation/length commands sent by the *libTuiles*. It then correspondingly activates/deactivates processes associated with the leaf tiles, these processes being nodes of an audio rendering graph.

Mainly two types of processes are handled by this engine. Sound file processes allow for the reading of sound files of any format handled by the libsndfile library. They also handle time stretching in order to match the changes in tempo and in tiles length without impacting the pitch of the sound, by relying on granular synthesis. At the initial speed, grains overlap by half and the position step between two grains is equal to half a grain. When the length of a tile increases, grain overlapping is increased and the step between grains is reduced and combined with a random offset in order to avoid artificial frequencies created by the proximity of grains. On the contrary, when the tile length decreases, the position step is increased together with the overlapping between grains in order to reduce amplitude variations between successive grains. This synthesis method, despite its quality being lower than other common time stretching methods, allows for both real-time stretching at a very low processing cost and also for click-free repositioning in sound files.

Leaf tiles may also be associated with FAUST processes. Connections can then be made between processes or with the sound card inputs and outputs. Processing is only done when the input process and FAUST process temporally overlap, i.e. when the associated tiles are both active. Therefore the composition and properties of tiles allow for a fine temporal adjustment of the audio rendering graph.

3.3 Multi-scale object oriented system architecture

One important aspect of the *libTuiles* architecture is the use of Commands, as depicted on Figure 8. These software modules allow for efficient communication between the event-based scale, the asynchronous real-time scale and the synchronous real-time scale, each of these scales being handled by a separate thread. In particular, the synchronous real-time thread that renders the audio signal does not tolerate interruptions that might be created by memory allocations and locking mechanisms. The proposed architecture relies on well-known object-oriented design patterns among which are the Prototype, the Abstract Factory and the Command. It also makes use of the ring buffer mechanism provided by the JACK library.

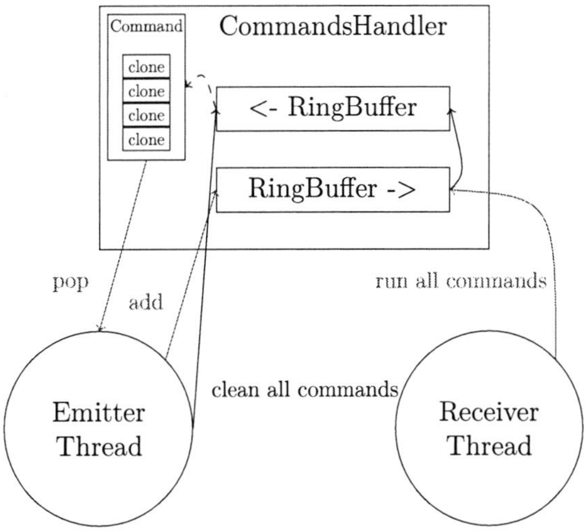

Figure 8. Software architecture for passing commands between two threads at different time scales.

An instance of the *CommandsHandler* class handles the creation and manipulation of instances of classes that inherit from the *Command* class as well as their transmission from a sender thread to a receiver thread. This instance is therefore shared between the two threads. Mappings between commands names and commands are first added to this class. For example the synchronous engine *CommandsHandler* includes commands such as *ActivateProcess* and *DeactivateProcess*. When a mapping is added, a prototype of the Command class is created. This prototype creates and holds a list of pointers to clones. In turn, each clone keeps a pointer to its prototype. For each message that needs to be passed from one thread to the other, a command can be simply defined by inheriting from the *Command* class and by redefining the *run()* method in order to manipulate data structures handled by the receiver thread, for example activating / deactivating processes.

During runtime, the emitter thread gets a pointer to a clone of a specific *Command* by calling the *popCommand(commandName)* method of the *CommandsHandler*. The requested instance is then removed from the list of clones in the *Command* prototype and can be tweaked with various parameters, in our case the tile identifier, the new length of the tile and so on. As all clones are generated beforehand, no memory allocation is done in this call. The pointer to the clone is then given to the *CommandsHandler* and shared with the receiver thread using a ring buffer, in order to avoid locking mechanisms.

The receiver thread periodically calls the *runCommands()* method of the *CommandsHandler*. This method reads the *Commands* in the ring buffer, calls their *run()* method and send them back to the emitter thread through a second ring buffer. Finally, the emitter thread periodically calls the *cleanCommands* of the *CommandsHandler* which reads pointers from the second ring buffer and puts each clone back in the list of available clones of its prototype.

This object-oriented software architecture allows for passing commands between threads without memory allocation nor locking mechanisms. In addition, only pointers are passed through the ring buffer thus minimizing the memory consumption and transferring time. The *Commands* architecture is therefore particularly efficient for applications mixing different time scales, especially if these do not tolerate interruptions.

4. INTERACTIVE EXPERIMENTS

In this section we describe the interactive experiments conducted with the libTuiles. This is done via the *LiveTuiles* interface. Completing the text given below, a presentation video of this interface is also provided [1] .

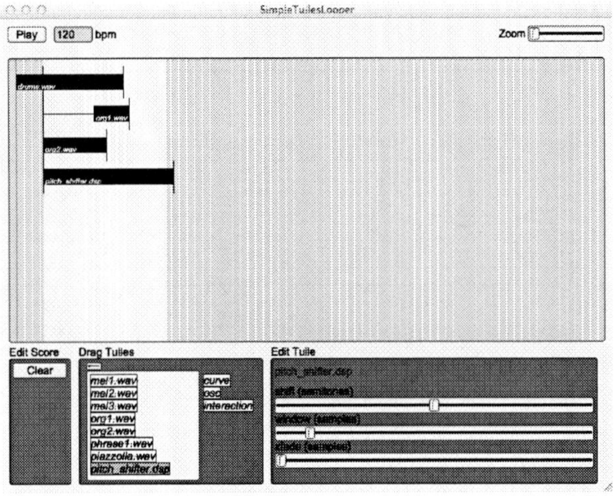

Figure 9. Screen shot : LiveTuiles with four leaf tiles among witch are three sound file tiles and one FAUST tile.

4.1 The *LiveTuiles* Interface

As depicted on Figure 9, *LiveTuiles* is an application that allows for the experimentation of temporal composition of sound processes, relying on *libTuiles* and on the synchronous engine described in the previous section.

This application sets a *Loop* tile as the root of a tiles tree, with a first leaf as child. All the other tiles added in the application are synchronized with this first leaf tile. Its synchronization interval, dynamically manipulable, defines the synchronization interval of the loop and therefore the looped interval when playing the tree. *LiveTuiles* allows one to create tiles associated with sound files and FAUST dsp files and to combine these tiles in order to build the tree using a *drag and drop* metaphor. These files are dragged from a file browser and dropped onto the score. Either they are placed freely on the score and internally composed using a fork operator with the root tile, or they are placed in fork, seq or join composition with an existing tile and properly inserted in the tiles tree.

The interface also allows for tweaking the FAUST effects parameters and for defining the connections between processes. The tree can then be played and dynamically modified by applying the *Resync* and *Stretch* operators directly on the graphical tiles.

4.2 Monitoring tiled inputs and conditional tiles

Interactive dynamic tree manipulations are made possible by the use of monitoring tiles. These tiles are attached to listener processes that receive flows of audio samples or of MIDI or OpenSoundControl events and compares them with a number of predefined conditions. When one of these conditions is matched, a command can be sent to the *TuilesManager* to control either a monitor tile or a switch tile.

The monitor tile allows for dynamic sequential composition of tiles. It is similar to what can be done with trigger points in the i-score sequencer. When activated, this tile waits for a trigger event (or for the end of its realization interval). During that time, it does not play its child tile. When the event arrives, the monitor tile sets the length of its synchronization interval so that the end is at the current position, it then sequentially composes its child tile, and plays it when the child enters its realization window. The monitor tile therefore provides a way to adapt the progression in the composed tree to external events, for example coming from a musician or from the conductor.

The switch tile only plays one of its children, set by a method or command, and uses the synchronization interval of the chosen child. Therefore, this tile allows for dynamic selection of a subtree among several subtrees, which is interesting for example in the case of structured improvisation with conditional branchings.

4.3 Loop tiles

A Loop tile is defined as an infinite sequential composition of a child tile with themselves. However, this tile does not only repeatedly play its child, and therefore the associated subtree, within the synchronization interval. It also allows for interesting overlapping effects as described in [12], when a *Resync* operator is applied to its child. In the case of sound processes, this overlapping results in multiple instances of the audio result being played at the same time. It is therefore essential to provide a *polyphony* parameter for loop tiles. Interestingly, this parameter somehow provides a control over the resulting musical complexity. On the contrary to existing loop based formalisms such as the hierarchical live-looping [14] and to looping implementations in popular software instruments, here the looping mechanisms inherits from the properties of the composition operation defined within the tiles

[1] http://hitmuri.net/LiveTuiles

model, allowing for rich musical variations of simple patterns.

4.4 A *LiveTuiles* session

A simple example session of *LiveTuiles* with interactive editing and real time playing is depicted in Figure 10. From two tiled signals of drums $d1$ and $d2$

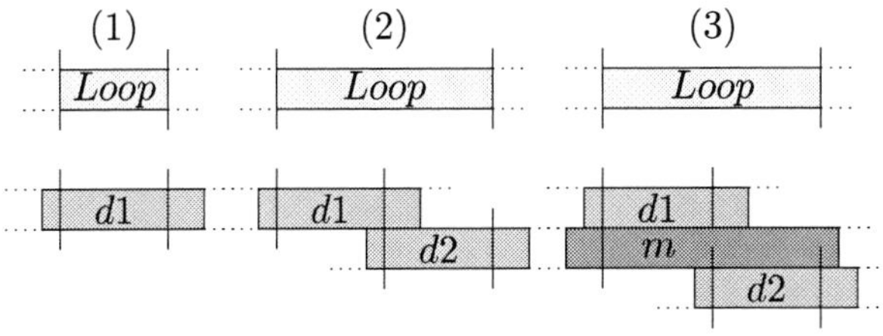

Figure 10. Live editing/playing

and from a lead tiled signal m, we start the session, at stage (1) by playing *Loop*($d1$), i.e. repeatedly playing the tile $d1$ synchronized with itself.

By dropping the tiled signal $d2$ at the right of the *Loop* operator, we reach stage (2) and we play *Loop*(*Seq*($d1, d2$)), i.e. repeatedly playing the combined tile $d1; d2$.

Last, by dropping the lead tile m at the left of the drum tile $d1$, we reach stage (3) and we play *Loop*(*Seq*(*Fork*($m, d1$), $d2$)), i.e. repeatedly playing the combined tile $d1; d2$ together with playing the lead tile m in parallel at every loop.

Provided the synchronization windows of the tile $d1$ and the tile $d2$ are of equal length, the underlying pulse is preserved in all three stages, regardless of the length of (the synchronization window of) the lead tile m. Tiled faust effects can also be added and applied still preserving the underlying pulse.

5. CONCLUSION

We described the implementation of an advanced synchronization algebra for audio or musical patterns. This software library, called the *libTuiles*, allows for the interactive creation, manipulation and execution of trees of tiled signals that embed a synchronization mechanism. Furthermore, it offers new musical possibilities, thanks to the underlying algebra, which can be experimented through a dedicated graphical interface *LiveTuiles*. One of the perspectives of this work is to adapt the *libTuiles* so that it becomes the execution engine for the T-calculus [13] that extends the synchronization algebra.

Acknowledgments

This work is partially supported by the french project INEDIT, ANR-12-CORD-0009.

6. REFERENCES

[1] S. Wilson, *The SuperCollider Book*. Cambridge: The MIT Press, 2011.

[2] D. Fober, Y. Orlarey, and S. Letz, "FAUST architectures design and OSC support," in *14th Int. Conference on Digital Audio Effects (DAFx-11)*. IRCAM, 2011, pp. 231–216.

[3] A. Cipriani and M. Giri, *Electronic Music and Sound Design - Theory and Practice with Max/Msp*. Contemponet, 2010.

[4] P. Teehan, M. R. Greenstreet, and G. G. Lemieux, "A survey and taxonomy of GALS design styles," *IEEE Design & Test of Computers*, vol. 24, no. 5, pp. 418–428, 2007.

[5] A. Allombert, M. Desainte-Catherine, and G. Assayag, "Iscore: a system for writing interaction," in *Third International Conference on Digital Interactive Media in Entertainment and Arts (DIMEA 2008)*. ACM, 2008, pp. 360–367.

[6] F. Lerdahl and R. Jackendoff, *A generative theory of tonal music*, ser. MIT Press series on cognitive theory and mental representation. MIT Press, 1983.

[7] D. Janin, "Vers une modélisation combinatoire des structures rythmiques simples de la musique," *Revue Francophone d'Informatique Musicale (RFIM)*, vol. 2, 2012.

[8] M. V. Lawson, *Inverse Semigroups : The theory of partial symmetries*. World Scientific, 1998.

[9] D. Janin, "Quasi-recognizable vs MSO definable languages of one-dimensional overlapping tiles," in *Mathematical Found. of Comp. Science (MFCS)*, ser. LNCS, vol. 7464, 2012, pp. 516–528.

[10] ——, "Overlaping tile automata," in *8th International Computer Science Symposium in Russia (CSR)*, ser. LNCS, vol. 7913. Springer, 2013, pp. 431–443.

[11] ——, "Algebras, automata and logic for languages of labeled birooted trees," in *Int. Col. on Aut., Lang. and Programming (ICALP)*, ser. LNCS, vol. 7966. Springer, 2013, pp. 318–329.

[12] F. Berthaut, D. Janin, and B. Martin, "Advanced synchronization of audio or symbolic musical patterns: an algebraic approach," *International Journal of Semantic Computing*, vol. 6, no. 4, pp. 409–427, 2012.

[13] D. Janin, F. Berthaut, M. DeSainte-Catherine, Y. Orlarey, and S. Salvati, "The T-calculus : towards a structured programming of (musical) time and space," LaBRI, Université de Bordeaux, Tech. Rep. RR-1466-13, 2013.

[14] F. Berthaut, M. Desainte-Catherine, and M. Hachet, "Drile : an immersive environment for hierarchical live-looping," in *Proceedings of New Interfaces for Musical Expression (NIME10)*, 2010, pp. 192–197.

REAL-TIME NOTATION USING BRAINWAVE CONTROL

Joel Eaton
Interdisciplinary Centre for Computer Music Research (ICCMR)
University of Plymouth
joel.eaton@postgrad.plymouth.ac.uk

Eduardo Miranda
Interdisciplinary Centre for Computer Music Research (ICCMR)
University of Plymouth
eduardo.miranda@plymouth.ac.uk

ABSTRACT

We present a significant extension to our work in the field of Brain-Computer Music Interfacing (BCMI) through providing brainwave control over a musical score in real time. This new approach combines measuring Electroencephalogram (EEG) data, elicited via generating Steady State Visual Evoked Potentials (SSVEP), with mappings to allow a user to influence a score presented to a musician in a compositional and/or performance setting.

Mind Trio is a generative BCMI composition based upon a musical game of 18th century origin. It is designed to respond to the subjective decisions of a user allowing them to affect control over elements of notation, ultimately directing parameters that can influence musical dramaturgy and expression via the brain. We present the design of this piece alongside the practicalities of using such a system on low-cost and accessible equipment.

Our work further demonstrates how such an approach can be used by multiple users and musicians, and provides a sound foundation for our upcoming work involving four BCMI subjects and a string quartet.

1. INTRODUCTION

The aim of our research is to develop musical systems with creative applications for users of all physical abilities. Specifically, we are concerned with the control of brain signals and the application of this feature for musical performance and composition.

The idea of applying brainwaves to music is not new. Experimental composers of the 1960's incorporated amplified brain signals measured via EEG into their work after the reported discovery of voluntary alpha wave (electrical signals of approximately 8-12Hz) control by Dr Joe Kimaya [1, 2]. The composer Alvin Lucier applied this method of neurofeedback in his 1965 piece *Music for a Solo Performer,* and David Rosenboom expanded the field of biofeedback and the arts throughout the 1970s [3]. Until recently using alpha and other low frequency rhythms as input to a musical system dominated applications of music performance technologies and composing with brainwaves [4] [5].

The last decade has brought about strong advances in the fields of Brain-Computer Interfacing (BCI) and brain signal processing techniques to the extent that computer based musical engines can now be directly controlled via harnessing EEG signals in real-time. Brainwave control of musical parameters has already been researched in [6] [7], and the SSVEP technique we present here has previously been used in musical applications for therapeutic and creative purposes [8] [9]. In Sections 4 and 5 of this paper we outline some considerations in our design of a portable BCMI platform, and introduce a proof-of-concept composition using SSVEP to affect a musical score, for presentation to a pianist.

2. BCMI SYSTEMS

BCMI systems vary in regard to the nature of human-computer interactivity. Computers in user-orientated systems attempt to learn the meaning of the input, a users' EEG, in an attempt to adapt to its behaviour. These systems are useful when variable or unpredictable brain information exists; variable either by lack of control, individual user differences in response to stimuli or the type of the input signal being read. For example a time locked Event Related Potential (ERP) such as a P300 response may vary across a range of amplitudes per user [10], or a generative musical system could be designed based on unpredictable activity across a range of frequency bands. Early musical systems with EEG input are regarded as user-orientated systems, such as Richard Teitelbaum's *In Tune* [11] whereby an analogue synthesiser adapts to the incoming alpha via the EEG, albeit via a human operator. Computer-orientated systems require a user to adapt to the functions of the computer; the success of the system relies on the users' ability to learn how to perform the tasks that translate to musical control. Mutually-orientated systems are a combination of the previous two.

If user control of a system's input range is achievable then a computer-orientated approach can be deemed suitable for systems designed with finite control in mind. The system presented here adopts this computer-orientated approach; a user controls the notation through the pre-determined rules of the computer's mappings. In our future work aside from the aforementioned use of user-orientated systems for interpreting non-meaningful data recording, incorporating a mutually-orientated approach to measure other unpredictable, but perhaps meaningful information, such as emotional arousal **[12]** within EEG may provide further layers of musical expression.

2.1 Musical Applications of BCMI

Musical engines of BCMI systems are designed for either the sonification or musification of EEG data, or for musical control. Some complexity can be added to systems through applying a combination of these approaches, depending on the objective. Sonification, the process of mapping data to sound, is often used in medical BCMI systems, for example to audibly identify deficiencies or abnormalities in brain signals; in a way not too dissimilar to the function of a stethoscope amplifying a heartbeat. This approach has been used in research into treating illnesses such as ADHD [13] and epilepsy [14]. Musification of brainwave information is the process of mapping brain signals to musical parameters and this is often the case when brain signals are largely uncontrollable and random in nature. Musical control systems utilise a user's cognitive ability to affect control over their brain waves. This provides a framework for designing BCMI tools that can respond to the subjective choices of a user, a *mental gesture*, so to speak.

2.2 BCMI Components

Our BCMI system is built using the following elements:

- *EEG Input* – Electrodes placed on the scalp, in the form of a headband.
- *EEG Analysis* - Amplification of electrical activity, and data extraction to isolate meaningful information.
- *Transformation Algorithm* - Mapping EEG information to control parameters within a musical engine.
- *Visual Stimuli* – This elicits the EEG data and provides real-time feedback to the user.
- *Musical Engine* – This is the musical interpretation of the EEG data, which is presented as a score to a musician.

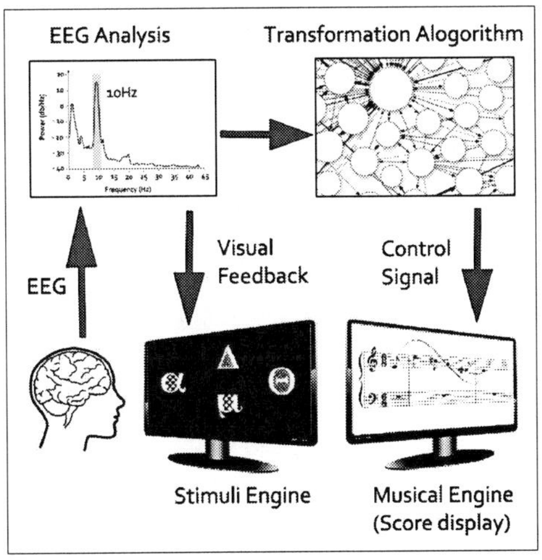

Figure 1. The components of the Brain-Computer Music Interfacing system. This diagram illustrates how EEG data is mapped to a separate computer screen for displaying the score, and a stimuli display with visual feedback.

3. SSVEP

Aside from the use of alpha rhythms BCMIs have utilised other techniques of harnessing brainwave information to control music. These include stimulating P300 ERPs [15], auditory imagery [16] and different methods of data classification [6] [17]. A recent survey of BCI techniques by the commercial company G.tec has validated SSVEP as currently the most accurate and responsive method for BCI user control [18] confirming it to be ideal for real-time control over precise values.

The issue of interpreting meaning in EEG signals for control has long been a focus within BCMI research [7]. The SSVEP technique allows for such precise control that meaning can be injected into the design of a system, allowing for simplicity or complexity dependant on the requirements of the application.

3.1 Eliciting Potentials

ERPs are spikes of brainwave activity produced by perception to stimuli presented to a subject. They are time locked to the event of the stimuli and as such the ERP response to a single event is problematic to detect in EEG on a single trial basis, as it becomes lost in the general noise of on-going electrical brain activity. However, if a user is subjected to repeated visual stimulation at short intervals (at rates approximately between 5Hz – 30Hz), then before the signal has had a chance to return back to its unexcited state the rapid introduction of the next flashing onset elicits another response. Further successive flashes induce what is known as the steady-state response, a continuously evoked amplification of the brainwave [19]. This negates a need for performing numerous delayed trials as the repeated visuals are consistently providing the stimuli required for a constant potential, translated as a consistent increased amplitude level in the associated EEG frequency.

This technique, SSEVP, was adopted in a BCMI system designed for testing with a patient with locked in syndrome [8] as a tool for providing recreational music making. Here four flashing icons (between 6 – 15Hz) were presented on a computer screen, their flashing frequencies relative to the frequencies of corresponding brainwaves. A user selects an icon by gazing at one and as a result of this action the amplitude of the corresponding brainwave frequency, measured in the visual cortex, increases. Here the EEG is analysed continuously, looking for amplitude changes within the four frequencies. The icons represent four choices, always available to the user at the same time. These icons are in turn mapped to commands within a musical engine providing explicit meaning to each icon. The instantaneous speed of the EEG response to the stimuli offers real-time control of a BCMI, which requires no user or system training beyond the task of visual focusing. When the analysis software detects an increase in an SSVEP channel a control signal is feedback to the visual interface providing feedback to the user.

3.2 Amplitude Control

As well as the selection of commands a second dimension of control was gathered through the level of visual focusing. This elicited a relative linear response within the amplitude of the corresponding brain wave. This allows users to employ proportional control methods akin to intrinsically analogue tasks such as pushing a fader or turning a dial. This differs from previous selective, more digital tasks in BCMIs, such as a switch or a toggle function. In previous implementations we utilised this control to trigger a series of defined notes within a scale [8] and for more complex mapping techniques [9].

Our SSVEP approach requires the presence of 3 electrodes (using the 10-20 placement system), training comprising verbal instructions and a calibration time of approximately 2 minutes per user.

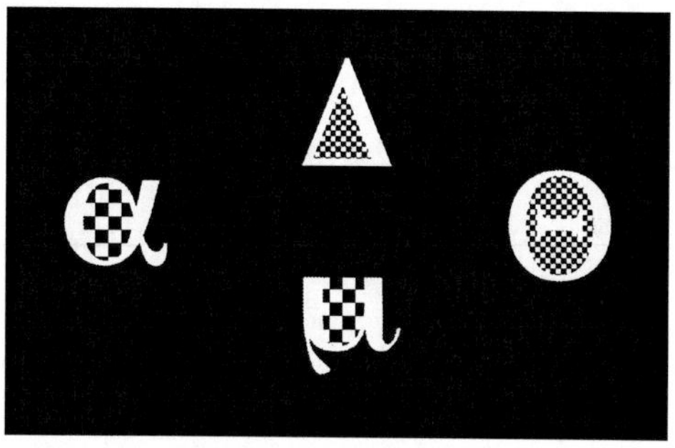

Figure 2. The visual stimuli screen as presented to a user. Note the differences in spatial frequency of checker patterns and the feedback ring around the left hand icon which increases in size and colour intensity relative to the power of the corresponding EEG frequency.

4. PRACTICALITIES IN BCMI DESIGN

We are keen to take BCMI research out of the laboratory and into more practical settings. Consequently, for the system presented here we were keen to use portable laptop computers and EEG systems with wireless electrodes. Currently high-end medical EEG systems are expensive, delicate and inefficient to transport and setup. In recent years headsets aimed at the pro-sumer market from companies such as NeuroSky and Emotiv offer affordable EEG platforms, but at the expense of accuracy. We have therefore bypassed more advanced amplitude control, discussed in Section 3, in favour of a simpler method using single threshold values where a value rising over a set threshold acts as a switch. In the system presented here we have adopted the Emotiv headset with bespoke signal processing software to drive the JMSL MaxScore notation platform.

4.1 Visual Interface Considerations

To elicit SSVEP a stable visual interface is required that updates precisely, without frame drops or variations in frequency. A good quality graphics card can, by todays standard, provide the processing required for this, but for laptop computers (high-end gaming laptops aside) this can be a struggle.

There are two options available for SSVEP stimuli design. Single graphics stimuli have icons that alternate between a pair of colours (black and white and red and green being the two pairs most suitable). These flicker between two alternations per frequency cycle. Pattern reversal icons with a checkerboard pattern only require one alternation per cycle, whereby the pattern is reversed [20]. Icons that use pattern reversal require particular attention to the spatial frequency of the patterns used, and this should be optimised for best results with each frequency band. The icons in Figure 2 display different spatial frequencies for different frequency bands; a larger spatial frequency for faster flashing rates and vice versa [21].

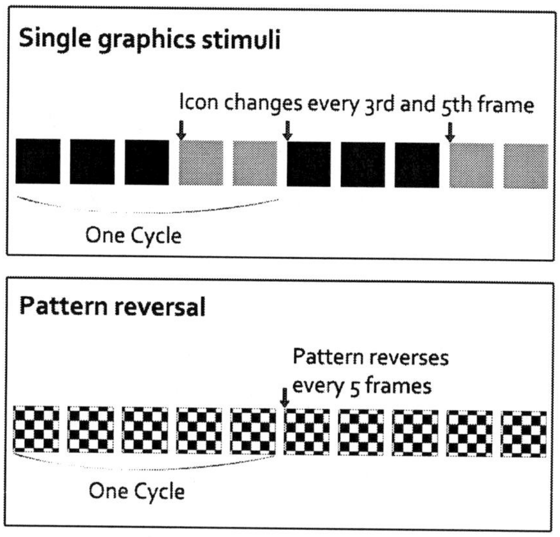

Figure 3. Diagram displaying the frame combination to elicit a 12Hz SSVEP response with single graphics stimuli and pattern reversal.

Calculating the rate of flashes in both cases requires dividing icon onset instances into integers of the screen's refresh rate [22]. For example a 12Hz single graphics stimuli with a 60Hz screen refresh rate would complete one full cycle (two alternations) every 5 frames, whereas pattern reversal stimuli would require only one alternation over the same period to elicit SSVEP (see Figure 3). As shown in Figure 3 there are 50% fewer alternations required per cycle using the pattern reversal stimuli. This reduction diminishes the graphics processing required providing a more stable technique for the laptops we used.

5. MIND TRIO

Musikalisches Würfelspiel, a music style of German origin, can be considered as an early form of generative music that was popularised in 18th Century Europe. Composing employed a system that used dice to randomly select small sections of pre-composed music resulting in a piece that would differ upon every iteration. Mozart's K6.516f, for instrumental trio, is widely thought to be derived from this method, and in another work attributed to him the score's accompanying commentary begins its instructions with the line 'To compose, without the least knowledge of music, so many [scores] as one pleases...'[23]. We have adapted this idea and twisted our interpretation to allow for composing with knowledge of what one is doing to the music.

The BCMI user plays the part of composer in Mind Trio, arranging the structure of the musical score. The purpose of our game is to choose from a selection of musical phrases, which in turn builds the score of the piece. From user selection via icon gazing a score is arranged then visually updated on a separate computer screen at regular intervals in time.

Figure 4 illustrates the concept of the compositional game. With the current musical phrase set to 56 the four icon choices represent the next four possibilities in the pathway matrix. By selecting the left hand icon Phrase 73 is selected as the next element in the composition, and the game repeats. With Phrase 73 as the current Phrase the icons will then switch to represent choices of phrase 59, 42, 54, 16, and so on.

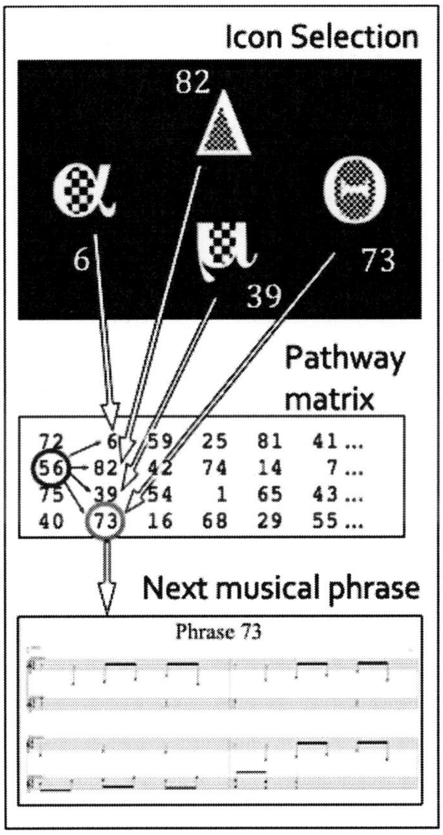

Figure 4. The compositional strategy for playing Mind Trio shows how to build a continuous score from Phrase 56 to Phrase 73. Note that the diagram shows only an excerpt of the pathway matrix.

5.1 System Design

Mind Trio is a musical piece designed for BCMI user and solo pianist. The BCMI user, wearing a wireless headset, sends EEG data to a primary laptop. Signal processing software analyses the incoming EEG data stream assessing relevant SSVEP activity using Fast Fourier Transform (FFT) analysis of frequency bandwidths held in the stimuli. EEG data is converted into a control signal sent to the visual interface displayed to the performer via the primary laptop. The control signal is sent to a secondary laptop where the transformation algorithm handles the mappings of the control data to direct the notation, which is presented for the pianist via the laptop's display screen (see Figure 1).

5.2 Real-Time Notation

For Mind Trio an array of 96 pre-composed musical phrases are allocated sequentially into four pathways in the pathway matrix. During playback the BCMI user selects a pathway using the associated icon and the score presented on screen updates to shift to this pathway at the next display onset time. Here, the musician does not know what is on the next page until it is automatically (digitally) turned.

In order for a system with a continuously updating score to function successfully a musician must be able to read musical segments of at least a few seconds at once. The display is divided into two lines of two bars, and with a mean tempo of 60bpm and a 4/4 time signature the page display onset time equates to approximately 8 seconds; thi is adequate for a musician of a professional standard to work with.

As the mapping of icons to pathways is relatively straightforward there is little computation time required, allowing the BCMI user a large window during each page display during which to make their selection. The piece begins in pathway 1 and during any window if no selection is made then the current pathway remains. If a pathway reaches the end of its 24 phrases it simply continues in a circular style from the beginning.

It is worth noting that in more complex mapping systems the selection window may need to be shortened to account for algorithmic processing as well as account for multiple selections over a range of parameters. Also a more complex score is likely to coincide with less accuracy from a musician. This is also owing to the fact that there is no possibility to rehearse an exact piece, as each composition will differ from the last.

Figure 5. A prototype of the notation system in action. The user gazes at the icons on the left hand screen, which, seconds later, updates the score on the right hand screen.

6. MULTIPLE BCMI USERS

To further our work integrating BCMI users and musicians we aim to build a system whereby multiple users can control multiple scores within the same piece. We have successfully trialled a version of our system with multiple users controlling musical parameters of pre-composed electronic music. Figure 6 below shows two subjects affecting elements of the same electronic composition as a way of composing together, expanding the concept of neurofeedback. Here, feedback not only exists in single loops between subjects and computers as the paths of neurofeedback loops change as they influence and combine with other subjects at different times. The musical outcomes of this setting pose an exciting playground for experimentation and creative music making. Our aim is to integrate this collaborative approach into our notation system whereby four BCMI users control micro, meso, and macro features of a score for a string quartet. We hope to have this system ready for performance by early 2014.

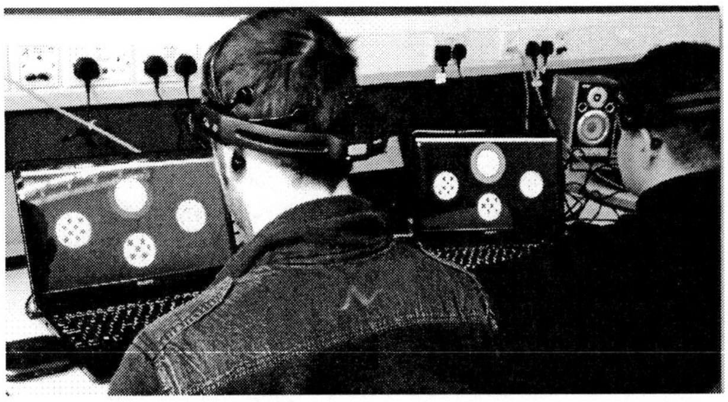

Figure 6. Two subjects enjoy composing music in a multi-user scenario. Each subject is controlling parameters of a group of instruments via the mappings of each icon. User 1 controls percussive sounds and user 2 controls melodic phrases.

7. DISCUSSION

Our research successfully demonstrates the suitability of the SSVEP technique for eliciting control over musical notation in the continuous fashion required for acoustic music performance. Furthermore our system highlights that SSVEP control is achievable using portable and affordable equipment that is subsequently more practical for use in real-world environments; it requires minimal calibration, apparatus and setup time. By harnessing brain signals in this manner the neurofeedback loop that is created between the BCMI user and the resulting music is extended to include a musician. This is a significant step in the design of new BCMI tools. We have demonstrated how SSVEP interfaces can be designed for consumer level laptop computers, widening access to the technologies required for BCMI, as well as for users with limited motor capabilities.

In practice the current iteration of the system is straightforward to use. The nature of MindTrio requires a user to be familiar with the musical pathways for the results of decisions to be pre-determined. For future iterations that affect more complex elements of notation the user interface requires adaption to translate the decisions simply alongside or within the stimulating icons.

There are still key issues that plague the stability of composing with brainwaves, which affect the usability and accuracy of measuring brain signals with this technology, more significantly than high-end medical systems and outside of the controlled environment of the laboratory.

Non-invasive EEG measures brain waves through electrodes placed on the scalp. Yet amplifying very low level electrical signals (as low as only a few microvolts) that are filtered through the skull, membrane, hair and skin results in significant noise levels alongside interference from other electrical sources and the continual electrical activity of non-related EEG. Although SSVEP provides relative high accuracy extracting meaning within EEG signals still requires complex signal analysis tools and is also largely reflected in the quality of the hardware components.

The system we have constructed here offers a compromising solution to these difficulties. The interface and signal processing software is robust and performs well in response to the real-time EEG data, but the Emotiv hardware offers a less stable interface for measuring accurate brain signals than more expensive and less portable platforms. This accuracy is noticeable in practice but is tolerable for MindTunes as real-time feedback is certainly present providing the response and feeling of control to a user. We predict that for embedding more complex control systems beyond straightforward selection then issues may arise.

Mind Trio presents a simple proof-of-concept system that paves the way for more advanced compositional techniques and mapping strategies using digital notation presented to musicians. By injecting more complex meaning within the design of such systems, higher levels of musical complexity can be offered and subsequently controlled. For example, a well as directing structural pathways, more expressive parameters and nuances such as harmonic structure, playing technique or dynamic and rhythmic changes, can be chosen via the BCMI. This expansion, coupled with multiple users poses an exciting platform for creative composition and BCMI design.

8. REFERENCES

[1] J. Kamiya, "Conditioned Discimination of the EEG Alpha Rhythm in Humans," presented at the Western Psychological Association, San Franscisco, USA, 1962.

[2] J. Kamiya, "Conscious Control of Brain Waves.," *Psychology Today,* vol. 1, pp. 56–60, 1968.

[3] D. Rosemboom, "Extended Musical Interface with the Human Nervous System," *Leonardo MonoGraph Series,* 1997.

[4] R. B. Knapp and H. Lusted, "A Bioelectric Controller for Computer Music Applications," *Computer Music Journal,* vol. 14, pp. 42-47, 1990.

[5] G. Baier, T. Hermann, and U. Stephani, "Multi-Channel Sonification of Human EEG,"

presented at the 13th International Conference on Auditory Display, Montréal, Canada, 2007.

[6] E. Miranda, K. Sharman, K. Kilborn, and A. Duncan, "On Harnessing the Electroencephalogram for the Musical Braincap," *Computer Music Journal,* vol. 27, pp. 80 - 102, 2003.

[7] E. Miranda, "Plymouth brain-computer music interfacing project: from EEG audio mixers to composition informed by cognitive neuroscience," *International Journal of Arts and Technology,* vol. 3, pp. 154-175, 2010.

[8] E. R. Miranda, W. L. Magee, J. J. Wilson, J. Eaton, and R. Palaniappan, "Brain-Computer Music Interfacing (BCMI): From Basic Research to the Real World of Special Needs," *Music and Medicine,* vol. 3, pp. 134-140, 2011.

[9] J. Eaton and E. Miranda, "New Approaches in Brain-Computer Music Interfacing: Mapping EEG for Real-Time Musical Control," in *Music, Mind, and Invention Workshop*, New Jersey, USA, 2012.

[10] R. Näätänen, "The role of attention in auditory information processing as revealed by event-related potentials and other brain measures of cognitive function," *Behavioral and Brain Sciences,* vol. 13, pp. 201-288, 1990.

[11] R. Teitelbaum, "In Tune: Some Early Experiments in Biofeedback Music (1966-74)," in *Biofeedback and the Arts: Results of Early Experiments*, D. Rosemboom, Ed., ed Vancouver: Aesthetic Research Centre of Canada Publications, 1976.

[12] A. Kirke and E. Miranda, "Combining EEG Frontal Asymmetry Studies with Affective Algorithmic Composition and Expressive Performance Models," in *International Computer Music Conference (ICMC 2011)*, Huddersfield, UK, 2012.

[13] R. R. Pratt, H. H. Abel, and J. Skidmore, "The Effects of Neurofeedback Training with Background Music on EEG Patterns of ADD and ADHD Chidren," *International Journal of Arts Medicine,* vol. 4, pp. 24 - 31, 1995.

[14] A. de Campo, R. Höldrich, A. Wallisch, and G. Eckel, "New sonification tools for EEG data screening and monitoring," in *13th International Conference on Auditory Display*, Montreal, Canada, 2007.

[15] M. Grierson, C. Kiefer, and M. Yee-King, "Progress Report on the EAVI BCI Toolkit for Music: Musical Applications of Algorithms for use with Consumer Brain Computer Interfaces," presented at the ICMC, Huddersfield, UK, 2011.

[16] E. Miranda and M. Stokes, "On Generating EEG for Controlling Musical Systems," *Biomedizinische Technik,* vol. 49, pp. 75-76, 2004.

[17] E. Miranda and A. Brouse, "Toward Direct Brain-Computer Musical Interfaces," in *2005 International Conference on New Interfaces for Musical Expression (NIME)*, Vancouver, BC, Canada, 2005.

[18] C. Guger, G. Edlinger, and G. Krausz, "Hardware/Software Components and Applications of BCIs," in *Recent Advances in Brain-Computer Interface Systems*, R. Fazel-Rezai, Ed., ed Rjeka, Croatia, 2011, pp. 1-24.

[19] D. Regan, "Human Brain Electrophysiology: Evoked Potentials and Evoked Magnetic Fields " *Science And Medicine. New York; London: Elsevier,* 1989.

[20] D. Zhu, J. Bieger, G. Garcia Molina, and R. M. Aarts, "A survey of stimulation methods used in SSVEP-based BCIs," *Comput Intell Neurosci,* p. 702357, 2010.

[21] K. Arakawa, S. Tobimatsu, H. Tomoda, J. Kira, and M. Kato, "The effect of spatial frequency on chromatic and achromatic steady-state visual evoked potentials," *Clinical Neurophysiology,* vol. 110, pp. 1959-1964, 1999.

[22] N. A. Mehta, S. H. S. Hameed, and M. M. Jackson, "Optimal Control Strategies for an SSVEP-Based Brain-Computer Interface," *International Journal of Human-Computer Interaction,* vol. 27, pp. 85-101, 2010.

[23] W. A. Mozart, "K. Anh 294d," ed. Berlin, Amsterdam: Johann Julius Hummel, 1793.

COMPOSING FOR CARS

Adam Parkinson
Department of Computing
Goldsmiths
University of London
a.parkinson@gold.ac.uk

Atau Tanaka
Department of Computing
Goldsmiths
University of London
a.tanaka@gold.ac.uk

ABSTRACT

The authors report on composing a piece for RoadMusic, an interactive music project which generates and manipulates music for the passengers and driver in a car, using sensor information gathered from the surroundings and from the movements of the car.

We present a literature review which brings together related works in the diverse fields of Automotive UI, musical mappings, generative music and sonification. We then describe our strategies for composing for this novel system, and the unique challenges it presented. We describe how the process of constructing mappings is an essential part of composing a piece of this nature, and we discuss the crucial role of mapping in defining RoadMusic as either a new musical instrument, a sonification system or generative music.

We then consider briefly the extent to which the RoadMusic performance was as we anticipated, and the relative success of our composition strategies, along with suggestions for future adaptations when composing for such an environment.

1. INTRODUCTION

Creating sound environments for automobiles is a complex and rich area of industrial and creative research. Historically, certain cars, notably Italian sports cars, are known for their unique engine and exhaust sound. Aftermarket exhaust pipes are a cottage industry where hobbyists can fine tune the sound of their cars. This was famously picked up by the manufacturer Mazda in the 1980s when they applied Kansei principles (emotional engineering to the sound produced by their MX5 Miata convertible) [10].

Silence is as important as the sound a car produces. While some manufacturers focus on the sound of a car, others focus on silencing exterior noise in the passenger compartment. Manufacturers like BMW use state of the art audio analysis and phase inversion noise cancellation technologies to create quieter environments for driver and passenger alike. A separate problem arises with the advent of the electric car where the car lacks a combustion engine to provide familiar points of reference for those inside, and outside the car.

For the driver, this means that there is no audio feedback from a revving engine to give a sense of acceleration and speed. More dangerously, the lack of external noise means that pedestrians simply do not hear the electric car approaching [12]. This problem has not gone unnoticed by electric car manufacturers, who have embarked ambitious development projects to create external sonification of electric cars.

While car sonification is a task that entails auditory display and sonic design for purposes of feedback (interior) and alerting (exterior), there is an enormous creative opportunity to create interesting, pleasant, yet useful sounds for the car. In effect, Mazdas Kansei engineering could be re-examined completely in the digital domain to produce personalizable, custom automobile audio habitats. Beyond sonic effects, principles of sonification could intersect with interactive music techniques to produce musical environments that are sensitive to a cars state and conditions on the road.

This paper reports on compositional strategies for an existing interactive car music system, RoadMusic, contextualising it within a discussion about the differences between sonification, generative music and the practices of developing new musical instruments [18]. We first describe research challenges, present related work, then describe the technical system. We finish by a discussion of the car as instrument, and strategies for composing for such a system.

2. COMPOSING FOR CARS?

RoadMusic is an interactive car music system developed by the sound artist Peter Sinclair. It deploys Pure Data on a single-board computer having roughly the same size and form factor as a car navigation system or radar-detector. It is attached with a standard suction cup typically used for this kind of automotive accessory to the windshield of the car. A range of sensors provides the computer with real time data generated during a drive. The data is preprocessed by Sinclairs host patch, and passed on to a musical patch that generates music. The computers audio output is connected to the car sound system. The RoadMusic hardware and software in effect replace the car stereo with an interactive music system.

Sinclair sought to create a platform from RoadMusic that could host a variety of different musical works composed for the system. With the idea to create a repertoire of car music, he created a modular software architecture that allows composers to create their own musical Pure Data patches that receive sensor data from the host RoadMusic data processing patch. In completing this composer/repertoire model, Sinclair commissioned a number of composers to compose pieces for the system, and presented them together as a body of work at the 2013 edition of the Reevox festival at the GMEM in Marseilles France.

The present authors were amongst the group of composers commissioned by Sinclair for the premier of RoadMusic. We were provided with a prototype hardware system and the common data-processing host patch given to all the composers. Within this context, we had carte blanche, or complete musical liberty, to create a musical piece that would be presented in a series of 20 minute drives in a fleet of cars during the festival.

This sets the context within which the research reported in this paper is situated. To what extent could we take the commission/composer paradigm as a guide to create a work for the RoadMusic system? What would our compositional strategies be? Would the musical output be generative, sonification-based, or interactive? Is RoadMusic a musical instrument, and if so, is the driver the performer? What areas of research in sound and music computing, such as mapping and interaction, could we apply to this context?

3. RELATED WORK

3.1 Automotive UI

Alongside the industry-led and creative applications mentioned above, Automotive User Interfaces is a growing area of HCI research. The Automotive UI conference began in 2009, and addresses all aspects of user interaction, thinking of the cars as complex interactive systems. [17] We have reported on the RoadMusic system within the context of Automotive UI concerns at the Automotive UI conference [18]. Within this community, there is also research into how much we can infer about a car's environment based upon sensor data gathered from that car: machine learning and data mining techniques have been used to classify road types based upon sensor data gathered from cars [20].

3.2 Sonification

Sonification is in many ways the default approach to making electric cars sonorous. Sonification allows for the transcoding of non-audio data and extra-musical phenomena into sound. An overview of the techniques and research areas of this representative mode of sonificiation, and the related area of auditory dispays, is given by Hunt et al [7].

Ben-Tal and Berger describe uses of sonification to represent data where visualization would be ineffective. By taking advantage of both the temporal nature of sound and human auditory perception capabilities, they suggest that sonification can facilitate pattern detection [2]. Software environments have been created to allow non-musicians to sonify data in this way: SonEnvir is aimed at users from scientific domains, enabling sonification for the presentation and analysis of data [3].

We also see the transformation of data into music in the field of generative music and algorithmic composition. Nick Collins provides an overview of generative and algorithmic musics, contemplating the ontological status of the softwares and creative potentials that might be realised as the composer/ performer's role changes [4].

There is a blurred area between generative composition and sonification. Similar to recent developments in data driven art that diverge from strict scientific visualization, Polansky notes a significant difference between artistic and scientific sonification, the former of which he calls manifestation. Describing how sonification might be used artistically, he suggests that a composer might use the Gaussian distribution not to hear the Gaussian distribution as much as we want to use the Gaussian distribution to allow us to hear new music. [14] Barrass and Vickers contextualise the relationship between the functional role of sonification and aesthetic concerns and the , proposing a design-oriented approach which integrates the two, enabling sonification to be a medium wherin data can be understood and even enjoyed [1]. Doornbusch also considers this artistic or creative end of sonification identifying as a salient example of this Xenakiss Pithoprakta, which used Brownian motion, amongst other phenomena, to score glissandi for strings. Importanly, Doornbusch (and Xenakis) considered this type of sonification as a form of composition [5]. Ben-Tal and Berger describe using sonification creatively in work in which they deliberately avoid representational aspects, with the data imparting a more organic feel to the music, helping to provide rich and varied textures of sound, a technique we came to use in our composition. [2]

3.3 Mapping

The relationship between data input and sound output is described by data mapping. While most literature covers the mapping of performer gesture to sound synthesis , these techniques can be extended to other sources of data, such as we encounter in sonification and related practices.

An overview, taxonomy and analysis of gesture mapping are provided by Hunt and Wanderley [9] Importantly, they note that mapping can actually be said to define the interactive instrument. In this sense mapping takes its place alongside interface hardware and sound synthesis software to comprise the make up of a new musical instrument. [8]

Doornbusch addresses the role of data mapping in algorithmic compositions and generative musics, noting differences with mapping in instrument design. Doornbusch describes how mapping in algorithmic composition is not a discrete process like it is in instrument design, rather it is an integrated part of the composition process and a process of experimentation [5]. However, this might depend upon the specific workflows of composers, performers and instrument designers (who might be one and the same person). Essl has looked at mapping in mobile music, arguing that on-the-fly construction of mapping become part of the creative music making process. [6]

3.4 Interactive car art

Cars have been the topic of interactive art works. Andreyev has explored the cars potential role in a work that draws on Situationist concepts in her project Four Wheel Drift [21]. stergren and Juhlins Sound Pryer used mobile technology and wireless networks to allow car users stuck in traffic to hear snippets of what other users in close proximity to them were listening to. [13]

3.5 Performance environments

Salter takes an environmental view of novel musical performance environments. He takes the notion of performance outside classical frontal stage setups, to think of immersive spaces that are ludic and playful. Roles of listener and player begin to merge, and the definition of the musical instrument extends beyond the sensor system worn by any one participant, to begin to include the smart or responsive space [16].

4. SYSTEM ARCHITECTURE

The RoadMusic hardware consists of sensors (3D accelerometer and webcam) fitted on a fitPC single-board computer, with audio output feeding the cars stereo system. The computer runs a Linux Mint distribution operating system, and Pure Data Extended software with some Pure Data externals, in particular the Gridflow library which is used to process the video input. The Pure Data host framework patch, out of which the composers work, can be broken down into three main components, a Sensor Engine, an Audio Engine and a Mapping Engine [Figure 1].

The accelerometers provide a continuous stream of data representing the acceleration and deceleration of the car, its movement around bends or over bumps, and general changes in the road surface. This data is analyzed to detect prototypical events such as a curve, slowing down or an acceleration of the car. These real-world events are used to send on-off messages to the software or to trigger events in the audio.

The system also keeps a log of the number of recorded events over time periods. This generates a slower stream of data that might describe something more general about a road, a driver or a journey, such as the number of stops and stars, the bumpiness or the bendiness of a road, etc. Sinclairs data cooking extracts further thresholds from these averages, turning them into events according to the characteristic of the drive, so a bendy journey will trigger an event in pure data for the bendiness event. There is also an event trigger sent when no change in input data has been detected over a time period.

In addition to the data from the accelerometers, visual information about the journey is picked up using the webcam which is positioned so that it is looking out of the front windscreen. The first level of this data is the relative RGB (red, green, blue) color balance. The images from the camera are also analyzed and blob tracking techniques are used. The system detects large moving objects, and outputs their relative x, y and z coordinates. The system also performs threshold detection, and outputs an event

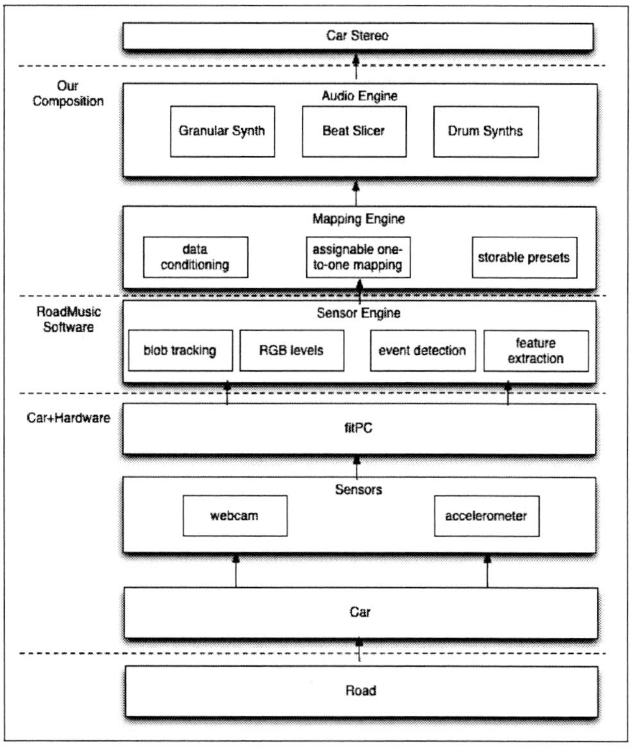

Figure 1. System Architecture.

trigger when there is a large change in the RGB levels, which might be indicative of transition from a built up or enclosed area onto an open road. [18].

We used Sinclairs Sensor Engine, but used our own Mapping Engine to connect this to our own Audio Engine, running on the fitPC, noted by the dotted lines demarcating different system components in Figure 1. At the heart of our Audio Engine is a granular synthesizer, a version of Nobuyasu Sakondas original patch for Max MSP which we have modified and ported to PD and which will play back, loop, and time stretch samples, with pitch and speed both being independently adjustable, and a freeze mode, which captures and repeats small fragments of the sample.

Other parts of the Audio Engine include a beat slicer, developed by one of the co-authors as the tutorial for sample-accurate beat displacement and re-ordering in the commercial MaxMSP distribution. A percussion synthesizer generated analog-like kick, hat and and snare drum sounds.

5. COMPOSITIONAL STRATEGY

Building a mapping environment that was idiomatic to the interactive system in question in turn defined the music composition environment. It is through combining very specific mappings and transformations with certain choices of samples that different sections of our work for the RoadMusic system were created. For this, we needed a Mapping Engine which allowed for quick experimentation with different mappings and transformations, and the ability to quickly save and recall mapping combinations.

In our Mapping Engine, the data is first transformed according to different scalings using objects and abstractions developed by Steiner [19]. These allow for different mapping modes: for instance, inverse relations, or exponential curves, describe the transformation of the input data before it is sent to a parameter. Data can thus only be sensitive in certain input ranges (for instance, only sudden slowing down might affect a parameter). The output range of the data can then be constrained, so that the input data will only affect certain ranges of a parameter. The data can then be smoothed, with different degrees of filtering. This processed data can then be mapped to musical parameters in the patch, with mapping combinations saved (and recalled) as presets.

This permitted us to work in a trial-and-error, improvisatory process of composition with this Mapping Engine. Sinclair had provided all the commissioned composers with example recordings of prototypical drives. These were archived sensor data and webcam video saved as a QuickTime movie, played back in a special simulator module of the RoadMusic host program. Sinclairs simulator combined with our Mapping Engine preset system enabled us to explore different combinations of mapping, transformations, and samples. We found different parameter combinations, and preserved these as presets and messages within the patch.

The composition is a series of these different mapping presets coupled with sample changes. We created a broad timeline for the different sections. In order to achieve a balance of control over the general structure of the piece whilst still having things being controlled by the data, we created systems of arming data, whereby a fixed timeline (score) armed sensors to execute musical section changes in response to specific driving events (eg a bump or a turn) only within specific time windows during the drive. This allowed us to impose a compositional trajectory to the piece, all while leaving the work responsive to events specific to a particular drive, and - we hoped- flexible to adapt to different drivers, cars, and routes.

6. DISCUSSION

6.1 Interaction, Sonification or Generative?

We conceived of three different yet related ways in which one might work with the RoadMusic system, defined by the mappings one would write: it could be treated as a new performance instrument, as a sonification system, or as a generative system. We found these models to be useful referents as we composed with RoadMusic and sought to integrate our own musical practices and compositional intent with the specifics we imagined that the car-as-instrument would demand. [Table 1].

6.1.1 RoadMusic as Performance Instrument

In this instance, the mappings would be used to create clear, immediate gesture-like correlations between the movements of the car and changes in the audio. For instance, accelerating might cause a sound to increase in pitch or amplitude, or a left turn might cause the music to pan to the right. Such correlations would be immediately perceivable to the driver and passengers, and the experience of driving the car with RoadMusic might feel akin to playing a musical instrument, as the drivers actions have an immediate effect on the sound.

This mode of mapping raises an immediate initial concern about safety. We were reluctant to encourage anyone driving the vehicle to make sudden maneuvers for the pure sake of musical satisfaction. This belongs to an area of general concern for those in the field of Automotive UI and a problem specific to the car-as-instrument which affects how we must think about composing for it. Interactive systems in the car must not be distracting, or encouraging of bad driving practice which could infringe upon road safety [11, 15]. In addition to safety concerns, Sinclair has suggested that from his previous work, clearly perceivable mappings can become rapidly incessant and uninteresting [18].

6.1.2 RoadMusic as Sonification

Another way of understanding RoadMusic is as a sonification system, understanding sonification here as the sonic representation of data; this would be the scientific sonification that is referred to by Polansky [14]. Some of this might be immediate, as a bumpy road could affect some synthesis parameter, or some of it might be revealed over time, such as the general bendiness of a journey.

To an extent, this corresponds with certain artistic intentions informing Sinclairs design and use of the RoadMusic system. Sinclair suggests that the system might communicate information to a user in a subliminal manner. This will only happen over time and long term use, as Sinclair notes; through the global recognition of a previous similar sound experience as opposed to the immediate, conscious tracking of a given signal. Furthermore, this may be through somewhat intangible parameters rather than simple, observable mappings and relations, expressed to the driver through the feel of the music as much as anything [18].

In debating how to work with the RoadMusic paradigm, we made a deliberate choice not to opt for any representative, data sonification, Our reasoning behind this was artistically and compositionally informed: we were attempting specifically to make a short (20 minute) piece of music, presumably to be experienced by individual listeners once: not long enough to begin to notice correlations between type of journey, feeling of road, and sound.

6.1.3 RoadMusic as Generative Composition

This category clearly blurs with Polansky's manifestation, or the creative- rather than scientific and representational- use of sonification [14]. While there is a degree of sonification in our RoadMusic composition, our own use of mapping for RoadMusic falls mostly within this category.

The generative nature of our work does not involve any algorithmic processes. Instead, incoming data is used to shape textures and trigger events, to add, as Ben-Tal and Berger [2] do, an organicness to textures that would otherwise be static, but without the intent to explicitly or subconsciously communicate anything to the listener about the car, the road or the journey through such sonic effects. Data is not generated by automatic computer processes, but by the drive itself, and shapes the piece, and may create

	INSTRUMENT	SONIFICATION	GENERATIVE
CORRELATION	correlation between drivers actions and sound perceivable	correlation between car movements and webcam/road data and sound are perceivable	correlation between car movements and sounds may be unclear
EXPRESSION	expressive for driver	expresses data	expresses intent of composer
MAPPING	legibly relates movements to sound	legibly translates data into sound	abstracts data before it affects sound

Table 1. Comparing Instrument, Sonification and Generative Composition.

musical formations that the composer would not otherwise have created, but there is no intentional representative correlation between data and sound. This is achieved through creating layers of abstraction within the mapping.

6.2 Mapping Strategies

We utilized two main techniques in order for the mapping to be a layer of abstraction between the sensor data and the sound produced, blurring many perceivable correlations for the driver/performer and avoiding representative sonification. These techniques were looping data sequences and limiting ranges that the data affected.

Looping data involves using the data to write sequences, which are then repeated and can be sent to any parameter within the Audio Engine. This is based on one of Peter Sinclairs techniques, which involves continuously writing g-force data into tables which are used as the wavetables within the synthesizers and thus affect the timbre and texture of sounds. Sinclair records 13 seconds of data into a 132 sample wavetable. We use an event-trigger from the Sensor Engine to periodically take low-resolution snapshots of these tables, reducing the 132 sample long table to a 16 sample long table. This is then treated as a 16 beat musically loop, continually read through.

Some of this data is used to trigger drum samples: values in certain ranges triggering synthesized kick, snare and hi-hat sounds, transforming into a two bar drum loop, the sequence for which is periodically rewritten. These tables are also used to change musical parameters and loop these changes over two bars. For instance, the pitch of the synthesized kick could be changed over the two bar loop, or another parameter, such as the grain-duration of a granular synthesizer, could be changed. This technique also allows for us to use patterns and repetition within the piece, which will always vary on each different performance of the piece.

Another technique we used to abstract the data in the mapping is choosing the ranges that the data can affect, or in which the data has the most effect. If the data is only affecting a small range of a parameter, it can have the effect of introducing small, continuous variation which may help add richness and a feeling of organicness to a texture, without there being any perceivable correlations between movement of the car and the sound produced for the driver/performer.

7. PRESENTATION AND EVALUATION

Our piece was presented at the Reevox festival of the Groupe de Musique Experimantal de Marseilles (GMEM) on the 9th February 2013. There were 6 cars, each carrying up to 7 people (including the driver) on one of two twenty five minute journeys around Marseille, with a rotating program of 6 pieces written for RoadMusic. This ran from 2pm until 7pm. The different cars, different drivers (with different driving styles), different routes (incorporating small city streets, motorways and tunnels), different audiences (ranging from young children to the elderly) and changing traffic conditions put our composition to the test.

This presentation was our first chance to test our aforementioned compositional strategies with a real audience in a real world setting. Like a composer writing a piece with no orchestra at their disposal and no chance for rehearsals, our first experience of the piece in a car was actually during the first performance itself. Only having being able to test the piece using recordings of data proved to be insufficient preparation for the experience RoadMusic inside a moving car. The experience is highly embodied, and jolts from the road, or the act of g-force upon the body, may be accompanied by a sonic experience. Without being in the car, it is difficult to understand the effectiveness of the mappings or the relationship between the sensor data and the sound.

We had adopted different compositional strategies from the other pieces. These generally involved more tangible correlations between sensor data and music, often with quite noticeable difference being brought about by stopping, by starting the car after pauses at traffic lights, or by bumps in the road surfaces. It felt as though the sensor data was sufficiently abstracted by our Mapping Engine, as intended, but it also became clear that there was perhaps too little correlation between sensor data and sound events in our piece. Anyone hearing the piece multiple times would hear that it was different each time and intimately tied to the data, but anyone hearing the piece only once may find little to distinguish it from a fixed piece of music. Further work on the piece might involve rewriting the mapping to provide some more legibility in correlations between the car's movements or the webcam footage and the sound.

Furthermore, our piece was in a minority that had used a timeline, and the timeline proved to be problematic. Some drives ended up being shortened, meaning that only the first part of our piece was heard by the audience. Also, a rewrite of the piece will be necessary should anyone wish to listen to the piece for anytime longer than 25 minutes. Replacing a strict timeline with a method for organically moving between different sections, would be a more appropriate method of composing, albeit one that might sacrifice some compositional control over structure. We also intend to investigate ways of using the data to provide the structure.

On the whole, the drivers followed the routes as though they were a score in a relatively straightforward way. However, we observed the drivers being expressive with RoadMusic pieces, contrary to our assumptions. They would look for ways of being expressive, perhaps by driving slightly faster at speed bumps or taking corners harder. Correlations between sound, mapping and driving styles are more complex than we anticipated within the context of RoadMusic.

These offer tangible challenges and future work for composing for this unique platform, that lies between being an expressive musical instrument, a system of sonification and a generative composition.

8. CONCLUSION

This paper documented the thoughts behind composing for a novel sound environment, RoadMusic, an interactive music system fitted in car. Mapping is an essential part of the artistic and compositional process. It is an integral part of the programming process (a versatile Mapping Engine has to be programmed), it forms part of an improvisatory compositional process (different mappings are experimented with and successful experiments preserved). It defines the difference between a new musical instrument, sonification and a generative composition, and through the mappings we created a generative composition, based upon our existing Audio Engine. However, there remains work to do be done in understanding the most effective manners of composing for this novel system.

9. BIBLIOGRAPHY

[1] S. Barrass and P. Vickers, "Sonification Design and Aesthetics," in T. Hermann, A. Hunt and J. Neuhoff (eds). *The Sonification Handbook*, Logos Publishing House, 2011.

[2] O. Ben-Tal and J. Berger, "Creative Aspects of Sonification," *In Leonardo Music Journal*, vol. 37, no. 3, pp. 229-233, 2004.

[3] A. Campo, C. Frauenberger and R. Hldrich, "Designing a Generalized Sonification Environment," in *Proc. International Conference on Auditory Display*, Sydney, 2004.

[4] N. Collins, "The Analysis of Generative Music Programs," it In Organised Sound, vol. 13, no. 3, pp. 237-248, 2008.

[5] P. Doornbusch, "A Brief Survey of Mapping in Algorithmic Composition," in it Proc ICMC, Gothenburg, 2002, pp. 205-210.

[6] G. Essl, "SpeedDial: Rapid and On-The-Fly Mapping of Mobile Phone Instruments," in it Proc. NIME, Pittsburgh, 2009, pp. 270-273.

[7] T. Hermann, A. Hunt and J. Neuhoff (eds). *The Sonification Handbook*, Logos Publishing House, 2011.

[8] A. Hunt, M. Wanderley and M. Paradiso, "The Importance of Parameter Mapping in Electronic Instrument Design," in *Proc. NIME*, Singapore, 2002.

[9] A. Hunt and M. Wanderley, "Mapping Performance Parameters to Synthesis Engines," in *Organised Sound*, vol. 7, no. 2, pp. 97-108, 2002.

[10] H. Katayose and S. Inokuchi, "The Kansei Music System," in *Computer Music Journal*, vol. 13, no. 4, pp. 72-77, 1989.

[11] A. Kun, T. Paek, Z. Medenica, N. Memarovi and O. Palinko, "Glancing at Personal Navigation Devices Can Affect Driving: Experimental Results and Design Implications," in *Proc. Automotive UI*, Essen, 2009, pp. 129-136.

[12] P. Nyeste and M. Wogalter, "On Adding Sound to Quiet Vehicles," in *Proc. Human Factors and Ergonomics Society Annual Meeting*, Raleigh, 2008, pp. 1747-1750.

[13] M. Ostergren and O. Juhlin, "Sound Pryer: Truly Mobile Joint Music Listening," in N. Kirisits, F. Behrendt, L. Gaye and A. Tanaka (eds) *Creative Interactions The MobileMusicWorkshop 2004 2008*, University for Applied Arts Vienna, 2008.

[14] L. Polansky, "Manifestation and Sonification," eamusic.dartmouth.edu/ larry/sonification.html, 2002, retrieved 10/02/2013.

[15] A. Rydstrom, C. Grane, and P. Bengtsson, "Driver behaviour during haptic and visual secondary tasks," in *Proc. Automotive UI*, Essen, 2009, pp. 121-127.

[16] C. Salter, M. Baalman and D. Moody-Grigsby, "Between Mapping, Sonification and Composition: Responsive Audio Environments in Live Performance," in R. Kronland-Martinet, S. Ystad and K. Jensen (eds) *Computer Music Modeling and Retrieval: Sense of Sounds*, Springer Verlag Berlin Heidelberg, 2008, pp. 246-262.

[17] A. Schmidt and A. Dey, Preface to *Proc. Automotive UI*, Essen, 2009.

[18] P. Sinclair, A. Tanaka and Y. Hubnet, "RoadMusic: Music For Your Ride From Your Ride," in *Adjunct Proc. Automotive UI*, Salzburg, 2011.

[19] H. Steiner, "Towards a Catalog and Software Library of Mapping Methods" in *Proc. NIME*, 2006, Paris, pp. 106-109.

[20] P. Taylor, S. Anand, N. Griffiths, F. Adamu-Fika, A. Dunoyer, T. Popham, X. Zhou and A. Gelencser, "Road Type Classification through Data Mining," in *Proc. Automotive UI*, Portsmouth, 2012, pp. 233-240.

[21] P. Watson and J. Andreyev, "Four Wheel Drift," in R. Adams, S. Gibson, and S, Mller (eds) *Transdisciplinary Digital Art*, Springer Verlag Berlin, Heidelberg, 2008.

DOWNY OAK: RENDERING ECOPHYSIOLOGICAL PROCESSES IN PLANTS AUDIBLE

Marcus Maeder
Zurich University of the Arts,
Institute for Computer Music and
Sound Technology,
Zurich, Switzerland
marcus.maeder@zhdk.ch

Roman Zweifel
Swiss Federal Institute for Forest,
Snow and Landscape Research WSL,
Birmensdorf,
Switzerland
roman.zweifel@wsl.ch

ABSTRACT

In our research project *trees: Rendering Ecophysiological Processes Audible*, we are working on the acoustic recording, analysis and representation of ecophysiological processes in plants and studying the acoustic and aesthetic requirements for making them perceptible. Measurements of acoustic emissions in plants are only interpretable in relation to climatic and physiological dynamics such as microclimatic conditions, sap flow and changes in trunk radius and water potential within the plants—all measurement data that is not auditory per se. Therefore, our work involves analysing the acoustic emissions mathematically, on one hand, and sonifying ecophysiological data on the other. How can phenomena that are beyond our normal perception be made directly observable, creating new experiences and opening a new window on the processes of nature? The sound installation *trees: Downy Oak*, exhibited at swissnex in San Francisco in summer 2012, is a first approach to a spatial audio sonification and research system. Our experiments show that immediate and intuitive access to measurement data through sounds and their spatial positioning is very promising in terms of new forms of data display as well as generative art works.

INTRODUCTION

The link between trees and various climatic processes is usually not immediately apparent. Plants, in general, do not live merely on moisture from rain, sunlight (which drives gas exchange) and nutrients from the soil: they also absorb carbon dioxide from the air and produce the oxygen that we breathe, maintaining our climate and biosphere. Hence the interest in cooperation between a biologist and an artist to conduct research and measurements to study the complex relationship between tree physiology and the climate on one hand and to explore the possibilities of acoustic and artistic representations of ecophysiological processes in trees on the other. Rendering audible the way in which water transport or trunk diameter, for example, are influenced by sunlight, humidity and wind allows us to identify and better understand plants' responses to climatic processes.

1.1 "Phytoacoustics"

Plant physiologists have known that plants emit sounds for several decades now 0. Many of these sounds are of transpiratory/hydraulic origin 0 and are therefore related to the circulation of water and air within the plant as part of the transpiration process. The frequencies of these acoustic emissions lie mostly in the ultrasonic range, depending on the species-specific characteristics of the plant tissues.

Fig. 1: An acoustic sensor (under the yellow tape) and a sap flow sensor (covered by reflective insulation material) mounted on a branch of a Scots pine in the Swiss Alps in summer 2012.

Some of the acoustic emissions are indications of embolism in the water transport system, which occurs when a plant is subjected to drought stress and desiccation 0. The excessive water tension in the water-conducting system leads to the rupture of the water columns in the plant vessels. Many studies have analysed these acoustic emissions in quantitative terms (number of emissions over time) 0 but few have focused on the signal properties (frequencies, waveforms and amplitudes) so far 0 or on the spatial distribution within the plant.

Each plant species—in fact each plant individual—has its own acoustic signature, related to its structure and to the local climatic conditions. Investigating the acoustic emissions of a tree in response to dynamically changing climatic conditions might reveal biological or physical properties that place them in a broader ecophysiological context and enable us to explain processes that are not yet fully understood.

Various artistic projects have subjected plant sounds to an artistic investigation with a view to revealing a world that is normally inaudible. These include Justin Bennett's *Hoor de Boomen* 0, Alex Metcalf's *Tree Listening* 0 and Christa Sommerer and Laurent Mignonneau's *Data Tree* 0 to name just a few. Our project (which is situated between the domains of artistic research and natural science) examines the aesthetic means of illustrating phenomena in nature but also aims to generate new knowledge through exploration using artistic and sound technology tools, systems and practices.

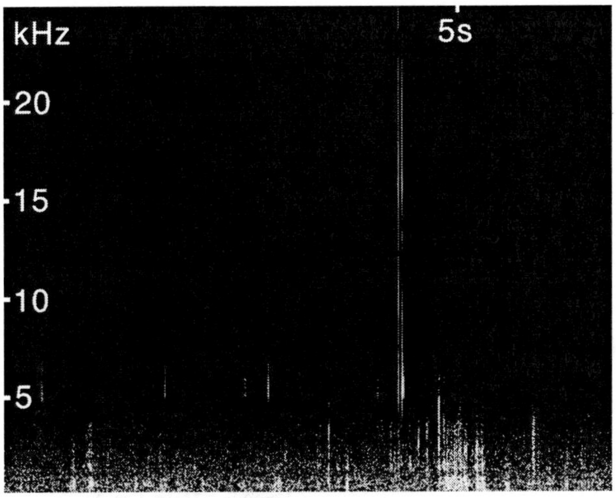

Fig. 2: Acoustic emissions of a sunflower fully exposed to sunlight. The high frequency signals represent the supposed cavitation pulses.

1.2 Sonification of ecophysiological data

The representation of data using sound (among other means) can help to exploit the effectiveness of our sense of hearing in grasping complex contexts both through immediate orientation in space and intuitive classification of sound characteristics 0. Sonification offers a deep and broad insight into multidimensional data, enabling us to recognize patterns and providing an aesthetic and emotional experience of scientific discoveries.

Gathering ecophysiological data (i.e. conducting measurements of the local climatic and environmental conditions and of the physiological processes within a plant in response to these) has become an important method in research on climate change and vegetation dynamics. It helps to determine physiological thresholds of plants in terms of increasing temperature and consequently drought stress. A downy oak in the central Alps, for example, is able to withstand the current climatic conditions of the air and soil whereas a Scots pine is pushed beyond its physiological limits despite the fact that both tree species have coexisted there for thousands of years 0. Consequently, shifts in the abundance of tree species are observed, and the ecophysiological knowledge acquired explains the underlying processes 0.

In our project, we began by combining field recordings of meteorological phenomena, recordings of acoustic emissions in trees and acoustic representations (sonifications) of ecophysiological data in a single auditory experience and making their correlation acoustically and aesthetically experienceable and explorable. We conducted a number of sonification experiments based on ecophysiological data collected by Roman Zweifel (WSL) and Fabienne Zeugin of the Swiss Federal Institute of Technology (ETH) on an ongoing basis on a downy oak (Quercus pubescens) at Salgesch in the Swiss mountains in 2003 and 2004. Zweifel and Zeugin measured relative air humidity, sap flow, stem radius changes and ultrasonic acoustic emissions (UAE) throughout an entire tree growth cycle and recorded the data at ten-minute intervals throughout the day and night.

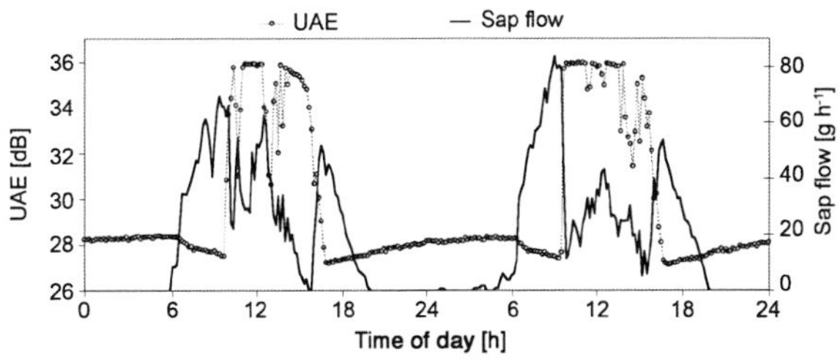

Fig. 3: Typical diurnal courses of acoustic emissions (UAE; cycles) in relation to branch sap flow rate (line) of a downy oak (Quercus pubescens) at Salgesch from 24 to 25 June 2004.

As the data relating to the ecophysiological processes was multidimensional, an analytical system was needed that focused on the key factors and the interrelations between these and rendered them intuitively perceptible. In terms of sound technology, the use of a spatial audio system immediately suggested itself for the sonification experiments as a means of spatially separating, distributing and conveying sounds and sound sequences. We were aware of comparable systems being developed at the Institute for Electronic Music and Acoustics (IEM) in Graz (Data Listening Space) 0 and at the ZKM in Karlsruhe (Cube) 0.

2. DOWNY OAK: A PROTOTYPE OF A SPATIAL AUDIO SONIFICATION SYSTEM

The sound installation *trees: Downy Oak,* exhibited at swissnex in San Francisco in summer 2012, is a preliminary approach to our intended research system and a work of art at the same time. It is the prototype of a spatial audio matrix that we will use during our future sonification experiments.

2.1 The audio system

The system (the *trees: Downy Oak* installation) consists of a grid of 36 self-built omni-directional speakers. It is designed as a cube matrix with an additional layer of speakers on top. Visitors can walk around the installation freely and explore it.

The Institute for Computer Music and Sound Technology has conducted research and development in Ambisonics-based surround technology since its foundation in 2005 0. One of the limitations concerning placement and moving of virtual audio sources in an Ambisonics sound field is that the perceived positions of the sources remain outside the speaker system. The virtual sound sources are projected onto the surface of a virtual (usually) half sphere, which is mapped on and distributed through a multichannel speaker system. The perceptual situation is comparable to listening to what is going on outside through an open window: An Ambisonics system is not able to project virtual sound sources onto a spot within the system's boundaries.

Fig. 5: The sound installation *trees: Downy Oak* at swissnex in San Francisco in summer 2012.

Our idea consisted in creating a three-dimensional speaker array in which virtual sound sources could be moved and placed *within* a defined space, allowing listeners to walk around inside the system. The speaker matrix that we developed for the *trees: Downy Oak* installation is currently a hybrid sound system: The Ambisonics sound field is mapped onto the outer surface of the cube matrix. The vertical speaker line in the middle is driven discretely. Our goal with newer versions of the system is to implement cross-fading algorithms between the speakers of the matrix so as to allow free placement and movement of virtual sound sources within the cube.

2.2 Downy Oak: Data sonification

The sonification system is based on a combination of different sonification techniques, i.e. playback of audifications 0 of original acoustic emission recordings (by transposing them into the audible domain) and parameter mapping sonification 0, whereby the sound parameters of a sample player (amplitude, pitch and filters) and the sound distribution system (spatial position or movements of virtual sound sources) are controlled by the data flow.

The different sonification modules are implemented in a set of Max Patches, which replays the measurement data of a downy oak throughout an entire growth cycle (April-October 2004). For an adequate (temporal) experience of the key processes, the speed of the running system is increased up to 36 times the normal speed to take into account the ten-minute measuring intervals. Environmental data is mapped onto the outside of the cube, while tree data is played back on the vertical speaker line in the middle of the array.

A larger number of ecophysiological and meteorological phenomena do not manifest themselves acoustically, and it was a challenging task to generate metaphorical sounds to portray a single phenomenon, such as sunlight or air humidity effectively. The following table shows the phenomena (i.e. the data), the kind of sounds that represent them and the individual playback parameters, controlled by the data flow and mapping:

Data	Sound characteristics	Playback parameters
Sun position [azimuth, altitude]; sunlight [W/m^2]	String-like, synthetic sound	Spatial position; amplitude
Temperature [°C]	-	Main volume
Rel. air humidity [%]	Water-like, synthetic sound	Pitch, amplitude
Rain [mm]	Field rec.: rain	Amplitude, spatial position
Wind [m/sec., azimuth]	Field rec.: wind	Amplitude, spatial position
Soil water potential [kPa]	Field rec.: seeping water	Amplitude
Tree trunk diameter [μm]	-	High pass filter, applied on sap flow sound
Tree sap flow [g H_20/h]	Floating water, transposed up and filtered	Amplitude
Tree ultrasonic acoustic emissions/cavitation pulses [dB]	Field rec.: ultrasonic acoustic emissions, transposed down	Amplitude

3. PRELIMINARY CONCLUSIONS

For us as well as for visitors, it was and still is a fascinating experience to spend time in the system, listening to the interplay of sounds and the related phenomena throughout an entire growth period, which lasts about 40 minutes. Besides the diurnal course of the tree's response to sunlight, there are many other recognizable patterns: As it gets drier in the summer, the cavitation events become longer, sometimes lasting deep into the night; the stressed plant needs more time to refill with water from the soil. In addition, the number of cavitation sounds is greater when a plant is well drained and exposed to full sunlight than in very dry periods.

Immediate and intuitive access to measurement data through sound and its spatial positioning is very promising as it offers new forms of data display and observation of processes in nature as well as generative art works. The representation and sonification of our tree data needs to become more complex: At present, there are just three parameters mapped onto a single vertical line of the audio matrix: sap flow, cavitation and trunk diameter, measured at the stem of the tree. We would like to include more information about the spatial distribution of the acoustic emissions and the related physiological measurements within a whole plant, including the crown, the root and some branches at various locations on the tree.

Our intention in presenting a first prototype of the sonification system at a public exhibition was to determine whether or not our initial experiments would be comprehensible to a broader audience, i.e. whether or not the ecophysiological phenomena and their interrelations could be identified through the chosen sounds and the design of our experiential space. Visitors had no major problems identifying most of the field recordings, but it became evident that the different sounds and their meanings needed to be explained. We set up a computer with a blog explaining the sounds and corresponding phenomena and their interplay. In addition, visitors were encouraged to leave comments about their experience of the installation. We also realized that additional elements were needed within the installation, particularly information about the time of day and season. We solved that problem on site by projecting the date and time of the sonified measurements onto the floor next to the installation.

Regarding the further development of our system, we are currently examining different forms of visual information as supportive elements. We think it would be helpful to have video information about the time of day, the coarse of the sun, the weather conditions etc. Daniel Bisig and Jan Schacher have been working on immersive audio-visual environments since 2010 0. In their recent research project *Immersive Lab* at the ICST, they are experimenting with an audio-visual setup that offers haptic interaction with generative art pieces. Alongside further development of our 3D speaker-matrix, we intend to integrate our sonification processes with the *Immersive Lab* installation adding panoramic/hemispheric video recordings.

4. ACKNOWLEDGEMENTS

The research project *trees: Rendering Ecophysiological Processes Audible* is funded by the Swiss National Science Foundation (SNSF) (100016_143958/1). The production and presentation of the prototype of the *trees: Downy Oak* installation was generously financed by the Swiss Arts Council Pro Helvetia and ThinkSwiss as well as swissnex San Francisco and the ICST. We would like to thank Jan Schacher for his help in getting the sonification software running for the entire duration of the exhibition.

5. REFERENCES

[1] Bennett, J. (2009): Hoor de Boomen, http://www.hoordebomen.nl/ from 01.06.2013

[2] Bisig, D., Schacher, J. C. (2011): Flowspace – A Hybrid Ecosystem, Proceedings of the International Conference on New Interfaces for Musical Expression, Oslo, Norway, 2011

[3] Hermann, T., Hunt, A., Neuhoff, J. G. (Ed.) (2011): The Sonification Handbook, Berlin: Logos

[4] Kawamoto, S., Williams, S. R. (2002): Acoustic Emission and Acousto-Ultrasonic Techniques for Wood and Wood-Based Composites, Gen. Tech. Rep. FPL-GTR-134. Madison, WI: U.S. Department of Agriculture, Forest Service, Forest Products Laboratory

[5] Metcalf, A. (2007/2010): Tree Listening, http://www.alexmetcalf.co.uk/Site/Tree-Listening.html, from 01.06.2013

[6] Milburn, J. A., Johnson, R. P. C. (1966): The conduction of sap. II. Detection of vibrations produced by sap cavitation in Rhicinus xylem, Planta (Berl.) 69, p. 43-52

[7] Milburn, J. A., Ritman, K. T. (1988): Acoustic emissions from plants: Ultrasonic and audible compared, Journal of Experimental Botany, vol. 39, no. 206, p. 1237-1248

[8] Ramakrishnan, Ch., Goßmann, J., Brümmer, L. (2006): The ZKM Klangdom, NIME 06, Proceedings of the 2006 conference on New interfaces for musical expression, IRCAM — Centre Pompidou Paris, France, 2006

[9] Schacher, J. C. (2010): Seven Years Of ICST Ambisonics Tools For MaxMSP, Proceedings of the 2nd International Symposium on Ambisonics and Spherical Acoustics May 6-7, Paris, France, 2010

[10] Sommerer, Ch., Mignonneau, L. (2009): Interactive Art Research, Wien: Springer

[11] Tyree, M. T, Dixon M. A. (1983): Cavitation Events in Thuja occidentalis L. Ultrasonic Acoustic Emissions from the Sapwood Can Be Measured, Plant Physiol. 72, p. 1094-1099

[12] Vogt, K., Pirrò, D., Rumori, M., Höldrich, R. (2012).: Sounds of simulations: data listening space, Proceedings International Computer Music Conference 2012, Ljubljana, Slovenia, p. 525

[13] Zweifel R., Zeugin F. (2008): Ultrasonic acoustic emissions in drought-stressed trees – more than signals from cavitation? New Phytologist, 179, p. 1070-1079

[14] Zweifel R., Rigling A., Dobbertin M., (2009). Species-specific stomatal response of trees to drought – a link to vegetation dynamics, Journal of Vegetation Science 20, p. 442-454

[15] Rigling, A., Bigler, C., Eilmann, B., Feldmeyer-Christe, E., Gimmi, U., Ginzler, C., Graf, U., Mayer, P., Vacchiano, G., Weber, P., Wohlgemuth, T., Zweifel, R., Dobbertin, M. (2013): Driving factors of a vegetation shift from Scots pine to pubescent oak in dry Alpine forests. Global Change Biology 19 (1): 229-240.

The Influence of Graphical User Interface Design on Critical Listening Skills

Josh Mycroft, Joshua D. Reiss, Tony Stockman
Centre for Digital Music,
Queen Mary's, University of London.
j.b.mycroft@qmul.ac.uk

ABSTRACT

Current Digital Audio Workstations include increasingly complex visual interfaces which have been criticised for focusing user's attention on visual rather than aural modalities. This study aims to investigate whether visual interface complexity has an influence on critical listening skills. Participants with experience mixing audio on computers were given critical listening tests while manipulating Graphical User interfaces of varying complexity. Results from the study suggest that interfaces requiring the use of a scroll bar have a significant negative effect on critical listening reaction times. We conclude that the use of scrolling interfaces, by requiring users to hold information in working memory, can interfere with simultaneous critical listening tasks. These results have implications for the design of Digital Audio Workstations especially when using small displays.

1. BACKGROUND

In current Digital Audio Workstation (DAW) design, unlimited track counts, multiple effects plug-ins and a large number of conceptual additions have resulted in increasingly complex interfaces [1]. It has been suggested that this increased interface complexity risks focusing user's attention on the visual display to the cost of aural engagement [2], with many DAW users opting to turn off the VDU at times during mixing [3].

This paper highlights some of the perceptual and creative implications of mixing using screen based interfaces then proceeds to report the findings from a study designed to quantify the influence of Graphical User Interfaces (GUI) design on aural acuity. Participants with experience mixing audio on computers were given critical listening tests while manipulating GUIs of varying complexity. The results were analysed to see whether the visual presentation style influenced the critical listening skills typical of those required in audio mixing workflows.

2. INTRODUCTION

The increasing visual complexity of current DAWs has potential consequences for the successful mixing of audio. In creative terms, the need to navigate through several windows risks inhibiting the engagement and 'flow' of the mixing process. For example, they may impede the user's ability to make requisite adjustments such as pan, level and effects changes [4]. Furthermore, the interface may compromise the realisation of creative ideas, which due to their fleeting nature are 'lost' when the user has to negotiate a badly implemented GUI. [5].

In perceptual terms, the large amount of information on the screen and the navigation required to access it across multiple windows can place high cognitive load on short-term and working memory [6] and overload the limited capacities of the visual mechanism [7]. The large amount of visual detail within the interface may also bias the perception of auditory information in favour of visual information [8]. For example, Macdonald and Lavie [9] found that when test subjects made either a low or high-load visual discrimination concerning a cross shape (respectively, a discrimination of line colour or of line length with a subtle length difference) the participant's ability to notice the presence of a simultaneously presented brief pure tone was significantly reduced (79% in the high-visual-load condition, significantly more than in the low-load condition). In a similar study Dehais et al [10] found a link between complexities of the GUI and reduced aural awareness. In flight simulations 57 % of trained pilots failed to notice auditory alarms under high visual load conditions. The authors suggest that visual information processing interfered with concurrent appraisal of auditory alarms, thereby inducing 'Inattentional Deafness' [9]. In order to ameliorate the effect of visual overload when using these GUIs, they suggest a temporary simplification of the user interface (Cognitive Countermeasures) to redress this problem [11].

Given the complex visual presentation of many contemporary DAWs (with scrolling and window switching a major part of the interface navigation) and the increased use of small screen displays for music and audio mixing (such as Cubasis, Auria, Nanostudio and FL Studio Mobile) it may prove insightful to quantify how GUI complexity influences the speed and accuracy of critical listening tasks typical of audio mixing workflows. In so doing it is hoped that heuristics may be realised that acknowledge the perceptual limitations of the user, decrease cognitive load and minimise the extraneous complexity of the interface encroaching on the intrinsic complexity of the user's main task [12].

3. STUDY DESIGN

3.1 Participants

There were eighteen participants recruited (eight from the Centre for Digital Music, Queen Mary, University of London and ten from second year 'A level' Music Technology Students at City and Islington College, London). All participants were experienced using DAWs. All gave informed consent to participate in the study. The study was conducted in accordance with the guidelines of the University. The Ethics Committee of Queen Mary, University of London, approved the details of the study.

3.2 Procedure

Participants were played an excerpt of a mix of eight audio tracks which they monitored on headphones. They were asked to listen to specified instruments from the mix (strings, guitar and tambourine) to ascertain which of these instruments was being panned (changing the apparent position of the sound between the headphone speakers). All files began panned centrally (pan position 0) and one of the three specified files was panned over the duration of the excerpt (two minutes) till it was panned hard left or right (pan position -60 or +60). The participants were asked to respond to the panning by pressing one of three response button (labelled strings, guitar or tambourine) as a timed response task. The excerpt was played twelve times in total, during which each of the specified instruments was panned three times.

At the same time as completing this critical listening task, the participants were asked to match the frequency curves of a four band equaliser (the target) with a pre-equalised four band equaliser (the source) so that the target and source frequency curves were as visually close as possible. This was done using four interfaces (figures 1-4):

Control interface: This consisted of a play button and three response buttons labelled guitar, strings and tambourine. There was no source or target equaliser, and the participants were not required to complete any interface manipulation task during the excerpt other than selecting a response button.

Interface one: This consisted of a play button, the three response buttons and the source and target equalisers.

Interface two: This consisted of a play button, the three response buttons, a source and target equaliser and three moving meters (a gain meter, a phase meter and a frequency analyser) placed between the source and target.

Interface three: This consisted of a play button, the three response buttons, the source and target equaliser as well as five additional equalisers placed between them. Due to the additional equalisers the source and target equalisers did not fit on the same screen and participants were required to scroll between them.

Participants were asked to begin matching the source and target as soon as they pressed the play button, but were informed they could stop at any point at which they clarified which instrument was panning, even if they had not completed matching the target equaliser curve to the source curve. Prior to the study participants were given a test patch so they could acquaint themselves with manipulating the equaliser.

The four interfaces and panning file types were arranged in a randomised order and presented to the participants. The time it took to respond to the panned file was recorded for each interface, though this information was not visible to the participants and they were not told they were being timed.

Due to the increased aural acuity required to hear small panning amounts and the potential distraction of visual feedback, it was hypothesised that interfaces which impact negatively on critical listening skills would result in participants taking longer to hear the panning (which becomes easier to identify at extremes).

Figure 1: Control interface only displays response buttons.

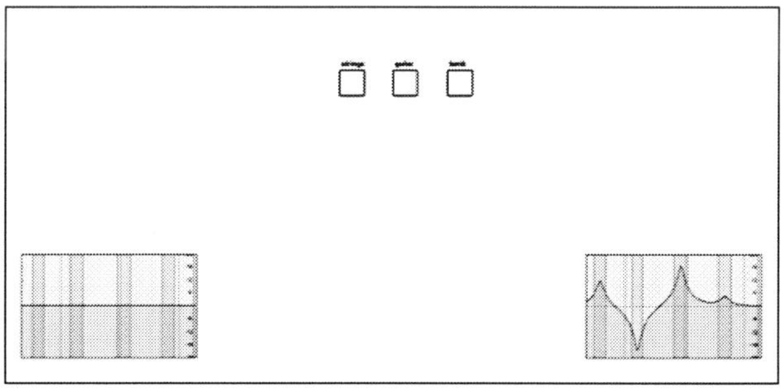

Figure 2: Interface 1 includes the addition of source and target equalisers.

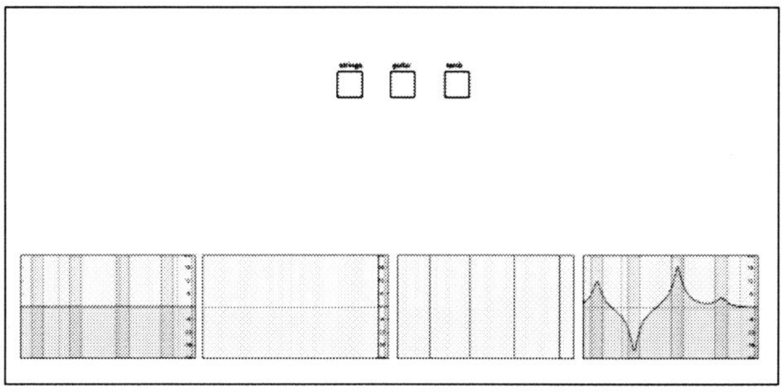

Figure 3. Interface 2 includes the addition of moving meters between the source and target equalisers.

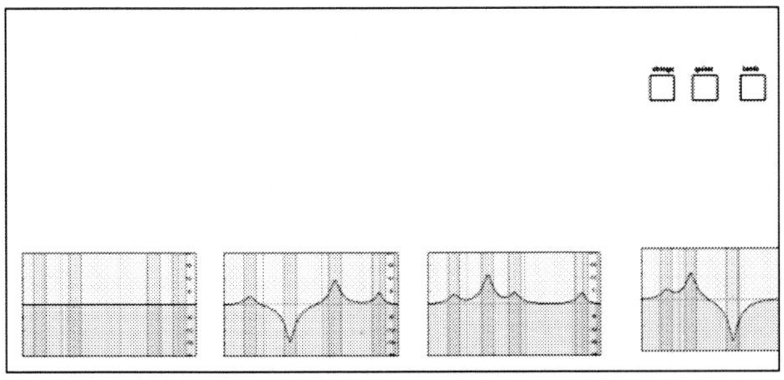

Figure 4. Interface 3 includes the addition of several equalisers, requiring scrolling.

4. ANALYSIS

Of the eighteen participants recruited, four were discounted due to incorrectly identifying some of the panning instruments, one was discounted due to an inability to clearly hear the panning instruments within the mix, and a further participant was discounted for failing to attempt matching the source and target equalisers.

Of the twelve remaining participants the time taken to correctly identify panning was compared between the four interface types. As all three of the specified instruments (tambourine, guitar and strings) were panned in each of the interface types it was possible to directly compare the response times for each instrument across interface types.

The mean time and standard deviation was calculated for the response times of all the interfaces and file types (see table one). A dependent *t*-test was then conducted between the control interface and the independent variable interfaces. The dependent *t* test generated a *P* value, where values of 0.05 or less reject the null hypothesis (that the interfaces design does not have any effect on critical listening skills).

5. RESULTS

While Interfaces one and two had slower response times across all three of the specified instruments compared to the control, none of these were statistically significant, with *P* values from the dependent *t*-tests being greater than 0.05 ($p>0.05$). See table two.

However there were significantly slower response times for all three instruments in interface three (requiring scrolling) compared to the control interface. The dependent *t*-test consistently generated *P* values less than 0.05, thereby rejecting the null hypothesis at the 95% confidence level.

The time difference between the Control and the interfaces was also calculated to discern how the interface affected the ability to complete the task. The analysis (table three) shows that interface 3 (at 95% confidence level) has a range for the true population mean that is greater than the control across all three file types.

The analysis also reveals that overall the Control provided the fastest response for the majority of participants on all file types (overall being the quickest interface 58 % of the time), while interface 3 provided the quickest response only 4% of the time (figure 5).

File		Interface type			
		Control	1	2	3
GUITAR	Mean	36.3	46.1	45.33	52.3
	SD	14.5	15.17	22.9	15.38
	CI (90%)	±6.88 29.41 To 43.19	±7.2 38.9 to 53.3	±10.87 34.46 to 56.2	±7.3 43.36 to 57.96
STRINGS	Mean	37.3	44.58	49.41	50.66
	SD	15.7	18.39	15.47	15.38
	CI (90%)	±7.45 29.85 to 44.75	±8.73 35.85 to 53.31	±7.35 42.06 to 56.76	±7.3 43.36 To 57.96
TAMB	Mean	49.0	51.9	53.83	66.41
	SD	16.94	19.49	18.68	21.78
	CI (90%)	±8.04 40.96 to 57.04	±9.25 42.65 to 61.15	±8.87 44.96 to 62.7	±10.34 56.07 to 76.75

Table 1. Mean time for task completion using the different interfaces.

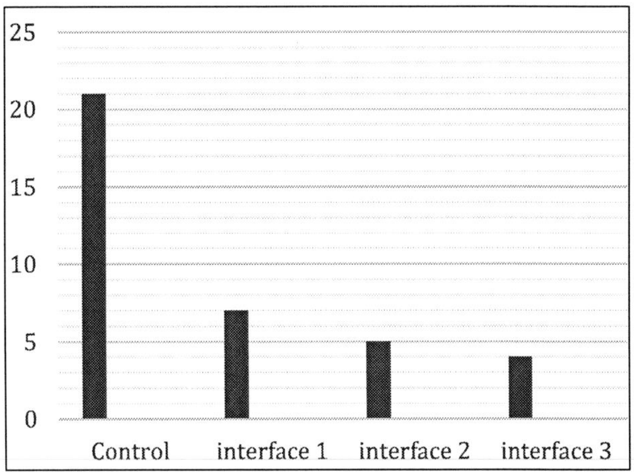

Figure 5. Occurrences of interface types being fastest across all participants and file types.

File Type	*P* values at 95% Confidence Intervals		
	Control to interface 1	Control to interface 2	Control to interface 3
Guitar	P = 0.120	P = 0.261	P= 0.033
Strings	P = 0.308	P= 0.070	P = 0.047
Tamb	P = 0.701	P = 0.514	P= 0.040

Table 2. The *P* values for time difference between Control and interface type.

6. DISCUSSION

The analysis of the data suggests that increased visual load by itself does not have a statistically significant effect on reaction time to the critical listening, though it is interesting to note that the control interface had the quickest reaction time across all the files. This result confirms a previous study by the authors [13] and aligns with research which postulates the independence of attentional resources for vision and audition [14, 15, 16].

However, as noted, introducing a scrolling interface has a significant effect on participant's critical listening reaction time. This may be due in part to the ergonomic issues of having to access information 'off the page', and future work will explore the influence of improving interface ergonomics on mixing workflow (see below). However, the negative effect on critical listening skills invoked by scrolling may be compounded by further cognitive issues, which require consideration. For example, Janata et al [17] found that attentive listening to multi-channel music employs neural circuits underlying 'multiple forms of working memory, attention, semantic processing, target detection, and motor imagery' (page 9). Thus, attentive listening to music appears to be enabled by areas that serve general functions rather than by "music specific" areas. In this way the use of working memory and attention to process the visual task may consume most of attentional capacity, leaving little or none remaining for processing other modalities [18]. This notion is further supported by Tano et al [5] who consider the fragility of Short Term Memory (STM) as being at odds with complex Graphical User Interfaces, especially in creative support software (ibid). They suggest that software built for creativity support (in their case Design software) should be designed with the 'fragility' of STM as a corner stone of the design process.

Another factor to consider is the disorientation caused by scrolling, which may compound the problems of STM. Sanchez and Wiley [19] found disorientation an issue with scrolling interfaces since they lack a static 'place on a page' [19, p.731]. The context switching between the two views may result in users becoming disoriented or lost during reading. In a more recent study, Sanchez and Branaghan [20] found that by simply rotating small screen device displays by ninety degrees, and thus minimising the need to scroll, reasoning was significantly improved.

File type	Interface type	Mean	S.D.	Confidence Interval (95%).
Guitar	Interface 1	9.83	18.33	±10.37 -0.54 to 20.2
	Interface 2	9	20.88	±11.81 -2.81 to 20.81
	Interface 3	16	19.12	±10.82 5.18 to 26.82
String	Interface 1	7.25	17.03	±9.64 -2.39 to 16.89
	Interface 2	12.08	15.90	±9 3.08 to 21.08
	Interface 3	13.33	10.59	±5.99 7.34 to 19.32
Tamb	Interface 1	3.58	19.58	±11.08 -7.5 to 14.66
	Interface 2	4.83	22.68	±12.83 -8 to 17.66
	Interface 3	17.41	22.65	±12.82 4.59 to 30.23

Table 3. The time difference for task completion between Control and interface types.

Being aware of the cognitive and perceptual factors of GUIs may contribute to the optimal use of DAWs, especially when limited display area is a factor. In so doing it is hoped that the users will be better able to engage in "high-level planning, integrative thinking, and problem solving" rather than being sidelined by the interface itself [12, p.3].

7. FUTURE WORK

Future studies will explore the design and use of scrolling interfaces against modifications or alternatives that reduce STM load and disorientation. As noted in section 6, the problems of access caused by scrolling may contribute to disrupting the mixing workflow. To measure this influence, future studies will use alternative scrolling designs (such as vertical scrolling) which support the use of the scroll wheel. Additionally Overview + Detail designs will be evaluated to quantify to what extent this may reduce any disorientation caused by scrolling [19]. User definable displays will be trialed to reduce the amount of information on screen, thereby reducing the need to scroll. Future studies will also explore other interface objects frequently found in DAWs, such as dials and faders, so that a broader range of interface elements can be investigated. By so doing it is hoped further refinements can be made toward possible design heuristics for interfaces which allow monitoring of multiple sources of visual information while simultaneously supporting critical listening.

8. REFERENCES

[1] K. Golkhe, M, Hlatky, S. Heise, D. Black, J. Loviscach. “Track Displays in DAW Software: Beyond Waveform Views”. In: *Proc. Audio Engineering Society,* London, 2010.

[2] L. Crane, L. “This is your Brain Creating and Recording Music”. *Tape Op,* No.74, p.12, 2010

[3] N. Porter. “Mixing With your Eyes Closed” http://audio.tutsplus.com/tutorials/mixing-mastering/quick-tip-mixing-with-your-eyes-closed. Accessed 5/7/2012

[4] W. Szalva. Behind the Gear. *Tape Op Magazine,* No.73, pages 10-11, 2009.

[5] S. Tano, S. Yamamoto, M. Dzulkhiflee, J. Ichino, T. Hashiyama, M. Iwata. (2012). “Three Design Principles Learned through Developing a Series of 3D Sketch Systems: ‘Memory Capacity’, ‘Cognitive Mode’, and ‘Life-size and Operability’” *IEEE International Conference on Systems, Man, and Cybernetics.* COEX, Seoul, Korea, 2012,

[6] B. Schneiderman, & B. Bederson. “Maintaining Concentration to Achieve Task Completion”. *Proceedings DUX,* 2005.

[7] R. Rensink. “The Management of Human Attention in Visual Displays”. *In Human Attention in Digital Environments.* Edited by Claudia Roda. Cambridge University Press, 2012.

[8] M. Schutz, S. Lipscomb. "Hearing gestures, seeing music: Vision influences perceived tone duration" *Perception 36(6) 888 – 897,* 2007.

[9] J. Macdonald, N. Lavie. “Visual perceptual load induces inattentional deafness.” *Atten Percept Psychophys.* 73(6): 1780–1789, 2011

[10] F. Dehais, M. Causse, N. Régis,E. Menant, P. Labedan, F. Vachon, S. Tremblay. “Missing Critical Auditory Alarms in Aeronautics: Evidence for Inattentional Deafness”? *Proceedings of the Human Factors and Ergonomics Society Annual Meeting* 56: 1639, 2012.

[11] F. Dehais, C. Tessier, L. Chaudron. “GHOST: experimenting conflicts countermeasures in the pilot’s activity.” *Proceedings of the International Joint Conference on Artificial Intelligence (IJCAI) 18, 163-168,* 2003.

[12] S.L. Oviatt. “Human-centered design meets cognitive load theory: Designing interfaces that help people think”. *Proceedings of the Conference on ACM Multimedia* New York, 871–880, 2006

[13] J. Mycroft, J.D. Reiss, T. Stockman. “The Influence of Visual Feedback on the Speed and Accuracy of Music Equalisation Tasks”. *Unpublished study,* 2012.

[14] A. Treisman, A. Davies. “Dividing attention to ear and eye”. In S. Kornblul (Ed.*), Attention and Performance IV (pp. 101- 117).* New York: Academic Press., 1973

[15] D. Alais, D. Burr. “The ventriloquist effect results from near optimal bimodal integration”. *Current Biology 14*: 257- 62, 2004.

[16] V. Santangelo, C. Spence. “Crossmodal attentional capture in an unspeeded simultaneity judgment task”. *Visual Cognition,* 16, 155–165, 2010.

[17] P. Janata, B. Tillmann, J. Bharucha. “Listening to polyphonic music recruits domain-general attention and working memory circuits”. *Cogn Affect Behav Neurosci* 2:121–140, 2002

[18] Lavie, N.“Perceptual load as a major determinant of the locus of selection in visual attention.” *Percept. Psychophys.* 56, 183–197, 1994.

[19] C. Sanchez, J. Wiley.“To scroll or not to scroll: scrolling, working memory capacity and comprehending complex text”. *Human Factors,* 51(5), 730–738, 2009.

[20] A. Sanchez, R. Branaghan.“Turning to learn: Screen orientation and reasoning with small devices”. *Computers in Human Behavior.* 27 793–797, 2011.

Discrete Isomorphic Completeness and a Unified Isomorphic Layout Format

Brett Park
University of Regina
park111b@uregina.ca

David Gerhard
University of Regina
gerhard@cs.uregina.ca

ABSTRACT

An isomorphic layout can be used to position pitches on a grid of hexagons. This has many beneficial musical properties such as consistent fingering and spatial harmonic consistency. A Unified Isomorphic Layout (UIL) format is presented in order to create a common specification for describing hexagonal isomorphic layouts. The UIL format provides an unambiguous description of relative pitch orientations and is easily visualized. The notion of complete and degenerate isomorphic layouts (along with a proof) is introduced to narrow down the number of valid isomorphic layouts used for exhaustive evaluations.

1. INTRODUCTION

There are many ways to arrange the available notes on a tone-centric musical instrument. A piano uses a linear layout of notes with a subset of notes (the accidentals) vertically offset. A guitar has a relatively consistent layout with the notes increasing by a semitone in one direction (along each string) and a perfect fourth in the other direction (from one string to the next) with the exception of one string at a major third. With these irregular note layouts, the musician has to learn a different set of fingerings for each key they play in. Piano students must practice scales in multiple keys, but the scales themselves are musically identical regardless of key, with the same pattern of musical intervals (tones and semitones, for example) from one note in the scale to the next. The difficulty of learning multiple scales stems from the note arrangement itself.

Some instruments (such as bass guitars) use a note layout that is *isomorphic*, which means that the distance (i.e. the number of keys) and direction of any musical interval is the same no matter which note you start on. A bass player can transpose to any key just by moving the fingerings being used to play a sequence of notes. This property of isomorphic layouts means that fingerings for playing a musical construct (such as a specific type of chord or scale) is independent of the root key. The "shape" of a major triad is the same for every major triad, which is why these layouts are called "isomorphic" (iso = same; morph = shape).

A hexagonal isomorphism is an isomoprhic arrangement of notes on a hexagonal grid rather than a rectangular grid. Each note has six adjacent tones allowing for more compact note layouts. Although hexagonal isomorphisms have been around for hundreds of years, there is not a lot of publicly available information on the many possible layouts and their properties. As well, only a few researchers are actively studying isomorphisms. In this paper, we present a unified framework for studying isomorphic layouts, which we call the *Unified Isomorphic Layout* (UIL) specification, This specification helps to identify and compare characteristics of layouts. We apply this framework to a number of "standard" isomorphic layouts, and present a method to guarantee completeness of any isomorphism. We also present a visualization system which allows detailed exploration of any isomorphism.

2. BACKGROUND

Hexagonal isomorphic layouts appear to have great potential, and many researchers have explored aspects of a set of specific layouts, but there is limited summative research bringing the field together as a whole. One of the biggest concerns with the existing hexagonal isomorphic research literature is that individual researchers have their favourite layouts, and commercial products tend to be focused on one particular isomorphism. There is, as yet, no public central repository of descriptions, evaluations, and visualizations of the many possible layouts. The research literature is sparse, and significant portions of the information are found within patents rather than research papers. We have created a tablet application that allows users to experiment with any possible isomorphic layout, and through public access to this application (Musix [1]) we have encountered many people who are interested in isomorphic layouts and are looking for more in-depth information. The focus of this paper, then, is a framework around which to centralize, summarize and visualize existing layouts, and to generate detailed analytical information about any hexagonal isomorphic note layout.

This paper continues with an itemized list of existing research (and researchers) into isomorphic layouts and their utility; a motivation of isomorphic research in a musical context; a proposal for a unified isomorphic layout notation to describe any layout and (more importantly) describe the relationships between different layouts; and a proof of isomorphic completeness both for and beyond western 12-tone scales; followed by a number of examples of common layouts described in the new UIL notation.

2.1 Research into Hexagonal Isomorphisms

Hexagonal isomorphic musical note layouts have been of interest for decades, although individual researchers have tended to focus on a specific layout or layouts, and much of the information available is presented in patents rather than research papers.

2.1.1 Harmonic Table

Peter Davies was awarded the patent for the Harmonic Table layout [2] which he filed in 1990. The harmonic table layout is equivalent to the Euler's Tonnetz [3] described in 1739, and is currently in use in the C-Thru AXiS commercial device. Davies discovered the layout during his analysis of notes contained in augmented and diminished chords. Although the patent describes information about his finding for the harmonic table, there is no known public material on his original analysis of other layouts.

2.1.2 Wicki-Hayden

Brian Hayden is credited with a patent for the Wick-Hayden layout [4] which was issued in 1986. The layout was developed for use on a concertina and was previously patented by Kaspar Wicki in 1896 (Swiss patent no. 13329). Several published conversations with Hayden can be found on the internet where he discusses concertina layouts [5] as well as describing a number of possible isomorphic layout combinations [6]. Hayden's research remains largely unpublished aside from his conversations with a few websites and magazines.

In Hayden's discussion with Woehr [6], he introduces an ordering of a largest absolute interval, smallest absolute interval, and the difference of the two as a method of describing layouts. Hayden concludes that only eleven interesting layouts exists and that their mirrors are not fundamentally different.

2.1.3 Notation and Alternate Tunings

Andrew Milne, William Sethares, and James Plamondon are important contributors to current research on isomorphic keyboards especially in the areas of isomorphic notation [7] and alternative tunings [8]. Their research goes into depths in regards to properties of layouts that make them good candidates for alternative tunings, compactness, and generic description. Tunings are described by periods, generators, syntonic commas, and temperament maps. A complete physical layout can be specified by a number of basis vectors and a series of matrix representations for button-lattices, layouts, and transformations. Proofs are also provided for their mappings in regards to linearity and transposition invariance [9]. Their description of isomorphic layouts is robust but does not easily allow the layouts to be visualized or implemented using the matrices.

Milne et al describe the isotone axis and the pitch axis of a layout. The isotone axis is a line that intersects all pitches of the same tone. The pitch axis is orthogonal to the isotone axis and shows the direction of uniform increasing pitch (from one isotone, say C to the next, say C♯). This allows a user to immediately visualize the "direction" of the layout without having to know which layout they are in. The pitch axis also has the property that the distance from the isotone axis along the pitch axis is equal to the pitch of the note.

2.1.4 Analysis and Reconfigurable Instruments

Brett Park, David Gerhard, Steven Maupin have been exploring hexagonal isomorphisms [10] based on their musical properties (melodic and harmonic) and fittings for specific musical styles. The analysis of layouts was conducted based on directions and distances for diatonic scales as well as major and minor triads. In addition to layout analysis, Park and Gerhard have been developing the commercially available isomorphic layout software called Musix [1] as well as creating a physical isomorphic keyboard with the ability to dynamically change isomorphic layouts while providing visual feedback. The device is named the Rainboard [11].

2.2 Why isomorphic layout research

Isomorphic note layouts have many potential advantages over non-isomorphic layouts such as transpositional invariance (fingerings are identical for different musical keys) and spatial / interval consistency (a relative interval is always in the same physical location relative to the base note). Hexagonal isomorphic layouts provide the tightest possible clustering of musical intervals [12]. Because of the many beneficial properties of hexagonal isomorphic layouts, they may provide the best opportunity for democratizing music creation.

Although many layouts have been "discovered" or analyzed, very few have empirical evidence to justify choosing one layout over another, and the benefits claimed by most researchers for their particular layout are, in fact, benefits of hexagonal isomorphisms in general. Most layouts are justified as being "good" because they group common music patterns in a close physical area. Although this may be true, there is no empirical evidence given that such groupings improve playability, learnability or other features of the instrument. As well, the layouts are generally considered to be unique based on the interval numbers that make up the layout. Additional properties, such as interval direction, are often not considered when evaluating layouts, however, the direction of the intervals can have a significant impact on playability and fingering. In fact, there exist some distinct traditional layouts are directional transpositions of each other, as will be shown later. Additional properties besides the identifying intervals should be considered as they may contribute to the ergonomic efficiency of the instrument.

2.3 Studying and evaluating all isomorphic layouts

There are two types of valid isomorphic layouts: complete and degenerate. Complete layouts contain at least one instance of every note in the given tonal system. For example: in a 12-tone musical system, all twelve tones will appear somewhere on the layout for the layout to be considered "complete". This does not guarantee playability or proximity of the notes, just that they will be present. Theoretical considerations can be made to prove completeness of a particular isomorphic layout, and therefore to list all complete layouts. Degenerate layouts, on the other hand, do not contain an instance of every tone in a musical system. Depending on the neighbouring intervals to a specific note, there may be no way to create all notes in the given tonal system. Even though some of the tones may be missing, however, the layout is still considered a valid isomorphism (based on the previous definition) in that fingerings are still identical in different keys and relative intervals are always in the same location.

Degenerate isomorphic layouts have limited musical utility, although they should not be completely discounted. When a scale is degenerate, note intervals will be missing in regularized patterns, due to the underlying isomorphic nature of the system. For example, it is possible to create an isomorphism of a 12-tone equal tempered scale where only every third semitone is present, resulting in a sequence of minor thirds, or a diminished 7th chord. This makes sense in the context of isomorphic note layouts, because the diminished 7th chord is root-ambiguous. Most musical scales (i.e. specified subsets of a given tonal system) are not equally distributed (like the diminished 7th is), instead consisting of a pattern of whole tones and semitones (the counter-example of course being the whole tone scale itself).

2.3.1 Classes of Degenerate Layouts

The number of possible degenerate layouts depends on the intervals which are missing in the layout, or alternatively which present interval is the smallest. Because of the properties of isomorphisms, this interval must be a divisor of the number of tones in the system. This is not to say that the smallest interval is necessarily adjacent to the root note.

For a 12 tone system, there are 4 classes of degenerate layouts. If the smallest available interval is the semitone, the layout is complete. If the smallest interval is 2 semitones (i.e. the semitone interval is missing from the isomorphism), then the layout is a whole tone scale. If the semitone and whole tone are both missing, the result is a diminished chord layout; if the minor third is also missing, the result is the augmented triad; if all intervals but the tritone are missing, the result is a two-note layout, and if all intervals are multiples of the octave, then only one note is available. Because these degenerate layouts are missing some notes, there are also a number of sub-classes of each degenerate layout depending on which notes are present. For the whole tone scale, there are two subclasses: scales which include C and those which include C♯.

Since degenerate layouts provide a significant limitation to an isomorphism, it is useful to be able to test for completeness or to generate layouts that are complete. We therefore develop a proof of completeness, presented in Section 7, based on co-prime intervals. This proof also allows all possible complete layouts to be generated by using a series of increasing co-primes.

Theoretically, there are an infinite number of isomorphic layouts, since intervals greater than the octave can be represented. In order to compare, represent, and evaluate these layouts, it is important to have an unambiguous representation for each layout that allows it to be placed in context with other layouts. Brian Hayden has suggested a representation method which labels the greatest interval as G, the lowest non-negative interval as L, and the difference between the smallest and the largest as D. By using the intervals G and L, the intervals composing the layout can be determined, but this description does not specify the direction of G or the relative direction of L. In order to further disambiguate between layouts, we have developed a complete notation which can fully specify any hexagonal isomorphic layout. Given a disambiguated layout format, the location and orientation of relative pitches should be unambiguous, allowing comparison between different layouts.

Once an exhaustive list of layouts with a reasonable interval range (less than a few octaves) can be generated and represented in an unambiguous manner, it is possible to begin analyzing their properties in a more formalized manner, taking isomorphic research from individual conjecture to empirical truth.

3. A UNIFIED ISOMORPHIC LAYOUT (UIL) NOTATION

In order to unambiguously describe hexagonal isomorphic layouts, a Unified Isomorphic Layout (UIL) notation is presented , based on Hayden's initial *GLD* notation. The UIL format adds to Hayden's specification by also specifying interval listing order, rotation, mirroring, and shear, and allows for microtonal layouts and non-12-tone scales. The interval directions for a base representation of the *LGD* format, as well as a mirrored, rotated version, are shown in Fig. 1.

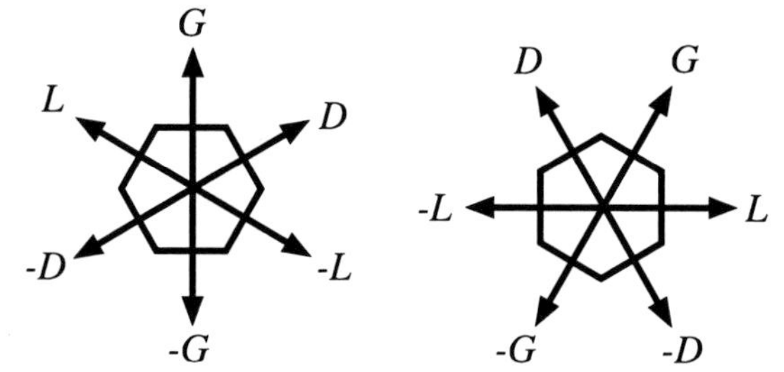

Figure 1. LGD format. (a) base representation; (b) mirrored and rotated by 30°.

The UIL notation format specification. $L, G, D; RMS; T$

L. *The lowest positive interval value. For the base layout, L is in the north-west direction and is to the left of G.*

G. *The greatest positive interval value. For the base layout, G will always point north. For all layouts (both complete and degenerate), the direction of G will be between the directions for L and D, since the interval values L and D must sum to G for the isomorphism to be valid.*

D. *The difference between G and L. It is possible for* $D = L$*. For the base layout, D is in the north-east direction and is to the right of G.*

R. *The clockwise rotation of the layout, in degrees (for both mirrored an non-mirrored layouts). $R = 0$ when the interval G is pointing directly north.*

M. *Indicates if the layout is mirrored. In a mirrored layout, the L and D axis are swapped, mirroring the layout about G.*

S. *Indicates the amount of shear after rotation as described by A. Prechtl et al [13]. In most cases, the shear will be 0 and may be omitted. A rotation can be applied to create the same result as a shear, with the only limitation being the shape of the note actuators (which can be stretched or otherwise modified under shear).*

T. *Indicates the number of tones in the scale. Other tuning parameters such as temperament can also be written directly after T. In the standard western 12-tone equal tempered case, ($T12TET$), the T value can be omitted.*

Base Representation. *A UIL layout representation where $R = 0$ and the layout is not mirrored.*

3.1 Special cases

Two special cases exists for UIL layouts. The first is when $G = D$, which only happens for intervals $0,1,1$. We refer to this as the zero case. In this case $L = 0$ and $D = 1$, and G is equal to the interval 1 that occurs between 0 and 1.

The second special case occurs where $L = D$ and is referred to as the equality case. The only equality case which results in a complete layout is $1,2,1$. In this case the interval direction chosen for L or D is irrelevant.

In both the zero case and the equality case, the mirror designation is meaningless.

4. REASONINGS FOR UIL FORMAT

One of the motivations for establishing a UIL format is to show when two layouts which may seem different are, in fact, within a rotation and mirroring of each other. It is therefore important to impose a restriction on the ordering of the *LGD* parameters so it is easier to identify related layouts. Without a strict ordering of intervals, rotation would be defined by both the degrees of rotation and interval order. The ordering restriction serves to disambiguate the rotation and mirroring of a layout, when given three intervals. Two layouts with the same *LGD* (within the same tuning) will have identical musical construct shapes (to within a rotation and mirroring). The use of *L*,*G*, and *D* also have some historic precedence from their use by Brian Hayden [6] although his definition was not order-restricted.

It is possible to represent the musical relations of the layout with only L and G since $D = G - L$. We chose to leave the D value in the format as it allows the adjacent intervals to be immediately visible without mentally performing the calculation for D. The inclusion of D also makes the interval directions visually similar to the interval directions in the base representation.

Although the inter-note relationships of a layout are completely specified by L, G, D, more information (mirroring and rotation) is required to fully define the physical layout.

Layout Name	UIL Format	L	G	D	R	M
Wicki-Hayden	2,7,5;R30M	2	7	5	30	1
Harmonic Table	3,7,4;R0	3	7	4	0	0
Gerhard	1,4,3;R60	1	4	3	60	0
Park	2,5,3;R90M	2	5	3	90	1
Janko	1,2,1;R90	1	2	1	90	0
C-System	1,3,2;R270M	1	3	2	270	1
B-System	1,3,2;R270	1	3	2	270	0
Bajan	1,3,2;R90M	1	3	2	90	1

Table 1. UIL notations for common isomorphic layouts. L = Least, G = Greatest, D = Difference, R = Rotation, M = Mirrored.

The mirroring and rotation parameters allow manipulation of the ergonomic aspects of the layout which may have a significant impact on playability. The size of the hexagons is not included in the UIL specification, since it simply introduces a scalar distance between intervals that is constant for all interval relations. It should be noted, however, that different layouts benefit from different hexagon sizes based on the compactness of the layout. A compact representation may need bigger hexagons to improve playability.

Scale intervals were chosen as the standard unit of *LGD* since it shows the musical relationship to the surrounding hexagons and allows for quick completion validation. If two of the interval values of the *LGD* are co-prime, then the layout will contain all intervals in the scale and be considered complete. A proof of this completeness is presented in Section 7.

4.1 Common UILs

Most interval sets that create a complete layout (with a reasonable interval size) have been named or patented. Some of the more common isomorphic layouts are listed in UIL format in Table 1, and are visualized in Section 6.1. An example of "different" layouts with the same *LGD* are the C-System, B-System, and Bajan layout. The difference between the three layouts can easily and clearly be seen by looking at the rotation and mirror properties of the three layouts.

4.2 Non 12-TET Scales

For the 12-tet scale the values for *LGD* are simple semitone intervals between 0 (unison / octave) and 11 (Major 7th), but nothing in the UIL format requires a 12-tone scale. This representation is useful for determining valid layouts and visualizing their relation, however, alternate equivalent representations of *LGD* can be given for different purposes. In these cases the values of *LGD* can be represented as cents, ratios, or roman numerals. The interval, roman, and shorthand format may be useful for musicians familiar with these notational systems. The cent and ratio representations are useful for comparing layouts across different tunings and will be suitable for microtonal music. Example alternate formats can be found in Table 2.

UIL Interval Format (12TET)	2,7,5;R30M
UIL Interval Format (7TET)	1,4,3;R30M;T7
UIL Interval Format (19TET)	3,11,8;R30M;T19
UIL Cent Format	200,700,500;R30M
UIL Ratio Format	9:8,3:2,4:3;R30M
UIL Roman Format	II,V,IV;R30M
UIL Shorthand Format	M2,P5,P4;R30M

Table 2. Alternate UIL LGD representations for interval representations and tunings

5. INFERENCES FROM UIL

5.1 Horizontal and Vertical alignment

Two common ways of visualizing a grid of hexagons is in a horizontal or vertical alignment [10]. The hexagon alignment can easily be discerned from the rotation angle of the UIL (Fig. 2). Vertical alignment occurs when the layout is rotated in increments of 60 degrees $(0, 60, 120, 180, 240, 300)$ and horizontal alignment occurs when the layout is rotated in increments of 60 degrees plus an initial 30 degree offset $(30, 90, 150, 210, 270, 330)$.

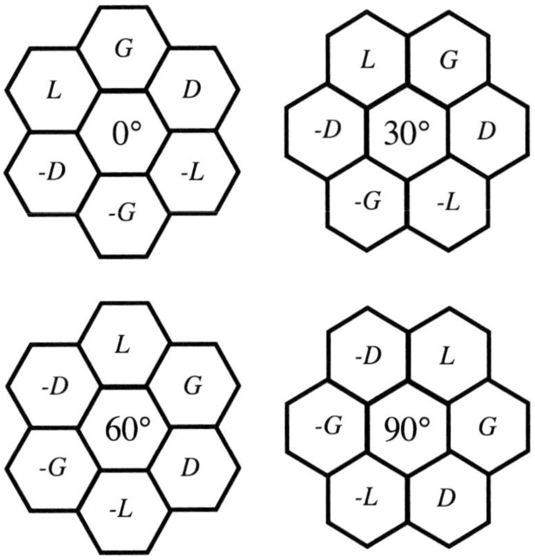

Figure 2. Vertical grid alignment (left) at 60 degree increments and Horizontal grid alignment (right) at 60 degree increments plus an initial 30 degree offset

5.2 Isotone and Pitch Axis

The *isotone axis* defines a line in an isomorphic layout which passes through all notes of a particular pitch [8]. If you draw a line between two instances of "A_4" and extend that line to infinity, all other instances of A_4 will appear only on that line. Further, all isotones are parallel. One important property that derives from the isotone axis is that the orthogonal distance of any note from this axis is directly related the pitch of the note. This orthogonal line, called the pitch axis [8], denotes the general direction in which pitches ascend.

Due to the strict interval order of the *LGD*, it is possible to infer information about the pitch axis and distance between isotones. In *LGD* base format (no rotation or mirroring), the pitch axis will always be between 0 and 30 degrees (Fig. 3). This results in the pitch axis being between R and $R+30$ degrees for non-mirrored layouts and the pitch axis being between $R-30$ and R for all mirrored layouts. The precise pitch axis angle (relative to R) can be can be calculated by $30 * \frac{D-L}{G}$. Since the pitch axis and the isotone axis are orthogonal, the isotone axis angle is equal to the pitch axis angle plus 90°.

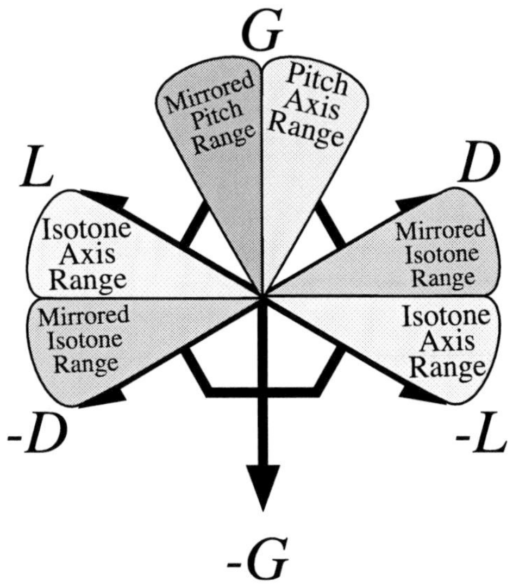

Figure 3. Normal and mirrored ranges for the pitch axis and isotone axis (without rotation).

6. VISUALIZATION OF LAYOUTS

Using the codebase we initially developed for the Musix iOS app, we constructed a system that allows the visualization of any isomorphic layout, including the isotone and the pitch axis, as well as the parallelogram which contains a single complete 12-note octave. This visualization is particularly useful for judging alignment of pitch axis, compactness of the representation, and similarity to other isomorphisms. The results of this visualization, as well as a set of example layouts and their analysis, are presented here.

6.1 Examples

The following figures present visualizations of some of the more common hexagonal isomorphic layouts in use today, as well as representations in the base UIL format. In these figures, notes are coloured with the root note of the scale in red, intervals in the major scale of that key coloured in white, and the other intervals coloured in black. Notes are labeled as N_o^i, where N is the the number of semitones from the root note, o is the octave of that note, and i is the common interval abbreviation. For example, 6_4^{tt} is the tritone in the 4th octave, 6 semitones from the root.

Figure 4 shows Wicki-Hayden, a popular layout discussed in Section 2.1.2. This layout collects "white" notes together, making whole tone and pentatonic melodies easy to play. Figure 5 shows the Janko keyboard, an early isomorphic layout related to the piano. Like the piano, pitches ascend to the right. The base UIL format visualization shows the pitch axis rising to the north. The harmonic table layout (Figure 7), discussed in Section 2.1.1, is already in base format, and makes plain one of the complaints about this layout: while major and minor triads are compact, whole tones are quite distant, and the layout as a whole is not as compact as, for example, the Bajan.

Figure 6 shows that three traditional isomorphic layouts, the Bajan, C-system, and B-system, are in fact mirrored and rotated versions of the same base layout. Figure 8 shows two additional layouts, the Gerhard and the Park, which have been studied in detail by the authors.

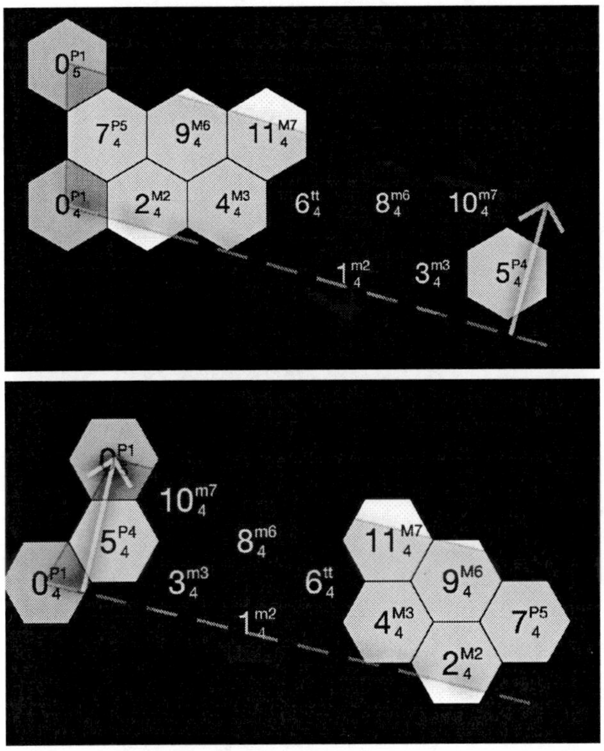

Figure 4. Wicki-hayden layout: 2,7,5;R30M (top) and the corresponding base representation 2,7,5;R0

7. PROOF OF ISOMORPHIC COMPLETENESS

In the following proof, hexagonal isomorphic intervals are listed as x, y, and z. The UIL format of *LGD* is a subspecification of any hexagonal isomorphism, and L, G, and D can each be any one of x, y, and z.

In order to create a valid hexagonal isomorphism (H), three note intervals x, y, and z are chosen that represent the neighbouring interval distances for each linear direction. The sum of these three intervals must be zero,

$$H = \{x, y, z \in \mathbb{Z} \mid x + y + z = 0\} \tag{1}$$

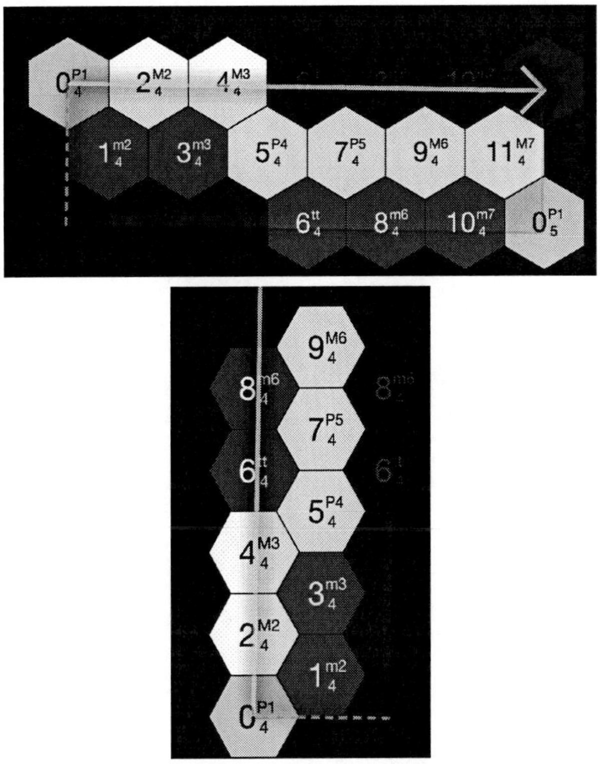

Figure 5. Janko layout: 1,2,1;R90 (top) and the corresponding base representation: 1,2,1;R0

since progressing once in each of three directions will return to the original note. By simplification, $z = -x - y$.

Theorem 7.1. *Isomorphic Completeness: Given two interval vectors x,y that define a unidirectional isomorphism, the isomorphism is complete (contains all note intervals) if and only if x and y are co-prime.*

Proof of Isomorphic Completeness. An isomorphism is complete if and only if some scalar combination of x, y, z exists such that all integers can be produced

$$(\forall n \in \mathbb{Z})(\exists a, b, c \in \mathbb{Z}) \mid ax + by + cz = n \tag{2}$$

First lets consider the case where $n = 1$.

$$ax + by + cz = 1 \tag{3}$$

We can simplify equation 2 to $hx + iy = 1$ by the following process:

$$\begin{aligned} 1 &= ax + by + cz \\ 1 &= ax + by + c(-x - y) \\ 1 &= ax + by - cx - cy \\ 1 &= x(a - c) + y(b - c) \\ \text{Let } h &= a - c \\ \text{Let } i &= b - c \\ 1 &= hx + iy \end{aligned} \tag{4}$$

Two cases then exists: x and y are coprime (they do not share a positive factor other than 1) or they are not coprime.

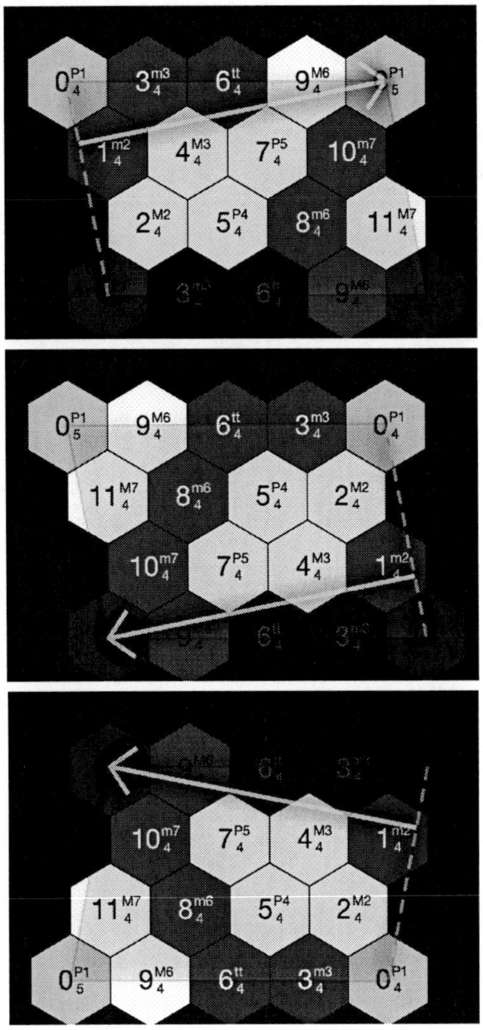

Figure 6. Bajan (top), C-system, and B-system, all of which use the intervals 1,3,2 with different rotations and mirrorings. C-system and B-system are mirrored versions of each other.

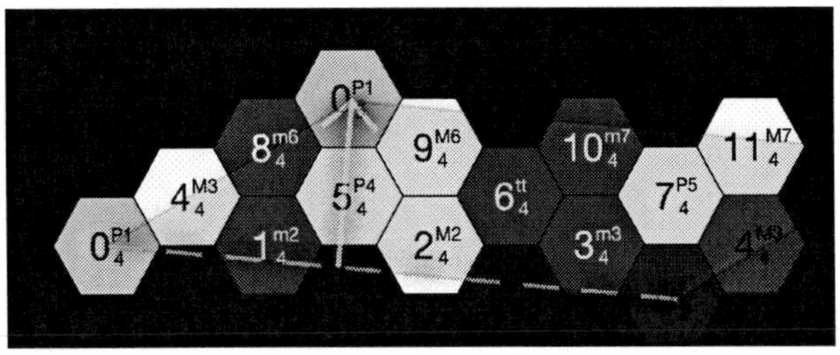

Figure 7. Harmonic Table layout: 3,7,4;R0

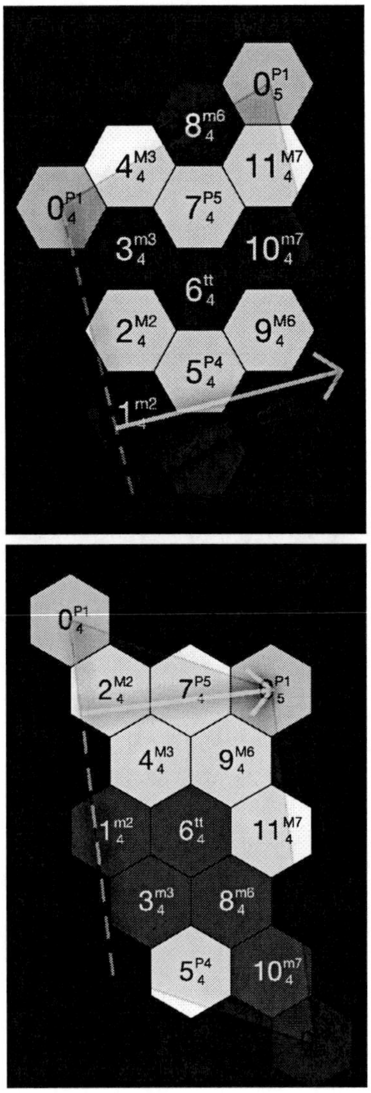

Figure 8. Gerhard (top): 1,4,3;R60; Park: 2,5,3;R90M

Case 1: (x and y are coprime)
If $x \perp y$ then hx + iy = 1 by Bézout's identity [1].

Case 2: (x and y are not coprime)
If x and y are not coprime they must share a prime factor e such that $x = ej$ and $y = ek$ where j and k are integers.

$$(\exists e, j, k \in \mathbb{Z}) \mid x = ej, y = ek \tag{5}$$

If we assume this is true for the case where $n = 1$:

$$\begin{aligned} 1 &= hej + iek \\ 1 &= e(hj + ik) \\ \text{Let } m &= hj + ik \\ 1 &= me \\ e &= 1/m \\ \text{since } e \in \mathbb{Z}, m &= \pm 1 \\ e &= \pm 1 \end{aligned} \tag{6}$$

Then we can substitute and simplify to determine $e = \pm 1$. Since the only positive common factor is $e = 1$, x and y are coprime which contradicts the assumption.

We must now extend the proof for all n. Equation 3 can be multiplied by an integer scalar t in order to produce the entire range of integers for n.

$$(\forall n \in \mathbb{Z})(\exists t \in \mathbb{Z}) \mid t(ax + by + cz) = t * 1 = n \tag{7}$$

If x, y, z can be multiplied by integer scalars to equal 1, then the scalars can also be multiplied by any integer t in order to produce the entire integer set n.

□

8. CONCLUSIONS AND FUTURE WORK

By considering the notion of complete and degenerate layouts, along with formalization of the criteria for each type of layout, it is possible to iterate through intervals that create complete layouts. These intervals can then be represented in UIL notation in order to disambiguate musical properties and pitch orientation. The Unified Isomorphic Layout notation provides an unambiguous textual representation of an isomorphic layout that can be easily visualized, resulting in a useful tool for isomorphic research.

Now that the UIL is established, we plan to iterate through all of the non-degenerate base layouts and explore their properties independent of rotation and mirroring. Such properties include pitch axis angle, isotone axis angle, isotone axis length (between two notes), pitch axis length (orthogonal distance for an octave), octave parallelogram area, and parallelogram squareness. After these properties are calculated, ergonomics of the layouts will be evaluated for various intervals, rotations, and mirrors. The ergonomic data will be used to develop a suggested fingering for playing in various UILs, as well as a recommendation system for which specific isomorphic layout would be best suited to any particular musical context or task.

[1] `http://en.wikipedia.org/wiki/Bezout's_identity`

9. REFERENCES

[1] B. Park, D. Gerhard, and M. Potts, "Musix." [Online]. Available: http://shiverware.com

[2] P. Davies, "Method of and means for producing musical note relationships," *US Patent 5415071*, Aug. 1991. [Online]. Available: http://www.google.com/patents/US5415071

[3] L. Euler, *Tentamen novæ theoriæ musicæ*, 1739.

[4] B. Hayden, "Arrangements of Notes on Musical Instruments," *British Patent GB2131592*, 1986.

[5] W. Williams. (2001, Jan.) CONCERTINA.net - Brian Hayden and Duet Concertina Systems. [Online]. Available: http://www.concertina.net/ww_hayden_interview.html

[6] J. Woehr. (2005, Oct.) Brian Hayden on the Reuther Uniform System and other self-transposing systems. [Online]. Available: http://www.well.com/~jax/rcfb/Hayden_on_Reuther.html

[7] J. Plamondon, A. J. Milne, and W. Sethares, "Sight-Reading Music Theory: A Thought Experiment on Improving Pedagogical Efficiency," *The Journal of Music Theory Pedagogy*, 2009. [Online]. Available: http://www.igetitmusic.com/papers/JIMS.pdf

[8] A. Milne, W. Sethares, and J. Plamondon, "Tuning continua and keyboard layouts," *Journal of Mathematics and Music*, vol. 2, no. 1, pp. 1–19, Mar. 2008.

[9] ——, "Isomorphic controllers and dynamic tuning: Invariant fingering over a tuning continuum," *Computer Music Journal*, vol. 31, no. 4, pp. 15–32, Dec. 2007.

[10] S. Maupin, D. Gerhard, and B. Park, "Isomorphic Tesselations for Musical Keyboards," *Proceedings of the 8th Sound and Music Computing Conference (SMC 2011)*, 2011. [Online]. Available: http://smcnetwork.org/system/files/smc2011_submission_169.pdf

[11] B. Park and D. Gerhard, "Rainboard and Musix: Building dynamic isomorphic interfaces," in *Proceedings of the 13th international conference on New interfaces for musical expression (NIME 2013)*, Daejeon, Korea Republic, May 2013.

[12] E. W. Weisstein. Circle Packing – from Wolfram MathWorld. [Online]. Available: http://mathworld.wolfram.com/CirclePacking.html

[13] A. Prechtl, A. J. Milne, S. Holland, R. Laney, and D. B. Sharp, "A midi sequencer that widens access to the compositional possibilities of novel tunings," *Computer Music Journal*, vol. 36, no. 1, pp. 42–54, 2012. [Online]. Available: http://www.mitpressjournals.org/doi/abs/10.1162/COMJ_a_00104

AMAROK PIKAP: INTERACTIVE PERCUSSION PLAYING AUTOMOBILE*

Selçuk ARTUT
Sabancı University
Faculty of Arts and Social Sciences
Istanbul, Turkey
sartut@sabanciuniv.edu

ABSTRACT

Alternative interfaces that imitate the audio-structure of authentic musical instruments are often equipped with sound generation techniques that feature physical attributes similar to those of the instruments they imitate. Amarok Pikap project utilizes an interactive system on the surface of an automobile that is specially modified with the implementation of various electronic sensors attached to its bodywork. Sur-faces that will be struck to produce sounds in percussive instrument modeling are commonly selected as distinctive surfaces such as electronic pads or keys. In this article we will carry out a status analysis to examine to what extent a percussion-playing interface using FSR and Piezo sensors can represent an authentic musical instrument, and how a new interactive musical interface may draw the interests of the public to a promotional event of an automobile campaign: Amarok Pikap. The structure that forms the design will also be subjected to a technical analysis.

Keywords: Interaction, Physical Computing, Human-Technology Interaction, Outdoor Interfaces, Musical Interfaces, Music Performance

1. INTRODUCTION

Throughout history, musical instruments have been ordered and classified according to methods of playing, or their sound intervals. However, DIY productions and hard-ware hacking techniques that are now increasingly widespread as information technologies rapidly become part of everyday life in the 2000s have led to a differentiation of standards and allowed for the wider production of musical instruments that do not conform to convention. Musical instruments could also be described as sound generators; and the means of technology allow sound generation to be carried out not only through acoustic methods, but also with a sensor structure triggering a sound that exists in the processor to generate sound. One criterion of success in sound synthesis methods is the degree of semblance to the original sound of the sound generated by the triggering of the sound sensor.

The sound sampling method used widely today in sound synthesizing is based on the principle of playing back pre-recorded sounds, and is thus used in generating simulated sounds. However, a recorded sound library features limited options. Potential sounds that musical instruments may produce can vary according to the approach and interaction of the performer with the instrument. As for percussion instruments, many factors, ranging from the impetus of the force exerted on the surface that generates the sound, to the material qualities of the object that is used to establish contact with the surface serve to increase the number of possible timbres. Since various gestures may generate different sounds from musical instruments, the number of recorded sounds depending on probable scenarios in instrument modeling is theoretically infinite. However, although interactive units known as gestural controllers allow the transfer of the movements of the performer to the digital instrument [1] the number of gestural movements achieved via sensors still remains limited. Therefore, although the modeled new instrument features common attributes with the original instrument it imitates in terms of its sound, it is nevertheless impossible to compare these two instruments on a one-to-one basis other than according to their fundamental features.

Attempting to produce the same performance as a traditional percussion instrument using the different surface of a simulated instrument poses a number of difficulties for the performer. Often, the surfaces of the percussion instruments played using hands do not fully absorb the impact exerted upon them and respond with their own physical tension to the hand that carries out the movement. Therefore, certain interactive surfaces, such as pads, that are designed to simulate such events, are made of materials that feature natural-like qualities. However, the reaction of the playing surface to the surface that applies the pressure may be different from that of the original musical instrument, and such differences must be considered both with their advantages and their disadvantages [2]. As we observed in the Volkswagen Amarok Pikap Truck project, musicians who play a percussion instrument can easily develop mastery of the new types of instruments that are produced by the application of a different interface by blending different techniques.

2. MOTIVATION

The Amarok Pikap Project that we examine in this article aimed at developing a concept that would allow it to become the focus of attention at events organized for product promotion –for a reason other than its most significant feature as a transport vehicle. The aim was to dispel the prejudice that since Amarok was a pickup, it would not be the vehicle of choice for metropolis dwellers. The design was planned so that users would physically interact with the various sensors installed on the outer shell of the car to play percussion with an interface they were not accustomed to. The purpose of this study was to determine how participants' interaction with this new musical interface is empowering the perception of the promotional campaign of the product.

3. RELATED WORK

There are various examples of making music using the automobile as an object. In Alessandra Camnasio's project titled Music From A Car [3], acoustic sounds retrieved by strikes to the outer surface of an automobile are recorded using various microphones to form a sound library; and these sounds are then used to compose a predominantly rhythmical musical piece. Another project is featured in the music video for the band OK Go's song Needing/Getting [4] where various extensions in-stalled on the outer surface of the automobile in motion collide with the surfaces around the automobile and produce a variety of sounds. The objects in the environment of the automobile have been pre-organized, and as the automobile drives through the planned-route, the musical composition is performed. However, in both projects, the sounds produced are acoustic sounds that 'belong' to the automobile. A similar approach can be observed as in the Smack Attack project. In Smack Attack [5] a peripheral device is attached to the wheel of a car, and the device is connected to the hi-fi system via Bluetooth. Several sensors on the peripheral device enables the users to produce musical sounds while driving.

4. CONCEPT DESCRIPTION

Two different types of sensors were used on the surface of the automobile. At the front of the automobile, on the hood of the engine, Force Sensing Resistor (FSR) sensors were used to allow sensitive response to the finger strikes of the performer; these sensors also did not form an extra, thick layer on the hood. FSRs act as analogue transformers of the applied force into variable resistance of electrical current. FSRs are usually used for such applications as input devices, musical instruments, or interactive applications.

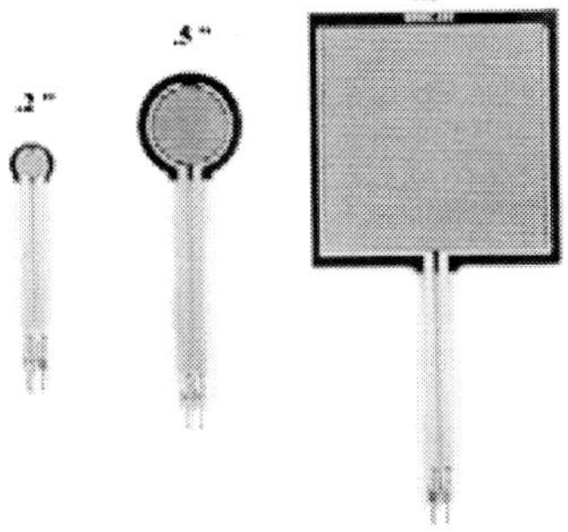

Figure 1. FSR Sensors.

For the Amarok Pikap Project several holes were drilled in the hood for cable pas-sage to carry out cable connections for the FSR sensors fixed to the outer surface of the hood. The fourteen FSR sensors fixed to the hood transmit the data they obtain to the computer in the car via their connection cables that are hidden under the surface of the cabinet.

In addition to the sensitive sensor system on the front shell of the car, Piezo sensors were affixed to the front and back windows on both sides of the car, the shell area below the windows and the shell area above the rear wheels. Piezo sensors feature a system that transforms vibrations on the surface into electrical energy. However, they do not provide the same level of sensitivity as FSR sensors. Also, since the interaction surface of Piezo sensors is not restricted to the surface of the sensor as in FSR sensors, undesired data might be collected from other, causing cross talk between the neighboring sensors.

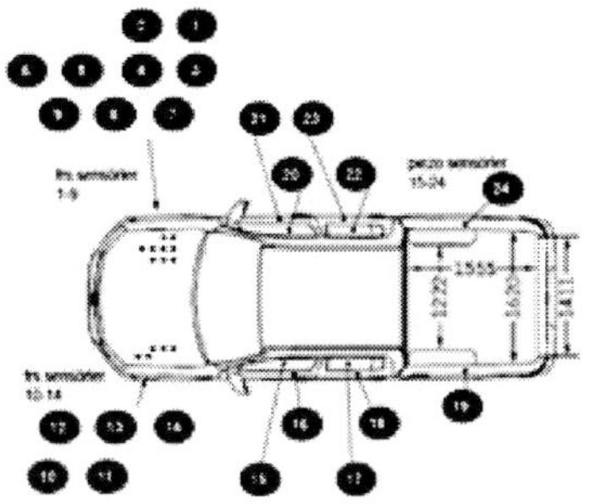

Figure 2. Sensor Positioning.

In order to obtain different gestures from the percussion played with the new inter-face, because of the restricted perception qualities of the sensors, parameters such as the attack duration and pitch of the force applied to the sensors are used in producing different alternatives when recalling the sound sample stored in the sound library. It might prove insufficient if sensors that source the spectrum of sound operate with an on-off logic, therefore an analogue structure allows for a wealth of data production. The sensors applied to the front part of the automobile allowed for a certain level of sensitivity in the playing of the instrument. This was not the case for the Piezo sensors used on the sides. Since the data produced due to the interaction of the users on the sides of the car did not allow for sensitivity because of reasons stated above, an on-off logic was deemed suitable for their use, and for values over a certain threshold, the contribution to the music of single-strike sounds in the percussion family such as a bell or a whistle were introduced.

Participants were given the chance to accompany with percussion sounds the high-tempo music played during the event from the DJ booth that was installed in the luggage department of the automobile. This allows for the automobile to become, in addition to its main use as a vehicle of transport, a sound-generating instrument –a veritable surprise for the viewers.

Amarok Pikap project, thanks to the car's ability to move easily, enabled the project to be a center of attention and to reach a wider audience in several places. The project has circulated in different public spaces where thousands of people experienced with amusement. Participants explained their experience extraordinary and as being at a level close to the real experience of playing a percussion instrument. Moreover professional percussion players also noted that the system works much better than they have expected in realizing gestural sensitivity.

5. DEVELOPMENT

Force data obtained when performers strike the sensor areas with their fingers –'play' a percussion instrument- is transformed into digital data in the Arduino development card. Then, the digital data is transformed into Midi data in the Max/MSP/Jitter application and a valid protocol standard for sound generation is achieved. The obtained midi data is transferred via Max/MSP/Jitter to the Ableton Live application and the percussion simulator that operates as a plug-in of the application is transformed into percussion sounds.

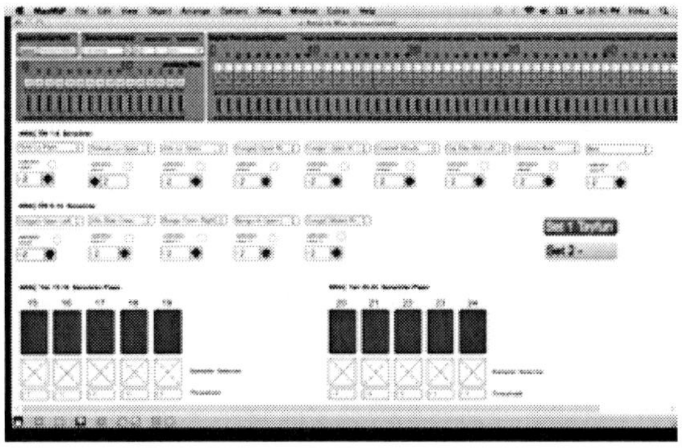

Figure 3. Max/MSP Jitter Patch.

The system progresses as a series of data transformation and transfers; and the obtained interaction data is transmitted to the Midi transformer application not via Serial Protocol but by OSC (Open Sound Control Protocol), so the delay in the sound that responds to the physical interaction is very short. The performance features of the sound module and the computer are factors that influence the delay parameter. The interactive system produced for the Amarok Pikap Project received highly positive feedback for its performance from various users including professional percussionists.

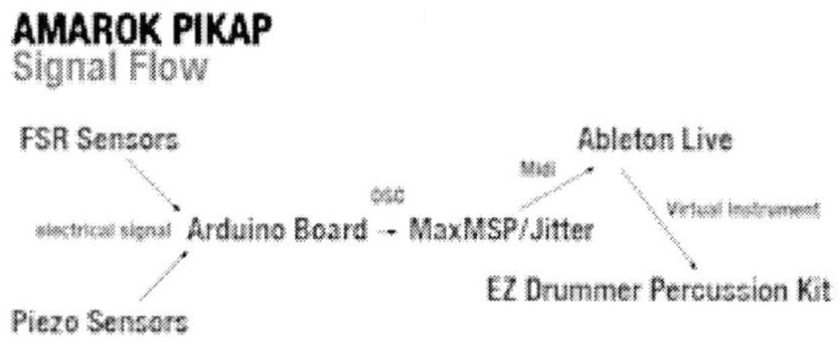

Figure 4. Signal Flow.

Amarok Pikap, the interactive percussion-playing automobile, was showcased in four beaches (Burç Beach, Alaçatı, Bodrum, Caddebostan) in Turkey during the summer months of 2012, switched location easily thanks to being a vehicle, and the interactive percussion system was easily set up and presented for use very easily set up and quickly presented for use. Although the temperature levels of the surface areas were quite high due to direct sun light exposure, there was no failure of FSR sensors.
In addition to the outdoor popularity of the activity, the event documentation video was viewed over a thousand times in a month on Youtube, and the project has been listed third on Cycling74's Popular Projects website.

6. CONCLUSION

In interaction design, the presentation of familiar phenomena in unfamiliar ways results in a human-technology relationship that swiftly produces results; since it creates curiosity in users at a level they are accustomed to. New interfaces produced for sound generators allow attractive implementations in brand promotions that create significant surplus value.

Figure 5. User Interaction.

At the end of the project, a distinct increase in brand awareness in terms of poten-tial buyers was observed. Today, music is among methods most widely used to con-vey a message to the masses. In this context, to allow the user/potential buyer to get involved in the event was among the main success criteria of the project that created difference.

The Amarok Pikap Project that presents a new interface for percussion, a widely used family of musical instruments, is important since it is the first of its kind. There are various examples of making music via acoustic sounds generated by striking various surfaces of an automobile. However, research has revealed no previous examples of playing a real instrument via strikes to the body of the car.

7. REFERENCES

[1] Marcelo M. Wanderley and Philippe Depalle. "Gestural Control of Sound Synthe-sis". Proceedings of the IEEE, vol. 92, No. 4 (April), Special Issue on Engineering and Music - Supervisory Control and Auditory Communication, G. Johannsen, Ed., pp. 632-644, 2004.

[2] A. Bouënard, M. M. Wanderley and S. Gibet. "Advantages and Limitations of Simulating Percussion Gestures for Sound Synthesis." Proceedings of the Internation-al Computer Music Conference (ICMC), pp. 255-261, Montreal, Qc., Canada, August 2009.

[3] Alessandro Camnasio - MUSIC FROM A CAR [Video]. Retrieved November 08, 2012, http://www.youtube.com/watch?v=H4d7GTLQTCY

[4] OK Go - Needing/Getting - Official Video [Video]. Retrieved November 02, 2012, http://www.youtube.com/watch?v=MejbOFk7H6c

[5] Smack Attack - Retrieved June 02, 2013, http://news.cnet.com/8301-17938_105-57580738-1/steering-wheel-music-pad-lets-you-drum-and-drive/

** See www.youtube.com/watch?v=wynafHRGk9A for the documentary of the project*

FULL AUTOMATION OF REAL-TIME PROCESSES IN INTERACTIVE COMPOSITIONS: TWO RELATED EXAMPLES

Dr. Javier Alejandro Garavaglia
Sir John Cass Faculty of Art, Architecture and Design
London Metropolitan University
41 Commercial Rd. E1 1LA, London, UK
j.garavaglia@londonmet.ac.uk

ABSTRACT

This article analyses two interactive compositions of my own authorship: both include live instruments and a fully automated programming of live electronics using MAX. On the one hand, the paper introduces *Intersections (memories)* for clarinet in B*b*, (2007/8); on the other hand, a comparison is offered, about how *Confluences (Rainbows II)* for flute, clarinet, violin, cello and piano (2010/12), is an amplification of the former piece with regard to not only its compositional further development, but also as a much more complex case of full automated live-electronics. The subject of full automation, including a historical perspective is explained in an article by the author in 2010 [1]. From a purely compositional perspective, both works share also a similar type of music dramaturgy due to their common *something to hold on to factors* (*STHotF*), as described by Landy [2], and later, also by Weale [3]. Hence, the *poiesis* and *aesthesis* [4] of both compositions are also hereby shortly introduced, to shed more light about the reasons for the full automation of their electronic parts, as these two aspects are solidly united to the electronics used and their relationship to the intended dramaturgy embedded in the two works.

1. INTRODUCTION

This article explains the technical and compositional facts that surround the pieces *Intersections (memories)* for clarinet in B*b*, from the years 2007/8 and *Confluences (Rainbows II)* for quintet (flute, clarinet, violin, cello and piano) from 2010/12, both compositions by the author of this paper. The latter composition is actually an amplification of the first piece, with several changes in the instrumentation, composition and electronics, although the main core structure of the original piece is maintained.

The main reason for the utilisation of complete automation of the live-electronics processes in both pieces rely upon the facts already explained in a former article of my authorship, *Raising Awareness About Complete Automation of Live-Electronics: a Historical Perspective* [1], and I would refer the reader to that article for full details. Herewith enunciated however, the main reasons therein exposed, which demonstrate clear advantages in the usage of fully automated live-electronics:

a. Concentration and reduction of unnecessary activities during the performance, allowing the performer or performers to purely concentrate on the musical aspects of the performance.
b. Relative independence of the electronics from the composer's presence during the performance, as the live electronics do not need further manipulation during the performance, just to be activated at the start of the piece.
c. Better combination of processes and lesser risks during the actual performance, as full automation allows for accurate and more complex combinations of different real-time processes such as multiple textures made of several simultaneous layers of real-time DSP functions, which are rather limited in those cases in which only manual manipulation is applied during a performance.
d. Principal means for the synchronisation is the usage of time-code (SMTPE) to follow events specified with an exact time position on the music score with the help of a SMPTE display on the stage (and eventually, a mirror of SMPTE times on the computer).
e. Accurate synchronisation of events and processes at the time of performing the pieces such as, for example, an accurate recording of a specific music motive or melody. A typical example of this case the case can be found in the first bar of *Confluences (Rainbows II)*.
f. Effective way of testing electronics beforehand: if the different DSP functions run steadily at the exact same set-times, they can be entirely tested while the work is being programmed and composed, resulting in less, or even no danger of exceeding, for example, CPU's or memory limits, as the real-time electronics can be fully monitored beforehand.
g. Frequent distribution of interactive pieces for performance purpose: thanks to the evolution of computing technology since the 1990s, pieces using full automation of their live-electronics have the advantage of an easier, costless, more effective and more frequent distribution, as the only requirements for their performance are the score and the patch/software. These advantages have also a beneficial impact on rehearsals and their organisation, as the full automation should normally allow for faster set-up times as well as faster rehearsal times.

In spite of the fact, that there are minor disadvantages in the usage of full-automated live-electronics, which are referred to in full in the article alluded to above [1], I shall not develop on them herewith, as they are not relevant to this article.

It is however important to stress upon the absolute accuracy of the programming required for a fully automated electronic part. Although this is already the case for *Intersections (memories)*, the addition of four more instruments in *Confluences (Rainbows II)*, turns the programming of the electronics into a much more complex process, in the particular case of this piece, with a total of more than 1000 function calls. Both compositions include several different types of DSP processes for a constant output in 5.1 surround image, such as surround diffusion, different types granulation, pitch shifting, several reverberation effects (including a variation of the Schroeder reverberation), spectral multiplication (convolution), pitch recognition, ring modulation of comb filtered sources and several recordings of each of the instruments into separate buffers for further manipulation during the performance.

Both compositions follow the same pattern for the writing of the general score: there is one staff for each instrument, another staff for the SMPTE times and a final staff, reserved to described the DSP functions occurring at precise times in the live-electronics part. Figures 1 and 3 below show examples of this in *Intersections*. The inclusion of the description of DSP functions in the score is meant hereby for information purposes only, as, due to the full automation of those processes, such indications are not needed for the performance of the piece to take place.

In order to finish this introduction, it is also worth mentioning, that the programming of the automatic real-time processes is absolutely entwined with the intended dramaturgy embedded in the pieces, and therefore, it must be seen as an essential and indissoluble component of the compositional process, as it is explained in section 2 below.

2. DRAMATURGY AND COMPOSITIONAL TECHNIQUES IN BOTH COMPOSITIONS

Revisiting the last topic of the former section, it must be stated upfront, that the composition processes in both works –and therefore their full dramatic content (as it is also the case in any other work of my authorship)– are conceived as a full unity, in which the full automation of the real-time processes does not only offer all of the advantages mentioned above, but also, that the absolute accuracy of them happening in exactly the way the have been programmed/composed is a constitutive part of the intended dramaturgy, notwithstanding the type of electronic DSP functions used in each particular case.

Although different similar meanings to the verb 'intersect' can be found in English, the title of the first piece indicates *something sharing a common area.*[1] The composition has its origin in a secret story, which is therefore not immediately apparent to the listener: there are three musical motives representing two different characters, all of which interact with one another forming new motives by intersecting at different points of the piece, with the results still sharing the original materials (their genetic identity) of each one in these combinations. Two of these motives represent the first character, the first one being of predominantly melodic nature, constituted by the pitches A, B, B, B*b*, A and E*b*, whilst the second motive for this character is purely rhythmical. The second character is represented by only one motive, which includes rhythmic and melodic attributes.

The story is based upon a real life experience of human relationship of a love affair, thus the reason for the two characters with their own motives and the transformations acting upon each other through time, forming in some cases, –as displayed in figure 4 later in this section– a new unity by the merge of those motives *intersecting* with one another. The three motives for the two characters can be found in figures 1 to 3.

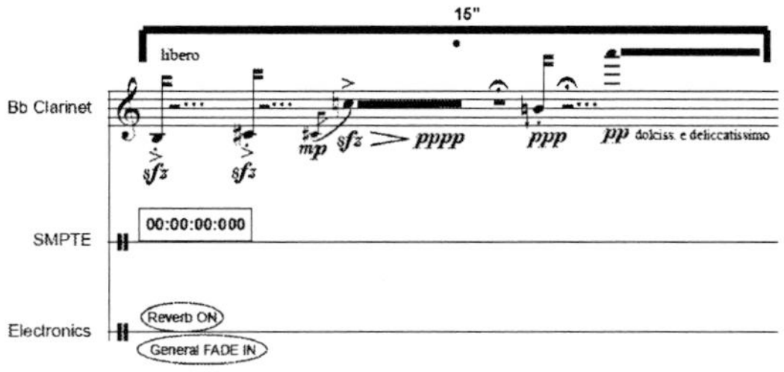

Figure 1. First character: motive No 1 (melodic)

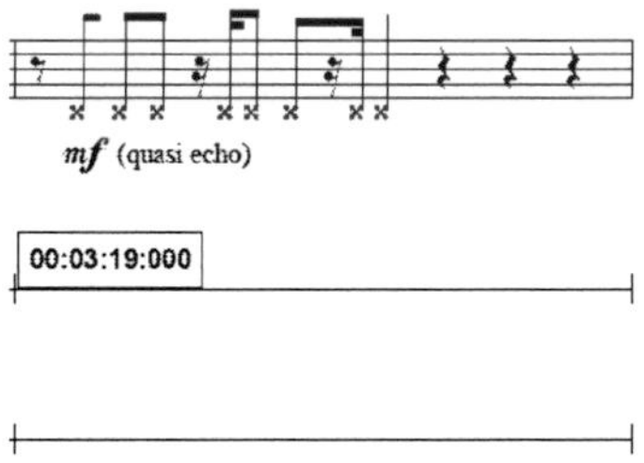

Figure 2. First character motive No 2 (rhythmic)

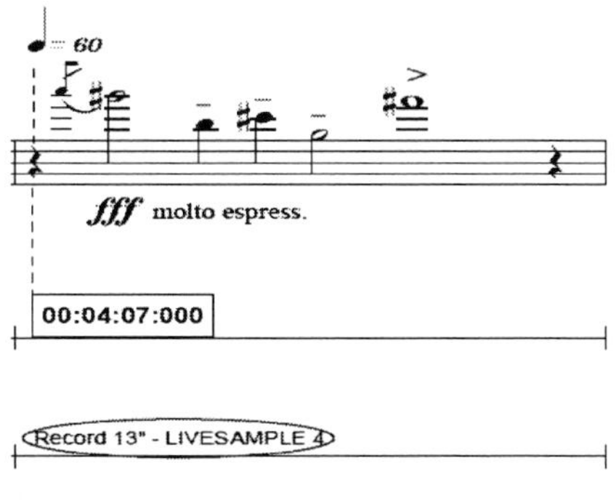

Figure 3. Second character motive

[1] 'Intersect: to share a common area'. (http://www.merriam-webster.com/dictionary/intersect)

There is also a third character, which appears transformed at different times during the piece. One of the most important of these transformations is the dissection of this third character melody into its constitutive notes, played isolated by the clarinet at different moments, each of which is recorded separately and individually by the electronics into a cumulative buffer; toward the end of the piece, this motive is played for the first time in its original full form only by the electronics, with the addition of granular synthesis, revealing the first Leitmotiv from the opera *Parsifal* by Richard Wagner (*Liebesmotiv*)[2]. This is one of the several examples in these two pieces of the *indissoluble* relationship during the composition process between writing the music and programming the full automated electronic. In this case, such a cumulative buffer adds events that are played across the first and middle parts of the piece, merging them together in order to play Wagner's melody in full length and in granulated form (bar 49 of the score). Without the accuracy of full automation, examples such as the one just explained, which require the full reconstruction of 18 separate recordings into one single melodic motive, would be difficult or even impossible to achieve with the precision required by its dramatic intention.

The musical motives cannot be taken as significant *STHotFs* for this piece though, as they are not evident to the listener, although the constant repetition and transformation (and intersections) of these three elements (the Leitmotiv and the two musical characters) may allow for the listener to perceive them in a rather recursive manner, becoming increasingly familiar with them during the performance of the piece. For those listeners familiar with Wagner's work, the Leitmotiv included herein should be a strong point of reference with regard to the dramaturgic intention of the piece though.

Following the idea of an *act of merging*,[3] *Confluences (Rainbows II)* keeps the main dramatic core of the clarinet piece, but enhances it not only with the addition of four new instruments, but also with the amplification of the motivic textures highly enriched by a rather complex programming of real-time DSP functions in the live-electronics part, as it is explained in full detail in the next section. In this piece, the *Parsifal* motive is removed from the piece, one of several issues that insure that, in spite of the shared core, the two works should be listened to as separate and individual entities. As it can be gathered from the above, in both cases, the most significant *STHotF* is the title of each of the compositions, mostly the first word, although the second word helps to give an idea of what else can be expected.[4] The love story suggested in the first piece is replaced by the confluence of several 'voices' of those characters in the second, which, possessing different timbres (due to the richer instrumentation), form a much more complex net or context, rather than the sole existence of two main characters and what unifies them (Wagner's Leitmotiv) intersecting with one another, as in the first composition.

According to another article of my authorship [5], based upon the concept of *Intention/Reception* in music by Weale and Landy [3], I amplified the *intention* and *reception* aspects of music dramaturgy by adding subcategories to both of them. The intention, called therein *Intrinsic Dramaturgy* [5], is divided into two subgroups: *a-priori* and *a-posteriori*. The first subgroup *–a-priori–* includes those works in which the dramatic elements of the piece are known beforehand by the listener, such as, for example, in the case of an opera or due to the text of a song.[5] The second subgroup *–a-posteriori–* includes those pieces where the dramatic element is not evident to the listener, and therefore additional information (such as *STHotFs*) is required for a minimal understanding of the intended dramatic plot. *The two pieces herein explained belong to this second subcategory of Intrinsic Dramaturgy.*

From the point of view of the instrumental techniques utilised, although more obvious in the clarinet piece, the two compositions rely mostly on the usage of advanced techniques, many of which are conceived in order to blend with the programmed electronics. The most common techniques utilised are: micro-intervallic; multiphonics (including multiphonic-trills); toneless articulation (woodwind instruments); key strokes; toneless playing (blowing through the clarinet, with an embouchure not enough to produce the fingered normal pitch); slap-tongue notes; playing notes with teeth on the reed of the clarinet with flutter tongue (which should produce a high pitch whistling sound); very fast tremolo over all 4 strings at the same time (for violin and cello, as in Berio's *Sequenza VI* for viola); playing with the hair of the bow on the side of the bridge of the cello, and so forth.[6]

Figure 4 shows not only an example of some these techniques for the clarinet in bars 29 and 30 in *Intersections*, but also the intersections of the three main motives of the two characters into one single motive in bar 29.

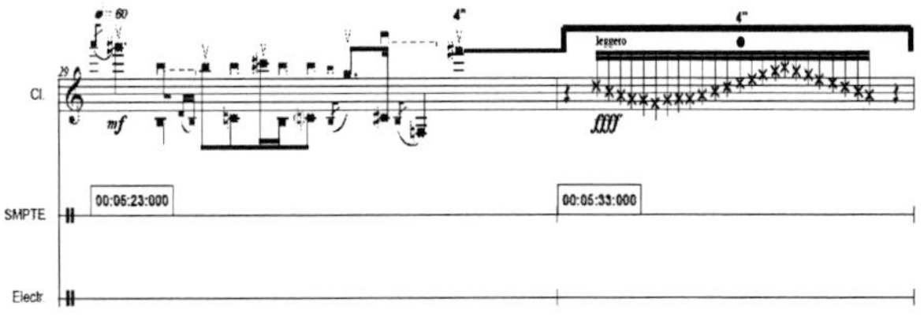

Figure 4. Example of advanced techniques (both bars) including and intersection of motives in *Intersections* in bar 29.

3. REAL-TIME DSP IN BOTH COMPOSITIONS – USE OF FULL

[2] Love motive.

[3] Confluence: 'a coming or flowing together, meeting, or gathering at one point'. (http://www.merriam-webster.com/dictionary/confluence)

[4] This, of course, without mentioning, that a possible program note in a concert could make the idea clearer to the listener.

[5] I thereafter divide this subcategory into three further subgroups: stage drama, non-stage drama and preconceived musical forms.

[6] A full description of these techniques is offered in each of the scores of these two compositions.

AUTOMATION IN THE PROGRAMMING OF THE 2 WORKS

The main reasons for the usage of full automation in these two compositions have been already explained in the former sections, hence, this section is dedicated to the explanation of how the fully automated electronics work, with a description of some of the DSP functions involved and how the automation in each case proves extremely useful for both dramatic and musical purposes.

However, before discussing some of those processes, a general description of how the full automation works in both cases must be introduced.

The two pieces were composed and programmed in order to completely avoid any type of extra-musical activity on the stage for the solely purpose of activating the electronics, such as pressing pedals or keys, manipulation of faders and so on during the performance. Hence, the audience can concentrate on the music played by the instrumentalist eliminating in this manner distraction or even loss of interest (avoiding therefore Delalande's sixth listening behaviour **[6]**)[7] caused by extra activities on the stage not related with playing a musical instrument. With regard to the dramaturgic aspect of this, it is my goal, that the performance of this type of pieces must create an environment allowing listeners for a full concentration on sound, mostly on its morphological, dramaturgical and spatial aspects.

In order to achieve that set of goals in these pieces, the computer is not on the stage, but with a second person (normally the composer) sitting at the mixing desk. The only device required on the stage is a SMPTE[8] display, showing the time-code send by MAX, which permits the player to follow it while reading the score of the piece.[9] The MAX patch begins by pressing a 'start' button (sending a MAX '*bang'*) and from then onwards, *no further manipulation on the computer is necessary*. The MAX patch is provided its own full score[10], in which each and every DSP function is thereafter automatically started, as a chain reaction to the initial '*bang'*. After the start point is activated, there are fifteen seconds (beginning by SMPTE 23:59:45:00) before the piece begins, which give more than enough time to the musician/s to prepare for the performance. Thus, any DSP function programmed for the composition starts at SMPTE 00:00:00:00, the actual start of the piece.

The person in charge of activation the live-electronics and balancing the overall sound via the mixing desk (normally the composer, but, as indicated before, full automation allows for anyone to perform this role) is required only to follow the SMPTE on the MAX main patch (a mirror of what is being sent to the SMPTE display) and concentrate purely on the input and output levels on the mixing console, in order to achieve the best possible sound balance inside the concert hall. Hence, automation allows here potentially for an optimal overall sound result, as the focus is on the sound balance during the performance, and not on the activation of several DSP functions.

Having said that, this section continues with a description of some of the DSP functions utilised in the pieces, with a fair amount of detail about how they were programmed and an explanation about how full automation is invaluable for an overall satisfactory performance of these two compositions.

3.1 – Surround sound (5.1)

Both compositions have a final output of a typical 5.1 Surround sound (L, C, R, SR, SL and LFE[11]). The LFE becomes the signal of all other channels via a *low-pass* filter with a cut-off frequency of 120 Hz although it can too, if required, process its own, independent low frequency signal.

The panning system between the 5 loudspeakers is programmed with an automatic combination of algorithms, which can either (a) maintain a constant time in the panning speed or (b) constantly change the time of circulation of sound between the speakers using a linear function between two given durations (in milliseconds): the start and end *inter-speaker-times*. The panning movement can be programmed in two directions: clockwise and anticlockwise. A third option is the random selection of one loudspeaker at a time, with the same options for time manipulation formerly explained (*a* and *b*) in this paragraph.

It should be made clear to the reader, that surround panning (despite the inclusion of joysticks in some advanced digital mixers such as the Yamaha DM2000, which offer some flexibility in the matter) is rather difficult to be manually controlled when several and simultaneous events are at work. Thus, automation is a solid and flexible option to obtain a constant speed between changing speakers, especially in cases of very short *inter-speaker-times*, which are impossible to be reproduced manually due to their short duration. The advantage of automation offers herewith the following options:

- *effective and full control of the panning speed*: the constant change of *inter-speaker-times* can be controlled from fast to slow or vice-versa (or even be left at a fixed rate), whilst very fast panning movements of less than 150 milliseconds produce a spatial granulation of the diffused sounds;
- *control of the panning direction*: clockwise, anticlockwise or random;
- *increase and decrease of panning speed*: by controlling the panning speed, imperceptible changes

[7] Delalande categorised the listening experience in six different behaviours, where the sixth is called 'non-listening behaviour'.

[8] The SMPTE is read by MAX in a subpatch, which contains the byphase modulated signal already recorded in an AIFF audio file. The output of the audio file comes out of the audio interface from a 7th channel and enters the SMPTE display on the stage, which decodes the information of the audio byphase modulated signal.

[9] See figures 1, 2 and 3, which shows examples how the musical score is written.

[10] The score in MAX consists of different timelines, which trigger each DSP function at the given time in the general music score.

[11] LFE is the short version of *Low Frequency Effect*, basically the signal sent to the subwoofer of the 5.1 system.

in the panning speed can be introduced, which respond in absolute accuracy to the parameters programmed;

- the already mentioned *avoidance of manual surround panning,* which is rather unpredictable and not always possible.
- *smooth and constant change of channel/speaker* in the surround panning, by the addition fade-in/fade-out envelopes for each channel, which make a constant crossover at any change of channel, whether clockwise or anti-clockwise or in random motion.

Particularly for the two pieces explained in this paper, the implementation of the surround sound and therefore, of the surround image in 5.1 is rather different in each case: while in *Intersections*, the surround movement and image is only at the end of the output chain, just before reaching the *DAC, Confluences* is so programmed, that several of the DSP functions in the MAX patch, such as pitch-shifting, ring modulation of comb filtered signals, multiple sample playback, and spectral multiplication (convolution), all possess their *own* individual surround options, which can be played simultaneously, therefore creating a texture of different surround/panning layers with different panning speeds within the general 5.1 image. This is impossible to be achieved without the aid of a fully automated programmed panning system. Figure 5 below, shows and example of the pitch-shifting function in *Confluences*.

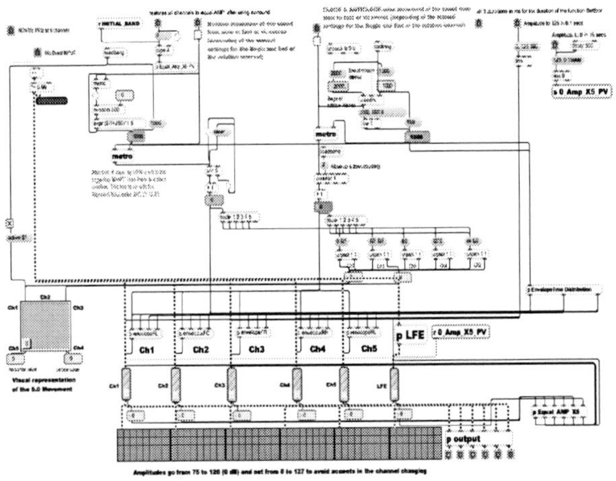

Figure 5. Automatic panning in 5.1 surround sound sub-patch (MAX 5) in *Confluences (Rainbows II)*

The results of this MAX sub-patch are sent subsequently directly to the general 5.1 output in the main patch. The main dramatic reason for the presence of surround textures, as explained above for *Confluences*, is the amplification of the environment in which the five different instruments develop their dramatic network of different combinations of the main motives, showing different aspects, which are not intended to be exposed in such a way in *Intersections.*

3.2 - The usage of a cumulative buffer in 'Intersections (memories)' for sample playback

This case applies only to the former piece, and not only depends on full automation, but also the precision required herewith cannot be achieved by any other means. Parsifal's *Liebesmotiv* (as described by Kurt Pahlen [7]) is the first to appear in the Overture of Wagner's work. It is shown in figure 6.

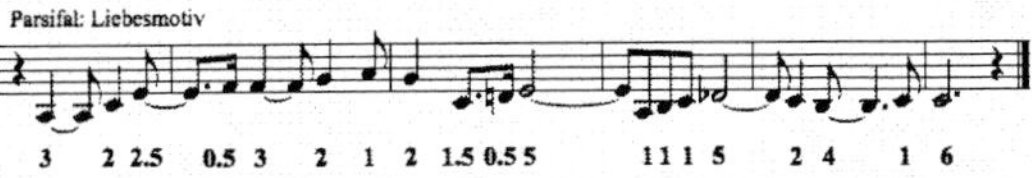

Figure 6. *Liebesmotiv* from the opera *Parsifal*, by Wagner. The numbers below each note indicate the duration of each note in quavers, which are translated into seconds in MAX for a cumulative buffer made of single recordings of each note during the performance.

In order to be able to record all of these notes in the right order and duration, each of the pitches from this melody needed to be composed within *Intersections*, not only with regard to their individual duration, but also taking under consideration, that the dynamic (amplitude level) of each note had to be as similar as possible to allow for a full playback of the Leitmotiv by the computer alone. Each time one of these notes is played at different moments between SMPTE: 00:02:10:00 and 00:08:17:00, the clarinet is accompanied only by a smooth reverberation of each note, which accentuates its intended dramatic meaning by extending its duration in time and at the same time, in the space.

MAX allows for a cumulative buffer to be used, which, from a first sample, recorded at the start of the buffer, all of the other notes are appended one after the other. In this way, a forty-five seconds long buffer is finished after 18 samples have been recorded (the final sample is recorded in bar 48, at SMPTE: 00:08:17:00), shortly afterwards, at SMPTE: 00:08:35:00, the electronics play it alone and repeatedly in full duration, granulating each note in a circular surround panning.

The required precision for the recording of each note, so that the duration and the sound of each note are recorded, was only possible by the implementation of full automation in MAX: while the clarinettist has only to follow the SMPTE displayed on the stage in order to play the notes accurately on the given time and without having to care about the activation of each recording (and therefore, allowing for a maximum in concentration on how to play those tender notes, marked always *mf* and *dolce* in the score), the electronics record and append each note/sample automatically into the buffer, adding in the process a short fade-in and fade-out of 195 milliseconds, in order to avoid clicks. Hence, the dramatic intention of playing the Leitmotiv in its complete and original form toward the end of *Intersections* is completely fulfilled, something which may not be possible if automation is not utilised. At this particular point, the musical score gives a very strong *STHotF*, by quoting Kurt Pahlen's words [7] at bar 49.[12]

[12] "Das erste Motiv ... bedeutet ... eine höhere, sublimierte Liebe, die durch eine Vereiningung mit Gott ihre Erfüllung erfährt." Translated freely into English: "The first motive ... means ... a higher, sublime love, which experiences its fulfillment through its union with God".

3.3 – Dynamic delays

The usage of this type of delays is already a common issue in several pieces I composed before these two. Although each piece uses them in different ways, the main idea of this DSP function is to produce delays across the 5.1 diffusion system, which, normally from the front to the rear, delay the sound by a random amount of time, which is herewith given in samples, and therefore dependant on the actual sampling rate for their actual time in ms[13]. The amplitude of each delay in the chain decreases (between 10% and 15% each time), and the algorithm works in such a way that, in spite of the random time selected by each activation of the patch, the second delay will always be longer than the first, the third longer than the second, and so forth. The output of each delay is sent thereafter to an individual reverb unit (slightly different for each of the five outputs) and further sent to a fixed output in the 5.1 surround image. Hence, this process is not included in any surround movement, as the surround image is fixed. Figure 7 shows the interior of this patch.

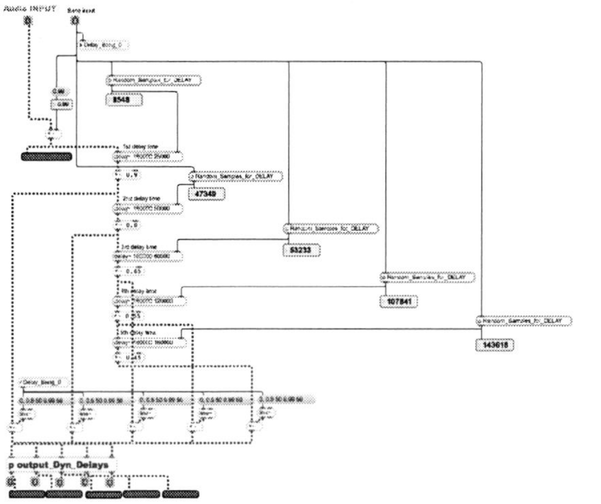

Figure 7. *Dynamic Delays* sub-patch in MAX, showing the calculation of each delay time in samples, the decrease of each subsequent delay in amplitude and the five individual outputs, corresponding to the 5.0 surround image. The smooth envelopes just before the output are there (*line~* objects) in order to avoid possible clicks.

Again, as shown in the former examples, this type of DSP function requires a level of precision in its activation, calculation and diffusion, which can only be achieved completely satisfactorily with the usage of full automation.

The intended dramaturgy embedded in this effect is to emphasise the second word of the title of the composition: *memories*, which seem to fade away with each repetition, as time passes by.

[13] Both pieces use a 44.1 kHz sampling rate, and therefore, the number of samples shown in Fig. 7 for each delay correspond to that rate. For example, the first delay showing a random caculation of 8548 samples, is, at a SR of 44.1 Khz, ca. 194 ms. long.

3.4 – Real Time Random Granulation using Pitch-Tracking and Phase modulation

The *Real Time Random Granulation* utilised herewith is a complex process which includes phase modulation in one of the three granular generators, whilst the overall grain generation depends on the incoming microphone signal(s) (from the live instruments), which is/are pitch-tracked by a pitch-recognition algorithm (external *fiddle~* object in MAX).

The granulation occurs between the interaction (ring modulation) of the incoming microphone signal and the sum of three cosine oscillators. These three oscillators are combined in such a manner, that the first receives the actual pitch value from the microphone signal from the pitch-tracker, while the second receives the same information, but this time multiplied by factor 2.5; the third oscillator receives its frequency input information directly from the output of oscillator No 2. All of these three oscillators are additionally phase modulated by the microphone signal. The output of the addition of these three oscillators is thereafter ring modulated with the incoming microphone signal, before being sent to the grain envelope generator, which calculates not only the *grain time*, but also the *inter-grain times*. Before the grains are sent to their output, they are filtered by a filter bank (the MAX object *svf~*), a combination of *low-pass* + *notch* + *high-pass* + *band-pass* filters, and then sent to a stereo output via delays (so that each channel has its own grain) and also to a reverb unit, with the purpose of adding some final colour to the overall sound. The reason for the stereo output from this patch, is that this granulation has the musical function of a rather established cloud within the surround image. Hence, the signal from each of the two channels is diffused only in quadrophony, in a crossing stereo image between the loudspeakers pairs L, R and SR, SL.

Thus, grains are a combination of multiple events, in which their frequency is mainly determined by the incoming frequency played by the live instruments, while the colour of the grains is mainly affected by the phase modulation and afterwards, by the ring modulation, whilst the filters add to the colour and create a certain illusion of multiple grain voices. The grain shape is a Gaussian-like envelope stored in a buffer, which also includes the *inter-grain time*.

It must be said though, that the last part of the chain, including the filter-bank, the delays and the final reverb were added for *Confluences*, while in *Intersections,* these features are missing (except for the filter-bank, which is nevertheless reduced to only a *low-pass* and a *notch* filter). In both cases however, the effect is of a smooth cloud of isolated grains appearing at each time in which there is an impulse coming from the live instrument(s). In *Confluences*, this type of granulation appears for the first time in bar 43, at SMPTE 00:06:03:00, triggered by the signals of the violin and the cello, whilst in *Intersections,* the first appearance is at SMPTE 00:01:17:00. Automation helps herewith for accurately switching on and off this DSP function at very exact moments without further notice. The sound-cloud formed by this specific type of granulation creates a rather ethereal atmosphere, which helps to underline the main dramatic ideas set by the music played by the instruments at those precise instances.

Figure 8 below shows the sub-patch for this type of granulation.

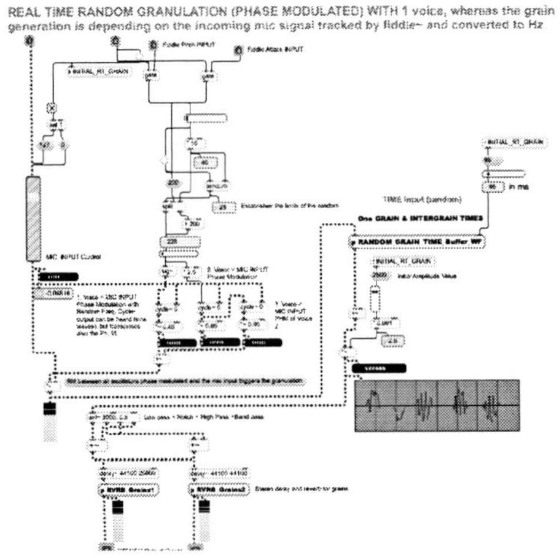

Figure 8. *Real Time Random Granulation* sub-patch in MAX. Most of the processes described above can be recognised in this figure. The pitch-tracking algorithm however is not included herewith, as it is an external sub-patch placed just before this one.

3.5 – Special Reverb Design for 'Confluences (Rainbows II)'

A special reverb was specially programmed for *Confluences.*

Although the main schema of the utilisation of a chain of *all-pass* filters (see Figure 9 below) for the reverb model is applied herewith –in a similar way as used in the Schroeder reverb, a combination of *comb* filters followed by a chain or normally five *all-pass* filters– there are special differences compared to the original Schroeder model. These differences are mostly evident in the lack of *comb* filters at the start of the chain, which creates a slightly different reverb effect, but far from the tap effect, which was sought to be avoided herewith.

The reverb design for *Confluences* is made of eight *all-pass* filters, which are accessed by the original signal at once *and* in chain, with in some cases, feedback on some of the filters (between filter 4 and 1, see Figure 9). The result is a rather smooth and natural reverb, due to the fact that *all-pass* filters transmit all frequencies of steady state signal equally well [8]; therefore the amplitude response is 1 at each frequency, while the phase response, which determines the delay versus frequency, can be arbitrary, as Smith states [9].

In *Intersections,* on the other hand, only *taps* with feedback –basically *comb* filters without the *feed-forward* property of *all-pass* filters– are used, which result in frequency cancellations which, in spite of being in a position to imitate rather closely room effects, they can also yield ringing and instability, and therefore, are unfortunately not as satisfactory as the system described above.

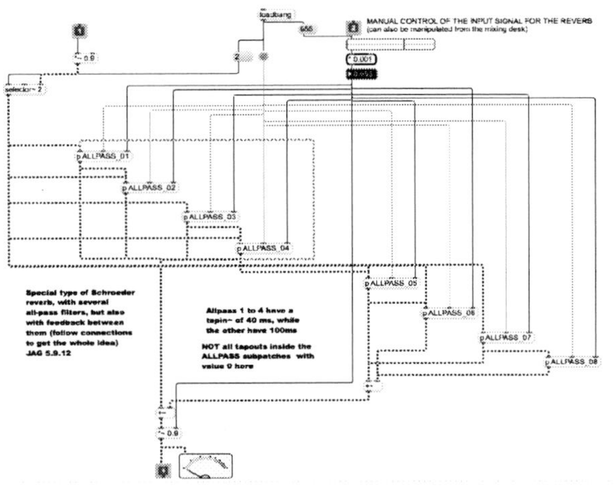

Figure 9. Reverb system in *Confluences,* made of eight *all-pass* filters.

In both pieces however, reverb is used for the dramatic purpose of creating a special environment independent from the natural reverberation of the eventual venue. In particular, reverb is used herewith to keep the sound of the instrument(s) in the concert space longer after the player(s) have ceased to play those notes. In this manner, those sounds are projected into the 5.1 surround image independently from their original source, particularly in *Intersections*, alluding to the 'memories' in the title. As the special reverb design for *Confluences* was only programmed in 2012, it is possible, that *Intersections* will use it too in future performances, due to its obvious advantages, most compatible with its dramaturgic intention rather than the *taps* with feedback of the original version.

As the reverb parameters change throughout the length of both pieces, there is the constant danger of feedback occurring during the performance. Despite a fixed input value for each of the different microphones given automatically within the MAX patch in both compositions, there is still the need for additional manual level control during the performance from the mixing desk in order to avoid feedback, which is the only exception of automation for both pieces.

4. CONCLUSIONS

The aim of this article –as it was in my former writings about the topic of full automation of live electronics [1]– is, on the one hand the fact that applying complete automation to the real-time processes of the electronics of a piece of music has a tangible beneficial impact on the performance of interactive works as much as on the achievement of their dramaturgical intentions; and, on the other hand, there is also an evident beneficial impact on the rehearsal of such pieces and on their eased circulation in different venues. Herewith, the usage of full automation of DSP functions is described extensivelly through the comparison between two different practical examples.

This article shows also the required progression of the complexity embedded in this type of programming between a solo and an ensemble piece: *Confluences (Rainbows II)* is up to date the most complex example of automation of live-electronics in my production. As demonstrated in those examples in section 3, several and simultaneous complex DSP processes were programmed in both compositions with no restrictions apart from those given by the CPU performance (and/or memory capacity) of the computer employed. And with the strong performance of computers in the past ten years, this has indeed ceased –in most cases– to be a limitation.

Moreover, the synchronisation between the performer (or performer) [14] and the electronics in these compositions is achieved with extreme simplicity by following a SMPTE display on the stage showing a precise time-code which is written periodically in the score every time DSP functions are automatically activated. As a result, much more demanding activities on stage such as, for example, activating pedals or the usage of click-tracks with headphones (and the usual leakage of sound that accompanies it) can be simply avoided.

The benefits for both the musical performance and the staging of these pieces are evident, as less attention can be dedicated to the synchronisation of several DSP events and nevertheless, those DSP functions can be played with extreme accuracy in real time without the need of further requirements or activities. In this manner, performers can focus much more (or exclusively) on the musical aspects of the pieces and much less (or not at all) on those technological aspects, therefore, enhancing the chances of a satisfactory delivery of the intended dramaturgy and an optimum result for the output of the algorithms utilised in the electronics.

The paper also demonstrates with diverse examples, that the dramaturgy intended in the pieces depends strongly on the absolute accuracy of the electronic processes, and therefore, these pieces cannot be performed as intended without a full automation of their electronics. Said in other words, as Landy remarks in *Understanding the Art of Sound Organization* [4], Molino's approaches to analysis, the *poiesis* (related to the construction of the work) and the *aesthesis* (related to the reception of the piece) cannot be completely fulfilled with regard to these two compositions if any other type of electronic activation were to be used.

Intersections (memories) had its premiere at the 18th (and last) Annual Florida Electroacoustic Music Festival (University of Florida, USA) in April 2008[15]. *Confluences (Rainbows II)* was premiered in September 2012 in Ljubljana, Slovenia during the ICMC 2012.[16]

5. REFERENCES

[1] Garavaglia, J., "Raising Awareness About Complete Automation of Live-Electronics: a Historical Perspective, in Auditory Display", in *6th International Symposium CMMR/ICAD 2009, Copenhagen, Denmark, May 2009. Revised papers - LNCS 5054.* Springer Verlag. Berlin, Heilderberg, 2010, pp. 438-465.
DOI=
http://www.springerlink.com/content/77q5w164360847g8

[2] Landy, L., "The 'something to hold on to factor' in timbral composition" in *Contemporary Music Review 10 (2)*, 1994, pp. 49-60.

[3] Weale, R., "Discovering How Accessible Electroacoustic Music Can Be: the Intention/Reception project" in *Organised Sound: Vol. 11, No. 2.* Cambridge. Cambridge University Press, 2006, pp. 189-200.

[4] Landy, L., *Understanding the Art of Sound Organization.* London. MIT Press, 2007, p. 197.

[5] Garavaglia, J., "Music Dramaturgy and Human Reactions: Music as a Means for Communication" in *Proceedings of the 9th International Symposium on Computer Music Modelling and Retrieval (CMMR 2012). Music and Emotions.* Editors: Mitsuko Aramaki, Mathieu Barthet, Simon Dixon, Richard Kronland-Martinet & Solvi Ystad, Queen Mary - University of London and Laboratory of Mechanics and Acoustics (LMA, France), 2012, pp. 112-127. Available at: http://www.cmmr2012.eecs.qmul.ac.uk/sites/cmmr2012.eecs.qmul.ac.uk/files/pdf/CMMR2012ProcceedingsFinal.pdf

[6] Delalande, F., "Music Analysis and Reception Behaviours: Someil by Pierre Henry" in *Journal of New Music Research 27 (1-2)*, Routledge, London, 1998, pp. 13-66.

[7] Pahlen, K., *Parsifal : Textbuch / Richard Wagner. Einf. und Kommentar von Kurt Pahlen unter Mitarb. von Rosmarie König.* München - Piper-Schott, 1993, p. 10.

[8] Roads, C., *The Computer Music Tutorial.* London: the MIT Press, 1996, p. 478.

[9] Smith, Julius O. III. PHYSICAL AUDIO SIGNAL PROCESSING.
https://ccrma.stanford.edu/~jos/pasp/Allpass_Filters.html

---

14 Or even conductors, as in the case of the premiere of *Confluences*)

15 The clarinet part was played by Jorge Variego.

16 The premiere was performed by: Anja Brezavšček (flute, Slovenia); Matjaž Porovne (violin, Slovenia); Jože Kotar (clarinet, Slovenia); Milan Hudnik (cello, Slovenia); Nina Prešiček (piano, Slovenia); Steven Loy (conductor, USA).

MOCAP TOOLBOX – A MATLAB TOOLBOX FOR COMPUTATIONAL ANALYSIS OF MOVEMENT DATA

Birgitta Burger **Petri Toiviainen**
Finnish Centre of Excellence in Interdisciplinary Music Research, Department of Music, University of Jyväskylä, Jyväskylä, Finland
birgitta.burger@jyu.fi petri.toiviainen@jyu.fi

ABSTRACT

The *MoCap Toolbox* is a set of functions written in Matlab for analyzing and visualizing motion capture data. It is aimed at investigating music-related movement, but can be beneficial for other research areas as well. Since the toolbox code is available as open source, users can freely adapt the functions according to their needs. Users can also make use of the additional functionality that Matlab offers, such as other toolboxes, to further analyze the features extracted with the *MoCap Toolbox* within the same environment. This paper describes the structure of the toolbox and its data representations, and gives an introduction to the use of the toolbox for research and analysis purposes. The examples cover basic visualization and analysis approaches, such as general data handling, creating stick-figure images and animations, kinematic and kinetic analysis, and performing Principal Component Analysis (PCA) on movement data, from which a complexity-related movement feature is derived.

1. MOTIVATION AND OVERVIEW

The *MoCap Toolbox* is a Matlab[1] toolbox dedicated to the analysis and visualization of motion capture (MoCap) data. It has been developed for the analysis of music-related movement, but is potentially useful in other areas of studies as well. It is open source, distributed under GPL license, and freely available for download at:

www.jyu.fi/music/coe/materials/mocaptoolbox.

The *MoCap Toolbox* is mainly intended for working with recordings made with an infrared marker-based optical motion capture system. Such motion capture systems are based on an active source emitting pulses of infrared light at a very high frequency, which is reflected by small, usually spherical markers attached to the tracked object (e.g., a participant dancing or playing an instrument). With each camera capturing the position of the reflective markers in two-dimensional, a network of several cameras can be used to obtain position data in three dimensions. Besides optical motion capture, the *MoCap Toolbox* can also be used for analyzing data captured with other tracker technologies, such as inertial or magnetic trackers. However, some features of the toolbox will be limited, since such trackers do not produce position data, but derivative data, (e.g., acceleration). Furthermore, the toolbox is optimized for the use of 3-dimensional position data, so using data with six degrees of freedom (position and rotation) might require customized adjustments of functions.

There are proprietary (closed source) software solutions available for motion capture analysis and visualization, such as Visual3D[2] or MotionBuilder[3], and applications that are primarily used for recording data (such as Qualisys Track Manager[4] or Vicon Nexus[5]). However, such applications are usually either too limited in their functionality, too focused on visualization and/or too restrictive to adapt to the needs of the researcher, such as developing new movement features useful for their individual research questions. To overcome these issues, we implemented this toolbox in Matlab, a generic scientific computing environment, and made it available to other researchers to be used in favor of their needs. The *Mocap Toolbox* is not the only Matlab toolbox available for motion capture analysis; one other toolbox worth mentioning is the toolbox created by Charles Verron [1]. This toolbox is more limited than the *MoCap Toolbox*, but offers a graphical user interface (GUI).

Matlab offers pre-built visualization opportunities and gives access to a large range of other functionality. Some functions included in the *MoCap Toolbox* use, for example, the *Signal Processing Toolbox* provided by MathWorks, or the *FastICA* package[6], a freely available third-party toolbox for Independent Component Analysis. Furthermore, the users themselves can make immediate use of the additional functionality and toolboxes provided by Matlab, for example the *Statistics Toolbox*, to further analyze features extracted with the *MoCap Toolbox* without the need to switch between different applications. *MoCap Toolbox* code is written using the generic Matlab syntax and is openly assessable, so users can add and adapt functions to their own needs.

[1] www.mathworks.com

[2] www.c-motion.com/products/visual3d/
[3] www.autodesk.com/motionbuilder
[4] www.qualisys.com/products/software/qtm/
[5] www.vicon.com/products/nexus.html
[6] www.cis.hut.fi/projects/ica/fastica/

The *MoCap Toolbox* supports various motion capture data formats, in particular the .c3d[7] file format (which, e.g., Vicon[8] or OptiTrack[9] optical motion capture systems can produce), the .tsv format and the .mat format, both produced by the Qualisys motion capture system[10], and the .wii data format produced by the *WiiDataCapture* software[11].

The *MoCap Toolbox* provides 64 functions for analyzing and visualizing motion capture data. The main categories can be summarized as data input and edit functions, coordinate transformation and coordinate system conversion functions, kinematic and kinetic analysis functions, time-series analysis functions, visualization functions, and projection functions. Furthermore, it uses three different data structures, the *MoCap data structure*, the *norm data structure*, and the *segm data structure*. To convert between the different data representations and enable certain visualizations, three different parameter structures are used, the *m2jpar*, the *j2spar*, and the *animpar structures*. Both the data and the parameter structures will be discussed and explained in the next section.

2. DATA REPRESENTATIONS

The *MoCap Toolbox* uses three different data structures, the *MoCap data structure*, the *norm data structure*, and the *segm data structure*. A *MoCap data structure* instance is created when mocap data is read from a file to the Matlab workspace using the function `mcread`. A *MoCap data structure* contains the 3-dimensional locations of the markers (in the `.data` field) as well as basic information, including the type of structure, the file name, number of frames of the recording, the number of cameras used for the recording, the number of markers in the data, the frame rate, the names of the markers, and the order of time differentiation of the data. Additionally, the *MoCap data structure* contains fields for data captured with analog data, such as EMG. Finally, the time stamp of the recording and the data type (e.g., 3D) can be added.

A *MoCap data structure* instance is also created when the function `mcm2j` is used. This function transforms a marker representation to a joint representation. These two representations use the same data structure, although they are conceptually different: the marker representation reflects the actual marker locations, whereas the joint representation is related to locations derived from marker locations. A joint can consist of one marker, but it can also be derived from more than one markers. It can, for example, be used for calculating the location of a body part where it is impossible to attach a marker. The midpoint of a joint, for instance, can be then derived as the centroid of four markers around the joint.

The *norm data structure*, created by the function `mcnorm`, is similar to the *MoCap data structure*, except that its `.data` field has only one column per marker. This column contains the Euclidean norm of the vector data from which it was derived. If, for instance, `mcnorm` is applied to velocity data, the resulting *norm data structure* holds the magnitudes of velocities, or speeds, of each marker.

The third data structure, the *segm data structure*, is not, like the other two, related to points in space (markers or joints), but to segments of the body (see, e.g., [2]). The function `mcj2s` performs a transformation from a joint representation to a segment representation and produces as output a *segm data structure* instance. Most fields of a *segm data structure* are similar to the ones of a *MoCap data structure*, however, the `.data` field is replaced by four other fields. The `.parent` field contains information about the kinematic chains of the body, i.e., how the joints are connected to form segments, and how segments are connected to each other. The fields `.roottrans` and `.rootrot` store the location and orientation of the center of the body, the root. The `.segm` field consists of several subfields that store the orientation of the body segments in several ways. The `.eucl` subfield contains for each segment the Euclidean vector pointing from the proximal to the distal joint of the segment. The length of each segment is stored in the `.r` subfield. The `.quat` subfield includes the rotation of each segment as a quaternion representation (see, e.g., [3] and [4]). Finally, the `.angle` subfield contains the angles between each segment and its proximal segment.

To convert between the different representations and to enable certain visualizations, the *MoCap Toolbox* offers three different parameter structures: *m2jpar, j2spar*, and the *animpar structures*.

The *m2jpar structure* is used by the function `mcm2j` and contains the information needed to perform the transformation from marker to joint representation. Besides fields holding the number of joints and the names of the joints, it includes a field with the numbers of the markers defining the location of each joint.

The *j2spar structure* is used by the function `mcj2s` and contains the information needed to perform the transformation from joint to segment representation. Besides the fields containing the segment names and the number of the root (center of the body) joint, it includes fields with the numbers of the three joints that define the frontal plane of the body and a vector indicating the number of the parent segment (the segment that is proximal in the kinematic chain) for each segment.

The *animpar structure* is used by the functions `mcplotframe` and `mcanimate` and contains the information needed to create frame (stick figure) plots and animations. The structure includes fields for the screen size, limits of the plotted area, viewing angles, marker sizes, plotting colors, connection line configurations and widths, and plotting of marker and frame numbers. Additionally, the structure contains fields related to creating animations, such as the frames per second, a substructure for perspective projection parameters, and settings for plotting marker traces.

[7] www.c3d.org
[8] www.vicon.com
[9] www.naturalpoint.com/optitrack/
[10] www.qualisys.com
[11] www.jyu.fi/music/coe/materials/mocaptoolbox

3. USING THE TOOLBOX

In what follows, we will give an introduction to the use of the toolbox for research and analysis purposes.

The *MoCap Toolbox* manual, provided with the download of the toolbox, offers an example chapter with eleven demos explaining the basic usage of the toolbox. Additionally, a demo data set called `mcdemodata`, including motion capture data and associated parameter structures, is provided with the download. The *MoCap data structures* `dance1` and `dance2` used below are available in the `mcdemodata` data set.

3.1 Reading Data and Filling Gaps

Recorded motion capture files can be imported into Matlab using the function `mcread` storing the content of the file as a *MoCap data structure*, i.e.,

```
d = mcread('file.tsv');
```

An essentially useful first step is usually to check for missing frames in the recording. Taking the *mocap data structure* d, we can use

```
mcmissing(d)
```

to detect missing frames in the recording. In case of missing data, we can fill them using linear interpolation with the function `mcfillgaps`:

```
d = mcfillgaps(d);
```

From this point onwards, we will use the two *MoCap data structures* `dance1` and `dance2` from the `mcdemodata`. Since they are already available as *MoCap data structures* and do not contain missing data, both importing and gap filling are not required anymore.

3.2 Visualizing and Animating Data

A good approach to get an overview of the data is to visualize and animate data. Using the *MoCap Toolbox*, mocap data can be plotted in different two ways: as a time series or as single frames. As a function of time, marker location data can be plotted with the function `mcplottimeseries`, e.g.,

```
mcplottimeseries(dance1,[1 20 28],
  'dim',3)
```

which plots the third/vertical dimension of markers 1, 20, and 28 (left front head, right hand, and right foot) (see Fig. 1).

Marker locations as single frames can be plotted using the function `mcplotframe` (using the (x,y) projection of the markers):

```
mcplotframe(dance1,450);
```

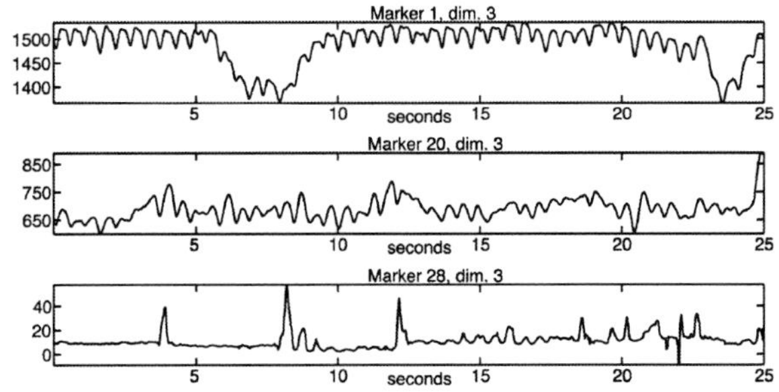

Figure 1. Marker location data plotted as function of time using `mcplottimeseries`.

This call, plotting the 450th frame of the recording (see Fig 2a), uses the default *animation parameter structure*. However, if a customized *animpar* structure is used, we can, for instance, set the connection lines between the markers to obtain a visualization that is easier to understand and that looks more human-like (see Fig. 2b):

```
ap = mcinitanimpar;
ap.conn = [1 2; 2 4; 3 4; 3 1; 5 6; 9
  10; 10 12; 11 12; 11 9; 8 9; 8 10; 8
  5; 8 6; 5 9; 5 11; 6 10; 6 12; 7 11;
  7 12; 7 5; 7 6; 5 13; 13 15; 13 16;
  16 19; 15 19; 6 14; 14 17; 14 18; 17
  20; 18 20; 9 21; 11 21; 10 22; 12 22;
  21 23; 23 25; 23 26; 25 26; 22 24; 24
  27; 24 28; 27 28];
mcplotframe(dance1,450,ap);
```

In case users collected the data with a Qualisys motion capture system and created a bone structure during the labeling process in the Qualisys software, they can export the so-called label list (which contains the marker connections) and use this file to create the connection matrix by employing the function `mccreateconnmatrix`.

We can change the general color scheme and the colors of individual markers, connector lines, traces, and numbers by adjusting the values of the respective fields of the *animpar* structure, for example (see Fig. 2c):

```
ap.colors = 'wrbgy';
ap.markercolors = 'bmgyrrrrrrrkk';
mcplotframe(dance1,450,ap);
```

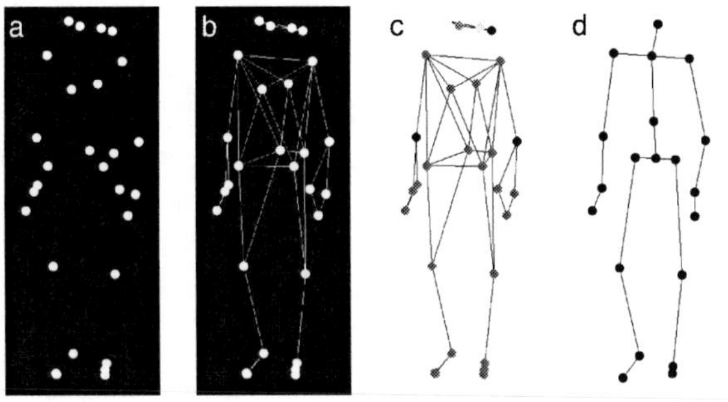

Figure 2. Marker location data plotted as frame using `mcplotframe`: a) using the default parameters; b) using a connection matrix; c) changing colors; d) joint transformation.

The function `mcanimate` is used to create animations:

```
mcanimate(dance1,an);
```

The *MoCap Toolbox* produces the single animation frames as .png files. They have to be compiled into a movie using other software, such as QuickTime Pro on Mac, or MovieMaker on Windows.

Animations can be created as 2D projections in two ways, either orthographic (default) or perspective, the latter one by including the perspective projection parameter:

```
mcanimate(dance1,an,1);
```

3.3 Kinematic Analysis

Kinematic variables, such as velocity and acceleration, are estimated using the time-derivative function `mctimeder`:

```
d1v = mctimeder(dance1,1); %vel.
d2v = mctimeder(dance2,1);
d1a = mctimeder(dance1,2); %acc.
d2a = mctimeder(dance2,2);
```

To analyze such time series, we can calculate their means and standard deviations using `mcmean` and `mcstd` (ignoring eventual missing frames). For this sample analysis, we will take the norm data, that is, the magnitudes of the 3-dimensional data of velocity and acceleration. To simplify the approach, we first combine the data from marker 1 (left front head) of the four *MoCap data structures* using mcconcatenate:

```
dva = mcconcatenate(d1v,1,d1a,1,d2v,1,
 d2a,1);
dva_mean = mcmean(mcnorm(dva));
dva_std = mcstd(mcnorm(dva));
```

The results (see Table 1) show that both mean and standard deviation of velocity and acceleration of the left front head marker are higher for `dance2` than for `dance1`, so the dancer in `dance2` moved faster and at a wider range of speeds and also used more and larger directional changes.

		mean	SD
velocity	dance1	235.85	110.79
	dance2	520.24	192.27
acceleration	dance1	2233.66	1326.55
	dance2	3347.21	1423.19

Table 1. Means and standard deviations of velocity and acceleration (magnitudes) of the left front head marker data of `dance1` and `dance2`.

The cumulative distance travelled by a marker can be calculated with the function `mccumdist` (returning a *norm data structure*):

```
d1dist = mccumdist(dance1);
d2dist = mccumdist(dance2);
```

We use the Matlab function `barh` for plotting markers 1 (left front head), 20 (right finger), and 28 (right foot) (see Fig. 3):

```
figure, barh([d1dist.data(1500,[1 20
 28]); d2dist.data(1500,[1 20
 28])],'b');
```

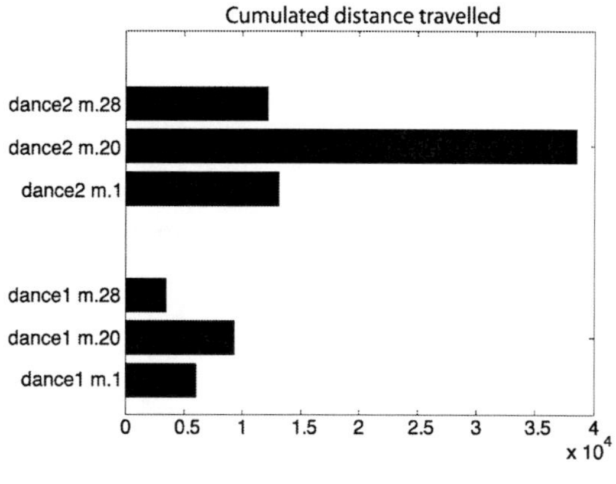

Figure 3. Cumulated distance travelled by markers 1, 20, and 28 of mocap data `dance1` and `dance2` (labels and title were added separately).

We can see in Figure 3 that the three markers, especially the right hand marker, travelled more for `dance2` than for `dance1`, so we can assume that the amount of movement was higher in `dance2`.

A measure related to the amount of movement is the area covered by the movement, which can be calculated using `mcboundrect`. If we want to calculate the bounding rectangle of the four hip markers, we do:

```
br1 = mean(mean(mcboundrect(dance1,[9
 10 11 12])));
br2 = mean(mean(mcboundrect(dance2,[9
 10 11 12])));
```
[12]

The bounding rectangle value for `dance1` equals .1806 and for `dance2`, it equals .9724. Since the value for `dance2` is higher, `dance2` not only had a higher amount of movement, but also used more space than `dance1`. The bounding rectangle measure was found to be a relevant movement feature in [5] and [6].

We can also calculate distances between markers using `mcmarkerdist`. The standard deviation of the distance between left and right finger,

```
md1 = std(mcmarkerdist(dance1,19,20));
md2 = std(mcmarkerdist(dance2,19,20));
```

gives us information about the variability of the marker distance. The standard deviation of the finger marker distance for `dance1` equals 49.0 and for `dance2` 175.65, so the fingers in `dance2` exhibited more variable distances.

Periodicity of movement can be estimated using the function `mcperiod`. It is based on autocorrelation, and

[12] `mcboundrect` uses window decomposition. The function output here is averaged across the windows and the four markers.

either the first or highest peak of the autocorrelation function is taken as periodicity estimation dependent on the parameter input. With

```
d1m1 = mcgetmarker(d1a,20);
d2m1 = mcgetmarker(d2a,20);
[per1 ac1 eac1] = mcperiod(d1m1,2,
  'highest');
[per2 ac2 eac2] = mcperiod(d2m1,2,
  'highest');
```

we calculate the periodicity of the acceleration of the right finger marker. `mcperiod` resulted in a periodicity estimate for each dimension being [1.04, 0.53, 0.52] for `dance1` and [1.04, 1.01, 1.06] for `dance2`. While the first dimension is similar, the second and third dimensions are roughly half for `dance1`, suggesting that in this case the finger moved in double tempo in y and z directions.

A more accurate periodicity analysis can be performed using windowed autocorrelation:

```
[per1 ac1 eac1] = mcwindow(@mcperiod,
  d1m1,2,0.25);
[per2 ac2 eac2] = mcwindow(@mcperiod,
  d2m1,2,0.25);
```

To allow visual inspection of the time development of the periodicity, the enhanced autocorrelation (eac) matrix can be plotted as an image (see Fig. 4). The colors indicate the regularity of periodic movement, with warm colors corresponding to regions of regular periodic movement in the period-time plane:

```
figure, imagesc(eac1(:,:,3)), axis xy
set(gca, 'XTick',0:4:46, 'XTickLabel',
  0.5*(0:4:46), 'YTick',[0 30 60 90
  120], 'YTickLabel',[0 0.5 1 1.5 2.0])
figure, imagesc(eac2(:,:,3)), axis xy
set(gca, 'XTick',0:4:46, 'XTickLabel',
  0.5*(0:4:46), 'YTick',[0 30 60 90
  120], 'YTickLabel',[0 0.5 1 1.5 2.0])
```

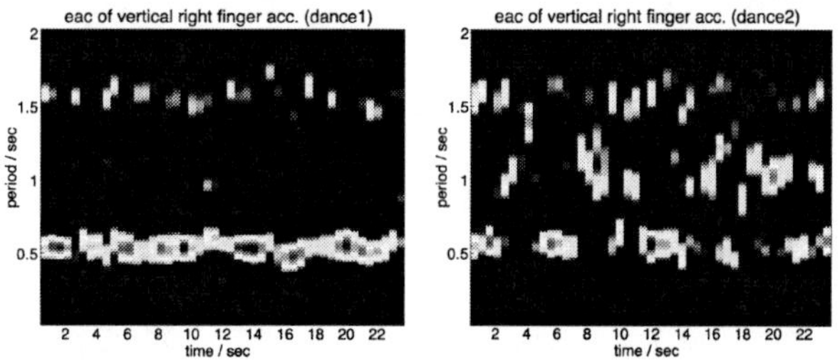

Figure 4. Enhanced autocorrelation function of the vertical components of the right finger acceleration in `dance1` and `dance2`.

We can see in Figure 4 that the vertical component of the right finger acceleration of `dance1` shows quite clear periodic movement with a period of about 500 milliseconds, whereas the periodicity for `dance2` is weaker and more irregular.

3.4 Kinetic Analysis

The *MoCap toolbox* offers the possibility to calculate kinetic variables using Dempster's body-segment model [7]. To make our present data compatible with Dempster's model, we first have to reduce the amount of markers from 28 to 20. We will accomplish this with a marker-to-joint transformation, implemented in the function `mcm2j`. The *m2jpar parameter structure* required for this transformation is created like this:

```
m2j = mcinitm2jpar;
m2j.nMarkers = 20;
m2j.markerNum = {[9 10 11 12],[9 11],
  21,23,26,[10 12],22,24,28,[7 8 7 8 9
  10 11 12],[5 6],[1 2 3 4],5,13,[15
  16],19,6,14,[17 18],20};
m2j.markerName = {'root', 'lhip',
  'lknee','lankle','ltoe','rhip',
  'rknee','rankle','rtoe','midtorso',
  'neck','head','lshoulder','lelbow',
  'lwrist','lfinger','rshoulder',
  'relbow','rwrist','rfinger'};
```

The joint `'root'`, for example, is obtained by calculating the centroid of markers 9, 10, 11, and 12. The marker-to-joint transformation is carried out as follows:

```
d1j = mcm2j(dance1,m2j);
d2j = mcm2j(dance2,m2j);
```

Figure 2d visualizes frame 450 of the joint representation of `dance1`. The next step is to do the joint-to-segment transformation. The *j2spar parameter structure* required for the transformation is created like this:

```
j2s = mcinitj2spar;
j2s.rootMarker = 1;
j2s.frontalPlane = [6 2 10];
j2s.parent = [0 1 2 3 4 1 6 7 8 1 10
  11 11 13 14 15 11 17 18 19];
j2s.segmentName = {'lhip','lthigh',
  'lleg','lfoot','rhip','rthigh',
  'rleg','rfoot','ltorso','utorso',
  'neck','lshoulder','luarm','llarm',
  'lhand','rshoulder','ruarm','rlarm',
  'rhand'};
```

The joint-to-segment transformation is accomplished using the function `mcj2s`:

```
d1s = mcj2s(d1j,j2s);
d2s = mcj2s(d2j,j2s);
```

In order to calculate kinetic variables, such as energy, each body part has to be associated to its parameter (i.e., masses and lengths) specified by the Dempster model. Therefore, a variable is created specifying the types of the segments[13]:

[13] For a list of the segment types, see the *MoCap Toolbox* manual.

```
s_ind = [0 0 8 7 6 0 8 7 6 13 12 10 11
 3 2 1 11 3 2 1];
```

This variable associates each joint with a segment type. Each component indicates the type of body segment for which the respective joint is a distal joint. Joints that are not distal to any segment have zero values.

The parameters for each body segment can be then obtained using the function `mcgetsegmpar`:

```
spar = mcgetsegmpar('Dempster',s_ind);
```

With this body-segment representation we can estimate kinetic variables for each segment individually. The time-average of the kinetic energy of the whole body, for example, can be calculated like this:

```
[trans1 rot1] = mckinenergy(d1j,d1s,
 spar);
[trans2 rot2] = mckinenergy(d2j,d2s,
 spar);
kinEn1 = sum(mcmean(trans1)) +
 sum(mcmean(rot1));
kinEn2 = sum(mcmean(trans2)) +
 sum(mcmean(rot2));
```

The value for the overall kinetic energy of `dance1` equals 2.21, and the value for `dance2` is 11.37, thus more energy was used in `dance2`, which supports our argumentation drawn earlier, that there is more movement in `dance2` than in `dance1`.

3.5 Principal Component Analysis (PCA)

Principal component analysis can be used to decompose motion capture data into components that are orthogonal to each other. By using

```
[pc1 p1] = mcpcaproj(d1j,1:5);
[pc2 p2] = mcpcaproj(d2j,1:5);
```

we calculate the first five principle component projections of the position data (as joint representations) of `d1j` and `d2j`. `p1.l` and `p2.l` contain the amount of variance explained by each component. From these variances, we can derive, for instance, a measure of movement complexity, defined as the cumulative sum of the proportion of explained variance contained in the first five PCs (see, e.g., [5] and [8]):

```
pcapropvar1 = cumsum(p1.l(1:5));
pcapropvar2 = cumsum(p2.l(1:5));
```

The results, presented in Table 2, indicate that, in case of `pcapropvar1`, most movement is already explained with the first component, and the first five components explain almost all movement. In case of `pcapropvar2`, however, only about 50% of the movement is explained with the first component, and the first five components explain less than the first five components of `pcapropvar1`, so more components are needed to fully explain the movements of `dance2`. Such a movement would be characterized as complex, since a high number of PCs is needed to explain the movement sufficiently, whereas a low proportion of unexplained variance (`dance1` case) implies a simpler movement.

	pcapropvar1	pcapropvar2
cumsum(1)	0.79	0.48
cumsum(1:2)	0.90	0.78
cumsum(1:3)	0.95	0.85
cumsum(1:4)	0.97	0.90
cumsum(1:5)	0.98	0.93

Table 2. Cumulative variances of the first five principle components for `dance1` (`pcapropvar1`) and `dance2` (`pcapropvar2`).

4. CONCLUSION

The *MoCap Toolbox* is a Matlab toolbox dedicated to the analysis and visualization of motion capture data. It has been developed for the analysis of music-related movement, but is potentially useful in other areas of studies as well. It has attracted researchers' attention working in various fields and has been downloaded for being used in a wide range of different research purposes; music-related, but also, for instance, face recognition, sports, gait, or biomechanics research. It has also gained attraction in artificial intelligence research, such as robotic motion, human-robot interaction, and machine learning.

The *MoCap Toolbox* has continuously been developed further since its first launch in 2008 by both the authors and the users, whose bug reports and suggestions for new functionality has greatly helped to improve and extend it.

In the future error handling will be improved, for instance, when wrong data structures are used. Toolbox functions usually recognize the mistake, but in the present version, some functions do not return sufficiently clear error messages.

Furthermore, some functions will be adapted to standard Matlab conventions, as it is already done in, for instance, `mcplottimeseries` (specifying the plotting parameters as a strings-value combination).

Individual functions will be improved, such as `mcfillgaps`, that would benefit from the implementation of more advanced gap-filling methods than linear filling, for example spline interpolation. Additionally, more body segment models besides Dempster's model will be included, such as models proposed in [9] or [10].

As commercial tools (e.g., Visual3D) commonly provide GUIs instead of operating on a command-line basis, a graphical user interface could also be implemented for the *MoCapToolbox*. It would make the toolbox more user-friendly – for example, connection matrices of stick figures could be drawn in the GUI, or gap filling could be graphically supported.

Acknowledgments

This study was supported by the Academy of Finland (project 118616).

5. REFERENCES

[1] C. Verron, Traitement et Visualisation de Vonnées Gestuelles Captées par Optotrak. IDMIL Report, 2005.

[2] D.G.E. Robertson, G.E. Caldwell, J. Hamill, G. Kamen, and S.N. Whittlesey, Research Methods in Biomechanics. Human Kinetics, 2004.

[3] P. Kelland, Introduction to Quaternions, with Numerous Examples. Rarebooksclub.com, 2012.

[4] A.J. Hanson, Visualizing Quaternions. Morgan Kaufmann Publishers, 2005.

[5] B. Burger, S. Saarikallio, G. Luck, M.R. Thompson, and P. Toiviainen, "Relationships between perceived emotions in music and music-induced movement," in Music Perception 30, 2013, pp. 519-535.

[6] G. Luck, S. Saarikallio, B. Burger, M.R. Thompson, and P. Toiviainen, "Effects of the Big Five and musical genre on music-induced movement," in Research in Personality 44, 2010, pp. 714-720.

[7] W.T. Dempster, Space Requirements of the Seated Operator: Geometrical, Kinematic, and Mechanical Aspects of the Body with Special Reference to the Limbs. WADC Technical Report 55-159, Wright-Patterson Air Force Base, 1955.

[8] S. Saarikallio, G. Luck, B. Burger, M.R. Thompson, and P. Toiviainen, "Dance moves reflect current affective state illustrative of approach-avoidance motivation," in Psychology of Aesthetics, Creativity, and the Arts, in press.

[9] C.E. Clauser, J.T. McConville, and J.W. Young, Weight, volume and center of mass of segments of the human body. AMRL Technical Report 69-70, Wright-Patterson Air Force Base, 1969.

[10] C.L. Vaughan, B.L. Davis, and J.C. O'Connor, Dynamics of Human Gait. Human Kinetics, 1992.

RELATIONSHIPS BETWEEN SPECTRAL FLUX, PERCEIVED RHYTHMIC STRENGTH, AND THE PROPENSITY TO MOVE

Birgitta Burger **Riikka Ahokas** **Aaro Keipi** **Petri Toiviainen**

Department of Music, University of Jyväskylä, Jyväskylä, Finland

{birgitta.burger@, j.riikka.ahokas@student., aaro.j.keipi@student., petri.toiviainen@}jyu.fi

ABSTRACT

The tendency to move to music seems to be built into human nature. Previous studies have shown a relationship between movement and the degree of spectral flux in music, particularly in the lower sub-bands. In this study, listeners' perceptions of a range of frequency-restricted musical stimuli were investigated in order to find relationships between perceived musical aspects (rhythm, melody, and fluctuation) and the spectral flux in three different frequency bands. Additionally, the relationship between the perception of features in specific frequency bands and participants' desire to move was studied. Participants were presented with clips of frequency-restricted musical stimuli and answered four questions related to musical features. Both perceived strength of the rhythm and the propensity to move were found to correlate highly with low-frequency spectral flux. Additionally, a lower but still significant correlation was found between these perceived musical features and high-frequency spectral flux. This suggests that the spectral flux of both low and high frequency ranges can be utilized as a measure of perceived rhythm in music, and that the degree of spectral flux and the perceived rhythmic strength in high and low frequency bands are at least partly responsible for the extent to which listeners consciously desire to move when listening to music.

1. INTRODUCTION

When listening to rhythmic music we tend to move our bodies with it. Movements induced by music might be subconscious, with almost indistinguishable trappings, or deliberate, strong and intentional. The proclivity to move with music seems to be built into human nature, which is described in the literature as groove (see, e.g., [1]-[3]). These studies propose that the functional role of rhythmic music and the construct of groove are related to the evolution of entrainment and social behavior and state that synchronizing is the simplest form of entrainment from a psychological point of view. "Synchronization" is also the concept that Leman [4] suggests as the most fundamental component in bodily engagement with music. He proposed three concepts of (co-existing) corporeal articulations – "Synchronization", "Embodied Attuning", and "Empathy" – that differ in the degree of musical involvement and in the kind of action-perception couplings involved. "Synchronization" forms the fundamental component, as synchronizing to a beat is easy and spontaneous. As the first step in engaging with the music, movements could be used for imitation and prediction of beat-related features in the music. The second component, "Embodied Attuning", concerns the linkage of body movement to musical features more complex than the basic beat, such as melody, harmony, rhythm, tonality, or timbre. Following this idea, movement could be used to reflect, imitate, and navigate within the musical structure. Finally, "Empathy" is seen as the component that links musical features to expressivity and emotions.

Thus, music-induced movements seem to be associated with rhythmic features of music, such as periodic and regular patterns of beats and pulses. In basic western popular music settings the rhythm section (the drummer and bass player) are responsible for providing the rhythm. Van Dyck et al. [5] studied the effect of the dynamics of the bass drum on dancers in order to find if the bass drum is a feature that dominates music-induced movements. The authors concluded that the dynamic changes of the bass drum have an underlying effect on the intensity of movement while dancing. Burger and colleagues (see [6] and [7]) conducted a motion capture study, in which participants were asked to move to various pop music stimuli. They performed computational feature extraction on both the movement and the music data and found several relationships between movement characteristics and rhythm- and timbre-related musical features. Their results indicate that clear pulses in the music encouraged participants to move their whole body with low spatial complexity, while spectral flux in the low and high frequency ranges was more distinctly related to certain body parts. With an increasing amount of flux in the low and high frequencies, the authors discovered an increase in head and hand movement as well as an increase in temporally regular movement synchronized to different metrical levels, whereas more complex, irregular rhythmic structures resulted in temporally less regular movement. The authors concluded that spectral flux was related to the perception of rhythm of the music – flux of the low frequencies being associated with kick drum and bass guitar and high frequency flux being influenced by hi-hat and cymbal sounds – and therefore considered important for inducing movement. However, the perceptual dimension of spectral flux of restricted frequency bands has only been studied so far in connection to polyphonic timbre (see [8] and [9]) and music information retrieval related applications, such as automatic classification (see [10] and [11], both slightly differing in their technical implementation), but not strictly in relation to rhythm perception.

The spectral flux of restricted frequency bands, or sub-band flux, is a computational measure indicating the extent to which the spectrum changes over time. When computing this feature (see [8]), the stimulus is divided into 10 frequency bands, each band containing one octave in the range of 0 to 22050 Hz. After that the sub-band flux is calculated for each of these ten bands by taking the average of the Euclidean distances of the spectra for each pair of two consecutive frames of the signal (for more information about the derivation of the feature, see [8]). Two spectrograms of sub-band no. 2 (50-100 Hz) are displayed in Figure 1 to show the difference between high and low amounts of sub-band flux.

The purpose of this study was to investigate listener's perception of a range of frequency-restricted musical stimuli. The original versions of the stimuli have already been used in the movement studies cited previously (see [6] and [7]), however the present study included both the original version and three different frequency restricted versions of the original stimuli (low, mid, and high frequencies). We aimed to find relationships between specific musical aspects (such as rhythm, melody, and fluctuation) and the spectral flux in the different frequency bands. Additionally, we were interested in the relationship between the perception of musical features in specific frequency bands and participants' desire to move. We hypothesized that the perceived strength of the rhythm is positively correlated with the spectral flux, especially for the stimuli restricted to low frequencies (sub-band 2), so participants would perceive the low-frequency sub-band flux as being related to rhythm. Furthermore, we assumed positive correlations between the desire to move and the spectral flux for sub-band 2 and 9, as the spectral flux in these bands was found to be related to several characteristics of human movement (see [6] and [7]).

2. METHOD

2.1 Participants

A total of 38 participants (26 females; average age: 26.42, SD of age: 4.95) took part in the experiment. Participants were international students from the University of Jyväskylä, Finland. Participants were compensated with a movie ticket.

2.2 Stimuli

The stimuli consisted of 30-second segments from 30 different popular songs from various genres including Techno, Pop, Rock, Latin, Funk, and Jazz (the same musical stimuli as in [6] and [7] – a list of stimuli is included in these publications). They were all non-vocal and in 4/4 time, but differed in their rhythmic complexity and pulse clarity. In order to present participants with frequency-restricted stimuli, each clip was modified using MATLAB MIRToolbox 1.4 (see [12]): The clip was first divided into ten frequency bands, each band containing one octave in the range of 0 to 22050 Hz. Then the sub-bands of interest (sub-band 2: 50-100 Hz, sub-band 6: 800-1600 Hz, and sub-band 9: 6400-12800 Hz) were extracted and saved as .wav files.

2.3 Apparatus

To gather the perceptual ratings, a special patch was created in Max/MSP 5, a graphical programming environment, running on Max OS X. The setup enabled the participants to repeat excerpts as often as they wished and to move forward at their own speed. The stimuli were played back through active studio monitors (Genelec 8030A). The participants could themselves adjust the volume to a preferred level.

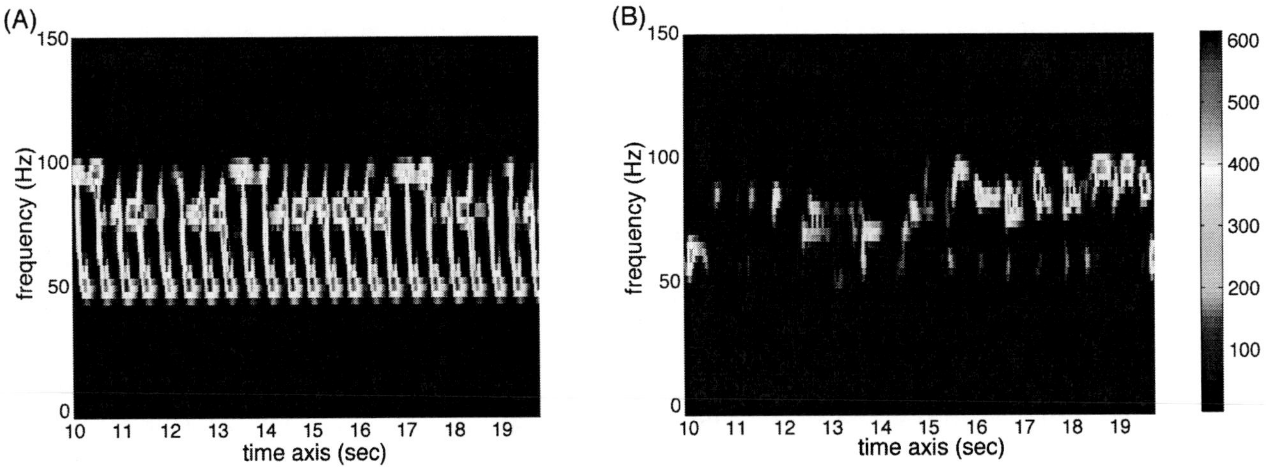

Figure 1. Spectrograms of sub-band no. 2 (50-100 Hz) (sec. 10 to 20 of two stimuli used in the study presented). (A) High amount of temporal change (red represents high energy at the respective time and frequency, whereas blue represents low energy; see color bar) resulting in high value for Sub-Band Flux. (B) Low amount of temporal change resulting in low Sub-Band Flux.

2.4 Procedure

The experiment was divided into four sections: one section containing the stimuli restricted to sub-band 2, a second section containing the stimuli restricted to sub-band 6, a third section containing the stimuli restricted to sub-band 9, and a fourth section containing the original stimuli. Each section was presented separately; first, the three sub-band restricted sections in random order, followed by the section containing the original clips. This section was always presented last to avoid a biased rating due to knowing the whole stimuli. The stimuli were also randomized within each section. Participants accomplished the experiment individually. They were asked to answer four questions, rating each on a seven-step scale (from "not at all" to "very much"):

1. *How prominent is the rhythm?*
2. *How prominent is the melody?*
3. *How much fluctuation is there in the music (How much is "going on" in the music)?*
4. *How strongly does it make you want to move?*

Preceding the experiment, there was a practice section with one example to allow participants to become familiar with the interface and the questions. The average duration of the experiment was 75 minutes.

2.5 Spectral flux extraction

For each of the four versions of each stimulus (three frequency-restricted and the original stimuli), the spectral flux was computed (using MATLAB MIRToolbox 1.4 [12]) by calculating the Euclidean distances of the spectra for each pair of consecutive frames of the signal, using a frame length of 25 ms and an overlap of 50% between successive frames. Subsequently, we averaged across the resulting time-series of flux values to receive one value for each of the four versions of the stimuli.

3. RESULTS

The first step of the analysis comprised checking the consistency of the ratings of the participants by calculating intraclass correlations (cf., [13]) for each question and stimulus type separately. The results are presented in Table 1.

	SB 2	SB 6	SB 9	Orig.
Question 1: ***rhythm?***	.95 ***	.97 ***	.96 ***	.96 ***
Question 2: ***melody?***	.94 ***	.95 ***	.93 ***	.95 ***
Question 3: ***fluctuation?***	.87 ***	.90 ***	.88 ***	.93 ***
Question 4: ***movement?***	.93 ***	.93 ***	.91 ***	.94 ***

*** $p < .001$

Table 1. Intraclass correlations for each question and stimulus type.

As these correlation coefficients indicate sufficiently high inter-participant consistency, we averaged the ratings across participants to receive one value per stimulus. Such high intraclass correlations, especially for question 1 ("*How prominent was the rhythm?*"), also suggest that the concepts of rhythm and melody were understood in a coherent way by the participants (despite findings related to cultural dependencies of rhythm perception, see [14] and [15]). Worth noting is that the correlation coefficient for question 3 ("*How much fluctuation is there in the music*") showed the lowest value for each stimulus type.

To investigate the relationship between the spectral flux data (calculated for each of the four versions of the stimuli as described in section 2.5) and the perceptual evaluations of the stimuli, we correlated the rating scores of the four questions for the music clips per stimulus type (averaged across participants) with the respective flux data. The results of the correlations are displayed in Table 2. Correlations with significance values less than $p < .01$ are indicated with asterisks.

	SB 2	SB 6	SB 9	Orig.
Question 1: ***rhythm?***	.79 ***	.20	.47 **	.54 **
Question 2: ***melody?***	-.01	-.28	.27	.03
Question 3: ***fluctuation?***	-.15	.01	.37	.11
Question 4: ***movement?***	.65 ***	.20	.52 **	.57 ***

** $p < .01$, *** $p < .001$

Table 2. Correlations between spectral flux and ratings on questions 1-4 for each stimulus type.

The strongest correlation ($r(30) = .79$, $p < .001$) for question 1 ("*How prominent is the rhythm?*") was found for the sub-band 2 stimuli. Question 4 ("*How strongly does it make you want to move?*") was also relatively highly correlated ($r(30) = .65$, $p < .001$) to these stimuli. Not quite as strong – though still significant – were the correlations between the same two questions and sub-band 9 flux ($r(30) = .47$, $p < .01$, for question 1, and $r(30) = .52$, $p < .01$, for question 4, respectively) and between these two questions and the flux of the original stimuli ($r(30) = .54$, $p < .01$, for question 1, and $r(30) = .57$, $p < .001$, for question 4, respectively). As all correlations were positive, these results suggest that participants rated stimuli with an increasing amount of flux in both low and high frequency ranges and overall flux with higher prominence of rhythm and with higher desire to move to the presented stimuli.

Meanwhile, the values for question 2 ("*How prominent is the melody?*") showed non-significant correlations with flux data of all stimulus types, suggesting that there is no relationship between the perceived melody prominence and the amount of (sub-band) flux in the stimuli.

Interestingly, the values for question 3: "*How much fluctuation is there in the music (How much is "going on" in the music)?*" showed no significant correlation to the (sub-band) flux data. This suggests that there was no relation between the fluctuation participants perceived in the stimuli and the computationally extracted flux in the sub-bands and the original clips.

Subsequently, we performed correlations between the ratings, segregated by each stimulus type. The results are shown in Figure 2.

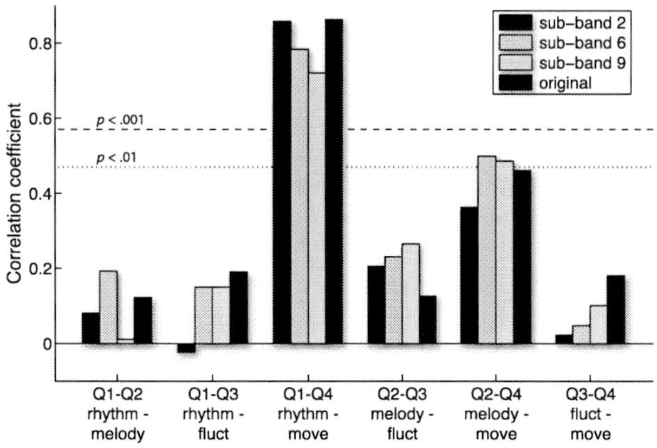

Figure 2. Correlations between the four ratings for each stimulus type separately.

The correlations between the questions show a similar pattern across the different stimulus types: for all stimulus types, question 1 (*"How prominent is the rhythm?"*) correlated positively with question 4 (*"How strongly does it make you want to move?"*) (sub-band 2: $r(30) = .86, p < .001$; sub-band 6: $r(30) = .78, p < .001$; sub-band 9: $r(30) = .72, p < .001$; original: $r(30) = .86, p < .001$) suggesting that the perception of a prominent rhythm was related to participants' eagerness to move to such stimuli regardless of its frequency range. For sub-band 6 and 9, additionally, question 2 (*"How prominent is the melody"*) correlated moderately high with question 4 (*"How strongly does it make you want to move?"*) (sub-band 6: $r(30) = .50, p < .01$; sub-band 9: $r(30) = .49, p < .01$). Thus, in the stimuli restricted to both the mid and high frequencies, the melody also appears to contribute to the willingness to move to such stimuli. The remaining correlations were non-significant.

4. DISCUSSION

We conducted an experiment to investigate participants' perceptions of rhythm, melody, fluctuation, and the desire to move in full-frequency and frequency-restricted musical stimuli. The participants' answers were consistent with our hypothesis: for stimuli restricted to the low frequency band (sub-band 2), stimuli having a higher amount of sub-band flux were perceived as being stronger related to the rhythm of the music than stimuli with a lower amount of sub-band flux, as suggested by the high correlations of flux data in sub-band 2 with the question *"How prominent is the rhythm?"*. These correlations are likely due to the frequency range of specific rhythmic instruments in this sub-band, such as kick drum and low bass notes. Additionally, a greater amount of low frequency spectral flux would induce the desire of movement in participants, as was suggested by the positive correlation with the question *"How strongly does it make you want to move?"*.

In addition, these two questions were also highly correlated to the spectral flux in sub-band 9. These correlations are likely due to the frequency range of specific rhythmic instruments in sub-band 9, such as hi-hat and some snare drum partials. These findings corroborate the results reported in [6] and [7], which showed higher amounts of specific bodily movements related to the amount of spectral flux in sub-bands 2 and 9. Spectral flux in sub-bands 2 and 9 may therefore be potentially more effective than spectral flux in other sub-bands in encouraging people to move to music.

The low correlations for question 3 (*"How much fluctuation is there in the music (How much is "going on" in the music)?"*) with all sub-bands, however, showed that participants could not perceive the amount of fluctuation in the stimuli. There are two possible explanations for this: 1) the participants were simply unable to accurately and consistently hear the amount of fluctuation in the individual sub-bands; or 2) participants did not understand the concept of fluctuation in this context. The intraclass correlation results for this question (see Table 2) showed that the answers for this question were less consistent compared to the other questions, so the latter explanation seems likely. Interestingly, none of the participants asked about the term during the data collection, thus it could be assumed that the participants understood the term fluctuation, but that this notion differed across participants. Future studies on a similar topic should make certain that the concept of fluctuation is clearly understood by participants.

Rhythmic content has been found to be strongly related to movement (see [5]-[7]). The high correlations between the questions *"How prominent is the rhythm?"* and *"How strongly does it make you want to move?"* for all the four stimulus types suggests that the perception of a prominent rhythm is related to participants' eagerness to move to stimuli regardless of its frequency range. Future studies could analyze the actual differences of participants' movement for specific frequency ranges, for instance in a motion capture setting.

The relationship found between perceived rhythm and desire to move (see previous paragraph) could also serve as support for Leman's theory of corporeal articulations [4]. Stimuli that participants rated to contain a strong rhythm, were also rated high on desire to move, suggesting a connection between both. That could be seen as being in line with the concepts of "Synchronization" and "Embodied Attuning", in which beat/musical features, such as the rhythm, are proposed to induce body movement.

There was a weaker – but still apparent – correlation between the two questions *"How prominent is the melody"* and *"How much does it make you want to move?"*, which points to a relationship between melodic strength and music-induced desire to move. The effect of melodic content on movement could also be the subject of future studies.

It could be argued that some of the participants' answers (especially to question 4: *"How much does it make you want to move?*") may have been skewed by prior experience with the particular stimuli since the stimuli used were clips from western popular music. However, it could be assumed that the wide range of backgrounds of participants, as well as the modification of the sub-band clips to within a certain frequency range (which often made the source music difficult to distinguish), helped to minimize the possible effects of familiarity on the ratings. Nevertheless, it might be valuable for future data acquisitions to include collecting both familiarity and preference ratings of the stimuli. This would give more insight into relationships between music characteristics and movement propensity, as it could be assumed that participants still rate certain stimuli high on "desire to move" although they do not like them.

We excluded extreme genres in our stimuli selection – such as death metal for example – as such music might be more prone to familiarity and preference than other popular music. Although musical styles such as death metal could contain high spectral flux and be considered rhythmic, not everybody would probably feel the urge to dance to such music. Thus, if such extreme genres were considered in the stimuli selection, relationships between spectral flux and movement propensity might be less linear than presented in this paper.

The presented analysis utilized one value – the average of the flux time-series – as measure for the spectral flux. As such, this could be regarded as an over-generalization, since taking the mean disregards information about the temporal regularity that the flux series should exhibit in order to induce movement. In general, a random use of, for instance, the kick drum would also result in a high amount of low-frequency flux, but it would fail to evoke a sensation of rhythm or movement in the listener. However, our stimuli were throughout the whole stimulus duration all metrically regular, had a sensation of pulse, and were steady in most of the musical characteristics. Thus, we believe that temporal averaging of the flux time-series was a suitable way to receive a relevant measure of spectral flux for each stimulus.

In conclusion, the results of this study show that for stimuli being restricted to low frequencies and, to a lesser extent, for stimuli being restricted to high frequencies, a high amount of spectral flux was perceived as having a more prominent rhythm. This suggests that the sub-band flux of both low and high frequency ranges can be utilized as a possible measure of perceived rhythm in music. Furthermore, the significant correlation between the answers to the questions "*How prominent is the rhythm*" and "*How much does it make you want to move*" to the spectral flux in sub-bands 2 and 9 point to an important role of the spectral content in these sub-bands; in essence, it suggests that the degree of flux and the perceived rhythmic strength in sub-bands 2 and 9 are at least partly responsible for the extent to which listeners consciously desire to move when listening to music. This is consistent with previous research (see [6] and [7]) that identified spectral flux in these particular sub-bands as correlating with various characteristics of bodily movements.

Acknowledgments

This study was supported by the Academy of Finland (project 118616).

5. REFERENCES

[1] G. Madison, "Experiencing groove induced by music: Consistency and phenomenology," in Music Perception 24(2), 2006, pp. 201-208.

[2] G. Madison, F. Gouyon, F. Ullén, and K. Hörnström, "Modeling the tendency for music to induce movement in humans: first correlations with low-level audio descriptors across music genres," in Journal of Experimental Psychology: Human Perception and Performance 37(5), 2011, pp. 1578-1594.

[3] P. Janata, S. T. Tomic, and J. M. Haberman, "Sensorimotor coupling in music and the psychology of the groove", in Journal of Experimental Psychology: General 141(1), 2011, pp. 54-75.

[4] M. Leman, Embodied Music Cognition and Mediation Technology. Cambridge, MA/London, UK: MIT Press, 2007.

[5] E. van Dyck, D. Moelants, M. Demey, P. Coussement, A. Deweppe, and M. Leman, "The impact of the bass drum on body movement in spontaneous dance," in Proceedings of the 11th International Conference in Music Perception and Cognition, Seattle, WA, 2010, pp. 429-434.

[6] B. Burger, M. R. Thompson, G. Luck, S. Saarikallio, and P. Toiviainen, "Music moves us: Beat-related musical features influence regularity of music-induced movement," in Proceedings of the 12th International Conference in Music Perception and Cognition and the 8th Triennial Conference of the European Society for the Cognitive Sciences for Music, Thessaloniki, Greece, 2012, pp. 183-187.

[7] B. Burger, M. R. Thompson, S. Saarikallio, G. Luck, and P. Toiviainen, "Influences of rhythm- and timbre-related musical features on characteristics of music-induced movement," in Frontiers in Psychology, 4:183, 2013.

[8] V. Alluri, and P. Toiviainen, "Exploring perceptual and acoustical correlates of polyphonic timbre," in Music Perception 27(3), 2010, pp. 223-242.

[9] V. Alluri, and P. Toiviainen, "Effects of enculturation of the semantic and acoustic correlates of polyphonic timbre," in Music Perception 29(3), 2012, pp. 297-310.

[10] D.-N. Jiang, L. Lu, H.-J. Zhang, J.-H. Tao, and L.-H. Cai, "Music type classification by spectral contrast feature," in *Proceedings of the IEEE International*

Conference on Multimedia and Expo, 2002, pp. 113-116.

[11] R. Cai, L. Lu, A. Hanjalic, H.-J. Zhang, L.-H. Cai, "A flexible framework for key audio effects detection and auditory context inference," in IEEE Transactions on Audio, Speech and Language Processing 14(3), 2006, pp. 1026-1039.

[12] O. Lartillot, and P. Toiviainen, "A Matlab toolbox for musical feature extraction from audio," in Proceedings of the 10th International Conference on Digital Audio Effects, Bordeaux, France, 2007, 1-8.

[13] P. E. Shrout, and J.L. Fleiss, "Intraclass correlations: uses in assessing rater reliability," in Psychological Bulletin 86(2), 1979, pp. 420-428.

[14] A. D. Patel, J. R. Iversen, and K. Ohgushi, "Cultural differences in rhythm perception: what is the influence of native language?" In Proceedings of the 8th International Conference on Music Perception and Cognition, Evanston, IL, 2004, 88-89.

[15] G. Soley and E. E. Hannon, "Infants Prefer the Musical Meter of Their Own Culture: A Cross-Cultural Comparison," in Developmental Psychology 46(1), 2004, 286-292.

Programming Interactive Music Scores with INScore

D. Fober, S. Letz, Y. Orlarey
GRAME
Lyon - France
fober, letz, orlarey@grame.fr

F. Bevilacqua
IRCAM
Paris - France
Frederic.Bevilacqua@ircam.fr

ABSTRACT

INSCORE is an environment for the design of interactive music scores that includes an original event-based interaction system and a scripting language for associating arbitrary messages to these events. We extended the previous version by supporting scripting languages offering a great flexibility in the description of scores and in the interactions with scores. The textual format is directly derived from the OSC message format that was defined in the original INSCORE version. This article presents the scripting language and illustrates its ability to describe interactions based on events, while remaining in the temporal space. It also introduces the IRCAM gesture follower and how it is embedded into INSCORE to provide gestural interaction capabilities.

1. INTRODUCTION

INSCORE is a dynamic music score viewer that can be controlled in real-time via OSC messages as well as using OSC based scripts. It supports extended music scores [1], combining symbolic notation with arbitrary graphic objects. All the objects of a score have a time dimension and can be synchronized in a master/slave relationship i.e. any object can be placed in the time space of another object [2]. It can be used in concert, notably for interactive music pieces, for music analysis, for pedagogical applications, etc.

INSCORE has been designed in response to a lack of computer tools for music notation, which did not evolved in proportion to the new forms of musical creation (see eg [3] [4]). In particular, there is a significant gap between interactive music and the way it is statically written.

Music notation generated in interaction with live performance exists for more than a decade. As mentioned by Freeman [5], numerous approaches exist: selection of predetermined score excerpts [6], mixture of symbolic and graphic elements [7], use of unconventional graphical notation [8], complex staff based notation [9].

These works are based on custom tools, sometimes designed using Max, that are generally specifically suited to a composer approach. Didovsky used JMSL [10] to design interactive scores, but JMSL should be considered more as a programming language for Java applications developers than an environment for composers. Baird is using Lilypond [11] for audience interaction [12], that can't be considered as a real-time environment for generating music scores, although it works in Baird's context due to relaxed time constraints.

With the recent Bach [13] or MaxScore [14] environments, the symbolic dimension of the music notation starts to be accessible to interaction, first using Max and next the Live environment. However, they are not designed to support unconventional graphical notation, although it could be implemented in Max using Jitter for example.

A unified environment, covering symbolic and graphic notation, opened to real-time interaction is missing and INSCORE aims at fulfilling the needs emerging from the contemporary creation.

Designed to be controlled by OSC messages, INSCORE is naturally turned to an interactive use. The approach to music score programming is also supported by a scripting language based on an extension of the OSC messages, and providing interaction primitives based on *events*. These events are similar to those typically available for user interfaces management (e.g. via Javascript DOM [15]), with an extension in the time domain.

The next section shows two examples of interactive scores, implemented in recent creations using INSCORE. Then it presents the message system and the interaction events, that allow both to describe the music score and to interact with it. Examples of uses are finally given, to illustrate the expressive capabilities of the system.

2. INTERACTIVE MUSIC SCORES

Today, interactive music is subject of convergent artistic and scientific interests. Interaction raises issues for the artistic work composition, description and performance as well. These issues are addressed in the temporal aspects of interactive scores [16] or control [17], and are related to the music piece computation.

For interactive pieces notation, two recent works have used INSCORE to create dynamic scores with original approaches, that also reflect the needs of the contemporary music creation. These works are *Calder's Violin* and *Alien Lands*.

2.1 Calder's Violin

Calder's violin, composed by Richard Hoadley, has been created in Cambridge in October 2011. The piece is defined as a composition for violin and automatic piano. Dynamic symbolic music notation is generated algorithmically and presented to the musician (figure 1) in real-time. This score is played by the musician in parallel to sounds generated by the computer. The technological environment includes SuperCollider for the audio programming and INScore for the music notation. For more details, you can refer to [18].

Figure 1. Calder's Violin: sample of music notation.

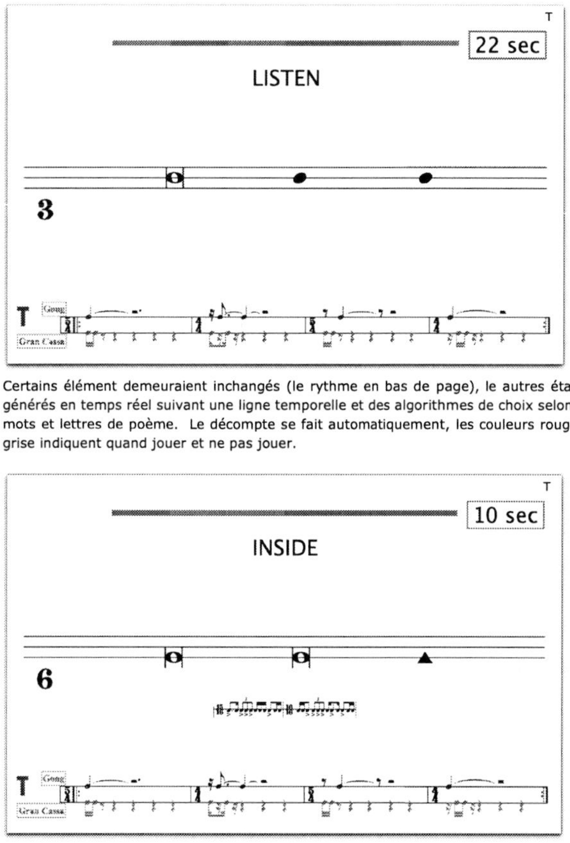

Figure 2. Alien Lands : a complex automatic music score.

3. MUSIC SCORE DESIGN USING MESSAGES

The basic principle for the description of a music score consists in sending OSC messages to the system to create the different score components and to control their attributes, both in graphic and time spaces.

3.1 Format of the messages

The global format of the INScore messages is illustrated in figure 3 in a syntax diagram specified in EBNF. It consists in a specialization of the OSC specification that may be viewed as *object oriented*, where the address indicates the target object of the message, `method` indicates a method of the target object and `params`, the method parameters. An INScore message could be viewed as a method call of an object of the score.

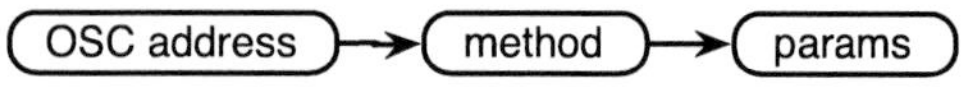

Figure 3. Format of the INScore messages.

The system includes messages to control the objects graphical attributes (position, color, scale, rotation, effects ...) to control their temporal attributes (date, time), to express the relationship between graphic and time spaces, to synchronize different score components, to draw *graphic* signals, and to manage interaction events.

Example 1

Changing the `x` position of an object named `obj`. The address describes the objects hierarchy: `obj` is embedded in a score named `scene` that is included in the application which address is `ITL`.

```
/ITL/scene/obj x -0.5
```

3.2 Scripting

Although intended to be sent as packets over a network, the OSC messages can be expressed under a textual form, which constitutes the file storage format of a score. This textual form has been extended to enforce the scripting capabilities of the system. The INScore viewer supports loading or drag & drop of scripts files, which is equivalent to send the enclosed or evaluated OSC messages to the system.

3.2.1 Extended adresses

The OSC addresses have been extended to support targeting external applications and/or stations (Figure 4). It allows to initialize both the music score and external resources as well using the same script.

Figure 4. Addressing scheme extension.

Example 2

Initializes a score with a Guido Music Notation file [19] and sends a message to an external application listening on port `12000` on a station named `host.adomain.net`. The semicolon (;) is used as a message terminator in a script.

```
/ITL/scene/score set gmnf 'myscore.gmn';
host.adomain.net:12000/run 1;
```

3.2.2 Variables

Variables have been introduced to allow sharing of parameters between messages. A variable associates an identifier and a parameter list or a list of messages (Figure 5). Variables can be used as message parameter using the form `$identifier`.

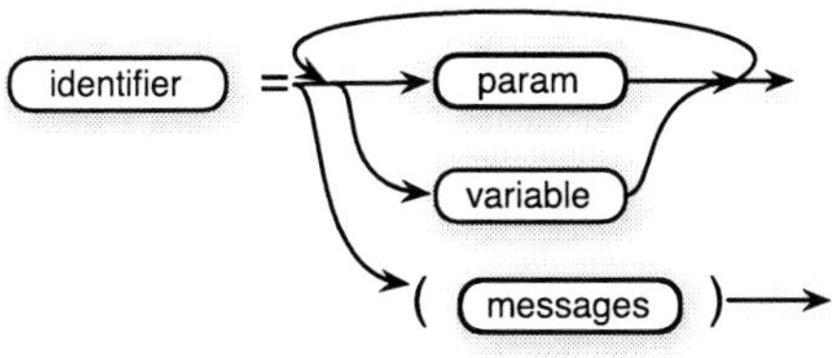

Figure 5. Variables.

Example 3
Variable declaration and use. The exclamation point (!) starts a line comment.

```
color = 200 200 200;
! using the previous color variable
colorwithalpha = $color 100;
/ITL/scene/obj color $colorwithalpha;
```

3.2.3 Languages

INSCORE scripts support programming languages like javascript (default) or lua. The corresponding sections are indicated by angle brackets as in html (Figure 6). The code is evaluated at parse time and the output of the evaluation should be a set of INSCORE messages that will be next parsed in place of the corresponding section.

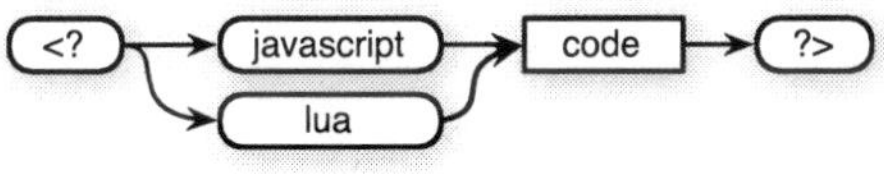

Figure 6. Languages.

4. EVENTS BASED INTERACTION

Interaction is based on associations between events and messages. The messages are sent when the event occurs. The general format of the messages to create such associations is described in Figure 7.

Figure 7. Format of an interaction message.

4.1 Events typologie

Events defined by the system are basically 1) typical user interface events (e.g. mouse click and mouse move) and 2) events defined in the time domain (table 1). This typology has been extended to *gesture events*, described in section 6.3.

Graphic domain	Time domain
mouseDown	timeEnter
mouseUp	timeLeave
mouseEnter	durEnter
mouseLeave	durLeave
mouseMove	

Table 1. Main events of the system.

In the time domain, an event is triggered when an object date enters (`timeEnter`) or leaves (`timeLeave`) a time interval defined by 2 dates, or when an object duration enters (`durEnter`) or leaves (`durLeave`) an interval bounded by 2 durations.

4.2 Contextual variables

A *contextual variable* is a variable which value depends on an event context (unlike script variables that are evaluated when loading the script). Most of these variables concern the graphic domain and are associated to user interface events; they give the mouse position at the time of the event occurrence and expressed in different reference spaces (`$x $y $sx $sy`). A variable can also give the date corresponding to the current mouse position (`$date`). When an event occurs, the associated messages are evaluated because they may refer to contextual variables.

Example 4
Asking an object to follow the mouse down. The comma (,) is used as separator in a messages list.

```
/ITL/scene/obj watch mouseDown (
      /ITL/scene/obj x '$sx',
      /ITL/scene/obj y '$sy' );
```

4.3 Managing interaction states

Every score component includes a stack to store interaction states. The methods `push` and `pop` are provided to push the current interaction state to the stack and to pop and restore a state from the top of the stack. Examples are given in section 5.3.

5. USE CASES

5.1 Page turning

A simple use case consists in automatic page turning. An object can watch the time intervals corresponding to the different pages and recall a page when it enters its time interval. Time is specified in music time where 1 is a whole note. Note that the `obj` object could be a cursor moving on the score as well.

```
!  first page duration is 12 whole notes
/ITL/scene/obj watch timeEnter 0 12
            (/ITL/scene/score page 1);
/ITL/scene/obj watch timeEnter 12 24
            (/ITL/scene/score page 2);
etc.
```

5.2 Sequence of interactions

Interaction messages described in figure 7 accept arbitrary messages to be associated to an event. Thus it is possible to associate an interaction message to an event and to describe sequences of interaction.

Example 5
Decription of an interaction sequence based on mouse clicks: the first click changes the object color, the second affects the scaling, the third rotates the object, the fourth modifies the scale too...

```
/ITL/scene/obj watch mouseDown (
  /ITL/scene/obj color 100 100 255,
  /ITL/scene/obj watch mouseDown (
    /ITL/scene/obj scale 1.4,
    /ITL/scene/obj watch mouseDown (
      /ITL/scene/obj angle 45.  ,
      /ITL/scene/obj watch mouseDown (
        /ITL/scene/obj scale 0.8 ))));
```

5.3 Looping a sequence of interactions

A sequence of interactions can be executed n times using the `push` and `pop` methods.

Example 6
Executing a sequence of 2 interactions 3 times.

```
/ITL/scene/obj watch mouseDown (
  /ITL/scene/obj color 255 0 0,
  /ITL/scene/obj watch mouseDown (
    /ITL/scene/obj color 0 0 255,
    /ITL/scene/obj pop ))
/ITL/scene/obj push;
/ITL/scene/obj push;
```

Example 7
Executing a sequence of 2 interactions in an infinite loop.

```
/ITL/scene/obj watch mouseDown (
  /ITL/scene/obj push,
  /ITL/scene/obj color 255 0 0,
  /ITL/scene/obj watch mouseDown (
    /ITL/scene/obj color 0 0 255,
    /ITL/scene/obj pop ))
```

5.4 Interaction in the time domain

The sequence of interactions described above (section 5.2) could be defined in the time domain using associations between messages and time events and by moving the object in time. With this approach, it is possible to access the events in a random order but also to control the time flow of the events.

This kind of description combines event based approach, non-sequential access and temporal control.

Example 8
Description of an interaction sequence using time events that are triggered when the object enters consecutives time zones, which duration is a whole note.

```
/ITL/scene/obj watch timeEnter 1 2
     (/ITL/scene/obj color 100 100 255);
/ITL/scene/obj watch timeEnter 2 3
     (/ITL/scene/obj scale 1.4);
/ITL/scene/obj watch timeEnter 3 4
     (/ITL/scene/obj angle 45.);
/ITL/scene/obj watch timeEnter 4 5
     (/ITL/scene/obj scale 0.8);
```

6. INTERACTION WITH GESTURES

INScore may embed the IRCAM gesture follower as an external plugin. The corresponding objects are similar to signals from input viewpoint. They provide specific interaction events and may also generate streams of messages.

6.1 Principle of the gesture follower

The IRCAM gesture follower if a tool to perform template-based recognition [20, 21]. Technically, the algorithm is available as a C++ library that can be implemented in various environments (up to now the objet called *gf* was the most common instantiation of the library in the Max environment). The gestures can be any type of temporal multidimensional times series, that must be regularly time-sampled. Typically, a drawing is a two-dimensional signal, but other signal types can be used such as three, six or nine dimension data obtained from inertial measurement units.

The gesture follower, as most recognition system, is based on two steps. The first step, called *learning*, corresponds to setting a series of "templates". Each template is used to set a Markov Chain modeling the times series. The second step, called *following*, corresponds to "compare" incoming data flow with the stored templates. Technically, the decoding is based on the forward procedure to estimate *likelihoods* of the incoming data to match each templates (note that the forward procedure is incremental compared to a standard Viterbi algorithms). The gesture follower also outputs the *position* (or *temporal index*) that is an estimation of the corresponding current position within the templates, and the estimated *speed* (relative to their templates).

6.2 Gesture follower object

Provided that the corresponding plugin is available, a *gesture follower* object may be embedded in a score. It is created with a fixed set of named gestures to be recognized and thus, its address space is automatically extended to the set of named gestures.

Example 9
Address space of a gesture follower named *myFollower* created to handle 2 gestures named *gestureA* and *gestureB*

```
/ITL/scene/myFollower
/ITL/scene/myFollower/gestureA
/ITL/scene/myFollower/gestureB
```

A gesture follower may take 3 states: a learning state, a following state and an idle state. It receives values that are stored to the corresponding gesture when in learning state, analysed to recognize a gesture when in following state and ignored when idle. Each time the follower receives data in the following state, it produces a set of likelihood, position and speed for each of the gestures.

6.3 Gestures events

Specific events are available from gestures and depends on the gesture state. A gesture may be *active* or *idle*: it is active when its likelihood is greater or equal than a given threshold, otherwise it is idle (figure 8).

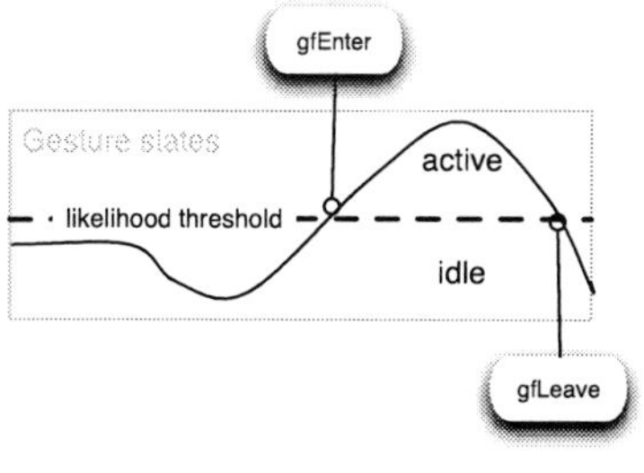

Figure 8. A gesture states and events.

Two specific events are associated to gestures :

- `gfEnter`: triggered when a gesture state moves from idle to active,
- `gfLeave`: triggered when a gesture state moves from active to idle.

6.4 Gesture streams

A gesture supports messages streaming, depending on its state. Figure 9 presents the `send` method that associates a list of messages to the `active` or `idle` state of a gesture. The messages are sent when the gesture follower state is refreshed i.e. when it is in following mode and each time it receives data.

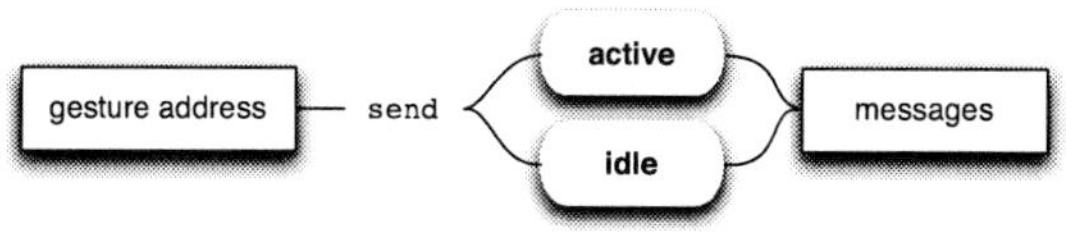

Figure 9. Associating messages to gesture states.

6.5 Variables defined in the context of gestures

Specific variables may be used by messages associated to gesture events or streams:

- `$likelihood` : gives the current gesture likelihood,
- `$pos` : indicates the current position in the gesture,
- `$speed` : indicates the current speed of the gesture.

These variables support scaling and translation of their values when suffixed using an interval. The values denoted by `$pos[1,5]` represents the current position scaled between 1 and 5.

Example 10

Using a gesture to move a cursor date from 0 to 1.

```
/ITL/scene/gf/gesture send active
        (/ITL/scene/cursor date $pos);
```

7. CONCLUSION

Using the OSC protocol to design a scripting language constitutes an original approach which is simple to apprehend for people familiar with OSC. While none of classical programming languages constructs exists in INSCORE scripts, programming capabilities emerge from the objects behavior and leads to new conceptions of music score design.

The association of messages to events reveals to be a simple, powerful and homogeneous way to describe dynamic music scores. A single textual script serves the need of both the static and dynamic parts of the score, leading to new kind of programming e.g. moving of objects in the time domain using an external application when these objects are designed using behaviors linked to time intervals.

This system opens a new dimension to the score components that were previously passive objects: they could react to messages but didn't send messages by themselves. While becoming active and able to send messages, autonomous dynamic behaviors emerge and since each object may embed its own behavior, the system may be viewed as a parallel programmable music score.

However, an external application or the user interaction is necessary to move objects in time. This is currently not considered as a limitation since external applications remain also necessary for the music itself.

Acknowledgments

This research has been conducted in the framework of the INEDIT project that is funded by the French National Research Agency [ANR-12-CORD-009-03].

8. REFERENCES

[1] D. Fober, C. Daudin, Y. Orlarey, and S. Letz, "Interlude - a framework for augmented music scores," in *Proceedings of the Sound and Music Computing conference - SMC'10*, 2010, pp. 233–240.

[2] D. Fober, C. Daudin, S. Letz, and Y. Orlarey, "Time synchronization in graphic domain - a new paradigm for augmented music scores," in *Proceedings of the International Computer Music Conference*, ICMA, Ed., 2010, pp. 458–461.

[3] T. Magnusson, "Algorithms as scores: Coding live music," *Leonardo Music Journal*, vol. 21, pp. 19–23, 2011.

[4] J. Freeman, "Bringing instrumental musicians into interactive music systems through notation," *Leonardo Music Journal*, vol. 21, no. 15-16, 2011.

[5] ——, "Extreme sight-reading, mediated expression, and audience participation: Real-time music notation in live performance," *Comput. Music J.*, vol. 32, no. 3, pp. 25–41, Sep. 2008. [Online]. Available: http://dx.doi.org/10.1162/comj.2008.32.3.25

[6] D. Kim-Boyle, "Musical score generation in valses and etudes," in *Proceedings of the 2005 conference on New interfaces for musical expression*, ser. NIME '05. Singapore, Singapore: National University of Singapore, 2005, pp. 238–239. [Online]. Available: http://dl.acm.org/citation.cfm?id=1085939.1086007

[7] G. E. Winkler, "The realtime score. A missing link in computer music performance." in *Proceedings of the Sound and Music Computing conference - SMC'04*, 2004.

[8] J. Gutknecht, A. Clay, and T. Frey, "Goingpublik: using realtime global score synthesis," in *Proceedings of the 2005 conference on New interfaces for musical expression*, ser. NIME '05. Singapore, Singapore: National University of Singapore, 2005, pp. 148–151. [Online]. Available: http://dl.acm.org/citation.cfm?id=1085939.1085980

[9] N. Didkovsky, "Recent compositions and performance instruments realized in the java music specification language," in *Proceedings of the 2004 international computer music conference*, 2004, pp. 746–749.

[10] N. Didkovsky and P. Burk, "Java music specification language, an introduction and overview," in *Proceedings of the International Computer Music Conference*, 2001, pp. 123–126.

[11] H.-W. Nienhuys and J. Nieuwenhuizen, "LilyPond, a system for automated music engraving," in *Proceedings of the XIV Colloquium on Musical Informatics*, 2003.

[12] K. C. Baird, "Real-time generation of music notation via audience interaction using python and gnu lilypond," in *Proceedings of the 2005 conference on New interfaces for musical expression*, ser. NIME '05. Singapore, Singapore: National University of Singapore, 2005, pp. 240–241. [Online]. Available: http://dl.acm.org/citation.cfm?id=1085939.1086008

[13] A. Agostini and D. Ghisi, "Bach: An environment for computer-aided composition in max," in *Proceedings of International Computer Music Conference*, ICMA, Ed., 2012, pp. 373–378.

[14] N. Didkovsky and G. Hajdu, "Maxscore: Music notation in max/msp," in *Proceedings of International Computer Music Conference*, ICMA, Ed., 2008.

[15] B. Höhrmann, P. Le Hégaret, and T. Pixley, "Document object model (dom) level 3 events specification," World Wide Web Consortium, Working Draft WD-DOM-Level-3-Events-20071221, December 2007.

[16] A. Allombert, "Aspects temporels d'un système de partitions musicales interactives pour la composition et l'exécution," Ph.D. dissertation, Université Bordeaux 1, Oct. 2009. [Online]. Available: http://tel.archives-ouvertes.fr/tel-00516350

[17] A. Cont, "Antescofo: Anticipatory synchronization and control of interactive parameters in computer music." in *Proceedings of International Computer Music Conference*, ICMA, Ed., 2008.

[18] R. Hoadley, "Calder's violin: Real-time notation and performance through musically expressive algorithms," in *Proceedings of International Computer Music Conference*, ICMA, Ed., 2012, pp. 188–193.

[19] H. Hoos, K. Hamel, K. Renz, and J. Kilian, "The GUIDO Music Notation Format - a Novel Approach for Adequately Representing Score-level Music." in *Proceedings of the International Computer Music Conference*. ICMA, 1998, pp. 451–454.

[20] F. Bevilacqua, B. Zamborlin, A. Sypniewski, N. Schnell, F. Guédy, and N. Rasamimanana, "Continuous realtime gesture following and recognition," in *In Embodied Communication and Human-Computer Interaction, volume 5934 of Lecture Notes in Computer Science*. Springer Berlin / Heidelberg, 2010, pp. 73—84.

[21] F. Bevilacqua, N. Schnell, N. Rasamimanana, B. Zamborlin, and F. Guédy, "Online gesture analysis and control of audio processing," in *Musical Robots and Interactive Multimodal Systems*, ser. Springer Tracts in Advanced Robotics, J. Solis and K. Ng, Eds. Springer Berlin Heidelberg, 2011, vol. 74, pp. 127–142. [Online]. Available: http://dx.doi.org/10.1007/978-3-642-22291-7_8

Real-time event sequencing without a visual interface

Tiago Fernandes Tavares
University of Campinas
School of Electrical and
Computer Engineering
tavares@dca.fee.unicamp.br

Adriano Monteiro
University of Campinas
Interdisciplinary Nucleus for
Sound Communication
monteiro_adc@gmail.com

Jayme G. A. Barbedo
EMBRAPA Agricultural Informatics
jbarbedo@gmail.com

Romis Attux
University of Campinas
School of Electrical and
Computer Engineering
attux@dca.fee.unicamp.br

Jônatas Manzolli
University of Campinas
Interdisciplinary Nucleus for
Sound Communication
manzolli@nics.unicamp.br

ABSTRACT

In electronic music, it is often useful to build loops from discrete events, such as playing notes or triggering digital effects. This process generally requires using a visual interface, as well as pre-defining tempo and time quantization. We present a novel digital musical instrument capable of looping events without using visual interfaces or explicit knowledge about tempo or time quantization. The instrument is built based on a prediction algorithm that detects repetitive patterns over time, allowing the construction of rhythmic layers in real-time performances. It has been used in musical performances, where it showed to be adequate in contexts that allow improvisation.

1. INTRODUCTION

Drum machines are electronic instruments frequently used to create rhythm sections in musical pieces using loops of drum notes. A generalization of this concept involves looping not simply drum notes, but generic discrete-event-related messages, allowing the periodic execution of actions such as switching timbre or triggering audio effects. To build a loop sequence, it is common to use a grid interface, like the one shown in Figure 1, which is also used to define the desired tempo and the time quantization in the excerpt.

In order to properly interact with other musicians, a drum-sequencer player must pre-define (or, at least, detect) the musical tempo and an adequate time quantization. This aspect is also present in novel interfaces that do not use the grid display but use the same paradigm, such as the Rhythmicator [2] or the Sinkapater [3]. Those interfaces are used to plan beats and beat sequences, which is significantly different from playing drums or even tapping rhythms.

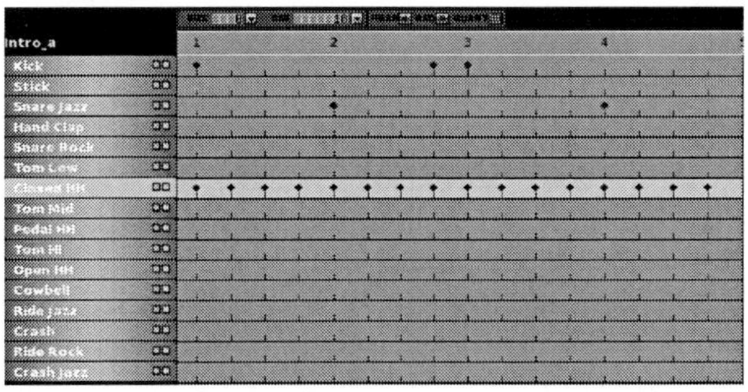

Figure 1. Drum sequencing interface in Hydrogen [1] software.

Another technique that can be used to create meaningful repetitions is to apply carefully arranged delay lines and feedback so that an audio sample is played in a pattern defined by the musician, as in RhythmDelay [4] or SDelay [5]. Using this technique, a musician can build audio loops on-the-fly, without the need of a grid interface. However, delay lines lack the symbolic-level flexibility of drum machines, as it is hard to change events (for example, changing all kick drums for cymbals) or to modify the musical tempo without affecting the timbres.

In this paper, we present a novel digital musical instrument that is capable of looping general event sequences that are played by the musician, without predefining or quantizing tempo. The instrument may be played using any interface that generates discrete events, from high-end MIDI drum interfaces to low-cost game controllers. It is implemented as a patch for PureData [6] and can be freely downloaded.

The event looping process is based on an online-learning algorithm that is used as follows. As the musician plays a sequence of events, a continuation for that is predicted by a string matching algorithm. When the user triggers the automation, the system starts yielding the predicted continuations and feeding them back into itself, creating an event sequence that corresponds to continuing the pattern played previously by the musician, without any explicit inputs regarding tempo or time-quantization.

The proposed method relies on a discrete-symbol representation for audio, which means that it possesses the flexibility of drum machines. To use it, however, the musician must employ skills that are closer to playing drums or tapping rhythms than to using visual interfaces. Also, the implementation in a free, open-source environment allows it to be used in several creative ways.

This paper is organized as follows. In Section 2, previous approaches on the automatic detection of patterns in music are presented. The event forecasting algorithm is described in Section 3, and implementation issues are discussed in Section 4. Experiments showing advantages and limitations of the proposed instrument are discussed in Section 5. Section 6 brings further discussions on the results. Last, Section 7 brings some conclusive remarks.

2. PREVIOUS WORK

The metaphor of a grid-looping environment, such as the usual drum machine [1], has been employed in many innovative systems. Two remarkable examples are the Rhythmicator [2], which uses a probabilistic model to create drum tracks directly from audio analysis, and the Sinkapater [3], which allows each drum track to use a different measure length, creating polyrhythms that are usually hard to be played by a human being [7]. In both cases, there is an inherent need to predefine tempo and beat, which, as discussed above, is a skill that is foreign to the playing of drums itself.

To avoid using these concepts – tempo and beat – it is necessary to automate the process of building the event loops. As shown in early studies by Shannon [8] and Solomonoff [9, 10], sequences of symbols can be predicted, as long as they present a certain degree of repetition. This assumption is fit for event loops, as the same pattern is, in general, repeated many times over a musical piece.

Assayag *et al.* [11] developed a system capable of forecasting continuations for melodies. In their work, a codebook built from a data corpus is used to predict plausible continuations for a given piece. The outcomes of this system were evaluated as "repetitive", which may be expected from the deterministic nature of the prediction system. Also, building a codebook is a slow process that cannot be done in real time, and the system only supports quantized tempo.

To avoid the repetition problem, there has been an effort towards developing systems capable of learning rhythms from a corpus and predicting new patterns. Techniques such as rule-based probabilistic recombination [12], artificial life [13] and genetic algorithms [14] were used in this context. This gives rise to another form of human-computer interaction, in which the machine yields unpredictable outcomes.

A characteristic that is common to all musical prediction methods cited above is that they rely on an exact timing precision. This can be achieved if strict timing quantization is used. However, the quantization implies in a pre-definition of tempo and beat.

We propose a system that receives as input a sequence of events and yields a possible continuation for these events. The yielded events may be re-inserted into the system using feedback, thus creating a loop of events that do not rely on explicit definitions of tempo or beat. The continuations are quickly learned, so the system may be used in real-time performances, and its behaviour is highly predictable, which gives the user great control of its outcomes.

A thorough explanation about the algorithm is presented in the next section.

3. PROPOSED SYSTEM

The proposed system assumes that events repeat within a particular piece or excerpt. This assumption allows simple, intuitive interactions with the system, as the process of designing a new loop becomes similar to that of showing a rhythmic pattern to a human being. Hence, the musician can have great control on the outcomes of the system, as if the usual grid interface was being used.

In the context of this work, each musical event n is represented by its *onset* s_n, that is, the time it happens, and its *label* l_n, which identifies the event. Using labels, events may be related to any description of discrete musical gestures desired by the musician, such as "play cymbal", "strongly play cymbal", "play random drum" or "activate reverb effect". As will be shown, the flexibility of the event label allows many creative uses of the system.

The system receives event-related messages through any device that yields discrete messages (such as MIDI instruments, OSC controllers or HID devices). The label and onset of the events are stored in an internal buffer of arbitrary size. The information in the internal buffer is used to predict the following event, as described below.

The forecasting algorithm is based on the assumption that the musician is playing a loop, a condition that has to be intentionally caused. When the user desires, the predictions may be used as inputs to the forecast system, creating a feedback loop and allowing the continuation of the event sequence. Preliminary tests showed that adding a reset functionality, which clears the internal buffer, made it easier to switch between different beats.

In the context of the prediction algorithm, two events n and m are considered equivalent if their label is the same ($l_n = l_m$) and their inter-onset intervals (IOIs), that is, the difference between their onset and the previous onsets, are within an allowed deviation ($\|s_n - s_{n-1} - (s_m - s_{m-1})\| \leq \alpha$). The algorithm, shown in Figure 2, aims at searching, within the last N recorded events, the longest subsequence $[M - K +$

$1 \dots M]$ whose events are equivalent to those in the subsequence $[N-K+1 \dots N]$. After the subsequence $[M-K+1 \dots M]$ is found, it is reasonable to assume that the continuation of the recorded excerpt (that is, event $N+1$) will be equivalent to that of the subsequence (event $M+1$).

procedure FORECAST($N, \boldsymbol{s}, \boldsymbol{l}, \alpha$)
  $\boldsymbol{d} \leftarrow$ array of N zeroes
  for $M = N-1$ to 2 **do** ▷ Search for repetitions
    $k \leftarrow 0$
    while $M-k>0$ and $l_{N-k} = l_{M-k}$ and $|(s_{N-k} - s_{N-k-1}) - (s_{M-k} - s_{M-k-1})| < \alpha$ **do**
      $k \leftarrow k+1$
    $\boldsymbol{d}_M \leftarrow k$
  ▷ Check if a subsequence was found
  if MAX(D) > 0 **then** ▷ If found
    $\hat{M} \leftarrow \arg\max D$
  else
    $\hat{M} \leftarrow N$
  ▷ Yield events
  $s_{N+1} = s_{\hat{M}+1} - s_m + s_N$
  $l_{N+1} = l_{\hat{M}+1}$
  return

Figure 2. Pseudo-code for event forecasting.

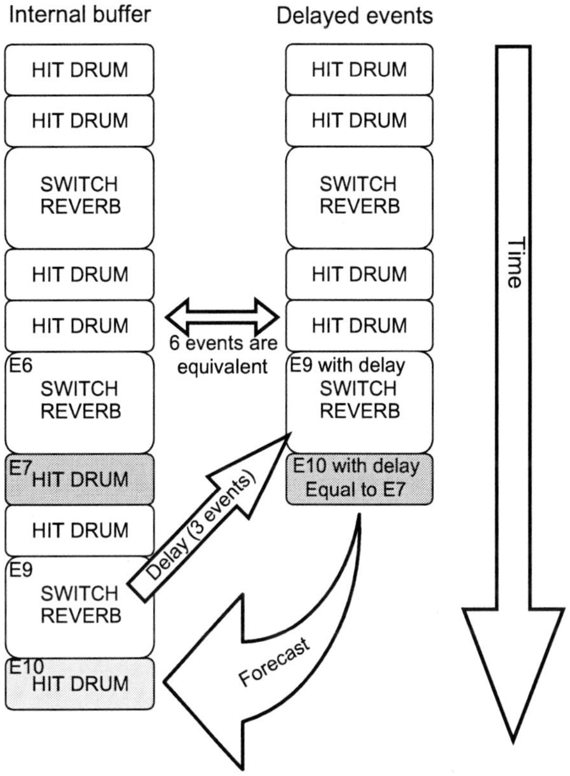

Figure 3. Example of a possible execution of the forecasting algorithm.

Figure 3 shows an example of a possible execution of the forecasting algorithm. The left column shows the internal buffer after the user has yielded a series of events, arbitrarily labeled "hit drum" and "switch reverb". After triggering event E9, the forecasting system detects that, if the buffer is delayed by three events, events E9 and E6, as well as the previous five events, are equivalent, which is a higher number of equivalent events than if any other delay was used.

In this example, event E7 is chosen as the most plausible continuation for the delayed sequence, generating the estimated E10 and is being used to build the yielded event. If event E10 is used by the system as an input, the next event to be yielded would be a "hit drum", then a "switch reverb", then a "hit drum" again, creating a cycle of repetitions. Hence, feedback may be used to create event loops in real time.

Next section discusses implementation and usability issues.

4. IMPLEMENTATION ISSUES

The proposed instrument was implemented as a patch for PureData [6]. This allows users to employ their favorite interfaces and sound designs, as well as their own compositional ideas. It is an open-source project, which means that the algorithm may be easily ported to other contexts.

The patch works in two modes: **observation**, or manual, and **prediction**, or automatic. In the observation mode, the system receives inputs from the user and tries to predict the next event that will be received. When the prediction mode is triggered, the system receives its own predictions, instead of user-generated events, as inputs.

Additional functionality may be easily implemented by the user, but not as part of the system itself. Several predictor instances in parallel, for example, may be used to achieve polyrhythms. Also, the actions related to an event must be defined by the user: playing a drum sample or switching the configurations of an effect, for example.

5. EXPERIMENTAL PERFORMANCES

The experiments in this section aim at highlighting interesting features and also drawbacks of the proposed system, gathering information on how it can be helpful to musicians and how it may be improved. For this purpose, the system was used in a solo and an accompanied performance. The recorded audio material can be listened to at the URL `http://www.dca.fee.unicamp.br/~tavares/Looper/index.html`.

The first performance – solo – aimed at showing the main capabilities of the instrument. The piece was intentionally composed so that a drum sequence and an effect switch were independently looped, allowing another layer of percussion to be freely played. Spectrograms are used to show the most important parts.

The second performance – duo – had the goal of showing that the drum loops could be quickly arranged and played in an arbitrary tempo. The piece was an improvisation in which digital effects were manually played while drums were looped using the proposed system. The piece was analyzed based on the impression of both musicians and on auditory characteristics of the recording.

5.1 Solo performance

The first experiment was based on composing and playing a short piece using the proposed instrument. The composer and performer was one of the authors of this paper. A low-cost gamepad controller was used to tap rhythms and to control the behaviour of the prediction algorithm.

The piece is based on two drum synthesizers that yield samples to a clip-based distortion that, in turn, yields a change in timbre. The drum onsets and the use of the distortion are controlled by the musician and can be individually looped using separated instances of the proposed system. By looping drum patterns, a base rhythm for the piece can be generated, whereas looping switches in the distortion creates different electronic ambiences that give more variations to the piece.

Figure 4 shows the instant the looping process is triggered by the musician as a vertical black line – the previous events are manually controlled. After triggering the prediction mode, the musician stopped playing. As it can be seen, the algorithm successfully continued the manually-played pattern.

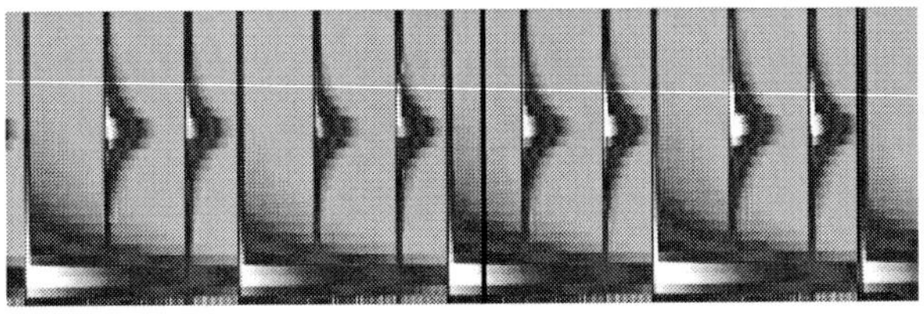

Figure 4. Spectrogram showing the prediction of a drum loop.

Figure 5 depicts the results of looping the distortion switch, which is triggered in the moment displayed as a vertical black line. As it can be seen, when the distortion is used more harmonics are present. This adds to the drum loops, creating a more complex rhythm.

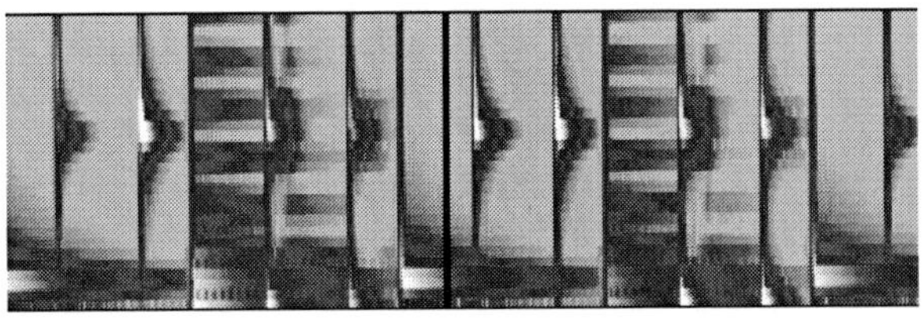

Figure 5. Spectrogram showing the prediction of distortion triggers.

Last, Figure 6 shows a particular excerpt in which both the drum and the effect loops are active. The musician manually plays a new layer of drum events. These events are not looped, but contribute to create a rhythm that would be hard to achieve by manual playing without the overlap of automated loop patterns.

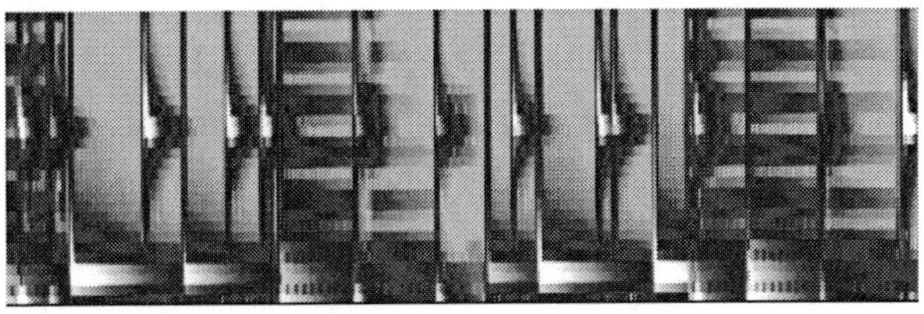

Figure 6. Spectrogram showing the use of an additional percussion layer on top of the event and the percussion loops.

In the audio recording, it could be noted that the developed rhythms tend to sound natural, despite of the lack of dynamics caused by the use of a low-cost controller. The transitions between musical sections were smooth, which is a consequence of having to play each new loop pattern that would be used – this prevented sudden transitions between complex patterns. These characteristics were also observed in the accompanied performance, as shown below.

5.2 Accompanied performance

In the second experiment, the proposed system was used in a guitar-electronics duo. The electronic percussion accompaniment, based on two tabla samples, was played over an improvised guitar. The guitar and the electronic parts were played, respectively, by an invited musician and by one of the authors of this paper, who used a low-cost gamepad controller to tap rhythms and control the behaviour of the prediction algorithm.

The guitar player stated that, while playing, there was no need to explicitly think about tempo or musical sections, because they emerged naturally from playing. According to the statement, this flexibility allowed the musician to enhance the focus on other musical aspects, such as dynamics and phrasing. Ultimately, this lead to a feel of flow, which is frequently not the case when playing with drum sequencers, as they are bounded to pre-defined tempo, swing and measures.

The electronics player observed that, as it is easy to switch between the automatic and the manual modes of operation, the percussion parts could be quickly rearranged. The interaction with the guitar player felt more natural than if a grid interface was used, because using the system with a game controller is more similar to tapping rhythms. Also, while the automatic operation was used, other actions could be performed – manually playing another percussion layer or triggering other digital effects.

In the audio recording, it was noticeable that the feeling of steadiness, often present when using drum machines, was only present in few passages. Hence the proposed instrument allows using steady beats, but not as a requirement of the instrument. In spite of the tempo flexibility, there was no variation in the loudness of the drum beats, as the physical interface (a game controller) did not capture dynamics.

In the audio recording, the feeling of steadiness, caused by the quantized tempo often present when using grid interfaces, was significantly reduced. Hence, the proposed instrument allows for a steady rhythm, but not as an imposition of the instrument (as it would be the case for a grid interface). However, due to the nature of the game controller used, no information on dynamics was gathered, so the percussion is clearly played with the same loudness at all times.

6. DISCUSSION

This section discusses characteristics of the proposed instrument, highlighting the main differences regarding the previous approaches.

A feature that must be considered is that the instrument does not pre-define a physical interface for usage nor a sound design. These parts of the interaction must be composed by the user, which allows for great flexibility, but also require the user to employ a certain level of expertise. A possible way to solve this is by developing pre-set configurations for common use cases, but it must be considered that developing own interfaces and sound designs is frequently an important part of modern musical composition processes.

The instrument allows a quick development of rhythm loops and does not require a visual interface or any pre-definition of tempo or beat. Also, the same interface that is used to develop the loops can be used to build a layer of freely improvised drums. This means that a the instrument is potentially more useful in contexts that allow for flexibility and improvisation.

Since there is no visual interface or explicit notations, there is no way to store rhythms for later use. This also indicates that the instrument is suitable for flexible and improvised scenarios. On the other hand, its applications in offline composition are limited, as there is no visual feedback regarding the stored sequences.

The instrument delivers great control of the sequence that will be played, because it simply continues patterns played by the musician. This behaviour is close, but not exactly the same as, the one yielded by the method proposed by Assayag *et al.* [11], as it is deterministic and learned from data yielded by a human being in real-time. Hence, the system does not aim at generating new sequences as the previous approaches discussed above [12–14].

However, it is possible to change the outcomes algorithm by increasing the onset tolerance α to values that are close to a typical inter-onset interval. In this case, the algorithm can yield unexpected continuations for a sequence. Although this is not the original purpose of the system, interesting sequences can emerge from this phenomenon.

Overall, the proposed system has presented great musical potential in improvised performances. It reinforces the paradigm of using multiple layers to build a piece. However, its applications to offline musical composition are limited, as there is no interface allowing the user to review the current content of the buffer.

Next section presents conclusive remarks.

7. CONCLUSION

We presented a novel digital instrument aimed at sequencing events without the need for visual interface or pre-definitions of tempo, measure or time quantization. The core of the instrument is a string matching algorithm that quickly learns patterns played by a human musician and continues them in real-time. The instrument was used in two musical performances, one solo and one duo, and was evaluated both by its user and by the accompanying musician.

The proposed instrument is shown to be adequate to improvised contexts, in which its quick response may be employed at its best. It allows the rapid generation of multi-layer rhythmic figures, as well as the automation of effect triggers. Also, allows using abilities that are closer to playing acoustic drums, such as tapping rhythms, which greatly favours its use in accompanied improvisation.

An aspect of the instrument that remains unexplored is the possibility of transforming its data, thus generating new sequences from user inputs. Doing this without using explicit time quantization and, at the same time, preserving the user's intention, is a topic that should be studied in future work.

8. REFERENCES

[1] Hydrogen. Hydrogen advanced drum machine for gnu/linux. [Online]. Available: http://www.hydrogen-music.org/

[2] G. Sioros and C. Guedes, "Automatic rhythmic performance in Max/MSP: the kin. rhythmicator," in *Proceedings of the International Conference on New Interfaces for Musical Expression*, Oslo, Norway, 2011, pp. 88–91. [Online]. Available: http://www.nime2011.org/proceedings/papers/B16-Sioros.pdf

[3] J. Harriman, "Sinkapater - an untethered beat sequencer," in *Proceedings of the International Conference on New Interfaces for Musical Expression (NIME)*, G. Essl, B. Gillespie, M. Gurevich, and S. O'Modhrain, Eds. Ann Arbor, Michigan: University of Michigan, May 21-23 2012.

[4] P. Community. Rhythmdelay. [Online]. Available: http://puredata.hurleur.com/sujet-8421-electronics-two-rhythm-delay-steroids/

[5] AudioMulch. Sdelay. [Online]. Available: http://www.audiomulch.com/help/contraption-ref/SDelay

[6] P. community. Puredata. [Online]. Available: http://puredata.info/

[7] J. J. Summers and T. M. Kennedy, "Strategies in the production of a 5 : 3 polyrhythm," *Human Movement Science*, vol. 11, no. 12, pp. 101 - 112, 1992. [Online]. Available: http://www.sciencedirect.com/science/article/pii/016794579290053E

[8] C. E. Shannon, "Prediction and entropy of printed english," *The Bell System Technical Journal*, vol. 30, pp. 50–64, 1951.

[9] R. Solomonoff, "A formal theory of inductive inference, part i," *Information and Control*, vol. 7, no. 1, pp. 1–22, Mar 1964.

[10] ——, "A formal theory of inductive inference, part ii," *Information and Control*, vol. 7, no. 2, pp. 224–254, Jun 1964.

[11] G. Assayag, S. Dubnov, and O. Delerue, "Guessing the composer's mind: Applying universal prediction to musical style," in *Proceedings ICMC 99*, Beijing, China, 1999.

[12] M. Dahia, H. S. E. Trajano, G. Ramalho, C. Sandroni, and G. Cabral, "Using Patterns to Generate Rhythmic Accompaniment for Guitar," in *Proceedings of the SMC 2004*, Paris, France, 2004.

[13] J. M. Martins and E. R. Miranda, "Breeding Rhythms with Artificial Life," in *Proceedings of the SMC 2008*, Berlin, Germany, 2008.

[14] G. Bernardes, C. Guedes, and B. Pennycook, "Style Emulation of Drum Patterns by Means of Evolutionary Methods and Statistical Analysis," in *Proceedings of the SMC 2010*, Oslo, Norway, 2010. [Online]. Available: http://smcnetwork.org/files/proceedings/2010/26.pdf

MELODY BOUNCE: MOBILE RHYTHMIC INTERACTION FOR CHILDREN

Stefano Baldan
University of Milan
stefano.baldan@unimi.it

Stefania Serafin
Aalborg University Copenhagen
sts@create.aau.dk

Amalia De Götzen
Aalborg University Copenhagen
ago@create.aau.dk

ABSTRACT

This paper presents an audio-based game for mobile devices, designed to develop rhythmical and timing abilities in elementary-school-aged children. Developing such skills is believed to be very important for social interaction and interpersonal coordination. Moreover, increasing evidence suggests that rhythmicity has a direct influence on other cognitive abilities such as motor coordination and sustaining attention. The game makes exclusive use of motion-based input and non-verbal audio feedback, being therefore equally enjoyable by children which might speak different languages and might or might not have visual impairments. The game logic is inherently collaborative and multiplayer, in order to promote a sense of inclusion of the child among the group of players. The game design is heavily inspired by observations of children's activities in schools, which are usually characterized by strong rhythmical patterns.

1. INTRODUCTION

Music plays a fundamental role in the life of every human being. Like verbal and visual languages, the art of organizing sounds has developed in every part of the world. There is wide agreement among music theorists and psychologists that our understanding of music is for the most part pre-cultural and wired in the structure of our auditory perceptual grouping [1].

Musical abilities are already present in very young children: even in the pre-kindergarten years children love to sing, play instruments, dance and listen to music [2]. As they grow up songs, rhymes and musical games become a crucial part of their social interactions and learning, with other children as well as with adults. Elementary-school-aged children eagerly sing full-voice songs learnt by their peers, by adults or through the media. They use musical utterances to make their playing activity more immersive and convincing, support the coordination of their movements with rhythmic chants or counting out loud. Those behaviors are found not only in organized games but also during free play, classroom work and any other kind of activity [3].

Figure 1. Children playing a rhythmic chant in the playground. Image courtesy: Mary Ann Moss

The value of these musical expressions often lays more in the social process they trigger rather than in the produced sound itself. To use the words of Christopher Small the act of *musicking* [4], namely the participation in a music-making activity in any capacity (for example by performing, listening, practicing, composing, or dancing), helps to create meaningful relations among all the participants. A performance which creates the right connections and fulfills the expectation of everyone involved, can be a very powerful framework to embed other activities such as teaching concepts belonging to different subjects, promoting positive social behaviors among the group, maintaining children physically and mentally engaged or asking for their attention.

Observing musical activities made by children, one of the most striking aspects is that they are characterized by very strong rhythmical patterns. Moreover, the rhythm is imposed not only through the production of sounds but also with the physical movement of the whole body. Starting from the 1920s, musical educators such as Dalcroze [5] and Orff [6] became aware of this, and started to base their teaching methods on these particular features of children play. Nevertheless, the importance of developing a good sense of rhythm and timing goes well beyond the context of playing games or music: work from Bernieri and Rosenthal shows how being rhythmically "in tune" with other people improves social relationships and what they call *interpersonal coordination* [7]. There is also evidence that rhythmicity directly influences other cognitive abilities like sustaining attention, controlling impulsivity and coordinating motion [8].

It is important to remember that in addition to actual world activities, like running in the playground or playing a musical instrument, today's children are getting more and more engaged with activities happening inside the digital world. A 2011 survey about 0 to 8-year-old children's media use in America indicates that while TV continues to be by far the most consumed medium by that age group, more than a quarter of screen time is spent on digital devices. At least half of all children now have access to a mobile device at home, and more than a quarter of all parents have downloaded *apps* for their children to use [9]. The motion-sensing and multimodal feedback capabilities offered by smartphones and tablet PCs open the possibility to develop digital games featuring a rich musical rhythmic interaction, which is so favored by children during their physical world activities.

2. RELATED WORK

From a Human Computer Interaction (HCI) perspective, rhythmical aspects and sound design for children are both relatively unexplored fields. In the work of Jylhä and Erkut [10], the potential of rhythmic interaction is investigated through the design of an application which uses rhythmical patterns generated by hand clapping to manipulate musical content. Their approach proves to be effective, especially in those cases where an eyes-free interaction is needed or desirable. Applications for mobile devices may fall in this category, because of the limited size of their display and because of the greater freedom of movement gained when performing motion-based gestures if the user is no more required to look at the screen.

The most promising efforts in sound design for children have probably been made in the context of audio-based games, namely computer games which rely on sound rather than on visual information as their primary feedback to the user. Eriksson and Gärdenfors [11] propose a set of guidelines for the design of computer games for visually impaired children, which they put into practice in the development of a collection of games for the Swedish Association of Talking Books and Braille. Even if not specifically addressed to children, research presented in [12] and [13] is interesting in that it investigates the use of non-verbal audio feedback in audio-based games. Avoiding spoken language allows the design of a game which is enjoyable by children who are not yet able to speak or which speak different languages.

The work of Michalowski et al. [14] concentrates on the relevance of rhythmic movements in general social interaction, through the design and implementation of a dancing robot for children. The system is capable to dance following a dominant rhythm, which can be extracted by the acoustic and visual information captured by its microphones and cameras. Observations of children's interactions with the robot at a public installation showed that when it was dancing in sync with the underlying music, users tended to spend more time with it and to behave themselves in a more rhythmically organized way.

Figure 2. The Whack-A-Mole arcade game

Digital systems focusing on rhythmic interaction are also being used for rehabilitation purposes. One example is the Interactive Metronome® [8], which combines motion sensing features, acoustic and visual feedbacks to provide a series of exercises designed to improve the timing abilities of the patients. The authors claim that training the sense of rhythm leads to appreciable improvements in many other skills like coordinating motion, sustaining attention, managing impulsivity and collaborating with others, and that patients suffering from disorders related to those skills (i.e. ADHD, dyslexia, autism and other similar conditions) benefit greatly from such a treatment.

3. GAME DESIGN

The work presented in this paper is a game which exploits rhythmic interaction to develop and improve children's musical abilities, sense of timing and social interactions. Particular efforts have been put in designing an experience which should be enjoyable per se but also suitable for basic musical education and ear training. To achieve this goals, design choices were driven by observing and trying to mimick the interactions that normally occur in self-organized playground games.

As already stated in section 1 sound production and rhythmic movement of the whole body are the most relevant aspects of such playground games, thus the decision to develop an application based on motion gestures as input and auditory feedback as output. This style of interaction seems to have great potentials in terms of ear training and enhancement of one's listening capabilities [15], enables accessibility to visual-impaired users [16] [17] and has relatively low requirements in terms of processing power compared to its visual-based counterparts [18] [19]. This last element makes audio-based games well suited for mobile or other embedded devices, which often have limited computing capabilities and very small displays.

Like children playground activities, the designed game needs to be played by multiple players at the same time. It should also engage children in a collaborative rather than competitive activity, in order to foster inclusion of every single member in the playing group and positive, constructive social connections. This is also one of the distinguishing features of the act of making music together: every single element contributes with his or her individual effort to build the common "voice" of the whole group.

The game logic needs to be simple enough to be immediately understandable and enjoyable by young children, yet provide for an engaging and amusing experience. In order to achieve that, we used the *Whac-A-Mole* arcade game (see Figure 2) as a source of inspiration. This all-time classic is around from the mid seventies, and since then has gathered a tremendous success in the physical as well as in the digital world. Lots of versions have been made, changing the subject to whack (moles, cartoon characters, celebrities and so on) or the "weapon" used to whack them (hammers, cakes, shotguns and much more). The notoriety of this game and the simplicity of its rules played a key role in the decision of using it as the starting point of our design.

The resulting game design is therefore an auditory variant of the Whac-A-Mole game for mobile devices. Children have to shake their devices whenever they hear a note coming from their speakers, and stay still when they hear notes coming from their neighbors. The goal is to "whack" as many notes as possible in sequence without mistakes in order to unfold the whole melody. Missed notes result in a failure sound and the restart of the melody from its beginning, while a full successful sequence triggers a high quality recorded version of the nursery rhyme as a reward sound.

4. IMPLEMENTATION

The game client is an app developed in Objective-C for iOS 4.3 or later, and communicates with a custom server developed in Python via text-based TCP messages. The client presents a minimal Graphical User Interface (GUI) (see Figure 3) consisting of two views: the main view is merely a wallpaper image occupying the whole screen, which serves mainly for aesthetic purposes and to give some visual feedback about the fact that the game is running. The settings view contains the controls to perform the match making: users can create a new game or join an already existing group. All in-game information is given uniquely by sound.

Gesture recognition is done processing raw data coming from the embedded accelerometer. When the sum of the magnitudes of the x, y, and z acceleration components raises above a certain threshold, a shake is detected. While

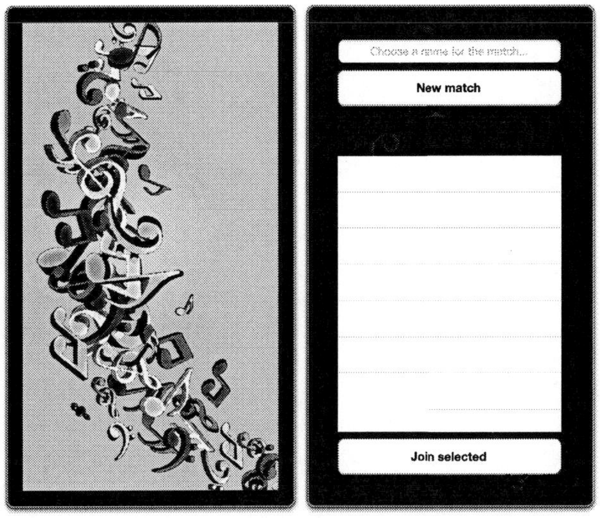

Figure 3. The Graphical User Interface of the game. Right side: the GUI, left side: the settings view.

the device keeps moving fast, no other gestures can be triggered. When the same quantity stated above goes under another threshold (lower than the previous one), quiet is detected and other gestures can be triggered again. Although iOS provides higher-level methods to detect device shakes, we decided not to use them in order to keep the system more flexible and to allow future detection of different kind of gestures (swings, rolls, thrusts and so on).

Musical notes are synthesized in real-time using the *libpd* framework [20]. This library enables the loading and processing of *PureData* patches inside the mobile application, providing a powerful, flexible and easy to program sound synthesis engine. Musical parameters like pitch, dynamics and timbre can be manipulated in different and creative ways, and other sound effects can be generated to reflect the performed gestures or just to add a funny, cartoonish touch to the game.

5. PRELIMINARY EVALUATION

The presented work is just in its preliminary steps and no extensive testing of the platform has been made yet. A preliminary evaluation was performed by presenting the game to First two four-year old girls and one six-year old boy and observing their behavior. Observations showed that the game was quite hard for them to play. The first prototype handled errors in a draconian way, making the melody stop and restart from the beginning as soon as a single note was missed. The fact they could never win the game was very frustrating for them, and after just a couple of minutes they got bored and stopped playing. Possible improvements might be allowing a greater number of errors before stopping the melody, or relaxing the time boundaries in which a note can be "hit".

6. CONCLUSIONS AND FUTURE WORK

This paper presents the first steps towards the development of rhythmic based collaborative sonic interaction games for children, that use current mobile technologies. It is important for the technology to be meaningful as part of the game and enhance the gaming experience.

This can be achieved by adding further developments of the games will include the recognition of a greater number of gestures, which will then be used to drive the sound synthesis engine and manipulate notes and sound effects accordingly. Another interesting feature to is the possibility for teachers to add new melodies to the game, by extending the existing mobile application and/or through a web-based interface. Groups of children and teachers could sing and record their favorite tunes, then make them available in the game to be discovered and enjoyed by other groups of children and teachers all around the world.

7. REFERENCES

[1] J. A. Sloboda, *The musical mind: the cognitive psychology of music*. Clarendon Press, 1985.

[2] C. A. Lindeman, *Musical Children: Engaging Children in Musical Experiences*. Prentice Hall, 2011.

[3] C. Lum and P. S. Campbell, "The sonic surrounds of an elementary school," *Journal of Research in Music Education*, vol. 55, no. 1, pp. 31–47, 2007.

[4] C. Small, "Musicking: a ritual in social space," *On the sociology of music education. Norman: University of Oklahoma*, pp. 1–12, 1997.

[5] E. Jaques-Dalcroze, *Rhythm, music and education*. GP Putnam's sons, 1921.

[6] C. Orff and K. G., *Musik fr Kinder*. Schott, 1950, vol. I.

[7] F. J. Bernieri and R. Rosenthal, "Interpersonal coordination: Behavior matching and interactional synchrony," *Fundamentals of nonverbal behavior*, p. 401, 1991.

[8] R. J. Shaffer, L. E. Jacokes, J. F. Cassily, S. I. Greenspan, R. F. Tuchman, and P. J. Stemmer, "Effect of interactive metronome® training on children with adhd," *The American Journal of Occupational Therapy*, vol. 55, no. 2, pp. 155–162, 2001.

[9] V. Rideout, "Zero to eight: Children's media use in america," Common Sense Media, Tech. Rep., October 2011.

[10] A. Jylhä and C. Erkut, "A hand clap interface for sonic interaction with the computer," in *Proceedings of the 27th international conference on Human Factors in Computing Systems (CHI), extended abstracts*. ACM, 2009, pp. 3175–3180.

[11] D. Archambault and D. Olivier, "How to make games for visually impaired children," in *Proceedings of the 2005 ACM SIGCHI International Conference on Advances in computer entertainment technology*. ACM, 2005, pp. 450–453.

[12] M. Liljedahl, S. Lindberg, and J. Berg, "Digiwall: an interactive climbing wall," in *Proceedings of the 2005 ACM SIGCHI International Conference on Advances in computer entertainment technology*. ACM, 2005, pp. 225–228.

[13] S. Targett and M. Fernström, "Audio games: Fun for all? all for fun," *ICAD2003*, 2003.

[14] M. P. Michalowski, S. Sabanovic, and H. Kozima, "A dancing robot for rhythmic social interaction," in *Human-Robot Interaction (HRI), 2007 2nd ACM/IEEE International Conference on*. IEEE, 2007, pp. 89–96.

[15] J. Friberg and D. Gärdenfors, "Audio games: new perspectives on game audio," in *Proceedings of the 2004 ACM SIGCHI International Conference on Advances in computer entertainment technology*. ACM, 2004, pp. 148–154.

[16] G. Andersen, "Playing by ear: using audio to create blind-accessible games."

[17] F. Winberg and S. Hellström, "Investigating auditory direct manipulation: sonifying the towers of hanoi," in *CHI'00 extended abstracts on Human factors in computing systems*. ACM, 2000, pp. 281–282.

[18] N. Röber and M. Masuch, "Leaving the screen: New perspectives in audio-only gaming," in *In: 11th Int. Conf. on Auditory Display*. Citeseer, 2005.

[19] N. Röber, "Playing audio-only games: A compendium of interacting with virtual, auditory worlds," 2005.

[20] P. Brinkmann, P. Kirn, R. Lawler, C. McCormick, M. Roth, and H. Steiner, "Embedding pure data with libpd," in *Proc Pure Data Convention 2011*, 2011.

PLUCKING BUTTONS: AN ALTERNATE SOFT BUTTON INPUT METHOD ON TOUCH SCREENS FOR MUSICAL INTERACTION

Edward Jangwon Lee
Audio & Interactive Media Lab
Graduate School of Culture Technology, KAIST
291 Daehak-ro, Yuseong-gu, Daejeon, Korea
noshel@kaist.ac.kr

Woon Seung Yeo
Audio & Interactive Media Lab
Graduate School of Culture Technology, KAIST
291 Daehak-ro, Yuseong-gu, Daejeon, Korea
woony@kaist.edu

ABSTRACT

This article introduces *plucking buttons*, an alternate method of interacting with soft buttons on touch screens that can provide more sound parameters that are expected to enhance expressiveness in digital music. Rather than pushing buttons, users are required to start and end touches inside and outside of the button, respectively, in order to activate the button. This gesture is similar to flicking (swiping) gestures on touch screens and plucking strings on musical instruments. Advantages of this button and gesture include providing extra sound parameters, preventing accidental input, and not requiring additional screen space. The largest challenge of this gesture to be used in music is the possible delay and inaccuracy of input due to relatively complex interaction, and this is tested by comparing two input types: plucking vs. pushing buttons. Test results suggest that plucking can be used, but can be efficiently used after training. Melodic musical tasks are also executed, and users were able to successfully play a simple song.

1. INTRODUCTION

The introduction of programmable touch screen interfaces has provided a versatile platform to build various types of digital musical interfaces with a very low production cost. Moreover, nowadays touch interfaces are widely adopted on mobile devices, such as smartphones and tablet PCs, and offers high computation power – powerful enough to synthesize and play real-time audio [1], and this has enabled digital musicians to have a powerful, programmable, and yet affordable digital musical interface with extreme mobility.

The versatility of touch screen programming and continuous multitouch features of these devices enabled the development of various types of user interface control components and input gestures. Nevertheless, buttons, that require tapping interaction in a predefined and restricted space on screen, seem to be the most popular control in touch screens. However, buttons on touch screens (soft buttons) differ from their real-life counterparts (hard buttons), as most devices do not provide haptic feedback and are not pressure-sensitive. The absence of pressure sensing leaves buttons prone to accidental input and also exhibits a loss of touch information. In a musical context, touch screen buttons have a risk of playing unintended notes, and the loss of information results in less sound parameters, which in turn can imply reduced expressiveness.

As a remedy for these weaknesses, this research proposes an alternate method of interacting with soft buttons on touch screens: *plucking*, which involves swiping gestures from inside to outside of the button. Requiring the touch to start inside a button and to end outside is expected to prevent accidental touches, while providing extra touch information that will grant additional expressiveness. However, as the proposed gesture is more complex than tapping, user tests are required to determine whether this gesture is usable for musical needs.

2. PLUCKING GESTURES

Unlike traditional musical instruments with strings, touch screens do not have strings that can be plucked. This section describes the plucking gesture in traditional music, and sets an alternate definition of plucking that can be applied on touch screens.

2.1 Plucking Gestures in Musical Instruments

In music, plucking is done to generate sound by applying force on a string of instruments, such as the guitar. This force can be applied either by using fingers or plectrums (picks). In detail, the plucking gesture can be divided as a threefold process: (a) holding, (b) pulling, and (c) releasing. *Holding* initiates a pluck by selecting and holding a string that is to be excited, and *pulling* repositions the string to a different location, thereby accumulating force. Finally, *releasing* the string finalizes the gesture and sets the string into vibration, which is transferred throughout the instrument to emit sound. Figure 1 illustrates the plucking process.

Normally, musical instruments in the chordophone family maintain a high tension their stretched strings. Therefore, a minimum amount of force is required to accumulate enough force to generate sound. This enables the second step of plucking – pulling – to be a very short distance, and this causes the plucking process to go through the three

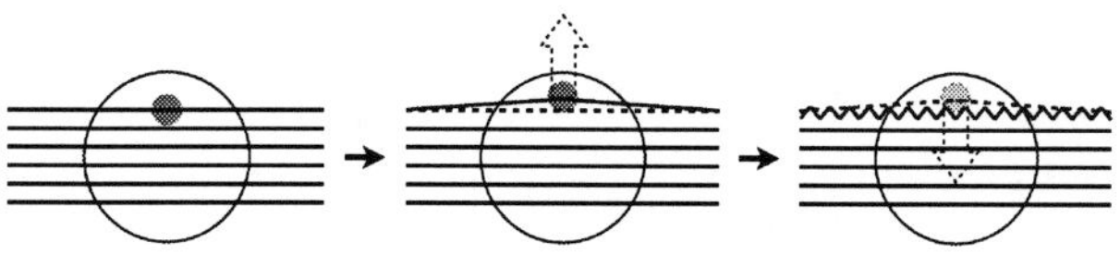

Figure 1. Holding, pulling and releasing.

steps almost instantly. However, varying the technique of any step results in tonal variety, which grants expressiveness and nuance to the player.

In terms of interaction, each step of plucking has its own role. *Holding* selects the target of interaction (string to be plucked), *pulling* determines the result variation (loudness and other tonal attributes), and *releasing* indicates that the user is ready to output a result, based on the two previous steps (set strings into vibration and generate sound).

2.2 Plucking Gestures in Touch Screens

In the context of touch screen environments, the threefold definition of plucking gestures – *holding, pulling, and releasing* – can be interpreted in terms of touch events: touch down (or touch start), touch move, and touch up (or touch end). Although this is a general lifespan of touchscreen interactions, the implications of each phase follow the three plucking stages. Starting a touch selects the control to be activated, moving the touch determines additional attributes, and finally, releasing the touch outputs a result calculated from the two previous steps.

The main difference between real string instruments and touch screens is that there is no real string to be plucked. Therefore, the user cannot feel any force being accumulated during the pull, nor the strings themselves. This characteristic can be used as an advantage to plucking gestures. While real strings normally are not to be pulled over adjacent strings, in touch interfaces, after a touch start point is decided, the touch can be pulled over other controls without activating them (Figure 2). This implies that no additional screen space is required to implement plucking gestures in touch screens – buttons, which serve as touch start (holding) points, can be placed nearly as that of ordinary types.

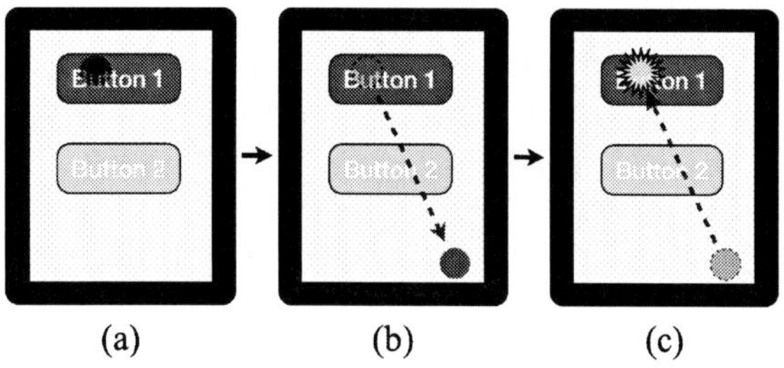

Figure 2. Plucking on touch screens. (a) Button 1 is pressed (touch down or *held*), (b) additional information is gathered while touch moves (touch move or *pull*), and (c) releasing triggers output combining Button 1 and the touch move data (touch end or *release*). Button 2 does not interact during the touch.

3. POSSIBILITIES OF PLUCKING GESTURES AS A MUSICAL GESTURE ON TOUCH SCREENS

In this section, we further discuss the qualifications of plucking gestures on touch screens, which is defined in the previous section. We believe that plucking grants additional musical expressiveness while not requiring extra screen space, and that users can easily execute plucking gestures, due to the similarity of plucking gestures to swiping.

3.1 Additional Sound Parameters

Nowadays, in the professional music industry, there is a trend of releasing touch interface versions of their previously released musical instruments. While this movement allowed users to purchase instruments at a more affordable price, the limitations of touch interfaces prevented those from the successful translation of certain aspects of the original hardware. For example, the well-known sampler AKAI MPC has its Apple iPad version, named iMPC. Although it is offered at a very low price, several features of the original MPC had to be omitted: velocity (pressure on pad when first pressed) and aftertouch (changing pressure during press). These two features use pressure information and enable users to input additional sound parameters when and while pressing a pad. However, the iPad version does not support this, as the device does not have sensors to dynamically measure pressure applied by users. As a remedy, AKAI sells an optional hardware named MPC FLY, which has external trigger pads with pressure sensors and an interface to the iPad and iMPC software (Figure 3). [1]

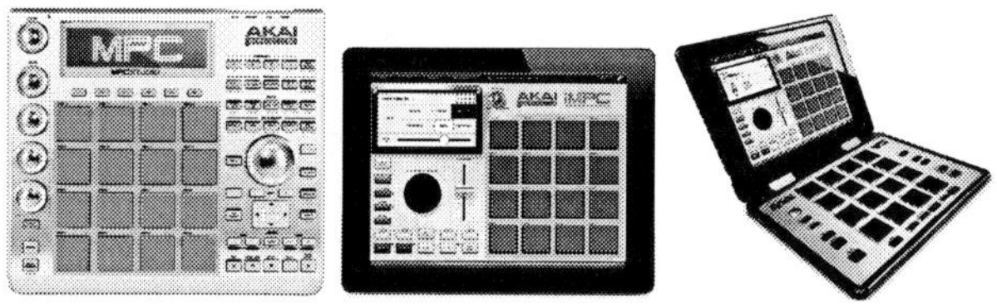

Figure 3. (left to right) AKAI MPC, iMPC and MPC Fly. Limitations of touch interfaces cause loss of gestural information, and external devices are in the market to mitigate such losses.

The example of iMPC – the AKAI MPC on iPad – illustrates the loss of gestural information during the translation from dedicated musical hardware to touch interface tablet PC software. Rather than fully using the pressure changes during pressing trigger pads, the tablet version generates sound upon touch events and prolonged touches can only control the length of sound – that is, on and off.

However, actual touch events convey more information than touch start and end. Between the beginning and ending of a touch, the touching finger is able to move to another location, and this movement contains a vast amount of information that can be used in designing a more complex interaction.

Dobrian (2006) argues that "expressive control relies on more sophisticated use of the control input information"

[1] Photographs of the MPC products are retrieved from AKAI Professional website, `http://akaipro.com`.

[2]. Pushing buttons and generating sound upon touch start on touch interfaces clearly discards gestural information that is generated after the touch starts. The most attractive aspect of plucking gestures on touch interfaces is that the three phases of touch events (touch down, touch move and touch up) are fully usable. Plucking gestures can incorporate touch movements and touch ending events as additional sound parameters, and thereby offer more expressiveness.

Compared to preexisting velocity simulation techniques such as touch size detection (harder touches activates a larger area on the screen) or accelerometer value changes (harder touches cause more movement of the device), plucking is a different approach. That is, rather than capturing the touch force itself, plucking requires additional interaction (pulling and releasing) in order to collect more data from one gesture.

3.2 Widely Used Gesture on Touch Interfaces

Although the proposed plucking gesture seems to be more complex than pressing buttons, the gesture itself is only a marginal cost added to *flicking*. Flicking gestures, which are mostly used in turning pages, takes all touch data (start, move and end) into account and accordingly scrolls the screen. Usually, flicking requires the user to move the touch quickly, and the velocity of movement should not decrease near touch end. The user executes flicking by touching an arbitrary point within the content, move to touch quickly towards a desired direction, and ends the touch without slowing down. Plucking gestures in this research slightly adds cost to flicking: (a) plucking requires the user to pinpoint the starting point of touch, so that the desired control to activate can be determined before the touch moves, and (b) the distance of pulling should be taken into account.

3.3 Avoids Accidental Input

One of the largest problems of touch interfaces is accidental input problems. In most real-life hard buttons, such as computer keyboards, users can place their fingers or hands on the button without activating it. However, on touch screens, buttons can be activated by the slightest touch, and this aspect is a risk to take in music, as well as other fields of applications.

Although the proposed gesture, *plucking buttons*, heighten the complexity of activating buttons, this complexity can serve as a mitigation to such accidental inputs. In order to activate a button with plucking, the user must start and end the touch inside and outside the button, respectively. Therefore, as real-life keyboards, users are able to place their hands on the buttons while they are unused, and no output is produced. Even after a button has been pressed *(holding)* and the finger has moved out of the button *(pulling)*, simply returning inside the button cancels the activation.

4. TEST DESIGN AND DATA COLLECTION

In this section, a test design that can determine whether plucking gestures can be used as a musical gesture on touch screen environments is described. After highlighting the anticipated difficulties of plucking, musical tasks [3] are devised to test each issue. Quantitative and qualitative methods are employed, in rhythmic and melodic musical tasks, respectively.

4.1 Challenges of Pulling Gestures in Music

Cost of Interaction. The highest obstacle of employing plucking gestures in music is the cost of interaction. In order to fully utilize touch data generated throughout the touch lifespan, the final sound output should be delayed until the touch event completes. Therefore, the total time required from player intention to sound output increases, and only a marginal amount of such time increase can be critical in real-time situations such as live performances. This test focuses on the human ability to rapidly execute plucking gestures enough to match their intentions and keep up to tempo.

Location of touch release. Among the three steps of plucking, *pulling* surely is the most time-consuming step. In order to minimize the cost of interaction described above, the time used in pulling should be as short as possible. Another challenging point stems from here: whether players can freely control the location of releasing. Choosing a point to touch on the screen is relatively easy, compared to pinpointing the location of releasing touch after rapid movement.

4.2 Rhythmic Musical Task

Staying *"in the pocket"*, that is, being able to keep up tempo, is one of the most important virtues of playing an instrument. Therefore, requiring additional time in musical interaction can be intolerable. As plucking gestures on touch interfaces clearly require more time compared to pushing buttons, proper user testing is crucial to approve the usability of plucking in music. To test the possibilities of keeping musical tempo while plucking, a quantitative test method is devised that records the time deviation between played notes (onsets) and prerecorded metronome pulses (click onsets). Many examples of this type of experiment, which require users to interact referring to auditory cues, can be found in the sensorimotor synchronization (SMS) literature [4] [5] .

4.2.1 Task Description

The objective of this task is to execute a simple test employing descriptive statistics to evaluate the rhythmic difference between pushing and plucking gestures.

A rhythmic musical task is prepared, requiring users to play notes at every one beat. A prerecorded common timed metronome track is played for a total of eight bars. The first four bars are pre-rolls, enabling users to become accustomed to the tempo. Although interaction details are recorded throughout the eight bars (32 beats), only the latter two (8 beats) are to be used in analysis. User tests are to be executed in three different tempi: 60, 120 and 180 beats per minute (bpm). Two versions of touch interface applications are prepared with one large button each, differing in interaction style: (a) sound generation upon pushing (touch down event) and (b) sound generation upon plucking gesture.

4.2.2 *Measurement and Hypothesis*

While the prerecorded metronome track is playing, every touch interaction is recorded. Afterwards, the recorded information is processed by hand in order to extract the final eight touches (onsets). Each touch time is measured as a millisecond representation of the current sample number of the metronome track (16bit, 44,100Hz sample rate) being played at the time of touch: that is, touch down time for pushing and touch up time for plucking. As the metronome onset time can be easily calculated, onset asynchronies can be calculated as the difference between metronome onset times and time of touches.

For each participant, mean onset asynchronies and standard deviations are calculated. As there are two different input methods (pushing and plucking) and three different tempi (60, 120, and 180bpm), each participant generates six sets of data.

We expect that the increased cost will increase a participant's mean asynchrony, as plucking is clearly a costlier interaction than pushing. However, as ending touches (lifting finger off screen) requires less physical movement than starting touches (placing finger on screen), in low tempi the standard deviation of plucking might be lower than pushing.

4.3 Melodic Musical Task

In addition to the quantitative rhythmic musical task, a melodic task to assess the playability is devised. This test is designed as a qualitative test, and feedbacks from users are collected during and after a time of exploring, free-playing, and being asked to play a simple song. Playing a simple song intends to determine whether users are able to play desired notes at a desired timing, without accidental input or misplayed notes.

4.4 Sample Demography and size

The test sample includes ten participants, including three professional musicians. Each participant was given three to five minutes of guided exploration of the interface, and the rhythmic test was executed afterwards. After the rhythmic musical task, users were asked to execute the melodic musical task.

5. IMPLEMENTATION

A simple touch application is implemented to meet our testing needs. The application, named *Pull*, is developed on Apple's New iPad with iOS 6.1 using Cocos2D/Box2D game development framework. [2] Multitouch feature is also included, to enable multi-note chords and drum patterns.

Timing. For precise interaction time recording relative to the metronome in rhythmic musical tasks, the MoMu toolkit [6] is used as the audio engine, running at 44,100Hz sample rate. Metronomes in each test tempo are pre-recorded and stored in .wav format (16bit, 44,100Hz sample rate), and user interaction timings are stored as the time elapsed since metronome start (calculated from the current sample number played). This method is similar to the method used in Kim et al. (2012) [7].

Sound generation. Instruments samples from Apple Logic Pro 9 were recorded as .wav files and preloaded. The samples include one octave of a marimba in C major scale (eight notes; C4 to C5), and a four-note TR808 drum kit (open and closed hi-hats, kick and snare drums).

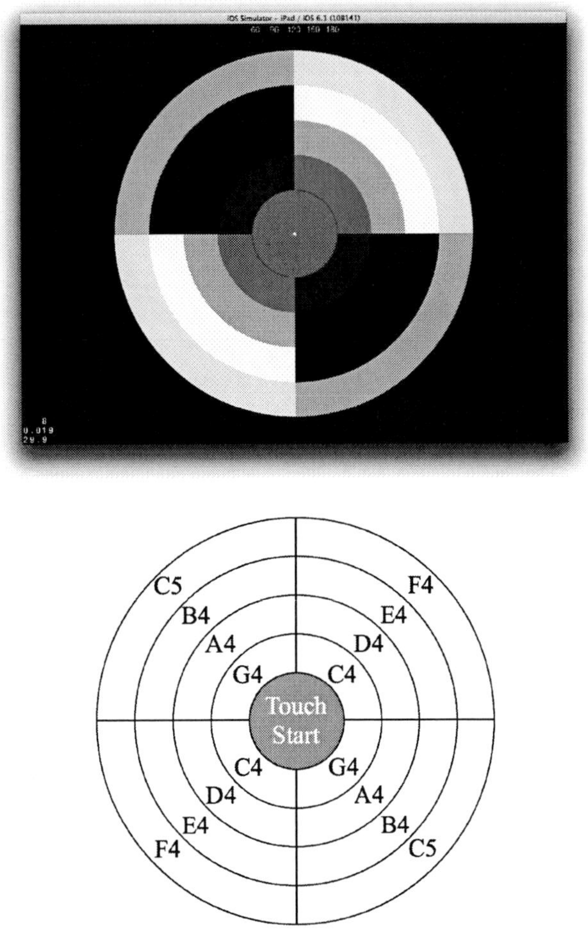

Figure 4. (upper) Prototype user interface. The grey circle in the center is the main button. After touching the innermost circle, the touch is moved to a desired arc, which each represents a different note, and releases the touch to generate sound with the corresponding pitch. Muti-touches are available. (lower) Pitch versus distance and angle mapping used in the initial melodic musical task.

5.1 User Interface

Figure 4 shows the prototype user interface. The grey innermost circle is the main button which users start the pulling gesture. The colored outer circles serve as a guideline for users to pinpoint their touch release location. After a *touch down, touch move, and touch up* event cycle is ended, the application calculates the move distance between the touch start and end points as well as the angle of movement in ra-

[2] `http://www.cocos2d-iphone.org`

dians, ranging between 0 and 2π. For each touch, a small ball is generated and follows the finger, to indicate the current touch position. On touch release, the ball rapidly returns to the original location.

5.2 Musical Mappings

The interface in upper portion of Figure 4 has only one button in the center of screen, with colored circle guidelines for plucking. Plucking gestures on this interface is implemented as follows. After starting the touch in the center, the touch is moved to a desired location in the outer circles, where each arc represents a different note. Arcs with the same color represent identical pitch. Releasing the touch inside the center circle does not produce sound; the touch *must* be moved outside the center circle and be released in order to play a note. Further details on the mappings can be found in the lower portion of Figure 4.

For the rhythmic musical task, an alternate one-button interface that generates sound upon touch down events is also implemented.

As this research focuses on the possibility of using plucking gestures on touch screens, only one button has been implemented. However, after user tests, another user interface employing several buttons has been developed, and will be introduced in section 6.

6. DATA ANALYSIS

6.1 Rhythmic Musical Task

The mean asynchronies and standard deviations of each participant are described in Table 1. Most of the participants showed a positive shift in mean asynchronies when plucking, suggesting that the increased cost of plucking gestures generates a systematic difference between the mean asynchronies of the two input methods. While most sensorimotor synchronization experiments exhibit negative asynchronies [5], frequent occurrence of positive means might imply that the increased interaction cost of plucking is larger than expected.

Standard deviations show less differences between the two input methods, which range between less than 1ms to 26ms. In 60bpm, most participants show an increase in variability while plucking. However, as the tempo increases, plucking begins to exhibit more stable results compared to pushing: six out of ten participants showed decreased standard deviation compared to pushing.

Data of full-time professional musicians can be found in participants 4, 6, and 7: a guitarist, drummer, and pianist, respectively. The guitarist (participant 4) was not able to pluck stably (SD = 56ms) in 60bpm, but in 120 and 180bpm plucking showed less standard deviation than pushing. The drummer (participant 6) showed superior performance in pushing, but relatively poor in plucking. Regarding the fact that the test began with 60bpm and towards higher tempi and that plucking is a newly introduced musical gesture, the test results might be handicapped with lack of training, as the drummer's standard deviation in 120bpm drastically rises (1ms to 25ms).

To further analyze the effects of training, participant 10 (non-musician) was offered several iterations of the experiment for fifteen minutes. After mentioning that he realized how it should be done, participant 10 was able to achieve stable results in both mean and variability. This suggests that the increased cost of interaction might be overcome through training.

6.2 Melodic Musical Task

Users were asked to freely explore the interface described in Figure 4 under our supervision and guidance for approximately five minutes, and play a popular song, *"Twinkle, Twinkle, Little Star"*. Most of the users claimed that although playing the song was not impossible, they could not play the song fast enough due to the difficulties of pinpointing the touch end location. As the initial musical mapping mapped pitch to pull distance, users had to concentrate on precisely ending touch moves at the next note to be played. This caused users to execute the plucking gesture extremely slowly.

Based on the feedbacks above, we concluded that the one-button plucking interface with pitch mapped to pulling distance (Figure 4) is inappropriate in a sense that pulling distance cannot be easily controlled, and another user interface with multiple buttons and different musical mapping has been implemented.

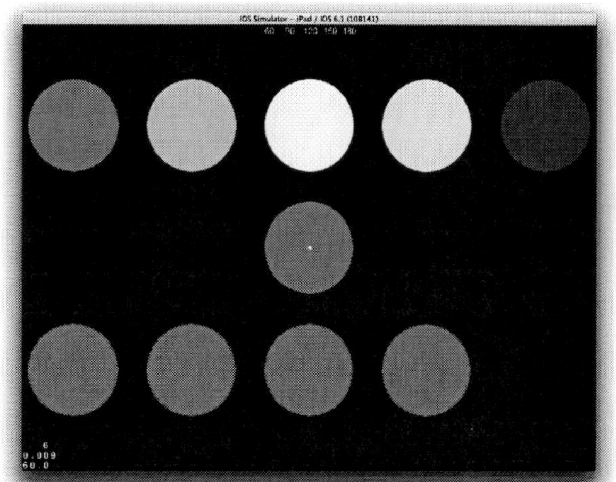

Figure 5. An alternate user interface with different musical mapping. Each circular button is mapped to a different pitch in the C major scale, and the pulling distance determines the amplitude gain.

The alternate interface, depicted in Figure 5, has seven colored buttons on the upper two lines, and four grey buttons on the lower line. Each of the colored button has been assigned a different pitch: C4 to C5, in C major scale. For the lower buttons, closed hi-hat, opened hi-hat, kick drum, and snare drum has been assigned. The pulling distance of pluck determines the gain of generated sound, ranging from 0 to 3. Further pulling results in louder sound.

An identical melodic musical task was executed with the new interface, and users commented that they were much

	Mean Asynchrony (ms)						Standard Deviation (ms)					
	60bpm		120bpm		180bpm		60bpm		120bpm		180bpm	
part.	push	pluck	push	pluck	push	pluck	push	pluck	push	pluck	push	pluck
1	**16**	-10	-17	**4**	-9	**28**	**25**	35	**17**	22	**11**	17
2	**-54**	-75	**-24**	-34	-24	**56**	31	**24**	**30**	39	**12**	20
3	**-9**	-18	-24	**27**	**-2**	-6	40	**25**	**21**	39	20	**8**
4^*	-5	**26**	3	**19**	-3	**17**	**19**	56	14	**12**	15	**14**
5	-56	**23**	**56**	1	-10	**-3**	**17**	30	18	**17**	28	**25**
6^*	-8	**26**	-14	**50**	-20	**52**	**20**	22	**1**	25	**12**	14
7^*	**-30**	-42	19	**25**	**9**	8	**22**	45	**15**	16	13	**9**
8	**-33**	-97	-15	**-12**	-30	**28**	**27**	35	**33**	34	42	**16**
9	-55	**-38**	-28	**-13**	9	**12**	36	**24**	14	**9**	9	**6**
10^{**}	-74	**43**	-87	**-73**	-61	**-31**	30	**19**	27	**25**	**17**	20

Table 1. Descriptive statistics of the collected data from ten participants. Higher mean asynchronies and lower standard deviations among the two input types, pushing and plucking, are highlighted in boldface. Most of the participants show a considerable amount of positive shift in their mean asynchronies while plucking, which suggest the increased cost of interaction. As the tempo increases, plucking gradually begins to exhibit lower standard deviations compared to pushing. Participants 4, 6, and 7 are professional musicians. Participant 10 has been trained through several iterations of the experiment.

more comfortable, as the interface had similarities with piano keys (left to right layout with higher pitches on the right) and trigger pads (grid layout of identically shaped buttons). Playability was also enhanced, and almost every test subject was able to play a simple song without difficulties.

7. CONCLUSIONS AND DISCUSSIONS

Plucking gestures on plucking buttons, which require the user to hold and pull a touch outside the button in order to generate output upon releasing, is a new type of musical interaction on touch screens. We believe that plucking buttons can contribute in the field of digital music by allowing more sound parameters to be mapped on a single button and providing a means of preventing accidental input – with an everyday gesture that is similar to flicking or swiping. Although the proposed gesture adds interaction cost, the costs are shown to be affordable through training, and the benefits cannot be neglected.

We are actively seeking for more possibilities of plucking. The plucking gesture implemented in this research only considers touch start and end points – the touch move path is not considered in the musical mapping. Adding parameters related to touch movement, such as acceleration, will surely produce interesting results. However, as plucking is a relatively small gesture, excessive sound parameters mapped to the gesture might cause confusion and difficulties to properly play, therefore caution is required.

8. ACKNOWLEDGMENTS AND ADDITIONAL INFORMATION

This research has been graciously supported by the funding of Korea Creative Contents Agency (KOCCA). Additional information on this research and video clips of plucking buttons and gestures can be found in the author's website: http://aimlab.kaist.ac.kr/~noshel/plucking.

9. REFERENCES

[1] G. Wang, G. Essl, and H. Penttinen, "Do mobile phones dream of electric orchestras?" in *Proc. Int. Conf. Sound and Music Computing (ICMC)*, Belfast, 2013.

[2] C. Dobrian and D. Koppelman, "The 'E' in NIME: Musical expression with new computer interfaces," in *Proc. Conf. New Interfaces for Musical Expression (NIME)*, Paris, 2006, pp. 277–282.

[3] M. M. Wanderley, "Evaluation of input devices for musical expression: Borrowing tools from hci," *Computer Music Journal*, vol. 26, no. 3, pp. 62–76, 2002.

[4] B. H. Repp and A. Penel, "Auditory dominance in temporal processing: New evidence from synchronization with simultaneous visual and auditory sequences," *Journal of Experimental Psychology: Human Perception and Performance*, vol. 28, no. 5, pp. 1085–1099, 2002.

[5] B. H. Repp, "Sensorimotor synchronization: A review of the tapping literature," *Psychonomic Bulletin & Review*, vol. 12, no. 6, pp. 969–992, 2005.

[6] N. J. Bryan, J. Herrera, J. Oh, and G. Wang, "Momu: A mobile music toolkit," in *Proc. Conf. New Interfaces for Musical Expression (NIME)*, Sydney, 2010, pp. 174–177.

[7] H. S. Kim, B. Kaneshiro, and J. Berger, "Tap-it: An ios app for sensori-motor synchronization experiments," in *Proc. Int. Conf. Music Perception and Coginition*, Thessaloniki, 2012, pp. 528–531.

ROBIN: AN ALGORITHMIC COMPOSER FOR INTERACTIVE SCENARIOS

Fabio Morreale
University Of Trento
morreale@disi.unitn.it

Raul Masu
University Of Trento
raul.masu@studenti.unitn.it

Antonella De Angeli
University Of Trento
deangeli@disi.unitn.it

ABSTRACT

The purpose of this paper is to present Robin, an algorithmic composer specifically designed for interactive situations. Users can interact in real time with the algorithmic composition by means of control strategies based on emotions. This study aims at providing a system for automatic music generation to be applied to interactive systems for music creation targeted at non-musicians. Robin adopts a rule-based approach to compose original tonal music in classical piano style. The first practical application of Robin is The Music Room, an interactive installation which enables people to compose tonal music in pairs by communicating emotion expressed by moving throughout a room.

1. INTRODUCTION

In 1978 Bischoff et al. stated the relevance of music: "*to bring into play the full bandwidth of communication there seems to be no substitute [...] than the playing of music live*" [1]. However, due to complexity which is intrinsic to playing, most people can only experience melodies created by somebody else. Research in Computer Music has been trying to simplify music creation, for the purpose of making this creative art accessible to an untrained audience [2,3]. Novel technologies, such as ubiquitous computers, touchscreen devices, visual tracking systems and physiological sensors, have been used to build new devices to complement or replace traditional instruments [4,5]. This technological advancement aroused a new set of issues, opening a challenging task to interaction designers and algorithm developers.

From an interaction design perspective, the challenge is to find new metaphors, as to detach the process of music composition from theoretical knowledge and practical skills that are the result of a formal musical education. There is a need for new interaction paradigms leveraging the communication forms, with the specific requirements of being available to everybody, intuitive and naturally connected with music. Emotion is probably the language that best meets the requirements mentioned above. In every culture, music is one of the arts that most effectively stir emotions [6,7] and music has always been associated with emotionality [9,26].

Being emotions the main composition medium, the involvement of the performer changes. Therefore, the traditional paradigm based on a note-to-note control is replaced by compositional decisions based on the emotions the user intends to elicit. This forces the system to include an algorithmic module, which can convert user input into musical language and generate music consequently.

In this paper we introduce Robin, an algorithmic composer designed to make the experience of musical creativity accessible to even untrained people. The main contribution introduced by Robin is the possibility of interacting with music in real time. Users can direct the composition in real time, conveying emotions that are translated into matching music in classical piano style. The potential lack of musical training of the users requires that the generated music should be understandable by everybody. In this connection, tonal music has the potential to reach a wider audience as it is the most common music in Western culture across different age groups and it is gradually spreading to other cultures.

Performing art provides the most important application field for the presented system. In fact, Robin can be used as a basis for interactive installations, where users can direct the music interacting with each other through their own body movements. Basing on this premise, we designed The Music Room, an installation where user couples can experience music creativity by moving throughout an area [5]. Robin also opens a number of possible practical applications in the most diverse fields. For example, movie directors and computer game developers could realize their own soundtracks instead of hiring professional musicians or licensing existing tracks. General technology users may adopt such a system to personalize their personal devices and online services, composing unique ringtones for mobile phones, creating a musical background for personal spaces on social networks (the musical equivalent to the so-called "status" which verbally describes somebody's moods and feelings), or for shared albums in image hosting websites. From a social perspective, a system that enables non-musicians to translate their own feelings and emotions into music might prove useful for therapeutic purposes.

The paper is organized as follows: in section 2 the related works are reviews; in section 3 Robin's architecture is described; in section 4 The Music Room is presented; in sections 5 and 6, finally, future developments are prefigured and some general conclusions are drawn.

2. RELATED WORKS

According to Todd and Werner, research on algorithmic music composition has based its own evolution on three approaches: evolutionary, learning-based and rule-based [10]. Evolutionary algorithms are particularly suitable to ensure an unpredictable outcome over the generative process [3]; the generated music, though, can result complex and unnatural. Learning-based algorithms compute music by training the system with pre-existing musical excerpts [12]. While the result is more natural, it strongly relies on the training set. The rule-based approach to a greater extent depends on human intervention, as compositional rules are manually coded [13]. Thus, a deep knowledge on music theory is required of algorithm designers, and the diversity and quality of musical outcomes depends on the amount of taught rules [14]. Recently, several algorithmic composition systems exploited the relation between music and emotion in the composition process [13,15,16]. In 2009, Hoeberechts and Shantz presented AMEE, a patented algorithmic composer that put the emphasis on automatic generation of soundtracks for video games [15]. In this system, the composition can be influenced in real time by altering the desired mood.

As regards the mapping between music and perceived emotions, research on the psychology of music suggests that the interpretation of emotions in music depends on acoustic cues embedded in composition and performance behaviours, whose combination stirs different emotional responses in the listener [8,9]. Researchers usually adopt a dimensional or a categorical approach to measure and classify emotions. In the categorical approach, emotions are discretized into a number of classes that correspond to the basic emotions. Several studies aimed at defining a set of musical variables, such as tempo, sound level, timbre, vibrato and consonance, that seemed typical of each of the basic emotions elicited by music such as anger, happiness, fear and solemnity [6,11]. The restricted number of categories, however, limits the fullness of emotional states evoked by music [17]. To overcome this limitation, most of the studies describe and measure emotions with a dimensional approach that allows combinations and gradients of emotions [9,13,16,18]. These studies are usually based on Russell's Circumplex theory [19], according to which emotions can be described as a continuum along two dimensions: valence, which refers to the positive vs. negative value of affective states, and arousal, which refers to the rest vs. activation difference.

2.1 Mapping music into valence and arousal

A general consensus suggests that mode and rhythm determine valence, while tempo and dynamics are determine arousal [9]. Other structural parameters that contribute to the elicitation of emotions are volume, melody direction, dissonance and expectation fulfillment. Table 1 shows how the combination of these elements determines the desired emotional expression by means of valence and arousal.

		Valence	Arousal
Mode	Major	Positive	
	Minor	Negative	
Tempo	Fast	Positive (less influential)	High
	Slow	Negative (less influential)	Low
Volume		Decrease in case of very low or very high volumes	Proportional to volume
Melody Direction	Rising	Positive	
	Falling	Negative	
Dissonance		Negative	
Note Density	High		High
	Low		Low
Expect. Fulfillment		Positive	

Table 1. Mapping between musical structures and the emotional dimensions of valence and arousal

Mode. Mode is the compositional factor which mostly influences valence. While minor mode elicits negative valence, major mode elicits positive valence. Mode does not directly impact on arousal [8, 18].

Tempo. Tempo influences the factor of arousal: in particular, fast tempo elicits high arousal, while slow tempo elicits low arousal [8]. Furthermore, to some extent, high tempo elicits positive valence, while slow tempo elicits negative valence [20]. A recent study showed that the influence of tempo on the dimension of valence dimension is to be particularly observed in non-musicians, as they attribute a greater importance to tempo than to mode when evaluating valence [18].

Volume. Volume is directly proportional to the arousal elicited in the listener. In case of very high and very low volume, however, valence is negatively influenced because the listening experience becomes unpleasant [8].

Melody direction. The direction of the melody in a sentence can influence the perceived valance. To some extent, rising melodies express positive emotions, while falling melodies express negative emotions [8].

Dissonance. Traditionally, dissonance can elicit negative valence, especially if the listener is a non-musician [21].

Note density. The density of notes impacts on the arousal dimension [8], which can be altered by the increased level of energy in the composition resulting from a dense melody.

Fulfillment of expectations. In his pioneering book, *Emotion and Meaning in Music,* Leonard Meyer explained how the fulfillment of expectations can elicit positive emotions while listening to a piece of music [22].

3. SYSTEM ARCHITECTURE

As Robin is intended to be used in interactive contexts available to everybody, two requirements must be met: i) the generated music needs to be accessible even to non-musicians; ii) the composition has to be influenced in real time. These requirements led to the adoption of a rule-based approach, as it guarantees an accurate control of the compositional process. The algorithm is taught a series of basic compositional rules of tonal music, which are used to create original compositions in Western piano music style. The choice of tonal music is consistent with the ultimate purpose of our research which is targeted at an untrained audience, that usually do not understand experimental, complex or atonal compositions [23]. To ensure consistency with user interaction, the system continuously listens to input changes, adapting the musical outcome accordingly.

Unlike AMEE [15], which outs the emphasis on soundtracks for computer games, Robin does not allow the definition of high-level musical structures, such as verses and sections. This choice was dictated by the fact that the evolution of user interaction with the system cannot be predicted.. AMEE tackles this issue by introducing forced abortion in the process of music generation. By contrast, we decided to avoid dramatic interruptions, as to guarantee a musical coherence and a natural evolution of the composition itself. The only high-level structural elements composed by Robin are theme repetitions, which simulate choruses and verses, that are typically present in most of contemporary genres, and cadences that define phrases. Robin is composed of three modules (Figure 1) that independently control different parts of the composition.

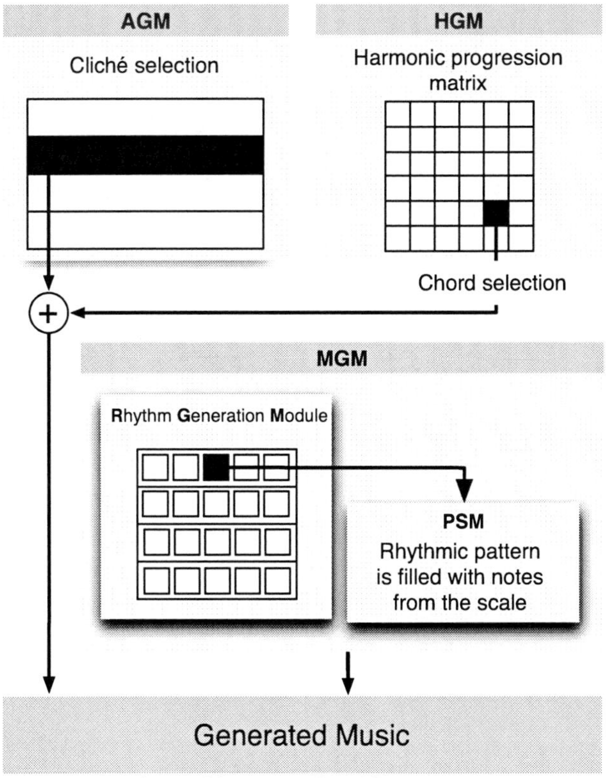

Figure 1. The architecture of Robin.

The Harmony Generation Module (HGM) determines the chord progression basing on a probabilistic approach. The generated chords are then fed to the Accompaniment Generation Module (AGM), that composes the *left hand* melody, and to the Melody Generation Module (MGM), that composes the *right hand* accompaniment. The MGM computes the melody notes by combining the rhythmic pattern chosen by the Rhythm Generation Module (RGM) with the pitches chosen by the Pitch Selection Module (PSM).

3.1 Harmony Generation Module

Traditionally, harmony is examined on the basis of chord progressions and cadences. Several algorithms for music compositions based on Generative Grammar implement chord progressions as stochastic processes [14,23]. The transition probabilities between successive chords are defined as Markov processes [23]. Chords transition data can be extracted analyzing existing music, surveying music theory or following personal aesthetic tastes and experiences [24].

In Robin, chords correlation does not depend on previous states of the system. A first-order Markov process determines the harmonic progression as a continuous stream of chords that is sometimes forced to go to a cadence or to modulate. The algorithm controls chord progression, starting from a random key and then iteratively processing a Markov matrix to compute the successive chords (Table 2). The 10x10 matrix contains the transition probabilities among the degrees of the scale. The entries are the seven degrees of the scale as triads in root position and three degrees (II, IV, V) set in the VII chord. The transition probabilities are based on the study of Harmony of Walter Piston [25] and from tonal music literature (mostly from Bach chorales).

	I	II	III	IV	V	VI	VII	IV7	V7	II7
I	0	0.05	0.05	0.30	0.20	0.05	0.1	0.05	0.15	0.05
II	0.04	0	0.04	0.04	0.45	0.08	0	0	0.35	0
III	0	0.07	0	0.21	0.07	0.65	0	0	0	0
IV	0.15	0.10	0.05	0	0.35	0.05	0	0	0.30	0
V	0.64	0.05	0.05	0.13	0	0.13	0	0	0	0
VI	0	0.40	0.10	0.10	0	0	0	0	0	0.40
VII	0.8	0	0	0	0	0	0	0	0	0.2
IV7	0	0.30	0	0	0.30	0.30	0	0	0.10	0
V7	0.9	0	0	0.05	0	0.05	0	0	0	0
II7	0	0	0	0	0.5	0	0	0	0.5	0

Table 2. Transition probability matrix among the degrees of the scale.

At each new bar the system analyzes the transition matrix and checks the row corresponding to the degree of the bar playing at that moment. At this point, the degree of the successive bar is computed: the higher the transition value, the higher the probability to be selected. The harmonic rhythm is one bar long and each bar measures $\frac{4}{4}$. In order to divide the composition into phrases, every eight bars the system forces the harmonic progression to a cadence (a conclusion of a phrase or a period) to a perfect or plagal mode. In order to generate compositions with more variations, Robin can switch between different keys and perform V and IV modulations.

3.2 Accompaniment Generation Module

The music generated by Robin consists of two voices: melody and accompaniment. At each new bar, the Accompaniment Generation Module (AGM) selects the new accompaniment. Four sets of clichés (accompaniment typologies) are available. The sets differ in the density of the notes in the arpeggio.

3.3 Melody Generation Module

Melody is computed by separately dealing with rhythm and pitch, thus maintaining coherence in the composition. At each new bar, the Rhythm Generation Module (RGM) selects a rhythmic pattern, which is consistent with the internal state of the system. The rhythmic pattern is then filled with pitches chosen by the Pitch Selection Module (PSM).

3.3.1 Rhythm Generation Module

The RGM is responsible for selecting the rhythmic patterns. A total of 38 possible rhythmic patterns are clustered into 3 sets, depending on the role of the bar in the phrase. The first set includes the rhythmic patterns suitable for the initial bars and for every bar in the phrase except the final one. The second set is responsible for lending an original character to each composition. The rhythmic patterns for all the bars except for the initial and the final ones belong to this set, that we divided into the following four subsets:

2a. Patterns with a predominance of quarter notes.
2b. Patterns with a number of 8th and 16th notes.
2c. Patterns with triplets.
2d. Patterns with syncopated rhythms.

The patterns belonging to the second category are selected with a stochastic approach. The computation of harmonic progression was defined as a stochastic process. Similarly, a probability-based squared matrix for rhythmic patterns is defined (Table 3). The rows and the columns represent the five rhythmic pattern subsets suitable for the internal bars (1, 2a, 2b, 2c, 2d), while the individual items of the matrix represent the transition probabilities. Unlike the harmonic progression, the conditional probability distribution of future rhythmic patterns depends on the sequence of events that preceded it. This choice aims at increasing the coherence in the composition, thus influencing the choice of rhythmic patterns on previous decisions. As a consequence, the rhythm probability matrix is dynamically updated at each step. For instance, when the algorithm repeatedly chooses patterns from the 2c subset, the probability of staying in the same subset increases at the expense of the other three subsets.

	1	2a	2b	2c	2d
1	0.20	0.20	0.20	0.20	0.20
2a	0.10	0.30	0.20	0.20	0.20
2b	0.05	0.1	0.35	0.20	0.30
2c	0.05	0.2	0.2	0.35	0.2
2d	0.05	0.2	0.2	0.2	0.35

Table3. Transition probability matrix for rhythmic patterns of internal bars. At each step, the matrix dynamically updates in relation to the history of the system.

The third set is composed of the rhythmic patterns used in the last bars of each phrase. This set is also divided into two subsets: the algorithm selects patterns from the 3a or 3b subset if most of the bars of the phrase were taken respectively from 2a, 2b or from 2c, 2d:

3a. Patterns of the cadences to 2a and 2b.
3b. Patterns of the cadences to 2c and 2d

3.3.2 Pitch Selection Module

The Pitch Selection Module (PSM) receives the rhythmic pattern and the current chord from RGM and HGM (Figure 2a). The selection of the notes of the melody occurs in two steps. In the first step (Figure 2b), all the significant notes in the bar are filled with notes of the chord. The notes regarded as significant are those whose duration is eighth or longer or that are in a relevant position in the bar (e.g. first and last place). At the second step (Figure 2b), the algorithm fills the remaining spaces with notes of the scale. Starting from the leftmost note, when the algorithm bumps into an empty space, it checks the note on the left and it steps one pitch up or one pitch down, depending on the value of the melody direction.

Figure 2. The selection of pitches for the melody. a) The PSM receives the rhythmic pattern and the chord. b) The relevant notes of the melody are filled with notes of the chord. c) The remaining spaces are filled with notes of the scale to form a descending or ascending melody.

3.4 User Intervention: emotional change

The theoretical foundations for the mapping between music and emotion adopted in our work were reviewed in 2.1. The concepts expressed in Table 1 are operationalized in Robin as follows:

Mode. The change between modes is supported by Robin in the HGM that populates the matrix with notes in the selected mode.

Tempo. Tempo is managed by Robin as a continuous variable measured in BPM.

Volume. Volume is a continuous variable that determines the intensity (velocity) of the musical outcome.

Melody direction. The direction of the melody is determined by the PSM as described in 3.3.2.

Dissonance. Dissonance is achieved by inserting a number of out-of-scale notes in both melody and harmony.

Note density. Note density is manipulated by means of clichés and rhythmic patterns.

Fulfillment expectations. We operationalized this concept by presenting a theme several times. Repeated themes, indeed, elicit positive valence as they builds memories and expectations in the listeners.

4. ROBIN IN THE CONTEXT OF PERFORMING ART: THE MUSIC ROOM

The Music Room is an interactive installation for collaborative music composition that represents the first interface to Robin [5]. Two people direct the composition of original piano music by moving throughout a room. Information about the emotionality of music is inferred from proxemics cues by following the analogy with love: high proximity is mapped into positive emotions and low proximity into negative emotions; high speed into intense emotions and low speed into mild emotions. The first versions of The Music Room were exhibited at the EU Researchers' Night, (Trento, Italy, September 28th 2012) and at the ICT Days (Trento, Italy, March 23th 2013[1]. The 5x5m room that hosted the installation was deliberately empty and minimally decorated, as to draw the attention of people to the musical cue.

The architecture consists of a Position Tracking Module and Robin. The acquisition of proxemic cues is performed through a camera in a bird eye position, fixed on the ceiling in the center of the room. Moving people are detected and followed through a visual tracking algorithm; their position is updated over time, processed and then sent to Robin. The cues of interest are the relative distance and average speed, computed according to the trajectory of each user over time. The information coming from the proxemic cues computed by the tracking system conveys the intended emotionality. By matching the values of speed and proximity to emotions, Robin adapts the musical flow, as has been previously described. The system is developed in SuperCollider, a programming language for audio synthesis and algorithmic composition. The software outputs a MIDI score that is transformed by Logic Pro, a Digital Audio Workstation, into piano music.

After each session, couples were given a link to a webpage where they could fill an evaluation questionnaire and download the song that Robin composed during their experience. The results of the questionnaire showed that most of the visitors (76%) greatly appreciated the installation and in particular the quality of the music (79%). Criticism was mostly aimed at the latency of the system response to user movements and at the lack of musical genres. Nevertheless, almost the 90% of the interviewees had an overall enjoyable experience.

5. FUTURE WORKS

Even though this system has already met with considerable appreciation, some limitations do exert an influence on the current version of the algorithm. In particular, the originality and the diversity of the compositions are affected by the absence of a bass line and by the lack of available genres. In order to improve the quality and diversity of the generated music, a number of new features are being currently developed. Among them, we are envisioning the possibility of extending the MGM to support multiple voices and the harmonic progression matrix to support chords in non-root position.

Furthermore, we are currently developing more musical genres and instruments, as to enable users to choose their favorite musical style before trying the installation. As regards the mapping of music with emotions, we are planning to increase the number of musical parameters that provoke a change in the elicited emotions. Among these parameters, we plan to include tensions and level of orchestration to map arousal, and timbre, number of harmonics and melodic range to map valence.

The latency between the user input and the musical output represents another limitation of the system. Even though the musical system is specifically designed to synchronize the user input with the generated music, we purposely decided to avoid sudden changes in music. This choice was mainly dictated by aesthetic reasons, requiring the phraseological structure of music to be preserved even in case of rapid changes in the emotional input. For this purpose, the successive musical phrase is computed at the last beat of the playing bar, currently fixed at $\frac{4}{4}$. This results in an approximately 4-second delay, in the worst-case scenario, occurring with a 60 BPM tempo and the bar at the first beat. Two solutions allow the new version of the algorithm to reduce this latency, while preserving musical coherence.

1. At every quarter, a new input from the user is checked. If it ranks above or below a specific threshold, a new bar starts straightaway.

[1] Some excerpts of the generated music can be found at http://goo.gl/Ulhgz

2. The tempo range is changed from 60-140 to 90-150 BPM. As a consequence, each beat lasts 0.75 seconds, while 90 BPM is still slow enough to be perceived as *andante*.

By implementing these solutions, the latency time drops to 0.75 seconds in the worst-case scenario: this figure can be regarded as sufficiently low even for interactive situations.

6. CONCLUSIONS

The importance of emotion-driven real-time algorithmic composition systems was already discussed by relevant studies [15,16]. In this connection, Robin represents a new approach in the context of interactive scenarios. The appreciation of the attendees of the two editions of the Music Rooms clearly witnesses to the quality of the music. Due to this success, a number of other installations based on Robin are currently being developed for educational, entertainment and therapeutic purposes.

7. REFERENCES

[1] Bischoff, J., Gold, R. and Horton, J. Music for an interactive Network of Microcomputers. Computer Music Journal, 2(3), (1978), pp. 24-29.

[2] Jordà, S., Geiger, G., Alonso, M., and Kaltenbrunner, M. The ReacTable: Exploring the synergy between live music performance and tabletop tangible interfaces. Proc. TEI 2007, (2007).

[3] Miranda, E.R., & Biles, J.A. Evolutionary Computer Music. Springer, (2007).

[4] Cope, D. Computer Models of Musical Creativity. The MIT Press, (2005).

[5] Morreale, F., Masu, R., De Angeli, A., Rota, P. The Music Room. CHI '13 Extended Abstracts. (2013).

[6] Gabrielsson, A, Juslin, P. N. Emotional Expression In Music Performance: Between the Performer's Intention and the Listener's Experience. Psychology of Music. (1996). 24(1), 68-91.

[7] Balkwill, L. L., Thompson, W. F., & Matsunaga, R. I. E. Recognition of emotion in Japanese, Western, and Hindustani music by Japanese listeners. Japanese Psychological Research, 46(4), (2004), pp. 337–349.

[8] Gabrielsson A., Lindrōm, E. The role of structure in the musical expression of emotions. In: P. N. Juslin, & J.A. Sloboda (Eds.), Handbook of music and emotion: Theory, research, applications, New York: Oxford University Press, (2010), pp. 367-400.

[9] Juslin P.N., Sloboda J.A. Handbook of music and emotion: theory, research, applications. Oxford University Press, (2010).

[10] Todd, P. M., & Werner, G. M. Frankensteinian methods for evolutionary music composition. Musical networks: Parallel distributed perception and performance, (1999) pp. 313–339.

[11] Juslin, P., Laukka, P. (2004). Expression, Perception, and Induction of Musical Emotions: A Review and a Questionnaire Study of Everyday Listening. Journal of New Music Research, 33(3), 217-238.

[12] Simon, I., Morris, D., & Basu, S. MySong: automatic accompaniment generation for vocal melodies. Proc. of the twenty-sixth annual CHI'08. ACM, (2008), pp. 725–734.

[13] Wallis,I., Ingalls,T., Campana,E., Goodman,J.: A Rule-Based Generative Music System Controlled By Desired Valence and Arousal. Proc. SMC 2011, (2011).

[14] Steedman, M. A Generative grammar for jazz chord sequences. Music Perception Vol. 2, No. 1, (1984).

[15] Hoeberechts, M., & Shantz, J. (n.d.). Real-Time Emotional Adaptation in Automated Composition. *Proceedings of Audio Mostly, 2009* (pp. 1–8).

[16] Livingstone, S., Mühlberger, R., Brown, A., & Loch, A. Controlling musical emotionality: an affective computational architecture for influencing musical emotions. *Digital Creativity*, *18*(1), (2007). 43–53.

[17] Scherer, K. R. Which Emotions Can be Induced by Music? What Are the Underlying Mechanisms? And How Can We Measure Them? Journal of New Music Research. (2004). 33(2), 239-251.

[18] Morreale, F., Masu, R., De Angeli, A., Fava, P. The effect of expertise in evaluating emotions in music. Proc. of the 3rd International Conference on Music & Emotion. (2013).

[19] Russell, J. A circumplex model of affect. Journal of personality and social psychology, (1980).

[20] Gagnon, L. Peretz I. Mode and tempo relative contributions to "happy-sad" judgments in equitone melodies. Cognition and emotions, 40, (2003), pp. 17-25.

[21] Fritz T., Jentschke S., Gosselin N., Sammler D., Peretz I., et al. Universal Recognition of Three Basic Emotions in Music. Current Biology, (2009), pp. 573–576.

[22] L. B. Meyer, Emotion and meaning in music. University of Chicago Press, (1956).

[23] Nierhaus, G. Algorithmic Composition: Paradigms of Automated Music Generation. Springer, (2009).

[24] Chai W. Vercoe B., Folk music Classification using Hidden Markov Models (2001), Proc. of ICAI 01, (2011).

[25] Piston W. DeVoto M, Harmony. Norton, (1941).

[26] Cooke D. The language of music: London: Oxford University Press, (1959).

x-OSC: A Versatile Wireless I/O Device For Creative/Music Applications

Sebastian Madgwick
University of Bristol, Bristol, UK
s.madgwick@bristol.ac.uk

Thomas Mitchell
University of the West of England, Bristol, UK
tom.mitchell@uwe.ac.uk

ABSTRACT

This paper introduces x-OSC: a WiFi-based I/O board intended to provide developers of digital musical instruments with a versatile tool for interfacing software to the physical world via OSC messages. x-OSC features 32 I/O channels supporting multiple modes including: 13-bit analogue inputs, 16-bit PWM outputs and serial communication. The optimised design enables a sustained throughput of up to 370 messages per second and latency of less than 3 ms. Access to settings via a web browser prevents the need for specific drivers or software for greater cross-platform compatibility. This paper describes key aspects x-OSC's design, an evaluation of performance and three example applications.

1. INTRODUCTION

The ubiquity of high-performance computational devices is raising the baseline expectations of computer literacy and the prioritisation of programming skills within school curricular [1]. As technology becomes increasingly familiar, an appetite for technological experimentation is giving rise to a new range of development platforms designed to make technological innovation accessible to all [2]. Principal examples include the Processing language/environment [3], which provides powerful abstractions for the development of cross-platform graphical software, and the Arduino development board, which has empowered artists, designers, and makers to create embedded hardware solutions [4].

Developers of digital musical instruments (DMIs) are notable users and creators of modern devices that are optimised to connect real-world electronics with music composition and performance software [5]. For example, Axel Mulder's I-Cube system [6], Fléty *et al*'s EtherSense [7] and Kartadinata's gluion [8] each represent solutions that have emerged from research into interactive music systems. Similarly, the interface device presented in this paper has been designed to meet the challenges associated with live music performance and represents a high-performance, robust, potable, low-latency and highly-compatible interface device suitable for a wide range of applications. The following sections of this paper will set out the context

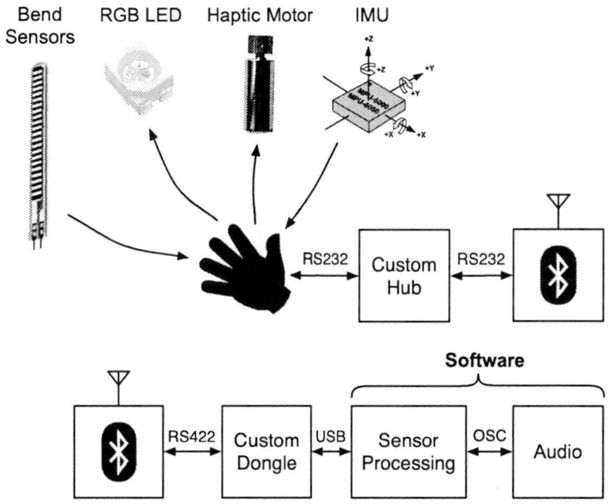

Figure 1. Data flow diagram for one of two data gloves in the current version of *The Gloves*

leading to the development of x-OSC with a review of related work; the implementation, specification and performance results will then be summarised; before closing with a range of example applications and concluding remarks.

2. BACKGROUND: THE GLOVES

The authors of this paper are developers of a glove-based gestural music interaction system built in collaboration with the singer/songwriter Imogen Heap [9, 10]. The current system structure and communication channels are shown in Fig. 1.

The system hardware transmits the current state of 16 bend sensors to measure the wearer's finger flexion, plus five inertial measurement units (IMUs) measuring orientations of the limbs and upper torso. In the opposite direction, the hardware responds to commands controlling LEDs and haptic motors to provide the wearer with primary feedback. These bidirectional data streams are encoded into a bespoke data protocol developed specifically for the system. The communications channel between the sensing of motion and the production of audio comprises five nodes, which each receive, translate and forward data to the next node. As each translation contributes to the overall latency of the system, it is reasonable to consider a more refined arrangement that implements open sound control (OSC) in hardware directly, an approach suggested by the inventors of OSC and developers of the uOSC platform [11].

3. RELATED DEVICES

Developers of DMIs require devices that have the capacity to connect software applications with a range of electronics that can measure control input and produce output actuation. There is an abundance of electronic devices appropriate for this task, which significantly differ in their intended use and design.

3.1 Development Boards

Many devices represent highly accessible development boards with accompanying software tools that simplify the embedded firmware development process. For example, Arduino [4] provides a range of development boards with a unique programming language (based on Wiring) and development environment (based on Processing [3]). Similarly, the Create USB interface may be programmed in either BASIC, the Arduino language or C, to cater for users with differing levels of expertise [12].

3.2 Interface Devices

Typically, developers of DMIs produce firmware that enables multiple analogue or digital I/O (input/output) channels to be accessed by software running on a host computer. However, a range of interface devices are designed to obviate the need for embedded development by enabling the device channels to be configured in firmware, communicating with the host software via a MIDI, USB or network link, often without the need for device drivers to be installed. In this sense, the device interface can be considered as a direct extension of the developer's host software [13].

MIDI Devices

The I-CubeX Digitizer [6] and the Eroktronix MidiTron [14] enable the reception of sensor readings and the delivery of actuator control messages via MIDI. Both devices enable configuration for different scenarios via MIDI SysEx commands. However, These devices are limited by their dependence on the MIDI hardware specification and consequently require additional peripherals for the host computer.

USB Devices

Modern MIDI-based interface devices, such as the Eobody3 [15], bypass this hardware limitation by using the USB MIDI standard to connect directly to the host computer. Further configurable USB interface devices include the GAINER [16] and Arduino installed with the Firmata library [13]. Both examples implement a serial protocol to enable I/O pins to be configured using commands from a compatible host application, without the need for user firmware development.

Open Sound Control (OSC) Devices

As modern computers come equipped with high-speed network support, OSC represents an ideal communications protocol for interface devices. OSC is a widely supported (over 80 languages/platform implementations [17]), lightweight network protocol designed specifically for communication between computers and multimedia devices [18]. Devices such as IRCAM's EtherSense [7] and glui's gluion [8], connect to a host computer via an Ethernet connection to exchange I/O and configuration messages. Schmeder and Freed's uOSC [11] provides a versatile firmware solution for connecting software with a range of development boards via a USB serial connection using the OSC protocol.

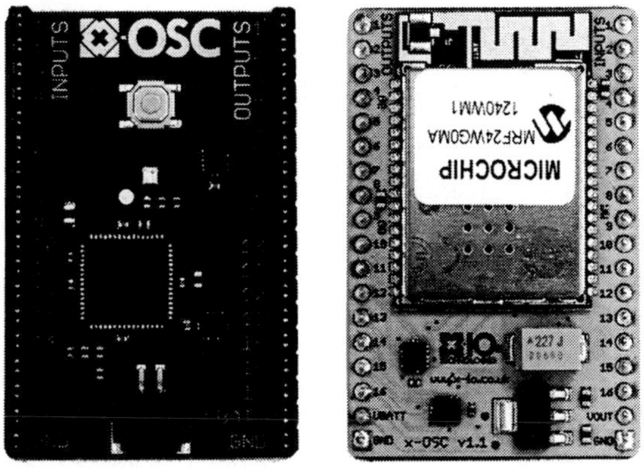

Figure 2. x-OSC board top (left) and bottom (right), size: 31 × 47 mm

Wireless Devices

The development boards and interface devices discussed above are limited by their dependence on wires (although serial connections may be tunnelled through Bluetooth, XBee or similar radio devices), however, many practical application scenarios demand untethered portable solutions. IRCAMs WiSe Box [19] digitiser provides host access to 16 analogue input readings at up to 333.3Hz via OSC when connected via a WiFi access point. The high message rate, small form factor and WiFi support make the WiSe Box ideal for collaborative interactive music system development. However, as the device is unable host ad-hoc networks, configuration is achieved over a custom USB serial connection/protocol. Furthermore, it is designed exclusively for the acquisition of sensor readings, making the WiSe Box unsuitable for actuation/feedback, a feature which is often considered essential for the development of DMIs.

4. X-OSC

x-OSC is a wireless I/O board that provides host software access to 32 multi-functional I/O channels via OSC messages over WiFi. There is no user programmable firmware or software to install making x-OSC immediately compatible with any WiFi-enabled platform.

As shown in Fig. 2, a simple hardware layout of two 18-way header sockets provide access to 16 inputs on the left hand side and 16 outputs on the right. The headers also provide a regulated 3.3 V output to power user electronics and an unregulated power input/output that provides direct access to the x-OSC battery. The standard pitch sockets are compatible with breadboards or direct connections using jumper wires. Other features include a battery connector, battery level measurement, an RGB status LED and a ping button. The on-board WiFi module incorporates a PCB antennae eliminating the need for an external antennae.

4.1 Inputs

16 dedicated inputs (0 V to 3.3 V) can be independently configured to be either analogue or digital. Digital inputs can be configured to use internal pull-up/down resistors and to minimise latency their state is only transmitted on change. All 16 analogue inputs are sampled with 13-bit resolution and sent simultaneously at a specified update rate up to 370 Hz. Analogue mode inputs also provide a *compare* function to send a message each time a specified threshold is crossed. This enables low-latency threshold detection without the need for a high message rate.

4.2 Outputs

16 dedicated outputs can be independently configured to digital, pulse or PWM modes. In digital mode, an output can be set to high or low enabling simple control of LEDs, relays, or generation of control logic signals. In pulse mode, an output can be triggered to generate a pulse with a period of 1 ms to 1 minute at a resolution of 1 ms. This may be useful for momentary actuators such a solenoid driving the strike mechanism of a percussive instrument. An output in PWM mode can generate a PWM waveform from 5 Hz to 250 kHz with a duty cycle resolution up to 16-bit. PWM is commonly used as a DAC where fixed frequency and variable duty cycle approximate an analogue signal. For example, this may be used to control the brightness of a light or the speed of a motor. Each 3.3V output is driven by a line-driver to protect the microcontroller outputs and source/sink up to 50 mA per channel.

4.3 Serial

In addition to modes described above, the first four inputs and outputs can be configured to serial mode with each transmit and receive pair utilising a dedicated hardware UART module. Each serial channel supports baud rates in the range 9600 to 1 M baud and incorporates a 2 kB buffer to ensure high throughput without loss of data. Received serial data is framed before being sent as *OSC-blob* messages. Framing boundaries are determined by a user defined buffer size, timeout and optional framing character.

4.4 Network modes

x-OSC can be configured to operate in one of two network modes: ad hoc or infrastructure. In ad hoc mode, x-OSC creates a network for other devices to join. Multiple devices can connect to a single x-OSC with simultaneous access to its I/O. Infrastructure mode allows x-OSC to connect to an existing network. The device IP address can be configured to be static or use DHCP to be assigned an appropriate IP address by the network server. The assigned IP address can be discovered by pressing the ping button,

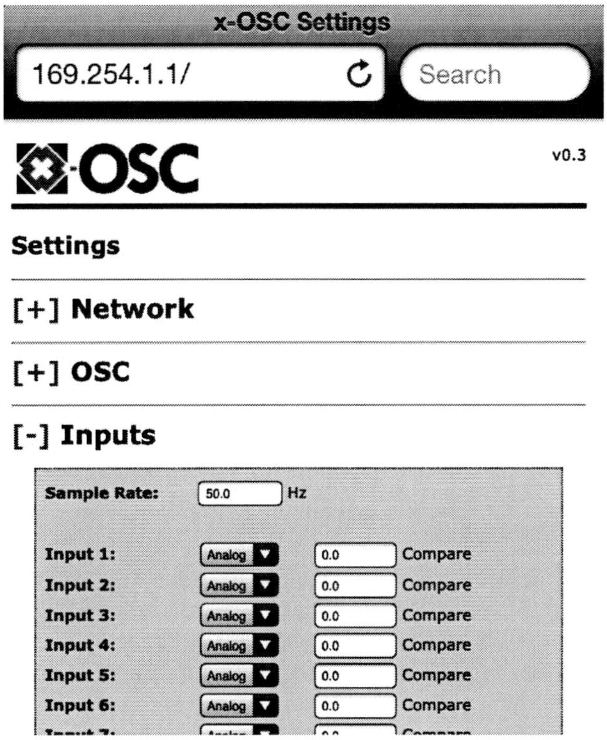

Figure 3. x-OSC settings viewed on web browser

which causes x-OSC to broadcast a message indicating the IP address over the network. Alternatively, a ping message can be sent to x-OSC by another network device. Infrastructure mode enables multiple x-OSCs to operate on the same network and be addressed by multiple host devices also connected to the network. A connection to a router can also provide an inherent interface to x-OSC via Ethernet or from remote internet connections.

4.5 Configuration via browser

An embedded web server enables all internal settings to be configured using a web browser, see Fig. 3. Settings may be viewed and modified during run-time without interrupting the OSC messages. Incorrect network settings can render x-OSC inaccessible; access can be re-established by pressing and holding the ping button to restart the device in ad hoc mode with default settings.

4.6 OSC messages

x-OSC transmits and receives OSC messages using the User Datagram Protocol (UDP) transport layer.

Although OSC is widely supported, many platforms fail to incorporate the full specification [11]. To maximise compatibility, x-OSC messages are limited to four of the fundamental data types: *int32*, *float32*, *OSC-string* and *OSC-blob*. For example, Boolean arguments are represented by an *int32* and *null* arguments by an argument value of zero. In addition to this, messages sent to x-OSC may use *int32* and *float32* interchangeably.

A set of OSC messages were defined that enable communication of I/O data to and from x-OSC as well as configuration of the internal x-OSC settings. Additional OSC messages include battery data, a ping message and override commands for the built in LED.

5. OPTIMISED DESIGN

x-OSC's design was optimised for throughput, latency and high-performance I/O. A key aspect of this design is the use of Microchip's TCP/IP stack, a networking library for Microchip microcontrollers and Microchip WiFi modules. Many competitor WiFi devices incorporate an internal networking stack to provide a self-contained and easy-to-use module compatible with any microcontroller. However, incorporation of the stack on the host processor provides the firmware with direct access to low-level stack processes and enables specific optimisations to be implemented.

5.1 Hardware

The key hardware components are Microchip's dsPIC33EP512MC806 digital signal controller and MRF24WG0MA WiFi module. The MRF24WG is Microchip's highest performing WiFi module, capable of up to 5 Mbit sustained throughput and maximum transmit power of +18 dBm. The dsPIC33E was specifically chosen for its high-performance and wide range of advanced peripherals:

- 16-bit architecture, 70 MIPS and 53 kB RAM represents one of Microchip's highest performing microcontrollers to minimise latency caused by heavy processing tasks such as maintaining the TCP/IP stack, processing OSC messages and floating-point operations.
- 512 kB of program space is enough to hold the main application, TCP/IP stack, and embedded webpage server content while leaving space for future developments. The current firmware size is 177 kB.
- Two ADCs (10-bit at 1.1 MHz and 12-bit at 500 kHz) and 9 direct memory access (DMA) channels enable the implementation of the 16 analogue inputs with minimal CPU loading.
- 16 PWM modules with dedicated timers in addition to nine general purpose timers for precise scheduling of I/O functionality with minimal CPU loading.
- Remappable peripherals are essential to enable the multifunctional modes of x-OSC's I/O channels.

5.2 Firmware

The firmware uses Microchip's TCP/IP Stack v5.42.06 with only essential application modules enabled. The stack's SPI library was modified to use the maximum 10 MHz full-duplex baud rate supported by the dsPIC33E. A key aspect of the optimised design is the extensive use of the advanced peripherals offered by dsPIC33EP so that most I/O functionality may be executed without CPU intervention.

Analogue sampling of the inputs utilises the 1.1 MHz 10-bit ADC, 16-channel multiplexer and DMA to yield measurements of all 16 inputs at 533 Hz with 13-bit resolution. This was achieved by configuring the ADC to continuously sample at 546 kHz while the multiplexer sequenced between each of the 16 inputs each ADC sample. A DMA channel assigned to the ADC writes each sample to a predefined pattern of address in RAM in *ping-pong* mode to alternate between two alternative blocks of RAM every 1024 samples (64 samples per channel) enabling the ADC to continue sampling uninterrupted without the risk of overwriting unprocessed samples. When analogue input data is required, the CPU computes a scaled mean of each channel's 64 samples to yield a 13-bit result through oversampling [20]. The battery voltage was measured in a similar way using the 12-bit ADC and computing the mean of 16 samples to attenuate noise.

The 16 independent PWM outputs utilise 16 16-bit PWM modules with dedicated timers and four of the nine general purpose timers as clock references. Each output channel is able to achieve both an independent frequency and duty-cycle between 5 Hz and 250 kHz and 8.1-bit to 16-bit resolution (dependent on the frequency) respectively. Use of 4 general purposes timers provides each PWM timer with simultaneous access to all possible prescaling options to maximise the PWM frequency resolution and range. The frequency range of 5 Hz to 250 kHz is divided by approx. 218,000 steps with a non-linear resolution of 3.66 μs at lower frequencies and 14.31 ns at higher frequencies. The output pulse mode is achieved by a 1 kHz CPU interrupt for 1 ms resolution and inherent synchronisation between pulses performed on different channels.

5.3 Power consumption

The optimisations of throughput, latency and I/O performance come at a cost in power consumption. The current consumption was measured as up to 225 mA in infrastructure mode or up to 300 mA in ad hoc mode. A 1000 mAh lithium polymer battery (of a similar physical size to x-OSC) may be expected to last approximately 3 hours.

6. EVALUATION OF PERFORMANCE

An important aspect of WiFi performance is the network connection delay. This may be critical if a connection is lost unexpectedly. The time taken to connect to a router was found to be approximately 30 seconds. The time taken for x-OSC to create an ad hoc network was found to be approximately 15 seconds, however recreating this network after another device had connected required only 6 seconds. Infrastructure configurations were found to provide better throughput and latency performance than ad hoc. The following investigations represent a host computer connected to a router via an Ethernet cable, the router hosts the WiFi network to which x-OSC is connected. The only network traffic was between x-OSC and the host machine.

6.1 Throughput

Throughput was quantified as the maximum sustained analogue input packet/s. Each packet contains an OSC message representing 16 floats, the complete UDP packet is 142 bytes long. The maximum throughput was found to be approximately 370 packets per second when sending

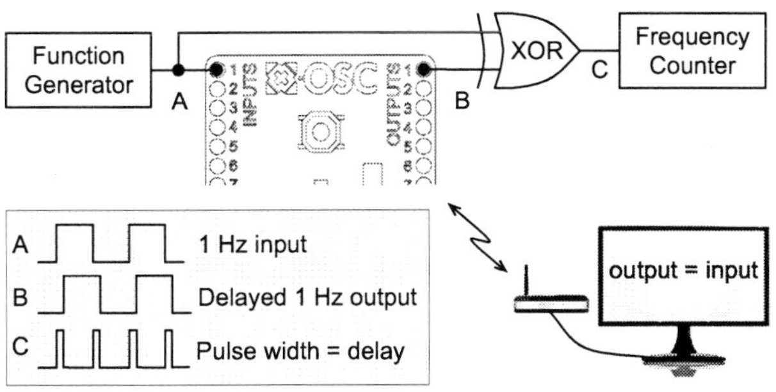

Figure 4. Experimental setup for evaluation of closed-loop latency

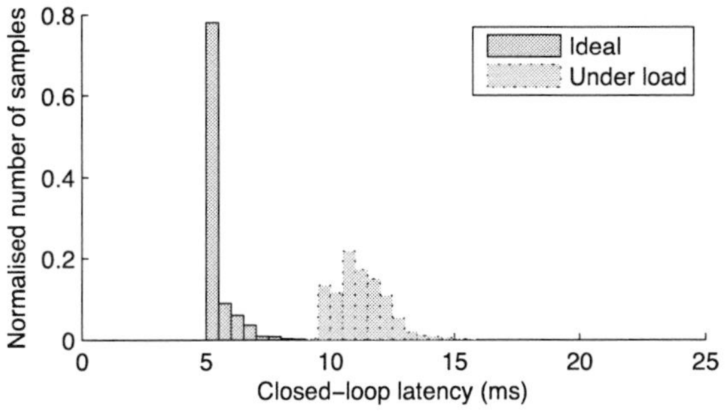

Figure 5. Closed-loop latency evaluation (distribution of approximately 50,000 samples)

alone and when three x-OSCs are sending to the same host machine simultaneously. As only three prototype modules were available at the time of writing, performance with more than three x-OSC devices could not be investigated.

6.2 Closed-loop latency

Closed-loop latency was quantified as the delay between a physical change on an input and the resulting physical change on an output. This measurement incorporates sampling jitter, sending to the host application via WiFi, processing by the host application and sending of the responding output change to x-OSC via WiFi. A 1 Hz square wave was used to create a changing input signal and a PC application was written to set an output equal to that input. Both the input and output signals were connected to the inputs of an XOR gate to generate a 2 Hz wave form with a pulse width equal to the closed-loop latency. This pulse width was logged using a frequency counter for several hours. This arrangement is shown in Fig. 4. Investigations were conducted for *ideal* conditions where only the waveform input and output messages were sent and received, and for *loaded* conditions where x-OSC was simultaneously sending analogue input messages to the host application at 200 packet/s. The results are shown in Fig. 5. Under loaded conditions the mean closed-loop latency was measured at 10.9 ms, for ideal conditions, this figure dropped to 5.5 ms. It is therefore assumed that under ideal conditions the latency for sending input data only is approximately 2.75 ms.

A previous x-OSC design used the older MRF24WB WiFi module in place of the MRF24WG. Investigations found

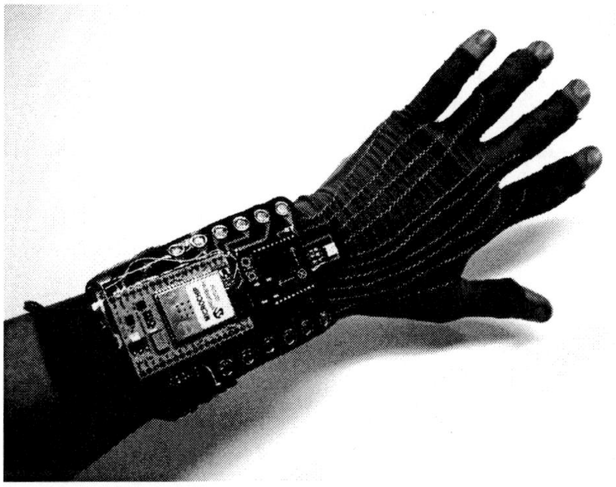

Figure 6. The x-OSC data glove, incorporating an IMU, RGB LED, vibration motors and e-textile flex sensors

the MRF24WB provided a maximum throughput of 290 packet/s which would reduce to 100 packet/s with three devices sending simultaneously. The closed-loop latency was found to be 8.4 ms in ideal conditions and 15.8 ms when also sending analogue input packets at 200 Hz.

7. EXAMPLE APPLICATIONS

In this section three example applications of x-OSC will be described to provide practical and divergent examples of its potential utility.

7.1 Data Gloves

The primary motivation for the development of x-OSC was to enhance the glove-based musical system discussed in section 2. Compatibility with the x-OSC glove (made by Hannah Perner-Wilson and shown in Fig. 6) was achieved using the oscpack C++ library [21]. Nine analogue inputs were used to take readings from the resistive e-textiles sensors, and one serial input was used to receive accelerometer, gyroscope, magnetometer and orientation data from an IMU. Five PWM outputs were used to control an RGB LED and a pair of haptic feedback motors.

Each x-OSC glove operates in infrastructure mode, connecting to a router positioned close to the performer to reduce the risk of WiFi interference [19]. The remaining six input, and 11 output channels provides scope for future development.

7.2 Solar Wind Chime

A second example application of x-OSC is in the context of an art/science communication project lead by the artist and designer Helen White. The aim of the project is to create a 'solar wind chime': an installation incorporating a physical chime which responds to readings of solar particle emissions provided in real-time by the National Oceanic and Atmospheric Administration. The chimes resonate and animate to produce an audio/visual manifestation of solar wind fluctuations. In this installation, 12 x-OSC output PWM channels are tuned to resonate the aluminium

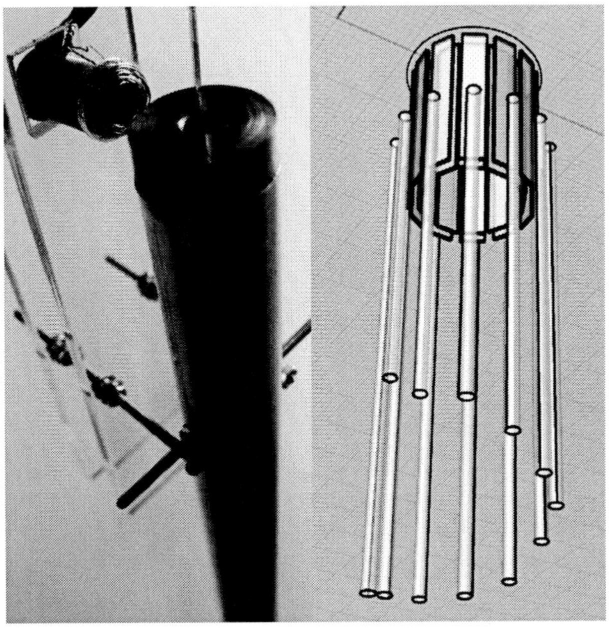

Figure 7. Solar wind chime: top of aluminium tube with electromagnet (left) and solar wind chime assembly design (right)

tubes of the solar wind chime, (shown in Fig.7). Furthermore, DC signals can be used to stimulate the physical displacement of the tubes. The solar wind readings are interpreted and remapped to OSC messages within a Processing sketch, using the oscP5 library [22].

7.3 Hexapod Robot

To demonstrate application of x-OSC beyond typical creative technology domains, x-OSC is used to connect software running on the host computer with a Sparkfun 12 servo hexapod robot, equipped with two IR range sensors as shown in Fig. 8. The software, written in C# using the Ventuz OSC library [23], implements a basic gait and avoidance algorithm which is used to drive twelve PWM output channels connected to each servo and two analogue input channels to take readings from the IR sensors.

8. CONCLUSION

x-OSC was developed for creative/music applications but its high-performance and versatility make it a valuable tool for any application requiring a real-time interface between software and electronic sensors or actuators. The hardware and firmware design has been optimised to achieve sustained throughput of up to 370 messages per second and latency of less than 3 ms. The widely supported OSC protocol enables any WiFi enabled platform to interface to the 32 multi-functional I/O channels without the need for specific drivers or software. Real-time access to settings via browser provides a convenient interface during development and eliminates the need for supporting software.

Acknowledgments

The authors would like to thank the Pervasive Media Studio, South West Microelectronics iNets, the European Regional Development Fund, the University of the West of England and the following individuals: Verity McIntosh, Clare Reddington, Imogen Heap, Helen White, Balazs Janko, Peter Bennett, Hannah Perner-Wilson, Kelly Snook and Adam Stark.

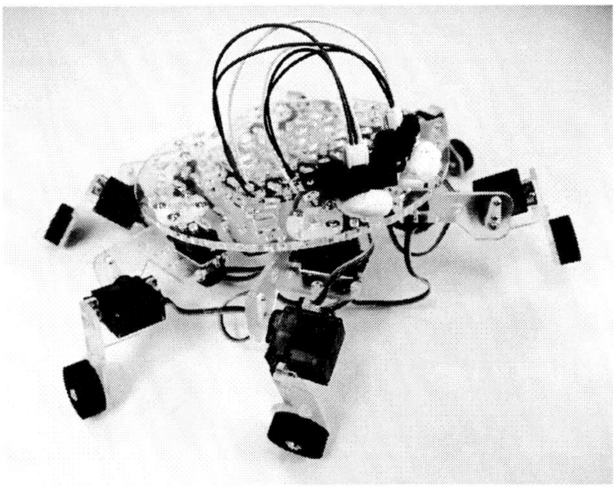

Figure 8. Sparkfun 12 servo hexapod robot with IR range sensors

9. REFERENCES

[1] R. Noss, R. Cox, D. Laurillard, R. Luckin, L. Plowman, E. Scanlon, and M. Sharples, "System upgrade: Realising the vision for UK education." London Knowledge Lab, London., Project Report, 2012.

[2] C. Anderson, *Makers: The New Industrial Revolution.* Crown Business, 2012.

[3] C. Reas, B. Fry, and J. Maeda., *Processing: A Programming Handbook for Visual Designers and Artists.* The MIT Press., 2007.

[4] D. Mellis, M. Banzi, D. Cuartielles, and T. Igoe, "Arduino: An open electronic prototyping platform," in *Proceedings of the Conference on Human Factors in Computing (alt.chi)*, 2007.

[5] E. R. Miranda and M. M. Wanderley, *New Digital Musical Instruments: Control And Interaction Beyond the Keyboard.* A-R Editions, 2006.

[6] A. Mulder, "The i-cube system: Moving towards sensor technology for artists." in *Proceedings of the 6th International Symposium on Electronic Art.*, 1995.

[7] E. Fléty, N. Leroy, J.-C. Ravarini, and F. Bevilacqua, "Versatile sensor acquisition system utilizing network technology," in *Proceedings of the International Conference on New Interfaces for Musical Expression*, 2004.

[8] S. Kartadinata, "The gluion: Advantages of an FPGA-based sensor interface," in *Proceedings of the International Conference on New Interfaces for Musical Expression*, 2006.

[9] T. Mitchell and I. Heap, "Soundgrasp: A gestural interface for the performance of live music," in *Proceedings of the International Conference on New Interfaces for Musical Expression*, 2011.

[10] T. J. Mitchell, S. Madgwick, and I. Heap, "Musical interaction with hand posture and orientation: A toolbox of gestural control mechanisms." in *Proceedings of the International Conference on New Interfaces for Musical Expression*, 2012.

[11] A. Schmeder and A. Freed, "uOSC: The open sound control reference platform for embedded devices," in *Proceedings of the International Conference on New Interfaces for Musical Expression*, 2008.

[12] D. Overholt, "A system for sketching in hardware: Do-it-yourself interfaces for sound and music computing," in *Proceedings of the Sound and Music Computing Conference*, 2012.

[13] H.-C. Steiner, "Firmata: Towards making microcontrollers act like extensions of the computer," in *Proceedings of the International Conference on New Interfaces for Musical Expression*, 2009.

[14] Eroktronix Labs, "Miditron." [Online]. Available: www.miditron.com

[15] E. Gallin and M. Sirguy, "Eobody3: a ready-to-use premapped and multi-protocol sensor interface," in *Proceedings of the International Conference on New Interfaces for Musical Expression*, 2011.

[16] S. Kobayashi, T. Endo, K. Harada, and S. Oishi, "Gainer: a reconfigurable i/o module and software libraries for education," in *Proceedings of the International Conference on New Interfaces for Musical Expression*, ser. NIME2006, 2006.

[17] The Center For New Music and Audio Technology (CNMAT), UC Berkeley, "Open sound control," 2013. [Online]. Available: www.opensoundcontrol.org

[18] M. Wright, "Open sound control: an enabling technology for musical networking," *Organised Sound*, vol. 10, no. 3, 2005.

[19] E. Fléty, "The wise box : a multi-performer wireless sensor interface using wifi and osc," in *Proceedings of the International Conference on New Interfaces for Musical Expression*, 2005.

[20] "Avr121: Enhancing adc resolution by oversampling," Atmel Corporation, Tech. Rep., 2005.

[21] R. Bencina, "A simple C++ open sound control (OSC) packet manipulation library," 2013. [Online]. Available: https://code.google.com/p/oscpack/

[22] A. Schlegel, "The oscp5 library," 2013. [Online]. Available: www.sojamo.de/libraries/oscP5

[23] Ventuz, "The ventuz OSC C# library," 2013. [Online]. Available: www.ventuz.com

THE AIRSTICKS: A NEW INTERFACE FOR ELECTRONIC PERCUSSIONISTS

Alon Ilsar
University of Technology, Sydney
alon.ilsar@student.uts.edu.au

Mark Havryliv
The Australian Institute of Music, Sydney
mhavryliv@ieee.org

Andrew Johnston
University of Technology, Sydney
andrew.johnston@uts.edu.au

ABSTRACT

This paper documents the early developments of a new interface for electronic percussionists. The interface is designed to allow the composition, improvisation and performance of live percussive electronic music using hand, finger, foot and head movements captured by various controllers. This paper provides a background to the field of electronic percussion, outlines the artistic motivations behind the project, and describes the technical nature of the work completed so far. This includes the development of software, the combination of existing controllers and senses, and an example mapping of movement to sound.

1. INTRODUCTION

The work presented in this paper is motivated by a desire to give percussionists control over complex sound textures at the same time as allowing them to time and execute precise rhythmic gestures. Such an interface takes advantage of the motor skills of an expert percussionist and combines it with all the real-time control over sound permitted by modern software.

In previous work, we developed an interface that allowed percussionists to manipulate sounds using head movements in a manner that did not interfere with the traditional four-limbed playing of their instrument. However, since then, we have shifted our focus to deconstructing the traditional approach to triggering sounds - namely, by striking a drum skin or a pad - and replacing it with sounds triggered by striking the air, allowing the performer to have more control over the sound both before and after the sound is triggered.

This paper will provide a brief background to the development of electronic percussion instruments, from the earliest electronic pads to the creation of gestural sensors, particularly the Radio Baton [1] [2]. The authors' own gestural interface, called the AirSticks, will be discussed, including a brief overview of the development of the design, how the design criteria has changed over the course of the instruments development and future plans for development and assessment.

1.1 Gestural Controllers

Gestural controllers, or 'open-air' controllers as they are referred to by Rovan and Hayward [3], allow tremendous freedom for sonic control. Such interfaces 'unchain the performer from the physical constraints of holding, touching, and manipulating an instrument' [3]. However, by their nature, they can weaken the perceptual relationship between gestures and sonic output. The relatively unlimited range of possible mappings of gesture to sound requires a performer to devote much time to learning different mapping scenarios and develop a routine of practicing to relate movements to change in sound [4]. This has given rise to much literature concerning the most effective design and pedagogical factors in designing novel instruments. See these papers for a rigorous treatment of these factors [5] [6].

The decoupling of physical contact with sonic output causes another perceptual issue relating to the feedback channel that helps performers regulate timing. It is well-established that accurate, repeatable and timely feedback -- whether it be physical or acoustic -- is required for a performer to comfortably deliver expressive performance [7] [8] [9] [10].

The technical innovation behind the development of the AirSticks is designed to take full advantage of the performance possibilities that open up when a percussionist is not required to strike a surface, but the speed and accuracy of the method for sensing when a strike occurs allows the perceptual feedback to be closed in a comfortable and satisfying way.

Position and rotation data for two 'sticks' is captured and analysed by a custom piece of software running on OSX which outputs MIDI data. This data is accompanied by MIDI data containing information about hand, finger, foot and head movements. Combined, these data provide the performer and composer with a plethora of mapping possibilities.

Mulder suggests that new musical instruments should be designed around the existing motor skills that a performer may already possess [11]. The AirSticks opens the door to creating a novel instrument that allows performers to utilise the hours of practice that traditional drum kit players have already dedicated, building on their existing technique in new ways to create an instrument that is both intimate for the performer [12] and transparent for the audience [13] [14]. The AirSticks also focus on maintaining the relationship between energy put in and the sonic output [15]. In other words, the AirSticks is an electronic drum kit that builds on traditional drum practice, celebrates advances in technology, is electronic in nature yet maintains a physically plausible relationship between movement and sound.

2. BACKGROUND

The term electronic percussion in this paper refers to instruments which are played like traditional acoustic percussive instruments, but instead have an electronic output. It could be argued that since the invention of the microphone, all acoustic percussion instruments in the studio and in bigger live contexts have had an electronic output which has led to the ability to manipulate each individual sound. Modern top-of-the-range electronic drum kits market themselves on giving the performer ultimate control over the drum samples they trigger, by allowing the editing of parameters such of virtual microphone placement, room size, drum skin tension, drum size and drum material. This culture of attempting to emulate acoustic drum kits with electronic percussion is not of interest to us, rather, we seek to build on the tradition of triggering sounds that an acoustic drum kit cannot produce, sounds that reflect the culture of the modern electronic producer. However, we also aim to incorporate the control of all four limbs gained by acoustic drummers into this completely different sounding instrument.

2.1 Early Electronic Pads

The earliest example of an electronic pad is Leon Theremin's Keyboard Electronic Timpani designed in 1932 though it wasn't until the 1960s and the invention of modular synthesis that electronic pads became more common place [16]. A particularly celebrated example of this is Schneider and Hutter's Electronic Percussion Musical Instrument, patented in 1977 and used in the seminal electronic band Kraftwerk [17]. It is a device made up of metallic pads and metal sticks connected to the pads with an electric chord. Upon striking the pad, the percussionist completes a circuit of white noise or a sinusoidal wave for the short time that the stick and pad are in contact, similar to plugging a lead into a modular synthesizer and quickly pulling it out. This simple device is a good example of merging physical movement with electronic sound in a new way.

2.2 The Electronic Drum Pad

In more recent years, with the increase in speed of computers and the introduction of MIDI, electronic pads have been used to trigger samples as opposed to closing circuits. This has meant that any sound can be assigned to a strike of the electronic pad. Though there has been many recent advances in this technology, very little information other than velocity and the precise location of the strike on the surface can be captured [18].

2.3 The Radio Baton

Some musicians have decided that more information needs to be captured by the computer to enable the creation of electronic percussive instruments that may be as expressive as acoustic ones. One example of this is the Radio Baton, a gesture sensor that allows the tracking of a mallet-like stick in three dimensional space [2]. Instead of sending a trigger over MIDI on impact, this instrument sends a MIDI note-on message when the mallet crosses an invisible plane above an antenna board. Boulanger calls this plane the hit-level [2]. A second plane, called the set-level, is positioned just above the hit-level. This plane acts as a note-off trigger to avoid double-triggering. As well as generating note-on triggers this instrument also captures and sends XYZ position data. Schloss uses all this data to allow three levels of control: a timbral level, a note level and the control of a musical process [1]. It is this control of a musical process that gives the electronic percussionist greater control over musical expression than can be gained from a two dimensional surface. Since the computer is constantly receiving XYZ position data, control changes can be made before and after a strike, giving the performer of the Radio Baton extra control and expressivity.

3. CAPTURING MOVEMENT

The AirSticks uses a similar principle to the Radio Baton in capturing both trigger commands and XYZ data[1]. The primary difference is that instead of using invisible planes, the AirSticks uses rotation around the X-axis to send note-on and note-off information. This change brings the triggering gesture far more in line with the actual performance of a drummer [19] [20]. In this section we will describe the evolution of this project and why we came to our particular conclusions.

3.1 Project History

We would like to note that so far in this project we have not developed a formal experimental framework. Instead we have decided to develop the new instrument over the past ten years through Ilsar's creative practice as a full time drummer and performer. Before meeting Havryliv, Ilsar pursued new ways of playing electro-acoustic percussion. He designed what he called the EAPP (electro-acoustic percussive pads) which featured an array of small junk percussion bits attached to a Perspex drum, with Piezo transducers glued to each item. The idea was that these sounds, since they were all acoustic in nature as opposed to being samples from a computer, would give the percussionist an experience more related to that of playing an acoustic instrument, yet still enable the manipulation of the sounds using audio effects. At first, Ilsar used a Kaoss Pad, an effect unit that allows the user to

[1] Where the X axis parallel to the ground running across the performer

change different parameters of the effect using a touch pad. Ilsar performed gigs playing miked up hi-hats and bass drum with his feet, the EAPP with one hand and the Kaoss Pad with the other. This obviously impeded his ability to play more complicated cross-rhythms.
Around the same time Havryliv designed a jacket he used to manipulate other performers in his own live performance situations [21]. The jacket used mercury tilt sensors that enabled a performer, with the movement of their arms, to change the parameters of a Pure-Data patch as audio went into his computer. Havryliv designed a similar wearable item for Ilsar, in the form of a hat. Ilsar replaced his Kaoss Pad with his hat, and could now perform with all four limbs and manipulate sounds by tilting his head. He went on to perform with this set up at the Great Escape Festival with Comatone and Foley, and at the Sydney Opera House with Gauche. For those acts, Ilsar mapped sampled sounds from these bands' respective albums to the Roland SPD20 electronic multi-pad and Roland KD7 foot triggers.

We then pursued designing a new open-air controller system where instead of triggering samples off a laptop by hitting a pad, samples could be triggered by striking the air. This led us to the three different technologies.

3.2 Infrared and Cameras

We experimented with infrared tracking by placing four infrared LED lights on the end of a mallet forming a square shape. This is based on technology developed by Kim [22]. An infrared camera connected to the computer would then track these four lights, and according to the size and shape created, information would be sent to another software to provide the XYZ position and limited rotation data. This solution had its problems:

- A suitable lighting environment may not always be available, a device that could be used in the standard club, pub or concert hall was desired.
- The tracking of two of these mallets at the same time could cause serious interference to the data.
- Though the latency was relatively low (10msec), it was not low enough to enable the percussionist to feel like they could be confident that a sound would be triggered at the precise moment they expect.

3.3 Exoskeleton

The idea with an exoskeleton was that all the different rotation of joints from the shoulder, elbow and wrist, would result in the location of the sticks held by the percussionist [23]. After attempting to build an exoskeleton, we decided to trial the Gypsy 6 Suit. Problems with this interface were:

- The six sensors on each arm did not give us an exact location of the hands.
- It was cumbersome to wear, restrictive to move in and easy to break.
- It needed calibrating before each performance.

3.4 Gaming Controllers

The Razer Hydra Gaming Controllers comprise of two joysticks tethered to a base station, which connects to a computer using USB (see Figure 1). The joysticks can be moved freely in space (so far as the tethering cables permit) and their position and orientation is determined by their relationship to a sphere on the base station, which uses some magnetic sensing system amongst other sensors. The device has a sampling rate of 250 Hz, with measurement precision to the millimeter and degree for position and orientation, respectively. These controllers are cheap and an open source gaming community has already developed online with members releasing MIDI software which the authors began to experiment with. These controllers also come with an SDK, a set of C++ APIs which allow the developer to read the state of the motion controllers. The state comprises position and orientation (6-DOF), and the button states. An OSX application was developed based on this SDK which translates the user's movements to a graphical representation (see Figure 2). Other advantages such as weight, ease of set up, low-to-no interference and extra buttons for control meant the authors could commit to designing a new triggering system with these controllers.

4. THE AIRSTICKS

At first, we attempted to take the information of velocity and acceleration to decipher what the performer meant as a strike. Trigger detection was based on detecting spikes in acceleration and jerk (the time derivative of acceleration). This method was inspired by the performance gesture associated with a real drum kit: a stick would be moving downward at a reasonably constant velocity, would hit the drum skin and experience a large change in velocity which is detected as a peak in acceleration. The velocity and acceleration derivatives are constantly calculated from the position data sent from the device, and when an acceleration value that exceeds a particular threshold is recorded, a trigger was detected.

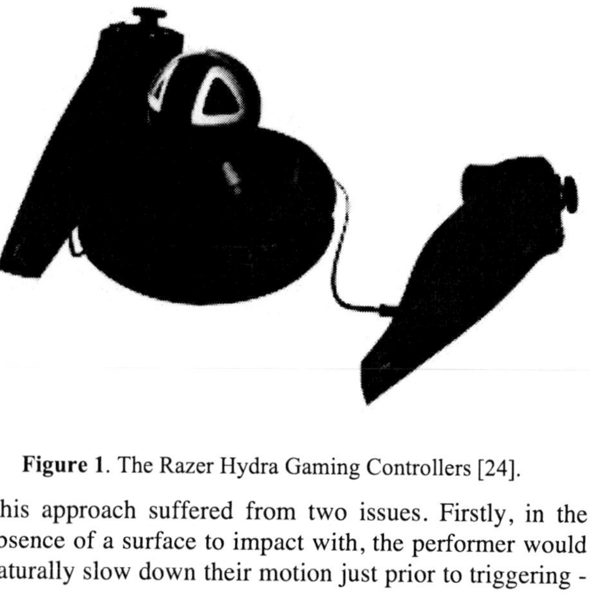

Figure 1. The Razer Hydra Gaming Controllers [24].

This approach suffered from two issues. Firstly, in the absence of a surface to impact with, the performer would naturally slow down their motion just prior to triggering -

this diminished the magnitude of potential acceleration peaks. Secondly, setting a constant threshold for trigger detection from acceleration data made it difficult to detect triggers across the range of potential gestures. In lowering the threshold intentional smaller movements would warrant a strike, but unintended jitters and shocks would also trigger a sound.

A machine learning method based on Neural Networks was developed that analysed velocity data alongside acceleration data. Upon recognising a peak in acceleration data, the velocity gesture leading up to that peak was analysed to see if it matched the velocity profile of a large range of strikes that had been recorded and learned in the past. This improved the performance of the trigger-detection, but even minor inconsistencies made it a frustrating and uncomfortable experience for the performer trying to accurately control musical performance timings.

4.1 Triggering System

The breakthrough occurred when we realized that instead of training the technology to enable the instrument to learn what the performer's intentions are, the performer should learn how to play a consistent non-complicated instrument. This is in line with the literature on instrument design and mappings. We devised a system of imaginary planes, similar to that of the Radio Baton, but instead of having a hit-level and a set-level, the rotation data sent from the gaming controllers is used. When the performer's wrist passed through a particular angle of rotation around the X axis, resembling the movement of a strike, a note-on would be triggered. The XYZ position data would determine the note-on number, splitting the 3D space into a 4x2x2 grid (see Figure 2). The performer quickly found consistency in finding this trigger angle, and could even anticipate it. An auditory response in this new instrument had replaced the tactile one of the electronic pads.

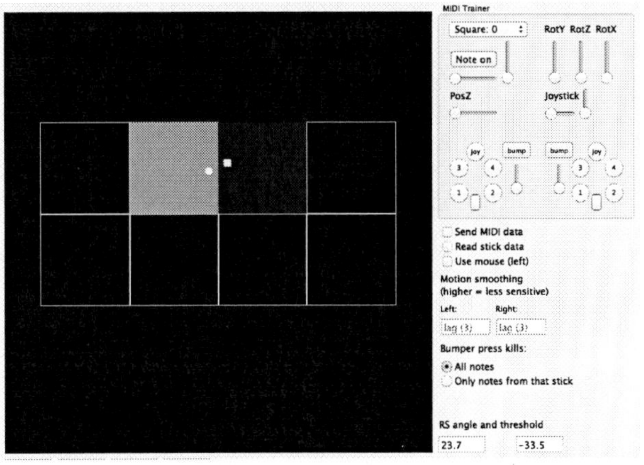

Figure 2. The AirSticks' Graphic User Interface.

This also allowed us to permit striking up and down through a point to improve the speed at which the instrument could be played. Velocity of the strike could still be interpreted, as the speed at which the controller passes through this point was also captured and sent to the computer. The angle of trigger was set to different degrees depending on the height of the strike. A strike high up would use a trigger angle of close to 90 degrees, or perpendicular to the ground, whereas the lowest angle trigger points would be set to 0 degrees, or parallel to the ground, with all other trigger angles in between being scaled appropriately, as if the performer was playing an invisible concave plane (see Figure 3).

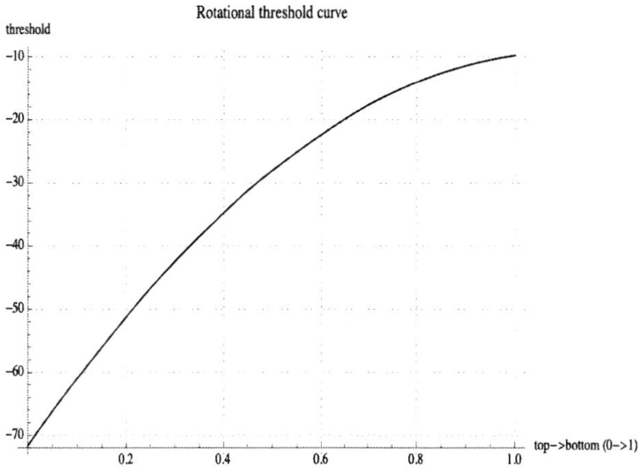

Figure 3. The threshold of the trigger angle against the distance from the bottom of the virtual space.

4.2 Thumb, Finger, Foot and Head Movements

Having created a consistent system for capturing the performer's movements using the Razer Hydra Gaming Controllers, we embarked on capturing other movements by the percussionist, particular those that would not take away from being able to play the AirSticks with the hands. Like all modern gaming controllers, the Razer Hydras consist of a thumb joystick, a trigger button controlled with the index fingers, and several buttons on each hand. This gives the performer the ability to send information to the computer with more subtle gestures, movements that either need to be more easily made than large ones, or ones that the performer decides should be hidden from the audience. Foot movements are captured using the SoftStep Foot MIDI Controller (see Figure 4) which enables the performer to trigger up to ten sounds with the back of the toe or heel or make up over forty more controller changes. Finally, head movements are captured using an accelerometer placed on top of the performers head that acts as a tilt sensor.

4.3 Graphic User Interface

The gaming controllers interface to an application designed for Mac OSX built on the Razer Hydra SDK, which provides a user interface for using the controllers and which outputs MIDI data based on position/orientation and gesture analysis (continuous and discrete, respectively). This arrangement provides the highest possible sampling rate and fidelity from the device, which in turn permits the use of sophisticated engineering techniques to analyse motion, and provide performance-time gestural analysis and response. A predictive filtering scheme based on Kalman state estimation is used to effectively up-sample the gestural analysis system to 1kHz, well beyond the perceptual limit for the sensation of causal association between gesture and aural result [25].

Figure 4. Keith McMillen's SoftStep Foot Controller [26].

The Graphic User Interface or GUI, is made of a grid and two floating points that represent the middle of each controller. This enables a simple visual representation of the virtual space. The performer can see in which grid each hand is in, and note that when they tilt past the trigger angle, the grid lights up, signaling a note-on message. The GUI also provides a MIDI trainer, a function extremely useful when using programs such as Ableton Live for the sound mapping. The MIDI trainer function enables a simple way to map control changes in the GUI to ones in Albeton Live. Another way of mapping sounds and control changes is by noting which numbers they are being sent on. This facilitates an easy way to sending MIDI to all sorts of other instruments and programs.

4.4 Mapping

Currently, all information from all sensors makes it way into Ableton Live 9. Here a world of possible mappings exists. We will now outline an example of one of the mappings of movement to sound we have made for the AirSticks, tying in to Schnell and Battier's concept of a 'composed instrument' [27]. We will focus on the way the gestures correspond to sound triggering and manipulation and avoid much of the technical work.

4.4.1 The AirSticks 16 Drum Rack

This mapping is the most developed to date and aims to allow the performer as much choice for solo or group improvisation as possible, while maintaining intimacy and transparency, keeping with the literature. The AirSticks 16 Drum Rack mapping utilises the 4x4x2 grid (see Figure 1) to allow the performer to trigger any of sixteen sounds in a virtual space around them. The GUI is compatible with Ableton Live's Drum Rack virtual instrument which also defaults to a sixteen sample array. The mapping allocates a group of samples for each box of the grid and foot triggers, and makes it possible to switch through different sounds using various buttons on the controllers. Rotating past a predetermined point on the X rotation triggers the sound that corresponds to the box the AirStick is in, mimicking a percussive strike. The velocity is determined by the speed at which this rotation is made and is mapped to volume and brightness. Aside from Note On and Off messages, control change information correlating to finger, thumb, hand, foot and head movements also makes its way into Ableton Live through the GUI. There are a large number of modes of effects that can be called up using the buttons on the controllers. Different modes basically switch on different effects, whose parameters are mapped to some of the below in Table 1.

Movement	Parameter(s)
LPosX	Reverb Input Filter Frequency
LPosY	Reverb Input Filter Width; Noise Gain Left
LPosZ	All Effects Gains
LRotX	Chorus Delay 1 Time; Grain Delay Pitch; Fragulator Playback Speed: Ping Pong Delay Time Delay
LRotY	Chorus Delay 1 High Pass Frequency; Grain Delay Frequency; High Pass Filter Frequency
LRotZ	Panning Of Respective Effect
LJoyX	Fragulator Amp Variation; Ping Pong Delay Filter Frequency
LJoyZ	Chorus LFO Amount; Reverb Decay Time; Grain Delay Feedback; Fragulator Repetition; Noise Centre Frequency Left; Ping Pong Delay Filter Width
LTrig	Sends into Same Respective Returns
RPosX	Reverb Early Reflections Spin Rate
RPosY	Reverb Early Reflections Spin Amount; Noise Gain Right; Noise Track Volume
RPosZ	Pitch
RRotX	Chorus Delay 2 Delay Time; Grain Delay Random Pitch
RRotY	Low Pass Filter Frequency
RRotZ	Panning Of Respective Effect
RJoyX	Chorus LFO Rate
RJoyZ	Chorus LFO Amount; Reverb Decay Time; Grain Delay Spray; Grain Delay Time Delay; Noise Centre Frequency Right
RTrig	Microphone Audio Track Sends to Respective Returns
HeadX	Master Panning
HeadZ	Master Volume

Table 1. Mapping of movement[2] to sound.

In general, movements to the right and down result in lower pitch manipulation, while movements upwards and towards the audience result in an increase in intensity. Of particular interest with this mapping is the use of the right trigger button, controlled by the movement of the index figure, to turn the gain up of a microphone placed near the performer, and the use of the left trigger button to turn

[2] L – Left; R – Right; Pos – Position; Rot – Rotation; Joy – Joystick; Trig – Trigger.

up an internal feedback loop. This allows the performer to 'tune' the room, using the acoustics of the room to create feedback tones and drones. It is our intention to develop this approach further as it brings an electro-acoustic element to a purely electronic instrument. It also means that if the performer does not react to the feedback created by their movements they can lose control of the sound. This creates a greater dialogue between the instrument and performer. It also allows the performer to manipulate other sounds in their environment, whether it be their voice, other musicians, the audience, or the surrounding sounds. To best understand this mapping there is a demonstration at

www.alonilsar.com/composer/airsticks

5. FUTURE RESEARCH

We are interested in not only using the current set up of the AirSticks in a variety of ways, but also continually changing aspects of the instrument to suit different pieces of work. Other mappings for the AirSticks that have been conceived are listed here below. All of these attempt to maintain the relationship between physical energy input and sound output.

- *FerguCircles* – designed to allow the performer to play samples using granular synthesis by forming circles with their hands around any of the three planes.
- *Bouncy Balls* – an experiment with physical modeling and perpetual motion.
- *Synthesiser n* – designed to allow the performer to play melodies on any soft synth across a number of virtual boxes.
- *Spinning Plates* – designed for a piece of virtual spinning plates which each make different changing pitches.

Other uses and ideas for the AirSticks include:

- Working with sound convolution.
- Performing with other traditional and non-traditional instruments.
- Using the AirSticks in children's theatre.
- Working with visual artists in creating a new Graphic User Interface that may be projected during performances.
- Establishing a set of rudiments to best practice and learn the instrument.
- Continually looking for new hardware devices that could potentially work even better with the GUI.

We will also soon invite other percussionists to play the instrument and get their feedback. We feel this is invaluable to create a more intimate instrument. We have also ready begun to put on performances using the AirSticks and asking for feedback from the audience in order to improve its transparency. We have also been gathering data on how musicians have reacted to playing in an ensemble that contains the AirSticks.

6. REFERENCES

[1] W. A. Schloss, "Recent advances in the coupling of the language Max with the Mathews/Boie Radio Drum," in *Proceedings of the International Computer Music Conference*, 1990.

[2] R. Boulanger, "The 1997 Mathews Radio-Baton & Improvisation Modes," in *Proc. of ICMC*, 1997.

[3] J. Rovan and V. Hayward, "Typology of tactile sounds and their synthesis in gesture-driven computer music performance," *Trends in Gestural Control of Music,* pp. 297-320, 2000.

[4] T. Winkler, "Making motion musical: Gesture mapping strategies for interactive computer music," in *ICMC Proceedings*, 1995, pp. 261-264.

[5] S. O'Modhrain, "A framework for the evaluation of digital musical instruments," *Computer Music Journal,* vol. 35, pp. 28-42, 2011.

[6] J. Malloch, S. Sinclair, A. Hollinger, and M. M. Wanderley, "Input Devices and Music Interaction," in *Musical Robots and Interactive Multimodal Systems*, ed: Springer, 2011, pp. 67-83.

[7] M. S. O'Modhrain and C. Adviser-Chafe, *Playing by feel: incorporating haptic feedback into computer-based musical instruments*: Stanford University, 2001.

[8] J.-L. Florens, A. Luciani, C. Cadoz, and N. Castagné, "ERGOS: Multi-degrees of freedom and versatile force-feedback panoply," in *Proceedings of EuroHaptics*, 2004, pp. 356-360.

[9] E. Berdahl, G. Niemeyer, and J. O. Smith, "Using haptics to assist performers in making gestures to a musical instrument," in *9th International Conference on New Interfaces for Musical Expression-NIME, Pittsburgh PA*, 2009, pp. 177-182.

[10] C. Chafe, "Tactile audio feedback," in *Proceedings of the International Computer Music Conference*, 1993, pp. 76-76.

[11] A. Mulder, "Towards a choice of gestural constraints for instrumental performers," *Trends in gestural control of music,* pp. 315-335, 2000.

[12] S. Fels, "Designing for intimacy: Creating new interfaces for musical expression," *Proceedings of the IEEE,* vol. 92, pp. 672-685, 2004.

[13] T. Mitchell, "SoundGrasp: A gestural interface for the performance of live music.," *International Conference on New Interfaces for Musical Expression (NIME)* vol. 2011, Oslo,

Norway, 30 May - 1 June 2011 . Oslo, Norway: UNSPECIFIED, 2011.

[14] T. J. Mitchell, S. Madgwick, and I. Heap, "Musical interaction with hand posture and orientation: A toolbox of gestural control mechanisms," 2012.

[15] A. Hunt, M. M. Wanderley, and M. Paradis, "The Importance of Parameter Mapping in Electronic Instrument Design," *Journal of New Music Research,* vol. 32, pp. 429-440, 2003.

[16] R. M. Aimi, "New expressive percussion instruments," Massachusetts Institute of Technology, 2002.

[17] P. Bussy, *Kraftwerk: Man, machine and music*: SAF Publishing Ltd, 2004.

[18] A. R. Tindale, A. Kapur, G. Tzanetakis, P. Driessen, and A. Schloss, "A comparison of sensor strategies for capturing percussive gestures," in *Proceedings of the 2005 conference on New interfaces for musical expression*, 2005, pp. 200-203.

[19] R. I. Godøy, E. Haga, and A. R. Jensenius, "Playing “air instruments”: mimicry of sound-producing gestures by novices and experts," in *Gesture in Human-Computer Interaction and Simulation*, ed: Springer, 2006, pp. 256-267.

[20] S. Fels, A. Gadd, and A. Mulder, "Mapping transparency through metaphor: towards more expressive musical instruments," *Organised Sound,* vol. 7, pp. 109-126, 2002.

[21] G. Schiemer and M. Havryliv, "Viral firmware: what will I wear tomorrow," in *Australasian Computer Music Conference*, 2004.

[22] J. Kim, G. Schiemer, and T. Narushima, "Oculog: playing with eye movements," 2007.

[23] N. Collins, C. Kiefer, M. Patoli, and M. White, "Musical exoskeletons: Experiments with a motion capture suit," *Proceedings of New Interfaces for Musical Expression (NIME), Sydney, Australia,* 2010.

[24] (7/4/13). *Razer Hydra*. Available: http://www.razerzone.com/gaming-controllers/razer-hydra

[25] M. Havryliv, "Haptic-rendered practice carillon clavier," 2012.

[26] K. McMillen. (7/4/13). *Keith McMillen Instruments - SoftStep*. Available: http://www.keithmcmillen.com/softstep/overview

[27] N. Schnell and M. Battier, "Introducing composed instruments, technical and musicological implications," presented at the Proceedings of the 2002 conference on New interfaces for musical expression, Dublin, Ireland, 2002.

A COMPUTATIONAL METHOD FOR EXPLORING MUSICAL CREATIVITY DEVELOPMENT

A. Alexakis
Dept. of Music Studies
University of Athens
tonisq
@music.uoa.gr

A. Khatchatourov
Sony Computer Science Laboratory
armen.khatchatourov
@gmail.com

A. Triantafyllaki
Dept. of Music Studies
University of Athens
a_triant
@music.uoa.gr

C. Anagnostopoulou
Dept. of Music Studies
University of Athens
Chrisa
@music.uoa.gr

ABSTRACT

The development of musical creativity using non-standard methods and techniques has been given considerable attention in the last years. However, the use of new technologies in teaching improvisation and thus development of creativity has received relatively little attention to date. The aim of this paper is two-fold: firstly to propose a way of formalising the measurement of creativity, and secondly to test whether the use of a particular interactive system built to support musical improvisational dialogues between the user and the computer (MIROR IMPRO), can develop creativity. First, based on previous research, we define a set of variables aiming at evaluating creativity, and we create a computational model to automatically calculate these variables in order to assess the development of creative abilities. Second, we assess the advancement of creativity in 8-10 year-old children, who spent six weeks interacting with MIROR-IMPRO. We used two groups of children in assessing this advancement: a group of children with no musical background (n=20) and a group of young pianists (n=10). We carried out a free improvisation test before the start and after the end of six sessions with the system. The results suggest a potential progress related to a number of these variables, which could be indicative of creativity advancement. The issue of measuring creativity is discussed in the light of these findings.

1. INTRODUCTION

Creativity is a fundamental human ability, and at the same time a particularly challenging concept to define. Various attempts exist to date, and its meaning tends to shift across the various disciplines. Yet however vague and slippery its definition may be, its core features are shared across domains, which makes it possible to model, and in general to become the subject of scientific investigation.

One of the first attempts to formally describe creativity is found in [26], where *Creativity Thinking* is modeled as a four-step process: *preparation* – information, specific knowledge and ideas about the case/problem under question are gathered, *incubation* – work proceeds unconsciously, *illumination* – suddenly the solution emerges, and *verification* – the solution is verified and elaborated. Another step-wise model suggested in [9] where a five-step approach is proposed in problem solving and creative thinking. The idea of problem solving is also closely related with the eminent contribution of J.P. Guilford in the field. Guilford in [11] introduced the idea of *convergent* and *divergent thinking* and associated the latter with creative thinking.

The above approaches to creativity focus mainly on the processes involved in creative thinking. Another aspect of creativity, closely related with attempts to measure or assess creativity, is focused mainly, but not solely, on the product. Creativity as 'product' is defined by Amabile in [5] as one whereby *"...appropriate observers independently agree it is creative. Appropriate observers are those familiar with the domain in which the product was created or the response articulated"*, hence introducing the idea of how a creative product is received and assessed by (as well as situated in) its environment.

But how can creativity be assessed? Guilford in [10] created a test to measure creativity, by assessing divergent thinking. The subjects were given 180 ordinary life objects (e.g. a pencil, a spoon, a cap) that they were asked to score across four dimensions: originality, fluency, flexibility, and elaboration. Extending Guilford's ideas, Torrance developed the Torrance Tests of Creative Thinking (TTCT) [25], while Amabile proposed the Consensual Assessment Technique (CAT) for ranking the creativity of art objects [5]. CAT is based on the idea that expert judges within a field will have a valid opinion regarding the creativity values of an object of art. Gathering and examining such expert opinions may provide a good estimation of the creative worth of an object. A well described application of CAT can be found in [12].

In the field of music creativity, Webster's work [29] continues to be prominent among scholars. Webster built on Guilford's ideas and created a tool to evaluate the creative aptitude of children (ages 6-8), the *Measurement of Creative Thinking in Music (MCTM)* [27]. The MCTM evolved into MCTM-II in [30]. Children's creative thinking is evaluated through a ten-task session, of about 20-25 minutes. The qualities that are scored are musical expressiveness (ME), musical flexibility (MF), musical originality (MO) and musical syntax (MS) [29]. In the specific field of ethnomusicology, Lomax developed the *"cantometrics"* [14]. They are comprised of a set of 37 items measuring group organization, level of cohesiveness, rhythmic features, melodic features, dynamic features, ornamentation and vocal qualities. Later, McPherson in [15] developed measures to assess a musician's ability to perform music creatively. These new measures are pertained to evaluate music learner's performance from memory, by ear and through improvising.

Simonton in [21] performed computerized content analysis to assess the melodic originality of 15,618 themes of 479 classical composers, from Josquin des Pres to Shostakovich. Simonton defined a number of variables each of which pertain to different qualities of the case under investigation. Similarly in [22] he investigated 1919 compositions of 172 classical composers, spanning almost 500 years. A panel of experts manually scored several of the above variables, prior to the computer analysis.

Regardless of how well they approach the notion of creativity, the above measures require more or less the engagement of (often numerous) human experts in scoring. They also employ statistical averages in order to eliminate human errors and individual particularities.

At the same time, the broad introduction of computer technology in music educational processes created the possibility to computationally automate the whole process. Hence it becomes more and more pertinent to come up with proposals that require no human intervention, even if the range of the investigated qualities is decreased.

The introduction of new music technologies in the educational process involves also the introduction of new interaction paradigms between the user and the machine. An example of new interaction paradigms are Interactive Reflexive Music Systems (IRMS) [18], and in particular the MIROR IMPRO system [20], which was developed within the MIROR project [1] as the evolution of *The Continuator* [2][3][4][17][19]. The core concept in such a system is that basic musical elements can be taught and musical cognitive processes can be developed not only by the traditional teacher/learner dipole but also by the direct interaction of the learner with the system, without the involvement of a human instructor.

The application generates different kinds of output melodies based on the user's musical input, stimulating the reflexive interaction between the user and the application. This generation is based on a specific Markovian mechanism designed by Sony CSL Paris, allowing a meaningful musical output. Namely, the output is composed of what the user could have played herself, i.e. a constrained recombination of musical elements previously played by the user. In this way, each response of the system is composed of musical material close to the user's style, but at the same time proposes to the user to explore, as the next, step, new ways to express musical ideas.This study explores the use of MIROR IMPRO in developing young children's improvisational skills - recognised as a central component of musical creativity [29]. Therefore, it would seem important to develop a methodology of evaluating the creativity that arises as a result of engaging with such a system. This may later be integrated into the system in order to give real time information to the user and to record such information for a traditional trainer/learner session that may subsequently follow. The aim of the paper is to propose a way of measuring creativity in children playing the keyboard; and to use this model in order to assess creativity in children with and without musical background, comparing their pre and post tests (before and after an intervention of 6 improvisation sessions using the MIROR IMPRO system).

The paper is structured in the following way: in the **Methods** section, the technical description of the work is laid out, including the data collection process, the knowledge representation schemata, computational details and the description of the variables used to assess creativity. In the **Results** section, the results of the work are presented and subsequently discussed in the last section (**Discussion**).

2. METHODS

2.1 The Goal

In this section, a model and a computational method to measure creativity is introduced. Specifically, we describe the musical corpus we used, the knowledge representation schema, algorithmic details and particularities, and finally the creativity measuring model, realized as a set of measures/variables.

2.2 Data collection

Within the framework of the psychological experiments related to the MIROR project, a number of children's musical improvisations on a MIDI keyboard were performed. The keyboard was connected to MIROR IMPRO system. Each improvisation session is comprised of a dialogue of music phrases that are alternately human and machine generated. Each of these phrases is recorded onto a different MIDI channel and thus it becomes straight-forward to extract all human phrases.

The data we used comes from two experiments with MIROR IMPRO and young children - one with non-musicians and one where children had been studying the piano from between 1-4 years.

The reasoning behind this sampling is the following. In our initial work with non-musicians we found that the keyboard as an object (rather than the interaction with the system itself) seemed to draw the attention of the children. We then introduced a second sample of children who were already familiar with the keyboard, as a way to eliminate the effect the keyboard may have on the interaction and hence the musical output from this interaction. In this paper we present the analysis from both groups of children.

The study with the young pianists took place in a small music school and involved 10 children (six girls and four boys) playing alone with the MIROR IMPRO system for six weeks (that is six sessions of 15 to 20 minutes). The study with the non-musicians took place in a primary school and involved 20 children (sixteen boys and four girls) playing with MIROR IMPRO across six weeks, in similar conditions. In both studies we proceeded to conduct a pre- (before the six weeks) and post-test (after the six weeks) with the children. This consisted of asking each child individually to improvise a short tune (1-2 minutes long) on the keyboard.

We compare the pre-test sessions to the post-test sessions of both the young pianists' and the non-musicians' sessions, in order to find out if their creativity developed by their post-test session. In this way, we might begin to attribute such development to their in-between sessions where they interacted with the MIROR IMPRO system, in order to explore further the use of IRMS in the development of children's musical improvisations and creativity.

The young pianists pre-corpus consists of 5218 note events having duration of 2,359,916 msecs. The post-corpus consists of 2427 note events having duration of 662,627 msecs. The non-musicians pre-corpus consists of 8990 note events having duration of 2,022,753 msecs. The post-corpus consists of 6477 note having duration of 1,030,853 msecs.

2.3 Knowledge Representation

The concept of a symbolic musical corpus raises the issue of music knowledge representation. Having in mind the data manipulation task, the viewpoint representation formalism was chosen to be used [8], as it offers great flexibility in surfacing the attributes of the musical objects. It also offers a direct and straight forward representation on corresponding data structures. The concept of viewpoint is lately gaining popularity among researchers, due to its capability to capture in a well-defined representation set of symbols, a big variety of the musical features of musical data.

The musical object on which a viewpoint is defined can here be a single note or a sequence of notes, viz. a segment. Here the notion of a segment is used to describe the whole melody played by the child.

On the note level, several viewpoints were calculated: pitch (as MIDI number), pitch class, onset, duration, ioi (interon-set time interval), trail (time interval between a NOTE OFF event and the consecutive NOTE ON), fnitioid (time interval from first note in track), seqint (melodic interval – pitch distance from previous event), contour (rising: 1, static: 0, falling: -1) and several others.

Segmental viewpoints [7] are also constructed. For each segment a set of segmental viewpoints is calculated, such as the number of notes in the segment, the duration etc.

Segmental Viewpoint	Description
`sd[seq]`	Standard deviation of sequence seq
`uniq_patt[seq]`	Number of unique patterns in sequence seq
`diff_patt[seq]`	Number of different patterns in seq
`tot_patt[seq]`	Number of total patterns in seq
`Avg_sise[seq]`	Average size in number of note events of seq
`Avg_dur[seq]`	Average duration
`Tot_size[seq]`	Total size in number of note events of seq
`Tot_dur[seq]`	Total duration
`Inteval (small,medium,large) [seq]`	Percentages of interval divisions
`Note (small,medium,large) [seq]`	Percentages of pitch divisions
`Rhythm (small,medium,large) [seq]`	Percentages of rhythm divisions
`velocity (small,medium,large) [seq]`	Percentages of dynamic divisions
`Texture[seq]`	Measures how "thick" is the music
`Cluster[seq]`	Number of chords in seq

Table 1. Segmental viewpoints used.

2.4 Computational Processing

The computation proceeds by reading one by one all MIDI files in a directory (a directory with MIDI files is considered a corpus) and building from the corresponding MIDI events a sequence of viewpoints. Consecutively, repeated patterns within each viewpoint sequence are extracted.

Thus, the identification of patterns can be seen as a problem within the stringology domain. As such, in order to identify common patterns suffix arrays [16] are employed. Suffix arrays provide an easy to implement and fast way to locate each and every common substring within a string. In [24], suffix arrays technique proves its capability and its efficiency on a much larger corpus.

For constructing the suffix array, the well-known QuickSort comparison sort algorithm is used in this work. The suffix array can be scanned and common patterns can be reported, along with their frequency, their length and their locations within the corpus.

2.5 Creativity Variables

In order to assess creativity we used a set of variables that we calculated for each subject, for the improvisation tests that took place before and after the training. The idea of assessing creativity through a set of metrics (realised as variables) is drawn directly from the creativity literature, as most of the scholars are proposing to measure creativity based on a set of measures, scored by one or more experts. Our aim is to come up with a set of metrics that are scored automatically, eliminating thus the need of experts. As evidenced in the creativity literature, we assume that advancement in musical variation and diversity is an indicator of musical creativity.

The following variables were used:

V1 – Standard Deviation. Standard deviation is a metric on how much away from the average falls most of the values. A low standard deviation means that data tend to be close to the average. We calculate this for the sequence of three viewpoints – MIDI numbers, intervals and rhythmic values. It indicates the diversity of the musical vocabulary.

V2 – Number of patterns with frequency 1. We identify all sequences of the 3 viewpoints (notes, intervals, rhythmic values) that appear only once in the corpus. We borrowed this idea from the lexical analysis in [23], as it seems to indicate novelty and musical variety. Suffix arrays make straight forward the identification of those patterns, since we count the number of rows in the array that has no common with their next.

V3 – Average Size, Duration. The idea of this indicator is taken from Webster's MCTM [27][28]. We calculate two variants of this variable. First, we calculate the segmental viewpoints size (in number of notes) and duration (in msecs) for each subject. Then we calculate the average of all segments per subject. Second, we calculate the total size and total duration for each subject.

V4 – Ratio of different per total patterns. This variable is drawn by analogy from lexical content analysis in psychotherapy [13] and is used also in [23]. There are evidence that the greatest the ratio of different words per total words the greatest the lexical diversity [13]. So we assume that the greatest the above ratio the greatest the musical variability and hence the musical creativity. We identify all sequences of the 3 viewpoints (notes, intervals, rhythmic values)

V5 – Interval Variation. This is an indicator on musical intervals diversity. We calculated the segmental viewpoint `interval(small, medium, large)`. Then we calculate for each subject's music (viz. each MIDI file) the percentages of small, medium and large intervals. We assume that small intervals are less than 4 steps and large ones more than 8 steps – a step is a semitone.

We assume that the more evenly distributed the percentages are that more variation we have. This applies also to V6, V7 & V8

V6 – Pitch Variation. We calculated the segmental viewpoint `note(low, medium, high)`. Then we calculate for each subject's music the percentages of low, medium and high pitches. We assume that low pitches are below F3 (MIDI number 53) and high ones over C#5 (MIDI number 73).

V7 – Rhythm Variation. We calculated the segmental viewpoint `rhythm(slow, medium, fast)`. Then we calculate for each subject's piece of music the corresponding percentages. We assume that medium rhythmic values are with the notes that has more or less the quarter note duration; that is 500 msecs for our MIDI files. Hence we take +/- 10% of that for identifying the slow and fast rhythms.

V8 – Dynamics Variation. We calculated the segmental viewpoint `velocity(soft, normal, hard)`. For identifying the dynamics of notes we take into consideration the velocity recorded along with the notes within the MIDI file. The velocity takes values in [0, 127] range. We calculate for each subject's music the percentages, similar to the above variables. We assume the piano range lays below velocity value of 40 and the forte one above 60.

V9 – Texture Richness. For all notes in each subject's corpus we sum up their duration. Then we divide the duration of each piece of music with the total duration of all notes. The more notes we have (and the more lengthy they are) the less the value of V9 will be. It indicates how much populated with notes the music is.

V10 – Clusterness. For each segment we calculate the number of simultaneities. It is an indicator of the number of chords and consequently the richness of harmony produced. A simultaneity occurs when a `"note on"` MIDI event is transmitted while others `"note on"` events are still alive.

3. RESULTS

Table 2 reports the mean values on pre and post conditions for the two groups, non-musicians and musicians. The general trends indicate advancement in creativity when we compare mean values on pre and post sessions.

	Non-musicians		Musicians	
	Pre	Post	Pre	Post
V1 pitch SD	10.75	13.16	8.84	9.65
V1 interval SD	10.08	10.75	9.36	9.24
V1 rhythm SD	0.93	0.97	15.11	19.84
V2 unique pitch	23.90	30.00	20.3	17.8
V2 unique interval	39.70	40.3	27.5	24.9
V2 unique rhythm	23.85	24.15	46.4	40.0
V3 Nb notes / segmented	48.70	48.42	42.62	29.42
V3 duration /segmented	12324	7598	25299	9822
V3 Nb notes / total	449.5	323.85	521.8	242.7
V3 duration/ total	10113 8	51543	235992	66263
V4 different pitch	0.35	0.37	0.29	0.31
V4 different interval	0.32	0.35	0.25	0.35
V4 different rhythm	0.29	0.30	0.31	0.38
V5 variation interval small	57.87	59.00	50.45	49.92
V5 variation interval medium	15.30	18.13	25.05	25.09
V5 variation interval large	26.82	22.79	24.50	24.98
V6 variation pitch low	13.85	20.09	12.25	15.62
V6 variation pitch medium	58.30	50.71	55.35	55.00
V6 variation pitch high	27.84	29.20	32.40	29.37
V7 variation rhythm slow	12.22	11.60	69.99	53.60
V7 variation rhythm medium	4.42	3.52	7.13	10.35
V7 variation rhythm fast	83.36	84.90	22.88	36.05
V8 variation dynamics soft	37.26	15.59	14.76	8.11
V8 variation dynamics normal	27.30	14.93	31.13	26.89
V8 variation dynamics hard	35.44	69.49	54.10	64.99
V9 texture richness	0.89	0.70	1.35	0.66
V10 clusterness	17.43	21.60	19.56	26.39

Table 2. Variables mean values for non-musicians and musicians, on pre and post session.

However, due to a small sample size and limited number of treatment sessions, not all of shifts are statistically significant.

The pre – post treatment comparison was performed with asymptotic Wilcoxon signed rank test with Pratt zero handling (with *coin* package in *R* software [31]). The two groups were assessed in a separate manner, so that no direct statistical comparison between groups was made.

The tables below report only statistically significant differences between pre- and post-conditions, for the variables not reported below no significant difference was found. For variables V1, V2, V4, V5medium, V6 we predicted greater values in post session. i.e. greater values indicating the progress of creativity. For variables V5small and V5large we predicted smaller values in post session (see the explanation in the **Discussion** section). Accordingly, a one-tailed test was used for these variables. For variables V3, V7, V8, V9, V10 no directional hypothesis was made. Accordingly, a two-tailed test was used.

3.1 Non-musicians

	MEAN	STD DEV	MEDIAN
Pre	10.75	3.34	10.87
Post	13.16	2.88	13.72
	Z = -2.65, p-value = 0.004 (one-tailed)		

Table 3. V1 – Standard Deviation on pre- and post-corpus.

As seen in Table 3, the average pitch SD was higher in the post-session than in the pre-session, indicating that greater variety in the notes used.

	MEAN	STD DEV	MEDIAN
Pre	101137.65	36301.93	96031.50
Post	51542.65	19238.46	49255.00
	Z=3.40, p-value=0.001 (two-tailed)		

Table 4. V3 – Duration, total.

As it can be seen from Table 4, the average total duration was almost two times shorter in the post-session than in the pre-session.

	MEAN	STD DEV	MEDIAN
Pre	15.30	6.51	16.20
Post	18.13	6.00	18.45
	Z = -1.75, p-value = 0.039 (one-tailed)		

Table 5. V5 – Percentages of medium intervals

As it can be seen from Table 5, the average medium intervals were more present in the post-session than in the pre-session.

	MEAN	STD DEV	MEDIAN
Pre	37.26	25.40	29.98
Post	15.59	12.32	11.93
	Z = 2.65, p-value = 0.008 (two-tailed)		

Table 6. V8 – Dynamics Variation, soft.

As it can be seen from Table 6, on the average, "soft" dynamic was more than two times less present in the post-session than in the pre-session.

	MEAN	STD DEV	MEDIAN
Pre	27.31	9.11	28.06
Post	14.93	9.58	14.07
	Z = 3.06, p-value = 0.002 (two-tailed)		

Table 7. V8 – Dynamics Variation, normal.

As it can be seen from Table 7, on the average, "normal" dynamic was more two times less present in the post-session than in the pre-session.

	MEAN	STD DEV	MEDIAN
Pre	35.44	24.67	34.40
Post	69.49	19.54	70.40
	Z = -2.99, p-value = 0.003 (two-tailed)		

Table 8. V8 – Dynamics Variation, hard

As it can be seen from Table 8, on the average, "hard" dynamic was more than two times more present in the post-session than in the pre-session.

	MEAN	STD DEV	MEDIAN
Pre	0.89	0.26	0.86
Post	0.70	0.07	0.72
	Z = 3.92, p-value = 0.001 (two-tailed)		

Table 9. V9 – Texture Richness

As it can be seen from Table 9, on the average, the musical excerpt played by the child is more "populated" in the post-session than in the pre-session (smaller values of this variable reflect more "populated" excerpt).

3.2 Musicians

	MEAN	STD DEV	MEDIAN
Pre	235991.60	111207.17	257527.50
Post	66262.70	31756.15	57980.50
	Z= 2.60, p-value = 0.009 (two-tailed)		

Table 10. V3 – Duration, total

As it can be seen from Table 10 average total duration was more than three times shorter in the post-session than in the pre-session

	MEAN	STD DEV	MEDIAN
Pre	0.25	0.06	0.26
Post	0.35	0.07	0.38
	Z = -2.29, p-value = 0.021 (two-tailed)		

Table 11. V4 – Ratio of different per total, intervals.

As it can be seen from Table 11, the average ratio of different intervals was higher in the post-session than in the pre-session.

	MEAN	STD DEV	MEDIAN
Pre	22.88	6.51	16.20
Post	36.05	22.17	31.60
	Z = -2.09, p-value = 0.037 (two-tailed)		

Table 12. V7 – Rhythm variation, fast.

As it can be seen from Table 12, the average percentage of fast rhythm was almost twice higher in the post-session than in the pre-session.

	MEAN	STD DEV	MEDIAN
Pre	1.35	0.66	1.21
Post	0.66	0.04	0.68
Z = 2.80, p-value = 0.005 (two-tailed)			

Table 13. V9 – Texture Richness.

As it can be seen from Table 13, on average, the musical excerpt played by the child is almost twice more "populated" in the post-session than in the pre-session (smaller values of this variable reflect more "populated" excerpt).

4. DISCUSSION

Both musicians and non-musicians improvised on the keyboard. In general, it was observed that musicians, who were keyboard players, improvised by creating musical sequences based on their previously known pieces. Non-musicians, who were not familiar with the keyboard, played mostly in the form of gestures, such as upward and downward melodic movement, oscillation between two notes, continuous repetition of a pattern etc. (for more information see [6]).

The students' teachers were supportive of our sample's participation in the study, although their role in the process was not studied nor was the impact of children's participation measured in some way, when they returned to their 'normal' musical activities. A follow-up study may be able to explore this aspect, particularly teachers' perceptions of students' musical skills after having participated in such activities.

Webster in [29] suggests that certain divergent, imaginative skills among others, are also critical to creative thinking, such as musical extensiveness (the amount of time invested in creative imaging), flexibility (the range of musical expression in terms of dynamics, tempo, and pitch) and originality (the unusualness of expression). Our variables explored mostly variance in flexibility, between the pre and the post test.

4.1 Non-musicians

The pre tests and post tests for the players without any musical background show some differences, which could potentially be attributed to the use of the MIROR IMPRO system. More specifically, the standard deviation of the pitches used increases in the post test. This shows that the children start to be more adventurous and explorative in their choice of pitches, using a bigger range of the piano.

While the pitch standard deviation increases, the medium intervals also increase, compared to small and large intervals. This fact could indicate that children stop playing at random, in all the registers (i.e. they don't make huge intervals any more between high and low register), and they avoid repetitions of the same note (i.e. they don't use very small intervals any more). Instead they use intervals that are more or less typically used in music, of medium size.

Another interesting difference between pre and post test is that children play louder, which could indicate a stronger confidence in their playing, and at the same time use more notes in the same amount of time, to create a thicker texture. However, it is interesting that in the post test they also play for significantly less time. This could be seen in two ways: the first suggests that they play in a more focused way, given the above significant results, for less time, while the second proposes that they might be getting tired by the time they reach the post test, and decide to play less.

4.2 Musicians

Before discussing the results of the pianists, there is one fact that needs to be explained in order to better evaluate the results. Children with a background in piano playing, during the pre test, played mainly their known pieces from the piano lesson, and improvised less. Therefore, their pre test has a lot of features that we would normally find in known music. By the time the children reach the post test, all of the children leave the security of the known pieces and prefer to play more freely their own tunes. We believe that this can be attributed to the use of the MIROR IMPRO system, as there was scant interaction with the researcher throughout the study. The post test improvisation session is also significantly shorter. As they played more freely, it could be explained as more focused improvisational playing.

In the post test, their ratio of different per total intervals used is higher, which means that there is less repetition and more originality in their playing. At the same time, pianists play almost twice as fast as in the pre test, which could indicate more confident playing, especially as this is coupled with less soft and timid playing. Like the non-musicians, they also use more notes per unit of time, to create a thicker texture.

4.3 General discussion

The work described here is introducing a model for measuring creativity and creativity development. This model in essence defines and describes musical creativity via a set of attributes realised as distinct variables. While the utilization of a set of variables for describing creativity is something that most of the scholars in the field are employing (see section 1), the appropriateness of a particular variable can always be under question. For example, is it valid to hypothesise that different distribution in the (small, medium, large) range of intervals (that is variable V5) indicates musical creativity advancement? Of course in general, in the borderline cases this hypothesis holds true; for instance if a `interval(95, 3, 2)` tuple is becoming a `interval(40, 40, 20)`, the player is musically exploring a larger interval range and this seems to be consistent with musical creativity development in the literature. But in most in-between cases the extent to which changes in the variables indicates creativity development is open to discussion. In general the concept of creativity evades a clear definition and the issue of assessing creativity development is a challenging topic which can be dealt with in many ways. Future work will include fine tuning of variables, eventually defining significant limits on experimental basis.

5. CONCLUSION

This study firstly proposed a set of variables to measure creativity in music, based on existing literature on creativity assessment, and secondly investigated the development of creative music improvisations of young children, after playing an Interactive Reflexive Music System called the MIROR IMPRO. It drew on two examples, a group of 20 non-musicians and a group of 10 young pianists, and measured the development of their creativity in free improvisation before and after six sessions of using the system.

The non-musicians' post test free improvisations include higher diversity of musical vocabulary, more medium intervals and richer texture, indicating a sensible progress in improvisational creativity. At the same time, they include more intensity in dynamics, indicating more confident playing behaviour. Interestingly this seems also to be the case with the young pianists, as their post tests include similar features. In their post tests, however, there is more use of different intervals with less repetition and faster playing, even though they move away from the familiarity of their known piano pieces by this final session. It can be argued that the differences between pre and post tests observed in the musicians and non-musicians may be due to more than increased familiarity with the keyboard, that is the differences observed may be due to the use of the MIROR IMPRO system to develop creativity.

Further analysis of the in-between six sessions with MIROR IMPRO may provide more ideas regarding the precise variables that seem to shift across sessions in both groups of melodies. Future work also includes the direct comparison of the two groups, to investigate the differences between the young pianists and the children with no musical background, as well as the introduction of a control group to assess an eventual development of creativity without MIROR-IMPRO.

This would allow also fine tuning of the creativity assessment model and its testing in various new settings in order to improve the definition of the variables used, as well as the introduction of new related variables.

Acknowledgments

The work described in this paper forms part of the MIROR European project [1], co-funded by the European Community under the Information and Communication Technologies (ICT) theme of the Seventh Framework Programme. (FP7/2007-2013). Grant agreement n° 258338

6. REFERENCES

[1] **M**usical **I**nteraction **R**elying **O**n **R**eflexion official website: http://www.mirorproject.eu/.

[2] A. R. Addessi and F. Pachet, "Childen's Interaction with a Musical Machine" in Proceedings of the 3rd Conference "Understanding and Creating Music", Caserta, 2003, pp. 11-15.

[3] A. R. Addessi and F. Pachet, "Experiment with a Musical Machine: musical style replication in 3 to 5 years old children" in B. J. Music Ed., 22, 1, 2005, pp. 21-46.

[4] A. R. Addessi, F. Pachet and R. Caterina, "Children Confronting an Interactive Musical System" in Proceedings of 8th International Conference on Music Perception & Cognition (ICMPC8), Adelaide, 2004.

[5] T. M. Amabile, The social psychology of creativity. Springer-Verlag, 1983.

[6] C. Anagnostopoulou, A. Alexakis and A. Triantafyllaki, "A Computational Method for the Analysis of Musical Improvisations by Young Children and Psychiatric Patients with No Musical Background" in Proceedings of 12th International Conference on Music Perception & Cognition, Thessaloniki, 2012

[7] D. Conklin and C. Anagnostopoulou, "Segmental pattern discovery in music" in INFORMS Journal on computing, 18, 3, 2006.

[8] D. Conklin and I. Witten, "Multiple viewpoint systems for music prediction" in New Music Research, 24, 1, 1995, pp. 51-73.

[9] J. Dewey, How We Think. Heath, 1933.

[10] J. P. Guilford, "Creativity" in American Psychologist, 5, 1950, pp. 444–454.

[11] J. P. Guilford, The nature of human intelligence. McGraw-Hill, 1967.

[12] M. Hickey, "An Application of Amabile's Consensual Assessment Technique for Rating the Creativity of Children's Musical Compositions" in J. of Research in Music Education, 49, 3, pp. 234-244.

[13] O.R. Holsti, "Content Analysis" in G.Lindzey & E.Aronson (Eds.), The Handbook of Social Psychology, 2nd ed., vol. II, Amerind Publishing Co, 1968, pp.596-692.

[14] A. Lomax, Cantometrics: A method in musical anthropology. University of California Extension Media Center, 1976.

[15] G. E. McPherson, "The Assessment of Musical Performance: Development and Validation of Five New Measures" in J. Psychology of Music, 23, 1995, pp. 142-161.

[16] U. Manber and G. Myers, "Suffix arrays: a new method for on-line string searches" in SIAM Journal on Computing, 22, 5, 1993, pp. 935-948.

[17] F. Pachet, "Interacting with a musical learning system: the Continuator" in C. Anagnostopoulou, M. Ferrand, and A. Smaill (Eds.), Music and artificial intelligence: Lecture notes in artificial intelligence 244.5, Springer-Verlag, 2002, pp. 119–132.

[18] F. Pachet, "Enhancing individual creativity with interactive musical reflexive systems" in I. Deliège and G. A. Wiggins (Eds.), Musical Creativity: Multidisciplinary Research in Theory and Practice, Psychology Press, 2006, pp. 359–376..

[19] F. Pachet and A. R. Addessi, "When Children Reflect on Their Playing Style: Experiments with the Continuator and Children" in ACM Computers in Entertainment, 2, 1, 2004

[20] F. Pachet, P. Roy and G. Barbieri, "Finite-Length Markov Processes with Constraints" in Proceedings of the 22nd International Joint Conference on Artificial Intelligence, IJCAI, pp. 635-642, Barcelona, Spain, July 2011.

[21] D. K. Simonton, "Thematic Fame, Melodic Originality, and Musical Zeitgeist: A Biographical and Transhistorical Content Analysis", in J. of Personality and Social Psychology 38, 6, 1980, pp. 972-983.

[22] D. K. Simonton, "The swan-song phenomenon: Last-works effects for 172 classical composers" in J. of Psychology and Aging, 4, 1, 1989, pp. 42-47.

[23] D. K. Simonton, "Lexical choices and aesthetic success: A computer content analysis of 154 Shakespeare sonnets" in Computers and the Humanities, 24, 1990, pp. 251-264.

[24] I. Knopke and F. Jürgensen, "A System for Identifying Common Melodic Phrases in the Masses of Palestrina" in Journal of New Music Research, 38, 2, 2009, pp. 171-181.

[25] P. E. Torrance, Torrance tests of creative thinking. Scholastic Testing Services, 1966.

[26] G. Wallas, The Art of Thought. Harcourt Brace, 1926.

[27] P. R. Webster, "An assessment of musical imagination in young children" in P. Tallarico (Ed.) Contributions to symposium: The Bowling Green State University symposium on music teaching and learning, Bowling Green, 1983, pp. 100–123.

[28] P. R. Webster, "Refinement of a measure of creative thinking in music" in C. K. Madsen & C. A. Prickett (Eds.), Applications of research in music behaviour, Tuscaloosa, AL, 1987, pp. 257–271.

[29] P. R. Webster, "Creativity as Creative Thinking" in Music Educators J. 76, 9, 1990, pp. 22–28.

[30] P. R. Webster, Measure of creative thinking in music-II (MCTM-II). Administrative guidelines. Unpublished manuscript, Northwestern University, 1994.

[31] http://cran.r-project.org/web/packages/coin

THE ACTUATED GUITAR: A PLATFORM ENABLING ALTERNATIVE INTERACTION METHODS

Jeppe Veirum Larsen
Department of Architecture, Design and Media Technology
Aalborg University
Aalborg, Demark
jvl@create.aau.dk

Dan Overholt
Department of Architecture, Design and Media Technology
Aalborg University Copenhagen
Copenhagen, Denmark
dano@create.aau.dk

Thomas B. Moeslund
Department of Architecture, Design and Media Technology
Aalborg University
Aalborg, Denmark
tbm@create.aau.dk

ABSTRACT

Playing a guitar is normally only for people with fully functional hands. In this work we investigate alternative interaction concepts to enable or re-enable people with non-functional right hands or arms to play a guitar via actuated strumming. The functionality and complexity of right hand interaction with the guitar is immense. We therefore divided the right hand techniques into three main areas: Strumming, string picking / skipping, and string muting. This paper explores the first stage, strumming. We have developed an exploratory platform called the Actuated Guitar that utilizes a normal electrical guitar, sensors to capture the rhythmic motion of alternative fully functioning limbs, such as a foot, knee or the head, and a motorized fader moving a pick back and forth across the strings. A microcontroller is utilized for processing sensor data, which allows flexible mapping of user input to the actuation of the motorized fader. Our approach employs the flexibility of a programmable digital system, allowing us to scale and map different ranges of data from various sensors to the motion of the actuator – thereby making it easier adapt to individual users.

Author Keywords: Interactive performance systems; Interfaces for sound and music; Music and robotics; Social interaction in sound and music computing; Actuated instruments; Actuated guitar; Musical instruments for the disabled.

1. INTRODUCTION

Playing a musical instrument can be an interesting and worthwhile pursuit, but in many cases is impossible for someone with a disability. Those of us living without disabilities can just pick and choose an instrument of our liking. We may prefer the sound of a certain instrument, wish to follow in the footsteps of an idol, or learn to play specific songs from the radio. Some people succeed and actually learn to play an instrument, but many give up along the way when they realize what it takes in time and effort to learn to play an instrument well.

What about people with disabilities that wish to play musical instruments? In this work, we begin to address the question via the development of alternative interaction methods for playing the guitar. Disabilities can either be congenital, or caused by illness or accidents in any stage of life. If an arm or hand amputee, or anyone having a medical problem such as cerebral palsy wishes to play a traditional instrument, it is likely that they will be unable to reach the instrument's full potential (or possibly not be able to play an instrument at all). The obstacles while learning to play an instrument designed for those without disabilities can be too large to overcome.

We focus here on the use of technology to enable alternative methods of playing the guitar, specifically for those who have limited or no use of one hand or arm. The use of actuators, feedback systems, and flexible interaction design techniques present a novel design optimized for easy customization. Furthermore, playing music can be a good activity for "Forced Hand Use" training [1]. This method encourages those with cerebral palsy or stroke patients, for example, to use their affected arm, with the aim that they will begin using that arm more in daily life or regain control with the arm or hand.

2. RELATED WORK

Related work has included a wide range of approaches to either customizing existing instruments, or designing entirely new music interfaces. These have ranged from simple mechanical aids [2] (sold by companies such as A Day's Work, LLC[1]), to advanced bioelectric controllers allowing users to produce computer-generated music [3]. An example of a simple tap-pad interface developed for disabled users is the TouchTone [4]. However, we have chosen here to focus on string instruments – specifically the guitar – rather than percussion, wind, or other families of musical instruments.

Most traditional instruments require more than one limb to be used while playing. As there are millions of disabled who lack the use of one or more of their limbs in the world today, these people are excluded from many types of music making. While quite a number of efforts have been undertaken in the past to modify existing instruments for use by the disabled, there have not been many specifically targeting the guitar as an instrument for disabled users.

Our work involves creating a semi-robotic musical instrument. A historical view of robotic musical instru-

[1] http://www.adaysworkmusiceducation.com/

ments is included in [5]. Robotic instruments focused on the guitar include the League of Electronic Musical Urban Robots (LEMUR's) GuitarBot [6], among others. While the GuitarBot is much more capable of completely automating the motions needed to play a guitar than our current work, it discards any affordances of direct human playing skills, due to a design that places each string on a separate 'neck'. We purposefully aim our development at more traditional guitar bodies, thus enabling users to develops skills that are as close to the normal techniques as possible. It follows in some of the author's related work with actuated instruments [8].

3. INTERACTION METHODS

Playing a guitar traditionally requires the use of both hands. The right hand does the strumming and or picking of the strings, and fingers of the left hand are used for fretting the strings. As stated in the introduction, the scope for this research is to enable or re-enable people who are not able (or lost the ability), to play the guitar. Our first approach focuses on the right hand, and how it interacts with the guitar. The common interactions of the right hand have been identified and divided into three stages:

Stage 1: Strumming
Stage 2: String picking and string skipping
Stage 3: String muting

The research is thus divided into the three stages, based on the dexterous complexity of each type of interaction. This paper elucidates only the first stage, strumming. Strumming is the most basic right hand interaction technique, making it a good place to start, as well as a prerequisite for the following stages to build upon (see **Figure 1**). Next we describe and discuss our approaches to strumming a guitar when the user does not have full control of the right hand.

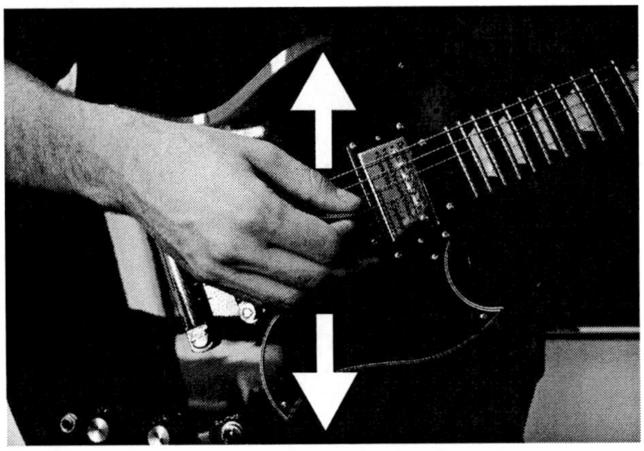

Figure 1. Strumming a guitar is the most basic right interaction possible with a guitar. Strumming is a near-perpendicular rhythmic motion across the strings.

3.1 Candidates for Rhythmic Movement

As the left hand is occupied fretting the strings, possible candidates for control of our motorized strumming actuator include various portions of the legs, the head, or possibly the remaining part an amputated arm, see **Figure 2**. Without mechanical aids, these parts of the body do not offer any realistic means of physically strumming across the strings in a normal playing position. However, the remaining part of an arm, the head or part of a leg (even a foot or toe) do offer the possibility to move in a rhythmic pattern.

Moving the arm or legs in a continuous rhythmic pattern are likely the best options, as humans are accustomed to naturally moving these body parts in rhythmic patters for long periods of time (for example when walking or running). For people with no control of their legs nor right arm, the head can also be used to move in a rhythmic pattern, albeit the muscles in the neck are not normally used for repeated rhythmic movements (and may quickly fatigue). Nevertheless, over shorter periods of time this would still give such individuals the ability to strum the actuated guitar.

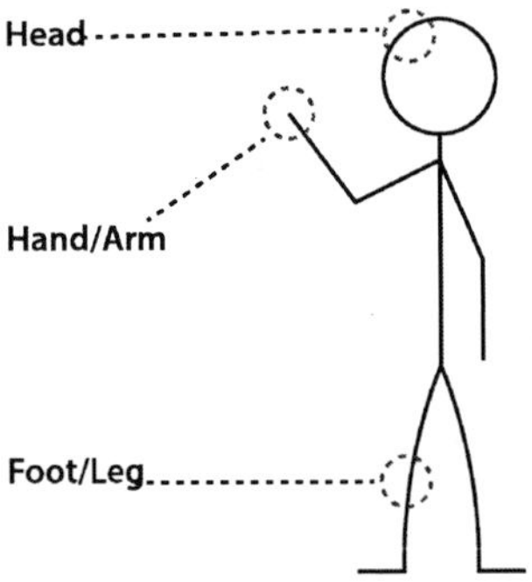

Figure 2. The different body parts that can be used instead of a paralyzed limb to interact with the instrument.

3.2 Gesture Capture and Motion Tracking

Because the rhythmic movement of these alternative parts of the body are not able to physically strum the strings in a normal fashion, our system needs to capture the motions and translate them into control signals for the actuator on the guitar. This can be done through the use of various sensors. The sensors can be mounted several different places on the body in order to optimize the experience for each individual.

Our initial experiments have made use of a simple accelerometer sensor that might be ideal for a person with an amputated right hand. It is fitted with a velcro armband and strapped onto various parts of the body. Many other types of sensors can also work as input for the actuated guitar, such as gyroscope sensors, which capture rotational movements. An individual that can only rotate their head, for example, could use this type of sensor, with the rotational input translated to the actuator's linear output – robotic strumming of the strings via a motorized fader.

The authors have considered many other options as well, such as a full Inertial Measurement Unit (IMU) that combines data from an accelerometer, gyroscope and magnetometer to provide a more precise estimation of orientation and motion, or even commercial options such as the

Leap Motion device[2], which could be mounted in various locations to capture player inputs. In the next phase of this research we plan to incorporate a single-chip IMU, the MPU-9150 released by Invense, Inc. It is a 9-axis motion tracking solution with built-in sensor fusion algorithms combining data from a 3-axis gyroscope, a 3-axis accelerometer, and a 3-axis magnetometer.

3.3 Mapping Sensor Input to Actuation

When customizing the actuated guitar for people with various disabilities, our digital approach attempts to make it easy to perform the necessary mapping of data from various input sensors (simple filtering, scaling and offset operations) to control of the strumming actuator. This is especially true when compared to the wide variety of mechanical approaches that would be needed for different scenarios and users. At the moment, these changes are managed in the firmware of the microcontroller that our system uses, but these parameters could also be changed graphically via a visual programming environment such as MaxMSP[3] or PureData[4]. This approach, based on the FireFader system [8] would likely be preferable for individuals who wish to modify the system themselves.

One example would be a user with a partly paralyzed leg, but who can still stomp their foot. Mounting our sensor on the foot will translate that motion into input for a microcontroller, which can then map the input to fit the actuator's full range of motion. This gives us the possibility of amplifying small motions to move the output actuators an entire strum-length, translate rotation motions into linear motions (if using a gyroscope sensor), etc. Doing this by purely mechanical means will be a highly complex construction and difficult to quickly modify to fit different users with different needs.

4. LIMITATIONS

The fine motor control exhibited by a normal human arm, hand and fingers will be difficult if not impossible to replicate via low-cost robotic actuation. A human hand can move in almost a hemispherical fashion at the end of the wrist. Fingers can stretch, bend and move sideways. In addition to the physical movements, we also receive sensory feedback from our hands and fingers. Although we are in the initial stages of this research (focused only on strumming to date), it is already clear that custom actuators would need to be designed, if attempting to truly approach this kind of control and feedback. Therefore, we have so far only researched the types of movements that are the most crucial to maintain, in order to design a substitution for the hand strumming a guitar.

It is worth noting that we are working with an electrical guitar for this prototype, and that the actuator we are using (a small motorized fader) can cause electrical noise to bleed from the motor's electromagnetic field into the guitar's pickups. This occurs due to the proximity of the electrical guitar pickup, be it single coil or humbucker design, near the plucking location on the strings (a position required to best capture the sound). This electromagnetic noise problem can be substantially circumvented by running the pulse-width modulation (PWM) signal that controls the motorized fader at a frequency higher than normal human hearing (more than 20kHz). While an acoustic guitar would not have this problem, the more fragile body makes it somewhat difficult to mount actuators on the guitar's body without damaging or compromising its ability to produce a good acoustic sound.

5. EXPLORATORY PLATFORM

To help us explore the possibilities offered by this research, a proof-of-concept guitar was created as described below (see **Figur 3**). The device consists of an Epiphone SG Standard electrical guitar, Arduino Nano V.3 board with an ATmega328 microcontroller, a "2motor" controller board from Gravitech with an L298 dual H-Bridge driver, an Analog Devices ADXL322 accelerometer, and a Penny+Giles PGFM3200 motorized fader.

The Arduino Nano sits on top of the 2motor board, both of which are plugged into a breadboard that is adhered to the guitar's body. The accelerometer is connected to the microcontroller's analog input ports for processing. A USB cable powers the Arduino, motor board and the motorized slider, and allows for quick data access and easy upload of software to the Arduino during our development process. The system can also be battery powered.

Figur 3. Implementation of the proof-of-concept guitar, which consists of an accelerometer, guitar, microcontroller, motor controller, motorized fader, and a pick.

The data flow throughout the system is shown in **Figure 4**. A user interacts with the accelerometer, which sends a signal to the Arduino. The ADXL322 is capable of sensing two independent axes, but as seen on **Figure 1** the type of movement we are most interested in when approximating traditional playing technique is just a single axis of motion. We therefore omit one axis entirely. The axis in use is averaged over 30 samples, as the sensor produces somewhat noisy data, and we are primarily interested in lower frequency information. The microcon-

---

[2] Leap Motion, http://www.leapmotion.com/
[3] MaxMSP, http://cycling74.com/
[4] PureData, http://puredata.info/

troller also reads the current position from the fader's potentiometer.

The feedback from the fader position in combination with the target value from the low-pass filtered accelerometer data determines what control data to send to the motor controller, for example in which direction and how fast to move. To avoid jitter while the fader is idle, the micro-controller only commands it to move when a sufficient G-force threshold is applied to the accelerometer in a given direction. The motor controller then turns on the motor in the given direction, and the fader strums the guitar. This is similar to the 'Real-Time Feed-Forward Control paradigm' outlined in [9].

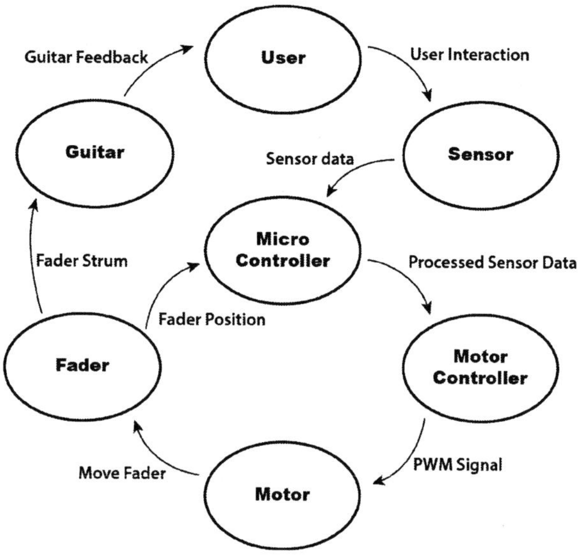

Figure 4. The data flow throughout the system. The user interacts with the sensor, which allows them to 'remote control' the position of the actuator – via internal feedback in the microcontroller that steers the system's output – thereby producing sound perceived by the user, completing the outer (interaction) feedback loop.

6. FUTURE WORK

There are many avenues of future work that would be interesting to pursue. For example, the initial studies shows that using a single accelerometer brings limitations. The constant pull of gravity of 1G is impossible to remove from such a sensor's output, making it difficult to get the same reading when strumming up and down (lateral motions are therefore preferable). The IMU mentioned in section 3.2 will help to resolve this issue, by allowing us to remove gravity effects through a calculation of the residual accelerations after subtracting the gravity vector. It should also enable us to explore much more detailed interaction due to the greater number of sensor types.

Trying completely different types of sensors, as mentioned in section 3.2, is also something we plan to pursue. Standard 'sip and puff' or simple force-sensitive resistor types of sensors would facilitate entirely different types of input, and could be interesting helps for more severely disabled people to strum the guitar.

7. CONCLUSIONS

We have shown that it is possible to enable or re-enable people to strum a guitar using an accelerometer as input controlling an actuated guitar using different body parts. Drawing on a range of inspiration we have shown that disabilities does not need to stop people to explore and experience normal instruments made for people without disabilities.

Acknowledgments
Funding for this work was provided in part by grants from Ludvig og Sara Elsass Fond in Copenhagen, Denmark.

8. REFERENCES

[1] M.D. Crocker, M. MacKay-Lyons, and E. McDonnell, "Forced Use of the Upper Extremity in Cerebral Palsy: A Single-Case Design," *American Journal of Occupational Therapy Volume 51*, November 1997 pp. 824-833.

[2] J. P. Snedeker, "Adaptive Engineering for Musical Instruments," in *Medical Problems of Performing Artists: Volume 20 Number 2*: Page 89 (June 2005).

[3] R. Benjamin Knapp and Hugh S. Lusted, "A Bioelectric Controller for Computer Music Applications," in *Computer Music Journal, Vol. 14, No. 1, New Performance Interfaces 1* (Spring, 1990), pp. 42-4, MIT Press.

[4] S. Bhat, "TouchTone: an electronic musical instrument for children with hemiplegic cerebral palsy," in *Proceedings of the fourth international conference on Tangible, embedded, and embodied interaction (TEI '10)*. ACM, New York, NY, USA, 305-306.

[5] A. Kapur, "A History of Robotic Musical Instruments," in *Proceedings of the International Computer Music Conference*. Barcelona, Spain, September 2005.

[6] E. Singer, K. Larke, and D. Bianciardi, "LEMUR GuitarBot: MIDI robotic string instrument," in *Proceedings of the 2003 conference on New interfaces for musical expression (NIME '03)*. National University of Singapore, Singapore, Singapore, 188-191.

[7] E. Berdahl and A. Kontogeorgakopoulos, "The FireFader Design: Simple, Open-Source, and Reconfigureable Haptics for Musicians", in *Proceedings of the ninth Sound and Music Computing Conference*, p.90-98 (2012)

[8] D. Overholt, E. Berdahl and R. Hamilton, "Advancements in Actuated Musical Instruments" in *Organised Sound*, 16, p. 154 – 165 (2011)

[9] E. Berdahl, J. Smith III and G. Niemeyer, "Mechanical Sound Synthesis: And the new application of force-feedback teleoperation of acoustic musical instruments" *in Proceedings of the 13th int. Conference on Digital Audio Effects* (September 2010)

Komeda: Framework for Interactive Algorithmic Music On Embedded Systems

Krystian Bacławski
Institute of Computer Science
University of Wrocław
krystian.baclawski@ii.uni.wroc.pl

Dariusz Jackowski
Institute of Computer Science
University of Wrocław
dariusz.jackowski@ii.uni.wroc.pl

ABSTRACT

Application of embedded systems to music installations is limited due to the absence of convenient software development tools. This is a very unfortunate situation as these systems offer an array of advantages over desktop or laptop computers. Small size of embedded systems is a factor that makes them especially suitable for incorporation into various forms of art. These devices are effortlessly expandable with various sensors and can produce rich audiovisual effects. Their low price makes it affordable to build and experiment with networks of cooperating devices that generate music.

In this paper we describe the design of Komeda – implementation platform for interactive algorithmic music tailored for embedded systems. Our framework consists of music description language, intermediate binary representation and portable virtual machine with user defined extensions (called modules).

1. INTRODUCTION

We believe that artists creating music installations are limited by the choice of platforms that can run their software. Personal computers, either desktops or laptops, can be too obstructive to the visual and spatial form of an installation. Mobile devices (i.e. phones and tablets) are not well suited for this purpose – problems like: device cost, replaceability, complex software stack, limited battery life, difficulties with expandability (i.e. no easy way to add custom external sensors and output devices) don't make them a great choice. Apparently the most viable option is to use small embedded systems, which could be easily incorporated into both static and movable parts of a music installation. Such systems should be build with affordable components and be easily expandable with peripherals. It is natural step forward to construct systems composed of handful or tens of such devices. An artist that desires to explore the idea of distributed music generation should be able to easily expand the system with communication capabilities and protocols. Hardware that matches the description above already exists, but it's not backed up by solid software framework that enables easy creation of musical applications.

Such platform should include:

- music notation language,
- hardware independent binary representation,
- portable virtual machine capable of playing music,
- communication protocol (also wireless),
- interface for sensors and output devices,
- support for music generation routines.

We would like to present the Komeda system, which currently provides only a subset of the features listed above, but in the future should encompass all of them.

2. OVERVIEW

Komeda consists of the following components: music description language, intermediate binary representation, virtual machine and module system. The language helps to create a musical score with place holders – so called "blanks" – which are filled in by the code running as a part of user defined module. The score takes a form of note sequence organized into patterns. In addition to that the language offers a limited set of control structures, pattern invocation and statements that allow communication with modules. Modules may represent instruments, note generator algorithms, sensors, etc. Each module is assigned a set of parameters and actions that a user can read, modify or invoke, respectively. The binary representation was designed to be platform independent bytecode for KomedaVM. The virtual machine provides player routine – or more specifically a scheduler and driver for instrument modules – and an interpreter for the bytecode.

3. LANGUAGE

3.1 Design

The first and the most important component of Komeda platform – at least from user's point of view – is the language. It is mainly focused on providing a succinct music notation description. However, it is not solely a data definition language like XML. It incorporates computation statements, control structures and other features specific to programming languages. We enable the user to express easily following concepts:

- music organized into parts (i.e. patterns, phrases, choruses),

- rich structure of music score (incl. loops, repetitions, alternatives),
- playback of score fragment in modified context (i.e. transposition, volume change),
- virtual player synchronisation (e.g. concerted transition to next music part),
- interaction with external world (e.g. sensors, controllers).

Having language users without much of a former experience, we would like them to find the concepts clear and the code readable. To help with adoption of Komeda, we decided to base its syntax on something widely known in both worlds – of music notation and programming languages. Hence, significant number of concepts were borrowed from LilyPond [1] and Java.

The main challenges we experienced while designing Komeda were:

- capturing all concepts needed to represent music score unambiguously – i.e. a user should be encouraged to express ideas in the least number of possible ways,
- balancing between having a readable syntax and concise notation – note that these two aspects collide with each other, as shorter constructs become more obscure,
- finding effective mapping to intermediate form (Komeda bytecode) – shape of binary data that represents the music to be executed in VM,
- simplicity of virtual machine and user modules.

Our design went a complete overhaul several times, as we were discovering dependencies between all three layers of Komeda environment: the language, the binary representation and the virtual machine.

At the time of writing we have working compiler from Komeda to intermediate representation. The implementation is written in Haskell, a purely functional language with strong static typing. Our choice is justified by a few arguments:

- Haskell [2] has set of rich abstractions and expressive types - our code looks clear and simple, there is little verbosity or boilerplate code, that obliterates the ideas,
- availability of great parser frameworks – Parsec [3] is used to express Komeda grammar.

3.2 Theoretical considerations

We choose to model the language after western music notation (with Helmholtz pitch notation). It has many drawbacks, nonetheless it is the most popular music notation which virtually anyone can read. Every person having former experience with western music notation should immediately recognize familiar structures in Komeda language. On the other hand we didn't try to create a music engraving language, so we had some flexibility in implementing musical concepts. In some cases we completely resign from some of them – most notable examples are key signatures, bars and time signatures. Here we would like to supply couple of arguments for these omissions.

The notion of key signature associated with tonality was made somewhat obsolete by atonal techniques or scales other than modes of the major system. Moreover, introducing the key signature could result in the decreased readability. Such is the case with Oliver Messaien's prelude *La colombe* notated in E major key in which most of the chords have more than one accidental, which makes hard to keep track of exact pitches in signatures with four sharps. Similarly notation of music based on the non-standard heptatonic scales requires custom key signatures (e.g. some of the pieces from Bela Bartok's *Microcosmos* which utilize both flats and sharps in the signature) or usage of accidentals instead of the key signature. Scales with more than seven pitch class appearing for example in the music of Bartok [4] [5] and Messaien (whose modes of limited transposition [6] mostly have more than seven tones) cannot be notated without accidentals. The same happens with works based on the serialism, dodecaphony and intervals pairings [7] or other atonal techniques. There is also another argument for foregoing the key signature even for tonal works. Contemporary composers often chose to notate them with only accidentals - great example here is the first movement of III Symphony by Henryk Górecki, who always notated F# with accidental in this E-minor piece.

Bars and metre are used in music mainly for three things: structuring, as a help for the performer in keeping track of the score and to introduce default accents in music. In Komeda the visual structure of music can be imposed using the white characters and comments. Obviously Komeda does not need any help in keeping track of the score, so we are left with only last application of measures. The problem of accent induced by metre is that there is not one standard of it. Underlying pulse of different time signatures is associated with genre, period and personal styles of both the composer and the performer. Moreover in the contemporary music the implicit accent is non-existent [8]. The lack of bars also simplify music generation.

3.3 Syntax concepts

3.3.1 Channels

Top-level construct of komeda language is a channel. It describes a behavior of monophonic audio source. Each channel is assigned an independent thread of execution that interprets Komeda language and in turn produces note sequence to be played.

```
channel 0 play @Pattern0
```

Listing 1: *Channel notation example*

The definition above states, that the channel number 0 will play a program defined by `Pattern0`. Number of channels is limited by the implementation of KomedaVM and may depend on hardware capabilities.

Note that the program executed by the channel may make use of certain sensor, voices or generator modules. That information has to be specified in channel initialization routine that is automatically added by the compiler. Thus code analysis has to be performed at compile time.

3.3.2 Identifiers and Parameters

Komeda programs will assign names to specific objects like patterns, voices, etc. Another group of names refer to certain playback parameters like tempo, volume, etc. Hence two groups of identifiers were conceived to capture these concepts. All user introduced identifiers begin with "@" sign, followed by uppercase letter (e.g. `@FooBar`). Parameters follow similar syntax, though they begin with lowercase letter (e.g. `@tempo`). Some of them are built into language (i.e. channel control), but others depend on modules imported into the scope of a channel.

3.3.3 Patterns

They are used to give music score a basic structure. Each pattern is given a unique name and can be referred to from other patterns, as if it was copied into the place of reference. Pattern execution interprets notes and control commands hold within its structure.

```
pattern @Pattern0 {
  ...
  @Pattern1
  ...
}

pattern @Pattern1 {
  ...
}
```

Listing 2: *Example of pattern invocation*

3.3.4 Notes, Rests and Slurs

Fundamental concept embraced by Komeda is a note. It is specified by pitch (semitone) and note length. Closely related to a note is a rest, which stops playback for a given unit of time. The timing is implicit – i.e. notes starts when a previous one stops. Pitch is expressed in Helmholtz notation with sharps only – we decided to drop flats. Length is represented as a fraction of default time unit, which allowed us to omit a concept of tuples (e.g. triplet) and dots from standard notation. The tempo is always expressed in quarter notes per minute.

```
@tempo 120
@unit 1/4

C#, D r a3/2 d'/2 e2
```

Listing 3: *Sample music score*

Komeda supports expressing slurs and ties as well, though they are immediately coalesced into a single note at compilation time.

```
a~a/2 c~d~e2~f
```

Listing 4: *Expressing slurs*

3.3.5 Control Structures

Usually a score consist of a few fragments that are repeated several `times`. Certainly one would like to express that concisely, possibly giving alternative endings – western music notation uses volta brackets for that purpose. Komeda is more flexible as it allows to designate alternative fragments (not only endings) `on` specified loop iteration. Note that alternative fragments don't have to be defined for each iteration, which can lead to repetitions of different lengths. It's also possible to nest repetitions as shown below:

```
times 8 {
  ...
  on 3 {
    ...
    times 2 {
      /* do it twice on 3rd repetition
         of outer loop */
      ...
    }
  }
  ...
  on 4 { ... }
}
```

Listing 5: *Nested loops and alternatives*

However sometimes one would like to express possibly infinite repetition that can be terminated under certain condition (e.g. user interaction). That is achievable using `forever` construct.

```
forever {
  ...
  if @Button.pressed()
    break
  ...
}
```

Listing 6: *Infinite loop with break on user action*

3.3.6 Context Changes

There are several cases, when a user would like to perform series of similar actions, captured by a pattern, but with slightly different settings. Example of such situation is when a user wants to play a pattern representing some phrase with a transposition.

```
with @pitch +3 @volume +10% {
  @NoteSequence
}

with @pitch -2 {
  @NoteSequence
}
```

Listing 7: *Temporary parameters modification*

The `with` statement can be used to temporarily change a set of parameters for the commands placed in its scope.

3.3.7 Synchronisation

Channels are inherently independent. Hence, instructions interpreted within a channel have no way to obtain information about state of another channel. While this isolation is generally a good idea, it poses a problem when timing between channels is required to achieve desired effect (e.g. smooth transition from one music part to another). To synchronize players, we introduced simple, but effective mechanisms based on the idea of notifications and rendezvous points.

In example below we devise a meeting point for two players. They will only advance to the next part of music, when they both arrive at `@Part2`.

```
rendezvous @Part2 for 2

pattern @PatA {
  times 3 { ... }
  ...
  arrive @Part2
  ...
}

pattern @PatB {
  ...
  times 2 { ... }
  arrive @Part2
  ...
}
```

Listing 8: *Use of meeting points for synchronization*

Another example requiring synchronization is two players, who improvise at the beginning and afterwards want to transition to main theme of work.

```
signal @StopImprovisation

pattern @PatC {
  ...
  /* to drummer: stop improvisation! */
  notify @StopImprovisation
  ...
}

pattern @PatD {
  ...
  until @StopImprovisation {
    // some crazy beats :)
  }
  ...
}
```

Listing 9: *Communication through signalling*

3.3.8 Instruments

Currently only simple DDS [9] instruments are supported for simplicity's sake. Simple DDS instrument is generated by a single oscillator (e.g. "sine", "triangle", "square", "noise") and ADSR [1] envelope. Such instruments can be supported on even the simplest hardware and are a good starting point for generation of more advanced sounds.

```
voice @SomeWave = @SimpleDDS {
  @osc "sine"
  @adsr 0.1 0.1 0.8 0.9
}
```

Listing 10: *Example voice definition*

In the example above a new instrument is created by calling constructor of imported *SimpleDDS* module.

[1] Attack-Decay-Sustain-Release

4. VIRTUAL MACHINE

KomedaVM is a small piece of software residing in flash memory of an embedded device. It is responsible for loading (from flash, RAM or if applicable some external sources such as SD cards) binary representation of Komeda language and executing it. For this purpose the machine has to maintain a global state and for each channel a private state. Additionally, it manages modules currently in use and schedule execution of instruments playback. Certain assumptions described in this chapter influenced shape of the language or imposed particular constraints on the design (e.g. number of available channels).

4.1 Binary representation

Almost all Komeda language concepts have their counterparts in binary representation. Some of composite high-level instructions are split down into simpler constructs as the compiler lowers the code. At the very bottom each channel behaves as an independent state machine – a very simple microprocessor with specialized set of instructions. We will not provide details of instruction set architecture (ISA) employed by KomedaVM, as it is still undergoing significant changes.

Having spent considerable amount of time analyzing contemporary micro-controllers ISAs, we decided to keep close to these designs. Affinities we would like to preserve are:

Reduced number of orthogonal instructions. If we keep virtual instruction design close enough to existing ISA, for instance AVR [10], we possibly could provide one-to-one mapping between Komeda and native instructions. That could reduce the size of interpreter as the processor is able to execute some instructions directly. While it is tempting to follow such path, certainly specialization hinders portability of virtual machine, which at the moment is our priority goal. Thus, we decided to take opposite approach, and deliver instructions that can be interpreted easily on most popular embedded processors, which tend to have RISC-like ISAs [11].

Sizeable register file and a stack. Komeda language is mainly oriented towards expressing control flow – it is not suitable for data processing. Thus, we decided to drop concept of program's memory, which anyway is a scarce resource in embedded systems. Instead, we use virtual registers and stack to store state of the program. The requirement for virtual stack emerged as we considered situation, when a pattern invokes another pattern – in some sense it mimics concept of function calls and activation records from general purpose programming languages.

Uniform size of instructions i.e. 2 bytes. If Komeda binary representation is going to be interpreted in software, the interpreter must be able to quickly decode and dispatch instructions. Such representation is also convenient, if we allow any arbitrary Komeda code processing (e.g. decompilation or whole pattern generation by native code).

4.2 Modules

From the virtual machine point of view, modules are independent entities. The communications with them is performed via specialized structure, which has to be initialized by KomedaVM before execution of a program. The machine is allowed to call a specific action assigned to a module. This is the only conceivable moment in which we allow the control to be transferred out of KomedaVM to native code.

Lets consider a single module. Firstly, we would like to avoid exposing the state of a module to the virtual machine, if possible. Secondly, when you consider module's internal state, it may be too large to be represented by the interface visible to KomedaVM – i.e. virtual registers. Thus the machine has to maintain the state that is not visible to Komeda code directly. Each module may be subjected to non-trivial initialization. Finally, a program may use same module but differently initialized or used in two different independent contexts.

As a consequence, we decided to design modules in spirit of object oriented paradigm, but without inheritance for now. Lots of similarities emerged – clearly modules are classes, modules with attached state are class instantiations (i.e. objects), parameters are public properties of an object, and remote procedures – just methods. Such model can be efficiently mapped onto C language which lacks of object oriented features.

4.3 Execution engine

Runtime system is composed of three components characterized shortly below.

NotePlayer Central subsystem of Komeda runtime. It is a scheduler that takes care of updating the state of channels (i.e. note pitch and length, slur mode, instrument number) and reprogramming AudioPlayer respectively. For each note being played NotePlayer maintains an alarm clock, which is triggered when the note is about to stop being played. Next note is then fetched and AudioPlayer reprogrammed to play it. Secondary functionality is related to the maintenance of synchronization state between channels.

AudioPlayer Its main task is to continuously generate and mix all audio inputs into a stream suitable to be digested by audio playback device. This subsystem is considered to be the most platform dependant constituent. Playback device implementation may vary greatly for each hardware platform. It can be implemented as a DAC with or without DMA (i.e. DAC capable of feeding itself with consecutive samples without involving processor), a simple PWM generator, FM synthesis sound chip, etc. AudioPlayer may be programmed to perform certain non-trivial computation like direct digital sound synthesis, or system interaction like fetching samples from storage device. It seems to be the only subsystem that needs to be called synchronously by the system clock.

Interpreter Subsystem invoked by NotePlayer to update the state of a channel. Each interpreter invocation has to end up producing a note information or a rest, eventually forcing interpreter to enter wait state on that channel. The result is obtained by executing compiled Komeda language statements.

NoteGenerator An optional subsystem written in C language that either was assigned to a channel by a programer or temporarily suppressed Komeda interpreter and intercepted its execution. It employs certain algorithm to deliver notes or rests upon channel update action.

5. FUTURE WORK

5.1 Features currently in development

At the time of writing Komeda is under active development. That means some of its interesting features undergo implementation process and are being evaluated with regards to language and virtual machine design. Our long term focus is the support for embedded platforms, such as Arduino [12], 8-bit and 16-bit microcontrollers (PIC, DSPIC, AVR, etc.) with built-in or attached digital-to-analog converters.

One of currently identified design issues is platform specific instruments support. For many embedded devices, especially those without D/A converter, implementation of DDS-based instruments is either cumbersome or utterly impractical (overhead of using PWM for DDS is too high). On the other hand, those devices are likely to have some native support for generation of simple waves, e.g. PWM-based square wave generator. Other conceivable platform specific instruments are external devices controlled via MIDI interface or mechanical devices that control real instruments. Whole range of possibilities is available here – from simple sine wave generator, through MIDI synthesizers, to another embedded device controlling servo arm playing xylophone.

Extending Komeda with flexible DDS instruments is not trivial and requires careful review of module system. Direct digital synthesis can consume virtually all computing resources and may affect note scheduling, which we want to avoid at all cost.

Interface delivered by modules should be flexible enough to extended the system beyond proposed purposes. Two more types of pluggable modules, other than instruments, are envisioned: sensors and generators.

- Sensors purpose is to measure physical quantities such as light intensity, magnetic field direction, temperature, etc.; and interpret them in a context of music. The values coming from sensors could be used to play a note, set new tempo rate or voice volume — i.e. control virtually any other music parameter available. Example mapping could translate room temperature into music tempo (i.e. hotter or cooler into faster or slower respectively) or light intensity into base pitch of notes being played (i.e. lighter or darker into higher or lower respectively).
- Generators are additional mechanism for employing generative music techniques. Their role is to deliver a number of values upon request – a user has

freedom to use these values as she wishes. Alternatively the channel could be forced to execute code generated by the module until the generator returns control. At the moment of writing music generation can only be achieved by external code modifying Komeda pattern binary representation. While this method is the most powerful one, almost certainly is the most difficult to use properly.

5.2 Planned features

Arguably the most needed feature of Komeda is language supported rich sound synthesis – instead of just simple DDS instruments implemented as external modules. There are a few issues worth mentioning:

- There is a need to extend the language to easily supply required synthesis arguments in a concise way.
- In chosen model the notes are the only acoustic events. They are mutually independent, save slurs, and take parameters only at initialization time. Though suitable for representing musical score this approach is somewhat limited. Especially when it comes to representing sounds with continuously changing spectra or indefinite pitch, etc.
- Last but not least, if Komeda was to support synthesis techniques, it would be necessary to extend the language with instrument specification. There are two possibilities to incorporate this into the main language. First option is to extend voice definitions with a new language for instrument specification. Such language could be modelled after CSound orchestra [13] or Nyquist `.alg` [14] files. Second option is to extend Komeda language with extra constructs expressing additional sonic events inside patterns. The later approach would greatly increase the expressive power of the language, but could lead to performance loss and increased complexity of the system.

Another important deficiency of Komeda is absence of continuous parameter control. That makes it impossible to express portamento and similar effect. Create ritardando or accelerando and crescendo or decrescendo is very problematic, as it needs assignment of different tempo or volume to each consecutive note. We find three possibilities to solve that – to allow only linear function, piecewise linear (i.e. envelopes) or arbitrary functions implemented as arrays.

For implementation of some non essential features we could add source code macros. Examples are: symbolic description of tempo or volume levels, flats, mordents and other ornaments. In addition, given enough expressive power, the macros could be used to create tools for generating or transforming score according to some compositional system. We are considering both text-substitution and compile time macros.

To increase expressive power we could introduce microtones and tunings other than equal temperament. The later is easier, as we represent pitch by discrete number.

6. CONCLUSIONS

Komeda is a complex system and describing its intricacies goes way beyond the scope of this paper. Instead we decided to present its philosophy and design decisions. We also chose to list ideas encountered during development stages. We hope that people creating similar platforms will find these information useful.

As for the future of Komeda, we hope to release a first public version in the next few months. As more and more planned features are being incorporated, the platform calls for a full evaluation in the form of an installation or a novel instrument. We are going to choose several artists for cooperation. Moreover, we would like to reiterate some concepts from the Komeda, to provide an even more flexible and easy to use platform.

7. REFERENCES

[1] [Online]. Available: http://www.lilypond.org/

[2] [Online]. Available: http://www.haskell.org/

[3] [Online]. Available: http://www.haskell.org/haskellwiki/Parsec

[4] E. Antokoletz, *The Music of Bela Bartok: A Study of Tonality and Progression in Twentieth-Century Music.* University of California Press, 1990.

[5] E. Lendva, *Bela Bartok: An Analysis of His Music.* Pro Am Music Resources, 1991.

[6] O. Messiaen, *Technique de mon langage musical.* Alphonse Leduc, 1944.

[7] J. C. B. Rae, *Pitch organisation in the music of Witold Lutoslawski since 1979.* PhD thesis, University of Leeds, 1992.

[8] V. Persichetti, *Twentieth-Century Harmony: Creative Aspects and Practice.* W. W. Norton & Company, 1961.

[9] T. Holmes, *Electronic and Experimental Music: Technology, Music, and Culture.* Routledge, 2008.

[10] [Online]. Available: http://www.atmel.com/products/microcontrollers/avr/default.aspx

[11] [Online]. Available: http://en.wikipedia.org/wiki/Reduced_instruction_set_computer

[12] [Online]. Available: http://www.arduino.cc

[13] [Online]. Available: http://www.csounds.com/manual/html/OrchTop.html

[14] [Online]. Available: http://www.cs.cmu.edu/~rbd/doc/nyquist/part16.html

Sound Hunter

Developing a Navigational HRTF-Based Audio Game for People with Visual Impairments

Sebastian Wolfgang Brieger
School of Computer Science and Communication
Royal Institute of Technology (KTH)
Stockholm, Sweden
brieger@kth.se

***Abstract*— In this article, a framework is proposed for designing 3D-based audio-only games in which all navigation is based on perceiving the 3D-audio, as opposed to relying on other navigational aids or imagining the audio as being spatial, where additional sounds may be added later on in the development process. To test the framework, a game named *Sound Hunter* was developed in an iterative process together with both sighted and visually impaired participants. The results indicate that the suggested framework might be a successful guidance tool when wanting to develop faster perception-based 3D-audio games, and the learning curve for the navigation was approximately 15 minutes, after which the participants navigated with high precision. Furthermore, with only small alterations to game menus and the iPhone's accelerometer function, both older and younger visually impaired people can navigate through 3D-audio environments by using simple hand movements. Finally, the results indicate that *Sound Hunter* may be used to train people's spatial hearing in an entertaining way with full experimental control. Two main factors seem to affect the learning curve for adapting to a foreign HRTF during virtual interactive gaming experiences; the adaptation to the navigational controls, and the experience of front/back confusion, where control adaptation is promoted by having a strong default setting with customizable sensitivity, and the experience of front/back confusion can be greatly reduced by introducing complex distance-dependent meta-level communication in synthesized sounds.**

***Keywords*— Audio games, HRTF-synthesis, 3D-audio, game development, visually impaired, blind, HCI.**

I. INTRODUCTION

Between 1996 and 2006, around 400 audio games had been developed, which is a very small number compared to visual computer games. The development teams were also small, usually consisting of one to four persons [1]. However the development has been more substantial over previous years, and the role of researchers, game developers, as well as sound designers has become more important in order to find more pleasant audio rendering techniques, as well as new exciting methods and technologies to use in audio games [14, 1]. There has been a rapid development of audio chips and 3D sound engines for computer games, and today, users as well as developers pay more attention to the audio content in computer games [7]. Sound is an expressive narrative medium, and sonic landscapes, or "soundscapes", may very well be as immersive and engaging as powerful 3D-based graphical environments [7].

Still, even though audio games are developed more sophistically these days, there is nonetheless very restricted access to an important part of the youth culture for people being visually impaired, and it could be argued that including this user group is of great importance, as it will aid their participation in society [1]. Accessibility to software applications is another area in which the visually impaired have more difficulties than sighted users. However, recent developments of various frameworks intended to make software applications more accessible has greatly aided the visually impaired, examples of which are *Microsoft Active Accessibility*, *VoiceOver* for the iPhone, as well as similar frameworks for Mac and Linux desktop environments [1]. By focusing more attention to game audio, new possibilities of designing games for people with visual impairments have emerged. However, this also requires that the games be developed with regard to their abilities and needs [7]. Games may also be used as a means to train the various senses and abilities in a person. For example, handicapped children may benefit largely both from using music [8] and computer games in order to aid their psychomotor and cognitive development [15, 1].

Despite the growing focus on audio in computer games, the audio content of mainstream computer games is still largely underdeveloped in comparison to the visual content [7]. This also applies to games being completely based on audio, which are extremely rare compared to audio-visual games. Almost all audio-only games on the market today are made for PC computers, where some of the popular titles are *SuperDeekout* [5] and *Terraformers* [18]. Still, as the number of blind iPhone users today is over 100 thousand and rapidly growing [23], it therefore seems as if there is a significant and highly unfulfilled market potential for audio-only games intended for smartphone users. Furthermore, as most of the popular audio-only games are created in the first-person perspective, it also seems important to examine whether or not it would actually be possible to navigate in a game environment solely by using 3D-audio. This could possibly help in creating more exciting audio games, where the player no longer needs to rely on their own imagination of spatial audio, but instead is able to actually perceive the audio as being spatial.

In this article, a framework is presented on how to design navigational 3D-audio games, in which all navigation is based on perceiving the 3D-audio, as opposed to using sonification, auditory icons, earcons or other navigational aids [7, 3, 21], all of which may be added later on in the development process. In this proposed rethink of the design process of 3D-audio games, the focus is shifted from creating complex auditory environments in which 3D-audio is used as a complementary spatial effect, to creating a functional 3D-audio navigation being complemented by carefully enriching the auditory environment. By following this design principle, games may be made to respond more rapidly and accurately to the player's navigational input, as well as give the player a sense of full control and feeling of immediate response from the auditory environment, which could help bridge the gap between the hasty action-filled visual games and the slower tempo audio games we have today. In order to test the framework, a game named Sound Hunter was developed, in which all navigation is based on perceiving sounds through synthesized head-related transfer function (HRTF) filtering. The filter used in Sound Hunter is the Pure Data external [earplug~], created by Pei Xiang, David Camargo, and Miller Puckette [24], featuring 368 (or 722 if mirrored to each ear) impulse responses, covering a spherical surface with an elevation of -40 to 90 degrees and an azimuth of 0 to 360 degrees, all of which are interpolated using linear interpolation. The generalized HRTF's are gathered from KEMAR (dummy head) data sets [10], and the amount of impulse responses used in [earplug~] was considered more than acceptable, seeing as both listening tests and error analyses have shown that 128 impulse responses give satisfactory localization abilities in the azimuth plane [22]. The distance simulation was programmed separately in Pure Data, with the logarithmic loudness function $L=log\ (1/r)$, where r is the maximum distance of 8m. Sound Hunter currently features 20 different levels (audio loops and synthesized sounds) varying in difficulty, where the player's objective is to capture each sound as quickly as possible, by using the iPhone to control player movement. As suggested in the framework, the game was developed in an iterative process, together with both older and younger visually impaired people.

II. BACKGROUND

Audio-based games are similar to video-based games, with the exception that they are played and perceived through sound and acoustics only [21]. Audio games have many advantages making them interesting for gameplay experimentation. For example, they allow an increased degree of spatial freedom, as no screens are necessary. Furthermore, the computational complexity is usually lower, meaning that less hardware is necessary, making them suitable for portable devices and mobile gaming [21]. Another common favourable argument is that they may lead to an increased level of immersion due to the lacking graphical representation, where the player has to rely more on their own imagination, similar to when reading books [21]. Apart from the earlier mentioned positive effects on physical and cognitive development, audio games can also be used to train a person's hearing and teach the player how to focus more on what they hear [9].

When building an audio-only game, it is important not only to use self-explanatory sounds, but also to establish agreements early on in the game to convey information correctly to the player [7]. These agreements should build upon metaphors and associative patterns to make it easier for the player to get a sense of what information is important in the game (e.g. the difficulty of the challenge ahead, the current success rate, or scores awarded when completing a game task). It is also important to emphasize the difference between various types of auditory information. For graphics, variations in colours, borders, buttons and other types of design principles are used to label and categorize different types of information. For auditory information, different models have been proposed, where one example is the SITREC categorization system suggested for audio game interfaces [7].

It is also important to distinguish auditory information generated by player activity from the information generated by other sources in the game. This player feedback informs the player whether or not the action was registered by the system [7], and has led to the development of three well-established design methods for auditory interfaces. *Auditory icons* are recognizable sounds, such as voices or confirmatory sounds [11, 12], and *earcons* are short musical phrases [3], both of which are associated with various types of information to inform the player of their actions [7]. The third design method, *sonification*, can be seen as sub-part of the auditory icon, and is the process of mapping abstract data to non-speech sound [21].

It is also possible for game sounds to have several layers of information, often when wanting to enhance the complexity or function of the sound. This additional information may be communicated on a meta-level [7]. In Sound Hunter, distance-dependent meta-level communication was conveyed by altering the cut-off frequency in square waves (to create complex motor-like sounds for easier levels), and by altering the frequency in sine waves (to create distance-dependent audibility for more difficult levels).

When considering the sound characteristics, it is also important that each sound is intelligible and distinguishable. Often, the sounds are accompanied by a musical context. The latter of which seldom is emphasized, but rather added as a backdrop in order to create a scene and set the mood [7, 14]. Another aspect of sound characteristics is that of looping sounds, which may reduce the level of realism in the sound, but is often still desirable in audio games, as it gives the player an overview of the game space [7].

In many action-based audio games, the success of the player depends on interaction based on precise timing [1]. Examples of audio-only action games including 3D-audio are most commonly found in the first-person shooter genre, for example *Shades of Doom* [13], *Terraformers* [18], and *Demor* [4], all of which are made for the PC. Another popular audio game category is that of adventure games, or exploration games, where three key features are combined: an interesting scenario, the exploration of new worlds, as well as activities of riddle solving [1]. Examples of audio-only exploration games including 3D-audio are *Blindside* [6], and *Escape The House: A 3D Sound Experience* [19], both of which are available for iOS users.

Röber and Masuch [21] attempted to prototype various game ideas for audio-based gaming by using individualized HRTF's, head-tracking, and a joystick or keyboard for player movement. They created three action-based games (*The Frogger Game Remake*, *Mozquitos*, and *MatrixShot*) and one exploration game (*The hidden Secret*). Röber and Masuch pointed out several future improvements, such as extending their framework with more advanced sonification and interaction techniques, as well as developing a truly mobile solution, allowing the player not to be bound by webcams, head-tracking devices and other stationary equipment. These issues are also present in the more mainstream audio game *Demor* [4, 21].

In his Master's degree project, Graeme [14] developed a 3D-based audio-only game called *Blind Fear*, featuring advanced auditory environments. However, similar to the previous studies mentioned here, Graeme found that the more effort he put into creating auditory environments being as advanced and rich as possible, the more difficult it became to actually manage to navigate in the auditory world. During various parts of the development process, Graeme managed to play through the entire game from beginning to end using only audio, but only after simplifying it by sacrificing additional sounds, thus compromising the aesthetical effort [14]. This example not only shows the difficulties that may arise when trying to balance functionality and aesthetics in an audio game, but also the need of including the intended users as early on as possible in the game's development process to minimize compromises between usability and aesthetics.

One of the more promising games is *Blindside* [6], requiring only a smartphone and headphones, where only a few sounds are focused on at a time, making the 3D-audio easier to perceive. However, there are still problems with this game. For example, it is quite static and slow, just as many other audio games (e.g. press forward button to move in the game at a pre-determined speed). Blindside also relies on the iPhone's gyroscope (where the player needs to stand up and spin around), which on the one hand gives more spatial freedom, but on the other hand makes it difficult to play when sitting up or lying down.

For the more mainstream 3D-audio-only games not relying on stationary equipment (e.g. *Shades of Doom* [13], *Terraformers* [18], or *Escape The House: A 3D Sound Experience* [19]), the actual 3D-effects are very difficult to perceive. The games give the impression to have been developed as if they were intended for stereo usage, with some additional binaural sound introduced to the mix. As there are many tools and programming libraries available for creating 3D-audio environments, such as FMOD's head related transfer function [14], and it can be expected that developers and sound designers decide to enhance stereo environments with various binaural sounds, rather than relying on only stereo.

III. PROPOSED FRAMEWORK: RETHINKING THE DESIGN OF 3D-AUDIO GAMES

All of the above mentioned audio-only games based on 3D-audio claim to present the player with exciting 3-dimensional sound-environments, either through surround sound systems, or by 3D-audio through headphones. However, the focus is usually not on the player's ability to perceive the 3D-audio in order to use this cue as the main tool for navigation, but rather on enhancing the perceived quality of the stereo environment in order to make it richer and more life-like. For the games focusing more on the navigational purposes of the 3D-audio, the problem instead seems to be their reliance on head-tracking devices or other stationary equipment [4, 21], making them highly inappropriate for relaxed gaming (e.g. lying down as opposed to walking around), or mobile gaming with only a smartphone and earphones.

In order to truly make use of 3D-audio for the purpose of navigation, however, it becomes very important not only to create the 3D-audio environments themselves, but to also understand our natural abilities and limitations when it comes to perceiving spatial sounds as human beings. For example, when filtering a sound using an HRTF filter in order to place the sound in a certain position in a 3D space (e.g. in front of the listener and slightly to the right), the sound will not automatically be perceived as being in front and slightly to the right of the listener without involving movement, either by moving the player's (head) position, or the sound source's position, creating dynamic localization cues. The effect has been named the *cone of confusion*, and arises when sounds in different positions in a vertical circle around either side of the listener's head have equal inter-aural time differences (ITD's), and the confusion is eliminated when moving the head (i.e. causing the sound's relative position to the listener to change, thus altering the ITD's) [17].

Furthermore, additional stereo sounds being used in audio games may disturb the player's ability to perceive the HRTF filtering. This is because our ability to perceive a sound as being spatial depends on the above mentioned ITD's, as well as interaural intensity differences (IID's), and further qualities of the sound, such as spectral differences, or room qualities simulated by reverberation, all of which may be masked, interfered, or in other ways become inaudible in either ear, causing severe inability to localize the sound object [14, 16]. As many audio-only games using 3D-audio can have over 30 different tracks playing simultaneously [13, 14], where some are in stereo (e.g. game music, instructions, auditory icons or earcons, usually at a relatively high volume), and some may be HRTF filtered, it is therefore not surprising that the 3D-effect becomes difficult to perceive.

There is usually a trade-off whether to use more sounds to enrich the auditory environment, or to use fewer sounds to aid navigation [7, 14]. Most common, however, is to add more sounds, such as auditory icons and earcons, in order to aid navigation through the already over-complex auditory environments [21, 7]. The framework for Sound Hunter was therefore developed in a way ensuring that perception-based 3D-audio navigation was the most important aspect of the game, with further sounds being added only later on in the development process (see *Figure 1*).

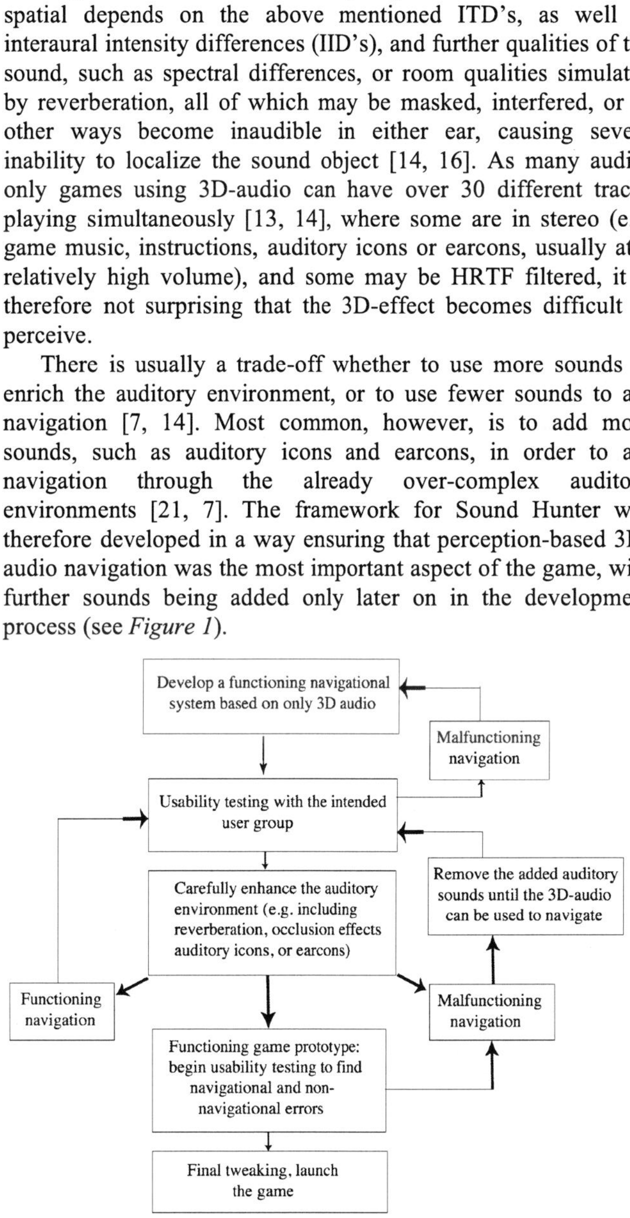

Figure 1: Proposed framework for developing navigational audio-only games based on 3D-audio.

Finally, there exist, to the best of the author's knowledge, no examples of audio games where it is clearly stated that the game was developed in an iterative process together with visually impaired people (or other intended user groups for that matter). As modern technology-oriented development processes based on Human Computer Interaction (HCI) strongly suggest that the intended users should be part of even the earliest Lo-Fi prototypes (e.g. paper prototypes, workshops) [20], the including of the users is therefore suggested as one of the key aspects of importance in developing a highly functional and entertaining audio game, being effective, efficient, and also satisfying its intended user group.

The framework proposed to ensure a more successful design of 3D-audio games can be viewed in *Figure 1.* Especially important are the recurring evaluations of in-game navigation, used to update the sound design aspects. These iterations should be made with the target user group.

IV. METHOD

Sound Hunter's game development process consisted of four parts involving 10 participants: 1) a pre-study in which other 3D-audio games were evaluated in order to create a framework for developing navigational 3D-based audio games and come up with the initial game idea, 2) three focus group sessions with two visually impaired participants, 3) usability testing with eight (new) participants: four visually impaired, and four sighted participants, and lastly 4) a final evaluation of the game with a participant from the usability tests; a visually impaired commercial audio-only game developer, also highly knowledgeable in the field of HRTF synthesis. Due to the great difficulties in acquiring visually impaired participants for the development of an audio game, the evaluation methods were mainly qualitative. However, some quantitative data-collection was also acquired during the usability tests to determine the game level order by difficulty, as well as to find trends in how the players gaming abilities improved over time. The initial game idea for Sound Hunter is presented first, followed by the adjustments having been made to the game throughout the development process.

V. SOUND HUNTER: THE ORIGINAL GAME IDEA

The original game idea for Sound Hunter was relatively simple. The intention was to create a single-player arcade-based game in which a sound is placed at the maximum distance (8m) and random location in a 3D-space, utilizing the azimuth angle. The player's objective is to capture the sound as quickly as possible by using 3D-audio as the only navigational aid. All player movement is controlled by the iPhone's accelerometer data, where leaning the iPhone forward or backwards (the accelerometer's y-data) leads to the player moving forward or backwards in the game, and leaning the iPhone left or right (the accelerometer's x-data) corresponds to the player's head turning either to the left or to the right. Once the sound is reached, a confirmatory auditory icon is heard, and the next level begins, where the levels become progressively more difficult. The game is programmed in *Pure Data.*[1]

VI. FOCUS GROUP SESSIONS 1–3

The participants were the same for all three focus group sessions.

Participant	Sex	Blindness	Age	Smartphone
P1	M	Born blind	31	Yes, iPhone
P2	M	Legally blind	57	No, Nokia
HRTF/binaural sound experience: P1, P2				
Notable HRTF/binaural sound knowledge: None				

P1 had played the occasional audio-based game, but never in depth. He also worked as a usability expert for utilities intended for blind people. P2 had played simple arcade-based games in his youth, but had no experience with audio-only games.

A. Focus group session 1

The first session began by presenting HRTF technology and its capabilities. In order not to bias the participants, an open discussion was held related to the types of games that might be created by using synthesized HRTF filtering, after which the initial game idea for Sound Hunter was presented and discussed. This allowed the gathering of general data and data being specific to the initial game idea.

Results: After some open discussion, both participants suggested that basically anything using this technology that is fun, entertaining and functioning has the potential of becoming a great success. P2 also pointed out that more simple games could be fun, such as the old-school arcade games he had played in his youth, in which the player reaches higher levels under various constraints (e.g. time, enemies). When presenting the game idea for Sound Hunter, both participants regarded the navigational aspect of being able to locate and control sounds in a 3D-based sound-environment as exciting (e.g. being able to hear sounds approach or appear behind the player) – *"We are a bit like virgins in this sense. Everybody else has played all of these cool games, but we don't have this experience, so I think most games using this technology could be fun"* (P2). An important conclusion from this focus group session was that all non in-game sounds (e.g. instructions, highscore) can be displayed as text on the iPhone instead of being pre-recorded, as this allows the user to control the language and *VoiceOver* reading speed as they prefer. Furthermore, we concluded that 20 game levels would be enough for further tests, which could be altered in difficulty by:

- *Varying the level of realism* in the sound (realism as in its connection to a real-life scenario e.g. crying baby vs. growling tiger),
- *Inserting different amounts of temporal silence* in the sound,
- *Varying the complexity* in the sound (e.g. dynamic drum-set vs. sine wave),
- *Varying frequency* (e.g. different ranges or by approaching our perceptual limitations), and
- *Using additional cues related to distance changes* being communicated on a meta-level (e.g. varying the level of activity or frequency in a sound object depending on its distance).

B. Focus group session 2

The intention with the second focus group session was to let the users test the navigation to see if it was intuitive, and to get an

[1] Pure data, http://pure-data.info. A planned development is to use *libPd* to have the application running on a mobile device.

understanding of the learning curve for blind users using the iPhone's accelerometer to manipulate sounds in a 3D space.

Results: First, the participants' passive azimuth localization abilities were tested to see if they experienced front/back-confusion. For simultaneous listening two pairs of in-ear earphones were used (*Pioneer-CL711-G*, frequency range 8Hz-22kHz). The sound was positioned and moved forward, backwards and around the listener using a graphical interface. The participants were told to point in the direction of the sound source when being asked of its location. This was done ten times unless an error was made. Both participants pointed in the correct direction all ten times, and expressed that they had a clear perception of the position at all times. Following this, the iPhone navigation was explained and practiced for about one minute. The sound was then repositioned at the maximum distance and random azimuth location, and the participants were asked to capture the sound as quickly as possible. The sound could only be captured within a range of 2% of the total radius, or 0.32m of 16m in width (i.e. the sound had to be almost exactly straight in front or behind the listener in order to be captured in a straight run). After some open discussion, the following conclusions were made:

Improvement	**Reason**
1. The iPhone should be held horizontally, using two hands – *"It takes a while to get used to, but it is the most logical way of working with it"* (P1).	1. Promotes easier hand movement, and the *VoiceOver* function alerts the user of the holding position already in the game menu, making it a more intuitive game control.
2. There should be a training option in the menu. – *"It takes a while so if you practice first you'll get a confidence boost"* (P2)	2. Allows the user to train their navigation during an unlimited period of time with a complex and easily heard sound.
3. The sensitivity should be increased, and the sound's movement should accelerate when leaning the iPhone more.	3. Promotes easier captures at close distances. – *"When it's close you want to be able to get it fast and not wait for it to spin"* (P2)
4. The game levels should vary in time, with longer times at the first levels and shorter times as the game progresses.	4. To promote a sense of confidence in the player. – *"You want to complete at least some of the first levels to get started"* (P2)
5. The sound should decrease more in intensity at further distances.	5. To give a greater illusion of externalization
6. Apart from the notification sound alerting the player that the sound has been captured, further auditory icons should be included.	6. Countdown to the next level, new highscore, new time record, game over, and dynamic sonification representing the score amounts for each level.

During the navigation, hand and head movements were observed and task completion time was registered. P2's hand movements were calm and sequential, while P1's were more rolling, as if using a joystick. P2 captured the sound within 73 seconds, while P1 needed more than 120 seconds. Both P1 and P2 held their heads still.

C. Focus group session 3

During the third focus group session, the participants tested the re-programmed navigation, as well as the current version of the game, featuring 20 levels varying in difficulty and time.

Procedure and results: When re-testing the navigation, the participants felt that the controls were more intuitive. However, they still had difficulties capturing the sound. The score radius was therefore broadened from 2% to 5%, which led to drastic improvements. When playing the game for the first time, they both came to the fifth level. However, as the placement of the levels was based on initial subjective impression of their independent difficulties, as well as the fact that both P1 and P2 expressed that the level difficulties varied a lot, they were allowed to play some of the later levels in the game (note that these levels had shorter times). When beginning at level 11, they both managed to reach level 13. Interestingly, they both accomplished the same amount of levels in both tests, and the atmosphere was clearly competitive. The main conclusions from this focus group were the following:

Improvement	**Reason**
1. Further usability tests were necessary to determine the correct level order.	1. Mixed level difficulty – *"I'm not sure exactly why, but some of the levels were much more difficult"* (P1).
2. The score radius should remain at 5%.	2. – *"I think 5% is the perfect normal difficulty level"* (P1)
3. The time decrease should be mentioned in the instructions.	3. Increases excitement and immersion – *"When I knew this it became much more fun playing"* (P2).

VII. USABILITY TESTS

The usability tests were conducted to determine the correct game level order, but also to see how well the participants perceived the HRTF filtering and how they used it interactively. Further reasons were to find out which levels were the most difficult and why they were considered difficult, to see if the participants improved in the game over time, to make observations of the participants movements and interactions, as well as to get qualitative feedback on the game in general.

Participant	**Sex**	**Blindness**	**Age**	**Smartphone**
P1	F	Sighted	24	Yes, iPhone
P2	M	Legally blind	52	Yes, iPhone
P3	F	Born blind	50	Yes, iPhone
P4	M	Sighted	16	Yes, other
P5	M	Sighted	15	Yes, iPhone
P6	M	Born blind	23	No
P7	M	Sighted	24	Yes, iPhone
P8	F	Born blind	18	Yes, iPhone

HRTF/binaural sound experience: P1, P2, P3, P4, P5, P6, P7
Notable HRTF/binaural sound knowledge: P6, P7

Procedure: After explaining how the game worked, the participants' passive HRTF perception was tested similarly as in focus group 2. The participants then got familiarized with the navigation, and were allowed to practice as long as they wanted.

When they captured the sound, it was replaced to let them capture it again until they felt comfortable enough to start playing the game. Each participant played through the entire game including all 20 levels five times each. Simultaneous listening was conducted throughout the test, and the time restrictions had been removed, thus allowing the participants to play each level as long as they needed in order to complete it. The quantitative data analysis consisted of analysing the amount of tips that had to be given for each level to be completed, as well as the level times retrieved through automatic data-collection, to determine level difficulty, and to see how the participants improved between gaming sessions. The qualitative data analysis consisted of observations and a semi-structured post-game interview, in order to obtain additional information regarding game improvements.

Tips: The tips were categorized into amount, participant, level and session. A tip was given if the participant communicated uncertainty connected to something previously explained (e.g. how the navigation worked), or if 90 seconds had passed without level completion. The given tip was always connected to the navigation (e.g. *"Try leaning forward"*), regardless of what caused the uncertainty, such as a certain level being more difficult, front/back-confusion, or if the participant could not hear the sound object (being the case for levels 19 and 20, where the frequency only becomes audible at closer distances). Almost all the tips were given in the first gaming session, indicating that it took about one session for the participants to properly understand the controls. The exceptions were the final two levels, where the frequencies were more difficult to perceive for the two older participants (P2 and P3), and the tips were therefore spread out between sessions. P2 had a documented hearing impairment on the right ear, and could barely hear level 19 and 20. The completion times were therefore set to 100s for P2 on these two levels for the quantitative data analysis. Furthermore, P8 had severe difficulties concentrating, and could therefore not finish the test. The results were also too biased by tips and uncompleted levels, and P8 was therefore excluded from the quantitative data analysis. Apart from this, no adjustments had to be made, and the quantitative data analysis was performed with seven participants.

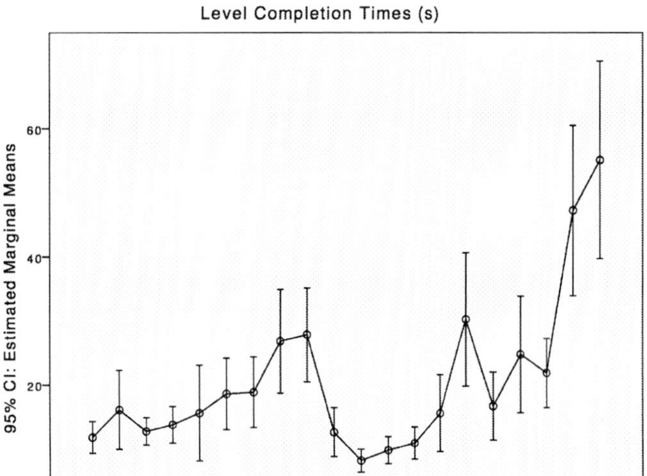

Figure 2: The comparable difficulty difference between each level.

Level difficulty: The new level order was determined by comparing the level completion times using a Oneway Repeated Measures Anova in SPSS. The within-level difference in level completion time was significant F(5.322, 180.958)=14.31, p<0.01, and 29.6 per cent of the total variance could be explained by completion time (using the Greenhouse-Geisser correction, sphericity assumed). As expected, the levels' difficulties did not match the order in which they had been placed (see *Figure 2*).

As seen in *Figure 2*, the easiest and most stable levels, were levels 11 to 13, which were the synthesized levels communicating complex distance-dependent meta-level information (level of activity in a motor-like sound depending on distance), and the most difficult levels (despite the broad confidence intervals caused by audibility differences between age groups) were levels 19 and 20, which communicated inaudible to audible frequency changes in sine waves, also depending on distance (20kHz to 5kHz for level 19, and 20Hz to 150Hz for level 20). It should also be mentioned that ITD's could not be utilized in level 19 due to the high frequency content, and IID's could not be utilized in level 20 due to the low frequency content, which was part of the experiment to indicate which of these static localization cues are the most important in virtual interactive gaming experiences.

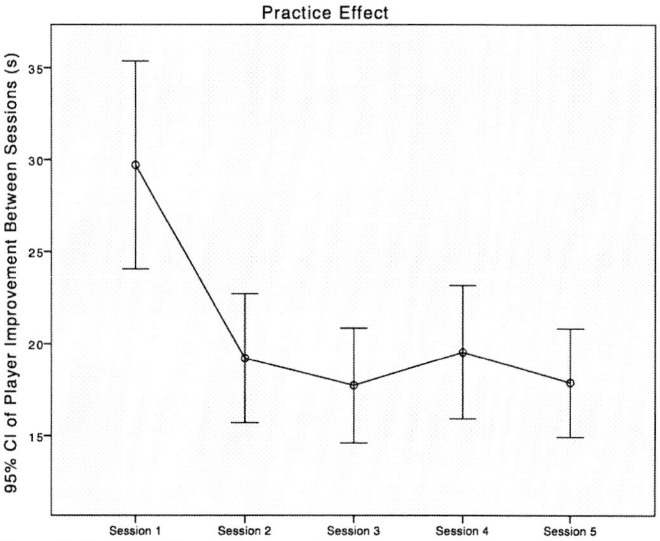

Figure 3: Practice effect between sessions.

Practice effect: The level times were also used to analyse the practice effect between gaming sessions, performed similarly as level difficulty, using a Oneway Repeated Measures Anova in SPSS. The within-subjects effects were significant F(2.441, 339.331)=11.572, p<0.01, and 10.6 per cent of the total variance in game completion time could be explained by the different gaming sessions (using the Greenhouse-Geisser correction, sphericity assumed). The differences between gaming session one and two t(139)=3.90, p<0.01, one and three t(139)=4.46, p<0.01, one and four t(139)=3.62, p<0.01, and one and five t(139)=4.41, p<0.01 were significant. All other differences and pairwise comparisons between gaming sessions were non-significant (see *Figure 3*).

Observations: To get an understanding of how the participants behaved when playing the game, special attention was paid to their hand and head movements, passive and interactive front/back-confusion, as well as their overall improvement and immersion in the game (see *Figure 4*). Two participants (P5 and P8) experienced front/back-confusion in the passive HRTF perception test, where P5 adapted immediately while playing, and P8 only adapted while playing levels 11 to 13 (including additional dynamic meta-level localization cues). All the participants used the navigation to eliminate front/back-confusion while playing the game (i.e. by spinning the sound, simulating the dynamic localization cue of head movement). The participants held their heads still, but their hand movements differed, where some used rolling movements, and some used calm and sequential hand movements. As indicated by the quantitative data analysis, it seemed to take about one gaming session (≈15 min including practice time) to fully understand the navigation. Five participants expressed signs of immersion (e.g. laughter, expressions of disgust for insect levels, or through threatening statements directed to the hunted sound object).

Figure 4: Participant playing Sound Hunter in their natural home environment.

Post-game interview: The post-game interview consisted of a semi-structured questionnaire with 51 questions, either being nominal, open, or measured on a 7-point Likert scale. The results confirmed most of the observations and quantitative results. The controls were seen as easily understood, and none of the participants considered front/back-confusion a problem, as long as it could be corrected by navigating. Sounds were perceived as more externalized than lateralized, and the overall sound quality and 3D rendering was seen as extremely good. All the participants, even the blind, stated that they improved in the game as a result of focusing attention to their hearing more than usual, or even training their hearing, rather than remembering the game levels. Five participants were highly immersed in the game, whereas three participants were more in a state of deep concentration (or flow). They all felt happy while playing the game, and stressed as a form of adrenaline rush, except P8, who stated that she was currently being examined for ADHD, and therefore always felt stressed and also had great difficulties concentrating or sitting still. This was clearly noticeable also during the observations. Finally, the game in itself was highly appreciated, mainly due to the 3D-audio experience, and all the participants would recommend Sound Hunter to others:

– *"The best part was being able to play a game with motion as a visually impaired person, and I would recommend the game to others, even sighted people, as it shows how important our hearing is"* (P2)

– *"It felt very interesting. I hardly ever play computer games and I thought it was very fun. I think it is good also to train one's hearing, and I can imagine that you could use this for all kinds of other things. It would probably be a great game for kids with special needs"* (P3)

– *"I thought the various sounds as well as the whole experience of the 3D sound in the game was cool and fun"* (P7)

– *"I've never played anything like it, and I would recommend it to others because of this* (P5)

– *"The best part was the 3D audio and your fantastic simulation! It was really easy to localize sounds. Other games do not provide this. I have never heard anything like what you have done here, and I have tested everything, and of everything I've heard, you have come the closest to providing real 3D audio"* (P6)

As the results from the focus group sessions and the usability tests showed that the participants could accurately use the 3D audio to navigate by using simple hand movements, the framework was considered applicable for similar developments.

VIII. Final Evaluation

The final evaluation was conducted with P6 from the usability tests, a 23 year-old blind audio-only game developer, also highly knowledgeable in the field of HRTF synthesis (will be referred to as P6 also in this section to avoid confusion). After letting P6 test the finished game with the correct level order, a semi-structured interview was held covering the development process and its results, how Sound Hunter may be optimized, as well as what future developments might be made by following Sound Hunter's framework.

Optimizing Sound Hunter: P6 was first asked whether he thought there was a need for audio-only smartphone games – *"Yes, absolutely, the amount of games and game developers for iOS increases all the time, so the interest is definitely there. I am completely convinced that you could capture the market there if you intend to develop a fully functioning iPhone game"*. We also concluded that when optimizing the controls for blind users, it is better to include a strong default setting with customizable sensitivity, rather than offering full customizability – *"You often want a default setting that you know works well and that is also generalizable for a large number of people. In my experience, sensitivity is the most important adjustment"* (P6). Front/back-confusion was greatly reduced in Sound Hunter through complex distance-dependent communication, and we discussed additional ways of accomplishing this, such as to introduce front/back sound bounces, or directional beeps. We also concluded that the frequency ranges towards 20Hz and 20kHz should be tighter – *"To avoid the unfair difficulties between age groups, and because most normal headphones do not support these ranges"* (P6). Furthermore, silence should be used with clear progression and never exceed 5s, which seems to be the border of confusion, where additional helping sounds (e.g. directional beeps) should never be necessary to guide through silence – *"This would equal trying to solve a self-introduced problem"* (P6). Finally, tiredness could be avoided by including more levels and a "Pause"/"Save" button, depending on the amount of levels.

Future development: Regarding future development, the game could be split into several unlockable "Sound hunting missions", each of which would correspond to ways of progressively making the game more difficult (e.g. silence, audibility, meta-level communication) – *"This is a classic way of getting people to play more"* (P6). Also, more sounds could be introduced, as well as simple forms of artificial intelligence (e.g. threatening or shooting objects). However, the most important conclusion was that all future developments should be made with Sound Hunter's underlying framework in mind, such that navigating is still possible.

IX. Conclusions

When playing an action-based game, whether it is graphical or auditory, the player wants to be transported into another world and perceive that world as if it were real. Arguably, an increased level of immersion due to increased imagination is not necessarily the reason behind the success of action-based graphical video games, and there is little reason why this should be the case for audio games. Creating a sense of auditory spatial presence can only be accomplished properly by connecting our real-world perceptions with the actions and responses in that of the game. Today, audio games based on 3D-audio are extremely rare, with only a handful being available for smartphone users. For these games, the main problems seem to be the inability to use 3D-audio as the only means of navigation, reliance on stationary equipment or physical movement by the player, as well as insufficient usage of HCI methods in the development processes.

In this article, a framework has been proposed for designing navigational perception-based 3D-audio games without relying on imagination or additional navigational aids, all of which may be added later on in the development process. To test the framework, the game *Sound Hunter* was developed in an iterative process together with both sighted and visually impaired participants. The results indicate that the suggested framework is a successful guidance tool when developing navigational 3D-audio games, and that the need for navigational 3D-audio smartphone games may be met by introducing proper design processes directed to the user group. The results also indicate that *Sound Hunter* may be used to train a person's spatial hearing, where complex distance-dependent meta-level communication in synthesized sounds greatly reduces front/back-confusion. Finally, all of the participants would recommend *Sound Hunter* to others, due to the fast and accurate interaction made possible by the way in which the 3D-audio was perceived and could be used to navigate.

Acknowledgment

The author is sincerely thankful to Kjetil Falkenberg at the Sound and Music Computing Group (supervisor), Funka Nu, Synskadades Riksförbund, Unga Synskadade Stockholm, and Blastbay Studios.

More in depth information regarding Sound Hunter and its development is available in the equally named master's thesis listed in the references [2].

References

[1] Archambault, D., Ossman, R., Gaudy, T., Miesenberger, K. (2006). Computer Games and Visually Impaired People. Institute for Integrated Study, University of Linz, Austria, p. 1-21J. Clerk Maxwell, A Treatise on Electricity and Magnetism, 3rd ed., vol. 2. Oxford: Clarendon, 1892, pp.68–73.

[2] Brieger, W.S. (2013). Sound Hunter: Developing a Navigational HRTF-Based Audio Game for People with Visual Impairments, Msc in Media Technology, Department of Computer Science and Communication, KTH, Royal Institute of Technology, Stockholm, Sweden.

[3] Brewster, S. A. (1988). Using non speech sounds to provide navigation cues. ACM Transactions on Computer-Human Interaction, 5(3):224–259, September 1998.

[4] Cohoen, Y., Dekker, J., Hulskamp, A., Kousemaker, D., Olden, T., Taal, C., Verspaget, W. (2004). Demor – Location based 3D Audiogame. http://student- kmt.hku.nl/_g7/site/, 2013.

[5] Danz Games. SuperDeekout. http://www.danzgames.com/superdeekout.htm, 2004. PC.

[6] epicycle Games. Blindside. http://boingboing.net/2012/05/24/blindside-a-new-3d-audio-on.html, 2012, iOS.

[7] Friberg, J. & Gärdenfors, D. (2004). Audio games: New perspectives on game audio. In Advances in Computer Entertainment Technology '04, Singapore, 2004, p. 1-7.

[8] Hansen, K. F., Dravins, C. & Bresin, R. (2012). Active Listening and Expressive Communication for Children with Hearing Loss Using Getatable Environments for Creativity *Journal of New Music Research, 41*, 365-375.

[9] Hansen, K. F.; Li, Z. & Wang, H. (2012). A music puzzle game application for engaging in active listening *SIG Technical Reports: Proceedings of 97th Information Science and Music (SIGMUS) Research Conference.*

[10] Gardner, WG & Martin, KD. (1995). 'HRTF Measurement of a KEMAR', *Journal of the Acoustical Society of America*, vol. 97, pp. 3907-3908.

[11] Gaver, W. W. What in the world do we hear? An ecological approach to auditory event perception. Ecological Psychology, 5(1):1–29, 1993.

[12] Gaver, W. W. Auditory interfaces. In M. G. Helander, T. K. Landauer, and P. V. Prabhu, editors, Handbook of Human-Computer Interaction, 2nd ed, pages 1003–1041. Elsevier, Amsterdam, 1997.

[13] GMA. Gma games. http://www.gmagames.com/sod.html, 2004.

[14] Graeme. E. A. (2011). Designing the Sonic Gameplay Environment. Msc Sound Design Final Project. Edinburgh College of Art. University of Edinburgh, p. 1-49.

[15] Hildén, A. and Svensson, H. (2002). Can All Young Disabled Children Play at the Computer. In Miesenberger, K., Klaus, J., and Zagler, W., editors, Proc. ICCHP 2002. International Conference on Computers Helping People with Special Needs, vol. 2398 of LNCS, Linz, Austria. Springer.

[16] Moore, B. C. J. (2008). An Introduction to the Psychology of Hearing, p. 233-238.

[17] Moore, B. C. J. (2008). An Introduction to the Psychology of Hearing, p. 249.

[18] Pin. Pin interactive. http://www.terraformers.nu/eng/, 2004.

[19] Relativity Media. Escape The House: A 3D Sound Experience. http://www.houseattheend.com/escape/, 2012, iOS.

[20] Rettig, M. (1994). Prototyping for tiny fingers. Communications of THS ACM, vol. 37, p. 21-27.

[21] Röber, N., Masuch, M. (2005). Playing audio-only games a compendium of interacting with virtual , auditory worlds. Games Research Group. Department of Simulation and Graphics. University of Magdeburg, Germany, p. 1-7.

[22] Sontiacchi, A., Noisternig, M., Majdak, P., & Höldrich, R. (2002). 'An Objective Model of Localisation in Binaural Sound Reproduction Systems', *Proceedings in AES 21st International Conference: Architectural Acoustics and Sound Reinforcement*, St. Petersburg, Russia.

[23] Texas School for the Blind and Visually Impaired. EyeNote research (BEP). http://www.tsbvi.edu/component/content/article/182-fall-2011/3617-eyenote, 2013.

[24] Xiang, P., Camargo, D & Puckette, M. (2005). 'Experiments on Spatial Gestures in Binaural Sound Display', *Proceedings of ICAD 05-Eleventh Meeting of the International Conference on Auditory Display*, Center for Research in Computing and the Arts, Institute for Telecommunication and Information Technology, University of California, Limerick, Ireland.

ENERGY HARVESTING POWER FLOWER BELL – A CYBERNETIC SOUND INSTALLATION DRIVEN BY A DIRT-BATTERY

Josef Schauer
TU Graz
`josef_s@sbox.tugraz.at`

Winfried Ritsch
KUG Graz
`ritsch@algo.mur.at`

Lothar Fickert
TU Graz
`lothar.fickert@tugraz.at`

ABSTRACT

This work describes the art-driven development of an energy harvesting system in sound installations. The used energy source is a dirt-battery. It is built by digging a piece of copper and a piece of zinc in a soil. Sound is generated when there is sufficient energy to trigger a bell. In the described sound installation, such a system looks like a flower and the bell represents its bloom. With its *roots* (electrodes) dug into the soil, it generates electrical energy to make sound. It is shown that this concept works. It is possible to make sound by dirt-energy. In a further step, many of such devices which are called Power Flower Bells (PFBs) should be spread in a meadow, communicating with low-power Radio Frequency (RF) technology, realizing musical compositions.

1. INTRODUCTION

The project was initiated by the artist Winfried Ritsch. His idea is to realize a cybernetic flower meadow, made up by a field of robotic flowers as a kind of cybernetic organism. These flowers should be powered by dirt-batteries and/or other energy sources [1]. Because other sources are well known and documented, the motivation of this project is to run the PFB just with a dirt-battery. Additional sources, as long as they have a matching ($\leq$3 V) Direct Current (DC) output, can be applied easily in order to fulfill the artistic vision of obtaining a robotic device that behaves quite like a natural flower because it needs water, light and space. There is a direct link between the energy they can harvest and the musical output they deliver. The musical performance depends on the state of each flower.

Thinking further this approach, the artist expresses the perception of the Power Flower Bells by visitors and gardeners as an independent life-form which is nourished by the environment [1]. A dirt-battery needs to be watered, otherwise its output gets a lot weaker and the PFB could stop running its Real Time Clock and Calender, which is the time basis for activities like clinking the bell. Also the RF communication uses this time base to be synchronized.

1.1 Problem Statement

Nowadays, there are some projects working with dirt-batteries, like the Soil Lamp [2]. The Soil Lamp is based on several cells of dirt-batteries connected in series to obtain a higher output voltage. To run a PFB, just one cell is needed which has a measurable output of about 0,8 V. The multiplication of the surfaces of the electrodes in this cell comes up to a parallel connection of many cells. For the here presented project it is essential that the installation of a flower meadow with many PFBs is an easy task. It is much less work to install one cell than to install many cells, especially because the zinc-halfs and the copper-halfs have to be separated from each other in one cell to prevent electron flow through the soil. The use of just one cell requires a circuit which is enable to convert the low voltage to a higher value, because even low-power micro-controllers need a minimum voltage of 1,8 V. To buffer energy for energy-intensive tasks like ringing the bell or RF-activities, an energy storage like a supercap is needed.

1.2 Scientific Interests

Because of the modular flexibility, the access to solutions for realizing energy harvesting sound installations or sensor/actor nodes increases by analyzing the technology. The great advantage of energy harvesting systems which is noticed by the industry is the fact that there are no costs for changing batteries any longer. Obviously, most of artists doing sound installations based on unwired devices would appreciate this quality too.
The knowledge of how to apply energy available in the direct environment of a system to build up a sound installation which is networked via RF can help to develop a wide spread of useful systems which do not just serve as sensors like as already applied in a lot of cases in industry, but also as actors which of course can just act when there is enough energy available. For a swarm or a cluster of items, this also requires research on how they can communicate. Another motivating fact is that by running a copper-zinc galvanic element in a copper-polluted soil – as you can find it for example on many traditional wine yards – the zinc will be left in the soil and the copper will be united with the copper-electrode, so the Power Flower Bell represents a nice-sounding detoxification method for copper-contaminated soils.

2. OVERVIEW

A block diagram of the system is shown in figure 1. It shows up the essential blocks of the PFB. The low output voltage of the dirt-battery (about 0,8 V) has to be converted to a higher level to enable the rest of the system to work properly. This happens in the power handling block. The increased voltage is loaded to a storage element, currently a supercap with a capacity of 10 mF is in use.
A dirt-battery can be too weak to even rise the voltage in the supercap to 1,8 V, which is the minimum voltage for getting the micro-controller started. When the dirt-battery is strong enough, the micro-controller starts, but immediately a sleep-instruction is given by the firmware.
When the voltage in the supercap reaches 3,5 V, the VBAT_OK pin of the bq25504 rises to high. Since this pin is connected to an interrupt-pin of the micro-controller, this one wakes up, acts if necessary and changes to sleep mode again. It is essential that the micro-controller spends as much time as possible in sleep mode to work efficiently. The Real Time Clock and Calender (RTCC) implemented on the micro-controller keeps running all the time and means the time basis for all actions of the device.

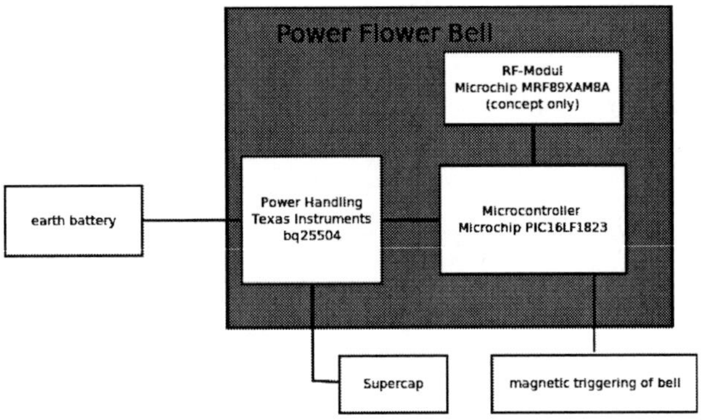

Figure 1. Block diagram to summarize the Power Flower Bell (PFB)

3. ENERGY GENERATION

Since the used hardware is able to handle various types of electrical energy generators, some of them are described in the Master Thesis [3], but this work is focused on the dirt-battery as an energy source.

3.1 Redox Reaction

Oxidation is a chemical reaction in which a material electrons are abstracted, reduction is a chemical reaction in which a material electrons are added. Redox reaction is the term for a chemical reaction in which electrons from one material are transferred to another one. This results in a change of the oxidation number of the materials involved in the reaction. The transport of electrons is the most important effect in a redox reaction, but besides, there can occur a transfer of atoms and ions. The reducer is the electron donor, and the oxidizer is the so-called electron acceptor.

By putting a piece of zinc in a solution with Cu^{2+} ions, a spontaneous redox reaction in which metal copper is sedimented on the piece of zinc, is obtained. The zinc in this process is dispersed.

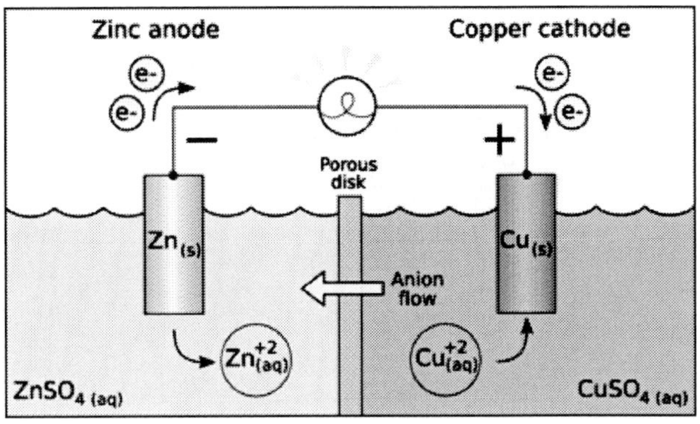

Figure 2. Galvanic cell [5]

In figure 2, you can see a galvanic cell which works with the same redox reaction of zinc and copper, but there is no direct conductance between the zinc and the Cu^{2+} ions. In one tank, the zinc electrode is in contact with the Zn^{2+} ions, while in the other one, the copper is in contact with the Cu^{2+} ions. That is why the reaction can just take place due to electrons moved from one electrode to the other by connecting them externally. By separating the reduction and oxidation half-reaction, electrons are forced to move externally. The electrode on which the oxidation takes place is called anode and the one on which the reduction is situated is named cathode. The oxidation of the zinc in the one half-cell leads to an increasing concentration of the Zn^{2+} solution and a decreasing mass of the zinc electrode. In the other half-cell, the reduction of copper leads to a decreasing concentration of the Cu^{2+} solution and a mass growth of the copper electrode [4]. Materials like platinum or graphite permit electron migration without mass losses. To keep the reaction running, the solutions have to be kept electrically neutral. The overload of Zn^{2+} has to be compensated by positive ions that leave the half-cell, or negative ions have to be added. In the other half-cell, the reduction of Cu^{2+} ions in the solution means a deficit of positive charges in the solution. This has to be compensated by adding positive ions or removing negative ones.
For this reason, a diaphragm, which allows ions to move from one half to the other but prohibits electrons to pass is necessary. Such a diaphragm can be a porous disk or – in the case of the dirt-battery – a pot made of clay.

3.2 Dirt-Battery

A dirt battery is nothing than a galvanic cell. The soil acts as the electrolyte. A dirt-battery was first shown by Alexander Bain in 1841 [6]. The output power of an earth-battery is not constant, it depends on factors like the connected load, the state of the electrodes, the state of the soil, in which they are planted in, as the distance between the electrodes. *Earth-battery* is another synonym for naming the same thing as *dirt-battery*.
Some humidity in the soil is necessary, so a PFB *living* indoors without being watered sometimes might not make any sound.

Figure 3. Dirt-battery *photo: Christoph Staber*

Figure 3 shows the used dirt-battery. It is built by a bucket made of plastic and filled with flower-soil. The copper electrode is a shield with a length of 70 cm and a width of 20 cm. In the center of the bucket, a flower pot made of clay is placed. This represents a diaphragm to isolate the two electrodes electrically. In the center of the pot, the zinc-electrode which exists in a solid block of zinc, is dug into soil.

The power that can be exploited from such a source strongly depends on the load connected to it. That for, the behavior of the dirt-battery is investigated by connecting resistors with different values between 1 Ω and 10 kΩ to it. The obtained curve can be seen in figure 4. Obviously, there is a specific resistor that permits the maximum output power. A dirt battery delivers the maximum output power when the connected load leads to an output voltage which is the half of the open-circuit voltage. This operation point is called *Maximum Power Point*. A theoretical explanation for this is given in [3].

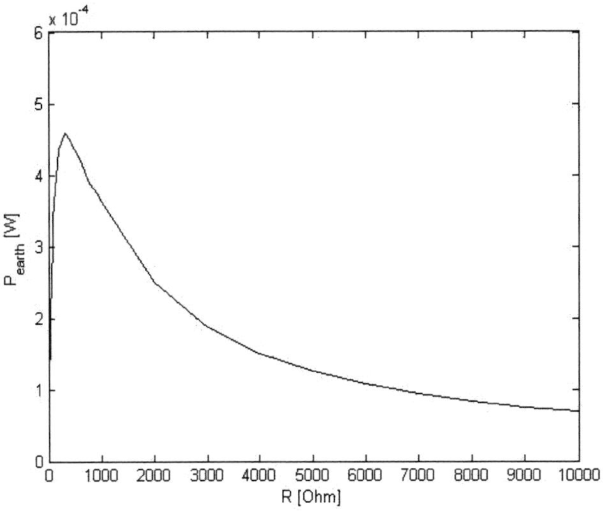

Figure 4. Sweep over resistance loads applied to the dirt-battery

3.3 Power Management

The low output power of the dirt battery is converted to 3,6 V by a Texas Instruments bq25504 Ultra Low Power Boost Converter with Battery Management for Energy Harvester Applications.
An important feature of the bq25504 is Maximum Power Point Tracking. This technology is commonly used in systems supplied by photo voltaic. The relation $\frac{V_{\text{out\_oc}}}{V_{\text{out\_MPP}}}$ can be set-up dimensioning two resistors. As mentioned in subsection 3.2, for the dirt-battery, this value is $\frac{1}{2}$.
The chip permits control over the storage element. The lower limit of the battery voltage, as the upper limit can be programmed. Further, there is a pin that signals a battery ready status at a programmable voltage measured at the supercap. This pin is connected to an interrupt pin of the micro-controller.

3.4 Effects on the Environment

The dirt-battery is thought to be applied in a free-field scenario. The intention is, in the best case, just to put a piece of copper and a piece of zinc into the soil and start harvesting electrical energy.
In a society in which the ecological footprint is becoming a more and more important factor in making decisions for people in their buying-behaviour, as in times of decreasing availability of resources on one hand, but increasing demand for resources on the other hand, the question has to be asked how ecologically sense- or harmful a technology is.
An article by Greenpeace [7] calls attention to this topic, especially when copper is used. It is not broken down but stays in the soil and does harm the biodiversity. For example, the earthworm is banished by copper. In France, 1885 copper was becoming a common fungicide. Up to now it has been known as an almost perfect substance for this application. Especially ecological wine farmers in the European Union are very dependent on the use of copper, since they are not allowed to use other fungicides. Mainly it is applied as copper-sulphate of which 3 kg/ha are allowed to be applied every year in Austria. In the 1960 of the last century, in some zones up to 60 kg/ha were applied annually.
The dirt-battery would leave zinc in the earth, while copper is brought from the soil to the copper electrode. That means, a dirt-battery could accumulate copper from a copper-polluted soil, lowering the copper-concentration in the contaminated soil.

4. NETWORK

An important feature is the low-power RF module, with which the PFB is equipped. It is a Microchip MRF89XAM8A 868 Hz Ultra-Low Power Sub-GHz Transceiver Module that includes a transceiver controller, peripherals and a Printed Circuit Board (PCB) antenna. Being synchronized by a Real Time Clock and Calender (RTCC) implemented on the micro-controller, the devices can communicate with each other. The synchronization is necessary, because RF communication is an energy-intense process and that for it should be inactive most of the time. At certain time-slots, the PFBs are enabled to receive data and exchange information. In order to be able to realize compositions, a newly planted flower starts sending data at defined time-slots. It starts with the lowest transmitting power. After sending a request to its environment, it waits for an answer of another PFB. If there is an answer, an ID of the other device, as the transmitting power necessary for contacting it are stored. Additionally, the Received Signal Strength Indicator feature of the low-power RF module permits an estimation of the distance to the device that has sent the response. Of course, more data, for example the key tone of the bell of each PFB can be stored. Like this, knowledge of the environment is earned. This knowledge can be exchanged again with other PFBs which are in the coverage of each other. So, if there is enough memory, a PFB can reproduce how the meadow is organized in a plane. The choice to use a module that comes up all-in-one with a PCB antenna was made because exhaustive development of the low power RF circuit would mean a lot of additional effort. The micro-controller controls the module by Serial Peripheral Interface (SPI).

5. COMPUTING

All the computing necessary is done by a micro-controller. In the first development step, this is a PIC16LF1823 micro-controller from Microchip®. The controller represents a minimalistic solution in terms of the resources of the device as its pin count (all in all 14 pins). The advantage of this choice is little energy consumption. Very important in the context of the Power Flower Bell is the current in sleep mode, because the device will spend most of the time in this mode. Powered with 1,8 V, the sleep current is rated with 20 nA and the operating current with 34 µA@1 MHz.

6. SOUND GENERATION

Electric generation of sound is a critical task in terms of energy consumption. Common loudspeakers have a weak efficiency, particularly small speakers [1]. Bells appeared the first time about 5000 years ago in Asia [8]. Up to today they are used to send acoustic signals to wide areas in many cultures. A big effort using a bell is that it produces a quite loud output with just a single hit on it. The hit corresponds to a control-signal which ideally looks like an impulse, but since the used motor is not ideal, it needs a control signal which looks like a unit step stopped after a small period of time (about 1 s). Because of this small period, the hammering on the bell is supposed to be very energy-efficient compared with loudspeakers, for which further amplifiers would be necessary as well.

For this reason, the simple method of bells for sound generation was chosen for the Power Flower Bell.
In future development steps, small loudspeakers might be implemented. The additional computing power that is necessary to reproduce music represents a challenge. In the case of a bell it is just a variable that has to be set if a current through the coil of the used motor is desired.

6.1 Pipe Bells

Pipe Bells were chosen by Ritsch because of it's sound. Hueber [9] and Rossing [10] described the bending vibrations of circular cylinders as not harmonic, they rather produce "nearly harmonious" partials. Hueber measured that the fundamental frequency one hears, physically is not present but rather is formed psychologically. Fletcher and Rossing documented the use of Flugges formula to pipe bells [11]. They also discussed the model of the virtual pitch which is important in the context of bells, because all of them show the feature of a strike tone. The strike tone is heard more or less clearly, depending on the quality of a bell. By convention, the part tones of a contemporary church bell are intended to come as close as possible to the frequency ratios 1:2:2,4:5:6:8, the higher part tones are not defined that strictly. Although the ratios 1:2:3:4:5:6:8 and 2:4:6:8 are quite familiar, the minor third between 2 and 2,4 does not fit into the harmonic series nor the series. The strike tone is the *holistic* pitch that a sound of a bell is associated by the ear immediately after the bell is striked. It is not possible to find a period of a fundamental frequency in the time signal or in the part-tone spectrum. The strike note is the most prominent one of multiple pitches that are elicited by a bell sound. Terhardt [12] explains the assigning of several pitches to just *one* pitch with the hierarchically organized perception of humans. An object may appear as a collection of multiple elements (spectral pitches) at the bottom of the hierarchy but may be represented by just one perceptual object (virtual pitch). The pitch ordinarily heard, is not dependent on the audibility of the fundamental. The auditory system extracts the fundamental from a range of the Fourier spectrum that extends above the fundamental [12].

6.2 Playing Music

Ritsch first was thinking of a lot of small devices that generate sound and are placed in a quite silent environment, as a meadow for example. The devices should act like musicians accumulated to a swarm. He describes the sound they would produce as an *endlessly distributed composition in time and space*.
For example, the PFBs can trigger their bells in spacial propagating waves. Also the performing of rhythmical dialogues and complex algorithmic interactions are possible [1]. Further Ritsch mentions the influence of former projects like *The House of Sounds*. Actually, *The House of Sounds* is a computer program that permits listening to a *sound world* built by *soundobjects* which are stored on computers. This computers are part of a *data-network*. The *soundobjects* age, can move from one computer to another one without external input, form groups, duplicate or die. Their existence is based on computers running the *House of Sounds* program connected to a data-network [13].

The clinking of the bells should have the opportunity to become a kind of spacial composition. Rhythmics and dynamics, as different bells for different flowers are the ways to express musical structures [1]. With different types and sizes of bells, harmonic variations can be performed. Playing few or no tones for some while enables a PFB to collect

Figure 5. Christmas bell that helped to estimate the required energy

more electrons into the supercap, as long as this one has enough capacitance. Later, the flower can realize faster rhythms, because there is more energy available before the device has to change to its energy-harvesting mode. A human can manipulate the performance by updating one Power Flower Bell which then signals to its neighbors how to continue, the neighbors send this information to their neighbors and so on. In future, it is also planned to construct different Instruments and sound-generators. For example, a chord can easily be used by hammering on it. A vision is to realize an orchestra with drums, strings and bells played with energy that comes from dirt-batteries, photo voltaic cells and similar sources.

6.3 Interfacing to the Environment

Applying different energy sources and sensors, the Music played by a PFB will be dependent on the surrounding. As mentioned in 3.2, in the current version a PFB for example needs water. Without watering it, it will get weaker and weaker, which in the actual programmed setups means, that the hits on the bell occur with more temporal distance, because it takes longer to collect energy. Imagine a PFB driven by photo voltaic, *living* outdoors: During a sunny day, it might play very fast variations, but during the night it will not be able to ring any time. In another way sensors could be applied, which measure parameters like the temperature of the air, loudness etc. The artist then is free to determine, in which way the measured signals will be used to manipulate the musical performance of one or more PFBs.

6.4 Estimation of Energy

The kinetic energy which is necessary to be given to a bell in order to produce a well hear able sound was estimated doing an experiment with a Christmas bell as shown in figure 5.

By measuring the mass of a clapper (m), mounting it to a piece of twine, deflecting it to a certain height (h) and releasing the clapper from this height, the energy stored in it in the moment when it touches the bell is W_{kin}.

$$W_{\text{kin}} = W_{\text{pot}} = m \cdot g \cdot h \qquad (1)$$

Because all losses are neglected, the potential energy is supposed to be the same as the kinetic energy in the moment of the impact between the clapper and the bell. It was possible to hear the bell at adequate loudness when the clapper with a mass of 5 g was deflected to a height of 5 cm and released. This means, an energy of 2,9 mW was given to the bell by the impact. This value was important to get an idea for dimensioning the whole system.

7. IMPLEMENTATION

The triggering of the bell is implemented by an extra n-channel Metal Oxid Semiconductor Field Effekt Transistor (MOSFET) on the PFB board. Its gate is connected to a General Purpose In-/Output (GPIO) of the Micro-controller. Configured as an output, it can be used to control the hammering of the clapper on the bell.
The actor in the first version is a low-cost vibration motor like used in mobile phones. On its spindle, a thin piece of stiff wire is soldered. The interior of a luster terminal is fixed on this wire. Different sounds with one bell can be obtained by the firmware, which controls how long the motor is connected to the supply voltage stored in the supercap. Other possibilities are varying the point on the wire where the luster terminal is mounted as the distance to the bell and the point of the bell where the clapper (luster terminal) hits the bell. In future works, this parameters should be investigated. Figure 6 helps to get an idea of how a Power Flower Bell can look like. This device was built together with Winfried Ritsch.

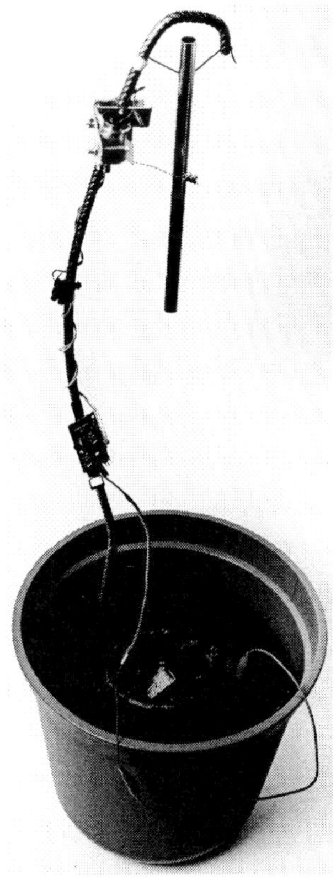

Figure 6. The first sounding Power Flower Bell *photo: Christoph Staber*

8. CONCLUSIONS

The work on the presented project showed that, in principle, it is possible to run low-power electronic devices like sensors or actors by a dirt-battery. A PFB device can be seen as such a device. Even if the amount of extracted energy is quite low, it can be a model for other applications. The dirt-battery, in its current state, can be developed further by optimizing the composition of the soil and the used diaphragm. Moreover, there might be applications, where galvanic energy is available as an unused source.

This work is one of a few available publications describing dirt-batteries. Much of the information about this topic found in the Internet is not scientific but sometimes even esoteric. All other systems found are driven by a serial set up of dirt batteries. The here presented system is based on *one* single cell of a dirt-battery, which is much easier to install.

The designed circuit can also be powered by many other kinds of DC low-power sources. There are certainly new possibilities for artists who want to realize a wireless networking, energy harvesting driven sound installation.

The integration of the RF part into the PFB circuit was not done during the project. However, the basics of this part of the system are described in the present document.

Even if the dirt-battery is not yet optimized, the functionality of the whole system could be shown.

Acknowledgments

My thanks go to DI Winfried Ritsch who works with me on his project. I am much obliged to Univ.-Prof. Dipl.-Ing. Dr.techn. Lothar Fickert from the Institute of Electrical Power Systems at the Graz University of Technology and DI Dr.techn. Alois Sontacchi from the Institute of Electronic Music and Acoustics at the University of Music and Performing Arts Graz for supporting me to participate at the SMAC/SMC 2013. Early steps of the PFB project took place at the Institute for Applied Microelectronics at the University of Las Palmas de Gran Canaria where Dr. Francisco Javier del Pino Suárez was my coordinator. Finally I want to thank Carmela for listening to me talking about the Power Flower Bell like she does and my parents for everything.

9. REFERENCES

[1] W. Ritsch, "Vision and context of the power flower bells network," 13.1.2012. [Online]. Available: http://algo.mur.at/projects/powerflowerbells/vision

[2] M. staps, "Soil lamp," 09.05.2012. [Online]. Available: http://www.mariekestaps.nl/?/Design/Soil-Lamp-2/

[3] J. Schauer, "Networked power flower bell - energy harvesting system for a cybernetic sound installation," Master's thesis, Technische Universität Graz, pp. 30-53, 2013.

[4] Institut für Physikalische und Theoretische Chemie der Technischen Universität Carolo-Wilhelmina zu Braunschweig, "Elektrodenreaktionen und galvanische Zellen," 06.12.2012. [Online]. Available: http://www.pci.tu-bs.de/aggericke/PC1/Kap_VI/Elektrodenreak_Galvanische_Ketten.htm

[5] Wikipedia, "Galvanic cell," 20.02.2013. [Online]. Available: http://en.wikipedia.org/wiki/Galvanic_cell

[6] J. Layton, "How soil lamps work," 31.03.2012. [Online]. Available: http://science.howstuffworks.com/environmental/green-tech/sustainable/soil-lamp.htm

[7] C. G. Hönck, "Kupfer satt," 14.01.2013. [Online]. Available: http://www.greenpeace-magazin.de/index.php?id=5347

[8] "Die glocken und ihre anfänge," 10.06.2013. [Online]. Available: http://www.glocken-online.de/glockenkultur/anfaenge.php

[9] K. A. Hueber, "Simulation of bell tones with the help of pipe-bells and piano sounds," *Acustica*, vol. 26, pp. 334–343, 1972.

[10] T. D. Rossing, "Editors comments on paper 20 and 21," *Acoustics of Bells*, pp. 336–339, Van Nostrand Reinhold Company Inc., 1984.

[11] J. Pan and S. Bergmann, "An experimental study of acoustical properties of tubular tower bells," *Proc. 20th International Congress on Acoustics*, Sydney, 2010.

[12] E. Terhardt, "Strike note of bells," 2000. [Online]. Available: http://www.mmk.e-technik.tu-muenchen.de/persons/ter/top/strikenote.html

[13] W. Ritsch, "The house of sound - soundlives," 07.04.2013. [Online]. Available: http://iem.at/ritsch/art/netart/sndlives/

Artificial Affective Listening towards a Machine Learning Tool for Sound-Based Emotion Therapy and Control

Alexis Kirke
Interdisciplinary Centre for Computer Music Research,
Plymouth University, UK
alexis.kirke@plymouth.ac.uk

Eduardo Miranda
Interdisciplinary Centre for Computer Music Research,
Plymouth University, UK
Eduardo Miranda@plymouth.ac.uk

Slawomir J. Nasuto
University of Reading, Reading, UK
s.j.nasuto@reading.ac.uk

ABSTRACT

We are extending our work in EEG-based emotion detection for automated expressive performances of algorithmically composed music for affective communication and induction. This new system will involve music composed and expressively performed in real-time to induce specific affective states, based on the detection of affective state in a human listener. Machine learning algorithms will learn: (1) how to use EEG and other biosensors to detect the user's current emotional state; and (2) how to use algorithmic performance and composition to induce certain affective trajectories. In other words the system will attempt to adapt so that it can – in real-time - turn a certain user from depressed to happy, or from stressed to relaxed, or (if they like horror movies!) from relaxed to fearful. As part of this we have developed a test-bed involving an artificial listening affective agent to examine key issues and test potential solutions. As well as giving a project overview, prototype design and first experiments with this artificial agent are presented here.

1. INTRODUCTION

The aim of our research is to develop technology for implementing innovative intelligent systems that can monitor a person's affective state and induce a further specific affective states through music, automatically and adaptively. [1] investigates the use of EEG to detect emotion in an individual and to then generate emotional music based on this. These ideas have been extended into a 4.5 year EPSRC research project [2] in which machine learning is used to learn, by EEG emotional feedback, what types of music evoke what emotions in the listener. This paper introduces the key background elements behind the project: Music and Emotion, Emotional Expressive Performance and Algorithmic Composition, and EEG Affective Analysis; then details some preparatory work being undertaken, together with the future project plans.

2. MUSIC AND EMOTION

Music is commonly known to evoke various affective states (popularly referred to as "emotions") [3]. There have been a number of questionnaire studies supporting the notion that music communicates affective states (e.g., [4, 5]) and that music can be used for affect regulation and induction (e.g., [6, 7]). However the exact nature of these phenomena is not fully understood. The literature makes a distinction between perceived and induced affectivity with music being able to generate both types [4]. The differences between induced affective state and perceived affective state have been discussed by Juslin and Sloboda [3]. For example a listener may enjoy a piece of music like Barber's Adagio, which most people would describe as a "sad" piece of music. However, if they gain pleasure from listening, the induced affective state must be positive, but the perceived affective state is sadness; i.e., a negative state. Despite the differences between perceived and induced affective state, they are highly correlated [4, 8]. Zentner et al. [9] reported on research into quantifying the relationship between perceived and induced affective state in music genres.

3. EMOTION-BASED ALGORITHMIC COMPOSITION

One area of algorithmic composition which has received more attention recently is affectively-based computer-aided composition. A common theme running through some of the affective-based systems is the representation of the valence and arousal of a participant's affective state [11]. Valence refers to the positivity or negativity of an affective state; e.g., a high valence affective state is joy or contentment, a low valence one is sadness or anger. Arousal refers to the energy level of the affective state; e.g., joy is a higher arousal affective state than happiness. Until recently the arousal-valence space was a dominant quantitative two-dimensional representation of emotions in research into musical affectivity. More recently, a new theory of emotion with the corresponding scale, referred to as GEMS (Geneva Emotional Musical Scale) has been proposed [9].

Many of the affective-based systems are actually based around re-composition rather than composition; i.e. they focus on how to transform an already composed piece of music to give a different emotional effect – e.g. make it sadder, happier, etc. This is the case with the best known and most thoroughly tested system - the Computational Music Emotion Rule System (CMERS) [11]. The rules for expressing emotions map valence and arousal onto such elements as modes and pitch class. These rules were developed based on the combining a large number of studies by psychologists into music and emotion. However it was found these needed to be supplemented by rules for expressive performance of the transformed music to express the emotion successfully. Hence CMERS is actually an integrated composition and expressive performance. CMERS key limitation as a composition system is that it is designed for re-composition, not for generating new material.

Oliveira and Cardoso [13] also perform affective transformations on MIDI music, and utilize the valence-arousal approach to affective specification. These are to be mapped on to musical features: tempo, pitch register, musical scales, and instrumentation. A knowledge-base of musical features and emotion was developed based on musical segments with a known affective content. This knowledge-base was then used to train a generalized mapping of affective state to required music and a model was then generated based on Support Vector Machine regression. The model was tested for transforming the emotion of classical music – the current results are not as good as CMERS.

Although Legaspi et al. [14] utilize pre-composed music as its heart, it is more fo-cused on composing new music. An affective model is learned based on score fragments manually labeled with their appropriate affective perception – this maps a desired affective state on to a set of musical features. The model is learned based on the machine learning approaches Inductive Logic Programming and Diverse Density Weighting Metric. This is then used as a fitness function for a Genetic Algorithm – however the GA is also constrained by some basic music theory. The GA is then used to generate the basic harmonic structure, and a set of heuristics are used to generate melodies based on the harmonic structure. The system was trained with emotion label dimensions "favourable-unfavourable", "bright-dark", "happy-sad", and "heartrending-not heartrending". Listening tests were done on a series of eight bar tunes and the results obtained were considered promising, but indicated more development was needed.

4. EEG AND EMOTION

EEG measurements have been found to be useful in a clinical setting for diagnosing brain damage, sleep conditions and epilepsy; e.g. [17]. It is well known in the literature that it is possible to relate different EEG spectral bandwidths (often referred to as "EEG rhythms") to certain characteristics of mental states, such as wakefulness, drowsiness, etc. As early as the 1970s researchers have reported on the relationship between EEG asymmetry and affective state. Reviews of EEG asymmetry and affective state can be found in [18, 19] and one of the most recent sets of results can be found in [20]. Davidson [21] proposed a link between asymmetry of frontal alpha activation and the valence and arousal of a participant's affective state.

Musha and co-workers [22] developed one of the earliest computer EEG affective state detection systems and a number of detection methods have been investigated since then; e.g., [23]. More recently detection and analysis of weak synchronization patterns in EEG have been shown to be indicators of cognitive processing; growing evidence suggests that synchronization may be a carrier of information about the information processing in the brain [24]. There are different ways in which signals may co-vary. For instance, there is the hypothesis that information about many cognitive phenomena is preserved not necessarily in the intensity of the activation, but rather in the relationship between different sources of activity. There are an in-creasing number of studies investigating the role of synchronization in cognitive processing using various techniques, e.g. [25]. A particularly promising form of synchronization is called Phase–locking, which has been studied extensively by the third author and co-workers, e.g. [26]. Moreover, there is growing evidence supporting the role of synchronization in music perception [27] and also in response to affectively charged non-musical stimuli [28].

5. EMOTIONAL FEEDBACK EEG MUSIC

The above sections show that there is increasing evidence in the literature that musical traits such as rhythm, melody, tonality and expressive performance, can communicate specific affective states. There is also increasing evidence (e.g. [12]) that these states are detectable in the EEG of the listener. There are fewer studies into establishing which musical traits are useful for implementing a system to induce affective states. Amongst the techniques available, the analysis of synchronisation patterns in the EEG signal is a promising option for detecting affective states induced by music. Other techniques (as discussed in the literature) will also be considered in the project and the most suitable will be adopted. Thus the detection of affective state by EEG is a research area which this project will contribute to as well. Although initially a valence-arousal model will be used in development, other models will be utilized if found to be more effective. The valence-arousal model will be calibrated using tests involving marked-up emotional picture databases.

As was mentioned earlier, [1] investigates the use of EEG to detect emotion in an individual and to then generate emotion-inducing music based on this. The work done previously in [1] was not real-time and did not involve any machine learning process. The research and implementation of a real-time version of a more advanced detection method would allow us to monitor affective states induced by music on the fly. We hypothesise that once we establish specific musical traits associated with specific affective states, then we will be able to parameterise such traits in order to exert control in a musical composition; e.g., speed up the tempo to induce affective state X, use a "harsher" timbre to induce state Y, etc. The parameterisation of musical traits will allow for the design of algorithms capable of generating music (e.g., rule-based) embodying musical traits aimed at inducing specific EEG-observed trajectories correlated to affective states. Such a generative system can be rendered intelligent and adaptive by means of machine learning techniques (e.g., case-based reasoning and reinforcement learning) that are able to learn to recognize complex patterns and make decisions based on detected patterns in real-time.

6. AFFECTIVE LISTENING PROTOTYPE

For full real-time tests to be run, a controlled laboratory environment will need to be available together with EEG lab assistants and various types of equipment. Given the project is geographically spread it was decided to investigate the development of a simulated testing environment. In addition to providing a potential way of testing elements of the system without a human lab set-up, these investigations would help to highlight issues which may come up in the listening tests, and allow these to be included earlier in design discussions.

One potentially useful element of a simulated testing environment would be a virtual "emotional listener". Such a listener would take as input music, and respond to the music with artificial emotions. This would not be useful for simulating EEG results. However once the artificial listener became sufficiently developed through iterative design to give advanced and adaptive responses, it could be placed in the machine learning and algorithmic composition / performance loop as a way of prototyping strategies without having to find a human test subject and use an EEG lab for all phases of development.

Figure 1 shows the schematic for the prototype machine listening test-bed, labeled the Affective Reactive Trajectories Harnessing Unit Response (ARTHUR). The main purpose of ARTHUR is to receive as input a MIDI tune and output an affective response to the tune. The units in ARTHUR are now described.

6.1 Music Feature Affective Response

The Affective Linear Estimator (ALE) [29] is the heart of the ARTHUR system which takes as input a monophonic tune, and responds with an estimate of the tunes' valence and arousal. A linear equation is used to model agent B's the affective estimate of a Tune A – this is shown in equations (1) and (2):

$$valenceEst = x_p mean(pitchA) + x_l mean(loudA) + x_k mean(keyModeA) + x_{IOI} mean(IOIA) + x_0 \quad (1)$$

$$arousalEst = y_p mean(pitchA) + y_l mean(loudA) + y_{IOI} mean(IOIA) + y_0 \quad (2)$$

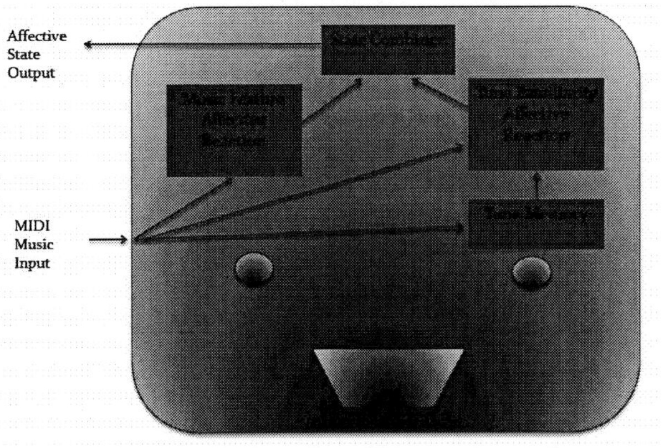

Figure 1. ARTHUR Schematic

6.2 Music Feature Affective Response

The Affective Linear Estimator (ALE) [29] is the heart of the ARTHUR system which takes as input a monophonic tune, and responds with an estimate of the tunes' valence and arousal. A linear equation is used to model agent B's the affective estimate of a Tune A – this is shown in equations (1) and (2):

$$valenceEst = x_p mean(pitchA) + x_l mean(loudA) + x_k mean(keyModeA) + x_{IOI} mean(IOIA) + x_0 \quad (1)$$

$$arousalEst = y_p mean(pitchA) + y_l mean(loudA) + y_{IOI} mean(IOIA) + y_0 \quad (2)$$

The parameters of ALE were estimated in a one-off process as follows. A set of 1920 random MIDI files was generated, of random lengths between 1 and 128 notes. Each MIDI file was transformed for 10 known and equally spaced valence and arousal values between -1 and 1 using transformation equations developed from a well-tested system for generating emotion-communicating music features [11] (there is not space here to detail these transformations).

	x	y
Pitch	-0.00214	0.003025
Loudness	0.012954	0.052129
keyMode	1.1874	-1.4301
IOI	-0.6201	0.59736
Constant	0.61425	-4.5185

Table 1. Regression Results

Then a linear regression was run on the resulting transformed MIDI files against the known arousal and valence values. The resulting coefficients are shown in Table 1. The average percentage errors – when tested on a separate 1920 transformed random files - were 10% for valence and 9% for arousal. These are considered to be sufficiently accurate. Actual human musical emotion recognition error rates can be as high as 23% [30]; and other far more complex artificial musical emotion detection systems have rates such as 81% [31].

ARTHUR does not wait until it has heard the whole tune to respond emotionally. It has an input buffer of fixed size. Once the buffer is filled it processes the music segment, then the buffer is cleared and the next segment of the music is shifted into the buffer.

6.3 Tune Familiarity Affective Reaction

ARTHUR stores all past buffer content in its memory. When hearing a new tune T*, having heard a series of tunes T_i in the past, ARTHUR adjusts its valence reaction based on both the tune affective features using equations (1) and (2), and the tune familiarity. The "mere exposure effect" is the effect that suggests that tune familiarity increases a listener's liking ratings on a tune [32]. Krugman [33] observed that valence increases with familiarity. Others have proposed a balance is needed between predictability and novelty [34]. ARTHUR's familiarity calculation is now explained.

First the similarity is compared between new tune segment T* and all past tunes T_i. The similarity is only calculated up to the length of the shortest tune. So if T* is 10 seconds long and T_i is 20 seconds long, only the first 10 seconds are compared. The system also does a simple form of pattern recognition. Rather than simply comparing each pitch and onset step by step, it moves through T* and then finds the notes that are closest in time to the notes in Ti. Then it looks at the pitch direction from a note to its next note in T*, does the same for the closest note in Ti, and compares the two. For onset times the system finds the closest note in Ti in time to each note in T* and for each of these notes compares the onsets. For similarity purposes, more weighting is given to pitch than to timing. Equations (3) to (6) detail the similarity calculations.

$$pitchDistance = distance(closest\ pitch\ directions) \quad (3)$$

$$onsetDistance = distance(closest\ onsets) \quad (4)$$

$$distance = 0.75*pitchDistance + 0.25*onsetDistance \quad (5)$$

$$similarity = 1-distance \quad (6)$$

The mean similarity of the new tune T* to all other tunes is calculated, denoted *sim*. Then this is compared to the mean similarity of all previous tunes to each other and a delta is calculated, as in equation (7). This delta is added to ARTHUR's estimate of the valence communicated by the tune on the basis of its musical features, to give the valence update.

$$deltaFamiliarity = W * (sim-meanSim) \quad (7)$$

$$valenceDelta = valenceFeatures + deltaFamiliarity \quad (8)$$

W in equation (8) is the variable which instantiates the balance between novelty and familiarity. It is calculated as in conditional equation (9).

$$W = \begin{cases} sim - (meanSim + 0.1 * stdSim) & [sim < meanSim + 0.1 * stdSim] \\ -sim + meanSim + stdSim & [sim > meanSim + stdSim] \\ 1 & [Otherwise] \end{cases} \quad (9)$$

To show how the tune familiarity and feature affective reaction elements combine, a couple of examples are now given.

6.4 Tune Familiarity Example

In these examples ARTHUR starts with 8 tunes in its memory, of length 12 notes, generated so that they have a variety of affective features. ARTHUR is then played a tune with a specific set of affective features repeatedly (32 times). Figure 2 shows a tune whose features are predominantly of higher valence. The pitches are fairly high and suggest a major key profile.

ARTHUR's valence reaction to being played this tune 32 times is shown in Figure 3. To understand the response it is helpful to first look at Figure 4. In Figure 4 ARTHUR's internal valence response purely to the musical features is shown.

It can be seen in Figure 4 that ARTHUR responds uniformly positively to being played the tune, and in fact ARTHUR "feels" more and more positive the more times it hears the tune. However in Figure 3, where tune familiarity is included, it can be see that there is an initial period of very positive response from ARTHUR to the tune. In fact the gradient increases the first 4 or 5 hearings. However after this the gradient drops off very fast until there is no positive response. It fact it can be seen that ARTHUR reacts *negatively* on the 32nd play. So initially ARTHUR's rate of valence increase goes up, because it is being affected not only the positive music features, but because the tune is becoming more familiar. But eventually the tune becomes too familiar and ARTHUR becomes "sick" of it leading the reducing valence in spite of positive valence tune features.

A second example is shown in Figure 5. This tune is a lower pitch tune than in Figure 2. Also it has a pitch profile which indicates a minor key (C minor), so is a lower valence tune than that in Figure 2. When played repeatedly to ARTHUR the resulting valence response is that shown in Figure 6. It can be seen that valence initially decreases then increases and then drops off rapidly. The reason for this is clarified again by showing ARTHUR's internal response valence-wise to just the tune features, graphed in Figure 6.

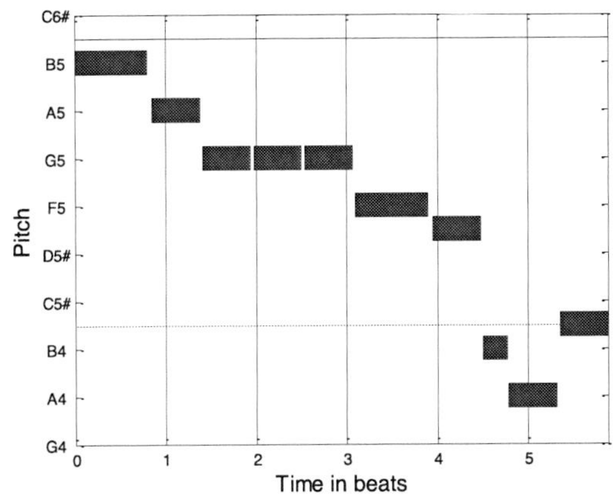

Figure 2. Higher Valence Tune 1 played to ARTHUR

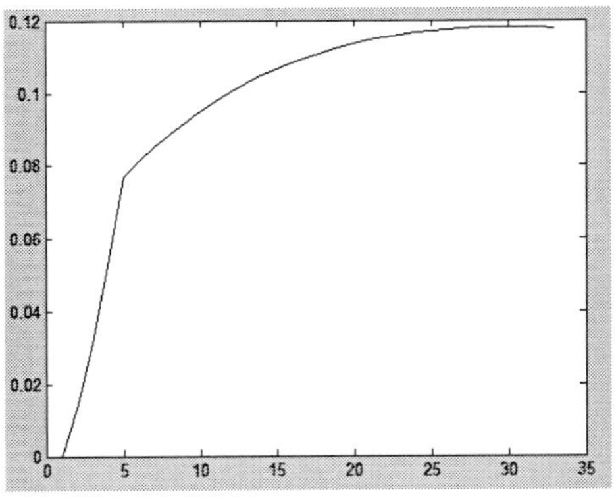

Figure 3. ARTHUR's Valence Response to repeatedly hearing Higher Valence Tune 1, with Familiarity response and Tune Memory

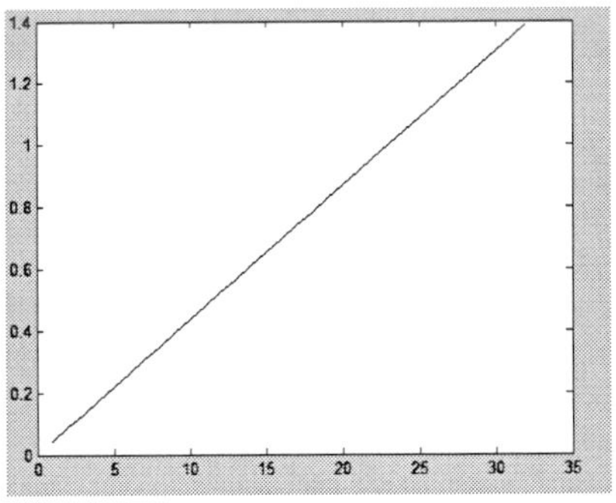

Figure 4. ARTHUR's Valence Response to repeatedly hearing Higher Valence Tune 1 without Tune Memory

It can be seen in Figure 7 that, as expected, ARTHUR's detection of the valence of the tune features will attempt to lower its valence repeatedly. So it is now possible to clarify that the initial decrease in valence in Figure 6 is partly due to ARTHUR being unfamiliar with the tune. Then there is a short period of valence increase where ARTHUR's increasing familiarity outweighs the low valence features of the tune. Then it can be seen that on repeated plays eventually the rate of valence decrease actually starts to increase, as ARTHUR gets "sick" of the tune.

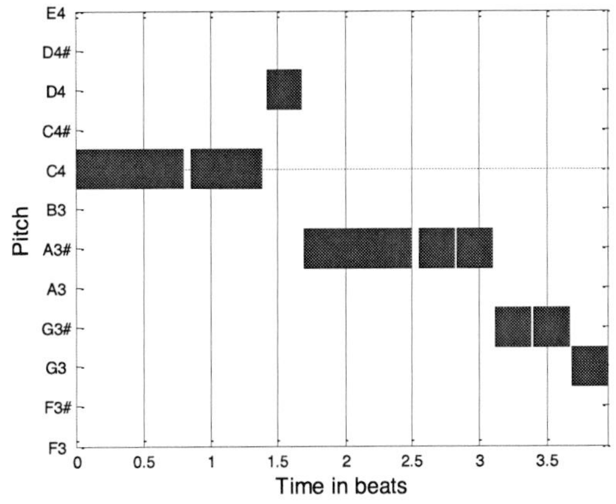

Figure 5. Lower Valence Tune 2 played to ARTHUR

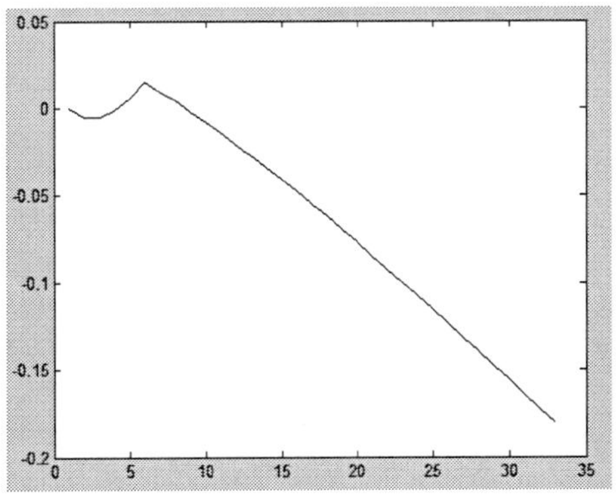

Figure 6. ARTHUR's Valence Response to repeatedly hearing Lower Valence Tune 2, with Familiarity response and Tune Memory

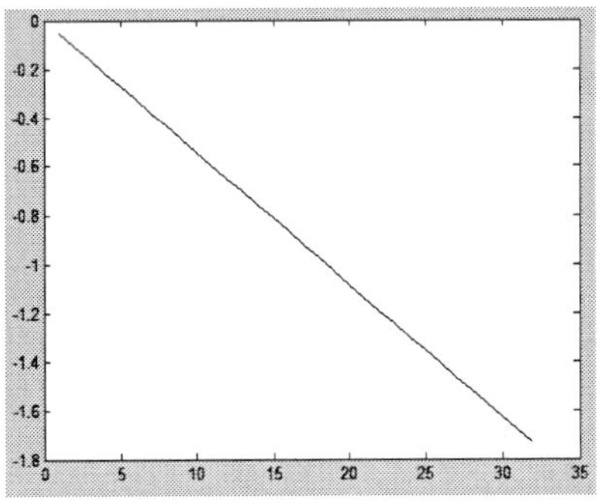

Figure 7. ARTHUR's Valence Response to repeatedly hearing Lower Valence Tune 2 without Tune Memory

This ability of ARTHUR to respond not only to the valence and arousal communicated by the tune as well as to the familiarity will hopefully make the system more useful as an offline test-bed for the brain-computer music interface system. Two key elements to highlight in ARTHUR's response are that it is highly dependent on the accuracy of simplified affective feature equations (1) and (2), and that it responds linearly. Furthermore it is based on communicated emotion research, rather than induced emotion research. However even in its simplified form ARTHUR has already highlighted some of the issues which will come up in testing, and directed the project team towards previous research on tune novelty. It also provides a starting point for developing a test bed with more advanced affective reactions.

7. CONCLUSIONS AND FUTURE WORK

A new method for utilizing the emotion-inducing nature of music and sound has been introduced. The background elements have been detailed, including affective representation, computer expressive performance, affective algorithmic composition and EEG-based machine learning. One of the initial steps in this research has been the develop of a prototype offline test bed based on a computer-listening music system (ARTHUR). This system is designed to allow for quicker and lower cost experiments to be done to test out machine learning and algorithm composition frameworks. Just as importantly it also helps to highlight and address key issues such as tune novelty response, early on in the research process.

Future work in the broader project includes characterising synchrony patterns corresponding to different induced affective states from the EEG recordings while participants listen to music stimuli. Initially, the analysis and the system for learning the emotional control music generation will be developed based on the valence arousal emotional scale, due to its widespread acceptance and availability of tagged databases. We will subsequently develop a GEMS representation for the images and will evaluate the usefulness of the two scales for developing our system.

Then, we shall progressively move towards the final goal of real-time assessment of affective states using reinforcement learning (RL). Initially, the affective state estimation will be updated at a slower time scale consistent with the computational demands of the synchronisation analysis. However, our aim is to create a system for a fast real-time assessment of affective state based on efficient analysis using feature selection and dimensionality reduction.

We plan to develop further algorithms for generating music featuring the various musical traits that have been discussed in the literature. Some musical features are more universal determinants of affective response, invariant across populations with common cultural background [9]. Other features may show more variation dependent on contextual effects of culture, personality and environment. Our initial results will be driven by more universal musical determinants of emotional response than context-specific. Thus, they will be based on results averaged across a test population. The later stages of the project will extend the former to include context-specific emotional responses.

We plan to test our initial generative music algorithms for inductive effects using an offline EEG affective state detector. The results of these tests will be used to initialize a case-based reasoning (CBR) system for affective induction by music. Then, we will extend the CBR system by investigating specific musical genres. A recent study [9] also suggested the importance of genre selection for the induction of certain affective states. The benchmark will be a classical solo piano genre, as classical music has well known computational approaches for eliciting certain affective states, but expansions on this will be investigated utilizing ideas from pop and electroacoustic music genres.

In order to have a real-time, dynamic assessment of the affective state – so as to increase accuracy and effectiveness - we will use the CBR system to initialise an automatic music generation system based on reinforcement learning (RL). RL has been successfully used in optimising the stimulation patterns in deep brain stimulation therapy of the epileptic seizures [35]. The RL system we plan to build will be used in action selection optimizing a desired affective response of this participant. The move towards more on-going assessment of affective state will be important because it will enable us to extend the system beyond the music composition based on manipulation of the musical traits eliciting generic affective responses, to a more adaptive individual-oriented system taking into account participants' states; thus utilising also the contextual effects of an individual and the environment.

Acknowledgments

This research was supported by EPSRC grant EP/J003077/1 "Brain-Computer Interface for Monitoring and Inducing Affective States".

8. REFERENCES

[1] A. Kirke, and E. Miranda, "Combining EEG Frontal Asymmetry Studies with Affective Algorithmic Composition and Expressive Performance Models", in *Proceedings of International Computer Music Conference*, Huddersfield, UK, 2011.

[2] S.J. Nasuto and E. Miranda, "Brain-Computer Interface for Monitoring and Inducing Affective States", *EPSRC Grant EP/J002135/1*, 2012

[3] P. Juslin and J. Sloboda, *Music and Emotion: Theory and Research.* Oxford University Press, 2001

[4] P. Juslin and P. Laukka, "Expression, perception, and induction of musical emotion: a review and a questionnaire study of everyday listening." *Journal of New Music Research*, vol. 33, pp. 216-237, 2004

[5] C. Minassian, C. Gayford and J. Sloboda, "Optimal experience in musical performance: a survey of young musicians", *Annual General Meeting of the Society for Education, Music and Psychology Research*, 2003

[6] A. Goethem, "The Functions of Music for Affect Regulation", *Proc. Int. Conf. on Music and Emotion*, Durham, UK, 2009

[7] P. Juslin, "Five Facets of Musical Expression: A Psychologist's Perspective on Music Performance", *Psychology of Music* vol. 31, pp. 273-302, 2003.

[8] E. Bigand, S. Vieillard, F. Madurell, J. Marozeau and A. Dacquet, "Multidimensional scaling of emotional responses to music: The effect of musical expertise and of the duration of the excerpts", *Cognition and Emotion*, vol. 19, pp. 1113-1139, 2005.

[9] M. Zentner, D. Gradnjean and K.R. Scherer, "Emotions evoked by the sound of music: characterization, classification, and measurement", *Emotion* vol. 8, no. 4, pp. 494-521, 2008.

[10] K.R. Scherer, "Which Emotions Can be Induced by Music? What are the Underlying Mechanisms? And How Can we Measure Them?" *Journal of New Music Research*, vol. 33, no. 3, pp. 239-251, 2004.

[11] S. Livingstone, R. Muhlberger, A. Brown and W.F. Thompson, "Changing Musical Emotion: A Computational Rule System for Modifying Score and Performance", *Computer Music Journal*, vol. 34, pp. 41-64, 2010.

[12] L. Schmidt and L. Trainor, "Frontal brain electrical activity (EEG) distinguishes valence and intensity of musical emotions", *Cognition and Emotion*, vol. 15, pp. 487-500, 2001.

[13] A.P. Oliveira and A. Cardoso, "Automatic Manipulation of Music to Express Desired Emotions", in *Proc. of Sound and Music Computing Conf.*, Porto, Brazil, 2009.

[14] R. Legaspi, Y. Hashimoto, K. Moriyama, S. Kurihara and M. Numao, "Music Compositional Intelligence with an Affective Flavor", In *Proc. of the Int. Conf. on Intelligent User Interfaces*, Honolulu, Hawaii, USA, 2007.

[15] A. Kirke and E.R. Miranda, *Guide to Computing for Expressive Music Performance*, Springer, UK, 2013.

[16] R. Bresin and A. Friberg, "Emotional Coloring of Computer-Controlled Music Performances", *Computer Music Journal*, vol. 24, pp. 44-63, 2000.

[17] M. Sheerani, A. Hassan, A. Jan and R. Zaka, "Role of Video-EEG Monitoring in the Management of Intractable Seizures and Non-epileptic Spells", *Pakistan Journal of Neurological Sciences*, vol. 2, no. 4, pp. 207-209, 2007.

[18] E.K. Silberman and H. Weingarter, "Hemispheric lateralization of functions related to emotion.", *Brain and Cognition*, vol. 5, pp. 322-353, 1986.

[19] J.J.B. Allen and J.P. Kline "Frontal EEG asymmetry, emotion, and psychopathology: the first, and the next 25 years", *Biological Psychology*, vol. 67, no. 1, pp. 1-5, 2004.

[20] M. Wyczesany, J. Kaiser and A. Coenen, "Subjective mood estimation co-varies with spectral power EEG characteristics", *Acta Neurobiologiae Experimentalis*, vol. 68, no. 2, pp. 180-192, 2008.

[21] R.J. Davidson, "The neuropsychology of emotion and affective style." In M. Lewis and J. M. Haviland (eds.) *Handbook of Emotion*. Guilford Press, 1993.

[22] T. Musha, Y. Terasaki, H. Haque and G Ivanitsky, "Feature extraction from EEGs associated with emotions", *Art. Life Robotics*, vol. 1, pp. 15-19, 1997.

[23] D.O. Bos, "EEG-based Emotion Recognition: The Influence of Visual and Auditory Stimuli", *Emotion*, vol. 56, no. 7, pp.1798-1806, 2006.

[24] P. Fries "A mechanism for cognitive dynamics: neuronal communication through neuronal coherence", *Trends in Cognitive Science*, vol. 9, pp. 474–480, 2005.

[25] P. Sauseng, W. Klimesch, M. Doppelmayr, T. Percherstorfer and S. Hanslmayr, "EEG alpha synchronization and functional coupling during top-down processing in a working memory task", *Hum. Brain Map*, vol. 26, pp. 148–155, 2005.

[26] C.M. Sweeney-Reed and S.J. Nasuto, "A novel approach to the detection of synchronization in EEG based on empirical mode decomposition", *Journal of Computational Neuroscience*, vol. 23, no. 1, pp. 79-111, 2007.

[27] J. Bhattacharya, H. Petsche and E. Pereda, "Long-range synchrony in the gamma band: role in music perception", *Journal of Neuroscience*, vol. 21, pp. 6329–37, 2001.

[28] M. Hu, J. Li, G. Li, X. Tang and W. Freeman, "Normal and Hypoxia EEG Recognition Based on a Chaotic Olfactory Model", *Lecture Notes in Computer Science*, LNCS 3973, Springer, 2006.

[29] A. Kirke, "Application of Intermediate Multi-Agent Systems to Integrated Algorithmic Composition and Expressive Performance of Music", Ph.D. Thesis, Plymouth University, Plymouth, UK, 2011.

[30] A. Camurri, R. Dillon, and A. Saron, "An Experiment on Analysis and Synthesis of Musical Expressivity", In *Proc. 13th Colloquium on Musical Informatics*, L'Aquila, Italy, 2000.

[31] R. Legaspi, Y. Hashimoto, K. Moriyama, S. Kurihara and M. Numao, "Music Compositional Intelligence with an Affective Flavor." In *Proc. of the Int. Conf. on Intelligent User Interfaces*, Honolulu, Hawaii, USA, 2007.

[32] C. S. Pereira, J. Teixeira, P. Figueiredo, J. Xavier, S.L. Castro et al, "Music and Emotions in the Brain: Familiarity Matters." *PLoS ONE*, vol. 6, no. 11, e27241. doi:10.1371/journal.pone.0027241, 2011.

[33] H.E. Krugman, "Affective response to music as a function of familiarity", *Journal of Abnormal and Social Psychology*, vol. 38, pp. 388-392, 1943.

[34] E.G. Schellenberg, K.A. Corrigall, O. Ladinig and D. Huron, "Changing the Tune: Listeners Like Music that Expresses a Contrasting Emotion", *Front Psychol.*, vol. 3, p. 574, Epub 24 Dec 2012.

[35] A. Guez, R. Vincent, M. Avoli and J. Pineau, "Adaptive Treatment of Epilepsy via Batch-mode Reinforcement Learning", *Innovative Applications of Artificial Intelligence*, pp. 1671-1678, 2008.

Music performance

MODELLING EMOTIONAL EFFECTS OF MUSIC: KEY AREAS OF IMPROVEMENT

Tuomas Eerola
University of Jyväskylä, Finland
tuomas.eerola@jyu.fi

ABSTRACT

Modelling emotions perceived in music and induced by music has garnered increased attention during the last five years. The present paper attempts to put together observations of the areas that need attention in order to make progress in the modelling emotional effects of music. These broad areas are divided into theory, data and context, which are reviewed separately. Each area is given an overview in terms of the present state of the art and promising further avenues, and the main limitations are presented. In theory, there are discrepancies in the terminology and justifications for particular emotion models and focus. In data, reliable estimation of high-level musical concepts and data collection and evaluation routines require systematic attention. In context, which is the least developed area of modelling, the primary area of improvement is incorporating musical context (music genres) into the modelling emotions. In a broad sense, better acknowledgement of music consumption and everyday life context, such as the data provided by social media, may offer novel insights into the modelling emotional effects of music.

1. INTRODUCTION

Emotions expressed or induced by music is one of the central aspects in music listening and is one of the main reasons why music appeals to people. The processes involved in emotional communication through music are complicated as they are related to different emotion induction mechanisms, emotion models, expectations, learning, individual differences, and music preferences. The purpose of this paper is to outline the central challenges Music Computing has to face to make advances in emotion modelling in music and outline the necessary steps to ensure forward movement in this field. These challenges can be broadly divided into *theory*, *data* and *context* – the traditional elements of any science – and covered in separate sections of the paper.

In the first section titled *Theory*, issues of theoretical development are discussed. Theory is not perhaps the strongest area of sound and music computing but should not be undervalued since all progress made in the topic requires advances in conceptual and theoretical issues. Issues with emotion models and their prevalence and underlying mechanisms are drawn from recent overviews of the field [1,2].

In the second section titled *Data*, I refer broadly to representation, collection, processing and interpretation of data. Each of these sub-topics has its own special issues and techniques, many of which have been the focus of studies during the last decade in *Music Information Retrieval* (MIR) and music psychology. The necessity of combining the knowledge and techniques from these separate fields is the central challenge music computing itself has acknowledged (see e.g. roadmap [1]) and the same holds for the field of music and emotion as well.

In the final third section, the *context* of the models and data will be examined. Here, context refers both to the context in which theories and data are supposed to hold and to the contextual constraints provided by the situation, music genre, and individual factors.

2. THEORY

Theoretical issues in music and emotions can be arranged in emotion models, focus, and mechanisms. For modelling, adhering to a particular theoretical framework naturally has vital importance, although the current state of art suggests that the field of music and emotions is not consistent in its use of emotion models, focus, and mechanisms [1,2]. There are terminological differences even within the field of affect sciences (e.g. mood/emotion/feeling) and within the vocabulary sound and music computing studies have adopted from other disciplines (e.g. human-computer interaction, marketing, engineering), whereas certain terms (e.g. mood and emotion) are used interchangeably in some contexts within MIR; these distinctions are important and meaningful when the are communicated across the disciplines. For this reason, I would advocate the conceptual and terminological clarifications drawn by Juslin and Sloboda in the *Handbook of Music and Emotions* [3].

2.1 Emotion models

An important theoretical issue is the notion of how emotions are construed. A plethora of theoretical proposals exist in the psychology of how emotions are divided into *discrete*, *low*- and *high-dimensional* models, and *other* notions for emotions (see Figure 1). According to the discrete emotion model, commonly used in non-musical contexts, all emotions can be derived from a few universal and innate basic emotions such as *fear*, *anger*, *disgust*, *sadness*,

[1] http://mires.eecs.qmul.ac.uk/wiki/index.php/Roadmap

and *happiness* [4]. In music-related studies many of these have been found to be appropriate [5], yet certain emotions have often been replaced by more appropriate ones. For instance, *disgust* is often replaced by *tenderness* or *peacefulness*. Discrete emotion model is commonly utilized in music and emotion studies because it is easy to evaluate in recognition studies, especially with special populations (children, clinical patients, and samples from different cultures) [1].

Low-dimensional models consist of 2 and 3-dimensional models, which propose that all affective states arise from separate independent, affect dimensions. The most common one of these, the two-dimensional circumplex model [6], has one dimension related to *valence* and the other to *arousal*. This particular model has received a great deal of attention in music and emotion studies, despite a number of drawbacks. For instance, it is unable to represent mixed emotions [7], and so several alternative, presumably better, dimensional models have been proposed in which affect the dimensions are chosen differently (e.g., *tension, energy*) [8] or by increasing the number of necessary dimensions to three [9, 10]. Recent studies in psychology have generally found formulations other than the valence-arousal dimensions to provide better fit to data [11].

In music, two recent studies of perceived and felt emotions [12, 13] found that the two-dimensional model was found to be a more parsimonious way to represent self-reported ratings of perceived and induced emotions conveyed by film soundtracks. Also, these same studies established that the discrete emotions ratings can be predicted from the ratings of emotion dimensions and vice versa, if the scales and the excerpts are organised in a manner that allows such comparisons.

High-dimensional models of emotions have recently been proposed by Zentner and his colleagues, called *Geneva Emotion Musical Scale* (GEMS) [14], which has from three to nine dimensions of experienced emotions. It has interesting spectrum of terms that emphasize the contemplative, positive and aesthetic nature of music-induced emotions (e.g., *wonder, trancendence*, and *nostalgia*). It is worth noting that the GEMS model construction is music-specific and the model construction was carried out with a wide range of participants, and has led to fascinating results on neurophysiological correlates [15]. A direct comparison of low and high-dimensional emotion models in music have, however, suggested that low-dimensional models often suffice to account for the main emotional experiences induced by music [13].

Other theoretical approaches to music and emotion studies include a collection of concepts such as preference, liking, intensity, and also such mood and emotion terms that have been the object of studies recently which have not been connected to theoretical framework. For instance, other types of discrete categories (*passionate, rollicking, humorous, aggressive*) are utilized in *MIREX Audio Mood Classification* task [16]. However, these concepts are not persistently theoretically motivated and may include isolated terms that have little to offer to our understanding of the emotions expressed and induced by music.

There are novel ways to probe which emotion model accounts for the emotions induced and expressed by music. The data provided by social media and online services of music is one such promising source. In the domain of music, social tags describe a variety of information (genre, geography, emotion, opinion, instrumentation, etc.), out of which emotions account for approximately 5% of the most used tags [17]. A number of studies have applied semantic computing to uncover emotion dimensions emerging from the semantic relationships between the tags [18], and some support for the valence-arousal formulation has been found [19]. Such observations have been formalized as *Affective Circumplex Transformation* (ACT) that provides an effective way of predicting the emotional content of music [20].

In sum, a variety of emotion models have been utilized in the sound and music studies and the most common ones have been adopted from psychology, although consensus about their utility has not yet been formed. Also, the models adopted from psychology focus on survival or utilitarian emotions. Music as a pleasurable leisure time activity therefore might be better served with a model that is grounded on terms that are relevant in music-induced emotions such as the ones provided by the GEMS model. Moreover, the emotion models need to be used in the manner consistent with the assumptions build into them. It makes little sense to study valence and arousal using two groups of extreme points within these continuums since the dimensionality cannot be established within such design.

2.2 Emotion focus

Two forms of emotional processes in relation to music can be distinguished – perception and induction of emotions. The first concerns listeners' judgments of emotional characteristics of the music, where listeners characterise the music in emotional terms (e.g., this music is solemn) or what the music may be expressive of (e.g., this music expresses tenderness). Modelling perceived emotions has been the main aim of sound and music computing studies and the most prevalent focus in the field of music and emotions. The latter concerns how music makes listeners feel, also referred to as *felt emotions*. This distinction is not only conceptually plausible, there is also mounting evidence to suggest these two modes of emotional responses can be empirically differentiated [21]. For the field, the problem lies in the often implicit assumption of this division and the induced emotions need to be further validated by indirect measures or psychophysiology. In many instances, we cannot be sure of the distinction. For instance, do emotion related tags or forced-choice selection of facial expressions express felt or perceived emotions?

2.3 Emotion mechanisms

Because the same music can express one emotion and induce another (e.g. cheesy love ballad after a break-up, or a national anthem in a wrong situation), there must be different mechanisms that are responsible for the emotions. The most comprehensive account of the mechanisms to date is the proposal by Juslin and Västfjäll [2], which attempts to

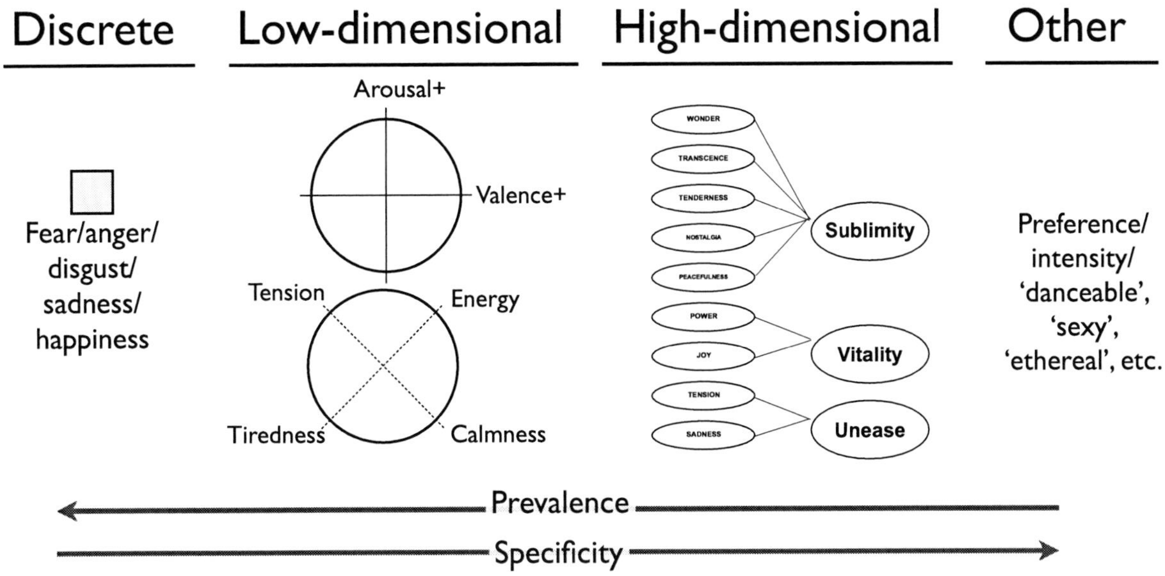

Figure 1. Prevalence and specificity of emotion models applicable to music.

account why music elicits an emotion and why this emotion is of a particular kind. This model, *BRECVEMA* [22], currently consists of eight mechanisms. Each mechanism has distinct response, information focus, possibly brain region, and way of elicitation. However, for sound and music computing, only some of these mechanisms are of central concern. Most past studies have studied *Contagion* mechanism, in which the listener mimics and thus perceives the emotional expression of another being through music, which is also presumed to account for the wide similarity of emotion recognition of music across cultures [23]. *Rhythmic entrainment* is of interest in such cases when the aspects of groove or dancibility have been included in the focus study [24]. Music computing can also attempt to solve the issue of *Musical expectancy*, in which early attempts have already been made [25]. Many other mechanisms are either too limited for application uses or need to be examined in individual settings.

2.4 Epistemological framework

It is also possible to challenge the above-mentioned theoretical issues which emphasise cognitive evaluation of emotions in lieu of other frameworks. Culturally-oriented frameworks would put the emotions in their historical and cultural context [26], and sociological accounts would emphasise how emotions are constructed within particular social groups according to commonly accepted norms constructed in daily lives. The intimate connection of emotions to the body makes embodied cognition a persuasive framework for research [27]. This would emphasise the ecological nature of sound communication and the role of corporeal responses and metaphors in this process. This, in turn, would have implications for what kind of issues will be pursued in emotion research; the process of meaning-generation, empathy, or the underlying neural architecture specialized for mimicry [28]. Finally, application-driven epistemology is something that may generate interesting research in itself, although I would not rank the priority of such research as high.

3. DATA

Sound and music computing is an inherently data-intensive field, and therefore the efforts in music and emotions are directed towards data in its many aspects, specifically (a) representations, (b) processing, (c) collection, and (d) evaluation.

3.1 Data representations

Data representation has specialised in its own areas related to music representations (mostly audio, occasionally midi) and ground-truth representations. In the former, the availability of large amount of good quality audio has widened the scope of studies to include almost any genre, and the number of examples used in studies is only limited by the amount of ground-truth data available for evaluation purposes. This limitation is significant, since availability of audio is meaningless unless it can be connected to listeners' emotions in one way or another. Traditional ground-truth sets contain limited amounts of audio examples carefully assessed by a number of participants in terms of their emotional qualities (self-reports of emotions). Another form of data comes from other measures (indirect, continuous, or physiological) and neural measurements of emotional processing taken during the music listening. These are even more difficult to obtain but have the benefits of being less affected by *demand characteristics*. Moreover, these data representations are more and more supplemented with textual, visual, movement, and social media data, all of which require different tools, algorithms and knowledge from specialized fields. However, combinations of the different data sources is still rare, although most researchers acknowledge the need for multimodal and multiple approaches in emotion research [29].

3.2 Data processing

Data processing borrows from the neighbouring (e.g., computer vision, neuroscience, speech) and technical disciplines (e.g. signal processing). This theme is however, the most advanced one of sound and music computing. However, the processing challenges lie in the realm of temporality of music-induced emotions and synchronisation of physiology and neural responses of the experienced emotions, which all require time-series techniques and behavioural validations. However, these challenges are not unique to music and emotions but pertinent to most neuroscience, physiology and multimedia (movies, particularly) research involved with emotions. Landmark example of how these challenges are solved come from a recent study of music-induced emotions, which correlated the haemodynamic response of the participants with the musical features [30]. Another challenge for data processing concerns the social media data, tags and online meta-data in general, how to obtain semantic structures from such freeform, unconstrained but large datasets [31].

3.3 Musical content estimation

The central limiting factor in predicting emotions from musical content is unreliable estimation of meaningful music-related concepts. Most of the low-level features (e.g. spectral centroid, zero-crossing, or attack slope) have been around for decades but mid to high-level concepts such as tension, mode, harmony and expectancy are demanding to model from audio representation. And this is not only a technical challenge, but rather a conceptual one; high-level concepts require some form of emulation of human perception (e.g. long frame of reference typically modelled with different memory structures, comparisons to typical data structures representing acquired knowledge of regularities in music and so on). Traditionally, there have been two different approaches to this dilemma. An engineering approach applies a combination of low-level features (e.g. MFCCs) and machine learning (e.g. Gaussian Mixture Models or Support Vector Machines) to solve the content problems [32, 33]. Another strategy is to model the perceptual processes faithfully [34], leading in some cases to less efficient models due to emulation of human hearing and all its perceptual constraints (e.g. masking, thresholding, streaming) [35]. Despite the strategy chosen, the need for new and reliable high-level features is strong [36] and reliable measures for syncopation, the degree of "majorness", and expectations are all top priority features that would increase the prediction rates for emotions [37,38].

Once the features can be estimated reliably, additional steps need to be taken to identify the key features that contribute to emotions. Typically, musical features from an existing music corpus are extracted and mapped into individually rated emotions. The mapping typically takes the form of regression analysis for emotions measurable in scalar terms [39, 40] and emotion categories by means of classification [38]. This approach is correlational because it associates certain features with certain emotions but what it fails to discover is the source of the differences. Another approach is to specifically manipulate musical structure to assess the true effect of these factors to emotions [41]. Unfortunately, the latter approach is time consuming and relatively rare, and typically focuses on few features at a time. Mercifully, combinations of correlational and causal approaches have yielded fairly consistent patterns of results on emotion features in music, summarised by Gabrielsson and Lindström [42].

Because the correlational approach is the most common and offers the largest sets of data, it is important to consider the feature selection before the construction of the model. Elsewhere, I have suggested four stages for this process [43]; (a) theoretically select plausible features, (b) validate the chosen features, (c) optimise the chosen features, and (d) evaluate the predictive capacity of the model. Theoretical selection is justified to eliminate dozens of technically possible features that may just increase noise. In the next step, the researcher should verify that the features are reliable and provide relevant information using a separate ground-truth dataset. In the third step, exploration of the independence of the features is useful in order to trim the feature set into separate, independent and preferably orthogonal entities using data reduction techniques. These steps decrease the danger of over-fitting and facilitate the interpretation of the subsequent models.

3.4 Data collection, evaluation and access

Finally, the data is as good as the collection and evaluation procedures allow it to be. In sound and music computing, rigorous data collection procedures are not always adhered to due to emphasis on algorithm development or data modelling, or in some cases, the researchers may not always have the expertise to follow the methodological requisites perfected in the behavioural sciences (e.g. psychology). Participant background descriptions (music preference and musical sophistication indices), and outlier screening, inter-rater reliability, and general replicability are often neglected in the data evaluation procedures in small-scale behavioural studies. Despite these traditional concerns, there are new innovative ways of getting participant data. Online games have been found to be a good way in obtaining mood ratings [44], crowd-sourcing platforms (e.g. *Amazon Mechanical Turk*), and large-scale online questionnaires that have certain practical limitations (sound setup, situation, listener background) but the large participant amount is assumed to compensate for these drawbacks. Another data collection issue is the annotation. Expert annotations are expensive and laborious, and crowd-sourced annotations may in some situations lead to equally coherent results [45]. Whether the data obtained from certain social online music services (e.g. *last.fm*, *Spotify* see *Million Song Dataset* [46]) can be harnessed to tackle the fundamental issues related to music and emotions, still remains to be seen but the results so far are promising in non-music related domains [47] and in music [20, 31].

Also, the modelled data needs to be assessed in a rigorous fashion. Whereas the studies adhering to psychology standards typically collect and evaluate the data properly, they often produce a final model that accounts for the handful of excerpts that are also the ones used to train the model in the study and no cross-validation and prediction with external datasets are used. Fortunately, sound and music studies normally pay attention to these issues and some researchers have taken the cross-validation steps particularly seriously [37, 38].

Finally, the effectiveness of the music and emotion research would be increased by establishing common repositories for open data-sharing (stimuli, features, evaluations, and protocols) and therefore facilitating replicability of the studies [48]. There are already shared tools (toolboxes such as *Marsyas*, *Sonic Visualiser*, and *MIR toobox* for musical feature extraction) and platforms for data sharing [49], and also possibilities of organising all this in an open and attributable manner (e.g. http://thedata.org/). In certain cases, this is routinely done [12,50] but the strength of sound and music computing is not fully capitalised before many different datasets are openly available.

4. CONTEXT

Theories and data only operate in the context in which they have been defined. In music psychology, the context of music and emotion studies have mainly been in Western art music and highly Western educated listeners in particularly restricted situations (concerts or laboratory setting), judging from the frequency of music genres, situations and participants utilised in the past ten years [1]. In sound and music computing, the context is more consumption oriented, that is, more studies utilising pop music and everyday listening situations and therefore closer to current music consumption habits [51]. However, context is much more; here broadly divided into socio-cultural, musical, individual and listening context.

4.1 Socio-cultural context

For modelling emotions in music, the cultural context is certainly the largest open issue that not only divides listeners in Western countries according to geographical areas and age groups, but to broad cultural differences across the globe. Few cross-cultural studies of emotion recognition have been conducted which explore the topic using music excerpts and listeners from multiple cultures [23, 52]. Fortunately, in sound and music computing, this issue has been acknowledged for some time now [53, 54] and datasets and applications of existing techniques to novel musical materials are at least applied to non-Western music collections [55]. This recent tendency has also highlighted the need for further development of musical feature extraction due to challenges offered by non-Western tuning systems and instruments. Within a culture, there are wide differences in musical practices, consumption habits, and meanings associated with music between different social and age groups. These socio-cultural differences have not received the attention they deserve, although they are known to have wide impact on music choices and emotions induced by music.

4.2 Musical context

As a smaller subset of the cultural context, the musical context – music genre, lyrics and videos – brings tangible differences for modelling emotions in music. Just consider genre differences; what is recognised as tender in piano music of *late romantic era*, probably does not have relevance in *gothic metal*, and happiness in *pop* may not be equivalent either as a concept or musical term in *electronica*. Recently, sobering results from the generalisibility of simple emotion predictions of valence and arousal across music genres was obtained [37]. According to the results, emotional valence did not transfer across genres although arousal did. In a small-scale study, the same musical features have been shown to operate differently if the underlying context is changed [56]. When the large materials provided by social media tags is harnessed for emotions in music, it has been found that genre information is able to bring significant improvements on model predictions [20]. For modelling emotions in music, the role of genre seems to be of utmost importance.

4.3 Individual context

With the context I also refer to individual differences such as personality, motivation and self-esteem, which all bring about significant differences between listeners. Such personality traits as neuroticism and extraversion are linked with negative and positive emotionality, leading to differences in music-induced emotions as well [57]. It is also known that specific personality traits, such as *openness to experience*, are linked with music-induced chills [58]. For modelling emotions in music, the individual differences have less important roles than say, music genre, but nevertheless, there is now a trend to incorporate the individuality of the user when creating personalised recommendation systems for music [59].

4.4 Listening context

A host of situational factors affect emotions induced by music. From everyday music listening studies [60] we know that differences in the listening contexts – whether at home, at a laboratory, on public transport, with friends, etc. – has a strong influence on what emotions are likely to be experienced. For instance, it is known that emotional episodes linked with music are most common at home and at evening, and occur during music listening, social interaction, or relaxation, working and watching movies or TV. These situational and social factors are challenging to incorporate into the emotion modelling. However, the contextual information provided by the situation is something that at least needs to be acknowledged in modelling emotions in music, even if it states that these results generally hold for people listening to music alone in laboratory conditions.

5. CONCLUSIONS

Significant advances in all areas of modelling emotional effects of music have been made during the last decade.

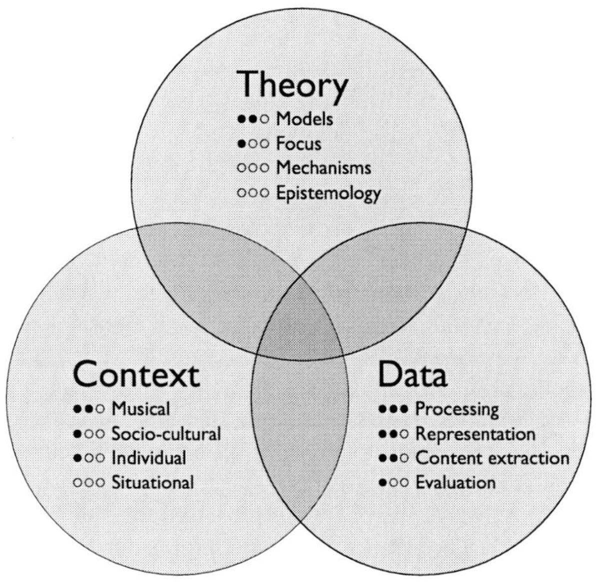

Figure 2. Key areas and their current status in modelling emotions in music (filled circles indicate advanced status).

Figure 2 emphasizes how the areas overlap and need to be developed in tandem. Figure also summarizes the current progress of the important areas. Those areas that are particularly well developed are ranked high (shown with small black indicators) and those key areas that require further attention can be summarized:

- commitment to emotion focus and mechanisms
- estimation of high-level music content
- robust evaluation procedures
- open data sharing conventions
- everyday listening (e.g. data and functions)
- sensitivity to musical context (e.g. genres)

These key areas of attention have been the subject of some studies detailed in earlier sections, but the progress in them is still limited. In the theoretical domain – which has lesser status in sound and music computing – future studies should adopt critical outlook to emotion models, focus and underlying theoretical assumptions. In the domain of data, cross-validation, appropriate behavioural data collection practices, creation of ways to measure high-level concepts from audio, and making all the efforts transparent by sharing the code and the data would greatly speed up the progress made in the field. Any advances in context-related issues would be a significant improvement, but to create better models of emotional effects of music, taking into account inherent differences in emotional values and functions of different music genres would provide the most imminent benefits.

6. REFERENCES

[1] T. Eerola and J. K. Vuoskoski, "A review of music and emotion studies: Approaches, emotion models and stimuli," *Music Perception*, vol. 30, no. 3, pp. 307–340, 2012.

[2] P. Juslin and D. Västfjäll, "Emotional responses to music: The need to consider underlying mechanisms," *Behavioral and Brain Sciences*, vol. 31, no. 05, pp. 559–575, 2008.

[3] P. N. Juslin and J. A. Sloboda, *Handbook of Music and Emotion.* Boston, MA: Oxford University Press, 2010, ch. Introduction: Aims, organization, and terminology, pp. 3–12.

[4] P. Ekman, "An argument for basic emotions," *Cognition & Emotion*, vol. 6, pp. 169–200, 1992.

[5] P. Juslin and P. Laukka, "Expression, Perception, and Induction of Musical Emotions: A Review and a Questionnaire Study of Everyday Listening," *Journal of New Music Research*, vol. 33, no. 3, pp. 217–238, 2004.

[6] J. A. Russell, "A circumplex model of affect," *Journal of Personality and Social Psychology*, vol. 39, no. 6, pp. 1161–1178, 1980.

[7] P. G. Hunter, E. G. Schellenberg, and U. Schimmack, "Mixed affective responses to music with conflicting cues," *Cognition & Emotion*, vol. 22, no. 2, pp. 327–352, 2008.

[8] R. E. Thayer, *The Biopsychology of Mood and Arousal.* Oxford University Press, New York, USA, 1989.

[9] U. Schimmack and A. Grob, "Dimensional models of core affect: A quantitative comparison by means of structural equation modeling," *European Journal of Personality*, vol. 14, no. 4, pp. 325–345, 2000.

[10] H. Lövheim, "A new three-dimensional model for emotions and monoamine neurotransmitters," *Medical Hypotheses*, vol. 78, no. 2, pp. 341–348, 2012.

[11] D. C. Rubin and J. M. Talarico, "A comparison of dimensional models of emotion: Evidence from emotions, prototypical events, autobiographical memories, and words," *Memory*, vol. 17, no. 8, pp. 802–808, 2009.

[12] T. Eerola and J. K. Vuoskoski, "A comparison of the discrete and dimensional models of emotion in music," *Psychology of Music*, vol. 39, no. 1, pp. 18–49, 2011.

[13] J. K. Vuoskoski and T. Eerola, "Measuring music-induced emotion: A comparison of emotion models, personality biases, and intensity of experiences," *Musicae Scientiae*, vol. 15, no. 2, pp. 159–173, 2011.

[14] M. Zentner, D. Grandjean, and K. R. Scherer, "Emotions evoked by the sound of music: Differentiation, classification, and measurement," *Emotion*, vol. 8, no. 4, pp. 494–521, 2008.

[15] W. Trost, T. Ethofer, M. Zentner, and P. Vuilleumier, "Mapping aesthetic musical emotions in the brain," *Cerebral Cortex*, vol. 22, no. 12, pp. 2769–2783, 2012.

[16] X. Hu, J. S. Downie, C. Laurier, M. Bay, and A. F. Ehmann, "The 2007 MIREX audio mood classification task: Lessons learned," in *Proceedings of the 9th International Conference on Music Information Retrieval*, 2008, pp. 462–467.

[17] P. Lamere, "Social tagging and music information retrieval," *Journal of New Music Research*, vol. 37, no. 2, pp. 101–114, 2008.

[18] M. Levy and M. Sandler, "A semantic space for music derived from social tags," in *Proceedings of 8th International Conference on Music Information Retrieval (ISMIR)*, 2007.

[19] C. Laurier, M. Sordo, J. Serra, and P. Herrera, "Music mood representations from social tags," in *Proceedings of 10th International Conference on Music Information Retrieval (ISMIR)*, 2009, pp. 381–86.

[20] P. Saari and T. Eerola, "Semantic computing of moods based on tags in social media of music," *IEEE Transactions on Knowledge and Data Engineering*, manuscript submitted for publication available at http://arxiv.org/, 2013.

[21] P. Evans and E. Schubert, "Relationships between expressed and felt emotions in music," *Musicae Scientiae*, vol. 12, no. 1, pp. 75–99, 2008.

[22] P. N. Juslin, "From everyday emotions to aesthetic emotions: Toward a unified theory of musical emotions," *Physics of Life Reviews*, in press.

[23] T. Fritz, S. Jentschke, N. Gosselin, D. Sammler, I. Peretz, R. Turner, A. D. Friederici, and S. Koelsch, "Universal recognition of three basic emotions in music," *Current Biology*, vol. 19, no. 7, pp. 573–576, 2009.

[24] D. Bogdanov, M. Haro, F. Fuhrmann, A. Xambó, E. Gómez, P. Herrera *et al.*, "Semantic audio content-based music recommendation and visualization based on user preference examples," *Information Processing & Management*, vol. 49, no. 1, pp. 13–33, 2012.

[25] M. M. Farbood, "A parametric, temporal model of musical tension," *Music Perception: An Interdisciplinary Journal*, vol. 29, no. 4, pp. 387–428, 2012.

[26] L. Kramer, *Music as cultural practice, 1800-1900*. Berkeley, US: University of California Press, 1990.

[27] M. Maiese, *Embodiment, emotion, and cognition*. New York, US: Palgrave, 2011.

[28] I. Molnar-Szakacs and K. Overy, "Music and mirror neurons: from motion to'e'motion," *Social cognitive and affective neuroscience*, vol. 1, no. 3, pp. 235–241, 2006.

[29] E. Douglas-Cowie, R. Cowie, I. Sneddon, C. Cox, O. Lowry, M. Mcrorie, J.-C. Martin, L. Devillers, S. Abrilian, A. Batliner *et al.*, "The humaine database: addressing the collection and annotation of naturalistic and induced emotional data," in *Affective computing and intelligent interaction*. Springer, 2007, pp. 488–500.

[30] V. Alluri, P. Toiviainen, I. P. Jääskeläinen, E. Glerean, M. Sams, and E. Brattico, "Large-scale brain networks emerge from dynamic processing of musical timbre, key and rhythm," *NeuroImage*, vol. 59, no. 4, pp. 3677–3689, 2012.

[31] M. Levy and M. Sandler, "Learning latent semantic models for music from social tags," *Journal of New Music Research*, vol. 37, no. 2, pp. 137–150, 2008.

[32] G. Tzanetakis and P. Cook, "Musical genre classification of audio signals," *Speech and Audio Processing, IEEE transactions on*, vol. 10, no. 5, pp. 293–302, 2002.

[33] Q. Claire and R. D. King, "Machine learning as an objective approach to understanding music," in *New Frontiers in Mining Complex Patterns*. Springer, 2013, pp. 64–78.

[34] A. Novello, S. van de Par, M. M. McKinney, and A. Kohlrausch, "Algorithmic prediction of inter-song similarity in western popular music," *Journal of New Music Research*, no. ahead-of-print, pp. 1–19, 2013.

[35] T. Lidy and A. Rauber, "Evaluation of feature extractors and psycho-acoustic transformations for music genre classification," in *Proc. ISMIR*, 2005, pp. 34–41.

[36] K. Markov and T. Matsui, "High level feature extraction for the self-taught learning algorithm," *EURASIP Journal on Audio, Speech, and Music Processing*, vol. 2013, no. 1, pp. 1–11, 2013.

[37] T. Eerola, "Are the emotions expressed in music genre-specific? an audio-based evaluation of datasets spanning classical, film, pop and mixed genres," *Journal of New Music Research*, vol. 40, no. 4, pp. 349–366, 2011.

[38] P. Saari, T. Eerola, and O. Lartillot, "Generalizability and simplicity as criteria in feature selection: Application to mood classification in music," *IEEE Transactions on Audio, Speech, and Language Processing*, vol. 19, no. 6, pp. 1802–1812, 2011.

[39] T. Eerola, O. Lartillot, and P. Toiviainen, "Prediction of multidimensional emotional ratings in music from audio using multivariate regression models," in *Proceedings of 10th International Conference on Music Information Retrieval (ISMIR 2009)*, K. Hirata and G. Tzanetakis, Eds. Dagstuhl, Germany: International Society for Music Information Retrieval, 2009, pp. 621–626.

[40] Y. Yang, Y. Lin, Y. Su, and H. Chen, "A regression approach to music emotion recognition," *IEEE Transactions on Audio Speech and Language Processing*, vol. 16, no. 2, pp. 448–457, 2008.

[41] P. N. Juslin and E. Lindström, "Musical expression of emotions: Modelling listeners' judgements of composed and performed features," *Music Analysis*, vol. 29, no. 1-3, pp. 334–364, 2010.

[42] A. Gabrielsson and E. Lindström, "The role of structure in the musical expression of emotions," *Handbook of music and emotion: Theory, research, applications*, pp. 367–400, 2010.

[43] T. Eerola, "Modeling listeners' emotional response to music," *Topics in Cognitive Science*, vol. 4, no. 4, pp. 607–624, 2012.

[44] Y. E. Kim, E. Schmidt, and L. Emelle, "Moodswings: A collaborative game for music mood label collection," in *Proceedings of the International Symposium on Music Information Retrieval*, 2008, pp. 231–236.

[45] P. Saari, M. Barthet, G. Fazekas, T. Eerola, and M. Sandler, "Semantic models of mood expressed by music: Comparison between crowd-sourced and curated editorial annotations," in *IEEE International Conference on Multimedia and Expo (ICME 2013): International Workshop on Affective Analysis in Multimedia (AAM)*, In press 2013.

[46] T. Bertin-Mahieux, D. P. Ellis, B. Whitman, and P. Lamere, "The million song dataset," in *Proceedings of the 12th International Conference on Music Information Retrieval (ISMIR 2011)*, 2011.

[47] T. Nguyen, D. Phung, B. Adams, and S. Venkatesh, "Mood sensing from social media texts and its applications," *Knowledge and Information Systems*, pp. 1–36, 2013.

[48] R. Mayer, A. Rauber, and S. B. Austria, "Towards time-resilient mir processes," in *Proceedings of the International Society for Music Information Retrieval Conference (ISMIR)*, 2012, pp. 337–342.

[49] K. West, A. Kumar, A. Shirk, G. Zhu, J. S. Downie, A. Ehmann, and M. Bay, "The networked environment for music analysis (nema)," in *Services (SERVICES-1), 2010 6th World Congress on*. IEEE, 2010, pp. 314–317.

[50] J. Skowronek, M. McKinney, and S. ven de Par, "Ground-truth for automatic music mood classification," in *Proceedings of the 7th International Conference on Music Information Retrieval (ISMIR)*, 2006, pp. 395–396.

[51] T. Lidy and P. van der Linden, "Report on 3rd chorus+ think-tank: Think-tank on the future of music search, access and consumption, midem 2011," CHORUS+ European Coordination Action on Audiovisual Search, Cannes, France, Tech. Rep., March 15 2011.

[52] P. Laukka, T. Eerola, N. S. Thingujam, T. Yamasaki, and G. Beller, "Universal and culture-specific factors in the recognition and performance of musical emotions," *Emotion*, in press.

[53] T. Lidy, C. N. Silla Jr, O. Cornelis, F. Gouyon, A. Rauber, C. A. Kaestner, and A. L. Koerich, "On the suitability of state-of-the-art music information retrieval methods for analyzing, categorizing and accessing non-western and ethnic music collections," *Signal Processing*, vol. 90, no. 4, pp. 1032–1048, 2010.

[54] G. Tzanetakis, A. Kapur, W. A. Schloss, and M. Wright, "Computational ethnomusicology," *Journal of interdisciplinary music studies*, vol. 1, no. 2, pp. 1–24, 2007.

[55] Y.-H. Yang and X. Hu, "Cross-cultural music mood classification: A comparison of english and chinese songs," in *Proc. ISMIR*, 2012.

[56] T. Eerola, "Analysing emotions in schubert's erlkönig: A computational approach," *Music Analysis*, vol. 29, no. 1-3, pp. 214–233, 2010.

[57] J. K. Vuoskoski and T. Eerola, "The role of mood and personality in the perception of emotions represented by music," *Cortex*, vol. 47, no. 9, pp. 1099–1106, 2011.

[58] E. C. Nusbaum and P. J. Silvia, "Shivers and timbres personality and the experience of chills from music," *Social Psychological and Personality Science*, vol. 2, no. 2, pp. 199–204, 2011.

[59] A. S. Lampropoulos, P. S. Lampropoulou, and G. A. Tsihrintzis, "A cascade-hybrid music recommender system for mobile services based on musical genre classification and personality diagnosis," *Multimedia Tools and Applications*, vol. 59, no. 1, pp. 241–258, 2012.

[60] P. Juslin, S. Liljeström, D. Västfjäll, G. Barradas, and A. Silva, "An experience sampling study of emotional reactions to music: Listener, music, and situation." *Emotion*, vol. 8, no. 5, pp. 668–683, 2008.

Human-Computer Music Performance: From Synchronized Accompaniment to Musical Partner

Roger B. Dannenberg, Zeyu Jin
Carnegie Mellon University
rbd@cs.cmu.edu
zeyuj@andrew.cmu.edu

Nicolas E. Gold, Octav-Emilian Sandu, Praneeth N. Palliyaguru
University College London
{n.gold,praneeth.palliyaguru.10,octav-emilian.sandu.10}@ucl.ac.uk

Andrew Robertson, Adam Stark
Queen Mary University of London
{andrew.robertson, adam.stark}@eecs.qmul.ac.uk

Rebecca Kleinberger
Massachusetts Institute of Technology
rebklein@mit.edu

ABSTRACT

Live music performance with computers has motivated many research projects in science, engineering, and the arts. In spite of decades of work, it is surprising that there is not more technology for, and a better understanding of the computer as music performer. We review the development of techniques for live music performance and outline our efforts to establish a new direction, *Human-Computer Music Performance* (HCMP), as a framework for a variety of coordinated studies. Our work in this area spans performance analysis, synchronization techniques, and interactive performance systems. Our goal is to enable musicians to incorporate computers into performances easily and effectively through a better understanding of requirements, new techniques, and practical, performance-worthy implementations. We conclude with directions for future work.

1. INTRODUCTION

Live performances increasingly use computer technology to augment acoustic or amplified acoustic instruments. The use of electronics in performance predates computing by many years, and there are many different conceptual approaches. The most obvious and popular approach is the simple replacement of acoustic instruments with digital ones. Another popular approach is the use of interactive systems that mainly react to input from human performers. In these systems, humans effectively "trigger" sound events or processes.

Two key aspects of live performance with computers are autonomy and synchronization. *Autonomy* refers to the ability of the computer performer to operate without direct control by a human, and *synchronization* refers to the ability to adapt a performance to the timing of humans. For example, interactive systems that are triggered by live performers are autonomous because they require little or no direct human control, and their synchronization is limited to computed responses to live events.

As we consider other forms of music, particularly traditional musical forms with scores and multiple parts, synchronization becomes essential. Performances with fixed recordings are used in many settings, but these are uncomfortable because they place the entire synchronization burden on humans. One of the promises of real-time sound synthesis was to eliminate fixed recordings, creating an opportunity to actively and adaptively synchronize computers to humans [1, 2].

An early system to address computer synchronization to live performers was the Sequential Drum [3]. The Sequential Drum assumes that a sequence of sound events to be played is mostly known in advance, but the timing and perhaps other parameters such as loudness are determined at performance time. A performer uses a drum-like interface where each drum stroke launches the next sound event in the sequence and perhaps also controls loudness and other parameters. A drawback of the Sequential Drum is its lack of autonomy – it requires a human's full attention during a performance.

Conducting systems are related to the Sequential Drum and a common theme in computer music research [4]. If a conductor exists anyway and a computer can follow the conductor's gestures, the computer could be considered an autonomous performer. Synchronization requires that the computer sense not only beats and tempo but start times and other cues as well. In practice, computers cannot follow "real" conducting intended for humans, but there is promise that conducting gestures can offer one mode of synchronization.

The difficulty of following conductors was one inspiration for Computer Accompaniment (CA) systems [5], which use score matching to synchronize computer accompanists to live performers. CA is autonomous and can synchronize to traditional scored music with high reliability. There are, however, some drawbacks. First, CA requires a score and for players to follow the score. Improvisation and rhythmic variation lead to timing problems, if not outright failures. Second, CA requires distinctive input to follow. When the followed instrument holds a long note or rests, there is no synchronization information. It is possible to follow multiple instruments [6], but this adds to the complexity. Finally, CA often has limited timing accuracy due to problems of accurate onset detection. CA generally works well for chamber music with expressive timing, but not well for different forms of popular music.

It is surprising that systems offering *autonomy* and *synchronization* for popular music performance have not been pursued more actively. Our goal is to create computer performers that play music with humans. We are particularly interested in music with fairly steady beats and where synchronization must be achieved through beats and measures rather than score following. This is a realistic problem that is characteristic of nearly all popular music, including rock, folk, jazz, and contemporary church music. It should be noted that score following systems are not a solution to this problem because (1) they require consistent playing at the note level to match to scores and (2) they do not synchronize with the precision required for steady tempo. The problem is broad in that it touches on music performance practice, music representation issues, machine listening, machine composition, human-computer interaction, sound synthesis, and sound diffusion. We refer to this overall direction as *Human-Computer Music Performance*, or HCMP.

Our goal here is to introduce the problems of HCMP, survey progress that we have made working together and individually, and describe future challenges and work to be done.

2. EXAMPLES OF HCMP SYSTEMS

To date, we have constructed a number of HCMP systems. The first system was a large project to create a virtual string orchestra to play with a jazz big band [7]. The system used tapping for synchronization, a small keyboard for cues (each key mapped to a different cue), and PSOLA [8] for time stretching a 20-track audio file in real-time. For this performance, an extra percussionist tapped her foot and entered cues.

This system was reimplemented and integrated with effects processing software and used by the first author in an experimental jazz quartet. This system was designed to be operated by the author who also plays trumpet in the quartet. Cues are given by a capacitive sensor worn on the index finger, and the system uses MIDI files rather than audio.

The B-Keeper system [9] is designed to follow the timing variations of a live drummer. Dedicated microphones are placed on the kick and snare drum, which are used to create an accurate representation of relevant drum events (Figure 1).

Figure 1. The band Higamos Hogamos performing with B-Keeper.

3. CHALLENGES OF HCMP

Active research is being carried out on many fronts. This section describes just a few interesting problems presented by HCMP and some of the approaches to solving them.

3.1 Detecting the Beat

Beat tracking algorithms aim to output the times of the tactus, the regular pulse with which humans would naturally tap in time with the music. Most beat tracking algorithms first process the signal to create an onset detection function [10]. Methods such as autocorrelation, comb filtering and interval clustering can be used to detect periodicity in this signal. The algorithm must also determine the phase, typically using dynamic programming or probabilistic methods, with the premise that musical events which correspond to peaks in the detection function are most likely to occur on the beat.

Real-time beat tracking algorithms might be used to provide a tempo and phase estimate for the underlying beat which can be used to synchronise HCMP systems. Whilst offline beat tracking algorithms have access to the full audio file and can operate non-causally, beat trackers for live performance must operate causally in real time. Examples of real-time algorithms released as external objects for MaxMSP are: btrack~ [11], beatcomber~ [12] and IBT~ [13].

Beat trackers are relatively successful on rock and pop examples, although they can exhibit errors such as tapping on the offbeat and tapping at double or half the tempo (octave errors). Complex passages, such as those featuring syncopation, can be problematic. Where the tempo changes, there is an inherent trade-off between reliability and responsiveness [14]. However, for a successful HCMP system, performers require full confidence that the system will behave as they expect.

An alternative to sensing the beat in audio is sensing the beat from foot-tapping or other gestures. We have successfully used a foot pedal in a number of performances and studied the foot pedal as an interface for communicating beat timing to a computer. In our measurements, the standard deviation of foot tap times is about 40 ms [15]. This alone is not satisfactory for music with a steady tempo, but we use the "steady tempo" feature to our advantage by using regression over previous beat times to predict the tempo and next beat time.

One of the difficult problems of tempo estimation is that tempo is normally steady but changes rather rapidly at times. We can minimize *average* error by using long regression windows, e.g. performing linear regression on the 20 previous beats, but then the *worst case* error where the tempo changes will be musically unacceptable. On the other hand, optimizing for the worst case tends to highlight special cases, often where synchronization is not musically necessary. In practice, we compromise with a window size of 5 to 7 previous tap times to predict the next tap time. This choice is sufficiently responsive that good synchronization, even in rock music, can be achieved, but it does require careful tapping. Some practice and musical skills are necessary, and the system has less-than-ideal autonomy, but this method can be reliable and effective.

We are also considering additional modes of acquisition (e.g. video) to augment audio analysis, drawing on instrumental technique (e.g. guitar strumming actions).

3.2 Score Representation

Synchronizing at the beat level is only the first step to musical synchronization. All performers need to be at the same musical position, e.g. "beat 2 of measure 5 of the chorus." Before we can talk about synchronization at this level, we need a formal model of what synchronization means.

In traditional music theory, a score provides an unambiguous sequence of beats and measures. Scores also indicate what each player should play in a given beat. In popular music, scores are treated much more casually, and the mapping from score notation to performances is sometimes specified informally, e.g. "play a 4-bar introduction, play an extra chorus at the end."

We could "solve" this problem by insisting on traditional scores, but the reality is that popular music performance often demands flexibility to adapt, even in the middle of a performance. It is not unusual for non-sectional changes also to be made, e.g. the band plays an extra measure by "intuition" before continuing with the next section. Systems that attempt to synchronize with a score need to identify the current score location within it. This requires identifying musical features in performance at the level at which the score is expressed. For example, a chord list requires chord identification, a lead sheet with melody may be able to use that in addition to chords, performances with lyrics may be able to follow the sung parts (using techniques such as that of Mauch et al. [16]).

To address some of these problems, we have recently developed a music notation display system for HCMP. The system can import images or photos of music notation, thus leveraging existing printed music. Users can manually annotate the music images with control information to mark measures, time signatures, section names, repeats, codas, etc. (See top of Figure 2.) The system can then compute the normal performance order of the score, essentially "flattening" the repeats into a linear sequence. This flattened score provides a reference mapping from measure numbers back to score locations. This mapping can be shared across different media (audio players, MIDI players, visual displays) to coordinate them.

Another representation issue is that users may want to reorganize the score for a particular performance. We call this process "arrangement." For example, an arrangement could be "play sections AABABA in that order, ignoring the structure implied by the score." Figure 2 (middle) shows how an arrangement is constructed. The row of boxes represents an editable sequence of sections. Clicking on a box highlights the corresponding section in the score just above.

While this work solves many representation problems, more work is needed to communicate arrangements to computer players. Implementing jumps in audio or MIDI files is tricky (consider that sections may have pickup notes that precede the section and notes that sustain into the next section). Ultimately, this illustrates the conceptual gap between human musicians who think of sections as high-level abstract objects to be realized in performance and computer players that model sections as immutable, concrete audio files or MIDI sequences. There are research opportunities here to raise the level of music abstraction offered by computers.

At performance time, the score is displayed in performance order using a "double-buffered" display allowing the performer to always look ahead in the score. (See Figure 2, bottom.) The performer can also use this display to give cues and indicate the current measure to the computer. This notation system is now complete, but work remains to integrate it with a performance system and to evaluate its use in live performances.

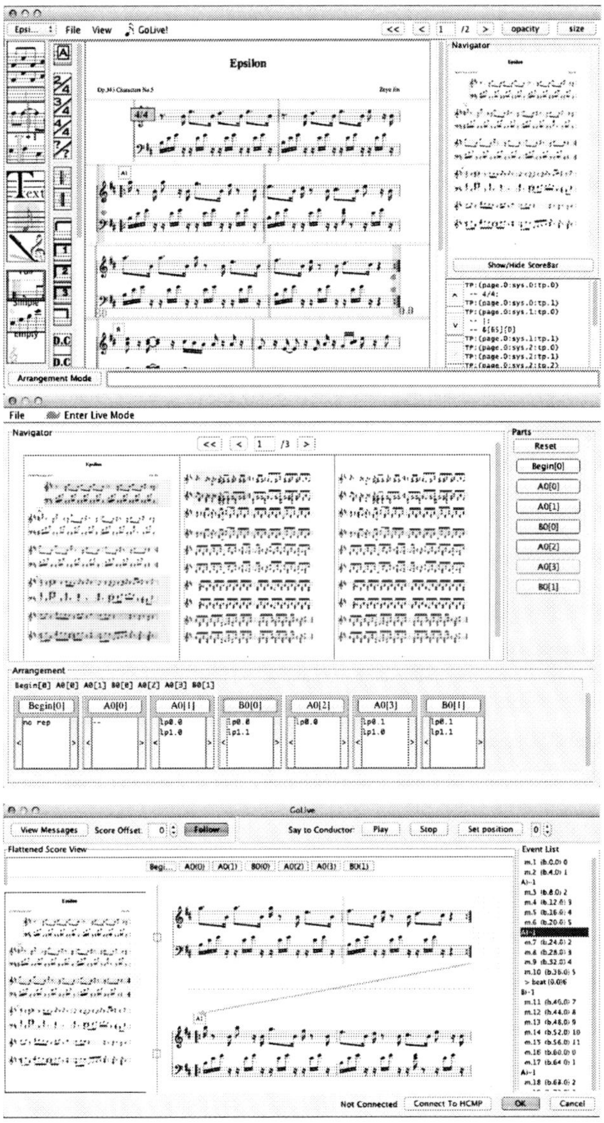

Figure 2. Digital music display system. Top is annotation system for indicating measures, sections, repeats, and other control structures. Middle is arrangement window showing original score and an editable sequence of sections constituting the arrangement. Bottom is live mode where score is displayed in performance order in real time with automatic page turning.

3.3 Synchronizing at Higher Levels

While our work on score representation offers a framework for coordinating performers, we still need to implement coordination. We propose the concept of cues as an approach to achieving synchronization in live performances. A cue is simply a signal that indicates a score location or directs a performer. Cues are typically given by humans to one another and take effect on the next section boundary. It is not uncommon to give cues many measures in advance because communication during a performance requires getting the attention of other performers and communication gestures may be unreliable.

In our systems, cues have several types [17]:

- *Position* cues indicate global position and indicate either when to start playing or that the computer and human(s) have diverged and need to resynchronize;
- *Intention* cues indicate a decision has been made about the future course of the performance; for example, this is the last repetition of a vamp;
- *Voicing* cues are not used for synchronization but indicate choices about how a player should render media. Volume changes or a request not to play can be indicated with voicing cues.

We have explored different means of giving cues. Our first system used a small MIDI keyboard where each key was labeled with a *position* cue that caused the computer to play a pre-recorded section of music. A later system used a wearable capacitive sensor attached to the index finger. By touching the sensor with the thumb, a cue can be given. This system detects cues reliably and does not intrude upon the human performer.

Currently, we are working on capturing gestures such as nodding your head in the direction of the computer performer. Detecting gestures from a continuous stream of sensor data is prone to false positives. We are evaluating the use of dynamic time warping and machine learning techniques to build a reliable system [18].

We are also exploring the potential of natural user interfaces to minimize disruption to performers. Ideally, a computer performer would not require explicit cuing but through understanding the performance norms of an ensemble and observing the gestures the human performers make, will be able to determine the intention and position cues for itself (i.e. full autonomy).

To that end, we have experimented with the Microsoft Kinect^{TM} sensor as an interface for various applications including use as a conducting system to set initial tempo, as a way to determine intention cues through counting raised fingers on one hand (a practice used in contemporary church-music leading to direct the band to a numbered score section), to observe guitarists' actions, and as a way to automate page turning. The latter project detects head tilt gestures that control the direction of a page turn in a PDF file displayed on a computer or (soon) iPad^{TM} , controlled over a network.

In all cases, the major challenge is the robustness of detection in noisy, realistic scenarios. Distinguishing the neck of a guitar from a player's arm has proved difficult, even in "near-mode" where the sensor tracks only the upper half of the body. The sensor is also very sensitive to angle, making it potentially difficult to deploy in realistic scenarios. Music stands, piano lids, microphones and other normal musical equipment found in stage environments all work to confound the clear picture required for easy detection.

The page turning system (evaluated by two of the authors in a laboratory setting, one acting as pianist) works well with the sensor placed in front of or behind a pianist (although is very sensitive to off-axis placement – front is best). Unfortunately, this precludes the typical "forward" nod for page turns because neck movement in that plane is not currently detectable from those sensor positions. Other challenges include differentiating expressive movement from directive gesture.

We are also developing chord sequence recognition systems to identify a score section based on the chord sequence played thus far (similar to [19]). There are challenges in synchronizing the incoming chord sequence to the "model sequence" in the score, particularly in the presence of inaccurately played, missed, substituted or mis-identified chords, and difficulties arising from the need to define a chord with reference to a beat where the beat is itself defined with less than 100% accuracy. In addition, there are many examples of popular music where the chord sequence is so repetitive as to offer little information alone as to which of the sections is currently being played. In these cases, alternative cues such as the texture of the music may be helpful. Our distributed approach (described below) can also produce conflicting chord and beat identifications from different instruments that require resolution.

A broader level of synchronization (and context knowledge) may also be required. It is not unusual for ensembles to move seamlessly from one work (or part of a work) to another without forward planning (e.g. see Benford *et al.*'s study of Irish folk music sequencing [20]). Recognizing when this occurs and shifting to the new work is similar to recognizing sections in general, albeit with a larger range of potential sections to select from.

Finally, another important possibility for detecting cueing gestures is the digital score display system described in the previous section. An interesting aspect of this interface is that music notation can be bi-directional: The display can show the computer's location in the score to the reader using a cursor or highlighting graphical areas, and the reader can indicate his or her location to the computer by pointing to notation (e.g. measures) in the score.

3.4 Adjusting Tempo

What does the computer player play? One approach is to play pre-recorded audio, using time-stretching techniques to adjust the playback tempo. We constructed one HCMP system in which the computer played the role of a 20-piece string orchestra. Each string part was recorded on a separate track so that high-quality pitch-synchronous overlap-add (PSOLA) time stretching could be used [7]. Other techniques such as the phase vocoder can be used on polyphonic recordings [4].

Another approach is MIDI, since MIDI sequences are easily time-stretched. A challenge with MIDI is to simulate sounds of acoustic instruments. Sample-based synthesis is good for isolated notes, but it has difficulty producing natural-sounding musical phrases. Progress has been made with large sample libraries and automated sample selection, but there is still much work to be done. Alternative techniques, including physical models and spectral models offer more flexible control, but expressive musical control is still an important problem.

Studies on latency in networked performance suggest that the just noticeable difference (JND), the latency setting at which the effect becomes noticeable to the performer, is between 20 and 30msec [21]. This also provides an estimate for the bounds within which the synchronization will be acceptable to human performers.

3.5 System Architecture

One lesson from building early systems is that robust interactive systems require careful design. The lack of a flexible program that supports new performances has hindered research, and we are working toward a more flexible, modular software architecture for HCMP.

HCMP systems decompose naturally into components:

- Input sensors for tapping and cueing,
- Beat and tempo estimation based on tapping or audio analysis,
- A virtual conductor that accepts position and tempo information and distributes it to players,
- Media players, including variable rate audio players based on time-stretching, and MIDI players.
- Score display (with automated page turning, position display)
- Development and configuration management system allowing users to combine media, define cues, make arrangements, and store everything so that it can be retrieved and used automatically in a performance.

We are developing components and plan to release a system based on "plug-ins" so that end-users can configure their own systems with just the features they need, and advanced users can extend the base system through scripting languages to provide custom features.

Our recent work [22] has shown that HCMP technology may be more likely to be adopted if it can be delivered quickly to users at low-cost and low-risk. We have therefore also been exploring the potential of mobile devices (such as smartphones) as a way to deliver HCMP systems. Each instrument in a band would be tracked by a smart device (e.g. resting on a music stand), undertaking its own audio processing and sending the results to a virtual conductor on another device for music generation.

This approach poses some interesting new problems. Since the audio processing for beat tracking and chord recognition is distributed among several devices, data fusion becomes paramount, especially in the absence of synchronous clocks. There are new opportunities also: textural detection may be easier (since the sound level can be more easily measured per instrument), beat tracking on an individual instrument may be better than on the ensemble as a whole (and could be based on knowledge of the individual instrument being tracked), and other device capabilities (e.g. video) may be usable. Additional equipment would not generally be needed by the users since we think it reasonable to assume that smart devices would be widely available to ensembles through personal phones. Where new technology is required (e.g. for gesture tracking) we are seeking to use off-the-shelf consumer devices such as Kinect™ (as described above) to minimise deployment complexity and cost.

To expose the research issues, we have undertaken a feasibility study to evaluate interactive performance technologies on consumer devices and in realistic performance environments. The aims were to evaluate the difficulty of repackaging this technology for smartphone, to assess the musical performance issues raised by doing so (e.g. where should the smartphone be placed while performing?), and to understand challenges to the state of the art and shape the future development of such techniques. We repackaged existing state-of-the-art beat tracking [12] and chord-estimation [23] software into smartphone apps using libpd [24]. The app was deployed to several iOS devices (see Figure 3) linked by a wireless network.

Figure 3. iOS app for beat/chord detection.

A local church's worship band area was used as a realistic physical evaluation environment, with a subset of the authors forming a band. Five genre-appropriate songs were used as test subjects and video, audio, and data from the systems were recorded. We also undertook "laboratory" evaluation using multi-track, multi-speaker recordings of the same songs to closely replicate live performance conditions, but allowing replication and experimental parameter control (see Figure 4). The gesture-control detection for band direction was also evaluated in this environment.

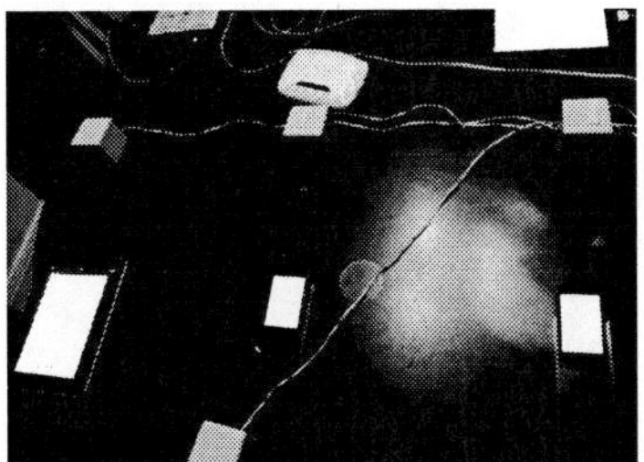

Figure 4. Simulation of live performance with multiple speakers and devices in a shared acoustic space.

Our analysis indicates that both platform and performance context provide significant challenges to state-of-the-art techniques. Problems include the distribution of tracking across multiple devices resulting in latency in reporting beats/chords, reconciling multiple independent timing streams, and the loss of the full mix at each tracker meaning the beat and chord tracking systems have less audio to work with. On the positive side, we also found evidence that beat tracking on an individual instrument track can outperform tracking on the whole mix.

4. HCMP EVALUATION

To measure progress, we need ways to evaluate HCMP systems. We have used a range of methods with varying levels of detail and rigour in the projects described in this paper. Evaluating HCMP research requires several approaches given the range of underpinning disciplines and potential outcomes. Interactive Music System (IMS) evaluation methods vary widely depending on the type of system and the particular interest of the researchers. Collins summarises three main evaluation forms for concert systems [25]: direct participant experience, indirect participant experience, and technical evaluation of algorithms. Hsu and Sosnick [26] address the first two aspects with a method based on the DECIDE framework. Stowell et al. [27] identify the difficulties in evaluating IMS, presenting and comparing qualitative and quantitative approaches including comparative listening tests, interaction analysis based on video, discourse analysis and the (somewhat controversial – see Ariza [28]) "musical Turing Test". They offer useful guidance on the application of these techniques: Discourse analysis may be used to assess direct participant experience (i.e. the musicians themselves), and the musical Turing Test (in effect, survey methods) used to assess indirect participant experience (i.e. the non-musicians supported by, or listening to the music). Rowe states that programs for machine musicianship should exhibit behaviour that can be observed as correct or incorrect [29]. In the HCMP case passing the musical Turing Test will require at least satisficing (i.e. satisfactory and sufficient) output.

Stowell et al. acknowledge that most evaluation methods are focused on the experience of performers [27] (e.g. Hsu and Sosnick's framework [26] does not address the third of Collins' criteria), thus the evaluation of HCMP systems (particularly the sub-components) will need to be supplemented by objective criteria (e.g. measuring latency of interaction in comparison to experimentally-derived musical synchronisation criteria [30, 31], and measures of beat-tracking accuracy [32] and chord recognition [23]). Adoptability issues will also need to be addressed [22].

The ensemble nature of popular music means that other than low-level laboratory tests of system components, the main evaluation activity will need to involve groups of musicians (or simulation of this scenario). In addition to work with live bands, as shown above, multi-track recordings can be used to simulate the live environment by replaying performances through electrical or acoustical signal paths to multiple speakers and detection systems..

5. FUTURE WORK

Human musicians are often expected to improvise, or at least perform from lead sheets, which give music structure and chords but not the details of notes and rhythms. Since human musicians may not have the skills to construct drum beats, bass lines, and other parts, HCMP is an excellent domain to investigate automated music composition. Perhaps music analogies are an interesting way to specify goals, i.e. "I want a bass part that sounds like the one in ...." Similarly, parts must be performed expressively and musically. Perhaps there are synthesis-by-rule approaches [33] or more general theories of expressive performance [34] for popular, beat-based music.

Ideally, an HCMP system would incorporate a learning mechanism that would allow it to extract useful information about the performance from rehearsals. This could make performances more reliable and more autonomous.

How can we evaluate general musicianship? Even synchronization is difficult to measure objectively: Once basic synchronization within 10 or 20 ms has been obtained, rhythmic "feel" that results from deliberate asynchrony [35] may be more important than precise synchronization. As we describe, a range of evaluation methods will likely be required, from measures of low-level performance (synchronization, chord identification) through to system-level evaluation methods involving performers considering their experiences alongside the systems, and audience-focused measures of reception. The standards required may vary depending on context: A computer that fills in for a human musician in a rehearsal or HCMP to facilitate practice at home may have modest requirements, while high-profile live performances in public may require virtuoso-level performance. The development of comprehensive and systematic top-to-bottom evaluation methodologies for HCMP is thus a key topic for future work.

6. CONCLUSIONS

HCMP has great potential to be widely used by many musicians. There are interesting scientific challenges as well as artistic ones. We are in the early stages of exploring possibilities and implementing systems that offer synchronization, interaction, and autonomy in live performance, with a focus on steady-tempo popular music, a problem which our research community has largely ignored. We believe that HCMP can become a practical, useful, and common way to make music, eventually used by millions. Ultimately, we hope that some of these users will leverage the unique properties of autonomous computer musicians to develop new musical genres.

Acknowledgments

Parts of this work were undertaken while Kleinberger was at University College London. This work was partly supported by the Arts and Humanities Research Council [grant number AH/J012408/1]; the Engineering and Physical Sciences Research Council [grant number EP/G060525/2]; the Department of Computer Science, UCL; Microsoft Research; the Royal Academy of Engineering; and the National Science Foundation [grant number 0855958]. Depending on the proposed use, some data from the RCUK-funded portions of this work may be available by contacting Nicolas Gold. Please note that intellectual, copyright and performance rights issues may prevent the full disclosure of this data.

7. REFERENCES

[1] R. B. Dannenberg, "An On-Line Algorithm for Real-Time Accompaniment," in *Proc. Int. Computer Music Conf.* Paris, 1985, pp. 193-198.

[2] B. Vercoe. "The Synthetic Performer in the Context of Live Performance," in *Proc. Int. Computer Music Conf.*, Paris, 1985.

[3] M. V. Mathews and C. Abbott. "The Sequential Drum," *Computer Music Journal*, vol. 4, no. 4, pp. 45-59, 1980.

[4] E. Lee, T. Karrer, and J. Borchers, "Toward a Framework for Interactive Systems to Conduct Digital Audio and Video Streams," *Computer Music Journal,* vol. 30, no. 1, pp. 21-36, 2006.

[5] R. B. Dannenberg and C. Raphael, "Music Score Alignment and Computer Accompaniment," *Comm. of the ACM*, vol. 49, no. 8, pp. 38-43, 2006.

[6] L. Grubb and R. B. Dannenberg, "Computer Performance in an Ensemble," in *Proc 3rd Int. Conf. for Music Perception and Cognition*, European Society for the Cognitive Sciences of Music, Liege, Belgium, 1994, pp. 57-60.

[7] R. B. Dannenberg, "A Virtual Orchestra for Human-Computer Music Performance," in *Proc. Int. Computer Music Conf.*, pp. 185-188, 2011.

[8] N. Schnell, G. Peeters, S. Lemouton, P. Manoury, X. Rodet, "Synthesizing a Choir in Real Time Using Pitch Synchronous Overlap Add (PSOLA)," in *Proc. Int. Computer Music Conf.*, Berlin, 2000.

[9] A. Robertson and M. D. Plumbley, "B-Keeper: A beat tracker for real-time synchronization within performance," in *Proc. of New Interfaces for Musical Expression (NIME 2007)*, New York, 2007, pp 234-237.

[10] J. P. Bello, L. Daudet, S. Abdallah, C. Duxbury, M. Davies, M. B. Sandler, "A Tutorial on Onset Detection in Music Signals," in *IEEE Trans. on Speech and Audio Processing,* vol. 13, no. 5, 2005, pp. 1035-1047.

[11] A. M. Stark, M. E. P. Davies and M. D. Plumbley, "Real-time beat synchronous analysis of musical signals," in *Proc. Digital Audio Effects Conf.*, 2009, pp. 299-304.

[12] A. Robertson, A. Stark, and M. Plumbley, "Real-Time Visual Beat Tracking Using a Comb Filter Matrix," in *Proc. Int. Computer Music Conf* Huddersfield, 2011.

[13] J. Oliveira, F. Gouyon, L. G. Martins and L. P. Reis, "IBT: A Real-time Tempo and Beat Tracking System", in *Proc. Int. Symp. on Music Information Retrieval (ISMIR)*, 2010, pp. 291-296.

[14] F. Gouyon, S. Dixon, "A Review of Automatic Rhythm Description Systems," *Computer Music Journal*, vol. 29, no. 1, pp.34-54, 2005.

[15] R. B. Dannenberg, and L. Wasserman, "Estimating the Error Distribution of a Single Tap Sequence without Ground Truth" in *Proc. Int. Symp. on Music Information Retrieval (ISMIR 2009)*, 2009, pp. 297-302.

[16] M. Mauch, H. Fujihara, and M. Goto "Lyrics-to-audio alignment and phrase-level segmentation using incomplete internet-style chord annotations," in *Proc. Sound and Music Computing Conf.*, Barcelona, 2010.

[17] N. E. Gold and R. B. Dannenberg, "A Reference Architecture and Score Representation for Popular Music Human-Computer Music Performance Systems," in *Proc. New Interfaces For Musical Expression*, Oslo, 2011.

[18] J. Tang *Extracting Commands From Gestures: Gesture Spotting and Recognition for Real-time Music Performance* (Master's Thesis), Carnegie Mellon Univ., 2013.

[19] Z. Duan and B. Pardo, "Aligning Semi-Improvised Music Audio with Its Lead Sheet," *Proc. Int. Symp. on Music Information Retrieval,* Miami, 2011.

[20] S. Benford, P. Tolmie, A.Y. Ahmed, A. Crabtree, T. Rodden, "Supporting Traditional Music-Making: Designing for Situated Discretion," in *Proc. ACM 2012 Conf. on Computer Supported Cooperative Work*, Seattle, 2012.

[21] N.P. Lago, and F. Kon, "The Quest for Low Latency," in Proc. Int. Computer Music Conf., 2004, pp. 33-36.

[22] N. E. Gold, "A Framework to Evaluate the Adoption Potential of Interactive Performance Systems for Popular Music," in *Proc. Sound and Music Computing Conf.*, Copenhagen, 2012.

[23] A. M. Stark and M. D. Plumbley, "Real-Time Chord Recognition for Live Performance," in *Proc. Int. Computer Music Conf.*, Montreal, 2009.

[24] P. Brinkman, *Making Musical Apps*. O'Reilly, 2012.

[25] N. Collins, *Introduction to Computer Music*. John Wiley & Sons, Inc., 2010.

[26] W. Hsu and M. Sosnick, "Evaluating Interactive Music Systems: An HCI Approach," in *Proc. New Interfaces for Musical Expression*, Pittsburgh, PA, 2009.

[27] D. Stowell, A. Robertson, N. Bryan-Kinns, M. D. Plumbley, "Evaluation of Live Human–Computer Music-Making: Quantitative and Qualitative Approaches," *International Journal of Human-Computer Studies*, vol. 67, no. 11, pp. 960–975, 2009.

[28] C. Ariza, "The interrogator as critic: The Turing Test and the Evaluation of Generative Music Systems," *Computer Music Journal*, vol. 33, no. 2, pp. 48–70, 2009.

[29] R. Rowe, *Machine Musicianship*. MIT Press. 2001.

[30] M. Gurevich and C. Chafe. "Simulation of Networked Ensemble Performance with Varying Time Delays: Characterization of Ensemble Accuracy," in *Proc. Int. Computer Music Conference*, Miami, 2004.

[31] R. A. Rasch. "Timing and Synchronization in Ensemble Performance," in *Generative Processes in Music: The Psychology of Performance, Improvisation, and Composition.* J.A. Sloboda, ed. Clarendon Press, pp. 70–90, 1988.

[32] M. Davies, N. Degara, and M.D. Plumbley. 2009. Evaluation methods for musical audio beat tracking algorithms, *Technical Report C4DM-TR-09-06, Centre for Digital Music,* Queen Mary University of London.

[33] J. Sundberg, A. Askenfelt and L. Frydén, "Musical Performance: A Synthesis-by-Rule Approach," *Computer Music Journal*, vol. 7, no. 1 (Spring), pp 37-43, 1983.

[34] P. N. Juslin, A. Friberg, and R. Bresin, "Toward a Computational Model of Expression in Performance: The GERM model," *Musicae Scientiae*, Special issue, pp. 63-122, 2001-2002.

[35] A. Friberg, and A. Sundström, "Swing Ratios and Ensemble Timing in Jazz Performance: Evidence for a Common Rhythmic Pattern," *Music Perception*, vol. 3, no. 19, pp. 333-349.

CONDUCTING A VIRTUAL ENSEMBLE WITH A KINECT DEVICE

A. Rosa-Pujazón, I. Barbancho, L. J. Tardón, A.M.Barbancho
Dpt. Ingeniería de Comunicaciones, E.T.S.I. Telecomunicacion
Universidad de Málaga, Campus de Teatinos s/n, 29071 Málaga, Spain
alejandror@uma.es, ibp@ic.uma.es, lorenzo@ic.uma.es, abp@ic.uma.es

ABSTRACT

This paper presents a gesture-based interaction technique for the implementation of an orchestra conductor and a virtual ensemble, using a 3D camera-based sensor to capture user's gestures. In particular, a human-computer interface has been developed to recognize conducting gestures using a Microsoft Kinect device. The system allows the conductor to control both the tempo in the piece played as well as the dynamics of each instrument set independently. In order to modify the tempo in the playback, a time-frequency processing-based algorithm is used. Finally, an experiment was conducted to assess user's opinion of the system as well as experimentally confirm if the features in the system were effectively improving user experience or not.

1. INTRODUCTION

Computers have become an extremely common tool in our everyday-life, to a degree that we are constantly interacting with them. Yet, standard human-computer interfaces show their shortcomings whenever trying to emulate interaction metaphors that do not naturally map easily to a keyboard-mouse setting, such as, for example, musical instrument simulation. However, the evolution of sensing and motion-tracking technologies has allowed for the development of new and innovative human-computer interfaces that improve user experience towards a more 'natural' interaction paradigm, thus bringing a new and vast array of computer-generated applications that fit much more accurately their real-life counterparts.

With regards to interactive music applications, these advanced human-computer interfaces have been used for a wide array of fields: new instruments creation/simulation [1], body motion to sound mapping [2] [3] [4] [5], gaming [6] [7], modification of visual patterns by using sung or speech voice [8], tangible and haptic instrument simulation [9] [10], drum-hitting simulation [11] [12] [13], etc.

One example of musical performance that is inherently linked to human body motion is that of the orchestra conductor, yet surprisingly there are only a handful of studies that address conducting simulation through the use of advanced human-computer interfaces. Conducting is required to coordinate and synchronize the performance of an ensemble. Therefore, the conductor must indicate musical parameters such as dynamics or tempo, using his hand and baton gestures to such purpose. Previous research has focused on capturing the conductor's hand or baton motion through the use of infrared sensors [14] [15] [16] [17], inertial sensors [18] or the Wiimote [19] [20], changing the tempo of the pieces performed accordingly. Some studies have also added some form of dynamics control [15] or heuristics [21] to provide a more satisfying user experience.

In this paper, we aim to present a new interaction paradigm for conducting gesture capturing, so that the user can effectively conduct a virtual orchestra, indicating the tempo and beat times of the piece performed, the overall dynamics and the specific volume levels for a concrete set of instruments in the ensemble. In order to achieve this, a Kinect sensing device is used, thus providing an inexpensive and off-the-shelf alternative for a non-intrusive experience for the user, as well as the possibility of tracking both user hands simultaneously. Additionally, we have conducted an experimental study to assess the usefulness of the application developed, as well as to find potential ways to further improve user experience.

The technical details of the system implemented will be discussed in the next section. Then, the following section will cover the details of the experiment performed, whose results will be presented and discussed in the subsequent sections. The conclusions drawn from the study will be depicted in the last section.

2. SYSTEM DESCRIPTION

As previously indicated, we opted for a Microsoft Kinect for XBOX device in our human-computer interface design. Kinect camera offers both a RGB-image and an depth image of the scene capture. By combining the depth map data with the OpenNI library and the NITE plugin, it is possible to extract 3D information to create an skeletal joint model to follow user movements. Concretely, the system is able to track the position in 3D space of up to 15 nodes or joints, corresponding to the head, neck, torso, hands, feet, etc. of the user. To provide some form of visual feedback, the application rendered a basic virtual environment coded in C/C++ using the OpenGL graphics library [22] and the OGRE graphics engine [23]. The environment was textured and modelled to resemble a concert hall (see figure 1). PortAudio library is used for sound management, and the tracks for each of the sets of instruments in the virtual

Figure 1. Virtual environment for the application

ensemble are stored and read from separate WAV files.

In order to adequately implement an ensemble conductor simulator, there are two main problems that need to be addressed: how to translate conducting gestures to changes in the performance, and how to smoothly change the tempo of the piece being played.

2.1 Changing the tempo of the piece: time-stretching

In order to change the tempo of the song being played, it is necessary to modify the playback speed according to the rate indicated by the conductor. Nevertheless, due to the duality of time and frequency domains, simply changing the playback speed also has an undesired effect in the form of changes in pitch of the music played. Thus, a slower playback time will result in a decrease of the pitch, while a faster one will make the pitch go higher. In order to smoothly play a musical piece at different playback speed without such pitch changing artifacts, it is necessary to resort to a time-stretching algorithm.

Time-stretching algorithms can be typically implemented in time-domain, using the so-called Synchronous Overlap-and-Add algorithm or SOLA [24]. This algorithm consists in dividing the data signal into successive segments, and then adding these segments together with a certain overlap, as can be seen in the figure 2. The overlapping is performed so that the last part of each segments "fades-out", while the the first part of the next segment "fades-in", taking into account the cross-correlation of both overlapping sections to maximize the smoothness in the transition.

SOLA time-domain algorith provides a computationally fast time-stretching alternative. However, the main problem with the SOLA algorithm is that it works at its best with structurally simple signals (such as speech [25]), but not so well with polyphonic data, and the time-stretching range is more limited. In order to achieve better quality output, it is necessary to resort to more complex techniques.

In particular, we have implemented a time-stretching algorithm based on the phase vocoder [24]. The phase vocoder is a time-frequency processing technique that uses short-time Fourier analysis and synthesis to transform a given

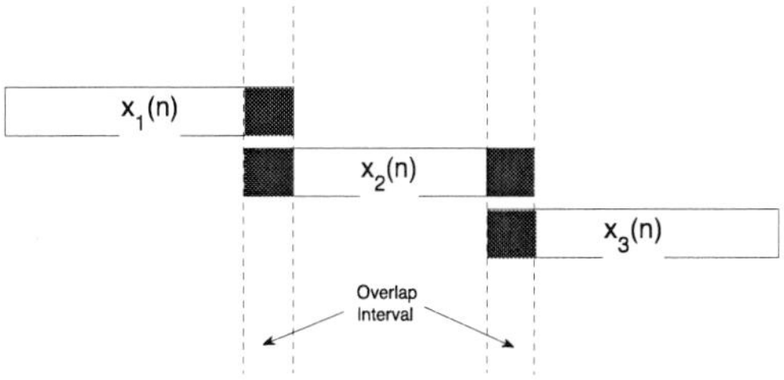

Figure 2. Time-stretching in time-domain

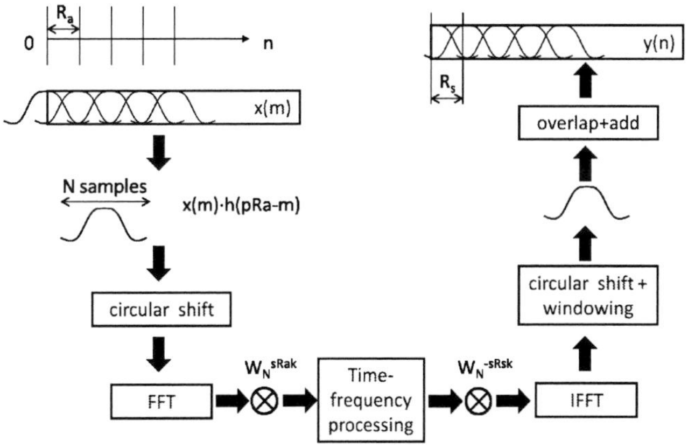

Figure 3. FFT/IFFT block implementation for phase vocoder

data signal, according to the equation of the short-time Fourier transform (STFT) with a window $h(n)$,

$$X(n,k) = \sum_{m=-\infty}^{\infty} x(m)h(n-m)W_N^{mk}$$

$$k = 0, 1, \dots, N-1, \quad W_N = e^{-j2\pi/N}$$

Working with this equation, it is possible to implement the phase vocoder using two different models [24]: the filter bank summation model and the block-by-block analysis/synthesis model. We have implemented our time-stretching algorithm following the latter. This model is based around the use of the fast fourier transform and its inverse (FFT/IFFT), dividing the input signal in overlapping segments (using a hop-size R_a). The FFT is performed then on each segment, as well as additional transformations to ensure phase coherency. After that, the data is processed as desired, and the output signal is synthesized using the inverse procedure, combining the successive processed segments by an overlap and add method with hop-size R_s. This process is portrayed in figure 3.

In order to implement time-stretching with a phase-vocoder, the hop-sizes for analysis and synthesis (R_a and R_s) are selected accordingly to the time-stretching factor desired (R_s/R_a), and the phase value for each frequency bin is adjusted accordingly [24]. In our application, the timestretching value ranged from 0.5 to 2.0.

2.2 Gesture recognition and interpretation

In order to conduct a given performance, an orchestra conductor gives a series of indications to the musicians by waving his hands, signalling the beat times, indicating the entry points, and controlling the dynamics of the whole ensemble. The role of the conductor is critical, as he is responsible for providing "expressiveness" to the performance. However, for a naïve user, giving the precise indications that a real conductor would give to the ensemble can easily become a daunting and nearly impossible task. For that reason, for the purpose of this application, we have focused on developing a gesture recognition system that can be used by expert and lay users alike. In particular, since the full-body skeleton-tracking functions of OpenNI/NITE provide the 3D coordinates for both hands of the user, we have assigned different functions to the right and left hand gestures respectively. Concretely, right-hand gesturing controls the tempo of the performance as well as the time positions of the beats, while left-hand gesturing controls the dynamics in the performance as well as the volume of each of the instruments taking part in the ensemble.

2.2.1 Conducting tempo

Beat times are indicated by moving the right hand in an horizontal waving motion; this gesture motion was selected as it was found in previous tests with users without musical background showed that they tended to wave their hands horizontally when asked to make conducting gestures, and, in general terms, users reported to be more comfortable with a horizontal motion rather than a vertical one when signalling high tempo. The system marks the time instant when the hand starts and stops a move (be it from left to right, or from right to left), and the time difference is then taken to calculate the new indicated conducting tempo in beats per minute. This time difference is then compared to the original tempo of the piece being played, thus calculating the time-stretching factor (T_s) that must be applied.

$$T_s = \frac{beatsPerMinuteOriginal}{beatsPerMinuteIndicated} \quad (1)$$

However, the system might give false positives if the measures are noisy. To ensure that detected motion does correspond to intended gestures indicated by the conductor, the length of the overall gesture is calculated, as per the following equations:

$$u(t) = \begin{cases} 1 & \text{if } |\frac{d\overrightarrow{p(t)}}{dt}| \geq V \\ 0 & \text{otherwise} \end{cases}$$

$$d(t) = \sum_{n=0}^{N_{start}} |(\overrightarrow{p(t-nT_f)} - \overrightarrow{p(t-(n-1)T_f)})| u(t)$$

where $\overrightarrow{p(t)}$ is the 3D vector position of the right hand at instant t, T_f represents the time between frames (roughly 30 milliseconds), N_{start} is the last known sample for which $u(t)$ changed to a value of 1 and V is a minimum velocity value (set at approximately 0.2 m/s). Thus, given a waving gesture, if that gesture is performed horizontally and the accumulated distance moved $d(t)$ exceeds a certain minimum value L, it is assumed that the user has performed a conducted gesture. L was set to a reasonable value for such waving gestures, but long enough so that no arbitrary noise could trigger a false positive (approximately 400 mm).

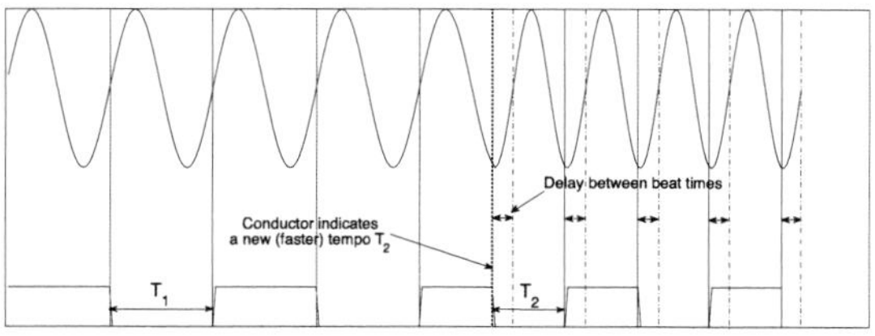

Figure 4. Delay effect when beat times are not properly synchronized

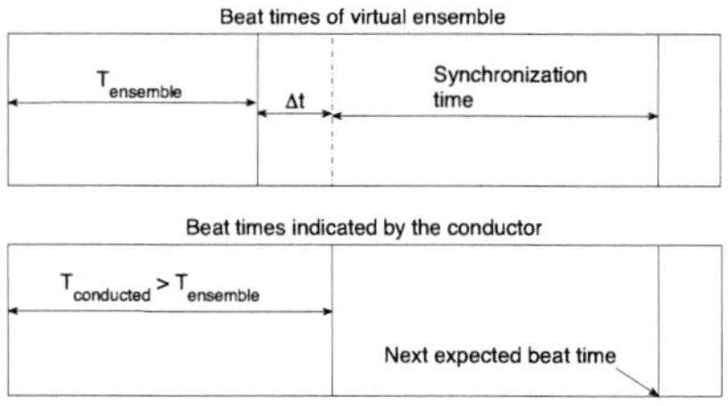

Figure 5. Beat time synchronization when the conductor indicates a slower tempo

However, the tempo conducted alone does not offer enough information for the system to adequately follow the conductor's indication, as just updating the system tempo without taking into consideration the actual position of the conducted beat times would result in a phase different between the beat times indicated by the conductor, and the actual beat times of the piece played. Such a situation creates the feeling that the orchestra is too slow and cannot follow the conductor gestures appropriately. This problem is better portrayed in figure 4, where the conductor's indicated tempo changes the period of a simple signal (a sinusoidal wave). If the conducted tempo only changes the playback tempo without taking the beat times into consideration (represented in the figure by the instants where the sinusoidal wave has a phase value of 0 radians), this introduces delay in the response of the system (the beat times of the piece played come at later time than the beat times indicated by the conductor).

To address this problem, it is necessary to synchronize the beat times of the piece played so that they match the next expected beat times that the conductor will most likely indicate. This assumption only makes sense if the tempo between beats is expected not to change too abruptly, but this is a reasonable assumption for the performance of an orchestra in real life. In particular, if the user conducts the virtual ensemble towards a slower tempo, the ensemble must actually play at an even slower tempo than the one indicated in order to synchronize its beat times with the ones of the conductor, and vice versa. This situation is portrayed in figure 6.

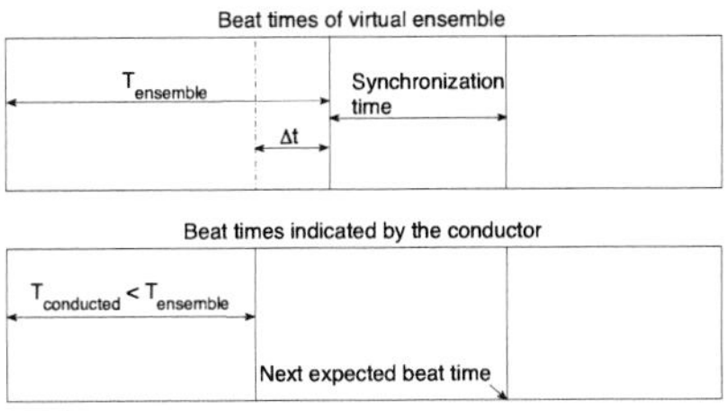

Figure 6. Beat time synchronization when the conductor indicates a faster tempo

In this figure, the user indicates a slower tempo with his gestures. However, the system does not realize this until a time of Δt seconds has passed. In order to match the conductor's next expected beat time, it is necessary to decrease even further the tempo of the piece played for the time period denoted as "synchronization time". The opposite situation is portrayed in figure 5, where the conductor indicates the system to increase the tempo.

Therefore, whenever the user conducts the orchestra to a change in tempo, the system takes into account this time difference Δt to properly synchronize its next expected beat time with the user indications, modifying the playing tempo accordingly. Thus, the timestretching factor T_s is updated according to the expected beat times by following these equations.

$$T_s = \begin{cases} \dfrac{T_{conducted}}{T_{conducted} - \Delta t} T_s & \text{if } T_{conducted} > T_{ensemble} \\ \dfrac{T_{conducted}}{T_{conducted} + \Delta t} T_s & \text{if } T_{conducted} < T_{ensemble} \end{cases}$$

Initially, the system followed these equations to instantly change the tempo in the piece played to match the beat times of the conductor. Nevertheless, we found that the changes occurred too abruptly, making the response of the virtual ensemble feel rather unnatural. In fact, given a real orchestra, the musicians would not probably change the tempo in their performance instantly with the motion of the conductor, but would rather do it over a period of time. Thus, in order to offer a more natural answer, a second iteration of the system was implemented. This second version still calculates the expected beat times for adequate synchronization, but instead of automatically updating the tempo to the new value indicated by the conductor, the system dynamically updates the tempo of the piece played until both system and conductor beat times are sufficiently synchronized. Concretely, the tempo is slowed or accelerated by adding a factor of ± 0.025 to the timestretching factor at a rate of 4 times per second (thus, the timestretching value is updated in intervals of 250 ms).

2.2.2 Control of dynamics

In this system, the conductor would use his left hand to indicate the system how to control the dynamics of the performance. In particular, by raising his left hand, the conductor indicates the system to raise the volume of the performance, while lowering the hand brings the volume down. The application also allows the user to select a specific instrument of the ensemble and modify the volume levels for that instrument exclusively. In particular, the user only has to point toward the instrument he wants to select, and raise or lower his left hand accordingly to whether he wishes to raise or lower the level of volume. The system determines which instrument the user is pointing at by calculating the pointing vector of his left arm, taking the left shoulder and left hand positions as references. The application indicates which instrument set is currently selected by placing a red arrow over the image that represents that instrument set (see figure 7).

Figure 7. Instrument selection for dynamics control

3. EXPERIMENTAL SETUP: METHODS AND MATERIALS

In this section, the different details of the experiment conducted will be presented, so that the same experiment can be easily reproduced by fellow researchers if needed.

3.1 Participants

A total of 24 participants took part in the experiment conducted, 3 female and 21 male, with ages ranging from 23 to 34 years (average 29,71 years, variance 10,30). There were 1 undergraduate, 15 graduates and 8 postgraduates. From the 24 participants, 2 had a strong formation in music, and 1 of these along with 2 more participants were actual professional musicians. Of the remaining 20 participants, 4 had played previously a musical instrument regularly. The rest of the participants (16) were nave musical users, with no previous formation or experience in music practice or music theory knowledge.

3.2 Materials

For the experiment, we used the previously discussed system. Thus, users were presented with a virtual reality application in which they had the possibility of modifying the tempo and/or the dynamics of the song played. For the purpose of the experiment, an excerpt of Peer Gynt's "In the hall of the mountain king" was played constantly in a loop while the system was tracking user's movements, and the playback was modified according to the motion detected. Two sets of instruments were considered for the tests with their corresponding WAV files: violin and trombone.

3.3 Procedure

The experiment was performed in a research lab in the School of Telecommunications of Málaga. Each participant performed the trials scheduled assisted by a researcher, who explained him/her the details of the tests as well as observed the participants behaviour during the experiment. Participants were instructed to use their right hand waving motion to conduct the tempo in the ensemble, and their left hand to indicate changes in dynamics (in the same way as described in the previous section). At the end of their performance, the researcher asked the participants to fill in a questionnaire concerning their opinion on the experience; additionally, the researcher also had a casual interview with the participants regarding their overall experience and their perception of the strengths and weak points of the system.

From a previous pilot study with a smaller sample of participants (4 in total), we had found that users did not notice the effects of the tempo synchronization algorithm in their experience, i.e., they seemed to be satisfied with just being able to change the tempo in the piece by "waving" their right hand, but did not pay attention to whether the beat times of the piece were synchronised or not with the hand motion's starting and ending points. Also, users had described the dynamic control interaction implemented to be sort of cumbersome and detrimental to the experience.

In order to further assess these issues, we defined two experimental factors in our study: a *tempo* factor and a *dynamics* factor. The *tempo* factor controls whether the synchronization algorithm previously described was present or not, while the *dynamics* factor controls whether the user can modify the dynamics in the piece being played, or just the tempo of the piece.

The combination of the two factors yields a total of $2 \times 2 = 4$ experimental conditions. A repeated measures approach was followed [26], so that there were 4 experimental sessions for each participant, each session corresponding to one of the aforementioned experimental conditions. To avoid order effects, the order in which the participants performed their sessions was fully counter-balanced. Each session was scheduled to last no less than 2 minutes and no more than 7 minutes. Each participant was told to spend as much time as they deemed necessary "playing" with the application at each experimental session, and were only instructed to stop or continue if the aforementioned time constraints were not met.

3.4 Data retrieval on user experience

The data was collected from the questions listed in the questionnaire which participants filled in at the end of the experiment. In extent, each participant was asked to evaluate the following aspects of their experience with a score from 0 (least satisfactory) to 10 (most satisfactory):

- Overall satisfaction with the application (*Satisfaction*)
- Level of control over the parameters of the piece played (*OverallControl*)
- Level of control over the tempo of the piece played (*TempoControl*)
- Synchronization between motion and the changes in the piece played (*Synchronization*)
- How intuitive was the interaction (*Intuitiveness*)
- Ease of use of the application (*EaseOfUse*)
- Level of realism perceived (*Realism*)

For each of this items, a dependent variable was created (with the name indicated in brackets). In addition to the aforementioned items, users were also encouraged to state personal comments and impressions regarding their experience with the application.

4. RESULTS

In order to analyze the variables, a repeated measures two-factors ANOVA 2×2 was performed on the factors *tempo* and *dynamics* previously defined. The principal effects analysis for the *tempo* factor had a significant effect on the variables *Satisfaction*($F_{1,23} = 25.09, p < 0.000$), *OverallControl*($F_{1,23} = 18.81, p < 0.000$), *TempoControl*($F_{1,23} = 21.49$, $p < 0.000$), *Synchronization*($F_{1,23} = 15.02$, $p < 0.001$) and *Realism*($F_{1,23} = 6.27$, $p < 0.020$). In the case of the *dynamics* factor, there was a significant effect on the variables *Satisfaction*($F_{1,23} = 9.75$, $p < 0.005$), *OverallControl*($F_{1,23} = 9.37$, $p < 0.006$), *Synchronization*($F_{1,23} = 15.02$,$p < 0.005$), *Intuitiveness*($F_{1,23} = 5.28$, $p < 0.031$) and *EaseOfUse*($F_{1,23} = 13.80$, $p < 0.001$). The estimated marginal means for the variables *Satisfaction*, *OverallControl*, *TempoControl* and *Synchronization* are presented in figure 8.

The quantitative effects that each of these factors had on the average values for each of the variables observed are summarized in table 1. Concretely, in the case of the *tempo* factor, every variable where it had a significant effect increases its value when the tempo synchronization algorithm is present. The same situation is found for the *dynamics* factor, with the exception of *Intuitiveness* and *EaseOfUse* variables, which offer lower values when the user is allowed to control the dynamics of the piece.

No significant second order interactions were found between the two experimental factors considered ($F_{1,23} <= 3.01$ for all the variables observed). Overall, user experience according to the variables observed was quite positive, with *Intuitiveness* being the variable that scored the highest values and *EaseOfUse* being the one that presented the highest variance. Figure 9 illustrates the average score for each variable and their standard deviations.

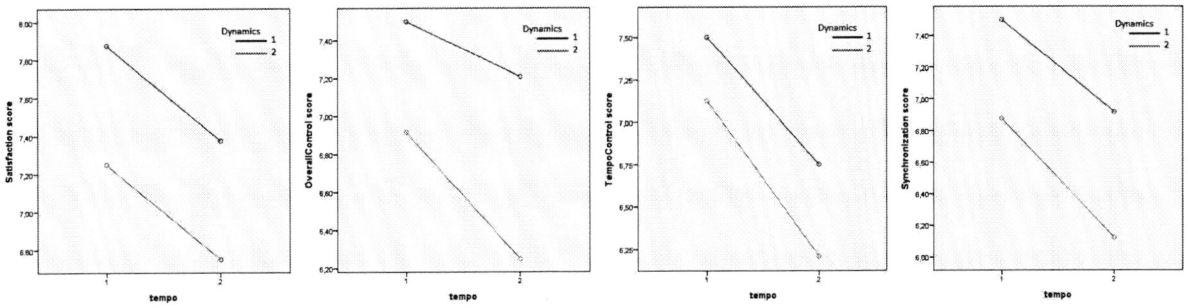

Figure 8. Estimated Marginal Means for the dependent variables Satisfaction, OverallControl, TempoControl and Synchronization. The *tempo* factor takes values 1 (tempo synchronization present) or 2 (tempo synchronization not present). The *dynamics* factor takes values 1 (dynamics control present) or 2 (dynamics control not present)

	Cond. 1	Cond. 2	Cond. 3	Cond. 4
Satisfaction	7.875	7.25	7.375	6.75
OverallControl	7.5	6.917	7.208	6.25
TempoControl	7.5	7.125	6.75	6.208
Synchronization	7.5	6.875	6.917	6.125
Intuitiveness	8.292	8.417	8.125	8.458
EaseOfUse	7.208	7.792	7	7.7917
Realism	7.25	7.083	7	6.833

Table 1. Average scores for each variable observed at each of the 4 experimental conditions: condition 1 (both tempo synchronization and dynamics control present), condition 2 (only tempo synchronization present), condition 3 (only dynamics control present) and condition 4 (none present)
.

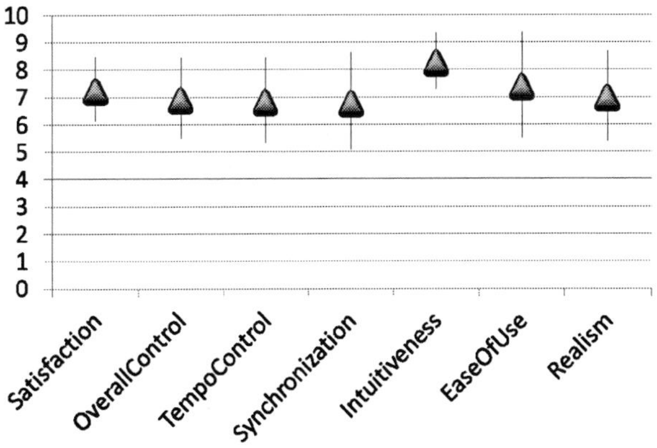

Figure 9. Average values for the variables considered, along with $\pm$ their standard deviations σ

5. DISCUSSION

The results yielded from the experiment conducted showed a quite positive response from the participants that took part in the experiment. As expected, an adequate synchronization between the beat times in the piece and the starting and final positions of user's "waving" motions was critical to the overall experience of the user. Interestingly though, from the interviews had with the participants, the vast majority of them did not consciously notice a significant difference between the two tempo conducting modes considered. Nevertheless, the results extracted from the analysis of the variables observed did show that user perception of satisfaction, control and realism among others was indeed significantly higher if the beat times of the piece were adequately synchronised with the beat times of the hand. In the case of the 4 participants that had a strongest musical background, they did acknowledge to have noticed this difference between the two conducting modes, yet no particular differences were found in the statistical analysis performed in this regard.

The presence of dynamics control showed also a positive income in user experience regarding satisfaction, control and synchronization. However, the added complexity of the interface made the system less intuitive and, especially, more difficult to use. In fact, from observation of user behaviour during the experiments, some of the participants found it difficult to control both tempo and dynamics at the same time, as their left hand might hamper their right hand motion when trying to select the violin. This is a flaw that comes mainly from the camera-based nature of the system, as it may be possible that one hand obscured the line of sight of the 3D sensor to the other one. In the particular case of the right hand, the system was highly sensitive to this kind of occlusion.

Previous work has focused mainly on capturing the conductor's gestures to modify the tempo of the piece played by applying the corresponding timestretching algorithm. A few studies, however, have also implemented the possibility of controlling the dynamics of the piece played, as is the case of Borchers et al. [15], offering a much more complete experience to the users. Our work also aims to offer this more complete experience, by adding the possibility of controlling the volume of the different instruments in the ensemble. However, as found in the tests performed, additional steps must be taken to ensure that users can actively used both hands without interfering the commands given by each other because of occlusion.

Most of the previous research has favored the use of infrared or inertial batons [15] [16] [17] [18], or, more recently, the use of Nintendo's Wiimote [19] [20]. However, this kind of devices is usually very expensive [17] or have ergonomic and usability issues (in the case of the Wii Remote, its shape is not that adequate for baton emulation, and its additional weight when compared with an infrared baton [21] might rise some issues in long sessions). By using a Kinect device as the basis of our system, we provide a non-intrusive interaction paradigm that minimizes the effects of such issues (both major and minor). Interestingly though, we would like to point out the fact that, in our user study, we also found that a small sample of the participants got "tired" after the experimental sessions and even reported arm pain because of the conducting gesture (2 cases). However, this can be explained in the unusual length of the experimental sessions.

Finally, one aspect that some participants criticized in the application was that they perceived some lag between their motion and the response given by the system. This is caused because of a delay introduced by the sensing device, and it is an issue where the system should be improved in its next iteration.

6. CONCLUSIONS AND FUTURE WORK

In this paper we have presented the work performed towards the implementation of an advanced human-computer interface for conductor simulation, using an off-the-shelf device that allows for optimal usability without involving a high purchase cost. We have implemented a time-stretching algorithm for tempo modification and developed a gesture recognition system for dynamics and tempo indication by the user. The application developed has been tested by musicians and naïve users, with positive impressions on the experience perceived by both types of users. Also, it has been experimentally confirmed that the addition of a better synchronization algorithm and dynamics control does indeed improve user experience, even if the users were not consciously aware of it. From the results yielded in the experiment, we conclude that the application developed provides a satisfactory exploratory experience in music interaction, which can be enjoyed alike by nave and expert users.

In future works we hope to improve further on the system designed. In particular, we intend on improving the gesture recognition module to expand the range of gestures identified from the already supported waving gesture to more complex gestures similar to the ones performed by orchestra conductors according to the time signature of the piece played. Also, as indicated in previous works [27], other features from the conductor's gesturing and body expression can have a significant effect on musician action. We also hope to expand the tests of the application by performing a larger user study to gather additional data in order to identify other key aspects where the application can be improved towards a better user experience. Last but not least, as satisfactory as the user response has been, we have found that issues like hand occlusion and lag perception need to addressed and improved upon for future implementations of the system.

Acknowledgments

This work has been funded by the Ministerio de Economia y Competitividad of the Spanish Government under Project No. TIN2010-21089-C03-02 and Project No. IPT-2011-0885-430000 and by the Junta de Andalucia under Project No. P11-TIC-7154. The work has been done at Universidad de Málaga. Campus de Excelencia Internacional Andalucía Tech.

7. REFERENCES

[1] S. Jordà, "The reactable: tangible and tabletop music performance," in *Proceedings of the 28th of the international conference extended abstracts on Human factors in computing systems.* ACM, 2010, pp. 2989–2994.

[2] A. Antle, M. Droumeva, and G. Corness, "Playing with the sound maker: do embodied metaphors help children learn?" in *Proceedings of the 7th international conference on Interaction design and children.* ACM, 2008, pp. 178–185.

[3] E. Khoo, T. Merritt, V. Fei, W. Liu, H. Rahaman, J. Prasad, and T. Marsh, "Body music: physical exploration of music theory," in *Proceedings of the 2008 ACM SIGGRAPH symposium on Video games*, 2008, pp. 35–42.

[4] G. Castellano, R. Bresin, A. Camurri, and G. Volpe, "Expressive control of music and visual media by full-body movement," in *Proceedings of the 7th international conference on New interfaces for musical expression.* ACM, 2007, pp. 390–391.

[5] M. Halpern, J. Tholander, M. Evjen, S. Davis, A. Ehrlich, K. Schustak, E. Baumer, and G. Gay, "Moboogie: creative expression through whole body musical interaction," in *Proceedings of the 2011 annual conference on Human factors in computing systems.* ACM, 2011, pp. 557–560.

[6] L. Gower and J. McDowall, "Interactive music video games and children's musical development," *British Journal of Music Education*, vol. 29, no. 01, pp. 91–105, 2012.

[7] C. Wang and A. Lai, "Development of a mobile rhythm learning system based on digital game-based learning companion," *Edutainment Technologies. Educational Games and Virtual Reality/Augmented Reality Applications*, pp. 92–100, 2011.

[8] G. Levin and Z. Lieberman, "In-situ speech visualization in real-time interactive installation and performance," in *Non-Photorealistic Animation and Rendering: Proceedings of the 3 rd international symposium on Non-photorealistic animation and rendering*, vol. 7, no. 09, 2004, pp. 7–14.

[9] S. Bakker, E. van den Hoven, and A. Antle, "Moso tangibles: evaluating embodied learning," in *Proceedings*

of the fifth international conference on Tangible, embedded, and embodied interaction. ACM, 2011, pp. 85–92.

[10] S. Holland, A. Bouwer, M. Dalgelish, and T. Hurtig, "Feeling the beat where it counts: fostering multi-limb rhythm skills with the haptic drum kit," in *Proceedings of the fourth international conference on Tangible, embedded, and embodied interaction*. ACM, 2010, pp. 21–28.

[11] S. Trail, M. Dean, T. Tavares, G. Odowichuk, P. Driessen, W. Schloss, and G. Tzanetakis, "Non-invasive sensing and gesture control for pitched percussion hyper-instruments using the kinect," 2012.

[12] K. Ng, "Music via motion: transdomain mapping of motion and sound for interactive performances," *Proceedings of the IEEE*, vol. 92, no. 4, pp. 645–655, 2004.

[13] A. Hofer, A. Hadjakos, and M. Mhlhuser, "Gyroscope-Based Conducting Gesture Recognition," in *Proceedings of the International Conference on New Interfaces for Musical Expression*, 2009, pp. 175–176. [Online]. Available: http://www.nime.org/proceedings/2009/nime2009_175.pdf

[14] H. Morita, S. Hashimoto, and S. Ohteru, "A computer music system that follows a human conductor," *Computer*, vol. 24, no. 7, pp. 44–53, 1991.

[15] J. Borchers, E. Lee, W. Samminger, and M. Mühlhäuser, "Personal orchestra: A real-time audio/video system for interactive conducting," *Multimedia Systems*, vol. 9, no. 5, pp. 458–465, 2004.

[16] L. Peng and D. Gerhard, "A wii-based gestural interface for computer-based conducting systems," in *Proceedings of the 2009 Conference on New Interfaces For Musical Expression*, 2009.

[17] E. Lee, T. Nakra, and J. Borchers, "You're the conductor: a realistic interactive conducting system for children," in *Proceedings of the 2004 conference on New interfaces for musical expression*. National University of Singapore, 2004, pp. 68–73.

[18] P. Bakanas, J. Armitage, J. Balmer, P. Halpin, K. Hudspeth, and K. Ng, "mconduct: Gesture transmission and reconstruction for distributed performance," in *ECLAP 2012 Conference on Information Technologies for Performing Arts, Media Access and Entertainment*. Firenze University Press, 2012, p. 107.

[19] D. Bradshaw and K. Ng, "Analyzing a conductors gestures with the wiimote," in *Proceedings of EVA London 2008: the International Conference of Electronic Visualisation and the Arts*, 2008.

[20] T. Nakra, Y. Ivanov, P. Smaragdis, and C. Ault, "The ubs virtual maestro: An interactive conducting system," *NIME2009*, pp. 250–255, 2009.

[21] T. Baba, M. Hashida, and H. Katayose, "virtualphilharmony: A conducting system with heuristics of conducting an orchestra," in *Proceedings of the 2010 Conference on New Interfaces for Musical Expression (NIME 2010)*, 2010, pp. 263–270.

[22] D. Shreiner, *OpenGL reference manual: The official reference document to OpenGL, version 1.2*. Addison-Wesley Longman Publishing Co., Inc., 1999.

[23] G. Junker, *Pro OGRE 3D programming*. Apress, 2006.

[24] U. Zölzer, X. Amatriain, and J. Wiley, *DAFX: digital audio effects*. Wiley Online Library, 2002, vol. 1.

[25] D. Malah, "Time-domain algorithms for harmonic bandwidth reduction and time scaling of speech signals," *Acoustics, Speech and Signal Processing, IEEE Transactions on*, vol. 27, no. 2, pp. 121–133, 1979.

[26] D. C. Howell, *Statistical methods for psychology*. Wadsworth Publishing Company, 2012.

[27] K. Parton and G. Edwards, "Features of conductor gesture: Towards a framework for analysis within interaction," in *The Second International Conference on Music Communication Science, 3-4 December 2009, Sydney, Australia*, 2009.

VIRTUAL CONDUCTOR FOR STRING QUARTET PRACTICE

R. Baez, A.M. Barbancho, A. Rosa-Pujazón, I. Barbancho, L.J. Tardón
Dpt. Ingeniería de Comunicaciones, E.T.S.I. Telecomunicación,
Universidad de Málaga, Campus de Teatinos s/n, 29071 Málaga, Spain
abp@ic.uma.es, ibp@ic.uma.es, alejandror@uma.es, lorenzo@ic.uma.es

ABSTRACT

This paper presents a system that emulates an ensemble conductor for string quartets. This application has been developed as a support tool for individual and group practice, so that users of any age range can use it to further hone their skills, both for regular musicians and students alike. The virtual conductor designed can offer similar indications to those given by a real ensemble conductor to potential users regarding beat times, dynamics, etc. The application developed allows the user to rehearse his/her performance without the need of having an actual conductor present, and also gives access to additional tools to further support the learning/practice process, such as a tuner or a melody evaluator. The system developed also allows for both solo practice and group practice. A set of tests were conducted to check the usefulness of the application as a practice support tool. A group of musicians from the Chamber Orchestra of Málaga including an ensemble conductor tested the system, and reported to have found it a very useful tool within an educational environment and that it helps to address the lack of this kind of educational tools in a self-learning environment.

1. INTRODUCTION

In recent years, our society has experienced a vast development of information and communication technologies as well as its integration in our everyday life. This phenomena has also spread to schools and educational models. Thus, for example, the use of internet has become an important asset in the classroom environment [1], as well as learning how to find a particular type of information among the different web resources as well as discriminating useful knowledge from redundant data. Furthermore, students are active users of many of the current Web 2.0 applications and emerging technologies, such as Facebook, Twitter and social networks in general, wikis, blogs, etc., and while the use of these resources in the classroom has not been yet consolidated, there is an intent and general agreement that the use of such tools could improve the learning process for the students, improving learning outcomes and/or creativity in the student [2], [3], [4], [5].

However, when it comes to the field of music studies, this array of tools might prove to be partially lacking. Of course, it is possible to make use of conventional web resources as a way to increase students' motivation towards learning, thus lowering potential barriers in regards to the abstract nature of music theory concepts. But music is a subject that relies heavily on practising and puts a special focus on interacting with other musicians to play complex pieces. With regards to this, the most conventional interaction paradigms and web 2.0 resources might prove to be insufficient, therefore requiring the use of more specialized tools and applications to provide a more specific interface for an adequate learning experience.

Looking into the research performed by the community in the field of human-computer interfaces for music interaction, there is a wide range of potential application fields and interaction models: virtual musical instrument creation/simulation [6], gaming and serious gaming [7], [8], [9], body-motion-to-sound mapping [10], [11], [12], guitar chords and frets detection [13], [14], singing voice interaction [15], tangible and haptic instrument simulation [16], [17], virtual drumkit emulation and drum-hitting simulation [18], [19], [20], etc. Particularly, with regards to orchestra conducting, there are a handful of systems and applications proposed that capture the conductor's gesture to control parameters of a virtual orchestra, such as tempo [21], [22], [23], [24] as well as dynamics [25], [26].

It is clear then that current technologies allow for the implementation of practice-oriented applications. Yet, from the perspective of a support tool for learning, most of these systems show some shortcomings that make them a less feasible solution. In extent, some of this interfaces are too exclusively focus on offering a recreational experience that can hardly be translated into a learning framework, and especially most of the examples cited require the use of very specialized hardware, thus limiting the potential target audience that can benefit from their use. Therefore, there is a need for more learning-oriented and accessible applications that can be used by students as a way to further improve their skills. Also, there is a lack of applications that make use of these technologies as a learning tool or to address concrete issues regarding musical practice.

In the case of string quartet groups, one problem typically found with regards to practising is that it can be difficult to coordinate all five members of the quartet for a given practice session. This can be specially critical if the conductor is not present, for in this case the rest of the musicians find it much more difficult to synchronize their

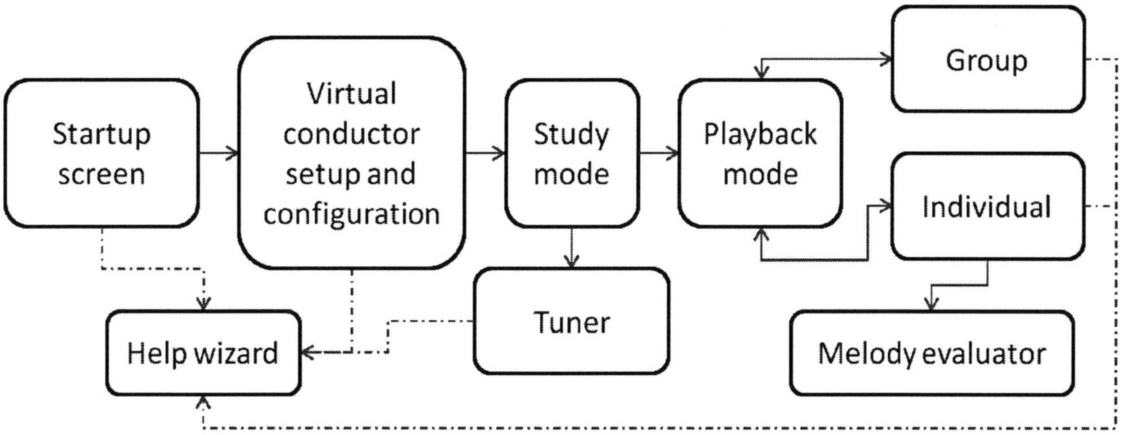

Figure 1. Modules of the Virtual Director application.

performances properly. This can ultimately make the value of the practice session diminish greatly. Thus, it would be quite useful to have a computer application that could provide beat and dynamics indications similar to those given by a real-life conductor. In this paper, we present an application developed to fulfil such purpose. In particular, this application implements a virtual orchestra conductor simulator for string quartet practice. Concretely, the system allows a musician to practise his/her performance either individually or in a group, and assess and evaluates the user's performance. In the next section, the details of the implementation of this virtual conductor will be covered, and later, the results of the tests performed will be briefly presented and discussed.

2. DESCRIPTION OF THE VIRTUAL CONDUCTOR SYSTEM

This application will emulate the role of a virtual conductor so that a musician can practise his performance as part of a string quartet ensemble. The application will assume a string quartet ensemble of four different instruments: violin, viola, cello and contrabass; however, the system can be configured to a different set of instruments, such as the more typical distribution of 2 violins, 1 viola and 1 cello. The system gives indications to the user regarding the beat times, changes in tempo, etc. The system also offers feedback to the user regarding his/her performance, evaluating the accuracy of the student when playing the corresponding piece. The application stores the information of each of melodies considered in MIDI format, and also allows for the playback of the MIDI data, so that the user can hear the piece as a whole for a better reference.

In this section, the general structure of the virtual conductor implemented will be presented, as well as the details of the components which the application consists of. A drawing of the different modules can be found in Fig. 1. The application will start with a presentation screen and then prompt a configuration menu to setup the virtual conductor parameters desired for the intended practice session. The system allows for two different study and playback modes, depending on whether the user wishes to perform solo or group practice. The application includes also a tuner module to ensure that the instruments are properly tuned before starting the practice session, as well as a melody evaluator that gives the user feedback on how accurate is his/her performance. A set of help menus are also provided to assist musicians in the use of the application.

The most relevant functionalities of the system will be described in the following subsections. In particular, the most important blocks in the application are the tuner, the melody evaluator and the virtual conductor emulation itself.

2.1 Tuner

When playing an instrument, it is extremely important to ensure that the notes played by the instruments are the ones that should be, in extent, that the instrument is properly tuned. In the case of string instruments, such as the violin or the viola, the musician must typically rely on his hearing acuteness and a tuning fork. To address this issue, the application includes a tuner module to assist the user in this procedure.

The music signal is recorded by a microphone, and then its spectrum is calculated with a sample frequency of 88200 Hz (thus allowing for a spectral resolution of 0.5 Hz). The tuner module was implemented following a similar detection method to the one presented in [27], analysing the spectrum of the signal recorded, and subsequently extracting the fundamental and partial frequencies. In order to do so, the peaks in the spectrum are detected by finding its local optima (using a window of 5 samples to the left and right of each potential peak candidate).

After that, a threshold value (set at a 20% of the maximum amplitude value found) is set to prune undesired peaks in the spectrum, following an iterative process: the sample with the highest magnitude is found, the 4 adjacent samples are erased (to account for the slopes of the peak), and a new iteration begins. Once the spectrum has been simplified this way, the distances between each successive peak $d(n_i, n_{i+1})$ are calculated and stored. In the standard frequency domain, the fundamentals and partials of a note would be found equally spaced along the spectrum, in frequencies f_{pitch}, $2f_{pitch}$, $3f_{pitch}$, $4f_{pitch}$ etc. Following this schema, it is possible to detect the fundamental

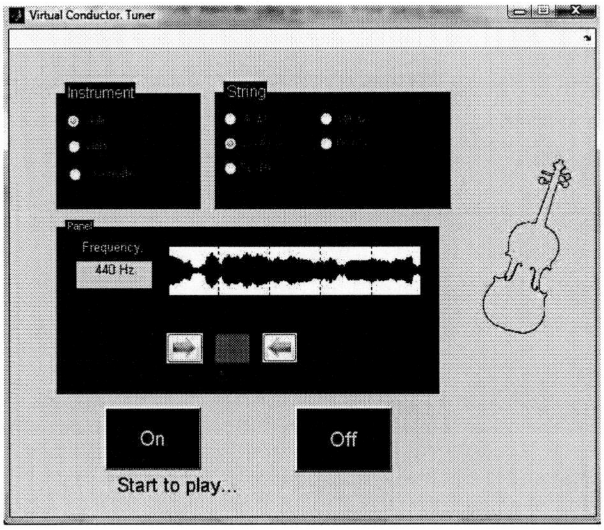

Figure 2. Tuner module interface.

and partial frequencies, thus effectively extracting the pitch of the note played. The system then evaluates each peak detected to determine whether it belongs to fundamental-partials set or not. If the system finds either the fundamental frequency and at least 2 partials, or, alternatively, 3 partials or more, then it proceeds to assess whether the string is tuned or not. If the fundamental frequency of the note detected is within 2.2 Hz of the expected value, it is assumed that the corresponding string is tuned. Otherwise, the string must be tuned accordingly.

Depending on the type of instrument that the musician is playing (violin, viola, contrabass or cello) and the string being tuned, the system indicates the user whether the string is properly tuned (by turning a red button into green) or if it is necessary to either tune up or down the string played (by lighting the corresponding arrow), as can be seen in Fig. 2.

2.2 Melody evaluator

The purpose of this module is to analyse the piece played by the user, extracting the melody from the signal sampled and checking whether the student is playing the right notes or not. In order to perform this analysis, the audio signal is windowed so that each window holds the audio samples corresponding to each of the beats given by the virtual conductor.

The system knows beforehand which notes should play at each beat/bar from the data stored in the MIDI files. Thus, for each beat in the time signature, the system checks the MIDI data to identify the notes that should be played at that particular beat. For each window, the application uses the same detection method as for the tuner to find the fundamental frequencies, and compares them to the ones that should be had according to the notes assigned to that beat.

It may be possible that a time delay were introduced in the processing stage of the signal, therefore creating a potential desynchronization in the alignment of the MIDI score and the actual performance of the user. To account for this lack of synchronization, the system not only checks for each note in the corresponding beat window, but also in

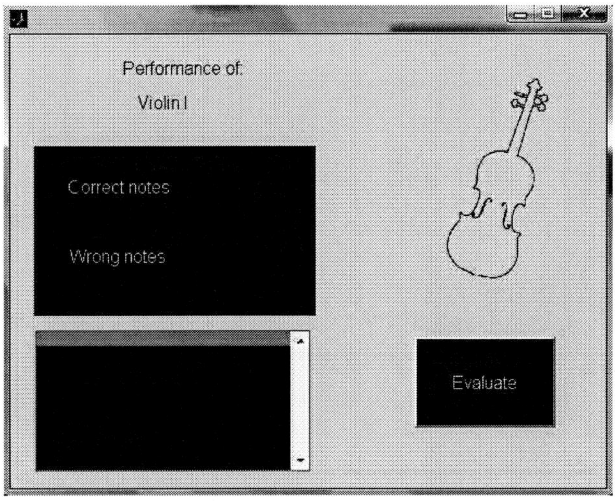

Figure 3. Melody evaluator dialog.

both the previous and next window.

Once the candidate notes have been detected, the system then evaluates if the notes played are the ones expected or if the user has made a mistake in his/her performance. For each note detected, it is assumed to be "correct" if the difference between the fundamental frequencies of the note detected and the expected one is lower to the minimum difference between the lowest note for the instrument considered and its sharp version. For example, in the case of the violin, the lowest note available is G3, and the difference between G3 and G#3 is 11 Hz. Thus, if a given detected note is within 11 Hz of the note expected for the time beat evaluated, the system labels it as a correct note, or as a mistake otherwise.

For each melody evaluated, the system indicates the user the amount of correctly played notes, as well as the number of notes which the user played wrong, and the corresponding beat times in the score. The dialog in the final application can be seen at Fig. 3).

2.3 Virtual Conductor

The main functionality of the system implemented is that of emulating the indications that an ensemble conductor gives to his/her fellow musicians when practising and playing a given piece. In order to implement this functionality, the system uses a virtual baton, represented by a set of four circles displayed on the computer screen. These circles change their colour and shape according to the beat and dynamics of piece played and the indication of the user in the configuration step. Each of the circles is placed in each of the four positions of the hands/baton that are typically used to signal beat times (up, down, left and right). At each beat time, the corresponding circle is coloured. The circles are coloured as if seen from the point of view of the musician, i.e. a 3/4 time signature would be signalled in the order down-right-up. The colour and size of each circle changes with the dynamics of the beat. Thus, for a *piano* or *pianissimo* nuance, there is a small light-coloured circle, while for a *mezzoforte-forte* intensity, the circle becomes larger and darker (see Fig. 4).

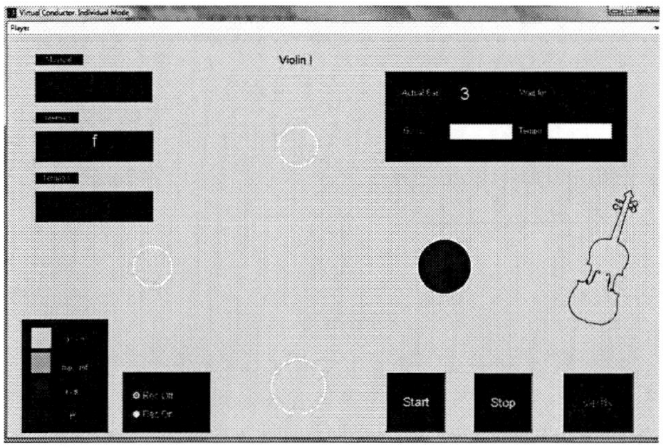

Figure 4. Virtual conductor for solo practice.

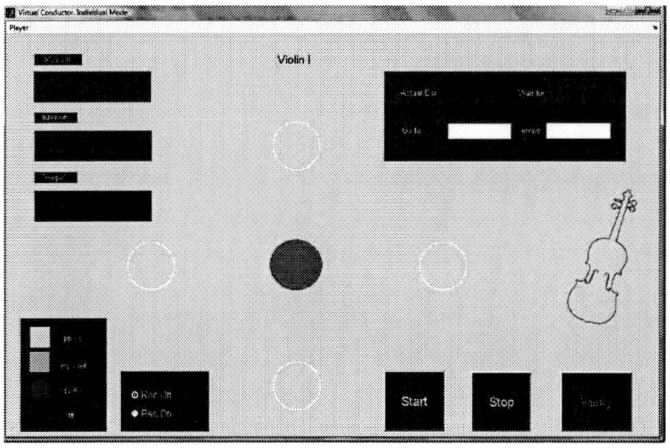

Figure 5. Indication of a *fermata*.

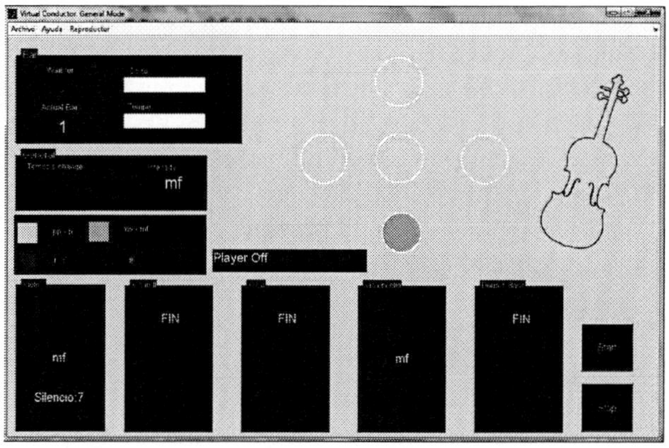

Figure 6. Virtual conductor for group practice.

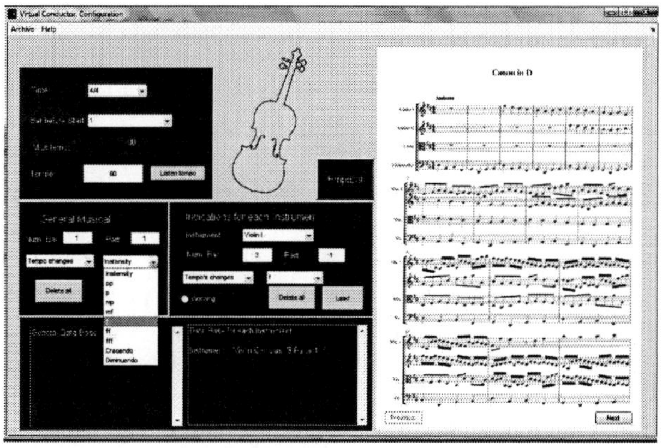

Figure 7. Configuration options with on-screen score.

In addition to the virtual baton, the application also gives additional visual feedback to the user to further guide his performance. In particular, dynamics nuances are also indicated in written form under the label "Intensity", as well as additional dynamics indications (such as *ritardando* or *fermata*) under the the label "Tempo"; in the case of indicating a *fermata*, this is further signalled to the user by painting a red circle in the center of the baton (as per Fig. 5). Furthermore, there might and will be bars in a piece where a given instrument is not played at all; such indications are given under the label "Musical".

The current bar number is also provided for further reference for the user. The user can also stop the performance at any time, restart at any given bar number, and manually change the tempo on the fly. This last option has been provided to specifically account for the fact that the tempo in rehearsals is usually initially lower to the actual tempo of the piece, and it is slowly increased as the musicians practise further.

The virtual conductor can be used for solo practice or group practice. In the case of the latter, the information provided by the system differs slightly from the previously commented features. Concretely, the space devoted to the virtual baton on the screen is more confined, and the indications given refer to the general indications that affect every single instrument globally. For specific indications for each of the instruments taking part in the performance, a set of panels are provided (first and second violin, viola, cello and contrabass) as seen in Fig. 6

2.4 Other modules

The virtual director tools has been design so that it can be fully configured to the needs of the student as well as providing an intuitive and easy to use interface. In that regard, the application also includes several modules and options to offer a more satisfying and complete experience to the user, such as a help menu, the possibility of loading music scores for reference on the screen, setting the tempo and speed nuances (*ritardando*,*fermata*, *crescendo*, *diminuendo* ect.), indicate a specific bar, an *anacrusis*, etc. An example of the configuration screen can be seen at Fig. 7

3. RESULTS AND DISCUSSION

3.1 Tuner

We conducted a set of tests to verify the correctness of the tuner implemented. In order to do so, we had access to a set of string instruments, and tuned them using the tuner module developed. Since the frequency of the notes for each string in a properly tuned instrument is known, checking the validity of the tuner application is immediate once the frequency peaks (fundamentals and partials) are extracted.

For the violin, it was found that the fundamental frequency for the G3 note could not be detected, but the string could still be tuned by detecting the first partial. The same result was obtained for the C3 note in the case of the viola. In the case of the cello, the fundamental frequency for the C2 note could not be found, nor could the first partial, but the note being played could still be detected by looking at the second partial. For all the other cases, the fundamental frequency of the note played was always detected, and thus it was possible to tune each string accordingly.

3.2 Melody evaluator

In order to test the viability of the melody evaluator implemented, we conducted a simple experiment in which a musician played a short piece, and the system gives a ratio of successfully played notes. For the tests, we used a set of melodies from pieces for the different string instruments considered (violin, viola, cello and contrabass).

The results yielded showed that the success rate oscillated between 100% and 84%, depending on the melody played and instrument used, with the best results found in the case of the cello (100% success rate with all the melodies), and the worst results (84% success rate) was found in the case of both the viola and the violin when playing Pachabel's Canon.

After analysing the spectrum of the melody played, it was found that the errors found in all cases were caused because of a lack of proper tuning of the instruments. For example, in the case of Pachabel's Canon for the violin, the error notes were F3 (739 Hz) and C3 (554 Hz); the fundamental peaks were not detected themselves, but the first partials detected for each note were at 1468 Hz and 1111.5 Hz respectively, while it should have been 1478 Hz and 1108 Hz had the instrument been properly tuned. After tuning all the instruments considered and repeating the tests with the same pieces, it was found that the melody evaluator had now a ratio of successfully detected notes of 100% in all cases.

3.3 Virtual conductor

To assess the effectiveness of the virtual conductor system as a learning tool, we presented the application to a set of musicians from the Chamber Orchestra of Málaga, as well to an ensemble conductor. Each participant learned how to use the application and was asked a total of 6 questions which they had to answer with a value ranging from 0 to 10, being the former the score given if they found no real utility to the tool, and the latter the one in case they found it extremely useful. The questions in particular were:

1. How useful did you found the tool developed?
2. Was the program easy to use?
3. Would you use this tool in your practice?
4. Do you find the tool useful as a way to enhance learning processes?
5. Are the indications given by the virtual conductor clear enough?
6. Please, state your personal opinion.

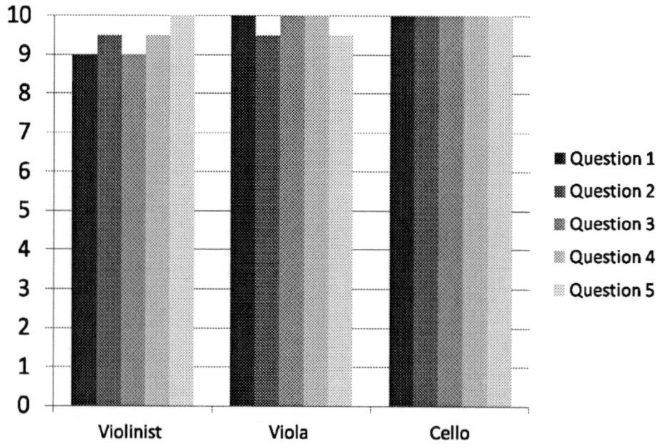

Figure 8. Virtual Conductor assessment from users' questionnaire.

The answers collected were overwhelmingly positive, with the average scores for all the items in the questionnaire being between 9 and 10. The average scores for each of the 5 questions are summarized in Fig. 8, in different sets according to the instrument played by the musicians that took part in the study. In their personal opinions, the participants also indicated that they found the tool especially useful both for solo and group practice, and that it would be desirable that there were more similar commercial products available, for it covers an important aspect with regards to music learning that is lacking in current paradigm.

The system was also tested by a professional ensemble conductor, who found the virtual conductor proposed to be an excellent pedagogical tool for musicians at any learning stage, as it addresses one important handicap in the learning process, which is solo rehearsing of chamber pieces. Furthermore, she found particularly enticing the group practice possibilities of the application, for it makes the learning process less lonely as well as it gives the student a much better context for his/her performance.

4. CONCLUSIONS AND FUTURE WORKS

In this paper we have presented the work conducted towards the development of a support tool for music learning that emulates the role of an ensemble conductor. The system does not only give indications similar to the ones given by a real-life conductor, but it also provides additional functionalities that further enhance or ease the learning experience, such as built-in tuner or a melody evaluator. To further validate the usefulness of the application developed, a set of experiments were conducted. The fellow musicians who tested the proposed system deemed it to be a really useful tool for the purposes of music learning, and highly encouraged that similar devices were available in the future, as there is a need for such kind of support tools that is not currently covered with the currently available resources.

While the response of the participants was quite positive, we would like to further improved the discussed tool in future iterations by integrating additional functionalities. The system can also be extended to account for a wider range of instrument than that of string instruments (e.g. wind instruments). Adapting the system to make use of real WAV files instead of MIDI files for playback would increase the audio fidelity of the system, providing more realistic sounds. The interface might be improved further with the addition of additional (such as changes over time on arousal and valence) as well as with the implementation of a more refined presentation of the cues (like, for example, having a virtual 3D model of the director giving indications in a more continuous, realistic way).

Acknowledgments

This work has been funded by the Ministerio de Economia y Competitividad of the Spanish Government under Project No. TIN2010-21089-C03-02 and Project No. IPT-2011-0885-430000 and by the Junta de Andalucia under Project No. P11-TIC-7154. The work has been done at Universidad de Málaga. Campus de Excelencia Internacional Andalucía Tech.

5. REFERENCES

[1] J. Schofield and A. Davidson, *Bringing the Internet to School: Lessons from an Urban District. The Jossey-Bass Education Series.* ERIC, 2002.

[2] H. Ajjan and R. Hartshorne, "Investigating faculty decisions to adopt web 2.0 technologies: Theory and empirical tests," *The Internet and Higher Education*, vol. 11, no. 2, pp. 71–80, 2008.

[3] R. Condie and B. Munro, "The impact of ict in schools: Landscape review," 2007.

[4] C. Harrison, C. Comber, T. Fisher, K. Haw, C. Lewin, E. Lunzer, A. McFarlane, D. Mavers, P. Scrimshaw, B. Somekh *et al.*, *ImpaCT2: The impact of information and communication technologies on pupil learning and attainment.* British Educational Communications and Technology Agency (BECTA), 2002.

[5] M. Resnick, "Sowing the seeds for a more creative society," *Learning and Leading with Technology*, vol. 35, no. 4, p. 18, 2007.

[6] S. Jordà, "The reactable: tangible and tabletop music performance," in *Proceedings of the 28th of the international conference extended abstracts on Human factors in computing systems.* ACM, 2010, pp. 2989–2994.

[7] L. Gower and J. McDowall, "Interactive music video games and children's musical development," *British Journal of Music Education*, vol. 29, no. 01, pp. 91–105, 2012.

[8] C. Wang and A. Lai, "Development of a mobile rhythm learning system based on digital game-based learning companion," *Edutainment Technologies. Educational Games and Virtual Reality/Augmented Reality Applications*, pp. 92–100, 2011.

[9] A. Barbancho, I. Barbancho, L. Tardón, and C. Urdiales, "Automatic edition of songs for guitar hero/frets on fire," in *Multimedia and Expo, 2009. ICME 2009. IEEE International Conference on.* IEEE, 2009, pp. 1186–1189.

[10] A. Antle, M. Droumeva, and G. Corness, "Playing with the sound maker: do embodied metaphors help children learn?" in *Proceedings of the 7th international conference on Interaction design and children.* ACM, 2008, pp. 178–185.

[11] E. Khoo, T. Merritt, V. Fei, W. Liu, H. Rahaman, J. Prasad, and T. Marsh, "Body music: physical exploration of music theory," in *Proceedings of the 2008 ACM SIGGRAPH symposium on Video games*, 2008, pp. 35–42.

[12] M. Halpern, J. Tholander, M. Evjen, S. Davis, A. Ehrlich, K. Schustak, E. Baumer, and G. Gay, "Moboogie: creative expression through whole body musical interaction," in *Proceedings of the 2011 annual conference on Human factors in computing systems.* ACM, 2011, pp. 557–560.

[13] A. Barbancho, A. Klapuri, L. Tardón, and I. Barbancho, "Automatic transcription of guitar chords and fingering from audio," *Audio, Speech, and Language Processing, IEEE Transactions on*, vol. 20, no. 3, pp. 915–921, 2012.

[14] I. Barbancho, L. Tardón, S. Sammartino, and A. Barbancho, "Inharmonicity-based method for the automatic generation of guitar tablature," *Audio, Speech, and Language Processing, IEEE Transactions on*, vol. 20, no. 6, pp. 1857–1868, 2012.

[15] G. Levin and Z. Lieberman, "In-situ speech visualization in real-time interactive installation and performance," in *Non-Photorealistic Animation and Rendering: Proceedings of the 3 rd international symposium on Non-photorealistic animation and rendering*, vol. 7, no. 09, 2004, pp. 7–14.

[16] S. Bakker, E. van den Hoven, and A. Antle, "Moso tangibles: evaluating embodied learning," in *Proceedings of the fifth international conference on Tangible, embedded, and embodied interaction.* ACM, 2011, pp. 85–92.

[17] S. Holland, A. Bouwer, M. Dalgelish, and T. Hurtig, "Feeling the beat where it counts: fostering multi-limb rhythm skills with the haptic drum kit," in *Proceedings of the fourth international conference on Tangible, embedded, and embodied interaction.* ACM, 2010, pp. 21–28.

[18] S. Trail, M. Dean, T. Tavares, G. Odowichuk, P. Driessen, W. Schloss, and G. Tzanetakis, "Non-invasive sensing and gesture control for pitched percussion hyper-instruments using the kinect," 2012.

[19] K. Ng, "Music via motion: transdomain mapping of motion and sound for interactive performances," *Proceedings of the IEEE*, vol. 92, no. 4, pp. 645–655, 2004.

[20] A. Hofer, A. Hadjakos, and M. Mhlhuser, "Gyroscope-Based Conducting Gesture Recognition," in *Proceedings of the International Conference on New Interfaces for Musical Expression*, 2009, pp. 175–176. [Online]. Available: http://www.nime.org/proceedings/2009/nime2009_175.pdf

[21] L. Peng and D. Gerhard, "A wii-based gestural interface for computer-based conducting systems," in *Proceedings of the 2009 Conference on New Interfaces For Musical Expression*, 2009.

[22] E. Lee, T. Nakra, and J. Borchers, "You're the conductor: a realistic interactive conducting system for children," in *Proceedings of the 2004 conference on New interfaces for musical expression*. National University of Singapore, 2004, pp. 68–73.

[23] D. Bradshaw and K. Ng, "Analyzing a conductors gestures with the wiimote," in *Proceedings of EVA London 2008: the International Conference of Electronic Visualisation and the Arts*, 2008.

[24] T. Nakra, Y. Ivanov, P. Smaragdis, and C. Ault, "The ubs virtual maestro: An interactive conducting system," *NIME2009*, pp. 250–255, 2009.

[25] J. Borchers, E. Lee, W. Samminger, and M. Mühlhäuser, "Personal orchestra: A real-time audio/video system for interactive conducting," *Multimedia Systems*, vol. 9, no. 5, pp. 458–465, 2004.

[26] T. Baba, M. Hashida, and H. Katayose, "virtualphilharmony: A conducting system with heuristics of conducting an orchestra," in *Proceedings of the 2010 Conference on New Interfaces for Musical Expression (NIME 2010)*, 2010, pp. 263–270.

[27] I. Barbancho, C. de la Bandera, A. Barbancho, and L. Tardon, "Transcription and expressiveness detection system for violin music," in *Acoustics, Speech and Signal Processing, 2009. ICASSP 2009. IEEE International Conference on*. IEEE, 2009, pp. 189–192.

ACOUSTIC SCORE FOLLOWING TO MUSICAL PERFORMANCE WITH ERRORS AND ARBITRARY REPEATS AND SKIPS FOR AUTOMATIC ACCOMPANIMENT

Tomohiko Nakamura, Eita Nakamura† and Shigeki Sagayama†
Graduate School of Information Science and Technology, The University of Tokyo
7-3-1, Hongo, Bunkyo-ku, Tokyo, 113-8656, Japan
{nakamura, enakamura, sagayama}@hil.t.u-tokyo.ac.jp

ABSTRACT

We discuss acoustic score-following algorithms for monophonic musical performances with arbitrary repeats and skips as well as performance errors, particularly focusing on reducing the computational complexity. Repeats/skips are often made arbitrarily during musical practice, and it is desirable to deal with arbitrary repeats/skips for wide application of score following. Allowing arbitrary repeats/skips in performance models demands reducing the computational complexity for score following. We show that for certain hidden Markov models which assume independence of transition probabilities from and to where repeats/skips are made, the computational complexity can be reduced from $O(M^2)$ down to $O(M)$ for the number of notes M, and construct score-following algorithms based on the models. We experimentally show that the proposed algorithms work in real time with practical scores (up to about 10000 notes) and can catch up with the performances in around 3.8 s after repeats/skips.

1. INTRODUCTION

Audio score following is the real-time alignment of acoustic signal of musical performance to the performance score, and has wide application such as automatic accompaniment, automatic score page turning and automatic captioning to music videos. It is particularly essential for automatic accompaniment, which synchronizes the accompaniment automatically to human performances in real time and helps music performers and lovers practice ensemble music by themselves.

Human performances have tempo fluctuation due to performers' physical limitation and their expression of musical ideas. Musical performers, both amateurs and professionals, also make performance errors such as pitch errors and note insertions and deletions. In addition to these, acoustic signals of musical performances are of complex nature because of possible noise and acoustic variation of musical instruments. According to these features of human performances and their acoustic signals, score following is a challenging task in musical signal processing and has been a field of research since [1, 2] and further explored in [3–12] (see [13] for a review).

Particularly during music practice, performers often repeat and/or skip sections for correcting errors or for practicing specific sections again and again, and it is desirable to handle such repeats/skips for application of score following in practical situations. In [5, 6, 12], score following algorithms allowing repeats/skips from and to specific score positions were studied. Although there are performers' tendencies on from and to where repeats/skips occur, estimation of the specific score positions is generically difficult, especially in practical situations where scores are prepared in musical instrument digital interface (MIDI) data or performances by various performers are necessary to be dealt with. Therefore it is attractive to have score following algorithms which can handle arbitrary repeats/skips from and to any score positions.

Allowing arbitrary repeats/skips leads to a large search space and results in two problems: (i) large computational complexity and (ii) a risk of lowering score-following accuracy. As we later discuss in detail, simply-generalized versions of algorithms in [3, 5, 6] are difficult to work in real time for practical scores with $O(1000)$ to $O(10000)$ notes, [1] and it is unavoidable to reduce the computational complexity.

Statistical approach to score following has advantages in handling acoustic variation of musical performances and was used in many previous works [13]. In this approach, one can either estimate the score position first and the tempo [3, 4], or estimate simultaneously the score position and the tempo [9, 10, 12]. Since the search space is too large in the latter case when dealing with arbitrary repeats/skips, we adopt the former method.

In the following, we discuss certain hidden Markov models (HMMs) for musical performance, which explicitly models performance errors and arbitrary repeats/skips. We show, when assuming independence of transition probabilities from and to where repeats/skips are made, the computational complexity can be reduced significantly, enabling us to construct acoustic score-following algorithms which handle arbitrary repeats/skips and work in real time. We experimentally evaluate the performance of the proposed algorithms for human performances in practice and also

† Presently with National Institute of Informatics
2-1-2 Hitotsubashi, Chiyoda-ku, Tokyo, 101-8430, Japan

[1] For example, there are around 1900 notes in the first movement of the clarinet part in Mozart's Clarinet Quintet.

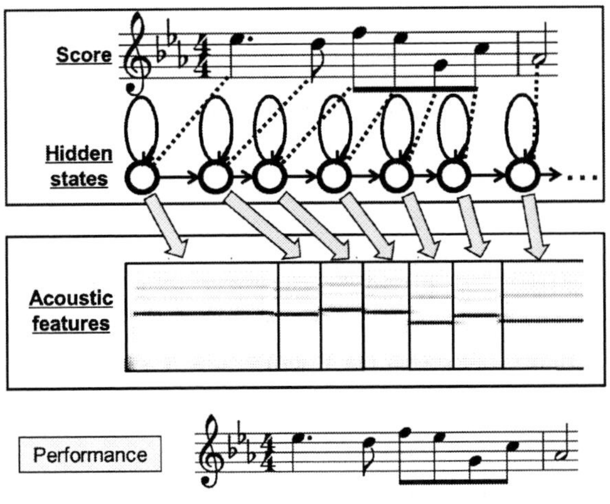

Figure 1. The performance HMM consists of states corresponding to notes, and the state emits acoustic features of the performed note.

examine whether there is any significant lowering of score-following accuracy. We confine ourselves to monophonic performances for the sake of simplicity.

2. HMM-BASED PERFORMANCE MODEL

2.1 HMM for Score Following

We regard score following as an inverse problem of estimating score positions from acoustic signals by modeling human performances. The human performance without errors and repeats/skips can be seen as a process of making a transition to the next note, and emitting an acoustic feature of the performed note. By associating the notes on score with hidden states, the performance is also interpreted as a state transition sequence. The performance often includes changes in tempos and note durations because of physical limitation and musical expression, and acoustic signals of the performance include noise and acoustic variations. These state transitions and emission of acoustic features are described as a stochastic process [3]. Assuming that the transitions depend only on the current state, the performance is represented by an HMM as shown in Fig. 1.

A performance with insertion/deletion errors are also described by an HMM [3]. Insertion is represented by a self transition and deletion is represented by a transition to the state after the next as shown in Fig. 2. These are described as

$$A_{i,i} = a_i + (1 - a_i)A_i^{(\text{ins})}, \; A_{i,i+2} = (1 - a_i)A_i^{(\text{del})}. \quad (1)$$

Here, $\{A_{i,j}\}_{i,j=1}^{M}$ is the state-transition probability matrix, and the durational self-transition probability a_i is determined by matching the expected staying time with the duration d_i of the i-th note, which yields

$$d_i = \sum_{k=1}^{\infty} k a_i^{k-1}(1 - a_i) = \frac{1}{1 - a_i}. \quad (2)$$

These errors are expressed as transitions to neighboring states and the HMM topology is left-to-right.

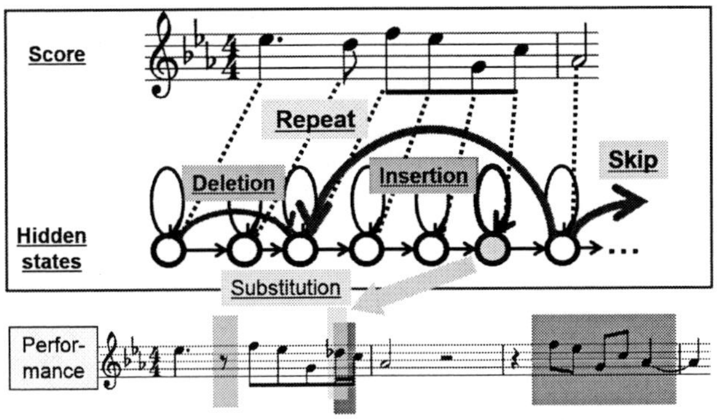

Figure 2. Representation of errors and repeats/skips in the performance model. Deletion (green arrows) is represented by a transition to the state after the next. Insertion (purple arrows) is described as a self transition, and substitution (orange objects) is represented by emission of CQF spectrum of incorrect pitch. Repeat/skip is expressed as a transition to a remote state (red arrows).

2.2 Feature Extraction from Acoustic Signal

The variation in acoustic signals of the performance is large even within the same pitch. For score following, therefore, features are preferred to be sensitive to pitch information and less sensitive to timbre and volume. As stated in [8], this requirement is matched by the normalized output of constant-Q filters (CQFs) with central frequencies at semitone intervals (CQF spectrum). For shorter calculation time, the CQF spectrum was calculated with a fast frame-wise algorithm [14]. Since a spectrum changes significantly at the onset time and is otherwise stationary, spectral flux is employed to distinguish successive notes of the same pitch [15].

2.3 Emission Probability

As shown in Fig. 2, substitution is represented by emission of CQF spectrum of incorrect pitch, and the corresponding probability is described as a mixture weight of a Gaussian mixture model for emission probability. The emission probability $b_i(y_t)$ at the i-th state of a CQF spectrum y_t at time t is thus

$$b_i(y_t) = \sum_{k \in \mathcal{K}} \omega_k(i) \mathcal{N}(y_t | \mu_k, \Sigma_k) \quad (3)$$

where $\mathcal{N}(\cdot|\mu_k, \Sigma_k)$ denotes a multidimensional normal distribution with mean μ_k and covariance matrix Σ_k, $\mathcal{K}$ is the set of all pitches, and $\omega_k(i)$ stands for the mixture weight.

3. MODELING OF ARBITRARY REPEATS/SKIPS AND THE COMPUTATIONAL COMPLEXITY

3.1 Topology of the Performance HMM

As discussed in Sec. 2, a performance with insertion/deletion/substitution errors is represented by left-to-right transitions to neighboring states and emission of acoustic features of incorrect pitch. On the contrary, repeats/skips from and to arbitrary notes are represented by transitions from each state to all the states, including remote ones (two examples are shown in Fig. 2.). Therefore, the topology of the performance model with arbitrary repeats/skips, which generalizes the models in [3, 5, 6], is complex, resulting in a large search space.

3.2 Computational Complexity of Score Following

The score position is estimated by calculating the most probable state given the CQF spectrums up to the time of estimation. In equations,

$$\hat{s}_t = \underset{s_t}{\operatorname{argmax}}\, p(s_t|y_{1:t}) = \underset{s_t}{\operatorname{argmax}}\, p(y_{1:t}, s_t) \quad (4)$$

where s_t and $\hat{s}_t$ denote the state random variable at time t and its estimated value, and $y_{1:t}=\{y_\tau\}_{\tau=1}^{t}$ stands for the CQF spectrum sequence. The second equation is derived from the Bayes' theorem.

(4) can be solved by applying the online forward algorithm, and its update rule is described as

$$\alpha_t(i) = b_i(y_t) \sum_{j=1}^{M} \alpha_{t-1}(j) A_{j,i} \quad (5)$$

where $\alpha_t(i){:=}p(y_{1:t}, s_t{=}i)$ is the forward variable. Here, the initial value $\alpha_1(i){=}b_i(y_1)\pi_i$ is calculated with the initial distribution π_i. (5) indicates that the computational complexity for score following is $O(M^2)$ since there are M summations over M states. As shown in Sec. 4, the $O(M^2)$ complexity is too large for the score follower to work in real time for scores with a number of notes larger than a few hundreds, and therefore it is crucial to reduce the complexity for processing practical scores.

3.3 Algorithms for Reducing Computational Complexity

In order to reduce the computational complexity, some constraints on the state-transition probability matrix are necessary. In this section, we propose two models and algorithms reduced the complexity to linear orders.

Human performers probably perform with their tendencies of pausing before repeats/skips and resuming after them. We can represent the tendencies at each state as the probabilities of pausing and resuming, or C_j and D_i. The distribution of where human performers resume is also probably dependent on where they pause. However, allowing the dependence results in $O(M^2)$ computational complexity as shown in Sec. 3.2, and thus we assume that the distribution of where human performers resume is independent of where they pause. With this assumption, the transition matrix can be written as

$$A_{j,i} = B_{j,i} + C_j D_i \quad (6)$$

where $B_{j,i}$ is a band matrix with bandwidth three representing the straight performance and deletion/insertion errors. Note that the normalization conditions $\sum_i A_{j,i}{=}1$ and $\sum_i D_i{=}1$ yield $C_j{=}1 - \sum_i B_{j,i}$.

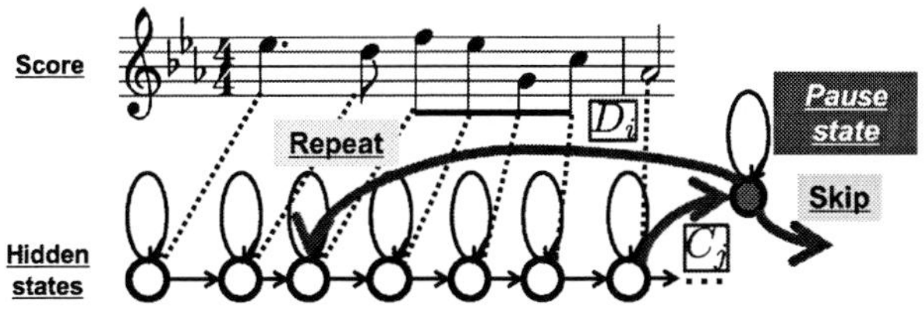

Figure 3. Representation of repeats/skips in the proposed performance model with the pause state (a blue disk) corresponding to pause sections at repeats/skips. Those are expressed as two-step transitions via the pause state (red arrows).

Substituting (6) into (5), we have

$$\alpha_t(i) = b_i(y_t) \left[\sum_{j=i-2}^{i} \alpha_{t-1}(j) B_{j,i} + \Big(\sum_{j=1}^{M} \alpha_{t-1}(j) C_j \Big) D_i \right]. \quad (7)$$

Since the sum in parentheses in the second term on the right-hand side is independent of i, it is sufficient to calculate this once at each estimation. The computational complexity of the sum is $O(M)$ and that of the rest of (7) is $O(M)$. Thus, we can reduce the computational complexity required for the estimation from $O(M^2)$ down to $O(M)$.

We obtain a similar model by focusing on a silent pause which is often made at repeats/skips before resuming performance. Such a pause can be represented by an additional state (the pause state). Since the repeats/skips are described as two-step transitions via the pause state as shown in Fig. 3, the tendencies of pausing and resuming the performances can be expressed as the transitions probabilities to the pause state and those from the pause state. In equations, the transition matrix of the model is

$$\tilde{A}_{j,i} = B_{j,i},\ \tilde{A}_{j,N} = C_j,\ \tilde{A}_{N,i} = (1 - \tilde{A}_{N,N}) D_i \quad (8)$$

for $i, j \in [1, M]$ where the N-th state is the pause state and $N{=}M + 1$.

Naively, the computational complexity for updating the forward variable in the model is $O(N^2)$. However, since the transition probabilities to the note states except for those from neighboring notes and the pause state are zero, the complexity for updating the forward variable for the note states is reduced to $O(M)$. For the pause state, we must deal with transitions from all the states, and the complexity for calculating its forward variable is $O(N)$. Therefore, the overall computational complexity is reduced to $O(N) \simeq O(M)$.

While the above discussion of computational complexity is based on the forward algorithm, a similar discussion is valid for the Viterbi algorithm. With a slight modification, the discussion can also be generalized for Mealy-type emission probabilities of the form similar to $A_{j,i}$ in (6).

3.4 Comparison of the Two Models

The two models discussed in the previous section has a similar structure as seen in (6) and (8). In both models, one can describe tendencies of performance on the distributions of notes to which repeats/skips are made. Both the models rely on the independence of the distribution from the notes before them. The difference is the explicit modeling of the pause state in the latter model. In actual performances, silent pauses at repeats/skips often exist and their duration is long to some extent. Therefore, the latter model is expected to be more suited for score following. However, since quantitative comparison of both the models is difficult, we provide experiments for evaluating the performances of the models in Sec. 4.

4. EVALUATION OF COMPUTATIONAL COMPLEXITY AND SCORE-FOLLOWING PERFORMANCE

4.1 Experimental Conditions

4.1.1 Overall Conditions

To evaluate our algorithms, we conducted three experiments. The first experiment examines quantitatively whether the proposed algorithms works in real time with the practical scores, the second one evaluates the performance of the proposed algorithms in following repeats/skips, and the third one evaluates score-following accuracy and examines whether there is a lowering of accuracy in modeling arbitrary repeats/skips for performances without repeats/skips.

In all the experiments, we used acoustic signals of monophonic performances at 16 kHz sampling rate and the scores were prepared in MIDI format. CQF spectrums were extracted by using 128 ms frames with a 20 ms hop-size, and the emission probabilities of the performance models were trained by clarinet performances in RWC musical instrument sound database [16]. The parameters of the proposed algorithm without the pause state were set as $\pi=[1,0,0,\cdots,0]^\top$, $A_i^{(\mathrm{ins})}=A_i^{(\mathrm{del})}=\exp(-500)$, $C_i=\exp(-1000)$, and $D_i=1/M$ for $i\in[1,M]$. For the other proposed algorithm, the parameters were set as $\tilde{A}_{N,N}=0.98$ in addition to the above. The probabilities of making errors of semitone, whole tone and perfect 12th were set as 0.001, 0.001, and 0.0001, respectively.

4.1.2 Condition on the First Experiment

Since the computational complexity mainly depends on the number of notes, and not on pitches and durations, artificially prepared scores with various numbers of notes were used in the first experiment. The machine had an Intel Core 2 Duo P9400 2.40 GHz with 6 MB of cache and 2 GB of RAM, and the operating system was Ubuntu 12.04LTS. The evaluation measure was the real time factor (RTF) defined as the ratio of the processing time and the hop-size, which is less than one if and only if the algorithms work in real time.

4.1.3 Condition on the Second Experiment

In the second experiment, for evaluating the score-following performance under practical situations, we used acoustic signals of 14 recorded performances (total 1687 s) by an amateur clarinet performer during his musical practice. Seven different songs were performed including classical and popular music pieces and nursery rhymes, partially from RWC music database [16]. 43 repeats/skips and 45 insertion/deletion/substitution errors were made naturally in the performances, and the ranges of repeats/skips were distributed from 0.1 s to 85 s in score time (0 bars to 43 bars). The performer did not waited the score follower's catching up with his performance. As evaluation measures, the detection rate of repeats/skips and the following time were employed. The following time is defined as the time interval (in units of seconds and notes) between the repeat or skip and the time when the score follower caught up with the performance within a range of Δ ms.

We compared the proposed algorithms with the algorithm without modeling of repeats/skips which corresponds to the previous work [3]. While Cano *et al.* used slightly different acoustic features of pitch and energy, CQF spectrums were employed as acoustic features in this experiment. The difference does not result in lowering the score-following accuracy, and rather improves it as stated in [8], and we believe that our choice of the acoustic features is adequate.

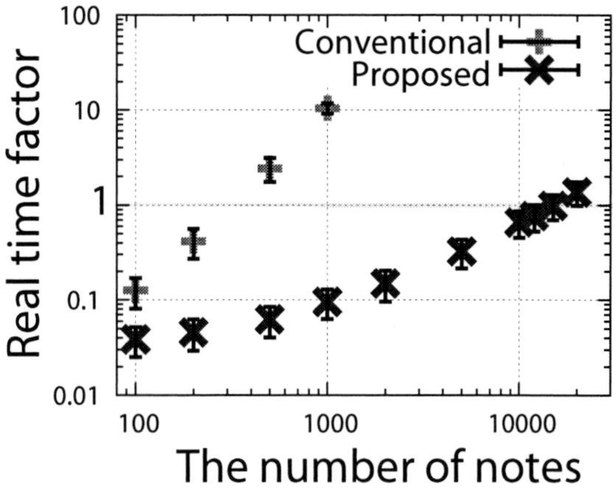

Figure 4. Real time factor (RTF) and its standard deviation of score following with the various number of notes in the performance score. The red points represent RTFs of the conventional algorithm, and the blue ones represent RTFs of the proposed algorithm with the pause state.

4.1.4 Condition on the Third Experiment

In the third experiment, a sufficient amount of real performances could not be prepared, and we used monophonic acoustic signals converted from MIDI signals. For the MIDI signals, the melody parts of 112 popular music pieces and royalty-free ones without repeats/skips in RWC music database were employed [16]. Evaluation measures were the piecewise precision rate and the overall precision rate used in the MIREX contest [17]. The piecewise precision rate (PPR) is the average of detection rates of notes in each piece, and the overall precision rate (OPR) is the detection rate of notes in all pieces.

4.2 Results and Discussions

4.2.1 First Experiment

The result of the first experiment is shown in Fig. 4, where the RTF was averaged over 95 calculations for each con-

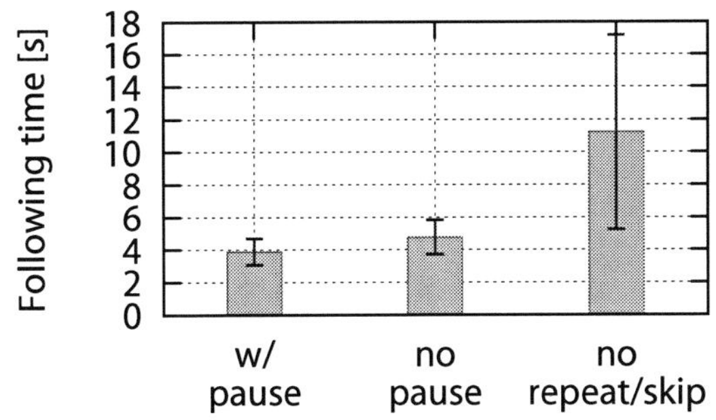

(a) Following time in second.

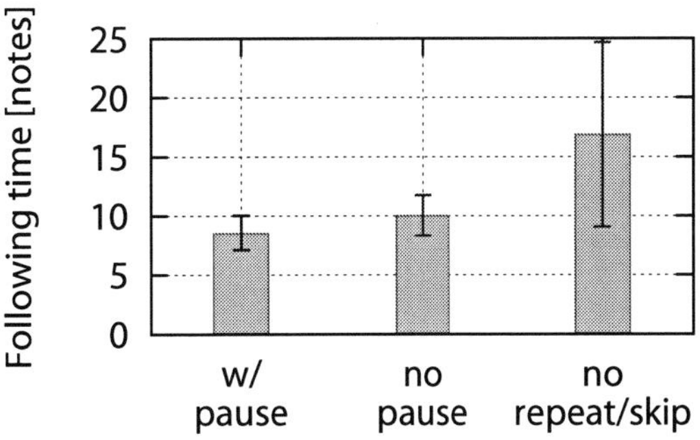

(b) Following time in notes.

Figure 5. Following time (both (a) in second and (b) in notes) of the proposed algorithm with the pause state (w/ pause), that without the pause state (no pause) and the conventional algorithm (no repeat/skip) in left-to-right fashion.

Evaluation Measure	w/ pause	no pause	no repeat/skip
Detection rate of repeats/skips	$32/43$	$29/43$	$8/43$

Table 1. Detection rate of repeats/skips by the proposed algorithm with the pause state (w/ pause), that without the pause state (no pause) and the conventional algorithm (no repeat/skip).

dition. Only the result of the proposed algorithm with the pause state is shown, since the result was similar for the other. The figure shows that in the proposed algorithm, the RTF increases asymptotically in proportion to M and, in the conventional algorithm, asymptotically in proportion to M^2, which is consistent with the theoretical result in Section 3.3. The result shows that the score follower worked in real time on the computer up to around 10000 notes, and the conventional one up to around 300 notes. The conventional algorithm is difficult to handle the practical scores with over $O(100)$ notes, and for those with 10000 notes, the computation time is around 2 s, or ten times the hopsize. On the other hand, the computational time is reduced to around 0.02 s, or one hundredth, by the proposed algorithms, and almost all the practical scores can be used. Although the detail of the upper bound of the number of notes for real-time working may be changed on other computers because of difference in processing power, the reduction of the computational complexity by the proposed algorithms always remains effective.

4.2.2 Second Experiment

In the second experiment, the algorithm with the pause state detected 32 repeats/skips of 43, and its following time was 3.9 ± 0.8 s (8.0 ± 1.5 notes) for Δ=500 ms as shown in Fig. 5 and Table 1. On the other hand, the algorithm without the pause state detected 29 repeats/skips, and its following time was 4.9 ± 1.0 s (10 ± 2 notes) for Δ=500 ms. As we conjectured in Sec. 3.4, the proposed algorithm without the pause state followed repeats/skips later than that with the pause state. In contrast to those algorithms, the conventional algorithm corresponding to the one in [3] detected only eight repeats/skips, and followed those with 11 ± 3 s and 17 ± 8 notes delay. It is obvious that modeling repeats/skips significantly improves the performance in following repeats/skips.

The algorithm with the pause state had 11 undetected repeats/skips. Some of the undetected repeats/skips were caused by the existence of similar sections and phrases such as choruses in popular music. Others happened in the cases where only a few notes were performed between the repeats/skips. Such scores and performances are generally difficult to follow both for computers and humans. Because human accompanists would need comparable following time, the proposed algorithms are applicable to practical use.

4.2.3 Third Experiment

In the third experiment, all the PPRs were 0.839 ± 0.009, the OPRs by the algorithms except that without the pause state were $30073/36051$ and the other was $30070/36051$. There were only the slight difference between the proposed algorithms and the conventional one in PPR and OPR, and this result shows that the modeling of repeats/skips did not lower the accuracy significantly.

4.3 Implementation to Automatic Accompaniment

We also implemented the proposed score-following algorithms to automatic accompaniment. As an accompaniment playback module, a tempo estimation [18] and a playback speed conversion of acoustic signals of accompaniment [19] were employed. Fig. 6 shows the accompaniment result to the performances with repeats by the algorithm with the pause state, and videos for such performances are available at `http://hil.t.u-tokyo.ac.jp/~nakamura/demo/automatic_accompaniment.html`.

5. CONCLUSION

We have proposed two score-following algorithms for monophonic performances with both insertion/deletion/substitution errors and arbitrary repeats/skips. (i) Assuming the independence of transition

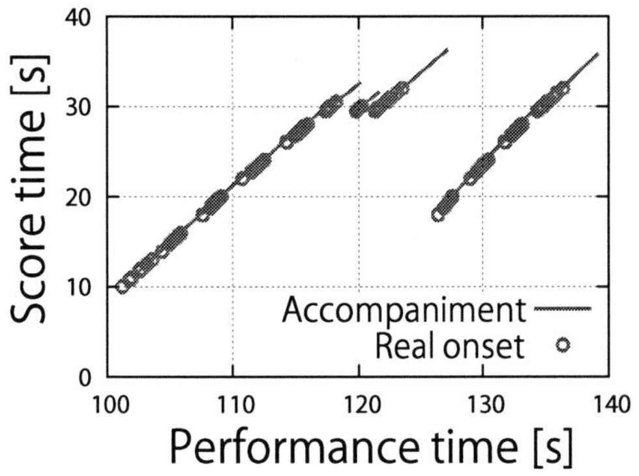

Figure 6. The automatic accompaniment result for a human performance with repeats by the algorithm with the pause state. The gray circle expresses a real onset, and the red line represents the played accompaniment.

probabilities from and to where repeats/skips are made, we have shown that the computational complexity is reduced from $O(M^2)$ down to $O(M)$. (ii) Focusing on a silent pause which are often made at repeats/skips before resuming performance, we have revealed that the computational complexity is also reduced down to $O(M)$ by explicit modeling of the existence of the pause. We have experimentally shown that the proposed algorithms work in real time for the practical scores up to 10000 notes and can catch up with performances in around 3.8 s after repeats/skips. The experiment has indicated that there is not a significant lowering of the score-following accuracy originating in modeling arbitrary repeats/skips.

As future works, an extension to polyphonic music is important to enable the score followers to process more scores and performances by other instruments as discussed in [7, 17]. Using tempo information is important to improve the performance of the algorithms and to help us to use beat information as discussed in [9–11].

Acknowledgments

We thank Naoya Ito for playing the clarinet, and Hirokazu Kameoka for useful discussions. This research has been partly supported by the Grant-in-Aid from JSPS (#23240021).

6. REFERENCES

[1] R. Dannenberg, "An on-line algorithm for real-time accompaniment," in *Proc. of ICMC*, 1984, pp. 193–198.

[2] B. Vercoe, "The synthetic performer in the context of live performance," in *Proc. of ICMC*, 1984, pp. 199–200.

[3] P. Cano, A. Loscos, and J. Bonada, "Score-performance matching using hmms," in *Proc. of ICMC*, 1999, pp. 441–444.

[4] C. Raphael, "Automatic segmentation of acoustic musical signals using hidden Markov models," *IEEE TPAMI*, vol. 21, no. 4, pp. 360–370, 1999.

[5] M. Tekin, C. Anagnostopoulou, and Y. Tomita, "Towards an intelligent score following system: Handling of mistakes and jumps encountered during piano practicing," in *Proc. of CMMR*, 2004, pp. 211–219.

[6] B. Pardo and W. Birmingham, "Modeling form for on-line following of musical performances," in *Proc. of AAAI*, vol. 2, 2005, pp. 1018–1023.

[7] A. Cont, "ANTESCOFO: Anticipatory synchronization and control of interactive parameters in computer music," in *Proc. of ICMC*, 2008.

[8] C. Joder, S. Essid, and G. Richard, "A comparative study of tonal acoustic features for a symbolic level music-to-score alignment," in *Proc. of IEEE WASPAA*, 2010, pp. 409–412.

[9] Z. Duan and B. Pardo, "A state space model for on-line polyphonic audio-score alignment," in *Proc. of ICASSP*, 2011, pp. 197–200.

[10] T. Otsuka, K. Nakadai, T. Takahashi, T. Ogata, and H. Okuno, "Real-time audio-to-score alignment using particle filter for coplayer music robots," *EURASIP JASP*, vol. 2011, p. 2, 2011.

[11] C. Joder, S. Essid, and G. Richard, "A conditional random field framework for robust and scalable audio-to-score matching," *IEEE TASLP*, vol. 19, no. 8, pp. 2385–2397, 2011.

[12] N. Montecchio and A. Cont, "A unified approach to real time audio-to-score and audio-to-audio alignment using sequential Montecarlo inference techniques," in *Proc. of ICASSP*, 2011, pp. 193–196.

[13] N. Orio, S. Lemouton, D. Schwarz, and N. Schnell, "Score following: State of the art and new developments," in *Proc. of NIME*, 2003, pp. 36–41.

[14] J. Brown and M. Puckette, "An efficient algorithm for the calculation of a constant Q transform," *JASA*, vol. 92, pp. 2698–2701, 1992.

[15] P. Masri, "Computer modelling of sound for transformation and synthesis of musical signal," Ph.D. dissertation, University of Bristol, 1996.

[16] M. Goto, "Development of the RWC Music Database," in *Proc. of ICA*, 2004, pp. l–553–556.

[17] A. Cont, D. Schwarz, N. Schnell, and C. Raphael, "Evaluation of real-time audio-to-score alignment," in *Proc. of ISMIR*, 2007.

[18] H. Takeda, T. Nishimoto, and S. Sagayama, "Automatic accompaniment system of MIDI performance using HMM-based score following," in *Proc. of the SIG Technical Reports on Music and Computer of IPSJ*, Aug. 2006, pp. 109–116, in Japanese.

[19] Y. Mizuno, H. Tachibana, and S. Sagayama, "Real-time Time-scale Modification of a Music Signal Using Phase Reconstruction for Synchronous Playback in Conducting/Accompaniment System," in *Proc. of ASJ Autumn Meeting*, Sep. 2011, pp. 897–898, in Japanese.

A CONTOUR-BASED JAZZ WALKING BASS GENERATOR

Rui Dias
University of Porto
INESC-Porto
School of Applied Arts,
Polytechnic Instituteof Castelo Branco
(ESART-IPCB)
ruidias@ipcb.pt

Carlos Guedes
School of Music and Performing Arts,
Polytechnic of Porto (ESMAE-IPP)
INESC-Porto
carlosguedes@esmae-ipp.pt

ABSTRACT

This paper describes a contour-based algorithm for the real-time automatic generation of jazz walking bass lines, following a given harmonic progression. A brief description of the walking bass procedure will be presented, and also a brief survey on some common implementations and techniques.
This algorithm was implemented in the Max/MSP graphical programming environment.

1. INTRODUCTION

1.1 The Walking Bass Practice

The walking bass is a very common playing procedure used in jazz music, in which the bass walks through the chord and scale notes in a regular pulse. This is especially used when accompanying a solo, firmly setting the base pulse like a metronome, and simultaneously exposing the underlying harmony of the song. This procedure has its roots deep in the first decades of the twentieth century, and was developed through the years with bass players like Jimmy Blanton, Ray Brown, Ron Carter and Charlie Mingus, amongst many others. A very good insight on the evolution of the bass role and many of the key innovators in jazz history can be found in The Jazz Bass Book, Technique and Tradition, by John Goldsby [1].

The basic idea of a walking bass line is to go from one chord to the next, linking them by filling the middle beats with notes of the chord or scale, typically describing a smooth melodic line or pattern. Far from being completely passive, however, the roll and behavior of the walking bass can dramatically change from almost neutral smooth lines to very abrupt register changes and energized rhythms, dynamically contributing to the overall group energy and musical result. The continuous flow of the regular walking bass notes, together with its harmonic and melodic content, form one of the most charismatic and important elements in traditional jazz playing.

The learning of this technique usually implies the learning of melodic licks, for each of the commonly used chord progressions. These licks are small melodic phrases that are particularly efficient and musical, and are usually related both to the available notes of the current chord and underlying scale and to physical placement of the notes and fingers on the bass. Bass learning methods like the ones by Ron Carter [2], Ray Brown [3], Bob Magnusson [4] and Steven Mooney [5] lead the student through a series of these licks, covering most common harmonic progressions, in order to provide the student with the basic formulae that can then be adapted to any song. As the walking bass player develops his technique and gains more experience, however, he will be able to use these phrases more articulately. More importantly, he will be able to move away from them, intuitively creating more natural sounding lines and integrating several other elements like ornaments, theme-specific elements and group feedback.
"(...) musicians string together a sequence of motifslicks as they used to be calledmodified to meet the constraints of the chord sequence. (...) Yet, the motif theory cannot be the whole story." [6]

1.2 Implementations

Due to the non-repetitive nature of the walking bass technique, its use in computer software is actually quite limited. Commonly, walking bass lines in use are pre-recorded or manually written for the entire song length, whether as audio recordings or MIDI events. This practice has its roots in play-along recordings, like the widely known Jamie Aebersold [7] long list of score + CD Play-A-Long albums, with comping tracks recorded by real jazz musicians, allowing the practitioner to play-along with the recording. Computer software facilitates this method by easily allowing the independent mixing for each track, as well as change the tempo and transpose an audio or MIDI track, even on iOS devices with apps like Smudge Apps Band [8] with multi-track recordings and mixer.
More advanced software use pre-recorded small phrases for each chord-type and/or chord progressions, which are then transposed and chained together according to some more or less intelligent algorithm. This seems to be the case with software like the extensive Band-in-a-box [9], and more recently iReal b [10], on the iPad. This kind of implementation can use audio or MIDI clips. While audio

clips keep all of the little nuances, sound and groove of the original player, the MIDI clips allow more flexibility for editing notes, instrument, and even tempo and phrase elements.

These implementations based on the use of pre-recorded phrases, whether audio or MIDI, have however some limitations:

- If the number of pre-programmed phrases is small, the output will easily sound repetitive;
- The larger the number of pre-programmed phrases, the larger the chances of melodic inconsistencies and non-musical results;
- In order to obtain smooth transitions between chords, the pre-programmed phrases have to be very neutral, resulting in a very neutral sounding bass line;
- It is not easy to handle less conventional harmonic progressions.

2. A CONTOUR-BASED APPROACH: TECHNICAL DESCRIPTION

The work presented in this paper stems directly from the research that led to the development of the GimmeDaBlues app [11]. It describes the algorithmic generation of melodic phrases that connect the chords in a previously defined harmonic grid, by calculating a path from the current chord to the next, according to user-defined settings controlling the direction and range of the melodic contour.

The phrase generation algorithm consists basically in three stages: Target Note calculation, Trajectory calculation, and an event manager (Player). The general structure is showed in Fig.1.

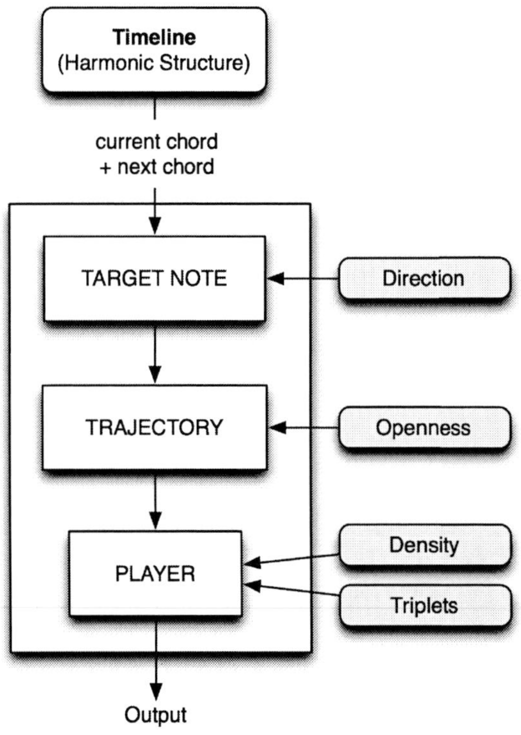

Figure 1. Algorithm structure.

2.1 Target note calculation

The algorithm needs to know the current chord and the next one in order to be able to calculate a phrase. The target note is the last note of the phrase to be generated. A simple probabilistic algorithm chooses which of the notes belonging to the next chord will be used e.g. fundamental, 3rd, 5th, 7th, etc.. Currently, in order to maintain a strong sense of the base harmony, a setting of 100% probabilities of choosing the fundamental note of the chord is used. Then, according to the current note and to a direction parameter, the algorithm will find the chosen chord note in the right octave.

The direction parameter defines whether the target note will be selected up or down, relatively to the current note, and there are five different settings: lowest, down, nearest, up, and highest. The down and up settings tell the algorithm to search for the nearest note in that direction, while with the lowest and highest settings, the algorithm will select the lowest and highest note in the instruments range. This parameter can be defined manually or automatically. So, for example, considering a double bass instrument defined with a range from E0 to G3 (having C3 as the middle C), if the current note is a C2, and the target note is an F, the direction parameter will define which F will be selected. The down setting would select F1, while the up setting would select F2. The lowest note setting will return F0 - the lowest F on the defined range - and the highest setting will return F3 the highest F on the defined range.

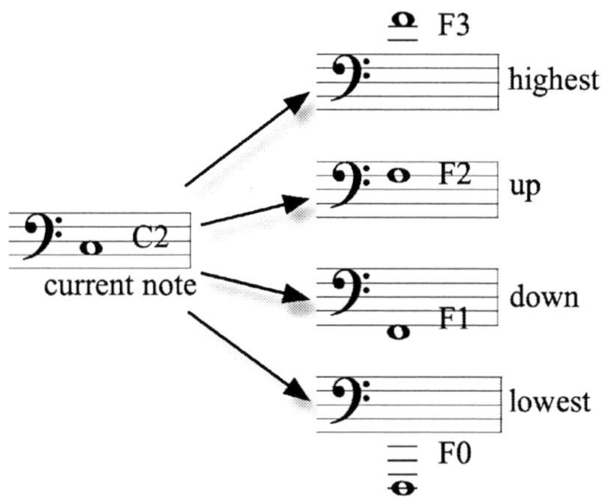

Figure 2. Possible target notes for the four direction settings.

With the "nearest" setting selected, the algorithm will automatically go up or down, choosing the F that is nearest to the current C2, which will be F2, because its a Perfect 4th interval, while F1 would be a Perfect 5th.

2.2 Trajectory

The trajectory is constituted by a selection of notes that define the path the bass line will take from the starting (current) note to the final (target) note. In a typical case for a chord duration of one bar in a 4/4 measure with the bass playing quarter notes, the complete generated bass line will have five notes, in which the fifth is the first note of the next

measure. The three passing notes between the starting note to the target note are calculated recursively, going from the strongest beats of the measure to the weakest, and depending on the trajectory calculation algorithm.
An openness parameter will set how direct or indirect the path will be, influencing the selection of the middle notes in the calculated bass line. The name relates to the notion of closed and open forms of a chord. The closed position will be the more direct path to the target note, while more open path will tend to use a wider trajectory, using chord notes in an open form.
The notes to use will be drawn from chord tones, scale degrees and chromatic inflections, according to each steps beat position. The stronger beats of the bar will tend to have chord tones, while the weak beats will tend to have scale notes acting as passing notes from one chord note to the next. The last beat of the bar can also be a chromatic approximation to the target note. This is a very commonly used technique, as the chromatic passing note creates a strong attraction to the target note, emphasizing it as well as the sense of direction in the melodic phrase.
Fig. 3 shows four examples of possible trajectories of the calculation of a bass line for a C7 F7 progression, where the initial note is C2, and the target note is F2.

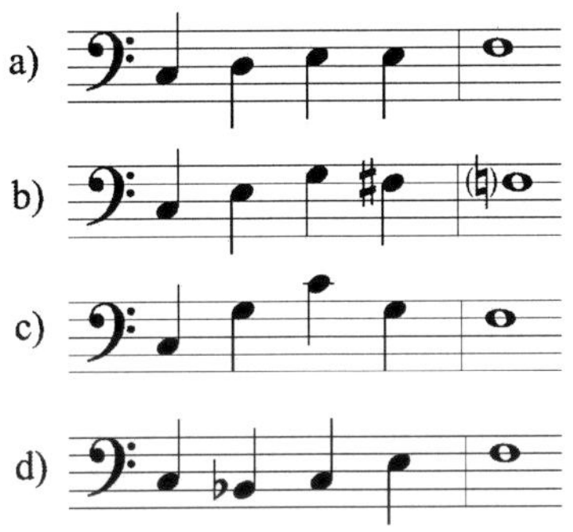

Figure 3. Phrase b) is the same as a) but with an ornamental triplet repeating the G in the third beat.

2.3 Ornaments

Although the construction of the phrases are the base of the walking bass technique, there are several other aspects regarding the notes, rhythm and articulations that have an important role in a good performance. These aspects, here referred to as ornaments, are little nuances and additions to the phrases that dont change nor define the main contents of the phrases, but nevertheless can contribute considerably to the quality and the dynamic of the walking bass lines.
The current implementation allows for the use of eighth-note triplet variations (or eighth-notes with a swing feeling) that can be set probabilistically. This is one of the most common rhythmic variations in the walking bass technique, in which some of the notes are anticipated by one triplet (or swinged eighth) with the same or another pitch. The control is done by a single percentage value, setting the probability factor.

Figure 4. Phrase b) is the same as a) but with an ornamental triplet repeating the G in the third beat.

2.4 Control

The combination of the direction selection and the trajectory openness provide a contour-based definition of the walking bass line, which not only creates smooth and natural lines but also allows an effective and intuitive control in interactive real-time implementations.
A simple example of a possible manual controller for this walking bass generator would be a joystick type controller, where the vertical axis would control the direction parameter, while the horizontal would control the openness parameter.

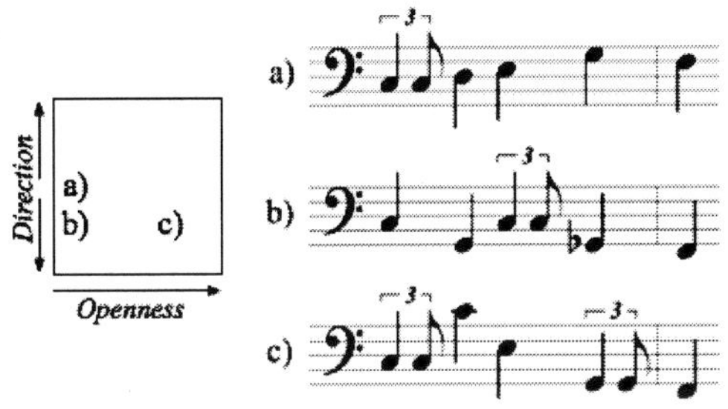

Figure 5. Example phrases with different settings.

Figure 5 shows three example phrases with different settings:
- a) direction: nearest / openness: low;
- b) direction: down / openness: low;
- c) direction: down / openness: high.

3. CONCLUSIONS AND FUTURE DEVELOPMENTS

The overall outcome of the described algorithm is quite effective and promising, mainly due to its flexible nature, by adapting to any arbitrary harmonic progression and by allowing a meta-control over the bassist behaviour.
Future implementations will focus on the way the phrase generation can be controlled algorithmically, exploring the contour shapes for the creation of motivic oriented groups of phrases. Several strategies can be approached, like Markov models and genetic algorithms, to control the succession of phrase parameters musically.
Due to its recursive nature, the current algorithm only deals with multiples 2/4, 2/2 and 4/4 measures. In metrical terms, the beat hierarchy in measures with an odd number of beats is not so clear, and thus the algorithm has to know how

to handle them appropriately. Also, and relating to metrical aspects in the phrase calculation, is the notion that the phrases played by good bass players tend to have very often a length of two measures instead of just one. This creates more fluent lines contributing to the smoothness of the musical form but also to the musical dynamics and movement by relieving the measure-by-measure step size.
Regarding harmony, some interesting developments can include the introduction of harmonic variations like chord substitutions and alternate chord progressions, which is a very common practice with advanced players, described in books like the ones by Nettles and Graf [12], or Felts [13], and addressed in the work by Steedman [14] [15].
Also, in order to make it sound more human and active, the ornaments features regarding rhythm, dynamics and articulation will have to be addressed.

4. REFERENCES

[1] John Goldsby, "The Jazz Bass Book Technique and Tradition". Backbeat Books, 2002.

[2] Ron Carter, "Building Jazz Bass Lines". Hal Leonard, 1998.

[3] Ray Brown, Ray Brown's Bass Method". Hal Leonard, 1999.

[4] Bob Magnusson, "The Art of the Walking Bass". Hal Leonard, 1999.

[5] Steven Mooney, "Constructing Walking Jazz Bass Lines" (book series). Waterfall Publishing House, 2011.

[6] P. Johnson-Laird, "How jazz musicians improvise", in Music Perception, Spring 2002, Vol. 19, No. 3.

[7] a list of the Jamie Aebersold publications can be found at en.wikipedia.org/wiki/List_of_songs_in_Aebersold's_Play-A-Long_series (consulted in March 17th 2013).

[8] Smudge Apps - *Band*. www.smudgeapps.com (consulted March 14th 2013)

[9] PG Music - *Band-in-a-box*.www.pgmusic.com (consulted in March 17th 2013)

[10] Technimo LLC, *iReal b*. www.irealb.com (consulted March 14th 2013)

[11] R. Dias, T. Marques, G. Sioros and C. Guedes, "GimmeDaBlues: an intelligent Jazz/Blues player and comping generator for iOS devices". in Proc. Conf. Computer Music and Music Retrieval (CMMR 2012). London 2012.

[12] Barrie Nettles and R. Graf, "The Chord Scale Theory and Jazz Harmony". Rottenburg: Advance Music, 2002.

[13] Randy Felts, "Reharmonization Techniques". Boston: Berklee Press, 2002.

[14] Mark Steedman, "A Generative Grammar for Jazz Chord Sequences", in Music Perception 2, 1984. pp. 52-77.

[15] Mark Steedman, "The Blues and the Abstract Truth: Music and Mental Models", in A. Garnham & J. Oakhill (eds.), Mental Models In Cognitive Science. Mahwah, NJ: Erlbaum 1996, pp. 305-318.

LANdini: a networking utility for wireless LAN-based laptop ensembles

Jascha Narveson
Princeton University
narveson@princeton.edu

Dr. Dan Trueman
Princeton University
dtrueman@princeton.edu

ABSTRACT

Problems with OSC communication over wireless routers are summarized and the idea of a separate networking utility named LANdini is introduced. LANdini's models and current structure are explained, and data from tests is presented. Future improvements are listed.

1. BACKGROUND MOTIVATION

1.1 Wireless routers are good

The two laptop ensembles of which we are a part - the Princeton Laptop Ensemble (PLOrk) and Sideband - both use wireless routers for group networking. This is a decision based on convenience and logistics: not having to worry about cables dramatically reduces set-up and take-down time for performances and rehearsals, and makes it easy to scale the ensemble up or down in size. In the case of PLOrk, which has at times exceeded 30 simultaneous performers, these are extremely valuable features. Avoiding networking cables also allows for a freedom of location, both on a performer basis (up in balconies, spread out around the audience, etc...), and on an ensemble basis (such as playing out-doors or in non-traditional venues). Even confined to on-stage setups, the presence of cables can impede fluid re-arrangement of performer stations from piece to piece, which is a common element in both PLOrk and Sideband concerts. In order to stay as flexible as possible, both PLOrk and Sideband intend to use wireless routers for the foreseeable future.

1.2 Wireless routers are bad

As a trade-off for all of the logistical convenience afforded by wireless routers, PLOrk and Sideband have had to deal with the less reliable performance of UDP protocols over wireless systems for OSC [1] communication, as well as the propensity of routers to occasionally drop users from the network. Latency and dropped packets have been a constant source of trouble for any piece in our repertoire that uses networking and, while some pieces can suffer a dropped packet and/or timing inconsistencies, others may be structured such that enough networking errors result in the piece failing. This is a well-known fact amongst laptop-ensemble musicians, and has been the subject of other academic inquiries [2]. Because of this, ensembles such as LSU's LOL and Virginia Tech's L2Ork choose to make the tradeoff in the other direction and perform with a wired router and a mass of ethernet cables [3, 4].

1.3 Previous solutions have left us unsatisfied

Composers who have worked with PLOrk and Sideband have approached the problems of wireless unreliability in different ways from piece to piece:

- To deal with dropped packets, some pieces take a shotgun approach by sending redundant OSC messages in short bursts in hopes that one of them will make it to its destination. This method is not guaranteed to work, and has the potential to create a lot of overhead, depending on the number and density of messages that need to be transmitted in this fashion.
- For network sync, some pieces have tried a simple server-side broadcast which either gets picked up or not on the client computers, with predictable results in terms of reliability and timing. Other pieces have employed versions of Cristian's algorithm [1] to coordinate execution time across different computers, and these solutions are often paired with the shotgun approach to set up timed messages in a network, again with imperfect results.
- Pieces requiring a specific spatial ordering of the players often require the players to select their user number manually before launching the patch - in one memorable case, a guest composer had written a piece that required everyone to change the network sharing name of their laptop to an integer and re-log-in in order to run the piece!

All of the methods above (with the exception of the username change) have worked well enough for composers to keep using them, but the current situation has three main drawbacks:

- Composers are wasting time solving problems of userlist maintenance, reliable message delivery, and useable timing anew with each piece. PLOrk and Sideband have both experienced lost rehearsal time and significant individual coding-time because of these problems.
- In addition to regular idiosyncratic behavior within the piece itself, each composer's approach to solving

the above mentioned networking issues potentially introduces another layer of erratic behavior.

- Composers sometimes avoid certain networking strategies altogether for fear of failure in a live situation. While this is pragmatic, this is obviously bad for the state of the art as a whole.

2. A PROPOSED SOLUTION

A solution to the above situation is to relegate all networking duties to a separate application which would run in the background for the duration of a rehearsal or concert. This modular approach directly addresses the three problems listed at the end of the previous section:

- Composers would no longer need to worry about how to deal with networking problems.
- Faults with basic networking issues would be easily traceable back to one common application. Assuming a stable enough application, this would make networking problems both rarer and easier to address as they come up.
- Composers could feel free to explore uses of networking that had hitherto felt too risky or complicated.

Our current attempt at addressing these problems is a software utility we've named LANdini. It is still in an early stage of development, but has to date been used in performance three times with encouraging results. It addresses issues with delivery and timing, as well as implementing some extra features that we thought would be useful, such as the "stage map" (see section 3.8).

2.1 Pre-existing solutions

There are other laptop ensembles who have also worked on solutions. One prominent example is OSCthulhu [5], a similarly motivated application developed by the group Glitch Lich (in particular Curtis McKinney). Its absence of clear documentation was an initial hurdle in its being adopted, but it also focussed on a state-based model of information flow which we didn't feel drawn to, and lacked some of the features which we envisioned, such as the "stage map" feature (see section 3.8).

Neil Cosgrove's LNX Studio [6] is quite a different type of application, being a collaborative music making environment that can work over LANs and internet connections. It's extremely well implemented, but it isn't designed to be a networking utility. What it does have is an impressively resilient network sync and message delivery system and excellent network time synchronization. It also boasts admirably open source code, and many of the features of LANdini were the result of studying and adapting solutions that were used in LNX Studio.

Ross Bencina's OSCGroups [7] is a core component of LNX Studio, but in that context is used for internet connections, which it was primarily designed for. Neil Cosgrove's code for LAN connections uses classes of his own making which feature the same API. Since the authors of this paper are interested in LAN-based music, we elected to follow Neil Cosgrove's example and implement our own solutions, leaving OSCGroups to those who are working over internet connections.

3. LANDINI'S IMPLEMENTATION

The following is a list of features that we felt would be reasonable demands to make of any networking utility that was going to be truly useful, along with explanation of how they are currently implemented in LANdini. It should be noted that, while LANdini was developed primarily for wireless networks, some of the features described could be useful for laptop ensembles on wired networks as well.

3.1 Self-contained

LANdini is a simple double-clickable application that doesn't require any extra installs. At the moment, LANdini is implemented in SuperCollider [8] to run on Mac OS 10.6+. SuperCollider was used because it was the language Narveson knew best, it has the potential of being cross-platform (though this hasn't been implemented and tested, due to a lack of Linux and PC machines), and it is easy to create stand-alone applications. SuperCollider doesn't currently support sending OSC via TCP, so UDP was used, and TCP-style behavior implemented directly. Narveson suspects this is better than the built-in latency that comes with TCP, but a parallel version in a TCP-enabled language would need to be tested to be sure.

3.2 No client/server differentiation

For simplicity and flexibility, LANdini is the same on each computer in the ensemble. In this way, members of the group can simply start LANdini at the beginning of a session and then let it run without worrying about having an extra server laptop on hand.

3.3 Dynamic user list

Each running copy of LANdini maintains a dynamically updated list. The details of how this is done are summarized in Figure 1, but involves each user broadcasting their name, ip, and port number once per second, and using incoming messages from other users to assemble a list of active LAN participants. Each user replies with a copy of their entire list, so that the sender of the original broadcast message can compare and add any users they haven't detected yet.

Once connected, each user creates local user profiles of everyone on the network and sends regular status pings to everyone on their user list. These pings contain positional information as well as info pertinent to the "guaranteed delivery" and "ordered guaranteed delivery" protocols (see sections 3.5 and 3.6 for details on the message protocols and status pings, respectively). The most recent ping time is also stored and used for removing that user from the list if too much time elapses without an update. This is currently set to 2 seconds, but can be adjusted.

Local applications can ask LANdini for a copy of the current user list either as a simple set of names or as a "stage map," as described below in section 3.8.

3.4 Minimal change to pre-existing OSC messages

In order to facilitate the updating of old pieces and the happy adoption of LANdini in to new pieces, we wanted to change as little as possible about the way OSC messages were sent and received by composers' patches.

Incoming OSC messages are, from the perspective of the receiving patch, completely unchanged, requiring no updating in the composer's code.

Outgoing OSC messages are sent through LANdini and are simply prefaced with two extra strings: a protocol and a destination. The protocol tells LANdini how to send the message, and the destination tells LANdini where to send the message. Other outgoing OSC messages are sent to LANdini to request specific information, like the current network time or user list.

3.5 Message protocols for different tasks

LANdini uses three message protocols that are based off of a subset of the many to be found in Neil Cosgrove's LNX Studio, mentioned above (see 2.1). In adopting the code, changes were made to accommodate the different internal organization of LANdini's data structures, but the general strategies are similar. Each protocol is referred to by a name that is used as a prefix in outgoing OSC messages from locally running applications:

- `/send` - this is just normal OSC
- `/send/GD` - this is the "guaranteed delivery" method, which indexes outgoing messages and stores local copies in a look-up dictionary in order to re-send upon request. Messages known to have been safely received are deleted on the sending computer, to save memory. A more detailed summary can be seen in Figure 2.
- `/send/OGD` - this is the "ordered guaranteed delivery" method, which works in a manner similar to `/send/GD`, with the addition that incoming messages are stored in an intermediate queue and passed on to the local application strictly in order. As above, the sending computer deletes messages that are known to have arrived safely, and the receiving computer deletes messages as they're performed and leave the queue.

3.6 Status Pings

The network's current state is maintained through frequent status pings that are sent between all active users who are running LANdini. At the time of writing, these pings default to 3 pings per second. A breakdown of the contents of the ping and how they're used is provided below:

- name: The sender's name is used so that the receiver can put the rest of the info in to the appropriate user profile. **All variables mentioned below are stored in the receiver's user profile for that particular sender** and appear in **bold** - analogous ones exist for every separate user profile on the receiver's machine. The underscores used in the variable names have been omitted for formatting purposes.
- update position: The sender sends an updated current x/y location on the "stage map" (see section 3.8)
- check `/send/GD` IDs:
  - The sender includes the ID of the last outgoing `/send/GD` ID they sent the receiver. This is compared against the receiver's **last incoming GD ID** variable: if their last outgoing ID is bigger, **last incoming GD ID** is updated to equal it.
  - The ID of the `/send/GD` message beneath which all other messages have been safely received is included so that the receiver can delete locally stored copies of those messages it sent the sender. This keeps memory usage at a minimum.
  - The receiver looks at all the IDs in the range from (**min GD** + 1) to **last incoming GD ID**, and ask for re-sends of the ones whose IDs don't appear in the **performed GD IDs** list.
- check `/send/OGD` IDs:
  - The sender includes the ID of the last `/send/OGD` from the receiver that they performed, allowing the receiver to delete locally stored copies of those messages.
  - The ID of the last `/send/OGD` the sender sent the receiver is compared to the receiver's **last performed OGD ID**. As above, all IDs between the receiver's **last performed OGD ID** and the sender's last sent `/OGD` ID are collected, and ones that don't appear in the receiver's **msg queue for OGD** are requested to be re-sent.
- check network time server: Every status ping message includes the name of the current network time server. In the event that the network time server leaves the group, the next user in alphabetical order is automatically chosen to take up the role. There is no deep reason for choosing alphabetical order as the organizing principle for this role: better methods will be explored and implemented in future versions of LANdini.

3.7 Synched network time

LANdini automatically establishes a shared network time on boot. At the moment, this is a simple implementation of Cristian's algorithm (see Figure 3), with the commonly added refinement of using the shortest recorded round-trip time. Once more than one player is on the network, the

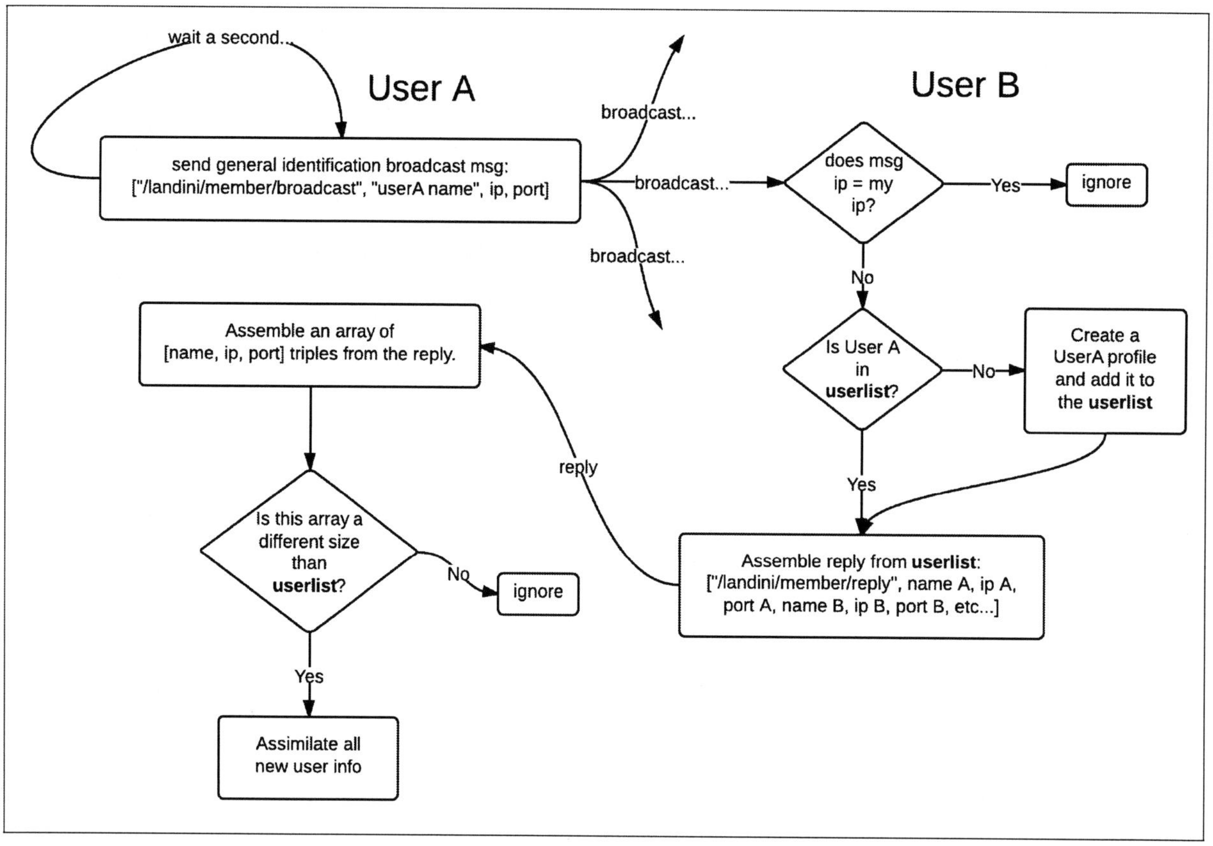

Figure 1. how LANdini assembles a user list

user with the first name in alphabetical order becomes the network time server. If this server goes offline, the next highest in alphabetical order takes over with minimal interruption. Network time can be polled and used as a reference when sending messages that need to be executed at a certain point in the future.

3.8 Stage Map

This feature is, to our knowledge, unique to LANdini. Up until this point, composers have required players to choose a player number at the startup of their patch; this is clearly vulnerable to human error, and can result in lost rehearsal time or incorrect performances with missing and/or redundant parts. Moreover, requiring players to choose a player number doesn't necessarily scale well - some patches are hard wired to expect N number of players, sometimes with no better reason than the server needing to know ahead of time how many players there are.

LANdini's stage map window (when opened) represents each user on the LAN with a simple named square. Imagining the window to represent the stage or area they're in, users arrange themselves in the window in relation to the other LAN members. This information is updated through the regular ping messages, and is therefore always current. Local applications can request a copy of the stage map as an OSC message containing ordered triples of name/x/y for each user. Once this data is received, it can be sorted and used to send commands to the ensemble in whatever order the local application specifies: left-to-right, front-to-back, or other, more subtle constructions, such as those found in Gil Weinberg's paper on network topologies [9].

Asking users to arrange themselves on the stage-map is also vulnerable to human error, of course; the thinking here is that having the ensemble do this at the start of a performance is safer and more convenient than choosing player numbers for every piece that requires a specific order.

3.9 Traffic monitoring windows

LANdini has windows for monitoring incoming OSC traffic on both the local and LAN ports. Text fields on the top of the windows allow users to filter the displayed messages by typing the text of the relevant messages, allowing users to search for specific messages. For instance, if one was interested only in seeing messages sent from a performance patch that used the OSC path texttt/drums, typing drums in the filter would cause all other messages to stop being printed. This is useful functionality for debugging.

4. PERFORMANCE

At the moment, LANdini has been used in several rehearsals and three concerts, with encouraging results. Background network traffic for the upkeep of the user lists and user status peaked at about 17 KB/sec for a group of 8 laptops, which is acceptably light background usage. As of this writing there has been no chance to test LANdini with a large group of 20+ laptops, although this is a necessary and planned future step.

Narveson did run a smaller-scale test, the results of which are summarized in Figure 4. The test consisted of four

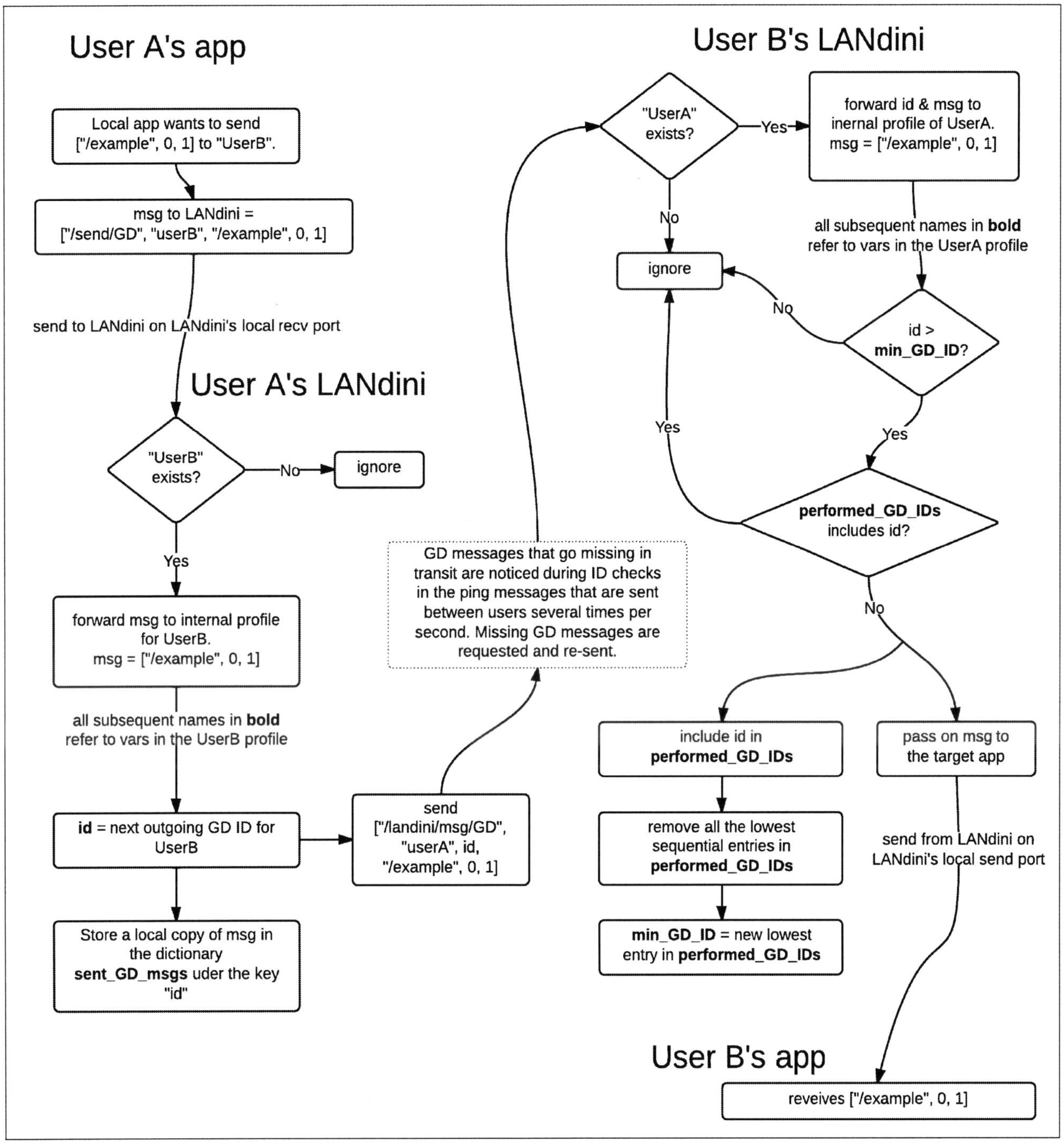

Figure 2. LANdini's `/send/GD` protocol

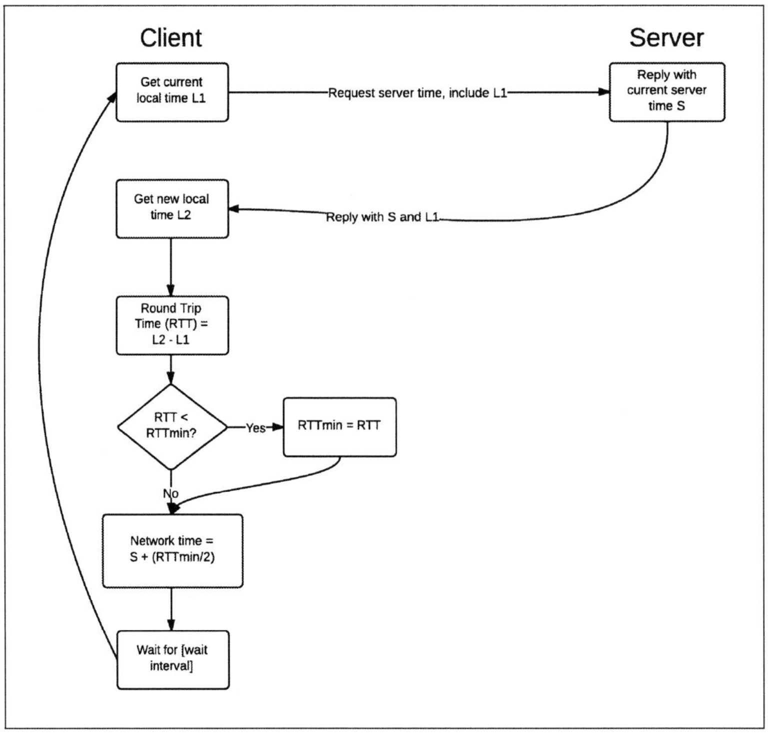

Figure 3. LANdini's simplified version of Cristian's Algorithm

rounds, one for regular OSC without LANdini, and one each for LANdini's `/send`, `/send/GD`, and `/send/OGD` protocols. The tests were performed with a D-Link Dir655 router (802.11n, 2.4Ghz), a 15" MacBookPro from 2011 running OS 10.8.2 as the server, and two 13" white plastic MacBooks from 2009 running OS 10.6.8 as the clients. Each round consisted of 50 tests of 1000 messages from a server laptop to two client laptops. The tests were simple patches written in SuperCollider - each round of 1000 messages was separated by 3 seconds, and the messages themselves used a 5ms spacing. The test patches recorded message ID, protocol, and arrival time.

The results show a clear performance advantage to using the `/send/GD` and `/send/OGD` protocols, which managed a 100% arrival rate without any appreciable cost in terms of average message spacing or total time between the arrival of messages 1 and 1000 in a given test. As expected, regular non-LANdini OSC and LANdini's `/send` protocol were matched in performance, with an arrival rate in the mid-to-high 90% range, depending on the machine.

The chart in the bottom left of Figure 4 shows outliers for the between-message deltas in these tests, reaching 1.4 seconds for the `/send/OGD` protocol on machine B in the worst case. This points to further work that needs to be done to make timing issues more reliable.

A positive side-effect of the LANdini GUI is that rehearsals and concerts are sped up by making it easy to confirm that everybody is on the network simply by looking at the user list. Previously, connection problems only showed up once we started playing and noticed unresponsive behavior.

5. EXAMPLE IMPLEMENTATIONS

As of this writing, three pieces in our repertoire have been converted to make use of LANdini - below are short summaries of how this has worked so far.

5.1 Beepsh

Narveson's piece Beepsh involves the group passing around pitch and rhythm sequences. The pre-LANdini implementation used its own method for establishing the player list and for establishing group pulse synchronization. The new version uses LANdini to get the list of available participants, and uses the simple `/send` protocol and network time for sending out the rapid pulse metronome messages. Pulses are scheduled for half a pulse of latency using LANdini's network time, and this provides good synchronization. The `/send/GD` protocol is used for players to update the server about the beginning and end of their sequences, since these are more important pieces of information. The Stage Map functionality makes easy to arrange the player messages in order so that sequences can be heard traveling around the group from one side of the stage to the other.

5.2 In Line

Narveson's other piece, In Line, also involves group synch. In this case, a regular metronomic pulse at 1 pulse/second is sent to the entire group using the `/send` protocol with a scheduling latency of 100ms, which performs well. Earlier versions of this piece relied on setting up an internal metronome which would be constantly corrected by `/pulse` messages from the Server as they came in, which resulted in occasional jitter. Other, crucial messages about state-change in certain players are handled using the `/send/GD`

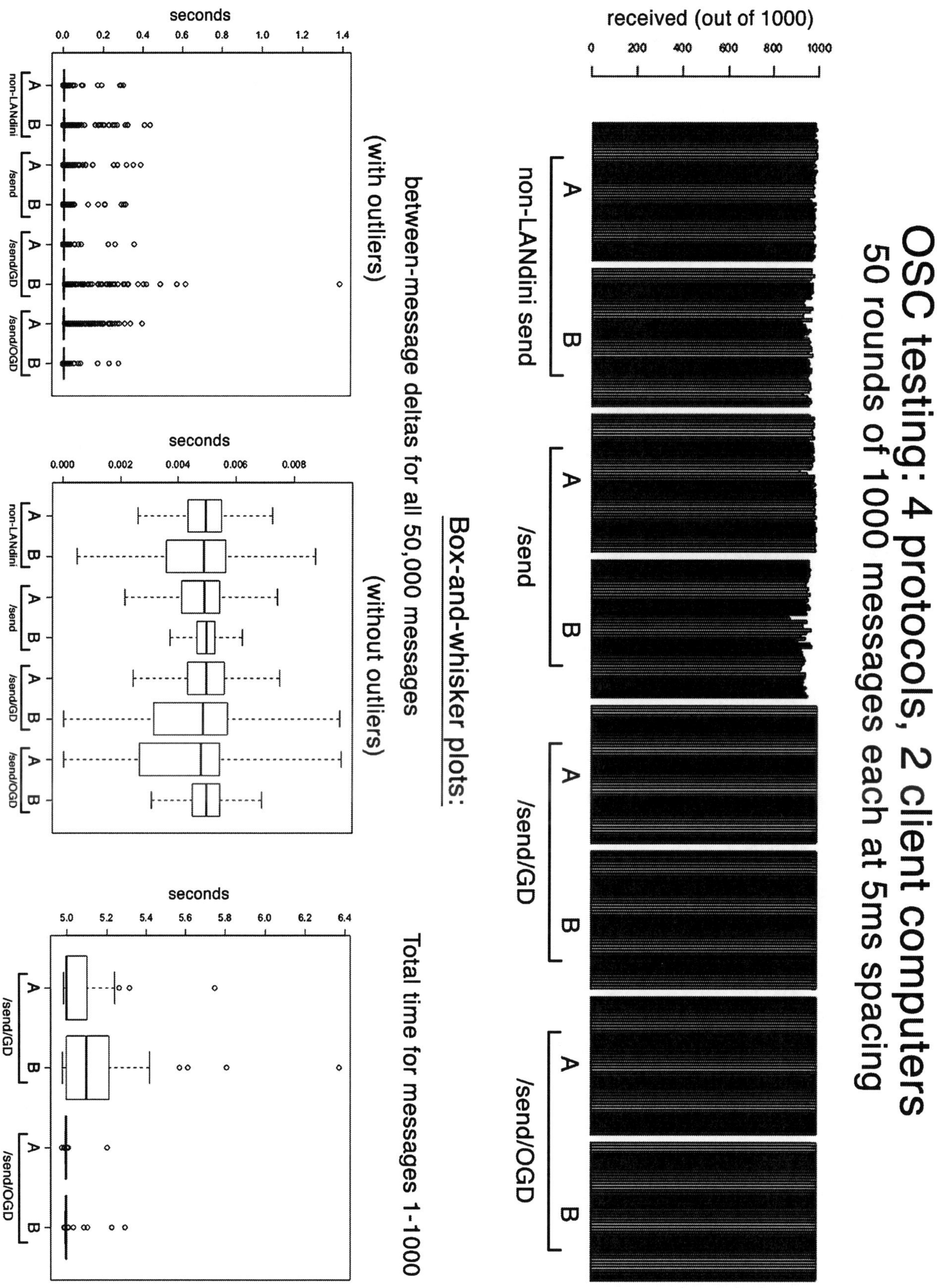

Figure 4. Test results for 50 bursts of 1000 OSC messages at 5ms intervals using four protocols across two machines

protocol, again with very encouraging results; earlier versions of the piece relied on a "shotgun" approach to ensuring the arrival of these messages, with occasional glitches. This piece has a history of crashing the router, which the current LANdini-enabled version has not done to date.

5.3 CMMV

Trueman's piece CMMV also uses a mixture of `/send` and `/send/GD` protocols, the former for time-sensitive beat information and the latter for less time-sensitive but musically important pitch information. Again, the performance of both has been very encouraging, with noticeable savings in rehearsal time due to the absence of networking problems.

5.4 Linked List test

Trueman has long tried to implement a simple "linked list" style OSC test in ChucK [10] in which two (or more) computers on a LAN pass a "play" message around a list: computers wait for the message and then, upon receiving it, play a simple sound and send a "play" message to the next user on the list. This deceptively simple test has so far failed to work, likely due to dropped packets. Using LANdini's `/send/GD` protocol solves this particular issue and enables the test to run smoothly.

6. FUTURE WORK

LANdini is currently being developed in SuperCollider, though porting it to other languages and environments is something that could be done if the need arose. One imminent future application is a port to iOS for Daniel Iglesia's new mobile music platform MobMuPlat [11].

There is currently a SuperCollider class - LANdiniWatcher.sc - which takes care of regularly polling LANdini for network time and user list info. This has the advantage of saving composers working in SuperCollider the need to setting up their own OSC loops to and from LANdinin to access network information, thus cutting down on time and potential problems with implementation from piece to piece. Skeletal classes for Max and ChucK exist which currently handle polling for network time, but need to be fleshed out to handle the "stage map" information.

While LANdini has been used in performance with 8-9 players, it has yet to carefully tested with groups that size or larger. Testing large group sizes is important because LANdini's background traffic currently grows in quadratic time: a group of size N sees (N * (N-1)) ping messages being sent every ping interval, which is set to 3 pings/second by default. For a group of 8 people this results in 8*7*3 = 168 pings per second - for 10 people that number goes up to 270 pings/sec, and, for 30 people, it would be 2610 pings/sec (!). Alternatives that get LANdini closer to "N log N" performance are clearly required, either in the form of automatic or manual throttles to the status ping frequency, a dynamic centralized server model (as is currently the case with network time, as explained in section 3.7), or something else entirely. In general, more tests related to timing and latency need to be done, as well.

At the time of writing, `/send/GD` looks for missing messages at each status ping, whereas `/send/OGD` looks for missing messages at the receipt of each new message. This should be changed since `/send/GD` currently shows marginally slower total-completion times than `/send/OGD` (see Figure 4).

Improvements to the implementation of synced network time include possible tweaks to the algorithm and the addition of visual feedback on the GUI about which machine is currently the time server. A manual over-ride of this function should be implemented in the event that the current time server machine is faulty in some way. As already stated, using alphabetical order as an organizing principle for determining the time server is an ad-hoc solution, and better methods need to be explored and implemented.

7. REFERENCES

[1] M. Wright, A. Freed, and A. Momeni, "Open sound control: State of the art 2003," in *International Conference on New Interfaces for Musical Expression*, Montreal, 2003, pp. 153–159.

[2] M. M. Cerqueira, "Synchronization over networks for live laptop music performance," 2010, senior thesis for Princeton University. [Online]. Available: http://lorknet.cs.princeton.edu/cerqueira_thesis.pdf

[3] S. D. Beck, August 2011, private communication.

[4] I. I. Bukvic, September 2011, private communication.

[5] C. McKinney and C. McKinney, "Oscthulhu: Applying video game state-based synchronization to network computer music," in *Proceedings of the 2012 International Computer Music Conference*, Ann Arbor, MI: MPublishing, University of Michigan Library, 2012.

[6] N. Cosgrove, "LNX Studio, version 1.4," 2012, open source software. [Online]. Available: http://lnxstudio.sourceforge.net

[7] R. Bencina, "Oscgroups," 2005, software utility. [Online]. Available: http://www.rossbencina.com/code/oscgroups

[8] J. McCartney, "Rethinking the computer music language: Supercollider," *Computer Music Journal*, vol. 26, pp. 61–68, 2002.

[9] G. Weinberg, "Interconnected musical networks: Toward a theoretical framework," *Computer Music Journal*, vol. 29, pp. 23–39, 2005.

[10] G. Wang and P. Cook, "Chuck: A concurrent, on-the-fly, audio programming language," in *Proceedings of the 2003 International Computer Music Conference*, San Francisco, California: International Computer Music Association, 2003, pp. 219–226.

[11] D. Iglesia, "Mobmuplat," 2013, mobile music platform for iOS. [Online]. Available: http://mobmuplat.com

MOTION RECURRENCE ANALYSIS IN MUSIC PERFORMANCES

Euler Teixeira, Hani Yehia, Mauricio Loureiro
Universidade Federal de Minas Gerais, CEFALA
Av. Antonio Carlos 6627, Belo Horizonte, Brazil
euler.teixeira@cpdee.ufmg.br

Marcelo Wanderley
McGill University, IDMIL - CIRMMT
555 Sherbrooke St. W., Montreal, Canada
marcelo.wanderley@mcgill.ca

ABSTRACT

This work presents a method to represent, segment and analyze the recurrence patterns on motion data during musical performances. Physical gestures were extracted during clarinet performances and analyzed according to gestural features, comparing different musicians, musical passages and performance styles. The gestural aspects of the performances were related to the musical structure and its expressive content, and an acoustical analysis validated the results. Results show a recurrent sequence of clarinet gestures inside a defined region of interest, shown to be a key moment in the music.

1. INTRODUCTION

Musical expressiveness is a concept that is hard to be formalized by objective data. There has been recently a growing search for methods to describe and analyze it according to a set of quantitative parameters. This has been done mainly through the audio analysis of musical performances, extracting musical content information directly from the acoustical data [1, 2]. Studies have shown that musicians make use of small deviations, regarding note durations, articulations, intensity, pitch and timbre, in order to convey their musical intentions [3, 4].

This study expands acoustical analysis methods for investigating musicians' expressive intentions, incorporating information about their body movements during musical performances. We present a method to define and analyze the physical gestures executed by the musicians while playing their instruments, and to extract motion parameters that can be objectively related to their expressive intentions and to the musical structure [5, 6]. This sort of multi-modal investigation has also been successfully employed in studies related to the analysis of speech [7] and dance [8], examining the coupling between their acoustical and visual components.

Observing a musical performance, it is possible to notice that the body movements executed by the musicians, besides being in many cases essential to the instrument's sound production itself, are also closely related to the musician's expressive intentions in a particular performance [9, 10]. Even with some recent studies in this direction [11–14], there is not so far a unique and objective method that can be widely used to extract and analyze such information from the motion capture data. Despite this, there is strong evidence that such expressive information is present in musicians' body movements, providing valuable information to better comprehend expressiveness from a multimodal point of view [15, 16].

In order to establish relations between performers' body movements and their expressive musical intentions, there are three key steps [6, 17]. The first step is to track points of interest in the musicians' body and instrument, during several musical performances, searching for patterns of temporal and spatial evolution, in order to define significant and recurrent physical gestures. After that, it is necessary to compare the gestures of different performers, performance styles and musical passages, taking into account spatial, temporal and musical parameters. The final step is to conduct an analysis over the corresponding acoustical data, searching for related parametric patterns coupled with the motion analysis.

With this method, it is possible to investigate where the expressive content can be found in the musicians' body movements, what is its behaviour, and how it relates to the musical structure, ultimately defining a musical significance for the physical gestures of musicians during performances. In this paper, the proposed method is applied to clarinet players' body movements, performing solo pieces of the classical repertoire.

2. EXPERIMENTAL METHODOLOGY

The objective of the study is to analyze the expressive content of musical performances by a group of clarinet players, based on the corresponding motion and acoustical data. In the proposed experiment, motion tracking is done with a high-end 3D motion capture device, the Optotrak Certus. It consists of a tracker, built with three infra-red cameras positioned along one axis, tracking the spatial position of active infra-red LED markers, inside a tridimensional measurement volume, together with synchronous audio recording.

The studied group of musicians consists of 10 classical clarinet players, 8 males and 2 females. The selected musical excerpt is presented in Figure 1. The musicians were asked to perform it according to two distinct performance styles. First, in the standard style, each musician performed the music freely. After that, they were asked to follow a metronome, set to a tempo estimated from the previous standard performances. The goal was to obtain an objec-

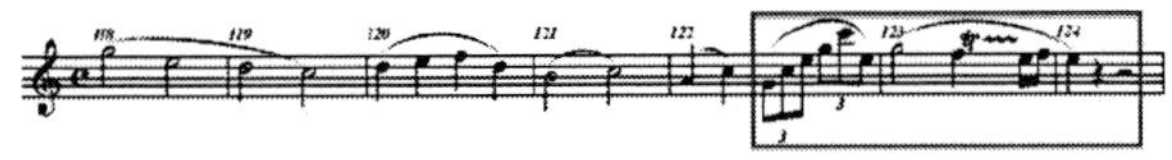

Figure 1. Theme from the first movement of Mozart's Quintet for Clarinet and Strings in A Major, Kv 581. Final part highlighted.

Figure 2. Photograph of the data acquisition experiment, from the motion capture sensor viewpoint.

tive way to compare between free and expressive musical performances, and controlled performances, restrained by the metronome beat.

Each of the 10 clarinet players performed the excerpt 6 times, 3 according to each of the 2 performance styles. They played standing up, sideways to the Optotrak tracker. Motion capture markers were placed on their bodies and clarinets, according to Figure 2. The motion capture tracker was placed vertically, about 2 meters away from the musician, using a sampling rate of 100 frames per second. The sound was recorded synchronously at 44.1 kHz to digital audio files, through a condenser microphone positioned about one meter away from the clarinet.

The audio of each performance was processed to extract its pitch and energy envelope curves. Note onsets and offsets were detected using the developed system described in [1], in order to visualize the evolution of each performance, according to the musical structure and the individual aspects of each execution.

3. MOVEMENT REPRESENTATION AND SEGMENTATION

Movement analysis in this study will be based on the clarinet bell motion. The clarinet motion has been the object of previous studies [9, 12] and it is believed to be an important expressive tool used by expert clarinet players. In order to analyze the evolution of clarinet bell tridimensional motion in conjunction with the acoustical data, we need a strong scalar representation of the motion data in time. A simple way to do that is to use the tangential velocity of

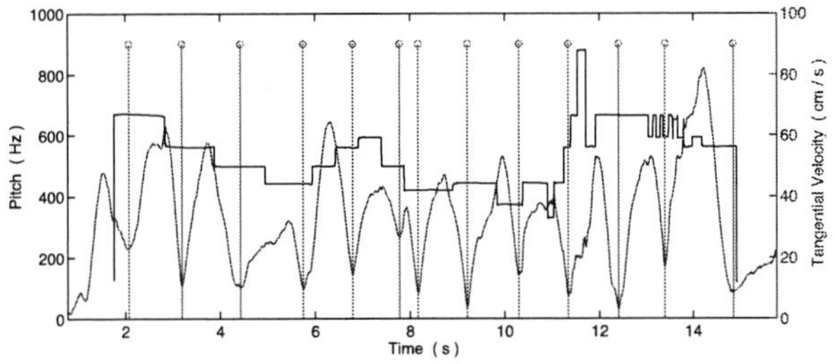

Figure 3. Movement segmentation for a clarinet performance. The blue curve shows the pitch (Hz), the green curve shows the tangential velocity of the clarinet bell (cm/s) and the red lines mark the movement segments.

the clarinet bell marker's trajectory, calculated in this case using the Euclidian distance between the positions of the marker in two subsequent samples. This unidimensional parameter captures a large amount of information from the musician's movements [11].

Through the extraction of pitch and energy envelope curves from the audio signal, it is possible to determine all note onsets and offsets, and thus to segment the acoustical data into musical notes and phrases. It is also very important to develop a procedure to segment the movement data accordingly. Unlike the acoustical data, there are no basic units established to segment the movements into, but it is possible to divide those movements into representative segments, according to their geometrical and temporal attributes.

This can be done based on the tangential velocity representation of movement, shown in Figure 3 after appropriate filtering, assuming that its local minima corresponds to inflection points in the musician's movement, where the motion direction or character is most likely to suffer a sudden change [11]. These points were thus used as a basis for the segmentation procedure, defining movement segments between subsequent local minima in the tangential velocity curve.

4. MOVEMENT RECURRENCE

In order to relate the musicians' movements to their expressive intentions and to the musical structure, we analyzed the recurrence of movements within the excerpt, along different performances by the same musician. The search for recurrent patterns in the movements of the musicians was made by using the instantaneous correlation algorithm developed in [18]. It calculates the correlation coefficient between a pair of signals for each instant in time and also for different time offsets between them, generating a bidimentional correlation map between the two signals, as shown in the bottom half of Figure 4. The horizontal axis represents time, from the first note onset to the last note offset of the music, and the vertical axis represents the time offset between the two analyzed signals, from -0.5 to +0.5 seconds. The blue areas on the map indicate low correlation values between the signals, while the red areas indicate high correlation values.

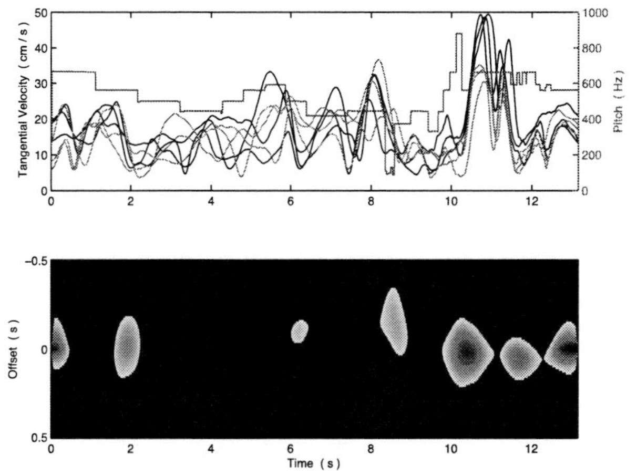

Figure 4. Clarinet bell motion recurrence map for the 6 performances by Musician 1. Top: tangential velocity curves, standard performances in blue, metronome performances in red. Bottom: motion recurrence map, blue indicates low recurrence, red indicates high recurrence.

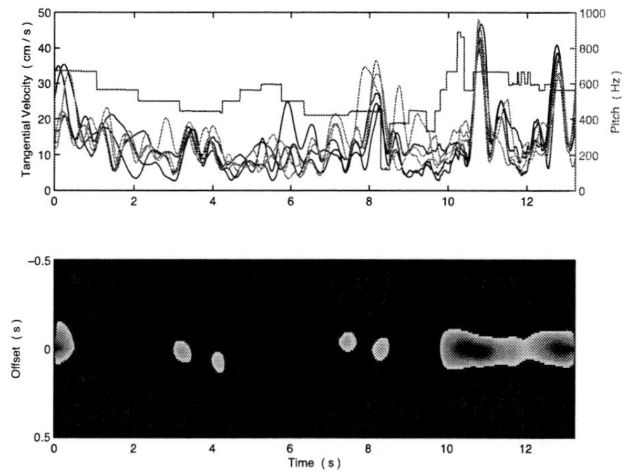

Figure 5. Clarinet bell motion recurrence map for the 6 performances by Musician 9.

For each musician, a correlation map was calculated for each of the 15 possible signal pairs of the 6 clarinet tangential velocity curves. These 15 correlation maps had their negative correlation values truncated to 0 and were then summed and normalized to 1, generating a resulting map that provides a recurrence measure for that musician's clarinet bell movement over his/her 6 performances. In order to highlight the regions of interest, of high recurrence, an empirical threshold was applied to the recurrence map, removing values below 0.7. Also, to guarantee a perfect temporal alignment between the signals, in accordance with the musical structure of the excerpt, the 6 velocity curves were time-warped [19], using the note onsets as reference points in the timing model. Figure 4 illustrates the result of this recurrence map analysis for Musician 1.

Analyzing Figure 4 it is possible to see the regions in the music where this musician employs recurrent movements along his performances. Most noticeably at the final part, after the 10 seconds mark, where all the 6 velocity curves at the top plot are all highly correlated. This is confirmed by the large dark red areas in the corresponding region of the recurrence map. Some moderate recurrence can also be identified in other regions, but for most of the excerpt, the blue areas on the map indicate the absence of recurrent movement patterns.

This motion recurrence map analysis was conducted for all 10 clarinet players. Figure 5 shows another example. Six of these musicians exhibited high movement recurrence regions in the final part of the music, similarly to the examples shown, two exhibited varying movement recurrence regions, especially during standard performances, and two exhibited no significant movement recurrence. As the four players who did not follow the dominant movement recurrence pattern are students with less expertise, they were discarded on further analysis.

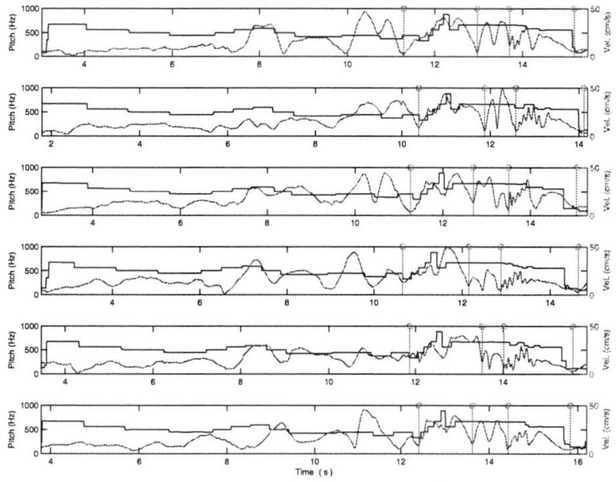

Figure 6. Regions of interest for the 6 performances by Musician 4, and their 3 constituent gestures, marked by the vertical lines. Standard performances on top 3 plots.

5. REGIONS OF INTEREST

The 6 expert musicians with similar recurrence patterns were selected for a detailed movement analysis over their high recurrence regions. The movement segments obtained by the tangential velocity minima criteria, and the motion recurrence map analysis were used together to define regions of interest in each of these 6 musicians' performances. These regions of interest were defined along the final part of the excerpt and consist of the movement segments contained inside the high recurrence areas, for each of the performances selected. The 3D spatial trajectory of the clarinet bell was analyzed along each region of interest, in order to group its constituent movement segments into representative physical gestures, based on visual inspection of their geometrical and temporal characteristics. Figure 6 illustrates the definition of the regions of interest and their constituent gestures for Musician 4. Figure 7 shows a 2D frontal view of each of their spatial trajectories, according to the reference plane shown in Figure 2.

According to figures 6 and 7, the musician executes recurrent and well defined gestures with the clarinet, inside

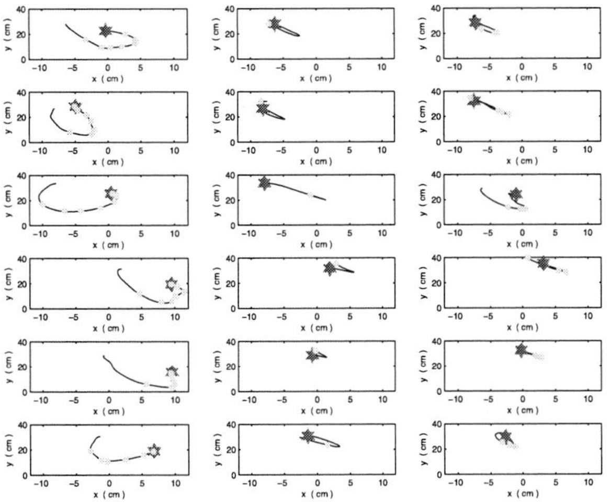

Figure 7. Spatial trajectories of the 3 gestures defined in each region of interest for the performances by Musician 4. The red star marks the initial point and the green circles indicate the note onsets. Each row represents one of the 6 performances.

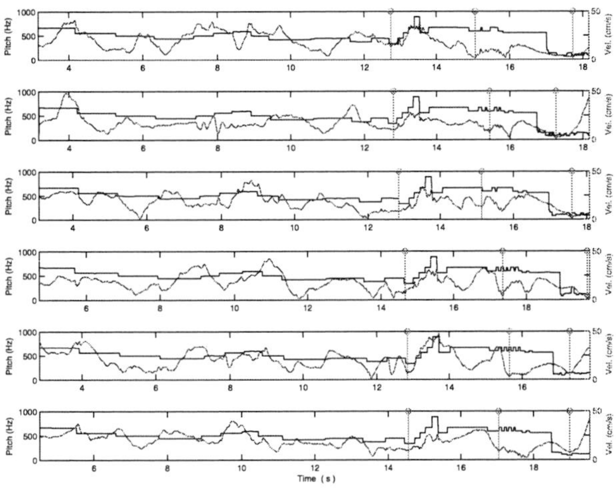

Figure 8. Regions of interest for the 6 performances by Musician 7, and their 2 constituent gestures.

the region of interest. The number, sequence, geometry and duration of these gestures are all highly recurrent along the performances. Most noticeably, the first gesture of the sequence, shown in the left column, always starts at the beginning of the same musical phrase, and consists of a clockwise partial elliptical movement, with significant extension and duration.

This analysis was conducted over the other 5 selected players, with similar results. Figures 8 and 9 show another example. In each case, the musician executed a recurrent sequence of gestures with the clarinet, showing that the tangential velocity based movement segmentation and recurrence analysis reveal highly representative music related gestures. The occurrence of such recurrent gestures and their strong relation to the musical structure, specially for the most skilled players, constitute strong evidences of the musical significance in the musician's physical movements and their relevance to music performance.

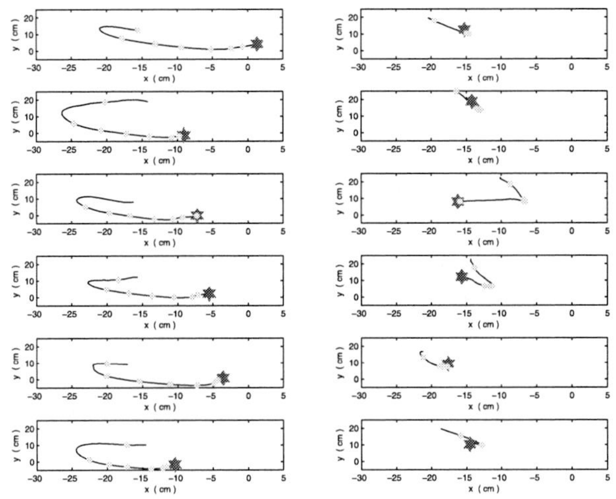

Figure 9. Spatial trajectories of the 2 gestures defined in each region of interest in the performances by Musician 7.

6. RECURRENT GESTURES

The definition of proper regions of interest in the musical performances, and their subdivision into representative and recurrent physical gestures, made possible a further local parametrical analysis on these gestures.

The resulting gestures were subjected to Principal Component Analysis (PCA), in order to investigate the spatial dimensionality of their trajectories. Calculating the percentage of total variance accounted for by the first principal component alone, by the first two principal components, and then by the three components, it is possible to define if the gesture trajectory is mainly unidimentional, mainly bidimentional or tridimensional. The percentage of variance accounted for by the first two principal components in each gesture represents a planarity index for its trajectory, while the percentage of variance accounted for by the first principal component represents a unidimentionality index for its trajectory. The results reveal that all recurrent clarinet gestures are highly planar, with planarity indexes always above 97%, and above 99% in 80% of the cases. They also show that a significant part of these gestures is also highly unidimentional, since 50% of them exhibit unidimentionality indexes above 95%, and 80% exhibit unidimentionality indexes above 80%.

A comparison was also established between the two performance styles, based on three gestural features: the total spatial distance covered along its trajectory (cm), the time duration of the gesture (s), and the mean tangential velocity along its trajectory (cm/s). The results indicate that during standard performances, within the defined regions of interest, the clarinet players execute recurrent clarinet gestures with greater spatial amplitude (28% larger on average) and at larger mean velocities (26% larger on average) than in the metronome controlled performances. The use of the metronome as a control device makes the musicians' gestures and their respective mean velocities smaller in general, but exerts little effect over their time durations, which became only slightly smaller.

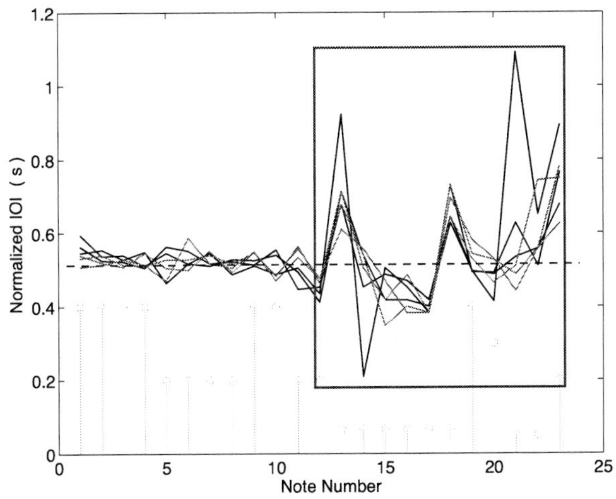

Figure 10. Note intra-onset intervals for Musician 1, normalized relative to a quarter-note. Standard performances in blue, metronome performances in red, relative nominal score value of the notes in green. The black dashed line shows the expected values. The region of interest is highlighted in red.

7. ACOUSTICAL ANALYSIS

The movement analysis indicated that the most significant recurrent clarinet gestures occurred during the final part of the musical excerpt, according to Figure 1. In order to further investigate the importance of this final part of the music, the relative note durations were also analyzed along the performances. To do that, the intra-onset intervals (IOI's) were calculated, based on the note onsets extracted from the audio signals. In order to get a relative idea of the note durations, according to their expected nominal durations in the score, the IOI's were normalized relative to a quarter-note. This way, if all notes were executed precisely with the note durations defined in the score, the plot representing the evolution of note IOI's along the performance would show a straight horizontal line. Any deviation from this expected horizontal line indicates a note duration manipulation by the musician. Figure 10 exemplifies this analysis for Musician 1.

The evolution of the note intra-onset intervals also reveals a great contrast between the initial and final part of the excerpt. In the initial part, there is little manipulation of the note durations by the musician, while in the final part, inside the red rectangle, the musician executes significant and recurrent manipulation over the note durations, indicated by the large deviation of the IOI curves around the black horizontal dashed line. This sort of behaviour was observed for almost all of the musicians in the study. Figure 11 shows another example. This validates the previous assumption of a strong expressive content being imposed by the musicians in this final part of the music, and being reflected in their corresponding clarinet gestures, since both movement and note duration analysis led to related results.

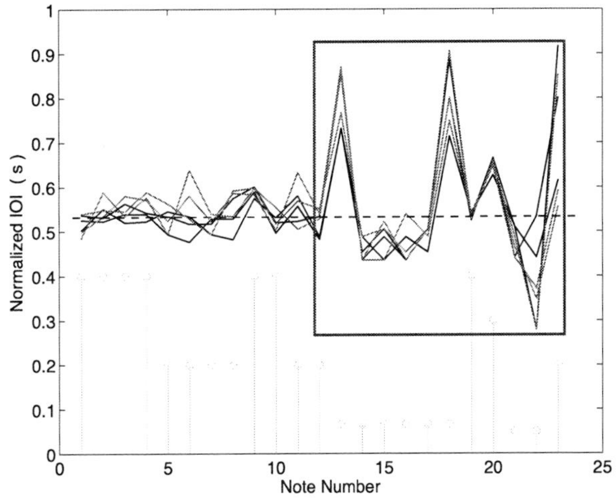

Figure 11. Note intra-onset intervals for Musician 7, normalized relative to a quarter-note.

8. CONCLUSION

The method defined for movement representation, segmentation and recurrence analysis led to consistent and representative clarinet gestures. Based on it, preliminary relations were pointed between gestural and musical aspects during the performances, and also between the two proposed performance styles, regarding gestural features. A recurrent sequence of planar gestures, more restrained in the metronome guided performances, was found in each region of interest, which was shown to be a key moment in the musical excerpt.

The strong recurrence and relation to the musical structure found in these physical gestures reinforce the assumption of a musical significance in the musicians ancillary movements, related to their expressive intentions and important for the desired musical outcome.

This method will now be applied to a quite larger data set, including new musical excerpts and groups of musicians, aiming at a detailed musical analysis and characterization of individual musicians, musical passages and performance styles.

Acknowledgments

The authors would like to thank the brazilian agencies CNPq, CAPES and FAPEMIG for funding this research.

9. REFERENCES

[1] T. Campolina, M. Loureiro, and D. Mota, "Expan: a tool for musical expressiveness analysis," *Proceedings of the 2nd International Conference of Students of Systematic Musicology*, pp. 24–27, 2009.

[2] M. Loureiro, H. Yehia, H. de Paula, T. Campolina, and D. Mota, "Content analysis of note transitions in music performance," *6th Sound and Music Computing Conference*, pp. 355–359, 2009.

[3] A. Gabrielsson, "Expressive intention and performance," in *Music, Mind and Machine*, Steiner, Ed. New York: Springer, 1995, pp. 35–47.

[4] P. Juslin, "Cue utilization in communication of emotion in music performance: relating performance to perception," *Journal of Experimental Psychology: Human perception and performance*, vol. 26, pp. 1797–1813, 2000.

[5] D. Fenza, L. Mion, S. Canazza, and A. Rodà, "Physical movement and musical gestures: A multilevel mapping stategy," *Proceedings of Sound and Music Computing*, 2005.

[6] A. Camurri, B. Mazzarino, M. Ricchetti, R. Timmers, and G. Volpe, "Multimodal analysis of expressive gesture in music and dance performances," *Springer-Verlag Berlin Heidelberg*, 2004.

[7] A. Barbosa, H. Yehia, and E. Vatikiotis-Bateson, "Temporal characterization of auditory-visual coupling in speech," *Proceedings of Meetings on Acoustics*, vol. 1, pp. 1–14, 2008.

[8] L. Naveda and M. Leman, "Representation of samba dance gestures, using a multi-modal analysis approach," *5th International Conference on Enactive Interfaces*, pp. 68–74, 2008.

[9] M. Wanderley, B. Vines, N. Middleton, C. McKay, and W. Hatch, "The musical significance of clarinetists' ancillary gestures: An exploration of the field," *Journal of New Music Research*, vol. 34, no. 1, pp. 97–113, 2005.

[10] B. Vines, C. Krumhansl, M. Wanderley, and D. Levitin, "Cross-modal interactions in the perception of musical performance," in *Cognition*, E. B.V., Ed., 2006, vol. 101, pp. 80–113.

[11] E. Teixeira, M. Loureiro, and H. Yehia, "Methodological aspects of the research in musical expressiveness based on corporal movement information," 2010, unpublished Report. Retrieved from http://hal.archives-ouvertes.fr/hal-00611660/en/.

[12] B. Caramiaux, M. Wanderley, and F. Bevilacqua, "Segmenting and parsing instrumentalists' gestures," *Journal of New Music Research*, vol. 41, no. 1, pp. 13–29, 2012.

[13] F. Desmet, L. Nijs, M. Demey, M. Lesaffre, J. Martens, and M. Leman, "Assessing a clarinet player's performer gestures in relation to locally intended musical targets," *Journal of New Music Research*, vol. 41, no. 1, pp. 31–48, 2012.

[14] N. Rasamimanana, "Towards a conceptual framework for exploring and modelling expressive musical gestures," *Journal of New Music Research*, vol. 41, no. 1, pp. 3–12, 2012.

[15] J. Davidson, "Visual perception and performance manner in the movements of solo musicians." *Psychology of Music*, vol. 21, pp. 103–113, 1993.

[16] J. W. Davidson, "What type of information is conveyed in the body movements of solo musician performers?" *Journal of Human Movement Studies*, vol. 6, pp. 279–301, 1994.

[17] S. Dahl and A. Friberg, "Visual perception of expressiveness in musicians' body movements," *Music Perception*, vol. 24, no. 5, pp. 433–454, 2007.

[18] A. Barbosa, R. Déchaine, E. Vatikiotis-Bateson, and H. Yehia, "Quantifying time-varying coordination of multimodal speech signals using correlation map analysis," *Journal of the Acoustical Society of America*, vol. 131, no. 3, pp. 2162–2172, 2012.

[19] P. Senin, "Dynamic time warping algorithm review," Information and Computer Science Department, University of Hawaii at Manoa, Honolulu, USA, Tech. Rep., 2008.

OBSERVED DIFFERENCES IN RHYTHM BETWEEN PERFORMANCES OF CLASSICAL AND JAZZ VIOLIN STUDENTS

Enric Guaus, Oriol Saña
Escola Superior de Música de Catalunya
{enric.guaus,oriol.sana}@esmuc.cat

Quim Llimona
Universitat Pompeu Fabra
quim.llimona01@estudiant.upf.edu

ABSTRACT

The aim of this paper is to present a case study that highlights some differences between violin students from the classical and jazz traditions. This work is part of a broader interdisciplinary research that studies whether classical violin students with jazz music background have more control on the tempo in their performances. Because of the artistic nature of music, it is difficult to establish a unique criteria about what this control on the tempo means. The case study here presented quantifies this by analyzing which student performances are closer to some given references (i.e. professional violinists). We focus on the rhythmic relationships of multimodal data recorded in different sessions by different students, analyzed using traditional statistical and MIR techniques. In this paper, we show the criteria for collecting data, the low level descriptors computed for different streams, and the statistical techniques used to determine the performance comparisons. Finally, we provide some tendencies showing that, for this case study, the differences between performances from students from different traditions really exist.

1. INTRODUCTION

In the last centuries, learning musical disciplines has been based on the personal relationship between the teacher and the student. Pedagogues have been collecting and organizing such a long experience, specially from the classical music tradition, for proposing learning curricula in conservatories and music schools. Nevertheless, because of the artistic nature of music, it is really difficult to establish an objective measure between performances from different students, so, it is very difficult to objectively analyze the pros and cons of different proposed programs.

In general, a musician is able to adapt the performance of a given score in order to achieve certain musical and emotional effects, that is, provide an *expressive musical performance*. There exists a huge literature for the analysis of expressive musical performances. Widmer [1] provides a good overview on this topic. Under our point of view, one of the most relevant contributions is the Performance Worm for the analysis of performances by Dixon [2]. It shows the evolution of tempo and perceived loudness information in a 2D space in real time, with a decreasing brightness according to a negative exponential function to show past information. Saunders [3] analyzed the playing styles from different pianists using (beat-level) tempo and (beat-level) loudness information. In the opposite direction, different systems have been developed to allow machines create more expressive music, which are summarized by Kirke [4]. Then, according to the literature, most of the studies related to expressive performance are based on loudness and rhythmic properties of music.

This research is part of a PhD thesis on art history and musicology. Its aim is to present evidences in differences of performances for violin students from jazz and classical traditions, in terms of rhythm. We decided focusing on rhythm of music because is one of the key aspects to work with classical violin students, and it is coherent with the existing literature. For that, we propose a methodology based on multimodal data collection from different pieces, students and sessions and analyze it using state-of-the-art techniques from statistics and Music Information Retrieval (MIR) fields.

This paper is organized as follows: Section 2 explains the experimental setup for data acquisition. Section 3 shows the statistical analysis we used for further discussion in Section 4. Finally, the conclusions and future work are presented in Section 5.

2. EXPERIMENTAL SETUP

The aim of this setup is to capture rhythmic properties of the proposed performances. It is specially designed to make our future analysis independent of the played violin, the played piece, the particular student and the particular playing conditions of a specific session. We are only interested on the musical tradition of the two groups of students: those coming from the jazz tradition and those coming from the classical tradition.

2.1 Participants

We had the collaboration of 8 violin students (Students $A \dots H$) from the Escola Superior de Msica de Catalunya (ESMUC), in Barcelona. Some of them are enrolled in classical music courses (subjects A, G) while others are enrolled both in classical and jazz music courses (subjects B, C, D, E, F, H). We also recorded two well known professional violinists as a reference, one from the classical tradition (subject I) and the other from the jazz tradition (subject J).

2.2 Exercises

We asked students to perform different pieces from the classical and jazz tradition as in a concert situation. Pieces were selected according to their rhythmic complexity, according to the criteria of both classical and jazz tradition professional violinist.

W. A. Mozart . Symphony n.38 in Eb Maj, 1st. movement, KV 543: Rhythmic patterns with sixteenth notes and some eighth notes in between. This excerpt presents high rhythmic regularity.

R. Strauss . Don Juan, op. 20, excerpt: Rhythmic excerpts that are developed through out the piece. There exists small variations on the melody but rhythm remains almost constant.

R. Schumann . Symphony n. 2 in C Maj, Scherzo, excerpt: Rhythmic complexity is higher than the two previous pieces. This excerpt does not present a specific rhythmic pattern.

Schreiber . Rhythm exercise proposed by jazz violin professor Andreas Schreiber, from Anton Bruckner University, Linz.

Charlier . Rhythm exercise proposed by drums professor Andr Charlier, from Le centre des musiques Didier Lockwood, Dammarie-Ls-Lys, France.

Gustorff . Rhythm exercise proposed by jazz violin teacher Michael Gustorff from ArtEZ Conservatory Arnhem, The Netherlands.

All students played classical tradition pieces but only jazz students were able to perform jazz tradition pieces. Because of that, for the further analysis, we only use classical tradition exercises and we only compute distances from student performances to the professional violinist from the classical tradition.

2.3 Sessions

We follow the students through 10 sessions in one trimester, from September to December 2011, in which they had to play all the exercises. With that, we want to make results independent of particular playing conditions in a specific session. Reference violinists were asked to play as in a concert situation, and they were recorded only once.

2.4 Data acquisition

For all the exercises, students and sessions, we created a multimodal collection with video, audio and bow-body relative position information. Position sensors were mounted on a unique violin. We asked students to perform twice, first with their own violin to obtain maximum richness in expressivity recording audio and video streams, and a second performance on the violin and bow with all the sensors attached. In this last case, all the participants performed on the same violin. We also recorded audio and video streams using both violins. In this research, we only include position and audio streams.

2.4.1 Audio

We recorded audio stream for the two types of violin for each exercise, student and session. We collected audio from (a) ambient microphone located at 2m far away from the violin, and clip-on microphone to capture timbre properties of the violin, and (b) a pickup attached to the bridge to obtain more precise and room independent data from the violin. We only use pickup information in our analysis.

2.4.2 Position

As detailed in previous research, the acquisition of gesture related data can be done using position sensors attached to the violin [5]. Specifically, we use the Polhemus [1] system, a six degrees of freedom electromagnetic tracker providing information on localization and orientation of a sensor with respect to a source. We use two sensors, one attached to the bow and the other attached to the violin obtaining a complete representation of their relative movement. From all the available data, we focus on the following streams that can be directly computed: Bow position, bow force and bow velocity.

This data is sampled at $sr = 240Hz$ and converted to audio at $sr = 22050Hz$ to allow feature extraction, as will be described in the following section. Video, audio and position streams are partly available under a Creative Commons License [6].

3. ANALYSIS

Right now, we collected the audio and position streams for each exercise, student, session and violin type. Now, we compute a set of rhythmic and amplitude descriptors from the collected streams and search for the dependence between them and the groups of students.

3.1 Feature extraction

We start computing descriptors from the audio recorded from the pickup (1 stream @ $sr = 22050Hz$) and from the position data from the sensors attached to the violin (3 streams @ $sr = 240Hz$). Data from Polhemus sensors is resampled to $sr = 22050Hz$. After some preliminary experiments, descriptors obtained through this resampling were determined to be related with rhythm, even assuming what we compute is not exactly the expected descriptor. We compute two sets of descriptors using MIR toolbox for Matlab [7]: (a) a set of compact descriptors for each audio excerpt including length, beatedness, event density, tempo estimation (using both autocorrelation and spectral implementations), pulse clarity, and low energy; and (b) a *bag of frames* set of descriptors including onsets, attack time and attack slope [2].

[1] `http://www.polhemus.com/`

[2] Attack time and attack slope are considered timbric descriptors, but we also include them in our analysis.

Descriptor	Student		Session		Exercise		Type	
length	9.20e-03	xxx	2.43e-01	-	1.69e-49	xxx	6.39e-01	-
beatedness	3.79e-01	-	1.52e-01	-	1.45e-15	xxx	2.01e-01	-
event density	3.54e-03	xx	1.49e-02	x	9.78e-27	xxx	6.42e-01	-
tempo estimation (autoc)	1.20e-01	-	5.16e-01	-	5.93e-18	-	6.68e-01	-
tempo estimation (spec)	9.14e-02	-	9.21e-01	-	7.98e-36	xxx	7.21e-01	-
pulse clarity	1.31e-02	x	4.47e-01	-	4.63e-99	xxx	5.24e-01	-
low energy	2.81e-02	x	6.93e-01	-	5.25e-89	xxx	4.96e-01	-
onsets	1.96e-01	-	4.25e-01	-	2.04e-01	-	1.44e-10	xxx
attack time	2.80e-03	xx	7.81e-01	-	2.24e.01	-	3.84e-01	-
attack slope	9.92e-05	xxx	2.30e-01	-	7.30e-01	-	7.17e-02	-

Table 1. Results of 1-way ANOVA analysis of the differences between the students and the classic tradition reference with the computed descriptors from the audio from the pickup.

Descriptor	Student		Session		Exercise	
length	2.67e-01	-	7.73e-01	-	7.84e-34	xxx
beatedness	8.86e-01	-	8.52e-01	-	1.15e-02	x
event density	9.84e-01	-	9.08e-01	-	1.41e-66	xxx
tempo estimation (autoc)	5.35e-01	-	8.52e-01	-	6.72e-23	xxx
tempo estimation (spec)	8.33e-01	-	8.66e-01	-	2.71e-13	xxx
pulse clarity	6.24e-01	-	6.35e-01	-	8.35e-09	xxx
low energy	7.59e-01	-	9.26e-01	-	2.15e-76	xxx
onsets	7.41e-01	-	9.52e-01	-	3.19e-10	xxx
attack time	1.14e-01	-	3.45e-01	-	9.05e-02	-
attack slope	6.70e-01	-	9.50e-01	-	2.87e-02	x

Table 2. Results of 1-way ANOVA analysis of the differences between the students and the classic tradition reference with the computed descriptors from the bow displacement.

Descriptor	Student		Session		Exercise	
length	2.67e-01	-	7.73e-01	-	7.84e-34	-
beatedness	1.74e-01	-	7.08e-02	-	3.51e-02	x
event density	3.39e-01	-	8.13e-01	-	3.27e-51	xxx
tempo estimation (autoc)	3.46e-01	-	9.51e-01	-	1.07e-13	xxx
tempo estimation (spec)	7.36e-01	-	7.10e-01	-	4.24e-13	xxx
pulse clarity	3.99e-01	-	8.24e-01	-	2.45e-25	xxx
low energy	5.93e-01	-	4.52e-01	-	4.70e-26	xxx
onsets	7.21e-01	-	8.72e-01	-	2.53e-11	xxx
attack time	8.47e-01	-	9.75e-01	-	3.20e-15	xxx
attack slope	9.76e-01	-	7.59e-01	-	2.14e-18	xxx

Table 3. Results of 1-way ANOVA analysis of the differences between the students and the classic tradition reference with the computed descriptors from the bow force.

Descriptor	Student		Session		Exercise	
length	2.67e-01	-	7.73e-01	-	7.84e-34	xxx
beatedness	1.85e-01	-	5.84e-01	-	1.65e-02	x
event density	7.53e-01	-	8.95e-01	-	6.27e-40	xxx
tempo estimation (autoc)	2.38e-01	-	9.75e-01	-	1.08e-08	xxx
tempo estimation (spec)	4.57e-01	-	2.92e-01	-	1.74e-17	xxx
pulse clarity	6.65e-01	-	4.23e-01	-	1.82e-14	xxx
low energy	6.84e-01	-	9.38e-01	-	1.07e-51	xxx
onsets	6.56e-01	-	2.84e-01	-	2.85e-04	xxx
attack time	9.52e-01	-	1.17e-01	-	2.14e-01	-
attack slope	7.52e-01	-	1.68e-01	-	4.08e-01	-

Table 4. Results of 1-way ANOVA analysis of the differences between the students and the classic tradition reference with the computed descriptors from the the bow velocity.

Descriptor	Pickup		Bow disp.		Bow force		Bow vel.	
length	9.08e-05	xxx	8.70e-01	-	8.70e-01	-	8.70e-01	-
beatedness	6.82e-03	xx	9.62e-02	-	5.66e-01	-	3.27e-04	xxx
event density	5.03e-01	-	4.27e-01	-	2.14e-02	x	2.34e-01	-
tempo estimation (autoc)	6.30e-04	xxx	9.39e-04	xxx	5.64e-04	xxx	3.39e-01	-
tempo estimation (spec)	2.75e-03	xx	9.71e-04	xxx	3.40e-01	-	5.49e-01	-
pulse clarity	5.91e-10	xxx	2.66e-01	-	8.44e-05	xxx	8.08e-04	xxx
low energy	5.04e-17	xxx	3.52e-01	-	1.11e-01	-	2.98e-02	x
onsets	1.90e-01	x	6.07e-01	-	1.17e-01	-	1.22e-01	-
attack time	1.76e-02	x	3.67e-02	x	3.53e-01	-	4.61e-01	-
attack slope	4.33e-02	x	3.94e-01	-	1.37e-01	-	4.92e-01	-

Table 5. Results of 2-way ANOVA analysis (student and exercise) of the differences between the students and the classic tradition reference with the computed descriptors from different streams

As mentioned in Section 1, according to pedagogic criteria, our work is based on the existing differences between the student performances (participants $A \dots H$) and the professional references (participants I, J). As detailed above, after the analysis of the recorded data, we observed that all the students played the exercises from the classical tradition with a high quality, while only those with jazz background played properly the exercises from the jazz tradition. Then, all the comparisons are computed in relation to the classical tradition professional violinist (participant I).

For the first set of (compact) descriptors, we compute the euclidean distance between the obtained descriptors of all the recordings from the students and their relative value from the professional performance.

For the frame-based descriptors, as the student and reference streams are not aligned, we use Dynamic time warping (DTW) [8] which also proved to be robust in gesture data [9]. Specifically, we use the total cost of warping path as a distance measure between two streams.

In summary, we have a set of descriptors related to the rhythmic distance between students and the reference for 4 streams of data (one from audio and three from position).

3.2 Statistical analysis

One-way Analysis of variance (ANOVA) is used to test the null-hypothesis within each variable, assuming that sampled population is normally distributed. Null hypothesis are defined as follows:

H_0: Descriptor X do not influence the definition of variable Y.

being X one of the rhythmic descriptors detailed in Section 3.1, and Y one of the four variables in our study (student, session, exercise, and type). Results shown in Tables 1, 2, 3, 4 represent the probability of null hypothesis being true. Then, we consider that descriptor X is representative for $p(H_0) \leq 0.05$. We also include a graphic marker to detect when the descriptor has a certain influence according to the following criteria: (a) – for $0.01 \leq p(H_0) \leq 0.05$, no influence; (b) x for $0.001 \leq p(H_0) < 0.01$, small influence; (c) xx for $0.0001 \leq p(H_0) < 0.001$, medium influence; (d) xxx for $p(H_0) < 0.0001$, strong influence.

It is also interesting to analyze results of two-way ANOVA analysis for the student and exercise variables of our study. Results are shown in Table 5, also including graphical markers.

4. DISCUSSION

As detailed in the Section 3.2, Table 1, 2, 3 and 4 show the results of the 1-way ANOVA analysis of the differences between the performances played by the students and the reference for different streams and descriptors. *Type* variable is only taken into account in the analysis of pickup data because Polhemus streams are only recorded using one violin, as described in Section 2.4.2. Nevertheless, as the null hypothesis can not be rejected for most of the descriptors, we conclude that the violin type has no influence in our analysis. Moreover, the probabilities of null hypotheses for *Session* variable are also high. The null hypotheses can not be rejected, then, we conclude that the *Session* variable has no influence in our analysis.

Focusing on the *Exercise* and *Student* variables in Tables 1, 2, 3, and 4, we observe a high dependence of the *Exercise* variable in most of the descriptors and streams, as expected. Our goal is to analyze the behavior of the students. Table 5 shows the results of the two-way ANOVA analysis for *Student* and *Exercise* joint variables (Note how, in this table, columns represent different streams, not variables, for space restrictions). Null hypotheses can be rejected for different descriptors and variables, but we observe a high accumulation of 'xxx' graphic markers for tempo estimation (auto-correlation) and pulse clarity descriptors [3]. We guess that these descriptors are the best to explain differences between the two groups of students.

Moreover, according to Tables $1 \dots 5$, we observe how the most representative stream is the audio recorded from the pickup. For that, from now to the end, we focus only on this stream.

Assuming ANOVA shows these descriptors present some statistically significant dependency with the two groups of students, we can go back to the original data and analyze

[3] Pulse clarity is considered as a high-level musical dimension that conveys how easily in a given musical piece, or a particular moment during that piece, listeners can perceive the underlying rhythmic or metrical pulsation [10].

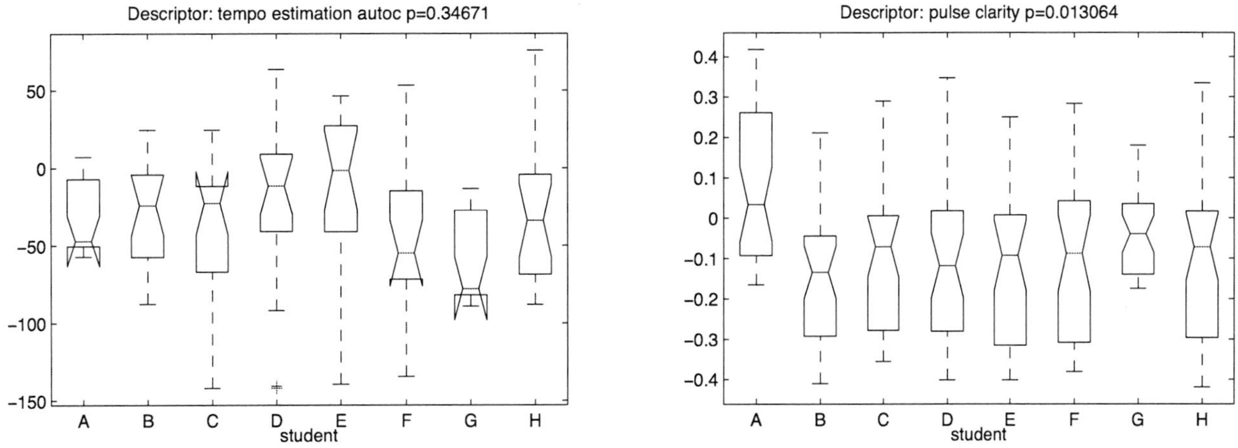

Figure 1. 1-way anova analysis plots for (a) tempo estimation (auto-correlation) descriptor on student variable, using bow-force estimation stream, and (b) pulse clarity descriptor on student variable, using pickup stream.

its behavior. Figure 1 shows the statistics for tempo estimation (auto-correlation) and pulse clarity descriptors (those who presented a high dependence in the ANOVA analysis) with respect to the classical tradition reference. Even with the *Exercise* variable information scrambled in these plots, we observe how student A and G present a different behavior with respect to the other ones. As described in Section 2.1, students A and G are those without jazz musical background.

Focusing on the tempo estimation (auto-correlation) shown in Figure 1 (a), we can derive some partial conclusions:

- Mean of the relative tempo estimation for students from the jazz tradition are far from the professional violinist, except for the participant F. Assuming a negative value of the difference means that the student plays faster than the reference, we observe a tendency on classical students playing faster than the reference.
- The lower limit (25th. percentile) of the relative tempo estimation for students from classical tradition are close to their mean. This could mean classical tradition students are more stable in their tempo.

Focusing on the pulse clarity shown in Figure 1 (b), we can derive some partial conclusions:

- Mean values of the relative pulse clarity for students from the classical tradition are closer to zero. We deduce the pulse-clarity for students from the classical tradition is closer to the professional violinist.
- Mean values of the relative pulse clarity for students from the jazz tradition are far and negative. Assuming a negative value of the difference means that the student plays with a higher pulse clarity than the reference, we could deduce that students from the jazz tradition show a clearer pulse than the reference.
- The lower limit (25th. percentile) of the samples for students with jazz background is lower than the lower limit of the samples for students with classical background. As in the previous case, assuming a negative value of the difference means that the student plays with a higher pulse clarity than the reference, we could deduce that students from the jazz tradition show a clearer pulse than the reference.

It is not the goal of this paper to pedagogically define what does it mean *to perform better*, but we guess that, in our scenario, students with jazz musical background can be objectively identified in terms of tempo and pulse clarity with respect to those students without this background. For all, we conclude that the two groups of students can be objectively identified.

5. CONCLUSION

In this paper, we presented a case study for the comparison of musical performances in terms of rhythm of two groups of students. Specifically we proposed a methodology to determine which parameters may best identify rhythmic properties of performances carried out by a given set of students under specific conditions, based on multimodal data, an analyzed whether they are closer to a given reference. The novelty of this methodology is the obtention of rhythmic properties related to a group of students instead of a specific student, piece, session, or violin. Data from the pickup resulted being more effective than gesture data from the position sensors. Pulse clarity and tempo estimation showed to be the descriptors that have a major influence in the student behavior. Then, by analyzing them in detail, we observe how the two separable groups they provide coincide with the groups of students defined by their musical background, as shown in Figure 1. This can be a controversial conclusion for pedagogic and artistic research. In order to make these conclusions more general, our next step is to increase the number of subjects to analyze, including more scores, participants and instruments.

Acknowledgments

The research leading these results has received funding from the European Union Seventh Framework Programme FP7 / 2007-2013 through the PHENICX project under grant agreement n 601166.

6. REFERENCES

[1] G. Widmer and W. Goebl, "Computational models of expressive music performance: The state of the art," *Journal of New Music Research*, vol. 33, no. 3, pp. 203–216, 2004.

[2] S. Dixon, W. Goebl, and G. Widmer, "The performance worm: Real time visualization of expression based on langner's tempo-loudness animation," in *Proceedings of the International Computer Music Conference (ICMC)*, Gteborg, Sweden, 2002, pp. 361–364.

[3] C. Saunders, D. Hardoon, J. Shawe-taylor, and W. Gerhard, "Using string kernels to identify famous performers from their playing style," in *Proceedings of the 15th European Conference on Machine Learning (ECML)*, 2004.

[4] A. Kirke and E. Reck Miranda, "A survey of computer systems for expressive music performance?" *ACM Surveys*, vol. 42, no. 1, 2009.

[5] E. Maestre, M. Blaauw, J. Bonada, E. Guaus, and A. Perez, "Statistical modeling of bowing control applied to violin sound synthesis," *IEEE Transactions onAudio, Speech, and Language Processing*, vol. 18, no. 4, pp. 855–871, May 2010.

[6] O. Mayor, J. Llop, and E. Maestre, "Repovizz: A multimodal on-line database and browsing tool for music peformance research," in *Proceedings of the 12th International Society for Music Information Retrieval Conference (ISMIR)*, Miami, USA, 2011.

[7] O. Lartillot and P. Toiviainen, "A matlab toolbox for musical feature extraction from audio," in *Proceedings of the International Conference on Digital Audio Effects*, Bordeaux, France, 2007.

[8] H. Sakoe and S. Chiba, "Dynamic programming algorithm optimization for spoken word recognition," *IEEE Transactions on Acoustics, Speech and Signal Processing*, vol. 26, no. 1, pp. 43–49, 1978.

[9] M. Muller, "Efficient content-based retrieval of motion capture data," *ACM Transactions on Graphics*, vol. 24, no. 3, 2005.

[10] O. Lartillot, T. Eerola, P. Toiviainen, and J. Fornari, "Multi-feature modeling of pulse clarity: Design, validation and optimization," in *Proceedings of the 9th International Society for Music Information Retrieval Conference (ISMIR)*, Philadelphia, PA, USA, 2008, pp. 521–526.

STUDY OF THE *TREMOLO* TECHNIQUE ON THE ACOUSTIC GUITAR: EXPERIMENTAL SETUP AND PRELIMINARY RESULTS ON REGULARITY

Sérgio Freire
School of Music
Federal University of Minas Gerais (UFMG)
sfreire@musica.ufmg.br

Lucas Nézio
School of Music (UFMG)
lucasnezio@gmail.com

ABSTRACT

This paper presents an experimental setup for the study of right hand techniques on the acoustic guitar, and describes the main features of our apparatus regarding the extraction of audio descriptors. A preliminary case study on the *tremolo* technique is also discussed, where four different musicians played five versions of the same musical excerpt. These versions are compared on the basis of the regularity of the rhythmic pattern, the note durations, and the uniformity of the amplitudes. The comparison results suggest a direct relationship between rhythmic regularity and the player's level of expertise. Nevertheless, this relationship does not apply to the note durations or the dynamic regularity. Finally, some concerns regarding the difficulties in listening to the discovered (ir)regularities are addressed, and some steps for further research are pointed out.

1. INTRODUCTION

The development of increasingly refined tools for audio processing, video analysis and motion capture has opened new methods for studying music performance. Several of these tools and methodologies can be seen in the multimodal (exploring more than one stream of data related to the same performance) projects developed at the Input Devices and Music Interaction Laboratory [1], McGill University, Canada.

On the other hand, the extraction of features and descriptors from only audio signals still receives much efforts and generates significant results [1–3].

The analysis of audio recordings of polyphonic or ensemble performances pose additional difficulties, especially in source and voice separation [4, 5]. Studies in this field are usually accomplished through independent recording of each musician or, as in the case of the piano, by using instruments such as the Disklavier, which can generate MIDI (or similar) data [6–8].

Fewer studies have focused on polyphonic performances on an acoustic guitar. Thus far, most of the existing literature deals with electric or commercial MIDI guitars, and some of them are not directly concerned with detailed features of the performance [9–12]. This paper presents the experimental setup and tools developed for studying the right hand techniques of an acoustic guitar player, along with the results and discussion of an experiment focused on the *tremolo* technique.

2. DESCRIPTION OF THE SYSTEM

The setup used for this study consisted of the following components: a Spanish acoustic guitar Alhambra (model E-533, year 1978), hexaphonic acoustic pickups made by LR Baggs, a multi-cable with six independent audio paths, an audio interface with preamplification Focusrite Saffire Pro40, and the Max programming environment. Developing the system with real-time capabilities provides the potential not only to use it as a didactic tool, but also for interactive applications of the acoustic-digital interface. In non real-time applications, the software Digital Performer is used for the multi-track recording; these recordings may be later fed into Max through an internal audio driver.

The basic data related to signal levels in the system are presented in Table 1. The RMS values are expressed in dBFS (dB full scale), where 0 dB corresponds to the maximum undistorted signal admitted by the system. The calculation is done for each of the 1024 samples (corresponding to 21.3 ms at a sampling frequency of 48 kHz), with a hop size of 512 samples. These data were averaged from several informal performance sessions on this instrument. They also showed that the pickup system was sufficiently reliable and uniform to allow for comparison of the signal levels from different strings. The amplitude range, with an average of 39 dB, is consistent with the data collected by Gieseler [13] for an acoustic guitar (ca. 35 dB).

The mechanical and acoustic coupling is very strong in the guitar used in this setup, and deserves special attention in the routines of attack detection. Two general values were calculated for each string (see Table 2), using the same strategy of averaging informal performance sessions. The first value is the maximum influence suffered by one string due to a simultaneous attack on the remaining five strings. The second is the maximum influence of the attack on one string on the combined levels of the five remaining strings. The presence of sympathetic resonance may elevate these values somewhat.

string	tunning (Hz)	background noise(dB)	intensity attacks pp (dB)	intensity attacks ff (dB)
first (E4)	330	-89.6	-60	-23
second (B3)	247	-89	-62	-23
third (G3)	196	-88.7	-62	-20
fourth (D3)	147	-88.8	-60	-23
fifth (A2)	110	-89.4	-60	-23
sixth (E2)	82.5	-90	-60	-20

Table 1. Basic amplitude values in the system.

string	maximum influence from remaining strings (dB)	maximum influence on remaining strings (dB)
first	-48	-34
second	-45	-35
third	-44	-42
fourth	-45	-45
fifth	-45	-49
sixth	-45	-46

Table 2. General amplitude levels due to mechanical coupling in the system.

The audio signal generated by the pickups was compared to the sound captured by a condenser microphone of median sensibility [14]. Two main results are worth mentioning here. First, a consistent positive correlation was found in the different dynamic levels between signals from the two sources. Second, the differences in sonority were more noticeable, mainly in the bass and medium registers. The typical resonances of an acoustic guitar, due to the soundboard and sound hole, are missing in the pickup signals, as expected. However, the attack transients are more defined in these signals, and help the extraction of descriptors (see next section).

Currently, the system can produce several low-level audio descriptors in real-time: moment of attack detection and note offset (with an error margin of 10 ms), amplitude, pitch, articulation (staccato - legato), and pitch bending. Efforts are being made to characterize the brightness (taking in account the string and fret in use) and sympathetic resonance (both in amplitude and pitch effects).

Simple visual interfaces for the real-time monitoring of amplitudes, beat/pulse duration, and the effective duration of each note (a kind of piano-roll display) were developed. Preliminary studies have focused on right hand techniques like arpeggios, plaqué (block chords), repeated notes, and *tremolos*. Such studies were important not only for the development of analytical methods and tools, but also for the calibration and progressive refinement of the system. They are discussed in detail in Nezio's dissertation [14]. Somewhat unexpected results from the analysis of two performances of a *tremolo* excerpt encouraged the realization of the present work, which has a larger number of interpreters and will be discussed later.

3. EXTRACTION OF NOTE ONSETS, OFFSETS AND AMPLITUDES

The majority of the sounds produced on the guitar may be characterized by a sharp attack followed by a resonance, with no sustained section. Therefore, it is not necessary for the purposes of this paper to distinguish between the onset and attack portions of the audio signal: on the guitar, an attack always presents a clear transient and a definite peak in the signal.

The extraction of note attacks, offsets and amplitudes is a crucial task in this system, and led to the development of a dedicated algorithm. The basic idea is to compare the peak amplitude value of the signal generated by one string with its RMS amplitude value (normally calculated on every 1024 samples). This RMS value may be re-placed by a variable floor value, depending on the signal levels present on the remaining strings. Figure 1 shows a general view of the processes and stages involved in this work, each of which will be discussed in detail below.

The first step is the filtering of the signal of the focused string, a stage called pre-processing by Bello [15]. Two band-pass filters are applied in parallel, the first in the low-medium register and the other in the high register. This contributes simultaneously to the diminution of the sympathetic resonances and to the amplification of transients. From this filtered signal, the peak value is extracted every 5 ms, and the average of the last two (sometimes three) values is calculated. This averaging avoids short bursts due to finger displacement or percussion to be interpreted as an attack.

The averaged peak value is then compared with the RMS signal of the same string or with a variable floor value, the chosen being the higher one. The floor value remains -60 dB (the low threshold of pp attacks, see Table 1) as far as the peak value of the combined signal of the remaining strings, calculated every 10 ms, does not exceed -50 dB. When this value surpasses -50 dB, a non-linear function, heuristically defined, generates a new floor value continuously.

For the comparison between the peak and the RMS (or floor) values, a two-step threshold detector is used (a digital version of a Schmitt trigger). The high threshold is determined by the RMS (or floor) value multiplied by a user parameter. In the process of fine tuning the algorithm, it was found that linking the low threshold to the high one was helpful; thus, the low value is calculated from the high value through a "release depth" factor, varying between 1.001 and 2.0. The higher this factor, the lower the incoming value must be to retrigger the detection. A minimum waiting time for the recognition of a new attack (re-attack) may also be set by the user.

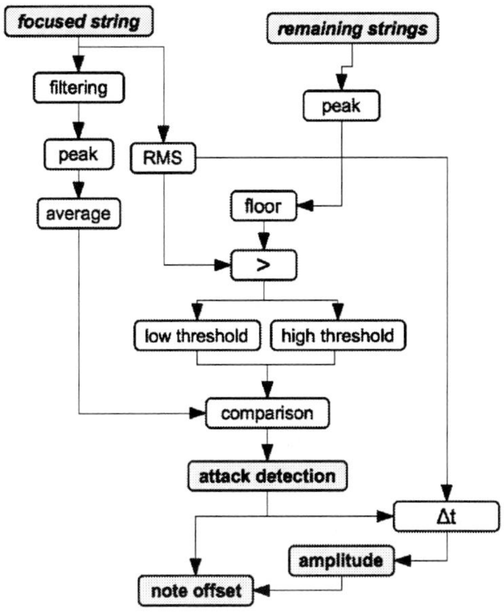

Figure 1. Flowchart of the algorithm developed to extract note attacks and offsets and to estimate the amplitude.

Once an attack is detected, the process of amplitude calculation is started. Because of the unavoidable delay in the RMS calculation and psychoacoustic reasons (integration of sound intensity in the ear), the amplitude is defined as the maximum RMS value of the non-filtered signal that occurs between 0 and 80 ms after the attack detection. We believe that this value represents the dynamics intentions of the performer quite well, based on the comparisons between the signals generated by the pickups and a microphone, mentioned earlier in this paper.

The detection of the offset of notes is accomplished in one of the following ways: either the RMS value of the focused string has dropped below a predefined value, or a new attack has occurred before this happens.

The routine just described is applied to all strings simultaneously. With these three audio descriptors, it is possible to do a detailed analysis of the rhythmic and dynamic patterns of performances on an acoustic guitar.

4. ANALYSIS AND COMPARISON OF THE REGULARITY IN FIVE INTERPRETATIONS OF A *TREMOLO* EXCERPT

On the guitar, the *tremolo* technique consists of playing fast and repeatedly the same note on one string, searching for a more sustained sonority, which does not make part of the regular sound palette of the instrument. When using the finger-picking, this effect is achieved through the rapid alternation of the right hand fingers, indicated by the letters *p* (thumb, from the Spanish pulgar), *i* (index), *m* (middle) and *a* (ring or annulary). A very common texture in the guitar literature is the use of the *tremolo* with the fingering *p a m i*, where the three last fingers make the *tremolo* using a treble string and the thumb plays a melody in a lower register. This is what happens in the musical excerpt chosen for this study was the opening bars of the Scherzino - the third movement of Alexandre Tansman's Cavatina (1951), as shown in Figure 2.

Figure 2. Initial bars of the Scherzino from Tansman's Cavatina, for guitar.

The musicians were asked to play it as normally expected in a music context, without any special instructions regarding tempo or dynamics. The guitarists were two undergraduate students (versions A e B), one graduate student (version C) and one professional guitarist (version D). One musician (A) played the excerpt twice, with an interval of about eight months, which is indicated by A1 and A2. The data generated by the real-time algorithm in Max were subsequently edited manually to bring the margin of error to a quasi sample-level precision. For the discussion that follows, is useful to name the set of four successive notes (*p a m i*) as a cycle; therefore, the excerpt has 4 bars, 24 cycles and 96 notes. [1]

4.1 BPM Calculation

The general tempo of the excerpt may be calculated from inter-onset intervals (IOI) between the eighth notes played by the thumb (lower voice in Figure 2). All versions exhibit the pattern 4-2-2-3-2-4-2-3-2-4-3-2 (repeated twice) for the choice of the strings played by the thumb in every cycle. The *tremolo* proper is always played on the first string, with the left hand finger kept in a fixed position on the fretboard.

Figure 3 shows the BPM (beats per minute) curve for each version. Note that the first value in the graphic is calculated when the second note is attacked, and this applies to all subsequent values. There is no general beat pattern among these versions, although the alternation of pulse acceleration and deceleration (in a triangular shape) may be detected to some extent in some of them. The peak (on the onset of the fifth cycle) and the valley (onset of the sixth cycle) present in the otherwise quite regular execution C are due to the anticipation of the attack on the fourth string in the fifth cycle. This is followed immediately by a much delayed attack of the annular, which contributes to a lower BPM value in the sixth cycle. These irregularities can be seen in Figure 4 version D, which plots all notes against IOIs, as an inverted curve (valley and peak). The slowest version B shows the most regular pulse, and the irregularity of the remaining versions may be attributed to the difficulties of playing *tremolos* in a faster tempo. Nevertheless,

[1] Recordings of these versions can be downloaded at: https://dl.dropbox.com/u/25793338/versionsAtoD.zip

version D shows a high level of technical control and regularity in each cycle, as will be seen in the next subsection.

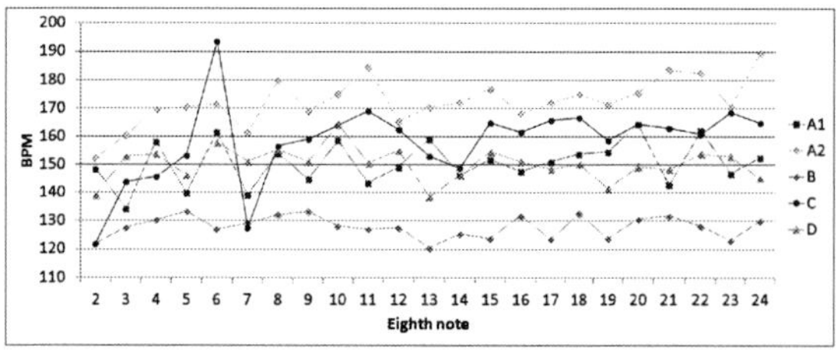

Figure 3. BPM curves for each version.

4.2 IOI Calculation

Figures 4 depict the IOIs between every attack in all versions. In some of them, clear regular patterns can be seen, especially in versions B and D. These graphics may lead to the supposition that these musicians have a highly internalized, quasi-mechanized way of executing this technique, which, owing to its speed, does not allow a conscious control of every attack. In the versions B and D, the peaks are always connected to a thumb attack, meaning that some extra time is interposed between each cycle. Version C also sometimes follows this pattern, but it is not systematic as the former ones. Another very distinct characteristic of version D is that the valleys in the curve always correspond to attacks made by the median finger (third note in the cycle). This feature points to a performance strategy based on an irregular regularity: the cycle is not played with constant interval times, although a clear time pattern can be observed. In each cycle, there is an acceleration from the thumb to the median finger attack (passing by the annulary), then a deceleration from the middle to the thumb (passing by the index).

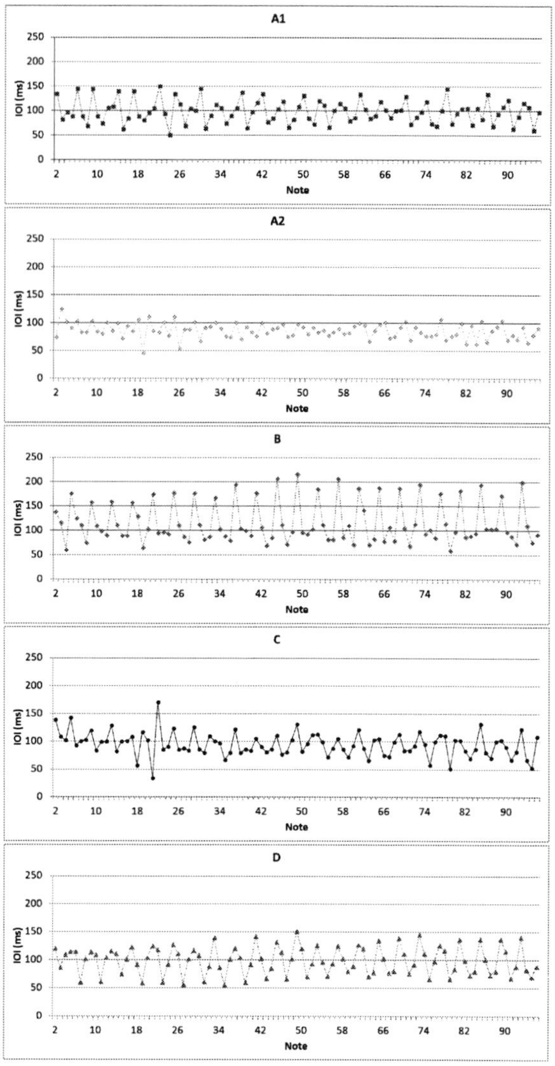

Figure 4. IOIs in ms from (a) version A1, (b) version A2, (c) version B, (d) version C, (e) version D.

4.3 Normalized Durations on the First String

Relevant information about performance strategies may also be drawn from the effective duration (interval be-tween the note attack and offset) of each note played on the first string. This may be related not only to the bio-mechanical aspect of this technique, but also to the desired sonority. The longer the duration the more sustained is the whole effect of the *tremolo*. Figure 5 shows a normalized value for the durations on the y-axis, which means that the duration of the note attacked by the index finger (the fourth in the cycle) is halved.

Versions A1 and D both exhibit longer durations in the last note of the cycle, which is expected, since the next attack is made on another string. Nevertheless, the shorter durations show different behaviours: while A1, on the average, produces two different durations for the notes played by the annulary and median fingers in each cycle, musician C maintains almost systematically equally very short durations for these notes. The waveforms representing typical cycles from these versions can be seen in Figures 6(a) and 6(b).

4.4 Amplitudes in Each Layer of the Excerpt

As in the former analysis of note durations, the amplitudes series can also help the analysis of the performance in both technical and interpretative terms. On the technical side, the main feature is again the uniformity observed in the first string. On the musical side, two different ways of interpreting the lower voice of the excerpt showed up: one considers the voice as one single stream, the other splits the notes in two melodies, one acting as a bass line (on the fourth string) and the other as a tenor line (on strings 3 and 2).

Figure 7 shows the amplitudes on the first string in versions A2 and D. It can be noted that version A2 is more uniform in this respect: its values are distributed across a narrower dynamic range and neighbor notes have more similar amplitude values. On the other hand, version D, the most regular on timing patterns, shows a very irregular amplitude series.

Figure 8 plots the amplitudes of the lower layer of the versions A1, B, and D. Version B clearly divides this layer in two voices, the bass line being the softer. Version A1

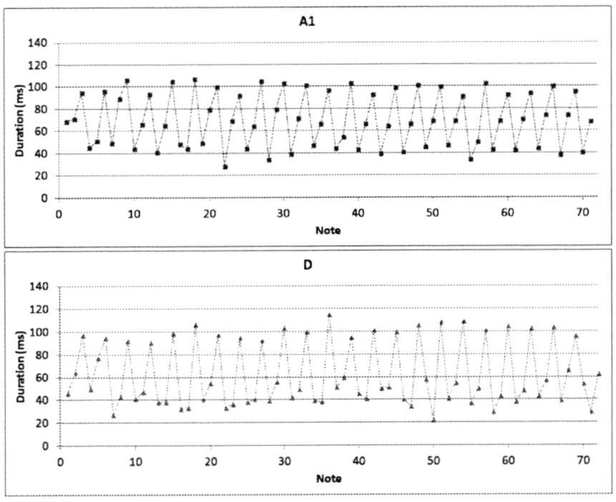

Figure 5. (a) Normalized note durations on the first string from version A1. (b) Normalized note durations on the first string from version D.

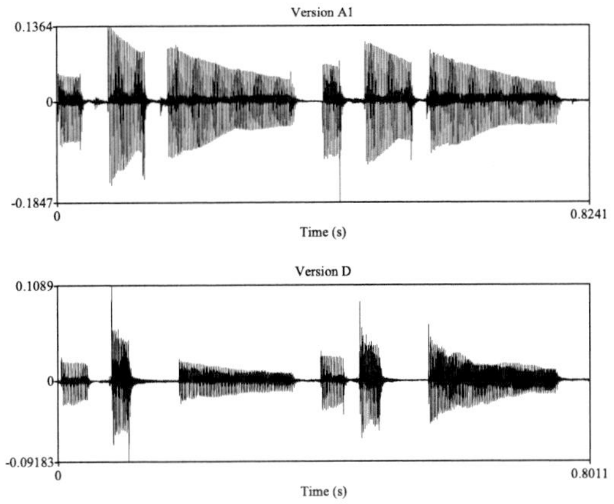

Figure 6. (a) Waveform of the notes played on the first string in cycles 9 and 10 in version A1. (b) Waveform of the notes played on the first string in cycles 4 and 5 in version D.

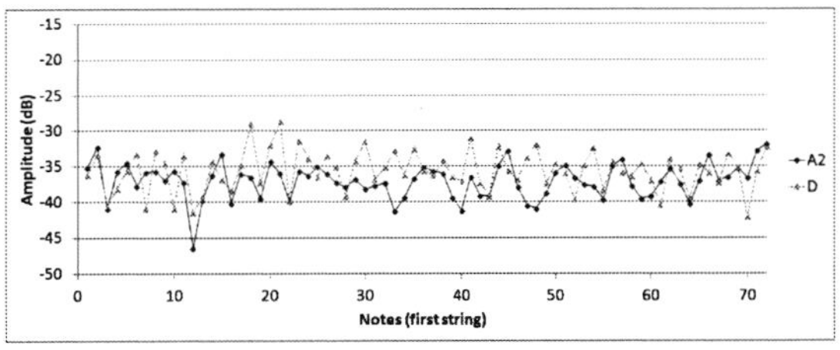

Figure 7. Amplitude curves on the first string in versions A2 and D.

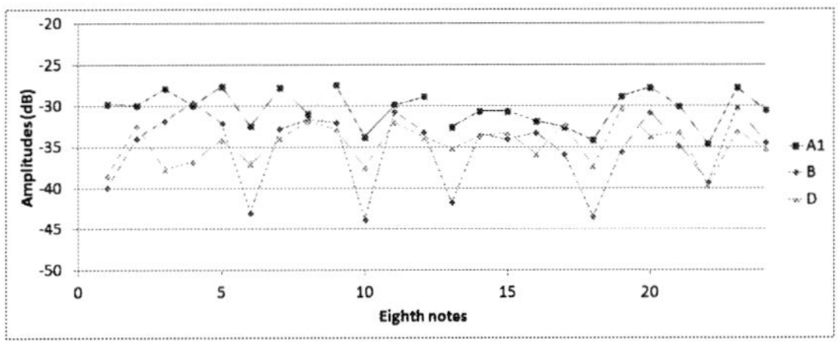

Figure 8. Amplitude curves on the lower layer (fourth, third and second strings) in versions A1, B and D.

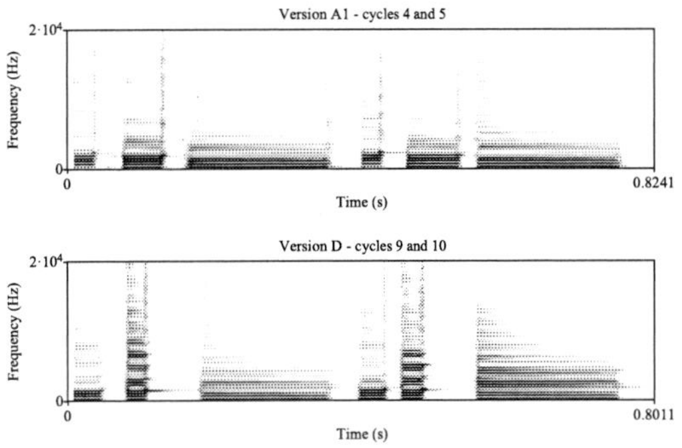

Figure 9. (a) Sonogram of cycles 4 and 5 from version A1. (b) Sonogram of cycles 9 and 10 from version D.

makes no such subdivision, and version D is somewhere in between the former two.

4.5 Spectral Features

We have not yet developed a method to study the regularity of timbre in the *tremolo* technique, although the sharpness of the attacks has certainly a strong influence on the spectrum of such short sounds. The balance between the attacks played by three different fingers (index, medium and annulary) is surely another technical challenge for guitarists playing *tremolos*. The sonograms of the recordings shown in Figures 6(a) and 6(b) illustrate some aspects of this issue, as can be seen in Figures 9(a) and 9(b). It is worth noting the very dissimilar spectra of each note in the cycles of version D, and the salient offset transients in version A1.

5. FINAL REMARKS

The above discussion has indicated some relevant characteristics of the *tremolo* technique on an acoustic guitar. None of the versions scored equally high in the different parameters related to regularity and uniformity. Nevertheless, the more trained musicians demonstrated a very fine control and regularity of movements. The less skilled performers in this technique have somehow brought into play relevant interpretative features, like longer durations and more regular amplitudes.

It is very difficult to perceive some of the characteristics described above during the performances. It is also hard to accept some of these results, which disagree strongly with a naïve, but theoretically justified, assumption of very regular IOIs in this excerpt. Listening to a single rhythmic structure - constructed with filtered audio clicks featuring the timing and amplitudes from the discussed versions - provides a better way for the perceiving such irregularities.

When both recordings – the performance on guitar and the rhythmic audio reduction – are superimposed, the missing factors in the analysis come into play. First, a stream segregation process is certainly taking place, dividing the excerpt in two (or three) streams, and preventing a unified perception of the global rhythm. The tiny differences in each note of the *tremolo* – type of attack, amplitude, duration – may also contribute to a more diffuse perception of the rhythm. Finally, the fact that the lower voice keeps sounding above the rapid *tremolos* also helps integrating the silences present in between these notes.

Future works may tackle the *tremolo* technique in a multimodal environment, using video images with high frame rates and 3D motion capture, where the correlations between the mechanical execution of the gestures and the effective production of sound may be traced.

Acknowledgments

We received financial support for this research, which was done during the last three years, from the Brazilian funding agencies CNPq and Fapemig.

6. REFERENCES

[1] "Input devices and music interaction laboratory," *accessed 22/03/2013*. [Online]. Available: http://www.idmil.org/performer_movement_analysis_and_synthesis

[2] G. Peeters, "A large set of audio features for sound description (similarity and classification) in the cuidado project," *IRCAM, Analysis/Synthesis Team*, 2004.

[3] "Centre for the history and analysis of recorded music," *accessed 22/03/2013*. [Online]. Available: http://www.charm.rhul.ac.uk/index.html

[4] A. Klapuri and M. D. (eds.), *Signal processing methods for music transcription*. Springer, 2006.

[5] A. Cont, S. Dubnov, and D. Wessel, "Realtime multiple-pitch and multiple-instrument recognition for music signals using sparse non-negative constraints," in *10th Int. Conference on Digital Audio Effects (DAFx-07)*, Bordeaux, France, 2007, pp. 24–27.

[6] W. Goebl and R. Bresin, "Are computer-controlled pianos a reliable tool in music performance research? recording and reproduction precision of a yamaha disklavier grand piano," in *MOSART Workshop*, Barcelona, 2001.

[7] L. Shaffer and N. Todd, *The Interpretive Component in Musical Performance*. New York: Oxford University Press, 1994.

[8] B. REPP, "Patterns of note onset asynchronies in expressive piano performance," *Jounal of the Acoustical Society of America*, vol. 100, pp. 3917–3932, 1996.

[9] M. Puckette, "Patch for guitar," *Pd Convention*, pp. 1–5, 2007.

[10] E. T. d. Lima and G. Ramalho, "On rhythmic pattern extraction in bossa nova music," *ISMIR*, 2008.

[11] C. Frisson, L. Reboursière, W. Chu, O. Lähdeoja, M. Anderson, C. Picard, A. Shen, and T. Todoroff, "Multimodal guitar: Performance toolbox and study workbench," vol. 2, no. 3, pp. 67–84, 9 2009. [Online]. Available: http://www.numediart.org/projects/07-1-multimodal-guitar/

[12] L. Reboursière, C. Frisson, O. Lähdeoja, M. Anderson, C. Picard, and T. Todoroff, "MultimodalGuitar: a toolbox for augmented guitar performances," June 15-18 2010. [Online]. Available: http://www.numediart.org/projects/07-1-multimodal-guitar/

[13] W. Gieseler, L. Lombardi, and R. Weyer, *Instrumentation in der Musik des 20. Jahrhunderts: Akustik, Instrumente, Zusammen-wirken*.

[14] L. Nézio, "Regularidade e simultaneidade na técnica violonística de mão direita: uma abordagem quantitativa de arpejos, sons plaqué e tremolos," 2012. [Online]. Available: http://www.bibliotecadigital.ufmg.br/dspace/bitstream/handle/1843/AAGS-95LJVL/lucas_n_zio_malta___disserta__o.pdf

[15] J. P. Bello, L. Daudet, C. bdallah, Samer anda Duxbury, M. Davies, and M. B. Sandler, "A tutorial on onset detection in music signals," *IEEE Transactions on speech and audio processing*, 2005.

A PRELIMINARY COMPUTATIONAL MODEL OF IMMANENT ACCENT SALIENCE IN TONAL MUSIC

Richard Parncutt
Centre for Systematic Musicology
University of Graz, Austria
parncutt@uni-graz.at

Erica Bisesi
Centre for Systematic Musicology
University of Graz, Austria
erica.bisesi@uni-graz.at

Anders Friberg
CSC, Dept. Speech, Music and Hearing
Royal Institute of Technology, Stockholm
afriberg@kth.se

ABSTRACT

We describe the first stage of a two-stage semi-algorithmic approach to music performance rendering. In the first stage, we estimate the perceptual salience of immanent accents (phrasing, metrical, melodic, harmonic) in the musical score. In the second, we manipulate timing, dynamics and other performance parameters in the vicinity of immanent accents (e. g., getting slower and/or louder near an accent). Phrasing and metrical accents emerge from the hierarchical structure of phrasing and meter; their salience depends on the hierarchical levels that they demarcate, and their salience. Melodic accents follow melodic leaps; they are strongest at contour peaks and (to a lesser extent) valleys; and their salience depends on the leap interval and the distance of the target tone from the local mean pitch. Harmonic accents depend on local dissonance (roughness, non-harmonicity, non-diatonicity) and chord/key changes. The algorithm is under development and is being tested by comparing its predictions with music analyses, recorded performances and listener evaluations.

1. INTRODUCTION

The music rendering competition Rencon (Hiraga et al., 2004) has shown how difficult it is to simulate the expressive performance of familiar Western classical music. Despite decades of research, automatically generated musical expression is often unconvincing - even in shorter musical excerpts, in which relatively intractable contextual factors such as genre-specific expressive devices and the music's programmatic meaning can be neglected in a first approximation.

Our approach is based on the analysis-by-synthesis approach of Sundberg (1988) and Friberg (1991), and their rule-based performance rendering system *Director Musices*. Like them, we begin with the score and adjust the timing and dynamics of an automatically generated performance by applying rules to selected structural features.

Inspired by Sundberg and Friberg, Parncutt (2003) developed a new theoretical foundation. In a broad definition, an *accent* is any musical event that seems important or attracts the attention of a listener. An *immanent* accent is an accent that is determined by the musical structure as suggested by the musical score; a *performed* accent is added to the music by the performer by manipulating dynamics, timing, articulation or timbre. In both cases, the perceptual *salience* of an accent is its perceptual or subjective importance, or the degree to which it attracts a listener's attention.

Many of the performance rules of Sundberg and Friberg can be reinterpreted in terms of this general concept of accent. The accent concept unifies the theory under a new general umbrella and establishes a stronger connection between performance rendering and the academic discipline of music theory and analysis.

The accent approach is ultimately based on the psychoacoustics of musical event perception. The noteheads in a musical score may be equal in size, but when the music is performed, they do not sound equally important. Imagine that a score is performed completely deadpan, with timing corresponding exactly to the score and all tones played at a sound level that would make them equally loud if played alone. In context, those tones will seem to differ in loudness, because they mask each other to different extents (Egan & Hake, 1950). On average, the outer voices typically seem louder or clearer than the inner voices since the (fundamental frequencies of the) outer voices are primarily masked on one side, but the inner voices are masked on both sides.

Now imagine that the performer adjusts the loudness of the tones so that they are equally loud in spite of masking. The tones will still seem unequally important due to the musical structure (phrasing, meter, melody, harmony). Because these effects arise initially from the structure and not from the performance, they may be considered immanent to the score.

Immanent accents may be divided into several kinds, which Parncutt (2003) identified as *grouping, metrical, melodic* and *harmonic*. Note that Lerdahl and Jackendoff's (1983) term *structural accent* has essentially the same meaning as Drake and Palmer's (1993) *grouping accent*. We adopt the latter; Lerdahl and Jackendoff's term is inappropriate insofar as all immanent accents may be considered "structural". The term "grouping accent" is also problematic, since a group of tones or sound events can be either *serial* (like a phrase) and *periodic* (like a metrical pattern or pulse); but the alternative term "phrasing accent" is equally problematic, because it may be misleading to describe a whole piece as one long "phrase" (the word "phrase" suggests a time period equivalent to one breath, while singing or playing an instrument).

Everyday usage of the word "accent" suggests that all notes in a score can be classified either as accented or unaccented - just as all tones, intervals or chords can be classified as consonant or dissonant. In fact, both consonance and accentuation vary on a continuous scale. The salience of an immanent accent may be compared with its perceptual importance when the music is heard in a dead-pan performance - before the performer manipulates accent salience with performed accents.

On this basis, Parncutt (2003) developed a new approach to modeling expression (timing, dynamics, articulation, timbre and so on) in Western classical music. The procedure involved first estimating the perceptual salience of the main immanent accents in the score, and second exaggerating or bringing out those accents in a computer-generated performance. Performers tend to clarify or disambiguate the structure of a piece of music for the listener by adding extra salience to selected immanent accents (Bisesi et al., 2012). Common expressive manipulations include slowing the tempo (or adding extra time) and increasing the loudness in the vicinity of immanent accents. It is also possible to unexpectedly reduce loudness to attract attention to an event. Important events are typically delayed, played louder, or both. Of course there are exceptions, but they happen less often.

In order to model such effects convincingly, we must address several questions. According to what general principles can immanent accents be identified? What general principles determine their salience? How are tempo, dynamics and other parameters typically varied in the vicinity of accents? Over what time period before and after an accent are they varied? What is the shape of the timing or dynamic curve leading up to and away from the accent? This proceedings contribution addresses the first two questions by identifying the main principles and sketching a computer algorithm to identify and evaluate immanent accents.

2. GROUPING ACCENTS

A phrase is a temporally contiguous series of tones or musical events that are grouped in our perception by the Gestalt principle of temporal proximity. Grouping accents occur at the start and end of phrases or sections. The listener's attention is drawn to structural boundaries for the simple reason that they delineate the structure; we assume that a listener only "understands the music" if s/he intuitively parses the structure "correctly", i.e. more or less as a composer, performer or theorist would do. The first note of a phrase or section is important because it announces something new; the last note is important because it announces the end of a group (closure). Performers tend to slow at phase boundaries; listeners consequently expect these tempo fluctuations (Repp, 1998). Bisesi et al. (2012) found a general agreement about the position of phrase beginnings, endings and climaxes across performances and listeners.

Grouping accents often coincide with other accents. Consider for example metrical accents. If the start of a phase coincides with the start of a measure, metrical and grouping accents coincide. We may assume that a compound accent is created, whose salience is greater than that of each of the two accents considered separately. If phrasing and metrical accents do not coincide, there is an upbeat or anacrusis. In that case, we may hear the start of the phrase as more or less important than the following upbeat – depending e.g. on how we are listening, or whether we are singing or playing percussion.

To analyse grouping accents in a score, it is necessary first to parse the piece according to its hierarchical phrasing structure. The outcome is sometimes ambiguous: different theorists might offer different analyses for the same passage. For this reason, we have not attempted an automatic analysis here. Instead, we describe the basic subjective principles according to which a theorist might segment a passage of music into phases and group these together to make a hierarchical structure. A semi-algorithmic approach of this kind was also adopted by Lerdahl and Jackendoff (1983).

The first step is to regard the entire piece or excerpt as one long phrase. The next is to divide this long phrase into a number (normally 2 or 3) of subphrases of nominally equal importance. Then divide each subphrase into sub-subphrases, and so on until arriving at the level of individual notes. This process is similar to the process of parsing speech utterances or written text in linguistics.

How exactly is the subdivision decided at each level? Musicians and theorists know intuitively how to do this; if we are to create a more objective procedure, we need to make those intuitive processes explicit. First, consider inter-onset intervals (IOIs) – the time interval between the onset of a note and the onset of the next note. The IOI of the last note in a phrase (i.e. the IOI between that note's onset and the onset of the first note in the next phrase) is often relatively long by comparison to IOIs within the phrase. Moreover, rests are more likely to occur between phrases than within them. Second, there might be a relatively large leap in pitch between the last note of a phrase and the start of a new one. Third, phrases often rise in pitch near the start and fall in pitch near the end, so a parsing that produces such phrase shapes may be preferred. Fourth, if a melody includes repetitions of recognizable motives, the phrasing should not break these motives up.

A final rule to observe is that subphrases of a given phrase should have roughly equal length; the longest subphrase should in any case not be more than twice as long as the shortest subphrase. If this rule is broken, the problem can be solved by joining together two shorter subphrases and dividing that phrase again at the next level down the hierarchy.

The phrasing structure of a piece may be ambiguous – different interpretations are possible and may even seem equally valid. In this case, different possible interpretations may be considered separately, and the validity of each interpretation may be estimated quantitatively in a comprehensive algorithm. We might e.g. consider interpretation A to be 70% valid and interpretation B to be 30% valid, and retain both alternatives in further analyses or applications.

Once the phrasing structure has been determined, the grouping accents can be located and their salience estimated. A grouping accent occurs at the start and end of a phrase at any hierarchical level. In a first approximation, the salience is simply the number of levels at which a given event marks the start or end of a phrase (cf. Todd, 1985). In a more sophisticated approach, the salience of a grouping accent may be the sum or another combination of such salience values.

In musical scores, phrasing is often explicitly marked by the composer, arranger or editor. Examples of phrasing and corresponding accents are shown in Figures 1a and 1b. In both cases, we have simply followed Chopin's phrase marks. In Figure 1a, the passage has been divided into two phrases. The relatively large time gap between the phrases and the similarity of the two phrases makes the phrasing quite unambiguous. Because the two phrases combine into one phrase at the next hierarchical level, the grouping accent at the start of the first phrase is stronger than that at the start of the second phrase. The start of the first phrase is also the start of phrases at two higher levels (groups of four and eight phases respectively), which accounts for the large difference in salience between the two grouping accents. The grouping accents at the ends of the phrases are determined by the same logic in reverse: the biggest phrase-ending grouping accent occurs at the end of the piece. Figure 1b spans a single phrase marked in the score, so it begins and ends with a grouping accent. The phrase is difficult to divide unambiguously into two or three shorter phrases, so we treat Chopin's phrasing as the lowest (fastest) level). In an analysis of the whole piece, we would have marked further phrases at higher (slower) hierarchical levels.

3. METRICAL ACCENTS

Like the phrasing, the meter of a piece of music usually has a hierarchical structure. Consider a piece in ¾ time. There is a basic ¼ note pulse; ¼ notes are grouped into threes making a ¾ note pulse at the barline. These are two adjacent levels of a hierarchy. The hierarchy can be extended both upwards and downwards: if note values smaller than a ¼ note are used, they can create faster pulses, and if groups of measures produce new, perceptible periodicities, they can be regarded as slower pulses called *hypermeter*.

In Figure 1a, there is a bigger metrical accent at the start of the first measure than at the start of the third measure, and both these accents are stronger than at the start of measures 2 and 4. We already encountered this 4-1-2-1 pattern in hierarchical phrasing analysis. However is not always clear whether these groupings are being perceived as phrases or hypermeter. For the purpose of performance rendering, phrases are already accounted for. For these reasons we do not consider higher-level hypermeters. But we do consider groups of two measures. For example, the metrical accent at measure 1 of Figure 1b is greater than the metrical accent at measure 2.

If a piece remains in the same time signature throughout and there are no obvious ambiguities (i.e. if the composer evidently intends the listener to perceive the notated meter), then the analysis of metrical accent within measures is straightforward. The salience of the metrical accents can be estimated in the same way as the grouping accents were determined above. In a first approximation, the salience of a metrical accent is the number of different level of pulsation to which it belongs. In a second approximation we include the dependence of pulse salience on tempo (pulses near about 100 per minute are the most salient) and add the salience of the pulses to which each event belongs.

If the piece stays in the same meter and has little or no syncopation, we can establish a complete metrical hierarchy. Any change in the meter causes a temporary weakening of the hierarchy as the new meter is established. Syncopations typically make other interpretations possible. This has not yet been modeled, but a systematic approach might be to present the different possible structures and weight them relative to each other: interpretation A might be the more likely with a probability of 70% and interpretation B with 30%.

Our algorithm currently works as follows. We first mark four metrical levels. The note value assigned to each beat level is given in Table 1 for the most common time signatures. The table could easily be extended to other time signatures. The conventional "beat" generally corresponds to level 1 in the table. The barline corresponds to level 2 for simple metres in which the measure is 2 or 3 beats, and to level 3 for compound metres in which the measure is 4 or 6 beats.

	Metrical level			
Time signature	Level 0	Level 1 (beat)	Level 2	Level 3
4/4	1/8	1/4	2/4	4/4
2/2	1/4	1/2	2/2	4/2
4/2	1/4	1/2	2/2	4/2
2/4	1/8	1/4	2/4	4/4
¾	1/8	1/4	¾	6/4
3/8	1/16	1/8	3/8	6/8
6/8	1/8	3/8	6/8	12/8
9/8	1/8	3/8	9/8	18/8

Table 1. The period of each metrical level expressed as note values for different time signatures.

Next, we compute the salience of each metrical level. Following Parncutt (1994), we assume that the function of pulse salience against period is a Gaussian function relative to a logarithmic scale of period:

$$\text{Salience}_i = e^{-0.5*(\frac{logX-logM}{logS})^2},$$

where X is the period of the metrical level in seconds, M = 1.0 seconds is the centre (mean) of the Gaussian distribution, S = 1.65 is the standard deviation of the distribution, and i is the metrical level (0..3). In Parncutt (1994) the mean M was smaller (0.6..0.7 seconds); we found that increasing it improves modeling of hypermetre.

Finally, we calculate the metrical accent salience of each point in time in the score. It is simply the sum of the salience of all metrical levels including that note.

4. MELODIC ACCENTS

Melodic accents are marked "C" in Figure 1. The C stands for contour (or melodic contour accents) and avoids confusion with M for metrical accents. For an overview of research on melodic accent, see Huron and Royal (1996).

In Figure 1a, the first melodic accent is at the start of measure 1. The accent is evidently due to the (rising) leap before the accent, which attracts attention to it. The next two marked accents also follow rising leaps. Figure 1b also shows examples of melodic accents in the bass line. In all these cases it appears that the salience of the accent is due to a combination of two factors: the size of the leap preceding the accent, and the distance of the accent from the centre of the melody's range or ambitus. Further principles determining melodic accents appear to be the following: only local peaks or valleys, and only tones following leaps (3 semitones or more), can bear a melodic accent; melodic accent salience depends on a combination of leap size and distance from local mean pitch; the first and/or last in a group of repeated notes may be accented; and melodic peaks generally receive stronger accents than melodic valleys.

Our computer implementation works as follows. First, the mean pitch is calculated for each track individually. Then each tone is assigned a salience S_1 for the pitch deviation from the mean:

For notes above the mean:

S_1 = |interval from mean in semitones|

For notes below the mean:

S_1 = |interval from mean in semitones| * 0.7

Then each tone is assigned a salience S_2 is according to the size of the preceding interval:

For rising intervals:

S_2 = |preceding interval in semitones|

For falling intervals:

S_2 = |preceding interval in semitones| * 0.7

The final value for melodic salience = $(S_1 + S_2) / 15$.

5. HARMONIC ACCENTS

Harmonic accents are marked "H" in the figures. To begin again with some examples: The harmonic accent in measure 1 of Figure 1a is due to the (mildly) dissonant 6th interval above the root, which resolves to the consonant 5th. Since this is a rather weak dissonance, the estimated salience of the harmonic accent is rather low. The accent in measure 3 is due to the diminished triad, two of whose tones do not belong to the prevailing diatonic scale. The accent depends partly on the dissonance of the diminished triad (independent of context) and partly on the double departure from diatonicity. In Figure 1b, the first harmonic accent announces the start of a new harmonic region. The preceding passage is in F# major; the D# minor chord heralds a passing transition to the key of C# major followed by a sequential repetition that suggests B major. Later harmonic accents are due to the relative dissonance of specific chordal sonorities.

These examples suggest that harmonic accent has several components. First, the dissonance of a chord (considered in isolation, but also relative to the dissonance of preceding and following chords) may attract attention and hence produce an accent. This is difficult to formulate in an algorithm since there is no accepted general model for the dissonance of a sonority in western music (Parncutt & Hair, 2011). If we assume that the dissonance of a sonority is a combination of its roughness and (lack of) harmonicity, dissonance could be estimated most simply by counting the number of clearly dissonant intervals (minor seconds, tritones, major seconds) and harmonicity could be estimated by the presence of clearly harmonic intervals such as perfect fifths and fourths, or the salience of the root according to Parncutt (1988). But there are further complications: a chord may be merely implied, and implied chords are often ambiguous. At the start of measure 1 of Figure 1a, do we have an inverted A-major chord or a suspension above an E-major chord? A simple algorithm is more likely to predict the former, whereas a (Schenkerian) theorist will indicate the latter.

Second, harmonic accents in major-minor tonal music are produced by tones foreign to the prevailing key. If the key of a passage is relatively clear, the salience of this kind of accent can be predicted using the key profiles of Krumhansl and Kessler (1982). These profiles may be considered as quantitative estimates of the harmonic stability of each tone in the chromatic scale in a given major or minor key. The lower the stability of a tone, the greater the harmonic accent at that tone. The harmonic accent of a chord may be estimated by combining accents for individual tones.

Third, harmonic accents are produced by important harmonic shifts. This aspect could be modeled by a key-tracking algorithm. Where modulations are predicted to occur, the chord announcing the modulation may be accented. But this procedure may not work for pivot chords, which belong to both a preceding and a following key; and music theorists differ markedly in their interpretation of modulations. At one extreme, any accidental may be considered to suggest a modulation, while at the other extreme, a whole extended piece may be considered to stay in the same key in spite of extensive chromaticism (chromaticisms may be instead function as tonicizations). This theoretical debate can be avoided by focusing on performance expression in modulating passages: if a performer brings out a modulation, it exists. The theoretical debate about modulation versus tonicization could be resolved by considering "real music" rather than the score.

We have not yet implemented the above approach. For the moment we are using the existing approach of Director Musices. The current implementation requires that a functional harmonic analysis is manually provided in the score. The salience of a harmonic accent is computed at each chord change as follows:

$$Salience = 1.5 * \sqrt{Harmonic\ charge}$$

Harmonic charge is a measure of the tonal perceptual distance of the chord from the prevailing key; see Friberg (1991) for a technical description.

6. EXAMPLES

In Figure 2 and we have tentatively applied the algorithm to the passages illustrated in Figure 1.

7. CONCLUSION

This has been a preliminary sketch of the main principles behind a new algorithm to estimate the perceptual salience of immanent accents in tonal western music - a step toward a new semi-algorithmic approach to performance rendering. We say "semi-algorithmic" because we are currently cautious about completely automatizing the procedure. Even when our algorithms for predicting the salience of different kinds of accents are refined and consistently make feasible predictions, some details of the algorithms will remain dependent on style. We also anticipate that the relative importance of different kinds of accents will depend on stylistic context.

We are testing versions of the algorithm in several ways. First, we are comparing its predictions with our music-theoretical intuitions, and judging the musical naturalness of the resulting performance renditions (analysis by synthesis). Given the large number of options at the beginning of such a project and the impossibility of considering all options systematically, this is the most practical way to proceed. We are then comparing predictions of a prototype with analyses of music theorists and our analyses of expression in recorded performances, and making improvements based on the data (cf. Thompson et al., 1989). Finally, the "musicalness" (musical quality, expressive content) of performances generated by the algorithm will be tested in listening experiments in which expert listeners judge the quality of performance renditions.

8. REFERENCES

Bisesi, E., MacRitchie, J. & Parncutt, R. (2012). Recorded interpretations of Chopin Preludes: Performer's choice of score events for emphasis and emotional communication. In E. Cambouropoulos et al. (Eds.), *Proceedings of the 12th International Conference on Music Perception and Cognition* (pp. 106-107).

Drake, C., & Palmer, C. (1993). Accent structures in music performance. *Music Perception, 10,* 343–378.

Egan, J. P., & Hake, H. W. (1950). On the masking pattern of a simple auditory stimulus. *Journal of the Acoustical Society of America, 22,* 622-630.

Friberg, A. (1991). Generative rules for music performance. *Computer Music Journal, 15* (2), 56–71.

Hiraga, R., Bresin, R., Hirata, K., & Katayose, H. (2004). Rencon 2004: Turing test for musical expression. In *Proceedings of the 2004 conference on New interfaces for musical expression* (pp. 120-123).

Huron, D., & Royal, M. (1996). What is melodic accent? Converging evidence from musical practice. *Music Perception, 13,* 489-516.

Krumhansl, C. L., & Kessler, E. J. (1982). Tracing the-dynamic changes in perceived tonal organization in a spatial representation of musical keys. *Psychological Review, 89,* 334-368.

Lerdahl, F., & Jackendoff, R. (1983). *A generative theory of tonal music.* Cambridge, MA: MIT Press.

Parncutt, R. (1988). Revision of Terhardt's psychoacoustical model of the root(s) of a musical chord. *Music Perception, 6,* 65-94.

Parncutt, R. (1994). A perceptual model of pulse salience and metrical accent in musical rhythms. *Music Perception, 11,* 409-464

Parncutt, R. (2003). Accents and expression in piano performance. In K. W. Niemöller (Ed.), *Perspektiven und Methoden einer Systemischen Musikwissenschaft* (pp. 163-185). Frankfurt/Main, Germany: Peter Lang.

Parncutt, R., & Hair, G. (2011). Consonance and dissonance in theory and psychology: Disentangling dissonant dichotomies. *Journal of Interdisciplinary Music Studies, 5* (2), 119-166.

Repp, B. H. (1998). Variations on a theme by Chopin: Relations between perception and production of timing in music. *Journal of Experimental Psychology Human Perception and Performance, 24,* 791-811.

Sundberg, J. (1988). Computer synthesis of music performance. In J. A. Sloboda (Ed.), *Generative processes in music.* Oxford: Clarendon.

Thompson, W. F., Sundberg, J., Friberg, A., & Frydén, L. (1989). The use of rules for expression in the performance of melodies. *Psychology of Music, 17,* 63-82.

Todd, N. P. McA. (1985). A model of expressive timing in tonal music. *Music Perception, 3,* 33-58.

Figure 1. Subjective analysis of immanent accents and their salience in music of Frédéric Chopin. (a) The first four measures of Prelude Op. 28 No. 7. (b) The first two measures of the central section of Prelude Op. 28 No. 13.

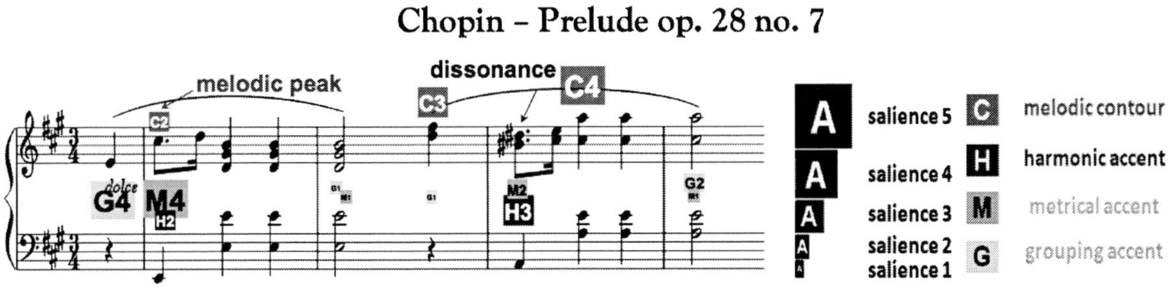

Figure 2. Model predictions for Prelude Op. 28 No. 7 and No. 13 (central section) by Frédéric Chopin.

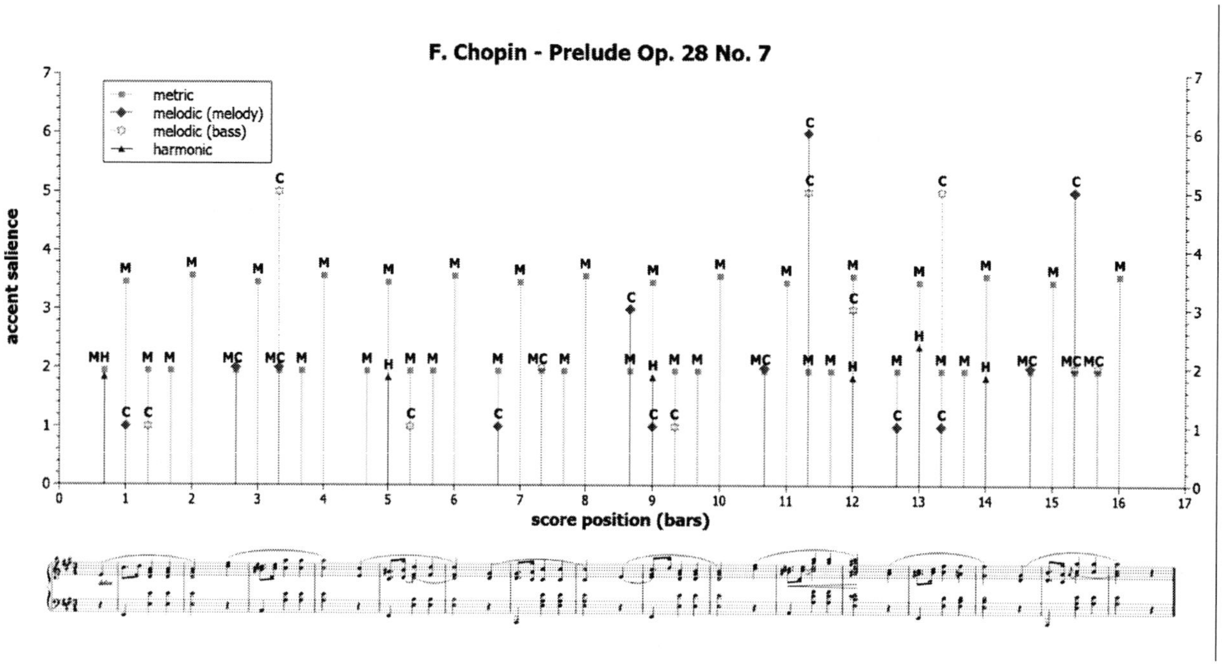

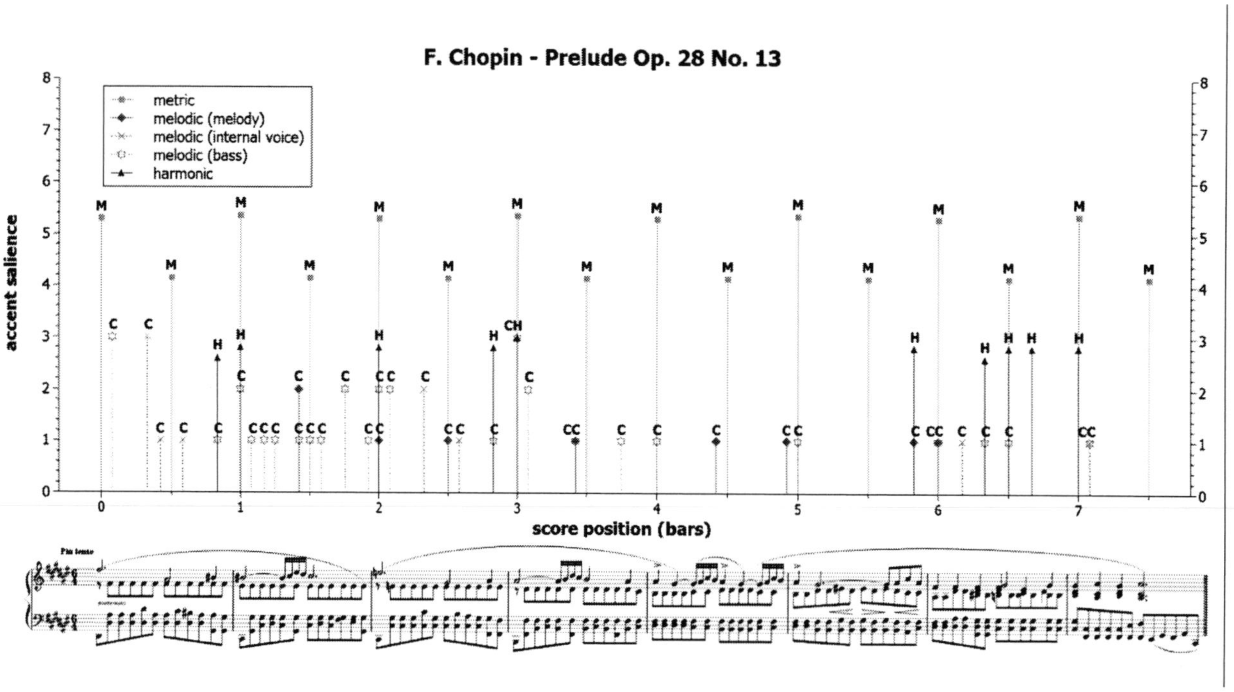

EXPRESSIVE PRODUCTION OF PIANO TIMBRE: TOUCH AND PLAYING TECHNIQUES FOR TIMBRE CONTROL IN PIANO PERFORMANCE

Michel Bernays
CIRMMT/BRAMS/OICRM
Université de Montréal, Canada
`michel.bernays@gmail.com`

Caroline Traube
CIRMT/BRAMS/OICRM
Université de Montréal, Canada
`caroline.traube@umontreal.ca`

ABSTRACT

Timbre is an essential expressive parameter in piano performance. Advanced-level pianists have integrated the palette of timbres at their artistic disposal as abstract concepts and multimodal images. A correspondingly imaged vocabulary composed of various adjectival descriptors is used in discussing and designating precise timbral nuances. However, the actual means of production and control of timbral nuances at the piano are not always explicitly expressed. This study explores the precise performance parameters used in producing different timbral nuances. For this aim, four short pieces were composed. Each was performed by four pianists, who highlighted five timbral nuances most representative of the piano timbre-describing vocabulary: dry, bright, round, velvety and dark. The performances were recorded with the Bösendorfer CEUS system, a high-quality piano equipped with high-accuracy sensors and an embedded computer. Fine-grained performance features were extracted from the data collected. The features that significantly differed between different-timbre performances were identified. The performance space resulting from a principal component analysis revealed an average organization of timbral nuances along a circular arc. Thirteen essential, timbre-discriminating performance features were selected. Detailed descriptions were thus obtained for each timbral nuance, according to the fine characteristics of their production and control in piano performance.

1. INTRODUCTION

Musical performance is essential to the art and experience of music. Classical performers in particular will apply their expressive creativity towards enlightening a composition. An extensive, empiric body of knowledge was thus developed amongst musicians to best serve the art and technique of performance, for every instrument, and especially in the context of this article, for the piano.

Among the many expressive musical attributes available to pianists, timbre has been widely acknowledged within the pianistic community [1]. Beyond its widely-understood function as a characteristic inherent to an instrument or sound source, timbre is also envisioned by pianists as a refined quality of sound, over which they hold control by way of expressive nuances in their performances. As such, pianists believe in their ability to produce different timbral nuances that can suit their expressive intentions [2]. This palette of piano timbre nuances has been associated with an extensive vocabulary, which includes numerous adjectival descriptors that pianists use to convey a precise conception of a timbral nuance [3, 4]. However, the precise technique and ways of production of piano timbre nuances has generally been subdued to abstraction, mental conception, imitation and aural modelling [5] in piano pedagogy and treatises [6, 7].

Moreover, scientific studies on piano performance and timbre production concluded long ago that piano timbre control would be limited by the mechanical constraints of the action to sheer keystroke velocity, thus making timbre inseparable from intensity [8]. However, when instead of considering a single, isolated key, the subtleties of tone combinations involved in a polyphonic musical context are taken into account, expressive piano performance parameters (such as articulation, synchrony and dynamic differentiation between tones, and pedalling) become involved in governing the emergence of performer-controlled composite timbres. Then, in order to measure and quantify piano performance with the level of precision at which the subtle nuances of timbre production can be identified, high-accuracy piano performance-recording tools are required. While extensive scientific research on piano performance has made used of MIDI digital recording pianos (and before that, mechanical apparatus such as piano rolls [9] and embedded cameras [10]) and acoustical analysis to learn more about specific technical aspects and general expressive models of piano performance [11], the intricacies of timbre production have essentially remained out of the reach and/or concern of piano performance studies. Yet in a notable exception, Ortmann investigated the relations between piano touch and timbre on a single tone [12]. He associated, to several 'tone-qualities' (each described by an adjectival descriptor), precise key depression profiles aimed at highlighting the key velocity and touch percussiveness from which could stem the tone-quality.

This study aims at following in these steps, by systematically investigating the strategies and technical nuances of gestural control involved in pianists' use of timbre as an expressive device in piano performance. With the high-accuracy Bösendorfer CEUS digital piano performance-recording system, the study explores piano timbre production in a polyphonic, ecologically valid musical context.

2. METHOD

In order to explore the expressive production of piano timbre nuances in a musically relevant framework that could mirror a genuine musical experience, the study was designed with respect to the following steps: selection of the most relevant verbal descriptors of piano timbre to designate the timbral nuances to explore; conception of musical pieces to be expressively performed according to these different timbral nuances; use of non-invasive, high-accuracy piano performance-recording equipment; timbre-coloured performance recordings; and extraction therein of meaningful piano performance and touch descriptors.

2.1 Piano timbre descriptors

The verbalization of piano timbre was studied quantitatively [13], according to judgements of semantic similarity between the 14 descriptors of piano timbre most cited by pianists in [3]. These evaluations were mapped into a semantic space, whose first two, most salient dimensions formed a plan in which descriptors were grouped in five distinct clusters — which was confirmed by hierarchical cluster analysis. In each cluster, the descriptor judged the most familiar was selected. The five most familiar, diverse and representative timbre descriptors thus highlighted — **Dry**, **Bright**, **Round**, **Velvety** and **Dark** — appear (in that order) along a circular arc in the semantic plan.

These five descriptors defined the timbres for which to seek out the production patterns in piano performances.

2.2 Musical pieces

In order to set a musical context adequate to expressive timbre production in performances, four short solo piano pieces were selected, among 15 specially composed for the study following instructions on the timbral nuances to be expressed (cf. Figure 1). Each selected piece could allow for a meaningful, consistent-throughout expression of each of the five timbral nuances, and featured many aspects of piano technique that we wanted to explore. Each just a few bars long (from four to seven, with different meters), their duration at score tempo ranged between 12 and 15 seconds.

2.3 Equipment

To investigate the fine-grained nuances of pianists' performance control and touch that let them express different timbral nuances, highly precise data were required, from which to thoroughly assess the intricacies of key strokes. In this aim, we had the opportunity to use the Bösendorfer CEUS piano digital recording system. Equipped with optical sensors behind the keys, hammers and pedals, microprocessors, electronic boards (cf. Figure 2), and a computer system, the CEUS system can track key and pedal positions and hammer velocities at high resolution (8-bit)

Figure 1. Scores of the four pieces composed and selected for the study.

and high sampling rate (500 Hz). The system we used was embedded in the Imperial Bösendorfer Model 290 grand piano installed at BRAMS.

The CEUS recording system constitutes an extremely precise tool to measure the subtleties in pianists' touch, in finer detail than was ever accessible to mechanical or MIDI piano performance-recording systems.

2.4 Performances

Four pianists [1] participated in the study. Each participant had received in advance the pieces scores and timbral nuances to explore, and were given time to practice. Rehearsal sessions were allotted on the Bösendorfer piano, to allow for familiarization with the instrument and the room. They were then asked to perform each of the four pieces, with each of the five timbres. Three such runs of 20 perfor-

[1] One female, three male; one Canadian, two French, one Italian; age from 22 to 46; all had extensive professional experience and advanced-level piano performance diploma. They are further referred to by their initials: PL, RB, BB and FP.

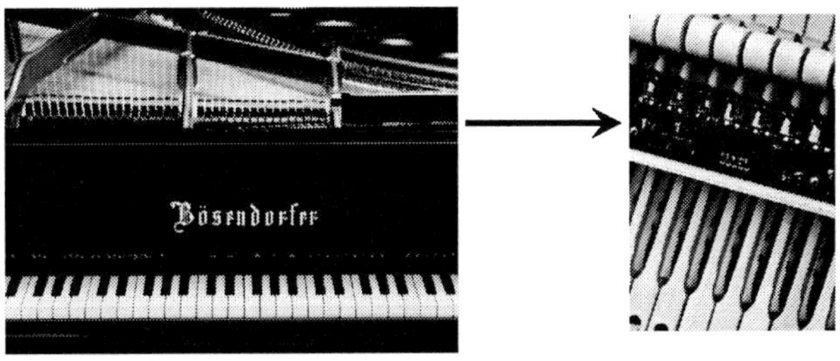

Figure 2. Details of the CEUS system: fallboard display interface and embedded electronics (©L.Bösendorfer Klavierfabrik GmbH).

mances were conducted successively so as to get three performances for each condition (piece × timbre). Each of the 60 performances per participant was recorded through the CEUS system. We thus collected 240 CEUS `boe`-format recordings of 4 pianists performing 4 pieces with 5 different timbres, 3 times each.

2.5 Performance analysis

In order to extract meaningful piano performance and touch features from CEUS-acquired data, a `Matlab` toolbox was specifically developed [14]. From the high-frequency, high-resolution key/pedal positions and hammer velocities, note and chord structures were retrieved, and an exhaustive set of quantified features spanning several broad areas of piano performance and touch were computed for each note (46 features) and chord (168 features [2]): dynamic levels; attack speed, depth, type, percussiveness and synchrony; sustain, release durations and synchrony (within chords); articulation, intervals and overlaps (between chords); and detailed use of pedals. Averages and deviations per performance (overall, and for the left and right hands separately) were calculated for all features, so as to enable comparisons between performances expressing different timbral nuances. In total, $322 \times 3 = 966$ features were calculated to characterize each of the 240 recorded performances.

3. RESULTS AND DISCUSSION

3.1 Significant, timbre-discriminating piano performance features

Statistical analyses of variance were performed over this 966-features-by-240-performance dataset. The data was organized in a repeated-measures design, with 80 samples (one for each same-pianist, same-piece, same-timbre condition, which includes 3 performances), timbre as factor (five groups) and the performance features as dependent variables. Different tests of analysis of variance (repeated-measures ANOVA, Welch robust test of equality of means, Kruskal-Wallis rank analysis) were performed, depending on the assumptions respected for each feature.

In the end, amongst the 966 performance features, 192 proved significant at the 5% level [3] in rejecting the null hypothesis of equal variance between the five timbre groups.

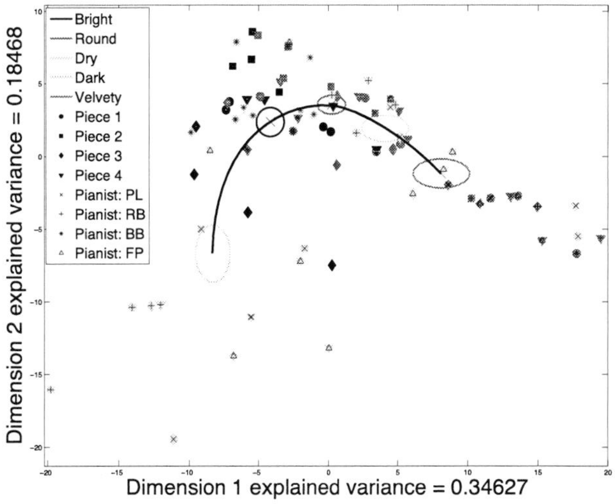

Figure 3. Principal Component Analysis over 80 samples (3-repetition performance means) for 192 significant features. Coloured crosses and ellipses indicate averages per timbre and ±1 S.E. (resp.).

3.2 Performance spaces of piano timbre

Principal Component Analysis was applied to the subset of 192 significant performance features. The first two principal components — which combined explained 53.1% of the variance in the input dataset (34.63% + 18.47% resp.) — and the position of each performance [4] according to their coordinates in these two dimensions, are represented in Figure 3. In this performance space, the five mean positions of performances sharing the same timbre appear along a circular arc. This arrangement of the five timbres is mostly consistent with their arrangement in the semantic similarity space [13], yet with an inversion of order along the arc of timbral nuances Dark and Velvety.

Scattering effects of performances can be observed, imputable to each of the three experimental factors. Performances tend to be grouped by performer (most especially for BB's, concentrated in the upper right region) and by piece (essentially in interaction with timbre). Yet the most salient grouping effect is due to timbre. A timbre-by-timbre account of performance positions shows that all Dry-timbre performances are situated on the left side of the space (mostly bottom-left), while most Velvety-timbre performances are positioned on the far-right side. Bright, Round and Dark-timbre performances are closely scattered around their respective means, except for one outlier among Bright performances and two outliers among Dark performances. [5] The loadings (weights attributed to each performance feature) for dimensions 1 and 2 do not show any predominant weight associated to one or a few features, yet they reveal that dimension 1 represents above all the dynamics, attack and soft pedal features, while dimension 2 mostly represents sustain pedal features.

[2] Including the means and standard deviations between the notes constituent of the chord, plus its chord-specific features.

[3] Including 145 features significant at the 1% level ($p < 0.01$) and 83 features significant at the 0.1% level ($p < 10^{-3}$).

[4] For the sake of display clarity, only the 80 means over the three same-pianist, same-piece, same-timbre repetitions are plotted, instead of the complete 240-performance set.

[5] Outliers are defined according to 95% confidence intervals, *i.e.* more than 1.96 standard deviations apart from the mean.

PCA performance spaces were also produced and studied separately for each piece and each performer. In each case, the first two principal components accounted for more than half of the variance in the input datasets, and the corresponding planar spaces all showed the same organization of five mean positions of same-timbre performances along a circular arc. However, the PCA loadings differed between cases, as different groups of features were most represented in the two dimensions depending on the piece or the performer.

Overall, the production of each timbral nuance was shown in the performance spaces as fairly consistent between performers (and between same-performers repetitions). However, this consistency was less salient for timbres Dry and Velvety, and could be affected by the scattering effects due to pieces and performers.

3.3 Characterization of piano timbre production

In order to obtain a minimal, unique performance portrait for each of the five piano timbre nuances explored in this study, the set of 192 significant features was reduced to 13 essential features. In this aim, the 192 features were divided into four broad, technically independent categories: (1) dynamics/attack, (2) soft pedal, (3) sustain pedal, and (4) articulation. Correlations between features were sought out within each group. The correlations coefficients were then submitted to cluster analysis. For each category, an optimal and meaningful number of clusters was empirically defined. With regards to pianistic/technical meaning, the most statistically significant feature was conserved in each cluster. This allowed us to identify, with hardly any loss of relevant information, a minimal set of 13 performance features to adequately describe each of the five timbral nuances in a unique way. These results are presented in the Kiviat (radar) chart of Figure 4. Below are the descriptions and statistical scores [6] of these 13 most relevant features.

- **Hammer velocity** ($\chi^2(4) = 23.195$, $p < 10^{-3}$, effect size $r = 0.294$ overall; $\chi^2(4) = 20.935$, $p < 10^{-3}$, effect size $r = 0.265$ left hand; $\chi^2(4) = 25.156$, $p < 10^{-3}$, effect size $r = 0.318$ right hand): maximum hammer velocity for each note, as directly measured by the piano sensors. As a direct correlate to intensity, it makes for a descriptor of dynamic level.
- **Key depression depth** ($\chi^2(4) = 21.412$, $p < 10^{-3}$, effect size $r = 0.271$): indicates how deep (close to the keybed) the key gets depressed for each note.
- **Variations in key attack speed** ($F(4, 75) = 3.117$, $p = 0.02$, effect size $r = 0.062$): indicate which timbres present the largest ranges in attack speed.
- **Attack duration** ($F(4, 75) = 3.881$, $p = 0.006$, effect size $r = 0.133$ overall; $F(4, 75) = 3.591$, $p = 0.01$, effect size $r = 0.149$ left hand; $F(4, 75) = 3.432$, $p = 0.012$, effect size $r = 0.105$ right hand): durations of note attacks, from the start of key depression to the instant of hammer launch. While primarily inversely proportional to intensity (the faster the attack, the shorter its duration), it also depends on nuances of touch and articulation at note onsets.
- **Soft pedal depression** ($F_W(4, 110.994) = 4.629$, $p = 0.002$, effect size $r = 0.291$): its amount of depression along the performance.
- **Sustain pedal use** ($F(4, 75) = 9.916$, $p < 10^{-3}$, effect size $r = 0.315$): duration of sustain pedal depression during performances.
- **Sustain pedal depression** ($F_W(4, 116.114) = 7.727$, $p < 10^{-3}$, effect size $r = 0.438$): its amount of depression along the performance.
- **Release duration** ($F_W(4, 115.91) = 13.795$, $p < 10^{-3}$, effect size $r = 0.32$): time taken for key release. This mostly accounts for articulation: a note released slowly (thus slowed by the finger) may probably overlap with the next.
- **Right-hand chords overlap** ($F(4, 75) = 2.561$, $p = 0.045$, effect size $r = 0.111$): descriptor of right-hand articulation: the more overlap, the more *legato* in right-hand play.

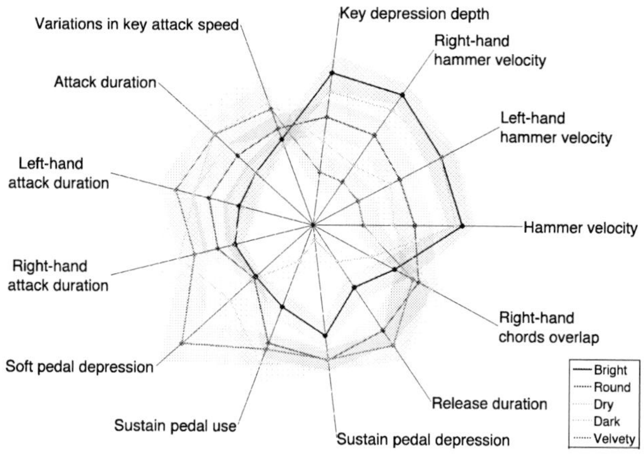

Figure 4. Kiviat chart of the 13 performance features giving a minimal and unique description of the five timbral nuances explored in the study. Z-scores per timbral nuance for each feature are indicated with colour-coded dots. The five colour-coded, dot-linking closed lines portray each timbral nuance. Shades around each closed line shows the ± 1.96 S.E. intervals (95% confidence interval).

Performance descriptions of the five timbral nuances were also assessed separately for each piece, according to the features significant for the piece. In each case, the piece-wise performance portrayals of the five timbral nuances were obtained according to a subset of the same features as overall (or equivalent ones). This indicates that, although the technical and compositional characteristics of a piece can bear an influence upon the efficiency of performance features to differentiate between timbral nuances, there exists an overall frame of performance features from which timbral nuances can be portrayed.

[6] Depending on the adequate statistical test as dictated by the assumptions met, the statistic reported can be the ANOVA F-ratio F(df1,df2), the Welch F-ratio F_W(df1,df2') or the Kruskal-Wallis Chi-square χ^2(df1).

Table 1. Summary of performance features significant in Post-hoc pairwise timbre comparisons.

Timbres		Significant descriptors pairwise	
Timbre #1	Timbre #2	*Timbre #1 > Timbre #2*	*Timbre #1 < Timbre #2*
Dry	**Bright**		Sustain pedal depression
Dry	**Round**		Sustain pedal use and depression
Dry	**Dark**		Right-hand attack duration
			Sustain pedal use and depression
			Left-hand chord durations
		Variations in right-hand overlap durations	Release durations
Dry	**Velvety**	Hammer velocity	
		Attack speed	Right-hand attack duration
		Key depression depth (esp. left hand)	
			Soft pedal depression
			Sustain pedal use and depression
			Release durations
Bright	**Round**	*none*	
Bright	**Dark**	Hammer velocity	
		Right-hand attack speed	Right-hand attack duration
		Key depression depth	
			Sustain pedal use
Bright	**Velvety**	Hammer velocity	
		Key attack speed	Right-hand attack duration
		Key depression depth	
			Soft pedal depression
Round	**Dark**	*none*	
Round	**Velvety**		Soft pedal depression
Dark	**Velvety**	*none*	

Furthermore, the evolution in time of those timbre-characteristic performance features were analyzed with regard to the musical structure of the pieces. Timbre profiles according to performance features were shown to follow certain patterns segmented per phrase/motif, with feature values either constantly increasing, decreasing or remaining stable along each phrase. At phrase transition, those patterns would either change in direction, remain the same, or be drastically reset (*e.g.* sustain pedal released at the end of a phrase). Such patterns would differ between timbres, in average feature value, in direction and amount of increase or decrease, in fluctuations within the phrases, and they especially differed in behaviour at phrase transitions.

3.4 Pairwise comparisons between timbres

The statistical analyses of variance were followed up by post-hoc pairwise comparisons, with Tukey's Honest Significant Difference test to estimate features significance, in the aim of assessing which performance features most significantly differ between each of the ten timbre pairs. Those results, once reduced for each timbre pair to a set of non-redundant (both in meaning and values), significant features, are presented in Table 1. This description is consistent with the PCA performance space and the arrangement patterns of timbres, with Round in the middle, Dry and Bright at one end and Dark and Velvety at the other.

3.5 Summary: Description of piano timbre nuances production

Thus, in the light of an exhaustive exploration of piano performance and touch, the five timbral nuances examined in this study could be portrayed according to the specificities of their production at the piano.

The production of each timbral nuance, as defined according to one verbal descriptor, could be characterized, in the context of this experiment, by a unique combination and pattern of utilization of certain control parameters:

- **Dry**: high intensity (slightly more with the left hand), very short and constantly fast attacks; keys are not fully depressed, which favours a very *staccato* articulation; both soft and sustain pedals are hardly used.
- **Bright**: high intensity (slight right-hand emphasis), very short attacks; keys deeply depressed down to the keybed; intermediate, *non-legato* articulation; the soft pedal is barely used; the sustain pedal is used sparingly, but is strongly depressed when in use.
- **Round**: the most average nuance in its production, with no salient trait: moderate, well-balanced, and constant intensity and attacks; key depressions are not very deep, yet well below escapement point; the soft pedal is barely used; the sustain pedal is used frequently and massively; and the articulation is quite *legato*.
- **Dark**: sharp contrast between hands in intensity and attack, very light in the right hand while much more marked in the bass, left hand; keys lightly depressed; fair use of the soft pedal; massive, quasi-constant use of the sustain pedal; and a very *legato* articulation, especially right-hand.
- **Velvety**: very low intensity, long attacks (especially with the right hand); very shallow key depression, very *legato* articulation (much more so in the left hand); prominent use of the soft and sustain pedals.

These features are overall characteristics of the production of each of the five timbral nuances examined in this study, independently of the performer and the musical context — as least to the extent of musical diversity represented in the four pieces composed for this study. Therefore, in the context of this study, the production and control of different timbral nuances in piano performance involved differences in dynamics, attack (and balance between hands), key depression depth, pedalling and articulation. On the other hand, the performance features of synchrony between notes in chords, note sustains, intervals between chords, and left-hand overlaps were not used in significantly different ways for producing each timbral nuance.

4. CONCLUSIONS

In exploring the expressive production of piano timbre, this study has revealed the differences in the production of five timbral nuances described by the terms Dry, Bright, Round, Velvety and Dark, and has identified specific patterns in the precise control of fine-grained performance features, through nuances in intensity, attack, key depression depth, articulation and pedalling, that let those timbral nuances arise in expressive piano performance. This quantified understanding of piano timbre production and control ought to be envisioned as a complement to the empiric body of knowledge that pianists have come to develop, both individually and as transmitted through teaching in a pedagogical context. With this study, the hope is to build a bridge between the pianistic and scientific perspectives on expressive piano performance and timbre production.

In complement to the study and results that were presented in this article, other related research questions are currently being investigated. First, the audio recordings of the performances are being used in perception tests, in order to determine whether the timbral nuances that the performers intended to express can be correctly identified. Acoustical analyses of the audio recordings will seek out the acoustical correlates of the piano timbre nuances performed. Correlations between the production and control patterns, the perceptual identification, and the acoustical correlates of piano timbre nuances will be examined, in particular to determine which performance features have an actual effect on sound production. Moreover, the individual strategies of expressive performance employed by each of the four participant pianists, overall and for producing the five different timbral nuances, are being explored.

In the future, this work could be applied to piano pedagogy. New methods could complement the traditional approach to piano timbre — through mental conception, imitation and careful self-actualization in performance as guided by the musical ear — with the devising of precise, tangible advice on the gesture to use in producing specific timbral nuances. Moreover, the results could be applied to the digital sound synthesis of piano timbre, and more precisely to the control of timbral nuances in piano synthesis engines. More subtle control parameters could be obtained — either with high-accuracy digital keyboard interfaces or with a software augmentation of the MIDI data sent by standard keyboard controllers — and used in conveying a more realistic simulation of an actual piano performance, coloured in timbre.

Acknowledgments

We wish to thank the pianists who took part in this study, the composers, and Bernard Bouchard for his invaluable technical and pianistic help. BRAMS (International Laboratory for Brain, Music and Sound Research) provided material support and access to the Bösendorfer CEUS. This work was made possible by funding from FRQSC (*Fonds de recherche du Québec – Société et culture*), CIRMMT (Centre for Interdisciplinary Research in Music Media and Technology) and OICRM (*Observatoire interdisciplinaire de création et recherche en musique*).

5. REFERENCES

[1] M. Bernays, "Expression et production du timbre au piano selon les traités: Conception du timbre instrumental exprimée par les pianistes et professeurs dans les ouvrages à vocation pédagogique," *Recherche en éducation musicale*, vol. 29, pp. 7–27, 2012.

[2] G. Sandor, *On piano playing*. New York: Schirmer Books, 1995, (First edition: 1981).

[3] M. Bellemare and C. Traube, "Verbal description of piano timbre: Exploring performer-dependent dimensions," in *Digital proceedings of the second Conference on Interdisciplinary Musicology (CIM05)*. Montreal, QC: OICRM, 2005.

[4] P. Cheminée, "«Vous avez dit «clair» ? » le lexique des pianistes, entre sens commun et terminologie," *Cahiers du LCPE: Dénomination, désignation et catégories*, vol. 7, pp. 39–54, 2006.

[5] R. Woody, "The relationship between explicit planning and expressive performance of dynamic variations in an aural modeling task," *Journal of Research in Music Education*, vol. 47, no. 4, pp. 331–342, 1999.

[6] H. Neuhaus, *The art of piano playing*. London, UK: Barrie and Jenkins, 1973, translated from Russian by K.A. Leibovitch.

[7] G. Kochevitsky, *The art of piano playing: A scientific approach*. Secaucus, NJ: Summy-Birchard, 1967.

[8] H. Hart, M. Fuller, and W. Lusby, "A precision study of piano touch and tone," *Journal of the Acoustical Society of America*, vol. VI, pp. 80–94, 1934.

[9] L. Vernon, "Synchronization of chords in artistic piano music," in *Objective Analysis of Music Performance*, C. Seashore, Ed. Iowa City, IA: University of Iowa Press, 1936, pp. 307–345.

[10] M. Henderson, J. Tiffin, and C. Seashore, "The Iowa piano camera and its use," in *Objective Analysis of Music Performance*, C. Seashore, Ed. Iowa City, IA: University of Iowa Press, 1936, pp. 252–262.

[11] W. Goebl, S. Dixon, G. DePoli, A. Friberg, R. Bresin, and G. Widmer, "'Sense' in expressive music performance: Data acquisition, computational studies, and models," in *Sound to Sense — Sense to Sound: A State of the Art in Sound and Music Computing*, P. Polotti and D. Rocchesso, Eds. Berlin, Germany: Logos, 2008, pp. 195–242.

[12] O. Ortmann, *The Physiological Mechanics of Piano Technique*. New York: E.P. Dutton, 1929.

[13] M. Bernays and C. Traube, "Verbal expression of piano timbre: Multidimensional semantic space of adjectival descriptors," in *Proceedings of the International Symposium on Performance Science (ISPS2011)*, A. Williamon, D. Edwards, and L. Bartel, Eds. Utrecht, Netherlands: European Association of Conservatoires, 2011, pp. 299–304.

[14] ——, "Piano touch analysis: A MATLAB toolbox for extracting performance descriptors from high-resolution keyboard and pedalling data," in *Proceedings of Journées d'Informatique Musicale (JIM2012), Gestes, Virtuosité et Nouveaux Medias*, T. Dutoit, T. Todoroff, and N. d'Alessandro, Eds. Mons, Belgium: UMONS/numediart, 2012, pp. 55–64.

Composing Social Interactions for an Interactive-Spatial Performance System

Adam Parkinson
Department of Computing
Goldsmiths
University of London
a.parkinson@gold.ac.uk

Koray Tahiroğlu
Department of Media
Aalto University
School of Arts, Design and Architecture
koray.tahiroglu@aalto.fi

ABSTRACT

This paper describes a recent composition, *No More Together*, in which performers' interactions directly influence the sound of the piece. The composition provides a structure for group interactions, and is performed with the *on-body* and *in-space* components of 'PESI', an interactive spatial performance system. Our composition attempts to compose social interactions, drawing upon notions of *participatory sense-making*, and the idea that these interactions are best construed as emergent systems, possessing their own internal dynamics. The composition is contextualised as part of the repertoire for the PESI system, exploring embodied, social and spatial interactions in sound and music computing.

1. INTRODUCTION

Implicit in any interactive system is a model for what constitutes interaction. Contemporary theories of social interaction offer new models for understanding social interactions, portraying interaction processes as autonomous, dynamic systems [1]. Group musical performances are unique social and collaborative environments, supporting a diverse range of interactions and group or individual goals. Novel technologies in sound and music computing, along with developments in human computer interaction, have brought about new possibilities for both designing and studying the social aspects of interactive performance systems [2]. The composition presented here explores these contemporary theories about the nature of these interactions.

This paper discusses the thinking behind a composition of a piece for an interactive, spatial and collaborative performance system developed as a part of the PESI research project. The system has unique affordances through the way it relates sonic, social and spatial interactions. Our composition represents an effort to develop a repertoire for this novel performance system which engages with these affordances. The composition consists of several components: the PESI system itself, the mappings (that relate performers movements to the manipulation of sounds), a set of nine audio samples and a short text score. Unlike what might often be understood by a musical score, our score attempts to compose social interactions rather than specific arrangements of sounds.

PESI is an interactive-spatial performance system that consists of two main parts; *on-body* and *in-space* (figure 1). We have previously described and presented the technical architecture in [3, 4] . Our discussion there focused on the technical details of the system. The process of composing for its affordances discussed here. The system is designed for co-located collaboration, encouraging reflections about space and movements. The combined *on-body* and *in-space* components create an environment wherein musicians are not only free to move and interact with each other but in which their social interactions contribute to the sonic outcome.

This paper is structured as follows. Section 2 discusses the related work and section 3 defines models for social interaction and participatory sense-making which resonate with our experiences of group improvisation and music-making. Section 4 describes the PESI interactive spatial performance system itself. Section 5 presents our composition, *No More Together*, in detail and how it relates to the affordances for interaction in the PESI system. In section 6 we report upon a performance, and describe the way in which we engage with interaction theory through the composition. We indicate our future work and conclude the paper in section 7. A video of the performance is available at http://vimeo.com/63524617.

2. RELATED WORK

We have seen in the sound and music computing field a range of design strategies for enabling different types of interaction and collaboration in art and music making, along with a range of proposals for what form musical interactions can take, which is expanded to include those interactions that do not directly affect the sound- producing actions [5–7].

Some, such as Nick Bryan-Kinns Daisyphone, have specifically addressed the issue of collaboration. The DaisyPhone allows players to modify loops without being in the same space, and Bryan-Kinns explores the social and musical aspects of their collaborations and interactions. Some of the notions explored in DaisyPhone, such as identity, *mutual awareness, mutual modifiability*, and localization of sounds, have informed the design of PESI. [8]. Like the DaisyPhone, Smules Ocarina is an iPhone instrument which facilitates remote collaboration and musical-social interaction, allowing one to hear other Ocarina players throughout the world [9].

Similar to the PESI system, Le Groux and Verschure describe The SMUSE, an interactive performance system which applies ideas of emergence and situatedness, asking questions about cognition whilst still being a creative tool [10]. Their system differs from our own work in that the computer is biomimetic and imbued with more intelligence than our own.

Murray-Browne et al and Magnusson [11, 12] describe the process of composing for new systems, extending the idea of composition to include aspects of designing instruments and mappings; we take a similarly expanded view of composition. Relatedly, Schnell and Battier introduce the term composed instruments, for the very design of instruments and the constraints and affordances they offer might be seen as constituting the composition [13]. Young et al describe the process of composing for the Hyperbow controller, explaining how the development of a new repertoire can feed into the evolution of the instrument itself [14].

Hanne De Jaegher's work on social interaction presents a novel approach, framing interaction as an autonomous process and the idea of participatory sense making [1]. David Borgo has brought similar ideas to studies of improvised music, drawing upon ideas of emergence and swarm intelligence to interrogate the relationships and interactions between musicians and the group as a whole in improvised music performances [15].

We drew upon these previous works in interactive, collaborative music-making, and developed a composition which explored the models of social interaction that we found in de Jaegher's work.

3. DYNAMICS OF INTERACTION

Hanne de Jaegher and Ezequiel Di Paulo propose that the interaction process between individuals should be seen as emergent and autonomous. They reject the model of individuals in an encounter trying to figure each other out, instead noting how the encounter itself has its own internal dynamics which, in turn, influences the behaviour of those involved [1].

De Jaegher et al introduce the concept of *participatory sense making*. Sense-making is understood as the processes by which an organism creates and appreciates meaning through its interactions with the world. Meaning and signification emerge out of our encounters and interactions with the world: de Jaegher uses the example of the softness of a sponge, something which is only revealed to us through our interactions with the sponge (squeezing) [1].

We gravitate to their work because it offers a convincing model for the dynamics we witness emerging in collective, improvised music performances in general, and in performances on the PESI system specifically. It offers an open yet rigorous notion of social interaction that is suited to the inherent complexities of interactions we find in musical improvisation. Their model has strong similarities with literature which attempts to articulate the often ephemeral qualities of group interactions in improvised music. Musicologist David Borgo notes that a performing group, like

Figure 1. PESI interactive-spatial performance system.

a hive, has emergent properties that cannot be reduced to any one individual within the group, and the creativity of the group cannot be to individual psychological processes. We can see how these ideas relate to de Jaegher et als description of social interactions as being an emergent and autonomous. A complex feedback occurs between performers and sound, much as the interaction processes that de Jaegher et al describe feedback into the actions of the individual agents involved [15].

We also find that de Jaegher et als definition of interaction and coordination is wide enough to account for the subtleties and complexities we find in musical interactions. They describe how synchronization is not the only kind of co-ordinated behaviour, and other interactions such as mirroring or anticipation are also co-ordinated. Theorists defining modes of interaction and 'togetherness' in musical performances take a similar approach: Nick Bryan-Kinns uses the concept of mutual engagement to describe the interactions we might find in group musical performance. His concept goes beyond an oversimplification of what constitutes interacting or playing together, and accounts for some of the diverse forms that might take, such as mirroring or carefully editing other's work [16].

We wanted to create a composition that would explore these models of social interaction, enabling different types of co-ordination and allowing interactions to develop their own dynamics.

4. PESI SYSTEM

The social interactions in the PESI system that affect the sound are the spatial location and coordination of the performers. During performance, these interactions provide dynamic control features, and performers are able to affect the sounds through changing their distance from the other performers. The design of the *on-body* component is intended to allow participants to focus more on their interactions with other participants and with the environment, increasing mutual engagement and decreasing cognitive overload [16].

Sharing a space brings awareness of the others and their presence, which is reinforced by being able to control others' sounds through one's spatial relation to them. Space and social action are therefore deeply interconnected in the system [17]. In this way the PESI system is a novel collaborative system that aims to open up new ways of musical exploration in group music activity.

We also bring a novel approach to the spatialisation of sound, which occurs both through multiple speakers in the *in-space* component and through the speakers attached to the performers bodies in the *on-body* component.

5. COMPOSITION: *NO MORE TOGETHER*

5.1 Repertoire

No More Together builds up a repertoire for a novel music system, which responds creatively to the specific affordances of that system. Many advances in musical technologies exist purely as isolated developements in technology, without a thorough investigation of the specific musical and expressive possibilities that these new technologies beget.

Atau Tanaka has written about the development of repertoires and idiomatic writing for new electronic instruments [18]. Performance practices must often be created for new musical instruments. With traditional instruments, idiomatic writing engages with the affordances of the instrument, such as the pitch range and timbres it is designed to play. The affordances that PESI provides include its relation of the movements of performers and intersubjective relations with the sound produced, and thus writing idiomatically for the piece, and *No More Together* is intended to explore and engage with this.

We have been developing a repertoire to be performed with the PESI system (see table 1). The first piece, *InHands*, was an improvisation for three musicians. Each instrument possessed different sonic characteristics, varying from squarewave generators to granular synthesis of sampled sounds. Spatial distances between performers further manipulated the sounds by changing the grain sizes and the modulation values of the frequencies. The piece was performed in SOPI research group's studio in December 2012. The second piece, *Test Tone*, was a combination of three pure sine waves playing a single frequency, each modulated, with the harmonic values based on the musicians' distance between each other. The third piece, *Trad Ensemble*, was composed for a traditional ensemble, and the sonic characteristics of the instruments were designed to be digital models of traditional instruments; piano, bell and bowl instrument. The distance between musicians is mapped to create beating patterns. Both the second and the third piece were performed in Goldsmiths, University of London in January 2013. Following that what emerged was a composition *No More Together*. It differed from previous work with PESI through the addition of a score to further influence the social interactions of the players, which we describe in detail in this paper.

5.2 The Score

A significant part of the latest composition is the score (see Figure 2). Conventionally, a score is understood as the organisation of sounds through musical notation. The twentieth century saw the rise of increasingly diverse ways of doing this, such as the graphic scores of Xenakis (UPIC)

	InHands	Test Tone	Trad Ensemble	No More Together
Description	free improvisation	pure tones	traditional ensemble set-up	manipulate social interaction
Musical Materials	granular synth	sine wave	digital model bell, perc., bowl	granular harp samples
Performer Instructions	free improvisation	free improvisation	free improvisation	score
Spatial Mapping	grain size & freq. mod.	harmonic values	beating patterns	grain size & freq. mod
Tuned / Pitch	open	tuned	tuned	tuned

Table 1. Composed pieces listed according to their sound mapping strategies, musical materials used, performer instructions, spatial mapping effect and tuned-pitch constraints.

NO MORE TOGETHER

For three performers and PESI system

Choose one of the following three states, and remain in it until the music asks you to change. Performers need not aim to be in the same state as each other.

1. *Play a constant sound. Only move in the space when someone else is moving.*
2. *Investigate a point of change in the sound. Only move in the space when no-one else is moving.*
3. *Move and play freely.*

Figure 2. The Score.

or Stockhausen, and the text-based scores of the Fluxus movement [19]. Some of these scores departed from the relatively strict instructions about rhythm and pitch that we find in most modern European staff notation, and on occasion focusing on giving tasks or actions to performers. Our own effort with the score here is not to compose sounds, but to compose social encounters.

Through the score, the performers are given three states to choose from, with the instruction that they change state when the music tells them to, this being intended to make sure they remain listening to and responding to their collective sound. The intention is not that the performers are all in the same state at the same time, but that they drift in and out of synchrony. The third state, move and play freely, is intended to enable the performers to explore the sonic, interactive, social and expressive possibilities of the system with relative freedom. This, along with their ability to change state at will, contributes to ensuring the autonomy of the players.

The score is designed not solely to facilitate smooth social interaction, but to create moments of social interaction that might develop their own dynamics. In a sense, the score is intended to trick the performers and to produce moments of social interaction outside their immediate control, so that the piece is not simply the performers acting out their ideas of social interaction. The performers may believe that the score is intended to produce synchronicity: however, de Jaegher et al suggest that it is often through failed encounters that we witness the social as an autonomous object with its own dynamics that transcends the apparent intentions of the agents involved. In particular, de Jaegher uses the example of two people passing each other in a corridor, and accidentally getting into a situation where, rather than passing smoothly, they continually mirror each others actions. In such an instance, the interaction can often continue despite the individual's efforts to break from it (and pass each other), having its own dynamics, and being an emergent object.

It is in these moments of failed interaction where the internal dynamics and relative autonomy of social interactions might be revealed to the audience and the performers. For this reason, the three states specified in the score are all potentially contradictory to each other, designed to create narrow corridor moments. State one asks that performers only move when someone else is moving, and state two asks that performers only move when no-one else is moving.

We opted for a score that functioned in this problematising manner because it was important to us that the score encouraged interactions, but did not attempt to structure them too much, nor disrupt the emergent autonomy of the interactions. In early performances of the piece there was no score, and so the performers improvised with the piece and explored the instruments, space, mappings and sounds. Observing the evolution of the performers interactions with the PESI system, the space and each other was of great interest, and we were keen that the score should not provide too much structure or constraint and prevent such evolutions from occurring.

De Jaegher et al note that the individuals involved in an interaction must be autonomous. It was therefore importance that the composition maintained as much of the autonomy of the performers as possible, whilst providing a structure within which interactions could occur and be maintained. Hence, there is a great deal of freedom for the performers in terms of how they move and interact in the space, and what sounds they produce. Essentially, the performers can choose to follow certain rules (eg not moving unless someone else is moving), but discard these rules should they wish (and move to state 3, move and play freely)

We find a related approach to scoring in John Zorns Game Pieces. As Zorn desribes,

> "My pieces are written as a series of roles, structures, relationships among players, different roles that the players can take to get different events in the music to happen. And my concern as a composer is only dealing in the abstract with these roles like the roles of a sports game like football or basketball. You have the roles, then you pick the players to play the game and they do it " [15]

.

Drawing upon this, our initial thoughts for the composition involved giving each of the performers a role, possibly based upon a contested model of psychological types (such as the Myerrs-Briggs Type Indicators). The piece could then potentially be a playful interrogation of a model of social interactions routed in individuals and types, as oppose to the dynamics of interactions themselves. However, we were concerned that this might make the performers too aware of social interactions or simply act out roles, potentially stiffling the sort of emergent dynamics of interaction that we are interested in.

5.3 Audio Engine

The soundworld of the piece is in large part determined by the samples and the granular synthesiser running in Pure Data [1] which plays them, along with the mappings. The granular synthesiser is based upon Noboyasu Sakonda's Max MSP granular synthesiser [20], modified by us and adapted to run in Libpd [2] on the iPhone and Pure Data on the computer.

The granular synthesiser is permanently in freeze mode, indefinitely stretching a single fragment of the sample, with x and y axis of the accelerometer changing the point in the buffer which is being frozen, and the degree of randomness which allows for fragments of the sample on either side of the buffer to be played. The mappings contribute to the sonic character of the piece. Because nothing is mapped to pitch, and all the samples are relatively in tune with each other, we have a degree of control over the tonal and melodic nature of the piece. The mappings afford the creation of shimmering soundscapes with the granular patch.

6. SONIFICATION OF INTERATIONS

As well as running on the mobile devices (the *on-body* component), the granular synthesisers run on a central computer and are spatialised through the *in-space* component. The mobile devices send accelerometer data via Open Sound Control (OSC) [3] network module to the host machine, which runs three versions of the granular synthesiser (one for each device), which are controlled by the movements of the device, effectively mirroring the *on-body* sounds.

The *in-space* sound is processed in two ways. Two Microsoft Kinects are used to track the locations of the three players in the space. The spatial location of each player moves the sound through multiple speakers in the space. In addition to this, we extract information about relations between performers, such as relative distances, velocity, acceleration and alignment, which we discuss further in [21]. These relations between the players cause the sounds to be further processed by an additional granular synthesiser. In this way, social interactions contribute to the overall sonic output, and the sonic output feeds back into social interactions. The *in-space* sounds are processed by a granular synthesiser, with grain length increasing when the distance

[1] `http://puredata.info/`
[2] `http://libpd.cc`
[3] `http://opensoundcontrol.org/`

between the musicians gets smaller. Similarly, when the musicians move away from each other the *in-space* audio module produces shorter length grains of sound. At the same time if the musician gets closer to the the third musician the frequency response range exponentially increases. The movements of the three performers are therefore intertwined with the sound of the piece.

7. DISCUSSION: SOCIAL INTERACTIONS AND SENSE-MAKING

During the performance, the musicians were drawn into interactions through which they participated in the collective generation of meaning, as well as sound, within the environment. During the perfomance, we witness the participatory sense-making activity of the musicians as they sonically and socially engage with the each other and the environment itself. The composition becomes a way of exploring interaction-theory through practice, and this theory in turn becomes a way for the audience and the performers to access the practice.

It is through a process of participatory sense-making that gestures and actions acquire meaning within social interactions, the meaning anchored to the interaction. During performances of our composition, we see gestures and themes emerge over time and acquire meaning within the context of the performance; for instance, a performer may find a certain part of the space that they can play, moving slowly towards the centre and back to granulate the sound produced, repeating this gesture and feeding back into both the music (the gesture changes the sound) and the social dynamics (the movements of the other players are influenced by the stop-start, back-forward motion of the performer, as it potentially affects how they can behave depending upon their state).

Co-ordination in the performance of *No More Together* does not always manifest itself as a simple sychronization or entrainment. As we noted, our score is not aimed at producing synchronizations of performers' actions, and total synchronization may actually be construed as a draw back. Differences emerging during the interaction enable performers to continue the process in a different direction. If sychronization is total and there are no negotiations nor emerging differences, then any sense of true autonomous interaction quickly dissipates.

We informally discussed performer's experiences of the piece with them. Of performing the composition, performers said "I like the way that we really co-ordinated each other in the space". The score gave the performers a way to try and block others movements, or regulate their own. Performers attempted to follow the score more closely at the beginning, but in the end moved more freely and took more liberties. One performer saw the score as optional, following it only when they chose to (which is effectively permitted within the score). The score also encouraged performers to listen; as one noted, "the score makes you listen to the others to understand what's going on". The score, then, was successful, producing a blend of synchronized interactions and more problematic 'failed' interactions, with the interaction itself being foregrounded in the performance.

8. CONCLUSION AND FUTURE WORK

In this paper we presented the composition *No More Together* that we have developed as a part of the repertoire for the PESI system. We also described contemporary theories of social interaction, and demonstrated how our score provided a way to engage with these theories. Building up a repertoire provides a very strong justification for our system's use in allowing for interaction dynamics to be explored within composition. We further discussed compositional approaches for using the system as opposed to underlying design ideas that lead to system's development.

We intend to find more composers to work with the PESI system, developing a repertoire to further investigate the unique social-musical interactions it facilitates. We are also interested in working with more performers, and perform with different audience, to investigate how our score and the models of interaction resonate with them. Dan Stowell [22] has shown the Discourse Analysis techniques can be used to interrogate performers' experiences of new musical instruments. We intend to bring similar techniques to explore experiences of the PESI system.

Acknowledgments

We would like to acknowledge Atau Tanaka for the discussions we had on the paper, Baptiste Caramiaux and Alessandro Altavilla for the performance of the composition *No More Together*. This work is supported by the Academy of Finland (project 137646).

9. REFERENCES

[1] H. D. Jaegher and E. D. Paolo, "Participatory sense-making an enactive approach to social cognition" in *Phenomenoogy and the Cognitive Sciences*, 2007.

[2] X. Serra, R. Bresin, and A. Camurri, "Sound and Music Computing: Challenges and Strategies", *Journal of New Music Research. 36*(3), 185-190, 2007.

[3] R. Pugliese, K. Tahiroğlu, C. Goddard, and J. Nesfield, "Qualitative evaluation of augmented human-human interaction in mobile group improvisation", in *Proceedings of the International Conference on New Interfaces for Musical Expression*, 2012.

[4] N.N. Correia, K. Tahiroğlu and M. Espada, "PESI: Extending mobile music instruments with social interaction", in *Seventh International Conference on Tangible, Embedded and Embodied Interaction (TEI)*, Work in Progress, Barcelona, Spain, 2013.

[5] S. Benford. "Performing musical interaction: Lessons from the study of extended theatrical performances", *Comput. Music J., 34*(4):49-61, 2010.

[6] C. Dobrian and D. Koppelman. "The E in NIME: Musical Expression with New Computer Interfaces", in *Proceedings of the International Conference on New Interfaces for Musical Expression*, 2006.

[7] M. Gurevich and J. Treviño, "Expression and Its Discontents : Toward an Ecology of Musical Creation", in *Proceedings of the International Conference on New Interfaces for Musical Expression*, 2007.

[8] N. Bryan-Kinns and P. Healey, "Daisyphone: support for remote music collaboration", in *Proceedings of the International Conference on New Interfaces for Musical Expression*, 2004.

[9] G. Wang, "Designing Smule's Ocarina : The iPhone's Magic Flute", in *Proceedings of the International Conference on New Interfaces for Musical Expression*, 2009.

[10] S. Le Groux and P. Verschure, "The Smuse: An Embodied Cognition Approach to Interactive Music Composition", in *Proceedings of the International Computer Music Conference*, 2012.

[11] T. Magnusson, "Designing constraints: Composing and performing with digital musical systems", *Computer Music Journal, 34*(4):62-73, 2010.

[12] T. Murray-Browne, D. Mainstone, N. Bryan-Kinns, M. Plumbley, "The Medium is the Message: Composing Instruments and Performing Mappings", in *Proceedings of the International Conference on New Interfaces for Musical Expression*, 2011.

[13] N. Schnell and M. Battier, "Introducing Composed Instruments, Technical and Musicological Implications", in *Proceedings of the International Conference on New Interfaces for Musical Expression*, 2002.

[14] D. Young, P. Nunn and A. Vassliev, "Composing for Hyperbow: A Collaboration Between MIT and the Royal Academy of Music", in *Proceedings of the International Conference on New Interfaces for Musical Expression*, 2006.

[15] D. Borgo, "Sync or Swarm: Musical improvisation and the complex dynamics of group creativity", *Algebra, Meaning, and Computation* (pp. 1-24). Springer Berlin Heidelberg.

[16] N. Bryan-Kinns, "Mutual Engagement in Social Music", *LNICST 78*, 260-266, 2012.

[17] A. Williams, E. Kabisch, and P. Dourish, "From Interaction to Participation: Configuring Space Through Embodied Interaction", in *Proceedings of UbiComp*, 2005.

[18] A. Tanaka, "Musical Performance Practice on Sensor based Instruments", In Wanderley, M., Battier, M. (Eds.) *Trends in Gestural Control of Music (CD-ROM)*. IRCAM, Paris. 2000.

[19] C. Cox, "Visual Sounds: On Graphic Scores", in C. Cox and d Warner(eds) *Audio Culture: Readings in Modern Music*, Contiuum, 2004.

[20] Sakonda's patch is available at `http://formantbros.jp/sako/download.html`

[21] K.Tahiroğlu, N. N. Correira and M. Espada, "PESI Extended System: In Space, On Body, with 3 Musicians", in*Proceedings of the International Conference on New Interfaces for Musical Expression*, 2013.

[22] D. Stowell, A. Robertson, N. Bryan-Kinns, and M. D. Plumbley. "Evaluation of live human-computer music-making: Quantitative and qualitative approaches", *International Journal of Human-Computer Studies, 67*(11):960-975, 2009.

HOW DO PEOPLE ASSESS COMPUTER GENERATED EXPRESSIVE MUSIC PERFORMANCES?

Sergio Canazza
CSC-DEI, Univ. Padova
canazza@dei.unipd.it

Giovanni De Poli
CSC-DEI, Univ. Padova
depoli@dei.unipd.it

Antonio Rodà
CSC-DEI, Univ. Padova
roda@dei.unipd.it

ABSTRACT

Music performance has being studied since long time and several computational systems were developed for generating expressive music performances. These models are generally evaluated by comparing their predictions with actual performances, both from a quantitative and a subjective point of view, often focusing on very specific aspects of the model. However little is known about how listeners evaluate the generated performances and which are the factors influencing their judgement and appreciation.

In this paper we present two experiments, conducted during two dedicated workshops, to start understanding how the audience judges the entire performances. In particular we analyzed possible different preferences and expectations of the listeners and influencing factors, such as cognitive styles.

1. INTRODUCTION

Many researchers analyzed and modeled human performance of musical scores, and the results led to the development of several computational systems for the so called computer generated expressive music performance (see e.g. [1] and [2] for a review). This area has drawn much attention from computer science researchers because of the challenge of emulating human competence. These systems are generally evaluated by comparing their predictions with actual performances, both from a quantitative and a subjective point of view, often focusing on very specific aspects of the model, such as a single rule, a phrasing rendering, a conveyed emotion [3]. The main evaluation aim is to validate or improve the system. However little is known how listeners evaluate the generated performances and which are the factors influencing their judgement and appreciation.

In order to analyze more deeply the subjective effectiveness of computer generated performances, the Performance Rendering Contest (Rencon) was initiated in 2002 [4] by Katayose and colleagues as a form of competition among different systems. During the years the Rencon contest evolved toward a more structured format. Now it is conducted in two stages. In the first one, a panel of experts rates both the scientific novelty of the entrant systems and their usefulness. In the second one, the performances generated during a dedicated workshop are openly evaluated by the audience and Internet viewers (see [5] for details).

The purpose of this paper is to investigate an aspect which has been overlooked by recent research, i.e. how subjects evaluate computer generated performances. Only recently has empirical research started to investigate the factors that influence human performance evaluations and the interactions among these factors. This research has typically focused on formal settings, such as competitions, or on educational practices [6–8]. It is thus worth studying more in detail how listeners evaluate and appreciate automatic performances, which factors influence their preferences and expectation. To this purpose we present a preliminary experiment carried out during Rencon-SMC11, which will be summarized in section 3, and a second one carried out during the meeting of the musicological society of Italy (GATM) on April 2012. In particular we analyze possible different preferences and expectations of the listeners and influencing factors, such as cognitive styles [9].

2. MUSIC APPRECIATION AND COGNITIVE STYLES

Individuals are different and we could therefore expect them to react differently to music just as they react differently to other stimuli. Research on individual differences has already explained between-person differences to identical psychological tasks. These individual differences also affect the way we react to music. Recently, Kreutz et al. [9] demonstrated the existence of top-down strategies during listening to music using a questionnaire survey. They found that listeners may be classified as *music-empathizers* (ME) when they focus on the affective aspects of the music and try to get tuned to the emotions of the composer or as *music-systemizers* (MS) who are rather interested in finding structures and organization behind the music. Moreover they developed an instrument for the measurement of music empathisizing. This scale was designed to investigate empathy as a cognitive style of processing music, rather than as a general trait. The authors reported that their scales were found to be internally consistent and reliable and results aligned with that of the general empathy scale [9]. Using this scale, it was found that listeners who enjoy computer music based genres demonstrated a trend towards a higher mean score on the music-systemizing scale than those who enjoy love songs [10].

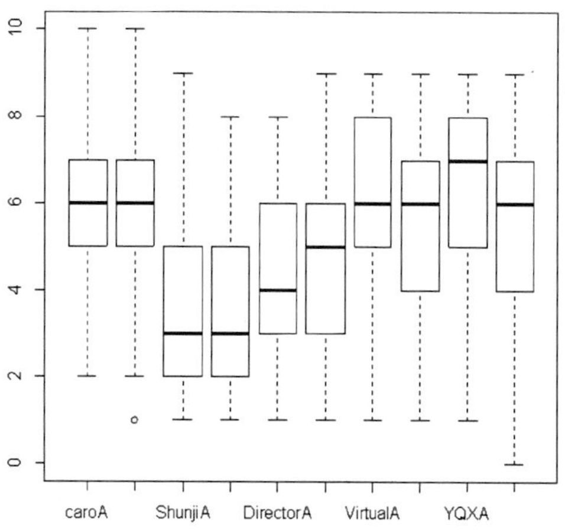

Figure 1. Boxplot of performance ratings of Rencon-SMC11 participants.

We can hypothesize that the cognitive style also may influence the preferences when evaluating computer generated performances. To this purpose we submitted of the participants of our experiment the questionnaire in order to measure their cognitive style.

3. RENCON-SMC11 EXPERIMENT

3.1 Material and method

During the final phase of Rencon-SMC11, five systems generated two expressive performances and were evaluated by the workshop attendants, who were experts on Sound and Music Computing. The five systems were:

- E1 uses two algorithms: *YQX* [11], developed by Dept. of Computational Perception, J. Kepler University, Linz (Austria) for tempo and Basis mixer [12] for dynamics;
- E2 *CaRo 2.0*, developed by the Sound and Music Computing group, Dept. of Information Engineering, University of Padova (Italy) [2];
- E3 *DirectorMusices*, developed by the Music Acoustics Group, KTH Royal Institute of Technology, Stockholm (Sweden) [13];
- E4 *VirtualPhilharmony*, developed by Katayose Lab., Dept. of Human and Systems Interaction, Kwansei Gakuin University (Japan) [14].
- E5 *Shunji*, developed by Katayose Lab., Dept. of Human and Systems Interaction, Kwansei Gakuin University (Japan) [15].

E1, E3, E5 are autonomous systems, while E2 and E4 are interactive performance systems [5].

The method and the results of the contest are discussed in [3, 5]; a new analysis of the ratings is presented below.

Just after the audience listened and evaluated the automatic performances, we distributed a questionnaire to the attendees. The purpose was to collect more information on the criteria used by the adjudicators and suggestions for future Rencon contests.

3.2 Results

The results are discussed in [5]. Here we summarize the most interesting results for our aims.

3.2.1 Analysis of ratings

Fig. 1 shows the box plot of ratings with estimated density traces. All the distributions are unimodal.

In order to explore the preferences of the listeners, we projected each listener rating on a 2D plane, by a PCA of the expressed evaluations of the system performances; the first two components explains respectively 46,4% and 20,7% of the total variance (Fig. 2). We may observe that the point are very scattered in the plane and don't show any clustering. Then we evaluated the correlation among each performance and the two-dimensional coordinates of the listeners. Fig. 2 shows the direction and strength of the maximal correlation of the listener preferences with the PCA positions of the performances. We may observe that the judgements of Caro system tend to be orthogonal to the Shunji one and that some subjects tend to evaluate similarly Caro and YQX systems, while others tend to agree in the evaluations of DirectorMusices and VirtualPhilarmony.

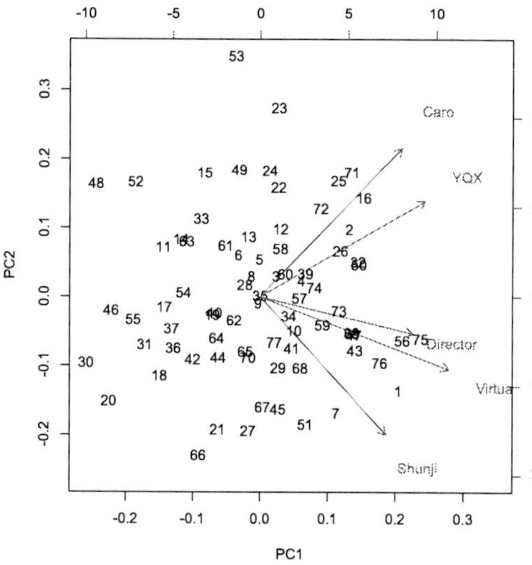

Figure 2. Biplot of a Principal Component Analysis of the performances ratings of Rencon-SMC11 participants. Numbers represent the ID of each listener, whereas arrows represent the correlation among the systems.

3.2.2 Analysis of listeners' preferences

The first question was intended to identify the expectation level of the listeners and was formulated as follows: *Your evaluation was made with reference to:* with three alternative answers: masters degree music student, music teacher, or top-level performer. The majority (58.3%) of the participants, who answered this question, indicated masters degree student as the reference used in their performance evaluations, while professional performers and music teachers were specified by 30.6% and 11.1% of the respondents, respectively. Thus, we can conclude that although the majority of the participants realistically expected a student-quality performance, approximately 2/5 of the participants had higher expectations. This expectation might be influenced by the contest setting and by the qualification level of the entrants, which may induce high expectations in the attendants. The non-answer rate of 10% may indicate that the question was not fully understood, and thus it was not included in the next experiment.

n.	Factors influencing the judgment	Freq.
b1	is able to highlight elements related to the musical structure (phrasing, counterpoint)	77.5%
b2	contains unexpected but interesting choices	40.0%
b3	is consistent with the suitable musical style (from an historical point of view)	52.5%
b4	is consistent with the favorite style (from a subjective point of view)	12.5%
b5	is consistent with the style of a famous performer	5.0%
b6	is able to convey emotional content	57.5%
b7	contains evident musical errors (that a human would never perform)	52.5%
b8	is consistent with the actual performance context (concert hall, classroom, or automatic performance contest)	7.5%

Table 1. Frequency of the main factors influencing the judgment of Rencon-SMC11 participants.

The second question, *Which of the following are the main factors that influenced your judgment?*, was intended to encourage subjects to reflect on the criteria that they used, either consciously or subconsciously. Different possible factors were proposed, and the subjects were told that they could select more than one option. The proposed factors tended to cover technical, interpretative/communicative, and stylistic aspects of the performances. The frequency of responses is reported in Tab. 1. We can observe that technical and interpretative/communicative factors predominate, whereas stylistic factors are much less frequently considered. No significant correlations were found between the answers to these questions and musical training, age, or gender.

Figure 3 shows the biplot of the Correspondence Analysis of these factors, as expressed by Rencon-SMC11 participants. The first two components explains 24.7% and 22.2% of total variance. We can notice that the main difference is due by factors b4, b5 and b8, which were less frequently indicated by attendants and were probably interpreted as mutually exclusive. A more interesting differentiation is characterized by factors b1, b2 and b3 respectively. We can hypothesize that they may contribute to diverse attitudes in evaluating generated performance. Instead factors b6 and b7 are almost superimposed, even if they represent two quite different assessment categories i.e. emotional vs. technical. We can conjecture that both factors are felt equally important in the assessment.

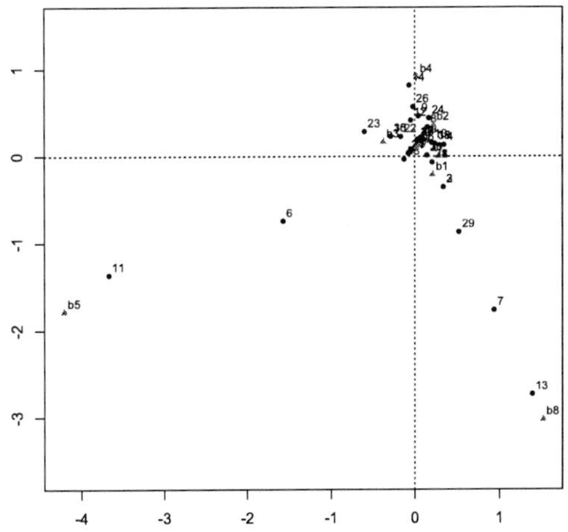

Figure 3. Biplot of a correspondence analysis of the factors influencing the judgement of Rencon-SMC11 participants.

4. GATM 2012 EXPERIMENT

4.1 Participants

On Sunday, 22nd, April, 2012 at Liszt Institute in Bologna (Italy) the annual assembly of the italian Analysis and Music Theory Group (*Gruppo Analisi e Teoria Musicale*, GATM) was held. In that occasion, a workshop on musical performance analysis took place. This workshop focused on expressive performance rendering computer systems. All the participants were Italian musicologists, specialized in musical analysis. Total = 23; 17 male; 6 female; 9 younger ($\leqslant$ 50 years); 14 older ($>$ 50 years).

The assessors' age is surveyed in categories (21-30; 31-40; 41-50; ...). The mean age falls in the interval 51-60 years; the overall range is between 31-40 to 71-80 years.

4.2 Materials

Four different performances of a short classical musical piece were proposed to the workshop participants. Several Sonatas (by Cherubini, Clementi, Gotifredo Ferrari da Rovereto, Kuhlau and Beethoven) were considered. First of all, the first movements (exposure of Sonata form) were discarded because it is both too long and quite trivial. At the end, the Op. 88, n. 3, *Allegro Burlesco* by Kuhlau was chosen because it lasts just over two minutes, it is not too complex and it possesses an expressive character.

The authors asked the teams classified in the first four positions at the final phase of Rencon-SMC11 to prepare the stimuli (files in MIDI format) using their systems for automatic expressive performance. All the four MIDI files were played by the same piano Yamaha Disklavier MarkIV. Finally, they were recorded by two AKG 414 microphones and transferred to the digital domain by a FireFace 800 A/D converter (96kHz, 24bit). The systems E1-E4 of the Rencon-SMC11 Experiment were used. E1 used Basis mixer [12] for dynamics, tempo, and articulation.

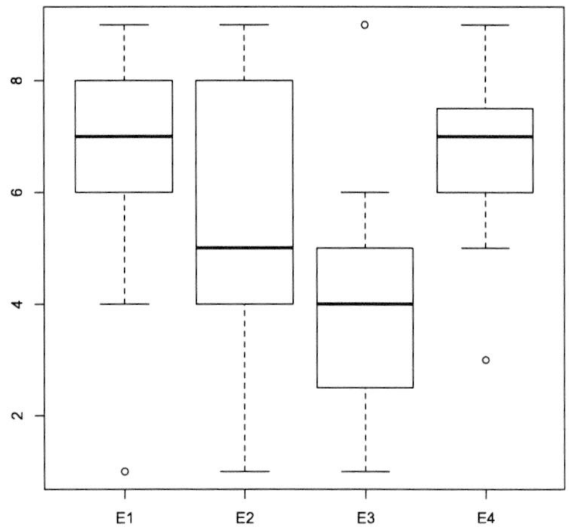

Figure 4. Boxplot of performance ratings in GATM experiment. Performance E2 shows a bimodal distribution.

4.3 Method

The attendees were invited to rate each stimulus and to fill an assessment questionnaire (see Appendix A), which was divided into three parts. At the end of the workshop the results were presented and discussed. Then, we presented the mathematical models used in the four performance rendering systems and communicated the ranking of the performances. Finally, we played two recorded performances, one was the winner and the other was a human performance, played by a concert artist and piano teacher. We told the assessors that they were listening the winner and another automatic performance and we asked them to express which one they prefer, by rising their hand.

4.4 Results

4.4.1 Analysis of performances evaluation

The average ratings of the performances (part A of the assessment questionnaire), considering the total of the participants, the male and the females, are presented in Tab. 2. The range of ratings is large: E1, E2 and E3 were rated between 1 and 9. The performance E4 was rated between 3 and 9. In addition, 9 participants express their preference for E1; 6 for E2; 1 for E3; 7 for E4. Fig. 4 shows the boxplot of ratings with estimated density. All the distribution of the assessors rates were unimodal, but E2 which shows a bimodal distribution, probably indicating two distinct taste categories.

	E1	E2	E3	E4
Total (M)	6.78	5.52	3.91	6.59
Total (SD)	1.86	2.39	1.90	1.37
Female (M)	6.17	5.83	4.17	5.6
Female (SD)	1.17	3.19	2.64	1.95
Male (M)	7.00	5.41	3.82	6.88
Male (SD)	2.03	2.15	1.67	1.05

Table 2. Analysis of the part A of the assessment questionnaire on the total participants, on females and on males. Mean (M) and Standard Deviation (SD).

Fig. 5 shows the biplot computed from the Principal Component Analysis (PCA) on the performances ratings. We may notice that E2 is orthogonal to the other performances. In addition, we may observe that the assessors are clustered in three groups: (i) assessors that likes E2, (ii) assessors that likes E1, E3 and E4 and (iii) subjects that tend to refuse all the automatic performances.

Comments to the GATM performances are listed in Appendix B, divided in three categories, according to [16]. In some cases there is a total disagreement in the assessment of the same performance. E.g., E1 has been judged both "regular" and "irregular"; E4 sounds at the same time "very pleasant" and "not at all suitable". Of course, many of these differences are due to the subjective nature of the evaluation of any artistic work. Others may depend from the experimental setup: the audience listened the entire performance only once, before to judge it, as in a live concert scenario. In some cases, this fact could be the cause of hasty and inaccurate judgments.

To better evaluate the subjective judgments of the public, we report some objective features calculated from the performances, regarding tempo and dynamics. Performance E1 has been played with an average tempo of 122 BPM; the middle section has been played at 108 BPM; a dynamic range of 40.6 dB with a maximum RMS amplitude of -13.46 dBFS. E2 is characterized by an average tempo of 132 BPM with a middle section at 124 BPM; a dynamic range of 49.4 dB and a maximum RMS amplitude of -9.9 dBFS. E3 has an average tempo of 102 with a middle part at 94; a dynamic range of 47.7 dB and a maximum RMS amplitude of -12.2 dBFS. Finally, E4 has been played at 128 BPM on average with a middle section at 88 BPM; a dynamic range of 47.0 dB and a maximum RMS amplitude of -12.5 dBFS.

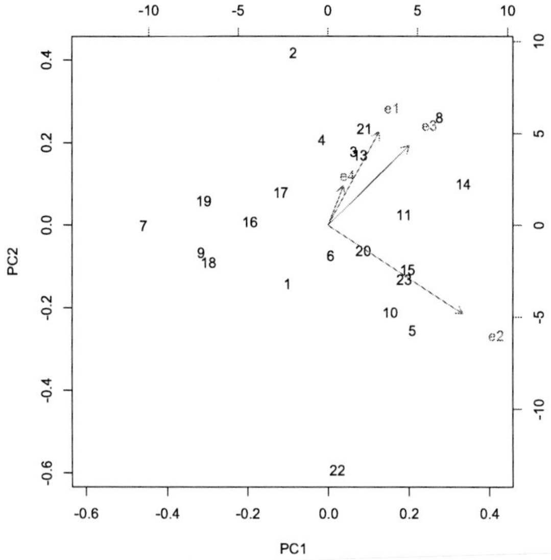

Figure 5. Biplot of a Principal Component Analysis of the performance ratings in GATM experiment. Numbers represent the ID of each listener, whereas arrows represent the correlation among the systems.

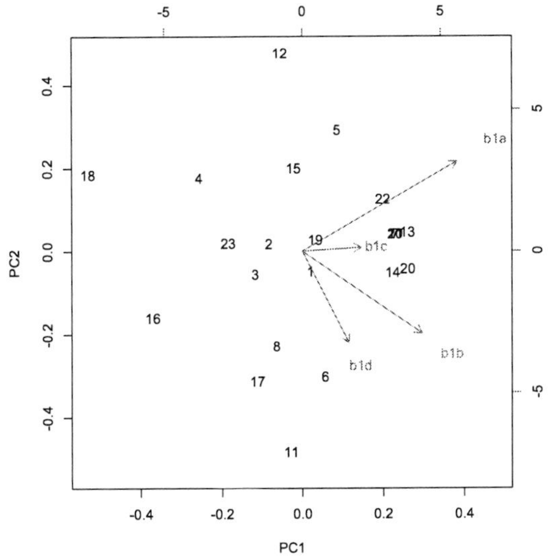

Figure 6. Biplot of a Principal Component Analysis on the factors presented in part B1.

	b1a	b1b	b1c	b1d
Total (M)	4.23	5.09	5.27	5.39
Total (SD)	1.74	1.59	0.98	1.62
Female (M)	4.50	4.83	5.17	4.50
Female (SD)	2.07	1.60	0.98	2.07
Male (M)	4.13	5.18	5.31	5.71
Male (SD)	1.67	1.63	1.01	1.36

Table 3. Analysis of the factors (part B1 of the assessment questionnaire) on the total participants, on females and on males. Mean (M) and Standard Deviation (SD).

Comparing these values with the afore mentioned comments, it is possible to note that when there is an agreement among the subject, the judgment is often coherent with the measured features. E. g., many subjects agree in considering exaggerated the dynamic variations of performance E2, which actually has the greatest dynamic range. On the contrary, performance E1 is generally considered too scholastic and little expressive, probably due to the small dynamic and agogic differences.

The overall balance of the performances is not always considered sufficient by the assessors. This is due to the fact that the systems pay more attention to the phrasing levels, than to the interpretation of the song in its entirety. This comment can be a useful hint for systems developers.

Finally, there are some interesting comments characterized by a comparison with human performances. Despite the audience was aware that all the performances were computer generated, some subjects used verbal expressions such as "seems to remember an unmusical student", "if it were a person it would seem inaccurate", or "boy playing so fast because he likes run", denoting the tendency to attribute to the automatic performances a human personality.

About the evaluation between E1 and the human performance: our experience has been that it is good, or at least interesting, to include a human performance among synthesized ones in the performances sample (and thus made the experiment a bit more as a sort of a Turing test) because it gives a perspective of how far away or close to the ecologically valid performance the synthesized ones lie. The result is that the human one was very slightly preferred, by only one preferences. And this may be in favor to not exclude in the future a sort of Turing test like experiment.

4.4.2 Analysis of assessors' preferences and cognitive style

The average rating of the factors that influence the enjoyment of the performances (part B1 of the assessment questionnaire, see Appendix A), considering all the participants, only male and only females, is listed in Tab. 3. It can be noticed that there are distinct genre behavior in factors b1b and b1d. The mean values are not quite distinct, apart factor b1a (related to technical accuracy of the performance) that received less importance: maybe the assessors, knowing that stimuli were generated performances, were less concerned by technical precision (b1a) and payed more attention to the interpretative factors.

Fig. 6 shows the biplot computed from the Principal Component Analysis (PCA) on the factors presented in the part B1. The first two components explains 49.4% and 24.8% of total variance. The factor b1a is orthogonal to b1d, as it was to be expected because b1a is related to technical aspects and b1c to emotional aspect.

Tab. 4 shows the ME and MS Simplified Unit Weight (SUW) values [9], describing the cognitive styles. The low empathising score (ME) reflects a philosophical/training/conditioning stance that some who are convinced that the role of music was not to express emotions – a 'formalist' perspective. This is particularly true in older generation analytic musicologists: it seems that this has been changing in the last couple of decades, at least in Anglo-Saxon school. Our experiment confirms this trend: the younger group is associated to a ME SUW value (-10.67), which is less negative than older group (-14.29).

MS scores: *music systemizing*					
	Total	Female	Male	Younger	Older
M	1.70	2.00	1.59	3.44	0.57
SD	7.47	5.62	8.18	4.22	8.95
M [9]	3.46	2.35	5.09		
SD [9]	8.04	7.93	8.09		
ME scores: *music empathizing*					
	Total	Female	Male	Younger	Older
M	-12.87	-14.00	-12.47	-10.67	-14.29
SD	10.39	10.81	10.55	12.70	8.80
M [9]	2.50	4.00	0.29		
SD [9]	7.20	5.89	8.47		

Table 4. Means (M) and Standard Deviation (SD) of music cognitive styles SUW scores [9] for all the assessors, male, female, younger ($\leqslant$ 50 years) and older ($>$ 50 years). All the data are compared with the results obtained by [9] for the "Professional" level of music performance experience (Mean [9] and SD [9]).

5. CONCLUSIONS

Two experiments, conducted during two dedicated workshops, were presented. The first one was carried out on a uneven population, the second one on a homogeneous population (musicology analysts). This allowed us to observe how this particular population stands on generated performances. The aim is to understand how the audience judges computer generated music performances. In particular, we analyzed possible different preferences and expectations of the listeners and influencing factors, such as cognitive styles.

The analysis of the ratings allows us to see (i) how preferences are distributed among the various performances and (ii) whether any orthogonalities and/or correlations exist.

If we compare the analysis of the factors in the two experiments, we can observe that general audience tends to give the same importance to emotional and technical factors (b6 and b7), and the difference depends on the remaining factors. On the contrary, for analyst audience, the emotional and technical factors (b1a and b1d) are very distinct and the remaining factors are situated between them.

It should be noted that, even if the performances are computer generated, there is a human contribution: in automatic systems this is given by the choice of the model and by the parameters (e.g., in the rules systems is given by the weights assigned to the rules); in interactive systems, in addition to the choice of the parameters, the contribution of the performer during the real-time control should also be considered. In this sense, the assessment includes also a judgment on the interpretative choices and depends on the experience of the assessors.

The analysis of the cognitive styles pointed out how the assessors stands on generated performances. The results of the GATM 2012 experiment show that all the assessors were systemizers, and young people had a less negative value of ME. It is important to conduct experiments with other populations of assessors, in order to point out the behavior of other typologies of assessors and study their preferences.

From the perspective of scientific progress, these judgments are useful not only for the purpose of ranking the systems but also for providing the researchers with information about the direction in which they should focus efforts to improve their systems. Specific measurements of performance quality can explicitly and precisely reveal the strengths and weaknesses of a system, and this information can, in turn, suggest short- and medium-term goals for improvement. This study helps to understand the relationship between art and technology.

Appendix A: Assessment questionnaire

There are many factors that can impact on one's enjoyment of a musical performance. The survey is intended to find out which of these are most important for you when you are listening to a generated music performance.
The survey is divided into three parts: part A must be filled after listening the music performances obtained by automatic methods. Parts B1 and B2 must be filled at the end.

The detailed instructions given to the participants are shown below.

PART A – *Instructions to fill the form:*

> You will listen to four different generated performances, one after the other, of the same musical piece. Then the performances will be played again, one-by-one, and at the end of each performance you will be requested to fill the corresponding section. How much do you give applause to the performance? (1: nothing – 10: ovation)

PART B1 – *Instructions to fill the form:*

> How much did the following factors influenced the (high or low) enjoyment of the listened generated performances?
> 1: no influence – 7: very high influence
>
> b1a. Technical accuracy of the performance
>
> b1b. Coherence with the concert performance style
>
> b1c. Presence of choices that are original and interesting
>
> b1d. Capacity of arousing an emotional involvement in the listener
>
> Are there any other factors that are important in determining your personal enjoyment of the performance?
> (If there are several, please list in order: most important → least important)

PART B2 – *Instructions to fill the form:*

> This questionnaire is about the so-called cognitive style. Some people are slightly more interested in other people than they are, for example, in technology. For other people, the opposite is true. Either way, there is no 'right' or 'wrong' cognitive style in that sense. They can just be different.
> Here we would like to invite you to fill in a questionnaire that will inform us about your cognitive style. The purpose of this research is to find out what aspects of music are more or less important to different people when listening to or thinking about music.
> While filling in your responses, please read the lines carefully and circle the number in each line that is most appropriate for you: (1: completely disagree, 2: partially disagree, 3: partially agree, 4: completely agree).

The statements are the same presented in [9, Appendix B].

Appendix B: Assessors' comments to the GATM performances

Comments to the GATM performances divided in the three following categories, according to [16].

Technical mastery and control

E1: phrasing balanced, low dynamic range, little agogic, if it were a person it would seem inaccurate, mechanical, distinction legato/staccato, clumsy performance, regular, irregular, balanced but not rigid.

E2: extreme dynamics, excessive sforzato, boy playing so fast because he likes to run, too varied, non-flexible dynamic, little physical plausibility, inadequate ritardandi and rubati, performance more technical (professional?).

E3: the pianist strikes too strong, unacceptable grace notes, excessive appoggiaturas, too slow, laborious performance (student awkward?), misplaced accents and weighting, mechanical.

E4: little physical responses, little phrasing, tempo too slow in the second section, good tempo, too excessive agogic, rhythmic variations between phrases, some technical stumbling, full of swing, not perfect technically.

Sound quality

E1: effect of sound without weight, muffled timbre, weight left hand, timbre quality.

E2: bright.

E3: regular touch, softness, touch too hard, heavy sound.

E4: nice touch.

Convincing musical understanding

E1: beginner student, reliefs of the parts, fluid and with the right amount of irony, elegant, pleasant, little expressive, too scholastic, not too expressive, good the form, adequate for this kind of music, switable, expressive, elegant, monotonous, delicate, perhaps a bit too caressing.

E2: instinctive choices, scherzoso, almost gestural, exaggerated and awkward, look brilliant, rhapsodic, right alternation, interesting, makes the sense of burlesque, performance uneven.

E3: first reading, balance, out of style, performance quite expressive, very pleasant, not at all suitable, seems to remember an unmusical student, enjoyable, point to emotional communication, simulation of a scholastic performance, it is grainy, not unitary, rigid and cold, scholastic, disorganized, poorly developed phrasing, lack of elegance, inappropriate, inadequate to express correct emotions.

E4: nice, close to a human performance, passages more credible, makes concertistic the performance, good emotional communication, there is no balance, exaggerated changes, loss of equality, burlesque, but excessive, passages more credible, no unitary perception of the musical piece, balanced in the first part, emphatic the middle and the final parts, very natural, expressiveness acceptable, good ideas with moments mannerist.

6. REFERENCES

[1] A. Kirke and E. R. Miranda, Eds., *Guide to Computing for Expressive Music Performance*. Springer-Verlag, 2012.

[2] S. Canazza, G. De Poli, A. Rodà, and A. Vidolin, "Expressiveness in music performance: analysis, models, mapping, encoding," in *Structuring Music through Markup Language: Designs and Architectures*, J. Steyn, Ed. IGI Global, 2012, pp. 156–186.

[3] R. Bresin and A. Friberg, "Evaluation of computer systems for expressive music performance," in *Guide to Computing for Expressive Music Performance*, A. Kirke and E. Miranda, Eds. London: Springer-Verlag, 2013, pp. 181–203.

[4] R. Hiraga, M. Hashida, K. Hirata, H. Katayose, and K. Noike, "Rencon: towards a new evaluation method for performance," in *Proceedings of International Computer Music Conference (ICMC)*, Gothenburg, Sweden, 2002, pp. 357–360.

[5] H. Katayose, M. Hashida, G. De Poli, and K. Hirata, "On evaluating systems for generating expressive music performance: the Rencon experience," *J. of New Music Research*, vol. 41, no. 4, pp. 299–310, 2012.

[6] G. McPherson and W. Thompson, "Assessing music performances: Issues and influences," *Research Studies in Music Education*, vol. 10, no. 1, pp. 12–24, 1998.

[7] S. Thompson and A. Williamon, "Evaluating evaluation: Musical performance assessment as a research tool," *Music Perception*, vol. 21, no. 1, pp. 21–41, 2003.

[8] B. H. Repp, "The aesthetic quality of a quantitatively average music performance: two preliminary experiments," *Music Perception*, vol. 14, no. 4, pp. 419–444, 1997.

[9] G. Kreutz, E. Schubert, and L. Mitchell, "Cognitive styles of music listening," *Music Perception*, vol. 26, no. 1, pp. 57–73, 2008.

[10] S. Garrido and E. Schubert, "Personality and computer music," in *Proc. Sound and Music Comp. Conf.*, 2011.

[11] G. Widmer, S. Flossmann, and M. Grachten, "YQX plays Chopin," *AI Magazine*, vol. 30, no. 3, pp. 35–48, 2009.

[12] M. Grachten and G. Widmer, "Linear basis models for prediction and analysis of musical expression," *J. of New Music Research*, vol. 41, no. 4, pp. 311–322, 2012.

[13] E. Bisesi, R. Parncutt, and A. Friberg, "An accent-based approach to performance rendering: Music theory meets music psychology." in *Proc. Symposium on Performance Science (ISPS 2011)*, 2011, pp. 27–32.

[14] H. Katayose and K. Gakuin, "Using an expressive performance template in a music conducting interface," in *Proceedings of the 2004 Conf. on New Instruments for Musical Expression (NIME 2004)*, 2004, pp. 3–5.

[15] S. Tanaka, M. Hashida, and H. Katayose, "Shunji: A case-based performance rendering system attached importance to phrase expression," in *Proc. Sound and Music Computing Conf. (SMC-11)*, 2011.

[16] W. J. Wrigley and S. B. Emmerson, "Ecological development of a music performance rating scale for five instrument families," *Psychology of Music*, vol. 41, no. 1, pp. 97–118, 2013.

TOWARDS COMPUTABLE PROCEDURES FOR DERIVING TREE STRUCTURES IN MUSIC: CONTEXT DEPENDENCY IN GTTM AND SCHENKERIAN THEORY

Alan Marsden
Lancaster University, UK
a.marsden@lancaster.ac.uk

Keiji Hirata
Future University Hakodate, Japan
hirata@fun.ac.jp

Satoshi Tojo
Japan Advanced Institute of Science and Technology
tojo@jaist.ac.jp

ABSTRACT

This paper addresses some issues arising from theories which represent musical structure in trees. The leaves of a tree represent the notes found in the score of a piece of music, while the branches represent the manner in which these notes are an elaboration of simpler underlying structures. The idea of multi-levelled elaboration is a central feature of the *Generative Theory of Tonal Music* (GTTM) of Lerdahl and Jackendoff, and is found also in Schenkerian theory and some other theoretical accounts of musical structure. In previous work we have developed computable procedures for deriving these tree structures from scores, with limited success. In this paper we examine issues arising from these theories, and some of the reasons limiting our previous success. We concentrate in particular on the issue of context dependency, and consider strategies for dealing with this. We stress the need to be explicit about data structures and algorithms to derive those structures. We conjecture that an expectation-based parser with look-ahead is likely to be most successful.

1. BACKGROUND

It is common to regard the structure of a piece of music as in some way hierarchical. Heinrich Schenker [1] was not the first to propose the idea that a piece of music contains different levels of elaboration or reduction, but his influence has been so great as to mean that 'Schenkerian' is almost a synonym for hierarchical in music theory. The later *Generative Theory of Tonal Music* (GTTM), by Lerdahl & Jackendoff [2], explains musical structure as explicitly hierarchical and tree-structured, borrowing concepts from formal linguistics.

More recent work also uses trees to represent musical structure. One well known, and again explicitly linguistic-inspired, example is Steedman's chord grammar [3, 4] which represents the structure of a complex chord sequence as a tree showing the derivation of the sequence from a simple model such as a twelve-bar blues. Rizo has used trees as a basis for a model of melodic similarity [5].

Recent theories such as those of Steedman and Rizo are defined in formal terms, allowing an analysis to be systematically derived from a sequence of chords or notes. Schenker was writing before the birth of formal cognitive science, and did not express his theory in this kind of systematic fashion. (Indeed, it is clear that it was never his intention to take music theory in this direction—that is the result of appropriations by scholars of later generations [6].) Lerdahl & Jackendoff, on the other hand, were writing on the explicit basis of theories of linguistic grammar and also took account of some of the early work in musical computing (e.g., [7]). Their theory is accordingly expressed in more formal terms, but still without the degree of precision required for derivation of analyses from a score without expert musical knowledge. Lerdahl & Jackendoff are quite explicit about this: 'our theory cannot provide a computable procedure for determining musical analyses' [2, p. 55]. Yet earlier they 'conceive of [their] theory as being in principle testable by the usual scientific standards' [p. 5]. A theory is only testable if it can make precise predictions, and the only logical resolution of these two statements is that Lerdahl & Jackendoff considered that suitable extension of the theory would produce a computable procedure for determining musical analyses.

Over the past decade, the authors have developed computer software to derive analyses in accordance with Schenkerian theory [8] and GTTM [9]. The results have been only partially successful. The ATTA software of Hamanaka, Hirata and Tojo requires the user to adjust parameters in order to arrive at acceptable analyses in accordance with GTTM. Marsden's Schenkerian analysis software can only make analyses for short extracts of music, and the results only partially match those of experts.

In view of this limited success, and the enduring popularity of the idea of reduction in musical computing, we believe it is worth stepping back to reconsider some of the fundamental issues concerning the derivation of tree structures in music. In particular, we aim to consider some of the details around context dependency which complicate the formulation of an effective computable procedure to automatically derive trees from the notes in the score of a piece of music.

Figure 1. Analysis of the theme from the first movement of Mozart's piano sonata in A major, K.331.

2. TREE REPRESENTATIONS

Formally, a tree is a connected graph of nodes and arcs in which there are no cycles. Some additional properties are considered to be essential when representing music, however. Firstly, arcs have a direction, connecting 'parents' to 'children'. The parent is the 'reduction' of the children, and the children the 'elaboration' of the parent. Secondly, child nodes in a musical-structure tree have an explicit order: 'left' children occur before 'right' children. In principle there is no restriction to the number of children a parent may have, and it is not uncommon for trees representing musical structure to have parents with three or more children. The simplest trees, however, have no more than two children per parent (called *binary trees*), and it is common to restrict discussion and the definition of procedures to this case. Nothing is lost by this, because it is always possible to convert any finite tree to a binary tree which represents exactly the same information, and to convert it back again to the original tree

In GTTM, Time-span reduction and prolongational reduction are explicitly represented in trees. They are often binary, but the theory does allow cases of parents with more than two children. Schenkerian analyses are notated in music-notation-like 'graphs' using noteheads and slurs rather than trees, but parent-child relations can be derived from these, and equivalent tree structures generated [10].

Figure 1 shows Lerdahl & Jackendoff's time-span reduction of the first eight bars of the theme from the first movement of Mozart's piano sonata in A major, K.331. (For clarity, not all of the lowest levels of branching are shown in the figure.) Schenker's analysis of this theme is somewhat different, but for present purposes we can point out that a Schenkerian analysis would look rather like the notation in the four lower staves, but with the vertical order reversed and the addition of slurs joining notes into groups more or less in accordance with the grouping shown by the corresponding level of branching in the tree.

2.1 Trees and Cognition

Schenker believed that his analyses showed the 'background and middleground' of a piece of music, which were the 'indispensable prerequisites to a musical work of art' [1, p. 3–4]. Background and middleground were, for Schenker, the genesis of a work not literally in the sense of the sequence of events (real or mental) which led to its composition, but in a metaphysical sense, constituting something of the reality of the piece.

Lerdahl & Jackendoff state the goal of theory to be a 'formal description of the musical intuitions of a listener who is experienced in a musical idiom' [2, p.1] and later make clear that they are concerned with 'the final state of his understanding' and not the mental processes which lead to this state.

Both Schenker and Lerdahl & Jackendoff, therefore, consider their reductions to correspond to a cognitive conception of the piece, but neither is directly concerned with how that conception is created in the act of listening.

2.2 Musical Grammar

On the other hand, both Schenker and Lerdahl & Jackendoff aim to show a systematic relationship between the notes of the score and the reduction. Schenker writes of musical 'laws', though he does not explicate

Figure 2. Recomposition of Figure 1 to place a copy of bar 4 at the beginning.

them in a precise fashion. (Instead, one is given the strong impression that only geniuses have true understanding of the laws!) Lerdahl & Jackendoff, by contrast, give a large set of rules to relate notes to analyses. However, as frequently pointed out, some of these are irregular rules in that they state only a 'preferred' relation between notes and structures, which need not hold if other rules imply a different relation. How conflicts between preference rules are to be resolved is not specified in the theory.

It is our conviction that music theories such as GTTM and Schenkerian theory form a useful ground for building computational systems which are capable of automatically deriving the structure of a piece of music from the notes in the score. Furthermore, we believe that such derivation of structure is essential for some effective musical processing in such tasks as finding similarity or segmenting pieces of music. In the following, we examine some difficulties in employing GTTM and Schenkerian theory as such a basis for computational structure-finding systems.

3. CONTEXT DEPENDENCY

Schenker was clear that the *Ursatz* (the simplest structure at the top level of every great piece of music) governed every aspect of the structure of a piece of music. The details of how a passage is reduced, therefore, depend in part on where that passage comes in the *Ursatz*. A fundamental problem of Schenkerian analysis is that one cannot know what the *Ursatz* is, and how it relates to the details of the piece, until one has analysed the structure: one needs to know the context to properly analyse the structure, but one cannot know what the context is before the structure is analysed. For example, it is common to find the same passage of music analysed in two different ways in a Schenkerian analysis according to where it comes in the piece. The typical case is for the melody of a passage to be analysed as an elaboration of the third or fifth degree of the scale when it occurs early in the piece, but for the same melody to be analysed as the descending 3-2-1 or 5-4-3-2-1 of the *Urlinie* late in the piece.

Marsden's Schenkerian analysis software [8] overcomes the difficulty of not knowing the location of the *Ursatz* in advance by effectively generating many possible analyses of the structure, then selecting those which contain an *Ursatz*, and finally selecting the one which appears best. This is an extremely costly procedure in computational terms, and cannot form the basis of a practical system.

GTTM similarly contains many instances of context-dependency. The preference rules for 'cadential retention' and 'structural beginning', TSRPR 7 and 8, cause reductions to depend on the grouping structure not just for the time-span where the reduction takes place, but for the enclosing time-span(s) also. In other words knowledge of higher-level structure is required before the lower level structure can be determined. In this case the structures are in different components of GTTM (grouping and time-span reduction), but a preference rule for grouping structure, GPR 7, completes the circle by stating that grouping structures are preferred which result in more stable time-span reductions.

Lerdahl & Jackendoff point out the importance of such context dependency in discussion of bar 4 (measure 4) of the Mozart theme in Figure 1 [2, p. 118–120, 134–35, 167]. Out of context, the opening chord of the bar would be considered the 'head' to which the entire bar reduces, because it is on the strong beat (TSRPR 1) and because it is closer to the tonic (TSRPR 2; in fact it is the tonic!). The correct reduction, which makes sense of the phrase, is instead to take the dominant chord at the end of the bar as the head, as indicated in Figure 1.

3.1 Recomposition of Contexts

Figure 2 illustrates the context dependency in the reduction of bar 4 of the Mozart theme. The theme has been rewritten to start with a copy of bar 4 and a new bar 2 to retain the overall pattern of descending sequence in the first two bars. Here it is clear that the pattern of notes in bar 4 is reduced in different ways according to the context, as shown by the tree structure in Figure 2. A Schenkerian graph of Figure 2 would also show a difference between the reduction of bar 4 in Figure 2 and the copy of it in bar 1 of that figure. In the reduction of bar 4 a slur which has its beginning earlier in the piece would end on

Figure 3. Recomposition of Figure 1 to make five-bar phrases.

Figure 4. Recomposition of Figure 3 to echo cadence.

Figure 5. Recomposition of Figure 3 to recreate four-bar phrase.

Figure 6. Recomposition of Figure 2 to prevent cadence at bar 4.

the melody note B while in bar 1 a slur would begin on the first C sharp and end somewhere beyond the end of bar 1. (In making this claim, we follow the procedure of music theorists who rely on their own intuition about the structure of a piece of music, tested by repeated listening and introspection. We furthermore assume that other listeners will have the same intuitions as ours. We judge that for our present purposes the cost of proper scientific listening tests is not warranted, but we would be interested to hear if other listeners do not share our intuitions.)

In the case of Figure 2, the new context for the pattern of bar 4 is evident from the fact that it occurs at the beginning. However, it is not only this which can cause a different reduction of this bar. Figure 3 shows a different recomposition of the Mozart theme to make the phrases five bars long. Here bar 4 is reduced differently because a new bar follows which takes the role of cadence. (Some might prefer the reduction of bar 4 to be connected to the branch from bar 5 rather than the one from bar 3, but this does not change the assignment of the tonic chord at the beginning of bar 4 as head for that bar rather than the dominant.)

From Figure 3, one might conclude that so long as the pattern of bar 4 does not occur at the end of a phrase, it should be reduced to tonic harmony, but this is contradicted by the example in Figure 4, which replaces the new cadential bar 5 by a copy of bar 4. Here the new bar 5 sounds like an echo of the cadence in bar 4.

Figures 5 and 6 illustrate the affect of other contexts for bar 4. Figure 5 illustrates that the possibility of splitting ten bars into two phrases of five bars each does not necessarily lead to a tree structure congruent with a division into two phrases of five bars. Here the new bar 5, while having the same outline of I-V and C sharp to B in the melody, groups with the beginning of the next phrase, partly by virtue of the similarity of rhythm. In Figure 6, which recomposes the music in Figure 2, bar 4 is prevented from acting as a cadence not by the insertion of a stronger cadence (as in Figure 3), but by a continuation which causes it to sound once again like a beginning.

To illustrate the significance of the difference in these structural analyses, imagine a software system designed to separate music into segments, and to report the degree to which a segment will sound finished or unfinished.

Such a system should segment Figures 1 and 2 into bars 1–4 and 5–8, Figures 3 and 4 into bars 1–5 and 6–10, Figure 5 into bars 1–4 and 6–10, and Figure 6 into bars 1–3 and 4–7. It should report that the first segments made up of bars 1–4 or 1–5 will sound finished but less final than the second segments 5–8 or 6–10, and that the first segment in Figure 6, bars 1–3, will not sound finished. All of these could be concluded directly from the graphs by taking the highest-level branching to indicate the segmentation, the presence of a retained cadence to indicate strong finality, and the presence of right-branching on the right-most branch (as would be the case in bar 3 of Figure 6) to indicate sounding unfinished.

3.2 Strategies for Context Dependency

3.2.1 Separation of bottom-up and top-down

GTTM includes two kinds of tree: time-span reduction and prolongational reduction. Time-span reduction is characterised as concerning 'relative stability within rhythmic units', and prolongational reduction 'relative stability expressed in terms of continuity and progression' [2, p. 123]. What this means precisely is not entirely clear, especially since rhythmic units are partially defined by time-span reduction in view of the interdependence between time-span reduction and grouping. Furthermore, the concepts of 'cadential retention' and 'structural beginning' clearly concern continuity and progression to some degree.

Another distinction between time-span reduction and prolongational reduction, not explicitly stated by Lerdahl & Jackendoff but clearly implied in their presentation, is that time-span reductions are made mostly bottom-up while prolongational reductions are made top-down. Perhaps a strategy to deal with context dependency is to make this bottom-up/top-down distinction absolute and revise time-span reduction to disregard top-down rules such as cadential retention and structural beginnings. This would reduce the pattern in bar 4 of the examples above always using right-branching and yielding tonic harmony as the head. A top-down process like prolongational reduction would then modify the tree to reflect context dependencies, for example replacing right branching by left branching at cadences.

Marsden's Schenkerian-analysis software [8] also operates in a two-step bottom-up then top-down process. It uses a version of the CYK parsing algorithm which fills a table with information about possible parses in a bottom-up process (the Schenkerian-analysis software also collects information about possible *Ursatz* membership) and then uses this information to build a parse top-down.

3.2.2 Expectation-based parsing

Most of our listening to music is to pieces we have heard before, or if not, at least to pieces similar to others we have heard before. Perhaps a reduction mechanism can take two inputs: the notes of the score, and a sequence of expectations based on the last time the piece was heard and the structure derived from that hearing, whether expressed in the fashion of GTTM as a prolongational and time-span tree, or in the manner of Schenkerian theory, or some other manner (e.g., expectation expressed in a numerical value [11]). If the piece has not been heard before, expectations can be generated on the basis of memories of similar pieces or a style [12]. Even if one's memory is not sufficiently accurate to expect what the next note will be, a trace of a previously derived tree structure might remain, or melodic expectation might be generated based on a familiarity with a style. Thus, on arriving at bar 4 in the Mozart theme, the listener will expect that the next bar will be a return to the opening, so bar 4 must function as a cadence.

Indeed in every case in the examples given above, the correct parsing of a structural unit is not clear until the next unit has begun. It would seem that parsing takes place after the event rather than while the music is being heard, but it is not clear how long the delay is. (Clearly limits to short-time and working memory will have an impact on this.) Possibly the delay is long enough for a rough parse to be made for an entire phrase before the detail of a reduction is completed.

Top-down information is known to influence visual object recognition, and experimental evidence suggests that high-speed processing of low-spatial-frequency information is instrumental in this process [13]. Perhaps similar low-bandwidth information or approximations in listening to music provide the same kind of top-down control. For example, it is possible that the listener rapidly extracts the main harmonies from a passage, and uses these to generate an outline tree to capture the I-V, I-V-I structure of the Mozart theme. This outline tree is then filled in with the rest of the detail of the reduction.

3.2.3 Category labels

Similar phenomena of context dependency occur in language, but we are not aware of any musical examples which have the force of 'garden-path sentences' which require the reader or hearer to undo an existing parse and re-parse the sentence for it to make sense. [14] shows how a Definite Clause Grammar can be used to parse the sentence 'That man that whistles tunes pianos.' The word 'whistles' is initially parsed as a transitive word with 'tunes' taken to be a noun and its object. The occurrence of the word 'pianos', however, causes the parsing to backtrack and then take 'whistles' to be intransitive and 'tunes' as a verb. Techniques therefore exist in natural language processing to cope with similar context dependency, but they cannot be naively transferred to music. For example, [15] reports that a backtracking parser, without additional features to guide it towards the correct parse, frequently failed to find a correct parse for jazz chord sequences within a reasonable time.

A characteristic of linguistic grammars is that they associate labels, such as 'noun phrase', with internal nodes of a parse tree. This allows for more efficient and reliable parsing because it disambiguates words or sequences of words which can have different functions, such as the word 'tunes' in the garden-path sentence mentioned above. In the incorrect parsing it is categorised as a noun, whereas it should be a verb.

Perhaps the use of category labels in musical reduction trees could similarly disambiguate cases which behave differently in different contexts. Each putative head in a reduction, for example, might have one of the categories *b*, *m*, or *c* attached, for 'beginning', 'middle' or 'close'. The pattern in bar 4, then, could produce the alternative reductions I(*b*) and V(*c*), where I and V stand as shorthand for the tonic at the beginning of the bar and the dominant at the end respectively. The grammar for categories could then be as follows:

$b \rightarrow b\ m$
$c \rightarrow m\ c$
$b\ b \rightarrow b\ c\ b$
$c \rightarrow b\ c$
$m\ c \rightarrow m\ c\ c$ [only when the second *c* is a copy of the first]
$b \rightarrow b\ b$ [only if no other parsing is possible]

The bars of the original theme (Figure 1) would be initially categorised as *b*, *m*, *m*, *b/c*, *b*, *m*, *m*, *c*. The alternative reduction for bar 4 with the label *c* will be selected in parsing because there is no rule to accept *m b* and selecting *c* allows the non-preferred sequence *b b* to be avoided.

The grammar also leads to the correct reductions for the other examples to be selected. Figure 6, for example, has initial categories *b/c*, *m*, *m*, *b/c*, *m*, *m*, *c*. The reduction with category *b* will be chosen for bar 4 because there is no following *b* which would allow *c* here to be absorbed by the third rule, and this bar is not copied by the final *c*.

Grammars using categories have been applied to music (e.g., [4]) but even for chord sequences, which are simpler than collections of notes, this alone does not lead to a successful analysis system. [14] shows greater success in analysing chord sequences when category labels assigned in a probabilistic fashion so that the label most likely to lead to a correct parse is used first, or at least early in backtracking.

3.3 A Tension-Relaxation Grammar

Category labels in language function not only to indicate syntactic position but also function. We suggest that in music this function might relate to the commonly used concepts of tension and relaxation. Lerdahl & Jackendoff relate prolongational reduction to the sense of tension and relaxation in a piece of music [2, 16]. Schenker does not use the same language, but his metaphor of a piece of music as a living organisms is not so far from these ideas. For him pieces grow and exhibit intention, cause and effect. A grammar of tension and relaxation, if such a thing is possible, could provide a basis for category labels, for expectation, and for outline parsing. The grammar might look something like this (where *S* is a complete 'sentence', *T* tension and *R* relaxation):

$S \rightarrow S\ S$
$S \rightarrow T\ R$
$T \rightarrow T\ S$
$R \rightarrow S\ R$

Other rules would indicate how tension and relaxation were related to, for example, harmonies:

$T \rightarrow$ I V
$R \rightarrow$ V I
$R \rightarrow$ IV V I
$R \rightarrow$ ii V I
etc.

Tension and relaxation could be derived from rhythmic characteristics of the music also, or from dynamics and timing. The function of the grammar is precisely to take information from whatever source seems useful and use it to guide derivation of structure and meaning from the music. Studies of performers' bodily movements while playing have shown that even these convey information about tension and structure to an audience (e.g., [17]). Even bodily movements might therefore provide input to the tension-relaxation grammar.

4. CONCLUSIONS

This discussion has focused on the general principles of tree structures in music and their derivation. Research which draws directly and only from music theory is unlikely to progress further than the authors' earlier work because Schenkerian theory, GTTM and the like are not expressed with the degree of precision required for computational implementation. They also lack empirical validation. Further progress will depend on derivation from examples (preferably large sets of them) and other empirical data.

Data from listening experiments is costly to obtain, and the structural intuitions which Schenker and Lerdahl & Jackendoff believed their theories revealed do not correspond to overt measurable behaviours. Experiments which test the match of reductions to tunes ask listeners to perform an unfamiliar task without any clear relation to other musical behaviours [18, 19]. The results are therefore of dubious validity. In our view a more solid basis for empirical data relevant to tree structures in music comes from four sources:

1. *Existing analyses by musical experts*. There are not many published examples of analyses according to GTTM, but the second and third authors have a test set of melodies analysed by experts. A sizeable quantity of published Schenkerian analyses exist in journals and textbooks.
2. *Variations*. In many cases, a theme and variation share a common underlying structure. What a theme and set of variations has in common therefore provides information about the proper tree-structure representation of the theme or variation.
3. *Music similarity data*. In the same way, melodic similarity, on which a quantity of data is emerging from MIR research, provides suggestive information about underlying tree structures. Similar pieces of music often share similar structures.

4. *Operational effectiveness in music processing*. Music-processing tasks often require structural information. (Examples include performance rendering, segmentation, and summarisation.) We conjecture that embedding systems for deriving tree structures from pieces of music within software to perform such tasks will provide empirical validation of the structures derived: if the task is performed well, the structure-derivation is likely to be correct.

We do not wish to discount the value of sophisticated music theory to music computing. On the contrary we believe that it has much to offer but that successful employment of ideas from music theory will also require the application of concepts and procedures from modern computational science. In particular, we believe that employment of the ideas of category labels, expectation, look-ahead and initial tracing of an over-arching structure of tension and relaxation will be useful for future progress.

It is common in computing to separate data structures from algorithms, and we suspect that music theory would benefit from a similar separation. Both GTTM and Schenkerian theory, in their textual expositions, describe the data structures in which musical structure is embodied (despite the fact that many of the rules of GTTM are expressed in a quasi-procedural fashion, using formulations such as 'prefer a reduction which ...'). As pointed out above, the algorithmic part—how to derive the structures from a score—is not made explicit but remains implicit in the theorists' examples. Computational linguistics, by contrast, makes a clear distinction between grammars and the parsers which use grammars, employing processes such as backtracking, decomposition/recomposition, and expectation, as we have seen. We believe that advances in the theory of musical structure will depend on similar clarity about data structures and explicit algorithms. It is our conjecture that in the case of deriving tree structures from musical scores, some kind of expectation-based parser, coupled with a look-ahead buffer, is most likely to be successful.

Acknowledgments

The authors are grateful to the anonymous reviewers' valuable comments that improved the manuscript. This research was supported by a Short-Term Invitation Fellowship in December 2012 funded by the Japan Society for the Promotion of Science.

5. REFERENCES

[1] H. Schenker, *Der freie Satz*. Universal Edition, 1935. Published in English as *Free Composition*, translated and edited by E. Oster, Longman, 1979.

[2] F. Lerdahl and R. Jackendoff, *A Generative Theory of Tonal Music*. MIT Press, 1983.

[3] M. Steedman, "A generative grammar for jazz chord sequences," *Music Perception*, vol. 2, no. 1, pp. 52–77, 1984.

[4] M. Steedman, "The blues and the abstract truth: music and mental models," in A. Garnham & J. Oakhill (eds.), *Mental Models in Cognitive Science*. Psychology Press, pp. 305–318, 1996.

[5] D. Rizo, Symbolic music comparison with tree data structures, PhD thesis, University of Alicante, 2010.

[6] N. Cook, *The Schenker Project: Culture, Race, and Music Theory in Fin-de-siècle Vienna*. Oxford University Press, 2007.

[7] J. Tenney and L. Polansky, "Temporal gestalt perception in music," *Journal of Music Theory*, vol. 24, no. 2, 205–241.

[8] A. Marsden, "Schenkerian analysis by computer: a proof of concept," in *Journal of New Music Research*, vol. 39, no. 3, pp. 269–289, 2010.

[9] M. Hamanaka, K. Hirata, and S. Tojo, "Implementing 'A Generative Theory of Tonal Music'", *Journal of New Music Research*, vol. 35, no. 4, pp. 249–277, 2006.

[10] A. Marsden, "Generative Structural Representation of Tonal Music," *Journal of New Music Research*, vol. 34, no. 4, pp. 409–428, 2005.

[11] M.T. Pearce and G.A. Wiggins, "Expectation in melody: The influence of context and learning," *Music Perception*, vol. 23, no. 5, pp. 377-405, 2006.

[12] W.E. Caplin, *Classical Form: A Theory of Formal Functions for the Music of Haydn, Mozart, and Beethoven*, Oxford University Press, 1998.

[13] M. Bar, K.S. Kassam, A.S. Ghuman, J. Boshyan, A.M. Schmidt, A.M. Dale, M.S. Hamalainen, K. Marinkovic, D.L. Schacter, B.R. Rosen and E. Halgren, "Top-down facilitation of visual recognition," *Proceedings of the National Academy of Science*, vol. 103, no. 2, pp. 449–454, 2006.

[14] F.C.N. Pereira and D.H.D. Warren, "Definite Clause Grammars for Language Analysis—A Survey of the Formalism and a Comparison with Augmented Transition Networks," *Artificial Intelligence* vol. 13, pp. 231–278, 1980.

[15] M. Granroth-Wilding and M. Steedman, "Statistical parsing for harmonic analysis of jazz chord sequences," *Proc. International Computer Music Conference (ICMC)*, Ljubljana, 2012, pp. 478–485.

[16] F. Lerdahl, *Tonal Pitch Space*, Oxford University Press, 2001.

[17] M.M. Wanderley, B.W. Vines, N. Middleton, C. McKay, W. Hatch, "The musical significance of clarinetists' ancillary gestures: An exploration of the

field," *Journal of New Music Research*, vol. 34, no. 1, pp. 97–113, 2005.

[18] Y. Oura and G. Hatano, "Identifying melodies from reduced pitch patterns," *Psychologica Belgica*, vol. 31, no. 2, pp. 217–237, 1991.

[19] N. Dibben, "The cognitive reality of hierarchic structure in tonal and atonal music," *Music Perception*, vol. 12, no. 1, pp. 1–25, 1994.

Situating the Performer and the Instrument in a Rich Social Context with PESI Extended System

Callum Goddard
Department of Media
Aalto University
School of Arts, Design and Architecture
callum.goddard@aalto.fi

Koray Tahiroğlu
Department of Media
Aalto University
School of Arts, Design and Architecture
koray.tahiroglu@aalto.fi

ABSTRACT

In this paper we present our solutions to the design challenges of facilitating awareness of actions and development of self-identities within *The notion of Participatory Enacting Sonic Interaction* (PESI) project. The PESI system is a modular framework for participatory music making with three performers. We present a brief technical overview, design considerations and revisions resulting from a user study conducted during the system's development. Through the development process of the PESI project a design approach we term: Non-Behaviourally Restrictive Digital Technology became apparent. In this approach, the shifting focus that embodied agents have in relation to the environment is accounted for and the development of sound-action relationships are encouraged. This is achieved through providing mappings relating to individual sensor values and movement information from motion tracking data. Our approach to the implementation of the PESI system can shift the collaborative music activity to a more engaging and active experience.

1. INTRODUCTION

Designing systems in which social interaction is the primary focus is challenging as it requires consideration of additional factors along side the social interaction. An awareness and understanding of the evolving nature of the performer-instrument relationship within specific contexts and cultures is needed to inform how these relationships may be facilitated through the technology. The idea of performance ecosystems helps to address these design challenges by emphasising how social factors effect and facilitate changes in the function of technology and music. Through the consideration of performance ecosystems, we highlight the importance of usage in technology which allows for the blurring of phenomenological and epistemic distinctions between acoustic and digital technology [1,2]. In blurring these traditionally held distinctions, we are able to focus directly on investigating the ideas of social interaction in collaborative music. Through investigating these ideas, we have implemented our own system that is capable of supporting collaborative and creative activities in group music practices.

This paper presents our design approach to *The notion of Participatory Enacting Sonic Interaction* (PESI) project, a modular framework for participative music making with three performers. The project incorporates new generation mobile phones and group motion tracking technology to create an environment in which performers' individual and social actions contribute to and affect the sonic output. We have briefly presented previous versions of the PESI system in [3–5]. The system has been developed on the iOS platform along with the use of the Microsoft Kinect System. Mobile phones enable individual action within the system and the Kinect system tracks participants, enabling augmentation of the social space within the system. The result is that the PESI system can facilitate group music practices that exploit social action in combination with the use of everyday devices for allowing musical action.

Compared to other approaches based upon analysis of social behaviours within musical practice, such as [6] and the EU-ICT SIEMPRE project, [1] the PESI project instead has focused on facilitating social action through technology within a musical context. As such, the design challenges of the PESI system relate to the ideas of awareness and mutual engagement within Human Computer Interaction (HCI). Finding solutions to these challenges has guided the design and development process, and in doing so, we have identified a design approach which we call: behaviourally non-restrictive digital technology.

This paper begins with an overview of related work on the performance ecosystem approach. Section 3 presents the design challenges and section 4 provides an technical and design overview of the PESI system. Section 5 outlines our idea of behaviourally non-restrictive digital technology, which is discussed in section 6, where the approach is compared with the work described in section 2. The paper is concluded in section 7.

2. RELATED WORK

2.1 Ecological Perspectives Towards Music

The ecological perspective has been used within the design and implementation of interactive digital music systems as

[1] http://siempre.infomus.org/

a way to contextualise and investigate relationships that develop when using these systems [7–11]. One approach, which has been given notable attention, is that of performance ecosystems. Based on ideas suggested by Simon Waters [12], a performance ecosystem is a tool to understand current musical activity. The central idea is that "understanding music making as a complex dynamic system puts it in terms of the process of creation, but also its consolidation into culture specifically as a social practice embodying behaviours, beliefs and actions" [12]. Here music making is seen as an activity that produces artefacts as well as being part of social practice.

Two projects that embrace the performance ecosystem perspective are the Audible Eco-Systemic Interface (AESI) project [7] and in 'Infra-instruments' [8]. Within both these projects the notion and design practices of interaction within interactive systems are questioned. The AESI project questions the performers' role in interactive systems. In many interactive systems the performer is the person providing external conditions that the dynamic behaviour of a system is driven by. The system is depended on the performer. Within the AESI project the need for a performer is removed. The relationship of performer, instrument and environment is reduced to only being between the instrument and the environment. This is accomplished through a feedback loop in which the system generates the controls from analysis of its ambient surroundings.

Similarly, the Infra-instruments project draws comparisons to and diverges from the approaches used within the development of 'hyper' and 'meta' instruments. Hyper and meta instruments are approaches that extend traditional instruments' interactive capabilities, expressive nature and virtuosity through the addition of sensors. Instead of extending the instrument, Bowers and Archer see value in simplifying and limiting the interaction. Their approach creates a space within the performance setting for the additional capabilities of computers [8].

The ecological perspective has also been taken by [9–11] to investigate the relationships between performers and spectators of interactive digital music system performances. Their research has highlighted considerations within the design of digital musical instruments (DMIs) to improve spectator experience within these performances. The improvement of experiences with DMIs and music technology is also a concern within the area of embodied music cognition and mediation [13]. Whilst not explicitly drawing upon ecological ideas, the focus is upon how we interact with music. The ideas developed within the field of embodied music cognition have been used to inform the development of an interface exploring musical experience and creativity [14]. The Musical Paint Machine extends the performance space of a player so that the sonic output of the instrument is visually represented. In this way, additional feedback modalities are introduced to the player as a method of stimulating creativity.

2.2 Blurring Distinctions Between Instruments

The works presented have followed Waters' main ideas on performance ecosystems; however, work by Green has extended these ideas further towards musical creation. Green emphasises the influence that social factors have in the use of technology and musical practice. When players and instruments are situated within a social world *'the categorical distinctions between the acoustic and the digital dissipate somewhat, and that such differences in practice are contingent upon the shifting intersections between the technical and social'* [2]. Thus the influence that social factors have on the usage of technology results in the distinctions [2] between acoustic and digital being blurred.

Accounting for relationships between the different parts of a system, from a conceptual stand point, is one of the main challenges in adopting an ecological perspective. In adopting Greens contingency view on musical instruments we can direct our own focus towards the consideration of social factors and their influences on the design of interactive systems. In the following section we briefly address these challenges in the PESI project by considering and accounting for the performers' relationship to the technology and to each other within the design of the system.

3. DESIGN CHALLENGES

To account for forms of embodied interaction in the implementation of the PESI system we have investigated the design challenges surrounding the role of meaning in relation to collaborative interactive systems. This has directed our focus to concerns relating to intersubjectivity, and the design of technology that facilitates co-operative processes.

Intersubjectivity is the way in which two people can share understanding of the world, or how meaning can be shared between two people [15–17]. To establish and allow for intersubjectivity within a collaborative system, users need to be able to interpret and understand the action of others. This is required for a communication flow to be established, thus enabling collaboration within the activity. Similarly participants need to be aware of what others are doing or have done, also known as having public awareness of actions [18]. Facilitating awareness in collaborative systems is very important in allowing for multiple users to interact with each other. This is emphasised by both the fields of HCI [15] and Computer-Supported Collaborative Work (CSCW) [18]. Awareness of actions is also an important design feature in facilitating mutual engagement, allowing for a more socially engaging experience [19, 20].

Issues of awareness within areas of HCI and CSCW and in research into mutual engagement in social music have mainly focused on activities in which participants are not co-located. Within the PESI system the participants are co-located, to account for this we extended the ideas of awareness and mutual engagement through considering the experiences of individual users. We draw on ideas of optimal experience, Flow [21], for this.

The exact conditions for achieving a Flow state are still being investigated, however, a key component of obtaining a Flow state within an activity is the maintenance of ones own personal identity [21]. The importance of self-identity within optimal experiences has prompted us to ex-

[2] These are the phenomenological and epistemic distinctions between acoustic and digital instrument technology [1]

Figure 1. Three musicians using the PESI system in a free form improvisation.

tend ideas of awareness and mutual engagement so that users area able to retain the ability to develop and act through their own self-identities within the system. This requires enabling users to be identifiable as other identities within the system, and that these identities can be influenced by others, through a their own self identities [21]. It also requires that each user be able to detach themselves, and their actions, from the overall interactive system.

We believe that facilitating the building of identities aids in, and strengthens, awareness within collaborative systems of co-located participants. Therefore, the design challenges of the PESI system are focusing on facilitating both awareness of actions, and allowing users to create their own identities within the system.

4. THE PESI SYSTEM

In the PESI system mobile devices run custom software that allows for them to be used as musical instruments that are usable within an improvised musical group performance [4]. The relationship and interaction between the performer and their mobile instrument is extended into the physical and social space through the use of motion tracking software and group analysis.

4.1 Technical Justifications

From the start of the project, the PESI system was designed with a modular structure. The modular structure aided in development by allowing for rapid system reconfiguration as well as the testing of ideas. This structure also makes the system more accessible to others to modify or to extend for their own uses. In that concern, we used readily available technology: Apple iPhones as the mobile phones, Microsoft Kinect as the motion tracking system and Pure Data [3] for the sound synthesis.

Including mobile phones allows us to emphasise the role of social communication within the system as they represent communication within our society. iPhones also have the additional benefit of being association with music practice. iDevices are largely connected with music listening as well as music production through the ever increasing number of musical applications available on the platform. They also contain the technology required by the PESI system: sensor input feedback mechanisms, enriched computational possibilities for sound processing and wireless communication.

The decision to use the Microsoft Kinect system within the PESI system was determined in a similar manner to the iPhones. The Kinect system is a cultural object that is primarily used within games that require whole body interaction. It allows us to emphasise the playful nature of the system as well as being able to visual track and allow for detailed evaluation of a group of people.

Pure data was the audio programming language of choice for the PESI system's sound synthesis. The primary reason pure data was chosen over other audio programming languages is due to its portability. The development of Libpd [4] has made it possible to run Pure Data on many different platforms. Within the PESI system this meant that the same sound synthesis patch can run on both iPhones and Laptop Computer. It also sufficiently fulfils the sound synthesis needs of the PESI system.

4.2 The Initial System and the Design Outcomes Arising from it's User Study

Development of the PESI system has gone through multiple iterations. Work began on a simple system in which only mobile phone instruments were augmented with relational parameters generated from a Microsoft Kinect system. Through a user test we were able to assess the effect extending the controls into the social domain had on the playability of the mobile phone instrument [3]. This resulted in an extension of the system, to allow for further ideas relating to development of the mobile phone instruments to be explored and implemented.

Figure 2. A group of three participants taking part in first user study of the PESI system.

The first user study used an initial simple system implementation and was primarily conducted to gain insight into the effect socially control parameters had on the interaction. 21 participants: 8 female and 13 male, aged 25-48 were involved in the study. Test participants were divided into 7 groups of three players, each group participated in a separate session (see Fig. 2). In each session we asked the users to use the system in two scenarios. In the first

[3] `http://puredata.info/`

[4] `http://libpd.cc`

scenario there were no social parameters effecting the mobile instruments, in the second scenario, a parameter calculated from the average distance between group members altered an amplitude distortion effect. The evaluation of the user test included a quantitative survey and qualitative interviews. We presented our findings in detail in [3].

In conducting this user study two design issues were highlighted. The first issue related to the average distance value of the group, participants found it was very hard to perceive and understand. Using the individual distance parameters between participants was much more understandable. We believe this is due to the fact that the interaction is obscured when using an average distance parameter. The behaviour is only revealed when the group synchronises, causing the actions to not be publicly available when the group is not synchronised. Thus, the difficulties in perception of the distance parameter's effect on the sound. We believe this is due to a breakdown of awareness from the lack of public availability of the actions relating to this parameter.

As an additional step we chose to reinforce and separate the interaction controlled by social parameters and individuals. For this, we decided to have the mobile instruments only controllable by the person playing it, and use an extended system for socially controlled sound synthesis. These became the *on-body* and *in-space* components of the PESI system respectively (see section 4.3).

The second issue was a technical problem that arose due to occlusion. Occlusion occurred when one or more participants blocked the Kinect's view of another participant and resulted in the Kinect temporarily losing track of the occluded participant.

The main problem that occlusion caused was technical. Within our implementation of the final PESI system there is a requirement to track the identities of performers. For the initial user test we were able to mitigate the problem that occlusion caused by removing the need to user IDs. This was not possible with the final implementation as IDs were required to ensure sonic cohesion between the *on-body* and *in-space* components .

Each user is assigned a unique ID value by the Kinect system, when the Kinect loses track of a user the ID is unassigned. Once the user reappears a new ID is assigned to that user. Thus, when occlusion occurred, a new ID is assigned by the Kinect to the occluded performer causing the PESI system to miss match the sound synthesis between the *on-body* and *in-space* components causing a breakdown in sonic cohesion. This further compounds the problems of awareness, particularly relating to self-identify within the system.

The issues relating to occlusion and social mapping that arose from the user study indicated that the system had not provided solutions to the design challenges mentioned in section 3, particularly those relating to awareness. However, in revealing these problems potential solutions were also presented, for example: not using average distance mappings and developing methods to prevent or at least reduce occlusion. These solutions where implemented when refining and continuing the development of the system, which we assessed in a second user study (see section 4.3.3).

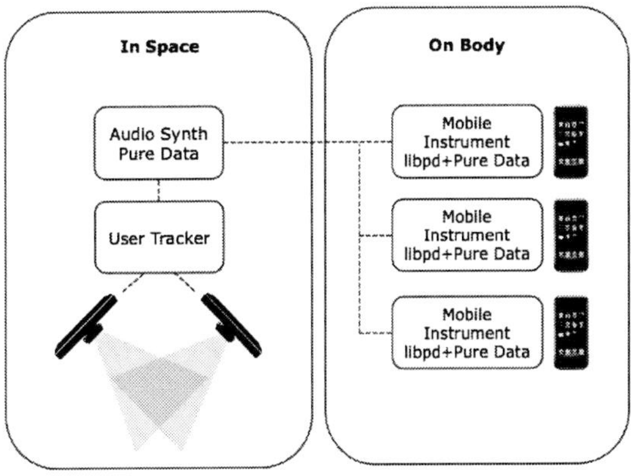

Figure 3. PESI extended system module diagram.

4.3 Design Report

The current system has two main parts: *on-body* and *in-space* components (see Fig. 3) [4, 5].

4.3.1 The on-body Component

The *on-body* component consists of a custom native iOS application built with Objective-C and using Libpd, designed to run on iPhones. This component also includes portable speakers that are directly connected to the mobile phones. Running the sound synthesis on the mobile phone allowed for the co-location of the performer's action and sonic results, reinforcing the embodiment of the interaction. Accelerometer, gyroscope and touch data are retrieved from the sensors in the mobile phone. This data is used to generate the parameters for the sound synthesis modules.

The design of the mobile instruments were based upon participants' comments from the initial systems' user test. The performers have a choice between three different sound modules. Only one module can be played at a time, however, it is possible to switch between each module when playing the mobile phone instrument. Each module has its own sonic characteristics, associated colour and a 'tuning' system that lets users alter static parameters within the instrument for further customisation.

The first instrument *Green* switches between pulse-width modulation (PWM) or wave shaping of a square wave depending on the orientation of the device. The tuning system allows for manipulation of two constant square waves with PWM. Tilt controls frequency and touch controls timbre. The second, *Red*, and third, *Blue*, instruments are based upon a granular synth. Tilting the X axis accelerometer controls the grain playback in both, however, in the *Red* instrument tilting the Y axis accelerometer changes the grain size. The Y axis on the touch screen allows for the playback pitch of the *Blue* instrument to be controlled. The tuning system in both allows for changing default settings within the granular synth in each instrument. For detailed technical descriptions of each instrument see [5].

4.3.2 The in-space Component

The idea behind the *in-space* component was to use a generated layer of sound, related but, external to the perform-

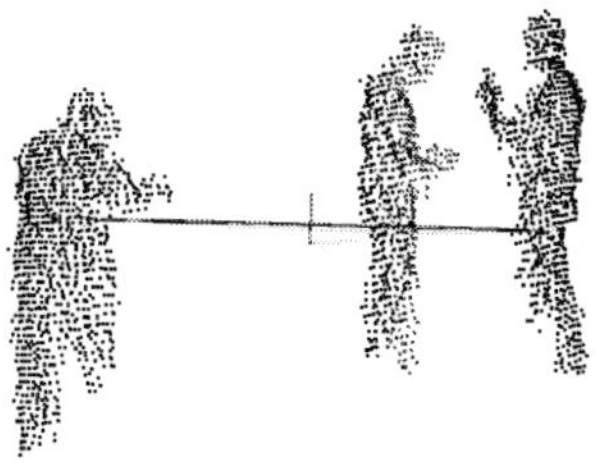

Figure 4. Point-cloud image generated by two Kinect sensor bars showing the motion tracking of three performers.

ers individual mobile instruments. Through this layer the social interactions within the system are represented and manifest as sounds.

The *in-space* component is based around a central control module that receives sensor information from a multi-user motion tracking system as well as from each mobile phone. This information is used to control the sound synthesis of the *in-space* component. The multi-user motion tracking system has been built with two kinect sensor bars (see Fig. 4), the OpenNI[5] library with Processing[6] and openFrameworks.[7] Multiple Kinects were used as single Kinect solutions to occlusion proved unreliable, two Kinects provided a robust solution to the ID switching by dramatically reducing occlusion within the system.

This system continuously tracks the spatial positions of three performers. From their positional information, relative distances between performers, velocity, acceleration and alignment are calculated. Sensor data from the motion tracking system and each mobile phones is sent to the central control module via Open Sound Control (OSC).[8] A robust network module was developed that managed the connections between each component in the system. This module allows the central control unit to re-establish connections, sort sensor information and track the devices that the information was sent from.

The sensor data from the mobile phones is used to generate identical copies of the sounds being played by the performers within the *in-space* component. These sounds are then processed with a granular synth, controlled by socially generated parameters and played back over a multichannel speaker ring that surrounds the performers. The processed sounds are associated to the instrument they have been produced from, thus are unique to each individual performer, to further reinforce the idea of self-identity.

The granular synthesis is mapped as follows (from the perspective of a performer using the system): the grain size and density vary depending on the distance to one performer and the frequency range of the playback scales exponentially depending on the distance to the second performer. The speed of an individuals movement within the space controls the amplitude of the synth. For further technical details see [5].

[5] `http://openni.org/`
[6] `http://processing.org/`
[7] `http://www.openframeworks.cc/`
[8] `http://opensoundcontrol.org/`

4.3.3 A User Study of the Current System

We invited three skilled-musicians for a user test jam session with the current PESI system (see Fig. 5). Similar to the previous user test, the evaluation was based on survey and interview analysis. Detailed findings from this user study were presented in [5]. In summary, musicians comments and feedback were positive regarding the *on-body* and *in-space* component; especially for the sound characteristics and the responsiveness of each module. This was supported with the following comments directly quoted from participants:

> *" ...pretty impressive... I liked the idea of the extended system. It gives a nice ambient and supporting feeling that you have sound around you...."*

> *".... I have been using sensor based instruments more with traditional music and tonal structures . It would actually be very interesting to implement this system for a traditional kind of music that you could improvise with. The system is actually quite interactive and the instrument is very good. You can do all kinds of stuff with small gestures. This system could be open to all kinds of directions.... "*

Figure 5. Skilled musicians performing with the current version of the PESI system in the user test jam session.

5. BEHAVIOURALLY NON-RESTRICTIVE DIGITAL TECHNOLOGY

In solving the design issues which occurred in the various stages of the PESI system's development, an idea arose, which we term: Behaviourally Non-Restrictive Digital Technology (BNDT). For the *in-space* component of the PESI system to operate, performers are not required to direct or focus their attention towards it or make explicit changes to their behaviour. Yet similarly users are able to act through the *in-space* component when their attention is directed towards it. When attention is directed towards this component, it is able to reveal itself to participants, in relation to theirs as well as other users' actions, allowing them to determine how they wish to deal with it. This can be leaving the system in ones peripheral perceptions or developing couplings with it.

We see the approach of BNDT as a method of accounting for the differing modes of use and shifting of focus that occurs between embodied agents and the environment [15]. The shifting of focus can also be related to the ideas of identity creation, discussed in section 3, as the design of the system allows for the detachment of the user from the system. In allowing for detachment and coupling, users are able to reconfigure their focus and understanding of the system - which we believe aids in the development of identities within the system.

However, accounting for differing modes is only one part of our idea of BNDT. Actions are still an important part of our investigation into design solutions surrounding the ideas of intersubjectivity and awareness within collaborative digital music systems.

5.1 Being Social in the World

Actions themselves are not a kind of act, they are instead properties of individuals at times [22], and are grounded in our movements. We effect objects around us by moving our bodies and we are able to produce different movements to fit a large range of circumstances. The effect these movements will have is also generally understood, as the results of movements are dependent upon the context and situation in which they occur [22].

An important idea relating to the understanding of actions within the context in which they arise from, is the notion of accountability. The notion of accountability is a fundamental feature of the ethnomethodological perspective, and is concerned with what is available to members as situated practice. Members being those who have common sense understandings relating to the situation [15]. In particular, situated practice is the context in which the action arises and thus can be part of the means by which action can be interpreted. Therefore, actions relating to situated practice are understood as normal, rational action by members. The availability of these actions depends on them being able to be observed by members and reported upon: observable-and-reportable [15].

The methods of understanding an action are also the methods for engagement with it. As such being competent with an action requires that it is engaged in ways that are recognised by members. Therefore, an action is needed to be organised in such a way that it is understood as being rational within the context it has emerged from. In the case of the PESI project, the focus was on the sound and action relationships that occur in the context of music.

5.2 Musical Gestures

The relationship between sound and action is being investigated within the field of musical gesture, which focuses on classifying musically related actions. Within this field actions are separated into two categories: sound-producing and sound-accompanying. [23]

Sound-producing actions are the actions used in the process of making sound. Godøy et al. [23] make a distinction between excitation action - which triggers the sound, and modulation action - which modifies the sound. Sound-accompanying actions are the other types of actions which are performed along to sound/music, but are not part of its production; for example playing air guitar or tracing the dynamics of the music. Sound-accompanying actions normally have a readily observable sound matching feature to them [23]. Within the PESI system we have primarily concerning ourselves with sound-producing gestures. However, we also accept the need to be aware of all musically related action that may arise within the PESI system.

One of the main aesthetic considerations we had in relation to the system was that it would not be using traditional acoustic instrument sounds. The sounds being used would be synthesised to create new sounds, to be interacted with and used within a musical context. Therefore, we encountered the problem of there being no established sound-action relationships for the sounds being synthesised with the PESI system. This required the design of new sound-action relationships for the PESI system.

We see sound-action relationships as inherently cultural. Associations of gestures that relate to the production of specific sounds are developed through the combination of cultural practice and physical constraints of the musical instrument [13]. This adds an additional level of complexity if we were to design new sound-action relationships. Instead we have continued to follow our idea of BNDT and decided to not predefine any sound-action, or musical gestures within the system. Instead we have used movement mappings to sound parameters.

5.3 No-predefined Gestures

We facilitate action through allowing movements to have an effect within the system. Performers can develop their own actions through the movements that the system can track. By combining motion tracking information with sensor data from mobile phones it is possible for many movements - both individual (through moving the mobile device) and social (through movement in space) to be used to generate sound responses. Actions can then arise in response to the sounds, caused through individual and social movements, and through this, gestures are able to be developed by performers within the system. We believe that this is possible when the resulting actions are made publicly available, allowing for all actions to be interpreted and accounted within the interaction.

In having no-predefined gestures, the idea of BNDT is further enforced, and the interaction is able to become fully situated, aiding in the potential for adoption into practice. As a further result of our approach we see the possibility to investigate formations of musical gestures from movement within a controlled and traceable environment. Our research interest lies in a similar direction to [24] in that it does not to look for stated understanding of gesture, but to understand how movements are actually employed in the interfaces that researchers have built.

6. DISCUSSIONS

When we compare the PESI system to the work discussed in section 2, we can highlight many common themes. Comparing to the work of Di Scipio [7] and the AESI system, both the PESI system and the AESI system have a focus on the performer and their role within the system. However, unlike the AESI system which questions if the performer is even needed, we take the opposite approach in which the performer's role is strengthened becoming an integral part of the PESI system.

Our approach to having no-predefined gestures could be seen as following Bowers and Archer's [8] ideas relating to infra-instruments. In only focusing on movements our overall mapping strategies have been reduced and somewhat restricted - like those of infra-instruments. We have also allowed for greater flexibility within the social practices of the PESI system, as well as providing space for the technology and computing that enables and enhances the musical activity.

Comparing the work of the PESI project to that of Gurevich and Trevino, Gurevich and Cavan Fyans and Cavan Fyans et al. [9–11] and their work directed towards spectator experience, we can see benefit in having actions publicly available. However, we can foresee a potential challenge faced by spectators of the PESI system. This is due to actions being created within the use of the PESI system. Those who are not a part of the improvised practice may struggle from a spectators stand point to grasp or understand the actions within the system, as they would not be members of the practice. This is a side-effect for primarily focusing on facilitating improvised musical practice and not on performances that feature spectators.

The musical paint machine takes the biggest depart from the ideas we have been using with the PESI system. This is because it has been designed to investigate musical practice, musical gesture, Flow and stimulation of creativity [14]. Here, an element that has not been part of our designs within the PESI system has been used: the addition of multi-modal feedback. Within the PESI system we have only focused on sonic feedback; however, the sonic feedback within the PESI system also provides information on social actions of the group, not just on each individuals personal action. We do see some parallels to the idea of behaviourally non-restrictive digital technology within the musical paint machine project. When using the musical paint machine one can chose their focus between the instrument and the feedback provided by the musical paint machine. This is similar to the PESI system, however, performers can chose between the social, personal or neither to direct their focus.

We acknowledge that there has been little discussion surrounding the sounds and music the system creates. Music itself is an aesthetic form and throughout the design of the system we have drawn upon our own aesthetic preferences to drive the development of the sound synthesis within the system. In theory, we see, our approaches implying a generality in assigning sound mappings to the interaction as the suitably of such mappings is determined through the emergent action-meaning relationship that, we believe, we have facilitated within the PESI system. The effect this has on aesthetic preferences within a social context requires further exploration and experimentation.

7. CONCLUSIONS

In this paper we presented our solutions to the design challenges that were faced within the development of the PESI extended system. In viewing the technology and practices that relate to music from an ecological perspective, the relationships between performers themselves and their instruments became our focus. Drawing upon work within the fields of HCI, CSCW and research into Flow the need to account for awareness and creation of identities were identified as key considerations when designing the PESI system.

Two evaluations were carried out at different stages in the PESI systems development. It was identified within the first evaluation that relational parameters between all three group members were not as perceivable. We hypothesise this was due to the actions of an individual no longer being publicly available due to the other group members obscuring a single members contribution. Within the development of the *in-space* component these considerations where accounted for and solutions were implemented. Relational parameters were relational between each group member but never related to the whole group. This was done to allow for better public availability of actions as well as to enable a stronger development of self-identity within the system. The results from the second evaluation support our design choices.

Through the development of the PESI system we developed an idea of non-behaviourally restrictive digital technology. Within this approach, the shifting focus that embodied agents have in relation to the environment is accounted for, and sound-action relationships are encouraged to be developed through providing mappings relating to individual sensor values and movement information from motion tracking data. Through the situatedness of the performer and instrument, we believe that musical gestures will arise that could not have been anticipated within the design of the system due to the influence social factors have on the usage of the mobile instruments. When discussing these ideas in relation to the related works discussed within section 2 the ideas we have developed can be see within many of these projects.

The contextualisation of sounds within social settings is still an open question within the PESI system and within collaborative digital music systems. Further investigation into the idea of behaviourally non-restrictive digital technology is also required, not only within the design of digital music systems, but in a wider context of digital technology. Both these points are to be considered within further work on the PESI system which will be moving to focus upon long-term movement behaviour between performers.

Acknowledgments

This work is supported by the Academy of Finland (project 137646).

8. REFERENCES

[1] T. Magnusson, "Of epistemic tools: musical instruments as cognitive extensions," *Organised Sound*, vol. 14, no. 2, pp. 168–176, 2009.

[2] O. Green, "Agility and playfulness: Technology and skill in the performance ecosystem," *Orangised Sound*, vol. 16, no. 2, pp. 134–144, 2011.

[3] R. Pugliese, K. Tahiroğlu, C. Goddard, and J. Nesfield, "A qualitative evaluation of augmented human-human interaction in mobile group improvisation," in *Proceedings of the International Conference on New Interfaces for Musical Expression*, University of Michigan, Ann Arbor, May 21 – 23 2012.

[4] N. N. Correia, K. Tahiroğlu, and M. Espada, "Pesi: Extending mobile music instruments with social interaction," in *Seventh International Conference on Tangible, Embedded and Embodied Interaction (TEI), Work in Progress*, Barcelona, Spain, 2013.

[5] K. Tahiroğlu, N. N. Correia, and M. Espada, "Pesi extended system: In space, on body, with 3 musicians," in *Proceedings of the International Conference on New Interfaces for Musical Expression*, Daejeon, Korea, May 27-30 2013.

[6] A. Camurri, D. Glowinski, M. Mancini, G. Varni, and G. Volpe, "The 3rd international workshop on social behaviour in music: Sbm2012," in *Proceedings of the 14th ACM international conference on Multimodal interaction*, Santa Monica, California, 2012.

[7] A. D. Scipio, "'sound is the interface': from interactive to ecosystemic signal processing," *Organised Sound*, vol. 8, no. 3, pp. 269–277, 2003.

[8] J. Bowers and P. Archer, "Not hyper, not meta, not cyber but infra-instruments," in *Proceedings of the 2005 International Conference on New Interfaces for Musical Expression (NIME05)*, Vancouver, BC, Canada, 2005.

[9] M. Gurevich and J. Treviño, "Expression and its discontents: Toward an ecology of musical creation," in *Proceedings of the International Conference on New Interfaces for Musical Expression*, New York City, NY, United States, 2007, pp. 106–111.

[10] A. C. Fyans and M. Gurevich, "Perceptions of skill in performances with acoustic and electronic instruments," in *Proceedings of the International Conference on New Interfaces for Musical Expression*, Oslo, Norway, 30 May - 1 June 2011.

[11] A. C. Fyans, A. Marquez-Borbon, P. Stapleton, and M. Gurevich, "Ecological considerations for participatory design of dmis," in *Proceedings of the 2012 Conference on New Interfaces for Musical Expression*, University of Michigan, Ann Arbor, May 21 – 23 2012.

[12] S. Waters, "Performance ecosystems: Ecological approaches to musical interaction." in *EMS : Electroacoustic Music Studies Network Performance*, 2007.

[13] M. Leman, *Embodied Music Cognition and Mediation Technology*. The MIT Press, 2008.

[14] L. Nijs, B. Moen, M. Lesaffre, and M. Leman, "The music paint machine: Stimulating self-monitoring through the generation of creative visual output using a technology-enhanced learning tool," *Journal of New Music Research*, 2012.

[15] P. Dourish, *Where the Action Is*. The MIT Press, 2004.

[16] H. D. Jaegher and E. D. Paolo, "Participatory sense-making an enactive approach to social cognition," *Phenomenoogy and the Cognitive Sciences*, 2007.

[17] T. Fuchs and H. D. Jaegher, "Enactive intersubjectivity: Participatory sense-making and mutual incorporation," *Phenom Cogn Sci*, vol. 8, pp. 465–486, 2009.

[18] T. Robertson, "The public availability of actions and artefacts," *Computer Supported Cooperative Work*, vol. 11, pp. 299–316, 2002.

[19] N. Bryan-Kinns, "Mutual engagement in social music making," *LNICST*, vol. 78, pp. 260–266, 2012.

[20] ——, "Mutual engagement and collocation with shared representations," *International Journal of Human-Computer Studies*, 2012.

[21] M. Csikszentmihalyi, *Flow: The psycology of optimal experiance*. HarperCollins Publishers Inc., 1990.

[22] D. Israel, J. Perry, and S. Tutiya, "Actions and movements," in *Proceedings of IJCAI*, 1991.

[23] R. I. Godøy, A. R. Jensenius, A. Voldsund, K. Glette, M. Høvin, K. Nymoen, S. Skogstad, and J. Tørresen, "Classifying music-related actions," in *Proceedings of the 12th International Conference on Music Perception and Cognition and the 8th Triennial Conference of the European Society for the Cognitive Sciecnes of Music*, July 23-28 2012.

[24] J. Donovan and M. Brereton, "Movements in gesture interfaces," in *Critiacal Computing 2005 - Between Sense and Sensibility, the Fourth Decennial Aarhus Conference, Proceeding of the Workshop : Appraoches to Movement- Based Interaction*, 2005.

Refined Spectral Template Models for Score Following

Filip Korzeniowski, Gerhard Widmer
Department of Computational Perception, Johannes Kepler University Linz
{filip.korzeniowski, gerhard.widmer}@jku.at

ABSTRACT

Score followers often use spectral templates for notes and chords to estimate the similarity between positions in the score and the incoming audio stream. Here, we propose two methods on different modelling levels to improve the quality of these templates, and subsequently the quality of the alignment.

The first method focuses on creating more informed templates for individual notes. This is achieved by estimating the template based on synthesised sounds rather than generic Gaussian mixtures, as used in current state-of-the-art systems.

The second method introduces an advanced approach to aggregate individual note templates into spectral templates representing a specific score position. In contrast to score chordification, the common procedure used by score followers to deal with polyphonic scores, we use weighting functions to weight notes, observing their temporal relationships.

We evaluate both methods against a dataset of classical piano music to show their positive impact on the alignment quality.

1. INTRODUCTION

Score following, in particular its application for automatic accompaniment, is one of the oldest research topics in the field of computational music analysis. First approaches [1,2] worked with symbolic performance data, and applied adapted string matching techniques to the problem. With the availability of sufficient computational power, the focus switched to directly processing sampled audio streams, widening the possible application areas. Systems for tracking monophonic instruments [3], especially singing voice [4–7] and finally polyphonic instruments [8–12] have emerged. Their common main task is, given a musical score and a (live) signal of a performance of this score, to align the signal with the score, i.e. to compute the performers' current position in the score.

The tonal content is the most important source to determine the current score position, an obvious commonality of most score following systems. One of the central problems a music tracker needs to address is thus how to create the connection between the tonal content extracted from the audio and what is expected according to the score. This task can be divided into three parts: computing features on the incoming signal to estimate the tonal content; modelling the score and expected tonal content for every score position; defining the likelihood of the signal for a score position, usually by employing a similarity measure between expected and actual tonal content.

First-generation score following systems for audio signals focused on tracking monophonic instruments. In this cases the score is simply a sequential list of pitches, which can be easily transferred into formal frameworks like Hidden Markov Models. Since robust and accurate pitch tracking methods exist for monophonic audio, the feature extraction yields exact pitch information for the incoming audio stream. The expected pitch for a score position is given directly by the score model, and the likelihood is defined by a Gaussian distribution to take the performer's expressiveness (e.g. vibrato) into account.

Score followers for polyphonic audio introduce another level of complexity. On the one hand, polyphonic scores no longer resemble linear sequences of pitches. On the other hand, real-time music transcription for polyphonic audio signals is far from solved. Hence, score following systems usually utilise features other than the extracted pitch content, less precise but easier to compute.

A prominent method for estimating the similarity between score and audio signal is to create spectral templates for score positions and use a distance measure to compare the template to the signal's spectrum, as done in [13,14]. While most systems use generic templates to model the expected tonal content (features) according to the score, in this paper we propose modelling techniques which incorporate instrument-specific properties to improve the alignment quality. One concerns the spectral modelling of individual notes, the other one the composition of these into combined templates representing polyphonic score positions. We evaluate both methods on a set of classical piano recordings.

The remainder of this paper is organised as follows: Section 2 describes our proposed methods and compares them to the current state of the art. Our experiments are described in Section 3. Finally, we present and discuss the results in Section 4.

2. SPECTRAL TEMPLATES

In general, methods to model the expected tonal content of a score heavily depend on the design of the feature extractor, i.e. on how information regarding the tonal content is computed from the incoming audio stream. Usually the signal's magnitude spectrum or related representations like chroma vectors or semitone spectra are used. Here, we assume that the magnitude spectrum is used directly as an estimator for the actual tonal content. However, the methods presented here can easily be adapted to any other representation.

We assume that the signal's spectrum is computed using the short-time Fourier transform (STFT) with a window size of N_{win}. Using the STFT we can compute the magnitude spectrum Y for frame t, resulting in a vector $Y_t = (y_1, \dots, y_{N_b})$, where $N_b = N_{win}/2$ is the number of frequency bins. Each value y_n contains the magnitude of the nth frequency bin of the spectrum of frame t. We denote as $F = (f_1, \dots, f_{N_b})$ the centre frequencies of each frequency bin of the spectrum.

The score is available in a symbolic representation, e.g. as MIDI file. Let G be the set of all score notes, then for all $g \in G$ we have the start position s_g and end position e_g in beats, and the note's fundamental frequency $f_0(g)$ in Hz.

We differentiate two levels of spectral templates: "note templates" are spectral templates for individual notes, denominated formally by ϕ; "score templates" represent spectral templates on the score level, including all sounding notes at a specific score position, and are denoted as Φ.

Having clarified the nomenclature, the next section describes our method to create spectral templates for individual notes.

2.1 Note Templates

Spectral templates for individual notes are the basic building blocks of spectral score models in most state-of-the-art score followers. Usually, these templates are generated using Gaussian mixtures in the frequency domain, where each Gaussian represents the fundamental frequency or a harmonic of a tone, as introduced by [15]. Similar methods are also used in [13] and [14], as these generic models have proven to work well in practice, and to some degree generalise over instrumental configurations.

However, it is reasonable to assume that adjusting the templates to the sonic characteristics of the currently tracked performance should improve the alignment. Attempts have been made to adapt basic templates on the fly using latent harmonic allocation in [11], however the method's complexity makes it currently unusable in real-time settings, as [11] reports computation times of about 10 seconds for one second of audio.

If we assume that the instrumentation of a performance is known beforehand (e.g. defined by the score), we could create instrument-specific models in advance. The authors of [16] introduced an improved method to compute chromagram-like representations of both score and audio by learning transformation matrices based on a diverse musical dataset. Given that their method could be extended to the spectral representation used in this paper, feeding their system with training data containing solely specific instruments could result in templates specialised for this instrument. In [9], templates are learned using non-negative matrix factorisation on a database of instrument sounds, an idea similar to what we propose in this paper. However, no comparison to the generic Gaussian mixture approach is given, and the method was dropped in subsequent publications of the author.

Here, we present two methods for modelling the spectral content of a note. The first one, which represents the standard approach inspired by the work of [15], is presented in the following section. The second one constitutes our proposed method, in which we try to incorporate characteristics of the tracked instrument. It is described in Section 2.1.2.

2.1.1 Gaussian Mixture Spectral Model

The first template modelling technique we present resembles the state-of-the-art methods used in most score following systems. Assuming a perfectly harmonic sound created by the instrument, we use Eq. 1 to create a spectral template for a note $g \in G$:

$$\hat{\phi}^g_{GMM}(f) = \sum_{i=1}^{N_h} \sqrt{i^{-1}} \mathcal{N}\left(f; i \cdot f_0^g, (\sigma_\phi \cdot s_\phi^i)^2\right), \quad (1)$$

where N_h is the number of modelled harmonics, $\mathcal{N}(f; \mu, \sigma^2)$ is the probability density at f of the Gaussian distribution with mean μ and variance σ^2, f_0^g is the fundamental frequency of note g, σ_ϕ is the standard deviation of the Gaussian representing the fundamental frequency, and s_ϕ is the spreading factor, defining how the variance of the components increases for each harmonic. For the experimental evaluation, we empirically chose the parameters to be $N_h = 5, \sigma_\phi = 5, s_\phi = 1.1$.

We then need to discretise the continuous model $\hat{\phi}^g_{GMM}$ to compare it to the actual tonal content of the signal. As written above, we use the magnitude spectrum to represent the audio's tonal content, which gives us the magnitudes for discrete frequency bins. Therefore, we discretise the model at the frequency bin centres in F, resulting in a vector

$$\begin{aligned} \phi^g_{GMM} &= (z_1, \dots, z_{N_b}), && \text{and} \\ z_i &= \hat{\phi}^g_{GMM}(f_i), && 1 \le i \le N_b, \end{aligned} \quad (2)$$

where f_i is the ith element of F, thus the centre frequency of the ith frequency bin, and N_b is the number of frequency bins. Figures 1a and 1b show examples of this model.

2.1.2 Synthesised Spectral Model

As stated above, the Gaussian mixture note model shown in Section 2.1.1 is a generic approximation of how the magnitude spectrum looks like when a note is played. However, harmonic structures strongly vary depending on the instrument, instrument model, individual pitch and playing dynamics. Adapting generic templates on-line to the current sound texture is possible, as shown in [11], but currently computationally unfeasible for real-time applications.

We try to reach a compromise by leaving out the costly on-line adaption, and instead learning initial models which are already adjusted to the instrument they are representing. Similar ideas have already been described in the field of polyphonic music transcription [17], and as stated above, also for score following [9]. While in these papers the templates are learned using non-negative matrix factorisation, we apply a simpler and more direct method to derive those. Furthermore, we provide a quantitative analysis on the effect of using informed templates compared to the generic templates based on Gaussian mixtures, which was missing so far in the context of score following.

To create the spectral note templates we utilise a software synthesizer [1] to generate short sounds for each MIDI-representable note. These sounds are then analysed using the STFT with the same parameters as used for estimating the tonal content of the performance audio. Finally, for each note g we average its spectrogram over time, resulting in a vector of the same form as in Eq. 2:

$$\phi_S^g = (z_1, \ldots, z_{N_b}) . \qquad (3)$$

Here, z_i stands for the mean of the ith frequency bin in the magnitude spectrogram of the training sound.

Clearly, this still is a very rough approximation, since the harmonic structure of a played note is all but invariant in time. Additionally, the dynamics have a considerable impact on the harmonics for certain instruments. However, as we will show experimentally, it seems to resemble the true magnitude spectrum generated by a specific instrument better than the unadapted manually designed model based on Gaussian mixtures, at least for instruments where the aforementioned problems have a lower impact, like the piano. Still, there's space for further improvements in future work. Figures 1c and 1d show exemplary synthesised spectral templates.

Figure 1 reveals considerable differences between templates generated by the two methods outlined before, especially regarding the number of harmonics and the harmonic structure. The shown examples resemble the general trends we saw examining a larger set of templates. For lower notes, the synthesised templates contain more harmonics than their GMM counterparts. The number of harmonics is comparable for higher notes, however their structure differs notably. As preliminary experiments showed, simply increasing the number of harmonics for the GMM templates did not improve the alignment quality of our score follower. On the contrary, we chose to model 5 harmonics due to these preliminary experiments - using more harmonics degraded the results.

Having discussed methods for creating spectral templates for individual notes, the following section elaborates on how to combine those to obtain templates representing the expected spectral content at polyphonic score positions.

2.2 Score Templates

Score models for monophonic scores can easily be represented as sequences of consecutive pitches. This facilitates the usage of established formal frameworks like Hidden

[1] specifically, we use the commonly available TiMidity++ software with its standard sound font

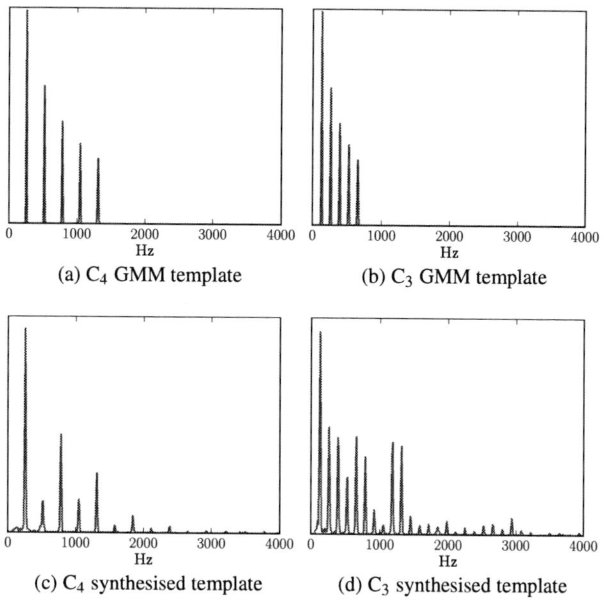

Figure 1. Spectral templates for two different notes. The left column shows the template for middle C, while the right column the C one octave lower. The upper row, shown in red, are templates computed by the GMM approach, the lower row, in blue, depicts the synthesised templates. As our evaluation database consists of piano music, we used piano sounds for the synthesised templates.

Markov Models for score following. However, polyphonic scores in general no longer resemble linear sequences of notes. Hence, for polyphonic score following so-called chordification is generally applied to transform polyphonic scores into a series of concurrently sounding sets of notes, called concurrencies. The score can then be seen as a sequential list of concurrencies, and the well-known methods used for monophonic instrument tracking can be applied directly on the problem. Figure 2 shows an example chordification of a short snippet of piano music.

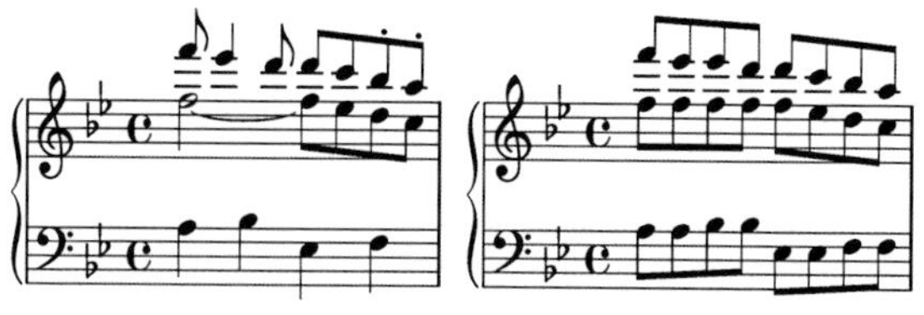

(a) Original (b) Chordified

Figure 2. Original and chordified version of the 11th bar of Mozart's Sonata in B (KV 333)

From a musical point of view, reducing polyphonic scores to their concurrencies seems unnatural. The information on how long a note is sounding, and hence how prominent it appears to a listener, is lost. In Figure 2, the F4 in the inner voice of the right hand is an exemplary case for this issue: a single note is separated into five.

We believe this approximation is superfluous and present a method to avoid it. The method itself is not necessarily tied to our system, where we use a continuous state space for the score position, but can be adapted for approaches with an explicit state space discretisation, like HMMs. We introduce a "weighting function" for each score note $g \in G$, which is inspired by the common "Attack-Decay-Sustain-Release" (ADSR) amplitude envelopes used in sound synthesisers to model the volume dynamics of generated sounds (see Figure 3). The attack phase defines how fast the tone reaches the initial maximal volume. The decay phase defines how the tone's volume decreases until it finally reaches the volume of the sustain phase. The release phase models how the volume dies away after the musician has stopped playing the note.

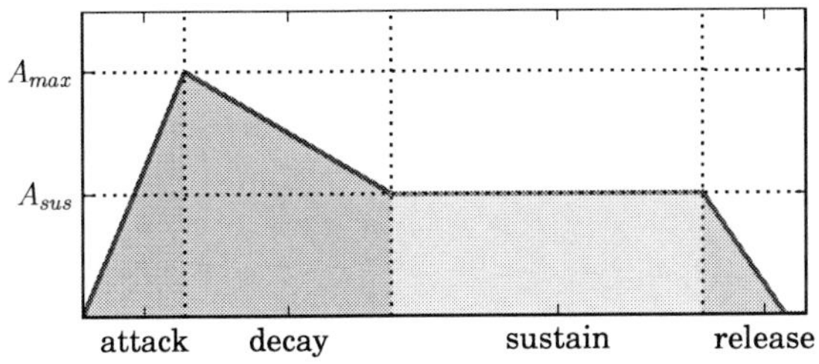

Figure 3. A generic linear ADSR (Attack-Decay-Sustain-Release) envelope.

Different instruments can be characterised using different ADSR envelopes, and thus different weighting functions. Our main focus is the tracking of classical piano music, hence we defined a weighting function designed to resemble piano sounds. We ignore the attack phase, and assume the volume reaches its maximum instantly. The volume then decays following an exponential function until it reaches a level defined by the sustain phase. The release follows as a rapid linear decrease of volume. Figure 4 shows the weighting function for an exemplary note, according to our method.

More formally, given a score position x in beats and playing tempo v in beats per second, we compute the mixing weight of each note g as

$$\psi(x, v, g) = \psi_{ds}(x, v, g) \cdot \psi_r(x, v, g). \quad (4)$$

Effectively, we split the function into two parts: the fundamental weight defined by the decay and sustain phase ψ_{ds}, and the cut-off specified by the release phase, ψ_r. Both depend on the time passed after the performer moved past the note start or note end respectively. Note that the actual *time* difference rather than difference in position between note start/end and the performer's current score position is taken into account, since this is what the note's volume depends on. We thus define the time difference between note start and score position as Δ_s and note end and score position as Δ_e:

$$\Delta_s(x, v, g) = \frac{x - s_g}{v} \quad \text{and} \quad (5)$$

$$\Delta_e(x, v, g) = \frac{x - e_g}{v}, \quad (6)$$

where s_g is the note's starting position and e_g the note's ending position in beats. For convenience, we will write Δ_s and Δ_e for $\Delta_s(x, v, g)$ and $\Delta_e(x, v, g)$ respectively. The decay/sustain-weight ψ_{ds} can then be written as

$$\psi_{ds}(x, v, g) = \begin{cases} 0 & \text{if } \Delta_s < 0 \\ \max\left(\lambda^{\Delta_s}, \eta\right) & \text{else} \end{cases}, \quad (7)$$

where $\lambda = 0.1$ is the decay parameter and $\eta = 0.1$ is the sustain weight. Figure 4a shows the decay/sustain portion of the weighting function. Finally, we define the release cut-off:

$$\psi_r(x, v, g) = \begin{cases} 1 & \text{if } \Delta_e < 0 \\ \max(1 - \beta \cdot \Delta_e, 0) & \text{else} \end{cases}, \quad (8)$$

where $\beta = 20$ is the release rate. This part of the weighting function is shown in Figure 4b.

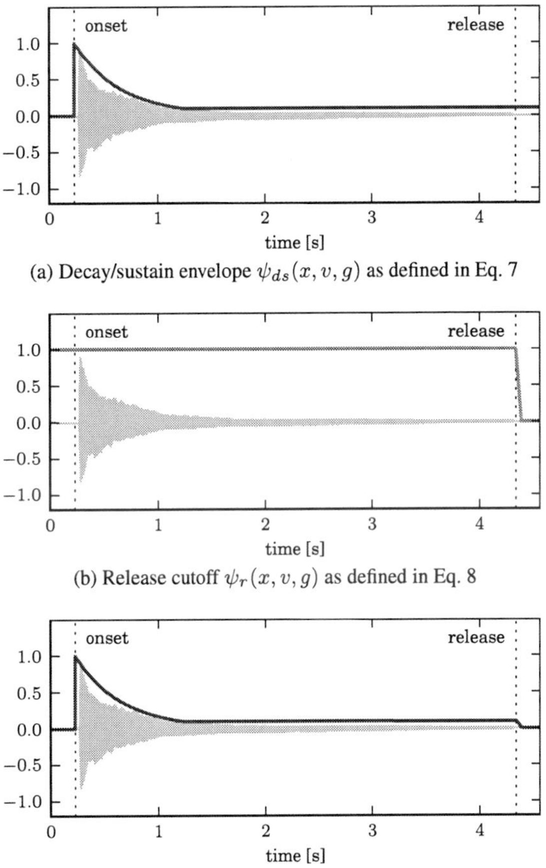

(a) Decay/sustain envelope $\psi_{ds}(x, v, g)$ as defined in Eq. 7

(b) Release cutoff $\psi_r(x, v, g)$ as defined in Eq. 8

(c) Weighting function $\psi(x, v, g)$ as defined in Eq. 4

Figure 4. Example of a weighting function as defined by Eq. 4: (a) shows the decay/sustain part, (b) the release cut-off, and (c) the combination of the two. The backgrounds show the waveform of a recorded piano note.

Now, to compute the spectral template for score position x at tempo v we just have to compute a weighted sum over all note note templates:

$$\Phi(x, v) = \frac{1}{Z(x, v)} \sum_{g \in G} \psi(x, v, g) \cdot \phi(g), \quad (9)$$

$$Z(x, v) = \sum_{g \in G} \psi(x, v, g)$$

ID	Composer	Piece	# Perf.	Eval. Type
CE	Chopin	Etude Op. 10 No. 3 (excerpt until bar 20)	22	Match
CB	Chopin	Ballade Op. 38 No. 1 (excerpt until bar 45)	22	Match
MS	Mozart	1_{st} Mov. of Sonatas KV279, KV280, KV281, KV282, KV283, KV284, KV330, KV331, KV332, KV333, KV457, KV475, KV533	1	Match
RP	Rachmaninoff	Prelude Op. 23 No. 5	3	Man. Annotations

Table 1. Performances used during evaluation

where ϕ is either ϕ_{GMM} or ϕ_S, depending on which type of spectral models are used for individual notes (see sections 2.1.1 and 2.1.2).

As mentioned above, the weighting function we defined in Eq. 4 is especially designed to reflect the volume envelope of recorded piano notes, which is depicted in Figure 4. It is conceivable to define individual weighting functions for different instruments, determined by their particular sonic characteristics. While instruments with percussive onsets can be naturally modelled using this technique, it is difficult to define a static envelope for instruments which allow the performer to continuously control the volume, like brass or strings.

The proposed method can be seen as a generalisation of the standard chordification approach. We can use a specifically designed weighting function to simulate the chordification process: If we define ψ in a way that it returns 1 between the note start and end positions, and 0 everywhere else, the resulting score template corresponds to the one yielded when chordification is applied. This generic weighting function is a natural fall-back option when it is difficult to define a specialised function for an instrument.

3. EXPERIMENTS

We evaluated the methods outlined above using our score following system to track a variety of classical piano pieces. The probabilistic framework of a Dynamic Bayesian Network (DBN) establishes the theoretical foundation for this process. Exact inference is only possible on a subset of DBNs. Since our system does not fall into this category, we apply approximate Monte-Carlo methods to estimate the artist's current score position. Specifically, we utilise Rao- Blackwellised particle filtering, where parts of the model are computed exactly, while intractable portions are approximated using a standard particle filter. Besides the spectral content we use an onset function to capture transients and the signal's loudness to detect rests as additional features. Since there is plenty of literature on this topic, we will not dwell on the inference methods, but refer the reader to [18] for a comprehensive tutorial on particle filtering, and to [19] for a more detailed elaboration on the application in our system.

We use the same dataset of piano music as in [20] (see Table 1) for evaluation. Two different types of ground truth data are available: For pieces performed on a computer-monitored piano full matches exist, where the exact onset time for each note in the performance is known; for the performances of Rachmaninoff's Prelude Op. 23 No. 5 we only have manual annotations at the beat level. We group the performances as shown in Table 1 and evaluate the alignment quality for each group. This way we are able to grasp the impact of our methods depending on the type of composition and recording situation.

From the alignment quality measures introduced by [21], we use the misalign rate to evaluate our experiments. In short, the misalign rate is the percentage of notes for which the computed alignment differs from the correct alignment by more than a specified threshold. In our evaluation, we set this threshold to 250 ms. Due to the inherently probabilistic nature of particle filters, results necessarily vary between multiple alignments of the same performance. Hence, we repeated each experiment 10 times and used the averaged misalign rate for each piece.

To assess the influence of each proposed method, we ran our score follower in four different configurations. The baseline setup used the Gaussian mixture note models and score chordification (GC). One configuration included our method to aggregate note models using mixing functions, but still relied on the baseline note models (GM). The synthesised note models were used together with score chordification in the third configuration (SC). Both proposed methods were applied in the last configuration (SM). Table 2 shows an overview of the evaluated configurations.

ID	Note Model	Score Model
GC	Gaussian mixture	Chordified
GM	Gaussian mixture	Mixture function
SC	Synthesised	Chordified
SM	Synthesised	Mixture function

Table 2. Evaluated configurations

4. RESULTS AND DISCUSSION

Tables 3 and 4 show the results of our experiments, indicating that both proposed methods improve alignment quality.

Using synthesised note templates instead of those based on Gaussian mixtures improves alignment quality for three of four piece groups (GC vs. SC and GM vs. SM). The quality degradation when aligning Chopin's Etude Op. 10

ID	GC	GM	SC	SM
CB	8.65%	7.75%	8.23%	**7.56%**
CE	7.39%	**4.09%**	7.53%	4.69%
MS	2.25%	2.16%	1.76%	**1.48%**
RP	23.17%	12.17%	8.98%	**7.13%**

Table 3. Mean misalign rates for the performance groups

ID	GC	GM	SC	SM
CB	0.91	0.73	0.72	**0.59**
CE	1.19	0.79	1.19	**0.68**
MS	0.60	**0.42**	0.61	0.54
RP	12.31	3.25	**0.75**	1.45

Table 4. Standard deviation of misalign rates per piece, averaged over performance groups, in percentage points (pp)

No. 3 is marginal but noticeable. The reasons for this discrepancy are to be investigated. A good clue could be that the harmonic structure of piano sounds, especially inharmonic components, can vary considerably for individual instruments. However, a real-time capable way to cope with such problems, e.g. by adapting the templates on-line, is yet to be found.

Our proposed method for creating spectral templates for score positions using mixing functions impacts the aligning process in a positive way, as suggested by our experimental results (compare GC vs. GM and SC vs. SM in Table 3). This corresponds to our expectations based on the argumentation in Section 2.2. Further examinations will analyse how mixing functions can be defined for other instruments than the piano, and whether their impact in these cases is comparable to what we were able to show here.

Table 4 shows the standard deviation of the piecewise misalign rate, averaged for each piece group. High deviations would indicate that the alignment quality differs considerably over multiple runs of the algorithm on the same piece. The results suggest that the proposed methods have also a positive effect on the score follower's robustness.

5. CONCLUSION

We presented two novel methods for instrument-specific spectral modelling of musical scores, intended to improve the alignment quality of score following systems. The first method assumes that the harmonic structure of a played tone is static over time. The second can be applied if the instrument exhibits a fixed volume envelope of a tone, once a note is played. Thus, the methods are especially useful for pitched percussive and plucked or struck string instruments. The methods are not specific to our score following system, but can be easily adapted and applied to any spectral-template-based music tracker. Systematic experiments on a variety of classical piano pieces showed their positive impact on our score follower's misalign rate, indicating their meaningfulness. Future work could examine how the methods can be used for different instruments and if they can uphold their positive impact.

Acknowledgments

This research is supported by the Austrian Science Fund (FWF) under project number Z159, and by the European Union Seventh Framework Programme FP7 (2007-2013), through the project PHENICX (grant agreement no. 601166).

6. REFERENCES

[1] R. B. Dannenberg, "An On-Line Algorithm for Real-Time Accompaniment," in *Proceedings of the International Computer Music Conference (ICMC)*, 1984.

[2] B. Vercoe, "The Synthetic Performer in the Context of Live Performance," in *Proceedings of the International Computer Music Conference (ICMC)*, 1984.

[3] C. Raphael, "Automatic Segmentation of Acoustic Musical Signals Using Hidden Markov Models," *IEEE Transactions on Pattern Analysis and Machine Intelligence*, vol. 21, no. 4, pp. 360–370, 1999.

[4] M. Puckette, "Score Following Using the Sung Voice," in *Proceedings of the International Computer Music Conference (ICMC)*, 1995.

[5] P. Cano, A. Loscos, and J. Bonada, "Score-Performance Matching using HMMs," in *Proceedings of the International Computer Music Conference (ICMC)*, 1999.

[6] A. Loscos, P. Cano, and J. Bonada, "Low-Delay Singing Voice Alignment to Text," in *Proceedings of the International Computer Music Conference (ICMC)*, 1999.

[7] L. Grubb and R. B. Dannenberg, "Enhanced Vocal Performance Tracking Using Multiple Information Sources," in *Proceedings of the International Computer Music Conference (ICMC)*, 1998.

[8] N. Orio and F. Déchelle, "Score Following Using Spectral Analysis and Hidden Markov Models," in *Proceedings of the International Computer Music Conference (ICMC)*, 2001.

[9] A. Cont, "Realtime Audio to Score Alignment for Polyphonic Music Instruments Using Sparse Non-negative constraints and Hierarchical HMMs," in *Proceedings of the IEEE International Conference in Acoustics and Speech Signal Processing (ICASSP)*, 2006.

[10] D. Schwarz, N. Orio, and N. Schnell, "Robust polyphonic midi score following with hidden markov models," in *Proceedings of the International Computer Music Conference (ICMC)*, 2004.

[11] T. Otsuka, K. Nakadai, T. Takahashi, T. Ogata, and H. Okuno, "Real-Time Audio-to-Score Alignment Using Particle Filter for Coplayer Music Robots," *EURASIP Journal on Advances in Signal Processing*, vol. 2011, no. 1, 2011.

[12] A. Arzt, G. Widmer, and S. Dixon, "Automatic Page Turning for Musicians via Real-Time Machine Listening," in *Proceeding of the 18th European Conference on Artificial Intelligence (ECAI)*, 2008.

[13] A. Cont, "A Coupled Duration-Focused Architecture for Real-Time Music-to-Score Alignment," *IEEE transactions on pattern analysis and machine intelligence*, vol. 32, no. 6, pp. 974–987, Jun. 2010.

[14] C. Raphael, "Music Plus One and Machine Learning," in *Proceedings of the International Conference on Machine Learning (ICML)*, 2010.

[15] ——, "Aligning music audio with symbolic scores using a hybrid graphical model," *Machine Learning*, vol. 65, no. 2-3, pp. 389–409, May 2006.

[16] O. Izmirli and R. B. Dannenberg, "Understanding Features and Distance Functions for Music Sequence Alignment," in *Proceedings of the 11th International Society for Music Information Retrieval Conference (ISMIR)*, 2010.

[17] B. Niedermayer, "Non-negative Matrix Division for the Automatic Transcription of Polyphonic Music," in *Proceedings of International Conference on Music Information Retrieval (ISMIR)*, 2008.

[18] A. Doucet and A. M. Johansen, "A Tutorial on Particle Filtering and Smoothing : Fifteen years later," in *The Oxford Handbook of Nonlinear Filtering*, D. Crisan and B. L. Rozovsky, Eds. Oxford University Press, 2008, vol. 1, no. December, ch. 8.2, pp. 656–704.

[19] F. Korzeniowski, F. Krebs, A. Arzt, and G. Widmer, "Tracking Rests And Tempo Changes: Improved Score Following With Particle Filters," in *International Computer Music Conference (ICMC)*, 2013.

[20] A. Arzt, G. Widmer, and S. Dixon, "Adaptive Distance Normalization for Real-Time Music Tracking," in *Proceedings of the European Signal Processing Conference (EUSIPCO)*, 2012.

[21] A. Cont, D. Schwarz, N. Schnell, and C. Raphael, "Evaluation of Real-Time Audio-to-Score Alignment," in *Proceedings of 8th International Conference on Music Information Retrieval (ISMIR)*, 2007.

A HISTORY OF SEQUENCERS: INTERFACES FOR ORGANIZING PATTERN-BASED MUSIC

Raphael Arar
California Institute of the Arts
raphaelarar@alum.calarts.edu

Ajay Kapur
California Institute of the Arts
akapur@calarts.edu

ABSTRACT

This paper presents a history of sequencers for musical performance and creation. A sequencer is a musical interface designed to record, edit and playback audio samples in pattern format for both music composition and performance. Sequencers have evolved over the years to take many forms including mechanical and analog sequencers, drum machines, software sequencers, robotic sequencers, grid-based sequencers and tangible sequencers. This vast array of sequencer types brings forth a number of technological approaches including hardware fabrication, software development, robotic design, embedded electronics and tangible interaction design.

1. INTRODUCTION

Throughout history, patterns have permeated music. From ancient chant to modern electronic music, a sense of rhythm and repetition appears in music of diverse genres. This notion of structure relates to various mathematical principles, ranging from the golden section[1] to the matrix, and their sonic applications have been manifold. The idea of a grid has been one of the most prevalent characteristics of music throughout the past few centuries. The reliance on a sonic grid with repeating rhythmic and melodic motives has become imbued into the human ear, and the sequencer in its many forms has become a popular interface for music creation and sound music computing.

In their most common modern form, sequencers play rigid patterns of notes using a grid of sixteen steps with each step corresponding to one-sixteenth of a measure. Patterns are then chained together to form longer rhythmic and/or melodic motives. Most commercial sequencers are monophonic and play one note or sample per step. However, many are capable of storing multiple samples, allowing for multi-timbral composition and playback.

The sequencer is a commonplace interface for popular electronic music composition and production. Its greatest benefit is its ability to rapidly construct pattern-based sequences that are tightly locked to a meter. Patterns can be layered to create multiple voices that play simultaneously.

In this paper, sequencers of every type are surveyed. Section 2 discusses mechanical sequencers. Section 3 discusses analog sequencers. Section 4 discusses drum machines. Section 5 discusses software sequencers. Section 6 discusses sound sculpture sequencers, while Section 7 discusses grid-based sequencers followed by Section 8, which discusses tangible sequencers.

2. MECHANICAL SEQUENCERS

Sequenced music appeared in history long before the advent of modern-day electronics. In fact, the earliest known sequencers are mechanical in nature. The following section explores two early mechanical sequencers, the music box and player piano, which have influenced the development of modern-day sequencers.

The music box (**Figure 1.** Music Box (a) and Weber Pianola Piano (b) can be considered one of the first sequencers and was popularized as a toy during the 18th century. The vibration of steel teeth cut into a comb produce sounds that occur with the revolution of a pin-studded cylinder underneath them. A full revolution completes the melodic pattern and results in a musical phrase [2].

The player piano is yet another form of mechanical sequencer that is powered by foot pedals or a hand-crank. Fourneaux invented the first player piano in 1863, which was then iterated on by other inventors including Edwin Scott Votey, who created the Pianola (**Figure 1.** Music Box (a) and Weber Pianola Piano (b)) in 1896, followed by Edwin Welte's loom-based player piano created in 1897. The melodic sequence is most commonly triggered by paper punch-cards that automatically operate the hammers on the piano [3].

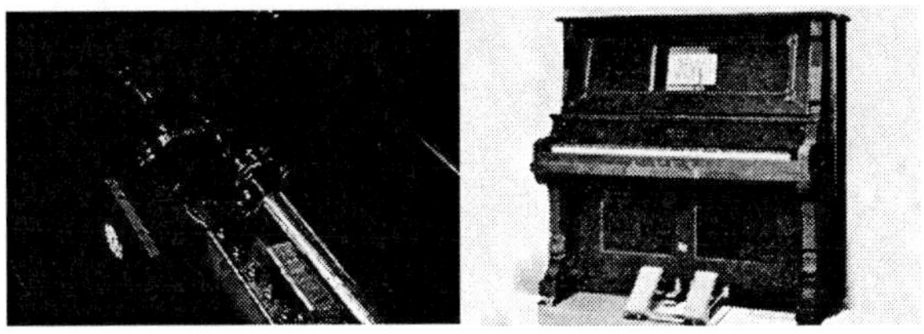

(a) (b)

Figure 1. Music Box[1] (a) and Weber Pianola Piano[2] (b)

[1] http://upload.wikimedia.org/wikipedia/commons/7/79/Baud_museum_
[2] http://www.pianola.org/history/history_playerpianos.cfm

3. ANALOG SEQUENCERS

Musical paradigms set forth by the player piano and music box made their way into future musical developments. Technological growth led composers and engineers to experiment with generating sound by way of electro-mechanical technology. Raymond Scott was one of the most notable composers to incorporate new technology in his work and the forefather of modern-day commercial sequencers.

In the mid-1940s, Raymond Scott created his "Wall of Sound" (**Figure 2**). It has been noted as one of the first and largest electro-mechanical sequencers spanning over thirty feet in length and stretched from his apartment floor to ceiling. The sequencer operated with mechanical relays that triggered solenoids, control switches and various tone circuits with sixteen individual oscillators. The sequencer could be manually adjusted by Scott to alter the sound patterns [4].

Scott's work with sequencers led to the development of fully analog sequencers that utilize analog electronics. The RCA[3] Mark II Sound Synthesizer designed by Herbert Belar and Harry Olson at RCA was created in 1957 and installed at the Columbia-Princeton Electronic Music Center. The synthesizer was the first analog electronic sequencer and used paper tape to automate playback by sending instructions back to the synthesizer [5].

Figure 2. Raymond Scott's "Wall of Sound"[4]

As a student, Robert Moog took inspiration from Scott's "Wall of Sound" to create his first analog sequencer, the Moog 960 in 1968. Moog created this particular sequencer as a module for his modular synthesizer. The 960 was one of the first analog step sequencers released for the commercial market. It contained three rows of eight value knobs and allowed for a three-value sequence of up to eight steps controlled by a clock. Each of the three banks could steer three different voltage-controlled oscillators (VCO), amplifiers (VCA) and filters (VCF) [4].

These early analog sequencers have affected electronic music production profoundly. Their developments led to the rise of a wide variety of electronic music. Many of the rudimentary sequencing implementations they utilized have served as paradigms for future electronic sequencers.

[3] http://www.rca.com/
[4] http://raymondscott.com/

4. DRUM MACHINES

This section explores the drum machine, a particular instance of a sequencer used to create percussive patterns. Since its inception, the drum machine has become a common interface for music creation and performance in electronic music.

The Rhythmicon is the earliest known drum machine invented by Léon Theremin in 1931. Having already established credibility and success with the creation of the theremin, Henry Cowell commissioned Theremin to build him a polymetrical instrument. The Rhythmicon was developed to produce up to sixteen different rhythms, each associated with a particular pitch (either individually or in combination). Despite its capabilities, the Rhythmicon was largely forgotten until the1960s [6].

Another instrumental drum machine was the Chamberlin Rhythmate created in 1957 by inventor Harry Chamberlin. This machine operated using fourteen tape loops. Each tape loop contained a sliding head, which enabled playback of different tracks on each piece of tape. The machine also contained volume, pitch and speed controls as well as a separate amplifier [7].

In 1959, Wurlitzer created the Sideman [8], which was the first commercial drum machine. It was electro-mechanical in nature and used a motor-driven wheel that would operate electrical contact points. These contact points could turn on up to twelve different preset rhythms, all of which contained ten drum sounds that were triggered using valve technology.

Shortly after the Wurlitzer Sideman, Ace Electronics began to prototype a new rhythm machine, the R1 Rhythm Ace, offering sixteen preset patterns that could be mixed together by pressing two buttons simultaneously allowing for over one hundred rhythm combinations. Ace changed the name to the FR-1 Rhythm Ace[5] (**Figure 3**) in 1967 when it was released for the commercial market.

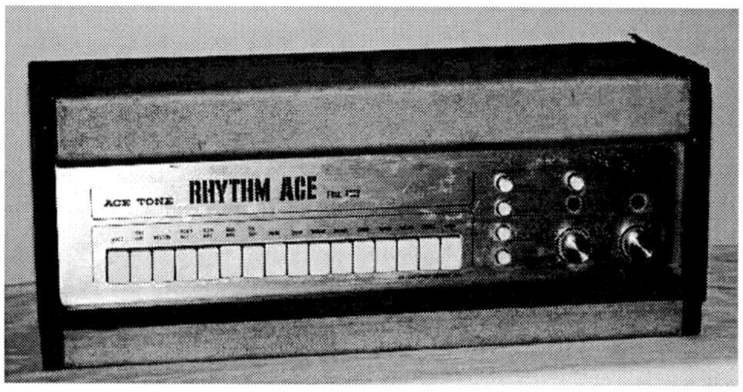

Figure 3. Ace Electronics' FR-1 Rhythm Ace[5]

5. SOFTWARE SEQUENCERS

With technology's exponential growth, software sequencers began to be developed. While the earliest software sequencers were used in conjunction with hardware synthesizers, modern software sequencers extend the physical metaphors set forth with analog sequencers described in Section 3. This section surveys early software

[5] http://www.soundonsound.com/sos/nov04/articles/roland.htm

sequencers to more contemporary ones included in many Digital Audio Workstations (DAWs).

The first software sequencer emerged as part of the ABLE computer created in 1975 by New England Digital. The computer contained a data processing unit developed for the Dartmouth Digital Synthesizer created two years prior. The ABLE computer served as the predecessor for the Synclavier I created in 1977, which was one of the earliest digital music workstations complete with a multi-track sequencer [9].

Three years later, the Page R was developed as part of the Fairlight CMI Series II synthesizer. This particular software-based sequencer combined sequencing with sample playback. It was commercially successful and its popularity led to the development of trackers.

In 1987, the first tracker software "Ultimate Soundtracker" was written by Karsten Obarski and released for the Commodore Amiga. The software supported only four channels of 8-bit samples and stepped through samples numerically. This structure became popular and led to the development of a slew of trackers including the OctaMED, ScreamTracker and others. The onset of computer games further popularized their use, as many game development companies leveraged tracker music for gameplay audio.

In the 1990s, DAWs such as Pro Tools[6], Logic[7], Digital Performer[8], Cakewalk[9] and many others began to hit the commercial market. Many of these DAWs dueled as production tools due to their MIDI capabilities and software instruments. As their companies developed the capabilities brought forth with MIDI, sequencing techniques became commonplace within most DAWs. Users now had the ability to loop patterns and build sequences directly with MIDI data. Ableton Live[10] (**Figure 4**) further extended software sequencing with the creation of Session View, which allows users to play back loops in a non-linear fashion utilizing scenes and clips.

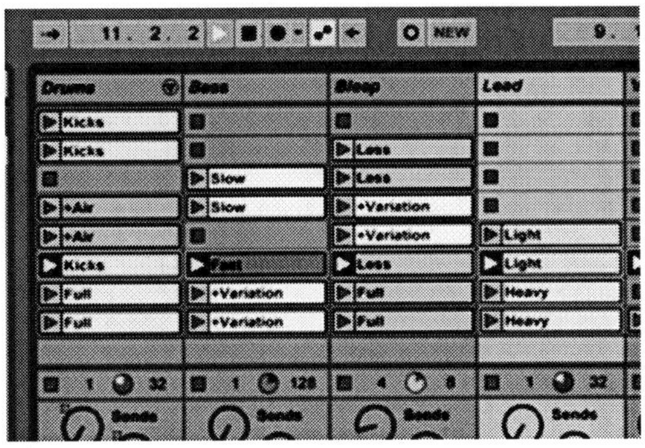

Figure 4. Ableton Live's Session View

6. SOUND SCULPTURE SEQUENCERS

The sequencer has also made its way into more of a contemporary art context. The following section explores Tim Hawkinson's *Uberorgan* and Trimpin's *Sheng High*, two artistic works that explore sequencer functionality in more of an aesthetic installation setting. Both of these sound sculptures incorporate fundamental sequencer design tactics set forth by the music box and the player piano and extend them based on the artists' unique visions.

Tim Hawkinson's *Uberorgan* (**Figure 5** (a)), commissioned by MASS MoCA in 2000, was one of the largest indoor sound sculptures ever created. The installation consisted of thirteen large, inflated bags; twelve of them corresponded to the tones in the musical scale and one acted as a control that fed air into the other twelve by long tubular ducts. Each of the twelve bags contained a long nozzle with a cardboard horn on one end, which produced sound. Playback was triggered in a manner similar to a player piano, and in the center of the gallery was a continuous sheet of marked paper fed over a sensor. The sensor then read the sheet and triggered playback on the corresponding horn [10].

Trimpin's *Sheng High* (**Figure 5** (b)), installed in 2005, is a sound sculpture based on the original Chinese instrument the sheng. The sheng is a reed instrument that relies on air pressure to produce sound through bamboo pipes. The sheng predates both the pipe and mouth organs. In *Sheng High*, Trimpin uses a similar concept to the sheng's playback; however, instead of a human player, he uses water pressure to push air in and out of the bamboo pipe in order to activate the reed. In the installation, thirty bamboo pipes are precisely tuned and each one hangs from a tripod to be centered in a vessel of water. By raising or lowering the pipe into water, air is pushed over the reed and produces sound. A wall scanner equipped with infrared sensors, one for each pipe, serves as the main sequencer clock. Trimpin uses recycled CDs to act as a visual notation system. Patterns created by the CDs are used to trigger the various pipes, since their reflections signal the infrared sensors and scanning device. As a result, the installation acts as a robotic sequencer, allowing visitors to witness a dialogue between the visual and aural patterns created by the sculpture [11].

(a) (b)

Figure 5. Tim Hawkinson's Uberorgan at MASS MoCA[10] (a) and Trimpin's Sheng High[11] (b)

7. GRID-BASED SEQUENCERS

The development of the MIDI specification in 1983 brought forth a great shift in musical devices. Now musicians and engineers had the ability to network devices together and use hardware controllers to trigger software audio samples. Synthesizers, samplers and sequencers begin to use MIDI to communicate with each other in

[6] http://www.avid.com/US/products/family/pro-tools
[7] http://www.apple.com/logicpro/
[8] http://www.motu.com/products/software/dp/
[9] http://www.cakewalk.com/
[10] https://www.ableton.com/
[11] http://www.artelectronicmedia.com/artwork/sheng-high

addition to software. With the ubiquity of MIDI and the establishment of OSC, these devices and their use began to rise.

The gradual progression of these devices led to a more recent movement known as "controllerism"[12]. Coined by Matt Moldover in 2007, controllerism can be thought of as the practice of using software controllers (commonly using MIDI and/or OSC) to create and modify music. This section will explore the Monome family of grid-based controllers, which serves as one of the key developments in this movement.

Brian Crabtree created the original Monome in 2005 at the California Institute of the Arts. The Monome is characterized by a minimal design and takes shape as a box with a grid of LED back-lit buttons. The box is simply an interface for software-based audio and must be connected to a computer. The most common Monome controllers range from 64 to 256 buttons [12].

Custom software, such as MLR, dictates how the Monome is used. The function of each button is completely customizable based on the software, which communicates over OSC messages. Sequencing audio is a very common application of the Monome based on the layout of its controls. The MLR software in particular allows for sample manipulation and sequencing through the interface.

Since its inception, the Monome has contributed to a movement of grid-based controllers. Many commercial products have evolved as a result of its creation. Notable controllers following the Monome include the Novation Launchpad released as well as the Akai APC40 both released in 2009. The development of the Monome also brought forth an array of open-source projects including the Arduinome (**Figure 6** (a)), Chronome(**Figure 6** (b)) and the Lumi [13].

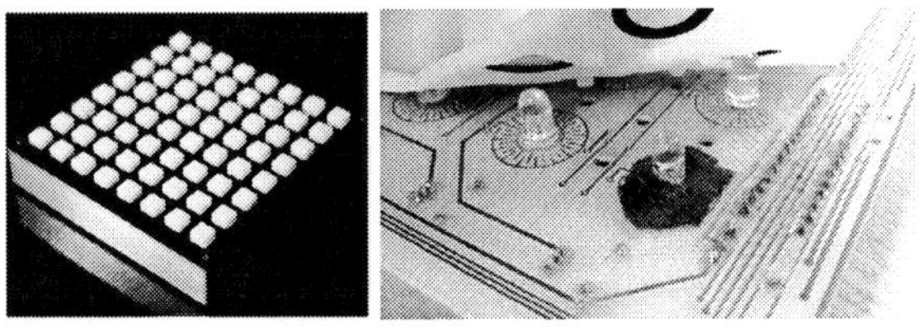

(a) (b)

Figure 6. Arduinome [12] (a) and Conductive Fabrics for Pressure Buttons on Chronome[13] (b)

8. TANGIBLE SEQUENCERS

The following section explores the development of tangible sequencers. A brief history of interaction design and its child discipline of tangible interaction design are discussed followed by two subsets of tangible sequencers: multi-touch tangible sequencers and computer vision tangible sequencers.

The principles of interaction design have played a large part in the future development of musical hardware including sequencers. Bill Moggridge and Bill Verplank first coined the term "interaction design" in the 1980s, and since its inception there have been many branches, all of which encompass the design of digital devices for human use.

Goal-oriented design is one of the primary methodologies surrounding interaction design. This facet of design is concerned with the creation of systems and devices that satisfy particular goals of its intended users. When viewed in a musical controller context, goal-oriented design can be seen as a musician's ability to easily create, edit and playback musical compositions and sequences. These design principles led to various branches of interaction design in order to make products more intuitive and easier to use [14].

Popularized by Hiroshi Ishii and his Tangible Media Group (TMG) at the MIT Media Lab, tangible user interfaces are those that allow a user to interact with digital information through physical controls. These interfaces seek to establish a metaphor between the physical world and the digital world; thus transforming intangible information into tangible, concrete objects [15].

8.1 Multi-touch Tangible Sequencers

Beginning in the early 21st century, touch surfaces began to become prevalent in many technology-based research endeavors. Musical instruments and systems were no exception, and multi-touch sequencers emerged out of many music technologists' research. Notable multi-touch sequencers include the reacTable, scoreTable (created with reacTable technology), Lemur, ZooZBeat, Gliss and the SmartFiducial.

The reacTable (**Figure 7** (a)), created in 2003, uses a tabletop tangible user interface for musical creation. The instrument has the ability to be collaborative and is versatile as a kind of tangible modular synthesizer [16]. The scoreTable, developed shortly after the initial reacTable, uses the same physical elements of the reacTable; however, its software is set up to retain basic sequencing functionality in that asynchronous interaction is combined with real-time performance [17].

The LEMUR (**Figure 7** (b)) created by JazzMutant[13] in 2004 is a modular multi-touch audio and multimedia controller. The controller has a plethora of sonic and visual capabilities including synthesizers, virtual instruments, lights and audio sequencers. The controller makes use of a multi-touch sensor on top of a 12" TFT display. The LEMUR predated many smartphone sequencer applications and incorporated multi-touch sequencing combined with visual feedback.

Shortly after the LEMUR, smartphones and tablets with touch-screens began to imbue the consumer electronic marketplace. This shift in computing led to a number of new musical interfaces including sequencers, as most platforms created application marketplaces to distribute these applications. Many musical sequencers have been developed for smartphones and tablets that incorporate multi-touch interaction including the Korg iElectribe[14], Figure[15], iMaschine[16], NodeBeat[17], and a number of others.

[12] http://www.controllerism.com/

[13] http://www.jazzmutant.com/lemur_overview.php

[14] http://www.korg.com/ielectribe

[15] http://www.propellerheads.se/products/figure/

[16] http://www.native-instruments.com/

ZooZBeat is a gesture-based mobile music studio presented at NIME in 2009, which uses not only multi-touch, but also the full gestural capabilities provided in most modern smartphones including accelerometer data. The interface makes use of a looping sequencer that is forgiving of user error from gestural input, allowing for constant real-time editing. The interface was designed to encourage immediate engagement and self-expression for novice players as well as room for growth and improvement in more advanced players [18].

Gliss is an iOS-based sequencer that allows for sequencing of up to five separate instruments. The interface takes inspiration from Xenakis' UPIC (Unite Polyagogique Informatique du CeMaMu) system, and allows users to create sequences by drawing on the screen in real-time. Another feature is the ability to randomize the playhead from that of the drawings, or allow for gestural control of the playhead using the iPhone's accelerometer [19].

The SmartFiducial is a wireless tangible user interface that makes use of multi-touch and multi-modal features [20]. The interface incorporates both infrared proximity sensing and resistive-based force-sensors as controls for the interface and its included software Turbine. This sequencer makes use of sixteen nodes that can be dragged to affect pitch. Z-depth sensing adds further sonic control by morphing among wavetable single-cycle waveforms. Furthermore, these sonic manipulations are reflected with visual feedback in the software.

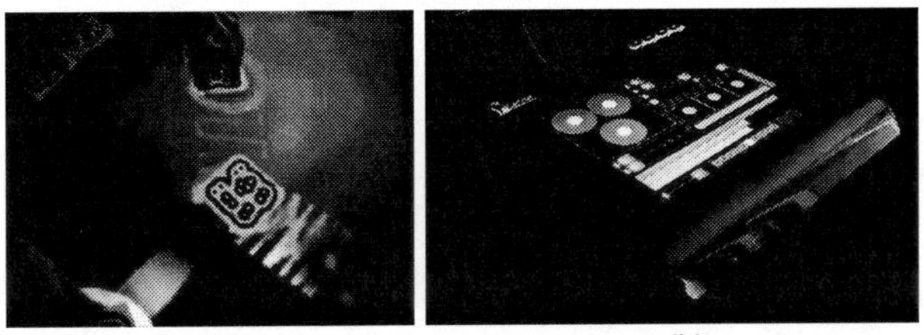

(a) (b)

Figure 7. The reacTable [16] (a) and the LEMUR[13] (b)

8.2 Computer Vision Tangible Sequencers

Many tangible sequencers make use of computer vision to aide human interaction. A variety of research projects have been conducted to address new tactics for musical control. Four notable tangible interfaces that use computer vision include the Music Table, d-Touch Sequencer, spinCycle, Bubblegum Sequencer and the Tactus.

The Music Table is one of the first tangible sequencers to use computer vision for tracking of steps. Basic use involves arranging cards on a tabletop that are then detected by an overhead camera. The camera allows the computer to track position and movement in order to affect sonic parameters as well as provide visual feedback [21].

The d-Touch sequencer (**Figure 8** (a)) uses a similar paradigm to that of the Music Table. The crux of interaction involves positioning a set of blocks on a flat surface that are then tracked with a camera connected to a computer. In order to convey both user feedback and camera tracking, the playing surface and blocks are marked with printed pieces of paper that contain graphic symbols. Four markers are placed on the corners of the surface in order to calibrate the playing area, while one marker is attached to each block to track in real time. The position of a block is then mapped to software parameters, which triggers audio playback [22].

Another sequencer that utilizes computer vision tactics is spinCycle. The crux of the interface is a turntable and camera that use color tracking to denote different audio samples and instruments. Tokens take the shape of translucent colored discs positioned on a larger rotating disc. The camera acts similarly to a turntable needle and follows the rotation of the disc in order to map visual input to audio output. A computer next to the interface shows a visual representation of the camera's input, which provides additional feedback to the audience [23].

The Bubblegum Sequencer (**Figure 8** (b)) is a sequencer that uses physical mapping to correspond to sample playback. The physical interface contains a 4 x 16 array of holes, and the physical objects are gumballs comprised of five different colors, which correspond to different samples. Each of the sixteen columns represents one-sixteenth note, while the rows allow for multi-timbral playback by stacking gumballs together [24].

Using the Bubblegum Sequencer as inspiration, the Tactus is a tangible tabletop synthesizer and sequencer that was created at UC Berkeley. Its premise is similar in that it uses an optical camera coupled with Max/MSP/Jitter to detect patterns among tangible tokens. Yet, it extends the ideas set forth in the Bubblegum Sequencer by its ability to turn almost any matrix-like object into a step sequencer [25].

(a) (b)

Figure 8. The d-Touch Sequencer [22] (a) and The Bubblegum Sequencer [24] (b)

9. FUTURE DIRECTIONS

The sequencer has evolved drastically since the music box in the 18th Century. Technology has progressed rapidly and musical devices and systems have progressed with them. It is interesting to note the transition to electronic music devices beginning with Raymond Scott's "Wall of Sound" into analog sequencers such as the RCA Mark II followed by the rise of software sequencers (**Figure 9**).

While the end of the 20th century saw a rise in digital devices and systems, the start of the 21st century has been marked by a desire for more intuitive interfaces and a return to tangible controls. The rise of mobile computing has also enabled anyone to make music. There are countless musical interfaces—everything from synthesizers to sequencers to mobile DAWs. While the smartphone and

[17] http://nodebeat.com/

tablet market has brought forth a slew of musical applications, many of these interfaces serve as great complements to music composition and performance. As new technology is invented, sequencers will continue to play a large role in the evolution of the electronic artist, and as a community we will continue to find new ways of organizing and expressing sound and music.

SEQUENCER TIMELINE

YEAR	DEVELOPMENT
1700s	Music Box
1863	Player Piano
1896	Pianola
1897	Loom-based Player Piano
1931	Rhythmicon
1940s	Raymond Scott's "Wall of Sound"
1957	Chamberlin Rhythmate
1957	RCA Mark II Sound Synthesizer
1959	Wurlitzer Sideman
1967	R1 and FR-1 Rhythm Ace
1968	Moog 960
1975	ABLE Computer Software Sequencer
1977	Synclavier I
1980	Page R
1987	Ultimate Soundtracker
1990s	Popular DAW Sequencers
2000	Tim Hawkinson's Uberorgan
2003	reacTable
2003	d-Touch
2003	Music Table
2004	LEMUR
2005	Trimpin's Sheng High
2005	Monome
2008	Arduinome
2008	Bubblegum Sequencer
2008	iPhone App Store Release
2009	Tactus
2009	Akai APC40 & Novation Launchpad
2009	LUMI
2010	Chronome

Figure 9. Sequencer Timeline

10. REFERENCES

[1] S. Olsen and S. Olson, *The Golden Section: Nature's Greatest Secret.* Walker & Company, 2006.

[2] T. D. Group, *Musical Instruments of the World: An Illustrated Encyclopedia with more than 4000 original drawings.* Sterling Publishing, 1997.

[3] A. Kapur, "A History of Robotic Musical Instruments," in *ICMC*, 2005.

[4] P. D. Miller, Ed., *Sound Unbound: Sampling Digital Music and Culture*, PAP/COM. The MIT Press, 2008.

[5] H. F. Olson and H. Belar, "Electronic Music Synthesizer," in *JASA*, vol. 27, no. 3, pp. 595–612, 1955.

[6] M. Schedel, "Anticipating interactivity: Henry Cowell and the Rhythmicon," *Organised Sound*, vol. 7, no. 3, pp. 247–254, 2002.

[7] T. Holmes, *Electronic and experimental music : technology, music, and culture.* New York: Routledge, 2008.

[8] H. E. Holman and J. H. Hearne, "RHYTHM DEVICE," U.S. Patent 3,207,835.

[9] M. Vail, "Vintage Gear - The Synclavier pioneered high-end technologies that we take for granted today.," *Keyboard.*, p. 128, 2002.

[10] N. Kernan, "Unnatural Science. North Adams, MA," *The Burlington Magazine*, vol. 142, no. 1172, pp. 720–722, 2000.

[11] Trimpin and A. Focke, *Trimpin : contraptions for art and sound.* Seattle [Wash.]: University of Washington Press, 2011.

[12] O. Vallis, J. Hochenbaum, and A. Kapur, "A Shift Towards Iterative and Open-Source Design for Musical Interfaces," in *NIME*, 2010.

[13] O. Vallis, J. Hochenbaum, J. Murphy, and A. Kapur, "THE CHRONOME: A CASE STUDY IN DESIGNING NEW CONTINUOUSLY EXPRESSIVE MUSICAL INSTRUMENTS."

[14] B. Moggridge, *Designing Interactions*, 1st ed. The MIT Press, 2007.

[15] M. J. Kim and M. L. Maher, "The Impact of Tangible User Interfaces on Designers' Spatial Cognition," *Human–Computer Interaction*, vol. 23, no. 2, pp. 101–137, 2008.

[16] S. Jorda, M. Kaltenbrunner, G. Geiger, and R. Bencina, "The reactable*," in *ICMC,* Barcelona, Spain, pp. 579–582, 2005.

[17] S. Jordà and M. Alonso, "Mary had a little scoreTable* or the reacTable* goes melodic," in *NIME*, 2006, pp. 208–211.

[18] G. Weinberg, A. Beck, and M. Godfrey, "ZooZBeat: a gesture-based mobile music studio," in *NIME*, pp. 312–315, 2009.

[19] J. Trutzschler, "Gliss: An Intuitive Sequencer for the iPhone and iPad," in *NIME*, Oslo, Norway, 2011, pp. 527–528.

[20] J. Hochenbaum and A. Kapur, "Adding Z-Depth and Pressure Expressivity to Tangible Tabletop Surfaces," in *NIME*, Oslo, Norway, 2011, pp. 240–243.

[21] R. Berry, M. Makino, N. Hikawa, and M. Suzuki, "The augmented composer project: the music table," in *Mixed and Augmented Reality, 2003. Proceedings. The Second IEEE and ACM International Symposium on*, 2003, pp. 338 – 339.

[22] E. Costanza, "D-touch: A consumer-grade tangible interface module and musical applications," in *HCI*, 2003, pp. 8–12.

[23] S. Kiser, "spinCycle: a Color-Tracking Turntable Sequencer," in *NIME*, 2006, pp. 75–76.

[24] H. Hesse and A. McDiarmid, "The Bubblegum Sequencer," in *CHI*, 2008.

[25] Y. Mann, J. Lubow, and A. Freed, "The Tactus: a Tangible, Rhythmic Grid Interface Using Found-Objects," in *NIME 2009*, Pittsburgh, PA, 2009.

Tale following: real-time speech recognition applied to live performance

Jean-Luc Rouas
CNRS - LaBRI
UMR 5800
F-33400 Talence, France
rouas@labri.fr

Boris Mansencal
Univ. Bordeaux - LaBRI
UMR 5800
F-33400 Talence, France
mansenca@labri.fr

Joseph Larralde
Univ. Bordeaux - LaBRI
UMR 5800
F-33400 Talence, France
larralde@labri.fr

ABSTRACT

This paper describes a system for tale following, that is to say speaker-independent but text-dependent speech recognition followed by automatic alignment. The aim of this system is to follow in real-time the progress of actors reading a text in order to automatically trigger audio events. The speech recognition engine used is the well known Sphinx from CMU. We used the real-time implementation pocketsphinx, based on sphinx II, with the French acoustic models developed at LIUM.

Extensive testing using 21 speakers from the PFC corpus (excerpts in "standard french") shows that decent performances are obtained by the system – around 30% Word Error Rate (WER). However, testing using a recording during the rehearsals shows that in real conditions, the performance is a bit worse : the WER is 40%.

Thus, the strategy we devised for our final application includes the use of a constrained automatic alignment algorithm. The aligner is derived from a biological DNA sequences analysis algorithm.

Using the whole system, the experiments report that events are triggered with an average delay of 9 s ($\pm$ 8 s).

The system is integrated into a widely used real-time sound processing software, Max/MSP, which is here used to trigger audio events, but could also be used to trigger other kinds of events such as lights, videos, etc.

Index Terms: tale following, text-dependent speech recognition, real-time, live performance

1. INTRODUCTION

This paper describes the application of a speech recognition system to a live performance. The kind of live performance we are interested in in this case involves acting and musical interpretation. There may be several actors – and they may speak at the same time – but the text should be previously known, but not necessarily in the exact interpretation – we indeed want the actors to have some acting freedom.

The aim of this project is to equip the computer with a *tale follower* which listens to the actors' performance in order to trigger basic audio events in real time. This performance situation problem is related to the well-known score following problem in the domain of computer music [1–4].

Thus, the designed system may be similar to what one would call *augmented tale telling*, where automatically triggered audio illustrations emphasise the actors' performance. Using such a system, actors are not directed by the musical score but are in command of the show. Additionally, a musician or a band may improvise on the audio track triggered by the actors' performance.

This paper is organised as follows: first, we present the motivations for building such a system and which requirements should be met. In section 3 we briefly describe the speech recognition engine and how we adapted it to our problem. The next section is dedicated to the text alignment procedure. The integration of the system into a audio processing environment is addressed in section 6. Application to a live performance is described in section 7.

2. OBJECTIVES

Score following has been studied since the early eighties in order to use the computer as a virtual musician able to play a score and accompany a musician in real time. The computer knows the score that is played by the musician and also knows the score it has to play to accompany the musician. Following the tempo of the musician, the computer anticipates the events coming from the musician in order to optimise the synchronisation between it and the musician, just like real musicians.

Our objective is to address the same problem by replacing the musician by an actor, thus considering as input the voice of an actor reading a text instead of a melody played by a musician. In our project, the computer knows the text that will be told by the actor as well as the score it has to play. The computer has to analyse the voice to extract phonemes, build words and align them with the text in order to know where the actor is situated in the text at any time.

The problems addressed are the following: efficiency, robustness, precision and reusability. Firstly, as the system is to be executed during live performances, it has to be efficient enough to work in real-time (as a score follower) for a good synchronisation between inputs and outputs – triggering a sound too early or too late is to be avoided at all cost. Secondly, in live situations, the system has to be robust to mispronunciations, forward jumps, as well as repetitions and everything that may occur in the context of actors interpretation. Thirdly, the precision of the temporal synchronisation between inputs and outputs depends of course on the algorithms global efficiency but also on the confidence of the alignment. For example, as will be detailed later in the paper, when the signal corresponds to a portion of a word, confidence is low, whereas confidence increases after the completion of a word or a sentence. Thus, this consideration provides constraints on the score to be played by the computer in order to optimise the precision of the synchronisation. Finally, we want to design a system as general as possible in order to be able to reuse it for quite different artistic contexts. For example, it has to be independent from the voice of the actor, whether male or female, so that different actors may perform on different occasions. It also has to be easily connected to the musical tools that are usually used in live performances in order not to add too much complexity for sound engineers or musicians.

3. SPEECH RECOGNITION

The speech recognition engine we choose to use is CMU Sphinx [5] for its real-time capabilities and the availability of French acoustic models. The aim of the system is to recognise words as they are said, find their position in the (known) text, and trigger audio events that are used to support the actors' playing and help the musician to focus on her improvisation.

3.1 Sphinx

We chose to use Sphinx as it is freely available and a real-time implementation – pocketsphinx – exists [6]. We will however not extensively describe the Sphinx system as it is fairly complex. Nevertheless, we remind that a speech recognition system has two main processing steps:

- An acoustic processing step, which uses phoneme models in order to transcribe audio features in a string of phones. The model used in this step is language-specific since phonemes differ in each language, and may or may not be speaker specific - it depends on how many speakers were used to train the models, though models may be speaker adapted in order to achieve better recognition.

- A "phoneme to words" step, which aims at transforming the string of phones into sequences of words. This step make use of a pronunciation dictionary, which indicates to the system how the words may be pronounced, and a language model which works as a sort of grammar by defining which word should follow another. The language model is usually trained on a large database of texts (i.e. newspaper articles) and statistics are extracted corresponding to the most frequent sequences of words. The length of those sequences may vary from one to three, we then speak of unigrams (word occurences statitics), bigrams (sequences of one or two words) or trigrams (sequences of one, two or three words).

The Sphinx system was used with success on French data during the ESTER evaluation [7] by the Laboratoire d'Informatique de l'Université du Maine (LIUM). The LIUM developed French acoustic and language models to be used with Sphinx for this evaluation [8]. They managed to achieve a performance of 18.2% WER on broadcast data from a number of television and radio channels [9]. The LIUM models are available both from the Sphinx repository on Sourceforge [1] and from the LIUM website [2]. It is worth noting that the LIUM French acoustic models are speaker independent.

3.2 Text Adaptation

In spite of these available models, we need to create our own language model and add some words and their pronunciation to the dictionary. There is indeed a specific vocabulary that may be used in poetry but that is not frequently found in the sources usually employed for training language models – i.e. newspapers.

3.3 Preliminary experiment

We wanted to test this system on a read speech corpus, the read text being the ideal case of a fake newspaper article read by several native speakers. The data we used come from the PFC (Phonologie du Français contemporain) Corpus [10]. The text is composed of 406 words and for this experiment we used a total of 21 speakers (11 female and 10 males) from the towns of Brecey and Brunoy which are usually used to represent "standard french". The total duration of the 21 files is approximately 57 minutes (i.e. 2:42 per file).

On these recordings, the system, without any adaptation, achieved surprisingly poor performances – 91.1% Word Error Rate (WER), as shown on the first line of table 1. These poor performances may be due to the fact that the LIUM-Sphinx system was trained for broadcast news transcription, which is particularly important considering the language model, which was trained on newspaper data (e.g. excerpts from "Le Monde"). However, the text used in this experiment, which is considered to be similar to a newspaper article, may not reflect well the training data used for the language model. It is also worth noting that the best performing LIUM system mentioned earlier in the paper is fairly complex since it makes use of a speaker segmentation algorithm, a 4-gram language model and works in several passes, which are options that we have not considered here due to real-time constraints.

Considering these facts, we therefore decided to train a new statistical language model on a combination of concatenations of phrases from the text. We did not use a fixed grammar as language model, because actors may change the text slightly during a live performance.

Using this language model, specific to the text of the poem, we managed to decrease the WER to 41.1%. Restricting the language model and dictionary to the original

[1] http://sourceforge.net/projects/cmusphinx/files/AcousticandLanguageModels/

[2] http://www-lium.univ-lemans.fr/en/content/data

Adaptation Method	Corr	Sub	Del	Ins	Err
none	9.5	30.1	60.4	0.7	91.1
LM only	59.9	3.9	36.2	1.4	41.5
MAP+LM	63.8	2.6	33.6	1.2	37.4
MAP+MLLR+LM	72.1	1.4	26.5	1.7	29.7

Table 1. Performance obtained using Sphinx with the LIUM acoustic models and different kinds of adaptation on PFC data

Take	Corr	Sub	Del	Ins	Err
#1	81.9	14.5	3.6	19.7	37.8
#2	79.8	15.6	4.6	20.6	40.7

Table 2. Performance obtained using Sphinx with the LIUM acoustic models on rehearsal data

text also has the welcome effect of speeding the speech recognition process. Besides, this result could probably be further improved by training an acoustic model specific to the speaker or channel. Using Maximum A Posteriori (MAP) adaptation combined with MLLR (Maximum Log Likelihood Ratio), we obtained a much more decent WER of 29.7%. The speaker/channel adaptation works quite well since recording conditions vary greatly in this database: the microphone is most of the time placed on a table and the room is not always very quiet.

3.4 Experiments using rehearsal data

The aim of our system is however to be speaker independent, since we may want to switch actors if necessary. There should not be any channel effect in our setup since we use close capture microphones.

Using the LM-only setup, we thus have tested the performance of the system on rehearsal data. The text of the poem is in that case told by the two actors (one male, one female) that will perform during the live show. We have recorded two sessions of the performance. Each recording has a duration of approximately 40 minutes, the theoretical length of the text being 1779 words. Since one of the aims of the system is to leave as much freedom as possible to the actors, they obviously took advantage of it. Instead of simply reading the poem, they played with it, sometimes speaking together, repeating words that were mentioned only once etc. The performance of the system is described in table 2. Even though we did not experiment with several actors, we are confident that the results should be similar with any interpreter since the acoustic models were not adapted here.

The performances are surprisingly better than with the PFC data in terms of number of correctly transcribed words (around 80%, to be compared with 70%) , but the number of insertions (20%) is much greater than in the previous test (around 1.2%). Although some of these insertions may be caused by the actors interpretation, this is quite unfortunate because we certainly do not want to trigger an event at a wrong time. The figure for the deletions is however much better on the rehearsal recordings than on the PFC data, which is encouraging.

These results show that we cannot rely only on the speech recognition alone to perform the task we want: the quite high error rate will certainly have some undesired consequences on the triggering of the events. Thus, we have chosen to use an algorithm for automatically aligning the recognised words with the text of the poem that allow for incomplete matching. This algorithm is described in the next section.

4. ALIGNMENT

The alignment algorithm is issued from research on DNA sequences. The starting point is the algorithm described in [11], which allows to transform a character string u in a string v using different operations: insertions, deletions, substitutions. Dynamic programming is used to find the optimal series of operations. As an example, the two following sequences can be aligned using this algorithm :

```
A T - G T T A T
A T C G T - A C
```

The algorithm from [12] works on the same principle but at a local level. This algorithm can find the two sub-strings of stronger similarity as in the example below:

```
G T G G A T - G T T A T G T G G
C C A C A T C G T - A C A A C A
```

It has been successfully applied on audio data for music similarity purposes [13].

We decided to apply this algorithm to our problem as the output from the speech recognition system might not be the exact researched text.

As input to the alignment procedure, we use both the recognised text and the confidence score given by the speech recognition system. If this recognition score is over a certain threshold, we use the algorithm to see if the recognised text may be aligned with the original text. To this end, we define a search window on the original text, which has a size proportional to the recognised sentence length. This window is used to restrict the search space for the alignment. The best approximate match, given by [12] algorithm, gives an alignment score. If this alignment score is greater than a second threshold, we consider that we have a valid alignment of a valid recognition and thus advance the start of search window to the end of the aligned sequence. If the alignment score is below this threshold, the size of the search window is increased without changing its starting point. This procedure is designed for the reading of a text: the progression of the reading should be linear – i.e. the reader must not go back to a previous element in the text.

5. EVENTS TRIGGERING PERFORMANCE EVALUATION

The timing of the events that the system should trigger is a very important point in our system. In order to assess that every event we designed to be triggered is effectively detected by the system, we have measured the time delay

Take	Average Delay (s)	Standard Deviation (s)
#1	9.20 (s)	$\pm$ 8.01 (s)
#2	10.42 (s)	$\pm$ 12.04 (s)

Table 3. Average delay for ten events on the two rehearsal recordings (average for four trials)

between the real occurrence of the triggering word in the recording and the time at which this word is effectively detected by the system.

To do this, we devised a list of ten words distributed along the text on which we measured the mean square of the delays. The result of this test, for the two rehearsal recordings is given in table 3. Since the performances may vary slightly between two tests using the same recording, the measurements are averaged on 4 trials.

As seen on table 3, the average delay is quite important. However, the delay can vary greatly between events, as illustrated by the confidence intervals. For instance, the best performing trial on both recordings is given in table 4. Note that the measured delays may be negative – the event is triggered before the word is actually pronounced – because of errors in the recognised stream of words leading to a false alignment.

The difficult passages are indeed mainly linked to moments where the actors play a lot with the text. We hope to improve that point in the future, but the performances are very dependent on the actors pronunciation and interpretation. Thus, in the actual state of the system, we had to select the proper words to trigger events efficiently.

word#	Take 1 delay (s)	Take 2 delay (s)
#1	10.936	-0.510
#2	8.038	-28.745
#3	1.818	-1.036
#4	21.446	-11.447
#5	0.185	0.915
#6	0.901	0.448
#7	0.807	0.953
#8	4.589	9.749
#9	21.135	26.157
#10	18.469	13.064

Table 4. Delay measured for each triggering word on take 1 and take 2

6. INTEGRATION WITH A MUSIC PROCESSING SOFTWARE

Max/MSP is a visual data-flow programming language which is widely used to program sound and music processing for live performances. Indeed, most of the interactive music composers consider that this language is the standard to process music in real time. Thus, we made a connection between our tale follower and Max/MSP to integrate it in a convenient environment and we developed our own sound modules in MAX.

The integration of the system has been achieved using the framework described on figure 1. Two HF microphones are used as input for a first computer (noted "Text follower" on the figure). The microphones are connected to the sphinx engine via Jack. Recognised words are then fed into the text aligner which indicates the progress of the reading. This information is then transferred via OSC to an audio processing second computer running Max/MSP. On this computer, switches triggering events are activated according to the received information and a cue list.

The sound coming from the instrument(s) played by the musician(s) is also processed using the second computer, which renders different effects and spread the sound on eight loudspeakers – the effects and the sound spatialisation characteristics may also be changed using the information from the tale follower).

7. THE FLUXUS SHOW

The whole system has been used for two performances of "Fluxus". "Fluxus" is the name of a poem in French by author Donatien Garnier. The performance consisted in the reading of this poem by two actors (a man and a woman), and the playing of a musical accompaniment by a musician and a computer. The musical part played by the computer was determined before the performance whereas the musician improvised his own part.

Composer and musician György Kùrtag Jr. composed a specific music for this poem. The musical illustrations designed to be played by the computer were previously recorded in a studio. The musician was also present and improvising during the show. Although we still have troubles with the accuracy of the speech recognition system, with carefully chosen target words, the system did perform almost flawlessly and the performance was a success – though this is unfortunately not quantifiable.

8. CONCLUSION

In this paper, we have described a *tale-following* system based on a speech recognition system and an automatic aligner. The performances of the speech recognition system in text-dependent mode are quite average – around 40 % WER – in studio conditions. These numbers are quite different from the results obtained by LIUM using the same acoustic models because we used the real-time implementation of Sphinx – pocketsphinx – and 3-gram language models (as opposed to 4-grams). Using the "regular" sphinx implementation (of sphinx III), we managed to obtain a WER of 6.4% on the PFC data – but not in real-time. This is to be compared to the 29.7% WER obtained using the same training method with pocketsphinx. We will have to investigate why the performance gap is so important between the two implementations.

Anyway, as we needed real-time speech recognition, the system takes advantage of a post-processing using an automatic alignment algorithm designed to be able to cope with these errors. But, even with the complete system, trial events were triggered with a delay that can vary from 0.1 to 20 seconds. Extensive testing allowed us to choose the most appropriate words to trigger the events, providing a great experience from the audience point of view.

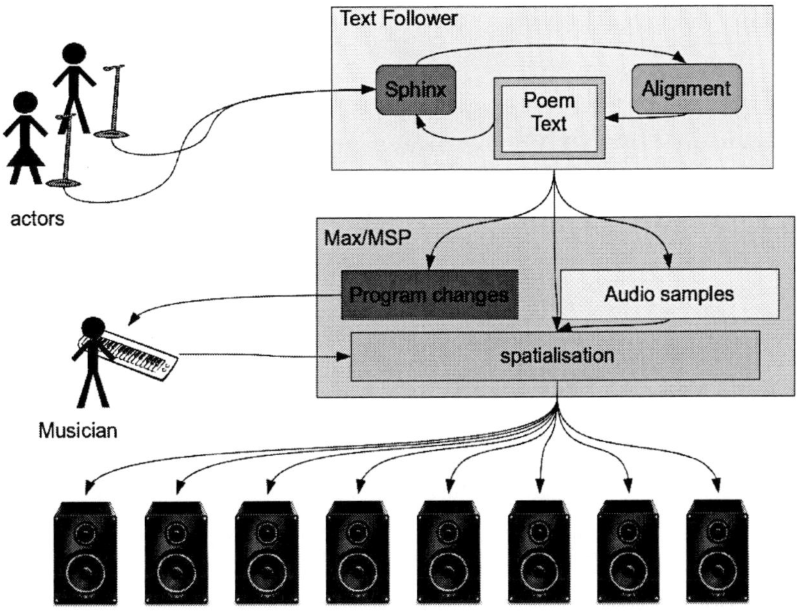

Figure 1. integration of the system

9. PERSPECTIVES

In this project, we have addressed only the temporal synchronisation between actors and musical accompaniment. An interesting perspective of this work is to extract voice and interpretation characteristics in order to use them for shaping the musical part. For example, we can consider adapting the energy of the music to the volume of the voice to enhance emotional impact. Intonation and speech rate could be used to modify musical and sound parameters and musical tempo. Effects could also be applied to the voice to transform it depending on the words and the sentences that are said by actors. For this purpose, we plan to use the iscore interactive sequencer [14, 15] which was developed during the virage project [16] to make the definition of the temporal organisation of musical events and the interconnection of different processes easier.

We also plan to adapt this system to singing voice following. The problem of speech recognition on singing voice is however still a challenge. We will adapt the speech recognition system to the singing voice by using specific data, but the intrinsic models may also need to be modified as singing voice characteristics differ from speech, particularly in terms of vowel durations, articulatory strategies and formant spanning. Nevertheless, by knowing the lyrics beforehand, we hope to be able to design an efficient system with real-time capabilities.

10. ACKNOWLEDGEMENTS

This work is partly supported by a grant from the ANR (Agence Nationale de la Recherche) with reference ANR-12-CORD-0022.

This research was carried out in the context of the SCRIME project (Studio de Création et de Recherche en Informatique et Musique Electroacoustique – Electroacoustic Music and Computer Science Research and Creation Studio, `scrime.labri.fr`) which is funded by the DGCA of the French Culture Ministry and the Aquitaine Regional Council. The SCRIME project is the result of a cooperation convention between the Conservatoire of Bordeaux, ENSEIRB-Matmeca (electronic and computer scientist engineering school) and the Bordeaux University of Sciences. It involves both electroacoustic music composers and scientific researchers and is managed by the LaBRI (Computer Science Research Laboratory at Bordeaux University, `www.labri.fr`). Its main missions are research and creation, diffusion and pedagogy thus extending its influence.

11. REFERENCES

[1] B. Vercoe, "The synthetic performer in the context of live performance," in *Proceedings of International Computer Music Conference (ICMC)*, 1984.

[2] M. Puckette and C. Lipp, "Score following in practice," in *Proceedings of International Computer Music Conference (ICMC)*, 1992.

[3] A. Cont, "Antescofo: Anticipatory synchronization and control of interactive parameters in computer music," in *Proceedings of International Computer Music Conference (ICMC)*, 2008.

[4] N. Orio, S. Lemouton, and D. Schwarz, "Score following: State of the art and new developments," in *In New Interfaces for Musical Expression (NIME)*, 2003.

[5] P. Lamere, P. Kwok, W. Walker, E. Gouvêa, R. Singh, B. Raj, and P. Wolf, "Design of the cmu sphinx-4 de-

coder," in *8th European Conf. on Speech Communication and Technology (EUROSPEECH 2003)*, 2003.

[6] H. D. Daines, M. Kumar, A. Chan, A. W. Black, M. Ravishankar, and A. I. Rudnicky, "Pocketsphinx: A free, real-time continuous speech recognition system for hand-held devices," in *IEEE International Conference on Acoustics, Speech, and Signal Processing (ICASSP)*, 2006.

[7] G. Gravier, J. Bonastre, S. Galliano, E. Geoffrois, K. M. Tait, and K. Choukri, "The ester evaluation campaign of rich transcription of french broadcast news," in *Language Resources and Evaluation Conference (LREC)*, 2004.

[8] P. Deléglise, Y. Estève, S. Meignier, and T. Merlin, "The lium speech transcription system: a cmu sphinx iii-based system for french broadcast news," in *9th European Conf. on Speech Communication and Technology (INTERSPEECH'2005 - EUROSPEECH)*, 2005.

[9] S. Galliano, E. Geoffrois, G. Gravier, J.-F. Bonastre, D. Mostefa, and K. Choukri, "Corpus description of the ester evaluation campaign for the rich transcription of french broadcast news," in *Language Resources and Evaluation Conference (LREC)*, 2006.

[10] J. Durand, B. Laks, and C. Lyche, *Phonologie, variation et accents du français*. Hermès, 2009, ch. Le projet PFC: une source de données primaires structurées, pp. 19–61.

[11] S. B. Needleman and C. D. Wunch, "A general method applicable to the search for similarities in the amino acid sequences of two proteins," *Journal of Molecular Biology*, vol. 48, pp. 443–453, 1970.

[12] T. Smith and M. S. Waterman, "Identification of commuon molecular subsequences," *Journal of Molecular Biology*, vol. 147, pp. 195–197, 1981.

[13] J. Allali, P. Ferraro, P. Hanna, and M. Robine, "Polyphonic alignment algorithms for symbolic music retrieval," *Lecture Notes in Computer Science*, vol. 5954, pp. 466–482, 2010.

[14] M. Desainte-Catherine and A. Allombert, "Interactive scores: a model for specifying temporal relations between interactive and static events," *Journal of New Music Research*, vol. 34, pp. 361–375, 2005.

[15] A. Allombert, M. Desainte-Catherine, and G. Assayag, "Iscore : Writing the interaction," in *Proceedings of the 3rd Digital Interactive Media in Entertainment and Art (DIMEA)*, 2008.

[16] A. Allombert, P. Baltazar, R. Marczak, and M. Desainte-Catherine, "Virage : Designing an interactive intermedia sequencer from users requirements and theoretical background," in *International Computer Music Conference (ICMC)*, 2010.

Technical Report on a Short Live-action Film whose Story with Soundtrack is selected in Real-time based on Audience Arousal during Performance

Alexis Kirke, Duncan Williams, Eduardo Miranda, Amanda Bluglass, Craig Whyte, Rishi Pruthi, Andrew Eccleston
Plymouth University, Plymouth, UK
{Alexis.Kirke, Duncan.Williams, Eduardo Miranda, Amanda.Bluglass, Craig.Whyte, Andrew.Eccleston}@plymouth.ac.uk; rishi.pruthi@students.plymouth.ac.uk

ABSTRACT

'many worlds' is a short narrative live-action film written and directed so as to provide four optional linear routes through the plot and four endings. At two points during the fifteen minute film, decisions are made based on audience biosignals as to which plot route to take. The use of biosignals is to allow the audience to remain immersed in the film, rather than explicitly selecting plot direction, as done in most interactive films. Four audience members have a bio-signal measured, one sensor for each person: ECG (heart rate), EMG (muscle tension), EEG ("brain waves") and Galvanic Skin Response (perspiration). The four are interpreted into a single average of emotional arousal. This is used to decide which route to select at each of the two plot selection points. The film starts with a binaural soundscape composed to relax the audience, and depending on which clip is selected at the decision points, a different soundtrack is played under the visual action as well. 'many worlds' is the first live action linear plotted film to be screened in a cinema in front of the general public which utilizes the above reactive approach.

1. INTRODUCTION

This paper documents the design and implementation of an engine for real-time detection of biosignal responses from an audience which can drive live editing of a film and its soundtrack. This generates streaming video for the purpose of audience affective manipulation whist they watch the narrative of an algorithmic short film written and directed by Alexis Kirke: 'many worlds'. A key vision behind the film is that at fixed points in the plot the audience's arousal level will be sampled and if is below a pre-determined threshold, a more intense version of the next scene will be selected.

There has been much previous work in algorithmic live action film, mostly database cinema [1]. There has also been a lot of work in interactive cinema [2, 3], in which the audience select plot lines. However most of this work has involved the audience consciously selecting film behaviour. This has the effect of destroying the immersion in the story [4]. [4] has begun to attempt to address this in a simple computer-generated graphical drama using single viewers at a workstation. A brain-influenced film installation has been developed which was displayed in a museum [5], also leading to further research in cinema and neuroscience [6]. [7] measured peoples' biosignals while they sat in a cinema to see if their emotional reactions could be detected. The result indicated that the detection was possible. [8] attempted to detect audience interest during movies scenes using various bio-signals but could not quantify the precise nature of "interest". A related study is found in [9] which attempted to detect "boredom" in people playing a video game. The power of such approaches is that not only can they maintain peoples' immersion, but can potentially increase it, by reactively manipulating them using plot, edit or soundtrack elements which respond to the audience dynamically.

1.1 Metering affect

The various models of emotion proposed by affective sciences offer complex, and still evolving, representations which can be used to map musical features to mood and vice versa. The dimensional approach to specifying emotion utilizes an n-dimensional space made up of emotion "factors". Any emotion can be plotted as some combination of these factors. The 2-Dimensional 'circumplex' model of affect [10], with emotion comprised of valence and arousal, is often utilized in emotional evaluation for music [11, 12, 13, 14]. In many emotional music creation systems [15] these dimensions are used. In this model, emotions are plotted on a graph with the first dimension being how positive or negative the emotion is (valence), and the second dimension being how physically excited the emotion is (arousal). For example "Happy" is high valence high arousal affective state, and "Stressed" is low valence high arousal state.

Self-reporting arousal on such a model [16,17] presents problems for the presentation and development of responsive, immersive music — and particularly as in this case, responsive immersive cinema — in that they force the interruption of any narrative. The use of a range of biosensors to meter affective responses [18, 19] from the cinema audience and respond accordingly presents the opportunity to bypass self-reporting or self-selection of material (for example, in the feature film world when DVD audiences can select alternative endings by a root level navigation menu) in favour of an affectively driven, emotion-synchronous model.

'many worlds' attempts this with a pilot system that does not currently utilize valence, focusing on the measurement of arousal as a time-based vector. Important factors of the movie experience (beside emotions) fall outside of what such a system can take into account. Aspects of the viewers' cognitive processes, of aesthetic dimensions, evaluative reactions, etc. – which are central parts of the movie experience – fly under the radar of the system. However arousal was chosen for this initial implementation because most biosensor research in the past has been more successful in detecting emotional arousal than emotional valence [20], and there are no current forms of measurement available for the other elements of the cinema-going experience such as those mentioned.

As has been mentioned, in emotional measurement, arousal is what distinguishes Happy from Relaxed, and Angry from Depressed. It measures the physical activity of the emotion. So if a watcher is feeling positive about a film, an arousal-maximizing strategy will make them feel Happy rather than Relaxed, or Angry rather than Depressed. This is obviously a fairly blunt instrument but provides a first in-road into implementing emotion-control strategies.

The arousal vector is involved in a constant feedback loop, as ongoing arousal is continuously 'pinged' in real-time within the limits of a preset buffer. This vector is evaluated at various time values, mapping the arousal and time value to a video selection, creating a range of possible narrative routes through the film for the audience. The entities involved in this process are time and a high-level arousal estimate (at a lower level, raw biosignal data), with the relationship between these entities determined by the director in order to sustain or increase audience arousal whilst watching the film.

This pilot system has possible applications in affective algorithmic soundtrack selection for film and television, as well as affective metering for standalone computer music or film.

2. SYSTEM OVERVIEW

Four sensors are used to monitor participating audience members physiological reactions in real-time. These responses are combined in an affective estimation algorithm to give a moving average value for audience arousal, which is compared with an arousal threshold at various decision points in the narrative to give control data that maps the next part of the narrative the audience will watch, seamlessly creating an edit 'on-the-fly'. Previous computer music research has made use of similarly collected biosignal data as control inputs for music with emotional correlations. Such affective correlations to the selected biosignals are well documented in literature [21, 22]. A flow-chart illustrating the complete signal flow is given in Figure 1 (at the end of this paper). The system broadly comprises three sections: Biosignal metering, Arousal estimation, and Video editing (arousal synchronous narrative selection). These sections are explained in more detail below.

Four biosensors were utilized, all of which have implicated in detecting affective arousal:

1. Electrocardiograph (EKG), indicating mean heart rate from the participant above calibration threshold, averaged over 2-10 beats [22]
2. Electromyograph (EMG), indicating muscle tension from the right forearm of the participant, as a mean within each buffer(n) [23]
3. Electroencephalograph (EEG), using three electrodes to indicate frontal brain activity, filtered to give only the alpha region using a band-pass 8-12kHz two-pole filter [24]. As in [24] the natural logarithm of the alpha data was calculated and multiplied by -1
4. Galvanic skin response (GSR), giving a normalized value for perspiration on the left wrist and forefinger of the participant [22]

2.1 Bio-signal metering

Sensor responses are digitized and passed to Max/MSP as raw data in real-time. Each data stream is calibrated to remove background noise using adjustable maximum and minimum input level outliers with EEG and GSR responses, and a simple noise-gating threshold for EKG and EMG responses. The responses from each sensor were then passed to an affective estimation routine to determine an instantaneous audience arousal value with which to carry out video selection.

2.2 Arousal estimation routine

Affective arousal is estimated from the four biosensors as a moving average. The output from each sensor is normalized before being summed across a nominal buffer, as shown in Equation 1, where A(n) = estimated arousal for buffer (n):

$$A(n) = \frac{\Sigma\, EEG(n)+EKG(n)+EMG(n)+GSR(n)}{n} \quad (1)$$

Results from the arousal estimation algorithm are compared with a pre-determined arousal threshold (AT) in order to generate a control message for selection of video playback in the video mapping portion of the code.

2.3 Video editing: arousal-synchronous narrative selection

The first iteration of the Jitter-based video playback engine was designed in order to switch between three different narratives 'on-the-fly' by direct comparison of arousal values with the pre-determined arousal threshold (AT). In the finished system, video timecode is also used as a mapping entity such that time and arousal are mapped to video selection and playback, creating an arousal-synchronous method of video narrative selection. 7 clips in total are used in this system, as illustrated in Figure 2.

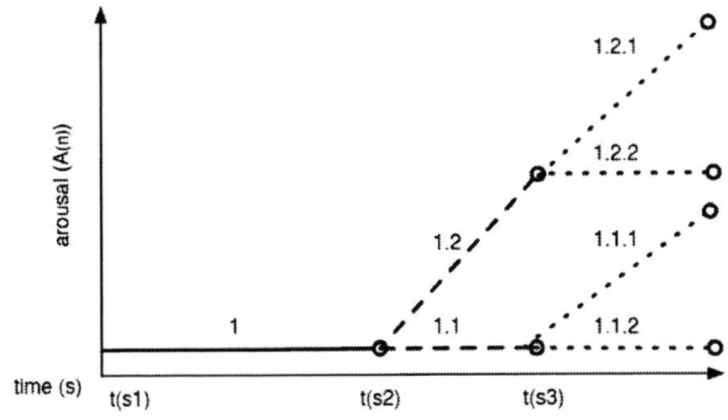

Figure 2. Illustrating arousal threshold and 'split' points – editing decisions are made at predetermined timecodes by comparing the estimated audience arousal from the four biosensors to an arousal threshold and selecting a bipolar route through to four separate narratives.

Table 1 and Figure 2 shows that the 7 clips present four possible 'routes' for the audience, through two branches or 'split' points based on timecode values, t(s2) and t(s3) respectively. The arousal buffer, (n), is reset after each of the split points as part of the affective estimation algorithm. This real-time detection of arousal allows the filmmaker to select narrative according, and in direct response to, the audience's arousal. This allows the film to adapt to the audience, and the filmmaker to discretely target the induction of arousal in the audience, maintaining or increasing arousal through the narrative. The choice of trying to increase audience arousal was an artistic decision by the filmmaker (writer / director). Other strategies that could have been chosen include minimizing arousal or creating a certain arousal trajectory.

The marking-up of video clips as to which expressed higher or lower arousal, was done by the filmmaker. This was a subjective process and part of the artistic decision making, as there are no agreed methodologies for measuring such "plot arousal". The story involves three lead characters, and takes place in two locations: one outside and one inside in a single room. Clips 1.1 and 1.2 in Figure 2 are differentiated by action taking place with one or with two people respectively. The two-person clip was considered to have a higher arousal due to their interactions. Clip 1.2.1 was considered to be higher arousal than Clip 1.2.2 for reasons which will not be documented here, so as not to reveal the endings: the writer / director judged Clip 1.2.1 to be higher arousal for dramatic reasons. Similarly with the decision that Clip 1.1.1 was higher arousal than Clip 1.1.2.

Four modifier values were applied to ensure correct clip selection at the pre-determined split point timecode values:

[beginning of film +1]
[first clip reached timecode +1]
[reached first split point +2]
[reached second split point +3]

Pathway	Clips Played	Arousal <> Arousal Threshold
1	1, 1.2, 1.2.1	Low arousal, Low arousal
2	1, 1.2, 1.2.2	Low arousal, High arousal
3	1, 1.1, 1.2.1	High arousal, Low arousal
4	1, 1.1, 1.2.2	High arousal, High arousal

Table 1. Showing four possible routes through seven video clips, with corresponding arousal estimations

which, combined with a modifier value for arousal (determined by comparing the moving average arousal with the selected arousal threshold):

[arousal >= arousal threshold +1]
[arousal < arousal threshold +0]

generate a unique reference number for each of the decision points. This unique reference is used as a control message to select the relevant clip and begin playback in the Jitter video engine.

clip URN 1 = +1 (beginning of film, no arousal)
clip URN 2 = +1 (beginning of film) +1 (first clip reached timecode)
clip URN 3 = +1 (beginning of film) +1 (first clip reached timecode) +1 (arousal>threshold)
clip URN 4 = +1 (beginning of film) +1 (first clip reached timecode) +2 (reached first split point)
clip URN 5 = +1 (beginning of film) +1 (first clip reached timecode) +2 (reached first split point) +1 (arousal>threshold)
clip URN 6 = +1 (beginning of film) +1 (first clip reached timecode) +2 (reached first split point) +3 (reached second split point)
clip URN 7 = +1 (beginning of film) +1 (first clip reached timecode) +2 (reached first split point) +3 (reached second split point) +1 (arousal>threshold)

3. SOUNDTRACK GENERATION

A soundtrack was composed by the writer / director for each of the film clips had been marked up for arousal. The electronic composition was generated with binaural beats. These involve two pure tones with frequencies that are slightly different. This creates the psychoacoustic effect of a beating slowly modulating their frequencies. The apparent frequency of modulation increases as the difference in pure tone frequencies increases. Although there has been work suggesting that binaural beats can affect mood [25], they are used here as an aesthetic choice by the composer, not with any scientific claims of mood manipulation. The use of such an abstract soundtrack is not so unusual. One key example of how audiences are becoming more used to such soundtracks is the sparse sub-bass soundtrack found in the mainstream feature film Paranormal Activity 2.

The composition for 'many worlds' was done intuitively based on scene drama, not based on the arousal markups. However an interesting structure emerged, as shown in Figure. Given that Clip 1.2.1 was marked up as having a higher arousal than Clip 1.2.2, it was found in post-analysis that the soundtrack had a maximum higher energy peak for the clip whose arousal was marked up as being higher (i.e. Peak 0.105 > Peak 0.052). Similarly with Clip 1.1.1 being marked up as higher arousal than Clip 1.1.2, the peak energy of the soundtrack turned out to have a higher energy in the higher arousal-marked clip (i.e. Peak 0.0975 > Peak 0.0920).

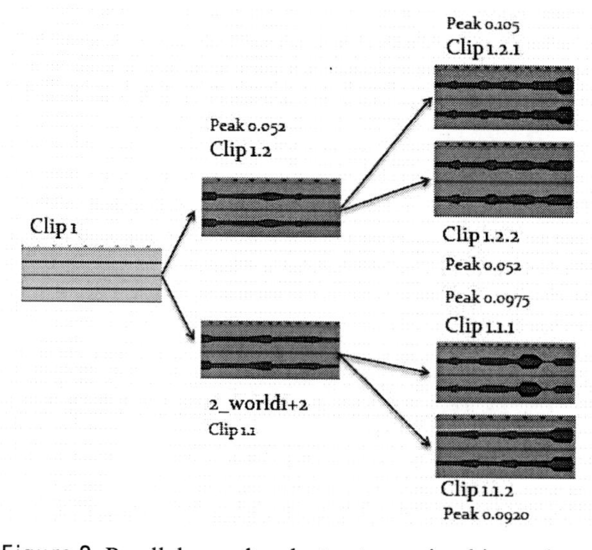

Figure 3. Parallel soundtrack structure using binaural beats sounds. Peaks indicate the maximum sample peak in the soundtrack in a clip.

4. SCRIPT

Little is mentioned here about the script, as it is desired to not reveal key storyline elements except when the film is viewed. The actual script was provided to the actors in a branching form, with all four routes in one script, as shown in Figure 4. (The figure is deliberately unreadable so as not to give away key story elements.) In summary: two students Charlie and Olivia arrive at the apartment of their friend to try and cheer her up on her 19th birthday. They find Connie, a physics student, has sealed herself in a coffin-sized box with a cyanide gas-capsule connected to a Geiger counter. At any time a large enough burst of cosmic rays in the atmosphere could trigger the cyanide and kill Connie; in fact it could already have happened. Charlie – also a physics student – realises Connie is performing a twisted version of a famous quantum physics experiment about the nature of reality, but one that was never meant to be performed in real-life. Over the next 10 minutes – through clips from their phones and a mysterious camera observing the room – the audience learn the true reason for the experiment.

A key inspiration for the film's creator was that the story refers to unresolved philosophical issues in quantum mechanics concerning how the observer effects the observed in physics experiments. This is paralleled by the audience sample affecting the observed story as they watch the film. Thus the mode of presentation of the story (live biosignal based editing) parallels the story content itself.

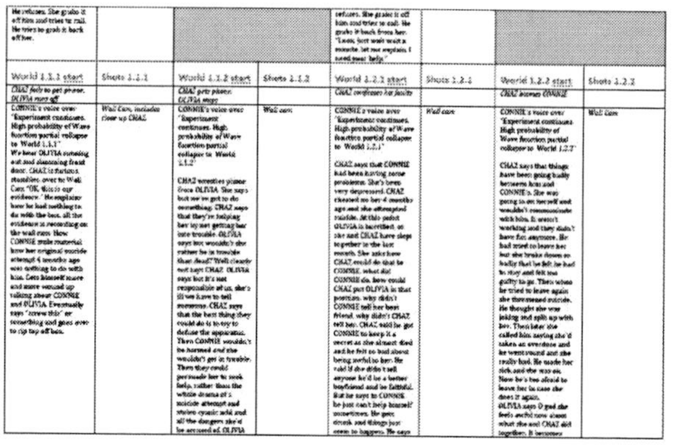

Figure 4. Section of script used by actors; near the top of this page the two possible paths each split into two again.

5. DISCUSSION

The system allows time-synchronous mapping of biosignal responses from four sensors to audio and video material, for the purpose of 'editing' a short film on the fly in direct response to a simple real-time metric of the participating audience's arousal. Four narrative structures are implemented, though many more are possible with the appropriate processing power — a version making use of distributed processing has been developed using User Datagram Protocol to send and receive control data and trigger video playback via a local area network. Larger numbers of sensors might reasonably be implemented by similar means.

In terms of sensor usage in the cinema environment, some people found the EEG headset uncomfortable, and one person found the muscle tension monitor uncomfortable. The sensors most amenable to calibration were heart rate, and also the muscle tension monitor, as the audience member could be asked to directly flex the area of muscle involved. EEG was the most difficult to calibrate because of the noisiness of the data and its artifacts, in fact a key addition to the system in future would be an artifact removal algorithm. GSR was also difficult to calibrate quickly because it was such a slow moving signal. The GSR also contributed the least to story pathway selection because of its slow-moving nature. The heart rate sensor, as well as being simple to calibrate, was the simplest to use. The downside was there was sometimes a false triggering of a heartbeat, so a suitably long averaging window needed to be used to filter these out.

The system might provide a useful platform for further work evaluating audience arousal through different narrative structures, (i.e., for emotional metering of real-world test material), or adapted to soundtrack-only manipulation, building on existing research into the affective changes which sound-tracking can induce [26, 27]. There remains a significant window for further work devising a method for incorporating valence metering to the affective estimation algorithm, applicable both to the real-time affective video system described here, and more widely to affective composition, music psychology, and emotional performance algorithms in computer music.

6. CONCLUSIONS

Affective mapping of arousal and timecode to video and sound selection, by means of a moving average estimation from four biosignal sensors (EKG, EEG, GSR, and EMG) allows the filmmaker to meter and respond to audience arousal in real-time with this system. The system described is capable of playing back full HD video and synchronous audio whilst monitoring and calculating the arousal estimate in real-time and was demoed to a live cinema audience at the Peninsula Arts Contemporary Music Festival, UK, on February 23rd 2013. Footage from the premier can be seen here: http://www.bbc.co.uk/news/technology-22436014

Acknowledgments

'many worlds' was commissioned by Peninsula Arts Contemporary Music Festival 2013, Sensing Memory.

7. REFERENCES

[1] L. Manovich, *Database as a Symbolic Form*, Cambridge, MIT Press 1998.

[2] F. Beacham, "Movies of the Future: Storytelling With Computers" *American Cinematographer*, April, p 4 - 12. American Society of Cinematographers 1995.

[3] P. Lunenfeld "The Myths of Interactive Cinema" In *Narrative Across Media: The Languages of Storytelling* ed. M.-L. Ryan, University of Nebraska Press, 2004.

[4] S. W. Gilroy, J. Porteous, F. Charles, and M. Cavazza, "PINTER: Interactive Storytelling with Physiological Input", *Proceedings of the 2012 ACM international conference on Intelligent User Interfaces*, Lisbon, Portugal, ACM 2012.

[5] P. Tikka. "Enactive Cinema Installation 'Obsession'" *Museum of Contemporary Art Kiasma, Helsinki*: Oblomovies and University of Art and Design. 2005.

[6] P. Tikka, A. Väljamäe, A. W. de Borst, R. Pugliese, N. Ravaja, M. Kaipainen, and Tapio Takala, "Enactive cinema paves way for understanding complex real-time social interaction in neuroimaging experiments" *Frontiers of Human Neuroscience*, vol. 6, p. 298, 2012.

[7] T. Castermans, M. Duvinage, and N. Riche, "Emotive Cinema", *QPSR of the numediart research program*, vol. 5, no. 1, March 2012.

[8] J. Kierkels and T. Pun, "Towards detection of interest during movie scenes", in *Proc. PetaMedia Workshop on Implicit, Human-Centered Tagging (HCT'08)*, 2008.

[9] D. Giakoumis, D. Tzovaras, K. Moustakas, and G. Hassapis, "Automatic Recognition of Boredom in Video Games Using Novel Biosignal Moment-Based Features", *IEEE Transactions On Affective Computing*, vol. 2, no. 3, July-September, IEEE 2011.

[10] J. A. Russell, "A circumplex model of affect.," *Journal of personality and social psychology*, vol. 39, no. 6, p. 1161, 1980.

[11] E. Schubert, "Measuring Emotion Continuously: Validity and Reliability of the Two-Dimensional Emotion-Space," *Australian Journal of Psychology*, vol. 51, no. 3, pp. 154–165, Dec. 1999.

[12] A. Mattek, "Emotional Communication in Computer Generated Music: Experimenting with Affective Algorithms," in *Proc. 26th Annual Conf. of the Society for Electro-Acoustic Music in the United States*, Miami, Florida, 2011.

[13] J. Doppler, J. Rubisch, M. Jaksche, and H. Raffaseder, "RaPScoM: towards composition strategies in a rapid score music prototyping framework," in *Proc. of the 6th Audio Mostly Conf.: A Conference on Interaction with Sound*, pp. 8–14, 2011.

[14] J. Rubisch, J. Doppler, and H. Raffaseder, "RAPSCOM - A Framework For Rapid Prototyping Of Semantically Enhanced Score Music." *Proceedings of Sound and Music Conference*, 2011.

[15] A. Kirke, "Application of Intermediate Multi-agent Systems to Integrated Algorithmic Composition and Expressive Performance of Music", PhD Thesis, Plymouth University, 2011.

[16] J. K. Vuoskoski and T. Eerola, "Measuring music-induced emotion: A comparison of emotion models, personality biases, and intensity of experiences," *Musicae Scientiae*, vol. 15, no. 2, pp. 159–173, Jul. 2011.

[17] T. Eerola and J. K. Vuoskoski, "A comparison of the discrete and dimensional models of emotion in music," *Psychology of Music*, vol. 39, no. 1, pp. 18–49, Aug. 2010.

[18] W. Trost, T. Ethofer, M. Zentner, and P. Vuilleumier, “Mapping Aesthetic Musical Emotions in the Brain,” *Cerebral Cortex*, Dec. 2011.

[19] M. Rossignac-Milon, "Affective Computing: A Survey Internship Report", *MIRALab*, University of Geneva, Switzerland, 2010.

[20] D. Sammler, M. Grigutsch, T. Fritz, and S. Koelsch, “Music and emotion: Electrophysiological correlates of the processing of pleasant and unpleasant music,” *Psychophysiology*, vol. 44, no. 2, pp. 293–304, 2007.

[21] S. Le Groux and P. Verschure, “Neuromuse: Training your brain through musical interaction,” in *Proceedings of the International Conference on Auditory Display, Copenhagen, Denmark*, 2009.

[22] V. Salimpoor, M. Benovoy, G. Longo, J. Cooperstock, and R. Zatorre, "The Rewarding Aspects of Music Listening Are Related to Degree of Emotional Arousal". *PLoS ONE*, vol. 4, no. 10, e7487. doi:10.1371/journal.pone.0007487, 2009.

[23] R. Hoehn-Saric, R. Hazlett, T. Pourmotabbed, and D. McLeod, "Does muscle tension reflect arousal? Relationship between electromyographic and electroencephalographic recordings", *Psychiatry Research*, vol. 71, no. 1, pp. 49–55, Elsevier 1997.

[24] L. Schmidt and L. Trainor, "Frontal brain electrical activity (EEG) distinguishes valence and intensity of musical emotions", *Cognition and Emotion*, vol. 15, no. 4, pp.487–500, Taylor & Francis 2001

[25] J. Owens, E. Justine and G. Marsh, "Binaural auditory beats affect vigilance performance and mood", *Physiology and Behavior*, vol. 63, no. 2, pp.249-52, Elsevier 1998.

[26] S. K. Marshall and A. J. Cohen, “Effects of musical soundtracks on attitudes toward animated geometric figures,” *Music Perception*, pp. 95–112, 1988.

[27] A. J. Cohen, “Music as a source of emotion in film,” *Music and emotion: Theory and research*, pp. 249–272, 2001.

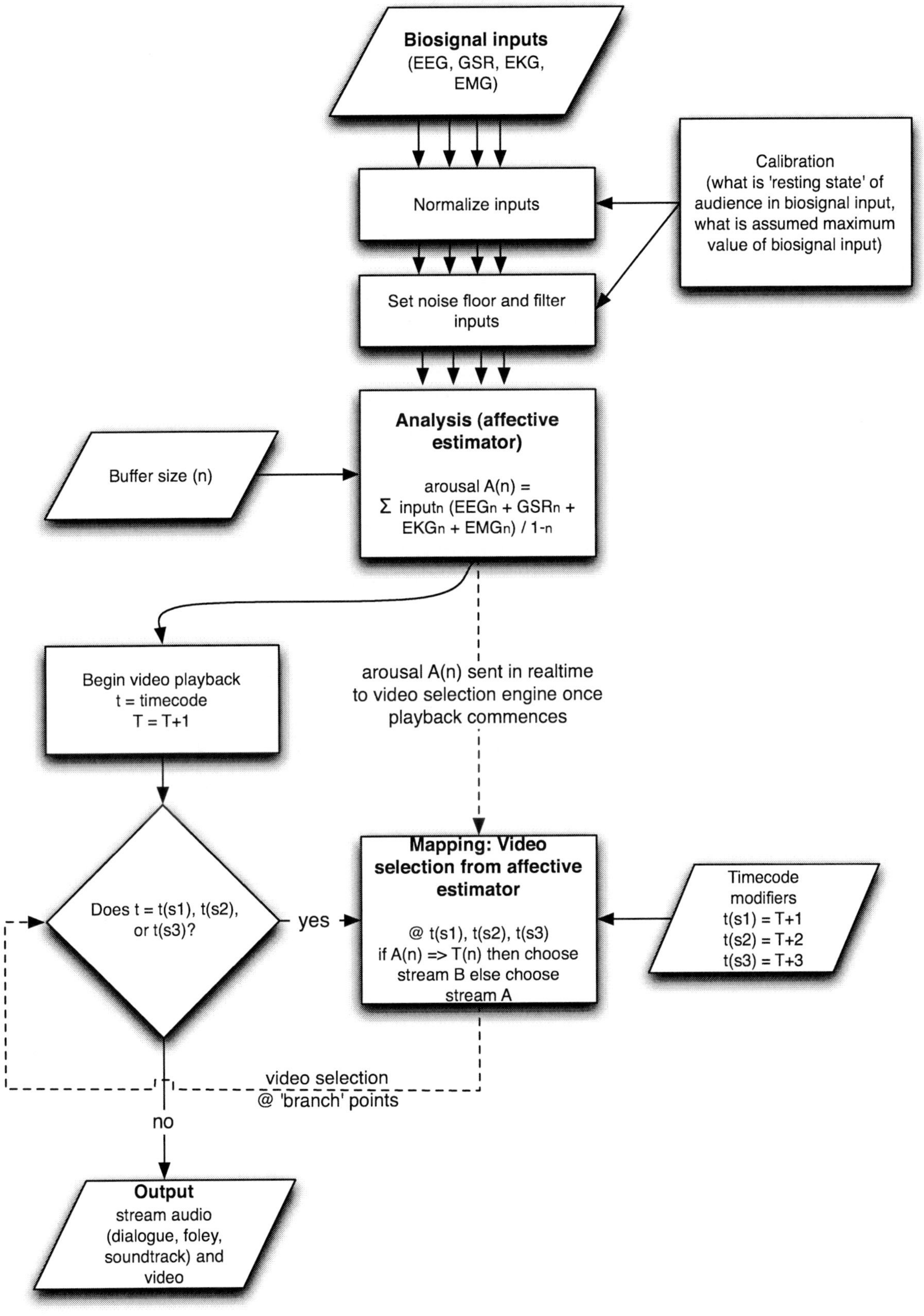

Figure 1. Flow chart overview of system: Biosignal inputs are calibrated, normalized, and averaged to determine values for synchronously selecting video outputs

IMPROVING THE REAL-TIME PERFORMANCE OF A CAUSAL AUDIO DRUM TRANSCRIPTION SYSTEM

Marius Miron
INESC TEC, Porto, Portugal
mmiron@inescporto.pt

Matthew E.P. Davies
INESC TEC, Porto, Portugal
mdavies@inescporto.pt

Fabien Gouyon
INESC TEC, Porto, Portugal
fgouyon@inescporto.pt

ABSTRACT

In this paper we analyze and improve an audio drum transcription system with respect to real-time constraints. Furthermore, we propose a novel evaluation method, which allows us to systematically explore situations which are likely to occur in real-life drum performances. Then, we evaluate the architecture on a drum loops database, and discuss the influence of the size of the evaluation window, and of the classification method. Finally, we present the implementation in Pure Data and Max MSP, and propose a "do-it-yourself" technique which allows anyone to modify, and build a drum transcription system.

1. INTRODUCTION

Drum transcription aims to extract symbolic drum notation from audio signals. The task involves detecting a set of event candidates and labeling them. Additionally, a drum transcription system must face challenges related to the overlapping of events, presence of different sounds, or variation in timbre and amplitude of the drum events.

Assigning labels to drum sounds in audio recordings has been applied to two types of data: drum loops [1], [2], [3], [4], [5], and polyphonic music including a mixture of instruments [6], [7], [8], [9]. All of these systems work offline, and each one of them has a different way of solving the challenges of drum transcription. A classifier is used in [3] and [6], while other approaches rely on using a set of adaptive templates [8] and [9], or non-negative matrix factorization [7]. The issue of overlapping sounds was addressed in [5] by using decoy spectral templates along with the learned Gamma Mixture Model templates. Other methods, as [2] and [7], detect events in different frequency bands to separate different classes of sounds that might overlap.

Regarding online processing, a real-time classification algorithm for isolated percussion sounds, implemented in Pure Data, was proposed in [10]. The method trains a classifier using 300 features across ten overlapping windows, and does not address the subject of drum performances which are made of a mixture of sounds. Furthermore, another algorithm [11, p 101] implemented in Super Collider, is used for approximate bass drum and snare drum detection, as a part of a real-time beat-tracking system. This algorithm does not transcribe hi-hats, and was not evaluated in the scope of drum performance transcription. Both the Pure Data [1] and Super Collider [2] implementations are available as open-source.

We proposed a real-time system [12], along with an implementation for Pure Data and Max MSP. The algorithm detects drum onsets, extracts a set of features, and classifies each event as either bass drum (BD), snare drum (SD), or hi-hat cymbal (HH), from a mixture of the three classes, plus toms. Additionally, it uses an instance filtering (IF) stage to filter overlapping events fed to the three K-nearest neighbor (KNN) classifiers. Similar to other past methods,([6] and [8]) a global onset detector is used but the overall performance is improved by the IF stage.

The offline algorithms have a set of advantages because they can post-process the data, or use a large buffer. For instance, they can adjust onset times by shifting them backwards in order to start the analysis closer to the real onset of the drum, as in [8]. Tanghe et al. [6] proposed a system that works with streaming audio, but onset computation is not causal and the buffer used for onset detection is 105 ms, which is very large for drums. Moreover, during the MIREX 2005 contest, the time frame to locate an onset was $\pm$ 30 ms. Because of the symmetric window, the evaluation does not assume causality.

On the other hand, a system which can transcribe drums online can be useful in building machine listening driven interactive systems, in tasks such as instrument syncopation, or real-time beat tracking. This task is particularly challenging because a real-time system needs to be causal, and works under real-time constraints. Such a system faces several challenges. First, it should reliably transcribe audio as fast as possible. Furthermore, the minimum time necessary to detect a drum onset or compute features, might be lower than the time between two consecutive events. Additionally, the events might not be aligned to the metrical grid, and they might overlap.

We present an audio drum transcription system which responds to the challenges addressed above and has a better real-time response than the system discussed in [12]. Morevoer, we propose a novel evaluation of real-life situation, sound overlapping, and systematically explore it. For this purpose we design a database which comprises different levels of overlapping events. Additionally, we test

[1] http://williambrent.conflations.com/pages/research.html/
[2] http://www.sussex.ac.uk/Users/nc81/bbcut2.html

the system with a sequential K-means clustering algorithm which doesn't require a training phase, and classifies the instances on the fly. This algorithm requires less processing time, hence is a faster alternative when it comes to classifying data in real-time.

This paper is structured as follows. In Section 2, we present an overview of the existing system, as well as the system improved for real time. In Section 3, we evaluate the improved system along with the existing system. First we present a novel method, which allows us to systematically evaluate different levels of sound overlapping, which are likely to occur in real-life situations. Additionally, we evaluate both of the systems on a drum loops database. In Section 4, we introduce a modular implementation of the drum-transcription system, which can be easily modified for multiple live setups. Section 5 concludes this paper.

2. METHOD

2.1 Overview Of The Existing System

The existing transcription system, as described in [12], works with real-time stereo audio, sampled at 44100 Hz, and is implemented in Pure Data and Max MSP. The architecture of the system is depicted in Figure 1.

The algorithm uses a high frequency content onset detection stage to detect global onset candidates for the BD, SD and HH classes. For each detect event, it extracts three feature vectors, in the BD, SD, and HH frequency bands. These bands have fixed cutoff frequencies determined empirically: for BD we have a low-pass filter at 90 Hz, for SD we have a band-pass filter at 280 Hz with 20 Hz bandwidth, and for HH we have a high-pass filter at 9000 Hz.

The features are extracted over 10 overlapping frames of size 43 ms. The feature vectors are averaged with the energy in each frame. The salient part for extracting the features is 132 ms after the onset detection, but can be as small as 54 ms, if a new event comes earlier.

An instance filtering (IF) stage, for each of the BD, SD, and HH, comes next and filters the event candidates. The filtered event candidates are then fed to three KNN classifiers. The IF stage deploys a second onset detection stage, with higher frequency resolution in each of the BD, SD and HH frequency bands. Because for this stage we use a larger window size (1024 samples, 23.2 ms) and hop size (256 samples, 5.8 ms), thus there is better spectral discrimination, the IF is more efficient at filtering instances. The evaluation shows that the IF stage increases the performance of the existing system.

2.2 Improving The Existing System For Real-Time

There are three major improvements on the original system, which increase the real-time performance, and which are explained in this Section.

First, using separate onset detectors is a better solution when detecting class specific onsets because we are able to control the parameters of each onset detector separately.

Secondly, the system can give an output at any time, rather than waiting a response from the classifier. This is particulary useful when the interval between consecutive events

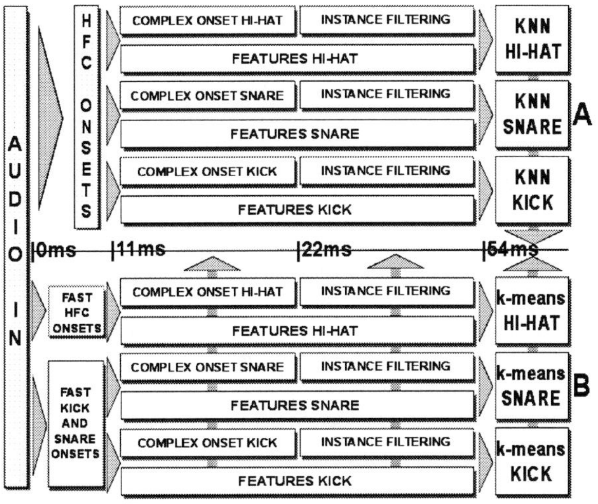

Figure 1: Comparison of the existing architecture (A), and the architecture improved for real-time (B), regarding the minimum response time

is smaller than the time to compute features or perform the IF. Additionally, during feature extraction, we do not take 10 overlapping 43 ms frames, but just one.

Thirdly, we use a sequential K-means clustering algorithm which is faster than the KNN classifier in a real-time situation [13, p 210].

2.2.1 Event Detection

Because the global onset detection can overdetect events for a class and misdetect for others, we propose an alternative to this system, using separate onset detectors than a single global one. By these means, it is less rather to have an overlapping situation since the event candidates are detected separately.

This fast onset detector uses a window size of 512 samples (11.6 ms) and hop size 128 samples (2.9 ms). Using such a small window does not yield a good enough frequency resolution to correctly separate between BD and SD. Moreover, the attack of the BD occurs at a higher frequency than the decay, and roughly in the same frequency band as the SD. Thus, we use a single complex onset detector in the SD band, 280 Hz with 20 Hz bandwidth, which captures the attacks of the BD and SD. We keep the high frequency onset for HH, since this type of drum has significant high frequency content.

2.2.2 Architecture

The architectures of the exiting system and of the one improved for real-time are portrayed in Figure 1, with respect to real-time constraints.

First, regarding the response time, the existing system can give a response in "maximum" of 143 ms. Because we need to give an answer as fast as possible, we extract features in a single window of 43 ms, instead of taking 10 overlapping frames. Thus, the improved system will give a response in maximum 54 ms: 11 ms, the time to detect an onset, plus 43 ms, the time needed to extract the features.

Secondly, the existing system has a "minimum" time response of 54 ms, the time needed to compute the features for the first window. Therefore, when a new onset occurs in the interval [0-54] ms, the analysis for the current event stops and the current event is missed. Thus, the existing system can not deal with situations when an event occurs earlier than 54 ms, and it misses events.

In the improved version, we would rather have an answer from the system rather than failing to detect events. If a new event occurs between 11 ms and 22 ms, then the system stops the current analysis, and offers the detected onset as an output. Similarly, if another onset is received between 22 ms and 54 ms, the system stops the current analysis, and offers as output the event filtered by IF stage. Thus, we reduced the minimum response time to 11 ms, the time needed to detect an onset.

In this way, the improved version deals properly with cases where the interval between two consecutive events is lower than the time needed to compute onsets or features.

2.2.3 Sequential K-Means Clustering

The existing system uses a binary KNN classifier for each BD, SD, and HH, in order to assign a class to each feature vector. Each instance is classified as member or non-member of the BD, SD and HH class.

The real-time performance of the classification algorithm depends on the number of points trained p. In this case, during the classification, finding the nearest neighbor takes $O(pn)$ time [13, p 210]. A faster alternative would be to have an algorithm which learns from the data gradually, rather than storing a database of learned instances. The sequential K-means clustering allows updating the centers of the clusters as new data points arrive. The time needed to classify an instance is $O(2n)$, assuming that we have two clusters. Thus, we obtain a faster, more real-time response by using the online K-means clustering rather than the KNN classifier.

The algorithm, as presented in [14], starts with the initialization of the initial means m_k, where k is the number of clusters. Having a new instance x, a distance is computed from x to each mean of each cluster. The closest cluster i is picked and its mean is updated with thew newly classified value $m_i = m_i + \frac{1}{n_i} * (x - m_i)$, where n_i is the number of the instances in a class. A "forgetful" K-means assumes replacing the counts $\frac{1}{n_i}$ with a constant $\frac{1}{a}$, and, thus, forgetting the older means by giving more weight to the recent instances.

We have three sequential k-means binary classifiers which can start with initial random means or can be initialized. Because we have binary classifiers, looking for either BD, SD, and HH, we initialize them with the features extracted from white noise filtered in the corresponding bands for BD, SD and HH. The parameters of the filters are as follows: the cutoff frequency for the low-pass filter is at 90 Hz, for the band-pass filter at 280 Hz with 20 Hz bandwidth, and for the high-pass filter at 7000 Hz. Because we are using a common onset detector for the BD and SD, both of the corresponding classifiers are initialized with white noise in BD and a SD bands. The HH classifier is initialized with white noise in HH and a SD bands.

3. EVALUATION

In Section 3.1, we present a novel method of evaluation for a drum transcription system by systematically analyzing the overlapping between events. We evaluate the existing architecture, and the one improved for real-time on the overlapping sounds database. Then, in Section 3.2, we test both of the architectures on the original drum loops database presented in [12]. Finally, we compare the performance of the k-means classifier with the one of the KNN classifier.

The evaluation window gives the maximum time deviation of a detected onset from the actual event. Because we impose real-time constraints, we set the size of the window to 18 ms, hence smaller than 35 ms, the one used in [12]. We analyze the consequences of choosing a smaller window size in Section 3.2.

The evaluation metrics, F-measure, F, precision, p, and recall, r, are described in [13, p 270]. Because we want to see distribution of precision across the BD, SD, and HH classes, we plot the $1 - p$ value instead of p. If this value is closer to 1, then the algorithm detects a high number of incorrect instances.

3.1 Drum Sounds Overlapping Analysis

Live performances are different from simple drum loops in terms of varying amplitudes and event displacement. We want to determine in which ways the existing transcription system described in [12] can be improved for real-time situations.

Furthermore, when building our system, we do not wish to make any assumptions about the metrical positions for any of the drum classes. We want to analyze every possible case. Thus, we build a database which contains systematic overlapping between BD, SD, or HH events. This database allows us to detect possible problems with our algorithm, when facing various situations that often appear in drum performances.

Moreover, the database is generated with sounds from a single drum kit. We are not using other drum kits because the only variable we want to analyze with this database is the sound overlapping. For the same reason, the effect of using the k-means classifier will be evaluated separately in Section 3.2.2. Therefore, we are using a KNN classifier for both of the evaluated systems.

Fewer instances in a KNN model result in faster performance [13, p 208] . In order to have a faster answer from the KNN classifier, we reduced the number of the training instances to 373, compared to 884 in [12], by removing different loudness excerpts when the sounds have the same timbre.

3.1.1 Database

We introduce a database made of different overlapping levels between various combinations of BD, SD and HH. Let $C = \{BD, SD, HH\}$ be an event with a duration of 100 ms. For each permutation of three C, we generate one file with a different interval between the events. Thus, we have a combination of events $E_i(a, b, c)$, where $a, b, c \in C =$

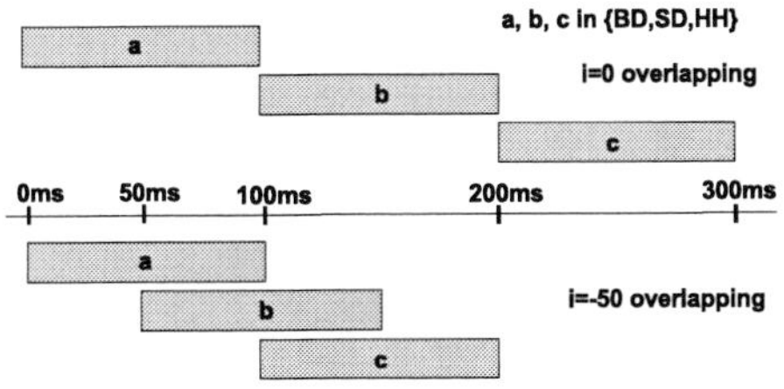

Figure 2: Two cases of overlapping sounds , $i = 0$ and $i = -50$

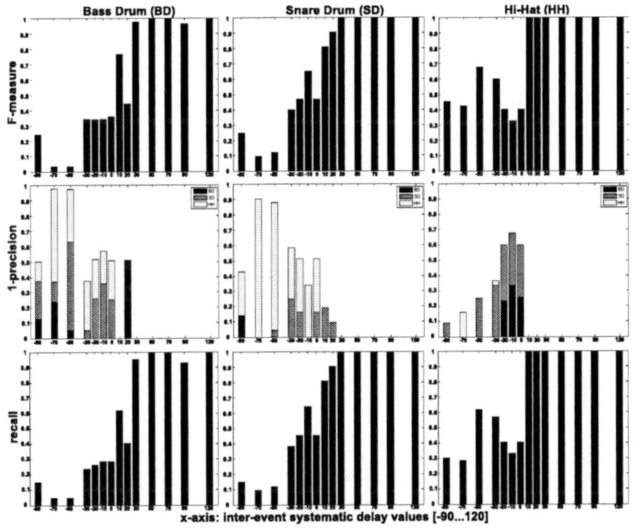

Figure 3: The original architecture, used in [12], tested with the overlapping sounds database

$\{BD, SD, HH\}$, and $i \in \{-90, -70, -50, -30, -20, -10, 0, 10, 20, 30, 50, 70, 90, 120\}$. For $i = 0$ an event starts where a previous event ends. For $i < 0$ the events overlap with i ms. For $i > 0$ there is no overlapping between events. An example of two situations is represented in Figure 2.

The database contains 210 MIDI files and the corresponding audio files, having nine events per file, in different combinations. The audio for the evaluation part is generated using Timidity++ [3] , by rendering midi drum loops from different genres, through a single drum kit.

3.1.2 Existing System Evaluation

Evaluating the existing system proposed in [12] , on this sound overlapping database, allows us to systematically analyze the behavior of the system along different variables. For instance, we can look at how the system performs when we have audio made of a single class of sounds, a combination of two sounds, or a combination of three different sounds. Furthermore, by comparing the performance on different overlapping levels, we can tell how well the system reacts in real-time.

The performance of the existing system when testing it on the overlapping sounds database is depicted in Figure 3. The system has few errors when sounds are not overlapping, $i > 0$. On the other hand, events are missed when

[3] http://timidity.sourceforge.net/

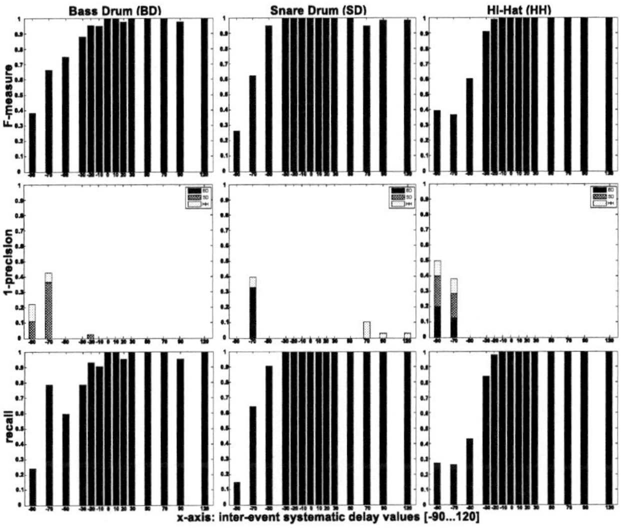

Figure 4: Results for testing the improved architecture with IF on the systematic sound overlapping database

sounds are overlapping, $i < 0$, even if the recall for onset detection is greater than 0.9 across all classes and delay times.

Furthermore, we can find important information about the system by analyzing the $1 - p$ distribution across all drum classes. For instance, we can tell that some events are wrongly classified as snares when we have hi-hats in audio. Moreover, there are few false positives in the -90 ms delay times because the interval between the two onsets, 10ms, is lower than the time resolution of the onset detection function. Thus, the onsets are detected simultaneously.

3.1.3 Real-time Architecture Evaluation

We tested the improved architecture, with the IF stage, on the overlapping sounds database. The results are presented in Figure 4. There is clear an improvement, in rejecting wrongly classified instances, and decreasing the number of the events missed.

The number of false positives significantly drops, especially for -50 ms delay time, when the system does not have the necessary time to compute the first feature window and classify the event. In this case, the interval between two consecutive events is 50 ms, and the minimum time to compute the features is 56 ms. For the -70 ms delay time, the interval between two consecutive events is 30 ms, and the algorithm exits with the output of the fast onset detector, because the IF stage needs 35 ms for processing. Finally, for event delay values of -90 ms, the interval is 10 ms, lower than the time needed to compute an actual fast onset, thus a lot of events are missed. In Figure 4, this yields a low value for recall.

3.2 Evaluation On The Drum Loops Database

The existing system [12] was originally tested on a drum loops database, comprising 177 drum loops, from different genres, at different tempi, and generated with 50 drum kits. First, we test the improved and the existing systems on this

	18 ms window			35 ms window		
	F	p	r	F	p	r
BD OG	0.76	0.88	0.67	0.81	0.93	0.71
BD RT	0.81	0.88	0.75	0.87	0.94	0.81
BD RTv	0.55	0.58	0.52	0.89	0.95	0.83
SD OG	0.74	0.85	0.66	0.78	0.88	0.69
SD RT	0.81	0.89	0.75	0.82	0.91	0.76
HH OG	0.77	0.90	0.67	0.81	0.93	0.71
HH RT	0.78	0.89	0.69	0.81	0.93	0.72

Table 1: The results of the original system (OG), and the improved systems (RT) with respect to the size of the evaluation window

database, by discussing the consequences of a smaller evaluation window, which imposes more real-time constraints. Secondly, we evaluate the k-means clustering method.

3.2.1 Evaluation Window Constraints

In [12], the size of the evaluation window was 35 ms, which is enough to capture all onsets, but not adjusted to the real-time constraints. Therefore, we want to see the if we can reduce this window to 18 ms, approximately half of the original size. We test the improved system (RT), along with the original architecture (OG), on the original drum loops database presented in [12], with window sizes of 18 ms and 35 ms. Furthermore, we test the hypothesis of using a separate onset detector for BD (RTv), which detects complex onsets below 90 Hz. We show that using a single onset detector for BD and SD is a better option, when dealing with real-time constraints.

As we mentioned in Section 2.2, because the attack of the BD occurs roughly in the same frequency band as the attack of SD, there is no reason to use separate onset detectors for BD and SD. This hypothesis is supported by the results in Table 1, when comparing the BD RT, the system with a common onset detector, with BD RTv, the system with separate onset detectors for BD and SD. There is a significant drop of performance when looking for the BD onsets in time intervals smaller than 18 ms. In the case of BD RTv, most of the correct BD events are detected in the [18-35] ms interval, on the decay of the sound, rather than on the attack.

Furthermore, the performance does not drop significantly for SD and HH, when comparing the OG and the RT systems across different window sizes. The onsets for the BD class are better detected in larger time span. As we showed above, this can be explained by the acoustic features of this drum.

3.2.2 Evaluation Of The Classification Method

We compare the performance of the system using a sequential K-means clustering algorithm (KM), with the one using a KNN classifier (KNN).

First we transcribe every file sequentially. This configuration is called KM ALL. The system learns continuously, as the means for each class are updated correspondingly when a new instance is classified.

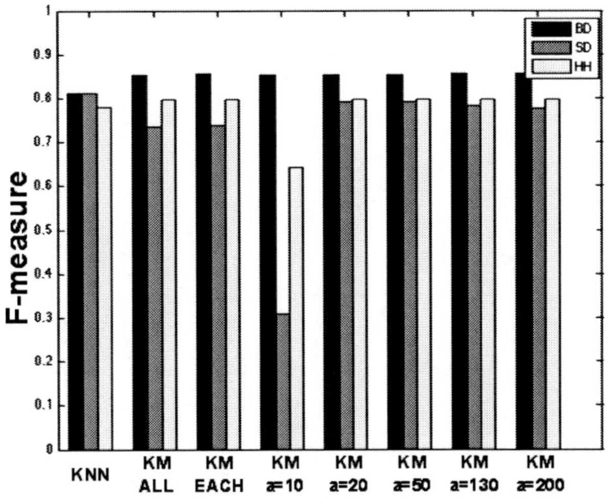

Figure 5: Comparison of the system using a KNN classifier (KNN), with the same system using the sequential K-means clustering (KM), in different configurations. ALL is running all all files through the K-means, EACH is resetting the K-means clustering before transcribing each file. Then we test the "forgetful" K-means configuration for different values of a

Secondly, in a real-life situation one has to use the sequential classification to detect the drum events performed with a single drum kit. We want to know how a sequential classifier performs regardless of the previous file. Thus we reset the K-means classifier each time a new file is transcribed. This configuration is called KM EACH.

Thirdly, we analyze the case of the "forgetful" K-means, as described in Section 2.2.3, and the influence of the constant a on the performance. We want to see how giving more weight to the recent instances affects the results. We assign several values for $a \in \{10, 20, 50, 130, 200\}$.

The results are presented in Figure 5. Using the K-means clustering algorithm gives better results than the KNN, when classifying BD. The F-measure is 4% higher for the KM. The results for the SD are lower with 3%, since other drums as toms occur in the same frequency band, thus classifying this type of drum requires some apriori knowledge about the spectrum of the sound. The results for the HH are similar for both of the KNN and KM. Additionally, resetting the K-means for each file KM EACH, does not decrease the performance.

Regarding the influence of the parameter a, the performance of the BD classifier is constant, regardless of the values of a. For the SD, the F measure shows that we need at least $a = 20$ instances for a good performance, but we get the highest value for $a = 130$. This happens because the SD needs to separate between many classes of events, including toms, thus it requires some long-term learning, rather than using the most recent instances. Furthermore, the HH class as well requires at least $a = 20$.

4. IMPLEMENTATION

The implementation of the transcription system can be downloaded as open-source from the Github repositories for Pure

Data [4] and Max MSP [5].

Users can choose from already built transcription patches or decide to built a new one. They can patch together different versions of the main modules: onset detection, feature computation, and classification. In this way, they can choose from different versions of the algorithm presented in this paper. For instance, they can use KNN classifier, or the sequential K-means. In the same way, the BD, SD and HH parts can use separate or common onset detectors, and different resolutions for the feature computation.

5. CONCLUSIONS

In this paper we proposed an audio drum transcription system improved for real-time performance. Additionally, we presented a novel evaluation which allowed us to systematically analyze the overlapping level between sounds. We discussed the problems of an existing causal drum transcription system, when facing real-time audio drum performances, and we proposed several improvements.

The evaluation shows that the improved system achieves better performance when dealing with different situations of overlapping sounds, which can occur frequently in real-life drum performances. Furthermore, the improved system achieves better performance than the original when tested on a drum loops database.

Finally, we proposed a "do-it-yourself" implementation in Pure Data and MaxMSP, which allows non-experts to build and customize their own drum transcription systems.

Acknowledgments

This work is supported by the ERDF – European Regional Development Fund through the (FCOM-01-0124-FEDER-014732) COMPETE Programme (operational programme for competitiveness) and by National Funds through the FCT – Fundacao para a Ciencia e a Tecnologia (Portuguese Foundation for Science and Technology) within project Shake-it, Grant PTDC/EAT-MMU/ 112255/2009. Part of this research was supported by the CASA project with reference PTDC/EIA-CCO/111050/2009 (FCT), and by the MAT project funded by ON.2.

6. REFERENCES

[1] D. Fitzgerald, R. Lawlor, and E. Coyle, "Drum transcription using automatic grouping of events and prior subspace analysis," *Proceedings of the 4th European Workshop on Image Analysis for Multimedia Interactive Services*, pp. 306–309, 2003.

[2] G. Tzanetakis, A. Kapur, and R. McWalter, "Subband-based Drum Transcription for Audio Signals," *2005 IEEE 7th Workshop on Multimedia Signal Processing*, pp. 1–4, Oct. 2005.

[3] O. Gillet and G. Richard, "Automatic transcription of drum loops," *International Conference on Acoustics, Speech, and Signal Processing ICASSP04, Montreal, Quebec, 2004*, pp. 269–272, 2004.

[4] ——, "Drum track transcription of polyphonic music using noise subspace projection," *Proceedings of the 6th International Conference on Music Information Retrieval*, pp. 92–99, 2005.

[5] E. Battenberg, V. Huang, and D. Wessel, "Toward live drum separation using probabilistic spectral clustering based on the itakura-saito divergence," in *AES 45th Conference: Applications of Time-Frequency Processing in Audio*, Helsinki, Finland, 2012.

[6] K. Tanghe, S. Degroeve, and B. De Baets, "An algorithm for detecting and labeling drum events in polyphonic music," in *Proceedings of the first Music Information Retrieval Evaluation eXchange (MIREX)*, 2005.

[7] J. Paulus and T. Virtanen, "Drum transcription with non-negative spectrogram factorisation," *13th European Signal Processing Conference*, 2005.

[8] K. Yoshii, M. Goto, and H. Okuno, "Drum sound recognition for polyphonic audio signals by adaptation and matching of spectrogram templates with harmonic structure suppression," *IEEE Transactions on Audio, Speech and Language Processing*, vol. 15, no. 1, pp. 333–345, Jan. 2007.

[9] V. Sandvold, F. Gouyon, and P. Herrera, "Drum sound classification in polyphonic audio recordings using localized sound models." in *ISMIR*, 2004.

[10] W. Brent, "Cepstral analysis tools for percussive timbre identification," *Proceedings of the 3rd International Pure Data Conference*, 2009.

[11] N. Collins, "Towards autonomous agents for live computer music: Realtime machine listening and interactive music systems," Ph.D. dissertation, 2006.

[12] M. Miron, M. Davies, and F. Gouyon, "An open-source drum transcription system for pure data and max msp," in *The 38th International Conference on Acoustics, Speech, and Signal Processing*, Vancouver, Canada, 2013.

[13] D. Hand, *Principles of data mining*. The MIT Press, Jan. 2001, vol. 30, no. 7.

[14] R. Duda, P. Hart, and D. Stork, *Pattern classification*, ser. Pattern Classification and Scene Analysis: Pattern Classification. Wiley, 2001.

[4] http://github.com/SMC-INESC/drumtranscription_pd

[5] http://github.com/SMC-INESC/drumtranscription_maxmsp

Creating Expressive Piano Performance Using a Low-dimensional Performance Model

Yupeng Gu
Indiana University
yupgu@indiana.edu

Christopher Raphael
Indiana University
craphael@indiana.edu

ABSTRACT

A model is presented for representing and generating piano performance. The model has far fewer parameters than the number of notes. This model explicitly addresses one of the fundamental characteristic of music performance that different areas in a performance have very different kinds of objectives or strategies that are employed. A graphical model is introduced to represent the evolution of the discrete strategies and tempo and dynamic progression. We design interactive procedures that allow users to modify the model intuitively. An algorithm is described to estimate parameters from partial performances that represent the skeleton of the music. Experiments are presented on the two-piano version of Rhapsody in Blue by George Gershwin.

1. INTRODUCTION

Music performance is an indispensable link in the chain connecting composer and listener. Performers use their skills, passions, expressions and desires to bring the music to life. Musicians have been serving this honored role for centuries. With the rapid development of computer technology, a growing interest appears over the role of the computer in this process. We propose an attempt to structure the problem. Although the idea could be generalized to many types of music, this work concerns itself in the context of Western classical music.

Musical performance usually does not have as many parameters to it as there are notes in a piece. We believe a performance is *much lower* dimensional than the note-by-note detail level (e.g. the parameters used in MIDI). Most notes are not acting independently, they are guided by higher-level notions or "inner motion" [1, 2]. There are usually strong correlations within a group of notes. This higher-level notion fits how musicians think of and communicate about music.

Many works have been done for modeling piano performances. While some [3–5] focus on providing methods of performance analysis, we want to design a performance model that is aiming for reproducing, modifying and creating expressive performances. Thus, it is not necessary for our model to have an understanding of musical structures that are often described by musicians. Rather, we seek a mathematical model to represent performance with a higher-level notion that can adapt to most situations. The model will consist of discrete states that describe different performance behaviors and continuous variables that describe tempo, timing and dynamic details of the different states.

Applications of such a generative performance models are numerous. One of the motivations of this work is to provide an easier way for more people to perform music, though the model could be applied broadly.

While almost all of us enjoy listening to music, being able to play music is also a very rewarding experience. However, it is not as easy to perform as to listen. To fill the gap between musical ideas and performance, musicians usually spend decades learning, developing, practicing and refining their techniques. Take piano as an example, the technique includes how to hit the correct notes at correct times, how to balance the volume within a group of notes, how to figure out the fingering etc. To make it even harder, a pianist once exaggerated, "It is not considered ready for a pianist to be able to play something right, you need to play everything 10 out of 10 times right to be ready for a performance." As a result, non-professionals can hardly enjoy performing music that requires certain level of technique to play. This left us singing, humming, describing and roughly playing to express and exchange our musical ideas. These methods are not ideal, but they require much less skill. iPad apps that allow one to play complicated music just by tapping the screen also gain a lot of attention recently including the million sold app "magic piano" [6]. These apps fulfilled people's needs to play but they don't allow much expressive control from the individual. Practicing still seems to be the only way towards good expressive performance. But it is fair to say some parts of practicing are quite "mechanical". It would be great if we can have a performance model that will always generate correct notes and reasonable correlation among them, but still capable of being expressive. We attempt to use such model to ease the process of practicing and hope to bring the joy of performing to more people. Our goal is to create a complete performance based on music ideas in few simple and incomplete reductions played by an user.

As a sub-problem, the question of how to systematically change a digital performance meaningfully can find a possible solution using our performance model. For a very long time, the only way to create an expressive performance digitally is having someone perform on an electronic instrument and record it directly. In this case often we may have a decent performance recorded with some parts of the performance unsatisfying. The only thing we could do to improve such performance is to "tweak" parameters at the individual note level and hope some combinations might work. This is clearly an unnatural and unmusical way to modify an expressive performance. It would be better to operate on a higher-level representation of the interpretation such as our proposed performance model that understands the notion of gestures and phrases. For instance, when we modify the timing or dynamic of a single note, some other parameters must compensate to retain a musical sense as specified in the performance model. Score-writing and MIDI-creating program are two of the obvious examples that could benefit from this method.

Such a method for creating performances could be considered as a special example of the expressive rendering problem. The rendering problem comes with growing interest in generating performances that can match the level of trained musicians along with the development of the computer technology. The existing rendering systems are mostly rule-based or case-based. Some systems include extracting and applying rules with parameters [7, 8], while others take advantages of statistical model that can learn from a large dataset and generate predictions for new performances based on similar music context from the dataset [9, 10].

While building an artificial performer from scratch could be very difficult [7, 8], creating expressive performance from a performance model can be an easier task to address. Although it is less ambitious, we think this approach has its own advantages. The first advantage of our performance model is that it is much lower dimensional than the MIDI performances. Hence it is easier to estimate our model parameters than to estimate all the details for every note. The second is that we can use such a performance model in an interactive system that can learn and improve from more specified inputs. Our model is not an answer to the original rendering problem since it may require many explicit information from human input. But it is capable of rendering expressive music without a professional performer.

A musically meaningful model of performance can also be used as a visualization tool. It is often an interesting experience for musicians to listen to a recording of themselves. As a listener, one has a different perspective and judges the performance more objectively. However, listening to a recording is time consuming, and we can only access a small amount of information at one time. Our model can be used to visualize rhythmic interpretation in a discrete way, so musicians can see and explore an entire performance at once. Furthermore, such visualization can also be used to compare different performances, so it will be easier for musicians to compare with other players.

Another possible application of such model is in creating an accompaniment system. A traditional accompaniment system seeks to create a flexible accompaniment to a live soloist that follows the player [11–13]. It could be useful in many music collaboration scenarios. Most Western classical music involves a collection of instruments. So activities such as practice, rehearsal and performance require multiple people to coordinate time and space with one another. A computer music accompanist could provide an alternative solution. A musician would practice with such a computer system when it is difficult to arrange a real rehearsal. This will be a better experience than practicing alone since a more realistic music context is provided. For amateurs and young students, such a system may enable them to play certain music in a complete form which would otherwise be impossible, making the musical experience more accessible and enjoyable. The accompaniment problem can be considered as an estimation problem for the performance model with an incomplete performance (e.g. a single instrument from an ensemble).

We present a mathematical model in section 2. There is a large literature on models that combine discrete state variables with Gaussian variables in fields such as economics, medical science and control engineering [14–17]. These models are known alternately as Markov jump process, hybrid models, state-space models with switching and switching Kalman filter. We think this type of model suits our purpose of creating a model for a piano performance. An interactive process that uses user input to complete the model is presented in section 3. Experiments are demonstrated in section 4.

2. THE MODEL

We only consider piano music in this work. Thus, a piano roll type of representation is most suitable here. A music score is represented as a series of music notes $r = \{r_1, r_2, ..., r_N\}$. Where $r_n = \{p_n, b_n, v_n, t_n, d_n, s_n\}$. p_n indicates the pitch of note r_n. b_n indicates the music time of note r_n and is expressed in terms of measure and beat. v_n is the MIDI velocity of r_n that describes the volume. It is a integer number between 1 and 127. t_n denotes the performed onset time of note r_n and is expressed in terms of seconds. d_n describes the duration of note r_n in terms of seconds. s_n is the discrete state associated with the note. The possible discretes states are described by the set $\Sigma = \{\alpha_1, \alpha_2, \alpha_3, \alpha_4\}$ which indicate different tempo behaviors.

Although piano music is often polyphonic and has many voices, we start with a simpler case first. If a part or a voice is ***monophonic***, we introduce a switching Kalman filter model.

One of the most important ideas of our model is the discrete states. Here is a brief explanation of the meaning of the 4 states. α_1**: constant speed** – represents the scenario where the performer plays in a steady rhythm; α_2**: slowing down**– represents a section of music where the performer gradually slows down; α_3**: speeding up**– represents a section of music where the performer gradually speeds up; α_4**: stress** – This is a common technique to make an emphasis of a certain note by taking a little extra time before playing that note. The time variables are modeled differently in each different discrete state setup.

The mathematical definition of timing and tempo behaviors in the 4 discrete states are:

α_1. **constant speed**

If for a segment where $s_l = s_{l+1} = ... = s_m = \alpha_1$, we set the tempo o (measured in seconds per beat) to be constant

$$t_{k+1} = t_k + (b_{k+1} - b_k) \times o$$

for $k = l, .., m$ with an initial $o \sim N(\mu_o, \sigma_o^2)$ with an unknown mean μ_o that is only effective in this segment.

α_2. **slowing down**

If for a segment where $s_l = s_{l+1} = ... = s_m = \alpha_2$, the tempo inherited from last section $o = (t_l - t_{l-1})/(b_l - b_{l-1})$ is increasing with a constant unknown rate $a \sim N(\mu_a, \sigma_a^2)$ that applies only to this segment:

$$t_{k+1} = t_k + (b_{k+1} - b_k) \times (o + (b_{k+1} - b_l) \times a)$$

for $k = l, .., m$.

α_3. **speeding up**

If for a segment where $s_l = s_{l+1} = ... = s_m = \alpha_3$, similar to α_2, $o = (t_l - t_{l-1})/(b_l - b_{l-1})$ is increasing with a constant unknown rate $a \sim N(\mu_a, \sigma_a^2)$,

$$t_{k+1} = t_k + (b_{k+1} - b_k) \times (o - (b_{k+1} - b_l) \times a)$$

for $k = l, .., m$. a is also only relevant for this segment.

α_4. **stress**

The stress state is modeled to only last for one note and its previous and successor states must both be state α_1. So if $s_{m-1} = \alpha_1$, $s_m = \alpha_4$, $s_{m+1} = \alpha_1$, $o = (t_{m-1} - t_{m-2})/(b_{m-1} - b_{m-2})$,

$$t_m = t_{m-1} + (b_m - b_{m+1}) \times o + c$$

$$t_{m+1} = t_m + (b_{m+1} - b_m) \times o$$

$c \sim N(\mu_c, \sigma_\epsilon^2)$ is a variable relevant only for this note.

The sequence of the discrete state is modeled as a Markov chain. Figure 1 shows the Markov model.

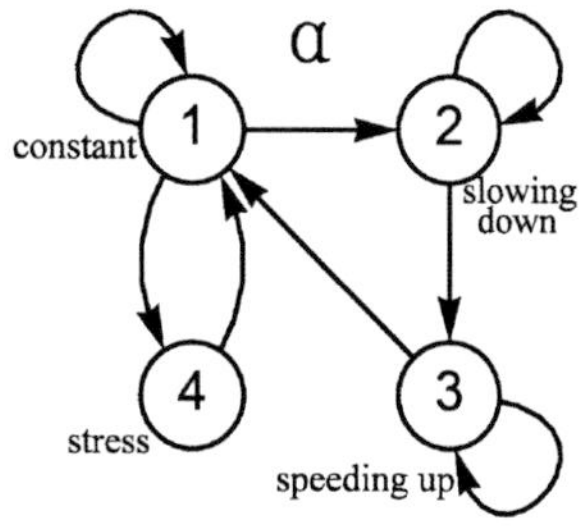

Figure 1. A Markov model showing possible transitions between the discrete states.

The assumptions are: 1) The states can stay in either constant speed state, slowing down state or speeding up state; 2) Before speeding up. there must be a slowing down process; 3) before slowing down the performance must be in constant speed and 4) the constraint for stress as mentioned in its definition.

One of the main reasons we choose these assumptions is that the state space of switching Kalman filter grows exponentially with time [18]. Even with approximation schemes, we want the number of possible state transitions in our model to be as small as possible. We think the first three states with enough transitions that can cycle through them are capable of capturing most tempo behaviors. We add the 4th state to have the ability to "remember" an intended tempo after a single note tempo variation. We also think these assumptions are suitable for capturing local tempo behavior changes that are within few notes. For large scale tempo behaviors such as an accelerando over couple measures, our model can explain them with a combination of several state changes.

The directed acyclic graph (DAG) of the graphical model is represented in figure 2. The model has both discrete and Gaussian variables. For every fixed configuration of the discrete variables, the continuous variable have a multivariate Gaussian distribution. Thus, the $s_1, .., s_N, t_1, ..., t_N$ collectively have a conditional Gaussian distribution [19].

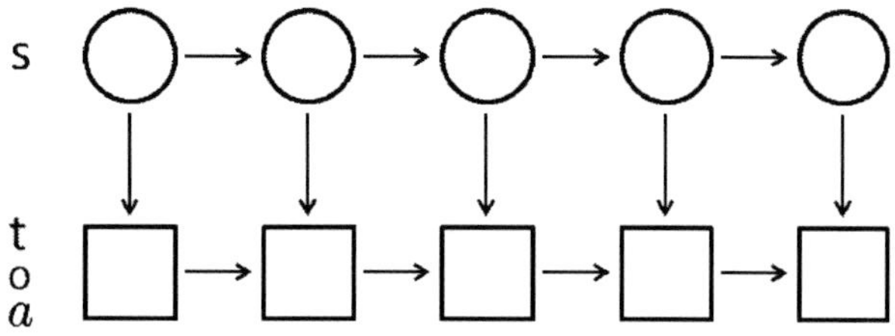

Figure 2. The DAG describing the dependency structure of the time variables in monophonic case. Circles represent discrete variables while squares represent continuous variables.

If a section of music contain ***polyphonic*** elements, we can always categorize them into one of the following two types. The first type is "chord". A chord here means a group of notes that should be played at the same time. We model the time variables of such event in a straightforward way – the time variables in a chord are exactly the same.

The second type is "multiple voices". There are occasionally notes that share a same music time belong to different voices (or even different instruments). As a result, we shouldn't assume they will be played at the same time. In the case of more than one voice, we choose one of the voices as the leading voice (usually the melody), which operates exactly the same as the switching Kalman filter in the monophonic case we introduced earlier. As for the other voices, they are also similar switching Kalman filters but subjected to constraint that the timing of certain notes have to be the same with some notes in the leading voice. These notes are called "anchor points", the parameters of the voices are independent if the timing of these anchor points is given.

Figure 3 is an example of a section of music with many chords and two voices.

Figure 3. An excerpt and its DAG describing the dependency structure of the time variables in polyphonic case. Circles represent discrete variables while squares represent continuous variables. Although the arrows from discrete variables to continuous variables are omitted in the graph for the sake of clarity, they are present in the actual model.

Figure 3 shows the dependency structure if we consider the 1st and 5th groups (the 1st and 5th chords in bass clef) of notes that share same music times to be the "anchor points" while the 2nd-4th groups of notes are considered to be in two voices.

At the first glance, specifying the "anchor points" could be a complicated problem itself and require a lot of manual labor. However, we will introduce an interactive process to choose them semi-automatically in the next section.

Now let's introduce the model for dynamic and duration. Since we set them to be exactly the same, only dynamic model is discussed here. The modeling assumption for these two variables can be summarized as "if something similar happened before, it will most likely act the same". Here is an example: figure 4 shows a music excerpt and one of its possible dependency structure. We will introduce how to construct the dependency structure in the next section too.

The variables without a predecessor such as $d_{a1}, d_{a2}, d_{a3}, d_{a4}, d_{b1}, d_{c1}$ are modeled as independent. In this example $d_{bk} = d_{b1} + (d_{ak} - d_{a1})$ for $k = 2, 3, 4$; $d_{ck} = d_{c1} + (d_{bk} - d_{b1})$ for $k = 2, 3, 4$ and so on. This model assumes that the balance within a chord is fixed for this excerpt.

Here is another example: figure 5 shows a music excerpt and it dynamic variables with dependency structure.

Again, the variables without a predecessor such as $d_{a1}, d_{a2}, d_{a3}, d_{a4}, d_{b1}, d_{c1}$ are modeled as independent. In this example $d_{bk} = d_{b1} + (d_{ak} - d_{a1})$ for $k = 2, 3, 4$; $d_{ck} = d_{c1} + (d_{bk} - d_{b1})$ for $k = 2, 3, 4$ and so on. This model assumes that similar short sections should have same relative dynamics.

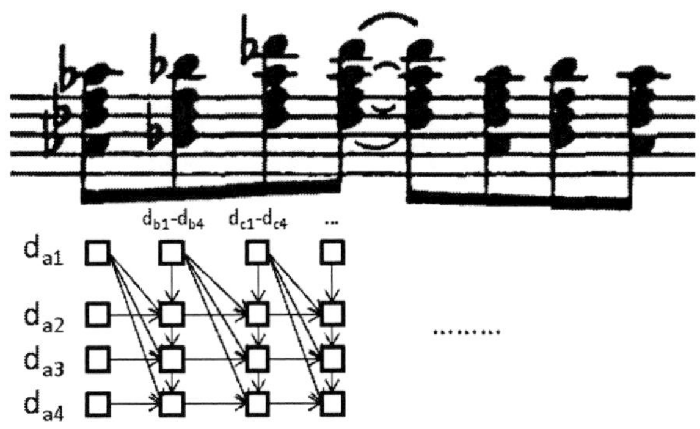

Figure 4. An excerpt and its DAG describing the dependency structure of the dynamic variables.

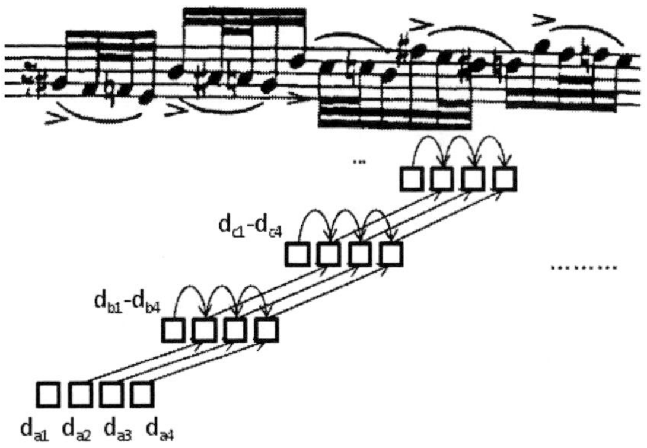

Figure 5. An excerpt and its DAG describing the dependency structure of the dynamic variables.

3. SYNTHESIZE PERFORMANCE

In the previous section, there is a very important missing part that we are going to introduce now – how to construct the dependency structures for timing, dynamic models. These structures are not specified by hand. Rather, besides the hidden parameters, we use an algorithm to retrieve the structures from user input of incomplete performances that represent the skeleton of the music.

Let's look at an example of the idea first, figure 6 shows the excerpt we want to play.

Figure 6. An excerpt from Rhapsody in Blue

Even a trained pianist needs quite some time to play this excerpt fluently. But the music ideas behind this excerpt is not so complicated. Here are two expected reductions for our model from an user: 1) a theme as shown in figure 7 :

2) a rhythm voice on the left hand as shown in figure 8 :

Anyone with a little piano knowledge can play the two parts shown in figure 7, 8 and play them expressively. Our goal is to complete the performance in figure 6 – specify the model and estimate the parameters – based on these

Figure 7. The theme of the excerpt

Figure 8. The second voice of the excerpt

two reductions.

Here are the procedures:

1) Data preparation

We use MIDI file exported from a score writing program as our starting point. Then we will have an user play the reductions that are representative in terms of musical ideas such as those shown in figure 7, 8.

2) Match the reductions to the score

This is a performance alignment problem – given a performance and a score, we want to find out what and when notes are being played. This can be achieved using Hidden Markov Model (HMM) type of approach. [20] provided an algorithm based on HMM to match a performance with a large portion of missing notes (e.g. a reduction like we have here) to the score.

3) Construct the timing model

The tasks of constructing the timing model are how to divide voices and specifying the "anchor points". Our assumptions are: if there are multiple reductions being played for a same excerpt and they have different rhythm structures, they are considered to belong to different voices (e.g. if music shown in figure 7 and figure 8 are played separately, they are considered to be in two voices); the notes that are being played in multiple reductions are considered to be the "anchor points" where voices meet (e.g. the low notes in three chords in figure 7); the notes that are never played in any reduction belong to the voice with closest pitch. Although the last one is a naive assumption, it has a chance of work because the hand of human can only cover a small range of pitches.

4) Construct the dynamic model

The tasks of constructing the dynamic model are specifying the independent notes and creating the dependency structure. Our assumptions are: for notes that are being played in any of the reductions, their dynamics are considered to be independent; for a group of consecutive notes that are never being played in any of the reductions, they depend on the nearest note played previously in the same voice parsed in the last procedure; for this group of notes, we search for the nearest played group of notes with the exact same rhythm structure. If found, dependency relationships will be established as well. Figure 4 shows the results of applying these assumptions to the first 4 chords of reduction in figure 7.

Figure 4 and figure 5 are two examples that work well with our assumptions. This works with many other cases as well. But we acknowledge that there are also many cases where these naive assumptions don't apply well. Currently we don't have a general sophisticated parameter reduction scheme for dynamics. So we simply treat notes in those cases to be independent and require user to specify them. We will work on automating this process without human input in the near future.

5) Parse the discrete variables for timing model

After we have the voices divided, each voice can be considered a monophonic excerpt and will be modeled as a switching Kalman filter introduced in section 2. Let $T_1, T_2, ..., T_N$ be the observed timings from reductions. We define the data model for timing variables $T_n = t_n + \epsilon_n$ where $\epsilon_n \sim N(\mu_\epsilon, \sigma_\epsilon^2)$. We can address the problem as finding the most likely configuration of both discrete variables and continuous variables $\hat{s_1}, .., \hat{s_N}, \hat{t_1}, ..., \hat{t_N} =$
$\arg\max_{s_1,..,s_N,t_1,...,t_N} P(s_1, .., s_N, t_1, ..., t_N | T_1, ..., T_n)$.
Then we can use the method known as the "beam search" to compute the discrete variables that guide the timing variables [21].

Note:

At this point, we finally have the complete model. For real world uses, we can manually refine the model structure and improve the discrete variables without too much effort to make the model more "realistic" since the model provides a lower dimensional structure that relates to how musicians talk about music. But for experimental purposes, we'll proceed with algorithmically generated model.

6) Estimating & computing the parameters

With the fixed discrete variables $\hat{s_1}, .., \hat{s_N}$ we obtained in previous procedure, estimating $\hat{t_1}, ..., \hat{t_N}$ is a standard smoothing problem for Kalman filter: $\hat{t_1}, ..., \hat{t_N} =$
$\arg\max_{t_1,...,t_N} P(t_1, ..., t_N | s_1, .., s_N, T_1, ..., T_n)$. We can use the recursive algorithm of Kalman filter to compute the timing variables [22].

For dynamics, we treat $v = (v_1, v_2, ..., v_N)$ as a random vector where we observe a subset of the variables $\{v_{k_1}, v_{k_2} ...\}$. Then we can compute the rest using the dynamic model we introduced in section 2.

4. EXPERIMENT

We choose the two piano version of Rhapsody in Blue by American composer George Gershwin as our experiment material. The MIDI score is exported from a score-written program. In general, the data can be collected from any reproducing piano or digital piano. We use a high quality hybrid piano AvantGrand N2 made by YAMAHA. The reason we choose such an instrument is to ensure that the reproduction will be exactly as performed. The piano keyboard is the same as YAMAHA C3 grand piano which provides the same touch of a real grand piano.

For demonstration of how the model works, we choose 3 excerpts from the piece and have an user play some reductions of these excerpts. The reductions represent the user's idea of the model structure which will be captured using the methods described in section 3. There could be multiple performances of a same reduction but we let the user pick the best one. These examples can be heard at https://dl.dropbox.com/u/6449856/Web/smc2013.html.

The following table shows the number of timing and dynamic parameters in MIDI file, the reductions played by an user and the result of our model for the three excerpts Ex1, Ex2 and Ex3.

# of timing Parameters	Ex1	Ex2	Ex3
MIDI	244	446	240
Played reductions	93	73	53
Our model	20	22	10

Table 1. The comparison of number of timing parameters in MIDI file, the reductions and the result of our model

# of dynamic Parameters	Ex1	Ex2	Ex3
MIDI	244	446	240
Played reductions	99	97	60
Our model	99	97	60

Table 2. The comparison of number of dynamic parameters in MIDI file, the reductions and the result of our model

The examples show that with far fewer parameters than the MIDI file as shown in the table, we still capture much expressiveness from human input and use them to render a complete expressive performance accordingly. Our timing model is capable of reducing the # of parameters in a performance to 10% - 20% of those in MIDI files. With further development, we are expecting a more advanced dynamic model that can achieve a similar percentage.

5. DISCUSSION

This performance model definitely needs more development. There are many assumptions made because of their simplicity. It is also not the most intelligent model either since it requires a lot of human-computer interaction. However, this model makes an attempt to capture the low-dimensional nature of music performances and creates a framework for reproducing and synthesizing expressive performance. This model explicitly addresses the way that different areas in music performance have very different kinds of objectives or strategies that are employed. This is a fundamental characteristic of music performance that has not been developed much. We try to make mathematical scientific sense out of this important aspect of performance. The model along with procedures introduced in section 3 provide a computer system that allows anyone with some basic piano skills to play very technical pieces such as the Rhapsody in Blue with their own music ideas. The model also offers a platform for systematically changing a performance meaningfully and intuitively.

This is our first step towards a good performance model. We believe there are many aspects that can be researched and improved. The discrete states for timing model are clearly something we can work on to make it better. Tempo can progress quadratically instead of linearly. We are also developing more sophisticated model for dynamics which now is almost solely rely on human input. There are much more dynamic relations among notes that wait for us to explore.

Another possible follow-up for this model is accompaniment system. Our proposed model can be considered as an offline version of accompaniment system. Since the goal of an accompaniment system is essentially generating a complete musical performance with partial performance data that is played by one soloist. We hope with proper modifications, an online version of our model can be used as an accompaniment system and play concerto type of music in real time.

This model also opens a new way of approaching expressive rendering problem. With this model, what we need for constructing an expressive performance is the different areas and few key numbers that represent the performing strategy in those areas. Hence we have far fewer parameters to estimate. But of course for fine detail of performance, the model may need to be more sophisticated than simple linear ones.

We look forward to presenting more generally useful applications of the performance model framework as it develops.

6. REFERENCES

[1] A. Truslit, *Gestaltung und Bewegung in der Musik* (Chr. Friedrich Vieweg, Berlin-Licherfelde), 1938

[2] B. H. Repp and P. Shove, "Musical motion and performance: theoretical and eimpirical perspectives," in *The practice ofr performance: Studies in Musical Interpretation,* edited by J. Rink (Cambridge U.P., Cambridge), 1995, pp. 55–83.

[3] N. P. McA. Todd, "The Dynamics of Dynamics: A Model of music expression," *J. Acoust. Soc. Am., vol.91, no.6* , 1992, pp. 3540–3550.

[4] J. Feldman, D. Epstein and R. Whiteman, "Force Dynamics of Tempo Change in Music," *Music Perception, vol.10, no.2* , 1992, pp. 185–204.

[5] A. Friberg and J. Sundberg, "Does music performance allude to locomotion? A model of final ritardandi derived from measurements of stopping runners," *J. Acoust. Soc. Am., vol.105, no.3* , 1999, pp. 1469–1484.

[6] Smule, *http://www.smule.com/magicpiano.*

[7] R. Hiraga, R. Bresin, K. Hirata, and H. Katayose, "Turing test for musical expression," *Proceedings of International Conference on New Interfaces for Musical Expression, in Proc. of NIME 2004*, 2004, pp. 120–123.

[8] T. Suzuki, "The second phase development of case based performance rendering system kagurame," *Proc. of the IJCAI-03 Rencon Workshop*, 2003, pp. 17–25.

[9] G. Grindlay, "Modeling expressive musical performance with hmms," *Musical Information Processing Systems (MIPS 2004). Neural Information Processing Systems (NIPS 2004)*, 2004.

[10] S. Flossmann, M. Grachten, and G. Widmer, "Expressive performance with bayesian networks and linear basis models," *Extended abstract, Rencon Workshop 2011: Musical Performance Rendering competition for Computer Systems*, 2011.

[11] R. Dannenberg, "An on-line algorithm for real-time accompaniment," *Proceedings of ICMC 1984*, Paris, France, 1984, pp. 193–198.

[12] B. Baird, D. Blevins, and N. Zahler, "Artificial intelligence and music: Implementing an interactive computer performer," *Computer Music Journal, vol.17, no.2*, 1993, pp. 73–79.

[13] C. Raphael, "A probabilistic expert system for automatic musical accompaniment," *Journal of Comp. and Graph. Stats. vol.10, no.3*, 2001, pp. 487–412.

[14] J. Hamilton, "A new approach to the economic analysis of nonstationary time series and the business cycle." *Econometrica, 57*, 1989, pp. 357–384.

[15] R. Shumway and D. Stoffer, "Dynamic linear models with switching," *J. Amer. Stat. Assoc. 86*, 1991, pp. 763–769.

[16] C. Kim, "Dynamic linear models with markov-switching," *J. Econometrics, 60*, 1994, pp. 1–22.

[17] Z. Ghahramani and G. Hinton, "Variational learning for switching state-space models," *Neural Computation, 12(4)*, 1998, pp. 963–996.

[18] K. P. Murphy, "Switching Kalman Filters," *Compaq Cambridge Research Lab Tech Report 98-10*, 1998.

[19] S. Lauritzen and F. Jensen, "Stable local computation with conditional gaussian distributions," *Technical Report R-99-2014, Department of Mathematic Sciences, Aalborg University*, 1999.

[20] Y. Gu and C. Raphael, "Orchestral accompaniment for a reproducing piano," *Proceedings of ICMC 2009*, 2009, pp. 501–504.

[21] ——, "Modeling piano interpretation using switching Kalman filter," *Proceedings of ISMIR 2012*, 2012, pp. 145–150.

[22] J. Hamilton, *Time Series Analysis*. Princeton Universtiy Press. Chapter13, 'The Kalman Filter', 1994.

SKALLDANS, AN AUDIOVISUAL IMPROVISATION FRAMEWORK

PerMagnus Lindborg
School of Art, Design, Media
Nanyang Technological University, Singapore
permagnus@ntu.edu.sg

ABSTRACT

Skalldans is an audiovisual improvisation framework for a solo laptop performer. The framework is an instrument for performance, developed in Max[2]. Sound and video syntheses are piloted with a MIDI interface, a camera, and a Wiimote; also, audiovisual streams influence each other. The present text discusses some of the hardware and software points of interest, for example, how audio and video syntheses are piloted, how the streams interact, and the camera tracking method with a linear regression stabiliser. It also touches upon the sources of inspiration for the piece.

1. INTRODUCTION

Occasionally laptop performers, stony faces lit by the computer screen and secretive to the point of incredulity, seem to demand from the audience a willing suspension of disbelief ("is he really playing or is he on Facebook?"). Live coders showcase their creative innards, perhaps mixing in a live video of their hands pecking away at the keyboard. By and large, audiences at concert events are thrilled by the body language and facial expression of performers. In the context of computer music, I felt that one way to make my laptop act more interesting was to involve myself a bit more, and to use visuals. In late 2007, I had an accident: walked straight into a glass pane and went unconscious. The doctors decided to take a MRI scan to check if the cranium was cracked (apparently it wasn't). The bash and the scan procedure were sonically amazing experiences. I was able to get a copy of the scan data, and thought that this must be used for a performance piece. Holbein's famous painting *The Ambassadors*, an excerpt of which is shown in Figure 1, inspired a *vanitas*, a study of a skull to reflect upon the meaningless of life. Sculptures of *Shiva Tandava* suggested the idea of a dance with death (Figure 2).

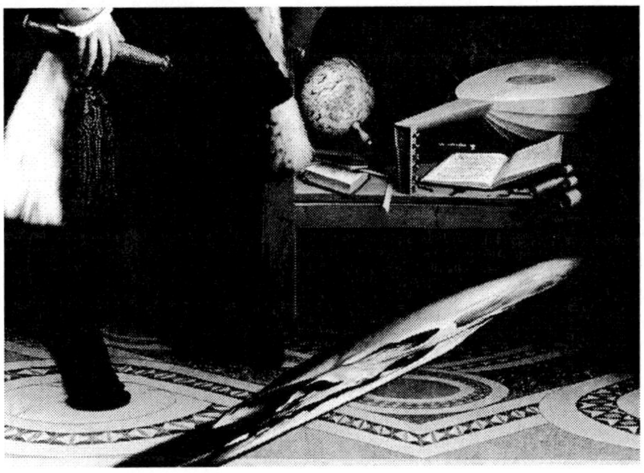

Figure 1. Detail of *The Ambassadors* (Holbein, H. y., 1533), showing the skewed image of a cranium.

2. HARDWARE-SOFTWARE

Skalldans has developed over a couple of years (2008-11), in different stages of software-hardware solutions, seeking to create a responsive hybrid instrument with a a 'rich' control [1]. The initial versions used a joystick to control the 'dance' of the 3D skull (see section 5, below). The problem was that this demanded at least one hand to be dedicated to piloting the visuals, which had the inconvenience of reducing the amount of control over audio. On one occasion, a second performer was engaged to control visuals only, but this was felt to be unsatisfactory. A solution was to mount a Wiimote onto a set of headphones, to capture 2 axes of head orientation: pitch (nod) and yaw (left-right turn). The Wiimote was eventually hidden in a large cap.

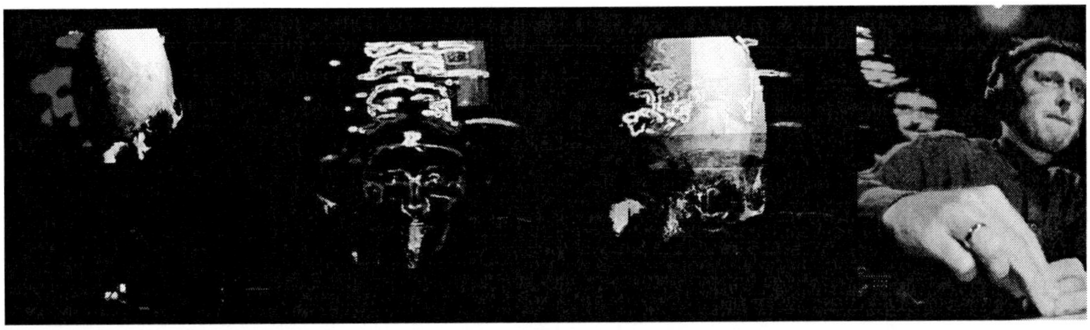

Figure 2. Shots from a performance of Skalldans at Open Ears Festival in Kortrijk, 2008, showing the 'analog video delay' and other visual effects. Photos by Finnbogir Péturson.

In its current version, the performer sits on stage in front of the projection screen, which allows for video feedback effects. In addition to the physical gesture capture device, control is offered by a uc33e USB MIDI interface, which has 9 sliders and 24 knobs. Figure 3 gives an overview of the flows of audio, video and control data in the framework. Processing is implemented in Max [2]. For reasons of portability, in particular to be able to run it on one computer only, syntheses are kept simple.

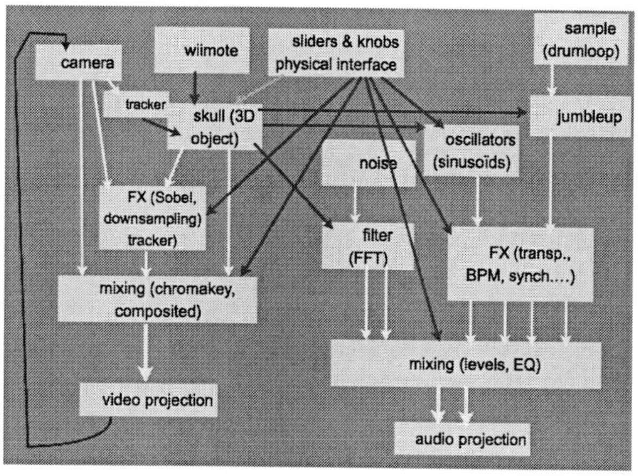

Figure 3. Audio, video, and control data flows.

3. AUDIO SYNTHESIS

The audio synthesis is influenced by the aesthetics of genres such as noise music and drum'n'bass. Audio synthesis and mixing are controlled by 7 sliders and 17 knobs on the uc33a interface. There are three instruments:

3.1. Drone

Two channels of additive synthesis, each with 32 oscillators, create a bass drone. The performer can adjust fundamental frequency, (in-)harmonicity, randomise phases with a keyboard click, and introduce small frequency distortions unequally to right and left channels. Figure 4 shows the Max GUI.

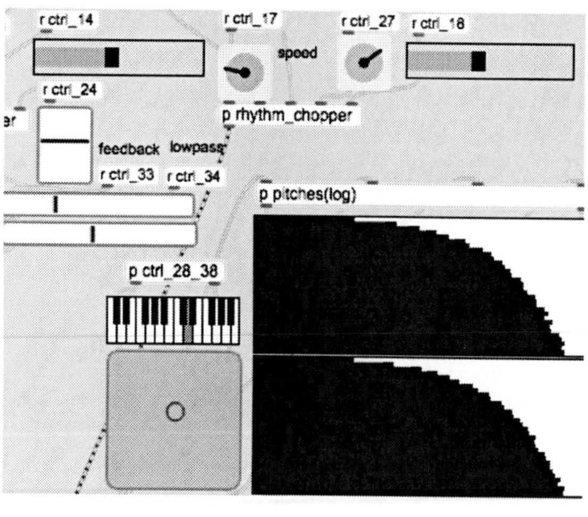

Figure 4. Drones with slightly inharmonic partials, illustrated by the jagged contours. In the upper part of the illustration is the Rhythm Choppers interface.

These parameters control the 'hollowness' of the sound and how much the stereophonic image is 'floating'.

3.2. Coloured Noise

This instrument is created with subtractive synthesis of white noise. The skull video, down-sampled skull image yields data for two FFT filters: the left side of the image for the left-channel filter, and vice versa. See Figure 5. In parallel, there is a feedback-delay loop, to prolong the ringing of tones of 'coloured noise'.

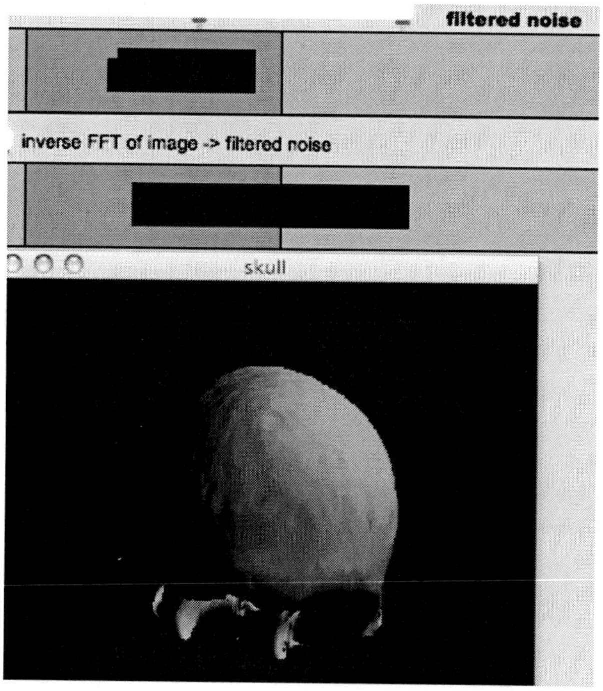

Figure 5. Skull image data are sampled and mapped to two FFT filters for the Noise instrument as well as for the Rhythm Choppers.

3.3. Rhythm

Two parallel 'Reloopers', wrapped around the "ModSquad" patcher [4], each take as input either the Drone, Coloured Noise, or a short percussion sample (Tanaka's original "jongly", the only non-synthesis element of the audio instrument). The Relooper is a step sequencer, a rhythm machine that cuts up and meshes audio according to a 16-step transfer function. In *Skalldans*, the transfer function is determined by the video. As with the FFT filters, each side of the skull video frame yields data for one audio channel. The skull image is mapped onto the cut'n'mesh transformation function from the centre line and towards the edge, i.e. the left side is read 'backwards'. This means that the Relooper rhythms are similar just as the image is symmetric around the centre line. Since the skull will often be in the centre of the image, the first step of the Relooper will often include the actual downbeat of the input, for example, the sample's kick drum.

4. CAMERA TRACKING

The built-in iSight camera of my MacBook Pro was used for camera tracking of the performer's head position in 2 dimensions, left-right and up-down. The camera tracking method builds on frame differencing and 'blob' sorting [3]. Further, there is a linear regression method to improve the stability of tracking. The (x, y) positions of the 'top 5 candidate blobs' from are compared with the predicted position based on the 5 previous tracking frames, and the best match (smallest Euclidian distance) is picked. Figure 6 shows parts of the Max implementation. The system was developed for *Walking Bach Slowly* (2011), an interactive installation where 3 people were tracked simultaneously with one birds-eye camera and the system needed to be able to "lock on", e.g. to distinguish targets crossing paths.

5. VIDEO SYNTHESIS

The MRI scan of my cranium was used to create a 3D object in Maya, adding appropriate smoothing, texturing and shading. In Max (Jitter), the 3D "skull" object is mixed together with concurrent video streams: the raw camera input, the "hairpin" of the tracked performer's head, and the linear regression line, thus visualising the innards of the tracking method. Compositing effects are added in real-time.

5.1. Chromakeying and Sobel Outlining

This allows the skull to be mixed into the camera live input (treated or not). A central 'poetic' idea of the performance is to illustrate the struggle that the performer has to 'fit' the live head and the skull together. The Sobel outlining effect creates a thin outline based on connecting points of equal image contrast. See Figure 7 for an example. This effect seems to suggest the idea of how fragile the cranium is.

5.2. Compositing Effects and Video Delay

Basic VFX such as downsampling, compositing effects (cellwise multiplication, maximum, difference etc of two streams) allow the performer to make the video flow more or less abstract. An analog video delay is created by tilting the computer screen upwards so that the camera input includes what is projected onto the screen behind the performer. See Figure 2 for an example.

In earlier versions, the skull object could also be plastically transformed, e.g. flattened and stretched, much as in Holbein's painting. However, this option was eventually taken out, because it was felt that such manipulations distracted from the more subtle control enabled by simply following - albeit sometimes imperfectly - the dancing movements of the performer's head. Therefore, skull movement is now entirely piloted by the Wiimote and camera tracking, except for one slider to zoom in or out. All visual effects and mixing are piloted by 2 sliders and 4 knobs on the uc33e interface, and a few computer keys.

6. AUDIO-VISUAL INTERACTION

The skull video is downsampled, and greyscale values (alpha channel) of two rows are read into audio buffers, that will act as FFT-bin filters. The performer can select a portion of the lines that will function as amplitude modulators of the Noise and Drone instruments in order to 'chop up' a rhythm that may or may not be in synch with the Relooper rhythm machine. See Figure 5 above. A switch allows the audio of the Relooper to affect settings of the visual effects; when an amplitude threshold is crossed (hi-lo gate), a new preset is selected at random, and in this way, rhythmic alterations between VFXs follow those of the musical beat.

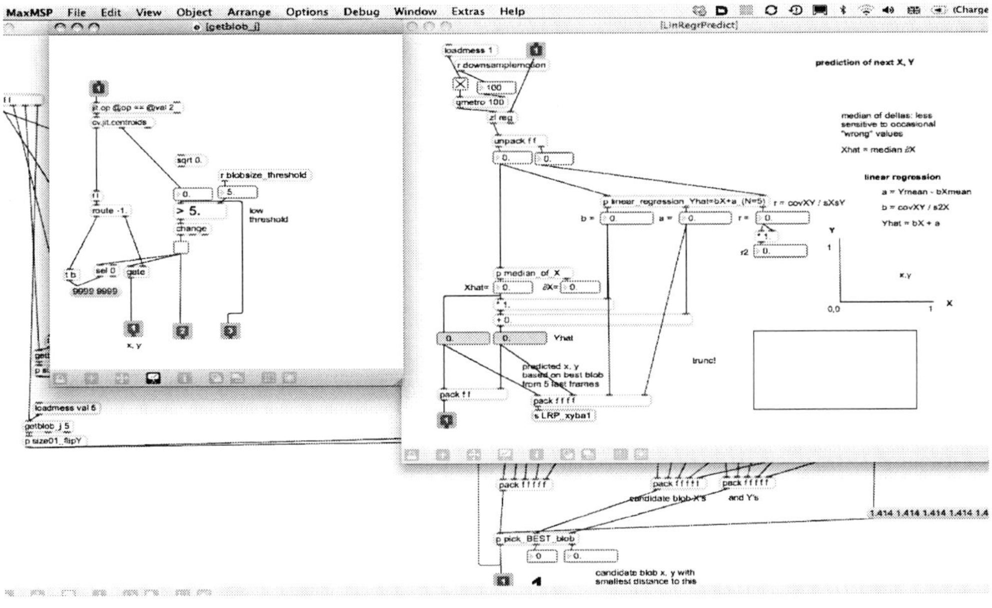

Figure 6. Linear regression prediction for blob tracking.

7. PERFORMING SKALLDANS

Skalldans has been included in performances in Singapore (Choppa Festival 2008), Belgium (Happy Ears 2008), see Figure 2, and Iceland (Nordic Music Days 2011), a shot from which is shown in Figure 7. Because the framework is a rather complex audiovisual instrument and still in development, these performances have been varied in expression, but the improvisation outline (the "composition", as it were) has followed roughly the same narrative: the first section focusses on noise and details of the rather mysterious skull object; the next section reveals that it is a cranium and it starts to dance; then more musical elements are added, i.e. the Drone, eventually with rhythmic chopping; a section follows where tempo picks up and the two other video streams (live, tracking) join, in various guises; at the opportune moment, the drum'n'bass takes off and video includes more colour; towards the end, rhythms tend to synchronise and simplify while the performer 'live head' fuses visually with the skull; video delay is introduced, the performer stands up and dances; before the whole audio-visual thing runs into a wall - or at least, this is the feeling that I wish to convey - and the performance ends.

There would be little point in writing a score, and I prefer the piece to change from one occasion to the next. Perhaps this is the best antidote I can find to death, and to continue dancing. Parts of the framework, in particular VFX and live mixing of video, have gone into in *Nosferatu Extemporations - The Ship* (2012), a piece for computer and saxophone. More about this can be found on my webpages [5]. Future work on the *Skalldans* improvisation framework will attempt to further improve the head (and perhaps hand) tracking with technologies such as Kinect and Leap, as well as more ways for interaction between the audio and video syntheses.

8. REFERENCES

[1] Lindborg, PerMagnus (2008). "Reflections on aspects of music interactivity in performance situations". eContact, 4.10, 1-20, Chippewa, J., editor.

[2] Cycling74 (). *Max*. http://www.cycling74.com.

[3] Pelletier, J.-M. (2010). *Cv.jit, Computer Vision library for Jitter.* http://jmpelletier.com/cvjit/ (February 2013).

[4] Tanaka, A. (2003) "Modsquad Relooper". In Max software distribution.

[5] Lindborg, PerMagnus (). *Skalldans*. http://www.permagnus.net/pm/artwork/multimedia/Skalldans/index.html (February 2013)

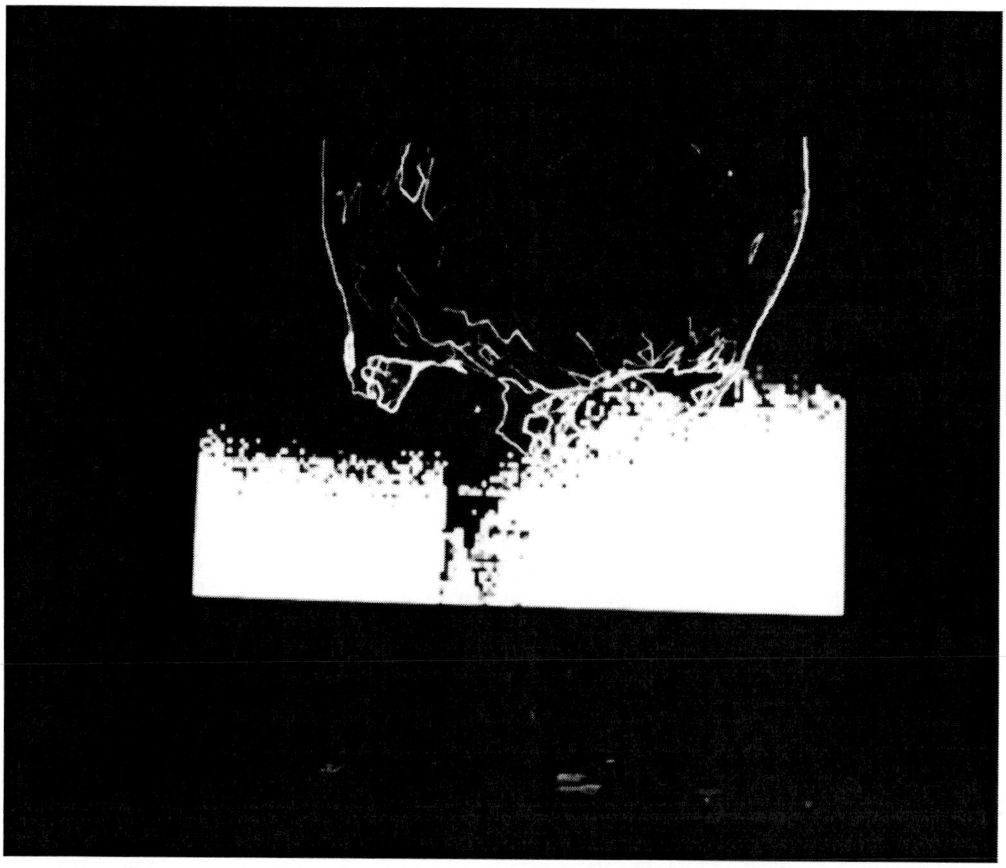

Figure 7. Shot from a performance of *Skalldans* at Nordic Music Days festival in Reikjavijk 2011. Sobel outlining of the skull is clearly visible. Photo by Bonnie Right.

NETWORK MUSIC WITH MEDUSA: A COMPARISON OF TEMPO ALIGNMENT IN EXISTING MIDI APIS

Flávio Luiz Schiavoni
Institute of Mathematics and Statistics
University of São Paulo
fls@ime.usp.br

Marcelo Queiroz
Institute of Mathematics and Statistics
University of São Paulo
mqz@ime.usp.br

Marcelo Wanderley
IDMIL/CIRMMT
McGill University
marcelo.wanderley@mcgill.ca

ABSTRACT

In network music, latency is a common issue and can be caused by several factors. In this paper we present MIDI network streaming with Medusa, a distributed music environment. To ease the network connection for the end user, Medusa is implemented using different MIDI APIs: Portmidi, ALSA MIDI and JACK MIDI. We present the influence of the MIDI API choice in the system latency and jitter using the Medusa implementation.

1. INTRODUCTION

Network music tools can provide an easy way to facilitate cooperation and collaboration in music. Computer networks can be used to connect applications and devices in live music performances, music recording sessions or rehearsals.

To integrate music tools, different data types can be transmitted, such as audio and MIDI. Despite some criticism [1] about the usage of MIDI in Digital Music Instruments, MIDI continues to be popular because it is a standard protocol present in several applications and music devices.

In this paper we will present the network MIDI distribution using Medusa. Medusa is a distributed music environment that allows users to share audio and MIDI streams through computer networks [2]. [1]

Currently, different MIDI APIs can be used to implement a MIDI application in a Linux system, such as ALSA MIDI, Portmidi and JACK MIDI. The Medusa MIDI implementation recently started running on these APIs in order to simplify integration of different tools over a computer network. Moreover, different APIs can influence system latency. In this paper we will present how these APIs can be used and a pragmatic comparison of these APIs in the Medusa implementation.

There are a few other related tools that allow realtime network music content distribution. Netjack [3] is an internal JACK client in JACK2 that is monitored by JACK and synchronized by JACK sample rate and JACK transport. This tool runs over UDP/IP multicast using JACK MIDI only, and allows redundancy in data transmission to avoid glitches [4].

Other network music tools are similar but their music content is limited to a specific musical data type. QmidiNet [2] is a network music tool that uses UDP/IP multicast to distribute MIDI streams. Jacktrip [5] and SoundJack [6] are network music tools that use UDP/IP and provide audio only music streams.

Another popular music data type used for device communication in music is OSC [7]. OSC does not necessarily pack MIDI or audio data and it is a network ready musical protocol. For this reason, we will not discuss OSC in this paper.

The remainder of this paper is organized as follows: Section 2 discusses the MIDI protocol and presents the MIDI APIs used to develop Medusa. Section 3 presents Medusa and our proposed MIDI stream implementation. Section 4 presents measurements done with the Medusa MIDI implementation over the previously explained MIDI APIs and their results. Section 5 presents our conclusion and future work.

2. WHY MIDI?

MIDI is one of the most widely-used standard protocols for interconnecting electronic music devices. Proposed as a unidirectional talker-listener network, MIDI was probably the first music standard protocol that created possibilities for music instrument networking [8].

The MIDI protocol facilitates integration between different music applications and devices in a single computer. Some reasons that motivated the development of MIDI in Medusa are:

- The MIDI protocol enables using digital music interfaces and synthesizers as an alternative or complement to audio transmission channels by reducing network bandwidth usage.
- MIDI messages can control several music devices and equipment like mixers and software plugins.
- MIDI Machine Control (MMC) controls recorders and provides messages that include Play, Fast Forward, Rewind, Stop, Pause, and Record.

[1] The source code of Medusa is available on the project website: http://sourceforge.net/projects/medusa-audionet

[2] http://qmidinet.sourceforge.net/qmidinet-index.html

- MIDI Time Code (MTC) is a time protocol that can be used to sync applications and devices such as loopers and sequencers.
- MIDI Show Control (MSC) is a protocol developed to control equipment in theaters, live performance, multimedia installations and similar environments.

These messages can be used to sync and control MIDI applications and devices that are usually directly connected. The usage of network MIDI streams can expand the control and integration possibilities of the MIDI protocol to a network distributed sound-processing software/hardware environment.

Different MIDI APIs help software developers to integrate MIDI in music applications.

2.1 MIDI APIs

Initially Medusa was implemented with JACK MIDI only [2]. Since some applications do not implement a JACK MIDI channel, two other MIDI APIs were integrated in Medusa: ALSA MIDI and Portmidi.

Since a MIDI event is supposed to be delivered immediately, the MIDI protocol does not have time-tagging [9]. On the other hand, the MIDI APIs here discussed have complements to the MIDI protocol that allow synchronizing different applications. How the application deals with event sync is an important feature in order to achieve low latency.

2.1.1 ALSA MIDI

ALSA, the Advanced Linux Sound Architecture, is the part of the Linux kernel that provides support to USB and PCI audio / MIDI devices. One of the basic components of ALSA system is the device driver for sound equipment.

ALSA also provides an API for application development. This API includes all the required features for developing audio and MIDI applications that run over ALSA drivers.

ALSA provides two different MIDI event types for MIDI application development: seq and raw. ALSA seq (sequencer) timestamps MIDI messages and monitors ALSA MIDI software that is bypassed. ALSA raw just operates MIDI drivers without timestamping.

In ALSA, all MIDI applications are mapped as virtual devices and there is no significant difference between physical and virtual devices. Once the application has created a virtual device, this port stream can be routed to other devices through a port connection. Some applications can be used to manage MIDI connections in ALSA, e.g. qjackctl [3].

In ALSA seq MIDI, an event uses MIDI ticks for timestamping (a discrete time measure related to a track-specific tempo). Other timestamp information is the relative note time in seconds and nanoseconds.

2.1.2 Portmidi

Portmidi is part of Portmedia project, a cross-platform API for music application development. This library supports real-time input and output of MIDI data and runs on Windows, MacOS, and Linux [10].

Using Portmidi API, it is possible to list the MIDI devices, physical or virtual, and present their input and output ports.

Portmidi in Linux runs over ALSA, but differently from ALSA MIDI it creates a data stream directly connected to a MIDI device port. This port connection cannot be changed or routed differently during the application execution.

In Portmidi, a MIDI event has a timestamp related to a Portmidi internal clock time.

2.1.3 JACK MIDI

JACK (JACK Audio Connection Kit) is a real time low-latency sound server that allows the creation of audio and MIDI connections between applications that run on the JACK API [3]. This sound server runs over different operating systems such as Linux, Windows and MacOS.

Like ALSA MIDI, JACK MIDI can be used to connect JACK MIDI capable applications and route MIDI streams between them. However, Jack MIDI does not access ALSA MIDI hardware but only FFADO (firewire) MIDI hardware.

Some software bridges, like a2jmidi / j2amidi [4], can interface Jack MIDI with ALSA MIDI devices in Linux systems. These applications are an alternative for connecting ALSA MIDI hardware to JACK MIDI capable applications.

Regarding its performance, there is virtually no jitter in JACK MIDI and it is sample accurate. JACK MIDI event process runs with audio sample blocks and for that reason the system latency can be tuned by adjusting JACK sample rate and process block size.

JACK MIDI event has a timestamp concept that is not directly associated with a time clock. It is associated with the sample position in the audio block associated to this MIDI event. For this reason, this concept of MIDI event time depends on JACK audio block size and sample rate.

2.1.4 Theoretical comparison

Despite the fact that these APIs have different approaches and features, we have grouped some of these features for a theoretical comparison. A summary of this comparison is presented in Table 1.

Feature	ALSA MIDI	Portmidi	JACK
Multi-stream	Yes	No	Yes
Cross-platform	No	Yes	Yes
Virtual devices	Yes	Yes	Yes
Multiples devices	Yes	No	Yes
Multiple connections	Yes	No	Yes
Hardware devices	ALSA	ALSA	FFADO

Table 1. MIDI APIs theoretical comparison

ALSA and JACK are the default sound server + driver in Linux audio context. Being complementary and not concurrent, the choice between one of these APIs depends on the hardware and software involved. Portmidi in Linux is

[3] http://qjackctl.sourceforge.net/

[4] http://home.gna.org/a2jmidid/

implemented over ALSA MIDI and combines the possibility of a direct device connection and porting the application to other operating systems.

3. MEDUSA

Medusa is a music network environment tool developed to simplify multichannel audio and MIDI distribution in computer networks. The Medusa development is divided into two main lines: 1) a common library (libmedusa) that contains the network connections, audio and MIDI pack and transformation, and 2) some specific implementations to connect libmedusa with different sound APIs [11].

The development is organized in a three layer architecture, as depicted in Fig 1.

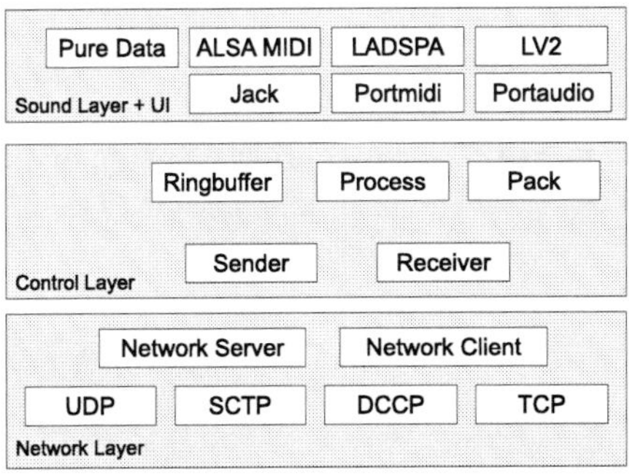

Figure 1. Medusa architecture

The **Network layer** is responsible for creating the network connection and data transmission. Rather than using only UDP for communication, Medusa implements different network transport protocols, namely UDP [12], DCCP [13], TCP [14] and SCTP [15]. Thus, the user can choose between a faster and unreliable protocol, namely UDP or DCCP, or a slower and reliable protocol such as TCP or SCTP. We grouped the protocol dependent implementations using two abstractions: a server that sends data to the network and a client that receives data from the network.

The **Control layer** is responsible for data management, data packing / unpacking, and data transformation. Medusa has two main roles in this layer: sender and receiver. Thus, a user can choose to provide a network resource as a sender or to consume a networked resource as a receiver.

Different sounds APIs have different ways to play / capture audio or MIDI data and need special implementations. The **Sound layer** is outside libmedusa and is responsible for connecting Medusa to specific audio / MIDI systems. For example, Pure Data uses its own object graphic interface, and a LADSPA plugin has a particular GUI; the sound layer puts together the sound API and the user application interface.

3.1 Medusa data flow

To implement MIDI communication, we developed two different data flows inside Medusa, one for audio and other for MIDI, as presented in Fig. 2. While audio can be processed, fragmented, converted from different sample rate, bit depth and byte order, MIDI data flow packs the data with meta-data to transmit it through the network. The audio data flow converts the audio data to a common format. With this feature, Medusa can interchange audio and MIDI data between applications with different audio configurations or be connected through different sound APIs.

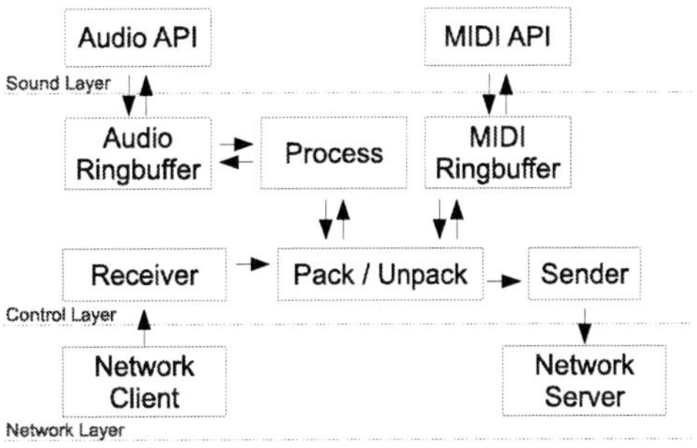

Figure 2. Internal Audio and MIDI data flow

3.2 Medusa package

The Control layer packs the sound data for transmission. This application package has additional meta-data that helps Medusa management. A field in Medusa package identifies the data type (audio or MIDI) and the data channel number. The Medusa_package header is presented in Fig. 3.

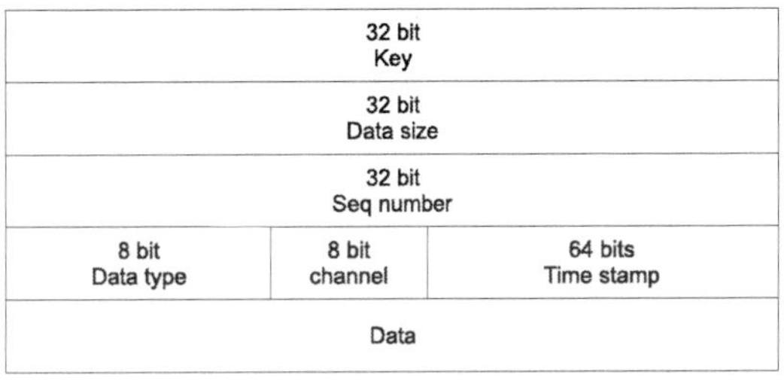

Figure 3. Medusa Package

In addition to the data identification and channel addressing, the package contains a sequential number to verify data loss, a timestamp to measure latency and synchronization, and a key to separate Medusa data from some possible network interference.

3.3 Medusa loopback channel

Every network socket is full duplex. Once we have separated the sender and receiver roles, this socket feature was used to implement a loopback channel.

The Medusa loopback channel allows senders and receivers to measure network performance during data transmission. When loopback mode is enabled, for every Medusa package sent by the server, the client will reply with a loopback message. The structure of a loopback message, as presented in Fig. 4, adds two new fields to the Medusa package. These fields represent the time when the client received the data package and the time when the client played the data from the package.

With this implementation it is possible to measure a network performance in different stages: a) the sender adds

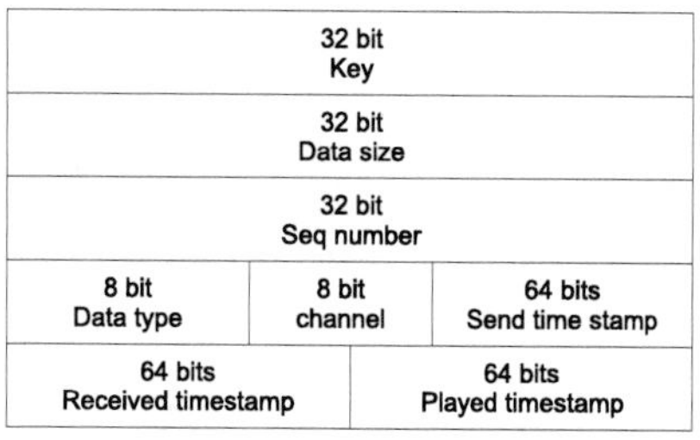

Figure 4. Medusa Loopback Package

the sending timestamp when the data is ready to be sent; b) when the receiver acquires the package, it creates a loopback package using the same packet header timestamped with the receiving time; c) when the receiver plays the package data it timestamps the loopback package and sends it back to the sender; d) the sender returns all the loopback information to a callback function including the time it was received.

Thus, a Medusa application can implement a loopback callback function to measure latency in different communication stages.

4. PRACTICAL PERFORMANCE MEASUREMENT

Using Medusa loopback channel we can compare time performance variations between Medusa implementations using the different MIDI APIs, thus verifying how the choice of MIDI API influences system latency.

4.1 Measurement environment

To measure the system latency a MIDI sequencer was used to produce note-on and note-off commands. We chose Qmidiarp[5] for these tests because it is a MIDI sequencer that runs over ALSA MIDI and JACK MIDI. Thus, we did not need to run an extra software bridge to interface between different APIs.

We set the test loop time to 120 bpm playing two half notes per bar, which means one note-on and one note-off per second. The note duration was set to zero which should result in one note-off event immediately following the note-on. The test was done by executing the loop 1300 times which lasted approximately 11 minutes.

We ran two Medusas in the same machine connected using localhost address. We decided to run these tests on localhost because the sender and receiver can thus use the same clock to timestamp the packages. The first Medusa was sending the MIDI events generated by Qmidiarp and receiving them back from the second instance which was set up as a loopback channel.

Theoretically every note-on should be played one second apart from the preceding and the succeeding note-on, the same being true of each note-off. We will call this theoretical time "expected_t(i)" and the actual time when each event was measured "t(i)". We assumed that the first event would happen at time 0 and so all the other expected note times are integer times relative to the first note. Since the first note can also have some latency, we calculated the minimum difference between all actual note times and corresponding expected note times, as presented in Eqn.1.

$$min\_t = |min(t(n) - expected\_t(n))| \quad (1)$$

We calculated the latency as an average difference between the relative note time and the expected note time adding the minimum latency to all values (Eqn. 2).

$$latency(\Delta t) = \frac{1}{n}\sum_{i=1}^{n}(t(i) - expected\_t(i) + min\_t) \quad (2)$$

The jitter was calculated as the mean latency deviation (Eqn. 3).

$$jitter = \frac{1}{n}\sum_{i=1}^{n}|rt(i) - \Delta t| \quad (3)$$

We also measured the note-off time based on the average difference between note-off and note-on (4).

$$\Delta Note\_off = \frac{1}{n}\sum_{i=1}^{n}(note\_off(i) - note\_on(i)) \quad (4)$$

4.2 Performance tests results

We calculated the system latency in 4 different stages: 1) sender transmission time, 2) receiver acquiring time, 3) receiver playing time and 4) sender loopback receiving time, as depicted in Table 2.

API	Time 1	Time 2	Time 3	Time 4
ALSA MIDI	0.268	0.370	0.745	3.045
Portmidi	2.380	2.574	2.907	5.196
JACK MIDI	3.923	4.033	14.374	14.590

Table 2. Latency measurements (times in ms)

Since the latency varied during the performance, we also calculated the latency deviation, or jitter, as presented in Table 3.

API	Time 1	Time 2	Time 3	Time 4
ALSA MIDI	0.284	0.295	0.674	1.939
Portmidi	0.609	0.936	0.937	2.016
JACK MIDI	2.749	3.950	2.748	2.759

Table 3. Jitter measurements (times in ms)

The average time difference between a note-on and a note-off is presented in Table 4. This table also presents the percentage of note-off events with the same time of the note-on event and latency jitter.

4.3 Data analysis

The "Time 1" column in Table 2 and Table 3 presents the latency and jitter in the server. This data represents how accurately the API would play the notes locally. These tables

[5] http://qmidiarp.sourceforge.net/

API	note-off	jitter	% of same time
ALSA MIDI	0.008	0.009	56%
Portmidi	0.033	0.046	49.5%
JACK MIDI	0.002	0.003	86%

Table 4. Note-off time and jitter (times in ms)

confirm that JACK is the biggest latency adder for playing each note. The data do not confirm the JACK MIDI theoretical features regarding event synchronization. Analyzing the chosen tool documentation, we observed that Qmidiarp does not use JACK's MIDI event sample alignment feature. We repeated the experiment with other MIDI tools such as j2a, j2amidi_bridge and Hydrogen, but since they also do not implement this sample alignment feature, they all present the same issue.

Some other tools implemented over JACK use it only for audio streams, and use other APIs for MIDI connection; examples of these tools are Pure Data, QTractor, RoseGarden and LMMS. Even if we had chosen one of these tools to obtain a more precise MIDI event time, this accuracy would be lost in the MIDI bridge between ALSA MIDI and JACK MIDI. The only implementation/setup that presented MIDI event sample alignment with JACK was the FFADO driver with a firewire sound interface.

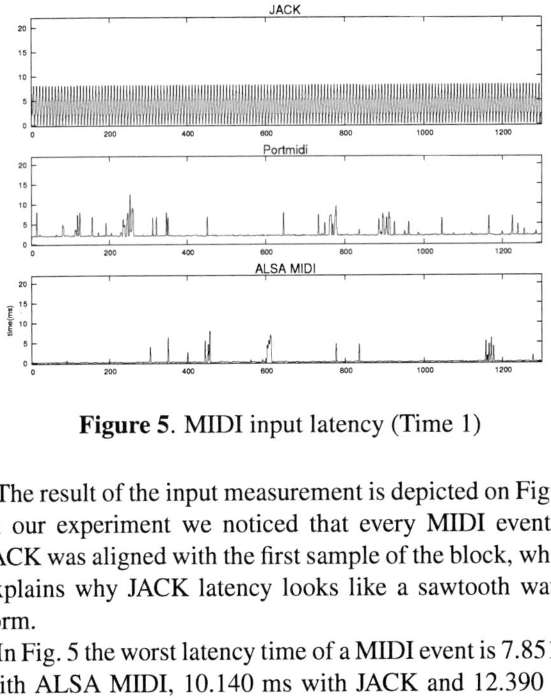

Figure 5. MIDI input latency (Time 1)

The result of the input measurement is depicted on Fig. 5. In our experiment we noticed that every MIDI event in JACK was aligned with the first sample of the block, which explains why JACK latency looks like a sawtooth waveform.

In Fig. 5 the worst latency time of a MIDI event is 7.851 ms with ALSA MIDI, 10.140 ms with JACK and 12.390 ms with Portmidi.

Portmidi is just a wrapper for developing portable music applications. In Linux, it runs over ALSA MIDI. Because Portmidi uses ALSA MIDI through a wrapper interface, it is predictable that ALSA MIDI performance would exceed Portmidi. In spite of ALSA's better outcome, its implementation is not portable and can not be used in other operating systems.

The second column, "Time 2", presents the time that Medusa spent to send the event from the server to the receiver. Subtracting Time 1 from "Time 2", Medusa latency is between 0.1 ms and 0.2 ms for every API. Since we are running on the localhost, this time can be understood as the time that the system spends to pack the MIDI data, copy the data to the kernel space, copy it back to user space and finally unpack the data. Medusa transmission time can be considered small if compared with the API latencies.

The third measured latency is the receiver playing time ("Time 3"), presented in Fig.6. Again, JACK performance can be understood as a simplistic implementation of JACK MIDI sync. Moreover, JACK default is to sync MIDI events with audio blocks and because of this the JACK configuration influences MIDI latency. In our tests, JACK was configured with 48Khz sample rate and a block size of 512 samples, meaning that every JACK block is about 10.67ms long. Since Medusa is not implemented as a JACK internal client, all received data has to wait for the next JACK block to be executed. At this stage, ALSA MIDI and Portmidi latency is very close.

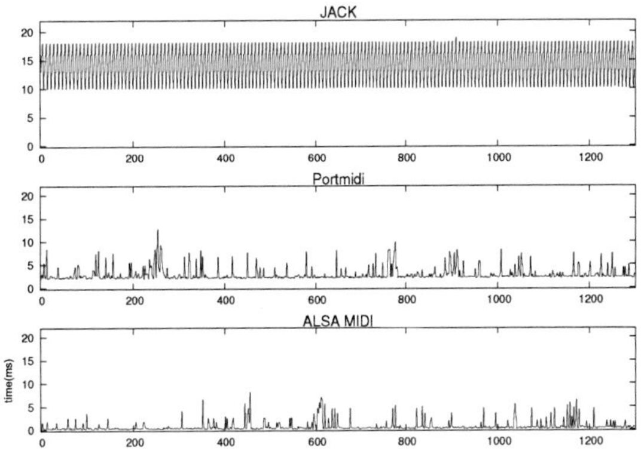

Figure 6. MIDI output latency

The last latency measured, "Time 4", is the loopback time. Since the Medusa loopback package is bigger than a Medusa MIDI package, the time to receive a loopback message is bigger than the time to receive a MIDI message. These data show that a round trip time to send both MIDI data and a loopback package is not simply twice the time to send a package. Furthermore, the loopback time in Medusa also includes the time to process the data in the receiver.

The note-off time, presented in Table 4, can be interpreted as how fast an API responds to two MIDI events occurring at the same time. Knowing that the application was programmed to send a note-on and a note-off at the same time, the way the application reads these events defines how synchronized the events really are. Since JACK aligns both events with the same sample, it will always be more precise having the majority of events occurring simultaneously.

5. CONCLUSIONS

In this paper we presented the Medusa MIDI implementation using different MIDI APIs. We presented these API's features and some theoretical comparisons between them. We also presented the Medusa architecture and how this tool can be used to obtain feedback about the data transmission. We used the Medusa loopback channel and a

MIDI sequencer to measure the latency in a network session.

Regardless of the best time synchronization advertised by JACK MIDI, in our measurements we discovered that the majority of JACK MIDI applications do not use the event synchronization features present in this API. In our tests, the JACK MIDI sync feature was present only in a firewire MIDI interface driver. Unfortunately, several MIDI interfaces use a USB connection and are available in Linux only by ALSA API. Future work should include proposing a better implementation for JACK MIDI applications concerning the JACK MIDI event sample alignment.

In the latency tests, ALSA MIDI presented the best latency performance. Unfortunately this API exists exclusively for Linux and its implementation cannot be ported to other operating systems.

Portmidi is a portable API and a solution for porting Medusa to other operating systems. Portmidi creates a wrapper to the operating system's native API and helps developers in creating portable music applications. Future work includes testing Portmidi performance in other operating systems.

Our experiments also presented how the different stages of network communication influence latency. Another important result was to verify that round trip time does not reflect directly the time between the data capture in the sender and the data playing in the receiver.

Since each MIDI API has a different approach and use context, the present paper does not intend to judge these APIs but to present some limits to MIDI network streaming using Medusa.

It is also important to affirm that different implementations using these APIs may have different results depending on how the API is implemented or how the application is executed.

In the future, we intend to consider sending MIDI timestamp events in the Medusa package to ensure a better network MIDI synchronization between these different APIs.

6. ACKNOWLEDGMENTS

The authors would like to thank the Linux Developers community and all open source software authors. Without their anonymous help this project would not have been possible.

Some friends helped with ideas, feedback and reviews: Wissam Saliba, Pedro Henrique de Faria, Siddhartha Shankar Rana, Egor Sanin, Marcello Giordano and Stephen Sinclair. A special thanks to R. Michael Winters for proofreading.

The authors would like also to thank the support of the funding agencies CNPq (grant no 141730/2010-2), FAPESP - São Paulo Research Foundation (grant no 2008/08623-8) and CAPES (grant no BEX 1194/12-7).

7. REFERENCES

[1] F. R. Moore, "The dysfunctions of MIDI," *Computer Music Journal*, vol. 12, no. 1, pp. 19–28, 1988.

[2] F. L. Schiavoni, M. Queiroz, and F. Iazzetta, "Medusa - a distributed sound environment," in *Proceedings of the Linux Audio Conference*, Maynooth, Ireland, 2011, pp. 149–156.

[3] S. Letz, N. Arnaudov, and R. Moret, "What's new in JACK2?" in *Proceedings of the Linux Audio Conference*, LAC, Ed., Parma, Italy, 2009, pp. 1–9.

[4] A. Carôt, T. Hohn, and C. Werner, "Netjack–remote music collaboration with electronic sequencers on the internet," in *Proceedings of the Linux Audio Conference*, Parma, Italy, 2009, pp. 118 – 122.

[5] C. Chafe, S. Wilson, A. Leistikow, D. Chisholm, and G. Scavone, "A simplified approach to high quality music and sound over IP," in *In Proceedings of the COST G-6 Conference on Digital Audio Effects (DAFX-00*, 2000, pp. 159–164.

[6] A. Carôt, A. Renaud, and B. Verbrugghe, "Network Music Performance (NMP) with Soundjack," in *In Proceedings of NIME 2006 Network Performance Workshop*, 2006.

[7] M. Wright, "Open Sound Control: an enabling technology for musical networking," *Organised Sound*, vol. 10, pp. 193–200, 2005.

[8] G. Loy, "Musicians make a standard: The MIDI phenomenon," *Computer Music Journal*, vol. 9, no. 4, pp. pp. 8–26, 1985. [Online]. Available: http://www.jstor.org/stable/3679619

[9] MIDI Manufacturers Association, "White paper: Comparison of MIDI and OSC," http://www.midi.org/aboutmidi/midi-osc.php, Nov. 2008.

[10] R. Bencina and P. Burk, "Portaudio - an open source cross platform audio api," in *Proceedings of the International Computer Music Conference*, 2001.

[11] F. L. Schiavoni and M. Queiroz, "Network distribution in music applications with medusa," in *Proceedings of the Linux Audio Conference*, Stanford, USA, 2012, pp. 9–14.

[12] J. Postel, "User Datagram Protocol," RFC 768 (Standard), Internet Engineering Task Force, Aug. 1980. [Online]. Available: http://www.ietf.org/rfc/rfc768.txt

[13] E. Kohler, M. Handley, and S. Floyd, "Datagram Congestion Control Protocol (DCCP)," RFC 4340 (Proposed Standard), Internet Engineering Task Force, Mar. 2006, updated by RFCs 5595, 5596. [Online]. Available: http://www.ietf.org/rfc/rfc4340.txt

[14] M. Padlipsky, "TCP-on-a-LAN," RFC 872, Internet Engineering Task Force, Sep. 1982. [Online]. Available: http://www.ietf.org/rfc/rfc872.txt

[15] L. Ong and J. Yoakum, "An Introduction to the Stream Control Transmission Protocol (SCTP)," RFC 3286 (Informational), Internet Engineering Task Force, May 2002. [Online]. Available: http://www.ietf.org/rfc/rfc3286.txt

mono2eN: A Multi-Channel Autospatialisation Performance System

Callum Goddard
Department of Media
Aalto University
School of Arts, Design and Architecture
callum.goddard@aalto.fi

ABSTRACT

This paper presents the mono2eN system, a multi-channel autospatialisation performance system. Developed through a practice-led research approach, the system was originally developed for a multi-channel solo acoustic bass performance. Central to the system is an autospatilisation algorithm that controls the multi-channel spatialisation parameters of a spatialised mono sound source as well as applying a magnitude freeze audio effect. The behaviour of both the spatialisation and freeze effect is dependent upon the audio content of the signal. The motivation behind the system and a technical overview of the autospatialisation algorithm is provided. Two studies are detailed, a performance case study and a user study. These were conducted to gain insight into and to convey the impressions and experience of practitioners and users of the system. Although some concerns over the audio effect triggering were raised, overall the results indicated a positive response to the system. This suggests that the mono2eN system has potential as an easy to understand multi-channel performance system that is able to spatialise any mono audio source, allowing for its use within a large number of contexts.

1. INTRODUCTION

The mono2eN system is a multi-channel autospatialisation performance tool developed through a practice-led research approach. Originally developed to augment a solo acoustic bass performance, it is possible to use any mono audio signal as the input to the system. This allows for it to be used within a large number of contexts. Central to the system is an autospatilisation algorithm that controls the multi-channel spatialisation parameters of a spatialised mono sound source as well as applying a magnitude freeze audio effect. The behaviour of both the spatialisation and magnitude freeze effect is dependent upon the audio content of the signal.

Taking a practice-led approach opens up playful and artistic approaches to the use of technology as well as promoting and encouraging unexpected and innovative applications [1]. The experiential aspect, both in the artefact produced, and the relationship between researcher and research problem, is emphasised. In many cases practice-led research does not start with an identified problem and "enthusiasm of practice" leads instead [2]. Due to the significance experience has within the work, evaluation must happen through (either direct or indirect) experience of the research [2]. Commonly, work is shared with the appropriate communities of practice. A works' adoption into practice, further development by users or new inspired works allow for the impact and effect of the work to be measured. [1]

The the mono2eN system has been shared with, modified and used by practitioners of spatial music (see Section 3.1). The code of the initial system [1] has also been distributed to, and modified by others. [2]

This paper presents the development process of the mono2eN autospatilization performance system from a practice-led perspective. The inspiration and intentions relating to the system and a technical overview of the system primarily focusing on the spatialisation control algorithm are given in section 2. An investigation into the system via a performance case study and user study is detailed and results arising from both are discussed in section 3. Finally, conclusions and the direction of further development to mono2eN system are presented in section 4.

2. THE MONO2EN SYSTEM

The work leading to the mono2eN system was motivated by a personal desire of the author to create a multi-channel performance for an 8-channel concert. [3] The performance intended to use an acoustic bass, on which a solo improvised composition was to be played. As such, both the acoustic bass part and the mono2eN system needed to be developed to complement each other.

Several design challenges presented themselves in the system's development. The pieces central identity and aesthetic was an improvised solo acoustic bass performance, thus, any method of enabling multi-channel performance required that the core character of the piece remained. [4] Also, no permanent alterations or augmentations were wished to be made to the acoustic bass as the piece was originally intended as single performance. Any additional controls

[1] http://sccode.org/1-4T6
[2] http://sccode.org/1-4T8
[3] http://tai-studio.org/index.php/projects/4for8/4for82012/
[4] That it still sounded like an acoustic bass guitar being played

could also not hinder the playability of the instrument, due to the playing and performance style of the piece.

The acoustic bass would be played and heard along side the multi-channel mix, having the acoustic bass sound spatialised to varying positions around the performance space was found to best complemented the acoustic sound from the bass guitar.

Due to the piece being improvised, having a static or predetermined mix was not desirable. As the musical content was to be improvised, dynamic and variable, it was wished that the spatialisation also contained these characteristics. This raised the question of how to develop a control method that would allow for the performer to improvise the mixing of the output channels whilst performing.

The solution settled upon was to develop an autospatialisation algorithm that would respond to the acoustic bass's signal (a mono audio signal) and use this to control the spatialisation parameters. This solution accounted for the aesthetic considerations, and provided an adequate solution to the design challenges faced relating to control over the spatialisation.

2.1 Spatialisation Techniques

Spatialisation methods have ever increasingly been used within electroacoustic music as multi-channel systems have become readily available [3]. Practitioners today have many potential methods for spatialisation which can be applied to a variety of contexts. Two potential methods of spatialisation which were considered within the implementation of the mono2eN system were Vector Base Amplitude Panning (VBAP) [4] and Wave Field Synthesis (WFS) [5,6].

VBAP uses changes in the relative volume levels of audio channels to determine the spatial positions of a sound. As this method of spatialisation is based upon altering the amplitude of the sound, is transparency, allowing the performance to retain its sonic character. Spatialisation is however, very dependent on speaker positioning relative to the listener.

WFS attempts to overcome this shortcoming through synthesising the wave front of a sound source [6]. In this respect overcoming the requirement for a 'sweet spot' where accurate spatialisation is heard. There as also been work into interactions with sound sources generated through WFS [7].

2.2 Implementation

The mono2eN system prototype was developed using SuperCollider.[5] Being developed through a practice-led approach, the exact algorithm that was implemented has been developed and tuned according to the authors personal preferences. In the process of developing the initial spatialisation algorithm, it was desired that an additional audio effect be added. Inspired by the idea of sound artefacts being left behind as the sound is spatialised, an algorithmically triggered magnitude freeze effect was implemented along side the autospatialisation algorithm.

[5] `http://supercollider.sourceforge.net/`

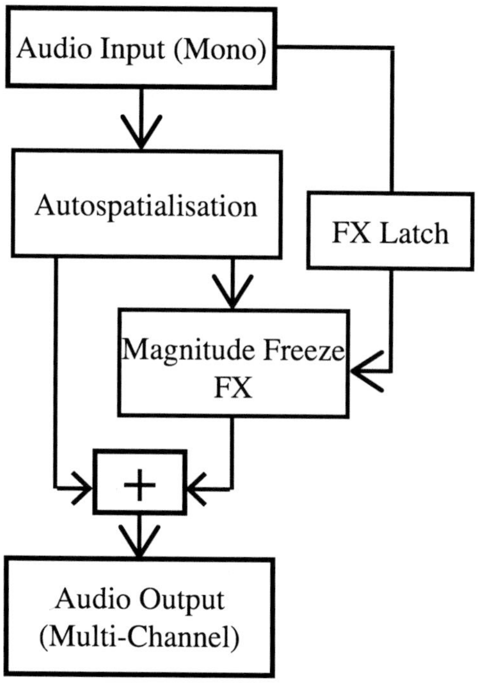

Figure 1. A structural overview of the mono2eN algorithm

The overall structure of the system can be seen as containing three parts: the autospatilisation, the FX latch and the magnitude freeze FX. The overall structure of the mono2eN system can be seen in Figure 1.

2.2.1 Autospatilaization

Autospatialisation (see Fig. 2) is achieved by panning the mono signal around a ring of speakers. This is achieved in SuperCollider by using the `PanAz`[6] function. Whilst more precise spatialisation could potentially be achieved by using VBAP or WFS, this project was primarily focusing on the interaction with the spatialisation. For this `PanAz` provided the perfect compromise between ease of use, only requiring one parameter, the panning azimuth, as well as providing effective spatialisation for the purpose of the performance.

Spectral analysis is performed on the incoming signal through the use of the SuperCollider `FFT`.[7] The centroid value of the input audio signal is calculated continuously. This value is used to determine the panning azimuth (angle) for the `PanAz` function, and thus the position the sound is panned to around the speaker ring. Once the sound has been panned the resulting audio channels are randomised in order to mitigate the inherent circling present in panning around a ring of speakers. This also reduces the multichannel chorus like sound that can be produced when the signal is panned around the speaker ring too quickly. Whilst doing this means that exact spatial positions are unable to be specified, the overall result is a perceptually more spatial system.

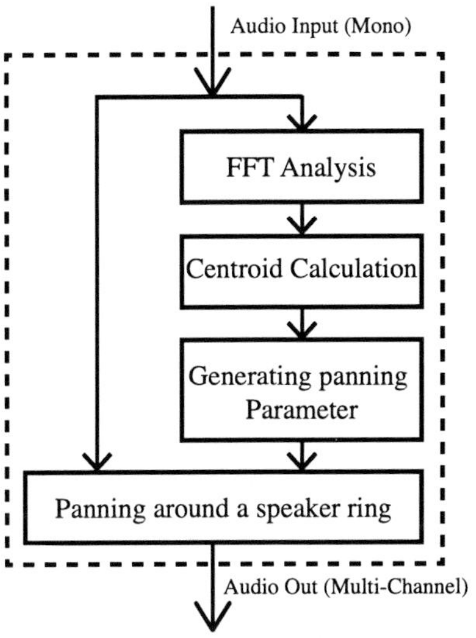

Figure 2. A structural overview of the autospatialisation part of the mono2eN system

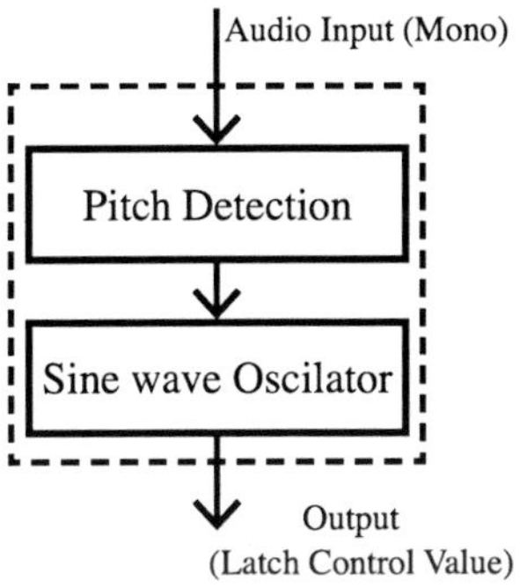

Figure 3. A structural overview of the FX Latch part of the mono2eN system

2.2.2 FX Latch

The FX latch (see Fig. 3) generates a control signal that turns the magnitude freeze FX on and off. A pitch value (p) is calculated using `Pitch`[8] with an amplitude threshold of 0.7 and median value of 7. When the input signal is above the amplitude threshold of the pitch detector. This value, p, is scaled and then used to set the frequency of a sine wave oscillator. The instantaneous amplitude value from the sine wave oscillator is then used as the trigger value for the magnitude freeze FX.

The sine wave oscillator also functions as a latch. When the input signal is below the pitch detector's amplitude threshold the sine wave oscillator's frequency is set to zero. The instantaneous amplitude of the oscillator remains constant until the frequency is set to a non-zero value, producing the latch behaviour.

Whilst the frequency of the oscillator is non-zero the instantaneous amplitude will vary between -1 and 1, the speed this occurs at is dependent on the frequency of sine wave oscillator (which is based on the input signal). This offers a degree of perceived instability to the latch, as well as offering the potential for skilled users of the system to trigger the magnitude freeze FX and develop rhythmic patterns.

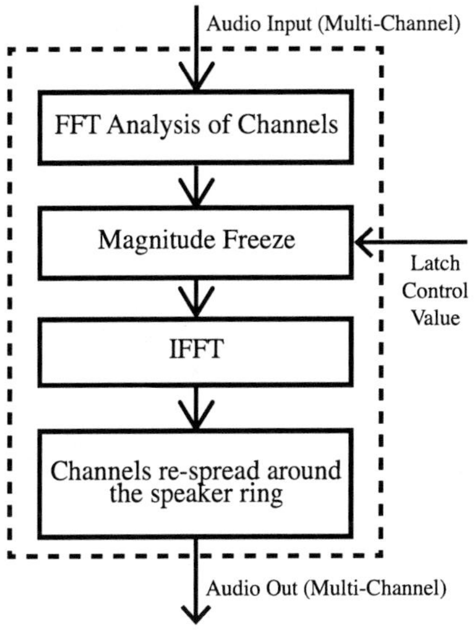

Figure 4. A structural overview of magnitude freeze FX part of the mono2eN system

2.2.3 Magnitude Freeze FX

The magnitude freeze FX (see Fig. 4) is applied to the spatialised audio signal. The output audio channels from the `PanAz` function (also corresponding to each output speaker) are individually spectrally analysed with an `FFT`. This analysis is done continuously. When the latch control value is above zero the magnitudes of the analysed values are frozen. This is achieved by using `PV_MagFreeze`.[9] An inverse `FFT` (`IFFT`) is performed to reconstruct the signal, and the channels are re-distributed around the speaker ring using the `SplayAz`[10] SuperCollider function. Finally, both the output of the spatialised signal and the frozen signal and added together and passed to the output.

2.3 Example Audio Files

Audio examples of the mono2eN system can be found at: `https://soundcloud.com/callumgoddard/sets/mono2ensamples`. An electric bass guitar and a Doepfer Dark Energy Synthesiser[11] have been used as the mono sound sources. An 8 channel output has been spread across a stereo field, both mono and processed audio examples are provided for comparison.

3. INVESTIGATION INTO THE SYSTEM

The evaluation of digital performance tools is becoming a much more important factor within the field of sound and computer music (SMC) and New Interfaces for Musical Expression (NIME). Whilst earlier methods within the

[6] `http://doc.sccode.org/Classes/PanAz.html`
[7] `http://doc.sccode.org/Classes/FFT.html`
[8] `http://doc.sccode.org/Classes/Pitch.html`
[9] `http://doc.sccode.org/Classes/PV_MagFreeze.html`
[10] `http://doc.sccode.org/Classes/SplayAz.html`
[11] `http://www.doepfer.de/Dark_Energy_e.htm`

Figure 5. Picture of Cartes Flux Performance of wosawip

field have followed ideas from the field of Human Computer Interaction (HCI) [8], more recent approaches have questioned their suitability in assessing musical interfaces [9, 10]. This has lead to the assessment of other evaluation methods, from quantitative to qualitative [9], to considering multiple perspectives [11]. Common to both [9, 11], is understanding what is wanted to be evaluated and why.

The investigation into the mono2eN system has been undertaken for two main reasons. The first, to gain insight into the immediate views and experiences of users of the system. Understanding and being aware of the users perspective, to inform and inspire further developments of the system. The second reason is to convey the experiential aspects of the system through presenting users views. These views, combined with audio files (Section 2.3, are hoped to provide sufficient indirect access to the mono2eN system to enable an insight into the experience the system provides.

The investigation draws on two cases. The first is a case study of an individual who adopted and used the mono2eN system into their performance practice. The second is a qualitative user study to gain insight into the initial impressions of musicians when using the system.

3.1 Performance Case Study

The mono2eN prototype system was given to, adapted and used by Till Bovermann within the performance wosawip, an improvised 4-channel duet. [12] The performance was performed as part of the Cartes Flux Festival [13] and CARPA 3. [14] Within the performance Till Bovermann played a monophonic synth called Benjolin [15] through a slightly altered version of the mono2eN patch. This was played alongside Chi-Hsia Lai who was performing with her own performance system WanderOnStage [12, 13].

Bovermann used the patch for a period of 6 months leading up to the first wosawip performance. During this period he made his own aesthetic adjustments to the patch via parameter values. He was interviewed after the Cartes Flux performance to gain insights into his experiences of using and performing with the mono2eN system.

Overall his experience was a positive one. It was noted that the system was easy to play at first and that it *"takes care of the spatialisation aspects in a way I like"*. More interestingly was that in using the mono2eN system with the Benjolin the original sound of the Benjolin was forgotten - with Bovermann stating: *"I honestly forgot how the Benjolin sounds"*. This resulted in the Benjolin + mono2eN system being perceived as a single instrument.

The sound of the magnitude freeze effect was also enjoyed once it activated. However, the transitions between it switching on an off were criticised due to their abrupt nature. So too was the control over the triggering, due to its perceived randomness in action. These factors meant that whilst the effect was enjoyed the control over it was mostly ignored, and the system was left to behave by itself.

Bovermann has continued to used the Benjolin through the mono2eN system in a second performance. Whilst more control over the magnitude freeze effect was desirable, his comments indicated that a lack of control did not render the system unusable or dramatically detract from the experience.

3.2 User Study

A qualitative user study was carried out to gain insight into the initial impressions musicians have when using the system. This was undertaken to inform the future developments of the mono2eN system.

3.2.1 Experimental Methodology

In total there were 4 participants, all musicians, 3 male, 1 female. The sample size was small due to the need for participants to both be able to play an instrument and have familiarity with interactive music systems. Participants brought their own instruments to use with the system, these included: both an electric and an acoustic guitar, a tactile synthesiser and percussion bowls/blocks.

Each participant was invited, in individual sessions, to play their instrument through the system. The structure of each session was as follows:

1. Participants were asked to sign a consent form.
2. Participants were asked to describe their musical background.
3. Participants were invited to play their instrument through the mono2eN system.
4. Semi-structured interview was conducted asking participants about their experiences and impressions of the mono2eN system.

Within the interview priority was given to participants discussions of the system in their own terms. Due to the possibility for misconceptions or misunderstandings to arise in this scenario, the following was decided:

[12] `http://tai-studio.org/index.php/projects/compositions/wosawip/`
[13] `http://cartes-art.fi/flux/en/ohjelma-programme/`
[14] `http://www.teak.fi/Tutkimus/carpa/`
[15] `http://casperelectronics.com/finished-pieces/benjolin/`

- All participants were allowed to ask questions when using the system, about how it works or on anything they were unsure of.
- If a participant wanted to know the details of the system it would be explained.
- Participants were allowed to play for as long as they wanted with no interruption to their playing.
- If they requested, they were allowed to have a second session after the interview.

The nature of the session was informal and planned to last 30 minutes. 10 minutes being allocated for participants to play with the system and 20 minutes allocated for the interview. In reality the playing times varied from around 6 minutes to 30 minutes, and with interviews lasting around 10 minutes. All performances were recorded. The mono input and multi-channel output of each performance were recorded through the MacBook Pro running the SuperCollider patch. A portable audio recorder with microphone also recorded the whole session, specifically to record the interview for transcription.

3.2.2 *Analysis*

The interviews were transcribed, then analysed based upon a grounded theory approach. [16] Here the data drives the theory formation. The interviews were compared for commonalities; these commonalities were then used to indicate the users' initial impressions and experience of the mono2eN system.

3.2.3 *Results*

The main areas of interest that arose from the interviews related to understanding, focus and enjoyment of the system. The overall comments indicated that the system was enjoyable to use. All participants when asked, were able to describe what the system was doing and were able to provide an explanation that approximated what the mono2eN system did. Participants did not find that the focus on their playing was disrupted by the system.

These results suggest that the system, as it stands, is easy to learn or at least intuitively understood when used. Playing times also indicate that the system encouraged playing, especially as 3 of the 4 participants wished to play a second time. The participant who did not wish to play again was satisfied with the playing session as well as with their understanding of the system deciding that no further playing was needed. They did however, express an interest in the code used for the system.

The comments from the case study relating to the instrument and system being perceived as one continued with the use of each instrument. The system also appeared to reveal parts of the instrument sound that participants were not aware of. This being indicated through a comment were a participant stated that they were: *"hearing things I hadn't heard before coming from my instrument when playing it through the system"* and that it *"...brings out details you wouldn't have heard so obviously..."*.

As in the case study, concerns over the FX latch triggering were raised. Participants responses varied from having some understanding of control, to not being aware they had any control over the trigger for the magnitude freeze effect.

The last thing to arise from this user study was the inaccessibility of code to musicians. Those participating within the study were offered a copy of the patch and half declined due to their unfamiliarity with SuperCollider. This is a consideration needed when the system is further developed and distributed.

4. CONCLUSIONS

This paper presented the mono2eN autospatialisation performance system which algorithmically spatialises a mono audio signal around a speaker ring. The design challenges and implementation were described from a practice-led research approach and the system algorithms described. A case and user study were conducted to gain insights into musicians views of the system and to inform and inspire further development.

The mono2eN system used a relatively simple method for spatialisation, however, the result was an effective system for musical performance which does not requiring any specialised speaker setup (beyond position speakers within a ring). The effect of using a more sophisticated spatialisation method within in the system is uncertain and maybe interesting to explore. However, the main focus of the system's development was to allow for automated control over sound spatialisation for a musical performance, which the system has achieved.

The interest of practitioners was positive as were the comments gained through the user tests and suggest the mono2eN system has the potential as a multi-channel performance tool. Comments indicated, that whilst the system is easy to use and understand in terms of the spatialisation algorithm, the method of control over the FX trigger caused concern. This concern however, did not prevent users from enjoying using the system.

The systems accessibility is also a concern and the way the final system is shared is an important consideration. Distributing the system as SuperCollider code allows for greater flexibility and user customisation of the algorithm, however, it also isolates the system from those who are not as technically inclined. Reducing the technological barrier of access, whilst encouraging adoption into practice, will need to be carefully considered as the system is further developed.

Practice-led development of the mono2eN system will continue. Finding solutions to these newly presented challenges will direct further development of the mono2eN system. In addressing these challenges it is hoped further spatial effects and interactions will emerge.

Acknowledgments

The author would like to thank Julian Parker and Till Bovermann for their suggestions and advice.

[16] `http://www.aral.com.au/resources/grounded.html`

5. REFERENCES

[1] C. Lawson, "Practice-led research: Examples from artists working with technology," in *cumulushelsinki2012.org*, 2012, pp. 1–11.

[2] B. Haseman, "A manifesto for performative research," *Media International Australia incorporating Culture and Policy, theme issue "Practice-led Research"*, no. 118, pp. 98–106, 2006.

[3] F. Otondo, "Contemporary trends in the use of space in electroacoustic music," *Organised Sound*, vol. 13, no. 1, pp. 77–81, 2008.

[4] V. Pulkki, "Virtual source positioning using vector base amplitude panning*," *J. Audio Eng. Soc.*, vol. 45, no. 6, pp. 456–466, 1997.

[5] G. Theile, "Wave field synthesis - a promising spatial audio rendering concept," in *Proc. of the 7th Int. Conference on Digital Audio Effects (DAFx'04)*, Naples, Italy, October 5-8 2004.

[6] E. Corteel and T. Caulkins, "Sound scene creation and manipulation using wave field synthesis," IRCAM, Paris, France, Tech. Rep., 2004.

[7] W. Fohl and M. Nogalski, "A gesture control interface for a wave field synthesis," in *Proceedings of the International Conference on New Interfaces for Musical Expression*, Daejeon, Korea, May 27-30 2013.

[8] M. M. Wanderley and N. Orio, "Evaluation of input devices for musical expression: Borrowing tools from hci," *Computer Music Journal*, vol. 23, no. 3, pp. 62–76, Fall 2002.

[9] D. Stowell, A. Robertson, N. Bryan-Kinns, and M. Plumbley, "Evaluation of live human–computer music-making: Quantitative and qualitative approaches," *International Journal of Human-Computer Studies*, vol. 67, pp. 960–975, June 23 2009.

[10] A. Johnston, "Beyond evaluation : Linking practice and theory in new musical interface design," in *Proceedings of the International Conference on New Interfaces for Musical Expression*, Oslo, Norway, 2011.

[11] S. O'Modhrain, "A framework for the evaluation of digital musical instruments," *Computer Music Journal*, vol. 35, no. 1, pp. 28–42, Spring 2011.

[12] C.-H. Lai, "Wanderonstage: the convergence of percussion performance and media technology," in *Proceedings of the 7th Audio Mostly Conference: A Conference on Interaction with Sound*, Corfu, Greece, September 24-26 2012.

[13] C.-H. Lai and T. Bovermann, "Audience experiance in sound performance," in *Proceedings of the International Conference on New Interfaces for Musical Expression*, Daejeon, Korea, May 27-30 2013.

MODELING AND SIMULATION: THE SPECTRAL CANON FOR CONLON NANCARROW BY JAMES TENNEY

Charles de Paiva Santana, Jean Bresson, Moreno Andreatta
UMR STMS, IRCAM-CNRS-UPMC
1, place I.Stravinsly 75004 Paris, France
{charles.de.paiva, jean.bresson, moreno.andreatta}@ircam.fr

ABSTRACT

This paper presents an approach for the analysis of musical pieces, based on the notion of computer modeling. The thorough analysis of musical works allows to reproduce compositional processes and implement them in computer models, opening new perspectives for the their exploration through the simulation and generation of variations derived from the original model.

1. INTRODUCTION

During the analysis of a musical work, musicologists wonder how different decisions in the elaboration of a composition would have affected the final score. For instance: how would certain serial piece be affected if the composer had followed the base series or tone-rows without any deviations, or how a different starting parameter would affect a process-based composition, and so on. In order to face these situations and investigate the corresponding hypotheses, the more or less conscious, accurate and comprehensive simulation of the pieces' generative processes is often essential. The modeling of a musical work requires the explicit formulation of the underlying relations existing between different aspects of its compositional process. Computer tools and environments can be of a precious help here, and the implementation of carefully designed models may allow to simulate, explore and compare the potential results of different possible compositional "choices" or alternatives for a work. We call such alternatives the different *instances* of the piece, and will use this concept as a base for our computer-aided analysis approach. We believe that the study and analysis of musical works through computational modeling and the generation of alternative instances may bring to light new interesting knowledge about the compositional processes and attitudes at their origins.

The pioneering works by Riotte and Mesnage [10] thoroughly explored the idea of modeling compositional processes with the computer.The Morphoscope software they developed permitted the implementation of computer processes considering scores jointly with the analytical and compositional models. However their results laid upon formalisation and validation of constructed models, while the study of compositional decisions and the simulation of alternatives was not a major concern.

Closer to our working perspective, previous works have also been carried out for the computer-assisted modeling and analysis of Xenakis' music in Patchwork [8] and OpenMusic [1], or for the analytical "re-composition" of Boulez' *Structures Ia* [2] in the OpenMusic and Rubato software environments. The approach we propose inherits from these previous works and develops the concept of model to produce alternative instances of the pieces.

We consider this idea of modeling and simulating pieces for the generation of alternative instances, and discuss its consequences on the musicological approach. We choose as a starting point the piece *Spectral CANON For CONLON Nancarrow* by James Tenney (1974) and develop a methodology to question some of Tenney's compositional choices and envisage expansions and his use of the "spectral" techniques.

This paper is organized as follows. In Section 2 we present the model and give preliminary elements for the analysis of James Tenney's piece. Section 3 describes the implementation of our model in the OpenMusic environment, which is then studied and extended in Section 4 in order to generate alternative instances of the piece. We conclude with some perspectives on this musicological approach and its possible use in future musicological projects.

2. THE MODEL OF JAMES TENNEY'S *SPECTRAL CANON FOR CONLON NANCARROW*

This piece *Spectral CANON For CONLON Nancarrow* by James Tenney (1932-2006) [11] for player piano is based on the idea of a correspondence between rhythmic and pitch interval ratios which recalls us of Henry Cowell's homologous ideas described in his book *New Musical Resources* [5].

Several versions of the piece are known to date. The original one by James Tenney dates back from 1974. It has been rewritten and extended by composer Clarence Barlow in 1990. [1] Previous analyses of the piece include for instance Polanski's (1983) [9] and Wannamaker (2012) [12].

[1] See http://conlonnancarrow.org/symposium/ClarenceBarlow.html. More recently, the Irish composer Ciarán Maher created some other variations based on Tenney instructions. See http://rhizomecowboy.com/spectral_variations/

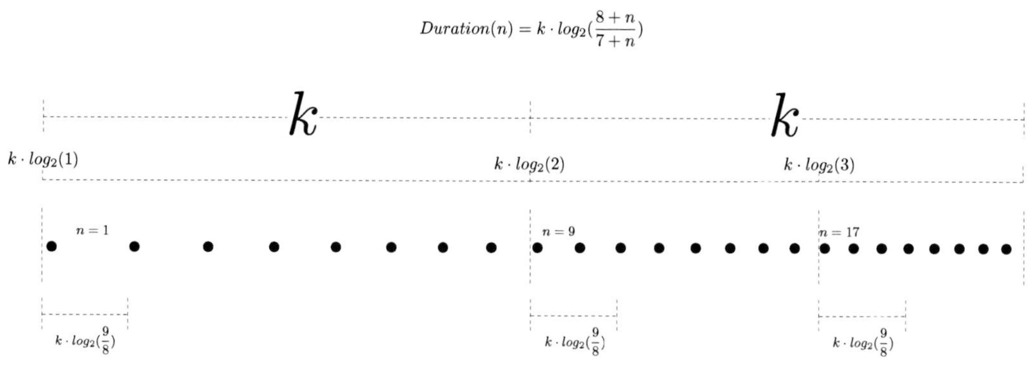

Figure 1. Representation of the series of durations (seen as the intervals between points). Its proportions are exactly the same of an harmonic series starting with the eighth overtone (9:8 ratio). k is an arbitrary duration value equivalent with the first octave. Subsequent octaves are equivalent of $k \cdot log_2(2)$, $k \cdot log_2(3)$ and so forth.

2.1 General Structure of the Piece

The piece consists of a 24 voices canon, where all voices share a same series of decreasing durations (*accelerando*), and superimpose to one another following a precisely determined pattern. When a voice reaches the end of the series, it begins playing its own retrograde.

2.2 Series of Durations

The series of durations is obtained by calculating the intervals between successive partials of the harmonic series, starting with the eighth one (9:8, corresponding to a major second). The general formula to obtain these intervals in the pitch domain multiplies the value of one octave in cents (1200) by the binary logarithm of each interval. To calculate series of durations, we replace the octave in cents by an arbitrary value in seconds, which we call the constant k:

$$duration(n) = k \cdot log_2(\frac{8+n}{7+n})$$

Tenney chose the precise value of k aiming the first interval to last four seconds:

$$k \cdot log_2(\frac{9}{8}) = 4, \quad k = 4\, log_2(\tfrac{9}{8}), \quad k = 23.539797$$

As the original series begins with the eighth interval in the harmonic series, it takes 8 durations to sum the value of k (or one octave). Figure 1 resumes the previous properties of durations and intervals. The total number of durations in the series is related to the number of voices (see next section).

2.3 Voice entries

The 24 voices enter at the successive "octaves" in the initial series of durations (hence, every eight elements in the series). The second voice enters when the first voice is twice faster, the third voice enters when the first voice is thrice faster and so forth. Figure 2 shows a reduced scheme of the voice entries. After 184 durations (8×23), the 24th voice enters and the first voice stops its 'forward' motion.

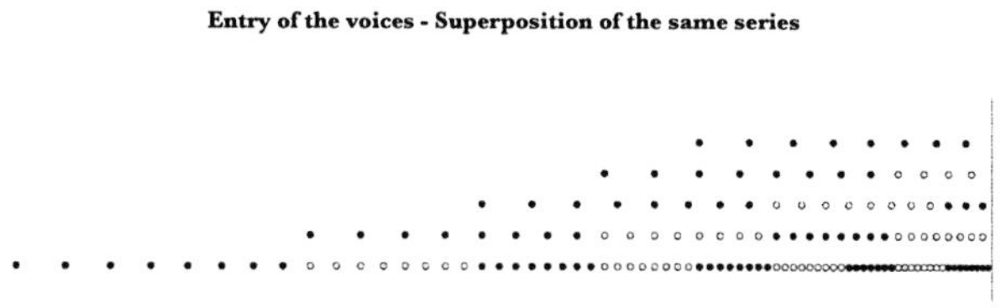

Entry of the voices - Superposition of the same series

Figure 2. Reduced representation of the voices entries. Each group represents a cycle of eight durations (the space of one 'durational octave')

2.4 Retrograde voices

The series retrograde is systematically appended to every voice in the canon.In the original version, the piece ends when the first voice completes its retrograde, and when the 24th voice ends its regular series, which is a point when all voices share the same attack.

Barlow's extended version of the canon continues until the last voice also finishes a complete retrograde. Since each voice starts its retrogradation and consequently decelerates at different moments, new unexpected textures emerge, forming melodic patterns, harmonic *glissandi* and chords due to occasional points of synchronism.

2.5 Pitches

Each voice plays repeatedly one single tone corresponding to its position in the canon (and in the harmonic series): the second voice plays twice the frequency of the first voice (octave), the third voice plays thrice the frequency of the first voice (fifth), and so forth. In this way, this piece is also a melodic canon (even if a very elementary one) where each voice plays a transposition of the first one at a precise interval, starting with the traditional ones (transposition at the octave, fifth) and going up to the most unusual intervals, smaller than one semitone.

3. IMPLEMENTATION OF THE MODEL

Our present work mostly takes place in the OpenMusic computer-aided composition environment [3, 4]. Open-

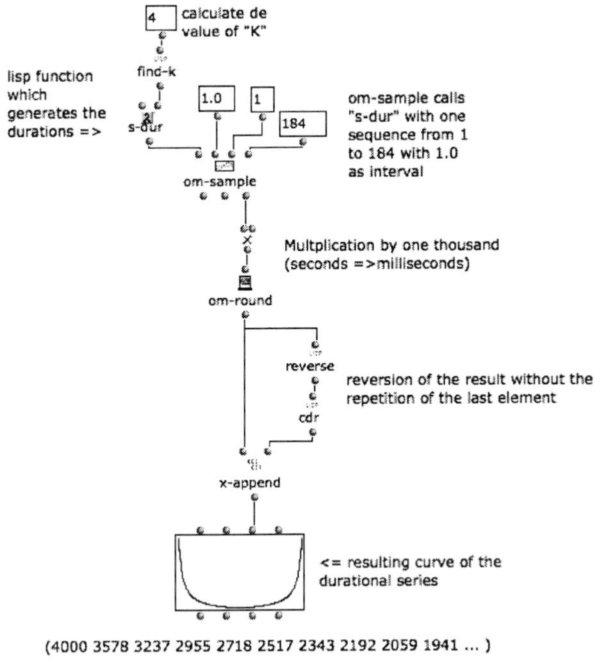

Figure 3. Generating the series of durations for *Spectral CANON for CONLON Nancarrow* in OpenMusic. The *s-dur* and *find-k* modules at the top of the figure refer to the functions implementing respectively the formulas for the series and first duration given in section 2.2.

Music is a visual programming language allowing to define and connect together functions and data structures in graphical programs, and to evaluate these programs to produce and transform musical data.

From the specifications given above we can easily implement functions in OpenMusic to generate the durations for one voice of the canon and to determine k for any chosen value for the first duration. The process of retrogradation is also implemented by simply appending the resulting series of durations with its reversion. This whole process is illustrated in Figure 3. Figure 4 shows the computation of the voices' entry times and of the pitches via the implementation of the specification given in section 2.3, and using an harmonic series generator for the pitches.

Starting from this implementation of the canon's generative process, we build a global model allowing to generate the piece, and highlighting a number of parameters identified in the previous sections: first duration of the series, pitch fundamental, number of voices, number of elements in the series, application (or not) of the retrograde, etc. (see Figure 5). These parameters (and others to be described in the next sections) will allow us to control and generate the score instances. With Tenney's original parameters, we obtain the score in Figure 6.

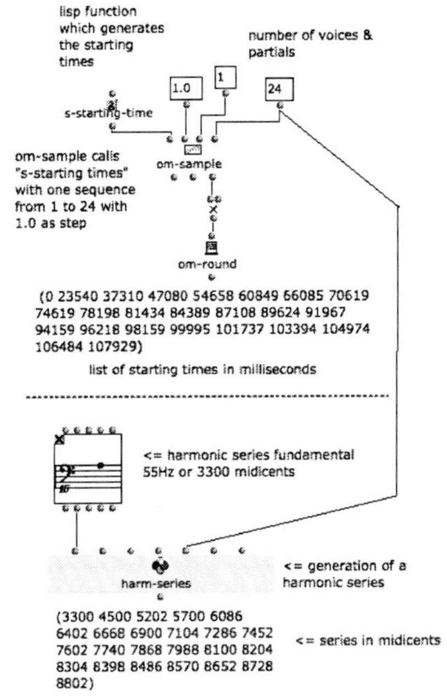

Figure 4. Computation of the voice entries and pitches for *Spectral CANON for CONLON Nancarrow* in OpenMusic. The *s-starting-time* module at the left refers to the function calculating the voice entries as specified in section 2.3. The *harm-series* module calculates the n (here, 24) first partials or harmonics of a fundamental pitch.

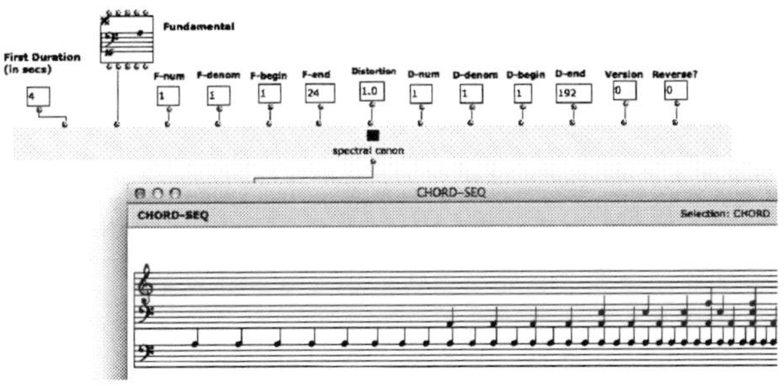

Figure 5. The model of *Spectral CANON for CONLON Nancarrow* in OpenMusic. The *spectral canon* box is an abstraction containing the previous implemented aspects of the canon.

4. EXPLORING THE MODEL

4.1 Compositional Choices and Parameters of the Models

Through the parametrization of the model we can explore the implication of the decisions and choices made by the composer at creating the piece.

We can for instance examine the compromise of an initial duration of 4 seconds, and the number of elements in the series of durations (184) related to the number of voices. Thanks to the modeling process, every simulation produces musical data structures (scores) which can be stored, visualized and listened in the computer environment. Quantitative elements of analysis could be for instance the total duration of the resulting score and the minimal (last) duration in a given parametrized sequence.

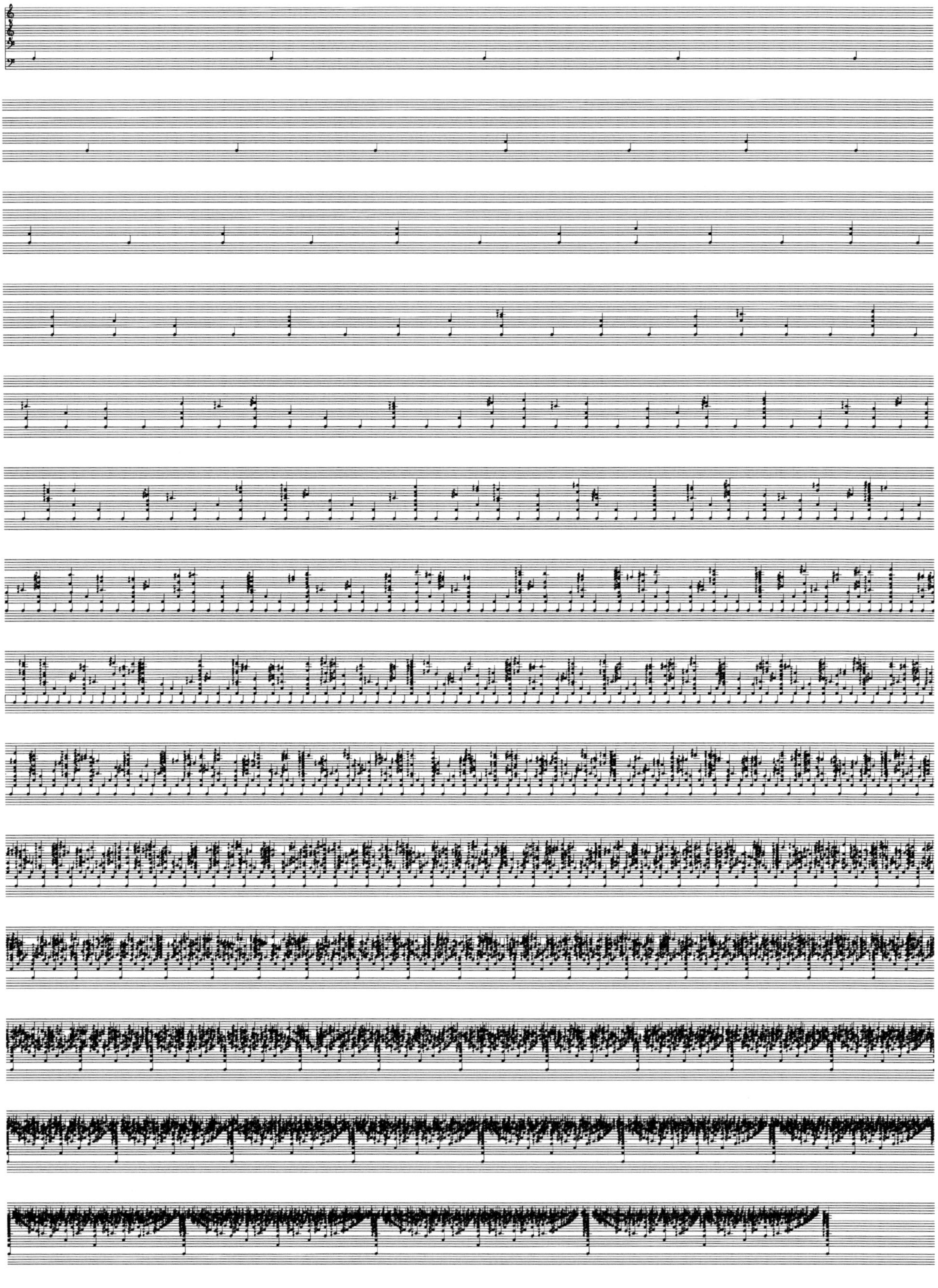

Figure 6. Complete score of the original version of *Spectral Canon For Conlon Nancarrow* generated from the implementation of the model, without any score edition. Interested readers can compare with the published score [11].

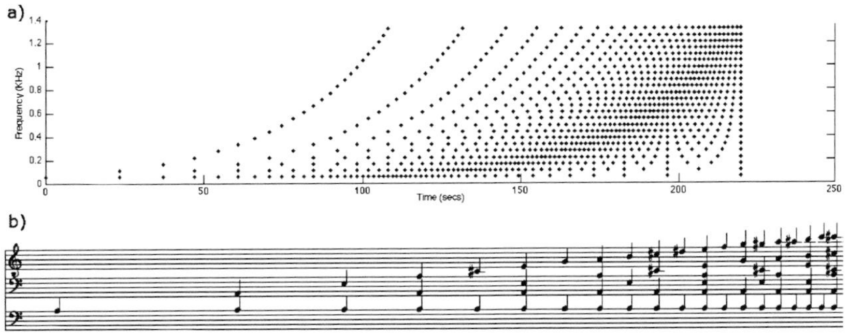

Figure 7. An instance of the canon with initial ratio of 2:1. a) Schematic 2D visualization of the pitches and onsets. b) Beginning of the score.

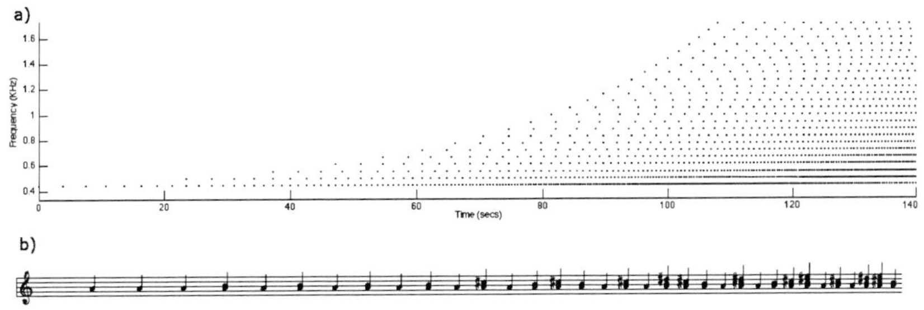

Figure 8. An instance of the canon beginning the harmonic series with the interval 9:8. a) Schematic 2D visualization of the pitches and onsets (0"-140"). b) Excerpt of the score from (appx. 44" to 60").

With Tenney's values, we obtain at total duration around 216 seconds, and a minimal duration for the last element in the series of about 176 ms. This minimal value is still long enough for a sensible perceptual appreciation, and generally speaking the acceleration and subsequent *ritardando* have an adequate variation rate to keep the attention from the listener. This would not be the case, for instance, with an initial duration of more than 6 or less than 3 seconds. (see [7] for a deeper discussion about the perception of continuous accelerations). Experiments in varying these parameters (while maintaining the others) actually show very few interesting score results: we therefore suppose that Tenney's choices for these values correspond to some kind of an ideal state for the model.

A more flexible parameter to explore through the model is the initial superparticular number at the origin of the series of durations' formula. As we have seen, Tenney begins the series of durations with the eighth interval of the harmonic series (corresponding to the ratio 9:8), when he could have chosen any of them, including the first one (2;1, the octave). By tuning this initial value as a parameter in our implementation, we can experiment with possible variations. Figure 7 shows an instance of the piece generated with an initial ratio of 2:1. This ratio equals the initial one used for the series of frequencies and voice entries. [2]

We see that while the piece is equally well structured, its texture in the "forward segment" is more of a "choral" (i.e., mostly constituted of chords and/or synchronized attacks) than the polyrhythmic texture that Tenney was probably looking for in his homage to Nancarrow.

In Figure 8 at the contrary, we keep the initial 9:8 ratio for the series of durations, but we apply it for the pitches as well, so that the first pitch of the first voice is not the fundamental but the the eighth partial in the harmonic series. In this case, however, we see that pitch ambitus becomes too narrow and the canon looses most of its timbre richness and perceptual features (although this can be of an aesthetic interest, or compensated with the manipulation of other parameters).

4.2 Generalizing the model

A second step in our modeling and simulation approach, enabled by the computer implementation, is to explore and modify the functional definitions in its generative processes. In particular for Tenney's canon, we can integrate additional "spectral" processes such as filtering and distortion, and expand the realm of the possible instances produced by this model, yet still driven by the same compositional concepts. These two examples are envisaged below.

4.2.1 Spectral distortion.

The interest in spectral distortion comes from the well-know fact that the overtone series we calculate is actually an ideal model, which is rarely found as such in natural phenomena. In the sounds of acoustic instruments, partials usually deviate more or less from the exact multiples of the perceived pitch or fundamental (this distortion is easy to hear in the low notes of the piano). To model the spectral distortion we use the formula:

$$partial = fundamental \cdot rank^{dist}$$

[2] This configuration gives us a more compact version of the piece. For a better visualisation, we will use this 2:1 ratio in the other examples given later on in this paper.

A distortion index $dist < 1$ causes a compression of the harmonic series, and at the contrary $dist > 1$ causes a dilatation of the series. (see also [6], p. 93).

In our model of Tenney's *Spectral Canon*, and following the principle of correspondence between pitches and durations, we use this formula to compute the harmonic and duration series, as well as the voice offsets (in order to stay in the "default" configuration, we simply set $dist = 1$). This extension of the model enables slight deviations in the voices entries, sweetening the mechanical character of the polyrhythms in the *accelerando* and changing our perception of the harmonic intervals. More radical deviations from the default configuration lead to surprising, unexpected versions of the piece. Figures 9 and 10 are examples of the possible results of these distortions.

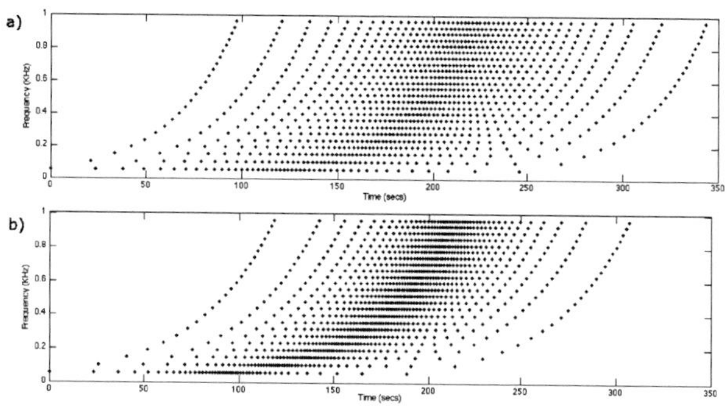

Figure 9. Slight distortions of the canon. a) $dist = 0.9$; b) $dist = 1.1$. Both examples have 24 voices and begin the series of durations with the ratio 2:1.

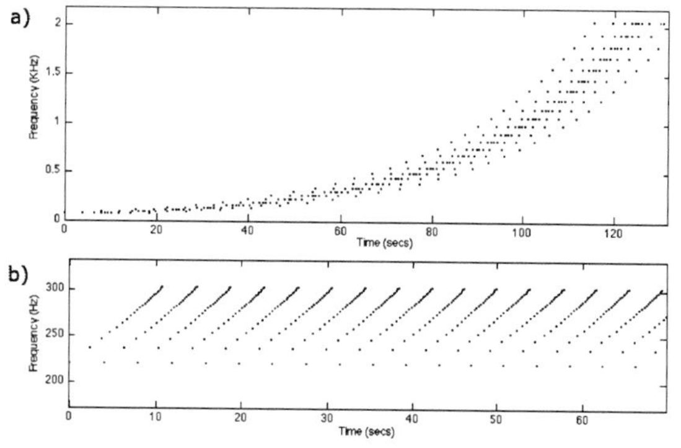

Figure 10. Extreme distortions of the canon. a) $dist = 2.5$; b) $dist = 0.1$. In this case the canon is perceived as a sequence of repeating patterns.

While maintaining the relative integrity of the model, the distortion either moves the voices entries and durations nearer to the beginning of the piece, or away from it. It is therefore likely compensate some undesirable effects produced by other previous choices in the model parametrization (e.g. the duration of the first note in the series).

4.2.2 Filtering.

Another possibility for expanding the model is the filtering of the series. This procedure, commonly used in the the

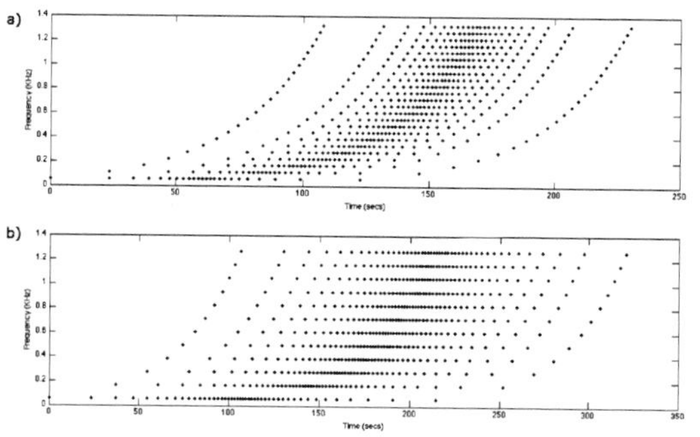

Figure 11. Illustration of the filtering process. a) Durations (filter = 1/2), and b) pitches (harmonic series) (filter = 1/2). (a) has 24 voices, and (b) has 12 voices. In both instances the initial ratio of the series of durations is 2:1.

harmonic domain, can also apply to the duration series in the canon.

The filtering of harmonic series is present as an option in the OpenMusic function *harm-series* [3] which we used to compute the pitches in our model (see Figure 4). In this function partials can be selected according to a pair of attributes given in the form of a fractional expression (for instance, 1/1 selects all partials; 1/2 selects every other partial; 2/5 selects the first two partials of each group of five, etc.) We therefore added this feature and corresponding parameters in our model (see Figure 5). In the default configuration the two filtering parameters are both equal to 1, hence selecting all the partials and all the elements in the duration series. Figure 11 shows two instances of the canon, generated respectively with the duration and frequency filtering processes.

5. CONCLUSION

We showed with the example of James Tenney's *Spectral Canon* that the modeling and simulation of a work could bring new light on its internal processes, and reveals that the potentialities of a piece are not necessarily limited to the composer's version of the score. In our approach, the model is a fundamental means toward the more comprehensive understanding of the musical work: At each step we give towards the complete implementation, we can inquire compositional choices with the advantage of easily simulating the results. Our work distinguishes itself from the conventional approaches in musicology where analysis and composition are two different disciplines. It leads us to permanently rethink the model, its parameters and their relative configurations, which enables creativity and dynamism in the musicological process.

Spectral CANON For CONLON Nancarrow is a relatively simple composition illustrating important aspects in our approach, which we believe constitutes a relevant basis

[3] *Harm-series* is a tool from the *Esquisse* library, developed by composers involved in the spectral school, such as Tristan Murail and Jean-Baptiste Barrière.

for the study of more complex works. Despite its apparent complexity, it can be generated entirely with relatively few simple functions, so that compositional decisions have a straightforward relations to the results. However, we showed how the concrete instances obtained from modifications of the functional processes and parameters could produce radically diverging aspects, forms and perceptive feelings.

An interesting aspect in computer modeling is the possibility to implement systematic approaches in the exploration of the different variations enabled by the model. By producing and observing exhaustive sets of instances produced by different parametrizations, we can test and evaluate until which point the characteristics of the piece, or of the composer's style or intention, is preserved. This question leads us to aesthetic considerations, whether or not the instances of a model are to be considered as part of the composer's work and which are their artistic and creative potentialities. The means and methodologies to explore this complexity in the compositional process, and its relation to the results' aesthetic and perceptive characteristics are some of the main challenges we plan to address in future works.

6. REFERENCES

[1] Agon, C., Andreatta, M., Assayag, G., Schaub, S.: Formal Aspects of Iannis Xenakis "Symbolic Music": A Computer-Aided Exploration of Compositional Processes. Journal of New Music Research, 33(2) (2004)

[2] Ahn Y.-K., Agon, C., Andreatta, M.: Structures Ia pour deux pianos by Boulez: towards creative analysis using OpenMusic and Rubato. Proc. Mathematics and Computation in Music, Berlin, Germany (2007)

[3] Assayag, G., Rueda, C., Laurson, M., Agon, C., Delerue, O.: Computer assisted composition at IRCAM: From PatchWork to OpenMusic. Computer Music Journal, Vol. 23(3) (1999)

[4] Bresson, J., Agon, C., Assayag, G.: OpenMusic. Visual Programming Environment for Music Composition, Analysis and Research. Proc. ACM MultiMedia: OpenSource Software Competition, Scottsdale, USA (2011)

[5] Cowell H.: New Musical Resources. Cambridge University Press, (1996) (original edition: 1930)

[6] Fineberg, J.: Guide to the Basic Concepts and Techniques of Spectral Music. Contemporary Music Review, Vol. 19(2). London: Routledge (2000)

[7] Grisey, G.: Tempus ex Machina: A composer's reflections on musical time. Contemporary Music Review, Vol. 2(1) (1987)

[8] Keller, D., Ferneyhough, B.: Analysis by Modeling: Xenakiss ST/10-1 080262. Journal of New Music Research, Vol. 33(2) (2004)

[9] Polansky, L.: The Early Works of James Tenney. In Garland, P. (ed.) Soundings 13: The Music of James Tenney (1983)

[10] Riotte, A., Mesnage, M.: Formalismes et modles musicaux (2 volumes). Editions Delatour France (2006)

[11] Tenney, J.: Spectral CANON for CONLON Nancarrow. In Byron, M. (Ed.) Pieces: An anthology, Vancouver : Aesthetic Research Centre (1976)

[12] Wannamaker, R. A.: The spectral music of James Tenney. Contemporary Music Review, Vol. 27(1) (2008)

Capacitive Left Hand Finger and Bow Sensors for Synchronization and Rhythmical Regularity Analysis in String Ensembles

Tobias Grosshauser
ETH Zurich
grotobia@ETHZ.ch

Sebastian Feese
ETH Zurich
sfeese@ETHZ.ch

Gerhard Tröster
ETH Zurich
troester@ife.ee.ethz.ch

ABSTRACT

In this paper bow and fingerboard sensors for measurements of synchronization between musicians in group music making are introduced. They are evaluated in several performing situations from advanced musicians in a new founded string trio up to a professional, long time experienced string quartet. The small form factor of the sensors allowed to measure synchronization in musicians' daily life situations. These are a rehearsal, tuition in chamber music class, and a concert situation. Additionally, the musicians filled out a questionnaire rating their grade of preparation, the influence of the sensor while playing, and some more data in each recording session. With the sensors, different rhythmic inaccuracies in seemingly simultaneous bow and note changes between the musicians while making music together are measured and quantified. Further a possibility for sensor based rhythmical regularity measurement while playing equal notes is presented. The results of the questionnaire confirm the unobtrusiveness of the setup and the possible use of it in daily performing situations and even on stage. At the end of this paper an outlook for synchronization skills is introduced and possible impacts into the field of new music is shown.

1. INTRODUCTION

A sensor setup for data acquisition and measurements of musical instrument playing parameters, here synchronization in group music making, which is often discussed among musicians, but difficult to objectify. These are synchronization related parameters like rhythmic inaccuracies (delay and anticipation times) in simultaneous finger changes, cues and bow changes and rhythmical regularity of isochronous notes. Several technologies for motion and gestures' detection during instrumental musical playing exist. Diverse works e.g. by Maestre in [1] show several approaches to objectively capture gestures, particularly those associated to the bowing of string instruments. The most used measuring methods are based on the use of acceleration sensors and gyroscopes. Among others, the first sensors applied to violin, bow, and violin gestures were the acceleration sensor on the bow by Bevilaqua et al. [2]. Wearable, left hand pressure, and position sensors were introduced by Grosshauser et al. in [3]. First measurements of fingers and hand coordination and synchronization between two violinists are carried out in Grosshauser et al. in [4] and of tongue and finger coordination in saxophone playing (Goebl et al. in [5]). Compared to the latter, in this paper a more flexible and partly wireless setup for group measurements is evaluated. To round up the field of musical instrument sensing, hyperinstruments with similar technologies (see Machover in [6]) and the commercially available K Bow by McMillen have to be mentioned. Nevertheless, sensing of synchronization of two or more musicians playing music together is clearly underrepresented in the literature, especially with unobtrusive sensors, allowing unhindered playing and ready for real-life, on stage measurements.

The sensors presented here are small 9 degree-of-freedom (DOF) sensor boards with onboard batteries and SD-card slots, described in sec. 2.2 and shown in Fig. 1 and flexible capacitive left hand finger position sensors (sec. 2.1).

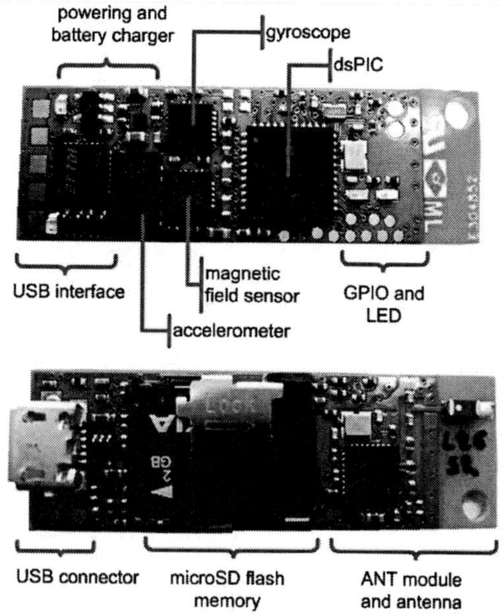

Figure 1. The 9DOF ETHOS module, with the dimensions of 14x45x4 mm and a weight of 4.2 $gr.$ without battery.

They are fixed on the bows and fingerboards and used for measuring rhythmic inaccuracies in synchronized cueing and performing situations of string ensembles. The setup allows precise measurements of the synchronization of two and more musicians while playing together. The setup was evaluated with advanced musicians in a recently launched music group and a professional, long time experienced group. The test subjects range from amateur violinists up to professional musicians. We measured different performing situations, ranging from rehearsal, tuition in chamber music class, and a concert situation. We show that the present setup allows unhindered playing while measuring. It further works with a high temporal resolution and can be used in the field of string players, from beginners up to professionals alike. To support musicians and music teachers in daily exercising, particularly during their technical training, here, the sensors allow to show synchronization inaccuracies and regularity parameters, difficult to detect and quantify, but meaningful for music making. The results achieved in the measurements could lead to teaching and practicing support in string instruments. Also the integration of the final set-up into electronic music scenarios and new playing techniques is possible.

2. SENSOR SETUP

For the right hand bowing the 9 DOF ETHOS sensors are used and for the continuous left hand finger position measurement flexible capacitive sensor stripes.

2.1 Flexible Capacitive Finger Position Sensor Stripes

The left hand finger sensors are thin stripes fixed on the fingerboard between the strings of each participant's instrument of the higher strings (Cello not yet). For the capacitive sensor the MPR121 chip from Freescale Semiconductor is used (2 each stripe) and the working principle is shown in Fig. 2. An Arduino Mini connected via I2C is used for data collection and for data transmission to a laptop computer via USB. This solution showed lower and more stable latency than the cap sense library for Arduino (around 25 ms, 40 Hz).

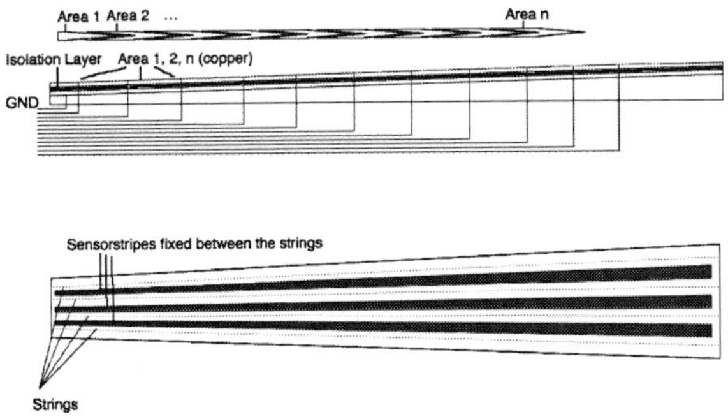

Figure 2. Working principle of the capacitive sensor stripes. Each red area (Area 1, Area 2, ... Area n copper areas) on the top layer is read out independently. This allows continuous finger position detection of each finger with a median sampling frequency of 50 Hz.

The resolution of the final setup is, but not limited to, around 2 mm depending on the placement of the fingers more between or on the strings, but enough for position and note detection, the scanning frequency is around 100 Hz. If a finger is put on the fingerboard, one or two of the stripes are touched. With this information the actually played string is detected.

Figure 3. Capacitive sensor stripes are fixed on the fingerboard for continuous finger position capturing.

2.2 ETHOS 9DOF Sensors

The used ETHOS sensor (see Harms et al. in [7]) is a 9DOF miniature board with 3 axes acceleration, 3 axes gyroscopes, and 3 axes magnetometer. A three-axis accelerometer (Linear Technology, LIS3LV02DL) is implemented and can be configured to resolve 2/6 G with a 16-bit resolution. Earth magnetic field is sensed by an integrated digital compass IC (Honeywell, HMC5843) in all three axes. A three-axes gyroscope (Invensense, ITG-3200) allows sensing of the rate of change with a maximum measurement range of $2000\,degr./s$ at resolution of 16-bit. We use a sampling frequency of $500\,Hz$, meaning temporal resolution of $2\,ms$. It is powered with a $140\,mAh$ LiPo battery for at least 3 hours recording time at this sampling frequency. The ETHOS unit dimensions are WxLxH of 14x45x4 mm^3. The central processing unit of ETHOS is a 16-bit dsPIC. The ETHOS sensors are fixed on the bow of each musicians for motion capturing (see Fig. 4).

It features an integrated real time clock, which is crucial for tagging of data and synchronization of multiple ETHOS units. The system gathers the individual information by three MEMS devices: an accelerometer, a gyroscope and a magnetic field sensor. Moreover a temperature sensor and system power monitor are implemented for automatic self-calibration. The maximum difference of the clocks are $40\,msec$ each $3600\,sec$. In our study we only used the data of $600\,sec$, meaning a deviation based on the run time difference of the real time clocks of max-

Figure 4. The ETHOS sensors fixed on the bow.

imum 6.67 $msec$. Grosshauser et al. in [4] demonstrated, that there is no delay between the bowing initial acceleration and the sound generation at the musical instrument. Based on this measurement we estimated, that our setup is precise enough for synchronization measurements. For the synchronization measurement, only the bow acceleration data are analyzed.

Each board further comprises an 8-channel ultra low power ANT module for wireless communication. ANT allows interconnection of multiple ETHOS units for creation of wireless body area networks (BAN). This network could be extended by other ANT or ANT+ enabled devices, e.g. a heart rate belt, step counter, or GPS module. Moreover, it allows to interface the unit with mobile computers. While the ANT standard is impractical for streaming of raw data, the bandwidth would allow a transmission of gathered orientation data at a maximum frequency of up to $200Hz$. For the study introduced in this paper, the sampling rate was too low. Due to this fact, ANT was not used, therefore the data were recorded on a SD card. The onboard microSD card slot was used (see Fig. 1) to store data, timestamps and system configuration. MicroSD flash memory is of small dimensions, available with high capacities and can be easily replaced in case of low memory. System power is provided by an external lithium-polymer battery with a nominal voltage of 3.7 V. If the system is connected to an USB port the system battery is loaded by an integrated Li-Ion battery charger. In our standard configuration we use a miniature 300 mAh battery with W x L x H dimensions of 20 x 30 x 3 mm^3. In the test setup of this experiment, we used a smaller battery with 140 mAh to reduce the weight in the bows.

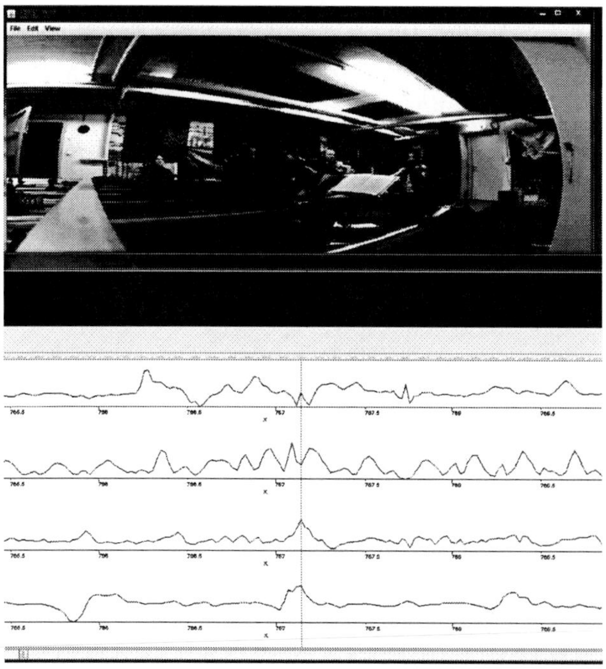

Figure 5. Screenshot of the bow acceleration data synchronized with the video recording. The data show additionally to the video the acceleration peaks of the bow changes of each player. This example shows an accurate bow change with no delays of all four musicians.

3. MEASUREMENTS AND RESULTS

A string trio and a string quartet was measured in different playing situations for one hour each. The string trio is a new founded group with advanced and professional musicians. The string quartet is an experienced group with four professional musicians. The music pieces were all of classicism from Haydn and Beethoven. The situations were daily rehearsals, tuition in a chamber music class, and a concert situation. The different situations should proof that unhindered playing with the presented setup is possible. This was evaluated with a questionnaire, results see in sec. 3.1. The sampling frequency of the capacitive left hand finger sensor will be increased due to low temporal resolution of around 10 ms. Each recording session was recorded with an A/V camera. The recorded data were analyzed per hand with a labeling tool, see Fig. 5. The acceleration peaks of the bow changes are easy recognizable in the data viewer. You simply mark the clear bow change points and if two, the time between these two points is calculated. The additional A/V view simplifies this task and helps to find the key points.

3.1 Results of the Questionnaire

To obtain information about the unobtrusiveness of the setup, a questionnaire was filled out before and after each recording session by the musicians of each test group. First a self estimation about their own mood and tiredness was ask to avoid e.g. negative influence of these factors to the reaction times. No noticeable extreme conditions were indicated, other than an increase of excitement before the concert. The participants were between 31 and 44 years old. The over all average age was 34.71 years (Trio: 38, Quartet: 32.25), the average experience of musical instrument playing was 24.85 years (Trio: 24.33 and Quartet: 25.25). There was one advanced musician and 6 professionals. All participants state no or positive influence of the measurement setup and the usefulness of the data. For further information please see Fig. 6. The sensors were not distracting, but still were noticed by 4 of 7 musicians. The new founded trio stated positive influence of the setup while playing with it. According to the trio members, this is due to the fact, that they concentrated more on synchronized playing, knowing that it is measured. All participants agreed, that the measured data are useful, 2 two of them rated the data as "very useful". An interesting aspect is, that even the professional quartet did not feel hindered while playing and suggested a data recording in a real concert situation.

3.2 Measurement of Temporal Inaccuracies in Synchronized Music Making

The stacked sensors are synchronized with clear acceleration movements in front of the camera, allowing a later re-synchronization of sensor and video data with the data labeling tool (see Fig. 5). The synchronization is done before and after the recording.

The measurement of the string quartet showed significantly lower delay times while playing together in com-

				The sensor setup was/had		Value of the data,
	Age	Instrument	Status	distracting?	influence?	useful, useless?
AverageQuartet	32.25					
Violin1	33	Violin	Professional	noticed but nondistracting	no infl	very useful
Cello	33	Cello	Professional	nondistracting	no infl	useful
Violin2	31	Violin	Professional	noticed but nondistracting	no infl	very useful
Viola	32	Viola	Professional	nondistracting	no infl	useful
TrioCello	34	Cello	Advanced	noticed but nondistracting	pos influence	useful
TrioViolin	36	Violin	Professional	nondistracting	pos influence	useful
TrioViola	44	Viola	Professional	noticed but nondistracting	pos influence	useful
Average Trio	38					
Average Overall	34.71					

Figure 6. Statistical data of the test subjects. Each participant filled out a questionnaire after each measurement.

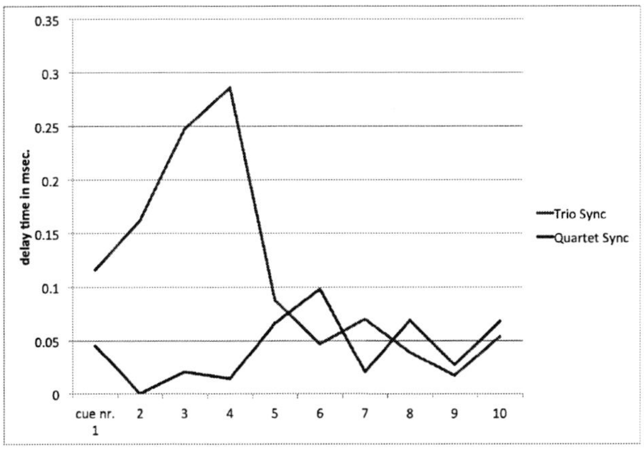

Figure 7. Delay between the earliest and latest musician in synchronized cueing.

parison to the trio. The average delay between the musicians of the string quartet was 19 ms, maximum is 98 ms, minimum 0 ms. The average delay of the trio is 43 ms, maximum is 171 ms, minimum is 0.05 ms. Also the delay in cueing situations is higher in the trio compared to the quartet (see Fig. 7). The left hand sensor data are collected via USB and recorded with a laptop computer without delay. The temporal resolution of around 20 ms was not good enough to find reliable left hand synchronization data. Only the bow changes are considered in the analysis.

In Fig. 8 the temporal deviations of bow changes are shown. In a straight series of eighth notes, faint delays are recognizable. This could be due to expression reasons, but e.g. in rhythm training situations, this temporal analysis is crucial. The sampling frequency of the capacitive sensor stripes is too slow to get precise synchronization information, especially of the experienced quartet. Delay higher than 20 ms can be detected. Also coordination measurements between left hand fingers and right hand bowing of each musician are possible, again with the above mentioned temporal limitation.

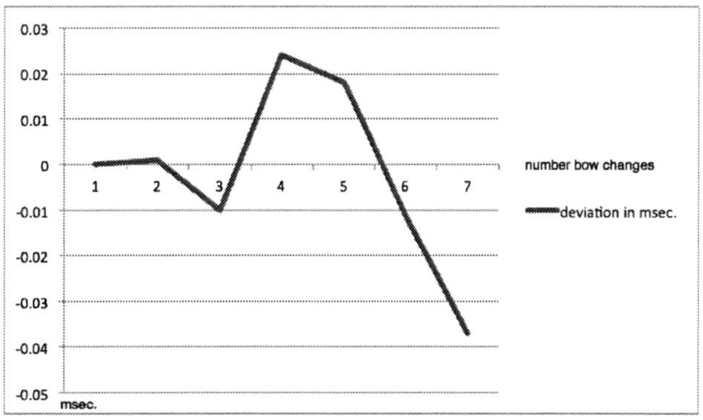

Figure 8. Rhythmical regularity: Delays of bow and note changes of isochronous, equally long notes.

4. POSSIBILITIES FOR NEW MUSIC INTERFACES IN PERFORMANCE AND TEACHING

If the musicians control synchronization delays, this playing method could be used for musical expression. Live data transmission with the integrated ANT rf transmitter Bluetooth allows beside the visualization of the acceleration, magnetometer, and gyroscope data the mapping of these data with musical effects or sound generation. Augmenting the sensor data with additional feedback e.g. sonification could be useful for synchronization training. Furthermore the sonification itself could be used as an expression parameter e.g. like micro-rhythmical patterns. The simplicity of the setup further allows easy integration of the measurement method in the course of daily practicing and rehearsing. Without wireless data transmission, every sensor can be fixed on the bows after calibration and after rehearsing, the data can be visualized and observed in standard chart programs.

5. CONCLUSIONS

The setup presented in this paper is a further step into getting more objective data in music making and performing. Beside the unobtrusiveness of the setup (based on the statements given in written form on the questionnaire filled from the participants in every measurement session and on interviews and discussions), findings of latencies between musicians while playing together are shown. Although synchronization is just one parameter of many, it is a very significant one. Measurements in different playing situations and different levels will allow comparisons, not only between two or more groups, but also for progress tracking in learning and exercising situations. In this direction, also the effectiveness of exercises can be observed. The individual observation of rhythmical regularity provides useful information in daily exercising.

In the future observations, tests for the importance and the stability of the measurement will be made. When combining measurements with the right exercises, the latency factor could help beginners or new-formed music groups to improve their playing skills. To do so, the resolution of the left hand sensors will be increased.

Furthermore, the work represents a new step towards novel measurement setups to quantify usually hidden parameters pivotal to music making, which are difficult to be objectively shown. While usually the individual impression of "uncoordinated" or "not in time" playing may be right, its objective depiction and quantifying is a challenge. By using the presented measurement setup and sensors it is possible to measure parameters like rhythmic inaccuracies and irregularities.

The next steps will also include the simplification of the present setup and its refinement to still enhance its already high acceptability among musicians and especially the increase of the sampling frequency, spatial resolution and the size of the capacitive left hand finger sensor. Easily understandable real-time feedback modalities and the use of the sensor setup in other types of musical instruments will be a long-term goal. This may ultimately contribute to the development of new methods of instrumental training and provide new interfaces based on traditional instrument for musical expression.

6. REFERENCES

[1] E. Maestre, "Statistical modeling of violin bowing parameter contours," Montreal, Canada, 2009. [Online]. Available: static/media/maestre-esteban-ICMC-2009.pdf

[2] F. Bevilacqua, N. Rasamimanana, E. Fléty, S. Lemouton, and F. Baschet, "The augmented violin project: research, composition and performance report," in *6th International Conference on New Interfaces for Musical Expression, NIME06*. Paris, France, France: IRCAM — Centre Pompidou, 2006, pp. 402–406.

[3] T. Grosshauser, "Low force pressure measurement: Pressure sensor matrices for gesture analysis, stiffness recognition and augmented instruments," in *8th International Conference on New Interfaces for Musical Expression, NIME08*, S. G. Volpe, A. Camurri, Ed., 2008.

[4] T. Grosshauser, V. Candia, H. Hildebrand, and G. Troester, "Sensor based measurements of musicians' synchronization issues," in *Proceedings of the International Conference on New Interfaces for Musical Expression (NIME)*. Ann Arbor, Michigan: University of Michigan, 2012.

[5] W. Goebl and C. Palmer, "Synchronization of timing and motion among performing musicians," in *Music Perception*, 2009.

[6] C. J. Machover, "Hyperinstruments: Musically intelligent and interactive performance and creativity systems," in *International Computer Music Conference*, 1989.

[7] H. Harms, O. Amft, R. Winkler, J. Schumm, M. Kusserow, and G. Troester, "Ethos: Miniature orientation sensor for wearable human motion analysis," in *Proceedings of IEEE Sensors conference*, 2010.

ACOUSTIC RETROREFLECTORS FOR MUSIC PERFORMANCE MONITORING

Heikki T Tuominen, Jussi Rämö, and Vesa Välimäki
Department of Signal Processing and Acoustics
Aalto University, Espoo, Finland
htuo@iki.fi

ABSTRACT

This paper is concerned with acoustic retroreflectors, which reflect sound back towards any sound source. They are constructed here of two reflecting panels connected with hinges and placed on a hard reflecting floor. Acoustic retroreflectors can replace electroacoustic monitoring in music performance when sufficiently large panels are placed at an appropriate distance from performers. A good distance is between about 3 and 8 m from a player, corresponding to propagation delays of between approximately 20 ms and 50 ms from a player to the retroreflector and back. We have conducted acoustic measurements in an anechoic chamber using various retroreflector structures, including symmetric V-shaped and asymmetric L-shaped reflectors of two different heights with various opening angles and incident angles. Our data show that the 90° opening angle produces the strongest reflection. Surprisingly, increasing the opening angle to 100° or more decreases the magnitude of reflection by more than 10 dB, while a smaller angle, such as 80°, mainly weakens the reflection at high frequencies. User tests with musicians indicate that acoustic retroreflectors can provide the desired feedback in performance spaces in which natural reflections to the stage are missing, such as in large halls far away from the walls or outdoors.

1. INTRODUCTION

For a performer, some places are easy to play in while others are difficult. This ease or difficulty is related to the reflections of the performance space sending the player's own sound back to her or his ears [1]. Without such auditory feedback provided by the walls or other reflective structures, the performer does not hear her or his playing well, which feels uncomfortable. This influences especially amateurs. Professionals notice this as well, but they are more competent to make adjustments. Through experience they look for a better position to stand or sit and their muscle memory helps them to maintain good ergonomics even when the space does not support the sounds they are making. Reflections that are too early or too late do not help (see Fig. 1).

This paper considers a light-weight acoustic arrangement corresponding to 'stage monitor speakers' used in amplified music performances. The function of monitoring is for players to hear their own performance and also a mix of other performers. How much monitoring feedback is needed, and how can this be implemented acoustically without building heavy structures on the stage? Can a portable set of good reflectors be made which can be carried by performers themselves to schools, museums, outdoor places, and other environments not allowing a loudspeaker-based monitoring system?

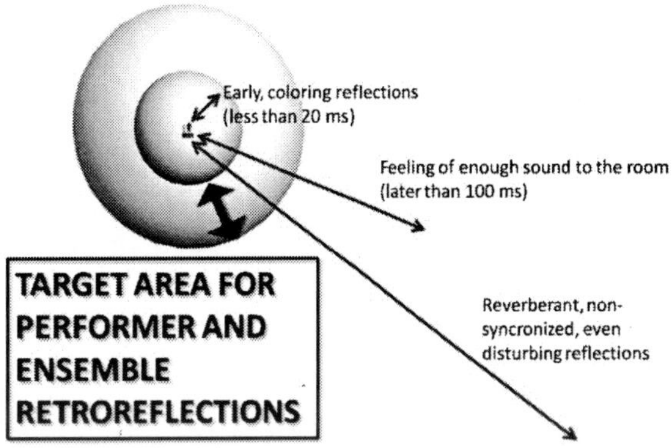

Figure 1. Rough division of usefulness of retroreflections in music and speech performances.

This paper suggests acoustic retroreflectors, which are constructed of three orthogonal acoustically reflective boards: two boards connected together at a right angle placed on a hard floor, which acts as the third board. Such a retroreflector echoes sound back towards a sound source placed at any angle in its vicinity [1, 2]. The best location for a retroreflector is inevitably in front of the performers, i.e., between the players and the audience. This implies that the construction must not be visually intrusive. The main emphasis in this work is to find low, ramp-like constructions, that can be hidden among chairs and music stands. Furthermore, knowing how far on the side of an ensemble a retroreflector can be installed while still working efficiently, is of interest. This is, in practice, connected to finding out how wide a horizontal range of angles can be covered with one retroreflector, i.e., how large a group of performers can benefit from each reflector. This paper does not consider what the audience hears, although good stage acoustics may greatly improve a music performance.

The rest of this paper is organized as follows. Sections 2 and 3 discuss the basics of reinforcing sound reflections and acoustic reflectors. Section 4 explains our arrangements for measuring the performance of acoustic retroreflectors. Section 5 analyzes the results of the acoustic measurements, section 6 presents user experiments conducted with performers, and section 7 concludes the paper.

2. REFLECTIONS ARE IMPORTANT

General room acoustics theory has shown that the listener's impression of a room, its envelopment by music and other similar features is formed by sound information (preferably lateral) that arrives 30 to 100 ms after the direct sound [1, 3, 4]. This has been corroborated in many ways through studies of audience experience.

Some literature on stage acoustics exists [4] but noticeably less. Even less can be found about music making in smaller ensembles and in non-concert-hall environments.

If the first reflected sound reaches the performer only after 50ms (corresponding to a distance of 8.5 m), the risk that the performer perceives an audible echo is greatly increased, making singing, playing and even talking very difficult. This phenomenon is not uncommon in long festivity halls of the 19th and 20th centuries. To free performers of this bad situation, it often suffices to add an extra reflection in the range 30--40 ms. Additional delayed sound in this range does not produce coloring to the spectrum as earlier reflections would.

3. ACOUSTIC RETROREFLECTORS

This paper considers only retroreflectors, *i.e* those returning the incident sound to the direction of the source (Fig. 2). Such reflectors have been in use also in electromagnetic waves, *e.g* with navigation radars [1, 2]. The phenmenon of retroreflection occurs with light as well, as can be seen in Fig. 3.

The minimum size of the reflector is determined by the longest wavelength to be reflected efficiently. The frequency range that is the most important for this application is the middle audio range from about 400 Hz to about 2 kHz, where the perception of spatial characteristics are at its best. This was verified in a series of field tests, where the reflection was artificially produced with a (guitar) loudspeaker.

4. TEST ARRANGEMENT

Measurements were conducted in a semi-anechoic chamber to collect data to answer the following questions:

- What geometrical features are needed to get an adequate reflection?
- How do reflectors of different shapes and in different placements operate acoustically?
- What is the operative coverage angle of a single reflector?

The right-angled retroreflector made of water-tight veneer of size 60 cm x 60 cm was used as a reference.

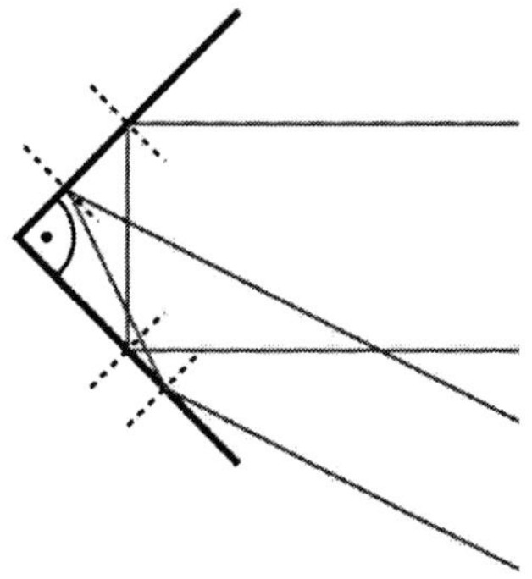

Figure 2. Principle of the corner retroreflector illustrated with sound rays [2].

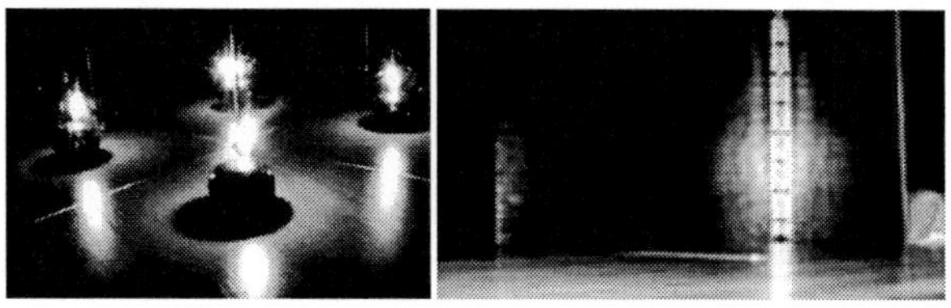

(a) (b)

Figure 3. (a) An optical retroreflector, consisting of two mirrors at right angles, displaying the single-reflection mirror images of a candle on the sides and the double-reflection image behind the hinge of the mirrors. In this case the floor reflections are not specular but diffuse and thus blurred. (b) A single and double retroreflection from the reference device as seen from a camera with flashlight. The strong double reflection is around the hinge and at the left edge, the single reflection is visible partially (90° opening and oblique incidence).

This material was used in all tested devices. Only the corner reflector construction, as in Fig. 2, was tested.

The study methodology was to compare the frequency responses of the reflections from the retroreflector in different configurations. The reflection response was computed from the impulse responses obtained from a Farina-type sweep signal [5]. The magnitude axis in all figures is scaled so that the average magnitude of the direct sound corresponds to 0 dB.

The measurements were conducted in the large anechoic chamber of the Aalto University. The measurement setup consisted of a Genelec 8030A active monitor, a Brüel&Kjaer 4191 free-field microphone, and a MOTU UltraLite mk3 audio interface. The used measurement and analysis software was Matlab. Furthermore, the metal-net floor of the anechoic chamber was covered with 2 m by 7 m laminate flooring in order to create a semi-anechoic chamber for the reflectors. Figure 4 shows photos of the measurement setup.

The loudspeaker and microphone were positioned at one end of the laminate flooring with the reflector at the other end. The distance between the microphone and the reflector was approximately 4 m. As shown in Fig. 4(a), the microphone was positioned just in front of the loudspeaker in order to capture the reflected sound waves before being scattered by the loudspeaker.

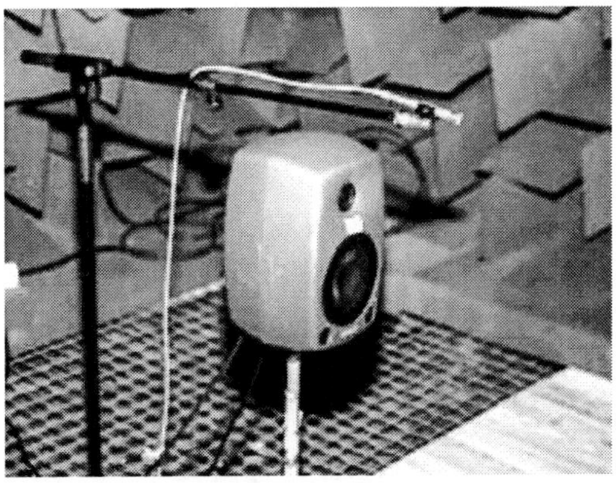

(a)

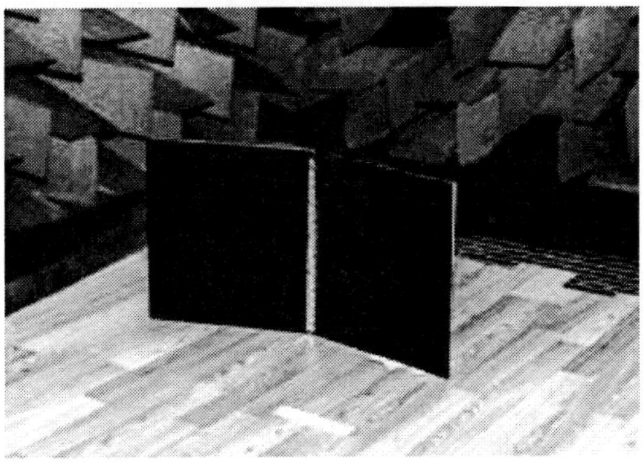

(b)

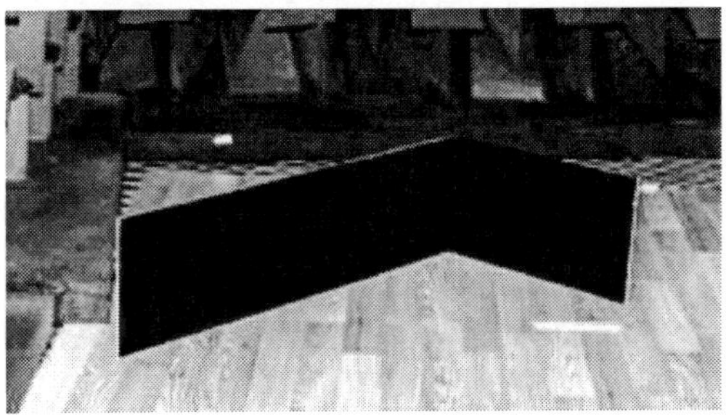

(c)

Figure 4. (a) Microphone and sound source, (b) a V-shaped reference retroreflector, widely opened (over 170°), and (c) an L-shaped retroreflector with differing wing lengths.

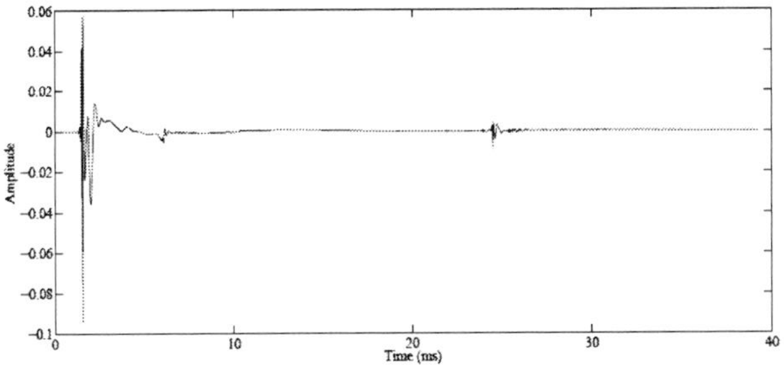

Figure 5. Example of impulse response with emitted sound on the left and the reflected sound well after 20 ms.

Figure 5 shows an example impulse response of a measurement, where the direct and reflected sounds are clearly separated. As can be seen, the direct sound starts around 1 ms, whereas the reflected sound appears around 24.5 ms. Thus, the delay between the direct and reflected sound is approximately 23.5 ms, which corresponds to sound traveling 8 m at the speed of 340 m/s.

5. MEASUREMENTS

We tested three basic types of retroreflectors. Figures 6 and 7 show the frequency responses from a test series with the reference device, and figures 8 and 9 a test series with lower but longer devices, with the incidence angle being varied.

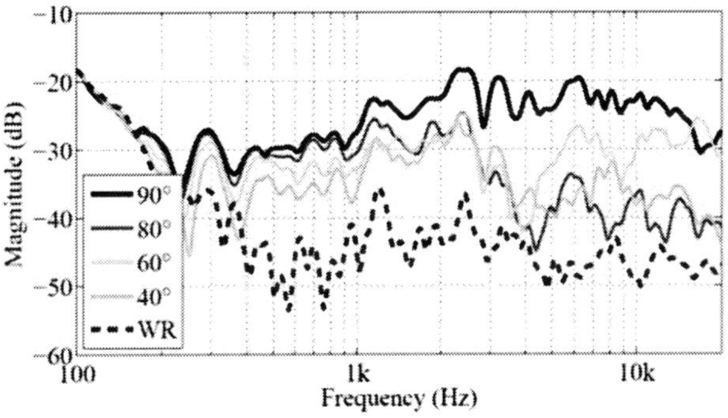

Figure 6. Reflection responses of the reference device with opening angles smaller than 90°. The black lines show the cases of 90° and without reflector (WR).

Figure 6 shows that in the range of interest, from 400 Hz to 2 kHz, the reflection response decreases systematically as the 'receiving area' of the reflector becomes smaller. Above 3 kHz the response drops quickly. The opening angle of 60° makes an exception and is better than others. This may be explained by the fact that this angle creates a formation of six coinciding images, just as 90° forms four efficient coinciding mirror images. Other opening angles do not create such simple image formations.

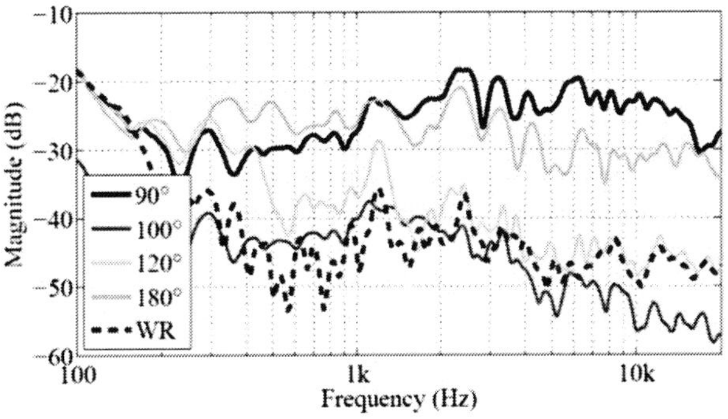

Figure 7. Reflection responses of the reference device with opening angles larger than 90°. The black lines show the cases of 90° and without the reflector (WR).

In Fig.7, a dramatic drop in the reflection response is apparent in the frequency range of interest and beyond for opening angles exceeding 90° upto the angle 180°, which corresponds to a single board with one mirror image. In fact, an opening of 100° gives the weakest reflection of all the measured opening angles, despite it physical similarity to a 90° reflector.

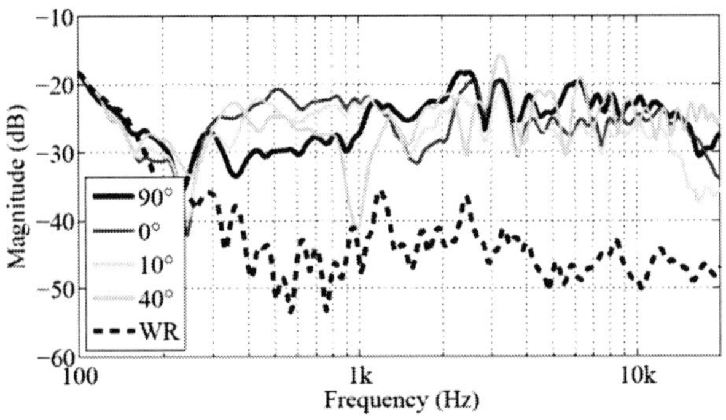

Figure 8. Reflection responses of a lower but longer reflector with equal wings for different incident angles. The black lines show the cases of 90° and without the reflector (WR).

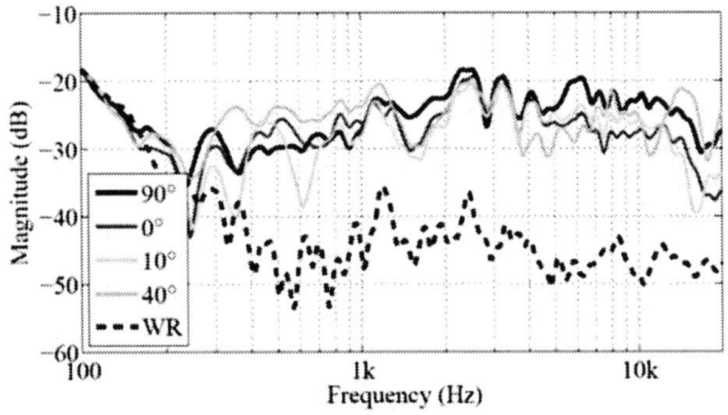

Figure 9. Reflection responses of a lower but longer reflector with unequal wings for different incident angles. The black lines show the cases of 90° and without the reflector (WR).

For incidence angle tests with lower but longer retroreflectors (responses in Figures 8 and 9), we used a scale where 45° means that one of the wings points directly towards the sound source and thus is invisible from the source.

Figure 8 indicates that the reflectivity of a symmetrical retroreflector is excellent for a wide range of incident angles (80° wide in practical use) with only the extreme of 40° showing more peaks and dips in the frequency response. Also, the L-shaped retroreflector keeps the reflection strong over a wide incidence angle range, as seen from the response in Fig. 9. Interestingly, it shows less peaks and dips and less variance between the incidence angles. This makes the L-shaped retroreflector more suitable than the symmetrical, V-shaped reflector. At 10° there is a significant dip just above 600 Hz, but so was there a similar dip in the V-shaped retroreflector as well, but at 40° incidence. Furthermore, dips in the frequency response are not perceived as clearly as peaks, if at all.

6. USER EXPERIMENTS

The same reflectors were also tested in real situations: in real music and festivity halls, the rehearsal room of a symphony orchestra, in outdoor performance venues and in an anechoic chamber.

Figure 10. A right-angled V-shaped retroreflector tested with the Jyväskylä Sinfonia in the rehearsing room among chairs and music stands.

Players of Jyväskylä Sinfonia stated that in a group performance the panels opened the possibility to hear all the performers. In a quartet formation the Viola player heard the first violin 'for the frist time', not only the adjacent players, and in an orchestra configuration, all players noted an improvement in hearing the ensemble as a whole. Four reflectors of the type shown in Fig.10 and wider were tested.

Antoher test series was made with professional viola player Teemu Kupiainen, who has an extensive side career in playing Bach on the streets, including in Africa, China and India.

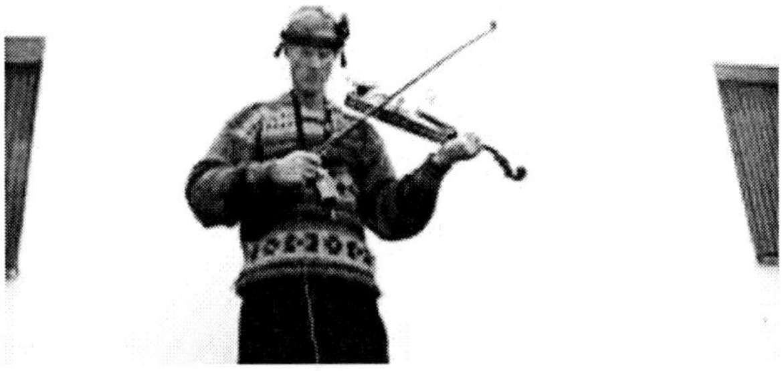

Figure 11. Violist Teemu Kupiainen with document microphones at both ears and the sound recorder for the simulated reflection signal in front. The cable leads the reflection signal to the loudspeaker.

For the tests, we created artificial reflection with loudspeaker at twice the distance of a retroreflector from the performer. The level was thus controllable and could be played back separately. The sound at the musician's ears was recorded (see Fig.11). The results in Fig.12 show that in an anechoic room a much weaker reflection is needed (-40 to -70 dB) and tolerated (-20 to -40 dB) than in a more normal and reverberant room. Even -5 dB is tolerable and as loud a reflection level as -15 dB may be needed to have a noticeable effect. The signal spectrum in both cases is the total sound coming to the ears of the performer, with adjustments for less bass and treble, which were found annoying.

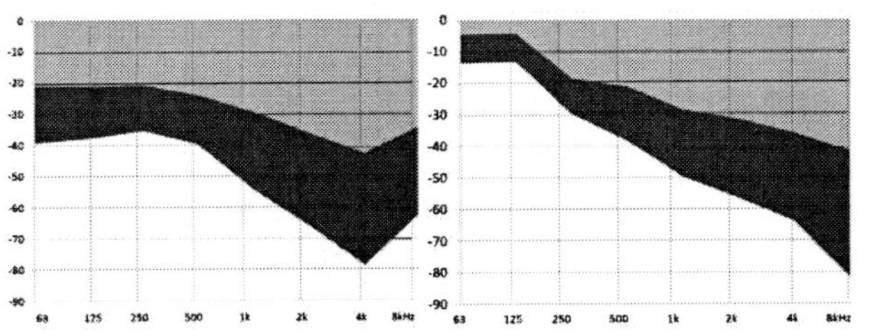

(a) (b)

Figure 12. Empirical SPL range of a favourable added reflection for a violist 5 m away from reflector (a) in an anechoic chamber and (b) in a room with 1.5 s long reverberation time. The lower edge of the red area represents the threshold level of noticing the reflection and the upper edge the level that is experienced as too loud and annoying.

Thus, the study implies that simple, portable retroreflectors can be successfully used in performance situations where the performers feel that the acoustics have inadequate ensemble balance or timbre control. The most promising construction is L-shaped two-board corner reflector, with opening angle not exceeding 90° (Fig. 13). This reflector is effective if all performers are within 80° seen from the reflector.

Figure 13. A low L-shaped retroreflector being tested by a speech coach in the Festivity hall of Helsinki University.

7. CONCLUSION

This paper has focused on the use of acoustic retroreflectors to replace monitor loudspeakers in music performances. The retroreflectors consist of two reflecting panels placed on a hard floor at a right angle. When a retroreflector is positioned at a suitable distance from the performers, it can reflect each player's own sound back to them, thus providing an unplugged approach to stage monitoring. An appropriate distance is one where the reflections arrive at the player with a delay of about 20 to 50 ms, since then the player's own sound is reinforced but a distinct echo is not perceived.

Acoustic measurements on retroreflectors were conducted in an anechoic chamber, which was converted to a semi-anechoic space by using laminate flooring. We measured the impulse response of a basic V-shaped retroreflector made of two 60 cm x 60 cm boards. The opening angle of the hinged retroreflector could be freely adjusted. The best reflection was observed the boards were at the right angle. When the opening angle was decreased, the reflection weakened mainly at frequencies above 3 kHz. However, at lower frequencies, the retroreflector still worked fairly well with the magnitude of the reflection decreasing by less than 10 dB even in the case of a very narrow 40° opening angle. However, increasing the opening angle quickly destroys the reflection. A 100° opening angle leads to 10 to 25 dB weaker reflections, depending on the frequency, than of a right angle, making such a configuration useless in practice. It is recommended that the angle between the panels be adjusted very close to 90° or slightly smaller but not larger.

Additionally, longer and lower, 30 cm tall, retroreflectors were investigated. The dependence of the magnitude of the reflection on the incident angle of sound was varied. The data show that the retroreflector produces a strong reflection for a wide range of incident angles, with only narrow notches appearing in the magnitude response at some frequencies. This verifies the basic assumption that a retroreflector can send the sound back to (almost) any direction.

User tests with professional and amateur musicians and with a speech coach confirm our belief that a retroreflector placed in front of the performer can provide helpful auditory feedback, when other natural reflections are missing. Retroreflectors can indeed replace electro-acoustic monitoring in a music performance, when microphones are undesirable or electricity is unavailable. The most obvious uses for acoustic retroreflectors are acoustic music performances in large halls or outdoors in a square or in a park, for example.

8. ACKNOWLEDGMENTS

The authors would like to thank SKR (Finnish Cultural Fund Uusimaa) for financing the construction phase of the portable set of retroreflectors, and the participants in the study as well as plus gambist/barytonist Dr Markus Kuikka, double bass player Johannes Raikas, speech coach Ina Virkki, and all the other participants in the field studies for valuable comments.

9. REFERENCES

[1] E. J. Heller, Why You Hear What You Hear. Princeton University Press, Princeton, NJ, 2013.

[2] Retroreflector, Corner reflector - Wikipedia

[3] T. Lokki and J. Pätynen, Lateral reflections are favorable in concert halls due to binaural loudness. Journal of the Acoustical Society of America, vol. 130, no. 5, pp. EL345-EL351, Nov. 2011.

[4] J. Dammerud, Stage acoustics - a Literature review. Akutek Info, 2006. http://www.akutek.info/Papers/JJD_stage_acoustics.pdf

[5] A. Farina, Simultaneous measurement of impulse response and distortion with a swept-sine technique, in AES 108th Convention, Paris, France, February 2000.

MIXING SYMBOLIC AND AUDIO DATA IN COMPUTER ASSISTED MUSIC ANALYSIS

A Case study from J. Harvey's *Speakings* (2008) for Orchestra and Live Electronics

Stéphan Schaub
University of Campinas
Interdisciplinary Nucleus of Sound Communication
schaub@nics.unicamp.br

Ivan Simurra
University of Campinas
Interdisciplinary Nucleus of Sound Communication
iesimurra@nics.unicamp.br

Tiago Fernandes Tavares
University of Campinas
School of Electrical and Computer Engineering
tavares@dca.fee.unicamp.br

ABSTRACT

Starting from a (music) analytical question arising from the study of Jonathan Harvey's *Speakings* for orchestra and electronics (2008) we propose a computer-based approach in which score (symbolic) and recorded (audio) sources are considered in tandem. After extracting a set of relevant features we used machine-learning algorithms to explore how compositional and auditory dimensions articulate in defining the identity of certain sound-events appearing in the first movement of the composition and how they contribute to their similarity with events occurring in the second movement. The computer-assisted approach was used as basis for discussing the metaphor that inspired this particular piece, but has the potential to be extended to other compositions in the repertoire.

1. INTRODUCTION

A significant part of the orchestral music composed since the end of World War 2 has made extensive use of non-standard playing techniques, of microtonal tuning systems and/or elaborated complex "sound masses". The corresponding works have stretched the capacity of the written score to provide a complete mental "image" of a composition's overall sound to its limits. When orchestral and electro-acoustic sounds are superimposed in a single performance or, even more so, when they are intentionally seamlessly blended together, the gap between the written score and the sounding results may become even more acute. In the effort to analyze such compositions, the possibility to include and articulate information extracted from both the written score and the recording of its performance becomes a crucial issue.

Today's computer technology provides important resources that can be applied to tackle either audio or symbolic (MIDI) data. The transcription of a recorded performance into visual representations can serve as "proto-scores" that can be annotated and, if need be, aligned with a written score [1, 2]. MIR techniques permit to extract specific aspects of an audio file and have thus paved the way towards more differentiated perspectives on recorded sources [3, 4]. Comparable resources can also be found in the processing of written information. Specialized libraries exist that extract "statistical" features, such as density or degrees of inharmonicity, from a MIDI file and retrace their evolutions in time [5]. Despite such resources, few examples can be found in the music analytical literature that explicitly seeks to articulate observations obtained from (and referable back to) the musical score and the recording of its performance.

In this article we present and discuss an example of such an attempt based on a (music) analytical question that arises from the study of Jonathan Harvey's *Speakings* for orchestra and electronics (2008).

This work cumulates both characteristics mentioned above. It makes extensive use of non-standard playing techniques deployed in complex textural structures and blends orchestral and electronic sounds together, at times in such a way as to make them indistinguishable from one another. When considering questions of identity and similarity between sound-events occurring in the piece, features extracted from both written and recorded sources bear, *a priori*, equal weight as a basis for investigation.

As it turns out, a wealth of information exists about this composition's genesis [6]. This has not only provided a basis for a preliminary analysis of the work but has also quite straightforwardly suggested questions of the type just mentioned. These, together with a brief description of Harvey's composition, will be presented in the first section of the present article.

How computer support was brought in, first to extract "global features" from the sound events considered and then to decide on how to classify and compare them within the context of our analysis, are the subjects of sections 3 and 4.

Although the questions underlying our discussion heavily rely on information provided by the composer – thus making them quite specific to the work at hand – the application of the suggested approach to a wider context should also be viable. This possibility will be the subject of the discussion provided in the closing section.

2. ABOUT J. HARVEY'S *SPEAKINGS*

2.1 Form and General Characteristics

Composed in 2008, *Speakings* is the result of collaboration between composer Jonathan Harvey and researchers at the IRCAM. As a byproduct of this collaboration, an article was published [6], describing some of the technological means applied to its realization (spatialization, real-time transformations, synchronization between orchestral and electronic sounds…).

From this source, we learn that: "*an evolution of speech consciousness* […], starting *from baby screaming, cooing and babbling, through frenzied chatter to mantric serenity* [provides] *the basic metaphor of the half-hour work's trajectory*". As it turns out, this metaphor actually operates at two different levels.

First, as mentioned in the above quote, it provided an "abstract narrative" to the work's overall three-movements structure (played without interruptions) of, respectively, 5'30, 14'00 and 8'30 durations. The first movement, dominated by the string instruments, occupies the lower dynamic range (up to *f*) and displays a darker and more "agitated" activity than the other two. The second movement involves more brass and woodwind instruments and progresses through an extended orchestral crescendo that culminates at *fff*. The last movement, finally, displays an overall calmer mood that mixes all the orchestral colors encountered during the previous two movements.

At a second level, the metaphor entered directly in the elaboration of some of the musical material appearing in the composition. In a way reminiscent to the *spectralist* approach, the composer used computer analyses of complex sounds to derive some of his material. The "*baby screaming, cooing and babbling,*" mentioned in the quote were obtained from recordings of actual baby sounds. As detailed in [6], these (the sounds, not the babies) were subjected to automatic transcription of speech signals into symbolic (melodic and harmonic) musical notation and the result transcribed to the orchestra so as to mimic the voice's rhythm and natural inflections. In order to render the corresponding passages even more speech-like, a real-time transformation was applied during the performance to a selection of (solo) instruments within the orchestra. Another example of a similar procedure used a recording of the composer singing a short mantra. The corresponding "transcription" for orchestra enters gradually towards the end of the second movement and announces the "serenity" of the work's concluding section.

The present analysis concentrates on the *baby sounds* that appear in the first movement and relates them to sound-events that bear similar characteristics and occur in the second movement. We now describe these in more details.

2.2 The "Baby Sounds" and their Categorization

The *baby sounds* appear in the first movement of the composition starting at measure 39. Whether they are "*screams*", "*cooings*" or "*babbles*", they all share a set of clearly identifiable characteristics:

- They are played by the violins accompanied by two (transformed and amplified) solo instruments;
- They occur in the high to very high register;
- The dynamic markings are between *ppp* and *mf* following a crescendo-decrescendo overall shape;
- The string parts always include a high proportion of glissandi, often played *tremolo*, with sounds often produced as *harmonics*.

With few exceptions, labels (actually instructions related to the electronic part) appear in the score that indicate the "category" to which the corresponding sound belongs. In accordance with the composition's underlying metaphor, the first are *baby screams*, the second *baby cooings* and the last are *baby babbles*. They appear, respectively, 6, 4 and 8 times over the course of the movement. Although they are quite clearly distinguishable aurally as pertaining to separate categories their general features as read from the score are very similar and the factors contributing to their differences are far from obvious.

During the second movement, between measures 133 and 190, a series of 30 sound-events can be heard, each of between 1.5 and 4 seconds in duration, which share very similar orchestration, playing modes, register etc. as the *baby sounds* of the first movement. As no real-time transformation is applied at that particular moment of the piece, no label appears alongside their appearance in the score.

The two questions that will provide the main thread through the remainder of this article are as follow: considering elements from the score as well as from the recording of the piece [7] is there a way to identify the differences between the three categories of *baby sounds* that appear in the first movement? Based on this information, is it possible to determine to what kind of baby sounds, if any, the events in the second movement pertain?

3. FEATURES EXTRACTION

3.1 Preliminary Remarks

To tackle these questions, features were extracted from each of the *baby sounds* of the first movement as well as from the "potential" ones of the second movement. Acoustic features, which are often used for genre classification and instrument identification tasks, were calculated directly from the audio excerpts as found in [7]. Symbolic features were calculated using MIDI files obtained from the score *via* its transcription using a music-editing software.

In all the tests performed acoustic and symbolic features were first considered as forming separate data sets before being combined into a single one (which will be called the "comprehensive set"). In all three cases, the quantification not only allowed for computerized treatment but also offered the common ground on which audio and symbolic aspects could be brought together. The following two subsections describe the specific features that have been extracted.

3.2 Audio Features

The acoustic classification process was based on calculating features that not only can describe audio excerpts in a vector space, but also correlate to human perceptual aspects (described below).

To obtain the features for each excerpt, we first divided each audio file in frames of 43ms, multiplied it by a Hanning window and calculated its DFT. Each feature, briefly described below, was calculated for each frame.

- The energy (which is closely related to the loudness) [8], is the sum of the squared absolute values of the samples of a frame.
- The spectral roll-off [8, 9] is the frequency under which 95% of the energy of the signal lies. It gives an idea of the roughness of the sound.
- The spectral flux [9] depicts the spectral difference between the current frame and the previous one. It tends to highlight note onsets and quick spectral variations.
- The pitch [10] is also calculated for every frame. The algorithm used, based on autocorrelation, retrieves the most prominent pitch in the frame. If no pitches are found, the algorithm yields zero.

The mean, variance and the time-domain centroid of each feature are calculated [8, 9] along the frames. At the end of this process, each audio excerpt is described by a 12 dimensional feature-vector. As is shown in works related to audio classification, the Euclidian distance between two vectors tends to be small when the related audio excerpts sound alike [9].

3.3 Symbolic Features

The symbolic features extracted were obtained using the OpenMusic library called SOAL [5, 11]. It allows for the extraction of quantified measures on symbolic (MIDI) data relating to the statistical dimensions such as densities, inharmonicity and relative-range, either considered "a-chronically" (i.e., spatial, vertical or out of time) or "diachronically" (in time). More details about this library can be found in [5].

All the symbolic features extracted here are related to "textural" qualities of the excerpts considered. These were established as the following:

- Virtual-fundamental: gives the "fundamental" note obtained by evaluating the distance between the first two lowest pitches of each except;
- E-deviation in harmonicity: corresponds to the deviation between the file's total pitch-content and the harmonic series deduced from the virtual fundamental.
- Relative density: is obtained by dividing the total number of pitches by the theoretical maximum possible number of them within the total range of the excerpt. A typical chromatic cluster, for instance, would correspond to the maximum relative density.
- Absolute Range: corresponds to the difference between the highest and the lowest note present in the excerpt.
- Relative Range: the range occupation of the excerpt considered with respect to the range spanned by all the excerpts considered. In the case of *Speakings*, this total range goes from F_4 (or 6500 Midicents) to $G\#_7$ (or 10400 Midicents).

The symbolic features extracted considered each single excerpt a-chronically.

4. CLASSIFICATION AND EXTENSION

The experiments described in this section aimed at obtaining a classification of the features that best represented each of the *baby-sound* categories. For this purpose all data was normalized to zero mean and unity variance, so that all features would be considered with equal weight.

General-purpose computer-based classification processes are frequently based on vector descriptions of data points. They highlight correlations in the data that are usually hard to identify manually. Although such general-purpose algorithms ignore specialist knowledge they have achieved important results in many fields.

Two different algorithms were used and compared: support vector machines (SVM) and C4.5 binary decision trees (BDT).

A SVM is a supervised machine-learning algorithm that yields a classification based on the maximization of a decision margin [12]. Although it has been used to generate efficient classifiers from data, its internal parameters are hard to interpret. SVMs are especially important because of their known ability to find hidden relationships between features [12]. They tend, furthermore, to yield models that generalize well, usually leading to better results in testing data at the expense of a lower performance when the model is executed over the training data.

A BDT is a supervised machine-learning algorithm whose training process consists of selecting features from data that yield an optimal entropy classification [13]. For this reason, the classification model is easy to interpret but, at the same time, may have limited generalization ability. The BDT may reveal decision processes that can be hard to obtain manually but, crucially in the present context, are easy to interpret [13].

4.1 The Classification of the Baby Sounds in the 1st Movement

In a first experiment both algorithms were trained using the labeled data from the first movement and the resulting systems applied to the classification of that same training data. This test aimed at detecting if the features made sense for classification. The accuracy of this process is shown in Table 1.

Number (and %) of correctly classified baby sounds	SVM	BDT
Audio	**14** (77%)	**17** (94%)
Symbolic	**11** (61%)	**14** (77%)
Comprehensive	**15** (83%)	**17** (94%)

Table 1. Classifications of the Baby Sounds in the first movement.

We note that the results obtained by the SVM are notably worse than those obtained by the BDT, in spite of the former being a more sophisticated model. This, however, is in line with the fact that its training process aims at optimizing the *generalization* capability of the system. The BDT, on the other hand, maximizes its results considering the training data alone.

Furthermore, the BDTs training process showed the most discriminative features in both sets. In the symbolic features set, the algorithm selected the relative density and the relative occupation while in the acoustic set as well as in the comprehensive set, it selected the average energy, the average spectral flow and the average spectral roll-off.

4.2 Extension to the Second Movement

The systems resulting from the training of both algorithms were then used to determine the category to which the *baby sounds* that appear in the second movement could be said to belong to. The results are shown in Table 2.

	Binary Decision Tree				Support Vector Machine		
	Symb.	Symb. 2	Audio	Comp.	Symb.	Audio	Comp.
1	B	B	C	C	B	C	B
2	B	C	S	S	B	B	B
3	B	B	S	S	B	B	B
4	B	B	S	S	B	B	B
5	B	C	C	C	B	B	B
6	C	B	S	S	B	B	B
7	B	C	C	C	B	B	B
8	B	C	S	S	B	B	B
9	B	B	C	C	B	B	B
10	B	B	S	S	B	B	B
11	B	B	B	B	B	B	B
12	B	B	S	S	B	B	B
13	B	B	B	B	B	C	B
14	B	B	S	S	B	C	B
15	B	B	S	S	B	C	B
16	B	B	C	C	B	C	B
17	S	B	S	S	B	B	B
18	B	B	S	S	B	B	B
19	B	B	C	C	B	B	B
20	B	B	S	S	B	B	B
21	B	B	S	S	B	B	B
22	B	B	S	S	B	B	B
23	B	B	S	S	B	B	B
24	B	B	S	S	B	B	B
25	B	B	S	S	B	B	B
26	B	B	C	C	B	B	B
27	C	C	S	S	B	B	B
28	B	B	S	S	B	B	B
29	S	B	S	S	B	B	B
30	B	B	S	S	B	B	B
S	2	0	21	21	0	0	0
C	2	5	7	7	0	5	0
B	26	25	2	2	30	25	30
S	6,67%	0,00%	70,00%	70,00%	0,00%	0,00%	0,00%
C	6,67%	16,67%	23,33%	23,33%	0,00%	16,67%	0,00%
B	86,67%	83,33%	6,67%	6,67%	100,00%	83,33%	100,00%

Table 2. Classifications of the Baby Sounds in Second movement.

Although data from the second movement is not labeled (no ground-truth is provided) it can be observed that the results of most executions are consistent between themselves. This means that, considering the specific features selected (both acoustic and symbolic), the sound events of the second movement are closer to the first movement's *baby babbles* than to the others baby sounds. Since this is true for all three feature-sets, it is important to discuss this result more thoroughly.

The classification of excerpts of the second movement, using the BDT only matched the results yielded by the SVMs when symbolic features were considered. This is to be expected, as the auditory similarity depends on the correlations between acoustic features, while symbolic features are meaningful even if analyzed individually.

The BDT decision process considered only two features from the symbolic dataset: Relative Range and Relative Density. In order to explore the combinations further, these two features were removed from the set and a new learning process initiated. The remaining features formed the "Symbolic 2" set. When training was based on this set, the algorithm considered two further features: E-harmonic Deviation and Relative Range.

The results in the second movement, shown in Table 2, are consistent with the ones obtained previously with a clear prominence of *baby babble* sounds.

5. DISCUSSION

Looking back at the music analytical questions formulated at the beginning of this article the results may now be interpreted within the "*basic metaphor*" underlying the composition. Leaving aside all considerations about what the composer's actual interpretation has been, the "reminiscences" of the *baby sounds* that precede the process leading to the "mantra" can be argued to correspond to the last of the three types of baby sounds. Remaining at the metaphorical level, the *baby babbling*, albeit in a more discreet form, become part of the "frantic chatter" through which the music – and the speech consciousness – evolves until reaching its final "serenity".

Such an observation, of course, does not in itself constitute an analysis of the composition. How it would fit into a more extensive study of the work would also greatly depend on the particular angle taken in such an endeavor. The results to be underlined here have more to do with the method employed and, in particular, with the dual role the computer played in reaching our conclusion.

The first of these roles is to be found in the increase in precision and in the associated extension in the number of "parameters" that can be taken into consideration in the analytical process. As a correlate, the quantification process that underlies these new possibilities offers a more objective basis for discussion and for communication of results.

The second role played by the computer is more obvious: namely in systematization of the exploration of these parameters. In this context, the fundamental difference between the two algorithms should be stressed again. The SVM generalizes user-labeled data but does so without providing any feedback as to the reasons that underlie its decisions. The BDT, on the other hand, provides an explicit hierarchy of features that can be discussed independently and may become the basis of a new set of experiments.

In both cases, the results provided by the algorithms depend, in two distinct senses, on the particular features that have been extracted. First, at the algorithmic level, a poor selection of features may lead to unsatisfactory classification. Second, at the analytical level, the same may weaken the interpretability of the results or their meaningfulness.

In the analysis presented here questions of segmentation and categorization were directly suggested by information provided by the composer. In a more general context, such data would have to be obtained from other sources, including independent (music) analytical decisions. Questions of identity and similarity, however, are bound to arise in a variety of contexts. In the face of the increasing complexity of a certain type of repertoire, the help of computerized processes such as the ones described here are likely to become increasingly important.

6. CONCLUSIONS

The computer-based music analytical approach proposed here, albeit still being in its preliminary stages, provided concrete support in tackling musical repertoire in which both written and recorded sources are best considered in tandem.

None of the features extracted was obtained by a method new to either the field of music information retrieval or to that of music analysis *per se*. Their handling, however, opened the way for a more comprehensive approach, in which information obtained form different sources could be considered simultaneously. The use of the machine learning techniques also showed the computer's potential as a tool to explore and make sense of the multiplicity of data that such an approach implies.

Amongst the tasks envisioned in the future are: the elaboration of further analytical examples, more detailed discussions of the methodological issues that may arise from the extension of the method as well as a harmonization of the computational tools involved.

Acknowledgments

The present research has been made possible by support of FAPESP and CNPq.

7. REFERENCES

[1] P. Couprie, "Cartes et Tableaux Interactifs: Nouveaux Enjeux pour l'Analyse des Musiques Electroacoustiques", in Journées d'Informatique Musicale 2013, http://www.mshparisnord.fr/JIM2013/actes/jim2013_12.pdf

[2] Y. Geslin and A. Lefevre, "Sound and musical representation: the Acousmographe software", in in Proc. INA - Groupe de Recherches Musicales, Paris. ICMC 2004.

[3] C. Cannam, C. Landone, and M. Sandler, "Sonic visualizer: An Open Source Application for Viewing, Analysing, And Annotating Music Audio Files", in Proc. of the ACM Multimedia 2010 International Conference, Firenze, Italy. October 25–29, 2010.

[4] M. Malt and E. Jourdan, "Zsa.Descriptors: a library for real-time descriptors analysis", in 5th Sound and Music Computing Conference, Berlin, Allemagne, 2008.

[5] D. Guigue, SOAL – Sonic Object Analysis Library – OpenMusic Tools for analysing musical objects structure. http://www.cchla.ufpb.br/mus3/index.php?option=com_content&view=article&id=7&Itemid=5

[6] J. Harvey, G. Nuono, A. Cont, G. Carpentier, "Making an Orchestra Speak" in Proc. Int. Conf. Sound and Music Computing (SMC2009), Porto, 2009, SMC 2009.

[7] British Broadcasting Corporation Scottish Symphony Orchestra (BBCSSO), conductor: Ilan Volkov. Aeon, 2010. http://www.outhere-music.com/aeon.

[8] J. G. A. Barbedo and A. Lopes, "Automatic Genre Classification of Musical Signals", in EURASIP Journal on Advances in Signal Processing, no. 1, 2007.

[9] G. Tzanetakis, and P. Cook, "Musical genre classification of audio signals", in Speech and Audio Processing, IEEE transactions on 10, no. 5, 2002, pp.293-302.

[10] D. Gerhard, "Pitch Extraction and Fundamental Frequency: History and Current Techniques, technical report", in Dept. of Computer Science, University of Regina, 2003.

[11] G. Assayag, C. Rueda, M. Laurson, C. Agon, and O. Delerue, "Computer-assisted composition at ircam: From patchwork to OpenMusic", in Computer Music Journal, vol. 23, no. 3, 1999, pp. 59 – 72.

[12] C. Cortes, and V. N. Vapnik, "Support-Vector Networks", Machine Learning, 20, 1995. http://www.springerlink.com/content/k238jx04hm87j80g

[13] R. Quinlan, "C4.5: Programs for Machine Learning". Morgan Kaufmann Publishers, San Mateo, CA. 1993.

BRAZILIAN CHALLENGES ON NETWORK MUSIC

Julian Jaramillo Arango
Department of Music/University of São Paulo/Brazil
xirrete@gmail.com

Marcio Tomiyoshi
Computer Science Department/University of São Paulo/Brazil
mtomiyoshi@usp.br

Fernando Iazzetta
Department of Music/University of São Paulo/Brazil
iazzetta@usp.br

Marcelo Queiroz
Computer Science Department/University of São Paulo/Brazil
mqz@ime.usp.br

ABSTRACT

This paper presents an overview of research and development of Network Music in Brazil, and particularly the production of two concerts at the University of São Paulo in partnership with the Sonic Arts Research Centre in Belfast, Northern Ireland. We present technical issues encountered that were of substantial impact on the realization of rehearsals and concerts, and also discuss aesthetic issues related to composition, performance and perception on distributed environments. From these concerts we emphasize the lessons we learned and also the perspectives for future research, always from both technical and artistic points-of-view.

1. INTRODUCTION

Since the appearance of the Internet there has been several approaches for using it for music creation and performance, ranging from network transmission of purely symbolic information, with all heavy processing (such as analysis and synthesis of digital signals) carried out locally on each node, to full-duplex high-quality multi-channel Audio/Video transmission, frequently resorting to high-end dedicated network infrastructures [1],[2],[3],[4].

A handful of musical works for the Internet unveils the different ways composers have adopted the new medium to place their musical knowledge. Online pieces such as "Cathedral" (1997) or "Auracle" (2004), by recently deceased composers William Duckworth and Max Neuhaus respectively, have proposed networked multi-user environments where musicians and nonmusicians are able to interact through sound. Installations such as Ataú Tanaka`s "Global String" (2000) and Chris Chafe`s "Ping" (2001) have suggested the metaphor of a string that resonates over the Internet between geographically distant points. Taking advantage of non-synchronic interaction and social network paradigms, new musical experiments are being proposed for the Web 2.0, such as "Graph Theory" (2005) by Jason Freeman, "It Space" (2007) by Peter Traub or "In B flat 2.0" (2009) by Darren Salomon. Since Internet connection has become an ubiquitous facility and bandwidth has expressively increased, network musical performance has became a reality. In the last decade, regular collaboration projects have been created, mainly in North America and Europe, establishing dispersed groups of musicians exploring the network as a musical performance platform. Remarkably, Telematic Circle project, conducted by American composer Pauline Oliveiros, has been organizing and staging network performance collaborations and concerts over Internet2.

Despite the enormous potential for artistic exploration and technical development related to Network Music, the currently available infrastructure in Brazil still imposes limitations and difficulties, both for the home user and Academia, accounting for the fact that networked musical collaboration hasn't yet gained widespread popularity here after nearly 20 years of research.

1.1 Brazilian challenges on Network Music

When the Internet first appeared, expectations on its potential for musical use were high. Although dial-up 56 kbps connections could barely sustain a lossy-encoded voice transmission without occasional drop-outs, let alone reasonable 128 kbps MP3-encoded music signals or 1411 kbps CD-quality stereo signals, bandwidth has largely increased ever since, reaching 30~100 Mbps for a home user and 1~10 Gbps within Universities nowadays in Brazil. Despite this obvious improvement, home users still face severe download fluctuations, because Internet providers are only required by law to ensure 20% of the nominal acquired speed, and also very low upload rates, usually about 3~5% of the corresponding download rates.

Technological difficulties have not prevented many attempts of bringing together music and networks among the general public in Brazil. A few very recent examples outside research circles are the joint rehearsals of the Deutsches Symphonieorchester Berlin and the Orquestra Jovem do Estado de São Paulo [5], a Rock/Rap distributed concert in São Carlos [6] and the event "Challenges of Network Art" with A/V exchange between Fortaleza and Rio de Janeiro [7].

Turning to research circles in Brazil, back in the 1990's Iazzetta and Kon were concerned with two main issues that affected musical performance on the Internet: time discontinuity (latency and jittering) and the lack of a suitable musical representation specifically designed for network transmission [8], [9]. Miletto and Pimenta started out in 2003 what would become the CODES Web-based environment for collaborative musical composition [10],[11]. Also in 2003 other works dealing with symbolic network transmission have appeared in the archives of the Brazilian Symposium on Computer Music, addressing problems such as distributed musical instruments [12], distributed performance [13] and multiagent distributed music processing [14]. In 2004 Kon and Lago studied the perceptual influence of latency on musical performance [15], suggesting that tolerable latencies are highly dependent on users perceptions and stimulus type (rhythmic/melodic, visual and haptic).

1.2 Network Music at University of São Paulo

From 2001 onwards there has been a continuous convergence of interests between research groups in the music and computer science departments at the University of São Paulo (USP). Music research with a technological component, spanning topics such as electroacoustic and interactive creation and performance, psychoacoustics and sonology, had clear potential interrelations with computer science research on digital sound processing, numerical simulation, distributed systems and artificial intelligence. A collaborative effort was created, first centered on room acoustics [16], then on technologically-mediated interactive music performance that ultimately grew into a research organization called NuSom (Research Center on Sonology). Over the years, this group produced several works both with scientific/technological as well as artistic contributions and creations.

As far as technological solutions for network performances are concerned, a few shortcomings were identified for every available software, either regarding cost, unavailability of source code or lack of specific functionalities (e.g. data compression, delayed local feedback or graphical user interfaces). Two parallel projects were launched, one aimed at adding compression and a delayed feedback option to JackTrip (in collaboration with its authors), and another (the Medusa project) based on JACK and aimed at transparently managing shared audio resources in a heterogeneous network [17], [18].

Academic exchange of students and researchers between the SARC (Sonic Arts Research Centre) at Queen's University Belfast and the Mobile group at USP has motivated a series of artistic collaborations. Among these two networked concerts (nicknamed NetConcerts) have been carried out, aiming the incorporation of an academic network as the platform for music performance and composition. The preparation phase preceding these concerts has involved a set of tests, rehearsals and the setup of an interconnected stage, put into effect by a team of graduate students from both institutions.

This text focuses on the problems that appeared in attempting to carry out these projects and concerts, and the solutions devised to overcome or bypass some of the difficulties that may (or may not) be specific to this Brazilian scenario. The following section discusses the main technical and artistic challenges that were addressed in putting together the NetConcerts. Section 3 presents details of each NetConcert, including preparations and rehearsals, compositions included and also some of the lessons learned. Finally, section 4 presents some perspectives and unsolved problems for further research.

2. TECHNICAL AND ARTISTIC CHALLENGES

There are a few general and well-known technical problems that impact a distributed concert, such as bandwidth limitations, latency and jitter. Other problems may be specific to a particular setting, for instance the need to think of mixing console control also as a distributed problem, since an operator on one stage doesn't know how a particular sound mixture is perceived on another stage due to acoustical differences. The choice of software for signal streaming may also be specific to the type of network connection available and the musical paradigm adopted.

The distribution of performers, instruments and roles also bring important challenges on composition and performance. Some specific issues have been identified and discussed [19], [20], and taken into consideration in our network performance practice such as the perception of time, the remote interactivity, the distributed nature of performance space, the notation and control resources for the network. Artistic intentions have started from the premise that in a networked concert, performance not only takes place in the physical space, but also in a non-physical one, a virtual space of communication that can be embodied by specific audiovisual clues on each site. Thus, the representation of this interconnected space has leaded to a particular concern about the staging process in networked musical contexts. The search for stage resources that enhance the interconnected nature of the performance has been our main artistic goal.

2.1 Technical issues

Several software solutions are available for performing music in different places using the Internet, but some applications are meant only for asynchronous symbolic information exchange (such as netpd [21], the Pd object netsend and JAM with Chrome [22], whereas others are concerned with synchronous audio streaming, such as SoundJack- [23], JackTrip- [24], eJamming- [25], netjack- [26], llcon [27] and the Pd external netsend~ [28], and also NINJAM [29], which has a very particular approach towards synchronization (players are synchronized with previous bars played by remote users). There have also been extreme cases where musicians performed through a Skype# call, but since it is a VoIP solution its audio quality is poor (it uses speech codecs aiming at intelligibility) and it may produce latencies up to 250 ms [30], whereas network music performances ideally require less than 50 ms [31].

In the NetConcerts between USP and SARC, both SoundJack and JackTrip were used. Initially, JackTrip was chosen because it is capable of interacting with the JACK audio server, but after some connection difficulties (as discussed in the sequel), performances were made using SoundJack. These alternatives differ in many aspects, which will be described briefly.

The SoundJack software was created by Alexander Carôt for his Ph.D thesis providing interesting options for network music performances. Despite its name, it currently doesn't connect to JACK (a feature that was available in earlier versions), but uses the PortAudio library instead. It allows sending uncompressed 48 kHz 16-bit audio streams, or OPUS-compressed streams (OPUS is an IETF standard defined on the RFC 6716 that gives high quality lossy audio compression with low algorithmic latency [32]) with 48, 96 or 192 kbps. The user also chooses the size of the audio block (64, 128, 256 or 512) and the number of samples in each network packet (128, 256 or 512). The lower these settings, the smaller the latency, provided that the audio block size is not set too low so that the computer can't handle it. The size of the network packet directly influences the amount of bandwidth needed. It is possible to adjust the buffer size during performance to avoid audio glitches caused by buffer underruns. There are two ways of connecting to other nodes: automatically or manually. In the automatic mode the application connects to a server that helps finding other users and works as a hub, helping in the NAT traversal process, whereas in the manual mode the user is required to set the IP address and port of the remote host.

The JackTrip project was developed at the CCRMA by Juan-Pablo Cáceres and Chris Chafe, and provides high-quality audio streaming while maintaining low latencies. It allows accessing the sound card through the JACK audio server, allowing the musician to connect it directly to any other software compatible with the JACK API (e.g., Pure Data patches). It is also possible to use the RtAudio library to access the audio device directly, as SoundJack does. It uses 8/16/24/32 bits per sample and any sampling rate desired, but it doesn't use audio compression, requiring fairly large amounts of network bandwidth in exchange for high audio quality. Theoretically, it allows the user to transmit as many audio channels as he/she wishes. There is no central server to help locating other users, so it requires the manual adjustment of IP address and port.

JackTrip's buffer size cannot be adjusted during performance, but only on startup. When the buffer becomes empty during a session, the current implementation starts to playback the audio received as soon as possible, which actually negates the buffer's main purpose. However, when JackTrip is used on academic research networks this is not much of an issue, since the jitter observed in these conditions is very low, and not enough to cause buffer underruns and/or audio glitches. For instance, when analyzing the network conditions between USP and SARC over 24 hours with the ping tool, a mean latency of 257.96 ms was observed, but with only 0.786 ms standard deviation.

From a non-technical user point-of-view, SoundJack is much more user-friendly, by including a graphical user interface and offering an automatic connection scheme, while limiting some configuration options that would appeal to musicians with access to a high-end network infrastructure. On the other hand, JackTrip is a command-line tool which require a little more user skill, but allows greater flexibility and can be considered a better choice in the context of academic music performances. As will be seen in the next section, it hasn't been favored over SoundJack due to a practical limitation on the number of channels. It turned out that depending on the JackTrip and audio device settings, the packet size may become bigger than the maximum allowed on the TCP/IP protocol (65535 bytes), causing the software to fail to transmit data appropriately, and effectively limiting the number of channels being streamed.

2.2 USP network infrastructure and required tests

University of São Paulo is a strategic point of connectivity in Brazil since it has been a founding partner of the ANSP (Academic Network of São Paulo) and manages, as from 2004, one of the Brazilian backbone Points of Presence (PoP). It facilitates the integration of the Brazilian National Research Network (RNP - Rede Nacional de Pesquisa) with foreign high-end networks that serve other regions of the globe, such as Clara, Internet2, Geant or, as was the case in the NetConcerts, with Janet in the UK. Broadband connection within the RNP backbone called "ipê" achieves 10 Gbps, and receives privileges and monitoring services.

During the NetConcerts preparations, connectivity issues between USP and SARC were observed. While trying to connect using JackTrip, only SARC was able to receive the stream correctly, which made it seems like there was a firewall on the USP side blocking UDP traffic, since changing port or public IP wasn't helping establishing the connection. After contacting USP central network administrators, they guaranteed that there never was any kind of firewall blocking, which made those issues were completely unexpected (testing with netcat on the same ports confirmed that indeed there was no firewall at all). It was possible to transmit UDP messages between the sites but, for some unknown reason, no connection was possible using JackTrip.

Another suspicion was that the bandwidth required could be part of the problem, triggering some behavior that blocked UDP traffic on this route. To test this hypothesis, the number of channels were lowered and, indeed, the connection with mono audio could be made successfully between USP and SARC. Further investigations showed that the bandwidth needed, while related to the issue, wasn't the cause of it. Inspecting the network traffic with Wireshark showed that the packet size used was the main problem. Since the network packet sent by JackTrip depends directly on the number of samples per frame and the quantity of channels, depending on the settings chosen, the packets were being fragmented by the IP layer of the protocol stack.

With only one channel and 512 samples per frame, the packet was sent without being split and everything worked fine. Increasing the number of channels, the packet had 2140 bytes, becoming too big to be sent at once and was fragmented in two segments, one with 1514 bytes and other with 626 bytes. Interestingly, the larger one would arrive without issues, but the smaller one wouldn't arrive at all. This also explains why SoundJack was able to connect without issues, since, by default, it transmits an OPUS stream, using much smaller network packets and avoiding fragmentation on the IP layer.

With the problem completely characterized, the network administrators at USP were called for again to finally solve this issue. To avoid their understandable tendency of blaming the software (since they don't know JackTrip), a simple Python script was written that sent increasingly bigger UDP packets and showed that, on the USP↔SARC route the packets were only correctly transmitted until a certain packet size, whereas with other routes no problems were observed at all. With this important piece of information, they were able to investigate the issue, identifying that the cause of the problem was outside of the USPnet backbone, and fixed it with the collaboration of external partners, making it possible to send up to 32 uncompressed audio channels between the concert sites. Unfortunately, such a solution was only found after the concerts, which explain the use of SoundJack in both NetConcerts.

In this case there were problems on the infrastructure that required much more investigation than it is generally needed, but it shows how important it is to be able to contact your network administrators and to be able to work with them to perform networked music, since it is not unexpected for the user to face at least some security restrictions or NAT issues.

The problem described in this section could also have been solved by adding features to the JackTrip code that could circumvent the issue, since it is an open-source software. Allowing JackTrip to split and join the network packets inside the application itself would have offered a quick solution, but would also mask the real underlying network infrastructure problem instead of solving it.

2.3 Artistic issues

The process of selecting, designing and adapting the performance space for different network music pieces was especially rewarding. Performers' and audiences' geographic displacement challenged the way we used to set up the live stage. In order to represent the shared space of communication between musicians, some aspects were taken into consideration.

Stagecraft elements such as screens and projections help audiences become aware of the interconnected nature of the performance. Fed with live content, they intensify the sense of community and enhance the liveness experienced in a telematic event. Live video resources on stage suggest a televisual reference that helps the audience strengthen causal relations between sound and performers' activity.

The above-mentioned difficulties in connecting Jacktrip between the two sites limited the audio setup to a bidirectional 44.100 Khz stereo Soundjack connection. Thus, it required the creation of three local sound mixtures related to the different sound outputs needed in a telematic event. The first mix was defined with the criterion of leaving, as intelligible as possible, the sound produced on stage in São Paulo. This stereo audio signal was sent to Belfast via Soundjack. The second mix was created for the stereo PA in São Paulo, and gathered the local sound and the incoming stereo signal from Belfast. A third mixture was created in order to produce a recording, and it was also used to transmit the concert by an online audio-streaming channel.

Notation resources have also been considered as an important concern in network performance and composition. Through live scores, graphic environments running locally on each side of the connection, the composer is able to conduct the performance remotely. Performers are able to follow the movements and changes in the graphical environment as musical directions or instructions sent by the composer (in our case through OSC messages).

Live video processing procedures have also been incorporated. Such strategy suggests a quite different approach with respect to live scores, since the goal here is metaphorically resizing the performance space in order to find new boundaries for the musical stage. Rather than creating a visual content for the music or a graphic score, the manipulation of live images from the remote stage reinforces performers' and audiences' sense of a shared space.

3. ARTISTIC CONTRIBUTIONS AND NETCONCERTS

NetConcert is a series of networked events hosted by the Mobile research group at the University of São Paulo (USP). Through live concerts with remote partners, NetConcert project aims to create an interdisciplinary laboratory for experimental work on the subject of interconnected musical performance, composition and distributed creativity. It intends to build a technical framework at the School of Arts and Communication that allows staging and commissioning Networked Music pieces. Among other transmissions and participations on networked events, two concerts have been carried out in cooperation with the Sonic Arts Research Centre (SARC) at the Queen's University Belfast (QUB), the former on June 6th, 2011 and the latter on March 23rd, 2012.

The repertoire was chosen keeping the balance between new commissioned pieces for the event and existing network music pieces by contemporary composers. Some pieces by SARC members that have already been played with other partners were performed whereas others were premiered. An adaptation for a geographically distributed laptop ensemble was made from a work composed originally for a local area network environment. Postgraduate students from USP Music Department engaged in the Mobile project were commissioned to compose pieces for the events.

3.1 NetConcert 1 (June 2011)

The first NetConcert took place on June 6th, 2011, and it was the first public experience with the network infrastructure installed in the LAMI laboratory at the Music Department. We performed pieces recently composed by SARC members such as Pedro Rebelo's "NetGraph" (2010) and Felipe Hickmann `s "Summer Snail" (2010). They included live score resources with different intentions; in the case of NetGraph remote controlled images become a platform for musical socialization. In the case of Hickmann, live score followed a game-like direction. New pieces were composed for the event: "Paulista" (2011) by Rui Chaves, that included the image from a live earth-cam# located at the Paulista Avenue (one of the main streets in São Paulo) and "Disparity" (2011) by Julián Jaramillo where the live images of two sax players are cut in vertical fragments and reassembled, creating a new live image from the two dislocated performances. The resultant image is different on each site because local video processes are driven by remote performance. Specific coincidences between pitch and amplitude are routed to video events.

Performers and collaborators engaged with the Mobile group were invited to participate in the first NetConcert. The improvisatory structure of the pieces implied that many rehearsals were devoted to jam sessions controlled by the composer. As temporal discontinuity used to be the main drawback in networked environments, periodical time structures and idiomatic musical languages were deliberately eluded. On the other hand, the preparation phase aimed towards the search for an appropriate scenography, thus two screens were disposed on the stage. One of them showed the performance space in Belfast. This element worked better when the camera was taking a close view of the remote performance space. The incoming video signal was projected next to the musicians trying to preserve the one-to-one scale. The existence of such a crude, unprocessed, remote live image from the partner stage granted an evidence of the interconnected status of performance. The other screen was dedicated to represent the communication space in specific ways for each piece.

Figure 1. São Paulo view of SARC composer Pedro Rebelo performing "NetGraph" with USP double bass student Miguel Antar.

3.2 NetConcert 2 (March 2012)

The second concert was carried out on March 2nd, 2012, with closer academic relations between SARC members and the Mobile group. We performed Pedro Rebelo`s "Cipher Series" (2011-2012) and Felipe Hickmann's new version of "Summer Snail" (2011) from SARC. Automatic live score resources were included in the pieces we commissioned in São Paulo. "Scratch-shot" (2012), by young Brazilian composer Andre Damião Bandeira, proposed a Pure Data Patch whose aleatoric behavior and chance directions guided the performance. The USP Music Department laptop ensemble was invited to perform "VAV" (2008) by Californian composer and The Hub member Chris Brown. The performance included six laptop players in São Paulo, two in Belfast, and a conductor. Performing "VAV" over the Internet was a great experience. A very simple dynamic notation environment was also created exclusively for the performance. The goal here was visualizing and making evident the rules of interaction and improvisation the piece called for.

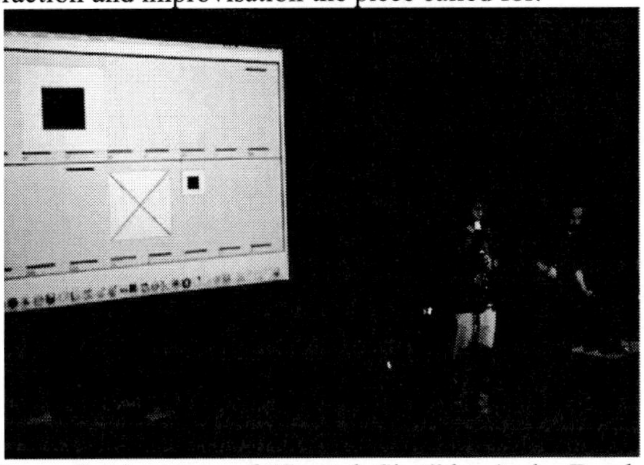

Figure 2. Live score of "Scratch-Shot" by Andre Bandeira.

"Ser Voz" ("To Be Voice", 2012) was commissioned to Michelle Agnes and Julián Jaramillo and performed with Mobile members Lilian Campesato and Vitor Kisil. The piece suggests a strategy to deal with latency since timing is dictated by a system of cued vocal events between performers. From gutturalities, onomatopoeia and imitative sounds, a vocal soundscape is progressively created by two pair of geographically displaced duets. As opposed to the first NetConcert preparation process, in the case of "Ser Voz", rehearsals were devoted to determine regions of synchronicity through specific vocal events. Video processing resources were also adopted but in this case, the one-to-one scale was not adopted. Each performer of "Ser Voz" had a webcam close to his face, thus by computer vision means the lips of each performer were isolated from the background and relocated in a new abstract image including the four performers' mouths.

	NetConcert 1	**NetConcert 2**
Preparation phase (weeks)	5	7
Total Number of pieces	4	5
Original pieces by SARC members	3	2
Original pieces by USP members	1	2
Original pieces by other composers	0	1
Rehearsals	2	3
Performers at SARC	5	4
Performers at USP	4	14
Technical collaborators at SARC	3	4
Technical collaborators at USP	5	6

Table 1. Human resources of the NetConcerts.

Academic Network at SARC	Janet	Janet
Academic Network at USP	RNP	RNP
Institutional support at SARC	QUB	QUB
Institutional support at USP	USP/FAPESP	USP/FAPESP
Software	SoundJack, Max/Msp, Unreal Media, Processing	SoundJack, Jacktrip, Max/Msp, Pure Data

Table 2. Technical resources of the NetConcerts.

4. PERSPECTIVES AND FURTHER RESEARCH

In this article we presented some issues regarding experiences in the field of networked music in Brazil. Although Brazilian researchers and artists have been concerned about it since the 1990s, it is only recently that this subject has been regularly researched. Particularly the Mobile project at the University of São Paulo has held a regular work in producing NetConcerts in recent years.

One of our main challenges has been to carry out a multidisciplinary investigation that takes into account both technical and aesthetical issues.

We have devoted a lot of attention to the solution of traditional technical problems of networked contexts (delay, connectivity, jittering) because we believe that stability in music network environments is a crucial point to be addressed, with an obvious impact on artistic performance. However, our main concern is related to the aesthetic possibilities brought by this context. More than relying on the remote connection between musicians performing on different locations, our main concern is to explore the creative potential of networked environments. This leads to many interesting open questions.

One of our major concerns is related to the control of networked environments. Achieving connection stability is fundamental to provide a background for the development of a creative use of the Internet. Since most of this production is essentially based on collective interaction, the development of a common platform that could be efficiently employed in different environments is a key point. Also, the integration and synchronization of audio, video and metadata is very important since it improves the communication between musicians during performance, and allows the development of complex strategies of music coordination that go beyond free improvisation.

Events held with SARC left us an important artistic experience and many lessons. They pointed out problems to be solved and future perspectives. On one hand, as a consideration of our experience with networked dynamic scores, we could assert that this new kind of notation suggests new connotations for the musical stage. Live scores create an instance of communication where the composer or conductor participates in the performance. Since notation is strongly related to sound and live score symbols usually do not resemble traditional musical notation, audience will take it as a clue to better understand the performance. On the other, the creation of an interconnected perspective for both performers and audiences encounters particular challenges in the setting up of the stage. Although each piece demands a specific set of connections, a common technical framework should be prepared for a telematic concert, thus, depending on the configuration of each piece, a proper order should be previously defined and rehearsed.

One of the main perspectives for our NetConcert project is to carry out an event that involves more than two sites by establishing a multisite connection. In collaboration with Icesi University, in Cali, Colombia and Universidad de Caldas in Manizales, Colombia, a multisite collaboration is being prepared. As part of the 2013 musical program at the Festival de la Imagen a version of John Cage "Four6" (1992) is being adapted for a network performance. The setup incorporates a multi-site jacktrip connection over colombian Renata and brazilian RNP network infrastructure.

The NetConcerts served as a laboratory for experimentation with different systems and platforms required to transmit and synchronize various information channels, but this very diversity was one of the main obstacles in assembling the performances. In our own experience the problem of remotely connecting musicians using distinct hardware and software platforms proved to be very difficult, and for practical reasons several choices have had to be made in order to guarantee the feasibility of those concerts. It seems that a clean solution to this problem depends on a more thorough abstraction with respect to operating systems and sources of stream data.

5. ACKNOWLEDGEMENTS

This work has been supported by the funding agencies CAPES and FAPESP (grant 2008/08632-8 and 2010/1254-0).

6. REFERENCES

[1] D. Konstantas, Y. Orlarey, S. Gibbs and O. Carbonel. "Distributed musical rehearsal," In: *Proc. of the ICMC*, 1997, pp.279–282.

[2] A. Tanaka. "Network Audio Performance and Installation". In: *Proc. of the ICMC*, 1999, pp.519-522,

[3] W. Woszczyk, J. Cooperstock, J. Roston and W. Martens. "Environment for immersive multi-sensory communication of music using broadband networks". In: *23. Tonmeistertagung VDT International Audio Convention*, 2004

[4] J.P. Cáceres, R. Hamilton, D. Iyer, C. Chafe and G. Wang. "To the edge with China: Explorations in

network performance" In: *ARTECH, 2008 Proceedings of the 4th International Conference on Digital Arts,* 2008, pp.61–66

[5] J. L. Sampaio. "Musicians have a rehearsal today over the Internet" (in Portuguese: Músicos fazem hoje ensaio pela Internet). In: *O Estado de São Paulo, May 3, 2012.*

[6] L.S. Roça and M. Tramontano. "Hybrid surroundings: sound, space and simultaneity" (in Portuguese: Entornos híbridos: som, espaço e simultaneidade). *Seminário Música Ciência Tecnologia,* vol.4. no 1, 2012.

[7] F.A.F. Silva. "Telematic Music: latency, compositional attitude and presence" (in Portuguese: Música telemática: latência, atitude composicional e presentidade). *Seminário Música Ciência Tecnologia,* vol.4. no 1, 2012.

[8] F. Kon and F. Iazzetta. "Internet Music: Dream or (virtual) Reality?". In: *Proceedings of the 5th Brazilian Symposium on Computer Music,* 1998.

[9] Iazzetta, Fernando & Kon, Fabio. "Downloading Musical Signs". In: *European Journal for Semiotic Studies,* no 1-2, vol 13, pp. 273-284, 2001.

[10] E. Miletto and M. Pimenta. "Towards a Web-based environment for collective musical composition" (in Portuguese: Rumo a um Ambiente para Composição Musical Coletiva Baseado na Web). In: *Proc. of the Brazilian Symposium on Computer Music,* 2003.

[11] E. Miletto, M. Pimenta, F. Bouchet, J.-P. Sansonnet and D. Keller. "Music Creation by Novices should be both Prototypical and Cooperative - Lessons Learned from CODES". In: *Proc. of the Brazilian Symposium on Computer Music,* 2009.

[12] F. Ramos, M. Costa and J. Manzolli. "Virtual Studio: Distributed Musical Instruments on the Web". In: *Proc. of the Brazilian Symposium on Computer Music,* 2003.

[13] A. Almeida and R. Furtado. "Distributed Musical Environment: Interactive Music Performance on the Internet" (in Portuguese: AMD Ambiente Musical Distribuído: Performance Musical Interativa na Internet). In: *Brazilian Symposium on Computer Music,* 2003.

[14] L. Ueda and F. Kon. "Andante: A Mobile Musical Agents Infrastructure". In: *Proc. of the Brazilian Symposium on Computer Music,* 2003.

[15] N. Lago and F. Kon. "The Quest for Low Latency". In: *Proc. of the ICMC,* 2004. pp. 33-36

[16] M. Queiroz, F. Iazzetta, F. Kon, M. Gomes, F. Figueiredo, B. Masiero, L. Ueda, L. Dias, M. Torres, L. Thomaz. "AcMus: an open, integrated platform for room acoustics research." In: *Journal of the Brazilian Computer Society,* no 3, vol 4, pp. 87-103, 2008.

[17] F. Schiavoni, M. Queiroz, and F. Iazzetta. "Medusa: a Distributed Sound Environment." In: *Proceedings of the Linux Audio Conference,* 2011, pp. 149-156.

[18] F. Schiavoni and M. Queiroz. "Network distribution in music applications with Medusa". In: *Proceedings of the Linux Audio Conference,* 2012, pp. 9-14

[19] J.J. Arango. "Musical creation, networks and Web 2.0." (in Spanish: Creación Musical, redes e Internet 2.0). *Revista EIMAS.* Universidade Federal de Juiz de Fora. 2010

[20] J.J. Arango. "Three narratives of space in music" (in Spanish: Tres narrativas del Espacio en Música). *Anais do XX Congresso da Anppom,* Florianópolis, SC, 2010

[21] http://www.netpd.org/

[22] http://www.jamwithchrome.com

[23] http://www.soundjack.eu/

[24] http:/code.google.com/p/jacktrip/

[25] http://www.ejamming.com/

[26] http://netjack.sourceforge.net/

[27] http://sourceforge.net/projects/llcon/

[28] http://www.remu.fr/sound-delta/netsend~/?p=22

[29] http://www.ninjam.com/

[30] http://www.skype.com/

[31] A. Percy. *Understanding latency in IP telephony.* Brooktrout Technology, Needham, MA, 1999.

[32] N. Schuett and C. Chafe. "The Effects of Latency on Ensemble Performance". 2002.

[33] J.M. Valin, K. Vos and T. Terriberry. "Definition of the Opus Audio Codec. RFC 6716" (*Proposed Standard*), 2012.

Sonic interaction design

SONIFICATION AND AUDITORY DISPLAYS IN ELECTRONIC DEVICES

Bruce N. Walker
Sonification Lab
Georgia Institute of Technology
bruce.walker@psych.gatech.edu

ABSTRACT

Sonification is the intentional use of sound to represent data. As visual displays both shrink and grow, as datasets grow in size and complexity, and as mobile data access increases, sophisticated auditory displays become crucial. Computers and devices that support audio are widespread, but there remains relatively little knowledge and experience among user interface designers in how to use auditory displays effectively. This paper present a taxonomy of auditory display methods, and discusses implementation and design issues in multimodal interaction. Some examples of auditory displays developed by the author's research group, the Georgia Tech Sonification Lab, are presented.

1. BACKGROUND

Sonification is the intentional use of sound to represent data, analogous to scientific visualization. As screen sizes for visual displays shrink (e.g., mobile devices) and grow (e.g., wall-sized displays), there arise new communication challenges to the information architect or interface designer. Further, it is increasingly common for data to be consumed by users who are moving, have their hands or eyes busy, or are in environments where visual displays are difficult to access. Using sound to present data in these situations where a user is unable to look at or unable to see a visual display, has been shown to have great success. It should also be noted that sonification and auditory displays actually have other advantages over visual displays. Auditory displays exploit the superior ability of the human auditory system to recognize temporal changes and patterns. As a result, auditory displays may be the most appropriate modality when the information being displayed has complex patterns, changes in time (both of these are often associated with large data sets), includes warnings, or calls for immediate action. For a more detailed overview of sonification theory and design, see Walker and Nees' chapter [1], and also see [2-10].

Auditory displays and sonification is a field that has been around for several decades, with considerable advances in both theory and design practice. Clearly, given the brief nature of this paper and presentation, the main aim is to open up the world of sonification to those who may have been more focused on visual display of information and data, or on the non-data uses of computer-generated sounds (e.g., computer music) to help them with terminology and provide pointers to more extensive research results and design guidelines. It is hoped that a more sophisticated and scientifically grounded understanding of what sonification and auditory displays are, and the range of ways they can be implemented, will help to make all displays more effective—especially given that multimodal is really how all user interfaces and experiences must be designed now—and encourage wider deployment and adoption of auditory interfaces.

2. TAXONOMY OF SONIFICATION

As detailed more thoroughly in [1], the use of sound in user interfaces can be roughly categorized into three types: (1) alarms, alerts, and warnings; (2) status and monitoring messages; and (3) data displays. These sounds can supplement visual interaction, or in many cases, replace it.

Alerts and notifications are sounds that indicate something has occurred, or is about to occur, or that the listener should immediately pay attention to something in the environment or in the display. They are usually quite simple, and quite obvious, but do not convey much information other than that something requires attention. For example, the doorbell is a clear signal that a guest is outside, but does not indicate exactly who has arrived.

Alarms and warnings indicate that one of a few types of events has happened. The sounds convey the general urgency of the situation, and are very good at capturing the auditory attention of a listener. There can certainly be degrees of urgency, so a simple alert is often less acoustically arresting than, say, a radiation leak warning sound. More sophisticated alarm sounds can encode more information into the auditory signal, such as actual location or type of problem. These so-called trendsons blur the line between alarms and status indicators. An example of a trendson use is the warning indication designed to convey irregular rotor speed in a helicopter—the warning sound is, itself, modified on the fly to convey information about the percentage over- or under-speed, so the pilot does not have to immediately consult a visual gauge, nor guess about how bad the problem is.

Status and progress indicators communicate what is happening with a system, and what changes are occurring in various system parameters and variables. They leverage the listener's ability to detect small changes in sounds, and allow a user to know what is happening, without needing to look at a visual display. This enables more eye-free operation. We have seen examples ranging from health care monitoring, to telephone hold times, to sophisticated interfaces for mobile devices.

Data exploration sounds are those that are intended to represent data with sound, so a listener can explore or interpret a dataset. These sounds are generally described as "sonification", and offer a more holistic sense of the data in the system, rather than momentary states, as is usually the case with alerts and process indicators. Stock market data or weather information or web server traffic are just a few examples of what can be represented via sonification. There are also plenty of examples of scientific data being sonified, such as solar flare activity and physics particle models, so that researchers can understand patterns and cycles and irregularities in the dataset.

Entertainment, sports, and leisure applications of sound are also certainly prevalent. For all the reasons listed above, sound can be used effectively and enjoyably in fitness, games, competitive sports, and travel applications. It is also true that auditory displays can open up all these activities to people with visual impairment. In fact, there is a whole subfield of audio-only games, very popular with both visually impaired and sighted players. Art is another area where the intentional use of sound is clearly important, and whole compositions can be developed to produce (musical) sounds based on climate, movement, or other kinds of data.

Within each of the categories above, there are many specific techniques that can be used to produce meaningful auditory displays and sonifications. Some are simple, such as speeding up speech even to the point it is no longer recognized as speech ("spearcons"), whereas other methods require the development of sophisticated models of physical systems (e.g., a molecule), and then "driving" that model with data to produce sound via perturbations of the model. It is important that those who are contemplating the use of sound in, or as, an interface, be aware of the many approaches, along with the times and places where their use is optimal.

3. DESIGN ISSUES

Auditory display and sonification designers must consider many factors, as do visual designers. In general, these include elements of the data or information to be represented, and aspects of the listener's task. In particular, as detailed in [1], designers must know: (1) what the user needs to do (i.e., the task); (2) what information the user needs to accomplish the task; (3) what kind of (auditory) display to use (e.g., simple alert, status indicator, or full sonification); and (4) how the user will need to filter, transform, or otherwise manipulate the information or data. The details of these issues will constrain how the auditory (or any) display is developed, and will make it more clear what elements and functionalities the designer needs to include. Consider, for example, a meteorologist who needs to know what the current temperature, humidity, barometric pressure, and wind speed are, and then predict the weather for later that day. She will need to know specific values of individual variables (e.g., what is the current outside temperature?). She will also need to compare that value to a specific value of another variable (e.g., is the temperature above or below the dewpoint?). Then she will need to understand trends in the data variable (e.g., is the temperature rising or falling?), and consider the rate of change and compare that to the rate of change in the other variables (e.g., wind speed). All these subtasks contribute to the larger task of understanding current conditions, in advance of predicting future conditions. And all may require different displays (whether auditory or visual), and methods for interacting with the data (selecting, choosing, filtering, zooming, playing, pausing, comparing, etc.).

3.1 Multimodal Displays

While unimodal auditory displays can often be effective (as can unimodal visual displays), it is much more common to utilize a combination of sounds, visuals, and even tactile components into a multimodal display. This will require the designer to understand the capabilities, limitations, and needs of each modality individually, as well as to consider how the display components interact with each other, to maximize display bandwidth and avoid confusions. As just one small example, the use of a rising pitch to represent increasing temperature may be perfectly reasonable on its own, but if a visual display uses a horizontally-oriented bar to represent the same concept, there may arise "compatibility" conflicts between the visual and auditory components of the display. Designers need to be aware of these multimodal interactions, and (1) avoid them through good design, and (2) evaluate the design to check for unintended conflicts or mismatches. On the other side of the same coin, designers can often leverage redundancies in multimodal displays, so that users get the same information in multiple modalities, with each reinforcing the other.

3.2 Mappings and Scalings

Once the nature of the data and the task are determined, sonification involves mapping data source(s) onto auditory variables. For example, a designer might choose to represent temperature with pitch: as temperature changes, so, too, does the pitch of the sounds in a sonification. Some auditory dimensions are better for representing certain types of data variables. For example, pitch is generally good for representing temperature, but tempo is not as effective [11]. Tempo can be more effective for speed. Once an effective mapping has been chosen, it is important to determine how much change in the pitch of the sound is used to convey a given change in the temperature. This is known as scaling. That is, if the pitch goes up an octave (a doubling of frequency), does that mean that the temperature has also doubled? In some cases, yes, but this is not a universally recognized relationship. Scaling values can be determined from studies that have been conducted, or by experimentation by the designer. In all cases, it is important to have a representative sample of listeners provide feedback about the mappings and scalings in the display, during the development phase.

3.3 Context and Aesthetics

Other issues arise, such as how the data sonifications are set into an auditory context. That is, what are the auditory equivalents to axes, tick marks, labels, trend lines, etc.? And will there be background noise (or music?) competing with the display? Will the device be used while a pedestrian walks along a busy urban street, or perhaps in a factory assembly line? Finally, designers always need to consider the aesthetics of the display. It is important for a sonification or auditory display to sound nice, as well as effective. Otherwise, the listener will simply turn it off. Of course, this also applies to visual displays!

4. SOME EXAMPLES FROM THE GT SONIFICATION LAB

4.1 SWAN: System for Wearable Audio Navigation

Blind pedestrians need to know where they are, how to get to their destination, and what is around them along the way. The System for Wearable Audio Navigation (SWAN) [12] uses a variety of sensors and algorithms to determine the user's exact location, and then uses an auditory display to convey location, route, and surroundings. Route information is presented via a 3D auditory display, such that the listener simply faces the apparent location of the beacon sound, and walks toward it. The user's orientation/heading is tracked via several sensors, and the sound is played via bone conduction headphones, to leave the ears uncovered. Objects of interest in the environment (e.g., stairs, doors, obstacles, coffee shops) are represented using non-speech sounds that evoke the object (e.g., a descending three-note arpeggio to indicate descending stairs).

4.2 Sonification Sandbox

This is a software package that supports the import and editing of a multi-column data set (via a spreadsheet), visual graphing, and auditory graphing. The Sonification Sandbox program [13-14] is written in cross-platform Java on top of the flexible and powerful Accessible Graphing Engine (AGE), and supports a wide range of import and data ingestion methods, and a wide variety of export formats (images, MIDI, WAV, movies). The MathGNIE [15] software package is another Java application that was built on top of the AGE platform, and is being successfully used by blind students in their mathematics classrooms.

4.3 Spearcons

Auditory menus are often used to allow a user to navigate through a list or menu of items (e.g., songs on an MP3 player, or the menu of a desktop computer's operating system). Typical auditory menus use text-to-speech (TTS) technology to speak aloud the menu items. However, this results in a very slow interaction, even when the speech rate is increased. Spearcons are non-speech sounds that are created by speeding up TTS-generated words (typically via a SOLA-type algorithm). The spearcons can then be used in place of, or in front of, the TTS items, resulting in a much faster and more enjoyable user experience. [16]

4.4 Spindex

When there are very long lists in an auditory menu, such as the list of fonts or hundreds or thousands of songs on a device, TTS, and even TTS+spearcons are not a very fast way to choose an item. The spindex, or "speech-based index" is a set of sounds that represent the first sounds of the TTS items, typically the "a", "b", "c", etc. sounds. [17] Prepending these spindex cues to the TTS allows the users to scroll very quickly through the list, arriving at the section of the list that interests them. For example, they can quickly get to the songs that start with "T", without having to listen to the TTS for all the songs that start with A, B, and so on. These sounds are especially useful in longer lists, and work well on mobile devices that employ swiping, flicking and wheeling input gestures. [18]

4.5 StockScapes

Some displays that use sound can serve as ambient displays, in that they are always present in the environment (e.g., in an office), and can be listened to or "tuned out" by the room's occupant. If the sounds are driven by data (e.g., recent stock market data [19-20]), the person can listen to the sounds, and determine what is happening in the market. The sounds can be ignored again, and simply serve as background music. Any sudden changes in the sounds/music (i.e., in the stock market) will be noticed by the person, simply because the auditory system is tuned to detect changes. Of course, aesthetics are crucial in this kind of ambient display. We have developed software that can ingest data and generate a range of interesting, nice-sounding, and informative soundscapes that are always fresh and can be listened to for long periods, because they have built in variety and randomness, based on sounds occurring in nature.

5. CONCLUSIONS

Electronic systems with visual displays are having sounds added to them all the time. For the most part, there really are only multimodal devices being developed. Unfortunately, the hardware engineers, software developers, and interaction designers of many of these systems have little or no knowledge of modern theory and methods for sonification and auditory displays. It is hoped that this overview, with hooks into the sonification literature, will help introduce visual display designers, sound designers, musicians, and researchers into the auditory realm, and thus improve the inevitable new multimodal displays. The few examples presented here are really only a tiny sample of the breadth and depth of all the great work happening in the auditory display community. Through this talk and paper, it is hoped that we can continue to build bridges between the communities of computer music and auditory display researchers, including sessions at conferences such as SMAC/SMC, and encouraging interested researchers and designers to attend the annual International Conference on Auditory Display (www.ICAD.org).

6. ACKNOWLEDGEMENTS

Portions of this research have been supported by grants from the National Science Foundation (IIS0644076), Department of Education (NIDRR: H133E060061), and other sources. This paper (and talk) is an expansion of a talk (and accompanying paper) presented by the author at the Society for Information Display (SID) conference, in Vancouver, 2013.

7. REFERENCES

[1] Walker, B. N., & Nees, M. A. "Theory of Sonification". In T. Hermann, A. Hunt, & J. Neuhoff (Eds.), *The Sonification Handbook* (pp. 9-39). Berlin, Germany: Logos Publishing House. (2012). http://sonification.de/handbook/download/TheSonificationHandbook-chapter2.pdf

[2] Barrass,S. "A perceptual framework for the auditory display of scientific data." *ACMTransactions on Applied Perception*, 2(4), 389–402 (2005).

[3] Brazil, E. "A review of methods and frameworks for sonic interaction design: Exploring existing approaches." *Lecture Notes in Computer Science*, 5954, 41–67 (2010).

[4] Brown, L. M., Brewster, S. A., Ramloll, R., Burton, M., & Riedel, B. "Design guidelines for audio presentation of graphs and tables." *Proceedings of the International Conference on Auditory Display (ICAD2003)* (pp. 284–287), Boston, MA (2003).

[5] de Campo, A. "Toward a data sonification design space map." *Proceedings of the International Conference on Auditory Display (ICAD2007)* (pp. 342–347), Montreal, Canada (2007).

[6] Frauenberger, C., & Stockman, T. "Auditory display design: An investigation of a design pattern approach." *International Journal of Human-Computer Studies*, 67, 907–922 (2009).

[7] Frauenberger, C., Stockman, T., & Bourguet, M.-L. "Pattern design in the context space: A methodological framework for auditory display design." *Proceedings of the International Conference on Auditory Display (ICAD2007)* (pp. 513–518), Montreal, Canada (2007).

[8] Kramer, G. "An introduction to auditory display." In G. Kramer (Ed.), *Auditory Display: Sonification, Audification, and Auditory Interfaces* (pp. 1–78). Reading, MA: Addison Wesley (1994).

[9] Kramer, G., Walker, B. N., Bonebright, T., Cook, P., Flowers, J., Miner, N., et al. "The Sonification Report: Status of the Field and Research Agenda." Report prepared for the National Science Foundation by members of the International Community for Auditory Display. Santa Fe, NM: International Community for Auditory Display (ICAD) (1999).

[10] Nees, M. A., & Walker, B. N. "Listener, task, and auditory graph: Toward a conceptual model of auditory graph comprehension." *Proceedings of the International Conference on Auditory Display (ICAD2007)* (pp. 266–273), Montreal, Canada (2007).

[11] Walker, B. N. "Magnitude estimation of conceptual data dimensions for use in sonification." *Journal of Experimental Psychology: Applied*, 8, 211–221 (2002).

[12] Wilson, J., Walker, B. N., Lindsay, J., Cambias, C., & Dellaert, F. (2007). SWAN: System for wearable audio navigation. In Proceedings of the 11th International Symposium on Wearable Computers (ISWC 2007) (pp. 91-98). Boston, MA: IEEE. 10.1109/ISWC.2007.4373786

[13] Walker, B. N., & Cothran, J. T. (2003). Sonification Sandbox: A graphical toolkit for auditory graphs. In Brazil, E. & Shinn-Cunningham, B., *Proceedings of the Ninth International Conference on Auditory Display ICAD2003*, Boston, MA (6-9 July) pp 161-163. Boston, MA: Boston University Publications.

[14] Davison, B., & Walker, B. N. (2007). Sonification Sandbox overhaul: Software standard for auditory graphs. In Scavone, G. P., *Proceedings of the International Conference on Auditory Display (ICAD 2007)*, Montreal, Canada: ICAD (26-29 June). pp. 509-512.

[15] Davison, B. K., Suh, H., & Walker, B. N. (2012). Math GNIE: Visually impaired students creating graphs and number lines on a computer. *Proceedings of the AER2012 Conference*. Bellevue, WA (18-22 July).

[16] Walker, B. N., Lindsay, J., Nance, A., & Nakano, Y., Palladino, D., Dingler, T., & Jeon, M. (2013). Spearcons (speech-based earcons) improve navigation performance in advanced auditory menus. *Human Factors*, Vol. 55 Issue 1 February 2013 pp. 157 - 182. Published online 2 July 2012. DOI: 10.1177/0018720812450587

[17] Jeon, M., & Walker, B. N. (2011). Spindex (speech index) improves auditory menu acceptance and navigation performance. *ACM Transactions on Accessible Computing (TACCESS)*. 3(3),10:1-26. DOI: http://doi.acm.org/10.1145/1952383.1952385

[18] Jeon, M., Walker, B. N., & Srivastava, A. (2012). "Spindex" (Speech Index) Enhances Menus on Touch Screen Devices with Tapping, Wheeling, and Flicking. *ACM Transactions on Computer-Human Interaction (TOCHI)*. Vol. 19, No. 2, Article 14, Publication date: July 2012. DOI: 10.1145/2240156.2240162

[19] Mauney, B. S., & Walker, B. N. (2004). Creating functional and livable soundscapes for peripheral monitoring of dynamic data. *Proceedings of the Tenth International Conference on Auditory Display ICAD2004*, Sydney (6-10 July).

[20] Mauney, B. S., & Walker, B. N. (2004). Designing systems for the creation and evaluation of dynamic peripheral soundscapes: A usability study. *Proceedings of the Annual Meeting of the Human Factors and Ergonomics Society (HFES2004)*. New Orleans, LA (20-24 September) pp 764-768.

CONTROLLING A SOUND SYNTHESIZER USING TIMBRAL ATTRIBUTES

Antonio Pošćić
Faculty of Electrical Engineering and Computing,
University of Zagreb, Croatia
antonio.poscic@fer.hr

Gordan Kreković
Faculty of Electrical Engineering and Computing,
University of Zagreb, Croatia
gordan.krekovic@fer.hr

ABSTRACT

In this paper we present the first step towards a novel approach to visual programming for sound and music applications. To make the creative process more intuitive, our concept enables musicians to use timbral attributes for controlling sound synthesis and processing. This way, musicians do not need to think in terms of signal processing, but can rely on natural descriptions instead. A special point of interest was mapping timbral attributes into synthesis parameters. We proposed a solution based on fuzzy logic which can be applied to different synthesizers. For a particular synthesizer, an audio expert can conveniently define mappings in form of IF-THEN rules. A prototype of the system was implemented in Pure Data and demonstrated with a subtractive synthesizer. A survey conducted among amateur musicians has shown that the system works according to their expectations, but descriptions based on timbral attributes are imprecise and dependent on subjective interpretation.

1. INTRODUCTION

The visual programming paradigm became very popular among computer musicians and multimedia artists in the last decade. One of the main reasons for the increasing acceptance of this approach is a faster learning curve compared to traditional textual programming [1]. Graphical representations of computer programs are closer to the way how humans mentally represent problems, so it is easier to understand and develop programs using the visual approach [2]. Many visual programming editors support direct manipulation of graphical objects which further helps users to perceive how their actions affect the program [3]. The visual programming paradigm also brings other psychological benefits which are particularly important for musicians and artists as they usually do not have strong backgrounds in programming [4].

Besides these benefits, there is one more factor specifically related to computer music, multimedia, and interactive art. In this domain, digital processing of audio signals, images, and videos is a fundamental part of every application. Many modern visual programming environments offer ready-to-use program elements which implement digital signal processing algorithms and facilitate integration with peripheral devices. In the context of music and sound processing, such elements are oscillators, filters, audio effects, score following algorithms, auto-tuners, etc. Using prepared elements, musicians and artists do not need to cope with low-level signal processing. Thanks to the general psychological benefits of the visual programming paradigm and visual programming environments designed to meet practical needs, visual programming is now widely recognized among computer musicians and multimedia artists.

In visual programming environments for sound and music processing, audio signals usually participate in the data flow. Pure Data, Max/MSP, Kyma, AudioMulch, and Reaktor are some of the most popular environments which rely on this paradigm. While visual programming based on signal flow ensures maximal flexibility, it forces the user to think about music and sound art in terms of signal processing. Musicians have to understand how certain program elements affect the audio signal and which parameter values should be chosen to achieve the desired sound quality.

With regards to these benefits of visual programming and to make the creative process more straightforward for musicians, within this research we present our vision and the foundations of a novel approach to visual programming for sound and music applications. One of the cornerstones of this concept relies on the notion that control over sound synthesizers, audio effects, and other elements for generating or modifying audio signals is established through timbral attributes. Instead of manipulating audio signals and parameters of program elements, musicians can focus on their musical ideas and realize them by describing timbral characteristics of a desired sound. For example, a musician can specify that the sound needs to be "metallic", "bright", and "harsh". Besides the target timbre, it is also possible to define timbral changes through time. The focus of this paper is, thus, on the usage and transformation of timbral characteristics. The approach presented in this research will be later used as one of the main building blocks of the aforementioned innovative visual programming language and environment.

There are two main factors which make the described concept challenging. The first one is a lack of theoretical and notational support related to timbre [5]. While other characteristics such as pitch and rhythm have more formal notations, timbral attributes are not standardized.

They are meaningful to musicians, but not convenient as an input to computer systems.

The second big challenge is mapping timbral attributes into parameters of sound synthesizers or audio effects. Such relations are usually complex and ambiguous. Additionally, mappings should work for different synthesis techniques and different types of audio effects so they have to be adequately generic. Existing works include several attempts at synthesizing sound specified by timbral attributes. Miranda used a machine learning algorithm to induce relations between quasi-timbral attributes and synthesis parameters [6]. However, the available attributes were always associated with the structure of a sound synthesizer so Miranda's approach would not work for any synthesizer other than the one designed as a part of his system. A research conducted by Gounaropoulos and Johnson employed a neural network to learn mappings between timbral attributes and audio features of a sound characterized by such attributes. This research used the backward-propagation algorithm to control the synthesizer [7]. As the algorithm was specifically designed to work in the case when synthesis parameters are directly related to audio features, it can be only applied to additive synthesis. The problem of controlling synthesis parameters with timbral attributes was not sufficiently explored nor solved in such a way that the solution could be adapted to different synthesis techniques.

Since this is also one of the central problems in our concept of a visual programming language and environment based on attribute flow, as mentioned before, in this paper we primarily focused on that issue. We devised, implemented, and evaluated a novel approach for mapping timbral attributes into synthesis parameters using fuzzy logic. Such a solution can be applied to an arbitrary sound synthesizer. The concrete implementation and demonstration was done using the programming language C and the visual programming environment Pure Data. We developed an external (Pure Data plugin) which enabled using a fuzzy logic library within Pure Data and demonstrated the solution on a subtractive synthesizer.

2. ATTRIBUTE-BASED VISUAL PROGRAMMING FOR MUSICAL COMPOSITION

The encompassing approach and concept presented in this paper are based on the notion that combining intuitive inputs (such as timbral characteristics) with visual programming elements and time-dependent control flow will enable musicians and other users to innovate their approaches towards music, sound creation, and sound modeling. Similar concepts based on a fusion of different paradigms can be observed throughout various works and designs in the field. One notable example is the sound design language Kyma [8] which enables the manipulation of sound objects in the domain of time.

Our concept defines that timbral attributes should be used in a way that can be usually found in the field of dataflow languages while also allowing time-based control of sound flows. This duality of our approach, not found in similar works, results in a visual programming language and environment relying on two paradigms [9]: icon based [10] and diagram based [11] visual programming. The icon based programming portion is linked with defining and selecting the timbral attributes through various possible user interfaces. On the other hand, the diagram based side of the concept is related to the links and interdependence between various manipulation objects such as synthesizers, VST plugins, etc. The time-bound connection between portions of the target sequence of sounds is established in a manner that resembles audio editing software such as Audacity [12].

Considering the aforementioned concepts, it's important to stress that attribute-based flow has not been selected by accident but it's rather a design choice made to enhance symbiosis with the targeted visual programming paradigm. The paradigm thus contains user interface elements derived from tools such as the aforementioned Audacity as well as elements belonging to visual programming languages such as Pure Data. By combining these traits, we enable the users to efficiently explore the possible synthesized sounds both in the time domain and in the different domains of sound characteristics. Using concepts that are usually present in diagram and dataflow languages, such as the possibility to connect blocks that manipulate the attribute flow, the user will be able to architect sound sequences and define links between sounds. On the other hand, the user will have means to change and adapt the individual generated sounds by directly influencing the behavior of sound synthesizing blocks. The approach based on fuzzy logic that is demonstrated in this article should be seen as one of the possible methods encapsulated in these blocks. Our preliminary research has shown that attribute flow is best suited to achieve these objectives and desired characteristics. These ideas and implementations will be further explored in future works.

One of the crucial characteristics of the system is also the ability to include a variety of different approaches with regards to mapping timbral attributes into synthesis parameters. The possible methods, beside the fuzzy logic method described in this research, include neural networks, classifier cascades, regression tree analysis, etc.

3. PROOF OF CONCEPT

The first and very important step towards the concept of visual programming based on attribute flow was to establish mappings between timbral attributes and synthesis parameters. To solve this problem, we suggest an approach which uses an expert system based on fuzzy logic. Within this research we implemented that solution and tested it with a subtractive sound synthesizer.

3.1 Mapping timbral attributes into synthesis parameters

Previous attempts to synthesize sounds from their timbral descriptions relied on machine learning algorithms [6, 7]. The idea was to induce relations between timbral attributes and synthesis parameters by learning from examples of synthesized sounds. Such a problem is hard to solve for a general case, since there can be more than one solution in the space of synthesis parameters for a certain sound quality. Relations between timbral attributes and synthesis parameters are therefore ambiguous. To formulate the problem so that it can be solved with known machine learning techniques, both previous researches were limited to one specific sound synthesizer. As described in the first chapter, authors used a priori knowledge about employed synthesizers and adapted algorithms to work with them.

To find a solution which could be applied to sound synthesizers with different structures, we decided to use an expert system based on fuzzy logic instead of a machine learning technique. Fuzzy logic is a form of probabilistic logic derived from the mathematical branch of fuzzy sets [13]. Compared to the traditional two-value logic where variables can be either true or false, fuzzy logic supports the concept of partial truth so variables can have a truth value that ranges between 0 and 1. This concept makes fuzzy logic convenient for quantifying imprecise information and making decisions based on incomplete data [14]. Furthermore, facts and rules can be described using linguistic terms which make the concept closer to human reasoning.

Linguistic variables are subjective and context-dependent variables whose values are words. For example, if the timbral attribute "warmth" is observed in the role of a linguistic variable, its values could be "very high", "high", "moderate", "low", and "very low" as shown in Figure 1. Inputs in a fuzzy logic system are usually numeric so it is necessary to convert these numeric values into linguistic terms. The linguistic terms can be considered fuzzy sets since an input value can have partial membership in more sets at the same time. For example, if the attribute "warmth" has the numeric value 0.85, it is situated between "very high" and "high" according to Figure 1. Therefore, the value belongs to both sets but not by the same degree. Fuzzy sets can use different types of membership functions such as triangular, trapezoidal, bell-shaped, and sigmoid functions.

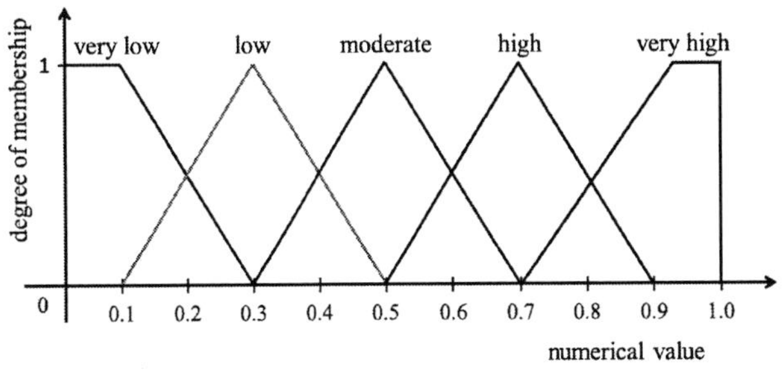

Figure 1. Fuzzy membership functions for the attribute "warmth".

A model for making decisions based on fuzzy logic uses a rule set defined by linguistic variables. Typically, fuzzy rules are specified in the form of IF-THEN statements:

```
IF (x1 IS S1) AND/OR ..., (xn IS Sn) THEN y IS T,
```

where x_i represents input fuzzy variables, y is the output variable, while S_n and T stand for input and output fuzzy sets. The first step of applying the model is to convert input variables into fuzzy logic variables using membership functions. Subsequently, output variables are calculated by evaluating the rules. In most applications, outputs have to be numerical values so fuzzy output variables must be defuzzified. Algorithms used for evaluating the rules and for the defuzzification process are explained in [14, 15].

Fuzzy rule sets are appropriate for representing expert knowledge of a certain domain. As the rules have a simple form, they can be conveniently written, discussed, and tuned by human experts. Systems based on fuzzy logic have been used in many different fields such as engineering, economics, finance, geology, meteorology, and sociology. Various problems from the musical domain were also approached using fuzzy logic. It has been employed for evaluating computer music [16], recognizing rhythmic structures [17], coding of musical gestures for interactive live performances [18], analyzing the emotional expression in music performance and body motion [19], mapping visual information into aural information and vice-versa [20], sound synthesis [21], and several other applications.

For setting synthesis parameters, Hamandicharef and Ifeachor employed an expert system based on fuzzy logic [22]. The purpose of their system was to find such synthesis parameters so that the synthesized sound mimics the target sound. The inputs of the expert system were audio features extracted from the target sound, while the outputs were parameters for the sound synthesizer. Audio experts were involved in building the fuzzy model and specifying relations between audio features and synthesis parameters.

We believe that having experts define rules is also beneficial in our case. Namely, for each synthesizer intended to be controlled using timbral attributes, a fuzzy model has to be defined once. Since the model is stored outside the program code, there is no need for programming, so the model can be easily defined and tuned by sound synthesis experts. In practice, such experts could be synthesizer manufacturers or users who thoroughly understand the architecture of a specific synthesizer. Once the model is ready, other users can control the synthesizer by adjusting timbral attributes without writing or changing the fuzzy model.

This way, the expert system based on fuzzy logic can be used for sound synthesizers with various structures. The only requirement to adapt the system to work with a different synthesizer is to write a new fuzzy model. On the other hand, the previous solutions based on machine learning algorithms were not capable of such adaptation. Those solutions relied on a priori knowledge about the synthesizer structures, so training machine learning algorithms to work with different synthesizers was impossible.

We expect an expert system based on fuzzy logic to work well with synthesis techniques for which the relations between timbral attributes and synthesis parameters are continuous or semi-continuous. Most of the popular synthesis techniques, such as subtractive and additive synthesis, satisfy the criterion. On the other hand, frequency modulation is not one of the supported synthesis techniques since the ratio of modulator and carrier frequencies is in a very complex relation with the perception of harmonicity. For that reason, we will limit this research to subtractive synthesis and extend it to other synthesis techniques in the future.

The selection of attributes used to describe the desired sound in our system was taken from [7]. Those attributes are: bright, warm, harsh, thick, metallic, woody, hit, plucked, and constant amplitude. The set of timbral attributes is not supposed to be orthogonal and it should instead only serve as an intuitive vocabulary for defining target sounds. In the sound description, an absolute value between 0 and 1 is assigned to each attribute. A value of 0 means that the particular quality is not presented in the sound, while the value 1 indicates that the quality is very prominent.

3.2 Implementation

Within this research we have developed a system for mapping timbral attributes to synthesis parameters which can be used in the Pure Data visual programming environment. To create an interface between Pure Data and a fuzzy logic library, we have implemented an external Pure Data component. It accepts a list of timbral attributes as input and calculates defuzzified outputs for the variables declared in the Fuzzy Control Language file. The Fuzzy Control Language (FCL) is a standardized (International Electrotechnical Commission standard, IEC 61131-7) language used to define and implement fuzzy logic models.

A similar implementation of a Pure Data external exists which is based on the *libfuzzy* library and the Fuzzy Inference System (FIS) notation [23]. However, the FIS notation is inferior both in usability and flexibility when compared to FCL. One example of the characteristics which make FIS less ergonomic is the requirement for each rule to be written using variable indices. This kind of deficiency could prove to be an insurmountable obstacle for typical users such as musicians when creating a large rule set.

The fuzzy logic implementation described in this paper relies on the *jFuzzyLogic* library [24]. Since Pure Data externals are natively written in C, a number of different C/C++ fuzzy logic libraries had been evaluated before we chose the *jFuzzyLogic* library. For example, the aforementioned *libfuzzy* library presents a valid fuzzy logic implementation in cases when the FIS input format is acceptable. None of the available open source C/C++ libraries were adequate due to obsolescence and improper or incomplete support for the Fuzzy Controller Language.

Since *jFuzzyLogic* was written in Java, wrapper functions that rely on Java Native Interface calls [25] have been implemented. These functions serve as glue code between the main functions of the external written in C and the *jFuzzyLogic* library. Proper error handling is also provided through these wrapper functions. To improve performance, a caching system based on the *sglib* library [26] has been implemented to reduce the number of output recalculations.

For demonstration and evaluation of the system we used a simple subtractive synthesizer with one oscillator and sub-oscillator, a noise generator, two filters (low-pass and band-pass), an amplitude envelope generator, two low-frequency oscillators, and a chorus effect. The block diagram of the synthesizer is shown in Figure 2.

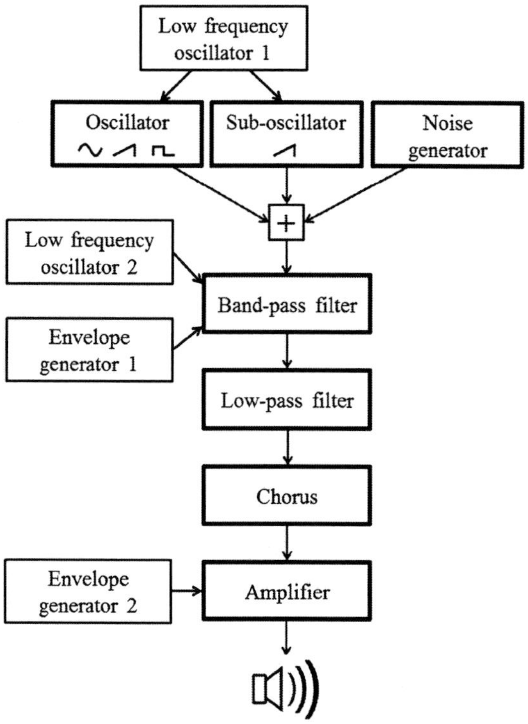

Figure 2. Block diagram of the subtractive synthesizer used in the experiments.

This is obviously a simple synthesizer which is not completely capable of producing sound qualities for all chosen timbral attributes as one might expect. However, it should not be considered a limitation, because the main goal of our system is to mimic a human expert and do the best with a given sound synthesizer regardless of its structure and capabilities. For the purposes of the evaluation, we implemented the synthesizer as a Pure Data patch and connected it to our external object as shown in Figure 3.

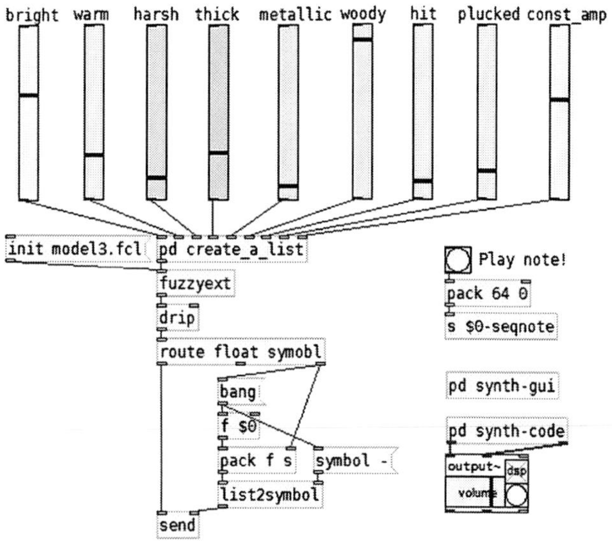

Figure 3. Example of using the external object within a Pure Data patch. The external object for fuzzy logic is called *fuzzext*.

The fuzzy logic model for mapping timbral attributes into synthesis parameters was defined in the FCL language. Inputs of the model are 9 timbral attributes ranging from 0 to 1 and there are 24 outputs with different ranges representing synthesis parameters. For the fuzzification and defuzzification processes, we defined triangular and trapezoidal functions specifically for each input and output variable. As the defuzzification technique, the model uses center of gravity. The rule set for calculating synthesis parameters consists of 85 rules in IF-THEN form. Some examples of the rules are as follows:

```
IF harsh IS little THEN filterlfo_r IS small;

IF plucked IS very_prominent OR hit IS prominent OR
hit IS very_prominent THEN volume_s IS very_small;

IF warm IS prominent OR warm IS very_prominent THEN
filterfreq_r IS moderate;

IF warm IS prominent OR warm IS very_prominent THEN
osc1type_r IS square;

IF woody IS very_prominent OR woody IS prominent OR
woody IS moderate THEN osc1type IS square;
```

4. EVALUATION

The purpose of the evaluation was twofold: to test the functionality of our system and to assess to what extent the chosen timbral attributes are appropriate for describing sounds. The evaluation was conducted among 6 amateur musicians who were asked to manually set synthesis parameters for 5 given sound descriptions. These descriptions were formed in the same way as the inputs in our system. For example:

bright 0.8, warm 0.6, harsh 0.1, thick 0.2, metallic 0.1, woody 0.7, hit 0.1, plucked 0.1, constant amplitude 0.6

The participants did not receive any further explanations regarding the attributes so they had to interpret the given descriptions entirely by themselves. To compare the results of manual parameter manipulation with the results obtained algorithmically, we used the same descriptions as inputs in our system and generated the sounds.

After the participants finished their tasks of manual sound design, they received the sounds generated by our system and a survey. In the first set of questions they were asked to evaluate how the sounds synthesized by our system fit the sound descriptions. The second set of questions regarded the similarity between their sounds and the sounds generated using our system. All these questions were of rating scale type with 5 available options. For the first set of questions the scale included a range from very poor (1) to very well (5), while the second set included options ranging from very different (1) to very similar (5). Finally, the third set consisted of the following general questions:

1. How clear were the given descriptions based on attributes? (1 - very unclear, 5 - very clear)
2. How difficult was setting the parameters manually? (1 - very easy, 5 - very difficult)
3. How helpful the system for automatic synthesis from timbral attributes can be helpful for musicians? (1 - very little, 5 - very much)

5. RESULTS

The average grade for the questions concerning how the generated sounds met the given descriptions was 3.9 and the median grade was 4. These statistical values were calculated taking into consideration all 6 participants and all 5 sounds. The best rated sound with the prominent "plucked" attribute had an average grade of 4.2, while all other sounds had averages 4.0 or below. The questions regarding perceptual similarity to their sounds were graded by the participants with an average of 2.7. The median was 4. Distribution of all grades is shown in Figure 4.

The average grades on last three questions were 3.7, 3.2, and 3.9 respectively for clarity of such descriptions, difficulty of manual parameter setting, and potential usefulness of our approach.

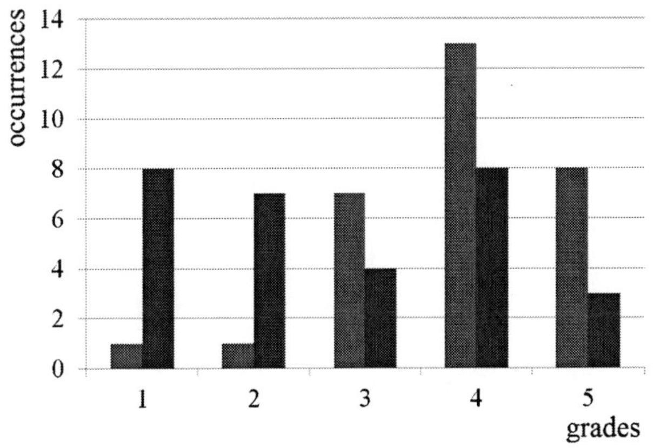

Figure 4. For each grade from 1 to 5 this chart shows how many times that grade appeared in the answers from all participant and for all sounds. The blue bars represent grades for achieving given sound descriptions, whilst the red ones represent grades for perceptual similarity to participants' sounds.

6. DISCUSSION

The results have shown that descriptions based on timbral attributes are somewhat imprecise for synthesizing exact sounds. The sounds that were created manually are perceptually different from automatically generated examples, but the participants were still quite satisfied with the results. To overcome this problem, our system could be improved to generate more than one option for any given description, thus allowing musicians to choose the most accurate instance of a sound.

The answers on the last three questions suggest that the problem of synthesizing sounds from timbral attributes is relevant to musicians and that our approach could be viable.

7. CONCLUSION

Parameters of a sound synthesizer can be successfully controlled from timbral attributes using an expert system based on fuzzy logic. For different types of synthesizers, fuzzy models can be defined by audio experts and later used without adaptation. Using an example based on a subtractive synthesizer, we have shown that the system satisfies expectations of target users. The main problem of this approach is the lack of unified and strict relations between the chosen timbral attributes and the general perception of the sound. For that reason, future research could examine other sets of timbral attributes and improve the system so that it can generate several options for a given description.

The results of this research are generally encouraging with regards to our intention to develop a visual programming environment for music and sound processing based on attribute flow.

8. REFERENCES

[1] K.N. Whitley, "Visual programming languages and the empirical evidence for and against," *Journal of Visual Languages and Computing*, vol. 8, no. 1, pp. 109–142, 1997.

[2] O. Clarisse and S.-K. Chang, "VICON: A Visual Icon Manager" in *Visual Languages*. Plenum Press, 1986.

[3] B. Shneiderman, "Direct Manipulation: A Step Beyond Programming Languages," *IEEE Computer*, vol. 16, no. 8, pp. 57–69, 1983.

[4] D.C. Smith, *Pygmalion: A Computer Program to Model and Stimulate Creative Thought*. Birkhaüser-Verlag, 1977.

[5] T. Wishart, *On Sonic Art*. Taylor & Francis Group, 1996.

[6] E. Miranda, "An Artificial Intelligence Approach to Sound Design," *Computer Music Journal*, vol. 19, no. 2, pp 59–75, 1995.

[7] A. Gounaropoulos and C. Johnson, "Synthesising Timbres and Timbre Changes from Adjectives/ Adverbs" in *Applications of Evolutionary Computing*. Springer-Verlag, 2006.

[8] C. Scaletti, "Composing sound objects in Kyma," *Perspectives of New Music*, pp. 42–69, 1989.

[9] E.J. Golin and S.P. Reiss, "The Specification of Visual Language Syntax," *Journal of Visual Languages and Computing*, vol. 1, no. 2, pp. 141–157, 1990.

[10] C. Frasson and M. Erradi, "Principles of an icons-based language," in *Proc. of the 1986 ACM SIGMOD int. conf. on Management of data*, New York, 1986, pp. 144–152.

[11] G. Engels and R. Heckel, "From trees to graphs: defining the semantics of diagram languages with graph transformation" in *ICALP Satellite Workshops*, Geneva, 2000, pp. 373–382.

[12] The Audacity Team. (2012). Audacity: Free Audio Editor and Recorder [Online]. Available: http://audacity.sourceforge.net/

[13] L.A. Zadeh, "Fuzzy sets," *Information and Control 8*, pp. 338–353, 1965.

[14] B. Kosko, *Fuzzy Thinking. The new science of fuzzy logic*. Hyperion, 1993.

[15] G.J. Klir and B. Yuan, *Fuzzy Sets and Fuzzy Logic: Theory and Applications*. Prentice Hall PTR, 1995.

[16] M. Miličević, "Aesthetics of Designing an Adaptive Fuzzy System for the Evaluation of the Computer Music" in *Proc. of the Int. Computer Music Conf.*, Beijing, 1999, pp. 538–541.

[17] T. Weyde, "Grouping, Similarity and the Recognition of Rhythmic Structure" in *Proc. of the Int. Computer Music Conf.*, Havana, 2001.

[18] N. Orio and C. De Piro, "Controlled Refractions: A Two Levels Coding of Musical Gestures for Interactive Live Performances" in *Proc. of Int. Computer Music Conf.*, Ann Arbor, 1998.

[19] A. Friberg, "A Fuzzy Analyzer of Emotional Expression in Music Performance and Body Motion" in *Proc. of the Music and Music Science*, Stockholm, 2004.

[20] R. Cádiz, "A Fuzzy-Logic Mapper for Audiovisual Media," *Computer Music Journal*, vol. 30, no. 1, pp. 67–82, 2006.

[21] E. Miranda and A.J. Maia, "Granular Synthesis of Sounds Through Markov Chains" in *Proc. of the Int. Computer Music Conf.*, Barcelona, 2005.

[22] B. Hamandicharef and E. Ifeachor, "Intelligent and Perceptual-Based Approach to Musical Instruments Sound Design", *Expert Systems and Applications*, vol. 39, no. 7, pp. 6476–6484, 2012.

[23] R. Cádiz and G. Kendall, "Fuzzy Logic Control Tool Kit: Real-Time Fuzzy Control for Max/MSP and Pd" in *Proc. of the Int. Computer Music Conf.*, New Orleans, 2006.

[24] P. Cingolani and J. Alcalá Fernández, "jFuzzyLogic: A Robust and Flexible Fuzzy-Logic Inference System Language Implementation" in *Proc. of the 2012 IEEE Int. Conf. on Fuzzy Systems*, Brisbane, 2012, pp 1–8.

[25] Oracle. (2011). Java Native Interface [Online]. Available: http://docs.oracle.com/javase/6/docs/technotes/guides/jni/

[26] M. Vittek, P. Borovansky, and P.-E. Moreau, "A Simple Generic Library for C, in Reuse of Off-the-Shelf Components" in *Proc. of the 9th Int. Conf. on Software Reuse*, Turin, 2006, pp. 423–426.

A Quantitative Review of Mappings in Musical iOS Applications

Thor Kell
IDMIL / CIRMMT, McGill University
thor.kell@mail.mcgill.ca

Marcelo M. Wanderley
IDMIL / CIRMMT, McGill University
marcelo.wanderley@mcgill.ca

ABSTRACT

We present a quantitative review of the mappings and metaphors used across the most popular musical iOS applications. We examined 337 applications in terms of both the metaphor they present to the user (piano, guitar, etc), and the exact nature of their mappings (pitch mapped horizontally, time mapped vertically, etc). A special focus is given to applications that do not present a well-known interaction metaphor to the user. Potential reasons for the popularity of certain metaphors are given. We further suggest that this data could be used to help explore the iOS design space, and offer some examples.

1. INTRODUCTION

iOS is the dominant platform for touch-based musical applications [1] [2], and more and more musicians are using iOS devices and applications to perform, produce, and practice their music. In any sort of instrument or interface for making music, mappings are important [3], as are the metaphors for those mappings.

On iOS devices, the hardware inputs being mapped are very limited: a capacitive multi-touch surface, an accelerometer, and a microphone. Yet the software to capture these inputs is limitless - does the application capture each touch, complex gestures, or somewhere in between?. The sonic output generated by the application software is also essentially limitless: anything from simple sample playback to complex synthesis techniques can be used to create sound.

Hunt et al. have written about the value of mappings in mediating between these two layers [4], and Jacob et al. have also written about the value of mapping parameters that are related in an integral way [5]. On iOS, the integrality of parameters largely rests on the metaphor presented by the application.

Fels et al. have written about the value of metaphor in human-machine interactions, and how it can improve a performer's understanding of the mapping and the instrument [6]. On iOS devices, as will be seen, the metaphors tend to be exceedingly obvious: pianos and guitars abound. Some applications, however, have non-obvious mappings (tone control based on where a piano key is touched, for example) that a metaphorical piano does not have. Furthermore, the wide range of abstract applications make the question of metaphor (or lack thereof!) a key one. Wessel and Wright have also written about more abstract control metaphors, in terms of the relationship of gesture and metaphor to the acoustic results [7]. Finally, McGlynn et al. have written about the expressive possibilities of interfaces that are not modelled on existing metaphors [8]. Their paper does not explicitly mention mapping, but mapping choices are inherent in each interface they discuss.

We hope to provide real-world insight into how metaphors and mappings are used for music making on iOS devices. We examined the most popular iPhone and iPad music applications (as of February 2013), categorized them in terms of the metaphor used by the application, e.g. a piano keyboard or synthesizer console, and reviewed the exact mappings used, e.g. pitch mapped horizontally via discrete buttons, with low pitches on the left. Based on this overview, we offer suggestions as to how to best use this data to create effective iOS music applications (apps), in terms of both standard and non-standard mappings.

2. METHOD

From the approximately 800,000 apps on the iOS app store [9], 1,200 music apps were chosen for review. These were selected by examining the 'Top Paid', 'Top Free', and 'Top Grossing' subsections of the iOS music app page, Each of those subsections lists 200 apps and differs across iPhone and iPad, giving 1,200 applications. Of these music apps, 337 deal with music creation in some way. These 337 apps were looked at in detail. "Music creation" is given a broad scope here: any application that allows creative interaction with music, in real time or not, is counted. This includes karaoke applications, but does not include radio applications, simple sound recorders, fingerprinting apps, or artist themed apps.

A cursory overview of the apps indicated that they could be organized into categories based on overarching metaphor - the most obvious being piano apps. Each app was assigned a metaphor, and then the total number of apps for each metaphor were added up. The goal of this classification was to delimit categories that would have broadly similar mappings. As the numbers for each app were added, it became clear that there were ten main categories, and then a large number of varied, heterogenous apps. Indeed, outside of the ten categories (all of which had at least thirteen apps), the largest metaphor was that of a violin, with two apps.

The final list of categories was as follows: Piano, DJ, Digital Audio Workstation (DAW), Music Production Controller (MPC), Guitar, Drum Kit, Synthesizer, Sequencer,

Karaoke, Amp Sim, and Other. For each category, the metaphor and the general mappings for the metaphor were examined. A number of apps from each category were looked at in detail in order to discover novel or additional mappings. All apps in the Other category were looked at in detail. Regardless of category, each app was analyzed in terms of the direction and layout of its mappings, giving an overview of how musical parameters are mapped regardless of metaphor.

Note that only a subsection of the applications with standard metaphors were downloaded and tested; their mappings are assumed to be consistent across the category. A larger subset of these applications were examined via their websites. However, *every* app in the Other category was looked at in detail. When an application could not be downloaded and tested by hand (due to hardware or price restrictions), it was examined via screenshots and video. Specifically, those applications are: *Korg iKaosillator, Rockmate, Ocarina 2*, and *Live FX*.

3. METAPHORS

Table 1 contains an overview of the number of applications in each category. Note that we have split the Other category into apps that represent known acoustic instruments (a trumpet, for example), and apps that have no acoustic referent. It must also be noted that apps that appeared on both the iPhone and iPad are counted twice.

Table 1. Metaphors

Metaphor	iPhone	iPad	Total
Piano	25	43	68
DJ	17	15	32
DAW	14	16	30
MPC	14	14	28
Guitar	12	13	25
Drum Kit	7	14	21
Synthesizer	4	16	20
Sequencer	6	13	19
Karaoke	9	9	18
Amp Sim	5	8	13
Other	21	34	55
Other (Acoustic Instruments)	4	4	8
Total	138	199	337

As can be seen, piano apps are the standout category, followed somewhat surprisingly by DJ apps. The other two acoustic instruments, Guitar and Drum Kit, are below DAWs and MPC apps. This primacy of the electronic is perhaps not surprising given that iOS is an electronic platform, but it is belied by the massive popularity of piano applications. The piano may simply be such a well-known metaphor that it transcends the limitations of the iOS platform (lack of easy volume and timbre control, etc).

Continuing down the list, we find Synthesizers, Sequencers, Karaoke apps, and then Amp Sims - applications that mimic guitar amplifiers and effects pedals. In the Other category, a small subsection of apps mimics other acoustic instruments, against suggesting that non-acoustic metaphors are more dominant. The rest of the Other apps present no consistent metaphor.

The following sub-sections detail each category in terms of its metaphor and mappings, and discuss some of the variations within each category.

3.1 Piano

Piano apps display a traditional keyboard that plays discrete pitches. Pitches are mapped from left to right, low to high, in steps of one semitone. The vast majority of apps display a keyboard, though some simply display abstract circles (*Smule Magic Piano*) Playback of multiple pitches is possible. Volume control is generally not possible, nor is timbre control, though some apps offer a 'pedal' button, for sustained notes (*Piano Infinity*), or give control over the amount of reverberation added (*Piano Complete*). Some apps provide a toggle to switch between instruments - piano, grand piano, harpsichord, cat, dog, and so on (*Real Piano HD, Piano Infinity, Cat Piano Concerto*). Exact tuning control (A440 vs. A442, for example) is also sometimes available (*Real Piano HD*), and some apps give access to a synthesizer-esq pitch bend wheel and a mod wheel for real-time volume control (*Pianist Pro*). Solutions for volume control include a 'force based' volume control (*Real Piano HD*), and a volume control based on where the user strikes each key - higher up the key is softer, near the bottom of the key is louder (*Pianist Pro*). Some programs include teaching modes where notes fall from the top of the screen to the bottom, and must be played as they hit the bottom (*Smule Magic Piano, Piano Infinity*).

Figure 1. *Cat Piano Concerto*, a typical piano app

3.2 DJ

These apps provide two virtual turntables, with a virtual mixer. The volume of each turntable is controlled by a vertical fader, with louder being higher. The mix between turntables is controlled by a horizontal fader. Play, stop, and pause commands are controlled by buttons. The speed of each turntable is controlled by a pitch fader; faster is towards the user for some apps (*djay*), matching a traditional turntable, and away from the user for other apps (*DJ Rig Free*). This fader is generally in percent. 'Pitch bends', small corrections to the speed of each turntable, are controlled by buttons. The user can touch the 'turntable' to scratch or backspin, but not to change the speed (*DJ Rig Free*).

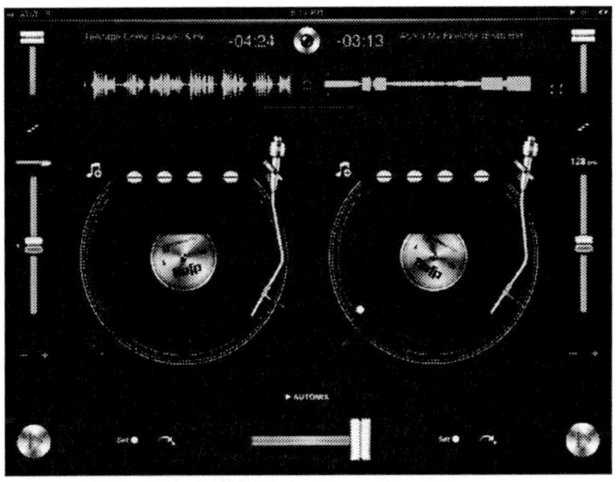

Figure 2. *djay*, a typical DJ app.

3.3 Digital Audio Workstation

DAW apps provide a complete solution for producing music and working with audio. They often include synthesizers, sequencers, and MPCs, as well as effect sections and mixers. Some go so far as to include auxiliary sends (*Auria*). The key distinction between a DAW app and a full-featured sequencer is that DAWs work with recorded audio: audio is recorded with a traditional red 'Record' button, and represented in clips wherein time moves from left to right, and amplitude is represented vertically (*FL Studio Mobile HD, Music Studio Lite*).

Figure 3. *Auria*, a typical DAW app.

3.4 MPC

These apps are based on the Akai **M**usic **P**roduction **C**enter line, a classic of hip-hop production. They have some number of trigger buttons in a grid - traditionally 16 buttons in a 4 x 4 grid. These buttons play a user-configurable sample when triggered. The user typically records one line, then loops it and records another line. Tempo can be tapped in (*iMPC*) or set with a slider (*BeatPad Lite*). The app may have a dedicated mixer (*iMPC*), or set volume via a slider on each pad (*Rhythm Pad*). There may be a separate FX section (*DJ Soundbox Pro*), or deep synthesis control of each drum sound (*Impaktor*). Finally, instead of the traditional 4x4 grid, some MPC apps have fewer buttons (*Rhythm Pad* has 8).

Figure 4. *iMPC*, a typical MPC app.

3.5 Guitar

A guitar, with 'strummable' strings and a fretboard. Frets are selected by holding down the appropriate area, and lower notes are placed to the left, as when holding a guitar. The lowest string is likewise placed closest to the user, and the strings are mapped vertically, again as when holding a guitar. Some apps provide direct access to complex chords via buttons (*Guitar!, Real Guitar Free*). Some apps provide vibrato by shaking the device (*Smule Magic Guitar*), and others allow effects via virtual pedals, with the timbre controlled by rotary knobs (*PocketGuitar*). Most apps do not provide timbral control or volume control.

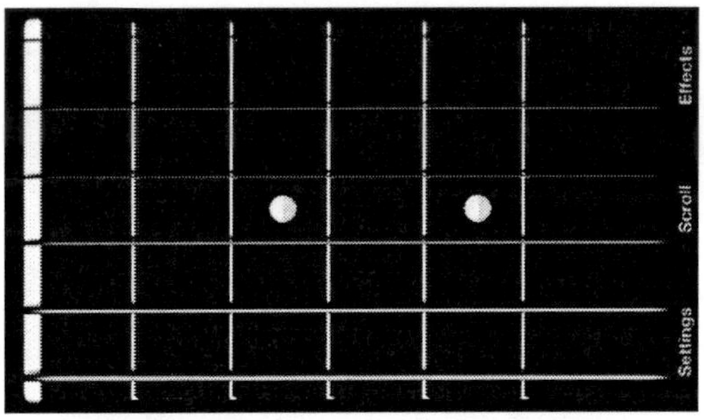

Figure 5. *Pocket Guitar*, a typical guitar app.

3.6 Drum Kit

A traditional drum kit, with some number of drums. Tapping each drum plays an appropriate sample, or one of a set of appropriate samples for that drum, and rolls can sometimes be performed by sliding a finger on a drum head; a faster slide leads to faster rolls (*Ratatap Drums Free*). As with the piano apps, volume and exact timbre control are generally not available. However, some applications provide force-based volume control (*Ratatap Drums Free*), and some play differing samples based on the exact location of the tap - playing the bell vs. the edge of a cymbal, for example (*Drums!*). Finally, the user can often switch between drum kits or drum kit layouts (*Drum Kit Pro, Drums!*)

Figure 6. *Ratatap Drums*, a typical drum app.

3.7 Synthesizer

A synthesizer app exposes a selection of controls to a synthesis engine, and provides a piano-style keyboard for triggering the synthesized sounds. Control of the synthesis parameters is typically done with rotary knobs, but horizontal (*Alchemy*) or vertical (*Minisynth*) sliders, and XY pads (*Alchemy*) are also often used. Common parameters include:

- Wave type - sawtooth, sine, square, etc (*Magellan*)
- Filters - cutoff, type, resonance (*Alchemy*)
- Frequency modulation (*iMS20*)
- ADSR envelope control (*iMS20*)

In addition to triggering sounds with a piano keyboard, sequencers are included in some synthesizers (*Magellan, iMS20*), as are grids with volume mapped vertically (*Magellan*), and XY pads (*iMS20*). Indeed, some synthesizers can set the scale used by the keyboard or XY pad (*Animoog, iMS20*). In the case of the *Animoog*, this changes the layout of black and white keys! Finally, some synthesizers apps include extra effects, which are controlled with rotary knobs (*Magellan*) or with virtual patching environments (*iMS20, Audulus*).

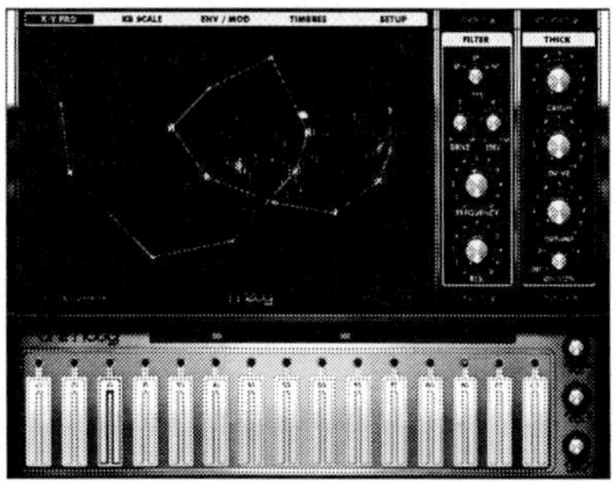

Figure 7. *Animoog*, a typical synthesizer app.

3.8 Sequencer

This category is inclusive of both drum machines and step sequencers. Time is divided into some number of discrete steps (16, 32, or 64), and time then moves step-by-step from left to right, according to a set tempo. One or more sounds or drum can be triggered on each step. Some sequencers model traditional drum machines (*Korg iElectribe*), and only allow access to a single track at a time, whereas others offer a grid with multiple tracks (*EasyBeats 2 Pro*). Some include DAW-style mixers with vertical sliders (KeyZ), some add effects sections with rotary control (*Molten Drum Machine*), and some have an MPC-style interface for adding events to the grid (*FunkBox Drum Machine*). The mapping of time also varies: some only display a single bar of time, whereas others allow a bar to be sequenced, and then allow the bar itself to be sequenced with other bars (*Genome MIDI Sequencer, DM1*). Zooming in time is occasionally provided by a rotary knob that controls the subdivision of a beat (*Molten Drum Machine*). Finally, volume per sound is sometimes controlled by the vertical position of the sound in the grid (*Looptastic Producer*).

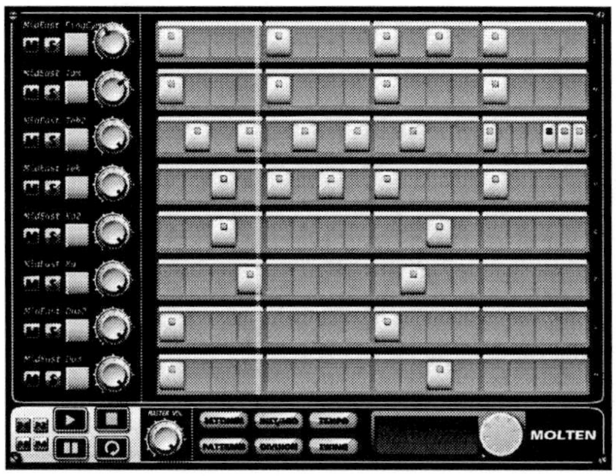

Figure 8. *Molten Drum Machine*, a typical sequencer app.

3.9 Karaoke

Karaoke apps allow the user to sing along to the instrumental track of a known song. At the very least, they present and somehow highlight the lyrics to be sung. Some provided visible pitch mapping, usually with pitch mapped vertically (higher notes are higher in pitch, lower notes are lower) and time moving from left to right (*StarMaker: Karaoke+*). Other options include additional reverb or echo (*Soulo Karaoke*), automating tuning effects that can be toggled on and off (*Sing! Karaoke, StarMaker: Karaoke+*), and toggles and level sliders for guide vocals (*StarMaker: Karaoke+*).

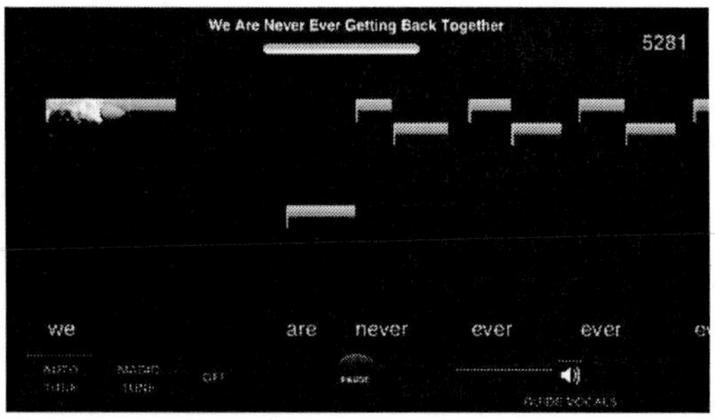

Figure 9. *StarMaker: Karaoke+*, a typical karakoae app.

3.10 Amp Sim

These apps provide some sort of model of a hardware FX box, usually a guitar pedal or guitar amplifier. Control of the effect is provided by rotary knobs (*AmpliTube*) horizontal faders (*AmpKit*), and on/off switches (*AmpliTube, AmpKit*). Some examples of the effects & parameters under control, from *AmpliTube*, are:

- Octave Pedal: direct level, octave level
- Delay: Delay time, feedback, delay level
- Phaser: speed

Some apps additionally allow the user to position a virtual microphone in front of the virtual amplifier, providing non-linear, two dimensional control of timbre (*Ultimate Guitar Amps and Effects*).

Figure 10. *AmpliTube*, a typical amp sim app.

3.11 Other

The Other category ranges from touch-based implementations of acoustic instruments to wildly abstracted music applications. Violin, harmonica, and trumpet applications were examined, along with gravity-based sequencers, isomorphic pitch-space controllers, and granular synthesizer experiments. In general, the most atypical mappings appeared in this category. For example, *Rework* maps pitch radially out from the centre, and *ThumbJam* allows the user to add vibrato and tremolo by shaking the device.

4. MAPPINGS

Beyond the metaphors listed above, we examined the raw mappings behind each app. For example, a standard piano application maps pitch horizontally from left to right (all directions given imply an increase), with discrete buttons. Likewise, a standard DAW application has a mixer

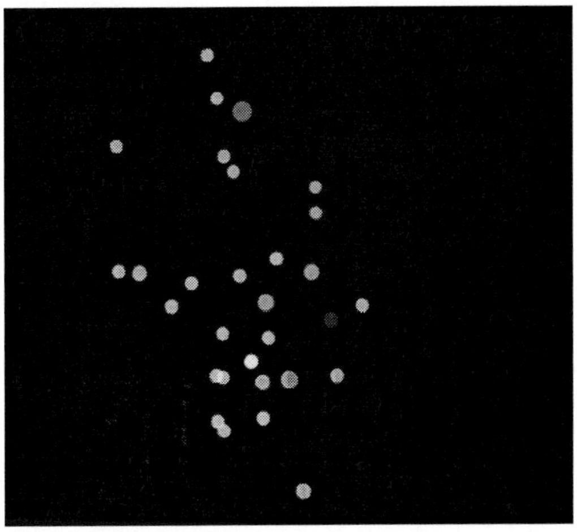

Figure 11. *Borderlands*, an app from the Other category.

that maps volume vertically, from bottom to top, continuously. Table 2 breaks down mappings in terms of pitch, trigger, time, volume, and timbre, across the ten metaphors listed above: Piano, DJ, DAW, MPC, Guitar, Drum Kit, Synthesizer, Sequencer, Karaoke, and Amp Sim.

It is important to note that some apps contain multiple mappings for a given parameter. Thus, the numbers in Table 2 will not add up to the total number of apps listed in Table 1. Secondly, despite the fact that many applications present rotary knobs or dials to control parameters (especially for timbral controls), these are not controlled in a rotary manner. They are in fact controlled as a vertical slider, and are notated here as such. Finally, some apps do not rotate when the device rotates. If the app presented a know metaphor (such as with guitar apps), the device was oriented to match the way the metaphorical instrument would be held. If the app presented no known metaphor, a best guess was taken, based on orientation of text, icons, and so on.

In Tables 2 and 3, each column refers to the parameter to be mapped. Pitch, Trigger, Volume, and Timbre should be self-explanatory. The Time column applies to applications like sequencers and DAWs that allow a user to queue or schedule events in time, and to tempo controls in DJ apps and sequencer apps. Each row refers to the mapping used. Most mappings should be self-explanatory. The Known Layout mapping is less clear: it refers to controlling a parameter through some visual layout that does not fit in a simple horizontal or vertical mapping, but is nevertheless clear to the user. For example, a drum kit app would control timbre via a known layout - that of a drum kit. Likewise, a trumpet app that mimics the valves of a trumpet would control pitch via a known layout.

4.1 Results

As can be seen from Table 2, the mappings for those standard categories do not cover a wide range of the possibilities. The runaway winner for pitch input, for example, is discrete pitches mapped left to right - almost certainly on a piano keyboard. It is important to note that mappings based on the keyboard are so common because users understand

Table 2. Mappings for standard categories

Mapping	Pitch	Trigger	Time	Volume	Timbre
Horizontal: Left-to-Right	143		67	32	
Horizontal: Right-to-Left				32	
Vertical: Top-to-Bottom	32				
Vertical: Bottom-to-Top	73			142	114
Continuous	50		48	174	114
Discrete	178		19	174	114
Known Layout					49
Toggle		45			50
Touch		243			
Gesture		43			
Microphone		18		18	

them instantly, without having to build up their own model for how an app maps pitch. Mapping pitch using a system of gestures would be interesting and novel, but would not be easy to use.

4.2 Other

In order to get a clearer view of potentially novel mappings, the raw mappings for each of the apps in the Other category (from Table 1) are listed in Table 3.

Most mappings listed in Table 3 should be self-explanatory. The Touch Area mapping refers to the width-times-height area touched, in terms of the size: a tap with a pinky finger covers a smaller area than a thumb, for example. The Physics mapping refers to some model of the physical world: virtual balls bouncing with pitch matched to their speed, for example. Finally, the Location mapping refers to placing a virtual object at a certain XY location in the app: Moving an virtual loudspeaker closer to a virtual microphone, for example.

4.3 Results

As can be seen from Table 3, these mappings are substantially more creative than the mappings for known metaphors. Indeed, many new mappings appear, and some of them are used for only single apps! Standard horizontal and vertical mappings remain very popular, but in general, these apps are more interesting - though they may also be correspondingly more difficult for an end user to grasp.

Table 3. Mappings for Other category

Mapping	Pitch	Trigger	Time	Volume	Timbre
Horizontal: Left-to-Right	22		15	4	11
Horizontal: Right-to-Left					1
Horizontal: Edge-to-Center				1	
Vertical: Top-to-Bottom	2		1		1
Vertical: Bottom-to-Top	16		6	12	16
Rotation: Clockwise	2		5		
Rotation: Counter-Clockwise	1				
Radial: Center-to-Edge	2		1	1	1
Radial: Edge-to-Center					
Diagonal: Bottom-Left-to-Top-Right	1				
Continuous	9		18	17	28
Discrete	40		9	2	2
Known Layout	3				4
Toggle	1	7			16
Touch		26			
Touch Area				1	
Gesture		1			
Microphone		9		3	
Shake	1	2		1	
Tilt	4	2		1	2
Physics	2	2			
Location		4	1		1
Colour	3				2

5. DISCUSSION

Our categorization of applications has shown that the majority of iOS music applications are based on known metaphors, and that piano applications are by far the most popular, followed by emulation of electronic music interfaces: DJ rigs, DAWs, and MPCs. Taken as a single class, the Other category would be the second most popular category, just behind piano apps. However, as these apps vary from simple percussion apps (*iMaracas*) to sophisticated isomorphic pitch controllers (*SoundPrism*), it would be disingenuous to group them together and point to their high number as evidence of the power of novel metaphors. Further investigation of this category would be needed in order to draw more accurate conclusions.

To the contrary, this research indicates that simple or known mappings and metaphors, such as the all-powerful piano keyboard, are the most popular. Even complex synthesis applications emulate physical synthesizers, with sundry dials and faders for timbral control. In the Other category, where apps lack a common metaphor, standard horizontal or vertical mappings still appear. However, numerous apps present novel mappings and novel inputs, indicating that there is more design space to be explored outside of keyboards and drum kits. Indeed, regardless of their lack of known metaphor, apps like *Figure, Borderlands* and *Samplr* show that successful applications can be made with novel mappings.

The importance of metaphor cannot be overstated. The massive popularity of piano apps, DJ apps, and so on, can be explained by Fels et al. [6] and their discussion of how a metaphor provides the user with a "literature" of common knowledge about the interface. This leads to transparency between the mappings and the user, which makes the mappings more effective for beginners. Wessel and Wright [7] discuss the value of metaphors in terms of organizing musical material. They also discuss the value of more abstract and creative metaphors across parameters like pitch and timbre. As has been shown in the above tables, most iOS applications lack such a creative metaphor: only 55 out of 337, just less than a sixth of the examined apps, do not fit in to known categories. It may be possible to bring new categories to life, however. The lack of success of, say, iPhone violins could be because no app has made the correct set of mappings with which to emulate a violin.

In terms of mappings, Tables 2 and 3 could be used to aid the design of new iOS applications. While it seems premature to relate these mappings directly to profitability and financial success (especially as the App Store does not provide sales numbers for each app), the fact that the vast majority of applications map pitch from left to right indicates that an app aimed at widespread success should at least include such a mapping as an option. The same can be said for the mapping of volume vertically, and of time from left to right. Tables 2 and 3, however, could also be used to create spectacularly atypical iOS apps, simply by utilizing mappings that are under-represented. Such an app might map pitch from right to left, continuously, while controlling timbre via the microphone, and selecting rhythms via certain gestures. Or, the app might run time counter-clockwise, control pitch via the area of each touch, and map volume radially. These examples highlight the possibilities for deeply creative mapping solutions that exist on the iOS platform.

The most successful use of these tables, however, is probably in a combination of these two approaches. A scattergun, unfocused collection of novel mappings will probably result in a scattergun, unfocused app. However, an app with some traditional mappings and some novel mappings, especially in underutilized areas such shaking and tilting, or with underutilized parameters such as timbre, may be both more of a research success and more of a popular success

Finally, it is also important to note the limitations of the iPhone and iPad hardware, and how those limitations impact mappings. Though capable of exceptional capacitive multi-touch input, iOS devices lack the ability to easily tell how hard a user is tapping them, or any way of giving the user tactile feedback on their input. In some cases, this leads to creative mappings to work around these limitations. For instance, *Smule Magic Piano* maps the tone of each note vertically: touching higher up a key plays a darker sound. Likewise, *Ratatap Drums* uses data from the accelerometer to detect the force of a tap, and adjusts the volume accordingly.

6. CONCLUSION

We have summarized the most popular categories, mappings, and metaphors for musical iOS apps, as of February 2013. It must be noted that the iOS App Store is an ever-changing world: the top 200 apps of February 2013 are almost certainly not the top 200 apps of July 2013 - and are without question not the top 200 apps of 2015.

As of February 2013, however, we found a massive prevalence of piano apps, and of apps that show known metaphors to the user. We also found a subset of apps with no known metaphor, which were, as a rule, the applications with the most creative mappings. Across all apps, the vast majority used simple mappings: pitch from left to right, volume from top to bottom, and so on. Even within the Other subset of apps, these simple mappings were the most popular. However, this subset also included deeply creative mappings, making use of tilting, physics models, radial lines, and more. We then suggested that these lists of mappings could be used to explore underutilized designed spaces on iOS and similar platforms.

Touch applications for music, on iOS and on other platforms, will only become more popular as such technology becomes more and more available. It is hoped that this report has helped expose how mappings and metaphors are currently used on these devices, and helped shine a light on mappings that have not yet been investigated.

7. ACKNOWLEDGEMENTS

This work is partially funded by a Natural Sciences and Engineering Research Council of Canada (NSERC) Discovery Grant to the second author.

8. REFERENCES

[1] E. van Buskirk, "Developer Explains Why Android Sucks for Some Audio App," http://evolver.fm/2012/05/23/developer-explains-why-android-sucks-for-some-audio-apps/, 05 2012, accessed: 24/02/2013.

[2] M. R. Team, "The best Android music making apps in the world today," http://www.musicradar.com/news/tech/the-best-android-music-making-apps-in-the-world-today-276167, 02 2013, accessed: 24/02/2013.

[3] A. Hunt, M. M. Wanderley, and M. Paradis, "The importance of parameter mapping in electronic instrument design," *Journal of New Music Research*, vol. 32, no. 4, pp. 429–440, 2003.

[4] A. Hunt, M. Wanderley, and R. Kirk, "Towards a model for instrumental mapping in expert musical interaction," in *Proceedings of the 2000 International Computer Music Conference*, 2000, pp. 209–212.

[5] R. J. Jacob, L. E. Sibert, D. C. McFarlane, and M. P. Mullen Jr, "Integrality and separability of input devices," *ACM Transactions on Computer-Human Interaction (TOCHI)*, vol. 1, no. 1, pp. 3–26, 1994.

[6] S. Fels, A. Gadd, and A. Mulder, "Mapping transparency through metaphor: towards more expressive musical instruments," *Organised Sound*, vol. 7, no. 2, pp. 109–126, 2002.

[7] D. Wessel and M. Wright, "Problems and prospects for intimate musical control of computers," *Computer Music Journal*, vol. 26, no. 3, pp. 11–22, 2002.

[8] P. McGlynn, V. Lazzarini, G. Delap, and X. Chen, "Recontextualizing the multi-touch surface."

[9] Apple, "Apple Updates iOS to 6.1," http://www.apple.com/pr/library/2013/01/28Apple-Updates-iOS-to-6-1.html, 01 2013, accessed: 24/02/2013.

Acoustics-like dynamics in signal-based synthesis through parameter mapping

Brendan Bernhardt Gaffney, Tamara Smyth
University of California, San Diego
bbgaffne,trsmyth@ucsd.edu

ABSTRACT

To ideally expand a sound synthesis parameter mapping strategy is to introduce complexity and capability without sacrificing its ease of use. Following work done with dynamical systems and catastrophe theory by René Thom, Sir E.C. Zeeman and others, we are able to create a general purpose model for introducing extended behaviors, akin to the dynamics of acoustic instruments, in low complexity interfaces without adding control parameters or losing the possibility of reverting to a simple, near-linear mapping.

Herein, we explore the principles of catastrophe theory, paying particular attention to the cusp model in which two input parameters yield a third and fourth describing the "catastrophic" events after which the theory is named. As acoustic systems possess several attributes of the catastrophic models, we experiment using the cusp model to enhance mapping of control parameters to FM synthesis parameters, in an attempt to give these signal-based virtual instruments the nuance and capability of their acoustic counterparts.

1. INTRODUCTION

The quality of a parametric sound synthesis model is not only determined by its produced sound, but also by the richness, depth, and intuitiveness of its control. As is the case with their acoustic counterparts, virtual musical instruments should engage users with music and sonic possibilities, allowing for exploration, discovery, and expression, with increased use, practice, and familiarity. A mapping strategy, therefore, may be evaluated by its "virtuosic ceiling" (potential for maturation with extended use) and its "entry fee" (ease of initial interaction) [1]. Balancing these two attributes is an important aspect in designing a system whereby performative gestures will be translated into synthesis parameters.

Physics-based synthesis models often have a myriad of possible synthesis parameters, offering possibilities in the produced sound akin to their acoustic counterparts. Though the complete set of possible parameters is usually too large to be effectively controlled by the user in realtime, there is usually a subset of "control parameters" that is naturally intuitive, largely because they are physical and relate to acoustic instruments with which the user has some familiarity and experience: blowing harder produces a louder sound; shortening the string produces a higher pitch. In addition to offering a low "entry fee" (ease of use) without requiring additional mapping, a quality physics-based model implements the dynamics of the system (the produced sound being dependent on both the current state of the model/parameters and their change over time), which also, by nature, offers possibilities that raise the "virtuosic ceiling" (maturation): blowing harder produces not only a louder sound, but also one that is brighter, harsher, detuned, or even the octave above (overblowing).

In signal-based models, the relationship between control and synthesis parameters is far less obvious (to both developer and user), and a mapping strategy is required to achieve a balance between ease of use and maturation. These mappings can be difficult to create, due to both their abstraction from a more obvious linear mapping, and their potential to create densely connected and difficult to debug and describe interactions. Existing strategies have incorporated generative methods to produce these mappings [2–4] and many have developed taxonomies to enable the decryption and development of these complex mappings [5, 6]. In this work we present an approach to parameter-mapping that, by borrowing concepts and models from catastrophe theory, aims to enrich signal-based models with the inherent complexities/intuitiveness of those that are based on some more natural, physically based musical interaction.

In an attempt to further the current mapping toolset, we have chosen to examine catastrophe theory as a potential set of theorems and models. Work done to extend the toolset available in creating these mappings is valuable to performer, composer and designer alike, as creating new primitives in mapping strategies yields a better set of design choices for the development of new mappings of control to synthesis, and therefore a more dynamic and nuanced interaction between instrument/interface designer, composer and performer.

In Section 2, we will examine catastrophe theory, its models and those attributes that indicate its potential value to parameter mapping development. In Section 3, we discuss its implementation, specifically in code via Pure Data and in a parameter mapping paradigm within frequency modulation synthesis. In Section 4 we discuss the results of these initial implementations, in Section 5 we examine the research to suggest possible topics for expansion and investigation, and in Section 6 we discuss the conclusions derived from our research.

2. CATASTROPHE THEORY

René Thom, a twentieth-century French mathematician, developed catastrophe theory as a means of explaining a set of complex singularities in geometry and mathematics. [7] [8] Thom's work inspired many to pursue the conclusions of catastrophe theory, not only in mathematics, but across disciplines. In his book *Catastrophe Theory*, Sir E.C. Zeeman, a British mathematician and champion of the relevancy of catastrophe theory across disciplines, presents several examples of simple, catastrophic systems outside mathematical fields [9]. A number of other researchers have used Thom's work in modeling a number of sociological [10], economic [11], physical [12], and biological [13] systems.

Catastrophe theory describes simple geometric models to explain systems that yield drastic changes in state in response to slowly changing attributes or parameters. These models have been developed from theorems proposed by Thom, that describe higher-dimensional geometry, specifically that of bifurcating sets of higher-order polynomials. His work concerned itself specifically with the discontinuities yielded by a number of special multi-dimensional geometric equations he termed *elementary catastrophes*, which are classified by the dimensions of their behavior and parameter spaces. The models Thom and Zeeman use to describe these systems are eloquent in that they are simple polynomials, whose real roots yield the stable states of the system, and whose coefficients shape the attributes of the thresholds and surface of the models [14].

While these previous implementations of catastrophe theory have little to prove for our mapping here, they point to the validity of catastrophe theory models in a range of applications and disciplines.

The elementary catastrophe we will concern ourselves with herein will be a lower dimensional model, due to its potential for representation on paper and its relative ease of comprehension and application. The model is the cusp catastrophe, which is described by a simple cubic polynomial, and from a two dimensional control space yields a third, potentially bimodally distributed behavior axis, whose value is dependent on previous states and trajectory through our control space. The cusp is manipulated by adjusting the coefficients of a polynomial, using two of these coefficients as navigational axes of a control space.

2.1 The Cusp Catastrophe

Catastrophe theory comprises a number of models that relate or map "attributes" to "behavioral" states. One such model, called the cusp catastrophe, is given by

$$c_h x^3 + b c_w x + a = 0, \tag{1}$$

where c_h and c_w are used to change the cusp height and width, respectively, and coefficients a and b are input control parameters. The surface C in Figure 1 is the control surface created by axes a and b, while the *manifold cusped* surface M (above C) is defined by the *real* roots of (1). The positive and negative values of x create the two *sheets* (upper and lower regions) of M.

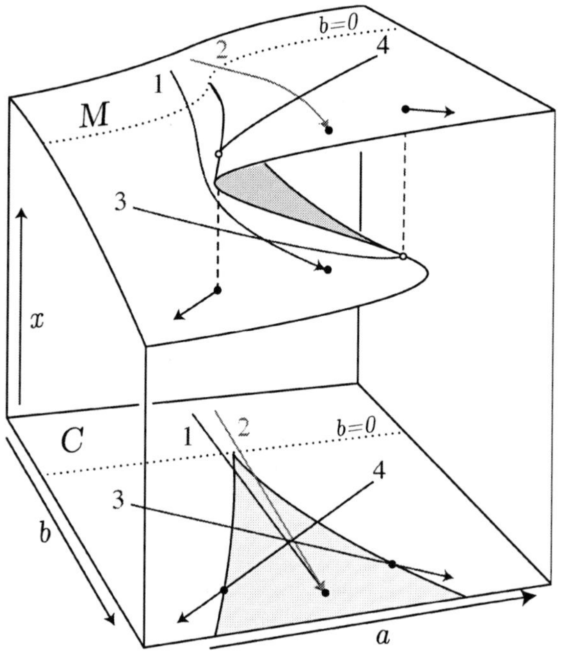

Figure 1. The elementary cusp catastrophe. Our variable axes b (splitting factor) and a (normal factor) and behavior axis x are labeled in the control surface C, and several trajectories through this control surface are traced both on C and their resulting values for x are traced on the behavior manifold M.

Since (1) is a cubic polynomial, it has three roots. The shaded area on control surface C, indicates values of a and b for which all three of these roots are real—*the bifurcating set*. These three real roots define the folded or "cusped" region of the manifold surface M. Outside the shaded region in C lie values for a and b yielding only a single real value for x. The two curved lines outlining the shaded area are thus thresholds for which a and b yield single or multiple (bifurcating) values of x. Bifurcating values of x appear for values of $b > 0$. For $b < 0$, x increases continuously with a. Static coefficients, c_h and c_w, effectively scale the coefficients a and b, thus skewing the dimensions of the cusp.

Fig. 1 shows several trajectories, labeled 1-4, of linearly changing values for a and b. Trajectories 1 and 2 on C, which originate on either side of the bifurcating set, produce different values for x, shown by corresponding trajectories 1 and 2 on M, despite a common destination point and similarly changing values of a and b. This exemplifies the first of the catastrophe model's attributes:

Attribute 1. *The behavior resulting from a given set of control values is dependent both on initial conditions and previous behavior.*

Trajectories 3 and 4 illustrate the characteristic jumps, or "catastrophes," after which the models are named, which occur when moving from the bifurcating set to the non-bifurcating set (jumps are illustrated in Fig. 1 using dashed lines on M and occur at points on C when the trajectory moves from inside to outside the shaded area). Furthermore, if a trajectory exits across the same threshold from

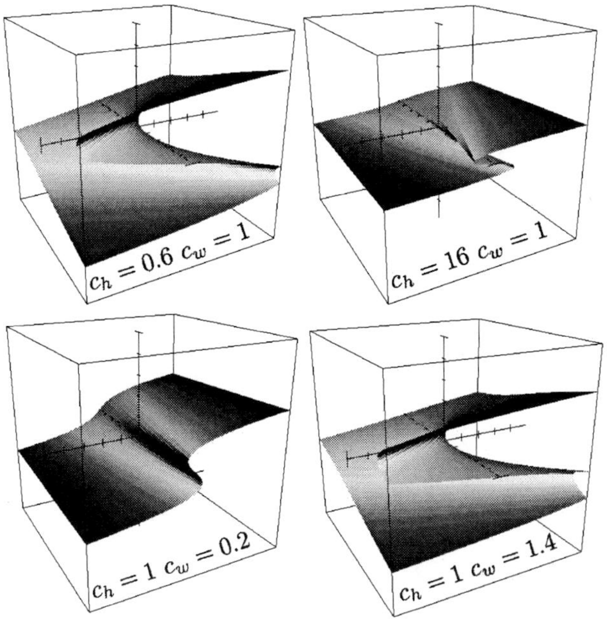

Figure 2. The effects of different values of c_h and c_w on the shape of our cusped surface. Axes are the same scale in all four plots.

which it entered, i.e. remains on the same "sheet", no jump occurs. This exemplifies the second of the model's attributes:

Attribute 2. *Jumps in the value of x occur only upon exiting the bifurcating set onto a new sheet.*

2.2 Applying to Dynamic Systems

Though the cusp model has two input parameters, it generates another two, yielding a total of four possible synthesis/application parameters: a, b, location x on the cusp manifold surface, and a binary value indicating whether x is on the upper or lower sheet. This increase indicates a potential value in parameter mapping, as it suggests a possible mapping of a simple control space to a more complex dynamic or sound synthesis system.

Any system that exhibits:

1. bimodal distributions of behavior for a dynamic input (relating to Attribute 1),
2. drastic changes in behavior despite slowly changing control parameters (relating to Attribute 2).

is a potential candidate for representation by a catastrophe model. Several such systems exist in music applications. In particular, blowing into the mouthpiece of a saxophone presents an example of an acoustic system that exhibits these two attributes: slowly varying embouchure and blowing pressure (corresponding to control axes a and b) for a given fingering, produces a sound that can leap in register/octave—a bimodality in state (Attribute 1) that can result in a jump in x (Attribute 2). That is, the tendency of the horn to lock into an upper or lower register, based on its previous state, exhibits Attribute 1. The tendency for a horn to jump *catastrophically* in register despite slow changes in control exhibits Attribute 2.

This simple catastrophic model of the saxophone shows the natural and musical behavior of control parameters fed through a cusp model. This nuanced behavior, coupled with the simplicity of the mathematics and rules of behavior, point to a potentially rewarding mapping strategy.

3. IMPLEMENTATION

In implementing catastrophe theory and polynomial equations in a mapping strategy, we are looking for complexity and capability in expression without diminishing the ability to use an interface effectively and easily. Furthermore, we hope to reward maturation with an interface, providing a more complex and nuanced interaction with the interface over time, more so than previously available without a complex mapping. The cusp model (1) is implemented as a Pd external object (written in C) [15], which offers a real-time interactive programming environment popular among computer musicians. Several patches from our experimentation, and the `cusp~` external, are available for download [16].

The first step in implementation is to fully understand the effects of manipulating the coefficients of (1). Initial tests were run in graphing programs to illustrate the width and height of the cusp for different values of c_h and c_w (see Figure 2). Following this, implementation is straightforward. First, the Cusp model is coded as a function having four input parameters, two static (c_w and c_h) and two dynamic (a and b), and two returned values, x and a binary indicating on which sheet, HIGH or LOW, x lies. Through experimentation, c_h was deemed unnecessary as it was *nearly* a scaling of x that could instead be more effectively and predictably applied as a linear scaling of the output (reducing required inlets in the Pd external to three).

The function uses the cubic polynomial solver in the GNU Scientific Library, as it returns only real values (and not complex values that have nothing to do with surface M). This function takes our three coefficients above and three pointers to memory locations in which it stores the returned roots of our equation. It also returns an integer indicating whether there is one or three real roots, effectively indicating whether we are in a bifurcating or non-bifurcating set of values for a and b.

Finally, a state variable is used to "remember" on which sheet of the cusp surface x resided in the previous time step, determining which of the roots of x, lower or upper, should be returned (the middle value is not considered in these models). Therefore, in this example we have a doubling of possible control parameters: the original a and b, plus two more given by the cusp model, x and sheet of x.

This code can be further optimized by implementing our own polynomial solver instead of calling an outside function (which itself makes several outside function calls). Furthermore, a number of other techniques can be used to determine the correct root, and some of these may be more optimal. Because this code, wrapped as a Pd external, is computed for every sample, it may be used in waveshaping and audio-rate modulation, as well as control rate paradigm.

4. APPLICATION AND RESULTS

Here, we choose to explore its use in the context of an FM (frequency modulation) synthesizer, to see how acoustic behavior as described in Section 2.2 can be incorporated in a signal-based model. A very simple implementation can be observed in Figure 3, where the index of modulation is controlled by both x and the binary HIGH/LOW sheet variable, while the carrier and modulator frequency are controlled by a and b, respectively.

The patch illustrated in Fig. 3 was used as an experimentation platform for determining the effect of our two generated parameters in very minimal signal-based synthesis system. Frequency modulation was chosen for our familiarity with its common control mappings and produced sound.

The interface chosen for initial experimentation was a touch sensitive trackpad, which returned an x and y value for a finger moved about its surface. By implementing our mapping with the cusp modeling, we essentially are able to traverse the lower and upper sheets of the model with our finger, and dictate the behavior based on our trajectory across and around the thresholds of the model, much as the paths in Fig. 1. This allows nuanced control of the output values, as it is immediately possible for a novice user to locate, empirically, the location of these thresholds and quickly learn to exploit or avoid their happening.

4.1 Cusps in Timbre, Amplitude and Pitch Control Paradigms

The cusp in the above patch maps timbre to our cusp model and pitch to our input a and b. Several other implementations were made systematically to determine by isolation the effect of cusp models on signal-based synthesis's most often used parameters, timbre, amplitude and pitch.

In Fig. 3 we have mapped our FM timbral parameter, the index of modulation, to the x output by the cusp model. We also tested this same system without the changing pitch, and therefore isolated timbral control with the cusped model. This yields an interesting, pseudo-vocal behavior, jumps in sideband presence and spread affecting a dynamic, albeit it expressively limited, control of timbre.

In other experiments, amplitude and pitch were controlled with the new complex yielded parameters x and sheet of x. An interesting result of this experimentation was the effect of the changing x without leaving the current sheet. The effect was to obtain a vernier control of a small subset of the accessible control space, effectively enabling a magnification of the values of x available on a given sheet. When mapping to amplitude, at higher values of b, where the sheets are most distant and the values of x therefore more disparate, this amounts to an ability to make nuanced changes in loudness at either a lower *piano* dynamic or, after jumping sheets, fine adjustments at a higher *forte* dynamic.

It is in our mapping of this model to pitch that the aforementioned "magnification" of certain subsets of the con-

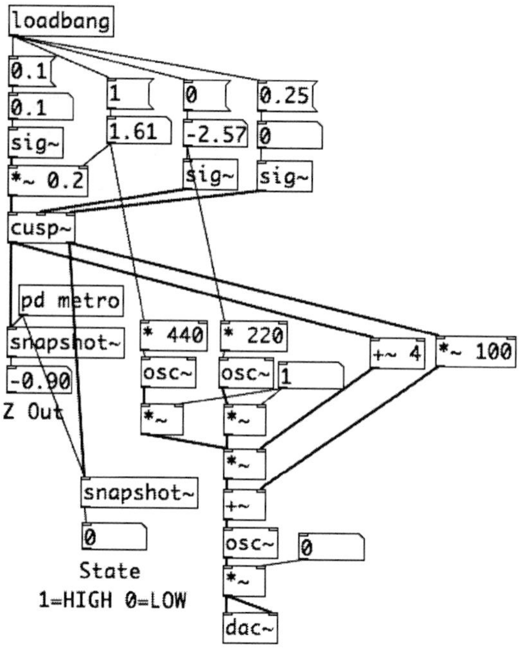

Figure 3. A simple patch illustrating the mapping of our four synthesis parameters (two generated by our cusp model, two direct from control) to a simple FM-based synthesis algorithm.

trol space is most notable. The lower portion of the control space allowed minute control of a lower pitch subset, and after a jump, minute control of a higher pitch subset. As the middle pitches can be accessed by simply decreasing b, this introduces a very interesting paradigm of control. A scale running from lowest to highest pitch sets therefore runs in a horseshoe shape, retreating around the bifurcating set of values of a and b and back out to the higher sheet, without encountering catastrophic jumps but increasing the nuance of control at all points. Furthermore, jumps of different sizes between registers can be made easily and with some precision by simply locating the proper crossing point of the threshold to take a path through.

These mappings to signal-based synthesis parameter primitives helped illustrate the value of these models to the expansion of available parameter mapping strategies. To our initial goal of introducing acoustic-like behavior to these simpler signal based models, it points to observed behaviors, like the selective magnification, that may map to acoustic-like paradigms.

4.2 Introducing Acoustic-like Behavior to a Signal Model

The main purpose of these experiments is to determine if the two additional parameters generated by the cusp model, x and sheet of x, are useful and intuitive synthesis parameters. As previously illustrated, it can be shown that acoustic systems have a tendency to behave like the cusped model, so our aim was to investigate the presence of some more natural or acoustic-like behavior in the mapping.

We can show this behavior by observing Attributes 1 and 2 in the process of using the interface, and determine if they are related as predictable and controllable features to a user.

By default a simple FM synthesis model has no inherent acoustic-like qualities, as FM linearly mapped to the control parameters of a trackpad or other continuous controller is dissimilar from any existing acoustic system. This allows us to track the effect of introducing the cusp mapping, and evaluate it independently of the synthesis algorithm's behavior. This isolation of a mapping is key to evaluating its worth, as many synthesis algorithms behave naturally and effectively without an intermediate mapping between control and synthesis parameters.

First, the implementation of this model effectively enlarges the parameter space of our sound synthesis system, as Attribute 1 shows that a large portion of our control surface has two possible values of x. By introducing this bifurcating behavior, like that found in acoustic systems, the parameter space of our interface widens, and therefore a larger portion of the sound space of the synthesis algorithm is available to a performer.

Furthermore, by using cusp-generated parameters x and sheet of x to control the index of modulation, an abstract synthesis parameter without an acoustic analog, we introduced a way of jumping between timbres of the synthesis algorithm. Each sheet of the cusp maps to two different sound spaces, with finer adjustments accessible using x, and a user can switch purposefully from one to another. These jumps, described by Attribute 2, introduce a triggered, more dynamic behavior to our previously linear interface.

Also, the complex behaviors of wind instruments discussed in Section 2.2 can be modeled with careful application of the cusp model in mapping control parameters. In experimentation, the sheet of x was mapped to pitch, while x was mapped to index of modulation. This mapping closely resembles the articulation of a single keying of the saxophone, where an increase in embouchre and blowing pressure will push the horn to both jump in octave (a catastrophic jump in pitch) and harshen in timbre (an accompanying increase in x).

The selective magnification also has many acoustic analogs. Jumps between registers as desribed above, with some small, more nuanced adjustments available on either end of these jumps, also closely resembles paradigms present in wind instruments. Again, the jumps can be associated with pitch, but if mapped with proper scaling of x instead of the binary sheet of x, small adjustments in intonation can be made in each register with some precision.

By identifying and exploiting these acoustic behaviors in our new mapping, which introduce more complex expression and control in an otherwise simple system, we have increased the potential for engagement and discovery in the process of learning a musical interaction with a digital system. We have done this by relating the interaction with a digital musical instrument to interactions a performer and composer are more likely to have some experience with. Furthermore, we have helped mediate the potential expressiveness of the vast sound space available in signal-based models to a much smaller and simpler control space.

4.3 Balancing Complexity and Cost

Another main focus of these experiments is to determine the ability for a user to easily acquire the mapping and behavior of the interface, and if maturation with the system is rewarding over time. While the initial experiments are basic, results indicate that the mapping has the potential to fulfill our two desired features of a new mapping, namely the low entry fee and high virtuosic ceiling.

By scaling and offsetting our input parameters, the bottom half of the trackpad can be kept near-linear, or without bifurcation (by keeping $b < 0$, as shown in Fig. 1), and therefore more immediately intuitive, while still allowing the top half to exhibit the more complex bifurcating behavior. By building this duality into the interface, it is possible for a simple interface to yield both easily accessible and more complex behaviors.

Furthermore, several cusps can be implemented with differing dimensions and locales on the control surface by simply adding more of these models in the intermediary mapping layer. These additional mappings afford the same designed duality in simplicity and complexity. We can therefore introduce the complexity in behavior available with several cusps without accumulating complexity in the lower half of our mapping and eliminating its ease of acquisition. These two conditions satisfy the desire to find mappings both easy to acquire and rich in complexity and nuance that can be acquired over time.

5. CONCLUSIONS

Catastrophe theory, as laid out by Thom and others, allows us the means by which to extend the currently available tools used in parameter mapping. It does so by supplying models in which a low number of parameters yield new and complex output behaviors.

The cusp model from catastrophe theory is ideal for several reasons. First, it is relatively easy to understand, due to its ease of representation in three dimensions on paper, and its low order polynomial description. It is also easy to implement in code, and easier still to include in a mapping strategy once encapsulated into an external or its equivalent outside of Pd.

The likeness of the cusp model to acoustical systems further extends the implemented mappings, by extending their behaviors, size of control space, and introducing control that is intuitive and nuanced like that of an acoustical system. It allows for an acoustics-like dynamic for a signal based synthesis algorithm, by introducing an intermediary mapping layer. We can see the real mapping benefits of introducing both dynamic jumps in parameter range and the effect of bifurcating control surfaces in both ease of control and likeness to acoustic analogs.

Furthermore, the cusp model, and other polynomials like it, is possible to implement in a non-complicating manner. It can be subtle or drastic, with or without linear mapping possibilities behind some threshold, and multiplied in number, all potentially without cost to the initial acquisition of the interface's function and the ease that simple mappings allow novice users to begin making sound in a purposeful manner. It is this introduction of complexity without cost that highlights the possibilities of these equations as tools in the mapping strategies of larger, more complex algorithms.

6. FURTHER RESEARCH

While this paper focuses on a simple implementation of a lower complexity model of catastrophe theory, there is still more to do in terms of applying these models and evaluating their wider uses and conclusions.

First and foremost, examination of all of catastrophe theory's models, not simply those more conveniently laid out on paper, is called for. While they do not guarantee the possibility of nuanced or simple behavior like the cusp catastrophe does, their higher level of input and output parameters suggest their potential relevancy. One such model, the butterfly model, is suited for further research, as its surface can also be traced with two parameters, and its coefficients and behaviors are more complex. Initial experimentation with the butterfly model's behaviors show some promise for parameter mapping.

Second, catastrophe theory itself may well be worth examining in music and sound synthesis outside of parameter mapping. Its relevancy in physics to describe complex behaviors resembling resonance point to its potential use in modeling the behavior of musical instruments, in terms of musical information retrieval or parameter estimation techniques.

In effect, catastrophe theory's implementation herein has only been the initial stages of applying a theory to a new discipline. The scope of this article was necessarily smaller in scope to more carefully explore a single implementation, and without expansion outwards, this topic is not fully explored or tested.

7. REFERENCES

[1] M. Wanderley and N. Orio, "Evaluation of input devices for musical expression: Borrowing tools from hci," *Computer Music Journal*, vol. 26, no. 3, pp. 62–76, 2002.

[2] C. G. Johnson, "Exploring the sound-space of synthesis algorithms using interactive genetic algorithms." *Interface*, 1999.

[3] P. Dahlstedt, "Free Flight in Parameter Space: A Dynamic Mapping Strategy for Expressive Free Improvisation," *Applications of Evolutionary Computing*, 2008.

[4] ——, "Creating and exploring huge parameter spaces: Interactive evolution as a tool for sound generation," in *Proceedings of the 2001 International Computer Music Conference*, 2001, pp. 235–242.

[5] A. Hunt, M. M. Wanderley, and R. Kirk, "Towards a Model for Instrumental Mapping in Expert Musical Interaction," *Proceedings of the 2000 International Computer Music Conference*, pp. 209–212, 2000.

[6] A. Hunt, M. M. Wanderley, and M. Paradis, "The Importance of Parameter Mapping in Electronic Instrument Design," *Journal of New Music Research*, vol. 32, no. 4, pp. 429–440, Dec. 2003.

[7] R. Thom, *Structural stability and morphogenesis*. Addison Wesley Publishing Company, 1989.

[8] ——, "Structural Stability, Catastrophe Theory, and Applied Mathematics," *SIAM review*, vol. 19, no. 2, pp. 189–201, 1977.

[9] E. Zeeman, *Catastrophe theory, Selected papers 1972-1977*. Addison Wesley Publishing Company, 1977.

[10] A. Wilson, *Catastrophe Theory and Bifurcation (Routledge Revivals): Applications to Urban and Regional Systems*. Routledge, 2012.

[11] H. R. Varian, "Catastrophe theory and the business cycle," *Economic Inquiry*, vol. 17, no. 1, pp. 14–28, 1979.

[12] T. B. Benjamin, "Bifurcation phenomena in steady flows of a viscous fluid. i. theory," *Proceedings of the Royal Society of London. A. Mathematical and Physical Sciences*, vol. 359, no. 1696, pp. 1–26, 1978.

[13] L. Cobb and S. Zacks, "Applications of catastrophe theory for statistical modeling in the biosciences," *Journal of the American Statistical Association*, vol. 80, no. 392, pp. 793–802, 1985.

[14] P. T. Saunders, *An introduction to catastrophe theory*. Cambridge University Press, 1980.

[15] M. Puckette *et al.*, "Pure data: another integrated computer music environment," *Proceedings of the Second Intercollege Computer Music Concerts*, pp. 37–41, 1996.

[16] (2013, April). [Online]. Available: http://www.burnheartsynth.com/files/cusp_tilde.zip

Real, Foley or synthetic? An evaluation of everyday walking sounds

Amalia de Götzen **Erik Sikström** **Francesco Grani** **Stefania Serafin**
Aalborg University Copenhagen
Department of Architecture, Design and Media Technology
`(ago, es, fg, sts)@create.aau.dk`

ABSTRACT

The aim of this paper is to evaluate whether foley sounds, real recordings and low quality synthetic sounds can be distinguished when used to sonify a video and if foley sounds can be rated as more expressive than real sounds. The main idea is to find a motivation for having such a solid tradition in using foley sounds for a film track. In particular this work focuses on walking sounds: five different scenes of a walking person were video recorded and each video was then mixed with the three different kind of sounds mentioned above. Subjects were asked to recognise and describe the action performed, to evaluate their confidence, the realism of the action and its expressiveness. Early results shows that foley sounds and real sounds cannot be distinguished by the subjects. A preliminary audio-only test was performed with the sounds used in the audio-video test in order to assess the recognition rate without the visual help.

1. INTRODUCTION

While existing for several decades, Foley sound effects (cf. [1]) are still an elusive research topic. They are widely used in the movie and video industries because the direct location recordings of scene sounds are simply not good enough or plagued anyway with all sorts of noises that are bound to appear on a crowded set, but their techniques of production are still considered an art which defies explanation (cf. [1,2]). In general, Foley artists learn by experience and know what to do in every particular situation they have to represent, but they hardly know *why* the sounds they produce work well in a given context – being often far more expressive than the direct recording materials. Furthermore, scientific literature about Foley effects is quite scarce (cf. [3–5]) and a wide area of investigation, ranging from multi-modal perception to audio feature evaluation, is available to researchers. However, several experimental studies can be found on the identification and classification of environmental sounds [6], for instance comparing different kind of synthesis [7], introducing the concept of *types of similarities* that can be used as a strategy in a classification task [8, 9], or analysing in depth the lexicon that is used for different environmental sound categories [10]. In [11] the authors claim that according to listener expertise and their confidence scores the similarity approach that they used can be predicted quite well: expert participants usually refer to acoustical similarities, while non experts refer to causal similarities. Following the results of the mentioned work, we decided to ask our *non expert* subjects to identify the action performed, implicitly suggesting to find a causal similarity to identify the sounds they had to judge.

The sounds of walking over different surfaces and materials occupy a special place within the domain of everyday sounds (or environmental sounds) present in video sequences. This everyday life task is really quite complex to reproduce faithfully in a virtualized environment (cf. [12, 13]) but its ubiquity constitutes an indispensable know–how in the idiomatic repertoire of any professional foley artist. Thus, in this experiment walking sounds were considered the most fitted to investigate the current status of sound perception in a direct confrontation between foley, real and synthetic sounds.

The main purpose of this investigation is to compare user recognition and appreciation of footstep sounds in an AV production context. The starting idea was to assert the recognition capabilities and their precision first with audio–only stimuli and then with audio–video ones. In order to do that, an experiment was conducted by asking subjects to express preference and confidence ratings over a group of stimuli presented both in audio–only and audio–video forms. The subjects were also asked to describe the action generating the sounds they were hearing and complete freedom was left to them for the description. A large majority of subjects ended up describing both an action *and* the supposed material over which it was performed. A very crude early semantic analysis was then applied to the descriptions of the audio–only sounds in an attempt to discern whether the subjects were actually recognizing actions and materials at all or whether they were recognizing appropriately one or the other.

2. METHOD

To achieve the goal stated in the last paragraph of Sec.1, we recorded footstep sounds on several surfaces, and we also reproduced their Foley counterpart, using techniques adopted from the movie industry. Moreover, we re–synthesized a low–quality version of the original sounds to be used as a control condition in the assessment of sound quality.

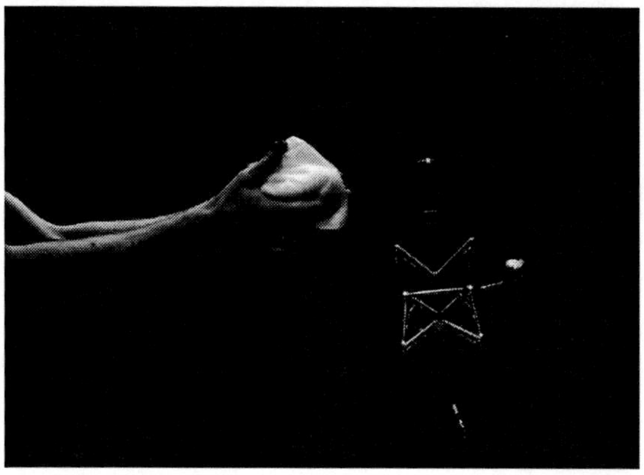

Figure 1. Recording footsteps on sand by massaging and squeezing a little bag filled with salt.

Figure 2. Recording footsteps on wood by walking in place.

2.1 Visual stimuli

The videos were recorded with a Canon 7D camera. They all last about 20 second and they represent 5 different scenes: a man walking on a wooden pavement, a men walking outside on concrete, a men walking outside on sand, a men walking outside on gravel, a men walking outside on grass.

2.2 Auditory stimuli

2.2.1 Foley sounds

All audio recordings were performed inside the anechoic chamber at AAU Copenhagen, Multisensory experiences lab. The "foley artist" was not a professional one, but a well documented PHd student, that used the same acknowledge techniques and the same professional equipment that is usually used in a foley recording studio. On the floor in the anechoic chamber a platform consisting of two large wooden boards with slices wall-to-wall carpeting in between was placed. The platform was resting on six legs that were fixed below the wire floor. Footsteps were produced with a walking-in-place-like treading. A Neuman U87 microphone was used for the recording, connected to an RME Fireface 800 audio interface.

- Footsteps on Sand:
  Salt was put into a shoe bag made of thin fabric. The final footstep sounds consisted of two recordings: one where the bag with salt was patted in a waving motion. This was to emulate the impact of the foot. The other recording was with the bag being held in one hand while being moved in circular patterns with the other hand. This was to emulate the sand being moved around by the foot. See fig. 1

- Footsteps on Gravel:
  A Foley pit created with a wooden box (16mm MDF boards, dimensions 60, 100, 15 cm) was built. The insides were covered with polystyrene material to help dampening the wooden resonance of the wooden construction. A thick felt blanket was also added on top of the polystyrene. The box was filled with approximately 25 Liters of gravel (8-16 mm stones).

- Footsteps on Concrete: A concrete slab was placed into the Foley pit filled with gravel (described above).

- Footsteps on Wood: A wooden pallet was placed on the platform. Thick felt blankets were stuffed under the boards of the pallet to alter the resonance of the pallet, see fig. 2

- Wooden creaks: Creaks were recorded by using a partially broken wooden pallet. The wooden creaks were added to the recordings of footsteps by manual editing during postproduction.

- Footsteps on grass: Tape from a VHS cassette was placed on the platform and patted on with waving strokes to emulate the walking on grass.

2.2.2 Real sounds

The following real recordings were chosen because they were recorded on actual locations (but different from where the videos were recorded) and not Foley:

- Grass sounds were taken from Freesound.org user Zoom H4 ;

- Gravel sounds were taken from user Spleencast ;

- Sand was taken from user DasDeer;

- Concrete was taken from user conleec

- Wooden floor was taken from user sinatra314.

2.2.3 Environmental sounds

To compensate the cleanliness of the foley sounds (recorded in anechoic conditions) and of the synthesized sounds versus the real sound samples, a fake background was added to them. The purpose was to avoid accidental recognition of the foley/synthesized sounds related to the difference in noise content between audio samples.

The two environment sounds used in the experiment were recorded with a Zoom H4n recorder. One recording is of an outdoor environment with distant traffic noises, the other recording was made inside an apartment living room.

The editing and synchronizing of the all the footstep sounds to the videos were done in Adobe Audition CS6. The editing of the Foley recordings were done as would have been normally edited in a film mix with post-production applied where it was deemed necessary.

2.2.4 Synthesized sounds

In order to assess whether subjects rated a lower quality reproduction of the recorded sounds with a lower mark, a set of synthetic footstep sounds was created. The sounds were created as follows. First of all the amplitude envelope of the original recordings (real sounds) was extracted, by using the following simple non-linear low-pass filter proposed by Cook ([14]):

$$e(n) = (1 - b(n))|x(n)| + b(n)e(n-1)$$

where

$$b = \begin{cases} b_{up} & \text{if } |x(n)| > e(n-1) \\ b_{down} & \text{otherwise} \end{cases}$$

with $b_{up} = 0.8$ and $b_{down} = 0.995$.

The original sounds were also passed through a 48th order LPC filter, in order to estimate the main resonances.

The synthetic sounds were obtained by using white noise as input, which became filtered through the LPC filter and with the amplitude obtained by multiplying sample-wise the original amplitude to the values of the estimated amplitude envelope.

The resulting synthetic footsteps present a similar amplitude evolution of the original ones, but the content is significantly noisier given the input signal used for the LPC filter. This can be easily perceived in the simulated footsteps on solid surfaces such as wood, where the sharp attack obtained in the original sounds is lost in the synthesis.

2.3 Testing interface and procedure

The same testing interface has been used for both the audio-video test and the preliminary audio only one. It was created using Max/MSP: subjects could see the video (or a black window in the audio test) and listen to the sound, make their evaluation on the same window and switch to the next trial when done, see fig. 3. The order of presentation of the stimuli (both audio and audio–video) was randomized for each participant. They were asked to describe the action that they were looking/listening to, to rate how confident they were with their identification, how realistic and how expressive was the scene in the likert scale from 1 to 5. No further explanation were given to them, letting them free to describe as much (or as little) as they wanted. We wanted to investigate how much they were going to describe the scene in the two different tests: will they focus on the action or also something else, like the materials involved, the environment, the speed walking etc.). There were 16 subjects (7 female and 9 male) who participated to the preliminary audio test. The mean age was 27 years, and the range was 21 to 42 years. All participants reported normal hearing and either normal or corrected-to-normal vision. All the participants completed the test. The same

Figure 3. The Max/MSP patch dispensed to the subjects for evaluation of video and audio.

16 subjects plus other 14, for a total of 30 subjects (10 female and 20 male) participated to the audio-video test. The mean age for this test was 28 and the range was from 21 to 46 yars old. The test lasted around 20 minutes for each condition.

The test was performed using a HP ProBook 6460b with a 14 inch screen along with the RME Fireface 800 and Sennheiser 600HD. The videos were presented at a resolution of 960*540 pixels.

3. DATA ANALYSIS

The audio and audio–video tests produced two very dissimilar overall results: the audio–video tests featured of course a solid recognition both in terms of actions and materials, while in the audio–only test recognition was much more of an issue. Therefore, we decided to supplement the analysis of the audio tests with an evaluation of the quality of the recognition through the textual description proposed by the subjects.

3.1 Audio test

In order to qualify appropriately the evaluation given by subjects about the sound stimuli that were dispensed to them, it was necessary to discern the extent to which the subjects themselves had recognized the action and/or the material present within each stimulus. The audio-only test shows some preliminary and qualitative results concerning this aspect: most of the subjects could not identify correctly the action performed *both* the action (walking) *and* the material (concrete, gravel, grass, sand, wood), but we found out that many of them could identify just one of the two aspects.

Since the subjects were left completely free to describe what they were hearing both in terms of the action performed and in terms of the materials on/over/with which the action was performed, we then re-processed all free-form answers attributing to them two different scores, one concerning the action and one concerning the recognition of the material. ¡¡¡¡¡¡¡ .mine =======

Given the preliminary status of this work and the (small) amount of data collected, we did not perform a fully detailed statistical analysis of the results (such as that found, for example, in [11]). However, we are fully aware that

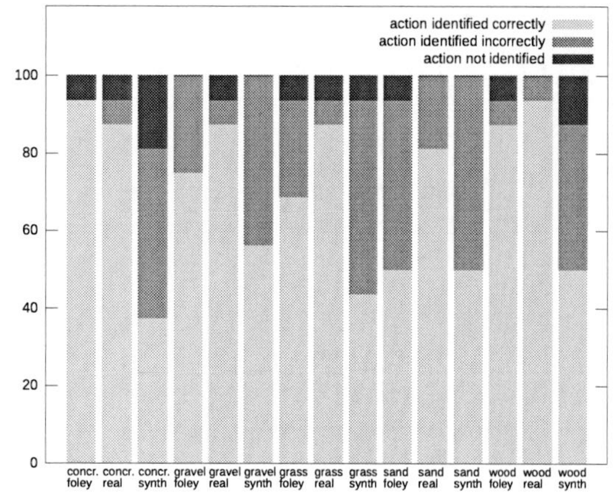

Figure 4. Correctness of the answers of the participants concerning actions.

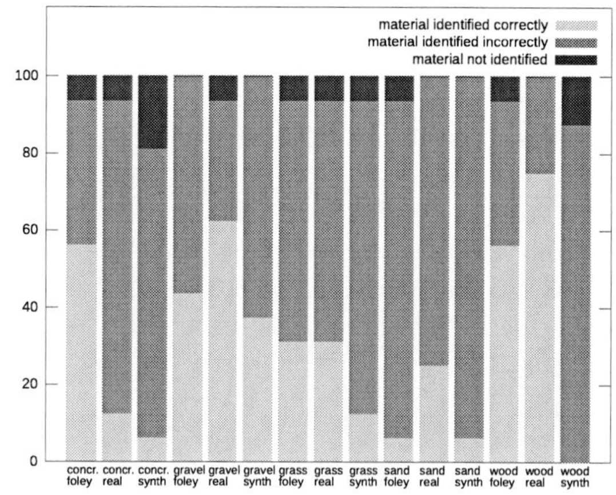

Figure 5. Correctness of the answers of the participants concerning materials.

such an analysis is to be carried out on a more definitive statement on this subject.

The scores were attributed on a scale from 0 to 2 in the following way:

0 was attributed to the text when the subject expressed the impossibilty of discerning anything out of the stimulus proposed (i.e. phrases like "I don't know" or "..." or "I cannot figure it out" etc.)

1 was attributed to the text description when the subject was actually able to provide an explanation as to what kind of action was being performed and what kind of material was being used, but the explanation was clearly wrong (i.e. the subject did not recognize either the action and/or the material)

2 was attributed to the text description when the subject was actually able to provide an explanation as to what kind of action was being performed and what kind of material was being used, and the explanation was correct to some extent (i.e. the subject provided a description that was amenable to let us understand that she/he indeed *did* recognize the action and/or the material used in the given stimulus)

The rationale behind this scoring system is that in this case a wrong answer is better that no answer at all, and this is reflected in the way grades are applied to each text description.

Figg.4 and 5 show quite distinctly some specific features of these results:

a) in general, actions (cf. fig.4) are better recognized than materials (cf. fig.5);

b) the stimulus "walking on wood" (columns 13, 14 and 15) is distinctly the better recognized one both in terms of action and of material by most subjects, at least as far as foley and real sound actions are concerned

c) the stimuli "waking on concrete" (columns 1 – 3) and "walking on gravel" (columns 4 – 6) come next in terms of recognition

d) the stimuli "walking on grass" (columns 7 – 9) and "waking on sand" (columns 10 – 13) give the worst results in terms of recognition; the difficulty comes mostly from the recognition of the material, but this very often jeopardizes the recognition of the action too

e) the recognition of synthetic sound probes (columns 3, 6, 9, 12 and 15) is much more difficult and unstable

An early conjecture regarding these results is that there seems to be some correlation between the quantity of acoustic resonance present in a stimulus and the capability of recognition: more resonating materials (wood, concrete, gravel) stand a larger chance of being recognized than less resonating ones. However, this conjecture has not been investigated further at this time as it has been left for future research.

3.2 Audio-Video test

The audio-video test was analysed starting from the media and its variance. The variance was found to be too large to further proceed with anova tests over it. The median values were then evaluated and the Wilcoxon–Mann–Whitney test performed. Figures 6, 7, 8 shows the median values for each trial:

1. Walking on concrete with foley sounds, real and synthesized sounds
2. Walking on gravel with foley sounds, real and synthesized sounds
3. Walking on grass with foley sounds, real and synthesized sounds
4. Walking on sand with foley sounds, real and synthesized sounds
5. Walking on wood with foley sounds, real and synthesized sounds

A preliminary observation of the data already shows some interesting results:

- given the video of the action the confidence 6 of the subject on their answers were quite high showing always better confidence on videos with foley and real sounds then on synthesised sounds.

- this trend is even more evident looking in figures n. 7

and 8 where both the expressiveness and the realism of the action are rated higher for the first two kinds of sounds.

- the realism of the videos on walking on sand and on grass where rated lower than the others (gravel, concrete and wood).
- the expressiveness of the video with gravel sounds as feedback is the highest

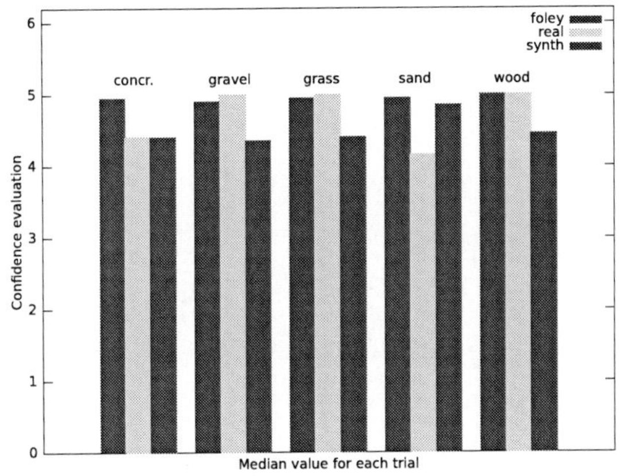

Figure 6. Median values of the confidence ratings for each trial

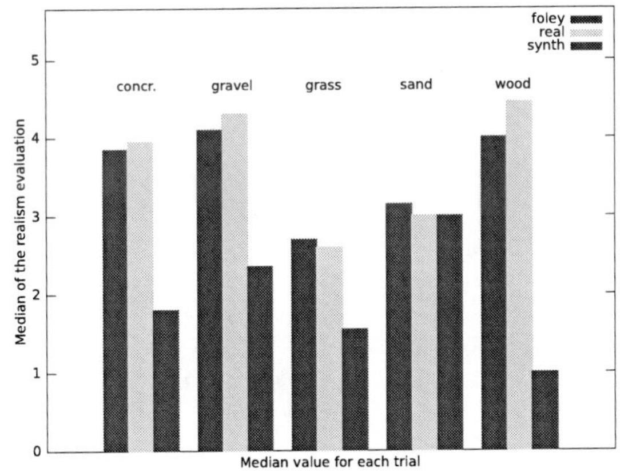

Figure 7. Median values of the realism ratings for each trial

4. DISCUSSION

The Wilcoxon–Mann–Whitney test was performed to test the null hypothesis that data of two trials are samples from continuous distributions with equal medians, against the alternative that they are not. For each material (concrete, gravel, grass, sand, wood) the p value has been computed between the 3 possible combination of the sound feedback: foley and real, foley and synthetic, real and synthetic. For the confidence rate it was always possible to confirm the null hypothesis, giving the analysis always high p values, while the analysis was slightly more interesting for the evaluation of the action realism and expressiveness. It was

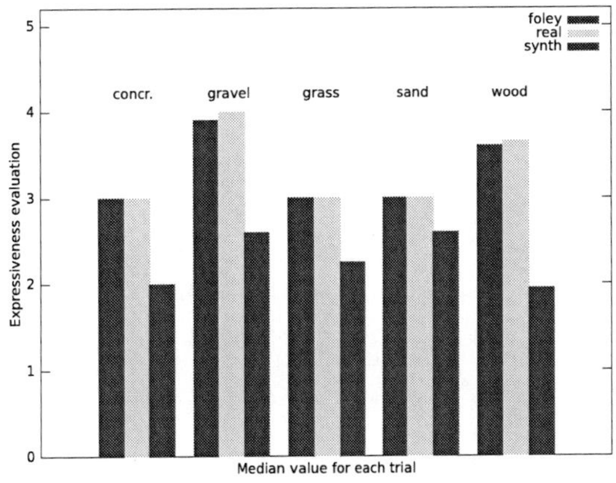

Figure 8. Median values of the expressiveness ratings for each trial

always possible to reject the null hypothesis comparing real or foley sounds with the synthetic ones, showing that even with the video, subjects could recognise the poor audio feedback, while subjects could not really distinguish between real and foley sounds. This was true both for the actions that got quite high median values and for the actions that got bad evaluation in terms of the median value (in particular sand and grass). It is interesting to notice that walking on gravel and walking on wood were the two actions with the higher expressiveness median value: the same behaviour can be noticed in the evaluation of the realism of the scene, showing a correlation between the two aspects.

5. CONCLUSIONS

This work is a preliminary study on foley walking sounds. The analysis of the data shows that recognizing the walking action by just listening to the sounds is a really difficult task. Very few subjects could recognise both the action and the material upon which the action was performed, without any significant difference between real and foley sounds. The same result was achieved in the audio-video test: in this case the action was recognised for all trials, but realism and expressiveness of the action were dramatically dependent on the sound feedback used and on the material used for the walking surface. Subjects could recognise the synthetic sounds and expressed their preferences for real/foley sounds; walking on sand and walking on grass were the two lowest rated actions as they were the hardest to recognize. This aspect is particularly interesting because these two actions were performed in some awkward way as foley, using other materials-gestures to mimic the sound of a walking gesture. That was the way they are usually performed when foleys of such sounds are required. So, the original idea was that for some reason these sounds should be more expressive, since that is the way these foleys are usually performed. But this was not the case. Further investigation should be carried out in order to analyze why some materials-gestures work better than others and what kind of information about the walker or the walking gesture can be conveyed using the different surfaces.

6. REFERENCES

[1] A. V. Theme, *The Foley Grail: The Art of Performing Sound for Film, Games, and Animation.* Elsevier, 2009.

[2] D. L. Yewdall, "Foley: the art of footsteps, props, and cloth movement," in *Practical Art of Motion Picture Sound.* Focal Press, Elsevier, 2003, pp. 294–328.

[3] S. Trento and A. de Götzen, "Foley sounds vs. real sounds," in *Proceedings of the Sound and Music Computing Conference - Padova 2011.* Padova, Italy: Padova University Press, 2011.

[4] T. L. Bonebright, "Were those coconuts or horse hoofs? visual context effects on identification and veracity of everyday sounds," in *Proceedings of the International Conference on Auditory Displays*, 2012.

[5] M. L. Heller and L. Wolf, "When sound effects are better than the real thing," *Journal of the Acoustical Society of America*, no. 111, p. 2339, 2002.

[6] J. A. Ballas, "Common factors in the identification of an assortment of brief everyday sounds," *Journal of experimental psychology: human perception and performance*, vol. 19, no. 2, pp. 250–267, 1993. [Online]. Available: http://dx.doi.org/

[7] E. Murphy, M. Lagrange, G. Scavone, P. Depalle, and C. Guastavino, "Perceptual evaluation of a real-time synthesis technique for rolling sounds," in *Proceedings of 5th International Conference on Encative Interfaces*, Pisa, Italy, 2008.

[8] C. Guastavino, "Categorization of environmental sounds," *Canadian Journal of Experimental Psychology*, vol. 61, pp. 54–63, 2007.

[9] M. Marcell, D. Borella, M. Green, E. Kerr, and S. Rogers, "Confrontation naming of environmental sounds," *Journal of clinical and experimental neuropsychology*, vol. 22, pp. 830–864, 2000.

[10] O. Houix, G. Lemaitre, N. Misdariis, P. Susini, and I. Urdapilleta, "A lexical analysis of environmental sound categories." *Journal of Experimental Psychology Applied*, vol. 18, no. 1, pp. 52–80, 2012.

[11] G. Lemaitre, O. Houix, N. Misdariis, and P. Susini, "Listener expertise and sound identification influence the categorization of environmental sounds." *Journal of experimental psychology. Applied*, vol. 16, no. 1, pp. 16–32, 03 2010. [Online]. Available: http://europepmc.org/abstract/MED/20350041

[12] Y. Visell, F. Fontana, B. Giordano, R. Nordahl, S. Serafin, and R. Bresin, "Sound design and perception in walking interactions," *International Journal of Human-Computer Studies*, vol. 67, no. 11, pp. 947–959, 2009.

[13] A. Lécuyer, M. Marchal, A. Hamelin, D. Wolinski, F. Fontana, M. Civolani, S. Papetti, and S. Serafin, "Shoes–Your–Style: Changing sound of footsteps to create new walking experiences," in *Workshop on Sound and Music Computing for Human-Computer Interaction (CHItaly)*, Alghero, Italy, 2011.

[14] L. Peltola, C. Erkut, P. Cook, and V. Valimaki, "Synthesis of hand clapping sounds," *IEEE Transactions on Audio, Speech, and Language Processing*, vol. 15, no. 3, pp. 1021–1029, 2007.

Urb: urban sound analysis and storage project

José Alberto Gomes
j@jasg.net

Diogo Tudela
contact@diogotudela.com

Research Center for Science and Technology of the Arts (CITAR)
Portuguese Catholic University - School of the Arts
Rua Diogo Botelho 1327, 4169-005 Porto, Portugal

ABSTRACT

This paper introduces Urb, a system for automated analysis and storing of an urban soundscape. Urb complements traditional sound maps, allowing the direct access of its features at any arbitrary moment since the system's boot, thus facilitating the study of the soundscape's evolution and the differences between specific timeframes, and facilitating artistic approaches to such data. In this paper, we will describe the creative and technical aspects considered during its early development, whilst addressing its three fundamental parts: the hardware and software for capturing and transmitting audio recordings, the software for analyzing the soundscape and the management of the database.

Keywords: Sound Scape, sound analysis, Networked Music, Timeline; Database.

1. INTRODUCTION

The youth has been completely conquered by this electronic world that is acoustic, intuitive, "holistic", this is, global and total, a new world that put in the shelve the old scientific world with its quantities, its immensities, our "First World" super-industrialized. The youth prefers the Third World because he is still acoustic and oral, and invites to total immersion (…)"[1]. According to McLuhan's critical thought, the 60's and 70's electronic revolution marked the return of the ear as a sovereign organ for cultural human perception. This socio-cultural transformation underlined the Western man's necessity of constant absorption. It is within this frame that the soundscape studies become more systematic and its presence as an artistic tool more persistent. This was not a new subject, but rather a new one that found fresh stable grounds within the constant multidirectional cultural and ecologic awareness that dictates the Electronic Era.

The notion of soundscape is increasingly relevant not only in contemporary culture and acoustic ecology, but also in many other fields, such as artistic productions.

The soundscape concept and movement were presented to us and based on Schafer's considerations of environment studies in the early 70's [2]. According to Iges, Murray Schafer's utopia, with some similarities of Pierre Schaeffer's analyses about the sound, it would be to impose some kind of order in the sound environment with the aim of achieving a "sound ecology"[3].

With the development of studies and sound collections, near the turn of the century, is made aware that the soundscape depends on the listeners' understanding and interpretation of a soundscape[4]. With sound files so freely available, like freesound project[1], and portable memory-based recorders so inexpensive, sound maps have become increasingly common on the Internet. Usually the sound maps are based on a Google-style map that is used to situate the geographic origin of the recordings, e.g. World Listening Project[2]. *However, lacking any coherent temporal perspective, and usually lacking any interpretative analysis, the listener is left trying to imagine what has been recorded and what significance it has.*[5]. An interesting variant of this approach is a live microphone in a fixed location that is constantly streaming audio like the Locustream Sound Map developed[3] [6].

Given the project relevance, in partnership with artists and research center interested in networked music and sonic performance, is developed as one of the important parts in the recent created NMSAT (Networked Music & Soundart Timeline) to support important collaborations in this area as Eu-phonic (with SARC Belfast, CRiSAP LCC University of the Arts London, CultureLab University of Newcastle, LORNA Reykjavik, KIBLA Malibor, Le Hangar Barcelona, STEIM Amsterdam), Audio Ambiances (LAMES CNRS Universite′ de Provence, CRESSON CNRS E′ cole d'Architecture de Grenoble, ENST/Telecom Paristech/Eurocom Sophia-Antipolis/EHESS), TransatLab puf— Franco-American academic partnership (School of the Art Institute of Chicago SAIC), Locustream (in collaboration with communities of field recordists and phonographers such as WLP—World Listening Project)[7].

To support the project, they developed an autonomous «LocustreamBox» - a small computer dedicated to task of streaming audio and configured to connect automatically to their server and related systems such as online interfaces or setups for installations[8].

The Locustream sound map has a very interesting approach to the soundscape but still has the time problem. It is very hard to have a good description if you cannot compare with different moments of the past. So,

---

[1] www.freesound.org

[2] www.worldlisteningproject.org

[3] http://locusonus.org/soundmap/034/)by de Locus Sonus project

combining the problem of temporal coherence presented by most of the Sound Maps with conceptual and physical path shown by Locus Sonus, we started to develop a plan to work a complementary access to a sound map that is discrete in time.

2. PROPOSAL

Urb claim to be a complement to the approach of the sound environment study, presenting a proposal for a system based on available and cheap hardware and open source software. Thus, it may be a tool with a very large ramp of development and flexibility to be used, not only by environmentalists and urban planners, but also by artists with creative intentions.

The implementation of the project is divided into 3 phases:

1st: design, prototyping and development of a listening point and database;

2nd: Create 4 listening points in the city of Porto; develop tools to access the database; invite artists from different areas to develop work with the data in real time and non real-time.

3rd: Make the site, database and the software public; make integration with Project Locustream Sound map; present approaches to data processing systems for artistic purposes; encourage spontaneous initiative for the multiplication of listening points.

3. HARDWARE

3.1 Raspberry Pi

The first approach to the microcomputer choice was analyzing the Locustream Box. They used a PC Engines 500 MHz AMD Geode LX800 using Gentoo Linux distribution[9].

This hardware was sufficient for what we need. The problem is that it would be needed to order the different parts and put them together, plus the total cost is around 150€. For us this seemed to be a major problem to a project that wants to grow spontaneously under the individual motivation. The Raspberry Pi is a credit-card-sized single-board computer developed in the UK by the Raspberry Pi Foundation with the intention of promoting the teaching of basic computer science in schools. It has an ARM1176JZF-S 700 MHz processor VideoCore IV GPU, and 512 megabytes of RAM. It does not include a built-in hard disk or solid-state drive, but uses an SD card for booting and long-term storage.[10]

The Raspberry Pi presents a solution for most of our needs. It is quite cheap, it is already built, and it has a very enthusiastic community working to develop the hardware and system. Most of them, around the Pure Data[4] on Rasperry, a fundamental tool for our project.

3.2 USB ADC

The Raspberry PI does not have an analogic input, so it is necessary a USB sound card. Not all the USB Analog to Digital Converters work with the Raspberry Pi and it's important to slow down the speed device to 1.1 adding

```
$>> dwc_otg.speed=1
```

to the string in the file /boot/cmdline.txt [11].

As we are only using the computer as a listening point, we change the USB ADC to default changing the /etc/modprobe.d/alsa-base.conf file replacing the

```
$>> options snd-usb-audio index=-2
```

string to

```
$>> options snd_bcm2835=-2
```

and creating a /.libao in the home directory with

```
$>> driver=alsa
$>> dev=default
```

strings.

3.3 Electret Microphone

This is a critical point, because it is very complicated to found a microphone that resists to the weather conditions and with an enough small size to put in places like windows or breathers and not expensive enough to be in a public place. We decide to use the Peter Sinclair suggestion for the Locus Sonus Project with a DIY microphone, Figure1, that only needs 5v power (perfect for the USB connections) using a electret microphone.[12]

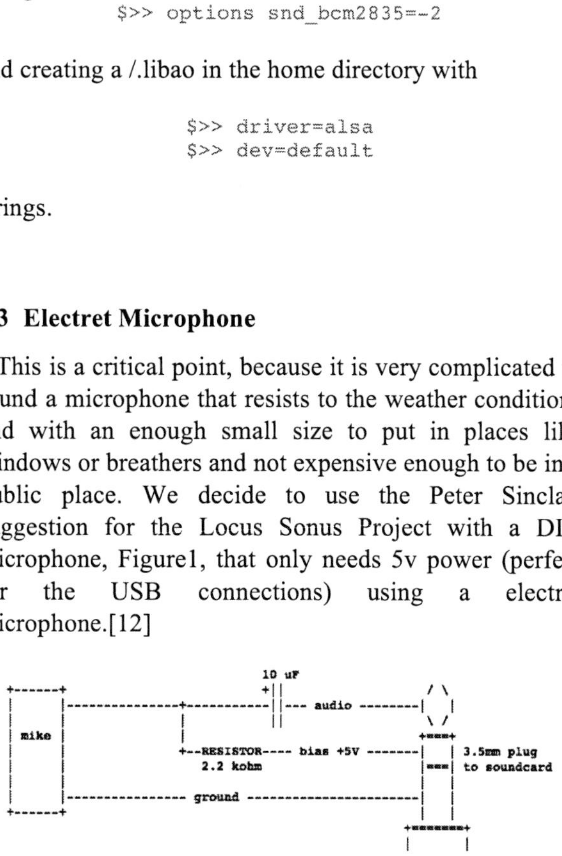

Figure 1. The Locus Mic DIY circuit.

4. SOFTWARE ARCHITECTURE DESCRIPTION

4.1 Sending and Storing Data

When sending and storing data on-line, Urb relies on Python and MySQL to preform the tasks. The Python module works as an outside agent, responsible for building a query out of a float package put together by Pure Data, and sending it to a MySQL database. This second component introduces a concurrent programming paradigm[5] into Urb's software architecture, as Python

4 http://puredata.info/

5 *"A concurrent application will have two or more threads in progress at some time. This can mean that the application has two threads that are being swapped in and out by the operating system on a single core*

and Pd are seemingly working simultaneously through unidirectional message passing communication, via [shell] object. The presence of a second programming language on the client side of the system is deeply connected to the aesthetical and functional aspirations of the project. While is advisable to keep a clean architecture and, therefore, avoid the presence of additional languages, the presented solutions for a Pd based project led to the decision of using a second language as a mean of keeping the project intentions intact facing technical distortion.

As a programming environment focused on media and artistic production, Pure Data relies on community developed externals and libraries in order to preform SQL connections. At the moment, communication between Pd and SQLite or PostgreSQL databases are ensured by some externals[6], which is still a far from optimal set of solutions when, like in Urb, as we will explain, using MySQL as a relational database management system is a binding need.

Although PostgreSQL presents itself as the most advanced open-source database system available[7], its usage implies the necessity of a dedicated server[8]; a service that exceeds the dimensions of an embryonic project like Urb. On the other hand, SQLite lacks the user and permissions management needed[9] to build a much-needed community around this project. As was underlined before, Urb's aesthetical agenda comprises easy access to the database in order to progressively build a clear picture of the city's soundscape and promote a consistent usage of that material within the composition scope. Therefore, between PostgreSQL's over complexity and SQLite's deficiency on social tools, MySQL turns out to be the fittest solution to Urb's data storage necessities, being a system that guarantees the possibility of social management with a simple shared server hosting service. Also, MySQL is a quite popular database system, which in the long term implies a much more rapid and responsive community, and a rather extensive collection of web articles and forum threads, both positive attributes for a development tool.

With MySQL laid down as a vital option for the project, Pure Data's insufficiencies towards this database system needed to be overthrown. Without any available externals and with C's development time being drawback to the challenge of writing some new ones, the usage of additional languages became a viable hypothesis. Within Max, connecting to a MySQL database is a process that needs the support of Java. Queries are sent through Nick Rothwell's MySQL Java class[10] loaded into the [mxj] object; an approach easily ported to Pd through its [pdj] object, whose API is based on the [mxj] implementation[11], making classes transferable between the two environments. So within Max, Java works as an interpreted language just like his host, using Java Virtual Machine as an interpreter for the loaded code[12]. Every time a message passes through the [pdj] inlet an access to the JVM is taking place, which can turn out to be minor step back in terms of performance, even though in this specific case, the message being passed is a list containing all the needed values.

In addition, and most importantly, by using these objects, one is importing into the patch the connection time needed for the code to access the on-line database with its query. So, this means that Pd would be responsible for handling both analysis and connection, being the second an obstacle to the first. Although this freezing time represents no significant disadvantage for a patch with a sampling rate of 5'', the same cannot be said to a patch with a dynamic sampling rate, responsive to significant audio events captured at the input.

With C representing an unnecessary amount of time in development and Java a blockage within the patch, Python revealed himself as a reasonable solution. Python is a high-level easy to learn multi-purpose language that is historically known for its harmonious cooperation with Linux and MySQL, a fact that in part led to the formation of the LAMP software bundle[13]. One can argue that Java's inclusion in the system through the [pdj] object is not mandatory. OSC could easily serve the purpose without damaging the performance of the patch. However, when developing for Raspberry Pi, not only Python is officially the primary programming language

processor. These threads will be "in progress"—each in the midst of its execution—at the same time." [21]

[6] Listed on Pd's official website are two different collections of externals whose purpose is to provide connection to a variety of relational databases. SQL library has no external to connect to a MySQL database and psql is reserved to PostgreSQL [22]

[7] *"PostgreSQL is the hammer of the database world (...) It has plug-ins for natural-language parsing, multidimensional indexing, geographic queries, custom datatypes, and much more. It has sophisticated transaction handling, has built-in stored procedures for a dozen languages, and runs on a variety of platforms."* [23]

[8] Right now, Urb is being hosted at a Hostgator's shared server. According to Hostgator's services PostgreSQL is only available for Dedicated and VPS servers upon request.
https://support.hostgator.com/articles/specialized-help/postgresql

[9] *"An SQLite database has no authentication or authorization data. Instead, SQLite depends on file system permissions to control access to the raw database file. This essentially limits access to one of three states: complete read/write access, read- only access, or no access at all. Write access is absolute, and allows both data modification and the ability to alter the structure of the database itself."* [24]

[10] net.loadbang.sql.mxj.MySQL
http://www.maxobjects.com/?v=objects&id_objet=3571&PHPSESSID=09ef5816e5d955699b350dedd401d647

[11] *"PDJ enables you to write java code to interact with pure-data objects. The API is totally based on Cycling74 Max/MSP 'mxj' object implementation. This will enable java mxj objects to run on pure-data with pdj."* [25]

[12] *"The class files that live in the classes folder are what are known as byte code files. Unlike C externals, which are compiled into platform-specific machine code, Java byte code can be executed on any system that will run the JVM (Java Virtual Machine)."* Max6/java-doc/tutorial

[13] *"MySQL is the dominant open source database management system: it is being used increasingly to build very significant applications based on the LAMP (Linux-Apache-MySQL-PHP/Perl/Python)(...)"* [26]

for the hardware[14], but also, interpreter and packages are available by default on both Debian and Gentoo distributions[13]. The readiness of Python when compared to the strict hardware and software specifications to make Java to compile builds a scenario where Python outstands as a much more robust and pragmatic solution than Java. [14]

Python's easy and flexible syntax allied to a stable MySQL library, MySQLdb, result on a fast implementation of a straight-forward yet effective script to send queries to a MySQL database that is easily accessible through the shell thanks to the language's script mode. Assuming that Urb's python script is in the /home/pi directory, the following command sends the appended list of 12 floats, one for each audio feature, to the MySQL database.

```
$>> python home/pi/urbsql.py   0 0 0 0 0 0 0 0
0 0 0 0 0
```

When run from Pd, the command can be constructed with a combination of [pack], [list] and [prepend] objects resulting on a string that is ready to be passed through the [shell] object, figure2.

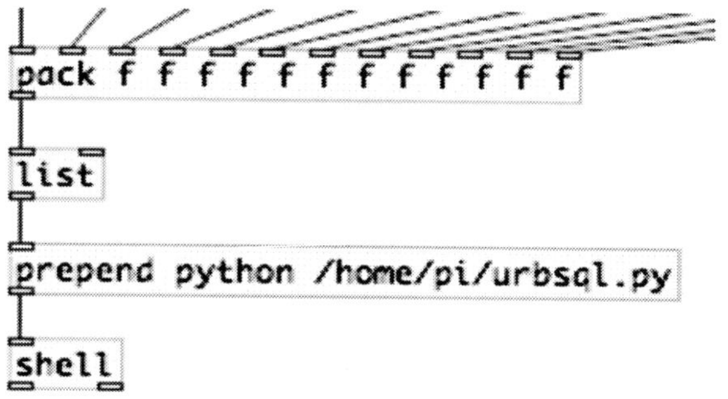

Figure2. Construction of the shell command on a Pd patch.

4.2 The Database

At the moment, since Urb is still on a prototype phase, the amount of data being produced and stored is minimal and as so, database management is yet to become a challenge. It is well established for now that each location, each sound recollection point will have its own table on the database, being that each table will take the name of its actual urban location, figure3.

The structure of each table is rather simple. Thirteen columns, one for each audio feature plus a first row that is using Unix Timestamp as a mean of identification and time localization of the event described in the row. The continuous nature of the timestamp provides not only a stable sequence to order entries but also enclosures meaningful information in itself by tagging the exact moment of the event and allowing further readings by crossing data from other sources. For the exception of the first column that takes integers with a display width of 11, all the other columns store varchar data width a display width of 255.

#	Coluna	Tipo	Agrupamento (Collation)	Atributos	Nulo	Omissão	Extra
1	id	int(11)			Não	None	AUTO_INCREMENT
2	pitch	varchar(255)	utf8_unicode_ci		Não	None	
3	amp	varchar(255)	utf8_unicode_ci		Não	None	
4	brightness	varchar(255)	utf8_unicode_ci		Não	None	
5	centroid	varchar(255)	utf8_unicode_ci		Não	None	
6	flatness	varchar(255)	utf8_unicode_ci		Não	None	
7	flux	varchar(255)	utf8_unicode_ci		Não	None	
8	kurtosis	varchar(255)	utf8_unicode_ci		Não	None	
9	rolloff	varchar(255)	utf8_unicode_ci		Não	None	
10	skewness	varchar(255)	utf8_unicode_ci		Não	None	
11	spread	varchar(255)	utf8_unicode_ci		Não	None	
12	zerocrossing	varchar(255)	utf8_unicode_ci		Não	None	
13	irregularity	varchar(255)	utf8_unicode_ci		Não	None	

Figure3. Structure of a generic Urb MySQL table

Along side with Urb's database, a series of data visualization and retrieval tools are being designed in order to keep the dialogue sustainable even for the non-technical user. It is of the most importance that Urb's data remains relevant and useable for the musician, composer or citizen without computational expertise, furthermore, all records are intended to be cleared of any composition methodology. The handling of Urb's data does not mean to be programmatically defined in any way.

Already implemented are two different PHP scripts that play a small part on what is expected to be a stable and refined project of data visualization and retrieval. For now, these two scripts are responsible for the following outputs:

— Displaying the data of a specific table as an HTML table. Regarded as a production tool, this allows monitoring the data flux without needing to log in to the host control panel.

— Export the data of a specific table as a .csv file. Due to safety constraints, the direct accesses to the contents of a MySQL database are often not possible. This is the case with Javascript and other JS based languages and frameworks like ProcessingJS. The way to avoid this technical predicament is to build a server side script that queries the database and exports the result as text file. Urb's actual script exports all the data on a database; each call o to the PHP script downloads the .csv file with the most recent set of data, making it accessible through Javascript.

Multiple users and restrictions strategies are yet to be defined and such decisions will be taken according to what the project itself dictates as more appropriate. Software architectural foundations have been set in a way that the gathering and distributing functions of the system work fluently and in a robust way, keeping options open as how exactly accesses will be managed in the future. For now, the main intention is to keep Urb as an inviting platform for the users of the so-called creative programming frameworks such as Max/MSP, Pure Data, Processing, ProcessingJS, openFrameworks, Cinder, Nodebox, Shoebot, among others.[15] With the already implemented code, Urb has reached a maturity state that guarantees a fast and thorough development and

---

[14] *"Does it have an official programming language? By default, we will be supporting Python as the educational language. Any language which will compile for ARMv6 can be used with the Raspberry Pi, though; so you are not limited to using Python."* [10]

evolution of the project into a ready-to-use tool and sharp investigation document.

5. SOUND ANALYSIS AND INFORMATION FOR THE DATA BASE

All the sound analysis is made on the Pure Data patch.

The first part of the patch is about the audio input. It is for adjusting the level, figure 4, and to equalize the sound in case that you have some problems with noise, as from a vent or electricity, figure 5.

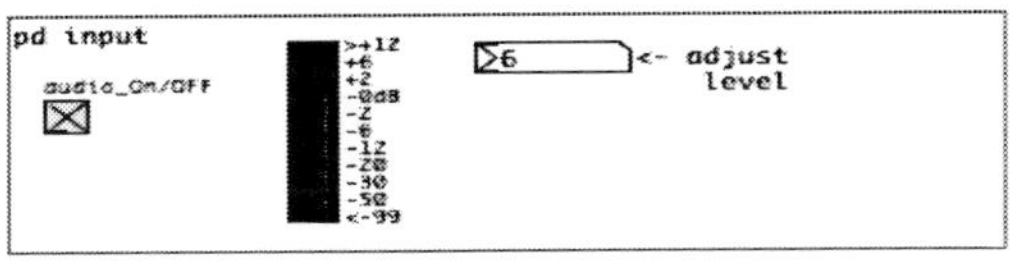

Figure 4. pd input

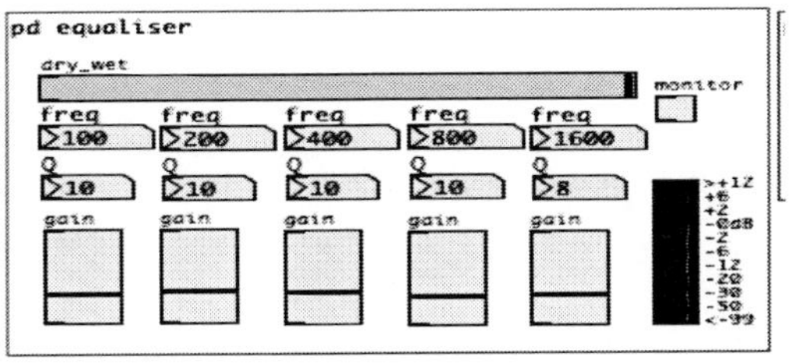

Figure 5. pd equalizer

The second part is where the analysis happens. The patch analyzes 12 different elements or descriptors of the sound. The first two are *Pitch* and *Amplitude.*

Pitch: using the native Pd-extemded object *sigmund~*.

Sigmund~ analyzes an incoming sound into sinusoidal components, which may be reported individually or combined to form a pitch estimate.[15]

Amplitude: using another native object *avg~* that computes the mean amplitude of its input signal since it last received a bang. The mean amplitude is the sum of the absolute values of the input divided by the number of samples received.[16]

The other 10 features are from the *timbreID*[17].

timbreID is a Pd external collection developed by William Brent. *It is composed of a group of objects for extracting timbral features, and a classification object that manages the resulting database of information. The objects are designed to be easy to use and adaptable for a number of purposes.*[16]

It implements a collection of low-level spectral audio descriptors, such as:

Centroid is defined as the center of gravity of the magnitude spectrum,

Kurtosis gives a measure of the flatness of a distribution around its mean value,

Flatness is the ratio of the geometric mean of magnitude spectrum to the arithmetic mean of magnitude spectrum. A very noisy spectrum without clear shape should have a high flatness value,

Flux is defined as the squared difference between the normalized magnitudes of successive spectral distributions,

Irregularity is the comparison of how much each frequency bin compares to its immediate neighbors. A jagged spectrum, irregularity will be high, and for smooth contoured spectra, it will be low,

Mfcc represents the shape of the spectrum with few coeficients,

Roll-off is a measure of spectral shape, which is used to distinguish between voiced and unvoiced speech.

Skewness is a measure of the asymmetry of a distribution around its mean value,

Spread is the spread of the spectrum around mean value,

Zero-crossing rate is the number of times the signal cross the zero axe. [16][17][18]

The reasons that we are using are *timberID* are: the Open Source nature, is very robust and stable, and was already tested and validated in other projects like earGram[19].

Such complete timbral features increase the project ability to respond to future demands or needs leaving the project scope flexible to ecological or artistic exploration and investigation.

Every five minutes the patch calculates the main value of each feature of that time and sends that value for the database, figure 6. During our tests we realize that the five minutes window is a sustainable amount of time to provide a clear "image" of the urban soundscape in a larger scale of time. It is a manageable number of entries to the database and doable to its storage in a long-term situation. It is around 553MB for a century of information for each listening point.

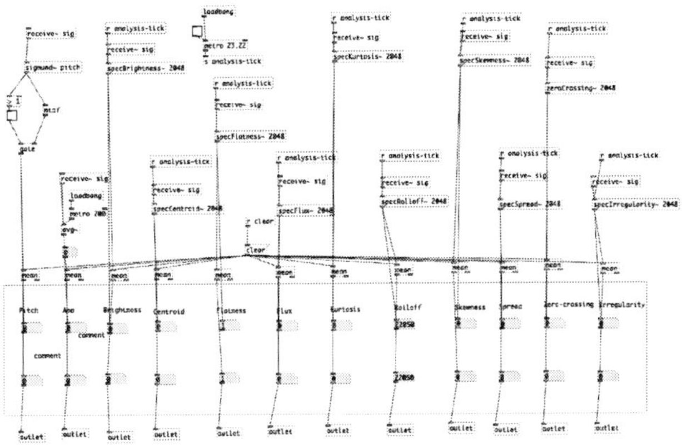

Figure 6. pd descriptors

As a future work we are studying a possible interest in developing an intelligent window that changes its duration, according the sound characteristics.

This descriptors data is a very powerful information. In the last years, the research about sound classification and genre identification is increasing exponentially. With the classification and similarity tools, Urb, in very near

[15] sigmund~ object's help patch
[16] avg~ object's help patch
[17] http://williambrent.conflations.com/pages/research.html.

future, can give detail information about every 5 minutes of a soundscape, not only quantitative information but also especially qualitative information. Saying if the sound is more industrial or natural, speech or non-speech, noisy or pitched, and compare with other moments or with other soundscapes.

This is not only an ecological and social tool but also an artistic tool. The classification tools are already used in concatenative sound synthesis[19][16][20] for example, and with Urb this process can be controlled by a sound scape. Eco-Structuralism[18] already uses sound and ecological structures to apply in music creation, and with Urb you have a repository of eco structures from soundscapes that you can use to music or visual creation.

The final patch part is the connection to the database previously described in section 4.

6. FUTURE WORK AND PERSPECTIVES

The first tests to assess the resistance of the hardware have shown a very positive outlook about the data sent to the database. With about 24 hours of analysis, and even with a brief look, it was easy to draw some conclusions, as the peak times of loudness (8:13 – 8:23) or silence (4:53 – 5:03) during that day,

```
Year month day hour min amp
2012 12    13  4    53  0.228982;
2012 12    13  4    58  1.114694;
2012 12    13  5    3   3.069494;
(…)
2012 12    13  8    13  48.119511;
2012 12    13  8    18  50.113361;
2012 12    13  8    23  46.514568;
```

or that the rain around 20:00 increases spectrum's frequency center and size.

```
Year month day hour min centroid spread
2012 12    12  20   18  1432     2.104941;
2012 12    12  20   23  1487     2.042615;
2012 12    12  20   28  1398     2.102901;
(…)
2012 12    13  4    43  1218     1.732905;
2012 12    13  4    48  1167     1.8436;
```

With the system working it will be possible to develop and link to tools that use the maximum capacity in having such detailed descriptors of sound. And thus, we have access to accurate sound characteristics of a particular location, not only during a certain time window, but also since the Urb's boot.

It will be possible to access to the database, not only through a temporal index, but also through some sound characteristics. For example, moments that the sound exceeded certain intensity, number of times that the sound had a more clear pitch, situations mainly constituted by the sound of voices, …

Using the data will serve to feed an adaptable viewer where you can graphically assess the soundscape evolution.

Anyway, the project is very focused on developing research and finding ways on how this data can be used in a creative and artistic process and we will spend great part of our efforts in this area of the investigation. Some experiments in this field are already ongoing and we are simultaneously interact with artistic communities that work with sonorization, visualization and composition from data to systematize approaches to this material and create or adapt tools to facilitate this process. Although the results are promising, it is still too early to propose systems and draw conclusions.

The next steps will be the multiplication of listening points and dissemination of the project to get, as much as possible, to interested communities in order to study and understand the specific needs and approaches.

7. REFERENCES

[1] P. Babin and M. McLuhan, *Autre homme, autre chrétien à l'âge électronique*. Chalet, 1978, p. 191.

[2] R. M. Schafer, *The Soundscape*, vol. 26, no. 3. Destiny Books, 1977.

[3] J. Iges, "Soundscapes: A historical approach," *Anais do VII Simpósio de Música Eletroacústica–En Red*, 1999.

[4] B. Truax, "Handbook for Acoustic Ecology," *sfuca*. Vancouver: Cambridge Street Publishing, CSR-CDR 9901., 1999.

[5] B. Truax, "Sound, Listening and Place: The aesthetic dilemma," *Organised Sound*, vol. 17, no. 3, 2012.

[6] P. Sinclair, "Locus Sonus," *Autumn Leaves–Sound and the Environment in Artistic ...*, 2007.

[7] J. Joy and P. Sinclair, "Networked Music & Soundart Timeline (NMSAT): A Panoramic View of Practices and Techniques Related to Sound Transmission and Distance Listening," *Contemporary Music Review*, vol. 28, no. 4–5, pp. 351–361, Aug. 2009.

[8] J. Joy, "Networked sonic spaces," pp. 2–4, 2008.

[9] "http://locusonus.org - Locus Sonus WiKiLab - Locustream Streambox." [Online]. Available: http://nujus.net/~locusonus/wikils/?page=Locustream Streambox. [Accessed: 26-Mar-2013].

[10] "FAQs | Raspberry Pi." [Online]. Available: http://www.raspberrypi.org/faqs. [Accessed: 26-Mar-2013].

[11] "FrontPage — PD Community Site." [Online]. Available: http://puredata.info/docs/raspberry-pi. [Accessed: 26-Mar-2013].

[12] "http://locusonus.org/ -Locustream LocusMic." [Online]. Available: http://locusonus.org/w/index.php?page=Locustream+LocusMic. [Accessed: 26-Mar-2013].

[13] N. Gift and J. Jones, *Python for Unix and Linux System Administration*. O'Reilly Media, 2008.

[14] A. B. Downey, *Think Python*. O'Reilly Media, 2012.

[15] B. Fry, *Visualizing Data: Exploring and Explaining Data with the Processing Environment*. O'Reilly Media, 2008.

[18] *Eco-structuralism is a new approach to music composition designed to maintain the characteristics and context of a sound whilst not necessarily using the original recording data directly.* [27]

[16] W. Brent, "A timbre analysis and classification toolkit for pure data."

[17] X. Zhang and Z. Ras, "Analysis of sound features for music timbre recognition," ... *and Ubiquitous Engineering, 2007. MUE'07 ...*, 2007.

[18] G. Peeters, "A large set of audio features for sound description (similarity and classification) in the CUIDADO project," *CUIDADO IST Project Report*, vol. 54, no. version 1.0, pp. 1–25, 2004.

[19] G. Bernardes, C. Guedes, and B. Pennycook, "EarGram: an Application for Interactive Exploration of Large Databases of Audio Snippets for Creative Purposes," *cmmr2012.eecs.qmul.ac.uk*, no. June, pp. 19–22, 2012.

[20] D. Schwarz, "Concatenative sound synthesis: The early years," *Journal of New Music Research*, vol. 35, no. 1, pp. 3–22, 2006.

[21] C. Breshears, *The Art of Concurrency: A Thread Monkey's Guide to Writing Parallel Applications*. O'Reilly Media, 2009.

[22] "psql — PD Community Site." [Online]. Available: http://puredata.info/downloads/psql/?searchterm=sql. [Accessed: 02-Apr-2013].

[23] E. Redmond and J. R. Wilson, *Seven Databases in Seven Weeks: A Guide to Modern Databases and the NoSQL Movement*. Pragmatic Bookshelf, 2012.

[24] J. A. Kreibich, *Using SQLite*. O'Reilly Media, 2010.

[25] "pdj — PD Community Site." [Online]. Available: http://puredata.info/downloads/pdj. [Accessed: 02-Apr-2013].

[26] G. Harrison and S. Feuerstein, *MySQL Stored Procedure Programming*. O'Reilly Media, 2009.

[27] T. Opie and A. R. Brown, "An Introduction to Eco- Structuralism," in *Proceedings International Computer Music Conference, pages pp. 9-12, New Orleans, USA.*, 2006, pp. 9–12.

Non-Realtime Sonification of Motiongrams

Alexander Refsum Jensenius
University of Oslo, Department of Musicology, fourMs lab
a.r.jensenius@imv.uio.no

ABSTRACT

The paper presents a non-realtime implementation of the sonomotiongram method, a method for the sonification of motiongrams. Motiongrams are spatiotemporal displays of motion from video recordings, based on frame-differencing and reduction of the original video recording. The sonomotiongram implementation presented in this paper is based on turning these visual displays of motion into sound using FFT filtering of noise sources. The paper presents the application ImageSonifyer, accompanied by video examples showing the possibilities of the sonomotiongram method for both analytic and creative applications.

1. INTRODUCTION

Motiongrams were originally developed for analysing the motion of dancers and musicians, with the aim of visualising spatial motion features over time [1]. Due to the visual similarity of motiongrams to spectrograms, motiongrams have also been used as the basis for sonification, through a method I call *sonomotiongram* [2]. The first implementation of the sonomotiongram method was focused on creating *realtime* sonifications of the motiongrams, and the sonification was based on an interpolated oscillator bank. Realtime here means that it is possible to listen to the sonification while watching the original video, hence listening to the sound of motion as it unfolds.

A realtime implementation is useful for realtime applications, such as in sonic feedback or in creative applications. It is less useful, however, for applications in which long video recordings need to be analysed. For such material it would be better to use the high temporal capacity of our auditory system to listen through long video recordings at a much higher speed than the video could be watched.

This paper presents a non-realtime implementation of the sonomotiongram method, based on FFT filtering of a noise source. This implementation allows for (much-)faster-than-realtime sonification of the input motiongrams. The paper starts with an overview of the motiongram and sonomotiongram methods, before the non-realtime implementation of the sonomotiongram method is shown. Finally, some examples of how the method can be used for analytical and creative applications are presented and discussed.

2. BACKGROUND

2.1 Motiongrams

A motiongram is a visual display of (human) motion, created by frame differencing and averaging a video file, as illustrated in Figure 1. This makes it possible to see the temporal unfolding of motion features on the X axis, and the vertical location of the motion on the Y axis. Motiongrams therefore give a holistic representation of the spatiotemporal unfolding of motion from a video recording, albeit only in one spatial dimension. This is because information about the spatial distribution of motion in the plane that is averaged over is represented by only one pixel for each row (see [1] for details). Thus a horizontal motiongram visualises vertical motion, while a vertical motiongram visualises horizontal motion.

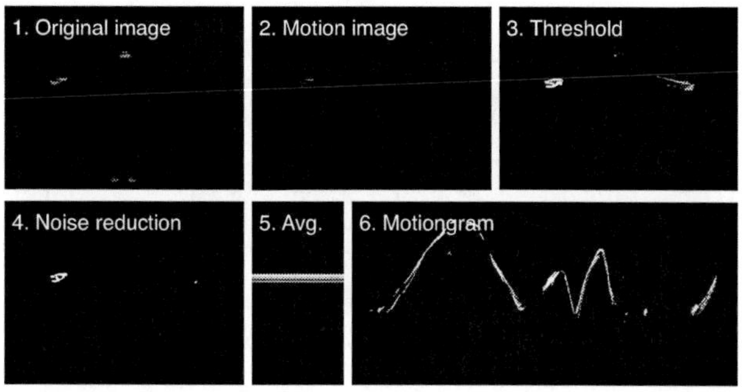

Figure 1. The steps involved in creating a motiongram: (1) original video image, (2) frame differencing, (3) thresholding, (4) noise reduction, (5) averaging over each row, (6) drawing the average matrices over time.

2.2 Sonomotiongrams

The sonomotiongram method is based on what could be called an "inverse FFT" process. The idea here is to treat a motiongram as if it were a spectrogram, with frequency information on the Y axis and time on the X axis, as illustrated in Figure 2. In the first implementation of the method, this was accomplished using an interpolated oscillator bank [2]. The implementation presented in this paper is based on doing FFT filtering of a noise source based on the matrix values of the motiongram. Both implementations result in a direct sonification of the image, in which lower sound frequencies are based on pixel values in the lower part of the image, and vice versa.

Even though they may appear to be visually similar, a motiongram is, in fact, very different from a spectrogram.

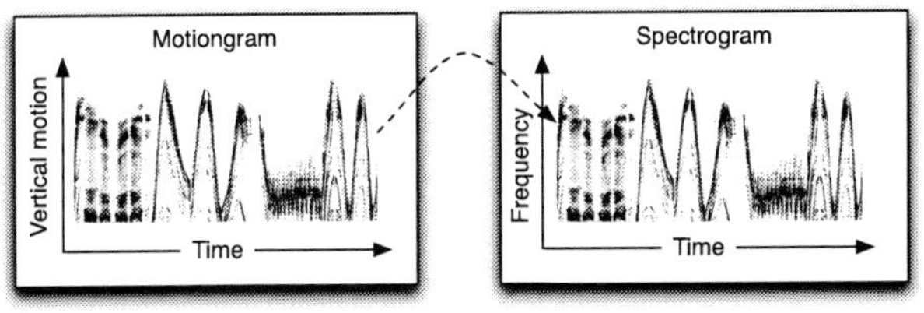

Figure 2. A sketch of the sonomotiongram method, showing how the motiongram matrix is "mapped" to spectral audio data.

A spectrogram of an audio recording displays the energy level of the frequency bands resulting from doing a Fourier transform on the audio. A motiongram, on the other hand, is a reduced display of a series of motion images. There is no analysis being done when creating a motiongram, it is only based on a reduction algorithm. The simplicity of the approach may be seen as a problem, but it is also what has made motiongrams useful in several different application areas [3].

Despite the fact that motiongrams and spectrograms represent different features, they share one property: the temporal unfolding of shapes of either motion or sound. Furthermore, the Y axis in a motiongram represents vertical motion, which is often associated with pitch/frequency [4], meaning that there is also a conceptual link between the Y axes in a motiongram and a spectrogram.

2.3 Image sonification

While the idea of using a motiongram as the basis for sound synthesis is novel, the general idea of sonifying an image has been around for decades. An early example of such an idea is the Pattern Playback machine built by a group of speech researchers in the late 1940s [5]. This system made it possible to "draw" shapes that could afterwards be played back as sound. Iannis Xenakis developed the UPIC system in 1977, which made it possible to create complex timbres by drawing with a digital pen on a computer screen [6]. Nowadays, the idea of making sound from drawings is available in the Metasynth software, along with the possibility of sonifying any type of images and photos [7].

There are also examples of how audio analysis software, like AudioSculpt [8] and SPEAR [9], allow for screen-based manipulation of spectrograms and resynthesis of the manipulated image into sound. This makes it possible for researchers and composers to edit the timbral content and development of sounds in the visual domain.

Closer to the non-realtime sonification approach presented in this paper are examples of how image sonification strategies are used in art installations and realtime applications. One example here is the installation SoundView allowing the user to move a pointer device over an image while listening to the sound [10]. Here the pointer can be thought of as a "tape-head" that scans through the image following an auditory information seeking principle [11]. Other related projects include the 2D spatiotemporal mapping strategies presented in the case of EEG sonification [12] and video sonification based on Hilbert curves [13].

3. IMAGESONIFYER

The original implementation of the sonomotiongram method was presented in [2], and was developed in Max/MSP/ Jitter as modules for the open framework Jamoma [14]. The non-realtime version presented here has been created as a standalone Max patch and application called ImageSonifyer [15]. A screenshot of the user interface of the application is shown in Figure 3.

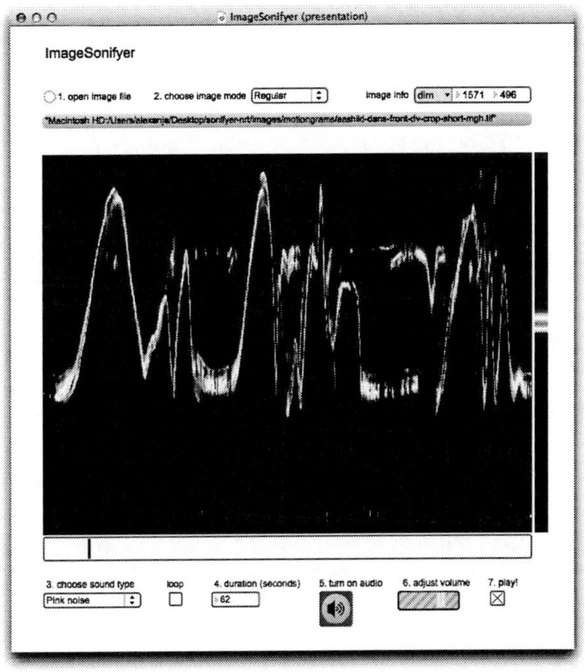

Figure 3. Screenshot of the ImageSonifyer application.

3.1 Features

The ImageSonifyer application is based on opening pre-made image files of motiongrams, and use these images as the starting point for the sonification. Motiongrams can be created in Max using the above-mentioned Jamoma modules, and can also be created using the standalone application VideoAnalysis [16]. It is also possible to use other types of images as input to ImageSonifyer, which will lead to more "traditional" image sonifications. The following features are available:

Load image file Any image file supported by QuickTime can be loaded and displayed. There is no limit on the pixel size of images that can be loaded, but the image will always be displayed at a fixed 4:3 ratio to get a full view of the image and to avoid scrolling. The sonification will still be based on the original image data and not on the reduced image presented on the screen.

Image mode A raw motiongram usually has a white foreground (pixel value 255) on a black background (pixel value 0). For visual reasons, however, it may be convenient to invert the motiongrams so that they

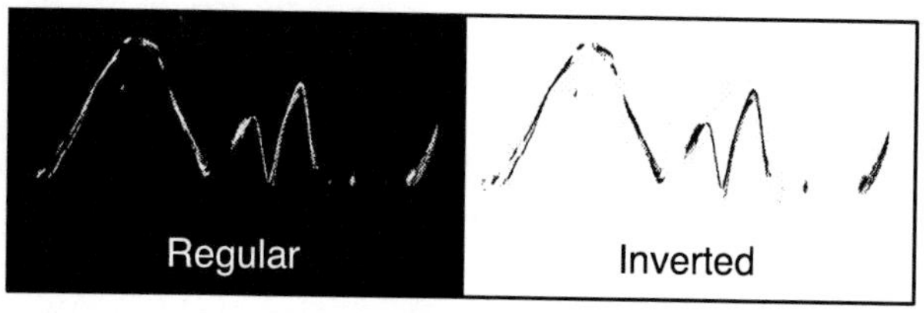

Figure 4. Illustration of the difference between a regular and inverted motiongram.

end up with a black foreground on a white background, as illustrated in Figure 4. There is an option to (re)invert the motiongram in ImageSonifyer in case a user loads an inverted motiongram and wants to sonify it as a regular motiongram.

Sound source The current implementation only allows for choosing between pink and white noise as the source material for the synthesis. In future research it will be interesting to explore other sounds as source material for the synthesis.

Panning Since motiongrams have a temporal direction from left to right, the horizontal location in the image is used to control the panning from left to right in ImageSonifyer. Hence, the sound starts in the left channel, and then gradually pans over to the right side when moving through the image.

Playback Sound can be played back by hitting the space bar button on the keyboard. Looping of the playback can be turned on and off with a toggle.

Duration The ability to freely select the duration of the sonification allows the user to experiment with both fast and slow sonifications of the same material. The duration value will default to the duration of the original video recording, assuming that the video was recorded at 25 fps. This means that an image file with a width of 1500 pixels will be played back over 1 minute. The user is free to set other durations (in seconds) to alter the playback speed.

Scrubbing As an alternative to a linear and clocked playback of the image file, it is also possible to scrub through the image using the mouse. Then the horizontal position of the mouse will control the location of the sonification, and the vertical position will control the sound level.

An example of ImageSonifyer in use can be seen in Video 1. [1]

3.2 Implementation

The sonification part of the ImageSonifyer application is inspired by the Metasynthy patch presented in [17], and the Max pseudo patch in Figure 5 shows an overview of the implementation. The first step is to load an image file into a `jit.qt.movie` object, and read individual matrix columns from this image using a `jit.submatrix` object. These numbers are passed to an MSP buffer using `jit.buffer~`, and used as the basis for an inverse FFT process using the `pfft~` object. There is also a simple crossfade function used to pan the sound from left to right following the position in the image.

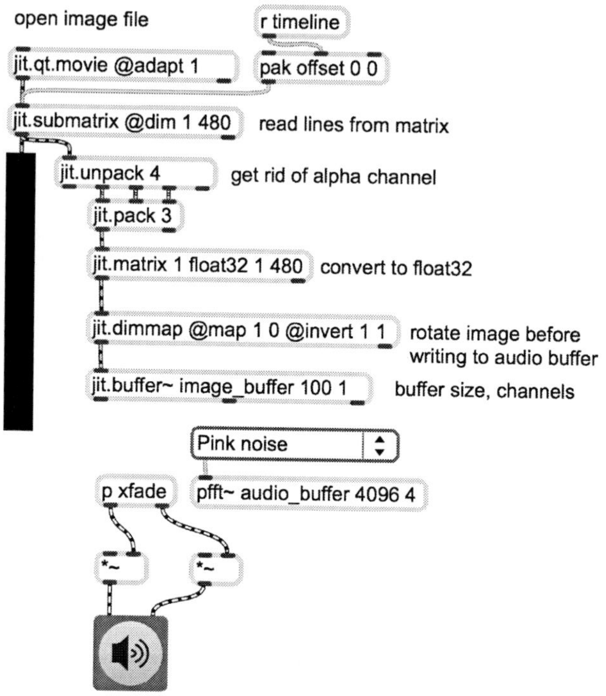

Figure 5. Pseudo Max patch showing the sonification process from input image file.

In the current implementation of the sonomotiongram method there is no use of the colour information in the image. Some experimentation has been done in using the colour information to alter the timbral quality, but this has not ended up working particularly well. After all, the main aim of this method has been to sonify motion features, and quite often the colour information in a motiongram is not particularly relevant. It will, however, be interesting to explore the use of colours at a later stage.

4. SONIFICATION EXAMPLES

The following sections will present some examples of how different types of video material can be sonified using the ImageSonifyer.

4.1 Sonification of standing still

What type of motion can be observed when a person attempts to stand physically still? This has been the topic of some recent experiments in our lab, using a high quality motion capture system able to detect motion at the scale of millimetres [18]. An alternative measurement approach is to place a video camera on the head of a person standing still, since even small motion in the head will lead to a large amount of changing pixels in the recorded image. Figure 6 shows the motiongram resulting from a 10-minute recording of a person standing still with a sports camera (GoPro

[1] Video examples are available from www.arj.no/smc2013/

Hero 2) attached to the head. The recorded image is not interesting in itself, but the motiongram and the sonification are able to represent the rhythmic pattern and the temporal development of the micromotion (Video 2).

4.2 Sonification of a high-speed guitar recording

How does a sonification of moving guitar strings sound like? Figure 7 shows a motiongram of a high-speed recording of a single strumming of the strings on an acoustic guitar. The recordings were made with a high-speed video camera (Phantom V711), at a speed of 7 500 frames per second and with an image resolution of 1280 x 800 pixels. Due to the memory limitations of the camera (21 GB), the maximum recording duration was 1.1 second, which results in a video file with more than 8 000 frames.

Video 3 shows a playback of the video file at 100 frames per second, and Video 4a and 4b shows sonifications of the recording with durations of 10 and 1 seconds, respectively. These sonifications were created slightly different than the other sonifications presented in this paper. Motiongrams are usually created by averaging over the rows in the video matrix. A regular motiongram, however, would not work so well for this particular recording, since the strings are not entirely horizontal in the recording. Thus the averaging happening when creating the motiongram would make the "height" of each string larger than they really were, and will lead to an imprecise rendition of the actual motion. The solution has therefore been to create a motiongram using a slit-scan approach, selecting a single pixel column in the middle of the sound hole on the guitar, and using this pixel column for drawing the motiongram before doing the sonification.

4.3 Sonification of long videos

While the sonomotiongram method was mainly developed for studying music-related body motion, it may be relevant for other applications as well. One example is that of the sonification of long video recordings. Such sonifications may be used to listen to rhythmic patterns and structural changes in the recordings, which may not otherwise be easily recognisable by watching the video in its entirety, or looking at different types of compact visualisations.

Figure 8 shows a motiongram and Video 5 shows a 60-second sonification of a 7.5 hour documentary film of the scenic train ride from the city of Bergen on the west coast of Norway to the capital Oslo. Fortunately, the Norwegian broadcasting company NRK has decided to release a full HD recording of the documentary, with a creative commons license allowing the reuse of the material [19].

When creating a sonification of the Bergensbanen recording, I decided to start out with what I call a *videogram* instead of a motiongram. The difference between the two is that a videogram is based on averaging the input video image instead of the motion image, that is, skipping step (2) in Figure 1. The end result is a videogram in which the colours reflect the colours of the original image, which is more meaningful for a recording in which movement of the camera is as prominent as movement within the image.

4.4 Sonification of abstract images

It is, of course, also possible to sonify other types of images than motiongrams or videograms, thereby using the ImageSonifyer application more like MetaSynth. Although this was never the intended use of the application, it can be creatively interesting to explore how different types of abstract images sound like, such as shown in Video 6a, b, c, and d. Such images are also interesting to explore through the scrubbing functionality of ImageSonifyer.

5. DISCUSSION

Although still in an exploratory state, the sonomotiongram method, and its implementation presented in this paper, has been versatile for both analytic and creative applications. On the analytic side, the possibility to create fast sonifications of long videos is useful, since it allows for listening to long videos in a much shorter time than it would have taken to watch through the recordings. I also find that listening to the sonifications reveal other features than what can be seen from the motiongrams, particularly when it comes to rhythmic and periodic elements in the material.

On the creative side, the scrubbing functionality of ImageSonifyer has proven creatively inspiring to work with. Here the application can be used for image-based improvisations, or using an image as a "score" for a fixed composition. This has already been tested in a concert, and will be explored further in future performances.

One of the positive sides of the sonomotiongram method is its flexibility, being able to sonify image files based on all sorts of video material: long and short recordings, different types of image resolution and qualities, different image framing (close-ups of hands to full body motion). The implementation in Max has been stable and reliable, and it runs comfortably on a normal laptop.

That said, there are also several issues that will have to be explored further in future research:

Dimensions Since they are based on averaging over each row in the video matrix, motiongrams are limited to displaying the distribution of motion in only one spatial dimension [1]. It will be interesting to explore different ways of sonifying multiple spatial dimensions, including two dimensions for regular video recordings and three dimensions for recordings from depth-cameras. This could, for example, be done through spatial or harmonic relationships.

Time and temporal resolution A challenge when working with video recordings as the source material for sonification is how to handle the temporal aspect. This is particularly apparent when working with realtime sonification of video recordings, due to the poor temporal resolution of video as compared to audio. Faster-than-realtime sonifications may overcome this problem, and allows for utilising the potential of our auditory system. Still it is important to find a balance between the temporal aspects of motion features in the video recording and the audio features of the sonification.

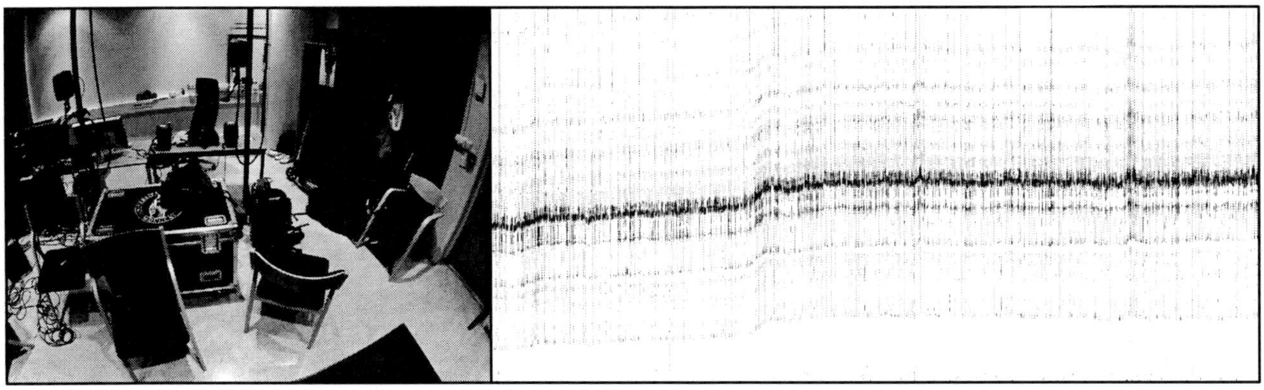

Figure 6. One frame from the video (left) and motiongram (right) of a person standing still for 10 minutes with a camera on the head. The motiongram illustrates the micromovements in the head of the person standing still. The sonification can be heard in Video 2.

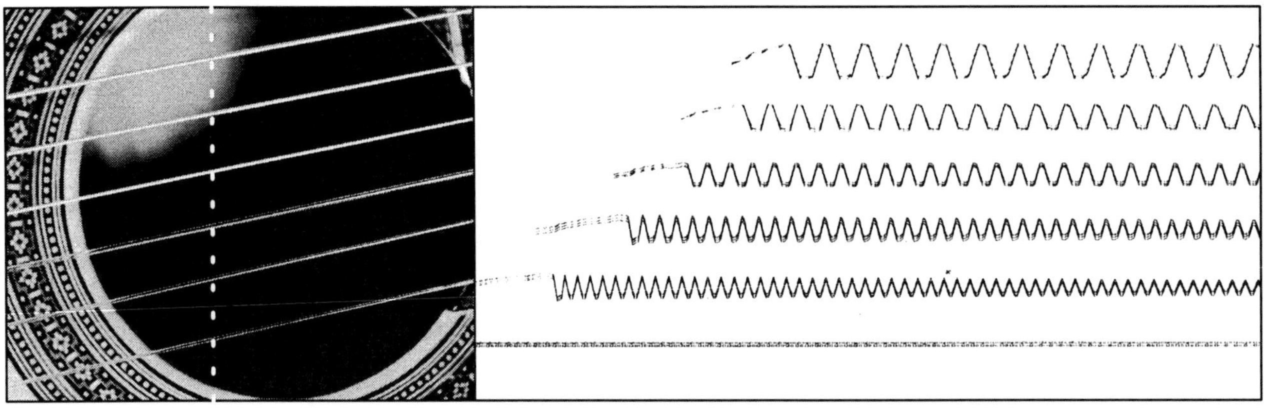

Figure 7. Motiongram of a high-speed guitar recording: one frame from the original video (left), motiongram of the first 1000 frames of the video recording (right). The motiongram has been inverted for visual clarity (black on white). The dotted line in the original video frame indicates the pixel column that was used for creating the motiongram. The original video can be seen in Video 3, and sonifications can be heard in Video 4a and 4b.

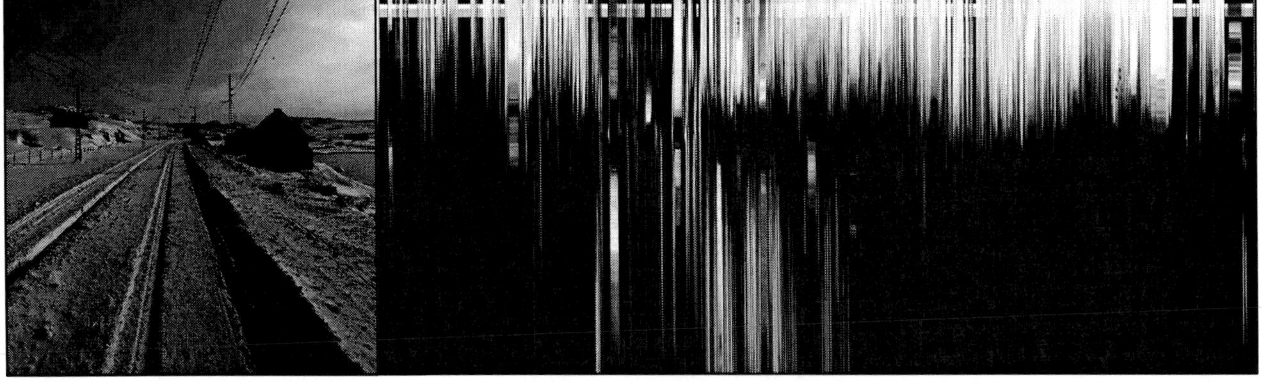

Figure 8. An image (left) and videogram (right) of the 7.5 hour documentary Bergensbanen, a recording of the entire train ride from Bergen to Oslo. The black vertical lines represent when the train were travelling inside tunnels, and the white horizontal stripe near the top is the NRK logo. The sonification can be heard in Video 5.

Analysis and/or performance The original idea of the sonomotiongram method came from an analytic point of view: creating a tool to help in the analysis of various types of music-related motion. While the method certainly works for this type of application, I find that it may be even more interesting from a creative point of view. Here the scrubbing functionality provides the user with a tool for creating what could be called interactive sonifications [20]. It would be interesting to take this one step further by using a realtime motiongram as the basis for such a scrubbing process, which makes it possible to create an interactive loop between motion and sound features.

Colour The current implementation of the sonomotiongram method does not make use of the colour information in the image. Future experiments will look into how the colour information can be used to change, for example, the timbral features of the sound.

Acknowledgments

This research has been funded by the Norwegian Research Council through the project Sensing Music-related Actions. Niko Plath assisted in making the high-speed recording used in Figure 7 at the Department of Musicology at the University of Hamburg. NRK has generously provided a CC license for the Bergensbanen documentary (Figure 8).

6. REFERENCES

[1] A. R. Jensenius, "Using motiongrams in the study of musical gestures," in *Proceedings of the International Computer Music Conference*, New Orleans, LA, 2006, pp. 499–502. [Online]. Available: http://urn.nb.no/URN:NBN:no-21798

[2] ——, "Motion-sound interaction using sonification based on motiongrams," in *Proceedings of the International Conference on Advances in Computer-Human Interactions*, Valencia, 2012, pp. 170–175. [Online]. Available: http://urn.nb.no/URN:NBN:no-30588

[3] ——, "Some video abstraction techniques for displaying body movement in analysis and performance," *Leonardo*, vol. 46, no. 1, pp. 53–60, 2013.

[4] K. Nymoen, "Methods and technologies for analysing links between musical sound and body motion," Ph.D. dissertation, University of Oslo, 2013. [Online]. Available: http://hdl.handle.net/10852/34354

[5] F. Cooper, A. Liberman, and J. Borst, "The interconversion of audible and visible patterns as a basis for research in the perception of speech," *Proceedings of the National Academy of Sciences of the United States of America*, vol. 37, no. 5, p. 318, 1951.

[6] G. Marino, M.-H. Serra, and J.-M. Raczinski, "The upic system: Origins and innovations," *Perspectives of New Music*, vol. 31, no. 1, pp. 258–269, 1993.

[7] E. Wenger, "Metasynth [computer program]. http://www.uisoftware.com/metasynth/," 1998.

[8] N. Bogaards, A. Röbel, and X. Rodet, "Sound analysis and processing with Audiosculpt 2," in *Proceedings of the International Computer Music Conference*, Miami, FL, 2004, pp. 462—465.

[9] M. Klingbeil, "Software for spectral analysis, editing, and synthesis," in *Proceedings of the International Computer Music Conference*, Barcelona, 2005, pp. 107–110.

[10] K. van Den Doel, "Soundview: Sensing color images by kinesthetic audio," in *Proceedings of the International Conference on Auditory Display*, Boston, MA, 2003, pp. 303–306.

[11] H. Zhao, C. Plaisant, B. Shneiderman, and R. Duraiswami, "Sonification of geo-referenced data for auditory information seeking: Design principle and pilot study," in *Proceedings of the International Conference on Auditory Display*, Sydney, 2004, pp. 33–36.

[12] T. Hermann, G. Baier, U. Stephani, and H. Ritter, "Vocal sonification of pathologic EEG features," in *Proceedings of the 12th International Conference on Auditory Display*, London, 2006, pp. 158–163.

[13] F. Grond, "Organized data for organized sound. Space filling curves in sonification," in *Proceedings of the 13th International Conference on Auditory Display*, Montreal, 2007, pp. 476–482.

[14] T. Place and T. Lossius, "Jamoma: A modular standard for structuring patches in Max," in *Proceedings of the International Computer Music Conference*, New Orleans, LA, 2006, pp. 143–146. [Online]. Available: http://hdl.handle.net/2027/spo.bbp2372.2006.032

[15] A. R. Jensenius, "ImageSonifyer [computer program]," 2013. [Online]. Available: http://www.fourms.uio.no/software/

[16] A. R. Jensenius and K. Nymoen, "VideoAnalysis [computer program]," 2009. [Online]. Available: http://www.fourms.uio.no/software/

[17] B. Moon, "Pad 28 - metasynthy," 2011. [Online]. Available: http://www.youtube.com/watch?v=rnERzPwRa4g&lr=1

[18] A. R. Jensenius and K. A. V. Bjerkestrand, "Exploring micromovements with motion capture and sonification," in *Arts and Technology, Revised Selected Papers*, ser. LNICST, A. L. Brooks, Ed. Berlin: Springer, 2012, vol. 101, pp. 100–107. [Online]. Available: http://www.springerlink.com/content/j04650123p105646/

[19] Ø. Solstad, "Download Bergensbanen in HD," 2009. [Online]. Available: http://nrkbeta.no/2009/12/18/bergensbanen-eng/

[20] T. Hermann, A. Hunt, and J. G. Neuhoff, *The Sonification Handbook*. Berlin: Logos Verlag, 2011.

Impulse Response Estimation for the Auralisation of Vehicle Engine Sounds using Dual Channel FFT Analysis

Simon Shelley and Damian Murphy
Audio Lab,
University of York, UK
damian.murphy@york.ac.uk

Simon Goodwin
Central Technology Department,
Codemasters Software Company, UK
simon.goodwin@codemasters.com

ABSTRACT

A method is presented to estimate the impulse response of a filter that describes the transformation in sound that takes place between a close-mic recording of a vehicle engine and the sound of the same engine at another point in or near to the vehicle. The proposed method makes use of the Dual Channel FFT Analysis technique and does not require the use of loudspeakers, computer modelling or mechanical devices. Instead, a minimum of two microphones is required and the engine itself is used as the source of sound. This is potentially useful for virtual reality applications or in sound design for computer games, where users select their virtual position at points inside or outside the vehicle. A case study is described to examine the method in practice and the results are discussed. The described method can be readily extended for surround sound applications using spatial microphone array recording techniques.

1. INTRODUCTION

In this work, we are interested specifically in the accurate auralisation of the sound of an engine at points inside and near to its vehicle, using a close-mic recording of the engine as the source signal. The idea is that using a single set of engine sounds recorded at only one point, Finite Impulse Response (FIR) filters can be used to accurately recreate the sound at other points in the vehicle in real-time. In virtual reality applications such as computer driving simulations, this reduces the need for multiple sets of sound assets recorded at different points around the vehicle. Also, multi-channel surround-sound auralisation can be achieved without drastically increasing the amount of memory and disk space that is required by the application. Another advantage of such an approach is that a recorded engine sound from one car can be easily transplanted into another virtual vehicle, while preserving the acoustic characteristics of the vehicle. In addition, using only one sound source for the engine means that any sound design, audio effects or alterations that might be applied to the engine recording, for example to simulate a damaged or enhanced engine in a computer game, need only be applied once.

In order to implement the auralisation of a vehicle engine at different points in space around the vehicle, appropriate predetermined acoustic impulse responses are required. These impulse responses, known as *acoustic transfer functions* when transformed into the frequency domain, describe the relation between the close-mic recording of the engine and the sound of the same engine at the points of interest around the vehicle. This article presents a method to obtain the impulse responses that describe the filters required for the auralisation process.

The work described in this paper is designed to be applied in gaming, computer simulation and virtual reality applications that require the design of filters to describe complex vibro-acoustic systems for auralisation purposes. The use of FIR filters is particularly useful in applications where users are given the choice of switching in real-time between multiple listener positions. In driving computer games, for example, users are often given the choice of multiple camera positions, either internal or external to the vehicle, from which to observe the action. The proposed technique may also have use in other areas relating to sound and music computing. One potential such application could be the estimation of vibro-acoustic transfer functions that take place in a classical string instrument such as a violin. In this case the string of the instrument would act as the sound source for the measurement, perhaps recorded at close distance by an electric pick-up.

The measurement and prediction of the acoustic transfer function between the engine of a vehicle and the driver's ears in the cockpit has been investigated in some detail in the area of *Noise, Vibration and Harshness* (NVH), also known as *Noise and Vibration* (N&V) [1, 2]. The aim of aforementioned work is to study the noise and vibration characteristics experienced in vehicles in order to then modify them according to specific design goals. Typically, a combination of vibratory and acoustic (vibro-acoustic) energy is considered to travel from one point in a vehicle to another through both air-borne and structure-borne pathways. The analysis of these vibro-acoustic pathways by which the energy is transferred from one point to another is known as Transfer Path Analysis (TPA) [3–6].

One approach to measure the air-borne acoustic transfer function between two points is to use a loudspeaker and a microphone. A broadband transfer function can then be acquired using a number of possible methods. One robust and reliable approach is to drive the loudspeaker with a swept-sine wave, as described in [7].

Unfortunately both the loudspeaker, and to a lesser extent the microphone, take up space within the measurement environment. This means that their presence not only has some effect on the transfer function itself, but also that there are limitations on where in the vehicle they can be placed. With current technology it is possible to build high quality microphones that take up very little space, however high quality loudspeakers with a wide frequency range and a flat frequency response can be difficult to fit into small awkward spaces. A common solution that is employed to deal with this problem is to exploit the *acoustic reciprocity theorem*, which dictates that the positions of the loudspeaker and microphone are interchangeable [8, 9]. This means for example that to measure the transfer function between a point in a car engine bay and the ears of the driver, the loudspeaker can be placed in the driver's position where there is plenty of space, and the microphone can be placed under the bonnet of the car in the engine bay.

Transducers that are used to measure the acoustic transfer function in this way should ideally have omni-directional characteristics, or at least have a known directivity pattern that is frequency independent. They should also have a flat frequency response and cover a wide spectrum of audible frequencies. This presents another problem, because in practice it is highly difficult to build a loudspeaker that meets these specifications and the introduction of inaccuracies are inevitable.

In addition to these issues, measurements using loudspeakers and microphones do not take into account the structure-borne contribution of the acoustic transfer function. The structure-borne contribution is mostly made up of acoustic energy transferred through the chassis of the car via the connecting power-train mounts. This makes up a significant part of the overall sound experienced in a vehicle interior [10]. Calculation of the structure-borne contribution is not trivial, and can be done using predictive models [11] or measurement using mechanical devices [12]. Both approaches have limitations and require considerable time and effort to implement.

Contrary to the requirement of Transfer Path Analysis techniques, to meet the goals of this work the separation of air-borne and structure-borne components of the acoustic transfer function is not a necessity. Instead, the goal is to generate a filter that integrates all components and results in a realistic sounding and immersive auralisation of the engine at different points around the vehicle. As an alternative, the use of *Dual Channel Fast Fourier Transform (FFT) Analysis* is investigated as a relatively fast and simple method to obtain a broadband transfer function that can be used to derive a transformation filter [13, 14]. With the proposed technique, the engine itself is used as the sound source, removing any requirement for a loudspeaker or mechanical devices, and instead using only microphones. Although a minimum of two microphones is required, and this basic case is considered in this paper, the method can be readily extended to measure multiple points in and around the vehicle simultaneously, and also to capture spatial information at the points of interest using a microphone array such as the coincident tetrahedral *soundfield* microphone [15] or a spaced multichannel array [16].

The paper is organised as follows: Section 2.1 introduces the dual channel FFT analysis technique. In Section 2.2 the proposed method is described using a case study in which an impulse response is measured in a car. Section 2.3 presents an analysis of the results of the case study, demonstrating the validity of the method. Finally, conclusions and future work are found in Section 3

2. METHOD

2.1 Dual Channel FFT Analysis

Using dual channel FFT analysis, it is possible to calculate the transfer function that describes the relationship between two signals, with the assumption that they are coupled by a *linear time-invariant* (LTI) system [13, 14]. This relationship is described by (1) where $a(t)$ is the input signal, $b(t)$ is the output signal and $h(t)$ is the impulse response of the linear time-invariant system that describes the relationship between the two signals.

$$b(t) = a(t) * h(t) = \int_{-\infty}^{\infty} a(t-\tau).h(\tau)\mathrm{d}\tau \qquad (1)$$

The LTI system can also be described in the frequency domain by its transfer function $H(\omega)$, which can be calculated by taking the Fourier Transform of the impulse response $h(t)$. The convolution theorem states that the output of the LTI system in the frequency domain $B(\omega)$ is the product of the input spectrum $A(\omega)$ and the transfer function of the system $H(\omega)$. The transfer function of the system can therefore be calculated by dividing the output spectrum $B(\omega)$ by the input spectrum $A(\omega)$, as follows:

$$H(\omega) = \frac{B(\omega)}{A(\omega)} \qquad (2)$$

In theory, by applying a broadband signal to the input of the system that covers the frequency range of interest, the transfer function of the system can be directly measured using (2). However real-world measurements can be contaminated with noise which causes a degree of error. The effect of this noise can be greatly reduced by repeating the measurement and performing a complex average [13]. This is done in practice by multiplying both the numerator and the denominator of (2) by the complex conjugate $A^*(\omega)$ in order to give the cross spectrum G_{AB} and the input auto spectrum G_{AA}. Averages are taken for G_{AB} and G_{AA} over a number of measurements in order to calculate the transfer function $H(\omega)$, as described by (3). This complex averaging process has the effect of reducing the level of random noise introduced in the output signal $b(t)$.

$$H(\omega) = \frac{\overline{G_{AB}}}{\overline{G_{AA}}} \qquad (3)$$

Finally the impulse response of the system $h(t)$ can be calculated, if required, by performing an Inverse Fourier Transform on the transfer function $H(\omega)$.

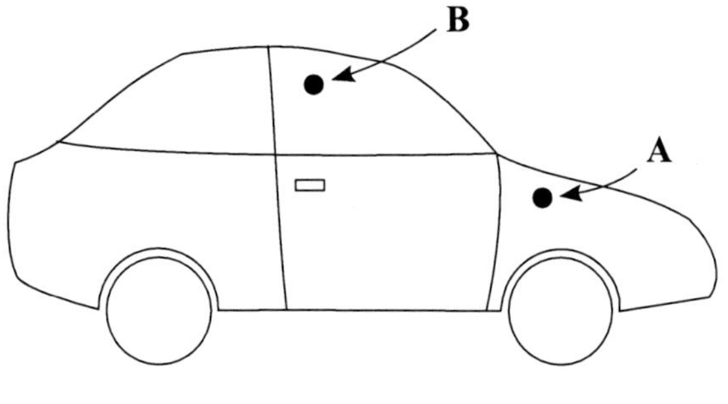

Figure 1. Diagram showing positions of microphones in the car used for the case study.

To demonstrate how the Dual Channel FFT Analysis technique can be used to obtain the transfer function between two recordings of an engine made at different points within a vehicle, a case study is described in the following section.

2.2 Case Study

To describe the method, we look at the specific case where the aim is to auralise the engine sound in the cockpit of a real car, a Subaru Impreza, using a close-mic recording of the engine. In order to obtain the data required to perform the dual channel FFT analysis, the engine must first be simultaneously recorded at a close location and at any other locations where the sound will be auralised. In practice, to record the engine at a close distance, an omni-directional Behringer ECM8000 microphone was suspended under the bonnet of the car in a small pocket of open space near the engine, position **A**. A second omni-directional microphone, an Earthworks M30, was mounted on a microphone stand inside the cockpit at the position of the driver's head, position **B**. Figure 1 illustrates the microphone positioning inside the car. The two measurement microphones have relatively flat frequency responses in the frequency range of interest, and although ideally they should be perfectly matched, they were considered close enough in specification for this case study.

Measurements were performed by recording the engine simultaneously at both microphone positions while controlling the throttle of the engine in a neutral gear with the car standing still. In order to measure the full frequency range of sound that the engine of the car can produce, the *revolutions per minute* (RPM) of the engine were increased from a low idling level to a relative high rate and back to idling speed for a duration of about 23 seconds. The process was repeated 12 times and recordings were made at position **A** and **B** simultaneously, resulting in 12 recordings of the engine from each microphone, 24 in total. All recordings were made at a sampling rate of 96 kHz, and a bit depth of 24 bits per sample.

The sweep of the RPM of the engine was performed by the driver while monitoring a stopwatch and the tachometer of the car in order to attempt to produce similar recordings in each of the 12 measurements. It should be noted that the exact reproduction of engine sweep in each measurement was not a requirement during this process. The aim of repeating the measurements was to provide a large amount of data in order to attempt to improve the signal to noise ratio of the result using the averaging process described in in Section 2.1.

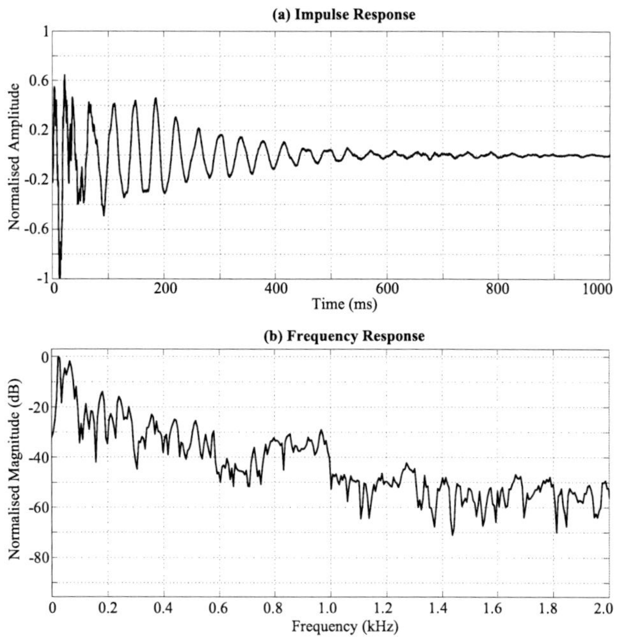

Figure 2. (a) Impulse response and (b) frequency response of derived FIR filter.

2.3 Analysis

For each of the 12 recordings, the two signals **A** and **B** were split into overlapping segments with a length of M=262144 samples and an overlap of $M/2$ samples. Each segment was windowed using a Hann function and then zero padded at the end to a length of $2M$ before calculating the discrete Fourier Transform. The cross spectrum G_{AB} and the input auto spectrum G_{AA} were then estimated for each segment and averages were taken over all measurements, according to the Welch method [17]. The transfer function was then calculated using (3) and finally the signal was cleaned by removing information at frequencies above 22 kHz and below 22 Hz. These limits were chosen to ensure that the measured frequency range lies comfortably within the operational frequency limits of the two microphones. The impulse response $h(t)$ and frequency response of the resulting filter are illustrated in Figure 2.

In order to auralise the engine sound inside the cockpit, the engine recording at microphone position **A** is convolved with the impulse response illustrated in Figure 2(a). The filtered engine sound can then be directly compared with the real engine sound recorded simultaneously in the cockpit itself. The real recording made in the cockpit consists mostly of the engine sound, however it is also contaminated slightly by microphone self-noise and environmental sounds such as the movement of the accelerator pedal and some creaking and rattling sounds from the body of the car, caused by engine vibration and changes in temperature.

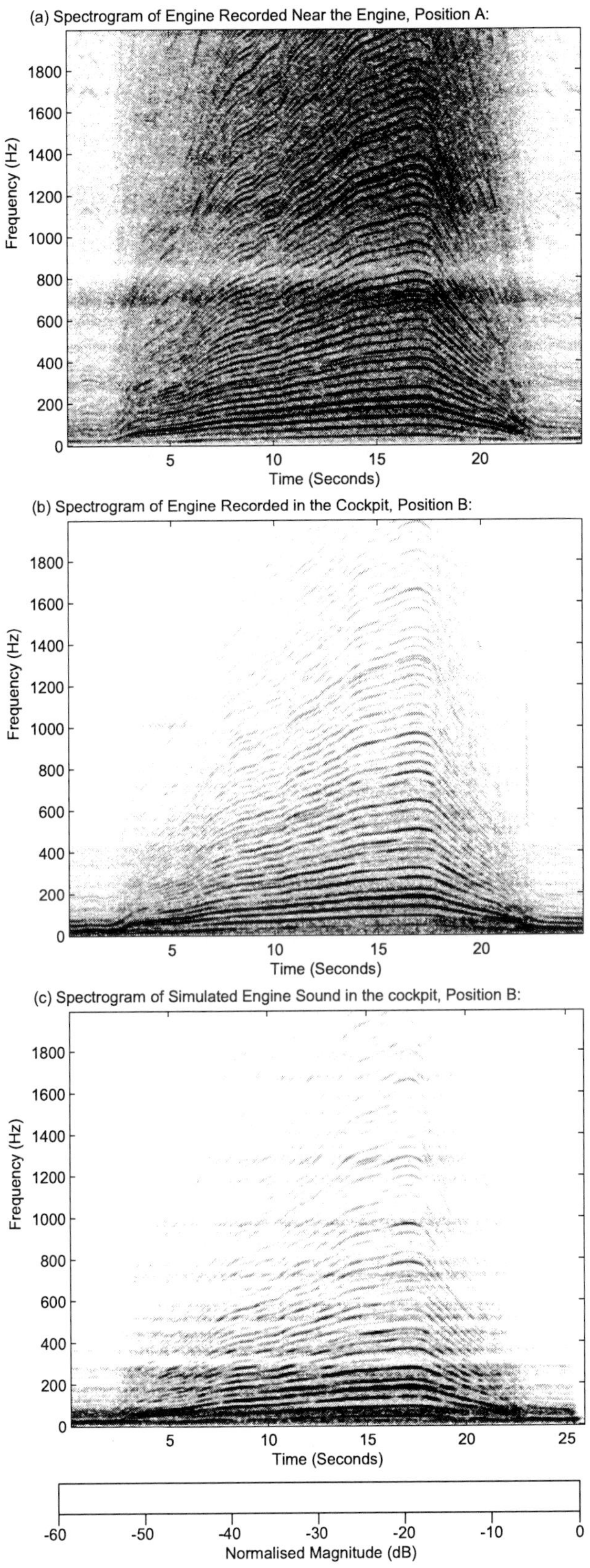

Figure 3. Spectrograms of the car engine (a) recorded at position **A**, (b) recorded at position **B** and (c) auralised at position **B** using the recording at position **A** as the source.

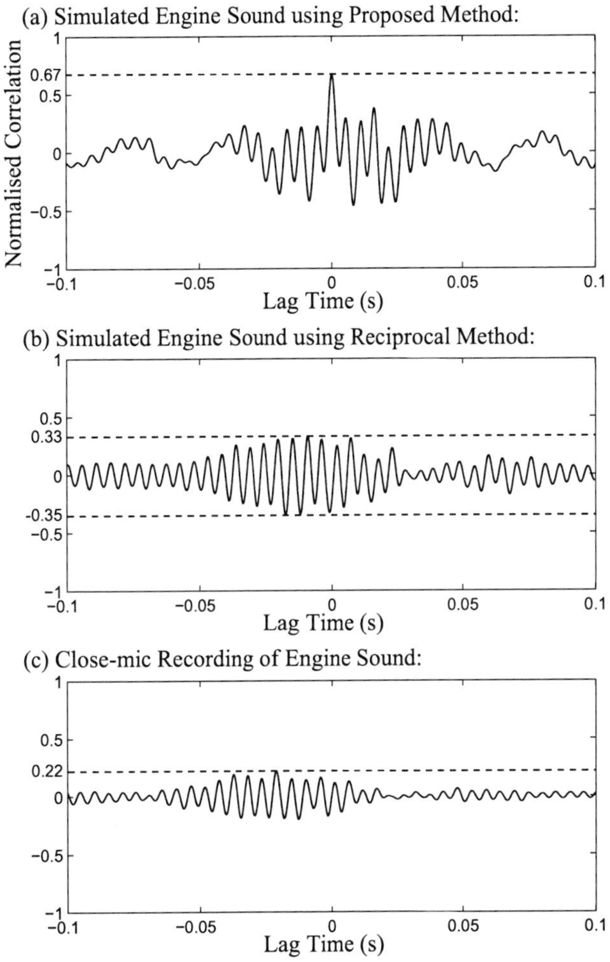

Figure 4. Normalised cross-correlation of the recording of engine at position **B** with (a) the auralised sound at the same point using the proposed method (b) the auralised sound using the reciprocal method and (c) the unprocessed recording of engine at position **A**.

Demonstration audio files relating to this work can be accessed online at [18] on the OpenAIR website [19].

Figure 3(a) and (b) are spectrograms of the engine sound recorded at microphone positions **A** and **B** respectively for one of the 12 measurements, presented over a frequency range of between 0 and 2000 Hz. Figure 3(c) is the spectrogram of the virtual auralised engine sound at position **B**, that has been generated by processing the signal recorded at position **A**.

A similarity in the spectral content between the real and the auralised sounds is evident from comparing spectrograms in Figure 3(b) and (c), and this similarity is further confirmed by listening to the files themselves. However it is evident from the spectrograms in Figure 3 and the frequency response of the filter, illustrated in Figure 2(b), that certain frequency bands are suppressed. In addition the auralised sound appears to be low-pass filtered in comparison with the actual recorded sound in the cockpit.

The comparison between the real recordings and auralised sounds is further investigated by measuring the normalised cross-correlation of the signals. Figure 4(a) shows the result of the cross-correlation between the real sound recorded in the cockpit and the auralised sound prepared using the filter described in Figure 2 for one of the 12 measurements. For this measurement, the correlation between the two signals is 0.67 at 0 s lag (1 would be exactly the same and 0 would indicate no similarity at all). Calculated for all 12 measurements, the mean peak correlation is 0.59 with a standard deviation of 0.09.

To compare the proposed method with an alternative technique, a third auralisation was prepared using the *reciprocal* method. For this method, an impulse response describing the sound transformation between positions **A** and **B** in the car was obtained by placing a loudspeaker at position **B**, in the cockpit of the car, and an omni-directional microphone at position **A**. A sine sweep measurement technique was then used to obtain the impulse response, as described in [7]. This method is a potential alternative to the one described in this paper, however it is not expected to perform as well mainly because it does not measure the structure-borne contribution to the transfer function. Note that this approach also has the disadvantage that it is not trivial to obtain coincident spatial impulse response measurements, as can be readily measured with the Dual Channel FFT method via a microphone array such as a soundfield microphone.

Figure 4(b) shows the result of the cross-correlation between the real sound recorded in the cockpit and the auralised sound prepared using the reciprocal method, using data from one of the 12 recordings. Using this method, the mean peak correlation for all 12 measurements is 0.26, with a standard deviation of 0.06. The relatively low value of correlation is supported by the audible quality of the auralised sound, which reveals a lack of low frequency content in comparison with the actual sound recorded in the cockpit.

Finally, Figure 4(c) shows the cross-correlation between the unprocessed engine sound recorded at position **A** and the sound recorded in the cockpit, recorded at position **B**, for one set of measurement data. The unprocessed engine sound results in a mean peak correlation of 0.15 for all 12 measurements, with a standard deviation of 0.04. As expected, the unprocessed engine sound shows the least correlation with the sound recorded in the cockpit.

3. CONCLUSIONS

This paper presents a method to auralise the sound of a vehicle's engine at selected points in the vehicle's interior, such as the cockpit or passenger compartment. The method is designed to be used in virtual reality applications and computer games. The aim is to provide a realistic and immersive audio experience to users both in terms of how the engine is filtered by both airborne and structure-borne transfer paths before reaching the ear, and in terms of the spatial characteristics and reverberation of the sound within the virtual space. At the same time, the method allows sound designers and developers of such applications full flexibility in designing and manipulating car engine sounds.

The first stage of the method is to measure the transfer functions that describe the relationship between a close-mic recording of the engine and the sound of the engine at the points of interest in the vehicle's interior. Once the transfer functions are determined, the derived impulse responses can be used to provide real-time audio from any recorded engine using auralisation techniques. The method is described here for a single channel output, however it can be readily extended for multi-channel systems in order to provide a surround sound experience from an engine recorded at a single point. The simplest way to achieve this would be to replace the single microphone in the cockpit with a microphone array, such as a Soundfield microphone, and calculate the transfer functions for each microphone channel.

Results from the case study show that the method works well, providing an auralised signal that exhibits a relatively high correlation with an actual recorded signal measured at the same point in the cockpit of a car. However, although the auralised signal sounds similar to the real signal, there are some audible differences meaning that there is room for improvement. Observations of the signals in the frequency domain reveal that certain frequency bands appear to be suppressed in the auralised signal, and that the auralised signal is low-pass filtered in comparison to the real signal recorded in the cockipit. Further investigation is required to understand the cause of these errors.

One explanation could be that the method assumes that the relationship between a close-mic recording of an engine and the sound of the engine in the vehicle interior can be described by a linear time invariant system, but in fact non-linearity is inevitable in such a system a complex vibro-acoustic system. Another cause of difference between auralised and measured audio would be the influence of other sounds and noises in either the cockpit of the car or the engine bay that are not correlated with sounds coming from the engine. Examples of such sounds are creaking in the bodywork of the car, fan noise and noise from the exhaust.

In future work, we would like to investigate if and how the method could be improved by taking into account other sources of sounds that are experienced in a vehicle interior, for example from the exhaust pipe. We would also like to investigate causes of error with the method, and the possibility of improving the results using post-processing techniques. We would like to apply the method to a variety of different vehicles in order to further test its validity and flexibility. Finally we would like to conduct a series of listening tests in order investigate how the difference is perceived between the virtually auralised engine sounds and recorded engine sounds recorded under the same conditions.

Acknowledgments

This work has been supported by AHRC Grant AH/J013838/1. We thank Andrew Chadwick for his help with the in-car measurements. We also thank the sound teams at Codemasters, as well as Steve Oxnard from the Audio Lab at York, for their inspiration and discussion in the planning stages of this work.

4. REFERENCES

[1] M. P. Norton and D. G. Karczub, *Fundamentals of Noise and Vibration Analysis for Engineers*. Cambridge University Press, 2003.

[2] S. Jha, "Characteristics and sources of noise and vibration and their control in motor cars," *Journal of Sound and Vibration*, vol. 47, no. 4, pp. 543–558, 1976.

[3] J. Plunt, "Finding and fixing vehicle NVH problems with transfer path analysis," *Sound and Vibration Magazine*, vol. 39, no. 11, pp. 12–16, 2005.

[4] K. Genuit and J. Poggenburg, "The design of vehicle interior noise using binaural transfer path analysis," in *SAE Technical Paper*, no. NCV19, 1999.

[5] S. Xiumin, Z. Shuguang, Z. Shiwei, and L. Lin, "Transfer path analysis of fuel cell vehicle interior air-borne noise," in *Vehicle Power and Propulsion Conference, 2008. VPPC '08. IEEE*, 2008, pp. 1–6.

[6] N. Alt, N. Wiehagen, and M. W. Schlitzer, "Interior noise simulation for improved vehicle sound," in *SAE Technical Paper*, no. 2001-01-1539, 2001.

[7] A. Farina, "Simultaneous measurement of impulse response and distortion with a swept-sine technique," in *108th AES Convention*, 2000, pp. 18–22.

[8] L. Rayleigh, "On the application of the principle of reciprocity to acoustics," *Proceedings of the Royal Society of London*, vol. 25, pp. 118–122, 1876.

[9] R. Sottek, P. Sellerbeck, and M. Klemenz, "An artificial head which speaks from its ears: Investigations on reciprocal transfer path analysis in vehicles, using a binaural sound source," in *Proc. 2003 Noise & Vibration Conference and Exhibition*, no. 2003-01-1635, Michigan, United States, 2003.

[10] G. Eisele, K. Wolff, and N. Alt, "Application of vehicle interior noise simulation (VINS) for NVH analysis of a passenger car," in *SAE Technical Paper*, no. 2005-01-2514, 2005.

[11] M. Smith, "Prediction methodologies for vibration and structure borne noise," in *Alberta Acoustics and Noise Association Spring Noise Conference*, Baff, Germany, 2011.

[12] R. Craik, "The measurement of structure-borne sound transmission using impulsive sources," *Applied Acoustics*, vol. 15, no. 5, pp. 355 – 361, 1982.

[13] H. Herlufsen, "Dual channel FFT analysis (part I)," in *Brüel & Kjær Technical Review*, no. 1984-1, 1984.

[14] ——, "Dual channel FFT analysis (part II)," in *Brüel & Kjær Technical Review*, no. 1984-2, 1984.

[15] M. A. Gerzon, "The design of precisely coincident microphone arrays for stereo and surround sound," in *Audio Engineering Society Convention 50*, 1975.

[16] M. Williams and G. L. Du, "Multichannel microphone array design," in *Audio Engineering Society Convention 108*, 2000.

[17] P. Welch, "The use of fast Fourier transform for the estimation of power spectra: A method based on time averaging over short, modified periodograms," *IEEE Transactions on Audio Electroacoustics*, vol. 15, no. 2, pp. 70–73, 1967.

[18] S. Shelley and D. T. Murphy. (2013) Audio demonstration of the auralisation of a car engine. [Online]. Available: www.openairlib.net/resources/vehicle-engine-auralisation

[19] D. T. Murphy and S. Shelley, "Openair: An interactive auralization web resource and database," in *Audio Engineering Society Convention 129*, 2010.

IMAGE SONIFICATION BASED ON OBJECT AND FEATURE EXTRACTION

Keunhyoung Luke Kim **Woon Seung Yeo**
Audio and Interactive Media Lab,
Graduate School of Culture Technology,
KAIST, Korea
doiluvu@gmail.com woony@kaist.edu

ABSTRACT

We introduce a new paradigm for image sonification based on extraction of abstract features. Unlike most image sonification examples that convert low-level raw data into sound, this method utilizes scale invariant feature transform (SIFT) for image abstraction to obtain higher-level information, thereby producing more robust results with a variety of images and visual transformations. To separate visual components from an image and enhance hierarchical information to SIFT features, the sonification also utilizes an image structure analysis algorithm. Being invariant to object-level changes such as rotating, moving, or scaling, sonified sound describe the characteristics of different polygons well. We first describe our sonification model with SIFT features, and discuss its performance.

1. INTRODUCTION

Sonification of visual information is a popular subject with many application areas. In addition to creating audiovisual art, image sonification techniques can provide a special "augmented reality" environment for the visually impaired by presenting live camera view as sound [1]. Moreover, certain visual features of images that are hardly noticeable by eyes can be easily heard and detected. This shows that auditory display an effective tool for diagnostics and/or data exploration of visual information

Sonification of "high-level" features abstracted from an image usually reduces sensitivity to minor visual changes and, compared to the raw data (e.g., bitmap pixels), can provide more meaningful information. When the level of abstraction becomes too high, however, it may become too purpose-specific and not generally applicable.

This paper deals with sonification of abstract image features – local key points that are used to recognize objects in computer vision techniques, and aims to suggest a new method for sonification of abstracted images which a) produces results that are reasonably invariant to visual transformations of abstract objects, and b) performs reasonably well with different kinds of images (e.g., typical photos, still-life, abstract paintings, etc.). The method separates visual objects in an image and sonifies local features of each object using additive synthesis. Since local features lack of structural information, we used Suzuki's structure analysis algorithm [2] to group them into objects. Each object is regarded as a tone that consists of one or more harmonics that are determined by the features of the object. Then the tones are placed separately in time and properly localized.

To obtain desired features and design characteristic timbre for each object, we use scale invariant feature transform (SIFT) – a well-known visual object recognition algorithm that produces abstracted image features to compare or find out objects in images [3]. SIFT uses differences between multiple Gaussian-blurred images to find the "key features", and the direction, magnitude and position of each key feature are used as parameters. Image features generated by SIFT are invariant to image translation, scaling, rotation, and are partially invariant to illumination changes as well as affine or 3-D projection: this is analogous to the properties of neural responses in inferior temporal cortex in primate vision [3], an allows us to extract more invariant and meaningful information from images.

2. RELATED RESEARCH

2.1 Image Sonification

Image Sonification is a relatively recent branch of data sonification. The idea of data transformation from image to sound is interesting and challenging for their dimensional and perceptional differences.

Examples of direct, low-level image to sound mapping include raster scanning [4], which is one of the most deeply studied techniques of image sonification with notable follow-up research. The mechanism is bidirectional and reversible: each image pixel corresponds to an audio sample in a row-by-row manner. This technique is useful for analysis of pitch- or frequency-related features of audio, but its linear scanning paradigm limits the feature of displaying information on visual "objects" in images.

Some researchers tried to extract more "abstract" information from images to overcome this limitation of sonifying raw data. Payling et al used basic image processing techniques to extracted local color information to generate music clips [5]. However, the information extracted was too simple and results were not generally applicable. A more advanced approach can be found in

[6]: here the authors extracted and sonified the edge information to help visually impaired "hear" the overall structure of images. It worked partially for simple and nicely processed images, but had problems with rather complex ones. Edwards et al worked on a purpose-specific image sonification of problematic biological cells from medical imaging data for diagnostic purpose [7].

2.2 Object Sonification

Similar to our work featured in this paper, some techniques have been suggested to enhance data exploration experience by providing auditory displays of virtual objects for sonification of symbolic information. For example, Shelley et al provided multimodal feedback for interaction with a virtual object [8]: they proposed four categories of sound abstraction and sonification methods from physical models to earcons. Despite the lack of detailed research on sonification method, this work presents a useful insight into levels of abstraction for object sonification.

3. SONIFICATION MODEL

Our sonification process takes two steps: 1) data extraction from images and 2) sonification of extracted data.

3.1 Data Extraction

While the major ingredient of this sonification is SIFT feature data, it represents only local characteristics of an image and lacks structural information. Sonified results from these features altogether may sound very chaotic and unrecognizable. Here we use image structure analysis techniques to obtain more "object level" point-of-view and conserve generality of application.

Once SIFT features are extracted, they are grouped into objects according to their positions and the result of structure analysis.

3.1.1 SIFT

With SIFT algorithm, image features are extracted in the following steps.

First, a "pyramid" of the original image, which consists of differences between multiple level Gaussian blurred images, is constructed. Each level of pyramid is a difference image of two adjacent levels.

Second, local maxima and minima from the pyramid are detected. The pyramid is three-dimensional; two dimensions are analogous to the dimensions of the original image, and one comes from the level of the pyramid. These points are stored as candidates of local image features.

Third, "weaker" points, including those with too low contrast or those whose gradients are along the edges of the image, are removed. Then the remaining points are finally marked as local features.

Lastly, the directions and the magnitudes of image gradients at each feature point are calculated. These properties are used as image comparison cue in object detection application, and as harmonics of tones representing each object in this sonification.

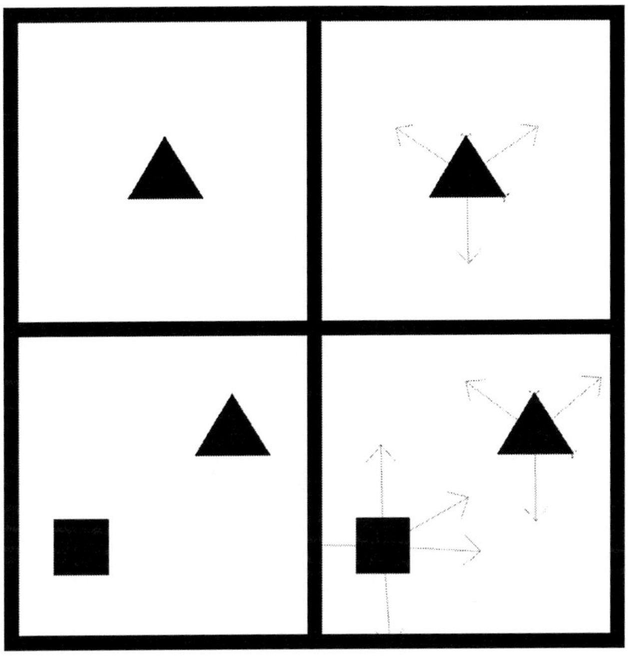

Figure 1. Original images (left) and their SIFT features shown as arrows (right).

SIFT feature describe characteristics of objects using color gradient and it successfully find the same object from different images even they are scaled or transformed. Example of SIFT extraction is shown in figure 1. The features found from the original images on left are shown on right. For polygon objects, SIFT features usually have directions according to each side of polygons. Upper two images show a triangle and SIFT features of a triangle. Each arrow represents a brightness change from dark to bright color. The size of arrow means amount of change. In the triangle, there are three sudden color changes, or gradients, since there are three sides in a triangle. In the lower images, there is a rectangle with 5 large arrows. The arrow heading to 2 o'clock is an exceptional one, which comes from position of the rectangle. These exceptional features can be rejected by limiting the SIFT feature extracting algorithm. Still, the four orthogonal large arrows strongly represent presence of a rectangle.

3.1.2 Representation of Objects

Objects represented by SIFT feature are high identifiable, but SIFT feature itself does not store edge or structural information and it cannot be determined whether a feature is in an object or not, where a need for image processing to extract structural information arises. Edge information is retrieved by the difference of Gaussian method [9]. With edge information, the structure of the image is analyzed by Suzuki's algorithm [2]. If an edge makes a closed loop, it is regarded as an object and features inside the loop become characteristic of the object. Result of structure analysis is a tree-like data of detected closed loops. Figure 2 shows the outlines of each object and which SIFT features belongs to which objects.

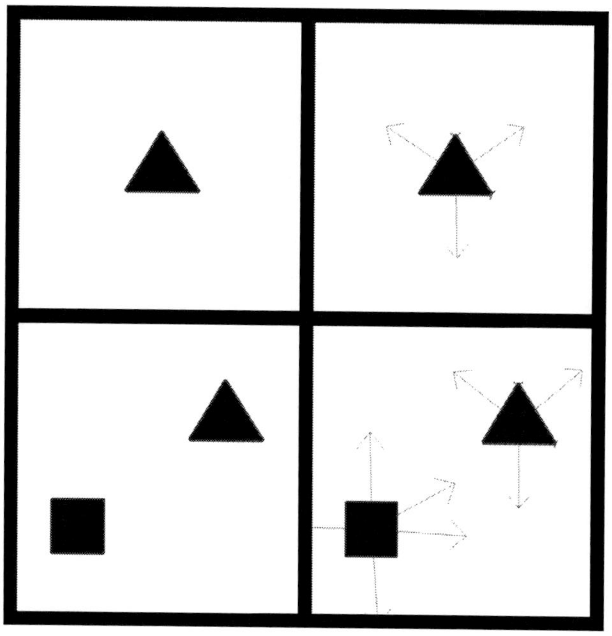

Figure 2. Borders of object area marked in red (left), and the SIFT features with object borders (right).

Finally we obtain a list of the objects that contains SIFT features. Additionally, magnitudes of each feature are normalized so that they do not exceed 1. Direction values are also scaled to fit into the range from 0 to 4. In the sonification step, each object is interpreted as a musical note played by an instrument. Features of an object determine the frequency and harmonics of its tone.

3.2 Sonification

3.2.1 Sonification of Each Object

We use additive synthesis method for sonification, where each feature corresponds to a sinusoid. Frequency of a sinusoid is determined by the gradient direction of its according feature, as

$$f = f_{base} \cdot 2^{direction}, \tag{1}$$

where f_{base} is the fundamental frequency and *direction* is the normalized direction value of each feature. Since the direction value ranges from 0 to 4, a 90 degree difference between two features results in separation by one octave in frequency. Likely, an ideal rectangle will have a fundamental frequency, the second, the third, and the fourth octave sinusoids.

The amplitude of each sinusoid determined by the gradient magnitudes and decreases gradually. Sinusoids of an objects rings simultaneously, which makes them heard as a tone with various harmonics. For a single triangle (see figure 1 and 2), there are 3 major features with different directions. Figure 3 shows the sonified result of a triangle: here we can notice three major frequency peaks in the spectrum.

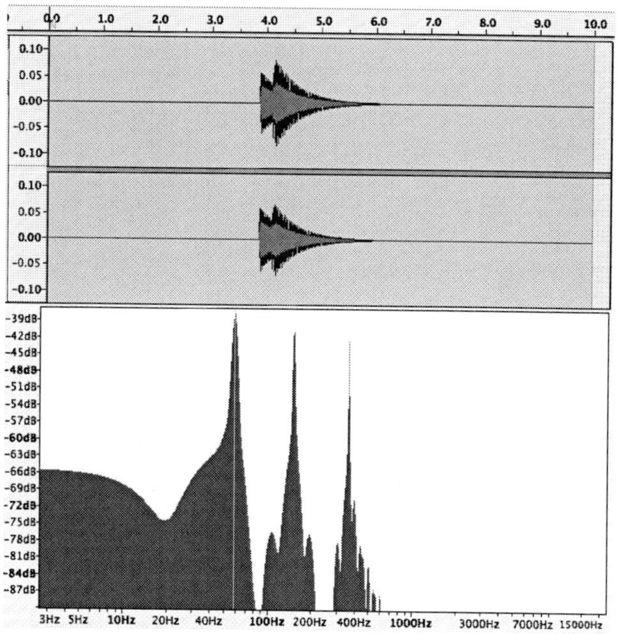

Figure 3. Sonification result of a single triangle (See figure 1 for the original image): the waveform (top) and the spectrum (bottom). Screenshots were taken using Audacity.

3.2.2 Composition of Objects

Objects in the 2-dimensional space of visual domain should be arranged over time in the auditory domain. Here, the vertical position of an object in an image determines when its corresponding sound will be played. More specifically, playback of an object sound is delayed according to how far it is placed from the top edge of the image. Horizontal position of an object is used for stereo panning. The position information of objects can be also used for more sophisticated sound localization.

Figure 4 shows the sonified result of an image with two different objects, which is shown in figure 1 (bottom left). In this example, it is clearly shown that the tone of the triangle comes before that of the rectangle with panning characteristics determined by their horizontal positions.

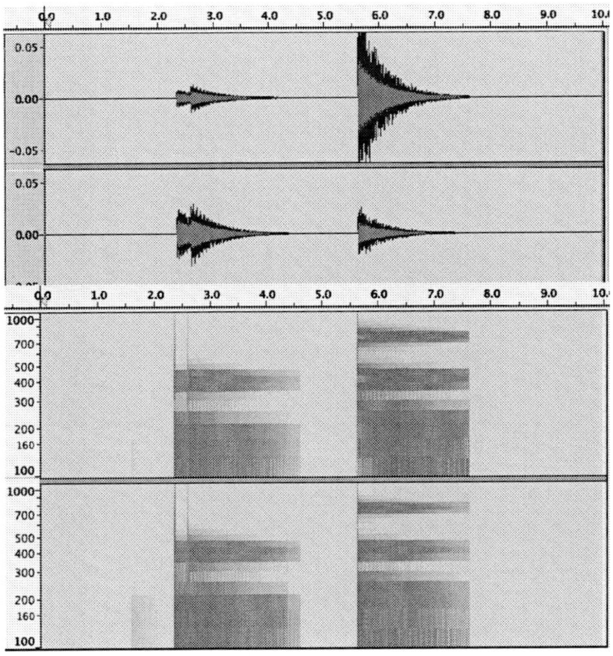

Figure 4. Sonification result of a triangle and a rectangle (see figure 1, bottom left for the original image). The waveforms (top) and their spectrograms (bottom) are shown. The tone for the triangle rings first from right, then the tone for the rectangle rings from left. Screenshots were taken using Audacity.

4. RESULT

We used five different sets of images to test the performance of the sonification model. Sonified results as well as the original images can be found at the author's website. [1]

4.1 Basic Shapes

Images with simple shapes (i.e., triangles and rectangles) were tested for comparison of basic transformations. Test image sets were created by transposing, rotating, and scaling the original images.

The results show that, in spite of these geometric transformations applied to generate the test image sets, we can obtain very similar sounds from the same shape, and distinguishable ones between different shapes. Transposition featured results with the least different (except timing and panning). While rotation may affect spectral distribution of the sound, the results are still recognizable. Scaling, obviously, can change the loudness of the sonified result.

4.2 Combination of Basic Shapes

This time we put two or more shapes in each image. Combinations include 1) two squares, 2) two triangles, 3) one square and one triangle, 4) two square and one triangle, 5) one square and two triangle, and 6) two squares and two triangles. From the sonified results, we can easily tell if the image contains two or more shapes. In addition, the listener should be able to notice the type of the shapes and their positions with basic information on the mapping mechanism.

4.3 More Complex Basic Shapes

We further tested more complex forms of triangles and rectangles. Some of them were "decorated", some were abstract paintings, while others were real photos of simple objects. Simpler examples result in sounds that are highly similar to the first set of examples. More complex shapes such as abstract paintings produce quite different tones, but certain level of similarity can still be found.

4.4 Patterns

General application to objectless images (such as patterns) is one of the important long-term objectives of this research. While polygon-based patterns generate stable and shape-representing sounds, line-based and irregular patterns are less recognizable. However, similarity between similar patterns can also be noticed from the results. At this point, our conclusion is that this method can generate a tune of pattern images with unique characteristics: this will be investigated further.

4.5 Complex Images

Some highly-complex images, such as photos of complex objects and paintings, were also sonified for comparison. While it can hardly be said that the results are generally evocative for complex images, some of them featured sound that are reminiscent of certain local characteristics of the images. If the complex images can be more simplified using filters or image processing techniques such as "posterize" or "cartoon filter", they should produce more recognizable sounds.

5. CONCLUSIONS

This research aims to propose a sonification method that enables the listener to recognize objects in image regardless of their positions and visual transformations. To this end, we proposed the use of SIFT features as a new way to sonify feature-level information of images. The suggested model partially achieved the goal for sonification of simple objects, and showed certain characteristics of mid-level abstracted images.

In summary, sonification of image feature information showed advantages in keeping object-level characteristic as it is more robust to object-level changes such as scaling, moving, or transposing an object. It can also deal with certain level of image textures. Not only these characteristics are useful for previously attempted image sonification works, but also they show a strong potential for new application areas. The technique catches essential visual characteristics and makes identifiable sound, which can be used for audio support for the visually impaired, or generation of earcons from simplified images.

For further research, more object recognition techniques (including as edge detections) will be introduces to the model to provide even more abstraction to the data. Other sonification models and synthesis methods will also be

[1] http://aimlab.kaist.ac.kr/~dilu/research/SIFTSonification

incorporated and tested to find out methods with more natural and evocative results.

6. REFERENCES

[1] Augmented reality for the totally blind. Available: http://ww.seeingwithsound.com/

[2] S. Suzuki, "Topological structural analysis of digitized binary images by border following," *Computer Vision, Graphics and Image Processing*, vol. 30, pp. 32-46, 1985.

[3] D. G. Lowe, "Distinctive image features from scale-invariant keypoints," *International Journal of Computer Vision*, vol. 60, pp. 91-110, 2004.

[4] W. S. Yeo and J. Berger, "Raster scanning: a new approach to image sonification, sound visualization, sound analysis and synthesis," in *Proc. International Computer Music Conference*, 2008.

[5] D. Payling, S. Mills, and T Howle, "Hue music – creating timbreal soundscapes from coloured pictures," in *Proc. International Conference on Auditory Display*, 2007.

[6] T. Yoshida, K. M. Kitani, H. Koike, S. Belongie, and K. Schlei, "Edgesonic: image feature sonification for the visually impaired," in *Proc. the 2nd Augmented Human International Conference*, pp. 11:1-11:4, 2011.

[7] A. D. N. Edwards, A. Hunt, G. Hines, V. Jackson, A. Podvoiskis, R. Roseblade, and J. Stammers, "Sonification strategies for examination of biological cells," in *Proc. International Conference on Auditory Display*, 2010.

[8] S. Shelley, M. Alonso, D. Hermes, and A. Kohlrausch, "On the use of sound for representing geometrical information of virtual objects," in *Proc. International Conference on Auditory Display*, 2008.

[9] John Canny, "A computational approach to edge detection," *IEEE Transactions on Pattern Analysis and Machine Intelligence*, vol. PAMI-8, pp. 679-698, 1986.

REAL-TIME HALLUCATINATION SONIFICATION AND SIMULATION THROUGH USER-LED DEVELOPMENT OF AN IPAD AUGMENTED REALITY PERFORMANCE

Alexis Kirke
Interdisciplinary Centre for Computer Music Research,
Plymouth University, UK
alexis.kirke@plymouth.ac.uk

Joel Eaton
Interdisciplinary Centre for Computer Music Research,
Plymouth University, UK
joel.eaton@students.plymouth.ac.uk

Eduardo Miranda
Interdisciplinary Centre for Computer Music Research,
Plymouth University, UK
eduardo.miranda@plymouth.ac.uk

ABSTRACT

The simulation of visual hallucinations has multiple applications. For example in helping diagnosis, in helping patients to express themselves and reduce their sense of isolation, for medical education, and in legal proceedings for damages due to eye / brain injuries. We present a new approach to hallucination simulation, which was developed initially for a performance but proved to have potential uses to sufferers of certain types of hallucinations. The system allows real-time audio and visual expression, using an iPad. An individual can overlay their hallucinations in real-time on the iPad screen over the iPad's video camera image. The system has been developed focusing on the visual symptoms of Palinopsia, experienced by the first author, and hence has initially been user-led research. However such an approach can be utilized for other conditions and visual hallucination types. The system also allows the hallucinations to be converted into sound through visual sonification, providing another avenue for expression for the hallucinating individual. A musical performance is described which uses the system, and which has helped to raise awareness and to comfort some people who have Palinopsia symptoms. Although no formal experimentation was done outside of performance preparation, we report on a number of unsolicited informal responses to the simulator from palinopsia sufferers and a palinopsia charity.

1. INTRODUCTION

Palinopsia is a visual symptom involving trails in the visual field [1], as shown in Figure 1. In addition to this it can lead to very strong after-images [2], similar to when anyone stares at the sun and looks away – but this can be much stronger for Palinopsics and can be caused by objects which are not particularly bright – for example a door. One interesting aspect of Palinopsia is that it can occur in individuals who show no other ill effects. Palinopsia is a symptom rather than a condition. Oliver Sacks the author and neuroscientist, has had the symptoms of Palinopsia [3].

The academic study of Palinopsia is still in the early stages. Scientists are divided in their terminology, using differing terms such as Polyopia and Visual Perservation [4]. They also have different ideas about the causes of the condition. One possibility is a reduction of inhibition function in certain neurons in the visual cortex [5]. This could both explain how the after-image of a moving object is not cancelled out more firmly, and why the evolving patterns seem to come from nowhere, perhaps from under-supressed random firing of cortical neurons. There have also been interesting initial results concerning a common "visual trail rate" of 15-20Hz [6].

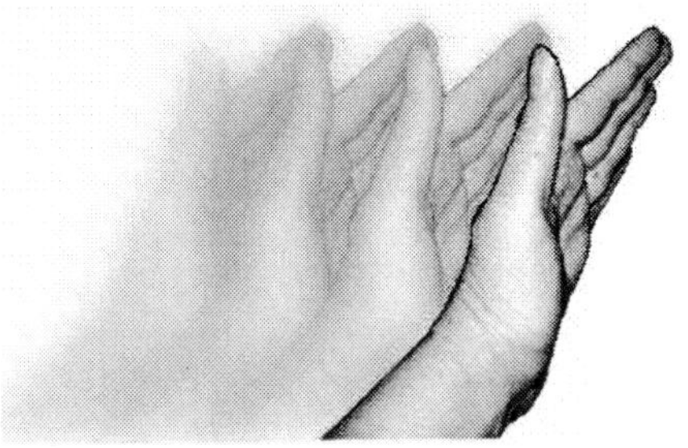

Figure 1. Visual Trails in Palinopsia

This lack of understanding of the condition could perhaps be aided by tools to enable Palinopsics to express their visual hallucinations more clearly to others. The Palinopsia Foundation in the USA have said that the "therapeutic uses for this application are endless. It could significantly help spread awareness of Palinopsia and understanding for those living with Palinopsia."[7] Thus software that can enable some of these people to express and discuss their visual disturbances with a close friend, or perhaps a therapist or medical professional they are working with, may be beneficial. It could help medical professionals and neuroscience researchers to gain a deeper insight into visualising precisely what the subjects are seeing.

For some the condition of Palinopsia is debilitating, for others they fail to realise the images are not real, and for many it is a lonely condition they are afraid to reveal to anyone. Oliver Sacks estimates that up to 90% of people with the hallucination condition Charles Bonnet syndrome do not mention their hallucinations to others [8].
In addition an artistic performance involving this software by a Palinopsic may help to raise awareness of the condition and help those who have the condition, and are

unaware they are not alone, to seek help if they need it; or just feel comfort if the symptoms are not debilitating.

2. SIMULATORS AND AUGMENTED REALITY

Static hallucination simulators are used to help people express exactly what hallucinations they have. There has been some work in the use Virtual Reality to model hallucinations to help in teaching people about schizrophrenia [9] and the pharmaceutical company Janssen Pharmaceuticals have actually developed a system for laptop and stereo glasses to simulate hallucinations [10] for training. But neither of these systems are truly interactive, or based on real-time augmented reality.

Augmented reality is a method of combining live camera data on a smartphone or tablet with real-time generatively generated images, both appearing on the screen simultaneously [11]. There are many applications available involving this. What is more rare are applications which manipulate the visual field to simulate what people are subjectively seeing. This is the application which was developed here, which has been labeled the "Hallucliphone".

3. HALLUCIPHONE

The Halluciphone was originally developed for a performance called "Insight". The basic system used in the performance consisted of an iPad with custom software allowing the first author to attempt to represent his hallucation effects. This data was sent to a laptop which then had MAX/MSP software for sonifying the visual effects. There has been previous work on sonification of visuals [12, 13] and also the sonification of medical data [14, 15]. The initial purpose of the sonification here was performative, and to draw attention to the hallucinations, giving them more 'reality'. However it may be that such sonification could help people to express their hallucations helpfully in a multi-modal way.

The augmented reality application that was developed could be made to 'hallucinate' in ways similar to the first author's vision. Whatever the iPad camera is seeing can be manipulated by my using the iPad multi-touch screen. Effects that can be controlled includes having groups of pixels randomly switch on and off. When these are combined with other elements related to Palinopsia, including visual after-images (see Figure 2) and trails on the iPad, the screen will be able to show a representation of the experienced visuals. This includes a simple interface to allow the performer to indicate where he is seeing patterns and images by touching the screen. Thus the audience is enabled to see some semblance of what is being experienced internally in what is usually "private" vision. It was this expression of private visual states which was the artistic motivation for the performance, but as time went on it became clear that many sufferers of hallucinations and their carers could gain benefits from having access to such a system.

3.1 iPad

The openframeworks development platform has advanced image processing features that can be integrated into the iOS platform for mobile deployment. This allows the Insight application to display a continuous video feed from the iPad's camera. The feed acts as input to the hallucination algorithms and provides a background layer to the hallucination effect layers which are overlaid. This provides a real-time projection of a reality layer and also hallucination effects, which are updated in-line with the video feed.

Figure 2: Halluciphone simulation of after-images

The hallucination controls are split into three modes that can overlap creating multi-layers of hallucinations. These modes are defined by their methods of user control and their resultant visual and audio functions and effects. Modes are entered via display-area specific touch commands on the reality layer. This allows for a continuous reality layer on screen, avoiding the need for any navigation menus or buttons that may obstruct an audiences' view of the projected mirrored display and detract the conductor from the hallucination experience. Mode specific commands provide control for instigating and manipulating layers of hallucinations. The three modes; single touch, multi-touch and visual echo; dictate the type of hallucination that can be applied to the display.

Single touch mode allows for an area of the video feed to be mapped into an after-image layer. The location of a users' touch dictates the on screen position of the after-image. The size of the after-image is defined by the time of the touch command, and the on-screen duration of the after-image is defined by the distance of a swipe movement after the initial touch command. Multiple instances of single touch commands can be initiated and overlapped.

Commands in multi-touch mode generate clusters of small after-image areas akin to stochastically arranged groups of circles. The cluster size and duration are, again, user definable, whereas individual after-image positioning within a cluster is fixed to a random ordering to mirror the randomness and blurring that occurs within Palinopsia.

Within the visual echo mode the video input is processed and generates echoes of delayed images. This creates the effect of visual trails surrounding a moving object whilst motionless background content is unaffected. Controls allow for speed of echoes and the duration of the effect. A feature of the visual echo mode is layers containing clusters of after-images, triggered and still visible before any echoes have been initiated, are also echo affected and echo simultaneously with the primary visual trails.

The technical implications of a software algorithm designed to emulate states envisioned only by a subject of Palinopsia offers a number of design and implementation issues. Successfully interpreting a neurological condition based upon text and conversational based descriptions requires considerable attention to detail as development is undertaken using limited references. A descriptive framework defines one persons' ultimate reality so wide margins for constant adjustment and refining need to be employed.

3.2 Laptop

The performances' success lay in the communication of the visual effects of Palinopsia to an audience. This allows for experimentation in how the visual effects of the condition can be musified. A dynamic framework of mapping visual effects to audio parameters allows for the user to select controls based on aesthetics. This assisted in creating a more engaging experience for an audience, where the performance is true to the condition, whilst allowing for creative artistic interaction

Figure 3 shows a view of a MAX patch to give an idea of how the various hallucination effects could be mapped onto the parameters of the synthesis units on the laptop. Figure 4 shows one of the 5 units which were available to the composer. Each unit could be loaded with a WAV file, which was then processed live by the mapped information from the iPad.

The actual mappings for the performance were selected through experimentation by the composer. This involved a process of setting up possible MAX/MSP mappings using a patch of the form shown Figure 3 (though the patch has been compressed here to fit into page) and trying them out in rehearsal. The top half of Figure 3 shows the various inputs from the iPad touchscreen. For example the brightness and variation on average across the screen, or the size of area over which an afterimage was switch on. These can be mapped onto the filter or effects parameters below. One of the most perceivable effects, in terms of linking it to hallucinations, turned out to be the delay at the bottom of Figure 3 – in particular as feedback loops built up. Levels of loudness were also significantly affected by the various visuals.

4. SCORES

The score has three elements. The performance involved a flute player, the first author controlling electronics via his laptop and the Halluciphone, together with lighting design so as to create a contrasting set of visuals for the Halluciphone. The audio score style was motivated by the commission being from a contemporary classical music festival, and a desire to create a "mysterious" sound that would echo the "mystery" of our internal perceptions and how they relate to other peoples'.

The purpose of the flute was to make the performance more organic, and sonically and visually dynamic for the audience, as well as more accessible for those coming to it as a contemporary classical concert. The flute also had an element of ephemerality which it was felt captured the unreal feel of the hallucinations. The flute score was in the idiom of contemporary classical music.

The first and third movements of the flute were constructed using motifs quoting classical electronic dance music from the late 1980s and 1990s. The second movement was written with some help from DJ Pierre, credited with developing the first "Acid House" [16] bass-line for the track "Acid Trax" as a member of the band Phuture. He sent an acapella version of a higher tempo version of the bassline from Acid Trax which was used as raw material for electronics in the third movement. The second movement was actually loosely based on the approach taken in DJ Pierre's bassline in Acid Trax. In acid house music, filtering is often used to change bassline characteristics – sometimes called "filter sweeps". The filter sweeps in the "Acid Trax" bassline can be seen in Figure 4. An excerpt from the 2nd Movement is shown in Figure 5. The second movement was largely made up of the flute playing the repetitive bass loop from Acid Trax. Parts of the line are played with notes having extended or reduced duration and loudness, reminiscent of the effect of filter sweeps.

The electronics utilized the audio provided by DJ Pierre directly, and also simple sounds which were chosen by the composer / first author for aesthetic reasons, but also because he knew from past experience that he found them hypnotic and they could therefore potentially focus him on any hallucinations. They were Binaural Beats, Sub-bass and White Noise. These were loaded into three of the sample channels shown in Figure 6. It was these electronics which were manipulated by the Halluciphone signals' patching using Figure 3.

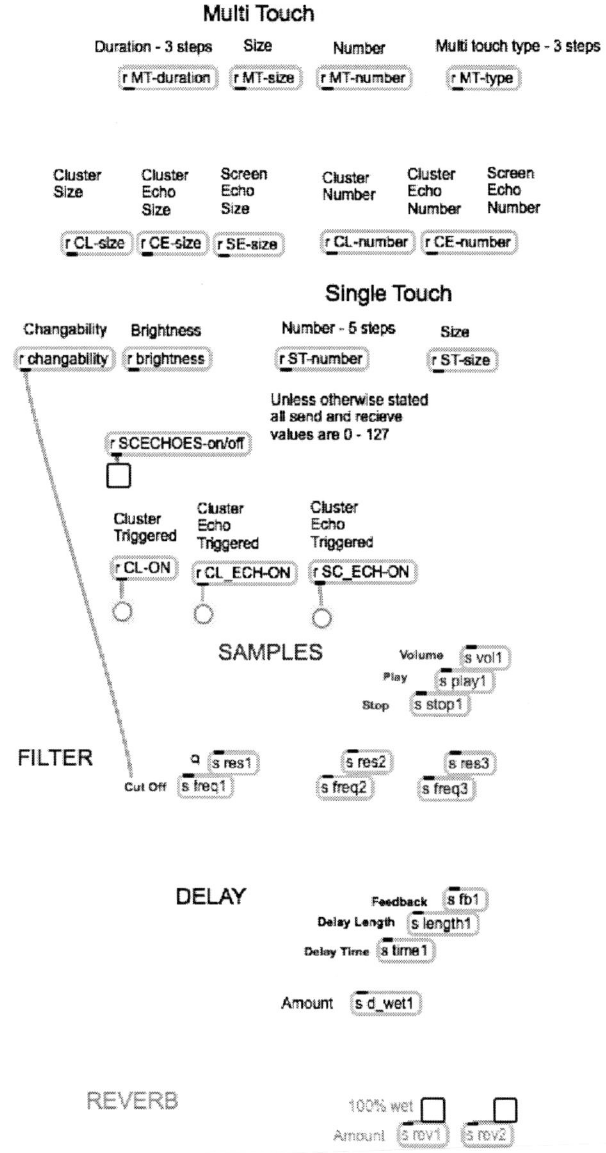

Figure 3: Mappings Available for Visuals Sonification

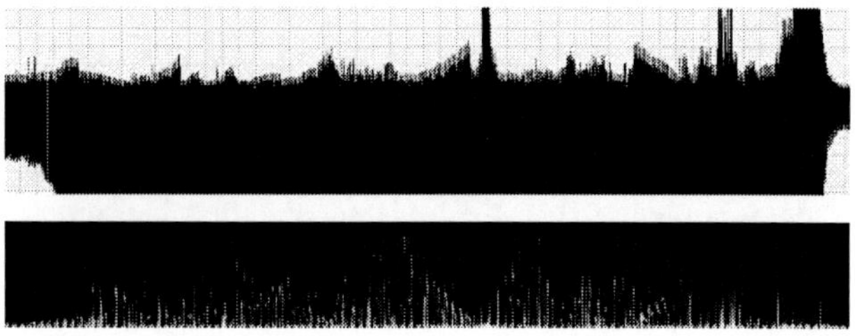

Figure 4: Waveform of Acid Trax bassline, plus spectragram of Filter Sweeps

Figure 5: Excerpt from 2nd Movement

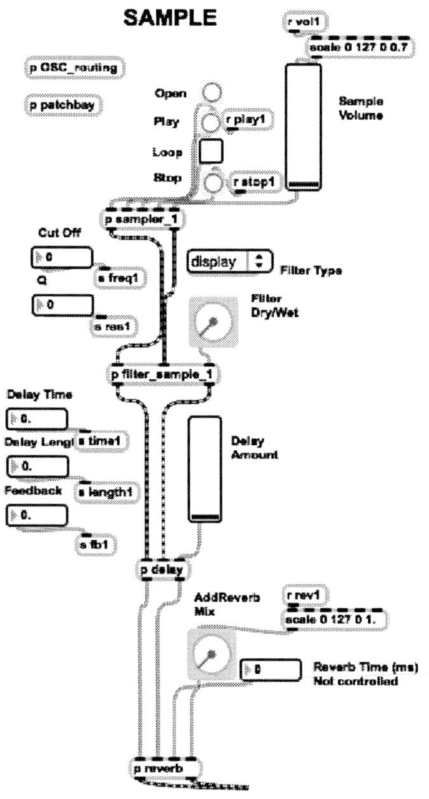

Figure 6: One of the Sonification channels on the Laptop

Cue	Track Time (sec)	State	Uptime (sec)	Previous state Downtime (sec)	Dwell time (sec)
0.5	0	Preset			
1	0	Blackout	0	0	30
2	30	Flute only	8	5	35
3	73		8	5	15
4	96		8	5	16
5	120	All audience at 45%	8	5	7
6	135	Just flute	5	8	105
7	248	Just flute	8	5	0
8	262	Stage flood-ed with light	1	0	1.5
9		Just Flute	0	0	0
10	284	Stage flood-ed with light	1	0	1.5
11		Just Flute	0	0	0
12	305	Stage flood-ed with light	1	0	1.5
Etc...					

Figure 7: Part of the Lighting Score use in the Performance

The lighting was designed so as to give a variety of visual effects to trigger and highlight hallucinations. They were controlled live by the lighting technician who knew the score and timings, and followed a lighting score, part of which is shown in Figure 7. An example photo of the visual echoes effect, highlighted by the lighting, is showing in Figure 8.

5. FEEDBACK

Because the project has so far been primarily performative in nature, no formal results are reported on the usage of the system as a hallucination simulator. However informal commentary from the Palinopsia Foundation and a number of sufferers of Palinopsia provide initial feedback together with motivation to extend the study into more formal realms.

The USA Palinopsia Foundation [17] are using a video demo of the iPhone version of our software to introduce their webpage. The following is a quote from a comment received anonymously as a result of the writer viewing a video of the Insight performance (sic): "*I have been suffering from these visals for about 14 years now, its only been in last few months that ive been learning about palinopsia and also hppd, i felt relieved knowing there was a name for something i have been suffering with for many years and just thought i was going mad... im really interested in talking to you i have just gone on the website you provided and was amazed by what you have done its exactly what i see.*" (sic) This also shows how the performance itself can be an effective vehicle for education as well as for raising awareness about the symptoms. A link to the video the person is referring to is given at the end of this paper. The next three quoted messages are from people who watched a demo of the simulator on Youtube: "*hi, I watched your iphone/ipad hallucination software video. Never ever thought I would find anyone else with this condition. I too have been suffering with it for almost a year now. I don't experience the trails but definitely the afterimages.*" "*I have had visual echoes for a month now and this is comforting that this isn't something much more serious.*" "*Thank you so much for this video... it allowed me to show people i love what i see when i have palinopsia, which is quite hard to describe just with words. Thanks!!*" (sic)

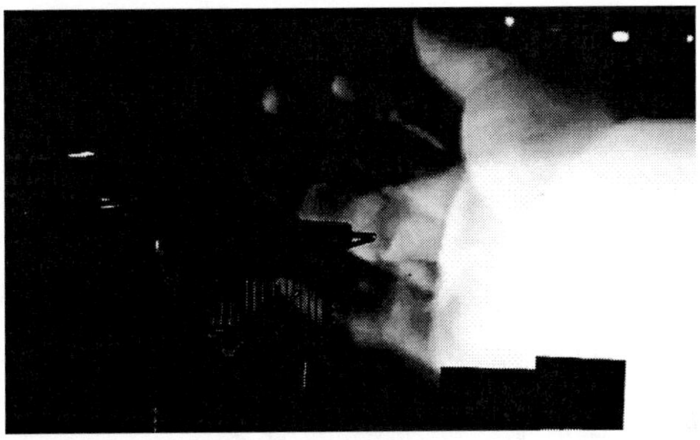

Figure 8: Visual Echo Simulation during the Performance Premiere

The performance premiered at Peninsula Arts Contemporary Music Festival 2012 at Plymouth University. It was found that the synthesizer at times suffered from feedback instability which needs to be investigated. It was also found that to create a sufficiently interesting performance the visual effects of the Palinopsia had to be slightly over-emphasized by the performer. However, allowing for this over emphasis, the performer in particular found that the visual echoes and the after images were quite often reasonable simulations, especially with the lighting score was implemented. The performance can be seen here:
http://www.youtube.com/watch?v=a5cKUkDyR1U

6. CONCLUSIONS

We have introduced a performance which highlights a new approach to hallucination simulation, allowing real-time audio and visual expression, using an iPad. An individual can overlay their hallucinations in real-time on the iPad screen over the iPad's video camera image. Such an approach could be utilized for other conditions and visual hallucination types. The system also allowed the hallucinations to be converted into sound through visual sonification. The musical performance – for which the system was initially developed - was described, which has helped to raise awareness and comfort some people who have Palinopsia symptoms. Because the project has so far been primarily performative in nature, no formal results were reported on the usage of the system as a hallucination simulator. However informal commentary from the Palinopsia Foundation and a number of sufferers of Palinopsia provide initial feedback together with motivation to extend the study into more formal realms.

7. REFERENCES

[1] H. Pomeranz and S. Lessell, "Palinopsia and polyopia in the absence of drugs or cerebral disease", *Neurology*, vol. 54, no. 4, pp. 855-859, 2000.

[2] S. Van der Stigchel, T. Nijboer, D. Bergsma, J. Barton, and C. Paffen, "Measuring palinopsia: characteristics of a persevering visual sensation from cerebral pathology", *J Neurol Sci.*, vol. 316, no.1-2, pp.184-8, 2012.

[3] O.Sacks, *The Minds Eye*, Alfred A. Knopf, 2010.

[4] D. Kömpf, H.Piper, B. Neundörfer and H. Dietrich "Palinopsia (visual preservation) and cerebral polyopia--clinical analysis and computed tomographic findings" *Fortschr Neurol Psychiatr.* Vol. 51, No. 8 pp.270-281, 1983.

[5] S. Van der Stigchel, T. Nijboer, D Bergsma, J Barton and C. Paffen, "Measuring palinopsia: Characteristics of a persevering visual sensation from cerebral pathology", *Journal of the Neurological Sciences*, vol. 316, pp. 184–188, 2012.

[6] J. Dubois and R. VanRullen, "Visual Trails: Do the Doors of Perception Open Periodically?" *PLoS Biology*, Vol. 9, No. 5, 2011.

[7] Palinopsia Foundation, Personal Communication, Non-profit Foundation, USA, 2011.

[8] O. Sacks, *Hallucinations*, Alfred A. Knopf, 2012.

[9] S. Brown, "Implementing a Brief Hallucination Simulation as a Mental Illness Stigma Reduction Strategy", *Community Mental Health Journal*, vol. 46, no. 5, pp. 500-504, 2010.

[10] F. Mantovani, G. Castelnuovo, A. Gaggioli, and G. Riva, "Virtual Reality Training for Health-Care Professionals", *CyberPsychology & Behavior*, vol. 6, no. 4, pp. 389-395, 2003.

[11] D. Van Krevelen and R. Poelman, "A survey of augmented reality technologies, applications and limitations", *Journal of Virtual Reality*, vol. 9, no. 2, pp. 1-20, 2010.

[12] J. Clemons, Y. Bao, M. Bagra, T. Austin and S. Savarese, "Scene Understanding for the Visually Impaired Using Visual Sonification by Visual Feature Analysis and Auditory Signatures", *Journal of Vision*, vol. 12, no.9, 2012.

[13] M. Bujacz, P. Skulimowski and P. Strumillo, "Sonification of 3D scenes using personalized spatial audio to aid visually impaired persons", In *Proc. Int. Conf. on Auditory Display*, Budapest, Hungary, 2011.

[14] C. Giller, A. Murro, Y. Park, S. Strickland and J. Smith, " EEG Sonification For Epilepsy Surgery: A Clinical Work-In Progress", *Proc. Int. Conf. on Auditory Display*, Atlanta, GA, 2012.

[15] T. Kagawa, H. Kudo, S. Tanoue, H. Mori, H. Nishino and K. Utsumiya, "A Supporting Method of Medical Imaging Diagnosis with Sonification", *Conf. on Complex, Intelligent and Software Intensive Systems*, pp.699-704, Palermo, 2012.

[16] P. Blashill, "Six Machines That Changed the Music World", *Wired Magazine*, 10.05, 2002.

[17] www.palinopsiafoundation.org, *Palinopsia Foundation*, Non-profit Foundation, USA.

Sound processing

Spectral Distortion Using Second-Order Allpass Filters

Greg Surges, Tamara Smyth
Music Department
University of California, San Diego
{gsurges, trsmyth}@ucsd.edu

ABSTRACT

This work presents a technique for detuning or applying phase distortion to specific spectral components of an arbitrary signal using a cascade of parametric second-order allpass filters. The parametric second-order allpass provides control over the position and slope of the transition region of the phase response, and this control can be used to tune a phase distortion effect to a specific frequency range. We begin by presenting the phase response of a cascade of first-order filters, which we relate to that of the parametric second-order allpass. Time-varying parameters and the time-varying phase response are derived for the second-order case, and we provide examples demonstrating the frequency-selective phase distortion effect in the context of processing of instrumental sounds.

1. INTRODUCTION

Allpass filters are a fundamental synthesis building-block, and have many applications in computer music. Allpass filters have been studied with applications to both synthesis and effects processing, often in cascaded form or with modulation of the filter coefficients. In [1], the dispersive effects of a cascade of first-order allpass filters are exploited to produce a frequency-dependent delay effect, called a spectral delay filter. Kleimola et al., in [2], propose the use of a cascade of filters, with audio-rate modulation of coefficients, to obtain complex AM- and FM-like spectra, with applications to synthesis, physical modeling, and effect processing. The dispersive effects of cascaded allpass filters have been used in physical modeling of piano strings [3] and spring reverberators [4]. Finally, Lazzarini et al. describe the use of a first-order allpass filter in phase distortion synthesis [5], where the authors modulate the filter coefficient with a modulation function designed to create a desired time-varying phase shift.

In this paper, we describe the use of cascaded parametric second-order allpass filters in detuning and phase distortion applications. The parametric second-order allpass used here has some important advantages over the first-order, as it offers greater control over the phase transition region - the range of frequencies where the largest amount of phase distortion will occur. Instead of directly modulating coefficients, we focus on modulating the filter parameters which control the placement and size of this transition region. This makes it possible to apply phase distortion to specific spectral bands, independently of others.

This work is part of a larger investigation into the use of cascaded allpass filters in generative self-oscillating feedback systems. By making the phase response of the feedback system time-varying, it is possible to avoid the static timbres characteristic of some feedback systems, and introduce more dynamic musical behaviors. Though the applications discussed in this work do not involve feedback systems, the techniques introduced here are a first step toward that goal.

In Section 2 of this paper, we derive the first-order allpass filter, and the phase response of a cascade of first-order filters. We also relate the first-order filter to the second-order allpass filter used in this work. In Section 3, we describe how the filter parameters and phase response can be made time-varying. A basic example of the detuning/phase distortion effect is provided. Applications to synthesis and processing of instrumental sounds are presented in Section 4.

2. THE ALLPASS FILTER

It is well known that an allpass filter has unity gain at all frequencies. It is, therefore, frequently used in situations where a frequency-dependent phase shift is desirable, without imparting any gain or attenuation.

2.1 First-Order Allpass Filter

A first-order allpass filter, given by

$$H_1(z) = \frac{c + z^{-1}}{1 + cz^{-1}}, \tag{1}$$

has a single pole and zero at $-c$ and $-1/c$, respectively, where $|c| < 1$ for stability. Because of the stability constraint, the pole at $-c$ lies inside the unit circle, while the reciprocal zero lies outside the unit circle (making the filter maximum phase). If the coefficient c is real, both pole and zero will lie on the real axis, with $|c|$ controlling the spacing of the pole-zero pair from the unit circle—a magnitude of c close to 1 positions the pole and its reciprocal zero closer to (as well as more equidistant from) the unit circle (see Fig. 1 for example of $c = 0.9$ and $c = -0.6$).

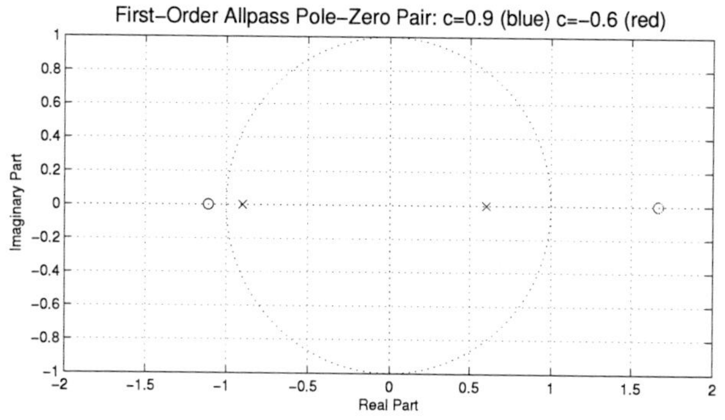

Figure 1. The position of the pole-zero pair for the first-order allpass filter (1). A coefficient of $c = 0.9$ yields the pair on the real axis to the left (blue) and $c = -0.6$ yields the pair to the right (red).

The magnitude of (1), is given by:

$$|H_1(\omega)| = \left| \frac{c + e^{-j\omega T}}{1 + ce^{-j\omega T}} \right| = 1, \quad (2)$$

where f_s is the sampling rate and $T = 1/f_s$ is the sampling period. A sampling rate of $f_s = 44100$ Hz was used throughout this paper.

The phase of (1) is given by

$$\begin{aligned} \angle H_1(\omega) &= \frac{\angle(c + e^{-j\omega T})}{\angle(1 + ce^{-j\omega T})} \\ &= \angle e^{-j\omega} + \angle(1 + ce^{j\omega}) - \angle(1 + ce^{-j\omega}) \\ &= -\omega + 2\tan^{-1}\left(\frac{c\sin(\omega)}{1 + c\cos(\omega)}\right), \end{aligned} \quad (3)$$

where the final result is obtained using the fact that $\angle z = \tan^{-1}(\Im(z)/\Re(z))$. Since the denominator inside the $\tan^{-1}(\cdot)$ is always positive (for $|c| < 1$), and the numerator can change sign, the contribution due to the $\tan^{-1}(\cdot)$ term has a possible range of $\pm\pi/2$ rad (and $\pm\pi$ rad for $2\tan^{-1}(\cdot)$), and thus contributes an oscillation around the first linear-phase term [6]. The result, as shown in Figure 2, is a phase response that is monotonically decreasing, with an overall decrease of 2π rad as ω increases by 2π rad / sample.

Rearranging (3) yields the following expression for the coefficient:

$$c = -\frac{\tan\left(\frac{\angle H_1 + \omega}{2}\right)}{\tan\left(\frac{\angle H_1 + \omega}{2}\right)\cos(\omega) - \sin(\omega)}, \quad (4)$$

which, for $\angle H_1 = -\pi/2$, conveniently reduces to

$$c = \frac{\tan(\omega/2) - 1}{\tan(\omega/2) + 1}. \quad (5)$$

That is, the behaviour of the phase response can be controlled to some extent using (5), by specifying the angular frequency

$$\omega = 2\pi\frac{f_{\pi/2}}{f_s} \text{ rad/sample}, \quad (6)$$

where $f_{\pi/2}$ is the frequency in Hz at which 90° ($\pi/2$) phase shift is reached.

A general higher-order all-pass filter can be made by cascading several first-order allpass sections

$$H_k(z) = \prod_{k=0}^{K} \frac{z^{-1} - a_k^*}{1 - a_k z^{-1}}, \quad (7)$$

where if the allpass filter has real coefficients, for each complex root a_k, there must be a corresponding complex conjugate root a_k^*, making the phase anti-symmetric about $\omega = 0$ [6]. The phase response for the overall filter is the sum of the phases for each section, and is given by

$$\angle H_k(\omega) = -K\omega - 2\sum_{k=1}^{K} \tan^{-1}\left(\frac{R_k \sin(\omega - \theta_k)}{1 - R_k \cos(\omega - \theta_k)}\right), \quad (8)$$

for $a_k = R_k e^{j\theta_k}$. In the following, we consider a special second-order case.

2.2 Second-Order Allpass Filter and its Cascade

Though there is some control over the behaviour of the first-order filter by using (5) to specify the frequency $f_{\pi/2}$ at which the phase response is $-90°$, more control is afforded using a special case of the second-order allpass filter, for which there is an additional "bandwidth" parameter [7].

The transfer function of a second-order allpass filter may be expressed using (7) for $k = 2$, but a more convenient formulation is given in [7] by:

$$H_2(z) = \frac{-c + d(1 - c)z^{-1} + z^{-2}}{1 + d(1 - c)z^{-1} - cz^{-2}}, \quad (9)$$

which allows for specification of coefficients

$$d = -\cos\left(\frac{2\pi f_\pi}{f_s}\right) \quad (10)$$

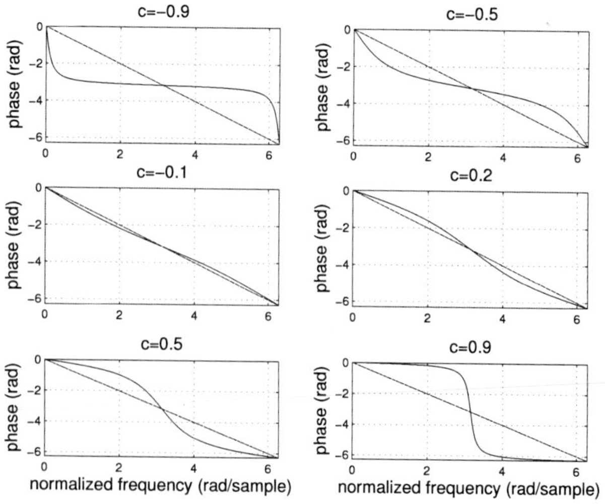

Figure 2. The phase response (blue), monotonically decreasing by 2π with an increase in ω of 2π, is shown with the linear-phase term - ω from (3).

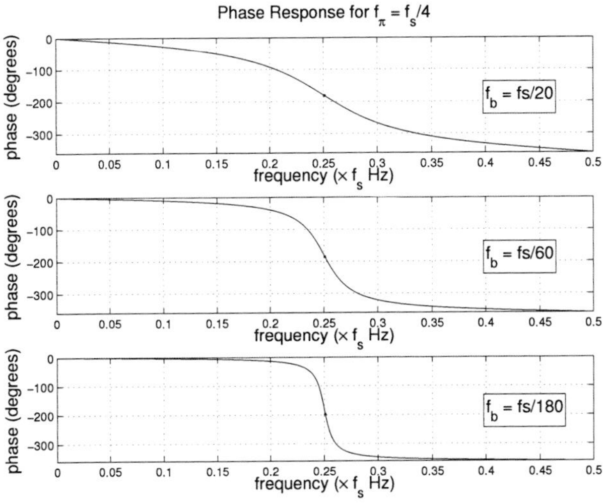

Figure 3. The phase response of the second-order allpass filter with $f_\pi = fs/4$ and with varying bandwidths f_b.

and

$$c = \frac{\tan(\pi f_b/f_s) - 1}{\tan(\pi f_b/f_s) + 1} \qquad (11)$$

according to the frequency f_π (in Hz) at which the phase response is -180° (or $-\pi$), and a bandwidth of the phase transition region f_b.

Figure 3 shows an example of the monotonically decreasing phase response where $f_\pi = f_s/4$ and several values are used for f_b. The curves begin with a gentle change in phase, followed by an increased downward slope reaching -180° at f_π, before tapering off again to a more gentle slope toward maximal delay. Adjusting f_π and f_b allows for both placement of the frequency point at which a 180° phase shift is reached, and control over the slope of the phase transition region.

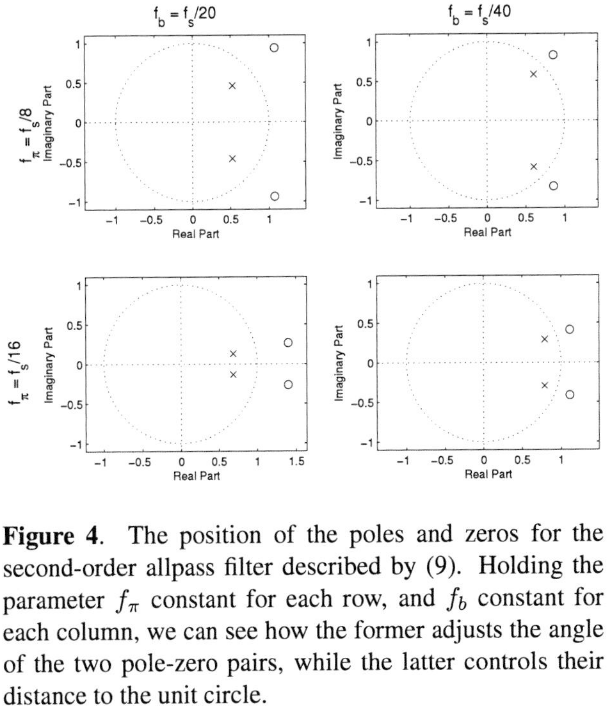

Figure 4. The position of the poles and zeros for the second-order allpass filter described by (9). Holding the parameter f_π constant for each row, and f_b constant for each column, we can see how the former adjusts the angle of the two pole-zero pairs, while the latter controls their distance to the unit circle.

The effect of the f_π parameter can also be seen in Figure 4 by how it adjusts the angle of the two pole-zero pairs on the unit circle. The bandwidth f_b controls the distance of the pole and zero to the unit circle.

3. PHASE DISTORTION WITH THE SECOND-ORDER ALLPASS

Through careful tuning of second-order allpass filter (9), it is possible to apply a time-varying phase distortion effect to a specific band of the spectrum.

3.1 A time-varying allpass filter

In order to make (9) time varying, it is necessary to redefine coefficients d and c as functions of time. In this work, rather than modulating the coefficients directly, it is the parameter f_π that is made time varying:

$$\tilde{f}_\pi(n) = f_\pi + M\cos\left(\frac{2\pi f_m n}{f_s}\right), \qquad (12)$$

where $\tilde{\cdot}$ indicates a function made time varying, f_π is as previously defined, M is the depth of modulation, f_m is the modulation frequency, and n is the discrete time index. Here, $\tilde{f}_\pi$ is modulated sinusoidally (though this is not a requirement), and can be seen as an FM signal, with f_π being the carrier frequency (which it will be subsequently called when referred to in the time-varying case).

The coefficient d from (10) is then replaced with

$$\tilde{d}(n) = -\cos\left(\frac{2\pi \tilde{f}_\pi(n)}{f_s}\right), \qquad (13)$$

yielding the filter's difference equation

$$\begin{aligned} y(n) &= -cx(n) + \tilde{d}(n)(1-c)x(n-1) + x(n-2) \\ &\quad -\tilde{d}(n)(1-c)y(n-1) + cy(n-2). \end{aligned} \qquad (14)$$

Expressing (9) as the difference equation in (14) follows the example of [2], in which filter output $y(n)$ is a combination of delayed versions of input $x(n)$ which are ring modulated with sinusoidally-varying coefficients. Here, in contrast, coefficient *parameters* are sinusoidally modulated yielding time-varying coefficients that are effectively FM signals as shown in (13). Following (8) for the phase of the general allpass, it can be easily be shown that the time-varying second-order allpass has a family of phase responses given by

$$\theta_A(\omega, n) = -2\omega + 2\tan^{-1}\left[\frac{\tilde{d}(n)(1-c)\sin(\omega) - c\sin(2\omega)}{1 + \tilde{d}(n)(1-c)\cos(\omega) - c\cos(2\omega)}\right] \qquad (15)$$

To gain some intuition for the effect of this new time-varying parameter $\tilde{f}_\pi(n)$, consider the effect of the parameters f_π, f_b, and M on this group of phase responses. Figure 5 illustrates an example for $f_\pi = f_s/4$ Hz, $f_b = f_s/40$

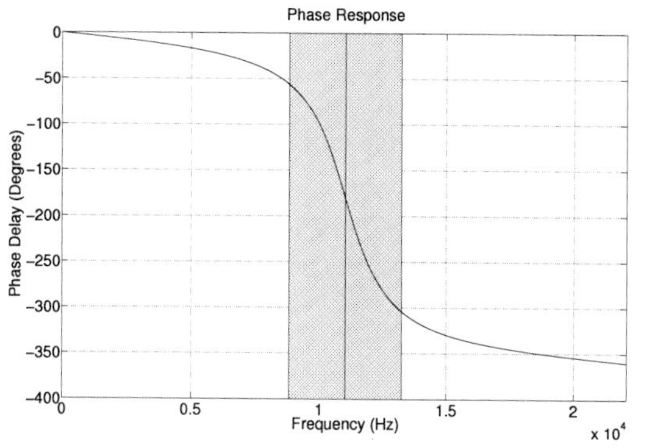

Figure 5. Effect of modulation depth and transition region on phase distortion. Vertical shaded region indicates range of $\tilde{f}_\pi(n)$, i.e. $f_\pi - M \leq \tilde{f}_\pi(n) \leq f_\pi + M$.

Hz, and $M = f_s/10$. Recalling (12), we can imagine the transition region centered on $\tilde{f}_\pi(n)$ being shifted up and down in frequency - left and right in Figure 5 - at a rate corresponding to f_m. The upper and lower limits of this shift are provided by M, and indicated by the shaded box in Figure 5. Spectral components in the shaded region will experience significant time-varying phase shift as f_π is modulated, while components outside of that region will experience relatively less. Components below the transition region will be delayed by a small and relatively stable amount, while those above the transition region will be delayed by a larger, but still relatively stable amount. By placing f_π at some frequency of interest, and tuning f_b and M to generate the appropriate transition region, we can apply phase distortion to components which fall into the transition region, while leaving others (relatively) unmodified.

Given a desired frequency deviation $|\tilde{f}_\pi(n)| - f_\pi$, there is a dependency between M and f_m. This can be explained by the interaction between the modulation frequency f_m and modulation index M in determining the instantaneous frequency of an FM signal. Following [8], and assuming a constant modulation index M, the instantaneous frequency of $\tilde{f}_\pi$ is given by:

$$\tilde{f}_\pi(n) = f_\pi - M f_m \sin(2\pi f_m n + \phi_m) \qquad (16)$$

By substituting a cosine modulation function (which allows us to disregard time, since the cosine will begin at maximum deviation), and rearranging (16) to solve for M, we obtain:

$$M = \frac{|\tilde{f}_\pi| - f_\pi}{f_m} \qquad (17)$$

where $|\tilde{f}_\pi|$ is the desired peak frequency deviation, and f_π and f_m are the carrier frequency and modulation frequency as defined above. Equation (12) then becomes:

$$\tilde{f}_\pi(n) = f_\pi - M f_m \cos\left(\frac{2\pi f_m n}{f_s}\right) \qquad (18)$$

As shown in (8), a cascade of identical allpass filters will produce an overall phase response that is the sum of the phases of each section. In addition, the composite filter will have a phase response with a similar curve to one section, with the only difference being a greater range between minimum and maximum delay (the range increasing by a factor of K, the cascade length). This is an important consideration, as the cascade length corresponds to the maximum possible amount of phase distortion. It is often necessary to adjust the cascade length to obtain the desired amount of distortion. In the following discussion, K is the cascade length in terms of second-order filters.

The bandwidth of a modulated cascade is similar to that of FM synthesis, but with a different dependency on the modulation index M. Whereas for classical FM synthesis, the bandwidth can be approximated by

$$BW_{fm} = 2(M + 1) f_m, \qquad (19)$$

the approximate maximum bandwidth of a modulated second-order allpass is given by:

$$BW_{ap} = 2(M + 2) f_m \qquad (20)$$

Thus, given an input signal with a single component with frequency f_0, the resulting spectrum will consist of

$$f_0 \pm k f_m, \text{ where } k = \{0, 1, ...M + 2\}. \qquad (21)$$

The cascade length K has a small effect on the overall bandwidth, by introducing additional, smaller amplitude sidebands. It has been shown that cascades of allpass filters can become unstable due to numerical error when larger values of K are used [9], so K generally should not be used as a bandwidth parameter. Both f_b and K affect the relative amplitudes of f_0 and the generated sidebands. In the case of a single second-order allpass filter, as f_b decreases, the amplitudes of the sidebands increase while that of f_0 decreases. As K increases, the amplitudes are affected in a more complex manner, due to the recursive processing at each stage in the allpass cascade. If each allpass stage is modulated at the same rate, the output of each stage will contain sidebands at the same frequencies. The generated sidebands sum to produce more complex spectra, with slightly larger bandwidths, as further sidebands are generated around components from earlier allpass stages. It is important to note that the above measures only apply when input components fall into the transition region controlled by f_b. Input components which fall to either side of this region will be affected to a lesser extent or hardly at all, as described above.

In summary, the parameters of the modulated second-order filter cascade are as follows:

- f_π: modulated filter "carrier" frequency - controls placement of frequency band affected by modulation.
- f_b: filter "bandwidth" - affects width of frequency band affected by modulation, and amplitudes of sidebands.
- f_m: modulation frequency - controls spacing of sidebands at audio rate / speed of vibrato at sub-audio rates.

- M: modulation depth - controls maximum bandwidth of spectrum at audio rate / depth of vibrato at sub-audio rates.
- K: filter cascade length - affects amount of phase distortion applied to frequencies in phase transition region, also affects overall bandwidth. Large K can lead to instability.

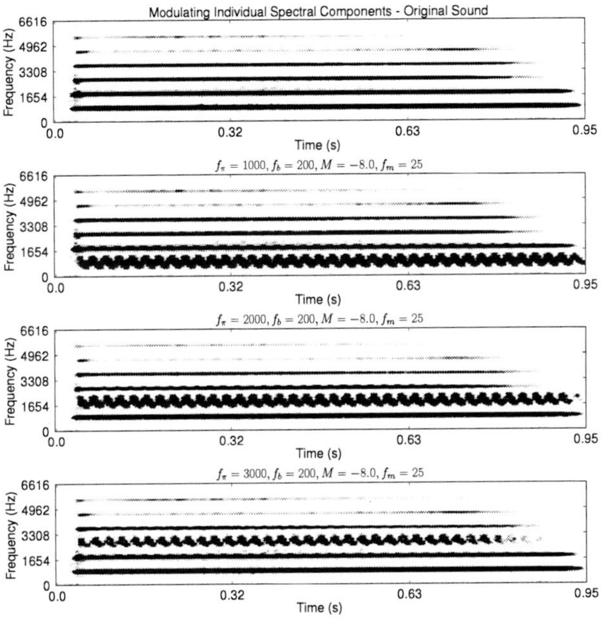

Figure 6. Modulating individual components of clarinet tone. From top to bottom: spectrograms of the original signal and processed versions in which frequency modulation was applied to the fundamental, first, and second harmonics, respectively. In all cases, $\tilde{f}_\pi(n) = f_\pi - Mf_m \cos(2\pi f_m n/f_s)$, $K = 10$.

3.2 Simple Application to a Clarinet Sample

To demonstrate the frequency-selective nature of this effect, consider a clarinet tone, which contains primarily odd harmonics. Figure 6 shows the effect of a modulated allpass cascade on the spectrum. The allpass cascade has been tuned to affect only specific harmonics of the clarinet sound. The carrier frequency f_π is set to the frequency of the ith harmonic and the bandwidth f_b is set to 200 Hz. This creates a narrow transition region with a steep slope centered around the frequency of the harmonic. The carrier f_π is modulated by a 25 Hz sinusoid.

4. APPLICATIONS

As a basic signal processing effect, it is possible to use this technique to animate the spectra of steady-state tones (as in the clarinet example of above). As shown previously in Figure 6, specific spectral components can be modulated independently. This effect could be useful to add interest to otherwise static timbres, perhaps as a post-processing stage applied to common "analog" waveforms. Here we discuss other musical applications.

4.1 Modulation at Sub-Audio Rates

As described above, through careful tuning of the filter parameters, it is possible to apply a frequency modulation effect to specific frequency ranges independently of others. With sub-audio coefficient modulation rates, this produces a selective vibrato effect. Various partials can be modulated independently of the rest, as illustrated in Figure 7. A recording of a clarinet improvisation was processed with a cascade of second-order allpass filters, adding a $f_m = 2$ Hz vibrato to a selected portion of the spectrum. The filter carrier frequency f_π was set to 3674 Hz (the visual midpoint of the spectrum), and a wide filter bandwidth $f_b = 800$ was used in order to affect a range of frequencies. The modulation depth M was set to 300, producing a 600 Hz swing for $\tilde{f}_\pi(n)$ (17), and it was necessary to use a filter cascade of length $K = 15$ in order to obtain the amount of phase distortion necessary to produce dramatic changes in frequency. Referring back to Figures 3 and 5, we see how f_b affects the slope of the phase transition region. As f_b is increased, producing a more shallow slope, the amount of phase distortion applied to any particular frequency component will decrease. By increasing K, we can compensate for this by increasing the maximum phase delay of the system - and consequently the phase delay applied to any given input component.

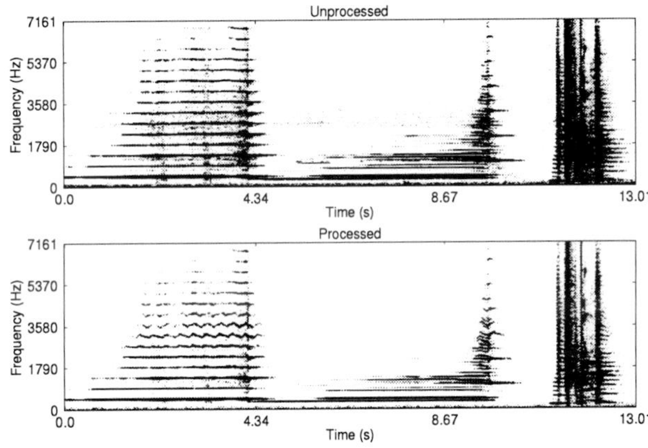

Figure 7. Clarinet passage with spectral modulation of selected harmonics for $f_\pi = 3674$ Hz, $M = 300$, $f_b = 800$ Hz, $f_m = 2$ Hz. Length of allpass cascade $K = 15$.

4.2 Audio-Rate Phase Distortion

In addition to sub-audio modulation, it is possible to modulate the filter parameters at audio rates. As described in Section 3, this has the effect of building FM-like sidebands around component frequencies present in the original signal because of the ring-modulation and FM terms in (14), and therefore can produce very rich spectra. Figure 8 provides a spectrogram of a clarinet performance through a single cascade of identical second-order allpass filters, which are driven by a fundamental frequency estimator. The carrier frequency f_π is set to the estimated fundamental.

In this case, the upper harmonics of the sound are left relatively unmodified, while the lower components (those nearest to the estimated fundamental frequency) are significantly modulated. FM-like sidebands appear around at 100 Hz intervals around the distorted frequencies. The amplitude envelopes of new components follow those of the originals. Temporal aspects are also preserved, but a smearing effect is added. There is a possible trade-off that may need to be considered as greater cascade lengths produce a more pronounced "smearing" effect.

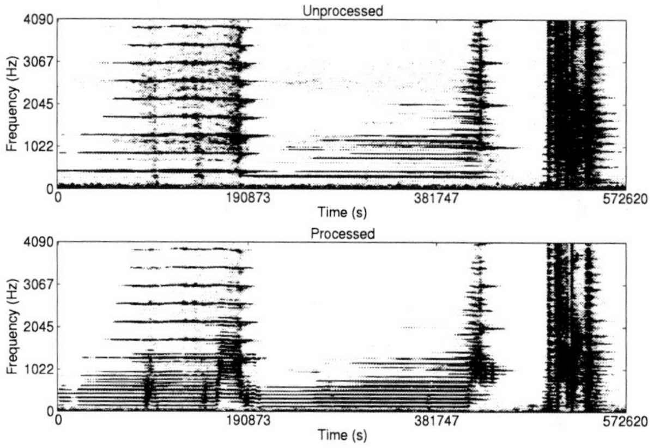

Figure 8. Clarinet passage with $\tilde{f}_\pi(n)$ driven by fundamental frequency estimator. Here, $f_m = 100$ Hz, $M = 1$, $f_b = 500$ Hz, and f_π is the estimated fundamental. Cascade length is $K = 5$.

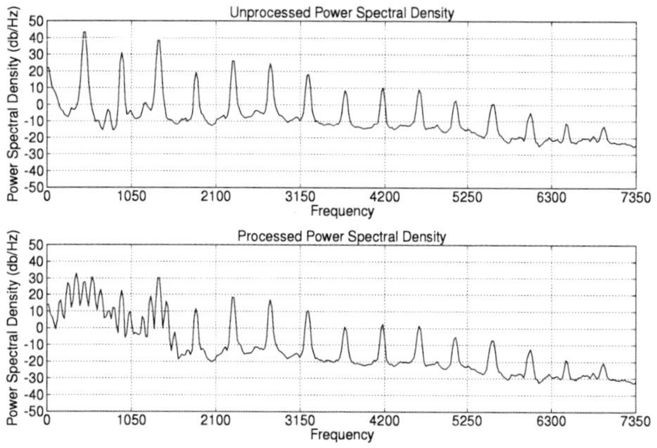

Figure 9. Example of audio-rate modulation of $\tilde{f}_\pi(n)$ on clarinet tone. Parameters used are the same as those in Figure 8.

Figure 9 provides another view of this effect on a portion of the clarinet passage used above. The excerpt used is approximately the first sonority of Figure 8 (approximately the first 4 seconds). Here, we see spectra of both the distorted and undistorted clarinet tone. The estimated fundamental frequency and a few of the surrounding components exhibit significant sidebands, while the remainder of the spectrum is left relatively unmodified. The effect of the interaction between M and f_b is to control the range of affected components (see Figure 5).

The spectrum of the modulated tone is dense, and contains subharmonics not present in the original signal. The overall spectral envelope follows that of the original tone.

5. CONCLUSION

Cascaded and coefficient-modulated second-order allpass filters have useful applications in detuning and phase distortion applications. The second-order allpass provides a greater amount of control over the transition region of the phase response than does the first. This property can be used to apply phase distortion to only specific frequency ranges. The parametric second-order allpass filter was presented, along with a means of making the parameters - and therefore the coefficients - time-varying. This allows for the use of the filter as a frequency-selective phase distortion effect, and a simple example of this effect applied to a clarinet tone was provided. Some more realistic example applications were also provided. The first example demonstrated a low-frequency detuning effect applied to the upper harmonics of a recorded clarinet passage, and the second applied a high-frequency phase distortion to the same passage.

These filters are also being studied as components in self-oscillating feedback systems, where they provide a method of avoiding static timbres without introducing unwanted gain or attenuation into the system. By introducing a time-varying, frequency-dependent phase shift, the system function changes over time, thus producing dynamic and evolving sonic behavior.

This technique could also be extended to modulation of the filter bandwidth parameter f_b, the use of non-sinusoidal parameter modulation functions, and the use of second-order allpass cascades as a synthesis technique - whether driven by a sinusoid or some other signal. Finally, multiple cascades with different time-varying parameters could be used in series, applying differing amounts of phase distortion to various spectral bands.

6. REFERENCES

[1] V. Välimäki, J. S. Abel, and J. O. Smith, "Spectral delay filters," *Journal of the Audio Engineering Society*, vol. 57, pp. 512–531, 2009.

[2] J. Kleimola, J. Pekonen, H. Penttinen, V. Välimäki, and J. S. Abel, "Sound synthesis using an allpass filter chain with audio-rate coefficient modulation," in *Proceedings of the 12th International Conference on Digital Audio Effects (DAFx-09), Como, Italy*, 2009, pp. 305–312.

[3] J. Ruahala and V. Valimaki, "Tunable dispersion filter design for piano synthesis," in *Signal Processing Letters, IEEE*, vol. 13.5, 2006.

[4] J. S. Abel, D. P. Berners, S. Costello, and J. O. Smith, "Spring reverb emulation using dispersive allpass filters in a waveguide structure," in *Audio Engineering Society Convention 121*, 2006.

[5] V. Lazzarini, J. Timoney, J. Pekonen, and V. Välimäki, "Adaptive phase distortion synthesis," in *Proceedings of the 12th International Conference on Digital Audio Effects (DAFx-09), Como, Italy*, 2009, pp. 1–8.

[6] P. Kabal, "Minimum-phase & all-pass filters," Department of Electrical & Computer Engineering, McGill University, Tech. Rep., 2011.

[7] U. Zölzer, *DAFX: Digital Audio Effects*. Wiley Publishing, 2011, ch. 2.

[8] T. Smyth. Modulation index cont. [Online]. Available: http://musicweb.ucsd.edu/~trsmyth/modulation/Modulation_Index_cont.html

[9] J. S. Abel and J. O. Smith, "Robust design of very high-order allpass dispersion filters," in *Proceedings of the 9th International Conference on Digital Audio Effects (DAFx-06), Como, Italy*, 2006.

[10] M. Cherniakov, *An Introduction to Parametric Digital Filters and Oscillators*. Wiley Publishing, 2004.

[11] B. Schottstaedt. An introduction to fm. [Online]. Available: https://ccrma.stanford.edu/software/snd/snd/fm.html

[12] A. V. Oppenheim, R. W. Schafer, and J. R. Buck, *Discrete-Time Signal Processing*. Prentice Hall, Englewood Cliffs, NJ, 1989, vol. 2.

MULTICHANNEL CONTROL OF SPATIAL EXTENT THROUGH SINUSOIDAL PARTIAL MODULATION (SPM)†

Andrés Cabrera
Media Arts and Technology
University of California
Santa Barbara, USA
andres@mat.ucsb.edu

Gary Kendall
Artillerigatan 40
Stockholm, Sweden
garyskendall@me.com

ABSTRACT

This paper describes a new sound processing technique to control perceived spatial extent in multichannel reproduction through artificial decorrelation. The technique produces multiple decorrelated copies of a sound signal, which when played back over a multichannel system, produce a sound image that is spatially enlarged. Decorrelation is achieved through random modulation of the time-varying sinusoidal components of the original signal's spectrum extracted using a modified version of the Loris sinusoidal modeling technique. Sinusoidal partial modulation (SPM) can be applied in varying measure to both frequency and amplitude. The amount of decorrelation between channels can be controlled through adjusting the inter-channel coherency of the modulators, thus enabling control of spatial extent. The SPM algorithm has lent itself to the creation of an application simple enough for general users, which also provides complete control of all processing parameters when needed. SPM provides a new method for control of spatial extent in multichannel sound design and electroacoustic composition.

1. INTRODUCTION

Multichannel reproduction poses challenges to sound designers and electroacoustic composers that do not exist in traditional stereo. In particular, how does one control the listener's perception of spatial imagery across an expanded reproduction space, especially attributes like spatial extent. When listening to sounds in the real world, it is often easy to judge the size and extent of a sonic event. For example, the auditory image of a truck is larger, not only louder, than a cell phone, both of which appear smaller than the sound of the city in the background. If these three sounds were to be recorded and played back over a single loudspeaker, they would no longer be differentiated by the size of their auditory images. Most importantly, the background sound of the city would no longer be surrounding the listener.

The most straightforward idea for controlling spatial extent is to spread a signal across multiple loudspeakers, but this fails almost completely due to the influence of the precedence effect [2]. Controlling the relative distribution of amplitude across loudspeakers, as provided variously by VBAP [3], DBAP, and changing the order of Ambisonics [4], does nothing to address the influence of precedence, which varies with the source material and the relative size of the reproduction setting [2]. What can have an effect is the interaction of the loudspeaker signals with the acoustics of the room, but changes in spatial extent are rather like side effects. Wavefield Synthesis [5] can reconstruct complete acoustic soundfields, but provides no methodology for the control of perceived spatial extent.

The work presented here aims to provide a practical tool for controlling spatial extent in multichannel settings, from 5.1 and octophonic systems to three-dimensional loudspeaker arrays. Audio source material is manipulated to produce multiple decorrelated copies of a sound signal for distribution over a multichannel system. Decorrelation is achieved through random modulation of the time-varying sinusoidal components of the original signal's spectrum, extracted employing sinusoidal modeling. Additionally, by employing parameters outside their normative range, this technique can also be used for unusual creative sound processing.

2. BACKGROUND

2.1 Auditory Spatial Impression

Auditory Spatial Impression (ASI) is the characteristic of human auditory sensation associated with the acoustics of sources in a physical space. It attempts to group together all the sensations related to the spatial qualities and characteristics of the perceived sound. It has been described as composed of three distinct components: "spaciousness", "size impression," and reverberation [6]. It is generally accepted that "spaciousness" itself consists of at least two separate and distinct components [7,8]:

1. Apparent Source Width (ASW) is defined as the "width of a sound image fused temporally and spatially with the direct sound image
2. Listener envelopment (LEV) is defined as "the degree of fullness of sound images around the listener".

† This paper is based on material presented in [1].

ASW includes the sensations of broadness, blurriness and ambiguity of localization, while LEV imparts the sensation of fullness and surrounding [9]. ASW has also been called by some authors *perceived spatial extent* [10] and *individual source width* [11] in the context of loudspeaker reproduction.

An alternative approach to describing spatial impression has been proposed by Griesinger, who from the perceptual perspective of a recordist partitioned spatial impression into three components Continuous Spatial Impression (CSI), Early spatial impression (ESI) and Background spatial impression (BSI) [12]. These concepts and terminology, however, are not as widely used and cited as the previous.

The concept of Apparent Source Width is well accepted within the acoustics community, and it has been shown that the phenomenon is related the perception of spatial extent that occurs in multi-channel reproduction of incoherent or decorrelated signals [13]. However, to distinguish it from the acoustic phenomenon, the term "spatial extent" will be employed here for the phenomenon experienced in loudspeaker reproduction.

2.2 Incoherent Signals in Reproduction

The similarity of signals played back over multiple loudspeakers is instrumental in the perceptual fusion of these signals into a single auditory image in the phenomenon known as the *precedence effect*. However, if the signals are different, they will be perceived as separate sources originating from separate spatial locations. A particular and important case occurs when signals contain the same spectral components and energy distribution, but differ in their on-going phase relationships. Their time domain representations can be so different that there is no coherent temporal relationship between them. The simplest example is two independent noise signals, which will have the same spectrum but a wholly different and unrelated time-domain waveforms. When incoherent and spectrally identical signals are played back over two loudspeakers, the spatial image can vary from two identical sounding sources in two locations to one image with a broad spatial extent. There are three parameters that have been shown to influence the perception of spatial extent of the sound. They are:

1. The location of loudspeakers with respect to the listener and each other.
2. The amount of decorrelation between the signals in the speakers and its corresponding effect on the decorrelation between the signals at each ear.
3. The level difference between the loudspeakers.

As shown by Damaske [14], the broad spatial extent produced by incoherent noise is very clear when the loudspeakers are separated by a narrow angle. When the angle becomes wider, the image tends to dissociate and will be split between both loudspeakers, with less sound material perceived in between. For example, according to Damaske an angle of 90° between two frontal loudspeakers can result in dissociated and independent images. Damaske also investigated the effect of varying the amount of decorrelation in quadraphonic reproduction, and found that when the degree of incoherence for a band of noise increased, so did the perception of spatial extent. Wagener showed that the degree of envelopment could also be controlled with relative signal levels using delayed incoherent reflections. As the level of the incoherent reflections increased, so did the perceived envelopment [14].

2.3 Fluctuations of ITD and ILD

It has also been shown that modulation of interaural time difference (ITD) and interaural level difference (ILD) can affect the perception of spatial extent in a similar way. Aschoff showed that fast moving sources can produce wide images when the speed of movement is too fast for the auditory system to track [14]. Griesinger found that fluctuations of ITD and ILD with frequencies lower than 3Hz have the effect of making the perceived sound move [15]. However frequencies greater than this will result either in a wider image, or the perception of a narrow image in the presence of a surrounding ambiance. Mason et al has showed that the magnitude of fluctuations in the ITD is related to the perception of ASW [16].

Mason et al. later showed that the relation between decorrelation and ASW is mediated by frequency, as some frequency areas, like the mid range, require more decorrelation to be perceived as wide as lower frequencies with less decorrelation [17].

3. SINUSOIDAL PARTIAL MODULATION (SPM)

3.1 Rationale

There is a long history of audio techniques that aim to enhance perceived spatial extent. The vast majority of these techniques involve manipulations in the time domain, though many produce spectral artifacts such as coloration and phasiness. Of these, particularly noteworthy is that of using random-phase all-pass filters first proposed by Kendall [10], because the technique is able to produce controlled levels of decorrelation among multiple audio channels. These decorrelation filters were shown to affect the precedence effect as well as perceived source width. Potard and Burnett [18] enhanced Kendall's all-pass filtering technique by decomposing the sound into three sub-bands (Low 0-1 kHz, Mid 1-4 kHz and High 4-20 kHz) that enabled different amounts of decorrelation to be applied. Both techniques suffer artifacts due to their static filtering, because the localization cues for any particular band of frequencies is static.

Discussed here is an innovative technique especially appropriate to multi-channel reproduction called Sinusoidal Partial Modeling (SPM). This technique applies controllable amounts of dynamic modulation to the partials of a source signal. Through the technique of sinusoidal modeling a set of time-varying sinusoidal partials together with residual energy information can be extracted from a source signal. Decorrelation can then be introduced at the resynthesis stage through modulation of the frequency and amplitude of the partials, which are resynthesized using oscillator banks, one for each output channel. Thereby any number of decorrelated copies of a monophonic source signal can be created. In multichannel reproduction, they produce a wide image. This approach to decorrelation can offer the following advantages over previous techniques:

1. Any number of output channels can be produced.
2. Since there is no time-domain filtering involved and modulation can be kept below perceptual thresholds while still achieving decorrelation, only spatial characteristics of the source, i.e. source width, should be affected.
3. Because the decorrelation is dynamic, the typical artifacts of static decorrelation like phasiness or static location cues will not be present. The product of this technique can resemble natural spatial widening occurring due to reverberation because of this dynamic nature.
4. SPM can provide control over the source width for multichannel playback, as the decorrelation can be carefully tailored to different circumstances, by affecting parts of the spectrum in different ways or controlling the relation between decorrelation and speaker location
5. The algorithm can also be used as a creative sound design tool to modify the sound drastically through extreme modulation (beyond the point where it is clearly audible as pitch deviation) that will have spatial effect as it is different for every channel.

There are also some disadvantages to this approach. Sinusoidal modeling is applicable to processing a wide variety of sources although it tends to be less successful at capturing full mixes, which might include frequent complex transients and quickly varying noise and sinusoidal components. It will generally perform better with individual tracks or submixes which can be mixed together. However, in the present implementation, effort was made to minimize artifacts through custom improvements, so that full mixes are rendered more successfully given appropriate settings.

3.2 The Algorithm

Sinusoidal Modeling is well suited to allow independent modulation of each of the components with the knowledge that the perceived source identity will be preserved if the modulation stays within perceptually detectable thresholds. Additionally, the amount of decorrelation among different regions of the spectrum within a single channel or between channels can be precisely controlled through controlling the similarity between the modulating signals for the bands.

The algorithm presented here attempts to avoid the obvious drawbacks of sinusoidal modeling by adopting and enhancing the Loris model [19]. The Loris technique for analysis/resynthesis was chosen because it uses the time-frequency reassignment method, which produces greater precision in time and frequency for a particular window size than other frequency estimation techniques. This means the analysis can use smaller windows with better frequency resolution than regular FFT, while also reducing time and transient smearing through time reassignment. This allows for a very high precision of sinusoidal tracking while giving adequate transient representation. Additionally, Loris provides a method for representing the residual/stochastic energy of a signal in the form of energy "band-width," which is assigned to partials then recreated using "band-width enhanced" oscillators. Consequently, the inter-channel decorrelation level of the stochastic energy can be controlled as precisely as the deterministic part. These two characteristics make Loris a good starting point for the system discussed here, as it is best able to represent most types of practical signals.

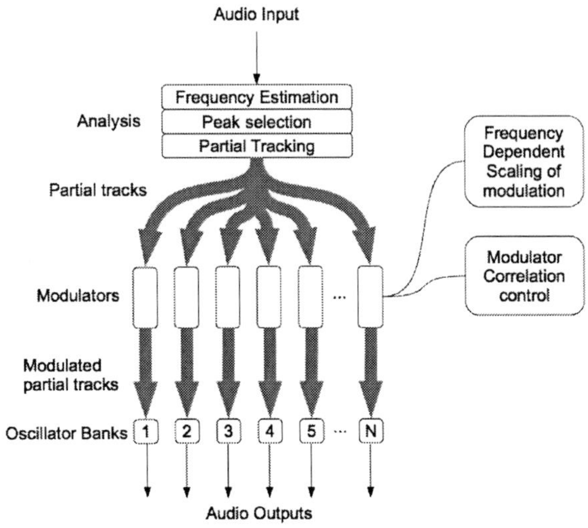

Figure 1. Overview of algorithm for Sinusoidal Partial Modulation.

3.3 Resynthesis and Decorrelation

A set of oscillator banks, one for each output channel, resynthesizes the input signal based on its sinusoidal analysis. As specified in Loris, the basis for resynthesis is the bandwidth-enhanced oscillator, which has frequency, amplitude and bandwidth as parameters for each breakpoint in the partial tracks. It is at this stage that the frequency and amplitude are modulated to produce inter-channel decorrelation. The modulator curves for partial track modulation need to have the following characteristics:

1. They must be random but low-passed to sub-audio frequencies to avoid audible sidebands.
2. The values must be clamped within +/- *max* to limit the maximum deviation from the original frequency and to have no DC offset.
3. They should be economical in terms of CPU usage, as a great number of them need to be calculated.
4. The signal must not make big sudden jumps that could easily stand out.

The random modulators could be constructed by low-pass filtering white noise, which would generate band-limited signals, but having that many filters running continuously would have a huge impact on CPU load. Additionally, although the range can be easily limited, there would be no way of preventing large jumps in the signal other than reducing the range. Because of this, an alternative simple method for generating low-passed modulator signals was developed. The signal is constructed by performing quadratic interpolation between random value breakpoints that are produced at regular intervals. How the random breakpoint generator works is shown in Figure 2. The maximum frequency of the modulator signal can be controlled and will be half the rate at which new breakpoints are produced. Each new random breakpoint is limited to a range around the previous one, in a sort of random walk algorithm. This guarantees that the jumps are never too large. Additionally to make sure the random values stay within the upper and lower limits, it is necessary to clamp the edges of the random range, forcing the breakpoint values to tend toward the center when they are close to the edges. This can be seen in Figure 2 at point 5, where the top of the range from point 4 has been reduced.

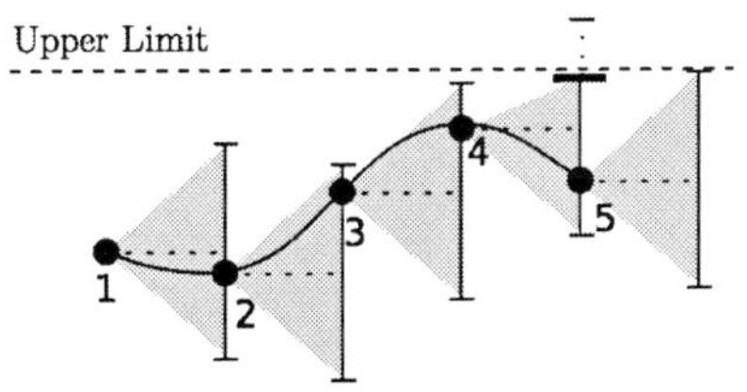

Figure 2. Random value generation constraints applied to one modulator signal.

The starting "phase" of the random modulator update function are randomized, so that each modulator will produce points at a different moments in time. This is necessary to avoid having high likelihood of the modulators peaking and having minimums at the same point in time, or other parallel motion that could be perceived.

An example of an actual modulator signal is shown in Figure 3, where random points are generated every 512 points, with a maximum jump of 1. Due to the interpolation, the modulator curves can occasionally and briefly cross the limits. This is not a problem as it would only mean a minor temporary increase in frequency or amplitude deviation.

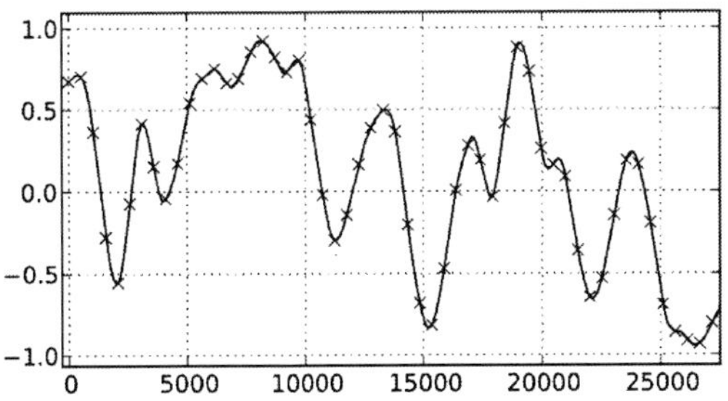

Figure 3. Resulting random modulation curve.

The coherency of the modulators and therefore the coherency between the output signals can be controlled by having a modulator bank which can be mixed together in any desired way to produce the final modulators. In this way coherency between output signals can be carefully controlled. Although not a widely studied subject, it seems likely that random modulation occurring within a critical band could cancel out or be diminished within the ear. To ensure this does not happen, one independent modulator is used per critical band (24 in total) so that sinusoidal partials falling within the same channel and same critical band are modulated by highly correlated signals.

3.4 SPM Implementation

The SPM algorithm was implemented in C++ to be able to reuse as much code from Loris as possible, though many parts of Loris still needed to be rewritten or modified. The resulting program is called Sprokit (SPatial PROcessing KIT) is designed for multiple platforms, including Linux, OS X and Windows. Any audio processing like Sprokit that involves FFT-based processing will introduce latency as a window of samples must be accumulated before any process can take place. Additionally, this process must accumulate the output of at least two windows in order to do the partial tracking as trajectories to the peaks of the second window start already during the resynthesis time of the first window.

Because the calculations for the modulators require more CPU time than current systems can provide, the program currently runs offline, that is, it must load a file and write the output files to disk, rather than streaming to an audio card. However, it is internally designed to eventually meet real-time requirements. It implements streaming analysis and resynthesis, which has the benefit for offline processing of enabling the processing to stop at any moment, while still producing a valid output audio file.

The interface has a main window showing the most important parameters that affect the spatial properties of the sound like relative level of the output signals and amount of decorrelation. The rest of the parameters are in a separate "properties" dialog window which is available if the user requires more advanced control. Figure 4 shows the final graphic user interface running on Linux. A set of sliders to allow per-channel adjustment of level (trim) and wet/dry mix. This was deemed useful as level and mix enable an engineer or composer to adjust the spatial image, a clearly desirable and practical feature. This particular implementation is limited to eight output channels, which was considered sufficient for most practical uses, although the algorithm itself has no such enforced limit.

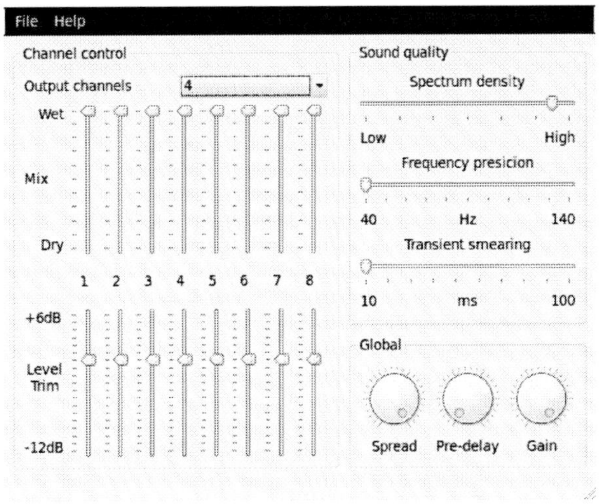

Figure 4. Main graphical user interface for Sprokit.

The algorithm parameters not presented in the main window of the application are accessible in the properties dialog window from the application's menus. This dialog window, has an initial page containing the parameters for analysis and resynthesis, and two additional pages with the specific parameters for frequency and amplitude modulation.

A simple preset mechanism was developed to be able to quickly switch between different configurations for consistent testing. Separate presets for the analysis and the resynthesis parameters are implemented to allow holding one constant while experimenting with the results of the other.

3.5 Objective Evaluation of SPM

A comparative objective study was performed to determine the effects of the SPM technique on interaural cross correlation (IACC) and other computational measures predicting spatial extent. The tests were conducted to verify that the algorithm produced interaural effects in a similar way to other techniques known to produce an enlarged source width, such as incoherent noise or sound processed through all-pass random-phase filters. To perform the tests, a set of typical audio signals were prepared in addition to coherent and incoherent noise. These signals were passed through the Kendall decorrelation algorithm [10] and the SPM multichannel decorrelation. Then, all the processed and original signals were rendered binaurally using convolution of HRIRs positioning them according to five selected loudspeaker configurations and simulating the effect of the cross-talk that would occur if the signals were played back over loudspeakers in the specified locations. These binaural signals were evaluated using three different metrics (Interaural cross-correlation coefficient, Interaural cross-correlation fluctuation function and Mason's Perceptually Motivated Measurement of Spatial Sound Attributes (PMMP)) to verify that the algorithm affects predictors of source width. The result confirmed that SPM affected predictors of spatial extent as expected and in ways comparable to Kendall decorrelation.

3.6 Strategies for Multichannel Sound Design

A wide image width is obtained when decorrelated signals are routed to each separate loudspeaker. The most continuous impression of width is likely to be achieved when loudspeakers are not too far apart; otherwise, there might be an empty space perceived between the speakers. Using a higher density of loudspeakers tends to produce a better impression of width and of being surrounded by the sound.

For a 5.1 setup, when the source is monophonic, the original source can be placed on the center speaker, with decorrelated copies on the other four. This creates a frontal bias, because transients will be stronger and sharper in the original signal, and the decorrelated copies will spread the sound around the listener. If a center loudspeaker is not available, the original sound can be mixed into the front channels. Using pre-delay in this case can help the center channel stand out, or blend better if desired.

A useful strategy when processing a stereo sound source for an octophonic layout is to place the original stereo signal in the front pair of speakers without transformation (dry only), and then on the other three speakers on the left, decorrelated copies of the left channel, and similarly for the right. This has the effect of preserving the original transients of the signal, with strong bias towards front localization, while still producing an effective spread of the sound in all directions. The lateral (left-right) separation of the original stereo source is also accurately preserved.

Since the processing works best for individual sources, it can be used as part of the compositional process to treat individual elements independently. The decorrelated copies of elements can then be positioned and used as desired, allowing for different width parameters, spread and spatial locations and for each source. The processed and unprocessed signals can be distributed across space by treating them as independent objects using techniques like VBAP or ambisonics. This would allow moving sources as well as potentially interesting spatial effects like adjusting source width dynamically or merging and separating sources.

4. CONCLUSIONS

This paper has presented a novel method for controlling apparent spatial extent in multichannel reproduction. The Sinusoidal Partial Modulation (SPM) method produces and controls the multichannel decorrelation of audio signals, through bringing together in an unusual way two usually separate areas of audio signal processing: sinusoidal modeling and decorrelation. The SPM algorithm is suitable for processing as wide a variety of audio material as sinusoidal modeling is. For the most satisfying results, the algorithm should be applied to individual tracks or submixes.

Most existing decorrelation techniques are based either on static phase shifts (generally using time domain filtering) or on applying modulation across the time domain signal as a whole. The SPM decorrelation technique is in a way a mixture between the two since the amount of phase shift varies through random modulation and is different for different areas of the spectrum. Thus, the decorrelation produced by this technique is both frequency dependent and dynamic. The SPM technique also allows very fine control over the decorrelation in relation to frequency. This opens new possibilities for the exploration of the frequency dependence of decorrelation. Then too, dynamic decorrelation is less prone to the kind of artifacts typical of other techniques. For example, the timbre of the output appears less colored.

Finally, the algorithm lent itself to the creation of an application simple enough for general users, but providing complete control of all processing parameters when needed.

5. REFERENCES

[1] A. Cabrera, *Control of Source Width in Multichannel Reproduction Through Sinusoidal Modeling*, Ph.D. dissertation, Queen's University Belfast, 2012.

[2] G. Kendall and A. Cabrera, "Why Things Don't Work: What You Need To Know About Spatial Audio," *Proceedings of the International Computer Music Conference,* Huddersfield, England, 2011.

[3] V. Pulkki, "Virtual sound source positioning using vector base amplitude panning," *J. Audio Eng. Soc.,* vol. 45, no. 6, pp. 456–466, 1997.

[4] D. G. Malham and A. Myatt, "3-d sound spatializationambisonic techniques," *Computer Music Journal,* vol. 19, no. 4, pp. 58–70, 1995.

[5] M. M. Boone and E. N. Verheijen, "Multichannel sound reproduction based on wavefield synthesis," in *Audio Engineering Society Convention 95*, 1993.

[6] T. Okano, L. Beranek, and T. Hidaka, "Relations among interaural cross-correlation coefficient (IACCE), lateral fraction (LFE), and apparent source width (ASW) in concert halls," *J. Acoust. Soc. Am.*, vol. 104, no. 1, pp. 255–265, July 1998.

[7] M. Morimoto and Z. Maekawa, "Effects of low frequency components on auditory spaciousness," *Acustica*, vol. 66, pp. 190–196, 1988.

[8] J. S. Bradley and G. A. Soulodre, "Objective measures of listener envelopment," J. *Acous. Soc. Am.*, vol. 98, no. 5, pp. 2590–2597, November 1998.

[9] A. M. Sarroff and J. P. Bello, "Toward a computational model of perceived spaciousness in recorded music," *J. Audio Eng. Soc.,* vol. 59, no. 7/8, pp. 498–513, 2011.

[10] G. Kendall, "The decorrelation of audio signals an its impact on spatial imagery," *Computer Music Journal*, vol. 19:4, pp. 71–87, 1995.

[11] F. Rumsey, "Spatial quality evaluation for reproduced sound: Terminology, meaning, and a scene-based paradigm," *J. Audio Eng. Soc.*, vol. 50, no. 9, pp. 651– 666, September 2002.

[12] D. Griesinger, "The psychoacoustics of apparent source width, spaciousness and envelopment in performance spaces," *Acta Acustica*, vol. 83, no. 4, pp. 721–, July/August 1997.

[13] R. Mason and F. Rumsey, "A comparison of objective measurements for predicting selected subjective spatial attributes," in *112th AES Convention*, May 1013 2002.

[14] J. Blauert, *Spatial hearing: the psychophysics of human sound localization*, revised ed. MIT press, 1997.

[15] D. Griesinger, "The psychoacoustics of Apparent Source Width, spaciousness & envelopment in performance spaces," Lexicon, Tech. Rep., 1997.

[16] R. Mason, F. Rumsey, and B. de Bruyn, "An investigation of interaural time difference fluctuations, Part 1: the subjective spatial effect of fluctuations delivered over headphones," in *110th AES Convention*, 2001.

[17] R. Mason, T. Brookes, and F. Rumsey, "Frequency dependency of the relationship between perceived auditory source width and the interaural cross-correlation coefficient for time-invariant stimuli," *J. Acous. Soc. Am.,* vol. 117, no. 3, pp. 1337–1350, 2005.

[18] G. Potard and I. Burnett, "Control and measurement of apparent sound source width and its applications to sonification and virtual auditory displays," in *Proceedings of ICAD 04-Tenth Meeting of the International Conference on Auditory Display*, 2004.

[19] K. Fitz and L. Haken, "On the use of time-frequency reassignment in additive sound modeling," *J. Audio Eng. Soc*, vol. 50, no. 11, pp. 879–893, 2002.

Real time digital audio processing using Arduino

André Jucovsky Bianchi
Computer Science Department
University of São Paulo
ajb@ime.usp.br

Marcelo Queiroz
Computer Science Department
University of São Paulo
mqz@ime.usp.br

ABSTRACT

In the search for low-cost, highly available devices for real time audio processing for scientific or artistic purposes, the Arduino platform comes in as a handy alternative for a chordless, versatile audio processor. Despite the fact that Arduinos are generally used for controlling and interfacing with other devices, its built-in ADC/DAC allows for capturing and emitting raw audio signals with very specific constraints. In this work we dive into the microcontroller's structure to understand what can be done and what are the limits of the platform when working with real time digital signal processing. We evaluate the behaviour of some common DSP algorithms and expose limitations and possibilities of using the platform in this context.

1. INTRODUCTION

Arduino is the name of a hardware and software project started in 2005 which aims to simplify the interface of electric-electronic devices with a microcontroller [1]. It evolved from the *Processing* software IDE [1] (2001) and the *Wiring* software and hardware prototyping platform [2] (2003). Hardware, software and documentation designs are published under free licenses (Creative Commons BY-SA 2.5, GPL/LGPL and CC BY-SA 3.0, respectively) and a large community has grown to provide code and support for newcomers. Nowadays, many Arduino hardware designs are available and range from more limited 8-bit microcontrollers to fully featured 32-bit ARM CPUs. Besides, other advantages of Arduino for academic and artistic use are its mobility (because of its low power needs and possibility of running on batteries for hours, if not days depending on the use), expandability (because of its standardized interface for attaching so called hardware *shields*) and price (selling for under 20 US dollars online).

Despite all these advantages, the Arduino platform has a somewhat limited processing power when compared to standard processors available in the market, as for example DSP chips such as Analog Device's Blackfin 32-bit RISC processors [3] and FPGA-based processors such as Xilinx Virtex-7 family [4]. Research and industry advances have led to optimized computational performance and power consumption for these platforms [2], but we could not find a thorough examination of the use of a low-tech device such as the Arduino.

In this work, we aim to systematically expose the microcontroller-based Arduino platforms' possibilities for carrying real time digital audio processing tasks so there can be more accurate elements to be taken into account when making the choice for a platform. Code examples can be downloaded from the IME/USP Computer Music Group webpage [5].

1.1 Related work

Arduino has been experimentally used as a real time audio processor for sampling audio and control signals with an effective rate of 15.125 KHz [3], which provided the base for our investigation. Also, an ALSA audio driver was implemented to use the Arduino Duemilanove [4] as a full-duplex, mono, 8-bit 44.1 KHz sound card under GNU/Linux.

2. METHODS

In order to meet the needs for real time audio processing, the microcontroller has to be tweaked so we can capture, process and output analog audio. Each of these tasks can be performed in a variety of ways, and for this examination we chose to go with the basic functionalities of the platform.

In this investigation, we used an Arduino Duemilanove with an ATmega328P microcontroller from Atmel, a very modest version of the platform. It has an 8-bit RISC central processor, operates with a base frequency of 16 MHz, and has memory capacity of 32 KB for program storage and 2 KB for random access [5]. From now on, whenever we refer to *the microcontroller*, we are in fact talking about this specific model from this specific manufacturer.

2.1 Microcontroller's elements

To be able to know how to configure the platform to suit our needs, a general understanding of the inner workings of a microcontroller is needed. The Atmel megaAVR series

[1] http://www.processing.org/
[2] http://wiring.org.co/

[3] http://www.analog.com/en/processors-dsp/blackfin/products/index.html
[4] http://www.xilinx.com/products/silicon-devices/fpga/virtex-7/index.htm
[5] http://compmus.ime.usp.br/en/arduino

microcontroller is comprised of several components, some of which are fundamental for our investigation and so will be briefly covered in this section.

2.1.1 Clocks

Many *clocks* provide the frequencies in which the different parts of the microcontroller work. They are basically either emitters or dividers of square wave signals that provide the frequency of operation of the CPU, the ADC, the memory access and other components of the microcontroller. Possible sources of clock frequencies are crystal and RC oscillators.

A useful concept associated with clocks is the one of a *prescaler*. Prescalers are dividers for clock frequencies that either actually lower the frequency of a clock or at least trigger specific interrupts on a (power of two) fraction of a clock's frequency.

The *system clock* provides the system's base frequency of operation. Other important clocks are the *I/O clock* and the *ADC clock* used for feeding a frequency to most of the input/output mechanisms. It is possible to choose which clock will feed a frequency to some parts of the system, as well as select prescaler values independently. In our study, we make use of the *timer clock* prescaler to control the PWM frequency that drives our DSP mechanism, as we will see in Section 2.3.

2.1.2 Registers and interrupts

The microcontroller's CPU is comprised of an arithmetic logic unit that works with 32 *registers* – portions of memory that provide data for computation as well as determine the execution flow of the program. An *interrupt* is an attempt of deviation from the current execution flow that can be triggered by a variety of events in the system, usually by setting reference values on specific registers.

In our case, interrupts are of extreme value as they are the low level structures that allow us to execute code with a somewhat fixed frequency (at least if we assume that the clock frequencies are indeed constant in relation with real time).

2.1.3 Timers/counters

A *timer*, or *counter*, is a register whose value is automatically incremented according to a specific clock. When a counter hits its maximum value it is reset to zero and signals an overflow interrupt, which may cause a certain function to be called.

Timers are important in the context of DSP because they provide a natural way to perform many of the DSP chain tasks, as for example to periodically launch the input signal sampling function (that fills the input buffer) and to emit a PWM square wave which, after analog low-pass filtering (through an integrator), corresponds to a smooth analog signal. The ATmega328P has two 8 bit counters and one 16 bit counter, each having different sets of features but all being capable of doing PWM.

2.1.4 Input and output pins

Microcontrollers can receive and emit digital signal through *I/O pins*, which in the case of the Arduino board are conveniently mounted in such a way that it is easy to plug other components and boards. These pins are read from and written to according to frequencies governed by different clocks (I/O, ADC and others).

In principle, the microcontroller pins are designed to work with binary signals represented by two different voltages (0 V and 5 V with a threshold value to account for small deviations). Despite that, I/O pins come equipped with handy mechanisms for sampling band limited input signals whose voltages vary between the reference extremes, and also for generating waveforms that, after being filtered, output varying signals of the same nature. These mechanisms are, respectively, the analog-to-digital converter (ADC) and the pulse-width modulation (PWM), which will be seen in the next sections.

2.1.5 Memory

The microcontroller has 3 manageable memory spaces for storing the program and working data, and the following table summarizes the different characteristics and purposes for each type of memory:

Type	Size (KB)	Data persistency	Write time (clock ticks)	Endurance (write/erase cycles)
Flash	32	yes	1	10,000
SRAM	2	no	2	n/a
EEPROM	1	yes	30	100,000

Usually, the Flash memory stores the program, the SRAM memory stores volatile data used along the computation, and the EEPROM is used for longer-term storage between working sessions. Notice that the amount of SRAM memory represents a hard limit for many DSP algorithms. A 512 point lookup table filled with precalculated sinewave bytes, for example, represents 25% of all available working space. Thus, it might be interesting to store hardcoded data in the program memory whenever possible if memory working space is lacking.

2.2 Audio in: ADC

Data can flow into the microcontroller in a variety of ways, the most basic being embedded mechanisms for digital serial communication and analog-to-digital conversion using the input pins. The former mechanism can feed digital data directly into memory, while the latter can either read 1 bit from an input pin (as explained in the last section) or sample an analog value between the reference voltages using 8 or 10 bits resolution.

Rather than providing the microcontroller with digital data, our setup uses the embedded analog-to-digital conversion to sample an audio signal using the microcontroller pins' ADC mechanism. This choice was made so the signal can be directly connected to the microcontroller (i.e. no external device has to be used for sampling) and we can study the device's performance taking into account this crucial step in the digital audio processing chain.

The ADC uses a *Sample and Hold* circuit that holds the input voltage at a constant level until the end of the conversion. This fixed voltage is then successively compared with reference voltages to obtain a 10 bit approximation. If a faster conversion is desired, precision can be sacrificed and the first 8 bits can be read before the last 2 are computed. Conversion time takes between 13 and 250 μs, depending on several configuration parameters that influence the precision of the result.

As noted before, the ADC mechanism has a dedicated clock to ensure conversion can occur independently of other microcontroller parts. Also, the mechanism can be triggered manually (on demand) or automatically (a new conversion starts as soon as the last one has finished).

2.3 Audio out: PWM

Once the input signal has been sampled and processed, one way to convert it back to analog is to use the embedded *pulse-width modulation* (PWM) mechanism that is available in some of the output pins of the microcontroller, followed by an analog filtering stage. A PWM wave encodes a determined value in the width of a square pulse. In order to do this, it defines a *duty cycle* as the percentage of time that the square wave has its maximum value in relation to the total time between square pulses (see Figure 1). The encoding of a value x ranging from X_1 to X_2 is just the enforcement of a duty cycle with a percentage equal to $\frac{x-X_1}{X_2-X_1}$.

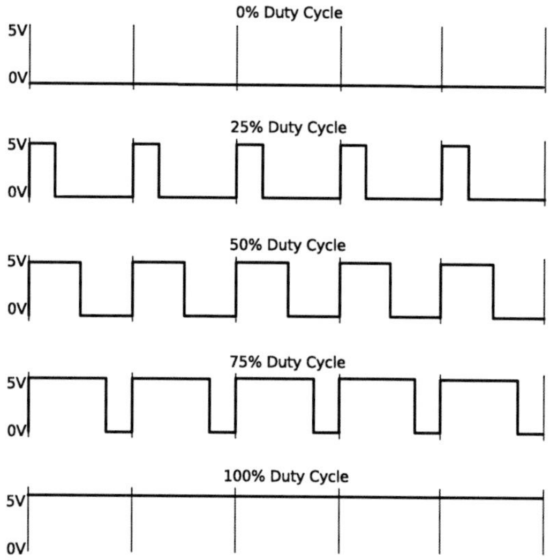

Figure 1. Examples of PWM waves with different duty cycles. The left alignment of the waves corresponds to the Fast PWM mode.

The final analog filtering stage is needed to remove high frequency components present in the square wave spectrum to reconstruct a band limited signal. In our case, this filtering is made from a simple RC integrator circuit that stands between the output pin and a normal speaker.

The PWM mechanism can operate in different modes which vary according to how the reference value to be encoded relates with a counter's signal to generate the output values of the modulated wave. In *Fast PWM* mode, the output signal is set to 1 in the beginning of the cycle and becomes 0 whenever the reference value becomes smaller than the counter value (see Figure 2). This mode has the disadvantage of outputting the square pulses aligned to the left of the PWM cycle, and so the *Phase correct* mode is available to solve this problem at the expense of cutting the signal generation frequency in half. It works by making the counter count back to zero instead of being reset when it hits its maximum value.

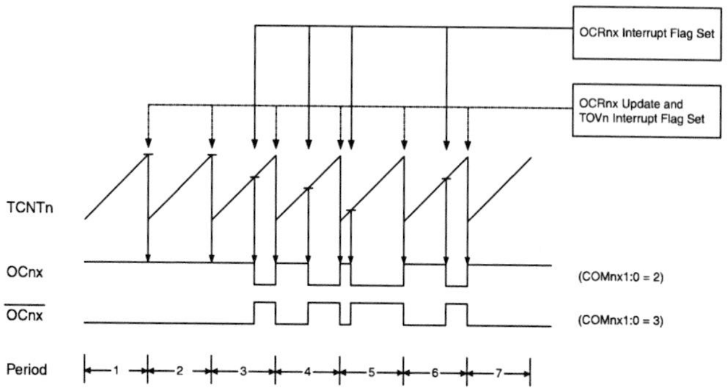

Figure 2. Time evolution of register values in the PWM mechanism. `TCNTn` is the value of the counter and `OCnx` is the value of the output pin. Note how changes in the reference value determine the duty cycle on each wave period.

The output frequency of the PWM signal is a function of the clock selected to be used as input for the counter, the counter prescaler value, the size of the counter (in bits) and the PWM mode. For a b bits counter with input clock of f_{clock} Hz and prescaler value of p, an output pin configured to operate in fast PWM mode overflows with a frequency of $\frac{f_{clock}}{p \times 2^b}$ Hz. This provides us with a way to output the processed signal while using the same infrastructure to schedule periodic actions, such as querying for ADC values and signaling that blocks of samples are ready to be processed.

Also notice that the counter size determines the output signal resolution, as the duty cycles of the square waves correspond to the ratio between the current counter value and its maximum possible value. We will see more about parameters choice for PWM on section 2.5.2.

2.4 Real time processing

The main constraint in real time DSP is, of course, the amount of time available for the computation of output samples: they must be ready to be consumed by the playback hardware or else glitches and other unwanted artifacts will possibly be introduced in the signal. One round of sample analysis, processing and calculation of a new sample is called a *DSP sample cycle*. Many algorithms, though, operate in blocks of samples, consuming and producing a whole block of samples in each round. If the DSP block has N samples and the sample rate is R Hz, then the *DSP block cycle period* is given by $T_{DSP} = \frac{N}{R}$ seconds.

In order to implement this behaviour in the microcontroller, we have to find a way to (1) accumulate input samples in a buffer, (2) schedule a periodic call to a function that will process the samples in this buffer, and (3) output modified samples in a timely fashion. Components are at hand: ADC for reading the input signal, counters and their interrupts for running periodic tasks, and PWM for outputting the resulting signal. In addition, the Arduino library provides a `loop()` function that is called repeatedly which we can use to process the block of samples when it becomes available.

As we saw in section 2.3, the PWM mechanism provides an overflow interrupt frequency that may be used to schedule a function for periodic execution. In our setup we use this mechanism to periodically read samples from the ADC mechanism and accumulate them in an input buffer, while also writing the computed samples from the last DSP cycle to the PWM output buffer. In this same function, whenever the buffer is full and ready to be processed, a flag is set and the `loop()` function is released to work on the samples.

Note that for some critical applications, the term "real time execution" might mean that the application should be interrupted whenever its time for computation is up. In the case of real time digital audio, if no output sample could be computed before the output hardware tries to read it, audible artifacts may be unavoidable had the computation been interrupted or not. Thus, our approach concentrates on measuring the time taken by certain algorithms and comparing it with the DSP cycle period, and does not account for what happens should the time not be sufficient.

2.5 Implementation

Putting all the elements together is a matter of choosing the right parameters for configuring different parts of the microcontroller.

2.5.1 ADC parameters

ADC conversion takes about 14.5 ADC clock ticks, including sample-and-hold time. If the CPU clock frequency is 16 MHz and the ADC prescaler has a value of p, then the ADC clock period is $p/16$ and the conversion period is then $T_{\text{conv}} = (14.5 \times p)/16$. Below we can see a table with the theoretical values for the conversion period T_{conv} for all prescaler values available and also the results $\tilde{T}_{\text{conv}}$ of measured conversion times using each prescaler value. Also depicted in the table are the measured conversion frequencies $\tilde{f}_{\text{conv}} = 1/\tilde{T}_{\text{conv}}$.

ADC prescaler	T_{conv} (μs)	$\tilde{T}_{\text{conv}}$ (μs)	$\tilde{f}_{\text{conv}}$ ($\approx$KHz)
2	1.8125	12.61	79.302
4	3.625	16.06	62.266
8	7.25	19.76	50.607
16	14.5	20.52	48.732
32	29	34.80	28.735
64	58	67.89	14.729
128	116	114.85	8.707

These measurements were made using the `micros()` function of the Arduino library API, which has a resolution of about 4 μs. This might explain part of the deviation of measured values from the expected values for lower values of prescaler. 8 bit approximation was used, and for obtaining a 10 bit approximation we can expect an overhead of about 25% in conversion time.

It is important to note that the choice for ADC prescaler value limits the sampling rate of the input signal. As our setup uses a counter's overflow interrupt to obtain samples from the ADC mechanism, the ADC conversion period must be smaller than the the PWM's cycle period. Any prescaler choice that leads to a frequency higher than the PWM's overflow interrupt frequency is valid, but the lower the prescaler value the lower the quality of the conversion.

2.5.2 PWM

From Section 2.3 we can see that in a 16 MHz CPU, an 8 bit counter with prescaler value of p has an overflow interrupt frequency of $f_{\text{overflow}} = 10^6/(p \times 2^4)$ Hz. Below we can see a table with the overflow interrupt frequency for all possible values of prescaler:

PWM prescaler	f_{incr} (KHz)	f_{overflow} (Hz)
1	16.000	62500
8	2.000	7812
32	500	1953
64	250	976
128	125	488
256	62,5	244
1024	15,625	61

The choice of PWM and ADC prescaler values determine directly the sampling rate of our DSP system. If we set the ADC prescaler in a way that the ADC conversion period is smaller than the PWM overflow interrupt period and synchronize reads from the input with writes to the output, then the PWM overflow interrupt frequency becomes the DSP system's sample rate. We will see this with more details in the next section.

For the PWM mechanism, we chose to use Fast PWM mode on an 8-bit counter with prescaler value of 1. That would give us a sample rate of 62500 Hz, which is enough for representing the audible spectrum. Nevertheless, if we need more time to compute we may artificially lower the frequency by only executing the sampling/outputting bit in a fraction of the interrupts. For our tests, we chose to cut the sample rate in half using the rationale that the payoff of having more time to compute is larger than the one of ensuring we can represent the upper fifth part of the audible spectrum. Therefore, our final choice of sample rate is 31250 Hz, with a sample period of 32 μs.

2.5.3 Putting it all together

Having chosen a value for the PWM counter size and PWM prescaler, we are left with the choice for ADC parameters. As noted, it suffices to choose a value that ensures ADC conversion period is smaller than the desired sample period. We chose to use 8 bit conversion to match the PWM resolution and to provide for a faster conversion time. Also, we chose an ADC prescaler value of 8, with a measured conversion time of 19.76 μs which, when compared with the a sample period of 32 μs ensures that conversion will be finished before the input ADC is queried for the sample.

Below we can see the code for the *interrupt service routine* (ISR) DSP controller function. Variable x is the input buffer, ADCH maps to the ADC register holding the input sample, OCR2A maps to the PWM output register and y is the output buffer. Some of the code is index wizardry and the rest we comment below.

```
// Timer2 Interrupt Service at 62.5 KHz
ISR(TIMER2_OVF_vect) {
  static boolean div = false;
  div = !div; // divide frequency to 31.25 KHz
  if (div){
    // 1. read from ADC input
    x[ind] = ADCH;
    // 2. write to PWM output
    OCR2A = y[(ind-MIN_DELAY)&(BUFFER_SIZE-1)];
    // 3. signal availability of new sample block
    if ((ind & (BLOCK_SIZE - 1)) == 0) {
      rind = (ind-BLOCK_SIZE) & (BUFFER_SIZE-1);
      dsp_block = true;
    }
    // 4. increment read/write buffer index
    ind++;
    ind &= BUFFER_SIZE - 1;
    // 5. start new ADC conversion
    sbi(ADCSRA,ADSC);
  }
}
```

Note that in step 3 we test if the input index is a multiple of the block size and, if it is, we set a read index rind and signal that there is a new DSP block available for calculation. Meanwhile, the loop() function is running concurrently and will eventually catch that signal and start to work on samples. Finally, we increment buffer indexes and perform the call to start a new ADC conversion by calling the sbi() function.

2.6 Benchmarking

We are interested in evaluating the performance of the Arduino board on some common sound processing tasks, in order to gain insight on its real time stream processing capabilities. Note that our interest lies in high-level DSP operations; for instance, we'd prefer to know how many simultaneous sinusoids can be synthesized in real time rather than how many multiplications and additions fit between successive DSP blocks (even though the former follows from the latter).

Some questions arise immediately from the real time constraint:

- What is the maximum amount of DSP operations that can be carried in real time?
- Which implementation details make a difference?

We try to answer these questions by running 3 different DSP algorithms in the microcontroller environment described in the last section. The chosen tasks are additive synthesis, time-domain convolution and FFT computation, and are discussed in the following sections.

2.6.1 *Additive synthesis*

An additive synthesis is the process of constructing a complex waveform by adding together several basic waveforms (see Figure 3). This technique has been widely used for synthesizing new sounds as well as resynthesizing signals after they have been processed (e.g. via spectral methods).

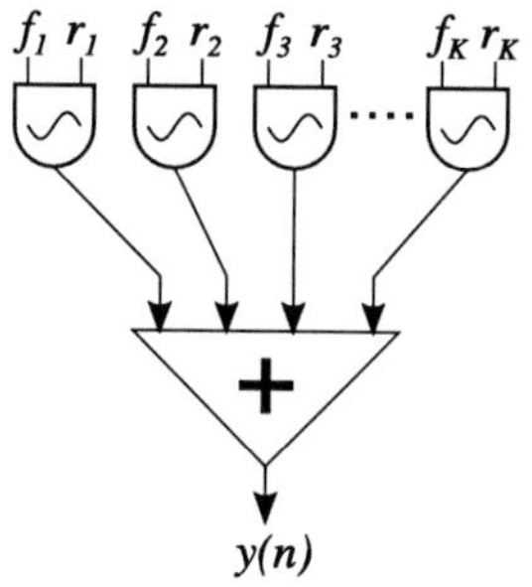

Figure 3. Additive synthesis: many basic oscillators governed by independent phase (f_i) and amplitude (r_i) functions are combined to form a complex signal.

The high level code for a simple additive synthesis can be seen below:

```
for (n = 0; n < N; n++)
{
  angle = 2.0 * M_PI * t;
  y[n] = 0.0;
  for (k = 0; k < numFreqs; k++)
    y[n] += r[k]*sin(f[k] * angle);
  t += 1.0 / SR;
}
```

2.6.2 *Time-domain convolution*

Frequency-domain multiplication of spectra correspond to time-domain convolution of signals, and such an operation allows for some techniques of frequency filtering. The time-domain implementation of convolution is a widely used technique in many computer music algorithms, being particularly efficient when the filter order N is small. The general scheme can be seen in Figure 4.

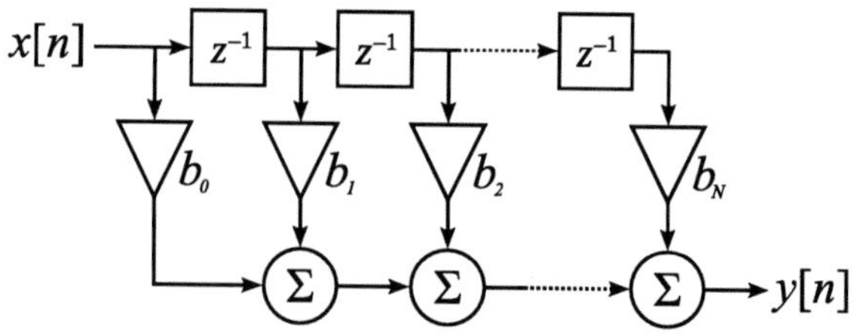

Figure 4. Time-domain convolution: the input signal $x[n]$ is convolved with the filter's impulse response defined by the coefficients b_i to generate the output signal $y[n]$. This is the general scheme for FIR filtering.

The high-level code for a time-domain convolution with a FIR filter of order N is:

```
for (k = 0; k < N; k++)
  y[n] += b[k]*x[n-k];
```

2.6.3 Fast Fourier Transform

The Fast Fourier Transform (FFT) is a clever implementation of the traditional Fourier Transform that brings its complexity down from $O(n^2)$ to $O(n \log(n))$, where n is the number of time-domain digital samples or, equivalently, the number of frequency bins that describe the frequency spectrum of the signal after the Transform computation [6]. The FFT algorithm takes advantage of redundancy and symmetry on intermediary steps of the calculation and is used in many signal processing algorithms. The general scheme of the FFT can be seen in Figure 5.

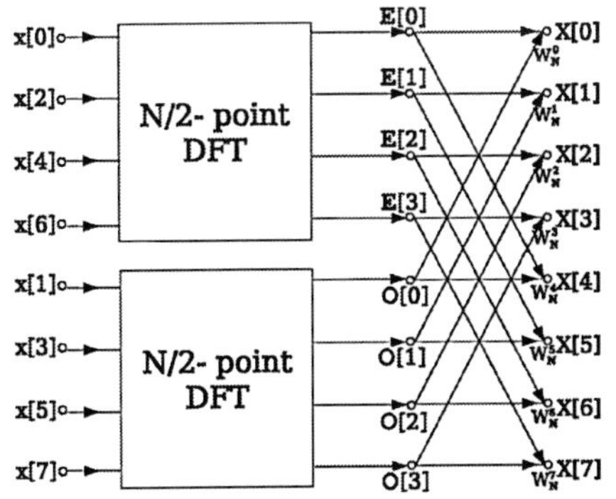

Figure 5. The FFT uses a divide-and-conquer approach and saves intermediate results to accelerate the calculation of a signal spectrum. The figure shows one step of an 8-point FFT calculation and how the results map to frequency bins.

2.6.4 Benchmarking

Each of the algorithms mentioned in the last sections have different computational costs in terms of number of integer and floating-point operations, and quantity/size of memory reads and writes.

In the context of real time audio processing in Arduino, these algorithms bring natural questions regarding feasibility of processing:

- Additive synthesis: what is the maximum number of oscillators that can be used to compute a new waveform in real time?
- Time-domain convolution: what is the maximum length of a filter that can be applied to an audio signal in real time?
- FFT: what is the maximum length of an FFT that can be computed in real time?

3. RESULTS

3.1 Additive synthesis

The first experiment tries to answer the question of how many oscillators can be used when performing real time additive synthesis inside the platform. In the beginning of the DSP cycle, an additive synthesis algorithm is run using a determined number of oscillators and the mean of the synth time is taken over ten million measurements. Block sizes used had 32, 64 and 128 samples (more showed to be unfeasible in real time) and the number of oscillators was increased until the DSP cycle period was exceeded.

The first result has to do with the use of loop structures. Because looping usually requires incrementing and testing a variable in each iteration, the use of one loop structure may have strong influence in the amount of oscillators that can be used in real time for additive synthesis inside the Arduino.

In any DSP algorithm that works over a block of samples there is at least one loop structure, that loops over all samples of the block. This loop could be eliminated at the cost of having to recompile the code every time the length of the block is changed, which is highly inconvenient. Usually more loops will be used, for instance in additive synthesis for summing the result of several oscillators. We investigate the alternative of removing this inner loop, by explicitly writing the sum of oscillators. Figure 6 shows the maximum amount of oscillators feasible in real time by making use of a loop and by making use of inline code. By removing the inner loop we were able to increase from 8 oscillators to 13 or 14 depending on the block size.

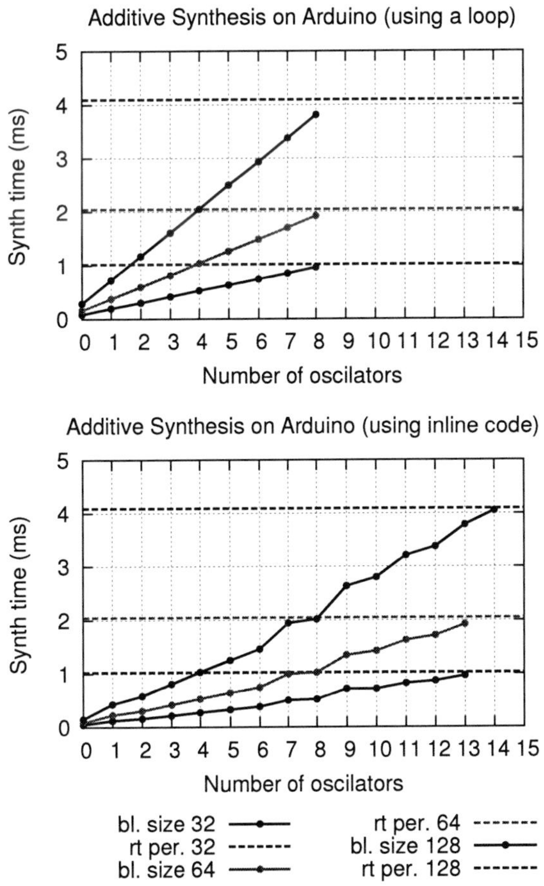

Figure 6. Additive synthesis results using loops (above) and inline code (below).

While implementing this experiment, a first attempt was made using the standard API `sin()` function. As that proved to be unfeasible in real time, we focused on table lookup implementations. At this point we noticed that even the smallest implementation difference can have large impact on the results. Therefore, we decided to test and plot the results for slightly different implementations.

Two parameters are used to calculate the value of each oscillator: phase and amplitude. Phase is handled by updating the index for sine table reads, and then the amplitude has to be multiplied by the value obtained by the lookup. Floating point operations are also extremely expensive in the platform we are using, so we implemented 3 different ways of multiplying the amplitude: (1) by using one integer multiplication and one integer division (2 integer operations), (2) by using only one integer division (1 integer operation), and (3) by using variable bit padding for performing bitwise power of 2 divisions or multiplications. Figure 7 shows the time used by the additive synthesis algorithm using these variants. By making use of lower level operations (that achieve less precise results) and inline coding we were able to raise the number of oscillators from 3 (when using 2 integer operations and a for loop) to 15 (when using a variable pad and inline code).

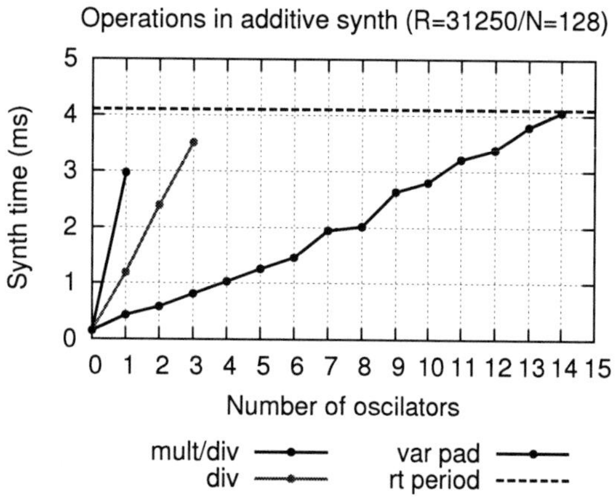

Figure 7. Time taken for additive synthesis algorithm with block size of 128 samples, using different number and kinds of operations and variable number of oscillators.

3.2 Time-domain convolution

Our second experiment tries to clarify what is the maximum size of a FIR filter that can be applied in real time to an input signal by use of time-domain convolution algorithms. Following lessons learned on the first experiment, we implemented the filtering loop using different types of operations for multiplying each coefficient by the sample values: (1) using one integer multiplication and one integer division, (2) using variable pad, and (3) using a constant hardcoded pad. The results for each of these implementations can be seen in Figure 8. This experiment was run with a sample rate of 31250 Hz and block sizes of 32, 64, 128 and 256 samples.

Results again show that small implementation differences make a big difference on computing power. When using integer division, the maximum order obtained for the filter was 1, while by using a variable pad the order raised to 7 and with constant padding we could achieve an order of 13 or 14 depending on the block size.

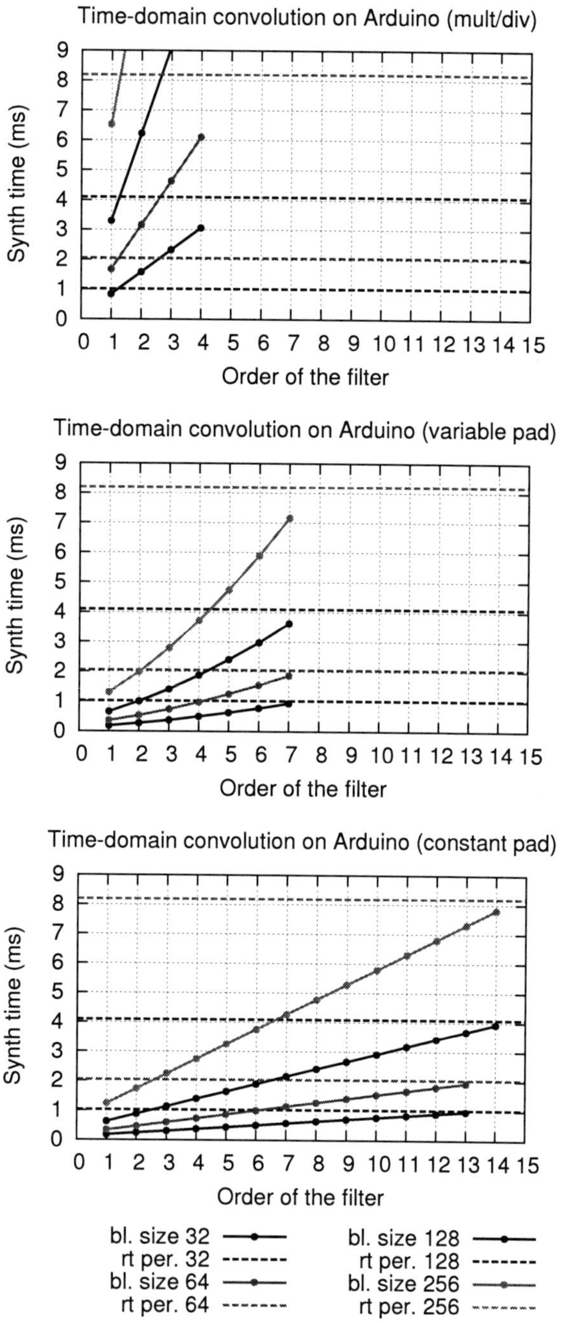

Figure 8. Time-domain convolution using 2 integer operations (top), variable padding (middle) and constant padding (bottom).

3.3 FFT

The third experiment is concerned with the maximum length of an FFT that can be computed in real time inside an Arduino. In this case we chose to evaluate a standard implementation of the FFT without further modifications.

It turned out that calculating an FFT using the same sample rate we used in the other experiments (31250 Hz) was unfeasible, so we had to tweak the microcontroller's parameters to reach a state where we had a longer DSP cycle period for the same amount of samples and the FFT was indeed feasible. By measuring the amount of time taken to compute the FFT given the number of samples, we could determine that the maximum FFT frequency for a 256 samples block is of about 2335 Hz. So by raising the PWM prescaler value to 32, we could reach a sample rate of about 1953 Hz.

Figure 9 shows the FFT analysis time at a sample rate of 1953 Hz for different block sizes. We can see that in this scenario the maximum block size for which an FFT can be computed in real time in our DSP setup in the Arduino is 256 samples. This was expected because we actually forced a sample rate small enough so that the 256 samples FFT was feasible. Note that, even though we can actually perform the FFT for block sizes smaller or equal to 256, there's not much time left for doing anything else with these results. An additive synthesis for reconstructing the signal, for example, is unfeasible as the maximum number of oscillators we could use was 14 (by restricting the type and number of operations), while here we would need the same number of oscillators as the number of samples in the block size.

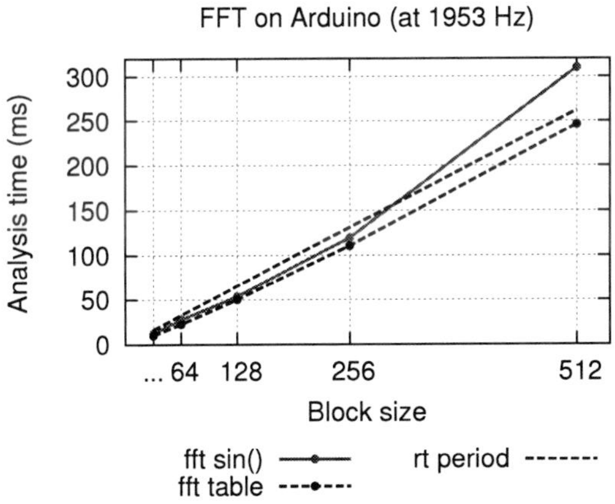

Figure 9. Time taken to compute the Fast Fourier Transform on the Arduino for different block sizes. The red line depicts the implementation using the `sin()` library function and the blue line shows a lookup-table implementation

4. DISCUSSION AND CONCLUSION

From the results of our experiments, it becomes clear that implementation details, such as choice of data type and number and type of operations, make a big difference in the amount and quality of computation, as described in Sections 3.1 and 3.2. Integer multiplication and division, for example, take double the time than integer sum. The amount of loops also proved to make a big difference. In Section 3.1, we nearly doubled the amount of oscillators that can be used in additive synthesis by only substituting one loop with inline code. The mere use of variables also showed to influence performance.

These experiments may serve as illustrations of the type of concern that must be kept in mind when implementing sound processing tasks in Arduino, and also serve as general guidelines for the limitations on the complexity of those tasks when real time functioning is required.

4.1 Future work

There are many possibilities of investigation in the realm of microprocessors like Arduino for real time sound processing, such as:

- Use of 10-bit ADC input and adapting tests for performing 2 byte operations. We should expect each operation to cost much more time because of the 8 bit nature of the processor.
- Determine of the amount of noise introduced in the signal by the ADC sampling/PWM synthesis process.

5. ACKNOWLEDGEMENTS

We would like to thank the members of the Computer Music Group [6] of the University of São Paulo for valuable discussions and contributions. This work has been supported by the funding agencies CAPES and FAPESP (grant 2008/08632-8).

6. REFERENCES

[1] "Arduino homepage," http://www.arduino.cc/, [Online; accessed 12-Jun-2013].

[2] R. Oshana, *DSP for Embedded and Real-Time Systems*. Newnes, 2012.

[3] M. Nawrath, "Arduino realtime audio processing," http://interface.khm.de/index.php/lab/experiments/arduino-realtime-audio-processing/, [Online; accessed 12-Jun-2013].

[4] S. Dimitrov and S. Serafin, "Audio Arduino – an ALSA (Advanced Linux Sound Architecture) audio driver for FTDI-based Arduinos," in *Proceedings of the International Conference on New Interfaces for Musical Expression*, A. R. Jensenius, A. Tveit, R. I. Godøy, and D. Overholt, Eds., Oslo, Norway, 2011, pp. 211–216. [Online]. Available: http://www.nime2011.org/proceedings/papers/G01-Dimitrov.pdf

[5] "Atmel ATmega48A/48PA/88A/88PA/168A/328/328P datasheet," http://www.atmel.com/devices/ATMEGA328P.aspx?tab=documents, [Online; accessed 12-Jun-2013].

[6] W. H. Press, S. A. Teukolsky, W. T. Vetterling, and B. P. Flannery, "Numerical recipes in C: The art of scientific computing. second edition," 1992.

[6] http://compmus.ime.usp.br/en/

AUDIO INTERPOLATION AND MORPHING VIA STRUCTURED-SPARSE LINEAR REGRESSION

Corey Kereliuk
McGill University
CIRMMT†
corey.kereliuk@mail.mcgill.ca

Philippe Depalle
McGill University
CIRMMT†
depalle@music.mcgill.ca

Philippe Pasquier
Simon Fraser University
SIAT*
pasquier@sfu.ca

ABSTRACT

We present a method of audio interpolation suitable for the restoration of missing and/or corrupted audio samples. Our method assumes that the missing/corrupted samples can be easily identified and are subsequently treated as missing data. We then model the audio signal as a linear combination of elementary waveforms (referred to as atoms) and estimate the values of the missing samples by solving a penalized linear regression problem. A first work in this direction was recently presented using the moniker 'audio inpainting' (in deference to similar work in the image processing community). We extend this avenue of research by incorporating additional continuity constraints into the problem, which leads to improved estimates of the missing data. Furthermore, we show how our method leads to a natural framework for morphing/transitioning between two sounds. Finally, we present several examples that illustrate the effectiveness of our interpolation strategy and the quality of morphing that can be attained.

1. INTRODUCTION

It is not uncommon for audio signals to suffer some form of degradation during the various stages of recording, transmission, and playback. For example, a scratched compact disc or dropped network packet can lead to chunks of missing samples. Likewise, impulsive clicks, clipping, and noise are common forms of audio degradation. In this work we focus specifically on localized types of distortion. In other words, we assume that the distorted samples are surrounded by undistorted ones (which occurs in many practical situations). Furthermore, we assume that the distorted samples can be easily identified, either manually, or through some other process (e.g., by detecting regions of silence, clipping, and so on). The task at hand is then one of interpolation, i.e., we aim to estimate the missing samples at known locations using the surrounding data.

There are several works in the literature aimed at audio interpolation [1–5]. In Janssen et al. the sound was modelled as an autoregressive (AR) process and the unknown parameters are estimated from the known data [1]. The missing/corrupted samples can then be interpolated using the AR model.

The work presented in Adler et al. [5] was inspired by related research in the image processing community on 'inpainting' (a process whereby missing pixels are interpolated from the surrounding ones [6]). We may also view the inpainting problem as a regression problem when the signal is modeled as a linear combination of elementary functions (atoms).

In the following sections we describe an extension of the audio inpainting work in [5] using recent results in structured sparse modelling of audio [7]. We compare our approach to those presented in [5] and [1] and show that in both cases we achieve superior reconstruction of the missing samples (in terms of minimizing the estimation error). We also demonstrate how the proposed method leads to a natural framework for morphing/transitioning between two sounds.

The remaining sections are laid out as follows. We first present our model and then outline a sketch of the interpolation problem. We then propose an estimation algorithm based on penalized linear regression with continuity constraints. Finally, we present several examples illustrative of our interpolation and morphing results.

2. THE ADDITIVE MODEL

We adopt the following additive sound model

$$y(t) = \sum_m \sum_n x_{m,n}\phi_{m,n}(t) \tag{1}$$

In other words, the audio signal $y(t)$ is modelled as a linear combination of elementary waveforms $\phi_{m,n}(t)$ referred to as atoms. The double indices (m, n) typically have a time-frequency interpretation (and their extent depends on the signal length and bandwidth). For example, we use Gabor atoms

$$\phi_{m,n}(t) = h(t - am)\exp(j2\pi bnt) \tag{2}$$

which are generated by translating and modulating a smooth and compact window function $h(t)$. In this model the parameters a and b are the time and frequency sampling intervals, m and n are integer indices, $j = \sqrt{-1}$ is the imaginary unit, and t is time. Gabor atoms are a natural choice for modelling audio since they have a compact time-frequency footprint (and thus represent distinct elements

† Centre for Interdisciplinary Research in Music Media and Technology
* School of Interactive Arts + Technology

of the time-frequency plane). The synthesis coefficients $x_{m,n}$ in this model can be calculated using the short-time Fourier transform (STFT). However, when the set of atoms is redundant (e.g., when the Gabor atoms are oversampled in time and/or frequency) there is, strictly speaking, no unique way to determine the synthesis coefficients. In fact, in recent years considerable effort has been invested into examining alternative methods for estimating the synthesis coefficients. In particular, sparse representations are increasingly seen in the literature (see [8] for a review). There are many advantages to sparse models, chiefly data reduction and increased salience of the model parameters (i.e., there is a clearer correspondance between the atoms and the sound signal). Furthermore, many natural signals are inherently sparse which has spurred on much of the growth in this area. For example, in the field of compressive sensing it has been shown that sparse signals can be reconstructed using a small number of measurements [9]. We show in the following sections how sparsity can be used in a similar way to regularize the interpolation procedure.

3. PROBLEM FORMULATION

3.1 Interpolation

In discrete-time the sample values are known at a distinct set of locations and thus the model in Eq. (1) can be rewritten as

$$\mathbf{y} = \mathbf{\Phi x} \tag{3}$$

where $\mathbf{y}$ is a vector containing the audio samples, the columns of the dictionary $\mathbf{\Phi}$ are Gabor atoms, and $\mathbf{x}$ is a vector of synthesis coefficients. When the signal is degraded/distorted we lose information about $\mathbf{y}$. When interpolating audio samples we assume that only some of the samples from $\mathbf{y}$ are reliable and that the others should be treated as missing data (to be re-estimated). We can model this scenario as

$$\mathbf{z} = \mathbf{My} \tag{4}$$

where $\mathbf{z}$ is the observed signal and $\mathbf{M}$ is a diagonal (binary) mask matrix that indicates which samples from $\mathbf{y}$ are reliable and which should be treated as missing data. Replacing $\mathbf{y}$ in Eq. (4) with the model from Eq. (3) leads to

$$\mathbf{z} = (\mathbf{M\Phi})\mathbf{x} = \mathbf{\Psi x} \tag{5}$$

where we use $\mathbf{\Psi}$ to represent the degraded dictionary. If we can accurately estimate $\mathbf{x}$ from $\mathbf{\Psi}$ and $\mathbf{z}$, then we may reconstruct the missing samples via linear regression, i.e., using the linear model in Eq. (3). This summarizes the interpolation setup, however, we have not yet considered how to estimate $\mathbf{x}$. We withhold this discussion until Sec. 4.

3.2 Morphing/Transitioning

We can use the same setup described in the previous section to morph/transition between different sounds. For example, we can generate a new sound by concatenating a source sound, silence, and a target sound together. We may then treat the samples between the source and target as missing data (by generating an appropriate mask matrix). In this case performing the interpolation procedure will create a morph or transition between the two sounds.

We note that this type of morphing is based on waveform interpolation as opposed to feature (or descriptor) interpolation [10]. Descriptor interpolation (e.g., interpolating between partials [11]) is more common in the literature, however, recent examples of waveform interpolation can be found as well. For example in Olivero et al. [12] the authors examined how to find a time-frequency multiplier capable of transforming one sound into another.

Many morphing techniques aim to create several hybrid sounds lying somewhere between the source and target [13]. Our approach, on the other hand, is a simple technique for smoothly transitioning between two sounds and, in this sense, bears more similarity to a cross-fade. However, our morphing results are quite audibly different from cross-fading in many cases (as we demonstrate in the results section). In essence we propose to use (or maybe more accurately abuse) the interpolation procedure in order to produce large chunks of new samples based on the surrounding data.

4. ESTIMATION PROCEDURE

4.1 Penalized linear regression

As we noted in Sec. 2, when the Gabor atoms are oversampled in time and/or frequency (which is typically the case), there is no unique way to determine the synthesis coefficients. Furthermore, even if the Gabor atoms were critically sampled, the degraded dictionary would still be rank deficient due to the multiplication by $\mathbf{M}$ (which discards data). This means that the system of equations in Eq. (5) is underdetermined and there is no unique way to determine $\mathbf{x}$. In this case, we can regularize the problem by introducing an objective function that penalizes certain types of solutions. In other words, we seek a solution that is consistent with our a priori knowledge of what a "good" solution should look like by penalizing solutions that deviate from this expectation. For example, we could attempt to solve

$$\min \|\mathbf{x}\|_2^2 \quad \text{subject to} \quad \|\mathbf{z} - \mathbf{\Psi x}\|_2^2 \leq \epsilon \tag{6}$$

where the second term expresses our desire for a solution that is consistent with the observed data and the first term penalizes large coefficients (in this case the goal is to find a minimum energy representation). When $\epsilon = 0$ the solution to this set of equations corresponds to the pseudo-inverse. Unfortunately, the pseudo-inverse tends to result in solutions which contain many small non-zero coefficients (and this tends to complicate the interpretation and use of the additive model) [14].

Another approach to counteract the ill-posedness of the interpolation problem is to penalize non-sparse solutions. There are many reasons for preferring sparse solutions as highlighted at the end of Sec. 2. We may leverage the fact that musical signals tend to be relatively sparse when represented using Gabor atoms and the additive model. For example, it is well-known that sparse signals can be reconstructed using a limited set of measurements (this is the basis of compressive sensing) [9].

In Adler et al. [5] sparse approximation was suggested as a tool to regularize the audio interpolation process. In particular, the orthogonal matching pursuit (OMP) algorithm was used to estimate the additive model coefficients in Eq. (5).

An alternative way to find sparse representations is to replace the 2-norm in Eq. (6) with the 1-norm which leads to the basis pursuit denoising (BPDN) optimization problem [15]:

$$\min \|\mathbf{x}\|_1 \quad \text{subject to} \quad \|\mathbf{z} - \mathbf{\Psi x}\|_2^2 \leq \epsilon \tag{7}$$

The 1-norm is attractive seeing as it is convex (so convergence to a local minimizer is guaranteed) and because it often induces sparse solutions [16].

In [7] it was shown that additional structure exists between the non-zero coefficients in sparse atomic models of audio. Specifically, it was shown that time-frequency representations of audio tend to exhibit a high degree of continuity between temporally adjacent atoms. This result is due to the fact that musical sounds tend to be somewhat stable (e.g., the decay time of a resonant mode tends to be longer than the length of individual atoms, and therefore multiple adjacent atoms tend to be activated simultaneously). In the following section we describe how recent results on structured-sparse modelling of audio can be applied to the interpolation problem. We begin by reviewing the proposed optimization problem and then discuss algorithms for its solution (a more detailed treatment of this formulation can be found in [7]).

4.2 Structured-sparse estimation

We would like to modify the BPDN optimization problem in order to exploit joint relationships between the representation coefficients. To this end we propose the following generalization of the BPDN problem (termed G-BPDN) for structured-sparse estimation:

$$\min \|f(\mathbf{x})\|_1 \quad \text{subject to} \ \|\mathbf{z} - \mathbf{\Psi x}\|_2^2 \leq \epsilon \tag{8}$$

Ideally, the function f should sparsify $\mathbf{x}$. This in turn allows us to use a BPDN-like formulation with coefficient vectors that are sparse after some transformation. This formulation is similar to the co-sparse analysis formulation from [17], however, we do not restrict f to be a linear operator. For the task of audio interpolation we propose using then following G-BPDN objective function:

$$\|f(\mathbf{x})\|_1 = \|\mathbf{L}|\mathbf{x}|\|_1 \tag{9}$$

where $|\mathbf{x}| = [|x_1|, |x_2|, \ldots, |x_n|]^{\mathrm{T}}$ is a vector containing the magnitudes of $\mathbf{x}$ and

$$\mathbf{L} = \begin{bmatrix} \tilde{\gamma}\mathbf{D} \\ \gamma\mathbf{I} \end{bmatrix} \tag{10}$$

In our case the analysis operator $\mathbf{D}$ is a matrix designed to calculate the amplitude difference between temporally adjacent pairs of coefficients and $\tilde{\gamma} = 1 - \gamma$. The parameter $\gamma \in [0, 1]$ can be used to emphasize either sparsity or amplitude continuity, however, in this work we simply fix $\gamma = 0.5$ (in which case it drops out of the optimization problem).

In this form, the G-BPDN optimization problem can be used to emphasize sparsity of the time-frequency coefficients as well as the sparsity of their time derivative (which should produce solutions with greater temporal continuity). It should be noted that the proposed optimization problem is quite similar to both the fused-lasso [18] and total-variation denoising [19] which are well-known in the statistics and image processing literature, respectively.

We propose solving this problem via smoothed projected gradient descent as outlined in [7]. We note that other techniques, such as the alternating direction method of multipliers (ADMM), could be used as well [20]. Projected gradient descent is a two-step procedure: a gradient descent step is taken and the result is projected onto the set of feasible solutions [21, 22]. The steps of this algorithm are outlined in Alg. 1.

Algorithm 1 Projected Gradient G-BPDN

```
1: init: x^(0) = Φ^H z, n = 0
2: repeat
3:    u^(n) = x^(n) − μ · diag(S_∞(x/e)) L^T S_∞(L|x|/e)
4:    λ^(n) = max(0, ε^(−1/2) ||z − Ψu^(n)||_2 − 1)
5:    x^(n+1) = u^(n) + (λ^(n) / (1+λ^(n))) Ψ^H (z − Ψu^(n))
6:    n = n + 1
7: until stopping condition
```

In Alg. 1, line 3 corresponds to the gradient descent step and line 5 corresponds to a projection onto the feasible set [1]. The operator $\mathcal{S}_\infty$ denotes projection onto the inf-norm ball and e is a smoothing parameter (as outlined in [7]). In general we stop this algorithm when the change in the objective function from one iteration to the next is small (e.g., less than 10^{-6}), however, a maximum number of iterations may be enforced as well.

5. RESULTS

5.1 Interpolation results

In this section we provide results that demonstrate the efficacy of our structured-sparse estimation approach. We focus specifically on an experiment outlined in Adler et al. [5] so that we may directly compare our results against a recent (and similar) approach. The test data consist of 10, five seconds music signals sampled at 16kHz which are available from [5]. Each of these audio excerpts was corrupted periodically (every 100ms) by setting an interval of samples to zero. The size of the missing interval duration was varied from a fraction of a millisecond up to 10ms in order to gauge how the performance would change with respect to the amount of missing data. A mask matrix was manually created to identify the missing samples. In the

[1] Provided $\mathbf{\Psi}$ is a Parseval tight frame as outlined in [7].

following experiments we used a tight frame Gabor dictionary created using Hann windows of length 64ms with 75% time overlap [2]. Furthermore, we set the parameter $\epsilon = 10^{-10}$ in order to force our model to represent the known samples with virtually no error [3].

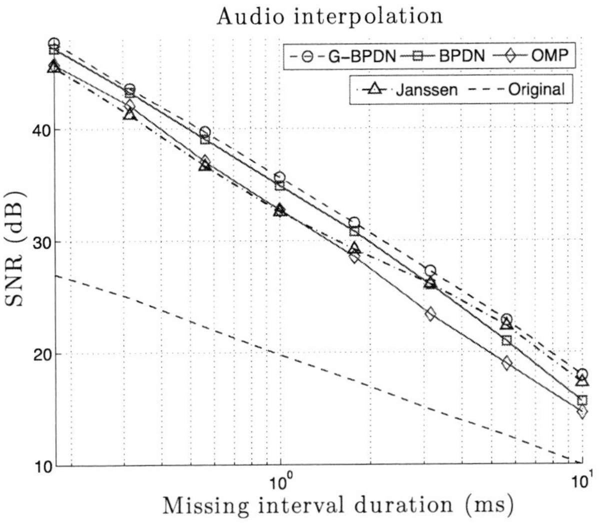

Figure 1. Results of interpolation for missing intervals of various durations. Results averaged over 10 test signals.

The interpolation performance was evaluated by measuring the signal-to-noise ratio (SNR) between the true signal and the residual error:

$$\text{SNR} = 10\log_{10}\frac{\|\mathbf{y}\|_2^2}{\|\mathbf{y}-\mathbf{\Phi}\hat{\mathbf{x}}\|_2^2} \tag{11}$$

where $\hat{\mathbf{x}}$ is the vector of estimated model coefficients.

Fig. 1 illustrates the SNR vs. missing interval duration averaged over all 10 test signals for both sparse and structured sparse interpolation (e.g., the solutions to Eq. (7) and Eq. (8), respectively). This graph also shows the results obtained using code from [5] (labelled as OMP) and the AR model from [1] (labelled as Janssen). The G-BPDN interpolation obtains the highest SNR in all cases. The benefit of G-BPDN (over the purely sparse estimation) is also more readily apparent as the missing interval duration grows. This illustrates that solutions with greater temporal continuity are indeed beneficial for bridging larger gaps of missing samples. The AR model from Janssen [1] also performs well for large gaps and even outperforms the purely sparse solution in this case. This is presumably because the AR model contains a memory of the previous samples (and therefore better models the temporal structure of the signal).

Fig. 2 illustrates the interpolated waveforms for a missing interval of 10ms (for a single test sound). It is evident that the G-BPDN solution is slightly closer to the true waveform than the other estimates. However, one can not automatically conclude that an improvement will be perceived when listening to the interpolated sounds. Indeed, when listening to sounds interpolated with BPDN and G-BPDN the results are very similar. This may, however, be a consequence of the fact that the auditory system is capable of filling in short gaps in missing sounds, which is a well-known fact (see for example, [23]). We have included several examples of interpolated sounds on the companion website [24].

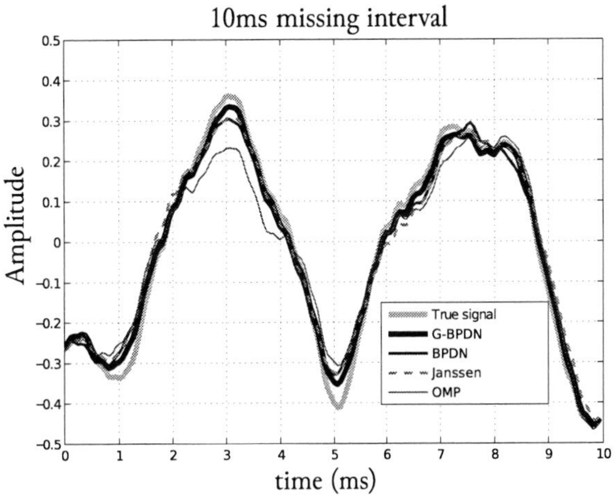

Figure 2. Waveform plot showing the interpolated results for a single test signal over a missing interval of 10ms.

From a computational point-of-view BPDN and G-BPDN have approximately the same complexity (each is dominated by two matrix vector products with the dictionary at each iteration). The overall complexity will depend on the number of iterations required for convergence which is difficult to predict a priori. A possible advantage of our approach is that after each iteration the coefficients $\mathbf{x}$ will satisfy $\|\mathbf{z}-\mathbf{\Psi}\mathbf{x}\|_2^2 \leq \epsilon$. In other words, the representation error is always bounded. An analysis of the computational complexity of OMP can be found in [25]. Quite informally we note that BPDN and G-BPDN both ran much faster (between 5-10× faster for a full run) than OMP on the same computer (all algorithms were implemented in Matlab and run on the same data).

5.2 Morphing results

As mentioned in Sec. 3.2 we can use the interpolation framework in order to transition between a source and target sound. To recap: we simply include a gap of missing samples between the two sounds which is subsequently treated as missing data to be interpolated. In general, the amount of data we want to estimate is much greater when transitioning between two sounds (in comparison to typical restoration tasks). The atoms in the Gabor dictionary should, at minimum, span the interval we wish to interpolate. As a rule of thumb we have found that atoms anywhere from 2 to 4× the gap length produce good results. As this leads to very long atoms in practice, it is wise to ensure that the number of known samples is at least this large as well.

[2] In this work the set of dictionary atoms span the space of the input signal. Block/frame-based processing was not used.

[3] We note that the value of ϵ we use is smaller than the one used in [5]. It is difficult to say whether or not this effects the results since the algorithms used are completely different. The value of ϵ used in this work was optimized to obtain the best result for the algorithm we considered (and we assume the authors in [5] would have done the same as well).

When estimating the additive model coefficients using Eq. (8) we have some flexibility with regard to the parameter ϵ, which controls the degree of approximation error that we are willing to tolerate (with respect to the known samples). As we increase the value of ϵ the set of feasible solutions grows, which in turn means that solutions with a greater degree of temporal continuity may be found (although these solutions will no longer perfectly match the known data). This flexibility can be beneficial when transitioning between two sounds since we often want the transition to be as smooth as possible. We have also found that novel sounds/timbres can be created with large values of ϵ (these can be heard online as discussed below).

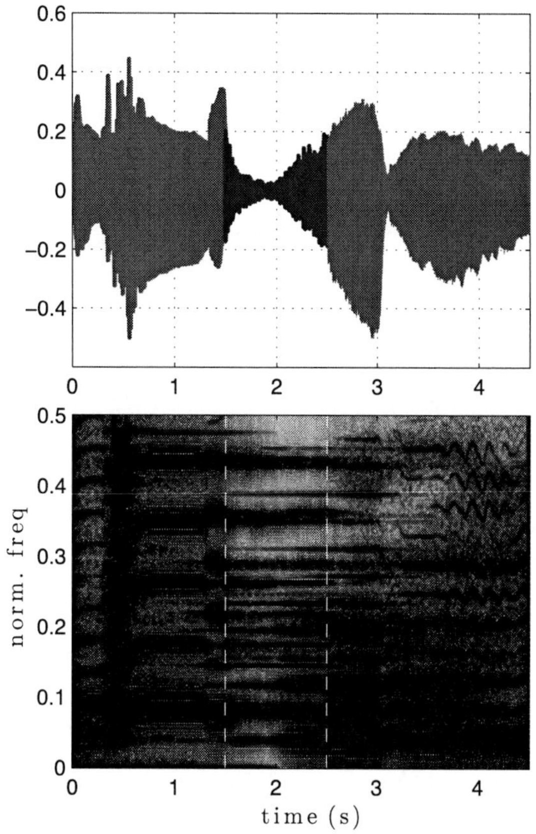

Figure 3. A one second transition between a saxophone passage and a female vocal excerpt (the sampling rate was 16kHz). Top: known data (light gray), interpolated data (dark gray). Bottom: spectrogram.

Fig. 3 shows a one second transition between a saxophone passage and a female vocal excerpt. For this example a Gabor dictionary with 2s long atoms was used and ϵ was set to 10^{-10}. The spectrogram seems to indicate an extension and averaging of the partials from each sound in the transition region. The audible impression for this particular transition is that the start/end of each sound has been extended into the transition region by adding reverb and preverb (i.e., reverb that precedes the sound).

We cannot quantitatively assess the morphing results (since no ground truth data exists for such a task). In order to qualitatively test the morphing results we have experimented with a wide variety of sources/targets including relatively stable sounds (e.g., clarinet, trumpet, tuba) and sound textures (drums, noise, abstract sounds). We also tested several missing interval durations from very short durations (250 ms) to extremely long durations (3 s). We have posted several audio examples on the companion website [24].

We make the following qualitative observations regarding these sounds. Firstly, for stable smooth sounds the morphing is quite similar to a simple cross-fade, although our transition appears to be slightly smoother. However, for more complicated sounds the results are quite audibly different from a simple cross-fade (the timbre during the transition appears to be more of a hybrid than a simple sum of the two signals). As mentioned above the effect sometimes sounds as though the source and target have been extended into the transition region by adding reverb and preverb. Indeed, since the atoms used are very long, their tails extend into the transition region, which helps to create this effect.

In our examples the cross-faded sounds are somewhat shorter than the interpolated sounds. This is because we must overlap the source and target sounds when we make a cross-fade. This could certainly be remedied by using more data for the cross-fade, however it brings to light a benefit of our interpolation approach: since we generate entirely new data for the transition, we can create longer transitions using less source material. This might be valuable in certain situations where the amount of available data is limited (for example, transitioning between tiny slices of sound which is common in some genres, e.g., 'microhouse').

We also note that tuning the value for ϵ allows us to create a wide variety of different sounds (some of which sound more 'wet' and others which sound more 'dry'). The ability to tune ϵ is a major advantage of our technique since it leads to many interesting transition effects.

6. CONCLUSION

We have presented a method of audio interpolation that can be used to restore missing or corrupted audio data. We began by modelling the sound as a linear combination of time-frequency atoms. Then, based on the observation that many musical signals are simultaneously sparse and structured (in terms of temporal continuity between the additive model coefficients), we proposed a structured-sparse optimization problem for estimating the model parameters. This model was subsequently used to synthesize an estimate of the missing samples. We compared our strategy to several state-of-the-art interpolation schemes and showed that, on average, our approach leads to an improvement in terms of the SNR. We also highlighted how this process can be used to morph/transition between sounds and provided several audio examples representative of the kind of results which may be achieved. Future work will examine additional types of structure/constraints that can be leveraged to improve the interpolation procedure. Finally, it would be interesting to consider a non-local approach to interpolation, especially for signals that are highly non-stationary. For example, one could try to integrating the ideas in [26] within the sparse approximation framework.

Acknowledgments

The authors gratefully acknowledge the support of the Natural Sciences and Engineering Research Council of Canada (NSERC).

7. REFERENCES

[1] A. Janssen, R. Veldhuis, and L. Vries, "Adaptive interpolation of discrete-time signals that can be modeled as autoregressive processes," *IEEE Transactions on Acoustics Speech and Signal Processing*, vol. 34, no. 2, pp. 317–330, 1986.

[2] W. Etter, "Restoration of a discrete-time signal segment by interpolation based on the left-sided and right-sided autoregressive parameters," *IEEE Transactions on Signal processing*, vol. 44, no. 5, pp. 1124–1135, 1996.

[3] S. Godsill, P. Rayner, and O. Cappé, *Digital audio restoration.* Springer, 2002.

[4] M. Lagrange, S. Marchand, and J. Rault, "Long interpolation of audio signals using linear prediction in sinusoidal modeling." *J. Audio Eng. Soc.*, vol. 53, pp. 891–905, 2005.

[5] A. Adler, V. Emiya, M. Jafari, M. Elad, R. Gribonval, and M. Plumbley, "Audio inpainting," *IEEE Transactions on Audio, Speech, and Language Processing*, vol. 20, no. 3, pp. 922–932, 2012.

[6] M. Elad, J. Starck, P. Querre, and D. Donoho, "Simultaneous cartoon and texture image inpainting using morphological component analysis (MCA)," *Applied and Computational Harmonic Analysis*, vol. 19, no. 3, pp. 340–358, 2005.

[7] C. Kereliuk, "Sparse and structured atomic modelling of audio," Ph.D. dissertation, McGill University, defended on March 28th, 2013.

[8] C. Kereliuk and P. Depalle, "Sparse atomic modeling of audio: A review," *Proceedings of the International Conference on Digital Audio Effects (DAFx)*, pp. 81–92, 2011.

[9] D. Donoho, "Compressed sensing," *IEEE Transactions on Information Theory*, vol. 52, no. 4, pp. 1289–1306, 2006.

[10] F. O'Reilly Regueiro, "Evaluation of interpolation strategies for the morphing of musical sound objects," Master's thesis, McGill University, 2010.

[11] K. Fitz, L. Haken, S. Lefvert, and M. O'Donnel, "Sound morphing using LORIS and the reassigned bandwdith-enhanced additive sound model: Practice and applications," in *Proc. International Computer Music Conference*, 2002, pp. 393–400.

[12] A. Olivero, B. Torrésani, P. Depalle, and R. Kronland-Martinet, "Sound morphing strategies based on alterations of time-frequency representations by Gabor multipliers," in *Proceedings AES 45th International Conference on Applications of Time-Frequency Processing in Audio*, 2012.

[13] M. Caetano and X. Rodet, "Sound morphing by feature interpolation," in *IEEE International Conference on Acoustics, Speech and Signal Processing*, 2011, pp. 161–164.

[14] M. Goodwin, "Matching pursuit with damped sinusoids," in *Proceedings of the IEEE Conference on Acoustics, Speech and Signal Processing (ICASSP)*, vol. 3, 1997.

[15] S. Chen, D. Donoho, and M. Saunders, "Atomic decomposition by basis pursuit," *SIAM review*, vol. 43, no. 1, pp. 129–159, 2001.

[16] D. Donoho, "For most large underdetermined systems of equations, the minimal ℓ_1-norm solution approximates the sparsest solution," *Communications on Pure and Applied Mathematics*, vol. 59, no. 7, pp. 907–934, 2006.

[17] S. Nam, M. Davies, M. Elad, and R. Gribonval, "Cosparse analysis modeling-uniqueness and algorithms," in *Proceedings of the IEEE Conference on Acoustics, Speech and Signal Processing (ICASSP)*, 2011, pp. 5804–5807.

[18] R. Tibshirani, M. Saunders, S. Rosset, J. Zhu, and K. Knight, "Sparsity and smoothness via the fused lasso," *Journal of the Royal Statistical Society: Series B (Statistical Methodology)*, vol. 67, no. 1, pp. 91–108, 2005.

[19] L. Rudin, S. Osher, and E. Fatemi, "Nonlinear total variation based noise removal algorithms," *Physica D: Nonlinear Phenomena*, vol. 60, pp. 259–268, 1992.

[20] M. Afonso, J. Bioucas-Dias, and M. Figueiredo, "Fast image recovery using variable splitting and constrained optimization," *Image Processing, IEEE Transactions on*, vol. 19, no. 9, pp. 2345–2356, 2010.

[21] S. Becker, J. Bobin, and E. Candès, "NESTA: a fast and accurate first-order method for sparse recovery," *SIAM Journal on Imaging Sciences*, vol. 4, no. 1, pp. 1–39, 2011.

[22] A. Beck and M. Teboulle, "A fast iterative shrinkage-thresholding algorithm for linear inverse problems," *SIAM Journal on Imaging Sciences*, vol. 2, no. 1, pp. 183–202, 2009.

[23] R. M. Warren *et al.*, "Perceptual restoration of missing speech sounds," *Science*, vol. 167, no. 3917, pp. 392–393, 1970.

[24] C. Kereliuk. (2013). [Online]. Available: http://www.music.mcgill.ca/~corey/smc2013

[25] B. Mailhé, R. Gribonval, P. Vandergheynst, and F. Bimbot, "Fast orthogonal sparse approximation algorithms over local dictionaries," *Signal Processing*, vol. 91, no. 12, pp. 2822–2835, 2011.

[26] M. Niediwiecki and K. Cisowski, "Smart copying-a new approach to reconstruction of audio signals," *Signal Processing, IEEE Transactions on*, vol. 49, no. 10, pp. 2272–2282, 2001.

Warped Frames: dispersive vs. non-dispersive sampling

Gianpaolo Evangelista
Media and Information Technology,
Linköping University,
Campus Norrköping,
Sweden
giaev24@ad.liu.se

ABSTRACT

Conventional Time-Frequency and Time-Scale Representations are often too rigid to capture fine details of sound or musical signals. Adaptation of ideal time-frequency tilings is often desirable in order to represent the signal in terms of components that are meaningful from a physical or perceptual point of view.

Remapping of the time and frequency axes by means of time and frequency warping can help achieve the desired flexibility of the representation. However, in the general case, the conjugate variable is affected as well, so that the resulting representation plane is distorted. In this paper we show methods to redress the conjugate distortion introduced by warping, both in the unsampled case of the integral Short-Time Fourier Transform and in the sampled case of generalized Gabor frames.

Ultimately, the methods illustrated in this paper allow for the construction and computation of Gabor-like non-uniform time frequency representations in which the new frames are obtained from uniform Gabor frames by frequency warping both the time variable and the time index. This provides a very general design procedure based on a prescribed warping map that can be derived, e.g., from a tonal scale.

1. INTRODUCTION

Time-frequency representations play a central role in the analysis, synthesis, coding and processing of sound signals. In this context, the most commonly used representation is the phase vocoder or Short-Time Fourier Transform (STFT), which has uniform time and frequency resolutions. However, non-uniform resolution is desirable in several applications. For example, the analysis and synthesis frequency bands can be adapted to a perceptual scale, achieving clear advantages in synthesis and coding due to the direct psycho-acoustic relevance of each component. In synthesis-by-analysis schemes, the frequency bands can be adapted to characteristics of the signal suggested, for example, by the frequencies of the partials of the tones, which in many instruments, such as the piano in the low register or percussions, are not harmonically related.

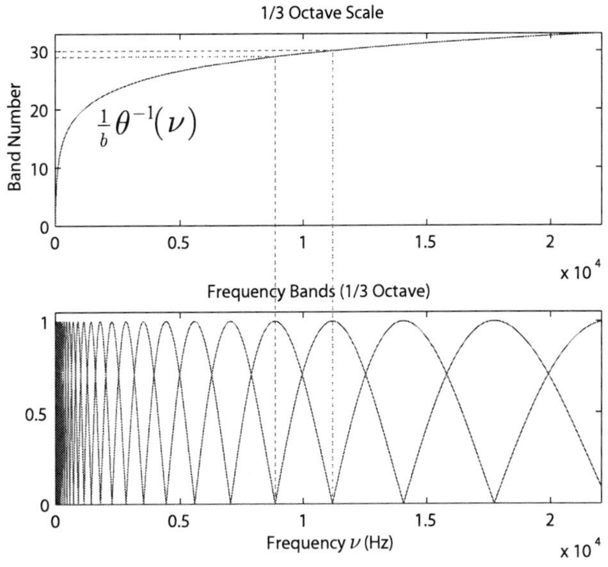

Figure 1. Frequency warping uniform frequency bands according to a $1/3$ of octave scale (top); resulting frequency band characteristics (bottom). Here b is the frequency shift in Hz of the original uniform bands.

Non-uniform frequency bands can always be thought of as obtained from uniform bands through a frequency map, i.e. a monotonically increasing function remapping the frequency axis. In certain cases, e.g. critical bands, the frequency map is given by experimentally fitted curves. In other cases, such as in the vibration of stiff strings or bars, the frequency map is derived from a wave dispersion characteristic. Sometimes the map is only specified at a finite number of points; a continuous curve can be obtained by interpolation. The application of a frequency map is known in filter design as frequency warping, a practice dating back to Constantinides's spectral transformations [1]. Frequency warping applied to a uniform system of bands is shown in Fig. 1 for adaptation to an equally tempered scale.

In a similar way, non-uniform analysis time intervals can be prescribed by remapping the time axis of the signal before performing uniform time-frequency analysis. The uniform analysis of the time warped signal achieves non-uniform time resolution and can be employed, e.g., to increase the time resolution close to signal transients and to reduce the time resolution in stationary portions of the signal.

However, frequency warping is not a time-shift invariant operation: it actually disrupts the time organization of signals. Uniform time-frequency analysis of the frequency warped signal results in a frequency dependent distortion of the time axis in the warped time-frequency representation. Similarly, the time warped time-frequency representation shows time dependent distortion of the frequency axis. Thus, warping one variable prior to uniform time-frequency analysis affects the conjugate variable in the representation plane.

In this paper, we address the problem of eliminating or mitigating the distortion of the conjugate variable in warped representations. We focus on the integral Short-Time Fourier Transform (STFT) and on its sampled version of Gabor frames. The method is quite general and can be applied to other representations such as time-scale.

Based on recently developed results [2–4], we address the problem of building perfect reconstruction structures for the time-frequency representation of signals that allow for arbitrary selection of bands specified according to a frequency map. Mathematically this amounts to constructing flexible frames that allow for parametric selection of the frequency bands of their atoms.

Just as Gabor frames can be obtained by uniformly sampling the integral STFT, the warped frames can be obtained as a result of nonuniform sampling in time-frequency. Nonuniform sampling theorems based on a time warping map were introduced in [5] and their adaptation to frequency sampling is immediate. Applications of frequency warping to time-frequency analysis date back to [6]. However, work previous to our paper did not take dispersion into account, which blurs the results of the analysis.

Orthogonal wavelets and wavelet frames [7], especially in their complex form [8], can be thought of as an example of nonuniform sampling of the time-frequency plane where the sampling grid is the time-scale grid $\{ma^n\}_{n\in\mathbb{N},m\in\mathbb{Z}}$. Further adaptation leading to more flexible time-frequency resolution settings were introduced in [9,10] for frequency and in [11] for time. The methods found in this paper do not make any assumption on the sampling grid. Rather, the grid is derived from the warping map, which can be assigned arbitrarily within smooth and one-to-one functions.

The paper is organized as follows. In Section 2 we review the concept of applying time and frequency warping to time-frequency representations derived from the continuous time Short-Time Fourier Transform, pointing out the problems introduced by dispersion. In Section 3 we illustrate how dispersion can be counteracted by means of further warping operations in the time-frequency domain. In Section 4 we attempt to apply the same redressing methods to frames, which allow for sampled time-frequency analysis and synthesis, and we provide the conditions by which the redressing of dispersion is exact. In Section 5 we illustrate the redressing method for frames, providing design examples and applications to audio signals. In Section 6 we draw our conclusions.

2. WARPED TIME-FREQUENCY

A uniform time-frequency representation is obtained by applying the Short-Time Fourier Transform (STFT) operator $\mathcal{S}$ to the signal s:

$$[\mathcal{S}s](\tau,\nu) = \langle s, h_{\tau,\nu}\rangle = \langle s, \mathbf{T}_\tau \mathbf{M}_\nu h_{0,0}\rangle = \int_{-\infty}^{+\infty} s(t)\overline{h_{0,0}(t-\tau)}e^{-j2\pi\nu(t-\tau)}dt, \quad (1)$$

where $\mathbf{T}_\tau s(t) = s(t-\tau)$ is the time-shift operator, $\mathbf{M}_\nu s(t) = e^{j2\pi\nu t}s(t)$ is the modulation operator and the overbar denotes complex conjugation. The operator $\mathcal{S}$ acts over time signals and the angular frequency ν is considered as a parameter. In (1), the analysis windows

$$h_{\tau,\nu}(t) = [\mathbf{T}_\tau \mathbf{M}_\nu h_{0,0}](t) = h_{0,0}(t-\tau)e^{j2\pi\nu(t-\tau)} \quad (2)$$

are modulated and shifted versions of a unique time window $h_{0,0}$. Their Fourier transforms are related to the Fourier transform of the original window $\hat{h}_{0,0}$ as follows:

$$\hat{h}_{\tau,\nu}(f) = \hat{h}_{0,0}(f-\nu)e^{-j2\pi f\tau}. \quad (3)$$

Since $[\mathcal{S}s](\tau,\nu) = s(\tau) * \overline{h_{0,\nu}(-\tau)}$, where the symbol $*$ denotes convolution, one can rewrite (1) in the frequency domain w.r.t. τ as follows:

$$\left[\widehat{\mathcal{S}s}\right](f,\nu) = \overline{\hat{h}_{0,\nu}(f)}\hat{s}(f) = \overline{\hat{h}_{0,0}(f-\nu)}\hat{s}(f). \quad (4)$$

Non-uniform time-frequency representations can be obtained from uniform ones via time and / or frequency warping, as discussed in Section 2.2, after we formally introduce warping operators in the next section.

2.1 Warping Operators

A 1D warping operator performs a remapping of the abscissae, as obtained through function composition. A time warping operator $\mathbf{W}_\gamma$ is completely characterized by a function composition operator in the time domain:

$$s_{tw} = \mathbf{W}_\gamma s = s \circ \gamma, \quad (5)$$

where γ is the time warping map and s_{tw} is the time-warped signal. Similarly, a frequency warping operator $\mathbf{W}_{\tilde{\theta}}$ is completely characterized by a function composition operator $\mathbf{W}_\theta$ in the frequency domain:

$$\hat{s}_{fw} = \widehat{\mathbf{W}_{\tilde{\theta}} s} = \hat{\mathbf{W}}_{\tilde{\theta}}\hat{s} = \mathbf{W}_\theta \hat{s} = \hat{s} \circ \theta, \quad (6)$$

where θ is the frequency warping map, which transforms the Fourier transform $\hat{s} = \mathcal{F}s$ of a signal s into the Fourier transform $\hat{s}_{fw} = \mathcal{F}s_{fw}$ of another signal s_{fw}, where $\mathcal{F}$ is the Fourier transform operator and the hat over a symbol denotes the Fourier transformed quantity (signal or operator). We affix the ˜ symbol over the map θ as a reminder that the map operates in the frequency domain. Accordingly, we have $\mathbf{W}_{\tilde{\theta}} = \mathcal{F}^{-1}\hat{\mathbf{W}}_{\tilde{\theta}}\mathcal{F} = \mathcal{F}^{-1}\mathbf{W}_\theta\mathcal{F}$.

If the warping map is one-to-one and almost everywhere differentiable then a unitary form of the warping operator can be defined by amplitude scaling, as given by the square root of the derivative of the map (dilation function). For example, a unitary frequency warping operator $\mathbf{U}_{\tilde{\theta}}$ has frequency domain action

$$\hat{s}_{fw}(\nu) = \left[\widehat{\mathbf{U}_{\tilde{\theta}} s}\right](\nu) = \sqrt{\left|\frac{d\theta}{d\nu}\right|}\hat{s}(\theta(\nu)), \qquad (7)$$

where ν is angular frequency. We assume henceforth that all warping maps are almost everywhere increasing so that the magnitude sign can be dropped from the derivative under the square root.

Unitary frequency warping ensures that the original signal energy is preserved. While bands are stretched or shrunk, the amplitudes are correspondingly reduced or increased so that the areas under the magnitude square Fourier transform in the warped bands are the same as the areas under the magnitude square Fourier transform of the original signal in the original bands.

Frequency warping generally disrupts the time organization of signals. Indeed, the time-shift operator $\mathbf{T}_\tau$ does not commute with the frequency warping operator:

$$\left[\widehat{\mathbf{W}_{\tilde{\theta}}\mathbf{T}_\tau s}\right](\nu) = \left[\mathbf{W}_\theta \widehat{\mathbf{T}_\tau s}\right](\nu) = e^{-j2\pi\theta(\nu)\tau}\hat{s}(\theta(\nu)), \qquad (8)$$

which is different from $\left[\widehat{\mathbf{T}_\tau \mathbf{W}_{\tilde{\theta}} s}\right](\nu) = e^{-j2\pi\nu\tau}\hat{s}(\theta(\nu))$, unless the map θ is the identity map. Thus, an event that starts at time T in the original signal, is dispersed into events starting at times $\phi_d(\nu)T$, where $\phi_d(\nu) = \theta(\nu)/\nu$ is the phase delay of the warping map, which depends on frequency unless the map is linear. This time dispersion results in audible de-synchronization of the signal and, as we will see, also in a distorted warped time-frequency representation. Similarly, time warping disrupts the frequency organization of signals resulting in time dependent frequency dispersion.

2.2 Warped Time-Frequency Representations

Remapping signals prior to STFT allows for a reinterpretation of the representation elements: while the organization of the representation (tiling) remains the same, the elements capture different components of the signal. Time warping dilates / shrinks and displaces the characteristic analysis time intervals (resolution and centers) w.r.t. signals. Frequency warping remaps the characteristic analysis frequency bands w.r.t. signals (bandwidths and centers).

Given a (time or frequency) warping operator $\mathbf{W}_\gamma$, the warped STFT is defined through the operator $\mathcal{S}_\gamma$ as follows

$$\begin{aligned}[\mathcal{S}_\gamma s](\tau,\nu) &= [\mathcal{S}\mathbf{W}_\gamma s](\tau,\nu) = \\ \langle \mathbf{W}_\gamma s, h_{\tau,\nu}\rangle &= \langle s, \mathbf{W}_\gamma^\dagger h_{\tau,\nu}\rangle,\end{aligned} \qquad (9)$$

which is indeed a warped version of (1), where $\mathbf{W}_\gamma^\dagger$ is the adjoint of the warping operator. If the warping operator is unitary then we have $\mathbf{W}_\gamma^\dagger = \mathbf{W}_\gamma^{-1} = \mathbf{W}_{\gamma^{-1}}$. In that case, warping the signal prior to STFT is perfectly equivalent to perform STFT analysis with inversely warped windows. The warped STFT is unitarily equivalent to the STFT so that a number of properties concerning conditioning and reconstruction hold [12].

If $\mathbf{W}_\gamma$ is a unitary time warping operator, the warped STFT analysis elements are

$$\begin{aligned}\tilde{h}_{\tau,\nu}(t) &= \left[\mathbf{W}_{\gamma^{-1}} h_{\tau,\nu}\right](t) = \\ &\sqrt{\frac{d\gamma^{-1}}{dt}} h_{0,0}(\gamma^{-1}(t) - \tau)e^{j2\pi\nu(\gamma^{-1}(t)-\tau)}.\end{aligned} \qquad (10)$$

These elements are formed by time warped windows centered at times $t = \gamma(\tau)$, as desired. However, the analysis frequencies are time-dependent. In fact, the instantaneous frequencies of the elements in (10), which are given by the time derivative of the phase of the complex exponential, are $\nu\frac{d\gamma^{-1}}{dt}$.

Similarly, if $\mathbf{W}_{\tilde{\theta}}$ is a unitary frequency warping operator, the Fourier transforms of the warped STFT analysis elements are

$$\begin{aligned}\hat{\tilde{h}}_{\tau,\nu}(f) &= \left[\widehat{\mathbf{W}_{\tilde{\theta}^{-1}} h_{\tau,\nu}}\right](f) = \\ &\sqrt{\frac{d\theta^{-1}}{df}} \hat{h}_{0,0}(\theta^{-1}(f) - \nu)e^{-j2\pi\theta^{-1}(f)\tau},\end{aligned} \qquad (11)$$

which shows how the analysis elements are obtained from frequency warped modulated windows centered at frequencies $f = \theta(\nu)$. The windows are time-shifted with dispersive delay, where the group delay is $\tau\frac{d\theta^{-1}}{df}$.

In the applications we would like to produce spectrograms with non-uniform time or frequency resolution but the dispersion introduced by warping results in misalignment and spreading of the time-frequency components in the conjugate variable of the warped one. In the next section we will show how further warping in the time-frequency plane can redress the warped representations.

3. REDRESSING THE WARPED STFT

To address the problem of realigning the frequency warped STFT $\left[\mathcal{S}_{\tilde{\theta}} s\right](\tau,\nu)$, consider its Fourier transform w.r.t. the time variable τ. This can be written in the form (4) by replacing the Fourier transform of the signal with that of the frequency warped signal:

$$\left[\widehat{\mathcal{S}\mathbf{W}_{\tilde{\theta}} s}\right](f,\nu) = \overline{\hat{h}_{0,0}(f-\nu)}\sqrt{\frac{d\theta}{df}}\hat{s}(\theta(f)). \qquad (12)$$

Recall that f is the angular frequency variable conjugate to time τ in the time-frequency plane. Performing unitary frequency warping on this variable by means of the inverse frequency map θ^{-1} one obtains:

$$\left[\mathbf{W}_{\tilde{\theta}^{-1}}\widehat{\mathcal{S}\mathbf{W}_{\tilde{\theta}} s}\right](f,\nu) = \overline{\hat{h}_{0,0}(\theta^{-1}(f) - \nu)}\hat{s}(f), \quad (13)$$

where we have used the fact that

$$1 = \frac{d\left[\theta(\theta^{-1}(f))\right]}{df} = \left.\frac{d\theta}{d\alpha}\right|_{\alpha=\theta^{-1}(f)}\frac{d\theta^{-1}}{df}. \qquad (14)$$

The redressed frequency warped STFT (13) is again in the form of a time-invariant filtering operation (convolution in time domain) where the filters are frequency warped versions of the modulated windows in (4). As a result, the dispersive delays in the analysis elements (11) are brought back to non-dispersive delays, the Fourier transform of the redressed analysis elements being

$$\hat{\tilde{\tilde{h}}}_{\tau,\nu}(f) = \left[\mathbf{T}_\tau \widehat{\mathbf{W}_{\tilde{\theta}} h_{0,\nu}}\right](f) = \hat{h}_{0,0}(\theta^{-1}(f) - \nu)e^{-j2\pi f\tau}. \tag{15}$$

It is possible to interpret (13) as the similarity transformation $\mathbf{W}^\dagger_{\tilde{\theta}} \mathcal{S} \mathbf{W}_{\tilde{\theta}}$ on the STFT operator, which is time-shift covariant.

A similar procedure for realigning the time-warped STFT can be derived by considering the inverse Fourier transform w.r.t. angular frequency in the time-frequency plane (second argument of the STFT) and by applying inverse time warping to the time variable conjugated to frequency in time-frequency. To simplify the result, the inverse Fourier transform can be taken with respect to time origin τ. This leads to a conjugate time covariant version of the time warped STFT in which frequency dispersion is eliminated.

4. WARPED GABOR FRAMES

4.1 Gabor frames

Given a window function h and two sampling parameters $a, b > 0$, the set of functions

$$\mathcal{G}(h, a, b) = \{\mathbf{T}_{na}\mathbf{M}_{mb}h : q, n \in \mathbb{Z}\} \tag{16}$$

is called a *Gabor system*. A signal s can be projected over a Gabor system by taking the scalar products $\langle s, \mathbf{T}_{na}\mathbf{M}_{mb}h\rangle$. These are exactly evaluations of the STFT of a signal with window h at the time-frequency grid of points (na, qb). Here we have defined the Gabor system using the same convention as in the definition (1) of the STFT. Usually, Gabor systems are defined with a reverse order of time-shift and frequency modulation operators, i.e. $\{\mathbf{M}_{mb}\mathbf{T}_{na}h : q, n \in \mathbb{Z}\}$. However, the extra phase factors that are introduced to convert from one definition to the other are perfectly irrelevant when establishing properties of the system. Even in the computation the extra phase factors cancel out in the analysis-synthesis algorithm, so they can be ignored.

A sequence of functions $\{\psi_l\}_{l\in I}$ in the Hilbert space $\mathcal{H}$ is called a frame if there exist both positive constant lower and upper bounds A and B, respectively, such that

$$A\|s\|^2 \leq \sum_{l\in I} |\langle s, \psi_l\rangle|^2 \leq B\|s\|^2 \quad \forall s \in \mathcal{H}, \tag{17}$$

where $\|s\|^2 = \langle s, s\rangle$ is the norm square or total energy of the signal. Frames generate signal expansions, i.e., the signal can be perfectly reconstructed from its projections over the frame.

A Gabor system that is a frame is called a *Gabor frame*. In this case, the signal can be reconstructed from the corresponding samples of the STFT. While not unique, reconstruction can be achieved with the help of a dual frame, which in turn is a Gabor frame generated by a dual window $\tilde{h}$. Perfect reconstruction depends on the choice of the window and the sampling grid. One can show that there exist no Gabor frames when $ab > 1$.

4.2 Warping Gabor frames

From (17) it is easy to see that any unitary operation on a frame results in a new frame with the same frame bounds A and B [12]. In particular, unitary operators can be applied to Gabor frames to obtain new frames. Depending on the operator, the resulting frames are not necessarily of the Gabor type, as the atoms are not generated by shifting and modulating a single window function.

Conceptually, starting from a Gabor frame (analysis) $\{\varphi_{n,q}\}_{q,n\in\mathbb{Z}}$ and dual frame (synthesis) $\{\gamma_{n,q}\}_{n,q\in\mathbb{Z}}$:

$$\begin{aligned} \varphi_{n,q} &= \mathbf{T}_{na}\mathbf{M}_{qb}h \\ \gamma_{n,q} &= \mathbf{T}_{na}\mathbf{M}_{qb}g, \end{aligned} \tag{18}$$

where h and g are dual windows, warped frames can be generated by unitarily warping the signal s prior to analysis and unitarily unwarping it after the synthesis:

$$\begin{aligned} s = \mathbf{U}^\dagger_{\tilde{\theta}} \sum_{n,q\in Z} \langle \mathbf{U}_{\tilde{\theta}} s, \varphi_{n,q}\rangle \gamma_{n,q} = \\ \sum_{n,q\in Z} \left\langle s, \mathbf{U}^\dagger_{\tilde{\theta}} \varphi_{n,q}\right\rangle \mathbf{U}^\dagger_{\tilde{\theta}} \gamma_{n,q}, \end{aligned} \tag{19}$$

where $\mathbf{U}_{\tilde{\theta}}$ is a unitary frequency warping operator. Defining the frequency warped frame (analysis) $\{\tilde{\varphi}_{n,q}\}_{q,n\in\mathbb{Z}}$ and dual frame (synthesis) $\{\tilde{\gamma}_{n,q}\}_{n,q\in\mathbb{Z}}$ as follows:

$$\begin{aligned} \tilde{\varphi}_{n,q} &= \mathbf{U}^\dagger_{\tilde{\theta}} \varphi_{n,q} = \mathbf{U}_{\tilde{\theta}^{-1}} \mathbf{T}_{na}\mathbf{M}_{qb}h \\ \tilde{\gamma}_{n,q} &= \mathbf{U}^\dagger_{\tilde{\theta}} \gamma_{n,q} = \mathbf{U}_{\tilde{\theta}^{-1}} \mathbf{T}_{na}\mathbf{M}_{qb}g, \end{aligned} \tag{20}$$

one obtains the signal expansion

$$s = \sum_{n,q\in Z} \langle s, \tilde{\varphi}_{n,q}\rangle \tilde{\gamma}_{n,q}. \tag{21}$$

However, warped Gabor frames suffer from the same problem as the warped STFT: as a result of frequency warping, the time organization of the analysis and synthesis systems is disrupted; the windows are time-shifted with frequency dependent shifts. Indeed the Fourier transforms of the warped Gabor frame elements are

$$\hat{\tilde{\varphi}}_{n,q}(f) = \sqrt{\frac{d\theta^{-1}}{df}}\hat{h}(\theta^{-1}(f) - qb)e^{-j2\pi\theta^{-1}(f)na}, \tag{22}$$

which bear frequency dispersive delays. In other words dispersive time samples are produced by the direct application of the warped frame analysis. Similar problems are encountered when time-warping Gabor frames.

The magnitude Fourier transforms $\hat{h}(\theta^{-1}(f) - qb)$ of a set of frequency warped modulated windows corresponding to $1/3$ octave frequency resolution is shown in Fig. 1, together with a scaled version $\frac{1}{b}\theta^{-1}$ of the warping map, which maps warped frequency to fractional band number, i.e., the integer values of $\frac{1}{b}\theta^{-1}$ correspond to the center frequencies of the bands.

In the next section we are applying a similar procedure to the one we introduced in the warped STFT in order to realign the time-frequency samples.

4.3 Redressing Warped Gabor Frames

The evaluation of the warped Gabor expansion coefficients

$$\tilde{c}_{n,q} = \langle s, \tilde{\varphi}_{n,q} \rangle \tag{23}$$

is identical to that of a time-frequency sampled warped STFT. In order to redress the frequency warped STFT into a time covariant representation we have introduced additional inverse frequency warping with respect to the time variable τ in the time-frequency plane. However, in the warped Gabor frames (20) this variable is sampled at instants na. Therefore, in order to parallel our warped STFT redressing procedure in the warped Gabor frames, one can only apply a discrete-time form of frequency warping to the time index n.

It is possible to show [13,14] that if the discrete-time frequency warping map ϑ is one-to-one and onto $[-\frac{1}{2}, +\frac{1}{2}[$, and almost everywhere differentiable there, then the set of sequences

$$\eta_m(n) = \int_{-\frac{1}{2}}^{+\frac{1}{2}} \sqrt{\frac{d\vartheta}{d\nu}} e^{j2\pi(n\nu - m\vartheta(\nu))} d\nu, \tag{24}$$

where $n, m \in \mathbb{Z}$, forms an orthonormal basis of $\ell^2(\mathbb{Z})$. These are recognized as generalized Laguerre sequences [9, 10, 15], which are the inverse discrete-time Fourier transforms of warped harmonic complex sinusoids in the frequency domain interval $[-\frac{1}{2}, +\frac{1}{2}[$. The map ϑ can be extended over the entire real axis as congruent modulo 1 to a 1-periodic function.

Given a sequence $\{x(n)\}$ in $\ell^2(\mathbb{Z})$, the scalar products

$$\tilde{x}(m) = \langle x, \eta_m \rangle_{\ell^2(\mathbb{Z})} \tag{25}$$

generate another sequence $\{\tilde{x}(m)\}$ in $\ell^2(\mathbb{Z})$, which satisfies

$$\hat{\tilde{x}}(\nu) = \sqrt{\frac{d\vartheta^{-1}}{d\nu}} \hat{x}(\vartheta^{-1}(\nu)), \tag{26}$$

where the $\hat{}$ symbol, when applied to sequences, denotes discrete-time Fourier transform. Thus, $\eta_m(n)$ defines the nucleus of an inverse unitary frequency warping $\ell^2(\mathbb{Z})$ operator $\mathbf{D}_{\tilde{\vartheta}^{-1}} = \mathbf{D}^{\dagger}_{\tilde{\vartheta}}$. Clearly, the transposed conjugate sequences $\mu_m(n) = \eta_n(m)$ form the nucleus of a unitary frequency warping $\ell^2(\mathbb{Z})$ operator $\mathbf{D}_{\tilde{\vartheta}}$.

In order to limit or eliminate time dispersion in the frequency warped Gabor expansion, one can apply the discrete-time frequency warping operator $\mathbf{D}_{\tilde{\vartheta}^{-1}}$ to the time sequence of expansion coefficients over the warped Gabor frame (23), i.e., with respect to index n. Since the operator is applied only on the time index, for generality, one can include dependency of the map and of the sequences η_n on the frequency index q, which will be useful in the sequel. The new coefficients are obtained as follows:

$$\tilde{\tilde{c}}_{n,q} = \left[\mathbf{D}_{\tilde{\vartheta}_q^{-1}} \tilde{c}_{\bullet,q}\right](n) = \sum_{m \in \mathbb{Z}} \overline{\eta_{n,q}(m)} \langle s, \tilde{\varphi}_{m,q} \rangle = \left\langle s, \sum_{m \in \mathbb{Z}} \eta_{n,q}(m) \tilde{\varphi}_{m,q} \right\rangle. \tag{27}$$

In order to reconstruct the signal from the coefficients $\tilde{\tilde{c}}_{n,q}$ one can first recover the coefficients $\tilde{c}_{n,q}$, which stems from the completeness and orthogonality of the set $\{\eta_{n,q}\}_{n \in \mathbb{Z}}$, and then combine them with the dual warped frame elements:

$$s = \sum_{n,q \in \mathbb{Z}} \tilde{c}_{n,q} \tilde{\gamma}_{n,q} = \sum_{n,q \in \mathbb{Z}} \sum_{m \in \mathbb{Z}} \tilde{\tilde{c}}_{m,q} \eta_{m,q}(n) \tilde{\gamma}_{n,q}. \tag{28}$$

Hence, defining the redressed frequency warped Gabor analysis and synthesis frames as follows:

$$\begin{aligned} \tilde{\tilde{\varphi}}_{n,q} &= \mathbf{D}_{\tilde{\vartheta}_q^{-1}} \tilde{\varphi}_{\bullet,q} = \sum_m \eta_{n,q}(m) \tilde{\varphi}_{m,q} \\ \tilde{\tilde{\gamma}}_{n,q} &= \mathbf{D}_{\tilde{\vartheta}_q^{-1}} \tilde{\gamma}_{\bullet,q} = \sum_m \eta_{n,q}(m) \tilde{\gamma}_{m,q}, \end{aligned} \tag{29}$$

from (27) and (28) we have:

$$s = \sum_{n,q \in Z} \tilde{\tilde{c}}_{n,q} \tilde{\tilde{\gamma}}_{n,q} = \sum_{n,q \in (Z)} \langle s, \tilde{\tilde{\varphi}}_{n,q} \rangle \tilde{\tilde{\gamma}}_{n,q}. \tag{30}$$

Indeed, the redressing discrete-time warping transformation is based on an orthonormal and complete expansion in $\ell^2(\mathbb{Z})$, which leads to the unitary equivalence of the redressed warped frames with the warped frames.

In order to verify the extent of our redressing method, we compute the Fourier transforms of the redressed frame. Exploiting the periodicity of the discrete-time redressing frequency warping map one can show that:

$$\hat{\tilde{\tilde{\varphi}}}_{n,q}(f) = A(f) \hat{h}(\theta^{-1}(f) - qb) e^{-j2\pi n \vartheta_q(a\theta^{-1}(f))}, \tag{31}$$

where

$$A(f) = \sqrt{\frac{d\theta^{-1}}{df}} \sqrt{\frac{d\vartheta_q}{d\nu}} \Bigg|_{\nu = a\theta^{-1}(f)}. \tag{32}$$

Hence, the effect of the dispersive delays would be counteracted if

$$\vartheta_q(a\theta^{-1}(f)) = d_q f \tag{33}$$

for any $f \in \mathbb{R}$, where d_q are positive constants controlling the time scale in each frequency band. In this case, the Fourier transforms of the redressed frame elements simply become:

$$\hat{\tilde{\tilde{\varphi}}}_{n,q}(f) = \sqrt{\frac{d_q}{a}} \hat{h}(\theta^{-1}(f) - qb) e^{-j2\pi n d_q f}. \tag{34}$$

Furthermore, if all d_q are identical, all the time samples would be aligned to a uniform time scale throughout frequencies.

However, each map ϑ_q is constrained to be congruent modulo 1 to a 1-periodic function, while the global warping map θ can be arbitrarily selected. Furthermore, having to be one-to-one in each unit interval, the functions ϑ_q can at most experience an increment of 1 there.

In the general case, a perfect time realignment of the components is not guaranteed. However, locally, within the essential bandwidths of the warped modulated windows it is possible to linearize the phase of the complex exponentials in (31).

We remark that, by construction, the redressed warped Gabor systems are guaranteed to be frames for any choice of the maps ϑ_q satisfying the stated periodicity conditions, even when the phase is not completely linearized.

5. EXAMPLES AND APPLICATIONS

The redressing method is a powerful technique to generate exact time-frequency representations adapted to non-uniform grids using arbitrary warping maps. In this section we illustrate two examples based on non-uniform frequency resolution adapted to a tempered scale. In the first case, the chosen windows have compact support in the frequency domain. In the second case, the windows are compactly supported in the time domain. The methods applies, however, also to windows that are not compactly supported in either domain.

In both our examples we define the redressed analysis and synthesis frames as in (29) and try to enforce condition (33). Actually, since we start with tight Gabor frames [16], analysis and synthesis frames coincide.

5.1 The Painless Case

In the so called "painless" case, where the window h is chosen to have compact support in the frequency domain, one can exactly eliminate the dispersive delays with the help of (29). In fact, to fix our ideas, suppose that the bandwidth of the window h is Kb, with K a positive integer, i.e., $\hat{h}(f) = 0$ for $|f| \geq Kb/2$. This corresponds to an overlap-add scheme in the frequency domain [4] – for example, the choice $K = 2$ corresponds to the case of half window length overlap in the frequency domain (see Fig. 1) – which allows one to satisfy the frame condition (17) even tightly ($A = B = 1$) with a simple choice of the window [4]. In particular, one could use the frequency domain cosine window:

$$\hat{h}(\nu) = \begin{cases} \sqrt{\frac{2a}{K}} \cos \frac{\pi\nu}{\beta} & \text{if } -\frac{\beta}{2} \leqslant \nu < +\frac{\beta}{2} \\ 0 & \text{otherwise} \end{cases} \qquad (35)$$

where $\beta > 0$ is the total bandwidth of the window and $K > 1$ is an integer, a is the time sampling interval and we let $b = \beta/K$. In that case the warped modulated windows $\hat{h}(\theta^{-1}(f) - qb)$ will be nonzero only for $\theta((q - K/2)b) < f < \theta((q + K/2)b)$.

In the painless case, condition (33) only needs to be satisfied by the map ϑ_q in this interval. Equivalently, we require

$$\vartheta_q(a\nu) = d_q\theta(\nu), \quad (q - \tfrac{K}{2})b < \nu < (q + \tfrac{K}{2})b, \qquad (36)$$

which is possible if on one hand the variation of the argument of the map ϑ_q in (36) satisfies

$$a[(q + \tfrac{K}{2})b - (q - \tfrac{K}{2})b] = Kab \leq 1 \qquad (37)$$

and, on the other hand, if also the variation of the map ϑ_q over the warped modulated window bandwidth satisfies

$$d_q[\theta((q + \tfrac{K}{2})b) - \theta((q - \tfrac{K}{2})b)] = d_q B_q \leq 1, \qquad (38)$$

where $B_q = \theta((q + \frac{K}{2})b) - \theta((q - \frac{K}{2})b)$ is the full bandwidth of the warped modulated window. The first of these conditions only requires $ab \leq 1/K$, which does not depend on q and can be satisfied assigning sufficient redundancy (oversampling) of the initial Gabor frame. Incidentally, this is the same condition for the original Gabor system to form a frame. A valid choice is $K = 2$, which

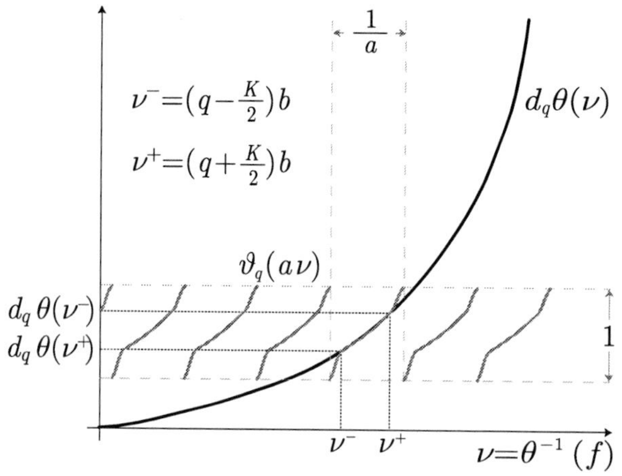

Figure 2. Locally eliminating dispersion by means of discrete-time frequency warping. Black line: curve derived from the original map θ by amplitude scaling. Gray line: discrete-time frequency warping characteristics for local delay linearization.

requires $ab \leq 1/2$. For the second condition, one needs to select $d_q \leq 1/B_q$, as intuitively clear from the sampling theorem. If there is an upper bound B to the bandwidths B_q then one can choose identical $d_q = 1/B$, $q \in \mathbb{Z}$, to satisfy the sampling condition with uniform rates.

An example of local linearization of the phase is shown in Fig. 2, plotted in the abscissa $\nu = \theta^{-1}(f)$, where the black curve is the amplitude scaled warping map $d_q\theta(\nu)$ and the gray curve represents the map $\vartheta_q(a\nu)$, which is $1/a$-periodic. Amplitude scaling the warping map θ allows the values of the map to lie in the range of the discrete-time warping map ϑ_q. The amplitude scaling factors are the new time sampling intervals d_q of the redressed warped Gabor expansion.

The choice of the initial sampling interval a allows all the maps $\{\vartheta_q\}_{q\in\mathbb{Z}}$ to be arbitrarily specifiable to match $d_q\theta(\nu)$ in the intervals where the Fourier transforms of the warped modulated windows (warped frame elements) are nonzero. Therefore, the warping map design method to eliminate dispersive sampling in the frequency warped Gabor elements is consistent when the elements are compactly supported in the frequency domain.

The score and the analysis of a singing phrase using a redressed warped Gabor frame adapted to the 12-tone scale are reported in Fig. 3. It is easy to see that the score of the singing part can be easily extracted from the non-uniform spectrogram.

5.2 Redressing in the Painful Case

In the painless case, the obtained redressed warped Gabor frame elements are identical in form to the ones generated in [4] by means of an ad-hoc procedure, where aliasing is canceled in the frequency domain. However, the redressing method by means of (29) for the warped frames presented in this paper can be applied to any frame.

For example, one can start from windows that are compactly supported in the time domain, where aliasing is canceled in the time-domain through overlap-add, such as the

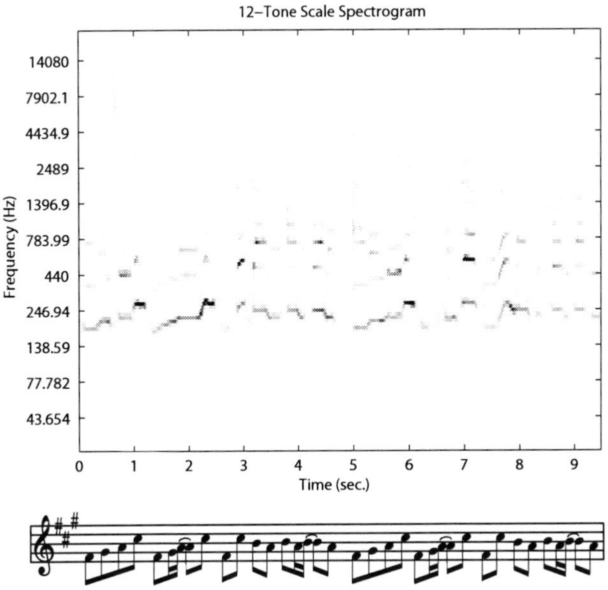

Figure 3. Nonuniform 12-tone scale spectrogram of the singing phrase represented in the score line [from *Tom's Diner*, Suzanne Vega], in which it is possible to track in tempered time-frequency scale the score and even the glissando introduced by the singer.

time-domain cosine window. This window is given by

$$h(t) = \begin{cases} \sqrt{\frac{2b}{R}} \cos \frac{\pi t}{T} & \text{if } -\frac{T}{2} \leqslant t < +\frac{T}{2} \\ 0 & \text{otherwise} \end{cases} \quad (39)$$

where T is the total duration of the window, $R > 1$ is an integer, b is the frequency sampling interval and we let the time shift parameter $a = T/R$.

The Fourier transform of the cosine window, given by

$$\hat{h}(\nu) = \sqrt{\tfrac{b}{2R}}(\text{sinc}(\nu T - \tfrac{1}{2}) + \text{sinc}(\nu T + \tfrac{1}{2})), \quad (40)$$

is plotted in Fig. 4, from which one can see that the main lobe has bandwidth $3/T = 3/Ra$. Assuming this as the essential bandwidth in which to linearize the phase, in order to satisfy (33) here, one needs to select $R \geq 3$, which is the analogon of (37), and $d_q B_q \leq 1$, which is the analogon of (38), where now $B_q = \theta(qb + \frac{3}{2T}) - \theta(qb - \frac{3}{2T})$.

Concurrently, the parameter T can be selected according to the smallest required essential bandwidth. For example, in the case of a tempered scale warping map, in order to have sufficient frequency resolution one can select $\frac{3}{2T} = f_0$, where f_0 is the frequency of the smallest tone to be represented, so that adjacent tones fall away from the main frequency lobe of the window, which gives $a = \frac{3}{2Rf_0}$.

The frequency shift parameter b must be chosen so that $ab \leq 1/R$ for the original Gabor system to be a frame. For $R = 3$ and the chosen value of a, this gives $b \leq 2f_0/3$. However, in practice one would like the tones of the scale to be adequately represented by the warped bands; in our examples we chose $b = f_0/3$.

A zoom of the analysis of the same phrase as in Fig. 3 by means of a redressed warped Gabor frame generated by a

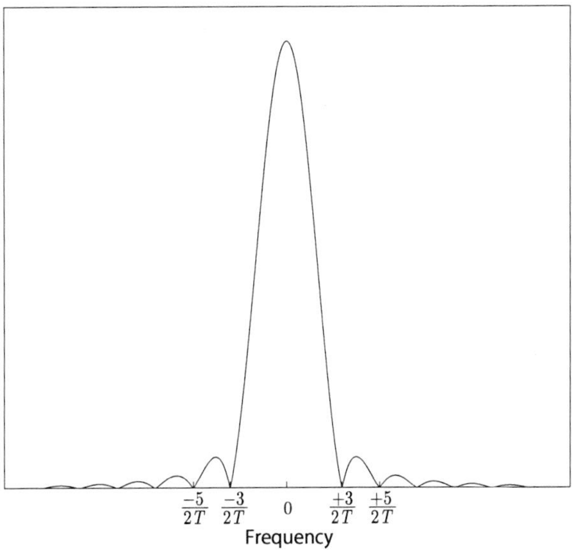

Figure 4. Magnitude Fourier transform of the cosine window.

cosine shaped time domain window is shown in Fig. 5. In spite of the fact that the phase is linearized only in the support of the main lobes of the warped widows, the quality of the result is not appreciably different form that obtained in the painless case. Moreover, perfect reconstruction is still guaranteed.

6. CONCLUSIONS

In this paper, we have introduced a new method to design time-frequency representations with arbitrary non-uniform time or frequency resolutions, based on frequency and time warping. The problems arising from the dispersive sampling introduced by warping are solved by introducing a further warping operation in time-frequency.

The procedure was first applied to the unsampled Short-Time Fourier Transform and, with further constraints, to Gabor frames. In the latter, perfect elimination of dispersion is only possible in particular cases, e.g., when the Gabor frame elements have compact support in the frequency domain (for frequency warping) or in the time domain (for time warping).

The design extends the methods presented in [4] by making use of warping maps to generate a full class of suitable frames with assignable non-uniform time and frequency resolutions and with non-dispersive sampling. It also paves the way to approximations in which the effect of dispersion is minimized within the essential bandwidths of the frame elements when these are not selected, possibly for real time computational needs, to have compact support in the frequency domain.

7. REFERENCES

[1] A. Constantinides, "Spectral transformations for digital filters," *Proceedings of the Institution of Electrical Engineers*, vol. 117, no. 8, pp. 1585–1590, 1970.

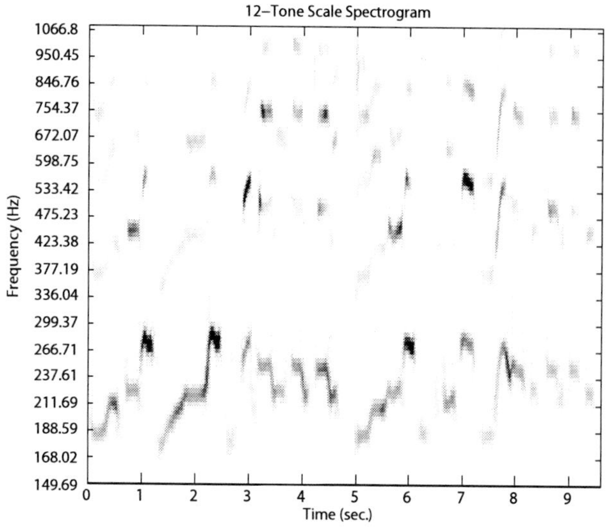

Figure 5. Zoom of the nonuniform 12-tone scale spectrogram of the same singing phrase as in Fig. 3 using a redressed warped Gabor frame generated by a cosine window in the time domain.

[2] G. A. Velasco, N. Holighaus, M. Dörfler, and T. Grill, "Constructing an invertible constant-Q transform with non-stationary Gabor frames," in *Proceedings of the Digital Audio Effects Conference (DAFx-11)*, Paris, France, 2011, pp. 93–99.

[3] P. Balazs, M. Dörfler, F. Jaillet, N. Holighaus, and G. A. Velasco, "Theory, implementation and applications of nonstationary Gabor Frames," *Journal of Computational and Applied Mathematics*, vol. 236, no. 6, pp. 1481–1496, 2011.

[4] G. Evangelista, M. Dörfler, and E. Matusiak, "Phase vocoders with arbitrary frequency band selection," in *Proceedings of the 9th Sound and Music Computing Conference*, Copenhagen, Denmark, 2012, pp. 442–449.

[5] J. Clark, M. Palmer, and P. Lawrence, "A transformation method for the reconstruction of functions from nonuniformly spaced samples," *Acoustics, Speech and Signal Processing, IEEE Transactions on*, vol. 33, no. 5, pp. 1151–1165, 1985.

[6] C. Braccini and A. Oppenheim, "Unequal bandwidth spectral analysis using digital frequency warping," *IEEE Transactions on Acoustics, Speech, and Signal Processing*, vol. 22, pp. 236–244, 1974.

[7] I. Daubechies, *Ten lectures on wavelets*, ser. CBMS-NSF Regional Conference Series in Applied Mathematics. Philadelphia, PA: Society for Industrial and Applied Mathematics (SIAM), 1992, vol. 61.

[8] N. Kingsbury, "Complex Wavelets for Shift Invariant Analysis and Filtering of Signals," *Applied and Computational Harmonic Analysis*, vol. 10, pp. 234–253, 2001.

[9] G. Evangelista, "Dyadic Warped Wavelets," *Advances in Imaging and Electron Physics*, vol. 117, pp. 73–171, Apr. 2001.

[10] G. Evangelista and S. Cavaliere, "Frequency Warped Filter Banks and Wavelet Transform: A Discrete-Time Approach Via Laguerre Expansions," *IEEE Transactions on Signal Processing*, vol. 46, no. 10, pp. 2638–2650, Oct. 1998.

[11] S. Azizi, D. Cochran, and J. McDonald, "Reproducing kernel structure and sampling on time-warped spaces with application to warped wavelets," *IEEE Transactions on Information Theory*, vol. 48, no. 3, pp. 789–790, 2002.

[12] R. G. Baraniuk and D. L. Jones, "Unitary equivalence : A new twist on signal processing," *IEEE Transactions on Signal Processing*, vol. 43, no. 10, pp. 2269–2282, Oct. 1995.

[13] P. W. Broome, "Discrete orthonormal sequences," *J. ACM*, vol. 12, no. 2, pp. 151–168, Apr. 1965. [Online]. Available: http://doi.acm.org/10.1145/321264.321265

[14] L. Knockaert, "On Orthonormal Muntz-Laguerre Filters," *IEEE Transactions on Signal Processing*, vol. 49, no. 4, pp. 790 –793, apr 2001.

[15] G. Evangelista and S. Cavaliere, "Discrete Frequency Warped Wavelets: Theory and Applications," *IEEE Transactions on Signal Processing*, vol. 46, no. 4, pp. 874–885, Apr. 1998, special issue on Theory and Applications of Filter Banks and Wavelets.

[16] S. Mallat, *A Wavelet Tour of Signal Processing*. Academic Press London, 1998.

IMPROVED POLYNOMIAL TRANSITION REGIONS ALGORITHM FOR ALIAS-SUPPRESSED SIGNAL SYNTHESIS

Dániel Ambrits and Balázs Bank
Budapest University of Technology and Economics,
Dept. of Measurement and Information Systems,
H-1521 Budapest, Hungary
ambrits.daniel@gmail.com, bank@mit.bme.hu

ABSTRACT

One of the building blocks of virtual analog synthesizers is the oscillator algorithm producing simple geometric waveforms, such as saw or triangle. An important requirement for such a digital oscillator is that its spectrum is similar to that of the analog waveform, that is, the heavy aliasing that would result from a trivial modulo-counter based implementation is reduced. Until now, the computationally most efficient oscillator algorithm with reduced aliasing was the Polynomial Transition Regions (PTR) method. This paper shows that the efficiency can be increased even further by eliminating the phase offset of the PTR method. The new Efficient PTR (EPTR) algorithm produces the same output as the PTR method, while requiring roughly 30% fewer operations, making it the most efficient alias-reduced oscillator algorithm to date. In addition to presenting an EPTR sawtooth algorithm, the paper extends the differentiated parabolic wave (DPW) triangle algorithm to the case of asymmetric triangle waves, followed by an EPTR implementation. The new algorithm provides continuous transition between triangle and sawtooth signals, while still remaining computationally efficient.

1. INTRODUCTION

Analog synthesizers produced in the 60s and 70s are still very popular among musicians for their characteristic timbre, and the sound of these classic synthesizers has become an inherent part of many modern musical genres. However, the original synthesizers are hard to find, expensive, and usually do not provide sufficient control (e.g., via MIDI) as required by today's musicians. Therefore, some companies provide modern analog synthesizers with digital control, but an even more cost-effective solution is to simulate the analog signal chain via digital signal processing. The first such synthesizer was the Clavia NordLead, which paved the way for virtual analog synthesis. For an excellent overview on related research, see [1].

In an analog synthesizer the signal flow starts with an oscillator generating geometric waveforms, such as square, sawtooth, triangle, sine, and sometimes a noise generator

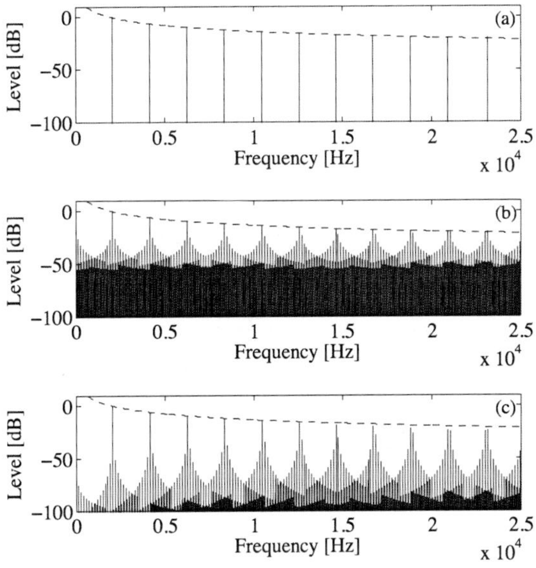

Figure 1. Spectrum of (a) the ideal, (b) the trivial and (c) the DPW sawtooth signals. The dashed line is the envelope of the ideal spectrum.

is also provided. Then this signal is fed to a filter that is controlled by envelope generators, low frequency oscillators (LFO), etc., and finally its gain is adjusted by an amplifier, again controlled by an envelope and LFO. This paper concentrates on the first part, that is, the digital modeling of the oscillator.

The trivial option for creating a digital replica of a geometric signal is to generate samples that correspond to the sampling of the analog waveform. In the case of the sawtooth signal, this results in a simple modulo counter, which can be implemented very effectively. However, as expected, this results in a heavy aliasing due to the non-bandlimited nature of the analog signal from which it originates [2]. This is displayed in Fig. 1 (b), together with the spectrum of the ideal (analog) sawtooth in Fig. 1 (a). A general remedy to the problem of aliasing is oversampling, that is, running the modulo counter at a significantly higher sampling rate, and then decimating. However, this leads to a considerable increase of computational complexity.

Therefore, special algorithms have been developed that reduce the aliased components while still keeping the computational requirements low. Note that it is not required to eliminate aliasing completely, since aliased components below a certain level are not audible due to masking effects [3].

The approaches include waveform generation based on a band-limited impulse train [4, 5] and band-limited step function [2, 6, 7], and the distortion and filtering of sine waves [8]. The simplest, yet still practically usable method is the differentiated parabolic wave (DPW) algorithm [9], that is based on the spectral tilt modification of the continuous-time signal before sampling. Later the higher-order extension of the method has also been presented [10], providing better alias suppression at the expense of greater complexity.

By noting that the DPW algorithm modifies only the samples around the discontinuity of the analog signal, a more efficient implementation is possible [11]. This algorithm is called Polynomial Transition Regions (PTR), and is based on precomputing correction polynomials for the samples in the transition, while the linear regions of the signal are offset by a constant value [11].

This paper presents an even more efficient version of the PTR algorithm, which will be called EPTR throughout the paper. The method is based on the fact that the offset of DPW and PTR waveforms compared to the trivial (modulo-counter generated) waveform is due to a phase shift of the DPW and PTR signals. When this phase shift is removed, the linear regions of the waveform can be taken simply as the trivial waveform values, eliminating the need for an extra addition. For the sawtooth signal this leads to the reduction of the number of operations by around 30%.

By modulating the pulse width of a square wave, very interesting sonic variations can be created. Accordingly, many classic and virtual analog synthesizers offer this kind of pulse-width modulation (PWM) signal. A similarly interesting effect can be achieved by modulating the symmetry of triangle waves. This way the triangle signal can be continuously transformed into a sawtooth waveform. Two of the rare examples generating triangle waves with variable symmmetry are the Moog Little Phatty and Sub Phatty analog synthesizers [12]. This paper first extends the DPW algorithm for the case of asymmetric triangle waves, then provides a highly efficient implementation by the use of the new EPTR algorithm.

The rest of this paper is organized as follows. Section 2 reviews the DPW algorithm for the case of the sawtooth signal and provides an extension to the case of the asymmetric triangle wave. This is followed by the basic idea of the PTR method in Sec. 3, while Sec. 4 proposes the new EPTR algorithm for the saw and asymmetric triangle waves. Finally, Sec. 5 compares the computational complexity of the DPW, PTR and the EPTR algorithms.

2. DIFFERENTIATED POLYNOMIAL WAVEFORM ALGORITHM

First, let us consider the steps of generating an alias-suppressed signal with the Differentiated Polynomial Waveform (DPW) algorithm. In the Nth-order method the continuous signal is integrated $N-1$ times. This is equivalent to processing the sampled signal with an Nth-order polynomial waveshaper [10]. As a result, the spectrum of the integrated sawtooth signal decreases by $6N$ dB per octave instead of 6 dB. This way the aliasing is significantly reduced when the signal is sampled. Then the signal is differentiated $N-1$ times in the discrete-time domain to restore its spectral tilt, which means filtering by the $(1-z^{-1})^{N-1}$ transfer function. Finally it is scaled to the desired amplitude [10].

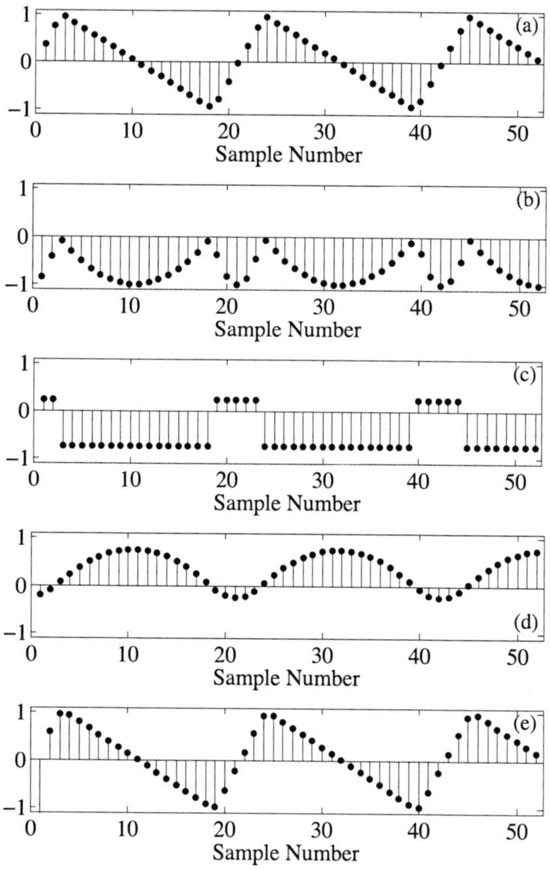

Figure 2. Generation of the triangle signal with variable symmetry by the DPW algorithm. The trivial signal (a) is first processed with the x^2-1 function. The result (b) is then multiplied with (c) a scaled rectangular wave to get (d) the parabolic waveform. Finally differentiating and scaling produce (e) the desired alias-suppressed waveform.

For $N = 2$ the integral of a piecewise linear signal is a piecewise parabolic ($x^2/2$) function. The trivial sawtooth signal corresponds to a periodic counter ranging from -1 to 1. The alias-suppressed sawtooth signal can be generated by squaring the signal, then differentiating the resulted piecewise polynomial waveform and finally scaling by a sufficient value [9].

While only symmetrical triangle wave is considered in the literature [10], it can be easily extended to asymmetric case. The method is explained by using Fig. 2. The gradient of the ascending region is $A > 0$, then the gradient of the descending region is $B = -A/(A-1) < 0$. Following the generation of the symmetric triangle signal for $N = 2$ [10], the trivial waveform Fig. 2(a) is first processed with the $x^2 - 1$ function, giving Fig. 2(b). (In the general case, when the value of the peak P_{peak} is not 1, the waveshaper would be $x^2 - P^2_{\text{peak}}$.) Then it is multiplied with a rectangular waveform with $1/A$ duty cycle so that the parabolic regions of the signal are alternately positive and negative. This rectangular wave is generated according to the counting direction of the trivial signal which, for the symmetric triangle holds the value 1 when the trivial waveform is ascending and -1 when it is descending. Note that by using this ± 1 rectangular wave the absolute values of the peaks are 1 in both regions but the width of these parabolic regions are not the same. Thus at the transition of two successive regions the gradients are different and this would cause jumps in the differentiated signal. This problem can be solved by scaling the regions with $1/|A|$ and $1/|B|$ factors so that the transition is smooth (see Fig. 2(c) and (d)). This step is the only difference between the symmetric and asymmetric case. Therefore the waveshapers are $(x^2 - 1)/A$ for the ascending region and $(x^2 - 1)/B$ for the descending region. Then the polynomial waveform is differentiated and multiplied by a scaling factor.

3. POLYNOMIAL TRANSITION REGIONS ALGORITHM

The signal generated with the Nth-order DPW algorithm differs from the trivial waveform by only $N-1$ samples per period. The differing samples are in the transition region, the linear sections only have an offset. This means unnecessary additional computation, since the integration and differentiation is computed even for the linear regions. The Polynomial Transition Regions algorithm was introduced to decrease the computation cost based on this observation. In the PTR method the sample values are derived in a closed form for each section, and the final signal is generated from the trivial signal using these general forms [11]. To show that the computational cost can be reduced even further, the linear section is discussed for $N = 2$.

Two successive samples in the linear section are $p[n] = p_n$ and $p[n-1] = p_{n-1} = p_n - 2AT$, where p_n is the current value of the trivial signal generator, and A is the gradient of the section. ($A = 1$, when the signal increases from -1 to 1 during one period. If $A < 0$, the signal decreases.) $T = f_0/f_s$, where f_0 is the fundamental frequency of the signal and f_s is the sampling frequency. For $N = 2$ the waveshaper is x^2 according to the DPW algorithm, then the differentiation and scaling leads to:

$$y[n] = \frac{p_n^2 - p_{n-1}^2}{4AT} = p_n - AT. \qquad (1)$$

For the linear section an addition operation is required for each sample. The value of the offset can be both positive and negative depending on whether the signal is ascending or descending. The $-AT$ offset represents a half sample delay compared to the trivial generator as seen in Fig. 3(a). This delay comes from the behavior of the discrete-time differentiation. We will see in the next section that a more efficient algorithm can be derived by eliminating this half sample delay, and so the need for the addition operation.

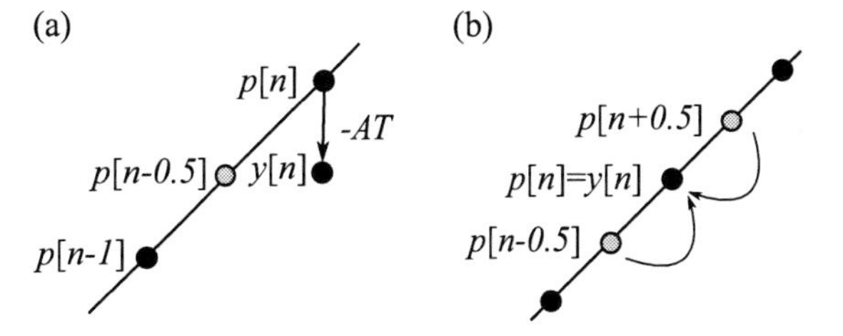

Figure 3. Discrete-time differentiation using (a) the trivial signal (dark dots) and (b) the waveform shifted with half sample (ligth dots).

4. EFFICIENT POLYNOMIAL TRANSITION REGION ALGORITHM

4.1 Eliminating the Half Sample Delay in the Linear Region

The simplest way to avoid the unnecessary computation in the linear region is using the trivial generator as the output. This is equivalent to using the differentiation on the adjacent samples which are at half sample distance from the origin as seen in Fig. 3(b). The $p_{n-0.5}$ and $p_{n+0.5}$ are the values of the continuous signal halfway between the samples.

$$\begin{aligned} y[n] &= \frac{p_{n+0.5}^2 - p_{n-0.5}^2}{4AT} = \\ &= \frac{(p_n + AT)^2 - (p_n - AT)^2}{4AT} = p_n. \end{aligned} \qquad (2)$$

In other words, the PTR algorithm is applied on a trivial signal which is with half sample in advance to the desired signal. Therefore also the samples in the transition region should be calculated from this shifted trivial waveform. However, this does not require that these samples are known during the wave generation, an explicit form of the correction can be calculated in advance.

For $N = 2$, the transition region is a one sampling time wide section. The shifted trivial signal causes that the samples to be corrected can be found before or after the break. So unlike in the PTR algorithm where this section was the [0,1] sample interval after the discontinuity, here it can be found in the [-0.5,0.5] interval with the transition in the centre. When we detect that the trivial signal generator is in this region, the position of the sample must be inspected and the correction must be applied according to the result. In the next section the transitions are derived for $N = 2$.

4.2 Sawtooth

4.2.1 Derivation of the sawtooth wave generation

The continuous signal with gradient A jumps from the value $P_{\max}$ to $P_{\min}$ as can be seen in Fig. 4. When the sample of the discrete trivial waveform is $p[n] = p_n$ before the discontinuity, the next sample is $p[n+1] = p_n + 2AT - (P_{\max} - P_{\min})$. These samples are processed by the x^2 waveshaper. The correction depends on whether the sample to be corrected is before or after the discontinuity of the continuous waveform.

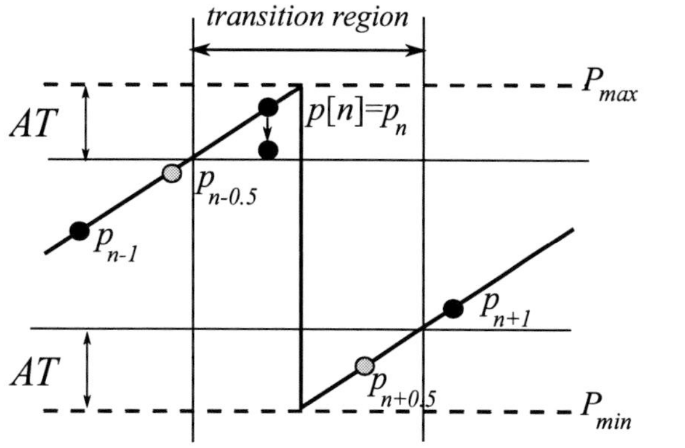

Figure 4. Correction of the sawtooth signal. During the derivation the half-sample delayed signal (light dots) is used instead of the trivial signal (dark dots). p_n is corrected to the desired value.

a) The sample is before the discontinuity ($p_n > P_{\max} - AT$), as in Fig. 4.

According to Section 4.1 the calculation must be applied using the adjacent samples at half sample distance from the output sample. The trivial sample has a value of $p[n] = p_n$, as seen in Fig. 4. The previous sample $p_{n-0.5} = p_n - AT$, the next sample would be $p_n + AT$ but it is higher than the maximum value, so $p_{n+0.5} = p_n + AT - (P_{\max} - P_{\min})$. Applying the DPW algorithm leads to the desired output:

$$y_A[n] = \frac{p^2_{n+0.5} - p^2_{n-0.5}}{4AT} = \\ = \frac{(p_n + AT + P_{\min} - P_{\max})^2 - (p_n - AT)^2}{4AT}. \tag{3}$$

For a sawtooth ranging from -1 to 1, we have $A = 1$, $P_{\max} = 1$, and $P_{\min} = -1$. In this special case the calculations lead to

$$y[n] = p_n - \frac{p_n}{T} + \frac{1}{T} - 1. \tag{4}$$

b) The sample is after the discontinuity ($p_n < P_{\min} + AT$).

The next sample is $p_{n+0.5} = p_n + AT$. The previous sample can be found before the discontinuity (since $p_n - AT < P_{\min}$), so it has a value of $p_{n-0.5} = p_n - AT + (P_{\max} - P_{\min})$.

$$y_B[n] = \frac{p^2_{n+0.5} - p^2_{n-0.5}}{4AT} \\ = \frac{(p_n + AT)^2 - (p_n - AT + P_{\max} - P_{\min})^2}{4AT}. \tag{5}$$

For the usual sawtooth signal $A = 1$, $P_{\max} = 1$ and $P_{\min} = -1$. In this special case the calculations lead to

$$y[n] = p_n - \frac{p_n}{T} - \frac{1}{T} + 1. \tag{6}$$

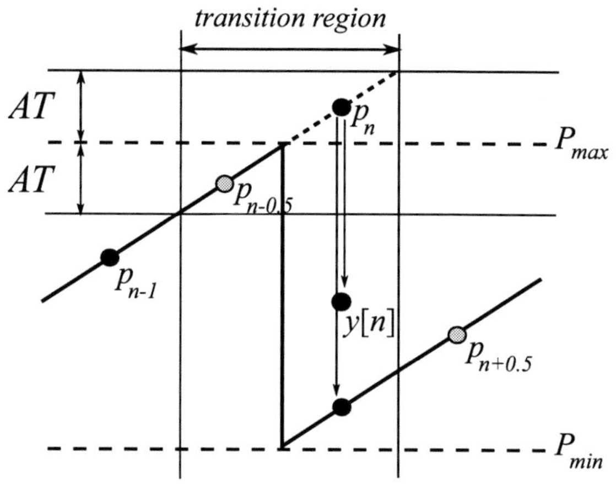

Figure 5. EPTR algorithm of the sawtooth signal. When the counter (dark dots) goes over $P_{\max} - AT$, the sample is in the transition region. First the correction is applied using the values of the half-sample delayed signal (ligth dots), then the counter jumps.

4.2.2 *The EPTR sawtooth wave algorithm*

The PTR algorithm assumes that the trivial sawtooth signal is given, that is, the trivial signal generation and correcting the samples in the transition region are handled separately [11]. If we were doing the same, then two branch operations would be required: one for detecting the jump of the trivial signal and one for finding the transition region. However, a computationally simpler algorithm can be realized by merging the trivial signal generation and sample correction.

A further advantage of this choice is that since the trivial signal is generated by us, we are able to run the trivial counter even over $P_{\max}$ without forcing it to jump and apply the correction using that value. Indeed, substituting $p_n - 2$ into (6) leads to (4). Therefore, there is no need to check whether the sample to be corrected is before or after the discontinuity and the two cases can be handled in the same way. When the transition region is detected, the corrected output sample is computed, and then the trivial signal jumps, while the relative position of the sample compared to the transition is irrelevant. This is shown in Fig. 5.

The next source code shows how the algorithm can be programmed to generate a sawtooth signal ranging from -1 to 1.

```
p = p + 2*T;
if p > 1 - T
   y = correct(p);
   p = p - 2;
else
   y = p;
```

The function $\text{correct}(p)$ is responsible for correcting the sample in the transition region. For the usual ± 1 sawtooth waveform we simply use (4):

$$\text{correct}(p) = p - \frac{p}{T} + \frac{1}{T} - 1. \tag{7}$$

region	A, $P_{\max}$, $P_{\min}$ (general case)	$A=1$, $P_{\max}=1$, $P_{\min}=-1$
linear region	p	p
correct(p)	$p+\frac{P_{\min}-P_{\max}}{2AT}p+\frac{P_{\min}-P_{\max}}{2}+\frac{(P_{\min}-P_{\max})^2}{4AT}$	$p-\frac{p}{T}+\frac{1}{T}-1$

Table 1. Correction functions for the EPTR sawtooth algorithm.

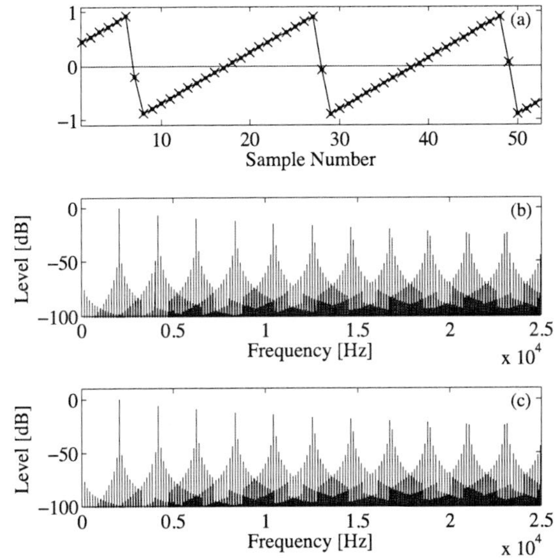

Figure 6. The DPW (crosses) and EPTR (dots) sawtooth waveforms (a), and the spectrum of the signal generated with the DPW (b) and EPTR (c) algorithms.

For the general case, see Table 1.

Note that the result would be the same if the trivial signal first jumped, then (6) was applied for correction. The resulting waveform is equivalent to the signal generated by the DPW and PTR algorithms as seen in Fig. 6. (The starting phase of the counter p was offset by a half sample for the EPTR algorithm so that the two curves match perfectly).

4.3 Triangle

4.3.1 Derivation of the asymmetric triangle wave generation

First let us consider computing the maximum peak of the triangle signal. Due to symmetry, the minimum peak can be calculated similarly. Around the maximum peak the trivial signal ascends to the value $P_{\max}$ with gradient A, then it descends with gradient B. When the trivial signal has a value of $p[n] = p_n$ before the peak, after its value is $p_{n+1} = P_{\max} + 2BT - (P_{\max} - p_n + 2AT) \cdot B/A$. The waveshapers are $(x^2 - P_{\max}^2)/A$ for the ascending and $(x^2 - P_{\max}^2)/B$ for the descending regions, as discussed in Section 2. Similarly to generating the sawtooth signal, the two adjacent values of the continuous signal are used which are at half sample distance from the output sample.

When the sample to be corrected is before the maximum peak ($p_n > P_{\max} - AT$), the two adjacent values used are $p_{n-0.5} = p_n - AT$ and $p_{n+0.5} = P_{\max} + BT - (P_{\max} - p_n) \cdot B/A$. The differentiation and scaling gives

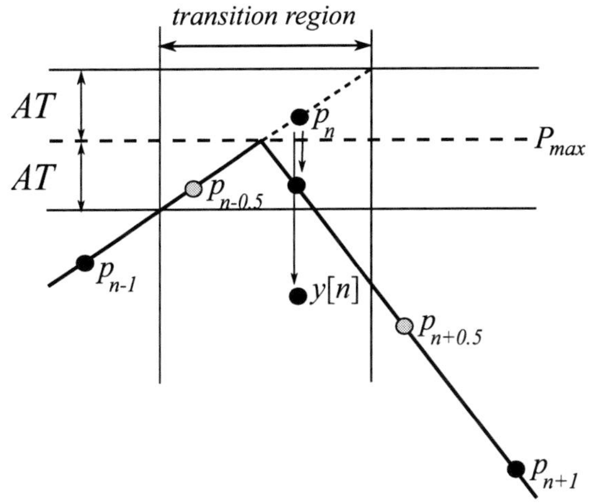

Figure 7. EPTR algorithm of the triangle signal. When the counter (dark dots) goes over $P_{\max} - AT$, the sample is in the transition region. The sample gets corrected by using the values of the half-sample delayed signal (ligth dots), then the counter jumps to the descending region. The method is the same for the correction around the minimum peak.

$$y[n] = \frac{(p_{n+0.5}^2 - P_{\max}^2)/B - (p_{n-0.5}^2 - P_{\max}^2)/A}{4T} = a_2 p_n^2 + a_1 p_n + a_0 \quad (8)$$

which is included as the correctMax function in Table 2. Similarly, when the sample is after the peak ($p_n > P_{\max} + BT$), the used value to the right is $p_{n+0.5} = p_n + BT$ and point to the left is still before the peak, so its value is $p_{n-0.5} = P_{\max} + AT - (P_{\max} - p_n + 2BT) \cdot A/B$. However, if we apply the same trick as in Sec. 4.2.2, that is, we are merging the trivial signal generation and sample correction, we are able to run the trivial counter p above $P_{\max}$ (see Fig. 7), and one function (8) can handle both cases.

The derivation is similar for the minimum peak. After determining the adjacent values, the differentiation and scaling gives

$$y[n] = \frac{(p_{n+0.5}^2 - P_{\min}^2)/A - (p_{n-0.5}^2 - P_{\min}^2)/B}{4T} = b_2 p_n^2 + b_1 p_n + b_0 \quad (9)$$

which is included as the correctMin function in Table 2.

It is possible that a high gradient section fits between two samples. The condition for this case is that $|A| \leq 1/T = f_s/f_0$. This is not equivalent to the sawtooth signal in which the gradient is infinite, thus this case should be

Linear region	p
correctMax(p)	$a_2p^2 + a_1p + a_0$
correctMin(p)	$b_2p^2 + b_1p + b_0$

Coefficient	General	Special
a_2	$\frac{B-A}{4A^2T}$	$\frac{-1}{4(A-1)T}$
a_1	$\frac{AT(A+B)+P_{\max}(A-B)}{2A^2T}$	$\frac{2AT-4T+2}{4(A-1)T}$
a_0	$\frac{(B-A)(AT-P_{\max})^2}{4A^2T}$	$\frac{-(AT-1)^2}{4T(A-1)}$
b_2	$\frac{A-B}{4B^2T}$	$\frac{-1}{4(B+1)T}$
b_1	$\frac{BT(B+A)+P_{\min}(B-A)}{2B^2T}$	$\frac{2BT+4T-2}{4(B+1)T}$
b_0	$\frac{(A-B)(BT-P_{\min})^2}{4B^2T}$	$\frac{-(BT+1)^2}{4T(B+1)}$

Table 2. The polynomial correcting functions for the EPTR asymmetric traingle algorithm. In the special case $B = -A/(A-1)$, $P_{\max} = 1$, $P_{\min} = -1$.

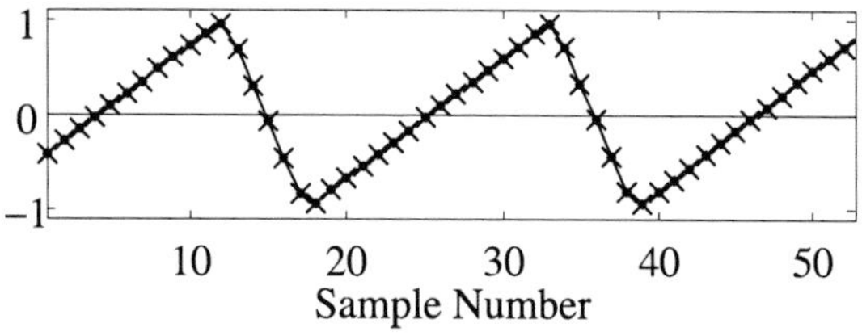

Figure 8. The PTR (crosses) and the EPTR (dots) asymmetric triangle waveforms. The starting phase of the counter p was offset by a half sample for the EPTR algorithm so that the two waves match perfectly.

handled separately. When the trivial signal has a value of $p[n] = p_n$ before the maximum peak, after it the value is $p[n+1] = p_n + P_{\min}(1 - A/B) - P_{\max}(1 - A/B)$. Since both of the adjacent samples are on linear sections with the same gradient, the calculation can be performed similarly to the sawtooth waveform.

4.3.2 *The EPTR asymmetric triangle wave algorithm*

Figure 7 explains the algorithm for generating an asymmetric triangle signal. Similarly to the sawtooth signal, the trivial waveform generation and the corrections are merged, thus checking whether the trivial generator is in the transition region is sufficient. The next code segment shows the implementation of the algorithm for a triangle waveform ranging from -1 to 1, with variable symmetry.

```
if dir == 1    // counting up?
  p = p + 2*A*T;
  if p > 1 - A*T
  //transition region?
    y = correctMax(p);
    p = 1 + (p - 1)*B/A;
    dir = -1;
  else  //linear region
    y = p;
else   // counting down
  p = p + 2*B*T;
  if p < -1 - B*T
  //transition region?
    y = correctMin(p);
    p = -1 + (p + 1)*A/B;
    dir = 1;
  else  //linear region
    y = p;
```

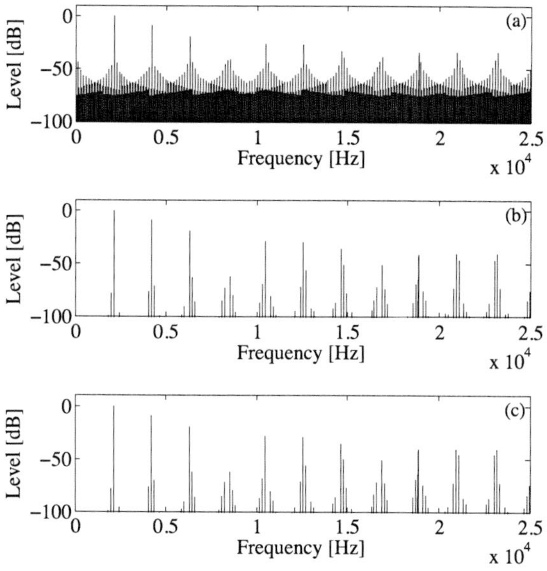

Figure 9. The spectrum of (a) the trivial, (b) the DPW and (c) the EPTR asymmetric triangle signal with 25% symmetry.

The correcting functions can be found in Table 2. First the counting direction must be determined, then the value of p is checked. When p is in the transition region, the corrected output sample is computed, the trivial counter is updated, and finally the counting direction is changed. If it is not in the transition region, the output simply equals the trivial counter $y = p_n$. The generated signal is equivalent to the DPW and PTR versions (see Fig. 8 and 9).

The previous code assumed that the values of $|A|$ and $|B|$ are not higher than f_s/f_0, so there is no region that fits between two samples. Although it is also possible to implement triangle waveforms with high gradient as discussed at the end of Sec. 4.3.1, it would result in a significantly more complicated algorithm. The allowed highest gradient case is close enough to the sawtooth waveform, therefore implementing the extra operations is not rewarding. Figure 10 shows the spectrum of a sawtooth with an infinitely sharp transition (a) and with a transition that lasts one sampling instant (b). The only drawback of limiting the gradient is a slight attenuation at high frequencies, on the other hand, the aliasing is reduced, since now we are correcting two samples around the transition. So the asymmetric triangle with a one sample-time transition can be safely used instead of the sawtooth signal. However, if there is still a need for the special case, the algorithm can be developed according to Sec. 4.3.1.

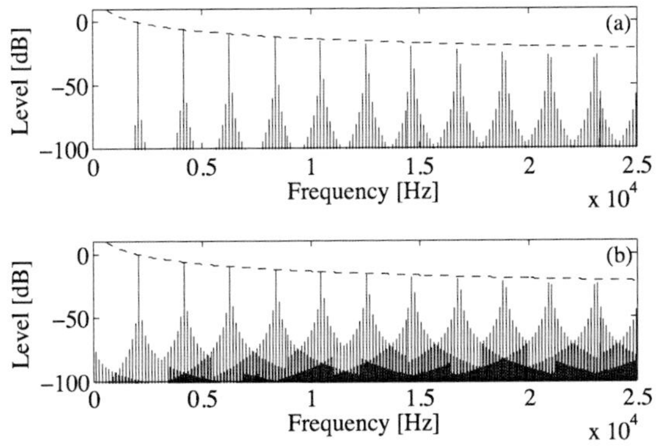

Figure 10. Spectrum of (a) the triangle signal with the highest allowed asymmetry and (b) the sawtooth signal. The dashed line is the envelope of the ideal spectrum.

Sawtooth	Add	Mul	Branch	Total
DPW	2	2	0	4
PTR	2	T	1	$3+T$
EPTR	$1+T$	T	1	$2+2T$
Triangle	**Add**	**Mul**	**Branch**	**Total**
DPW	3	3	0	6
PTR	$2+2T$	$6T$	2	$4+8T$
EPTR	$1+2T$	$6T$	2	$3+8T$

Table 3. Computational load of DPW, PTR and EPTR for sawtooth and triangle signals ($T = f_0/f_s$).

5. COMPARISON

The advantage of the EPTR method over PTR is the reduced computational load. For providing a fair comparison we merged the trivial signal generation and the correction also for the PTR algorithm, although [11] and the adherent source codes [13] were handling them separately, leading to even higher load for the PTR algorithm. Table 3 compares the two algorithms in operations per sample while generating sawtooth and asymmetric triangle waveforms.

The PTR algorithm uses an addition operation to increment the trivial counter. Then with a branch operation it decides whether the current sample is in the linear or the transition region. Finally, in the linear region an addition for the offset is applied and in the transition region a multiplication and an addition is necessary. When producing a sawtooth waveform with the EPTR algorithm, using the shifted trivial signal eliminates the addition operation in the linear region. Similarly, only the addition operation of the trivial counter is needed in the linear region during the asymmetric triangle signal generation. Note that this advantage of the EPTR algorithm vanishes for generating square waves.

The resulting waveforms generated with the two algorithms have are practically identical, as we have seen in Sec. 4.

6. CONCLUSIONS

This paper has proposed a new version of the PTR algorithm. The Efficient Polynomial Transition Regions Algorithm requires around 30% lower number of operations compared to the PTR algorithm, while results in exactly the same waveform as that of the DPW and PTR algorithms. Thus, it is the most efficient alias-reduced algorithm up to date, making it an ideal choice for systems with low computational power requirements. In addition, the paper has extended the DPW algorithm for generating triangle waves with variable symmetry, and its EPTR implementation was also presented, allowing continuous transition between symmetric triangle and sawtooth signals. Future research includes the extension of the algorithm to higher orders, and to arbitrary waveforms composed of line segments (e.g., trapezoidal waves).

Acknowledgments

The work of Balázs Bank has been supported by the Bolyai Scholarship of the Hungarian Academy of Sciences.

The authors are thankful to Prof. Vesa Välimäki for his valuable comments.

7. REFERENCES

[1] J. Pekonen and V. Välimäki, "The brief history of virtual analog synthesis," in *Proc. 6th Forum Acusticum.* Aalborg, Denmark: European Acoustics Association, June 2011, pp. 461–466.

[2] V. Välimäki and A. Huovilainen, "Antialiasing oscillators in subtractive synthesis," *IEEE Signal Processing Magazine*, vol. 24, no. 2, pp. 116–125, March 2007.

[3] H.-M. Lehtonen, J. Pekonen, and V. Välimäki, "Audibility of aliasing distortion in sawtooth signals and its implications for oscillator algorithm design," *Journal of the Acoustical Society of America*, vol. 132, no. 4, pp. 2721–2733, October 2012.

[4] T. Stilson and J. Smith, "Alias-free digital synthesis of classic analog waveforms," in *in Proc. International Computer Music Conference*, Hong Kong, August 1996, pp. 332–335.

[5] S. Tassart, "Band-limited impulse train generation using sampled infinite impulse responses of analog filters," *IEEE Transactions on Audio, Speech, and Language Processing*, vol. 21, no. 3, pp. 488–497, March 2013.

[6] E. Brandt, "Hard sync without aliasing," in *Proc. International Computer Music Conference*, Havana, Cuba, September 2001, pp. 365–368.

[7] V. Välimäki, J. Pekonen, and J. Nam, "Perceptually informed synthesis of bandlimited classical waveforms using integrated polynomial interpolation," *Journal of the Acoustical Society of America*, vol. 131, no. 1, pp. 974–986, January 2012.

[8] J. Lane, D. Hoory, E. Martinez, and P. Wang, "Modeling analog synthesis with DSPs," *Computer Music Journal*, vol. 21, no. 4, pp. 23–41, Winter 1997.

[9] V. Välimäki, "Discrete-time synthesis of the sawtooth waveform with reduced aliasing," *IEEE Signal Processing Letters*, vol. 12, no. 3, pp. 214–217, March 2005.

[10] V. Välimäki, J. Nam, J. O. Smith, and J. S. Abel, "Alias-suppressed oscillators based on differentiated polynomial waveforms," *IEEE Transactions on Audio, Speech, and Language Processing*, vol. 18, no. 4, pp. 786–798, May 2010.

[11] J. Kleimola and V. Välimäki, "Reducing aliasing from synthetic audio signals using polynomial transition regions," *IEEE Signal Processing Letters*, vol. 19, no. 2, pp. 67–70, February 2012.

[12] "Moog Slim Phatty user's manual," *Moog Music, Inc.*, 2010, URL: http://www.moogmusic.com/sites/default/files/slim_phatty_users_manual.pdf.

[13] J. Kleimola and V. Välimäki, "Polynomial Transition Regions [Online]," November 2011, URL: http://www.acoustics.hut.fi/go/spl-ptr.

Towards a discrete electronic transmission line as a musical harmonic oscillator

Kurijn Buys
Strange New Instruments
kurijn@gmail.com

Roman Auvray
LAM - D'Alembert
UPMC Univ Paris 06, UMR CNRS 7190,
Paris, France
auvray@lam.jussieu.fr

ABSTRACT

In analogy with strings and acoustic pipes as musical harmonic oscillators, a novice electronic oscillator is considered. The equivalent circuit of a discrete representation of strings and pipes, which takes the form of a discrete transmission line, is constructed with real electronic components. The proposed model includes the "equivalent series resistances", which seems to be the only relevant default for both capacitors and inductors for this application. In an analytical approach, the complex wave number is derived, allowing the study of both the wave's dispersion and attenuation in function of frequency and resulting in recommended and critical component values. Next, components are selected for a first eight-node prototype, which is numerically evaluated and then practically constructed and measured. The results prove a good match between theory and practice, with five distinguishable modes in the entrance impedance. A new prototype design is planned, which is expected to have much improved quality factors.

1. INTRODUCTION

The analogue dynamic theories between acoustics and electronics, allow an "equivalent electronic circuit" representation of linear oscillating mechanisms. A well-known example is the simple spring-mass system that can be represented by an equivalent capacitor-inductor or "LC" oscillator. While this concept is usually applied to facilitate calculations it also can serve as a source of inspiration to design new musical electronic circuits. The discrete ideal string or acoustic pipe representation consists of concatenated spring-mass systems. This leads to the idea to construct an equivalent circuit of this so called "discrete transmission line" model, with real components that could operate as a string or pipe. Such a circuit allows electronic charges to propagate and reflect at open or shorted endings as boundary conditions, which results in an electronic harmonic oscillator.

While the proposed electronic resonator is a first order approach of both a string and pipe, it is just the difference between these acoustic examples that illustrates the great variety in timbre and musical expression. Therefore, the proposed electronic sound propagative medium is expected to offer new potentials in this regard. The more detailed model of the electronic resonator such as electric losses and nonlinearities and the musician's access to control the instrument, will bring along its proper (unheard) character. Also, the electric medium allows its own transform possibilities (we can think of interaction with magnets, adding external circuits, easily switching between boundary conditions, designing a broad variety of mouthpiece models,...).

Historically, it is custom to use equivalent electrical circuits to study sound transmission through ducts under low frequency assumptions. For instance, every acoustic publication usually presents the Helmholtz resonator along with its equivalent electrical circuit [1]. A panel of "duct accidents", such as constrictions or tone holes, can also be described using equivalent electrical circuits if the different elements are assumed to interact by simple in- and outputs only. This is the lumped description that is opposed to an integral approach.

Passive [2, 3], as well as active [4], studies of musical instruments also benefited from their equivalent electrical description. Following the classical description of sound production as a coupling between an exciter, eventually non-linear, and a resonator [5,6], attempts have been made to model sound production with electrical circuits only [7]. Despite the theoretical studies that have been performed, no experimental, and academical, work seems, to the authors' knowledge, to be done on this issue, which could be explained by the only recently available low resistive capacitors.

As for the design objectives, as usual for musical instruments, a very resonant and harmonic system is desired. This allows for large dynamics and a long sustained sound with a wide timber variety. The low inharmonicity objective is also motivated by the fact that for self-sustained operation (like winds), the pitch of second register notes, mainly determined by the second harmonic, will be in better accordance with the first register note.

While several plucked and self-sustained excitation mechanisms can be imagined, this part of the complete electronic instrument is not treated in this article.

2. THEORETICAL STUDY

2.1 Deducing an appropriate model

Considering existing harmonic resonators such as strings and pipes, we can apply a discretization on a ideal model to become a finite element approximated representation consisting of N concatenated equal valued springs and masses leading to N normal modes. This can be interpreted as a two-terminal circuit which has both a Thévenin and Norton equivalent circuit form [8]. In the case of a string, the former translates force and velocity respectively as the voltage and current, while the springs and masses respectively relate to capacitors and inductors. The Norton equivalent has opposite relations but is further not concerned in our study. Using real components for this discrete transmission line, their own non-ideal characteristics will come into play, so that an adapted model is needed that takes in these relevant artefacts.

A first thing to note is that the discretization at the boundaries, using a first order approach, causes the inductor at a shorted boundary to be of half the inductance of the "in-line" inductors, and similarly, a half-valued capacitor is used at an open boundary. We will concentrate the study on a situation with an open entrance and shorted end boundary conditions, but similar results apply for all other situations as the electrical open and shorted conditions preserve the electrical charge and thus are acceptable approximations of the Dirichlet and Neumann conditions, respectively. While in mechanics and acoustics a considerable energy loss is typical at the boundaries, partly to make the instrument audible, in this electrical case, a high impedance connection can be used to pick up the signal and amplify the sound.

In order to analytically and numerically study the model, we look for an equivalent circuit that includes relevant component artefacts.

Most of the real capacitor defaults are not of importance for our application. The systems linearity allows a study and use at low voltages, under the maximum operation or "breakdown" voltage, and avoiding ripple currents. The inherent inductance and parallel conductance are negligible at audio frequencies [9]. It is only the "Equivalent Series Resistance" (ESR) that is of relevance. This factor is usually specified at 100 kHz and, according to datasheet observations, increases about 5 to 100 times at 100 Hz, which depends on the capacitor type.

The real inductor's magnetic saturation, parasitic capacitance and core hysteresis can be neglected for the same reasons. Besides inductance, it is also only the ESR (or "DCR" in datasheets), that plays a role in our application [10].

For the same type of capacitor (materials, voltage rating,...) and inductor (wire type, core material and dimension,...), the ESR, R_C and R_L, are related to their capacitance and inductance [9,10], respectively, by:

$$\begin{cases} R_C = ESR = \gamma_C / C \\ R_L = DCR = \gamma_L \sqrt{L} \end{cases} . \quad (1)$$

For different inductors, the remaining resistive factor γ_L stays around the order of 1 $\Omega/\sqrt{H}$, while the resistive capacitor factor γ_C takes the unit of seconds and varies in the orders of $[10^{-7} - 10^{-3}]$ s depending on the capacitor type and design.

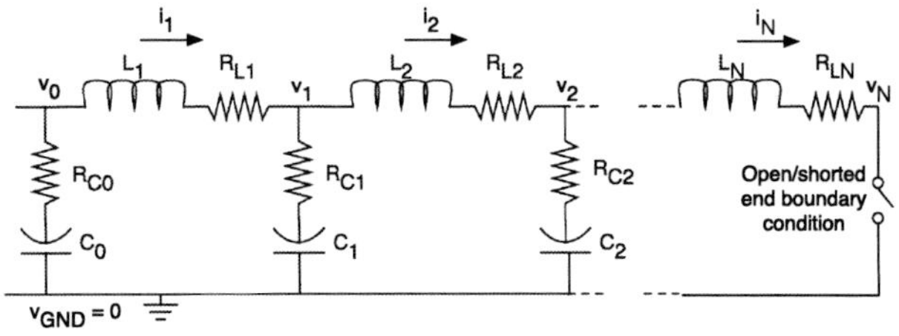

Figure 1. Outline of the discrete transmission line with the appropriate component models

Everything together, the appropriate model is presented in figure 1. It should be noted that all inductances L_i are equal except for $L_N = L_{i \neq N}/2$. The same applies for resistor R_{Li}, capacitor C_i and resistor R_{Ci} while $R_{LN} = R_{i \neq N}/\sqrt{2}$, $C_1 = C_{i \neq N}/2$, and $R_N = 2R_{i \neq N}$. This model is close to the classical electrical transmission line model based on the Telegrapher's equations [11]. However, here the capacitor's ESR is of importance, rather than its parallel conductance G.

2.2 Analytical approach

We develop a mathematical approach to study the proposed transmission line that partly corresponds to the typical transmission line derivation [11,12].
First we describe the wave propagation in an infinite "discrete" transmission line. Referring to figure 1 and applying elementary circuit analysis to each node we obtain a set of basic circuit equations that after a Fourier transform directly are expressed in the frequency domain as follows

$$\begin{cases} V_{n+1}(\omega) = V_n(\omega) - Z_s(\omega)\, I_{n+1}(\omega) \\ I_{n+1}(\omega) = I_n(\omega) - Y_p(\omega)\, V_n(\omega) \end{cases} , \quad (2)$$

with V_i and I_i the voltage and current in the corresponding nodes, and

$$\begin{cases} Z_s(\omega) = R_L + j\omega L & \text{series impedance} \\ Y_p(\omega) = \frac{1(\omega)}{R_C + \frac{1}{j\omega C}} & \text{shunt (parallel) admittance} \end{cases} . \quad (3)$$

To solve equations (2), we first can cast this array of coupled inhomogeneous equations in the form of a set of coupled, homogeneous algebraic equations that evidence a simple set of solutions, which may be written in the form:

$$\begin{cases} V_{n+1}(\omega) = V_n e^{-\Gamma(\omega)} \\ I_{n+1}(\omega) = I_n e^{-\Gamma(\omega)} \end{cases} , \quad (4)$$

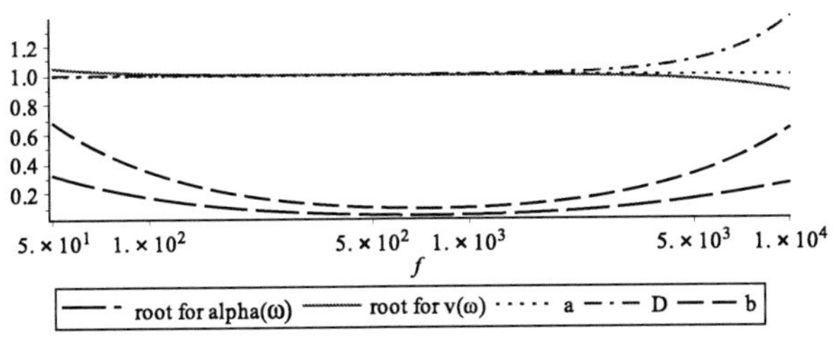

Figure 2. Frequency evolution of the losses contribution roots and its coefficients, for the typical component values: $\frac{\gamma_L}{\sqrt{L}} = 213\ s^{-1}$, $\frac{1}{\gamma_C} = 10^5\ s^{-1}$.

where Γ is the complex wave number. If these "constant phase solutions" are to be valid solutions, the nodal phase constant $\Gamma(\omega)$ must satisfy the equation:

$$Z_s(\omega)Y_p(\omega) = e^{-\Gamma(\omega)} + e^{\Gamma(\omega)} - 2. \quad (5)$$

This results in the dispersion relationship for a discrete, uniform transmission line:

$$\Gamma(\omega) = 2\ \text{arcsinh}\left(\frac{\sqrt{Z_s(\omega)\,Y_p(\omega)}}{2}\right). \quad (6)$$

For a lossless case, we can write $Z_s(\omega)\,Y_p(\omega) = -\omega^2 LC$. $\Gamma(\omega)$ is purely imaginary so that no evanescent waves appear and the nodal phase velocity $v_\varphi(\omega) = \frac{\omega}{Im(\Gamma(\omega))}$ remains constant at low frequencies. v_φ only decreases by 5% at $\omega = \omega_{0ll} = \frac{1}{\sqrt{LC}}$, the resonant frequency of a single lossless LC oscillator, which explains that a finer discretization reduces this "numerical dispersion".

Considering the losses, the wave number is complex and also comprises evanescent waves, described by a nodal attenuation coefficient $\alpha(\omega) = Re(\Gamma(\omega))$. Using eqs. (6) and (3), we obtain:

$$\begin{cases} v_\varphi(\omega) = \dfrac{\omega}{\text{arcsinh}\left(\omega\sqrt{LC}\sqrt{\frac{a+\sqrt{a^2+b^2}}{2D}}\right)} \\ \alpha(\omega) = \text{arcsinh}\left(\omega\sqrt{LC}\sqrt{\frac{-a+\sqrt{a^2+b^2}}{2D}}\right) \end{cases}, \quad (7)$$

where (using the "equal type" formulations (1))

$$\begin{cases} a = 1 - R_L R_C \frac{C}{L} = 1 - \frac{\gamma_L \gamma_C}{\sqrt{L}} \\ b = \frac{R_L}{\omega L} + \omega R_C C = \frac{\gamma_L}{\omega\sqrt{L}} + \omega\gamma_C \\ D = (\omega R_C C)^2 + 1 = (\omega\gamma_C)^2 + 1 \end{cases}. \quad (8)$$

Considering a constant nodal velocity and maintaining the same type of components, it is clear that L/C should be chosen as high as possible to reduce the influence of losses. The order of γ_L is about $1\ \sqrt{\Omega/s}$, γ_C lies between $[10^{-7} - 10^{-3}]\ s$ and L will have an order of $[10^{-6} - 10^{-2}]\ H$, so that a number of frequency values can be derived that will indicate critical lossy zones.
The frequency evolution of the roots and their coefficients is presented in figure 2. While a remains constant over frequency and near to 1, the coefficients b and D vary over frequency.

For $\omega < \frac{\gamma_L}{\sqrt{L}} = [3 - 300]\ s^{-1}$, b increases rapidly so that both the roots for v_φ and α increase.

When ω approaches $\frac{1}{\gamma_C} = [10^3 - 10^7]\ s^{-1}$, b also increases , but D raises by ω^2.
In the case of v_φ, the nominator increment is slower than D, so that the root reduces, and thus the phase velocity increases (counteracting on the numerical dispersion).
For $\alpha(\omega)$, the nominator first increases faster than D, increasing the root to a maximum close to $\omega = 1/\gamma_C$, where D will prevail and decrease the root again. However, the ω factor in the expression of α increases the attenuation factor with frequency.

When we now consider a finite number of N nodes with an open entrance and a shorted end condition, standing waves will appear. The near to ideal boundary conditions guarantee a simple reflection coefficient that only holds the medium losses, contained in the complex wave number: $R(\omega) = -e^{-2\Gamma N}$. Also in analogy with an acoustic cylinder (neglecting radiation) [13], the nondimensional entrance impedance can be derived as follows:

$$Z_e/Z_c = \frac{1 + R(\omega)}{1 - R(\omega)} = \tanh(\Gamma N), \quad (9)$$

with $Z_c = \sqrt{Z_s/Y_p}$, the characteristic impedance for a transmission line, which is close to the real constant $\sqrt{L/C}$ for $\frac{R_L}{L} \ll \omega \ll \frac{1}{R_C C}$, where losses are small [14].

The entrance impedance Z_e is characterized by a number of modes who's coefficients can be related to the wave number components (see Eq. (7)). The (anti-)resonant frequencies $\omega_n = 2\pi n v_\varphi/2N$ and $\omega_n = 2\pi(2n-1)v_\varphi/4N$ illustrate the direct relation of the inharmonicity to the change in phase velocity $v_\varphi \omega_{0ll}$ (which is constant when perfectly harmonic). These frequencies indicate the extrema of the impedance modulus, that depend on the attenuation coefficient α:

$$a_{(M,m)n} \approx \tanh(\alpha(\omega_n)N)^{\mp 1} \approx (\alpha(\omega_n)N)^{\mp 1}, \quad (10)$$

where the negative exponent applies to the maxima M and the positive one to the minima m.
The modal quality factor is proportional to the maxima but increases with the frequency, and is independent of N for low frequencies:

$$Q_n \approx a_{(M)n}\omega_n \frac{N}{2v_\varphi(\omega)}, \quad (11)$$

For equal components, apart from the $\alpha(\omega)$'s root deviation, the number of nodes does not affect both amplitude and quality factors of the harmonic series.

It is interesting to study the case where a fundamental frequency is maintained while increasing the number of nodes by choosing the same inductors and smaller capacitors of the same type. When doubling the number of nodes for example, we choose $C/4$ for the new capacitors, the coefficients in Eq. (8) remain equal so that the only change in numerical dispersion decreases the inharmonicity. As the attenuation coefficient is halved, both the a_n and Q_n remain equal. This means that a fine discretization can be applied with only the advantage of enhanced harmonicity.

To resume, apart from a preferable high L/C factor; concerning the inductor, $\frac{\gamma_L}{\sqrt{L}}$ should be chosen low enough under the fundamental frequency of the resonator, especially for (first register) self-sustained oscillation where the first resonant peak should be relatively high. As for the capacitor, $\frac{1}{\gamma_C}$ should be chosen as high as possible to promote a soft spectral decay of the impedance peaks.

To obtain sounds, an exciter will be needed. A simple initial voltage condition is sufficient to model a simple pluck-type excitation. However, for self-sustained control (which would be preferable if the resonator is very lossy), a convenient exciter model would need components that supply a voltage to current ratio in the same order as the characteristic impedance, just as for acoustic self-sustained mechanisms [5]. For now, we disregard the exciter part and concentrate on the independent validation of the electronic resonator.

3. STUDY OF A FIRST PROTOTYPE

In this section we will discuss the conception and measurement of a concrete transmission line. The aim is to compare the theory to a first practical prototype to allow more specific designs later on. We arbitrary choose an eight node line with ω_{0ll} around $2\pi 1200$ to become a fundamental frequency of about 230 Hz.

3.1 Selecting appropriate components

3.1.1 Inductors

The ESR of inductors depends on to the wire length and thickness [14]. Therefore, the variation on γ_L for a same cable thickness depends on the core design and permeability to the extent of space for windings. A classical inductor may have γ_L as low as 1.5. Special core materials, such as those used in "common mode chokes", can lower this value down to 0.5, but the core becomes easily magnetically saturated so that a linear use allows a very limited coil current. We could neglect this amplitude related aspect, which even might evoke a desirable saturation effect on the sound when experimenting with higher amplitudes later on. However, These coils have close windings so that the increased inherent capacitance can slightly decrease the coil reactance at high frequencies. For these reasons we opt for a standard coil type for our first prototype.
We choose a 22 μH Bourns $2305 - RC$ inductor with $R_L = 7\ m\Omega$ and $\gamma_L = 1.5$.

3.1.2 Capacitors

Many industrial applications have promoted the design of low ESR capacitors, but none of them are specifically designed for the audio domain, which explains the poor concerning information in datasheets. We consider three suitable types [15]:

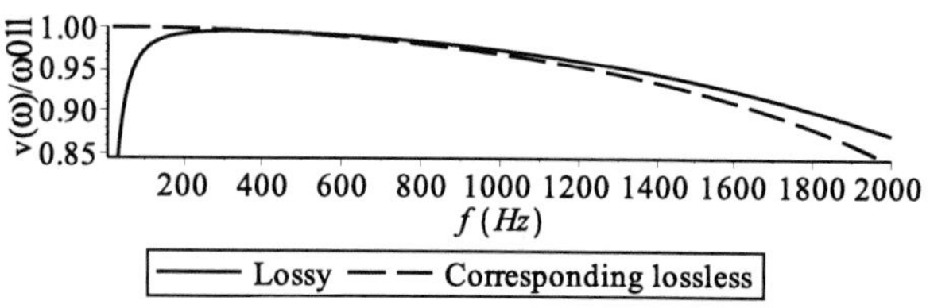

Figure 3. Evolution of the phase velocity relative to ω_{0ll} for the lossy and the corresponding lossless case.

- Polymers (dry electrolyte), with typical capacities of $[10{-}3000]\mu F$ and $\gamma_C = [10^{-6}{-}10^{-4}]\ s$ at $100\ Hz$.

- Ceramics, where the "MLCC" ceramic chips have the lowest ESR, about 1/3 of Polymers. However, it seems that ESR rapidly increases towards the audio domain and little information is available. Their capacities range between $[1\ pF - 100\ \mu F]$ but for the very low ESR $NP0$ type C is maximum $0.1\ \mu F$. It should be noted that these components are susceptible to contact noises due to their piezo-electric side-effect.

- Film capacitors, especially the Polypropylene type have very low ESR. But as the ceramics, no audio frequency information is provided. The capacity ranges between $[10\ pF - 1\ mF]$.

To obtain meaningful conclusions between theory and practice, we prefer a fully quantified Polymer capacitor. We choose a Nichicon $E5$ series 820 μF, 6.3 V capacitor with $R_C = 18\ m\Omega$ at 100 Hz (descending to 5 $m\Omega$ at 100 kHz) and $\gamma_C = 1.5 \times 10^{-5}$.

3.1.3 Conclusion

The resulting lossless single LC frequency is $\omega_{0ll} = 2\pi\ 1185$. While these components are far from the most optimal choice, the results will allow a clear comparison to the theory. The characteristic impedance is relatively low: $\sqrt{L/C} = 0.16\ \Omega$. $\frac{\gamma_L}{\sqrt{L}} = 2\pi\ 51$ is below the fundamental frequency of about 230 Hz and $\frac{1}{\gamma_C} = 2\pi\ 10^4$ lies far above ω_{0ll}.
Using equations (7), the frequency evolution of the phase velocity and attenuation coefficient is calculated for this case.
Figure 3 represents the evolution of the phase velocity relative to the constant lossless velocity, so that a constant value of 1 would indicate an absence of inharmonicity. A corresponding lossless case is added to illustrate the effect of the numerical dispersion. As predicted, below $\omega = \frac{\gamma_L}{\sqrt{L}}$ the velocity drops and at high frequencies, the dispersion due to losses counteracts on the numerical dispersion.
Figure 4 shows $\alpha(\omega)$ represented by the real part of Γ. The globally increasing progression is explained by the ω factor in its expression.

The resulting entrance impedance, as calculated by equation (11) is shown in figure 8, together with the numerical and measured curves.

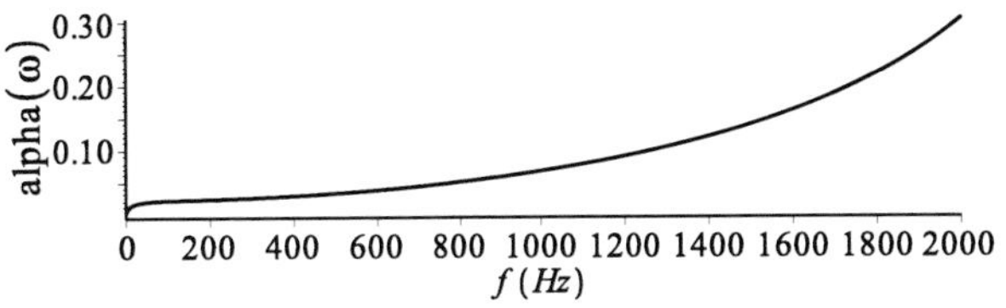

Figure 4. Evolution of the attenuation coefficient $\alpha(\omega)$ over frequency.

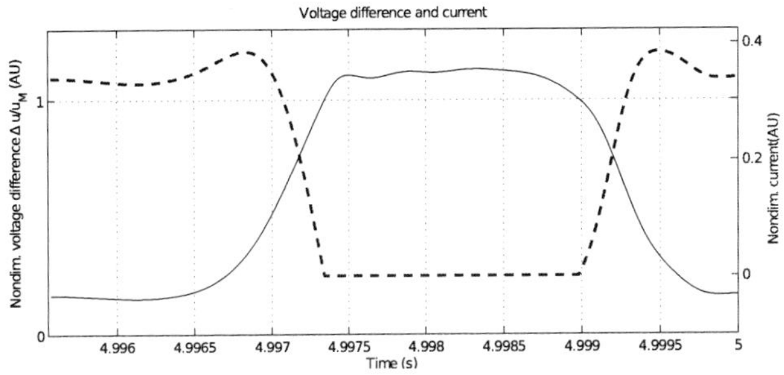

Figure 5. Temporal input voltage and current signals during a self-sustained operation with a nondimensional input voltage or "mouthpiece pressure" of 0.65.

3.2 Numerical simulation

Before the final construction, we used Matlab and Simulink to perform a numerical simulation on the proposed model with the chosen components. This allows to observe the eventual influence of aspects neglected in the analytical study, such as the approximated discretization at the borders, the inductor's inherent capacitance C_L and the capacitor's parallel conductance G. The entrance impedance curves are presented in figure 8.

We also added a single reed exciter model [16–18] and we empirically confirmed a self-sustained operation. The resulting input current and voltage signals are shown in figure 5 and the spectrum of the latter is represented in figure 6.

The nondimensional oscillation threshold is found to be minimum 0.6, which is above the usual clarinet thresholds [13], what can be explained by the relatively low modal amplitudes and quality factors and the prominent inharmonicity of our resonator. However, the spectrum, waveform and sound are similar to a simulated clarinet in the "beating reed" regime [16]. The fundamental frequency is found at $f_0 = 225.2\,Hz$, which is slightly below $230.7\,Hz$, the frequency of the first resonant peak. This may be clarified by the numerical dispersion that turns down the frequency of the higher resonant peaks.

3.3 Concrete realization and measurement

An actual realization of the proposed transmission line is constructed and is depicted in figure 7. Two equally valued capacitors are put in series to obtain the needed half-valued capacitance at the open entrance boundary. By measuring the voltages surrounding an additional appropriate resistance put in series with the transmission line entrance and

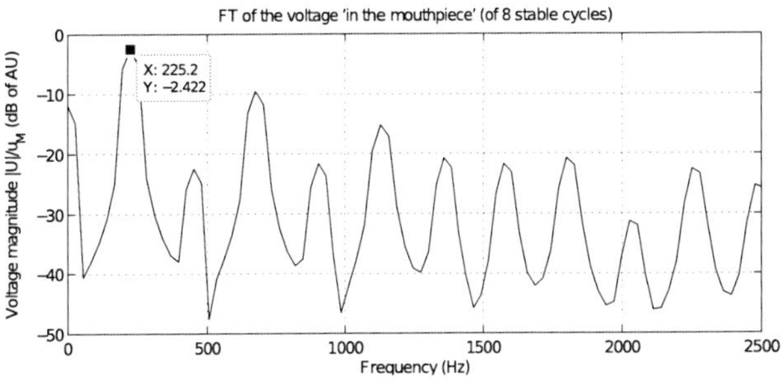

Figure 6. Spectrum of the input voltage signal with a nondimensional input voltage of 0.65.

Figure 7. First prototype of the discrete harmonic transmission line.

applying a voltage sweep, both the input voltage and current can be measured, so that the entrance impedance can be derived. The result is added to figure 8 and discussed in the next paragraph.

3.4 Theoretical and measured Z_e comparison

Figure 8 shows the spectral modulus and argument of the analytical, numerical and measured entrance impedances of the first discrete transmission line prototype with a shorted end condition. An open end condition is also verified and results in similar characteristics, but for even harmonics.

The analytical approach results in an entrance impedance with four clearly visible modes. The fundamental frequency is found at $f_0 = 230.7\,Hz$. The plotted lossless harmonics confirms the earlier shown inharmonicity curve: the second impedance peak is still very close to $3 \times f_0$, and later peaks diverge more and more downwards.

The first four nondimensional amplitude peaks are foud at $a_0 = 5.3, a_1 = 3.1, a_2 = 1.8, a_3 = 1.3$. And the corresponding modal quality factors are $Q_0 = 5$, $Q_1 = 7.2$, $Q_2 = 7.0$, $Q_3 = 6.6$. The quality factor is inversely related to the damping ratio $\zeta = \frac{1}{2Q}$, which should be smaller than 1 to obtain an underdamped system. While that condition is satisfied, this order of damping ratios only allows very short free oscillations, so that a self-sustained use is advised to obtain sounds. To compare with musical acoustic examples, the quality factor of clarinets lies between $10 - 50$ and wooden soundboards have their Q between $10 - 150$, while those of strings vary between $100 - 10^4$ [19].

Comparing the numerical with the analytic curves, we see that a very good match is obtained. This is found to be independent of the additional properties, C_L and G, of the concerned components.

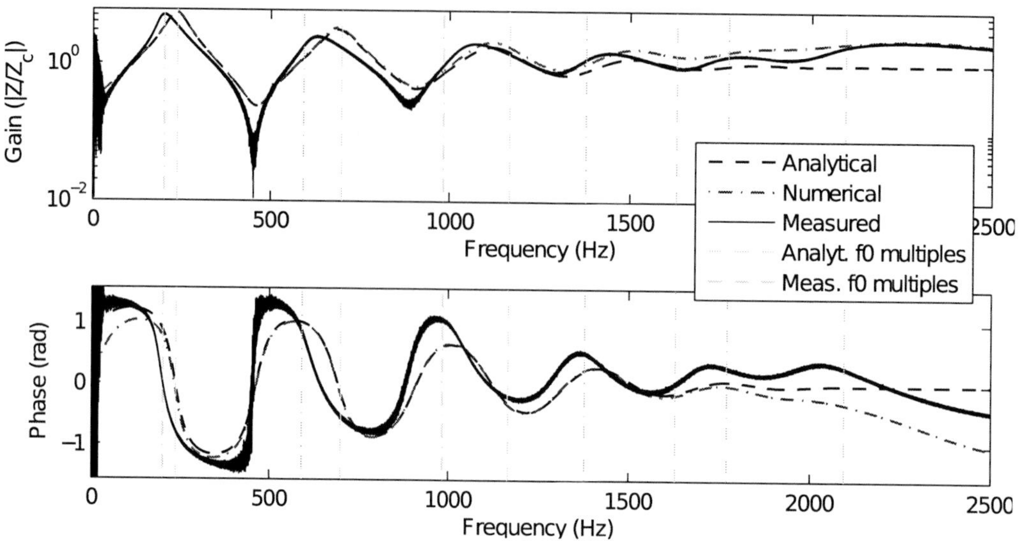

Figure 8. Input impedances of analytical, simulated and measured transmission lines.

Also the measured impedance is close to both predictions. At first sight, we observe an upwards inharmonicity. However, it is likely an actual higher R_L value that brings down the f_0 to $196.7\ Hz$. The amplitudes at the resonant frequencies and the quality factors closely correspond, while the anti-resonant peaks at low frequencies seem to descend more. Also, unlike the analytical and numerical approach a fifth harmonic is visible.

4. CONCLUSION AND PERSPECTIVES

The conception of a new electronic harmonic resonator with musical potentials is proved to be realizable. The measured entrance impedance of such a discrete transmission line with eight nodes is found to be very similar to the analytical and numerical approaches that use the corresponding datasheet values. This means that apart from capacitance and inductance, only the equivalent series resistance of both capacitors and inductors is to be considered for the design.

The lack of relevant ESR information in the audio frequency domain made us choose components with rather low characteristic impedance. However, more experimental models can be constructed that will likely feature much higher relative amplitudes and quality factors. Such an optimized model is already under construction, using eight $20\ mH$ inductors and $1\ \mu F$ film capacitors to obtain about the same fundamental frequency, a more convenient characteristic impedance of $Z_c = 140\ \Omega$ and roughly estimated quality factors of around 300! However, as it concerns "common mode" inductors, the current ratings are very low, especially for an additional direct current flux, so that a wind instrument design might be out of the question.

To cope with the numerical dispersion, we could add an adapted circuit at one of the boundaries that will introduce an opposite dispersion. However, as theoretically shown, increasing the node density, an equal relative losses and less dispersive model can be obtained by choosing the same inductors and smaller capacitors of the same type. This also is of interest when considering the perspective to play higher notes by moving the end boundary condition to a reduced number of nodes, just as releasing a key on a wind instrument...

Another perspective is the addition of electric circuits acting as convenient nonlinear exciters. These can be based on models of (single, double, free, lip or "flute") reeds, a bowing exciter [5, 19] or any other nonlinear relation that will result in a self-sustained oscillation. It would be desirable to use circuits with the same simplicity as the transmission line. However, equivalent circuits are not guaranteed for any nonlinear system. We think about FET's that might provide a single-reed mechanism equivalent, and also valves are considered, as they are reputed for their pleasing effect on sound.

5. REFERENCES

[1] A. D. Pierce, *Acoustics, an Introduction to its Physical Principles and Applications*. McGraw-Hill, 1981.

[2] J. W. Coltman, "Resonance and Sounding Frequencies of the Flute," *J. Acoust. Soc. Amer.*, vol. 40, pp. 99–107, 1966.

[3] D. H. Lyons, "Resonance frequencies of the recorder (English flute)," *J. Acoust. Soc. Amer.*, vol. 70, no. 5, pp. 1239–1247, 1981.

[4] A. W. Nolle, "Flue organ pipes: Adjustments affecting steady waveform," *J. Acoust. Soc. Amer.*, vol. 73, pp. 1821–1832, 1983.

[5] M. E. McIntyre, R. T. Schumacher, and J. Woodhouse, "On the oscillations of musical instruments," *J. Acoust. Soc. Amer.*, vol. 74, no. 5, pp. 1325–1345, 1983.

[6] B. Fabre and A. Hirschberg, "Physical Modeling of Flue Instruments: A Review of Lumped Models," *Acust. Acta Acust.*, vol. 86, pp. 599 – 610, 2000.

[7] J. W. Coltman, "Jet drive mechanisms in edge tones and organ pipes," *J. Acoust. Soc. Amer.*, vol. 60, pp. 725–733, 1976.

[8] D. Johnson, "Scanning Our Past - Origins of the Equivalent Circuit Concept: The Voltage-Source Equivalent," 2003.

[9] F. Mazda, *Discrete Electronics Components*. Cambridge University Press, 1981.

[10] A. Williams and F. Taylor, *Electronic filter design handbook*, ser. McGraw-Hill Handbooks. McGraw-Hill, 2006.

[11] R. V. Jones, "Transmission line theory," *Harvard University*, 2002.

[12] K. Nalty, "Transmission Lines, Stacked Insulated Washers Lines, Tesla Coils and the Telegrapher's Equation," 2008.

[13] J.-P. Dalmont, J. Gilbert, J. Kergomard, and S. Ollivier, "An analytical prediction of the oscillation and extinction thresholds of a clarinet," *Journal of the Acoustical Society of America*, vol. 118, no. 5, pp. 3294–3305, Nov. 2005.

[14] F. Ulaby, *Fundamentals of Applied Electromagnetics*. Pearson Educación, 2007.

[15] J. Wright, "Low ESR Capacitors," *Electro Sonic - E-Magazine*, 2004.

[16] K. Buys and C. Vergez, "A hybrid reed instrument: an acoustical resonator with a numerically simulated mouthpiece," *Acoustics 2012*, 2013.

[17] T. A. Wilson and G. S. Beavers, "Operating modes of the clarinet," *J. Acoust. Soc. Amer.*, vol. 56, pp. 653–658, 1974.

[18] A. Hirschberg, "Aero-acoustics of wind instruments," in *Mechanics of Musical Instruments*, J. K. A. Hirschberg and G. Weinreich, Eds. Wien: Springer, 1995.

[19] A. Chaigne and J. Kergomard, *Acoustique des instruments de musique*. Belin, 2008.

Solving interactions between nonlinear resonators

Joël Bensoam, David Roze
IRCAM - CNRS UMR 9912, Instrumental Acoustics team, 1 place Igor Stravinsky, F-75004 Paris
joel.bensoam@ircam.fr david.roze@ircam.fr

ABSTRACT

In the context of musical acoustics, physical models of musical instruments have to be more and more sophisticated. For string models, realism is obtained by taking into account tension, flexion, shear, rotation and coupling phenomena but also nonlinear effects due to large displacements. The sound synthesis modal method is extended to the nonlinear case using Volterra series. The inverse problem of interaction between two acoustical objects is solved by finding the roots of a polynomial at each time step.

1. INTRODUCTION

Modalys, a sound synthesis software developed at Ircam for research and musical applications, makes it possible to build virtual instruments based on physical models in order to obtain the broadest range of expressive variations in the instrument in response to intuitive controls. An instrument, as a complex structure, is described by the mechanical/acoustical interactions of its components (strings, tubes, soundboard, 3D FEM objects...). Propagation equations of each substructure are projected on the basis of its modes of vibration, which allows to obtain an infinite dimensional system of differential equations (time dependent). Limiting development in the first predominant modes (in practice, tens or hundreds modes), the system of equations becomes finite and provides a mathematical representation of the behaviour of a substructure irrespective of its nature: mechanical or acoustic. As a result, knowing the nonlinear coupling terms between each substructure, it is possible to characterise the dynamic behaviour of the overall system by assembling these elementary systems of equations. The use of this model requires therefore to have

- a solution for wave propagation (direct problem) in each substructure (depending on initial conditions and external actions),
- interaction models (which depend on the physical situation: contact, friction, reed model, lips, turbulent jet, ...) characterising the connection between substructures

Although, historically, the first stage of this sound synthesis process was done in the linear framework, the purpose of this article is to show that non-linear models can also be used in that context.

So, the linear framework for propagation is recalled in section 2 in order to be extended to the non-linear case (section 3). The mechanism of interaction will not be changed and used to produce an example in the last section.

2. SUBSTRUCTURE SOUND SYNTHESIS

2.1 Green formalism

Since each sub-structure is described by a linear model, a Green operator exists and allows to express the velocity vector field (or displacement field) as a function of applied forces. Formally [1], the wave propagation is obtained by

$$\mathbf{u}(\mathbf{x}, t) = \int \mathbb{G}(\mathbf{x}, \mathbf{y}, t) * f(\mathbf{y}, t)\, \mathrm{d}\mathbf{y} \tag{1}$$

which gives, in the numerical point of view, discrete instantaneous linear equations

$$u_i(t_i) = \tilde{u}_i(t_i)_{\to 0} + \sum_j \mathbb{G}_{ij} f_j(t_i) \tag{2}$$

The term $\tilde{u}_i(t_i)_{\to 0}$ determines the state of the system, at time t_i and at point i, in the absence of applied force at the same moment t_i. It characterises the effects of inertia and elasticity due to previous external actions. With this formulation, it is not necessary to obtain the dynamic evolution of all points $i \in [1, \ldots, N]$ of the system. When there are $m \leq N$ interactions (i.e., at most m interaction forces) the system is reduced to m linear equations of type (2). To solve the $2m$ unknowns, k types of interaction models ($k \leq m$) must be given in order to obtain well-posed problem. Finally, the system of equations (propagation & interaction)

$$\begin{cases} u_i(t_i) = \tilde{u}_i(t_i)_{\to 0} + \sum_{j=1}^{m} \mathbb{G}_{ij} f_j(t_i), & i = 1, \ldots, m \\ f_i = \mathcal{C}_{(k)}(u_i), & i = 1, \ldots, m \end{cases} \tag{3}$$

is in principle resolvable since, as pointed out by the tilde symbol, the historical term $\tilde{u}_i(n)_{\to 0}$ is computable. In the case where the interaction models $\mathcal{C}_{(k)}$ are all linear, solving this problem is trivial. If some models are nonlinear, the problem is more complex and the iterative Uzawa's algorithm for saddle point problem is used [2].

Since the interaction models, $\mathcal{C}_{(k)}$, depend on the physical problem, they are supposed to be given. The problem is to formulate the wave propagation in the form given by (2). This can be done by using, for each sub-structure, a modal decomposition, and a numerical simulation for the dynamic of each mode.

$$\mathbf{X}^{[k]}(t_{i+1}) = \frac{e^{-c_k T}}{\Omega_k} \begin{pmatrix} c_k \sin\Omega_k T + \Omega_k \cos\Omega_k T & \sin\Omega_k T \\ -\omega_k^2 \sin\Omega_k T & -c_k \sin\Omega_k T + \Omega_k \cos\Omega_k T \end{pmatrix} \mathbf{X}^{[k]}(t_i) + f^{[k]}(t_{i+1}) \begin{pmatrix} \frac{1}{\omega_k^2}[1 - \frac{e^{-c_k T}}{\Omega_k}(c_k \sin\Omega_k T + \Omega_k \cos\Omega_k T)] \\ \frac{e^{-c_k T}}{\Omega_k} \sin\Omega_k T \end{pmatrix}$$

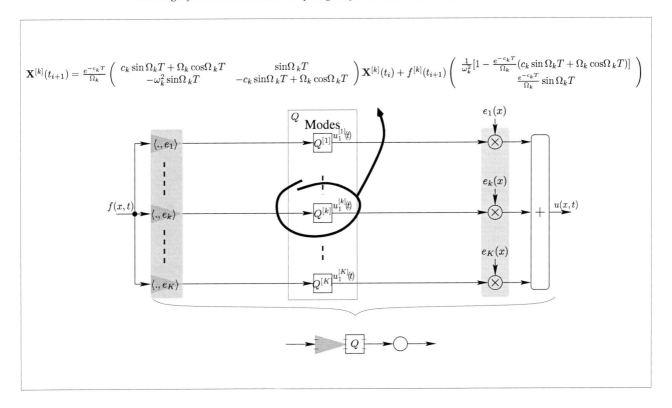

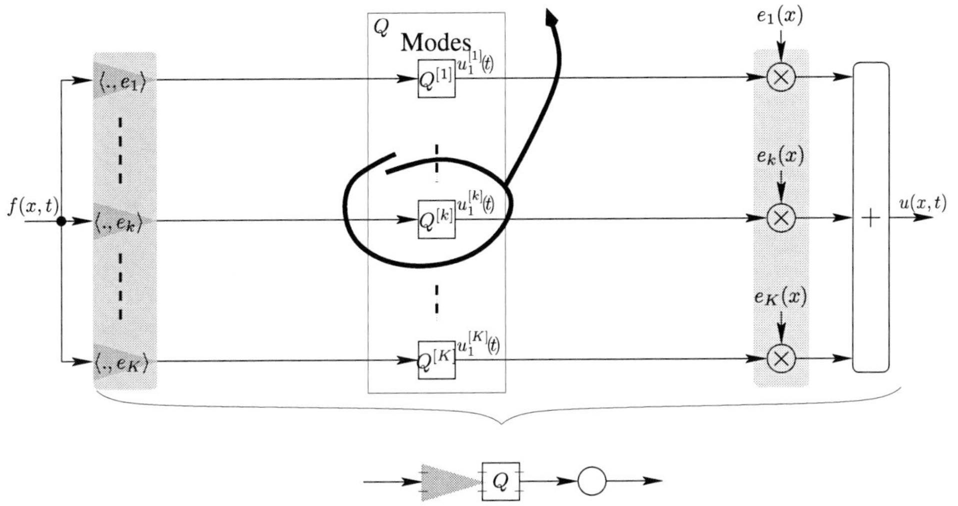

Figure 1. Linear sound synthesis: the propagation equation of each substructure are projected on its modal basis. Limiting the development in the first predominant modes (in practice, tens or hundreds modes), it allows to obtain a finite dimensional system of recursive filters and provides a numerical representation of the behaviour of a substructure irrespective of its nature: mechanical or acoustic.The set Q of filters performs the simulation for K modes. Each filter $Q^{[k]}$ computes a modal output as defined in equation (7) where $\mathbf{X}^{[k]}(t_{i+1})$ is a function of $\mathbf{X}^{[k]}(t_i)$ and input $f^{[k]}(t_{i+1})$ with $\Omega_k = \omega_k\sqrt{1 - \frac{c_k^2}{\omega_k^2}}$.

2.2 Modal synthesis

Given a modal decomposition, $u = \sum_{k=1}^{K} u^{[k]} e_k$, a second order boundary value problem

$$\frac{\partial^2 u}{\partial t^2}(x,t) + 2c(x)\frac{\partial u}{\partial t}(x,t) - \omega^2 \frac{\partial^2 u}{\partial x^2}(x,t) = f(x,t)$$

used to describe a wave propagation, can be written as a set [1] of first order differential equations

$$\begin{cases} \mathbf{X}^{[k]}(t) = \begin{bmatrix} u^{[k]} & \dot{u}^{[k]} \end{bmatrix}^T \\ \dot{\mathbf{X}}^{[k]}(t) = \mathbf{A}^{[k]}\mathbf{X}^{[k]}(t) + \mathbf{B} f^{[k]}(t) \\ \mathbf{A}^{[k]} = \begin{bmatrix} 0 & 1 \\ -\omega_k^2 & -2c_k \end{bmatrix}, \quad \mathbf{B} = \begin{bmatrix} 0 \\ 1 \end{bmatrix} \end{cases} \tag{4}$$

where the matrix $\mathbf{A}^{[k]}$ captures the modal datas (eigen pulsation ω_k, damping c_k), $f^{[k]}$ are the modal forces. This is the state space representation of the filter defined by the transfer function

$$Q^{[k]}(s) = \frac{1}{s^2 + 2c_k s + \omega_k^2}. \tag{5}$$

[1] a modal truncation is performed in order to obtain a finite dimensional set.

Using the exponential map, a solution can be formulated as

$$\mathbf{X}^{[k]}(t) = \int_0^t e^{\mathbf{A}^{[k]}(t-\tau)}\mathbf{B} f^{[k]}(\tau)\mathrm{d}\tau + e^{\mathbf{A}^{[k]}t}\mathbf{X}(0), \tag{6}$$

which gives, after a time discretization: $t_i = iT$ and a zeroth order approximation of the input force, a recursive filter formula

$$\mathbf{X}^{[k]}(t_{i+1}) = e^{\mathbf{A}^{[k]}T}\mathbf{X}^{[k]}(t_i) + \mathbf{B_0}^{[k]} f^{[k]}(t_{i+1}) \tag{7}$$

with $\mathbf{B_0}^{[k]} = -\mathbf{A}^{[k]^{-1}}\left[\mathbf{B} - e^{\mathbf{A}T}\mathbf{B}\right]$. A modal reconstruction $\sum_k \mathbf{X}^{[k]} e_k$ leads to a formalism in accordance with equation (2). Technically, the computation of the exponential gives rise to a sound synthesis process described in Fig. 1.

3. NONLINEAR WAVE PROPAGATION

Nonlinear wave propagation cannot be computed using the above mentioned tools (modal decomposition and the Green operator) as is. Then, in order to compute interactions between nonlinear resonators a system equivalent to (3) has to be found for the nonlinear case.

This section will introduce the Volterra series used to simulate the dynamics of weakly nonlinear models: a nonlinear equation is turned into an infinity of linear ones for which the simulation of the dynamics can be handled by the algorithm defined in section 2. The Volterra series can be used for all polynomial nonlinearities around an equilibrium point. This method is not also limited to scalar nonlinearities: fully coupled (transverse/longitudinal) string vibration can also be considered. A Reissner beam model with coupling between the degrees of freedom has been investigated using Volterra series in [6].

To be more pedagogical, only the Kirchhoff-Carrier string model will be used here to illustrate this method.

3.1 Kirchhoff-Carrier string model (KCM)

The equation, defined for $(x,t) \in [0,L] \times \mathbb{R}_+^\star$,

$$\frac{\partial^2 u(x,t)}{\partial t^2} + \delta \frac{\partial u(x,t)}{\partial t} - \kappa \frac{\partial^3 u(x,t)}{\partial t \partial x^2} = \left[c^2 + b \int_0^L \left(\frac{\partial u(x,t)}{\partial x}\right)^2 \mathrm{d}x\right] \frac{\partial^2 u}{\partial x^2} + f_{tot}(x,t) \quad (8)$$

describes the Kirchhoff-Carrier string model [3] [4]. Volterra kernels of this model have been computed in a previous work [5] and simulations were performed. The damping are specified by δ and κ (fluid and structural resp.). The sound speed is c and b is a coefficient of nonlinearity. Boundary conditions are homogeneous Dirichlet conditions (the string motion is null at the edges) and the string is at rest for $t \leq 0$.

3.2 Volterra series

For control engineers, a dynamical system, such as (8), is considered as a causal system with input f and output u (cf. Fig. 2). Using Volterra's series, the solution is defined

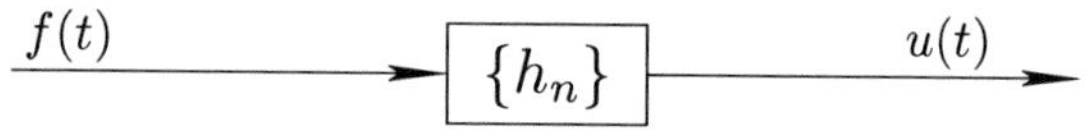

Figure 2. System with input f and output u described by a Volterra series $\{h_n\}_{n\in\mathbb{N}^\star}$.

as the infinite sum of multi-convolutions between the input and the Volterra kernels $\{h_n\}_{n\in\mathbb{N}^\star}$ of the model

$$u(t) = \sum_{n=1}^{\infty} \int_{(\mathbb{R}+)^n} h_n(\tau_{1:n}) f(t-\tau_1)\dots f(t-\tau_n) \mathrm{d}\tau_{1:n} \quad (9)$$

with for each (non)linear order n: $(\tau_{1:n}) = (\tau_1, \dots, \tau_n)$ and $\mathrm{d}\tau_{1:n} = \mathrm{d}\tau_1 \dots \mathrm{d}\tau_n$.

More precisely, Volterra's series were historically used to solve ordinary differential equations. Since equation (8) is a partial differential equation, the output of the system is a function of time and space. To respect formulation (9) Volterra kernels will be paremeterized in space and denoted $h_n^{(x)}(t_{1:n})$ in time domain ($H_n^{(x)}(s_{1:n})$ in the Laplace domain) and the input will be split as $f_{tot}(x,t) = \phi(x) f(t)$.

In practice, the simulation will not be performed using this definition of Volterra series, since multi-convolution would be too costly in computation time: First, the explicit expression of Volterra kernels which are a characteristic of the physical system, will be given. Then, a structure of numerical simulation will be made by identifying the Volterra kernels in order to compute the output (transverse displacement) as a function of the input (excitation force).

3.3 Solving the Volterra kernels

One method to find the Volterra kernels is to establish a recursive formula. This procedure is described in [5]§4.1 for the Kirchhoff-Carrier model giving the recurrence relation

$$(\widehat{s_{1:n}}^2 + \delta \widehat{s_{1:n}}) H_n^{(x)}(s_{1:n}) - (c^2 + \kappa \widehat{s_{1:n}}) \frac{\partial^2 H_n^{(x)}(s_{1:n})}{\partial x^2} = E_n^{(x)}(s_{1:n}) \quad (10)$$

where $(\widehat{s_{1:n}}) = (s_1 + \dots + s_n)$. The source $E_n^{(x)}$ is a function of lower order kernels (cf. (12)) and $E_1^{(x)} = \phi(x)$ is the spatial distribution of the input force. Modal decomposition on the modal basis, $e_k(x) = \sqrt{\frac{2}{L}} \sin(\frac{k\pi x}{L})$, is one option to solve the problem (10) by transforming the differential equations into algebraic ones. The modal projection of Volterra kernels then verifies $\forall (n,k) \in (\mathbb{N}^\star)^2$

$$H_n^{[k]}(s_{1:n}) = Q^{[k]}(\widehat{s_{1:n}}) E_n^{[k]}(s_{1:n}) \quad (11)$$

where $Q^{[k]}(s) = \left[s^2 + (\delta + \kappa \frac{k^2\pi^2}{L^2}) s + \frac{k^2\pi^2 c^2}{L^2}\right]^{-1}$ is the transfer function describing the linear part of the model. According to equation (5) each Volterra kernel is a filter where nonlinear effects are contained in the source terms $E_n^{[k]}$. For the particular case of KCM, this yields

$$\begin{cases} E_1^{[k]} = \langle \phi, e_k \rangle = \phi_k \\ E_n^{[k]}(s_{1:n}) = \gamma_k \sum_{\substack{p,q,r \geq 1 \\ p+q+r=n}} \\ \left[\sum_{\ell=1}^{K} \ell^2 H_p^{[\ell]}(s_{1:p}) H_q^{[\ell]}(s_{p+1:p+q})\right] H_r^{[k]}(s_{p+q+1:n}), \end{cases} \quad (12)$$

with $\gamma_k = -b\frac{k^2\pi^4}{L^4}$. Thus it can be seen that E_n depends only on the lower order kernels H_p, H_q, H_r since the principal sum is over $p+q+r=n$.

3.4 Structure of simulation based on Volterra kernels

The Volterra kernels are not explicitly computed. In practice, equation (11) is used in the multi-convolution (9) to identify a structure of simulation. This structure is composed of linear filters sets (each one representing a nonlinear order) connected with sums and products according to the combinatorics revealed in (12). To illustrate this, the general structure of this kind of simulation is presented in Fig. 3. To give a concrete realisation Fig. 4 represents this structure for the Kirchhoff-Carrier model limited to the third order: the output approximation has two components, $u(x,t) = u_1(x,t) + u_3(x,t)$ (since there is no quadratic nonlinearity).

The first part (well-known order 1 contribution) is $U_1^{[k]}(s) = H_1^{[k]}(s) F(s) = Q^{[k]}(s) \phi_k F(s)$ where $F(s)$ is the Laplace transform of excitation force $f(t)$. For the second part, knowing from (11) and (12) that

$$H_3^{[k]}(s_{1:3}) = Q^{[k]}(\widehat{s_{1:3}}) E_3^{[k]}(s_{1:3}) = Q^{[k]}(\widehat{s_{1:3}}) \gamma_k \sum_{\ell=1}^{K} \ell^2 H_1^{[\ell]}(s_1) H_1^{[\ell]}(s_2) H_1^{[k]}(s_3)$$

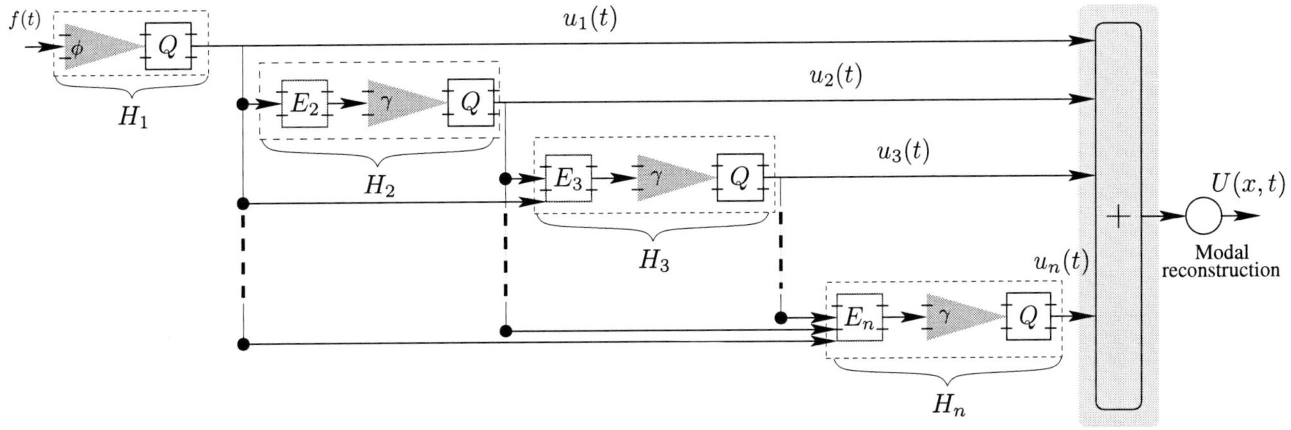

Figure 3. Recursive structure of simulation based on Volterra kernels. Each line represents the K modal projections of u_i. According to equation (11) and Fig. 1, E_i represents the combinatorics of lower order kernels on all K modes in order to compute H_i with the set of filters Q. The triangle γ contains all the nonlinear coefficients γ_k, as ϕ is the set of ϕ_k.

	N=1	N=3
N^f	$K(9+2N_x)-N_x$	$K(2\times 9+2N_x+5)-N_x$

Table 1. Number N^f of floating point operations to compute one sample of $u(x,t)$ with K modes for linear approximation ($N=1$) and third-order approximation ($N=3$) at N_x observation points.

and according to (9), u_3 is computed by

$$\begin{aligned} U_3^{[k]}(s_{1:3}) &= H_3^{[k]}(s_{1:3})F(s_1)F(s_2)F(s_3) \\ &= Q^{[k]}(\widehat{s_{1:3}})\gamma_k \sum_{\ell=1}^{K} \ell^2 H_1^{[\ell]}(s_1)H_1^{[\ell]}(s_2)H_1^{[k]}(s_3) \\ &\qquad F(s_1)F(s_2)F(s_3) \\ &= Q^{[k]}(\widehat{s_{1:3}})\gamma_k \sum_{\ell=1}^{K} \ell^2 U_1^{[\ell]}(s_1)U_1^{[\ell]}(s_2)U_1^{[k]}(s_3) \end{aligned}$$

This last relation gives the structure of simulation presented in Fig. 4 with K modes.

At this point, sound synthesis can then be performed for reasonable computation time: adding one nonlinear component to linear synthesis approximatively doubled the simulation time. Actually, the number of required floating point operations (flops) is evaluated in Table 1 using Fig. 4 and knowing that each filter $q^{[k]}$ requires 4 sums and 5 products (9 flops) for each time sample.

3.5 Green operator based on Volterra kernels

In order to perform sound synthesis and compute interactions with nonlinear resonators represented by Volterra series the algorithm presented in section 2 has to be extended. The relation (2) between force and displacement/velocity which was an affine function will become a polynomial of same order as the truncation of the Volterra series.

To see this, let be the vector $\mathbf{X}_n^{[k]}(t_i) = \begin{bmatrix} u_n^{[k]}(t_i) \\ \dot{u}_n^{[k]}(t_i) \end{bmatrix}$ the state-space representation used in section 2.2 where n is the nonlinear order and k the considerated mode. Since the final desired result is a modal reconstruction of all nonlinear contributions $\mathbf{X}_n^{[k]}$

$$\mathbf{X}(x,t_i) = \sum_{n=1}^{N}\sum_{k=1}^{K} \mathbf{X}_n^{[k]}(t_i)e_k(x), \tag{13}$$

and since according to formula (7) each nonlinear contribution (dotted rectangles in Fig. 3) can be written as

$$\mathbf{X}_n^{[k]}(t_i) = \tilde{\mathbf{X}}_n^{[k]}(t_i) + \mathbf{B}_0^{[k]} f_n^{[k]}(t_i), \tag{14}$$

it follows that the relation between force and displacement is a polynomial

$$\mathbf{X}(x,t_i) = \tilde{\mathbf{X}}(x,t_i) + \Pi\left(f(t_i)\right). \tag{15}$$

The modal excitation force $f_1^{[k]}(t_i)$ is the input of the system. For higher orders ($n \geq 2$) the source term $f_n^{[k]}(t_i)$ is a combination of variables $\mathbf{X}_p^{[k]}$ which are already known since the order $p < n$.

This yields for the Kirchhoff-Carrier model studied before (still limited to order $N=3$), the functions $f_1^{[k]}(t_i) = \phi_k f(t_i)$ that handle the modal decomposition of the spatial distribution $\phi(x)$ of the external force. For $n=3$, the terms $f_3^{[k]}(t_i) = \gamma_k \sum_{\ell=1}^{K}(\ell u_1^{[\ell]}(t_i))^2 u_1^{[k]}(t_i)$ (cf. equation (12)) capture the non linear effects due to the deformation of the string. Evaluating equation (14) for $n=1$ and $n=3$ turns equation (13) into an order 3 polynomial

$$\begin{aligned} \mathbf{X}(x,t_i) &= \tilde{\mathbf{X}}(x,t_i) + \mathbf{\Theta}_3(x)f^3(t_i) \\ &+\mathbf{\Theta}_2(x,t_i)f^2(t_i) + \mathbf{\Theta}_1(x,t_i)f(t_i) \end{aligned} \tag{16}$$

where the coefficient are described in appendix A.

Finally, in the general case (N can be higher than 3), the system propagation and interaction for a nonlinear resonator can still be represented by

$$\begin{cases} \mathbf{X}(x,t_i) = \tilde{\mathbf{X}}(x,t_i) + \Pi\left(f(t_i)\right) \\ f(t_i) = \mathcal{C}_{(k)}(\mathbf{X}(t_i)) \end{cases} \tag{17}$$

where Π is a polynomial of same order as the nonlinear truncation. This is an extension of the substructure coupling method defined in equation (3) to the nonlinear case.

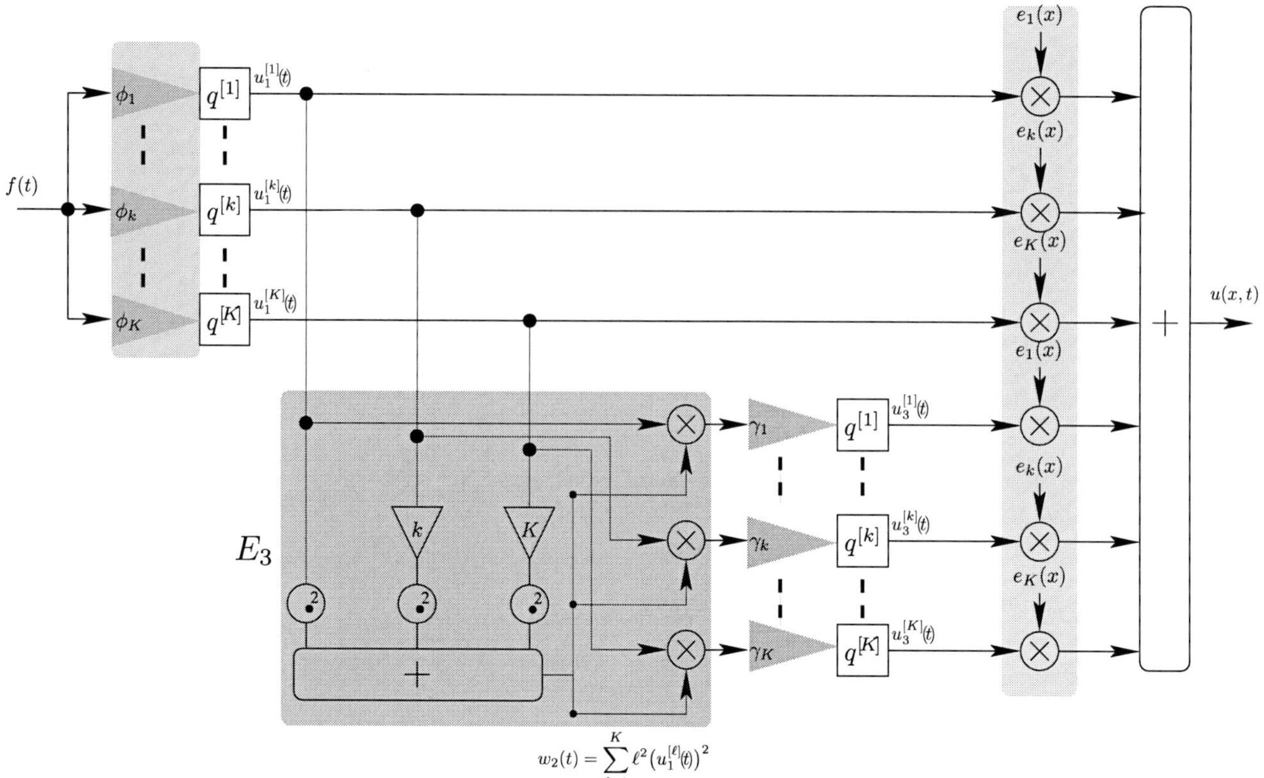

Figure 4. Structure of simulation of the Kirchhoff-Carrier model limited to the third order. Filters in the left column compute the linear response for each mode whereas the second column compute the order 3 response. Triangles are simple gains corresponding to spatial distribution of force for order 1, and nonlinear coefficient for order 3.

4. SIMULATION ON AN INTERACTION EXAMPLE: "ADHERE COUPLING"

In this section, the formalism (17) for propagation *and* interaction between nonlinear resonators is investigated with two strings glued together for a moment then released for free oscillation. In this example, the choice of the coupling C is shown in figure (9).

4.1 The "Adhere coupling"

When two substructures (here, two nonlinear strings) are glued together, the relative velocity at the interface point vanishes: the model of interaction is then represented by the vertical line in the force/velocity plane (Fig. 9).

Solving the interaction consists in finding the intersection point between this line and the polynomial of relative velocity defined by $v_r(t_i) = \dot{u}_r(t_i) = \dot{u}_a(x_a, t_i) - \dot{u}_b(x_b, t_i)$. For this type of contact where $v_r = 0$, this will gives the equation

$$\tilde{v}_r(t_i) + \Pi_a(f_a(t_i)) - \Pi_b(f_b(t_i)) = 0 \qquad (18)$$

that permits to compute the interaction force f for each time step. Note the sign reversal in the normal force $f_a = -f_b = f$ according to Newton's third law, where f_a (resp. f_b) is the interaction force applied to object A (resp. B). Those resulting forces are then used as inputs to the propagation simulation for the next time step.

	String A	String B
Length	1.8m	1.5m
Frequency	55Hz	68Hz
Interaction point	$\frac{\sqrt{2}}{2}L_A$	$\frac{\sqrt{2}}{2}L_B$
Nonlinear coefficient	$b_A = \frac{E}{2\rho L_A}$	$b_B = \frac{E}{2\rho L_B}$
Damping	$\delta = 3\text{s}^{-1}$, $\kappa = 0.01\text{m}^2\text{s}^{-1}$	
Young modulus	$E = 2.0 \times 10^{11}$Pa	
Material density	$\rho = 7800\text{kg m}^{-3}$	

Table 2. Physical parameters of the two strings used in the simulation.

4.2 Simulation

A simulation has been performed with two strings defined by Kirchhoff-Carrier model, one of them being excited by the force described in Fig. 5.

The strings physical parameters are described in Table 2. The simulation is performed with $K = 20$ modes at a sampling frequency $f_s = 44100$Hz. The interaction duration has been set to 5000 samples. Both strings are observed by a modal reconstruction at interaction points.

Simulation results are presented in Figs. 6 and 7. We can see that the first string (in blue) vibrates freely before the "Adhere interaction" is imposed, then the two strings velocities are equals, the relative error on displacement and velocity can be seen in Fig. 8: the error is lower for velocity than for displacement since, the interaction definition is based only on relative velocity.

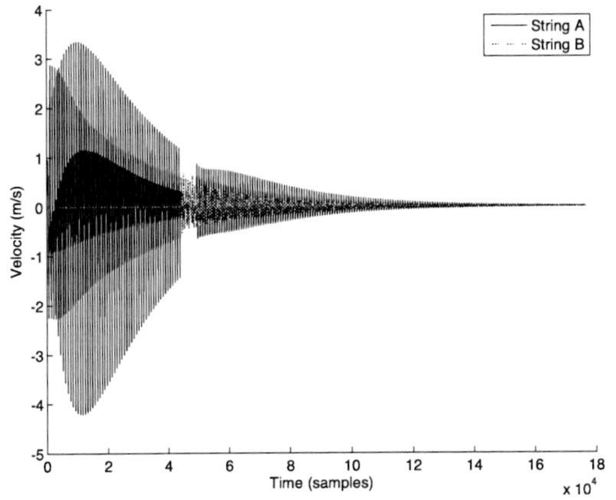

(a) Two strings in interaction: temporal velocity signals

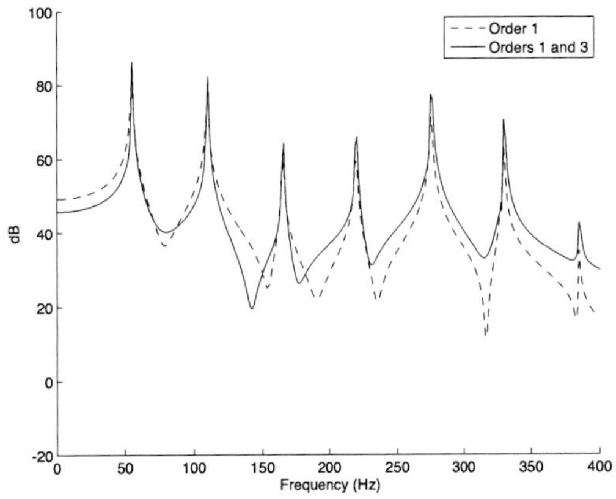

(b) String A spectrum before interaction: taking into account the nonlinearity, a spectral enhancement is obtained

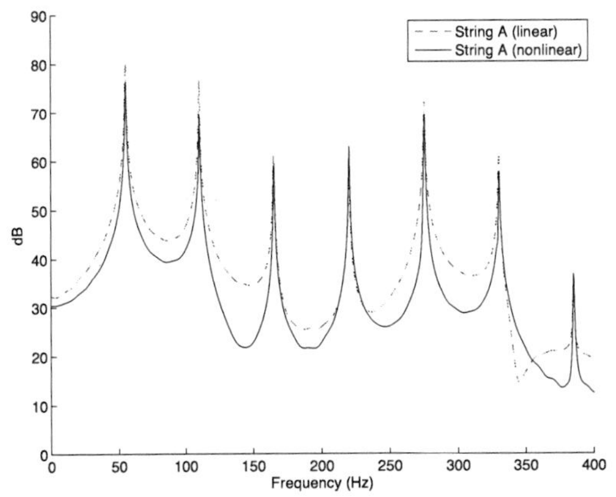

(c) String A spectrum after interaction: nonlinear effects are still present in the dynamics

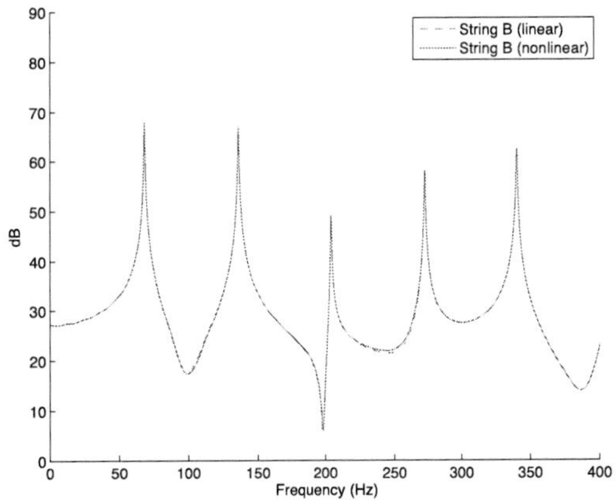

(d) String B spectrum after interaction, the contact force makes string B vibrate.

Figure 7. Interaction between two nonlinear strings: The first string A vibrates freely. An "Adhere coupling"interaction is then applied between the two strings during 5000 samples. The interaction force between the strings A and B, is computed from nonlinear dynamics of the two strings using the two first Volterra kernels. The nonlinear effects are still present in the string A after the interaction. A spectral enhancement can be observed on the spectra before and after the coupling. String B vibrates after the interaction using energy provided by the interaction force.

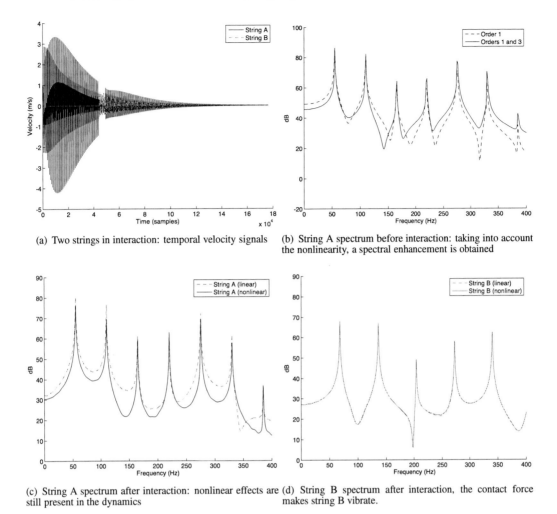

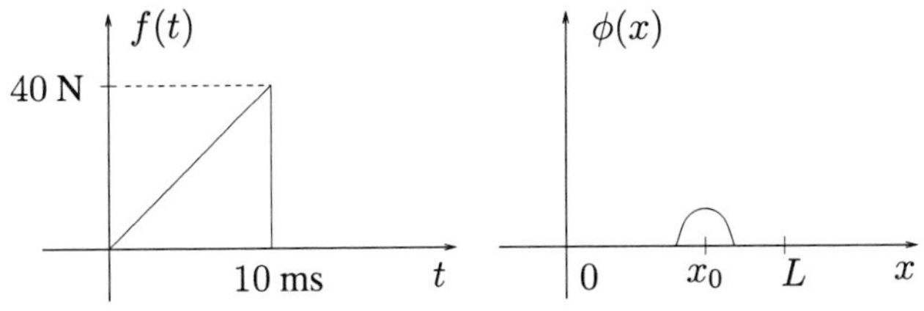

Figure 5. Functions $f(t)$ and $\phi(x)$ used to define the initial excitation force $f_{tot}(x,t) = f(t)\phi(x)$ for the simulation.

After 5000 samples the interaction is removed and the two strings vibrates freely at their own dynamics as shown in Figs. 7(c) and 7(d). This figure shows that for a sufficient excitation force, nonlinear effects appears: the linear and nonlinear part have the same magnitude for the first modes, but for higher frequencies the nonlinear part has an higher magnitude which can be heard in simulations sounds which are more brilliant when the nonlinear contribution is activated. This is noticeable for string A, but not for string B. It can be deduced that the interaction force to string B was not high enough to trigger nonlinear effects.

5. CONCLUSION

This paper introduced an extension of the Green formalism and problem inversion to the case of weakly nonlinear resonators. Using a Volterra series until order N to simulate the dynamics of a string, interactions can be computed the same way the sound synthesis software Modalys does, by solving an order N polynomial instead of a affine function.

The work presented here is based on a particular case where $f(x,t) = \phi(x)f(t)$. The polynomial roots and the convergence of the Volterra series will be studied in a future work before using a more general force $f(x,t)$. Furthermore, it will be possible to consider more realistic string or beam models with polarisation and coupling between transverse and longitudinal displacements and rotations.

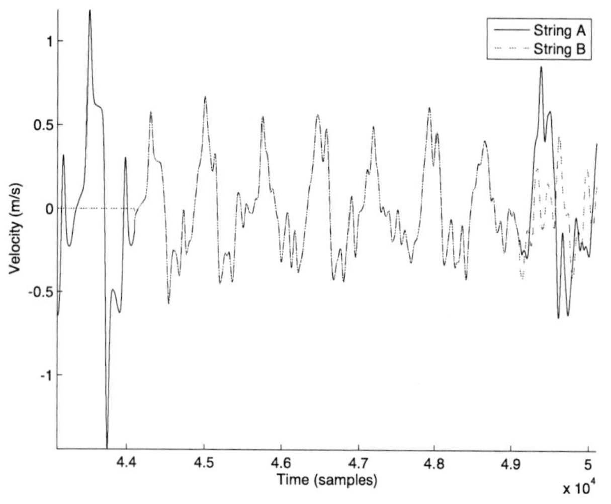

Figure 6. Zoom on the velocity of the two strings during the interaction ($44100 \leq t \leq 49100$ samples). As mentioned in section 4.1 the relative velocity ($v_r = v_A - v_B$) is null during the interaction.

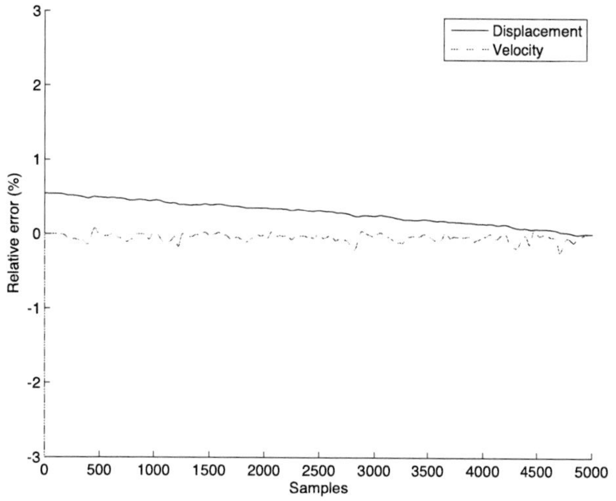

Figure 8. Relative error (for velocity and displacement) between string A and string B during the interaction.

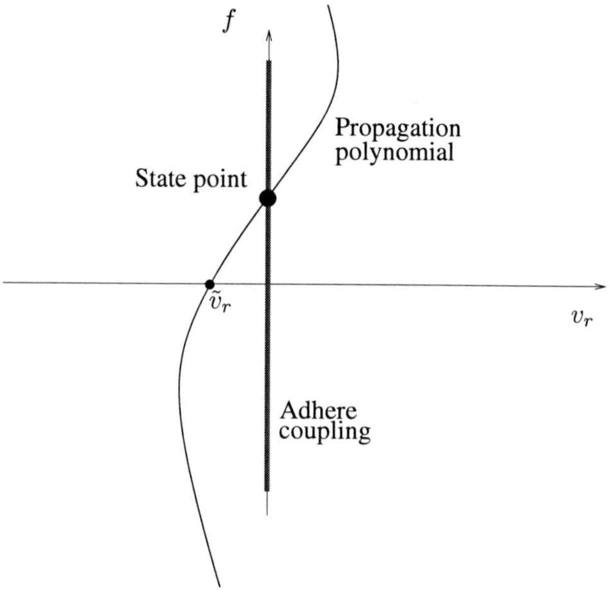

Figure 9. Interaction law (in thick red) for the "Adhere coupling" in the force/velocity plane: relative velocity vanishes when the substructure are glued. The state point is obtained by intersection of this law with the (relative) dynamics of the nonlinear resonators representing by a polynomial (in blue) whose order correspond to the Volterra series truncation order. In case of linear propagation it would be a straight line (first order polynomial).

A. COEFFICIENTS OF THE POLYNOMIAL

The coefficients of the polynomial (16) are

$$\boldsymbol{\Theta}_3^{[k]}(x) = \sum_{k=1}^{K} \gamma_k \mathbf{B}_0^{[k]} \sum_{\ell=1}^{K} (\ell \mathbf{C}\mathbf{B}_0^{[\ell]} \phi_\ell)^2 \mathbf{C}\mathbf{B}_0^{[k]} \phi_k e_k(x)$$

$$\boldsymbol{\Theta}_2^{[k]}(x, t_i) = \sum_{k=1}^{K} \gamma_k \mathbf{B}_0^{[k]} \left[\sum_{\ell=1}^{K} (\ell \mathbf{C}\mathbf{B}_0^{[\ell]} \phi_\ell)^2 \tilde{u}_1^{[k]}(t_i) \right.$$
$$\left. + \sum_{\ell=1}^{K} 2\ell^2 \tilde{u}_1^{[\ell]}(t_i) \mathbf{C}\mathbf{B}_0^{[\ell]} \phi_\ell \mathbf{C}\mathbf{B}_0^{[k]} \phi_k \right] e_k(x)$$

$$\boldsymbol{\Theta}_1^{[k]}(x, t_i) = \sum_{k=1}^{K} \left[\gamma_k \mathbf{B}_0^{[k]} \left[\sum_{\ell=1}^{K} (\ell \tilde{u}_1^{[\ell]}(t_i))^2 \mathbf{C}\mathbf{B}_0^{[k]} \phi_k \right.\right.$$
$$\left.\left. + 2\ell^2 \tilde{u}_1^{[\ell]}(t_i) \mathbf{C}\mathbf{B}_0^{[\ell]} \phi_\ell \tilde{u}_1^{[k]}(t_i) \right] + \mathbf{B}_0^{[k]} \phi_k \right] e_k(x)$$

$$\tilde{\mathbf{X}}(x, t_i) = \sum_{k=1}^{K} \left[\tilde{\mathbf{X}}_3^{[k]}(t_i) + \tilde{\mathbf{X}}_1^{[k]}(t_i) \right.$$
$$\left. + \gamma_k \mathbf{B}_0^{[k]} \sum_{\ell=1}^{K} (\ell \tilde{u}_1^{[\ell]}(t_i))^2 \tilde{u}_1^{[k]}(t_i) \right] e_k(x)$$

with $\mathbf{C} = \left[\begin{array}{cc} 1 & 0 \end{array} \right]$.

Acknowledgments

We would like to thank the CAGIMA project supported by the National French Research Agency (ANR).

B. REFERENCES

[1] J. Bensoam, "Représentation intégrale appliquée à la synthèse sonore par modélisation physique : méthode des éléments finis," Thèse de doctorat, Académie de Nantes Université du Maine, 2003.

[2] ——, "Mise en oeuvre des couplages non linéaires dans le logiciel de synthèse sonore : Modalys," in *8ème Congrès Français d'Acoustique CFA*, Tours, Avril 2006.

[3] G. Kirchhoff, *Vorlesungen über Mathematische Physik: Mechanik.* Leipzig: Teubner, 1877.

[4] G. F. Carrier, "On the non-linear vibration problem of the elastic string," *Quarterly of Applied Mathematics*, vol. 3, pp. 157–165, 1945.

[5] T. Hélie and D. Roze, "Sound synthesis of a nonlinear string using volterra series," *Journal of Sound and Vibration*, vol. 314, pp. 275–306, 2008.

[6] D. Roze, "Simulation de la propagation d'onde non linéaire par les séries de volterra," Thèse de doctorat, Université Pierre et Marie Curie - Paris VI, 2010.

AN ENERGY CONSERVING FINITE DIFFERENCE SCHEME FOR SIMULATION OF COLLISIONS

Vasileios Chatziioannou
Institute of Music Acoustics
University of Music and Performing Arts Vienna
chatziioannou@mdw.ac.at

Maarten van Walstijn
Sonic Arts Research Centre
Queen's University Belfast
m.vanwalstijn@qub.ac.uk

ABSTRACT

Nonlinear phenomena play an essential role in the sound production process of many musical instruments. A common source of these effects is object collision, the numerical simulation of which is known to give rise to stability issues. This paper presents a method to construct numerical schemes that conserve the total energy in simulations of one-mass systems involving collisions, with no conditions imposed on any of the physical or numerical parameters. This facilitates the adaptation of numerical models to experimental data, and allows a more free parameter adjustment in sound synthesis explorations. The energy preservedness of the proposed method is tested and demonstrated though several examples, including a bouncing ball and a non-linear oscillator, and implications regarding the wider applicability are discussed.

1. INTRODUCTION

Impact modelling is required in many engineering problems, for example during the simulation of colliding or bouncing objects [1]. Taking Hertz's contact law as a starting point [2] and denoting the compression along the displacement axis y with Δy, collision forces can generally be modelled using a one-sided power law

$$f(\Delta y) = \begin{cases} k_c \, \Delta y^{\alpha} & \text{if } \Delta y > 0 \\ 0 & \text{if } \Delta y \leq 0 \end{cases}, \qquad (1)$$

where the force f is active only for positive compression values, and where k_c and α are power law constants.

In the context of musical acoustics, collisions have often been studied in relation to hammer and mallet impacts. For example, experimental studies of hammer-string interaction in a piano have reported exponent values in the range of $\alpha \in [2,\ 5]$ [3], though, in principle, α may take on any value larger than 1 for impact modelling [4]. Collisions may also occur in a more spatially distributed manner, such as the string-bridge interaction in a sitar. In all cases, the impactive interaction represents an important nonlinear element in the system that is closely linked to the expressive control and characteristics of the instrument.

The musical acoustics and sound computing literature offers a variety of time-stepping methods for simulating collisions, most of which are based on finite differences (e.g. [2, 5]) or closely related methods such as the trapezoidal rule [6] or Verlet integration (e.g. [1, 7]). While many successful simulation results have been obtained, and stability can even be shown for some specific cases or under specific assumptions (see, e.g. [8]), the formulation of a more general class of provably stable algorithms for impact modelling is still considered as an open and difficult problem [1, 5]. This sets collision modelling problems somewhat apart from most other challenges naturally appearing in simulation of musical instruments. That is, the past decade has seen a significant development of energy methods in finite difference simulation of musical instruments and parts thereof, notably in [5] and further publications by the same author. As such, provably stable schemes have been derived for a wide range of systems, including nonlinearly vibrating drums [9] and shells [10]. The general approach taken herein is that difference operators are applied to the Newtonian description of the system, the stability bounds of which are established through defining an invariant representing the numerical counterpart of the Hamiltonian of the underlying system. However this way of deriving schemes has limitations in application to systems in which the force is a non-smooth function of the phase space variables, in which case the invariant can only be defined for specific model parameters [5].

The present authors propose to address this by first reformulating the system in its Hamiltonian form [11], and discretise this rather than Newton's equations of motion. Drawing from a wider research field, it can be said that Hamilton's equations can generally be discretised using two different approaches [12]. The first approach leads to numerical schemes that preserve the symplectic structure of the system and allow only canonical transformations in each integration step, while the second approach aims to preserve the Hamiltonian of the system; it has been shown that only one of these properties can generally be preserved [13]. A fundamental observation is that symplectic schemes impose a stronger constraint on the behaviour of the numerical solution while preserving a slightly perturbed Hamiltonian. Since symplecticness is more suited to the study of families of trajectories and long-term behaviour of dynamical systems, this approach has dominated much of the physics and engineering oriented research. There are however indications in the literature that energy-conserving schemes possess better stability properties than symplectic methods (see, e.g. [14]). This is particularly relevant for real-time sound synthesis applications, in which stability has to be guaranteed with minimal constraints on any of the model parameters. An energy-conserving approach is therefore adopted in this paper, focusing on a small set of simplified test problems involving a point mass colliding with a rigid barrier.

2. NUMERICAL MODELLING OF IMPACTS

The most basic model employing (1) is that of a point-mass colliding with a rigid barrier positioned at $y = 0$, where the mass approaches the barrier from below ($y < 0$). The motion of the mass is then governed by

$$m\frac{d^2y}{dt^2} + k_c\lfloor y\rfloor^\alpha = 0, \tag{2}$$

where m is the object mass and

$$\lfloor y\rfloor = \begin{cases} y & \text{if } y > 0 \\ 0 & \text{otherwise.} \end{cases} \tag{3}$$

Since we are aiming at the construction of energy preserving schemes, no dissipative components are included at this point, but as explained in Section 3, these can be added once the stability properties have been established. It has been shown in [5] that while simply applying a centered difference operator to the acceleration term in (2) leads to an unstable scheme, partially conservative behaviour can be ensured for the specific cases $\alpha = 1$ and $\alpha = 3$ with the use of an average operator. For instance if y_n denotes the value of variable y at time $n\Delta t$, with Δt being the sampling interval, then the following numerical scheme for a cubic power law

$$m\frac{y_{n+1} - 2y_n + y_{n-1}}{\Delta t^2} + k_c\lfloor y_n\rfloor^2\frac{y_{n+1} + y_{n-1}}{2} = 0 \tag{4}$$

preserves the energy-like function

$$H_n = \frac{1}{2}m\left(\frac{y_n - y_{n-1}}{\Delta t}\right)^2 + \frac{1}{4}k_c\lfloor y_n\rfloor^2\lfloor y_{n-1}\rfloor^2 \tag{5}$$

in the two main phases of the simulation ($y \leq 0$ and $y > 0$). The main downside of directly discretising the Newtonian equation of motion (2) is that nothing firm can be stated about stability of simulations with values of α other than 1 or 3, since an expression analogous to (5) is then not forthcoming [5].

2.1 Hamiltonian formulation

Aiming at a more general treatment of power-law nonlinearities, we attempt to construct an energy preserving scheme for an impact force of type (1) with arbitrary exponent $\alpha \geq 1$, starting from Hamilton's equations. The equivalent Hamiltonian formulation of (2) is

$$\frac{dy}{dt} = \frac{\partial H}{\partial p}, \tag{6a}$$

$$\frac{dp}{dt} = -\frac{\partial H}{\partial y}, \tag{6b}$$

where

$$H(y,p) = \frac{p^2}{2m} + \frac{k_c}{\alpha+1}\lfloor y\rfloor^{\alpha+1}, \tag{7}$$

is the Hamiltonian of the system and p is the momentum of the mass. Employing mid-point derivative approximations, system (6) can be discretised to yield the numerical scheme:

$$\frac{y_{n+1} - y_n}{\Delta t} = \frac{1}{2m}\frac{p_{n+1}^2 - p_n^2}{p_{n+1} - p_n}, \tag{8a}$$

$$\frac{p_{n+1} - p_n}{\Delta t} = -\frac{k_c}{\alpha+1}\frac{\lfloor y_{n+1}\rfloor^{\alpha+1} - \lfloor y_n\rfloor^{\alpha+1}}{y_{n+1} - y_n}. \tag{8b}$$

Now setting

$$\left\{\begin{array}{ll} q_n & = p_n\,\Delta t/m \\ \beta & = \Delta t^2 k_c/m \end{array}\right\}, \tag{9}$$

yields a scheme with just two parameters:

$$y_{n+1} - y_n = \frac{1}{2}(q_{n+1} + q_n), \tag{10a}$$

$$q_{n+1} - q_n = -\frac{\beta}{\alpha+1}\frac{\lfloor y_{n+1}\rfloor^{\alpha+1} - \lfloor y_n\rfloor^{\alpha+1}}{y_{n+1} - y_n}. \tag{10b}$$

Solving (10) is facilliated by defining the auxiliary variable

$$x = \frac{1}{2}(q_{n+1} + q_n), \tag{11}$$

which, from equation (10a), gives

$$\begin{aligned} q_{n+1} &= 2x - q_n, \\ y_{n+1} &= y_n + x. \end{aligned} \tag{12}$$

Substituting into equation (10b) we have:

$$\frac{\beta}{2(\alpha+1)}\left(\frac{\lfloor y_n + x\rfloor^{\alpha+1} - \lfloor y_n\rfloor^{\alpha+1}}{x}\right) + x - q_n = 0$$
$$\Rightarrow \qquad F(x) = 0. \tag{13}$$

Note that

$$\lim_{x\to 0} F(x) = \frac{\beta}{2}\lfloor y_n\rfloor^\alpha - q_n, \tag{14}$$

so there is no singularity in $F(x)$. To sum up, the Hamiltonian system is discretised in (8) and subsequently transformed in (10), whereas for the computation (13) is solved numerically to yield a physically correct root of $F(x)$ (see Section 2.1.2), which is used to update y and q using (12).

2.1.1 Conservation of Energy

The presented scheme can be shown to conserve the total system energy at each time step as follows. Rewriting (8) as

$$\frac{1}{\Delta t}(y_{n+1} - y_n)(p_{n+1} - p_n) = \frac{1}{2m}(p_{n+1}^2 - p_n^2) \tag{15a}$$

$$\frac{1}{\Delta t}(y_{n+1} - y_n)(p_{n+1} - p_n) = -\frac{k_c}{\alpha+1}(\lfloor y_{n+1}\rfloor^{\alpha+1} - \lfloor y_n\rfloor^{\alpha+1}) \tag{15b}$$

and substituting by parts yields

$$\left(\frac{p_{n+1}^2}{2m} + \frac{k_c}{\alpha+1}\lfloor y_{n+1}\rfloor^{\alpha+1}\right) = \left(\frac{p_n^2}{2m} + \frac{k_c}{\alpha+1}\lfloor y_n\rfloor^{\alpha+1}\right)$$
$$\Rightarrow H(y_{n+1}, p_{n+1}) = H(y_n, p_n). \qquad (16)$$

2.1.2 Existence and Uniqueness

The scheme relies on finding a solution to equation (13), which can be achieved numerically provided that a solution exists. From the definition of $F(x)$ it follows that

$$\frac{dF}{dx} = 1 + A\frac{(\alpha+1)\lfloor y_n + x\rfloor^{\alpha}x - \lfloor y_n + x\rfloor^{\alpha+1} + \lfloor y_n\rfloor^{\alpha+1}}{x^2}, \qquad (17)$$

with $A = \dfrac{\beta}{2(\alpha+1)}$ and $\lim_{x\to 0}\dfrac{dF}{dx} = 1 + \dfrac{\alpha\beta}{4}\lfloor y_n\rfloor^{\alpha-1}$. It can be shown that $dF/dx \geq 1$, meaning that $F(x)$ always has a single root. This is equivalent to showing that

$$G(y_n + x) \leq G(y_n) + x\,G'(y_n + x), \qquad (18)$$

where

$$G(y) = \lfloor y\rfloor^{\alpha+1}$$
$$G'(y) = dG/dy = (\alpha+1)\lfloor y\rfloor^{\alpha}. \qquad (19)$$

Given that $G(y)$ is a convex function, the inequality (18) holds $\forall\, y_n \in \mathbb{R}$, and this result is independent of the value of q_n. Hence under the condition $\alpha \geq 1$, a unique solution of (13) exists, regardless of the value of β. Since $F(x)$ is near-linear in the neighbourhood of its root, the solution can be found with excellent convergence using the Newton-Raphson method; the number of iterations required can be kept low (typically below 6) by using the previous value of x as the initial guess.

2.2 Energy preservedness under finite precision

Due to quantisation in finite-precision arithmetic, the Hamiltonian can be preserved only to machine precision in implementations on digital processors. The resulting energy error can be expressed in terms of the deviation of $H_n = H(y_n, p_n)$ from the initial energy H_0, which in normalised form reads

$$e_n = \left|\frac{H_n - H_0}{H_0}\right|. \qquad (20)$$

It is worth noting that quantisation generally results into a random-like signal e_n that is zero mean and as such will not cause an energy shift over time. Figures 1 and 2 show examples of the mass trajectory and the associated e_n obtained with the proposed scheme (8) (labeled FD_H for discretising Hamilton's equations using finite differences). For comparison, the corresponding results for $\alpha = 1$ and $\alpha = 3$ calculated with the partially stable finite difference schemes presented in [5] are also shown (labeled FD_N for discretising Newton's second law).

In order to get a more complete view of the energy preservation properties of the proposed scheme, its performance is analysed across a range of α and β values. The variations in these parameters correspond to different levels of

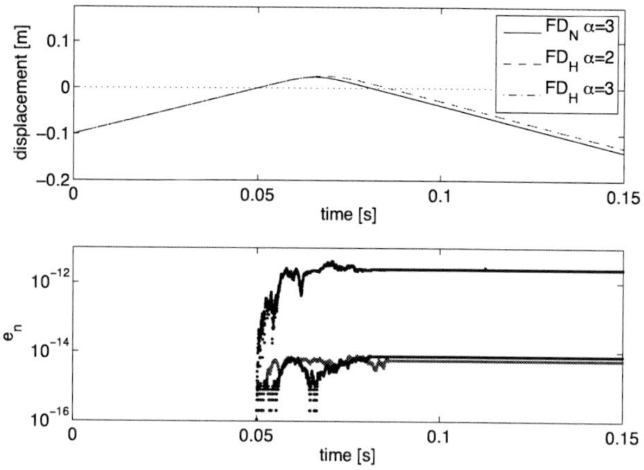

Figure 1. Simulation of a unit mass (m = 1 kg) colliding with a rigid barrier with initial position y_0 = -0.1 m and momentum p_0 = 2 kg m/s. The stiffness is chosen as $k_c = \sqrt{5000}^{\alpha+1}$. Top: mass displacement. Bottom: energy error by (20). All simulations were run at a 44.1 kHz sampling rate.

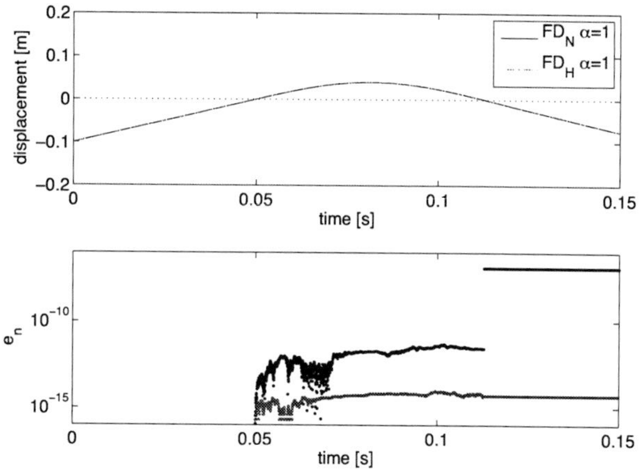

Figure 2. Simulation of a unit point-mass approaching a rigid barrier with initial position y_0 = -0.1 m and momentum p_0 = 2 kg m/s with k_c = 2.5e3 and a sampling rate of 44.1 kHz Top: mass displacement. Bottom: energy error.

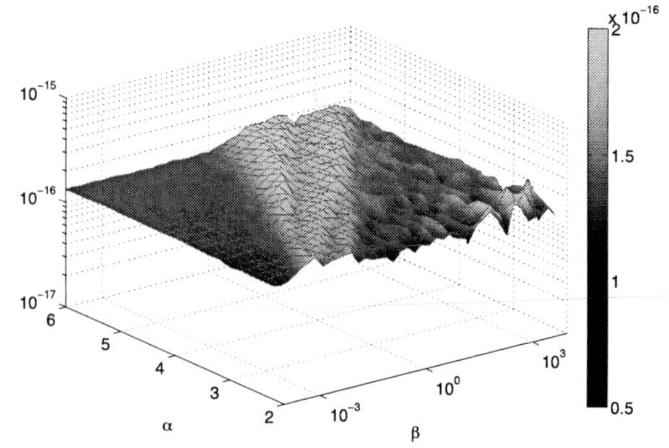

Figure 3. Simulation results of the energy preservation metric (21) as a function of α and β.

interaction between the mass and the barrier. To ensure a meaningful comparison, the calculations are made independent of the collision duration and the initial energy of the system, using the following energy preservation metric:

$$\mathcal{P} = \sum_{n=n_1}^{n_2} \frac{|H_{n+1} - H_n|}{(n_2 - n_1 + 1)H_0}, \tag{21}$$

where the collision occurs in the interval $[n_1, n_2]$. $\mathcal{P}$ can be thought of as the mean energy deviation per sample during the contact period, thus excluding periods during which energy deviations are expected to be negligible. As depicted in Figure 3 the preservedness is only mildly dependent on the model parameters, and structurally retains very low values. This result supports a strong confidence in the stability of practical implementations.

2.3 Effective repelling force

Having established the stability properties, the immediate next question to explore is how well the scheme approximates the original continuous-time model. While standard finite difference procedures may be used to show that the scheme is of second order accuracy, additional insight can be obtained by determining the extent to which Newton's second law $f = m\,\partial^2 y/\partial t^2 = \partial p/\partial t$ is adhered to. This can be done by defining the *effective repelling force* of the scheme as

$$\begin{aligned} f_{n+\frac{1}{2}} &= \frac{p_{n+1} - p_n}{\Delta t} \\ &= \frac{k_c}{\alpha+1}\left(\frac{\lfloor y_n + x \rfloor^{\alpha+1} - \lfloor y_n \rfloor^{\alpha+1}}{x}\right), \end{aligned} \tag{22}$$

where we made use of (8b) and (12). Note that $x = (q_{n+1} + q_n)/2$ can be thought of as the mid-point value $q_{n+\frac{1}{2}}$, thus representing a measure of momentum. In other words, the accuracy of equation (22) in approximating the underlying power-law depends directly on the impact momentum, and the scheme converges to (1) in the limit:

$$\lim_{x \to 0} f_{n+\frac{1}{2}} = k_c \lfloor y \rfloor^{\alpha}. \tag{23}$$

Given that $x \to 0$ when $\Delta t \to 0$, this also demonstrates that the numerical model is consistent with theory.

Figure 4 shows two examples of plotting the absolute value of effective repelling force, as directly evaluated from simulation data, against the mid-point displacement $(y_{n+1} + y_n)/2$, and comparing to the corresponding theoretical term $k_c \lfloor (y_{n+1} + y_n)/2 \rfloor^{\alpha}$. For visual clarity, the values for β and q_0 have deliberately been chosen high; the discrepancy between the effective repelling force and its theoretical counterpart is considerably smaller fow lower values. The more important notion that can be derived from these plots is that the scheme effectively smoothes the curve around $y = 0$, leading to a continuously differentiable force function, which can be shown to be of class C^{α}.

2.4 Generalisation

The conservation of energy can be shown to hold for a more general class of nonlinear one-mass oscillators, represented by a generic Hamiltonian. For an arbitrary $H(y, p)$,

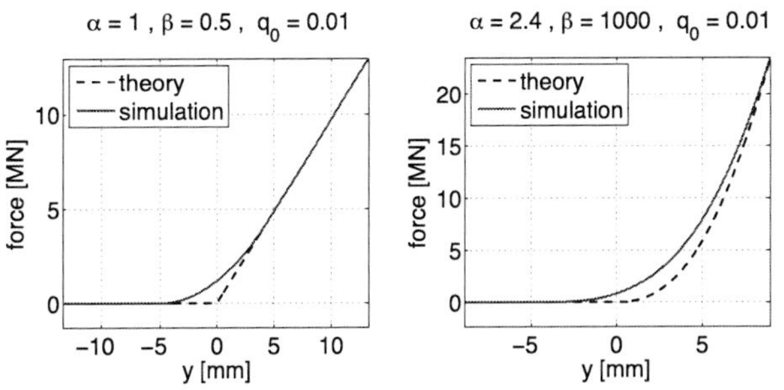

Figure 4. Examples of the effective repelling force for a power law of linear form (left) and cubic form (right). In both cases, a unit mass and a sampling rate of 44.1 kHz was used to evaluate the force curves. The model parameters used are shown above the plots.

applying the following mid-point derivative approximations

$$\frac{y_{n+1} - y_n}{\Delta t} = \frac{H(y_n, p_{n+1}) - H(y_n, p_n)}{p_{n+1} - p_n} \tag{24a}$$

$$\frac{p_{n+1} - p_n}{\Delta t} = -\frac{H(y_{n+1}, p_{n+1}) - H(y_n, p_{n+1})}{y_{n+1} - y_n}, \tag{24b}$$

yields a general numerical scheme for which, as previously, energy conservation follows from

$$\begin{aligned} &\frac{1}{\Delta t}(y_{n+1} - y_n)(p_{n+1} - p_n) = H(y_n, p_{n+1}) - H(y_n, p_n) \\ &\frac{1}{\Delta t}(y_{n+1} - y_n)(p_{n+1} - p_n) = \\ &\qquad -(H(y_{n+1}, p_{n+1}) - H(y_n, p_{n+1})), \end{aligned}$$

hence

$$H(y_{n+1}, p_{n+1}) = H(y_n, p_n). \tag{25}$$

A beneficial feature of the method is that - unlike equation (5) - the total energy at each time step n is calculated from the state space variables in exactly the same way as for the continuous system, and is evaluated using the values of a single time step. In other words, the operator H renders the energy invariant in both domains.

3. FURTHER EXAMPLES

With no specific constraints on the Hamiltonian, provably stable algorithms can be derived for a wider class of one-mass systems involving collisions. In order to demonstrate this, three further cases are discussed here, simulated using a sampling rate of 44.1 kHz. For each case, it can be shown that the nonlinear equation analogous to equation (13) always has a unique solution, but the proofs are omitted here for brevity.

3.1 Bouncing Ball

Consider a ball falling under gravity and bouncing on a floor (at $y = 0$), neglecting any frictional effects. The Hamiltonian of the system is [15]

$$H = \frac{p^2}{2m} + \frac{k_c}{\alpha+1}\lfloor -y \rfloor^{\alpha+1} + m\,g_0\,y, \tag{26}$$

where g_0 is the gravitational acceleration. The Hamiltonian formulation (6) is discretised in the same way as explained in section 2.1, yielding the nonlinear function

$$F(x) = \frac{\beta}{2(\alpha+1)} \frac{\lfloor -y_n - x \rfloor^{\alpha+1} - \lfloor -y_n \rfloor^{\alpha+1}}{x} + x - q_n + \Delta t^2\, g/2 = 0, \tag{27}$$

where for $x \to 0$ the first term is defined in a way similar to (14). Figure 5 shows the results of such a simulation with $\alpha = 4$; due to the lack of losses the ball bounces back to its initial height and the energy is conserved.

3.2 Oscillating mass with repelling force

So far, only a mass colliding with a barrier has been considered. The system begins to bear a little more resemblance to a musical instrument if the oscillating element can store potential energy in a spring of stiffness k. The repelling force is now set to become active above a specified displacement y_0. The Hamiltonian of this system is

$$H = \frac{p^2}{2m} + \frac{k}{2} y^2 + \frac{k_c}{\alpha+1} \lfloor y - y_0 \rfloor^{\alpha+1}. \tag{28}$$

The corresponding nonlinear function is now

$$F(x) = \frac{\beta}{2(\alpha+1)} \frac{\lfloor y_n - y_0 + x \rfloor^{\alpha+1} - \lfloor y_n - y_0 \rfloor^{\alpha+1}}{x} + x - q_n + \frac{\Delta t^2\, k}{4m}(x + 2y_n) = 0. \tag{29}$$

Figure 6 shows the result of an example simulation using $\alpha = 2$. As can be seen, the repetitive collisions do not cause an accumulative energy shift, and the energy is conserved to machine precision. This was observed for a large number of simulations with different parameters and long simulation times.

3.3 Non-conservative systems

In more realistic scenarios, the total energy of the system is not conserved. This can occur due to damping effects or the application of non-conservative external forces. For instance, the Newtonian equation of motion

$$m\frac{d^2y}{dt^2} + m\gamma\frac{dy}{dt} - k_c\lfloor -y \rfloor^{\alpha} + m\, g_0 = f, \tag{30}$$

describes the displacement of a bouncing ball subject to an external force f as well as to a resistive term that represents frictional losses, where γ is a damping constant. The corresponding Hamiltonian, which is now time-dependent, can be found using the so-called Caldirola–Kanai Lagrangian [16,17]:

$$H = e^{-\gamma t}\frac{p^2}{2m} + e^{\gamma t}\left(\frac{k_c}{\alpha+1}\lfloor -y \rfloor^{\alpha+1} + m\, g_0\, y\right) \tag{31}$$

and Hamilton's equations for this system, including the application of the external force, are

$$\frac{dy}{dt} = \frac{\partial H}{\partial p}, \tag{32a}$$

$$\frac{dp}{dt} = -\frac{\partial H}{\partial y} + e^{\gamma t} f, \tag{32b}$$

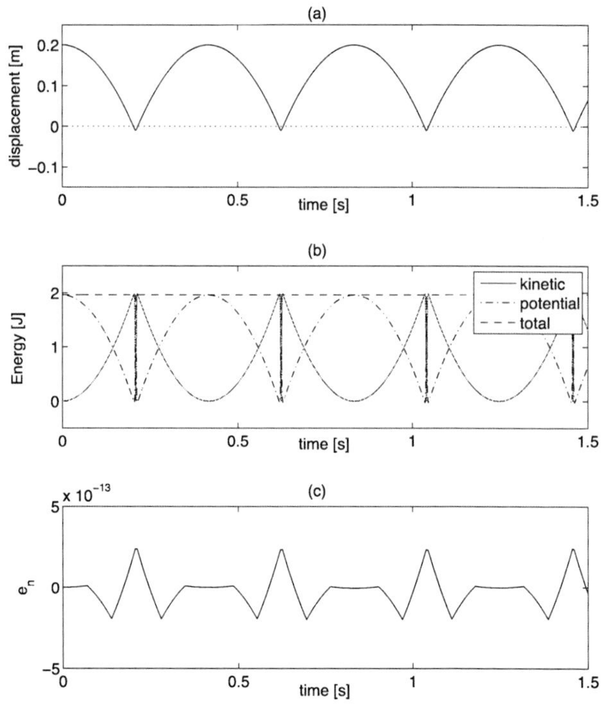

Figure 5. (a) Displacement of a lossless bouncing ball under a gravitational force with $k_c = 1e11$ and $\alpha = 4$. (b) The energy components. (c) The energy error.

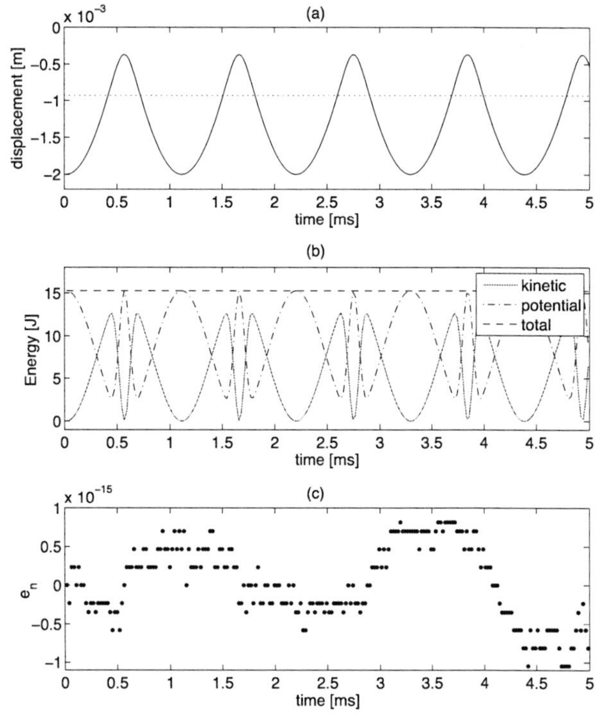

Figure 6. (a) Displacement of a lossless oscillating unit mass attached to a spring with stiffness $k = (2\pi 440)^2$ N/m and initial position y_0 = -2 mm. A repelling force becomes active when $y >$ -0.93 mm following a quadratic power law with $k_c = 2.5e10$. (b) The corresponding energy components. (c) The energy error.

Note that in this case p represents the generalised momentum and equals $\partial L/\partial \dot{y} = e^{\gamma t} m\dot{y}$, where L is the Lagrangian and $\dot{y} = dy/dt$. Hence the total (internal) energy of the system is given by $e^{-\gamma t}H$. The partial derivatives of the Hamiltonian are now defined at mid-point as:

$$\frac{\partial H}{\partial p}\Big|_{t=t+\Delta t/2} \approx e^{-\gamma(n+\frac{1}{2})\Delta t}\,\frac{1}{m}\,\frac{p_{n+1}+p_n}{2}, \tag{33a}$$

$$\frac{\partial H}{\partial y}\Big|_{t=t+\Delta t/2} \approx e^{\gamma(n+\frac{1}{2})\Delta t}\,\frac{k_c}{\alpha+1}\,\frac{\lfloor y_{n+1}\rfloor^{\alpha+1} - \lfloor y_n\rfloor^{\alpha+1}}{y_{n+1}-y_n}, \tag{33b}$$

and mid-point evaluation of the external force term yields

$$e^{\gamma t} f\big|_{t=t+\Delta t/2} \approx e^{\gamma(n+\frac{1}{2})\Delta t}\,\frac{f_{n+1}+f_n}{2}. \tag{34}$$

Appling these to (32) and defining

$$\left\{\begin{aligned} q_n &= \frac{\Delta t}{m} e^{-\gamma n\Delta t} p_n \\ w_n &= \frac{\Delta t^2}{m} f_n \end{aligned}\right\}, \tag{35}$$

allows to write the resulting scheme as

$$y_{n+1} - y_n = \frac{r q_{n+1} + r^{-1} q_n}{2}, \tag{36a}$$

$$r q_{n+1} - r^{-1} q_n = \frac{w_{n+1}+w_n}{2} - \frac{\beta}{2(\alpha+1)}\,\frac{\lfloor y_{n+1}\rfloor^{\alpha+1} - \lfloor y_n\rfloor^{\alpha+1}}{y_{n+1}-y_n}, \tag{36b}$$

where $r = e^{\gamma\Delta t/2}$ and β is defined again as in (13). Solution is now facilitated by defining the auxiliary variable as

$$x = \frac{1}{2}(r q_{n+1} + r^{-1} q_n), \tag{37}$$

which again yields a nonlinear equation to be solved:

$$F(x) = \frac{\beta}{2(\alpha+1)}\,\frac{\lfloor -y_n - x\rfloor^{\alpha+1} - \lfloor -y_n\rfloor^{\alpha+1}}{x} + x - q_n/r - \frac{w_{n+1}+w_n}{4} = 0. \tag{38}$$

Figure 7 shows the simulation results for a mass, initially driven by an external force, with its motion being damped by frictional forces. An energy preservation check does not apply now, but stability may still be observed in that

$$\frac{\partial\left(e^{-\gamma t}H\right)}{\partial t} \leq 0 \tag{39}$$

for any period during which $f = 0$. Regarding finite precision effects, checking the simulation after 20 seconds run time verified that the oscillations decay to zero, i.e. no limit cycles appear.

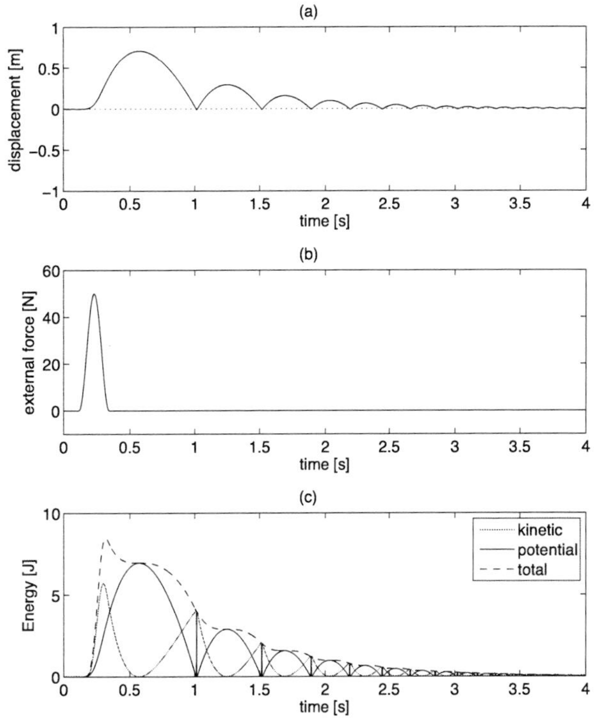

Figure 7. (a) Displacement of a unit mass driven by an external force, with initial conditions $y_0, p_0 = 0$ and internal damping $\gamma = 2$. (b) The profile of the external force. (c) The variation of the energy components.

4. CONCLUSIONS AND PERSPECTIVES

A method has been presented to formulate energy preserving schemes for the simulation of a point mass under the influence of a nonlinear force term. This has been achieved by discretising the Hamiltonian formulation instead of the Newtonian equation of motion. A proof of existence and uniqueness of the solution has been given for the case of an impactive interaction governed by a power law. The accuracy of the scheme has been investigated through the effective repelling force, which is dependent on the power-law constants and the impact velocity. Simulation results with several lossless example systems have confirmed that the system energy is conserved to machine precision, regardless of the model parameters.

For lossless one-mass systems, the proposed method is similar to that presented by Greenspan [18]. That is, for problems of the form

$$m\frac{d^2y}{dt^2} = f(y), \tag{40}$$

where the force f is a nonlinear function of y, scheme (24) is equivalent to Greenspan's method, which uses the potential function rather than the Hamiltonian as its starting point. A common feature between the proposed method and [18] is that finite difference operators are directly applied to an energy variable, as distinct from arriving at a scheme by applying difference operators to the variables of a Newtonian description, which has been the prevalent approach to derive numerical schemes for musical acoustics and sound computing applications. It is worth noting that for many musically relevant systems, including any of its linear components, such direct discretisation of energy variables holds no particular advantages; the specific merit of applying difference operators to the Hamiltonian itself only emerges in application to systems in which the force is a non-smooth function of the phase space variables, making it particularly suitable for simulation of collisions. In comparison to [18], the advantage of approximating partial derivatives of the Hamiltonian rather than the potential function is that it allows direct extension to problems of the form

$$m\frac{d^2y}{dt^2} = f(y,p), \tag{41}$$

such as collision models with nonlinear damping [19]. Given that all dynamic systems can be formulated in Hamiltonian form, one could go one step further here and conjecture that the approach can be applied to more complex systems, which would open up new possibilities for the simulation of musical instrument sounds. This would invariably involve impacting of spatially distributed elements (e.g. strings, membranes, plates). In order to gain some initial perspective of how the proposed method would apply to such systems, consider a problem of the form of (40) where $f(y) = ky$ is a simple linear spring restoring force. The generalised scheme (24) then reduces to

$$\frac{y_{n+1} - y_n}{\Delta t} = \frac{1}{m}\left(\frac{p_{n+1} + p_n}{2}\right) \tag{42a}$$

$$\frac{p_{n+1} - p_n}{\Delta t} = -k\left(\frac{y_{n+1} + y_n}{2}\right), \tag{42b}$$

which is equivalent to applying the trapezoidal integration rule to $\partial y/\partial t = p/m$, $\partial p/\partial t = -ky$, thus shifting the system resonance frequency $\sqrt{k/m}$ in the same way as the bilinear transform. This signifies that the proposed manner of discretisation results into rather heavy numerical dispersion for any linear subsystem. While it is straightforward to pre-compensate for such errors in the case of a one-mass system, the implications for a mass interacting with a spatially distributed object are more complex, and worthy of further investigation. Other key questions to be addressed in future research are whether any uniqueness issues would arise and how these may be resolved, and how the resulting conservative schemes compare to alternatives, in particular symplectic schemes.

5. REFERENCES

[1] S. Papetti and F. Avanzini and D. Rocchesso, "Numerical Methods for a Nonlinear Impact Model: A Comparative Study With Closed-Form Corrections," *IEEE Trans. Audio, Speech, and Language Processing*, vol. 19, no. 7, pp. 2146–2158, 2011.

[2] A. Chaigne and V. Doutaut, "Numerical simulation of xylophones. I. Time-domain modeling of the vibrating bars," *Journal of the Acoustical Society of America*, vol. 101, no. 1, pp. 539–557, 1997.

[3] D. Hall, "Piano string excitation. VI: Nonlinear modeling," *Journal of the Acoustical Society of America*, vol. 92, no. 1, pp. 95–105, 1992.

[4] D. Marhefka and D. Orin, "Simulation of contact using a nonlinear damping model," in *IEEE International Conference on Robotics and Automation*, vol. 2, 1996, pp. 1662–1668.

[5] S. Bilbao, *Numerical Sound Synthesis.* John Wiley and Sons, 2009.

[6] F. Avanzini and D. Rocchesso, "Physical modeling of impacts: theory and experiments on contact time and spectral centroid," in *Proceedings of the Conference on Sound and Music Computing*, 2004, pp. 287–293.

[7] F. Pfeifle and R. Bader, "Real-time finite difference physical models of musical instruments on a field programmable gate array (FPGA)," in *Proceedings of the 15th International Conference on Digital Audio Effects (DAFx 2012), York, UK*, 2012.

[8] M. Rath, "Energy-stable modelling of contacting modal objects with piece-wise linear interaction force," in *Proceedings of the 11th International Conference on Digital Audio Effects (DAFx 2008), Espoo, Finland*, 2008.

[9] S. Bilbao, "Time domain simulation and sound synthesis for the snare drum," *The Journal of the Acoustical Society of America*, vol. 131, no. 1, pp. 914–925, 2012.

[10] S. Bilbao, "Percussion synthesis based on models of nonlinear shell vibration," *IEEE Transactions on Audio, Speech, and Language Processing*, vol. 18, no. 4, pp. 872–880, 2010.

[11] V. Arnold, *Mathematical methods of classical mechanics.* Springer, 1978, vol. 60.

[12] J. Sanz-Serna, "Runge-Kutta schemes for Hamiltonian systems," *BIT Numerical Mathematics*, vol. 28, no. 4, pp. 877–883, 1988.

[13] G. Zhong and J. Marsden, "Lie-Poisson Hamilton-Jacobi theory and Lie-Poisson integrators," *Physics Letters A*, vol. 133, pp. 134–139, 1998.

[14] O. Gonzalez and J. Simo, "On the stability of symplectic and energy-momentum algorithms for nonlinear Hamiltonian systems with symmetry," *Computer Methods in Applied Mechanics and Engineering*, vol. 134, no. 3-4, pp. 197–222, 1996.

[15] K. Meyer, G. Hall, and D. Offin, *Introduction to Hamiltonian dynamical systems and the N-body problem.* Springer, 2008, vol. 77.

[16] P. Caldirola, "Forze non conservative nella meccanica quantistica," *Il Nuovo Cimento*, vol. 18, no. 9, pp. 393–400, 1941.

[17] E. Kanai, "On the quantization of the dissipative systems," *Progress of Theoretical Physics*, vol. 3, no. 4, pp. 440–442, 1948.

[18] D. Greenspan, "Conservative numerical methods for $\ddot{x} = f(x)$," *Journal of Computational Physics*, vol. 56, no. 1, pp. 28–41, 1984.

[19] K. Hunt and F. Crossley, "Coefficient of restitution interpreted as damping in vibroimpact," *Journal of Applied Mechanics*, pp. 440–445, 1975.

ON FINITE DIFFERENCE SCHEMES FOR THE 3-D WAVE EQUATION USING NON-CARTESIAN GRIDS

Brian Hamilton
Acoustics and Audio Group
University of Edinburgh
b.hamilton-2@sms.ed.ac.uk

Stefan Bilbao
Acoustics and Audio Group
University of Edinburgh
sbilbao@staffmail.ed.ac.uk

ABSTRACT

In this paper, we investigate finite difference schemes for the 3-D wave equation using 27-point stencils on the cubic lattice, a 13-point stencil on the face-centered cubic (FCC) lattice, and a 9-point stencil on the body-centered cubic (BCC) lattice. The tiling of the wavenumber space for non-Cartesian grids is considered in order to analyse numerical dispersion. Schemes are compared for computational efficiency in terms of minimising numerical wave speed error. It is shown that the 13-point scheme on the FCC lattice is more computationally efficient than 27-point schemes on the cubic lattice when less than 8% error in the wave speed is desired.

1. INTRODUCTION

Finite difference (FD) schemes have long been used to approximate solutions to the wave equation [1,2]. The wave equation can be used to model 3-D sound propagation in terms of pressure or velocity potential [3] and FD schemes provide an approximation to such acoustic fields. This has been used for 3-D room acoustics modelling [4], for the cavities of percussion instruments [5–7], and for artificial reverberation purposes [8,9]. Certain FD schemes are also known by an equivalent wave-scattering formulation called the *digital waveguide mesh* (DWM) [10], which has seen much use in the acoustics and audio signal processing community [8] due to its simplicity and passive construction.

Such FD approximations are carried out on temporal and spatial grids. The spatial grid is usually the Cartesian grid (the integer or cubic lattice [11]), but non-Cartesian grids (lattices) can also be used in 3-D [11], such as the body-centered cubic (BCC) grid [12], the face-centered cubic (FCC) grid [6,7], and the "diamond lattice" (not a lattice in the strict sense [11,13]), which is used in the "tetrahedral DWM" [14] . Furthermore, there are many approximations to the 3-D Laplacian operator that pertain to each grid [12,15]. Numerical dispersion in a FD scheme can give rise to audible artifacts [16,17] and this largely depends on the choice of the spatial grid and approximation to the Laplacian. Mitigating these effects in an efficient manner is critical for large-scale 3-D room acoustics simulations since these simulations can be prohibitively expensive in terms of memory and computation time, even with the use of graphical processing units (GPUs) [18,19]. Making sense of all these choices has been the subject of many studies [12,20–23], however, the treatment of non-Cartesian grids has been lacking important details, as will be seen in this paper.

It has recently been shown that one must consider the cell that tiles the wavenumber space, also known as the Brillouin zone of the lattice in crystallography [13], to properly analyse numerical dispersion and computational efficiency of FD schemes on the 2-D hexagonal grid [24]. While the Brillouin zone has long been considered in multidimensional sampling on non-Cartesian grids [25], it has yet to be considered in the context of FD schemes for the 3-D wave equation. The computational efficiencies of special cases of a 27-point stencil (approximation to the Laplacian) on a cubic lattice have been studied previously [23], and while this encompassed 13-point and 9-point special cases related to the FCC and BCC lattices respectively, it will be seen that it is necessary to consider both the stencil and the lattice on which it operates.

The main contributions of this paper are to consider the wavenumber cells on non-Cartesian grids to show how it relates to stability conditions and the analysis of numerical dispersion, and to compare computational efficiencies of FD schemes in terms minimising numerical dispersion for audio and acoustics applications.

The paper is organised as follows. In Section 2, we introduce the finite difference schemes and in Section 3, we discuss the discretisation of time and space. In Section 4, we consider the tiling of the wavenumber space for non-Cartesian grids and in Section 5, stability conditions are discussed with respect to the wavenumber tilings. Numerical dispersion and computational efficiency are analysed in Sections 6 and 7 respectively. Conclusions are given in Section 8.

1.1 3-D Wave Equation

Modelling 3-D room acoustics usually begins with the 3-D wave equation:

$$\left(\frac{\partial^2}{\partial t^2} - c^2\Delta\right) u = 0\,, \quad \Delta = \frac{\partial^2}{\partial x^2} + \frac{\partial^2}{\partial y^2} + \frac{\partial^2}{\partial z^2} \quad (1)$$

where c is the wave speed, Δ is the 3-D Laplacian operator, t is time, and $u = u(t, \boldsymbol{x})$ is the solution to be approximated for $\boldsymbol{x} \in \mathbb{R}^3$ ($\boldsymbol{x} = (x, y, z)$). The variable u can represent pressure or a velocity potential [3,20]. A room is not complete without walls but this study is only concerned with the interior (the bulk of the computation) so boundary conditions will not be considered here. At this point it is worth mentioning that the FD schemes considered in this paper are those that can be coupled to existing boundary conditions that model frequency-dependent walls [23,26].

2. FINITE DIFFERENCE SCHEMES

2.1 Time Difference Operator

In FD schemes, the variable u is replaced by an approximation to u, $\hat{u} = \hat{u}(t, \boldsymbol{x})$, and partial differential operators are replaced by finite difference operators. A standard FD approximation to $\frac{\partial^2}{\partial t^2}$ is the following:

$$\delta_{tt,k}\hat{u} = \frac{1}{k^2}(\hat{u}(t+k,\boldsymbol{x}) - 2\hat{u}(t,\boldsymbol{x}) + \hat{u}(t-k,\boldsymbol{x}))\,, \quad (2)$$

where k is the time-step, which could be chosen to be $k = 1/F_s$ where F_s is an audio sampling rate like 44.1 kHz.

2.2 Finite Difference Approximations to the Laplacian

Approximations to the 3-D Laplacian can be built using the following FD operator:

$$\delta_{\Delta,\Omega,h}\hat{u} = \frac{\kappa}{h^2}\sum_{i=1}^{|\Omega|}(\hat{u}(t,\boldsymbol{x}+\boldsymbol{v}_i h) - 2\hat{u}(t,\boldsymbol{x}) + \hat{u}(t,\boldsymbol{x}-\boldsymbol{v}_i h))\,, \quad (3)$$

where $\Omega \subset \mathbb{R}^3$ is a set of equal-norm vectors $\boldsymbol{v}_i \in \Omega$, and $|\Omega|$ denotes the cardinality of that set. The constant h is the spatial step, which will be chosen based on the time-step and stability constraints of the FD scheme. The FD operator in (3) becomes a $(2|\Omega| + 1)$-point second-order accurate approximation to the Laplacian (we also call this a *discrete Laplacian* or a *stencil*) for particular choices of Ω and κ. The standard 7-point stencil uses the standard unit vectors $\Omega_C = \{\hat{\boldsymbol{e}}_x, \hat{\boldsymbol{e}}_y, \hat{\boldsymbol{e}}_z\}$. We also consider a 13-point stencil that uses the following six vectors from the FCC lattice: $\Omega_F = \{\hat{\boldsymbol{e}}_x \pm \hat{\boldsymbol{e}}_y, \hat{\boldsymbol{e}}_x \pm \hat{\boldsymbol{e}}_z, \hat{\boldsymbol{e}}_y \pm \hat{\boldsymbol{e}}_z\}/\sqrt{2}$, and a 9-point stencil that uses the following four vectors from the BCC lattice: $\Omega_B = \{\hat{\boldsymbol{e}}_x \pm \hat{\boldsymbol{e}}_y \pm \hat{\boldsymbol{e}}_z, \hat{\boldsymbol{e}}_x \mp \hat{\boldsymbol{e}}_y \pm \hat{\boldsymbol{e}}_z\}/\sqrt{3}$. These stencils are shown in Fig. 1. For these choices of Ω we get the following condition for consistency:

$$\kappa = \frac{3}{|\Omega|\|\boldsymbol{v}\|^2}\,, \quad (4)$$

where $\|\boldsymbol{v}\|$ denotes the Euclidean norm of any $\boldsymbol{v} \in \Omega$.

We can also build a consistent approximation to the Laplacian as a weighted combination of these stencils:

$$\delta_{\boldsymbol{\Delta},\boldsymbol{\alpha},\Upsilon,h}\hat{u} = \sum_{j=1}^{|\Upsilon|}\alpha_j\delta_{\Delta,\Omega_j,h}\hat{u}\,, \qquad \sum_{j=1}^{|\Upsilon|}\alpha_j = 1\,, \quad (5)$$

where Υ is a set of sets and $\boldsymbol{\alpha} = (\alpha_1, \ldots, \alpha_{|\Upsilon|})$. In this study, we consider $\Upsilon_F = \{\Omega_F\}$, $\Upsilon_B = \{\Omega_B\}$, and a 27-point stencil with $\Upsilon_C = \{\Omega_C, \sqrt{2}\Omega_F, \sqrt{3}\Omega_B\}$.

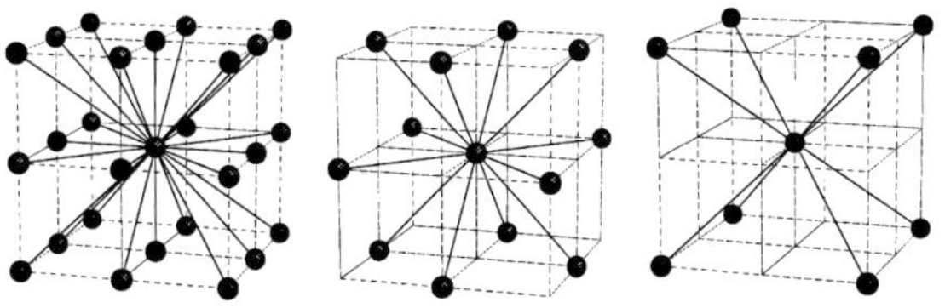

(a) Cubic (b) FCC (c) BCC

Figure 1: Some spatial points in the cubic lattice and scaled FCC and BCC lattices. Lines from center point denote vectors of associated stencils. The 27-point stencil $\delta_{\boldsymbol{\Delta},\boldsymbol{\alpha},\Upsilon_C,h}$ uses all the points in (a), whereas the 7-point stencil $\delta_{\Delta,\Omega_C,h}$ uses the black points and the center point.

2.3 Finite Difference Scheme for Wave Equation

Combining these operators we have a FD scheme for the 3-D wave equation:

$$\left(\delta_{tt} - c^2\delta_{\boldsymbol{\Delta},\boldsymbol{\alpha},\Upsilon,h}\right)\hat{u} = 0\,, \quad (6)$$

which is updated in time with the explicit recursion:

$$\hat{u}(t+k,\boldsymbol{x}) = (c^2k^2\delta_{\boldsymbol{\Delta},\boldsymbol{\alpha},\Upsilon,h} + 2)\hat{u}(t,\boldsymbol{x}) - \hat{u}(t-k,\boldsymbol{x})\,, \quad (7)$$

given some initial conditions.

3. DISCRETISING TIME AND SPACE

In practice, the FD approximation is calculated at a countable set of points in space and time, denoted by a lattice (a grid of points). The temporal grid is simply the integer lattice $\mathbb{Z}$ scaled by the time-step k:

$$\boldsymbol{T}_k = \{t_n = nk, n \in \mathbb{Z}\}\,. \quad (8)$$

A spatial lattice in 3-D is defined by:

$$\boldsymbol{G}_h = \{\boldsymbol{x}_{\boldsymbol{m},h} = \boldsymbol{m}^T\boldsymbol{V}h \in \mathbb{R}^3, \boldsymbol{m} \in \mathbb{Z}^3\}\,, \quad (9)$$

where $\boldsymbol{V}$ is a *generator matrix* [11] made up of any three column vectors chosen from Ω_C, Ω_F, and Ω_B for the cubic, FCC, and BCC lattices respectively. The approximated solution will have a certain bandwidth (spatial and temporal) given some time-step k, grid spacing h (spatial step), and discrete Laplacian $\delta_{\boldsymbol{\Delta},\boldsymbol{\alpha},\Upsilon,h}$. Given the bandwidth in the approximation, there will be a temporal and spatial lattice on which values of $\hat{u}(t,\boldsymbol{x})$ will have to be calculated so that the *continuous approximation* $\hat{u}(t,\boldsymbol{x})$ can be completely reconstructed [25]. For this reason, we only need to compute $\hat{u}(t,\boldsymbol{x})$ on a spatial and temporal grid, i.e., we calculate the set: $\{\hat{u}(t,\boldsymbol{x}) : t \in \boldsymbol{T}_k, \boldsymbol{x} \in \boldsymbol{G}_h\}$, where $\boldsymbol{T}_k$ and $\boldsymbol{G}_h$ are the appropriate grids for our FD scheme.

Choosing the appropriate grid for a given stencil is not always obvious and one must be careful so that only necessary values of $\hat{u}(t,\boldsymbol{x})$ are computed. For example, consider the FD scheme (6) with the 27-point stencil ($\Upsilon = \Upsilon_c$). Two special cases, among others, were analysed in a study on the computational efficiency of this scheme when employed on the cubic lattice: the *close-cubic packed* (CCP) scheme ($\boldsymbol{\alpha} = (0,1,0)$), and the *octahedral* scheme ($\boldsymbol{\alpha} =$

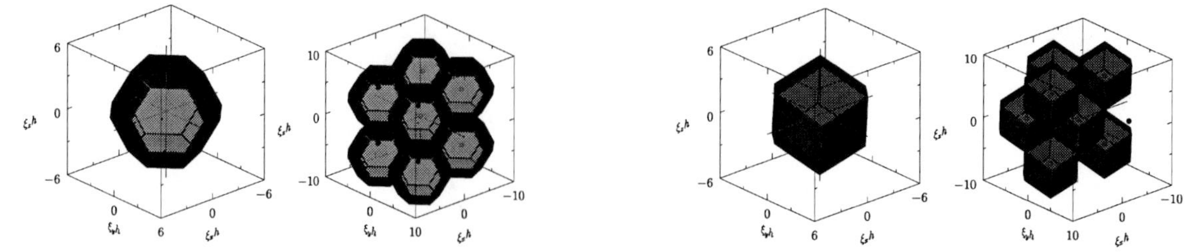

(a) FCC (b) BCC

Figure 2: Wavenumber cells, wavenumber tilings, and dual lattices (black dots) of FCC and BCC lattices.

$(0,0,1)$) [23]. As can be deduced from Fig. 1, the cubic lattice can be constructed with two scaled [1] and interleaved FCC lattices [11]. Note that the red points in Fig. 1(a) are part of one FCC lattice, and the blue and black points are part of another, shifted FCC lattice. As a consequence, the FD scheme with $\boldsymbol{\alpha} = (0,1,0)$ operates on two *disjoint* sets of points, each pertaining to one FCC lattice; this results in two *decoupled* schemes on FCC subgrids. [2] When such a scheme is employed on the cubic lattice, the FD approximation on half of the spatial points provides no additional information (bandwidth) that cannot be reconstructed from the values of $\hat{u}(t, \boldsymbol{x})$ on one FCC lattice. As such, the appropriate lattice for the CCP scheme is the FCC lattice. Similarly, the cubic lattice can be constructed from four scaled and interleaved BCC lattices [11], so, for the same reasons, the appropriate lattice for the octahedral scheme is a single BCC lattice. These features were not considered in [23], so we can improve on the reported computational efficiency, which depends on density of the spatial lattice, if we choose the appropriate lattices, as will be seen later.

4. TILING THE WAVENUMBER SPACE

It is well known that the Fourier transform of a discrete signal is periodic with period $2\pi/k$, where k is the sampling period, or time-step. The same applies to discrete multidimensional signals on spatial lattices, but the periodicity of the spatial frequencies, or wavenumbers $\boldsymbol{\xi} = (\xi_x, \xi_y, \xi_z) \in \mathbb{R}^3$, is more subtle. In general, the periodicity represents a regular tiling of the continuous frequency space which is given by the Voronoi tessellation of the *dual lattice*. The dual lattice has the generator matrix $(\boldsymbol{V}^{-1})^T$ when $\boldsymbol{V}$ is the generator matrix of the *direct lattice* and consists of unit-norm vectors [11]. The dual lattice is further scaled by 2π and the inverse of the time or spatial period [13]. This leads to the well-known sampling theorem in 1-D and this was extended to sampling in multiple dimensions [25]. The cell that makes up the tiling of the wavenumber space is known as the *Brillouin zone* of the direct lattice in crystallography [13] and the *wavenumber cell* of the lattice in the context of multidimensional sampling [25]. The cubic lattice is self-dual [11], so the wavenumber tiling is composed of cubic wavenumber cells with sides of length $2\pi/h$. Previous studies have assumed a cubic wavenumber cell for FD schemes for the 3-D wave equation on the FCC and BCC lattices, but this is not the case. The FCC and BCC lattices form a dual pair [11] and their wavenumber cells are the truncated octahedron and the rhombic dodecahedron respectively [11, 13]. These cells and their tilings are shown in Fig. 2.

We can determine how well a set of values on a spatial lattice can reconstruct an isotropic spatial signal (bandwidth cuts off at the same $|\boldsymbol{\xi}|$ in all directions) from the dual lattice and its associated wavenumber tiling [25]; this is called the *sampling efficiency* of the lattice. Some studies have chosen specific lattices for FD schemes solely based on sampling efficiency [28–30], but this can be misleading. Sampling efficiency is not a suitable metric in choosing a grid for a FD scheme because, aside from at the initial conditions, sampling is not part of the FD approximation. The solution $u(t, \boldsymbol{x})$ is unknown so it cannot be sampled (aside from the special case in 1-D [16]); it must be approximated by $\hat{u}(t, \boldsymbol{x})$ at points on a grid and the rest of $\hat{u}(t, \boldsymbol{x})$ can be reconstructed using multidimensional sinc interpolation. The efficiency in computing an accurate FD approximation depends on other factors besides the lattice on which it is employed, such as the stencil used, the combined density of the spatial and temporal grid set according to stability constraints, the number of arithmetic operations at each update, and most importantly, the particular metric used to measure efficiency, which could be in terms of order of accuracy given by a Taylor expansion or accuracy in the numerical wave speed.

We argue that the key to choosing a lattice is its rotational symmetry, which is related to the *kissing number* problem (how many non-overlapping spheres can touch or *kiss* a central sphere of the same size) [11]. We are essentially using points on the spatial lattice to approximate an isotropic (directionally-independent) operator, the Laplacian, so symmetry in the lattice plays a large role in emulating this isotropy. For example, two shells of points are required for an isotropic stencil (to the fourth-order error term) on the 2-D square lattice [31], but the lattice with the highest kissing number in 2-D, the hexagonal lattice, provides an isotropic stencil using only the first shell of points [31].

The lattice in 3-D with the highest kissing number and the most symmetry is the FCC lattice [11]. The 13-point stencil from the FCC lattice is not quite isotropic, but it has been observed that it is *nearly isotropic* [22, 23]. This can be seen in Fig. 3, where isosurfaces (surface of equal error, as a function of $\boldsymbol{\xi}$) of the second-order error terms in approximations to the Laplacian are shown. Among the

[1] We use the term "scaled" when a lattice generated with unit-norm vectors is multiplied by something other than the grid spacing h.

[2] The same observation has been made in the context of lattice Boltzmann simulations [27].

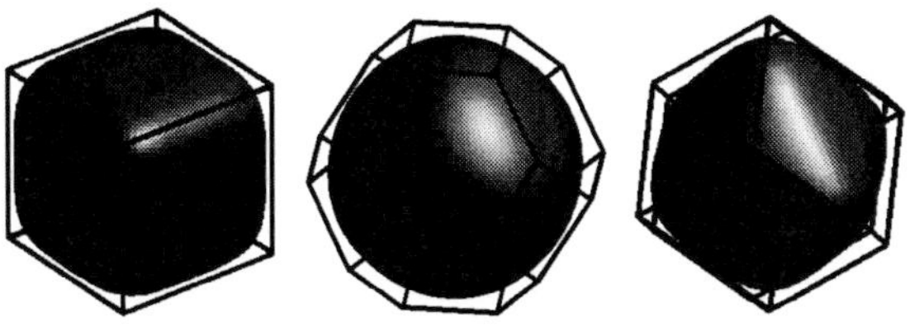

(a) 7-point stencil (b) 13-point stencil (c) 9-point stencil

Figure 3: Equal isosurfaces of first error-term in Taylor expansions of Fourier symbols of approximations to Laplacian. Isotropic error gives a sphere.

three isosurfaces displayed in Fig. 3 the isosurface pertaining to the 13-point FCC stencil is the closest to a sphere (isotropic). We also observe that they loosely conform to the wavenumber cells of their associated lattices. A rounder wavenumber cell is more amenable to an isotropic error since the full error must ultimately conform to the tiling of the wavenumber space.

Considering that the Fourier symbol of the Laplacian describes concentric spherical shells (isosurfaces of scalar values), we can take another point of view: in essence, we are trying to fit a sphere into the wavenumber cell. Thus, we require the roundest wavenumber cell. This problem could be formulated as finding the lattice whose wavenumber cell has a ratio of *inradius* (largest radius for a sphere contained by the cell) to *circumradius* (the smallest radius for a sphere that contains the cell) closest to unity (this ratio for a sphere). This is a combination of the kissing problem (maximise inradius) and the *covering problem* (what is the least dense arrangement of overlapping spheres that covers space; minimise circumradius) [11]. These ratios are approximately 1.29, 1.41, and 1.73 for the FCC, BCC, and cubic lattices respectively. This is similar, but different from finding the optimal sampling lattice for an isotropic signal, which is essentially the sphere packing problem in the wavenumber space [25], and for lattices, the kissing number problem [11]. The 2-D hexagonal lattice is self-dual, and solves both the kissing number problem and the covering problem, so sampling arguments [28], while unfounded, arrive at the same conclusion. This line of reasoning has also been used in 3-D to select the BCC lattice [29], which is optimal for sampling because its dual, the FCC lattice, is the lattice with the highest kissing number and sphere packing density [25]. However, it will be seen that the BCC lattice is not ideal in the context of FD schemes for the 3-D wave equation. It is interesting to note that a recent study also followed sampling arguments [30], but arrived at the FCC lattice by conflating the optimal sampling lattice with its dual.

5. STABILITY

Using von Neumann's method for determining stability conditions in FD schemes [32], it is sufficient to consider a plane wave of the form: $\hat{u}(t,\boldsymbol{x}) = e^{j(\omega t+\boldsymbol{\xi}\cdot\boldsymbol{x})}$, where ω is the temporal frequency and $(\omega,\boldsymbol{\xi}) \in \mathbb{R}^4$. It helps to define a normalised wavenumber $\boldsymbol{\xi}_h = \boldsymbol{\xi} h$ and normalised frequency $\omega_k = \omega k$. Inserting the plane wave into the FD

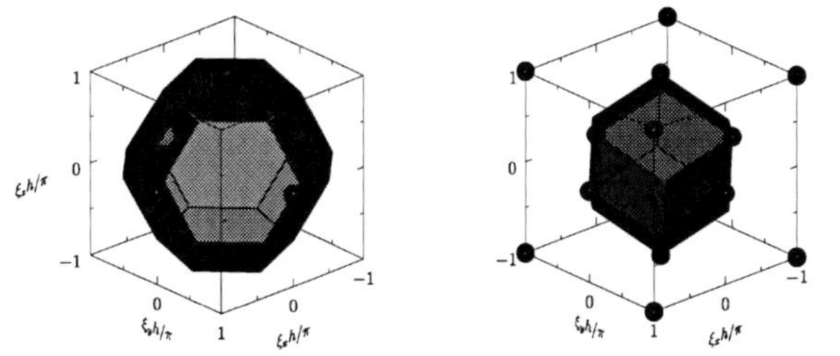

(a) FCC (b) BCC

Figure 4: Scaled FCC and BCC wavenumber cells inscribed in cubic wavenumber cell. Arguments of the maxima in $|\mathcal{D}_{\Delta,\sqrt{2}\Omega_F,h}|$ and $|\mathcal{D}_{\Delta,\sqrt{3}\Omega_B,h}|$ denoted by black spheres.

scheme then gives a dispersion relation of the form:

$$\mathcal{D}_{tt}(\omega_k) = \lambda^2 \mathcal{D}_{\boldsymbol{\Delta},\boldsymbol{\alpha},\Upsilon}(\boldsymbol{\xi}_h), \tag{10}$$

where $\lambda = ck/h$ is the Courant number and

$$\mathcal{D}_{tt}(\omega_k) = -4\sin^2(\omega_k/2), \tag{11}$$

$$\mathcal{D}_{\boldsymbol{\Delta},\boldsymbol{\alpha},\Upsilon}(\boldsymbol{\xi}_h) = -4\sum_{j=1}^{|\Upsilon|}\alpha_j\kappa_j\sum_{i=1}^{|\Omega_j|}\sin^2(\boldsymbol{\xi}_h\cdot\boldsymbol{v}_{j,i}/2) \tag{12}$$

for $\boldsymbol{v}_{j,i} \in \Omega_j$. The scheme is stable if we can ensure that no real wavenumbers produce growing solutions in time. This requires finding a maximum for $|\mathcal{D}_{\boldsymbol{\Delta},\boldsymbol{\alpha},\Upsilon}(\boldsymbol{\xi}_h)|$ and we get the following stability condition:

$$\lambda \le \lambda_{\max,\boldsymbol{\alpha}} = \sqrt{\frac{4}{\max_{\boldsymbol{\xi}_h}|\mathcal{D}_{\boldsymbol{\Delta},\boldsymbol{\alpha},\Upsilon}(\boldsymbol{\xi}_h)|}} \tag{13}$$

In deriving this condition we have not specified a grid, but $\mathcal{D}_{\boldsymbol{\Delta},\boldsymbol{\alpha},\Upsilon}(\boldsymbol{\xi}_h)$ is periodic according to the wavenumber tiling of the appropriate grid for the stencil. It is then sufficient to consider just one wavenumber cell of the appropriate lattice. So in the CCP and octahedral schemes on cubic lattices, the stability condition is found within the wavenumber cell of scaled FCC and BCC lattices respectively, but an exhaustive search over a larger domain will also locate the maximum. For the schemes considered here, $|\mathcal{D}_{\boldsymbol{\Delta},\boldsymbol{\alpha},\Upsilon,h}(\boldsymbol{\xi})|$ is *multilinear* in $\cos(\xi_x h)$, $\cos(\xi_y h)$, and $\cos(\xi_z h)$ variables, and it can be shown that the maximum occurs at either the faces, center of edges, or vertices of a cubic wavenumber cell [12]. As we can see in Fig. 4, the wavenumber cells of the scaled FCC and BCC lattices are neatly inscribed in a cube with sides of $2\pi/h$. The points where the maximum of $|\mathcal{D}_{\Delta,\sqrt{2}\Omega_F,h}|$ occurs line up with the square faces of the truncated octahedron wavenumber cell for the CCP scheme. Similarly, the points where the maximum of $|\mathcal{D}_{\Delta,\sqrt{3}\Omega_B,h}|$ occurs line up with vertices of the rhombic dodecahedron wavenumber cell for the octahedral scheme (the corners of the cube pertain to vertices of replicated dodecahedral cells).

It has been shown that the stability conditions for the 27-point stencil scheme are [12]:

$$-2\alpha_1 \le \alpha_2 \le 2\alpha_1 + 1, \tag{14}$$

$$\lambda \leq \lambda_{\max,\boldsymbol{\alpha}} = \min\left(1, \frac{1}{\sqrt{2\alpha_1+\alpha_2}}, \frac{1}{\sqrt{2\alpha_1-\alpha_2+1}}\right), \tag{15}$$

and from (15) we can get the stability conditions for the 13-point and 9-point FD schemes after we rescale the grid spacings. For the 13-point ($\Upsilon = \Upsilon_F$) and 9-point ($\Upsilon = \Upsilon_B$) schemes we have the respective stability conditions:

$$\lambda \leq \sqrt{1/2}, \quad \lambda \leq \sqrt{1/3}. \tag{16}$$

Note that the condition for the 13-point scheme is different from the Courant number used in the "dodecahedral DWM" [6], which means this case was not covered in a study comparing DWM topologies [22]. It was observed that the dodecahedral DWM had good numerical dispersion properties [22] and since numerical dispersion is minimised when the Courant number is set to $\lambda_{\max,\boldsymbol{\alpha}}$ [16] the FD scheme on the FCC lattice will provide less dispersion. [3]

6. NUMERICAL DISPERSION

Inserting the plane wave $u(t,\boldsymbol{x}) = e^{j(\omega t+\boldsymbol{\xi}\cdot\boldsymbol{x})}$ into the wave equation we get the dispersion relation $\omega^2 = c^2|\boldsymbol{\xi}|^2$, which tells us that the *phase velocity* ($\omega(\boldsymbol{\xi})/|\boldsymbol{\xi}|$) of each plane wave is the wave speed c. However, in the FD scheme the relationship is not linear and we get a frequency- and direction-dependent wave speed in the approximation $\hat{u}(t,\boldsymbol{x})$. The *relative phase velocity* (we will just call this the *numerical wave speed*) is:

$$\hat{\nu}(\boldsymbol{\xi}_h) = \frac{\omega_k(\boldsymbol{\xi}_h)}{\lambda|\boldsymbol{\xi}_h|}, \quad \omega_k(\boldsymbol{\xi}_h) = \mathcal{D}_{tt}^{-1}(\lambda^2\mathcal{D}_{\boldsymbol{\Delta},\boldsymbol{\alpha},\Upsilon}(\boldsymbol{\xi}_h)) \tag{17}$$

for $\omega_k \in (0,\pi]$ and $\boldsymbol{\xi}_h \in \mathbb{B}$, where $\mathbb{B}$ is the wavenumber cell of the grid. The wave speed error, defined as $|1-\hat{\nu}(\boldsymbol{\xi}_h)|$, is the main concern in audio and acoustics applications of FD schemes. Higher frequencies tend to travel slower and this causes transients to be smeared over space and time. It is therefore of interest to analyse numerical dispersion in such schemes, but a proper analysis of the wave speed error requires the correct wavenumber cell on non-Cartesian grids.

With 2-D schemes one can plot the wave speed error over the entire domain using a single contour plot [12, 24], but this is not possible for 3-D. Some possibilities to visualise the wave speed error include fixing two angles and plotting the error as a function of $|\boldsymbol{\xi}_h|$ [23]; fixing $|\boldsymbol{\xi}_h|$ and plotting the error as a function of two angles as a mapping of colours on a spherical shell [12, 22] or where the error denotes a polar radius [33]; plotting contours of two-dimensional slices of $\mathbb{B}$ [12, 23]; or fixing some error and plotting this as a three-dimensional isosurface of wavenumbers. In each of these representations one can encounter aliased wavenumbers if one does not consider the correct domain $\mathbb{B}$. If one assumes a cubic wavenumber cell for the 13- and 9-point schemes, as has been done in the past, the cell will contain aliased wavenumbers, as can be deduced from Fig. 4, or missing wavenumbers. [4] This can result in an incorrect numerical wave speed if the denominator in (17) is not adjusted accordingly to reflect the tiling of the wavenumber space.

Table 1 lists the parameters of the schemes analysed here, along with some acronyms sometimes employed in the literature [22, 23]. These acronyms stand for the standard leapfrog (SLF), interpolated wideband (IWB), interpolated isotropic (IISO2), [5] close-cubic packed (CCP), and octahedral (OCTA) schemes. The 27-point IWB and IISO2 schemes are analysed because they were identified as being the most effective 27-point schemes at reducing wave speed error [23]. Note that the CCP and OCTA schemes are analysed here on their native lattices for the reasons stated in Section 2.3, so we will refer to these as the "FCC scheme" and the "BCC scheme".

The density of a spatial grid is μ/h^3, where μ is the density of the unscaled lattice (unit grid spacing). The *computational density* (updates per unit time and space) of a scheme is then $\mu(h^3k)^{-1}$. Fixing the Courant number at the stability limit, we can write the computational density as $(c\mu/\lambda)h^{-4}$. Thus, to put schemes on an equal footing we use the spatial step $h = \sqrt[4]{\mu/\lambda}h'$ so that each scheme has the density ch'^{-4}. Similarly, we can write the computational density as $(\mu\lambda^3/c^2)k^{-4}$, so we can equalise the schemes by choosing the time-step as $k = \sqrt[4]{\mu\lambda^3}k'$. The parameter μ and the values μ/λ and $\mu\lambda^3$ for each scheme are listed in Table 1. We can now compare schemes on different grids and with different Courant numbers in terms of normalised wavenumbers $\boldsymbol{\xi}_{h'} = \boldsymbol{\xi}h'$ or normalised frequencies $\omega_{k'} = \omega k'$ by keeping h' or k' constant across all schemes.

The computational density is a metric for efficiency that has been used in previous comparisons [23] and is mostly a starting point to compare computational costs. It does not take into account specific operations like multiplications, additions, and memory reads, although these are simply an extra scaling factor. Ideally, such comparisons should be conducted in practice on specific computational hardware (see [34]).

In Fig. 5, we show isosurfaces of the 10% wave speed error, as a function of $\boldsymbol{\xi}_{h'}$. The surface displayed represents wavenumbers with 10% wave speed error, and since the wave speed error is monotonic in these schemes, any wavenumber inside the surface results in less than 10% error. These plots are normalised for computational density, but it is difficult to compare them since the wavenumber cells differ. However, it can be observed that the FCC scheme's isosurface (Fig. 5(d)) fills its wavenumber cell better than the other schemes fill their respective cells.

In Fig. 6, we show error surfaces where $|\boldsymbol{\xi}_{h'}|$ is fixed at $\pi/10$. We note that the relative comparison of Fig. 5(a) to Fig. 5(d) is more favourable to the FCC scheme than what is found in [30]. This is because we have also normalised for computations per unit time, but also because there is a mistake in the spatial density of the FCC lattice in [30].

[3] The dodecahedral DWM is left out for brevity, but a similar comparison can be found for 7-point FD scheme on the 2-D hexagonal grid and the "triangular DWM" [24].

[4] The wavenumber cells extend beyond the cube in Fig. 4 when the FCC and BCC lattices are not scaled.

[5] The second of three isotropic schemes that were examined in [23].

Table 1: Parameters for various schemes

Subfigure	lattice	# of points	Υ	α	μ	λ	μ/λ	$\mu\lambda^3$	Acronyms from [23]
(a)	cubic	7	Υ_C	$(1,0,0)$	1	$\sqrt{1/3}$	1.73	0.19	SLF
(b)	cubic	27	Υ_C	$(1/4,1/2,1/4)$	1	1	1.00	1.00	IWB
(c)	cubic	27	Υ_C	$(5/12,1/2,1/12)$	1	$\sqrt{3/4}$	1.15	0.65	IISO2
(d)	FCC	13	Υ_F	1	$\sqrt{2}$	$\sqrt{1/2}$	2.00	0.50	CCP*
(e)	BCC	9	Υ_B	1	$3\sqrt{3}/4$	$\sqrt{1/3}$	2.25	0.25	OCTA*

*These schemes are employed on the cubic lattice in [23] so μ and λ would change to $\mu = 1$ and $\lambda = 1$.

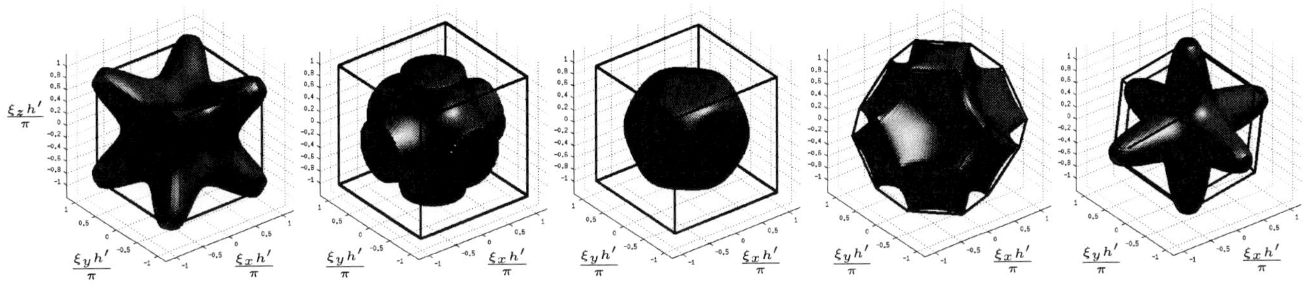

(a) SLF (b) IWB (c) IISO2 (d) FCC (e) BCC

Figure 5: 10% wave speed error isosurfaces.

From these plots we see that the FCC scheme has the lowest amount of error (for $|\boldsymbol{\xi}_{h'}| = \pi/10$).

In Fig. 7, we display volumetric slices of the wave speed error for specific planes. In these plots we can see that most of the error in the FCC scheme is less than 15%. The cubic schemes have large error near the face centers or corners of the cubic wavenumber cell. On the other hand, these wavenumbers are not represented on the scaled FCC lattice. The BCC scheme also has pronounced error near the diagonal vertices (those with a vertex figure consisting of three rhombi). The FCC scheme exhibits no numerical dispersion along the x,y, and z directions, similar to the IWB scheme; this is a useful feature for simulating axial room modes [23].

In Fig. 8, we have taken the same slices and reassigned the wave speed error to temporal frequencies ω_k and a fixed angle of propagation (polar angle) using the function $\omega_k(\boldsymbol{\xi}_h)$ in (10) [35]. We only show quadrants since these plots have four-fold symmetry. We have not normalised densities in Fig. 8 to show directionally dependent *cutoff frequencies*, of interest for audio applications. To generate Figs. 8(d) and 8(e) it is necessary to consider the correct wavenumber cell.

Finally in Fig. 9, we plot the wave speed error along the worst-case direction for each scheme as a function of normalised wavenumber $|\boldsymbol{\xi}_{h'}|$ and as a function of normalised frequency $\omega_{k'}$. Notice that the FCC scheme has slightly less dispersion than the IISO2 and IWB schemes until about 8% error. This gap will become more pronounced once we compare computational efficiencies.

7. COMPUTATIONAL EFFICIENCY

We use the relative efficiency measure introduced in [35] and employed in [23] to compare 3-D schemes for their computational efficiency in terms of minimising numerical dispersion. The basic idea is to determine how much one must increase the computational density (by reducing h or k; density scales to the fourth power) in a reference scheme (in this case, the SLF scheme) to maintain the wave speed error below some threshold in every direction. This is completely determined by the parameters in Table 1 and (17) if we increase the computational density by reducing h.[6] We plot these relative efficiencies in Fig. 10. It can be seen that if less than 8% wave speed error is desired up to some critical frequency, the FCC scheme has the best computational efficiency (using this particular metric), followed by the IISO2 and IWB schemes. If greater than 8% wave speed error is acceptable, the IWB scheme will have a smaller computational density. The data in Fig. 10 agree with the numbers reported in [23] after adjusting for the grid densities of the CCP and OCTA schemes. As such, the reported efficiencies for the CCP and OCTA schemes have been improved by a factors of two and four respectively. Nonetheless, the efficiency of the FD scheme on the BCC lattice is poor, which confirms our discussion about choosing a lattice based on sampling efficiency.

We have not taken into account the number of specific operations for each scheme and, as mentioned previously, we have left this out for brevity. However, we should point out that the FCC scheme employs less than half the neighbouring points of the 27-point stencil, so if one considers additions and memory bandwidth the FCC scheme is the most efficient scheme in a wider range of errors. Furthermore, the gap in Fig. 10 between the FCC scheme and 27-point schemes for less than 8% wave speed error increases by a factor of two. These implementation-specific details are further investigated in another study [34].

[6] This has previously been done by solving for $\boldsymbol{\xi}_h(\omega_k)$ using (10) and increasing the computational density by reducing k [23, 35], but the choice is immaterial because the measure is ultimately independent of h and k, which is apparent from the axes in Fig. 10.

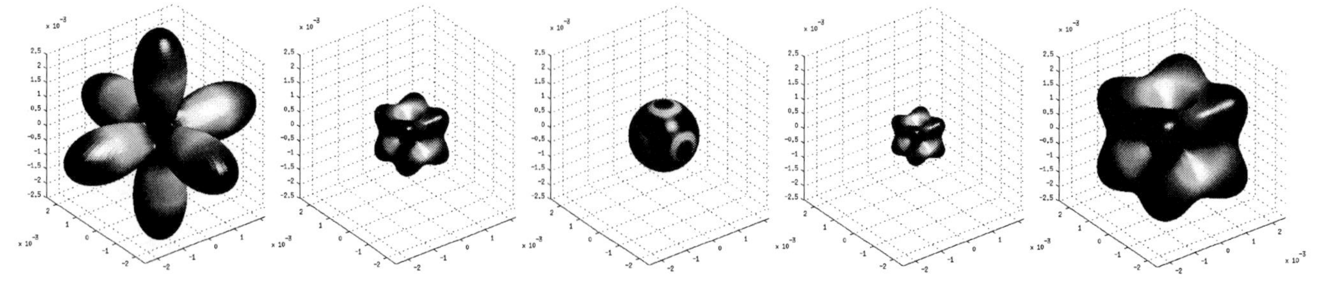

(a) SLF (b) IWB (c) IISO2 (d) FCC (e) BCC

Figure 6: Wave speed error surface for $|\boldsymbol{\xi}_{h'}| = \pi/10$. Colour mapping is relative to each plot to show detail.

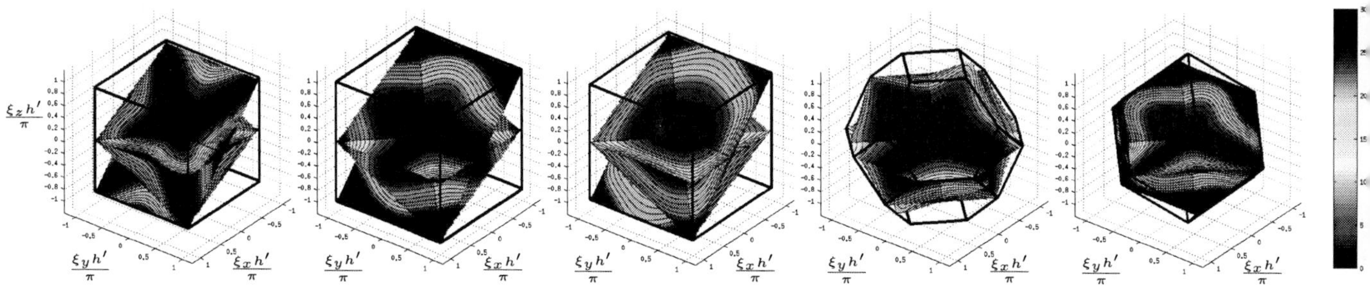

(a) SLF (b) IWB (c) IISO2 (d) FCC (e) BCC

Figure 7: Volumetric slices of wave speed error along three planes. 2% error contours.

8. CONCLUSIONS

In this paper, we have considered the wavenumber cell of non-Cartesian grids in order to compare 27-point FD schemes on the cubic lattice with a 13-point scheme on the FCC lattice and a 9-point scheme on the BCC lattice. These FD schemes have been compared in terms of numerical dispersion and using a metric of computational efficiency for minimising wave speed error. It has been shown that the 13-point scheme on the FCC lattice is the most computationally efficient scheme when less than 8% wave speed error in the approximated solution is desired up to some critical frequency. The demonstrated inefficiency of the BCC scheme confirms that sampling-based arguments are not suitable for FD schemes.

In future work, perceptual tests will be conducted to determine critical thresholds of wave speed error for the purposes of large-scale 3-D room acoustics simulations and artificial reverberation (some preliminary work can be found in [17]). The tetrahedral DWM was not considered in this paper, but it will be treated as a special case in a future study.

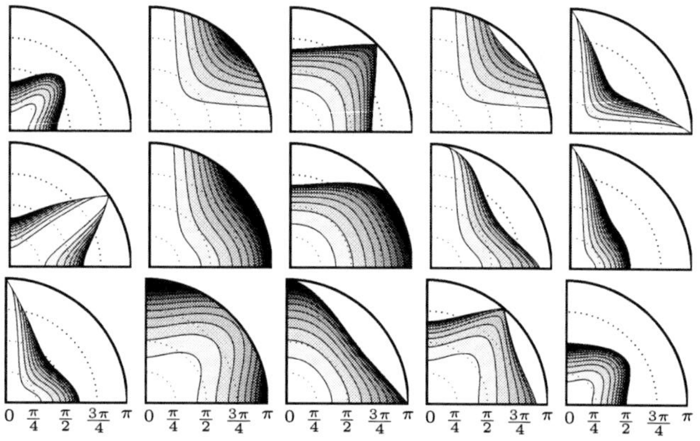

(a) SLF (b) IWB (c) IISO2 (d) FCC (e) BCC

Figure 8: Volumetric slices of wave speed error as a function of polar angle $\theta \in [0, \pi/2]$ on a plane and radius $\omega_k \in (0, \pi]$ with 2% error contours. First row: $\xi_z = 0$ plane, second row: $\xi_x = \xi_z$ plane, third row: the plane described by the zero point and the normal vector $\hat{\boldsymbol{n}} = (1, 1, 1)$.

Acknowledgments

This work was supported by the European Research Council, under grant StG-2011-279068-NESS, and by the Natural Sciences and Engineering Research Council of Canada.

9. REFERENCES

[1] R. Courant, K. Friedrichs, and H. Lewy, "Über die partiellen differenzengleichungen der mathematischen physik," *Mathematische Annalen*, vol. 100, no. 1, pp. 32–74, 1928.

[2] G. E. Forsythe and W. R. Wasow, *Finite-difference methods for partial differential equations*. New York: Wiley, 1960.

[3] P. M. Morse and K. U. Ingard, *Theoretical acoustics*. Princeton University Press, 1968.

[4] L. Savioja, T. J. Rinne, and T. Takala, "Simulation of room acoustics with a 3-D finite difference mesh," in *Proc. Int. Computer Music Conf. (ICMC)*, Danish Institute of Electroacoustic Music, Denmark, 1994, pp. 463–466.

[5] L. Rhaouti, A. Chaigne, and P. Joly, "Time-domain modeling and numerical simulation of a kettledrum," *J. Acoustical Society of America*, vol. 105, p. 3545, 1999.

[6] J. A. Laird, "The physical modelling of drums using digital waveguides," Ph.D. thesis, University of Bristol, 2001.

[7] M.-L. Aird, "Musical instrument modelling using digital waveguides," Ph.D. thesis, University of Bath, 2002.

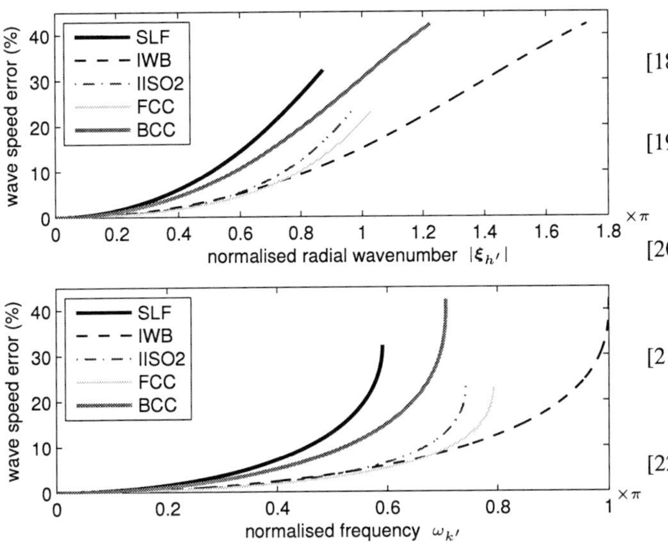

Figure 9: Wave speed error along worst-case direction for each scheme.

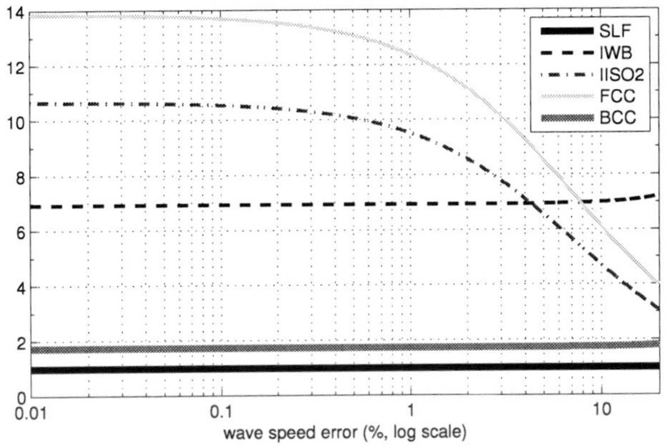

Figure 10: Efficiency for FD schemes relative to SLF.

[8] D. T. Murphy, A. Kelloniemi, J. Mullen, and S. Shelley, "Acoustic modeling using the digital waveguide mesh," *IEEE Sig. Proc. Magazine*, vol. 24, no. 2, pp. 55–66, 2007.

[9] V. Välimäki, J. D. Parker, L. Savioja, J. O. Smith III, and J. S. Abel, "Fifty years of artificial reverberation," *IEEE Trans. Audio, Speech, and Language Processing*, vol. 20, no. 5, pp. 1421–1448, 2012.

[10] S. A. van Duyne and J. O. Smith III, "Physical modeling with the 2-D digital waveguide mesh," in *Proc. Int. Computer Music Conf. (ICMC)*, Tokyo, Japan, 1993.

[11] J. Conway and N. J. A. Sloane, *Sphere packings, lattices and groups*. Springer-Verlag, 1988.

[12] S. Bilbao, "Wave and scattering methods for the numerical integration of partial differential equations," Ph.D. thesis, Stanford University, 2001.

[13] N. W. Ashcroft and N. D. Mermin, *Solid State Physics*. Saunders College, Philadelphia, 1976.

[14] S. A. van Duyne and J. O. Smith III, "The tetrahedral digital waveguide mesh," in *Proc. IEEE WASPAA*, 1995, pp. 234–237.

[15] L. Savioja, "Improving the three-dimensional digital waveguide mesh by interpolation," *Proc. Nordic Acoustical Meeting*, pp. 265–268, 1998.

[16] S. Bilbao, *Numerical sound synthesis: finite difference schemes and simulation in musical acoustics*. Wiley, 2009.

[17] A. Southern, D. T. Murphy, T. Lokki, and L. Savioja, "The perceptual effects of dispersion error on room acoustic model auralization," in *Proc. Forum Acusticum, Aalborg, Denmark*, 2011, pp. 1553–1558.

[18] L. Savioja, "Real-time 3D finite-difference time-domain simulation of low-and mid-frequency room acoustics," in *Proc. Digital Audio Effects (DAFx)*, vol. 1, 2010, p. 75.

[19] C. J. Webb and A. Gray, "Large-scale virtual acoustics simulation at audio rates using three dimensional finite difference time domain and multiple GPUs," in *Proc. Int. Cong. Acoustics (ICA)*, Montréal, Canada, 2013.

[20] S. Bilbao and J. O. Smith III, "Finite difference schemes and digital waveguide networks for the wave equation: Stability, passivity, and numerical dispersion," *IEEE Trans. Speech and Audio Processing*, vol. 11, no. 3, pp. 255–266, 2003.

[21] L. Savioja and V. Välimäki, "Interpolated rectangular 3-D digital waveguide mesh algorithms with frequency warping," *IEEE Trans. Speech and Audio Processing*, vol. 11, no. 6, pp. 783–790, 2003.

[22] G. R. Campos and D. M. Howard, "On the computational efficiency of different waveguide mesh topologies for room acoustic simulation," *IEEE Trans. Speech and Audio Processing*, vol. 13, no. 5, pp. 1063–1072, 2005.

[23] K. Kowalczyk and M. van Walstijn, "Room acoustics simulation using 3-D compact explicit FDTD schemes," *IEEE Trans. Audio, Speech, and Language Processing*, vol. 19, no. 1, pp. 34–46, 2011.

[24] B. Hamilton and S. Bilbao, "Hexagonal vs. rectilinear grids for explicit finite difference schemes for the two-dimensional wave equation," in *Proc. Int. Cong. Acoustics (ICA)*, Montréal, Canada, 2013.

[25] D. P. Petersen and D. Middleton, "Sampling and reconstruction of wave-number-limited functions in N-dimensional Euclidean spaces," *Information and control*, vol. 5, no. 4, pp. 279–323, 1962.

[26] S. Bilbao, "Modeling of complex geometries and boundary conditions in finite difference/finite volume time domain room acoustics simulation," *IEEE Trans. Audio, Speech, and Language Processing*, vol. 21, no. 7, pp. 1524–1533, Jul. 2013.

[27] K. Petkov, F. Qiu, Z. Fan, A. E. Kaufman, and K. Mueller, "Efficient LBM visual simulation on face-centered cubic lattices," *IEEE Trans. Visualization and Computer Graphics*, vol. 15, no. 5, pp. 802–814, 2009.

[28] X. Fei, T. Xiaohong, and Z. Xianjing, "The construction of low-dispersive FDTD on hexagon," *IEEE Trans. Antennas and Propagation*, vol. 53, no. 11, pp. 3697–3703, 2005.

[29] N. Röber, M. Spindler, and M. Masuch, "Waveguide-based room acoustics through graphics hardware," in *Proc. Int. Computer Music Conf. (ICMC)*, 2006.

[30] M. Potter, M. Lamoureux, and M. Nauta, "An FDTD scheme on a face-centered-cubic (FCC) grid for the solution of the wave equation," *J. Computational Physics*, vol. 230, no. 15, pp. 6169–6183, 2011.

[31] L. V. Kantorovich and V. I. Krylov, *Approximate methods of higher analysis. Translated by Curtis D. Benster.* Interscience Publishers, 1958.

[32] J. G. Charney, R. Fjörtoft, and J. von Neumann, "Numerical integration of the barotropic vorticity equation," *Tellus*, vol. 2, no. 4, pp. 237–254, 1950.

[33] Y. Liu, "Fourier analysis of numerical algorithms for the Maxwell equations," *J. Computational Physics*, vol. 124, no. 2, pp. 396–416, 1996.

[34] B. Hamilton and C. J. Webb, "Room acoustics modelling using GPU-accelerated finite difference and finite volume methods on a face-centered cubic grid," in *Proc. Digital Audio Effects (DAFx)*, Maynooth, Ireland, 2013.

[35] M. van Walstijn and K. Kowalczyk, "On the numerical solution of the 2D wave equation with compact FDTD schemes," in *Proc. Digital Audio Effects (DAFx)*, Espoo, Finland, 2008, pp. 205–212.

Automatic Tuning of the OP-1 Synthesizer Using a Multi-objective Genetic Algorithm

Matthieu Macret
School of Interactive Arts and Technology
Simon Fraser University, Surrey,
B.C., Canada V3T 0A3
mmacret@sfu.ca

Philippe Pasquier
School of Interactive Arts and Technology
Simon Fraser University, Surrey,
B.C., Canada V3T 0A3
pasquier@sfu.ca

ABSTRACT

Calibrating a sound synthesizer to replicate or approximate a given target sound is a complex and time consuming task for musicians and sound designers. In the case of the OP1, a commercial synthesizer developed by Teenage Engineering, the difficulty is multiple. The OP-1 contains several synthesis engines, effects and low frequency oscillators, which make the parameters search space very large and discontinuous. Furthermore, interactions between parameters are common and the OP-1 is not fully deterministic. We address the problem of automatically calibrating the parameters of the OP-1 to approximate a given target sound. We propose and evaluate a solution to this problem using a multi-objective Non-dominated-Sorting-Genetic-Algorithm-II. We show that our approach makes it possible to handle the problem complexity, and returns a small set of presets that best approximate the target sound while covering the Pareto front of this multi-objective optimization problem.

1. INTRODUCTION

Sound re-synthesis is the process of replicating a sound using electronics or software. Tuning a synthesizer for this purpose can be a very unintuitive task, since changes in input parameters can give rise, via nonlinearities and interactions among parameters, to unexpected changes in the output sound. Optimization techniques such as GAs have been successfully used to perform this tuning in the past for a variety of synthesis techniques [1–3] and synthesizers of increasing complexity [4–7]. It is now common for synthesizers to include several synthesis engines, FX and LFOs with large parameter complexity. A research partnership has been started by the authors in collaboration with Teenage Engineering (TE), with the goal of developing a system able to tune their synthesizer, the OP-1, to approximate any given target sound. Tuning this synthesizer presents all the characteristics of a real world problem. In comparison to previously studied synthesizers, the search space is larger, discontinuous and more difficult because of a large number of possible local minima. To the best of our knowledge, there is no system capable of successfully tuning sound synthesizers with the same complexity as the OP-1.

In collaboration with TE, we have developed a new system to select suitable parameters for the OP-1 to approximate a given target sound. In contrast with previously developed systems, we consider that the problem requires a multi-objective approach to be solved. We use a custom Non-dominated Sorting Genetic Algorithm (NSGA-II) to address this problem. An evaluation of the system with contrived and non-contrived target sounds is presented in Section 5. Sound examples are available for public audition [8].

2. RELATED WORKS

The complexity of a re-synthesis problem can vary tremendously according to the number and the nature of the synthesis parameters to search. First efforts focused on optimizing a limited number of synthesis parameters.

Horner et al. [2] used additive synthesis to replicate instrument sounds. A GA was used to better approximate the envelopes to apply to the oscillators. The number of oscillators to use and their frequencies were not determined by the GA but through spectral analysis.

Chan et al. [1] implemented and evaluated a hybrid sampling wavetable model. A GA adjusted some of the wavetable parameters in order to minimize phase cancellations during the crossfade between sampling and wavetable synthesis.

Wakefield and Mrozek [9] used subtractive synthesis to create artificial reverberation. A GA was used to search for low-order filter parameters so that the generated impulse response best matched that of a target room transfer function.

Horner et al. also used GA to optimize several FM parameters: the modulation indices, carrier and modulator frequencies for a variety of carriers [3]. The relative spectral error between the original and matched spectra served as a fitness function in guiding the GA's search for the best FM parameters to mimic instrumental sounds. The FM synthesis model was constrained to limit the complexity of the problem. In a previous work, we used a similar technique to optimize modulation indices, carrier and modulator frequencies for ModFM synthesizers [5].

Automatic optimization schemes were also used to solve another class of more complex re-synthesis problems. These problems involved searching every synthesis parameter. For example, Vuori et al. [6] built a GA system for estimating each parameter of a non-linear physical flute model. Each chromosome of this system represented 8 different parameters of the physical model. The relative spectral error between the original and matched spectra served as the fitness function. They showed that their algorithm converged smoothly and effectively with the desired sound.

Bozkurt and Yuksel [7] presented automatic parameter tuning experiments with genetic algorithms in application to multiple-modulator FM synthesis. Contrary to the FM synthesis systems previously presented [3,5], their synthesis model was not constrained and every FM parameter was estimated. Mitchell [10] applied an Evolutionary Strategy to tune the parameters of a FM synthesis model of similar complexity.

GAs were also used to determine the parameters of more complex synthesizers. Yee-King and Roth [4] used a GA to find the parameters of Virtual Studio Technology instruments (VSTi) synthesizers to match a given target sound. They evaluated their system on 2 VSTi synthesizers: the mdaDX10, a single modulator FM synthesizer with 16 parameters, and the mdaJX10, a substrative synthesizer with one noise oscillator and 40 parameters.

In this work, we apply an automatic optimization scheme to tune the parameters of a current commercial synthesizer: the OP-1. This synthesizer differs from the synthesizers previously presented in the number and the complexity of its parameters and in the number of available synthesis modules.

3. AN ALL-IN-ONE SYNTHESIZER: THE OP-1

The OP-1 is the all-in-one portable synthesizer, sampler and controller developed by Teenage Engineering (TE) [11]. TE provided us with a C++ library that embeds most of the functionalities of the OP-1. We had access to seven different synthesizer engines (FM, Digital, DrWave, String, Cluster, Pulse and Phase), four different FXs (Delay, Grid, Punch, Spring) and three different LFOs (Tremolo, Value, Element). In the following sections, the parameters selecting the engine, FX and LFO will be referred to as *type parameters*. Only one engine, one effect and one LFO can be used at a given time to produce a sound. An ADSR envelope is also always applied to the sound. Once chosen, the synthesizer engine, FX, LFO and ADSR are each controlled by 4 knobs. In the following sections, the parameters controlling the knobs will be referred to as *knob parameters*. The knob parameters are mapped to integers ranging from a minimum of 0 to a maximum of 32767, corresponding to the fine-tuning mode of the OP-1. The OP-1 has 24 physical keys and it is possible to change the octave from -4 to 4. Therefore, 120 different keys ($8 \times 12 + 24$) are available when using the OP-1. We refers as OP-1 presets a set of *knob parameters* and *type parameters*. More details about the functionalities can be found on the Teenage Engineering website [11].

Equation 1 gives the number of possible different combinations.

$$N_{\text{eng}} \times N_{\text{LFO}} \times N_{\text{FX}} \times N_{\text{k}}^{N_{\text{knobs}} \times N_{\text{t}}} \times N_{\text{key}} \quad (1)$$

where N_{eng} is the number of engines type, N_{LFO} the number of LFO types, N_{FX} the number of FX type, N_{t} the number of modules that can be controlled by knobs (engine, LFO, FX and ADSR), N_{k} the number of possible integer values for each knob and N_{key} the number of keys. Their numerical values are given in Table 1. An estimate of the total number of possible combinations for the OP-1 synthesizer is then 10^{76}.

4. AUTOMATIC CALIBRATION WITH A MULTI-OBJECTIVE GENETIC ALGORITHM

Searching the synthesizer parameters space to approximate a given target sound has all the characteristics of a real world problem. First, the search is very large (10^{76} possible different combinations). By comparison, the number of atoms in the observable universe is estimated at about 10^{80}. Second, the synthesizer is not fully determinist. The output sound can be slightly different for the same set of input parameters, which induces noise in the evaluation and can then slow down or even mislead the search. Third, there are discontinuities in the search space. For example, for a given individual, switching from an engine to another completely changes the nature of the output sound. As a result, its fitness objectives values also substantially changes causing a discontinuity in the fitness landscape. It also completely modifies the mapping of the *knob parameters*. For example, the *knob parameters* for a FM engine do not map to the same synthesis parameters than the *knobs parameters* for a Digital engine. Finally, our experiments showed that there is a large number of local minima (see Section 4.3). For instance, it is often possible to get a similar level of sound approximation using two different engines. Given these problem characteristics, it is not conceivable to use a random search or a simple optimization technique such as hill climbing or greedy algorithms to find a good set of parameters to match a given target sound. These techniques are highly dependant on the initial conditions and doesn't scale very well to large and difficult search spaces [12].

GAs are search algorithms that mimic the process of natural evolution. In a GA, a population of strings called chromosomes (which encode candidate solutions to an optimization problem) are evolved toward better solutions. GAs are especially well adapted to the characteristics of our problem. First, GAs scales very well to complex fitness landscapes [13]. Contrary to gradient search methods, they are less susceptible to converge prematurely to a local minima.

Second, GAs perform well in search space where the evaluation is approximative or noisy [14]. Adjustable selection pressure makes it possible to keep diversity in the population. A large number of individuals are evaluated for each generation. Because mutation and crossover are stochastic operators, it is common for an individual to be rediscovered several times during the evolution. The fact that the individual is re-evaluated each time it is rediscovered makes it possible to reduce the effect of the noise in the evaluation.

GAs are complex algorithms with a large set of parameters to tune (population size, stopping criteria, choice of the genetic operators...). In order to find the best configuration for the GA, we explored several options. In the following sections, we adopt the vocabulary developed by Mitchell et al. [15] and refer to the target sounds generated using the OP-1 as *Contrived sounds*. *Contrived sounds* were used as target sounds when exploring different GA configurations.

N_{eng}	N_{LFO}	N_{FX}	N_{k}	N_{knobs}	N_{t}	N_{key}
7	3	4	32767	4	4	120

Table 1. Synthesizer parameters complexity

Using these sounds as target sounds has two advantages. First, it ensures that a solution exists. Second, it is possible to easily track the performance of the algorithm because the target synthesis parameters are known.

We adopted an iterative design process and considered problems of increasing complexity. Table 2 describes these problems ordered by increasing complexity. From problem 1 to 4, we progressively added the knob parameters. In this first set of problems, we fixed the type parameters to limit the search space discontinuities. Finally, in problem 5, every type and knobs parameters were searched. At first, we limited the search to the 4 knobs controlling the engine parameters (Problem 1). We experimented with different GA configurations until we found one configuration able to either, in the best-case scenario, reverse engineer the target set of OP-1 parameters or, in the worst-case scenario, gave a perceptually satisfying approximation of the target sound. Once a satisfying GA configuration was found, the 4 knobs controlling the ADSR were added (Problem 2). The previous satisfying GA configuration was tested on the new problem. If this configuration was not satisfying anymore, we adjusted the GA parameters again until a satisfying one was found. This process was reiterated with the other problems until we obtained good performance when searching every parameter (Problem 5).

In the following subsections, we describe the final system implementation for searching all the parameters. We explain our design choices given the observations gathered during the different steps of our iterative design process.

4.1 Representation

The parameters in our synthesizer are integers. At first we decided to encode these parameters using a binary representation (which is a common choice in practice). However, our experiments using this representation on Problem 1 (see Table 2) seemed to indicate that the GA was always converging to the same local minima. Investigating further, we realized that, in order to improve the best individual fitness, 12 bits would have to be changed to go from 4095 to 4096 and improve the objective fitness values, which is very unlikely to happen. We then switched from a binary encoding to a Gray code encoding for both *type parameters* and *knob parameters*. The Gray code is based on the idea that two successive values differ by only one bit. Our experiments with this new encoding showed that the GA now converged toward the target set of parameters, thus we chose to keep this representation for our system. Our chromosome is made up of blocks representing the type and knobs parameters. The two first lines of Table 2 in bold letters show the final chromosome design.

4.2 Genetic operators

4.2.1 Crossover

Losing diversity during the evolution is a normal phenomenon given that we apply a selection pressure on the population. However, a lack of diversity can lead to premature convergence because there is not enough genetic material to explore the fitness landscape. One reason for the loss of diversity is the recombination of identical chromosomes. Indeed, when the same individual is selected twice for cross-over, two offsprings identical to this individual are produced. This phenomenon causes the diversity to go down. In order to avoid this situation, we apply a crossover operator that tests the parent chromosomes before recombining them. If they are identical, the first offspring will be a copy of the parents and the second offspring will be a new randomly generated chromosome. This simple technique is shown to be efficient in slowing down the diversity loss and prevent premature convergence [13]. Our system uses a 2-point crossover and a crossover rate of 60 %.

4.2.2 Mutation

The mutation operator participates in both exploration and exploitation (local search). Flipping one bit in a Gray code can either lead to a small change in the coded parameter (local search) or a relatively large change in the coded parameter (exploration: by jumping to another area of the fitness landscape). This flip-bit mutation operator is applied to every individual in the population whether recombined or not. In our system, the probability of flipping k bits in a N_{bits} long chromosome follows a binomial law with $p = \frac{1}{N_{\text{bits}}}$ and $n = N_{\text{bits}}$.

4.3 Fitness function

In our attempt to solve Problem 1, we used the Euclidian distance between the Short-Time Fourier Transform (STFT). The sampling rate was 44100 Hz and we set a window size of 1024 samples (23 ms) and an overlapping of 512 samples (11.5 ms). Our experiments showed that this fitness function worked well when we restricted the optimization to include only the 4 knobs which controlled the engine parameters (Problem 1).

However, when we added the 4 knobs controlling the ADSR parameters (Problem 2), the GA appeared to converge prematurely. A further investigation of this phenomenon showed that the weight of the temporal envelope in the Euclidian distance between the STFTs is significant. For example, consider a target sound T and two candidate sounds A and B. A has a similar spectrum to the spectrum of T for the first short-time windows but not for the last ones because the temporal envelope for A has a shorter release time than the one for T. Globally, the spectrum for B is not as similar to the spectrum for T but their temporal envelope is the same. The weight of these last short-time windows in the STFT distance can make B appear closer to T than A.

In this context, a right set of engine knobs parameters (A) can be discarded because the associated ADSR knobs parameters are not right. It slows down the evolution because some good genetic material is lost. It can even lead to a premature convergence if this set of engine knobs parameters is never recovered again later in the evolution.

It is not surprising that, in previous work [3, 5], the envelope was determined analytically for each individual in the population, however it is not possible to do this in our case because we do not know the mapping between the ADSR knob parameters and the resulting temporal envelope. Indeed, performing a local search to set the ADSR knobs parameters for each individual in the population would be too computationally expensive. Furthermore, given the non deterministic nature of our synthesizer, any classic local search algorithm such as greedy algorithm or hill climbing would likely fail because the noise in the evaluation would mislead the search.

Pb. Id	Engine		FX		Key / Octave	LFO		ADSR	N_{bits}
	Type	Knobs	Type	Knobs		Type	Knobs	Knobs	
1		X							60
2		X						X	120
3		X		X				X	180
4		X		X			X	X	240
5	X	X	X	X	X	X	X	X	257

Table 2. Problem descriptions

In order to avoid the premature convergence observed with Problem 2, we decided to uncouple the temporal envelope from the spectral components as much as possible. Thus, we chose to extract two separate sound features: 1) the FFT computed on the entire sound; and 2) the temporal envelope. Computing the FFT on the entire sound mitigates, to some extent, the effect of the temporal envelope on the spectrum. We extracted the temporal envelope using the Hilbert transform followed by a low-pass filter.

Our first idea was to put these two sound features in an aggregate fitness function (see Eq. (2)). However, it is difficult to choose the appropriate weights for the temporal envelope a_{env} and the FFT a_{FFT} to make the system converge.

$$f = \frac{a_{\mathrm{env}} f_{\mathrm{env}} + a_{\mathrm{FFT}} f_{\mathrm{FFT}}}{a_{\mathrm{env}} + a_{\mathrm{FFT}}} \quad (2)$$

Therefore, we chose to consider two objectives: FFT and temporal envelope instead of only one: the STFT. We implemented this new 2-objectives fitness function in a multi-objective framework, the Non-dominated-Sorting-Genetic-Algorithm-II. The experiments showed that this new system converged to the target set of parameters for Problem 2.

However, when we added the 4 knobs controlling the LFO or FX (Problem 3-4), our system was converging prematurely again. The explanation was that the addition of a LFO or FX made the spectrum of the target sound non-stationary. The FFT on the entire length of the sound was not able to capture the variation of the spectrum over time. In order to deal with this limitation, we added back the STFT as a third objective. Contrary to simple GA, the NSGA-II uses a selection operator based on non-domination sorting. Therefore, contrary to the simple GA using STFT as fitness function, an individual with a good set of engine knobs parameters would be more likely kept in the population even if it has wrong ADSR knobs parameters. Indeed, this individual would have a high fitness value for the FFT and a low fitness value for the envelope. It would be then kept in the population because it is dominating the population according to the FFT objective. In the simple GA, this individual would likely be discarded because its fitness value would be affected by a wrong temporal envelope.

4.4 Selection

Our system is based on a Non-dominated Sorting Genetic Algorithm II (NSGA-II). Details about this algorithm can be found in Deb's work [16]. The principal features of this algorithm are the following:

- *Elitism:* This property prevents the loss of good solutions once they are found by insuring that the fittest members of the population are kept in future generations.
- *Non-dominated sorting:* An individual is said to be non-dominated if there is no other individual that performs better for at least one of the objectives without performing worse for the remaining objectives. This principle is used to sort the population into non-dominated sets that are then used to form the next generation.
- *Diversity preservation:* The crowding distance is a measure of how close an individual is to its neighbours. A crowded-comparison operator guides the selection process at the various stages of the algorithm toward a uniformly spread-out Pareto front.

Our system uses a population of 500 individuals for each generation. This number of individuals was empirically determined as a good trade-off between performance and computational cost.

4.5 Stopping criteria

The optimization process terminates if the weighted change in the 3 objective fitness, given by Eq. (3), is less than 10^{-30} over 200 generations. δ_{n} is the weighted change at generation n, f_{k} is the best objective fitness score at generation k, N = 200 if $n \geq 200$ otherwise $N = n$. If this condition is never verified, the optimization process stops after 3000 generations.

$$\delta_{\mathrm{n}} = \sum_{i=1}^{N} \left(\frac{1}{2}\right)^{i-1} (f_{\mathrm{n+1-i}} - f_{\mathrm{n-i}}), \quad (3)$$

4.6 Pareto front

The Pareto front is the set of non dominated individuals for the 3 objectives.

4.6.1 Similarity rule

In our first experiments, the Pareto front was very large at the end of the evolution (more than 2000 individuals). Upon closer examination, we realized that strictly identical individuals were present in the Pareto front. This was due to the fact that the synthesizer is not fully deterministic and the non-domination, crowding selection is only made on objective fitnesses. We then added a similarity rule that tests whether the chromosome of an individual is already present before adding it to the Pareto front. This simple rule made it possible to cut the size of the final Pareto front by a factor of more than 2.

However, the size was still too large (around 1000 individuals) to be easily analyzed by a user. Further investigating the Pareto front, we realized that a large number of individuals sounded perceptually identical even if they were produced using different sets of parameters. In order to limit this kind of duplicate individuals in the Pareto front, we refined the similarity rule. We stated that 2 individuals are considered identical if they have the same engine/LFO/FX types, identical key/octave and the Euclidian distance between the knob parameters is less than 1000 (3 % of the knob parameter range). This value was defined by making tests on a large numbers of Pareto fronts. Depending on the target sound, this last change made it possible to reduce the size of the Pareto front to between 10 and 150 individuals while conserving its quality and diversity.

4.6.2 Post processing

A number of 150 individuals in the Pareto front is still very large to be handled by a user. We applied a technique developed by Chaudhari et al. [17] to select the most significant individuals in the Pareto front when its size is superior to 10 individuals. This approach consists of the following steps:

1. Apply a k-means clustering algorithm to cluster on the solutions enclosed in the Pareto set. The clustering is done on the OP-1 parameters because our goal is to help the user to identify different good OP-1 presets in the Pareto front, for example using different sound engines.

2. Determine the optimal number of clusters, k. The silhouette of an individual is a measure of how closely it is matched to other individuals within its cluster and how loosely it is matched to individuals of the neighbouring cluster. A silhouette $s(i)$ close to 1 implies that the individual i is in an appropriate cluster, while $s(i)$ close to -1 implies that i is in the wrong cluster. Thus the average $s(i)$ of the entire Pareto Front is a measure of how appropriately the Pareto Front has been clustered. A value of the average silhouette is obtained for several values of k with $k < 10$. The k that gives the highest average silhouette width is selected.

3. For each cluster, select a representative solution. For each cluster, the individual, within the cluster, that encodes the OP-1 presets that is the closest to the cluster centroid presets is selected as the representative solution.

4. Analyze the results. At this point, the user can analyze the k representative solutions of the clusters and then explore the individuals of the cluster that seems the most promising.

4.7 Full problem complexity

In Problem 5, we add the type parameters. These extra parameters to search induces discontinuities in the fitness landscape (see Section 4). However, our experiments show that adding the type parameters to the search (Problem 5) do not diminish the final solution quality when we compare them to final solutions found for Problem 4. The *right* type parameters are determined in early generations and become prominent in later generations. The evolution continues then as if it would be Problem 4 being solved. This phenomenon is induced by the selection pressure and mimics very well the behaviour of a human asked to perform the same task. One would broadly explore the possibilities of the synthesizer and quickly select an engine and key, after which one would fine tune the knob parameters. Another explanation to this phenomenon is that the chromosome size is not very different between problems 4 and 5 (240 bits against 257 bits) because every type parameters has a small range compared to the knobs (see Section 3).

4.8 Implementation

The implementation of the GA is done using the DEAP Python framework [18]. Sound features are extracted using the Python wrapper for Yaafe [19]. Yaafe is coded in C++ and has the advantage of being fast and memory-efficient. In our current implementation, the time to evaluate the 3 objectives for a 1 second-long mono sound sampled at 44100Hz is in average 314 milliseconds (SD= 1ms).

The bottlenecks of our algorithm are the fitness evaluation and the NSGA-II selection operator. The fitness evaluation is distributed between 100 processors on a supercomputer [20] to speed up the computation. It also make it possible to use larger populations than would have been feasible using only one processor for the same running time. We use the DEAP C++ version of the NSGA-II selection operator to further speed up our algorithm. In our current implementation, applying the genetic operator (crossover, mutation, selection) for a population of 500 individuals takes in average 243 milliseconds (SD=4 ms). The total computing time for a run is in average 34 min (SD=4min).

5. EVALUATION

We based our evaluation design on Johnson's recommendation about experimental analysis of algorithms [21]. We especially focused on ensuring reproducibility and comparability.

5.1 Sound collection

5.1.1 Contrived sounds

Using *contrived sounds* as target sounds allows us to validate our system design. It makes possible to show that our system is able to reverse engineer a given target sound generated by the OP-1.

Given the complexity of the algorithm and its running time, we chose to limit our evaluation to 12 contrived sounds. We selected these sounds in order to have a sample of spectrums that was diverse and representative of the the OP-1 possible outputs. We especially focused on having diversity in spectral variation, noisiness and spectral spread. The first half of the sounds has a stationary spectrum and the other half has a non-stationary spectrum, as measured by their respective spectral flux.

We made sure that we used each engine, LFO and FX at least once to generate this set of sounds. These contrived sounds are available to listen online [8].

5.1.2 Other sounds

A second evaluation was performed on 12 non-contrived sounds including synthetic sounds (DX-7 synthesizer, Moog synthesizer, lightsaber sound), instrument sounds (Violin, flute, bassoon, snare), a male voice sound and a natural sound (Cat meow). These sounds were carefully chosen to have a good diversity in spectral variation, noisiness and spectral spread.

5.2 Measurement

In these evaluations, we evaluated the solution quality and the running time.

The solution quality was measured differently for the contrived sounds and for the non-contrived sounds. For the contrived sounds, we already know what are the target OP-1 presets. In addition to the target sound, we generate ten other sounds using the target presets and compare them to the target sound. With a determinist synthesizer, their objective fitness values (FFT, envelope and STFT) would be equals to zero but it is not the case with the OP-1. We define the best possible objectives values as the minima of the 3 objectives fitness values over these 10 sounds. We calculate the relative error for each run subtracting these best possible objective values to the best objectives fitness values obtained in the particular run. For the non-contrived sounds, we are only able to measure the final fitness values for the 3 objectives at the end of the evolution. The running times are measured by the number of generations before the GA reaches the stopping criteria ($nbGen$).

5.3 Analysis

We ran the algorithm at least 10 times for each target sound. We used Bootstrapping to obtain estimates of summary statistics [21]. This method involves taking the original data set of size N, and sampling from it with replacement to form a new sample, called a bootstrap sample, that is also of size N and that is not identical to the original sample. This process is repeated a large number of times (1000 in our case) and for each of these bootstrap samples we compute the desired statistic. This provides an estimate of the distribution of the desired statistic. Questions about how this statistic varies or the standard error for this statistic can now be answered. This technique makes possible the extraction of more useful information when the sampling size is small, as is the case in our experiments due to the time complexity of the problem.

For each of the measures described above, we used Bootstrapping to get an estimate of its minimum, maximum, mean and standard deviation. We also used the bootstrap shift method test [21] to assess the significance of every comparison we performed. This test has the advantage of being distribution-free and of scaling well with small sample size.

6. RESULTS

Our experimental results for contrived sounds and non-contrived sounds are available online [8].

6.1 Contrived sounds

6.1.1 Module types selection

Table 3 describes some statistics about the proportion of module types in the population over the various generations. Prop. choice is the proportion of runs where one type was totally taking over in the population. Accuracy is the proportion of runs choosing the correct type when one type was taking over in the population. The Take over gen is the generation as from one type was taking over. Our results suggested that our system performed well at finding the right engine type (90 % prop. choice; 80 % accurate) and the right key/octave (77 % and 91 % prop. choice; 52% and 62% accurate). However, it was not the case for the LFO (43 % prop. choice; 22 % accurate) and FX type (42 % prop. choice; 18 % accurate). A possible interpretation of these results is that the engine type and key/octave have a greater influence on the output sound than the LFO or FX type. The LFO and FX type do not change the nature of the output sound but only alter it. It is then more challenging to determine the right type for the FX and LFO.

6.1.2 Pareto front

The number of different module combinations was very low in the Pareto front (μ = 3.0, SD = 0.2 over 10 080 possible combinations). These findings suggested that the GA successfully identified a limited number of promising locations in the parameter space that dominate all others. When listening to the sounds in the Pareto front, one can distinguish several clusters of perceptually similar sounds. Each of these clusters sounds perceptually similar to the target sound but the OP-1 presets it represents are sensibly different between clusters. A Pareto front affords more flexibility to the user who receives a set of similar sounds rather than a single sound with a simple GA. The user can then make the final choice.

Our system approximates very well the temporal envelope of the target sound as shown by the very low relative errors for the envelope objective (μ = 0.20, SD = 0.02). Figure 1 shows the relative error over the best possible FFT and STFT objectives values. As measured by their respective spectral flux, conf0, conf2, conf3, conf5, conf7 and conf10 are the configurations generating non-stationary spectra. The other configurations are generating stationary spectra. We see that the performances of the GA are not significantly better for the target sounds with stationary spectra than for the target sounds with non-stationary spectra; $p = 0.07$, $p = 0.08$. However, we can still observe differences in the GA performances for different groups of target sounds. A first group with negative relative errors (conf2, conf7, conf9) contains the OP-1 target configurations that are the most non-deterministic. Indeed, in this non-determinist context, the best possible objective fitness values are very difficult to determine precisely. Then, it is possible that the GA finds an OP-1 presets outperforming the best possible objective fitness values, resulting in a negative relative error. These negative relative errors induces a bias when comparing the performances of our system for target sound with stationary spectrum and with non-stationary spectrum. A second group (conf4, conf6, conf8, conf10 and conf11) contains mostly

	Prop. choice		Take over gen		Accu.
	C	NC	C	NC	C
Engine	0.90	0.74	139	129	0.80
FX	0.42	0.44	322	270	0.18
LFO	0.43	0.45	240	317	0.22
Key	0.77	0.38	122	265	0.52
Octave	0.91	0.57	109	174	0.62

Table 3. Statistics about modules types. C: Contrived sounds, NC: Non-contrived sounds, Accu.: Accuracy

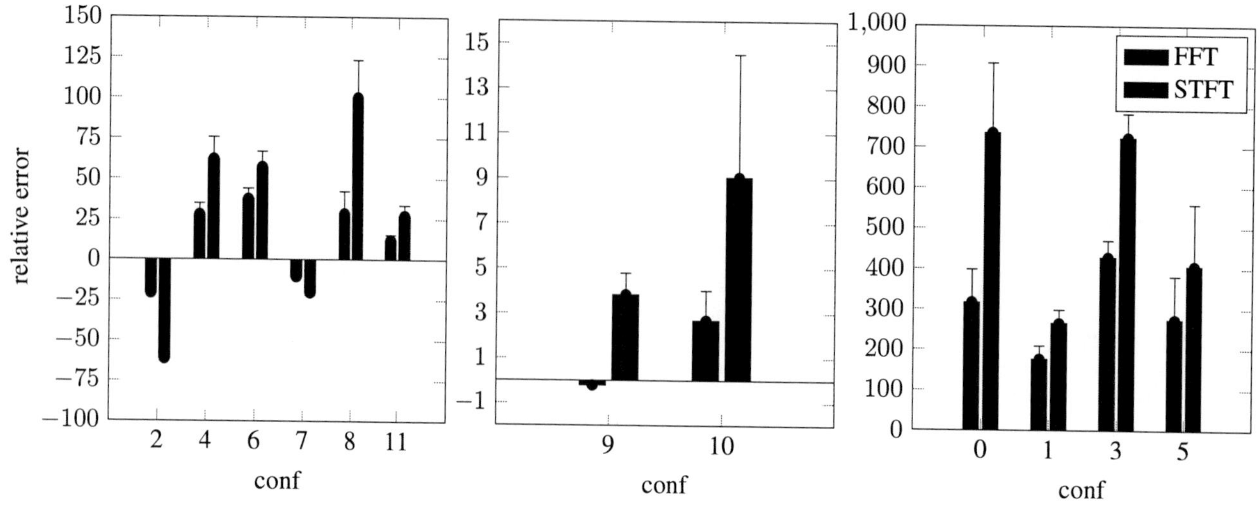

Figure 1. Objectives' relative error

target sounds with stationary spectrum at the exception of conf10. Our system is performing the best for this group as indicated by a very small relative error compared to the other groups. Conf10 presents a STFT under the form of a sawtooth wave over time. This common shape doesn't seem to be difficult to approximate for our system even if the spectrum is non-stationary. The last group (conf0, conf1, conf3, conf5) contains mostly target sounds with non-stationary spectra at the exception of conf1. The relative error for this group is the highest. The spectral energy of conf1 is mainly concentrated in a narrow frequency band. Our system seems to fall into a local minima for this particular kind of spectrum.

6.2 Non-contrived sounds

It is more challenging to evaluate the results of the non-contrived sounds experiments because we do not have any target parameters or parameter distances to refer to. Even if our system has shown good average performances for contrived sounds, it does not automatically mean that it would be good for non-contrived sounds. Indeed, the structure and complexity of the fitness landscape depends largely on the chosen target sound.

6.2.1 Number of generations to converge

The mean of *nbGen* was significantly superior for the contrived sounds (μ = 1431, SD = 86) than for the non-contrived sounds (μ = 1070, SD = 50); $p < 0.001$. This results may seem surprising as the resynthesis problem for a non-contrived sound is more complex than for a contrived sound.

	FFT		Env.		STFT	
	μ	SD	μ	SD	μ	SD
C	130.3	17.2	0.20	0.02	249.0	31.2
NC	3163.5	242.7	8.7	0.78	4299.5	262.6

Table 4. Objective best fitness values. C: Contrived sounds, NC: Non-contrived sounds

6.2.2 Module types selection

Table 3 describes some statistics about the proportion of module types in the population through the generations. As with contrived sounds, an engine was quickly taking over. However, contrary to the experiments with contrived sounds, no key was clearly taking over (Prop choice 38 % against 77 % for contrived sounds). It could be explained by the fact that most of the non-contrived sounds do not have a clearly identified pitch (cat meow, DX-7 and Moog synthesizer sounds with pitch modulation). FX and LFO types were, as with contrived sounds, still challenging to set for the GA (FX prop. choice 44 %, LFO prop choice 45 %).

6.2.3 Pareto front

First, we could hear that the Pareto front sounds were perceptually similar to the targets, which is of importance for real world applications. The Pareto fronts were also significantly more diverse (μ = 4.3, SD = 0.3) than the ones we got using contrived target sounds (μ = 3.0, SD = 0.2); $p < 0.001$. They were also significantly more populated (μ = 306, SD = 11; μ = 83, SD = 21); $p < 0.001$. These differences can be explained by a larger problem complexity and also by the fact that, at the difference with contrived target sounds, the existence of a OP-1 presets that would perfectly approximate the target sound is not insured anymore. In other words, there is no guaranteed global optimum, and likely many more local optima. With the concept of Pareto front, the user receive a set of OP-1 presets that produces sounds perceptually similar to the target sound. These OP-1 presets do not involve automatically the use of the same engine, LFO or FX, which gives the users several alternatives of variable quality to approximate a given target sound.

The objective best values for the 3 objectives, shown in Table 4, were, as expected, significantly worse for the non-contrived sounds than for the contrived sounds ($p < 0.001$, $p < 0.001$, $p < 0.001$).

7. CONCLUSIONS AND FUTURE WORKS

We developed an algorithm to automatically tune the parameters of a multi-engine synthesizer in order to reproduce a given target sound. We described the iterative design process that lead us to consider a multi-objective approach and to use a custom Non-dominated Sorting Genetic Algorithm-II to tackle this problem. This new approach gives more flexibility to the user who receives a set of presets rather than only one preset as with previous systems. An experimental study has been conducted to assess the performances and limitations of our system. Contrived and non-contrived sounds have been considered in this study. We showed that our system is able to explore a complex parameter space in order to find configurations producing sounds perceptually similar to the target. Disparities in performances have been highlighted with the system performing better for target sounds with stationary spectrum than for sounds with non-stationary spectrum. The comparisons between the system performances for non-contrived sounds and contrived sounds confirmed even more that the complexity of the re-synthesis problem are highly variable given the nature of the target sound. Future works will entail taking into account the characteristic of the target sound to adapt the parameters of our GA system using, for example, some sound pre-processing analysis and machine learning.

Acknowledgments

This research was funded by a grant from the Canada Council for the Arts, and the Natural Sciences and Engineering Research Council of Canada. We would like to thank Teenage Engineering for their collaboration and support. Special thanks goes to Laurent Droguet from IRCAM and Dr. Corey Kereliuk from McGill university.

8. REFERENCES

[1] S. Chan, J. Yuen, and A. Horner, "Discrete summation synthesis and hybrid sampling-wavetable synthesis of acoustic instruments with genetic algorithms," in *Proc. of the International Computer Music Conference (ICMC)*, 1996, pp. 49–51.

[2] A. Horner and J. Beauchamp, "Piecewise-linear approximation of additive synthesis envelopes: a comparison of various methods," *Computer Music Journal*, vol. 20, no. 2, pp. 72–95, 1996.

[3] A. Horner, J. Beauchamp, and L. Haken, "Machine Tongues XVI: Genetic Algorithms and Their Application to FM Matching Synthesis," *Computer Music Journal*, vol. 17, no. 4, pp. 17–29, 1993.

[4] M. Yee-King and M. Roth, "Synthbot: An unsupervised software synthesizer programmer," *Proc. of ICMC, Belfast, N. Ireland*, 2008.

[5] M. Macret, P. Pasquier, and T. Smyth, "Automatic Calibration of Modified FM Synthesis to Harmonic Sounds using Genetic Algorithms," in *Proc. of Sound and Music Computing Conference (SMC)*, 2012, pp. 387–394.

[6] J. Vuori and V. Välimäki, "Parameter estimation of non-linear physical models by simulated evolution-application to the flute model," in *Proc. of ICMC*, 1993, pp. 402–410.

[7] B. Bozkurt and K. Yüksel, "Parallel evolutionary optimization of digital sound synthesis parameters," *Appli. of Evolutionary Computation*, pp. 194–203, 2011.

[8] "Experimental results," last accessed: June 2013. [Online]. Available: http://metacreation.net/mmacret/SMC2013/

[9] G. Wakefield and E. Mrozek, "Perceptual matching of low-order models to room transfer functions," in *Proc. of ICMC*, 1996, pp. 111–113.

[10] T. Mitchell, "Automated evolutionary synthesis matching," *Soft Computing-A Fusion of Foundations, Methodologies and Applications*, pp. 1–14, 2012.

[11] "Teenage engineering website," last accessed: March 2013. [Online]. Available: http://www.teenageengineering.com/

[12] M. Roth and M. Yee-King, "A comparison of parametric optimization techniques for musical instrument tone matching," in *Proc. of Audio Engineering Society Convention*, 2011, pp. 18–26.

[13] M. Rocha and J. Neves, "Preventing premature convergence to local optima in genetic algorithms via random offspring generation," in *Multiple Approaches to Intelligent Systems*. Springer, 1999, pp. 127–136.

[14] Y. Jin and J. Branke, "Evolutionary optimization in uncertain environments: a survey," *IEEE Evolutionary Computation*, vol. 9, no. 3, pp. 303–317, 2005.

[15] T. J. Mitchell and D. P. Creasey, "Evolutionary sound matching: A test methodology and comparative study," in *International Conference on Machine Learning and Applications*. IEEE, 2007, pp. 229–234.

[16] K. Deb, A. Pratap, S. Agarwal, and T. Meyarivan, "A fast and elitist multiobjective genetic algorithm: NSGA-II," *IEEE Evolutionary Computation*, vol. 6, no. 2, pp. 182–197, 2002.

[17] M. P. Chaudhari, R. VDharaskar, and V. Thakare, "Computing the Most Significant Solution from Pareto Front obtained in Multi-objective Evolutionary," *International Journal of Advanced Computer Science and Applications*, pp. 63–68, 2010.

[18] F.-A. Fortin, F.-M. D. Rainville, M.-A. Gardner, M. Parizeau, and C. Gagné, "DEAP: Evolutionary algorithms made easy," *Journal of Machine Learning Research*, vol. 13, pp. 2171–2175, jul 2012.

[19] B. Mathieu, S. Essid, T. Fillon, J. Prado, and G. Richard, "Yaafe, an easy to use and efficient audio feature extraction software," in *ISMIR*, 2010.

[20] "Westgrid - Compute Canada," last accessed: June 2013. [Online]. Available: http://www.westgrid.ca/

[21] D. S. Johnson, "A theoreticians guide to the experimental analysis of algorithms," *Data structures, near neighbor searches, and methodology: 5th and 6th dimacs implementation challenges*, vol. 59, pp. 215–250, 2002.

An Open-source Framework for Time-domain Simulations

Clemens Bernhard Geyer
IWK - University of Music and Performing Arts Vienna
clemens.geyer@gmail.com

Wilfried Kausel
IWK - University of Music and Performing Arts Vienna
kausel@mdw.ac.at

ABSTRACT

In scientific research simulation of new or existing acoustical models is typically implemented using commercial numerical programming environments like Simulink/Matlab or expensive simulation packages like COMSOL or FLUENT. In this paper a new version of the open-source simulation library ART (Acoustic Research Tool) is presented where time-domain simulation capabilities have now been added to existing frequency domain models. The concept allows mixing of modeling elements belonging to different levels of abstraction and it relieves the user from tricky implementation details like scheduling, data dependencies and memory allocation. Starting with an equation in the z-Domain, signals can be described recursively as a function of other current or previous signal samples and local or global simulation parameters. Alternatively signals can also be generated by specifying a certain topology of predefined elements with certain input and output ports. The library can be called from any programming environment running on Microsoft Windows or on Linux which allows it to be integrated in any application software project. The examples shown here have been written in the open-source high-level programming language Python. They can be downloaded together with the library and documentation from the project site http://artool.sourceforge.net.

1. INTRODUCTION

The simulation and verification of acoustical models is usually done in commercial environments like Simulink/Matlab or implemented in a high-level programming language such as Java or Python. However, none of these tools perfectly fulfill the requirements of acoustical simulations, namely easy usage and extensibility. The Acoustic Research Tool, abbreviated *ART* was originally developed as an open-source library for frequency-domain simulations of acoustical models, see [1]. In 2012, ART was extended in order to allow users the possibility to do any kind of time-domain simulation. Although the focus of course lies on acoustical models, the implemented architecture provides the functionality of implementing any kind of signal processing in the time-domain.

The structure of this paper is the following: Section 2 presents a short overview of the history of ART and the previously existing features which could be reused for time-domain simulations. In Section 3, the overall architecture of the new simulator as well as some internal data structures are explained. Moreover, it gives an overview of the implemented acoustical models which are available in the simulation library. Two examples are presented in Section 4, one using modules from the previously mentioned library, the other showing the flexibility of ART to simulate acoustical models which are not available in the current library by the usage of generic time modules.

2. OVERVIEW OF ART

2.1 History of ART

ART is a platform-independent open-source library which provides users the ability to simulate existing models in the frequency-domain and to implement custom elements which can be added to the simulation. It was initiated by Wilfried Kausel in 2005 and has been under development since then. Over the last years, several contributors have added new simulation methods and optimized the simulation process. However, ART only covered frequency-domain simulations and thus only allowed to calculate impedances of musical instruments, but no sound synthesis.

During 2012, ART was extended in order to enable time-domain simulations for sound-synthesis and acoustical model simulation. Generally speaking, models in the time-domain can be based on any discrete signal or function and are thus not restricted to specific building blocks such as finite impulse response (FIR) filters. Consequently, an open approach had to be chosen giving users a means to make simulations on existing models and functions, but also implement their own time models without the need of recompiling any source code. ART is implemented in ANSI C++ and can be compiled with either commercial (e.g., MS Visual Studio) or open-source (e.g., GNU Compiler Collection) compilers on any platform. The output is either an executable or a dynamic library which allows the integration of ART into nearly all common high-level programming languages (current examples on the homepage make use of Delphi and Python).

2.2 Comparison to other Simulation Environments

Simulations of acoustical circuits are usually done in high level programming languages or simulation environments such as Matlab/Simulink, Python or C++. Moreover, there also exist several other scientific open-source projects like FAUST (Functional Audio Stream, [2]) or EIN as presented by Lansky and Steiglitz in [3]. In [4], Rabenstein et al. present a simulation approach, which is very similar to the one implemented by ART. They also use generic physical blocks with input and output ports and present a solution for the automatic dependency calculation.

ART is currently in an early development stage and not using any optimizations when compiled. Therefore, any comparison between the performance of ART with professional simulation environments like Matlab cannot seriously be conducted. It provides a library of well-known acoustical models in the frequency as well as in the time domain and can easily be integrated in every other high-level programming language. Thus, ART should not be seen as an alternative but rather an addition to traditional simulation environments because the user can focus on the physical model without the need of learning a new programming language or low-level programming.

2.3 Existing Simulation Framework

The previous version of ART already provided a set of functionality which could be reused for the implementation of time-domain simulations. First of all, *muParserX* [5], an open-source parsing library which provides a subset of Matlab or GNU Octave, was integrated into ART to set values of several simulation variables. Although not all of the features of the parser were extensively used, it made value assignments for variables much more flexible. For example, assignment expressions could contain complex mathematical formulas and even reference values of other variables.

The second important feature implemented in the frequency domain simulation was the creation of a *dependency graph* which is responsible for the following two points:

(1) Checking for circular variable or expression references
(2) Intelligent evaluation of expressions

Both functionalities may be easily demonstrated with an example: Assuming we want to calculate the wavelength of a given frequency, but also take the current temperature into account. Wavelength λ is based on the speed of sound c and frequency f:

$$\lambda = \frac{c}{f} \tag{1}$$

The speed of sound c depends on temperature T (in Celsius) as described in the following equation (see Equation(16) in [6]):

$$c \cong 20.06 \cdot \sqrt{T + 273.15} \tag{2}$$

If temperature T changes, the speed of sound and therefore also the wavelength have to be recalculated. ART therefore builds the previously mentioned dependency graph as shown in Figure 1 in order to efficiently evaluate expressions: If any of the variables gets assigned a new value or a new calculation expression, all dependent variables will be set invalid and reevaluated the next time the value is needed. This graph also detects cyclic dependencies, e.g., when c was defined by

$$c = \frac{\lambda}{f} \tag{3}$$

instead of Equation (1). When ART is triggered to evaluate λ, it will first try to calculate c. However, in order to get the value of c, λ has to be evaluated, thus resulting in an indefinite loop. ART automatically throws an exception any time such a cyclic dependency occurs during an evaluation. This is implemented by a simple flag which is set before the beginning of the evaluation and cleared after the value assignment has completed. Whenever ART tries to evaluate a variable with this flag set, a circular dependency has occurred.

ART also implements basic error handling, e.g., when there is a syntax error for an expression. The exception thrown by *muParserX* will be handled by ART and the error message passed to the calling function. The same is true for some exceptions specific to ART, e.g., the previously mentioned circular dependency. It is expected to improve the error-handling in future releases in order to simplify the debugging process for the user.

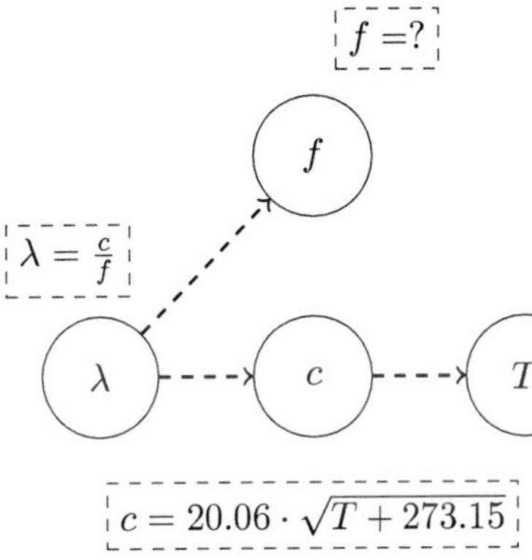

Figure 1. Dependency graph of wavelength variable λ.

3. IMPLEMENTATION OF TIME-DOMAIN SIMULATIONS

The previous section described the provided features by ART for frequency-domain simulations. Although these functions are quite useful for all kinds of simulations, time-domain simulations require additional data types and adaptions of existing interfaces and methods. This section first gives an overview of the newly implemented architecture in the time domain. After that, the two main functions to enable efficient simulations are discussed, namely resizable ring buffers and an easy-to-use convolution function. At the end of the section, the current state of implemented time-domain modules is shortly presented.

3.1 Architectural Overview of Time-domain Modules

A time-domain simulation consists of global parameters such as the sampling period T and several modules. These are added to the simulator and can be connected to each other. Figure 2 shows the template of such a time-domain module: It has a unique name, has the ability to save local parameters and consists of a number of input and output ports. Output ports save the prescribed calculation expression and may reference any global or local parameters as well as input and output ports of the current time module. Input ports only reference to output ports of other time-domain modules, but do not implement any calculations. Note that each output port cannot only access past time values from other input and output ports of the same module, but also past time values of itself (i.e., a difference equation) like it is the case for infinite impulse response (IIR) filters.

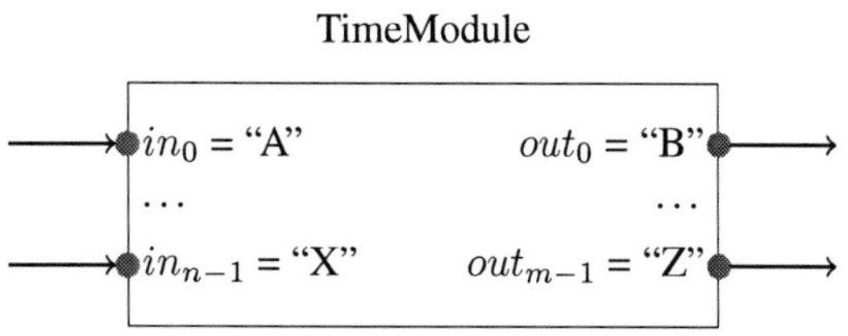

Figure 2. Basic idea of the time module concept: Each time module has a unique name, n input and m output ports. The time module may be seen as a black box – the calculation details of the ports are hidden from the user.

The generic black box is a template for any time-domain module and is implemented as an interface. It provides access to read out the current value of the output ports, associate input ports with output ports of other time modules and set local parameters. All modules can access global simulation parameters which opens the door to change usually fixed input values like the sound velocity during a simulation without much effort.

3.2 Resizable Ring Buffers and Convolution

As already mentioned, output ports may access a time step of any other port of its own module as long as this time step is not in the future. The naive way of implementing this functionality is to provide an array consisting of enough elements to save all values for the complete simulation. When simulating only 10 seconds for a sampling rate of 44.1 kHz including several modules with multiple input and output ports may thus quickly result in shortage of memory. A common solution to solve this problem is to use ring buffers as shown in Figure 3. As most acoustical models in the time-domain do not require filters of high order, a ring buffer with 10 to 20 elements will fit for usual applications and thus highly reduce memory usage.

However, some applications even require an automatic resizing of the ring-buffer. This is the case, e.g., for the discrete convolution which is commonly used in digital signal processing and defined by

$$y[t] = \sum_{k=-\infty}^{\infty} u[k] \cdot g[t-k] = \sum_{k=-\infty}^{\infty} u[t-k] \cdot g[t]. \quad (4)$$

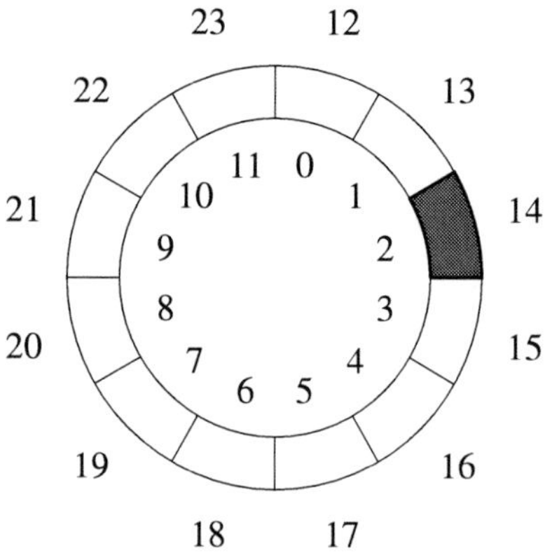

Figure 3. Accessing an element of a ring buffer of size 12: The inner circle shows the elements from index 0 to 11, whereas the outer circle starts from 12 and ends with 23. When accessing the 14th element, the ring buffer in fact returns element number $14 \bmod 12 = 2$.

Assuming that $g[t]$ is a finite transfer function with a fixed number of elements, the user usually has to make sure that the input function $u[t]$ consists of at least the same number of elements as $g[t]$. In case $u[t]$ will be convoluted with multiple transfer functions, the number of needed buffer elements is not easily determined and a common source of mistakes. In ART, this problem was solved with a resizable ring buffer which automatically increments the buffer size of an input function if the number of unused elements gets near a defined threshold. Consequently, the user only needs to define the correct mathematical model and does not need to deal with any implementation details. The description of the resize function of the ring buffer and the internal implementation of the convolution function can be found in [7].

3.3 Time-domain Module Library

One target of the time-domain simulator in ART was to provide a generic simulation library for any kind of discrete signal processing, not only limited to acoustical applications. [1] This is the reason why in the current version three types of modules have been implemented:

(1) General-purpose signal processing modules
(2) Digital Waveguide (DWG) modules of common acoustical elements
(3) Generic time module

The first type of modules covers simple mathematical functions like adding two input signals or a signal generating module for a single impulse or sine wave. The advantage of this kind of modules is that the user does not need to implement this modules on his or her own and they automatically generate proper signals for the globally defined sampling rate. For example, the sine wave module has three local parameters which can be set by the user:

[1] Note that there is no general rule about how acoustical models look like. In contrary, they are based on mathematical models of other disciplines like electrical engineering or mechanics.

amplitude, frequency (in Hz) and a phase delay given in seconds.

The second type of modules covers DWGs for cylindrical and conical bores as well as cylindrical and conical junctions as first presented in [8] and later evaluated, e.g., in [9]. However, ART currently does not provide any models which take viscothermal losses into account. The cylindrical bore module is based on a fractional delay filter – the user just has to specify the length the cylinder and the type of interpolation filter, namely Thiran or Lagrange. ART automatically calculates the correct filter parameters based on the selected type, the current sampling rate and the specified sound velocity. [2] Both types of fractional delay filters including stability considerations are presented in [10]. The cylindrical junction module is used to simulate wave scattering effects between any two cylindrical bores with different radii.

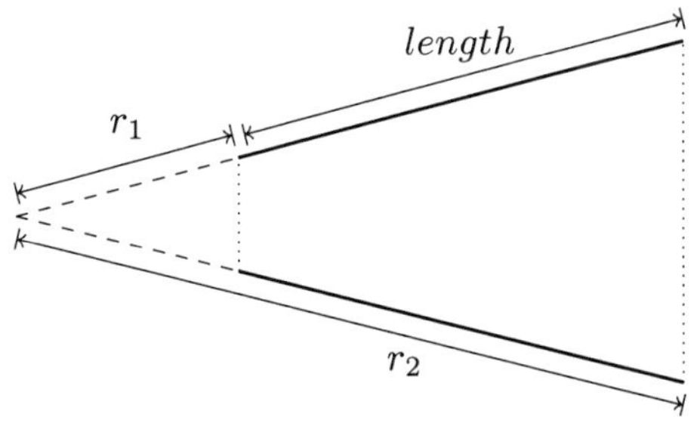

Figure 4. Parameter overview of the DWG cone module. The user has to provide both cone apex radii r_1 and r_2 whereas the $length$ parameter will be automatically calculated by ART.

The conical modules are more complex as they usually include the calculation of the cone apex radii as can be seen in Figure 4. Therefore, ART provides an alternative way of specifying the parameters of the cone as bore profile (radius on the left end, radius on the right end and length of the cone), see Figure 5. Like the cylindrical junction module, the conical junction module calculates the wave scattering between two cones or a cone and a cylinder with different radii. [3] Again, the user has two different ways of specifying the parameters, one with the cone apex radii and the spherical area of both cones at the junction, the other with the left and right radius as well as the length of the conical bores at the left and right side of the junction. Section 4.3 will present a small simulation with nearly all of the described DWG modules.

So far, the user could only refer to pre-implemented modules and only had little possibility to individualize them. This is the reason why the third type of modules has been introduced: The generic time module allows the user to create new input and output ports and define calculation

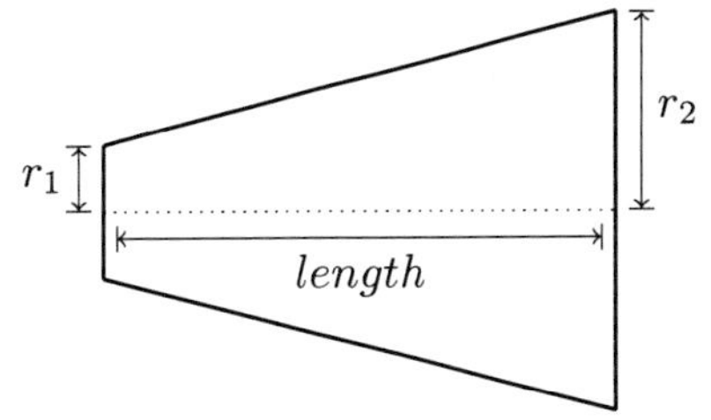

Figure 5. Alternative parameter specification of the cone module based on the left radius r_1, the right radius r_2 and the length of the cone $length$.

expression for them. They fully integrate with all other modules, but are more flexible and can even be used to solve difference equations or discretized differential equations.

All presented modules can be created by using the interface of ART without the need of re-compiling the library or implementing C++ code. However, the architecture of ART also allows other programmers to easily integrate new modules to the existing ones, giving them the full power of object oriented programming concepts. It is a future goal to engage other scientists to implement other acoustical models (e.g., Wave Digital Filters) and make them available to the users of ART.

4. EXAMPLES

This section gives an overview of the flexibility of ART and demonstrates how it eases the simulation in case of pre-implemented modules. Note that the focus lies on the implementation of the simulation in ART and not the mathematical theory which is presented in detail in the given literature.

4.1 Fibonacci Numbers

Although the Fibonacci numbers are no physical model, they are a good means of demonstrating the power and flexibility of ART. The standard definition of the Fibonacci numbers is given by

$$f_n = f_{n-1} + f_{n-2} \tag{5}$$

meaning that the current element is the sum of the previous two elements. Moreover, the most common definition sets the first element to zero and the second to one:

$$f_1 = 0,\ f_2 = 1 \tag{6}$$

For linear recursion equations like the Fibonacci numbers, there is an explicit formula to calculate an element without the need of knowing all previous elements. However, like for some types of non-linear differential equations, it is not always possible to find an explicit solution for a general (non-linear) difference equation. Thus, it is necessary to calculate each element separately in order to get the solution of the nth element.

[2] Fractional delay filters are used to interpolate values between any two time samples. As the spatial resolution of the simulation depends on the sampling rate and sound velocity, you can also use them to interpolate values between two spatial samples. Thus, the length of a cylindrical bore can be set to any value and does not need to be a multiple of the spatial resolution.

[3] The term *radius* in this context refers to the apex radius and not the radius at the junction between both elements.

```
# init simulation
pSim = ARTRootObject()

# create simulator
mySim = ARTCreateSimulator("MySimulator", "TimeDomain", "")

# create time module
timeModule = ARTCreateTModule(mySim, "FibonacciModule", "TimeModule")

# add output ports to time modules
ARTAddOPortToTModule(timeModule, "fib", "fib[t] = fib[t-1] + fib[t-2]")

# initialize fibonacci ports
ARTSetParameter(mySim, "FibonacciModule.fib[-1] = 1; FibonacciModule.fib[-2] = 0")

fibPort = ARTGetPortFromTModule(FibonacciModule, "fib")

# print fibonacci numbers
for i in range(0, 47):
  # get data structure
  fibonacci = ARTGetComplexFromPort(fibPort, i + 3)
  print "fib[{0:2d}] = {1:.0f}".format(i,fibonacci.re)

# destroy all previously allocated elements
ARTRootDestroy()
```

Figure 6. Calculation of the first 50 elements of the Fibonacci numbers in ART by using the generic time module.

Figure 6 shows a complete implementation of calculating the Fibonacci numbers in ART using the open-source programming language Python. In the first line, a so called *ARTRootObject* is created. This element is responsible for the complete memory administration of the simulation and contains all used simulators, modules and internal data structures. The user does not need to track any allocated objects as they will all be freed in the last line by calling the *ARTRootDestroy* function. After the creation of the root object, a time-domain simulator is added – note that you have to explicitly define the simulation domain as ART is also capable of creating a simulator in the frequency domain. The next steps are straight forward: a generic time-domain module with one output port is added to the simulator. The output port *fib* just contains the definition of the Fibonacci numbers and is initialized by the *ARTSetParameter* function. Note that the simulation starts at time $t = 0$ such that the first two elements are treated like past time values for $t = -1$ and $t = -2$. The last part of the example code retrieves the current value from the port using the *ARTGetComplexFromPort* function and prints the result on the standard output in a for-loop.

Although the calculation of the Fibonacci numbers could have been done much easier, this example shall demonstrate the usage and flexibility of ART: First, the user does not need to know anything about the calculation itself; if an output port depends on other values, these are determined automatically. Secondly, the user does not need to allocate any memory – ART automatically allocates the amount of memory needed. Even when calculating 1000 or more elements of the Fibonacci numbers, only the last 20 elements are kept in memory. Finally, the user could introduce several local parameters and other time modules to simulate much more complex acoustical models. Consequently, users do not need profound knowledge of programming in order to implement and simulate new models.

4.2 Numerical Solution of Differential Equations

This section only shows how ART can be used to even solve differential equations, but will not go into details on the mathematical background which can be found in [7].

The differential equation which will be numerically solved is given by

$$y''(t) + 2y'(t) + 5y(t) = t \tag{7}$$

with the known values

$$y(0) = 1,\ y'(0) = 0\ . \tag{8}$$

Using the method of finite differences, Equation 7 can be solved numerically with the following difference equation where T represents the sampling period:

$$y[t] = \frac{2y[t-1](1+T) - y[t-2] + T^3 \cdot t}{1 + 2T + 5T^2}\ . \tag{9}$$

Figure 7 shows the solution in ART including the initialization of $y[-1]$ and $y[-2]$ which is done using the `ARTSetParameter` function. At a sampling rate of 1 KHz, the numerical error to the exact solution is below 10^{-3} and converges towards 0.

4.3 Conical Bore Simulation

In [9, p 102-109], Walstijn sets up a simulation of conical bores based on DWG modules. The simulated part consists of a cone in the center and a cylinder on each the left and right side of the cone as shown in Figure 8.

The implemented setup of the simulation is slightly different to the original one of Walstijn: Instead of fractional delay modules, the DWG modules presented in Section 3.3 were used, [4] namely two cylindrical bores, one conical bore and two conical junctions. As previously described,

[4] Note that the fractional delay filters are implemented as part of the cylindrical and conical bore modules, but don't need to be added separately to the simulation.

```
# create time modules
numericModule = ARTCreateTModule(mySim, "numericSolution", "TimeModule")

# add output ports to time modules
ARTAddOPortToTModule(numericModule, "out",
  "out[t] = (2*out[t-1]*(1+T) - out[t-2] + T^3*t)/(1 + 2*T + 5*T^2)")

# fetch output port from the numeric module
outPort = ARTGetPortFromTModule(numericModule, "out")

# set the global sampling rate to 1kHz
ARTSetParameter(mySim, "T = 1/1000")

# initialize past values of y[t]
ARTSetParameter(mySim, "numericSolution.out[-1] = 1")
ARTSetParameter(mySim, "numericSolution.out[-2] = 1")

for i in range(0, 10000):
  # get data structure
  outVal = ARTGetComplexFromPort(outPort, i)
  # print value to standard output
  print "out[{0:2d}] = {1:.10f}".format(i,outVal.re)
```

Figure 7. Python code for simulating a differential equation with ART. Note that some steps like initialization and deallocation of all objects have been omitted for simplicity.

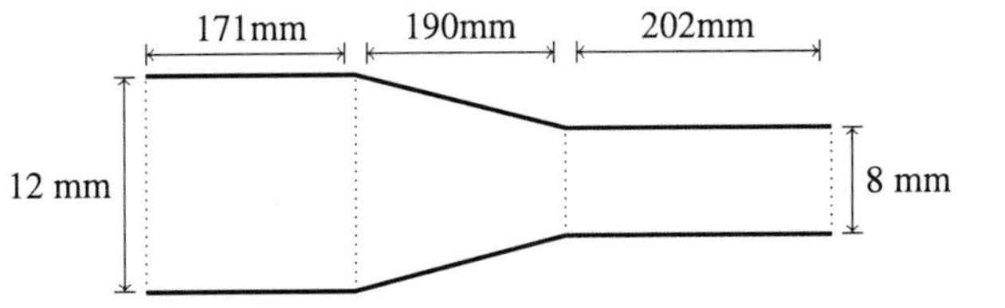

Figure 8. Measurements of the conical bore simulation. The original simulation can be found in [9, p 102-109].

it was not necessary to calculate any cone apex radii – providing the measurements of the bore profile was sufficient. Figure 10 shows the plotted output of the impulse response of the defined system. The results show high similarity with the plots in [9].

```
# create cone module
cone = ARTCreateTModule(sim, "Cone",
    "DWGConeModule")

# connect output ports of modules
ARTConnectPorts(sim, "LeftConeJunction.
    p2m = Cone.p1m; Cone.p1p =
    LeftConeJunction.p2p")
ARTConnectPorts(sim, "Cone.p2m =
    RightConeJunction.p1m;
    RightConeJunction.p1p = Cone.p2p")

# set local parameters of cone module
ARTSetParameter(sim, "Cone.r1 = 0.006;
    Cone.r2 = 0.004; Cone.length = 0.19;
     Cone.mode = 'boreprofile'; Cone.type
     = 'lagrange'")
```

Figure 9. Extract from the conical bore simulation implemented in Python accessing the ART library. The complete code is available in the *example* section on SourceForge, see [1].

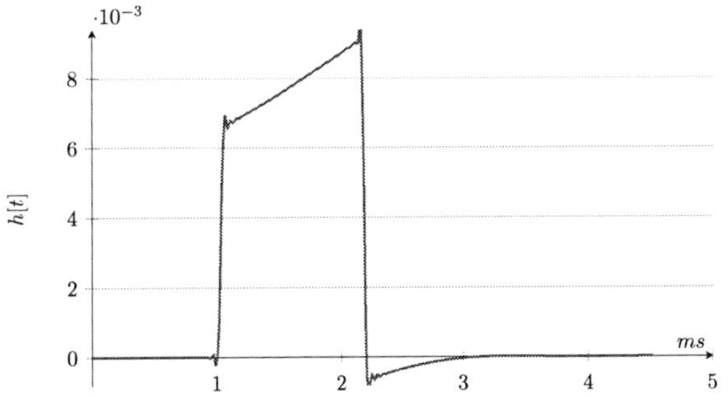

Figure 10. Impulse response of the anechoic (open loop) conical bore system with bilinear transformation used at the conical junction modules and Lagrange filters for the delay lines. The sampling frequency was 44.1 kHz, the speed of sound set to 331 m/s.

4.4 Simulation of Brassiness

Another simulation example shall demonstrate the flexibility of ART when using models which are currently not part of the library and covers *brassiness* in a cylindrical tube.

Brassiness is a phenomenon occurring in brass instruments when the volume is above a certain level. The resulting pressure wave includes periodic impulses causing the spectrum to contain high frequencies. This change in the high harmonics can be sensed, e.g., when listening to a recording of a trumpet played at different sound levels.

Brassiness has been studied for a long time and there are several existing models in the frequency domain based on general Burger's equations. In [11], the implementation of brassiness in a complete simulation of a trumpet is presented. Other approaches rely on models in the time domain and take the change of the sound velocity into account. The implemented approach for the simulation of this section is based on [12] where time-dependent delay modules are used to generate the effect, but also takes the fluid velocity into account.

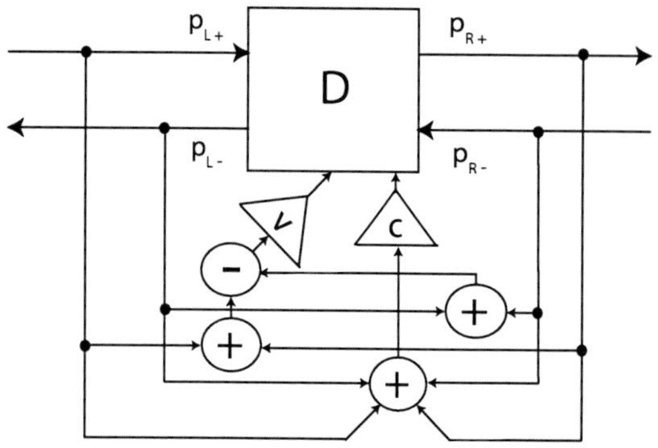

Figure 11. A delay module for the brassiness simulation: The delay value D is calculated based on the sound speed c and velocity difference v.

Figure 11 shows a block diagram of this delay module. When comparing this module with the generic time module in Figure 2, you can easily see the similarities: c and v are local parameters, p_{L+} and p_{R-} are input ports, p_{L-} and p_{R+} are output ports. All output ports and local parameters need explicit calculation expressions and can access past time values. Moreover, ART even allows the user to define simple if-then-else expressions which were used in this simulation to minimize interpolation errors by checking the sign of the current pressure values and use different expressions for each case. The details of this simulation including a description of the physical model and the implementation in ART can be found in [13].

Several other examples of time-domain simulations can be found in [7], including the non-linear simulation of lip movement in brass wind instruments as explained by Adachi and Sato in [14] and the reed movement of a clarinet mouthpiece presented by Chatziioannou and Walstijn in [15, 16].

5. CONCLUSION

In the previous section, several example simulations were presented, demonstrating the implemented features of ART. Although the provided functionality is good enough for small to medium simulation setups, future work will include the implementation of other well-known models in the time domain, increase the usability and performance and provide a proper documentation such that users with only fundamental knowledge in programming will be able to create their own simulations, too. Moreover, support from the open-source community to implement wrapper interfaces to other programming languages and improve the current integration of existing interfaces would be highly appreciated.

The usability of ART can be improved by providing a graphical user interface (GUI) which allows the user to easily set global and local parameters and create new templates for time-domain modules. Apart from the described restrictions, ART could become an interesting supplement to commercial applications like Simulink for time-domain simulations. Moreover, it could also be used for educational and experimental purposes due to its flexibility and the provided collection of implemented existing acoustical models.

6. REFERENCES

[1] "Acoustic Research Tool (ARTool) homepage," 2012. [Online]. Available: http://artool.sourceforge.net/

[2] "Faust: A signal processing language," 2013. [Online]. Available: http://sourceforge.net/projects/faudiostream/

[3] P. Lansky and K. Steiglitz, "Ein: A signal processing scratchpad," *Computer Music Journal*, no. 19:3, pp. 18–25, 1995. [Online]. Available: http://music.princeton.edu/~paul/ein.pdf

[4] R. Rabenstein, S. Petrausch, A. Sarti, G. De Sanctis, C. Erkut, and M. Karjalainen, "Blocked-based physical modeling for digital sound synthesis," *Signal Processing Magazine, IEEE*, vol. 24, no. 2, pp. 42–54, 2007.

[5] "muParserX project homepage," 2012. [Online]. Available: http://code.google.com/p/muparserx/

[6] E. A. Dean, "Atmospheric effects on the speed of sound," Defense Technical Information Center, Tech. Rep., August 1979.

[7] C. B. Geyer, "Time-domain simulation of brass and woodwind instruments," Master's thesis, University of Music and Performing Arts Vienna, 2012. [Online]. Available: http://iwk.mdw.ac.at/lit_db_iwk/download.php?id=16433

[8] J. O. Smith III, "Physical modeling using digital waveguides," *Computer Music Journal*, vol. 16, no. 4, pp. 74–91, 1992.

[9] M. v. Walstijn, "Discrete-time modelling of brass and reed woodwind instruments with application to musical sound synthesis," Ph.D. dissertation, University of Edinburgh, UK, 2002.

[10] V. Välimäki, "Discrete-time modeling of acoustic tubes using fractional delay filters," Ph.D. dissertation, Faculty of Electrical Engineering, Helsinki University of Technology, 1995.

[11] J. Gilbert, L. Menguy, and D. M. Campbell, "A simulation tool for brassiness studies (l)," *Journal of the Acoustical Society of America (JASA)*, vol. 123, no. 4, pp. 1854–1857, 2008.

[12] C. M. Cooper and J. S. Abel, "Digital simulation of "brassiness" and amplitude-dependent propagation speed in wind instruments," in *Proc. of the 13th Int. Conference on Digital Audio Effects (DAFx-10), Graz, Austria*, 2010.

[13] W. Kausel and C. B. Geyer, "Time domain simulation of standing waves in brass wind instruments taking non-linear wave steepening into account," in *Proceedings of the SMAC/SMC 2013*. Stockholm: Royal Swedish Academy of Music, 2013.

[14] S. Adachi and M. Sato, "Time-domain simulation of sound production in the brass instrument." *J. Acoust. Soc. Am.*, vol. 97, no. 6, pp. 3850–3861, 1995.

[15] V. Chatziioannou, "Forward and inverse modelling of single-reed woodwind instruments with application to digital sound synthesis," Ph.D. dissertation, Queen's University Belfast, 2010.

[16] V. Chatziioannou and M. van Wastijn, "Estimation of clarinet reed parameters by inverse modelling," *Acta Acustica united with Acustica*, vol. 98, no. 4, 2012.

AURALIZATION OF COUPLED SPACES BASED ON A DIFFUSION EQUATION MODEL

Paul Luizard
LIMSI-CNRS,
Orsay, France &
LAM-D'Alembert,
UPMC Univ Paris 06,
UMR CNRS 7190,
Paris, France
paul.luizard@limsi.fr

Jean-Dominique Polack
LAM-D'Alembert,
UPMC Univ Paris 06,
UMR CNRS 7190,
Paris, France
jean-dominique.polack@upmc.fr

Brian F.G. Katz
LIMSI-CNRS
Orsay, France
brian.katz@limsi.fr

ABSTRACT

Auralization of room acoustics consists in audio rendering based on the sound characteristics of a virtual space. It is defined by Vorländer [1] as "the creation of audible acoustic sceneries from computer-generated data", as the auditory equivalent of visualization techniques. Auralization is obtained by convolving a room impulse response with an anechoic recording, adding room presence to the reverberation-free excitation signal, providing subjective immersion in the considered space. Since acoustically coupled spaces are encountered in various venues such as large stairways distributing corridors or rooms, naves and side galleries in churches, even crossing streets in dense cities, it becomes interesting to produce accurate auralization in these types of venues. Such coupled room impulse responses can be synthesized using a recently proposed sound energy decay model based on a diffusion equation and adapted to coupled spaces. This paper presents the parametric model of sound energy decay and describes the impulse response synthesis process leading to auralization of coupled spaces.

1. INTRODUCTION

The term auralization has been used since the early twentieth century in the musical community in the sense of "prehearing" according to Summers [2]. It was later defined for the room acoustics community by Kleiner et al. [3] as "the process of rendering audible, by physical or mathematical modeling, the sound field of a source in a space". Thus the process of auralization is artificial and different than real reverberation experienced by a listener in an acoustical space. However it is interesting to create new acoustical environments or even to recreate lost ones, e.g. based on maps and descriptions of buildings which do not exist anymore. According to Lokki et al. [4], auralization process,

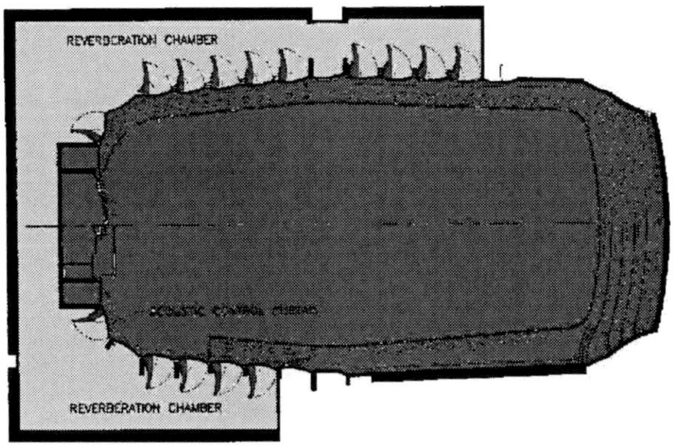

Figure 1. Example of coupled volume concert hall: KKL Lucerne, Switzerland (Top & bottom of the map: 4th and 3rd floors). Blue room: main room with stage and audience; yellow surrounding room: reverberation chamber; red doors: coupling surface. Picture from Beranek [5].

to be indistinguishable from the real auditory environment, requires simulation or reproduction of three issues: directivity of sound sources, sound propagation in a 3-D space, and reproduction of spatial sound. The present study focuses on sound propagation to obtain monaural impulse responses, possibly further adapted for spatialized rendering.

Pioneer studies used sound recording in scale models, played back at lower speeds with respect to the scale factor, as performed by Spandöck [6]. Nowadays computer modeling is often used to generate room impulse responses to be further convolved with anechoic recordings. These operations can be either pre-calculated for a given space or real-time convolution can be performed [7, 8], e.g. using the "waveguide" method [9]. A number of different means to generate impulse responses are available with various advantages and drawbacks in terms of sound quality and computation time. Those methods are either based on wave approach (e.g. BEM or FDTD) for small volumes whose acoustics have modal behavior, geometrical acoustics (e.g. ray-tracing, radiosity), or statistical acoustics for larger volumes. However, results can present important variations from one method to another when applied to coupled spaces, as shown by Luizard et al. [10]. Therefore, the choice of the employed simulation method is determinant and depends on characteristics of the venue.

Coupled spaces have particular acoustical characteristics due to the energy exchange between several architectural volumes (Fig. 1). A signature of this sort of system is the curved sound energy decay which can present several decay rates as opposed to most single volume rooms. The early decay, presenting a steeper slope than the late part, contributes to give an important sense of sound clarity while the lower late decay rate induces an impression of reverberation, although these concepts are usually antagonistic in single volume rooms. Therefore, coupled volume acoustics is worth being exploited, particularly for theater and music purpose, and auralization is a relevant means to virtually explore acoustically coupled spaces with various goals, e.g. design or entertainment.

This study first presents the proposed analytical model of sound energy decay and its application to coupled spaces, then the auralization process is described from room impulse response synthesis to final audible rendering. Furthermore, suggestions are proposed to improve auralization quality and listener engagement in the virtual room.

2. PARAMETRIC MODEL OF SOUND ENERGY DECAY

Previous research [11, 12] has been conducted in room acoustics to develop analytical models of sound energy decay in order to predict sound field behavior in various spaces. The present model is based on a diffusion equation under the hypothesis that sound behaves as moving particles in a uniformly scattering medium, as proposed by Ollendorff [13] who introduced the use of diffusion equation to model acoustic phenomena. The diffusion equation (eq. (1)) is expressed in terms of sound energy density $w(\mathbf{r},t)$ and is composed of four terms: a temporal derivative, a spatial derivative (Laplace term), an absorption term, and a source term with acoustical power F. Considering source-receiver distance $\mathbf{r}$ allows for estimating energy variation throughout the reverberant space.

$$\frac{\partial}{\partial t}w(\mathbf{r},t) - D\nabla^2 w(\mathbf{r},t) + \sigma w(\mathbf{r},t) = F(\mathbf{r},t) \quad (1)$$

Introducing the mean free path between two successive collisions $\lambda = \frac{4V}{S}$ makes it possible to express statistical quantities which influence the behavior of sound field, depending on architectural parameters such as the room volume and surface. Coefficients D (eq. (2)) and σ (eq. (3)) are related to sound diffusion and absorption, respectively:

$$D = \frac{\lambda c}{3} = \frac{4Vc}{3S}, \quad (2)$$

$$\sigma = \frac{c\overline{\alpha}}{\lambda} = \frac{c\overline{\alpha}S}{4V}, \quad (3)$$

where c is the speed of sound, $\overline{\alpha}$ is the mean absorption coefficient, V and S are the volume and surface of the room.

The proposed solution to eq. (1) is a heuristic approximation which accounts for two different regions defined within the considered space, namely the near and far fields, with a continuous transition from one another. In the neighborhood of the source, the sound energy decays with source-receiver distance (first term of the sum) until being less spatially dependent and becoming homogeneous enough to be associated to the concept of diffuse sound field as defined by Sabine [14] in the classical statistical theory (constant term of the sum). Coefficients defined in eqs (2 & 3) are part of this statistical model. Nevertheless, this expression is exact in steady state condition and for homogeneous energy decay as described by Sabine, asymptotically far from the sound source.

$$w(\mathbf{r},t) = \left(\frac{a}{r}e^{-\sqrt{\frac{\sigma}{D}}r} + b\right)e^{-\sigma t}H(t), \qquad t > \frac{r}{c}. \quad (4)$$

Function H is the Heaviside step function representing the fact that sound decay is described from the instant the direct sound reaches the receiver position at distance r from the source.

This model (eq. (4)) can be calibrated with respect to room characteristics by adapting its parameters a and b. The latter express the relative importance of spatially decaying sound energy as compared to homogeneous energy through space, governed by a and b respectively.

3. APPLICATION TO COUPLED SPACES

This sound energy decay model can be adapted to coupled spaces in combination with classical statistical theory [15, 16], allowing for simulation of various source-receiver configurations and coupling surface settings, whereas the classical theory does not consider sound level variations within a given subspace. Hence using this model provides finer estimation of sound fields in coupled spaces. First, initial uniform sound levels are estimated in each room for steady state conditions, governed by parameter b. The concept of coupling factor k_i is used to estimate the initial sound level in the reverberation chamber such that

$$\begin{cases} w_{1_0} = \frac{4P}{c\overline{\alpha}_1(S_1+S_c)} \\ w_{2_0} = k_2 w_{1_0} \end{cases}, \quad (5)$$

$$\text{with} \qquad k_2 = \frac{S_c}{\overline{\alpha}_2(S_2+S_c)}, \quad (6)$$

where P is the sound power, S_c is the coupling surface area, and subscripts 1 & 2 refer to the main room and chamber respectively. Then the spatially dependent energy is added, governed by parameter a. Finally, the sound energy emitted from the chamber is introduced with respect to the distance between the coupling surface and the receiver, considering the coupling surface as a secondary sound source. This process allows for estimating sound energy density and creating curved energy decays at any receiver position in the main room, according to the characteristics of the rooms.

An example, whose geometry is shown in Fig. 2 and specifics are detailed in Table 1, is performed in quasi-rectangular coupled spaces, the main room being larger but more damped than the reverberation chamber

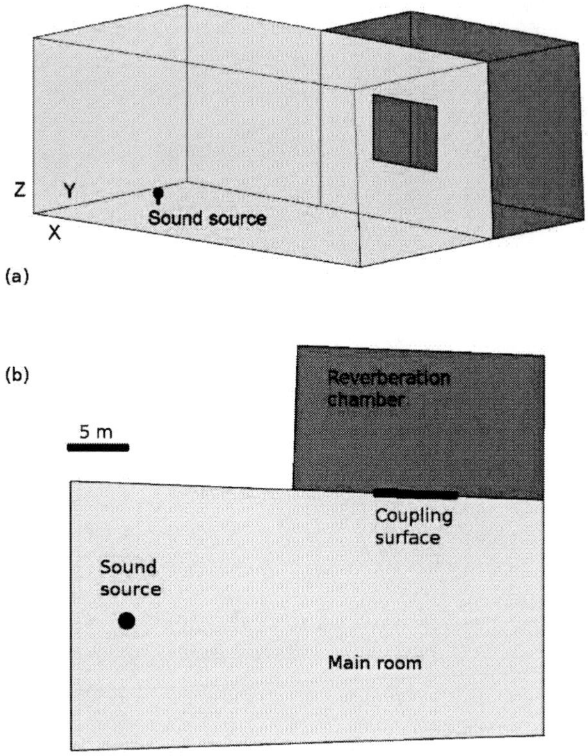

Figure 2. (a) View of the coupled room simple geometry used as example. The large blue room on the left is the main room and the orange room behind it is the reverberation chamber. (b) Floor plan of the same geometry.

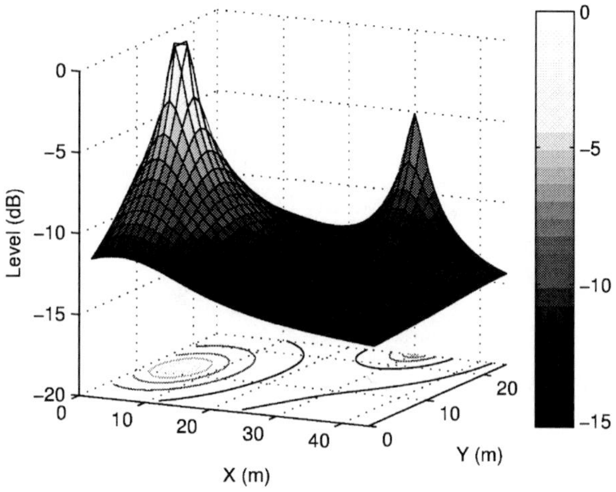

Figure 3. Illustration of the output of the model in the case of 2 coupled rooms shown in Fig. 2: sound energy density in the main room. The highest peak corresponds to the sound source on stage, the other one is due to the sound emitted back from the reverberation chamber. Lines on the horizontal plane represent equal energy levels as vertical projections.

such that reverberation time (RT) at mid-frequencies is larger in the latter. Opposite walls are slightly angled in order to avoid flutter echoes. Fig. 3 represents the sound energy density estimated on the ground floor in the main room of coupled volumes. Spatial variations are in the range of 15 dB between the source peak and the lowest energy in the room. The second peak next to a wall corresponds to the energy emitted from the chamber back in the main room.

Considering receivers along a line through the room length, on the axis such that $Y = 12$ m on Fig. 3 with 1 m-step from one another, Fig. 4 shows the temporal energy decays with increasing source-receiver distance. Darker decays stand for receivers nearer the sound source while lighter ones represent distant receivers. The curvature point appears at different levels under the initial level for various receiver positions, such that the further the receiver, the higher the decay curve. This means that the second slope, or late reverberation, appearing earlier and louder, has stronger effects on distant receivers than on ones nearer the sound source. The energy decay given by classical statistical theory, which is the same at every receiver position since no spatial variation is considered, appears as the blue dotted line. Fig. 4 represents normalized decays and distant receivers can provide decay curves with late decay levels above the reference one.

	Main room	Reverberation chamber
Length (m)	44	14
Width (m)	24	24
Height (m)	18	18
Surface (m^2)	4560	2040
Volume (m^3)	19000	6050
$\overline{\alpha}$	0.55	0.1
RT (s)	1.2	5.0

Table 1. Architectural and acoustical specifics of the geometry shown in Fig. 2 for each separate room, i.e. without the coupling surface.

A line of receivers different than the one considered above would lead to different results both in terms of total energy variation, as can be imagined from Fig. 3, and in terms of temporal decays because the room configuration is not symmetrical, with the coupling surface on one lateral side. This observation underlines the fact that sound energy decays, and thus impulse responses, generally vary throughout a given space, making it interesting to be able to generate auralization accounting for those differences. Hence using this proposed statistical model which is distance dependent leads to more precise results than the classical statistical model.

4. FROM SOUND ENERGY DECAYS TO IMPULSE RESPONSES

Auralization is based on an anechoic sound convolved with an impulse response. The present study deals more specifically with room impulse responses which add reverberation to the dry signal to give it a certain room presence. A room impulse response is the temporal equivalent of a transfer function of the room. It is composed of sound reflected on the walls and received at a specific position.

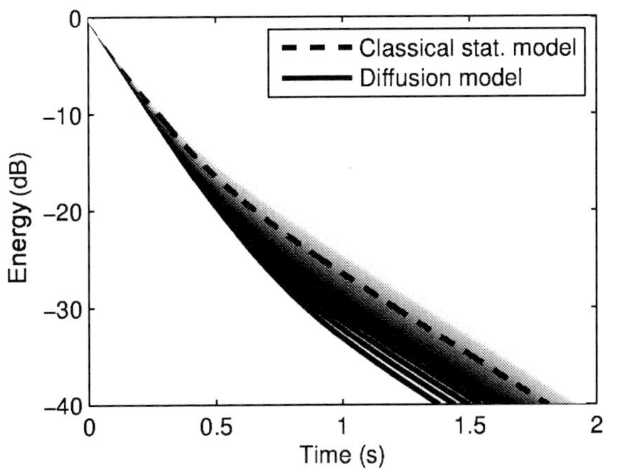

Figure 4. Normalized sound energy decays along the line such that Y = 12 m in Fig. 3, i.e. the center line of the main room, for various source-receiver distances $5 < r < 25$ m. Darker decays (below) correspond to small r while lighter decays (above) correspond to more distant receivers. The dotted line represents the classical model by Cremer et al. [16].

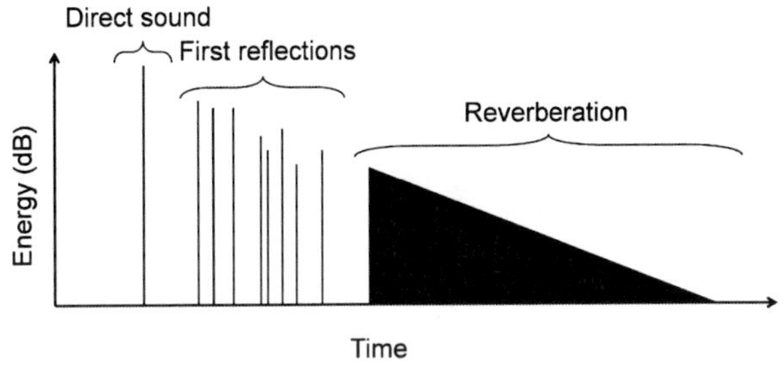

Figure 5. Schematic representation of a room impulse response in single volume.

An illustration of such a signal is shown in Fig. 5. The previously proposed model of sound energy decay can be used to synthesize room impulse responses using various processes. The idea is to apply the given energy decay to pre-filtered noise in order to obtain the reverberation part of impulse response (top of Fig. 6). An inverse Fourier transform of this decaying noise produces the temporal impulse response (bottom of Fig. 6). This sort of process has been used in previous research for perceptual experiments whose purpose was to estimate Just Noticeable Differences (JND) of single and double-slope reverberation from single and coupled spaces, allowing to change decay rates easily while keeping temporal distribution and frequency content unchanged. Frissen et al. [17] applied energy decays to a normally distributed random number sequence and Picard et al. [18] applied energy decays to pink noise.

Refinements can be performed along two different dimensions: the temporal or spectral distribution of energy. Measured room impulse responses show different trends along temporal segments. As can be seen in Fig. 5, the first part of received energy is the direct sound, then the first reflections from the walls and ceiling reach the listener before the density of reflection becomes too high

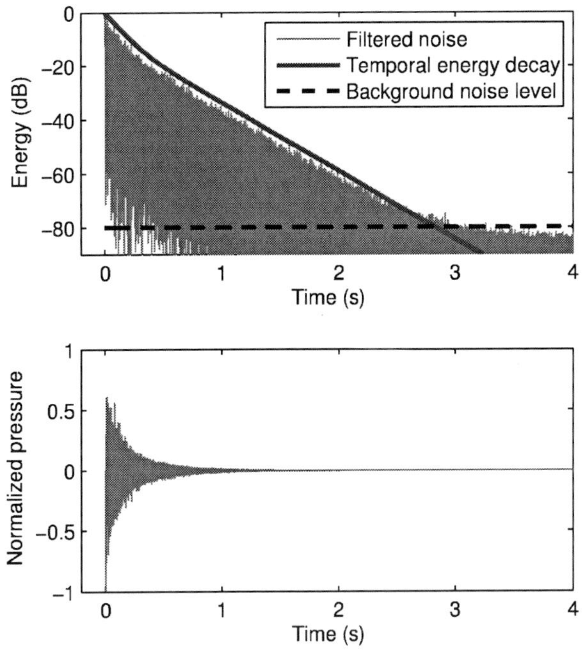

Figure 6. Impulse response synthesis process. Top: Decay curve applied to pre-filtered noise. Bottom: Resulting impulse response in linear amplitude scale.

to be considered as discrete, which is called reverberation. Hence simulated room impulse responses should include direct sound and possibly early reflections, which have been proved by Barron [19] to be perceptually influential, in order to sound more realistic. Fig. 7 shows the steps to construct impulse responses with reverberation only, added early reflections, and direct sound. While the room geometry is responsible for intensity and time of arrival of early reflections, intensity of direct sound relative to the rest of impulse response corresponds to the source-receiver distance. Therefore, adding the described steps can be seen as accounting for a type of room and a specific receiver position. Furthermore, the three decay curves presented in Fig. 7, which are backward integrations of the impulse responses as defined by Schroeder [20], are different in the sense that the early decay is steeper with the direct sound and early reflections. Depending on the proportion of change as compared to the case with reverberation only, the modification will be audible, possibly adding clarity to the sound.

Another refinement can be performed, in the frequency domain, consisting in setting different decay rates in the available octave bands. The proposed model of energy decay can be used with various absorption coefficient settings in order to obtain a collection of decay curves, as illustrated in Fig. 8. RT values in uncoupled rooms shown in Table 2 are set depending on the desired absorption in the main room and in the reverberation chamber. These decay curves can be applied successively to noise filtered in frequency bands. The obtained impulse response is closer to reality than before this process because measurements in actual concert halls always present a variation of decay rates, leading to total energy variations in the order

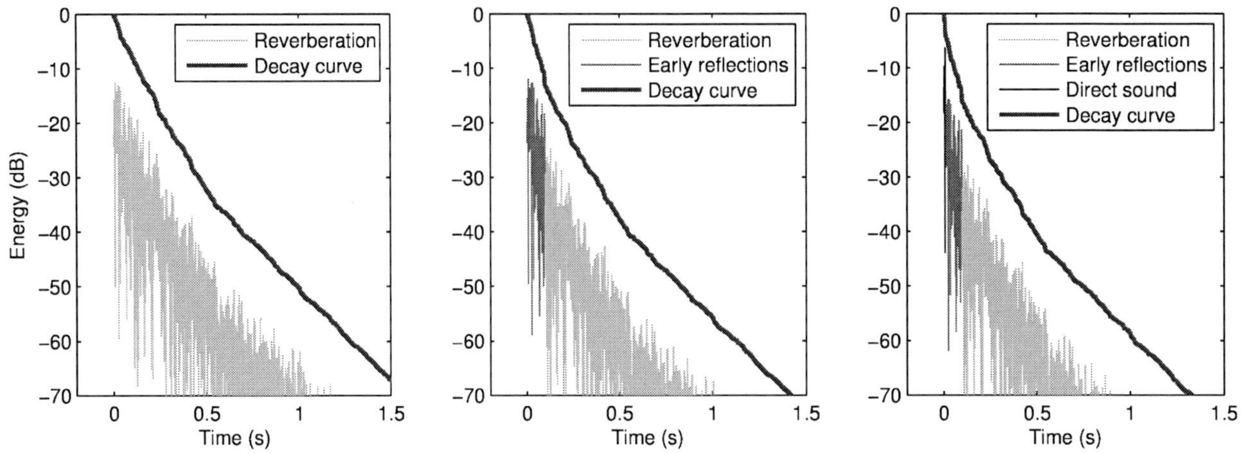

Figure 7. Possible refinements of room impulse response synthesis in temporal domain: addition of early reflections (center) and direct sound (right) to reverberation only (left).

	Main room						Reverberation chamber					
Center frequency (Hz)	125	250	500	1000	2000	4000	125	250	500	1000	2000	4000
RT (s)	3.12	2.82	2.11	1.74	1.34	0.96	13.67	10.87	8.46	4.8	3.31	2.63
$\overline{\alpha}$	0.19	0.24	0.32	0.39	0.50	0.61	0.03	0.04	0.06	0.10	0.14	0.16

Table 2. Reverberation times (RT) and mean absorption coefficients ($\overline{\alpha}$) per octave bands in uncoupled configuration, from measurements in a scale model of coupled spaces. Energy decay curves presented in Fig. 8 are generated with these values.

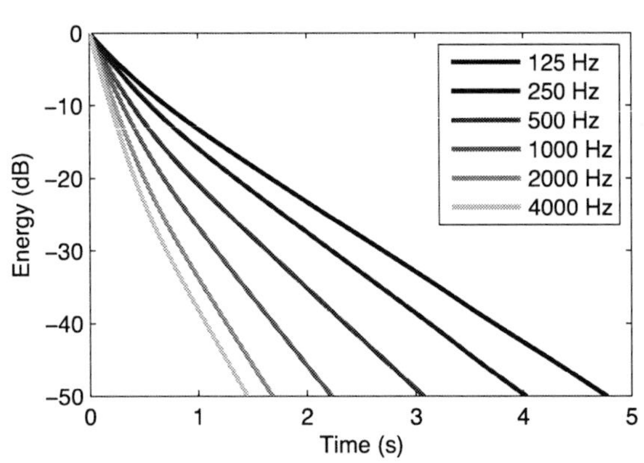

Figure 8. Example of double-slope decay curves per octave bands from a coupled volume system, at r = 20 m from the source.

of dozens of decibels over frequency bands.

5. CONCLUSION

A model of sound energy decay based on the diffusion equation in coupled spaces is proposed to perform auralization. The process which has been used in previous research consists in applying these sound decays to filtered noise with various possible refinements to produce realistic room impulse responses. Convolving the latter with anechoic sounds allows for hearing sound sources within virtual spaces. This process can be useful in several domains, e.g. virtual reality or architectural acoustic design, where acoustical immersion might be required to experience particular sound environments, among which coupled spaces are often encountered. Further research includes listening tests to estimate the level of sound quality which can be obtained with the proposed energy decay model, as compared to other auralization methods.

6. REFERENCES

[1] M. Vorländer, *Auralization: Fundamentals of Acoustics, Modeling, Simulation, Algorithms, and Acoustic Virtual Reality.* Springer, Berlin, 335 p., 2008.

[2] J. Summers, "What exactly is meant by the term "auralization"?" *J. Acoust. Soc. Am.*, vol. 124, p. 697, 2008.

[3] M. Kleiner, B. Dalenbäck, and P. Svensson, "Auralization - an overview," *J. Audio Eng. Soc.*, vol. 41, pp. 861–874, 1993.

[4] T. Lokki and L. Savioja, "State-of-the-art in auralization of concert hall models - what is missing?" in *Proc. of Baltic-Nordic Acoustics Meeting, Reykjavik, Iceland, 17-19 August*, 2008.

[5] L. Beranek, *Concert Halls and Opera Houses: Music, Acoustics and Architecture, 2nd ed.* Springer-Verlag, New York, 667 p., 2004.

[6] F. Spandöck, "Akustische modellversuche," *Ann. Phys.*, vol. 20, pp. 345–360, 1934.

[7] T. Smyth and A. Elmore, "Explorations in convolutional synthesis," in *Proc. of the* 6th *Sound and Music Computing Conference, Porto, Portugal, 23-25 July*, 2009.

[8] Huopaniemi, Karjalainen, Välimäki, and Huotilainen, "Virtual instruments in virtual rooms - a real-time binaural room simulation environment for physical models of musical instruments," in *Proc. of International Computer Music Conference, Aarhus, Denmark, 12-17 Sept.*, 1994.

[9] M. Karjalainen, "Digital waveguide networks for room modeling and auralization," in *Proc. of Forum Acusticum, Aug. 29 - Sept. 2*, 2005.

[10] P. Luizard, M. Otani, J. Botts, L. Savioja, and B. Katz, "Comparison of sound field measurements and predictions in coupled volumes between numerical methods and scale model measurements," in *Proc. of the* 21st *International Congress on Acoustics, Montreal, Canada, 2-7 June*, 2013.

[11] J. Picaut, L. Simon, and J. Polack, "A mathematical model of diffuse sound field based on a diffusion equation," *Acta Acustica United with Acustica*, vol. 83, pp. 614–621, 1997.

[12] V. Valeau, J. Picaut, and M. Hogdson, "On the use of a diffusion equation for room-acoustic prediction," *Journal of the Acoustical Society of America*, vol. 119, pp. 1504–1513, 2006.

[13] F. Ollendorff, "Statistical room-acoustics as a problem of diffusion: A proposal," *Acustica*, vol. 21, p. 236245, 1969.

[14] W. Sabine, *Collected papers on acoustics.* Harvard University Press, 1922.

[15] H. Kuttruff, *Room Acoustics.* Elsevier Science Ltd, London, 452 p., 1973.

[16] L. Cremer, H. Müller, and T. Schultz, *Die Wissenschaftlichen Grundlagen der Raumakustik / Principle and Applications of Room Acoustics.* Hirzel Verlag / Applied Science, New York, 651 p., 1978 / 1982.

[17] I. Frissen, B. Katz, and C. Guastavino, *Auditory Display.* Springer, New York, 493 p., 2010, ch. Effect of sound source stimuli on the perception of reverberation in large volumes.

[18] D. Picard, "Audibility of non-exponential reverberation decays," Master's thesis, Rensselaer Polytechnic Institute, 2003.

[19] M. Barron, "The subjective effects of first reflections in concert halls - the need for lateral reflections," *J. Sound Vib.*, vol. 15(4), pp. 475–494, 1971.

[20] M. Schroeder, "New method of measuring reverberation time," *Journal of the Acoustical Society of America*, vol. 37, pp. 409–412, 1965.

Warped low-order modeling of musical tones

Rémi Mignot, Heidi-Maria Lehtonen, and Vesa Välimäki
School of Electrical Engineering,
Department of Signal Processing and Acoustics, Aalto University
Otakaari 5A, 02150 Espoo, Finland

ABSTRACT

Source-filter modeling of musical tones requires a filter model for the spectral envelope of the signal. Since the perceptual frequency resolution is best at low frequencies, frequency warping has been previously shown to improve spectral envelope estimation of audio signals. In this paper, considering low-order modeling for harmonic tones, we investigate the perceptual performance of three warped models which extend the filter models: Linear Prediction Coding (LPC), True-Envelope based Linear Prediction (TE-LPC), and Discrete All-Pole method (DAP). The respective warped methods allow a continuous control of the warping factor, and here we are interested in the perceptual quality of the envelope estimation according to the warping factor for all methods. Results of our listening tests show that the frequency warping which best approximates the Bark scale, does not always give the best results.

1. INTRODUCTION

The *source filter* principle, which is popular in speech coding and synthesis, can also be applied to the harmonic tones of musical instruments (cf. e.g. [1,2]). In its basic version, a periodic excitation, the source, is processed by a filter, which aims to reproduce the spectral envelope of the original tone (cf. e.g. [3]). One benefit of the source-filter model is the possibility to independently vary the fundamental frequency and the spectral shape of the synthetic signal. Furthermore, the parametric representation of the source-filter model allows to reduce the number of parameters, which facilitates the synthesis control.

Here, the aim is to obtain very low-cost real-time simulations. Then, we investigate low-order filters which imitate the shape of the original spectrum of musical instrument tones closely in a perceptual sense. One possible method is the well known Linear Prediction Coding (LPC). Unfortunately, as pointed in [4], this method is suitable for continuous spectra but not for the discrete spectra of harmonic tones. To deal with the problem, the Discrete All-Pole (DAP) modeling method [5] and the TE-LPC method [6] have been proposed, both of which identify the coefficients of an autoregressive filter for a discrete spectrum.

In audio processing, one problem is that these prior methods use a linear frequency scale, which is suboptimal in terms of human perception. The frequency scale can be warped to better match the resolution of the human hearing. It has been proposed in [7–10] to apply the filter identification in a warped scale similar to the Mel scale or the Bark scale. Thanks to this modification, the spectral envelope approximation focuses on the low frequencies, and the details at higher frequencies, which are irrelevant in the perceptual sense, are naturally smoothed.

However, these warped methods increase the real-time simulation complexity and our informal perceptual tests have revealed that frequency warping which fits the Bark scale does not give the best results in all cases. The aim of this paper is the study of the influence of the warping for low-order filter estimations, according to a *warping* factor λ which continuously controls the frequency warping. The quality of the filter models as a function of λ is perceptually evaluated using listening tests.

As a general conclusion, we will observe that for low-order modeling, warping brings only a small perceptual advantage compared to the use of the linear frequency scale, which can even be a better choice in some cases.

This paper is organized as follows: section 2 presents the spectral envelope estimation techniques and their warped versions: WLPC (*Warped LPC*), WTLP (*Warped TE-LPC*), and WDAP (*Warped DAP*). Section 3 discusses the synthesis of test sounds which is based on a harmonic sine model of the periodic part, where the harmonic magnitudes and phases are modified according to the filter approximation. Then, the listening tests and results are presented in section 4, and finally, section 5 concludes this paper. Note that the new methods WLTP and WDAP are proposed in this paper by adapting previous methods to our problem. Additional materials are given in the companion web page [1].

2. LOW-ORDER ENVELOPE MODELING

2.1 Linear Prediction Coding (LPC)

2.1.1 Standard LPC

The LPC of order P consists of the prediction of a signal by a combination of the P past values: $\tilde{x}_n = \sum_{i=1}^{P} a_i x_{n-i}$. The coefficients $\{a_i\}$ minimize the expectation of the square of the residual $e_n = x_n - \tilde{x}_n$, and they are also the coefficients of the AR filter $H(z) = G/A(z)$ where $A(z) = 1 - \sum_{k=1}^{P} a_i z^{-1}$ and G is the prediction gain.

[1] http://www.acoustics.hut.fi/go/smac2013-warping

This standard method usually uses the autocorrelation sequence r_n of the weighted signal. In [4] it is shown that the optimal a_i's also maximise the spectral flatness of the residual. Then, the frequency response of the filter $H(z)$, gives an estimation of the spectral envelope of $|X(\omega)|$.

2.1.2 Warped LPC

In [7,10], it is proposed to realise a frequency mapping replacing z^{-1} by an all-pass filter $D(z)$. Then the Warped LP coefficients can be computed in a similar way by replacing the autocorrelation r_n by a warped correlation c_n.

For practical reasons, first-order all-pass filters are usually used: $D(z) = (1-\lambda z)/(z-\lambda)$ where the pole λ is the *warping factor*. For example, at a sampling rate $F_s = 44.1$ kHz, $\lambda = 0.756$ leads to a warping close to the Bark scale mapping, cf. [8,9]. Note that if $\lambda = 0$, then $c_n = r_n$.

2.1.3 LPC and Warped LPC of a discrete spectrum

Unfortunately, one well-known problem persits for discrete spectra, such as periodic signals. In [5] it is proved that the autocorrelation of a discrete spectrum is an aliased version of the original continuous case. Therefore, in the case of a high-order LPC, the estimated spectral envelope fits the whole magnitude spectrum, peaks and valleys, and in the case of low-order LPC, the estimated spectral envelope is attracted by the valleys between the peaks. Some methods deal with this problem, such as the TE-LPC and DAP methods presented below.

2.2 True Envelope based LPC

2.2.1 Standard TE-LPC

Most of cepstrum methods for spectral envelope estimation roughly consist of the filtering of a magnitude spectrum $|X(\omega)|$ by windowing its cepstrum with a mask in low quefrencies (cf. e.g. [11]). Since this operation does not solve the problem of discrete spectra, the True Envelope (TE, cf. [12,13]) iteratively computes the cepstral filtering $H_n(\omega)$ on $G_n(\omega) = \max(|X(\omega)|, H_{n-1}(\omega))$. In other words, at every iteration, the valleys of $|X(\omega)|$ are filled by the previously estimated envelope, then the envelope goes towards a smooth envelope passing close to the peaks.

To convert the TE estimation $H_e(\omega)$ to an AR filter $H(z)$, in [6] it is proposed to apply a standard LPC using the correlation ρ_n given by the inverse DFT of the power spectrum $H_e(\omega)^2$ instead of r_n (cf. sec. 2.1.1).

Note that the TE order is defined by the size of the cepstral mask. In the case of a periodic signal of frequency F_0, the optimal order is $\hat{o} = 0.5F_s/F_0$ where F_s is the sampling rate, cf. [14]. Concerning the LPC order of the TE-LPC, for high quality applications, it is shown in [15] that the same order $\hat{o}$ gives the best results. In the following, we always use this optimal TE order but in order to have low-order AR filters, the LPC order is chosen to be lower.

2.2.2 Warped TE-LPC

In [16], the Mel-based TE-LPC (also called MTELPC) is proposed to decrease the order using a warping. The estimate of the Mel-scaled True Envelope (MTE), with a reduced optimal order $0.15F_s/F_0$, is used to compute the coefficients of a warping filter. However, firstly this method uses a fixed frequency mapping adapted to the Mel scale only, and we want to study different warping scales, secondly its quality cannot outperform the MTE quality which is itself below the TE quality.

In this paper we propose two changes. On the one hand, we use a warping defined by the all-pass filter $D(z)$ with the parameter λ, and on the other hand, this warping is done after the estimation of the TE (normally scaled), done with the optimal order $0.5F_s/F_0$. So, the warped LP coefficients are computed starting from the warped correlation γ_n obtained by an inverse DFT of the power of the warped True Envelope $\mathcal{H}_e^2$. With ν the adimensional warped frequency, uniformly spaced in $[0, 2\pi[$, $\mathcal{H}_e(\nu)$ is given by an interpolation of $H_e(\omega)$, using the relation: $\omega(\nu) = \nu - 2\,\mathrm{atan}(\lambda \sin\nu/(1+\lambda\cos\nu))$. In the following, this method is called Warped TE-LPC (WTLP).

2.3 Discrete All-Pole methods

2.3.1 Standard Discrete All-Pole (DAP)

As pointed out in section 2.1.3, for a periodic signal an original spectral envelope is sampled by the harmonics, and its autocorrelation sequence is an aliased version of the original one. In [5] the DAP method is proposed to solve this bias by exploiting the frequency positions and the values of the spectral peaks only. For periodic signals these peaks are the harmonics, but the method is not restricted to harmonic spectra. This method is based on the minimization of the discrete version of the Itakura-Saito distance between the squared spectral envelope measured and estimated at the frequencies ω_m of the M spectral peaks. Then, an iterative minimization of E_{IS} leads to a P-order AR filter $H(z)$, which gives an estimate of the spectral envelope passing through the peaks in ω_m.

2.3.2 Warped DAP

In order to adapt this method to a warped frequency scale, we propose the WDAP method. This new version of the DAP method consists simply of computing the algorithm but replacing the linear frequency positions ω_n of the peaks, by their new frequency positions ν_m in the warped frequency scale, defined by: $\nu_m = -\angle D(\mathrm{e}^{j\omega_m})$. Note that it is possible because the DAP method does not assume the harmonic structure of the input peaks.

Nervertheless, in some cases the WDAP method can be ill-conditioned, which implies some variations, or "ripples", of the spectral envelope between the peaks. Even if the presented WDAP should not be used for spectral modifications, this paper shows its benefit at least for sound coding.

3. REFERENCE AND TEST SOUND COMPUTATION

The reference and test sounds have been computed from original recordings using a frame-by-frame additive synthesis (cf. [17,18]). Using a harmonic sine modeling of the signal, the attack and the noisy parts have been isolated

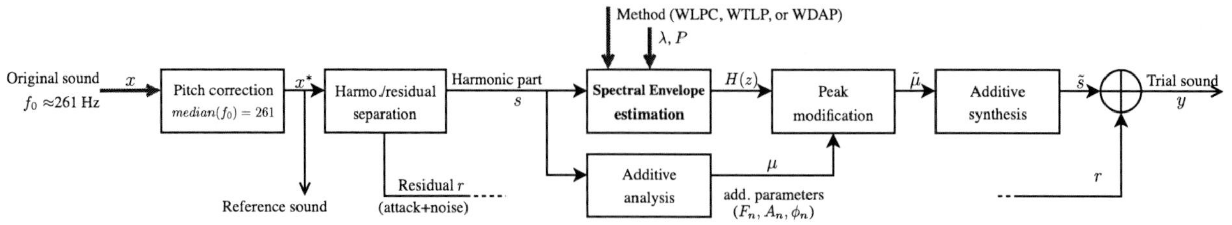

Figure 1. Block diagram of the sound computation.

from the harmonic part. The spectral envelope identification is realised for the harmonic part only. Figure 1 sums up the computation.

Reference sound: Because of the poor tuning of the used files, which come from the IOWA database [19], the fundamental frequency has been shifted in order to have a median value at 261 Hz (C4) for all sounds. Note that the natural vibrato is conserved. Then, the overlap-add synthesis of the harmonic part produces the reference sound by adding the original residual (a static sine synthesis is used for every frame, cf. [20]).

Test sounds: The AR filters $H_n(z)$ have been estimated using the three methods for all frames. Then the estimated spectral envelopes are applied to the test sounds by replacing the peak magnitudes by $|H_n(\mathrm{e}^{j\omega_{n,m}})|$ where $\omega_{n,m}$ is the (unchanged) frequency of the harmonic m of the frame n. For the peak phases, first the reference phases are changed to $\pi/2$ and the phases are unwrapped using a shape-invariant method, cf. e.g. [21]. Actually, this quarter cycle dephasing guarantees the centering of the signal avoiding clippings. Finally, $\angle H_n(\mathrm{e}^{j\omega_{n,m}})$ is added to the unwrapped phase.

Figure 2 shows some examples of spectral estimations for a frame of the clarinet signal. The spectra and the sound examples of all tones are given in the companion web page.

Simulation of a Warped filter The warped method returns the coefficients of the Warped AR filter $H_w(z) = G/A_w(z)$. To simulate the filter using the linear frequency scale, we can algebraically solve the standard ARMA filter $H(z) = B(z)/A(z) = H_w(D^{-1}(z)) = G/A_w(D^{-1}(z))$. Since the orders of the polynomials A and B are also P, the computation of the warped AR filter is as time consuming as a $2P$-order standard AR filter. That is why, in the following tests, we also study the quality of the standard methods with an order twice ($2P$ and $\lambda = 0$).

Note that because the (W)LPC methods are highly biased for discrete spectra, we automatically adjusted its level to the reference level using their dBA measure. Without this procedure, the WLPC method is always the worst method.

4. LISTENING TEST

The performances of the WDAP, WLPC, and WTLP methods and their non-warped versions were evaluated with a listening test. The task of the subjects was to compare each test tone against the reference tone.

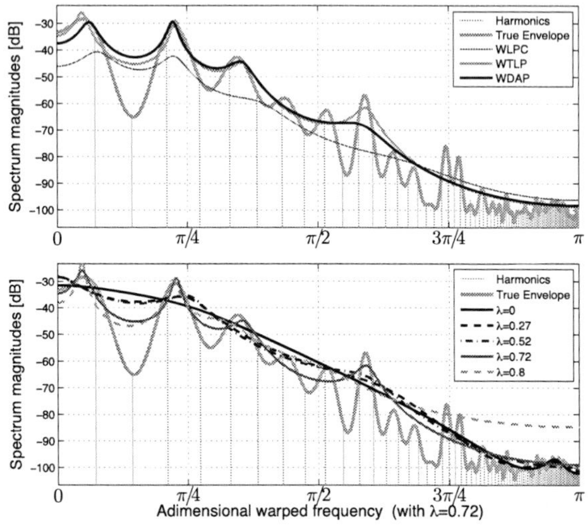

Figure 2. Spectral envelope estimations for a frame of the clarinet signal. Top fig.: comparison between the 3 methods and the True Envelope estimate, $\lambda = 0.72$ and $P = 8$. Note that the level of the WLPC is increased by equalizing the dBA measure. Bottom fig.: comparison of estimations with different values of λ for the WTLP method ($P = 8$).

Four warping factors were used: 0.27, 0.52, 0.72, and 0.8. Here we fixed the higher warping factor at 0.8, which is higher than 0.756, and we selected 3 other factors relatively uniformly spaced. Figure 4 presents these warpings, and a comparison with: the warping given by $\lambda = 0.756$, the Bark scale of [22] and the Mel scale of [23]. Remark that $\lambda = 0.756$ (for $F_s = 44.1$kHz) gives the warping closest to the Bark scale in the least-square sense, but as figure 4 shows, it is far from the Mel scale which is commonly used in speech recognition.

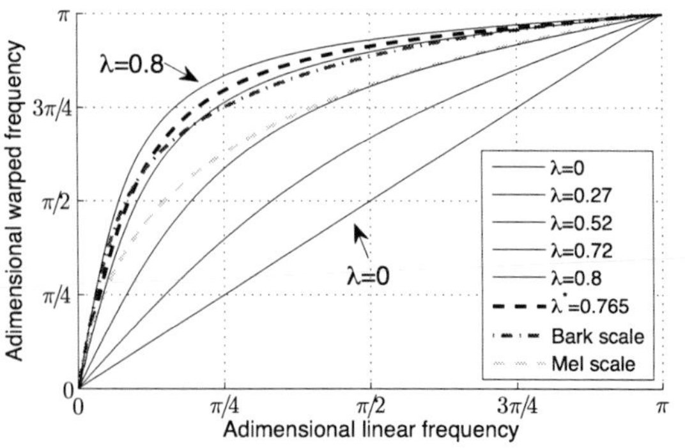

Figure 4. Frequency warpings used for the listening test and comparison with the “optimal warping” $\lambda = 0.756$, the Bark scale of [22] and the Mel scale of [23].

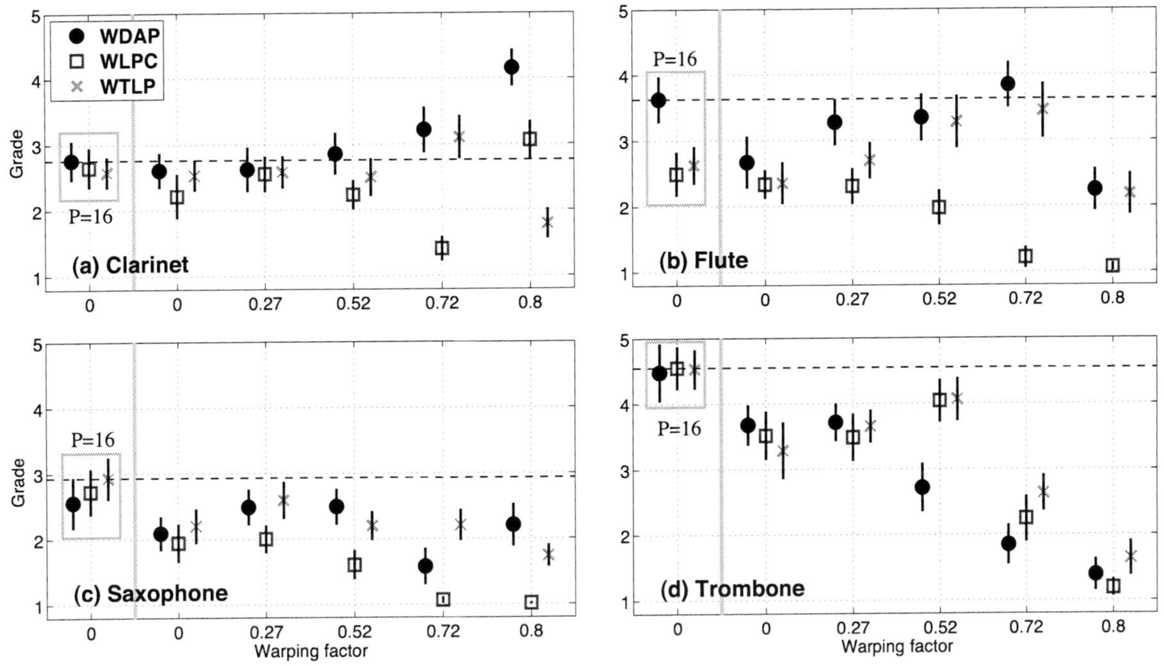

Figure 3. Marginal means and the 95% confidence intervals for the (a) clarinet, (b) the flute, (c) the saxophone, and (d) the trombone. The results for the WDAP, WLPC, and WTLP methods are presented with circles, rectangles, and crosses, respectively. The horizontal dashed lines present the performance of the best method without warping. The filter order is 8 unless indicated otherwise.

The filter order for the warped versions was 8, and for the non-warped versions two filter orders, 8 and 16 were used, resulting in six filter order/warping factor combinations. Tones from four musical instruments were included in the test: a clarinet tone, a flute tone, a saxophone tone, and a trombone tone. The fundamental frequency of each tone was 261 Hz (corresponds to the note C4).

4.1 Listening test environment, subjects, and the method

The listening tests were carried out in a sound-insulated listening booth at the Aalto University Department of Signal Processing and Acoustics. The tones were played back with Sennheiser HD 650 circum-aural reference headphones at 64 dBC SPL. The user interface was coded with Matlab. Ten volunteer subjects between 25 and 39 years of age participated in the test. They were personnel of the university, and all had previous experiences in participating in listening tests. None of them reported any hearing defects.

Before the actual test took place the subjects went through a practice test, which provided the subjects a possibility to familiarize themselves with the user interface and a preselected set of 20 test sounds representing extremes of the test tones in terms of quality. The actual test consisted of three rounds of 76 trials (three methods, six filter order/warping factor combinations, and four instruments results in $3 \times 4 \times 6 = 72$ trials, and additional 4 reference-reference comparisons as acid tests), and the order of the trials was randomized for each round and each subject. Each trial consisted of a tone pair, the first and second tone being always the reference and the test tone, respectively, separated with 500 ms of silence. The subjects were allowed to listen to the tone pairs twice and then asked to rate the quality of the test tone on a continuous five-step scale with resolution of 1 decimal place. The anchor points were as specified in the ITU-T BS.1284 standard [24]: Imperceptible (5), Perceptible, but not annoying (4), Slightly annoying (3), Annoying (2), and Very annoying (1).

4.2 Results

The performance of each subject was verified by the acid tests. It was required that the grade resulting from the reference-reference pair comparison should be at least 4 (perceptible, but not annoying) in each case. Based on this analysis 3 subjects were discarded from further analysis.

The results of the listening test were analyzed with a four-way analysis of variance (ANOVA). The method, the filter order/warping factor combination, and the instrument were modeled as fixed effects, while the subject was modeled as a random effect. The assumptions for validity of ANOVA were checked before the analysis. The Shapiro-Wilk test confirmed that the variances were equal ($p > 0.05$), but the normality of residuals could not be confirmed ($p < 0.05$). However, since the linear-mixed effects models have been found to be robust against violations of the assumptions [25], and the distribution was very close to normal, ANOVA test was performed.

ANOVA returned significant effects for the method [$F(2, 1434) = 145.91, p \ll 0.001$], the filter order/warping factor combination [$F(5, 1434) = 144.29, p \ll 0.001$], the instrument [$F(3, 1434) = 164.75, p \ll 0.001$], as well as for the interactions between the method and filter order/warping factor combination [$F(10,1434) = 21.61, p \ll 0.001$], between the method and the instrument [$F(6,1434) = 38.77, p \ll 0.001$], between the filter order/warping factor combination and instrument [$F(15, 1434) = 45.18, p \ll 0.001$], and the interaction between all three fixed effects [$F(30, 1434) = 10.10, p \ll 0.001$].

Figure 3 shows the marginal means and the 95% confidence intervals for the interaction between the method, the filter order/warping factor combination, and the instrument. Additionally, the Dunnett's post hoc test [26] with the significance level of 5% was performed. The figures show the grades as a function of the filter order/warping coefficient combination. The horizontal dashed line shows the best result obtained without warping and with an order 16, and it serves as a reference point showing whether warping brings any advantage (effectively, a non-warped filter of order 16 has the same amount of coefficients as a warped filter of order 8).

In the case of the clarinet, Fig. 3(a) reveals that the WDAP method clearly outperforms all other methods, when the warping factor is 0.8, thus producing the best result. For the flute (Fig. 3(b)), the WDAP method seems to achieve the highest scores, but as the confidence intervals overlap with the WTLP method, no conclusion can be drawn which one of these two methods is the best. In the case of the saxophone in Fig. 3(c) the non-warped versions of the three methods seem to produce the best results, although again the confidence intervals overlap with the results of WDAP and WTLP methods with the warping factors 0.27 and 0.52. For the trombone, warping does not bring any advantage, as can be seen in Fig. 3(d), although the confidence intervals of the case $P = 16$ of the non-warped versions overlap with the WLPC and WTLP methods with warping factor 0.52. All these findings were confirmed with the results of the post hoc test.

4.3 Listeners' thoughts about the test

All subjects reported that the test was fairly easy, the differences in the test tones were clearly audible, and it was easy to make decisions about the quality. Some subjects noted, however, that in some cases it was hard to apply the given scale, since the differences between the test tones varied. Indeed, some subjects judged artefacts as more severe degradation than changes in timbre, for example, and the others rated these degradations quite the contrary. Many subjects reported also that they used more the bottom of the scale than the top, which is also visible in the results (see Fig. 3).

4.4 Discussion

The results show that the WDAP method is the best or among the best methods in the case of the clarinet, the flute, and the saxophone. For the trombone the results show that warping does not bring any significant advantage. Also in the case of the saxophone this is somewhat questionable, since the non-warped methods with filter order 16 obtain the highest grades. The reason for this is the smooth overall shape of the spectrum. The clarinet has prominent odd harmonics resulting in valleys between adjacent harmonics, which implies that warping brings advantage since more effort is put to low frequencies. The situation is different especially for the trombone that has no prominent formant in the spectrum, as can be seen in Fig. 5.

Usually two major problems occur for high λ values: first, because of the ill-conditioning, especially with the WDAP

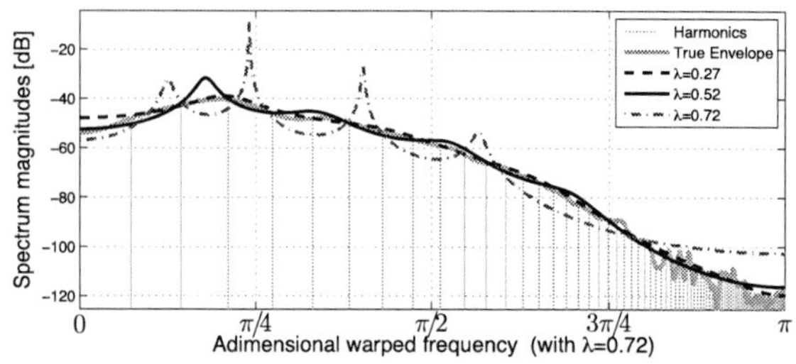

Figure 5. Spectral envelope estimations for a frame of the trombone signal. Comparison of estimations with different values of λ for the WDAP method ($P = 8$). The spectra of the other tones are presented in the companion web page.

method, the estimation spectrum can have artificial peaks at low frequencies (cf. Fig. 5). Second, the envelope usually decreases at high frequencies, then the spectral tilt increases with λ because of the frequency "compression" at high frequencies. In this case, as shown in fig. 5, the low-order estimation cannot follow the spectrum and the real envelope is over-estimated. Note that a pre-whitening filter can solve this problem but it usually produces unfitting side effects at low frequencies.

5. CONCLUSION

This article presents a new warped method called the WDAP for modeling the spectral envelope of musical instrument tones. In contrast to the standard DAP method [5], the algorithm is computed by placing the linear frequency points by their warped equivalents. Additionally, we introduced a modified version of the TE-LPC method [6], called the WTLP method, in which warping is realized with an all-pass filter with warping coefficient λ and performed after estimating the TE.

As partial conclusions of the results of the listening tests (cf. fig. 3): first, for low-order filters, it is obvious that it is sometimes preferable to use non-warped methods with a order twice, $P = 16$, rather than warped filters with $P = 8$ which has an equal CPU usage in time simulation. Second, we see that the WLPC, or the LPC, has no benefit compared to the two other tested methods. This observation is not surprising because this method is not adapted to discrete spectra, such as periodic signals. Third, the warping closest to the "optimal warping" in the sense of [8] ($\lambda = 0.756$ with $F_s = 44.1$ kHz) is not always the best one in a perceptual sense, and it is preferable in some cases to use a lower warping factor (cf. e.g. the saxophone in Fig. 4(c)).

For practical reasons, we could not do a detailed study with a high number of different instruments, with a higher number of warping factors, and with some different pitches. With 4 instruments and 6 order/warping factor combinations, we got 76 trials and the individual tests lasted almost 45 minutes. Hence, it is difficult to have a general conclusion, nevertheless these tests show that the perceptual optimal warping factor λ depends of the original timbre, or spectral envelope, and is not linked to the Bark scale. Note that the value $\lambda = 0.756$ gives the warping closest to the Bark scale (for $F_s = 44.1$ kHz), and is relatively far from the Mel scale which is commonly used in speech recognition (cf. Fig. 4). Then, it seems impossible to choose a unique λ, perceptually good for all instruments, in the case of low-order filters.

In next works, it would be interested to derive a objective criterion which allows to choose the best perceptual λ according to the considered instrument.

Acknowledgments

The work of Rémi Mignot is funded by the Marie Curie Action project ESUS 299781. The work of Heidi-Maria Lehtonen is supported by the Finnish Cultural Foundation. The authors wish to thank Marko Takanen for his help in the statistical analysis.

6. REFERENCES

[1] M. Caetano and X. Rodet, "A source-filter model for musical instrument sound transformation," in *IEEE ICASSP*, 2012, pp. 137–140.

[2] H. Hahn, A. Röbel, J. Burred, and S. Weinzierl, "Source-filter model for quasi-harmonic instruments," in *DAFx*, Graz, Austria, Septembre 2010.

[3] V. Välimäki and A. Huovilainen, "Oscillator and filter algorithms for virtual analog synthesis," *Computer Music Journal*, vol. 30, no. 2, pp. 19–31, Summer 2006.

[4] J. Makhoul, "Linear prediction: A tutorial review," *Proceedings of the IEEE*, vol. 63, no. 4, pp. 561–580, 1975.

[5] A. El-Jaroudi and J. Makhoul, "Discrete all-pole modeling," *IEEE Transactions on Signal Processing*, vol. 39, no. 2, pp. 411–423, 1991.

[6] F. Villavicencio, A. Röbel, and X. Rodet, "Improving LPC spectral envelope extraction of voiced speech by True-Envelope estimation," in *IEEE ICASSP*, 2006, pp. I869–I872.

[7] H. Strube, "Linear prediction on a warped frequency scale," *The Journal of the Acoustical Society of America*, vol. 68, no. 4, pp. 1071–1076, 1980. [Online]. Available: http://link.aip.org/link/?JAS/68/1071/1

[8] J. Smith and J. Abel, "Bark and erb bilinear transforms," *IEEE Transactions on Speech and Audio Processing*, vol. 7, no. 6, pp. 697–708, 1999.

[9] A. Härmä, M. Karjalainen, L. Savioja, V. Välimäki, U. Laine, and J. Huopaniemi, "Frequency-warped signal processing for audio applications," *J. Audio Eng. Soc.*, vol. 48, no. 11, pp. 1011–1031, 2000.

[10] A. Härmä, "Linear predictive coding with modified filter structures," *IEEE Transactions on Speech and Audio Processing*, vol. 9, no. 8, pp. 769–777, 2001.

[11] A. Oppenheim and R. Schafer, *Digital Signal Processing*. Prentice Hall, 1975, 585 pages.

[12] A. Röbel and X. Rodet, "Efficient spectral envelope estimation and its application to pitch shifting and envelope preservation," in *DAFx*, 2005, pp. 30–35.

[13] S. Imai and Y. Abe, "Spectral envelope extraction by improved cepstral method," *Electron. and Commun.*, vol. 62-A, no. 4, pp. 10–17, 1979, in Japanese.

[14] A. Röbel, F. Villavicencio, and X. Rodet, "On cepstral and all-pole based spectral envelope modeling with unknown model order," *Pattern Recognition Letters*, vol. 28, no. 11, pp. 1343–1350, 2007.

[15] F. Villavicencio, A. Röbel, and X. Rodet, "All-pole spectral envelope modelling with order selection for harmonic signals," in *IEEE ICASSP*, 2007, pp. I49–I52.

[16] ——, "Extending efficient spectral envelope modeling to Mel-frequency based representation," in *IEEE ICASSP*, 2008, pp. 1625–1628.

[17] R. McAulay and T. Quatieri, "Speech analysis/synthesis based on a sinusoidal representation," *IEEE Transactions on Acoustics, Speech and Signal Processing*, vol. 34, no. 4, pp. 744–754, 1986.

[18] X. Serra and J. Smith, "Spectral modeling synthesis: A sound analysis/synthesis system based on a deterministic plus stochastic decomposition," *Computer Music Journal*, pp. 12–24, 1990.

[19] University of IOWA, Electronic Music Studios, "Musical Instrument Samples." [Online]. Available: http://theremin.music.uiowa.edu/MIS.html

[20] X. Rodet and P. Depalle, "Spectral envelopes and inverse FFT synthesis," *93nd AES Convention*, 1992.

[21] R. Di Federico, "Waveform preserving time stretching and pitch shifting for sinusoidal models of sound," in *In Proceedings of the COST-G6 Digital Audio Effects Workshop*, 1998, pp. 44–48.

[22] E. Zwicker and E. Terhardt, "Analytical expressions for critical-band rate and critical bandwidth as a function of frequency," *The Journal of the Acoustical Society of America*, vol. 68, p. 1523, 1980.

[23] D. O'Shaughnessy, *Speech Communication: Human and Machine*. Addison-Wesley, 1987.

[24] I.-R. BS.1284-1, "General methods for the subjective assessment of sound quality."

[25] H. Jacqmin-Gadda, S. Sibillot, C. Proust, J.-M. Molina, and R. Thiébaut, "Robustness of the linear mixed model to misspecified error distribution," *Computational Statistics and Data Analysis*, vol. 51, no. 10, pp. 5142–5154, June 2007.

[26] C. W. Dunnett, "Pairwise multiple comparisons in the unequal variance case," *Journal of the American Statistical Association*, vol. 75, pp. 796–800, Dec. 1980.

Four-part Harmonization Using Probabilistic Models: Comparison of Models With and Without Chord Nodes

Syunpei Suzuki
Nihon University
syunpei@kthrlab.jp

Tetsuro Kitahara
Nihon Univercity
kitahara@chs.nihon-u.ac.jp

ABSTRACT

In this paper, we explore machine learning models that generate four-part harmonies according to the melody of a soprano voice. Although researchers have already tried to produce four-part harmonization through machine learning, the computational models that most studies have proposed already contain nodes or states that represent chords or harmonic functions. Explicitly introducing such nodes or states is suitable from the viewpoint of practically achieving musically acceptable harmonization, but it is unsuitable from the scientific viewpoint of acquiring the fundamental concepts of harmonies from actual music data. Therefore, we developed two kinds of computational models, one that contains chord nodes and another does not, and investigate to what extent the model without chord nodes acquires the fundamental concept of harmonies compared to the model with chord nodes. For our models, we describe musical simultaneity (i.e., the appropriateness of combinations of simultaneously played notes) and musical sequentiality (i.e., the smoothness of the melodic line within each voice) are described as dependencies between random variables in Bayesian networks. Both models learned 254 pieces taken from a Hymn corpus, and the results of this experiment show that the Bayesian network without chord nodes acquired some of the basic rules of harmony.

1. INTRODUCTION

Automatic music harmonization is an important subtask in automatic music arrangement. In general, this task is divide into two types of harmonization. The first type is a sequence of chord symbols, such as C-F-G7-C, a given melody [1–3]. The second type comprises concrete notes to voices other than the melody voice. The typical form in the latter type of harmonization is a four-part harmony, that consists of soprano, alto, tenor, and bass voices. The four-part harmonization is a traditional part of the theoretical education of Western classical musicians, so numerous researchers have attempted to generate automatically the four-part harmonization [4–10].

One of the most commonly used approach is to develop an expert system (rule-based system) [4]. Ebcioğlu, for example, implemented the knowledge of harmonization by using a logic programming language called BSL [4]. A rule-based harmonization system is difficult to develop, because this systems rules are various and hence often difficult to integrate without contradiction. For example, two note allocation rules include one rule that, considers consonance between the voices and another rule that considers the natural temporal connection within the voice. Given that these rules make different considerations, they might recommend different notes, in which case meta rules for resolving such contradictions are necessary. However, developing such rules is not easy. Some studies have attempted to achieve harmonization as a constraint satisfaction problem or with the genetic algorithm, instead of directly implementing note allocation rules. Researchers designed these constraints or fitness functions, according to basic some rules of harmonization [6, 7].

In recent years, the number of studies on four-part harmonization that use machine learning technologies has been increasing [5, 8, 9], thus increasing the difficulty of designing meta-rules. The scientific interest in these studies is to discover the principle of harmony from actual music data so that humans do not necessarily need to implement it on a computer. For example, Hild et al. developed a J. S. Bach-style choral harmonization system using several neural networks [5], Allan and Williams proposed a four-part harmonization method based on a hidden Markov model (HMM) [8], and Yi and Goldsmith proposed a four-part harmonization method based on a Markov decision process [9].

Researchers strive to address two issues while developing a computational model for four-part harmonization. The first issue is to take into account the simultaneity and sequentiality of harmonization. The simultaneity is the appropriate (e.g., non-dissonant) allocation of notes that are simultaneously sounding, while sequentiality is the smooth connection in a melodic line within each voice. The second issue is to take a limited number of training data into account. Because four-part harmonization has very complex dependencies both within and between voices, the model should describe all of the dependencies. As the complexity of the model increases, however, the number of training data required will exponentially increase. The quantity of available training data should therefore be considered while designing the model.

In Yi and Goldsmith's model [9], a state is defined as a 10-tuple $(S_1, A_1, T_1, B_1, S_2, A_2, T_2, B_2\ , S_3, P)$, where S_i, A_i, T_i, B_i are respectively the soprano, alto, tenor, and bass notes at time i, and P is a temporal position. The temporal sequence of such states is treated as a Markov decision process. This model has the potential of generating four-part harmony, because it considers both simultaneity and sequentiality. Unfortunately, it usually requires a tremendous amount of training data precisely because it has many states. Not surprisingly, Yi and Goldsmith do not report the results of learning with an actual corpus.

Hild et al. attempted four-part harmonization by integrating three kinds of neural networks [5], one that generates a sequence of harmonic functions called harmonic skeletons from a soprano melody, a second one that allocates concrete notes from the harmonic skeletons, and a third one that inserts eighth notes for ornamentation. They trained their neural networks separately on one set of Bach chorales in major key and another set in minor key, each set containing 20 chorales.

Allan and Williams used a hidden Markov model (HMM) [8]. This model's has hidden states represent chords that are designed to emit an observable melody line. The states are coded as a list of pitch intervals of the alto, tenor, and bass notes from the soprano note, such as 0:4:9:16 / T (T stands for tonic). This model takes into account simultaneity and sequentiality, but this model also requires a lot of training data due to its large number of states. In fact, Allan and Williams model distinguishes each unique voicing of the same chord.

Buys and Merwe adopted a weighted finite-state transducer (WFST) for four-part harmonization [10]. Their WFST consists of three graphical models for estimating chords, bass notes, and inner-voice(i.e., alto and tenor) notes. The alto, tenor, and bass notes are coded in separate nodes unlike the above-mentioned models.

Most of the above-mentioned studies introduced nodes or states that represent chords (e.g., C, G) or harmonic functions (e.g., tonic). In contrast, the present study introduces a computational model that does not explicitly contain the concept of harmony so that the researchers could investigate whether this model is able to acquire the concepts of harmony from actual music data. Specifically, we developed a computational model of four-part harmonization with and without chord nodes to investigate to what extent the model without chord nodes learns the harmony that the model with chord nodes was already programmed to know. For our computational model, we adopt a Bayesian network, because most of the existing methods can be generalized to Bayesian networks.

2. PROPOSED METHOD

In this section, we present our method of four-part harmonization that uses a Bayesian network.

2.1 Problem Statement

The problem that we aim to solve is how to generate melodic lines for the alto, tenor, and bass voices, according to the existing melody of the soprano voice. Based on the typical form of Chant Donné used in the theoretical education of harmony, we assume that the rhythm of all of the voices is the same, in other words, the number of notes and the onset and offset times for each note are the same for all of the voices.

2.2 Overview of the Procedure

The user provides the system with a melody in the MIDI format. Let $S_1, \cdots, S_N$ be the note numbers of the notes in the given melody. Then, the system determines the notes of the remaining voices (alto, tenor, and bass). Let A_i, T_i, B_i be the i-th notes of the alto, tenor, and bass voices, respectively. The i-th notes A_i, T_i, B_i are inferred after the previous notes A_{i-1}, T_{i-1}, B_{i-1} are determined, and this process is repeatedly performed until the last notes are inferred. Finally, the result is output in the MIDI format.

2.3 Design of Bayesian Networks

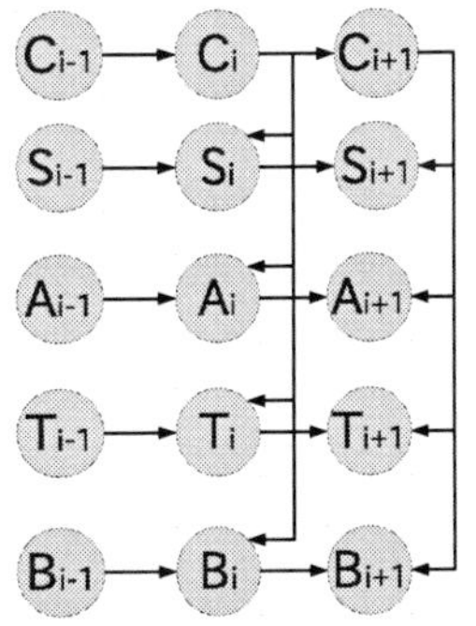

Figure 1. Chord model

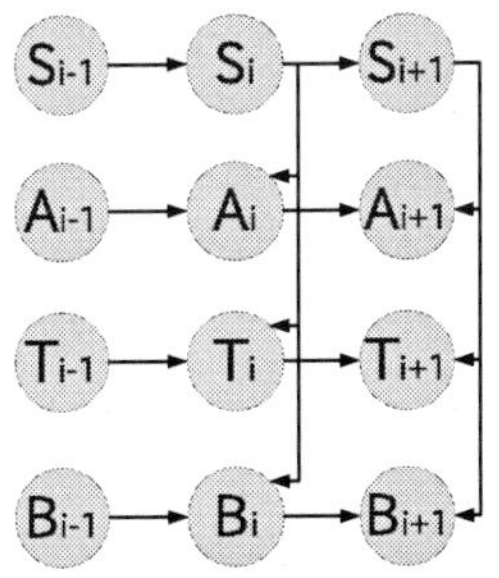

Figure 2. Non-chord model

The Bayesian networks that we designed for this experiment appear in Figures 1 and 2. Figure 2 shows a model that does not include chord nodes (called a non-chord model), while Figure 1 shows a model that includes chord nodes (called a chord model). S_i, A_i, T_i, B_i, C_i represent the note numbers of the i-th note in the soprano, alto, tenor, and bass part, and their ranges are [60, 81], [55, 76], [48, 69], and [41, 62], respectively. C_i represents the chord name for i-th note and takes an element of $\{\mathrm{C}, \mathrm{C}\sharp, \cdots, \mathrm{B}\} \times \{\mathrm{maj}, \mathrm{min}\}$. To all nodes, we introduced a special symbol "0", which means no notes or chords. When the first note and chord is inferred, there are no notes or chords for time $i-1$. The symbol "0" is set to the nodes S_{i-1}, A_{i-1}, $T_{i-1}, B_{i-1}, C_{i-1}$. Similarly, this symbol is set to the nodes $S_{i+1}, A_{i+1}, T_{i+1}, B_{i+1}, C_{i+1}$ when the last note and chord is inferred.

The common feature of these Bayesian networks is that they include nodes for the $(i+1)$-th note as well as nodes for the i-th note. While the i-th note is being inferred, the $(i+1)$-th note is also inferred at the same time. Because the likelihoods of all nodes are taken into account, we avoided the values for the i-th note that would decrease the likelihood of the $(i+1)$-th note. Thus, we have taken into account the sequentiality from the previous note to the next note.

There is a difference in the network design towards simultaneity between our two Bayesian networks. For the non-chord model, we assumed that the note for each voice depends on the note in the soprano voice. Ideally, all pairs of the nodes S_i, A_i, T_i, B_i should have arcs because all voices are mutually dependent. However, taking dependencies into account is difficult in practice, because a large amount of training data is required. We therefore simplified the dependencies between the voices. In the chord model, the note for each voice is assumed to depend on the chord. Ideally, the dependencies between the voices should be taken into account. It is also practically difficult to take dependencies into account in the non-chord model, due to a limited amount of training data.

The conditional probability tables (CPTs) were trained with a corpus. The details of the training are described in Section 3.1.

3. EXPERIMENTS

We conducted experiments on the generation of four-part harmonies using the two above-mentioned Bayesian networks and compared the results.

3.1 Learning CPTs

For the learning CPTs of the Bayesian networks, we constructed a melody corpus consisting of 254 four-part melodies that we took from a book of hymns [11]. We limited the hymns to major-key pieces in which the shortest notes are eighth notes. We then manually input the scores of the selected pieces, and Band-in-a-Box [13] automatically labeled the chord for each note.

Because we wanted to assume that the rhythms of the four voices are completely the same (i.e., the onset and offset times of four voices are the same), we had to modify the training data so that the data satisfied this condition. We therefore divided all notes that were longer than eighth notes into a sequence of eighth notes with the same pitch. The CPTs were trained with the data modified in this manner. By introducing this modification, however, the probability that each note is the same as the previous note artificially high, so we assigned a penalty coefficient (currently 0.2) to these probabilities.

3.2 Experimental condition

We used 32 soprano melodies [12] in the C-major key for the inputs of the four-part harmonization. After generating four-part harmonies for these 32 soprano melodies with the chord and non-chord models, we compared the results through the following criteria:

C1 The number of notes containing dissonance intervals.

The dissonance intervals are defined as minor 2nd, major 2nd, diminished 5th, minor 7th, and major 7th. The notes forming the G7 chord (e.g., Soprano: D, Alto: F, Tenor: B, Bass: G) were excluded even if they contained dissonance intervals. Because the relations of chords and notes are explicitly trained in the chord model, the number of notes containing dissonance intervals in the chord model would be less than that in the non-chord model.

C2 The number of non-diatonic notes.

The melodies used here are actually used for excises of harmonics at music colleges, so the melodies are orthodox and hence the results of harmonization should not contain non-diatonic notes. This number ended up being close to zero, so this result fit the criterion better than did the other results for their respective criteria.

C3 Whether the last chord is C.

All of the melodies used here should end with the C chord. If the results of the non-chord model meet this criterion, then we can conclude that this model appropriately acquired one of the important rules in harmonics: ending with the tonic chord. The results of the chord model, on the other hand, would easily meet this criterion because it was directly trained in the sequentiality of chord symbols.

C4 The number of notes containing the same note name in more than three voices.

Allocating the same note name to simultaneous notes in different voices (e.g., soprano: C, alto: C, tenor: E, bass: C) does not cause dissonance but rather does make the music monotonous. Such note allocation should therefore be avoided.

C5 The number of successive large (more than perfect 4th) note motions in the bass voice.

Successive, large note motions will decrease the smoothness in a sequence of notes within a voice. In particular, successive large note motions in the bass part should be avoided, because the conventional job of the bass voice is to keep the piece grounded. To avoid successive large note motions in the chord model, the model should train in chord inversions and infer appropriate inversions given the previous and/or next notes. If the model does not learn chord inversions sufficiently, then it would output the root note of each chord for the bass part, decreasing the sequential smoothness.

C6 The number of note names appearing in each voice.

When only two or three note names appear in a certain voice, the music is monotonous. This number should therefore not be low (e.g., less than three).

3.3 Experimental results

Table 1 lists the results of evaluation based on the above-mentioned criteria.

Concerning the dissonance of the output harmonies, 3% of all chords for the chord model and 18% of all chords for the non-chord model were dissonant. Because the chord model was directly trained in the relations between chords and notes, it successfully selected chord tones as long as it inferred an appropriate chord. Accordingly, this model generated harmonies with almost no dissonance. On the other hand, the results for the non-chord model feature more dissonant chords than do the results of the chord model, because the latter model was trained only in the relationship between the soprano voice and the other voices. However, we can conclude that the non-chord model acquired a basis of harmony to some extent, even though it

Table 1. Evaluation results (C: the chord model, N: the non-chord model; ○: satisfactory, ×: unsatisfactory). "Total" for C6 is averages, not summations.

	Total	C1		C2		C3		C4		C5								C6					
	# of	C	N	C	N	C	N	C	N	C				N				C			N		
	Note									2	3	4	5+	2	3	4	5+	Alto	Tenor	Bass	Alto	Tenor	Bass
Sample 1	15	1	1	0	0	○	○	8	3	2	1	0	0	0	1	1	0	2	2	3	4	3	6
Sample 2	14	0	4	0	0	○	○	5	4	0	0	0	1	0	1	1	0	2	3	4	5	5	4
Sample 3	14	0	1	0	0	○	○	7	4	1	1	0	0	0	1	0	0	2	2	3	4	6	6
Sample 4	15	1	0	0	0	○	○	5	3	1	0	0	1	1	0	0	0	2	4	3	4	3	4
Sample 5	14	1	3	0	0	○	○	6	3	0	1	0	1	1	0	0	1	2	2	3	4	5	6
Sample 6	14	2	2	0	0	○	○	6	5	2	0	0	1	1	1	0	0	2	2	3	5	3	5
Sample 7	14	1	0	0	0	○	○	4	5	2	1	0	0	0	1	1	0	2	2	2	4	3	5
Sample 8	13	0	2	0	0	○	○	6	2	2	0	1	0	1	0	0	0	2	3	3	4	4	5
Sample 9	13	1	2	0	0	○	○	7	2	1	1	0	1	2	0	0	0	2	1	2	3	5	4
Sample 10	15	0	2	0	0	○	○	7	5	0	0	0	1	1	0	1	0	2	4	3	5	3	5
Sample 11	15	1	3	0	0	○	○	6	2	1	0	0	1	1	1	0	0	2	3	3	5	5	5
Sample 12	13	0	1	0	0	○	○	5	7	0	1	1	1	2	0	0	0	2	2	3	5	3	4
Sample 13	14	0	3	0	1	○	○	4	2	0	1	0	2	0	1	0	0	2	4	3	5	6	4
Sample 14	14	0	5	0	0	○	×	7	3	1	0	2	0	0	2	0	0	2	2	3	4	6	6
Sample 15	14	0	1	0	0	○	×	7	4	1	0	2	0	1	0	1	0	2	2	3	4	5	7
Sample 16	14	2	4	0	0	○	○	2	4	3	0	0	0	2	0	0	0	2	4	3	4	4	5
Sample 17	14	0	6	0	1	○	○	5	2	0	0	0	0	0	1	0	0	2	2	4	4	6	4
Sample 18	13	2	2	0	1	○	○	5	5	1	0	1	0	1	1	0	0	2	2	3	6	6	4
Sample 19	14	0	1	0	0	○	○	3	3	2	1	0	0	0	0	1	0	2	2	4	4	3	4
Sample 20	14	0	1	0	0	○	○	6	6	0	1	1	1	1	0	1	0	2	4	3	5	3	5
Sample 21	14	0	5	0	0	○	○	3	1	0	1	0	1	1	1	0	0	2	4	3	4	4	5
Sample 22	14	0	3	0	0	○	○	4	3	0	0	0	2	2	1	0	0	2	3	3	3	3	4
Sample 23	14	0	5	0	0	○	○	4	5	0	1	0	1	0	1	0	0	2	2	3	4	7	7
Sample 24	14	1	1	0	0	○	○	6	2	2	0	0	1	0	0	0	0	2	3	4	5	4	4
Sample 25	14	1	0	0	0	○	○	3	3	1	1	0	1	0	1	0	0	2	4	3	5	4	5
Sample 26	14	2	1	0	0	○	○	3	4	1	0	0	1	0	1	0	0	2	4	3	6	6	6
Sample 27	14	0	5	0	1	○	○	5	3	0	0	0	1	1	0	0	0	2	4	4	4	7	5
Sample 28	14	0	5	0	1	○	○	5	4	0	0	0	1	0	1	0	0	2	3	4	4	7	4
Sample 29	14	1	1	0	0	○	○	5	4	4	1	0	0	1	1	0	0	2	1	3	3	3	4
Sample 30	14	0	3	0	0	○	○	4	3	1	0	0	1	3	0	0	0	2	4	3	3	3	5
Sample 31	11	0	3	0	1	○	○	4	3	0	0	0	1	1	0	0	0	2	2	4	2	5	4
Sample 32	14	0	3	0	1	○	○	7	2	1	0	0	1	0	0	1	0	2	2	4	3	3	4
Total	445	17	79	0	7	32	30	164	111	30	12	8	21	24	18	8	1	2	2.7	3.1	4.1	4.4	4.8

was not directly told the chord symbols, because less than 20% of its chords were dissonant. Most dissonant intervals appeared between voices in which the arcs are omitted (e.g, alto and tenor, alto and bass) due to a computational cost. Ideally, these arcs should be added but adding arcs exponentially increase the computational cost (in fact, a conventional PC needs more than 40 minutes to harmonize four-measure melodies, even though the present model takes only a few seconds). Given that the voices connecting to each other with arcs did not cause dissonant intervals in the non-chord model, we expect that the model's dissonant intervals would decrease if we were to add arcs to it.

The results of the chord model include no non-diatonic notes, and the non-chord model employed only a few non-diatonic notes. These results mean that both models were trained in the typical usage of notes in the C-major key. Out of the seven non-diatonic notes that the non-chord model selected, two were F♯ notes forming a sequence of E–F♯–G and one was an F♯ note forming a sequence of G–F♯–G together with the previous and next notes. The former F♯ note can be interpreted as a passing note and the later F♯ note can be interpreted as an auxiliary note.

All pieces written by the chord model and 97% of the pieces by the non-chord model ends with the chord of C major, meaning that both models knew a basic rule of harmony, which is to end with the tonic chord. In all three pieces that did not end with C major from the non-chord model, the bass part ended with A, which technically made the last chord Am. Ending with Am instead of C after G7 in the C-major key is known as a deceptive cadence and is often used in realistic music. Therefore these results are not necessarily inappropriate.

In the chord model, 37% of all chords contained the same note name in more than three voices (e.g, C-G-C-C), while only 24% did in the non-chord model. These results arose because the chord model does not consider the relation between voices. It may be improved by adding arcs between voices, but the network would become more complex, making it difficult to train with a limited amount of data.

The results for the chord model contained many successive, large (perfect 4th or more) note motions compared to the non-chord model, because the chord models simultaneous nodes for the chord (C_i) and bass (B_i) have a greater dependency than do its successive bass nodes (B_{i+1}, B_i, B_{i+1}).

The number of different note names appearing in each voice is between 2 and 4 for the chord model and higher than 4 on average for the non-chord model. In fact, some of the chord models outputs for the alto and tenor voices were monotonous repetitions of only a few notes, while the non-chord model smoothly connected notes within each voice.

3.4 Discussion

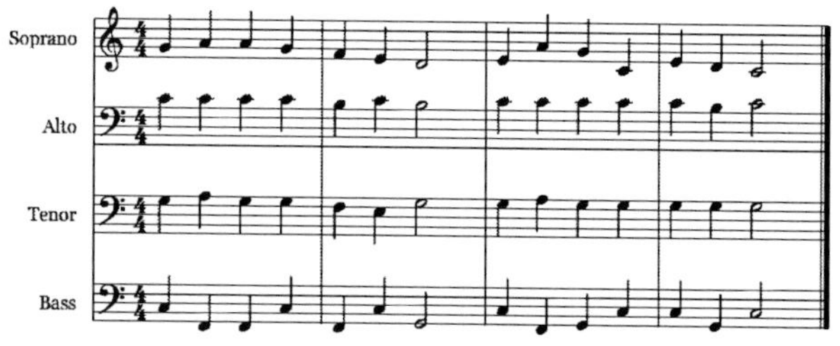

Figure 3. Sample 25 with the chord model

Figure 4. Sample 25 with the non-chord model

Figure 4 shows the result of Sample 25 for the non-chord model. This result has the following chord progression:

|C F F Em |Dm C G7 |C F C/E F |C/E G7 C/E |

From the fact that no voices have non-chord tones in this progression, we can deduce that this model successfully learned the chord tones of frequently used chords even though it was not given chord symbols during the training phase. In addition, the chord progression was based on functional harmony such as:

C (tonic) $\rightarrow$ F (subdominant) $\rightarrow$ Em (tonic counter parallel),

Dm (subdominant parallel) $\rightarrow$ C (tonic) $\rightarrow$ G7 (dominant).

In particular, the chord progression ends with a typical cadence, C $\rightarrow$ F $\rightarrow$ C $\rightarrow$ G7 $\rightarrow$ C. Using G7 instead of G as a previous chord of C was suitable because the tritone pushes towards a resolution. The bass line basically consists of conjunct motions and motions of 5th and therefore is a musically orthodox bass line; however, the bass note for the last C chord was E when it should have been C.

Table 2. Typical cadences generated with the non-chord model

Samples	Cadences		
Sample 1, 6, 9	F	Bm(-5)/D	C
Sample 2, 7, 10, 18, 28	C	Bm(-5)/D	C
Sample 3	Am	G	C
Sample 4, 16, 19, 29, 31	G7	G7	C
Sample 5, 8, 11, 13, 22	C	G7	C
Sample 20	C	F	C
Sample 23, 27	C	G/D	C
Sample 26	C/G	G7	C

Many other pieces also generated typical cadences. Examples are listed in Table 2. All of these cadences are commonly used in realistic music, so we consider our model to have learned most of the commonly used cadences.

The result of Sample 25 for the chord model is shown in Figure 3. The inferred chord progression consists of only three chords, C, F, and G, and this makes the harmony monotonous; however the actual chords are slightly different because the third note for the tenor voice is G instead of A and the fifth note for the alto voice is B instead of C. Every bass note is the root of the chord, and this makes the harmony more monotonous.

Figure 5. Sample 29 with the chord model

Figure 6. Sample 29 with the non-chord model

Figure 6 shows the result of Sample 29 for the non-chord model, which has an orthodox chord progression of ending the former half with G7 and the latter half with C. In successive G7 chords, the tenor note was D whether the soprano note was B, and vice versa. Taking different notes for the soprano and tenor voices avoided a monotonous harmony. The principal difference from the result for the chord model (Figure 7) was the chord progression in the third measure: | C F Bm(-5)/D C |. The result for the chord model includes only two chords, C and G, making the harmony very monotonous. Every note in the alto voice was C or B, and every note in the tenor voice was G. These are also reasons why the harmony is monotonous.

Next, we present an example of the non-chord model not generating a typical cadence (Figure 8). This piece ends with a deceptive cadence: | C G/B Am7 |. In addition, some chords sounded dissonant due to major 2nd or minor 2nd intervals between the tenor and bass voices. The chord model (Figure 7) produced no dissonant chords, but the harmony was monotonous similar to Sample 25 (Figure 4), because every chord was C, F, or G and because almost every bass note was the root of the chord.

To summarize, the non-chord model successfully achieved smooth harmonies by using various diatonic chords and in created a smooth bass line consisting mainly of conjunct motions and motions of 5th. In addition, the non-chord model generated typical and appropriate cadences in most pieces. The chord model generated monotonous harmonies in most pieces due to a combination of only C, F, and G and a bass line of almost all root notes.

Figure 7. Sample 14 with the chord model

Figure 8. Sample 14 with the non-chord model

4. CONCLUSIONS

In this paper, we report on our experiments with generating four-part harmonies for given soprano melodies by using Bayesian networks. Although related works have explicitly introduced to their machines the nodes or states that represent chords or harmonic functions, researchers should not explicitly introduce chords and nodes to the machine if they wish to determine whether the machine can acquire the principles of harmony from actual music data. Based on this idea, we attempted four-part harmonization with a Bayesian network that did not include chord nodes. The experimental results show that the non-chord model learned some basic rules in harmonics.

We suspect that machines take three steps while learning harmony: (1) avoiding dissonant notes, (2) avoiding prohibition in harmonics, and (3) exploring more musically aesthetic solutions. By reviewing the experimental results, we can see that our model without chord nodes attained the first step. To attain the second step (e.g., to avoid the prohibition of parallel 5th), our non-chord model will consider new dependencies, such as that between S_{i-1} and B_i. In the future, we will advance our computational model by constructing a larger-scale corpus and by adding new dependencies.

Acknowledgments

We thank Dr. Hiroko Terasawa and Dr. Masaki Matsubara(University of Tsukuba) for their invaluable comments on this project.

5. REFERENCES

[1] Hu. Jiarui, Guan Yin and Zhou Changle, “A Hierarchical Approach to Simulation of the Melodic Harmonization Process” , *Intelligent Computing and Intelligent Systems(ICIS)*, pp.780–784, 2010.

[2] Masanobu Miura, Seiji Kurokawa, Akihiro Aoi and Masezo Yanagida, “Yielding Harmony to Given Melodies”, *International Congress on Acoustic(ICA)* , pp.3417–3420, 2004. buys2012

[3] Takashi Kawakami, Mitsuru Nakai, Hiroshi Shimodaira and Shigeki Sagayama, “Hidden Markov Model Applied to Automatic Harmonization of Given Melodies”, *IPSJ SIG Notes 99-MUS-34*, pp.59–66, 2000.

[4] Kemal Ebcioglu, “An Except System for Harmonizing Chorales in the Style of J.S. Bach”, *Understanding Music with AI*, MIT Press, pp.294–333 1992.

[5] Hermann Hild, Johannes Feulner and Wolfram Menzel, “HARMONET: A Neural Net for Harmonizing Chorales in the Style of J.S.Bach”, *Neural Information Processing Systems Foundation(NIPS)*, pp.267–274, 1991.

[6] Francois Pachet and Pierre Roy, “Formulating Constraint Satisfaction Problems on Part-Whole Relations: The Case of Automatic Musical Harmonization”, *European Conference on Artificial Intelligence(ECAI)*, pp.1–11, 1998.

[7] Somnuk Phon-Amnuaisuk and Geraint A. Wiggins, “The Four-Part Harmonisation Problem: A comparison between Genetic Algorithms and a Rule-Based System”, *AISB’99 Symposium on Musical Creativity*, 1999.

[8] Moray Allan and Christopher K. I. Williams, “Harmonising Chorales by Probabilistic Inference”, *Advances in Neural Information Processing Systems*, 2004.

[9] Liangrong Yi and Judy Goldsmith, “Automatic Generation of Four-part Harmony”, *Proc. UAI-AW*, 2007.

[10] Jan Buys and Brink van der Merwe, “Chorale Harmonization with Weighted Finite-state Transducers”, *Twenty-Third Annual Symposium of the Pattern Recognition Association of South Africa(PRASA)*, pp.95–101, 2012.

[11] United Church of Christ in Japan Hymn committee, “Hymn Hymn the second edition Tomoni Utaou”, The Board of Publications The United of Church of Christ in Japan, 1982.

[12] Jou Shimaoka, et al.,“Harmonics Theory and Exercise -The Separate Volume- Enforcement of the task”, ONGAKU NO TOMO SHA CORP, 1967.

[13] “Band-in-a-Box”, PG music Inc., 2009.

A VERSATILE TOOLKIT FOR CONTROLLING DYNAMIC STOCHASTIC SYNTHESIS

Gordan Kreković
Faculty of Electrical Engineering and Computing,
University of Zagreb, Croatia
gordan.krekovic@fer.hr

Davor Petrinović
Faculty of Electrical Engineering and Computing,
University of Zagreb, Croatia
davor.petrinovic@fer.hr

ABSTRACT

Dynamic stochastic synthesis is one of the non-standard sound synthesis techniques used mostly in experimental computer music. It is capable of producing various rich and organic sonorities, but its drawback is the lack of a convenient approach to controlling the synthesis parameters. Several authors previously addressed this problem and suggested direct parameter control facilitated with additional features such as parameter automation. In this paper we present a comprehensive toolkit which, besides direct control, offers several new approaches. First, it enables controlling the synthesizer with an audio signal. Relevant audio features of an input signal are mapped to the synthesis parameters making the control immediate and intuitive. Second, the toolkit supports MIDI control so that musicians can use standard MIDI interfaces to play the synthesizer. Based on this approach we implemented a polyphonic MIDI-controlled synthesizer and included it in the toolkit along with other examples of controlling the dynamic stochastic synthesizer. The toolkit was developed in the widely used visual programming environment Pure Data.

1. INTRODUCTION

The usefulness of a sound synthesizer in practical tasks concerning musical composition depends not only on its capability to produce desired sonorities, but also on different aspects of its technical implementation [1]. Such aspects are, for example, suitability for a given hardware and software environment, intuitiveness of the user interface, flexibility in controlling the synthesis process, and many others. Nowadays composers have a wide range of possibilities when choosing sound synthesizers for their compositions.

Most well-known synthesis techniques have been implemented in various forms: as hardware synthesizers, software plugins, patches for music-specific programming languages, and applications for mobile devices. Interfaces for musical expression and parameter automation ensure convenient control over the synthesis parameters. Modern tools for sound synthesis generally open numerous opportunities in creating novel sonorities and successfully follow the growing ambitions of computer musicians.

However, there are still some insufficiently explored, yet interesting sound synthesis techniques which could widen the possibilities of musical expression, but have not yet been adapted for practical usage. One such example is dynamic stochastic synthesis devised by Iannis Xenakis in the early 1970s. This synthesis technique is characterized by distinctive and rich timbral qualities. Nevertheless, a convenient solution for controlling the synthesis parameters is still missing. We believe that the lack of an intuitive control is one of the reasons why this technique has not been employed in a larger number of compositions or further explored.

Dynamic stochastic synthesis (DSS) produces a waveform by interpolating a set of constantly varying breakpoints [2]. The waveform evolves over time in a nondeterministic manner which results in organic and complex sonorities. Composers can control the DSS process by restraining ranges, within which the waveform can change, and by specifying amounts and probability distributions of those changes. The problem is that manipulating the aforementioned ranges, amounts, and parameters of probability distributions is usually inconvenient for most practical tasks. Such synthesis parameters are not intuitive and do not allow the use of typical musical interfaces for playing. Moreover, the original implementation of the dynamic stochastic synthesizer did not even provide any kind of support for changing parameters during the synthesis process.

Several authors have already addressed the same problem and proposed various interface designs for direct parameter control [3-5]. They suggested graphical user interfaces, keyboard shortcuts, and MIDI controllers. One standout solution was a mobile application which obtained parameters from multi-touch gestures and accelerometers [6]. Even though these interfaces were straightforward and helpful, musicians still needed to cope with values of the synthesis parameters. To avoid numerical parameters and keep ideas in the musical domain, in our previous research we proposed an approach that uses an input audio signal for controlling the DSS process [7]. The algorithm was based on mapping selected audio features into the synthesis parameters, so that the control was as intuitive as possible.

The research described in this paper takes a few steps further in making DSS more suitable for the practical needs of computer musicians. Several approaches to controlling synthesis parameters were developed and packaged together in a comprehensive toolkit for the visual programming language Pure Data [8]. Besides direct parameter control and control using an audio signal, we introduced a new approach based on MIDI notes and controllers. This novel approach allows musicians to play a dynamic stochastic synthesizer using regular MIDI interfaces. The toolkit was designed so that it can be easily modified, extended, and integrated in compositions.

2. DYNAMIC STOCHASTIC SYNTHESIS

Before presenting the toolkit for controlling dynamic stochastic synthesis, here is a short overview of this synthesis technique. Dynamic stochastic synthesis was devised by Iannis Xenakis as a result of his ambition to achieve unified and simultaneous engagement on different time-scales within the composition, from the overall structure of the composition to its microstructure and tone quality. Before this breakthrough, he employed stochastic processes for choosing note attributes and forming musical structures. To expand the same principle on the microstructure level, Xenakis suggested applying stochastic processes to the sample level.

Dynamic stochastic synthesis generates samples by interpolating a set of breakpoints which change their amplitudes and positions in time stochastically. A breakpoint position is represented relatively to the preceding breakpoint in number of samples, so it is commonly called breakpoint duration. Initial amplitudes and durations are usually chosen randomly or taken from a trigonometric function. At every repetition of the waveform, these values are varied independently of each other using random walk. That means that both the amplitude and the duration of a certain breakpoint are changed by adding random steps to the values in the previous cycle as shown in Figure 1. A succession of random steps applied on all breakpoints causes the continuous variation of the waveform. The amount and character of the variation depend on a selected probability distribution and its parameters. Both amplitude and duration random walks are limited each with two reflecting barriers which bounce excessive values back into the predefined range. These barriers prevent breakpoints from going too far from their initial positions and therefore enable control over amplitude and frequency ranges of the overall waveform.

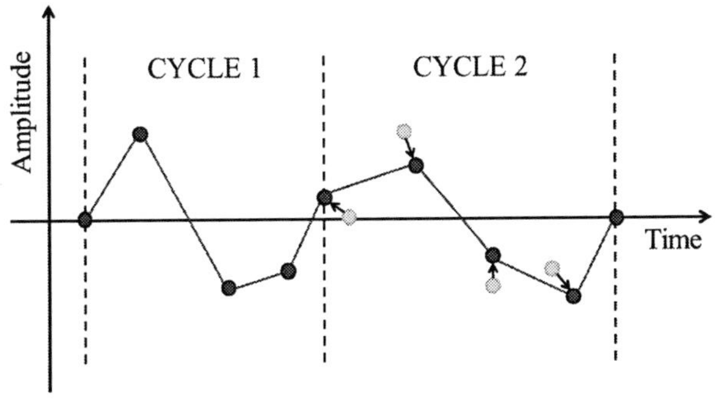

Figure 1. Breakpoints change their positions from one repetition to another. Light blue circles in the second represent positions from the first cycle, whilst darker circles represent new positions.

Parameterization of the algorithm is achieved through: (1) the number of breakpoints in a waveform, (2) barriers of the amplitude random walk, (3) probability distribution of the amplitude random walk and its parameters, (4) barriers of the duration random walk, and (5) probability distribution of the duration random walk and its parameters. The amplitude barriers provide control over the amplitude range of the generated waveform, whilst the duration barriers define minimal and maximal number of samples between two breakpoints. If changes in amplitude and duration in successive repetitions are small, the synthesized sound is relatively simple, but it can have interesting modulation effects. On the other hand, as the changes become larger, the sound becomes more complex and noisier. Detailed explanations of the original algorithm can be found in [9] and [10]. Several computer musicians later implemented this algorithm extending the basic concept with new ideas [3, 5, 11, 12].

3. TOOLKIT FOR PURE DATA

The motivation while developing this toolkit was to make DSS available to a wider community of computer musicians. Also, by providing several interfaces for controlling the DSS process, we wanted to bring this non-standard synthesis technique closer to the practical needs of composers and live performers. For implementation we chose Pure Data, a visual programming language which is freely available for different operating systems and which is popular among musicians and multimedia artists [8]. All parts of this library were developed as abstract patches, so that everyone familiar with Pure Data can easily modify and extend them.

3.1 gendyn~

The central patch in the toolkit is a straightforward implementation of the basic DSS algorithm. It was named *gendyn~* after the original program by Xenakis. The purpose of this patch is to synthesize audio signal accordingly to input parameters. Through the inlets it receives the number of breakpoints in a waveform n, frequency limits $f_{\min}$ and $f_{\max}$, amplitude range a, and statistical parameters for the both random walks p_1 and p_2.

Frequency limits $f_{\min}$ and $f_{\max}$ are used to calculate barriers of the duration random walk. Frequency limits expressed in Hertz are more meaningful then duration limits expressed in number of samples. They are also more convenient for direct integration with patches that provide DSS process control using audio or MIDI signals. For that reason, *gendyn~* receives frequency limits through the inlets and converts them to the duration limits using these simple formulae:

$$d_{\min} = \lceil f_S / (f_{\max} \cdot n) \rceil, \tag{1}$$

$$d_{\max} = \lceil f_S / (f_{\min} \cdot n) \rceil, \tag{2}$$

where d_{min} and d_{max} are the maximal and the minimal duration expressed in number of samples, f_S is the sampling frequency, f_{max} and f_{min} represent the frequency limits, whilst n stands for the number of breakpoints in a waveform.

The amplitude range of the waveform is controlled with the parameter a so that the amplitude random walk has reflecting barriers at $-a$ and $+a$. Therefore, this parameter defines the maximal absolute amplitude of the breakpoints.

The only probability distribution available in our current implementation is the normal distribution. Its mean value for both random walks is zero, because symmetrical probability densities generally prevent breakpoints from gravitating towards one of the barriers. The standard deviation of the distribution for the amplitude random walk is calculated by scaling the parameter p_1 proportionally to the amplitude range a. Similarly, for the duration random walk, its input parameter p_2 is scaled accordingly to the range contained between minimal and maximal duration. Extending the patch with more probability distributions is simple, but requires adding a new parameter for selecting among available distributions.

3.2 audio2gendyn~

An approach to controlling the dynamic stochastic synthesis with an audio signal was proposed in our previous work [7]. The purpose of that research was to reduce the need for manipulating numerical parameters and to allow musicians to control a synthesizer by playing a musical instrument, singing, or experimenting with different sound sources. The algorithm was designed to extract relevant audio features from the input signal and map them to the synthesis parameters so that the relation between the input signal and the synthesized signal is as natural as possible.

As our original implementation version was done in C++, for the Pure Data toolkit we developed a new patch from scratch and also introduced several improvements and simplifications. This new patch is called *audio2gendyn~* and uses features of the input audio to calculate synthesis parameters. The synthesis engine *gendyn~*, which is included in this patch, receives these parameters and produces the resulting sound accordingly. The amplitude, frequency, and timbral qualities of the synthesized sound are expected to follow the corresponding characteristics of the input audio signal. The aim was not to imitate the input signal (as it is not possible with DSS anyway), but to achieve intuitive control over the synthesis process.

The most appropriate audio features of the input signal for calculating the frequency limits f_{min} and f_{max} are fundamental frequency f_0 and spectral centroid f_C. Whilst for periodic signals the fundamental frequency works well, for noisy signals much better results are obtained by using the spectral centroid. Spectral centroid indicates the center of the gravity of a frequency spectrum and it is perceptually related to the impression of timbral brightness.

In case of the periodic input signal, the fundamental frequency is extracted using the object *sigmund~* which is one of the standard Pure Data extras. The frequency limits f_{min} and f_{max} are then defined as a perfect fifth below and a perfect fifth above the fundamental frequency, i.e.

$$f_{\min} = 2f_0/3, \quad f_{\max} = 3f_0/2. \tag{3}$$

In contrast to our initial algorithm [7], here the frequency limits are strictly related to the fundamental frequency by the given musical intervals (i.e. frequency ratios). Timbral qualities of the input sound are not considered for determining the frequency limits. The advantage of this simplification is that the frequency of the overall synthesized waveform depends only on the fundamental frequency of the input signal and never drifts too far from it. However, timbral qualities of the input signal are not neglected here; they affect the standard deviation of the probability distribution for the duration random walk as will be described later.

If the input signal does not show significant periodicity, the spectral centroid is used similarly as the fundamental frequency in the earlier case. First, the spectral centroid f_C is calculated using the object *specCentroid~* from *timbreID* toolkit [13]. Then the frequency limits are defined as:

$$f_{\min} = f_C/8, \quad f_{\max} = f_C/4. \tag{4}$$

The scaling factors were obtained experimentally so that switching between periodic and non-periodic input signals does not cause unpleasant glitches in the synthesized signal. These factors were chosen after numerous tests with different types of sounds including those with both periodic and non-periodic parts such as speech signals and sounds of plucked instruments.

Defining the barriers for the amplitude random walk was a much simpler task. The amplitude of the synthesized signal is expected to follow the amplitude of the input signal, so the algorithm uses the root mean square amplitude of an input frame to control the parameter a.

Finally, the only remaining parameters are p_1 and p_2. Standard deviations of the probability distributions in random walks significantly affect timbral qualities of the synthesized sounds. Wider probability density functions result with a less stable waveform and consequently less predictable frequency content of the synthesized signal. For that reason, the parameters p_1 and p_2 should be defined accordingly to the level of how tone-like the input sound is, as opposed to being noise-like. A suitable measure for this purpose is spectral flatness [14]. This feature is one of audio descriptors in the MPEG-7 standard and it is commonly used for robust retrieval of song archives. Spectral flatness quantifies amount of peaks or resonant structure, as opposed to the flat spectrum of white noise. A low flatness suggests that the spectral power is concentrated in a small number of spectral bands, whilst higher values indicate that the power is more equally distributed among all bands. The spectral flatness is defined as a quotient of the geometric and the arithmetic mean of the power spectrum, i.e.

$$S_F = \frac{\sqrt[N]{\prod_{n=0}^{N-1} x(n)}}{\frac{1}{N}\sum_{n=0}^{N-1} x(n)}, \tag{5}$$

where $x(n)$ stands for the magnitude of the n-th frequency bin.

To calculate the spectral flatness in *audio2gendyn~* we employed the object *specFlatness~* from *timbreID* toolkit [13]. The scaled spectral flatness is then used for the both parameters p_1 and p_2:

$$p_1 = p_2 = s \cdot S_F \,, \tag{6}$$

where s stands for a scaling factor and S_F denotes the spectral flatness. Many subjective tests proved the suitability of such mapping. The value of the scaling factor was obtained experimentally so that the character of the synthesized signal is notably affected by the spectral flatness of the input signal.

3.3 midi2gendyn~

The second solution for controlling DSS included in this toolkit is based on the standard MIDI interface. The usage of MIDI controls was suggested earlier [5], but only for direct parameter control. The musician could manipulate parameters with a MIDI controller and send values to the dynamic stochastic synthesizer in the same way as if using a graphical user interface. Evidently, this was not a different approach to control, but only facilitation.

Most sound synthesizers can be played with MIDI keyboards and other MIDI interfaces which generate notes and not just control values. To apply this traditional playing approach to DSS, we implemented *midi2gendyn~*. It is the first polyphonic MIDI synthesizer based on DSS. The patch receives MIDI notes, velocities, and other controls, maps them into synthesis parameters, and employs sound units based on *gendyn~* to generate the sound.

To determine frequency limits f_{min} and f_{max} from the input note, the algorithm converts the MIDI note number into the frequency and puts the limits symmetrically around it. This way, the frequency of the input note is in the middle between f_{min} and f_{max}. The width of that frequency range is specified with a separate MIDI control value. This approach is convenient in practical cases as the musician can play the synthesizer using a keyboard and simultaneously change the frequency width using a slider, knob, or pedal.

The amplitude range a is calculated by scaling the note velocity, whilst the parameters p_1 and p_2 are separately obtained from corresponding MIDI controls. The synthesizer also receives the pitch bend control which affects the tone frequency and therefore the frequency limits f_{min} and f_{max} accordingly.

4. EXPERIMENTS AND EXAMPLES

The patches from this toolkit can be used in different ways. For that reason we prepared several typical usage examples and included them in the package. Those examples can be reused, modified, and extended to meet specific practical needs.

4.1 Direct control and automation

The first two examples show how a dynamic stochastic synthesizer can be controlled by direct parameter manipulation. In the first example, sliders on the graphical user interface are connected to the inlets of *gendyn~* (Figure 2). These sliders also receive MIDI controls, so that they can be managed from a MIDI interface with physical sliders or knobs. Audio effects can be applied on the pure audio signal synthesized by a dynamic stochastic synthesizer. In these examples we added a simple reverb, which was very efficient in making the sound richer and characteristically colored.

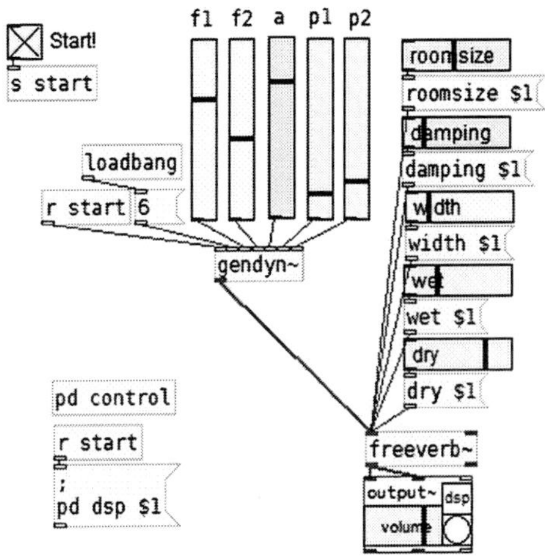

Figure 2. A patch which demonstrates direct parameter control using sliders. Beside sliders on the graphical user interface, it is possible to use MIDI controls defined in the subpatch called *control*.

The second example of direct parameter control demonstrates parameter automation (Figure 3). The patch reads parameter values from tables. As Pure Data supports drawing values on graphical representations of tables, such automation could be convenient both for composing and live performing.

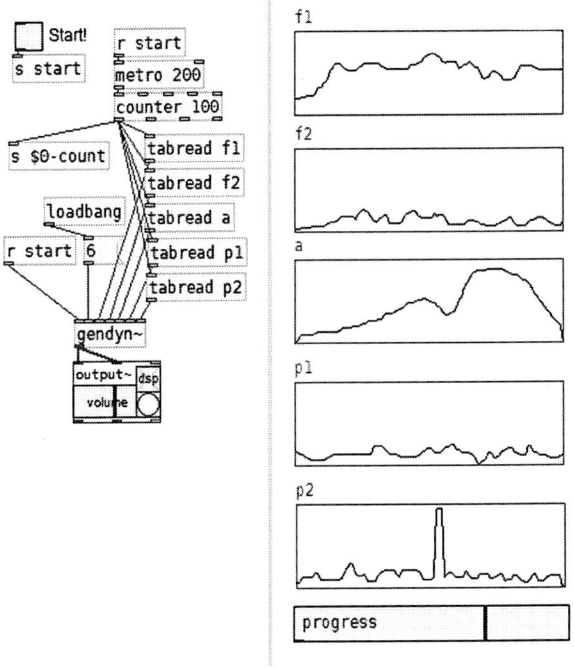

Figure 3. An example of parameter automation. Parameter values are stored in the tables on the right side.

4.2 Examples of audio control

Experimenting with different types of sounds for controlling the DSS showed that this synthesis technique can produce more than just buzzing sounds with characteristic drifts in frequency and amplitude. Mapping relevant audio features into the corresponding synthesis parameter enables the synthesizer to mimic some characteristics of the input sound. It is easier to make simultaneous and quick changes in parameter values than by direct parameter manipulation. The most interesting sounds for controlling the DSS are those with high variability of their audio features such as percussive sounds and human voice.

Within the toolkit we provided two examples of receiving an audio signal for controlling the DSS. The first one uses inputs from the audio interface, whilst the second one reads a wave file as shown in Figure 4.

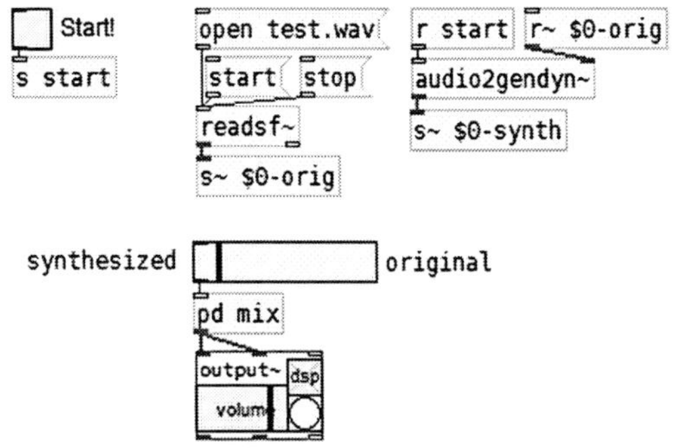

Figure 4. Controlling the dynamic stochastic synthesis with an audio signal from a wave file. It is possible to mix the synthesized and the original signals using the yellow slider.

4.3 Polyphonic MIDI-controlled synthesizer

To test the *midi2gendyn~* patch we used a MIDI keyboard. Phenomena which most strongly affected the playing experience were frequency drifts. They always occur when the frequency range $f_{max} - f_{min}$ and duration standard deviation obtained from the parameter p_2 are higher than zero. Changes in the waveform frequency are characteristic to DSS and result with buzzing, unstable and drifting sounds. One of the possible applications of such sounds in compositions is to layer them with the sounds generated by other synthesis engines.

Demonstration of the toolkit and highlights from all of the mentioned experiments are shown in the video which is available at the following link:
http://www.youtube.com/watch?v=1Uk6KeglvnI

5. CONCLUSIONS

By implementing several different approaches to controlling DSS in a single toolkit, we made the synthesis technique more convenient for particular use cases. This should motivate musicians to experiment further in their compositions and live performances. Since it is a non-standard synthesis technique, we cannot expect DSS to suddenly become popular in a wider range of music genres even when researches like this one are available. However, it is now more accessible to musicians than it was before and it is ready to be used in numerous ways.

6. REFERENCES

[1] D. A. Jaffe, "Ten Criteria for Evaluating Synthesis Techniques". *Computer Music Journal*, vol. 19, no. 1, pp. 76–87, 1995.

[2] I. Xenakis, *Formalized Music: Thought and Mathematics in Music*, Stuyvesant NY: Pendragon Press, 1992.

[3] P. Hoffman, "The new GENDYN program", *Computer Music Journal*, vol. 24, no. 2, pp. 31-38, 2000.

[4] S. Bokesoy and G. Pape. "Stochos: software for real-time synthesis of stochastic music", *Computer Music Journal*, vol. 27, no. 3, pp. 33-43, 2003.

[5] A. R. Brown, "Extending dynamic stochastic synthesis", *Proceedings of the International Computer Music Conference*, Barcelona, Spain, 2005, pp. 111-114

[6] N. Collins, "Implementing stochastic synthesis for SupperCollider and iPhone". *Proceedings of the Xenakis International Symposium*, London, 2011.

[7] G. Kreković, I. Brkić, "Controlling Dynamic Stochastic Synthesis with an Audio Signal", *Proceedings of the International Computer Music Conference*, 2012, pp. 100-104.

[8] M. Puckette, "Pure Data", *Proceedings of the International Computer Music Conference*, San Francisco, USA, 1996.

[9] M. H. Serra, "Stochastic composition and stochastic timbre: GENDY3 by Iannis Xenakis", *Perspectives of New Music*, vol. 31, no. 1, pp. 236-257, 1992.

[10] S. Loque, "The stochastic synthesis of Iannis Xenakis", *Leonardo Music Journal*, vol. 19, no. 1, pp. 77-84, 2009.

[11] S. Russell. (2012). *Gendyflext* [Online]. Available: https://github.com/ssfrr/gendyflext

[12] J. Young, "Rethinking synthesis: extending and exploring Gendyn", BA thesis, University of Sussex: Department of Informatics, 2010.

[13] W. Brent, "A timbre analysis and classification toolkit for Pure Data", *Proceedings of the International Computer Music Conference*, New York, USA, 2010

[14] J. Johnston, "Transform coding of audio signals using perceptual noise criteria", *IEEE Journal on Selected Areas in Communications,* vol. 6, no. 2, pp. 314-323, 1988.

Visions of sound: The Centro di Sonologia Computazionale, from Computer Music to Sound and Music Computing

Sergio Canazza
CSC-DEI, Univ. Padova
canazza@dei.unipd.it

Giovanni De Poli
CSC-DEI, Univ. Padova
depoli@dei.unipd.it

Alvise Vidolin
CSC-DEI, Univ. Padova
vidolin@dei.unipd.it

ABSTRACT

Centro di Sonologia Computazionale (CSC) scientific research was the premise for subsequent activities of musical informatics, and is still one of the main activities of the Centre. Today CSC activities rely on a composite group of people, which include the Center board of directors and personnel, guest researchers and musicians, and particularly on master students attending the course "Sound and Music Computing" at Dept. of Information Engineering (DEI), which is historically tightly linked to the CSC. The dissemination of scientific results as well as the relationship between art and science is hard and surely not trivial. With this aim, this paper describes an exhibition that illustrated the history of CSC, from the scientific, technological and artistic points of view. This exhibition is one of the first examples of "a museum" of Computer Music and SMC researches.

1. INTRODUCTION

Since the invention of musical instruments, art and technology have stimulated and benefit one another. The craftsmanship required to make a violin is a classic example, but the invention of music-writing techniques was also an achievement, often based on complex mathematics, which enabled musicians in the late Middle Ages to create intricate combinations of sounds.

Over the centuries, Padova institutes, musicians and scholars have helped to revolutionize the science and art of sound. During the late 20th century, the Centro di Sonologia Computazionale [1] (CSC, Center of Computational Sonology) of Padova University (Italy) and the Electronic Music class at the Conservatory "Cesare Pollini" in Padova gave birth to a unique scientific, technological, and artistic experience, which stemmed from individual collaborations and multidisciplinary exchanges.

Between the 1970s and 1990s, CSC emerged as one of the world leading centres for research into "Computer music". The design and development of software programs and hardware devices (filters, computers) conducted by Paduan researchers have since then produced state-of-the art results from both the technological and musical standpoints, and have generated collaborations with several renowned contemporary composers. CSC engineering skills have been used to build electronic and digital instruments, augmented reality systems, immersive video-games, and measuring instruments. It has also led to advances in such widely differing fields as sound design, musical cultural heritage preservation and promotion, and cognitive/physical rehabilitation.

The CSC is carrying out a project for the preservation and restoration of electrophone equipments and audio documents. An important (from both scientific and dissemination points of view) moment in this project was the realization of an exhibition by the University of Padova, in collaboration with the SaMPL Lab of the Conservatory "C. Pollini": *Visions of sound. Electronic music at the University of Padova*, open from April 3 to July 18, 2012 at the exhibition halls of the Botanical Garden. The exhibition showed the history of the computer music produced in Padova and was assisted by various events, including a series of educational seminars held by CSC researchers and some concerts. The dissemination of the Computer Music history is hard and complicated, because of its multi-faced nature. It is necessary to emphasize the communication of all its different aspects, in particular it is important that general public understand also the genesis of the computer music works. This paper presents our experience.

The exhibition illustrated the history of CSC, from scientific, technological and artistic points of view. From the first experiments by Teresa Rampazzi and by the group *Nuove Proposte Sonore* (NPS) in the sixties, the close collaboration among the Conservatory, the CSC and the Computing Centre of the University, to the present, it was possible to expose historic equipments, as the original magnetic tape recorder used by Teresa Rampazzi, a Synthi AKS, an ARP 2500 (now the last example in Italy), and the *4i System*, devices which allowed the realization of the electronic music of the last decades, art music as well as consumer music. It was also possible to listen to some major works realized at the CSC, e.g., *Prometeo* by Luigi Nono, *Perseo e Andromeda* by Salvatore Sciarrino, and *Medea* by Adriano Guarnieri: for this latter musical work the original multi-channel installation was recreated, for the first time after its première in 2002 at the *Teatro La Fenice* in Venice. The exhibition was enriched by numerous interactive installations, specially designed and realized by researchers

[1] CSC was founded by Giovanni Battista Debiasi (1928-2012): this paper is humbly and affectionately dedicated to his memory, a leading researcher and an outstanding teacher whose brightness and kindness we will always remember.

Figure 1. Giovanni Battista Debiasi, Vicenza (Italy), 4th June 1928 – Padova (Italy), 24th June 2012.

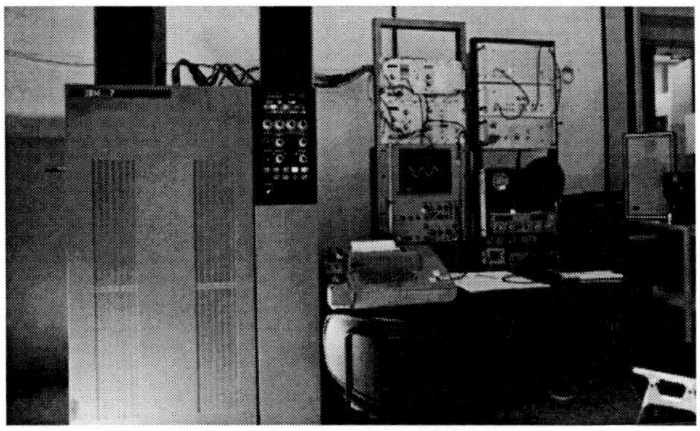

Figure 2. System panels for recording, sound synthesis and processing in 1979.

at CSC – which today is with the Department of Information Engineering (DEI) – to introduce visitors to the world of sound, applications of technology, the result of the novel research in the Sound and Music Computing field, in particular immersive reality systems, preservation and restoration of musical cultural heritage, information systems for enhanced learning and for rehabilitation of disabled people.

This exhibit aims at showing the deep connections between academic research and the multifaceted world of sound, and their influences on both art music and popular music, especially from the Seventies.

This exhibition was important (i) as a moment of cultural reflection, because it has led to the comparison of the different research areas that have occurred since the sixties to the present, and (ii) as a stimulus to overcome the problems related to the preservation and restoration of cultural heritage music the CSC.

In Sec. 2 the history of the Centre is concisely summarized. Then all the sections of the exhibition are detailed, as an example of dissemination to a general public, reported here for consideration by the SMC community.

2. CENTRO DI SONOLOGIA COMPUTAZIONALE

The CSC was born in 1979 [1], but it was already active since the late sixties as a point of reference for the birth and development of computer music in the world (the musical works realized in CSC are listed at `http://csc.dei.unipd.it/musical_productions.html`). At the same time, with its own set of electronic equipment (filters, digital signal processors, computers) specially designed and programmed by researchers at the Department of Information Engineering, it is a striking witness to the technological era and its evolution in recent decades (Sec. 4).

CSC, today directed by Giovanni De Poli, was founded by Giovanni Battista Debiasi (fig. 1). In 1957 Giovanni Battista Debiasi, at the University of Padova, proposed an original work about an electronic organ based on photodiodes. This was the first step of a multidisciplinary future for electric/electronic engineering and music in Padova. In the early seventies Debiasi carried out research on speech analysis and synthesis, in collaboration with Gian Antonio Mian and Carlo Offelli [2, 3]. In the eighties and nineties, in advance to the international scientific community, Debiasi studied issues related to the preservation and restoration of cultural musical heritage. He trained hundreds of students: his research fields are now everywhere, in Italy and in the world, and this gives the sign of the importance that he played in the birth and development of Sound and Music Computing (see, at least, [1, 4, 5]).

Fig. 2 shows the system panels for recording, sound synthesis and processing in 1979: this system was also used in the Summer Schools organized in CSC and that were considered as world references in the field of computer music. Among the various hardware systems of CSC, particularly important from the history and the musicology points of view, was the project – granted by the Laboratory for Computer Music at the La Biennale (LIMB) in Venice, in collaboration with IRCAM in Paris – that led to the realization of the *4i System* (fig. 3 and Sec. 7).

CSC has been mainly a centre of promotion and cultural diffusion of music informatics since its foundation. Thanks to close collaboration among experts of various disciplines, it has been possible to create an interdisciplinary group, which has become an international reference in the field, and has come to be part of contemporary music history. Activities of CSC can be grouped into four main areas: scientific research, music research, production and performance of music works, teaching and dissemination.

The rapid evolution known by computers and microelectronic devices in the second half of the last century has led to the development of several sound synthesis methods (Sec. 5) and to reduction the processing times, allowing to recover the performer-instrument relationship and then reintroducing the causality between gesture and sound typical of the musician with his/her instrument. This evolution permitted to integrate the electronic medium with traditional instruments, mixing freely the sound of mechanical devices with sound processing generated during the performance: arising the live electronics performer, which allowed to recover the absence of the performer typical of electroacoustic music (Sec. 7), when the public was confused in front of stages with only loudspeakers. The com-

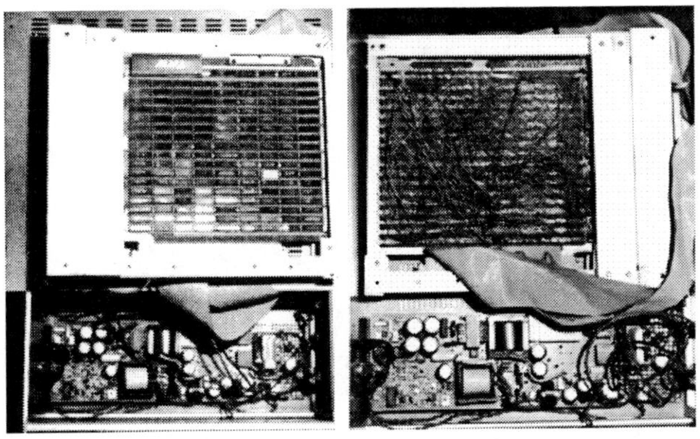

Figure 3. *4i System* developed by Giuseppe Di Giugno.

puter allows to control individual processes (synthesis and sound processing) to a more abstract level than that reached by the electrophone equipments of the sixties (generally based on voltage control). The use of systems with multiple speakers, thanks to which the sounds came from different directions (front, back, side, top, bottom) made obsolete the traditional concert halls and the placement of chairs lined up in the theater. Even at this stage the CSC played a pioneering role (see Sections 7, 8, and 9), becoming a leader in the opera *Prometeo* by Luigi Nono (Venice La Biennale, 1984; Teatro alla Scala, 1985) and the work *Perseo e Andromeda* by Salvatore Sciarrino (Staatstheater Stuttgart, 1991; Teatro alla Scala, 1992).
Now the CSC is carrying out researches in all the areas of SMC field (Sec. 6).

3. *WELL-CALCULATED MUSIC*: PREMISES

The first section of the exhibition introduces the roots of music in Padova. One of the major breakthroughs in the 14th century Italy was the development of written music and musical symbols. Music had traditionally been handed down orally, but musicians and composers had come to realize that complex musical constructs had to be written down and that symbols were needed to set the time-values between different sounds. The composer and theorist Marchetto da Padova pioneered these developments and his arithmetic- and geometry-based studies paved the way for musical notation, the forerunner of modern music scores. Mathematical studies are also at the core of Giuseppe Tartini's theories (1692-1770). He was "first violin and head of concerts" at St. Antonio's Basilica in Padova. He discovered a "terzo suono" (literally a "third sound"), which he heard when two different notes were played together on a violin. His work was devoted to linking the physics to a musical and metaphysical theory. Tartini is known for his art of bowing, as he used a specially design bow to create virtuoso effects.
In this section of the exhibition the following items were exhibited:

- original manuscripts (unique source worldwide) of the first half of 15th century;
- the original *Trattato di musica secondo la vera scienza dell'armonia* (Treatise on music according to the true science of harmony) by Giuseppe Tartini, 1754. In this treatise, published in 1754, the violinist and composer Giuseppe Tartini accounted for his research on the phenomenon of the third sound. He included elements of physics, arithmetic, and geometry, organized into a complex theory which sparkled a lively discussion;
- original ancient violins and bows.

4. *WELL-CALCULATED MUSIC*: THE 20TH CENTURY

When the first instruments able to generate "new" sounds appeared in the 1950s', composers and musicians welcomed enthusiastically this revolution. Electronic music was born, i.e. music realized with either analogue electronic (1950s' and 1960s') or digital (since the 1970s') devices. In the most important international research centre, technology was used to create new sounds, or to explore and process sounds recorded and produced with this equipment. The new music had no performers, and the loudspeaker – the main mean to deliver sound to listeners – became the new "star" of concert halls. Musical structures became more free, while the need for accurate control of durations and for adequate notation posed new problems.

At the CSC, Teresa Rampazzi [2] was an electronic-music pioneer. She and Ennio Chiggio set up the NPS Group *Nuove Proposte Sonore* (New Sound Proposals) in Padova in 1965. Chiggio was part of *Gruppo Enne*, a group which applied kinetics to visual art. The NPS Group conducted research into the timbre and density of "sound events", creating "sound objects" (or "sounding objects" according to Rampazzi's own terminology) and more or less complex tracks which explored acoustic phenomena. In 1972, Rampazzi donated her equipment to the Conservatory of Padova, which was one of the very first italian Conservatories where electronic music classes were started – following Firenze.
In this section of the exhibition the following equipments were exhibited:

- the original ARP 2500 (see fig. 4). It is an early 1970s analogue synthesizer: it was one of the most versatile and powerful professional synthesisers of its time. The synthesizer came with a wide range of compatible modules which could be connected to generate and manipulate sound;
- EMS Synthi AKS portable analogue synthesizer manufactured by Electronic Music Studios in London (fig. 5). Its built-in pin matrix, sequencer and keyboard pack the power of an electronic-music laboratory into a portable briefcase;
- TEAC A 3340 S (see fig. 4). Four-track tape recorder introduced in the mid-1970s. It played tracks through four loudspeakers and paved the way for modern "surround sound";

[2] The title of this section of the exhibition was an usual question by Teresa Rampazzi to her students: "but do you have it [your music] well calculated?"

Figure 4. The original ARP 2500, the stop-watch and the TEAC reel to reel tape recorder (4-tracks) used by Teresa Rampazzi.

Figure 5. The Synthi AKS used by Teresa Rampazzi.

- Junghans stop-watch – used by Teresa Rampazzi for the realization of her *well-calculated* music (see fig. 4);
- Teletype, electromechanical device used to transmit text messages and employed by early computers at CSC for data input/output purposes;
- Digital-to-analogue and analogue-to-digital converters at 12 and 16 bits, originally connected to the IBM System/7, with programmable clock filter, low-pass filters at 4.5 kHz, 7 kHz, and 14 kHz.

These items, following the musical instruments history (Sec. 3), allow the general public to understand the genesis of the Computer Music.

5. NUMBER AND SOUND

In the Seventies, composers discovered the potential of information technology and adopted computers and electronics devices: the born of Computer Music. in the international field sound synthesis had an extraordinary impact on music writing, allowing composers to better understand the way in which sounds are formed and their aural effect, transforming sometimes even the orchestral writing [6]. Sec. 3 showed how Padova in the 14th century has been a research laboratory in musical writing (in particular with Marchetto da Padova). In line with this, it is interesting to note that in the Seventies the CSC contributed to the development of a formal musical notation language for computer [7].
The CSC is among the pioneers of the most innovative and interesting methods of synthesis, based on sound source (e.g., a musical instrument) modeling, instead of signal modeling [8]. This synthesis uses algorithms that produce the sound as a side effect of a process of simulation of physical phenomena, i.e., reproducing what occurs in nature. The bow-string interaction in the physical reality, studied by Tartini in his treatise (Sec. 3), in this way becomes a mathematical model.

The results of the research conducted by computer music brings a terrific deepening of knowledge within the acoustic and psychoacoustic. It is with these studies that the foundations are laid for the development of auditory communication in multimedia and multimodal environments (virtual and augmented reality). In this section multimedia installations were exhibited, in which the visitors could interact with different sound synthesis techniques; a digital juke-box with some of the most important musical works realized in CSC, restored on purpose by the authors; a printout MARCR J578 A, the publication by Enore Zaffiri *Musica per un anno* (Music for a year), DUCHAMP Center; a folder NPS (*Nuove Proposte Sonore*), with various enclosed documents; a copy of the magazine *Oggetti Sonori* (Sound Objects), or *Oggetto Sonoro* (Sound Object); two original video works by Ennio Chiggio: small television in plexiglass display cabinet, with video board, and *Dischi a rotazione apparente* (Discs with apparent rotation) – *Marcel Rotour* (1967, Photographic tape, plexiglass and wooden frame, 50x50x20 cm). These different items helps general public to contextualize the musical works, showing the relationship among music and others arts.

6. SOUND AND SOCIETY

At the end of the Nineties, the international computer music research domain evolved into Sound and Music Computing (SMC), which also includes non-musical areas related to research on sound. The results are manifold.
Researchers in CSC developed multimodal interactive systems for teaching with special interfaces, specifically designed to enhance the learning of students with disabilities. The research on the preservation and restoration of audio documents (see [9] for a review) are combined with technology's innovations in information retrieval to meet the needs of today society where everything has to be stored, browsable, and available "anybody, anytime and everywhere". This implies the definition of new strategies for data storage and study of new techniques of content search (e.g., by humming) in data mining, as well as listening strategies appropriate to each situation (the living room, the concert hall, the walkman/iPod headphones). Innovative 3D audio techniques [10] allow to virtually recreate an environment in which various sound sources are located at different moving points in space, with important applications in virtual reality systems, from immersive video games

Figure 6. The model – as shown in the exhibition – of the original building designed by Renzo Piano in 1984 for *Prometeo* by Nono.

Figure 7. An interactive installation dedicated to explain the results of the 3D audio research domain. The visitor could appreciate the change of the sound spatialization depending on of his head movement.

to flight simulators (see an example in fig. 7). Microphones arrays systems with variable geometry are specifically designed for both monitoring of urban environments for homeland security and as musicians tracking system for live electronics [11].

7. MUSIC AND SPACE

The initial absence of typical performers in the electronic music repertoire is overcome with the development of computers able to generate electronic sounds in live contest and to process the sound signal (voices or musical instruments) in real time. Live electronics was born [12], which now is used in a large music repertoire all over the world and with it also grows new professional figures with a double training: musical and scientific.

The CSC also developed new interfaces to play these instruments, necessary to control the musical timbre and the virtual space and polarizing the interest of many composers. The traditional keyboard organ is not suited to control multiple parameters simultaneously, synthesis algorithms, and sound spatialization. In the Eighties, CSC in Padua, IRCAM in Paris and LIMB of the Venice La Biennale jointly developed the *4i System*, a digital signal processors based system for live electronics. This system was used in some of the most important musical works of the second half of the Twentieth century, including *Prometeo, la tragedia dell'ascolto* (1984-85) by Luigi Nono, based on the movement of sound in space. The fig. 6 shows the arrangement of the choir and orchestra of the *Prometeo* in a model (displayed in the exhibition) of the original building designed by Renzo Piano for the representation at the Venice La Biennale in 1984. In this section the following items were exhibited:

- *4i System* (see fig. 3). It is realized by means of a 128-kbyte memory PDP11 computer with a 4i digital sound processor (designed by Giuseppe Di Giugno), a 16-bit digital-to-analogue converter and a control interface for performance parameters;
- an interactive system (developed on purpose) in which the user can control the live electronics software of the *Prometeo* and contemporaneously observe the original gesture of the live electronics performer;
- original scores with notes handwritten by Luigi Nono;
- heliography of the Prologue of *Prometeo* (in the 1984 version), with several original corrections and annotations, probably added during the early rehearsals in Venice;
- a multimedia installation for the interactive listening of the *Perseo e Andromeda* (1990) by Salvatore Sciarrino, in which the synthesized sounds replace the traditional orchestra. The visitors can listen the entire work, some parts and/or the single sound object, observing the related score.

8. *MEDEA* BY ADRIANO GUARNIERI (2002)

In the exhibition two large and innovative musical works were showed: the musical theatre opera *Medea* (2002) by Adriano Guarnieri and the interactive multimedia installation *Casetta delle immagini* by Carlo De Pirro.

Medea is a video-opera in three part loosely based on Euripide's tragedy, for video sequences, soloists, chorus, orchestra and live electronics, in which the sound direction becomes almost *visual* and the spatial sound seems to alternate *close-ups* and *overviews*. It was showed in this exhibition (see fig. 8) by means of the original stage sound-design, using the eight-channel audio recording made during the first performance at the *PalaFenice* in Venice.

The mythical story of Medea, represented by three female voices, merges with the play of the dynamics of sound in space. The sound produced by the singers and by the orchestra is detected by 68 microphones, processed by live electronics software and finally diffused by dozens of speakers distributed among the public. The sound movement in the room, besides, is controlled in various ways (e.g.,musicians' gestures) and *reinterpreted* in real time by live electronics software. This work is one of the greatest artistic studies

Figure 8. The stage of *Medea* – as represented in the exhibition – using the original eight-channel audio recording as well as three video output. Guarnieri himself, visiting the exhibition, recognized this installation as "this is my **real** *Medea*".

in expressive gesture and sound interaction, a domain born in the late 90s, which bring interesting results even in the analysis of musical performance.

This section of the exhibition showed also some of the better models developed at CSC related to most recent research studying the possible connections between two universes that may seem antithetical, the emotions and the machines, deepening the procedures that enable the computers to communicate and simulate expressive components, emotions, intentions and affects [13].

9. *CASETTA DELLE IMMAGINI* BY CARLO DE PIRRO (2002)

This interactive multimedia installation was designed by the composer Carlo De Pirro [3] at the CSC for *Piazza Pinocchio*, the Italian space at the Expo 2002 in Neuchâtel (Switzerland), Section *Artificial Intelligence and Robotics*. The work uses the results of research in the fields of analysis, modeling and communication of expressive content and emotional non-verbal interaction, by means of multisensorial interfaces in mixed reality environments. The *Casetta delle immagini* (*Little house of the appearances*) is a sort of *magic room* for children, where every gesture becomes sound, images and colors. The visitors' movements were captured by cameras and analyzed by specially developed software able to process a virtual gesture model and thus generate projection images and rhythmic sequences of music.

A similar idea is now implemented in *Stanza Logo-motoria* [14], a systems for educational purposes used in many Italian schools, that exploits a multimodal interactive environment aimed at learning through the movement and can be used in situations of learning difficulties or for children with multi-disabilities.

[3] Adria, 1956 – Padova, 2008. Carlo, professor of Music Composition at Rovigo Conservatoire, collaborated with the CSC for more than fifteen years: his musical compositions were (and are) a great stimulus for the researches carried out in CSC, thanks to his innovative and artistic approach.

In this section the original *Casetta delle immagini* was exhibited, restored on purpose by the authors.

10. CONCLUSIONS

CSC scientific research was the premise for the other activities of musical informatics, and it is the main focus of the Centre. Today the CSC still supports production of musical works, thanks to significant investments in research that begun in 1979 when the Centre was officially founded. In the early days the research was mainly focused on sound synthesis. Nowadays, the Centre is working, in synergy with the SaMPL Lab of the Conservatory of Padova, on preservation and restoration of audio documents, new sound synthesis techniques, analytical tools, techniques of sound spatialization, complex dynamic systems and analysis and morphing of expressive content in music performances. Today CSC activities rely on a composite group of people, which include the Center board of directors and personnel, guest researchers and musicians, and particularly on master students attending the courses "Sound and Music Computing" at Dep. of Information Engineering of the University of Padova.

The CSC is carrying out a project for the preservation and restoration of electrophone equipments and audio documents. The principal output of this project is the realization of an interactive "museum" of Computer Music and of researches in SMC field. The first attempt was the exhibition *Visions of sound. Electronic music at the University of Padua*. In the authors' opinion, it is time to start a debate on how the scientific SMC community wants to preserve its history and what kind of access tools we are able to develop, in order to communicate the (scientific and applicative) potential of its researches to the general public and (no less important) to potential investors [15].

Acknowledgments

In the realization of the exhibition *Visions of sound* the efforts of the CSC researchers, of the entire University of Padova, of the Conservatory "C. Pollini", of Padova and of the Veneto Region were terrific. The authors deeply thank in particular the scientific and the organization boards of the exhibition, the Luigi Nono's Archive (in particular the president Nuria Schoenberg-Nono), the Rectorate and the Museums Center of the University of Padova, the director of the Conservatory Maria Nevilla Massaro and Nicola Bernardini (professor of Electronic Music), and Ivo Rossi (vice-Mayor of Padova).

11. REFERENCES

[1] G. B. Debiasi, G. De Poli, G. Tisato, and A. Vidolin, "Centro di Sonologia Computazionale C. S. C. University of Padova," in *Proc. of International Computer Music Conference*, 1984, pp. 287–294.

[2] G. Debiasi, G. De Poli, G. A. Mian, G. Mildonian, and C. Offelli, "Italian speech sinthesis from unrestricted text for an automatic answerback system," in *Proc. of 8th Inf. Congress of Acoustics, London*, 1974, p. 296.

[3] G. A. Mian, F. Morgantini, and C. Offelli, "An application of the linear prediction technique to efficient coding of speech segments," in *Proc. of 1976 IEEE Int. Conf. Acoustic, Speech, Signal Processing, Philadelphia, April 12-14*, 1976, p. 722.

[4] G. Francini, G. Debiasi, and R. Spinabelli, "Study of a system of minimal speech reproducing units for italian," *JASA*, vol. 43, pp. 1282–1286, 1968.

[5] G. B. Debiasi and M. Rubazzer, "Architecture for a digital sound synthesys processor," in *Proc. of ICMC*, 1982, pp. 225–231.

[6] G. De Poli, "A tutorial on digital sound synthesis techniques," *Computer Music Journal*, vol. 7, no. 4, pp. 8–26, 1991.

[7] G. B. Debiasi and G. De Poli, "MUSICA, A Language for the Transcription of Musical texts for Computers," *Interface*, vol. 11, no. 1, pp. 1–27, 1982.

[8] G. Borin, G. De Poli, and A. Sarti, "Algorithms and structures for synthesis using physical models," *Computer Music Journal*, vol. 16, no. 4, pp. 30–42, 1992.

[9] S. Canazza, "The digital curation of ethnic music audio archives: from preservation to restoration," *International Journal of Digital Libraries*, vol. 12, no. 2-3, pp. 121–135, 2012.

[10] S. Spagnol, M. Geronazzo, and F. Avanzini, "On the relation between pinna reflection patterns and head-related transfer function features," *IEEE Trans. Audio, Speech, and Language Process.*, vol. 21, no. 3, pp. 508–519, March 2013.

[11] D. Salvati and S. Canazza, "Adaptive time delay estimation using filter length constraints for source localization in reverberant acoustic environments," *IEEE Signal Processing Letters*, vol. 20, no. 5, pp. 507–510, 2013.

[12] A. Vidolin, "Musical interpretation and signal processing," in *Musical Signal Processing*, C. Roads, S. T. Pope, A. Piccialli, and G. De Poli, Eds. Lisse: Swets and Zeitlinger, 1997, pp. 439–459.

[13] S. Canazza, G. De Poli, A. Rodà, and A. Vidolin, "Expressiveness in music performance: Analysis, models, mapping, encoding," in *Structuring Music through Markup Language: Designs and Architectures*, J. Steyn, Ed. IGI Global, 2012, pp. 156–186.

[14] S. Zanolla, A. Rodà, F. Romano, F. Scattolin, S. Canazza, and G. L. Foresti, "When sound teaches," in *Proc. of Sound and Music Computing Conference*, 2011, pp. 64–69.

[15] N. Bernardini and G. De Poli, "The future of sound and music computing," *Journal of New Music Research (special issue)*, vol. 36, no. 3, pp. 139–239, 2007.

SMOOTHNESS UNDER PARAMETER CHANGES: DERIVATIVES AND TOTAL VARIATION

Risto Holopainen

ABSTRACT

Apart from the sounds they make, synthesis models are distinguished by how the sound is controlled by synthesis parameters. Smoothness under parameter changes is often a desirable aspect of a synthesis model. The concept of smoothness can be made more accurate by regarding the synthesis model as a function that maps points in parameter space to points in a perceptual feature space. We introduce new conceptual tools for analyzing the smoothness related to the derivative and total variation of a function and apply them to FM synthesis and an ordinary differential equation. The proposed methods can be used to find well behaved regions in parameter space.

1. INTRODUCTION

Some synthesis parameters are like switches that can assume only a discrete set of values, other parameters are like knobs that can be seamlessly adjusted within some range. Only the latter kind of parameter will be discussed here. Usually, a small change in some parameter would be expected to yield a small change in the sound. As far as this is the case, the synthesis model may be said to have well behaved parameters.

A set of criteria for the evaluation of synthesis models were suggested by Jaffe [1]. Three of the criteria seem relevant in this context: 1) How intuitive are the parameters? 2) How perceptible are parameter changes? 3) How well behaved are the parameters? The vague notion of smoothness under parameter changes (which is not the name of one of Jaffe's criteria) can be made more precise by the approach taken in this paper.

From a user's perspective, the mapping from controllers to synthesis parameters is important [2]. In synthesis models with reasonably well behaved parameters, there are good prospects of designing mappings that turn the synthesis model and its user interface into a versatile instrument. However, a synthesis model does not necessarily have to have well behaved parameters to be musically useful. Despite the counter-intuitive parameter dependencies in complicated nonlinear feedback systems, some musicians are using them [3]. Likewise, acoustic instruments may have far from smooth responses to changes in physical control variables (e.g. overblowing in wind instruments).

The smoothness of transitions has been proposed as a criterion for evaluating sound morphings [4]. As the morphing parameter is varied between its extremes, one would expect the perceived sound to pass through all intermediate stages as well. However, because of categorical perception some transitions may not be experienced as gradual. It may be impossible to create a convincing morph between, say, a banjo tone and a sustained trombone tone.

Quantitative descriptions of the smoothness of a synthesis parameter should use a measure of the amount of change in the sound, which can be regarded as a distance in a perceptual space. Similarity ratings of pairs of tones have been used in research on timbre perception, where multidimensional scaling is then used to find a small number of dimensions that account for the perceived distances between stimuli [5]. In several studies, two to four timbral dimensions have been found and related to various acoustic correlates, often including the attack time, spectral centroid, spectral flux and spectral irregularity [6]. The importance of spectrotemporal patterns was stressed in a more recent study [7] where five perceptual dimensions were found.

Most timbre studies have focused on pitched, harmonic sounds, in effect neglecting a large part of the possible range of sounds that can be synthesized. At the other extreme, the problem of similarity between pieces of music has been addressed in music information retrieval [8]. The difficulty in comparing two pieces of music is that they may differ in so many ways, including tempo, instrumentation, melodic features and so on. Most synthesis models of interest to musicians are also able to vary along several dimensions of sound, e.g., pitch, loudness, modulation rate and many timbral aspects. A thorough study of the perceived changes of sound would include listening tests for each synthesis model under investigation. A more tractable solution is to use signal descriptors as a proxy for such tests.

There are numerous signal descriptors to choose from [9], but the descriptors should respond to parameter changes in a given synthesis model. For example, in a study of the timbre perception of a physical model of the clarinet, the attack time, spectral centroid and the ratio of odd to even harmonics were found to be the salient parameters [10]. Since a synthesis model may be well behaved with respect to certain perceptual dimensions but not to others, the smoothness may be assessed individually for each of a set of complementary signal descriptors.

A synthesis model will be thought of as a function that

maps a set of parameter values to a one-sided sequence of real numbers, representing the audio samples. It will be assumed that all synthesis parameters are set at the beginning of a note event and remain fixed during the note. Dynamically varying parameters can be modelled by an LFO or envelope generator, but for simplicity we will consider only synthesis parameters that remain constant over time.

The effects of parameter changes may be studied either locally near a specific point in parameter space, or globally as a parameter varies throughout some range. The local perspective leads to a notion of the derivative of a synthesis model, which is developed in section 2. Parameter changes over a range of values are better described by the total variation, which is introduced in section 3. Then, sections 4 and 5 are devoted to case studies of the smoothness of FM synthesis and the Rössler attractor. Some applications and limitations of the methods are discussed in the conclusion.

2. SMOOTHNESS BY DERIVATIVE

In order to formalize the notion of smoothness, we will formulate a synthesis model explicitly as a function and describe what it means for that function to be smooth. First, we define a suitable version of the derivative. Then, in Sections 2.2 and 2.3, the practicalities of an implementation are discussed.

2.1 Definition of the derivative

Consider a synthesis model as a function $G : \mathbb{R}^p \to \mathbb{R}^\mathbb{N}$ that maps parameters $\mathbf{c} \in \mathbb{R}^p$ to a one-sided sequence of samples x_n, $n = 0, 1, 2, \ldots$, where the sample sequence will be notated $X(\mathbf{c})$ to indicate its dependence on the parameters. Then the question of smoothness under parameter changes is related to the degree of change in the sequence $X(\mathbf{c})$ as the point $\mathbf{c}$ in parameter space varies. In practice, the distance in the output of the synthesis model will be measured through a signal descriptor rather than from the raw output signal. If a distance were to be calculated from the signals themselves, two periodic signals with identical amplitude and frequency but different phase might end up being widely separated according to the metric, despite sounding indistinguishable to the human ear. Signal descriptors that are clearly affected by the synthesis parameters and that can be interpreted in perceptual terms are preferable.

In order to treat the synthesis model as a function, it will be assumed to be deterministic in the sense that the same point in parameter space always yields identical sample sequences. The idea of relating how much a function $f(x)$ changes as the independent variable x changes by a small amount leads to the concept of derivative. Functions that have derivatives of all orders are called smooth. A more refined concept is to say that a function is k times continuously differentiable; the larger k is, the smoother the function.

Now, we would like to apply some suitably defined derivative to synthesis models considered as functions. To this end, a distance metric is needed for points in the parameter space, and another distance metric is needed for points in the space of sample sequences. Let $d_p(\mathbf{c}, \mathbf{c}')$ be a metric in parameter space, and let $d_s(X(\mathbf{c}), X(\mathbf{c}'))$ be a metric in the sequence space. The derivative can then be defined as the limit

$$\lim_{\|\boldsymbol{\delta}\| \to 0} \frac{d_s(X(\mathbf{c}), X(\mathbf{c} + \boldsymbol{\delta}))}{d_p(\mathbf{c}, \mathbf{c} + \boldsymbol{\delta})} \tag{1}$$

where $\boldsymbol{\delta} \in \mathbb{R}^p$ is some small displacement in parameter space. The limit, if it exists, is the derivative evaluated at the point $\mathbf{c}$.

In general, synthesis parameters do not make up a uniform space. Different parameters play different roles; they affect the sound subtly or dramatically and may interact so that the effect of one parameter depends on the settings of other parameters. This makes it hard to suggest a general distance metric that would be suitable for any synthesis model. Our solution will be to consider the effects of varying a single synthesis parameter c_j at a time, so the distance $d_p(\mathbf{c}, \mathbf{c}')$ in (1) reduces to $|c_j - c_j'|$. Furthermore, consider a scalar valued signal descriptor $\phi^{(i)}(\mathbf{c}) \equiv \phi^{(i)}(X(\mathbf{c}))$ which itself is a signal that depends on the sample sequence and the parameter value. Thus, we arrive at a kind of partial derivative evaluated with respect to the parameter c_j using a signal descriptor $\phi^{(i)}$,

$$\frac{\partial \phi^{(i)} \circ G(\mathbf{c})}{\partial c_j} = \lim_{h \to 0} \frac{d_s(\phi^{(i)}(\mathbf{c}), \phi^{(i)}(\mathbf{c} + h\mathbf{e}_j))}{h} \tag{2}$$

where $\mathbf{e}_j$ is the jth unit vector in the parameter space. Clearly the magnitude of this derivative depends on the specifics of the signal descriptors used and which synthesis parameters are considered. In a finite dimensional space, all partial derivatives should exist and be continuous for the derivative to exist. Such a strict concept of derivative does not make sense in the present context where any number of different signal descriptors can be employed, so only the partial derivatives (2) will be considered.

Before discussing the implementation, let us recall some intuitive conceptions of the derivative. As William Thurston has pointed out [11], mathematicians understand the derivative in multiple ways, including the following.

- The derivative is the slope of a line tangent to the graph, if it has a tangent.
- In terms of symbolic operations, $\frac{d}{dx}x^n = nx^{n-1}$.
- The derivative is the best linear approximation to the function near a point.
- It is the limit of what you get by looking at a function under a microscope of higher and higher power.

Synthesis models are typically very complicated if considered as mathematical functions; hence the analytic approach to differentiation is out of the question and one has to rely upon numerical approximations. The various intuitions of what the derivative is may guide a practical numerical implementation in different directions, as will be further discussed in Section 2.3.

Numerical estimation of the derivative is highly sensitive to measurement noise. Here one source of measurement noise are the signal descriptors. Whereas one would like to magnify a curve in order to find its derivative at a point, doing so will also reveal more fine details caused by the noise, which may lead to false estimates. When properly estimated, the derivative will exaggerate irregularities and make them easier to detect.

2.2 Pointwise or time-average distance?

The distance metric d_s in sequence space has so far been left unspecified. We propose two alternatives, each suitable in different situations. The signal descriptors that will be used are based on short-time Fourier transforms of the signal $X(\boldsymbol{c})$ at regular intervals, using a hop size equal to the FFT window length, L. Hence, the signal descriptor is a sequence which we write concisely as $\phi_m(\boldsymbol{c})$, where $m = \lfloor n/L \rfloor$ is a time index.

Using a pointwise distance metric, one may follow the two signals over time and take the sum over their distances $|\phi_m(\boldsymbol{c}) - \phi_m(\boldsymbol{c}')|$ at each moment. Since these are infinite sequences, the sum may not converge. Therefore, an exponentially decaying weighting function is applied in the distance metric

$$d_s(X(\boldsymbol{c}), X(\boldsymbol{c}')) = \left[\sum_{m=0}^{\infty} \gamma^m \left(\phi_m(\boldsymbol{c}) - \phi_m(\boldsymbol{c}')\right)^2 \right]^{1/2} \tag{3}$$

where $\gamma \in (0, 1)$ controls the decay rate. Convergence is then guaranteed if the signal descriptors ϕ_m are bounded.

The second approach involves first taking an average over the sequence $\phi_m(\boldsymbol{c})$, $m = 0, 1, \ldots, M$ and then comparing averages of two sequences. Thus, the distance becomes

$$d_s(X(\boldsymbol{c}), X(\boldsymbol{c}')) = |\langle\phi(\boldsymbol{c})\rangle - \langle\phi(\boldsymbol{c}')\rangle| \tag{4}$$

where we take time averages

$$\langle\phi(\boldsymbol{c})\rangle = \lim_{M\to\infty} \frac{1}{M} \sum_{m=0}^{M-1} \phi_m(\boldsymbol{c}) \tag{5}$$

before computing the distance. For time-varying signals, the drawback of the second approach is that two different temporal sequences ϕ_m may average to the same value.

As an illustration, consider two signals of equal average amplitude, the first having constant amplitude and the second with a periodic amplitude modulation. Suppose we compare the RMS amplitudes of the two signals using the second approach (4). When averaged over sufficiently long time, both signals will appear to have the same average amplitude. In contrast, the pointwise distance measure (3) will detect their difference.

2.3 Estimation of the derivative

A numerical computation of the derivative may return a number even if the limit (1) or (2) does not exist. Therefore, a measure of the reliability of the estimate, or "degree of differentiability", should be added.

Although the synthesis model is assumed to be deterministic, all signal descriptors will introduce measurement noise. If a number of windowed segments of the signal are analyzed, then the spectrum of these segments will fluctuate unless some integer number of periods fit exactly into the window. The fluctuation can be reduced by using the time-averaged version of the distance metric (4).

Several methods for the estimation of derivatives exist [12]. Theoretically, it may be possible to arrive at analytical expressions for the derivative of a synthesis model considered as a function, at least in some trivial cases. In practice, numerical estimates have to be used. A simple approach would be to evaluate (2) directly at two points $\boldsymbol{c}$ and $\boldsymbol{c}'$. Another approach is to fit a polynomial to the curve $\phi(c)$, and then do a symbolic differentiation of the polynomial.

The method of estimation of derivatives that will be used here is similar to one described in ref. [12, p. 231] but slightly simpler. The derivative at a point c_0 is approximated by a sequence of symmetric differences with decreasing distance h. A linear regression of this sequence gives the derivative as the intercept. Suppose a sequence of slopes

$$y_i(c_0; h_i) = \frac{\phi(c_0 + h_i) - \phi(c_0 - h_i)}{2h_i} \tag{6}$$

are given. Then the limit as $h \to 0$ can be found as the y-intercept of the fitted line

$$y_i = d + bh_i + \eta_i, \tag{7}$$

which gives the estimated derivative d. This method also provides a hint about the badness of fit, for which the root mean square error (RMSE) of the residuals η can be used.

3. TOTAL VARIATION

Whereas the derivative is concerned with local behaviour of a function, an even more useful perspective on the smoothness of a synthesis model may be to look at its properties over intervals of a parameter. One possible way to do so is to measure the length of the curve that a signal descriptor traces out as the parameter traverses some interval. If this curve is highly wrinkled, the curve becomes rather long, whereas a straight line connecting the endpoints means that the parameter changes are smooth. The total variation of a function may be used for such a measure; intuitively, it measures the length travelled back and forth on the y-axis of a function $y = f(x)$, $x \in [a, b]$.

Let $f(x)$ be a real function defined on an interval $x_0 \leq x \leq x_k$, and suppose $x_0 < x_1 < \cdots < x_k$ is a partition of the interval. Then the total variation of $f(x)$, $x_0 \leq x \leq x_k$ is defined as

$$\mathcal{V}_{x_0}^{x_k}(f) = \sup \sum_{j=1}^{k} |f(x_j) - f(x_{j-1})| \tag{8}$$

taking the supremum over all partitions of the function. If f is differentiable, the total variation is bounded and can be expressed as

$$\mathcal{V}_{x_0}^{x_k}(f) = \int_{x_0}^{x_k} |f'(x)|\, dx. \qquad (9)$$

Also, recall that one way for a function to fail to be differentiable is that its total variation diverges to infinity.

The mesh of the partition, which is the greatest distance $|x_j - x_{j-1}|$, needs to be fine enough when estimating the total variation numerically. A global description of the function's smoothness is obtained from considerations of the limit of the total variation as the mesh gets finer. Suppose the partition of $[x_0, x_k]$ is uniform with each point separated from its nearest neighbours by $|x_j - x_{j-1}| = \Delta$. Then, the question is whether a limit exists as $\Delta \to 0$.

For the present purposes it will suffice to consider approximations of the total variation using a small but fixed mesh. Certain functions may appear to have different amounts of total variation when observed at different scales. A slow increase in total variation as the mesh is successively made finer indicates that the estimation process goes as intended.

An alternative to measuring the total variation would be to measure the arc length, which can be thought of as the length of a string fitted to the curve if it is continuous. Fractal curves on the plane have the property that their arc length grows as the measurement scale gets smaller.

When measuring the total variation of a signal descriptor over a range of synthesis parameter values, there are still two possible approaches to how the distance is measured. As discussed above in section 2.2, either a pointwise distance may be taken, or the distance may be taken over time averages of the signal descriptors. The latter approach will be used here because it is better suited for the case of static parameters. Applications of the derivative and total variation to two synthesis models will be demonstrated next.

4. FM SYNTHESIS

With only three synthesis parameters, basic FM synthesis is convenient for investigations of the smoothness of its parameter space. The formula that will be used is

$$x_n = \sin(2\pi f_c n/f_s + I \sin(2\pi f_m n/f_s)) \qquad (10)$$

with modulation index I, carrier frequency f_c, modulator frequency f_m and sample rate $f_s = 48\,\text{kHz}$. Since the spectrum of the signal (10) is governed by a sum of Bessel functions [13], it may actually be possible to estimate some related signal descriptors directly from the formula, although we will not attempt to do so. The oscillations of the Bessel functions give FM synthesis its characteristic timbral flavour of partials that fade in and out as the modulation index I increases, with the overall brightness increasing with the modulation index. Brightness is related to the spectral centroid, which will be used to study the effects of parameter changes.

In the top of Figure 1, the centroid is shown as a function of I at two different carrier to modulator (C:M) ratios. The centroid, given in units of normalized frequency, is measured as the time average over 25 FFT windows using a

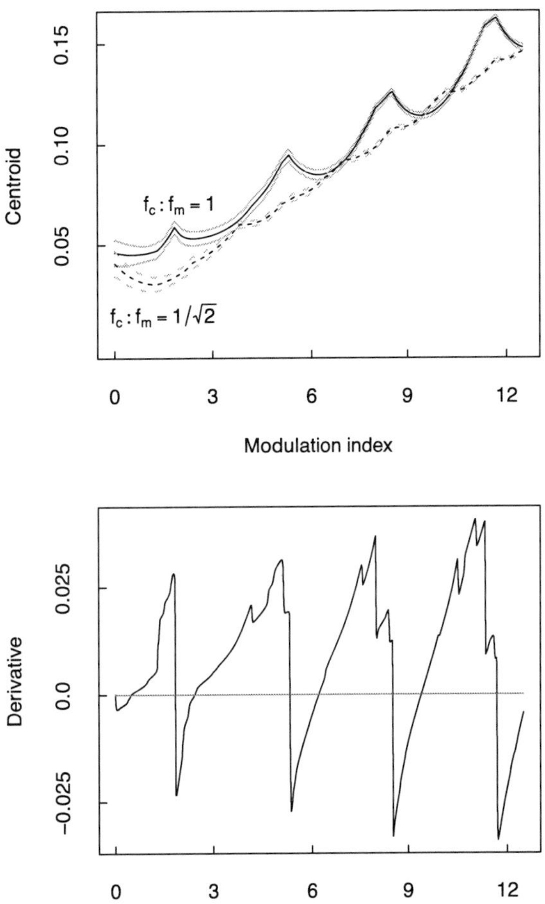

Figure 1. FM synthesis. Top: centroid as a function of modulation index for $f_c = f_m = 440$ Hz (solid line) and $f_c = 311.1$, $f_m = 440$ Hz (dashed line). The outer lines indicate one standard deviation of the centroid. Bottom: the derivative of the centroid at $f_c = f_m = 440$ Hz.

1024 point Hamming window. As can be seen, the C:M ratio 1 gives a rather bumpy curve with a general rising trend of the centroid, but with several local peaks. The bottom part shows the derivative, estimated with the method described in the end of Section 2.3. Evidently, the derivative is discontinuous at each of the peaks. The RMSE of the linear regression used in the estimation of the derivative is typically very small, but has sharp peaks around the discontinuities. It turned out to be necessary to re-initialize the oscillator's initial phase at the beginning of each run at a new parameter value, otherwise there would be oscillations in the centroid as a function of modulation index that would prevent the derivative from converging.

The total variation of the centroid over the range $0 < I \leq 12.5$ is about 0.127 for the inharmonic ratio $f_c/f_m = 1/\sqrt{2}$, and increases to about 0.188 for $f_c/f_m = 1$. We may now ask how the total variation changes as a function of the C:M ratio. This is shown in Figure 2. Narrow peaks arise at the simple C:M ratios 1 : 2, 1 and 3 : 2. Insofar as FM synthesis is reputed for its timbral variability as the modulation index varies, this phenomenon is more pro-

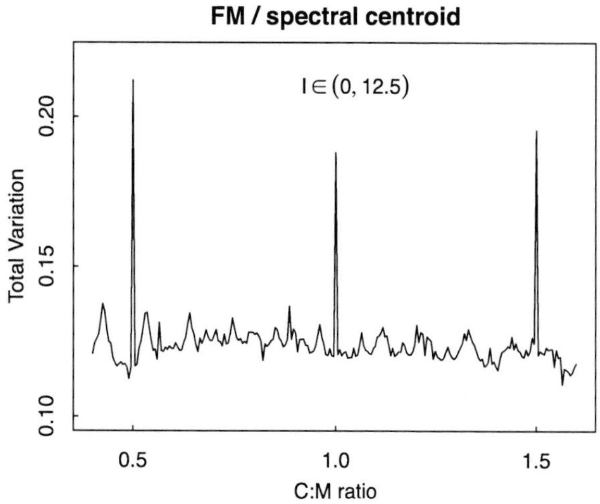

Figure 2. Total variation of the centroid of FM signals for $I \in [0, 12.5]$ as a function of the C:M ratio.

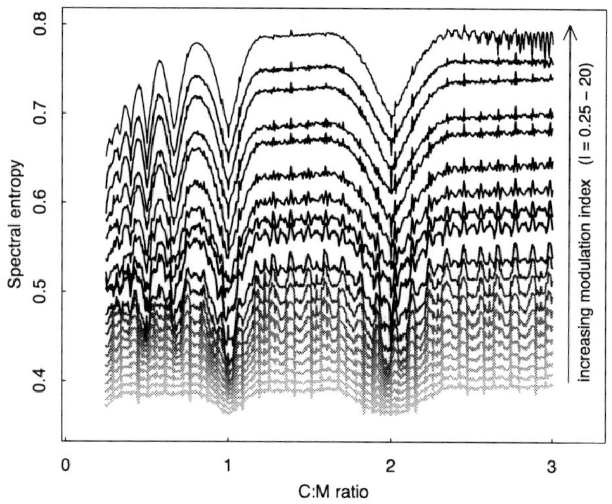

Figure 3. Spectral entropy of FM as a function of C:M ratio (horizontal) and modulation index (vertical).

nounced at the simple C:M ratios that result in harmonic spectra.

Since the density of the spectrum depends on the modulation index as well as on the C:M ratio, signal descriptors related to spectral density may provide additional insights. The spectral entropy will be used for this purpose. Spectral entropy is measured from the amplitude spectrum, normalized so that all bins a_k sum to 1. Then, the normalized entropy is

$$H = -\frac{1}{norm} \sum_k a_k \log a_k \qquad (11)$$

where a perfectly flat spectrum yields the maximum spectral entropy $H = 1$, and a sinusoid results in the smallest possible entropy of a signal that is not completely silent.

In Figure 3, the spectral entropy is shown as a function of the C:M ratio as well as the modulation index. Despite an even geometric progression of the modulation index $I \in [0.25, 20]$, the curves are slightly irregularly distributed. Two dips in spectral entropy can be seen at the simple ratios $C : M = 1, 2$. These dips can be understood to result from the fact that, at harmonic C:M ratios, several partials overlap (negative frequencies match positive frequencies), whereas for inharmonic ratios, there are more distinct partials in the spectrum.

The total variation of spectral entropy over the range of C:M ratios shown in Figure 3 is about 1 for $I = 0.25$, and it increases monotonically to a maximum value of 2.5 at $I = 1.25$. For higher modulation indices, the total variation decreases. These results can be interpreted as indicating that, if the modulation index is set at a fixed value and the C:M ratio is varied, then the sounds will change less for low modulation indices, and the maximum change occurs for $I = 1.25$.

5. THE RÖSSLER SYSTEM

Ordinary differential equations with bounded and oscillating solutions are good candidates for sound synthesis.

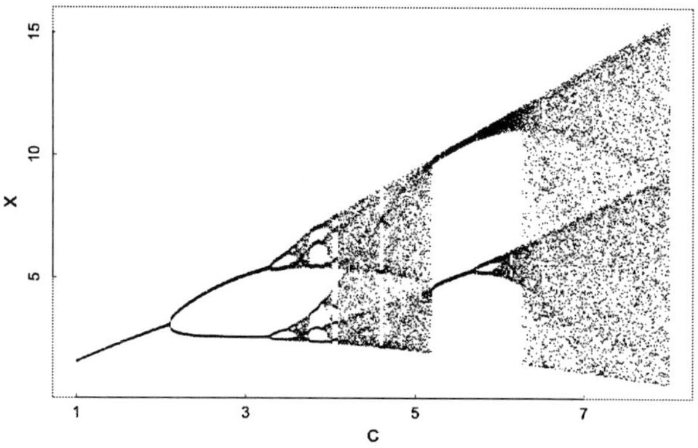

Figure 4. Poincaré section of the Rössler system showing bifurcations for $c \in [1, 8]$ and $a = b = 0.3$.

In particular, there are many nonlinear oscillators capable of both chaotic and periodic behaviour. Rössler's system [14],

$$\begin{aligned} \dot{x} &= -y - z \\ \dot{y} &= x + ay \\ \dot{z} &= b + z(x - c) \end{aligned} \qquad (12)$$

is known to have a chaotic attractor at $a = b = 0.2, c = 5.7$. For lower values of c there are periodic solutions. A Poincaré section across the ray $x = -y$, $x \geq 0$ at $a = b = 0.3$ and a range of values of c reveals a period doubling route to chaos, after which there is a period two window (see Figure 4). In the following, (12) is solved with the fourth order Runge-Kutta method. The system is allowed time to approach an attractor by iterating at least 25000 time steps of size 0.025 before any measurements are taken.

The system rotates in the xy-plane, with occasional spikes in the z variable. Therefore, the x and y variables are suitable for use as audio signals, after they have been suitably

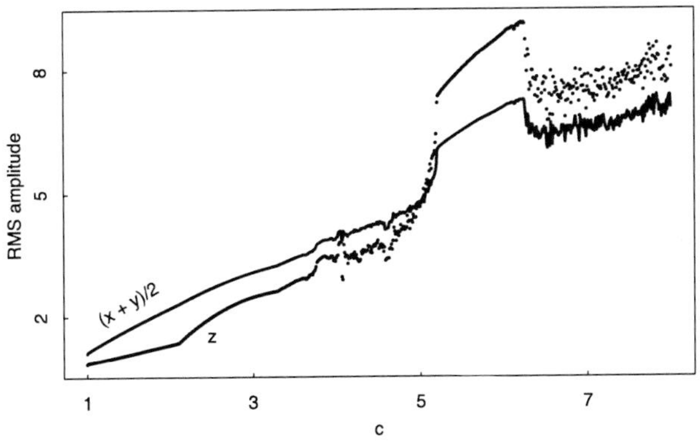

Figure 5. RMS amplitude of the Rössler system; the average of x and y is greater than z for low values of c.

scaled in amplitude. The first thing to check with an ordinary differential equation intended for use as an audio oscillator is its amplitude range and stability. As can be seen from Figure 4, the amplitude grows approximately linearly with c over the displayed range. By measuring the RMS amplitude of each coordinate, one gets a more detailed overview of the amplitude's dependence on the parameter c (see Figure 5). Because the amplitudes of x and y are typically not very different, their average has been plotted together with the amplitude of the z coordinate.

Bifurcation plots already reveal a few things about the smoothness under parameter changes. Each bifurcation is a point where the system's behaviour changes in a discontinuous way, whereas the behaviour between bifurcations can be expected to vary more smoothly.

Before going further, let us recall that dynamic systems may depend critically on the initial condition. Indeed, chaos is defined in terms of the exponential divergence of two orbits starting from infinitesimally separated initial conditions, which is measured with the largest Lyapunov exponent [15]. Even more dramatically, different initial conditions may lead to different kinds of behaviour. In conservative systems, orbits may be periodic, quasiperiodic or chaotic depending on the initial condition. Dissipative systems, such as Rössler's, have a basin of attraction of points that end up on the attractor, but should an orbit be started from outside the basin of attraction, it may wander off to infinity.

It is important to distinguish the properties of the orbit itself (chaotic versus regular) from the bifurcation scenarios as a parameter is varied. When looking at bifurcation diagrams, there are intervals of smooth change and intervals that are very irregular. It is tempting to guess that the irregular parts correspond to chaotic orbits, and the smooth parts to periodic orbits. This is only a half-truth; in fact, there are periodic windows interspersed with all the chaos.

As already seen, the RMS amplitude changes smoothly in some regions and irregularly in others. A quick comparison with the largest Lyapunov exponent λ indicates that the irregular parts correspond to chaotic regions (see Figure 6). Although it is easy to pick out "irregular regions" by visual inspection, a localized version of total variation can also achieve this. The local variation (LV) is defined as the total variation over a short interval of length δ centred about a point x:

$$LV(f;x,\delta) = \mathcal{V}_{x-\delta/2}^{x+\delta/2}(f) \tag{13}$$

A mathematical definition of the LV would probably involve taking the limit $\delta \to 0$, but for practical purposes a small but finite interval must be used. Now the smoothness of a curve may be described in the neighbourhood of any point x_0, which is computed by partitioning the interval into a suitably large number of points and proceeding as described above in Section 3. In the following example, $\delta = 0.02$ has been subdivided into 16 steps to find the local variation.

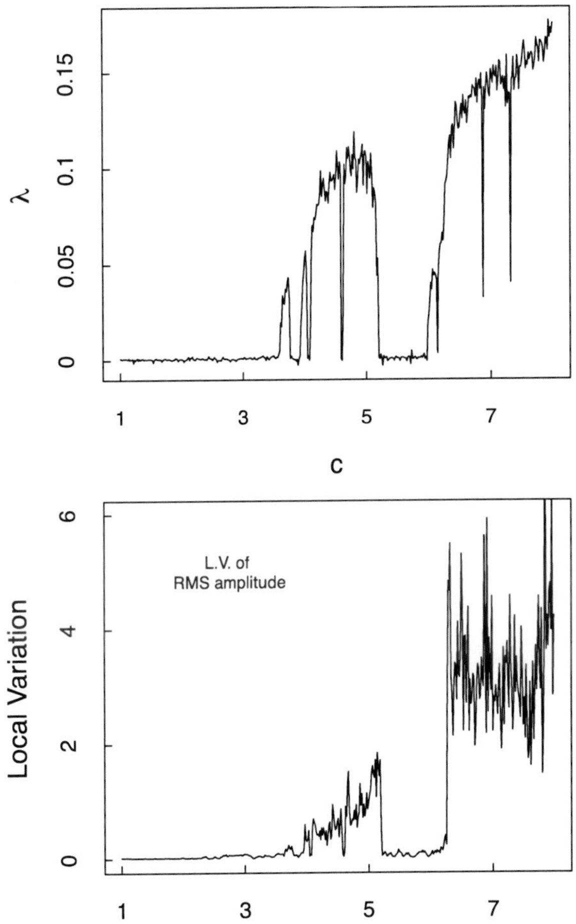

Figure 6. Greatest Lyapunov exponent (top) and local variation of the RMS amplitude (bottom) for the Rössler system as a function of the parameter c.

The local variation of the average RMS amplitude of the x and y coordinates of the Rössler system are shown in Figure 6 below a plot of the largest Lyapunov exponent over the same parameter range. When $\lambda = 0$, the dynamics is regular (either periodic or quasi-periodic), whereas $\lambda > 0$ indicates chaos. It is worth noting that regions of regular dynamics correspond to low values of the local variation, i.e., the amplitude changes smoothly. At chaotic regions, the local variation obtains higher values, although there is

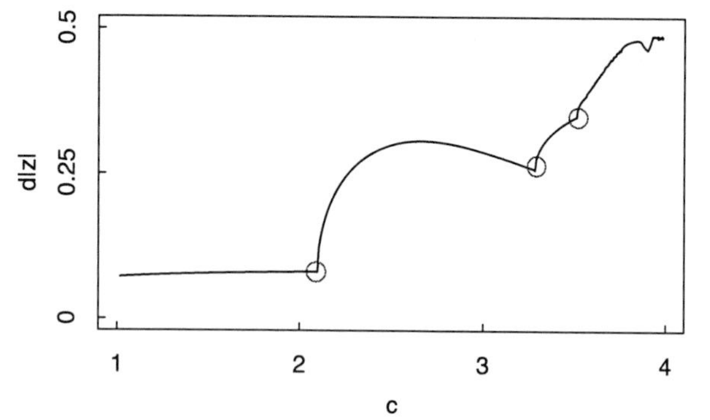

Figure 7. Derivative of the peak amplitude of the z coordinate as a function of c. Points of bifurcations are marked with circles.

no simple correlation between λ and LV. The higher values of LV in chaotic regions can be partly explained by the existence of periodic windows which may be very thin, yet are known to be dense in the chaotic regions.

In the interval $1 \leq c \leq 4$, there is a sequence of period doubling bifurcations. Most changes in amplitude are too subtle to notice directly (compare Figure 5), but taking the derivative, as shown in Figure 7, reveals points where the slope changes. In fact, the bifurcation points would be even easier to detect by plotting the second derivative of the peak amplitude.

In this study of the Rössler system, the effects of transients and dynamic parameter changes have been minimized. On the contrary, in a performance situation when using the Rössler system as an audio oscillator, its parameters would typically change over time. Then one may notice effects of hysteresis near bifucrations and in the chaotic regions. Approaching the same parameter value from different directions may then result in different behaviour.

6. CONCLUSION

By conceiving of a synthesis model as a function from points in parameter space to one-sided real sequences of audio samples, we have introduced a concept of derivative and total variation that can be used to describe the smoothness properties of the synthesis model. The derivative relates to local properties near specific points in parameter space, whereas the total variation characterizes the amount of change over intervals of a parameter. Interesting findings were that the total variation of the centroid with respect to the modulation index in FM synthesis is greater for simple harmonic C:M ratios than for other ratios. In other words, FM becomes smoother for inharmonic C:M ratios than for simple ratios. In the study of the Rössler system, we found that regular dynamics corresponds to smooth variation in the RMS amplitude. Chaotic regions are generally less smooth in parameter space, but there is some variation and relatively smooth parameter regions may exist where the system is chaotic as well.

The methods of characterizing the smoothness of synthesis models can be applied to analog synthesis and even to acoustic instruments using mechanical transducers to excite them. Mechanical transducers may be needed also for the automated control of acoustic instruments by MIDI or other means, but the response characteristics of the transducer and the instrument considered together may not be known in advance and need to be mapped out. Analog, voltage controlled synthesizers can be similarly studied by applying some control voltage to one of its inputs. Then, studying the signal's response to changes in control voltage can further elucidate input to output relations and the smoothness of the parameter. Although smoothness properties can be roughly assessed by visual inspection, the derivative, and the total and local variations provide quantitative measures of smoothness.

Comparisons of smoothness properties across different synthesis models are, however, not so straightforward. One might intuitively want to argue that the Rössler system is less smooth, on the whole, than FM synthesis, but the set of synthesis parameters have entirely different meanings in the two models, so a direct comparison will be problematic. The same signal descriptors and distance metrics must of course be used for both synthesis models, and one must decide what parameter ranges to compare.

Noise is used in many kinds of synthesis. If the noise is prominent in the output signal, it will increase the variance of the signal descriptors and make the estimation of derivatives and total variation more complicated. If the noise is mild enough not to alter the behaviour of the synthesis model altogether, one can take ensemble averages over many runs of the system. Stochastic synthesis such as Xenakis' Gendyn algorithm [16] may however be beyond the scope of the present methods.

Ordinary differential equations and nonlinear feedback systems may exhibit hysteresis. In synthesis models with hysteresis, there is no longer a unique correspondence between the point in parameter space and the resulting output signal. This fact invalidates the assumption that the synthesis model can be thought of as a function that maps points in parameter space to sequences in the sample sequence space. Sometimes a transition from one type of behaviour to another may depend not only on the direction of the changing parameter, but also the speed of its change.

We began by making the assumption that signal descriptors could be used instead of conducting listening tests. This is obviously an exaggeration. Firstly, one needs to know what perceptual characteristics of sound are captured by various signal descriptors. Second, we have been looking at rather small variations in these descriptors and magnified them with the derivative or considered their total variation. It is very easy to gain a false impression that minor variations or roughnesses in the curves would be audible. Listening tests would be necessary in order to assess how the smoothness and irregularity of parameter changes are really perceived.

The assumption that maximally smooth parameters are always preferable is not necessarily true. Monotonicity and smoothness may be good, because then the parameter can be remapped in a way that is more practical for the user. Nevertheless, the rugged appearance of the parameter space of a chaotic system should not detract musicians from using them.

7. REFERENCES

[1] D. Jaffe, "Ten criteria for evaluating synthesis techniques," *Computer Music Journal*, vol. 19, no. 1, pp. 76–87, Spring 1995.

[2] A. Hunt, M. Wanderley, and M. Paradis, "The importance of parameter mapping in electronic instrument design," in *Proceedings of the 2002 Conference on New Instruments for Musical Expression (NIME-02)*, Dublin, Ireland, 2002.

[3] D. Sanfilippo and A. Valle, "Towards a typology of feedback systems," in *Proc. of the ICMC 2012*, Ljubljana, Slovenia, September 2012, pp. 30–37.

[4] M. Caetano and N. Osaka, "A formal evaluation framework for sound morphing," in *Proc. of the ICMC 2012*, Ljubljana, Slovenia, 2012, pp. 104–107.

[5] J. Grey, "Multidimensional perceptual scaling of musical timbres," *J. Acoust. Soc. Am*, vol. 61, no. 5, pp. 1270–1277, May 1977.

[6] A. Caclin, S. McAdams, B. Smith, and S. Winsberg, "Acoustic correlates of timbre space dimensions: A confirmatory study using synthetic tones," *J. Acoust. Soc. Am*, vol. 118, no. 1, pp. 471–482, 2005.

[7] T. Elliott, L. Hamilton, and F. Theunissen, "Acoustic structure of the five perceptual dimensions of timbre in orchestral instrument tones," *J. Acoust. Soc. Am*, vol. 133, no. 1, pp. 389–404, January 2013.

[8] J.-J. Aucouturier and F. Pachet, "Music similarity measures: What's the use?" in *Proceedings of the International Symposium on Music Information Retrieval (ISMIR)*, Paris, France, October 2002.

[9] G. Peeters, B. Giordano, P. Susini, N. Misdariis, and S. McAdams, "The timbre toolbox: Extracting audio descriptors from musical signals," *J. Acoust. Soc. Am*, vol. 130, no. 5, pp. 2902–2916, November 2011.

[10] M. Barthet, P. Guillemain, R. Kronland-Martinet, and S. Ystad, "From clarinet control to timbre perception," *Acta Acustica united with Acustica*, vol. 96, pp. 678–689, 2010.

[11] W. Thurston, "On proof and progress in mathematics," *Bulletin of the American Mathematical Society*, vol. 30, no. 2, pp. 161–177, April 1994.

[12] W. Press, S. Teukolsky, W. Vetterling, and B. Flannery, *Numerical Recipes. The Art of Scientific Computing*, 3rd ed. Cambridge University Press, 2007.

[13] J. Chowning, "The synthesis of complex audio spectra by means of frequency modulation," *Journal of the Audio Engineering Society*, vol. 21, no. 7, pp. 526–534, September 1973.

[14] O. Rössler, "An equation for continuous chaos," *Physics Letters*, vol. 57A, no. 5, pp. 397–398, July 1976.

[15] T. Tél and M. Gruiz, *Chaotic Dynamics. An Introduction Based on Classical Mechanics.* Cambridge University Press, 2006.

[16] I. Xenakis, *Formalized Music. Thought and Mathematics in Music.* Stuyvesant: Pendragon Press, 1992.

Audio restoration of solo guitar excerpts using a excitation-filter instrument model

J. Parras-Moral, F. J. Cañadas-Quesada, P. Vera-Candeas, N. Ruiz-Reyes
Telecommunication Engineering Department, University of Jaén, Spain
jpm00031@red.ujaen.es, fcanadas@ujaen.es, pvera@ujaen.es, nicolas@ujaen.es

ABSTRACT

This work proposes a denoising algorithm for musical instruments based on the use of an excitation-filter instrument model. Firstly, frequency patterns for the musical instrument are learned. These patterns are trained in advance from the RWC database and classified into harmonic and transient components. The harmonic patterns of the target instrument are modelled with an excitation-filter approach. Frequency patterns from the beginning of different notes (onsets) are also learned. Secondly, frequency patterns from noise are trained. Two different types of global degradations from vinyl audio (hum and hiss), apart from localized degradations from crackle noise, are used in this work. Two different types of global degradations from vinyl audio (hum and hiss), apart from localized degradations from click, crackle and scratch noise, are used in this work. Two databases (click+crackle+scratch+hiss and click+crackle+scratch+hiss+hum) are collected in order to obtain different subsets for training and testing. Finally, an NMF approach is applied to separate instrument signal and noise from noisy performances. The proposed approach is compared with some commercial algorithms when denoising a vinyl degraded guitar database. The separation measures indicate that the proposed approach obtains competitive results.

1. INTRODUCTION

The improvement of the quality for the audio material degraded by non-stationary noise in old recordings has been a widely investigated problem over the last years [1–4]. Nowadays, audio restoration is an attractive research field from a commercial viewpoint (e.g. albums or movies audio remastering) but it is still an unsolved problem because the quality of restored audio is quite dependent of algorithm parameters. Hence, it is necessary the judgment of subjects trained in audio to evaluate the quality of the audio processed.

Audio restoration is the process of removing any degradation to the audio material, which occurs as a result of the recording process, in order to preserve the quality of the original one. In general, any degradation can be classified into localized or global. A localized degradation, which affects only certain samples of the audio, can be described as impulsive noise such as click, crackle or scratch. It is usually caused by dust, dirt, scratches or breakages on the surface of the recording medium. A global degradation, which affects all samples of the audio, can be described as background noise. The main global degradations are known as hum and hiss noise. While hum noise models a $50-60Hz$ low frequency harmonic signal (caused by electrical noise), hiss noise models broadband noise (caused by ambient noise from the recording environment) [5].

Recent techniques, based on Non-negative Matrix Factorization (NMF) [6], has been successfully applied to a wide range of music analysis tasks [7–10]. Specifically, NMF is able to decompose a magnitude spectrogram as a product of two nonnegative matrices, $\mathbf{X} \approx \mathbf{B} \cdot \mathbf{G}$. Each column of the basis matrix $\mathbf{B}$ represents a spectral pattern from an active sound source. Each row of the gains matrix $\mathbf{G}$ represents the time-varying activations of a spectral pattern factorized in the basis matrix. In this paper, we propose a supervised NMF approach to restore the target audio by means of the removal or attenuation of any degradation in vinyl audio. This approach trains a set of spectral patterns that represent the target audio and the most common noise active in these recordings. The training audio of the target source is composed by samples of isolated notes from a spanish guitar instrument [11]. The spectral patterns from the guitar is trained both from the harmonic and onset components. The harmonic patterns are learned using a excitation-filter instrument model [10]. In the same way, the training audio of the noise is the concatenation of a wide set of public samples recorded from the most common types of vinyl noise [12–17]. Part of this material is not used in training to preserve the testing subset for vinyl noises. Some experiments have been developed in order to show the benefits of the use of instrument models and the trained spectral patterns of vinyl noises. Results are compared with some commercial approaches.

In this paper some proposals are shown. We propose the use of spectral patterns for the harmonic component of the instrument based on an excitation-filter model. The transient component of the instrument is taken into account training a set of spectral patterns from note onsets. Also, the vinyl noise spectral patterns are trained from some public samples. A model for the degraded audio composed by harmonic and transient components for the instrument and vinyl noise is developed. Separation is performed using an NMF algorithm to estimate the time-varying activations for spectral patterns from vinyl degraded signals. The instrument contribution of the mixed signal is obtained as a result of the separation process.

The paper is structured as follows: Section 2 reviews the state-of-the-art theory that is used in this paper; Section 3 shows the proposal of this work. The comparison of the obtained results with those obtained by other state-of-the-art methods are described at section 4 ; finally, we draw some conclusions and discuss future work in Section 5.

2. BACKGROUND

2.1 Augmented NMF parameter estimation

Standard Non-negative Matrix Factorization (NMF), developed by Lee and Seung [6], is a technique for multivariate data analysis where an input magnitude spectrogram, represented by matrix $\mathbf{X}$, is decomposed as a product of two non-negative matrices $\mathbf{B}$ and $\mathbf{G}$,

$$\mathbf{X} \approx \mathbf{BG} \tag{1}$$

where $\mathbf{B}$ is the frequency basis and $\mathbf{G}$ represents the gains or activations of the active sources along the time, being $\hat{\mathbf{X}} = \mathbf{BG}$ the approximation of the input matrix. The magnitude spectrogram $\mathbf{X}$, composed of T frames and F frequency bins, of a music signal consists of a set of time-frequency units $\mathbf{X}_{f,t}$ or $x(f,t)$.

Constraining parameters to be non-negative has been efficient in learning the spectrogram factorization models. In fact, this constraint has been widely used in SS [8,18].

In the case of magnitude spectra, the parameters are restricted to be non-negative, then, a common way to compute the factorization is to minimize the reconstruction error between the observed spectrogram $x(f,t)$ and the modelled one $\hat{x}(f,t)$. This reconstruction error can be represented by a cost function.

The most used cost functions are the Euclidean (EUC) distance, the generalised Kullback-Leibner (KL) and the Itakura-Saito (IS) divergences. In this work, the KL cost function is used as is done in several systems [7,9,10].

An iterative algorithm based on multiplicative update rules is proposed in [6] to obtain the model parameters that minimize the cost function. Under these rules, $D_{KL}(x(f,t)|\hat{x}(f,t))$ is non-increasing at each iteration and it is ensured the non-negativity of the bases and the gains. These multiplicative update rules are obtained by applying diagonal rescaling to the step size of the gradient descent algorithm, more details can be found at [6]. The multiplicative update rule for each scalar parameter θ_l is given by expressing the partial derivatives of the $\nabla_{\theta_l} D_{KL}$ as the quotient of two positive terms $\nabla^-_{\theta_l} D_{KL}$ and $\nabla^+_{\theta_l} D_{KL}$:

$$\theta_l \leftarrow \theta_l \frac{\nabla^-_{\theta_l} D_{KL}(x(f,t)|\hat{x}(f,t))}{\nabla^+_{\theta_l} D_{KL}(x(f,t)|\hat{x}(f,t))} \tag{2}$$

The main advantage of the multiplicative update rule in eq. (2) is that non-negativity of the bases and the gains is ensured, resulting in an augmented non-negative matrix factorization (NMF) algorithm.

2.2 Multi-Excitation factorization Model (MEI)

The Multi-Excitation model proposed by Carabias et al. [10] is an extension of the source-filter model presented in [18]. This model achieves a good generalisation of the harmonic basis functions for a wide range of harmonic instruments [10], making its use a good alternative to obtain harmonic basis functions from a database of isolated sounds of the target instrument.

The source-filter model has origins in speech processing and sound synthesis. In speech processing, the excitation models the sound produced by the vocals cords, whereas the filter models the resonating effect of the vocal tract. In sound synthesis, excitation-filter (or source-filter) synthesis colors a spectrally rich excitation signal to get the desired sound.

The model proposed in [10] extend the source-filter model by defining the excitation as a weighted sum of instrument-dependent excitation patterns. Under this model, the spectrum of a note is generated by the harmonic excitation of the note multiplied by the filter transfer function of the instrument. Thus, the excitation $e_n(f)$ is different for each pitch and has harmonic nature. The pitch excitation is obtained as the weighted sum of excitation basis functions while the weights vary as the function of pitch.

Following this model, the pitch excitation can be obtained as

$$e_n(f) = \sum_{m=1}^{M} \sum_{i=1}^{I} w_{i,n} v_{i,m} G(f - m f_0(n)) \tag{3}$$

where $v_{i,m}$ is the i-th excitation basis vector (composed of M partials), and $w_{i,n}$ is the weight of the i-th excitation basis vector for pitch n. The basis functions $b_n(f)$ (or $\mathbf{B_{f,n}}$) are computed following the source-filter paradigm as

$$b_n(f) = h(f) e_n(f) \tag{4}$$

where $h(f)$ is the instrument-dependent instrument. Finally, the source-filter model with Multi-Excitation per Instrument (MEI) for magnitude spectra of the whole signal is the sum of instruments and pitches obtained as

$$\hat{x}(f,t) = \sum_n g_n(t) h(f) \sum_{m=1}^{M} \sum_{i=1}^{I} w_{i,n} v_{i,m} G(f - m f_0(n)) \tag{5}$$

where $n = 1, ..., N$ (N being the number of pitches), M represents the number of harmonics and I the number of considered excitations with $I << N$. Using a small number of excitation bases I reduces significantly the parameters of the model, which benefits the learning of parameters. The free parameter of the model are: the time gains $g_n(t)$ (or $\mathbf{G_{n,t}}$), the instrument filter $h(f)$, the basis excitation vectors $v_{i,m}$ and the excitation weigths $w_{i,n}$.

The framework presented in [6] can be used for MEI. For the sake of compact representation we present here the parameter update for the MEI model of (5). Multiplicative updates which minimize the divergence for each parameter of the MEI model are computed by substituting each parameter in eq. (2). More details can be obtained in [10].

3. DESCRIPTION

3.1 Signal factorization

Our proposal attempts to overcome the denoising problem learning in advance the harmonic and transient basis functions from the musical instrument and the spectral patterns from the vinyl noise. For that purpose, an objective function is defined to factorize a mixture spectrogram $X_{f,t}$ into three separated spectrograms, X_H (harmonic part of the musical instrument), X_T (transient part of the musical instrument) and X_N (vinyl noise part). We assume that each of them represents the specific spectral features demonstrated by the instrument and noise. In this manner, our factorization model is defined (see eq. 6),

$$\hat{\mathbf{X}} = \hat{\mathbf{X}}_H + \hat{\mathbf{X}}_T + \hat{\mathbf{X}}_N = \mathbf{B}_H\mathbf{G}_H + \mathbf{B}_T\mathbf{G}_T + \mathbf{B}_N\mathbf{G}_N \quad (6)$$

where all matrices are non-negative matrices.

In order to estimate basis functions or activation gains matrices, the iterative algorithm proposed in [6] can be applied. Using this algorithm, the update rule for the basis functions can be expressed as

$$\mathbf{B} = \mathbf{B} \odot \frac{[(\hat{\mathbf{X}})^{-1} \odot \mathbf{X}]\mathbf{H}'}{\mathbf{1}\mathbf{H}'} \quad (7)$$

where $'$ represents the transpose matrix operator, $\odot$ the element-wise multiplication of matrices, $\mathbf{1}$ is a all one elements matrix with F rows and T columns (or $\mathbf{1}_{f,t}$), $\mathbf{X}$ is the original spectrogram, $\hat{\mathbf{X}}$ is the modeled spectrogram and $\hat{\mathbf{X}}^{-1}$ is the inverse matrix regarding the modeled spectrogram. Eq. (7) can be used for each component of the proposed signal factorisation ($\mathbf{B}_H, \mathbf{B}_T, \mathbf{B}_N$).

The update rule for the activations gains can be written as

$$\mathbf{G} = \mathbf{G} \odot \frac{\mathbf{B}'[(\hat{\mathbf{X}})^{-1} \odot \mathbf{X}]}{\mathbf{B}'\mathbf{1}} \quad (8)$$

Both expressions are valid for each of the components represented in eq. (6).

In our approach, all basis functions ($\mathbf{B}_H$, $\mathbf{B}_T$, $\mathbf{B}_N$) are trained in advance from databases of guitar sounds or vinyl recorded noise.

3.2 Basis functions training

3.2.1 Instrument modeling for harmonic components

The model revised at section 2.2 requires to estimate the basis functions $b_n(f)$ for each note n defined in eq. (6) as the harmonic basis functions $\mathbf{B}_H$. The basis $b_n(f)$ are learned in advance by using the RWC database [11] as a training database of solo instruments playing isolated notes. Let the ground-truth transcription of the training data be represented by $r_n(t)$ as a binary time/frequency matrix. The frequency dimension represents the MIDI scale and time dimension t represents frames. $r_n(t)$ is known in advance for the training database, then it is used to initialize the gains for the training stage such that only the gain value associated with the active pitch n at frame t and played by instrument is set to unity, the rest of the gains are set to zero. Gains initialised to zero remain at zero because of the multiplicative update rules, and therefore the frame is represented only with the correct pitch.

The training procedure is summarised in Algorithm 1.

Algorithm 1 Training Harmonic Spectral Patterns

1. Compute $x(t,f)$ from a solo performance of the target instrument in the training database.
2. Initialise gains $g_n(t)$ with the ground truth transcription $r_n(t)$ and the rest of parameters $h(f)$, $v_{i,m}$ and $w_{i,n}$ with random positive values.
3. Update source-filter $h(f)$.
4. Update excitation basis vectors $v_{i,m}$.
5. Update the weights of the excitation basis vectors $w_{i,n}$.
6. Update gains $g_n(t)$.
7. Repeat steps 3-6 until the algorithm converges (or the maximum number of iterations is reached).
8. Compute basis functions $b_n(f)$ for the musical instrument from eq. (3) and (4) .

Basis function $b_n(f)$ are computed by this training algorithm resulting in a basis function for the complete pitch range n played by the instrument. The instrument-dependent basis functions $b_n(f)$ (or $\mathbf{B}_H$) are known and held fixed during the factorization process, and therefore, the factorization of new signals of the same instrument can be reduced to estimate the gains $g_n(t)$.

3.2.2 Learning transient basis functions

The transient spectral patterns from a musical instrument does not follow a harmonic behaviour. Here, our approach is to learn a representative set of transient basis functions from the note onsets of a training database. Again, the basis $\mathbf{B}_T$ are learned in advance by using the RWC database [11]. In order to initialize the gains for the training stage, lets define $ro(t)$ as a binary time/frequency vector that represents the frames in which a note onset is active. To obtain this vector the database of solo instruments playing isolated notes is annotated supposing that the transient components are active T_O frames from the beginning of each note. In our experiments, a value of $T_O = 5$ frames is used.

The training procedure is summarised in Algorithm 2, the number of transient basis functions is defined as O.

Algorithm 2 Training Transient Spectral Patterns

1. Compute $x(t,f)$ from a solo performance of the target instrument in the training database.
2. Initialise all gains $\mathbf{G}_T$ with random positive values for those frames in which a note onset is active using $ro(t)$.
3. Initialise transient basis functions $\mathbf{B}_T$ with random positive values.
4. Update basis functions $\mathbf{B}_T$.
5. Update gains $\mathbf{G}_T$.
6. Repeat steps 4-5 until the algorithm converges (or the maximum number of iterations is reached).

As in the harmonic case, transient basis functions $\mathbf{B}_T$ are known and held fixed during the factorization process.

3.2.3 Training basis functions from recorded vinyl noise

The vinyl noise used to train vinyl noise basis functions $\mathbf{B}_N$ was obtained from the concatenation of a wide set of public samples recorded from the most common types of vinyl noise [16] [17] [18] [19] [20] [21]. From this concatenation noise signal, two third of the total one was considered for training and the remainder for evaluation. Two groups of different degradations from vinyl noise are trained:

- clicks+crackles+scratches+hiss.
- clicks+crackles+scratches+hiss+hum.

The training procedure is summarised in Algorithm 3, the number of transient basis functions is defined as R.

Algorithm 3 Training vinyl Noise Spectral Patterns

1. Compute $\mathbf{X}$ from the training subset of the noise database.
2. Initialise all gains $\mathbf{G}_N$ with random positive values.
3. Initialise noise basis functions $\mathbf{B}_N$ with random positive values.
4. Update basis functions $\mathbf{B}_N$.
5. Update gains $\mathbf{G}_N$.
6. Repeat steps 4-5 until the algorithm converges (or the maximum number of iterations is reached).

Again, the two groups of noise basis functions $\mathbf{B}_N$ are known and held fixed during the factorization process.

3.3 Denoising application

In order to synthesize the denoised instrument signal, the magnitude instrumental spectrogram $\hat{\mathbf{X}}_H + \hat{\mathbf{X}}_T$ are estimated as the product of the factorization $\mathbf{B}_H\mathbf{G}_H + \mathbf{B}_T\mathbf{G}_T$. To assure a conservative reconstruction process, an instrumental mask $\mathbf{M}_J$ has been generated by means of Wiener filtering (the mask values are defined from 0 to 1).

Firstly, the magnitude spectrograms for the harmonic $\hat{\mathbf{X}}_H$ and transient $\hat{\mathbf{X}}_T$ components of the instrument are estimated using the factorization scheme proposed in eq. (6). In algorithmic approximation, the estimation of the instrumental spectrogram is detailed in Algorithm 4.

Algorithm 4 Estimation of instrumental components

1. Compute the magnitude spectrogram $\mathbf{X}$ of the degraded signal.
2. Initialise $\mathbf{G}_H$, $\mathbf{G}_T$ and $\mathbf{G}_N$ with random nonnegative values.
3. Initialise $\mathbf{B}_H$, $\mathbf{B}_T$ and $\mathbf{B}_N$ from the training algorithms.
4. Update $\mathbf{G}_H$.
5. Update $\mathbf{G}_T$.
6. Update $\mathbf{G}_N$.
7. Repeat steps 4-6 until the algorithm converges (or the maximum number of iterations is reached).
8. Compute the estimated instrumental spectrogram as $\hat{\mathbf{X}}_H + \hat{\mathbf{X}}_T$.

The instrumental mask is therefore defined as

$$\mathbf{M}_J = \frac{\hat{\mathbf{X}}_H + \hat{\mathbf{X}}_T}{\hat{\mathbf{X}}_H + \hat{\mathbf{X}}_T + \hat{\mathbf{X}}_N} \quad (9)$$

The phase information related to the instrumental signal is computed by multiplying the mask $\mathbf{M}_J$ with the complex spectrogram related to the degraded signal $x_J(t) + x_N(t)$. The inverse transform is then applied to obtain an estimation of the instrumental signal $\hat{x}_J(t)$.

4. EVALUATION

4.1 Material

Two test databases D1 and D2 of vinyl degraded guitar sounds were used to evaluate the performance of the proposal. Each database is composed of five degraded files. Each file [19–21] (see Table 1), 30-seconds duration, is created from a real-world Spanish guitar excerpt (with CD quality) degraded by typical noise in vinyl recordings. In the first database D1, degradations include clicks, crackles, scratches and hiss noise. In the second database D2, degradations include clicks, crackles, scratches, hiss and hum noise.

Identifier	Name
F1	Danza de los vecinos
F2	Iberia
F3	Albaicin
F4	Fuente y Caydal
F5	Rumba improvisada

Table 1. Real-world CD quality Spanish guitar excerpts used in experiments [19–21].

The degradation of the audio guitar excerpts was made using the concatenation signal of a wide set of public samples recorded from the most common types of vinyl noise [16] [17] [18] [19] [20] [21]. From this concatenation of vinyl noise, two thirds of the total was considered for training and the remainder for evaluation. So, different noise material was used for training and testing in order to validate the results. Specifically, the training material has durations of 228 seconds for clicks, crackles, scratches and hiss noise and 89 seconds for clicks, crackles, scratches, hiss and hum noise.

To evaluate different acoustic scenarios, the mixing process between guitar excerpts and vinyl noise was produced at 0, 5 and 10 dB of signal-to-noise ratio (see Table 2).

Name	Database	SNR (dB)
D1_0	D1	0
D1_5	D1	5
D1_10	D1	10
D2_0	D2	0
D2_5	D2	5
D2_10	D2	10

Table 2. Acoustic scenarios in the evaluation process.

4.2 Commercial audio restoration products

Three current and well-known commercial audio restoration products have been used to evaluate the performance of our proposal:

- Adobe Audition CS5.5 v4.0.

- Izotope RX 2 (Declicker, Decrackle, Denoiser and Hum removal).
- Waves V8 (X-Click, X-Crackle, X-Hum and Z-Noise).

Both Waves and Izotope plugins were used in Wavelab 6 audio editing and mastering suite from Steinberg [22]. Each audio restoration product has been manually tuned to provide the best results according to noise reduction and quality of the target audio.

4.3 Experimental setup

The proposed method has been evaluated by using the following parameters: frame size of $64ms$, hop size of $32ms$, frequency sampling rate of $44100Hz$, 100 iterations for NMF algorithm, number of transient basis functions $O = 10$ and number of vinyl noise basis functions $R = \{10, 100\}$ (see the following section). Sound source separation applications based on NMF algorithms usually adopt logarithmic frequency discretization. For example, uniformly spaced subbands on the Equivalent Rectangular Bandwidth (ERB) scale are assumed in [23]. In our method, we use the resolution of a quarter semitone by directly integrating the bins of the STFT similary to [10].

4.4 Results

For an objective evaluation of the performance of the separation method we use the metrics implemented in [23]. These metrics are commonly accepted by the specialised scientific community, and therefore facilitate a fair evaluation of the method. The metrics for each separated signal are the *Source to Distortion Ratio* (SDR), the *Source to Interference Ratio* (SIR), and the *Source to Artifacts Ratio* (SAR).

In an NMF framework, the unknown parameters are initialized randomly. Therefore, the spectra resulting from separation are different at each execution, giving different metric results per execution. Thus, the proposed method has been performed 50 times per audio file to demonstrate the statistical significance of the metrics. The 95% confidence interval for the metrics was always smaller than $1.1dB$ in the proposed method.

The SDR results for the denoised guitar signals when using the D1 and D2 databases at different SNRs are given in Table 3. The proposed methods are: P10 proposed method with $R = 10$ noise basis functions, UP10 unrealistic proposed method with $R = 10$ noise basis functions (the noise is directly trained from the same noise added to the degraded signal which is an unrealistic situation), P100 proposed method with $R = 100$ noise basis functions and UP100 unrealistic proposed method with $R = 100$ noise basis functions. The unrealistic approaches are used for estimating the loss produced in separation performance when training the vinyl noise in an implementation different from the real noise. The SDR value of the original input signal is also presented. As can be seen, Waves software obtains the best separation measures from the commercial restoration products. In our approach, the use of $R = 10$ bases is better than using $R = 100$, so we can conclude that the spectral richness of the vinyl noise can be captured with a reduced number of basis functions. Also, the proposed methods achieve better performance for the D2 database mainly because the hum noise is the most stable in frequency. Finally, we can state that our approach is competitive in relation to the commercial audio restoration software.

Name	Input	Audition	Izotope	Waves	P10	UP10	P100	UP100
D1_0	3.2	7.5	5.1	8.6	9.0	9.6	8.4	9.2
D1_5	8.3	11.8	11.2	11.7	12.4	12.9	11.4	12.2
D1_10	13.1	16.2	13.3	16.5	14.6	15.1	13.1	14.1
D2_0	4.7	-2.2	3.0	6.5	11.2	11.8	9.9	10.5
D2_5	9.7	-2.0	5.1	7.7	13.9	14.4	12.4	13.0
D2_10	14.6	-1.9	5.6	8.5	15.8	16.3	13.9	14.6

Table 3. *Denoised guitar SDR results in dB for D1 and D2 databases.*

The SIR results for the denoised guitar signals when using the D1 and D2 databases at different SNRs are given in Table 4. These results inform about the amount of noise present in the cleaned guitar. In all cases, the denoised signals with the proposed methods have less interferences from the vinyl noise.

Name	Input	Audition	Izotope	Waves	P10	UP10	P100	UP100
D1_0	3.3	8.7	8.7	11.7	11.5	12.3	11.1	12.3
D1_5	8.5	13.3	15.2	14.2	16.3	17.0	16.1	17.0
D1_10	13.3	18.3	20.6	20.0	20.6	21.1	20.4	21.2
D2_0	9.7	9.7	12.2	20.8	21.4	21.5	20.5	21.2
D2_5	14.7	14.3	17.6	21.8	25.4	25.4	24.8	25.5
D2_10	19.7	19.0	22.6	28.1	29.2	29.4	28.8	29.5

Table 4. *Denoised guitar SIR results in dB for D1 and D2 databases.*

The SIR results for the estimated vinyl noise component when using the D1 and D2 databases at different SNRs are given in Table 5. Now, the amount of original guitar eliminated from the denoised guitar is shown. On the contrary, in this case Audition and Waves approaches obtain much better results than the proposed approach for the D1 database.

Name	Audition	Izotope	Waves	P10	UP10	P100	UP100
D1_0	18.1	1.7	17.2	10.6	11.4	8.3	10.1
D1_5	19.8	6.7	23.4	5.5	6.4	3.1	4.9
D1_10	16.8	1.8	18.6	0.6	1.7	-1.9	-0.1
D1_0	-11.6	-8.5	-1.8	3.2	3.7	0.6	2.4
D2_5	-16.0	-10.7	-7.0	-1.7	-1.1	-4.1	-2.4
D2_10	-20.2	-14.8	-11.9	-6.1	-5.5	-8.4	-6.7

Table 5. *Estimated vinyl noise SIR results in dB for D1 and D2 databases.*

In order to give the reader the opportunity of listening the material a webpage for the results has been created. On this page, some audio examples (mixed, separated guitar and separated noise) from database D1 and D2 can be heard by the reader. The web page can be found at *http://dl.dropbox.com/u/22448214/SMC%202013/index.html*

5. CONCLUSIONS AND FUTURE WORK

In this work, a denoising technique based on an excitation-filter model for harmonic instruments is proposed. The instrumental part of the degraded signal is divided into harmonic and transient components and trained from the RWC database. The vinyl noise is trained from public recordings. Basis functions are fixed from the training algorithms and in the separation process the activation gains for each component are estimated following an NMF framework. The results show that the proposed approach are competitive in comparison with some commercial audio restoration softwares.

The main problem of the proposed approach is the similarity of the transient basis functions for the instrument and the spectral patterns of the localized degradations such as click, crackle and scratch noise. In our opinion, this issue causes the presence of instrument interferences in the estimated noise and, consequently, the loss of instrument signal in the denoised instrumental audio. This problem also occurs when training the vinyl noise from the original noise (UP10 and UP100 approaches).

For future work, an interesting idea to solve the interference problems can be the definition of sparseness and smoothness constraints [18] in the basis functions and activations gains of the signal factorization.

6. REFERENCES

[1] S. Godsill, P. Wolfe, and W. Fong, "Statistical model-based approaches to audio restoration and analysis," *J. New Music Research*, vol. 30, no. 4, pp. 323–338, 2001.

[2] P. Esquef, M. Karjalainen, and V. Valimaki, "Detection of clicks in audio signals using warped linear prediction," in *Proc. 14th IEEE Int. Conf. on Digital Signal Processing*, Santorini, Greece, 2002, pp. 1085–1088.

[3] H. Lin and S. Godsill, "The multi-channel ar model for real-time audio restoration," in *IEEE Workshop on the Applications of Signal Processing to Audio and Acoustics (WASPAA)*, New Paltz, NY, US, 2005, pp. 335–338.

[4] G. Cabras, S. Canazza, P. Montessoro, and R. Rinaldo, "he restoration of single channel audio recordings based on non-negative matrix factorization and perceptual suppression rule," in *Proc. 13th Int. Conf. Digital Audio Effects DAFx*, Graz, Austria, 2010, pp. 458–465.

[5] S. Godsill and P. Rayner, *Digital Audio Restoration A Statistical Model Based Approach*. Springer-Verlag, 1998.

[6] D. Lee and H. Seung, "Algorithms for non-negative matrix factorization," *in Advances in NIPS.*, pp. 556–562, 2000.

[7] P. Smaragdis and J. Brown, "Non-negative matrix factorization for polyphonic music transcription," in *IEEE Workshop on the Applications of Signal Processing to Audio and Acoustics (WASPAA)*, New Paltz, NY, US, 2003.

[8] G. Cabras, S. Canazza, P. Montessoro, and R. Rinaldo, "The restoration of low-quality audio recordings based on non-negative matrix factorization and perceptual assessment by means of the ebu mushra test method," in *Proc. of ACM Multimedia International Conference*, Firenze, Italy, 2010, pp. 19–24.

[9] N. Bertin, R. Badeau, and E. Vincent, "Enforcing harmonicity and smoothness in bayesian nonnegative matrix factorization applied to polyphonic music transcription," *IEEE Trans. Audio, Speech, Lang. Processing*, vol. 18, no. 3, pp. 538–549, 2010.

[10] J. Carabias, T. Virtanen, P. Vera, N. Ruiz, and F. Canadas, "Musical instrument sound multi-excitation model for non-negative spectrogram factorization," *IEEE Journal of Selected Topics in Signal Processing*, vol. 5, no. 6, pp. 1144–1158, 2011.

[11] M. Goto, H. Hashiguchi, T. Nishimura, and R. Oka, "Rwc music database: Music genre database and musical instrument sound database," in *Proceedings of the 4th International Conference on Music Information Retrieval*, 2003, pp. 229–230.

[12] http://bedroomproducersblog.com/2012/04/02/free-vinyl-noises-sample-pack-released-by-mad-ep.

[13] http://www.musicradar.com/news/tech/sampleradar-243-free-vinyl-style-samples-277010.

[14] http://daviddas.com/2011/01/vinyl-record-samples-for-free-download/.

[15] http://grillobeats.com/blog/downloads/samples-vinyl/.

[16] http://www.thecontrolcentre.com/diamondsanddust.htm.

[17] http://www.partnersinrhyme.com/blog/public-domain-vinyl-record-hiss-pop-crackle/.

[18] T. Virtanen and A. Klapuri, "Analysis of polyphonic audio using source-filter model and non-negative matrix factorizationn," *Advances in Models for Acoustic Processing, Neural Information Processing Systems Workshop*, 2006.

[19] Paco de Lucia plays Manuel de Falla, Record company: Polygram Iberica S.A, 1978.

[20] Concerto De Aranjuez, Record company: Polygram Iberica S.A, 1978.

[21] Paco de Lucia Antologia, Record company: Polygram Iberica S.A, 1995.

[22] Wavelab 6, Audio Editing and Mastering Suite from Steinberg. http://www.steinberg.net/en/products/wavelab/why_wave lab.html.

[23] E. Vincent, C. Févotte, and R. Gribonval, "Performance measurement in blind audio source separation," *IEEE Trans. Audio, Speech and Language Processing*, vol. 14, no. 4, pp. 1462–1469, 2006.

SPATIUM, TOOLS FOR SOUND SPATIALIZATION

Rui Penha
Universidade de Aveiro / INET-MD
rui@ruipenha.pt

João Pedro Oliveira
Universidade Federal de Minas Gerais
jppo@ua.pt

ABSTRACT

In this paper we present *spatium*, a set of free, open source and modular software tools for sound spatialization, describing the creative and technical aspects considered during its development. The system is comprised of spatialization renderers, spatialization interfaces, DAW plugins and Max objects that communicate via OSC (Open Sound Control). They aim to: facilitate the exploration of different approaches to sound spatialization, ease the integration of sound spatialization into diverse compositional workflows, smooth the transition from the studio to different performance environments and be easily expandable to cater for growing needs.

1. INTRODUCTION

Sound is always in space, in the sense that "there is no non-spatial hearing" [1], and the experimental placement of sounds in space as a musical parameter is something that dates back to at least the 16th century. Nevertheless, the intentional control of sound spatialization is undoubtedly amongst the most important conquests of electroacoustic music. It is thus without surprise that a survey of recent research (or even just a quick search online) reveals the existence of many tools for sound spatialization, either commercial or freely available, and several composers developing their own custom solutions for specific pieces. We aim to contribute to this field with the recent release of *spatium*, a set of free, open source and modular software tools for sound spatialization. It is comprised of: three spatialization renderers, ten spatialization interfaces, one Audio Unit plugin, two Max for Live devices and four Max objects. Both the software and its source are available for download at http://spatium.ruipenha.pt, were one can also find online documentation for all the elements, a short video tutorial and a musical example.

1.1 Why (yet) another spatialization tool?

Most composers still use the built-in panning devices of either their DAWs (Digital Audio Workstations) or hardware mixing consoles as their primary spatialization tools, albeit being conscious of their limitations [2]. As it is also a common practice amongst composers working with sound spatialization, we set out to build *spatium* as a custom-made system, with specific goals that existing tools did not fully address:

- simple integration with DAWs, including ones that are limited to stereo busses (e.g., Ableton Live), allowing the recording of spatial information as plugin automation;
- easy adjustment to different studio and performance environments, maximizing portability and taking advantage of increased spatial resolution at particular venues;
- ability to choose the most suitable interface paradigm for each musical intention, including gestural control of spatialization, kinematic spatialization and introducing some novel approaches to dynamic spatialization;
- ability to facilitate the realtime use of sound spatialization through intuitive interfaces, minimizing the need to fully grasp the technical details of a given spatialization technique in advance.

spatium is still a work in progress that can greatly benefit from the contribution of the community. We have therefore decided to share it as both free and open source software.

1.2 Why modular?

A stratified approach has been identified as fruitful solution to integrate sound spatialization into different compositional needs and to allow different combinations of rendering algorithms and controlling interfaces [3]. This modular approach also benefits from the current trend of multicore processors, by enabling the distribution of processing between multiple cores, processors or even machines. Being open source software, the modular architecture also caters for the users who may want to integrate the proposed interfaces with their own spatialization renderers or the other way around: the Processing community, e.g., has built many sketches that could easily be repurposed as spatialization interfaces for *spatium* [1].

2. ARCHITECTURE

As can be seen on Fig. 1, a simple *spatium* system is composed of three main elements:

- the spatialization renderer - which receives monophonic audio channels, the spatial information for

[1] Many examples can be found at http://www.openprocessing.org.

each channel and renders the result for a chosen loudspeaker layout;

- the spatialization interface - which generates spatial information to send, either via OSC to the spatialization renderer or via Midi to be stored as plugin automation at a specific DAW track;
- the Audio Unit plugin or the Max for Live device - which stores spatial information as automation and sends it, via OSC and synchronized with the audio, to the spatialization renderer.

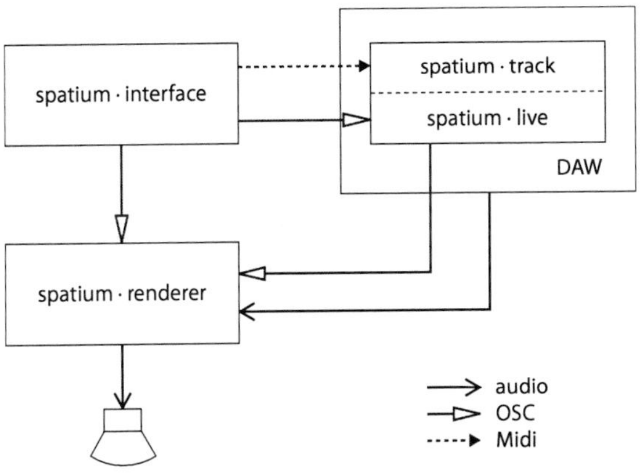

Figure 1. The modular architecture of *spatium*.

2.1 Coordinate System

spatium exclusively uses spherical coordinates: azimuth 0° is in front and increases clockwise; elevation 0° is at the horizontal plane at ear level and increases towards the top; radius goes from 0.0 at the origin to 1.0 at the surface of the soundfield. This is known as the navigational coordinate system and was chosen because of its familiarity, namely due to its previous use in other spatialization tools [4].

2.2 Communication protocol

Communication protocols to send spatialization data over OSC have been proposed, most notably SpatDIF [5]. We chose, however, to develop our own protocol, as in order to be compliant with SpatDIF, an audio renderer must understand and interpret all its core statements, which include descriptors that *spatium* does not use (e.g., orientation) and default position to Cartesian coordinates, as opposed to *spatium*'s exclusive use of spherical coordinates. SpatDIF was developed mainly to control several spatialization renderers from one common interface, whilst *spatium*'s main goal was to enable the control of a chosen spatialization renderer using several interfaces at once. As the audio renderers and the interfaces of *spatium* were developed in parallel within an integrated approach, their protocol requirements are much simpler than the ones needed to provide universal control over different approaches.

One can communicate with the spatialization renderers using four types of messages, send via UDP to port 11475:

- /spatium/#/aer *f1 f2 f3*
- /spatium/#/azimuth *f1*
- /spatium/#/elevation *f2*
- /spatium/#/radius *f3*

with # being the channel, from 1 to 16 [2], and *f1 f2 f3* being, respectively, its azimuth, elevation and radius.

3. SPATIALIZATION TECHNIQUES

spatium uses two spatialization techniques, one based on Ambisonics with distance encoding - used in *spatium·ambi*, along with its related renderers and of their underlying Max objects - and another one based on amplitude panning between stereo pairs - used in *spatium·panning* and its homonymous max object. Both techniques include some novel strategies for the placement of sounds inside of the soundfield that are specific to *spatium*.

3.1 Ambisonics with distance encoding

Ambisonics has recently regained much interest, in part for its ability to encode spatial audio independently of the reproduction setup. High Order Ambisonics can provide greater spatial resolution while maintaining scalability, backwards compatibility, superior immersiveness and reproduction of moving sound sources. The encoding format used in *spatium* is fixed as a mixed-order Ambisonics soundfield, using a 3rd order horizontal, 1st order vertical approach. The choice of having superior resolution on the horizontal plane was made due to the ubiquity of horizontal-only loudspeaker systems and also because our perception of localization has much better resolution on the horizontal plane than on the median plane [1]. By using mixed-order Ambisonics encoding, we are able to minimize the number of audio channels needed to encode the soundfield, whilst retaining periphonic capabilities. We chose, however, to use a 12-channel 3H1V instead of traditional 8-channel 3H1P, as originally proposed by Jérôme Daniel [6], in order to retain horizontal resolution even when going up in the soundfield.

To this 12-channel 3H1V mixed-order Ambisonics soundfield, an additional channel is added for distance encoding, as we have proposed before [7]. This approach is related to W-panning [8] and B Format Inside Panner [9], as they all encode sounds inside the speaker array by increasing the omnidirectional component while decreasing the directional components of the Ambisonics soundfield. Our proposal is distinguished by isolating the sounds at the center of the space in a specific channel, through the use of an additional angular coordinate. This system allows for the postponing of the application of cues for the perception of distance to the decoding stage, where they can be adapted to the characteristics of a specific space and sound system.

3.2 Amplitude panning between stereo pairs

This technique is used in *spatium* as an alternative to the main Ambisonics renderers and objects, using amplitude

[2] Using standard OSC notation, this number can be replaced by an asterisk $*$ to control all channels simultaneously.

panning with the least possible number of speakers, ideally only a stereo pair, to spatialize a sound inside a concentrical loudspeaker layout with an arbitrary number and placement of loudspeakers. When placing a sound close to the circumference defined by the loudspeakers, it will pan the sound between the two closest speakers, as it happens with 2D VBAP [10], using either sine or square root panning laws. When placing the sound inside the circle, it will use the azimuth to determine a stereo pair, the opposite azimuth (azimuth - 180°) to determine a second stereo pair and the radius to amplitude pan between them. Whilst these phantom images across the soundfield do not work as traditional stereo phantom images, due to the interference of the listener's head, this approach enables some spatialization effects such as the rotation around the vertical axis of a sound placed in the middle of the soundfield, by keeping its radius 0.0 whilst changing its azimuth. Three concrete scenarios can be seen on Fig. 2: to pan sound a, the algorithm will do an amplitude panning between speakers 1 and 2; to pan sound b, the algorithm will do an amplitude panning between speakers 1 and 5; to pan sound c, the algorithm will do an amplitude panning between speakers 3 and 4, an amplitude panning between speakers 7 and 8 and finally an amplitude panning between these two pairs.

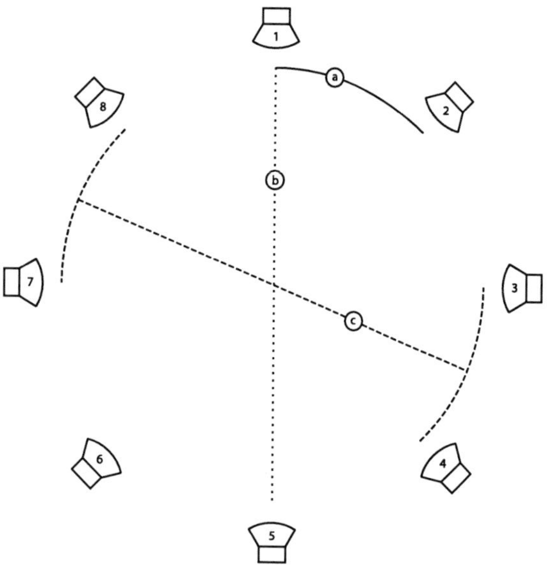

Figure 2. Three scenarios of amplitude panning between stereo pairs.

3.3 Max objects

These techniques were implemented as Max objects, including three Ambisonics-based objects - *spatium·encode*, *spatium·decode* and *spatium·rotate* - and one Amplitude panning-based object - *spatium·panning*, along with some auxiliary patches. They were used to develop *spatium*'s renderers and are documented on the included help files. As *spatium·panning* is a new technique, it required the development of a new object, but many objects have already been developed for Ambisonics-based spatialization in Max/MSP [11–14]. Any one of these existing libraries provides a very flexible and rich approach to Ambisonics spatialization and it would have been possible to implement *spatium·ambi* using them. We nevertheless felt the need to develop our own Ambisonics-based objects, not only to expand the encoding and decoding capabilities with our proposal for distance encoding, but also to incorporate some of the characteristics of the popular VBAP object [15] that we found particularly interesting. Most Ambisonics-based libraries of objects for Max require the user to have some previous knowledge about the idiosyncrasies of Ambisonics (e.g., spherical harmonic orders, order weighting). This knowledge is of course helpful to get good results, as it is true with any technique, but their complexity contrasts with VBAP's simplicity. *spatium*'s objects, as the VBAP object, do not process audio, relying instead on the standard matrix~ MSP object to render the audio. This makes the objects' code easier to maintain and their output simpler to hack for specific needs. Both the Ambisonics and Amplitude panning implementations of the *spatium* objects were designed to be easily interchangeable with the VBAP in existing Max/MSP patches.

4. SPATIALIZATION RENDERERS

spatium has four spatialization renderers, three based on Ambisonics with distance encoding - *spatium·ambi*, *spatium·player* and *spatium·diffusion* - and another one based on amplitude panning between stereo pairs - *spatium·panning*.

4.1 spatium·ambi

spatium·ambi receives mono audio channels and encodes them into an Ambisonics soundfield with distance encoding. The spatial information to encode each channel is received via OSC. The resulting soundfield can be decoded to several loudspeaker layouts, enabling the composition of spatial music with (almost) any loudspeaker setup and the fine-tuning of the piece to any given performance setup. As it was conceived to be used alongside other applications, the main goal when designing its GUI was to make it as compact as possible. As can be seen on Fig. 3, the top portion shows the renderer's 16 monophonic audio inputs, each with its own amplitude meter and three floating-point number displays showing its azimuth, elevation and radius. The bottom portion shows the controls over specific points of the audio engine, with the input to output path laid out from left to right.

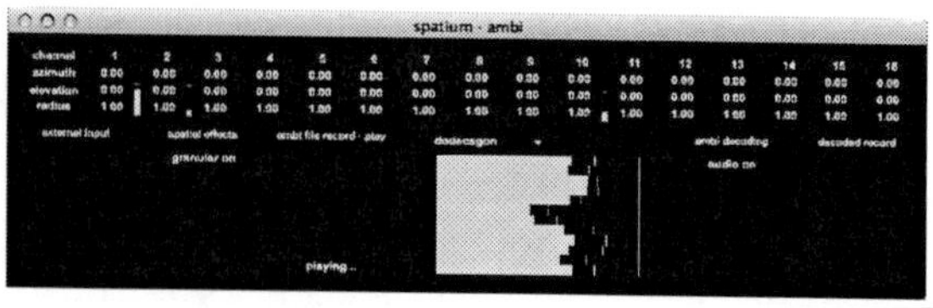

Figure 3. The GUI of the *spatium·ambi* renderer.

4.1.1 *Granular spatialization*

Some approaches have been proposed for the spatialization of granular audio, namely by using swarm-based algorithms to define the grains' positions in space [16, 17].

The granular settings' panel controls several parameters of a granular engine based on Nathan Wolek's granular toolkit [18]. This engine feeds a sound file into four granular generators whose output iterates through four outputs each, giving a total of 16 grain streams that can be individually assigned to any of the 16 channels available at the encoding stage.

4.1.2 Spectral spatialization

Some approaches have been proposed for spectral spatialization [16, 19], a technique that opens several possibilities to mingle timbre and space into cohesive gestures. When activated, the spectral engine divides the live audio input into 28 frequency bands that can be individually silenced or assigned to any of the 16 channels available at the decoding stage.

4.1.3 Decoding loudspeaker layouts

Concentric and equally spaced loudspeaker setups are the ideal means for the reproduction of a decoded soundfield. Regular polygons and Platonic solids are the most obvious solutions for equally spaced layouts and they constitute the major part of the presets of *spatium·ambi* (and of its underlying *spatium·decode* Max object). For the 3D (periphonic) layouts, we used four of the Platonic solids: hexahedron, octahedron, dodecahedron and icosahedron. For the 2D (horizontal) layouts, we used six of the regular polygons, based on the ones we most frequently found at performance venus: square, pentagon, hexagon, octagon, dodecagon and hexadecagon. The stereo output uses the traditional Ambisonic 2-channel UHJ format [20], with minor modification to include the distance decoding. We have found this stereo decoding very pleasing and capable of giving a reliable rendering of an horizontal-only environment, for when the composer is forced to work with solely the ubiquitous stereo monitoring. We have also included a decoder for the standard ITU 5.1 layout and a horizontal-only binaural option, using recent HRTF Measurements of a KEMAR manikin [21]. This binaural implementation is based on the decoding of the soundfield into a regular 24-gon loudspeaker, convoluted with stereo HRTF for each of these positions. By replacing the hrtf#.aif files included with the source code (with # being an integer from 1 to 24 representing the loudspeakers from azimuth 0° onwards with a 15° increment), one can easily use customized HRTF Measurements.

4.1.4 Decoder settings

The control of the order weights is something that is very important to control the reproduction characteristics, namely the spatial resolution or the size of the sweet spot. However, it can be a difficult concept to grasp for composers with little knowledge about the Ambisonics' underlying math. In *spatium·ambi*, each loudspeaker layout choice automatically adjusts which Ambisonic orders to use and with what weights, defaulting to a *max-rE* decoder [22]. In the decoder settings panel, one can adjust the rotation of the soundfield and the order weights. In order to simulate distance cues such as loudness, atmospheric absorption or near-field effect [23] at the decoding stage, one can also adjust the level of the center portion of the soundfield and its equalization.

4.1.5 Reverb settings

The natural reverberation is usually one of the most difficult characteristics to predict and control at performance venues. We have thus decided to include a reverb at the decoding stage, so its characteristics can be adjusted at the time of performance. It is a convolution reverb, using the B-format (i.e., 1st order Ambisonics) impulse responses available at the Open AIR Library [24], along with HISSTools' multiconvolve~ object [25] for realtime convolution. The fact that the impulse responses have less spatial resolution than the soundfield being decoded is not a big problem for diffuse reverberation purposes, but it does imply that, in order not to loose spatial resolution, the dry signal must always be present. After choosing the impulse response, one can manipulate its equalization, the reverb gain and, most importantly as a distance cue, the amount of reverb being applied to the center channel. Albeit using non-optimized impulse responses, this reverb implementation gives a satisfactory definition of acoustical spaces that appear to be bigger than the performance venue.

4.1.6 spatium·player and spatium·diffusion

These two renderers are based on *spatium·ambi*, both have the same output options and can share the same preset files, presenting a smaller GUI with a waveform display on top. *spatium·player* is a player for pre-encoded soundfields and *spatium·diffusion* can be used to perform live diffusion of pre-existing stereo works.

4.2 spatium·panning

Unlike the realtime, spatialization mixing-board concept of *spatium·ambi*, *spatium·panning* was designed for the spatialization of individual sound files before their sequencing and mixing in a DAW. This renderer thus takes an audio file and spatializes it to any 2D, concentrical loudspeaker setup (up to 24 channels) using amplitude panning between stereo pairs. The loudspeaker configuration does not have to be regular and the same sound and path can be rendered to different loudspeaker configurations by just enabling or disabling specific loudspeaker locations. The spatialization path can be constructed and edited as a polygonal chain synchronized with the original audio file, using the GUI visible on Fig. 4. *spatium·panning* can also receive OSC from *spatium*'s interfaces to be recorded as a spatialization path for further editing. The end result can then be rendered as a set of mono audio files, one for each loudspeaker feed.

5. SPATIALIZATION INTERFACES

Some existing stratified tools for sound spatialization focus on the possibility of controlling "different spatial rendering algorithms from one common interface" [3]. We believe that the most interesting capability of this modular approach, from a composer's perspective, is actually the

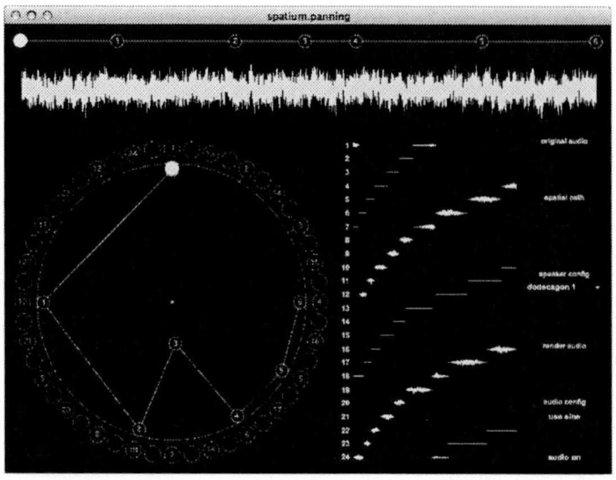

Figure 4. The GUI of the *spatium·ambi* renderer.

other way around. Each interface has its own interaction vocabulary and enforces a specific approach, even if solely by making the composer's vision cumbersome to implement. We have addressed this before, both in terms of designing GUIs specifically to explore this binding between interface and composition technique [26] and in terms of the dangers of confining to the idiosyncrasies of one interface when controlling a musical parameter [27].

We have therefore developed several interfaces (ten at the moment of this writing) that enable both traditional and novel approaches to sound spatialization and that are employable with all the spatialization renderers. We divide these into three categories: dynamic spatialization, kinematic spatialization and gestural spatialization. These interfaces send the spatial information either by OSC messages or by Midi controller values, with most of their parameters being also controllable via OSC. As Midi controller values are generic by nature and the OSC ip, port and addresses are customisable, these interfaces can also be used to generate data for purposes other than spatialization.

5.1 Dynamic spatialization

Dynamic spatialization is the spatialization of sound whose control is focused on the causes of movement, as opposed to the traditional focus on the geometry of motion, characteristic of kinematic spatialization. Inspired by several approaches with swarm spatialization [16, 17] and the Sound Swing series by Bernhard Leitner [28], we developed interfaces where the manipulation of forces like gravity or friction supersedes the traditional control over key frame positions and velocities.

spatium·pendulum and *spatium·flocking* are 3D spatialization interfaces that share some GUI characteristics, visible on Fig. 5. The control within a 3D space using a 2D computer environment is made possible by interacting with one of three 2D projections. These are, from bottom left and on clockwise order, the projection on the horizontal plane, the projection on the frontal plane and the projection on the median plane. The menu on the bottom right corner can be hidden to reveal a one-point perspective 3D view over the scene. The *spatium·pendulum* interface simulates

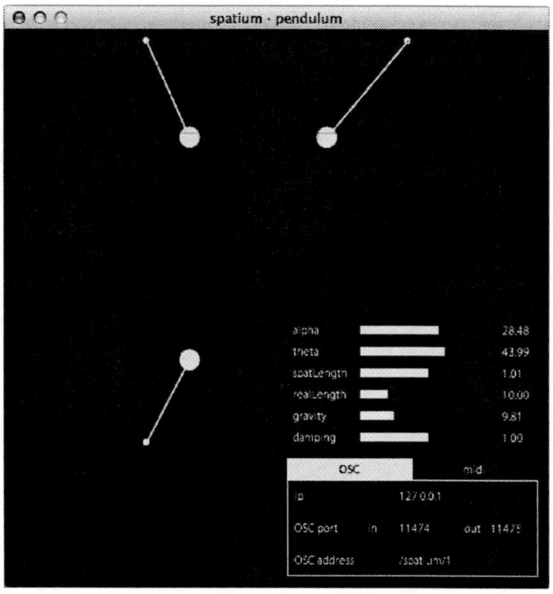

Figure 5. The GUI of the *spatium·pendulum* interface.

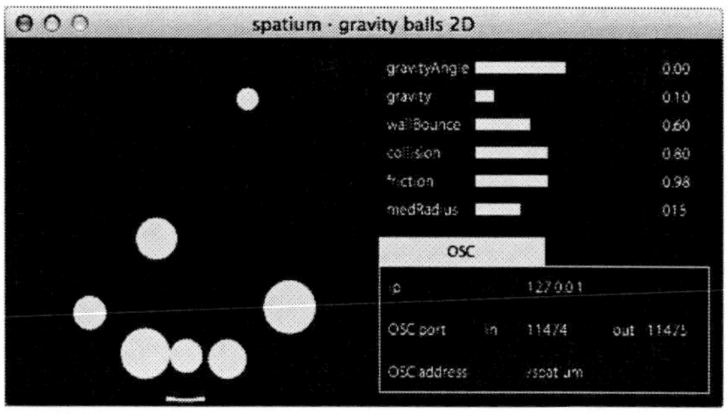

Figure 6. The GUI of the *spatium·gravityBalls2D* interface. The control over the azimuth of the gravitational force can be seen underneath the main circle.

a 3D pendulum, with controllable pivot position, gravity and damping. The *spatium·flocking* interface uses a flocking algorithm to move up to 16 birds in a 3D space, generating movements that work particularly well with granular synthesis, as suggested by previous research [16, 17].

spatium·pendulum2D, *spatium·gravityBalls2D* and *spatium·springs2D* are three interfaces for dynamic spatialization that work solely in the horizontal plane and share a similar GUI to the one visible on Fig. 6. The *spatium·pendulum2D* interface is simply a 2D version of the same algorithm used for the *spatium·pendulum* interface. The *spatium·gravityBalls2D* interface simulates up to 16 balls that are enclosed within the 2D soundfield. Each of these balls has a different radius and is attracted by a gravitational force whose azimuth is controllable, as seen on Fig. 6. The balls bounce on the walls, when they collide with eachother and can be launched against the other balls using a slingshot. The *spatium·springs2D* interface simulates up to 6 springs that connect as many anchors to the spatialization particle, which can be launched by dragging and releasing the mouse.

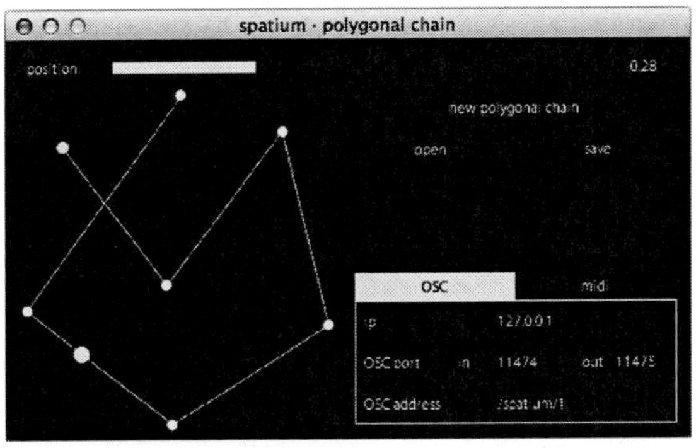

Figure 7. The GUI of the *spatium·polygonalChain2D* interface.

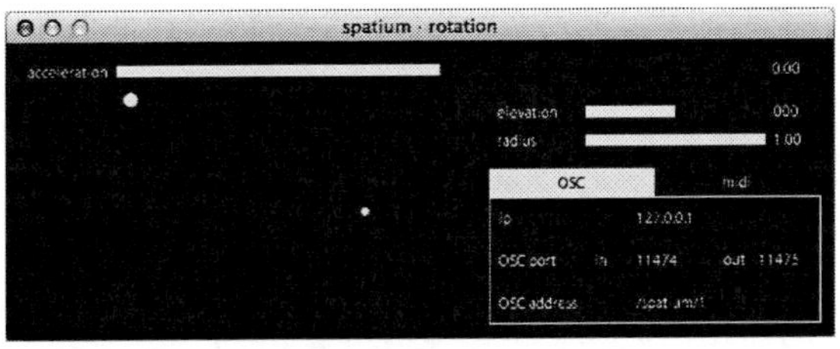

Figure 8. The GUI of the *spatium·rotation* interface.

5.2 Kinematic spatialization

Kinematic spatialization is the spatialization of sound whose control is focused on the geometry of motion (e.g., position, velocity, acceleration), without considering external causes for this movement. They are thus closer to some more traditional interfaces for spatialization. The *spatium·polygonalChain2D* interface, visible on Fig. 7, enables the creation of a spatialization path as a polygonal chain, that can be saved and retrieved for further editing. After creating the polygonal chain, the user can perform the movement by moving a horizontal fader with the mouse or by controlling its position along the timeline via OSC. With the *spatium·rotation* interface, visible on Fig. 8, one controls the angular acceleration on a horizontal plane, with controllable elevation and radius. The movement accelerates clockwise or counter clockwise, moving with either variable or uniform acceleration, when the fader is respectively moving or left in a fixed position, or with constant angular velocity, when the fader is reset to 0.

5.3 Gestural spatialization

Gestural spatialization refers to both the kind of interface and to the relation established between the spatialization and the musical gestures. The gestural spatialization interfaces focus on direct, real-time control over the spatialization particle. The *spatium·linearRotation* interface has a similar GUI to that of the *spatium·rotation* interface, visible on Fig. 8, with the topmost fader now directly controlling the azimuth, with two complete revolutions available. The main purpose is to facilitate the control over the rotation of the spatialization particle using the mouse, which we found to be easier to accomplish using a linear fader instead of a circular controller. With *spatium·trackpad*, one can use the laptop's trackpad as an absolute positioning touch controller. It controls solely one spatialization particle, as we found the trackpad too small for multi-particle control. The *spatium·controlOSC* interface has two modes that enable the use of Control [29], a free, open source and customizable touch controller that runs on both iOS and Android and outputs OSC via Wi-Fi. The first mode, called *multitouch*, is optimized for a tablet and enables the direct, multi-touch control over up to 16 channels in a 2D space. The second mode, called *gyroscope*, enables the control of the spatialization particle's position in a 3D space by pointing to the desired physical location with, e.g., an iPhone or Android phone.

6. PLUGINS

Both the Audio Unit plugin and the Max for Live devices developed for *spatium* are not actual audio effects and pass the audio untouched to the output. They simply send their parameters via OSC messages, thus enabling the recording and synchronization of spatial information as automation on any compatible DAW.

The *spatium·track* plugin can be placed in an audio track effects chain to send its three parameters - *azimuth, elevation* and *radius* - via OSC. Up to 16 instances of this plugin, which uses the generic Audio Unit GUI, can be used simultaneously, but only one can use a given channel at a given time to avoid conflicting information. By setting a spatialization interface to output Midi and configuring the DAW's automation control accordingly, one can record the spatial information generated by *spatium*'s interfaces on the same track as the audio being spatialized, enabling its reproduction and further editing.

The *spatium·live* device receives, displays, stores and/or controls spatialization information to be sent via OSC. It can be used instead of *spatium·track* when in Ableton Live, adding the possibility of being controlled directly via OSC.

The *OSCsend* is not a part of *spatium*, instead being a generic device that can record up to three automatable parameters to be sent via OSC to any ip address and port. It can be used to control *spatium*'s interfaces by setting the appropriate addresses as parameters.

7. CONCLUSIONS AND FUTURE WORK

We hope that *spatium* can successfully facilitate the integration of spatialization in other composers' workflows, at the same time catalysing the emergence of new and creative approaches to sound spatialization. We have been using it for almost a year and it has proven a trustworthy set of tools, capable of promoting some unorthodox approaches to sound spatialization. After its initial release, on October 2012, the feedback from the community has been very encouraging, leading to some of the developments that we have included in this paper, such as the *spatium·panning*, *spatium·player* and *spatium·diffusion* renderers, the control of the interfaces' parameters via OSC or the Max for Live devices. Although we do not have concrete data on the usage of *spatium*, in the first month after the release of the latest version at the time of this writing, in late March 2013, the website received circa 500 unique visitors.

We plan to release new interfaces, to upgrade the still very basic granular and spectral spatialization effects and to add some new decoding layouts in the near future. Amongst these, we plan to include 3D binaural rendering and potentiate its utility as both a mobile composition aid and as a distribution format. We also plan to implement the capability of imposing audio effects into specific points of the soundfield, as we have proposed before [7]. The first practical uses of *spatium* also revealed the need for a simple mixer that enables the amplitude manipulation and summing of several soundfields placed on a timeline. The *spatium·panning* object's algorithm will also be expanded with a 3D version.

Acknowledgments

We would like to thank Fundação para a Ciência e a Tecnologia for supporting our work.

8. REFERENCES

[1] J. Blauert, *Spatial Hearing*. The MIT Press, 1997.

[2] N. Peters, G. Marentakis, and S. McAdams, "Current technologies and compositional practices for spatialization: a qualitative and quantitative analysis," *Computer Music J.*, vol. 35, no. 1, pp. 10–27, 2011.

[3] N. Peters, T. Lossius, J. Schacher, P. Baltazar, C. Bascou, and T. Place, "A stratified approach for sound spatialization," in *Proc. SMC*, Porto, 2009.

[4] V. Schacher, "Seven years of ICST ambisonics tools for Max/MSP - a brief report," in *Proc. Ambisonics Symposium*, Paris, 2010.

[5] N. Peters, T. Lossius, and J. Schacher, "SpatDIF: Principles, specification, and examples," in *Proc. SMC*, Copenhagen, 2012.

[6] C. Travis, "A new mixed-order scheme for ambisonic signals," in *Proc. Ambisonics Symposium*, Graz, 2009.

[7] R. Penha, "Distance encoding in ambisonics using three angular coordinates," in *Proc. SMC*, Berlin, 2008.

[8] D. Menzies, "W-Panning and O-Format, tools for object spatialization," in *Proc. Int. Conf. Auditory Display*, Kyoto, 2002.

[9] M. Morrell and J. Reiss, "A comparative approach to sound localisation within a 3D sound field," in *Proc. 126th AES Convention*, Munich, 2009.

[10] V. Pulkki, "Virtual sound source positioning using vector base amplitude panning," *J. AES*, vol. 45, no. 6, pp. 456–466, 1997.

[11] J. Schacher and P. Kocher, "Ambisonics spatialization tools for Max/MSP," in *Proc. ICMC*, New Orleans, 2006.

[12] G. Wakefield, "Third-order ambisonic extensions for Max/MSP with musical applications," in *Proc. ICMC*, New Orleans, 2006.

[13] G. Wakefield and W. Smith, "Cosm: a toolkit for composing immersive audio-visual worlds of agency and autonomy," in *Proc. ICMC*, Huddersfield, 2011.

[14] J. Colafrancesco, "L'ambisonie d'ordre supérieur et son appropriation par les musiciens, présentation de la bibliotèque Hoa.lib." in *Journées d'Informatique Musicale*, Mons, 2012.

[15] V. Pulkki, "Generic panning tools for Max/MSP," in *Proc. ICMC*, Berlin, 2000.

[16] D. Kim-Boyle, "Spectral and granular spatialization with boids," in *Proc. ICMC*, New Orleans, 2006.

[17] S. Wilson, "Spatial swarm granulation," in *Proc. ICMC*, Belfast, 2008.

[18] N. Wolek, "A granular toolkit for Cycling'74's Max/MSP," in *Proc. SEAMUS Nat. Conf.*, Iowa City, 2002.

[19] R. Torchia and C. Lippe, "Techniques for multichannel real-time spatial distribution using frequency-domain processing," in *Proc. Int. Conf. NIME*, Hamamatsu, 2004.

[20] Wikipedia. Ambisonic UHJ format. Accessed on February 2013. [Online]. Available: http://en.wikipedia.org/wiki/Ambisonic_UHJ_format

[21] H. Wierstorf, M. Geier, A. Raake, and S. Spors, "A free database of head-related impulse response measurements in the horizontal plane with multiple distances," in *Proc. 130th AES Convention*, London, 2011.

[22] F. Hollerweger, "Periphonic sound spatialization in multi-user virtual environments," Master's thesis, IEM/CREATE, 2006.

[23] J. Daniel, "Spatial sound encoding including near field effect: Introducing distance coding filters and a viable, new ambisonic format," in *Proc. AES 23rd Int. Conf.*, Copenhagen, 2003.

[24] T. U. of York. OpenAIR library. Accessed on February 2013. [Online]. Available: http://www.openairlib.net

[25] A. Harker and P. Tremblay, "The HISSTools impulse response toolbox: Convolution for the masses," in *Proc. ICMC*, Ljubljana, 2012.

[26] R. Penha, "Towards a free, open source and cross-platform software suite for approaching music and sound design," in *Research, Reflections and Innovations in Integrating ICT in Education*, A. Méndez-Villas, A. S. Martín, and J. M. González, Eds. Badajoz: Formatex, 2009, pp. 1204–1208.

[27] J. Oliveira, "Tecnologia, fetichismo e crise de identidade," 2012, unpublished manuscript.

[28] B. Leitner, *Sound:Space*. Cantz Verlag, 1998.

[29] C. Roberts. Control. Accessed on February 2013. [Online]. Available: http://charlie-roberts.com/Control/

Dynamic FM synthesis using a network of complex resonator filters

Julian Parker
Department of Signal Processing & Acoustics
Aalto University
Espoo, Finland
julian.parker@aalto.fi

Till Bovermann
Department of Media
Aalto University
Helsinki, Finland
till.bovermann@aalto.fi

ABSTRACT

There is a strong analogy between the sinusoidal operator used in FM synthesis, and the resonator filter. When implemented in a direct-form structure, a resonator filter is not suitable for use as a substitute for an FM operator, as it is not stable under centre frequency modulation. Recent, more robust resonator filter structures have made this use a possibility. In this paper we examine the properties of this structure that makes it appropriate for this application, and describe how a network of these filters can be combined to form a dynamic FM synthesis network. We discuss the possible range of sounds that can be produced by this structure, and describe its application to a performance system for improvised electroacoustic music.

1. INTRODUCTION

FM synthesis [1,2] and resonator filters [3–5] are both mature topics in digital audio signal processing. Resonators can in some ways be thought of as a generalisation of a sinusoidal oscillator that can take arbitrary input. Indeed, in the physical world, oscillators are often resonators which are driven in some way. Hence, we have a strong analogy between resonators and the sinusoidal operators at the heart of FM synthesis. This raises the question – what would an FM synthesiser-like structure constructed out of resonators and driven by an audio-signal sound like? Digital filter design has traditionally been dominated by direct-form topologies, which generally have poor time-varying properties. This deficiency seems to have discouraged any development of this idea. This situation is in contrast to the analog synthesis world, where audio-rate modulation of filters has been part of the standard repertoire of techniques since the beginning.

Previous work on the use of time-varying linear filters outside of audio signal processing exists [6–8], and has recently been applied in the analysis of the behaviour of Feedback-AM synthesis [9]. Feedback-AM synthesis can be considered to a be technique based on time-varying filters, and this analogy has been extended to second-order filters, including the direct-form resonator filter [10]. However, the poor time-varying stability of the direct-form filter means that this exploration has been limited to very low modulation depths.

In 2003, the late Max Mathews proposed a better behaved implementation of a resonator based on the idea of complex multiplication [11]. This structure is anecdotally reported to be completely stable under modulation of its parameters. This work has unfortunately seen little attention in the time since, although some analysis of coefficient interpolation schemes has been performed [12]. The resonator design proposed by Mathews is termed the 'phasor filter' or the 'complex resonator', the latter of which is the term used hereforth.

In this work, the idea of an FM synthesiser-like configuration of complex resonators is explored - with arbitrary audio input and the natural decay of the resonators taking the place of envelopes in defining the dynamic behaviour of the sound. In Section 2, we review the complex resonator structure, derive some useful properties of the structure, and examine the output it produces under audio-rate modulation of its centre frequency. In Section 3 we describe how a number of complex resonators can be combined into an FM synthesis network, and qualitatively examine the range of sounds which this structure can produce. In Section 4, we describe how this system has so far been applied in practice to produce musical performance systems. In Section 5, we conclude.

2. THE COMPLEX RESONATOR

The complex resonator is a system first introduced by Mathews and Smith [11]. It arises from the observation that multiplication of a complex number by a complex coefficient is equivalent to rotation around the origin on the complex plane. If we take a complex number $x = re^{i\theta}$ and multiply it by itself, the result is $x^2 = r^2e^{2i\theta}$. If we repeat the multiplication n times, we have $x^n = r^ne^{ni\theta}$. It should be clear that this process represents a continuous rotation around the origin. If $|x| < 1$, this motion is an in-going spiral. If $|x| > 1$, the motion is an out-going spiral. If $|x| = 1$, the motion is a circle around the origin. We can see that this circular motion is analogous to a resonance, with the angular velocity of the motion (defined by θ) being the frequency of the resonance. We can write this process as a pair of difference equations in terms of the real and imaginary parts of the product, and hence derive a system that looks very much like a digital filter:

$$x_{\text{Re}}[n+1] = r\cos(\theta)x_{\text{Re}}[n] - r\sin(\theta)x_{\text{Im}}[n],$$
$$x_{\text{Im}}[n+1] = r\sin(\theta)x_{\text{Re}}[n] + r\cos(\theta)x_{\text{Im}}[n] \quad (1)$$

If we add an input $u[n]$ to the real part, and take an output $y[n]$ from the imaginary part we can write the system in state space form:

$$\underline{x}[n+1] = \boldsymbol{A}\underline{x}[n] + \boldsymbol{B}u[n]$$
$$y[n] = \boldsymbol{C}\underline{x}[n] \quad (2)$$

where

$$\boldsymbol{A} = \begin{bmatrix} r\cos(\theta) & -r\sin(\theta) \\ r\sin(\theta) & r\cos(\theta) \end{bmatrix}, \boldsymbol{B} = \begin{bmatrix} 1 \\ 0 \end{bmatrix}, \boldsymbol{C} = \begin{bmatrix} 0 & 1 \end{bmatrix}$$

As we intend in this paper to use the system as a resonator and not as a pure oscillator, it makes sense to parameterise r in a more intuitive way. Instead, we would like to specify a decay time for the response of the filter. Intuitively from understanding the system as a repeated rotation, we can see that the reduction in amplitude at each sample step is given by multiplying by r. This clearly describes an exponential decay. Therefore, we can calculate a desirable value of r from a decay time τ, using the equation $r = e^{-\frac{1}{\tau f_s}}$, where f_s is the sampling frequency. It is also worth noting that we can trivially convert from unity sampling period angular frequency θ to a centre frequency with arbitrary sampling period by the relation $\theta = \frac{f_c}{2\pi f_s}$ where f_c is the centre frequency and f_s is the sampling frequency.

2.1 Normalization

In the form described above, the resonator structure possesses a large gain at its resonant peak. For more predictable use of the resonator in larger signal processing structures, particularly those involving feedback, it is desirable to normalize the filter so that its peak gain is unity. Also, since we are planning on modulating the filter's centre frequency at audio rate, any fluctuations in peak amplitude will introduce additional sidebands due to amplitude modulation. The normalisation should minimise this problem. First, the system is expressed in transfer function form:

$$H_{\text{res}}(z) = \frac{r\sin\theta z^{-2}}{1 - 2r\cos\theta z^{-1} + r^2 z^{-2}} \quad (3)$$

Assuming unity sampling period, and that the peak gain is at the specified centre frequency of the filter (which is correct apart from very close to DC or Nyquist, where the poles interfere with each other), we have:

$$H_{\text{res}}(e^{i\theta}) = \frac{r\sin(\theta)e^{-2i\theta}}{1 - 2r\cos(\theta)e^{-i\theta} + r^2 e^{-2i\theta}}$$
$$= \frac{r\sin(\theta)}{(1-r)(e^{2i\theta} - r)} \quad (4)$$

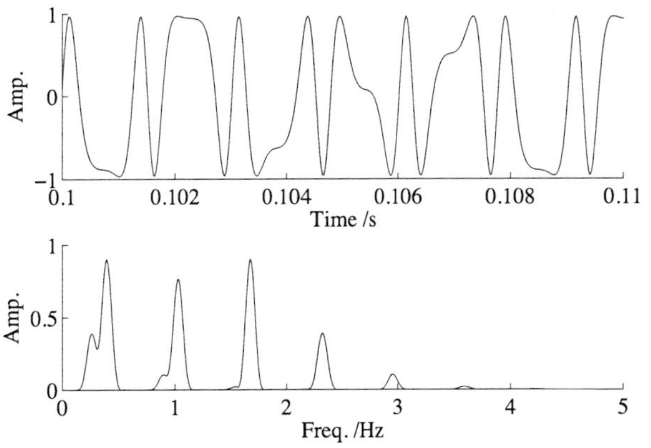

Figure 1. Extract from output of modulated complex resonator, excited with an impulse. Time-domain behaviour at a point near to the start of the decay (top), 4096 sample STFT taken at same point (bottom).

and therefore

$$|H_{\text{res}}(e^{i\theta})| = \left| \frac{r\sin(\theta)}{(1-r)(e^{2i\theta} - r)} \right|$$
$$= \frac{\sqrt{r^2\sin^2(\theta)}}{(1-r)\sqrt{(\cos(2\theta) - r)^2 + \sin^2(2\theta)}}$$
$$= \frac{r\sqrt{\frac{1}{2}(1-\cos(2\theta))}}{(1-r)\sqrt{1 + r^2 - 2r\cos(2\theta)}}. \quad (5)$$

This expression could be used to normalize the peak gain of the filter to unity, however it is rather complex and calculating it every time the coefficients are updated would be computationally expensive. With some further analysis, we can construct a simpler approximation to this expression. By observation, we can see that the maxima of the magnitude should occur at $\theta = \frac{\pi}{2}$. Taking a Taylor expansion around this point, we have:

$$|H_{\text{res}}(e^{i\theta})| \approx \frac{r}{1-r^2} - \frac{(1-r^2)}{2(1+r)^3}\left(\theta - \frac{\pi}{2}\right)^2 + O\left[\theta - \frac{\pi}{2}\right]^3 \quad (6)$$

Examining the first two terms of the series, we see that as $r \to 1$, $\left|\frac{r}{1-r^2}\right| \gg \left|\frac{(1-r^2)}{2(1+r)^3}\right|$. The same is true of the higher-order angle-dependent terms. For the purposes of this work, the resonator is generally used with τ on the order of 0.01 seconds and upwards. This corresponds to a resonance of $r = 0.9977$ or higher at a sampling rate of 44.1kHz. Therefore, for these purposes we can make the approximation

$$|H_{\text{res}}(e^{i\theta})| \approx \frac{r}{1-r^2} \quad (7)$$

which can be used to normalize the peak gain of the resonator. The peak gain will still fall to zero when the centre frequency is exactly at DC, but the normalization holds until very close to this point.

It is also possible to exactly normalise the filter with respect to varying centre frequency by using the method described by Smith et al. [3], and inserting two zeros at $z =$

$\pm\sqrt{r}$. This would be achieved by adding an un-attenuated path from the input to output of the system, and by inverting the input to the first state and dividing it by $\sin(\theta)$. However, this multiplication is problematic as it results in a divide-by-zero when the centre frequency is exactly at DC. Given that we may want to allow the centre frequency to take on negative values (to allow large modulation depths), this is unacceptable. This method also produces extremely large signal values at the input to the first state when the centre frequency is close to DC, which will cause numerical issues in fixed-point architectures.

2.2 Time-varying stability

As the filter will be modulated at audio rate, it is wise to examine its stability under time-varying conditions. Intuitively, it seems that it should be stable under arbitrary modulation of r and θ as long as $|r| < 1$, as the rotation that these parameters represent will always be following an in-going spiral. We can express this formally by applying the sufficient (but not necessary) condition for bounded-in bounded out (BIBO) stability of a time-varying filter described by Laroche [13] – which is that $||\boldsymbol{A}(n)||_2 = \sqrt{\lambda_{max}(\boldsymbol{A}^*\boldsymbol{A})} < 1,\ \forall n$ where * denotes the conjugate transpose and λ_{max} is a function which returns the maximum eigenvalue of its argument. Examining $\boldsymbol{A}$ in the case of the complex resonator, we have:

$$
\begin{aligned}
||\boldsymbol{A}(n)||_2 &= \sqrt{\lambda_{max}(\boldsymbol{A}^*\boldsymbol{A})} \\
&= \sqrt{\lambda_{max}\begin{pmatrix} r^2\cos^2(\theta) & -r^2\sin^2(\theta) \\ -r^2\sin^2(\theta) & r^2\cos^2(\theta) \end{pmatrix}} \\
&= \sqrt{r^2} \qquad (8)
\end{aligned}
$$

which gives us the condition that $|r(n)| < 1,\ \forall n$ which in this case is simply the normal time-invariant stability condition of keeping the eigenvalues of the state transition matrix within the unit circle.

2.3 Output of a frequency modulated complex resonator

Figure 1 shows a small extract from the signal produced by a resonator when the centre frequency of $f_c = 1028$ Hz is modulated with a 642 Hz sinusoid with a modulation depth of 998Hz. The decay time τ of the filter is 2 seconds. The filter is excited with an impulse. Note that we use absolute modulation depth to denote the amount of modulation, as the usual FM synthesis concept of modulation index is not meaningful in the general case where we do not know the content of the modulating signal.

The sound is like that of a simple struck bell. The response has an exponentially decaying envelope, as would be expected in the case of an unmodulated resonator. Using a different signal as input allows a variety of dynamic behaviours. As the bandwidth of the filters is very narrow, only very little of the input sound is recognisable. The input acts more as a way of controlling the amplitude and spectral balance of the output signal, with the sound output being dominated by distributions of sidebands of the carrier frequency (in this case centre frequency) consistent with those present in standard FM synthesis [1, 2].

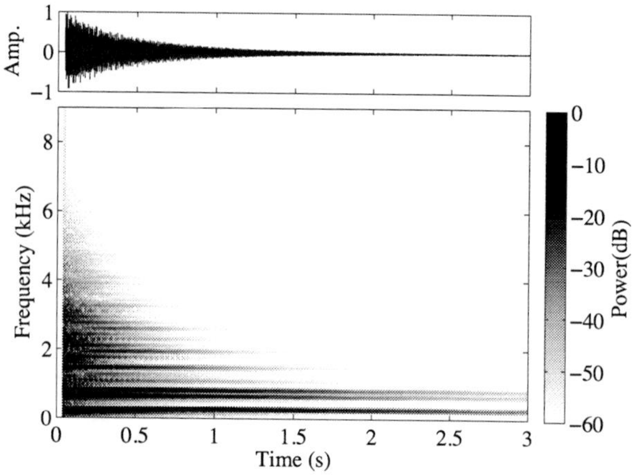

Figure 2. Waveform and spectrogram of cascaded four-resonator system, excited by an impulse.

3. RESONATOR FM NETWORKS

We define a resonator FM network as a vector $\underline{S}$ of resonator systems parameterised by a time-invariant (or slowly changing) centre frequency f_i, a time-varying frequency offset a_i and a decay time τ_i.

$$
\underline{S} = \begin{pmatrix} S_1(f_1 + a_1, \tau_1) \\ S_2(f_2 + a_2, \tau_2) \\ \vdots \\ S_i(f_i + a_i, \tau_i) \end{pmatrix} \qquad (9)
$$

This vector of systems has a state space representation of its own, given by:

$$
\begin{aligned}
\underline{\chi}[n+1] &= \boldsymbol{\alpha}[n]\underline{\chi}[n] + \boldsymbol{\beta}u[n] \\
\underline{\upsilon}[n] &= \boldsymbol{c}\underline{\chi}[n] \qquad (10)
\end{aligned}
$$

where

$$
\underline{\chi} = \begin{pmatrix} \underline{x}_1 \\ \underline{x}_2 \\ \vdots \\ \underline{x}_i \end{pmatrix}, \underline{\upsilon} = \begin{pmatrix} y_1 \\ y_2 \\ \vdots \\ y_i \end{pmatrix}, \boldsymbol{\alpha} = \begin{pmatrix} \boldsymbol{A}_1 & 0 & \dots & 0 \\ 0 & \boldsymbol{A}_2 & \dots & 0 \\ \vdots & \vdots & \ddots & \vdots \\ 0 & 0 & \dots & \boldsymbol{A}_i \end{pmatrix},
$$

$$
\boldsymbol{\beta} = \begin{pmatrix} b_1\boldsymbol{B} & 0 & \dots & 0 \\ 0 & b_2\boldsymbol{B} & \dots & 0 \\ \vdots & \vdots & \ddots & \vdots \\ 0 & 0 & \dots & b_i\boldsymbol{B} \end{pmatrix}, \boldsymbol{c} = \begin{pmatrix} \boldsymbol{C} & 0 & \dots & 0 \\ 0 & \boldsymbol{C} & \dots & 0 \\ \vdots & \vdots & \ddots & \vdots \\ 0 & 0 & \dots & \boldsymbol{C} \end{pmatrix}. \qquad (11)
$$

The $\underline{x}_i$ are the individual state vectors of each filter. The $\boldsymbol{A}_i$ are the state update matrices. The y_i are the filter outputs. $\boldsymbol{B}$ and $\boldsymbol{C}$ are as defined in (2), and the b_i are the coefficients representing the gain of the input signal to the input of each filter. We also define an expression for the overall output of the parallel systems:

$$
Y[n] = \underline{\kappa} \cdot \underline{\upsilon}[n] \qquad (12)
$$

Where $\underline{\kappa}$ is the time-invariant (or slowly varying) vector of output mixing coefficients κ_i.

The vector $\underline{a}$ of centre frequency offsets is calculated from the output of the resonators as follows:

$$\underline{a}[n+1] = \mathbf{\Gamma}\underline{v}[n] \quad (13)$$

We term $\mathbf{\Gamma}$ the FM feedback matrix. Since the outputs $\underline{v}$ are bounded by the maximum amplitude of the input signal (and likely much lower), the elements of $\mathbf{\Gamma}$ must be quite large – of the order of the depth of frequency modulation in Hz required. In fact, they are not absolute modulation depths but instead place an upper bound on the depth of modulation of a particular resonator by a particular output.

The behaviour of the system is governed by the vector of centre frequencies $\underline{f}$, decay times $\underline{\tau}$ and $\mathbf{\Gamma}$. Since each individual resonator system has unity peak gain and is completely stable under coefficient modulation, the overall system should also remain stable regardless of the values of $\mathbf{\Gamma}$. We can also make some general observations about the relationship between the output of the system and the content of $\mathbf{\Gamma}$. For example, $||\mathbf{\Gamma}||$ gives a measure of the overall depth of modulation, and hence the extent of the FM sidebands and the complexity of the timbre. Feedback loops are generated by entries along the diagonal of $\mathbf{\Gamma}$, and also by symmetrical patterns in the upper and lower triangular parts. When $\mathbf{\Gamma}$ contains only entries in the upper or lower triangular part of the matrix (with the diagonal empty), the system will be in a purely feedforward configuration.

Note that there is no connection between the outputs of the resonators and any of the inputs of the resonators. All of the resonators are excited only by the general input signal, albeit with different weightings. This is a specific choice, and is crucial to the use of the system as a musical instrument as it means that the overall envelope of the output of the system is predominantly a function of the input and the resonator ringing times. A user can therefore interact with the system in a relatively predictable way, in that it only produces sound when some kind of excitation is provided.

3.1 Results

Figure 2 shows the output of a system of four resonators configured in a simple feedforward configuration and excited by an impulse. The centre frequencies are distributed irregularly, and the modulation depths are around 1000Hz. The resulting sound is reminiscent of the idiophones used in Indonesian Gamelan music. Exciting the system with a more complex signal produces strong dynamic behaviour. Low amplitude inputs sound like brushing or blowing on a complex resonant object. Stronger inputs produce extremely dissonant and non-linear behaviour (although the system remains technically linear, just not LTI).

The dynamic behaviour of the sound is completely dependent on the nature of the input signal, and the natural exponentially decaying envelope of the resonators. This imparts a more organic quality to the sound than the precisely defined envelopes used in traditional FM synthesis. Standard FM synthesis strategies can be used when deciding on the topology of connections between resonators and their centre frequencies.

4. APPLICATIONS

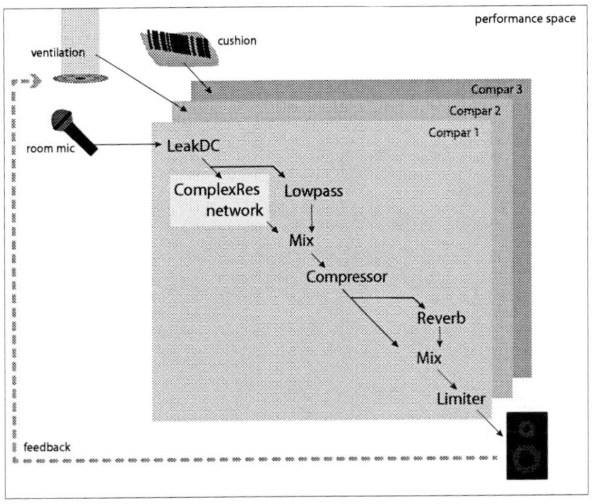

Figure 3. Overview of the performance setup.

The above described resonator network was implemented for practical use, and applied in a performance situation.

4.1 SuperCollider implementation

The complex resonator filter was implemented as a unit generator plugin (*UGen*) for SuperCollider [1] [14]. It has the interface

```
ComplexRes.ar(in, freq, decay)
```

where `in` is the source signal, `freq` the resonance frequency θ and `decay` the decay time τ in seconds.

Both SuperCollider code and sound examples for such networks can be found at the webpage accompanying this publication. [2]

4.2 Performance setup

The SuperCollider ComplexRes implementation was used in two consecutively developed setups: *Compar* is a feedforward resonator network featuring three `ComplexRes` nodes. Its successor *ComparFeedback* implements an FM feedback matrix. The number of nodes can be set when defining the synthesis engine. *ComparFeedback* implements a superset of the *Compar* system.

In both designs, the complex resonator network was embedded in a network of other processing structures. To remove unwanted DC offset, the input signal is processed by a high-pass filter (*LeakDC*). After a mixing stage in which the filter output is combined with the (low-passed) raw signal, it is fed through a compressor and processed by

[1] `http://supercollider.sourceforge.net/`

[2] `http://tai-studio.org/index.php/projects/complexres/`

a reverberation unit. A schematic overview of the setup is displayed in Figure 3.

Due to the increased complexity of the *ComparFeedback* unit, it became evident that an extended graphical user interface is needed compared to that for *Compar* (see Figure 5). However *Compar* features, despite its limitations compared to *ComparFeedback*, a unique way of performance which makes it a valuable instrument of its own.

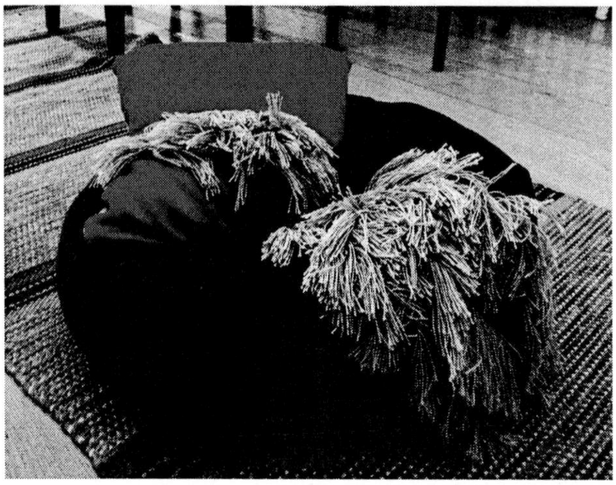

Figure 4. Cushion-shaped musical interface made of conductive yarn.

Both *Compar* and *ComparFeedback* were used as core parts of a feedback-based performance setup, similar to that described by Di Scipio in its general form [15]. These performance systems were designed and implemented as part of the project *Electronic Music Practice for Neurodiverse People* [3]. As shown in Figure 3, three copies of the synthesis engine were used, each with a different input: *Compar 1* connected to a microphone placed in the performance place, *Compar 2* was wired to a contact microphone attached to a ventilation outlet, and *Compar 3* processed the input of a cushion-shaped musical interface made of conductive yarn which, when touched, renders a noisy electrical signal (see Figure 4). The latter served as a source of direct interaction with the sound.

The combination of all three elements created a drone-like soundscape, grounded in the acoustic features of the environment in which it was played. Particularly, the room-modes of the performance space and the resonating frequencies of the (already prominent) ventilation system had a large impact on the resulting sounds. The setup was inspired by works such as Tudor's *Rainforest IV* (1973) and Lucier's *Music on a Long Thin Wire* (1977).

Parameters such as input gain, filter frequencies, modulation depths, decays and reverberation were controlled by the artist during performance. Overall, the implemented systems reacted in a stable manner and were intuitive to play. Sonically, it created organic, FM-like sounds that were highly dependent on the sound colour of the input source: If noisy (e.g. in the case of the cushions), the resulting sounds were noisy, too; the filter network mostly altered the noise colour and added short tonal elements. If the input has a less noisy character the FM becomes much more prominent, adding distinctive sidebands to the output.

[3] http://tai-studio.org/index.php/projects/deind/

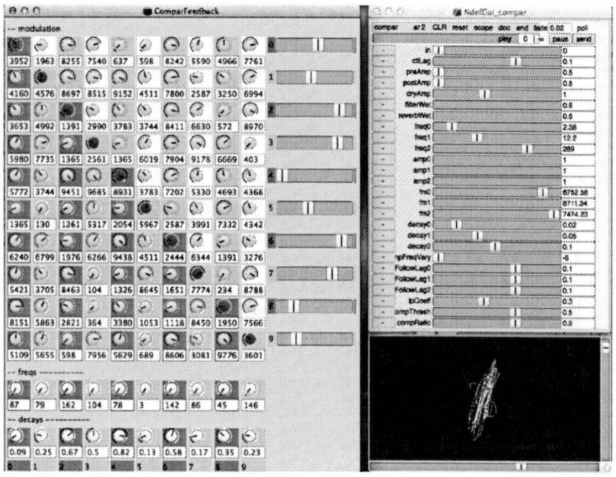

Figure 5. ComparFeedback (left) and Compar GUI (right)

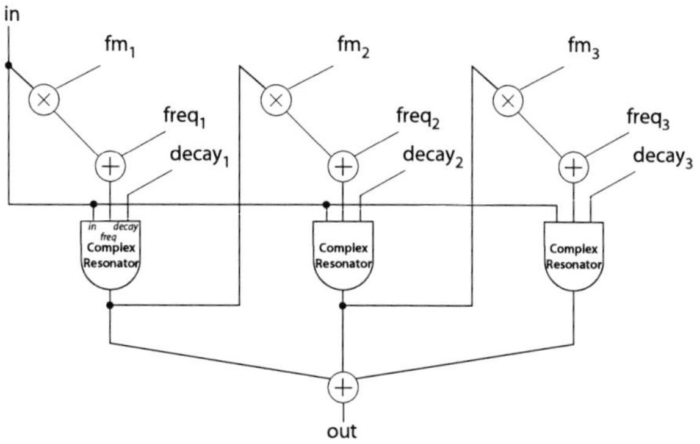

Figure 6. FM network in the Compar synthesis engine.

5. CONCLUSIONS

In this work the complex resonator filter has been examined, and results derived which are useful when applying it in a time-varying context. These results are an approximate normalisation of the filter to unity peak gain, and a derivation of the stability condition for the filter under parameter modulation. A new structure for dynamic FM synthesis was proposed, based on an arbitrary number of these filters configured to frequency modulate each other, and a formal description of this system given. The system is able to produce sounds within a very wide timbral space, and possesses a unique organic quality due to the natural exponential decay of the resonators and the use of audio input as excitation. The resonators were implemented as a SuperCollider UGen, and networks constructed from them within this environment. The resulting tools were applied within a performance system where the resonator network is excited by both the environmental sound of the space of the performance, and the signals generated by a cushion made of conductive thread.

Acknowledgments

This research was part of the DEIND project on designing electronic instruments for neurodiverse people, funded by the Aalto Media Factory of Aalto University, Helsinki.

6. REFERENCES

[1] J. M. Chowning, "The synthesis of complex audio spectra by means of frequency modulation," *J. Audio Eng. Soc.*, vol. 21, no. 7, pp. 526–534, 1973.

[2] M. Le Brun, "A derivation of the spectrum of fm with a complex modulating wave," *Computer Music J.*, vol. 1, no. 4, pp. 51–52, 1977.

[3] J. O. Smith and J. B. Angell, "A constant-gain digital resonator tuned by a single coefficient," *Computer Music J.*, vol. 6, no. 4, pp. 36–40, 1982.

[4] K. Steiglitz, "A note on constant-gain digital resonators," *Computer Music J.*, vol. 18, no. 4, pp. 8–10, 1994.

[5] J. Dattorro, "Effect design, part 1: Reverberator and other filters," *J. Audio Eng. Soc.*, vol. 45, no. 9, pp. 660–684, 1997.

[6] S. C. Scoular, I. B. Rogozkin, and M. S. Cherniakov, "Review of soviet research on linear time-variant discrete systems," *Signal Processing*, vol. 30, no. 1, pp. 85–101, 1993.

[7] M. Cherniakov, V. Sizov, and L. Donskoi, "Synthesis of a periodically time-varying digital filter," *IEE Proc. Vision, Image and Sig. Processing*, vol. 147, no. 5, pp. 393–399, 2000.

[8] M. Cherniakov, *An introduction to parametric digital filters and oscillators.* Wiley, 2003.

[9] J. Kleimola, V. Lazzarini, V. Välimäki, and J. Timoney, "Feedback amplitude modulation synthesis," *EURASIP J. Advances Sig. Processing*, vol. 2011, Dec. 2011.

[10] V. Lazzarini, J. Kleimola, and V. Välimäki, "Aspects of second-order feedback AM synthesis," in *Proc. of the Int. Computer Music Conf. (ICMC)*, Huddersfield, 2011.

[11] M. Mathews and J. O. Smith, "Methods for synthesizing very high Q parametrically well behaved two pole filters," in *Proceedings of the Stockholm Musical Acoustics Conference (SMAC 2003)*, Royal Swedish Academy of Music, August 2003.

[12] D. Massie, "Coefficient interpolation for the Max Mathews phasor filter," in *133rd Convention of the Audio Eng. Soc.*, 2012.

[13] J. Laroche, "On the stability of time-varying recursive filters," *J. Audio Eng. Soc.*, vol. 55, no. 6, pp. 460–471, 2007.

[14] J. McCartney, "Rethinking the computer music language: SuperCollider," *Computer Music J.*, vol. 26, no. 4, pp. 61–68, 2002.

[15] A. Di Scipio, "Listening to yourself through the otherself: On background noise study and other works," *Organised Sound*, vol. 16, no. 02, pp. 97–108, 2011.

Reconfigurable Autonomous Novel Guitar Effects (RANGE)

Duncan MacConnell
Computer Science
University of Victoria
Victoria, BC
duncanmacconnell@gmail.com

Shawn Trail
Computer Science
University of Victoria
Victoria, BC
trl77@uvic.ca

George Tzanetakis
Computer Science
University of Victoria
Victoria, BC
gtzan@cs.uvic.ca

Peter Driessen
Electrical Engineering
University of Victoria
Victoria, BC
peter@ece.uvic.ca

Wyatt Page
Electrical Engineering
Massey University
Wellington, NZ
w.h.page@massey.ac.nz

ABSTRACT

The RANGE guitar is a minimally-invasive hyperinstrument incorporating electronic sensors and integrated digital signal processing (DSP). It introduces an open framework for autonomous music computing eschewing the use of the laptop on stage. The framework uses an embedded Linux microcomputer to provide sensor acquisition, analog-to-digital conversion (ADC) for audio input, DSP, and digital-to-analog conversion (DAC) for audio output. The DSP environment is built in *Puredata (Pd)*. We chose *Pd* because it is free, widely supported, flexible, and robust. The sensors we selected can be mounted in a variety of ways without compromising traditional playing technique. Integration with a conventional guitar leverages established techniques and preserves the natural gestures of each player's idiosyncratic performing style. The result is an easy to replicate, reconfigurable, idiomatic sensing and signal processing system for the electric guitar requiring little modification of the original instrument

1. INTRODUCTION

Electric guitar players have utilized audio effects since their inception. An extensive variety of DSP guitar effects are offered commercially, some of which even provide a code environment for user modification of DSP algorithms [1]; however, in most cases the functionality of these devices is specific and their programmability is limited. These commercial audio effects are typically implemented either as foot pedals or as separate hardware devices. An alternative is the use of a laptop and audio interface to replace the dedicated guitar effects. This approach is generic in the sense that any audio effect can be implemented as long as the computer is fast enough to calculate it in real-time. Using a laptop is also completely open, flexible, and programmable. However such a setup requires more cables, more power, and is cumbersome to transport and awkward on stage [1]. In both of these cases (dedicated hardware or laptop) the control of the effects is separated from the actual guitar playing as shown in Figure 1.

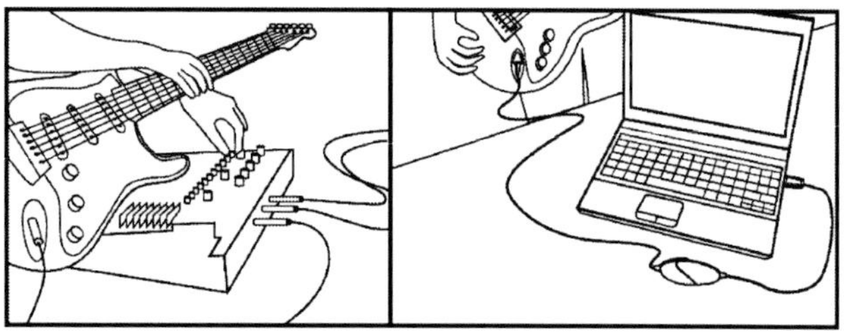

Figure 1. Typical guitar effect Interaction - note the separation of guitar playing vs. effect manipulation

2. RELATED WORK

Historic examples include the *Guitarorgans*, the analog synth controller *Stepp DGX MIDI guitar* [2], and the *Roland G 303*. Systems for mobile devices acting as the DSP host have also become common [3].

Augmented guitars have also been explored. MIT's *Chameleon Guitar* has multiple soundboards, each equipped with piezo sensors and DSP filtering to simulate the guitar tones offered from different wood [2]. Another example, the *Moog Guitar*, is an electric guitar with onboard sliders that control augmentation of the guitar's traditional sound by sending electro-magnetic energy into strings. This allows for infinite note sustain, while similarly pulling energy from the strings creates short staccato sounds. Edgar Berdahl introduced a similar idea in his *Feedback Guitar* [3].

The *DUL Radio* [4] from the Center for Digital Urban Living at Aarhus University, Denmark is a wireless accelerometer sensor package designed for artist's to use with

[1] http://line6.com/tcddk/

[2] http://www.stepptechnologies.co.uk/

[3] http://www.incidentgtar.com/, http://www.misadigital.com/

Puredata (Pd) [5] or *MAX/Msp* [4]. The group demonstrates the device by attaching an accelerometer to the headstock of the guitar for 3D gesture tracking. This makes for an easily removable, modular solution for 3D gesture tracking. Unfortunately we were not able to integrate it with the RANGES system at this time because of our LINUX requirement which isn't supported by the DUL drivers at this time.

3. MOTIVATION

In designing an augmented guitar instrument, consideration must be taken to ensure the extensions do not inhibit traditional guitar technique. Effort should be made to create intuitive control interfaces that take advantage of the guitar player's natural performance technique. Traditional audio effect units and commercial DSP solutions tend to disregard this, forcing the musician to interact with musical parameters by way of non-musical gestures: turning a knob or adjusting a fader [6]. This conflicts with the guitarist's normal gestural interaction, fails to convey any meaningful event information, and can even act as a distraction for the audience [7].

There has always been a union of guitar and effect despite a separation of guitar playing and effect control. To address this issue, we have integrated minimally invasive sensors on the body of the guitar to allow natural and intuitive DSP control. The RANGE system was designed for use in performance contexts to allow guitar players more expressivity in controlling DSP effects than conventional pedal controllers provide.

The proximity of the sensors to the guitarist's natural hand position is important, as it allows the guitarist to combine DSP control with traditional guitar playing technique. Like the *Moog Guitar*, the sensors sit flat on the guitar body, eliminating any interference with a guitarist's performance technique. Further, we have reduced the hardware dependencies, cabling, and power requirements to a minimal footprint. Design goals were motivated by the desire to shift away from the cumbersome and distracting laptop on stage in exchange for a smaller, open architecture. This framework is designed to take advantage of low-cost electronic components and free open-source software, facilitating reconfiguration and adaptation to the specific needs of different instruments and musicians.

4. SYSTEM DESCRIPTION

The RANGE system is based on a framework for developing robust hyperinstrument prototypes, which provides audio input, output, and sensor acquisition. The framework itself provides a completely open platform for designing and testing hyperinstruments. The hardware and software components that comprise this system are modular in nature and the configuration is designed so that any user can adapt this work for their own use. For this implementation, the sensor interface consists of three membrane potentiometer strips mounted on the body of the guitar which feed into the analog inputs of the embedded Linux computer. We have selected the *Beaglebone* [5] for it's flexibility and low cost. The guitar's audio signal goes directly into the *Beaglebone* for analysis and processing using an *Audio Cape* for ADC/DAC. Pitch tracking is performed on the incoming audio signal using Fiddle [8] and used to generate control data. The control data and DSP is managed in *Pd*. The potentiometer outputs are mapped to continuous controller values that modify the parameters of effect parameters, oscillators, and filters. These potentiometers offer the guitarist a broad range of interface solutions and sound design possibilities in a small embedded format that has previously been only possible with a laptop. The system has relatively low cost (all prices in US dollars): *Beaglebone* (89), audio cape (58), and membrane sensors ($3 \times 13 = 39$) for a total of 186 USD.

Figure 2 shows a schematic diagram of the system.

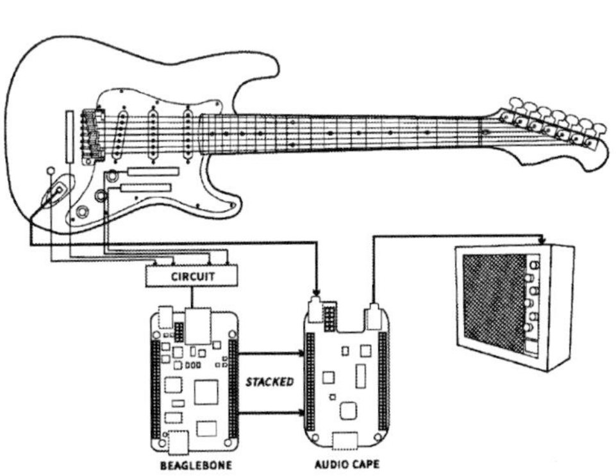

Figure 2. Schematic of RANGE

4.1 Analog Sensor Input

Membrane potentiometers are a common sensor for capturing musical data, and are often incorporated into hyperinstrument design. Adrian Freed [9] provides a detailed look at force sensing resistors, membrane potentiometers, and other sensors. His "Many and DuoTouch Augmented Guitar Prototype" [6] provides simple and elegant circuit solutions to achieve desired sensor behaviour for musical applications. The RANGE guitar is equipped with three $50mm$ *SoftPot* membrane potentiometers. These sensors are arranged on the body of the guitar, near the volume and tone controls. This arrangement allows the guitarist to easily access the sensors, and the orientation affords comfortable interaction. The sensors are limited to the body of the guitar corresponding to the expressive hand of the guitar player. The expressive hand, responsible for the rhythm and dynamics of the guitar, is most suited for acute sensor control. In addition to the three touch sensors, toggle switches are also mounted to the guitar to provide a simple method for switching software state.

Traditional potentiometers use the position of a sliding wiper to determine resistance. Membrane potentiometers function similarly, providing a variable resistance level based on the position of the user's finger. The main difference is

[4] `http://cycling74.com/`

[5] `http://elinux.org/BeagleBone`

[6] `http://cnmat.berkeley.edu/user/adrian_freed/blog/2009/05/09/AugmentedGuitar`

that membrane potentiometers only allow current to flow when the membrane is pressed, and so the value is lost when the user's finger is removed. The RANGE's sensor input behaviour must be consistent and stable in order to be used musically. Specifically, the instrument design requires that the analog input values remain when the membrane is not pressed.

In order to secure a stable and usable signal from the membrane potentiometers, pull-up resistors are used. This forces the potentiometer to open circuit when the finger is removed. A simple software solution is used within *Pd* for detecting when the membrane is forced open, and the previous buffered value is retained. Figure 3 shows the corresponding circuit.

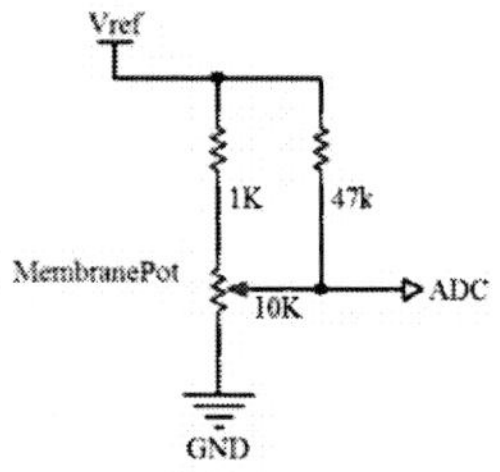

Figure 3. Membrane Potentiometer Circuit

4.2 Hardware, Software, and Latency

The RANGE uses a *Beaglebone* microcomputer, which provides on-board GPIO and ADC pin access, as well as UART, I2C and SPI. It features an ARM 600 MHz Cortex-A8 core using the ARMv7-Architecture, as well as full USB and Ethernet support. The *Beaglebone* is becoming widely supported in the embedded computing community [10], and many expansion "Capes" are being developed to provide an array of hardware interaction opportunities. The *Beaglebone Audio Cape* provides audio input and output by way of two 3.5 mm connectors, and supports sampling rates up to 96 kHz for capture and playback by way of the cape's TLV320AIC3106 codec. The system described provides a complete DSP platform, allowing users to connect to the *Beaglebone* via ethernet for rapid interface prototyping.

The *Beaglebone* hardware ships with the *Linux Angstrom Cloud9* operating system, however many users have experienced unsatisfactory audio output quality. For this framework, *Ubuntu 12.04* was used, which facilitates *Pd* installation and interfaces well with the audio codec provided by the *Beaglebone Audio Cape*. To provide access to the *Beaglebones* GPIO and ADC pins, a *Pd* external has been developed. The ADC provides 12-bit values, which are accessed by the external by directly reading the corresponding files in the userspace. The external is designed to report analog and digital pin values each time the object receives a "bang" message. In this way, pin values can be obtained at any rate, and can be coupled with other musically timed events within the patch. The control data is not altered in any way by the external that retrieves it, as it is meant to make any sensor's data available within *Pd*.

Control of digital audio effects has been a desired function of the RANGE from its inception. The stable sensor values allow for reliable control, while placing the sensors directly on the body allows the guitarist faster and more intuitive interaction. Analog values obtained by the *Pd* external can be scaled and mapped to any control. Therefore specific effect parameters (delay length, feedback level, filter frequency, etc.) are adjusted by the touch potentiometers. This simple prototyping system is robust but offers a lot of flexibility and potential. The potentiometers can also provide an intuitive control interface for synthesis applications. Some novel applications include controlling oscillator frequency, filter frequency/bandwidth, MIDI note attribute, and envelope values (attack, decay, sustain, release). This application allows the RANGE to be used as a versatile synthesizer controller while the guitar can still be played as usual. Figure 4 shows an example mapping, with sensor input controlling a typical electric guitar effect chain on the left and common DSP applications on the right.

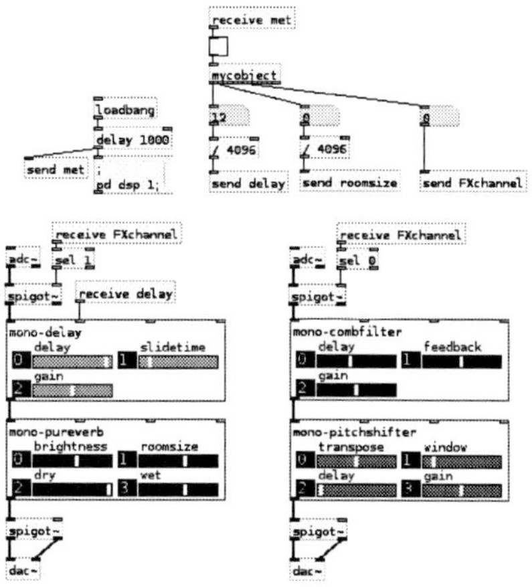

Figure 4. Common Guitar Effect Setup Built in Pd

In contrast to pure controller approaches that utilize a laptop for DSP, our goal is to use the *Beaglebone* for both control and DSP. Many modern guitar effects are actually internally implemented using a dedicated embedded DSP chip even though to a guitar player they appear similar to traditional analog pedals. RANGE makes this DSP functionality accessible providing a wide range of possibilities for both digital audio effects and their control. In order to be a viable platform for this purpose it is critical that the overall system latency is appropriate for music applications. The framework provides simple sensor and audio throughput, using *Pd* with the ALSA API.

For latency tests, it is important to perform measurements under different system (CPU/DSP) load applications [11]. For our system, all tests were performed in the "normal state" (audio throughput, no effects processing) as well as the "use state" (audio throughput, effects processing). In the normal state, audio latency for the system corresponds to the audio delay set by *Puredata*. With *Puredata* set to 10 ms audio delay, we measure a total system delay of 10 ms. With effects engaged, the use state latency is measured at

12 ms. This difference can be attributed to the system load increase from the signal processing. For pitch analysis, normal and use state behaved the same, measuring a total pitch analysis latency of 15 ms. All results reflect usable latency levels, for audio applications, as they approach the general latency goal of 10 ms [11, 12]. Figure 5 shows the audio and pitch-tracking latency.

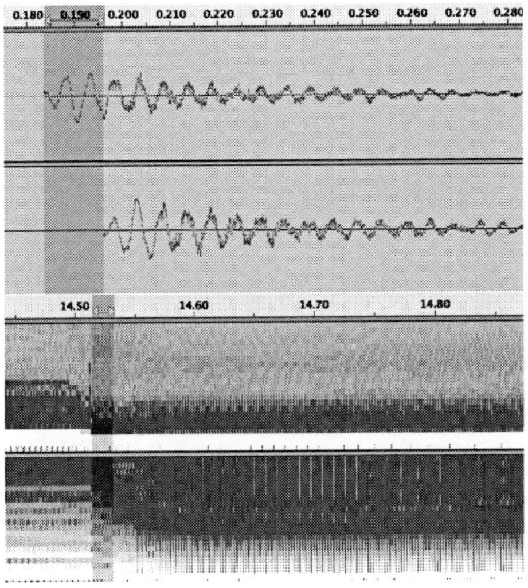

Figure 5. Audio Latency Measurements

5. CONCLUSIONS AND FUTURE WORK

RANGE successfully presents a reconfigurable, autonomous, and novel DSP and sensing framework for the guitar. The RANGE system has been used in concert several times, and has proved to be a novel, satisfying method of DSP interaction for the author who is a touring guitar player and computer musician. We plan to conduct a user study contrasting the proposed approach with a traditional electric guitar effect setup. We also plan to investigate polyphonic transcription using a surrogate sensing approach [13]. Lastly we intend to extend the platform to support magnets for robotic guitar string actuation building on the previous work by Berdahl [3], McPherson [14], on electromagnetic actuation of stringed instruments. Media related to the RANGE system can be viewed here [7].

6. ACKNOWLEDGMENTS

We'd like to especially thank: Calum MacConnell for the graphics; Stephen Harrison, Leo Jenkins and Gorkem Cipli for their technical support in the lab; Pat Metheny, Mike Gamble, Kevin Patton, Edgar Bergdahl, and Dan Overholt for their inspiration and support regarding extended guitar and string based hyperinstruments.. NSERC and SSHRC provided funding.

[7] `http://misticlabs.tumblr.com/RANGEguitar`

7. REFERENCES

[1] D. Wessel and M. Wright, "Problems and prospects for intimate musical control of computers," *Computer Music Journal*, vol. 26, no. 3, pp. 11–22, 2002.

[2] A. Zorana and J. A. Paradiso, "The chameleon guitar—guitar with a replaceable resonator," *Journal of New Music Research*, vol. 40, no. 1, pp. 59–74, 2011.

[3] E. Berdahl, G. Niemeyer, and J. O. S. III, "Active control of a vibrating string," in *Acoustical Society of America (ASA) and European Acoustics Association (EAA)*, 2008.

[4] M. Brynskov, R. Lunding, and L. S. Vestergaard, "Dul radio: A light-weight, wireless toolkit for sketching in hardware," in *Tangible and Embedded Interaction Work-in-Progress Workshop Proceedings*, 2011, pp. 67–72.

[5] M. S. Puckette, "Pure data: another integrated computer music environment," in *Proceedings Second Intercollege Computer Music Concerts*, 1996, pp. 37–41.

[6] S. Gelineck, "A quantitative evaluation of the differences between knobs and sliders," in *Proc. Int. Conf. New Interfaces for Musical Expression (NIME)*, 2009.

[7] J. Murphy, "The helio: A study of membrane potentiometers and long force sensing resistors for musical interfaces," in *Proc. Int. Conf. on New Interfaces for Musical Expression (NIME)*, 2010.

[8] M. Puckette, "Real-time audio analysis tools for pd and msp," in *Proc. Int. Computer Music Conf. (ICMC)*, 1998.

[9] A. Freed, "Novel and forgotten current-steering techniques for resistive multitouch, duotouch, and polytouch position sensing with pressure," in *Proc. Int. Conf. New Interfaces for Musical Expression (NIME)*, 2009.

[10] S. Barrett and J. Kridner, *Bad to the Bone Crafting Electronic Systems with BeagleBone*. Morgan and Claypool, 2013.

[11] M. Wright, R. J. Cassidy, and M. F. Zbyszynski, "Audio and gesture latency measurements on linux and osx," in *Proc. Int. Computer Music Conf. (ICMC)*, 2004, pp. 423–429.

[12] P. F. Driessen, T. E. Darcie, and B. Pillay, "The effects of network delay on tempo in musical performance," *Computer Music Journal*, vol. 35, no. 1, pp. 76–89, 2011.

[13] S. Trail, "Direct and surrogate sensing for the gyil african xylophone," in *Proc. Int. Conf. New Interfaces for Musical Expression (NIME)*, 2012.

[14] A. McPherson, "Techniques and circuits for electromagnetic instrument actuation," in *Proc. Int. Conf. New Interfaces for Musical Expression (NIME)*, 2012.

Music information retrieval

PHENICX: Performances as Highly Enriched aNd Interactive Concert Experiences

Emilia Gómez, Maarten Grachten, Alan Hanjalic, Jordi Janer, Sergi Jordà, Carles F. Julià, Cynthia Liem, Agustin Martorell, Markus Schedl, Gerhard Widmer (Authors in alphabetical order)
PHENICX consortium
phenicx@upf.edu

ABSTRACT

Modern digital multimedia and internet technology have radically changed the ways people find entertainment and discover new interests online, seemingly without any physical or social barriers. Such new access paradigms are in sharp contrast with the traditional means of entertainment. An illustrative example of this is live music concert performances that are largely being attended by dedicated audiences only.

This papers introduces the PHENICX project, which aims at enriching traditional concert experiences by using state-of-the-art multimedia and internet technologies. The project focuses on classical music and its main goal is twofold: (a) to make live concerts appealing to potential new audience and (b) to maximize the quality of concert experience for everyone. Concerts will then become multimodal, multi-perspective and multilayer digital artifacts that can be easily explored, customized, personalized, (re)enjoyed and shared among the users. The paper presents the main scientific objectives on the project, provides a state of the art review on related research and presents the main challenges to be addressed.

1. INTRODUCTION

In the current digital age, access to recorded music is readily available. This makes it very easy to serendipitously get confronted with unknown music genres on (social) streaming services. However, barriers can be experienced to really go out and experience a live performance of such an unknown music genre: the walls of an unknown concert venue put up a physical barrier, and at the local etiquette of the social community that identifies most strongly with the performed music puts up a social barrier. If people who would be interested in exploring live performances of unfamiliar music will be faced with an isolated, imposed and standardised concert situation they do not naturally identify with, they thus will remain 'outsiders' to the music and its entourage.

Present-day technologies can change the way we access and enjoy musical concerts today. A wealth of musical information is available on the web, ranging from artist information to scores and lead sheets or other related information about musical pieces. Employing automated analysis techniques, it is possible to find a way through all this supporting information, tailored to our backgrounds and interests. Linking this to live concert performance data, an enriched and deepened experience of the performed music can be created in a personalised way. This can trigger our curiosity to see more of such performances, and share the experience over social media to our friends who then can pick up interest in this as well.

Following these considerations, the PHENICX project was conceived. It focuses on researching how to improve the accessibility of live music concert performances by addressing two main objectives:

Transforming live music concert performances into enriched multimodal, multi-perspective and multilayer digital artefacts

With *multimodal*, we mean different musical modalities, such as audio, video, and symbolic scores. With *multi-perspective*, we mean that a concert performance can be considered from different viewpoints: physical viewpoints in a concert hall and different user perspectives dependent on their backgrounds and intents. With *multilayer*, we mean that multiple music concert performance descriptors can be relevant at the same time, working at differing levels of specificity (e.g. requiring general or sophisticated musical knowledge) and considering different time scale resolutions. Automated and multimodal music description techniques are relevant to this objective, such that they will yield meaningful descriptors from the considered musical pieces. In our approach, performance information is characterised along two dimensions: that of the *musical piece* (*objective* descriptors, valid for any rendition of the piece), as well as *its actual performance* (descriptors on individual expressive and interpretative aspects that make one performance different from another).

Presenting digital music artefacts as engaging digital experiences that can be explored, (re)enjoyed and shared in many customisable and personalised ways

For this, we need advanced user profiling and community characterisation techniques, which will pave the way for sophisticated personalisation techniques. Next to that, techniques for dedicated and adaptive information selection and

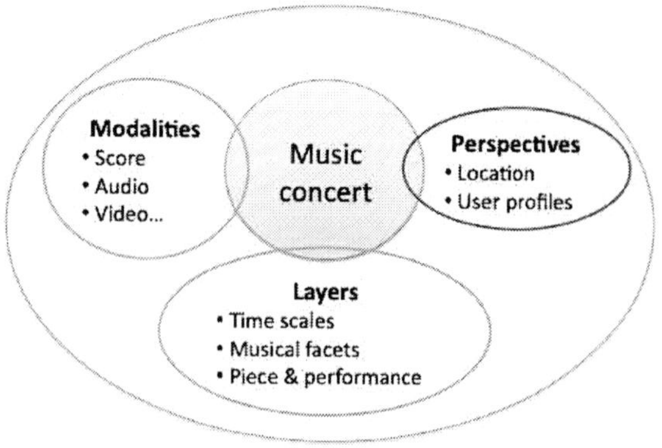

Figure 1. PHENICX view of a musical concert.

presentation has to be investigated, as well as interactive opportunities for audiences to engage even more with the performance.

By working towards these objectives as outlined above, we can transform the current audience experience of concert performances, break the physical and social barriers and decrease the perceived distance between musical performers and their concert audiences.

This transformation entirely takes place in the digital domain. Performing musicians themselves will therefore not have to change their way of performing, maintaining their original performance traditions.

2. PRACTICAL SETTING

The PHENICX project will mainly focus on Western classical music in large ensemble settings. Classical music is a very strong example of European cultural heritage, which suffers from very strong audience stereotypes, and the general image of being a complex and possibly boring genre. As such, it does not straightforwardly attract new audiences, and its live performance tradition may be endangered as outlined in our Motivation. As will be outlined in the remainder of this paper, Western classical music also poses several interesting research challenges that are not encountered for other musical genres, and thus can help in pushing scientific advances in music and multimedia information retrieval forward. The project will be structured in four different research and development areas.

Multimodal musical piece analysis: the project will research on suitable analysis techniques for automatic description and enrichment of the considered musical pieces.

Multimodal musical performance analysis: the project will also address performance aspects by extracting expression-related features from audio signals and other modalities (e.g. score, video), synchronizing performances with their score and with alternative performances of the same piece, and characterizing performer's or conductor's gestures.

Profiling and personalization, in order to adapt concert experiences to different user profiles.

Exploration and interaction, as a way to enhance the concert experience through music visualization, personalised musical information and interactive systems for conductor/performer impersonation.

In the following sections, we discuss relevant scientific state-of-the-art in these areas and corresponding challenges as foreseen for PHENICX. A discussion on how these challenges can be validated in real world end-user settings will be available in [1].

3. MULTIMODAL MUSICAL PIECE ANALYSIS

The main goal of the research related to musical piece analysis in the project is to provide the audience with meaningful information about the music material played in the concert, including musical descriptors (e.g. theme, melodic line, key, structure), semantic labels (e.g. mood), similar pieces, or links to existing online information about performers, composers or instruments. Moreover, the project will research on audio processing technologies to separate the different sections of the orchestra from mixed recordings in order to allow multi-perspective listening experiences.

3.1 Content-based feature extraction and similarity

Current techniques are capable of automatically obtaining features from music recordings related to different musical facets such as melody, harmony, rhythm and instrumentation. These descriptors are exploited by music retrieval and recommendation systems to compute similarity distances and to classify musical pieces according to e.g. artist, genre or mood [2].

However, there is a glass ceiling in current feature extractors. The accuracy of state-of-the-art methods for audio feature extraction does not go beyond 80% (results slightly vary for different tasks, e.g. onset detection, genre classification, chord detection, predominant melody extraction), even though they are not always evaluated on realistic situations (limited, e.g. to simple music material). In addition, there is a semantic gap between existing descriptors and expert musicological analyses. For instance, similarity algorithms have been traditionally based on low-level timbre descriptors, beat tracking is not accurate for expressive music with varying tempo, and melodic/harmonic descriptors are often limited to global key, which has shown to be poor to represent the tonal content of a musical piece. In the foreseen project, we will research on the best strategies for our particular repertoire, classical music in large ensemble settings. We will address the limitations of state-of-the-art methods for predominant melody estimation [3], rhythm description [4] and tonal analysis [5] to deal with our particular music material.

In the project, we should finally investigate to what extent differing application contexts may have different notions of similarity, both from a systems and user perspective, and we will consider hybrid approaches (integrating different descriptors and temporal resolutions) as proposed in [6]. For example, a scholar studying a particular piece may wish to gather many recordings of the piece and will consider these recordings to be dissimilar in comparison to each other, while to a novice unfamiliar with the piece, all these recordings will sound very similar to each other, and any differences between them are not as relevant. While this has not frequently been addressed in literature yet, it is an important topic to investigate since it will influence the ultimate success of a music information system.

3.2 Music auto-tagging

The process of automatically assigning semantically meaningful labels to representations of music is known as auto-tagging. So far, auto-tagging has mostly been performed on the level of artists (e.g. [7, 8]) or songs (e.g. [9, 10]); only few works [11, 12] have addressed tagging of segments within a song.

To the PHENICX project, it is useful to automatically obtain descriptions for recorded performances. However, this necessitates research beyond the current state-of-the-art. Current methods strongly focused on pop music. In classical music, a 'song' will typically be much longer than in pop music, which means that novel techniques are required to obtain segment-level descriptors. Furthermore, the multimodal and social setting of the project allows for additional data sources such as social tags, which can be gathered from collaborative tagging systems, textual features extracted from web pages or microblogs, or even simple visual features mined from images (e.g., album covers or photographs). However, once again, if these additional data sources were considered in previous work (which is uncommon, since the predominant focus has been on audio information only), this was in the pop music domain, and it has to be investigated to what extent they will be equally informative for classical music.

3.3 Linking web sources of music

In PHENICX, we will extract information about performers and instruments, aim for a multimodal approach which enriches the presentation with videos, images and other supporting material, including possible alternative performances of the same piece. This means that different sources of music information need to be linked together.

Classical music is more complex than pop music: in many cases, we are not just dealing with songs performed by artists, but with a piece consisting of multiple movements, written by a composer, and interpreted by varying groups of performing artists. In terms of Semantic Web technology facilities, the Music Ontology [13] is a rare example of an ontology which has been expanded to deal with classical music, and as such will be of active interest for PHENICX. However, in the imperfect real world, (metadata) information on classical music may not always be cleanly and consistently labeled, according to this ontology. We will hence elaborate techniques to cope with this imperfect data.

As an example of a multimodal music information system involving web-scale information, [14] should be mentioned, presenting a system offering information about similarities between music artists or bands, prototypicality of an artist or band for a genre, descriptive properties of an artist or band, band members and instrumentation, and images of album cover artwork. Once again, this system targets popular music, and it should be verified to what extent the approach will translate to the classical domain.

3.4 Multi-perspective audio description: source localisation and separation

One characteristic of orchestral music concerts compared to other amplified musical live performances is how sound is propagated from the performers to the audience. Sound sources are spread over a large stage area creating an acoustic image in front of the audience, which is affected then by the acoustics of the concert hall. A recording setup might consist principally of a stereo pair microphones placed near the conductor.

In a typical setup, however, this stereo track can be complemented with a number of ze—nithal microphones covering specific instrumental sections. These zenithal tracks are used to find the right balance in the final mastering mix.

One of the objectives of the project consists in obtaining the localisation of the active instruments on stage from a set of recorded tracks. This process shall include means of providing a source signal separation. In our scenario, we might take advantage of additional data such as the score or source positioning informations (e.g. instrument sections).

State of the art methods of source localisation include beamforming techniques, which take input signals from sensor arrays. Other specific techniques address the case of stereo signals [15]. Regarding source separation, state of the art techniques involve Non-negative Matrix Factorisation (NMF) and PLCA [16], but more recent techniques are also based on signal-models that exploit musical knowledge [17]. Score-informed techniques such as [18] are specially relevant in the context of the project.

4. MULTIMODAL MUSICAL PERFORMANCE ANALYSIS

The central purpose of research related to musical performance analysis in the PHENICX project is to give the audience or music consumer deeper insights into the subtle art of expressive performance, which is so central to classical music. This requires methods for computing expressive aspects (e.g., tempo and timing) from recorded or live performance – which in turn requires methods for aligning performances to scores, or to each other –, models for explaining, predicting, and visualising expressive aspects, and methods for recognising and characterising expressive actions by the musicians that are not readily apparent from the audio signal (for instance, gestures by the conductor). The latter will also be used to devise ways of directly interacting with performances via gestures.

4.1 Score-performance alignment, performance-to-performance matching, and real-time score following

Computing a one-to-one alignment between a performance and another representation of the same piece is important for several purposes in the project. We distinguish three cases: (1) aligning a recorded performance (audio recording) to the musical score ("score-performance alignment"), (2) aligning two or more performances (audio recordings) to each other ("performance-to- performance matching"), and (3) aligning an ongoing performance (coming in as an audio stream) to the score in real time ("performance tracking" or "real-time score following").

In the case of *score-performance alignment*, the score is usually either rendered to audio, or acoustic features are computed directly from the score. Most alignment algorithms then use some kind of Dynamic Time Warping (DTW) to find an optimal global alignment [19–21], or model the musical processes via statistical graphical models [22, 23]. PHENICX will focus on the DTW approach, starting from and improving the methods proposed in [21], which rely on the percussiveness of the considered instruments sounds. Although recent efforts towards timbre-invariant audio features are promising [24], generalising the above methods to the wide variety of orchestral instruments will require the design of new audio features, as well as fundamental modifications to the general top-down alignment strategy. A second class of challenges concerns the possibility of structural differences between score and performance, or between performances [25, 26]. We believe these problems can more easily solved in DTW-based methods.

With respect to *real-time score following*, there are also two competing approaches, again based on either (online) DTW (OLDTW) or graphical models and probabilistic inference (e.g., [27,28]. Recent research on DTW-based performance tracking [25] looks extremely promising – not only with respect to computational efficiency and low latency, but also w.r.t. robustness against playing errors, omissions and insertions.

The biggest challenge in real-time tracking of classical music is to design more effective predictive tempo models, for the system to be able to anticipate abrupt changes in local tempo, or the return of the soloist or orchestra after a long rest. Here, the above predictive performance models will play an important role.

4.2 Explanatory and predictive computational models of expressive performance

Despite considerable research over several decades, our knowledge of the factors that shape musical expression is still far from complete. Valuable explanatory models do exist, but they tend to focus on highly specific aspects of performance, such as the form of a final ritard [29] and the effect of phrase structure on tempo [30]. With advances in both sensor technology and automatic transcription of musical audio, much more substantial empirical data is now becoming available [31], and these now allow for a paradigm-shift from the classical music-theory driven approach to a data mining approach, inspiring new computational models of expressive performance.

In this context, Grachten and Widmer [32] recently proposed a framework for modeling expressive performance. It allows to estimate the contribution of arbitrary features of the musical score (including, but not limited to expressive markings annotated in the score) in shaping expressive characteristics of the performance, such as tempo, loudness, and articulation. Musical features are represented as basis functions, which are linearly combined over one or more performances, to approximate their expressive characteristics. This framework can be used for explanatory modeling, and thereby provide the users with precise characterisations and explanations (e.g. in what ways do different ensembles perform the same piece differently?). Moreover, as a computational model, the framework also allows for predictive modeling. Accurate hypotheses about the shape of musical expression in a performance can improve score-performance alignment and real-time score following [25].

4.3 Gesture recognition

The purpose of gesture recognition in the project is to provide additional insight into how expressive performances are realized, and to facilitate interactive music-making scenarios. In the literature on the recognition of body gestures, we can distinguish two main approaches: Machine learning (usually supervised – e.g., [33]) and analytical techniques. The analytical description of gestures in order to recognise them is the most used technique right now in commercial applications and devices that require gesture recognition. Other frameworks allow describing the gestures rather than program them directly, as in [34] that allows this description in a form of regular expressions.

In PHENICX we will consider an analytical approach to recognise the principal components of specific symbolic gestures for different instruments using a composition technique and an agent-based framework [35], as well as general features of the whole body movement, and try to recognise concurrent performances of these gestures at the same time for multi-user interaction. More precisely, in the field of studying body movement of music performers we can find several approaches, like recording precise movement of a violin bow to synthesise its sound [36] or (more related to our approach) studies about "Air playing" [37]. Our research will try to link body movements and gestures to high level properties of music, such as loudness, tonality, tempo and note density.

5. PROFILING AND PERSONALISATION

PHENICX strives to offer personalised music experiences. This means that adequate user and recommendation models need to be set up.

An important direction to consider here is that of profiling and personalisation through social media mining, in which we build forth on techniques proposed in existing work including [38–41]. Of these references, only [41] explicitly deals with music recommendation, showing that users prefer social recommendations (taking into account friends) over non-social ones, and that social recommendations are particularly well-suited to discover relevant and novel music. However, the proposed user model is relatively coarse. Furthermore, in general it is important to realize that apart from general taste, a person's preference for a certain item will also be influenced by ad hoc context and search intent.

In existing music-related work, the concept of 'context' has been defined and addressed in varying ways. In [42], a study is presented investigating if and how various context factors relate to music taste (e.g., human movement, emotional status, and external factors such as temperature and lighting conditions). Other work involving context e.g. includes temporal context [43], listening history and weather conditions [44], walking pace or heartbeat rate [45,46], geographical location [47], and driving circumstances [48]. As for the latter work, while eight different contextual driving factors are considered, the application scenario is quite restricted and the system relies on explicit human feedback. In PHENICX, upon establishing relevant context factors to the practical application scenarios of interest, we will rather aim to rely on implicit user feedback to adhere to the requirement of unintrusiveness, which is a prerequisite for wide user acceptance.

The concept of 'intent' deals with the 'why' behind an action. In terms of information search, moving beyond textual search, search intent is now increasingly being studied for the image and video domains, e.g. [49, 50]. In PHENICX, we strive to make another step forward in this field, by explicitly studying and considering search intent and particular information needs in the music domain as well.

Finally, there are two recommendation aspects which have not been studied extensively yet, but are well-known and deserve closer examination within our project. First of all, especially if different performances of the same piece are considered to be different entities in a recommender system (e.g. because the metadata does not fully match), 'long tail' issues [51] will occur, in which many musical items will have relatively low consumption counts. Furthermore, we wish to advance towards serendipitous findings, building forth on a model for serendipitous music retrieval and recommendation proposed by Schedl et al. [52], and establishing proper evaluation methodologies for this [53].

6. EXPLORATION AND INTERACTION

In the area of exploration and interaction, the project will research on two different areas. The first one is to provide meaningful visualization of musical pieces and performances from different layers as extracted by multimodal piece and performance analysis (Section 3-4). The second one is to allow the audience to interact with the concert from different perspectives according to source (section 3.4) and user profile (section 5).

6.1 Visualisation of music pieces and performances

We can distinguish two qualitatively distinct sources of information to be exploited in visualisation: the score itself, from which users can be informed about melodic lines, harmony, motifs or structure; and a specific performance, the specific way the written music was actually realized. Performance differences such as timing, phrasing and dynamics are quite notable for the symphonic repertoire, being one of the main sources of engagement and enjoyment for the audience. Moreover, both dimensions – score and performance – can inform and enrich each other. For users with different musical backgrounds (e.g. naive listeners, basic musical training, professional musicians), the most relevant musical descriptions and their corresponding visualisations will differ in terms of modalities, types and specificity levels. As outlined in section 3.1, we will employ different types of automatic music descriptors, which take different temporal scales into account, ranging from short-time melodic description to global key properties.

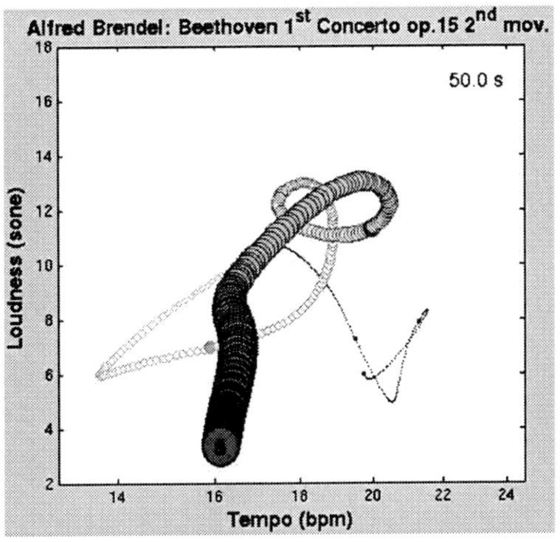

Figure 3. 'Performance Worm' visualisation of expressive timing and dynamics in Beethoven's First Piano Concerto.

Existing real-time music visualisation tools for tonality include dynamic tracking in both audio and symbolic domains [54], [55], but most of them are mostly intended to inform musicians (in music theory terms). We propose an extension of temporal multi-scale techniques for the analysis and representation of a variety of audio and/or symbolic features, through time-scale summarisation and mapping into feature spaces and geometrical colourspaces. This has been proposed for temporal multiscale tonality representations and interactive navigation of music pieces [5], illustrated in figure 2. For tonality, some of these models have been validated as perceptually relevant by cognitive psychology methodologies [56], and they have been used to inform real-time music performances, such as jazz improvisations. This approach is being currently extended beyond usual tonal simplifications, covering other musical (non-tonal) representation domains, and as interactive controllers for music creation.

In addition to properties of the music (the composition) itself, we also want to visualise interesting aspects to the specific *performance*. Examples of performance visualization are the Performance Worm [57] and more general phase plane representations [58]. While these uncover rather local timing and dynamics patterns, multi-level visualisations such as the Timescapes used in [59] can visualise how expressive timing shapes a piece at many levels simultaneously, making explicit also long-term developments and large-scale structure in a performance.

For live, real-time visualisation on stage, visualisation methods must be integrated with a real-time performance tracker, which is less trivial than it may seem. For instance, all of the above-mentioned methods rely on some kind of smoothing over time, and in doing so, effectively need to look 'into the future' of a given point in time. Predictive performance models may alleviate this problem. More-

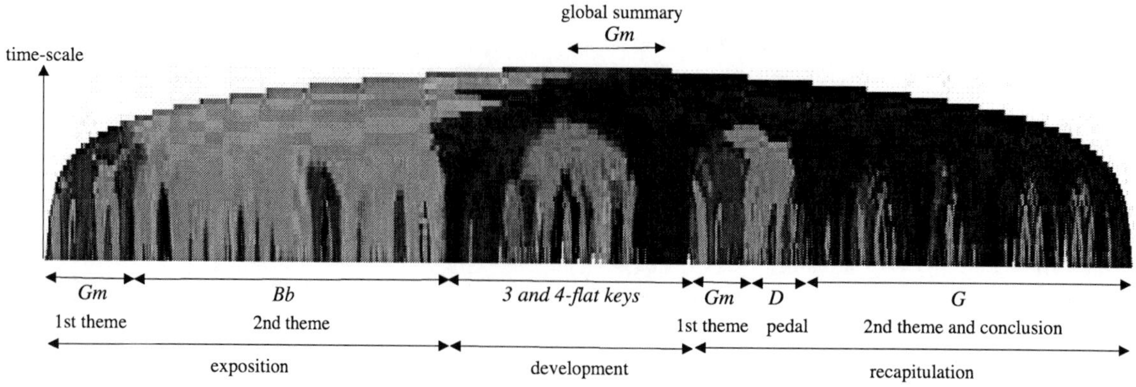

Figure 2. Multiscale tonality visualization of Finale of Haydn's "Rider" String Quartet, op.74 n.3 (in Gm).

over, timing and (global) dynamics are only two aspects of a much more complex and multi-faceted phenomenon. We will also investigate new ways of visualising dimensions such as articulation, balance of the voices/instrument sections in the orchestra, etc.

6.2 Multi-perspective audio processing: source auralisation

With the separated signals and information about the instruments location as presented in Section 3.4, we can attend a meaningful process of auralisation. Recent approaches have addressed the concept of upmixing (i.e. providing a spatial multi-channel output from a mono or stereo audio signal) by means of source separation techniques [60]. The challenge here is to provide a meaningful auralisation of the orchestral content by exploring different options from an acoustic zoom for a given instrument section, to virtually place the listener in a specific position on stage.

6.3 User-generated and multi-perspective concert video

Finally, it is of relevance to mention recent approaches regarding multi-perspective and user-generated concert video content. This topic has been emerging in several recent works, and since such content reflects collective strategies taking into account a particular person's view on a concert, it can be of interest for PHENICX too.

As for existing work,in [61] audio fingerprints are used to synchronise multiple user-generated concert video recordings, and key moments within a concert are detected based on the amount of overlap between multiple user clips. In [62], an automated video mashup system is presented, synchronising different user videos through camera flashes, and generating an aesthetic mashup result based on formalised requirements as elicited from video camera users. Finally, in [63] a concert video browser is demonstrated based on segment-level visual concept detectors, in which crowdsourcing mechanisms are used to improve the indexing results. It is striking that none of these existing methods actually base their analyses or evaluations on musical audio content, nor do they try to relate obtained results to musical content. In contrast, in PHENICX, since multi-perspective video and social information are to be used to get a better insight into the live musical performance, musical aspects will need to be taken into account explicitly.

Acknowledgments

The PHENICX consortium includes the Music Technology Group, Universitat Pompeu Fabra (project coordinator), Delft Multimedia Information Retrieval Lab - Technische Universiteit Delft (scientific coordinator), Department of Computational Perception, Johannes Kepler Universitt Linz, Royal Concertgebouw Orchestra, Video Dock BV, Austrian Research Institute for Artificial Intelligence and Escola Superior de Música de Catalunya. The project is funded by the European Union Seventh Framework Programme FP7 / 2007- 2013 under grant agreement n 601166.

References

[1] C. C. S. Liem, R. van der Sterren, M. van Tilburg, A. Sarasúa, J. Bosch, J. Janer, M. Melenhorst, E. Gómez, and A. Hanjalic, "The phenicx project: Towards interactive and social classical music performance consumption," in *Workshop on Interactive Content Consumption at EuroITV*, submitted.

[2] D. Bogdanov, J. Serrà, N. Wack, P. Herrera, and X. Serra, "Unifying low-level and high-level music similarity measures," *IEEE Transactions on Multimedia*, vol. 13, pp. 687–701, 08/2011 2011.

[3] J. Salamon and E. Gómez, "Melody extraction from polyphonic music signals using pitch contour characteristics," *IEEE Transactions on Audio, Speech and Language Processing*, vol. 20, pp. 1759–1770, 08/2012 2012.

[4] A. Holzapfel, M. Davies, J. Zapata, J. Oliveira, and F. Gouyon, "Selective sampling for beat tracking evaluation," *IEEE Transactions on Audio Speech and Language Processing*, 2012.

[5] A. Martorell and E. Gómez, "Two-dimensional visual inspection of pitch-space, many time-scales and tonal uncertainty over time," in *3rd International Conference on Mathematics and Computation in Music*, Paris, June 2011.

[6] K. Seyerlehner, G. Widmer, and T. Pohle, "Fusing

Block-Level Features for Music Similarity Estimation," in *International Conference on Digital Audio Effects*, Graz, Austria, September 2010.

[7] M. Schedl and T. Pohle, "Enlightening the Sun: A User Interface to Explore Music Artists via Multimedia Content," *Multimedia Tools and Applications: Special Issue on Semantic and Digital Media Technologies*, vol. 49, no. 1, pp. 101–118, August 2010.

[8] J. H. Kim, B. Tomasik, and D. Turnbull, "Using Artist Similarity to Propagate Semantic Information," in *International Society for Music Information Retrieval Conference)*, Kobe, Japan, October 2009.

[9] M. Sordo, "Semantic Annotation of Music Collections: A Computational Approach," Ph.D. dissertation, Universitat Pompeu Fabra, Barcelona, Spain, 2012.

[10] K. Seyerlehner, G. Widmer, M. Schedl, and P. Knees, "Automatic Music Tag Classification based on Block-Level Features," in *Sound and Music Computing Conference*, Barcelona, Spain, July 2010.

[11] M. I. Mandel, R. Pascanu, D. Eck, Y. Bengio, L. M. Aiello, R. Schifanella, and F. Menczer, "Contextual Tag Inference," *ACM Transactions on Multimedia Computing, Communications and Applications*, vol. 7S, no. 1, pp. 32:1–32:18, 2011.

[12] M. I. Mandel and D. P. W. Ellis, "A Web-Based Game for Collecting Music Metadata," *Journal of New Music Research*, vol. 37, no. 2, pp. 151–165, 2008.

[13] Y. Raimond, C. Sutton, and M. Sandler, "Interlinking Music-Related Data on the Web," *IEEE MultiMedia*, vol. 16, no. 2, pp. 52–63, 2009.

[14] M. Schedl, G. Widmer, P. Knees, and T. Pohle, "A music information system automatically generated via web content mining techniques," *Information Processing & Management*, vol. 47, 2011.

[15] A. Jourjine, S. Rickard, and O. Yilmaz, "Blind separation of disjoint orthogonal signals: demixing N sources from 2 mixtures," in *International Conference on Acoustics, Speech, and Signal Processing*, vol. 5, 2000, pp. 2985–2988 vol.5.

[16] P. Smaragdis and J. C. Brown, "Non-negative matrix factorization for polyphonic music transcription," *IEEE Workshop on Applications of Signal Processing to Audio and Acoustics*, vol. 3, no. 3, pp. 177–180, 2003.

[17] J. Durrieu, G. Richard, B. David, and C. Févotte, "Source/Filter Model for Unsupervised Main Melody Extraction From Polyphonic Audio Signals," *IEEE Transactions on Audio, Speech & Language Processing*, vol. 18, no. 3, pp. 564–575, Mar. 2010.

[18] S. Ewert and M. Müller, "Using Score-Informed Constraints for NMF-based Source Separation," in *IEEE International Conference on Acoustics, Speech, and Signal Processing*. Kyoto, Japan: IEEE, 2012.

[19] S. Dixon and G. Widmer, "MATCH: A Music Alignment Tool Chest," in *International Society for Music Information Retrieval Conference*, London, UK, 2005.

[20] M. Müller, H. Mattes, and F. Kurtz, "An Efficient Multiscale Approach to Audio Synchronization," in *International Society for Music Information Retrieval Conference*, Victoria, Canada, 2006.

[21] B. Niedermayer, "Accurate Audio-to-Score Alignment: Data Acquisition in the Context of Computational Musicology," Ph.D. dissertation, Johannes Kepler University Linz, Austria, 2012.

[22] A. Cont, "A Coupled Duration-focused Architecture for Real-time Music-to-Score Alignment," *IEEE TPAMI*, vol. 32, no. 6, pp. 974–987, 2010.

[23] C. Raphael, "Aligning Music Audio with Symbolic Scores Using a Hybrid Graphical Model," *Machine Learning*, vol. 65, no. 2-3, pp. 389–409, 2006.

[24] M. Müller and S. Ewert, "Towards Timbre-invariant Audio Features for Harmony-based Music," *IEEE Transactions on Audio, Speech and Language Processing*, vol. 18, no. 3, pp. 649–662, 2010.

[25] A. Arzt and G. Widmer, "Towards Effective 'Anytime' Music Tracking," in *STAIRS Conference*, Lisbon, Portugal, 2010.

[26] C. Fremerey, M. Müller, and M. Clausen, "Handling Repeats and Jumps in Score-performance Synchronization," in *International Society for Music Information Retrieval Conference*, Utrecht, Netherlands, 2010.

[27] A. Cont, "ANTESCOFO: Anticipatory Synchronisation and Control of Interactive Parameters in Computer Music," in *International Computer Music Conference*, 2008.

[28] C. Raphael, "Music Plus One and Machine Learning," in *International Conference on Machine Learning*, 2010.

[29] A. Friberg and J. Sundberg, "Does Music Allude to Locomotion? A Model of Final Ritardandi Derived from Measurements of Stopping Runners," *Journal of the Acoustical Society of America*, vol. 105, no. 3, pp. 1469–1484, 1999.

[30] N. P. Todd, "A Computational Model of Rubato," *Contemporary Music Review*, vol. 3, no. 1, pp. 69–88, 1989.

[31] S. Flossmann, W. Goebl, M. Grachten, B. Niedermayer, and G. Widmer, "The Magaloff Project: An Interim Report," *Journal of New Music Research*, vol. 31, no. 4, pp. 363–377, 2010.

[32] M. Grachten and G. Widmer, "Linear Basis Models for Prediction and Analysis of Musical Expression," *Journal of New Music Research*, vol. 41, no. 4, pp. 311–322, 2012.

[33] T. Schlömer, B. Poppinga, H. Henze, and S. Boll, "Gesture Recognition with a Wii Controller," in *International Conference on Tangible and Embedded Interaction*, New York, 2008.

[34] K. Kin, B. Hartmann, and T. DeRose, "Proton: Multitouch Gestures as Regular Expressions," in *CHI 2012*, 2012.

[35] C. F. Julià, S. Jordà, and N. Earnshaw, "Gestureagents: An agent-based framework for concurrent multi-task multi-user interaction," in *TEI 2013*. Barcelona, Spain: ACM, February 2013.

[36] E. Maestre, A. Perez, and R. Ramirez, "Gesture Sampling for Instrumental Sound Synthesis," in *International Computer Music Conference*, 2010.

[37] R. Godoy, E. Haga, and A. Jensenius, "Playing"Air Instruments": Mimicry of Sound-producing Gestures by Novices and Experts," in *Gesture in Human-Computer Intraction and Simulation*, 2006.

[38] Z. Cheng, J. Caverlee, and K. Lee, "You Are Where You Tweet: A Content-Based Approach to Geo-Locating Twitter Users," in *ACM International Conference on Information and Knowledge Management*, October 26-30 2010, pp. 759–768.

[39] B. Sriram, D. Fuhry, E. Demir, H. Ferhatosmanoglu, and M. Demirbas, "Short Text Classification in Twitter to Improve Information Filtering," in *Annual International ACM SIGIR Conference on Research and Development in Information Retrieval*, Geneva, Switzerland, July 19–23 2010.

[40] M. Clements, A. P. de Vries, and M. J. Reinders, "The Task Dependent Effect of Tags and Ratings on Social Media Access," *ACM Transactions on Information Systems*, vol. 2, no. 3, November 2008.

[41] S. D. Cedric S. Mesnage, Asma Rafiq and R. Brixtel, "Music Discovery with Social Networks," in *Workshop on Music Recommendation and Discovery*, Chicago, IL, USA, October 2011.

[42] S. Cunningham, S. Caulder, and V. Grout, "Saturday Night or Fever? Context-Aware Music Playlists," in *International Audio Mostly Conference of Sound in Motion*, October 2008.

[43] T. Cebrián, M. Planagumà, P. Villegas, and X. Amatriain, "Music Recommendations with Temporal Context Awareness," in *ACM Conference on Recommender Systems*, Barcelona, Spain, 2010.

[44] J. S. Lee and J. C. Lee, "Context Awareness by Case-Based Reasoning in a Music Recommendation System," in *Ubiquitous Computing Systems*, ser. Lecture Notes in Computer Science, H. Ichikawa, W.-D. Cho, I. Satoh, and H. Youn, Eds. Springer Berlin / Heidelberg, 2007, vol. 4836, pp. 45–58.

[45] B. Moens, L. van Noorden, and M. Leman, "D-Jogger: Syncing Music with Walking," in *Sound and Music Computing Conference*, Barcelona, Spain, 2010, pp. 451–456.

[46] H. Liu and J. H. M. Rauterberg, "Music Playlist Recommendation Based on User Heartbeat and Music Preference," in *International Conference on Computer Technology and Development*, Bangkok, Thailand, 2009, pp. 545–549.

[47] M. Kaminskas and F. Ricci, "Location-Adapted Music Recommendation Using Tags," in *User Modeling, Adaption and Personalization*, ser. Lecture Notes in Computer Science, J. Konstan, R. Conejo, J. Marzo, and N. Oliver, Eds. Springer Berlin / Heidelberg, 2011, vol. 6787, pp. 183–194.

[48] L. Baltrunas, M. Kaminskas, B. Ludwig, O. Moling, F. Ricci, K.-H. Lüke, and R. Schwaiger, "InCarMusic: Context-Aware Music Recommendations in a Car," in *International Conference on Electronic Commerce and Web Technologies (EC-Web)*, Toulouse, France, Aug–Sep 2011.

[49] M. Lux, C. Kofler, and O. Marques, "A classification scheme for user intentions in image search," in *ACM CHI '10*, 2010.

[50] A. Hanjalic, C. Kofler, and M. Larson, "Intent and its discontents: the user at the wheel of the online video search engine," in *ACM Multimedia*, 2012.

[51] O. Celma, *Music Recommendation and Discovery – The Long Tail, Long Fail, and Long Play in the Digital Music Space.* Berlin, Heidelberg, Germany: Springer, 2010.

[52] M. Schedl, D. Hauger, and D. Schnitzer, "A Model for Serendipitous Music Retrieval," in *16th International Conference on Intelligent User Interfaces: 2nd International Workshop on Context-awareness in Retrieval and Recommendation*, Lisbon, Portugal, February 14 2012.

[53] Yuan Cao Zhang, Diarmuid O Seaghdha, Daniele Quercia, Tamas Jambor, "Auralist: Introducing Serendipity into Music Recommendation," in *ACM Int'l Conference on Web Search and Data Mining.*

[54] E. Chew, "Towards a mathematical model of tonality," Ph.D. dissertation, Massachusetts Institute of Technology, 2000.

[55] P. Toiviainen, "Visualization of tonal content in the symbolic and audio domains," *Tonal theory for the digital age*, p. 187, 2007.

[56] P. Toiviainen and C. Krumhansl, "Measuring and modeling real-time responses to music: The dynamics of tonality induction," *Perception*, vol. 32, pp. 741–766, 2003.

[57] J. Langner and W. Goebl, "Visualizing Expressive Performance in Tempo-Loudness Space," *Computer Music Journal*, vol. 27, no. 4, pp. 69–83, 2003.

[58] M. Grachten, W. Goebl, S. Flossmann, and G. Widmer, "Phase-plane Representation and Visualisation of Gestural Structure in Expressive Timing," *Journal of New Music Research*, vol. 38, no. 2, pp. 183–195, 2009.

[59] C. Sapp, "Comparative analysis of multiple musical performances," in *International Conference on Music Information Retrieval*, Vienna, Austria, September 23-27 2007, pp. 497–500.

[60] D. Fitzgerald, "Upmixing from mono - a source separation approach," in *International Conference on DSP*, 2011, pp. 1–7.

[61] L. Kennedy and M. Naaman, "Less talk, more rock: automated organization of community-contributed collections of concert videos," in *WWW '09*, 2009.

[62] P. Shrestha, P. H. N. de With, H. Weda, M. Barbieri, and E. H. L. Aarts, "Automatic mashup generation from multiple-camera concert recordings," in *ACM Multimedia*, 2010.

[63] C. G. M. Snoek, B. Freiburg, J. Oomen, and R. Ordelman, "Crowdsourcing rock n' roll multimedia retrieval," in *ACM Multimedia*, 2010.

SEMI-AUTOMATIC MELODY EXTRACTION USING NOTE ONSET TIME AND PITCH INFORMATION FROM USERS

Antti Laaksonen
Department of Computer Science
University of Helsinki
ahslaaks@cs.helsinki.fi

ABSTRACT

Automatic melody extraction from music audio has proven to be challenging. In this paper we focus on semi-automatic melody extraction, where prior information produced by the user is used in the algorithm. Our experiment shows that users – even without a musical background – are able to produce useful approximations of both the note onset times and the pitches in the melody that is being extracted. We present a dynamic programming algorithm that takes this user-generated information and uses it for melody extraction. The algorithm is based on audio samples that are built around approximate note onset times. In addition to this, approximate note pitches can be used to constrain the set of possible melodies. We compare our algorithm with a state-of-the-art melody extraction algorithm using orchestral music material. In the evaluation we use simulated note approximations that could have been produced by a user without a musical background. In this setting, the accuracy of our algorithm is remarkably better than that of the automatic algorithm.

1. INTRODUCTION

In the automatic melody extraction problem, the input is an excerpt from a musical work as an audio signal, and the output is a symbolic representation of the most important melody line in the excerpt. Practical applications for automatic melody extraction include the construction of datasets for music search engines and sheet music production for individual pieces.

Automatic melody extraction is a difficult problem [1]. The difficulties lie in recognizing which frequencies in the audio signal are fundamental frequencies of musical notes and furthermore, which of the notes belong to the melody. Human listeners can easily follow different instruments and they have previous knowledge about melody structure. It is difficult to transmit these skills to a computer.

Most melody extraction systems share a common structure [4, 11, 14]. First, potential melody frequencies are filtered from the audio signal. After this, the melody is constructed using knowledge about the properties of typical melodies. Another popular approach to melody extraction has been separation of melody and accompaniment sources [2, 9]. More information of the proposed melody extraction systems can be found in [13, 15].

In this paper, we concentrate on semi-automatic melody extraction. To facilitate the melody extraction from the audio signal, a semi-automatic system uses additional musical information given by the user. First we study what kind of information can be gathered from users, both with and without a musical background. After that, we present and evaluate a melody extraction algorithm that uses this information.

Of course, semi-automatic systems have severe limitations compared to independent systems. They cannot be used to automatically process large datasets because they require user interaction. However, an important use case is the transcription of an individual piece for which there is no sheet music available. In this case, it may be acceptable for the user to take a significant amount of time to help the system produce the final transcription.

User information has already been used in some signal separation systems. For example, users can provide information about instruments playing the melody [6], give a partial transcription [7] or select the audio source corresponding to the melody [3]. In Songle [5], a first draft for the transcription is produced automatically, and after that the users can work on it collaboratively.

The organization of the rest of the paper is as follows: In Section 2 we study the ability of the users to recognize note onset times and the pitches in the melody. In Section 3 we present a semi-automatic melody extraction algorithm which uses approximate note onset times and the pitches produced by the user. In Section 4 we evaluate our algorithm and compare it with a state-of-the-art automatic melody extraction algorithm. Finally, in Section 5 we present our conclusions.

2. NOTE APPROXIMATIONS

We conducted an experiment where human listeners approximated note onset times and the pitches in the melody. The experiment shows that users can produce useful onset time and pitch approximations for semi-automatic melody extraction. Our melody extraction algorithm in Section 3 is based on these approximations. We also use the results of the experiment for estimating error distribution in the evaluation of the algorithm in Section 4.

Figure 1. The Star Wars melody in the first task.

Figure 2. The Parsifal melody in the second task.

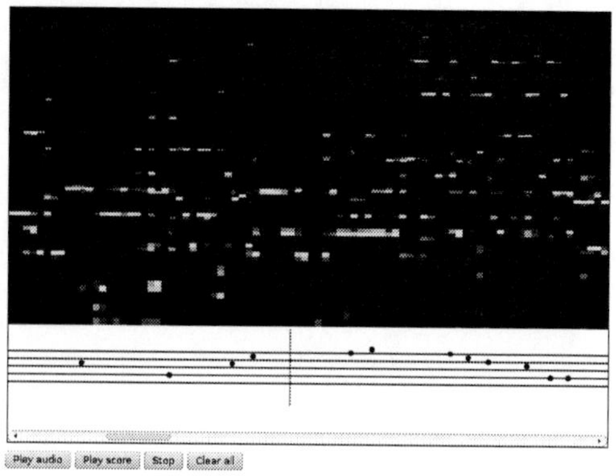

Figure 3. The user interface used in the experiment.

Task	Group	Participants	avg σ_T	min σ_T
Star Wars	A	6	0.19	0.03
	B	13	0.08	0.03
Parsifal	A	11	0.13	0.08
	B	15	0.14	0.09

Table 1. Number of participants with no more than one extra or missing note. The average and minimum error deviation of note onset times are calculated for those participants.

2.1 Experiment set-up

The experiment consisted of two tasks, both involving a short orchestral music excerpt containing a melody. The excerpt in the first task was a theme from Star Wars by John Williams (Figure 1), and the second excerpt was a theme from Wagner's Parsifal (Figure 2). We tried to select melodies that are clear and unambiguous. Furthermore, we presumed that the first excerpt would be familiar for the participants and the second excerpt would be unfamiliar.

We had 30 participants in our experiment. Group A consisted of 15 participants without a musical background. Those participants either had no experience playing an instrument or singing, or had only practiced music for a short period of time during their childhood. Group B consisted of 15 participants with a strong musical background who had practiced music actively for a long time. All the participants were university students, and none of the them were professional musicians or experienced transcribers.

Figure 3 shows the user interface used in the experiment. The window is divided into two parts: the upper part contains a spectrogram of the audio file and the lower part contains a staff line with the melody. Initially, the staff line is empty. The system allows one to play a selected segment of the audio file or the melody in the staff line. In the latter case, the melody is synthesized using a flute-like sound. Notes can be added to the staff line by pressing a key while listening to the audio file. After this, the pitches of the notes can be adjusted and the notes can also be moved or removed.

Both tasks in the experiment consisted of three subtasks. The first subtask was to mark down the pulse of the melody by pressing a key at regular intervals. This subtask served as an introduction to the user interface. After this, the second subtask was to determine the note onset times in the melody and finally, the third subtask was to adjust the note pitches. We report the results of the latter two subtasks because they are relevant for our algorithm.

The participants were briefly told how to use the system at the beginning of the experiment. They were asked to work carefully, but were also told not to use too much time if they could not hear something easily. The participants typically used 10–30 minutes for each of the two tasks. The participants's performance during a task was not commented on, and they had to decide themselves when they were ready.

The results in the Parsifal task were generally better than in the Star Wars task. This can be explained both by the nature of the melodies and by the structure of the experiment. The orchestration of the Parsifal melody is slower and lighter, which may make it easier to perceive and mark down. In addition to this, the Star Wars task was the first task in the experiment and the participants were more acquainted with the system when they started the Parsifal task.

2.2 Onset time determination

In the note onset time subtask, the participants placed notes on the staff line. The participants had to determine both the number of notes and the horizontal positions of the notes. The principal method for this was to press a key at each note while listening to the music. The participants were allowed to listen to the music an unlimited number of times and could move and remove notes afterwards.

Let $t_1, t_2, \dots, t_n$ denote the reference note onset times measured in seconds and $x_1, x_2, \dots, x_m$ the approximate onset times by the participant. If we assume that $n = m$, we can calculate the root mean squared error σ_T of the onset time using the formula $\sqrt{(\sum_1^n (t_k - x_k)^2)/n}$.

However, in practice, n and m may differ. For example, several participants ignored the C# note at the beginning of the Parsifal melody, probably interpreting it as a glissando. In the following, we regard a note onset time approximation as accurate if it contains the correct number of notes, or only has one extra or missing note.

Table 1 shows the numbers of participants with the correct number of notes, or just one extra or missing note. The average and minimum error deviation of these participants

Task	Group	$d = 0$	$d = 4$	$d = 7$	avg σ_P
Star Wars	A	1	2	7	2.41
	B	9	14	14	0.83
Parsifal	A	1	2	9	2.81
	B	11	12	15	0.71

Table 2. Number of participants who produced an d-approximation when $d \in \{0, 4, 7\}$. The average error is calculated for participants having a 7-approximation.

Task	Group	Intervals	Parsons code
Star Wars	A	1	2
	B	14	14
Parsifal	A	1	9
	B	11	14

Table 3. Number of participants having correct intervals and Parsons codes.

are also shown. If $n \neq m$, we calculate the error by excluding one note onset time in the data so that the error is minimized. About half of the participants in group A, and almost all in group B, produced accurate note onset time approximations.

Interestingly, in the Parsifal task the results of groups A and B are very similar to each other. This suggests that the musical background has a minor role in determining the onset times for a slow melody. Instead of this, a more important factor may be the experience in using the computer. Among the most accurate participants in this subtask were active computer gamers without any musical background.

Our melody extraction algorithm in Section 3 is based on note onset time approximations. It is important for the algorithm that the errors in Table 1 are small, ranging from 0.03 to 0.09 among the best participants without a musical background. In Section 4, we use an error deviation of 0.05 in producing evaluation material for the algorithm.

2.3 Pitch determination

In the note pitch subtask, the participants were given a template with correct note onset times. Their task was to determine a pitch for each of the notes. This was done by moving the note vertically using the keyboard while listening to the original audio file and the synthesized melody.

Musical background had a strong impact on this subtask. Most participants with a strong musical background (group B) determined the correct pitches easily. However, the participants in group A were in general unable to determine pitches accurately. Several participants commented that it was difficult to compare original and synthesized pitches because the timbre was different. This phenomenon has also been reported in previous studies [12].

Instead of exact pitches, we now focus on approximate pitches. Let $c_1, c_2, \ldots, c_n$ denote the correct pitches in the melody measured in semitones and $a_1, a_2, \ldots, a_n$ represent the approximate pitches, also in semitones, produced by the participant. Furthermore, we define a d-approximation as a sequence of pitches where the distance from the correct pitch is not more than d semitones, i.e. $|c_k - a_k| \leq d$, for every k. For example, $d = 7$ means that the pitch difference is no more than a perfect fifth. We also calculate the root mean squared error σ_P of the pitches using the formula $\sqrt{(\sum_1^n (c_k - a_k)^2)/n}$.

Table 2 shows the number of participants who produced d-approximations where $d \in \{0, 4, 7\}$ as well as the average errors of the pitches for participants with a 7-approximation. While the participants in group A could not recognize the pitches exactly, half of them produced a 7-approximation of the pitch sequence.

The intervals of consecutive pitches are another important aspect of the pitch sequence. The intervals of a pitch sequence are correct if $c_{k+1} - c_k = a_{k+1} - a_k$ for every k. Furthermore, the Parsons code is correct if the directions of the intervals are correct i.e. $c_k < c_{k+1}$ iff $a_k < a_{k+1}$, $c_k > c_{k+1}$ iff $a_k > a_{k+1}$, and $c_k = c_{k+1}$ iff $a_k = a_{k+1}$.

Table 3 shows the number of participants with the correct intervals and Parsons codes. Interval recognition was as difficult as exact pitch recognition: again only participants in group B were able to recognize correct intervals. However, in the Parsifal task, more than half of the participants produced a correct Parsons code.

Note pitch approximations can be used in our algorithm in Section 3, and they significantly enhance melody extraction results. In Section 4, we use an error deviation of 2.5 in producing evaluation material for the algorithm.

3. ALGORITHM

This section describes our melody extraction algorithm that uses musical information produced by the user. The algorithm exploits standard techniques for calculating pitch salience values for audio segments [13, 15]. However, the user information allows signal processing and dynamic programming methods that are usually not possible.

The algorithm selects relevant audio segments using the approximate note onset times, and approximate pitches can be used to constrain the search for the melody. The fundamental assumption in the algorithm is that the approximate note onset times are known beforehand. The results of Section 2 suggest that this assumption is meaningful when the user helps with the extraction.

The input of the algorithm consists of an audio file and the approximate note onset times retrieved from the user. As in Section 2.2, the sequence $t_1, t_2, \ldots, t_n$ denotes the note onset times. Each value t_k is the time in seconds where the kth note begins.

The algorithm assigns a pitch p_k for each note onset time. Each pitch is a note number in semitones, and it can be calculated from the note frequency f using the formula $12 \log_2(f/27.5)$. Then, for example, the note number of A = 440 Hz is 48, and the interval between pitches p_a and p_b is $|p_a - p_b|$ semitones.

3.1 Signal processing

The usual first step in melody extraction algorithms is to divide the audio signal into small frames that have a constant length. After that, a frequency spectrum for each frame is calculated using the Fourier transform or a similar method. However, our algorithm uses a different approach because the note onset times are available.

For each note onset time t_k the algorithm calculates the Fourier transform of the window $[t_k + w_1, t_k + w_2]$. The idea is to select the values w_1 and w_2 so that in the resulting window the frequencies of the melody are strong. If $t_k + w_2 > t_{k+1}$, the window is $[t_k \dots t_{k+1}]$. We evaluate different ways for selecting the parameters in Section 4.

After this, the algorithm calculates a salience value $s_{k,p}$ for each note onset time t_k and pitch p. The salience values will be used in the second phase of the algorithm, and the objective is that pitches with large salience values are strong candidates for melody pitches.

Let $a_{k,f}$ be the normalized amplitude of frequency f in the Fourier transform of note onset time t_k using linear interpolation. The algorithm calculates the salience value $s_{k,p}$ as a weighted sum of the harmonics [8] by the formula

$$s_{k,p} = \sum_{i=1}^{n} a_{k,if(p)} h_i \tag{1}$$

where $f(p) = 27.5 \cdot 2^{p/12}$ and h_i is the weight of the ith harmonics and n is the total number of harmonics. In this paper we use the values $n = 3$ and $h_i = 1/i$.

Note that we assume that the tuning is near A = 440 Hz and does not change during the excerpt. This is a realistic assumption in orchestral music that we focus on.

3.2 Dynamic programming

The melody selection procedure of our algorithm is based on dynamic programming. The salience value of a pitch sequence $p_1, p_2, \dots, p_n$ is the sum $\sum_{i=1}^{i=n} s_{i,p_i}$ of the individual salience values.

The algorithm selects a pitch sequence with a maximum salience value using the following recursive formula:

$$v_{k,p} = \begin{cases} -\infty & \text{if } p \notin P_k \\ s_{k,p} & \text{if } k = 1 \\ s_{k,p} + \max\limits_{r \in N_{k-1,p}} v_{k-1,r} & \text{if } k > 1 \end{cases} \tag{2}$$

Here $v_{k,p}$ is the maximum salience value of a pitch sequence for note onset times $t_1, t_2, \dots, t_k$ whose last pitch is p. The set P_k contains the possible values for p_k. Correspondingly, the set $N_{k,p}$ contains the possible values for p_k when p_{k+1} equals p. The construction of sets P_k and $N_{k,p}$ is the topic of Section 3.3.

The values $v_{k,p}$ can be computed efficiently using dynamic programming. Now $\max_{p \in P_n} v_{n,p}$ is the maximum salience value for the pitch sequences that satisfy the constraints given by sets P_k and $N_{k,p}$. The pitch sequence with maximum salience can be constructed in reverse order: first set $p_n = \arg\max_{p \in P_n} v_{n,p}$ and then for $k < n$, select p_k so that $v_{k,p_k} + s_{k+1,p_{k+1}} = v_{k+1,p_{k+1}}$.

3.3 Constraints

The sets P_k and $N_{k,p}$ constrain the set of possible melodies that the algorithm can produce. Let p_{min} and p_{max} be the lowest and highest possible pitches in the melody and $P_{all} = \{p_{min}, \dots, p_{max}\}$ the set of all possible pitches.

If we do not have any constraints for the pitches, we can define the sets P_k and $N_{k,p}$ simply as follows:

$$\begin{aligned} P_k &= P_{all} \\ N_{k,p} &= P_{all} \end{aligned} \tag{3}$$

Now suppose that we have some information about the note pitches produced by the user. As in Section 2.3, let $c_1, c_2, \dots, c_n$ be the correct pitches and $a_1, a_2, \dots, a_n$ be the approximate pitches. There may be numerous errors in the approximate pitches. However, the results of Section 2.3 suggest that they can still be used.

First we assume that the approximate pitch sequence is a d_P-approximation i.e. $|c_k - a_k| \leq d_P$ for every k. Now it is possible to construct the set P_k as follows:

$$P_k = \{p \in P_{all} : |a_k - p| \leq d_P\} \tag{4}$$

Furthermore, if we assume that the Parsons code of the approximate pitch sequence is correct, we can construct the set $N_{k,p}$ in the following way:

$$\begin{aligned} N_{k,p} = & \{r \in P_{all} : r < p, a_k < a_{k+1}\} \cup \\ & \{r \in P_{all} : r > p, a_k > a_{k+1}\} \cup \\ & \{r \in P_{all} : r = p, a_k = a_{k+1}\} \end{aligned} \tag{5}$$

4. EVALUATION

In this section we evaluate our algorithm using an orchestral music collection. We also compare our algorithm with a state-of-the-art automatic melody extraction algorithm. We present the best results of the algorithms and study the impact of the parameters in our algorithm.

4.1 Material

Dataset	Type	Excerpts	Length
Dvorak	Classical	11	319 s
Rota	Film	8	230 s
Tchaikovsky	Classical	11	335 s
Wagner	Classical	9	380 s
Williams	Film	10	348 s
Total		49	1621 s

Table 4. The material used in the evaluation. There were five datasets: three sets came from classical composers and two came from film composers.

The material used in the evaluation, as presented in Table 4, consists of 49 audio excerpts with a total length of 27 minutes. We extracted the excerpts from CD tracks into mono WAV files with a sample rate of 44,100 Hz.

The material differs from the material used in MIREX [10] in two ways. First, all the excerpts are from orchestral works, whereas most of the material in MIREX is vocal music with a light accompaniment. Second, all the excerpts are from real recordings.

To get the reference melodies, we manually annotated the melodies in the material. Each annotation consists of note onset times and pitch values. All the melodies are continuous, i.e., we interpret that there are no pauses between consecutive notes. We attempted to select melodies that are clear and unambiguous. However, there is always some subjectivity in determining the melody.

Details concerning the material and our annotations used in the evaluation are available on our website [1].

4.2 Algorithms

We evaluated four versions of the algorithm described in Section 3. We call the different versions of the algorithm A1, A2, A3 and A4. A1 uses only note onset time information. In addition to this, A2 uses note pitch approximations, A3 uses Parsons codes and A4 uses both pitch approximations and Parsons codes.

We generated the user information in the evaluation from the reference annotations. We assumed that the number of the notes is correct and used normal distribution for simulating the user error: $N(\mu_N, \sigma_N^2)$ and $N(\mu_P, \sigma_P^2)$ denote the distributions for note onset times and pitches. We used reference onset times and pitches as means and experimented with different standard deviations. Furthermore, we set the allowed pitch difference so that $d_P = 2\sigma_P$. The Parsons codes were always correct.

This simulation is, of course, a simplification compared to the real situation. However, a large-scale experiment with real users was not possible, and we expect that, despite its limitations, the simulation sheds light on the applicability of the approach.

We compared our algorithm with MELODIA [15] which is a state-of-the-art melody extraction algorithm. MELODIA is a fully automatic system and it does not utilize user information. The parameters for MELODIA are the voicing tolerance v_M and the monophonic noise filter n_M.

As opposed to our algorithm, MELODIA produces a pitch frequency for each frame in the audio and can identify frames without melody using a negative pitch value. We converted the pitch frequencies f to note numbers using the formula $12\log_2(f/27.5)$. Furthermore, we also interpreted the negative pitch values as melody pitches because the melodies in our material are continuous.

4.3 Results

First, we present the best results achieved by the algorithms. After this, we present the results of our algorithm using varying error deviations and window parameters.

We calculated the melody extraction accuracy using the formula l_c/l_t where l_c is the total length of segments where the output of the algorithm corresponds to the reference, and l_t is the total length of the data. The accuracy can be calculated for an excerpt, a dataset or the material as a whole. The formula is similar to the overall accuracy metric used in MIREX, except that in MIREX the accuracy is calculated frame by frame.

[1] http://cs.helsinki.fi/u/ahslaaks/smc13/

Dataset	A1	A2	A3	A4	M
Dvorak	0.15	0.42	0.20	0.57	0.21
Rota	0.27	0.70	0.35	0.75	0.47
Tchaikovsky	0.20	0.60	0.20	0.70	0.24
Wagner	0.26	0.52	0.32	0.62	0.41
Williams	0.33	0.62	0.39	0.70	0.32
Total	0.24	0.56	0.29	0.66	0.33

Table 5. The best results of the algorithms. The error deviations are $\sigma_N = 0.05$ and $\sigma_P = 2.5$ and all the other parameters are optimized.

$\sigma_P \backslash \sigma_N$	0	0.01	0.05	0.1	0.2	0.5
0	1.00	0.99	0.94	0.88	0.75	0.53
1	0.86	0.86	0.81	0.75	0.63	0.45
2	0.75	0.74	0.71	0.66	0.56	0.40
3	0.65	0.65	0.63	0.58	0.49	0.37
4	0.60	0.60	0.58	0.54	0.45	0.33
5	0.57	0.55	0.54	0.50	0.41	0.30

Table 6. The results of A4 for all of the material when the error deviations σ_N and σ_P change.

Table 5 shows the best results of the algorithms. For generating the user information from reference melodies, we used error deviations $\sigma_N = 0.05$ and $\sigma_P = 2.5$, which are realistic deviations based on Section 2. After this, we selected window parameters $w_1 = 0.5$ and $w_2 = 0.55$ that produced the best results on the evaluation material.

M denotes the automatic MELODIA algorithm. We chose parameters $v_M = 0.5$ and $v_F = 0$ that produced the best results on the evaluation material.

The results of A1 and A3 were equal or weaker than that of MELODIA, depending on the dataset. The results of A2 and A4, that use approximate pitch values, were substantially better. In MIREX, the overall accuracy of MELODIA was 0.70 [15] which suggests that our material is more challenging than the material used in MIREX.

Table 6 shows the results of A4 when the error deviations σ_N and σ_P change and where the window parameters are $w_1 = 0.5$ and $w_2 = 0.55$, as tehy were previously. It seems that accurate onset times are more important than accurate note pitches; even the results with $\sigma_P = 5$ were reasonable. As expected, the accuracy without deviation was 1.00.

Table 7 shows the results of A4 when the window parameters w_1 and w_2 change and the error deviations are $\sigma_N = 0.05$ and $\sigma_P = 2.5$, as they were previously. Here w_d is the length of the window i.e. $w_d = w_2 - w_1$. There were no big differences in the results in this case. The deviation in the onsert times of the approximate notes makes it difficult to determine the window parameters.

5. CONCLUSIONS

In the first part of the paper, we described an experiment in which the participants transcribed two melodies from orchestral music excerpts. As expected, most participants

$w_1 \backslash w_d$	0.05	0.1	0.25	0.5	1
0.05	0.51	0.55	0.59	0.58	0.56
0.1	0.60	0.60	0.61	0.57	0.56
0.25	0.63	0.64	0.61	0.58	0.57
0.5	0.66	0.66	0.62	0.59	0.59
1	0.63	0.63	0.61	0.58	0.58

Table 7. The results of A4 for all of the material when the window parameters w_1 and $w_d = w_2 - w_1$ change.

with a musical background were able to determine note onset times and pitches accurately. However, about half of the participants without a musical background also produced useful information about the melody, even if they could not determine note pitches exactly.

In the second part of the paper, we presented a semi-automatic algorithm for melody extraction. This algorithm is based on a dynamic programming scheme and assumes that approximate note onset times and the pitches in the melody are available. Thus, the algorithm requires help from the user to extract the melody.

The proposed algorithm is intended for users without a musical background because they can benefit from it the most. Even if they cannot determine note pitches accurately, they can provide approximations good enough for the algorithm. Constraining the range of possible pitches greatly simplifies the melody extraction problem.

When using simulated information from users without a musical background, the results of our algorithm are considerably better than that of a state-of-the-art automatic algorithm. Of course, a severe weakness in our algorithm is that it requires a lot of work on the part of the user, which limits its applicability in practice.

Our future work aims to constrain the pitch range of the melody notes by using less prior information or by limiting it automatically. One possible approach only requires the user to transcribe a subset of the notes, as in [7]. Another possibility is to assume that the approximate pitch range, i.e. the register of the melody, is known. For example, in orchestral music, it is often the case that the melody is located in the high register.

6. ACKNOWLEDGEMENTS

This work has been supported by the Helsinki Doctoral Programme in Computer Science and the Academy of Finland (grant number 118653).

7. REFERENCES

[1] E. Benetos et al, "Automatic music transcription: breaking the glass ceiling," in *Proceedings of the 13th International Society for Music Information Retrieval Conference*, 2012.

[2] J.-L. Durrieu et al, "Source/filter model for unsupervised main melody extraction from polyphonic audio signals," in *IEEE Transactions on Audio, Speech, and Language Processing*, 18(3), 564–575, 2010.

[3] J.-L. Durrieu and J.-P. Thiran, "Musical audio source separation based on user-selected F0 track," in *Proceedings of the 10th International Conference on Latent Variable Analysis and Signal Separation*, 2012.

[4] M. Goto, "A real-time music scene description system: predominant-F0 estimation for detecting melody and bass lines in real-world audio signals," in *Speech Communication*, 43(4), 311–329, 2004.

[5] M. Goto et al, "Songle: a web service for active music listening improved by user contributions," in *Proceedings of the 12th International Society for Music Information Retrieval Conference*, 2011.

[6] H. Kirchhoff, S. Dixon and A. Klapuri, "Shift-variant non-negative matrix deconvolution for music transcription," in *Proceedings of the 37th International Conference on Acoustics, Speech and Signal Processing*, 2012.

[7] H. Kirchhoff, S. Dixon and A. Klapuri, "Multi-template shift-variant non-negative matrix deconvolution for semi-automatic music transcription," in *Proceedings of the 13th International Society for Music Information Retrieval Conference*, 2012.

[8] A. Klapuri, "Multiple fundamental frequency estimation by summing harmonic amplitudes," in *Proceedings of the 7th International Conference on Music Information Retrieval*, 2006.

[9] M. Lagrange et al, "Normalized cuts for predominant melodic source separation," in *IEEE Transactions on Audio, Speech, and Language Processing*, 16(2), 278–290, 2008.

[10] MIREX wiki containing the Audio Melody Extraction task, http://www.music-ir.org/mirex/wiki/

[11] R. Paiva, T. Mendes and A. Cardoso, "Melody detection in polyphonic musical signals: exploiting perceptual rules, note salience, and melodic smoothness," in *Computer Music Journal*, 30(4), 80–98, 2006.

[12] M. Pitt and R. Crowder, "The role of spectral and dynamic cues in imagery for musical timbre," in *Journal of Experimental Psychology: Human Perception and Performance*, 18(3), 728–738, 1992.

[13] G. Poliner et al, "Melody transcription from music audio: approaches and evaluation," in *IEEE Transactions on Audio, Speech, and Language Processing*, 15(4), 1247–1256, 2007.

[14] M. Ryynänen and A. Klapuri, "Automatic transcription of melody, bass line, and chords in polyphonic music," in *Computer Music Journal*, 32(3), 72–86, 2008.

[15] J. Salamon and E. Gómez, "Melody extraction from polyphonic music signals using pitch contour characteristics," in *IEEE Transactions on Audio, Speech, and Language Processing*, 20(6), 1759–1770, 2012.

Joint f0 and inharmoncity estimation using second order optimization

Henrik Hahn
IRCAM-CNRS-UPMC UMR 9912-STMS
henrik.hahn@ircam.fr

Axel Röbel
IRCAM-CNRS-UPMC UMR 9912-STMS
axel.roebel@ircam.fr

ABSTRACT

A new method is presented for the joint estimation of the inharmonicity coefficient and the fundamental frequency of inharmonic instrument sounds. The proposed method iteratively uses a peak selection algorithm and a joint parameters estimation method based on nonlinear optimization. We further introduce an adapted tessitura model to evaluate our proposed method for piano sounds and to compare it with state-of-the-art techniques.

1. INTRODUCTION

The stiffness of instrumental strings effectuates the frequencies of the modes of vibration to be highly inharmonic. This effect is decisive for most string based instruments and marks a significant part of the perceptive sound characteristic of the piano [1]. Inharmonicity means that the partial frequencies are not exact integer multiples of their fundamental but located at increased positions. The amount of increase is reflected by the inharmonicity coefficient β, while the frequency f of a partial k can be expressed for all partials K present in a signal by the relation:

$$f_k = kf_0\sqrt{1+k^2\beta}, \quad k = 1 \ldots K \tag{1}$$

where f_0 denotes the signals fundamental frequency, which is in fact a theoretical value, as there is no partial with that specific frequency present in an inharmonic signal. Hence, the inharmonicity coefficient β as well as the fundamental frequency f_0 can not easily be measured from an instruments signal, but they need to be taken into account for a lot of different applications, like f_0-estimation and harmonic sinusoidal analysis, as well as for prior knowledge to control sound synthesis of string based instruments. And finally, demixing of sound mixtures is an emerging topic, which also relies on good estimations of the inharmonicity coefficient and the fundamental frequency.

In the following section we give a brief overview on three previous estimation methods and point out several drawbacks of them in section 3 before we give a detailed description of our approach, which aims to solve these drawbacks. An extensive evaluation of our approach with an adapted tessitura model, comparing it with the three other methods is presented in the 4th section.

2. PREVIOUS METHODS

Several methods for the automatic estimation of the inharmonicity factor β with according refinement of the fundamental frequency f_0 have been proposed in the past years. Galembo and Askenfelt proposed a method [2] based on inharmonic comb filtering (ICF). In this method, the parameters for the inharmonic comb filter have been found by an exploration of a vast range of possible parameter values within three consecutive steps and refining the parameter grid in each. The algorithm finally interpolates the best parameter sets to obtain its f_0 and β-coefficient. Hodgkinson et al. proposed a method [3] using median-adjustive trajectories (MAT). This algorithm works in an iterative manner in which a partial k of the inharmonic series is selected and used for improving the estimate of β and f_0. The improved estimates are then used to search the next partial k. The most recent approach is based on Non-negative matrix factorization by Rigaud et al. [4, 5] aiming at the joint estimation of f_0 and β-coefficients for several fundamental frequencies at once with a specific focus on the polyphonic case. Another approach has been proposed in [6] showing similar accuracy, but improved computational performance to the ICF method.

3. PROPOSED METHOD

3.1 Drawbacks in recent methods

All recent methods we studied so far share similar drawbacks. First of all, they usually work with a fixed maximum of around 30 partials or fixed amplitude thresholds to avoid using too noisy signal components for the estimation. But, especially low pitched piano tones may exhibit very rich spectra containing more than 200 partials. For an analysis which tries to reliably identify as much partials as possible in such a signal, the estimation of the β coefficient needs to be executed for far more partials, because slight deviations in the β estimation will remain unnoticed. Figure 1 illustrates how such small errors in the estimation of the β coefficient result in misleading partial detection. Increasing the amount of partials for the estimation of β is by no means a trivial task as it requires a suitable strategy for selecting reasonable spectral peaks and rejecting noisy signal components. Furthermore, some approaches need at least 5 partials for a reliable estimation, but high pitched piano notes or moderately high pitched but with very low intensity do not contain more than 3 to 4 partials. Especially low intensity signals require a robust distinction between noise and sinusoid within a peak selection process but also require the estimation to be robust against noisy

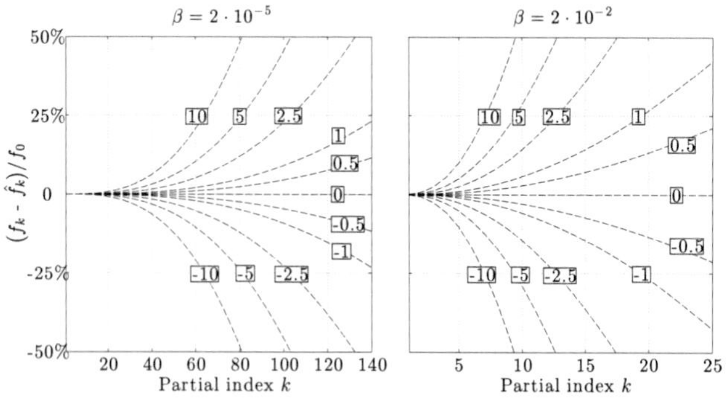

Figure 1. Analysis of the effect of the deviation in β. Boxed values indicate hypothetical deviations of the β value from its 'real' value in percent. Dashed curves demonstrate the resulting deviation in frequency estimation for respective partial index.

partials. Previous approaches often use heuristics to either neglect noisy partials during the peak selection or reduce their influence in the estimation process.

3.2 General method description

The proposed method estimates jointly the inharmonicity coefficient β and the fundamental frequency f_0 in an iterative manner, which can be used on several frames at once and is illustrated in figure 2. For the algorithm a signal segment $y(t)$ behind the signals attack point is selected to ensure, the algorithm analyses no transient components. A standard f_0 estimation [7] is applied and the f_0 information is then being used to set the analysis parameters for the STFT adaptively to guarantee suitable analysis window lengths according to the fundamental. The STFT is taken for N overlapping frames n yielding $Y(f,n)$ and all spectral bins are classified into the 3 classes: main lobe, side lobe or noise component using the *peak classification* method proposed by Zivanovic et al. [8]. The algorithms

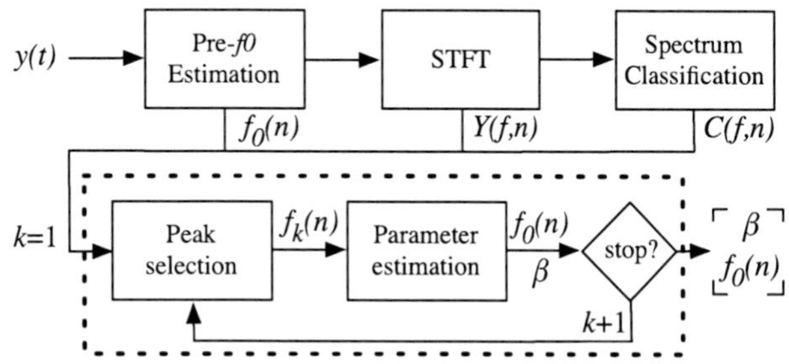

Figure 2. General scheme of proposed iterative method.

main loop identifies a valid peak for the current partial index within each frame and estimates a new f_0 for each frame n and a new β for all frames within each iteration until some abort criterion has been reached. With increasing partial index, the estimated parameters converge to our target values.

3.3 Peak selection step

The selection of a valid peak within the spectrum is done in 4 steps:

1. Estimate the frequency of the current partial $\hat{f}_k(n)$ by using eq. (1). Use the initial $f_0(n)$ and $\beta = 0$ for the first iteration, and the updated values in all later ones.

2. Select all spectral peaks classified as main lobe within a narrow band f_b around the estimated partials frequency $\hat{f}_k(n)$:

$$\hat{f}_k(n) - pf_0(n) \leq f_b \leq \hat{f}_k(n) + pf_0(n), p = .25$$

3. If two or more peak candidates have been found within at least one frame, we apply a logarithmic amplitude weighting function using a Hann window, centered at the estimated position $\hat{f}_k(n)$, with window length f_b and select the peak with the strongest logarithmic amplitude after weighting.

4. Refine the frequency of the selected peaks by QIFFT and bias correction as proposed by Abe et al. [9].

3.4 Estimation step

With at least 3 partials within one frame, we can estimate the parameters β and $f_0(n)$ for all frames n. As shown in eq. (2), we use the squared deviation of our estimated values from the measured partial frequencies normalized with the fundamental frequency to achieve equal error surface scalings for all possible fundamental frequencies. The final objective function with normalizations according to the number of frames N and amount of partials per frame $K(n)$ is given in eq. (3).

$$R = \frac{1}{2}\left(\frac{f_k(n) - kf_0(n)\sqrt{1+k^2\beta}}{f_0(n)}\right)^2 \quad (2)$$

$$O_1 = \frac{1}{N}\sum_{n=1}^{N}\frac{1}{K(n)}\sum_{k=1}^{K(n)} R \quad (3)$$

As the objective function (3) reflects the least–mean–squared (LMS) error of all f_0-normalized deviations of our partial frequency estimations with their measured peak frequency counterparts, optimization reflects a fitting of eq. (1) to the measured data in the LMS sense. The optimization is being done by a gradient descent approach, whereas we utilize the method of the scaled conjugate gradient [10], denoted CG throughout this document, for faster convergence compared with other methods. The gradient functions for both parameters are shown in eq. (4) and (5).

$$\frac{\partial R}{\partial \beta} = -\frac{k^3}{2\sqrt{1+k^2\beta}} \quad (4)$$

$$\frac{\partial R}{\partial f_0(n)} = -\frac{f_k(n)}{f_0(n)^2} \quad (5)$$

3.5 Stop criterion

We only use two disjunctive abort criteria: If the next partial $\hat{f}_k(n)$ in the peak selection process would raise above the Nyquist frequency within one frame n or if no valid partial has been found for 3 consecutive iterations in at least one frame of the main loop. This means, the algorithm tries to use as much partials as possible of the signal, since it only stops, if the signals maximum bandwidth or some supposed noise level has been reached.

4. EVALUATION

For the evaluation we will compare the results of our proposed method with the results of the 3 algorithms mentioned in chapter 2: ICF, MAT and NMF. Our proposed method will be denoted CG in the figures. We will use an artificial data sound of inharmonic sounds, created using an additive synthesis model and inharmonicity values taken from the tessitura model for the β coefficient shown in [5] as well as the 3 piano data sets from the RWC library [11] and a piano sound set taken from the IRCAM Solo Instruments library recorded with two microphones. The artificial data set will be used to compare all β coefficient estimation algorithms with a given ground truth. For the general evaluation of all data sets we will establish a tessitura model for the evolution of the coefficient for all sound samples contained in each data set. The tessitura model for the evolution of β over the MIDI index is derived from [5] and will be used to measure the variance of each estimation algorithm to quantify its accuracy. Furthermore, we will compare the computational efficiency of all algorithms by measuring their realtime factors. For each algorithm a MATLAB™ implementation has been used therefore the realtime factors are more suitable for a comparison in between the algorithms rather than to give an indication for the performance of native implementations. For all algorithms we used equal analysis parameters to ensure all algorithms analyze exactly the same frames of the signals and as most other algorithms also need a pre-f_0 estimation, we used the same pre-f_0 for all of them. The window length for the STFT was set to 6 times the roughly estimated fundamental with 4 times spectral oversampling and a *blackman* window. As our algorithm works on several frames, we took 3 consecutive frames with a hopsize of 1/8 of the analysis window length, whereas the other algorithms analyzed the 3 frames independently.

4.1 Tessitura model of the β coefficient

The tessitura model for the β coefficient introduced in [5] is a function of the MIDI value m representing its evolution for the whole keyboard of a piano. It can be represented as the sum of two linear asymptotes in the logarithmic scale, whereas these two asymptotes are being described as Treble (b_T) and Bass bridge (b_B) and are characterized as linear functions, parametrized by its slope and constant value, such that the model $\beta_\phi(m)$ can be described as:

$$\beta_\phi(m) = e^{b_B(m)} + e^{b_T(m)} \tag{6}$$

$$= e^{(\phi_1 m + \phi_2)} + e^{(\phi_3 m + \phi_4)} \tag{7}$$

with ϕ being a vector of four elements containing the slope and constant parameters of the linear functions b_B and b_T respectively. All algorithms apart from ours estimate 3 coefficients, denoted $\hat{\beta}$, for each input sound file according to the 3 signal frames which are being used by our algorithm to estimate a single value. A curve fitting is done in a least-squares sense by minimizing the variance of the model $\beta_\phi(m)$ according to (8) with M^* representing the estimates of a single algorithm for one data set. We are using the logarithm of β as well as $\hat{\beta}$ for the objective function to account for the logarithmic behavior of the β coefficient.

$$O_2 = \frac{1}{2} \sum_m^{M^*} |\log(\hat{\beta}(m)) - \log(\beta_\phi(m))|^2 \tag{8}$$

Again we are using the scaled Conjugate Gradient method [10] to obtain the tessitura model $\beta_\phi(m)$ with minimum variance using the gradients (9) and (10) for optimizing the parameters for the functions b_B and b_T with i either being set to 1 or 3 for eq. (9) or set to 2 or 4 for eq. (10). The four initial values for vector ϕ are choosen as $[-0.09, -6.87, 0.09, -13.70]^T$.

$$\frac{\partial O_2}{\partial \phi_{1|3}} = \sum_m^{M^*} |\log(\hat{\beta}(m)) - \log(\beta_\phi(m))| \frac{m e^{(\phi_i m + \phi_{(i+1)})}}{\beta_\phi(m)} \tag{9}$$

$$\frac{\partial O_2}{\partial \phi_{2|4}} = \sum_m^{M^*} |\log(\hat{\beta}(m)) - \log(\beta_\phi(m))| \frac{e^{(\phi_{(i-1)} m + \phi_{(i)})}}{\beta_\phi(m)} \tag{10}$$

As the estimation algorithms may give highly noisy results especially for the upper pitch range we delimit the usage of $\hat{\beta}$ values to a range which is logarithmically close to the initial value by accepting only values which are smaller than ten times the initial function value and bigger than one tenth of it. This is demonstrated in fig. 3, but to finally compute the variance $\sigma^2 = 2N^{-1}O_2$ we take all N estimations of $\hat{\beta}$ into account. The variance according

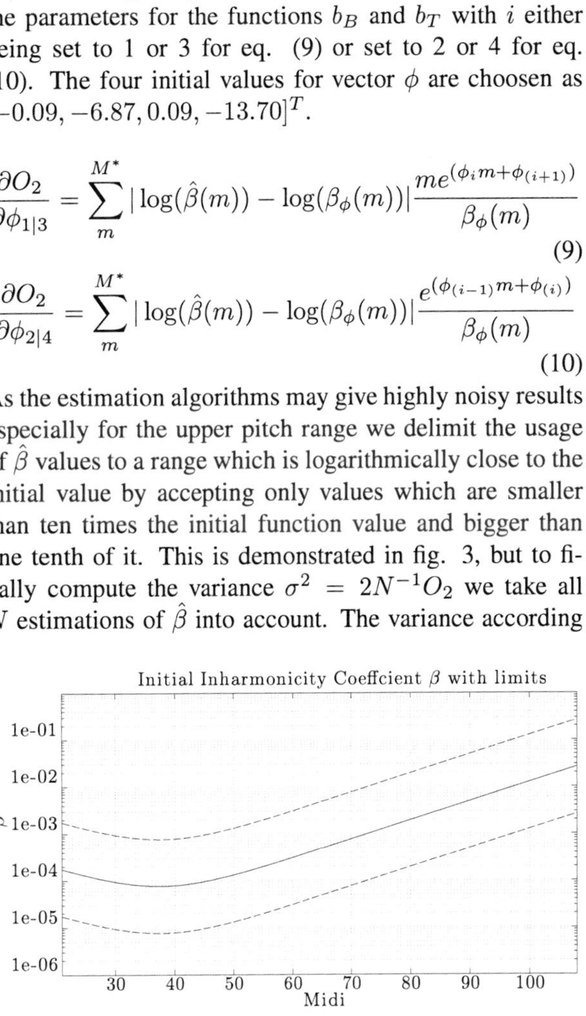

Figure 3. The initial model $\beta_\phi(m)$ (solid) and limits (dashed) for adaptation

to all estimations of $\hat{\beta}$ of one algorithm on data set can be used to determine its estimation accuracy, because we can assume the inharmonicity coefficient of one piano to roughly follow our tessitura model for β. We can further state, that the instruments original β coefficient is equal for all recordings of the same note of this instrument and constant along time. Therefore, each instrument exhibits a certain variance due to slight tuning errors of its inharmonicity. This variance is unknown and reflects the lower boundary for every estimation algorithm. As all our algorithms estimate either a single inharmonicity value per frame of each sound sample (MAT, ICF, NMF) or a single value per sound sample (CG), the more these values are varying, the less accurate this algorithm has to be. Therefore, we can use the overall variance of the inharmonicity estimations of one algorithm for one data set to determine its accuracy performance.

4.2 Evaluation on artificial data

The sounds have been generated by additive synthesis using eq. (1) to generate the partials frequencies with the β coefficients taken from the initial tessitura model $\beta_{\phi}(m)$ for each corresponding fundamental frequency, a decaying spectral envelope as well as a simple Attack–Release temporal envelope. The sounds do not include any kind of noise.

We estimated the β values with all methods for all synthesized sounds and measured their deviations from the original values used for synthesis. Fig. 4 shows the resulting relative errors as percentage of the original β value denoted $\bar{\beta}$. As can be seen in fig. 4 the MAT, NMF and CG meth-

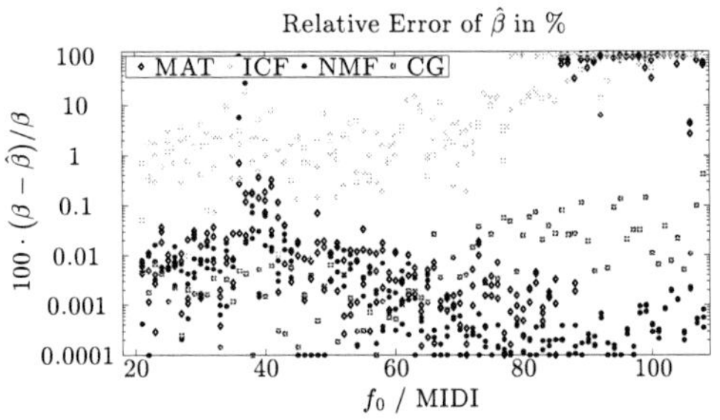

Figure 4. Error in estimation of β given as percentage.

ods outperform the ICF method with relative errors below 0.1% until MIDI index 86 (D6). Above that index, only the NMF and CG method stay below 0.1% or even drop further down. The estimated tessitura models of all algo-

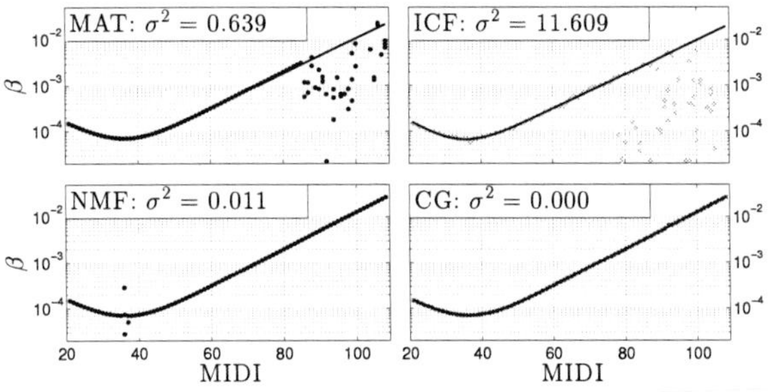

Figure 5. Estimated $\hat{\beta}$ for the artificial data set.

rithms for the artificial set are shown in fig. 5 and their resulting overall variance of the estimated $\hat{\beta}$ is depicted in fig. 6. The extremely high variance of the results for the MAT and ICF is especially caused by the low estimation accuracy for high pitches (MIDI index values above 85). The increased variance of the NMF method is due to estimation errors around MIDI index 35 at which the inharmonicity coefficient reaches its absolute minimum. Hence, our proposed CG outperforms the MAT and ICF methods significantly in terms of overall variance as it almost never shows an accuracy error of more than 0.1%.

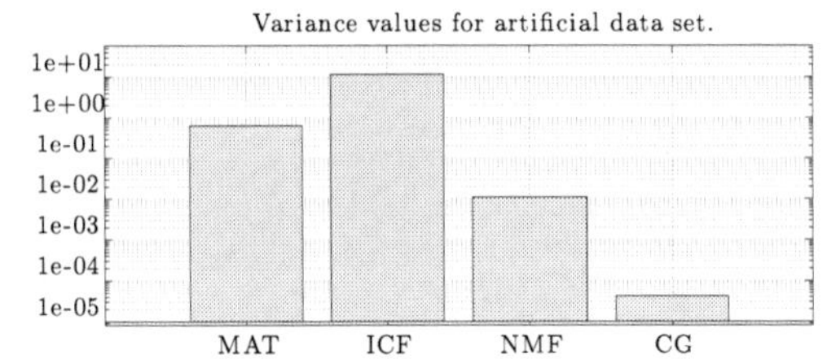

Figure 6. Variance of measurements on artificial data.

4.3 Evaluation on recorded data

The RWC piano library contains recordings of 3 different grand pianos. Each piano has been recorded for all pitches in 3 different intensity levels (*pp*, *mf* and *ff*). The piano set of the IRCAM Solo instruments library also contains recordings for all pitches but with up to 7 intensity levels per pitch and as it has been recorded with 2 discrete channels, we treat these separately. It can be seen in the figures

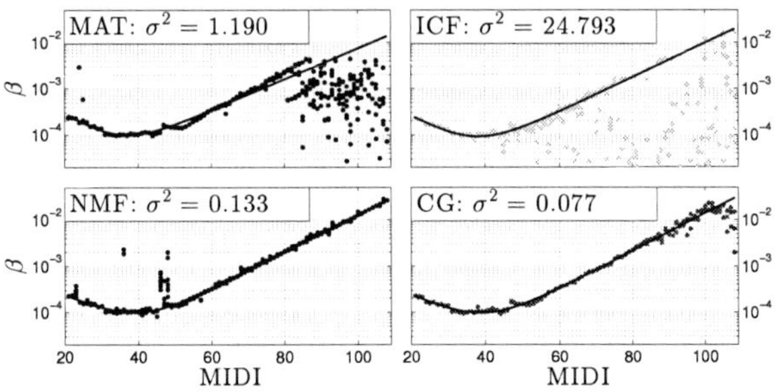

Figure 7. Estimated $\hat{\beta}$ for RWC piano 1

7 to 11, that the NMF as well as our proposed CG method show especially in the upper pitch range significantly less noise in the estimation of $\hat{\beta}$ compared to the ICF and MAT methods. This seems to be caused by the adaptive noise level used by the NMF method and the peak classification used by CG for selecting reasonable partials. Also, the use

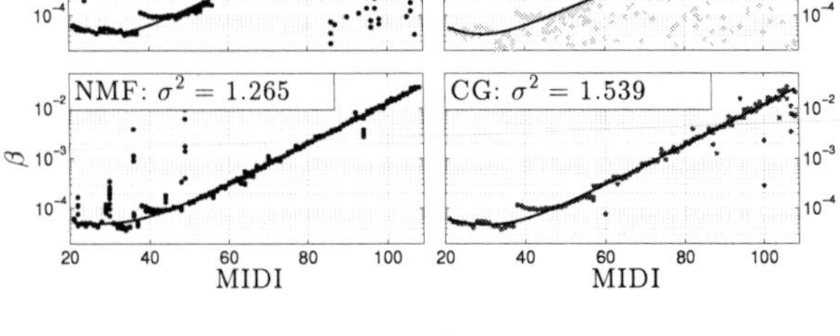

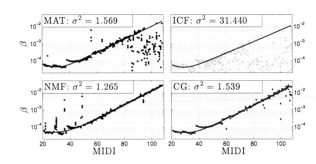

Figure 8. Estimated $\hat{\beta}$ for RWC piano 2

of a Kulback-Leibler-divergence with euclidean distance

(NMF) and a minimum variance method (CG) for estimating β shows to be clearly superior to a heuristic grid search (ICF) or a median method (MAT). The CG method only shows a slightly higher variance for the RWC 2 data set, whereas it outperforms NMF on all other data sets up to a factor of 20 for the RWC 3 data set . The overall estimation performance is demonstrated in fig. 12. Here, the averaged variance values from all data sets are shown as bars, whereas their minimum and maximum values are given as error bars. It can be observed, that the CG method has the least variance closely followed by the NMF method. The ICF method is far from being accurate, whereas the MAT method rates third. In terms of computational performance, as shown in 13, the MAT method is by far the fastest method, but it clearly lacks in estimation accuracy in the upper pitch range, whereas our proposed method CG outperforms NMF which showed similar estimation results as well as the ICF method.

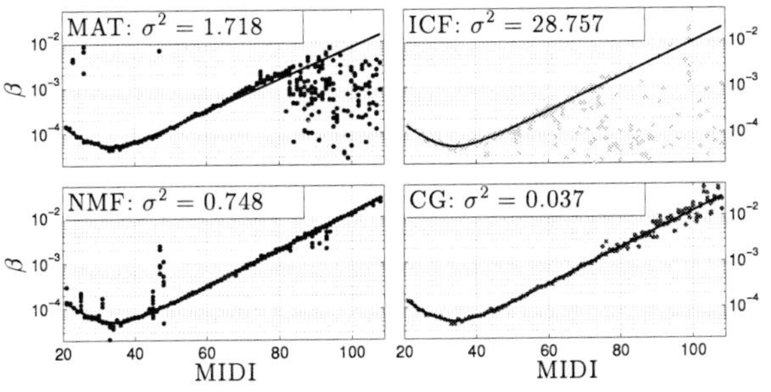

Figure 9. Estimated $\hat{\beta}$ for RWC piano 3

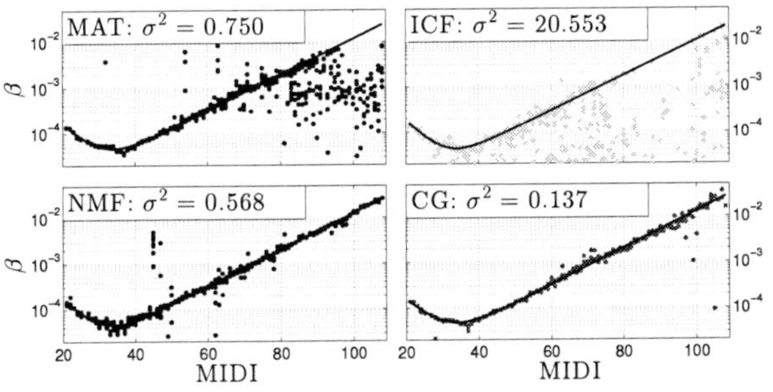

Figure 10. Estimated $\hat{\beta}$ for IRCAM Solo Instrument piano left channel

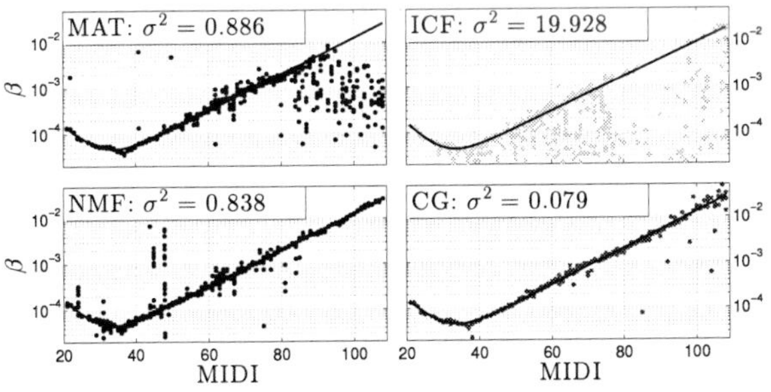

Figure 11. Estimated $\hat{\beta}$ for IRCAM Solo Instrument piano right channel

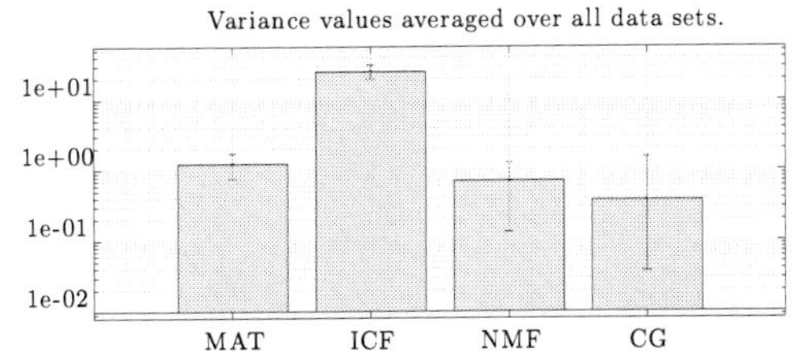

Figure 12. Averaged variance of measurements on real world data according to the tessitura model. The error bars indicate the minimum and maximum variance values among all data sets.

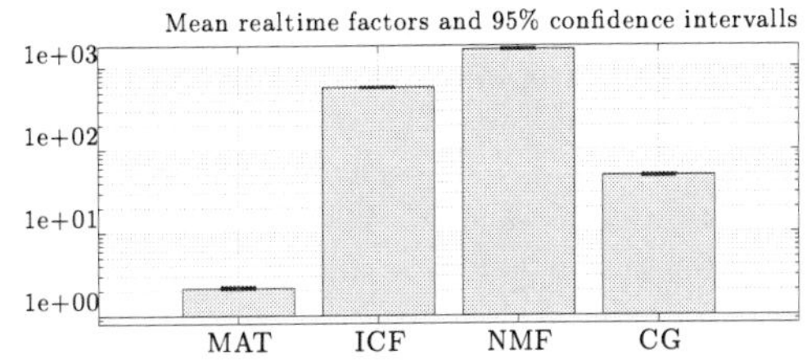

Figure 13. Processing real-time factors for all 4 algorithms averaged for all data sets with 95% confidence intervalls.

5. CONCLUSION

In this paper we gave an overview about three recent approaches (ICF, MAT and NMF) for the estimation of the inharmonicity coefficient and fundamental frequency of inharmonic instrument sounds. We pointed out some issues which are not well addressed in these previous methods and showed possible solutions for these drawbacks with our proposed algorithm. In the evaluation we have shown that for synthetic data with known inharmonicity our proposed algorithm works below an average estimation error in β of 0.1% which clearly outperforms the ICF and MAT method and showed similar accuracy as the NMF method. For real world signals our proposed method again significantly outperforms the MAT and ICF algorithms and showed superior performance in computational efficiency compared with the NMF method which showed a similar estimation accuracy.

Hence, this article shows that a peak selection algorithm with adaptive noise and sidelobe rejection paired with a minimum variance based parameter estimation is a suitable strategy for a robust detection of the inharmonicity coefficient and a signals fundamental frequency.

6. ACKNOWLEDGEMENTS

The authors would like to thank the authors of [3], namely Matthieu Hodgkinson as well as the authors of [4], namely François Rigaud for sharing their sources for the evaluation and their precious help sorting out problems using them. The authors also like to thank the numerous reviewers for their precious remarks and helpful suggestions for improving this document.

This research has been financed as part of the french ANR project Sample Orchestrator 2.

7. REFERENCES

[1] H.Fletcher, E. D. Blackham, and R. Stratton, "Quality of piano tones," *J. Acoust. Soc. Am.*, vol. 34, no. 6, pp. 749 – 761, 1962.

[2] A. Galembo and A. Askenfelt, "Signal representation and estimation of spectral parameters by inharmonic comb filters with application to the piano," *IEEE Transactions On Speech And Audio Processing*, vol. 7, no. 2, pp. 197 – 203, March 1999.

[3] M. Hodgkinson, J. Wiang, J. Timoney, and V. Lazzarini, "Handling inharmonic series with median-adjustive trajectories," in *12th International Conference on Digital Audio Effects (DAFx-09)*, September 2009.

[4] F. Rigaud, B. David, and L. Daudet, "Piano sound analysis using non-negative matrix factorization with inharmonicity constraint," in *Proc. of the 20th European Signal Processing Conference (EUSIPCO 2012)*, August 2012, pp. 2462–2466.

[5] ——, "A parametric model of piano tuning," in *14th International Conference on Digital Audio Effects (DAFx-11)*, September 2011.

[6] J. Rauhala, H.-M. Lehtonen, and V. Valimäki, "Fast automatic inharmonicity estimation algorithm," *J. Acoust. Soc. Am.*, vol. 121, no. 5, pp. EL184 – EL189, May 2007.

[7] A. de Cheveigné and H. Kawahara, "YIN, a fundamental frequency estimator for speech and music," *The Journal of the Acoustical Society of America*, vol. 111, no. 4, pp. 1917–1930, 2002.

[8] M. Zivanovic, A. Röbel, and X. Rodet, "A new approach to spectral peak classification," in *Proc. of the 12th European Signal Processing Conference (EUSIPCO)*, Vienna, Austria, Septembre 2004, pp. 1277–1280. [Online]. Available: http://articles.ircam.fr/textes/Zivanovic04a/

[9] M. Abe and J. Smith, "CQIFFT: Correcting bias in a sinusoidal parameter estimator based on quadratic interpolation of FFT magnitude peaks," Stanford University, Department of Music, Tech. Rep. STAN-M-117, 2004. [Online]. Available: https://ccrma.stanford.edu/STANM/stanms/stanm117/stanm117.pdf

[10] M. F. Møller, "A scaled conjugate gradient algorithm for fast supervised learning," *NEURAL NETWORKS*, vol. 6, no. 4, pp. 525–533, 1993.

[11] M. Goto and T. Nishimura, "Rwc music database: Music genre database and musical instrument sound database," in *ISMIR*, 2003, pp. 229–230.

LARGE DATA SETS & RECOMMENDER SYSTEMS: A FEASIBLE APPROACH TO LEARNING MUSIC?

Jamie Gabriel
Macquarie Univeristy
jamie.gabriel@mq.edu.au

ABSTRACT

One of the critical challenges in music teaching is providing ways for students to search easily across very large amounts of music data, in order that they can build intuition and gain experience around the ways in which different music styles are comprised. This paper demonstrates how MusicXML can be used to create large music data sets that can be utilized for searching and recommendation, in order to facilitate music learning.

1. INTRODUCTION

This paper will outline a methodology to facilitate exploration across large bodies of musical information. The methodology will utilize the data-format MusicXML, showing that it can by used to create data sets that are both amenable to searching, and for deriving recommendations. The motivation behind this methodology is to enhance the understanding that music learners can gain in regard to the mechanics that underlie different music styles, and to facilitate the exploration of music for those who have limited experience with complex music scores.

Having access to extremely large corpuses of music, rendered as data, is a growing phenomenon, especially in recent years. The field of Music Information Retrieval (MIR), here characterized as 'having access to increased bodies of music and the accompanying challenges of how to extract meaningful music content information' [1] is growing rapidly. Solutions that, up until recently, have been regarded as impossible (such as the automated transcription of complex music [2,3,4] and the automated optical recognition of music scores for the purpose of converting this into MIDI and MusicXML data [5] are becoming a reality. Music is also far more available than it has been in the past: there is a vast and growing amount of music scores and music recordings to be found online (seen in such initiatives as the IMSLP and Petrucci Music Library [6]. Additionally, the belief that the transcription of recorded music can only be accurately achieved through manual means is increasingly being challenged by a growing number of technological solutions that can accomplish this task [7]. The changing nature by which music data is obtained is part of the wider technological phenomenon of 'Big Data', characterised by vast data sets becoming available and being amenable to nuanced interrogation [8]. However, with the increased access to music in the form of data comes the increased challenge in finding ways to understand and iterate through this data.

This paper will show how MusicXML can be prepared as a mineable data set, provide examples of how data search functionality can be implemented across this data, and demonstrate a way in which prediction and recommendation can be implemented. It will suggest further applications and research that are applicable to both music teaching and music prediction. The code for this paper has been written in Python and can be downloaded and perused at the code repository service, GitHub[1].

2. DATA PREPARATION

MusicXML is a well-formed subset of the XML data format and was purpose designed to capture, as a data set, the various attributes that can be seen on a music score (in terms of western musical notation). Currently the data attributes number around 650, and include such things as: clef, time signature, tempo, lyrics, written annotations, part names etc. Since its introduction in 2004, MusicXML has become 'the most quickly adopted symbolic music interchange format since MIDI' [9]. MusicXML is now well established in the Music Information Retrieval field as a promising vehicle by which to drive the design and inform the data-stores of music related applications [5].

To prepare the MusicXML data-set under consideration, the data was first parsed using the python Music21 module, an API developed at MIT specifically for music analysis [10]. This allowed the MusicXML data to be transformed into a nested Python dictionary structure. The initial testing set of MusicXML data (forming the corpus) consisted of the music scores of two pieces of music: a movement from a Beethoven String quartet and a transcription of Keith Jarrett jazz piano solo[2]. Each of these pieces of music was divided into logically named parts, where each part can be regarded as what occurs on a single music stave on the score. For the Beethoven ex-

[1] https://github.com/jgab3103/music-app

[2] Beethoven's String Quartet No. 2, Op. 59, 4th Movement, and a transcription of Keith Jarrett solo on Autumn Leaves, taken from the Tokyo 1996 live album.

ample, the parts were named, vln_1, vln_2, vla, and vlc, signifying the instrumental parts within a string quartet.

Creating the parts in the jazz example was more complex, and the MusicXML data was prepared using not only the transcription but also the jazz lead sheet of the song under consideration, which listed the song's harmonic progression. Each voice in the harmonic progression was given its own part, consisting of root, third, fifth, seventh, ninth, eleventh and thirteenth. The transcribed solo was given its own part also. A visualization of this data, prior to being rendered into MusicXML, can be seen in Figure 1.

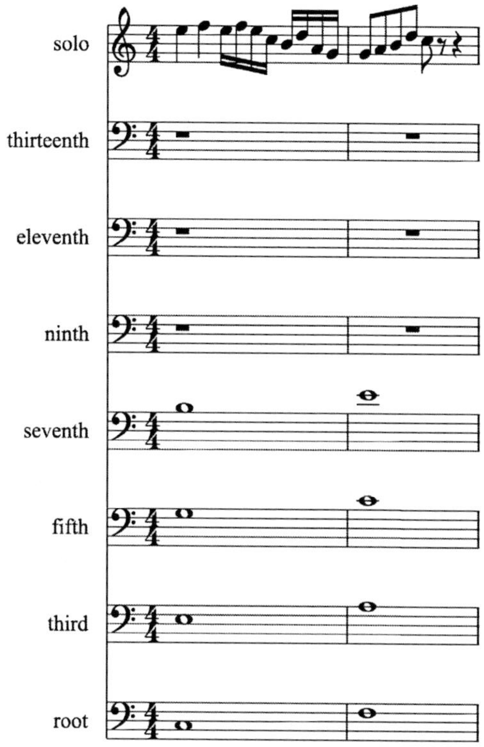

Figure 1

Each part was then broken up into a series of events (either note events or rest events) and these events can best be intuited as any occurring note or rest in a musical passage on a given music stave. Information regarding the note or rest event's duration, the midi-frequency (listed as -1 if it was a rest event) and the note or rest event's position was captured. The position of the note was regarded as being relative to the bar of music so, for example, if the time signature of the part was currently 4/4, and the note or rest event occurred on the 3rd beat of the bar, the value would be captured as .75 (being three quarters of the way through a 4/4 bar. The resulting data structure parts and note and rest events can be seen in Figure 2.

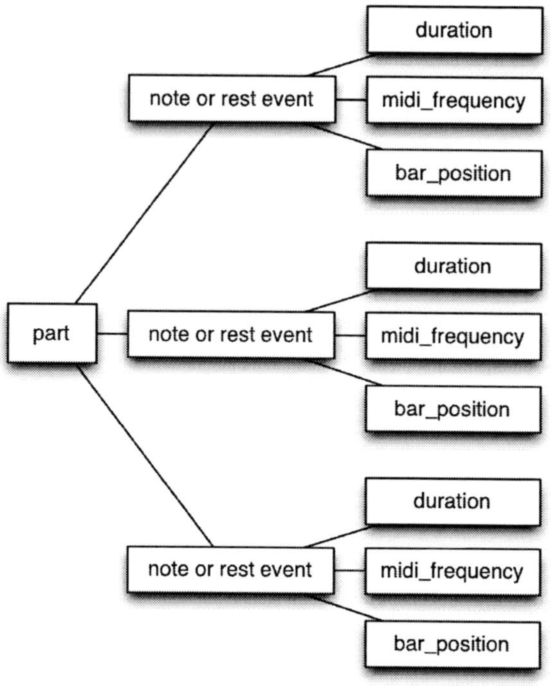

Figure 2

To facilitate the searching of this data set, each note or rest event was given a unique name that could act as an index. This name was created from a concatenation of various elements that were extracted from the parsed data. These elements were: 1) the bar in which the note or rest event occurred; 2) the relative position in the bar the note or rest event occurred and 3) the current tempo (in beats per minute). An example of such a concatenated string is "123_.75_120", here indicating the 123rd bar in a particular part, located at a position three quarters between the start and end of the bar, and having a current tempo of 120 beats per minute.

Although the sample data set is here quite limited, it is important to note that that this data set could be arbitrarily large. It could be all Beethoven's string quartets, or all string quartets, or all of Keith Jarrett's jazz solos. Regardless of what style pieces of music are perceived to be, they here form part of the same corpus.

During the data preparation stage a number of utility functions were also created. The most notable of these were, firstly, a graphing function (using Python's Matplotlib library) that allowed the visualization of a series of note or rest events within a part, similar to the piano roll view editor often found in digital audio workstation (DAW) software. Secondly, a write-to-MIDI function was created using the Python library MIDIutil that allowed the data set to be written to an output midi file, which can be heard, or easily converted back into MusicXML format in software packages such as Sibelius and MuseScore.

Considering the vast array of attributes that can be found in MusicXML as well as the sonic qualities of audio music generally, it is worth noting that there is a great deal that has been left out during the creation of the data set. Information regarding things such as timbre, score annotation and dynamics are absent. The data set has been purpose designed as a searchable index of frequencies, the relative time at which frequencies occur, and the speed (i.e. tempo) at which they occur. Collecting just this information is enough to inform a highly useful search engine.

3. DATA SEARCH TO FACILITATE LEARNING

With the data structured in the manner above, where each note or rest event was indexed, it became possible to search in order to seek specific and similar musical situations. It became possible to look for the occurrences of specific chords or harmonic progressions across a large corpus of music. It also became possible to see how things such as different tempo could influence note choice, or to examine similar passages in different key signatures. The design of the data set allowed multi-parameter searching across parameters such as piece name, part name, tempo, duration, time-signature, position in bar and time signature.

As an example of the kind of learning that could be facilitated with this data set, consider a student of jazz who wishes to search for all instances of minor 7 flat 5 chord that occurs in all jazz examples within a given corpus, regardless of key. The motivating question of the student is to gain an understanding of how different musicians improvise on this chord. To undertake such a search, it is possible to iterate through the parts, firstly finding any part named 'root'. If this part is found, it is possible to compare the distance between midi frequencies of the root part to other parts of the same piece of music (here the third, fifth and seventh part) that occur at the same time (i.e. same bar and position in bar). If the distances indicated are 3, 6 and 10 (respectively indicating a minor third, flattened fifth, and flattened seventh), a suitable candidate has been found, and can be returned to the user.

As an alternate learning example, consider a student of orchestration wishes to look across a large corpus, which could include all the orchestral works of Prokofiev, Mahler, Stravinsky, and Ravel. The student might wish to seek all the examples where there is a solo cello part that occurs in the cello's upper range (i.e. above G4), where the tempo is between 60bpm and 80bpm. This would return all examples of passages of solo cello in a slow tempo setting, and would allow the student to gain an intuition into the different ways composers write for solo cello at this tempo and range. Rather than relying on standard rules of thumb about how to orchestrate in this setting (i.e. that the violas will often take on the traditional role of cellos when the cello is playing in a higher range at a slow tempo) this provides the student with concrete examples and intuitions about those times composers choose to move away from things that are typically done.

These types of searches, while useful, are fairly simplistic. A student may not wish to have to rely on part names from which to derive information. What if a student, rather than seeking all minor 7 flat 5 chords in jazz pieces within the corpus, was seeking all instances of minor 7 flat 5 chords that occur, regardless of how they are voiced. (i.e. in root position or inversion). Because a minor 7th flat 5 chord can be characterised by the set of distances between the midi-frequencies of various parts, it is possible to calculate this, and search for it. For example, a C minor 7 flat 5 chord, consisting of the notes C, E flat, G flat and B flat can be characterised by the list of distances that occur between each note, in this case [3, 3, 4, 2] seen in Figure 3.

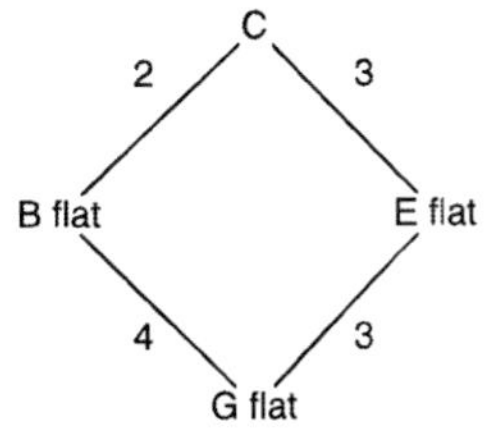

Figure 3

Note that in order to be able to locate a C minor 7 flat 5 chord from any voicing or inversion that may appear across various parts, the various frequencies under consideration need to first be collected and arranged in the manner of Figure 4, building chord structures by successively taking the note that is the shortest distance away. For example, if the note C is found in one part, and the notes B flat, E Flat and G flat are found in other parts at the same time, the chord can then be constructed by taking the note the shortest distance away from C (the B flat), and then by taking the note the shortest distance from the B flat (the G flat) and finally appending the E flat. This creates an ordered list of distances (being [3, 3, 4, 2]) that can be used to define a minor 7 flat 5 chord. If the chord appears in first inversion, the ordered list will hold, simply starting at a different point and wrapping around (becoming the list of distances of [3,4,2,3]).

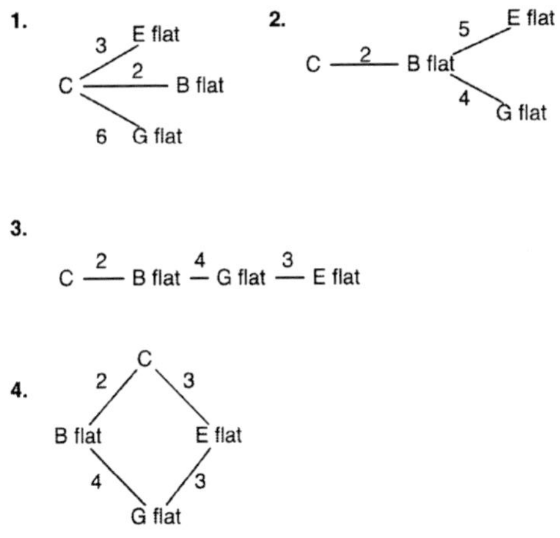

Figure 4

This kind of search makes it possible to interrogate the corpus in order to seek occurrences of a particular chord type, regardless of its voicing or the parts in which it occurs. One of the benefits of this type of searching is that it allows students to explore similar sonorities regardless of the style in which they are occurring, and hear different chord structures in different contexts. If, for example, the corpus included all of Wagner's operas as well as a large set of jazz improvisations, this search picks up not only the minor 7 flat 5 chords in the jazz examples, but the minor 7 flat 5 chords found in the opening bars in Tristan and Isolde (the so called "Tristan chord"). This would afford students a powerful insight into the ways in which similar sonorities are handled in different musical settings and styles.

As a final learning example, consider a scenario where a student wishes to find all examples of a minor 7th flat 5 chord that is followed by a dominant chord, in a II-V progression (i.e. in the key of C minor, a D minor 7th flat 5 chord followed by a G Dominant 7 chord). Using the same procedure as above to locate the chord structure, a dominant chord can be found. The challenge lies in finding where these two chords form a II-V progression. This can be accomplished by examining the distance between the frequencies located at the beginning of the set of distances characterizing the minor 7 flat 5 chord, and the frequency located at the beginning of the set of distances characterizing the dominant chord.

Searching data in this way allows some exciting possibilities in music pedagogy to start to emerge. It becomes far simpler to expose music students to correlations between different genres; it becomes far quicker to iterate through many differing examples. It allows students with different musical backgrounds (i.e. those with limited exposure to navigating complex orchestral scores) to explore different types of music.

Like any typical implementation of a search engine, it is also possible to keep a search history so students can track the things that have interested them most. If the database is linked to audio examples it also becomes possible to provide customized listening to students based on their searches (i.e. consider a scenario in where the examples returned from a student's search of all minor 7 flat 5 chords can be ported to an iPod or similar device). Finally, this type of searching allows user profiling to take place, (a growing phenomena preference systems [11,12]), so it becomes conceivable to data mine the searches that students undertake in order to create a shareable profile of those pieces of music in the corpus they prefer.

4. GOING FURTHER THAN SEARCHING: RECOMMENDATION

While it is useful to be able to implement a search engine for music data, is it possible to go further? Often it is productive to not only provide music students with a range of similar examples, but also with a mechanism by which to be able to directly compare their own work to composers and improvisers whose works they are studying. Consider the problem of teaching students how to carry out counterpoint or multi-part harmony. Theorist and educator Kent Kennan notes that it is critical in such a situation, to ensure students understand that, a 'good melodic line [consists of] a sense of direction and a climax point, both of which contribute to a clear cut and interesting melodic contour…[as well as a] pleasing balance between conjunct and disjunct motion and ascending and descending motion' [13]. This is typical statement of many instructive music texts. Yet what does it actually mean? Qualities such 'as sense of direction' and 'climax point' are subjective. It is possible then, to take a different route? What if students were placed in a position, whether they are composing or improvising, of being able to view a possible set of choices of the next note in a phrase whilst they are in the process of creating a phrase, given what is happening in the corpus as a whole?

Using this data set to build some kind of recommender system is in some ways a complicated enterprise. The data set is good in the sense that it has no issues one would usually expect in a large data set such as data sparsity or any kind of data inflation. However at the same time, this data set is problematic. The first reason for this is that, if the data set is normalized and plotted in multi-dimensional space, note and rest events that are quite different in terms of their behavior through the corpus would sometimes cluster together. Consider the notes at (a.) and (b.) in Figure 5. They are very similar in some respects (i.e. frequency and duration), however in musical passages on-beats (seen here at a.) and off-beats (seen here at b.) tend to behave quite differently.

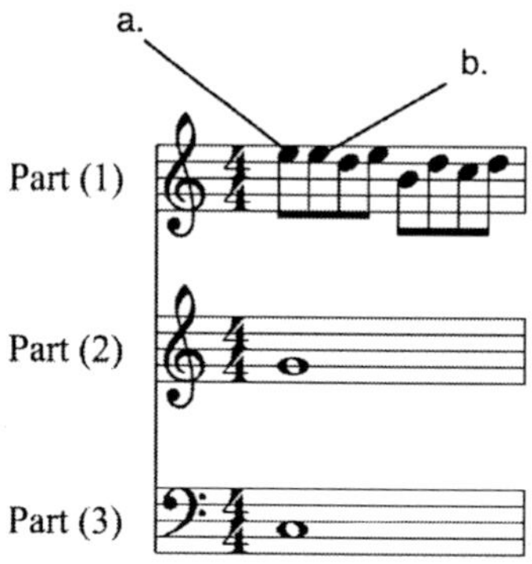

Figure 5

The second issue arises when considering those data points that should be regarded as similar, yet do not appear clustered closely when plotted in multi-dimensional space. Consider an example that was same in all respects as that listed in Figure 5, but transposed to key of F sharp major. Even though these would be very similar passages they would appear as markedly different. Related to this, consider how different absolute pitches operate depending on the setting in which they occur. The note middle C could be found in a passage that is in the key of G Major, C minor, or E flat major and would behave in markedly different ways. Consequently, being able to use this data in a predictive manner requires that these issues somehow be accommodated.

Rather than calculating distances between note and rest events in multi-dimensional space, one alternative approach to his problem could be to collect certain attributes found in the data set, locate them in a tuple, and then find identical tuples across the corpus with a view to creating a list of the next possible note and rest events these tuples could lead to. It would then be possible to use weighted probability to calculate the likelihood that any note or rest event defined with an identical tuple could lead to certain other notes.

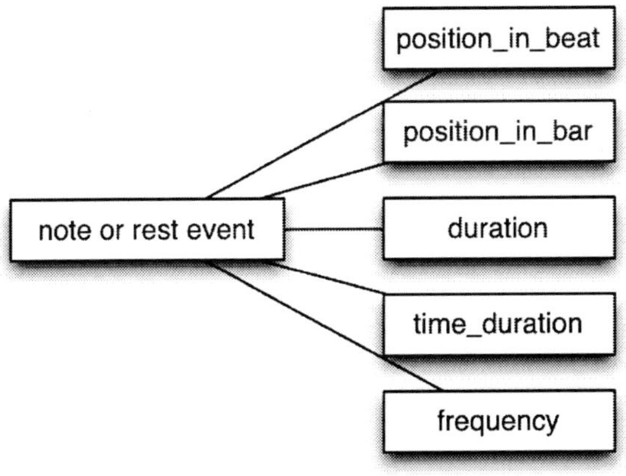

Figure 6

An example of a data structure to accommodate this is listed in Figure 6 and utilizes the same information found in the data set already converted from MusicXML. The attributes 'position_in_beat', 'position_in_bar' and 'duration', are drawn directly from the data set. The 'time_duration_of_beat' attribute is an actual time value, calculated using duration and tempo (being duration multiplied by tempo divided by 60).

Although previously the data set has utilized the attribute 'midi_frequency' to denote frequency, to implement recommendations, frequency will instead be denoted only in terms of a list of the minimized distances to other frequencies occurring at the same time in different parts of the same piece of music.

For example, if the note or rest event under consideration is the quarter note E (seen at (a.) in the Figure 7), its frequency is calculated by measuring the distance (modulo 12) between this note and any other notes occurring at the same in different parts time (seen at (b.) and (c.) Note also that this distance is minimized: the distance to the other notes (here being a C and a G) is the distance to the closest C and closest G).

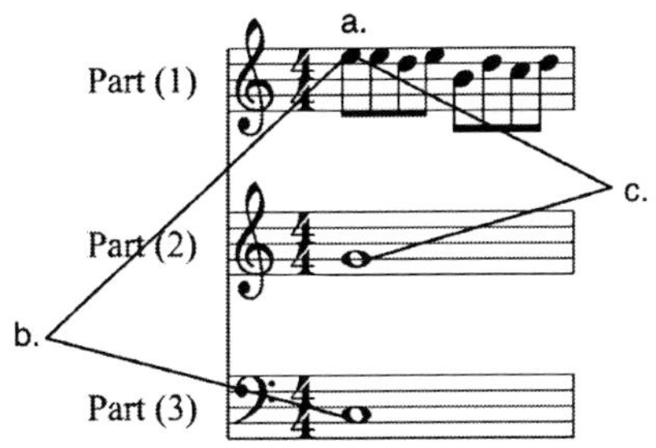

Figure 7

The data set is then converted into a set of tuples, an example of which can be seen in Figure 8. When looking over the entire corpus, it now becomes possible to find identical points at which this tuple occurs and to then investigate what happens next. If, for example, one hundred examples of the tuple were found across the corpus leading to three possibilities as to which note or rest events that could occur next, this could be returned to the user as a weighted probability to be used as recommendation.

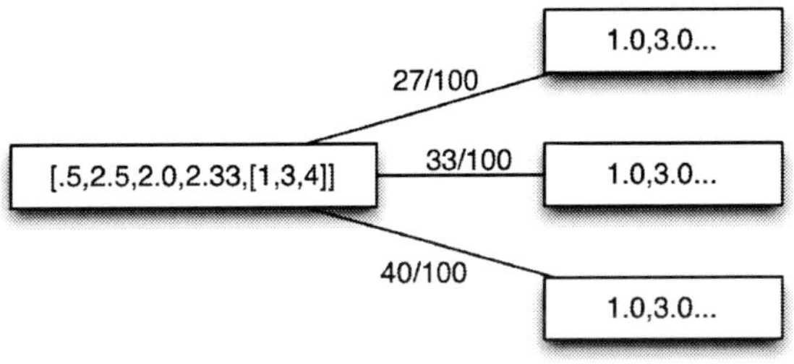

Figure 8

This is perhaps one of the simplest ways to differentiate between different note and rest events in a corpus in order to introduce a notion of recommendation. However it does make it possible to discern similar data points across the corpus and to see where these data points lead.

There are of course issues here. It is not an ideal solution to simply return to a recommendation based on the highest probability, as this will certainly limit variety. Additionally, if every note or rest event in the corpus can be rendered as a tuple upon which recommendations can be made, when there are tuples occurring at the same time (derived from note or rest events in different parts that occur at the same time), which tuple's recommendation should be given precedence? The challenge with this approach is how to adjust the probability weightings. Possible solutions could include utilizing different parts of the corpus to influence probability weightings, or identifying common sequences of tuples, which could suggest recurring themes in the music and adjusting the weights based on this.

The possibility of suggesting recommendation based on the data set offers some exciting opportunities. Increasingly, music software packages (such as Logic Pro,

Cubase etc.) provide composers with a range of automated music creation tools (such as pre-recorded loops) to facilitate composition. The approach outlined above introduces the possibility of taking this a step further: to allow composers to be presented with different options around how their compositions might unfold as they write them, and even to have these recommendations be derived from the behavior of their own customized corpus. Additionally, utilizing a data set drawn from MusicXML has ramifications for the way in which music preference systems can be designed. Consider music streaming services such as Pandora, which rely on the manual categorization of different types of music in order that it can be data-mined: is it feasible to use MusicXML data mining to speed up this process?

5. CONCLUSION

This paper has demonstrated a way in which MusicXML data can be used in order to create a mineable data set. It has shown how search functionality can be implemented across the data set and how it can be used for recommendation. This way of interacting with music provides a means by which students can gain very deep insights into a large corpus of music and develop strong musical intuitions based on concrete examples.

6. REFERENCES

[1] J.J. Bosch, J. Janer, F. Fuhrmann, P. Herrera, "A comparison of sound segregation techniques for predominant instrument recognition in musical audio signals", in ISMIR, 2012

[2] A.P. Klapuri, "Automatic music transcription as we know it today", Journal of New Music Research, Vol. 33, Issue 3, 2004

[3] E. Benetos, A. Klapuri, and S. Dixon. Score-informed transcription for automatic piano tutoring. In *EUSIPCO*, 2012.

[4] A. Hankinson, J.A Burgoyne, G. Viglienso, A. Porter, J. Thompson, W. Liu, R. Chiu and I. Fuginaga, "Digitial document image retrieval using optical music recognition, in ISMIR 2012

[5] E. Gomez, F.Canadas, J.Salamon, J. Bonada, P.Vera and P.Cabanas, "Predominantly fundamental frequency estimation vs. singing voice separation for the automatic transcription of accompanied Flamenco music", in ISMIR 2012

[6] V. Sebastien, H. Ralambondrainy, O. Sebastien, and N. Conruyt, "Score Analyzer: Automatically determining scores difficulty level for instrumental e-learning" in ISMIR 2012

[7] IMSLP, *Petrucci Music Library,* last viewed 30th March 2013, http://imslp.org/

[8] E. J. Humphrey, J. P. Bello and Y. Lacun, "Moving beyond feature design: deep architectures and automatic feature learning in music informatics" in ISMIR 2012.

[9] E. Dumbill, *Planning for Big Data,* O'Reilly Media, 2012.

[10] *Music21: a toolkit for computer-aided musicology,* last viewed 30th March 2013, http://mit.edu/music21/

[11] M. Good, "MusicXML in Practice: Issues in Translation & Analysis", in Procceedings in the first International Conference MAX 2002: music using XML.

[12] M. Schedl, A. Flexer, "Putting the user in the center of music information retrieval", in ISMIR, 2012

[13] K. Kennan, *Counterpoint,* (4th Edition), Pearson, 1998, p.34.

Comparing Timbre-based Features for Musical Genre Classification

Martin Hartmann, Pasi Saari, Petri Toiviainen and Olivier Lartillot
Finnish Centre of Excellence in Interdisciplinary Music Research, Department of Music, University of Jyväskylä
[firstname].[lastname]@jyu.fi

ABSTRACT

People can accurately classify music based on its style by listening to less than half a second of audio. This has motivated efforts to build accurate predictive models of musical genre based upon short-time musical descriptions. In this context, perceptually relevant features have been considered crucial but only little research has been conducted in this direction. This study compared two timbral features for supervised classification of musical genres: 1) the Mel-Frequency Cepstral Coefficients (MFCC), coming from the speech domain and widely used for music modeling purposes; and 2) the more recent Sub-Band Flux (SBF) set of features which has been designed specifically for modeling human perception of polyphonic musical timbre. Differences in performance between models were found, suggesting that the SBF feature set is more appropriate for musical genre classification than the MFCC set. In addition, spectral fluctuations at both ends of the frequency spectrum were found to be relevant for discrimination between musical genres. The results of this study give support to the use of perceptually motivated features for musical genre classification.

Introduction

Humans are very accurate at arranging music into genre classes, even when pieces were listened for the first time. Further, the correct genre might not be known by listeners, but they could still affirm to what genres a piece of music would definitely not belong to. In fact, less than half a second of music is enough information for people to classify the type of music with great accuracy and identify other information such as title and artist [1, 2].

This brings the question of how people perceive and recognize musical styles and what are the descriptions in the music that make it possible to categorically decide that a given song belongs to a specific genre. In other words, the question is how can humans confidently build hypotheses about the style of musical pieces based on such a limited evidence. It seems that the vertical structure of the music or short-time descriptions of musical polyphonic timbre could help us to understand these fascinating perceptual processes. However, it is not easy to build accurate predictive models of musical higher-level knowledge based on musical timbre descriptions. One reason is the lack of an acoustic explanation of polyphonic timbre. Pitch and loudness can be described as high or low, but musical timbre cannot be directly measured this way since it is possibly composed of multiple perceptual dimensions [3], such as dryness, brightness, or fullness. A second reason for this difficulty refers to the indirect path between musical descriptors and what is actually understood by humans about the musical content. In the particular case of content-based music information retrieval (MIR), this "semantic gap" refers to the insufficiency of low-level information extracted from the musical signal to arrange music based on cultural meanings and interpretations shared by communities [4]. Despite these problems, plenty of approaches to music genre classification have been suggested for more than a decade.

The aim of this study is to compare the performance of two timbre-based features for supervised music genre classification. The *mel-frequency cepstral coefficients* (MFCC) [5] come from the domain of speech and have been widely used for multiple music modeling purposes, whereas the *sub-band flux* set of features (SBF) has been recently suggested [6] and it is designed specifically for musical polyphonic timbre modeling. A main premise in this study is that perceptually relevant timbre-based features can help us understand better the acoustic foundation of polyphonic musical timbre and alleviate the constraints of the semantic gap in music genre classification. The performance of these two descriptors was comprehensively inspected using different data sets, feature combinations and learning algorithms for feature selection and classification.

1. BACKGROUND

Genre classification is widely studied in MIR perhaps because musical genres have been historically important in music stores and libraries for categorization based on essential similarities. In the digital era, automatic genre classification offers applications outside scientific areas, for example in radio playlists, music database systems or for content tagging in social networking services.

The task of genre classification has been reviewed, for example, in [7]. A great variety of musical features has been evaluated for music genre classification based on audio signal. Commonly extracted features are timbral, rhythmic and melodic [7]. The best results for this task seem to be obtained using timbre-based feature extraction. For example [8] obtained one of the highest performances for

Feature	Frequency Range (Hz)
Sub-band No. 1	0 - 50
Sub-band No. 2	50 - 100
Sub-band No. 3	100 - 200
Sub-band No. 4	200 - 400
Sub-band No. 5	400 - 800
Sub-band No. 6	800 - 1600
Sub-band No. 7	1600 - 3200
Sub-band No. 8	3200 - 6400
Sub-band No. 9	6400 - 12800
Sub-band No. 10	12800 - 22050

Table 1: Sub-Band Flux frequency ranges.

the data sets analyzed in this study using a feature extraction method that roughly consisted of the computation of modulation spectra from timbre-based features. There has been also research on combinations based on different musical representations, for example [9] using chord transition rules together with spectral, rhythmic and melodic features. As regards the number of features used for classification, it is important to reduce the feature space of models to ease their interpretation and avoid over-fitting, which might arise e.g. due to data noise. For instance, feature selection based on genre separation ability has been implemented to evaluate timbre features for music clustering [10].

Mel-Frequency Cepstral Coefficients

The MFCCs are widely used in plenty of MIR tasks to discard pitch information and describe the spectral shape of the musical signal. This set of features was designed in the 70s for speech recognition purposes [5] and were later implemented in music modeling [11]. Due to their widespread use, MFCCs are often selected as a timbral feature benchmark, so it is common to compare new timbre-based features against the MFCCs. For example, non-negative matrix factorization of spectrograms were introduced for genre classification and their performance was assessed against results obtained using MFCCs [12].

Sub-Band Flux

The SBF set of features is a descriptor of perceived polyphonic musical timbre and was pioneered by [6]. The set represents frequency and amplitude fluctuations as a function of time in ten octave-scaled frequency channels. High correlations between this feature set and perceptual ratings of polyphonic timbre were found in the study by [6]. 35 participants rated 100 very short musical excerpts using bipolar timbre semantic scales (Strong-Weak, Empty-Full, and so forth). Using factor analysis, the results were grouped into three perceptual dimensions: *Brightness*, *Activity* and *Fullness*. A regression analysis showed that some SBFs explained optimally these dimensions. Similar results were also found in a cross-cultural setting [13], and [14] recently found high correlations between SBFs and movement features in a study on music-induced movement.

Data Set	GTZAN	ISMIR04
Genre classes	blues (100) classical (100) country (100) disco (100) hip hop (100) jazz (100) metal (100) pop (100) reggae (100) rock (100)	classical (320) electronic (115) jazz/blues (26) metal/punk (45) rock/pop (101) world (122)
Excerpts	1000	729

Table 2: Music data sets used for data collection.

Primary Set	Features
SBF_{μ}	10
MFCC_{μ}	13
$\text{SBF}_{\mu\sigma}$	20
$\text{MFCC}_{\mu}+\text{SBF}_{\mu}$	23
$\text{MFCC}_{\mu\sigma}$	26
$\text{MFCC}_{\mu\sigma}+\text{SBF}_{\mu\sigma}$	46

Table 3: Feature combinations used in the study and their respective sizes. Means are represented with the symbol μ and the combination of means and standard deviations is represented as $\mu\sigma$.

The SBF derives from the spectral flux feature, which is defined as the Euclidean distance between successive spectral frames. For the calculation of the SBFs, the signal is firstly decomposed with an octave-scaled filter bank using the frequency ranges shown in Table 1. The spectral flux is computed for each of the resulting frequency channels.

2. METHOD

This section will explain in detail how the feature extraction and classification stages were performed in this study. Musical features were extracted from two data sets, and the descriptors were compounded into subsets of different sizes using feature combination and dimensionality reduction. Finally, a classification stage of distribution modeling and testing was implemented. The general design is illustrated in Figure 1.

Data Sets

In order to compare both timbre-based features, two data sets were used: the GTZAN set, originally developed for one of the first studies on musical genre classification [15], and the ISMIR04 set, which is a publicly available part of a bigger data set [16]. Before being subjected to feature extraction, the musical data was preprocessed by trimming audio down to 50 seconds from the middle of each file to reduce computational load in the ISMIR04 data set, which

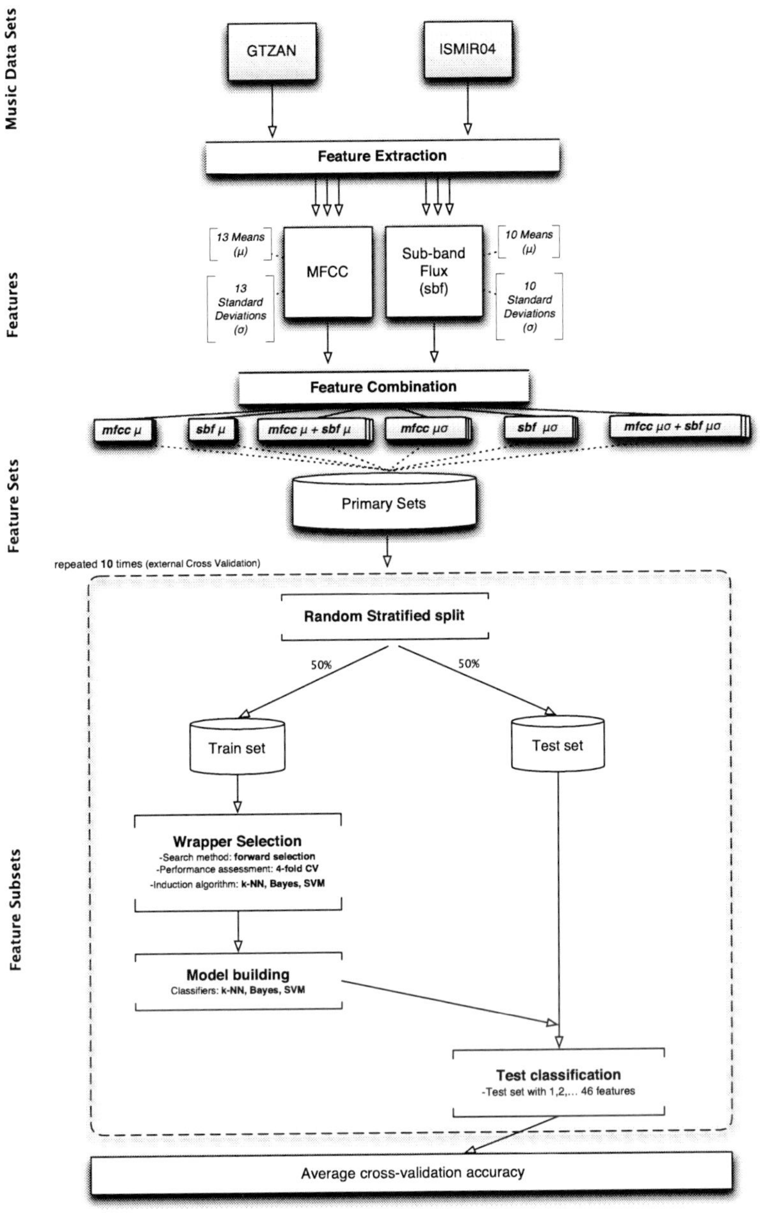

Figure 1: General design of the study.

consists of whole songs. Also the sampling rate was uniformed to 44100 Hz as a means to use the same algorithms for feature extraction in both data sets.

The main characteristics of the GTZAN and ISMIR04 data sets are presented in Table 2. The data sets differ in number and type of genre classes and in number of excerpts. Also the relative balance of the data sets, or the distribution of the examples into genres is fairly different. GTZAN is a balanced data set because each of the genres contains 100 musical examples. This differs from the imbalance of the ISMIR04 data set, which for example contains 320 classical songs but only 26 examples in the *jazz/blues* class.

Feature extraction

The frame-based extraction of MFCCs and SBFs was performed in MIRtoolbox 1.3 [17] using an analysis window of 25 milliseconds and a hop size of 50 % following previous studies such as [15]. Two feature statistics were obtained, the average (μ) and standard deviation (σ) along frames. In addition, a feature scaling to zero mean and unit variance was performed based upon the normality assumption. The aim of this standardization procedure was to prevent the classification results from getting distorted by the feature ranges.

The means and standard deviations of MFCCs and SBFs were combinated into different feature sets to assess classification upon different scenarios. Six primary sets of different feature size were generated, as presented in Table 3.

Feature Selection and Classification

Each of the six primary sets was subjected to the attribute selection and classification stage. Pattern recognition algorithms were run in Weka, a suite for machine learning [18]. First, optimal feature subsets were obtained using feature

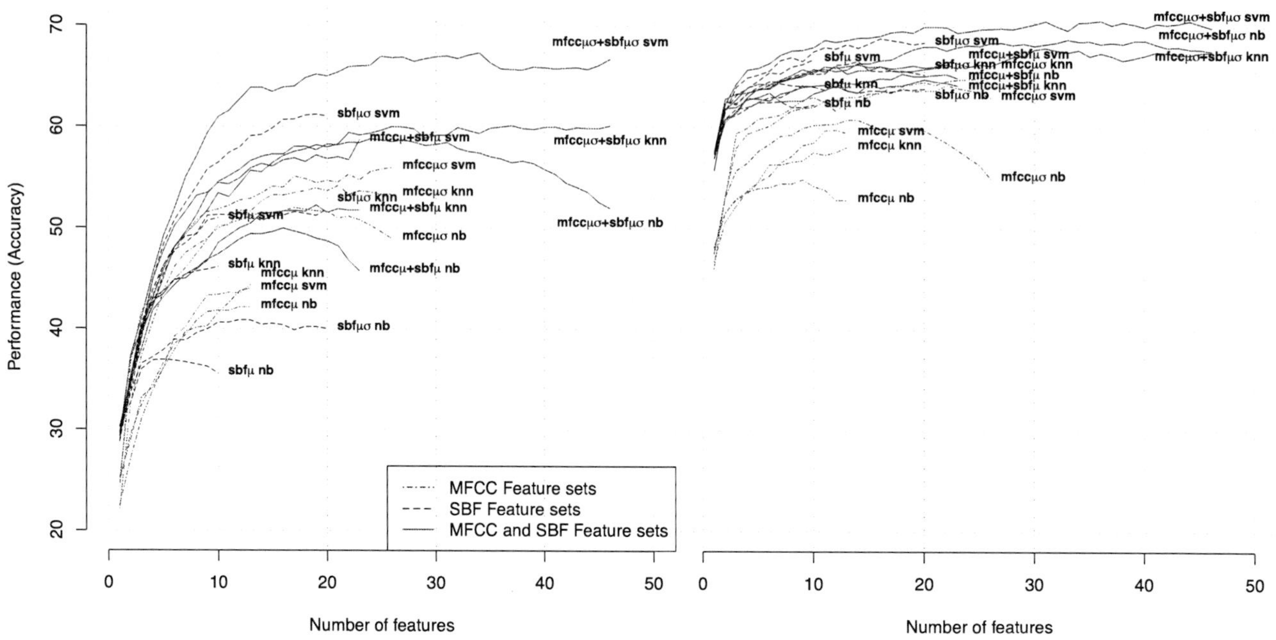

(a)

(b)

Figure 2: GTZAN (a) and ISMIR04 (b) accuracies as a function of feature cardinality.

selection. The final classification stage consisted of model building and testing of the subsets.

In order to perform feature selection and classification, a random division of the data into training and testing subsamples was undertaken. The music datasets were split into halves to ensure a good tradeoff between train and test data. Training data was used for the feature selection stage and for model training, whereas testing data was saved for further use in the final classification. The data splitting was stratified, i.e. a similar ratio of examples per class between training and testing sets was ensured.

The feature selection stage was performed using Wrapper forward selection algorithms. In Wrapper selection, the training set is used as a new primary set. This set is partitioned into training and testing data for the purpose of inner classification. Three algorithms were tested for feature selection using inner 4-fold CV: instance-based k-Nearest Neighbors (k==10) (k-NN), Support Vector Machines (SVM) and Naïve Bayes (NB). For each primary set, subsets of all possible sizes were generated. The features chosen for the subsets were the best ones for each subset size based on maximum classification rates.

Next, a model was built and tested for each of the feature subsets in a classification routine that consisted of the same learning algorithms used for feature selection. An outer CV loop was utilized to obtain final classification estimates by evaluating a maximum amount of instances. The loop consisted of a three-step sequence of random partition of the primary sets, feature selection and classification that was repeated 10 times. Finally and for each classification model, the CV accuracies were averaged.

3. RESULTS

The classification accuracy per CV split was calculated as the number of correctly classified instances divided by the total number of test music examples. A total of 828 classification estimates were obtained after averaging the accuracy values that were obtained from each cross-validation fold. The results are presented in Figures 2a and 2b, which show the classification estimates as a function of feature cardinality. Each of 18 profiles in the plots is grouped to indicate classification models using MFCCs, SBFs, or a combination of both. For both data sets, the highest accuracies were offered by the $\mathsf{MFCC}_{\mu\sigma}+\ \mathsf{SBF}_{\mu\sigma}$ feature set (SVM classification). The maximum CV accuracy obtained for the GTZAN set was 67.28 % using SVMs for classification of the best 34 features from the feature combination $\mathsf{MFCC}_{\mu\sigma}+\ \mathsf{SBF}_{\mu\sigma}$. For the ISMIR04 set, the maximum CV accuracy was 70.58 % using SVMs to classify the $\mathsf{MFCC}_{\mu\sigma}+\ \mathsf{SBF}_{\mu\sigma}$ best 36 features. The second highest accuracies were obtained using $\mathsf{SBF}_{\mu\sigma}$ (SVM classification). For any particular feature size, classification models consisting of feature means and standard deviations ($\mu\sigma$) performed better than models with only mean (μ) feature values. As regards the learning algorithm used, the best performances of each feature combination were obtained using SVMs. The minimum CV accuracies, obtained from the $\mathsf{MFCC}_{\mu\sigma}$ subsets of the best single feature using k-NNs, were 45.99 % in GTZAN and 22.10 % in ISMIR04.

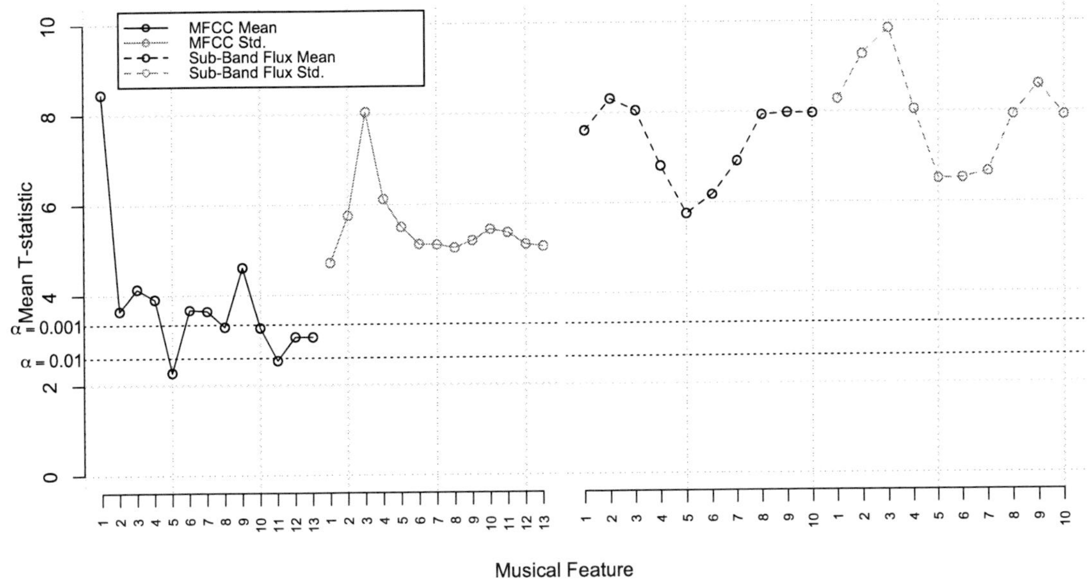

Figure 3: Mean t-value for each feature across all pairs of genres (GTZAN).

4. ANALYSIS

The MFCCs and SBFs were compared by performing statistical analyses of difference between classification model performances and by estimating the separation ability between genre classes that was yielded by the features. Only the GTZAN data set was chosen for most of the analyses; both sets are difficult to compare due to their differences in number of excerpts and in type and distribution of genre classes. GTZAN was preferred over ISMIR04 because it is widely used in MIR; another reason is that its balanced distribution made it possible to compare SBFs and MFCCs using t-tests for equal sample sizes, thus offering a relatively higher statistical power.

The separation ability is here understood as the level of discrimination between classes obtained using independent two-sided paired t-tests. Figure 3 offers an estimation of the feature relevance for overall discrimination between genres for the GTZAN data set. The plot shows, for each feature, a mean t-value that summarizes paired t-tests for assessment of separability between each possible pair of genres in GTZAN. The lowest and uppermost SBFs as well as the MFCC σ 3 yielded high mean t-statistic values.

For further analyses based on the classification accuracies, it was relevant to estimate if the obtained performance was above chance level. The baseline accuracy [19] of a data set is used as a benchmark for this purpose. It corresponds to the percentage of the class that is most frequent in the set. For both data sets, the obtained CV accuracies were found to surpass the accuracy that would be obtained by assigning all the examples to the most populated class. The GTZAN baseline is 10 %, while the obtained minimum CV accuracy was 22.10 %. In the case of the ISMIR04 set, the baseline is 43.9 %, while the minimum result obtained was 45.99 %. Since the minimum results were higher than baseline accuracies, the obtained performance exceeded chance level.

For the next analyses based upon classification results it was opted to utilize models based on the SVM learning algorithm. Only this classification technique was chosen because for each of the classifiers that were tested, the difference between the performance of MFCC and SBF models was found to be fairly similar.

The results of all the SVM classifications based on full-sized feature combinations were compared in order to find out whether the performance of MFCC and SBF models differed. Since the number of cross-validation folds was not large enough to meet normality assumption [19], the accuracies obtained for each full-sized feature combination were assessed running a non-parametric Friedman's test with post-hoc analysis following previous studies such as [20]. Figures 4a and 4b show the differences in performance between the classification models. Each box plot displays the per-fold performance distribution of a single feature combination. The figures show eleven differences between models at p-values lower than 0.05, out of which three were found for both GTZAN and ISMIR04 models: 1) The $\mathsf{SBF}_{\mu\sigma}$ set performed higher than the MFCC_{μ} set at $p < .001$ level; 2) the MFCC_{μ} set yielded lower results than the $\mathsf{MFCC}_{\mu\sigma}+ \mathsf{SBF}_{\mu\sigma}$ feature set ($p < .001$); 3) the $\mathsf{MFCC}_{\mu\sigma}+ \mathsf{SBF}_{\mu\sigma}$ feature set performed higher than the feature combination $\mathsf{MFCC}_{\mu\sigma}$ (ISMIR04: $p < .001$, GTZAN: $p < .05$).

Finally, an analysis based on SVM classification results obtained from full sized combinations of $\mathsf{MFCC}_{\mu\sigma}$ and of $\mathsf{SBF}_{\mu\sigma}$ was carried out for the GTZAN set data. These particular classification models were chosen in order to compare all the SBF descriptors against the totality of the extracted MFCC descriptors. The most accurately classified genres for the chosen models were classical, metal and jazz.

The $\mathsf{MFCC}_{\mu\sigma}$ and $\mathsf{SBF}_{\mu\sigma}$ models were compared by finding out if there were any genres for which one fea-

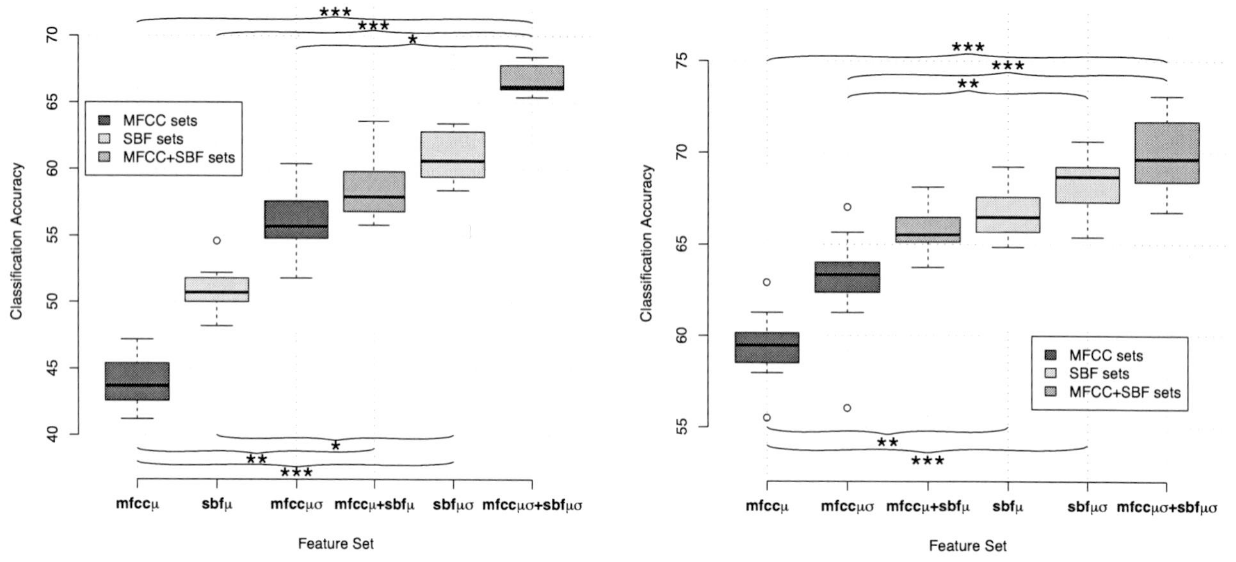

(a) (b)

Figure 4: Comparison of SVM classification results based on different feature set combinations using GTZAN (a) and ISMIR04 (b) music data sets. The boxes are presented in increasing order of median classification accuracy. A Friedman's test was utilized to find differences based on the CV accuracies of each full-sized feature set combination. Differences in performance of classification model pairs that exhibited p-values lower than 0.05 are shown with braces. The corresponding p-values for these cases are indicated with asterisks (*:$p < .05$, **: $p < .01$, ***:$p < .001$) .

ture combination offered good class separability but the other did not, and vice versa. The separability between classes was evaluated from the t-statistic of all the features for certain pairs of genres. The genre pairs shown in Figure 5 were chosen based upon the $\mathsf{MFCC}_{\mu\sigma}$ and the $\mathsf{SBF}_{\mu\sigma}$ SVM classification models and their differences in genre misclassification. In order to find the genre pairs, the confusion matrices corresponding to these classification models were modified by summing their respective upper and lower triangles in order to add the false positives of each possible genre pair together. Two triangular matrices were obtained; the triangle corresponding to $\mathsf{SBF}_{\mu\sigma}$ was subtracted from the $\mathsf{MFCC}_{\mu\sigma}$ triangle, and vice versa. The required genre pairs were chosen from the elements in the triangular matrices based on the maximum values that were obtained from each subtraction. It was found that country and jazz were relatively highly misclassified by $\mathsf{SBF}_{\mu\sigma}$ models and relatively lowly by $\mathsf{MFCC}_{\mu\sigma}$ models: as shown in Figure 5, the MFCC σ 3 descriptor showed a comparatively high t-statistic with regards to the separability between country and jazz. In contrast, hip-hop and reggae showed relatively high misclassification for $\mathsf{MFCC}_{\mu\sigma}$ and comparatively low for $\mathsf{SBF}_{\mu\sigma}$ models. As shown in the plot, the SBF σ 3 offered the highest t-values for the discrimination of these genres. A similar procedure with symmeterized confusion matrices was used in a genre classification study by [20].

5. DISCUSSION

The comparisons between the MFCC and SBF sets over different conditions showed that SBF sets performed better than MFCCs in the majority of the cases. This is observed for both music data sets despite variations in the general shape of the GTZAN and ISMIR04 plots (Figs. 4a and 4b) that might be due to differences in their baseline accuracies. To illustrate this, classical music comprises 10 % of the balanced GTZAN data set, which has 10 classes. In comparison, from the unbalanced ISMIR04 set with 6 classes, almost 44 % consists of classical music. This genre is in the latter case overrepresented, which would lead to relatively higher results in ISMIR04 if a naïve learner assigned all the examples to the most populated class.

As regards the use of different learning algorithms to find differences between MFCC and SBF model performance, it was found that the results were consistent for the three classifiers used. It can be suggested that the difference in performance between SBF and MFCC models is mostly invariant, at least with respect to the chosen classifiers.

Based on the analysis of mean separability, congruent results were found between the class discrimination obtained from certain features and prior findings regarding perceived polyphonic timbre dimensions. As shown in Figure 3, the mean separability of each feature for all possible combinations of genres yields fairly different profiles for MFCCs and SBFs, probably because the features themselves are fundamentally different. The high average t-statistic for the extreme SBFs suggests that the lower and

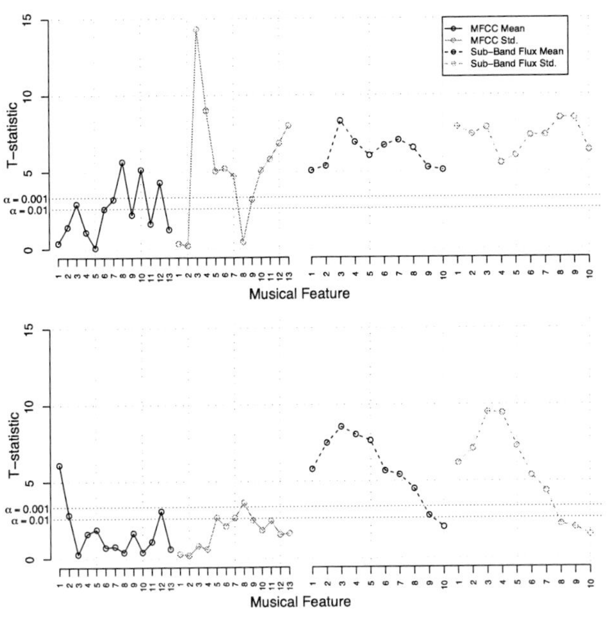

Figure 5: T-statistic of all features in genre pairs (country/pop in upper graph, hip hop/reggae in lower graph) for which $\mathsf{MFCC}_{\mu\sigma}$ and $\mathsf{SBF}_{\mu\sigma}$ models showed important differences in genre misclassification (GTZAN data set).

upper extremes of the spectrum are especially important for the purpose of genre classification. This tendency follows results by [6,13] regarding correlations between SBFs from the extreme frequency channels and the perception of polyphonic timbral Activity, Fullness and Brightness. Indeed, the SBF descriptors with the highest t-values in Figure 3 were found to correlate with perceptual dimensions in previous studies on polyphonic timbre perception [6]. It can be thus suggested that the perceived dimensions of Activity, Fullness and Brightness that are described by some SBFs are relevant for the purpose of musical genre classification. In this sense, perceptually motivated features have been considered potentially crucial for music classification [21], although few research has been conducted so far in this direction.

The aforementioned contemplation might be also valid for some MFCC descriptors, particularly MFCC μ 1 and MFCC σ 3. The relevance of perceived brightness is also suggested by the high average t-value of MFCC μ 1, which correlates with this timbral feature. As regards MFCC σ 3, which corresponds to energy at extreme low and mid-high frequencies, this descriptor exhibited a high mean t-statistic, implying that the lower spectrum end might be purposeful for genre classification. Based on the cosine basis function corresponding to MFCC 3, inter-class discriminations from this feature correspond to differences in energy covariance between the lower extreme of the mel spectrum and frequencies around 2500 Hz.

The MFCC σ 3 was also found to discriminate well jazz music from country, as shown in Figure 5. Since this feature is a standard deviation, it is plausible that the separability obtained between jazz and country is due to a relatively higher variance in low frequencies over time in the case of country music. As regards the discrimination between hip hop and reggae, the t-test results in Figure 5 showed that this appears to be a burdensome task using MFCCs. The SBFs that can separate better these two classes are the means and standard deviations of SBF 3 and SBF 4, which correspond to fluctuations at low frequencies. Perhaps the generally "fuller" sound that could be perceived in hip hop music when compared to reggae corresponds to the higher SBF μ 3 found in hip hop excerpts, as SBF 2 and SBF 3 represent perceived Fullness [6, 13].

Notably, standard deviations of features not only offered particularly good separability but also seemed to be favorable with regards to the obtained classification performance when compared to feature combinations that consisted only of mean values. With this respect, it might be that the addition of standard deviations increased the feature redundancy of the subsets, reducing its noise and improving the separation between classes [22]. In any case, the results raised the question of the relevance of standard deviations for music classification. While the feature means are a customary measure of central tendency, the feature standard deviations are less prevalent and could be considered as a problematic statistic for music description. These refer to changes over time, but do not give cues about the temporal evolution of the music because the time-scale of change is unknown. To illustrate this, the loudness of a musical piece that is *pp* during the first half and *ff* during the second half could have the same standard deviation as that of a piece whose dynamics varied periodically.

It is worthy to remark that the separability analyses were conducted for individual features and for pairs of genre classes, thus it is not possible to tell whether the features that yielded high t-values had an optimal individual contribution in the multi-class classification experiment with multiple features. In other words, descriptors that showed high separation ability might not have necessarily been decisive in the classification task.

6. CONCLUSIONS

The present findings showed that the SBF feature set, which has been designed specifically for modeling human perception of polyphonic musical timbre, is a promising feature for genre classification due to its satisfactory classification performance over a number of scenarios. For the analyzed cases, SBF models performed better than MFCC models. In addition, spectral fluctuations at both ends of the frequency spectrum were found to be relevant for discrimination between musical genres. Even though the classification results were comparatively lower than those obtained by other approaches using a higher number of features and pioneering classification methods, the outcomes of this study encourage the evaluation of perceptually motivated features for musical genre classification. The results follow previous ideas regarding the importance of global frequency distribution in genre discrimination [4], and support the hypothesis that the energy fluctuations within certain frequency channels, more specifically in lower and upper spectrum ends, can be very useful for the task of music genre classification. A possible extension of the presented work would be to test the SBF feature set in other MIR tasks such as music segmentation. Other natural directions for future studies in genre classification include the use of SBF with newer modeling techniques as well as experiments on more challenging music data sets. Finally, the design of perceptually interpretable features that boost efficiency through compact musical representations can provide critical insights for MIR.

Acknowledgments

The authors would like to thank Vinoo Alluri, Birgitta Burger, Tuomas Eerola, Rafael Ferrer Flores and Marc Thompson for their extensive contributions and insightful suggestions. This study and manuscript preparation were supported by doctoral research grants to the corresponding author (MH) from the Music Department and Faculty of Humanities of the University of Jyväskylä, and from the Ellen and Artturi Nyyssönen Foundation. The presentation of this article was supported by travel grants from the Finnish Doctoral Programme in Music Research and from the *Music Mining Plant* Project, funded by the Academy of Finland.

7. REFERENCES

[1] R. Gjerdingen and D. Perrott, "Scanning the dial: the rapid recognition of music genres." *Journal of New Music Research.*, vol. Vol. 37, no. 2, 2008.

[2] C. Krumhansl, "Plink: Thin slices of music," *Music Perception*, vol. 27, no. 5, pp. 337–354, 2010.

[3] J. M. Grey, "Multidimensional perceptual scaling of musical timbres." *Journal of the Acoustical Society of America.*, vol. 2, no. 61, pp. 1270–1277, 1977.

[4] J.-J. Aucouturier and F. Pachet, "Representing musical genre: A state of the art." *Journal of New Music Research*, vol. 32, no. 1, pp. 83–93, 2003.

[5] P. Mermelstein, "Distance measures for speech recognition, psychological and instrumental," *Pattern Recognition and Artificial Intelligence*, vol. 116, 1976.

[6] V. Alluri and P. Toiviainen, "Exploring perceptual and acoustical correlates of polyphonic timbre," *Music Perception*, vol. 27, no. 3, pp. 223–241, 2010.

[7] N. Scaringella, G. Zoia, and D. Mlynek, "Automatic genre classification of music content (a survey)," *IEEE Signal Processing Magazine*, vol. 23, no. 2, pp. 133–141, 2006.

[8] C.-H. Lee, J.-L. Shih, K.-M. Yu, and H.-S. Lin, "Automatic music genre classification based on modulation spectral analysis of spectral and cepstral features," *IEEE Transactions on Multimedia*, vol. 11, no. 4, pp. 670 –682, june 2009.

[9] A. Anglade, E. Benetos, M. Mauch, and S. Dixon, "Improving music genre classification using automatically induced harmony rules," *Journal of New Music Research*, vol. 39, no. 4, pp. 349–361, 2010.

[10] F. Morchen, A. Ultsch, M. Thies, and I. Lohken, "Modeling timbre distance with temporal statistics from polyphonic music," *IEEE Transactions on Audio, Speech, and Language Processing*, vol. 14, no. 1, pp. 81–90, 2006.

[11] B. Logan, "Mel Frequency Cepstral Coefficients for music modeling," in *International Symposium on Music Information Retrieval*, vol. 28. Citeseer, 2000, p. 5.

[12] A. Holzapfel and Y. Stylianou, "Musical genre classification using nonnegative matrix factorization-based features," *IEEE Transactions on Audio, Speech, and Language Processing*, vol. 16, no. 2, pp. 424–434, 2008.

[13] V. Alluri and P. Toiviainen, "Effect of enculturation on the semantic and acoustic correlates of polyphonic timbre," *Music Perception*, vol. 29, no. 3, pp. 297–310, 2012.

[14] B. Burger, M. R. Thompson, S. Saarikallio, G. Luck, and P. Toiviainen, "Influences of rhythm- and timbre-related musical features on characteristics of music-induced movement," *Frontiers in Auditory Cognitive Neuroscience*, 2013. In press.

[15] G. Tzanetakis and P. Cook, "Musical genre classification of audio signals." *IEEE Transactions on Speech and Audio Processing*, vol. 10, no. 5, pp. 293–302, 2002.

[16] P. Cano, E. Gómez, F. Gouyon, P. Herrera, M. Koppenberger, B. Ong, X. Serra, S. Streich, and N. Wack, "ISMIR 2004 audio description contest," *Music Technology Group of the Universitat Pompeu Fabra, Tech. Rep*, 2006.

[17] O. Lartillot and P. Toiviainen, "A Matlab toolbox for musical feature extraction from audio," in *International Conference on Digital Audio Effects*, Bordeaux, 2007.

[18] I. Witten and E. Frank, *Data mining: Practical machine learning tools and techniques*. Elsevier, 2005.

[19] A. Flexer, "Statistical evaluation of music information retrieval experiments," *Journal of New Music Research*, vol. 35, no. 2, pp. 113–120, 2006.

[20] A. Meng, P. Ahrendt, J. Larsen, and L. K. Hansen, "Temporal feature integration for music genre classification," *IEEE Transactions on Audio, Speech, and Language Processing*, vol. 15, no. 5, pp. 1654–1664, 2007.

[21] Z. Fu, G. Lu, K. M. Ting, and D. Zhang, "A survey of audio-based music classification and annotation," *IEEE Transactions on Multimedia*, vol. 13, no. 2, pp. 303 –319, April 2011.

[22] I. Guyon and A. Elisseeff, "An introduction to variable and feature selection," *Journal of Machine Learning Research*, no. 3, pp. 1157–1182, 2003.

SIMILARITY SEARCH OF FREESOUND ENVIRONMENTAL SOUND BASED ON THEIR ENHANCED MULTISCALE FRACTAL DIMENSION

Motohiro Sunouchi
Graduate School of Information Science and Technology, Hokkaido University,
North 13, West 8, Kita-ku, Sapporo, Japan
sunouchi@meme.hokudai.ac.jp

Yuzuru Tanaka
Meme Media Laboratory, Hokkaido University,
North 13, West 8, Kita-ku, Sapporo, Japan
tanaka@meme.hokudai.ac.jp

ABSTRACT

In this paper, we propose a new acoustic feature signature based on the multiscale fractal dimension extracted from sound signals for the content-based retrieval of environmental sounds such as field-recording sounds shared through Freesound. The multiscale fractal dimension de-rived from the fractal theory is known as a descriptor representing several features of the sound waveform. We report the basic characteristics of the enhanced multiscale fractal dimension (EMFD) extracted from each sound signal. Furthermore, we developed a similarity search system for environmental sounds using EMFD and Mel frequency cepstral coefficients 39 (MFCC39). We have compared the descriptiveness of EMFD signature and MFCC39 for the search purpose and found some competitive aspects of EMFD signature against MFCC39. These results show that EMFD signature is useful for describing the features of environmental sound and applicable to the search of large-scale sound databases.

1. INTRODUCTION

These days, handy PCM sound recorders are growing popular. Not only music creators but also many amateurs are enjoying recording environmental sounds, sharing them on the web and creating new music by utilizing them. In general, environmental sounds comprise various types of sound, such as those made by creatures, natural phenomenon and machines, city noise, music, speeches and so on. To analyze environmental sounds, various types of acoustic features have been proposed [1–4]. For promoting communications and music creations utilizing database of field-recording sounds on the web, it is important to find appropriate acoustic features for search-ing tasks that describe timbre, tone and texture of sounds more effectively.

In this paper, we show the method to compute the fractal dimension and the multiscale fractal dimension (MFD) of a sound signal in chapter 2. In chapter 3, we show the process of the development of EMFD based on MFD. In chapter 4, we demonstrate the basic characteristics of EMFD. In chapter 5, we show the method to evaluate the descriptiveness of EMFD signature and report the results of the evaluation.

2. MULTISCALE FRACTAL DIMENSION

2.1 Fractal Dimension of a Curve

Mandelbrot, who advocated a concept of fractal, demonstrated that some structures in nature could be modeled well by the theory of fractals [5]. Fractal dimension is one of the numerical values that can describe characteristics of a fractal. The fractal dimension of a straight line, which is a special case of a curve, is 1. In general, the fractal dimension of a curve is defined as a real number between 1 and 2. The fractal dimension of a curve in a two-dimensional space can be calculated as follows.

As an example of a curve, let's take the sound wave-form. A covering area can be drawn by a moving disk, whose radius is r, along the curve of waveform. The center of the disk should be at any position on the original waveform curve and the width of the covering area like a belt becomes $2r$. Fig. 1 shows the covering area obtained by moving the disk along the waveform. This covering area is called Minkowski Sausage.

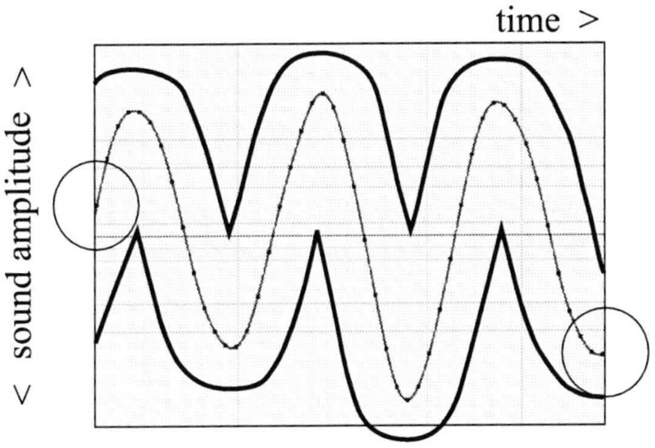

Figure 1. Sound waveform and Minkowski sausage

Let $A(r)$ be the area of Minkowski Sausage obtained by a disk of radius r. We plot $\log A(r)$ with respect to $logr$ to obtain Fig. 2. For curves in nature such as coastlines, the plot of $\log A(r)$ versus log r is often like a straight line. Equation (1) shows that the fractal dimension D can be defined as the gradient of the plotted line subtracted from 2.

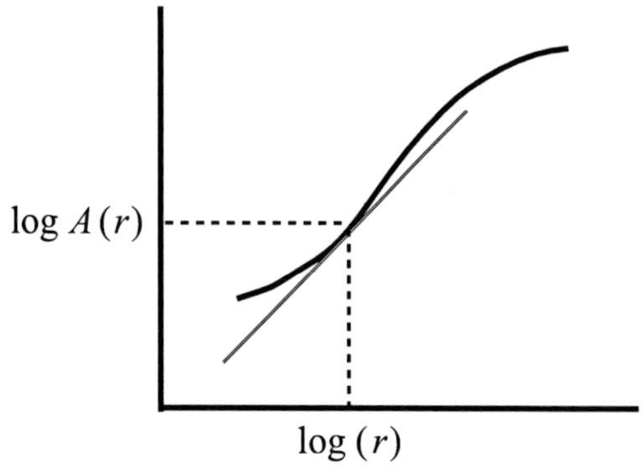

Figure 2. Double logarithmic plot of $A(r)$ vs. r of Minkowski Sausage

$$D = 2 - \lim_{r \to 0} \frac{\log A(r)}{\log r} \tag{1}$$

2.2 Multiscale Fractal Dimension of Sound Waveform

In practice, sound waveform may have different structures depending on its scale, therefor fractal dimension D may vary by the value of r. Let $\mathrm{grad}(r)$ be the gradient of $\log A(r)$ versus $\log r$, then multiscale fractal dimension (MFD) is defined as function of r by the equation (2).

$$D(r) = 2 - \mathrm{grad}(r) \tag{2}$$

MFD at time t denoted by $D(r,t)$ can be defined for a fixed short time scanning window, say 50msec in this paper, of target sound's waveform. The function $D(r,t)$ is called fractogram. P. Maragos utilized MFDs to reduce the error in speech recognition system using HMM and reported the modest improvement in recognition performance [6]. A. Zlatintsi used MFDs to analyze short-time music signal structures at multiple time scales and concluded that there is a strong evidence that MFDs can well describe the structure and properties of instrument sounds [7].

3. ENHANCED MULTISCALE FRACTAL DIMENSION

We developed the method to compute the signature "enhanced multiscale fractal dimension" (EMFD) of sound based on MFD. The following procedures are performed to compute EMFD. EMFD can be computed as follows.

3.1 Preprocessing a Target Sound

A target sound to analyze should be first normalized with its maximum amplitude to be -0.1db, and converted in the standard format based on the following specifications, the sampling rate (frequency) is chosen to be 44,100hz, while the bit depth is 16bits. We use only a single channel.

3.2 Creating MFDs Profile

To compute the area of Minkowski Sausage, we setup a unit disk vector C_r whose radius is r based on the equation

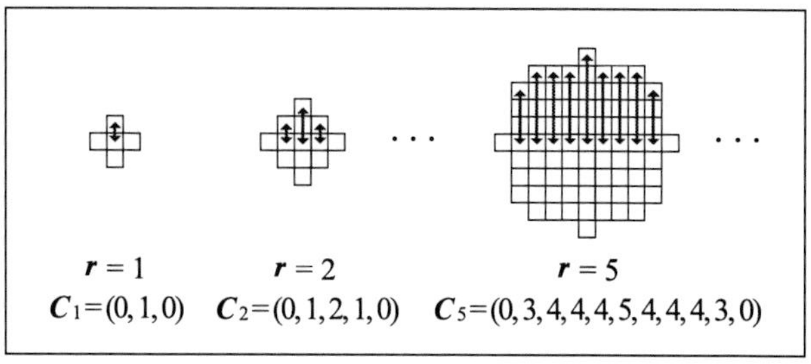

Figure 3. Mesh-Approximation of a unit disk

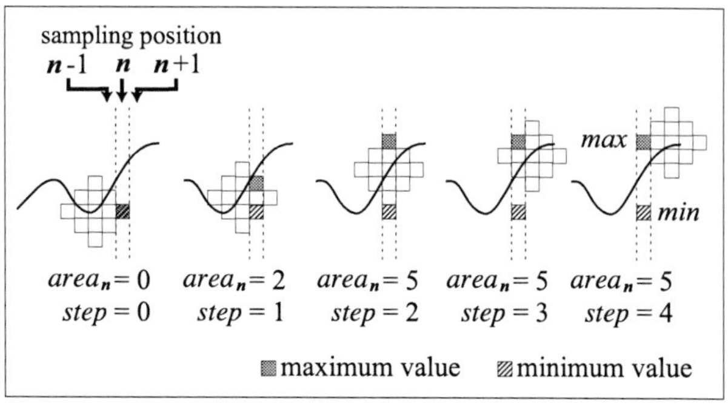

Figure 4. Steps for computing the area of Minkowski Sausage at n-th sampling position in the current scanning window by sliding the unit disk of r=2.

(3). Fig. 3 shows how the model of unit disk is built. The vector C_r, whose radius is r, includes $2r$ elements that denote the vertical distance from the top to the center of unit disk at each horizontal position.

$$C_r = \left\{ \mathrm{floor}\left(\sqrt{2ri - i^2}\right) \;\middle|\; i = 0 \to 2r, i \in \mathbb{N} \right\} \tag{3}$$

Fig. 4 shows how the area of Minkowski Sausage at the n-th sampling position is computed by sliding the unit disk along the sound signal in the current scanning window. The striped block corresponds to the minimum value at the n-th sampling position that is covered by the unit disk at each discrete step, whereas the gray block corresponds to the maximum value. At each discrete step of sliding the unit disk, the maximum and minimum values at each n-th sampling position are independently updated to keep respectively the maximum value and the minimum value. Let n be the sampling position, r be the radius of the unit disk, $area_n$ be the area of Minkowski Sausage at each sampling position n and $\mathrm{sig}(n)$ be the amplitude value of sound signal at each sampling position n, then $area_n$ is computed by equation (4). MFD is computed using the equation (5) for 132 different discrete values (r = 1, 2, ... , 132). The minimum radius (r = 1) corresponds to the sampling period of the sound signal (1/44.1 ms) and the range of different values of r corresponds to the range of the time scales from 1/44.1 to 3 ms.

$$area_n = \max_{step=0 \to 2r} \{\mathrm{sig}(n - r + step) + C_r(step)\} - \min_{step=0 \to 2r} \{\mathrm{sig}(n - r + step) - C_r(step)\} \tag{4}$$

$$MFD(r) = 2 - \frac{\log\{A(r+1)/A(r)\}}{\log\{(r+1)/r\}} \tag{5}$$

$$swp(sound) = \left\{0, 50, ..., \text{floor}\left(\frac{\text{the length of the sound in milliseconds}}{50} - 1\right) \times 50\right\} \tag{6}$$

$$\underset{\substack{dimbin=1\to 50\\ rbin=1\to 132}}{EMFD} = \left\{\frac{\text{card}\{t\,|1+0.02(dimbin-1) \le MFD_t(rbin) < 1+0.02dimbin, t \in swp(sound)\}}{\text{card}\{swp(sound)\}}\right\} \tag{7}$$

3.3 Enhanced Multiscale Fractal Dimension

In this paper, we use a fixed width scanning window of length 50ms. The set of fixed scanning windows of the target sound is defined as $swp(sound)$ by equation (6). MFD for each scanning window can be obtained as a vector of length 132, each of which takes a value between 2 and 1. To describe features of various types of environmental sounds using a single type of signature, we define a new signature, namely the enhanced multiscale fractal dimension (EMFD). EMFD is defined as a feature vector computed as the two-dimensional histogram of time-varying MFD values. Each bin contains the percentage of the scanning windows of the target sound. We define 50 bins with a width of 0.02 for the value of the fractal dimension of each scanning window and the 132 bins with a width of 1 for the radius of the unit disk. The value in each bin is computed by equation (7). In the equation (7), the $\text{card}(A)$ returns the cardinality of set A. And $dimbin$ is a counting number that corresponds to the bins for the value of the fractal dimension and $rbin$ is a counting number that corresponds to the bins for the radius of the unit disk. For example, the value of bin whose $dimbin$ is 1 and $rbin$ is 1 is *(the number of the scanning windows in which the MFD(1) is between 1 and 1.02) / (the total number of the scanning windows)*. The equation (8) is always true at each radius of the unit disk. The Fig. 5 is an image which visualizes the EMFD of a cuckoo sound. The higher the value of bin is, the darker the color of the bin is in the figure.

$$\sum_{dimbin=1}^{50} EMFD = 1.0 \text{ , at each radius of the unit disk} \tag{8}$$

3.4 Logarithmic EMFD with a Long Time Scale

Furthermore we developed a derived signature to utilize for similarity search task and for the evaluations of the descriptiveness of EMFD in chapter 5. We have analyzed various types of environmental sounds using EMFD and found that EMFD seems to have informative values for larger unit disks than the disk of 3ms radius (r=132). We extended the maximum radius of the unit disk to 218 that corresponds to 5 milliseconds (1/10 of the period of scanning window) and the discrete values to include $\{r = round(1.4^x), x = 1, ..., 16\}$. For the dimensionality reduction of the feature vector, we reduced the number of bins for the $dimbin$ from 50 to 32. We define this 32 ($dimbin$) x 16 ($rbin$) feature vector as EMFD-LL. Fig. 6 shows the EMFD-LL histogram of the same cuckoo sound as the one in Fig. 5.

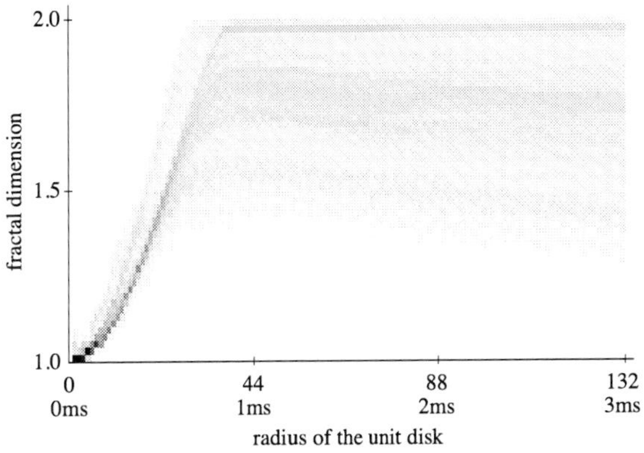

Figure 5. EMFD histogram of a cuckoo sound

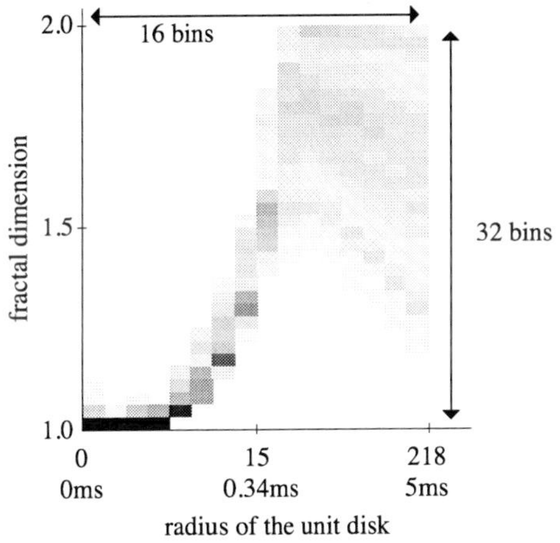

Figure 6. EMFD-LL histogram of a cuckoo sound

4. BASIC CHARACTERISTICS OF EMFD

To demonstrate the basic characteristics of EMFD and to estimate the robustness of EMFD as a signature, we applied EMFD to test sound signals.

4.1 EMFD of Single Sine Waves

Fig. 7 shows the EMFD histograms of single sine waves of 110hz, 220hz, 440hz, 880hz and 1760hz. The higher the frequency of a signal is, the smaller the value of the radius at the first peak of EMFD histogram becomes. The fractal dimension of a single sine wave converges to 2.0 at the

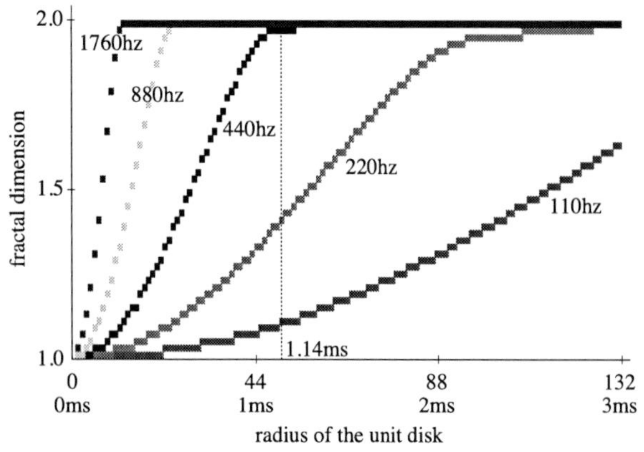

Figure 7. EMFD histograms of single sine waves of 110hz, 220hz, 440hz, 880hz and 1760hz

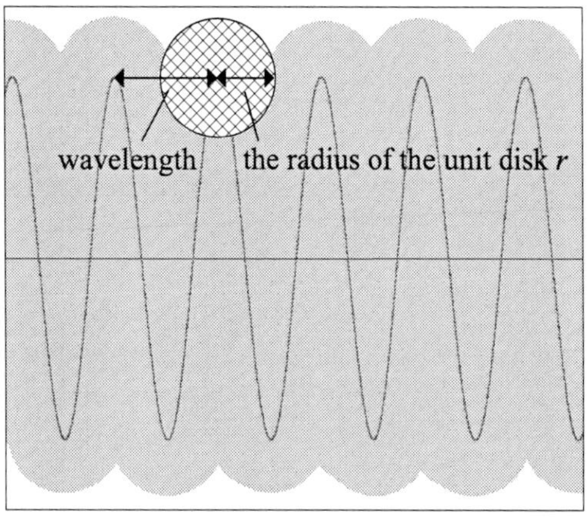

Figure 8. Minkowski Sausage by the unit disk with which the fractal dimension converges to 2.0

radius of the unit disk around the half of the wavelength of the signal. For a single sine wave of 440hz, the half of its wave length is $1000/440/2 = 1.14(ms)$. We can find that the EMFD histogram of 440hz sine wave converges 2.0 at around 1.14 (ms) in Fig. 7. Fig. 8 explains this property of EMFD. When the radius of the unit disk is more than $500/frequency$, even if the radius increases, the area of Minkowski Sausage becomes nearly constant. Therefore the fractal dimension converges 2.0 by equation (2).

4.2 Robustness of EMFD against Volume Level and Phase Shifting

To analyze various types of environmental sounds with EMFD and for more reliable evaluation of the descriptiveness of EMFD in chapter 5, we demonstrate the robustness of EMFD against changing volume levels and phase shifting of sound signals. To test sounds with different volume levels, we prepared 3 sine waves of 110hz, 440hz and 1760hz with maximum volume of -0.1db. We duplicated the sound files and damp the signal level to -12db ($\approx 1/4$) and -24db ($\approx 1/16$) for the test. In Fig. 9, the three of EMFD histograms in the upper row show the test results. The original signal (black line) and the signal damped to -12db (dark gray line) show almost the same EMFD at any frequency. There seems to be difference between the original signal and the signal damped to -24db (light gray line) especially with a large radius of the unit disk. The difference of the fractal dimension is no more than 3.12% ($r = 132, 440hz$). If the sound amplitude is reduced to 1/16, the impression in hearing the sound should be totally different. Therefore we may conclude that EMFD has enough robustness against changing volume levels.

Next we applied EMFD to single sine waves of 60hz, 180hz and 540hz with their phase shifted by 0 (black line), $\pi/4$ (dark gray line) and $\pi/2$ (ight gray line). In Fig. 9, the three of EMFD histograms in the lower row show the test results. The lower the frequency of signal is, the bigger its impact from the difference between the phase of signal and scanning window is. The difference of the fractal dimension is no more than 1.07% ($r = 132, 60hz$). And if the frequency is higher than 400hz, we can find vanishingly small difference only in the histograms. For practical purposes, EMFD has enough robustness against phase shifting to scanning window.

5. EVALUATION OF DESCRIPTIVENESS OF EMFD SIGNATURE

To evaluate the descriptiveness of EMFD signature, we have developed a similarity search system using the k-nearest neighbors method. As a sound dataset, sufficient numbers of environmental sounds with metadata have been imported to the search system via Freesound API [8]. We evaluated the descriptiveness of acoustic features based on the similarity index we defined between tag groups of search-key sound and that of the retrieved sounds.

5.1 Sound Dataset

To collect environmental sounds for the sound dataset, we chose the Freesound project [9]. The database of Freesound stores many types of sounds uploaded by users. Freesound allows users to share their recording sounds and to describe metadata about shared sounds on the web. Each sound in this database is labeled with a group of tags, and they are relatively well maintained as user generated contents [10]. By utilizing Freesound API, applications can access the database of Freesound easily.

Based on the rules we defined, the sounds and its metadata were imported to our search system. The rules are as follows. These imported sounds are tagged with field-recording. The length may be between 1 second and 600 seconds. We chose the top 3,000 sounds in descending order of downloaded number. After sounds were imported to the search system, each sound is converted to the uniformed format (1 channel, sampling rate at 44,100hz, bit depth is 16bits with volume adjustment) for normalization to extract acoustic features including EMFD. The average length of imported sounds is 70.4 seconds.

5.2 Acoustic Features

The most well known feature for speech recognition and music classification may be mel-frequency cepstral coeffi-

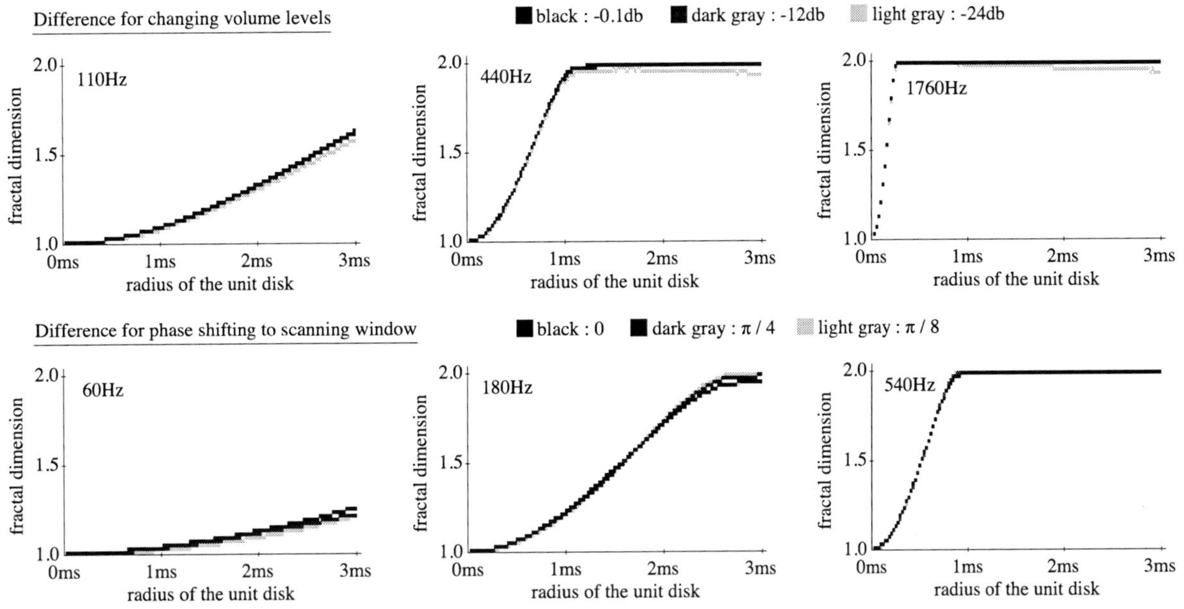

Figure 9. EMFD histograms to estimate the robustness. The upper row: Difference for changing volume levels. The lower row: Difference for phase shifting to scanning window.

cients (MFCC) [11]. We chose MFCC for the comparison of descriptiveness with our EMFD-LL. We computed the standard 13 MFCC coefficients with their first and second derivatives. It is called MFCC39. The EMFD-LL is a feature vector consisting of 512 elements as mentioned in the sub section 3.4. To achieve the best possible performance of searching tasks by k-NN method, we applied Principal Components Analysis (PCA) for feature vector of top 600 sounds (in descending order of downloaded number) in dataset to reduce their dimensionality. For the feature sets of EMFD-LL + MFCC39, PCA is applied for the concatenated original feature vectors. Table 1 shows the acoustic feature sets and the length of its feature vectors.

	Feature Sets	L1	L2
1	EMFD-LL	512	72
2	MFCC39 (13MFCC+13Δ+13ΔΔ)	39	12
3	EMFD-LL + MFCC39	551	74

Table 1. List of acoustic feature sets for the comparison of descriptiveness of them. L1 is the length of concatenated original feature sets. L2 is the length of the feature vector after applying PCA.

5.3 Evaluation Method

We have developed a similarity search system based on the k-NN method using respective features as mentioned above. When user chooses any sound in dataset and its feature set via web browser, the search result list based on the selected feature set is shown instantly.

To evaluate the descriptiveness of each feature set, we defined the similarity index between the tag group of the search-key sound and that of the retrieved sounds. To compute the similarity index between tag groups, we utilized the Natural Language Tool Kit (NLTK) [12] with a lexical database WordNet [13].

The similarity between tag_1 and tag_2 is defined as equation (9). The function of $path\_similarity$ provided by NLTK returns a score denoting how similar two synonym groups are, based on the shortest path that connects the meanings in the is-a taxonomy. Two synonym groups c_1 and c_2 denote those with tag_1 and tag_2 respectively as their elements. Then similarity between tag groups is defined by equation (10) and the similarity index between the tag group of the search-key sound and that of each retrieved sound in its search result list is defined as equation (11). The symbol s denotes the search-key sound and rs denotes the retrieved sounds in the search result list. The closer the meaning similarity of tag groups between search-key sound and each retrieved sound is, the bigger the similarity index is.

$$sim_{tag}(tag_1, tag_2) = \max_{c_1, c_2} \{path\_similarity(c_1, c_2)\} \quad (9)$$

$$sim_{taggroup}(tags_1, tags_2) = \frac{\sum_{t_1 \in tags_1} \max_{t_2 \in tags_2} \{sim_{tag}(t_1, t_2)\}}{\mathrm{card}(tags_1)} \quad (10)$$

$$sim_{sound}(s, rs) = \frac{\sum_{res \in rs} sim_{taggroup}(tags_s, tags_{res})}{\mathrm{card}(rs)} \quad (11)$$

5.4 Evaluation Results

For each of 3,000 sounds in the dataset, we computed the similarity index between itself as a search-key and each retrieved sound in search result list. Fig. 10 shows the average values of the similarity index for each feature set. The values in the column "top n" are the average values of the similarity indices that a search-key sound and retrieved sound(s) in the top n rank in search result list. For reference, the average value of the similarity indices between the two randomly chosen sounds is 0.230.

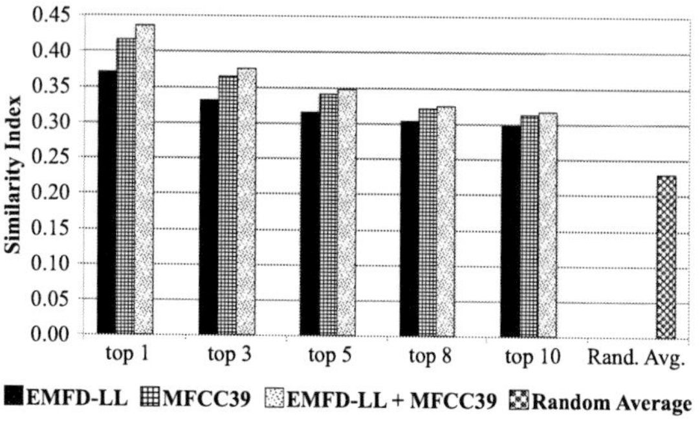

Figure 10. The evaluation results of the similarity index

Furthermore, to analyze for which kind of environmental sounds the EMFD-LL can have good descriptiveness, we picked up tag groups based on the following procedures. Let $simE$ be the similarity index between a search-key sound and its top 10 retrieved results using EMFD-LL and $simM$ be that of MFCC39. Next we created two groups of sounds in the dataset, EMFD-LL Group gE and MFCC39 Group gM defined by equation (12).

$$\begin{aligned} gE &= \{gE \in dataset \,|simE > simM\} \\ gM &= \{gM \in dataset \,|simE < simM\} \end{aligned} \tag{12}$$

Then we calculated the occurrence ratio for each tag labeling sounds in each group gE and gM. The occurrence ratio of each tag is defined as *(number of occurrences of the tag labels to sounds in the group) / (number of sounds in the group)*. Let $oct(g, tag)$ be the function returns the occurrence ratio of the tag in group g. We picked up tag groups based on the equation (13). The parameter a is an optional coefficient to narrow down the options to choose tags. It seems that EMFD-LL can describe well the features of sound labeled with some tags in $T(a)$.

$$T(a) = \{tag\,|oct(gE, tag) > oct(gM, tag) \times a\} \tag{13}$$

We made sound groups with tags picked up and compute the similarity index for each sound group. As a result, we found that sound groups that EMFD-LL is obviously effective include, for example, {frog, frogs}, {children, child} and {waves, beach, sea, ocean}. Fig. 11 shows the similarity index of each group.

6. CONCLUSIONS

In this paper, we proposed the acoustic feature signature EMFD based on the MFD and demonstrated the basic characteristics of EMFD. To evaluate the descriptiveness of

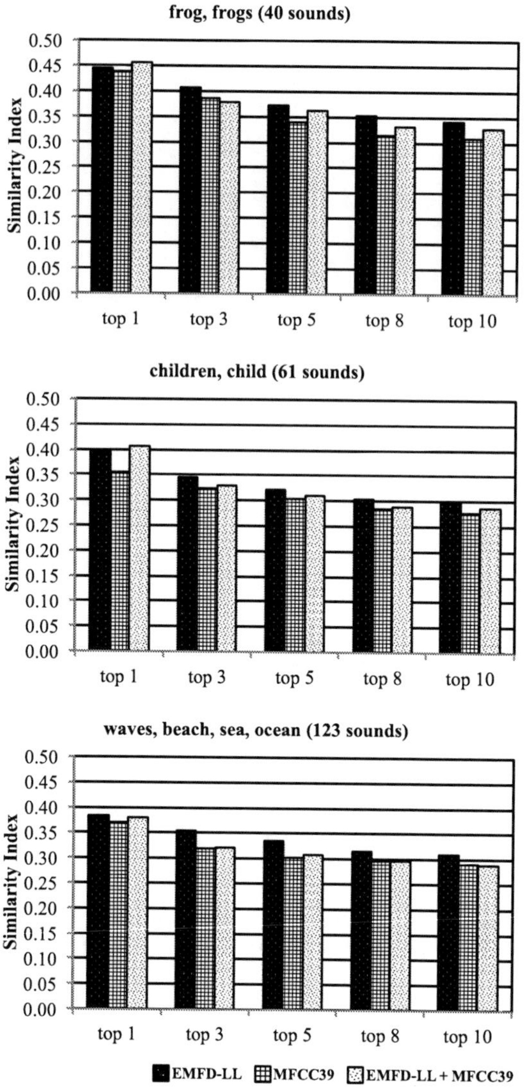

Figure 11. The evaluation results of the similarity index for sound groups for which EMFD-LL is obviously effective.

EMFD signature of the environmental sounds, we developed the similarity search system using k-NN method and the similarity index. From the evaluation results, we found that the descriptiveness of EMFD-LL+MFCC39 is higher than that of MFCC39. Furthermore, for the sounds tagged with, for example, flogs, children, waves, beach, sea and ocean, the descriptiveness of EMFD-LL is obviously higher than that of MFCC39. Our goal is to improve the method to utilize EMFD and to improve the descriptiveness of EMFD so that we achieve the similarity search system for the environmental sounds with better performance. For our future research, we intend to trace the unique properties of the descriptiveness of EMFD and develop the improved signature with lower dimensionality.

Acknowledgments

The authors would like to thank Masataka Goto, Prime Senior Researcher at the National Institute of Advanced Industrial Science and Technology (AIST), for the constructive comments that helped to improve this paper.

7. REFERENCES

[1] D. Mitrovic, M. Zeppelzauer, and H. Eidenberger, "On Feature Selection in Environmental Sound Recognition," in *Proc. 51st Int. Symposium ELMAR*, Zadar, Croatia, 2009, pp. 28–30.

[2] G. Roma, J. Janer, S. Kersten, M. Schirosa, P. Herrera, and X. Serra, "Ecological Acoustics Perspective for Content-Based Retrieval of Environmental Sounds," *EURASIP Journal on Audio, Speech, and Music Processing*, vol. 2010, pp. 1–11, Nov. 2010

[3] C. Lee, C. Han, and C. Chuang, "Automatic Classification of Bird Species From Their Sounds Using Two-Dimensional Cepstral Coefficients," *IEEE Transaction on Audio, Speech, and Language Processing*, vol. 16, no. 8, pp. 15411550, Nov. 2008.

[4] D. Mitrovic, M. Zeppelzauer, and H. Eidenberger, "Discrimination and Retrieval of Animal Sounds," in *Proc. The 12th Int. Multi-Media Modelling Conf.*, Beijing, China, 2006, pp. 339–343.

[5] B. Mandelbrot, *The Fractal Geometry of Nature*. W. H. Freeman and Company, 1982.

[6] P. Maragos and A. Potamianos, "Fractal dimensions of speech sounds: computation and application to automatic speech recognition," *The Journal of the Acoustical Society of America*, vol. 105, no 3, pp. 1925–1932, Mar. 2009.

[7] A. Zlatintsi and P. Maragos, "Musical Instruments Signal Analysis and Recognition Using Fractal Features," in *Proc. 19th European Signal Processing Conf. (EUSIPCO 2011)*, Barcelona, Spain, 2011, pp. 684–688.

[8] V. Akkermans, F. Font, J. Funollet, G. Roma, X. Serra, and S. Togias, "FREESOUND 2.0: An Improved Platform for Sharing Audio Clips," in *Int. Symposium on Music Information Retrieval*, Miami, FL, USA, 2011.

[9] Music Technology Group at Universitat Pompeu Fabra, "Freesound: collaborative database of creative-commons licensed sound," *Freesound.org*, 2005, http://www.freesound.org/

[10] E. Martinez, O. Celma, M. Sordo, B. de Jong, and X. Serra, "Extending the folksonomies of freesound.org using content-based audio analysis," in *Proc. SMC2009 - 6th Sound and Music Computing Conf.*, Porto, Portugal, Jul. 2009, pp. 65–70.

[11] T. Ganchev, N. Fakotakis and G. Kokkinakis, "Comparative Evaluation of Various MFCC Implementations on the Speaker Verification Task," in *Proc. 10th Int. Conf. Speech and Computer (SPECOM-2005)*, Patras, Greece, Oct. 2005, pp. 191–194.

[12] NLTK Project, "Natural Language Tool Kit," http://nltk.org/

[13] Princeton University, "WordNet: a lexical database for English," http://wordnet.princeton.edu/

USING SEMANTIC LAYER PROJECTION FOR ENHANCING MUSIC MOOD PREDICTION WITH AUDIO FEATURES

Pasi Saari and Tuomas Eerola
Finnish Centre of Excellence in Interdisciplinary Music Research
University of Jyväskylä, Finland
`firstname.lastname@jyu.fi`

György Fazekas and Mark Sandler
Centre for Digital Music
Queen Mary University of London
`firstname.lastname@eecs.qmul.ac.uk`

ABSTRACT

We propose a novel technique called Semantic Layer Projection (SLP) for predicting moods expressed by music based on audio features. In SLP, the predictive models are formed by a two-stage mapping from audio features to listener ratings of mood via a semantic mood layer. SLP differs from conventional techniques that produce a direct mapping from audio features to mood ratings. In this work, large social tag data from the Last.fm music service was analysed to produce a semantic layer that represents mood-related information in a low number of dimensions. The method is compared to baseline techniques at predicting the expressed Valence and Arousal in 600 popular music tracks. SLP clearly outperformed the baseline techniques at predicting Valence ($R^2 = 0.334$ vs. 0.245), and produced roughly equivalent performance in predicting Arousal ($R^2 = 0.782$ vs. 0.770). The difficulty of modelling Valence was highlighted by generally lower performance compared to Arousal. The improved prediction of Valence, and the increasingly abundant sources of social tags related to digital music make SLP a highly promising technique for future developments in modelling mood in music.

1. INTRODUCTION

The modern age of digital music consumption has brought new challenges in organising and searching rapidly expanding music collections. The popular appeal of music is often attributed to its striking ability to elicit or convey emotion. Therefore, managing large music collections in terms of mood has significant advantages that complement conventional genre-based organisation.

Social music services such as Last.fm [1] play an important role in connecting digital music to crowd-sourced semantic information. A prime advantage of using Last.fm data is in the large number of users worldwide applying semantic tags, i.e., free-form labels, to elements of the music domain, e.g. tracks, artists and albums. Tags are used in order to communicate users' music listening preferences that are also used for improving the service. The data is available to researchers through a dedicated API, which makes it possible to apply semantic computing to tags related to millions of tracks. Semantic computation of Last.fm tags has been found effective in characterising music information related to genre, mood, and instrumentation [1]. Parallel to analysing crowd-sourced tags, a tag set dedicated to music research purposes has also been collected in [2]. The importance of mood tags has been highlighted in several studies, including [3], claiming that mood tags account for 5% of the most commonly used tags. Applying semantic computation to tags can therefore yield effective mood-related semantic models for music.

The prominence of mood in music is reflected by the large number of studies modelling expressed or induced emotion. To this end, two prevalent techniques emerged: *i)* the dimensional model of Valence, Arousal and Tension; and *ii)* the categorical model of basic emotions such as happiness, sadness and tenderness. On one hand, these models have been found mutually inclusive to a large degree [4]. On the other hand, more general models of emotion have also been proposed, and refined using a taxonomy specifically designed for musically induced emotion [5].

These types of representations have been widely used in computational systems for predicting mood from audio. Feature extraction methods have been developed, for instance, in [6] and [7], providing a good basis for modelling and predicting perceived moods, genres and other characteristics of musical audio. The typical approach in most previous studies involves the use of computational algorithms, such as supervised machine learning, to predict perceived moods directly from audio features. For a more detailed overview of the advances of mood modelling and recognition, see e.g. [8].

Achieving high efficiency of these models, however, relies heavily on good quality ground-truth data. Due to the expense of human annotation, ground-truth is laborious to collect, and therefore typical data sets are limited to a few hundred tracks. This leads to challenges in mood prediction emerging from the high dimensionality of audio feature data and from the need for complex model parameter optimisation, often resulting in the lack of generalizability of the predictions to novel tracks [9]. One way of overcoming these challenges and increasing the efficiency of mood prediction is to utilise audio content related to a large number of tracks and associated crowd-sourced semantic tags.

In this work, we use multivariate techniques in a novel way to predict listener ratings of mood in 600 popular mu-

[1] Last.fm: `http://www.last.fm/`

sic tracks, using an intermediate semantic layer created from tag data related to a substantially large collection of tracks. This demonstrates how a large collection of tracks and associated mood tags can be used to improve prediction quality. The new technique involves mapping audio features (audio level) to a semantic mood space (semantic layer) first, and then mapping the semantic mood space to listener ratings (perceptual level). This differs from conventional methods that map audio directly to the perceptual level. Instead, we use direct mapping as baseline to assess the efficiency of the proposed technique.

2. RELATED WORK

This section summarises past research on connecting audio, as well as semantic and perceptual levels to represent music. Figure 1 illustrates how previous studies relate to the approach presented here.

2.1 Mapping from Audio Features to Semantic Layer

The challenge of auto-tagging music tracks can be considered analogous to our task. Gaussian Mixture Modelling (GMM) was used in [10], whereas [11] employed Support Vector Machines (SVM) for this purpose. Bertin-Mahieux et al. [12] proposed a boosting-based technique. This provided higher precision (0.312) and overall F-score (0.205) with somewhat lower recall (0.153) compared to hierarchical GMMs proposed in [10], when a set of general tag words were considered. In the context of mood tags, the authors reported 0.449, 0.176, 0.253 precision, recall and F-score, respectively, noting that, due to the specific experimental conditions, the results are bounded at a value lower than one. Miotto and Lanckriet [13] found that using semantic modelling of music tags improves auto-tagging compared to the conventional approach of treating each tag individually without any tag similarity information. The proposed Dirichlet mixture model (DMM) captured the broader context of tags and provided an improved peak precision (0.475) and F-score (0.285) compared to previous results using the same data set, when combining DMM with different machine learning techniques.

2.2 Mapping from Audio Features to Perceived Mood

Yang et al. [14] modelled moods represented in the Arousal-Valence (AV) plane using Support Vector Regression (SVR) with LIBSVM implementation [15] trained on audio features. Reported performance was lower for Valence ($R^2 = 0.281$) than for Arousal ($R^2 = 0.583$). Eerola et al. [16] compared various linear regression models at predicting multidimensional emotion ratings with acoustical features. A set of film soundtrack excerpts collected in [4] were used in this experiment. The best models based on Partial Least Squares Regression (PLS) showed high performance at predicting listener ratings of Valence, Arousal, and Tension ($R^2 = 0.72, 0.85, 0.79$). Especially for Valence, the performance was strikingly higher than in [14]. The same soundtrack data was utilised in classification of music to four basic emotion categories in [9], showing the maximum accuracy of 56.5%. Audio features related to tonality

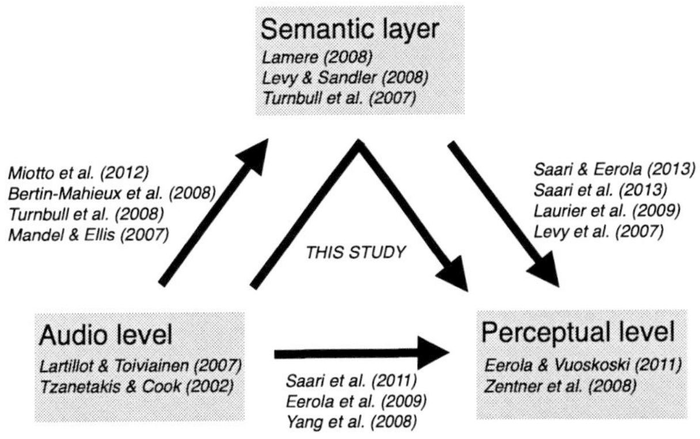

Figure 1. The difference of the present and past studies in mapping between audio features, semantic layer, and perceptual level. Selected past research is cited for each sub-task.

(average majorness of the mode and key clarity), as well as to the average slope of the onset attacks were found to be the most effective predictors of the perceived mood. SVM has been particularly popular in the annual MIREX mood classification challenge [2] representing the state-of-the-art in the field. Moreover, SVM together with ReliefF feature selection produced competitive results [17].

2.3 Mapping from Semantic Layer to Perceived Mood

The studies of Laurier et al. [18] and Levy et al. [19] compared semantic models of mood based on social tags to emotion models proposed by research in affective sciences, as well as expert-generated mood categories used in the MIREX challenge. The accuracy of tag-based semantic models at predicting listener ratings of musical mood was assessed in [20], proposing a technique called Affective Circumplex Transformation (ACT) for the task, based on previous research in affective sciences [21, 22].

ACT was used to predict perceived mood in 600 popular music tracks. The results showed promising performance ($R \approx 0.60$) for the ratings related to the dimensional emotion model as well as separate mood terms. Similar analysis across separate sources of curated editorial annotations for production music, and crowd-sourced Last.fm tags for commercial music, was performed in [23]. The results suggested that semantic models of mood based on tags can be used interchangeably to predict perceived mood across different annotation types and track corpora.

To apply the approach taken in [20] and [23] to new track corpora, semantic annotations need to be available for the corresponding tracks. In order to predict mood in unannotated track corpora, one must rely on other type of information, such as audio features. In the present study, we show how semantic tag data that was found to be promising and relevant in previous work can be used to enhance audio-based mood prediction.

[2] http://www.music-ir.org/mirex/wiki/MIREX_HOME

	# Tracks	# Terms	# Terms / track
Mood set	259,593	357	4.44
SET10K	9,662	357	5.53

Table 1. Statistics of the mood term sets.

3. METHODOLOGY

3.1 Semantic Computing of Mood in Music

The following procedures were applied to uncover a semantic space of mood in music. More detailed account on the analysis and data collection is given in [20].

3.1.1 Vector-Space Modelling

First, a mood vocabulary was collected by aggregating and lemmatising mood term lists from several research papers in affective sciences, music psychology and Music Information Retrieval (MIR), and term lists in the Allmusic.com web service (see [20] for details). Synonyms and inflected forms of the vocabulary terms were identified and aggregated or added manually (e.g., happy ≈ happiness), resulting in 568 unique terms.

Semantic computation was applied to audio tracks and mood tags collected in [20]. Mood vocabulary terms were identified in tags using a bag-of-words approach similar to [1], and terms were applied to associated tracks accordingly. We excluded tracks with less than 2 mood annotations, as well as terms associated to less than 100 tracks, to avoid working with overly sparse information. Table 1 shows the resulting data (mood set) (SET10K is described in Section 3.2). Finally, the mood data set was normalised by computing Term Frequency - Inverse Document Frequency (TF-IDF) weights: $\hat{n}_{i,j} = (n_{i,j}+1)\log(\frac{R}{f_i})$, where $n_{i,j}$ is the original frequency weight related to term w_i and track t_j, R is the total number of tracks, and f_j is the number of tracks term w_i is associated to.

3.1.2 Latent Semantic Modelling

A low-rank approximation of the TF-IDF matrix was computed by Singular Value Decomposition (SVD) and Multidimensional Scaling (MDS). SVD decomposes a sparse matrix N so that $N = USV^T$, where matrices U and V are orthonormal and S is the diagonal matrix containing the singular values of N. Rank k approximation of N is computed by $N^k = U^k S^k (V^k)^T$, where the i:th row vector U_i^k represents a term w_i as a linear combination of k dimensions. Similarly, V_j^k represents track t_j in k dimensions. Based on a rank k approximation, dissimilarity between terms w_i and $w_{\hat{i}}$ is calculated by using the cosine distance between $U_i^k S^k$ and $U_{\hat{i}}^k S^k$.

To represent mood terms explicitly in a low-dimensional space, non-metric MDS [24] with Kruskal's stress-1 criterion was applied on the term dissimilarities, obtained by the rank k approximation of mood TF-IDF using SVD.

Next, we used the Affective Circumplex Transformation (ACT) proposed in [20] to conform the MDS configuration to the space of Arousal and Valence (AV), using AV values of 101 mood terms given in [21, p. 1167] and [22, p. 54].

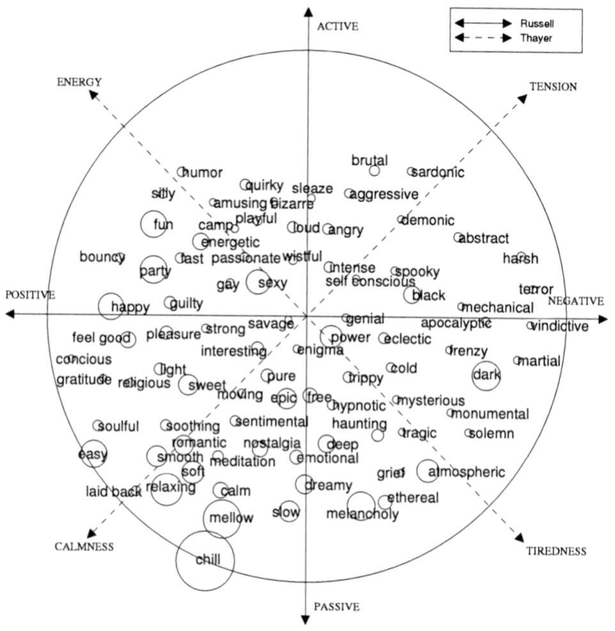

Figure 2. ACT with rank $k = 16$. Only the most frequently applied tags are shown for each part of the AV-space. Tag frequencies are reflected by the size of circles.

This technique is used here to *(i)* increase the interpretability of the MDS configuration; and *(i)* allow us to directly predict mood from the semantic layer. The first two dimensions of the resulting space represent Valence and Arousal as shown in Fig. 2 (with $k = 16$). The size of the circles reflects the frequencies of tags in the mood set, ranging from 110 tracks ("vindictive") to 79,524 tracks ("chill").

Finally, to represent a track in the MDS term space, we applied projection based on the positions of the associated terms. Given an MDS term configuration $y_i = (y_{i1}, y_{i2}, y_{i3})$, $i \in (1, ..., |w|)$, position of a track represented by a sparse term vector q is computed by the center-of-mass:

$$\hat{t} = \frac{\Sigma_i q_i y_i}{\Sigma_i q_i}. \tag{1}$$

3.2 Data set Description

Two data sets were used in our analysis: a 9,662 track subset of the mood set (SET10K), and a set of 600 tracks (SET600) collected in [20]. The audio tracks in both sets are non-overlapping.

SET10K was sampled from the mood set in a balanced manner by optimising mood variance in terms of track projections in the semantic space and including only unique artists. We use this set in successive analysis for mapping audio features to the semantic layer of mood. Audio content of the SET10K consists of 15-30s preview clips obtained from Last.fm. The clips are typically samples of full tracks in 128kB/s mp3 format starting from 30s-60s into the audio. Arguably, these samples contain relevant material that, up to a certain limit, characterise the full tracks.

SET600 was annotated in a listening test [20], where 59 participants rated 15s excerpts of 600 popular music tracks from Last.fm in terms of perceived mood expressed by music. Moods were rated in nine point Likert-scales for

Valence ("negative" / "positive"), Arousal ("calm" / "energetic"), Tension ("relaxed" / "tense"), Atmospheric, Happy, Dark, Sad, Angry, Sensual and Sentimental. The excerpts were sampled from full tracks corresponding to positions in the Last.fm previews. SET600 consists of 15s clips using 320kB/s mp3 format.

3.3 Audio Feature Extraction

Audio features describing dynamics, rhythm, pitch, harmony, timbre and structure were extracted from SET10K and SET600 using the MIRtoolbox [6]. Statistical means and standard deviations over features extracted from various short 50% overlapping time frames were computed to obtain song-level descriptors. The resulting set of 128 features is presented in Table 2. For the features describing rhythmic repetition (127-128) and zero crossing rate (43-44), we used long frame length of 2s, whereas for chromagram-based features such as the repetition of register (125-126), key clarity (19-20), centroid (17-18), mode (21-22), HCDF (23-24), and roughness (25-26) we used a frame length of 100ms. For other features the frame length was 46.4ms except for low-energy ratio (3), which was extracted directly from the full extent of the signal.

Features from SET10K were normalised using the z-score transform. All feature values more than 5 standard deviations from zero were considered outliers and truncated to the extremes $[-5, 5]$ (0.1% and 1.3% of the values in SET10K and SET600 respectively). SET600 was then normalised according to the means and standard deviations of SET10K. In particular, we discovered a slight discrepancy in mean RMS energy (1) between SET10K and SET600. The energy was generally higher in SET600, perhaps due to the use of different MP3 encoders. However, this was ignored in our study for simplicity.

Table 2. Extracted feature set. Feature statistics (m = mean, d = standard deviation) are computed across sample frames.

Category	No.	Feature	Stat.
Dynamics	1-2	RMS energy	m, d
	3	Low-energy ratio	–
	4-5	Attack time	m, d
	6-7	Attack slope	m
Rhythm	8-9	Fluctuation (pos., mag.)	m
	10	Event density	m
	11-12	Pulse clarity	m, d
	13-14	Tempo	m, d
Pitch	15-16	Pitch	m, d
	17-18	Chromagram (unwr.) centr.	m, d
Harmony	19-20	Key clarity	m, d
	21-22	Key mode (majorness)	m, d
	23-24	HCDF	m, d
	25-26	Roughness	m, d
Timbre	27-28	Brightness (cutoff 110 Hz)	m, d
	29-30	Centroid	m, d
	31-32	Flatness (< 5000 Hz)	m, d
	33-34	Irregularity	m, d
	35-36	Skewness (< 5000 Hz)	m, d
	37-38	Spectr. entropy (<5000 Hz)	m, d
	39-40	Spectr. flux	m, d
	41-42	Spread	m, d
	43-44	Zerocross	m, d
MFCC	45-46	1st MFCC	m, d
	⋮	⋮	⋮ ⋮
	69-70	13th MFCC	m, d
	71-96	1st -13th Δ MFCC	m, d
	97-122	1st-13th $\Delta(\Delta)$ MFCC	m, d
Structure	123-124	Repetition (spectrum)	m, d
	125-126	Repetition (register)	m, d
	127-128	Repetition (rhythm)	m, d

3.4 Regression Techniques and Model Evaluation

3.4.1 Semantic Layer Projection

We propose a novel technique for mood prediction in music termed Semantic Layer Projection (SLP). The technique involves mapping audio features to perceived mood in two stages using the semantic mood level as a middle layer, instead of the conventional way of mapping audio features directly to the perceived mood. SLP may be implemented with several potential mapping techniques. We choose to use PLS for the first mapping, due to its higher performance demonstrated in previous research, and linear regression for the second.

First, we apply PLS to the SET10K to produce a mapping from audio features to the 10-dimensional semantic mood representation obtained using ACT. We compare two variants of the semantic mood layer: (SLP_{10D}) track projections in all 10 dimensions of the mood space, and (SLP_{1D}) track projections in separate dimensions corresponding to Valence (1st dim.), and Arousal (2nd dim.). To map from audio features to the semantic layer, we apply PLS to each dimension separately. Then, we project the audio features of SET600 to the semantic layer using the obtained mappings. Finally, we apply linear regression between the 10-dimensional (SLP_{10D}) and 1-dimensional (SLP_{1D}) layer representations and the listener ratings.

We optimise the number of components used in the PLS mappings using 50 × 2-fold cross-validation. In each fold, we divide SET10K into training and test sets, and estimate how well the PLS mapping based on train set fits the test set. To decide on the number of components, we apply (50, 100)-fold cross-indexing proposed in [9]. Cross-indexing is a technique developed to tackle model over-fitting in choosing the optimal model parameterisation from several candidates. Finally, we use the selected number of components to form a model based on the whole SET10K.

3.4.2 Baseline Techniques

In this study, two baseline techniques – PLS and Support Vector Regression (SVR) – were compared with SLP. These techniques were chosen since they represent regression methods that were already found efficient in previous MIR studies. Baseline techniques were applied in the usual way, mapping audio features of SET600 directly to the ratings of perceived mood.

We use PLS in a conventional way with 2 components as in [16]. In SVR, we use the Radial Basis Function (RBF) kernel and apply grid search to optimise the cost ($C = 2^l$, $l \in [-3, ..., 3]$) and gamma ($\gamma = 2^l$, $l \in [-13, ..., 8]$) model parameters. Moreover, we optimise the set of audio features used in SVR by feature subset selection. To this end, we apply the ReliefF [25] feature selection algorithm adapted for regression problems. ReliefF produces relevance weights $\tau \in [-1, 1]$ for the individual features by taking into account their prediction potential and redundancy. To choose a subset of the features, we use a relevance weight threshold $\tau_0 = 0$ and include all features with $\tau > \tau_0$.

3.4.3 Cross-Validation Procedure

For validating the performance of the techniques, we use 50×2-fold cross-validation corresponding to 2-fold cross-validation run 50 times, and report the mean and standard deviation over the 100 performance estimates for each technique. All model optimisation and feature selection is based solely on the training set at each run.

4. RESULTS AND DISCUSSION

In SLP_{10D} and SLP_{1D} we use the rank $k = 16$ for SVD computation. This choice of k was found effective in [20], while other values had no consistent effect on the performance and did not improve the results.

Fig. 3 shows the performance of each technique at predicting the ratings for Valence and Arousal. For Valence, it is evident that SLP outperformed the baseline techniques. SLP_{10D} gave the highest performance ($R^2 = 0.334 \pm 0.035$), outperforming SLP_{1D} ($R^2 = 0.252 \pm 0.032$). SLP_{10D} performed at significantly higher level ($t(99) = 17.994, p = 5.63 \times 10^{-33}$)[3] than SVR ($R^2 = 0.245 \pm 0.048$), while the difference between SLP_{1D} and SVR was not significant. Conventional PLS was the least efficient with a performance of $R^2 = 0.152 \pm 0.045$.

Cross-indexing to optimise the number of PLS components in mapping from audio features to the semantic space yielded 7 components for SLP_{10D} and 13 components for SLP_{1D}. The number of components for SLP_{10D} is the average across 10 dimensions, while the latter relates to the first dimension of SLP_{10D}. The regression model used in the second-stage mapping of SLP_{10D} relied heavily on the first semantic dimension related to Valence: the first dimension showed an average significance of $p \approx 10^{-4}$ across cv-folds. SLP_{10D} model therefore bears a strong similarity to the SLP_{1D}. ReliefF feature selection to optimise the set of audio features used in SVR yielded on average 43 features ($SD = 11$).

In general, the fact that SLP_{1D} outperformed SVR shows the efficiency of SLP. In SLP_{1D} tracks are explicitly projected to Valence already in the first-stage mapping from the audio features to the semantic layer. Therefore minimal learning is required within SET600 for the second-stage mapping to perceived mood. This contrasts to the extensive adaptation to SET600 in SVR, which involves feature selection, cost and gamma optimisation, as well as support vector optimisation.

The overall performance for predicting Valence was at a significantly lower level than the performance of $R^2 = 0.72$ reported in [16]. Most notably, the PLS technique that was successful in [16] did not give convincing performance here. Since the set of audio features used in these studies is similar, the difference in performance is possibly due to the variety of genres covered by SET600. This is in contrast with the previous study using only film soundtracks. Film music is composed to mediate powerful emotional cues [4], which may provide higher variance in feature values so that better representations can be learnt. However, the performance in the present study is in line with other past research such as [14] ($R^2 = 0.281$).

All techniques gave notably higher performance for Arousal than for Valence. In this case, SLP_{10D} again yielded the highest values ($R^2 = 0.782 \pm 0.020$), but outperformed SVR ($R^2 = 0.770 \pm 0.028$) only marginally. PLS gave the third highest performance ($R^2 = 0.751 \pm 0.027$) outperforming SLP_{1D} ($R^2 = 0.745 \pm 0.019$). For Arousal, SLP_{1D} used five PLS components, while the performance of SVR was obtained with 37 features on average ($SD = 9$). Again, the second-stage regression model in SLP_{10D} relied mainly on the 2nd dimension ($p \approx 2 \times 10^{-9}$) related to the Arousal dimension used in SLP_{1D}. Despite more complex training within SET600, SLP_{10D} gave only slight, although highly significant ($t(99) = 5.437, p = 5.4 \times 10^{-7}$) performance gain over SVR. In fact, all techniques performed better than $R^2 = 0.7$, which corroborates past findings that audio features provide a robust basis for modelling perceived Arousal in music.

Similar patterns in the general performance levels between techniques were found in modelling ratings in the other seven scales related to individual mood terms. In general, moods that are characterised by high or low arousal, such as Angry and Atmospheric, performed at similar, yet slightly lower level than Arousal, whereas moods such as Happy and Sad – characterised by positive and negative valence – produced performance similar to Valence.

Since SLP_{10D} produced clearly the highest performance for Valence, while outperformed SVR by a more modest margin for Arousal, it is worth to compare the potential of these techniques in future approaches to mood prediction. SVR represents a sophisticated state-of-the-art technique that is efficient in learning characteristics of the training data relevant to the target mood, but requires complex optimisation of multitude of model parameters. Robust learning of SVR, and any method that could be used as baseline is solely dependent on high quality training data, which is typically laborious to collect. This also means that generalizability of these models to unknown music tracks, and possibly to new music genres, can not be guaranteed, as found in [26]. On the other hand, the efficiency of SLP is primarily based the first-stage mapping from audio to the semantic layer, and require only minimal adaptation to test data. This is suggested by the promising results of SLP_{1D} that produced explicit mood estimates already at the first-stage.

Semantic data required to built the semantic layer can be collected from online services by crowd-sourcing. Some services already make available data related to millions of tracks. Therefore, the cost of collecting training data for SLP is related mostly to obtaining the audio representation of the training set. Larger data for the semantic layer

[3] Pairwise Student's t-test across cv-folds.

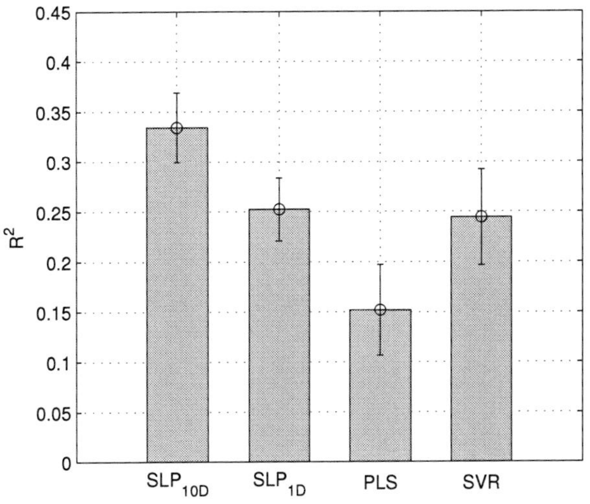

(a) Valence.

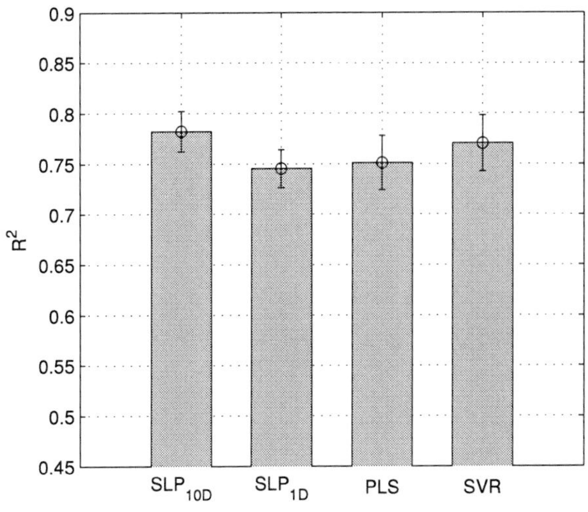

(a) Arousal.

Figure 3. Performance ($R^2 \pm sd$) for each technique in predicting the perceived mood.

enables more delicate learning and would presumably increase the model performance. We therefore claim that the potential of SLP in future mood prediction approaches is higher than that of SVR. Note, however, that as SLP in general can be implemented with any prediction model, SVR can in fact be implemented in the future as the mapping technique within SLP.

Finally, we seek to gain understanding of what audio features are the most useful for modelling Valence and Arousal. We apply SLP_{10D} using each audio feature category described in Table 2 separately. Table. 3 shows the results. Eight harmony-related features including Mode and Key clarity were found to be the most useful in predicting Valence ($R^2 = 0.186$), and in fact, the model using only these 8 features would have outperformed PLS using all features. Features describing timbre, structure, and MFCC showed modest potential for predicting Valence ($R^2 > .10$), whereas rhythm features were largely redundant in this particular task. Prediction of Arousal was on the other hand highly efficient with most feature categories. Timbre ($R^2 = 0.687$) and MFCC ($R^2 = 0.649$) features performed the best. Prediction with harmony-related features was also competitive ($R^2 = 0.653$), while even the four pitch-related features could predict Arousal at moderate level ($R^2 = 0.471$).

In general, these results support previous findings that harmony-related features are useful in mood prediction [9], and that timbre-related features are more useful for predicting Arousal. The results also highlight the need to either optimise existing harmony-related features, or to uncover and investigate a wider variety of audio descriptors for Valence prediction.

Table 3. Performance ($R^2 \pm sd$) of SLP_{10D} using different audio feature categories. Number of features in each category are presented in brackets.

	Valence	Arousal
Dynamics (7)	0.092 ± 0.031	0.536 ± 0.034
Rhythm (7)	0.056 ± 0.044	0.583 ± 0.028
Pitch (4)	0.074 ± 0.034	0.471 ± 0.031
Harmony (8)	$\mathbf{0.186 \pm 0.035}$	0.653 ± 0.030
Timbre (18)	0.141 ± 0.037	$\mathbf{0.687 \pm 0.027}$
MFCC (78)	0.123 ± 0.030	0.649 ± 0.026
Structure (6)	0.127 ± 0.043	0.547 ± 0.025

5. CONCLUSIONS

In this study we developed a novel approach to predict the perceived mood in music called Semantic Layer Projection (SLP). By introducing a two-stage mapping from audio features to semantic layer and finally to mood ratings, SLP provides a way to exploit semantic information about mood learnt from large music collections. It also facilitates building predictive models for disparate music collections. The proposed technique outperformed SVR, a sophisticated predictive model on the Valence dimension, and produced prediction performance roughly at the same level on the Arousal dimension.

The results highlight the difficulty of modelling the Valence dimension in music. However, SLP provides clear advantage compared to baseline techniques specifically in this task, which signifies its high potential that can be developed further in more general audio and semantics-based mood recognition models.

Future direction of the present study includes using more efficient collection of tracks to represent the semantic layer, and improving the prediction of Valence via an extension of the audio feature set. Moreover, a version of the proposed technique that takes musical genre into account – possibly by introducing a genre layer – will be developed to further generalise our model to many different types of music collections.

6. REFERENCES

[1] M. Levy and M. Sandler, "Learning latent semantic models for music from social tags," *Journal of New Music Research*, vol. 37, no. 2, pp. 137–150, 2008.

[2] D. Turnbull, L. Barrington, D. Torres, and G. Lanckriet, "Towards musical query-by-semantic-description using the CAL500 data set," in *Proceedings of the 30th international ACM SIGIR conference on information retrieval*, 2007, pp. 439–446.

[3] P. Lamere, "Social tagging and music information retrieval," *Journal of New Music Research*, vol. 37, no. 2, pp. 101–114, 2008.

[4] T. Eerola and J. Vuoskoski, "A comparison of the discrete and dimensional models of emotion in music." *Psychol. Music*, vol. 39, no. 1, pp. 18–49, 2011.

[5] M. Zentner, D. Grandjean, and K. Scherer, "Emotions evoked by the sound of music: Characterization, classification, and measurement," *Emotion*, vol. 8, no. 4, pp. 494–521, 2008.

[6] O. Lartillot and P. Toiviainen, "A matlab toolbox for musical feature extraction from audio," in *Proceedings of the 10th International Conference on Digital Audio Effects, Bordeaux, France*, September 2007.

[7] G. Tzanetakis and P. Cook, "Musical genre classification of audio signals," *IEEE Transactions on Speech and Audio Processing*, vol. 10, no. 5, pp. 293–302, Jul. 2002.

[8] M. Barthet, G. Fazekas, and M. Sandler, "Multidisciplinary perspectives on music emotion recognition: Recommendations for content- and context-based models," in *Proc. of the 9th Int. Symposium on Computer Music Modeling and Retrieval (CMMR)*, 2012, pp. 492–507.

[9] P. Saari, T. Eerola, and O. Lartillot, "Generalizability and simplicity as criteria in feature selection: Application to mood classification in music," *IEEE Transactions on Speech and Audio Processing*, vol. 19, no. 6, pp. 1802 –1812, aug. 2011.

[10] D. Turnbull, L. Barrington, D. Torres, and G. Lanckriet, "Semantic annotation and retrieval of music and sound effects," *IEEE Transactions on Audio, Speech, and Language Processing*, vol. 16, no. 2, pp. 467–476, 2008.

[11] M. I. Mandel and D. P. Ellis, "Multiple-instance learning for music information retrieval," in *Proceedings of 9th International Conference of Music Information Retrieval (ISMIR)*, 2008, pp. 577–582.

[12] T. Bertin-Mahieux, D. Eck, F. Maillet, and P. Lamere, "Autotagger: A model for predicting social tags from acoustic features on large music databases," *Journal of New Music Research*, vol. 37, no. 2, pp. 115–135, 2008.

[13] R. Miotto and G. Lanckriet, "A generative context model for semantic music annotation and retrieval," *IEEE Transactions on Audio, Speech, and Language Processing*, vol. 20, no. 4, pp. 1096–1108, 2012.

[14] Y. H. Yang, Y. C. Lin, Y. F. Su, and H. H. Chen, "A regression approach to music emotion recognition," *IEEE Transactions on Audio, Speech, and Language Processing*, vol. 16, no. 2, pp. 448–457, Feb. 2008.

[15] C.-C. Chang and C.-J. Lin, "Libsvm: a library for support vector machines," *ACM Transactions on Intelligent Systems and Technology (TIST)*, vol. 2, no. 3, p. 27, 2011.

[16] T. Eerola, O. Lartillot, and P. Toiviainen, "Prediction of multidimensional emotional ratings in music from audio using multivariate regression models," in *9th International Conference on Music Information Retrieval*, 2009, pp. 621–626.

[17] R. Panda and R. P. Paiva, "Music emotion classification: Dataset acquisition and comparative analysis," in *n 15th International Conference on Digital Audio Effects (DAFx-12)*, 2012.

[18] C. Laurier, M. Sordo, J. Serra, and P. Herrera, "Music mood representations from social tags," in *Proceedings of 10th International Conference on Music Information Retrieval (ISMIR)*, 2009, pp. 381–86.

[19] M. Levy and M. Sandler, "A semantic space for music derived from social tags," in *Proceedings of 8th International Conference on Music Information Retrieval (ISMIR)*, 2007.

[20] P. Saari and T. Eerola, "Semantic computing of moods based on tags in social media of music," *IEEE Transactions on Knowledge and Data Engineering*, manuscript submitted for publication available at http://arxiv.org/, 2013.

[21] J. A. Russell, "A circumplex model of affect," *Journal of Personality and Social Psychology*, vol. 39, no. 6, pp. 1161–1178, 1980.

[22] K. R. Scherer, *Emotion as a multicomponent process: A model and some cross-cultural data*. Beverly Hills: CA: Sage, 1984, pp. 37–63.

[23] P. Saari, M. Barthet, G. Fazekas, T. Eerola, and M. Sandler, "Semantic models of mood expressed by music: Comparison between crowd-sourced and curated editorial annotations," in *IEEE International Conference on Multimedia and Expo (ICME 2013): International Workshop on Affective Analysis in Multimedia (AAM)*, In press 2013.

[24] J. Kruskal, "Multidimensional scaling by optimizing goodness of fit to a nonmetric hypothesis," *Psychometrika*, vol. 29, pp. 1–27, 1964.

[25] M. Robnik-Sikonja and I. Kononenko, "An adaptation of relief for attribute estimation in regression," in *Proceedings of the Fourteenth International Conference on Machine Learning*, ser. ICML '97. San Francisco, CA: Morgan Kaufmann Publishers Inc., 1997, pp. 296–304.

[26] T. Eerola, "Are the emotions expressed in music genre-specific? an audio-based evaluation of datasets spanning classical, film, pop and mixed genres," *Journal of New Music Research*, vol. 40, no. 4, pp. 349–366, 2011.

BEAT-STATION: A REAL-TIME RHYTHM ANNOTATION SOFTWARE

Marius Miron, Fabien Gouyon, Matthew E.P. Davies
INESC TEC
Porto, Portugal
mmiron,mdavies,fgouyon@inescporto.pt

André Holzapfel
Boğaziçi University
Istanbul, Turkey
andre@rhythmos.org

ABSTRACT

This paper describes an open-source software for real-time rhythm annotation. The software integrates several modules for graphical user interface, user management across a network, tap recording, audio playing, midi interfacing and threading. It is a powerful tool for conducting listening tests, but can also be used for beat annotation of music or in a game setup. The parameters of this software, including the real-time constraints, are not pre-defined in the code but can be easily changed in a settings file. Finally, the framework used allows for scalability, as it was developed in openFrameworks. We show the usefulness of the software by applying it in a cross-cultural beat tapping experiment during the ISMIR 2012 conference. An analysis of the collected real-time annotations indicates that listeners encounter difficulties in synchronizing to music in presence of unfamiliar rhythmic structures and instrumental timbres.

1. INTRODUCTION

When analyzing a piece of music, an important initial step is to obtain an understanding of its temporal structure; to know: where boundaries between melodic phrases are, where the downbeats are located, where an instrument begins to play a note? Annotating such aspects of musical structure is a time-consuming task, but human annotations are often needed for the evaluation of automatic analysis approaches, or for obtaining insight into human perception of musical structure.

Tanghe et al. [1] described the process of annotating note onsets. They noted the absence of suitable annotation tools for their purposes. In their conclusion they underlined the importance of an easy-to-use, flexible, dedicated system for music annotation. Visual feedback, multi-layer annotations, connectivity to external user interfaces, flexible input and output, were found to be the key features of such a system.

Moreover, during the time-consuming and possibly boring process of manual annotation, the subjects can be motivated by designing the application as a game, providing the subjects with some goal to achieve. With one single exception [2], focused on collecting tags for music pieces, we are not aware of annotation systems which have been specically designed as a game.

Regarding annotation tools that integrate into existing software, Gouyon et al. [3] presented a semi-automatic rhythm annotation tool. This open-source tool is integrated into WaveSurfer [1]. It comprises a beat tracking algorithm, which sets the time values for the beats, and an annotation tool, which allows the editing of these time values. The annotator can stratify the beats into several metrical levels, however without the ability to simultaneously edit beats at several levels in real-time. MUCOSA [4] is a music content semantic annotator also based on WaveSurfer. The environment stores metadata at three different levels using an annotation client and a collection tagger. Additionally, it supports sharing annotations between various research groups via an administrative web interface. Li et al. [5] introduced editable audio and music segmentation layers into the Audacity editor [2]. While it offers important visual cues to the annotator, it is mainly focused on phrase segmentations, and not on rhythm or note onset annotation.

With respect to stand-alone annotation tools, Sonic Visualizer [6] is a music analysis and annotation platform developed in C++. In a similar way to MUCOSA, it structures information into several editable layers. It lacks the annotation sharing and user management capabilities of MUCOSA, but is highly expandable due to the integration of VAMP plug-ins which can provide automatically generated guides for annotation, *e.g.* by using an onset detection algorithm first, and then modifying its output by hand.

Most existing annotation tools were not designed for experimental conditions or games. For these systems, important settings such as the time sampling rate for user inputs are not available for editing. Other features, such as user management [4], or MIDI interfacing are present in some systems, but absent from others [5].

In this paper, we present *beatStation*, a software focused on (but not restricted to) rhythm annotation. The software can be applied in a game setup and provides functionalities for beat perception experiments. Compared to the other annotation software presented above, beatStation has multiple modules, and can be easily expanded as it was implemented in openFrameworks [3]. The application is open-source, flexible and scalable. It uses several popular openFrameworks add-ons for user and file management across network, audio playing, graphical user interface, process

[1] http://sourceforge.net/projects/wavesurfer/
[2] http://audacity.sourceforge.net
[3] http://www.openframeworks.cc/

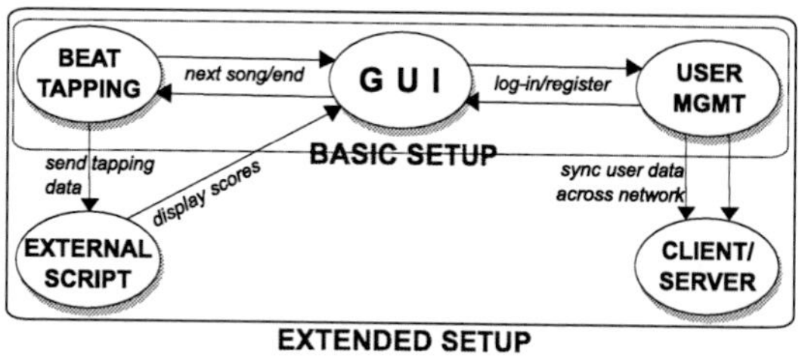

Figure 1: Software framework

threading, MIDI interfacing, and can be easily extended with more add-ons. Due to the flexibility of openFrameworks, it can be ported to any operating system platform, including mobile platforms.

Moreover, beatStation allows a user-friendly approach to conduct experiments by providing access to a range of parameters of the application from a simple settings file. Additionally, various stations can be simultaneously used in a client-server configuration, providing user management control. The software can be configured *e.g.* to annotate meter at several levels simultaneously in real-time, but also the annotation of melodic motif and phrase boundaries is possible. The data collected from the subjects is easily accessible and portable for analysis in the form of *xml*-files.

The beatStation was used during the ISMIR 2012 conference to gather sensorimotor synchronization [7] responses from subjects when asked to tap to Turkish and euro-genetic popular music. The experiment was designed as a game, in which attendants were motivated to tap the beat across a set of music stimuli to maximize their chances of winning a competition. This pilot experiment was a great success, and the software ran continuously for 5 days without incident. The results of the experiment provided us with some valuable insights into the ways listeners respond to musical styles they are not familiar with. These insights have already been used to design a dataset for a more thorough analysis of sensorimotor synchronization in Turkish music.

The remainder of the paper is structured as follows: In Section 2, we present the software framework with each module add-on. Section 3 presents details of our case study, and results are analyzed in Section 4. Finally, Section 5 concludes the paper.

2. SOFTWARE FRAMEWORK

As stated in [8] , openFrameworks introduced a framework which can be easily used by creative individuals, and also incorporates the strong assets of the C++ programming language. Since its introduction, a huge variety of applications has been developed and the community of developers has grown considerably. The framework grew as external code was added in the form of add-ons. Many of these add-ons can be combined in a single application, making it possible to connect various modules related to visuals, sensors and even algorithms for audio signal processing or sound synthesis.

The beatStation application has a basic setup, as depicted in Figure 1, including the core modules of beat tapping recording and storing, graphical user interface, and user management. Its extended setup includes external script calling and client-server communication.

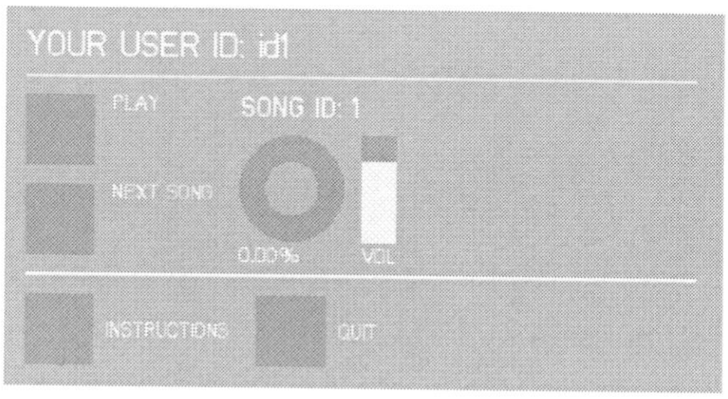

Figure 2: Screenshot of the *beatStation* interface

The add-ons used inside *beatStation* are as follows: *ofxUI* and *ofxTextSuite* for the graphical user interface, *ofxXMLSettings* for storing the data related to users and tapping, *ofxDirList* to load sound files or xml data files, *ofxTCPClient* and *ofxTCPServer* for tcp/ip communication. Additionally, the following pre-existing openFramework classes were used: *ofxMidi* for midi connectivity, *ofThread* for calling an external application to process the results, *ofSoundPlayer* for playing sounds.

2.1 Recording and storing real-time input

Our motivation was to create a software for real-time rhythm annotation, where the subject would be asked to tap to a musical stimulus. Hence, the tappings can capture various aspects such as beats, note onsets or downbeat structure – indeed any time-based information which can be meaningfully entered in real-time.

The subject is presented a set of songs, which is located in the `sounds` directory. Whether the songs are presented in a random or alphabetical order can be chosen by modifying the *randomFiles* variable in the `settings.xml` file. The number of times the subject can listen to a song can be set from the *noPlays* variable, in the same file. If a song is played more than once, then only the final set of annotations are retained. The subject's responses are saved in the `data` directory every time a user quits the interface or finishes annotating a song. Each user has an associated XML file where the tapping data is stored on the following structure:

```
<tapping userID="14" currentSound="1">
    <songIndexes>2 </songIndexes>
    <song songID="2" tryNo="1">
        <fileName>file1.aiff</fileName>
        <transcription></transcription>
        <transcription2></transcription2>
    </song>
</tapping>
```

The unique ID of each user and the number of sounds tapped are stored at the top level. The lower levels stores the IDs of songs tapped, and for each one of those, the name of the song, and transcription values in milliseconds.

Annotation can be performed using the keyboard or a MIDI interface, *e.g.* drum pads for beat annotation. The settings related to MIDI are *midiPort*, *midiChannel*, *midiNote*, and *midiNote2*. When using the computer keyboard, the subjects can tap various metrical levels using the SPACE

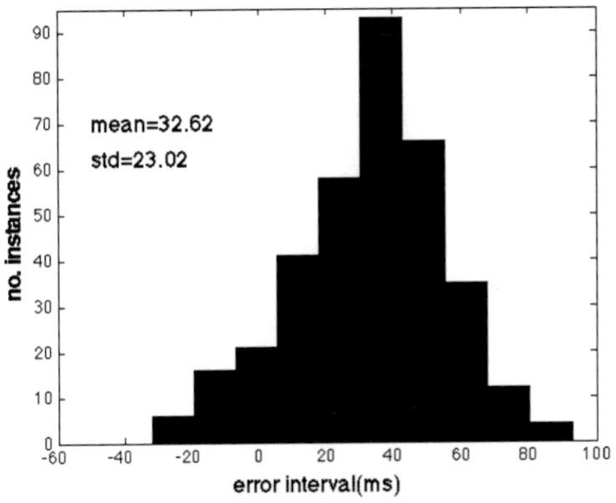

(a) KEYBOARD

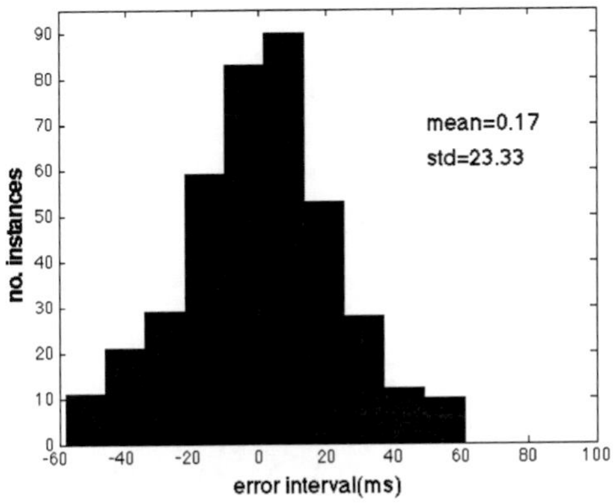

(b) MIDI INTERFACE

Figure 3: The histograms representing the delay between the onsets of the pulses in the signal and the time instances tapped on, using (a) the KEYBOARD, and (b) the MIDI INTERFACE

and TAB keys. The associated settings are *tapWithSpace*, and *tapWithTab*.

Regarding the real-time performance, the MIDI and the keyboard have associated event listener functions, which capture the events from the external interfaces. Checking for keyboard and MIDI interruptions with an event listener introduces a delay, which cannot be controlled using the application. This delay depends on the operating system, the MIDI drivers and the MIDI interface.

The unpredictable variability of the timing accuracy of general purpose computers was discussed in [9] . In this paper, we computed the tapping latency for our application when using a MIDI interface Roland Handsonic HPD-10 connected through a Digidesign USB sound card, and the keyboard, on a 2012 iMac computer. Five subjects were asked to tap along a sound example of 170 seconds duration, comprising equidistant pulses at a period of 500ms. Each subject tapped the sound example three times, first using the MIDI interface and then the keyboard.

In Figure 3, we depict a histogram of timing differences between the taps and the pulse locations in the signal. The delay using the keyboard is almost twice as large, but still lies within the tolerance demanded *e.g.* in beat tracking evaluation [10]. The standard deviation is similar for both interfaces and is in the range of the typically reported human variability [7] in sensorimotor synchronization.

2.2 Graphical User Interface

The graphical user interface (GUI) comprises several scenes for each stage of the application: user registration, user log-in, instructions, song annotation, and display of results. The user can move from one scene to another following a sequence of steps. First, the user has to register in the main GUI, where a basic description of the experiment is displayed. Then the application displays a set of instructions describing the task which is to be performed by the subject. After this, the tapping GUI is loaded. At this stage, the user can listen to songs and input their taps. A results page is displayed when the user finishes tapping all the songs or quits.

As depicted in Figure 2, the PLAY button is used to start playback of a song, after which the NEXT button can be used to move to the following sound example. All the buttons are disabled when a song is playing, except the QUIT button (provided the *canQuit* variable has been set in the settings file). The volume can be adjusted with the VOL slider. The instructions can be displayed with the INSTRUCTIONS button. The percentage played from a song can be seen in the rotary slider.

The software can be customized for various setups. The initial description can be edited in the `description.txt` file. In a similar way, the text for the instructions can be changed in the `instructions.txt` file.

The core of the GUI is the *ofxUI* add-on, which offers GUI scene management, widget layout, spacing, font loading, and several GUI widgets as buttons, input boxes, radio buttons etc. The absolute dimension of the GUI elements can be set by altering the value *itemDimGUI* in the settings file. Also, the application can be ran windowed or full screen by modifying the *fullscreen* variable in the same file. Users can be prevented to exit the application by setting a password in the field *passToExit*.

2.3 User Management

Before being presented with the audio stimuli, each subject is required to register in the application. For the prototype we only asked for a name, but more complex information could be gathered. Using the name, we generate a unique numeric ID and another ID based on the initials of the entered name. The latter can be used to log-in to the application and to resume the experiment at a future date, which is useful when the subject can perform the experiment in several parts. Additionally, we record the time and date of the registration. This data is stored in the `data/users.xml` file, with the following structure:

```
<users>
    <records>1</records>
    <maxID>0</maxID>
    <user>
        <ID>0</ID>
        <name>tt1</name>
        <fullname>tt</fullname>
        <date>2012-10-01</date>
    </user>
</users>
```

The number of records and the maximum ID in the XML is stored at the higher level, and the information concerning each subject, ID, name, full name, registration date, on the lower level.

2.4 Client-Server Communication

Within our specific experiment setup, we wished to have several stations operating in parallel. Therefore we implemented a client-server architecture which allows different computers to communicate over a network. This architecture allows users to login into different machines (e.g. with different datasets) without the need to create a new user account each time.

Each client station sends a message to the server each time a user authenticates or creates an account. The server listens on a port for incoming messages from the client stations. If a message is received, the server checks if the user exists, and if it needs to, adds the user to the `users.xml`. Then, the server sends a message back to the client which tells the client if the user already exists in the database, or if it has just been added. Using this information from the server, the client allows the user to proceed using the application.

A station can either be determined as client or server by modifying the *isClient* variable in the settings file. If set to a client, the port to communicate is set using the *tcpPort* variable, along with the IP address of the server, *ipServer*. All annotations are stored on the local machine, regardless of whether the station is a client or server.

2.5 Calling External Scripts

In order to process annotation data on the fly, external scripts can be called depending on certain values in the settings file. These values are $launchScript$, which tells the application to launch a script or not, $scriptDirectory$, the relative path to the directory where the script resides, and $appToLaunchPath$, the full command line of the external program which calls the script. For instance, during our ISMIR experiment, we called an Octave[4] script to evaluate the recorded taps as follows:

```
<appToLaunchPath>
   /Applications/Octave.app/Contents
   /Resources/bin/octave -qf --quiet
   --eval "clear all; cd path;
   tapping2('xmlin','xmlout');exit;"
</appToLaunchPath> -
```

The $tapping2$ script reads the tapping data file, $xmlin$, and outputs a results file $xmlout$.

2.6 Designing for various setups

The beatStation was designed to function as a game during the ISMIR 2012 conference, having two stations in a client-server architecture. In this setup, the subjects were encouraged to annotate all songs, in order to achieve a better position in the high-score table. The high-score table was displayed on the log-in/registration page. We imposed a lower limit of five songs that someone has to tap in order to enter the high-score, a value that can be modified using the $minTaps$ variable. The version of the beatStation used at ISMIR 2012 can be downloaded from the Github repository [5].

In general experimental setups, there may be no requirement for a high-score table. For this reason, we disabled the script launching possibility in the final version, which automatically disables the high-score table. Subjects can not quit the application ($canQuit = 0$), and an additional page with a questionnaire can be launched in the application. The related code is commented in the source code, but can be adapted and activated. The more generic, non-ISMIR, version of the beatStation can be obtained from the Github repository [6].

The beatStation can be used for annotating the beats or any other events in music in real-time. As it is primarily designed for listening tests, it does not offer additional visual cues, and it can record high resolution annotations, on two (in our case: metrical) levels simultaneously (see Section 2.1). It doesn't allow editing of the annotations but the data can be easily exported to any other framework that allows editing (e.g. Sonic Visualiser). Functions to read the data into a Octave structure are provided with the software.

3. CASE STUDY

The goal of our experiments at ISMIR 2012 with two beatStations was, (apart from a real-world test of functionality), to collect data recording the sensorimotor synchronisation of listeners to music stimuli from two different music cultures; Turkish Makam music and euro-genetic popular music. By analysis of the recorded tapping sequences and their relation to annotated ground truth, we aim to address the question of whether high mutual agreement between tapping sequences (*i.e.* which arises when users tap the same way to the stimuli) is indicative of accurate tapping compared to the ground truth. By comparing these findings between the recorded taps and ground truth for stimuli from the two music cultures, we can obtain first indications into how difficult following the rhythm in Turkish music is for listeners who are unfamiliar with it, compared to generally more familiar euro-genetic popular music. We also investigate which musical properties caused problems in synchronizing with the stimuli.

When registering at a beatStation, a subject was asked to "listen to some short samples of music and to tap your perception of the most prominent pulse". Subjects were allowed to tap to a stimulus a second time, if the subject was not satisfied with their initial taps. The taps were recorded using the space bar of the keyboard, and high-quality headphones were used. The whole setup took place in the registration hall of the conference venue. While we are aware that this was not an ideal environment for conducting experiments of this kind, no subject reported the background ambient noise to be a problem. In order to motivate subjects to tap as many stimuli as possible, the beatStation was set up as a game, a kind of informal tapping competition. To that end, we used the script functionality (see Section 2.5) to compare the subjects taps with existing ground

[4] http://www.gnu.org/software/octave/

[5] http://github.com/nkundiushuti/beatStationISMIR/

[6] http://github.com/SMC-INESC/beatStation/

truth, and a high score table was generated with the scores of the "best" tappers.

In this paper, the Information Gain evaluation measure [10] was applied for the computation of all comparisons between beat annotations. In this evaluation measure, local timing deviations between beat annotations are summarized in a beat error histogram. The beat error histogram is characterized by a concentration of magnitudes in one or a few bins if annotations are strongly related, and by a flatter shape if the two annotations are unrelated. The deviation of this histogram from the uniform distribution, the so-called Information Gain, is measured using K-L divergence. This Information Gain measure has a range from 0 to 4.7 bits using the parameters described in [10], with 0 bits implying lack of any relation between two sequences, and higher values indicating a strong relation.

On the server beatStation, the dataset in [11] was used. This dataset, referred to as ISMIR2012, consists of 48 audio excerpts of 15s length each, which form part of the MillionSongSubset from the Million Song Dataset [12]. For the other beatStation, we selected 36 excerpts of 15s length, which we refer to as the MAKAM dataset. For all excerpts contained in the two datasets, ground truth annotations of the beat were performed by the authors of the paper. For excerpts in additive meters, *e.g.* 9/8, the pulsation at the metrical level of the 1/8 notes was annotated.

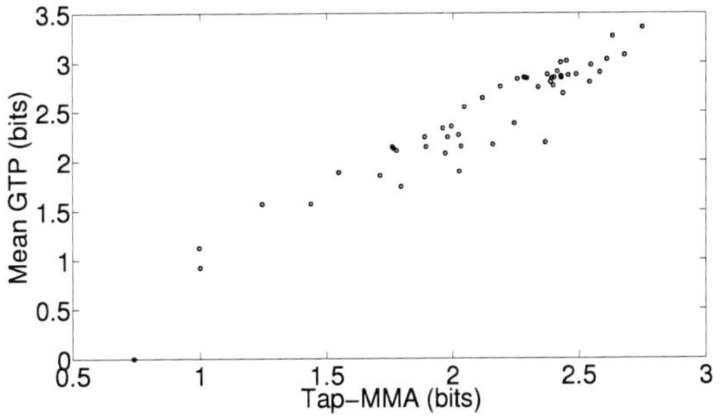

(a) ISMIR2012

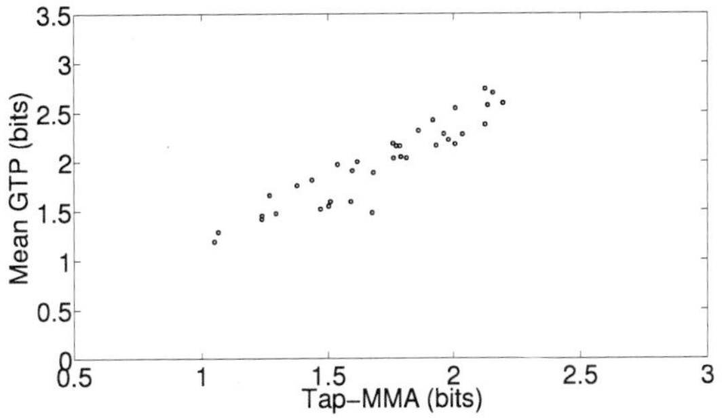

(b) MAKAM

Figure 4: Scatter plots of the mean GTP over the Tap-MMA for, (a) the ISMIR2012, and (b) the MAKAM dataset

4. DATA ANALYSIS

Throughout the ISMIR2012 conference a total of 157 users registered at the beatStations. While this number reflects the high interest that the experiment attracted, many users only tapped a small number of files. While we didn't ask for explicit feedback from users, we suspect this may have been due to limited time available within the conference. To simplify our analysis, we retained only those users who tapped all files, which was done for each tapping station separately. By pure coincidence, we ended up with a set of 21 subjects for both the ISMIR 2012 and MAKAM dataset. While some enthusiastic subjects tapped to both datasets, the two sets of subjects were not identical.

We first compute the degree of mutual agreement between tapping sequences by comparing all pairs of annotations for a song using the Information Gain measure. We also computed the ground truth performance of each tapping sequence by comparing it with the ground truth annotation using the same measure. Then, we computed the Mean Mutual Agreement between all tapping sequences for a recording (Tap-MMA), and the mean Ground Truth Performance among all tappers for a specific song (mean GTP). Figure 4 shows a very high correlation between these two measurements, with the correlation coefficients being 0.951 for the ISMIR2012 and 0.930 for the MAKAM dataset. This shows that on both datasets mutual agreement in synchronization to the sound is strongly related to a high agreement with the annotated ground truth. While the correlations are high, both the Tap-MMA and the mean GTP of the taps are lower for the MAKAM data than for the ISMIR2012 data. On the MAKAM dataset we measure total means of 1.70 bits and 1.98 bits for Tap-MMA and mean GTP, respectively, on the ISMIR2012 dataset we obtain 2.43 and 2.11 bits. This is reflected by the scatter plot depicted in Figure 4a reaching further up to the right upper corner than the scatter plot for the MAKAM dataset depicted in Figure 4b.

Based on this analysis we infer that the MAKAM dataset represented a higher degree of difficulty for the sensorimotor synchronization than the ISMIR2012 dataset. This conclusion is supported by considering how often the subjects chose to tap a sample for a second time; For the MAKAM dataset 41% of the tapped annotations stem from a second attempt, while for the ISMIR2012 dataset the subjects only chose to tap a file again in 25% of the cases. This indicates that subjects were more confident that their spontaneous taps correlate with the musical meter for the familiar styles of euro-genetic popular music.

Finally, we use the outcome of the experiments to obtain conclusions about what traits influence synchronization for human listeners on the MAKAM dataset. First, those excerpts with $4/4$ time signatures were tapped more accurately compared to the ground truth, and wtih greated mutual agreement. Secondly, samples having either no percussive accompaniment or where the rhythmic accompaniment is played by Western drums cause problems for the listeners as well. While the former can be attributed to a larger *rubato* style in those performences, the latter reveals an interesting problem. In many recordings, Western drums, often in the form of electronic MIDI drums, are introduced to accompany rhythmic idioms that were originally not connected with them (such as the 9/8 *Aksak*). Even though the instrumental timbre of the drums introduce clear phenomenal cues for the beat, their acculturation seems to present problems to the listeners.

5. CONCLUSIONS

We presented a real-time annotation software, used for an experiment designed as a beat tapping game during the ISMIR 2012 conference. We introduced every layer of the used framework and its role in the overall architecture. Furthermore, we showed how basic features can be controlled from a simple settings file, in order to design various experimental setups. Our case study indicates that the software is stable having run across two machines for five continuous days during the ISMIR conference. We found that for our task the small latency in the system was not problematic and did not effect our ability to evaluate tap sequences. Through an objective comparison of input interfaces we confirmed that external MIDI hardware offers lower latency than using the SPACE bar on a standard computer keyboard.

The software can be used to capture in real time any kind of information that requires tapping: beats, onsets, rhythmic patters, structure segmentation. On the other hand, currently the data analysis is only offerred for comparing beats using Matlab/Octave. Moreover, the future development of the application can take various directions. For instance, an annotation software with off-line editing of annotations could incorporate visual cues and editing features, as well as additional interaction with the audio, such as adding pause and stop buttons. In an experimental setup for *e.g.* sensorimotor synchronization, the additional questionnaire page can be activated in the application and the parameters can be set according to the user's needs.

The results of our case study show that Turkish Makam music poses different challenges to listeners when asked to follow the beat of a piece. These challenges seem to be related to rhythmic structures as well as instrumental timbres. This motivates us to conduct a more formal comparative study of tapping behavior on additive and divisive rhythm which addresses the influence of cultural background of the listener and examines the various possible ways humans synchronize to these rhythms. Such a study is an important contribution to widening the focus of current research in MIR to include rhythms from other cultures, and to incorporate adequate cultural concepts of beat and rhythm into processing tools.

Finally, serialization of data and client-server communication should be adapted to gather tapping data from distributed devices onto a server. The basic game setup can be redesigned to allow users to compete against each other, or work in teams to achieve higher mutual agreement.

Acknowledgments

This work is partly supported by the European Research Council under the European Union's Seventh Framework Program, as part of the CompMusic project (ERC grant agreement 267583), and by the ERDF – European Regional Development Fund through the (FCOM-01-0124-FEDER-014732) COMPETE Programme (operational programme for competitiveness) and by National Funds through the FCT – Fundacao para a Ciencia e a Tecnologia (Portuguese Foundation for Science and Technology) within project Shake-it, Grant PTDC/EAT-MMU/ 112255/2009. Part of this research was supported by the CASA project with reference PTDC/EIA-CCO/111050/2009 (FCT), and by the MAT project funded by ON.2. We would like to thank all participants of the test at ISMIR 2012.

6. REFERENCES

[1] K. Tanghe, M. Lesaffre, S. Degroeve, M. Leman, B. De Baets, and J. Martens, "Collecting ground truth annotations for drum detection in polyphonic music," in *Proc. ISMIR*, 2005, pp. 50–57.

[2] E. L. M. Law, L. V. Ahn, R. B. Dannenberg, and M. Crawford, "Tagatune: A game for music and sound annotation," in *Proc. ISMIR*, 2007, pp. 361–364.

[3] F. Gouyon, N. Wack, and S. Dixon, "An open source tool for semi-automatic rhythmic annotation," in *Proc. DAFx*, 2004, pp. 193–196.

[4] P. Herrera, Ò. Celma, J. Massaguer, P. Cano, E. Gómez, F. Gouyon, M. Koppenberger, D. Garcia, J. G. Mahedero, and N. Wack, "Mucosa a music content semantic annotator," in *Proc. ISMIR*, 2005, pp. 77–83.

[5] B. Li, J. A. Burgoyne, and I. Fujinaga, "Extending audacity for audio annotation," in *Proc. ISMIR*, 2006.

[6] C. Cannam, C. Landone, M. Sandler, and J. P. Bello, "The sonic visualiser: A visualisation platform for semantic descriptors from musical signals," in *Proc. ISMIR*, 2006.

[7] B. H. Repp, "Sensorimotor synchronization: a review of the tapping literature." *Psychonomic bulletin & review*, vol. 12, no. 6, pp. 969–992, Dec. 2005. [Online]. Available: http://view.ncbi.nlm.nih.gov/pubmed/16615317

[8] J. Noble, *Programming Interactivity: A Designer's Guide to Processing, Arduino, and Openframeworks.* O'Reilly Media, Incorporated, 2009.

[9] A. Wallace and G. Madison, "The timing accuracy of general purpose computers for experimentation and measurements in psychology and the life sciences," *The Open Psychology Journal*, 2010.

[10] M. E. P. Davies, N. Degara, and M. D. Plumbley, "Evaluation methods for musical audio beat tracking algorithms," Queen Mary University of London, Centre for Digital Music, Tech. Rep. C4DM-TR-09-06, 2009.

[11] J. R. Zapata, A. Holzapfel, M. E. P. Davies, J. Lobato Oliveira, and F. Gouyon, "Assigning a confidence threshold on automatic beat annotation in large datasets," in *Proc. ISMIR*, 2012, pp. 157–162.

[12] T. Bertin-Mahieux, D. Ellis, B. Whitman, and P. Lamere, "The million song dataset," in *Proc. ISMIR*, 2011, pp. 591–596.

MODELLING PERCEPTION OF SPEED IN MUSIC AUDIO

Anders Elowsson
KTH Royal Institute of Technology
CSC, Dept. of Speech, Music and Hearing
elov@kth.se

Anders Friberg
KTH Royal Institute of Technology
CSC, Dept. of Speech, Music and Hearing
afriberg@kth.se

ABSTRACT

One of the major parameters in music is the overall speed of a musical performance. Speed is often associated with tempo, but other factors such as note density (onsets per second) seem to be important as well. In this study, a computational model of speed in music audio has been developed using a custom set of rhythmic features. The original audio is first separated into a harmonic part and a percussive part and onsets are extracted separately from the different layers. The characteristics of each onset are determined based on frequency content as well as perceptual salience using a clustering approach. Using these separated onsets a set of eight features including a tempo estimation are defined which are specifically designed for modelling perceived speed. In a previous study 20 listeners rated the speed of 100 ringtones consisting mainly of popular songs, which had been converted from MIDI to audio. The ratings were used in linear regression and PLS regression in order to evaluate the validity of the model as well as to find appropriate features. The computed audio features were able to explain about 90 % of the variability in listener ratings.

1. INTRODUCTION

This study is focused on one of the major parameters in music, the overall speed of a musical performance. From a music theoretic background we are used to associate speed with the tempo of the music. However, as suggested earlier, the perceived speed is related to the tempo but may also be dependent on other aspects like the note density (number of onsets per second) [1]. An indirect indication of this was provided in [2] where it was found that the note density (and not the tempo) was constant for a certain emotional expression across different music examples. Madison & Paulin [3] asked listeners to rate the speed for 50 music examples spanning a variety of musical styles and rhythms. They found that speed correlated with tempo but also indicated that there must be other aspects involved in the perceptual judgment of speed. In Figure 1, three examples with different tempos and onset densities are shown. As outlined in Table 1, example *A* has a slow tempo but the hi-hat plays on 16th notes. As a result, the number of onsets coming from percussive instruments is high. Example *B* has a high number of onsets from harmonic instruments (e.g. vocals, piano, etc.) but a moderate tempo. Finally, example *C* has the highest tempo but the lowest overall note density. How do these different aspects affect the perceived speed? In this study we will model the perception of speed by extracting specifically developed features (such as tempo and onset densities) from music audio. An important idea is that the model should exploit the characteristics of the onsets to better understand the music.

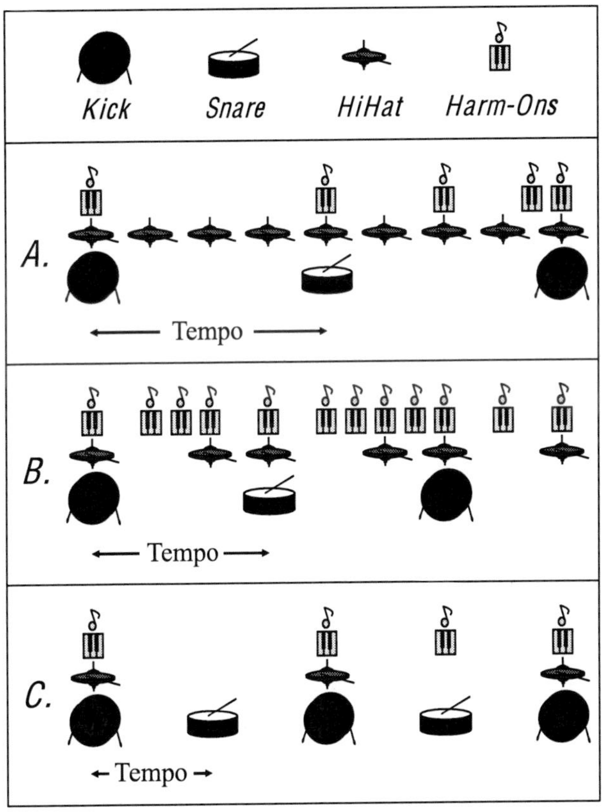

Figure 1. Several factors that can influence the perceived speed of a piece of music. The tempo is one important factor but onset density is relevant as well.

Example	Tempo	Drum-Ons	Harm-Ons
A	Slow	Fast	Mid
B	Mid	Mid	Fast
C	Fast	Slow	Slow

Table 1. Different characteristics of the music which are related to speed. A song may have a slow tempo but many onsets that increases the perceived speed.

The current work is part of an ongoing study about perceptually determined features in music information retrieval. In a previous study it was shown that speed could be modeled by a combination of tempo and different note densities of the instruments using symbolic data [4]. The explained variation was about 90 % using linear regression. This indicates that a similar result could in theory be obtained using audio data provided that the appropriate low-level audio features could be extracted.

A flowchart of the processes used in the model is shown in Figure 2. As a first step, source separation (Section 3) was used to separate harmonic content and percussive content in the audio as well as to cluster onsets into different groups. Features were computed from both the percussive and the harmonic part as well as from the original audio as described in Section 4. To find appropriate features as well to evaluate the validity of the model, regression was used, in which the audio features were mapped against ground truth data consisting of listener ratings of speed. This is described in Section 5.

2. SPEED DATA AND AUDIO EXAMPLES

The speed estimations were perceptually determined in a previous experiment in which 20 listeners rated speed for each music example on a quasi-continuous scale marked slow-fast with the range 1-9. The music examples were a set of 100 ringtones consisting mainly of popular songs, originally in MIDI format and converted to audio [5, 6].

3. SOURCE SEPARATION AND ONSET DETECTION

The intermediate processing steps between audio and feature extraction (green boxes in Figure 2) are described in this section.

3.1 HP-Separation

Source separation was used to separate harmonic and percussive content. Source separation has been used in the past in computational models related to rhythm [7]. The method proposed by FitzGerald [8] was used as the first step of the separation. The basic idea of the method is that percussive sounds are broadband noise signals with short duration and that harmonic sounds are narrow band signals with longer duration. To be able to separate these different sounds, the audio is transformed to the spectral domain by using a short-time Fourier transform (STFT). By applying a median filter across each frame in the frequency direction, harmonic sounds are suppressed. By applying a median filter across each frequency bin in the time direction percussive sounds are suppressed. After median filtering, the signal is transformed back to the time domain again using the inverse STFT.

To further suppress harmonic content in the percussive waveform a second separation stage incorporates a constant-Q transform (CQT) [9]. The CQT can be understood as an STFT with logarithmically spaced frequency bins, accomplished by varying the length of the analysis window. The implication relevant to this study is that a high frequency resolution can be achieved also in the low frequencies, at the expense of a poor time resolution.

The frequency resolution of the CQT was set to 60 bins per octave and each frame was median filtered across the frequency direction with a window size of 40 bins. After filtering, the percussive signal was transformed back to the time domain using an inverse CQT.

By transforming back to the time-domain, the underlying phase information is retained. The phase can be regarded as a mapping that connects a frequency bin to a certain point in time. This is especially useful in the CQT-stage as the filtering can be performed at a low

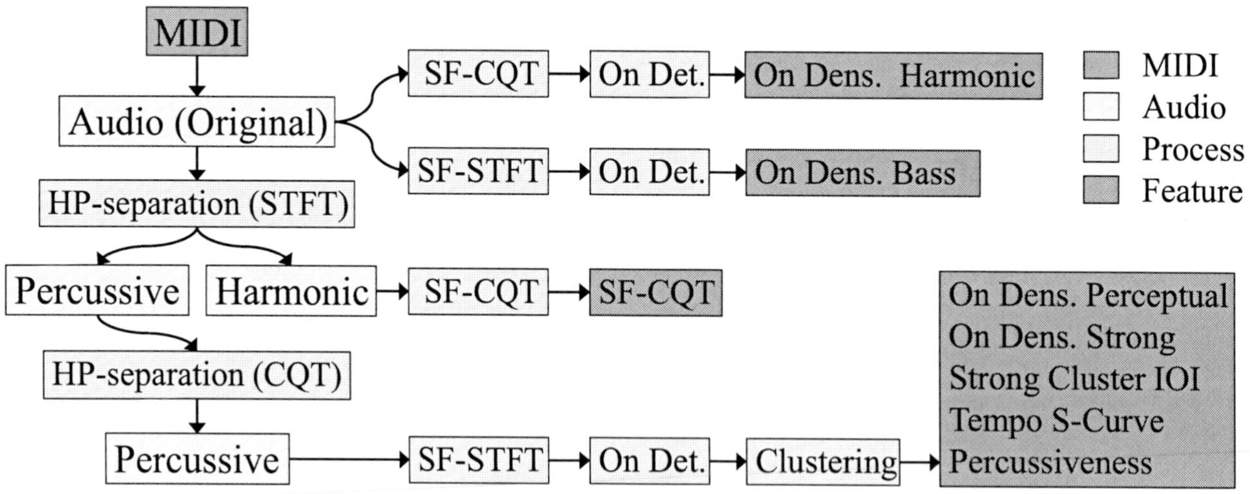

Figure 2. Flowchart of the processes used to compute audio features for the speed in music. Audio is generated from MIDI, the audio is filtered to separate harmonic and percussive content, onsets are detected from a spectral flux, and audio features are computed.

time-resolution (with window lengths up to a second); but subsequent onset detection algorithms can be computed at a higher time-resolution. The resulting percussive and harmonic waveforms are shown in Figure 3.

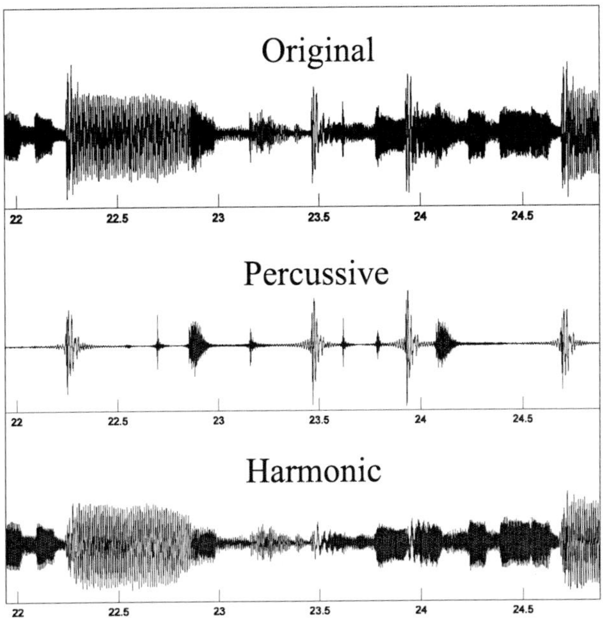

Figure 3. The result of the HP-separation. The original waveform is separated into a percussive and a harmonic waveform. The example is a 3-second section of the song *Candy Shop*, by *50 cent*, which will be used to visualize the feature extraction throughout this paper.

3.2 Onset Detection

Audio features were computed from all three waveforms (original, harmonic and percussive) by the scheme shown in Figure 2. The first step, independent of feature and waveform, was to compute a spectral flux (SF) [10], where spectral fluctuations along the time-domain are detected. The SF was computed several times in different ways. Some shared steps will be described here, with unique steps described in Sections 4.1-4.8. The power spectrum was computed with a CQT or an STFT and converted to sound level. A range of 30 dB was used. Thus, the maximum sound level of each band is set to 0 dB and sound levels below -30 dB are set to -30 dB. Let $L(n, i)$ represent the sound level at the ith frequency bin/band of the nth frame. The SF is given by

$$SF(n) = \sum_{i=1}^{b} H\big(L(n,i) - (L(n-s,i)\big) \qquad (1)$$

where b is the number of bins/bands. The variable s is the step size and H is a half-wave rectifier function, or for the percussive SF:

$$H(x) = \begin{cases} x & \text{if } x > 0 \\ 0.2x & \text{if } x \leq 0 \end{cases} \qquad (2)$$

The implication of Eq. 2 is that negative spectral fluctuations have a slight influence on the onset detection function. Onsets were detected by peak picking on a low-pass filtered curve of the spectral flux (see Figure 4).

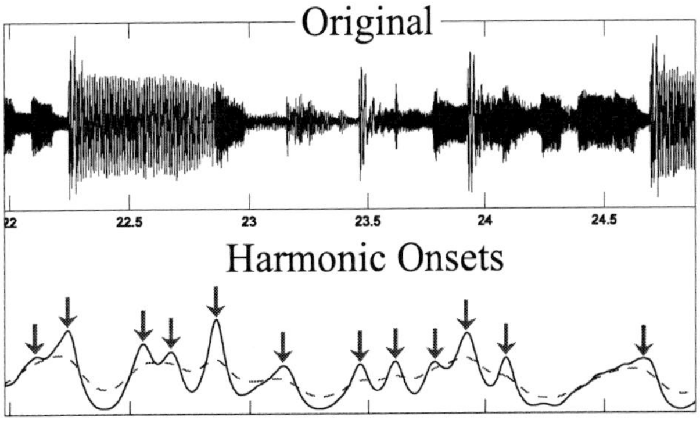

Figure 4. The onset detection functions that discover onsets by finding peaks in the SF. In this example harmonic onsets are tracked.

3.3 Clustering

To better exploit the characteristics of the percussive onsets they were clustered into groups. The clustering was based on sound level in 8 frequency bands, spaced approximately an octave apart, as well as the RMS sound level. As the appropriate number of clusters is unknown beforehand, three k-means clusterings [11, 12] were carried out, with the number of clusters k, set to 2, 3 and 4. The fit of each clustering attempt was defined by the smallest Euclidian distance between any two clusters, where a large smallest distance gave a higher fit. When choosing which clustering attempt to use, a higher number of groups (k) were premiered over a lower if their fit was similar. The result is shown in Figure 5.

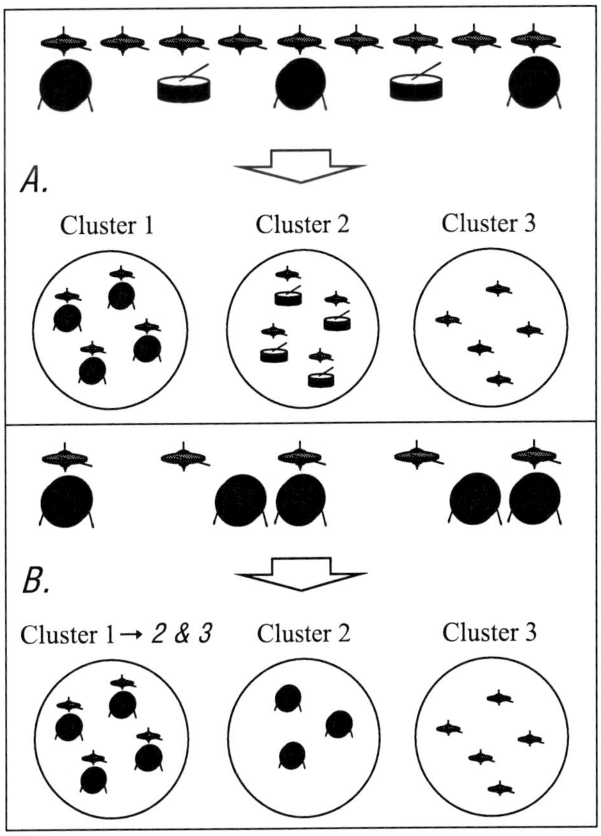

Figure 5. The clustering of percussive onsets. In example *A* the drums are clustered into three different clusters. In example *B* three clusters are initially discovered, but the onsets in Cluster 1 are assigned to Cluster 2 & 3.

When the clustering is completed the onsets have been divided into 2, 3 or 4 clusters. At this point the clusters are further analyzed to find out if the sound of the onsets in two of the clusters can be combined to form the sound of the onsets in a third cluster. This happens in example *B* of Figure 5. The k-means clustering has divided the onsets into three different clusters, corresponding to the sound of the kick and the hihat combined, as well as both played separately. The algorithm then compares the different clusters and discovers that Cluster 2 (the kick) and Cluster 3 (the hihat) can be combined to form the sound of Cluster 1 (the kick and the hihat). To account for this, each onsets belonging to Cluster 1 will instead be set as belonging to both Cluster 2 and Cluster 3, and Cluster 1 will cease to exist. This does not happen in example *A* of Figure 5 where 3 unique clusters have been identified.

4. FEATURE EXTRACTION

A total of 8 audio features were computed, 2 from the original waveform, 5 from the percussive waveform and 1 from the harmonic waveform. The audio features are shown as the end result in the flowchart in Figure 2. The 8 features are explained in Sections 4.1-4.8, with one subsection for each feature.

4.1 Onset Density – Harmonic

Onsets in harmonic instruments were tracked from the original waveform, with the SF of a CQT. The bins of the CQT were not combined into broader bands before the SF. This facilitates the detection of harmonic onsets, as a pitch shift of a semitone in an instrument will result in an increase in energy in the half wave rectified SF.

To avoid false onset detections at pitch glides from vibratos, shifts of a peak by 20 cents (one bin), without an increase in sound level, were restricted from affecting the SF. This was accomplished by subtracting the sound level of each bin of the new frame, by the maximum sound level of the adjacent bins in the old frame. The onset detection function for harmonic onsets is shown in Figure 4.

4.2 Onset Density – Bass

Onsets in the low register (frequencies between 40 Hz and 210 Hz) were tracked with an SF of the lower bins of an STFT. The frequency bins were summed to a single band before the SF.

4.3 Onset Density – Perceptual weighting

Percussive onsets were tracked with an SF of an STFT on the percussive waveform. The bins of the frequency domain representation were divided into 13 non-overlapping frequency bands (half-octave spacing). Subband processing for onset detection has been described in [13], and can be motivated by its similarity to human hearing [14]. The strength of each detected onset was calculated based on the average sound level of the first 50 ms from the onset position, where lower frequencies were given a higher relevance.

To further determine the perceived strength of the onsets, each onset was compared to the surrounding onsets within 1.5 seconds. This time span (3 seconds in total) was defined as the perceptual present of the particular onset. By comparing it with the strongest onset within the perceptual present its strength could be altered to represent its perceptual impact. The onset was given a higher strength if there were no significantly stronger onsets within the perceptual present. If there were onsets that were significantly stronger, its strength was lowered. The height of the cluster-bars in Figure 6 represents the perceptual strength of each onset. To derive at a measure of onsets density, the sum of the perceptual strength of the onsets was used.

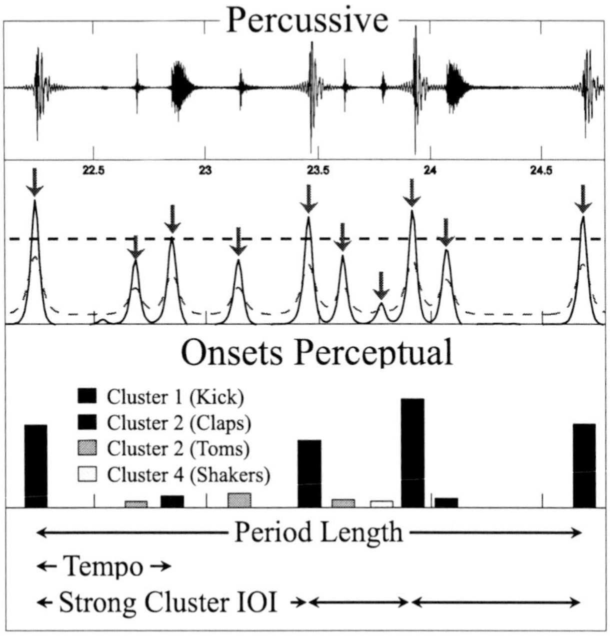

Figure 6. An overview of the processes involved in extracting 5 features (described in Section 4.3-4.7) from the percussive waveform. Onsets are detected and clustered into different components to gain an understanding of how the music will be perceived. *The perceptual weighting* of the onsets is represented by the height of the bars. In this particular song, *Tempo* is derived from the IOI between kick and handclaps and only the kick belonged to a *strong cluster*. The *percussiveness* feature is related to the height of the peaks in the onset detection function, as visualized by the dotted line.

4.4 Onsets Density – Strong

The strongest clusters of the clustering process were used to compute two features. The first feature was simply the number of onsets, belonging to a strong cluster, per second. This feature was only computed for periods of strong onsets within 1.5 seconds of each other.

4.5 Strong Cluster IOI

The second feature derived from the strong clusters was developed to catch the assumed perception of a *slow* speed, when the interonset intervals (IOIs) of onsets belonging to the same strong cluster are long. As an example, a song with equally spaced drum onsets consisting of "Kick, Snare, Kick, Snare, Kick Snare,.." was assumed to have a *higher* perceived speed than a song where the drums instead plays "Kick, Kick, Snare, Kick, Kick, Kick, Snare, Kick, etc..". This is accounted for in the *Tempo* feature as well, because the tempo in the second example would be half the tempo of the first example.

In Figure 6, this feature is derived from the IOI between onsets belonging to Cluster 1. Common IOIs are detected by peak picking in a low pass filtered histogram of cluster IOIs. Each found peak contributes to the feature based on its relative height as well as the cluster strength.

4.6 Tempo S-Curve

The tempo detection algorithm is part of an ongoing project, and a detailed description is in preparation. All distances between onsets within 5 seconds from each other are used to detect the tempo.

4.6.1 Period Length

First, the period length of the percussive waveform is detected. The period length corresponds to the length of the most prominent pattern of repeated rhythmic sounds in the music. A histogram over onset distances is generated, where the contribution of each onset-pair increases with increasing similarity in spectrum as well as increasing onset strength. The leftmost peak in the low pass filtered histogram, within 92 % of the highest peak, is chosen as the period length.

4.6.2 Tempo

Secondly, the tempo (beat length) is detected. A histogram over onset distances is once again generated, where the contribution of each onset-pair increases with increasing *dissimilarity* in spectrum as well as increasing onset strength. The final probability distribution for tempo is the Hadamard product of the histogram and several filters. One filter is based on the determined period length. The idea is that the beat will be a simple ratio of the period length, so Hanning windows are produced at positions

$$P_{len} \times \left(\frac{1}{2}\right)^n, \quad P_{len} \times \left(\frac{1}{2}\right)^n \times \left(\frac{1}{3}\right) \qquad n = 0,1,2,.. \tag{3}$$

Another filter is based on IOIs within strong clusters as described in Section 4.5. The general distribution of tempos in popular music is taken into account in one filter and several filters are connected to the onset density of the particular song. The highest peak in the final probability distribution was chosen as the tempo.

4.6.3 S-Curve

In compliance with the findings in [3], an S-Curve (Figure 7) was applied to the tempo value, giving differences in tempo a higher impact between 60 and 160 BPM.

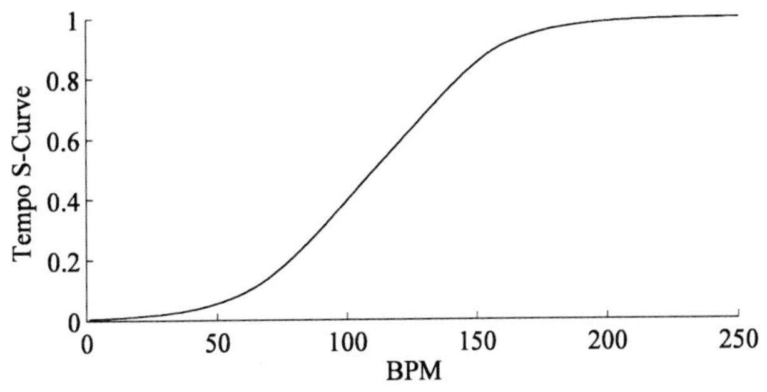

Figure 7. The S-Curve that gives differences in tempos between 60 and 160 BPM a higher impact.

4.7 Percussiveness

One feature was based on the percussiveness of the onsets. This estimate is derived from the height h of the peaks in the SF of the percussive waveform, as shown in Figure 6.

$$Percussiveness = \frac{\sum_{i=1}^{n} h(i)^{1+p}}{\sum_{i=1}^{n} h(i)^{p}} \tag{4}$$

Equation 4 gives the mean peak height when p is 0, an estimate closer to the lowest peaks when p is negative, and an estimate closer to the highest peaks when p is positive. In this study p was set to 0.4.

4.8 SF CQT

When extracting information from the harmonic waveform the integral of the SF was used; indicated as the colored area in Figure 8. The use of an onset detection function was avoided as the HP-separation had removed all transients from the harmonic waveform. The use of a CQT was motivated by the harmonic nature of the processed audio. Spectral changes in high frequencies were used for this feature.

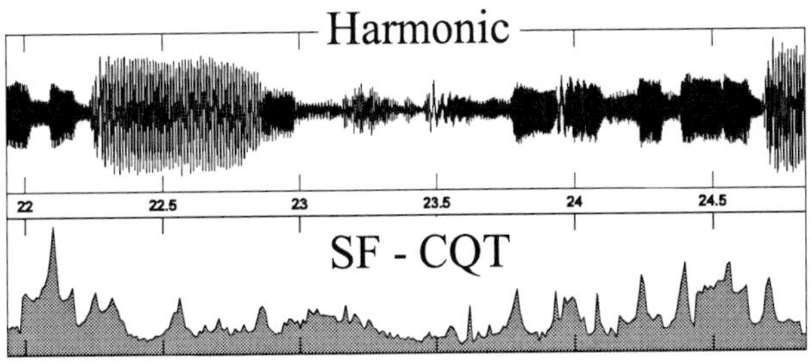

Figure 8. The integral of the spectral flux of the harmonic waveform.

5. PREDICTING SPEED FROM THE FEATURES

Two regression techniques were used to analyze the mapping between the computed audio features and the listener ratings of speed. First, a multiple linear regression was used, justified by a predictor-to-case ratio higher than 1:10. Secondly, PLS regression was used [15]. PLS regression carries out data reduction, whilst maximizing covariance between features and predicted data [16].

The multiple linear regression between listener ratings and computed audio features is presented in Table 2. As shown, a linear combination of the computed audio features was able to explain about 90 % of the variability. In comparison, the agreement among the listeners estimated by the mean intersubject correlation was 0.71 and Cronbach's alpha 0.98 [4].

Multiple Regression - Speed			
R^2 = 0.909	Adjusted R^2 = 0.900		
Variable	beta	sr^2	p-value
On Dens. - Harmonic	0.205	0.033	0.000***
On Dens. - Bass	0.130	0.007	0.016*
On Dens. - Perceptual	0.302	0.018	0.000***
On Dens. - Strong	-0.155	0.010	0.004**
Strong Cluster IOI	0.127	0.006	0.021*
Tempo S-Curve	0.430	0.056	0.000***
Percussiveness	-0.095	0.005	0.041*
SF CQT	0.107	0.004	0.053

Table 2. The prediction of the perceptual feature *speed* from computed audio features. The variable sr^2 is the squared semi-partial correlation coefficient.

The most important feature was *Tempo S-Curve*, followed by *Onset Density - Harmonic*, *Onset Density - Perceptual* and *Onset Density - Strong* (negative contribution). The independent contribution in terms of the squared semi-partial correlation coefficient sr^2 indicates that *Onset Density - Bass*, *Strong Cluster IOI*, *Percussiveness* and *SF CQT* each increased the explained variance with less than 1 %. The negative contribution of *Percussiveness* could be explained as a higher perceived speed when the percussive onsets are less clear.

A partial least square regression (PLS) of the same features is shown in Table 3. With 3 components, the cross-validated adjusted R^2 indicates that just below 90 % of the variability could be explained. Note also that the cross-validation procedure only lowers the result marginally, supporting the validity of the features.

PLS Regression - Speed		
Number of Components Used = 3		
R^2 = 0.907	Adjusted R^2 = 0.903	
R^2 cv = 0.883	Adjusted R^2 cv = 0.878	
Component	Explained variance	Cum. variance
1	0.853	0.853
2	0.042	0.895
3	0.011	0.907

Table 3. The prediction of the perceptual feature *speed* from computed audio features. The squared correlation coefficient R^2 was derived using Partial Least-square Regression (PLS), with 10-fold cross validation. In the lower part, R^2 as a function of the number of components is shown. Components 4-8 did not contribute and are not shown.

The fitted values of the linear regression from Table 2 are shown in Figure 9 below. As seen in the figure, the deviations from the target are rather evenly distributed across the range and with a maximal deviation of about one unit.

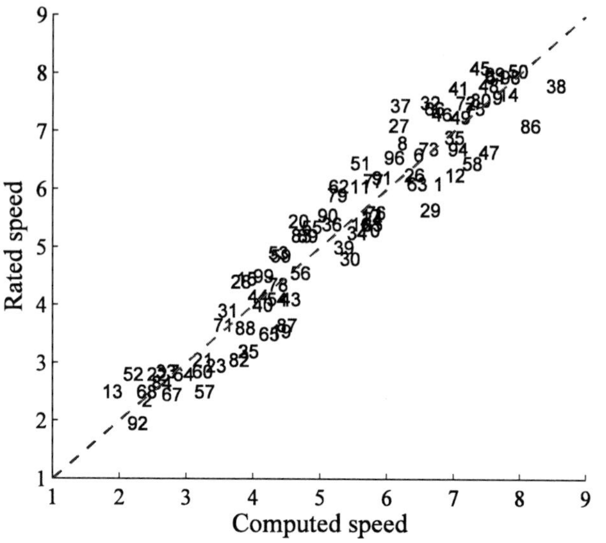

Figure 9. The fitted values in the prediction of the perceptual feature speed, where higher means faster. For each song (numbered for easier identification), the x-axis represents the estimated speed (derived from computed audio features), and the y-axis represents the ground truth (derived from listeners).

6. CONCLUSIONS AND DISCUSSION

The computed audio features were able to explain about 90 % of the variability in listener ratings. The most important features were tempo together with onset densities for different layers of the music. The validity of the features was supported by a cross-validation, and fitted values were relatively close to target values.

The results show that it was possible to reach the same high explained variance on audio data as on MIDI data using similar features [4]. This indicates that the appropriate low-level audio features have been extracted, which is reassuring for the ongoing study.

Since good results were achieved only after we applied source separation, both in terms of clustering and HP-separation, the segmentation of data seems to be a promising path forward. From an ecological point of view it seems reasonable to assume that the interaction between onsets of the same source is relevant; especially if the sound of this source is one of the most prominent ones. By clustering onsets we can detect onsets belonging to the same source and thus use the rhythmic pattern of this source in the model. By using several onset detection functions on separate parts of the audio, different aspects of the music can be captured. The CQT seems to be suitable for detecting onsets in harmonic instruments, while the better time-resolution of the STFT in lower frequencies facilitates the detection of percussive instruments. A drawback with the proposed system is that the computation of several STFTs and CQTs is relatively time consuming.

7. ACKNOWLEDGEMENT

This work was supported by the Swedish Research Council, Grant Nr. 2009-4285 and 2012-4685.

8. REFERENCES

[1] A. Gabrielsson, *Studies in Rhythm*, doctoral dissertation, Uppsala University, 1973.

[2] R. Bresin, and A. Friberg, "Emotion rendering in music: Range and characteristic values of seven musical variables," *Cortex*, Vol. 47, no. 9, pp. 1068-1081, 2011.

[3] G. Madison, and J. Paulin, "Ratings of speed in real music as a function of both original and manipulated beat tempo." *Journal of the Acoustical Society of America*, Vol. 128, no. 5, pp. 3032-3040, 2010.

[4] A. Friberg, E. Schoonderwaldt, A. Hedblad, M. Fabiani, and A. Elowsson "Perceptually derived features can be used in music information retrieval," submitted for publication.

[5] A. Friberg, E. Schoonderwaldt, and A. Hedblad, "Perceptual ratings of musical parameters," in von Loesch, H., & Weinzierl, S. (Eds.), *Gemessene Interpretation - Computergestützte Aufführungs-analyse im Kreuzverhör der Disziplinen*, Mainz: Schott, 2011, pp. 237-253.

[6] A. Hedblad, *Evaluation of Musical Feature Extraction Tools Using Perceptual Ratings.* Master thesis, KTH Royal Institute of Technology, 2011.

[7] M. Alonso, G. Richard and B. David, "Accurate tempo estimation based on harmonic + noise decomposition," *EURASIP Journal on Advances in Signal Processing*, vol. 2007, Article ID 82795, 14 pages, 2007.

[8] D. FitzGerald, "Harmonic/percussive separation using median filtering," in *Proc. of the 13th International Conference on Digital Audio Effects (DAFx-10)*, Graz, Austria, 2010.

[9] C. Schörkhuber and A. Klapuri, "Constant-Q transform toolbox for music processing," in *7th Sound and Music Conference (SMC'2010)*, Barcelona, 2010.

[10] S. Dixon, "Onset detection revisited," in *Proceedings of International Conference on Digital Audio Effects*, pages 133–137, 2006.

[11] G. A. F. Seber, *Multivariate Observations.* Hoboken, NJ: John Wiley & Sons, Inc., 1984.

[12] H. Spath, *Cluster Dissection and Analysis: Theory, FORTRAN Programs, Examples.* Translated by J. Goldschmidt. New York: Halsted Press, 1985.

[13] A. Klapuri, "Sound onset detection by applying psychoacoustic knowledge," in *Proc. IEEE Conf. Acoustics, Speech and Signal Processing (ICASSP,'99)*, 1999.

[14] C. Duxbury, J. P. Bello, M. Sandler, and M. Davies, "A comparison between fixed and multiresolution analysis for onset detection in musical signals," in *Proc. 7th Int. Conf. Digital Audio Effects (DAFx)*, Naples, Italy, 2004.

[15] P. Geladi, & B. R. Kowalski. Partial least-squares regression: a tutorial. *Analytica chimica acta*, Vol. 185, pp. 1-17, 1986.

[16] T. Eerola, O. Lartillot, P. Toiviainen. "Prediction of multidimensional emotional ratings in music from audio using multivariate regression models," in *10th International Society for Music Information Retrieval Conference (ISMIR 2009)*, 2009.

GLOBAL KEY EXTRACTION FROM CLASSICAL MUSIC AUDIO RECORDINGS BASED ON THE FINAL CHORD

Christof Weiß
Fraunhofer Institute for Digital Media Technology, Ilmenau, Germany
christof.weiss@idmt.fraunhofer.de

ABSTRACT

This paper presents a novel approach to global key extraction from audio recordings, restricted to the genre *Classical* only. Especially in this field of music, musical key is a significant information since many works include the key in their title. Our rule-based method relies on pre-extracted chroma features and puts special emphasis on the final chord of the piece to estimate the tonic note. To determine the mode, we analyze the chroma histogram over the complete piece and estimate the underlying diatonic scale. In both steps, we apply a multiplicative procedure to obtain high error robustness. This approach helps to minimize the amount of false tonic notes which is important for further key-related tonality analyses. The algorithm is evaluated on three different datasets containing mainly 18th and 19th century music for orchestra, piano, and mixed instruments. We reach accuracies up to 97 % for correct full key (correct tonic note and mode) classification and up to 100 % for correct tonic note classification.

1. INTRODUCTION

The key is an essential information about a musical work. Especially in Western art music, the usage of different keys shows some historical peculiarities that are connected to the evolution of the musical instruments and tuning schemes. Inspired by the ability to play all keys on keyboard instruments, J. S. Bach and several latter composers created series of works for every single key. In other works, musical keys obtain certain characteristics or special semantic meanings.

Therefore, automatized extraction of musical key is an important task in Music Information Retrieval (MIR). Besides applications for annotating classical music datasets, the key may also be necessary for further MIR tasks like genre classification or composer identification. For such scenarios, all key misclassifications constitute a problem. Especially, the system should avoid confusions of fifth-related keys that arise frequently in many common algorithms, e.g. in [1–4].

To this end, we first consider the special role of the final chord in this paper. For most pieces, the root of this chord (the first note in a cluster of ascending thirds) equals the tonic note of the written global key. We combine this information with a scale estimation of the complete piece. For this, we present the idea of multiplicative chroma processing to estimate a chord's root or a diatonic scale. We show that this reduces classification errors compared to template-based methods.

This rule-based approach is inspired by music theory and does not make use of machine learning techniques so far. We restrict ourselves to consider classical music only. For other genres like *Rock*, *Pop* or *Jazz*, such a method may not work since there may arise a considerable number of fade out endings or complex final jazz chords.

2. RELATED WORK

Since the concept of musical key is not defined precisely in many cases, automatic key extraction remains a challenging MIR task—also on classical music data. There are algorithms dealing with symbolic data only, as well as direct audio analysis methods on which we focus on in this paper. Recent overviews can be found in [2, 5], also comparing knowledge-based and data-driven algorithms—the two main approaches.

In general, the first step is an extraction of chroma features. Motivated by studies on human pitch perception [6, 7], many algorithms match the chroma statistics to pitch class profiles or use advancements of such approaches [1, 5, 8–10]. In the MIREX 2005 contest (1252 classical pieces synthesized from MIDI), the best results reached 87 % correctly identified keys [3].

Among the works concerning data-driven techniques, Hidden Markov Models (HMMs) are used most frequently [4, 11]. They also show promising results in localized tonality analysis and chord detection. Chai and Vercoe [4] combine HMMs with a two-step approach, considering diatonic scale and tonic note individually. Noland and Sandler [11] investigate the effect of the signal processing parameters and test their HMM-based approach on recordings of Bach's well-tempered piano, book 1 (48 tracks), yielding 98 % correct classification for the best parameter settings.

There are works considering special sections of the recordings: Izmirli [9] investigates the first seconds of 85 classical pieces by different composers (randomly chosen from a NAXOS dataset) with up to 86 % success. Chuan and Chew [12] test their geometrical approach on the beginning of several Mozart symphonies yielding up to 96 % success rate. Extending these tests to a wide stylistic range, they reach 75 % correct accuracy [13]. Van de Par et al. [14] combine profile training with special weighting of the beginning and ending section. They evaluate on piano music [1] with high accuracies up to 98 %.

3. SYSTEM OVERVIEW

In the presented key detection system, we make use of the final chord's significance in Western classical music applying a two-step approach: First, we estimate the final chord's root and the complete piece's dominating diatonic scale individually. Then, we combine these informations to obtain the most probable full key consisting of the tonic note and the associated mode (major/minor). An overview is shown in Fig. 1.

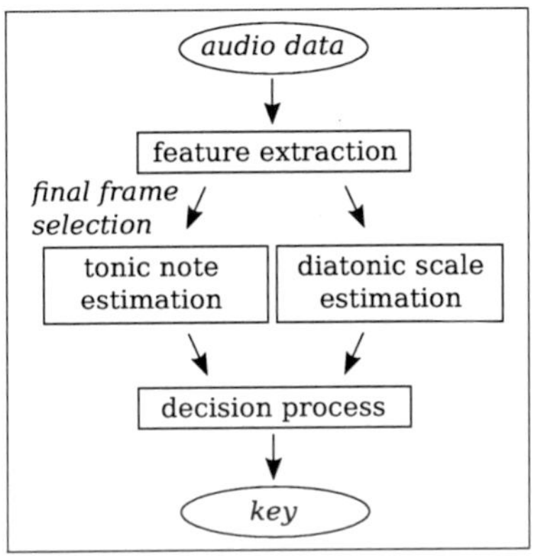

Figure 1. The key extraction process.

3.1 Feature Extraction

The system is based on chroma features which are commonly used to represent the harmonic content of music [15, 16]. We use the Chroma Toolbox of Müller and Ewert [17] to extract pitch and chroma features from the audio data in a preprocessing step. First, we calculate a pitch representation from the audio signals via a multi-rate filter bank, covering the pitch range of a grand piano (MIDI pitches Nos. 21–108). To account for the global tuning, we use the tuning estimation of this toolbox package and apply a shifted filter bank if the difference from a 440 Hz tuning exceeds 15 cent. We obtain a set of N_{tot} pitch feature vectors $\mathbf{p}$ (88-dim.), each covering a frame of length 50 ms:

$$\left(\mathbf{p}^1, \ldots, \mathbf{p}^i, \ldots, \mathbf{p}^{N_{\text{tot}}}\right) \quad (1)$$

To estimate the overall dynamics, we calculate the average L_1 norm of these vectors:

$$||\mathbf{p}||_{\text{mean}} = \frac{1}{N_{\text{tot}}} \sum_{i=1}^{N_{\text{tot}}} ||\mathbf{p}^i||_1 \quad (2)$$

[1] cf. Sec. 4.1 and [10] for details

Next, the energy of all pitch bands belonging to a pitch class (chroma) is summed up and normalized to obtain 12-dim. chroma vectors $\mathbf{c}$, where c_k^i is the k-th component of the i-th chroma vector:

$$\left(c_1^i, c_2^i, \ldots, c_{12}^i\right) \mathrel{\widehat{=}} (C, C\sharp, \ldots, B) \quad (3)$$

Then, we add up all vectors over the piece to obtain a normalized (using L_2 norm) chroma histogram $\mathbf{g}$:

$$\mathbf{g}' = \sum_{i=1}^{N_{\text{tot}}} \mathbf{c}^i\,, \quad \mathbf{g} = \frac{\mathbf{g}'}{||\mathbf{g}'||_2} \quad (4)$$

For all pitch- and chroma-related vectors, we identify flat and sharp notes ($C\sharp = D\flat$) and understand the indexing in a circular way ($k \to 1 + (k-1) \bmod 12$).

3.2 Tonic Note Estimation

3.2.1 Frame Selection

Starting from this feature set, we estimate the root of the piece's final chord. Since we do not want to consider frames containing silence, we take the last N final feature frames that exceed a defined energy threshold. To account for the overall loudness of the piece, we apply a dynamical adaption for the energy threshold. We calculate the L_1 norm of the pitch feature vectors [2] $\mathbf{p}^j$ and select only vectors fulfilling the condition

$$||\mathbf{p}^j||_1 > f_e \cdot ||\mathbf{p}||_{\text{mean}} \quad (5)$$

with a suitable factor f_e.

3.2.2 Chroma Processing

From the frame selection thus obtained (length N_{end}), we compute a 12-dim. chroma histogram $\mathbf{h}$:

$$\mathbf{h}' = \sum_{m=1}^{N_{\text{end}}} \mathbf{c}^m\,, \quad \mathbf{h} = \frac{\mathbf{h}'}{||\mathbf{h}'||_2} \quad (6)$$

Here, we are only interested in the root and not in the mode of the final chord, and thus ignore this chord's third. [3] To consider the tonal relationship between the chroma classes, we re-sort the entries of $\mathbf{h}$ according to a perfect fifth ordering by re-ordering the indices:

$$(1,\, 2, \ldots, 12) \to (2,\, 9,\, 4,\, 11,\, 6,\, 1,\, 8,\, 3,\, 10,\, 5,\, 12,\, 7)$$

$$\left(h_1^{\text{fifth}}, \ldots, h_{12}^{\text{fifth}}\right) \mathrel{\widehat{=}} (D\flat,\, A\flat, \ldots, C,\, G, \ldots, B,\, F\sharp)$$

We multiply these values for each two neighboring entries

$$h_k^{\text{prod}} = h_k^{\text{fifths}} \cdot h_{k+1}^{\text{fifths}} \quad (8)$$

to consider only such chroma peaks, where the respective upper fifths is also present. The principle is illustrated in Fig. 2.

[2] Since the chroma features are normalized, we compute the energy measure directly on the pitch features.

[3] In classical music, the final chord may not be representative for the overall mode of the piece: Many minor pieces end in the respective major chord ("Picardy third"), certain symphony movements show a development from minor to major, etc.

Since the majority of classical pieces' final chords—independently of their mode—contain strong energy in the root as well as in the fifth chroma, this procedure provides the final chord's root with a high reliability:

$$k^{\text{root}} = \arg\max_k h_k^{\text{prod}} \tag{9}$$

Also for third-less chords or even monophonic endings, this method works well, as the third partial of the root always produces some energy in the fifth chroma. To estimate the likelihoods, we calculate confidence measures P_k^{tonic} using the euclidean norm:

$$P_k^{\text{tonic}} = \frac{h_k^{\text{prod}}}{||\mathbf{h}^{\text{prod}}||_2} \tag{10}$$

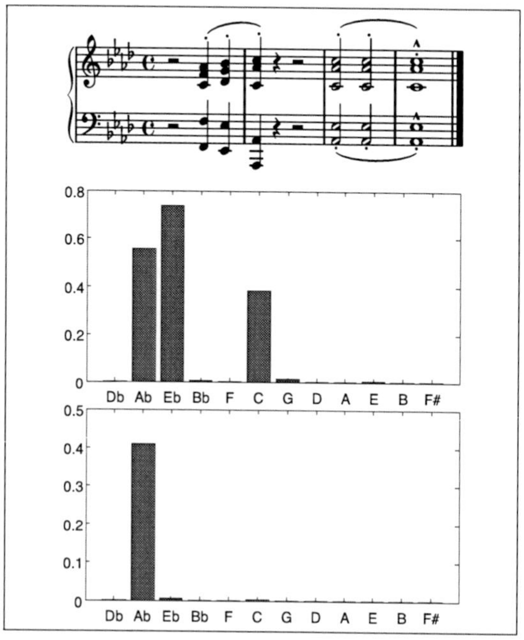

Figure 2. The final bars of Frédéric Chopin's Impromptu No. 1 for Piano, op. 29 in A♭ major. The upper plot shows the re-sorted chroma histogram $\mathbf{h}^{\text{fifths}}$ from the last $N = 30$ frames (cf. Eqs. 5–6), which results in the lower one $\mathbf{h}^{\text{prod}}$ after pairwise multiplication (cf. Eq. 8). From this, we identify the correct root A♭ even though the maximum value in the chroma histogram belongs to E♭.

3.3 Diatonic Scale Estimation

Since classical works or single movements may pass through certain tonal progressions, show parts in other keys, or even end in a key different from the global key [4], we consider the complete length data to identify the diatonic scale that corresponds to the global key's major or natural minor scale. To this end, we use the chroma histogram $\mathbf{g}$ from the preprocessing step (Sec. 3.1) and try to estimate the most probable diatonic scale or "tonal level". This concept, illustrated e.g. in [18], is suitable for various tonal analysis tasks. As an example, G major as well as E minor are denoted as "+1 level" (1♯), B♭ major and G minor as "-2 level" (2♭). As a diatonic scale consists of seven fifth-related notes (cf. Fig. 3), we again re-sort the histogram to a fifth ordering and compute a 12-dimensional vector by multiplying each seven fifth-related chroma energies corresponding to the respective diatonic scale (Indexing: $g_1^{\text{prod}} \to k = -5$ diatonic (= D♭ major scale), …, $g_{12}^{\text{prod}} \to k = +6$ diatonic):

$$g_k^{\text{prod}} = \prod_{l=1+k \bmod 12}^{1+(k+11) \bmod 12} \left(g_l^{\text{fifths}}\right)^{m_l^{(a)}} \tag{11}$$

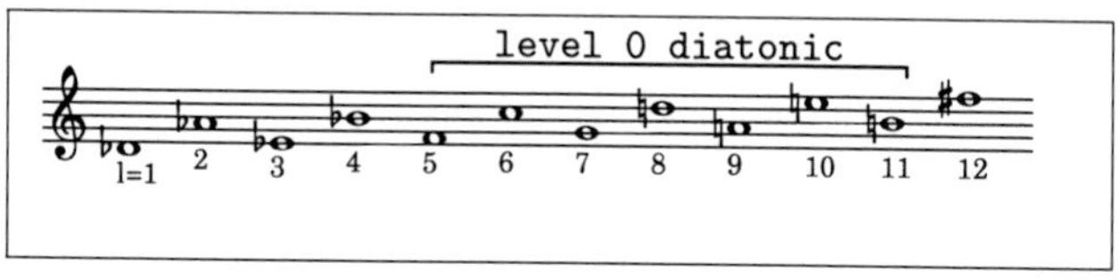

Figure 3. A diatonic scale (level 0) in a representation of neighboring fifths. The notes are signed with the indices of $\mathbf{m}^{(a)}$. The tonic note for the corresponding major scale is C ($l = 6$), for the minor scale A ($l = 9$).

To account for the individual relevance of the notes, we test a weighting [5] by five different templates of exponents $m_l^{(a)}$:

$$\mathbf{m}^{(1)} = (0\;0\;0\;0\;1\;1\;1\;1\;1\;1\;1\;0)$$
$$\mathbf{m}^{(2)} = (0\;0\;0\;0\;1\;3\;2\;1\;2\;3\;1\;0)$$
$$\mathbf{m}^{(3)} = (0\;0\;0\;0\;3.75\;4.75\;3.00\;3.75\;4.25\;4.50\;3.75\;0)$$
$$\mathbf{m}^{(4)} = (0\;0\;0\;0\;4.04\;5.87\;4.27\;3.51\;5.00\;4.57\;3.20\;0)$$

$\mathbf{m}^{(1)}$ corresponds to equal weighting. In $\mathbf{m}^{(2)}$, we emphasize the notes of the tonic chords (for the level 0 diatonic of Fig. 3, these are the C major and the A minor chord). $\mathbf{m}^{(3)}$ is computed from the templates of Temperley [7], where we summed up the major and the relative minor profile, multiplied with 0.5. $\mathbf{m}^{(4)}$ is the same for the Krumhansl templates [6]. The non-diatonic notes are exponentiated by 0 and thus not considered. Up to this, the scale estimation step basically equals a common template matching. [6] However, the multiplicative procedure leads to a high fidelity, since yet shifting by one fifth (i.e., one small g_l value in the product Eq. 11) leads to a small g_k^{prod} entry.

Again, we compute confidence measures for all 12 levels via

$$P_k^{\text{scale}} = \frac{g_k^{\text{prod}}}{||\mathbf{g}^{\text{prod}}||_2}. \tag{12}$$

[4] Most frequently, this is the corresponding minor/major key; cf. remarks to Sec. 3.2

[5] Note that for a product calculation, weighting has to be done by exponentiation and not by multiplication.

[6] The fifth ordering is just for visualisation: In this representation, all diatonic scale notes are neighbors.

3.4 Decision Process

To select the most probable key from the confidence measures computed before, we build a 24-dimensional confidence vector, combining every tonic note confidence with the associated major and minor scale confidences, where the exponent s serves as a tuning parameter between root and scale influence:

$$P_k^{\text{major}} = \left(P_k^{\text{tonic}}\right)^s \cdot P_k^{\text{scale}} \qquad P_k^{\text{minor}} = \left(P_k^{\text{tonic}}\right)^s \cdot P_k^{\text{mscale}} \tag{13a}$$

$$\mathbf{P}^{\text{combined}} = \left(\mathbf{P}^{\text{major}}, \mathbf{P}^{\text{minor}}\right) \tag{13b}$$

For the minor case, one has to shift the scale vector by three entries to associate the roots with the corresponding [7] minor scales:

$$\mathbf{P}^{\text{mscale}} = \left(P_{10}^{\text{scale}}, \ldots, P_{12}^{\text{scale}}, P_1^{\text{scale}}, \ldots, P_9^{\text{scale}}\right) \tag{14}$$

The highest P_k^{combined} provides the key:

$$k^* = \arg\max_k P_k^{\text{combined}} \tag{15}$$

The normalized confidence vector for the full key is

$$P_k^{\text{key}} = \frac{P_k^{\text{combined}}}{||\mathbf{P}^{\text{combined}}||_2}. \tag{16}$$

The confidence for the selected key is $P_{k^*}^{\text{key}}$.

4. EVALUATION

4.1 Description of the Datasets

To evaluate our algorithm, we consider three datasets of classical music audio recordings. The first one (*Symph*) contains classical and romantic symphonies (all movements) from 11 composers, 115 tracks in total (cf. Tab. 1), taken from a dataset of NAXOS recordings.

Composer	*Symphonies No.*
Beethoven, L. v.	2, 3, 8
Brahms, J.	2, 3
Bruckner, A.	3, 4, 8
Dvořak, A.	5, 7
Haydn, J.	22, 29, 60, 103
Mendelssohn-B., F.	3, 5
Mozart, W. A.	35, 39, 40, 41
Schubert, F.	2, 3, 8
Schumann, R.	2, 4
Sibelius, J.	3, 4
Tchaikovsky, P. I.	5, 6

Table 1. Contents of *Symph* dataset.

The second dataset (*SMD*) is a selection from Saarland Music Data Western Music, collected in a collaboration of Saarland University and MPI Informatik Saarbrücken with Hochschule für Musik Saar [19]. The dataset contains music for solo, voice and piano, as well as chamber and orchestral music. We annotated the key for the 126 tracks showing clear tonality. [8]

Third, we test our method on a dataset of piano music recordings (*Pno*). This data was used to investigate key determination in the publications [10] and [14] and thus, allows for a direct comparison. The set contains 237 piano pieces by Bach, Brahms, Chopin and Shostakovich which are explicitly dedicated to a special key, as in the "well-tempered piano". Detailed information about the recordings can be found in [10].

Dataset	*Symph*	*SMD*	*Pno*	**tot.**
major global key	70 %	57 %	49 %	**56 %**
minor global key	30 %	43 %	51 %	**44 %**
major final chord	72 %	55 %	70 %	**67 %**
minor final chord	12 %	20 %	14 %	**15 %**
third-less fin. chord	16 %	25 %	15 %	**18 %**
fin. chord ≙ gl. key	70 %	64 %	53 %	**60 %**
fin. root ≙ gl. tonic	99 %	98 %	98 %	**99 %**

Table 2. The datasets' properties with respect to global key and final chord.

Table 2 shows some properties of the datasets. Final chord and global key coinicide for only 60 % of the pieces. However, the final chord's root matches the global tonic note almost always. Most of the mode deviations are picardian thirds (20 %), where a minor piece ends in the relative major chord (The opposite case is rare). The rest is caused by third-less final chord (18 %) like empty fifths (1 %) or unisono endings (17 %). 71 % end in a full triad, 11 % end in a fifth-less chord.

4.2 Experimental Results

We investigate the influence of the system parameters in a large study (Tab. 3). First, we show selected results for different energy threshold factors f_e, where a value of $f_e = 0.15\,\%$ seems to separate best silence from music frames. In the test of the weight exponents $\mathbf{m}^{(a)}$, the emphasis of the chord notes in $\mathbf{m}^{(2)}$ and the template derived from Temperley $\mathbf{m}^{(3)}$ perform best. To estimate the individual influence of root and scale estimation, we also run the algorithm with different weight exponents s in the decision process, where a slight preference of the scale confidence yields best results. For the size of the final frame set, a value of $N = 40$ frames corresponding to 2 seconds performs best. This value seems to balance the requirements for short chords (no failures caused by previous chords) with a sufficiently high reliability. With the low dynamic threshold f_e, we are also including reverb to a certain extent. Because of this, and of the frequent occurence of final ritardando in classical music, we do not have to worry about choosing a fixed small number of final frames N independently of the tempo.

[7] We identify sharp and flat chromas (D♭ =C♯): E.g., the tonic confidence for C♯ is multiplied with the confidence of level −5 for the D♭ major likelihood, and with the confidence of level +4 for the C♯ minor case.

[8] To this end, we skipped works of Bellini, Berg, Debussy, Donizetti, Martin, Poulenc and Ravel as well as the first and second movement of Faure's op. 15. From Schumann's works, op. 15 and 48 have been removed, since they are work cycles and do not constitute separated pieces in some way. For detailed information, see http://www.mpi-inf.mpg.de/resources/SMD. The key annotations are also available on this website.

To check the influence of the individual steps, we perform single runs without the multiplicative procedure in the tonic note estimation and in the diatonic scale estimation, respectively (block (E) in Tab. 3). From this, we can see that the multiplication in the diatonic scale does not improve much. However, the multiplication in the tonic note estimation leads to a clear advancement, even when combined with a basic template matching with the Krumhansl profile (E4).

Parameters	*Symph*	*SMD*	*Pno*
(A)	$\mathbf{m} = \mathbf{m}^{(3)}$, $N = 40$, $s = 0.8$		
$f_e = 0.10\,\%$	92.2 %	94.4 %	96.2 %
$\boldsymbol{f_e = 0.15\,\%}$	**92.2 %**	**93.7 %**	**97.0 %**
$f_e = 0.25\,\%$	92.2 %	92.9 %	96.6 %
$f_e = 0.50\,\%$	92.2 %	92.1 %	94.9 %
(B)	$f_e = 0.15\,\%$, $N = 35$, $s = 0.75$		
$\mathbf{m} = \mathbf{m}^{(1)}$	88.7 %	92.1 %	94.1 %
$\mathbf{m} = \mathbf{m}^{(2)}$	**93.0 %**	**95.2 %**	**95.8 %**
$\mathbf{m} = \mathbf{m}^{(3)}$	92.2 %	93.7 %	96.6 %
$\mathbf{m} = \mathbf{m}^{(4)}$	89.6 %	91.3 %	95.4 %
(C)	$f_e = 0.15\,\%$, $N = 35$, $\mathbf{m} = \mathbf{m}^{(3)}$		
$s = 0.5$	89.6 %	91.3 %	95.8 %
$\boldsymbol{s = 0.8}$	**92.2 %**	**93.7 %**	**97.0 %**
$s = 1.0$	92.2 %	93.7 %	96.2 %
$s = 1.2$	92.2 %	92.9 %	96.2 %
(D)	$f_e = 0.15\,\%$, $s = 0.8$, $\mathbf{m} = \mathbf{m}^{(3)}$		
$N = 10$	90.4 %	89.7 %	93.2 %
$N = 30$	92.2 %	93.7 %	96.6 %
$\boldsymbol{N = 40}$	**92.2 %**	**93.7 %**	**97.0 %**
$N = 60$	90.4 %	90.5 %	96.6 %
(E)	$f_e = 0.15\,\%$, $s = 0.8$, $\mathbf{m} = \mathbf{m}^{(2)}$, $N = 35$		
(E1)	83.5 %	80.2 %	82.3 %
(E2)	91.3 %	92.0 %	92.0 %
(E3)	76.5 %	62.7 %	55.3 %
(E4)	90.4 %	91.3 %	93.7 %

Table 3. Correct full key classification results for different parameter sets. We test the influence of the energy threshold factor f_e (A), the weight exponent set $\mathbf{m}^{(a)}$ (B), the root–scale weight exponent s (C), and the size of the final frame set N (D). The best results for each parameter are printed bold. In (E1), the multiplication in the tonic note estimation Eq. 8 is replaced by a simple maximum-picking. In (E2), the product Eq. 11 is replaced by a weighted sum. (E3) considers both these changes at the same time. For (E4), we use the full combined (major + parallel minor) Krumhansl template (non-diatonic entries nonzero) and again calculate a sum instead of a product.

Most of the parameters discussed here show important impact especially on one of the databases. In our interpretation, this is caused by different acoustic behavior (orchestra vs. piano) as well as properties of the music (cf. Tab. 6) and its temporal dimensions (symphonic vs. solo/chamber music). Individual error rates for two of the best parameter sets are shown in Tab. 4. Hereby, we emphasize the small number of fifths errors that arise frequently in other approaches. Third errors include all tonic note relations of minor and major thirds, including the relative key. Especially

Dataset	*Symph*	*SMD*	*Pno*
Correct full key	**92.2 %**	**93.7 %**	**97.0 %**
Correct tonic note	98.3 %	96.0 %	97.5 %
Fifth errors	0.9 %	2.3 %	0.8 %
Third errors	0.9 %	1.6 %	1.7 %
Ø confidence	96.5 %	96.5 %	98.2 %
Correct full key	**93.0 %**	**95.2 %**	**95.8 %**
Correct tonic note	100 %	96.8 %	97.0 %
Fifth errors	0 %	1.6 %	0.4 %
Third errors	0 %	1.6 %	2.5 %
Ø confidence	96.1 %	96.2 %	97.1 %

Table 4. Key extraction results for $f_e = 0.15\,\%$, $N = 40$, $s = 0.8$, $\mathbf{m} = \mathbf{m}^{(3)}$ (upper block) and $f_e = 0.15\,\%$, $N = 35$, $s = 0.75$, $\mathbf{m} = \mathbf{m}^{(2)}$ (lower block).

Dataset	*Symph*	*SMD*	*Pno*
Correct full key	**73.0 %**	**71.2 %**	**62.9 %**
Correct tonic note	78.4 %	71.2 %	62.9 %
Fifth errors	9.0 %	12.8 %	13.1 %
Third errors	12.6 %	14.4 %	20.2 %

Table 5. Results of the `MIRtoolbox` key algorithm.

on symphonic data, identification of the correct tonic note is clearly more reliable than full key detection.

For our best parameter sets, we reach results slightly below the state-of-the-art [11, 12]. Taking into account that these algorithms are evaluated on music from one composer for one type of orchestration, our results may be comparable, since we considered a wide range of styles and instrumentations. On Bach's well-tempered piano, we reach 100 % full key identification for the upper settings in Tab. 4. On the *Pno* set, we almost reach the 98 % accuracy presented in [14]. To compare to a public algorithm, we run the key detection algorithm of `MIRtoolbox` from Univ. Jyväskylä [20] on our data, a common chroma- and template-based approach. Looking at the results in Tab. 5, we see that our method performs clearly better for detection of the full key and especially of the tonic note .

Epoch	1)	2)	3)	4)
No. in *Symph*	0	46	26	43
No. in *SMD*	11	49	20	46
No. in *Pno*	144	0	0	93
total No.	**155**	**95**	**46**	**185**
Correct full key	**98 %**	**96 %**	**96 %**	**92 %**
Correct tonic note	99 %	98 %	100 %	96 %

Table 6. Results by epoch: Baroque (1), Classical (2), Early Romantic (3) and Late Romantic / Modern (4) music. Parameters like in Tab. 4, lower block.

Last, we show the results by musical epoch in Tab. 6. To this end, we clustered the results by composer and aggregate music by Bach (Baroque), Haydn, Mozart and Beethoven (Classical), Schubert, Schumann and Mendelssohn (Early Romantic), and the rest (Late Romantic and Modern). We see the accuracy decreasing with composition time as expected because of the increase of tonal complexity during the centuries.

5. CONCLUSIONS

We presented a new rule- and theory-based approach to extract the key from classical music audio recordings. The method puts special emphasis on the final chord of the piece. After extracting chroma features, a number of final frames exceeding a dynamic threshold is selected. From this, the final chord's root is determined via a pairwise multiplication of fifth-related chroma values. From a full-piece chroma statistics, the system estimates the underlying diatonic scale. Finally, combining these results by multiplying corresponding confidence measures provides the full key.

For the evaluation, we considered three datasets on symphonic, mixed and solo piano music containing 478 recordings in total. We performed a parameter study and reach an average success rate of 95.0 % for full key detection and 97.7 % for tonic note detection for the best parameter settings. Hence, our results are in the range of most state-of-the-art approaches for automatic key detection, specialized on classical music.

Since our method provides the final chord's root with a high reliability, our approach can be combined with other chroma processing as well as machine learning techniques. So, this may be a helpful tool to facilitate renaming, browsing, and analyzing of classical music.

Acknowledgments

The authors thank M. Müller and S. Ewert for publishing their Chroma Toolbox. The research presented in this paper is part of the SyncGlobal project. SyncGlobal is a 2-year collaborative research project between Piranha Womex AG, Bach Technology GmbH, 4FriendsOnly AG and the Fraunhofer IDMT in Ilmenau, Germany. The project is co-financed by the Germany Ministry of Education and Research in the framework of the SME innovation program (FKZ 01/S11007).

6. REFERENCES

[1] E. Gómez and P. Herrera, "Estimating the tonality of polyphonic audio files: Cognitive versus machine learning modelling strategies," in *Proc. 5th Int. Conf. Music Inf. Retr. (ISMIR)*, 2004.

[2] B. Schuller and B. Gollan, "Music theoretic and perception-based features for audio key determination," *J. New Music Research*, vol. 41, no. 2, pp. 175–193, 2012.

[3] Ö. Izmirli, "An algorithm for audio key finding," in *Proc. 1st Annual Music Inf. Retr. Evaluation eXchange (MIREX '05)*, 2005.

[4] W. Chai and B. Vercoe, "Detection of key change in classical piano music," in *Proc. 6th Int. Conf. Music Inf. Retr. (ISMIR)*, 2005.

[5] H. Papadopoulos and G. Peeters, "Local key estimation from an audio signal relying on harmonic and metrical structures," *IEEE Transactions on Audio, Speech, and Language Processing*, vol. 20, no. 4, pp. 1297–1312, 2012.

[6] C. L. Krumhansl, *Cognitive Foundations of Musical Pitch.* Oxford University Press, 1990.

[7] D. Temperley, *The Cognition of Basic Musical Structures.* MIT Press, 2001.

[8] E. Gómez, "Key estimation from polyphonic audio," in *Proc. 1st Annual Music Inf. Retr. Evaluation eXchange (MIREX)*, 2005.

[9] Ö. Izmirli, "Template based key finding from audio," in *Proc. Int. Comput. Music Conf. (ICMC)*, 2005.

[10] S. Pauws, "Musical key extraction from audio," in *Proc. 5th Int. Conf. Music Inf. Retr. (ISMIR)*, 2004.

[11] K. Noland and M. Sandler, "Influences of signal processing, tone profiles, and chord progressions on a model for estimating the musical key from audio," *Comput. Music J.*, vol. 33, no. 1, pp. 42–56, 2009.

[12] C.-H. Chuan and E. Chew, "Polyphonic audio key finding using the spiral array CEG algorithm," in *2005 IEEE Int. Conf. Multim. and Expo*, 2005.

[13] ——, "Fuzzy analysis in pitch class determination for polyphonic audio key finding," in *Proc. 6th Int. Conf. Music Inf. Retr. (ISMIR)*, 2005.

[14] S. van de Par, M. F. McKinney, and A. Redert, "Musical key extraction from audio using profile training," in *Proc. 7th Int. Conf. Music Inf. Retr. (ISMIR)*, 2006.

[15] M. A. Bartsch and G. H. Wakefield, "To catch a chorus: Using chroma-based representations for audio thumbnailing," in *Proc. IEEE Workshop on Applications of Signal Processing to Audio and Acoustics*, 2001.

[16] M. Müller, F. Kurth, and M. Clausen, "Audio matching via chroma-based statistical features," in *Proc. 6th Int. Conf. Music Inf. Retr. (ISMIR)*, 2005.

[17] M. Müller and S. Ewert, "Chroma toolbox: Matlab implementations for extracting variants of chroma-based audio features," in *Proc. 12th Int. Conf. Music Inf. Retr. (ISMIR)*, 2011.

[18] Z. Gárdonyi and H. Nordhoff, *Harmonik.* Möseler, 1990. [in German]

[19] M. Müller, V. Konz, W. Bogler, and V. Arifi-Müller, "Saarland music data," in *Proc. 12th Int. Conf. Music Inf. Retr. (ISMIR)*, 2011.

[20] O. Lartillot and P. Toiviainen, "A toolbox for musical feature extraction from audio," in *Proc. 8th Int. Conf. Music Inf. Retr. (ISMIR)*, 2007.

PEVI: INTERFACE FOR RETRIEVING AND ANALYZING EXPRESSIVE MUSICAL PERFORMANCES WITH SCAPE PLOTS

Shota Miki
Kwansei Gakuin University
1339.czf78655@gmail.com

Takashi Baba
Kwansei Gakuin University
takashi-baba@kwansei.ac.jp

Haruhiro Katayose
Kwansei Gakuin University
katayose@kwansei.ac.jp

ABSTRACT

Although a variety of interfaces for music retrieval have been proposed so far, they are not always valid for retrieving classical music, a piece of which is recorded by many players. The lineup that current music retrieval systems suggest for a given musical piece is likely to be in order of sales. This is not always desired by classical music lovers, who are interested in various interpretations of a piece. In this paper, PEVI, a novel interface based on a scape plot for finding interpretations of classical music, is presented. The scape plot window, which visualizes the most similar performances of a specified scope (multiple layers) in a specified piece by using color tags, is used as the key to assigning a range of musical pieces to be referred to. Similar performances are displayed, on a different window, as their coordinates represent the similarity of two selected musical features in regard to tempo, dynamics, and delicate control within a beat. Users of PEVI are able to observe the transition of the indices of similar performances by changing the scope on the scape plot and each weight of the musical features. In this paper, the effectiveness of PEVI is discussed with an analysis of difference performances of "Romance de Amor."

1. INTRODUCTION

Recently, many music information retrieval systems have been proposed. We can easily find songs that are similar to a favorite piece or are cover songs. Popular music lovers enjoy the benefits of the service provided by music information retrieval systems, mainly the classifying of content on the basis of collaborative filtering approaches. By contrast, these services are not always scrupulous enough for classical music listeners. One of the big differences between classical music and popular mu-sic is that there exist plenty of performances of a particular musical piece in the genre of classical music. For classical music listeners, the differences of each performer's (conductor's) interpretations or expressions are important.

Recommendations made by existing music information retrieval systems, such as instrumentations that are similar to query tune or a lineup of bestselling performances, are often not those desired by classical music listeners.

The goal of this paper is to provide such classical music listeners with a music retrieval interface that can also be used as a tool for active music listening [1]. For this goal, musical features such as tempo, dynamics, and delicate control within a beat should be used as the indices of similarity. One such implementation is Maezawa et al.'s "Query-by-Conducting" [2]. It makes use of global tempo transition information given by a user's conducting actions in order to search for similar performances.

It is desirable that the user can specify the scope (part) of the performance to be searched. Interpretation or expression of an expressive musical performance is essentially multi-layered, from each note-level, phrase-level, and section-level expression. A function for assigning the scope of a performance is especially required for dealing with classical music. As a tool for visualizing expressive music performances, C. Sapp proposed a visualization called the "scape plot" that shows the most similar performances of a specified scope (multiple layers) in a specified piece by using color tags [3]. The "scape plot" it-self is static, and it does not show the second most similar data and below. In this paper, we propose an interface for retrieving and analyzing expressive performances of classical music called "PEVI." The main feature of PEVI is the ability to use the scape plot as an interface to indicate the scope of a performance that is specified.

This paper is organized as follows. In Section 2, the possibility of being able to use a scape plots as an interface for music information retrieval and as an analysis system for classical music is described. In Section 3, an outline of PEVI is described. The possibilities of PEVI are discussed on the basis of an analysis of different performances of "Romance De Amor" in Section 4, and conclusions are in Section 6.

2. SCAPE PLOT AS PERFORMANCE RETRIEVAL INTERFACE

2.1 Scape Plot

In classical music, many artists perform from the same printed scores, but there are many different musical expressions produced by various interpretations. In addition, a layered structure is also an important factor of musical expressions. There are cases when features of a microscopic structure are different from those of a macroscopic structure. In The Mazurka Project, C. Sapp proposed the scape plot as a way of visualizing the similarity between performances in multiple layers at the same time [3]. The scape plot has a triangular shape. Figure 1 is a sample of a scape plot.

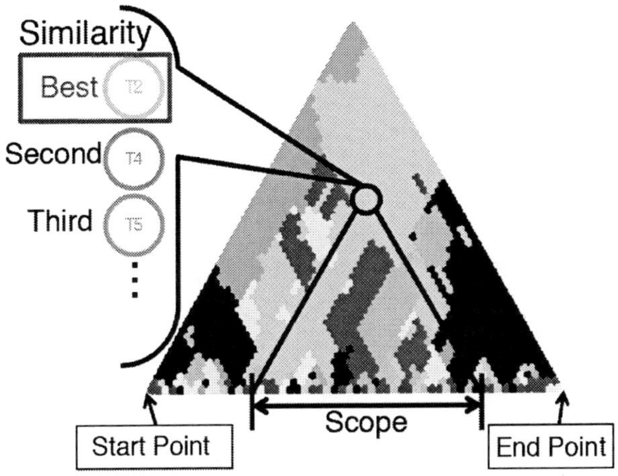

Figure 1. Sample of a scape plot. The base vertical line is the time axis of a piece. The index color of the most similar performance of the span to the query is plotted at the vertex of the equilateral triangle, the base of which is the "scope."

The base of the scape plot represents the time axis of a piece; in other words, the left vertex means the start, and the right vertex means the end of a piece. When a section of the piece or the base of a scape plot is chosen, a triangle that has a section specified as the base is decided, and the top vertex of the triangle is colored to indicate the most similar performance. Each performance is assigned a unique hue. The top vertex of the scape plot shows the most similar performance in regard to the whole piece. Thus, the scape plot shows the most similar performance in every time scale at the same time.

2.2 Using Scape Plot as Span Controller for Calculating Similarity

The scape plot is quite good for use as a visualizer of expressive musical performances. However, it can only visualize the most similar performance of each scope. The remaining performances are not visualized. We also cannot know how similar performances are. We solve these problems and propose a novel system that uses the scape plot as not only a way of visualizing but also as a user interface for giving a scope in order to calculate the similarity of performances, the results of which, including the invisible information on the scape plot, are displayed in another area. Thus, we will be able to understand the performances in detail by watching the real-time trajectories of similar performances while listening to the query performance.

Important features that identify an expression are, for example, tempo, dynamics, timbre, and expression within a beat. Above all, tempo and dynamic features have a large effect on musical expressions and are extracted relatively easily and correctly, so they are frequently used as tools for comparing expressions, as is also adopted in the scape plot. In addition to tempo and dynamic features, the proposed system is designed to deal with features related to delicate control within a beat.

3. PEVI

3.1 Overview

PEVI is a novel interface based on the scape plot for finding interpretations of classical music. An overview of PEVI is shown in Figure 2. The first thing that users of PEVI do is to give the query performance of a music piece. Then, the user can limit the number of performance examples retrieved, which contributes to improve time resolution of visualization. Users are allowed to give weight to each feature considered for similarity calculation.

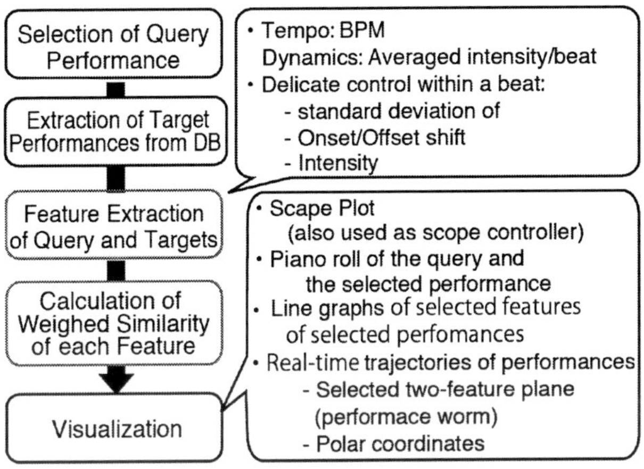

Figure 2. Overview of PEVI

The functions of visualization that PEVI offers are the scape plot, which is also used as a scope controller, the piano roll of the query and the selected performances which are retrieved, line graphs of the selected features, and real-time trajectories of the performances in a selected two-feature plane (so called the "performance worm" [4]) and in polar coordinates.

An example of the GUI of PEVI (top page) is shown in Figure 3. This figure is a snapshot of the visualizing of performances of Prelude Op. 28 No. 7 in A major by F. Chopin in the tempo-dynamics plane. The half-tone dot meshing area in the left figure is the span used for calculating similarity. When users push the play button, they can listen to the span of the query performance while watching animated visualizations of the trajectories of the performances that are retrieved.

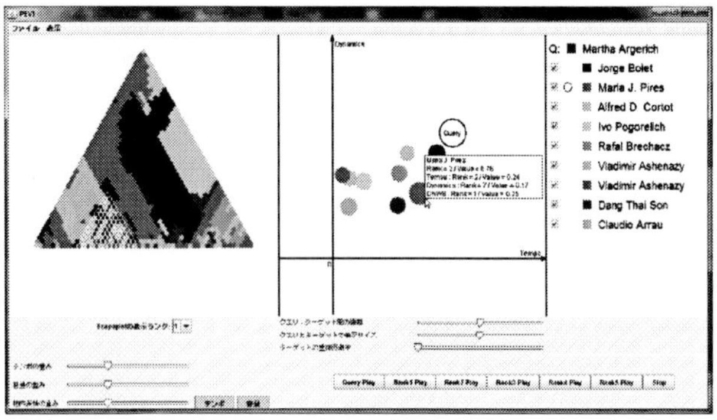

Figure 3. Main GUI of PEVI. Half-tone dot meshing area in the left figure is the span used for calculating similarity. Color index represents name of performer.

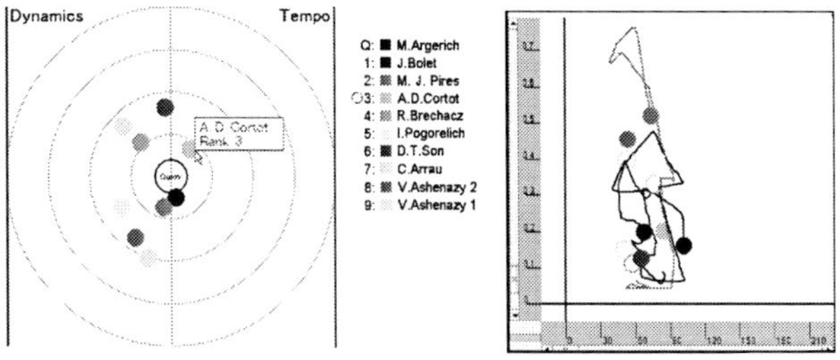

Figure 4. Sample of visualizations with PEVI

Figure 4 shows samples of visualization of the performances retrieved. The left shows the visualization in a polar coordinate, and the right shows the performance worm. Users of PEVI are able to change the query by selecting a colored index in these visualizations just like web-surfing.

3.2 Calculating Similarity

We use Pearson product-moment correlation as the similarity between each feature of performances. The sequence x means the data of a query, and the sequence y means the data of one of the target performances. $\bar{x}$ and $\bar{y}$ mean arithmetic averages of sequence $x = \{x_i\}$ and sequence $y = \{y_i\}$. Then, Pearson coefficient, often called an "r-value" in statistics, is defined as:

$$\mathrm{Peason}(x,y) = \frac{\sum_n (x_n - \bar{x})(y_n - \bar{y})}{\sqrt{\sum_n (x_n - \bar{x})^2 \sum_n (y_n - \bar{y})^2}} \quad (1)$$

The value range of Pearson correlation is −1.0 to +1.0. The 1.0 indicates an identical match between two performances.

Figure 5 shows an example of the Pearson correlation of tempo between two performances. It shows there is a strong correlation in the scope from beat 1 to 3, almost no correlation in the scope from beat 3 to 10, and a negative correlation in the scope from beat 7 to 10.

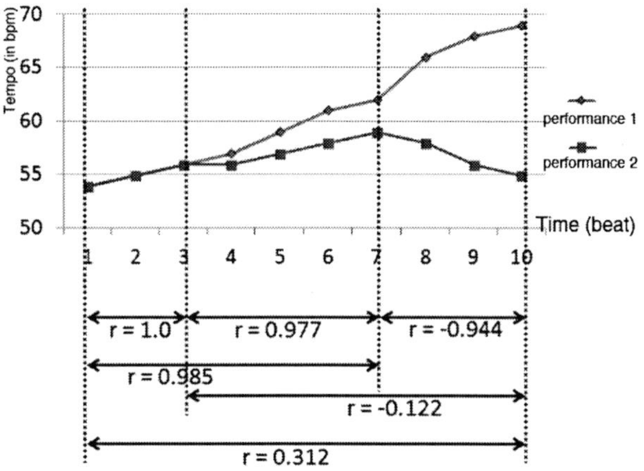

Figure 5. Sample of Pearson product-moment

3.3 Data Format of the Performances

PEVI accepts performance data that are written in compliance with the CrestMuseXML and DeviationInstanceXML formats, which are compatible with CrestMusePEDB[1], a database for expressive performances [5].

The objects of the collection stored in CrestMusePEDB are pieces of classical music up until the early twentieth century whose copyrights are expired, mainly piano pieces composed by J. S. Bach, W. A. Mozart, L. V. Beethoven, and F. Chopin, and pieces that are often covered by earlier studies or are interesting as research objects are chosen. Performance expressions are labeled by hand from recordings of excellent performances. Transitions of tempo and dynamics are extracted at the beat level, and timings and the shifts of the dynamics of each tone are extracted at the MIDI level. Deviations of each tone from a printed score are detected as a musical expression. The data are written in compliance with MusicXML. We obtain tempo and dynamics transitions in increments of a quarter note.

4. USER EVALUATION

In this section, a preliminary user evaluation of PEVI is described. The goal of implementing PEVI is to expand the possibility of using the scape plot to retrieve and analyze classical music, where expressing the notes of a score makes much sense. The effectiveness of the visualization, usability, possibilities, and problems were collected by using a questionnaire.

Seven university students (from 20 to 24 years of age), whose musical experience ranged from the novice level to more than 10 years of piano playing, participated in the evaluation. After an explanation of how to use PEVI, the participants were made to use it freely to access performances until they judged that they had fully used the functions of PEVI. The experimenters explained the meaning of some of the musical terms in the GUI to the novice participants during the procedure on demand. The average operation time was around one hour.

The participants were asked to score the following items on a scale of 1 to 6 (1: lowest, 6: highest): a) intuitiveness of visualizing two styles (polar coordinate and

[1] http://www.crestmuse.jp/pedb/

performance worm), b) effectiveness of visualizing delicate control within a beat to listen to the differences between performances, c) effectiveness of using the scape plot to assign a "scope" to calculate similarity, d) effectiveness of giving weight to each feature, and some items regarding the total usability of PEVI. In addition, participants were asked to write their opinions freely regarding the total usability.

As for the visualization, the participants preferred the performance worm style to the polar coordinate style.

The effectiveness of visualizing delicate control within a beat was given significantly high scores ($P < 0.05$) by the participants who had some musical experience.

In comparison, participants with little musical experience answered "I can hear the differences between performances, but I'm not sure what makes the differences. From the start, I have never listened to music knowing there exists differences among the performances." These results illustrate that PEVI is an effective tool for enhancing the pleasantness of listening to music for listeners with some musical experience rather than for novice listeners.

As for the total usability, the intuitiveness of the GUI and pleasantness were given high scores, 5.8 and 5.0 respectively. We may conclude that PEVI is a novel tool for active music listening, especially for classical music.

5. ANALYZING "ROMANCE DE AMOR"

PEVI is expected to be used to analyze how each of the performers (performances) affects each other, which is regarded as a typical theme of musicology. This usage was originally pointed out by C. Sapp as an application of the scape plot in [6]. However, PEVI, which is implemented as an interactive application that enables users to change weights for the features and the span, provides users with smoother operation in order to achieve this goal. In this section, the potential of PEVI is discussed by introducing examples of performances of "Romance de Amor" for guitar.

"Romance de Amor" is a Spanish folksong. The first eight bars at the beginning are shown in Figure 6. After being used as the theme of the French film "Jeux interdits," it has been one of the most famous pieces of music for guitar and has been performed by many guitar players, including professionals and amateurs. It is not so strange to frame the hypothesis that the relationship between master and disciple, nationalities, and age may cause there to be similarities in performances. This hypothesis is examined by retrieving performances of "Romance de Amor" by using PEVI.

Figure 6. Beginning part of "Romance de Amor"

The retrieved guitarists were Narciso Yepes, Kiyoshi Shomura, Kazuhito Yamashita, Shin-ichi Fukuda, Daisuke Suzuki, Yasuji Ohagi, and Kaori Muraji. First, "Romance de Amor" was made known to the world by the virtuoso performance of Yepes. Shomura is one of a few Japanese guitarists who studied under Yepes. Suzuki, Ohagi, and Muraji studied under Fukuda, who is a friend of Shomura. Both Yamashita and Fukuda and both Ohagi and Muraji are guitarists of the same generation, respectively. Suzuki is a Jazz guitar player as well as a classic guitar player. Ohagi and Muraji are the youngest among the seven guitarists and regarded to play the latest interpretation of the song. Muraji is the only female guitarist of the seven. Yamashita is known for his transcendent technique and is regarded as a unique guitarist by the others.

The performance data for this analysis were obtained with experienced guitar players' iterated listening and revision, using a tool[2] for creating a performance data

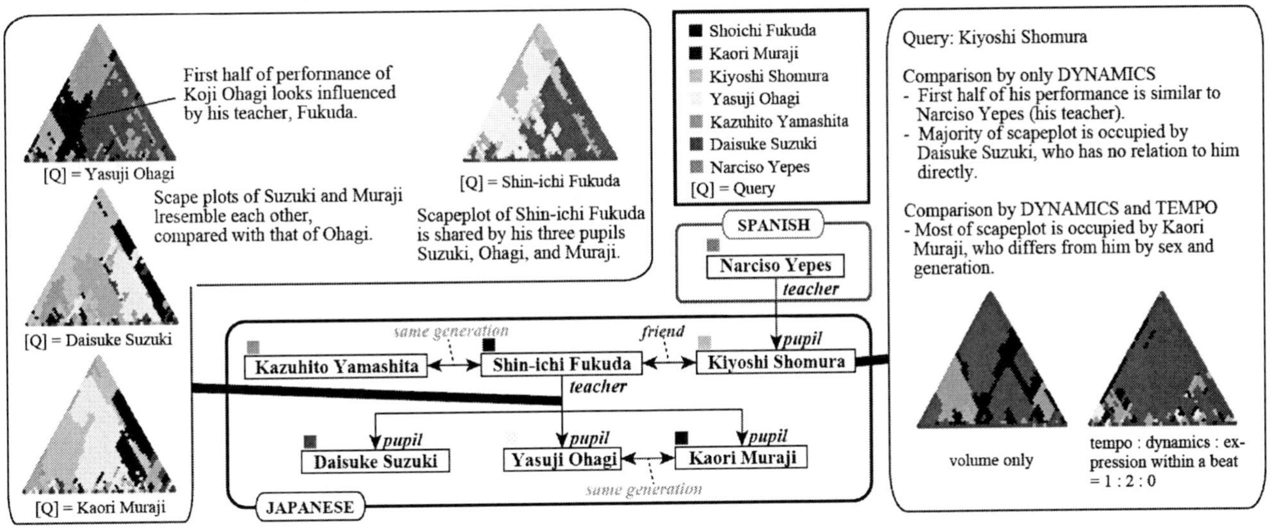

Figure 7. Analyzing guitar performances of "Romance de Amor"

[2] http://en.sourceforge.jp/projects/cmx/

provided by the CrestMusePEDB committee.

The result of the analysis is shown in Figure 7. The right side of Figure 7 shows the analysis when Shomura's performance was set as the query performance. There was no distinctive similarity between Yepes' and Shomura's performances when the weights for the tempo, dynamics, and delicate control within a beat were equally given. In accordance with a gain in the weight for dynamics, the area that shows Yepes' performance (magenta) in the scape plot expanded at the first half. We could find similarity in the expression of dynamics between Shomura and Suzuki's performances. When the weights for tempo, dynamics, and expression in a beat were set to 1:2:0, we could see similarity between Shomura's and Muraji's performances.

The left side of Figure 7 shows the results when queries were set to Suzuki, Ohagi, Muraji, and their teacher, Fukuda, respectively. Each weight for tempo, dynamics, and expression within a beat were set to 1:1:1. In the plot for Fukuda (around the center area), we could see a big yellow area that represented Ohagi and a big purple one that represented Muraji. We could see that red represented Suzuki, the area of which was small compared with those for yellow and purple, at the base of the triangle. This shows that Suzuki inherited local features of expression from his teacher Fukuda the most. The second and third performances most similar to Fukuda's were also those of his pupils. These observations suggest that Fu-kuda's pupils inherited features of expression from their teacher, Fukuda, the most. The next performance similar to Fukuda's was that of Yamashita, who is of the same generation as Fukuda.

The three scape plots at the most left side are those of Fukuda's three pupil guitarists. Some similarities were observed between Suzuki's and Muraji's performances. They were especially similar at the latter half, where expression in regard to dynamics was similar to that of their teacher, Fukuda. Compared with Suzuki's and Muraji's scape plot, Ohagi's one looked different. It seems that performers of the same generation may play in a different style, even when their teacher is the same.

Figure 8 shows snapshots of the transition of the performances, where Ohagi's performance was set as the query. This shows that Muraji's performance (in pink) got closer to Ohagi's, replacing Fukuda's (in blue) between bars 5 and 8.

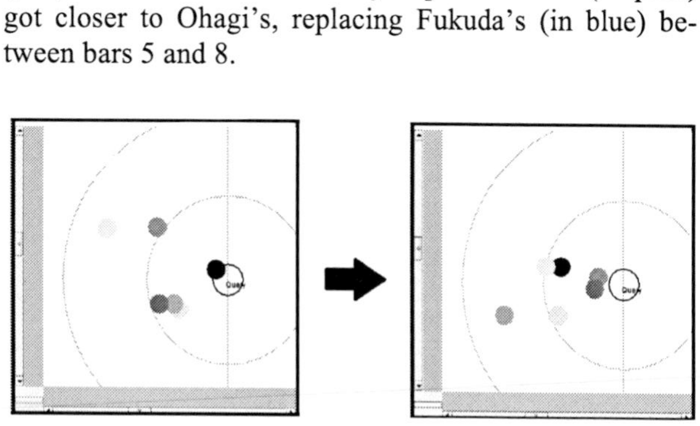

Figure 8. Transition of the performances, where Ohagi's performance was given as the query. Left and right figures are snapshots at bars 5 and 8, respectively.

6. DISCUSSION

PEVI enables interpretations to be retrieved and analyzed by focusing on factors of musical features. We expect that the main users of PEVI will be classical music enthusiasts and scholars. For example, PEVI could be used for an analysis of student/teacher similarities or genealogical studies of musical performers. PEVI will be useful for not only comparing the degree of similarity but also for knowing which factors of musical expressions or which part of a performance are affected by a teacher. For the player, the findings obtained by using our system can be used as a reference. The features in the macroscopic layers are especially difficult to understand only by ear.

Of course, PEVI will also be useful for those beginning to listen to classical music. Comparing expressions is one way to enjoy classical music, but it is difficult to find differences of expressions by using only one's own ear. PEVI enables these differences to be understood by listening to and "touching" the performances and by investigating specific factors. If our system can work on mobile devices, it will be of great use to many classical music listeners.

The database of musical expressions enabled us to make our system. Separating each tone from recordings is helpful for manipulating or understanding expressions. Recently, audio source separation techniques have been rapidly developing [7,8,9]. We can easily separate one note from recordings. This will encourage construction of separated music databases and advance automatic music-understanding technologies. If a bigger musical expression database were constructed, our system would be able to deal with many more performances in the future. Furthermore, if musical features can be detected perfectly and automatically from live performances, we can compare our own performances to those of virtuoso performances. PEVI will be able to help every performer who learns how to express themselves by listening to professional players and both music school students and amateur players.

If we use expression within a beat, we can compare the musical features of performances in detail. Pianists do not always play left- and right-hand notes together, according to aural traditions, although they are written as simultaneities in a printed score. Deviations of the left and right hand produce various expressions and characterize the performance. In addition, articulations such as legato and staccato are also important musical features for identifying interpretations. Individual performers will be characterized more minutely.

As future work to further develop our system, we would like to reflect on other important musical features when retrieving interpretations, for example, the timbre and expression within a beat. Currently, PEVI deals with only two musical features: tempo and dynamics transition. If we use timbre, PEVI is useful for investigating interpretations of performances played as instrumentals with instruments that have much more ability to change timbre than does the piano, for example, the guitar and other strings.

7. CONCLUSIONS

In this paper, PEVI, a novel interface based on the scape plot for finding interpretations of a specified piece, was presented. The scape plot has two problems: it is not able to visualize performances that are not the most similar and it cannot control the weights of musical features. The interface solves these problems by displaying the invisible information on another area and adding a function to change the weights of tempo and dynamics transition and to redraw the scape plot. As a result, we can easily find objective performances for any musical feature of a specified performer in a pool. As future work, we would like to add functions for selecting target performances, mixing expressions of multiple performances, playing new expressions, and reflecting other musical features, for example, timbre, expression within a beat, and articulations in interpretation retrieval.

Acknowledgments

This research was partially supported by CREST, JST, Japan.

8. REFERENCES

[1] M. Goto, K. Yoshii, H. Fujihara, M. Mauch, and T. Nakano, "Songle: A Web Service for Active Music Listening Improved by User Contributions," in International Conference on Music Information Retrieval (ISMIR), 2011

[2] A. Maezawa, M. Goto, and H. Okuno, "Query-by-Conducting: An Interface to Retrieve Classical-music Interpretations by Real-time Tempo Input," Music Information Retrieval Conference (ISMIR 2010), 2010

[3] C. Sapp, "Hybrid Numeric/Rank Similarity Metrics for Musical Performance Analysis," in International Conference on Music Information Retrieval (ISMIR), 2008

[4] S. Dixon,W. Goebl, and G.Widmer, "The performance worm: Real time visualisation of expression based on langner's tempo-loudness animation," ICMC2002, pp. 361-364, 2002

[5] M. Hashida, T. Matsui, and H. Katayose, "A New Music Database Describing Deviation Information of Performance Expressions," International Conference on Music Information Retrieval (ISMIR 2008), pp. 489–494, 2008

[6] Peter Grosche, Meinard Müller, Craig Stuart Sapp: "What Makes Beat Tracking Difficult? A Case Study on Chopin Mazurkas," International Conference on Music Information Retrieval (ISMIR 2010), pp. 649-654, 2010

[7] N. Yasuraoka, T. Yoshioka, K. Itoyama, T. Takahashi, K. Komatani, T. Ogata, and H. Okuno, "Musical Sound Separation and Synthesis Using Harmonic/Inharmonic GMM and NMF for Phrase Replacing System," Information Processing Society of Japan, 2011, Vol. 52, No. 12, 3839–3852, 2011

[8] Masahiro Nakano, Jonathan Le Roux, Hirokazu Kameoka, Nobutaka Ono, Shigeki Sagayama, "Infinite-State Spectrum Model for Music Signal Analysis," Proc. ICASSP, pp. 1972-1975, 2011

[9] Hideyuki Tachibana, Hirokazu Kameoka, Nobutaka Ono, Shigeki Sagayama, "Comparative evaluations of various harmonic/percussive sound separation algorithms based on anisotropic continuity of spectrogram," Proc. ICASSP2012, pp. 465-468, 2012

Segmentation and Timbre Similarity in Electronic Dance Music

Bruno Rocha
University of Amsterdam
BrunoMachadoRocha@gmail.com

Niels Bogaards
Elephantcandy
Niels@elephantcandy.com

Aline Honingh
University of Amsterdam
A.K.Honingh@uva.nl

ABSTRACT

In this paper we argue that the notion of music similarity should be expanded into sub-similarities, meaning that similarity of music has to be judged with respect to a certain context, such as melody, harmony, rhythm or timbre. We start by focusing on timbre similarity, restricted to the domain of Electronic Dance Music (EDM). We will assess the similarity of *segments* of music, thus we start by studying segmentation before we come to the topic of similarity. The segmentation algorithm performs well on an EDM dataset as well as on a standard MIREX dataset. Initial listening tests of the similarity model give promising results but will have to be further evaluated in future research.

1. INTRODUCTION

Similarity in music is a fascinating but complicated concept. Although most people clearly understand when a piece of music is similar to another, a good formalization of the concept of music similarity does not yet exist.

In the academic field of Music Information Retrieval, various systems have been developed that classify music according to a certain type of similarity [13,14,23,24,35,37]. On the other side, in industry, a number of tools have been released that can recommend similar music (Apple Genius, last.fm, Pandora). Such systems and tools, however, often (1) rely on metadata or listener ratings and not on the actual audio, (2) consider similarity as a holistic entity, and (3) consider only complete musical records. As a result, only limited functionality can be provided to the end user.

Let us briefly go through the shortcomings of existing systems.

Most existing music-recommendation apps use metadata (keywords tagged by the user which can include information about artist, title, genre and more [29]), or collaborative filtering (relevance of a song to a user is predicted based on similar users' ratings [25]), meaning that the music itself (the audio file) is not studied . Therefore, the amount of music that can be used as both input and output is limited, and the functionality is limited to finding matches that have the same label. The presented research in this paper focuses on content-based music retrieval, in which the audio is studied. In this way, we can use all music that we have, and have access to all musical information contained in the audio.

Musical similarity consists of many facets, for example, tempo, rhythm, meter, instrumentation and pitch contour. Current research and industrial tools often treat similarity as a monodimensional property, aiming for an arbitrary 'best match'. However, it is known that similarity depends on context [11]. By all means, we can imagine that a piece of music could be rhythmically similar to another piece, without being similar in melody or harmony (e.g. salsa music has a typical rhythm, similar for most salsa music, but different salsa tracks vary in melody/harmony/...) Therefore, it is useful to expand the notion of similarity into sub-similarities, meaning that similarity of music has to be judged with respect to a certain context, such as melody, harmony, rhythm or timbre. The research described in this paper is part of a larger project in which several sub-similarities are studied. This paper focuses on timbre similarity.

Most studies in the area of music similarity concentrate on the similarity of pieces of music or songs as a whole. We can, however, imagine that a piece of music is similar to only a part of another piece of music, for example its introduction. The overall similarity between the two pieces will be therefore not that high, while the similarity between the first song and the introduction of the second could be of great importance. Therefore, in this project, we have focused on the similarity of segments of music, and thus we start by studying segmentation before we come to the topic of similarity.

Since the topic of music similarity, even when restricted to just timbre similarity of music segments, remains a broad subject, we decided to treat it in the restricted domain of electronic dance music (EDM). The choice for this genre was motivated by the collaboration with audio software company Elephantcandy, which identified a specific need for similarity tools in this genre. After a brief introduction into EDM, this paper will report on our study on segmentation and timbre similarity.

The contributions of this paper are two-fold: (1) we present an algorithm for the detection of structural boundaries in EDM, of which the main innovations are the addition of a first downbeat detection and the implementation of musically informed rules; (2) an algorithm to perform polyphonic timbre similarity is presented, of which the main novelty is the modification of the concept of roughness.

2. ELECTRONIC DANCE MUSIC (EDM)

Electronic Dance Music (EDM) is a label that defines a metagenre encompassing a heterogeneous group of musics made with computers and electronic instruments [27]. Most EDM tracks are made with the expectation of being combined with other tracks and danced to. However, some genres, although drawing on the conventions of EDM, are not suitable for the dance floor or written intentionally for not dancing [9].

Until recently, EDM was (with some sporadic exceptions) an underground culture, i.e. cultivated outside the view of the general public eye [18], but it has risen to the mainstream charts of the music industry [20]. Today it has become common for established Top 40 artists and producers to infuse elements of popular EDM styles in their music. EDM "has broken free from the underground to become the driving beat behind pop music and product sales, the soundtrack of choice for a new generation" [17].

Almost all EDM share certain musical characteristics: (1) a steady tempo, mostly in the range of 120-150 BPM (dependent of genre); (2) a repeating bass drum pattern [9].

Timbre, often also referred to as texture, stands out as a primary compositional parameter in EDM. It is seen as the criterion by which patterns may be differentiated most easily [46]. Most of the timbral changes that occur in EDM involve an element either entering or leaving the mix. In Butler [9], DJs Shiva and Stanley described a prototypical structure of EDM tracks. They based their descriptions mainly on timbral changes. As the DJs Butler [9] interviewed stated, in EDM "everything happens in four", be it beats, measures, or hypermeasures. However, empirical analysis in the current project showed it has become increasingly common for producers to introduce an element of surprise, typically by adding one measure at the end of some segments.

3. UNSUPERVISED DETECTION OF STRUCTURAL CHANGES IN EDM

The segmentation of time series into meaningful, coherent units by automatically detecting their boundaries is a challenge crossing several scientific domains [39]. A musical segment is a region with some internal similarity or consistency in a given feature space, such as timbre or instrumentation, implying that it has temporal boundaries at its start and end [12]. Tzanetakis and Cook [43] stress the importance of segmentation in Music Information Retrieval (MIR), where it is better to consider a song as a collection of distinct regions than as a whole with mixed statistics. Performance in audio similarity can benefit from segmenting the tracks beforehand [12].

As pointed out before, timbral changes are essential for EDM producers when considering structural changes. Aucouturier and Sandler [2] argue that, to segment a song into its relevant sections, one should discard any pitch and harmonic information and focus on timbre alone.

To find structural segments in EDM we will (1) extract timbral features, and (2) divide the music into segments, based on these features. In order to take into account the dynamic evolution of a feature, the analysis has to be carried out on a short-term window that moves chronologically along the temporal signal; each position of the window is called a frame [28]. After extracting the relevant features on subsequent frames one has to calculate the distance between each frame and all the others, according to a certain distance measure. The largest calculated distances represent the segment boundaries. We will explain all steps of the segmentation algorithm below. The MIR Toolbox [28] was used to perform most of the steps.

3.1 Detection of first bass drum downbeat

Many EDM tracks begin with beatless intros and culminate in turning the beat around, a phenomenon that occurs when people perceive a certain metrical structure which is violated later (usually by introducing a beat on the perceived off-beat) [9]. For this reason, the entrance of the bass drum in an EDM track often results in a decisive metrical representation [9]. In some cases, DJs may even skip beatless intros and start playing from the first bass drum beat, representing the start of the main structure of the track, which makes its detection a critical step for the performance of the segmentation algorithm.

To detect the first bass drum downbeat, we start by applying a bandpass filter and then compute the global energy of the filtered signal by taking the root average of the square of the amplitude, also called Root Mean Square (RMS), on non-overlapping windows of 30 seconds, in order to find in which part of the audio file is the beat likely to start (beatless intros usually have low-energy in the low-frequency region). An onset detection is then performed on the thirty seconds window where the energy rises abruptly, leaving us with candidates for the first downbeat. We select the first that exceeds a given threshold and save the previous part as the first segment. See figure 1 for a visual explanation.

3.2 Tempo estimation and confidence measure

Tempo estimation is performed in order to detect the duration of a beat. This is important because all features (for both the segmentation and the similarity tasks) are extracted on beat-related frame lengths.

Looking at local correlation between samples we can evaluate periodicities in a signal. An autocorrelation function is computed on the onset detection curve and translated into the frequency domain in order to be compared to a spectral decomposition of the onset detection curve, and the two curves are subsequently multiplied [28]. The result is a curve with peaks as indications of the most predominant periodicities found in the track. We then perform peak picking and select the highest peaks above a certain threshold. The highest peak is selected as the tempo of the track.

A binary confidence measure telling us about the likeliness that the detected tempo is correct is then derived from the harmonic relation between the found peaks. When only one peak is detected or all the observed peaks are harmonically spaced (which would give alternative tempos that are for example two or three times as fast), the estimated confidence value is 1. If there are several peaks with no har-

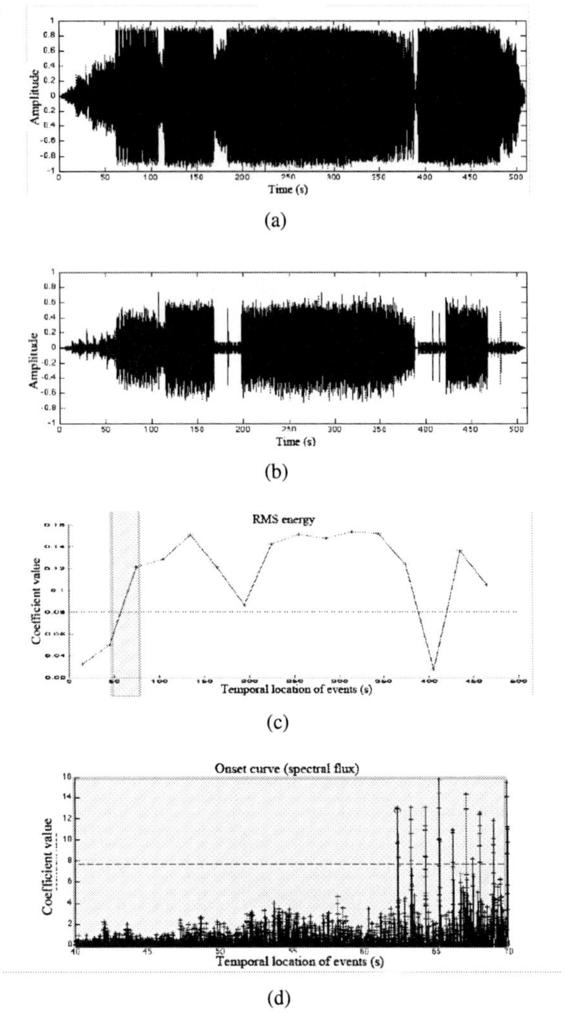

Figure 1. Detection of the first downbeat. (a) Audio waveform after downsampling, (b) audio waveform after bandpass filtering, (c) RMS energy curve, (d) Onset detection on 30 second window. Song: "Insomnia (Monster Mix)" by Faithless.

monic relation between the spacing of the peaks, the estimated confidence value is 0. This measure will be used later, on the level of fine-tuning the segment boundaries (section 3.4).

3.3 Novelty detection

After computing the tempo score in beats per minute (BPM) and building a vector with all the beat positions, we compute the magnitude spectrum of each frame of the signal. The frames are beat-aligned with 87.5% overlap so that we decompose the energy along frequencies for each beat of the track.

We perform a cepstrum analysis in order to find periodic sequences in the signal. This is motivated by the fact that timbre should be the most important characteristic for segmentation [2, 9], and by analysis on both MFCC and cepstrum-based segmentation.

Following Foote [19], we then compute the cosine distance between each possible pair of frames from the cepstrum data to get a self-similarity matrix (figure 2). Convoluting along the main diagonal of the similarity matrix results in a novelty curve that indicates the temporal locations of significant timbral changes by its peaks. These locations present the segment boundaries that we searched for.

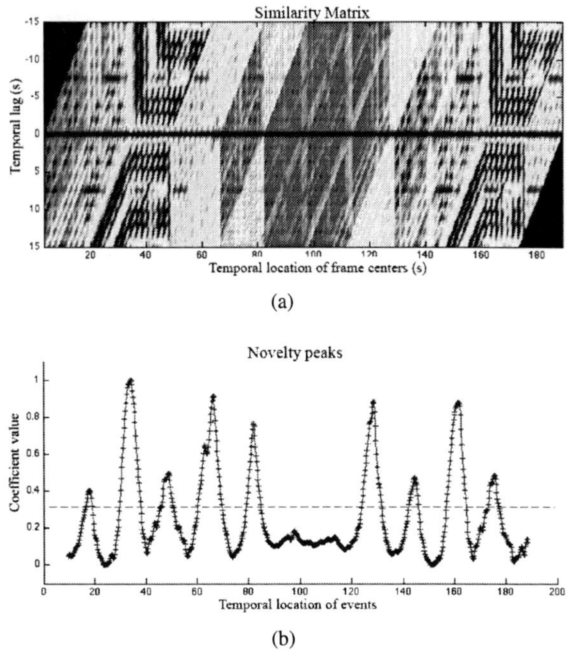

Figure 2. Novelty detection. (a) Similarity matrix with kernel size of approximately 30 seconds, (b) Novelty curve. Song: "& Down" by Boys Noize.

3.4 Musically informed rules

Although our algorithm located the segment boundaries based on timbral changes, we are not done yet. The nature of EDM requires us to fine-tune the segment boundary locations. Butler [9] categorizes sounds in EDM as rhythmic, articulative, or atmospheric. For the purpose of segmentation, articulative sounds, which are brief and intermittent, are very important. They usually appear before structural boundaries, such as the beginning of a measure or multi-measure group, in order to raise expectation for a segment boundary for the listener. As the novelty detection is based on textural changes and the timbres of articulative sounds are frequently quite distinct from the neighbours, novelty peaks are detected when these sounds occur. However, the relevant structural changes usually follow these sounds and start on a downbeat.

To overcome this displacement, we propose a set of heuristic rules to align the obtained novelty peaks with the most probable structural boundaries - for the tracks on which the tempo was estimated with confidence. We analyze the distances between peaks and update them at each iteration, forming a dynamic structure. Furthermore, to account for the extra measure issue (explained in section 2), an asymmetric weight was applied, such that the gravitation toward the 8th or 16th measure mark is stronger when a boundary

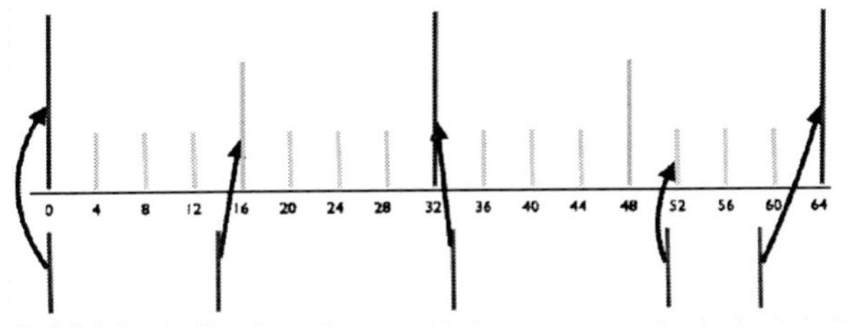

Figure 3. Application of musically informed rules to detected boundaries. The timeline is shown in beats (0 corresponds to the first detected beat; 4 beats = 1 measure). Heuristic rules dictate a dynamic and asymmetric weight towards the 8th and 16th measures.

is detected before than when it is detected after that mark. Figure 3 shows the effect of the rules on a hypothetical track.

For the tracks that had a tempo estimation with confidence=0, the detected boundaries remain unchanged, as the changes would most probably result in a less precise estimation of the segment boundaries. However, for the tested datasets, more than 90% of the tracks had confidence=1.

3.5 Evaluation of segmentation

The segmentation algorithm was evaluated using several datasets: (1) EDMs, an in-house EDM dataset specially created for this project [1], consisting of 35 songs - annotated by the authors - from 19 artists; (2) RWC Pop [21], annotated by two groups of researchers RWO corresponds to the annotations of the dataset creators and RWQ corresponds to the annotations made in the Quaero project [4]; (3) Eurovision dataset [5]. Found segment boundaries are considered correct if they are within ± 0.5 seconds (precise) or ± 3 seconds (relaxed) from a border in the ground truth annotations. Based on the matched hits, boundary retrieval recall rate, boundary retrieval precision rate, and boundary retrieval F-measure are calculated.

The results can be found in table 1. Of the EDMs dataset, we show the results both with and without the musically informed rules. On the other datasets, the rules did not make a significant difference and we show only the results where the musically informed rules have been applied. The algorithm performs well on the EDMs dataset. As can be seen from table 1, the musically informed rules increased the F-score with around 10 points on the 0.5s tolerance-window level. Although this method was created specifically for EDM, results on the RWC Pop dataset would be in the top 3 of best performing algorithms submitted to MIREX 2012, with its best performing algorithm having $F(3s) = 0.77$ on RWQ and $F(3s) = 0.71$ on RWO [32]. This suggests that structural changes in pop music might have the same periodicity as in EDM. This method does not reach high performance on the Eurovision dataset. An explanation for this might be that, in this song contest, pop music is usually mixed with traditional music from several European countries of which the structural boundaries may be quite distinct.

[1] The annotations are available for research purposes on request to the authors.

Dataset	P0.5s	R0.5s	F0.5s	P3s	R3s	F3s
EDMs (no rules)	37.10	51.48	41.63	63.62	86.34	73.80
EDMs	46.52	62.87	51.67	62.15	84.83	69.38
RWO	28.10	23.95	25.28	70.11	63.70	65.08
RWQ	31.40	27.86	28.99	66.74	61.25	62.59
EUR	9.27	9.15	8.86	43.85	43.55	42.39

Table 1. Boundary retrieval precision rate (P), recall rate (R) and F-score (F) with two tolerance windows: ±0.5 seconds and ±3 seconds. Three annotated datasets were used: in-house (EDM-set), RWC (original (RWO) and Quaero (RWQ) annotations) and Eurovision (EUR).

4. MUSIC SIMILARITY: TIMBRE

Cambouropoulos [11] explains that the concept of similarity always depends on context, such that we can only speak of similar music with respect to a certain context such as timbre, melody, rhythm etc. To make a start with defining musical similarity in this way, and since timbre is seen as the criterion by which patterns in EDM may be differentiated most easily [46], this paper focuses on timbre similarity.

Studies in timbre perception indicate that the phenomenon of timbre is multidimensional, with a number of factors interacting to produce the exact tone quality that is perceived by a listener [16]. These factors have been identified to include, among others, spectral flux, spectral centroid, and attack time [10, 26, 34]. These studies focused on monophonic timbres. However, here we want to describe polyphonic textures, which the aforementioned features cannot represent.

For our purposes, we have empirically made a selection of a small number of features to describe timbre in EDM. We will now describe the three types of features that we believe capture the most relevant dimensions of a polyphonic texture for comparison with other textures.

4.1 Mel-Frequency Cepstral Coefficients

Mel-Frequency Cepstral Coefficients (MFCCs) [15] are used to represent the spectral envelope of a given sound, which is one of the most salient components of timbre. We calculate them by first computing the power spectrum successively on frames with the duration of a beat, followed by logarithmically positioning the frequency bands on the Mel scale, and finally performing a discrete cosine transform on the bands [28].

The number of MFCCs that well represent a spectral envelope is subject to discussion. The low order MFCCs account for the slowly changing spectral envelope, while the higher order ones describe the fast variations of the spectrum [1]. Therefore, while it is true that the more MFCCs we compute, the more precise the approximation of the signal's spectrum is, a large number of MFCCs may not be appropriate, as we are only interested in the spectral envelope and not in the finer details of the spectrum [3]. The same authors reported an ideal value of 20 coefficients, which we selected.

For the computation of these features, we frame the signal into half-overlapping windows with duration of a beat and calculate the mean of each coefficient for each segment, ending up with twenty values per segment.

4.2 Spectral Flatness

Spectral flatness, also referred to as tonality coefficient, measures the sinusoidality of a spectrum [33]. It indicates whether the distribution of the spectrum is smooth or spiky, and provides a way to quantify how tone-like a sound is, as opposed to being noise-like. The spectral flatness is calculated by dividing the geometric mean of the power spectrum by the arithmetic mean of the power spectrum, i.e.:

$$\frac{\sqrt[N]{\Pi_{n=0}^{N-1} x(n)}}{\frac{1}{N}\sum_{n=0}^{N-1} x(n)}, \tag{1}$$

where $x(n)$ represents the magnitude of bin number n.

For the computation of the spectral flatness, we split the spectrum into four bands. Then we frame the signal into half-overlapping windows with the duration of a beat. Finally we calculate the mean spectral flatness for each band, ending up with four values per segment.

4.3 Dirtiness

Helmholtz [22] introduced the term auditory roughness, also referred to as sensory dissonance, in the psychoacoustics literature. It is related to the beating phenomenon that occurs whenever a pair of sinusoids is close in frequency [36]. Roughness can be considered as an attribute of timbre, as it is usually described as a function of a signal's amplitude envelope and corresponding spectral distribution [45].

We took the notion of roughness and approached it from a different perspective. Dirtiness is a term used by EDM listeners and producers when referring to a particular sound quality that is pervasive in synthesizers (as used in EDM) there is even a subgenre of EDM called Dirty Dutch [41] and numerous online videos teach how to achieve a dirty synth sound. Spectral analysis revealed that dirtiness might be (partly) explained by the detuning that producers apply to their synth sounds. This detuning is characterized by a varying stream of frequencies very close to the harmonics of the fundamental frequency we perceive as the pitch of the played sound, which can therefore be described using the concept of roughness.

We are not interested in the value of roughness at each instance but in its value over a larger period of time with a high frequency resolution. For this reason, we compute roughness values in half-overlapping windows of 8 beats. For the computation of roughness we use Vassilakis [44] model. Dividing the spectrum into four bands, we then calculate the mean for each band, ending up with four values per segment.

4.4 Feature vector for timbre similarity

The aforementioned features (20 MFCCs, 4 Spectral Flatness values, and 4 Dirtiness values) together make a feature vector that describes the timbre of a segment. The similarity between two different timbres is then described by calculating the Euclidian distance between the two associated feature vectors.

Initial listening tests on this similarity rating model gave promising results. Since no groundtruth database exists for timbre-similarity, we could not perform an evaluation of the model. We plan to do a full evaluation of this similarity measure by creating our own groundtruth corpus in the near future. The algorithm in its present form computes a similarity rating based on different timbral features with equal weighting. One might expect that some features may be more important than others and that the optimal weighting scheme is different from the one we have used here. Optimizing the weighting is planned for future research as well, but is however highly dependent on confident ground truth.

5. DISCUSSION AND CONCLUSIONS

We have presented our model for structural segmentation and timbre similarity for electronic dance music. The segmentation algorithm included a set of musically informed rules to account for the fact that segment boundaries in EDM are usually on the beat. The algorithm was evaluated on various corpora, and performed best on an inhouse dataset of EDM. Although this method was created specifically for EDM, results on the RWC Pop dataset can compete with the best performing algorithms submitted to MIREX 2012, suggesting that the structural boundaries underlying EDM follow the same principles as the boundaries in pop-music.

In the literature, the topic of segmentation has been approached from different angles, and can be interpreted as phrasing/grouping [6, 30], or structural segmentation [8, 31]. Structural segmentation is described as to identify the key structural sections in musical audio as for example verse and chorus, and should be accessible to everybody (needing no particular musical knowledge) [32]. The question however here is, whether there is indeed consensus on the concept of structural segmentation. One issue that we came across, for example, is the question whether it is necessary for a segment boundary to coincide with a downbeat. We found this to be the case for EDM, and in this case the "preference" for perceiving a new segment starting on a downbeat overruled the concept of timbral change that was underlying our algorithm, hence the introduction of the musically informed rules. One can wonder whether this is the case for other genres as well.

An issue related to this is how far phrase-segmentation and structural segmentation merge. If a phrase, starting with an upbeat, introduces the start of new structural segment, does the structural segment start with the start of the phrase (on the upbeat) or does it start on the downbeat following the upbeat?

The evaluation process of segmentation algorithms is important to consider as well. Several studies use only a ± 3 second tolerance window for evaluation. We would like to argue that this window is too large to be able to assess algorithms in a detailed way. If the large window is used to cover up misalignments like ones caused by issues that we outlined above (e.g. boundaries on upbeats or downbeats), then these are the issues that we should consult instead of hiding them with large tolerance windows. Problems like these have been discussed before [38] and we feel it is important to continue this discussion.

Besides the segmentation algorithm we have presented our model for timbre similarity in EDM. A feature vector has been created to describe a particular timbre, with the most novel feature being 'dirtiness', which accounts for the rough sound that is characteristic for some types of EDM. The selection of features for this feature vector was based on empirical tests on a reduced dataset, for which only the features described in section 4 seemed to reveal any particular relevance. Initial listening test gave promising results, but since no groundtruth dataset exist, a formal evaluation has not been done. We plan to do a full evaluation of this similarity measure by creating our own groundtruth corpus in the near future. This evaluation will also include statistical tests involving other features and comparisons between MFCC-only approaches (e.g. [42]) and ours.

Acknowledgments

The authors wish to thank three anonymous reviewers. This research has been funded by the Center for Digital Humanities (http://cdh.uva.nl/) and the Netherlands foundation of Scientific Research (NWO), grant no. 639.021.126.

6. REFERENCES

[1] Aucouturier, J. J., and Pachet, F. Music similarity measures: Whats the use. In Proceedings of the 3rd International Conference on Music Information Retrieval. Paris, France, 2002.

[2] Aucouturier, J. J., and Sandler, M. Segmentation of Musical Signals Using Hidden Markov Models. Proceedings of the 110th Convention of the Audio Engineering Society. Amsterdam, The Netherlands, 2001.

[3] Aucouturier, J. J., Pachet, F., and Sandler, M. The Way It Sounds: Timbre Models for Analysis and Retrieval of Music Signals. IEEE Transactions on Multimedia, 7(6), 2005: 1028-1035.

[4] Bimbot, F., Le Blouch, O., Sargent, G., and Vincent, E. Decomposition into autonomous and comparable blocks: a structural description of music pieces. Proceedings of the 11th International Society for Music Information Retrieval Conference. Utrecht, The Netherlands, 2010.

[5] Bimbot, F., Deruty, E., Sargent, G., and Vincent, E. Methodology and resources for the structural segmentation of music pieces into autonomous and comparable blocks. Proceedings of the 12th International Society for Music Information Retrieval Conference. Miami, FL, USA, 2011.

[6] Bod, R. Memory-based models of melodic analysis: Challenging the Gestalt principles. Journal of New Music Research, 31(1), 2002: 27-36.

[7] Bogert, B. P., Healy, M. J. R., and Tukey, J. W. The quefrency alanysis of time series for echoes: Cepstrum, pseudo-autocovariance, cross-cepstrum, and saphe cracking. In M. Rosenblatt (Ed.), Time Series Analysis 1963: pp. 209-243.

[8] Bruderer, M. J., McKinney, M., and Kohlrausch, A. Structural boundary perception in popular music. In Proc. of 7th International Conference on Music Information Retrieval 2006 (pp. 198-201).

[9] Butler, M. J. Unlocking the Groove: Rhythm, Meter, and Musical Design in Electronic Dance Music. Bloomington, IN, USA: Indiana University Press, 2006.

[10] Burgoyne, J., and McAdams, S. A meta-analysis of timbre perception using nonlinear extensions to CLASCAL. Computer Music Modeling and Retrieval. Sense of Sounds, 2008: 181202

[11] Cambouropoulos, E. How similar is similar?. Musicae Scientiae, 13(1 suppl), 2009. 7-24.

[12] Casey, M., Veltkamp, R., Goto, M., Leman, M., Rhodes, C., and Slaney, M. Content-Based Music Information Retrieval: Current Directions and Future Challenges. Proceedings of the IEEE, 96(4), 2008, pp. 668-696.

[13] Chew, E., Volk (Fleischer), A. and Lee. Dance Music Classification Using Inner Metric Analysis: a computational approach and case study using 101 Latin American Dances and National Anthems. Proceedings of the 9th INFORMS Computer Society Conference. Kluwer. ICS2005, Annapolis, MD, Jan 5-7. 2005

[14] Cilibrasi, R., Vitanyi, P., and de Wolf, R. Algorithmic clustering of music based on string compression. Computer Music Journal, 28(4):49-67. 2004

[15] Davis, S., and Mermelstein, P. Comparison of parametric representations for monosyllabic word recognition in continuously spoken sentences. IEEE Transactions on Acoustics, Speech and Signal Processing, 28(4), 1980: 357366.

[16] Fales, C. Heaviness" in the Perception of Heavy Metal Guitar Timbres The Match of Perceptual and Acoustic Features over Time. In P. Greene and T. Porcello (Eds.), Wired For Sound: Engineering And Technologies In Sonic Cultures (pp. 181-197). Middletown, CT, USA: Wesleyan University Press, 2004

[17] Ferguson, J. P. EDM is taking over the Chicago festival season. Time Out Chicago. Retrieved from http://timeoutchicago.com. Website accessed on May 31, 2012.

[18] Fikentscher, K. You Better Work!: Underground Dance Music in New York. Middletown, CT, USA: Wesleyan University Press, 2000.

[19] Foote, J. T. Content-based retrieval of music and audio. Proceedings of Multimedia Storage and Archiving Systems II 1997.

[20] Greenburg, Z. The worlds highest-Paid DJs 2012. Forbes. Retrieved from http://www.forbes.com. Accessed on August 2, 2012.

[21] Goto, M., Hashiguchi, H., Nishimura, T., and Oka, R. RWC Music Database: Popular, Classical, and Jazz Music Databases. Proceedings of the 3rd International Conference on Music Information Retrieval. Paris, France, 2002.

[22] Helmholtz, H. On the sensations of tone. New York: Dover, 1954.

[23] Hillewaere, R., Manderick, B., and Conklin, D. String quartet classification with monophonic models. In Proceedings of the 11th International Society for Music Information Retrieval Conference, Utrecht, Netherlands. 2010

[24] Honingh, A. and R. Bod. Clustering and classification of music using interval categories. In Proceedings of MCM 2011. Parijs June 15-17. 2011

[25] Kaminskas, M., and Ricci, F. Contextual music information retrieval and recommendation: state of the art and challenges. Computer Science Review, 2012.

[26] McAdams, S., Winsberg, S., Donnadieu, S., De Soete, G., and Krimphoff, J. Perceptual scaling of synthesized musical timbres: Common dimensions, specificities, and latent subject classes. Psychological Research 58, 1995: 17792.

[27] McLeod, K.. Genres, Subgenres, Sub-Subgenres and More: Musical and Social Differentiation Within Electronic/Dance Music Communities. Journal of Popular Music Studies, 13, 2001: 59-75.

[28] Lartillot, O., and Toiviainen, P. A Matlab Toolbox for Musical Feature Extraction from Audio. Proceedings of the 10th International Conference on Digital Audio Effects. Bordeaux, France, 2007.

[29] Lamere P. Social tagging and music information retrieval. Journal of New Music Research Vol. 37(2). pp 101-104, 2008

[30] Lerdahl, F. A., and Jackendoff, R. S. A generative theory of tonal music. The MIT Press, 1983.

[31] Levy, M., and Sandler, M. Structural segmentation of musical audio by constrained clustering. Audio, Speech, and Language Processing, IEEE Transactions on, 16(2), 2008, 318-326.

[32] MIREX evaluation task "Structural Segmentation", 2012. http://www.music-ir.org/mirex/wiki/2012:Structural_Segmentation

[33] Peeters, G. A large set of audio features for sound description (similarity and classification) in the CUIDADO project. Technical Report. IRCAM, France, 2004.

[34] Peeters, G., Giordano, B. L., Susini, P., Misdariis, N., and McAdams, S. The Timbre Toolbox: Extracting audio descriptors from musical signals. Journal of the Acoustical Society of America, 130(5), 2011: 2902-2916.

[35] Perez-Sancho, C., Rizo, D., and Inesta, J. Genre classification using chords and stochastic language models. Connection Science, 21(2-3):145-159. 2009

[36] Plomp, R., and Levelt, W. J. Tonal consonance and critical bandwidth. The journal of the Acoustical Society of America, 1965 38, 548.

[37] Pollastri, E. and Simoncelli, G. Classification of melodies by composer with hidden markov models. In Music and Artificial Intelligence. 2001

[38] Rocha, B., Smith, J.B., Peeters, G., Ross, J.C., Nieto, O., Balen, J. van. Report on Late-break session on Music Structure Analysis. ISMIR 2012. Available from http://ismir2012.ismir.net.

[39] Serrá, J., Muller, M., Grosche, P., and Arcos, J. L. Unsupervised Detection of Music Boundaries by Time Series Structure Features. Proceedings of the Twenty-Sixth AAAI Conference on Artificial Intelligence, 2012: 1613-1619. Toronto, Canada.

[40] Smith, J.O. "Hamming Window", in Spectral Audio Signal Processing, http://ccrma.stanford.edu/~jos/sasp/Hamming_Window.html, online book, accessed 29 March, 2013.

[41] Styles of house music. (2013, March 7). In Wikipedia, The Free Encyclopedia. Retrieved March 29, 2013, from http://en.wikipedia.org/w/index.php?title=Styles_of_house_music&oldid=542547435

[42] Terasawa, H., Slaney, M., and Berger, J. Perceptual distance in timbre space. In Proceedings of the International Conference on Auditory Display (ICAD05) pp. 1-8, 2005.

[43] Tzanetakis, G. and Cook, P. Audio information retrieval (AIR) tools. Proceedings of the 1st International Symposium on Music Information Retrieval. Plymouth, MA, USA, 2000.

[44] Vassilakis, P. N. Perceptual and Physical Properties of Amplitude Fluctuation and their Musical Significance. Doctoral Dissertation. University of California, Los Angeles, 2001.

[45] Vassilakis P. N. and Kendall, R. A. Psychoacoustic and cognitive aspects of auditory roughness: definitions, models, and applications. Proceedings of Human Vision and Electronic Imaging XV 2010 (SPIE 7527).

[46] Yeston, M. The Stratification of Musical Rhythm. New Haven, Conn.: Yale University Press, 1976.

Melodic Outline Extraction Method for Non-note-level Melody Editing

Yuichi Tsuchiya
Nihon University
tsuchiya@kthrlab.jp

Tetsuro Kitahara
Nihon University
kitahara@kthrlab.jp

ABSTRACT

In this paper, we propose a method for extracting a melodic outline from a note sequence and a method for re-transforming the outline to a note sequence for non-note-level melody editing. There have been many systems that automatically create a melody. When the melody output by an automatic music composition system is not satisfactory, the user has to modify the melody by either re-executing the composition system or editing the melody on a MIDI sequencer. The former option, however, has the disadvantage that it is impossible to edit only part of the melody, and the latter option is difficult for non-experts, musically untrained people. To solve this problem, we propose a melody editing procedure based on a continuous curve of the melody called a melodic outline. The melodic outline is obtained by applying the Fourier transform to the pitch trajectory of the melody and extracting low-order Fourier coefficients. Once the user redraws the outline, it is transformed into a note sequence by the inverse procedure of the extraction and a hidden Markov model. Experimental results show that non-experts can edit the melody to some extent easily and satisfactorily.

1. INTRODUCTION

Automatic music composition systems [1–6] give the user original music without requiring the user to perform musically difficult operations. These systems are useful, for example, in the situation that a musically untrained person wants original (copyright-free) background music for a movie. These systems automatically generate melodies and backing tracks based on the user's input such as lyrics and style parameters. In most cases, however, the generated pieces do not completely match those desired or expected by users because it is difficult to express the desire as style parameters. The common approach for solving this problem is to manually edit the generated pieces with a MIDI sequencer, but this approach is not an easy operation for musically untrained people.

The goal of this study is to achieve an environment that enables musically untrained users to explore satisfactory melodies by repeated trial-and-error editing of melodies generated by automatic music composition systems. There are two reasons why it is difficult for musically untrained people to use a conventional MIDI sequencer. The first reason is that musically untrained listeners understand music without mentally representing audio signals as musical scores [7]. The melody representation for melody editing should therefore not be based on musical notes; it should capture the coarse structure of the melody that an untrained person would recognize in an audio signal. The second reason is that it is difficult for untrained people to avoid dissonant notes in a MIDI sequencer. A certain support is therefore needed to avoid such notes using a computing technology.

In this paper, we propose a new sub-symbolic melody representation called a melodic outline. The melodic outline represents only the coarse temporal characteristics of the melody; the notewise information of the melody is hidden. This representation can be obtained by applying the Fourier transform to the pitch trajectory of the melody. Because low-order Fourier coefficients represent the coarse melodic characteristics and high-order ones represent the fine characteristics, we can obtain the melodic outline by applying the inverse Fourier transform to only low-order Fourier coefficients. Once the melodic outline is obtained, the user can redraw the outline with a mouse. The redrawn outline is transformed into a sequence of notes by the inverse procedure of melodic outline extraction. In this process, the selection of notes dissonant to the accompaniment are avoided to select by using a hidden Markov model (HMM).

The rest of the paper is organized as follows. In Section 2, we describe the concept of the melodic outline. In Section 3, we present a method for melodic outline extraction and conversion of the outline to a sequence of notes. In Section 4, we report experimental results. Finally, we conclude the paper in Section 5.

2. BASIC CONCEPT OF MELODIC OUTLINE

A melodic outline is a melody representation in which the melody is represented as a continuous curve. An example is shown in Figure 1. A melodic outline is mainly used for editing a melody with a three-step process: (1) the target melody represented as a sequence of notes is automatically transformed into a melodic outline, (2) the melodic outline is redrawn by the user, and (3) the redrawn outline is transformed into a note of sequence. The key technology for achieving this is the mutual transform of a note-level melody representation and a melodic outline. We think that this mutual transform should satisfy the following requirements:

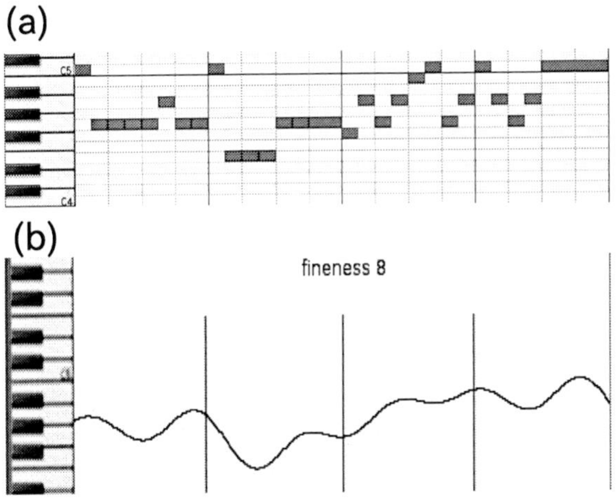

Figure 1. Example of melodic outline. (a) Input melody, (b) Melodic outline

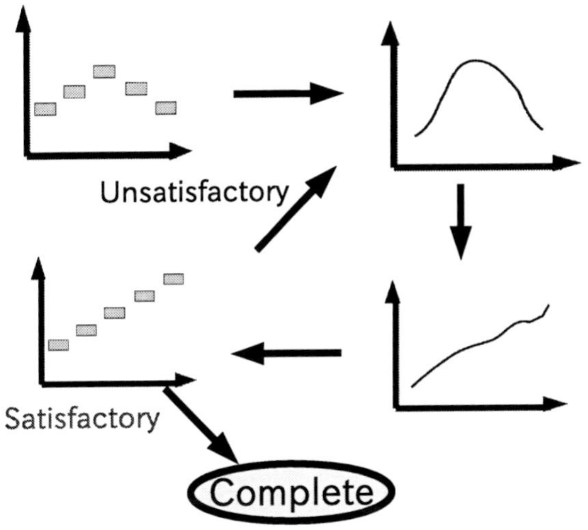

Figure 2. Flow of melody editing.

1. A melodic outline does not explicitly represent the pitch and note value of each note.
2. When a melodic outline is inversely transformed into a note sequence without any editing, the result should be equivalent to the original melody.
3. When a melodic outline edited by a user is transformed into a note sequence, musically inappropriate notes (e.g., notes causing dissonance) should be avoided.

No previous studies have proposed melody representations satisfying all these requirements. Various methods for transforming a melody to a lower-resolution representation have been proposed such as [8], but these representations are designed for melody matching in query-by-humming music retrieval, so they cannot be inversely transformed into a sequence of notes. OrpheusBB [9] is a human-in-the-loop music composition system, which enables users to edit automatically generated content when it does not satisfy their desire. When the user edits some part of the content, this system automatically regenerates the remaining part, but the editing is performed at the note level.

The flow of the melody editing is shown in Figure 2. The method supposes that the user composes a melody with an automatic music composition system. The melody is transformed into a melodic outline with the method described in Section 3.1. The user can freely redraw the melodic outline. Using the method described in Section 3.2, the melodic outline is inversely transformed into a note sequence. If the user is satisfied with the result, the user again edits the melodic outline. The user can repeat the editing process until a satisfactory melody is obtained.

3. METHOD FOR MUTUAL TRANSFORM OF MELODIC OUTLINE AND NOTE SEQUENCE

In the section, we describe our method for editing melodies developed using the process described above (Figures 3 and 4). Our melody editing method consists of three steps: (1) transform of a note sequence into a melodic outline, (2) editing of the melodic outline, and (3) inverse transform of the edited melodic outline into a note sequence.

3.1 Transform of a Note Sequence into a Melodic Outline

The given MIDI sequence of a melody (Figure 3 (a)) is transformed into a pitch trajectory (Figure 3 (b)). The pitch is represented logarithmically, where middle C is 60.0 and a semitone is represented by 1.0. (The difference from note numbers is that non-integer values are acceptable.) Regarding the pitch trajectory as a periodic signal, the Fourier transform is applied to this trajectory. Note that the input to the Fourier transform is not an audio signal, so the result does not represent a sound spectrum. Because the Fourier transform is applied to the pitch trajectory of a melody, the result represents the feature of temporal motion in the melody. Low-order Fourier coefficients represent slow motion in the melody while high-order Fourier coefficients represent fast motion. By extracting low-order Fourier coefficients and applying the inverse Fourier transform to them, a rough pitch contour of the melody, i.e., the melodic outline, is obtained (Figure 3 (c)).

3.2 Inverse Transform of a Melodic Outline into a Note Sequence

Once part of the melodic outline is redrawn, the redrawn outline is transformed into a note sequence. The overview of the procedure of the transform is shown in Figure 4.

First, the Fourier transform is applied to the redrawn outline (Figure 4 (a)). Then, the higher-order Fourier coefficients of the original pitch trajectory, which had been removed when the melodic outline is extracted, are added to the Fourier coefficients of the redrawn outline to generate the same pitch trajectory as the original melody from the non-redrawn part of the melodic outline. Next, the inverse Fourier transform is applied, producing the post-edit pitch trajectory (Figure 4 (b)).

Next, the pitch trajectory is transformed into a note sequence. In this process, notes that cause dissonance with the accompaniment should be avoided, which is achieved using a hidden Markov model. The HMM used here is shown in Figure 5. This model is formulated based on the idea that the observed pitch trajectory $O = o_1 o_2 \cdots o_N$ is emitted with random deviation from a hidden sequence of note numbers $H = h_1 h_2 \cdots h_N$ that does not cause dissonance.

The HMM consists of hidden states $\{s_i\}$, each of which corresponds to a note number.(Therefore, each h_n takes an element of $\{s_i\}$.) Each state s_i emits a value of pitch following a normal distribution $N(i,\sigma^2)$. For example, the state s_{60}, corresponding to the note number 60, follows the normal distribution with a mean of 60.0 and a variance of σ^2. The variance σ^2 is common among all states and is experimentally determined; it is set to 13 in the current implementation. In the current implementation, 36 states, from s_{48} to s_{84}, are used. The transition probability $P(s_j|s_i)$ is determined as follows:

$$P(s_j|s_i) = p_1(s_j)\, p_2(s_i, s_j),$$

where $p_1(s_j)$ is the probability that each note number appears in the target key (C major in the current implementation). This is experimentally defined based on the idea of avoiding non-diatonic notes as follows:

$$p_1(s_i) = \begin{cases} 16/45 & \text{(C)} \\ 2/45 & \text{(D)} \\ 8/45 & \text{(E)} \\ 3/45 & \text{(F, A)} \\ 12/45 & \text{(G)} \\ 1/45 & \text{(B)} \\ 0 & \text{(Non-diatonic notes)} \end{cases}$$

In addition, $p_2(s_i, s_j)$ is the probability that note numbers i,j successively appear. This probability is also experimentally defined based on the pitch interval between the two note numbers as follows:

$$p_2(s_i, s_j) = \begin{cases} 1/63 & \text{(Augmented fourth、} \\ & \text{Diminished fifth} \\ & \text{Major sixth, Minor seventh)} \\ & \text{Major seventh)} \\ 2/63 & \text{(Perfect prime)} \\ 4/63 & \text{(Minor sixth)} \\ 6/63 & \text{(Perfect fourth, Perfect fifth)} \\ 10/63 & \text{(Minor second, Major second、} \\ & \text{Minor third, Major third)} \end{cases}$$

Currently, the editing targets only the diatonic scale. These transition probabilities are applied only at each note boundary and no transitions are accepted between the onset and offset times of each note, because only pitch editing is currently supported for simplicity. As described above, the transition probabilities are manually determined so that non-diatonic notes in the C major scale are avoided. However, the transition probabilities can be learned using a melody corpus. If the transition probabilities are learned with melodies of a particular genre (e.g., jazz), they would reflects melodic characteristics of that genre.

By using the Viterbi algorithm on this HMM, we obtain a sequence of note numbers $H = h_1 h_2 \cdots h_N$ (which would not contain dissonant notes) from the pitch trajectory $O = o_1 o_2 \cdots o_N$. Finally, the result is output in the MIDI format.

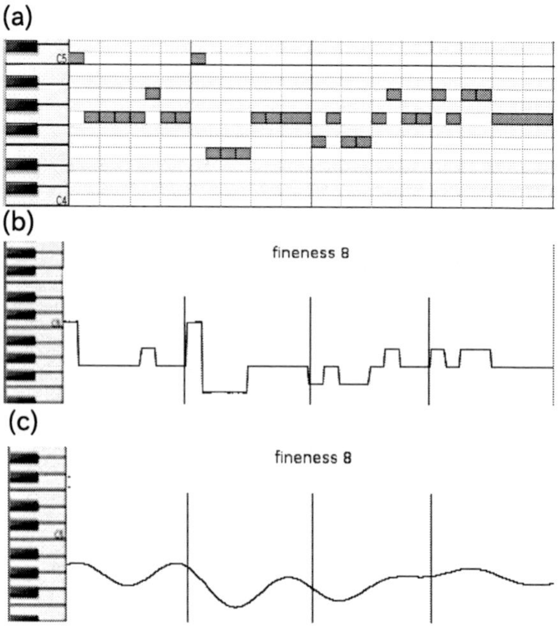

Figure 3. Overview method of extracting note sequence to melodic outline. (a) MIDI sequence of melody, (b) Pitch trajectory, (c) Melodic outline.

4. IMPLEMENTATION AND EXPERIMENTS

4.1 Implementation

We implemented a system for melody editing based on the proposed method. In this system, the original melody is assumed to be an output of Orpheus [4]. After the user creates a melody using Orpheus, the user inputs the melody's ID given by Orpheus into our system. Then, the system obtains a MIDI file from the Orpheus web server, and displays the melody both in a note-level representation and as a melodic outline(Figure 6 (a)). Once the user redraws the melodic outline, the system immediately regenerates the melody with the method described in Section 3 and updates the display(Figure 6 (b)). If the user is not satisfied after, listening to the regenerated melody, the user can redraw the melodic outline repeatedly until a satisfactory melody is obtained.

4.2 Example of Melody Editing

We demonstrate an example of melody editing using a melodic outline. As a target of editing, we used a four-measure melody generated by Orpheus [9], which generates a melody based on the prosody of Japanese lyrics. We input a sentence (*Yume mita mono wa hitotsu no kofuku / Negatta mono wa hitotsu no ai*) [1] taken from a Japanese poem "*Yume mita mono wa...*" by Michizo Tatehara, and obtained the melody shown in Figure 7 (a). Figure 7 (b) shows

[1] This literally means "All I dream is a piece of happiness. All I hope is a piece of love."

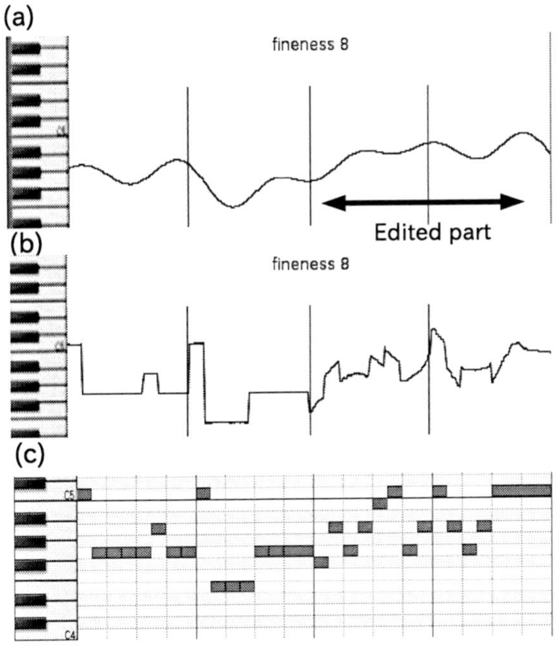

Figure 4. Overview of transforming melodic outline to note sequence. (a) Edited melodic outline, (b) Generated pitch trajectory, (c) Generated melody.

a melodic outline extracted from this melody. From this melodic outline, we can see the following: (1) this melody has disjunct motion in the second measure, (2) the pitch rises gradually from the third measure to the forth measure, (3) the melody ends with a downward motion in pitch.

We edited this melody with the melodic outline. The last half of the melodic outline is redrawn so that the gravity of the pitch motion is higher than that of the original melody. The redrawn melodic outline and the melody generated from it are shown in Figures 7 (c) and (d), respectively. The generated melody reflects the editing; it rises in higher pitch than the original melody.

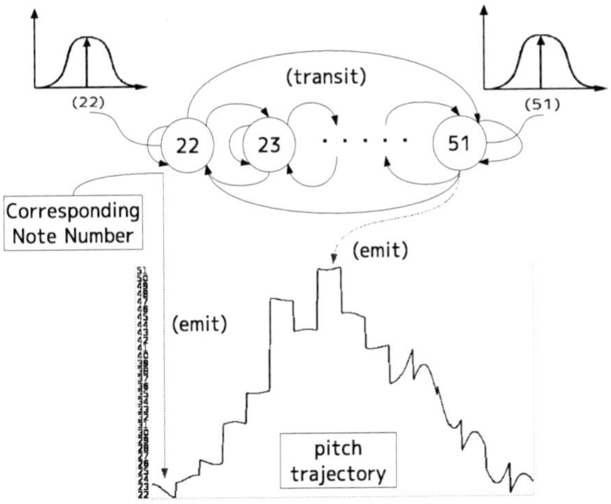

Figure 5. Overview of HMM for estimating note sequence from pose-edit pitch trajectory

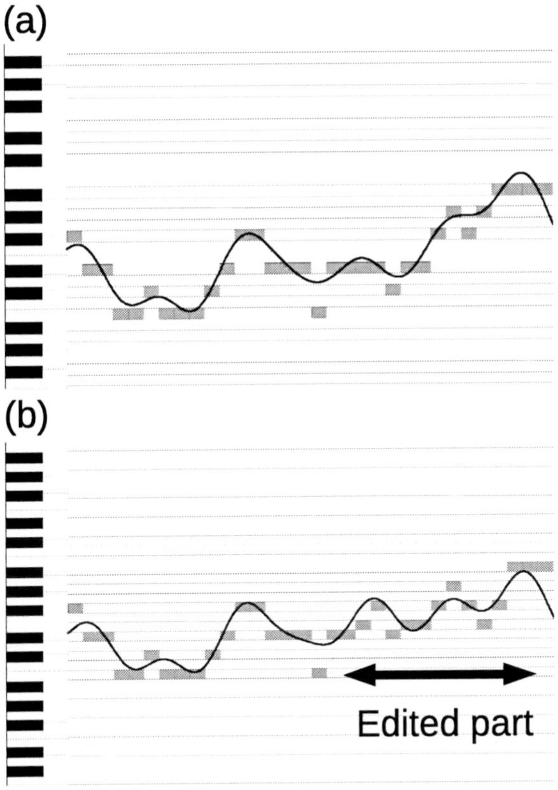

Figure 6. The user interface of edit display. (a)Input melody, (b)Edited the melodic outline.

Table 1. Questionnaire results (instructed editing).

	A	B	C	D	E	F	average
Q1	6	5	7	6	7	7	6.3
Q2	6	7	5	6	7	6	6.1
Q3	5	6	6	6	6	6	5.8

4.3 User Test

We asked human subjects to use this melody editing system. As with the previous section, the melody to be edited is prepared by giving a sentence (*Osake wo nondemo ii / Sorega tanosii kotodattara*)[2] taken from a Japanese poem "*Clover no harappa de* ..." by Junko Takahashi to Orpheus. The melody is shown in Figure 8 (a). We asked the subjects to edit this melody in two ways. The first way is based on the instruction to make all notes in the last measure higher. The second way is free editing. After each editing, we asked the subjects to answer the following questions:

Q1 Were you satisfied with the output?
Q2 Did you edit the melody without difficulty?
Q3 Were you able to edit the melody as desired?
(7: Strongly agree, 6: agree, 5: weakly agree, 4: neutral, 3: weakly disagree, 2: disagree, 1: strongly disagree)

The subjects were six musically untrained people (20–21 years old).

[2] This literally means "You may drink alcohol, if it makes you happy."

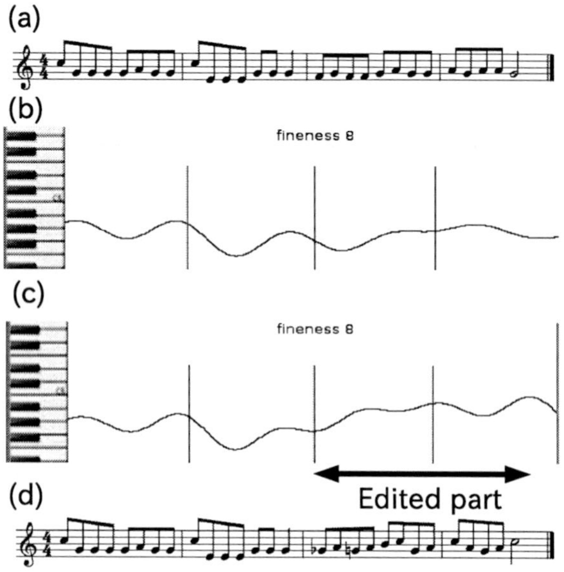

Figure 7. Example of melody editing. (a) Input melody, (b) Melodic outline of (a), (c) Edited melodic outline, (d) Note representation of generated melody.

Table 2. Questionnaire results (free editing).

	A	B	C	D	E	F	average
Q1	6	6	6	5	6	5	5.6
Q2	6	7	7	3	6	6	5.8
Q3	6	3	6	3	7	6	5.1

The results of the questionnaire for the instructed editing are listed in Table 1. Almost every subject agreed on all three questions. Figures 8 (b) and (c) show the melodies generated by Subjects C and F, respectively. The melody of Figure 8 (b), as instructed, has lower pitches in the last measure than in the last measure of the original melody, and is musically acceptable. Although the melody of Figure 8 (c) has some higher notes in the last measure than in the last measure of the original melody, it is also musically acceptable.

The results of the questionnaire for the free editing are listed in Table 2. Most subjects agreed on all the questions. Figures 8 (d) and (e) shows the melodies generated by Subjects A and E, which are mostly musically acceptable. The third measure of the melody of Subject E starts with A♭, which might cause a sense of incongruity because it is a non-diatonic note. The subject, however, is probably satisfied with this output because the subject's answer to Q1 is 7. Two subjects answered 3 for Q3, which could be because the time for the experiment is limited. In the future, we will conduct a long-term experiment.

5. CONCLUSION

In this paper, we proposed a method enabling musically untrained people to edit a melody at the non-note level by transforming the melody to a melodic outline. The melodic outline is obtained by applying the Fourier transform to the pitch trajectory of the melody and extracting only low-order Fourier coefficients. After the outline is redrawn by the user, it is transformed into a note sequence. In this transform, a hidden Markov model is used to avoid notes dissonant to the accompaniment. Experimental results show that both the editing user interface and the results are satisfactory to some extent for human subjects.

Figure 8. Melodies created by subjects.

In the content design field, it is said that controllers for editing content should be based on the cognitive structure of the content and at an appropriate abstraction level [10]. When a user interface for editing content satisfies this requirement, it is called directable. Melodic outlines are designed based on the insight that non-professional listeners cognize melodies without mentally obtaining note-level representations. The melody editing interface based on melodic outlines is therefore considered to achieve directability in editing melodies.

We have several future issues. First, we plan to extend the method to edit the rhythmic aspect of melodies. Second, we will try to learn the state transition probability matrix from a music corpus. In particular, we will try to achieve a matrix that has characteristics of a particular genre by learning the matrix with a corpus of that genre. Finally, we plan to conduct a long-term user experiment for investigating how users acquire or develop the schema of melodies through our system.

Acknowledgments

We thank Dr. Hiroko Terasawa and Dr. Masaki Matsubara (University of Tsukuba) for their valuable comments.

6. REFERENCES

[1] L. Hiller, L. Isaacson, "Musical composition with a high-speed digital computer", Journal of Audio Engineering Society, 1958.

[2] C. Ames, M. Domino, "Cybernetic composer: An overview," in Understanding Music with AI, M. Balaban, K. Ebcioglu, O. Laske, Eds. Association for the

Advancement of Artificial Intelligence Press, pp.186-205, 1992.

[3] D. Cope, "Computers and Musical Style", Oxford University Press, 1991.

[4] S. Fukayama, K. Nakatsuma, S. Sako, T. Nishimoto, S. Shigeki"Automatic song composition from the lyrics exploiting prosody of the japanese language", in Proc. Sound and Music Computing, 2010.

[5] D. Ando, P. dahlstedt, M. G. Nordaxhl, H. iba,"Computer aided composition by means of interactive gp", in Proc. The International Computer Music Association, pp.254–257, 2006.

[6] J. A. Biles,"Genjam: A genetic algorithm for generating jass solos", in Proc. The International Computer Music Association, 1994.

[7] M. Goto, "A Real-time Music-scene-description System: Predominant-F0 Estimation for Detecting Melody and Bass Lines in Real-world Audio Signals", Speech Communication (The International Speech Communication Association Journal), 2004.

[8] M. Marolt, "A Mid-level Representation for Melody-based Retrieval in Audio Collections", The Institute of Electrical and Electronics Engineers, Inc. Transactions on Multimedia, pp.1617–1625, 2008.

[9] T. Kitahara, S. Fukayama, H. Katayose, S. Sagayama, N. Nagata "An Interactive Music Composition System Based on Autonomous Maintenance of Musical Consistency", in Proc. Sound and Music Computing, 2011.

[10] H. Katayose, M.Hashida "Discussion on Directability for Generative Music Systems", The Special Interest Group Technical Reports of Information Processing Society of Japan, pp.99–104, 2007.

SoundAnchoring: Content-based Exploration of Music Collections with Anchored Self-Organized Maps

Leandro Collares
Department of Computer Science
University of Victoria
leco@cs.uvic.ca

Tiago Fernandes Tavares
School of Electrical and Computer Engineering
University of Campinas
tavares@dca.fee.unicamp.br

Joseph Feliciano
Department of Computer Science
University of Victoria
noelf@uvic.ca

Shelley Gao
Department of Computer Science
University of Victoria
syugao@gmail.com

George Tzanetakis
Department of Computer Science
University of Victoria
gtzan@cs.uvic.ca

Amy Gooch
Department of Computer Science
University of Victoria
amy.a.gooch@gmail.com

ABSTRACT

We present a content-based music collection exploration tool based on a variation of the Self-Organizing Map (SOM) algorithm. The tool, named SoundAnchoring, displays the music collection on a 2D frame and allows users to explicitly choose the locations of some data points known as anchors. By establishing the anchors' locations, users determine where clusters containing acoustically similar pieces of music will be placed on the 2D frame. User evaluation showed that the cluster location control provided by the anchoring process improved the experience of building playlists and exploring the music collection.

1. INTRODUCTION

Commonly used interfaces for organizing music collections, such as iTunes and Microsoft Media Player, rely on long sortable lists of text and allow listeners to interact with music libraries using textual metadata (e.g., artist name, track name, album name, genre, etc.). Text-based interfaces excel when the user is looking for specific tracks. However, these interfaces are not suited for indirect queries, such as finding tracks that sound like a given track. Furthermore, text-based interfaces do not give users the ability to quickly summarize an unknown music collection.

Content-Based music collection Visualization Interfaces (CBVIs), such as *Islands of Music* [1], *MusicBox* [2] and *MusicGalaxy* [3], use Music Information Retrieval (MIR) techniques to group tracks from a collection according to their auditory similarity. In these interfaces, acoustically similar tracks are placed together in clusters, whereas dissimilar tracks are placed further apart. Consequently, CBVIs can reveal relationships between tracks that would be difficult to detect using text-based interfaces.

A number of CBVIs rely on the Self-Organizing Map (SOM) [4] to organize the tracks of the music collection according to acoustic similarities. In the traditional SOM algorithm, however, users cannot determine the positions of clusters containing acoustically similar tracks on the music space. Additionally, the clusters' positions are randomized between different executions of the algorithm. We believe these characteristics can have a negative impact on the user experience.

In order to address the previously described issues, this paper presents *SoundAnchoring*, a CBVI that not only emphasizes meaningful relationships between tracks, but also allows users to determine the general placement of track clusters themselves. With SoundAnchoring, users can customize the layout of the music space by choosing the locations of a small number of tracks. These 'anchor' tracks and their respective positions determine the locations of clusters containing acoustically similar tracks on the music space. Such features allow users to create playlists easily without giving up control over which tracks are added. SoundAnchoring turns a music library into an interactive music space in three steps: feature extraction, organization and visualization.

Feature extraction involves calculating an n-dimensional 'feature' vector for each track. Since each element of the feature vector is an acoustic descriptor, tracks whose feature vectors are similar will be acoustically similar.

In the organization stage, we use AnchoredSOM, a variation of the traditional SOM algorithm. AnchoredSOM maps the music collection into a 2D representation that can be displayed on a screen. Moreover, AnchoredSOM gives users the power to determine the positions of clusters containing acoustically similar tracks on the 2D music space.

Lastly, the output of AnchoredSOM is used to render a visualization of the music collection. SoundAnchoring provides users with different ways to interact with the collection. If present, metadata is used to enrich the visualization. An outline of SoundAnchoring is depicted in Figure 1.

SoundAnchoring was evaluated through a user study. The anchoring process was evaluated positively. Ultimately, users felt that SoundAnchoring was easier to use than the control system, which was based on the traditional SOM algorithm. Thus, we conclude that the ability to choose

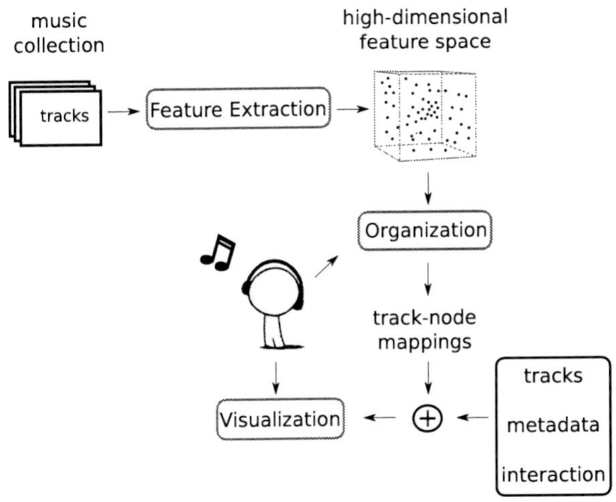

Figure 1: Outline of SoundAnchoring. A feature vector is computed for each track of the music collection. The set of feature vectors is a high-dimensional space that is mapped to two dimensions using the AnchoredSOM algorithm. The output of the algorithm is used to create a visualization of the music space. Users customize the positions of clusters containing acoustically similar tracks on the music space by choosing the locations of anchors.

anchors and their positions on the music space is an important feature in CBVIs that employ SOMs.

The remainder of the paper is organized as following:

- Section 2 contains related work on CBVIs that use SOMs.
- Section 3 describes the design of SoundAnchoring, with an emphasis on the organization and visualization stages.
- Section 4 describes the user study conducted to evaluate SoundAnchoring.
- Section 5 presents and discusses the results of the user study.
- Section 6 closes the paper with conclusive remarks and possible avenues of future work.

2. RELATED WORK

The SOM has been frequently employed in content-based interfaces to generate visualizations of music collections. Other dimensionality reduction techniques used for music collection organization include Principal Component Analysis (PCA) and Multidimensional Scaling (MDS), employed in *MusicBox* [2] and in *MusicGalaxy* [3], respectively.

In SoundAnchoring, SOM is employed to make optimum use of screen space on mobile devices. Tolos et al. [5] and Muelder et al. [6] showed that the music space produced by PCA presents problems regarding the distribution of tracks. Mörchen et al. [7] suggested that since the output of PCA and MDS are coordinates in a 2-dimensional plane, it is hard to recognize groups of similar tracks, unless these groups are clearly separated. By choosing suitable parameters for the SOM algorithm, we believe that the music space can be displayed in an aesthetic way and occurrences of regions completely devoid of tracks can be minimized.

The first interface for music collection exploration that employed SOMs, SOMeJB, was an adaption of a digital library system. Interfaces that employ SOMs have evolved since then by incorporating more possibilities of interaction and customization, and auditory feedback.

SOMeJB (SOM-*extended Jukebox*), devised by Rauber and Frühwirth [8], introduced the use of SOMs for music collection exploration but still relied heavily on text to represent the music space. SOMeJB extended the functionalities of the SOMLib digital library system [9], which could organize a collection of text documents according to their content. SOMeJB was aimed to enable users to browse a music collection without a particular track in mind. The music library visualization generated by SOMeJB comprised a grid with track names grouped according to acoustic similarities between tracks. Even though SOMeJB represented a major departure from metadata-based organization, text was still the principal element of the interface.

In *Islands of Music*, a SOM-based interface developed by Pampalk et al. [1], the importance of text was diminished. The goal of Islands of Music was to support the exploration of unknown music collections using a geographic map metaphor. Clusters containing similar tracks were visualized as islands, while tracks that could not be mapped to any of the islands were placed on the sea. Connections between clusters were represented by narrow strips of land. Within an island, mountains and hills depicted sub-clusters. It was also possible to enrich the visualization by adding text summarizing the characteristics of the clusters.

Islands of Music inspired several content-based interfaces that, in addition to employing the geographic metaphor, refined the possibilities of interaction between users and music collections. *PlaySOM*, developed by Neumayer et al. [10], relied on the same metaphor of Islands of Music. PlaySOM improved the interaction with the music library by allowing users to add all tracks of a SOM node to a playlist.

Further refinements in interfaces using SOMs employed audio to assist in navigating music collections. *Sonic SOM*, devised by Lübbers [11], featured spatial music playback to provide users with an immersing experience. Knees et al. [12] developed *nepTune*, a 3D version of Islands of Music [1]. In nepTune, the user would navigate the music collection with a video game controller while tracks close to the listener's current position were played using a 5.1 surround system. Metadata retrieved from the Internet, such as tags and artist-related images, were displayed on screen to describe the track being played. Lübbers and Jarke [13] conceived an interface similar to nepTune. Valleys and hills replaced islands and oceans, respectively. Auditory feedback was enhanced by attenuating the volume of the tracks that deviated from the user's focus of attention.

A system developed by Brazil et al. [14, 15] combines both visual and auditory feedback for navigation. In this system, a user would navigate a sound space by means of a cursor surrounded by an 'aura'. All sounds encompassed by the aura would be played simultaneously, but spatially arranged according to their distances from the cursor.

Although computer-based organization of music is an important tool for exploring of music collections, the perception of music is known to be highly subjective [16]. Thus, different listeners employ different methods to explore their music libraries. In order to accommodate these methods, interfaces should ideally adapt to the user's behaviour.

The previously described work of Lübbers and Jarke [13] allowed users to customize the environment by changing the positions of the tracks, adding landmarks, or building and destroying hills. These actions would modify the similarity model employed to organize the music collection and thus cause the system to re-build the environment to reflect the user's preferences.

A similar approach was adopted by Stober and Nürnberger [17], who developed *BeatlesExplorer*. In this interface, a music collection comprising 282 Beatles tracks was organized using SOMs. A user could drag and drop tracks between nodes, which would make the system relocate other tracks so that the collection organization could satisfy the user's needs.

Interfaces for music collection exploration with smartphones and tablets in mind were also developed. Such interfaces benefited from the increase in processing power and storage for mobile devices and new possibilities of user interaction provided by touch-based screens. *PocketSOMPlayer*, created by Neumayer et al. [10], was an interface derived from PlaySOM geared towards mobile devices. In PocketSOMPlayer, tracks could be added to a playlist by drawing trajectories on the music collection visualization.

Improvements in multi-touch gesture interaction stimulated the design of interfaces that allowed visually-impaired individuals to explore music collections without relying on the WIMP (window, icon, menu, pointer) paradigm. In the prototype developed by Tzanetakis *et al.* [18] for iOS devices, a random track would begin to play as soon as the user tapped on a square of the SOM grid. Moving one finger across squares would cause tracks from adjacent squares to cross-fade with each other, thereby generating auditory feedback.

With SoundAnchoring, users choose 'anchor' tracks and their positions on the music space. AnchoredSOM, a variation on the traditional SOM algorithm, places acoustically similar tracks on the neighbourhood of each anchor. Therefore, users are able to determine both the locations of clusters on the music space and their auditory content.

The concept of anchoring was introduced by Giorgetti et al. [19], who employed SOMs for localization in wireless sensor networks. The algorithm devised by Giorgetti et al. did not modify the weight vectors of nodes that contain anchors. Furthermore, Giorgetti et al.'s algorithm replaced the input vector with the node's weight vector when the input vector was mapped to an anchor node. In AnchoredSOM, weight vectors of all nodes are modified, while input vectors remain constant.

SoundAnchoring allows users to select tracks individually or by moving one finger over the music space, based on the implementation of Neumayer et al. [10]. While moving the finger on the device's surface, users receive auditory feedback derived from the mechanism designed by Tzanetakis *et al.* [18] for assistive browsing.

3. SOUNDANCHORING DESIGN

The design of SoundAnchoring is comprised of three steps: feature extraction, organization and visualization. Feature extraction consists of representing each track of the collection as a vector of features that characterize the musical content. Tracks that sound alike are close to each other in the feature space. In organization, the high-dimensional feature space is reduced to a 2-dimensional representation. The topology of the feature space is preserved during this step. Finally, the output of the organization stage is used to produce a visualization of the music space. Users can interact with this customizable music space visualization and build playlists.

Feature extraction is carried out on a desktop computer, as it is independent from user interaction. Organization and visualization take place on an iPad 2. The forthcoming subsections present details pertaining to each step.

3.1 Feature Extraction

Feature extraction is the computation of a single feature vector for each track of the music collection. Before performing feature extraction, the first and the last fifteen seconds of each track are removed to avoid lead-in and lead-out effects. The audio clips are then divided into 23-ms frames, with a 12.5-ms overlap. Each frame is multiplied by a Hanning window and has its Discrete Fourier Transform (DFT) calculated. After that, we calculate a set of features for each frame. Later, the value series for each feature is divided into a 1-second frame, with length of 12.5 milliseconds between the beginning of each frame. The mean and variance of each frame are computed, generating two series f_μ and f_σ. Finally, the mean and variance of f_μ and f_σ are calculated. Therefore, there are four elements in the feature vector for each acoustic feature calculated.

The sixteen acoustic features employed in SoundAnchoring are frequently used in automatic genre classification tasks: thirteen MFCCs (Mel-Frequency Cepstral Coefficients), Spectral Centroid, Spectral Rolloff and Spectral Flux [20]. After feature extraction, each audio clip yields a 64-dimensional feature vector. Tracks that have similar feature vectors sound alike. AnchoredSOM reduces the 64-dimensional feature space to two dimensions for easy visualization. Acoustically similar tracks are placed close to each other on the 2D music space.

3.2 Organization

The organization stage maps the 64-dimensional feature space to discrete coordinates on a grid using SOM. This dimensionality reduction technique preserves the topology of the high-dimensional space as much as possible; tracks that have similar feature vectors should be placed close to each other, whereas tracks that have dissimilar feature vectors should be apart in the 2-dimensional space. SoundAnchoring employs AnchoredSOM to allow the user to define the location of some specific tracks or anchors.

The traditional SOM is an artificial neural network in which nodes are arranged in a 2-dimensional rectangular grid. During the execution of the SOM algorithm, the neural network is iteratively trained with input vectors, namely the feature vectors computed during feature extraction. At the end of the execution, different parts of the network are optimized to respond to certain input patterns.

Each node of the SOM is characterized by two parameters: a position in the two-dimensional space and a weight vector of the same dimensionality as the feature vectors: 64. When a feature vector is presented to the network, the best matching node (BMN), i.e., the node whose weight vector is the most similar to the feature vector is determined. The feature vector, which corresponds to one track of the music collection, is mapped to the BMN. The BMN's weight vector is updated to resemble the feature vector. Weight vectors of the BMN's neighbouring nodes are also updated towards the feature vector. The magnitude of the change in the neighbouring nodes' weight vectors, which is determined by the learning rate, decreases with time and distance. The neighbourhood size also decreases with time. After several iterations, different parts of the network will have similar weight vectors and, consequently, will respond similarly to certain feature vectors.

In visualizations of music collections based on the traditional SOM algorithm, tracks that sound similar tend to be close to each other. The SOM algorithm, however, does not have information regarding genre labels as only feature vectors are used as input to the algorithm. Thus, the locations of genre clusters are an emergent property of the SOM.

The weight vectors are usually initialized with small random values. Consequently, the positions of clusters containing acoustically similar tracks on the music space cannot be determined in advance by the user. Moreover, the position of a given cluster containing similar tracks is likely to vary between executions of the traditional SOM algorithm, as shown in Figures 2a-2d. We believe this scenario has a negative impact on the user experience. In order to alleviate the situation, we introduce AnchoredSOM, a variation on the traditional SOM algorithm.

3.2.1 AnchoredSOM

AnchoredSOM allows users to choose the locations of 'anchor' data points on the SOM, which correspond to tracks in the music collection. The anchors will attract similar tracks to their neighbourhoods. AnchoredSOM consists of four stages, detailed below:

- **Stage 0.** This stage is analogous to the initialization of the traditional SOM. In AnchoredSOM, however, node weight vectors are initialized with feature vectors randomly chosen from the high dimensional feature space. This approach speeds up the convergence of the SOM algorithm.
- **Stage 1.** In this stage, only feature vectors of the anchors are presented to the SOM for i_1 iterations. Both the initial learning rate, L_0, and the initial neighbourhood size, σ_0, have high values to cause significant changes to the weight vectors of the entire SOM.
- **Stage 2.** Only feature vectors of the anchors are presented to the SOM for i_2 iterations. In stage 2, however, the initial learning rate, L_0, and the initial neighbourhood size, σ_0, are low to bring small changes to localized areas of the SOM.
- **Stage 3.** For each of the i_3 iterations, the input of the entire feature set to the SOM is followed by m occasions on which only the anchors' feature vectors are presented to the SOM. The input of anchors' feature vectors for m successive times within one iteration keeps the weight vectors of nodes surrounding the anchors' nodes similar to the anchors' feature vectors.

In our implementation, we employed the Euclidean distance for measuring the similarity between feature vectors. Learning and neighbourhood functions are exponentially-decaying with time. The values for the number of iterations, initial learning rate and initial neighbourhood size were empirically determined. The size of the grid is based on the number of tracks in the music collection.

Figures 2e-2h show that AnchoredSOM lends itself to setting the positions of clusters containing similar music. AnchoredSOM performs better with genres that are distinct and well-localized, such as the classical genre. With acoustically diverse genres, such as the pop genre, the tracks will be more loosely dispersed on the grid.

3.2.2 Number of Anchors

A pilot study was conducted to determine the number of anchors that would be used in SoundAnchoring. Participants were told that we had designed an interface able to organize their entire music collection on a 2D grid in a logical manner. They were also told that information was being collected regarding the number of music genres people needed to organized their collections. Participants received a sheet of paper containing a 10x10 grid and a table to make colour-genre associations.

Firstly, individuals had to complete the table with the minimum set of genres they deemed necessary to categorize their collection effectively. Some major categories were presented but they were encouraged to add more genres if any genres were unrepresented. After picking the genres, participants were asked to colour the squares next to the genres using a set of crayons. Later, participants were asked to choose one square of the grid to act as the centre point of each genre. Similar tracks would be grouped around that square. Glass tokens were provided to help participants space out the chosen squares before colouring them. Most participants chose five categories and thus SoundAnchoring uses five anchors of different genres.

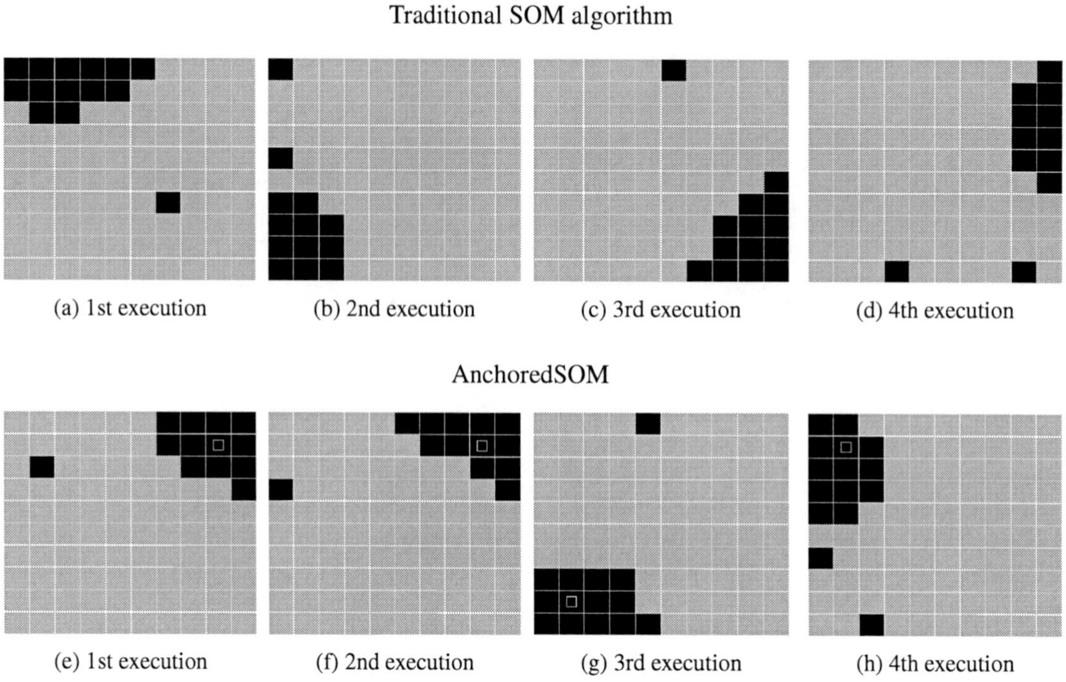

Figure 2: Topological mapping of clusters containing classical tracks, in blue. Traditional SOM, subfigures a-d: the location of the classical cluster varies drastically with each execution of the algorithm. AnchoredSOM, subfigures e-h: the same white-marked anchor track was used to maintain the position of the classical cluster in (e, f). When the same anchor track is placed on a different node, the other classical tracks remained clustered around it (g, h).

3.3 Visualization

The output of AnchoredSOM is employed to generate a visualization of the music collection. In our implementation, interactions with the music collection are based on the Apple Cocoa Touch API (Application Programming Interface). In order to get to the final screen, which contains the music space, users go through a sequence of screens and make choices that influence the organization and the appearance of the music space. The sequence of screens aims to lower the cognitive load on the user.

In SoundAnchoring, colours convey information on genres. As user studies have shown no basis for universal genre-colour mappings [21], SoundAnchoring allows users to make genre-colour associations using seven palettes, derived from Eisemann's work [22]. Eisemann built associations between colours and abstract categories such as 'capricious', 'classic', 'earthy', 'playful', 'spicy', 'warm', etc. The aforementioned categories referred to moods that each colour grouping evoked when utilized in advertisements, product packaging and print layouts. The colours of each grouping created by Eisemann were chosen from the Pantone Matching System, a de facto colour space standard in publishing, fabric and plastics. These predefined colour palettes give users some freedom to assign colours to genres and have a positive bearing on the aesthetics of the music space visualizations.

Classifying music by genre is challenging, as there is often overlapping between genres and disagreement on the label set used for classification [23]. Genres, however, are usually employed to narrow down the number of choices when browsing music for entertainment reasons [24]. Therefore, genres provide users with a familiar vantage point to start exploring their music collections.

After selecting a colour palette and building genre-colour associations, users choose five anchors from the music collection and place them on the grid. The anchors' feature vectors and locations are presented to AnchoredSOM, along with the feature vectors of the other tracks of the music collection. AnchoredSOM then maps the tracks to nodes of the SOM.

3.3.1 Interaction with Music Collection

The SoundAnchoring interface (Figure 3) displays the entire music collection on a grid. Users interact with the music collection using different gestures.

By tapping on one of the nodes of the grid, users will see a list of tracks mapped to that node by AnchoredSOM. Single-tapping on the track gives audio feedback. Double-tapping on the track adds it to the playlist. This action is similar to building a playlist by selecting tracks individually in text-based interfaces. With the SOM, however, acoustically similar tracks will be either in the same node or in neighbouring ones.

Instead of listing the tracks of a certain node and adding tracks to the playlist individually, users can alternatively moving one finger over the grid to add multiple tracks to the playlist. As the user performs this gesture, known as 'sketching', SoundAnchoring randomly adds one track of each node activated by the user's finger to the playlist. The user also receives aural and visual feedback while sketching. Excerpts of the randomly chosen tracks cross-fade with each other as the user moves the finger across nodes as a way of providing auditory feedback to users. The opac-

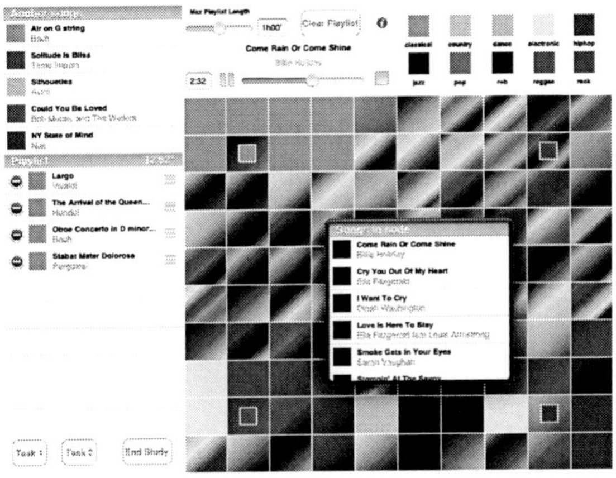

Figure 3: SoundAnchoring interface. Tapping on a node reveals tracks that have been mapped to that node. Genre buttons allow users to limit the number of genres displayed on the music space. Playlists can be built by selecting tracks individually or 'sketching' on the surface, which causes SoundAnchoring to randomly choose one track from each node.

ity of the nodes that have been activated oscillates for a few seconds giving the impression of a trail on the grid.

Finally, genre masks refine the use of genres as a familiar vantage point to explore music libraries. Genre buttons coloured according to the genre-colour associations previously made are employed to filter genres that are displayed. If a genre is filtered out, both the colour assigned to that genre and the tracks belonging to it disappear from the grid. Consequently, these tracks are not listed when the user taps on a node. Furthermore, sketching across nodes does not add tracks from the filtered-out genre to the playlist. Therefore, genre masks give users more flexibility to explore the music space.

4. EVALUATION

For evaluation we conducted a user study in which each one of the twenty-one participants (eleven females and ten males) performed tasks in two systems with the same visual interface: SoundAnchoring (SA), which allows individuals to determine the position of anchors on the music space, and a Control System (CS), which loads pre-calculated maps generated using the traditional SOM algorithm.

The study took place in a prepared office room. SoundAnchoring and the Control System were loaded in two iPads 2. Participants were randomly assigned to start working with either SA or CS to compensate for learning effects.

Subjects performed two tasks, with no enforced time limits. Task 1 was conceived to raise awareness for the mapping of similar tracks to the same node or neighbouring nodes of the SOM. Participants were required to tap on one square of the grid and listen to the tracks of that square, then its adjacent squares. These steps were repeated with two other squares, distant from the first square and from each other. Task 2 was the creation of a playlist. Slips of paper containing descriptions of different scenarios were placed face down. Participants were asked to pick one slip of paper and build a playlist of at least thirty minutes containing a minimum of three genres that would match the scenario described.

After using each system, subjects rated a set of eighteen statements using a 6-point scale (from zero to five). Subjects were also encouraged to write about positive and negative aspects of each system, as well as recommendations for improvement.

5. RESULTS AND DISCUSSION

The mean values for each statement were calculated and the statistical significance of the differences between systems were computed using Fisher's randomization test [25]. The statements, mean values and p-values are shown in Table 1.

In most statements, the mean rate difference is not statistically significant ($p > 0.05$). A remarkable exception is statement 10 ("Getting the system to do what I wanted was easy"), which shows that SoundAnchoring is consistently evaluated as easier to use than the Control System. However, most of the results are inconclusive, which necessitates a qualitative analysis of the textual feedback provided by the subjects.

Overall, both SA and CS were favourable reviewed by participants as shown by mean rates for statements 4-6, 9, 12, 15 and 18 (Table 1). Words employed to describe both SOM-based systems: "intuitive", "easy to use", "aesthetically appealing", "interesting", "flexible", "user-friendly", and "entertaining". More elaborate comments on the interface included: "easy to sample-listen to songs", "a fun way to browse a music collection", "good for exploring unfamiliar music collections", "easy to find songs similar to known ones you like", "similar songs are actually similar", "does a good job of grouping similar music", "great to access songs you have forgotten about" and "nice mapping from sounds to graphics".

Comments suggest that participants perceived the visualization of the music collection using SOMs and the grouping of acoustically similar tracks as positive. Therefore, the clustering process was able to retrieve useful information from the music collection and display it properly. Moreover, the feedback shows that content-based music collection visualization is an efficient approach to music collection exploration.

Playlist creation was mentioned in comments such as "It is easy to build accurate playlists for specific scenarios", "Making a playlist becomes fun instead of a chore" and "easy to take playlist in a new sound direction that suits your inspiration". By analyzing user-system interactions that were logged during the user study, we realized that most participants added tracks to the playlist by tapping on each node and selecting tracks individually. This behaviour was reflected in comments such as "It can be time-consuming to make a playlist", "I wanted to have total control over the songs added to the playlist, so I had to tap on all the grid boxes to get to know the songs". One participant particularly liked the sketching gesture for creating

Statement	Mean rate SA	Mean rate CS	p-value
1. Please rate the playlist you created in task 2.	**4.2**	4.1	0.83
2. The interactions with the interface were natural.	**3.8**	3.7	1.0
3. I was unable to anticipate what would happen next in response to the actions I performed.	**1.2**	1.4	0.67
4. The amount of controls available to perform the tasks was adequate.	4.0	**4.2**	0.22
5. The auditory aspects of the interface appealed to me.	**4.3**	4.2	0.74
6. The visual aspects of the interface were unappealing to me.	**0.9**	1.0	0.72
7. It was impossible to get involved in the experiment to the extent of losing track of time.	**1.2**	1.6	0.39
8. I felt proficient in interacting with the interface at the end of the experiment.	**3.6**	3.4	0.64
9. The interface was unresponsive to actions I initiated (or performed).	0.8	**0.6**	0.58
10. Getting the system to do what I wanted was easy.	**4.3**	3.8	**0.03**
11. I would consider replacing my current application for music exploration with one based on the system tested.	2.6	**3.2**	0.07
12. Learning how to use the system was difficult.	**0.8**	1.0	0.70
13. I disliked creating playlists with the system.	1.0	1.0	1.0
14. The system is unsuitable for managing and exploring my music collection.	1.7	**1.4**	0.46
15. I enjoyed exploring the music collection with the system.	4.2	**4.4**	0.67
16. I can create playlists quickly by using the system.	2.9	**3.1**	0.54
17. I disliked the playlists created by using the system.	0.8	0.8	1.0
18. Please provide an overall rate for the system.	4.0	**4.1**	0.52

Table 1: Statements' mean rates for SoundAnchoring (SA) and the Control System (CS), and p-values. Better rates for each statement and the statistically significant p-value are shown in bold.

playlists: "Adding songs to the playlist by dragging my finger on the surface and listening to audio was a really nice feature I was impressed with". A slightly different opinion was expressed by another participant: "I really liked to be able to explore the collection sliding my finger on the surface but I think it shouldn't add the songs to the playlist when I do that. I can add the songs individually later". Even though there is some disagreement with regard to interaction, playlist creation using the interface was seen as enjoyable. Feedback from participants is supported by the mean rates for statements 1, 13 and 17 in Table 1. Therefore, the goal of building an interface in which building playlists would be engaging was achieved.

As for the anchoring mechanism, opinions were in general positive. Most participants stated it was useful: "With anchor songs I knew where to start browsing my music collection", "Close songs were actually similar to each other in the version with anchor songs", "I did like knowing where my anchor songs were as it was easier to figure out which types of songs were in the various areas of the grid", "Anchor songs helped me decide where to look for songs suitable to the situation given", "I would be interested in using a conventional system (album, artist, title) to explore my music collection and then selecting the anchors to browse similar songs". Only one participant claimed that "anchoring didn't help much". These statements show that anchors helped participants navigating the music collection. Moreover, subjects were able to adapt the music collection organization to their individual preferences by setting the clusters' positions on the grid. Such conclusions are in agreement with mean rates for statement 10.

Participants also provided invaluable suggestions to further improve the user experience provided by SoundAnchoring. Among these suggestions are a zooming function to explore more thoroughly areas of the music space and a search function to locate specific tracks on the grid. Subjects would also like to add all the tracks of a node to the playlist with only one gesture. With regard to anchoring, participants would like the interface to recommend anchors based on listening habits. Therefore, SoundAnchoring should incorporate more possibilities of interaction to cater for different ways of exploring music collections, and learn from users' behaviour.

6. CONCLUSION

This paper presents SoundAnchoring, a content-based music visualization interface that maps the music library to a 2D space. With SoundAnchoring, users play an active role in the organization of the music space by choosing where clusters containing acoustically similar tracks will be located.

A user study was carried out to evaluate SoundAnchoring. The ability to modify the topology of the music visualization, along with gestural control and other interface-related features, delivered a positive user experience with regard to playlist creation. Despite encouraging results, SoundAnchoring can be improved in several ways. Immediate enhancements comprise the addition of new gestures suggested by user study participants.

As for future work, we intend to perform an objective evaluation of AnchoredSOM that takes different feature sets and algorithm parameters into consideration. A long-term user study involving a larger number of participants could more comprehensively evaluate the real-world applicability of SoundAnchoring. Further research avenues include the use of graphics processing units (GPUs) and cloud computing to improve the performance of the feature extraction and organization stages.

7. REFERENCES

[1] E. Pampalk, A. Rauber, and D. Merkl, "Content-based organization and visualization of music archives," in *Proceedings of the 10th ACM International Conference on Multimedia*. ACM, 2002, pp. 570–579.

[2] A. S. Lillie, "MusicBox: Navigating the space of your music," Master's thesis, Massachusetts Institute of Technology, 2008.

[3] S. Stober and A. Nürnberger, "Musicgalaxy - an adaptive user-interface for exploratory music retrieval," in *Proc of 7th Sound and Music Computing Conference*, 2010.

[4] T. Kohonen, "The self-organizing map," *Proceedings of the IEEE*, vol. 78, no. 9, pp. 1464–1480, 1990.

[5] M. Tolos, R. Tato, and T. Kemp, "Mood-based navigation through large collections of musical data," in *Consumer Communications and Networking Conference, 2005. CCNC. 2005 Second IEEE*. IEEE, 2005, pp. 71–75.

[6] C. Muelder, T. Provan, and K.-L. Ma, "Content based graph visualization of audio data for music library navigation," in *IEEE International Symposium on Multimedia (ISM)*. IEEE, 2010, pp. 129–136.

[7] F. Mörchen, A. Ultsch, M. Nöcker, and C. Stamm, "Visual mining in music collections," *From Data and Information Analysis to Knowledge Engineering*, pp. 724–731, 2006.

[8] A. Rauber and M. Frühwirth, "Automatically analyzing and organizing music archives," *Research and Advanced Technology for Digital Libraries*, pp. 402–414, 2001.

[9] A. Rauber and D. Merkl, "The SOMlib digital library system," *Research and Advanced Technology for Digital Libraries*, pp. 852–852, 1999.

[10] R. Neumayer, M. Dittenbach, and A. Rauber, "PlaySOM and pocketSOMplayer, alternative interfaces to large music collections," in *Proc. of ISMIR*, vol. 5, 2005.

[11] D. Lübbers, "SoniXplorer: Combining visualization and auralization for content-based exploration of music collections," in *Proc. of ISMIR*, 2005, pp. 590–593.

[12] P. Knees, M. Schedl, T. Pohle, and G. Widmer, "An innovative three-dimensional user interface for exploring music collections enriched with meta-information from the web," in *Proceedings of the ACM Multimedia*, 2006, pp. 17–24.

[13] D. Lübbers and M. Jarke, "Adaptive multimodal exploration of music collections," in *Proc. of ISMIR*, vol. 2009, 2009.

[14] E. Brazil, M. Fernström, G. Tzanetakis, and P. Cook, "Enhancing sonic browsing using audio information retrieval," in *International Conference on Auditory Display ICAD-02, Kyoto, Japan*, 2002.

[15] E. Brazil and M. Fernström, "Audio information browsing with the sonic browser," in *Coordinated and Multiple Views in Exploratory Visualization, 2003. Proceedings. International Conference on*. IEEE, 2003, pp. 26–31.

[16] J. S. Downie, "Music information retrieval," *Annual review of information science and technology*, vol. 37, no. 1, pp. 295–340, 2003.

[17] S. Stober and A. Nürnberger, "Towards user-adaptive structuring and organization of music collections," *Adaptive Multimedia Retrieval. Identifying, Summarizing, and Recommending Image and Music*, pp. 53–65, 2010.

[18] G. Tzanetakis, M. S. Benning, S. R. Ness, D. Minifie, and N. Livingston, "Assistive music browsing using self-organizing maps," in *Proceedings of the 2nd International Conference on PErvasive Technologies Related to Assistive Environments*. ACM, 2009, pp. 3:1–3:7.

[19] G. Giorgetti, S. Gupta, and G. Manes, "Wireless localization using self-organizing maps," in *Proceedings of the 6th international conference on Information processing in sensor networks*. ACM, 2007, pp. 293–302.

[20] G. Tzanetakis and P. Cook, "Musical genre classification of audio signals," *IEEE Transactions on Speech and Audio Processing*, vol. 10, no. 5, pp. 293–302, 2002.

[21] J. Holm, A. Aaltonen, and H. Siirtola, "Associating colours with musical genres," *Journal of New Music Research*, vol. 38, no. 1, pp. 87–100, 2009.

[22] L. Eisemann, *Pantone's Guide to Communicating with Color*. Grafix Press, Ltd., Florida, 2000.

[23] M. Sordo, Ò. Celma, M. Blech, and E. Guaus, "The quest for musical genres: Do the experts and the wisdom of crowds agree?" in *Proceedings of the 9th International Conference on Music Information Retrieval*, 2008, pp. 255–260.

[24] A. Laplante, "Users relevance criteria in music retrieval in everyday life: an exploratory study," in *Proceedings of the 11th International Society for Music Information Retrieval Conference*, 2010, pp. 601–606.

[25] R. A. Fisher, *The Design of Experiments*. Hafner Publishing Company, New York, 1935.

SmartDJ, An Interactive Music Player for Music Discovery by Similarity Comparison

First author
Aw Si Ying Maureen
Nanyang Technological University
50 Nanyang Avenue
Singapore 639798
maureenaw@outlook.com

Second author
Lim Chung Sion
Nanyang Technological University
50 Nanyang Avenue
Singapore 639798
limcs@me.com

Third author
PerMagnus Lindborg
Nanyang Technological University
50 Nanyang Avenue
Singapore 639798
permagnus@ntu.edu.sg

ABSTRACT

In this digital music era, sorting and discovery of songs is getting harder and more time consuming than before, due to the large pool of songs out there. Many music recommendation system and other similar applications in the market make use of collaborative filtering and social recommendation to suggest music to listeners. However, the problem arises when there is not enough information collected for the song, which happens mostly to new and less popular music. Other issues include missing or inaccurate metadata, the need for Internet connection, etc.

We present research on acoustic features to automatically classify songs according to user-friendly and high-level concepts that indicate social contexts for music listening, and a prototype application called "SmartDJ". We aim to provide novel ways that the user can browse her/his music collection, with a player that enhances interaction via a visual feedback, personalised DJ trajectories, smooth mix transitions and so forth. SmartDJ sorts the songs based on similarity by extracting low level features, then reducing feature space dimensionality with principle component analysis (PCA) and multidimensional scaling (MDS) methods, and plotting songs in a GUI for manual or automatic browsing, where song similarity is given by Euclidian distance in a lower-dimension song space. Users are able to visualise their music library and select songs based on their similarity, or allow the system to perform automation, by selecting a list of songs based on the selection of the seed song. Users can maneuver with the high-level descriptor on the interactive interface to attain the different song space desired.

1. INTRODUCTION

Music discovery system is essential for users to explore songs from a large collection of music. The idea of SmartDJ is to serve as a personal Deejay (DJ) to make the selection of song choices for users without having the skillset of a DJ. The system automatically generates a playlist of songs based on the seed song and/ or user can make selection of songs, all based on song similarity. We proposed a new and interactive way of visualizing a personal music library by translating all the songs into a song space to provide a form of visual feedback. The similarity between the songs is determined by its proximity.

In order to achieve the song similarity comparison, signal analysis is performed on individual song. Low-level descriptors are extracted for similarity measurement. The large dataset is then reduced with the use of dimension reduction techniques such as principle component analysis (PCA) and multidimensional scaling (MDS) methods, for easy viewing by users.

The song space model can be adjusted accordingly with different inputs from the user to suit the different scenarios or needs.

2. BACKGROUND

A well-know model that is applicable to the case of our song space model is Thayer's mood model (1989) as depicted in Figure 1. Thayer's mood model divides mood into two allegedly uncorrelated dimension vectors: arousal and valence [1]. Arousal can be described as the energy or activation of an emotion. Low arousal corresponds to feeling sleepy or sluggish while high arousal corresponds to feeling frantic or excited. Valence describes how positive or negative an emotion is. Low valence corresponds to feeling negative, sad or melancholic and high valence to feeling positive, happy or joyful.

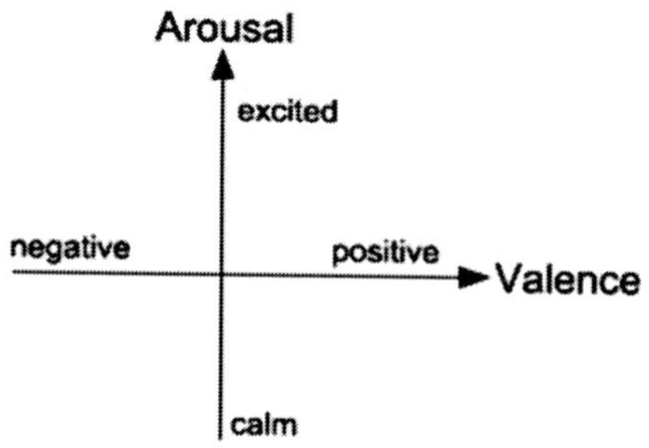

Figure 1. Thayer's Mood Model

Microsoft Research Asia (Liu, Lu, et al., 2003) proposed a method to properly use Thayer's model for music mood classification, in which mood was divided into four nominal classes resembling the four quadrants in the mood plane spanned by the two vectors. The first quadrant (excited & positive) corresponds to 'happy/ excited' emotion, second quadrant (excited & negative) corresponds to 'angry/ anxious' emotion, third quadrant (calm & negative) corresponds to 'sad/ bored' emotion and finally the last quadrant (calm & positive) corresponds to 'relax/ serene' emotion. This model is further elaborated with the various emotions as labeled on an Arousal-Valence (A-V) space [2] shown in Figure 2. We can aim to apply Thayer's mood model to our song space model. As such we will have a better feel of how the different songs are position in the space. Hence, manipulating the song space with different user input and the system can then select songs from the right space to suit the needs of the user.

Aside from mood model, many also suggest other forms of song classification, genre classification in particular. Davalos [3] suggests using Linear discriminant analysis for dimension reduction so as to project the data for optimum class separation. While Clark, Park and Guerard [4] suggested Growing neural gas (GNG) as a form of self-organizing map, Langlois and Marques [5] suggested Hidden Markov Models (HMMs) for genre classification. Keeping in mind that our objective is to project songs into a song space based on similarity and not based on genre or other features, the methods suggested can be explored and used as a form of reference for our work.

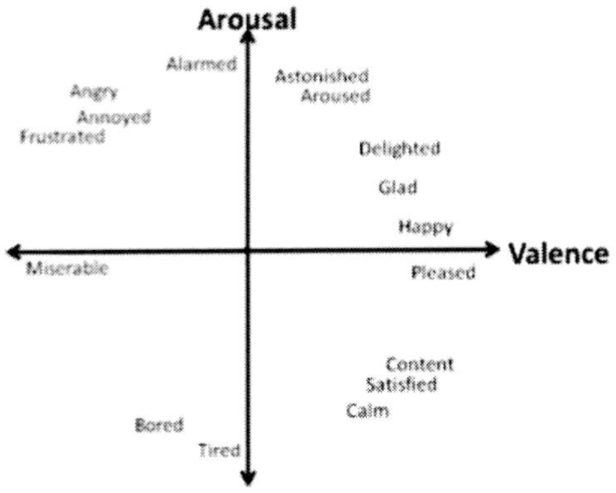

Figure 2. A-V Space Labeled with Different Emotions

3. PLATFORM

Matlab R2010b [6] serves as the main platform for developing the prototype of the song space model. Dimension reduction techniques such as PCA and plotting of the two-dimensional song space were performed with the use of Matlab. MIRtoolbox 1.4 [7] is an essential tool that rides on Matlab and is used for low- level features extraction in our work.

Max 6 (MSP) [8] is used to develop the GUI for our work, which involves interface design, data organization and processing. The working model developed from Matlab will be ported over to Max/MSP to serve as the backbone for our application, and will work hand-in- hand with the user interface. A third party component, ircam-descriptor [9] is a real-time descriptor analyser for Max/MSP. It is capable of performing features extraction and other signal processing analysis offline. Therefore, this allows songs to be imported to SmartDJ for analysis and to plot them onto the song space, without having the need of playing the songs unlike in the case of a real-time analysis.

4. SONG SPACE DEVELOPMENT

Similarity between songs is a subjective measure. Many software deals with this by defining based on a certain genres, artists, etc. And more often recommend songs to user based on the popularity of the song (play count) and by collaborative filtering, which means that, if listeners who like song A, B and C also like song E, then the system is likely to recommend song E to other listeners who listen to song A, B and C.

In the case of SmartDJ, it sorts out the similarity of songs by first extracting low-level features, such as brightness, centroid, roll-off, Mel-Frequency Cepstral Coefficient (MFCC), etc. This in total makes up 28 features, which is inclusive of the 13 MFCC coefficients. All features were extracted with the use of MIRtoolbox 1.4.

4.1 Features Extraction

A corpus of 310 songs was used in the training dataset. The audio files are in lossless WAVE format, encoded in linear pulse code modulation (PCM) of 16 bits in stereo channels with a resulting audio bit rate of 1411200 bit/s. Only an excerpt of 30 seconds of the middle segment of the songs was examined. The middle segment of the song was a sensible choice, as intuitively, it is where the gist of the song is, and in most cases it is the chorus of the music. Even though this may not always be the case, but most of the time true. Davalos however chose to analyze the first 30 seconds [3] of the song. The audio signal was then down-sampled to 22050Hz [10], which is similar to the case of Arenas-Garcıa, Petersen, and Hansen (2007). Even though the experiment was conducted in an ideal scenario, but in actual fact during implementation, users might be more prone to mp3 files due to its smaller file size and compactness. But further investigation will have to be done to determine if the end result will be affected, which will not cover in this paper.

4.2 Dimension Reduction

The large dataset collected from the corpus is then reduced in dimension and projected onto a two- dimensional song space as a form of visual feedback to the user. The similarity between the songs can be determined from the plot with similar songs being situated near each other and songs that are very different being plotted far away from one another. In order to reduce the dataset into a two-dimensional plot, dimension reduction techniques have to be employed. In our case, we chose principle component analysis (PCA) and multidimensional scaling (MDS) methods, where song similarity is given by Euclidian distance in a lower-dimension song space. With PCA, the highest variance is retained in the first and second principle component (PC) respectively, giving it the greatest spread. Hence, as shown in Figure 3, the data is plotted with PC2 against PC1, in order to retain most of the information.

With the 28 features, the percentage variability for the first two and three PCs account for only 24.99% and 32.43% respectively, which is fairly poor. To overcome overfitting issue and to improve the variability explained, the features employed were further streamline to nine spectral shapes features. The song space model obtained from spectral shape features is shown in Figure 3.

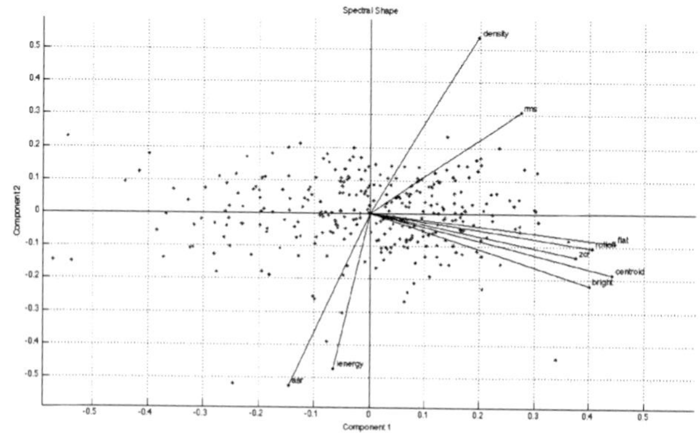

Figure 3. Song Space Model with spectral shape features.

Results from the first three PCs account for 51.05%, 72.87% and 81.64% (*See Figure 4*) of the variance respectively. A sharp bend at the second PC indicates that the variability explained by the third PC onwards is not as significant. Hence, a two-dimensional plot with the first two PCs is employed in our model.

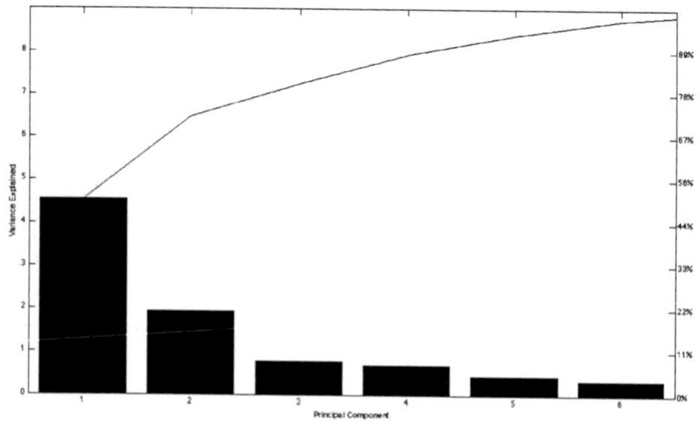

Figure 4. Percent variability explained by the first 6 PCs.

4.3 Song Space Model

A general trend of the song placement can be noticed from our song space model. The typical Pop, Rock and Techno songs take up the first quadrant (upper right). We would consider this quadrant to contain songs with higher danceability and are generally high, bright and nosier. Songs that are dark but rich in audio content takes up the second quadrant (upper left) and they are songs that are generally more Acoustic and Country. Songs from artists such as Taylor Swift, Jason Mraz and Bruno Mars tend to appear more often in this quadrant. Music that is dark and generally more melancholy takes up the third quadrant (lower left). They are songs that are more instrumental and jazzier for example songs from artists like Adele and Kenny G tend to appear in this quadrant. Finally, the fourth quadrant (lower right) contains songs that are generally melancholy but with a faster beat. Examples include Jazz and Country music with a hype. This division into the four quadrants draws back the relation to Thayer's mood model (Figure 1), which similarly categorizes the mood plane into four main sectors spanned by the two vectors. This suggests that the song space can be classified in terms of emotional mood and user can select the type of music on the song space based on their social context.

From the general trend observed above, we observed that as song progresses along the horizontal axis, it moves from a "quieter" zone to a "nosier" zone. And in terms of genre, this means that songs change from Jazz, Acoustics and light-hearted Country songs to Rock, Techno, Pop and House music. Thus, x-axis (PC1) corresponds to the noisiness of a song. The vertical axis increases in energy level as it progresses from bottom to top. Jazz music is generally located at the bottom, while Pop music is generally located at the upper half of the song space. Thus, y-axis (PC2) relates to the massiveness or heaviness of a song. This analysis is supported by the features' loadings as shown in Figure 3. It can be seen that the loadings for features like flatness, rolloff, zero crossing rate (ZCR), centroid and brightness lie closer to the horizontal axis, and they measure the amount of high frequency energy and how much the signal oscillate. Thus it corresponds with our analysis by saying that the horizontal axis is a measure of how noisy, or saturated with high-frequency content, the music is. Also the loadings of density and RMS point in the direction close to the positive y-axis while loadings of low energy and absolute silent ratio (ASR) point in the negative y-axis direction. Hence, corresponds with our analysis with the vertical axis being a measure of the amount of energy or how *massive/ heavy* the music is.

5. SMARTDJ INTERFACE

The idea of interface design for SmartDJ is focused on non-DJ users who utilise SmartDJ as their daily music player without too much hassle. The simplicity and interactivity is the design focus for SmartDJ.

5.1 Soundbar Mode

Soundbar Mode allows the user to simply play tracks with minimum action required. The Soundbar mode comes with three main panels for basic operation. SmartDJ panel provides trigger buttons for effect automation such as auto-crossfading and party mode. Visualiser, playlist editor and advanced setting are located under Features tab for triggering the pop-up window according to user's need.

Figure 5. Soundbar Mode

The main music player control includes essential controls and information to provide the ease of use to amateurs. Essential controls such as previous song, play, next song, loop, shuffle and additional information provide basic control for the music player. Information such as current playing track information and upcoming track are included to provide information feedback to the users. Upcoming track information tab that paired with next button to provide instant reselection for user who is not satisfy with the next song. He/she can change the upcoming track until he/she finds the desired song to cue.

5.2 DJ Mode

DJ mode is created to simulate the interface of conventional DJ software with simplified features for the non-DJ users such as cross-fader, volume, speed, pitch and parametric equaliser for individual play desk to perform manual manipulation. Users are able to achieve beat synchronization manually but changing the speed of both deck individual to match the song speed of both. Furthermore, the pitch of song can be maintained as original by manipulating the pitch slider. These manual features give better interaction without increase the difficulty of using SmartDJ.

Effects such as beat synchronisation and song structure detection can be applied on DJ mode. Beat synchronisation helps to match the speed of song for both tracks for the ease of song transition where it gives better song transition effect when both BPMs of song are nicely matched. Key lock feature allows the system to maintain the pitch of song while changing the speed. Song structure detection is the concept applies for finding best mixing points for users. Song structure detection separates song into different part such as verse, chorus, intro and outro. This information can be used for users to perform manual crossfading at desired point or serves as reference for the automation to pick the appropriate point for mixing. Currently, this component is considered as a part for future development.

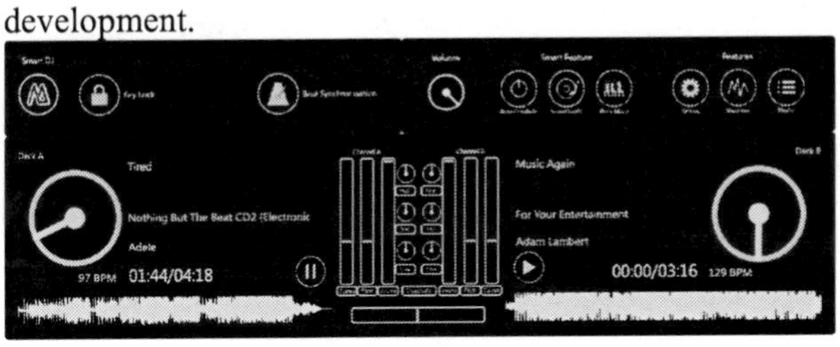

Figure 7. DJ Mode

6. INTERACTIVE FEATURES

The interface design for SmartDJ is focused on non-DJ users who utilise SmartDJ. The objective of developing SmartDJ is to create a new way of interaction between the users with music player. Therefore, interactive features are the main focus of the SmartDJ development. Song Space Visualiser and Smart Equaliser are the main features that emphasise on user interactivity. Advance Setting Panel provides further adjustment for the system to suit the users' need better.

6.1 Song Space Visualiser

Song Space Visualiser creates a new way of interaction between user and music player by providing a visual feedback regarding to the song similarity of songs that added into SmartDJ.

The analysed result after dimension reduction will then plot into smaller dimensional song space. This visual feedback helps the users to understand that what are the similar songs around the seed song. Alternatively, SmartDJ is able to select the subsequence songs based on seed song automatically if the users choose to activate the automation.

This is inspired by the work of CataRT [11] and MusicBox by Anita Lillie [12]. CataRT is a real-time sound synthesis system that allows display the corpus of songs data on a space based on its proximity in descriptor space. The concept of MusicBox is one step further from CataRT and closer to our idea. It projects a large corpus of songs in a space and the model can be adjusted by filtering different descriptors. Song Space Visualiser aims to improve the idea into a potential application that comes with higher usability, higher user interactivity and higher user friendliness.

The 3 different interfaces then evaluated by group of people who are amateur users that use music player very often. They verify these programmes based on the accuracy of the presentation, user interactivity and user friendliness. The result is SmartDJ scored the better overall score in terms of user interactivity and user friendliness.

In SmartDJ, there are 2 song spaces, which displaying the relationship of BPM against key of songs (Song Space 1) and the relationship of song similarity (Song Space 2). These 2 song spaces are formed by 5 dimension data, which include BPM, key, Brightness, Noisiness and Heaviness. With different dimension arrangement, these 2 song spaces provide different visual feedback to the user.

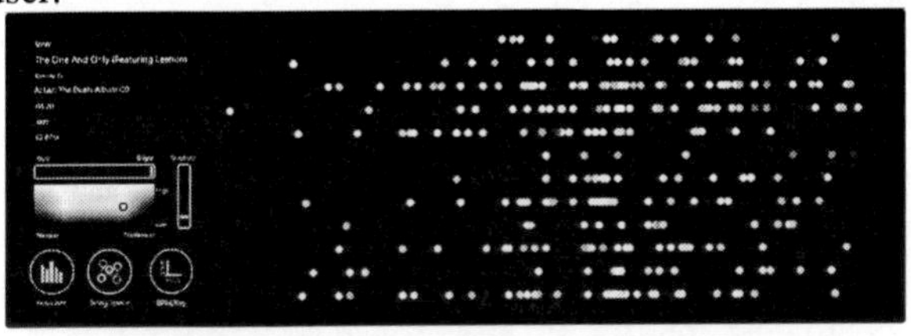

Figure 1. Song Space Based on BPM and Key

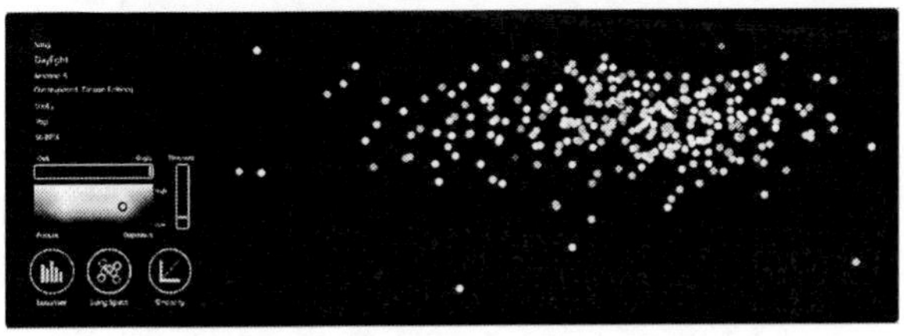

Figure 2. Song Space Based on Similarity

In the background, K-th Nearest Neighbour used to choose songs that are closest to the seed song with the inputs provided by the user. User can define the number of song selection as well to include more songs for the system to perform filtering. The system will have a higher chance to locate the best candidate to prevent the system falls into a loop where the seed song and selected song will keep playing repeatedly.

In order to overcome this issue, SmartDJ introduces *Social Input* as input parameter of song space for user to define direction for the song selection system to select subsequent songs based on seed song as center point. The social input can be categorised into 4 stages, which are slight increment, huge increment, slight decrement and huge decrement that can help to define how the system should choose the subsequent song across the song space.

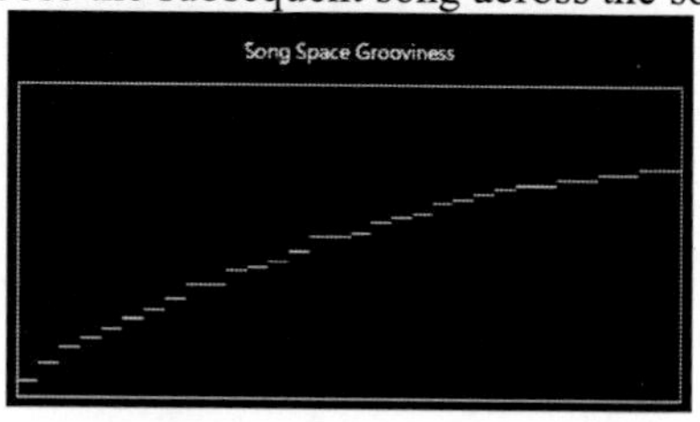

Figure 3. Social Input Panel

6.2 Smart Equaliser

Smart Equaliser creates a new approach for users to manipulate the equalization setting. There are 3 types of equaliser interface to suit different kinds of user.

Firstly, a set of parametric equalization is included for basic adjustment of low, mid and high frequencies.

Secondly, a typical 13 bands of graphic equaliser that is widely used in music players is prepared for users who prefer to have greater control yet it is simple to manipulate.

Thirdly, a fully customisable graphic equaliser gives more flexible adjustment for individual frequency bands. Users can draw a line across the space horizontally to increase or decrease the gain of specific bands. It is the most complex version but it also comes with the highest potential to discover new equalisation effect for audio tracks.

The algorithm is created by using convolution between the music signals with signals obtained from Fast Fourier Transform. The number of individual bands is 256 bands and equally divided from 20 Hz to 20kHz to give the maximum flexibility for the users yet it is not difficult to manipulate the music signals. Common equalisation presets are available for the ease of use while custom setting is also available for user to save as their personal preferences.

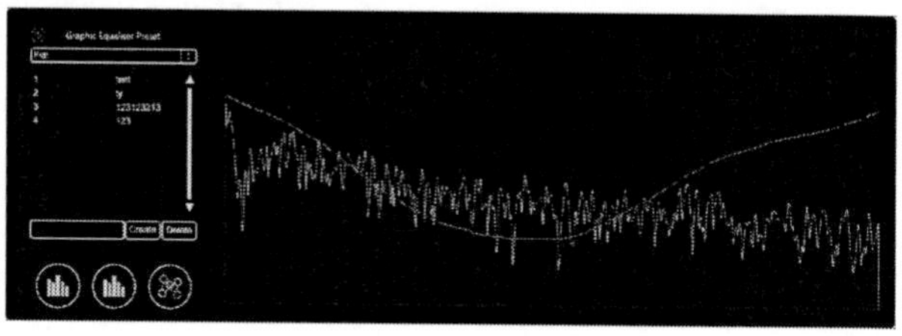

Figure 4. Smart Equaliser

6.3 Advance Setting Panel

Parameters for song space model, song selection and song transition are available for the system to determine a set of suitable songs for users.

The song space model can be varying based atmosphere mode which is targeting for the need of users while song recommendation is needed based on different scenario such as partying, house music for relaxing, chill and calm music before sleep and other possible scenarios. Different scenario setting generates the result of different space models based on different sets of feature combination.

Song selection automation features such as *Danceability*, *Grooviness* and proximity threshold help to customize the behaviour of system while generating playlist based on seed songs. Danceability is a high level descriptor that referred as the dance-ness of the song that can be defined as how significant the beat of the song that will make the listener feels like dancing. Grooviness is defined as the how the songs in the playlist build up or down the groove throughout the playtime.

7. SMART SONG TRANSITION

SmartDJ includes song transition features that it helps to transit from one song to another. The conventional DJ software focuses more on the manual features instead of automation. Therefore, we purposed several smart transition automation techniques inspired by the actual DJ skills for song transition. The transition comes in to amend where there is no perfect match for subsequence song by gradually pitching, adjusting BPM over the course of several minutes and creating equalisation mixing to prevent frequency band overlapping with each other.

7.1 Spectral Matching

Spectral matching is one of the basic DJ skills that apply the technique of tuning down the low frequency of current song while transiting to the next song. This technique helps avoiding the low frequency of both songs to overpower each other. This technique does not limit to only low frequency but mid and high frequency range as well. This techniques can simulate the actual DJ action which is turning up or down of the parametric equaliser.

EQ Blend [13] requires some equalization blending. The technique focuses on preventing the certain frequency bands of current song overpower the subsequence song. For an example, track A is an instrumental track with heavily concentrated on mid range of frequency spectrum while track B is a vocal track, mixing these 2 songs together will cause the frequency overpowering issue on mid range frequency band. DJs have to tune down the desired frequency band to make room for the next song to come in.

7.2 Beat Matching

Beat synchronization is another essential techniques that commonly used by DJs to do song transition. 3% rule applies where the tempo difference between 2 songs is within 3% when we change the tempo of the song. Two songs in F Minor that have BPM of 130 and 131 can be harmonically mixed together because the tempo difference is less than 3%. This helps to maintain the original pitch of the song without changing the speed significantly. Moreover, a purposed technique, "Modus Matching" helps to select the corresponding BPM for subsequence songs when there is not suitable songs fall within the 3% region. It selects the following song by twice or half of the tempo. [14]

7.3 Tonality Matching

The purpose of tonality matching is to ensure the transition can be done musically smooth. The concept of harmonic mixing is to ensure the song will be harmonically compatible based on certain conditions such as same key (Tonic), relative Major/Minor ket, sub-dominant key (Perfect 4th) and dominant key (Perfect 5th). This involved in musical context where a song in Cm can be easily compatible with other songs with same key, its relative major D#/Eb, its sub-dominant Fm or its dominant Gm. [15]

A matrix of weights that representing the proximity between tonalities applies to select the subsequence songs with best harmonic matching possible. This matrix can be derived based on Camelot Wheel Chart [16] that shows the similarity between different keys.

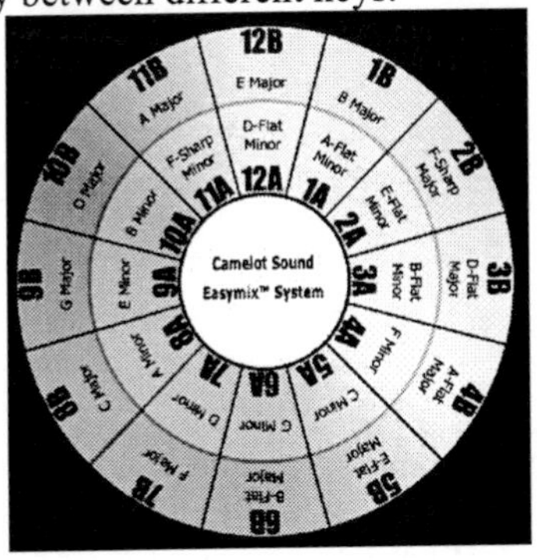

Figure 5. Camelot Wheel Chart

8. CONCLUSION

SmartDJ, other than a music player with DJ features, we proposed a novel way in which user can browse his/her music collection. With the implementation of the song space model, songs projected onto a Song Space Visualiser allows user to better understand the relationship between the music and to make a known song selection to better fit their current listening context. And with the DJ transition effects and automatic song selection, music listening will no long be the same.

The objective of SmartDJ project is not just about developing a prototype but creating potential commercial product or at least it prepares ground for commercial application. Therefore, our project focuses on developing the front end (user interface) and back end (features extraction and dimension reduction) concurrently to create a new way of interacting with music. There are additional features can be included for further development such as song structure detection and user rating system to further enhance and complete the software functionality.

Acknowledgments

This project served as part of final year project for undergraduate studies of Information Engineering and Media at Nanyang Technological University, Singapore. PerMagnus Lindborg from School of Art, Media and Design, and Associate Professor Andy Khong Wai Hoong from School of Electrical and Electronics Engineering supervised this project.

9. REFERENCES

[1] Schuller, Björn, Hage, Clemens, Schuller, Dagmar and Rigoll, Gerhard (2010) 'Mister D.J., Cheer Me Up': Musical and Textual Features for Automatic Mood Classification', Journal of New Music Research, 39: 1, 13-34.

[2] Watson, Diane & Mandryk, Regan L. (2012) "Modeling Musical Mood from Audio Features And Listening Context On An In-Situ Data Set", University of Saskatchewan, 2012 International Society for Music Information Retrieval.

[3] Pedro Davalos, "Automatic Music Genre Classification", CPSC 633-600, Final Project Report, May 13, 2009.

[4] Sam Clark, Danny Park, Adrien Guerard, "Music Genre Classification Using Machine Learning Techniques", 2012.

[5] Thibault Langlois, Gonc ¸alo Marques, "A MUSIC CLASSIFICATION METHOD BASED ON TIMBRAL FEATURES", 10th International Society for Music Information Retrieval Conference, ISMIR 2009

[6] MATLAB Release 2010b. Natick, Massachusetts: © 1984-2010 The MathWorks, Inc.

[7] Lartillot, Olivier, Toiviainen, Petri, "A Matlab Toolbox for Musical Feature Extraction From Audio", International Conference on Digital Audio Effects, Bordeaux, 2007.

[8] Max 6. © 2013 C'74. http://cycling74.com

[9] Schwarz, Diemo, "ircamdescriptors~ real-time descriptor analysis for Max/MSP", IRCAM Real-Time Music Interaction Team, France.

[10] Arenas-Garcıa, Jerónimo, Kaare Brandt Petersen, and Lars Kai Hansen. "Sparse kernel orthonormalized PLS for feature extraction in large data sets." Advances in Neural Information Processing Systems 19 (2007): 33-40

[11] Schwarz, Diemo, "CataRT, Real-Time Corpus Based Concatenative Synthesis", IMTR Team, IRCAM – Centre Pompidou, Paris, France, 2007.

[12] Lillie, Anita Shen, "MusicBox: Navigating the space of your music", Master Thesis, Massachusetts Institute of Technology, Cambridge, MA, 2008

[13] Cartledge, Chris, "EQ Mixing: Critical Techniques and Theory", DJ TechTools, http://www.djtechtools.com/2012/03/11/eq-critical-dj-techniques-theory/, 11 March 2012.

[14] "How to: Understanding key and tempo in harmonic matching", Harmonic Mixing Community, http://community.mixedinkey.com/Topics/1767/how-to- understanding-key-and-tempo-in-harmonic-mixing, October 2008.

[15] "Mixing Harmonically", MixShare: ReWiki, http://www.mixshare.com/wiki/doku.php?id=mixing_harmonically, 9 June 2011.

[16] Davis, Mark, "Harmonic Key Selection", Camelot Sound, http://www.camelotsound.com/Easymix.aspx.

Sound analysis based on phase information that connects time and frequency

Peter Pabon
Institute of Sonology
pabon@koncon.nl

Jordy van Velthoven
Institute of Sonology
c012934@koncon.nl

ABSTRACT

This paper intends to reveal some of the properties and possibilities for sound analysis combining the Fourier and Mellin transform. First, the general transforms are defined and it is introduced how these signal and spectrum representations relate to each other. Second, a central property of Mellin-based form of the Fourier transform; its affine scaling, which leads to the concept of a joined, logarithmic time/frequency-axis is introduced. Third, the concept of a time-frequency continuum that is perpendicular to the logarithmic time-frequency axis is introduced. Next is discussed how information guides itself through the time-frequency continuum and how components link and move together depending on their spectrum and signal characteristics. Finally, an attempt is made to connect the special features that characterize this analysis method to other signal analysis methods.

1. INTRODUCTION

The question of balancing between a time domain or frequency domain description is a fundamental issue in various areas like the design of band-limited oscillators, the description of wave-propagation, directional hearing, the modeling of excitation mechanisms, or the problem of sound source separation in general. Instead of focusing on one of these applications, this paper aims to reveal a general concept that direct this balancing. This is done by exploring the properties of a signal modeling concept intermediate to the Fourier and Mellin transform that puts the paradigm of time-frequency trade-off in a different perspective.

The Mellin transform essentially warps frequency content in conjunction with time. Its abstraction is generally promoted for its power to smoothly rescale and stretch either time or frequency content while preserving magnitude characteristics in the other domain. These elegant options are seen as accommodating abstractions for controlling our analysis, but they will not be the object of our investigations. What is often considered merely an intermediate form in the processing path to the Mellin abstraction; -the exponentially sampled signal and spectrum representations- are our real object of interest. In particular the intimate link of the exponential time representation with the exponentially sampled spectrum representation is rarely recognized, but it will proof here to be a crucial element in time-frequency thinking. The practical implementation of exponential time/frequency sampling is is far from trivial.

2. FOURIER AND MELLIN TRANSFORM

In Fourier analysis it is possible to present a function in the time domain or the frequency domain and to convert a function in the time domain to the frequency domain and vice versa with help of the Fourier transform and it's inversion. The Fourier transform $\mathcal{F}$ of a function $g(t)$ is defined as:

$$\mathcal{F}\{g(t)\} = \hat{g}(f) = \int_{-\infty}^{\infty} g\,(t)\,e^{-i2\pi ft}dt \qquad (1)$$

The Mellin transform $\mathcal{M}$ of a function $g(x)$ is defined as:

$$\mathcal{M}\{g(x)\} = \hat{g}(s) \;=\; \int_{0}^{\infty} g\,(x)\,x^{s-1}dx, \qquad s \in \mathbb{C} \qquad (2)$$

The Mellin transform is closely related to both the Laplace transform and the Fourier transform. Substitution of e^{-t} in (2) for the variable x gives the Laplace transform $\mathcal{L}$ of the function $g(e^{-t})$:

$$\mathcal{L}\{g(e^{-t})\} = \hat{g}(s) \;=\; \int_{0}^{\infty} g\left(e^{-t}\right)e^{-st}dt \qquad (3)$$

Since the Laplace transform can be seen as an extended form of the Fourier transform defined in (1), by substituting $i2\pi f$ for the variable s in (2) the Fourier transform of $g(e^{-t})$ is derived:

$$\mathcal{F}\{g(e^{-t})\} \;= \hat{g}(f) = \int_{0}^{\infty} g\left(e^{-t}\right)e^{-i2\pi ft}dt \qquad (4)$$

The Laplace transform and the Fourier transform that are derived from the Mellin transform are now both defined as an unilateral or one-sided transformation. Both transforms can also be defined as a bilateral or two-sided transformation by extending the limits of integration to all real numbers.

The relation between the Mellin transform and the Fourier transform can be written symbolically as:

$$\mathcal{M}\{g(x)\}_{s\,=\,i2\pi f} \;=\; \mathcal{F}\{g(e^{-t})\}_f \qquad (5)$$

It is from these definitions that the Mellin transform can be interpreted as the Fourier transform of an exponentially warped time signal or as a logarithmic-time Fourier transform [1]

3. TIME AND FREQUENCY SAMPLING

The definitions and relations between the integral transforms from the previous section doesn't take into account any later sampling of the variables. The variable f for which the transformed functional result $\hat{g}(f)$ is specified in (4) only specifies a frequency dependent result, where it does not matter if its plotted along a linear or an exponential frequency scale. The same frequency variable f reappears in the complex exponent $e^{-i2\pi ft}$ where it is scaled with the time variable t. The correlation between time and frequency that this integral transform is representing, is powered by the parallel development of frequency f and time t information in this complex exponent. [Note that the product of time and frequency is caught in the imaginary part of the complex exponent and in reality is expressing a phase angle. So, the integral actually sums phase differences, that are disguised as a sum of products.]

This leads to an ambiguity. Consider a sine signal with a frequency that changes logarithmically with linear time. When evaluated on an exponential time-scale, this signal will show a constant product of time and frequency tf in the complex exponent. Alternatively, a sine signal now with a linear frequency dependence on linear time, will in exponential time have an exponential frequency increment. If the frequency variable f is also allowed to have the same exponential increment, this will again lead to a constant product ft in the exponent. So, the formulation in (5) expresses a final result on a frequency scale, indifferent if the frequency term in the integral proceeds linear or exponentially. Apart from this ambiguity, the Mellin integral also implies that a change in time offset in relation to the starting frequency will largely change the outcome of the integral and thus also the observed frequency content.

3.1 Two forms for the Mellin integral

The correspondence between the Mellin integral and the Fourier integral seen in (5) lead to the expression of the transformed result as a function $\hat{g}(f)$ based in the frequency domain. This frequency domain function holds a spectrum representation, but one that is not necessarily comparable to the spectrum of the signal on a linear frequency axis. The general formulation of the Mellin integral seen in (2) offers some powerful abstractions in formulating derivatives of time functions. However in (4), these properties account for the magnitude information only, but do not apply to the phase/frequency information as this information is caught in the imaginary part of the complex exponent and is thus evaluated as the product $-ft$ against linear time. For true frequency derivatives that are comparable to those of the general Fourier representation, but with some of the Mellin properties, it is necessary to evaluate the exponentially sampled time function $g(e^t)$ against exponentially progressing time e^t and exponentially decaying frequency e^{-f} variables.

$$\hat{g}(e^f) = \int_0^\infty g\left(e^t\right) e^{i2\pi e^{(t-f)}} e^t dt \qquad (6)$$

Formula (6) describes a convolution with an exponentially frequency sweeping complex exponential. As only the imaginary part is involved and magnitude remains the same, this convolution process is thus comparable to an all-pass filtering. Apart from an offset, a sine wave with an exponentially changing instantaneous frequency over time $f_i = e^t$, is essentially identical to a sine wave with an exponentially changing instantaneous phase $\phi_t = e^t$ as a function of time. If now the instantaneous phase ϕ_t as it is expressed in the time domain is taken as the reference for the time variable, the dependency is reversed and thus $t = \ln(\phi_t)$.

Moreover, a sine wave with a constant frequency f can be observed over exponentially sampled time. If this frequency is taken to be the constant factor, whatever the moment in time, than still the amount of phase distance travelled at the sampling points will increase exponentially. The logarithm $\ln(\phi_f)$ of the series of phase ϕ_f observations will show a constant increase, that is directly proportional to the frequency f of the sine wave, so $f = \ln(\phi_t)$. This changes formula (6) into

$$\hat{g}(\phi_f) = \int_0^\infty g(\phi_t) e^{i2\pi e^{(\ln\phi_t - \ln\phi_f)}} e^t dt \qquad (7)$$

Note that a phase change over time is still frequency, and a phase change with constant frequency still denotes time, but time and frequency are now allowed to vary in relation to each other. Hence, the exponential time and frequency scaling from the Mellin integral can still be maintained, without the problematic effect that a shift in time will change the frequency content. Furthermore, by linking the exponential dependency exclusively to the phase, only the imaginary part of the complex exponent is warped. Thus, for the real part of the complex exponent that describes the amplitude, the exponential behavior is no longer implicitly linked to exponential time or exponential frequency. A dependency on exponential time is essentially a logarithmic dependency as the typical natural preset is that amplitude changes exponentially with linear time or with linear frequency. The modified transformation in (6) will thus have properties of all the general integral transforms that were defined in the previous section. It will have a property of the Mellin transform for any information that links to an exponential change in phase, have a property of the Fourier transform for the frequency and it will have a property of the Laplace transform for any amplitude information that varies exponentially with linear time or linear frequency. Under these modified conditions the Fourier transform still works as normal, but the derivatives of a phase change against time, will now no longer include an amplitude term as this was contained in the real part of the integral. The ability to derive on frequency without a gain change may seem an undesirable concept if ones intention is to evaluate or to process frequency content on base of amplitude, but the ability to still evaluate or process frequency content without changing the amplitude could prove to be a valuable option.

4. EXPONENTIAL SAMPLING AND THE MELLIN DOMAIN

An exponentially re-sampled time signal is the starting point for either one of the two flavours (4) or (6) of the Mellin

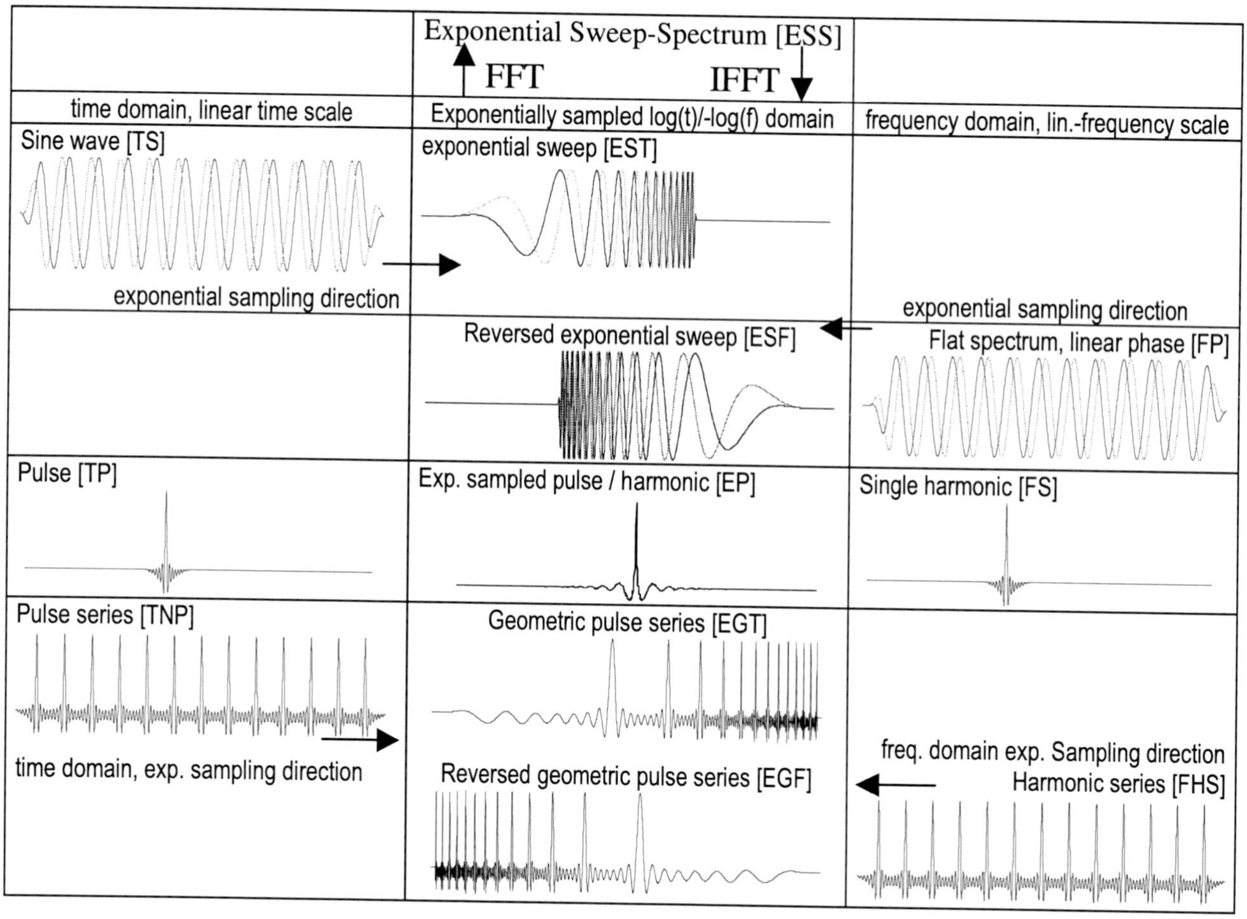

Figure 1. Signals in the time domain (left), related exponentially sampled series (middle) and connected linear frequency spectra (right).

transform. The two forms clearly separate when the spectrum content is to be considered. Formulation (6) essentially converts a logarithmic time representation to a logarithmic frequency representation, where both representations will appear to exist in one and the same exponentially sampled domain (see Figure 1, middle column). The familiar relationships that exist between the time domain and the frequency domain are invariable mathematical properties, but their interpretation is inseparable from the linear increment by which the information is distributed on either the time axis or the frequency axis. The exponential sampling followed by a presentation as a linear sequence gives the time axis a logarithmic interpretation. That the original linear association between the data points now proceeds on this proportional scale can however not be read from its now linear sequential storage. A Fast Fourier transform (FFT) procedure does not check for the original clock count and just assumes its time or frequency proceeding linearly. As a result, the FFT result of any such linear stored series, that before had the association of a logarithmical time signal representation, will lead to what in linear FFT terms is considered a frequency domain representation comparable to the Mellin formulation (4). This spectrum is not the logarithmic frequency spectrum of the logarithmic time signal as in (6).

This Mellin spectrum representation is comparable to a Mel-frequency cepstrum representation, as it is the linear Fourier transform of information that is logarithmically distributed along the dependent axis. This representation will be referred to as the Exponential Sweep Spectrum [ESS]. As mentioned before, the exponential sampling converts any narrow frequency band signal, i.e. a sine wave, to a regular exponential sweep [EST] (see Figure 1). On the other hand, the exponential sampling of a signal with a wide frequency band, i.e. a pulse [TP], will remain a pulse [EP] on the logarithmical-time axis. Both the exponential sweep [EST], and the pulse [EP] have the same magnitude distribution in the ESS, they only differ in their ESS-phase representation. The convolution of an exponential sweep with an identical, but time reversed exponential sweep [ESF] will convert the exponential sweep [EST] to a pulse [EP] in the exponentially sampled domain. This conversion, that complies to the convolution described in (6), is actually comparable to a linear scale Fourier analysis, as all constant frequency information is summed into one component with an offset on the axis that now has the identity of frequency.

What is valid for a single parallel sweep is also valid for a sum of parallel sweeps. This property of the formulation (6) which is called in general the superposition principle can symbolically written as:

$$\mathcal{F}(s_1 + s_2) \longrightarrow \mathcal{F}\ (s_1) + \mathcal{F}(s_2) \qquad (8)$$

Aside the superposition principle, the homogeneity principle is also valid. The homogeneity principle can symbolically written as:

$$as \longrightarrow a\mathcal{F}(s) \tag{9}$$

Due to the linearity of the Mellin transform [2], the convolution of any sum of shifted exponential sinusoid sweeps with the same basic time reversed exponential sweep that functions as a kernel [ESF] will pile up all exponentially warped sinusoids according to their own frequency offset.

The convolution of an exponential sampled signal with this time reversed exponential sweep kernel is the actual implementation of the transform (6). Note that a sine wave with a low frequency will, after its exponentially resampling, reach the fastest movement later, and thus reappear as an exponential sweep that is more displaced to the right on the frequency axis. As a result the spectrum has an opposite directed logarithmic frequency ordering. To be consistent, also in Figure 1 the exponential sampling from the linear frequency axis is done from right to left and the result is that the direction of the corresponding linear frequency axis is reversed. The pulse [EP] in the exponentially sampled domain can thus have two interpretations, that of an exponentially sampled pulse in the time domain or that of a single frequency band on an exponentially sampled frequency axis. The convolution with the reversed sweep [ESF] will bring any logarithmically sampled time signal to its spectrum on a logarithmic frequency axis, while the product of the convolution with the forward version [ESP] of the same sweep will bring any spectrum with a logarithmic frequency axis to its logarithmically sampled time signal. When staying in this exponentially sampled domain, this implementation of the transform thus has an inverse. The sweep [ESF] and its inverse [EST] both have an ESS with a flat magnitude characteristic. Both versions of the sweep can be seen as impulse responses of all-pass filters, with their convolution and deconvolution properties characterized by the opposite polarity of the phase in the ESS.

Moreover, also the exponentially sampled impulse series [EGT] and the exponentially sampled harmonic series [EGF] comprise essentially the same shape, only time reversed. As a result, both have identical ESS magnitude characteristics, and phase curves with opposite polarities. This implies that any convolution that is applied along this joint scale, using either one of the geometric series [EGT] or [EGF] as an impulse response, will be a magnitude pattern selection process (filtering) that searches periodicity in both the time domain and the frequency domain at the same time. This unifies the principle of periodicity detection over both domains.

5. A JOINED TIME-FREQUENCY AXIS

The relationship between time and frequency, $T = 1/f$, is in the Fourier representation generally associated with independent, perpendicular axes. The exponential sampling straightens out the $1/x$ curve and parallels the logarithmic time and logarithmic frequency axes. This paralleling means that also other reciprocal relationships between time and frequency that exist as a Fourier pair unify. An example of such a proportion is the length of the analysis window in the time domain that curtails the bandwidth in the frequency domain. This proportion becomes a linear distance on a shared logarithmic axis. The benefit of the definition of both the analysis window and the bandwidth on the same axis is that no longer the incommensurable relation between time and frequency will be a preset in the analysis, as it can be optimized by widening in either the time or frequency perspective. With the exponentially sampled domain, the notions of zero time and zero frequency are missing. Both time and frequency values can still be measured in an absolute sense, but their zeroes are never reached due to the logarithmic approach. When there are no scale zeroes to measure against, a transformation becomes affine, which means that the order along the scale is preserved by maintaining a fixed time-frequency product. This specific property turns up as an extra constraint that directs the exponential time sampling process. With progressively larger sampling periods (downsampling), something has to give in at the Nyquist frequency end. This means that, for a practical implementation, during the exponential re-sampling process the frequency range needs to be progressively band-limited. So, any signal that appears on the time entry point on the logarithmic time axis will at that moment be sampled at an extreme high rate and thus be spectrally rich and full of high frequency details. Note that this entry point behaves like a sort of zero scale mark as it connects the logarthmic time scale to a physical instant that exists in linear time. Over time the waveform squeezes by the downsampling while it at the same time loses high frequency detail by the progressive band-limiting. The signal will be muted when the lowest frequency components from the complex reach their Nyquist limit.

6. THE TIME-FREQUENCY CONTINUUM

As mentioned before, the joint time-frequency axis is a dual representation where the logarithmic time and the logarithmic frequency share the same axis. Despite this association, the notions of time domain and frequency domain remain to exist. The two identities are however not anymore that strictly incongruent as with the ordinary square-matrix of the Fast Fourier Transform (FFT). As an extra, the convolution process that brings the signal from its time identity to its spectrum identity can be sectioned. This is realized by using cascaded all-pass filters with impulse responses that each sweep over the full frequency range, but in a fraction of the time. For the inverse transform, the impulse responses are reversed.

This allows a fluent transformation from one to the other domain identity, with intermediate representations that are neither a pure time domain nor a pure frequency domain description. These intermediate representations can be seen as descriptions where frequency changes with constant time, or where time sampling changes with constant frequency. Note that it is possible to pass over the invariant-frequency or invariant-time horizontal by overdoing with an extra filter section.

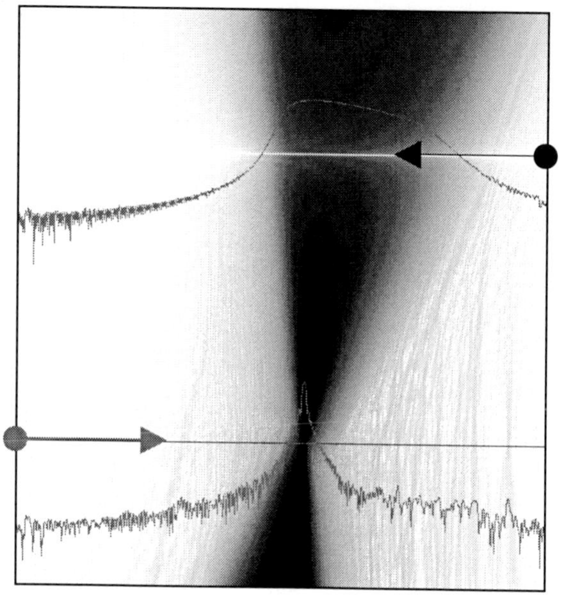

Figure 2. Magnitude distribution over the time-frequency-continuum for a sine wave. The black arrow indicates the exponential sampling direction and entry point for the signal. The red curve at this intersection shows the logarithmic signal magnitude (envelope) along a logarithmic time axis. The grey arrow marks the exponential sampling direction and entry point when starting from the linear spectrum. The red curve at this intersection shows now the logarithmic spectrum magnitude that at this vertical level has a logarithmic frequency axis interpretation.

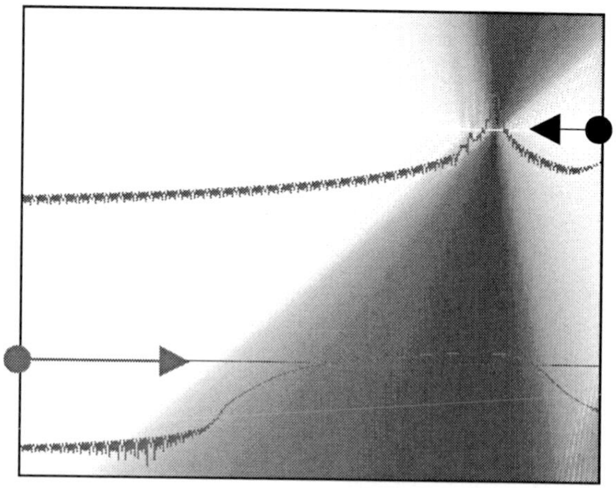

Figure 3. Magnitude distribution over the time-frequency-continuum for a pulse.

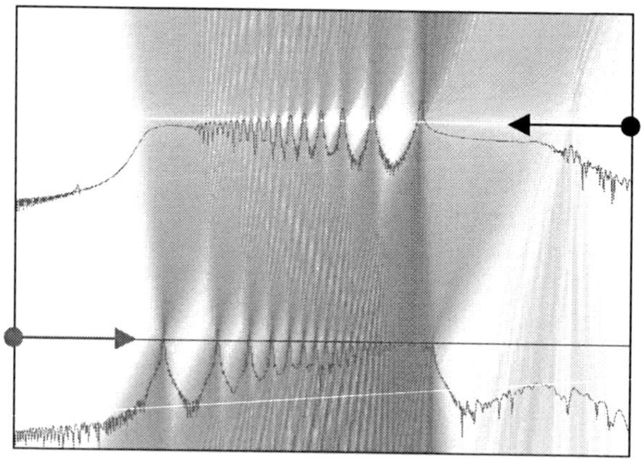

Figure 4. Magnitude distribution over the time-frequency-continuum for a periodic pulse series.

Figure 3 demonstrates how an exponentially sampled sine wave travels top-down through the time-frequency continuum and thereby integrates to becomes its own narrow spectral peak representation. At the stages in between it can not be said that its frequency or time information, simply because both orderings only exist by their constant sampling along the axis. If the incoming sinusoid would have had an increasing frequency already on the linear time scale, than after the exponential sampling its resulting sweep would have increased faster and the point of focus would have been reached at an earlier stage in the continuum. So, the intermediate horizontal intersections have the interpretation of lines with constant acceleration or deceleration of phase against time, or the other way around.

6.1 First derivatives

Any signal component with constant frequency that is exponentially re-sampled over the time line, will have an exponential increasing instantaneous frequency (see EST in Figure 1). This constant component behaves as a linear offset in the exponent that denotes the center frequency offset along the scale.

Taking the derivative against linear time will isolate the frequency as a constant component. This derivative, called the instantaneous frequency (IF), guides a tangent that linearly turns along the logarithmic time axis at the top. The turning is linear because time and frequency share the same exponential proportion. Note how in all time-frequency continuum plots (see figure 2, 3 and 4), beams or rays show up that, according to this IF-tangent, all focus on designated spots along the logarithmic frequency axis. For all the samples along the logarithmic time axis, the proportional phase change over time (the frequency) is constant, or in other words, the focusing point along the frequency axis marks where all information along the time axis that has a constant time frequency product integrates on.

Aside the derivative against time of the complex valued time function, there is also a derivative against frequency for the complex valued spectrum function. This derivative represents the group delay (GD). A pulse in time will have a flat spectrum with a phase spectrum that has a linear increasing term that describes the time-offset of the pulse. After exponential sampling along the frequency axis this first linear-phase term changes to an exponentially sweeping phase function (see Figure 1, ESF derived from FP). The derivative of this function against frequency isolates this linear offset as a constant factor that represents the group delay. This means, that all information along the frequency axis that is phase locked on the same point in time (and thus has the same group delay) will show beams or rays that now focus upward on this specific spot on the time axis (see Figure 3).

6.2 Binding factors

Both differentials, the IF and the GD, direct how the information as being either a time or frequency component, will focus within the time-frequency continuum. The property that the grouped components share in time or in frequency, is a constant fixed product of time and frequency, actually a fixed product of a time period and frequency distance. The same product appears in the complex exponential as $e^{i\pi tf}$ with either the signal or spectral description.

Note that the phase information, seen as a function of time or seen as a function of frequency, has in its absolute sense no further relevance as to precisely carry the differential (IF or GD) which codes the actual information how to focus in the time-frequency continuum.

6.3 Sharpness / resolution

The sharpness of the spectral peak at the point where all time information concentrates on the frequency axis (its bandwidth) is not determined by the frequency resolution entailed in the analysis procedure (the all-pass filter impulse response or the Mellin that convolves the signal to its spectrum), but by the actual width or length of its exposure over the logarithmic time line.

6.4 Second and higher order derivatives

As described in a section above, the derivate along the time axis known as instantaneous frequency (IF) and derivative along the frequency axis known as group delay (GD) both indicate how the information in either representation will focus on the other axis, or at an intermediate point within the time-frequency continuum. Information groups together along either axis on base of a shared linear IF or GD component or shared tf product. A constant linear increasing first derivative means a constant second derivative. Thus a flat second derivative along the time axis (DIF) or a flat second derivative along the frequency axis (DGD) indicates that successive information will focus at some point in the time-frequency continuum. When a first constant second derivative switches to a different offset than this marks the appearance of new information in the time-frequency continuum. A zero DIF or DGD would mean a lack of directivity to focus. Information that has a fixed, frequency counterbalanced phase difference along the frequency axis, or information that is spread over the time axis and shares a fixed frequency response, will always have a flat second derivative on its exposure along the axis. Grouping in either time or frequency means sharing the same offset pattern for the second derivative. This means that higher order derivatives will report on exclusive binding of different component groups over the continuum. For this to work, the grouped components need not to be sequentially ordered. Contributing to the same second derivative indicates mutual binding on base of correlation, while binding to a differently grouped second derivative can be interpreted as independency.

7. RANDOMNESS IN TIME AND FREQUENCY

Having a predominantly flat DIF means having only correlated components over time, and as a result only sharp peaks in the frequency distribution. Having a predominantly flat DGD means having only correlated components over frequency that in essence relate to sharp pulses in the time signal. Randomness can be defined as a zero prone DIF and zero prone DGD, which implies that both amplitude distributions in time or frequency have, on the average, not the tendency nor the mass/width to curve according to an e^{-t^2/σ^2} or e^{-f^2/σ^2} shape, thus no Gaussian trends in either domain. The result is that there is no preference value in either time or frequency that could lead to a centered value around a mean (see Figure 5). Peaked or pulsed information may still appear along either the time or frequency axis in the form of uniform randomly distributed spikes or uniform randomly distributed sinusoids. If the sharpness of information is not associated with a certain combined appearance of a correlation over a certain distance away from its focusing point, than there is randomness (see Figure 6). Note that a signal could be synthesized where there is focusing and thus correlation only in the middle between the pure time and frequency descriptions. It would be hard to characterize such a signal by using general signal and spectrum analysis methods that can not explore the options between these domains. One implication is that it is impossible to pinpoint randomness and thus noise by a single spectral or time domain description only. A specification of randomness must at least be a spectra-temporal description.

7.1 Gaussian properties and exponential sampling

When a Gaussian distributed data set is exponentially sampled along its dependent axis, than as a result the former e^{-x^2/σ^2} shaped distribution will, now on the logarithmically scaled dependent axis, change to a parabolic shaped distribution with a bending scaled by $-x^2/\sigma^2$. By calculating the second derivative, this second order (quadratic) factor can be isolated as a constant. A distribution can thus be tested on its non-Gaussianity by testing the average deviance from this second order parabolic model. This non-Gaussianity criterion, is an important binding factor in blind source separation techniques [3] [4]. This criterion complies closely with the earlier described criteria for independency as a grouped difference or deviance from a constant second derivative seen with the DIF or DGD. The Mellin transform is one-sided and for its operation it needs a complex valued signal at its input. This complex valued signal can be obtained for example by the Hilbert transform of a real valued signal. In contrast to a real valued signal that is ideally distributed around a zero mean, the now complex signal amplitude values distribute around an all-positive mean, which suits the affine property of the transform. Testing for non-Gaussianity using a Mellin-like transform has the advantage that also the third order term, called the skewness, is able to contribute and that not only the fourth order term, called the kurtosis, has to be used for deviance weighting and grouping. Furthermore, with

Figure 5. Magnitude distribution over the time-frequency-continuum for pink noise.

the DIF or DGD approach, frequency can be used as an offset and thus there are no requirements to precise assess the mean, neither is there a need for having at least one Gaussian distributed component in a mix before any contrasting independent component can be isolated.

8. SHIFTING INFORMATION IN THE TIME-FREQUENCY CONTINUUM

Sifting information in the TF-continuum The reason why a peak is able to stand out in the time/frequency continuum, is because somewhere higher up, over some wider region the phase curve showed a progression that matched to an exponential incrementing phase curve template. The sharpness or focussing of a magnitude peak over some width, is just an acknowledgement of the consistent grouping of information that is linked along the axis. As amplitude is preserved all over the continuum, we could choose to subtract this information at any point where it maximally peaks along the time axis, or any point along the frequency axis, or in between, while having in mind that this will be the point with least effects on other identities in the continuum. Just one isolated spectral peak can be reverse transformed to its related time signal representation. This signal can again be used as a phase as a function of time template, a kernel to cross-correlate all other signal information with and that will produce a maximum spectral focusing for all signal components that have a comparable frequency development with time. Here it is the specificity of the time progression of the template, the deviance from the normal, that determines the amount of focusing or isolation for all other information that is linked to it. As the normal linear progression of phase with time is non specific, as this is just frequency, the quadratic progression of phase with time will be the carrier, where again the higher powers/derivatives (the ones that specify the non-Gausianity) determine the amount of success or independence. Note the generality of the procedure, as one isolated peak on the time axis can be a template to isolate a spectral phase template that can be used to select all frequency information that has a comparable time development.

9. CONCLUSIONS

Due to the properties of the Mellin transform, the Fourier transform was reformulated to a transform from phase as a function of logarithmic time to phase as a function of logarithmic frequency. Phase is used as a binding factor that connects both domains as it is basically the same reference point in both domains. Due to the one-sidedness of the transform, domain circularity is no longer a feature of the transformation. Events may occur in the exponentially sampled time domain, or spectrum components may appear in the exponentially sampled frequency domain, without any preconditioned necessity for a (periodic) reappearance. The objective of searching for a fundamental periodicity can thus be replaced by a stronger, more flexible concept, that of a search for repetition, which may even be a one-time event only. With a sign directed integral, past and future will keep their annotation and also the notion of phase is no longer ambiguous as rotational direction remains preserved. A general Fourier description would offer the same options when applied one-sided, but it is the exponential warped scale that gives this integration the option to deal with time-variability also. The exponentially warped phase domain offers a linearization of time and frequency dependencies and presents a method to resolve grouped components in a time-frequency continuum based on their characteristic match to a second order dependency.

10. REFERENCES

[1] P. Flandrin, "Time-Frequency and chirps," in *SPIE-AeroSense'01*, Orlando(FL), 2001.

[2] V.N. Mahalle, A.S. Gudadhe and R.D. Taywade, "Generalization of Linear Scale Invariant System in the Fractional Domain and Some Properties of Fractional Complex Mellin Transform," *Int. J. Contemp. Math. Sciences*, vol. 6, no. 12, pp. 577 - 584, 2011.

[3] A. Hyvärinen, J. Karhunen and E. Ola, *Independent Component Analysis.* John Wiley & Sons, 2004.

[4] J.V. Stone, *Independent Component Analysis; a tutorial introduction.* MIT press, 2004.

Author index